LITERATURE

FOURTH EDITION

❧❧❧❧❧❧

JAMES H.
Pickering

University of Houston

JEFFREY D.
Hoeper

Arkansas State University

Macmillan Publishing Company
New York

Editor: D. Anthony English
Production Supervisor: Ann-Marie WongSam
Production Manager: Su Levine
Cover Designer: Tom Mack
Cover illustration: Edward Hopper (1882–1967), "Room in Brooklyn," 35.66. Oil on Canvas, 29 × 34 in. (73.6 × 86.3 cm.), The Hayden Collection, The Museum of Fine Arts, Boston, MA. Copyright 1993/All rights reserved.

This book was set in New Baskerville by Americomp and was printed and bound by Rand McNally. The cover was printed by New England Book Components, Inc.

Acknowledgments appear on pages iii–xi, which constitute a continuation of the copyright page.

Macmillan Publishing Company
866 Third Avenue, New York, New York 10022

Macmillan Publishing Company is part of the Maxwell Communications Group of Companies.

Maxwell Macmillan Canada, Inc.
1200 Eglinton Avenue East
Suite 200
Don Mills, Ontario M3C 3N1

Library of Congress Cataloging-in-Publication Data

Literature / [compiled by] James H. Pickering, Jeffrey D. Hoeper.—
    4th ed.
        p.   cm.
    Includes index.
        ISBN 0-02-395581-3 (paper)
        1. Literature—Collections.   I. Pickering, James H.   II. Hoeper,
Jeffrey D.
PN6014.L558   1994
808'.0427—dc20
                                                              93-34
                                                              CIP

Printing: 1 2 3 4 5 6 7   Year: 4 5 6 7 8 9 0

ACKNOWLEDGMENTS

"The Necklace" by GUY DE MAUPASSANT from *Boule de Suif and Other Short Stories* by Guy de Maupassant, translated by Marjorie Laurie. Reprinted by permission of The Bodley Head.

"The Darling" from *The Darling and Other Stories* by ANTON CHEKHOV. Translated from the Russian by Constance Garnett. Reprinted by permission of Macmillan Publishing Company.

"Araby" and "The Dead" from *Dubliners* by JAMES JOYCE. Copyright 1916 by B. W. Huebsch. Definitive text copyright © 1967 by the Estate of James Joyce. Used by permission of Viking Penguin, a division of Penguin Books USA Inc.

"A Jury of Her Peers" by SUSAN GLASPELL. Reprinted by permission of Daphne C. Cook and the Estate of Susan Glaspell.

"The Hunger Artist," from *The Penal Colony* by FRANZ KAFKA, translated by Willa and Edwin Muir. Translation copyright 1948 and renewed 1970 by Schocken Books, Inc. Reprinted by permission of Schocken Books, published by Pantheon Books, a division of Random House, Inc.

"The Fly," from *The Garden Party* by KATHERINE MANSFIELD. Copyright 1922 by Alfred A. Knopf, Inc. and renewed 1950 by John Middleton Murry. Reprinted by permission of Alfred A. Knopf, Inc.

"The Witness for the Prosecution" by AGATHA CHRISTIE. Reprinted by permission of The Putnam Publishing Group from *Witness for the Prosecution* by Agatha Christie. Copyright © 1924 by Agatha Christie Mallowan.

"Hills Like White Elephants" from *The Short Stories of Ernest Hemingway* by ERNEST HEMINGWAY. Copyright 1938 by Ernest Hemingway, renewed © 1966 by Mary Hemingway. Reprinted by permission of Charles Scribner's Sons, an imprint of Macmillan Publishing Company.

"A Rose for Emily," from *Collected Stories of William Faulkner* by WILLIAM FAULKNER. Copyright 1930 and renewed 1958 by William Faulkner. Reprinted by permission of Random House, Inc. "Barn Burning," from *Collected Stories of William Faulkner* by William Faulkner. Copyright © 1950 by Random House, Inc. and renewed 1977 by Jill Faulkner Summers. Reprinted by permission of Random House, Inc.

"The Rocking-Horse Winner" by D. H. LAWRENCE, copyright 1933 by the Estate of D. H. Lawrence, renewed © 1961 by Angelo Ravagli and C. M. Weekley, Executors of the Estate of Frieda Lawrence, from *Complete Short Stories of D. H. Lawrence*. Used by permission of Viking Penguin, a division of Penguin Books USA, Inc.

"The Astronomer's Wife," from *The White Horses of Vienna and Other Stories* by KAY BOYLE. Reprinted by permission of Watkins/Loomis Agency, Inc.

Hughes. Copyright 1926 by Alfred A. Knopf, Inc. and renewed 1954 by Langston Hughes. "Dream Deferred" ("Harlem") from *The Panther and the Lash* by Langston Hughes. Copyright © 1951 by Langston Hughes. Reprinted by permission of Alfred A. Knopf, Inc. "Theme for English B" and "Advice" by Langston Hughes from *Montage of a Dream Deferred*, 1951, published by Henry Holt & Co. Reprinted by permission of Harold Ober Associates Incorporated. Copyright 1951 by Langston Hughes. Copyright renewed 1979 by George Houston Bass.

From *The Collected Poems of William Butler Yeats* by WILLIAM BUTLER YEATS, copyright © 1956 by Macmillan Publishing Company: "The Lake Isle of Innisfree," (also appears in *The Poems of W. B. Yeats: A New Edition*, edited by Richard J. Finneran, 1983); "The Wild Swans at Coole," copyright 1919 by Macmillan Publishing Company, renewed 1947 by Bertha Georgie Yeats; "The Second Coming," copyright 1924 by Macmillan Publishing Company, renewed 1952 by Bertha Georgie Yeats; "Leda and the Swan" and "Sailing to Byzantium," copyright 1928 by Macmillan Publishing Company, renewed 1956 by Bertha Georgie Yeats. Reprinted by permission of Macmillan Publishing Company.

Sonnet XXX ("Love Is Not All") of *Fatal Interview* by EDNA ST. VINCENT MILLAY. From *Collected Poems of Edna St. Vincent Millay*, HarperCollins. Copyright © 1931, 1958 by Edna St. Vincent Millay and Norma Millay Ellis. Reprinted by permission of Elizabeth Barnett, literary executor. "Time Does Not Bring Relief," "Witch-Wife," and "Afternoon on a Hill," from *Collected Poems of Edna St. Vincent Millay*, HarperCollins. Copyright 1917, 1945 by Edna St. Vincent Millay.

"Résumé," copyright 1926, 1928, renewed 1954, © 1966 by DOROTHY PARKER from *The Portable Dorothy Parker* by Dorothy Parker, Introduction by Brendan Gill. Used by permission of Viking Penguin, a division of Penguin Books USA, Inc.

"E=mc²" by MORRIS BISHOP from *The Best of Bishop: Light Verse from the New Yorker and Elsewhere* (Ithaca, NY: Cornell University Press). Copyright © 1946, 1974 by Alison Kinsbury Bishop. This selection originally appeared in *The New Yorker*. Reprinted by permission of *The New Yorker*.

"Buffalo Bill's," "in Just-" "nobody loses all the time," "next to of course god america i," " my sweet old etcetera," "anyone lived in a pretty how town," and "pity this busy monster,manunkind" by E. E. CUMMINGS. Reprinted from *Complete Poems, 1904–1962*, by E. E. Cummings, edited by George J. Firmage, by permission of the Liveright Publishing Corporation. Copyright © 1923, 1925, 1926, 1931, 1935, 1938, 1939, 1940, 1944, 1945, 1946, 1947, 1948, 1949, 1950, 1951, 1952, 1953, 1954, 1955, 1956, 1957, 1958, 1959, 1960, 1961, 1962 by E. E. Cummings. Copyright © 1961, 1963, 1966, 1967, 1968, by Marion Morehouse Cummings. Copyright © 1972, 1973, 1974, 1975, 1976, 1977, 1978, 1979, 1980, 1981, 1982, 1983, 1984, 1985, 1986, 1987, 1988, 1989, 1990, 1991 by Trustees for the E. E. Cummings Trust.

"Reapers" by JEAN TOOMER. "Reapers" is reprinted from *Cane* by Jean Toomer, by permission of Liveright Publishing Corporation. Copyright 1923 by Boni & Liveright. Copyright renewed 1951 by Jean Toomer.

"Women" from *The Blue Estuaries* by Louise Bogan. Copyright © 1968 by Louise Bogan. Reprinted by permission of Farrar, Straus & Giroux, Inc.

"Black Tambourine" by HART CRANE. "Black Tambourine" is reprinted from *The Complete Poems and Selected Letters and Prose of Hart Crane*, edited by Brom Weber, by permission of Liveright Publishing Corporation. Copyright © 1933, 1958, 1966 by Liveright Publishing Corporation.

"Very Like a Whale," from *Verses from 1929 On* by OGDEN NASH. Copyright 1934 by The Curtis Publishing Company. By permission of Little, Brown and Company.

"Yet Do I Marvel," "For a Lady I Know," and "Incident" by COUNTEE CULLEN. Reprinted by permission of GRM Associates, Inc., Agents for the Estate of Ida M. Cullen. From the book *Color* by Countee Cullen. Copyright © 1925 by Harper & Brothers; copyright renewed 1953 by Ida M. Cullen.

"The Conquerors," copyright © 1958 by PHYLLIS McGINLEY, "The 5:32," copyright 1941 by Phyllis McGinley, "Reflections Outside a Gymnasium," copyright 1936 by Phyllis McGinley, from *Times Three* by Phyllis McGinley. "Portrait of Girl with Comic Book," copyright 1952 by Phyllis McGinley, originally appeared in *The New Yorker*, from *Times Three* by Phyllis McGinley. Used by permission of Viking Penguin, a division of Penguin Books USA, Inc.

"Reason" from *Poems 1930–1969* by JOSEPHINE MILES. Reprinted by permission of Indiana University Press.

"The Ladder" from *Naked Heel* by LEONORA SPEYER. Copyright 1931 by Leonora Speyer and renewed 1959 by Countess Pamela Moy and Mrs. Leonora Speyer, Jr. Reprinted by permission of Alfred A. Knopf, Inc.

"Disillusionment of Ten O'Clock," "Peter Quince at the Clavier," "Anecdote of the Jar," and "The Emperor of Ice-Cream," by WALLACE STEVENS from *The Collected Poems of Wallace Stevens*. Copyright 1923 and renewed 1951 by Wallace Stevens. Reprinted by permission of Alfred A. Knopf, Inc.

"Barter" from *Collected Poems* by SARA TEASDALE. Copyright 1917 by Macmillan Publishing Company, renewed 1945 by Mamie T. Wheless. Reprinted by permission of Macmillan Publishing Company.

"In a Station of the Metro" and "Ancient Music" from EZRA POUND, *Personae*. Copyright 1926 by Ezra Pound. Reprinted by permission of New Directions Publishing Corp. and Faber and Faber Ltd.

"Hurt Hawks," from *The Selected Poetry of Robinson Jeffers* by ROBINSON JEFFERS. Copyright 1928 and renewed 1956 by Robinson Jeffers. Reprinted by permission of Random House.

"Poetry" from *Collected Poems* by MARIANNE MOORE. Copyright 1935 by Marianne Moore, renewed 1963 by Marianne Moore and T. S. Eliot. Reprinted by permission of Macmillan Publishing Company.

"The Love Song of J. Alfred Prufrock" and "Journey of the Magi" from *Collected Poems 1909–1962* by T. S. ELIOT, copyright 1936 by Harcourt Brace & Company, copyright © 1963, 1964 by T. S. Eliot, reprinted by permission of the publisher.

"Harlem Dancer" and "If We Must Die" by CLAUDE MCKAY from *Selected Poems of Claude McKay*, published by Harcourt Brace Jovanovich, 1981. By permission of Archives of Claude McKay, Carl Cowl, Administrator.

"Those Winter Sundays" by ROBERT HAYDEN. "Those Winter Sundays" is reprinted from *Angle of Ascent, New and Selected Poems*, by Robert Hayden, by permission of Liveright Publishing Corporation. Copyright © 1975, 1972, 1970, 1966 by Robert Hayden.

"Drug Store" and "Auto Wreck" by KARL SHAPIRO. Copyright © 1987 by Karl Shapiro by arrangement with Wieser & Wieser, Inc., 118 East 25th St., New York, NY 10010.

"The Force That Through the Green Fuse Drives the Flower," "Fern Hill," and "Do Not Go Gentle into that Good Night," by DYLAN THOMAS, from *Poems of Dylan Thomas*. Copyright 1939, 1946 by New Directions Publishing Corp., 1945 by Trustees for the Copyrights of Dylan Thomas, 1952 by Dylan Thomas. Reprinted by permission of New Directions Publishing Corp.

"The Death of the Ball Turret Gunner" and "Eighth Air Force" from *The Complete Poems* by RANDALL JARRELL. Copyright © 1969 by Mrs. Randall Jarrell. Reprinted by permission of Farrar, Straus & Giroux, Inc.

"Skunk Hour" and "The Mouth of the Hudson" from *Life Studies* and *For the Union Dead* by ROBERT LOWELL. Copyright renewed © 1987, 1992 by Harriet Lowell, Caroline Lowell, and Sheridan Lowell. Reprinted by permission of Farrar, Straus & Giroux, Inc.

"Constantly Risking Absurdity" from LAWRENCE FERLINGHETTI, *A Coney Island of the Mind*. Copyright © 1958 by Lawrence Ferlinghetti. Reprinted by permission of New Directions Publishing Corp.

"A Smile for Her Smile" and "Museum Piece" from *Ceremony and Other Poems*, copyright 1950 and renewed 1978 by RICHARD WILBUR, reprinted by permission of Harcourt Brace & Company. "Sleepless at Crown Point" from *The Mind-Reader*, copyright © 1973 by Richard Wilbur, reprinted by permission of Harcourt Brace & Company. "The Star System," an excerpt from "Flippancies" in *The Mind-Reader*, copyright © 1975 by Richard Wilbur, reprinted by permission of Harcourt Brace & Company.

"I Am a Black Woman" by MARI EVANS, published by William Morrow & Co., 1970, by permission of the author.

"Love Song: I and Thou" by ALAN DUGAN, © 1961, 1962, 1968, 1972, 1973, 1974, 1983 by Alan Dugan. From *New and Collected Poems, 1961–1983* by Alan Dugan, first published by The Ecco Press in 1983. Reprinted by permission.

"More Light! More Light!" from *Collected Earlier Poems* by ANTHONY E. HECHT. Copyright © 1990 by Anthony E. Hecht. Reprinted by permission of Alfred A. Knopf, Inc. "The Dover Bitch" by Anthony E. Hecht. Reprinted by permission of Macmillan Publishing Company.

"At the Edge" from DENISE LEVERTOV, *Collected Earlier Poems, 1940–1960*. Copyright © 1959 by Denise Levertov Goodman. Reprinted by permission of New Directions Publishing Corp.

"First Snow in Lake County" by LISEL MUELLER from *Learning to Play by Ear*, Juniper Press, La Crosse, WI, 1990. © by Lisel Mueller.

"Together" by MAXINE KUMIN published in *The Nightmare Factory*, 1970. Reprinted by permission of Curtis Brown, Ltd. Copyright © 1970 by Maxine Kumin. "Woodchucks," copyright © 1971 by Maxine Kumin, from *Our Ground Time Here Will Be Brief* by Maxine Kumin. Used by permission of Viking Penguin, a division of Penguin Books USA, Inc.

"Bitch" by CAROLYN KIZER from *Mermaids in the Basement*. Copyright © 1984 by Carolyn Kizer. Reprinted by permission of Copper Canyon Press, P.O. Box 271, Port Townsend, WA 98368.

"I Know a Man" from *For Love: Poems 1950–1960* by ROBERT CREELEY. Reprinted by permission of Charles Scribner's Sons, an imprint of Macmillan Publishing Company.

"Curiosity" by ALASTAIR REID from *Weathering* (E.P. Dutton). © 1959, 1988 Alastair Reid, "Curiosity" originally appeared in *The New Yorker*. Reprinted by special permission.

"April Inventory," from *Heart's Needle* by W. D. SNODGRASS. Copyright © 1957 by W. D. Snodgrass. Reprinted by permission of Alfred A. Knopf, Inc.

"Meeting a Bear" and "Walking in a Swamp" by DAVID WAGONER from *Collected Poems, 1956–1976*, copyright 1976 by David Wagoner. Reprinted by permission of the author.

"A Blessing," "Autumn Begins in Martins Ferry, Ohio," "Lying in a Hammock at William Duffy's Farm in Pine Island, Minnesota" by JAMES WRIGHT from *The Branch Will Not Break*, copyright 1963 by James Wright. Reprinted by permission of Wesleyan University Press by permission of University Press of New England.

"Blackberry Eating" from *Mortal Acts, Mortal Words* by GALWAY KINNELL. Copyright © 1980 by Galway Kinnell. Reprinted by permission of Houghton Mifflin Company. All rights reserved.

"Leviathan," by W. S. MERWIN, from *Green with Beasts*, © 1956 by W. S. Merwin. "The Drunk in the Furnace," from *The Drunk in the Furnace*, © 1960 by W. S. Merwin. Reprinted by permission of Georges Borchardt, Inc., Literary Agency.

"Lullaby" and "Her Kind" from *To Bedlam and Part Way Back* by ANNE SEXTON. Copyright © 1960 by Anne Sexton. Reprinted by permission of Houghton Mifflin Company. All rights reserved. "The Truth the Dead Know" from *All My Pretty Ones* by Anne Sexton. Copyright © 1962 by Anne Sexton, copyright renewed 1990 by Linda G. Sexton. Reprinted by permission of Houghton Mifflin Company. All rights reserved.

"My Arkansas," from *And Still I Rise* by MAYA ANGELOU. Copyright © 1978 by Maya Angelou. Reprinted by permission of Random House, Inc. "The Health Food Diner," from *Shaker, Why Don't You Sing?* by Maya Angelou. Copyright © 1983 by Maya Angelou. Reprinted by permission of Random House, Inc. "On the Pulse of Morning" from *On the Pulse of Morning* by Maya Angelou. Copyright © 1993 by Maya Angelou. Reprinted by permission of Random House, Inc.

"Two Brothers in a Field of Absence," from *Living Wills* by CYNTHIA MACDONALD. Copyright © 1990 by Cynthia MacDonald. Reprinted by permission of Alfred A. Knopf, Inc.

"Oystering" by RICHARD HOWARD, from *The Damages*, copyright 1984 by Richard Howard. Reprinted by permission of Wesleyan University Press by permission of University Press of New England.

"Cross Ties," from *Cross Ties: Selected Poems* by X. J. KENNEDY. Reprinted by permission of the University of Georgia Press.

"Aunt Jennifer's Tigers," "Storm Warnings" and "The Knight" by ADRIENNE RICH. Reprinted from *Collected Early Poems, 1950–1970*, by Adrienne Rich, by permission of W. W. Norton & Company, Inc. Copyright © 1993 by Adrienne Rich. Copyright © 1967, 1963, 1962, 1961, 1960, 1959, 1958, 1957, 1956, 1955, 1954, 1953, 1952, 1951 by Adrienne Rich. Copyright © 1984, 1975, 1971, 1969, 1966 by W. W. Norton & Company, Inc.

"Pike," from *New Selected Poems*, by TED HUGHES. Copyright © 1959 by Ted Hughes. "An Otter," from *Lupercal* by Ted Hughes. Copyright © 1960 by Ted Hughes. Reprinted by permission of HarperCollins Publishers.

"Flower Feet" © 1989 RUTH FAINLIGHT. Originally in *The New Yorker*. Reprinted by special permission.

"Margaret Are You Drug," from "Translations From the English" from *White Paper* by GEORGE STARBUCK. Copyright © 1965 by George Starbuck. First appeared in *The Atlantic Monthly*. By permission of Little, Brown and Company.

"Advice to My Son" by PETER MEINKE. Copyright © 1965 by The Antioch Review, Inc. First appeared in *The Antioch Review*, Vol. 25, No. 3 (Fall 1965). Reprinted by permission of the editors.

"Jump Cabling" by LINDA PASTAN from *Light Year '85* (Bits Press). Reprinted by permission of the author. "Ethics" and "Marks" by Linda Pastan. Reprinted from *PM/AM: New and Selected Poems* by Linda Pastan, by permission of W. W. Norton & Company, Inc. Copyright © 1982 by Linda Pastan.

"Telephone Conversation" by WOLE SOYINKA. Reprinted by permission of Brandt & Brandt Literary Agents, Inc.

"To Be of Use," "A Work of Artifice," and "The Woman in the Ordinary" from *Circles on the Water* by MARGE PIERCY. Copyright © 1982 by Marge Piercy. Reprinted by permission of Alfred A. Knopf, Inc.

"The Lover Not Taken" by BLANCHE FARLEY. Reprinted by permission of the author.

"Rondeau: An Un-Love Song" by AMY JO SCHOONOVER. Originally appeared in *The Spoon River Quarterly*. Reprinted by permission of Amy Jo Schoonover and *The Spoon River Quarterly*.

"Middle Age: A Nocturne" by ROBERT PHILLIPS from *Personal Accounts*, 1986. Reprinted by permission of Ontario Review Press.

"Portrait," by PATTIANN ROGERS from *Expectations of Light*, 1981. Copyright © 1981 by Princeton University Press. Reprinted by permission of Princeton University Press.

"Sex Without Love" from *The Dead and the Living* by SHARON OLDS. Copyright © 1983 by Sharon Olds. Reprinted by permission of Alfred A. Knopf, Inc.

"Poetry" from *The Women and the Men* by NIKKI GIOVANNI. Copyright © 1975 by Nikki Giovanni. By permission of William Morrow & Company, Inc.

"Loo-Wit" by WENDY ROSE from *The Halfbreed Chronicles,* West End Press, published 1985, reprinted 1992. Reprinted by permission of the author.

"Back from the Word-Processing Course, I Say to My Old Typewriter," copyright 1984 by MICHAEL BLUMENTHAL from *Days We Would Rather Know: Poems by Michael Blumenthal,* published by the Viking Press. Reprinted by permission of Rosenstone/Wender, agents for the author.

"Dance of the Moon," from *For the Sleepwalkers* by EDWARD HIRSCH. Copyright © 1981 by Edward Hirsch. Reprinted by permission of Alfred A. Knopf, Inc.

"Exile" by RICK LOTT. First appeared in *Poetry*, May 1991, copyright © 1991 by The Modern Poetry Association. Reprinted by permission of the Editor of *Poetry* and the author.

"The White Porch" by CATHY SONG from *Picture Bride,* Yale University Press, 1983. Reprinted by permission of Yale University Press.

"Deer Harvest" by LESLIE ADRIENNE MILLER from *Staying Up for Love,* 1990. Reprinted by permission of Carnegie Mellon University Press.

Sophocles' King Oedipus by SOPHOCLES translated by William Butler Yeats from *The Collected Plays of W. B. Yeats.* Copyright 1934, 1952 by Macmillan Publishing Company, renewed 1980 by Macmillan Publishing Company. Reprinted by permission of Macmillan Publishing Company.

Lysistrata, by ARISTOPHANES, from *Lysistrata* by Aristophanes, translated by Douglas Parker. Translation copyright © 1964 by William Arrowsmith. Used by permission of New American Library, a division of Penguin Books USA, Inc.

The Cherry Orchard by ANTON CHEKHOV, from *Anton Chekhov: Four Plays,* translated by David Magarshack. Copyright © 1969 by David Magarshack. Reprinted by permission of Hill and Wang, a division of Farrar, Straus & Giroux, Inc.

Trifles by SUSAN GLASPELL. Reprinted by permission of Daphne C. Cook and the Estate of Susan Glaspell.

Desire Under the Elms, from *The Plays of Eugene O'Neill* by EUGENE O'NEILL. Copyright 1924 and renewed 1952 by Eugene O'Neill. Reprinted by permission of Alfred A. Knopf, Inc.

The Glass Menagerie, from *The Glass Menagerie* by TENNESSEE WILLIAMS. Copyright 1945 by Tennessee Williams and Edwina D. Willliams and renewed 1973 by Tennessee Williams. Reprinted by permission of Random House, Inc.

A Raisin in the Sun, from *A Raisin in the Sun* by LORRAINE HANSBERRY. Copyright 1958 by Robert Nemiroff, as an unpublished work. Copyright © 1959, 1966, 1984 by Robert Nemiroff. Copyright renewed 1987 by Robert Nemiroff. Reprinted by permission of Random House, Inc.

The Strong Breed by WOLE SOYINKA. © Oxford University Press 1964. Reprinted from Wole Soyinka's *Collected Plays 1* (1973) by permission of Oxford University Press.

Wine in the Wilderness, by ALICE CHILDRESS. Copyright © 1969 by Alice Childress. CAUTION: *Wine in the Wilderness,* being duly copyrighted, is subject to a royalty. The amateur acting rights in the play are controlled exclusively by the Dramatists Play Service, Inc., 440 Park Avenue South, New York, N.Y. 10016. No amateur performance of the play may be given without obtaining in advance the written permission of Dramatists Play Service, Inc. and paying the requisite fee.

True West, copyright © 1981 by SAM SHEPARD. From *Seven Plays* by Sam Shepard. Used by permission of Bantam Books, a division of Bantam Doubleday Dell Publishing Group, Inc.

Am I Blue? by BETH HENLEY. Copyright, 1982, by Beth Henley. Reprinted by permission of William Morris Agency, literary agent for the author. CAUTION: Professionals and amateurs are hereby warned that *Am I Blue?* is subject to a royalty. It is fully protected under the copyright laws of the United States of America, and of all the countries covered by the International Copyright Union (including the Dominion of Canada and the rest of the British Commonwealth), and of

PREFACE

❧❧❧❧❧❧❧

Literature is a comprehensive anthology of fiction, poetry, and drama designed to introduce students to the formal study of literature. Throughout its four editions, excellence has been the one indispensable criterion in our choice of stories, poems, and plays. We have sought to retain and to add works of outstanding literary merit that introductory students will find both entertaining and thought-provoking. The fourth edition includes 57 stories (17 of them new); over 400 poems (60 new); and 16 plays (6 new). As a matter of convenience, the selections within each section are arranged chronologically—except for the stories and poems used as examples in the chapters on the elements of fiction and poetry.

Within the scope of a single volume it would be presumptuous to attempt a complete survey of world literature, but we have cast a careful critical eye over the vast sweep of the literary landscape from the Greeks of the Golden Age (500 B.C.) to the minimalists of the present. In addition, we have attempted to choose works that illustrate the full range of literary possibilities in each of the three genres. We have also made an effort to mirror the cultural diversity characteristic of North America. Thus, over half of all the selections from the modern period are by women and minorities.

An introductory course in literature is perhaps most valuable because it can help students develop their abilities to read carefully and to articulate thoughtfully their responses to what they have read. This text facilitates such cognitive development by beginning with a chapter on "Reading, Studying, and Writing About Literature" that provides basic definitions, essential guidelines, and appropriate model essays for student writing assignments. Although we have kept our advice brief, we do introduce the student to the process of writing a literary analysis or explication and the use of MLA documentation.

Each of *Literature's* three sections is prefaced by a discussion of the elements that go into the making of a story, a poem, or a play and the way in which such elements relate to each other and to the work as a whole. The intention is to provide both a method of literary analysis and a useful critical vocabulary that can be transferred from one text to another. We believe that such an analytical approach—alone or in combination with thematic, historical, sociological, or psychological approaches—will encourage students to sharpen and clarify their responses to literature and equip them to articulate these responses.

Literature is intended to be a flexible text that presents the instructor with a generous assortment of literary works and encourages a variety of course structures to explore those works. The genre approach is but one of many possibilities. Our chronological arrangement of works within the genres encourages the historical study of literature. The "Thematic Contents" facilitates a focus on related themes and topics. The study of individual authors is also made possible by the inclusion of multiple works by such writers as Hawthorne, Poe, Faulkner, Oates, Walker, Shakespeare, Donne, Blake, Wordsworth, Keats, Dickinson, Housman, Yeats, Frost, Millay, cummings, Hughes, and Brooks. The alphabetically-arranged "Handbook for Literary Study" at the end of the text provides definitions, examples, and cross-references for everything from Old Comedy to New Criticism, from Renaissance to Deconstruction, and from Alliteration to Zeugma. Wherever possible, the definitions in this handbook are illustrated with examples taken from the works included in *Literature*. As an aid to library research, we have listed a number of the standard sources that students and faculty may wish to consult on advanced topics such as deconstruction, reader-response criticism, New Criticism, and their kin.

In editing the anthology, we have been governed by the desire to reprint authoritative versions of each work in a format that modern students will find understandable and enjoyable. Thus, we have consistently chosen to use modern prose translations of works originally written in foreign languages. Furthermore, we have made liberal use of footnotes and marginal glosses to ease the student's introduction to such early English masters as Chaucer and Shakespeare. We have also modernized punctuation, capitalization, and spelling wherever such changes would alter neither the pronunciation nor meaning. Where several versions of a particular poem are equally defensible, we have chosen the version we judged to have the greatest literary merit.

At the end of each selection, we have enclosed a date in brackets. For stories, this represents the date of first publication. For poems, it is the date of first publication in a book. And for plays, it is the date of first production. Because a poem's title is often important to its interpretation, we have bracketed those titles that have been imposed only by editorial tradition. When a poem's first line serves as its title, we have enclosed it in quotation marks unless it was used as the title by the author in the original published version.

This book owes much to our students, whose responses continue to guide the selection of stories, poems, and plays. We are also grateful to a number of colleagues across the country who have shared with us the fruits of their years of classroom experience. Those who offered comments and suggestions for the fourth edition include David R. Anderson, Texas A&M University; Judith Mattson Bean, Texas A&M University; Larry Beason, Eastern Washington University; Richard Bonin, Gonzaga University; Sherill Cobb, Collin Community College; Jeffrey N. Cox, Texas A&M University; Norma L. Gaskey, Jefferson Community College; Louis Gallo, Radford University; Ruth A. Gerik, University of Texas at Arlington; Giles Gregory Hall, Jr., Virginia State University; Dalla Lacy, The University of

Texas at Arlington; Jane Helm Maddock, Western Montana College; Louis J.
Masson, The University of Portland; Sherry Newell, Cameron University; Walter F.
Utroske, Eastern Montana College; Mark Vogel, Applachian State University; Lynn
West, Spokane Community College; Verity Whitley, Blackhawk College; David
Wickham, Mountain View College; and William Zak, Salisbury State University.
We have tried to incorporate as many suggestions as possible from these and other
instructors who have generously shared their thoughts and expertise with us.

Finally, we wish to acknowledge the contributions of the staff at Macmillan. We
are particularly grateful to D. Anthony English, the Editor-in-Chief of Macmillan's
College Division, who has worked closely with us over the past dozen years to make
sure that the text remains fresh and useable for each new class of college students.
With his help we are confident that the fourth edition of *Literature* is a better value
than ever before. In its twelfth year, we think this anthology presents students and
teachers with a generous "baker's dozen"—ample selections and high quality at
a very reasonable price.

JAMES H. PICKERING
Houston, Texas

JEFFREY D. HOEPER
Jonesboro, Arkansas

CONTENTS

❊❊❊❊❊❊❊

II POETRY 643

4 What Is Poetry? 645

5 Denotation and Connotation 654

6 Allusion 661

7 Repetition and Ambiguity 665

8 Puns and Paradoxes 673

III DRAMA 1055

Introduction

❧❧❧❧❧❧

Reading, Studying, and Writing About Literature

Our impulse to read literature is a universal one, answering a number of psychological needs that all of us, in certain moods and on certain occasions, share. Such needs, to be sure, vary greatly from individual to individual, for they are, in turn, the products of our separate tastes, experiences, and educations. They also vary *within* each of us; they shift and alter as we change and grow. Certain books that are "right" for us at one stage of life seem "wrong" or irrelevant later on. *The Wizard of Oz* and *Treasure Island* thrill us as children. While we may and do reread these classics in adulthood and find new pleasure in them, we are likely to find the quality of the experience quite different from the one remembered. Our reading tastes will also vary from one day to the next, depending on our current moods and intellectual and aesthetic needs. More than one professor of English, for example, has been known to teach Shakespeare or Melville by day, only to turn in the evening to the latest spy novel by John Le Carré. There is nothing particularly unusual in such a contrast for one may have many purposes in reading. Four of these purposes come at once to mind.

WHY WE READ

Reading for Escape

All of the works already mentioned—*The Wizard of Oz, Treasure Island,* the plays of William Shakespeare, and the novels and short stories of Herman Melville—offer exciting narratives that can be read uncritically simply because they allow us to escape the problems and responsibilities of our everyday lives and to participate, however briefly, in a world of experience that differs radically from our own. The average student is most likely to think of vicarious reading in terms of the spy or detective story or the science fiction or historical novel—any kind of fiction that is read for the fun of it. **But many works of literature, classics as well as pulps, survive precisely because they succeed in temporarily detaching us from time and place and transporting us to some imaginary world that we otherwise would never know.** Although some people tend to regard such a motive as adolescent or even anti-intellectual, the fact remains that literature flourishes, in part at least, because of the escape it affords our imaginations.

Reading to Learn

Literature offers the reader "knowledge" in the form of information. Part of our interest in works as different as Joseph Conrad's "The Secret Sharer," Geoffrey Chaucer's "The Miller's Tale," or Anton Chekhov's *The Cherry Orchard* lies in the fact that in reading them we gain a good deal of information about Southeast Asia, medieval England, or Czarist Russia—information that is all the more fascinating because it is part of the author's re-created world. Literature read in this way serves as a social document, giving us insight into the laws, customs, institutions, attitudes, and values of the time and place in which it was written or in which it is set.

When you think about it, there is scarcely a story, a poem, a play we read that doesn't offer us some new piece of information that broadens our knowledge of the world. Not all of this "knowledge" is particularly valuable, and much of it will be forgotten quickly. Some of it may, in fact, turn out to be misleading or even false—but history books, too, may be in error, and the errors in both sorts of literature at least teach us about the preconceptions of the times when such errors found their way into history and fiction.

Reading to Confront Experience

One of the most compelling aspects of literature is its relationship to human experience. **Reading is an act of engagement and participation. It is also, simultaneously, an act of clarification and discovery.** Literature allows us the chance to overcome, as perhaps no other medium can, the limitations of our own subjectivity and those limitations imposed by sex, age, social and economic conditions, and the times in which we live. Literary characters offer us immediate access to a wide range of human experiences we otherwise might never know. As readers we observe these characters' public lives, while also becoming privy to their innermost thoughts, feelings, and motivations. So intimate is this access that psychologists have traditionally found imaginative literature a rich source for case studies to illustrate theories of personality and behavior.

The relationship between literature and experience, however, is highly reciprocal. Just as literature allows us to participate in the experiences of others, so too it has the power to alter our attitudes and expectations. To know why we identify with one character and not another may tell us about the kind of person we are or aspire to be. If we are sensitive and perceptive readers, we can learn from these encounters to enrich the quality and alter the direction of our lives, though the extent of such learning is impossible to predict and will vary from one reader to the next. One mark of a "great" work of literature is its ability to affect nearly every reader, and this affective power of fiction, drama, and poetry helps to explain the survival of those works we regard as "classics." James Joyce's "The Dead," William Shakespeare's *Othello,* and the poems of Robert Frost, for example, survive as "classics" because they have offered generations of readers the opportunity to clarify and modify their views of life, and also because they shed light on the complexity and ambiguity of human existence.

Reading for Aesthetic Pleasure

We also read for the sheer aesthetic pleasure of observing good artistry. And if, as the poet John Keats insisted, "A thing of beauty is a joy forever," then well-ordered and well-chosen words are certainly one form of immortality. Whatever its other uses, a poem, a play, or a novel is a self-contained work of art, with a describable structure and style. Sensitive and experienced readers will respond to unified stylistic effects, though they may not be initially conscious of exactly what they are responding to, or why. When that response is a positive one, we speak of our sense of pleasure or delight, in much the same way that we respond to a painting, a piece of sculpture, or a musical composition. If we push our inquiry further and try to analyze our response, we begin to move in the direction of literary criticism.

LITERARY CRITICISM

Contrary to rumor, literary criticism is not always an exercise in human ingenuity that professors of English engage in for its own sake. Neither is the word *criticism* to be confused with the kind of petty faultfinding we sometimes encounter in caustic book reviews. **Literary criticism is nothing more or less than an attempt to clarify, explain, and evaluate our experience with a given literary work.** It allows us to explain what we see in a literary work that others may have missed or seen less clearly. It allows us to raise and then answer, however tentatively, certain basic questions about an author's achievement and about the ways in which he or she achieved it. It also allows us to form some judgments about the relative merit or quality of the work as a whole. Literary criticism is a method of learning about literature, and the more we learn about how to approach a story, poem, or play, the greater our appreciation of a truly great work becomes, and greater still the sense of pleasure and enjoyment we can derive from it.

Literary criticism is the inevitable by-product of the reading process itself, for if we take that experience seriously, then criticism of some sort becomes inevitable. The only question is whether the judgments we form will be sensible ones. Literary criticism begins the moment we close our book and start to reflect on what we have just read. At that moment, to be sure, we have a choice. If we have been engaged in light reading, say in a detective story, where our interest and curiosity are satisfied once the solution to the crime is revealed and the criminal apprehended, we may simply put the book aside without a second thought and turn to weightier matters. Such an act, in itself, is a judgment. But if our reading has moved us intellectually or emotionally, we may find ourselves pausing to explore or explain our responses. If, in turn, we choose to organize and define those responses and to communicate them to someone else—to a parent, a roommate, or a close friend—we have in that moment become a literary critic.

The nature of literary criticism and the role of the critic have been simplified in this example for the sake of making a point; however, the illustration is a perfectly valid one. **Criticism is the act of reflecting on, organizing, and then articulating, usually on paper, our response to a given literary work.** Such an activity does not, however, take place in a vacuum. Like all organized fields of academic study, the study of literature rests on at least three key assumptions that critics and readers must be willing to accept. Literary criticism, first of all, presupposes that a piece of literature contains relationships and patterns of meaning that the reader-critic can discover and share. Without such prior agreement, of course, there can be no criticism, for by definition there would be nothing worthy of communication. Second, literary criticism presupposes the ability of the reader-turned-critic to translate his or her experience of the work into intellectual terms that can be communicated to and understood by others. Third, literary criticism presupposes that the critic's experience of the work, once organized and articulated, will be generally compatible with the experience of other readers. This is not to imply that critics and other readers will always see eye to eye, for of course they don't and never will. It *is* to say that **to be valid and valuable the critic's reading of a work must accord, at least in a general way, with what other intelligent readers over a reasonable period of time are willing to agree on or at least accept as plausible.**

To move from this general consideration of the function of literary criticism to the ways in which it can profitably be applied to the study of a given work of fiction, poetry, or drama is our task in the pages that follow. The approach we have chosen in this book is an ***analytical*** one that attempts to increase the understanding and appreciation of literature by introducing students to the typical devices, or ***elements,*** that comprise a story, a poem, or a play and to the way in which these elements relate to each other and to the work as a whole. Such an approach has much to recommend it to the student coming to the formal study of literature for the first time.

To begin with, **the analytical approach provides a critical vocabulary of such key terms as** *point of view, character, image, scene,* **and** *protagonist.* Such a set of generally agreed-upon definitions is essential if we are to discuss a work intelligently. Without the appropriate vocabulary we cannot organize our responses to a work or share them. A common vocabulary allows us to move our discussion from one literary work to another—it allows us to discuss *literature,* not just individual and isolated literary works. The theory and vocabulary of the elements of literature, along with their application to literary analysis, are neither remote nor arcane. They are the working tools of authors, critics, and intelligent readers. **Their great virtue is the common ground they provide for discussing, describing, studying, and ultimately appreciating a literary work.**

A second advantage of the analytical approach follows from the first. In order to identify and describe the various elements in a text and their interrelationship, we must ask and then attempt to answer certain basic questions about the text itself: What is the story's point of view and how does it influence our knowledge of the characters? What are the central images of the poem and how do they relate to one another? How do each of the play's scenes contribute to our understanding of the protagonist? Such questions and their answers help us not only to determine what the work says and means but also to form value judgments about how effectively (or ineffectively) the author has used his or her material.

The analytical method is just one of a number of approaches that may be taken in the study of literature. It is, however, the cornerstone of literary criticism. In emphasizing a literary work itself and the terminology useful in describing that work, the analytical method provides a framework for other critical approaches. Just as some buildings—ranging from log cabins to castles—make their structural supports the focus of attention, so too many critical essays emphasize the formal and structural elements of literature. Other buildings, however, conceal their framing timbers behind walls of stucco, stone, or wood. Similarly, other forms of criticism use the analysis of a literary work's elements as support to emphasize the relationships between the literary work and its author, its reader, or its place in history. Each of these critical approaches deserves attention. In the beginning, however, we must give priority to literary analysis; before we can profitably turn to the larger implications of a literary work, that work itself must be understood.

WRITING ABOUT LITERATURE

Most of the writing you will be asked to do in this course will require you to understand and analyze the ways in which individual works of literature convey their meaning to readers. For this reason, you must understand the elements of literature and be able to explain how they work together to make up the meaning of the entire literary work. Ordinarily, however, you will not need to be thoroughly grounded in literary history, the history of ideas, the author's biography, or any other form of specialized knowledge. An assignment focusing on the elements of literature requires only careful study of the work itself, sensitivity to the uses of language, and recognition of the ways in which language affects readers. Instructors tend to favor this form of assignment precisely *because* it demands so little specialized information of students and makes the text itself sufficient for the task at hand.

Explication

Essays focusing on the literary work alone generally fall into two categories: explication and analysis. An *explication* **(a term derived from a Latin word meaning** *unfolding***) is a detailed attempt to explain or unfold the entire meaning of a work.** Because explication is so detailed, it is normally limited to short poems or short prose passages that seem in some way central to the meaning of a story or play. Shakespeare's "Sonnet LXXIII" ("That time of year thou may'st in me behold") or one of Othello's soliloquies would make a fine topic for an explication. But the student who attempts to explicate *all* of the sonnets or *all* of *Othello* will end up writing a book, not an essay.

Typically, an explication begins with a brief paragraph identifying the poem or prose extract and explaining its place within the context of any larger work of which it is a part. You may also wish to identify the speaker, the situation, the setting, and the tone in this introductory paragraph. Remember, however, that the goal of the introduction is to present a general thesis isolating the key ideas that unify the poem or passage—and therefore unify the explication itself.

The body of the explication often unfolds through a line-by-line or idea-by-idea commentary on the entire piece. Because the reader cannot be assumed to have memorized the poem or passage, it should be quoted either in its entirety before the beginning of the explication or in coherent units (perhaps sentences or stanzas) as the explication itself takes them up. You are expected to identify and comment upon everything unusual or important in the lines under consideration. Remember that in general your reader will not have studied the passage with as much care as you have. **Your goal in an explication is to help the reader to see everything that you have discovered through patient and meticulous analysis.** Thus, the denotative meanings of any unfamiliar words must be explained; important connotations should be discussed; allusions, ambiguities, puns, paradoxes, and ironies should be identified and explained; images and image patterns should be considered; the various forms of figurative language (such as metaphor and simile) should be pointed out and their contribution to the development of the imagery and hence to the meaning of the poem should be analyzed; any symbols or allegorical systems of symbols should be discussed; and finally the contributions of rhythm and sound to the unfolding meaning of the poem should be examined. Each of these elements of poetry is defined and discussed in the introductory chapters on poetry.

At times, too, you may wish to consider elements most frequently associated with the study of fiction or drama (and therefore defined and discussed in those chapters). For example, an explication of Othello's meditations before he smothers Desdemona in act 5, scene 2, would certainly need to examine the contribution of the lines to the plot and to the characterization of Othello. Such an explication might also show how Othello's rhetorical flourishes and poetic diction contribute to Shakespeare's conception of his character. Of course, not all of the elements of literature will have an important role in any particular line of a poem or passage of prose, and therefore not all of them must be discussed in your explication. But each element should be considered during the process of study and evaluation that precedes writing.

The explication of a brief passage from a play, a short story, or a novel can often be used to provide important insights into the entire work. For example, the many comparisons in Othello's speech at the beginning of act 5, scene 2, may be taken as evidence of his fertile poetic imagination. He describes Desdemona's skin as whiter than snow and "smooth as monumental alabaster." He somewhat chillingly compares the murder he contemplates with quenching a light or plucking a rose. Like a poet, then, Othello tends to see things that he only imagines and to feel more passionately than ordinary men. From such insights, it is but a small step to the assertion that perhaps Othello's most pitiable human flaw is bound up in just this poetic tendency. Because he so easily makes imaginary events vivid and real (as he did, for example, in courting Desdemona with stories of his "battles, sieges, fortunes"), he is easily able to imagine all that Iago falsely tells him about Desdemona's wanton infidelity. In this way the explication of the poetic language in a very brief passage can serve as a microcosm, revealing insights about the character of Othello that help one to better understand the causes of his tragedy.

There is no rigid formula guiding the organization of an explication, though individual instructors may have preferences that you should attempt to find out in advance. The explication may unfold, as we have indicated, through a stanza-by-stanza (or sentence-by-sentence) analysis of everything that seems important. It may, however, also be organized in terms of the elements of literature themselves, with separate sections, for example, on poetic diction, figurative language, imagery, versification, and form. Keep in mind, however, that **the purpose of your explication is to explain fully to your reader what makes the passage meaningful, interesting, and effective.** An explication is not simply a piece of writing in which one demonstrates an understanding of literary terminology. Nor is it a mere paraphrase—or restatement—of the poem's literal meaning. Like any good essay, it should be organized in such a way that it develops a coherent thesis, and the number of words spent in the discussion of any particular element of the passage should be roughly proportional to the importance of that element in creating the meaning and in proving the essay's thesis. Typically, the essay's concluding paragraph redirects the reader's attention to that thesis in a final effort to show how the explication of the entire passage has led to a better understanding of its artistry and achievement.

An Explication of Shakespeare's "Sonnet LXXIII"

That time of year thou may'st in me behold
When yellow leaves, or none, or few, do hang
Upon those boughs which shake against the cold,
Bare ruined choirs, where late the sweet birds sang.
5 In me thou seest the twilight of such day,
As after sunset fadeth in the west,
Which by and by black night doth take away,
Death's second self, that seals up all in rest.
In me thou seest the glowing of such fire,
10 That on the ashes of his youth doth lie,
As the death-bed whereon it must expire,
Consumed with that which it was nourished by.
This thou perceiv'st, which makes thy love more strong,
To love that well which thou must leave ere long.

[1609]

William Shakespeare's "Sonnet LXXIII" begins as a poignant meditation on approaching death. It was written when Shakespeare was somewhere between the ages of twenty-nine and forty-five and, hence, may reflect his own feelings at a time when he was (by Renaissance standards) decidedly middle-aged. However, it is not certain that the poem is in any way autobiographical. Indeed, it is not even certain that the poem is addressed to a woman. What is certain is that in "Sonnet LXXIII" the speaker's death grows more imminent in each quatrain, and simultaneously the warmth of his attachment to the one he loves (and must soon leave!) increases.

The first four lines create a metaphor comparing the speaker's age and the season of autumn. Because this metaphor extends beyond what is needed to identify the speaker's age, we immediately expect there to be correspondences between the autumn woods and the autumnal man. In looking more closely, we may note the unusual order of the words "yellow leaves, or none, or few." Clearly, this series does not simply describe the progressive dropping of the leaves. Shakespeare's word order and the repetition of the conjunction "or" suggest an observation followed by two clarifications. In the autumn of a man's years what begins to change color and fall out is hair, not leaves—a condition with which Shakespeare was quite familiar, judging from the famous Droeshout portrait of the balding poet. The hesitations and clarifications in the series "yellow leaves, or none, or few" give the image an immediacy, as if the speaker were seeing himself clearly for the first time in years: "I'm grey! And bald! Or nearly so!"

   The similarities between the aging man and the autumnal tree
continue in line 3 with the reference to "those boughs which shake
against the cold, / Bare ruined choirs, where late the sweet birds
sang." A tree denuded ("bare") of its leaves has the general
appearance of a man, and its boughs, like thin, shivering arms,
shake in the cold breezes. Furthermore, a leafless tree with its
crisscrossing branches looks something like the open woodwork
that frequently screens the choir in a cathedral, but in late fall the
members of that choir, the songbirds, have departed. Perhaps, too,
in late middle-age it may sometimes seem as if the sweet song of a
man's youth—the high spirits and carnal desires—have taken flight
like birds in winter.
   The second quatrain moves us from the season of autumn to the
hour of sunset. Just as late fall is the end of the year, so twilight is
the end of the day. Just as the leaves that hang upon wintry trees
linger after turning yellow, so too the light that brightens the west
lingers after the sun has set. This sense of lingering is well brought
out by the poem's meter. Consider, for example, the scansion of
lines 5 and 6:

         In̆ me̅/ thŏu se̅e̅st/ the̅ twi̅/li̅ght ŏf/ sŭch da̅y,

         As̆ a̅f/tĕr su̅n/sĕt fa̅/dĕth in̆/ the̅ we̅st.

Unless we choose to stress the prepositions "of" and "in," the last
half of each line is dominated by unaccented syllables so that the
line lingers after its central idea has been expressed. This impression is augmented by the words "seest" and "fadeth"—in each of
which the second syllable actually seems to fade away and be almost unpronounced. This correspondence between sound and sense
also carries over into consonance and assonance. In each line
vowel sounds are echoed or reflected in almost the same way that
twilight is reflected from the clouds. In line 5 the long "e" of "me"
is repeated in "seest," and a long "i" is repeated in the two syllables of the word "twilight." In line 6 the short "a" of "as" reoccurs
in "after" and a sibilant "s" reoccurs in "sunset." In line 7 the explosive consonant "b" is repeated in the phrase "by and by black
night." At the same time, a long "i" echoes as a result of its repetition in the two "by's" and in "night." "Doth" in line 7 alliterates
with "death" in line 8, where we also have the alliteration of "second," "self," and "seals." Thus, the sounds in this quatrain linger
on, just as the light it describes does.
   The season of autumn, which was reduced to the hour of sunset
in the second quatrain, is further reduced in the third to the final
glowing moments of a fire. The speaker makes his bed on the ashes
of a youth that presumably was full of romantic attachments. If
this is his deathbed, it is so only because he is consumed by that
love which also nourishes him. The lines are rich in paradoxical

possibilities. Most literally, the speaker compares himself to a fire which is put out by rising ashes ("that which it was nourished by"). In this sense, the speaker is like those dissipated youths who are said to shorten their lives by "burning the candle at both ends." At one further remove, the speaker's deathbed is a bed of ashes, which in religious symbolism would suggest remorse. Taken together these two senses imply that the excesses of youth are catching up with the speaker, shortening his life, and driving him toward repentance.

In yet another sense, however, it is a deep bed of ashes that holds the fire overnight and makes possible its Phoenix-like rebirth the next morning. So far from repenting his past is this speaker that all of these reflections have only served to intensify his passion. The progression of imagery throughout the poem does empha-size the brevity of the life remaining to the speaker, but it also creates a warm, romantic setting. The bleak, wintery exterior has become a hearth at sunset. And now we note, if we have not ear-lier, that the speaker uses the intimate pronoun "thou" (with its passionate connotations) throughout the poem. As the final couplet shows, the speaker has used these reflections about imminent death as a rhetorical (and hopeful) argument urging his mistress to "lŏve/ thăt wēll/ whĭch thōu/ mŭst lēave/ ĕre lōng." The seven stresses in the line drive home the speaker's urgent desire that this should be true.

Thus, the entire poem is a rhetorical argument, and as an argu-ment, the poem takes full advantage of the structure of a Shakespearean sonnet. Its three quatrains present three successive images of the brevity of an old man's life, but also three images of his lingering youthfulness—in the yellow leaves, the last daylight, and the glowing embers. If those three quatrains gradually close in on the poem's theme, the final couplet snaps it into clear focus. This is an old man's means of seduction, relying on pity and an engaging hopefulness that the dying embers can still brighten into the flame of love.

At the same time, however, the entire poem uses figurative lan-guage to suggest the outlines of a story, complete with time, place, situation, and anticipated consequences. On an autumn evening, a man settles down with his mistress before a warm hearth and be-moans his advancing years. After hearing such moving words, who can doubt that his mistress's sympathetic kisses will fan those fad-ing embers into flame once more?

Analysis

Although explication requires the careful examination of *each* element in a short passage, literary *analysis* requires a very thorough study of *one* element in a long and complex work. For example, one might analyze the rural dialect used in Eugene O'Neill's *Desire Under the Elms*, the plot of Guy de Maupassant's

"The Necklace," or the theme of Lord Tennyson's "Ulysses." A thorough explication of *Desire Under the Elms*, "The Necklace," or even "Ulysses" would run to many pages, but analysis imposes limitations that make the topics more manageable.

The formation of a specific thesis is one means of imposing such limitations and is even more important in an analysis than it is in an explication. After all, most of us intuitively see the value of a thorough explication of an important passage. Such writing helps us to understand the work more fully and to appreciate its richness and complexity. Analysis is different. For example, the use of dialect in *Desire Under the Elms* may at first seem peripheral, unimportant, and somewhat annoying. Thus, an analysis of the dialect will seem belabored and boring unless the writer's thesis is immediately presented to the reader and is made interesting. The contention that O'Neill uses a regional dialect because of the play's setting in rural New England in 1850 is so obvious that it would even put to sleep an instructor well fortified with coffee. More promising is the thesis that the characters' limited ability to communicate (or even understand) their thoughts and feelings is a sign of their limited development as human beings and one cause of their tragic downfall.

Yet how is one to discover an interesting and original thesis? No general guidelines can guarantee success. However, you can often make your writing more intriguing by considering the relationships between the literary work and other subjects that interest you. If you are interested in Freudian psychology, for example, you may observe that in *Desire Under the Elms* Eben Cabot has all of the characteristics of the classical Oedipal fixation. He prays for his father's death and lusts after women old enough to be his mother. From here it is only a short step to formulating a stimulating thesis about the role of the Oedipal fixation in Eben's character. Similarly, a student with an interest in the Greek classics may choose to write an analysis of the uses of the Phaedra legend in the plot of the play. A student with an interest in religion may wish to examine the many biblical allusions in order to show how Ephraim manipulates these allusions in creating a God that is as hard and lonely as he himself is. And a student with an interest in early American history may choose to examine the extent to which Ephraim Cabot's life and failings illustrate the influence of the Puritan heritage on the American character.

Be aware, however, that a literary analysis can rarely focus *entirely* on something so narrow as any of the topics listed in the preceding paragraph. Just as one cannot unravel a single thread from a tapestry without manipulating the entire fabric, so too **one cannot trace a single element through a work of literature without touching upon many of the other important elements.** An analysis of dialect in *Desire Under the Elms* would almost certainly examine (however briefly) the animal imagery, the biblical allusions, and the connotations of the word "purty," since each of these is a prevalent feature in the speech of the characters. Similarly, the following character analysis of John the Carpenter in Geoffrey Chaucer's "The Miller's Tale" develops frequent comparisons between the Carpenter and the other major characters in the poem. Even more intriguingly, the essay raises speculations about the character of the Miller (who narrates the story), Chaucer (who wrote it), and the reader (who enjoys it). Each aspect of this penetrating analysis is nicely unified by the essay's thesis that an "examination of the Carpenter and his fate . . . leads to the discovery that the reader's sense of justice and fair play may be disturbingly similar to the values of the coarse, repulsive Miller."

Just Deserts:
An Analysis of the Carpenter in
Chaucer's "The Miller's Tale"
by
Deborah Chappel

Chaucer's bawdy, well-timed "Miller's Tale" leaves a sweet taste
of satisfaction in the mouth. Each of the four lively and human
characters seems to get exactly what he or she deserves, so that
the reader, having been caught up for an hour or so in the "and
then?" excitement of good narrative, closes the book with contentment. A closer examination of the Carpenter and his fate, however,
leads to the discovery that the reader's sense of justice and fair
play may be disturbingly similar to the values of the coarse, repulsive Miller. What the reader is actually applauding at the end of
"The Miller's Tale" is the downfall of a character who is meek,
gentle, honest, loving, trusting, and moral.

The Carpenter stands in direct opposition to the other major
characters of the story. They are young, while he is old. In fact, he
is so old that, while Nicholas and Alisoun busy themselves with amorous play the whole night long, and even Absolon roams the
streets like any tomcat until daybreak, poor John can't stay
awake, not even in expectation of the second flood. The lustful temperaments of Absolon, Alisoun, and Nicholas seem natural to their
ages, so that John's jealous guarding of his young wife opposes the
inevitable forces of nature.

The Carpenter's attitude toward love and marriage is vastly different from the attitude of the other major characters. Love for Alisoun is practicality and lust. There is no evidence in the story that
she loves John or Nicholas. Love for Nicholas and Absolon is conquest and physical pleasure. Only the Carpenter is depicted as loving his wife "more than his lyf." When Nicholas warns him of the
second flood, this good man's first fear is for his wife. John is loving, too, toward those in his charge. When he fears that something
is wrong with Nicholas, John sends his knave to check on him, and
even visits Nicholas in his chamber.

Also in opposition to the other major characters, the Carpenter is
fervently religious. When he hears his knave's report of Nicholas'
condition, the Carpenter blesses himself and calls on St. Frideswide
for help: "Men sholde nat knowe of Goddes privitee, / Ye, blessed
be alwey a lewed man, / That noght but oonly his bileve can!"
When he visits Nicholas in his room, John makes the sign of the
cross on all four walls and the threshold and says a prayer. When
Nicholas tells the Carpenter of the coming of a second flood and
gives him instructions concerning preparation, Nicholas knows how
to give his story impetus. He makes biblical reference to Solomon,

since biblical references obviously carry great weight with John.

Never is the Carpenter obviously dishonest or immoral. He is gentle and considerate of his wife. When he hears Absolon wooing Alisoun in the middle of the night, John is so trusting that he does nothing about it except ask her if she hears it too. John is also so gullible that he believes both Nicholas' prophecy and his instructions for their survival, being perfectly willing to take the advice of a younger man. Not only does the poor Carpenter believe his young wife and lodger; they talk him into doing all of the work to prepare for the flood—and he never complains. When Nicholas sarcastically says, "Thou art so wys, it nedeth thee nat teche, / Go, save our lyf," poor John scurries to do his bidding.

The only actual criticism of John in the text of "The Miller's Tale" is that his wit was rough, and the reader can certainly perceive this to be the case. Not knowing of the wisdom of Cato, who "bad man sholde wedde his similitude," John was foolish enough to wed a lusty, attractive young girl. Having wed her, he was foolish enough to love her, and so was doomed to spend his life in the constant fear of being cuckolded. At no time does he exhibit the wit and understanding of any of the other major characters in the story. When Absolon is undone, he quickly conceives a plot for revenge. When Nicholas and Alisoun are on the brink of discovery and ruination, they turn the situation to their advantage by pretending that John is mad. Poor John, on the other hand, so precipitously cuts the rope on his boat at the first mention of water, that he doesn't even look to see if the supposed flood had indeed arrived. The Miller refers to John repeatedly as "this sely carpenter," and he seems to be always at the mercy of some powerful fear, from fear of being cuckolded to fear of drowning in the second flood.

In the end, then, the Carpenter's abiding flaw is great, overwhelming stupidity. This great fault is not compensated by his honesty, gentleness, love, and religious belief. We are made to feel that he deserves everything he gets—to be made the butt of Nicholas and Alisoun's jokes, to be cuckolded, and to have his wife and her lover convince his neighbors that he is mad. The Carpenter, the most virtuous character but the most stupid, suffers the worst fate of all: people laugh at him openly and he gets no revenge for his wrongs.

The reader can easily perceive why the Miller would be uncharitable toward the poor Carpenter, who is everything that he is not. The Miller is a rough, uneducated man, but a crafty one, as evidenced by his witty story. He is a thief, good at stealing grain—coarse and ugly, but, in his own way, a leader of his pack. The Miller is irreligious, tells filthy stories, drinks heavily, batters down doors with his head, and scoffs at fidelity in marriage. Nicholas, Alisoun, and even Absolon are scoundrels with whom the

Miller can identify, since they are cunning, deceitful, and cynical about marriage and religion. The Carpenter, being a stupid and virtuous man, is a man to be made a fool of. "The Miller's Tale" makes a fool of the Carpenter with gusto.

There may be a lot of the Miller in Chaucer, too, for Chaucer seems to share the Miller's view of the characters in this tale. Chaucer apparently didn't prize deep religious feeling, particularly when this feeling manifested itself in superstition or self-righteousness; religious folk are the most wickedly satirized of the characters in The Canterbury Tales. Several of Chaucer's tales, most notably that of the Wife of Bath, reveal further cynical views toward love and marriage. A practical, logical man, Chaucer evidently thought an excess of affection to be a foolish thing, and suspect. Chaucer was human enough, too, to mock anyone who would let himself be made the butt of a joke. The characters Chaucer draws with flair are original rogues and rascals, such as Alisoun, Nicholas, the Wife of Bath, and even Absolon. Chaucer seems to prefer these characters to the dull, virtuous ones like John the Carpenter. Perhaps Chaucer also felt that the Carpenter got exactly what he deserved.

To account for the Miller's satisfaction at the Carpenter's fate, and even to explore Chaucer's similarity to the Miller, doesn't end the story, however. There is still the matter of our response as readers. I laughed aloud as the Carpenter "got his" at the end of "The Miller's Tale." Perhaps there's more of the Miller in me than I would like to admit. Perhaps, too, part of the genius of Chaucer is his subtle appeal to that part of us that is like the Miller—coarse, bawdy, unloving, and irreligious.

As should be clear from the discussion and the accompanying examples, explication and analysis—each in its own way—forward the process of critical inquiry by providing an explicit occasion to explore, clarify, organize, and share our experience with a given literary work. Like all forms of writing, writing about literature involves the process of discovery, for as we write about what we have read, we almost inevitably enlarge our understanding and our appreciation in a way that is simply not possible with reading alone. The previous discussion has emphasized specific ways to approach the writing of an explication or analysis; the following general comments are included as broader guidelines to the writing process itself.

WRITING A PAPER: STEPS AND STAGES*

Even for good readers, getting ideas on paper can be sheer agony, and in many cases, it is those writers who set the highest standards for themselves who anguish

---

* Adapted from James H. Pickering, *Reader's Guide to the Short Story to Accompany FICTION 100: An Anthology of Short Stories,* 5th ed. (New York: Macmillan Publishing Company, 1988).

most over their writing. The causality is circular: writing is painful because it is done with such a sense of responsibility toward its reader and judge. In turn, because of this sensation of judgmental pressure, the next time you are asked to do any writing, your tendency will be to put it off until the last moment, and thus you find yourself again having to perform under the worst possible circumstances: trying to get everything right on the first draft, editing and polishing as you go, relying on pure association for the organization of your thoughts. All this while trying at the same time to guess which approach is most likely to appeal to this particular instructor.

Anyone who has ever attended college has had to rely from time to time on the night-before-due method of paper writing. Writing is a very personal activity, and in many instances, the best advice is to stay with what has worked best for you in the past. But anyone, no matter how experienced in writing, can get stuck staring at a blank page or word-processor screen for whatever reason.

The following discussion is based on the best *general* advice developed by modern composition theory for generating ideas about a topic and keeping them fluid until (but not before) they are developed fully enough to consider polishing for presentation to an audience. You may wish to eliminate or change the order of some of the recommended steps to fit your personal style, but **we believe that the principle of constructing most of the paper *prior to any thought toward an audience* is a sound one and should be seriously considered.**

1. The First Reading

We have discussed the reading of the work you plan to write about briefly. Whether you have a previously assigned topic or are free to choose your own, keep in mind as you read that the "casual" reader is one who makes ready and easy assumptions, filling in gaps and filtering out inconsistencies, trying to make "ordinary" sense out of an extraordinary text. However, **the *quality* of your attention should be quite different from that of a casual reader. Do not assume things so easily or take the "world" of literature for granted.** You will want to ask yourself what and how much the reader must grant to make that world possible. "Do people *really* talk like that?" How have we been led by the author to think that they might? How is the style of dialogue related to the setting? Through whom do we see the action? Do those eyes see everything? Read with a pencil in hand and mark your text (if you own it) or take notes on any feature of the story that you feel may have been overlooked by your "casual reader." Do not assume that any such observations are necessarily "deep." **Sometimes the most obvious features of a work are ignored precisely because they *are* obvious.**

2. Freewriting

After having read and considered the story you are planning to write about, it is helpful to put yourself through a stint (or several stints) of nonstop, freely associative writing. In this kind of writing don't concern yourself with logic or style or punctuation or any other standard of correctness. Freewriting in many respects resembles the way we think, which is in fragments. **The point of this exercise is to get down as many impressions as possible of the work you have just read without having to consider any particular use for what you are writing.** Try to keep in mind through *all* of these first stages of composition that if you find yourself stuck or spending long periods hovering over one sentence or paragraph, it is probably because you are prematurely considering an audience and feeling judged for what you are putting on paper. Note the way in which one student has attempted to capture and get down on paper some thoughts on Faulkner's "Barn Burning":

> The Snopeses seem mean and stupid. Especially the daughters seem stupid I dont know about the rest of them, the mother seems nice. I dont know why sarty is going to tell on his father. Why hes different than his father and more like his mother who wants to help him after the fight. But for some reason the father knows Sarty wants to tell on him but I dont know why. The mansion owner is right to try to make Pap clean the rug but I wouldn't have taken it to their house to get it cleaned. The father is so touchy that he will try to do something mean to anybody who tries to get back at him, but he always moves away to another place, so when he gets to Despains mansion he walks right in and ruins the rug. He makes very racist remarks but so does the man in the first lawsuit. On the night of the fire Sarty gets away and runs to the mansion to tell on his father and then he runs away into the forest.

3. Listing Ideas and Questions

It is impossible to tell in advance what your freewriting might produce, but *anything* is better than a blank page. **Go through what you have and underline whatever looks to you like a possible idea or a significant question.** There are no rules for this. All you are trying to do at this point is to lift fairly solid material from the irrelevant verbiage. Make a loose list of the items you have culled and arrange them in any order that seems logical to you. Here is the same student's list of remarks and questions derived from her freewriting.

1. Are the Snopeses stupid? The brother and two sisters are. The mother and the aunt just seem afraid. Pap is just mean and will do anything to get back at someone.

2. Sarty is more like his mother.

3. Why does Sarty want to tell and how does his father know that he does?

4. The father does mean things but nobody can get back at him because they can't prove anything.

5. Pap tracks manure on the expensive rug on purpose.

6. All the people in the story seem kind of racist.

7. Sarty and his mother know what Pap is going to do when he gets the oil cans.

8. Why does Sarty try so hard to tell on his father?

4. The Thesis Sentence

After reviewing the list of ideas and questions you have drawn from your freewriting, you should have a relatively clear notion of the concerns of the story that most attract your attention. Try to formulate in a full sentence, with complete subject and predicate, the point that you plan to explore or demonstrate in your paper. "Faulkner's attitude toward the Old South in 'Barn Burning' " is a *topic,* but "Faulkner's attitude toward the Old South in 'Barn Burning' is revealed by the ambiguity of the story's ending" is a ***thesis statement.*** Go back to your freewriting sessions if no central idea has formed itself solidly enough yet for you to produce a satisfactory thesis sentence. Eventually the tendency of your writing will help you discover the points of doubt in your reading of the story that you feel are in need of exploration and clarification. The student writing on "Barn Burning" found that she could not write a thesis sentence without first condensing her list of ideas:

1. The father does mean things to other people and they can't do anything about it because he has nothing to lose.

2. No matter how hard he tries, Sarty is more like his mother than like his father.

3. Why does Sarty want to tell on his father?

She was then able to formulate her thesis sentence:

Sarty wants to tell on his father because he is more like his mother

and doesn't want to be a "lone wolf" like his father all his life.

5. Rereading the Text

Once you have stated the thesis of your paper, it will probably be necessary for you to go back to the text of the story to find and note supporting evidence for your point of view. Don't be afraid to alter your thesis if you find that the facts are other than you remember them. The implications of the story will keep growing for you throughout your involvement with it. If you are planning a more formal study with references to the opinions of others, you should now have a firm enough sense of direction to begin your research. The time-honored system for keeping track of notes and the books and journals from which the notes are taken is to keep two sets of index cards (usually 3 × 5s and 5 × 8s), one set with full bibliographical information on each of the sources, and the other set with the notes keyed by number or letter to the source from which each was taken. The method may seem very fussy, but anyone who has ever painstakingly copied out quotations for a paper and was later unable to identify their source because of a failure to make an adequate bibliographical entry will appreciate the need. If there is even a remote chance that you may cite a work, make up a card on it. You never know what turns of argument your paper may take to bring you back to it.

6. The Rough Draft

Once you are satisfied with your thesis statement and feel that you have enough specific illustration for it from the text (and from whatever secondary sources you may have consulted), you are ready to try a rough draft. Once more, it is important to **keep in mind that you are still writing for yourself,** and writing as much to discover and explore ideas as to express them. Use as your organizing principle for this first full version of the paper the same list that you made after freewriting, with whatever additions and revisions your survey of the evidence has suggested. Once you have a sense of the major divisions of your argument, you should write fairly rapidly without fussing over style or grammar or spelling. What you should be aiming for at this point is mainly to "fill up" each section of the rough draft with as many associated ideas as possible. Cutting surplus material will always be easier later on than trying to eke out an anemic, underdeveloped section of the essay. Don't bother to copy quotations into this draft. Either number the location of each quotation as it occurs to you while writing, or go back after you have finished writing and note the strategic location for each reference. If you have taken notes on cards, you will now be able to arrange them in the order they will most likely be used in the later drafts.

Here is the rough draft of the paper on "Barn Burning" we have been following:

Pap Snopes is a mean man who always thinks he has to get even with somebody for one thing or another. He is like a lone wolf who doesn't care for anything and during the civil war he stole horses from both the North <u>and</u> the South. He was shot in the foot getting away with one. He is a sharecropper and hardly owns any thing. So he can always do something to people who own farms and they cant fight back because he hasnt got any thing that they can take from him. He doesnt even seem to love his family much because he's always yelling at them or hitting them like when he hits because he say Sarty would of told the truth.[1] Even though the story doesnt tell why Pap thinks so. He is like a flat tin figure because he doesn't feel anything.[2] He only cares for getting even, and thats what he has been doing all his life. The family has had to move from one place to another constantly because of Pap burning down barns. When the story starts there is a trial about the barn of a man named Harris that burned down. He made Pap pay a dollar to get a pig back that kept getting loose and going into Harrises yard. Sarty has to think very hard about what enemies these people are because he <u>thinks</u> he is on his father's side. When they ask Sarty to stand up and testify he becomes very frightened and confused.

Sarty is really more like his mother than he is his father, even though he keeps trying to think and act like his father. He gets in a fight with a bigger boy when the other boy calls him a barn burner. When he starts to get into the wagon his mother feels sorry for him and wants to wash the blood and dirt off his face but Pap wont allow it. Also the mother has kept a pearl-inlaid clock that she had from before she was married. Even though the clock no longer works.* She doesn't have any other pretty thing in her own life, but she is very much against her husband's destruction of other peoples property like the de Spain's rug.

When Sarty goes with his father to see their new landlord he is very impressed with the mansion. He believes that people who live in a house like this are out of reach of his father and that is father will finally have some respect for property. But this is just when his father decides to walk through some fresh manure. Pap pushes the de Spain's black butler out of the way and tracks the manure right onto an expensive rug in the hallway. When he leaves he turns on his foot and grinds the dirt further into the carpet. Outside he tells Sarty that this big house was built with "nigger sweat," meaning slavery, and that "white sweat" is supposed to make it even bigger.[3] Pap is not going to let anyone richer than he is push him around. But that is why he is always getting even and having to move.

When major de Spain brings the rug for Pap to clean, Pap goes out to the field and gets a sharp stone for his daughters to scrub it with. They also use strong lye on it. The major is going to make Pap pay for it with twenty bushels of corn from the fall harvest, but Pap sues de Spain instead. When the trial comes up Pap is only made to give five dollars worth of corn for a hundred dollar rug, but he still is not satisfied and decides to burn down de Spain's barn to get even with him. The mother tries to stop him but he won't listen. Sarty tries at first to believe that he is true to his father, but something makes him break away to warn the de Spains. He has turned away from his father because he wants to believe that people who have beautiful things are more like his mother than his father. They are more civilized. But we still have to think of the way the de Spains made their money, and we are not sure whether Pap was so much worse than they are.

7. *The First Revision*

Ideally you will have begun writing early enough to allow you time to put the rough draft away for a few days so that you may approach it again with a fresh eye and some objectivity. The reason you have been urged to produce so much loose, baggy writing in the first two stages of the paper is so that at this stage, the first revision, your problem will not be production but weeding and cutting. By now you should have an abundance of good ideas and they should be in a relatively logical order. The point is to accomplish most of the *creative* work of the paper on your own terms without having to consider a reader.

Now, **in your first revision, the major task is to turn private writing into public communication.** In most instances, your real and final audience is your instructor, the person who will be assigning grades. If you find it useful in your work of revising the rough draft to think of pitching your tone and style directly to that audience, then by all means do so. But many student writers find it more helpful to think of their peers as the audience of their writing. This does not mean simply people of your own age or scholastic level, but the members of your present literature class, who, even though they may not be much like you in background or even age, share in common the influence of the ideas of one another and of the same instructor. In other words, your class constitutes a community of readers, and when you think of them as an audience, you should also have in mind the agreements and disagreements that are current within the group. Another technique that some writers find helpful in establishing an appropriate tone and style for their argument is to imagine a "casual reader" who is not inattentive or insensitive, but understandably eager to brush aside irritating complications to the story's "ordinary" sense. Your rationale as "a more careful reader" is to point out that the story is not really following the paths we are accustomed to taking in our less attentive readings, and then to trace the resulting implications of this more tangled track.

However, to talk about such things as tone is to get somewhat ahead of ourselves. **The first concern in revising with a reader in mind is to get your material into its most effective argumentative order.** What this means in plain terms is **placing your generalizations in some close relationship with the particular evidence you plan to use in support of them.** Short papers can be organized in a simple *particular* to *general* pattern (usually the close *explication* or glossing of a brief section of the text followed by a discussion of the implications of this section for the rest of the story), or from the *general to the particular* (comments on some larger element of the fiction, such as character or setting, illustrated by quotations from relevant points in the text). But your audience should never be left wondering for very long "Why am I being asked to read all these quotations (or all this plot summary)?" or "What makes this person think *this* is so?" Some appropriate conclusion should be fairly close at hand following the citation of textual evidence, and any claim to a special understanding of the text or to knowledge of obscure facts of history requires a reasonably handy reference to some source for the idea or information. **In this phase of your writing you should cut mercilessly any unsupported assertions and any excess, functionless quotations or plot summaries.**

8. The Final Draft

Perhaps the single most important determining factor in the success or failure of your literary essay is the skill you show in moving between the level of generality and the level of specific detail. This is why you are urged to take such care with the arrangement of assertions and their support in the first revision of your paper. **In the final draft the main concern is with the *transitions* between those larger building-blocks of your paper:** how you introduce arguments and their supporting evidence, and how you follow up on them once they have been introduced. It is largely a matter of finding the best "voice" to suit the kind of material under discussion. As a general principle you should take care to be as sensitive as possible to the mood of the literary moments you are presenting. Worse than not quoting at all is to quote and then make some cute, anticlimactic comment that shatters the dignity of a passage (or bluntly misses its humor). It is not a bad idea to get a friend to listen to your paper read aloud. Someone who knows you should be able to tell whether you are sounding like yourself or putting on some pompous or coy vocal disguise. Your arguments may be cogent enough, but you still must

convince any reader that you are an honest and competent guide to the work
under discussion.

Following is the final draft of a student analysis of Faulkner's "Barn Burning."
It is by no means perfect, but it tries quite successfully to explain the motivation
of the boy, "Sarty" (whose actual name is Colonel Sartoris Snopes). One of its
real victories is that it catches the irony of the fact that the boy who wants so badly
to belong somewhere ends up running away from his own family.

Odd Son Out

The character of Pap Snopes in William Faulkner's story "Barn
Burning" is somewhat like that of a lone wolf. He has courage and
cunning and is unafraid of people who have power and money because he doesn't have anything to lose and they do. He seems to
have no love for anyone or anything, and Faulkner describes him
as always looking the same in his black coat, like "something cut
ruthlessly from tin" (40). The one thing that does matter to him is
getting even, and he does that with barn burning. The family has
had to move more than a dozen times in the last ten years.

The Story starts out with a trial in a country store where Pap is
accused of having burned the barn of a man named Harris. They
have no solid proof, but Harris wants Pap's youngest son, Sarty, to
testify. Sarty has been sitting there saying over and over to himself that these people are his enemies, but he is very confused
when they want him to tell the truth. Throughout the story he constantly tells himself that he feels the same way about things as his
father does, but Pap somehow knows he is different. After the trial
he takes Sarty aside and says, "You were fixing to tell them. You
would have told him" (39) and then hits the boy.

Sarty's mother is not at all like Pap, or like her twin daughters
or elder son either. When Sarty gets hurt in a fight with a much
bigger boy who calls him a "barn burner," the mother feels sorry
for him and wants to wash the blood and dirt off his face, but Pap
won't allow it. When they leave that place and finally reach the
next house they are going to live in, the mother and aunt begin unloading furniture while the two huge, "bovine" daughters just sit in
the wagon until Pap orders them out. In the load with the furniture
is a "clock, inlaid with mother-of-pearl which would not run,
stopped at some fourteen minutes past two o'clock of a dead and
forgotten day and time, which had been his mother's dowry" (37).
The clock seems to be the only pretty thing in the mother's life and
it is broken. It is all she has left of the home she had before she
met Abner Snopes.

The only child in the family at all like the mother is Sarty. When
Pap takes him along to meet their new landlord, Sarty is very impressed with the mansion where the de Spains live: "Hit's as big as
a courthouse he thought quietly" (40). He believes that people who

live in such a place can't be touched by his father. They are too far above him. But that's just when Pap decides to push his way in past the black butler, tracking fresh horse manure in on an expensive rug and grinding it in further as he turns on his heel to leave. Outside they stop for a moment to look back at the big house and Pap says, " 'Pretty and white, aint it? That's sweat. Nigger sweat. Maybe it ain't white enough yet to suit him. Maybe he wants to mix some white sweat with it' " (41). We now know that Major de Spain has made his fortune with slaves. Pap is never going to allow the wealthy to push him around, but that is why he is always getting even and having to move, too. Pap purposely ruins the rug Major de Spain brings for him to clean, and it is the lawsuit over the rug that leads Pap to another barn-burning party. Sarty's mother begs her husband not to do it, just as she begged him not to ruin the rug, but she is afraid to try and stop him. Sarty tries as usual to believe he will stick with his father, but his father knows better, and he's right. The story ends with Sarty being the cause of his own father's death and running away like a "lone wolf" himself. The reasons for his actions are never very clear in the story, but he seems to want most to belong somewhere. Perhaps he believes that people who care for pretty things are kind and sympathetic like his mother. But then again we have to remember how the de Spains got what they have.

9. The Finished Paper

In your final draft, questions of style are largely taken care of by the way in which you imagine yourself moving from point to point—as a teacher, as a guide, as a passionate advocate, as a somewhat removed skeptic—whatever you find the appropriate role for this particular exercise. But you have also to attend to all the fundamentals of composition from sentence structure to spelling before typing the copy that you plan to submit to your instructor.

Finally, as a last step, carefully *proofread* your paper and ink in whatever minor corrections may be necessary. In format, the finished paper should be typed and double-spaced (or the handwritten equivalent if allowed), with one-inch margins on all four sides—about 250 words per page.

QUOTATION AND DOCUMENTATION

Documentation Within Text

In most brief papers, your quotations will be taken from a single story, poem, or play and from an edition of that work used by the entire class as a text, in which case full bibliographical citation is not really necessary. **It should be obvious from your introductory paragraph which work you are about to discuss, so any direct quotation from the text needs only a page number in parentheses (outside the final quotation marks but within the closing punctuation of the sentence) to help your reader locate the passage in question.**

"During these last decades," states the narrator in the opening sen-

tence of Kafka's "A Hunger Artist," "the interest in professional

fasting has markedly diminished" (47).

Notice that the language of the quotation is woven into the sentence structure of the paper so as not to be too disruptive of the flow of the discussion.

To keep the verb tense scheme simplified, literary discussions are gener-ally conducted in the "literary present" tense, as if the action of the plot were a *continuing* one (the character "says," the character "does," the character "goes,"), even though stories are most often narrated in the *past* tense. Some-times it becomes necessary to change the grammar of the quoted material to make it fit into the context of your own discussion. Any such alterations of the original (or additions, as when vague pronoun references must be identified) are indi-cated by the use of square brackets.

Gregor sometimes "hear[s] [his parents] expressing their appre-

ciation of his sister's activities, whereas formerly they had fre-

quently scolded her for being as they thought a somewhat useless

daughter" (93).

For most general discussions of a work, it is wise to keep the number and length of direct quotations to a minimum. However, in those cases in which you find yourself having to quote more than four lines of uninterrupted prose, the con-ventional way to set off such passages is to single-space and double-indent. Quo-tation marks (except for those already present in the source) are unnecessary because the format already marks off the inserted material from your own writing.

Julian raised his eyes to heaven. "Yes, you should have bought it," he said. "Put it on and let's go." It was a hideous hat. A purple velvet flap came down on one side of it and stood up on the other; the rest of it was green and looked like a cushion with the stuffing out. He decided it was less comical than jaunty and pathetic. Everything that gave her pleasure was small and de-pressed him. (455)

Note that the parenthetical page reference is still used, but in this case with two spaces *following* the closing punctuation of the final sentence.

When you begin quoting sources from outside your course text, you will have to provide your reader with the information needed to locate the passages in ques-tion. If you are writing about a single story the title and author of which are clear from the context of your discussion, again, as with your course-text references, you must place the page number(s) in parentheses at the end of the quotation. But it is also necessary to identify, either at the foot of the page or at the end of your paper, the precise edition of the work to which your page numbers refer. (See also discussion of Footnotes and Endnotes below.) For example:

Charles Peacock, from V. S. Pritchett's "The Fall," reminds me in certain ways of Woody Allen, especially in the way that "crowds and occasions" frighten both of them, and engage them in "the fundamental battle of . . . life: the struggle against nakedness, the panic of grabbing for clothes and becoming someone" (81).[1]

------

[1] All quotations from "The Fall" are from V. S. Pritchett: Selected Stories (New York: Vintage, 1979).

The rules for quoting from literature are quite simple: either your quotations are direct (in which case you must indicate so with the proper punctuation and page reference) or they are not. If you are not quoting directly, you may paraphrase or summarize a work as much as you like without providing a page reference for every allusion to the plot. However, when you begin to incorporate materials from critical and scholarly texts into your papers, the rules are much more strict. Certainly you must continue to indicate in the usual ways any direct reproduction of the language of your source,

One introduction to The Red Badge of Courage points out that publication of the novel "made Crane a famous man" (Crews ix).

but along with acknowledgments of direct quotations from critical and scholarly works, you must also give fair credit for any material that you *paraphrase* or *summarize*. The original language of a passage from Ludwig Lewisohn's *The Story of American Literature* (New York: Random House, 1939) runs as follows:

Within nine years after the publication of "A Chance Acquaintance" Howells had not only made himself master of his craft and method but reached his highest point of power. The intervening novels, especially "The Undiscovered Country," which deals sanely and finely with spiritualism and "Dr. Breen's Practice," a spirited defense, within his limitations of course, of the professional woman, have in an increasing degree both his virtues and his graces as a novelist. (248)

A summary of Lewisohn's passage might read

Not many years after having written "A Chance Acquaintance" Howells had hit the stride of his style with such novels as The Undiscovered Country and Dr. Breen's Practice (Lewisohn 248).

Even if you completely rephrase the observation in your own language, you have not come to this judgment of the progress of William Dean Howells's art independently but have chosen to use even Lewisohn's example titles for the framing of the time scheme. Thus, you owe him an acknowledgment either by way of the parenthetical reference or, better yet, by beginning the above summary with "As Ludwig Lewisohn points out . . ." or other similar introductory phrase and concluding the paraphrase with the page number in parentheses. The failure to do so constitutes plagiarism just as much as if you had directly copied the passage, or even its key words or phrases.

If you really *need* another writer's key words and phrases for the sense of your own argument, go ahead, help yourself. Just be sure that there is always a clear boundary between your own and the other person's language, such as:

Lewisohn claims that "within nine years" after "A Chance Acquaintance" was published, Howells had reached the "highest point of his power" as a novelist with such books as The Undiscovered Country and Dr. Breen's Practice (248).

or even

Howells's Dr. Breen's Practice has been called a limited but "spirited defense" of the right of women to enter into the professions (Lewisohn 248).

If you will look again at the above examples of scholarly citation you will notice that the author's names are mentioned in the body of the paper or are included with the parenthetical page references. If you should happen to be citing *two* works by the same author in your paper, enough of each title should be included as well to make it distinguishable from the others when your reader turns to your list of Works Cited (discussed in more detail below). A reference to Chester Anderson's article, "The Sacrificial Butter," might be placed at the end of a quotation or paraphrase in your essay as,

(Anderson, "Butter" 52-53)

while a citation of his book *Word Index to Stephen Hero* could be shortened to

(Anderson, Index 98)

Works Cited

Finally, **all parenthetical references must be fully identified in a list of Works Cited,** alphabetically arranged according to the authors' last names, on a separate page at the end of your paper. There your reader should be able to find all the information needed to locate the sources to which your parenthetical notations refer. Following are the formats for some of the most common kinds of entries in a list of Works Cited:

A book by a single author

Beachcroft, Thomas Owen. The Modest Art: A Survey of the Short Story in English. London: Oxford UP, 1968.

A book by two authors

Pickering, James H., and Jeffrey D. Hoeper. Concise Companion to Literature. New York: Macmillan, 1981.

A book by more than three authors

Baugh, A. C. et al. A Literary History of England. New York: Appleton, 1948.

An introduction, preface, or foreword

Ziff, Larzer. Introduction. The Scarlet Letter. By Nathaniel Hawthorne. New York: Bobbs-Merrill, 1963.

A work from an anthology

Barthelme, Donald. "Cortés and Montezuma." Sixty Stories. New York: E. P. Dutton, 1982. 328-336.
Hirsch, Edward. "Fast Break." Wild Gratitude: Poems by Edward Hirsch. New York: Alfred A. Knopf, 1986. 8-9.
Ibsen, Henrik. Hedda Gabler. Literature 2nd ed. Ed. James H. Pickering and Jeffrey D. Hoeper. New York: Macmillan, 1986. 1232-1285.

A translation

Tolstoy, Leo. War and Peace. Trans. Louise and Aylmer Maude. New York: Simon and Schuster, 1942.

An article from a scholarly journal

Bauman, Michael. "Marvell's 'To His Coy Mistress.' " Explicator 31 (May 1973): 72.
Bryant, Hallman B. "Reading the Map in 'A Good Man Is Hard to Find.' " Studies in Short Fiction 18 (Summer 1981): 301-07.
Stirling, B. "Psychology in Othello." Shakespeare Association Bulletin 19 (1944): 135-44.

Footnotes and Endnotes

Of course, traditional footnotes or endnotes numbered sequentially through the paper are still acceptable, and even preferred by some writers, because the system allows them to take the reader aside for incidental commentary, and to end their sentences cleanly without parenthetical references dangling off the end. As its name suggests, the footnote is placed at the foot of the page on which its reference number occurs,[1] is single-spaced, and appears four spaces below the text.[2] In footnotes, the author's name appears in proper order, and the city of publication and publisher are placed within parentheses.

------
[1] Thomas Owen Beachcroft, The Modest Art: A Survey of the Short Story in English (London: Oxford UP, 1968) 112.

------
[2] As you are probably aware, considerable debate goes on over the question of when the short story as a true genre actually began.

Endnotes (as one would expect) are placed on a separate page at the end of the paper, but are double spaced. Both endnotes and footnotes have their *first lines* indented, in reverse fashion from items in the list of Works Cited.

A third alternative is to use parenthetical page references and a list of Works Cited for source documentation, *along with* foot- or end-notes. The numbered notes may serve either for extensions of the discussion too awkward to include in the main text, or for evaluative comments on sources that may or may not appear in the Works Cited list. Again, for more extensive examples see the *MLA Handbook for Writers of Research Papers,* 3rd edition.

Points to Remember

1. **Critical writing, like all writing, involves five stages of the writing process—prewriting, writing, revision, editing, and proofreading.** Be certain that your own writing schedule allows adequate time for each. This is particularly true of prewriting (the time you set aside to study the text and plan your essay) and revision (the time you set aside to rethink and rewrite what you have already written).

2. **As part of the prewriting stage, make sure that you fully understand just what is expected of you,** including your instructor's protocols governing length, format, and deadlines, as well as the standards against which your completed essay will be evaluated. If the topic or thesis (or given passage in the case of explication) has been assigned in advance by your instructor, your options are limited and your task, in some respects at least, is easier. If the assignment is more general, you must be extremely careful that the topic or thesis you choose (or the passage you choose to explicate) is of manageable size, and, of course, that it is worthy of study in the first place. If your essay takes the form of an analysis that focuses on one or more of the elements of literature, you would do well to review the questions posed at the end of the appropriate section(s) of *Literature.*

3. **Before you begin to write, be sure to reread the text as many times as necessary to make absolutely certain that you understand exactly what is there**—no more and no less. Proceed by taking notes, marking individual lines or passages, and making marginal notations to use later on as the source of ideas or evidence when you begin to organize and write your essay. The more times you reread the text, the more likely you are to understand it.

4. **Keep a dictionary handy and refer to it as often as necessary.** Many words have changed their meanings (sometimes dramatically) over time, and the correct *denotative* meaning of a particular word must be understood before any attempt is made to construct an explication or analysis around its *connotations.*

5. **In writing an analysis, it is essential that you supply sufficient evidence from the text to support your reading of it.** Individual words, phrases, lines, and passages should be properly quoted and either explicated or interpreted in support of your thesis. Quote directly when necessary, unless the passage quoted would be so long as to be obtrusive. Be sure to enclose the quoted materials in quotation marks. You can and should be selective here, using ellipsis to indicate omission. (Ellipsis consists of three periods—evenly spaced—or a fourth period where your omission includes the end of a sentence.)

6. **Don't summarize.** Explication and analysis depend upon interpretation, not summary. Some summary is, of course, necessary as a means of orienting the reader and organizing your ideas. But a mere summary of what happens (or what is said) in a story, poem, or play is not an adequate substitute for a discussion of what makes it effective or important. An exception is the review, a type of writing about literature that we have not yet touched on. Reviews, of the sort that commonly appear in newspapers and magazines, are intended for audiences who are usually not familiar with the work being discussed. Here some summary statements about what the work is all about, together with comments about the author and his or her other works, are highly appropriate and, in the case where the work being discussed is a new one, probably necessary in order to orient the reader. As such they will tend to occupy far more space than would be appropriate in either an explication or analysis where the reader's general familiarity with the work can be assumed.

7. **Organize your ideas.** An explication, as the example from Shakespeare makes quite clear, more or less organizes itself. In writing an analysis, on the other hand, the method of organization is one of the key decisions that must be made as you plan your paper. The question of how to organize an analysis is usually most easily resolved by allowing the major ideas marshalled in support of your thesis to become the controlling subjects of your individual paragraphs.

8. **Use the library when appropriate.** College and university libraries are filled with books and periodicals that provide explications and analyses of literary works, and the question of whether or not they should be consulted in approaching your own writing assignment is one that inevitably arises for most students. Your instructor should be regarded as the best authority here, for he or she can tell you not only whether or not such research is expected and appropriate, but if it is, just where you may most profitably begin. Remember always that published critics are simply intelligent readers who have practiced the art; they are never to be regarded as the final authority about a given work, though some tend to write with a degree of positiveness that might lead you to think otherwise. Remember, too, that if you do consult such sources and make use of their ideas, your indebtedness must be fully acknowledged in a format that conforms to a stylesheet recommended or required by your instructor or school.

I

FICTION

I

FICTION

1

❧❧❧❧❧❧❧

What Is Fiction?

When we speak of *fiction*, we are usually referring to the short story and the novel—the two genres that have dominated Western literary culture since the late eighteenth century. More generally, however, **the word *fiction* refers to any narrative, in prose or verse, that is wholly or in part the product of the imagination.** As such, plays and narrative poems (poems that tell a story) can be classified as fiction, as can folktales, parables, legends, allegories, satires, and romances—all of which contain certain fictional elements. When we talk about fiction in this sense, then, we are not talking about fiction as a genre (the short story and the novel) but about a way of treating subject matter. We are, that is, making a statement about the relationship between real life and the life depicted in literature.

The precise relationship between fiction and life has been debated extensively among critics and authors since classical times. Most modern critics agree, however, that **whatever its apparent factual content or *verisimilitude*, fiction is finally a structured imitation of life and is not to be confused with a literal transcription of life itself.** Fiction organizes and refines the raw material of fact to emphasize and clarify what is most significant in life. The world of fiction is a re-created world apart, a world of the possible or the probable, rather than the actual. It is a world governed by its own rules of internal completeness. To the extent that readers find such a world credible or believable, it is because that world has been made to be consistent in character and event.

The writer of fiction, however, may deliberately choose not to deal with the world of our everyday experience at all. His or her chosen manner of treatment may be comic, or satiric, or ironic, rather than serious. Writers of fiction, in short, are free to exercise tremendous freedom in their choice of subject matter and the fictional elements at their disposal and are free to invent, select, and arrange those elements so as to achieve any one of a number of desired effects. In every instance, the writer's success depends on how well he or she has succeeded in unifying the story and controlling its impact; it does not depend on how closely or

31

faithfully life is mirrored and copied. To quote Henry James, one of America's most successful and influential writers of novels and short stories, "The only obligation to which in advance we [as readers] may hold a novel, without incurring the accusation of being arbitrary, is that it be interesting. . . . We must grant the artist his subject, his idea, his *donnée:* our criticism is applied only to what he makes of it."*

* Henry James, "The Art of Fiction," *The Art of Fiction and Other Essays by Henry James* (New York: Oxford UP, 1948) 8, 14.

2

✣✣✣✣✣✣

The Elements of Fiction

PLOT

When we refer to the *plot* of a short story, we are referring to the *deliberately arranged sequence of interrelated events* that makes up its basic narrative structure. Most plots have an identifiable beginning, middle, and end.

In order for a plot to begin, some kind of catalyst is necessary. Some kind of existing state of equilibrium must be broken that will generate a sequence of events that taken together serve to "tell a story." **Most plots originate in some kind of significant *conflict*.** The conflict may be either external, when the *protagonist* (who is also often referred to as the *hero** or the *focal character*) is pitted against some outside object or force, or internal, in which case the issue to be resolved is one within the protagonist's own self. External conflict may take the form of a basic opposition between a person and nature or between a person and society. It may also take the form of an opposition between two people (between the protagonist and a human adversary, the antagonist). Internal conflict, on the other hand, focuses on two or more elements contesting within the protagonist's own character.

Some short story plots, it should be noted, contain more than one conflict. In Joseph Conrad's "Heart of Darkness," for example, while the basic conflict takes place within Kurtz, its resolution depends on Captain Marlow's determined efforts to forge his way upriver into the very heart of Africa and to rescue the man whose life and motives have become his fascination. Marlow longs, that is, to pit himself against a hostile natural environment and the barriers imposed by the trading company's ineptness. The conflicts of a story may exist prior to the formal initiation of the plot itself, rather than be explicitly dramatized. Some conflicts, in fact, are never made explicit and must be inferred by the reader from what the characters do or say as the plot unfolds (as is the case in the conflict between the young man and woman in Ernest Hemingway's "Hills Like White Elephants"). Conflict, then, is the basic opposition, or tension, that sets the plot of a short story in motion; it engages the reader, builds the suspense or the mystery of the work, and arouses expectation for the events that are to follow.

---

* In general, *protagonist* is a better term than *hero;* the latter implies a set of admirable and positive qualities that many protagonists do not have.

33

The plot of the traditional short story is often conceived of as moving through five distinct sections or stages, which can be diagramed roughly as follows:

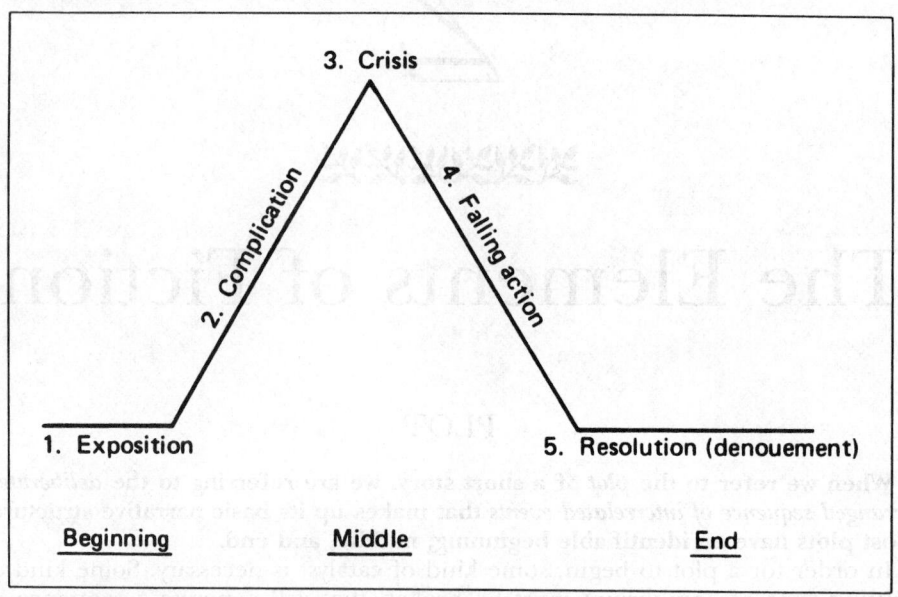

In some novels this five-stage structure is repeated in many of the individual chapters, while the novel as a whole builds on a series of increasing conflicts.

Exposition: The exposition is the beginning section in which the author provides the necessary background information, sets the scene, establishes the situation, and dates the action. It usually introduces the characters and the conflict, or at least the potential for conflict.

Complication: The complication, which is sometimes referred to as the rising action, develops and intensifies the conflict.

Crisis: The crisis (also referred to as the climax) is that moment at which the plot reaches its point of greatest emotional intensity; it is the turning point of the plot, directly precipitating its resolution.

Falling Action: Once the crisis, or turning point, has been reached, the tension subsides and the plot moves toward its conclusion.

Resolution: The final section of the plot is its resolution; it records the outcome of the conflict and establishes some new equilibrium. The resolution is also referred to as the ***conclusion*** or the ***denouement,*** the latter a French word meaning "unknotting" or "untying."

Highly plotted works, such as detective novels and stories, which contain distinct beginnings, middles, and ends, generally follow such conventional plot development. In the case of Arthur Conan Doyle's Sherlock Holmes stories, for example, the exposition is usually presented succinctly by the faithful (and convenient) Dr. Watson:

One summer night, a few months after my marriage, I was seated by my own hearth smoking a last pipe and nodding over a novel, for my day's work had been an exhausting one. My wife had already gone upstairs, and the sound of the locking of the door some time before told me that the servants had also retired. I had risen from my seat and was knocking out the ashes of my pipe, when I suddenly heard the clang of the bell. . . . I went out into the hall and opened the door. To my astonishment, it was Sherlock Holmes who stood on my step.

"Ah, Watson," said he, "I hoped that I might not be too late to catch you."

—From "The Crooked Man" [1893]

The *complication* comes about almost at once. The crime is reported, and with Holmes's famous "Come, Watson, the game is afoot," the period of rising action and suspense begins. Holmes, of course, is the *hero-protagonist;* Professor Moriarty, or some other suitably challenging opponent like *"the* woman," Irene Adler ("A Scandal in Bohemia," 1891), is the *antagonist*. For a time at least, the conflict of will and intellect seems almost even. Once Holmes solves the crime or mystery, the *crisis* or *climax* has been reached. The suspense and tension drop away, and the plot enters into the *falling action*, which is devoted to Holmes's detailed explanation of his method of detection. The *resolution* is short and belongs either to Watson ("A few words may suffice to tell the little that remains"—"The Final Problem," 1893) or to Holmes:

"And that's the story of the Musgrave Ritual, Watson. They have the crown down at Hurlstone—though they had some legal bother, and a considerable sum to pay before they were allowed to retain it. I am sure that if you mention my name they would be happy to show it to you. Of the woman nothing was ever heard, and the probability is that she got away out of England, and carried herself, and the memory of her crime, to some land beyond the seas."

—From "The Musgrave Ritual" [1893]

"A Scandal in Bohemia" represents perfectly this traditional dramatic structure. As Vincent Starrett notes:

It is practically all on exhibition: the Baker Street prologue with mystifications by the detective; the references to other cases whose secrets may not at the moment be revealed; the statement of the problem about to present itself, and discussion of the insufficient evidence at hand; the arrival of the illustrious client, with further mystifications and an elaboration of the problem; the adventure itself, and finally the fascinating if slightly anticlimactic, explanations of the detective, illustrating the ease with which it had all been accomplished.*

The terms *exposition*, *crisis*, *falling action*, and *resolution* are helpful in understanding the relationship among the parts of many kinds of narrative. But all plots, unfortunately, do not lend themselves to such neat and exact formulations. Even when they do, **it is not unusual for critics and readers to disagree among themselves about the precise nature of the conflict**—whether, for example, the protagonist is more in conflict with society than with himself or herself—or about where the crisis, or turning point, of the story actually occurs. **Nor is there any special reason that the crisis should occur at or near the middle of the plot. It can, in fact, occur at any moment.** In James Joyce's "Araby" and "The Dead" and in

* Vincent Starrett, *The Private Life of Sherlock Holmes* (New York: Haskell House Publishers, 1971) 22.

a number of the companion stories in *Dubliners,* the crisis—in the form of a sudden illumination that Joyce called an epiphany—occurs at the very end of the story, and the falling action and the resolution are dispensed with almost entirely. **Exposition and complication can also be omitted in favor of a plot that begins *in medias res* ("in the midst of things").** In many modern and contemporary stories the plot consists of a "slice of life" into which we enter on the eve of crisis, and the reader is left to infer beginnings and antecedents—including the precise nature of the conflict—from what he or she is subsequently able to learn.

This is the case in such stories as Ernest Hemingway's "Hills Like White Elephants" and Doris Lessing's "Wine," in which the author chooses to eliminate not only the traditional beginning, but also the ending in order to focus our attention on a more limited moment of time, the middle, which takes the form of a single, self-contained episode. Both stories offer little in the way of a traditional plot: there is very little description and almost no action. Rather, in both instances the reader overhears a continuous dialogue between two characters—a man and woman. Conflict and complication in each case are neither shown nor prepared for, but only revealed; the situation and the "story" are to be understood and completed through the active participation of the reader. Such **stories are sometimes referred to as "plotless" in order to suggest that the author's emphasis and interest have been shifted elsewhere, most frequently to character or idea.**

Understanding the plot on a schematic level becomes even more difficult when dealing with works, usually novels, that have more than one plot. Many novels contain one or more *subplots* that reinforce by contrast or parallel the main plot.

Selectivity

In deciding how much plot to include in a given work, how much emphasis to give individual episodes, and how these episodes are to be related to one another, the author's selectivity comes fully into play. In general, the shorter the narrative, the greater the degree of selectivity that will be required. The very economy of the short story, of course, limits the amount of plot that can be included. But no matter how much space is available, the author, in constructing the plot, will of necessity be forced to select those incidents that are most relevant to the story to be told. Those incidents that are the most significant will be emphasized and expanded into full-fledged dramatic scenes by using such devices as description, dialogue, and action. Other incidents will be given relatively less emphasis through deliberate subordination. In the latter case, the author may shorten the dramatic elements of the scene or eliminate them altogether in favor of summary—in favor of telling rather than showing. All these episodes, major or minor, need not advance the plot in precisely the same way or at the same pace, although the reader does have the right to expect that each will contribute in some way to the completed story.

The Ordering of Plot

The customary way of ordering the episodes or events in a plot is to present them chronologically, that is, in the order of their occurrence in time. Chronological plotting can be handled in various ways. It can be tightly controlled so that each episode logically and inevitably unfolds from the one that preceded it. It can also be loose, relaxed, and episodic, taking the form of a series of separate and largely self-contained episodes, resembling so many beads on a string. The latter is likely to be found, however, in a novel rather than a short story, simply because of the space required for its execution.

It is important to recognize that, even within plots that are mainly chronological, the temporal sequence is often deliberately broken and the chronological parts rearranged for the sake of emphasis and effect. Recall the Hemingway and Lessing stories cited above in which we encounter the characters in the middle of their "story" and must infer what has happened up to "now." In this case and others, **although the main direction of the plot may be chronological and forward, the author is under no obligation to begin at the beginning.** Hemingway and Lessing have us begin in the middle of things; other authors may begin at the end and then, having intrigued and captured us, work backward to the beginning and then forward again to the middle. In still other cases, the chronology of the plot may shift backward and forward in time, as for example in William Faulkner's "A Rose for Emily," where the author deliberately sets aside the chronological ordering of events and their cause/effect relationship in order to establish an atmosphere of unreality, build mystery and suspense, and underscore Emily Grierson's own attempt to deny the passage of time itself.

Perhaps the most frequently and conventionally used device for interrupting the flow of a chronologically ordered plot is the *flashback*, **a method of exposition that dramatically presents (often by means of a character's recollections, dreams, or reveries) scenes or incidents that took place prior to the beginning of the plot.** Flashbacks, such as young Robin's thoughts of home and family as he stands beside the dark church building in Hawthorne's "My Kinsman, Major Molineux," provide us with information that would otherwise be unavailable and thus increase our knowledge and understanding of present events.

The key point to remember about plot is that it is open to infinite variety. An author is under no obligation whatsoever to make his or her plot conform to any scheme or pattern but his or her own. The only requirement that the writer of fiction dares not shirk is that the plot be interesting.

Evaluating Plot

The customary test of a plot's effectiveness is its unity: the degree to which each episode bears in some necessary and logical (or psychological) way upon the resolution of the initial conflict. In considering a plot's unity **one can also raise questions about the plausibility of a given episode or, for that matter, about the plausibility of the plot as a whole.** The violation of plausibility—which is, in turn, a violation of the basic intelligence of the reader—is a quality we often associate with popular romantic commercial fiction, in which a happy ending seems to be grafted on a plot for the sake of convenience or propriety, when everything that preceded pointed toward an opposite conclusion.

One frequently used test of plausibility involves the author's use of *chance* (events that occur without apparent cause or sufficient preparation) and *coincidence* (the accidental occurrence of two events that have a certain correspondence). Although chance and coincidence do occur in real life, their use in literature becomes suspect if they seem to be merely an artificial device for arranging events or imposing a resolution. Such events tend to mar or even destroy a plot's plausibility and unity.

🌼 ANALYZING PLOT 🌼

1. What are the conflicts on which the plot turns? Are they external, internal, or some combination of the two?

2. What are the chief episodes or incidents that make up the plot? Is its development strictly chronological, or is the chronology rearranged in some way?

3. Compare the plot's beginning and end. What essential changes have taken place?

4. Describe the plot in terms of its exposition, complication, crisis, falling action, and resolution.

5. Is the plot unified? Do the individual episodes logically relate to one another?

6. Is the ending appropriate to and consistent with the rest of the plot?

7. Is the plot plausible? What role, if any, do chance and coincidence play?

The two stories by Nathaniel Hawthorne that follow—"My Kinsman, Major Molineux" and "Young Goodman Brown"—will serve as an introduction to plot, as well as to many of the other key elements of fiction to be discussed in the following pages. The plots of both stories utilize the familiar motif of the journey during which a young man undergoes a series of new and unsettling experiences that change his view both of himself and his world. Robin Molineux and Young Goodman Brown enter upon their adventures—one urban, the other rural—as initiates: as young men of good will who are as yet untried and untested in the ways of the adult world. Notice, as you read, how each separate incident of the plot serves in one way or another to advance the protagonist's education.

Nathaniel Hawthorne   1804–1864

MY KINSMAN, MAJOR MOLINEUX

After the kings of Great Britain had assumed the right of appointing the colonial governors, the measures of the latter seldom met with the ready and general approbation which had been paid to those of their predecessors, under the original charters. The people looked with most jealous scrutiny to the exercise of power which did not emanate from themselves, and they usually rewarded their rulers with slender gratitude for the compliances by which, in softening their instructions from beyond the sea, they had incurred the reprehension of those who gave them. The annals of Massachusetts Bay will inform us, that of six governors in the space of about forty years from the surrender of the old charter, under James II., two were imprisoned by a popular insurrection; a third, as Hutchinson inclines to believe,[1] was driven from the province by the whizzing of a musket-ball; a fourth, in the opinion of the same historian, was hastened to his grave by continual bickerings with the House of Representatives; and the remaining two, as well as their successors, till the Revolution, were favored with few and brief intervals of peaceful sway. The inferior members of the court party, in times of high political excitement, led scarcely a more desirable life. These remarks may serve as a preface to the following adventures, which chanced upon a summer night, not far from a hundred years ago.[2] The reader, in order to avoid a long and dry detail of colonial affairs, is requested to dispense with an account of the train of circumstances that had caused much temporary inflammation of the popular mind.

It was near nine o'clock of a moonlight evening, when a boat crossed the ferry with a single passenger, who had obtained his conveyance at that unusual hour by the promise of an extra fare. While he stood on the landing-place, searching in either pocket for the means of fulfilling his agreement, the ferryman lifted a lantern, by the aid of which, and the newly risen moon, he took a very accurate survey of the stranger's figure. He was a youth of barely eighteen years, evidently country-bred, and now, as it should seem, upon his first visit to town. He was clad in a coarse gray coat, well worn, but in excellent repair; his under garments were durably constructed of leather, and fitted tight to a pair of serviceable and well-shaped limbs; his stockings of blue yarn were the incontrovertible work of a mother or a sister; and on his head was a three-cornered hat, which in its better days had perhaps sheltered the graver brow of the lad's father. Under his left arm was a heavy cudgel formed of an oak sapling, and retaining a part of the hardened root; and his equipment was completed by a wallet, not so abundantly stocked as to incommode the vigorous shoulders on which it hung. Brown, curly hair, well-shaped features, and bright, cheerful eyes were nature's gifts, and worth all that art could have done for his adornment.

The youth, one of whose names was Robin, finally drew from his pocket the half of a little province bill of five shillings, which, in the depreciation in the sort of currency, did but satisfy the ferryman's demand, with the surplus of a sexangular

---

[1] Thomas Hutchinson (1711–1780), royal governor of Massachusetts from 1771 to 1774, and author of the *History of the Colony and Province of Massachusetts Bay,* published in three parts between 1764 and 1828.

[2] Hawthorne's story was first published in 1832.

piece of parchment, valued at three pence. He then walked forward into the town, with as light a step as if his day's journey had not already exceeded thirty miles, and with as eager an eye as if he were entering London city, instead of the little metropolis of a New England colony. Before Robin had proceeded far, however, it occurred to him that he knew not whither to direct his steps; so he paused, and looked up and down the narrow street, scrutinizing the small and mean wooden buildings that were scattered on either side.

"This low hovel cannot be my kinsman's dwelling," thought he, "nor yonder old house, where the moonlight enters at the broken casement; and truly I see none hereabouts that might be worthy of him. It would have been wise to inquire my way of the ferryman, and doubtless he would have gone with me, and earned a shilling from the Major for his pains. But the next man I meet will do as well."

He resumed his walk, and was glad to perceive that the street now became wider, and the houses more respectable in their appearance. He soon discerned a figure moving on moderately in advance, and hastened his steps to overtake it. As Robin drew nigh, he saw that the passenger was a man in years, with a full periwig of gray hair, a wide-skirted coat of dark cloth, and silk stockings rolled above his knees. He carried a long and polished cane, which he struck down perpendicularly before him at every step; and at regular intervals he uttered two successive hems, of a peculiarly solemn and sepulchral intonation. Having made these observations, Robin laid hold of the skirt of the old man's coat, just when the light from the open door and windows of a barber's shop fell upon both their figures.

"Good evening to you, honored sir," said he, making a low bow, and still retaining his hold of the skirt. "I pray you tell me whereabouts is the dwelling of my kinsman, Major Molineux."

The youth's question was uttered very loudly; and one of the barbers, whose razor was descending on a well-soaped chin, and another who was dressing a Ramillies wig,[3] left their occupations, and came to the door. The citizen, in the mean time, turned a long-favored countenance upon Robin, and answered him in a tone of excessive anger and annoyance. His two sepulchral hems, however, broke into the very centre of his rebuke, with most singular effect, like a thought of the cold grave obtruding among wrathful passions.

"Let go my garment, fellow! I tell you, I know not the man you speak of. What! I have authority, I have—hem, hem—authority; and if this be the respect you show for your betters, your feet shall be brought acquainted with the stocks by daylight, tomorrow morning!"

Robin released the old man's skirt, and hastened away, pursued by an ill-mannered roar of laughter from the barber's shop. He was at first considerably surprised by the result of his question, but, being a shrewd youth, soon thought himself able to account for the mystery.

"This is some country representative," was his conclusion, "who has never seen the inside of my kinsman's door, and lacks the breeding to answer a stranger civilly. The man is old, or verily—I might be tempted to turn back and smite him on the nose. Ah, Robin, Robin! even the barber's boys laugh at you for choosing such a guide! You will be wiser in time, friend Robin."

He now became entangled in a succession of crooked and narrow streets, which crossed each other, and meandered at no great distance from the waterside. The

---

[3] A type of wig with a long tail named after Ramillies in Belgium, site of a British military victory.

smell of tar was obvious to his nostrils, the masts of vessels pierced the moonlight above the tops of the buildings, and the numerous signs, which Robin paused to read, informed him that he was near the centre of business. But the streets were empty, the shops were closed, and lights were visible only in the second stories of a few dwelling-houses. At length, on the corner of a narrow lane, through which he was passing, he beheld the broad countenance of a British hero swinging before the door of an inn, whence proceeded the voices of many guests. The casement of one of the lower windows was thrown back, and a very thin curtain permitted Robin to distinguish a party at supper, round a well-furnished table. The fragrance of the good cheer steamed forth into the outer air, and the youth could not fail to recollect that the last remnant of his travelling stock of provision had yielded to his morning appetite, and that noon had found and left him dinnerless.

"Oh, that a parchment three-penny might give me a right to sit down at yonder table!" said Robin, with a sigh. "But the Major will make me welcome to the best of his victuals; so I will even step boldly in, and inquire my way to his dwelling."

He entered the tavern, and was guided by the murmur of voices and the fumes of tobacco to the public-room. It was a long and low apartment, with oaken walls, grown dark in the continual smoke, and a floor which was thickly sanded, but of no immaculate purity. A number of persons—the larger part of whom appeared to be mariners, or in some way connected with the sea—occupied the wooden benches, or leather-bottomed chairs, conversing on various matters, and occasionally lending their attention to some topic of general interest. Three or four little groups were draining as many bowls of punch, which the West India trade had long since made a familiar drink in the colony. Others, who had the appearance of men who lived by regular and laborious handicraft, preferred the insulated bliss of an unshared potation, and became more taciturn under its influence. Nearly all, in short, evinced a predilection for the Good Creature in some of its various shapes, for this is a vice to which, as Fast Day[4] sermons of a hundred years ago will testify, we have a long hereditary claim. The only guests to whom Robin's sympathies inclined him were two or three sheepish countrymen, who were using the inn somewhat after the fashion of a Turkish caravansary;[5] they had gotten themselves into the darkest corner of the room, and heedless of the Nicotian[6] atmosphere, were supping on the bread of their own ovens, and the bacon cured in their own chimney-smoke. But though Robin felt a sort of brotherhood with these strangers, his eyes were attracted from them to a person who stood near the door, holding whispered conversation with a group of ill-dressed associates. His features were separately striking almost to grotesqueness, and the whole face left a deep impression on the memory. The forehead bulged out into a double prominence, with a vale between; the nose came boldly forth in an irregular curve, and its bridge was of more than a finger's breadth; the eyebrows were deep and shaggy, and the eyes glowed beneath them like fire in a cave.

While Robin deliberated of whom to inquire respecting his kinsman's dwelling, he was accosted by the innkeeper, a little man in a stained white apron, who had come to pay his professional welcome to the stranger. Being in the second gen-

---

[4] A day set aside each spring throughout New England for public fasting, prayer, and sermonizing.
[5] An inn in eastern countries where caravans lodge for the night.
[6] Tobacco smoke, in reference to Jean Nicot, a diplomat on assignment to Spain, who introduced the use of tobacco to France in 1560.

eration from a French Protestant,[7] he seemed to have inherited the courtesy of his parent nation; but no variety of circumstances was ever known to change his voice from the one shrill note in which he now addressed Robin.

"From the country, I presume, sir?" said he, with a profound bow. "Beg leave to congratulate you on your arrival, and trust you intend a long stay with us. Fine town here, sir, beautiful buildings, and much that may interest a stranger. May I hope for the honor of your commands in respect to supper?"

"The man sees a family likeness! the rogue has guessed that I am related to the Major!" thought Robin, who had hitherto experienced little superfluous civility.

All eyes were now turned on the country lad, standing at the door, in his worn three-cornered hat, gray coat, leather breeches, and blue yarn stockings leaning on an oaken cudgel, and bearing a wallet on his back.

Robin replied to the courteous innkeeper, with such an assumption of confidence as befitted the Major's relative. "My honest friend," he said, "I shall make it a point to patronize your house on some occasion, when"—here he could not help lowering his voice—"when I may have more than a parchment three-pence in my pocket. My present business," continued he, speaking with lofty confidence, "is merely to inquire my way to the dwelling of my kinsman, Major Molineux."

There was a sudden and general movement in the room, which Robin interpreted as expressing the eagerness of each individual to become his guide. But the innkeeper turned his eyes to a written paper on the wall, which he read, or seemed to read, with occasional recurrences to the young man's figure.

"What have we here?" said he, breaking his speech into little dry fragments. " 'Left the house of the subscriber, bounden servant;[8] Hezekiah Mudge,—had on, when he went away, gray coat, leather breeches, master's third-best hat. One pound currency reward to whosoever shall lodge him in any jail of the province.' Better trudge, boy; better trudge!"

Robin had begun to draw his hand towards the lighter end of the oak cudgel, but a strange hostility in every countenance induced him to relinquish his purpose of breaking the courteous innkeeper's head. As he turned to leave the room, he encountered a sneering glance from the bold-featured personage whom he had before noticed; and no sooner was he beyond the door, than he heard a general laugh, in which the innkeeper's voice might be distinguished, like the dropping of small stones into a kettle.

"Now, is it not strange," thought Robin, with his usual shrewdness,—"is it not strange that the confession of an empty pocket should outweigh the name of my kinsman, Major Molineux? Oh, if I had one of those grinning rascals in the woods, where I and my oak sapling grew up together, I would teach him that my arm is heavy though my purse be light!"

On turning the corner of the narrow lane, Robin found himself in a spacious street, with an unbroken line of lofty houses on each side, and a steepled building at the upper end, whence the ringing of a bell announced the hour of nine. The light of the moon, and the lamps from the numerous shop-windows, discovered people promenading on the pavement, and amongst them Robin hoped to recognize his hitherto inscrutable relative. The result of his former inquiries made him unwilling to hazard another, in a scene of such publicity, and he determined

[7] Many French Protestants or Huguenots fled France to America after their freedom to worship was revoked with the Edict of Nantes in 1685.
[8] Indentured servants were bound over to their master's service for a period of years—often in return for having their passages to the colonies paid.

to walk slowly and silently up the street, thrusting his face close to that of every elderly gentleman, in search of the Major's lineaments. In his progress, Robin encountered many gay and gallant figures. Embroidered garments of showy colors, enormous periwigs, gold-laced hats, and silver-hilted swords glided past him and dazzled his optics. Travelled youths, imitators of the European fine gentlemen of the period, trod jauntily along, half dancing to the fashionable tunes which they hummed, and making poor Robin ashamed of his quiet and natural gait. At length, after many pauses to examine the gorgeous display of goods in the shop-windows, and after suffering some rebukes for the impertinence of his scrutiny into people's faces, the Major's kinsman found himself near the steepled building, still unsuccessful in his search. As yet, however, he had seen only one side of the thronged street; so Robin crossed, and continued the same sort of inquisition down the opposite pavement, with stronger hopes than the philosopher seeking an honest man, but with no better fortune. He had arrived about midway towards the lower end, from which his course began, when he overheard the approach of some one who struck down a cane on the flag-stones at every step, uttering, at regular intervals, two sepulchral hems.

"Mercy on us!" quoth Robin, recognizing the sound.

Turning a corner, which chanced to be close at his right hand, he hastened to pursue his researches in some other part of the town. His patience now was wearing low, and he seemed to feel more fatigue from his rambles since he crossed the ferry, than from his journey of several days on the other side. Hunger also pleaded loudly within him, and Robin began to balance the propriety of demanding, violently, and with lifted cudgel, the necessary guidance from the first solitary passenger whom he should meet. While a resolution to this effect was gaining strength, he entered a street of mean appearance, on either side of which a row of ill-built houses was straggling towards the harbor. The moonlight fell upon no passenger along the whole extent, but in the third domicile which Robin passed there was a half-opened door, and his keen glance detected a woman's garment within.

"My luck may be better here," said he to himself.

Accordingly, he approached the door, and beheld it shut closer as he did so; yet an open space remained, sufficing for the fair occupant to observe the stranger, without a corresponding display on her part. All that Robin could discern was a strip of scarlet petticoat, and the occasional sparkle of an eye, as if the moonbeams were trembling on some bright thing.

"Pretty mistress," for I may call her so with a good conscience, thought the shrewd youth, since I know nothing to the contrary,—"my sweet pretty mistress, will you be kind enough to tell me whereabouts I must seek the dwelling of my kinsman, Major Molineux?"

Robin's voice was plaintive and winning, and the female, seeing nothing to be shunned in the handsome country youth, thrust open the door, and came forth into the moonlight. She was a dainty little figure, with a white neck, round arms, and a slender waist, at the extremity of which her scarlet petticoat jutted out over a hoop, as if she were standing in a balloon. Moreover, her face was oval and pretty, her hair dark beneath the little cap, and her bright eyes possessed a sly freedom, which triumphed over those of Robin.

"Major Molineux dwells here," said this fair woman.

Now, her voice was the sweetest Robin had heard that night, the airy counterpart of a stream of melted silver; yet he could not help doubting whether that sweet voice spoke Gospel truth. He looked up and down the mean street, and then surveyed the house before which they stood. It was a small, dark edifice of two stories, the second of which projected over the lower floor, and the front apartment had the aspect of a shop for petty commodities.

"Now, truly, I am in luck," replied Robin, cunningly, "and so indeed is my kinsman, the Major, in having so pretty a housekeeper. But I prithee trouble him to step to the door; I will deliver him a message from his friends in the country, and then go back to my lodgings at the inn."

"Nay, the Major has been abed this hour or more," said the lady of the scarlet petticoat; "and it would be to little purpose to disturb him to-night, seeing his evening draught was of the strongest. But he is a kind-hearted man, and it would be as much as my life's worth to let a kinsman of his turn away from the door. You are the good old gentleman's very picture, and I could swear that was his rainy-weather hat. Also he has garments very much resembling those leather small-clothes. But come in, I pray, for I bid you hearty welcome in his name."

So saying, the fair and hospitable dame took our hero by the hand; and the touch was light, and the force was gentleness, and though Robin read in her eyes what he did not hear in her words, yet the slender-waisted woman in the scarlet petticoat proved stronger than the athletic country youth. She had drawn his half-willing footsteps nearly to the threshold, when the opening of a door in the neighborhood startled the Major's housekeeper, and, leaving the Major's kinsman, she vanished speedily into her own domicile. A heavy yawn preceded the appearance of a man, who, like the Moonshine of Pyramus and Thisbe, carried a lantern,[9] needlessly aiding his sister luminary in the heavens. As he walked sleepily up the street, he turned his broad, dull face on Robin, and displayed a long staff, spiked at the end.

"Home, vagabond, home!" said the watchman, in accents that seemed to fall asleep as soon as they were uttered. "Home, or we'll set you in the stocks by peep of day!"

"This is the second hint of the kind," thought Robin. "I wish they would end my difficulties, by setting me there to-night."

Nevertheless, the youth felt an instinctive antipathy towards the guardian of midnight order, which at first prevented him from asking his usual question. But just when the man was about to vanish behind the corner, Robin resolved not to lose the opportunity, and shouted lustily after him,—

"I say, friend! will you guide me to the house of my kinsman, Major Molineux?"

The watchman made no reply, but turned the corner and was gone; yet Robin seemed to hear the sound of drowsy laughter stealing along the solitary street. At that moment, also, a pleasant titter saluted him from the open window above his head; he looked up, and caught the sparkle of a saucy eye; a round arm beckoned to him, and next he heard light footsteps descending the staircase within. But Robin, being of the household of a New England clergyman, was a good youth, as well as a shrewd one; so he resisted temptation, and fled away.

He now roamed desperately, and at random, through the town, almost ready to believe that a spell was on him, like that by which a wizard of his country had once kept three pursuers wandering, a whole winter night, within twenty paces of the cottage which they sought. The streets lay before him, strange and desolate, and the lights were extinguished in almost every house. Twice, however, little parties

---

[9] An allusion to the comic play presented by the tradesmen in *A Midsummer Night's Dream* (1600) by William Shakespeare (1564–1616) in which a character named Moonshine appears with lantern in hand.

of men, among whom Robin distinguished individuals in outlandish attire, came hurrying along; but, though on both occasions they paused to address him, such intercourse did not at all enlighten his perplexity. They did but utter a few words in some language of which Robin knew nothing, and perceiving his inability to answer, bestowed a curse upon him in plain English and hastened away. Finally, the lad determined to knock at the door of every mansion that might appear worthy to be occupied by his kinsman, trusting that perseverance would overcome the fatality that had hitherto thwarted him. Firm in this resolve, he was passing beneath the walls of a church, which formed the corner of two streets, when, as he turned into the shade of its steeple, he encountered a bulky stranger, muffled in a cloak. The man was proceeding with the speed of earnest business, but Robin planted himself full before him, holding the oak cudgel with both hands across his body as a bar to further passage.

"Halt, honest man, and answer me a question," said he, very resolutely. "Tell me, this instant, whereabouts is the dwelling of my kinsman, Major Molineux!"

"Keep your tongue between your teeth, fool, and let me pass!" said a deep, gruff voice, which Robin partly remembered. "Let me pass, I say, or I'll strike you to the earth!"

"No, no, neighbor!" cried Robin, flourishing his cudgel, and then thrusting its larger end close to the man's muffled face. "No, no, I'm not the fool you take me for, nor do you pass till I have an answer to my question. Whereabouts is the dwelling of my kinsman, Major Molineux?"

The stranger, instead of attempting to force his passage, stepped back into the moonlight, unmuffled his face, and stared full into that of Robin.

"Watch here an hour, and Major Molineux will pass by," said he.

Robin gazed with dismay and astonishment on the unprecedented physiognomy of the speaker. The forehead with its double prominence, the broad hooked nose, the shaggy eyebrows, and fiery eyes were those which he had noticed at the inn, but the man's complexion had undergone a singular, or, more properly, a twofold change. One side of the face blazed an intense red, while the other was black as midnight, the division line being in the broad bridge of the nose; and a mouth which seemed to extend from ear to ear was black or red; in contrast to the color of the cheek. The effect was as if two individual devils, a fiend of fire and a fiend of darkness, had united themselves to form this infernal visage. The stranger grinned in Robin's face, muffled his party-colored features, and was out of sight in a moment.

"Strange things we travellers see!" ejaculated Robin.

He seated himself, however, upon the steps of the church-door, resolving to wait the appointed time for his kinsman. A few moments were consumed in philosophical speculations upon the species of man who had just left him; but having settled this point shrewdly, rationally, and satisfactorily, he was compelled to look elsewhere for his amusement. And first he threw his eyes along the street. It was of more respectable appearance than most of those into which he had wandered; and the moon, creating, like the imaginative power, a beautiful strangeness in familiar objects, gave something of romance to a scene that might not have possessed it in the light of day. The irregular and often quaint architecture of the houses, some of whose roofs were broken into numerous little peaks, while others ascended, steep and narrow, into a single point, and others again were square; the pure snow-white of some of their complexions, the aged darkness of others, and the thousand sparklings, reflected from bright substances in the walls of many; these matters engaged Robin's attention for a while, and then began to grow wearisome. Next he endeavored to define the forms of distant objects, starting away, with almost ghostly indistinctness, just as his eye appeared to grasp them; and finally he took a minute survey of an edifice which stood on the opposite side of the street, directly in front of the church-door, where he was stationed. It was a large, square mansion, distinguished from its neighbors by a balcony, which rested on tall pillars, and by an elaborate Gothic window, communicating therewith.

"Perhaps this is the very house I have been seeking," thought Robin.

Then he strove to speed away the time, by listening to a murmur which swept continually along the street, yet was scarcely audible, except to an unaccustomed ear like his; it was a low, dull, dreamy sound, compounded of many noises, each of which was at too great a distance to be separately heard. Robin marvelled at this snore of a sleeping town, and marvelled more whenever its continuity was broken by now and then a distant shout, apparently loud where it originated. But altogether it was a sleep-inspiring sound, and, to shake off its drowsy influence, Robin arose, and climbed a window-frame, that he might view the interior of the church. There the moonbeams came trembling in, and fell down upon the deserted pews, and extended along the quiet aisles. A fainter yet more awful radiance was hovering around the pulpit, and one solitary ray had dared to rest upon the open page of the great Bible. Had nature, in that deep hour, become a worshipper in the house which man had builded? Or was that heavenly light the visible sanctity of the place,—visible because no earthly and impure feet were within the walls? The scene made Robin's heart shiver with a sensation of loneliness stronger than he had ever felt in the remotest depths of his native woods; so he turned away and sat down again before the door. There were graves around the church, and now an uneasy thought obtruded into Robin's breast. What if the object of his search, which had been so often and so strangely thwarted, were all the time mouldering in his shroud? What if his kinsman should glide through yonder gate, and nod and smile to him in dimly passing by?

"Oh that any breathing thing were here with me!" said Robin.

Recalling his thoughts from this uncomfortable track, he sent them over forest, hill, and stream, and attempted to imagine how that evening of ambiguity and weariness had been spent by his father's household. He pictured them assembled at the door, beneath the tree, the great old tree, which had been spared for its huge twisted trunk and venerable shade, when a thousand leafy brethren fell. There, at the going down of the summer sun, it was his father's custom to perform domestic worship, that the neighbors might come and join with him like brothers of the family, and that the wayfaring man might pause to drink at that fountain, and keep his heart pure by freshening the memory of home. Robin distinguished the seat of every individual of the little audience; he saw the good man in the midst, holding the Scriptures in the golden light that fell from the western clouds; he beheld him close the book and all rise up to pray. He heard the old thanksgivings for daily mercies, the old supplications for their continuance, to which he had so often listened in weariness, but which were now among his dear remembrances. He perceived the slight inequality of his father's voice when he came to speak of the absent one; he noted how his mother turned her face to the broad and knotted trunk; how his elder brother scorned, because the beard was rough upon his upper lip, to permit his features to be moved; how the younger sister drew down a low hanging branch before her eyes; and how the little one of all, whose sports had hitherto broken the decorum of the scene, understood the prayer for her playmate, and burst into clamorous grief. Then he saw them go in at the door; and when Robin would have entered also, the latch tinkled into its place, and he was excluded from his home.

"Am I here, or there?" cried Robin, starting; for all at once, when his thoughts had become visible and audible in a dream, the long, wide, solitary street shone out before him.

He aroused himself, and endeavored to fix his attention steadily upon the large edifice which he had surveyed before. But still his mind kept vibrating between fancy and reality; by turns, the pillars of the balcony lengthened into the tall, bare stems of pines, dwindled down to human figures, settled again into their true shape and size, and then commenced a new succession of changes. For a single moment, when he deemed himself awake, he could have sworn that a visage—one which he seemed to remember, yet could not absolutely name as his kinsman's— was looking towards him from the Gothic window. A deeper sleep wrestled with and nearly overcame him, but fled at the sound of footsteps along the opposite pavement. Robin rubbed his eyes, discerned a man passing at the foot of the balcony, and addressed him in a loud, peevish, and lamentable cry.

"Hallo, friend! must I wait here all night for my kinsman, Major Molineux?"

The sleeping echoes awoke, and answered the voice; and the passenger, barely able to discern a figure sitting in the oblique shade of the steeple, traversed the street to obtain a nearer view. He was himself a gentleman in his prime, of open, intelligent, cheerful, and altogether prepossessing countenance. Perceiving a country youth, apparently homeless and without friends, he accosted him in a tone of real kindness, which had become strange to Robin's ears.

"Well, my good lad, why are you sitting here?" inquired he. "Can I be of service to you in any way?"

"I am afraid not, sir," replied Robin, despondingly; "yet I shall take it kindly, if you'll answer me a single question. I've been searching, half the night, for one Major Molineux; now, sir, is there really such a person in these parts, or am I dreaming?"

"Major Molineux! The name is not altogether strange to me," said the gentleman, smiling. "Have you any objection to telling me the nature of your business with him?"

Then Robin briefly related that his father was a clergyman, settled on a small salary, at a long distance back in the country, and that he and Major Molineux were brothers' children. The Major, having inherited riches, and acquired civil and military rank, had visited his cousin, in great pomp, a year or two before; had manifested much interest in Robin and an elder brother, and, being childless himself, had thrown out hints respecting the future establishment of one of them in life. The elder brother was destined to succeed to the farm which his father cultivated in the interval of sacred duties; it was therefore determined that Robin should profit by his kinsman's generous intentions, especially as he seemed to be rather the favorite, and was thought to possess other necessary endowments.

"For I have the name of being a shrewd youth," observed Robin, in this part of his story.

"I doubt not you deserve it," replied his new friend, good-naturedly; "but pray proceed."

"Well, sir, being nearly eighteen years old, and well grown, as you see," continued Robin, drawing himself up to his full height, "I thought it high time to begin the world. So my mother and sister put me in handsome trim, and my father gave me half the remnant of his last year's salary, and five days ago I started for this place, to pay the Major a visit. But, would you believe it, sir! I crossed the ferry a little after dark, and have yet found nobody that would show me the way to his dwelling; only, an hour or two since, I was told to wait here, and Major Molineux would pass by."

"Can you describe the man who told you this?" inquired the gentleman.

"Oh, he was a very ill-favored fellow, sir," replied Robin, "with two great bumps on his forehead, a hook nose, fiery eyes; and, what struck me as the strangest, his face was of two different colors. Do you happen to know such a man, sir?"

"Not intimately," answered the stranger, "but I chanced to meet him a little time previous to your stopping me. I believe you may trust his word, and that the Major will very shortly pass through this street. In the mean time, as I have a singular curiosity to witness your meeting, I will sit down here upon the steps and bear you company."

He seated himself accordingly, and soon engaged his companion in animated discourse. It was but of brief continuance, however, for a noise of shouting, which had long been remotely audible, drew so much nearer that Robin inquired its cause.

"What may be the meaning of this uproar?" asked he. "Truly, if your town be always as noisy, I shall find little sleep while I am an inhabitant."

"Why, indeed, friend Robin, there do appear to be three or four riotous fellows abroad to-night," replied the gentleman. "You must not expect all the stillness of your native woods here in our streets. But the watch will shortly be at the heels of these lads and"—

"Ay, and set them in the stocks by peep of day," interrupted Robin, recollecting his own encounter with the drowsy lantern-bearer. "But, dear sir, if I may trust my ears, an army of watchmen would never make head against such a multitude of rioters. There were at least a thousand voices went up to make that one shout."

"May not a man have several voices, Robin, as well as two complexions?" said his friend.

"Perhaps a man may; but Heaven forbid that a woman should!" responded the shrewd youth, thinking of the seductive tones of the Major's housekeeper.

The sounds of a trumpet in some neighboring street now became so evident and continual, that Robin's curiosity was strongly excited. In addition to the shouts, he heard frequent bursts from many instruments of discord, and a wild and confused laughter filled up the intervals. Robin rose from the steps, and looked wistfully towards a point whither people seemed to be hastening.

"Surely some prodigious merry-making is going on," exclaimed he. "I have laughed very little since I left home, sir, and should be sorry to lose an opportunity. Shall we step round the corner by that darkish house, and take our share of the fun?"

"Sit down again, sit down, good Robin," replied the gentleman, laying his hand on the skirt of the gray coat. "You forget that we must wait here for your kinsman; and there is reason to believe that he will pass by, in the course of a very few moments."

The near approach of the uproar had now disturbed the neighborhood; windows flew open on all sides; and many heads, in the attire of the pillow, and confused by sleep suddenly broken, were protruded to the gaze of whoever had leisure to observe them. Eager voices hailed each other from house to house, all demanding the explanation, which not a soul could give. Half-dressed men hurried towards the unknown commotion, stumbling as they went over the stone steps that thrust themselves into the narrow foot-walk. The shouts, the laughter, and the tuneless bray, the antipodes of music, came onwards with increasing din, till scattered individuals, and then denser bodies, began to appear round a corner at the distance of a hundred yards.

"Will you recognize your kinsman, if he passes in this crowd?" inquired the gentleman.

"Indeed, I can't warrant it, sir; but I'll take my stand here, and keep a bright lookout," answered Robin, descending to the outer edge of the pavement.

A mighty stream of people now emptied into the street, and came rolling slowly towards the church. A single horseman wheeled the corner in the midst of them, and close behind him came a band of fearful wind-instruments, sending forth a fresher discord now that no intervening buildings kept it from the ear. Then a redder light disturbed the moonbeams, and a dense multitude of torches shone along the street, concealing, by their glare, whatever object they illuminated. The single horseman, clad in a military dress, and bearing a drawn sword, rode onward as the leader, and, by his fierce and variegated countenance, appeared like war personified; the red of one cheek was an emblem of fire and sword; the blackness of the other betokened the mourning that attends them. In his train were wild figures in the Indian dress, and many fantastic shapes without a model, giving the whole march a visionary air, as if a dream had broken forth from some feverish brain, and were sweeping visibly through the midnight streets. A mass of people, inactive, except as applauding spectators, hemmed the procession in; and several women ran along the sidewalk, piercing the confusion of heavier sounds with their shrill voices of mirth or terror.

"The double-faced fellow has his eye upon me," muttered Robin, with an indefinite but an uncomfortable idea that he was himself to bear a part in the pageantry.

The leader turned himself in the saddle, and fixed his glance full upon the country youth, as the steed went slowly by. When Robin had freed his eyes from those fiery ones, the musicians were passing before him, and the torches were close at hand; but the unsteady brightness of the latter formed a veil which he could not penetrate. The rattling of wheels over the stones sometimes found its way to his ear, and confused traces of a human form appeared at intervals, and then melted into the vivid light. A moment more, and the leader thundered a command to halt: the trumpets vomited a horrid breath, and then held their peace; the shouts and laughter of the people died away, and there remained only a universal hum, allied to silence. Right before Robin's eyes was an uncovered cart. There the torches blazed the brightest, there the moon shone out like day, and there, in tar-and-feathery dignity, sat his kinsman, Major Molineux!

He was an elderly man, of large and majestic person, and strong, square features, betokening a steady soul; but steady as it was, his enemies had found means to shake it. His face was pale as death, and far more ghastly; the broad forehead was contracted in his agony, so that his eyebrows formed one grizzled line; his eyes were red and wild, and the foam hung white upon his quivering lip. His whole frame was agitated by a quick and continual tremor, which his pride strove to quell, even in those circumstances of overwhelming humiliation. But perhaps the bitterest pang of all was when his eyes met those of Robin; for he evidently knew him on the instant, as the youth stood witnessing the foul disgrace of a head grown gray in honor. They stared at each other in silence, and Robin's knees shook, and his hair bristled, with a mixture of pity and terror. Soon, however, a bewildering excitement began to seize upon his mind; the preceding adventures of the night, the unexpected appearance of the crowd, the torches, the confused din and the hush that followed, the spectre of his kinsman reviled by that great multitude,—all this, and more than all, a perception of tremendous ridicule in the whole scene, affected him with a sort of mental inebriety. At that moment a voice of sluggish merriment saluted Robin's ears; he turned instinctively, and just behind the corner of the church stood the lantern-bearer, rubbing his eyes, and drowsily enjoying the lad's amazement. Then he heard a peal of laughter like the ringing of silvery bells; a woman twitched his arm, a saucy eye met his, and he saw the lady of the scarlet petticoat. A sharp, dry cachinnation appealed to his memory, and, standing on tiptoe in the crowd, with his white apron over his head, he beheld the courteous little innkeeper. And lastly, there sailed over the heads of the multitude a great, broad laugh, broken in the midst by two sepulchral hems; thus, "Haw, haw, haw,—hem, hem,—haw, haw, haw, haw!"

The sound proceeded from the balcony of the opposite edifice, and thither Robin turned his eyes. In front of the Gothic window stood the old citizen, wrapped in a wide gown, his gray periwig exchanged for a nightcap, which was thrust back from his forehead, and his silk stockings hanging about his legs. He supported himself on his polished cane in a fit of convulsive merriment, which manifested itself on his solemn old features like a funny inscription on a tombstone. Then Robin seemed to hear the voices of the barbers, of the guests of the inn, and of all who had made sport of him that night. The contagion was spreading among the multitude, when all at once, it seized upon Robin, and he sent forth a shout of laughter that echoed through the street,—every man shook his sides, every man emptied his lungs, but Robin's shout was the loudest there. The cloud-spirits peeped from their silvery islands, as the congregated mirth went roaring up the sky! The Man in the Moon heard the far bellow. "Oho," quoth he, "the old earth is frolicsome to-night!"

When there was a momentary calm in that tempestuous sea of sound, the leader gave the sign, the procession resumed its march. On they went, like fiends that throng in mockery around some dead potentate, mighty no more, but majestic still in his agony. On they went, in counterfeited pomp, in senseless uproar, in frenzied merriment, trampling all on an old man's heart. On swept the tumult, and left a silent street behind.

"Well, Robin, are you dreaming?" inquired the gentleman, laying his hand on the youth's shoulder.

Robin started, and withdrew his arm from the stone post to which he had instinctively clung, as the living stream rolled by him. His cheek was somewhat pale, and his eye not quite as lively as in the earlier part of the evening.

"Will you be kind enough to show me the way to the ferry?" said he, after a moment's pause.

"You have, then, adopted a new subject of inquiry?" observed his companion, with a smile.

"Why, yes, sir," replied Robin, rather dryly. "Thanks to you, and to my other friends, I have at last met my kinsman, and he will scarce desire to see my face again. I begin to grow weary of a town life, sir. Will you show me the way to the ferry?"

"No, my good friend Robin,—not to-night, at least," said the gentleman. "Some few days hence, if you wish it, I will speed you on your journey. Or, if you prefer to remain with us, perhaps, as you are a shrewd youth, you may rise in the world without the help of your kinsman, Major Molineux."

[1832]

Nathaniel Hawthorne *1804–1864*

YOUNG GOODMAN BROWN

Young Goodman[1] Brown came forth at sunset, into the street of Salem village,[2] but put his head back, after crossing the threshold, to exchange a parting kiss with his young wife. And Faith, as the wife was aptly named, thrust her own pretty head into the street, letting the wind play with the pink ribbons of her cap, while she called to Goodman Brown.

"Dearest heart," whispered she, softly and rather sadly, when her lips were close to his ear, "prithee, put off your journey until sunrise, and sleep in your own bed to-night. A lone woman is troubled with such dreams and such thoughts, that she's afeard of herself, sometimes. Pray, tarry with me this night, dear husband, of all nights in the year!"

"My love and my Faith," replied young Goodman Brown, "of all nights in the year, this one night must I tarry away from thee. My journey, as thou callest it, forth and back again, must needs be done 'twixt now and sunrise. What, my sweet, pretty wife, dost thou doubt me already, and we but three months married!"

"Then God bless you" said Faith with the pink ribbons, "and may you find all well, when you come back."

"Amen!" cried Goodman Brown. "Say thy prayers, dear Faith, and go to bed at dusk, and no harm will come to thee."

So they parted; and the young man pursued his way until, being about to turn the corner by the meeting-house, he looked back and saw the head of Faith still peeping after him, with a melancholy air, in spite of her pink ribbons.

"Poor little Faith!" thought he, for his heart smote him. "What a wretch am I, to leave her on such an errand! She talks of dreams, too. Methought, as she spoke, there was trouble in her face, as if a dream had warned her what work is to be done to-night. But no, no! 't would kill her to think it. Well; she's a blessed angel on earth; and after this one night, I'll cling to her skirts and follow her to Heaven."

With this excellent resolve for the future, Goodman Brown felt himself justified in making more haste on his present evil purpose. He had taken a dreary road, darkened by all the gloomiest trees of the forest, which barely stood aside to let the narrow path creep through, and closed immediately behind. It was as lonely as could be; and there is this peculiarity in such a solitude, that the traveller knows not who may be concealed by the innumerable trunks and the thick boughs overhead; so that, with lonely footsteps, he may yet be passing through an unseen multitude.

"There may be a devilish Indian behind every tree," said Goodman Brown to himself; and he glanced fearfully behind him, as he added, "What if the devil himself should be at my very elbow!"

His head being turned back, he passed a crook of the road, and looking forward again, beheld the figure of a man, in grave and decent attire, seated at the foot of

---

[1] A respectful title of address for individuals not of gentle birth.

[2] Located some sixteen miles northeast of Boston, the Puritan village of Salem, first settled in 1626, was the site of the famous witchcraft hysteria of 1691–1692. John Hathorne, one of Nathaniel Hawthorne's ancestors, presided over the Salem witch trials as a judge. The author himself was born in Salem in 1804.

an old tree. He arose at Goodman Brown's approach, and walked onward, side by side with him.

"You are late, Goodman Brown," said he. "The clock of the Old South[3] was striking, as I came through Boston; and that is full fifteen minutes agone."

"Faith kept me back awhile," replied the young man, with a tremor in his voice, caused by the sudden appearance of his companion, though not wholly unexpected.

It was now deep dusk in the forest, and deepest in that part of it where these two were journeying. As nearly as could be discerned, the second traveller was about fifty years old, apparently in the same rank of life as Goodman Brown, and bearing a considerable resemblance to him, though perhaps more in expression than features. Still, they might have been taken for father and son. And yet, though the elder person was as simply clad as the younger, and as simple in manner too, he had an indescribable air of one who knew the world, and would not have felt abashed at the governor's dinner-table, or in King William's court,[4] were it possible that his affairs should call him thither. But the only thing about him that could be fixed upon as remarkable, was his staff, which bore the likeness of a great black snake, so curiously wrought, that it might almost be seen to twist and wriggle itself like a living serpent. This, of course, must have been an ocular deception, assisted by the uncertain light.

"Come, Goodman Brown!" cried his fellow-traveller, "This is a dull pace for the beginning of a journey. Take my staff, if you are so soon weary."

"Friend," said the other, exchanging his slow pace for a full stop, "having kept covenant by meeting thee here, it is my purpose now to return whence I came. I have scruples, touching the matter thou wot'st of."

"Sayest thou so?" replied he of the serpent, smiling apart. "Let us walk on, nevertheless, reasoning as we go, and if I convince thee not, thou shalt turn back. We are but a little way in the forest, yet."

"Too far, too far!" exclaimed the goodman, unconsciously resuming his walk. "My father never went into the woods on such an errand, nor his father before him. We have been a race of honest men and good Christians, since the days of the martyrs.[5] And shall I be the first of the name of Brown that ever took this path and kept"—

"Such company, thou wouldst say," observed the elder person, interrupting his pause. "Well said, Goodman Brown! I have been as well acquainted with your family as with ever a one among the Puritans; and that's no trifle to say. I helped your grandfather, the constable, when he lashed the Quaker woman so smartly through the streets of Salem. And it was I that brought your father a pitchpine knot, kindled at my own hearth, to set fire to an Indian village, in King Philip's war.[6] They were my good friends, both; and many a pleasant walk have we had along this path, and returned merrily after midnight. I would fain be friends with you, for their sake."

"If it be as thou sayest," replied Goodman Brown, "I marvel they never spoke of these matters. Or, verily, I marvel not, seeing that the least rumor of the sort

[3] Old South, the Third Church of Boston, was established in 1669.

[4] William of Orange (1650–1702) who together with Queen Mary II ruled England from 1689 until 1702.

[5] That is, since the period when Mary Tudor, the Catholic queen who ruled England from 1553 until 1558, systematically persecuted Protestants.

[6] The Wampanoag Indians led by Metacom or King Philip waged a short-lived uprising against the New England colonists (1675–1676).

would have driven them from New England. We are a people of prayer, and good works to boot, and abide no such wickedness."

"Wickedness or not," said the traveller with the twisted staff, "I have a very general acquaintance here in new England. The deacons of many a church have drunk the communion wine with me; the selectmen, of divers towns, make me their chairman; and a majority of the Great and General Court[7] are firm supporters of my interest. The governor and I, too—but these are state secrets."

"Can this be so!" cried Goodman Brown, with a stare of amazement at his undisturbed companion. "Howbeit, I have nothing to do with the governor and council; they have their own ways, and are no rule for a simple husbandman[8] like me. But, were I to go on with thee, how should I meet the eye of that good old man, our minister, at Salem village? Oh, his voice would make me tremble, both Sabbath-day and lecture-day!"[9]

Thus far, the elder traveller had listened with due gravity, but now burst into a fit of irrepressible mirth, shaking himself so violently, that his snakelike staff actually seemed to wriggle in sympathy.

"Ha, ha, ha!" shouted he, again and again; then composing himself, "Well, go on, Goodman Brown, go on; but, prithee, don't kill me with laughing!"

"Well, then, to end the matter at once," said Goodman Brown, considerably nettled, "there is my wife, Faith. It would break her dear little heart; and I'd rather break my own!"

"Nay, if that be the case," answered the other, "e'en[10] go thy ways, Goodman Brown. I would not, for twenty old women like the one hobbling before us, that Faith should come to any harm."

As he spoke, he pointed his staff at a female figure on the path, in whom Goodman Brown recognized a very pious and exemplary dame, who had taught him his catechism in youth, and was still his moral and spiritual adviser, jointly with the minister and Deacon Gookin.

"A marvel, truly, that Goody[11] Cloyse should be so far in the wilderness, at nightfall!" said he. "But, with your leave, friend, I shall take a cut[12] through the woods, until we have left this Christian woman behind. Being a stranger to you, she might ask whom I was consorting with, and whither I was going."

"Be it so," said his fellow-traveller. "Betake you to the woods, and let me keep the path."

Accordingly, the young man turned aside, but took care to watch his companion, who advanced softly along the road, until he had come within a staff's length of the old dame. She, meanwhile, was making the best of her way, with singular speed for so aged a woman, and mumbling some indistinct words, a prayer, doubtless, as she went. The traveller put forth his staff, and touched her withered neck with what seemed the serpent's tail.

"The devil!" screamed the pious old lady.

"Then Goody Cloyse knows her old friend?" observed the traveller, confronting her, and leaning on his writhing stick.

"Ah, forsooth, and is it your worship, indeed?" cried the good dame. "Yea, truly is it, and in the very image of my old gossip,[13] Goodman Brown, the grandfather

---

[7] Massachusetts' colonial legislature.   [8] Farmer; but here used in the sense of an ordinary citizen.
[9] New England Puritans set aside two days during the week for the preaching and hearing of sermons or lectures: the Sabbath, or Sunday, and lecture day, usually Wednesday or Thursday.
[10] Just.   [11] Short for "goodwife," the female equivalent of "goodman."
[12] Shortcut.   [13] Friend.

of the silly fellow that now is. But, would your worship believe it? my broomstick
hath strangely disappeared, stolen, as I suspect, by that unhanged witch, Goody
Cory,[14] and that, too, when I was all anointed with the juice of smallage and
cinque-foil and wolf's-bane—"[15]

"Mingled with fine wheat and the fat of a new-born babe," said the shape of old
Goodman Brown.

"Ah, your worship knows the recipe," cried the old lady, cackling aloud. "So,
as I was saying, being all ready for the meeting, and no horse to ride on, I made
up my mind to foot it; for they tell me there is a nice young man to be taken into
communion to-night. But now your good worship will lend me your arm, and we
shall be there in a twinkling."

"That can hardly be," answered her friend. "I may not spare you my arm,
Goody Gloyse, but here is my staff, if you will."

So saying, he threw it down at her feet, where, perhaps, it assumed life, being
one of the rods which its owner had formerly lent to the Egyptian Magi.[16] Of this
fact, however, Goodman Brown could not take cognizance. He had cast his eyes
in astonishment, and looking down again, beheld neither Goody Cloyse nor the
serpentine staff, but his fellow-traveller alone, who waited for him as calmly as if
nothing had happened.

"That old woman taught me my catechism!" said the young man; and there was
a world of meaning in this simple comment.

They continued to walk onward, while the elder traveller exhorted his companion to make good speed and persevere in the path, discoursing so aptly, that his
arguments seemed rather to spring up in the bosom of his auditor, than to be
suggested by himself. As they went he plucked a branch of maple, to serve for a
walking-stick, and began to strip it of the twigs and little boughs, which were wet
with evening dew. The moment his fingers touched them, they became strangely
withered and dried up, as with a week's sunshine. Thus the pair proceeded, at a
good free pace, until suddenly, in a gloomy hollow of the road, Goodman Brown
sat himself down on the stump of a tree, and refused to go any farther.

"Friend," said he, stubbornly, "my mind is made up. Not another step will I
budge on this errand. What if a wretched old woman do choose to go to the devil,
when I thought she was going to Heaven! Is that any reason why I should quit my
dear Faith, and go after her?"

"You will think better of this by and by," said his acquaintance, composedly.
"Sit here and rest yourself awhile; and when you feel like moving again, there is
my staff to help you along."

Without more words, he threw his companion the maple stick, and was as
speedily out of sight as if he had vanished into the deepening gloom. The young
man sat a few moments by the roadside, applauding himself greatly, and thinking
with how clear a conscience he should meet the minister, in his morning walk, nor

[14] Martha Cory, a member in good standing of the church at Salem, was accused, tried, and hung for
witchcraft on September 22, 1692; her husband, Giles, was pressed to death with stones three days
earlier for failing to plead guilty or not guilty to charges of wizardry. Sarah Cloyse (above) was jailed
for witchcraft but later released. Both she and Martha Cory are referred to in contemporary court
records as "Goody."

[15] Plants associated with the practice of witchcraft.

[16] The allusion is to the story of Aaron's rod, which when cast at the feet of Egypt's Pharaoh turns into
a serpent. Summoning his magicians, pharaoh orders them to follow Aaron's example: "For every
man cast down his rod, and they became serpents. But Aaron's rod swallowed up their rods." See
Exodus 7:8–12.

shrink from the eye of good old Deacon Gookin. And what calm sleep would be his, that very night, which was to have been spent so wickedly, but purely and sweetly now, in the arms of Faith! Amidst these pleasant and praiseworthy meditations, Goodman Brown heard the tramp of horses along the road, and deemed it advisable to conceal himself within the verge of the forest, conscious of the guilty purpose that had brought him thither, though now so happily turned from it.

On came the hoof-tramps and the voices of the riders, two grave old voices, conversing soberly as they drew near. These mingled sounds appeared to pass along the road, within a few yards of the young man's hiding-place; but owing, doubtless, to the depth of the gloom at that particular spot, neither the travellers nor their steeds were visible. Though their figures brushed the small boughs by the wayside, it could not be seen that they intercepted, even for a moment, the faint gleam from the strip of bright sky, athwart which they must have passed. Goodman Brown alternately crouched and stood on tiptoe, pulling aside the branches, and thrusting forth his head as far as he durst, without discerning so much as a shadow. It vexed him the more, because he could have sworn, were such a thing possible, that he recognized the voices of the minister and Deacon Gookin, jogging along quietly, as they were wont to do, when bound to some ordination or ecclesiastical council. While yet within hearing, one of the riders stopped to pluck a switch.

"Of the two, reverend Sir," said the voice like the deacon's, "I had rather miss an ordination dinner than to-night's meeting. They tell me that some of our community are to be here from Falmouth[17] and beyond, and others from Connecticut and Rhode Island; besides several of the Indian powwows,[18] who, after their fashion, know almost as much deviltry as the best of us. Moreover, there is a goodly young woman to be taken into communion."

"Mighty well, Deacon Goodkin!" replied the solemn old tones of the minister. "Spur up, or we shall be late. Nothing can be done, you know, until I get on the ground."

The hoofs clattered again, and the voices, talking so strangely in the empty air, passed on through the forest, where no church had ever been gathered, nor solitary Christian prayed. Whither, then, could these holy men be journeying, so deep into the heathen wilderness? Young Goodman Brown caught hold of a tree, for support, being ready to sink down on the ground, faint and over-burthened with the heavy sickness of his heart. He looked up to the sky, doubting whether there really was a Heaven above him. Yet, there was the blue arch, and the stars brightening in it.

"With Heaven above, and Faith below, I will yet stand firm against the devil!" cried Goodman Brown.

While he still gazed upward, into the deep arch of the firmament, and had lifted his hands to pray, a cloud, though no wind was stirring, hurried across the zenith, and hid the brightening stars. The blue sky was still visible, except directly overhead, where this black mass of cloud was sweeping swiftly northward. Aloft in the air, as if from the depths of the cloud, came a confused and doubtful sound of voices. Once, the listener fancied that he could distinguish the accents of townspeople of his own, men and women, both pious and ungodly, many of whom he

---

[17] Massachusetts seaport town on Cape Cod, located southeast of Boston and some seventy miles from Salem.
[18] Medicine men.

had met at the communion table, and had seen others rioting at the tavern. The next moment, so indistinct were the sounds, he doubted whether he had heard aught but the murmur of the old forest, whispering without a wind. Then came a stronger swell of those familiar tones, heard daily in the sunshine, at Salem village, but never, until now, from a cloud at night. There was one voice, of a young woman, uttering lamentations, yet with an uncertain sorrow, and entreating for some favor, which, perhaps, it would grieve her to obtain. And all the unseen multitude, both saints and sinners, seemed to encourage her onward.

"Faith!" shouted Goodman Brown, in a voice of agony and desperation; and the echoes of the forest mocked him, crying—"Faith! Faith!" as if bewildered wretches were seeking her, all through the wilderness.

The cry of grief, rage, and terror was yet piercing the night, when the unhappy husband held his breath for a response. There was a scream, drowned immediately in a louder murmur of voices fading into far-off laughter, as the dark cloud swept away, leaving the clear and silent sky above Goodman Brown. But something fluttered lightly down through the air, and caught on the branch of a tree. The young man seized it and beheld a pink ribbon.

"My Faith is gone!" cried he, after one stupefied moment. "There is no good on earth, and sin is but a name. Come, devil! for to thee is this world given."

And maddened with despair, so that he laughed loud and long, did Goodman Brown grasp his staff and set forth again, at such a rate, that he seemed to fly along the forest path, rather than to walk or run. The road grew wilder and drearier, and more faintly traced, and vanished at length, leaving him in the heart of the dark wilderness, still rushing onward, with the instinct that guides mortal man to evil. The whole forest was peopled with frightful sounds: the creaking of the trees, the howling of wild beasts, and the yell of Indians; while, sometimes, the wind tolled like a distant church bell, and sometimes gave a broad roar around the traveller, as if all Nature was laughing him to scorn. But he was himself the chief horror of the scene, and shrank not from its other horrors.

"Ha! ha! ha!" roared Goodman Brown, when the wind laughed at him. "Let us hear which will laugh loudest! Think not to frighten me with your deviltry! Come witch, come wizard, come Indian powwow, come devil himself! and here comes Goodman Brown. You may as well fear him as he fear you!"

In truth, all through the haunted forest, there could be nothing more frightful than the figure of Goodman Brown. On he flew, among the black pines, brandishing his staff with frenzied gestures, now giving vent to an inspiration of horrid blasphemy, and now shouting forth such laughter, as set all the echoes of the forest laughing like demons around him. The fiend in his own shape is less hideous, than when he rages in the breast of man. Thus sped the demoniac on his course, until, quivering among the trees, he saw a red light before him, as when the felled trunks and branches of a clearing have been set on fire, and throw up their lurid blaze against the sky, at the hour of midnight. He paused, in a lull of the tempest that had driven him onward, and heard the swell of what seemed a hymn, rolling solemnly from a distance, with the weight of many voices. He knew the tune. It was a familiar one in the choir of the village meeting-house. The verse died heavily away, and was lengthened by a chorus, not of human voices, but of all the sounds of the benighted wilderness, pealing in awful harmony together. Goodman Brown cried out; and his cry was lost to his own ear, by its unison with the cry of the desert.

In the interval of silence, he stole forward, until the light glared full upon his eyes. At one extremity of an open space, hemmed in by the dark wall of the forest, arose a rock, bearing some rude, natural resemblance either to an altar or a pulpit, and surrounded by four blazing pines, their tops aflame, their stems untouched, like candles at an evening meeting. The mass of foliage, that had overgrown the summit of the rock, was all on fire, blazing high into the night, and fitfully illuminating the whole field. Each pendent twig and leafy festoon was in a blaze. As the red light arose and fell, a numerous congregation alternately shone forth, then disappeared in shadow, and again grew, as it were, out of the darkness, peopling the heart of the solitary woods at once.

"A grave and dark-clad company!" quoth Goodman Brown.

In truth, they were such. Among them, quivering to-and-fro, between gloom and splendor, appeared faces that would be seen, next day, at the council-board[19] of the province, and others which, Sabbath after Sabbath, looked devoutly heavenward, and benignantly over the crowded pews, from the holiest pulpits in the land. Some affirm, that the lady of the governor[20] was there. At least, there were high dames well known to her, and wives of honored husbands, and widows a great multitude, and ancient maidens, all of excellent repute, and fair young girls, who trembled lest their mothers should espy them. Either the sudden gleams of light, flashing over the obscure field, bedazzled Goodman Brown, or he recognized a score of the church members of Salem village, famous for their especial sanctity. Good old Deacon Gookin had arrived, and waited at the skirts of that venerable saint, his reverend pastor. But, irreverently consorting with these grave, reputable, and pious people, these elders of the church, these chaste dames and dewy virgins, there were men of dissolute lives and women of spotted fame, wretches given over to all mean and filthy vice, and suspected even of horrid crimes. It was strange to see, that the good shrank not from the wicked, nor were the sinners abashed by the saints. Scattered, also, among their pale-faced enemies, were the Indian priests, or powwows, who had often scared their native forest with more hideous incantations than any known to English witchcraft.

"But, where is Faith?" thought Goodman Brown; and, as hope came into his heart, he trembled.

Another verse of the hymn arose, a slow and mournful strain, such as the pious love, but joined to words which expressed all that our nature can conceive of sin, and darkly hinted at far more. Unfathomable to mere mortals is the lore of fiends. Verse after verse was sung, and still the chorus of the desert swelled between, like the deepest tone of a mighty organ. And, with the final peal of that dreadful anthem, there came a sound, as if the roaring wind, the rushing streams, the howling beasts, and every other voice of the unconverted wilderness were mingling and according with the voice of guilty man, in homage to the prince of all. The four blazing pines threw up a loftier flame, and obscurely discovered shapes and visages of horror on the smokewreaths, above the impious assembly. At the same moment, the fire on the rock shot redly forth, and formed a glowing arch above its base, where now appeared a figure. With reverence be it spoken, the apparition bore no slight similitude, both in garb and manner, to some grave divine of the New England churches.

"Bring forth the converts!" cried a voice, that echoed through the field and rolled into the forest.

At the word, Goodman Brown stepped forth from the shadow of the trees, and

---

[19] The Governor's Council.
[20] The wife of Sir William Phips (1651–1695), Governor of Massachusetts, had been accused of witchcraft during the Salem hysteria.

approached the congregation, with whom he felt a loathful brotherhood, by the sympathy of all that was wicked in his heart. He could have well-nigh sworn, that the shape of his own dead father beckoned him to advance, looking downward from a smoke-wreath, while a woman, with dim features of despair, threw out her hand to warn him back. Was it his mother? But he had no power to retreat one step, nor to resist, even in thought, when the minister and good old Deacon Gookin seized his arms, and led him to the blazing rock. Thither came also the slender form of a veiled female, led between Goody Cloyse, that pious teacher of the catechism, and Martha Carrier, who had received the devil's promise to be queen of hell.[21] A rampant hag was she! And there stood the proselytes, beneath the canopy of fire.

"Welcome, my children," said the dark figure, "to the communion of your race! Ye have found, thus young, your nature and your destiny. My children, look behind you!"

Then turned; and flashing forth, as it were, in a sheet of flame, the fiend-worshippers were seen; the smile of welcome gleamed darkly on every visage.

"There," resumed the same form, "are all whom ye have reverenced from youth. Ye deemed them holier than yourselves, and shrank from your own sin, contrasting it with their lives of righteousness and prayerful aspirations heavenward. Yet, here are they all, in my worshipping assembly! This night it shall be granted you to know their secret deeds; how hoary-bearded elders of the church have whispered wanton words to the young maids of their households; how many a woman, eager for widow's weeds, has given her husband a drink at bedtime, and let him sleep his last sleep in her bosom; how beardless youths have made haste to inherit their father's wealth; and how fair damsels—blush not, sweet ones!—have dug little graves in the garden, and bidden me, the sole guest, to an infant's funeral. By the sympathy of your human hearts for sin, ye shall scent out all the places—whether in church, bed-chamber, street, field, or forest—where crime has been committed, and shall exult to behold the whole earth one stain of guilt, one mighty blood-spot. Far more than this! It shall be yours to penetrate, in every bosom, the deep mystery of sin, the fountain of all wicked arts, and which inexhaustibly supplies more evil impulses than human power—than my power, at its utmost!—can make manifest in deeds. And now, my children, look upon each other."

They did so; and, by the blaze of the hell-kindled torches, the wretched man beheld his Faith, and the wife her husband, trembling before that unhallowed altar.

"Lo! there ye stand, my children," said the figure, in a deep and solemn tone, almost sad, with its despairing awfulness, as if his once angelic nature could yet mourn for our miserable race. "Depending upon one another's hearts, ye had still hoped that virtue were not all a dream! Now are ye undeceived!—Evil is the nature of mankind. Evil must be your only happiness. Welcome, again, my children, to the communion of your race!"

"Welcome!" repeated the fiend-worshippers, in one cry of despair and triumph.

And there they stood, the only pair, as it seemed, who were yet hesitating on the

---

[21] Martha Carrier was another of the accused Salem witches. Cotton Mather (1663–1728), the famous Puritan minister who took an active role in the witchcraft controversies at Salem, concludes his account of her trial of August 2, 1692 in his *Wonders of the Invisible World* (1693) as follows: "This rampant hag . . . was the person of whom the confessions of the witches, and of her own children among the rest, agreed that the devil had promised her, she should be queen of hell." Martha Carrier was executed by hanging on Gallows Hill on August 19, 1692.

verge of wickedness, in this dark world. A basin was hollowed, naturally, in the rock. Did it contain water, reddened by the lurid light? or was it blood? or, perchance, a liquid flame? Herein did the Shape of Evil dip his hand, and prepare to lay the mark of baptism upon their foreheads, that they might be partakers of the mystery of sin, more conscious of the secret guilt of others, both in deed and thought, than they could now be of their own. The husband cast one look at his pale wife, and Faith at him. What polluted wretches would the next glance show them to each other, shuddering alike at what they disclosed and what they saw!

"Faith! Faith!" cried the husband. "Look up to heaven, and resist the Wicked One!"

Whether Faith obeyed, he knew not. Hardly had he spoken, when he found himself amid calm night and solitude, listening to a roar of the wind, which died heavily away through the forest. He staggered against the rock, and felt it chill and damp, while a hanging twig, that had been all on fire, besprinkled his cheek with the coldest dew.

The next morning, young Goodman Brown came slowly into the street of Salem village staring around him like a bewildered man. The good old minister was taking a walk along the grave-yard, to get an appetite for breakfast and meditate his sermon, and bestowed a blessing, as he passed, on Goodman Brown. He shrank from the venerable saint, as if to avoid an anathema.[22] Old Deacon Gookin was at domestic worship, and the holy words of his prayer were heard through the open window. "What God doth the wizard pray to?" quoth Goodman Brown. Goody Cloyse, that excellent old Christian, stood in the early sunshine, at her own lattice, catechising a little girl, who had brought her a pint of morning's milk. Goodman Brown snatched away the child, as from the grasp of the fiend himself. Turning the corner by the meeting-house, he spied the head of Faith, with the pink ribbons, gazing anxiously forth, and bursting into such joy at sight of him that she skipt along the street, and almost kissed her husband before the whole village. But Goodman Brown looked sternly and sadly into her face, and passed on without a greeting.

Had Goodman Brown fallen asleep in the forest, and only dreamed a wild dream of a witch-meeting?

Be it so, if you will. But, alas! it was a dream of evil omen for young Goodman Brown. A stern, a sad, a darkly meditative, a distrustful, if not a desperate man did he become, from the night of that fearful dream. On the Sabbath day, when the congregation was singing a holy psalm, he could not list, because an anthem of sin rushed loudly upon his ear, and drowned all the blessed strain. When the minister spoke from the pulpit, with power and fervid eloquence, and with his hand on the open Bible, of the sacred truths of our religion, and of saint-like lives and triumphant deaths, and of future bliss or misery unutterable, then did Goodman Brown turn pale, dreading lest the roof should thunder down upon the gray blasphemer and his hearers. Often, awaking suddenly at midnight, he shrank from the bosom of Faith, and at morning or eventide, when the family knelt down at prayer, he scowled, and muttered to himself, and gazed sternly at his wife, and turned away. And when he had lived long, and was borne to his grave, a hoary corpse, followed by Faith, an aged woman, and children and grand-children, a goodly procession, besides neighbors not a few, they carved no hopeful verse upon his tombstone; for his dying hour was gloom.

[1835]

---

[22] Curse.

CHARACTER

The relationship between plot and character is a vital and necessary one. **Without character, there would be no plot and, hence, no story.** For most readers of fiction the primary attraction lies in the characters, in the endlessly fascinating collection of men and women whose experiences and adventures form the basis of the plots of the stories and the novels in which they appear. Part of the fascination with the characters of fiction is that we often come to know them so well. In real life we come to know people for the most part only on the basis of externals—on the basis of what they say and what they do; the complexity of their inner lives can be inferred only after years of close acquaintance, if at all. Fiction, on the other hand, often provides us with immediate access, however brief and fleeting, to that inner life—to the intellectual, emotional, and moral complexities of human personality. And even when the author withholds that access, he or she usually provides sufficient information to allow us to make judgments about the internal makeup of the men and women to whom we are introduced. In either case, however, the ability to make such judgments—the ability to interpret correctly the evidence the author provides—is always crucial to our understanding.

When we examine character in literary analysis, we are concerned essentially with three separate, but closely connected, activities. We are concerned, first of all, with being able to establish the personalities of the characters themselves and to identify their intellectual, emotional, and moral qualities. Second, we are concerned with the techniques an author uses to create and develop characters. Third, we are concerned with whether the characters are credible and convincing. In evaluating the success of characterization, the third issue is a particularly crucial one, for although plot can carry a work of fiction to a point, it is a rare work whose final value is not intimately connected with the convincing portrayal of characters. Naturally, such an evaluation can only take place within the context of the story or novel as a whole, which inevitably links character to the other elements of fiction.

Characters in Fiction

The term *character* applies to any individual in a literary work. For the purpose of analysis, characters in fiction are customarily described by their relationship to plot, by the degree of development they are given by the author, and by whether or not they undergo significant character change.

The major, or central, character of the plot is the protagonist; his or her opponent, the character against whom the protagonist struggles or contends, is the antagonist. The protagonist is usually easy enough to identify: he or she is the essential character without whom there would be no plot in the first place. It is the protagonist's fate on which the attention of the reader is focused. The terms *protagonist* and *antagonist,* incidentally, do not (unlike the terms *hero, heroine,* or *villain*) imply a judgment about moral worth. Many protagonists embody a complex mixture of both positive and negative qualities, very much in the way their real life counterparts do.

Very often the title of the work identifies the protagonist: "The Death of Ivan Ilych," "Young Goodman Brown," "The Darling," "A Rose for Emily," and "Yellow Woman."

The antagonist can be somewhat more difficult to identify, especially if the antagonist is not a human being, as is the case with the marlin that challenges the courage and endurance of the old fisherman Santiago in Ernest Hemingway's famous short novel *The Old Man and the Sea*. In fact, as we noted earlier, the antagonist may not be a living creature at all, but rather the hostile social or natural environment with which the protagonist is forced to contend. The protagonist may not always manage to compete successfully with and defeat the antagonist, either; often, as in the case of Samuel L. Clemens's (Mark Twain's) "The Celebrated Jumping Frog of Calaveras County" and Stephen Crane's "The Blue Hotel," just the opposite is true.

To describe the relative degree to which fictional characters are developed by their creators, critics usually distinguish between what are referred to as *flat* and *round characters*. Flat characters are those who embody or represent a single characteristic, trait, or idea, or at most a very limited number of such qualities. Flat characters are also referred to as *type characters*, as *one-dimensional characters*, or, when they are distorted to create humor, as *caricatures*.

Flat characters usually play a minor role in the stories and novels in which they appear, but not always so. For example, Montresor and Fortunato are the protagonist and antagonist, respectively, in Edgar Allan Poe's "The Cask of Amontillado." Yet they are both flat characters: Montresor, who leads the unsuspecting Fortunato to be walled up in his family crypt, embodies nothing but cold-blooded revenge. And Fortunato, who appears dressed in the cap and motley of the jester, complete with bells, is quite literally a fool. Flat characters have much in common with the kind of *stock characters* who appear again and again in certain types of literary works: e.g., the rich uncle of domestic comedy, the hard-boiled private eye of the detective story, the female confidante of romance.

Round characters **are just the opposite. They embody a number of qualities and traits and are complex multidimensional characters of considerable intellectual and emotional depth. Most importantly, they have the capacity to grow and change.** Major characters in fiction are usually round characters, and it is with the very complexity of such characters that most of us become engrossed. The terms round and flat do not automatically imply value judgments. Each kind of character has its uses—witness Poe's successful use of flat characters to dramatize the theme of revenge in "The Cask of Amontillado." Even when they are minor characters, as they usually are, flat characters often help us to understand the personalities of characters who are more fully realized. Finally, round characters are not necessarily more alive or more convincing than flat ones. If they are, it is because the author has succeeded in making them so.

Characters in fiction can also be distinguished on the basis of whether they demonstrate the capacity to develop or change as the result of their experiences. *Dynamic characters* exhibit a capacity to change; *static characters* do not. As might be expected, the degree and rate of character change varies widely, even among dynamic characters. In some stories, the development is so subtle that it may go almost unnoticed; in others, it is sufficiently drastic and profound to cause a total reorganization of the character's personality or system of values. Change in character may come slowly and incrementally over many pages, or it may take place with a dramatic suddenness that surprises, and even overwhelms, the character.

Dynamic characters include the protagonists in most novels, which by virtue of their very size provide excellent vehicles for illustrating the process of change. So-called initiation novels, such as Charles Dickens's *David Copperfield* and Samuel L. Clemens's *Huckleberry Finn*, are examples. In each case the author has arranged the events of the plot so that they reveal the slow and painful maturing of the young protagonist coming into contact with the world of adult experience. But short stories can also illustrate character change, as in the case of Hawthorne's young country rustic Robin Molineux, who journeys to colonial Boston in search of his kinsman only to undergo an ordeal that leaves him on the threshold of maturity. What that maturity consists of, Hawthorne refuses to say, but there can be little doubt that by the story's conclusion Robin has passed into and through a significant emotional and spiritual crisis.

Static characters leave the plot as they entered it, largely untouched by the events that have taken place. Although static characters tend to be minor ones, because the author's principal focus is located elsewhere, this is not always the case. Olenka, the protagonist of Anton Chekhov's "The Darling," is a static character whose essential qualities are submissiveness and blind devotion. Without opinions, personality, or inner resources of her own, she passes through a series of relationships that leave her character essentially unchanged. But protagonists like Olenka are comparatively rare; for the most part, an author creates static characters as *foils* to emphasize and set off by contrast the development taking place in others.

Methods of Characterization

In presenting and establishing character, an author has two basic methods or techniques at his or her disposal. One method is *telling*, which relies on exposition and direct commentary by the author. In telling the guiding hand of the author is very much in evidence. We learn primarily from what the author explicitly calls to our attention. **The other method is the indirect, dramatic method of *showing*, which involves the author's stepping aside, as it were, to allow the characters to reveal themselves directly through their dialogue and their actions.** With showing, much of the burden of character analysis is shifted to the reader, who is required to infer character on the basis of the evidence provided in the narrative. Telling and showing are not mutually exclusive, however. Most authors employ a combination of the two, even when the exposition, as in the case of most of Hemingway's stories, is limited to several lines of descriptive detail establishing the scene.

Most modern authors prefer showing to telling, but neither method is necessarily better or more fruitful than the other. As with so many other choices that the writer of fiction must make, the choice of a method of characterization depends on the circumstances. These include the author's temperament, the particular literary conventions of the period in which he or she is writing, the size and scope of the work, the degree of distance and objectivity the author wishes to establish between himself or herself and the characters, the author's literary and philosophical beliefs about how a sense of reality can best be conveyed to the reader, and, of course, the kind of story the author wishes to tell.

Direct methods of revealing character—characterization by telling—include the following.

1. *Characterization through the use of names.* Names are often used to provide essential clues that aid in characterization. Some characters are given names that suggest their dominant or controlling traits, as for example, Young Goodman Brown, the naive young Puritan in Hawthorne's story, and Mr. Blanc, the reserved Easterner in Stephen Crane's "The Blue Hotel." Other characters are given names that reinforce (or sometimes are in contrast to) their physical appearance.

Names can also contain literary or historical allusions that aid in characterization by means of association. For example, the name Bonaparte, which Frank O'Connor gives to one of the young Irish soldiers in "Guests of the Nation," has clear and unmistakable (and ironic) historical overtones. One must also, of course, be alert to names used ironically which characterize through inversion. Such is the case with the foolish Fortunato of Poe's "The Cask of Amontillado," who surely must rank with the most *un*fortunate of men.

2. *Characterization through appearance.* In real life appearances are often deceiving. In the world of fiction, however, details of appearance (what a character wears and how he or she looks) often provide essential clues to character. Take, for example, the second paragraph of "My Kinsman, Major Molineux," in which Hawthorne introduces his protagonist to the reader. The several details of the paragraph tell us a good deal about Robin's character and basic situation. We learn that he is a "country-bred" youth nearing the end of a long journey, as his nearly empty wallet suggests. His clothes confirm that he is relatively poor. Yet Robin is clearly no runaway or rebel, for his clothes, though "well worn," are "in excellent repair," and the references to his stockings and hat suggest that a loving and caring family has helped prepare him for his journey. The impression thus conveyed by the total paragraph and underscored by its final sentence describing Robin's physical appearance, is of a decent young man on the threshold of adulthood who is making his first journey into the world. The only disquieting note—a clever bit of foreshadowing—is the reference to the heavy oak cudgel that Robin has brought with him. He later will brandish it at strangers in an attempt to assert his authority and in the process reveal just how inadequately prepared he is to cope with the strange urban world in which he finds himself.

As in the Hawthorne story, details of dress and physical appearance should be scrutinized closely for what they may reveal about character. Details of dress may offer clues to background, occupation, economic and social status, and perhaps, as with Robin Molineux, even a clue to the character's degree of self-respect. Details of physical appearance can help to identify a character's age and the general state of his physical and emotional health: whether the character is strong or weak, happy or sad, calm or agitated. Appearance can be used in other ways as well, particularly with minor characters who are flat and static. By common agreement, certain physical attributes have become identified over a period of time with certain kinds of inner psychological states. For example, characters who are tall and thin like Poe's Roderick Usher are often associated with withdrawn and introspective intellectual or aesthetic types. Portly or fat characters, on the other hand, suggest an opposite personality, one characterized by a degree of laziness, self-indulgence, and congeniality. Such convenient and economic shortcuts to characterization are perfectly permissible, of course, as long as they result in characters who are in their own way convincing.

3. *Characterization by the author.* In the most customary form of telling, the author interrupts the narrative and reveals directly, through a series of editorial comments, the personality of the characters, including the thoughts and feelings that pass through the characters' minds. By so doing the author retains full control over characterization. The author not only directs our attention to a given character, but tells us exactly what our attitude toward that character ought to be.

By contrast, there are two methods of indirect characterization by showing: characterization through dialogue (what characters say) and characterization through action (what characters do). Unlike the direct methods of characterization already discussed, showing involves the gradual rather than the immediate revelation of character. Such a process requires rather than excludes active participation by calling upon both the reader's intelligence and memory.

4. *Characterization through dialogue.* Real life is quite literally filled with talk. People are forever talking about themselves and between themselves, communicating bits and pieces of information. Not all of this information is important or even particularly interesting; it tells us relatively little about the personality of the speaker, except, perhaps, whether he or she is at ease in social situations. Some light fiction reproduces dialogue as it might occur in reality, but the best authors trim everything that is inconsequential. What remains is weighty and substantial and carries with it the force of the speaker's attitudes, values, and beliefs. We pay attention to such talk because it may consciously or unconsciously serve to reveal the speaker's innermost character and personality.

It is by no means easy for a reader to understand characters on the basis of dialogue alone. Some characters are careful and guarded in what they say: they speak only by indirection, and we must infer from their words what they actually mean. Others are open and candid: they tell us, or appear to tell us, exactly what is on their minds. Some characters are given to chronic exaggeration and overstatement; others to understatement and subtlety.

It is a rare work of fiction whose author does not employ dialogue in some way to establish and reinforce character. For this reason the reader must be prepared to analyze dialogue in a number of different ways: for (a) what is being said, (b) the identity of the speaker, (c) the occasion, (d) the identity of the person or persons the speaker is addressing, (e) the quality or character of the exchange, and (f) the speaker's tone of voice, stress, dialect, and vocabulary.

a. *What is being said.* To begin with, the reader must pay close attention to the substance of the dialogue itself. Is it small talk, or is the subject developing the plot? In terms of characterization, if the speaker insists on talking only about himself or only on a single subject, we may conclude that we have encountered either an egotist or a bore. If the speaker talks only about others, we have merely a gossip or busybody.

b. *The identity of the speaker.* Obviously, on balance, what the protagonist says must be considered to be potentially more important (and hence revealing) than what minor characters say, although the conversation of minor characters often provides crucial information as well.

c. *The occasion.* In real life, conversations that take place in private at night are usually more serious and, hence, more revealing than conversations that take place in public during the day. Talk in the bedroom, for example, is usually more significant than talk in the street or the supermarket. On the whole, this is probably also true in fiction as well, but the reader should always consider the likelihood that seemingly idle talk on the street or at the supermarket has been included by the author because it is somehow important to the story being told.

d. *The identity of the person or persons the speaker is addressing.* Dialogue between friends is usually more candid and open, and thus more significant, than dialogue between strangers. The necessary degree of intimacy is usually established by the author in setting a scene or through the dialogue itself. When a character addresses no one in particular, or when others are not present, his or her speech is called a *monologue,* although, strictly speaking, monologues occur more frequently in drama than in fiction.*

  e. *The quality of the exchange.* The way a conversation ebbs and flows is important, too. When there is real give-and-take, the characters can be presumed to be open-minded. When there is none, one or more of the characters are presumably opinionated, doctrinaire, or close-minded. When there is a certain degree of evasiveness in the responses, a character may be secretive and have something to hide.

  f. *The speaker's tone of voice, stress, dialect, and vocabulary.* The speaker's tone of voice (either stated or implied) may reveal the speaker's attitude toward himself or herself (whether, for example, he or she is confident and at ease or self-conscious and shy) and toward those with whom he or she is speaking. The speaker's attitude to others may, for example, be either warm and friendly or cold, detached, and even hostile. Moreover, the reader must also be alert to suggestions of irony in the speaker's voice, which would suggest that what is being said is quite the opposite from what is actually meant. Finally, dialect, stress, and word choice all provide important clues to character: they may reflect the character's origin, education, occupation, or social class.

  In evaluating what a given character says about himself or herself and others, one always faces (in the absence of clarifying comments by the author) the problem of the character's reliability and trustworthiness. Both deliberate deception and unconscious self-deception always lurk as distinct possibilities in fictional characters, as in real people. Although determining the reliability and veracity of characters can be difficult, most authors provide clues. When one character is contradicted in whole or in part by another, the accumulated evidence on both sides must be carefully weighed and examined. One can also test reliability by looking at the character's subsequent conduct and behavior to see if what he or she does somehow contradicts what he or she says. Finally, there is always the appeal to the subsequent events of the plot itself to see whether those events tend to support or contradict the character's statements. Any number of fictional plots turn, in fact, on the failure of one character to understand correctly the personalities of others. The badly frightened Swede in Stephen Crane's "The Blue Hotel," for example, is so steeped in the folklore of the frontier West that he convinces himself that his companions are conspiring to rob or to murder him, a misapprehension that triggers a chain of violent events that costs the Swede his life.

  5. *Characterization through action.* The idea that one's behavior is a logical and even necessary extension of one's psychology and personality is widely shared. What a given character *is* is revealed by what that character *does.* In brief, the single most important and definitive method of revealing character is through action.

  To establish character on the basis of action, it is necessary to scrutinize the events of the plot for what they seem to reveal about the characters. From these

---

* A specialized form of monologue is the stream-of-consciousness technique, in which the author enters the mind or consciousness of his or her character and directly expresses unfolding thoughts and emotions. Stream of consciousness implies a recognition that speech is inadequate to communicate inner psychological life.

events we learn about the unconscious emotional and psychological states of the characters as well as about their conscious attitudes and values. Some actions, of course, are inherently more meaningful in this respect than others. A gesture or a facial expression usually carries with it less significance than some larger overt act. But this is not always the case. Very often it is the small and involuntary action, by very virtue of its spontaneous and unconscious quality, that tells us more about a character's inner life than a larger, premeditated act. In either case, whether the action is large or small, conscious or unconscious, it is necessary to identify the common pattern of behavior of which each separate action is a part. One helpful way of doing so is on the basis of *motive*. In seeking motive, we attempt to trace certain effects back to their underlying causes. If we are successful in doing so and if a consistent pattern of motivation appears, then it is fairly safe to assume that we have made some important discoveries about the character.

Robin Molineux's responses to the events that befall him provide a good example of character revealed through action. Robin's adventure is a journey of moral and psychological initiation, a rite of passage from youth to adulthood, innocence to maturity, and ignorance to knowledge. Ironically, the provincial capital that Robin enters is on the brink of a political revolution whose first victim is none other than the very kinsman whom Robin is seeking. For all his self-proclaimed "shrewdness," Robin is not among the knowing. His country ways and naive-because-untested expectations leave him open and vulnerable to the world of the city, a world filled with danger, hostility, temptation, and violence. Through one event after another, including a meeting with a group of conspirators whose password Robin can neither understand nor return, Robin's ignorance, inadequacy, and lack of preparation are exposed. Taken together, the events of the plot, and Robin's response to them, reveal his essential character and prepare him for the climax of the story; his smug self-confidence is undermined while his confusion, anxiety, doubt, and sense of his own helplessness increase.

Evaluating Character

Having identified the essential personality of the characters in the work, we must also be prepared to evaluate how successful the author has been in their creation. Although it is unreasonable to expect that the characters of fiction will necessarily be close approximations of the kind of people that we know—for part of the joy of fiction is having the opportunity to meet new people—we can expect the author's creations to be convincing and credible on their own terms. **What we chiefly require in the behavior of fictional characters is** *consistency*. Characterization implies a kind of unspoken contract between author and reader; and the reader has the right to expect that a character, once established, will not then behave in ways contrary to his or her nature. The principle of consistency by no means implies that characters in fiction cannot undergo development and change, for, as we have noted, the plots of many works are organized precisely upon just such a possibility. Rather, when a character undergoes change, such change should be well motivated by events and consistent in some basic and identifiable way with the nature of the character. Thus, in seeking to test for consistency, we must frequently ask ourselves whether the motive for a particular action or series of actions is adequate and probable given what we know about that character.

🌿 ANALYZING CHARACTER 🌿

1.   Who is the protagonist of the work and who (or what) is the antagonist? Describe the major traits and qualities of each.

2.   What is the function of the work's minor characters?

3.   Identify the characters in terms of whether they are flat or round, dynamic or static.

4.   What methods does the author employ to establish and reveal the characters? Are the methods primarily of showing or telling?

5.   Are the actions of the characters properly motivated and consistent?

6.   Are the characters of the work finally credible and interesting?

SETTING

Fiction can be defined as character in action at a certain time and place. The first two elements of this equation, *character* and *action*, have already been discussed. Now we turn our attention to *setting*, **a term that, in its broadest sense, encompasses both the physical locale that frames the action *and* the time of day or year, the climatic conditions, and the historical period during which the action takes place.** At its most basic, setting helps the reader visualize the action of the work and thus adds credibility and authenticity to the story. It helps, in other words, to create and sustain the illusion of life, to provide what we call *verisimilitude*. There are, however, many different kinds of setting in fiction and they function in a variety of ways.

Some settings are relatively unimportant. They serve as little more than incidental and decorative backdrops, which have little or no necessary relationship to either the plot or the characters. Other settings are intimately connected with the meaning of the total work. It is with settings of this type that as critics we must be chiefly concerned.

In order to understand the function of setting, the reader must pay particular attention to the descriptive passages in which the details of setting are introduced. Generally speaking, unless such passages are intended merely as local color, the greater the attention given to them, the greater their importance in the total work. In most short stories, setting is established at or near the beginning as a means of orienting the reader and framing the action to follow. Where the emphasis on setting in such passages is slight, as it is, for example, in most of Hemingway's stories, or where the setting once established is then referred to again only incidentally, if at all, one can assume that setting is relatively unimportant. If, on the other hand, the emphasis on the setting in early passages is substantial, and if similar references to the setting recur periodically as a kind of echoing refrain, one can assume that the setting serves some important function.

The quality of the language by which the author projects the setting provides another clue as to his or her intention. When that intention is to invest the setting with a photographic vividness, the details of the setting will be rendered through language that is concrete and sensory. The author will pile specific detail on top of specific detail in an attempt to provide the illusion of reality. On the other hand, the author may want us to "feel" rather than simply "see" the setting, as is the case when setting is to be used as a means of creating atmosphere. In that case the appeal will be to the reader's imagination and emotions through language that is connotative and suggestive. The author will, that is, manipulate the poetic qualities of language to elicit from the reader the desired and appropriate response. Often the author will want the reader to *both* see and feel the setting and will use the resources of language to bring about both effects simultaneously.

The Functions of Setting

Setting in fiction is called upon to perform a number of specific functions. Among them are the following:

1. *Setting as a background for action.* Everything happens somewhere. For this reason alone, fiction requires a background of some kind, even if it only resembles a western stage set. Sometimes this background is extensive and highly developed. In other cases, and this includes many modern stories, setting is so slight that it can be dispensed with in a single sentence or must be inferred altogether from dialogue and action. When we speak of setting as background, we have in mind a setting that exists largely for its own sake, without necessary relationship to action or characters.

2. *Setting as antagonist.* Often, the forces of nature function as a causal agent or antagonist, helping to establish conflict and to determine the outcome of events. The Yukon wilderness with which Jack London's nameless tenderfoot tries unsuccessfully to contend in his famous story "To Build a Fire" is an example of a setting that functions as antagonist.

3. *Setting as a means of creating appropriate atmosphere.* Many authors manipulate their settings as a means of arousing the reader's expectations and establishing an appropriate state of mind for events to come. No author is more adept in this respect than Edgar Allan Poe, who not only provides the details of setting, but tells the reader just how to respond to them.

4. *Setting as a means of revealing character.* Very often the way in which a character perceives the setting, and the way he or she reacts to it, will tell the reader more about the character and his or her state of mind than it will about the setting itself. This is particularly true of works in which the author carefully controls the point of view. In "My Kinsman, Major Molineux," for example, there is no indication that the outlandishly attired conspirators, who move easily through the streets of colonial Boston, are confused in the slightest by the city. Yet Robin Molineux, Hawthorne's young protagonist, most certainly is. For Robin the city is scarcely real; he is "almost ready to believe that a spell was on him." The dark "crooked and narrow" streets seem to lead nowhere, and the disorienting moonlight, so perfect for carrying out clandestine activities, serves only to make "the forms of distant objects" fade away "with almost ghostly indistinctness, just as his eye appeared to grasp them." The urban landscape perfectly mirrors Robin's growing sense of isolation, loneliness, frustration, and confusion.

An author can also clarify and reveal character by deliberately making setting a metaphoric or symbolic extension of character. A case in point is found in Edgar Allan Poe's "The Fall of the House of Usher." Poe begins his story with the famous passage that includes a reference to the "barely perceptible fissure" extending the full length of the house "until it became lost in the sullen waters of the tarn." As the events of the story's plot proceed to make clear, Roderick and his house are mirror images of one another. Roderick is as remote and gloomy as the house itself: his eyes, like the windows, are vacant and lifeless; his hair has the same gossamer consistency as the fungi growing from the eaves; and there is within him the same perceptible and fatal fissure. As the action of the story proceeds to make clear, Roderick and his house are in an advanced state of decay. Setting and character are one; the house objectifies, and in this way serves to clarify, its master.

5. *Setting as a means of reinforcing theme.* Setting can also be used as a means of reinforcing and clarifying the theme of a novel or short story. In Stephen Crane's "The Blue Hotel," the Palace Hotel standing alone on the prairie, with its light blue color, is pictured as "always screaming and howling in a way that made the dazzling winter landscape of Nebraska seem only a grey swampish hush." The reader subsequently discovers that this setting has direct thematic relevance to Crane's conception of the relationship between humans and nature in which an individual's survival (and, ironically, at times his or her destruction) depends on a capacity for self-assertion, much in the way that the blue hotel asserts its lonely presence against the stark, inhospitable Nebraska landscape.

A Note on Setting in Time

In most of the preceding examples we have emphasized the physical aspects of setting at the expense of the temporal ones. But **the time of day, time of year, or period in history at which a given event or series of events occurs can also contribute importantly to setting.** The fact that the events of Hawthorne's "My Kinsman, Major Molineux" take place at night is a highly relevant part of the setting, for darkness is traditionally an appropriate cover for deeds of conspiracy and violence. In Poe's "The Cask of Amontillado," the action takes place not only in the evening, but "during the supreme madness of the carnival season" in the dark crypts beneath Montressor's palazzo. Poe could scarcely have conjured up a more effective setting in which to dramatize the way insanity emerges from beneath the surface of apparent respectability to consummate its single-minded desire for vengeance. Many of the most climactic moments in fiction, in fact, seem to take place at night (as, for example, in the meeting of "fiend worshippers" that Hawthorne's Young Goodman Brown attends in the woods outside his native Salem) as if to suggest that it is after the rest of the world is asleep that we stand most ready to reveal the essential truths about ourselves to the world.

In much the same way, certain seasons of the year lend themselves more to certain kinds of events than to others. Poe's narrator arrives at the "melancholy House of Usher" on "a dull, dark, and soundless day in the autumn of the year," a period we normally associate with the coming of winter and death. Winter also is an appropriate setting for the action of Crane's "The Blue Hotel," for the howling storm that swirls around the hotel is perfectly in keeping with the physical violence that soon overtakes and destroys the Swede. Authors will often use the cycle of the year and the cycle of the day to establish settings precisely *because* of the traditional associations with the successive cycles in human life: spring-morning-youth; summer-noon-maturity; fall-evening-old age; winter-night-death.

🌿 ANALYZING SETTING 🌿

1. What is the work's setting in space and time?

2. How does the author go about establishing setting? Does the author want the reader to see or feel the setting; or does the author want the reader to both see and feel it? What details of setting does the author isolate and describe?

3. Is the setting important? If so, what is its function? Is it used to reveal, reinforce, or influence character, plot, or theme?

4. Is the setting an appropriate one?

POINT OF VIEW

A story must have a plot, characters, and a setting. It must also have a storyteller: **a narrative voice, real or implied,** that **presents the story to the reader.** When we talk about narrative voice, we are talking about *point of view,* **the method of narration that determines the position, or angle of vision, from which the story is told.** The nature of the relationship between the narrator and the story, the teller and the tale, is always crucial to the art of fiction. It governs the reader's access to the story and determines just how much he or she can know at any given moment about what is taking place. So crucial is point of view that, once having been chosen, it will color and shape the way in which everything else is presented and perceived, including plot, character, and setting. Alter or change the point of view, and you alter and change the story.

The choice of point of view is the choice of who is to tell the story, who talks to the reader. It may be a narrator outside the work (*omniscient* point of view); a narrator inside the work, telling the story from a *limited omniscient* or *first-person* point of view; or apparently no one (*dramatic* point of view). These four basic points of view, and their variations, involve at the extreme a choice between omniscient point of view and dramatic point of view—a choice that involves, among other things, the distance that the author wishes to maintain between the reader and the story and the extent to which the author is willing to involve the reader in its interpretation. While moving away from omniscience along this spectrum of choices, the author progressively surrenders the ability to see into the minds of the characters.

Commonly Used Points of View

1. *Omniscient point of view.* **With the** *omniscient point of view* **an "all-knowing" narrator firmly imposes his or her presence between the reader and the story and retains complete control over the narrative.** The omniscient narrator is not a character in the story and is not involved in the plot. From a vantage point outside the story, the narrator is free to tell us much or little, to dramatize or summarize, to interpret, speculate, philosophize, moralize or judge. He or she can tell us directly what the characters are like and why they behave as they do; record their words and conversations and dramatize their actions; or enter their minds to explore directly their innermost thoughts and feelings. The narrator can move the reader from one event to the next, being just as explicit (or evasive) as he or

she wishes about their significance and meaning; he or she can skip backward and forward in time, now dramatizing, now summarizing as he or she chooses. When the omniscient narrator speaks directly to us, there is a natural temptation to identify the narrator's voice with the author's. Sometimes such an identification is warranted; at other times it may not be, for the voice that tells the story and speaks to the reader, although it may seem to reflect the author's beliefs and values, is as much the author's creation as any of the characters.

A typical example of the omniscient point of view is found in the brief passage that occurs near the beginning of Leo Tolstoy's "The Death of Ivan Ilych":

> Ivan Ilych had been a colleague of the gentlemen present and was liked by them all. He had been ill for some weeks with an illness said to be incurable. His post had been kept open for him, but there had been conjectures that in the case of his death Alexeev might receive his appointment, and that either Vinnikov or Shtabel would succeed Alexeev. So on receiving the news of Ivan Ilych's death the first thought of each of the gentlemen in that private room was of the changes and promotions it might occasion among themselves or their acquaintances.

The use of omniscient narration allows Tolstoy to establish in a concise way the nature of the "official" bureaucratic world in which Ivan Ilych has lived and worked, and how that world responds both to the news that he is incurably ill and then to the fact of his death.

As this example suggests, the great advantage of the omniscient point of view is the flexibility it gives its "all-knowing" narrator, who can direct the reader's attention and control the sources of information. As we move away from omniscient telling in the direction of dramatic showing, the narrator progressively surrenders these advantages. In choosing to move inside the framework of the story to merge his or her identity with that of any one of the characters (limited omniscient or first-person point of view) or to give up all identity (dramatic point of view), the narrator restricts the channels through which information can be transmitted to the reader. As a result, the reader becomes more and more directly involved in the task of interpretation.

2. *Limited omniscient point of view.* **With a** *limited omniscient* **(sometimes referred to as** *third-person*) *point of view,* **the narrator limits his or her ability to penetrate the minds of characters by selecting a single character to act as the center of revelation.** What the reader knows and sees of events is always restricted to what this focal character can know or see. This point of view differs significantly from the first-person point of view, discussed below. At times the reader may be given direct access to this focal character's own "voice" and thoughts, insofar as these are reproduced through dialogue or presented dramatically through monologue or stream of consciousness. On all other occasions, the reader's access is indirect: it is the narrator's voice, somewhere on the sidelines, that tells the story and transmits the action, characterization, description, analysis, and other informing details upon which the reader's understanding and interpretation depend. Although the focal character is a visible presence within the story in a way that a fully omniscient narrator is not, that character is only as available and accessible to the reader as the narrator will permit.

The character chosen as narrative center, and often referred to through the use of a third-person pronoun as he or she, may be the protagonist or may be some other major character (for example, Robin Molineux in Hawthorne's "My Kinsman, Major Molineux"). Sometimes, however, the assignment is given to a minor character who functions in the role of an onlooker, watching and speculating from the periphery of the story and only minimally involved, if at all, in its action. Once chosen, it is this character's mind and eyes that become the story's angle of vision and the point of entry for the reader. Henry James aptly refers to this character in his critical essays and prefaces as "the reflector" or "mirroring consciousness," for it is through the prism of his or her conscious mind that the story is filtered and reflected.

The advantages of the limited omniscient point of view are the tightness of focus and control that it provides. These advantages explain why the limited omniscient point of view is so admirably suited to the short story, whose restricted scope can accommodate full omniscience only with great difficulty. The limited omniscient point of view is used with good effect in Hawthorne's "Young Goodman Brown," in which the author is interested in the way in which progressive disillusionment and the conviction of sin can totally influence and distort an individual's outlook. Whether or not Goodman Brown's night in the forest, climaxed by his meeting with the devil, is dream or reality finally makes no difference; Goodman Brown is convinced that "Evil is the nature of mankind." Goodman's naive and untested faith is destroyed; his vision of life is darkened; and he goes to his grave a gloomy, distrustful, and lonely man. The limited omniscient point of view serves Hawthorne's purposes well, for it is Brown's personal vision of the way that things appear to be—rather than the way that things actually *are*—that is at the center of Hawthorne's story.

The limited omniscient point of view also works particularly well as a means of creating and sustaining irony, because it can exploit the disparity between what the focal character thinks he or she knows and the true state of affairs. Henry James, whose novels and stories make heavy use of a third-person "reflector" in the form of a "finely aware and richly responsible" character who prides himself or herself on these traits, is an excellent case in point. In James's "The Tree of Knowledge," for example, a story that turns, as its title suggests, on "knowledge" and "knowing," the reflector is the middle-aged bachelor Peter Brench, who has dedicated his life to making sure that Mrs. Mallow and her son Lancelot are kept ignorant of the "Master's" lack of artistic talent. Brench, James tells us, is an individual who "had judged himself once for all": "It was one of the secret opinions ... of Peter Brench that his main success in life would have consisted in his never having committed himself about the work, as it was called, of his friend Morgan Mallow." As it turns out, Peter Brench's heroic gesture has been an unnecessary one, for Mrs. Mallow and Lancelot know only too well that the Master's talent is impoverished. For years they have successfully kept from Brench the very knowledge that he would keep from *them*. This irony of situation is made possible by James's ability to narrate the story from Peter Brench's point of view while slowly revealing to the reader the extent of Peter's false assumptions.

3.   *First-person point of view.* The use of *first-person point of view* places still another restriction on the voice that tells the story. As already noted, the movement from full to limited omniscience essentially involves the narrator's decision to limit his or her omniscience to what can be known by a single character. **First-person point of view goes one step further by having that focal character address the reader directly, without an intermediary.** This character refers to himself or

herself as "I" in the story and addresses the reader as "you," either explicitly or by implication.

The first-person point of view thus combines the advantages and restrictions of limited omniscience with its own. As with limited omniscience, first-person narration is tightly controlled and limited in its access to information. The first-person narrator, like his or her limited omniscient counterpart, while free to speculate, can only report information that falls within his or her own firsthand knowledge of the world or what he or she comes to learn secondhand from others.* First-person narratives are necessarily subjective. The only thoughts and feelings that first-person narrators experience directly are their own, and authors sometimes explore and exploit this subjectivity by allowing their narrators' thoughts and feelings—their perceptions of the world—to become colored by unwitting prejudices and biases. The implications of this uncorrected subjectivity are crucially important, for it means that the reader can never expect to see characters and events as they actually are but only as they *appear* to be to the mediating consciousness of the "I"-narrator who stands between the reader and the work. For this reason it is always necessary to pay particular attention to the character that fills that role—to the character's personality, biases, and degree of awareness and perceptivity—in order to measure his or her reliability as a narrator. In this respect, of course, first-person point of view closely resembles the perspective from which each of us views our own life and times. Like the protagonist-narrator, we can *see* everything that falls within our line of vision, but we can only *know* the content of our own mind, and we must be constantly alert to the influences, large and small, that shape and possibly distort our outlook on the world.

Among the advantages of first-person point of view is the sense of immediacy, credibility, and psychological realism that autobiographical storytelling always carries with it. **No other point of view, in fact, is more effective in its capacity for eliciting the reader's direct intellectual and emotional involvement in the teller and the tale.**

First-person narrators are usually identified and differentiated on the basis of their degree of involvement with the events of the plot. They may be the protagonist, like Sammy, the engaging would-be hero of John Updike's "A&P," who tell stories of their own mishaps and adventures. In such works, the protagonist-narrator is always firmly in control of the content, pace, and method of presentation. Certain events will be fully or partially dramatized as the protagonist witnesses them; others will be transmitted to the reader indirectly through the use of summary and comment. Protagonist-narrators, not surprisingly, tend to dominate their works to the disadvantage of other characters, and by continually calling attention to their own presence, and to their own thoughts and feelings, fully characterize themselves in the process. To the extent that such characters are perceptive and intelligent and able to make sense (and even see the irony and humor) of the events in which they participate, their stories, like Sammy's, often illustrate growth and maturation. Where such sensitivity and intelligence are lacking, or where emotional clarity or even sanity are in question, as in Charlotte Perkins Gilman's "The Yellow Wall-Paper," the protagonist-narrator becomes the fit subject for irony or compassion and pity.

---

* Some authors get around this limitation by introducing letters, diaries, and journals into their narratives, thus giving the narrator (and the reader) direct and immediate access to the thoughts and feelings of others.

Protagonist-narrators may narrate events as they take place or in leisurely ret-
rospect, with the narrator looking backward over a period of time on adventures
that have already been concluded. In retrospective views, the extent to which the
narrator has managed in the interim to achieve appropriate distance and objectivity can be an issue as well. The unnamed protagonist-narrator of James Joyce's
"Araby," for example, looking backward at his own adolescent romanticism has
not reached such a position. In calling himself "a creature driven and derided by
vanity," he is clearly judging himself too harshly for an act that an older, and a
presumably wiser, adult would be willing to excuse as part of the inevitable process
of growing up.

Not all protagonist-narrators tell their own stories. Sometimes that narrator is
charged with the responsibility of telling someone else's story, as, for instance,
Melville's lawyer tells the story of the strange and "inscrutable" law clerk who
happens into his employment and into his life in "Bartleby the Scrivener." Sometimes the first-person narrator is not the protagonist at all, but rather a character
whose role in the plot is clearly secondary. He or she may, in fact, have almost no
visible role in the plot and exist primarily as a convenient device for transmitting
the narrative to the reader. Such is the case with Dr. Watson, the narrator of "A
Scandal in Bohemia" and the other Sherlock Holmes stories. From his position at
the periphery of the action, Watson is able to move easily among the other
characters, using them as sources to acquire information. Furthermore, like other
first-person narrators, Watson takes on the role of confidant, a genial and sympathetic personality whom Holmes treats almost as an alter ego, informing his
clients, "This is my intimate friend and associate, Dr. Watson, before whom you
can speak as freely as before myself." In a sense, however, the slow-witted Watson
is also Holmes's foil, allowing Arthur Conan Doyle to keep his readers in the dark
until the last moment about the problem-solving going on in the mind of Sherlock
Holmes.

First-person narrators are always subject to hidden biases and prejudices in their
telling of the story. Minor characters serving as narrators, no less than major ones,
must be watched constantly, especially if the reader has reason to suspect that they
may be other than totally reliable guides to the truth of what they report.

4. *Dramatic point of view.* **In the dramatic, or objective, point of view the
story is told ostensibly by no one.** The narrator, who to this point in the discussion has been a visible, mediating authority standing between the reader and
the work, now disappears completely and the story is allowed to present itself
dramatically through action and dialogue. With the disappearance of the narrator, telling is replaced by showing, and the illusion is created that the reader
is a direct and immediate witness to an unfolding drama. Without a narrator to
serve as mentor and guide, the reader is left largely on his or her own. There
is no way of entering the minds of the characters; no evaluative comments are
offered; the reader is not told directly how to respond, either intellectually or
emotionally, to the events or the characters. The reader is permitted to view the
work only in its externals, from the outside. Although the author may supply
certain descriptive details, particularly at the beginning of the work, the reader
is called on to shoulder much of the responsibility for analysis and interpretation. Based on the behavior and conversation of the characters, the reader must
deduce the circumstances of the past and present action and determine why the
characters act as they do.

The dramatic point of view appeals to many modern and contemporary writers because of the impersonal and objective way it presents experience and because of the vivid sense of the actual that it creates. Ernest Hemingway is a leading exemplar. The dramatic mode dominates Hemingway's short stories where it is used with great effectiveness to illustrate and reinforce the psychological and emotional detachment and self-control that many of his characters adopt as a means of coping with the reality of experience.

The following passage of dramatic narration occurs at the beginning of Hemingway's "Hills Like White Elephants."

The Hills across the valley of the Ebro were long and white. On this side there was no shade and no trees and the station was between two lines of rails in the sun. Close against the side of the station there was the warm shadow of the building and a curtain, made of strings of bamboo beads, hung across the open door into the bar, to keep out flies. The American and the girl with him sat at a table in the shade, outside the building. It was very hot and the express from Barcelona would come in forty minutes. It stopped at this junction for two minutes and went on to Madrid.

"What should we drink?" the girl asked. She had taken off her hat and put it on the table.

"It's pretty hot," the man said.

"Let's drink beer."

"Dos cervezas," the man said into the curtain.

"Big ones?" a woman asked from the doorway.

"Yes. Two big ones."

The woman brought two glasses of beer and two felt pads. She put the felt pads and the beer glasses on the table and looked at the man and the girl. The girl was looking off at the line of the hills. They were white in the sun and the country was brown and dry.

"They look like white elephants," she said.

"I've never seen one," the man drank his beer.

"No, you wouldn't have."

—From "Hills Like White Elephants,"
Ernest Hemingway [1927]

The action unfolds dramatically. The concrete, factual details are introduced without comment; and the action and the characters are allowed to present themselves directly to the reader without benefit of an intervening narrator. The effect is one of pure showing. What we are shown are two Americans, a man and a woman, sitting at a table next to a railroad station, waiting for the train from Barcelona. The weather is hot, they order two beers, and they begin a casual, listless conversation that gradually reveals the situation (the woman's pregnancy), the tension that exists between them (he wants her to have an abortion; she does not), and the underlying differences in attitudes and sensibilities (his selfishness and callousness, her sensitivity and imagination) that now threaten their entire relationship. The differences in sensibilities are first clearly signalled by her imaginative observation that the hills in the distance "look like white elephants," his indifferent response ("I've never seen one"), and the cynicism of her curt reply ("No, you wouldn't have"). Hemingway's story, telescoped into the forty minutes it takes for the train to arrive, unfolds slowly, inexorably, almost artlessly, through the medium of flat, unemotional dialogue. The story we witness and assemble largely by ourselves is one of two unhappy people caught up in a conflict which, given the differences in their respective characters and personalities, will not yield a clear-cut or satisfactory resolution.

✈ ANALYZING POINT OF VIEW ✈

1.   What is the point of view: who talks to the reader? Is the point of view consistent throughout the work or does it shift in some way?

2.   Where does the narrator stand in relation to the work? Where does the reader stand?

3.   To what sources of knowledge or information does the point of view give the reader access? What sources of knowledge or information does it serve to conceal?

4.   If the work is told from the point of view of one of the characters, is the narrator reliable? Does his or her personality, character, or intellect affect an ability to interpret the events or the other characters correctly?

5.   Given the author's purposes, is the chosen point of view an appropriate and effective one?

6.   How would the work be different if told from another point of view?

THEME

The *theme* is the central idea or statement about life that unifies and controls the total work. Theme is not the issue, or problem, or subject with which the work deals, but rather the comment or statement the author makes about that issue, problem, or subject.

Theme in literature, whether it takes the form of a brief and meaningful insight or a comprehensive vision of life, is the author's way of communicating and sharing ideas, perceptions, and feelings with his or her readers or, as is so often the case, of probing and exploring with them the puzzling questions of human existence, most of which do not yield neat, tidy, or universally acceptable answers. Although we cannot, as critics, judge a work solely on the basis of the quality of the ideas presented (or on their degree of complexity or sophistication), it is nevertheless true that one of the marks of a great work of literature—a work that we generally regard as a "classic"—is the significance of its theme.

Four important points about theme in fiction need to be made:

1.   *A theme does not exist as an intellectual abstraction that an author superimposes on the work like icing on a cake.* Rather, the theme necessarily and inevitably emerges from the interplay of the various elements of the work and is organically related to the work's total structure.

2.   *The theme may be less prominent and less fully developed in some works of fiction than in others.* This is especially the case in detective, gothic, and adventure fiction, where the author wants primarily to entertain by producing mystification, inducing chills and nightmare, or engaging the reader in a series of exciting, fast-moving incidents. Works of this type, in fact, often do not have a demonstrable theme at all. To identify the theme of a detective story with the idea that "crime doesn't pay" is not only to confuse theme with moral, but in all probability to misinterpret where the author has chosen to place the work's emphasis. One must, however, be careful. Many works of humor and satire—for example, stories

like Samuel L. Clemens's "The Celebrated Jumping Frog of Calaveras County," John Updike's "A&P," Garrison Keillor's "The Tip Top Club"—while they make us smile, and perhaps laugh, do have thematic content and offer the reader significant and sobering insights. As in Updike's case, these insights may cause us to ponder some of the vulgarities and absurdities of twentieth-century life that we all too often accept without comment or reaction. Much the same thing is true of gothic fiction. In the hands of genuine artists like Poe, Faulkner, and Flannery O'Connor, melodrama, terror, and horror are used not for their own sakes but to probe the recesses of the human soul.

3. *It is entirely possible that intelligent readers will differ, at times radically, on just what the theme of a given work is.* Critical disagreements often occur when the elements of the work are arranged in a way that yields two or more acceptable, yet mutually exclusive, statements. A case in point is "Young Goodman Brown," Hawthorne's story of a young Puritan who leaves his wife of three months (appropriately named Faith) and embarks on a nighttime journey into the forest to keep a prearranged appointment with the Devil. As he makes his way through the forest, first alone and then in the company of a stranger (presumably the Devil) who resembles his own father, Goodman Brown becomes increasingly convinced that his fellow townspeople, and finally even Faith, are members of the Devil's unholy communion. The story climaxes in a lurid rite of initiation, in which Goodman Brown cries out: "My Faith is gone! . . . There is no good on earth, and sin is but a name. Come Devil! for to thee is the world given."

In the aftermath, Brown's faith is destroyed; he shrinks from the bosom of his wife and goes to his grave convinced that "Evil is the nature of mankind." The final theme of the story, however, is anything but clear. Hawthorne's tale is made deliberately ambiguous through the use of a limited omniscient point of view; the narrator refuses to commit himself as to whether what Goodman Brown thinks he sees is really happening or whether it is merely the figment of Brown's distorted imagination.

As a result, the story has been analyzed by its various critics to yield a multitude of possible themes, all of them plausibly rooted in the facts of the story as the critics have interpreted those facts. Some have accepted Goodman Brown's own interpretation as the definitive statement of Hawthorne's theme; others have argued that Hawthorne is attempting to illustrate the failure of belief and the effects of moral scepticism. The story has also been variously interpreted as an attack on the hypocrisy of Puritan society, as an attack on Calvinistic theology, and as a psychoanalytic study of arrested sexual development that has nothing to do with the question of religious faith. Nor does Hawthorne's story stand alone as an example of protracted (and finally inconclusive) literary debate.

4. *The theme of a given work need not be in accord with the reader's particular beliefs and values.* We are under no obligation as readers, of course, to accept the story's theme as it is presented to us, especially if we believe that it violates the truth of our own experience and the experience of others. But we must remember that although literature is full of ideas that may strike us, at least initially, as unpleasant, controversial, or simply wrong-headed, literary sophistication and plain common sense should warn us against dismissing them out of hand. Many stories survive, in part at least, because of the fresh and challenging ideas and insights they offer. Such ideas and insights have the power to liberate our minds and our imaginations and to cause us to reflect critically about our own values, beliefs, and assumptions.

Identifying Theme

When we attempt to identify the theme of a work of fiction we are attempting to formulate in our own words the statement about life or human experience that is made by the total work. The task is often far from easy because it necessarily involves us in the analysis of a number of elements in their relation to one another and to the work as a whole. Part of the value of attempting to identify theme is that it forces us to bring together and to understand the various aspects of the work; in this process we may notice things we had previously ignored or undervalued. We will be successful in the task if we are willing to be open-minded and objective and resist the temptation to pay attention to *some* rather than *all* the elements of the work or, what is worse, to read into them what simply is not there. The identification of theme, then, is a way to test our own understanding, to focus our response, and to make the work finally and fully our own.

The ideas that constitute a work's theme may be relatively commonplace ones that easily fall within the framework of our own experience. They may also be fairly complex and abstract—somewhat hard to understand and put into words—either because we have not encountered them before or because they relate to concepts that are in themselves inherently difficult. Some themes are topical in nature (that is, they involve ideas that are valid only in relation to a specific time and place, or to a specific set of circumstances); others are universal in their application. On some occasions the theme may be explicitly stated by one of the characters (who serves as a spokesperson for the author) or by the author in the guise of an omniscient narrator. Even though such explicit statements must be taken seriously into account, a degree of caution is also necessary—for characters and narrators alike can be unreliable and misleading. In many cases, however, theme is not stated but rather implied by the work's total rendering of experience; it is only gradually revealed through the treatment of character and incident and by the development of the story.

Because different kinds of works will yield different themes in different ways, there is no one correct approach to identifying theme. The following suggestions and comments, however, may prove helpful:

1. *It is important to avoid confusing a work's theme with its subject or situation.* Theme is the abstract, generalized statement or comment that the work makes about a concrete subject or situation. Take the case of Hawthorne's "My Kinsman, Major Molineux." Its subject, young Robin Molineux, is easily enough identified. We will then want to ask ourselves a series of questions about what happens to Robin in the course of the story. What visible changes take place in his situation, in his character, or in both? What does he discover and learn as the result of his experiences? Having asked and answered such questions, we are in a position to propose a theme for the story and, having done so, to defend our thesis in the form of a critical analysis that will relate all the significant aspects of the story— especially plot, character, and point of view—in support of our interpretation.

2. *We must be as certain as we can that our statement of theme does the work full justice.* There is always the danger of either misunderstanding the theme by failing to discover its total significance or of overstating and enlarging it beyond what the elements of the story can be shown to support, and thus making the work appear more universally applicable than it is. The danger of the latter is probably greater than the danger of the former. Authors, like all intelligent people, know that universal, all-embracing statements about life are frequently refuted by the expe-

rience of individuals and they will usually restrict their claims accordingly. They know that most of the really important questions about human experience do not yield up easy answers. As readers, we must be careful not to credit literary works with solutions and answers where such issues and questions are only being explored or where only tentative answers are being proposed.

3. Theme was defined previously as a "statement about life that unifies and controls the total work." Therefore, *the test of any theme we may propose is whether it is fully and completely supported by the work's other elements.* If our statement of the theme leaves certain elements or details unexplained, or if those elements and details fail to confirm our statements, then unless the work itself is flawed, chances are we have been only partially successful in our identification.

4. *The title an author gives the work often suggests a particular focus or emphasis for the reader's attention.* Just as the title of a work sometimes serves to identify the work's protagonist or essential character, it may also provide clues about theme. For example, Joseph Conrad's "Heart of Darkness" refers not only to the uncharted center of Africa, the "dark" continent, but to the capacity for evil and corruption that exists in the human heart, a title relevant to both the plot situation and the theme of Conrad's story.

❧ ANALYZING THEME ❧

1. Does the work have a theme? Is it stated or implied?

2. What generalization(s) or statement(s) about life or human experience does the work make?

3. What elements of the work contribute most heavily to the formulation of the theme?

4. Does the theme emerge organically and naturally, or does the author seem to force the theme upon the work?

5. What is the value or significance of the work's theme? Is it topical or universal in its application?

SYMBOL AND ALLEGORY

Symbol

A *symbol,* according to Webster's Dictionary, is **"something that stands for or suggests something else by reason of relationship, association, convention, or accidental resemblance . . . a visible sign of something invisible."** Symbols, in this sense, are with us all the time, for there are few words or objects that do not evoke, at least in certain contexts, a wide range of associated meanings and feelings. For example, the word *home* (as opposed to *house*) conjures up feelings of warmth, security, and personal associations of family, friends, and neighborhood, while the American flag suggests country and patriotism. Human beings by virtue of their capacity for language and memory are symbol-making creatures.

Most of our daily symbol-making and symbol-reading is unconscious and accidental, the inescapable product of our experience as human beings. **In literature,**

however, symbols—in the form of words, images, objects, settings, events, and characters—are often used deliberately to suggest and reinforce meaning, to provide enrichment by enlarging and clarifying the experience of the work, and to help to organize and unify the whole. William York Tindall, a well-regarded scholar and author of *The Literary Symbol* (1955), likens the literary symbol to "a metaphor one half of which remains unstated and indefinite."* The analogy is a good one. Although symbols exist first as something literal and concrete within the work itself, they also have the capacity to call to mind a range of invisible and abstract associations, both intellectual and emotional, that transcend the literal and concrete and extend their meaning. A literary symbol brings together what is material and concrete within the work (the visible half of Tindall's metaphor) with its series of associations; by fusing them, however briefly, in the reader's imagination, new layers and dimensions of meaning, suggestiveness, and significance are added.

The identification and understanding of literary symbols require a great deal from the reader. They demand awareness and intelligence: an ability to detect when the emphasis an author places on certain elements within the work can be legitimately said to carry those elements to larger, symbolic levels, and when the author means to imply nothing beyond what is literally stated. They also make demands on the reader's maturity and sophistication, for only when we are sufficiently experienced with the world will the literal and concrete strike an appropriately symbolic chord. If, that is to say, we have not had the occasion to think much or think deeply about life and experience, it is not likely that we will be able to detect, much less understand, the larger hidden meanings to which symbols point. As Tindall observes, "What the reader gets from a symbol depends not only upon what the author has put into it but upon the reader's sensitivity and his consequent apprehension of what is there."**

Beginning readers must be particularly careful in approaching the subject of symbols and symbolism. Although the author's use of symbols may be unconscious, ours is very much an age in which the conscious and deliberate use of symbolism defines much of our literary art. There is, consequently, a tendency among students of literature to forget that all art contains a mixture of both the literal and the symbolic and to engage in a form of indiscriminate "symbol hunting" that either unearths symbols and symbolic meanings where none are intended or pushes the interpretation of legitimate symbols beyond what is reasonable. Both temptations must be avoided.

It is perfectly true, of course, that the meaning of any symbol is, by definition, indefinite and open-ended, and that a given symbol will evoke a slightly different response in different readers, no matter how discriminating. Yet there is an acceptable range of possible readings for any symbol beyond which we must not stray. We are always limited in our interpretation of symbols by the total context of the work in which they occur and by the way in which the author has established and arranged its other elements; and we are not free to impose—from the outside—our own personal and idiosyncratic meanings simply because they appeal to us. We must also be careful to avoid the danger of becoming so preoccupied with the larger significance or meaning that we forget the literal importance of the concrete thing being symbolized.

* William York Tindall, *The Literary Symbol* (New York: Columbia UP, 1955) 12.
** Tindall 17.

Types of Symbols

Symbols are usually classified as being *traditional* or *original*, depending on the source of the associations that provide their meaning.

Traditional symbols **are those whose associations are the common property of a society or culture and are so widely recognized and accepted that they can be said to be almost universal.** The symbolic associations that generally accompany the forest and the sea, the moon and the sun, night and day, the colors black, white and red, and the seasons of the year are examples of traditional symbols. They are so much a part of our culture that we take their significance pretty much for granted. A special kind of traditional symbol is the archetype, a term that derives from anthropologist James G. Frazer's famous study of myth and ritual *The Golden Bough* (1890–1915) and the depth psychology of Carl Jung. (Jung holds that certain symbols are so deeply rooted in the repeated and shared experience of our common ancestors—he refers to them as the "collective consciousness" of the human race—as to evoke an immediate and strong, if unconscious, response in any reader.) Hawthorne's use of blackness in "Young Goodman Brown," with its obvious overtones of mystery, evil, and satanism, is an example of an archetypal symbol. Stories that focus on the initiation of the young—for example, Nathaniel Hawthorne's "My Kinsman, Major Molineaux," James Joyce's "Araby," and Katherine Anne Porter's "The Grave"—all carry with them archetypal overtones. Frazer discovered that such rites of passage exist everywhere in the cultural patterns of the past and continue to exert a powerful influence on the patterns of our own behavior.

Original symbols **are those whose associations are neither immediate nor traditional; instead, they derive their meaning, largely if not exclusively, from the context of the work in which they are used.** Perhaps the most famous example of an original symbol is Herman Melville's white whale, Moby Dick. While whales are often associated in the popular imagination with brute strength and cunning, Moby Dick assumes his larger, metaphysical significance (for Captain Ahab he is the pasteboard mask behind which lurks all the pent-up malignity of the universe) only within the contextual limits of Melville's novel. Outside that novel, a whale is just a whale.

Use of Symbols

SETTING AND SYMBOL. In a number of the examples used above in the discussion of setting—Stephen Crane's snow-surrounded blue hotel, Roderick Usher's ancestral mansion, and the city streets through which Robin Molineux roams in search of his kinsman—we noted how the details of setting are used functionally to extend, clarify, and reinforce the author's larger intention and meaning. We also called attention to the fact that authors employ the seasons of the year and the time of day because of the traditional associations these have for the reader. These identifications are not arbitrary ones, for in each of the works cited, the author deliberately calls attention to the setting, not once but on several occasions, in a way that suggests that it is integrally related to his larger purposes. In the case of Crane, it is to call attention to the thematic implications of the work; in the case of Poe and Hawthorne, it is to help reveal the personalities of their characters. Setting in fiction that goes beyond mere backdrop is often used in such symbolic ways. Symbolic settings are particularly useful to authors when they frame and encompass the events of plot and thus provide the work as a whole with an overarching pattern of unity.

PLOT AND SYMBOL. Single events, large and small, or plots in their entirety often function symbolically. Even the most commonplace action or event—even to the level of gesture—can carry symbolic meaning, though it is often difficult, at least upon first reading, to tell for certain whether symbolism is involved. The symbolic nature of plot or plot elements may not, in fact, become clear until after we have finished the work and look backward to see how the individual parts of the plot relate to the whole. In Hawthorne's "My Kinsman, Major Molineux," for example, it may not be clear until the end of the story that each of the separate incidents that punctuate Robin's journey in search of his kinsman form a chain of symbolic events that are an integral part of his ritual of initiation.

When the entire sequence of events that constitute a plot falls into a symbolic pattern as in "My Kinsman, Major Molineux," the events are often archetypal. Such a plot, that is, conforms to basic patterns of human behavior so deeply rooted in our experience that they recur ritualistically, time and time again, in the events of myth, folklore, and narrative literature. In fiction, perhaps the most frequently encountered archetypal pattern is the journey or quest, in which young men and women undergo a series of trials and ordeals that finally confirms their coming of age and new-found maturity.

CHARACTER AND SYMBOL. Symbolism is frequently employed as a way of deepening our understanding of character. Some characters are given symbolic names to suggest underlying moral, intellectual, or emotional qualities. The name "Robin Molineux," for example, suggests springtime, youth, and innocence. The objects assigned to characters function in the same way: the heavy oak cudgel that Robin carries with him into the city functions as a symbol to suggest his youthful aggressiveness; Miranda's attention to the carved wedding ring that her brother has discovered in the grave in Katherine Anne Porter's "The Grave" symbolizes her vague intimations of the role in life she is destined to play; the gun that Dave covets in Richard Wright's "The Man Who Was Almost a Man" is the symbol of the masculine independence that is not yet his; and the house in which Emily Grierson has lived so long in William Faulkner's "A Rose for Emily" functions as an analog to Emily herself, "lifting its stubborn and coquettish decay" alone and apart.

But while the personalities of major characters are often revealed and clarified through the use of symbols rooted in the language that describes them, their very complexity as human beings usually prevents their being defined by a single symbol. This is not true of minor characters, especially those who are flat and one-dimensional and are constructed around a single idea or quality. Literature is filled with such individuals. For example, the girl in James Joyce's "Araby," significantly known only as "Mangan's sister," in whose service the narrator visits the bazaar, symbolizes the mystery, enchantment, and "otherness" that typifies and objectifies a young boy's first love.

Symbolism thus enhances fiction through helping readers to organize and enlarge their experience of the work. This is not to say that a work of fiction containing symbolism is necessarily better than one that does not. Nor is it to say that symbolism in and of itself can make a work successful. But symbolism, when employed as an integral and organic part of a work of fiction, can stimulate the imagination—which is, after all, one of the major goals of any form of art.

Allegory

Allegory is a technique for expanding the meaning of a literary work by having the characters, and sometimes the setting and the events, represent certain abstract ideas, qualities, or concepts—usually moral, religious, or political in nature. Unlike symbolism, the abstractions of allegory are fixed and definite and tend to take the form of specific ideas that, once identified, can be readily understood. Because they remain constant, they are also easily remembered. In their purest form, works of allegory operate consistently and simultaneously at two separate but parallel levels of meaning: one located inside the work itself, at the concrete level of plot and character; the other, outside the work, at the level of the particular ideas or qualities to which these internal elements point. Such works function best when these two levels reinforce and complement each other: we read the work as narrative, but are also aware of the ideas that lie beyond the concrete representations.

The most famous sustained allegory in the English language is John Bunyan's *The Pilgrim's Progress* (published in two parts, in 1678 and 1684). In Bunyan's book the didactic impulse, always latent within allegory, is very clear. *Pilgrim's Progress* is a moral and religious allegory of the Christian soul in search of salvation. It tells the story of an individual, appropriately named "Christian," who sets off in search of the Celestial City (heaven) and along the way is forced to confront obstacles whose names and personalities (or characteristics) embody the ideals, virtues, and vices for which they stand: Mr. Worldly Wiseman, Mistrust, Timorous, Faithful, Giant Despair, the Slough of Despond, the Valley of the Shadow of Death, and so on.

Although works of pure allegory like Bunyan's are relatively rare, many works do make occasional use of allegory, not infrequently combined with symbolism. As a fictional mode of presentation, however, allegory is unquestionably out of favor among modern and contemporary authors, for reasons that have to do with the nature of allegory itself. First of all, the didacticism of allegory and its tendency toward a simplified, if not simplistic, view of life is suspect in a world where there is very little common agreement about truth and the validity of certain once universally respected ideas and ideals. Second, the way allegory presents character is simply not in keeping with the modern conception of fictional characterization. In allegory the characters, and the ideas and ideals those characters embody, are presented as a given. The modern author, on the other hand, prefers to build characters and to develop and reveal their personalities gradually, in stages, throughout the course of the work.

Several of the stories included in *Literature* either contain clear instances of the use of allegory or lend themselves to allegorical readings. The name Faith, which Hawthorne gives to the wife of Young Goodman Brown, is certainly, in part at least, intended allegorically. "With Heaven above, and Faith below, I will yet stand firm against the devil!" Goodman Brown cries out as he approaches his midnight rendezvous, and in the pages that follow, his exhortations to "Faith" clearly refer not only to his wife, whom he fears is numbered among the devil's communion, but to his Puritan religious faith which is itself being tested. Franz Kafka's "A Hunger Artist," similarly, has been interpreted as an allegory treating the plight of the artist in the modern world. An allegorical reading has also been suggested for Hawthorne's "My Kinsman, Major Molineux." Read as a historical and political allegory of America's coming of age and maturation as a young and independent nation, Robin can be said to represent Colonial America, and his kinsman the traditional British authority that must be displaced and overthrown. Both Robin and colonial America share a number of common characteristics: both have rural, agrarian origins; both are young and strong, yet insecure and self-conscious because untested and inexperienced in the ways of the world; both are pious and proud (even arrogant) and given to aggressive behavior; and both have a reputation, deserved or not, for native "shrewdness." Just as Robin learns that he can "rise in the world without the help of (his) . . . kinsman, Major Molineux," so colonial America realizes that it can achieve its destiny as a mature and independent nation without the paternalistic control of Great Britain. In each of the preceding examples, an allegorical interpretation does seem to "work," in the sense that it allows us to organize the elements of the story around a central illuminating idea. Nevertheless, it would be a mistake to press such readings too far. To read these works *exclusively* as allegories is to oversimplify the internal dynamics of each story and to distort the author's vision.

__ ❧ ANALYZING SYMBOL AND ALLEGORY ❧ __

1.   What symbols or patterns of symbolism (or allegory) are present in the story? Are the symbols traditional or original?

2.   What aspects of the work (e.g., theme, setting, plot, characterization) does the symbolism (allegory) serve to explain, clarify, or reinforce?

3.   Does the author's use of symbolism (allegory) seem contrived or forced in any way, or does it arise naturally out of the interplay of the story's major elements?

STYLE AND TONE

Style

The distinctive quality of literature that sets it apart from all other forms of artistic expression is its reliance on language. Using words is the writer's craft. They are the writer's means of recovering and objectifying experience; and they are his or her means of presenting, shaping, and controlling subject matter. Language is also the means by which the writer controls and influences the reader: in responding to literature we are always responding to the author's words. The literary critic must pay close attention to those words; not only because they convey the substance of the author's message—the story he or she wishes to tell—but because they provide important clues to the author's emotional and psychological life, beliefs, and attitudes and to the way in which the author perceives himself or herself and the world around him or her.

When we talk about an author's words and the characteristic way he or she uses the resources of language to achieve certain effects, we are talking about *style*. In its most general sense, style consists of *diction* (the individual words an author chooses) and *syntax* (the arrangement of those words), as well as such devices as rhythm and sound, allusion, ambiguity, irony, paradox, and figurative language.

Each writer's style is unique. It constitutes the writer's "signature" in a way that sets his or her work apart. One test of the distinctiveness of an author's style is its ability to resist paraphrase. The test is relatively simple. Take a passage from any well-regarded work and paraphrase it. Although the underlying ideas may remain the same, the words themselves will probably register a quite different effect upon you.

By examining the style of a work of fiction we are seeking as critics to accommodate a number of objectives. First of all, we are seeking to isolate and identify those distinctive traits that comprise the author's "signature." Second, we are interested in understanding the effects produced by particular stylistic devices and techniques and how these effects influence our response to the work's other elements—particularly character, incident, setting, and theme—and to the work as a whole. Third, we are attempting, by way of evaluation, to arrive at a judgment based on a consideration of just how effectively the author has managed to integrate form and content. This examination is an attempt to measure just how well an author has succeeded in a given work with the style he or she has chosen.

Elements of Style

The following are some basic elements of style we examine in order to characterize an author's writing.

DICTION. Although words are usually meaningful only in the context of other words, stylistic analysis begins with the attempt to identify and understand the type and quality of the individual words that comprise an author's basic vocabulary. When used in connection with characterization, words are the vehicles by which a character's ideas, attitudes, and values are expressed. Words convey the details of outer appearance and inner state of mind. In dialogue they reflect the speaker's intelligence and sophistication, general level of conscious awareness, and socioeconomic, geographical, and educational background. When used to describe incidents, words help to convey the narrator's (or author's) attitude toward those events and the characters involved in them. When used to describe setting, words help to create and sustain an appropriate atmosphere.

The analysis of diction includes the following considerations: the *denotative* (or dictionary) meaning of words, as opposed to their *connotative* meaning (the ideas associated with or suggested by them); their degree of *concreteness* or *abstractness;* their degree of *allusiveness;* the *parts of speech* they represent; their length and construction; the *level of usage* they reflect (standard or nonstandard; formal, informal, or colloquial); the *imagery* (details of sensory experience) they contain; the *figurative devices* (*simile, metaphor, personification,* etc.) they embody; their *rhythm and sound patterns* (*alliteration, assonance, consonance, onomatopoeia*). In studying diction, we also need to pay close attention to the use of *repetition:* the way key words recur in a given passage or series of passages in such a way as to call special attention to themselves.

SYNTAX. When we examine style at the level of syntax, we are attempting to analyze the ways the author arranges words into phrases, clauses, and finally whole sentences to achieve particular effects. Although syntax is determined partly by the lexical content (or meaning) of the words and partly by the basic grammatical structure of the language, every writer enjoys considerable freedom to shape and control the syntactic elements of style. In looking at an author's syntax we want to know how the words have been arranged and particularly how they deviate from the normal and expected.

Although one can study syntactic units smaller than the sentence—for example, individual phrases that call attention to themselves by their length, content, and placement—syntax is probably most easily analyzed in sentences. Such an approach mirrors most closely the writing process itself, for sentences are the major units of thought, and it is on the crafting of sentences that most authors concentrate their creative energies. Sentences can be examined in terms of their length—whether they are short, spare, and economical or long and involved; in terms of their form—whether they are simple, compound, or complex; and in terms of their construction—whether they are *loose* (sentences that follow the normal subject-verb-object pattern, stating their main idea near the beginning in the form of an independent clause), *periodic* (sentences that deliberately withhold or suspend the completion of the main idea until the end of the sentence), or *balanced* (sentences in which two similar or antithetical ideas are balanced).

Each type of sentence will have a slightly different effect on the reader. Long, complicated sentences slow down and retard the pace of a narrative, whereas short, simple sentences hasten it. Loose sentences, because they follow the normal, predictable patterns of speech, tend to appear more natural and less contrived than either periodic or balanced sentences, particularly when they are used in the creation of dialogue. Moreover, the deliberate arrangement of words within individual sentences or groups of sentences can result in patterns of rhythm and sound (pleasant or unpleasant) that establish or reinforce feeling and emotion. Although an author will usually vary the kinds of sentences used in order to avoid monotony (unless monotony is intended), certain syntactic patterns will dominate and become characteristic of that author's style.

Stylistic Analysis

Because stylistic analysis is generally carried out by isolating and examining one or more representative passages from a given work, the following examples may prove illustrative.

During the whole of a dull, dark, and soundless day in the autumn of the year, when the clouds hung oppressively low in the heavens, I had been passing alone, on horseback, through a singularly dreary tract of country; and at length found myself, as the shades of evening drew on, within view of the melancholy House of Usher. I know not how it was—but, with the first glimpse of the building, a sense of insufferable gloom pervaded my spirit. I say insufferable; for the feeling was unrelieved by any of that half-pleasurable, because poetic, sentiment with which the mind usually receives even the sternest natural images of the desolate or terrible.

—From "The Fall of the House of Usher," Edgar Allan Poe [1839]

STYLISTIC ANALYSIS. In this first paragraph of the story, the unnamed narrator, Roderick Usher's boyhood acquaintance, first approaches the melancholy and decaying house. Poe's obvious intent is to establish, from the outset, the appropriate setting and atmosphere for the story—one that will simultaneously arrest the reader's attention and evoke an appropriate emotional response. The opening sentence, surely one of the most famous in all of American literature, is a long, periodic one, in which a series of rhythmic phrases and clauses are deliberately arranged to suspend, until the very end, and so prepare the way for, the object of the narrator's search. Within the sentence, Poe carefully intensifies his visual details with adjectives and adverbs and reinforces their effect through the use of alliteration and onomatopoeia. The second and third sentences, which record the narrator's response to the scene, continue to invite the reader to respond in the same way. Poe's emotion-charged prose is clearly excessive (note the use of such words as "oppressively," "dreary," "melancholy," "insufferable," "sternest," "desolate," and "terrible"), yet its very excess effectively establishes the mood that is to dominate the story from beginning to end.

I was pretty tired, and the first thing I knowed, I was asleep. When I woke up I didn't know where I was, for a minute. I set up and looked around, a little scared. Then I remembered. The river looked miles and miles across. The moon was so bright I could a counted the drift logs that went slipping along, black and still, hundred of yards out from shore. Everything was dead quiet, and it looked late, and *smelt* late. You know what I mean—I don't know the words to put it in.

—From *The Adventures of Huckleberry Finn*, Mark Twain [1885]

STYLISTIC ANALYSIS. When Ernest Hemingway wrote in his *Green Hills of Africa* (1935) that "All modern American literature comes from one book by Mark Twain called *Huckleberry Finn*," he was referring to the realism of Mark Twain's style, which differs so markedly from the heavy, "literary" prose of writers like Poe. The defining qualities of Mark Twain's style—which does, clearly, look ahead to the twentieth century—are very much in evidence in this passage. Huck Finn is speaking in a voice and manner appropriate to a largely self-educated rural adolescent. Note his informal, colloquial language, with its small grammatical flaws, his simple, uncomplicated, relaxed sentences, and the sparse, yet vivid, imagery he uses to discuss the moonlit river—all of which convey the impression of something real, honestly reported. His final confession of inadequacy, although hardly necessary, is perfectly in keeping with a character who constantly refuses to falsify his experience of the world.

When the short days of winter came dusk fell before we had well eaten our dinners. When we met in the street the houses had grown sombre. The space of sky above us was the colour of ever-changing violet and towards it the lamps of the street lifted their feeble lanterns. The cold air stung us and we played till our bodies glowed. Our shouts echoed in the silent street. The career of our play brought us through the dark muddy lanes behind the houses where we ran the gauntlet of the rough tribes from the cottages, to the back doors of the dark dripping gardens where odours arose from the ashpits, to the dark odorous stables where a coachman smoothed and combed the horse or shook music from the buckled harness. When we returned to the street light from the kitchen windows had filled the areas. If my uncle was seen turning the corner we hid in the shadow until we had seen him safely housed. Or, if Mangan's sister came out on the doorstep to call her brother in to his tea we watched her from our shadow peer up and down the street. We waited to see whether she would remain or go in and, if she remained, we left our shadow and walked up to Mangan's steps resignedly. She was waiting for us, her figure defined by the light from the half-opened door. Her brother always teased her before he obeyed and I stood by the railings looking at her. Her dress swung as she moved her body and the soft rope of her hair tossed from side to side.

—From "Araby," James Joyce [1914]

STYLISTIC ANALYSIS. Joyce's "Araby" is a love story, told, retrospectively, by an older, and presumably wiser, adult looking backwards on a bittersweet moment of adolescence. In the third paragraph of the story, Joyce describes the Dublin neighborhood (North Richmond Street) that makes up the boy's physical world. The details he uses are less important for their concrete, denotative qualities, however, than for the way they capture and reflect the boy's own subjective ap-preciation of life and its sensual pleasures. What Joyce provides is a series of rich, lyrical, and evocative images that appeal to the eye, to the touch, to the ear, and to the nose, as well as kinetic images that convey a sense of life in motion—images that are made all the more alive and poetic because they seem to spring from the crowded associations of memory. Joyce also employs a number of the devices we normally expect to find in poetry: personification, metaphor, and distinctive pat-terns of rhythm and sound. Note, for example, the final sentence describing "Mangan's sister," upon whom the focus of the passage finally and fittingly comes to rest. The swinging of her dress and the tossing metaphoric "rope" of her hair are emphasized by swishing alliterative "s" sounds that are used to suggest the hypnotic and sensual appeal she exercises on the imagination of a young man caught up in the infatuation of first love.

   The girl stood up and walked to the end of the station. Across, on the other side, were fields of grain and trees along the banks of the Ebro. Far away, beyond the river, were mountains. The shadow of a cloud moved across the field of grain and she saw the river through the trees.
   "And we could have all this," she said. "And we could have everything and every day we make it more impossible."
   "What did you say?"
   "I said we could have everything."
   "We can have everything."
   "No, we can't."
   "We can have the whole world."
   "No, we can't."
   "We can go everywhere."
   "No, we can't. It isn't ours any more."
   "It's ours."
   "No, it isn't. And once they take it away, you never get it back."
   "But they haven't taken it away."
   "We'll wait and see."
   "Come on back in the shade," he said. "You musn't feel that way."
   "I don't feel any way," the girl said. "I just know things."

                    —From "Hills Like White Elephants," Ernest Hemingway [1927]

   STYLISTIC ANALYSIS. The passage perfectly illustrates the famous Hemingway style—economical and terse. It is characterized by short, simple sentences and active verbs; by an informal, commonplace vocabulary of short, denotative words; the absence of unnecessary adjectives and adverbs; and by a concentration of particular concrete images that record the surface level of experience. Descriptive details of setting are sparse though important—in this case they juxtapose the sensuous fertility across the river with the hot, sterile foreground where the con-versation between the two characters takes place. Such details, however, are clearly subordinate to the dialogue, which carries the narrative movement of the story and explores the attitudes and temperaments of the characters. The objective point of view places the burden of interpretation on the reader, who must pay close attention to what is being said in order to identify correctly the verbal nuances that define both character and conflict.
   The dialogue itself is difficult to follow. It is random, indirect, and inexplicit, for Hemingway's characters, aware as they are that to expose oneself openly is to risk psychic injury, tend to approach each other obliquely, their real thoughts and

emotions hidden and held tightly in check. In this passage, the girl senses, though she cannot or will not articulate the fact, that it is not the matter of her pregnancy—or the "awfully simple operation" he proposes—that jeopardizes their relationship, but rather his failure to understand that human relationships themselves inevitably curtail and limit one's freedom. Her inability to communicate this message and his failure to understand it—the failure of dialogue, if you will—thus serves to underscore and explain both the differences in their attitudes and the size of the barrier existing between them.

The preceding examples illustrate how style can be used to serve characterization (Mark Twain, Joyce, and Hemingway), the creation of setting and atmosphere (Poe and Joyce), and the reinforcement of theme (Hemingway). They also illustrate the dynamic, changing nature of the language of fiction itself. In comparing the style of Poe and the style of Hemingway, for example, we can see a movement toward less formality and more concrete diction, as well as simpler syntax; the differences reflect the modern tendency toward realism in fiction. Generalizations about style, however, can be dangerous. Style is a highly personal and sometimes a highly idiosyncratic matter, open to endless opportunities for innovation and experimentation. Although some fictional styles are easier to read and understand than others, and although all readers sooner or later come to express stylistic preferences, there is, finally, no one style that is best or most appropriate. The critic's job is not to state preferences but to analyze and describe: to try to understand the distinctive elements that comprise an author's style, the various effects that those elements create, and the way in which they serve to reveal and reinforce the other elements of the work.

Tone

All of us are familiar with the term *tone* as it is used to characterize the special qualities of accent, inflection, and duration in a speaker's voice. From early childhood on we learn to identify and respond to these elements of speech. For example, a mother can tell her child to "Come here" in a manner that is angry, threatening, concerned, amused, sympathetic, or affectionate, simply by altering her tone of voice. In each case, the mother's meaning is the same—she wants her child to come. However, the relationship she creates with her auditor (the child) will differ dramatically according to her tone. **Tone, then, is a means of creating a relationship or conveying an attitude.** The particular qualities of a speaking voice are unavailable to a writer in creating tone, but to a certain extent rhythm and punctuation can substitute for a speaker's accent and inflection, while word order and word choice can influence tone as easily in prose as in speech.

Just as the tone of the mother's voice communicates her attitude of anger or concern, so tone in fiction is frequently a guide to the author's attitude toward the subject or audience and to the author's intention and meaning. As critics we infer the author's tone through close and careful study of the various elements within the work, including plot, character, setting, point of view, and style. No matter how hard an author tries to mask his or her attitudes and feelings, and to hide the authorial presence within the work, perhaps by taking refuge somewhere behind the narrative voice that tells the story, the author's tone can be inferred by the choices made in the process of ordering and presenting the material; by what is included and emphasized and what, by contrast, is omitted. The literary critic learns to look at such choices carefully— at the characters, incidents, setting, and details depicted; at the issues and problems that are raised and explored; at the style the author has employed; at every decision, in short, that the author has made—in order to infer from them the underlying attitudes and tone that color and control the work as a whole.

IRONY. When the young grocery clerk in John Updike's "A&P" addresses us, he is frank and open, and while he may not yet fully appreciate the implications of his story, there is little reason to believe that he means anything other than what he says. The same thing, however, is not always true of Updike himself, who is on most occasions far more circumspect and cautious and prefers to adopt a posture of detachment and objectivity. Authors like Updike know all too well that life is not always simple or straightforward; that the affairs of adults, and adolescent grocery clerks, are full of surprises, ambiguities, contradictions, and complexities; and that appearances can and often do deceive. In order to reflect the puzzling, problematic nature of experience, such authors choose to approach their subjects indirectly, through the use of irony. They use techniques to create within a work two separate and contrasting levels of experience and a disparity of understanding between them.

The three types of irony that occur most frequently in literature are *verbal irony* (in which there is a contrast between what a speaker literally says and what he or she means); *irony of situation* (in which an event or situation turns out to be the reverse of what is expected or appropriate); and *dramatic irony* (in which the state of affairs known to the reader or the audience is the reverse of what its participants suppose it to be).

Verbal irony is easily enough recognized in speech because of the intonation of the speaker's voice. For example, when Mark Anthony refers to Brutus in Shakespeare's *Julius Caesar* as "an honorable man," few members of the audience are likely to misunderstand the irony in his statement. When used in fiction, however, verbal irony is sometimes more difficult to identify because it is conveyed exclusively through the author's style, through the words on the printed page. Sometimes the author helps the reader by means of repetition, as Hawthorne does in "My Kinsman, Major Molineux," where Robin, the uninitiated youth from the country, prides himself on his native "shrewdness." Shrewd, at least in the way of the city, Robin is most certainly not.

Irony of situation, on the other hand, results from the careful manipulation of plot, point of view, setting, and atmosphere. Robin's prolonged and frustrating search for his kinsman, for example, is rendered ironic by the fact that his arrival in Boston coincides exactly with a revolutionary plot whose chief object is the very individual who Robin believes will help him rise in the world. Robin Molineux is but one in a long line of fictional characters whose expectations are altered or reversed by the events that overtake them. The situational irony in Hawthorne's story is sustained not only by the plot, but by the point of view, which reveals the true state of things only gradually both to Robin and the reader. In Shirley Jackson's well-known short story "The Lottery," irony of situation is established by the ostensibly gay and light-hearted atmosphere and festive scene on the June morning on which the story opens and by Jackson's use of a detached and matter-of-fact dramatic point of view. Only as the events of the morning unfold does the reader come to grasp the fact that the residents of this picturesque rural village are about to stone to death one of their fellow citizens.

Dramatic irony, like irony of situation, depends on the use of plot, character, and point of view. An omniscient narrator, for example, will sometimes reveal information to the reader that his or her characters do not know; this allows the narrator (and the reader) to judge the subsequent actions of those characters and to anticipate the likely outcome of events. Dramatic irony can also be established by means of characters whose innocence and naivete cause them to misperceive or misinterpret events whose significance is perfectly clear to the reader. The plots of such works frequently turn on the matter of knowing or not knowing, as in Henry James's "Four Meetings," and result in outcomes that are either comic or tragic in their final implication.

As critics Robert Scholes and Robert Kellogg note in their study of narrative literature, *The Nature of Narrative* (1966), there are "In any example of narrative art . . . broadly speaking, three points of view—those of the characters, the narrator, and the audience." When any of the three "perceives more—or less—than another, irony must be either actually or potentially present."* In any work of fiction, it is crucially important that we be able to determine if and how that potential has been exploited; to overlook or misinterpret the presence of irony can only lead to a misinterpretation of the author's attitudes and tone and the way he or she would have us approach the work.

𝒳 ANALYZING STYLE AND TONE 𝒳

1.   Describe the author's diction. Is the language concrete or abstract, formal or informal, literal or figurative? What parts of speech occur often?

2.   What use does the author make of imagery; figurative devices (simile, metaphor, personification); patterns of rhythm and sound (alliteration, assonance, consonance, onomatopoeia); repetition; allusion?

3.   Are the sentences predominantly long or short; simple, compound, or complex; loose, periodic, or balanced?

4.   Describe the author's tone. Is it, for example, sympathetic, detached, condescending, serious, humorous, or ironic? How is the tone established and revealed?

5.   What kind(s) or irony does the author use: verbal irony, irony of situation, dramatic irony? What purpose(s) does the irony serve?

6.   What are the distinctive characteristics of the author's style? In what ways is the style appropriate to the work's subject and theme?

---

* Robert Scholes and Robert Kellogg, *The Nature of Narrative* (New York: Oxford UP, 1966) 240.

3

※※※※※※

Stories

Washington Irving 1783–1859

RIP VAN WINKLE

Whoever has made a voyage up the Hudson must remember the Kaatskill Mountains. They are a dismembered branch of the great Appalachian family, and are seen away to the west of the river, swelling up to a noble height and lording it over the surrounding country. Every change of season, every change of weather, indeed every hour of the day, produces some change in the magical hues and shapes of these mountains, and they are regarded by all the good wives, far and near, as perfect barometers. When the weather is fair and settled, they are clothed in blue and purple, and print their bold outlines on the clear evening sky; but sometimes, when the rest of the landscape is cloudless, they will gather a hood of gray vapor about their summits, which in the last rays of the setting sun will glow and light up like a crown of glory.

At the foot of these fairy mountains the voyager may have described the light smoke curling up from a village, whose shingle roofs gleam among the trees just where the blue tints of the upland melt away into the fresh green of the nearer landscape. It is a little village of great antiquity, having been founded by some of the Dutch colonists in the early times of the province, just about the beginning of the government of the good Peter Stuyvesant (may he rest in peace!), and there were some of the houses of the original settlers standing within a few years, built of small yellow bricks brought from Holland, having latticed windows and gable fronts surmounted with weathercocks.

In that same village, and in one of these very houses (which, to tell the precise truth, was sadly time-worn and weather-beaten), there lived many years since, while the country was yet a province of Great Britain, a simple good-natured fellow of the name of Rip Van Winkle. He was a descendant of the Van Winkles who figured so gallantly in the chivalrous days of Peter Stuyvesant and accompanied him to the siege of Fort Christina.[1] He inherited, however, but little of the martial

---

[1] Peter Stuyvesant (1592–1672), the last Dutch governor of New Netherland, assumed that position in 1647 and held it until 1664. In the process of securing the borders of the colony, Stuyvesant laid seige to and captured, in 1655, Fort Christina, a Swedish fort on the Delaware River near what is now Wilmington, Delaware.

character of his ancestors. I have observed that he was a simple good-natured man; he was, moreover, a kind neighbor and an obedient henpecked husband. Indeed, to the latter circumstance might be owing that meekness of spirit which gained him such universal popularity; for those men are most apt to be obsequious and conciliating abroad who are under the discipline of shrews at home. Their tempers, doubtless, are rendered pliant and malleable in the fiery furnace of domestic tribulation, and a curtain lecture[2] is worth all the sermons in the world for teaching the virtues of patience and long-suffering. A termagant[3] wife may, therefore, in some respects, be considered a tolerable blessing; and if so, Rip Van Winkle was thrice blessed.

Certain it is that he was a great favorite among all the good wives of the village, who, as usual with the amiable sex, took his part in all family squabbles, and never failed, whenever they talked those matters over in their evening gossips, to lay all the blame on Dame Van Winkle. The children of the village, too, would shout with joy whenever he approached. He assisted at their sports, made their playthings, taught them to fly kites and shoot marbles, and told them long stories of ghosts, witches, and Indians. Whenever he went dodging about the village he was surrounded by a troop of them, hanging on his skirts, clambering on his back, and playing a thousand tricks on him with impunity; and not a dog would bark at him throughout the neighborhood.

The great error in Rip's composition was an insuperable aversion to all kinds of profitable labor. It could not be from the want of assiduity or perseverance; for he would sit on a wet rock, with a rod as long and heavy as a Tartar's lance,[4] and fish all day without a murmur, even though he should not be encouraged by a single nibble. He would carry a fowling-piece on his shoulder for hours together, trudging through woods and swamps and up hill and down dale, to shoot a few squirrels or wild pigeons. He would never refuse to assist a neighbor even in the roughest toil, and was a foremost man at all country frolics for husking Indian corn or building stone fences; the women of the village, too, used to employ him to run their errands, and to do such little odd jobs as their less obliging husbands would not do for them. In a word, Rip was ready to attend to anybody's business but his own; but as to doing family duty and keeping his farm in order, he found it impossible.

In fact, he declared it was of no use to work on his farm; it was the most pestilent little piece of ground in the whole country; everything about it went wrong, and would go wrong in spite of him. His fences were continually falling to pieces; his cow would either go astray or get among the cabbages; weeds were sure to grow quicker in his fields than anywhere else; the rain always made a point of setting in just as he had some out-door work to do; so that, though his patrimonial estate had dwindled away under his management, acre by acre, until there was little more left than a mere patch of Indian corn and potatoes, yet it was the worst-conditioned farm in the neighborhood.

His children, too, were as ragged and wild as if they belonged to nobody. His son Rip, an urchin begotten in his own likeness, promised to inherit the habits with the old clothes of his father. He was generally seen trooping like a colt at his mother's heels, equipped in a pair of his father's cast-off galligaskins,[5] which he had much ado to hold up with one hand, as a fine lady does her train in bad weather.

---

[2] A tirade or upbraiding delivered by a wife to her husband in the privacy of their curtained bed.
[3] Shrewish, quarrelsome.
[4] The Tartars were a war-like tribe of Mongolians.   [5] Loose breeches.

Rip Van Winkle, however, was one of those happy mortals, of foolish, well-oiled disposition, who take the world easy, eat white bread or brown, whichever can be got with least thought or trouble, and would rather starve on a penny than work for a pound. If left to himself, he would have whistled life away in perfect contentment; but his wife kept continually dinning in his ears about his idleness, his carelessness, and the ruin he was bringing on his family. Morning, noon, and night her tongue was incessantly going, and everything he said or did was sure to produce a torrent of household eloquence. Rip had but one way of replying to all lectures of the kind, and that, by frequent use, had grown into a habit. He shrugged his shoulders, shook his head, cast up his eyes, but said nothing. This, however, always provoked a fresh volley from his wife; so that he was fain to draw off his forces and take to the outside of the house—the only side which, in truth, belongs to a henpecked husband.

Rip's sole domestic adherent was his dog Wolf, who was as much henpecked as his master; for Dame Van Winkle regarded them as companions in idleness, and even looked upon Wolf with an evil eye, as the cause of his master's going so often astray. True, it is, in all points of spirit befitting an honorable dog he was as courageous an animal as ever scoured the woods; but what courage can withstand the ever-during and all-besetting terrors of a woman's tongue? The moment Wolf entered the house his crest fell, his tail drooped to the ground or curled between his legs, he sneaked about with a gallows air, casting many a sidelong glance at Dame Van Winkle, and at the least flourish of a broomstick or ladle he would fly to the door with yelping precipitation.

Times grew worse and worse with Rip Van Winkle as years of matrimony rolled on; a tart temper never mellows with age, and a sharp tongue is the only edged tool that grows keener with constant use. For a long while he used to console himself, when driven from home, by frequenting a kind of perpetual club of the sages, philosophers, and other idle personages of the village which held its sessions on a bench before a small inn, designated by a rubicund[6] portrait of His Majesty George the Third.[7] Here they used to sit in the shade through a long lazy summer's day, talking listlessly over village gossip or telling endless sleepy stories about nothing. But it would have been worth any statesman's money to have heard the profound discussions that sometimes took place when by chance an old newspaper fell into their hands from some passing traveller. How solemnly they would listen to the contents, as drawled out by Derrick Van Bummel, the schoolmaster, a dapper learned little man, who was not to be daunted by the most gigantic word in the dictionary, and how sagely they would deliberate upon public events some months after they had taken place!

The opinions of this junto[8] were completely controlled by Nicholas Vedder, a patriarch of the village and landlord of the inn, at the door of which he took his seat from morning till night, just moving sufficiently to avoid the sun and keep in the shade of a large tree; so that the neighbors could tell the hour by his movements as accurately as by a sun-dial. It is true he was rarely heard to speak, but smoked his pipe incessantly. His adherents, however (for every great man has his adherents), perfectly understood him, and knew how to gather his opinions. When anything that was read or related displeased him, he was observed to smoke his pipe vehemently, and to send forth short, frequent, and angry puffs; but when pleased, he would inhale the smoke slowly and tranquilly, and emit it in light and placid clouds; and sometimes, taking the pipe from his mouth and letting the

---

[6] Ruddy.   [7] King of England from 1760 to 1820.   [8] Ruling clique.

fragrant vapor curl about his nose, would gravely nod his head in token of perfect approbation.

From even this stronghold the unlucky Rip was at length routed by his termagant wife, who would suddenly break in upon the tranquility of the assemblage and call the members all to naught; nor was that august personage, Nicholas Vedder himself, sacred from the daring tongue of this terrible virago,[9] who charged him outright with encouraging her husband in habits of idleness.

Poor Rip was at last reduced almost to despair, and his only alternative, to escape from the labor of the farm and clamor of his wife, was to take gun in hand and stroll away into the woods. Here he would sometimes seat himself at the foot of a tree, and share the contents of his wallet[10] with Wolf, with whom he sympathized as a fellow-sufferer in persecution. "Poor Wolf!" he would say, "thy mistress leads thee a dog's life of it; but never mind, my lad—whilst I live thou shalt never want a friend to stand by thee!" Wolf would wag his tail, look wistfully in his master's face, and, if dogs can feel pity, I verily believe he reciprocated the sentiment with all his heart.

In a long ramble of the kind on a fine autumnal day Rip had unconsciously scrambled to one of the highest parts of the Kaatskill Mountains. He was after his favorite sport of squirrel-shooting, and the still solitudes had echoed and re-echoed with the reports of his gun. Panting and fatigued, he threw himself, late in the afternoon, on a green knoll, covered with mountain-herbage, that crowned the brow of a precipice. From an opening between the trees he could overlook all the lower country for many a mile of rich woodland. He saw at a distance the lordly Hudson, far, far below him, moving on its silent but majestic course, with the reflection of a purple cloud or the sail of a lagging bark here and there sleeping on its glassy bosom, and at last losing itself in the huge highlands.

On the other side he looked down into a deep mountain-glen, wild, lonely, and shagged, the bottom filled with fragments from the impending cliffs, and scarcely lighted by the reflected rays of the setting sun. For some time Rip lay musing on this scene; evening was gradually advancing; the mountains began to throw their long blue shadows over the valleys; he saw that it would be dark long before he could reach the village, and he heaved a heavy sigh when he thought of encountering the terrors of Dame Van Winkle.

As he was about to descend, he heard a voice from a distance hallooing, "Rip Van Winkle! Rip Van Winkle!" He looked round, but could see nothing but a crow winging its solitary flight across the mountain. He thought his fancy must have deceived him, and turned again to descend, when he heard the same cry ring through the still evening air: "Rip Van Winkle! Rip Van Winkle!"—at the same time Wolf bristled up his back, and giving a low growl, skulked to his master's side, looking fearfully down into the glen. Rip now felt a vague apprehension stealing over him; he looked anxiously in the same direction, and perceived a strange figure slowly toiling up the rocks and bending under the weight of something he carried on his back. He was surprised to see any human being in this lonely and unfrequented place, but supposing it to be some one of the neighborhood in need of his assistance, he hastened down to yield it.

On nearer approach he was still more surprised at the singularity of the stranger's appearance. He was a short, square-built old fellow, with thick bushy hair and a grizzled beard. His dress was of the antique Dutch fashion—a cloth jerkin[11] strapped round the waist—several pair of breeches, the outer one of ample volume, decorated with rows of buttons down the sides, and bunches at the knees. He bore

[9] Scolding woman.   [10] Knapsack.   [11] A short waistcoat or jacket.

on his shoulder a stout keg that seemed full of liquor, and made signs for Rip to approach and assist him with the load. Though rather shy and distrustful of this new acquaintance, Rip complied with his usual alacrity; and, mutually relieving each other, they clambered up a narrow gully, apparently the dry bed of a mountain-torrent. As they ascended, Rip every now and then heard long rolling peals, like distant thunder, that seemed to issue out of a deep ravine, or rather cleft, between lofty rocks, toward which their rugged path conducted. He paused for an instant, but supposing it to be the muttering of one of those transient thunder-showers which often take place in mountain-heights, he proceeded. Passing through the ravine, they came to a hollow, like a small amphitheatre, surrounded by perpendicular precipices, over the brinks of which impending trees shot their branches, so that you only caught glimpses of the azure sky and the bright evening cloud. During the whole time Rip and his companion had labored on in silence; for though the former marvelled greatly what could be the object of carrying a keg of liquor up this wild mountain, yet there was something strange and incomprehensible about the unknown that inspired awe and checked familiarity.

On entering the amphitheatre, new objects of wonder presented themselves. On a level spot in the centre was a company of odd-looking personages playing at nine-pins. They were dressed in a quaint outlandish fashion: some wore short doublets,[12] others jerkins, with long knives in their belts, and most of them had enormous breeches, of similar style with that of the guide's. Their visages, too, were peculiar: one had a large head, broad face, and small piggish eyes: the face of another seemed to consist entirely of nose, and was surmounted by a white sugar-loaf hat, set off with a little red cock's tail. They all had beards, of various shapes and colors. There was one who seemed to be the commander. He was a stout old gentleman, with a weatherbeaten countenance; he wore a laced doublet, broad belt and hanger,[13] high-crowned hat and feather, red stockings, and high-heeled shoes with roses in them. The whole group reminded Rip of the figures in an old Flemish[14] painting in the parlor of Dominie[15] Van Shaick, the village parson, and which had been brought over from Holland at the time of the settlement.

What seemed particularly odd to Rip was, that though these folks were evidently amusing themselves, yet they maintained the gravest faces, the most mysterious silence, and were, withal, the most melancholy party of pleasure he had ever witnessed. Nothing interrupted the stillness of the scene but the noise of the balls, which, whenever they were rolled, echoed along the mountains like rumbling peals of thunder.

As Rip and his companion approached them they suddenly desisted from their play, and stared at him with such fixed statue-like gaze, and such strange, uncouth, lack-lustre countenances, that his heart turned within him and his knees smote together. His companion now emptied the contents of the keg into large flagons, and made signs to him to wait upon the company. He obeyed with fear and trembling; they quaffed the liquor in profound silence, and then returned to their game.

By degrees Rip's awe and apprehension subsided. He even ventured, when no eye was fixed upon him, to taste the beverage, which he found had much of the flavor of excellent Hollands.[16] He was naturally a thirsty soul, and was soon tempted to repeat the draught. One taste provoked another, and he reiterated his visits to the flagon so often that at length his senses were overpowered, his eyes swam in his head, his head gradually declined, and he fell into a deep sleep.

On waking, he found himself on the green knoll whence he had first seen the

[12] A close-fitting jacket covering the entire torso.   [13] A short sword, hung from the belt.
[14] Belgian.   [15] Minister.   [16] A gin made in Holland.

old man of the glen. He rubbed his eyes—it was a bright sunny morning. The birds were hopping and twittering among the bushes, and the eagle was wheeling aloft and breasting the pure mountain-breeze. "Surely," thought Rip, "I have not slept here all night." He recalled the occurrences before he fell asleep. The strange man with a keg of liquor—the mountain-ravine—the wild retreat among the rocks—the woebegone party at nine-pins—the flagon. "Oh, that flagon! that wicked flagon!" thought Rip—"what excuse shall I make to Dame Van Winkle?"

He looked round for his gun, but in place of the clean, well-oiled fowling-piece, he found an old firelock lying by him, the barrel encrusted with rust, the lock falling off, and the stock worm-eaten. He now suspected that the grave roysterers of the mountain had put a trick upon him, and, having dosed him with liquor, had robbed him of his gun. Wolf, too, had disappeared, but he might have strayed away after a squirrel or partridge. He whistled after him and shouted his name, but all in vain; the echoes repeated his whistle and shout, but no dog was to be seen.

He determined to revisit the scene of the last evening's gambol, and if he met with any of the party to demand his dog and gun. As he rose to walk, he found himself stiff in the joints and wanting in his usual activity. "These mountain-beds do not agree with me," thought Rip, "and if this frolic should lay me up with a fit of the rheumatism, I shall have a blessed time with Dame Van Winkle." With some difficulty he got down into the glen: he found the gully up which he and his companion had ascended the preceding evening; but to his astonishment a mountain-stream was now foaming down it, leaping from rock to rock and filling the glen with babbling murmurs. He, however, made shift to scramble up its sides, working his toilsome way through thickets of birch, sassafras, and witch-hazel, and sometimes tripped up or entangled by the wild grapevines that twisted their coils or tendrils from tree to tree and spread a kind of network in his path.

At length he reached to where the ravine had opened through the cliffs to the amphitheatre; but no traces of such opening remained. The rocks presented a high impenetrable wall, over which the torrent came tumbling in a sheet of feathering foam, and fell into a broad, deep basin, black from the shadows of the surrounding forest. Here, then, poor Rip was brought to a stand. He again called and whistled after his dog; he was only answered by the cawing of a flock of idle crows sporting high in air about a dry tree that overhung a sunny precipice, and who, secure in their elevation, seemed to look down and scoff at the poor man's perplexities. What was to be done? The morning was passing away, and Rip felt famished for want of his breakfast. He grieved to give up his dog and gun; he dreaded to meet his wife; but it would not do to starve among the mountains. He shook his head, shouldered the rusty firelock, and with a heart full of trouble and anxiety turned his steps homeward.

As he approached the village he met a number of people but none whom he knew, which somewhat surprised him, for he had thought himself acquainted with every one in the country round. Their dress, too, was of a different fashion from that to which he was accustomed. They all stared at him with equal marks of surprise, and whenever they cast their eyes upon him, invariably stroked their chins. The constant recurrent of this gesture induced Rip, involuntarily, to do the same, when, to his astonishment, he found his beard had grown a foot long!

He had now entered the skirts of the village. A troop of strange children ran at his heels, hooting after him and pointing at his gray beard. The dogs, too, not one of which he recognized for an old acquaintance, barked at him as he passed. The very village was altered; it was larger and more populous. There were rows of houses which he had never seen before, and those which had been his familiar haunts had disappeared. Strange names were over the doors—strange faces at the windows—everything was strange. His mind now misgave him; he began to doubt whether both he and the world around him were not bewitched. Surely this was his native village, which he had left but the day before. There stood the Kaatskill Mountains—there ran the silver Hudson at a distance—there was every hill and dale precisely as it had always been. Rip was sorely perplexed. "That flagon last night," thought he, "has addled my poor head sadly."

It was with some difficulty that he found the way to his own house, which he approached with silent awe, expecting every moment to hear the shrill voice of Dame Van Winkle. He found the house gone to decay—the roof fallen in, the windows shattered, and the doors off the hinges. A half-starved dog that looked like Wolf was skulking about it. Rip called him by name, but the cur snarled, showed his teeth, and passed on. This was an unkind cut indeed. "My very dog," sighed poor Rip, "has forgotten me!"

He entered the house, which, to tell the truth, Dame Van Winkle had always kept in neat order. It was empty, forlorn, and apparently abandoned. This desolateness overcame all his connubial fears—he called loudly for his wife and children—the lonely chambers rang for a moment with his voice, and then all again was silence.

He now hurried forth, and hastened to his old resort, the village inn, but it too was gone. A large rickety wooden building stood in its place, with great gaping windows, some of them broken and mended with old hats and petticoats, and over the door was painted, "The Union Hotel, by Jonathan Doolittle." Instead of the great tree that used to shelter the quiet little Dutch inn of yore, there now was reared a tall, naked pole, with something on the top that looked like a red nightcap,[17] and from it was fluttering a flag, on which was a singular assemblage of stars and stripes. All this was strange and incomprehensible. He recognized on the sign, however, the ruby face of King George, under which he had smoked so many a peaceful pipe; but even this was singularly metamorphosed. The red coat was changed for one of blue and buff, a sword was held in the hand instead of a sceptre, the head was decorated with a cocked hat, and underneath was painted in large characters, GENERAL WASHINGTON.

There was, as usual, a crowd of folk about the door, but none that Rip recollected. The very character of the people seemed changed. There was a busy, bustling, disputatious tone about it, instead of the accustomed phlegm and drowsy tranquility. He looked in vain for the sage Nicholas Vedder, with his broad face, double chin, and fair long pipe, uttering clouds of tobacco-smoke instead of idle speeches; or Van Bummel, the schoolmaster, doling forth the contents of an ancient newspaper. In place of these, a lean, bilious-looking fellow, with his pockets full of handbills, was haranguing vehemently about rights of citizens—elections—members of Congress—liberty—Bunker's Hill—heroes of Seventy-six—and other words, which were a perfect Babylonish jargon[18] to the bewildered Van Winkle.

The appearance of Rip, with his long, grizzled beard, his rusty fowling-piece, his uncouth dress, and an army of women and children at his heels, soon attracted the attention of the tavern politicians. They crowded round him, eyeing him from

---

[17] The Phrygian cap, or liberty cap as it came to be called, was originally worn by slaves freed by the Romans. During the French Revolution of the 1790s it became a symbol of freedom. The "naked pole" referred to is a liberty pole.

[18] Irving apparently confuses Babylon with Babel. See Genesis 11:1–9.

head to foot with great curiosity. The orator bustled up to him, and, drawing him partly aside, inquired "on which side he voted." Rip stared in vacant stupidity. Another short but busy little fellow pulled him by the arm, and, rising on tiptoe, inquired in his ear, "Whether he was Federal or Democrat."[19] Rip was equally at a loss to comprehend the question; when a knowing, self-important old gentleman, in a sharp cocked hat, made his way through the crowd, putting them to the right and left with his elbows as he passed, and, planting himself before Van Winkle, with one arm akimbo, the other resting on his cane, his keen eyes and sharp hat penetrating, as it were, into his very soul, demanded in an austere tone, "What brought him to the election with a gun on his shoulder and a mob at his heels, and whether he meant to breed a riot in the village?"—"Alas! gentlemen," cried Rip, somewhat dismayed, "I am a poor, quiet man, a native of the place, and a loyal subject of the king, God bless him!"

Here a general shout burst from the bystanders—"A Tory! a Tory![20] a spy! a refugee![21] hustle him! away with him!" It was with great difficulty that the self-important man in the cocked hat restored order; and, having assumed a tenfold austerity of brow, demanded again of the unknown culprit what he came there for, and whom he was seeking. The poor man humbly assured him that he meant no harm, but merely came there in search of some of his neighbors, who used to keep about the tavern.

"Well—who are they?—name them."

Rip bethought himself a moment, and inquired, "Where's Nicholas Vedder?"

There was a silence for a little while, when an old man replied in a thin piping voice, "Nicholas Vedder! why, he is dead and gone these eighteen years! There was a wooden tombstone in the churchyard that used to tell all about him, but that's rotten and gone too."

"Where's Brom Dutcher?"

"Oh, he went off to the army in the beginning of the war; some say he was killed at the storming of Stony Point—others say he was drowned in a squall at the foot of Antony's Nose.[22] I don't know—he never came back again."

"Where's Van Bummel, the schoolmaster?"

"He went off to the wars too, was a great militia general, and is now in Congress."

Rip's heart died away at hearing of these sad changes in his home and friends and finding himself thus alone in the world. Every answer puzzled him, too, by treating of such enormous lapses of time, and of matters which he could not understand: war—Congress—Stony Point. He had no courage to ask after any more friends, but cried out in despair, "Does nobody here know Rip Van Winkle?"

"Oh, Rip Van Winkle!" exclaimed two or three. "Oh, to be sure! that's Rip Van Winkle yonder, leaning against the tree."

Rip looked and beheld a precise counterpart of himself as he went up the mountain, apparently as lazy, and certainly as ragged. The poor fellow was now completely confounded. He doubted his own identity, and whether he was himself

---

[19] The two political parties during George Washington's administration, 1789–1797.

[20] "Tories" was the name given to those who supported the British government during the period of the American Revolution.

[21] The "Refugees" were British supporters who fled their homes for the safety of the British lines.

[22] Stony Point, a fortification on the west bank of the Hudson below West Point, was captured by American general Anthony Wayne (1745–1796) in July 1779. Antony's Nose is a promontory on the Hudson near Stony Point; Irving named it after Peter Stuyvesant's trumpeter Antony Van Corlear.

or another man. In the midst of his bewilderment the man in the cocked hat demanded who he was, and what was his name.

"God knows," exclaimed he, at his wit's end; "I'm not myself—I'm somebody else—that's me yonder—no—that's somebody else got into my shoes. I was myself last night, but I fell asleep on the mountain, and they've changed my gun, and everything's changed, and I'm changed, and I can't tell what's my name, or who I am!"

The bystanders began now to look at each other, nod, wink significantly, and tap their fingers against their foreheads. There was a whisper, also, about securing the gun and keeping the old fellow from doing mischief, at the very suggestion of which the self-important man in the cocked hat retired with some precipitation. At this critical moment a fresh comely woman passed through the throng to get a peep at the gray-bearded man. She had a chubby child in her arms, which, frightened at his looks, began to cry. "Hush, Rip," cried she, "hush, you little fool! the old man won't hurt you." The name of the child, the air of the mother, the tone of her voice, all awakened a train of recollections in his mind. "What is your name, my good woman?" asked he.

"Judith Gardenier."

"And your father's name?"

"Ah, poor man! Rip Van Winkle was his name, but it's twenty years since he went away from home with his gun, and never has been heard of since—his dog came home without him; but whether he shot himself, or was carried away by the Indians, nobody can tell. I was then but a little girl."

Rip had but one question more to ask, but he put it with a faltering voice:

"Where's your mother?"

"Oh, she, too, had died but a short time since; she broke a blood-vessel in a fit of passion at a New England peddler."

There was a drop of comfort, at least, in this intelligence. This honest man could contain himself no longer. He caught his daughter and her child in his arms. "I am your father!" cried he—"young Rip Van Winkle once—old Rip Van Winkle now! Does nobody know poor Rip Van Winkle?"

All stood amazed, until an old woman, tottering out from among the crowd, put her hand to her brow, and peering under it in his face for a moment, exclaimed, "Sure enough! it is Rip Van Winkle—it is himself! Welcome home again, old neighbor! Why, where have you been these twenty long years?"

Rip's story was soon told, for the whole twenty years had been to him but as one night. The neighbors stared when they heard it; some were seen to wink at each other, and put their tongues in their cheeks: and the self-important man in the cocked hat, who, when the alarm was over, had returned to the field, screwed down the corners of his mouth and shook his head—upon which there was a general shaking of the head throughout the assemblage.

It was determined, however, to take the opinion of old Peter Vanderdonk, who was seen slowly advancing up the road. He was a descendant of the historian of that name, who wrote one of the earliest accounts of the province.[23] Peter was the most ancient inhabitant of the village, and well versed in all the wonderful events and traditions of the neighborhood. He recollected Rip at once, and corroborated his story in the most satisfactory manner. He assured the company that it was a fact, handed down from his ancestor the historian, that the Kaatskill Mountains

[23] Adriaen Van der Donck (1620–1655?) wrote a history of New Netherland which was published in Amsterdam in 1655.

had always been haunted by strange beings. That it was affirmed that the great Hendrick Hudson, the first discoverer of the river and country, kept a kind of vigil there every twenty years, with his crew of the Half-moon,[24] being permitted in this way to revisit the scenes of his enterprise and keep a guardian eye upon the river and the great city called by his name. That his father had once seen them in their old Dutch dresses playing at nine-pins in a hollow of the mountain; and that he himself had heard, one summer afternoon, the sound of their balls, like distant peals of thunder.

To make a long story short, the company broke up, and returned to the more important concerns of the election. Rip's daughter took him home to live with her; she had a snug, well-furnished house, and a stout cheery farmer for a husband, whom Rip recollected for one of the urchins that used to climb upon his back. As to Rip's son and heir, who was the ditto of himself, seen leaning against the tree, he was employed to work on the farm, but evinced an hereditary disposition to attend to anything else but his business.

Rip now resumed his old walks and habits; he soon found many of his former cronies, though all rather the worse for the wear and tear of time; and preferred making friends among the rising generation, with whom he soon grew into great favor.

Having nothing to do at home, and being arrived at that happy age when a man can be idle with impunity, he took his place once more on the bench at the inn-door, and was reverenced as one of the patriarchs of the village and a chronicle of the old times "before the war." It was some time before he could get into the regular track of gossip, or could be made to comprehend the strange events that had taken place during his torpor. How that there had been a Revolutionary war—that the country had thrown off the yoke of old England—and that, instead of being a subject of his Majesty George the Third, he was now a free citizen of the United States. Rip, in fact, was no politician; the changes of states and empires made but little impression on him; but there was one species of despotism under which he had long groaned, and that was—petticoat government. Happily, that was at an end; he had got his neck out of the yoke of matrimony, and could go in and out whenever he pleased, without dreading the tyranny of Dame Van Winkle. Whenever her name was mentioned, however, he shook his head, shrugged his shoulders, and cast up his eyes; which might pass either for an expression of resignation to his fate or joy at his deliverance.

He used to tell his story to every stranger that arrived at Mr. Doolittle's hotel. He was observed, at first, to vary on some points every time he told it, which was, doubtless, owing to his having so recently awaked. It at last settled down precisely to the tale I have related, and not a man, woman, or child in the neighborhood but knew it by heart. Some always pretended to doubt the reality of it, and insisted that Rip had been out of his head, and that this was one point on which he always remained flighty. The old Dutch inhabitants, however, almost universally gave it full credit. Even to this day they never hear a thunderstorm of a summer afternoon about the Kaatskill but they say Hendrick Hudson and his crew are at their game of nine-pins; and it is a common wish of all henpecked husbands in the neighborhood, when life hangs heavy on their hands, that they might have a quieting draught out of Rip Van Winkle's flagon.

[1819]

---

[24] Henry (not Hendrick) Hudson (?–1611) was the English captain employed by the Dutch who in 1609 discovered the river that would bear his name.

Edgar Allan Poe   *1809–1849*

THE FALL OF THE HOUSE OF USHER

Son coeur est un luth suspendu;
Sitôt qu'on le touche il résonne.
De Beranger[1]

During the whole of a dull, dark, and soundless day in the autumn of the year, when the clouds hung oppressively low in the heavens, I had been passing alone, on horseback, through a singularly dreary tract of country; and at length found myself, as the shades of the evening drew on, within view of the melancholy House of Usher. I know not how it was—but, with the first glimpse of the building, a sense of insufferable gloom pervaded my spirit. I say insufferable; for the feeling was unrelieved by any of that half-pleasurable, because poetic, sentiment, with which the mind usually receives even the sternest natural images of the desolate or terrible. I looked upon the scene before me—upon the mere house, and the simple landscape features of the domain—upon the bleak walls—upon the vacant eye-like windows—upon a few rank sedges—and upon a few white trunks of decayed trees—with an utter depression of soul which I can compare to no earthly sensation more properly than to the after-dream of the reveller upon opium—the bitter lapse into everyday life—the hideous dropping off of the veil. There was an iciness, a sinking, a sickening of the heart—an unredeemed dreariness of thought which no goading of the imagination could torture into aught of the sublime. What was it—I paused to think—what was it that so unnerved me in the contemplation of the House of Usher? It was a mystery all insoluble; nor could I grapple with the shadowy fancies that crowded upon me as I pondered. I was forced to fall back upon the unsatisfactory conclusion, that while, beyond doubt, there *are* combinations of very simple natural objects which have the power of thus affecting us, still the analysis of this power lies among considerations beyond our depth. It was possible, I reflected, that a mere different arrangement of the particulars of the scene, of the details of the picture, would be sufficient to modify, or perhaps to annihilate its capacity for sorrowful impression; and, acting upon this idea, I reined my horse to the precipitous brink of a black and lurid tarn[2] that lay in unruffled lustre by the dwelling, and gazed down—but with a shudder even more thrilling than before—upon the remodelled and inverted images of the gray sedge, and the ghastly tree-stems, and the vacant and eye-like windows.

Nevertheless, in this mansion of gloom I now proposed to myself a sojourn of some weeks. Its proprietor, Roderick Usher, had been one of my boon companions in boyhood; but many years had elapsed since our last meeting. A letter, however, had lately reached me in a distant part of the country—a letter from him—which, in its wildly importunate nature, had admitted of no other than a personal reply. The MS. gave evidence of nervous agitation. The writer spoke of acute bodily illness—of a mental disorder which oppressed him—and of an earnest desire to see me, as his best, and indeed his only personal friend,

---

[1] Lines from a peom by Pierre-Jean de Béranger (1780–1857): "His heart is a suspended lute;/ Whenever one touches it, it responds."
[2] A small mountain lake or pond.

with a view of attempting, by the cheerfulness of my society, some alleviation of his malady. It was the manner in which all this, and much more, was said—it was the apparent *heart* that went with his request—which allowed me no room for hesitation; and I accordingly obeyed forthwith what I still considered a very singular summons.

Although, as boys, we had been even intimate associates, yet I really knew little of my friend. His reserve had been always excessive and habitual. I was aware, however, that his very ancient family had been noted, time out of mind, for a peculiar sensibility of temperament, displaying itself, through long ages, in many works of exalted art, and manifested, of late, in repeated deeds of munificent yet unobtrusive charity, as well as in a passionate devotion to the intricacies, perhaps even more than to the orthodox and easily recognizable beauties, of musical science. I had learned, too, the very remarkable fact, that the stem of the Usher race, all time-honoured as it was, had put forth, at no period, any enduring branch; in other words, that the entire family lay in the direct line of descent, and had always, with very trifling and very temporary variation, so lain. It was this deficiency, I considered, while running over in thought the perfect keeping of the character of the premises with the accredited character of the people, and while speculating upon the possible influence which the one, in the long lapse of centuries, might have exercised upon the other—it was this deficiency, perhaps, of collateral issue, and the consequent undeviating transmission, from sire to son, of the patrimony with the name, which had, at length, so identified the two as to merge the original title of the estate in the quaint and equivocal appellation of the "House of Usher"—an appellation which seemed to include, in the minds of the peasantry who used it, both the family and the family mansion.

I have said that the sole effect of my somewhat childish experiment—that of looking down within the tarn—had been to deepen the first singular impression. There can be no doubt that the consciousness of the rapid increase of my super-stition—for why should I not so term it?—served mainly to accelerate the increase itself. Such, I have long known, is the paradoxical law of all sentiments having terror as a basis. And it might have been for this reason only, that, when I again uplifted my eyes to the house itself, from its image in the pool, there grew in my mind a strange fancy—a fancy so ridiculous, indeed, that I but mention it to show the vivid force of the sensations which oppressed me. I had so worked upon my imagination as really to believe that about the whole mansion and domain there hung an atmosphere peculiar to themselves and their immediate vicinity—an atmosphere which had no affinity with the air of heaven, but which had reeked up from the decayed trees, and the gray wall, and the silent tarn—a pestilent and mystic vapour, dull, sluggish, faintly discernible, and leaden-hued.

Shaking off from my spirit what *must* have been a dream, I scanned more narrowly the real aspect of the building. Its principal feature seemed to be that of an excessive antiquity. The discoloration of ages had been great. Minute fungi overspread the whole exterior, hanging in a fine tangled web-work from the eaves. Yet all this was apart from any extraordinary dilapidation. No portion of the masonry had fallen; and there appeared to be a wild inconsistency between its still perfect adaptation of parts, and the crumbling condition of the individual stones. In this there was much that reminded me of the specious totality of old wood-work which has rotted for long years in some neglected vault, with no disturbance from the breath of the external air. Beyond this indication of extensive decay, however, the fabric gave little token of instability. Perhaps the eye of a scrutinizing observer might have discovered a barely perceptible fissure, which, extending from the roof of the building in front, made its way down the wall in a zigzag direction, until it became lost in the sullen waters of the tarn.

Noticing these things, I rode over a short causeway to the house. A servant in waiting took my horse, and I entered the Gothic archway of the hall. A valet, of stealthy step, thence conducted me, in silence, through many dark and intricate passages in my progress to the *studio* of his master. Much that I encountered on the way contributed, I know not how, to heighten the vague sentiments of which I have already spoken. While the objects around me—while the carvings of the ceilings, the sombre tapestries of the walls, the ebon blackness of the floors, and the phantasmagoric armorial trophies which rattled as I strode, were but matters to which, or to such as which, I had been accustomed from my infancy—while I hesitated not to acknowledge how familiar was all this—I still wondered to find how unfamiliar were the fancies which ordinary images were stirring up. On one of the staircases, I met the physician of the family. His countenance, I thought, wore a mingled expression of low cunning and perplexity. He accosted me with trepidation and passed on. The valet now threw open a door and ushered me into the presence of his master.

The room in which I found myself was very large and lofty. The windows were long, narrow, and pointed, and at so vast a distance from the black oaken floor as to be altogether inaccessible from within. Feeble gleams of encrimsoned light made their way through the trellised panes, and served to render sufficiently distinct the more prominent objects around; the eye, however, struggled in vain to reach the remoter angles of the chamber, or the recesses of the vaulted and fretted ceiling. Dark draperies hung upon the walls. The general furniture was profuse, comfortless, antique, and tattered. Many books and musical instruments lay scattered about, but failed to give any vitality to the scene. I felt that I breathed an atmosphere of sorrow. An air of stern, deep, and irredeemable gloom hung over and pervaded all.

Upon my entrance, Usher arose from a sofa on which he had been lying at full length, and greeted me with a vivacious warmth which had much in it, I at first thought, of an overdone cordiality—of the constrained effort of the *ennuyé*[3] man of the world. A glance, however, at his countenance, convinced me of his perfect sincerity. We sat down; and for some moments, while he spoke not, I gazed upon him with a feeling half of pity, half of awe. Surely, man had never before so terribly altered, in so brief a period, as had Roderick Usher! It was with difficulty that I could bring myself to admit the identity of the wan being before me with the companion of my early boyhood. Yet the character of his face had been at all times remarkable. A cadaverousness of complexion; an eye large, liquid, and luminous beyond comparison; lips somewhat thin and very pallid, but of a surpassingly beautiful curve; a nose of a delicate Hebrew model, but with a breadth of nostril unusual in similar formations; a finely moulded chin, speaking, in its want of prominence, of a want of moral energy; hair of a more than web-like softness and tenuity; these features, with an inordinate expansion above the regions of the temple, made up altogether a countenance not easily to be forgotten. And now in the mere exaggeration of the prevailing character of these features, and of the expression they were wont to convey, lay so much of change that I doubted to whom I spoke. The now ghastly pallor of the skin, and the now miraculous lustre of the eye, above all things startled and even awed me. The silken hair, too, had been suffered to grow all unheeded,

[3] Bored.

and as, in its wild gossamer texture, it floated rather than fell about the face, I could not, even with effort, connect its Arabesque[4] expression with any idea of simple humanity.

In the manner of my friend I was at once struck with an incoherence—an inconsistency; and I soon found this to arise from a series of feeble and futile struggles to overcome an habitual trepidancy—an excessive nervous agitation. For something of this nature I had indeed been prepared, no less by his letter, than by reminiscences of certain boyish traits, and by conclusions deduced from his peculiar physical conformation and temperament. His action was alternately vivacious and sullen. His voice varied rapidly from a tremulous indecision (when the animal spirits seemed utterly in abeyance) to that species of energetic concision—that abrupt, weighty, unhurried, and hollow-sounding enunciation—that leaden, self-balanced and perfectly modulated guttural utterance, which may be observed in the lost drunkard, or the irreclaimable eater of opium, during the periods of his most intense excitement.

It was thus that he spoke of the object of my visit, of his earnest desire to see me, and of the solace he expected me to afford him. He entered, at some length, into what he conceived to be the nature of his malady. It was, he said, a constitutional and a family evil, and one for which he despaired to find a remedy—a mere nervous affection, he immediately added, which would undoubtedly soon pass off. It displayed itself in a host of unnatural sensations. Some of these, as he detailed them, interested and bewildered me; although, perhaps, the terms, and the general manner of the narration had their weight. He suffered much from a morbid acuteness of the senses; the most insipid food was alone endurable; he could wear only garments of certain texture; the odours of all flowers were oppressive; his eyes were tortured by even a faint light; and there were but peculiar sounds, and these from stringed instruments, which did not inspire him with horror.

To an anomalous species of terror I found him a bounden slave. "I shall perish," said he, "I *must* perish in this deplorable folly. Thus, thus, and not otherwise, shall I be lost. I dread the events of the future, not in themselves, but in their results. I shudder at the thought of any, even the most trivial, incident, which may operate upon this intolerable agitation of soul. I have, indeed, no abhorrence of danger, except in its absolute effect—in terror. In this unnerved—in this pitiable condition—I feel that the period will sooner or later arrive when I must abandon life and reason together, in some struggle with the grim phantasm, FEAR."

I learned, moreover, at intervals, and through broken and equivocal hints, another singular feature of his mental condition. He was enchained by certain superstitious impressions in regard to the dwelling which he tenanted, and whence, for many years, he had never ventured forth—in regard to an influence whose supposititious force was conveyed in terms too shadowy here to be restated—an influence which some peculiarities in the mere form and substance of his family mansion, had, by dint of long sufferance, he said, obtained over his spirit—an effect which the *physique* of the gray walls and turrets, and of the dim tarn into which they all looked down, had, at length, brought about upon the *morale* of his existence.

He admitted, however, although with hesitation, that much of the peculiar gloom which thus afflicted him could be traced to a more natural and far more palpable origin—to the severe and long-continued illness—indeed to the evi-

[4] Strange or exotic.

dently approaching dissolution—of a tenderly beloved sister—his sole companion for long years—his last and only relative on earth. "Her decease," he said, with a bitterness which I can never forget, "would leave him (him the hopeless and the frail) the last of the ancient race of the Ushers." While he spoke, the lady Madeline (for so was she called) passed slowly through a remote portion of the apartment, and, without having noticed my presence, disappeared. I regarded her with an utter astonishment not unmingled with dread—and yet I found it impossible to account for such feelings. A sensation of stupor oppressed me, as my eyes followed her retreating steps. When a door, at length, closed upon her, my glance sought instinctively and eagerly the countenance of the brother—but he had buried his face in his hands, and I could only perceive that a far more than ordinary wanness had overspread the emaciated fingers through which trickled many passionate tears.

The disease of the lady Madeline had long baffled the skill of her physicians. A settled apathy, a gradual wasting away of the person, and frequent although transient affections of a partially cataleptical character,[5] were the unusual diagnosis. Hitherto she had steadily borne up against the pressure of her malady, and had not betaken herself finally to bed; but, on the closing in of the evening of my arrival at the house, she succumbed (as her brother told me at night with inexpressible agitation) to the prostrating power of the destroyer; and I learned that the glimpse I had obtained of her person would thus probably be the last I should obtain—that the lady, at least while living, would be seen by me no more.

For several days ensuing, her name was unmentioned by either Usher or myself: and during this period I was busied in earnest endeavours to alleviate the melancholy of my friend. We painted and read together; or I listened, as if in a dream, to the wild improvisations of his speaking guitar. And thus, as a closer and still closer intimacy admitted me more unreservedly into the recesses of his spirit, the more bitterly did I perceive the futility of all attempt at cheering a mind from which darkness, as if an inherent positive quality, poured forth upon all objects of the moral and physical universe, in one unceasing radiation of gloom.

I shall ever bear about me a memory of the many solemn hours I thus spent alone with the master of the House of Usher. Yet I should fail in any attempt to convey an idea of the exact character of the studies, or of the occupations, in which he involved me, or led me the way. An excited and highly distempered ideality threw a sulphureous lustre over all. His long improvised dirges will ring forever in my ears. Among other things, I hold painfully in mind a certain singular perversion and amplification of the wild air of the last waltz of Von Weber.[6] From the paintings over which his elaborate fancy brooded, and which grew, touch by touch, into vaguenesses at which I shuddered the more thrillingly, because I shuddered knowing not why;—from these paintings (vivid as their images now are before me) I would in vain endeavour to educe more than a small portion which should lie within the compass of merely written words. By the utter simplicity, by the nakedness of his designs, he arrested and overawed attention. If ever mortal painted an idea, that mortal was Roderick Usher. For me at least—in the circumstances then surrounding me—there arose out of the pure abstractions which the hypochondriac contrived to throw upon his canvas, an intensity of intolerable

---

[5] Catalepsy is an illness characterized by a trance-like state in which the person loses the will or desire to move.
[6] Karl Maria von Weber (1786–1826), a famous composer of German operas. "The Last Waltz of Von Weber" was, however, the work of Karl Gottlieb Reissiger (1798–1859).

awe, no shadow of which felt I ever yet in the contemplation of the certainly glowing yet too concrete reveries of Fuseli.[7]

One of the phantasmagoric conceptions of my friend, partaking not so rigidly of the spirit of abstraction, may be shadowed forth, although feebly, in words. A small picture presented the interior of an immensely long and rectangular vault or tunnel, with low walls, smooth, white, and without interruption or device. Certain accessory points of the design served well to convey the idea that this excavation lay at an exceeding depth below the surface of the earth. No outlet was observed in any portion of its vast extent, and no torch, or other artificial source of light was discernible; yet a flood of intense rays rolled throughout, and bathed the whole in a ghastly and inappropriate splendour.

I have just spoken of that morbid condition of the auditory nerve which rendered all music intolerable to the sufferer, with the exception of certain effects of stringed instruments. It was, perhaps, the narrow limits to which he thus confined himself upon the guitar, which gave birth, in great measure, to the fantastic character of his performances. But the fervid *facility* of his *impromptus* could not be so accounted for. They must have been, and were, in the notes, as well as in the words of his wild fantasias (for he not unfrequently accompanied himself with rhymed verbal improvisations), the result of that intense mental collectedness and concentration to which I have previously alluded as observable only in particular moments of the highest artificial excitement. The words of one of these rhapsodies I have easily remembered. I was, perhaps, the more forcibly impressed with it, as he gave it, because, in the under or mystic current of its meaning, I fancied that I perceived, and for the first time, a full consciousness on the part of Usher, of the tottering of his lofty reason upon her throne. The verses, which were entitled "The Haunted Palace,"[8] ran very nearly, if not accurately, thus:

I

In the greenest of our valleys,
  By good angels tenanted,
Once a fair and stately palace—
  Radiant palace—reared its head.
In the monarch Thought's dominion—
  It stood there!
Never seraph spread a pinion
  Over fabric half so fair.

II

Banners yellow, glorious, golden,
  On its roof did float and flow;
(This—all this—was in the olden
  Time long ago)
And every gentle air that dallied,
  In that sweet day,
Along the ramparts plumed and pallid,
  A winged odour went away.

[7] Henry Fuseli (1741–1825), a Swiss-born English painter, was noted for his wildly romantic impressionism.

[8] Poe published the poem in the *American Museum* in April of 1839, some five months before the story itself appeared in *Burton's Gentleman's Magazine.*

III

Wanderers in that happy valley
    Through two luminous windows saw
Spirits moving musically
    To a lute's well-tuned law,
Round about a throne, where sitting
    (Porphyrogene![9])
In state his glory well befitting,
    The ruler of the realm was seen.

IV

And all with pearl and ruby glowing
    Was the fair palace door,
Through which came flowing, flowing, flowing
    And sparkling evermore,
A troop of Echoes whose sweet duty
    Was but to sing,
In voices of surpassing beauty,
    The wit and wisdom of their king.

V

But evil things, in robes of sorrow,
    Assailed the monarch's high estate;
(Ah, let us mourn, for never morrow
    Shall dawn upon him, desolate!)
And, round about his home, the glory
    That blushed and bloomed
Is but a dim-remembered story
    Of the old time entombed.

VI

And travellers now within that valley,
    Through the red-litten windows, see
Vast forms that move fantastically
    To a discordant melody;
While, like a rapid ghastly river,
    Through the pale door,
A hideous throng rush out forever,
    And laugh—but smile no more.

    I well remember that suggestions arising from this ballad, led us into a train of thought wherein there became manifest an opinion of Usher's which I mention not so much on account of its novelty, (for other men* have thought thus,) as on account of the pertinacity with which he maintained it. This opinion, in its general form, was that of the sentience of all vegetable things. But, in his disordered fancy, the idea had assumed a more daring character, and trespassed, under certain

[9] Of royal birth.
* Watson, Dr. Percival, Spallanzani, and especially the Bishop of Landaff.—See "Chemical Essays," vol. v. [Poe's note]
    The allusions are, specifically, to Richard Watson (1737–1819), the Bishop of Landaff, a British chemist; James Gates Percival (1795–1856), an American doctor and poet; and Lazzaro Spallanzani (1729–1799), an Italian professor of natural history.

conditions, upon the kingdom of inorganization. I lack words to express the full extent, or the earnest *abandon* of his persuasion. The belief, however, was connected (as I have previously hinted) with the gray stones of the home of his forefathers. The conditions of the sentience had been here, he imagined, fulfilled in the method of collocation of these stones—in order of their arrangement, as well as in that of the many *fungi* which overspread them, and of the decayed trees which stood around—above all, in the long undisturbed endurance of this arrangement, and in its reduplication in the still waters of the tarn. Its evidence—the evidence of the sentience—was to be seen, he said, (and I here started as he spoke,) in the gradual yet certain condensation of an atmosphere of their own about the waters and the walls. The result was discoverable, he added, in that silent, yet importunate and terrible influence which for centuries had moulded the destinies of his family, and which made *him* what I now saw him—what he was. Such opinions need no comment, and I will make none.

Our books—the books which, for years, had formed no small portion of the mental existence of the invalid—were, as might be supposed, in strict keeping with this character of phantasm. We pored together over such works as the Ververt et Chartreuse of Gresset; the Belphegor of Machiavelli; the Heaven and Hell of Swedenborg; the Subterranean Voyage of Nicholas Klimm by Holberg; the Chiromancy of Robert Flud, of Jean d'Indaginé, and of De la Chambre; the Journey into the Blue Distance of Tieck; and the City of the Sun of Campanella. One favourite volume was a small octavo edition of the *Directorium Inquisitorum,* by the Dominican Eymeric de Gironne; and there were passages in Pomponius Mela, about the old African Satyrs and Ægipans, over which Usher would sit dreaming for hours. His chief delight, however, was found in the perusal of an exceedingly rare and curious book in quarto Gothic—the manual of a forgotten church—the *Vigiliæ Mortuorum secundum Chorum Ecclesiæ Magun-tinæ.*[10]

I could not help thinking of the wild ritual of this work, and of its probable influence upon the hypochondriac, when, one evening, having informed me abruptly that the lady Madeline was no more, he stated his intention of preserving her corpse for a fortnight, (previously to its final interment,) in one of the numerous vaults within the main walls of the building. The worldly reason, however, assigned for this singular proceeding, was one which I did not feel at liberty to dispute. The brother had been led to his resolution (so he told me) by consideration of the unusual character of the malady of the deceased, of certain obtrusive and eager inquiries on the part of her medical men, and of

[10] The titles and authors which compose Roderick Usher's library are real: *Vairvert* and *Chartreuse* are light-hearted, anti-religious poems by Jean-Baptiste-Louis Gresset (1709–1777); *Belphegor* is a novel by Niccolò Machiavelli (1469–1527), in which a demon visits the earth to argue that women are man's damnation; *Heaven and Hell* by the Swedish mystic and scientist Emanuel Swedenborg (1688–1772) deals with the spiritual continuity of man and matter. The *Subterranean Voyage* by the Danish dramatist, novelist, and historian Ludwig Holberg (1684–1754) is an account of a voyage into the underworld; while chiromancy, or palm-reading, is the subject of books by English physician and pseudo-scientist Robert Flud (1574–1637) and two Frenchmen, Jean d'Indaginé (16th century) and Maria Cireau de la Chambre (1594–1669). The *Journey into the Blue Distance* by the German writer Ludwig Tieck (1773–1853) and the *City of the Sun* by Italian writer Tommaso Campanella (1568–1639) both deal with voyages to other worlds. Nicholas Eymeric de Gironne (1320–1399) served as Inquisitor-General of Castile and his book, *Directorium Inquisitorium,* is an account of the procedures to be used for torturing heretics. Pomponius Mela was a first-century Roman whose books of geography depicted the fabulously strange satyrs and aegipans (goat-men) of Africa. The last title, *The Vigils of the Dead according to the Choir of the Church of Mayence,* was printed at Basel in Switzerland about 1500.

the remote and exposed situation of the burial-ground of the family. I will not deny that when I called to mind the sinister countenance of the person whom I met upon the staircase, on the day of my arrival at the house, I had no desire to oppose what I regarded as at best but a harmless, and by no means an unnatural, precaution.[11]

At the request of Usher, I personally aided him in the arrangements for the temporary entombment. The body having been encoffined, we two alone bore it to its rest. The vault in which we placed it (and which had been so long unopened that our torches, half smothered in its oppressive atmosphere, gave us little opportunity for investigation) was small, damp, and entirely without means of admission for light; lying, at great depth, immediately beneath that portion of the building in which was my own sleeping apartment. It had been used, apparently, in remote feudal times, for the worst purposes of a dungeon-keep, and, in later days, as a place of deposit for powder, or some other highly combustible substance, as a portion of its floor, and the whole interior of a long archway through which we reached it, were carefully sheathed with copper. The door, of massive iron, had been, also, similarly protected. Its immense weight caused an unusually sharp grating sound, as it moved upon its hinges.

Having deposited our mournful burden upon trestles within this region of horror, we partially turned aside the yet unscrewed lid of the coffin, and looked upon the face of the tenant. A striking similitude between the brother and sister now first arrested my attention; and Usher, divining, perhaps, my thoughts, murmured out some few words from which I learned that the deceased and himself had been twins, and that sympathies of a scarcely intelligible nature had always existed between them. Our glances, however, rested not long upon the dead—for we could not regard her unawed. The disease which had thus entombed the lady in the maturity of youth, had left, as usual in all maladies of a strictly cataleptical character, the mockery of a faint blush upon the bosom and the face, and that suspiciously lingering smile upon the lip which is so terrible in death. We replaced and screwed down the lid, and, having secured the door of iron, made our way, with toil, into the scarcely less gloomy apartments of the upper portion of the house.

And now, some days of bitter grief having elapsed, an observable change came over the features of the mental disorder of my friend. His ordinary manner had vanished. His ordinary occupations were neglected or forgotten. He roamed from chamber to chamber with hurried, unequal, and objectless step. The pallor of his countenance had assumed, if possible, a more ghastly hue—but the luminousness of his eye had utterly gone out. The once occasional huskiness of his tone was heard no more; and a tremulous quaver, as if of extreme terror, habitually characterized his utterance. There were times, indeed, when I thought his unceasingly agitated mind was labouring with some oppressive secret, to divulge which he struggled for the necessary courage. At times, again, I was obliged to resolve all into the mere inexplicable vagaries of madness, for I beheld him gazing upon vacancy for long hours, in an attitude of the profoundest attention, as if listening to some imaginary sound. It was no wonder that his condition terrified—that it infected me. I felt creeping upon me, by slow yet certain degrees, the wild influences of his own fantastic yet impressive superstitions.

It was, especially, upon retiring to bed late in the night of the seventh or eighth

---

[11] The allusion is to the all-too-common contemporary practice of stealing fresh corpses and selling them to medical students and physicians for use in dissection and experimentation.

day after the placing of the lady Madeline within the donjon, that I experienced the full power of such feelings. Sleep came not near my couch—while the hours waned and waned away. I struggled to reason off the nervousness which had dominion over me. I endeavoured to believe that much, if not all of what I felt, was due to the bewildering influence of the gloomy furniture of the room—of the dark and tattered draperies, which, tortured into motion by the breath of a rising tempest, swayed fitfully to and fro upon the walls, and rustled uneasily about the decorations of the bed. But my efforts were fruitless. An irrepressible tremor gradually pervaded my frame; and, at length, there sat upon my very heart an incubus[12] of utterly causeless alarm. Shaking this off with a gasp and a struggle, I uplifted myself upon the pillows, and, peering earnestly within the intense darkness of the chamber, hearkened—I know not why, except that an instinctive spirit prompted me—to certain low and indefinite sounds which came, through the pauses of the storm, at long intervals, I knew not whence. Overpowered by an intense sentiment of horror, unaccountable yet unendurable, I threw on my clothes with haste (for I felt that I should sleep no more during the night), and endeavoured to arouse myself from the pitiable condition into which I had fallen, by pacing rapidly to and fro through the apartment.

I had taken but few turns in this manner, when a light step on an adjoining staircase arrested my attention. I presently recognised it as that of Usher. In an instant afterward he rapped, with a gentle touch, at my door, and entered, bearing a lamp. His countenance was, as usual, cadaverously wan—but, moreover, there was a species of mad hilarity in his eyes—an evidently restrained *hysteria* in his whole demeanour. His air appalled me—but anything was preferable to the solitude which I had so long endured, and I even welcomed his presence as a relief.

"And you have not seen it?" he said abruptly, after having stared about him for some moments in silence—"you have not then seen it?—but, stay! you shall." Thus speaking, and having carefully shaded his lamp, he hurried to one of the casements, and threw it freely open to the storm.

The impetuous fury of the entering gust nearly lifted us from our feet. It was, indeed, a tempestuous yet sternly beautiful night, and one wildly singular in its terror and its beauty. A whirlwind had apparently collected its force in our vicinity; for there were frequent and violent alterations in the direction of the wind; and the exceeding density of the clouds (which hung so low as to press upon the turrets of the house) did not prevent our perceiving the life-like velocity with which they flew careering from all points against each other, without passing away into the distance. I say that even their exceeding density did not prevent our perceiving this—yet we had no glimpse of the moon or stars—nor was there any flashing forth of the lightning. But the under surfaces of the huge masses of agitated vapour, as well as all terrestrial objects immediately around us, were glowing in the unnatural light of a faintly luminous and distinctly visible gaseous exhalation which hung about and enshrouded the mansion.

"You must not—you shall not behold this!" said I, shudderingly, to Usher, as I led him, with a gentle violence, from the window to a seat. "These appearances, which bewilder you, are merely electrical phenomena not uncommon—or it may be that they have their ghastly origin in the rank miasma of the tarn. Let us close this casement;—the air is chilling and dangerous to your frame. Here is one of your favourite romances. I will read, and you shall listen;—and so we will pass away this terrible night together."

---

[12] A demon or evil spirit.

The antique volume which I had taken up was the "Mad Trist" of Sir Launcelot Canning;[13] but I had called it a favourite of Usher's more in sad jest than in earnest; for, in truth, there is little in its uncouth and unimaginative prolixity which could have had interest for the lofty and spiritual ideality of my friend. It was, however, the only book immediately at hand; and I indulged a vague hope that the excitement which now agitated the hypochondriac, might find relief (for the history of mental disorder is full of similar anomalies) even in the extremeness of the folly which I should read. Could I have judged, indeed, by the wild over-strained air of vivacity with which he hearkened, or apparently hearkened, to the words of the tale, I might well have congratulated myself upon the success of my design.

I had arrived at that well-known portion of the story where Ethelred, the hero of the Trist, having sought in vain for peaceable admission into the dwelling of the hermit, proceeds to make good an entrance by force. Here, it will be remembered, the words of the narrative run thus:

"And Ethelred, who was by nature of a doughty heart, and who was now mighty withal, on account of the powerfulness of the wine which he had drunken, waited no longer to hold parley with the hermit, who, in sooth, was of an obstinate and maliceful turn, but, feeling the rain upon his shoulders, and fearing the rising of the tempest, uplifted his mace outright, and, with blows, made quickly room in the plankings of the door for his gauntleted hand; and now pulling therewith sturdily, he so cracked, and ripped, and tore all asunder, that the noise of the dry and hollow-sounding wood alarumed and reverberated throughout the forest."

At the termination of this sentence I started, and for a moment, paused; for it appeared to me (although I at once concluded that my excited fancy had deceived me)—it appeared to me that, from some very remote portion of the mansion, there came, indistinctly, to my ears, what might have been, in its exact similarity of character, the echo (but a stifled and dull one certainly) of the very cracking and ripping sound which Sir Launcelot had so particularly described. It was, beyond doubt, the coincidence alone which had arrested my attention; for, amid the rattling of the sashes of the casements, and the ordinary commingled noises of the still increasing storm, the sound, in itself, had nothing, surely, which should have interested or disturbed me. I continued the story:

"But the good champion Ethelred, now entering within the door, was sore enraged and amazed to perceive no signal of the maliceful hermit; but, in the stead thereof, a dragon of a scaly and prodigious demeanour, and of a fiery tongue, which sat in guard before a palace of gold, with a floor of silver; and upon the wall there hung a shield of shining brass with this legend enwritten—

Who entereth herein, a conqueror hath bin;
Who slayeth the dragon, the shield he shall win;

And Ethelred uplifted his mace, and struck upon the head of the dragon, which fell before him, and gave up his pesty breath, with a shriek so horrid and harsh, and withal so piercing, that Ethelred had fain to close his ears with his hands against the dreadful noise of it, the like whereof was never before heard."

Here again I paused abruptly, and now with a feeling of wild amazement—for there could be no doubt whatever that, in this instance, I did actually hear (although from what direction it proceeded I found it impossible to say) a low and

---

[13] A title of Poe's own invention.

apparently distant, but harsh, protracted, and most unusual screaming or grating sound—the exact counterpart of what my fancy had already conjured up for the dragon's unnatural shriek as described by the romancer.

Oppressed, as I certainly was, upon the occurrence of the second and most extraordinary coincidence, by a thousand conflicting sensations, in which wonder and extreme terror were predominant, I still retained sufficient presence of mind to avoid exciting, by any observation, the sensitive nervousness of my companion. I was by no means certain that he had noticed the sounds in question; although, assuredly, a strange alteration had, during the last few minutes, taken place in his demeanour. From a position fronting my own, he had gradually brought round his chair, so as to sit with his face to the door of the chamber; and thus I could but partially perceive his features, although I saw that his lips trembled as if he were murmuring inaudibly. His head had dropped upon his breast—yet I knew that he was not asleep, from the wide and rigid opening of the eye as I caught a glance of it in profile. The motion of his body, too, was at variance with this idea—for he rocked from side to side with a gentle yet constant and uniform sway. Having rapidly taken notice of all this, I resumed the narrative of Sir Launcelot, which thus proceeded:

"And now, the champion, having escaped from the terrible fury of the dragon, bethinking himself of the brazen shield, and of the breaking up of the enchantment which was upon it, removed the carcass from out of the way before him, and approached valorously over the silver pavement of the castle to where the shield was upon the wall; which in sooth tarried not for his full coming, but fell down at his feet upon the silver floor, with a mighty great and terrible ringing sound."

No sooner had these syllables passed my lips, than—as if a shield of brass had indeed, at the moment, fallen heavily upon a floor of silver—I became aware of a distinct, hollow, metallic, and clangorous, yet apparently muffled reverberation. Completely unnerved, I leaped to my feet; but the measured rocking movement of Usher was undisturbed. I rushed to the chair in which he sat. His eyes were bent fixedly before him, and throughout his whole countenance there reigned a stony rigidity. But, as I placed my hand upon his shoulder, there came a strong shudder over his whole person; a sickly smile quivered about his lips; and I saw that he spoke in a low, hurried, and gibbering murmur, as if unconscious of my presence. Bending closely over him, I at length drank in the hideous import of his words.

"Not hear it? yes, I hear it, and *have* heard it. Long—long—long—many minutes, many hours, many days, have I heard it—yet I dared not—oh, pity me, miserable wretch that I am!—I dared not—I *dared* not speak! *We have put her living in the tomb!* Said I not that my senses were acute? I *now* tell you that I heard her first feeble movements in the hollow coffin. I heard them—many, many days ago—yet I dared not—*I dared not speak!* And now—to-night—Ethelred—ha! ha!—the breaking of the hermit's door, and the death-cry of the dragon, and the clangour of the shield!—say, rather, the rending of her coffin, and the grating of the iron hinges of her prison, and her struggles within the coppered archway of the vault! Oh whither shall I fly? Will she not be here anon? Is she not hurrying to upbraid me for my haste? Have I not heard her footstep on the stair? Do I not distinguish that heavy and horrible beating of her heart? MADMAN!" here he sprang furiously to his feet, and shrieked out his syllables, as if in the effort he were giving up his soul "MADMAN! I TELL YOU THAT SHE NOW STANDS WITHOUT THE DOOR!"

As if in the superhuman energy of his utterance there had been found the potency of a spell—the huge antique panels to which the speaker pointed, threw slowly back, upon the instant, their ponderous and ebony jaws. It was the work of the rushing gust but then without those doors there DID stand the lofty and enshrouded figure of the lady Madeline of Usher. There was blood upon her white robes, and the evidence of some bitter struggle upon every portion of her emaciated frame. For a moment she remained trembling and reeling to and fro upon the threshold, then, with a low moaning cry, fell heavily inward upon the person of her brother, and in her violent and now final death-agonies, bore him to the floor a corpse, and a victim to the terrors he had anticipated.

From that chamber, and from that mansion, I fled aghast. The storm was still abroad in all its wrath as I found myself crossing the old causeway. Suddenly there shot along the path a wild light, and I turned to see whence a gleam so unusual could have issued; for the vast house and its shadows were alone behind me. The radiance was that of the full, setting, and blood-red moon which now shone vividly through that once barely-discernible fissure of which I have before spoken as extending from the roof of the building, in a zigzag direction, to the base. While I gazed, this fissure rapidly widened—there came a fierce breath of the whirl-wind—the entire orb of the satellite burst at once upon my sight—my brain reeled as I saw the mighty walls rushing asunder—there was a long tumultuous shouting sound like the voice of a thousand waters—and the deep and dank tarn at my feet closed sullenly and silently over the fragments of the "House of Usher."

[1839]

Edgar Allan Poe   *1809–1849*

THE CASK OF AMONTILLADO

The thousand injuries of Fortunato I had borne as I best could, but when he ventured upon insult I vowed revenge. You, who so well know the nature of my soul, will not suppose, however, that I gave utterance to a threat. *At length* I would be avenged; this was a point definitely settled—but the very definitiveness with which it was resolved precluded the idea of risk. I must not only punish but punish with impunity. A wrong is unredressed when retribution overtakes its redresser. It is equally unredressed when the avenger fails to make himself felt as such to him who has done the wrong.

It must be understood that neither by word nor deed had I given Fortunato cause to doubt my good will. I continued, as was my wont, to smile in his face, and he did not perceive that my smile *now* was at the thought of his immolation.

He had a weak point—this Fortunato—although in other regards he was a man to be respected and even feared. He prided himself on his connoisseurship in wine. Few Italians have the true virtuoso spirit. For the most part their enthusiasm is adopted to suit the time and opportunity, to practice imposture upon the British and Austrian *millionaires*. In painting and gemmary, Fortunato, like his countrymen, was a quack, but in the matter of old wines he was sincere. In this respect I did not differ from him materially;—I was skillful in the Italian vintages myself, and bought largely whenever I could.

It was about dusk, one evening during the supreme madness of the carnival season, that I encountered my friend. He accosted me with excessive warmth, for he had been drinking much. The man wore motley.[1] He had on a tight-fitting parti-striped dress, and his head was surmounted by the conical cap and bells. I was so pleased to see him that I thought I should never have done wringing his hand.

I said to him—"My dear Fortunato, you are luckily met. How remarkably well you are looking to-day. But I have received a pipe[2] of what passes for Amontillado,[3] and I have my doubts."

"How?" said he. "Amontillado? A pipe? Impossible! And in the middle of the carnival!"

"I have my doubts," I replied; "and I was silly enough to pay the full Amontillado price without consulting you in the matter. You were not to be found, and I was fearful of losing a bargain."

"Amontillado!"

"I have my doubts."

"Amontillado!"

"And I must satisfy them."

"Amontillado!"

"As you are engaged, I am on my way to Luchresi. If any one has a critical turn it is he. He will tell me————"

"Luchresi cannot tell Amontillado from Sherry."

---

[1] The multicolored attire of a court jester or fool.   [2] Wine cask with a capacity of 126 gallons.
[3] A pale dry Spanish sherry.

"And yet some fools will have it that his taste is a match for your own."

"Come, let us go."

"Whither?"

"To your vaults."

"My friend, no; I will not impose upon your good nature. I perceive you have an engagement. Luchresi————"

"I have no engagement:—come."

"My friend, no. It is not the engagement, but the severe cold with which I perceive you are afflicted. The vaults are insufferably damp. They are encrusted with nitre."[4]

"Let us go, nevertheless. The cold is merely nothing. Amontillado! You have been imposed upon. And as for Luchresi, he cannot distinguish Sherry from Amontillado."

Thus speaking, Fortunato possessed himself of my arm; and putting on a mask of black silk and drawing a *roquelaire*[5] closely about my person, I suffered him to hurry me to my palazzo.[6]

There were no attendants at home; they had absconded to make merry in honor of the time. I had told them that I should not return until the morning, and had given them explicit orders not to stir from the house. These orders were sufficient, I well knew, to insure their immediate disappearance, one and all, as soon as my back was turned.

I took from their sconces[7] two flambeaux, and giving one to Fortunato, bowed him through several suites of rooms to the archway that led into the vaults. I passed down a long and winding staircase, requesting him to be cautious as he followed. We came at length to the foot of the descent, and stood together upon the damp ground of the catacombs[8] of the Montresors.

The gait of my friend was unsteady, and the bells upon his cap jingled as he strode.

"The pipe," he said.

"It is farther on," said I; "but observe the white web-work which gleams from these cavern walls."

He turned towards me, and looked into my eyes with two filmy orbs that distilled the rheum of intoxication.

"Nitre?" he asked at length.

"Nitre," I replied. "How long have you had that cough?"

"Ugh! ugh! ugh!—ugh! ugh! ugh!—ugh! ugh! ugh!—ugh! ugh! ugh!—ugh! ugh! ugh!"

My poor friend found it impossible to reply for many minutes.

"It is nothing," he said at last.

"Come," I said, with decision, "we will go back, your health is precious. You are rich, respected, admired, beloved; you are happy, as once I was. You are a man to be missed. For me it is no matter. We will go back; you will be ill, and I cannot be responsible. Besides, there is Luchresi————"

"Enough," he said; "the cough is a mere nothing; it will not kill me. I shall not die of a cough."

---

[4] Saltpeter, a white or gray mineral composed of potassium nitrate.

[5] A man's knee-length cloak, popular during the eighteenth and early nineteenth centuries.

[6] Palace.

[7] Decorative wall brackets for holding candles, lights, or, as in this case, flambeaux or torches.

[8] Underground chambers or tunnels with recesses for entombing the dead.

"True—true," I replied; "and, indeed, I had no intention of alarming you unnecessarily—but you should use all proper caution. A draught of this Medoc[9] will defend us from the damps."

Here I knocked off the neck of a bottle which I drew from a long row of its fellows that lay upon the mould.

"Drink," I said, presenting him the wine.

He raised it to his lips with a leer. He paused and nodded to me familiarly, while his bells jingled.

"I drink," he said, "to the buried that repose around us."

"And I to your long life."

He again took my arm, and we proceeded.

"These vaults," he said, "are extensive."

"The Montresors," I replied, "were a great and numerous family."

"I forget your arms."

"A huge human foot d'or[10] in a field azure; the foot crushes a serpent rampant[11] whose fangs are imbedded in the heel."

"And the motto?"

Nemo me impune lacessit."[12]

"Good!" he said.

The wine sparkled in his eyes and the bells jingled. My own fancy grew warm with the Medoc. We had passed through long walls of piled skeletons, with casks and puncheons[13] intermingling, into the inmost recesses of the catacombs. I paused again, and this time I made bold to seize Fortunato by an arm above the elbow.

"The nitre!" I said; "see, it increases. It hangs like moss upon the vaults. We are below the river's bed. The drops of moisture trickle among the bones. Come, we will go back ere it is too late. Your cough————"

"It is nothing," he said; "let us go on. But first, another draught of the Medoc."

I broke and reached him a flagon[14] of De Grâve.[15] He emptied it at a breath. His eyes flashed with a fierce light. He laughed and threw the bottle upwards with a gesticulation I did not understand.

I looked at him in surprise. He repeated the movement—a grotesque one.

"You do not comprehend?" he said.

"Not I," I replied.

"Then you are not of the brotherhood."

"How?"

"You are not of the masons."[16]

"Yes, yes," I said; "yes, yes."

"You? Impossible! A mason?"

"A mason," I replied.

"A sign," he said, "a sign."

"It is this," I answered, producing from beneath the folds of my *roquelaire* a trowel.

"You jest," he exclaimed, recoiling a few paces. "But let us proceed to the Amontillado."

---

[9] A red Bordeaux wine.   [10] Of gold.   [11] Rearing its head.
[12] "No one attacks me with impunity."   [13] Casks which can hold 84 gallons.
[14] A vessel for holding wine.   [15] A white Bordeaux wine.
[16] A member of the Ancient Free and Accepted Masons, an international secret fraternal order dating from the early eighteenth century.

"Be it so," I said, replacing the tool beneath the cloak and again offering him my arm. He leaned upon it heavily. We continued our route in search of the Amontillado. We passed through a range of low arches, descended, passed on, and descending again, arrived at a deep crypt, in which the foulness of the air caused our flambeaux rather to glow than flame.

At the most remote end of the crypt there appeared another less spacious. Its walls had been lined with human remains, piled to the vault overhead, in the fashion of the great catacombs of Paris. Three sides of this interior crypt were still ornamented in this manner. From the fourth side the bones had been thrown down, and lay promiscuously upon the earth, forming at one point a mound of some size. Within the wall thus exposed by the displacing of the bones, we perceived a still interior crypt or recess, in depth about four feet, in width three, in height six or seven. It seemed to have been constructed for no especial use within itself, but formed merely the interval between two of the colossal supports of the roof of the catacombs, and was backed by one of their circumscribing walls of solid granite.

It was in vain that Fortunato, uplifting his dull torch, endeavored to pry into the depth of the recess. Its termination the feeble light did not enable us to see.

"Proceed," I said; "herein is the Amontillado. As for Luchresi————"

"He is an ignoramus," interrupted my friend, as he stepped unsteadily forward, while I followed immediately at his heels. In an instant he had reached the extremity of the niche, and finding his progress arrested by the rock, stood stupidly bewildered. A moment more and I had fettered him to the granite. In its surface were two iron staples, distant from each other about two feet, horizontally. From one of these depended a short chain, from the other a padlock. Throwing the links about his waist, it was but the work of a few seconds to secure it. He was too much astounded to resist. Withdrawing the key I stepped back from the recess.

"Pass your hand," I said, "over the wall; you cannot help feeling the nitre. Indeed, it is *very* damp. Once more let me *implore* you to return. No? Then I must positively leave you. But I must first render you all the little attentions in my power."

"The Amontillado!" ejaculated my friend, not yet recovered from his astonishment.

"True," I replied; "the Amontillado."

As I said these words I busied myself among the pile of bones of which I have before spoken. Throwing them aside, I soon uncovered a quantity of building stone and mortar. With these materials and with the aid of my trowel, I began vigorously to wall up the entrance of the niche.

I had scarcely laid the first tier of the masonry when I discovered that the intoxication of Fortunato had in a great measure worn off. The earliest indication I had of this was a low moaning cry from the depth of the recess. It was *not* the cry of a drunken man. There was a long and obstinate silence. I laid the second tier, and the third, and the fourth; and then I heard the furious vibrations of the chain. The noise lasted for several minutes, during which, that I might hearken to it with the more satisfaction, I ceased my labors and sat down upon the bones. When at last the clanking subsided, I resumed the trowel, and finished without interruption the fifth, the sixth, and the seventh tier. The wall was now nearly upon a level with my breast. I again paused, and holding the flambeaux over the mason-work, threw a few feeble rays upon the figure within.

A succession of loud and shrill screams, bursting suddenly from the throat of the chained form, seemed to thrust me violently back. For a brief moment I hesitated, I trembled. Unsheathing my rapier,[17] I began to grope with it about the recess; but the thought of an instant reassured me. I placed my hand upon the solid fabric of the catacombs, and felt satisfied. I reapproached the wall; I replied to the yells of him who clamoured. I re-echoed, I aided, I surpassed them in volume and in strength. I did this, and the clamourer grew still.

It was now midnight, and my task was drawing to a close. I had completed the eighth, the ninth and the tenth tier. I had finished a portion of the last and the eleventh; there remained but a single stone to be fitted and plastered in. I struggled with its weight; I placed it partially in its destined position. But now there came from out the niche a low laugh that erected the hairs upon my head. It was succeeded by a sad voice, which I had difficulty in recognizing as that of the noble Fortunato. The voice said—

"Ha! ha! ha!—he! he! he!—a very good joke, indeed—an excellent jest. We will have many a rich laugh about it at the palazzo—he! he! he!—over our wine—he! he! he!"

"The Amontillado!" I said.

"He! he! he!—he! he! he!—yes, the Amontillado. But is it not getting late? Will not they be awaiting us at the palazzo, the Lady Fortunato and the rest? Let us be gone."

"Yes," I said, "let us be gone."

"*For the love of God, Montresor!*"

"Yes," I said, "for the love of God."

But to these words I hearkened in vain for a reply. I grew impatient. I called aloud—

"Fortunato!"

No answer. I called again—

"Fortunato!"

No answer still. I thrust a torch through the remaining aperture and let it fall within. There came forth in return only a jingling of the bells. My heart grew sick; it was the dampness of the catacombs that made it so. I hastened to make an end of my labour. I forced the last stone into its position; I plastered it up. Against the new masonry I re-erected the old rampart of bones. For the half of a century no mortal has disturbed them. *In pace requiescat!*[18]

[1846]

---

[17] A long, slender, two-edged sword.   [18] "May he rest in peace!"

Herman Melville   *1819–1891*

BARTLEBY THE SCRIVENER

I am a rather elderly man. The nature of my avocations, for the last thirty years, has brought me into more than ordinary contact with what would seem an interesting and somewhat singular set of men, of whom, as yet, nothing, that I know of, has ever been written—I mean, the law-copyists, or scriveners.[1] I have known very many of them, professionally and privately, and, if I pleased, could relate divers histories, at which good-natured gentlemen might smile, and sentimental souls might weep. But I waive the biographies of all other scriveners, for a few passages in the life of Bartleby, who was a scrivener, the strangest I ever saw, or heard of. While, of other law-copyists, I might write the complete life, of Bartleby nothing of that sort can be done. I believe that no materials exist, for a full and satisfactory biography of this man. It is an irreparable loss to literature. Bartleby was one of those beings of whom nothing is ascertainable, except from the original sources, and, in his case, those are very small. What my own astonished eyes saw of Bartleby, *that* is all I know of him, except, indeed, one vague report, which will appear in the sequel.

Ere introducing the scrivener, as he first appeared to me, it is fit I make some mention of myself, my employes, my business, my chambers, and general surroundings; because some such description is indispensable to an adequate understanding of the chief character about to be presented. Imprimis:[2] I am a man who, from his youth upward, has been filled with a profound conviction that the easiest way of life is the best. Hence, though I belong to a profession proverbially energetic and nervous, even to turbulence, at times, yet nothing of that sort have I ever suffered to invade my peace. I am one of those unambitious lawyers who never addresses a jury, or in any way draws down public applause; but, in the cool tranquillity of a snug retreat, do a snug business among rich men's bonds, and mortgages, and title-deeds. All who know me, consider me an eminently *safe* man. The late John Jacob Astor,[3] a personage little given to poetic enthusiasm, had no hesitation in pronouncing my first grand point to be prudence; my next, method. I do not speak it in vanity, but simply record the fact, that I was not unemployed in my profession by the late John Jacob Astor; a name which, I admit, I love to repeat; for it hath a rounded and orbicular sound to it, and rings like unto bullion.[4] I will freely add, that I was not insensible to the late John Jacob Astor's good opinion.

Some time prior to the period at which this little history begins, my avocations had been largely increased. The good old office, now extinct in the State of New York, of a Master in Chancery,[5] had been conferred upon me. It was not a very

[1] Clerks who copy legal documents by hand.
[2] In the first place; a phrase often used to introduce a list of items in a legal document.
[3] John Jacob Astor (1763–1848), a German-born immigrant, created a fortune out of prudent investments in New York City real estate and from his monopolistic control of the fur trade in the American West. At the time of his death, Astor was the richest man in America. The Astor House, his fashionable hotel located opposite City Hall Park, opened its doors in 1836.
[4] Uncoined gold or silver bars or ingots.
[5] Decisions of chancery courts—which dealt with issues of equity (fairness) rather than common law (matters prescribed by statute)—were often arrived at through negotiation between the two opposing parties in return for which, no matter who "won," the judge himself was paid. The New York Court of Chancery was abolished by the "new Constitution" adopted in 1846.

arduous office, but very pleasantly remunerative. I seldom lose my temper; much more seldom indulge in dangerous indignation at wrongs and outrages; but, I must be permitted to be rash here, and declare, that I consider the sudden and violent abrogation of the office of Master in Chancery, by the new Constitution, as a—premature act; inasmuch as I had counted upon a life-lease of the profits, whereas I only received those of a few short years. But this is by the way.

My chambers were upstairs, at No. — Wall Street.[6] At one end, they looked upon the white wall of the interior of a spacious skylight shaft, penetrating the building from top to bottom.

This view might have been considered rather tame than otherwise, deficient in what landscape painters call 'life.' But, if so, the view from the other end of my chambers offered, at least, a contrast, if nothing more. In that direction, my windows commanded an unobstructed view of a lofty brick wall, black by age and everlasting shade; which wall required no spy-glass to bring out its lurking beauties, but, for the benefit of all near-sighted spectators, was pushed up to within ten feet of my window panes. Owing to the great height of the surrounding buildings, and my chambers being on the second floor, the interval between this wall and mine not a little resembled a huge square cistern.

At the period just preceding the advent of Bartleby, I had two persons as copyists in my employment, and a promising lad as an office-boy. First, Turkey; second, Nippers; third, Ginger Nut. These may seem names, the like of which are not usually found in the Directory. In truth, they were nicknames, mutually conferred upon each other by my three clerks, and were deemed expressive of their respective persons or characters. Turkey was a short, pursy[7] Englishman, of about my own age—that is, somewhere not far from sixty. In the morning, one might say, his face was of a fine florid hue, but after twelve o'clock, meridian—his dinner hour—it blazed like a grate full of Christmas coals; and continued blazing—but, as it were, with a gradual wane—till six o'clock, P.M., or thereabouts; after which, I saw no more of the proprietor of the face, which, gaining its meridian with the sun, seemed to set with it, to rise, culminate, and decline the following day, with the like regularity and undiminished glory. There are many singular coincidences I have known in the course of my life, not the least among which was the fact, that, exactly when Turkey displayed his fullest beams from his red and radiant countenance, just then, too, at that critical moment, began the daily period when I considered his business capacities as seriously disturbed for the remainder of the twenty-four hours. Not that he was absolutely idle, or averse to business, then; far from it. The difficulty was, he was apt to be altogether too energetic. There was a strange, inflamed, flurried, flighty recklessness of activity about him. He would be incautious in dipping his pen into his inkstand. All his blots upon my documents were dropped there after twelve o'clock, meridian. Indeed, not only would he be reckless, and sadly given to making blots in the afternoon, but, some days, he went further, and was rather noisy. At such times, too, his face flamed with augmented blazonry, as if cannel coal[8] had been heaped on anthracite. He made an unpleasant racket with his chair; spilled his sandbox;[9] in mending his pens, impatiently

---

[6] The fashionable street near the lower tip of Manhattan Island, which by Melville's time had become New York's commercial and financial center.

[7] Shortwinded from being overweight.

[8] Bituminous coal that burns very brightly; anthracite coal, by contrast, burns much more slowly with a clean, steady flame.

[9] A box with a perforated top for sprinkling sand as a blotter on wet ink.

split them all to pieces, and threw them on the floor in a sudden passion; stood up, and leaned over his table, boxing his papers about in a most indecorous manner, very sad to behold in an elderly man like him. Nevertheless, as he was in many ways a most valuable person to me, and all the time before twelve o'clock, meridian, was the quickest, steadiest creature, too, accomplishing a great deal of work in a style not easily to be matched—for these reasons, I was willing to overlook his eccentricities, though, indeed, occasionally, I remonstrated with him. I did this very gently, however, because, though the civilest, nay, the blandest and most reverential of men in the morning, yet, in the afternoon, he was disposed, upon provocation, to be slightly rash with his tongue—in fact, insolent. Now, valuing his morning services as I did, and resolved not to lose them—yet, at the same time, made uncomfortable by his inflamed ways after twelve o'clock—and being a man of peace, unwilling by my admonitions to call forth unseemly retorts from him, I took upon me, one Saturday noon (he was always worse on Saturdays) to hint to him, very kindly, that, perhaps, now that he was growing old, it might be well to abridge his labours; in short, he need not come to my chambers after twelve o'clock but, dinner over, had best go home to his lodgings, and rest himself till teatime. But no; he insisted upon his afternoon devotions. His countenance became intolerably fervid, as he oratorically assured me—gesticulating with a long ruler at the other end of the room—that if his services in the morning were useful, how indispensable, then, in the afternoon?

'With submission, sir,' said Turkey, on this occasion, 'I consider myself your right-hand man. In the morning I but marshal and deploy my columns; but in the afternoon I put myself at their head, and gallantly charge the foe, thus'—and he made a violent thrust with the ruler.

'But the blots, Turkey,' intimated I.

'True; but, with submission, sir, behold these hairs! I am getting old. Surely, sir, a blot or two of a warm afternoon is not to be severely urged against gray hairs. Old age—even if it blot the page—is honourable. With submission, sir, we *both* are getting old.'

This appeal to my fellow-feeling was hardly to be resisted. At all events, I saw that go he would not. So, I made up my mind to let him stay, resolving, nevertheless, to see to it that, during the afternoon, he had to do with my less important papers.

Nippers, the second on my list, was a whiskered, sallow, and, upon the whole, rather piratical-looking young man, of about five-and-twenty. I always deemed him the victim of two evil powers—ambition and indigestion. The ambition was evinced by a certain impatience of the duties of a mere copyist, an unwarrantable usurpation of strictly professional affairs, such as the original drawing up of legal documents. The indigestion seemed betokened in an occasional nervous testiness and grinning irritability, causing the teeth to audibly grind together over mistakes committed in copying; unnecessary maledictions, hissed, rather than spoken, in the heat of business; and especially by a continual discontent with the height of the table where he worked. Though of a very ingenious mechanical turn, Nippers could never get this table to suit him. He put chips under it, blocks of various sorts, bits of pasteboard, and at last went so far as to attempt an exquisite adjustment, by final pieces of folded blotting-paper. But no invention would answer. If, for the sake of easing his back, he brought the table lid at a sharp angle well up toward his chin, and wrote there like a man using the steep roof of a Dutch house for his desk, then he declared that it stopped the circulation in his arms. If now he lowered the table to his waistbands, and stooped over it in writing, then there was a sore aching in his back. In short, the truth of the matter was, Nippers knew not what he wanted. Or, if he wanted anything, it was to be rid of a scrivener's table altogether. Among the manifestations of his diseased ambition was a fondness he had for receiving visits from certain ambiguous-looking fellows in seedy coats, whom he called his clients. Indeed, I was aware that not only was he, at times, considerable of a ward-politician, but he occasionally did a little business at the Justices' courts, and was not unknown on the steps of the Tombs.[10] I have good reason to believe, however, that one individual who called upon him at my chambers, and who, with a grand air, he insisted was his client, was no other than a dun,[11] and the alleged title-deed, a bill. But, with all his failings, and the annoyances he caused me, Nippers, like his compatriot Turkey, was a very useful man to me; wrote a neat, swift hand; and, when he chose, was not deficient in a gentlemanly sort of deportment. Added to this, he always dressed in a gentlemanly sort of way; and so, incidentally, reflected credit upon my chambers. Whereas, with respect to Turkey, I had much ado to keep him from being a reproach to me. His clothes were apt to look oily, and smell of eating-houses. He wore his pantaloons very loose and baggy in summer. His coats were execrable; his hat not to be handled. But while the hat was a thing of indifference to me, inasmuch as his natural civility and deference, as a dependent Englishman, always led him to doff it the moment he entered the room, yet his coat was another matter. Concerning his coats, I reasoned with him; but with no effect. The truth was, I suppose, that a man with so small an income could not afford to sport such a lustrous face and a lustrous coat at one and the same time. As Nippers once observed, Turkey's money went chiefly for red ink. One winter day, I presented Turkey with a highly respectable-looking coat of my own—a padded gray coat, of a most comfortable warmth, and which buttoned straight up from the knee to the neck. I thought Turkey would appreciate the favour, and abate his rashness and obstreperousness of afternoons. But no; I verily believe that buttoning himself up in so downy and blanket-like a coat had a pernicious effect upon him—upon the same principle that too much oats are bad for horses. In fact, precisely as a rash, restive horse is said to feel his oats, so Turkey felt his coat. It made him insolent. He was a man whom prosperity harmed.

Though, concerning the self-indulgent habits of Turkey, I had my own private surmises, yet, touching Nippers, I was well persuaded that, whatever might be his faults in other respects, he was, at least, a temperate young man. But, indeed, nature herself seemed to have been his vintner, and, at his birth, charged him so thoroughly with an irritable, brandy-like disposition, that all subsequent potations were needless. When I consider how, amid the stillness of my chambers, Nippers would sometimes impatiently rise from his seat, and stooping over his table, spread his arms wide apart, seize the whole desk, and move it, and jerk it, with a grim, grinding motion on the floor, as if the table were a perverse voluntary agent, intent on thwarting and vexing him, I plainly perceive that, for Nippers, brandy-and-water were altogether superfluous.

It was fortunate for me that, owing to its peculiar cause—indigestion—the irritability and consequent nervousness of Nippers were mainly observable in the morning, while in the afternoon he was comparatively mild. So that, Turkey's paroxysms only coming on about twelve o'clock, I never had to do with their

[10] The Halls of Justice, the City prison, built in 1838 and quickly rechristened "the Tombs" because of its gloomy Egyptian exterior.
[11] Bill collector.

eccentricities at one time. Their fits relieved each other, like guards. When Nippers's was on, Turkey's was off; and *vice versa*. This was a good natural arrangement, under the circumstances.

Ginger Nut, the third on my list, was a lad, some twelve years old. His father was a carman,[12] ambitious of seeing his son on the bench instead of a cart, before he died. So he sent him to my office, as student at law, errand-boy, cleaner and sweeper, at the rate of one dollar a week. He had a little desk to himself, but he did not use it much. Upon inspection, the drawer exhibited a great array of the shells of various sorts of nuts. Indeed, to this quick-witted youth, the whole noble science of the law was contained in a nut-shell. Not the least among the employments of Ginger Nut, as well as one which he discharged with the most alacrity, was his duty as cake and apple purveyor for Turkey and Nippers. Copying law-papers being proverbially a dry, husky sort of business, my two scriveners were fain to moisten their mouths very often with Spitzenbergs,[13] to be had at the numerous stalls nigh the Custom House and Post Office. Also, they sent Ginger Nut very frequently for that peculiar cake—small, flat, round, and very spicy—after which he had been named by them. Of a cold morning, when business was but dull, Turkey would gobble up scores of these cakes, as if they were mere wafers—indeed, they sell them at the rate of six or eight for a penny—the scrape of his pen blending with the crunching of the crisp particles in his mouth. Of all the fiery afternoon blunders and flurried rashnesses of Turkey, was his once moistening a ginger-cake between his lips, and clapping it on to a mortgage, for a seal. I came within an ace of dismissing him then. But he mollified me by making an oriental bow, and saying "With submission, sir, it was generous of me to find you in stationery on my own account.'

Now my original business that of a conveyancer[14] and title-hunter, and drawer-up of recondite documents of all sorts was considerably increased by receiving the master's office. There was now great work for scriveners. Not only must I push the clerks already with me, but I must have additional help.

In answer to my advertisement, a motionless young man one morning stood upon my office threshold, the door being open, for it was summer. I can see that figure now pallidly neat, pitiably respectable, incurably forlorn! It was Bartleby.

After a few words touching his qualifications, I engaged him, glad to have among my corps of copyists a man of so singularly sedate an aspect, which I thought might operate beneficially upon the flighty temper of Turkey, and the fiery one of Nippers.

I should have stated before that ground-glass folding-doors divided my premises into two parts, one of which was occupied by my scriveners, the other by myself. According to my humour, I threw open these doors, or closed them. I resolved to assign Bartleby a corner by the folding-doors, but on my side of them, so as to have this quiet man within easy call, in case any trifling thing was to be done. I placed his desk close up to a small side-window in that part of the room, a window which originally had afforded a lateral view of certain grimy back-yards and bricks, but which, owing to subsequent erections, commanded at present no view at all, though it gave some light. Within three feet of the panes was a wall, and the light came down from far above, between two lofty buildings, as from a very small opening in a dome. Still further to a satisfactory arrangement, I procured a high

---

[12] A cart driver, teamster.   [13] A red and yellow variety of apples.
[14] An individual who draws up property deeds.

green folding-screen, which might entirely isolate Bartleby from my sight, though not remove him from my voice. And thus, in a manner, privacy and society were conjoined.

At first, Bartleby did an extraordinary quantity of writing. As if long famishing for something to copy, he seemed to gorge himself on my documents. There was no pause for digestion. He ran a day and night line, copying by sun-light and by candle-light. I should have been quite delighted with his application, had he been cheerfully industrious. But he wrote on silently, palely, mechanically.

It is, of course, an indispensable part of a scrivener's business to verify the accuracy of his copy, word by word. Where there are two or more scriveners in an office, they assist each other in this examination, one reading from the copy, the other holding the original. It is a very dull, wearisome, and lethargic affair. I can readily imagine that, to some sanguine temperaments, it would be altogether intolerable. For example, I cannot credit that the mettlesome poet, Byron,[15] would have contentedly sat down with Bartleby to examine a law document of, say, five hundred pages, closely written in a crimpy hand.

Now and then, in the haste of business, it had been my habit to assist in comparing some brief document myself, calling Turkey or Nippers for this purpose. One object I had, in placing Bartleby so handy to me behind the screen, was, to avail myself of his services on such trivial occasions. It was on the third day, I think, of his being with me, and before any necessity had arisen for having his own writing examined, that, being much hurried to complete a small affair I had in hand, I abruptly called to Bartleby. In my haste and natural expectancy of instant compliance, I sat with my head bent over the original on my desk, and my right hand sideways, and somewhat nervously extended with the copy, so that, immediately upon emerging from his retreat, Bartleby might snatch it and proceed to business without the least delay.

In this very attitude did I sit when I called to him, rapidly stating what it was I wanted him to do—namely, to examine a small paper with me. Imagine my surprise, nay, my consternation, when, without moving from his privacy, Bartleby, in a singularly mild, firm voice, replied, 'I would prefer not to.'

I sat a while in perfect silence, rallying my stunned faculties. Immediately it occurred to me that my ears had deceived me, or Bartleby had entirely misunderstood my meaning. I repeated my request in the clearest tone I could assume; but in quite as clear a one came the previous reply, 'I would prefer not to.'

'Prefer not to,' echoed I, rising in high excitement, and crossing the room with a stride. 'What do you mean? Are you moon-struck? I want you to help me compare this sheet here—take it,' and I thrust it toward him.

'I would prefer not to,' said he.

I looked at him steadfastly. His face was leanly composed; his gray eye dimly calm. Not a wrinkle of agitation rippled him. Had there been the least uneasiness, anger, impatience, or impertinence in his manner; in other words, had there been anything ordinarily human about him, doubtless I should have violently dismissed him from the premises. But as it was, I should have as soon thought of turning my pale plaster-of-paris bust of Cicero[16] out of doors. I stood gazing at him a while, as he went on with his own writing, and then reseated myself at my desk. This is very strange, thought I. What had one best do? But my business hurried me. I

---

[15] George Gordon, Lord Byron (1788–1824), the English Romantic poet.
[16] Cicero (106–43 B.C.), the Roman statesman, orator, and author, who initially gained his fame as a defense lawyer.

concluded to forget the matter for the present, reserving it for my future leisure. So calling Nippers from the other room, the paper was speedily examined.

A few days after this, Bartleby concluded four lengthy documents, being quadruplicates of a week's testimony taken before me in my High Court of Chancery. It became necessary to examine them. It was an important suit, and great accuracy was imperative. Having all things arranged, I called Turkey, Nippers, and Ginger Nut, from the next room, meaning to place the four copies in the hands of my four clerks, while I should read from the original. Accordingly, Turkey, Nippers, and Ginger Nut had taken their seats in a row, each with his document in his hand, when I called to Bartleby to join this interesting group.

'Bartleby! quick, I am waiting.'

I heard a slow scrape of his chair legs on the uncarpeted floor, and soon he appeared standing at the entrance of his hermitage.

'What is wanted?' said he mildly.

'The copies, the copies,' said I hurriedly. ''We are going to examine them. There' and I held toward him the fourth quadruplicate.

'I would prefer not to,' he said, and gently disappeared behind the screen.

For a few moments I was turned into a pillar of salt,[17] standing at the head of my seated column of clerks. Recovering myself, I advanced toward the screen, and demanded the reason for such extraordinary conduct.

'*Why* do you refuse?'

'I would prefer not to.'

With any other man I should have flown outright into a dreadful passion, scorned all further words, and thrust him ignominiously from my presence. But there was something about Bartleby that not only strangely disarmed me, but, in a wonderful manner, touched and disconcerted me. I began to reason with him.

'These are your own copies we are about to examine. It is labour saving to you, because one examination will answer for your four papers. It is common usage. Every copyist is bound to help examine his copy. Is it not so? Will you not speak? Answer!'

'I prefer not to,' he replied in a flute-like tone. It seemed to me that, while I had been addressing him, he carefully revolved every statement that I made; fully comprehended the meaning; could not gainsay the irresistible conclusion; but, at the same time, some paramount consideration prevailed with him to reply as he did.

'You are decided, then, not to comply with my request—a request made according to common usage and common sense?'

He briefly gave me to understand, that on that point my judgment was sound. Yes: his decision was irreversible.

It is not seldom the case that, when a man is brow-beaten in some unprecedented and violently unreasonable way, he begins to stagger in his own plainest faith. He begins, as it were, vaguely to surmise that, wonderful as it may be, all the justice and all the reason is on the other side. Accordingly, if any disinterested persons are present, he turns to them for some reinforcement for his own faltering mind.

'Turkey,' said I, 'what do you think of this? Am I not right?'

'With submission, sir,' said Turkey, in his blandest tone, 'I think that you are.'

'Nippers,' said I, 'What do *you* think of it?'

---

[17] See *Genesis* 19:26. Lot's wife was turned into a pillar of salt for disobeying God's injunction not to look back on the destruction of Sodom and Gomorrah.

'I think I should kick him out of the office.'

(The reader, of nice[18] perceptions, will here perceive that, it being morning, Turkey's answer is couched in polite and tranquil terms, but Nippers's replies in ill-tempered ones. Or, to repeat a previous sentence, Nippers's ugly mood was on duty, and Turkey's off.)

'Ginger Nut,' said I, willing to enlist the smallest suffrage in my behalf, 'what do *you* think of it?'

'I think, sir, he's a little *luny*,' replied Ginger Nut, with a grin.

"You hear what they say,' said I, turning toward the screen, 'come forth and do your duty.'

But he vouchsafed no reply. I pondered a moment in sore perplexity. But once more business hurried me. I determined again to postpone the consideration of this dilemma to my future leisure. With a little trouble we made out to examine the papers without Bartleby, though at every page or two Turkey deferentially dropped his opinion, that this proceeding was quite out of the common; while Nippers, twitching in his chair with a dyspeptic nervousness, ground out, between his set teeth, occasional hissing maledictions against the stubborn oaf behind the screen. And for his (Nippers's) part, this was the first and the last time he would do another man's business without pay.

Meanwhile Bartleby sat in his hermitage, oblivious to everything but his own peculiar business there.

Some days passed, the scrivener being employed upon another lengthy work. His late remarkable conduct led me to regard his ways narrowly. I observed that he never went to dinner; indeed, that he never went anywhere. As yet I had never, of my personal knowledge, known him to be outside of my office. He was a perpetual sentry in the corner. At about eleven o'clock though, in the morning, I noticed that Ginger Nut would advance toward the opening in Bartleby's screen, as if silently beckoned thither by a gesture invisible to me where I sat. The boy would then leave the office, jingling a few pence, and reappear with a handful of ginger-nuts, which he delivered in the hermitage, receiving two of the cakes for his trouble.

He lives, then, on ginger-nuts, thought I; never eats a dinner, properly speaking; he must be a vegetarian, then; but no; he never eats even vegetables, he eats nothing but ginger-nuts. My mind then ran on in reveries concerning the probable effects upon the human constitution of living entirely on ginger-nuts. Ginger-nuts are so called, because they contain ginger as one of their peculiar constituents, and the final flavoring one. Now, what was ginger? A hot, spicy thing. Was Bartleby hot and spicy? Not at all. Ginger, then, had no effect upon Bartleby. Probably he preferred it should have none.

Nothing so aggravates an earnest person as a passive resistance. If the individual so resisted be of a not inhumane temper, and the resisting one perfectly harmless in his passivity, then, in the better moods of the former, he will endeavour charitably to construe to his imagination what proves impossible to be solved by his judgment. Even so, for the most part, I regarded Bartleby and his ways. Poor fellow! thought I, he means no mischief; it is plain he intends no insolence; his aspect sufficiently evinces that his eccentricities are involuntary. He is useful to me. I can get along with him. If I turn him away, the chances are he will fall in with some less-indulgent employer, and then he will be rudely treated, and perhaps driven forth miserably to starve. Yes. Here I can cheaply purchase a delicious

---

[18] Accurate, precise.

self-approval. To befriend Bartleby; to humour him in his strange wilfulness, will cost me little or nothing, while I lay up in my soul what will eventually prove a sweet morsel for my conscience. But this mood was not invariable with me. The passiveness of Bartleby sometimes irritated me. I felt strangely goaded on to encounter him in new opposition—to elicit some angry spark from him answerable to my own. But, indeed, I might as well have essayed to strike fire with my knuckles against a bit of Windsor soap.[19] But one afternoon the evil impulse in me mastered me, and the following little scene ensued:—

'Bartleby,' said I, 'when those papers are all copied, I will compare them with you.'

'I would prefer not to.'

'How? Surely you do not mean to persist in that mulish vagary?'

No answer.

I threw open the folding-doors near by, and, turning upon Turkey and Nippers, exclaimed:

'Bartleby a second time says, he won't examine his papers. What do you think of it, Turkey?'

It was afternoon, be it remembered. Turkey sat glowing like a brass boiler; his bald head steaming; his hands reeling among his blotted papers.

'Think of it?' roared Turkey; 'I think I'll just step behind the screen, and black his eyes for him!'

So saying, Turkey rose to his feet and threw his arms into a pugilistic position. He was hurrying away to make good his promise, when I detained him, alarmed at the effect of incautiously rousing Turkey's combativeness after dinner.

'Sit down, Turkey,' said I, 'and hear what Nippers has to say. What do you think of it, Nippers? Would I not be justified in immediately dismissing Bartleby?'

'Excuse me, that is for you to decide, sir. I think his conduct quite unusual, and, indeed, unjust, as regards Turkey and myself. But it may only be a passing whim.'

'Ah,' exclaimed I, 'you have strangely changed your mind, then—you speak very gently of him now.'

'All beer,' cried Turkey; 'gentleness is effects of beer—Nippers and I dined together to-day. You see how gentle *I* am, sir. Shall I go and black his eyes?'

'You refer to Bartleby, I suppose. No, not to-day, Turkey,' I replied; 'pray, put up your fists.'

I closed the doors, and again advanced toward Bartleby. I felt additional incentives tempting me to my fate. I burned to be rebelled against again. I remembered that Bartleby never left the office.

'Bartleby,' said I, 'Ginger Nut is away; just step around to the Post Office, won't you? (it was but a three minutes' walk), and see if there is anything for me.'

'I would prefer not to.'

'You *will* not?'

'I *prefer* not.'

I staggered to my desk, and sat there in a deep study. My blind inveteracy returned. Was there any other thing in which I could procure myself to be ignominiously repulsed by this lean, penniless wight?[20]—my hired clerk? What added thing is there, perfectly reasonable, that he will be sure to refuse to do?

'Bartleby!'

No answer.

[19] Brown, aromatic toilet soap.
[20] Creature.

'Bartleby,' in a louder tone.

No answer.

'Bartleby,' I roared.

Like a very ghost, agreeably to the laws of magical invocation, at the third summons, he appeared at the entrance of his hermitage.

'Go to the next room, and tell Nippers to come to me.'

'I prefer not to,' he respectfully and slowly said, and mildly disappeared.

'Very good, Bartleby,' said I, in a quiet sort of serenely-severe self-possessed tone, intimating the unalterable purpose of some terrible retribution very close at hand. At the moment I half intended something of the kind. But upon the whole, as it was drawing toward my dinner-hour, I thought it best to put on my hat and walk home for the day, suffering much from perplexity and distress of mind.

Shall I acknowledge it? The conclusion of this whole business was, that it soon became a fixed fact of my chambers, that a pale young scrivener, by the name of Bartleby, had a desk there; that he copied for me at the usual rate of four cents a folio (one hundred words); but he was permanently exempt from examining the work done by him, that duty being transferred to Turkey and Nippers, out of compliment, doubtless, to their superior acuteness; moreover, said Bartleby was never, on any account, to be dispatched on the most trivial errand of any sort; and that even if entreated to take upon him such a matter, it was generally understood that he would 'prefer not to'—in other words, that he would refuse point-blank.

As days passed on, I became considerably reconciled to Bartleby. His steadiness, his freedom from all dissipation, his incessant industry (except when he chose to throw himself into a standing revery behind his screen), his great stillness, his unalterableness of demeanour under all circumstances, made him a valuable acquisition. One prime thing was this—*he was always there*—first in the morning, continually through the day, and the last at night. I had a singular confidence in his honesty. I felt my most precious papers perfectly safe in his hands. Sometimes, to be sure, I could not, for the very soul of me, avoid falling into sudden spasmodic passions with him. For it was exceeding difficult to bear in mind all the time those strange peculiarities, privileges, and unheard-of exemptions, forming the tacit stipulations on Bartleby's part under which he remained in my office. Now and then, in the eagerness of dispatching pressing business, I would inadvertently summon Bartleby, in a short, rapid tone, to put his finger, say, on the incipient tie of a bit of red tape with which I was about compressing some papers. Of course, from behind the screen the usual answer, 'I prefer not to,' was sure to come; and then, how could a human creature, with the common infirmities of our nature, refrain from bitterly exclaiming upon such perverseness—such unreasonableness. However, every added repulse of this sort which I received only tended to lessen the probability of my repeating the inadvertence.

Here it must be said, that according to the custom of most legal gentlemen occupying chambers in densely populated law-buildings, there were several keys to my door. One was kept by a woman residing in the attic, which person weekly scrubbed and daily swept and dusted my apartments. Another was kept by Turkey for convenience sake. The third I sometimes carried in my own pocket. The fourth I knew not who had.

Now, one Sunday morning I happened to go to Trinity Church, to hear a celebrated preacher, and finding myself rather early on the ground I thought I would walk round to my chambers for a while. Luckily I had my key with me; but upon applying it to the lock, I found it resisted by something inserted from the inside. Quite surprised, I called out; when to my consternation a key was turned from within; and thrusting his lean visage at me, and holding the door ajar, the apparition of Bartleby appeared, in his shirt-sleeves, and otherwise in a strangely tattered dishabille,[21] saying quietly that he was sorry, but he was deeply engaged just then, and—preferred not admitting me at present. In a brief word or two, he moreover added, that perhaps I had better walk round the block two or three times, and by that time he would probably have concluded his affairs.

Now, the utterly unsurmised appearance of Bartleby, tenanting my law chambers of a Sunday morning, with his cadaverously gentlemanly nonchalance, yet withal firm and self-possessed, had such a strange effect upon me, that incontinently I slunk away from my own door, and did as desired. But not without sundry twinges of impotent rebellion against the mild effrontery of this unaccountable scrivener. Indeed, it was his wonderful mildness chiefly, which not only disarmed me, but unmanned me as it were. For I consider that one, for the time, is a sort of unmanned when he tranquilly permits his hired clerk to dictate to him, and order him away from his own premises. Furthermore, I was full of uneasiness as to what Bartleby could possibly be doing in my office in his shirt-sleeves, and in an otherwise dismantled condition of a Sunday morning. Was anything amiss going on? Nay, that was out of the question. It was not to be thought of for a moment that Bartleby was an immoral person. But what could he be doing there?—copying? Nay again, whatever might be his eccentricities, Bartleby was an eminently decorous person. He would be the last man to sit down at his desk in any state approaching to nudity. Besides, it was Sunday; and there was something about Bartleby that forbade the supposition that he would by any secular occupation violate the proprieties of the day.

Nevertheless, my mind was not pacified; and full of a restless curiosity, at last I returned to the door. Without hindrance I inserted my key, opened it, and entered. Bartleby was not to be seen. I looked round anxiously, peeped behind his screen; but it was very plain that he was gone. Upon more closely examining the place, I surmised that for an indefinite period Bartleby must have ate, dressed, and slept in my office, and that, too, without plate, mirror, or bed. The cushioned seat of a rickety old sofa in one corner bore the faint impress of a lean, reclining form. Rolled away under his desk, I found a blanket; under the empty grate a blacking box and brush; on a chair, a tin basin, with soap and a ragged towel; in a newspaper a few crumbs of ginger-nuts and a morsel of cheese. Yes, thought I, it is evident enough that Bartleby has been making his home here, keeping bachelor's hall all by himself. Immediately then the thought came sweeping across me, what miserable friendlessness and loneliness are here revealed! His poverty is great; but his solitude, how horrible! Think of it. Of a Sunday, Wall Street is deserted as Petra;[22] and every night of every day it is an emptiness. This building, too, which of week-days hums with industry and life, at nightfall echoes with sheer vacancy, and all through Sunday is forlorn. And here Bartleby makes his home; sole spectator of a solitude which he has seen all-populous—a sort of innocent and transformed Marius brooding among the ruins of Carthage![23]

---

[21] Disheveled, partly dressed.

[22] The ancient city south of the Dead Sea in what is now Jordan rediscovered by explorers in 1812. Once an important trading center, Petra was surrounded by high cliffs of red stone rock, hence the comparison to Wall Street.

[23] Gaius Marius (157–86 B.C.), the Roman general and consul of plebian origins, who was betrayed and forced to flee by his patrician enemies, is often pictured as an old man brooding alone amidst the

For the first time in my life a feeling of overpowering stinging melancholy seized me. Before, I had never experienced aught but a not unpleasing sadness. The bond of a common humanity now drew me irresistibly to gloom. A fraternal melancholy! For both I and Bartleby were sons of Adam. I remembered the bright silks and sparkling faces I had seen that day, in gala trim, swan-like sailing down the Mississippi of Broadway; and I contrasted them with the pallid copyist, and thought to myself, Ah, happiness courts the light, so we deem the world is gay; but misery hides aloof, so we deem that misery there is none. These sad fancyings—chimeras,[24] doubtless, of a sick and silly brain—led on to other and more special thoughts, concerning the eccentricities of Bartleby. Presentiments of strange discoveries hovered round me. The scrivener's pale form appeared to me laid out, among uncaring strangers, in its shivering winding-sheet.

Suddenly I was attracted by Bartleby's closed desk, the key in open sight left in the lock.

I mean no mischief, seek the gratification of no heartless curiosity, thought I; besides, the desk is mine, and its contents, too, so I will make bold to look within. Everything was methodically arranged, the papers smoothly placed. The pigeon-holes were deep, and removing the files of documents, I groped into their recesses. Presently I felt something there, and dragged it out. It was an old bandanna handkerchief, heavy and knotted. I opened it, and saw it was a savings-bank.

I now recalled all the quiet mysteries which I had noted in the man. I remembered that he never spoke but to answer; that, though at intervals he had considerable time to himself, yet I had never seen him reading—no, not even a newspaper; that for long periods he would stand looking out, at his pale window behind the screen, upon the dead brick wall; I was quite sure he never visited any refectory or eating-house; while his pale face clearly indicated that he never drank beer like Turkey, or tea and coffee even, like other men; that he never went anywhere in particular that I could learn; never went out for a walk, unless, indeed, that was the case at present; that he had declined telling who he was, or whence he came, or whether he had any relatives in the world; that though so thin and pale, he never complained of ill health. And more than all, I remembered a certain unconscious air of pallid—how shall I call it?—of pallid haughtiness, say, or rather an austere reserve about him, which had positively awed me into my tame compliance with his eccentricities, when I had feared to ask him to do the slightest incidental thing for me, even though I might know, from his long-continued motionlessness, that behind his screen he must be standing in one of those dead-wall reveries of his.

Revolving all these things, and coupling them with the recently discovered fact, that he made my office his constant abiding-place and home, and not forgetful of his morbid moodiness; revolving all these things, a prudential feeling began to steal over me. My first emotions had been those of pure melancholy and sincerest pity; but just in proportion as the forlornness of Bartleby grew and grew to my imagination, did that same melancholy merge into fear, that pity into repulsion. So true it is, and so terrible, too, that up to a certain point the thought or sight of

---

ruins of the ancient north African city of Carthage. The image itself is traceable to the Greek historian Plutarch (46–120 A.D.), who in his *Parallel Lives of Illustrious Greeks and Romans* quotes a grieving and indignant Marius replying to the emissary of the Roman governor of Libya who has denied him refuge: " 'Tell him that you have seen Gaius Marius sitting as a fugitive among the ruins of Carthage'—thus quite cleverly putting together and comparing the fate of that city with the change in his own fortunes."

[24] Imaginary monsters.

misery enlists our best affections; but, in certain special cases, beyond that point it does not. They err who would assert that invariably this is owing to the inherent selfishness of the human heart. It rather proceeds from a certain hopelessness of remedying excessive and organic ill. To a sensitive being, pity is not seldom pain. And when at last it is perceived that such pity cannot lead to effectual succour, common-sense bids the soul be rid of it. What I saw that morning persuaded me that the scrivener was the victim of innate and incurable disorder. I might give alms to his body; but his body did not pain him; it was his soul that suffered, and his soul I could not reach.

I did not accomplish the purpose of going to Trinity Church that morning. Somehow, the things I had seen disqualified me for the time from church-going. I walked homeward, thinking what I would do with Bartleby. Finally, I resolved upon this—I would put certain calm questions to him the next morning, touching his history, etc., and if he declined to answer them openly and unreservedly (and I supposed he would prefer not), then to give him a twenty-dollar bill over and above whatever I might owe him, and tell him his services were no longer required; but that if in any other way I could assist him, I would be happy to do so, especially if he desired to return to his native place, wherever that might be, I would willingly help to defray the expenses. Moreover, if, after reaching home, he found himself at any time in want of aid, a letter from him would be sure of a reply.

The next morning came.

'Bartleby,' said I, gently calling to him behind his screen.

No reply.

'Bartleby,' said I, in a still gentler tone, 'come here; I am not going to ask you to do anything you would prefer not to do—I simply wish to speak to you.'

Upon this he noiselessly slid into view.

'Will you tell me, Bartleby, where you were born?'

'I would prefer not to.'

'Will you tell me *anything* about yourself?'

'I would prefer not to.'

'But what reasonable objection can you have to speak to me? I feel friendly toward you.'

He did not look at me while I spoke, but kept his glance fixed upon my bust of Cicero, which, as I then sat, was directly behind me, some six inches above my head.

'What is your answer, Bartleby?' said I, after waiting a considerable time for a reply, during which his countenance remained immovable, only there was the faintest conceivable tremor of the white attenuated mouth.

'At present I prefer to give no answer,' he said, and retired into his hermitage.

It was rather weak in me, I confess, but his manner, on this occasion, nettled me. Not only did there seem to lurk in it a certain calm disdain, but his perverseness seemed ungrateful, considering the undeniable good usage and indulgence he had received from me.

Again I sat ruminating what I should do. Mortified as I was at his behaviour, and resolved as I had been to dismiss him when I entered my office, nevertheless I strangely felt something superstitious knocking at my heart, and forbidding me to carry out my purpose, and denouncing me for a villain if I dared to breathe one bitter word against this forlornest of mankind. At last, familiarly drawing my chair behind his screen, I sat down and said: 'Bartleby, never mind, then, about revealing your history; but let me entreat you, as a friend, to comply as far as may be with the usages of this office. Say now, you will help to examine papers to-morrow or next day: in short, say now, that in a day or two you will begin to be a little reasonable:—say so, Bartleby.'

'At present I would prefer not to be a little reasonable,' was his mildly cadaverous reply.

Just then the folding-doors opened, and Nippers approached. He seemed suffering from an unusually bad night's rest, induced by severer indigestion than common. He overheard those final words of Bartleby.

'*Prefer not*, eh?' gritted Nippers—'I'd *prefer* him, if I were you, sir,' addressing me— 'I'd *prefer* him; I'd give him preferences, the stubborn mule! What is it, sir, pray, that he *prefers* not to do now?'

Bartleby moved not a limb.

'Mr. Nippers,' said I, 'I'd prefer that you would withdraw for the present.'

Somehow, of late, I had got into the way of involuntarily using this word 'prefer' upon all sorts of not exactly suitable occasions. And I trembled to think that my contact with the scrivener had already and seriously affected me in a mental way. And what further and deeper abberation might it not yet produce? This apprehension had not been without efficacy in determining me to summary measures.

As Nippers, looking very sour and sulky, was departing, Turkey blandly and deferentially approached.

'With submission, sir,' said he, 'yesterday I was thinking about Bartleby here, and I think that if he would but prefer to take a quart of good ale every day, it would do much toward mending him, and enabling him to assist in examining his papers.'

'So you have got the word too,' said I, slightly excited.

'With submission, what word, sir,' asked Turkey, respectfully crowding himself into the contracted space behind the screen, and by so doing, making me jostle the scrivener. 'What word, sir?'

'I would prefer to be left alone here,' said Bartleby, as if offended at being mobbed in his privacy.

'*That's* the word, Turkey,' said I—'*that's* it.'

'Oh, *prefer*? oh yes—queer word. I never use it myself. But, sir, as I was saying, if he would but prefer——,'

'Turkey,' interrupted I, 'you will please withdraw.'

'Oh certainly, sir, if you prefer that I should.'

As he opened the folding-door to retire, Nippers at his desk caught a glimpse of me, and asked whether I would prefer to have a certain paper copied on blue paper or white. He did not in the least roguishly accent the word prefer. It was plain that it involuntarily rolled from his tongue. I thought to myself, surely I must get rid of a demented man, who already has in some degree turned the tongues, if not the heads of myself and clerks. But I thought it prudent not to break the discussion at once.

The next day I noticed that Bartleby did nothing but stand at his window in his dead-wall revery. Upon asking him why he did not write, he said that he had decided upon doing no more writing.

'Why, how now? what next?' exclaimed I, 'do no more writing?'

'No more.'

'And what is the reason?'

'Do you not see the reason for yourself?' he indifferently replied.

I looked steadfastly at him, and perceived that his eyes looked dull and glazed. Instantly it occurred to me, that his unexampled diligence in copying by his dim window for the first few weeks of his stay with me might have temporarily impaired his vision.

I was touched. I said something in condolence with him. I hinted that of course he did wisely in abstaining from writing for a while; and urged him to embrace that opportunity of taking wholesome exercise in the open air. This, however, he did not do. A few days after this, my other clerks being absent, and being in a great hurry to dispatch certain letters by the mail, I thought that having nothing else earthly to do, Bartleby would surely be less inflexible than usual, and carry these letters to the Post Office. But he blankly declined. So, much to my inconvenience, I went myself.

Still added days went by. Whether Bartleby's eyes improved or not, I could not say. To all appearance, I thought they did. But when I asked him if they did, he vouchsafed no answer. At all events, he would do no copying. At last, in reply to my urgings, he informed me that he had permanently given up copying.

'What!' exclaimed I; 'suppose your eyes should get entirely well—better than ever before—would you not copy then?'

'I have given up copying,' he answered, and slid aside.

He remained as ever, a fixture in my chamber. Nay—if that were possible—he became still more of a fixture than before. What was to be done? He would do nothing in the office; why should he stay there? In plain fact, he had now become a millstone to me,[25] not only useless as a necklace, but afflictive to bear. Yet I was sorry for him. I speak less than truth when I say that, on his own account, he occasioned me uneasiness. If he would but have named a single relative or friend, I would instantly have written, and urged their taking the poor fellow away to some convenient retreat. But he seemed alone, absolutely alone in the universe. A bit of wreck in the mid-Atlantic. At length, necessities connected with my business tyrannised over all other considerations. Decently as I could, I told Bartleby that in six days time he must unconditionally leave the office. I warned him to take measures, in the interval, for procuring some other abode. I offered to assist him in this endeavour, if he himself would but take the first step toward a removal. 'And when you finally quit me, Bartleby,' added I, 'I shall see that you go not away entirely unprovided. Six days from this hour, remember.'

At the expiration of that period, I peeped behind the screen, and lo! Bartleby was there.

I buttoned up my coat, balanced myself; advanced slowly toward him, touched his shoulder, and said, 'The time has come; you must quit this place; I am sorry for you; here is money; but you must go.'

'I would prefer not,' he replied, with his back still toward me.

'You *must.*'

He remained silent.

Now I had an unbounded confidence in this man's common honesty. He had frequently restored to me sixpences and shillings carelessly dropped upon the floor, for I am apt to be very reckless in such shirt-button affairs. The proceeding, then, which followed will not be deemed extraordinary.

'Bartleby,' said I, 'I owe you twelve dollars on account; here are thirty-two; the odd twenty are yours—Will you take it?' and I handed the bills toward him.

But he made no motion.

'I will leave them here, then,' putting them under a weight on the table. Then taking my hat and cane and going to the door, I tranquilly turned and added—

[25] See Matthew 18:4–6.

'After you have removed your things from these offices, Bartleby, you will of course lock the door—since everyone is now gone for the day but you—and if you please, slip your key underneath the mat, so that I may have it in the morning. I shall not see you again; so good-bye to you. If, hereafter, in your new place of abode, I can be of any service to you, do not fail to advise me by letter. Good-bye, Bartleby, and fare you well.'

But he answered not a word; like the last column of some ruined temple, he remained standing mute and solitary in the middle of the otherwise deserted room.

As I walked home in a pensive mood, my vanity got the better of my pity. I could not but highly plume myself on my masterly management in getting rid of Bartleby. Masterly I call it, and such it must appear to any dispassionate thinker. The beauty of my procedure seemed to consist in its perfect quietness. There was no vulgar bullying, no bravado of any sort, no choleric hectoring, and striding to and fro across the apartment, jerking out vehement commands for Bartleby to bundle himself off with his beggarly traps. Nothing of the kind. Without loudly bidding Bartleby depart—as an inferior genius might have done—I *assumed* the ground that depart he must; and upon that assumption built all I had to say. The more I thought over my procedure, the more I was charmed with it. Nevertheless, next morning, upon awakening, I had my doubts—I had somehow slept off the fumes of vanity. One of the coolest and wisest hours a man has, is just after he awakes in the morning. My procedure seemed as sagacious as ever but only in theory. How it would prove in practice—there was the rub. It was truly a beautiful thought to have assumed Bartleby's departure; but, after all, that assumption was simply my own, and none of Bartleby's. The great point was, not whether I had assumed that he would quit me, but whether he would prefer so to do. He was more a man of preferences than assumptions.

After breakfast, I walked down town, arguing the probabilities *pro* and *con*. One moment I thought it would prove a miserable failure, and Bartleby would be found all alive at my office as usual; the next moment it seemed certain that I should find his chair empty. And so I kept veering about. At the corner of Broadway and Canal Street, I saw quite an excited group of people standing in earnest conversation.

'I'll take odds he doesn't,' said a voice as I passed.

'Doesn't go?—done!' said I; 'put up your money.'

I was instinctively putting my hand in my pocket to produce my own, when I remembered that this was an election day. The words I had overheard bore no reference to Bartleby, but to the success or non-success of some candidate for the mayoralty. In my intent frame of mind, I had, as it were, imagined that all Broadway shared in my excitement, and were debating the same question with me. I passed on, very thankful that the uproar of the street screened my momentary absent-mindedness.

As I had intended, I was earlier than usual at my office door. I stood listening for a moment. All was still. He must be gone. I tried the knob. The door was locked. Yes, my procedure had worked to a charm; he indeed must be vanished. Yet a certain melancholy mixed with this: I was almost sorry for my brilliant success. I was fumbling under the door-mat for the key, which Bartleby was to have left there for me, when accidentally my knee knocked against a panel, producing a summoning sound, and in response a voice came to me from within—'Not yet; I am occupied.'

It was Bartleby.

I was thunderstruck. For an instant I stood like the man who, pipe in mouth, was killed one cloudless afternoon long ago in Virginia, by summer lightning; at his own warm open window he was killed, and remained leaning out there upon the dreamy afternoon, till someone touched him, when he fell.

'Not gone!' I murmured at last. But again obeying that wondrous ascendency which the inscrutable scrivener had over me, and from which ascendency, for all my chafing, I could not completely escape, I slowly went downstairs and out into the street, and while walking round the block, considered what I should next do in this unheard-of perplexity. Turn the man out by an actual thrusting I could not; to drive him away by calling him hard names would not do; calling in the police was an unpleasant idea; and yet, permit him to enjoy his cadaverous triumph over me—this, too, I could not think of. What was to be done? or, if nothing could be done, was there anything further that I could *assume* in the matter? Yes, as before I had prospectively assumed that Bartleby would depart, so now I might retrospectively assume that departed he was. In the legitimate carrying out of this assumption, I might enter my office in a great hurry, and pretending not to see Bartleby at all, walk straight against him as if he were air. Such a proceeding would in a singular degree have the appearance of a home-thrust. It was hardly possible that Bartleby could withstand such an application of the doctrine of assumptions. But upon second thoughts the success of the plan seemed rather dubious. I resolved to argue the matter over with him again.

'Bartleby,' said I, entering the office, with a quietly severe expression, 'I am seriously displeased. I am pained, Bartleby. I had thought better of you. I had imagined you of such a gentlemanly organisation, that in any delicate dilemma a slight hint would suffice—in short, an assumption. But it appears I am deceived. Why,' I added, unaffectedly starting, 'you have not even touched that money yet,' pointing to it, just where I had left it the evening previous.

He answered nothing.

'Will you, or will you not, quit me?' I now demanded in a sudden passion, advancing close to him.

'I would prefer *not* to quit you,' he replied, gently emphasising the *not*.

'What earthly right have you to stay here? Do you pay any rent? Do you pay my taxes? Or is this property yours?'

He answered nothing.

'Are you ready to go on and write now? Are your eyes recovered? Could you copy a small paper for me this morning? or help examine a few lines? or step round to the Post Office? In a word, will you do anything at all, to give a colouring to your refusal to depart the premises?'

He silently retired into his hermitage.

I was now in such a state of nervous resentment that I thought it but prudent to check myself at present from further demonstrations. Bartleby and I were alone. I remembered the tragedy of the unfortunate Adams and the still more unfortunate Colt in the solitary office of the latter;[26] and how poor Colt, being dreadfully incensed by Adams, and imprudently permitting himself to get wildly excited, was at unawares hurried into his fatal act— an act which certainly no man

---

[26] A sensational and highly publicized New York murder case of 1841–1842, in which John C. Colt killed his creditor Samuel Adams with a hatchet and then tried to conceal the body by shipping it to New Orleans. Though Colt's plea of self-defense attracted much public support, he was convicted of murder. He committed suicide in his cell minutes before he was to be hung in a prison yard filled to capacity with sensation seekers.

could possibly deplore more than the actor himself. Often it had occurred to me in my ponderings upon the subject, that had that altercation taken place in the public street, or at a private residence, it would not have terminated as it did. It was the circumstance of being alone in a solitary office, upstairs, of a building entirely unhallowed by humanising domestic associations—an uncarpeted office, doubtless, of a dusty, haggard sort of appearance—this it must have been, which greatly helped to enhance the irritable desperation of the hapless Colt.

But when this old Adam[27] of resentment rose in me and tempted me concerning Bartleby, I grappled him and threw him. How? Why, simply by recalling the divine injunction: 'A new commandment give I unto you, that ye love one another.'[28] Yes, this it was that saved me. Aside from higher considerations, charity often operates as a vastly wise and prudent principle—a great safeguard to its possessor. Men have committed murder for jealousy's sake, and anger's sake, and hatred's sake, and selfishness' sake, and spiritual pride's sake; but no man, that ever I heard of, ever committed a diabolical murder for sweet charity's sake. Mere self-interest, then, if no better motive can be enlisted, should, especially with high-tempered men, prompt all beings to charity and philanthropy. At any rate, upon the occasion in question, I strove to drown my exasperated feelings toward the scrivener by benevolently construing his conduct. Poor fellow, poor fellow! thought I, he don't mean anything; and besides, he has seen hard times, and ought to be indulged.

I endeavoured, also, immediately to occupy myself, and at the same time to comfort my despondency. I tried to fancy, that in the course of the morning, at such time as might prove agreeable to him, Bartleby, of his own free accord, would emerge from his hermitage and take up some decided line of march in the direction of the door. But no. Half-past twelve o'clock came; Turkey began to glow in the face, overturn his inkstand, and become generally obstreperous; Nippers abated down into quietude and courtesy; Ginger Nut munched his noon apple; and Bartleby remained standing at his window in one of his profoundest dead-wall reveries. Will it be credited? Ought I to acknowledge it? That afternoon I left the office without saying one further word to him.

Some days now passed, during which, at leisure intervals, I looked a little into 'Edwards on the Will,' and 'Priestley on Necessity.'[29] Under the circumstances, those books induced a salutary feeling. Gradually I slid into the persuasion that these troubles of mine, touching the scrivener, had been all predestinated from eternity, and Bartleby was billeted[30] upon me for some mysterious purpose of an all-wise Providence, which it was not for a mere mortal like me to fathom. Yes, Bartleby, stay there behind your screen, thought I; I shall persecute you no more; you are harmless and noiseless as any of these old chairs; in short, I never feel so private as when I know you are here. At last I see it, I feel it; I penetrate to the predestinated purpose of my life. I am content. Others may have loftier parts to enact; but my mission in this world, Bartleby, is to furnish you with office-room for such period as you may see fit to remain.

I believe that this wise and blessed frame of mind would have continued with

---

[27] Adam of the Book of Genesis whose infidelity brought original sin into the world.
[28] Jesus to his disciples: John 15:12–13.
[29] American theologian Jonathan Edwards (1703–1758) in his *Freedom of the Will* (1754) rejects the idea of free will and argues the Calvinistic doctrine of predestination. Joseph Priestley (1733–1804), the English scientist who discovered oxygen, rejected Calvinism, but argues in his *Doctrine of Philosophical Necessity Illustrated* (1777) for determinism on the basis of nature's laws of cause and effect.
[30] Assigned, as if by official order.

me, had it not been for the unsolicited and uncharitable remarks obtruded upon me by my professional friends who visited the rooms. But thus it often is, that the constant friction of illiberal minds wears out at last the best resolves of the more generous. Though to be sure, when I reflected upon it, it was not strange that people entering my office should be struck by the peculiar aspect of the unaccountable Bartleby, and so be tempted to throw out some sinister observations concerning him. Sometimes an attorney, having business with me, and calling at my office, and finding no one but the scrivener there, would undertake to obtain some sort of precise information from him touching my whereabouts; but without heeding his idle talk, Bartleby would remain standing immovable in the middle of the room. So after contemplating him in that position for a time, the attorney would depart, no wiser than he came.

Also, when a reference[31] was going on, and the room full of lawyers and witnesses, and business driving fast, some deeply occupied legal gentleman present, seeing Bartleby wholly unemployed, would request him to run round to his (the legal gentleman's) office and fetch some papers for him. Thereupon, Bartleby would tranquilly decline, and yet remain idle as before. Then the lawyer would give a great stare, and turn to me. And what could I say? At last I was made aware that all through the circle of my professional acquaintance, a whisper of wonder was running round, having reference to the strange creature I kept at my office. This worried me very much. And as the idea came upon me of his possibly turning out a long-lived man, and keep occupying my chambers, and denying my authority; and perplexing my visitors; and scandalising my professional reputation; and casting a general gloom over the premises; keeping soul and body together to the last upon his savings (for doubtless he spent but half a dime a day), and in the end perhaps outlive me, and claim possession of my office by right of his perpetual occupancy: as all these dark anticipations crowded upon me more and more, and my friends continually intruded their relentless remarks upon the apparition in my room; a great change was wrought in me. I resolved to gather all my faculties together, and forever rid me of this intolerable incubus.[32]

Ere revolving any complicated project, however, adapted to this end, I first simply suggested to Bartleby the propriety of his permanent departure. In a calm and serious tone, I commended the idea to his careful and mature consideration. But, having taken three days to meditate upon it, he apprised me, that his original determination remained the same; in short, that he still preferred to abide with me.

What shall I do? I now said to myself, buttoning up my coat to the last button. What shall I do? what ought I to do? what does conscience say I *should* do with this man, or, rather, ghost. Rid myself of him, I must; go, he shall. But how? You will not thrust him, the poor, pale, passive mortal—you will not thrust such a helpless creature out of your door? you will not dishonour yourself by such cruelty? No, I will not, I cannot do that. Rather would I let him live and die here, and then mason up his remains in the wall. What, then, will you do? For all your coaxing, he will not budge. Bribes he leaves under your own paperweight on your table; in short, it is quite plain that he prefers to cling to you.

Then something severe, something unusual must be done. What! surely you will not have him collared by a constable, and commit his innocent pallor to the common jail? And upon what ground could you procure such a thing to be done?

[31] The act of referring an issue or case to the Court of Chancery.
[32] Evil spirit, nightmare.

—a vagrant, is he? What! he a vagrant, a wanderer, who refuses to budge? It is because he will *not* be a vagrant, then, that you seek to count him *as* a vagrant. That is too absurd. No visible means of support; there I have him. Wrong again: for indubitably he *does* support himself, and that is the only unanswerable proof that any man can show of his possessing the means so to do. No more, then. Since he will not quit me, I must quit him. I will change my offices; I will move else-where, and give him fair notice, that if I find him on my new premises I will then proceed against him as a common trespasser.

Acting accordingly, next day I thus addressed him: 'I find these chambers too far from the City Hall; the air is unwholesome. In a word, I propose to remove my offices next week, and shall no longer require your services. I tell you this now, in order that you may seek another place.'

He made no reply, and nothing more was said.

On the appointed day I engaged carts and men, proceeded to my chambers, and, having but little furniture, everything was removed in a few hours. Through-out, the scrivener remained standing behind the screen, which I directed to be removed the last thing. It was withdrawn; and, being folded up like a huge folio, left him the motionless occupant of a naked room. I stood in the entry watching him a moment, while something from within me upbraided me.

I re-entered, with my hand in my pocket—and—and my heart in my mouth.

'Good-bye, Bartleby; I am going—good-bye, and God some way bless you; and take that,' slipping something in his hand. But it dropped upon the floor, and then—strange to say—I tore myself from him whom I had so longed to be rid of.

Established in my new quarters, for a day or two I kept the door locked, and started at every footfall in the passages. When I returned to my rooms, after any little absence, I would pause at the threshold for an instant, and attentively listen ere applying my key. But these fears were needless. Bartleby never came nigh me.

I thought all was going well, when a perturbed-looking stranger visited me, inquiring whether I was the person who had recently occupied rooms at No.— Wall Street.

Full of forebodings, I replied that I was.

'Then, sir,' said the stranger, who proved a lawyer, 'you are responsible for the man you left there. He refuses to do any copying; he refuses to do anything; he says he prefers not to; and he refuses to quit the premises.'

'I am very sorry, sir,' said I, with assumed tranquillity, but an inward tremor, 'but, really, the man you allude to is nothing to me—he is no relation or appren-tice of mine, that you should hold me responsible for him.'

'In mercy's name, who is he?'

'I certainly cannot inform you. I know nothing about him. Formerly I employed him as a copyist; but he has done nothing for me now for some time past.'

'I shall settle him, then—good morning, sir.'

Several days passed, and I heard nothing more; and, though I often felt a charitable prompting to call at the place and see poor Bartleby, yet a certain squeamishness, of I know not what, withheld me.

All is over with him, by this time, thought I, at last, when, through another week, no further intelligence reached me. But, coming to my room the day after, I found several persons waiting at my door in a high state of nervous excitement.

'That's the man—here he comes,' cried the foremost one, whom I recognised as the lawyer who had previously called upon me alone.

'You must take him away, sir, at once,' cried a portly person among them, advancing upon me, and whom I knew to be the landlord of No. — Wall Street.

'These gentlemen, my tenants, cannot stand it any longer; Mr. B——,' pointing to the lawyer, 'has turned him out of his room, and he now persists in haunting the building generally, sitting upon the banisters of the stairs by day, and sleeping in the entry by night. Everybody is concerned; clients are leaving the offices; some fears are entertained of a mob; something you must do, and that without delay.'

Aghast at this torrent, I fell back before it, and would fain have locked myself in my new quarters. In vain I persisted that Bartleby was nothing to me—no more than to anyone else. In vain—I was the last person known to have anything to do with him, and they held me to the terrible account. Fearful, then, of being exposed in the papers (as one person present obscurely threatened), I considered the matter, and, at length, said, that if the lawyer would give me a confidential interview with the scrivener, in his (the lawyer's) own room, I would, that afternoon, strive my best to rid them of the nuisance they complained of.

Going upstairs to my old haunt, there was Bartleby silently sitting upon the banister at the landing.

'What are you doing here, Bartleby?' said I.

'Sitting upon the banister,' he mildly replied.

I motioned him into the lawyer's room, who then left us.

'Bartleby,' said I, 'are you aware that you are the cause of great tribulation to me, by persisting in occupying the entry after being dismissed from the office?'

No answer.

'Now one of two things must take place. Either you must do something, or something must be done to you. Now what sort of business would you like to engage in? Would you like to re-engage in copying for someone?'

'No; I would prefer not to make any change.'

'Would you like a clerkship in a dry-goods store?'

'There is too much confinement about that. No, I would not like a clerkship; but I am not particular.'

'Too much confinement,' I cried, 'why, you keep yourself confined all the time!'

'I would prefer not to take a clerkship,' he rejoined, as if to settle that little item at once.

'How would a bar-tender's business suit you? There is no trying of the eyesight in that.'

'I would not like it at all; though, as I said before, I am not particular.'

His unwonted wordiness inspirited me. I returned to the charge.

'Well, then would you like to travel through the country collecting bills for the merchants? That would improve your health.'

'No, I would prefer to be doing something else.'

'How, then would going as a companion to Europe, to entertain some young gentleman with your conversation—How would that suit you?'

'Not at all. It does not strike me that there is anything definite about that. I like to be stationary. But I am not particular.'

'Stationary you shall be, then,' I cried, now losing all patience, and, for the first time in all my exasperating connection with him, fairly flying into a passion. 'If you do not go away from these premises before night, I shall feel bound—indeed, I *am* bound—to—to quit the premises myself!' I rather absurdly concluded, knowing not with what possible threat to try to frighten his immobility into compliance. Despairing of all further efforts, I was precipitately leaving him, when a final thought occurred to me—one which had not been wholly unindulged before.

'Bartleby,' said I, in the kindest tone I could assume under such exciting circumstances, 'will you go home with me now—not to my office, but my dwelling—and remain there till we can conclude upon some convenient arrangement for you at our leisure? Come, let us start now, right away.'

'No; at present I would prefer not to make any change at all.'

I answered nothing; but, effectually dodging everyone by the suddenness and rapidity of my flight, rushed from the building, ran up Wall Street toward Broadway, and, jumping into the first omnibus,[33] was soon removed from pursuit. As soon as tranquillity returned, I distinctly perceived that I had now done all that I possibly could, both in respect to the demands of the landlord and his tenants, and with regard to my own desire and sense of duty, to benefit Bartleby, and shield him from rude persecution. I now strove to be entirely carefree and quiescent; and my conscience justified me in the attempt; though, indeed, it was not so successful as I could have wished. So fearful was I of being again hunted out by the incensed landlord and his exasperated tenants, that, surrendering my business to Nippers, for a few days, I drove about the upper part of the town and through the suburbs, in my rockaway;[34] crossed over to Jersey City and Hoboken, and paid fugitive visits to Manhattanville and Astoria. In fact, I almost lived in my rockaway for the time.

When again I entered my office, lo, a note from the landlord lay upon the desk. I opened it with trembling hands. It informed me that the writer had sent to the police, and had Bartleby removed to the Tombs as a vagrant. Moreover, since I knew more about him than anyone else, he wished me to appear at that place, and make a suitable statement of the facts. These tidings had a conflicting effect upon me. At first I was indignant; but, at last, almost approved. The landlord's energetic, summary disposition had led him to adopt a procedure which I do not think I would have decided upon myself; and yet, as a last resort, under such peculiar circumstances, it seemed the only plan.

As I afterward learned, the poor scrivener, when told that he must be conducted to the Tombs, offered not the slightest obstacle, but, in his pale, unmoving way, silently acquiesced.

Some of the compassionate and curious bystanders joined the party; and headed by one of the constables arm in arm with Bartleby, the silent procession filed its way through all that noise, and heat, and joy of the roaring thoroughfares at noon.

The same day I received the note, I went to the Tombs, or, to speak more properly, the Halls of Justice. Seeking the right officer, I stated the purpose of my call, and was informed that the individual I described was, indeed, within. I then assured the functionary that Bartleby was a perfectly honest man, and greatly to be compassionated, however unaccountably eccentric. I narrated all I knew, and closed by suggesting the idea of letting him remain in as indulgent confinement as possible, till something less harsh might be done though, indeed, I hardly knew what. At all events, if nothing else could be decided upon, the almshouse[35] must receive him. I then begged to have an interview.

Being under no disgraceful charge, and quite serene and harmless in all his ways, they had permitted him freely to wander about the prison, and, especially, in the enclosed grass-platted yards thereof. And so I found him there, standing all alone in the quietest of the yards, his face toward a high wall, while all around,

[33] A four-wheeled carriage.   [34] A light, open carriage.
[35] Poorhouse.

from the narrow slits of the jail windows, I thought I saw peering out upon him the eyes of murderers and thieves.

'Bartleby!'

'I know you,' he said, without looking round—'and I want nothing to say to you.'

'It was not I that brought you here, Bartleby,' said I, keenly pained at his implied suspicion. 'And to you, this should not be so vile a place. Nothing reproachful attaches to you by being here. And see, it is not so sad a place as one might think. Look, there is the sky, and here is the grass.'

'I know where I am,' he replied, but would say nothing more, and so I left him.

As I entered the corridor again, a broad meat-like man, in an apron, accosted me, and jerking his thumb over his shoulder, said, 'Is that your friend?'

'Yes.'

'Does he want to starve? If he does, let him live on the prison fare, that's all.'

'Who are you?' asked I, not knowing what to make of such an unofficially speaking person in such a place.

'I am the grub-man.[36] Such gentlemen as have friends here, hire me to provide them with something good to eat.'

'Is this so?' said I, turning to the turnkey.[37]

He said it was.

'Well, then,' said I, slipping some silver into the grub-man's hands (for so they called him), 'I want you to give particular attention to my friend there; let him have the best dinner you can get. And you must be as polite to him as possible.'

'Introduce me, will you?' said the grub-man, looking at me with an expression which seemed to say he was all impatience for an opportunity to give a specimen of his breeding.

Thinking it would prove of benefit to the scrivener, I acquiesced; and, asking the grub-man his name, went up with him to Bartleby.

'Bartleby, this is a friend; you will find him very useful to you.'

'Your sarvant, sir, your sarvant,' said the grub-man, making a low salutation behind his apron. 'Hope you find it pleasant here, sir; nice grounds—cool apartments—hope you'll stay with us some time—try to make it agreeable. What will you have for dinner to-day?'

'I prefer not to dine to-day,' said Bartleby, turning away. 'It would disagree with me; I am unused to dinners.' So saying, he slowly moved to the other side of the enclosure, and took up a position fronting the dead-wall.

'How's this?' said the grub-man, addressing me with a stare of astonishment. 'He's odd, ain't he?'

'I think he is a little deranged,' said I sadly.

'Deranged? deranged is it? Well, now, upon my word, I thought that friend of yourn was a gentleman forger; they are always pale and genteel-like, them forgers. I can't help pity 'em—can't help it, sir. Did you know Monroe Edwards?'[38] he added touchingly, and paused. Then, laying his hand piteously on my shoulder, sighed, 'he died of consumption at Sing-Sing.[39] So you weren't acquainted with Monroe?'

---

[36] An individual who provides prisoners with food, for a price.
[37] A jailor who has charge of the keys of a prison.
[38] Monroe Edwards (1808–1847), a swindler and forger whose 1842 trial had created a great deal of public excitement in New York City.
[39] The state prison built in 1825 at Ossining, a town on the Hudson River north of New York City.

'No, I was never socially acquainted with any forgers. But I cannot stop longer. Look to my friend yonder. You will not lose by it. I will see you again.'

Some few days after this, I again obtained admission to the Tombs, and went through the corridors in quest of Bartleby; but without finding him.

'I saw him coming from his cell not long ago,' said a turnkey, 'maybe he's gone to loiter in the yards.'

So I went in that direction.

'Are you looking for the silent man?' said another turnkey, passing me. 'Yonder he lies—sleeping in the yard there. 'Tis not twenty minutes since I saw him lie down.'

The yard was entirely quiet. It was not accessible to the common prisoners. The surrounding walls, of amazing thickness, kept off all sounds behind them. The Egyptian character of the masonry weighed upon me with its gloom. But a soft imprisoned turf grew under foot. The heart of the eternal pyramids, it seemed, wherein, by some strange magic, through the clefts, grass-seed, dropped by birds, had sprung.

Strangely huddled at the base of the wall, his knees drawn up, and lying on his side, his head touching the cold stones, I saw the wasted Bartleby. But nothing stirred. I paused; then went close up to him; stooped over, and saw that his dim eyes were open; otherwise he seemed profoundly sleeping. Something prompted me to touch him. I felt his hand, when a tingling shiver ran up my arm and down my spine to my feet.

The round face of the grub-man peered upon me now. 'His dinner is ready. Won't he dine to-day, either? Or does he live without dining?'

'Lives without dining,' said I, and closed the eyes.

'Eh! He's asleep, ain't he?'

'With kings and counsellors,'[40] murmured I.

*   *   *   *   *   *   *   *

There would seem little need for proceeding further in this history. Imagination will readily supply the meagre recital of poor Bartleby's interment. But, ere parting with the reader, let me say, that if this little narrative has sufficiently interested him, to awaken curiosity as to who Bartleby was, and what manner of life he led prior to the present narrator's making his acquaintance, I can only reply, that in such curiosity I fully share, but am wholly unable to gratify it. Yet here I hardly know whether I should divulge one little item of rumour, which came to my ear a few months after the scrivener's decease. Upon what basis it rested I could never ascertain; and hence, how true it is I cannot now tell. But, inasmuch as this vague report has not been without a certain suggestive interest to me, however sad, it may prove the same with some others; and so I will briefly mention it. The report was this: that Bartleby had been a subordinate clerk in the Dead Letter Office at Washington, from which he had been suddenly removed by a change in the administration. When I think over this rumour, hardly can I express the emotions which seize me. Dead letters! does it not sound like dead men? Conceive a man by nature and misfortune prone to a pallid hopelessness, can any business seem more fitted to heighten it than that of continually handling these dead letters, and assorting them for the flames? For by the cartload they are annually burned. Sometimes from out the folded paper the pale clerk takes a

[40] See Job 3:11–16.

ring— the finger it was meant for, perhaps, moulders in the grave; a bank-note sent in swiftest charity—he whom it would relieve, nor eats nor hungers any more; pardon for those died despairing; hope for those who died unhoping; good tidings for those who died stifled by unrelieved calamities. On errands of life, these letters speed to death.

   Ah, Bartleby! Ah, humanity!

[1863]

Samuel L. Clemens (Mark Twain)   *1835–1910*

THE CELEBRATED JUMPING FROG
OF CALAVERAS COUNTY

In compliance with the request of a friend of mine, who wrote me from the East, I called on good-natured, garrulous old Simon Wheeler, and inquired after my friend's friend, Leonidas W. Smiley, as requested to do, and I hereunto append the result. I have a lurking suspicion that *Leonidas W.* Smiley is a myth; that my friend never knew such a personage; and that he only conjectured that if I asked old Wheeler about him, it would remind him of his infamous *Jim* Smiley, and he would go to work and bore me to death with some exasperating reminiscence of him as long and as tedious as it should be useless to me. If that was the design, it succeeded.

I found Simon Wheeler dozing comfortably by the bar-room stove of the dilapidated tavern in the decayed mining camp of Angel's,[1] and I noticed that he was fat and bald-headed, and had an expression of winning gentleness and simplicity upon his tranquil countenance. He roused up, and gave me good day. I told him that a friend of mine had commissioned me to make some inquiries about a cherished companion of his boyhood named *Leonidas W.* Smiley—*Rev. Leonidas W.* Smiley, a young minister of the Gospel, who he had heard was at one time a resident of Angel's Camp. I added that if Mr. Wheeler could tell me anything about this Rev. Leonidas W. Smiley, I would feel under many obligations to him.

Simon Wheeler backed me into a corner and blockaded me there with his chair, and then sat down and reeled off the monotonous narrative which follows this paragraph. He never smiled, he never frowned, he never changed his voice from the gentle-flowing key to which he tuned his initial sentence, he never betrayed the slightest suspicion of enthusiasm; but all through the interminable narrative there ran a vein of impressive earnestness and sincerity, which showed me plainly that, so far from his imagining that there was anything ridiculous or funny about his story, he regarded it as a really important matter, and admired its two heroes as men of transcendent genius in *finesse*. I let him go on in his own way, and never interrupted him once.

"Rev. Leonidas W. H'm, Reverend Le—well, there was a feller here once by the name of *Jim* Smiley, in the winter of '49—or maybe it was the spring of '50—I don't recollect exactly, somehow, though what makes me think it was one or the other is because I remember the big flume[2] warn't finished when he first come to the camp; but anyway, he was the curiousest man about always betting on anything that turned up you ever see, if he could get anybody to bet on the other side; and if he couldn't he'd change sides. Any way that suited the other man would suit *him*—any way just so's he got a bet, *he* was satisfied. But still he was lucky, uncommon lucky; he most always come out winner. He was always ready and laying for a chance; there couldn't be no solit'ry thing mentioned but that feller'd offer to bet on it, and take ary side you please, as I was just telling you. If there was a horse-race, you'd find him flush or you'd find him busted at the end of it; if there was a dog-fight, he'd bet on it; if there was a cat-fight, he'd bet on it; if there was

---

[1] An early mining camp in Calaveras County, California, northeast of San Francisco.
[2] A slanting wooden trough through which water is directed during the placer mining of gold.

a chicken-fight, he'd bet on it; why, if there was two birds setting on a fence, he would bet you which one would fly first; or if there was a camp-meeting, he would be there reg'lar to bet on Parson Walker, which he judged to be the best exhorter about here, and so he was too, and a good man. If he even see a straddle-bug start to go anywheres, he would bet you how long it would take him to get to—to wherever he was going to, and if you took him up, he would foller that straddle-bug to Mexico but what he would find out where he was bound for and how long he was on the road. Lots of the boys here has seen that Smiley, and can tell you about him. Why, it never made no difference to *him*—he'd bet on *any* thing—the dangdest feller. Parson Walker's wife laid very sick once, for a good while, and it seemed as if they warn't going to save her; but one morning he come in, and Smiley up and asked him how she was, and he said she was considerable better— thank the Lord for his inf'nite mercy—and coming on so smart that with the blessing of Prov'dence she'd get well yet; and Smiley, before he thought, says, "Well, I'll resk two-and-a-half she don't anyway.'

"Thish-yer Smiley had a mare—the boys called her the fifteen-minute nag, but that was only in fun, you know, because of course she was faster than that—and he used to win money on that horse, for all she was so slow and always had the asthma, or the distemper, or the consumption, or something of that kind. They used to give her two or three hundred yards' start, and then pass her under way; but always at the fag end of the race she'd get excited and desperate like, and come cavorting and straddling up, and scattering her legs around limber, some-times in the air, and sometimes out to one side among the fences, and kicking up m-o-r-e dust and raising m-o-r-e racket with her coughing and sneezing and blow-ing her nose—and *always* fetch up at the stand just about a neck ahead, as near as you could cipher it down.

"And he had a little small bull-pup, that to look at him you'd think he warn't worth a cent but to set around and look ornery and lay for a chance to steal something. But as soon as money was up on him he was a different dog; his under-jaw'd begin to stick out like the fo'castle of a steamboat, and his teeth would uncover and shine like the furnaces. And a dog might tackle him and bully-rag him, and bite him, and throw him over his shoulder two or three times, and Andrew Jackson[3]—which was the name of the pup—Andrew Jackson would never let on but what *he* was satisfied, and hadn't expected nothing else—and the bets being doubled and doubled on the other side all the time, till the money was all up; and then all of a sudden he would grab that other dog jest by the j'int of his hind leg and freeze to it—not chaw, you understand, but only just grip and hang on till they throwed up the sponge, if it was a year. Smiley always come out winner on that pup, till he harnessed a dog once that didn't have no hind legs, because they'd been sawed off in a circular saw, and when the thing had gone along far enough, and the money was all up, and he come to make a snatch for his pet holt, he see in a minute how he'd been imposed on, and how the other dog had him in the door, so to speak, and he 'peared surprised, and then he looked sorter discouraged-like, and didn't try no more to win the fight, and so he got shucked out bad. He give Smiley a look, as much as to say his heart was broke, and it was *his* fault, for putting up a dog that hadn't no hind legs for him to take holt of, which was his main dependence in a fight, and then he limped off a piece and laid down and died. It was a good pup, was that Andrew Jackson, and would have made a name for hisself if he'd live, for the stuff was in him and he had genius—I know

---

[3] Andrew Jackson (1767–1845), the seventh president of the United States.

it, because he hadn't no opportunities to speak of, and it don't stand to reason that a dog could make such a fight as he could under them circumstances if he hadn't no talent. It always makes me feel sorry when I think of that last fight of his'n, and the way it turned out.

"Well, thish-yer Smiley had rat-tarriers, and chicken cocks, and tomcats and all them kind of things, till you couldn't rest, and you couldn't fetch nothing for him to bet on but he'd match you. He ketched a frog one day, and took him home, and said he cal'lated to educate him; and so he never done nothing for three months but set in his back yard and learn that frog to jump. And you bet you he *did* learn him, too. He'd give him a little punch behind, and the next minute you'd see that frog whirling in the air like a doughnut—see him turn one summerset, or maybe a couple, if he got a good start, and come down flat-footed and all right, like a cat. He got him up so in the matter of ketching flies, and kep' him in practice so constant, that he'd nail a fly every time as fur as he could see him. Smiley said all a frog wanted was education, and he could do 'most anything—and I believe him. Why, I've seen him set Dan'l Webster[4] down here on this floor— Dan'l Webster was the name of the frog—and sing out, "Flies, Dan'l, flies!" and quicker'n you could wink he'd spring straight up and snake a fly off'n the counter there, and flop down on the floor ag'in as solid as a gob of mud, and fall to scratching the side of his head with his hind foot as indifferent as if he hadn't no idea he'd been doin' any more'n any frog might do. You never see a frog so modest and straightfor'ard as he was, for all he was so gifted. And when it come to fair and square jumping on a dead level, he could get over more ground at one straddle than any animal of his breed you ever see. Jumping on a dead level was his strong suit, you understand; and when it come to that, Smiley would ante up money on him as long as he had a red.[5] Smiley was monstrous proud of his frog, and well he might be, for fellers that had traveled and been everywheres all said he laid over any frog that ever *they* see.

"Well, Smiley kep' the beast in a little lattice box, and he used to fetch him down-town sometimes and lay for a bet. One day a feller—a stranger in the camp, he was—come acrost him with his box, and says:

" 'What might it be that you've got in the box?'

"And Smiley says, sorter indifferent-like, 'It might be a parrot, or it might be a canary, maybe, but it ain't—it's only just a frog.'

"And the feller took it, and looked at it careful, and turned it round this way and that, and says, 'H'm—so 'tis. Well, what's *he* good for?'

" 'Well,' Smiley says, easy and careless, 'he's good enough for *one* thing, I should judge—he can outjump any frog in Calaveras County.'

"The feller took the box again, and took another long, particular look, and give it back to Smiley, and says, very deliberate, 'Well,' he says, 'I don't see no p'ints about that frog that's any better'n any other frog.'

" 'Maybe you don't,' Smiley says. 'Maybe you understand frogs and maybe you don't understand 'em; maybe you've had experience, and maybe you ain't only a amature, as it were. Anyways, I've got *my* opinion, and I'll resk forty dollars that he can outjump any frog in Calaveras County.'

"And the feller studied a minute, and then says, kinder sadlike, 'Well, I'm only a stranger here, and I ain't got no frog; but if I had a frog, I'd bet you.'

"And then Smiley says, 'That's all right—that's all right—if you'll hold my box

[4] Daniel Webster (1782–1852), the U.S. senator from Massachusetts.
[5] A "red cent," or penny.

a minute, I'll go and get you a frog.' And so the feller took the box, and put up his forty dollars along with Smiley's, and set down to wait.

"So he set there a good while thinking and thinking to himself, and then he got the frog out and prized his mouth open and took a teaspoon and filled him full of quail-shot—filled him pretty near up to his chin—and set him on the floor. Smiley he went to the swamp and slopped around in the mud for a long time, and finally he fetched a frog, and fetched him in, and give him to this feller, and says:

" 'Now, if you're ready, set him alongside of Dan'l, with his fore paws just even with Dan'l's, and I'll give the word.' Then he says, 'One—two—three—*git!*' and him and the feller touched up the frogs from behind, and the new frog hopped off lively, but Dan'l give a heave, and hysted up his shoulders—so—like a Frenchman, but it warn't no use—he couldn't budge; he was planted as solid as a church, and he couldn't no more stir than if he was anchored out. Smiley was a good deal surprised, and he was disgusted too, but he didn't have no idea what the matter was, of course.

"The feller took the money and started away; and when he was going out at the door, he sorter jerked his thumb over his shoulder—so—at Dan'l, and says again, very deliberate, 'Well,' he says, '*I* don't see no p'ints about that frog that's any better'n any other frog.'

"Smiley he stood scratching his head and looking down at Dan'l a long time, and at last he says, 'I do wonder what in the nation that frog throw'd off for—I wonder if there ain't something the matter with him—he 'pears to look mighty baggy, somehow.' And he ketched Dan'l by the nap of the neck, and hefted him, and says, 'Why blame my cats if he don't weigh five pound!' and turned him upside down and he belched out a double handful of shot. And then he see how it was, and he was the maddest man—he set the frog down and took out after that feller, but he never ketched him. And—"

[Here Simon Wheeler heard his name called from the front yard, and got up to see what was wanted.] And turning to me as he moved away, he said: "Just set where you are, stranger, and rest easy—I ain't going to be gone a second."

But, by your leave, I did not think that a continuation of the history of the enterprising vagabond *Jim* Smiley would be likely to afford me much information concerning the Rev. *Leonidas W.* Smiley, and so I started away.

At the door I met the sociable Wheeler returning, and he buttonholed me and recommenced:

"Well, thish-yer Smiley had a yaller one-eyed cow that didn't have no tail, only just a short stump like a bannanner, and—"

However, lacking both time and inclination, I did not wait to hear about the afflicted cow, but took my leave.

[1865]

Henry James   *1843–1916*

FOUR MEETINGS

I saw her but four times, though I remember them vividly; she made her impression on me. I thought her very pretty and very interesting—a touching specimen of a type with which I had had other and perhaps less charming associations. I'm sorry to hear of her death, and yet when I think of it why *should* I be? The last time I saw her she was certainly not—! But it will be of interest to take our meetings in order.

I

The first was in the country, at a small tea-party, one snowy night of some seventeen years ago. My friend Latouche, going to spend Christmas with his mother, had insisted on my company, and the good lady had given in our honour the entertainment of which I speak. To me it was really full of savour—it had all the right marks: I had never been in the depths of New England at that season. It had been snowing all day and the drifts were knee-high. I wondered how the ladies had made their way to the house; but I inferred that just those general rigours rendered any assembly offering the attraction of two gentlemen from New York worth a desperate effort.

Mrs. Latouche in the course of the evening asked me if I "didn't want to" show the photographs to some of the young ladies. The photographs were in a couple of great portfolios, and had been brought home by her son, who, like myself, was lately returned from Europe. I looked round and was struck with the fact that most of the young ladies were provided with an object of interest more absorbing than the most vivid sun-picture. But there was a person alone near the mantel-shelf who looked round the room with a small vague smile, a discreet, a disguised yearning, which seemed somehow at odds with her isolation. I looked at her a moment and then chose. "I should like to show them to that young lady."

"Oh yes," said Mrs. Latouche, "she's just the person. She doesn't care for flirting—I'll speak to her." I replied that if she didn't care for flirting she wasn't perhaps just the person; but Mrs. Latouche had already, with a few steps, appealed to her participation. "She's delighted," my hostess came back to report; "and she's just the person—so quiet and so bright." And she told me the young lady was by name Miss Caroline Spencer—with which she introduced me.

Miss Caroline Spencer was not quite a beauty, but was none the less, in her small odd way, formed to please. Close upon thirty, by every presumption, she was made almost like a little girl and had the complexion of a child. She had also the prettiest head, on which her hair was arranged as nearly as possible like the hair of a Greek bust, though indeed it was to be doubted if she had ever seen a Greek bust. She was "artistic," I suspected, so far as the polar influences of North Verona could allow for such yearnings or could minister to them. Her eyes were perhaps just too round and too inveterately surprised, but her lips had a certain mild decision and her teeth, when she showed them, were charming. About her neck she wore what ladies call, I believe, a "ruche"[1] fastened with a very small pin of

---

[1] A ruffle or pleat of lace or silk.

pink coral, and in her hand she carried a fan made of plaited straw and adorned with pink ribbon. She wore a scanty black silk dress. She spoke with slow soft neatness, even without smiles showing the prettiness of her teeth, and she seemed extremely pleased, in fact quite fluttered, at the prospect of my demonstrations. These went forward very smoothly after I had moved the portfolios out of their corner and placed a couple of chairs near a lamp. The photographs were usually things I knew—large views of Switzerland, Italy and Spain, landscapes, reproductions of famous buildings, pictures and statues. I said what I could for them, and my companion, looking at them as I held them up, sat perfectly still, her straw fan raised to her under-lip and gently, yet, as I could feel, almost excitedly, rubbing it. Occasionally, as I laid one of the pictures down, she said without confidence, which would have been too much: "Have you seen that place?" I usually answered that I had seen it several times—I had been a great traveller, though I was somehow particularly admonished not to swagger—and then I felt her look at me askance for a moment with her pretty eyes. I had asked her at the outset whether she had been to Europe; to this she had answered "No, no, no"—almost as much below her breath as if the image of such an event scarce, for solemnity, brooked phrasing. But after that, though she never took her eyes off the pictures, she said so little that I feared she was at last bored. Accordingly when we had finished one portfolio I offered, if she desired it, to desist. I rather guessed the exhibition really held her, but her reticence puzzled me and I wanted to make her speak. I turned round to judge better and then saw a faint flush in each of her cheeks. She kept waving her little fan to and fro. Instead of looking at me she fixed her eyes on the remainder of the collection, which leaned, in its receptacle, against the table.

"Won't you show me that?" she quavered, drawing the long breath of a person launched and afloat but conscious of rocking a little.

"With pleasure," I answered, "if you're really not tired."

"Oh I'm not tired a bit. I'm just fascinated." With which as I took up the other portfolio she laid her hand on it, rubbing it softly. "And have you been here too?"

On my opening the portfolio it appeared I had indeed been there. One of the first photographs was a large view of the Castle of Chillon by the Lake of Geneva. "Here," I said, "I've been many a time. Isn't it beautiful?" And I pointed to the perfect reflexion of the rugged rocks and pointed towers in the clear still water. She didn't say "Oh enchanting!" and push it away to see the next picture. She looked a while and then asked if it weren't where Bonnivard, about whom Byron wrote, had been confined. I assented, trying to quote Byron's verses, but not quite bringing it off.

She fanned herself a moment and then repeated the lines correctly, in a soft flat voice but with charming conviction. By the time she had finished, she was nevertheless blushing. I complimented her and assured her she was perfectly equipped for visiting Switzerland and Italy. She looked at me askance again, to see if I might be serious, and I added that if she wished to recognise Byron's descriptions she must go abroad speedily—Europe was getting sadly dis-Byronised. "How soon must I go?" she thereupon enquired.

"Oh I'll give you ten years."

"Well, I guess I can go in *that* time," she answered as if measuring her words.

"Then you'll enjoy it immensely," I said; "you'll find it of the highest interest." Just then I came upon a photograph of some nook in a foreign city which I had been very fond of and which recalled tender memories. I discoursed (as I suppose) with considerable spirit; my companion sat listening breathless.

"Have you been *very* long over there?" she asked some time after I had ceased.

"Well, it mounts up, put all the times together."

"And have you travelled everywhere?"

"I've travelled a good deal. I'm very fond of it and happily have been able."

Again she turned on me her slow shy scrutiny. "Do you know the foreign languages?"

"After a fashion."

"Is it hard to speak them?"

"I don't imagine you'd find it so," I gallantly answered.

"Oh I shouldn't want to speak—I should only want to listen." Then on a pause she added: "They say the French theatre's so beautiful."

"Ah the best in the world."

"Did you go there very often?"

"When I was first in Paris I went every night."

"Every night!" And she opened her clear eyes very wide. "That to me is"—and her expression hovered—"as if you tell me a fairy-tale." A few minutes later she put to me: "And which country do you prefer?"

"There's one I love beyond any. I think you'd do the same."

Her gaze rested as on a dim revelation and then she breathed "Italy?"

"Italy," I answered softly too; and for a moment we communed over it. She looked as pretty as if instead of showing her photographs I had been making love to her. To increase the resemblance she turned off blushing. It made a pause which she broke at last by saying: "That's the place which—in particular—I thought of going to."

"Oh that's the place—that's the place!" I laughed.

She looked at two or three more views in silence. "They say it's not very dear."

"As some other countries? Well, one gets back there one's money. That's not the least of the charms."

"But it's *all* very expensive, isn't it?"

"Europe, you mean?"

"Going there and travelling. That has been the trouble. I've very little money. I teach, you know," said Miss Caroline Spencer.

"Oh of course one must have money," I allowed; "but one can manage with a moderate amount judiciously spent."

"I think I should manage. I've saved and saved up, and I'm always adding a little to it. It's all for that." She paused a moment, and then went on with suppressed eagerness, as if telling me the story were a rare, but possibly an impure satisfaction. "You see it hasn't been only the money—it has been everything. Everything has acted against it. I've waited and waited. It has been my castle in the air. I'm almost afraid to talk about it. Two or three times it has come a little nearer, and then I've talked about it and it has melted away. I've talked about it too much," she said hypocritically—for I saw such talk was now a small tremulous ecstasy. "There's a lady who's a great friend of mine—she doesn't want to go, but I'm always at her about it. I think I must tire her dreadfully. She told me just the other day she didn't know what would become of me. She guessed I'd go crazy if I didn't sail, and yet certainly I'd go crazy if I did."

"Well," I laughed, "you haven't sailed up to now—so I suppose you *are* crazy."

She took everything with the same seriousness. "Well, I guess I must be. It seems as if I couldn't think of anything else—and I don't require photographs to work me up! I'm always right *on* it. It kills any interest in things nearer home—things I ought to attend to. That's a kind of craziness."

"Well then the cure for it's just to go," I smiled—"I mean the cure for this kind.

Of course you may have the other kind worse," I added—"the kind you get over there."

"Well, I've a faith that I'll go *some* time all right!" she quite elatedly cried. "I've a relative right there on the spot," she went on, "and I guess he'll know how to control me." I expressed the hope that he would, and I forget whether we turned over more photographs; but when I asked her if she had always lived just where I found her, "Oh no sir," she quite eagerly replied; "I've spent twenty-two months and a half in Boston." I met it with the inevitable joke that in this case foreign lands might prove a disappointment to her, but I quite failed to alarm her. "I know more about them than you might think"—her earnestness resisted even that. "I mean by reading—for I've really read considerable. In fact I guess I've prepared my mind about as much as you *can*—in advance. I've not only read Byron—I've read histories and guide-books and articles and lots of things. I know I shall rave about everything."

" 'Everything' is saying much, but I understand your case," I returned. "You've the great American disease, and you've got it 'bad'—the appetite, morbid and monstrous, for colour and form, for the picturesque and the romantic at any price. I don't know whether we come into the world with it—with the germs implanted and antecedent to experience; rather perhaps we catch it early, almost before developed consciousness—we *feel*, as we look about, that we're going (to save our souls, or at least our senses) to be thrown back on it hard. We're like travellers in the desert—deprived of water and subject to the terrible mirage, the torment of illusion, of the thirst-fever. They hear the splash of fountains, they see green gardens and orchards that are hundreds of miles away. So we with *our* thirst—except that with us it's *more* wonderful: we have before us the beautiful old things we've never seen at all, and when we do at last see them—if we're lucky!—we simply recognize them. What experience does is merely to confirm and consecrate our confident dream."

She listened with her rounded eyes. "The way you express it's too lovely, and I'm sure it will be just like that. I've dreamt of everything—I'll know it all!"

"I'm afraid," I pretended for harmless comedy, "that you've wasted a great deal of time."

"Oh yes, that has been my great wickedness!" The people about us had begun to scatter; they were taking their leave. She got up and put out her hand to me, timidly, but as if quite shining and throbbing.

"I'm going back there—one *has* to," I said as I shook hands with her. "I shall look out for you."

Yes, she fairly glittered with her fever of excited faith. "Well, I'll tell you if I'm disappointed." And she left me, fluttering all expressively her little straw fan.

II

A few months after this I crossed the sea eastward again and some three years elapsed. I had been living in Paris and, toward the end of October, went from that city to the Havre, to meet a pair of relatives who had written me they were about to arrive there. On reaching the Havre I found the steamer already docked—I was two or three hours late. I repaired directly to the hotel, where my travellers were duly established. My sister had gone to bed, exhausted and disabled by her voyage; she was the unsteadiest of sailors and her sufferings on this occasion had been extreme. She desired for the moment undisturbed rest and was able to see me but five minutes—long enough for us to agree to stop over, restoratively, till the morrow. My brother-in-law, anxious about his wife, was unwilling to leave her room; but she insisted on my taking him a walk for aid to recovery of his spirits and his land-legs.

The early autumn day was warm and charming, and our stroll through the bright-coloured busy streets of the old French seaport beguiling enough. We walked along the sunny noisy quays and then turned into a wide pleasant street which lay half in sun and half in shade—a French provincial street that resembled an old water-colour drawing: tall grey step-roofed red-gabled many-storied houses; green shutters on windows and old scroll-work above them; flowerpots in balconies and white-capped women in doorways. We walked in the shade; all this stretched away on the sunny side of the vista and made a picture. We looked at it as we passed along; then suddenly my companion stopped—pressing my arm and staring. I followed his gaze and saw that we had paused just before reaching a café where, under an awning, several tables and chairs were disposed upon the pavement. The windows were open behind; half a dozen plants in tubs were ranged beside the door; the pavement was besprinkled with clean bran. It was a dear little quiet old-world café; inside, in the comparative dusk, I saw a stout handsome woman, who had pink ribbons in her cap, perched up with a mirror behind her back and smiling at some one placed out of sight. This, to be exact, I noted afterwards; what I first observed was a lady seated alone, outside, at one of the little marble-topped tables. My brother-in-law had stopped to look at her. Something had been put before her, but she only leaned back, motionless and with her hands folded, looking down the street and away from us. I saw her but in diminished profile; nevertheless I was sure I knew on the spot that we must already have met.

"The little lady of the steamer!" my companion cried.

"Was she on your steamer?" I asked with interest.

"From morning till night. She was never sick. She used to sit perpetually at the side of the vessel with her hands crossed that way, looking at the eastward horizon."

"And are you going to speak to her?"

"I don't know her, I never made acquaintance with her. I wasn't in form to make up to ladies. But I used to watch her and—I don't know why—to be interested in her. She's a dear little Yankee woman. I've an idea she's a school-mistress taking a holiday—for which her scholars have made up a purse."

She had now turned her face a little more into profile, looking at the steep grey house-fronts opposite. On this I decided. "I shall speak to her myself."

"I wouldn't—she's very shy," said my brother-in-law.

"My dear fellow, I know her. I once showed her photographs at a tea-party." With which I went up to her, making her, as she turned to look at me, leave me in no doubt of her identity. Miss Caroline Spencer had achieved her dream. But she was less quick to recognise me and showed a slight bewilderment. I pushed a chair to the table and sat down. "Well," I said, "I hope you're not disappointed!"

She stared, blushing a little—then gave a small jump and placed me. "It was you who showed me the photographs—at North Verona."

"Yes, it was I. This happens very charmingly, for isn't it quite proper for me to give you a formal reception here—the official welcome? I talked to you so much about Europe."

"You didn't say too much. I'm so intensely happy!" she declared.

Very happy indeed she looked. There was no sign of her being older; she was as gravely, decently, demurely pretty as before. If she had struck me then as a thin-stemmed mild-hued flower of Puritanism it may be imagined whether in her present situation this clear bloom was less appealing. Beside her an old gentleman was drinking absinthe; behind her the *dame de comptoir*[2] in the pink ribbons called "Alcibiade, Alcibiade!" to the long-aproned waiter. I explained to Miss Spencer that the gentleman with me had lately been her shipmate, and my brother-in-law came up and was introduced to her. But she looked at him as if she had never so much as seen him, and I remembered he had told me her eyes were always fixed on the eastward horizon. She had evidently not noticed him, and, still timidly smiling, made no attempt whatever to pretend the contrary. I stayed with her on the little terrace of the café while he went back to the hotel and to his wife. I remarked to my friend that this meeting of ours at the first hour of her landing partook, among all chances, of the miraculous, but that I was delighted to be there and receive her first impressions.

"Oh I can't tell you," she said—"I feel so much in a dream. I've been sitting here an hour and I don't want to move. Everything's so delicious and romantic. I don't know whether the coffee has gone to my head—it's *so* unlike the coffee of my dead past."

"Really," I made answer, "if you're so pleased with this poor prosaic Havre you'll have no admiration left for better things. Don't spend your appreciation all the first day—remember it's your intellectual letter of credit. Remember all the beautiful places and things that are waiting for you. Remember that lovely Italy we talked about."

"I'm not afraid of running short," she said gaily, still looking at the opposite house. "I could sit here all day—just saying to myself that here I am at last. It's so dark and strange—so old and different."

"By the way then," I asked, "how come you to be encamped in this odd place? Haven't you gone to one of the inns?" For I was half-amused, half-alarmed at the good conscience with which this delicately pretty woman had stationed herself in conspicuous isolation on the edge of the sidewalk.

"My cousin brought me here and—a little while ago—left me," she returned. "You know I told you I had a relation over here. He's still here—a real cousin. Well," she pursued with unclouded candour, "he met me at the steamer this morning."

It was absurd—and the case moreover none of my business; but I felt somehow disconcerted. "It was hardly worth his while to meet you if he was to desert you so soon."

"Oh he has only left me for half an hour," said Caroline Spencer. "He has gone to get my money."

I continued to wonder. "Where *is* your money?"

She appeared seldom to laugh, but she laughed for the joy of this. "It makes me feel very fine to tell you! It's in circular notes."

"And where are your circular notes?"

"In my cousin's pocket."

This statement was uttered with such clearness of candour that—I can hardly say why—it gave me a sensible chill. I couldn't at all at the moment have justified my lapse from ease, for I knew nothing of Miss Spencer's cousin. Since he stood in that relation to her—dear respectable little person—the presumption was in his favour. But I found myself wincing at the thought that half an hour after her landing her scanty funds should have passed into his hands. "Is he to travel with you?" I asked.

[2] Barmaid.

"Only as far as Paris. He's an art-student in Paris—I've always thought that so splendid. I wrote to him that I was coming, but I never expected him to come off to the ship. I supposed he'd only just meet me at the train in Paris. It's very kind of him. But he *is*," said Caroline Spencer, "very kind—and very bright."

I felt at once a strange eagerness to see this bright kind cousin who was an art-student. "He's gone to the banker's?" I enquired.

"Yes, to the banker's. He took me to an hotel—such a queer quaint cunning little place, with a court in the middle and a gallery all round, and a lovely landlady in such a beautifully fluted cap and such a perfectly fitting dress! After a while we came out to walk to the banker's, for I hadn't any French money. But I was very dizzy from the motion of the vessel and I thought I had better sit down. He found this place for me here—then he went off to the banker's himself. I'm to wait here till he comes back."

Her story was wholly lucid and my impression perfectly wanton, but it passed through my mind that the gentleman would never come back. I settled myself in a chair beside my friend and determined to await the event. She was lost in the vision and the imagination of everything near us and about us—she observed, she recognized and admired, with a touching intensity. She noticed everything that was brought before us by the movement of the street—the peculiarities of costume, the shapes of vehicles, the big Norman horses, the fat priests, the shaven poodles. We talked of these things, and there was something charming in her freshness of perception and the way her book-nourished fancy sallied forth for the revel.

"And when your cousin comes back what are you going to do?" I went on.

For this she had, a little oddly, to think. "We don't quite know."

"When do you go to Paris? If you go by the four o'clock train I may have the pleasure of making the journey with you."

"I don't think we shall do that." So far she was prepared. "My cousin thinks I had better stay here a few days."

"Oh!" said I—and for five minutes had nothing to add. I was wondering what our absentee was, in vulgar parlance, "up to." I looked up and down the street, but saw nothing that looked like a bright and kind American art-student. At last I took the liberty of observing that the Havre was hardly a place to choose as one of the aesthetic stations of a European tour. It was a place of convenience, nothing more; a place of transit, through which transit should be rapid. I recommended her to go to Paris by the afternoon train and meanwhile to amuse herself by driving to the ancient fortress at the mouth of the harbour—that remarkable circular structure which bore the name of Francis the First and figured a sort of small Castle of Saint Angelo. (I might really have foreknown that it was to be demolished.)

She listened with much interest—then for a moment looked grave. "My cousin told me that when he returned he should have something particular to say to me, and that we could do nothing or decide nothing till I should have heard it. But I'll make him tell me right off, and then we'll go to the ancient fortress. Francis the First, did you say? Why, that's lovely. There's no hurry to get to Paris; there's plenty of time."

She smiled with her softly severe little lips as she spoke those last words, yet, looking at her with a purpose, I made out in her eyes, I thought, a tiny gleam of apprehension. "Don't tell me," I said, "that this wretched man's going to give you bad news!"

She coloured as if convicted of a hidden perversity, but she was soaring too high to drop. "Well, I guess it's a *little* bad, but I don't believe its *very* bad. At any rate I must listen to it."

I usurped an unscrupulous authority. "Look here; you didn't come to Europe to listen—you came to *see!*" But now I was sure her cousin would come back; since he had something disagreeable to say to her he'd infallibly turn up. We sat a while longer and I asked her about her plans of travel. She had them on her fingers' ends and told over the names as solemnly as a daughter of another faith might have told over the beads of a rosary: from Paris to Dijon and to Avignon, from Avignon to Marseilles and the Cornice road; thence to Genoa, to Spezia, to Pisa, to Florence, to Rome. It apparently had never occurred to her that there could be the least incommodity in her travelling alone; and since she was unprovided with a companion I of course civilly abstained from disturbing her sense of security.

At last her cousin came back. I saw him turn toward us out of a side-street, and from the moment my eyes rested on him I knew he could but be the bright, if not the kind, American art-student. He wore a slouch hat and a rusty black velvet jacket, such as I had often encountered in the Rue Bonaparte. His shirt-collar displayed a stretch of throat that at a distance wasn't strikingly statuesque. He was tall and lean, he had red hair and freckles. These items I had time to take in while he approached the café, staring at me with natural surprise from under his romantic brim. When he came up to us I immediately introduced myself as an old acquaintance of Miss Spencer's, a character she serenely permitted me to claim. He looked at me hard with a pair of small sharp eyes, then he gave me a solemn wave, in the "European" fashion, of his rather rusty sombrero.

"You weren't on the ship?" he asked.

"No, I wasn't on the ship. I've been in Europe these several years."

He bowed once more, portentously, and motioned me to be seated again. I sat down, but only for the purpose of observing him an instant—I saw it was time I should return to my sister. Miss Spencer's European protector was, by my measure, a very queer quantity. Nature hadn't shaped him for a Raphaelesque or Byronic attire, and his velvet doublet and exhibited though not columnar throat weren't in harmony with his facial attributes. His hair was cropped close to his head; his ears were large and ill-adjusted to the same. He had a lackadaisical carriage and a sentimental droop which were peculiarly at variance with his keen conscious strange-coloured eyes—of a brown that was almost red. Perhaps I was prejudiced, but I thought his eyes too shifty. He said nothing for some time; he leaned his hands on his stick and looked up and down the street. Then at last, slowly lifting the stick and pointing with it, "That's a very nice bit," he dropped with a certain flatness. He had his head to one side—he narrowed his ugly lids. I followed the direction of his stick; the object it indicated was a red cloth hung out of an old window. "Nice bit of colour," he continued; and without moving his head transferred his half-closed gaze to me. "Composes well. Fine old tone. Make a nice thing." He spoke in a charmless vulgar voice.

"I see you've a great deal of eye," I replied. "Your cousin tells me you're studying art." He looked at me in the same way, without answering, and I went on with deliberate urbanity: "I suppose you're at the studio of one of those great men." Still on this he continued to fix me, and then he named one of the greatest of that day; which led me to ask him if he liked his master.

"Do you understand French?" he returned.

"Some kinds."

He kept his little eyes on me; with which he remarked: "Je suis fou de la peinture!"[3]

"Oh I understand that kind!" I replied. Our companion laid her hand on his arm with a small pleased and fluttered movement; it was delightful to be among people who were on such easy terms with foreign tongues. I got up to take leave and asked her where, in Paris, I might have the honour of waiting on her. To what hotel would she go?

She turned to her cousin enquiringly and he favoured me again with his little languid leer. "Do you know the Hôtel des Princes?"

"I know where it is."

"Well, that's the shop."

"I congratulate you," I said to Miss Spencer. "I believe it's the best inn in the world; but, in case I should still have a moment to call on you here, where are you lodged?"

"Oh it's such a pretty name," she returned gleefully. "A la Belle Normande."

"I guess I know my way round!" her kinsman threw in; and as I left them he gave me with his swaggering head-cover a great flourish that was like the wave of a banner over a conquered field.

III

My relative, as it proved, was not sufficiently restored to leave the place by the afternoon train; so that as the autumn dusk began to fall I found myself at liberty to call at the establishment named to me by my friends. I must confess that I had spent much of the interval in wondering what the disagreeable thing was that the less attractive of these had been telling the other. The *auberge* of the Belle Normande proved an hostelry in a shady by-street, where it gave me satisfaction to think Miss Spencer must have encountered local colour in abundance. There was a crooked little court, where much of the hospitality of the house was carried on; there was a staircase climbing to bedrooms on the outer side of the wall; there was a small trickling fountain with a stucco statuette set in the midst of it; there was a little boy in a white cap and apron cleaning copper vessels at a conspicuous kitchen door; there was a chattering landlady, neatly laced, arranging apricots and grapes into an artistic pyramid upon a pink plate. I looked about, and on a green bench outside of an open door labelled Salle-à-Manger, I distinguished Caroline Spencer. No sooner had I looked at her than I was sure something had happened since the morning. Supported by the back of her bench, with her hands clasped in her lap, she kept her eyes on the other side of the court where the landlady manipulated the apricots.

But I saw that, poor dear, she wasn't thinking of apricots or even of landladies. She was staring absently, thoughtfully; on a nearer view I could have certified she had been crying. I had seated myself beside her before she was aware; then, when she had done so, she simply turned round without surprise and showed me her sad face. Something very bad indeed had happened; she was completely changed, and I immediately charged her with it. "Your cousin has been giving you bad news. You've had a horrid time."

For a moment she said nothing, and I supposed her afraid to speak lest her tears should again rise. Then it came to me that even in the few hours since my leaving her she had shed them all—which made her now intensely, stoically composed.

---

[3] "I am crazy about painting!"

"My poor cousin has been having one," she replied at last. "He has had great worries. His news was bad." Then after a dismally conscious wait: "He was in dreadful want of money."

"In want of yours, you mean?"

"Of any he could get—honourably of course. Mine *is* all—well, that's available."

Ah it was as if I had been sure from the first! "And he has taken it from you?"

Again she hung fire, but her face meanwhile was pleading. "I gave him what I had."

I recall the accent of those words as the most angelic human sound I had ever listened to—which is exactly why I jumped up almost with a sense of personal outrage. "Gracious goodness, madam, do you call that his getting it 'honourably'?"

I had gone too far—she coloured to her eyes. "We won't speak of it."

"We *must* speak of it," I declared as I dropped beside her again. "I'm your friend—upon my word I'm your protector; it seems to me you need one. What's the matter with this extraordinary person?"

She was perfectly able to say. "He's just badly in debt."

"No doubt he is! But what's the special propriety of your—in such tearing haste!—paying for that?"

"Well, he has told me all his story. I *feel* for him so much."

"So do I, if you come to that! But I hope," I roundly added, "he'll give you straight back your money."

As to this she was prompt. "Certainly he will—as soon as ever he can."

"And when the deuce will that be?"

Her lucidity maintained itself. "When he has finished his great picture."

It took me full in the face. "My dear young lady, damn his great picture! Where is this voracious man?"

It was as if she must let me feel a moment that I did push her!—though indeed, as appeared, he was just where he'd naturally be. "He's having his dinner."

I turned about and looked through the open door into the salle-à-manger. There, sure enough, alone at the end of a long table, was the object of my friend's compassion—the bright, the kind young art-student. He was dining too attentively to notice me at first, but in the act of setting down a well-emptied wine-glass he caught sight of my air of observation. He paused in his repast and, with his head on one side and his meagre jaws slowly moving, fixedly returned my gaze. Then the landlady came brushing lightly by with her pyramid of apricots.

"And that nice little plate of fruit is for him?" I wailed.

Miss Spencer glanced at it tenderly. "They seem to arrange everything so nicely!" she simply sighed.

I felt helpless and irritated. "Come now, really," I said; "do you think it right, do you think it decent, that that long strong fellow should collar your funds?" She looked away from me—I was evidently giving her pain. The case was hopeless; the long strong fellow had "interested" her.

"Pardon me if I speak of him so unceremoniously," I said. "But you're really too generous, and he hasn't, clearly, the rudiments of delicacy. He made his debts himself—he ought to pay them himself."

"He has been foolish," she obstinately said—"of course I know that. He has told me everything. We had a long talk this morning—the poor fellow threw himself on my charity. He has signed notes to a large amount."

"The more fool he!"

"He's in real distress—and it's not only himself. It's his poor young wife."

"Ah he has a poor young wife?"

"I didn't know—but he made a clean breast of it. He married two years since—secretly."

"Why secretly?"

My informant took precautions as if she feared listeners. Then with low impressiveness: "She was a Countess!"

"Are you very sure of that?"

"She has written me the most beautiful letter."

"Asking you—whom she has never seen—for money?"

"Asking me for confidence and sympathy"—Miss Spencer spoke now with spirit. "She has been cruelly treated by her family—in consequence of what she has done for him. My cousin has told me every particular, and she appeals to me in her own lovely way in the letter, which I've here in my pocket. It's such a wonderful old-world romance," said my prodigious friend. "She was a beautiful young widow—her first husband was a Count, tremendously high-born, but really most wicked, with whom she hadn't been happy and whose death had left her ruined after he had deceived her in all sorts of ways. My poor cousin, meeting her in that situation and perhaps a little too recklessly pitying her and charmed with her, found her, don't you see?"—Caroline's appeal on his head was amazing!—"but too ready to trust a better man after all she had been through. Only when her 'people,' as he says—and I do like the word!—understood she _would_ have him, poor gifted young American art-student though he simply was, because she just adored him, her great-aunt, the old Marquise, from whom she had expectations of wealth which she could yet sacrifice for her love, utterly cast her off and wouldn't so much as speak to her, much less to _him_, in their dreadful haughtiness and pride. They _can_ be haughty over here, it seems," she ineffably developed—"there's no mistake about that! It's like something in some famous old book. The family, my cousin's wife's," she by this time almost complacently wound up, "are of the oldest Provençal noblesse."

I listened half-bewildered. The poor woman positively found it so interesting to be swindled by a flower of that stock—if stock or flower or solitary grain of truth was really concerned in the matter—as practically to have lost the sense of what the forfeiture of her hoard meant for her. "My dear young lady," I groaned, "you don't want to be stripped of every dollar for such a rigmarole!"

She asserted, at this, her dignity—much as a small pink shorn lamb might have done. "It isn't a rigmarole, and I shan't be stripped. I shan't live any worse than I _have_ lived, don't you see? And I'll come back before long to stay with them. The Countess—he still gives her, he says, her title, as they do to noble widows, that is to 'dowagers,' don't you know? in England—insists on a visit from me _some_ time. So I guess for _that_ I can start afresh—and meanwhile I'll have recovered my money."

It was all too heart-breaking. "You're going home then at once?"

I felt the faint tremor of voice she heroically tried to stifle. "I've nothing left for a tour."

"You gave it _all_ up?"

"I've kept enough to take me back."

I uttered, I think, a positive howl, and at this juncture the hero of the situation, the happy proprietor of my little friend's sacred savings and of the infatuated _grande dame_ just sketched for me, reappeared with the clear consciousness of a repast bravely earned and consistently enjoyed. He stood on the threshold an instant, extracting the stone from a plump apricot he had fondly retained; then he put the apricot into his mouth and, while he let it gratefully dissolve there, stood looking at us with his long legs apart and his hands thrust into the pockets of his velvet coat. My companion got up, giving him a thin glance that I caught in its passage and which expressed at once resignation and fascination—the last dregs of her sacrifice and with it an anguish of upliftedness. Ugly vulgar pretentious dishonest as I thought him, and destitute of every grace of plausibility, he had yet appealed successfully to her eager and tender imagination. I was deeply disgusted, but I had no warrant to interfere, and at any rate felt that it would be vain. He waved his hand meanwhile with a breadth of appreciation. "Nice old court. Nice mellow old place. Nice crooked old staircase. Several pretty things."

Decidedly I couldn't stand it, and without responding I gave my hand to my friend. She looked at me an instant with her little white face and rounded eyes, and as she showed her pretty teeth I suppose she meant to smile. "Don't be sorry for me," she sublimely pleaded; "I'm very sure I shall see something of this dear old Europe yet."

I refused however to take literal leave of her—I should find a moment to come back next morning. Her awful kinsman, who had put on his sombrero again, flourished it off at me by way of a bow—on which I hurried away.

On the morrow early I did return, and in the court of the inn met the landlady, more loosely laced than in the evening. On my asking for Miss Spencer, "*Partie, monsieur,*" the good woman said. "She went away last night at ten o'clock, with her—her—not her husband, eh?—in fine her Monsieur. They went down to the American ship." I turned off—I felt the tears in my eyes. The poor girl had been some thirteen hours in Europe.

IV

I myself, more fortunate, continued to sacrifice to opportunity as I myself met it. During this period—of some five years—I lost my friend Latouche, who died of a malarious fever during a tour in the Levant. One of the first things I did on my return to America was to go up to North Verona on a consolatory visit to his poor mother. I found her in deep affliction and sat with her the whole of the morning that followed my arrival—I had come in late at night—listening to her tearful descant and singing the praises of my friend. We talked of nothing else, and our conversation ended only with the arrival of a quick little woman who drove herself up to the door in a "carry-all" and whom I saw toss the reins to the horse's back with the briskness of a startled sleeper throwing off the bedclothes. She jumped out of the carry-all and she jumped into the room. She proved to be the minister's wife and the great town-gossip, and she had evidently, in the latter capacity, a choice morsel to communicate. I was as sure of this as I was that poor Mrs. Latouche was not absolutely too bereaved to listen to her. It seemed to me discreet to retire, and I described myself as anxious for a walk before dinner.

"And by the way," I added, "if you'll tell me where my old friend Miss Spencer lives I think I'll call on her."

The minister's wife immediately responded. Miss Spencer lived in the fourth house beyond the Baptist church; the Baptist church was the one on the right, with that queer green thing over the door; they called it portico, but it looked more like an old-fashioned bedstead swung in the air. "Yes, do look up poor Caroline," Mrs. Latouche further enjoined. "It will refresh her to see a strange face."

"I should think she had had enough of strange faces!" cried the minister's wife.

"To see, I mean, a charming visitor"—Mrs. Latouche amended her phrase.

"I should think she had had enough of charming visitors!" her companion returned. "But *you* don't mean to stay ten years," she added with significant eyes on me.

"Has she a visitor of that sort?" I asked in my ignorance.

"You'll make out the sort!" said the minister's wife. "She's easily seen; she generally sits in the front yard. Only take care what you say to her, and be very sure you're polite."

"Ah she's so sensitive?"

The minister's wife jumped up and dropped me a curtsey—a most sarcastic curtsey. "That's what she is, if you please. 'Madame la Comtesse!' "

And pronouncing these titular words with the most scathing accent, the little woman seemed fairly to laugh in the face of the lady they designated. I stood staring, wondering, remembering.

"Oh I shall be very polite!" I cried; and, grasping my hat and stick, I went on my way.

I found Miss Spencer's residence without difficulty. The Baptist church was easily identified, and the small dwelling near it, of a rusty white, with a large central chimney-stack and a Virginia creeper, seemed naturally and properly the abode of a withdrawn old maid with a taste for striking effects inexpensively obtained. As I approached I slackened my pace, for I had heard that some one was always sitting in the front yard, and I wished to reconnoitre. I looked cautiously over the low white fence that separated the small garden-space from the unpaved street, but I descried nothing in the shape of a Comtesse. A small straight path led up to the crooked door-step, on either side of which was a little grass-plot fringed with currant-bushes. In the middle of the grass, right and left, was a large quince-tree, full of antiquity and contortions, and beneath one of the quince-trees were placed a small table and a couple of light chairs. On the table lay a piece of unfinished embroidery and two or three books in bright-coloured paper covers. I went in at the gate and paused halfway along the path, scanning the place for some further token of its occupant, before whom—I could hardly have said why—I hesitated abruptly to present myself. Then I saw the poor little house to be of the shabbiest and felt a sudden doubt of my right to penetrate, since curiosity had been my motive and curiosity here failed of confidence. While I demurred a figure appeared in the open doorway and stood there looking at me. I immediately recognised Miss Spencer, but she faced me as if we had never met. Gently, but gravely and timidly, I advanced to the door-step, where I spoke with an attempt at friendly banter.

"I waited for you over there to come back, but you never came."

"Waited where, sir?" she quavered, her innocent eyes rounding themselves as of old. She was much older; she looked tired and wasted.

"Well," I said, "I waited at the old French port."

She stared harder, then recognised me, smiling, flushing, clasping her two hands together. "I remember you now—I remember that day." But she stood there, neither coming out nor asking me to come in. She was embarrassed.

I too felt a little awkward while I poked at the path with my stick. "I kept looking out for you year after year."

"You mean in Europe?" she ruefully breathed.

"In Europe of course! Here apparently you're easy enough to find."

She leaned her hand against the unpainted doorpost and her head fell a little to one side. She looked at me thus without speaking, and I caught the expression visible in women's eyes when tears are rising. Suddenly she stepped out on the cracked slab of stone before her threshold and closed the door. Then her strained smile prevailed and I saw her teeth were as pretty as ever. But there had been tears too. "Have you been there ever since?" she lowered her voice to ask.

"Until three weeks ago. And you—you never came back?"

Still shining at me as she could, she put her hand behind her and reopened the door. "I'm not very polite," she said. "Won't you come in?"

"I'm afraid I incommode you."

"Oh no!"—she wouldn't hear of it now. And she pushed back the door with a sign that I should enter.

I followed her in. She led the way to a small room on the left of the narrow hall, which I supposed to be her parlour, though it was at the back of the house, and we passed the closed door of another apartment which apparently enjoyed a view of the quince-trees. This one looked out upon a small wood-shed and two clucking hens. But I thought it pretty until I saw its elegance to be of the most frugal kind; after which, presently, I thought it prettier still, for I had never seen faded chintz and old mezzotint engravings, framed in varnished autumn leaves, disposed with so touching a grace. Miss Spencer sat down on a very small section of the sofa, her hands tightly clasped in her lap. She looked ten years older, and I needn't now have felt called to insist on the facts of her person. But I still thought them interesting, and at any rate I was moved by them. She was peculiarly agitated. I tried to appear not to notice it; but suddenly, in the most inconsequent fashion—it was an irresistible echo of our concentrated passage in the old French port—I said to her: "I do incommode you. Again you're in distress."

She raised her two hands to her face and for a moment kept it buried in them. Then taking them away, "It's because you remind me," she said.

"I remind you, you mean, of that miserable day at the Havre?"

She wonderfully shook her head. "It wasn't miserable. It was delightful."

Ah, was it? my manner of receiving this must have commented. "I never was so shocked as when, on going back to your inn the next morning, I found you had wretchedly retreated."

She waited an instant, after which she said: "Please let us not speak of that."

"Did you come straight back here?" I nevertheless went on.

"I was back here just thirty days after my first start."

"And here you've remained ever since?"

"Every minute of the time."

I took it in; I didn't know what to say, and what I presently said had almost the sound of mockery. "When then are you going to make that tour?" It might be practically aggressive; but there was something that irritated me in her depths of resignation, and I wished to extort from her some expression of impatience.

She attached her eyes a moment to a small sunspot on the carpet; then she got up and lowered the window-blind a little to obliterate it. I waited, watching her with interest—as if she had still something more to give me. Well, presently, in answer to my last question, she gave it. "Never!"

"I hope at least your cousin repaid you that money," I said.

At this again she looked away from me. "I don't care for it now."

"You don't care for your money?"

"For ever going to Europe."

"Do you mean you wouldn't go if you could?"

"I can't—I can't" said Caroline Spencer. "It's all over. Everything's different. I never think of it."

"The scoundrel never repaid you then!" I cried.

"Please, please—!" she began.

But she had stopped—she was looking toward the door. There had been a rustle and a sound of steps in the hall.

I also looked toward the door, which was open and now admitted another person—a lady who paused just within the threshold. Behind her came a young man. The lady looked at me with a good deal of fixedness—long enough for me to rise to a vivid impression of herself. Then she turned to Caroline Spencer and, with a smile and a strong foreign accent, "*Pardon, ma chère!* I didn't know you had company," she said. "The gentleman came in so quietly." With which she again gave me the benefit of her attention. She was very strange, yet I was at once sure I had seen her before. Afterwards I rather put it that I had only seen ladies remarkably like her. But I had seen them very far away from North Verona, and it was the oddest of all things to meet one of them in that frame. To what quite other scene did the sight of her transport me? To some dusky landing before a shabby Parisian *quatrième*[4]—to an open door revealing a greasy ante-chamber and to Madame leaning over the banisters while she holds a faded wrapper together and bawls down to the portress to bring up her coffee. My friend's guest was a very large lady, of middle age, with a plump dead-white face and hair drawn back *à la chinoise.* She had a small penetrating eye and what is called in French *le sourire agréable.*[5] She wore an old pink cashmere dressing-gown covered with white embroideries, and, like the figure in my momentary vision, she confined it in front with a bare and rounded arm and a plump and deeply-dimpled hand.

"It's only to spick about my café," she said to her hostess with her *sourire agréable.* "I should like it served in the garden under the leetle tree."

The young man behind her had now stepped into the room, where he also stood revealed, though with rather less of a challenge. He was a gentleman of few inches but a vague importance, perhaps the leading man of the world of North Verona. He had a small pointed nose and a small pointed chin; also, as I observed, the most diminutive feet and a manner of no point at all. He looked at me foolishly and with his mouth open.

"You shall have your coffee," said Miss Spencer as if an army of cooks had been engaged in the preparation of it.

"C'est bien!" said her massive inmate. "Find your bouk"—and this personage turned to the gaping youth.

He gaped now at each quarter of the room. "My grammar, d'ye mean?"

The large lady however could but face her friend's visitor while persistently engaged with a certain laxity in the flow of her wrapper. "Find your bouk," she more absently repeated.

"My poetry, d'ye mean?" said the young man, who also couldn't take his eyes off me.

"Never mind your bouk"—his companion reconsidered. "To-day we'll just talk. We'll make some conversation. But we mustn't interrupt Mademoiselle's. Come, come"—and she moved off a step. "Under the leetle tree," she added for the benefit of Mademoiselle. After which she gave me a thin salutation, jerked a measured "Monsieur!" and swept away again with her swain following.

---

[4] Fourth floor (though actually the fifth).   [5] "Pleasant smile."

I looked at Miss Spencer, whose eyes never moved from the carpet, and I spoke, I fear, without grace. "Who in the world's that?"

"The Comtesse—that *was:* my *cousine* as they call it in French."

"And who's the young man?"

"The Countess's pupil, Mr. Mixter." This description of the tie uniting the two persons who had just quitted us must certainly have upset my gravity; for I recall the marked increase of my friend's own as she continued to explain. "She gives lessons in French and music, the simpler sorts—"

"The simpler sorts of French?" I fear I broke in.

But she was still impenetrable, and in fact had now an intonation that put me vulgarly in the wrong. "She has had the worst reverses—with no one to look to. She's prepared for any exertion—and she takes her misfortunes with gaiety."

"Ah well," I returned—no doubt a little ruefully, "that's all I myself am pretending to do. If she's determined to be a burden to nobody, nothing could be more right and proper."

My hostess looked vaguely, though I thought quite wearily enough, about: she met this proposition in no other way. "I must go and get the coffee," she simply said.

"Has the lady many pupils?" I nonetheless persisted.

"She has only Mr. Mixter. She gives him all her time." It might have set me off again, but something in my whole impression of my friend's sensibility urged me to keep strictly decent. "He pays very well," she at all events inscrutably went on. "He's not very bright—as a pupil; but he's very rich and he's very kind. He has a buggy—with a back, and he takes the Countess to drive."

"For good long spells I hope," I couldn't help interjecting—even at the cost of her so taking it that she had still to avoid my eyes. "Well, the country's beautiful for miles," I went on. And then as she was turning away: "You're going for the Countess's coffee?"

"If you'll excuse me a few moments."

"Is there no one else to do it?"

She seemed to wonder who there should be. "I keep no servants."

"Then can't I help?" After which, as she but looked at me, I bettered it. "Can't she wait on herself?"

Miss Spencer had a slow headshake—as if that too had been a strange idea. "She isn't used to *manual* labour."

The discrimination was a treat, but I cultivated decorum. "I see—and you *are.*" But at the same time I couldn't abjure curiosity. "Before you go, at any rate, please tell me this: who *is* this wonderful lady?"

"I told you just who in France—that extraordinary day. She's the wife of my cousin, whom you saw there."

"The lady disowned by her family in consequence of her marriage?"

"Yes; they've never seen her again. They've completely broken with her."

"And where's her husband?"

"My poor cousin's dead."

I pulled up, but only a moment. "And where's your money?"

The poor thing flinched—I kept her on the rack. "I don't know," she woefully said.

I scarce know what it didn't prompt me to—but I went step by step. "On her husband's death this lady at once came to you?"

It was as if she had had too often to describe it. "Yes, she arrived one day."

"How long ago?"

"Two years and four months."

"And has been here ever since?"

"Ever since."

I took it all in. "And how does she like it?"

"Well, not *very* much," said Miss Spencer divinely.

That too I took in. "And how do *you*—?"

She laid her face in her two hands an instant as she had done ten minutes before. Then, quickly, she went to get the Countess's coffee.

Left alone in the little parlour I found myself divided between the perfection of my disgust and a contrary wish to see, to learn more. At the end of a few minutes the young man in attendance on the lady in question reappeared as for a fresh gape at me. He was inordinately grave—to be dressed in such particoloured flannels; and he produced with no great confidence on his own side the message with which he had been charged. "She wants to know if you won't come right out."

"Who wants to know?"

"The Countess. That French lady."

"She has asked you to bring me?"

"Yes sir," said the young man feebly—for I may claim to have surpassed him in stature and weight.

I went out with him, and we found his instructress seated under one of the small quince-trees in front of the house; where she was engaged in drawing a fine needle with a very fat hand through a piece of embroidery not remarkable for freshness. She pointed graciously to the chair beside her and I sat down. Mr. Mixter glanced about him and then accommodated himself on the grass at her feet; whence he gazed upward more gapingly than ever and as if convinced that between us something wonderful would now occur.

"I'm sure you spick French," said the Countess, whose eyes were singularly protuberant as she played over me her agreeable smile.

"I do, madam—*tant bien que mal*,"[6] I replied, I fear, more dryly.

"Ah violà!" she cried as with delight. "I knew it as soon as I looked at you. You've been in my poor dear country."

"A considerable time."

"You love it then, *mon pays de France*?"

"Oh it's an old affection." But I wasn't exuberant.

"And you know Paris well?"

"*Yes, sans me vanter*,[7] madam, I think I really do." And with a certain conscious purpose I let my eyes meet her own.

She presently, hereupon, moved her own and glanced down at Mr. Mixter. "What are we talking about?" she demanded of her attentive pupil.

He pulled his knees up, plucked at the grass, stared, blushed a little. "You're talking French," said Mr. Mixter.

"*La belle découverte!*"[8] mocked the Countess. "It's going on ten months," she explained to me, "since I took him in hand. Don't put yourself out not to say he's *la bêtise même*,"[9] she added in fine style. "He won't in the least understand you."

A moment's consideration of Mr. Mixter, awkwardly sporting at our feet, quite assured me that he wouldn't. "I hope your other pupils do you more honour," I then remarked to my entertainer.

---

[6] "After a fashion."   [7] "Without boasting."   [8] "Quite a discovery!"
[9] "Stupidity itself."

"I have no others. They don't know what French—or what anything else—is in this place; they don't want to know. You may therefore imagine the pleasure it is to me to meet a person who speaks it like yourself." I could but reply that my own pleasure wasn't less, and she continued to draw the stitches through her embroidery with an elegant curl of her little finger. Every few moments she put her eyes, near-sightedly, closer to her work—this as if for elegance too. She inspired me with no more confidence than her late husband, if husband he was, had done, years before, on the occasion with which this one so detestably matched: she was coarse, common, affected, dishonest—no more a Countess than I was a Caliph. She had an assurance—based clearly on experience; but this couldn't have been the experience of "race." Whatever it was indeed it did now, in a yearning fashion, flare out of her. "Talk to me of Paris, *mon beau Paris* that I'd give my eyes to see. The very name of it *me fait languir*.[10] How long since you were there?"

"A couple of months ago."

"*Vous avez de la chance!*[11] Tell me something about it. What were they doing? Oh for an hour of the Boulevard!"

"They were doing about what they're always doing—amusing themselves a good deal."

"At the theatres, *hein?*" sighed the Countess. "At the cafés-concerts? *sous ce beau ciel*[12]—at the little tables before the doors? *Quelle existence!*[13] You know I'm a Parisienne, monsieur," she added, "to my finger-tips."

"Miss Spencer was mistaken then," I ventured to return, "in telling me you're a Provençale."

She stared a moment, then put her nose to her embroidery, which struck me as having acquired even while we sat a dingier and more desultory air. "Ah I'm a Provençale by birth, but a Parisienne by—inclination." After which she pursued: "And by the saddest events of my life—as well as by some of the happiest, hélas!"

"In other words by a varied experience!" I now at last smiled.

She questioned me over it with her hard little salient eyes. "Oh experience!—I could talk of that, no doubt, if I wished. *On en a de toutes les sortes*[14]—and I never dreamed that mine, for example, would ever have *this* in store for me." And she indicated with her large bare elbow and with a jerk of her head all surrounding objects; the little white house, the pair of quince-trees, the rickety paling, even the rapt Mr. Mixter.

I took them all bravely in. "Ah if you mean you're decidedly in exile—!"

"You may imagine what it is. These two years of my *épreuve—elles m'en ont données, des heures, des heures!*[15] One gets used to things"—and she raised her shoulders to the highest shrug ever accomplished at North Verona; "so that I sometimes think I've got used to this. But there are some things that are always beginning again. For example my coffee."

I so far again lent myself. "Do you always have coffee at this hour?"

Her eyebrows went up as high as her shoulders had done. "At what hour would you propose to me to have it? I must have my little cup after breakfast."

"Ah you breakfast at this hour?"

"At mid-day—*comme cela se fair*.[16] Here they breakfast at a quarter past seven. That 'quarter past' is charming!"

"But you were telling me about your coffee," I observed sympathetically.

[10] "Makes me pine." [11] "How lucky you are!" [12] "Under the beautiful sky."
[13] "What a life!" [14] "One has all kinds—"
[15] "These two years have given me hours and hours of trial!" [16] "As is the fashion."

"My *cousine* can't believe in it; she can't understand it. *"C'est une fille charmante,* but that little cup of black coffee with a drop of *'fine,'*[17] served at this hour—they exceed her comprehension. So I have to break the ice each day, and it takes the coffee the time you see to arrive. And when it does arrive, monsieur—! If I don't press it on *you*—though monsieur here sometimes joins me!—it's because you've drunk it on the Boulevard."

I resented extremely so critical a view of my poor friend's exertions, but I said nothing at all—the only way to be sure of my civility. I dropped my eyes on Mr. Mixter, who, sitting cross-legged and nursing his knees, watched my companion's foreign graces with an interest that familiarity had apparently done little to restrict. She became aware, naturally, of my mystified view of him and faced the question with all her boldness. "He adores me, you know," she murmured with her nose again in her tapestry—"he dreams of becoming *mon amoureux.* Yes, *il me fait une cour acharnée*[18]—such as you see him. That's what we've come to. He has read some French novel—it took him six months. But ever since that he has thought himself a hero and me—such as I am, monsieur—*je ne sais quelle dévergondée!*"[19]

Mr. Mixter may have inferred that he was to that extent the object of our reference; but of the manner in which he was handled he must have had small suspicion—preoccupied as he was, as to my companion, with the ecstasy of contemplation. Our hostess moreover at this moment came out of the house, bearing a coffee-pot and three cups on a neat little tray. I took from her eyes, as she approached us, a brief but intense appeal—the mute expression, as I felt, conveyed in the hardest little look she had yet addressed me, of her longing to know what, as a man of the world in general and of the French world in particular, I thought of these allied forces now so encamped on the stricken field of her life. I could only "act" however, as they said at North Verona, quite impenetrably— only make no answering sign. I couldn't intimate, much less could I frankly utter, my inward sense of the Countess's probable past, with its measure of her virtue, value and accomplishments, and of the limits of the consideration to which she could properly pretend. I couldn't give my friend a hint of how I myself personally "saw" her interesting pensioner—whether as the runaway wife of a too-jealous hair-dresser or of a too-morose pastry-cook, say; whether as a very small bourgeoise, in fine, who had vitiated her case beyond patching up, or even as some character, of the nomadic sort, less edifying still. I couldn't let in, by the jog of a shutter, as it were, a hard informing ray and then, washing my hands of the business, turn my back for ever. I could on the contrary but save the situation, my own at least, for the moment, by pulling myself together with a master hand and appearing to ignore everything but that the dreadful person between us *was* a "grande dame." This effort was possible indeed but as a retreat in good order and with all the forms of courtesy. If I couldn't speak, still less could I stay, and I think I must in spite of everything, have turned black with disgust to see Caroline Spencer stand there like a waiting-maid. I therefore won't answer for the shade of success that may have attended my saying to the Countess, on my feet and as to leave her: "You expect to remain some time in these *parages?*"[20]

What passed between us, as from face to face, while she looked up at me, *that* at least our companion may have caught, that at least may have sown, for the aftertime, some seed of revelation. The Countess repeated her terrible shrug.

[17] "Brandy.   [18] "Yes, he has courted me ardently—"
[19] "I know not what kind of shameless woman!"   [20] "Parts."

"Who knows? I don't see my way—! It isn't an existence, but when one's in misery—! *Chère belle*," she added as an appeal to Miss Spencer, "you've gone and forgotten the '*fine*'!"

I detained that lady as, after considering a moment in silence the small array, she was about to turn off in quest of this article. I held out my hand in silence—I had to go. Her wan set little face, severely mild and with the question of a moment before now quite cold in it, spoke of extreme fatigue, but also of something else strange and conceived—whether a desperate patience still, or at last some other desperation, being more than I can say. What was clearest on the whole was that she was glad I was going. Mr. Mixter had risen to his feet and was pouring out the Countess's coffee. As I went back past the Baptist church I could feel how right my poor friend had been in her conviction at the other, the still intenser, the now historic crisis, that she should still see something of that dear old Europe.

[1877]

Guy de Maupassant   *1850–1893*

THE NECKLACE*

She was one of those pretty and charming girls who are sometimes, as if by a mistake of destiny, born in a family of clerks. She had no dowry, no expectations, no means of being known, understood, loved, wedded by any rich and distinguished man; and she let herself be married to a little clerk at the Ministry of Public Instruction.

She dressed plainly because she could not dress well, but she was as unhappy as though she had really fallen from her proper station, since with women there is neither caste nor rank: and beauty, grace, and charm act instead of family and birth. Natural fineness, instinct for what is elegant, suppleness of wit, are the sole hierarchy, and make from women of the people the equals of the very greatest ladies.

She suffered ceaselessly, feeling herself born for all the delicacies and all the luxuries. She suffered from the poverty of her dwelling, from the wretched look of the walls, from the worn-out chairs, from the ugliness of the curtains. All those things, of which another woman of her rank would never even have been conscious, tortured her and made her angry. The sight of the little Breton peasant[1] who did her humble housework aroused in her regrets which were despairing, and distracted dreams. She thought of the silent antechambers hung with Oriental tapestry, lit by tall bronze candelabra, and of the two great footmen in knee breeches who sleep in the big armchairs, made drowsy by the heavy warmth of the hot-air stove. She thought of the long *salons*[2] fitted up with ancient silk, of the delicate furniture carrying priceless curiosities, and of the coquettish perfumed boudoirs made for talks at five o'clock with intimate friends, with men famous and sought after, whom all women envy and whose attention they all desire.

When she sat down to dinner, before the round table covered with a tablecloth three days old, opposite her husband, who uncovered the soup tureen and declared with an enchanted air, "Ah, the good *pot-au-feu!*[3] I don't know anything better than that," she thought of dainty dinners, of shining silverware, of tapestry which peopled the walls with ancient personages and with strange birds flying in the midst of a fairy forest; and she thought of delicious dishes served on marvelous plates, and of the whispered gallantries which you listen to with a sphinxlike smile, while you are eating the pink flesh of a trout or the wings of a quail.

She had no dresses, no jewels, nothing. And she loved nothing but that; she felt made for that. She would so have liked to please, to be envied, to be charming, to be sought after.

She had a friend, a former schoolmate at the convent, who was rich, and whom she did not like to go and see any more, because she suffered so much when she came back.

But one evening, her husband returned home with a triumphant air, and holding a large envelope in his hand.

"There," said he. "Here is something for you."

She tore the paper sharply, and drew out a printed card which bore these words:

---

* *Translated by Marjorie Laurie.*
[1] A native of Brittany, a region (historically a province) in northwest France.
[2] Drawing rooms.   [3] Stew.

"The Minister of Public Instruction and Mme. Georges Ramponneau request the honor of M. and Mme. Loisel's company at the palace of the Ministry on Monday evening, January eighteenth."

Instead of being delighted, as her husband hoped, she threw the invitation on the table with disdain, murmuring:

"What do you want me to do with that?"

"But, my dear, I thought you would be glad. You never go out, and this is such a fine opportunity. I had awful trouble to get it. Everyone wants to go; it is very select, and they are not giving many invitations to clerks. The whole official world will be there."

She looked at him with an irritated glance, and said, impatiently:

"And what do you want me to put on my back?"

He had not thought of that; he stammered:

"Why, the dress you go to the theater in. It looks very well, to me."

He stopped, distracted, seeing his wife was crying. Two great tears descended slowly from the corners of her eyes toward the corners of her mouth. He stuttered:

"What's the matter? What's the matter?"

But, by violent effort, she had conquered her grief, and she replied, with a calm voice, while she wiped her wet cheeks:

"Nothing. Only I have no dress and therefore I can't go to this ball. Give your card to some colleague whose wife is better equipped than I."

He was in despair. He resumed:

"Come, let us see, Mathilde. How much would it cost, a suitable dress, which you could use on other occasions. Something very simple?"

She reflected several seconds, making her calculations and wondering also what sum she could ask without drawing on herself an immediate refusal and a frightened exclamation from the economical clerk.

Finally, she replied, hesitatingly:

"I don't know exactly, but I think I could manage it with four hundred francs."

He had grown a little pale, because he was laying aside just that amount to buy a gun and treat himself to a little shooting next summer on the plain of Nanterre,[4] with several friends who went to shoot larks down there, of a Sunday.

But he said:

"All right. I will give you four hundred francs. And try to have a pretty dress."

The day of the ball drew near, and Mme. Loisel seemed sad, uneasy, anxious. Her dress was ready, however. Her husband said to her one evening:

"What is the matter? Come, you've been so queer these last three days."

And she answered:

"It annoys me not to have a single jewel, not a single stone, nothing to put on. I shall look like distress. I should almost rather not go at all."

He resumed:

"You might wear natural flowers. It's very stylish at this time of the year. For ten francs you can get two or three magnificent roses."

She was not convinced.

"No; there's nothing more humiliating than to look poor among other women who are rich."

But her husband cried:

"How stupid you are! Go look up your friend Mme. Forestier, and ask her to lend you some jewels. You're quite thick enough with her to do that."

---

[4] A town west of Paris.

She uttered a cry of joy:

"It's true. I never thought of it."

The next day she went to her friend and told of her distress.

Mme. Forestier went to a wardrobe with a glass door, took out a large jewel-box, brought it back, opened it, and said to Mme. Loisel:

"Choose, my dear."

She saw first of all some bracelets, then a pearl necklace, then a Venetian cross, gold and precious stones of admirable workmanship. She tried on the ornaments before the glass, hesitated, could not make up her mind to part with them, to give them back. She kept asking:

"Haven't you any more?"

"Why, yes. Look. I don't know what you like."

All of a sudden she discovered, in a black satin box, a superb necklace of diamonds, and her heart began to beat with an immoderate desire. Her hands trembled as she took it. She fastened it around her throat, outside her high-necked dress, and remained lost in ecstasy at the sight of herself.

Then she asked, hesitating, filled with anguish:

"Can you lend me that, only that?"

"Why, yes, certainly."

She sprang upon the neck of her friend, kissed her passionately, then fled with her treasure.

The day of the ball arrived. Mme. Loisel made a great success. She was prettier than them all, elegant, gracious, smiling, and crazy with joy. All the men looked at her, asked her name, endeavored to be introduced. All the attachés of the Cabinet wanted to waltz with her. She was remarked by the minister himself.

She danced with intoxication, with passion, made drunk by pleasure, forgetting all, in the triumph of her beauty, in the glory of her success, in a sort of cloud of happiness composed of all this homage, of all this admiration, of all these awakened desires, and of that sense of complete victory which is so sweet to a woman's heart.

She went away about four o'clock in the morning. Her husband had been sleeping since midnight, in a little deserted anteroom, with three other gentlemen whose wives were having a very good time. He threw over her shoulders the wraps which he had brought, modest wraps of common life, whose poverty contrasted with the elegance of the ball dress. She felt this, and wanted to escape so as not to be remarked by the other women, who were enveloping themselves in costly furs.

Loisel held her back.

"Wait a bit. You will catch cold outside. I will go and call a cab."

But she did not listen to him, and rapidly descended the stairs. When they were in the street they did not find a carriage; and they began to look for one, shouting after the cabmen whom they saw passing by at a distance.

They went down toward the Seine[5] in despair, shivering with cold. At last they found on the quay one of those ancient noctambulant coupés[6] which, exactly as if they were ashamed to show their misery during the day, are never seen round Paris until after nightfall.

It took them to their door in the Rue des Martyrs, and once more, sadly, they climbed up homeward. All was ended, for her. And as to him, he reflected that he must be at the Ministry at ten o'clock.

She removed the wraps which covered her shoulders, before the glass, so as

---

[5] The river that flows through Paris.   [6] A closed four-wheeled carriage.

once more to see herself in all her glory. But suddenly she uttered a cry. She no longer had the necklace around her neck!

Her husband, already half undressed, demanded:

"What is the matter with you?"

She turned madly towards him:

"I have—I have—I've lost Mme. Forestier's necklace."

He stood up, distracted.

"What!—how?—impossible!"

And they looked in the folds of her dress, in the folds of her cloak, in her pockets, everywhere. They did not find it.

He asked:

"You're sure you had it on when you left the ball?"

"Yes, I felt it in the vestibule of the palace."

"But if you had lost it in the street we should have heard it fall. It must be in the cab."

"Yes. Probably. Did you take his number?"

"No. And you, didn't you notice it?"

"No."

They looked, thunderstruck, at one another. At last Loisel put on his clothes.

"I shall go back on foot," said he, "over the whole route which we have taken to see if I can find it."

And he went out. She sat waiting on a chair in her ball dress, without strength to go to bed, overwhelmed, without fire, without a thought.

Her husband came back about seven o'clock. He had found nothing.

He went to Police Headquarters, to the newspaper offices, to offer a reward; he went to the cab companies—everywhere, in fact, whither he was urged by the least suspicion of hope.

She waited all day, in the same condition of mad fear before this terrible calamity.

Loisel returned at night with a hollow, pale face; he had discovered nothing.

"You must write to your friend," said he, "that you have broken the clasp of her necklace and that you are having it mended. That will give us time to turn round."

She wrote at his dictation.

At the end of a week they had lost all hope.

And Loisel, who had aged five years, declared:

"We must consider how to replace that ornament."

The next day they took the box which had contained it, and they went to the jeweler whose name was found within. He consulted his books.

"It was not I, madame, who sold that necklace; I must simply have furnished the case."

Then they went from jeweler to jeweler, searching for a necklace like the other, consulting their memories, sick both of them with chagrin and anguish.

They found, in a shop at the Palais Royal,[7] a string of diamonds which seemed to them exactly like the one they looked for. It was worth forty thousand francs. They could have it for thirty-six.

So they begged the jeweler not to sell it for three days yet. And they made a bargain that he should buy it back for thirty-four thousand francs, in case they found the other one before the end of February.

[7] At the time the story was written the shops in the vicinity of the Palais Royal included many of the most famous jewellers in Paris.

Loisel possessed eighteen thousand francs which his father had left him. He would borrow the rest.

He did borrow, asking a thousand francs of one, five hundred of another, five louis[8] here, three louis there. He gave notes, took up ruinous obligations, dealt with usurers and all the race of lenders. He compromised all the rest of his life, risked his signature without even knowing if he could meet it; and, frightened by the pains yet to come, by the black misery which was about to fall upon him, by the prospect of all the physical privation and of all the moral tortures which he was to suffer, he went to get the new necklace, putting down upon the merchant's counter thirty-six thousand francs.

When Mme. Loisel took back the necklace, Mme. Forestier said to her, with a chilly manner:

"You should have returned it sooner; I might have needed it."

She did not open the case, as her friend had so much feared. If she had detected the substitution, what would she have thought, what would she have said? Would she not have taken Mme. Loisel for a thief?

Mme. Loisel now knew the horrible existence of the needy. She took her part, moreover, all of a sudden, with heroism. That dreadful debt must be paid. She would pay it. They dismissed their servant; they changed their lodgings; they rented a garret under the roof.

She came to know what heavy housework meant and the odious cares of the kitchen. She washed the dishes, using her rosy nails on the greasy pots and pans. She washed the dirty linen, the shirts, and the dishcloths, which she dried upon a line; she carried the slops down to the street every morning, and carried up the water, stopping for breath at every landing. And, dressed like a woman of the people, she went to the fruiterer, the grocer, the butcher, her basket on her arm, bargaining, insulted, defending her miserable money sou by sou.[9]

Each month they had to meet some notes, renew others, obtain more time.

Her husband worked in the evening making a fair copy of some tradesman's accounts, and late at night he often copied manuscript for five sous a page.

And this life lasted for ten years.

At the end of ten years, they had paid everything, everything, with the rates of usury, and the accumulations of the compound interest.

Mme. Loisel looked old now. She had become the woman of impoverished households—strong and hard and rough. With frowsy hair, skirts askew, and red hands, she talked loud while washing the floor with great swishes of water. But sometimes, when her husband was at the office, she sat down near the window, and she thought of that gay evening of long ago, of that ball where she had been so beautiful and so fêted.

What would have happened if she had not lost that necklace? Who knows? Who knows? How life is strange and changeful! How little a thing is needed for us to be lost or to be saved!

But, one Sunday, having gone to take a walk in the Champs Elysées[10] to refresh herself from the labor of the week, she suddenly perceived a woman who was leading a child. It was Mme. Forestier, still young, still beautiful, still charming.

Mme. Loisel felt moved. Was she going to speak to her? Yes, certainly. And now that she had paid, she was going to tell her all about it. Why not?

She went up.

---

[8] A French coin worth twenty francs.   [9] A small French coin worth one-twentieth of a franc.
[10] Paris' most famous avenue, lined with trees and gardens.

"Good-day, Jeanne."

The other, astonished to be familiarly addressed by this plain goodwife, did not recognize her at all, and stammered:

"But—madam!—I do not know—You must be mistaken."

"No. I am Mathilde Loisel."

Her friend uttered a cry.

"Oh, my poor Mathilde! How you are changed!"

"Yes, I have had days hard enough, since I have seen you, days wretched enough—and that because of you!"

"Of me! How so?"

"Do you remember that diamond necklace which you lent me to wear at the ministerial ball?"

"Yes. Well?"

"Well, I lost it."

"What do you mean? You brought it back."

"I brought you back another just like it. And for this we have been ten years paying. You can understand that it was not easy for us, us who had nothing. At last it is ended, and I am very glad."

Mme. Forestier had stopped.

"You say that you bought a necklace of diamonds to replace mine?"

"Yes. You never noticed it, then! They were very like."

And she smiled with a joy which was proud and naïve at once.

Mme. Forestier, strongly moved, took her two hands.

"Oh, my poor Mathilde! Why, my necklace was paste. It was worth at most five hundred francs!"

[1884]

Leo Tolstoy   *1828–1910*

THE DEATH OF IVAN ILYCH*

I

During an interval in the Melvinski trial in the large building of the Law Courts the members and public prosecutor met in Ivan Egorovich Shebek's private room, where the conversation turned on the celebrated Krasovski case. Fedor Vasilievich warmly maintained that it was not subject to their jurisdiction, Ivan Egorovich maintained the contrary, while Peter Ivanovich, not having entered into the discussion at the start, took no part in it but looked through the *Gazette* which had just been handed in.

"Gentlemen," he said, "Ivan Ilych has died!"

"You don't say so!"

"Here, read it yourself," replied Peter Ivanovich, handing Fedor Vasilievich the paper still damp from the press. Surrounded by a black border were the words: "Praskovya Fedorovna Golovina, with profound sorrow, informs relatives and friends of the demise of her beloved husband Ivan Ilych Golovin, Member of the Court of Justice, which occurred on February the 4th of this year 1882. The funeral will take place on Friday at one o'clock in the afternoon."

Ivan Ilych had been a colleague of the gentlemen present and was liked by them all. He had been ill for some weeks with an illness said to be incurable. His post had been kept open for him, but there had been conjectures that in case of his death Alexeev might receive his appointment, and that either Vinnikov or Shtabel would succeed Alexeev. So on receiving the news of Ivan Ilych's death the first thought of each of the gentlemen in that private room was of the changes and promotions it might occasion among themselves or their acquaintances.

"I shall be sure to get Shtabel's place or Vinnikov's," thought Fedor Vasilievich. "I was promised that long ago, and the promotion means an extra eight hundred rubles a year for me besides the allowance."

"Now I must apply for my brother-in-law's transfer from Kaluga," thought Peter Ivanovich. "My wife will be very glad, and then she won't be able to say that I never do anything for her relations."

"I thought he would never leave his bed again," said Peter Ivanovich aloud. "It's very sad."

"But what really was the matter with him?"

"The doctors couldn't say—at least they could, but each of them said something different. When last I saw him I thought he was getting better."

"And I haven't been to see him since the holidays. I always meant to go."

"Had he any property?"

"I think his wife had a little—but something quite trifling."

"We shall have to go to see her, but they live so terribly far away."

"Far away from you, you mean. Everything's far away from your place."

"You see, he never can forgive my living on the other side of the river," said Peter Ivanovich, smiling at Shebek. Then, still talking of the distances between different parts of the city, they returned to the Court.

* Translated by Louise and Aylmer Maude.

Besides considerations as to the possible transfers and promotions likely to result from Ivan Ilych's death, the mere fact of the death of a near acquaintance aroused, as usual, in all who heard of it the complacent feeling that, "it is he who is dead and not I."

Each one thought or felt, "Well, he's dead but I'm alive!" But the more intimate of Ivan Ilych's acquaintances, his so-called friends, could not help thinking also that they would now have to fulfill the very tiresome demands of propriety by attending the funeral service and paying a visit of condolence to the widow.

Fedor Vasilievich and Peter Ivanovich had been his nearest acquaintances. Peter Ivanovich had studied law with Ivan Ilych and had considered himself to be under obligations to him.

Having told his wife at dinner-time of Ivan Ilych's death, and of his conjecture that it might be possible to get her brother transferred to their circuit, Peter Ivanovich sacrificed his usual nap, put on his evening clothes, and drove to Ivan Ilych's house.

At the entrance stood a carriage and two cabs. Leaning against the wall in the hall downstairs near the cloak-stand was a coffin lid covered with cloth of gold, ornamented with gold cord and tassels, that had been polished up with metal powder. Two ladies in black were taking off their fur cloaks. Peter Ivanovich recognized one of them as Ivan Ilych's sister, but the other was a stranger to him. His colleague Schwartz was just coming downstairs, but on seeing Peter Ivanovich enter he stopped and winked at him, as if to say: "Ivan Ilych has made a mess of things—not like you and me."

Schwartz's face with his Piccadilly whiskers, and his slim figure in evening dress, had as usual an air of elegant solemnity which contrasted with the playfulness of his character and had a special piquancy here, or so it seemed to Peter Ivanovich.

Peter Ivanovich allowed the ladies to precede him and slowly followed them upstairs. Schwartz did not come down but remained where he was, and Peter Ivanovich understood that he wanted to arrange where they should play bridge that evening. The ladies went upstairs to the widow's room, and Schwartz with seriously compressed lips but a playful look in his eyes, indicated by a twist of his eyebrows the room to the right where the body lay.

Peter Ivanovich, like everyone else on such occasions, entered feeling uncertain what he would have to do. All he knew was that at such times it is always safe to cross oneself. But he was not quite sure whether one should make obeisances while doing so. He therefore adopted a middle course. On entering the room he began crossing himself and made a slight movement resembling a bow. At the same time, as far as the motion of his head and arm allowed, he surveyed the room. Two young men—apparently nephews, one of whom was a high-school pupil—were leaving the room, crossing themselves as they did so. An old woman was standing motionless, and a lady with strangely arched eyebrows was saying something to her in a whisper. A vigorous, resolute Church Reader, in a frock-coat, was reading something in a loud voice with an expression that precluded any contradiction. The butler's assistant, Gerasim, stepping lightly in front of Peter Ivanovich, was strewing something on the floor. Noticing this, Peter Ivanovich was immediately aware of a faint odour of a decomposing body.

The last time he had called on Ivan Ilych, Peter Ivanovich had seen Gerasim in the study. Ivan Ilych had been particularly fond of him and he was performing the duty of a sick nurse.

Peter Ivanovich continued to make the sign of the cross, slightly inclining his head in an intermediate direction between the coffin, the Reader, and the icons[1] on the table in a corner of the room. Afterwards, when it seemed to him that this movement of his arm in crossing himself had gone on too long, he stopped and began to look at the corpse.

The dead man lay, as dead men always lie, in a specially heavy way, his rigid limbs sunk in the soft cushions of the coffin, with the head forever bowed on the pillow. His yellow waxen brow with bald patches over his sunken temples was thrust up in the way peculiar to the dead, the protruding nose seeming to press on the upper lip. He was much changed and had grown even thinner since Peter Ivanovich had last seen him, but, as is always the case with the dead, his face was handsomer and above all more dignified than when he was alive. The expression on the face said that what was necessary had been accomplished, and accomplished rightly. Besides this there was in that expression a reproach and a warning to the living. This warning seemed to Peter Ivanovich out of place, or at least not applicable to him. He felt a certain discomfort and so he hurriedly crossed himself once more and turned and went out of the door—too hurriedly and too regardless of propriety, as he himself was aware.

Schwartz was waiting for him in the adjoining room with legs spread wide apart and both hands toying with his top hat behind his back. The mere sight of that playful, well-groomed, and elegant figure refreshed Peter Ivanovich. He felt that Schwartz was above all these happenings and would not surrender to any depressing influences. His very look said that this incident of a church service for Ivan Ilych could not be a sufficient reason for infringing the order of the session—in other words, that it would certainly not prevent his unwrapping a new pack of cards and shuffling them that evening while a footman placed four fresh candles on the table: in fact, that there was no reason for supposing that this incident would hinder their spending the evening agreeably. Indeed he said this in a whisper as Peter Ivanovich passed him, proposing that they should meet for a game at Fedor Vasilievich's. But apparently Peter Ivanovich was not destined to play bridge that evening. Praskovya Fedorovna (a short, fat woman who despite all efforts to the contrary had continued to broaden steadily from her shoulders downwards and who had the same extraordinarily arched eyebrows as the lady who had been standing by the coffin), dressed all in black, her head covered with lace, came out of her own room with some other ladies, conducted them to the room where the dead body lay, and said: "The service will begin immediately. Please go in."

Schwartz, making an indefinite bow, stood still, evidently neither accepting nor declining this invitation. Praskovya Fedorovna recognizing Peter Ivanovich, sighed, went close up to him, took his hand, and said: "I know you were a true friend to Ivan Ilych . . ." and looked at him awaiting some suitable response. And Peter Ivanovich knew that, just as it had been the right thing to cross himself in that room, so what he had to do here was to press her hand, sigh, and say, "Believe me. . . ." So he did all this and as he did it felt that the desired result had been achieved: that both he and she were touched.

"Come with me. I want to speak to you before it begins," said the widow. "Give me your arm."

Peter Ivanovich gave her his arm and they went to the inner rooms, passing Schwartz who winked at Peter Ivanovich compassionately.

[1] Traditional religious paintings.

"That does for our bridge! Don't object if we find another player. Perhaps you can cut in when you do escape," said his playful look.

Peter Ivanovich sighed still more deeply and despondently, and Praskovya Fedorovna pressed his arm gratefully. When they reached the drawing-room, upholstered in pink cretonne[2] and lighted by a dim lamp, they sat down at the table—she on a sofa and Peter Ivanovich on a low pouffe,[3] the springs of which yielded spasmodically under his weight. Praskovya Fedorovna had been on the point of warning him to take another seat, but felt that such a warning was out of keeping with her present condition and so changed her mind. As he sat down on the pouffe Peter Ivanovich recalled how Ivan Ilych had arranged this room and had consulted him regarding this pink cretonne with green leaves. The whole room was full of furniture and knick-knacks, and on her way to the sofa the lace of the widow's black shawl caught on the carved edge of the table. Peter Ivanovich rose to detach it, and the springs of the pouffe, relieved of his weight, rose also and gave him a push. The widow began detaching her shawl herself, and Peter Ivanovich again sat down, suppressing the rebellious springs of the pouffe under him. But the widow had not quite freed herself and Peter Ivanovich got up again, and again the pouffe rebelled and even creaked. When this was all over she took out a clean cambric handkerchief and began to weep. The episode with the shawl and the struggle with the pouffe had cooled Peter Ivanovich's emotions and he sat there with a sullen look on his face. This awkward situation was interrupted by Sokolov, Ivan Ilych's butler, who came to report that the plot in the cemetery that Praskovya Fedorovna had chosen would cost two hundred rubles. She stopped weeping and, looking at Peter Ivanovich with the air of a victim, remarked in French that it was very hard for her. Peter Ivanovich made a silent gesture signifying his full conviction that it must indeed be so.

"Please smoke," she said in a magnanimous yet crushed voice, and turned to discuss with Sokolov the price of the plot for the grave.

Peter Ivanovich while lighting his cigarette heard her inquiring very circumstantially into the prices of different plots in the cemetery and finally decide which she would take. When that was done she gave instructions about engaging the choir. Sokolov then left the room.

"I look after everything myself," she told Peter Ivanovich, shifting the albums that lay on the table; and noticing that the table was endangered by his cigarette-ash, she immediately passed him an ashtray, saying as she did so: "I consider it an affectation to say that my grief prevents my attending to practical affairs. On the contrary, if anything can—I won't say console me, but—distract me, it is seeing to everything concerning him." She again took out her handkerchief as if preparing to cry, but suddenly, as if mastering her feeling, she shook herself and began to speak calmly. "But there is something I want to talk to you about."

Peter Ivanovich bowed, keeping control of the springs of the pouffe, which immediately began quivering under him.

"He suffered terribly the last few days."

"Did he?" said Peter Ivanovich.

"Oh, terribly! He screamed unceasingly, not for minutes but for hours. For the last three days he screamed incessantly. It was unendurable. I cannot understand how I bore it; you could hear him three rooms off. Oh, what I have suffered!"

"Is it possible that he was conscious all that time?" asked Peter Ivanovich.

___

[2] Heavy cotton or linen fabric.   [3] A rounded ottoman.

"Yes," she whispered. "To the last moment. He took leave of us a quarter of an hour before he died, and asked us to take Volodya away."

The thought of the sufferings of this man he had known so intimately, first as a merry little boy, then as a school-mate, and later as a grown-up colleague, suddenly struck Peter Ivanovich with horror, despite an unpleasant consciousness of his own and this woman's dissimulation. He again saw that brow, and that nose pressing down on the lip, and felt afraid for himself.

"Three days of frightful suffering and then death! Why, that might suddenly, at any time, happen to me," he thought, and for a moment felt terrified. But—he did not himself know how—the customary reflection at once occurred to him that this had happened to Ivan Ilych and not to him, and that it should not and could not happen to him, and that to think that it could would be yielding to depression which he ought not to do, as Schwartz's expression plainly showed. After which reflection Peter Ivanovich felt reassured, and began to ask with interest about the details of Ivan Ilych's death, as though death was an accident natural to Ivan Ilych but certainly not to himself.

After many details of the really dreadful physical sufferings Ivan Ilych had endured (which details he learnt only from the effect those sufferings had produced on Praskovya Fedorovna's nerves) the widow apparently found it necessary to get to business.

"Oh, Peter Ivanovich, how hard it is! How terribly, terribly hard!" and she again began to weep.

Peter Ivanovich sighed and waited for her to finish blowing her nose. When she had done so he said, "Believe me . . . ," and she again began talking and brought out what was evidently her chief concern with him—namely, to question him as to how she could obtain a grant of money from the government on the occasion of her husband's death. She made it appear that she was asking Peter Ivanovich's advice about her pension, but he soon saw that she already knew about that to the minutest detail, more even than he did himself. She knew how much could be got out of the government in consequence of her husband's death, but wanted to find out whether she could not possibly extract something more. Peter Ivanovich tried to think of some means of doing so, but after reflecting for a while and, out of propriety, condemning the government for its niggardliness, he said he thought that nothing more could be got. Then she sighed and evidently began to devise means of getting rid of her visitor. Noticing this, he put out his cigarette, rose, pressed her hand, and went out into the anteroom.

In the dining-room where the clock stood that Ivan Ilych had liked so much and had bought at an antique shop, Peter Ivanovich met a priest and a few acquaintances who had come to attend the service, and he recognized Ivan Ilych's daughter, a handsome young woman. She was in black and her slim figure appeared slimmer than ever. She had a gloomy, determined, almost angry expression, and bowed to Peter Ivanovich as though he were in some way to blame. Behind her, with the same offended look, stood a wealthy young man, an examining magistrate, whom Peter Ivanovich also knew and who was her fiancé, as he had heard. He bowed mournfully to them and was about to pass into the death-chamber, when from under the stairs appeared the figure of Ivan Ilych's schoolboy son, who was extremely like his father. He seemed a little Ivan Ilych, such as Peter Ivanovich remembered when they studied law together. His tear-stained eyes had in them the look that is seen in the eyes of boys of thirteen or fourteen who are not pure-minded. When he saw Peter Ivanovich he scowled morosely and shame-facedly. Peter Ivanovich nodded to him and entered the death-chamber. The service began: candles, groans, incense, tears, and sobs. Peter Ivanovich stood looking gloomily down at his feet. He did not look once at the dead man, did not yield to any depressing influence, and was one of the first to leave the room. There was no one in the anteroom, but Gerasim darted out of the dead man's room, rummaged with his strong hands among the fur coats to find Peter Ivanovich's and helped him on with it.

"Well, friend Gerasim," said Peter Ivanovich, so as to say something. "It's a sad affair, isn't it?"

"It's God's will. We shall all come to it some day," said Gerasim, displaying his teeth—the even, white teeth of a healthy peasant—and, like a man in the thick of urgent work, he briskly opened the front door, called the coachman, helped Peter Ivanovich into the sledge,[4] and sprang back to the porch as if in readiness for what he had to do next.

Peter Ivanovich found the fresh air particularly pleasant after the smell of incense, the dead body, and carbolic acid.

"Where to, sir?" asked the coachman.

"It's not too late even now. . . . I'll call round on Fedor Vasilievich."

He accordingly drove there and found them just finishing the first rubber, so that it was quite convenient for him to cut in.

II

Ivan Ilych's life had been most simple and most ordinary and therefore most terrible.

He had been a member of the Court of Justice, and died at the age of forty-five. His father had been an official who after serving in various ministries and departments in Petersburg had made the sort of career which brings men to positions from which by reason of their long service they cannot be dismissed, though they are obviously unfit to hold any responsible position, and for whom therefore posts are specially created, which though fictitious carry salaries of from six to ten thousand rubles that are not fictitious, and in receipt of which they live on to a great age.

Such was the Privy Councillor and superfluous member of various superfluous institutions, Ilya Epimovich Golovin.

He had three sons, of whom Ivan Ilych was the second. The eldest son was following in his father's footsteps only in another department, and was already approaching that stage in the service at which a similar sinecure would be reached. The third son was a failure. He had ruined his prospects in a number of positions and was now serving in the railway department. His father and brothers, and still more their wives, not merely disliked meeting him, but avoided remembering his existence unless compelled to do so. His sister had married Baron Greff, a Petersburg official of her father's type. Ivan Ilych was *le phénix de la famille*[5] as people said. He was neither as cold and formal as his elder brother nor as wild as the younger, but was a happy mean between them—an intelligent, polished, lively and agreeable man. He had studied with his younger brother at the School of Law, but the latter had failed to complete the course and was expelled when he was in the fifth class. Ivan Ilych finished the course well. Even when he was at the School of Law he was just what he remained for the rest of his life: a capable, cheerful,

---

[4] A low, sled-like vehicle on runners, drawn by horses.
[5] The phoenix (e.g., rare bird) of the family.

good-natured, and sociable man, though strict in the fulfilment of what he considered to be his duty: and he considered his duty to be what was so considered by those in authority. Neither as a boy nor as a man was he a toady, but from early youth was by nature attracted to people of high station as a fly is drawn to the light, assimilating their ways and views of life and establishing friendly relations with them. All the enthusiasms of childhood and youth passed without leaving much trace on him; he succumbed to sensuality, to vanity, and latterly among the highest classes to liberalism, but always within limits which his instinct unfailingly indicated to him as correct.

At school he had done things which had formerly seemed to him very horrid and made him feel disgusted with himself when he did them; but when later on he saw that such actions were done by people of good position and that they did not regard them as wrong, he was able not exactly to regard them as right, but to forget about them entirely or not be at all troubled at remembering them.

Having graduated from the School of Law and qualified for the tenth rank of the civil service, and having received money from his father for his equipment, Ivan Ilych ordered himself clothes at Scharmer's, the fashionable tailor, hung a medallion inscribed *respice finem*[6] on his watch-chain, took leave of his professor and the prince who was patron of the school, had a farewell dinner with his comrades at Donon's first-class restaurant, and with his new and fashionable portmanteau, linen, clothes, shaving and other toilet appliances, and a travelling rug, all purchased at the best shops, he was off for one of the provinces where, through his father's influence, he had been attached to the Governor as an official for special service.

In the province Ivan Ilych soon arranged as easy and agreeable a position for himself as he had had at the School of Law. He performed his official tasks, made his career, and at the same time amused himself pleasantly and decorously. Occasionally he paid official visits to country districts, where he behaved with dignity both to his superiors and inferiors, and performed the duties entrusted to him, which related chiefly to the sectarians,[7] with an exactness and incorruptible honesty of which he could not but feel proud.

In official matters, despite his youth and taste for frivolous gaiety, he was exceedingly reserved, punctilious, and even severe; but in society he was often amusing and witty, and always good-natured, correct in his manner, and *bon enfant*,[8] as the governor and his wife—with whom he was like one of the family—used to say of him.

In the province he had an affair with a lady who made advances to the elegant young lawyer, and there was also a milliner; and there were carousals with aides-de-camp who visited the district, and after-supper visits to a certain outlying street of doubtful reputation; and there was too some obsequiousness to his chief and even to his chief's wife, but all this was done with such a tone of good breeding that no hard names could be applied to it. It all came under the heading of the French saying: *"Il faut que jeunesse se passe."*[9] It was all done with clean hands, in clean linen, with French phrases, and above all among people of the best society and consequently with the approval of people of rank.

So Ivan Ilych served for five years and then came a change in his official life.

[6] A Latin motto: "Regard the end."
[7] A religious sect which had broken with the Russian Orthodox Church in the seventeenth century and whose activities were legally restricted.
[8] A good child.   [9] Youth must have its fling. (Translators' note)

The new and reformed judicial institutions were introduced, and new men were needed. Ivan Ilych became such a new man. He was offered the post of Examining Magistrate, and he accepted it though the post was in another province and obliged him to give up the connexions he had formed and to make new ones. His friends met to give him a send-off; they had a group-photograph taken and presented him with a silver cigarette-case, and he set off to his new post.

As examining magistrate Ivan Ilych was just as *comme il faut*[10] and decorous a man, inspiring general respect and capable of separating his official duties from his private life, as he had been when acting as an official on special service. His duties now as examining magistrate were far more interesting and attractive than before. In his former position it had been pleasant to wear an undress uniform made by Scharmer, and to pass through the crowd of petitioners and officials who were timorously awaiting an audience with the governor, and who envied him as with free and easy gait he went straight into his chief's private room to have a cup of tea and a cigarette with him. But not many people had then been directly dependent on him—only police officials and the sectarians when he went on special missions—and he liked to treat them politely, almost as comrades, as if he were letting them feel that he who had the power to crush them was treating them in this simple, friendly way. There were then but few such people. But now, as an examining magistrate, Ivan Ilych felt that everyone without exception, even the most important and self-satisfied, was in his power, and that he need only write a few words on a sheet of paper with a certain heading, and this or that important, self-satisfied person would be brought before him in the role of an accused person or a witness, and if he did not choose to allow him to sit down, would have to stand before him and answer his questions. Ivan Ilych never abused his power; he tried on the contrary to soften its expression, but the consciousness of it and of the possibility of softening its effect, supplied the chief interest and attraction of his office. In his work itself, especially in his examinations, he very soon acquired a method of eliminating all considerations irrelevant to the legal aspect of the case, and reducing even the most complicated case to a form in which it would be presented on paper only in its externals, completely excluding his personal opinion of the matter, while above all observing every prescribed formality. The work was new and Ivan Ilych was one of the first men to apply the new Code of 1864.[11]

On taking up the post of examining magistrate in a new town, he made new acquaintances and connexions, placed himself on a new footing, and assumed a somewhat different tone. He took up an attitude of rather dignified aloofness towards the provincial authorities, but picked out the best circle of legal gentlemen and wealthy gentry living in the town and assumed a tone of slight dissatisfaction with the government, of moderate liberalism, and of enlightened citizenship. At the same time, without at all altering the elegance of his toilet, he ceased shaving his chin and allowed his beard to grow as it pleased.

Ivan Ilych settled down very pleasantly in this new town. The society there, which inclined towards opposition to the Governor, was friendly, his salary was larger, and he began to play *vint* (a form of bridge), which he found added not a little to the pleasure of life, for he had a capacity for cards, played good-humoredly, and calculated rapidly and astutely, so that he usually won.

[10] Proper.

[11] The emancipation of the serfs in 1861 was followed by a thorough all-round reform of judicial proceedings. (Translators' note)

After living there for two years he met his future wife, Praskovya Fedorovna Mikhel, who was the most attractive, clever, and brilliant girl of the set in which he moved, and among other amusements and relaxations from his labours as examining magistrate, Ivan Ilych established light and playful relations with her.

While he had been an official on special service he had been accustomed to dance, but now as an examining magistrate it was exceptional for him to do so. If he danced now, he did it as if to show that though he served under the reformed order of things, and had reached the fifth official rank, yet when it came to dancing he could do it better than most people. So at the end of an evening he sometimes danced with Praskovya Fedorovna, and it was chiefly during these dances that he captivated her. She fell in love with him. Ivan Ilych had at first no definite intention of marrying, but when the girl fell in love with him he said to himself: "Really, why shouldn't I marry?"

Praskovya Fedorovna came of a good family, was not bad looking, and had some little property. Ivan Ilych might have aspired to a more brilliant match, but even this was good. He had his salary, and she, he hoped, would have an equal income. She was well connected, and was a sweet, pretty, and thoroughly correct young woman. To say that Ivan Ilych married because he fell in love with Praskovya Fedorovna and found that she sympathized with his views of life would be as incorrect as to say that he married because his social circle approved of the match. He was swayed by both these considerations: the marriage gave him personal satisfaction, and at the same time it was considered the right thing by the most highly placed of his associates.

So Ivan Ilych got married.

The preparations for marriage and the beginning of married life, with its conjugal caresses, the new furniture, new crockery, and new linen, were very pleasant until his wife became pregnant—so that Ivan Ilych had begun to think that marriage would not impair the easy, agreeable, gay and always decorous character of his life, approved of by society and regarded by himself as natural, but would even improve it. But from the first months of his wife's pregnancy, something new, unpleasant, depressing, and unseemly, and from which there was no way of escape, unexpectedly showed itself.

His wife, without any reason—*de gaieté de cœur*[12] as Ivan Ilych expressed it to himself—began to disturb the pleasure and propriety of their life. She began to be jealous without any cause, expected him to devote his whole attention to her, found fault with everything, and made coarse and ill-mannered scenes.

At first Ivan Ilych hoped to escape from the unpleasantness of this state of affairs by the same easy and decorous relation to life that had served him heretofore: he tried to ignore his wife's disagreeable moods, continued to live in his usual easy and pleasant way, invited friends to his house for a game of cards, and also tried going out to his club or spending his evenings with friends. But one day his wife began upbraiding him so vigorously, using such coarse words, and continued to abuse him every time he did not fulfil her demands, so resolutely and with such evident determination not to give way till he submitted—that is, till he stayed at home and was bored just as she was—that he became alarmed. He now realized that matrimony—at any rate with Praskovya Fedorovna—was not always conducive to the pleasures and amenities of life but on the contrary often infringed both comfort and propriety, and that he must therefore entrench himself against such infringement. And Ivan Ilych began to seek for means of doing so. His official

---

[12] Out of wantonness.

duties were the one thing that imposed upon Praskovya Fedorovna, and by means of his official work and the duties attached to it he began struggling with his wife to secure his own independence.

With the birth of their child, the attempts to feed it and the various failures in doing so, and with the real and imaginary illnesses of mother and child, in which Ivan Ilych's sympathy was demanded but about which he understood nothing, the need of securing for himself an existence outside his family life became still more imperative.

As his wife grew more irritable and exacting and Ivan Ilych transferred the centre of gravity of his life more and more to his official work, so did he grow to like his work better and became more ambitious than before.

Very soon, within a year of his wedding, Ivan Ilych had realized that marriage, though it may add some comforts to life, was in fact a very intricate and difficult affair towards which in order to perform one's duty, that is, to lead a decorous life approved of by society, one must adopt a definite attitude just as towards one's official duties.

And Ivan Ilych evolved such an attitude toward married life. He only required of it those conveniences—dinner at home, housewife, and bed—which it could give him, and above all that propriety of external forms required by public opinion. For the rest he looked for light-hearted pleasure and propriety, and was very thankful when he found them, but if he met with antagonism and querulousness he at once retired into his separate fenced-off world of official duties, where he found satisfaction.

Ivan Ilych was esteemed a good official, and after three years was made Assistant Public Prosecutor. His new duties, their importance, the possibility of indicting and imprisoning anyone he chose, the publicity his speeches received, and the success he had in all these things, made his work still more attractive.

More children came. His wife became more and more querulous and ill-tempered, but the attitude Ivan Ilych had adopted towards his home life rendered him almost impervious to her grumbling.

After seven years' service in that town he was transferred to another province as Public Prosecutor. They moved, but were short of money and his wife did not like the place they moved to. Though the salary was higher the cost of living was greater, besides which two of their children died and family life became still more unpleasant for him.

Praskovya Fedorovna blamed her husband for every inconvenience they encountered in their new home. Most of the conversations between husband and wife, especially as to the children's education, led to topics which recalled former disputes, and those disputes were apt to flare up again at any moment. There remained only those rare periods of amorousness which still came to them at times but did not last long. These were islets at which they anchored for a while and then again set out upon that ocean of veiled hostility which showed itself in their aloofness from one another. This aloofness might have grieved Ivan Ilych had he considered that it ought not to exist, but he now regarded the position as normal, and even made it the goal at which he aimed in family life. His aim was to free himself more and more from those unpleasantnesses and to give them a semblance of harmlessness and propriety. He attained this by spending less and less time with his family, and when obliged to be at home he tried to safeguard his position by the presence of outsiders. The chief thing however was that he had his official duties. The whole interest of his life now centered in the official world and that interest absorbed him. The consciousness of his power, being able to ruin anybody he wished to ruin, the importance, even the external dignity of his entry into court, or meetings with subordinates, his success with superiors and inferiors, and above all his masterly handling of cases, of which he was conscious—all this gave him pleasure and filled his life, together with chats with his colleagues, dinners, and bridge. So that on the whole Ivan Ilych's life continued to flow as he considered it should do—pleasantly and properly.

So things continued for another seven years. His eldest daughter was already sixteen, another child had died, and only one son was left, a schoolboy and a subject of dissension. Ivan Ilych wanted to put him in the School of Law, but to spite him Praskovya Fedorovna entered him at the High School. The daughter had been educated at home and had turned out well: the boy did not learn badly either.

III

So Ivan Ilych lived for seventeen years after his marriage. He was already a Public Prosecutor of long standing, and had declined several proposed transfers while awaiting a more desirable post, when an unanticipated and unpleasant occurrence quite upset the peaceful course of his life. He was expecting to be offered the post of presiding judge in a University town, but Happe somehow came to the front and obtained the appointment instead. Ivan Ilych became irritable, reproached Happe, and quarrelled both with him and with his immediate superiors—who became colder to him and again passed him over when other appointments were made.

This was in 1880, the hardest year of Ivan Ilych's life. It was then that it became evident on the one hand that his salary was insufficient for them to live on, and on the other that he had been forgotten, and not only this, but that what was for him the greatest and most cruel injustice appeared to others a quite ordinary occurrence. Even his father did not consider it was his duty to help him. Ivan Ilych felt himself abandoned by everyone, and that they regarded his position with a salary of 3,500 rubles [about £350] as quite normal and even fortunate. He alone knew that with the consciousness of the injustices done him, with his wife's incessant nagging, and with the debts he had contracted by living beyond his means, his position was far from normal.

In order to save money that summer he obtained leave of absence and went with his wife to live in the country at her brother's place.

In the country, without his work, he experienced *ennui* for the first time in his life, and not only *ennui* but intolerable depression, and he decided that it was impossible to go on living like that, and that it was necessary to take energetic measures.

Having passed a sleepless night pacing up and down the veranda, he decided to go to Petersburg[13] and bestir himself, in order to punish those who had failed to appreciate him and to get transferred to another ministry.

Next day, despite many protests from his wife and her brother, he started for Petersburg with the sole object of obtaining a post with a salary of five thousand rubles a year. He was no longer bent on any particular department, or tendency, or kind of activity. All he now wanted was an appointment to another post with a salary of five thousand rubles, either in the administration, in the banks, with the

[13] St. Petersburg, the Imperial capital of Russia. Renamed Leningrad in 1924. Renamed St. Petersburg in 1991.

railways, in one of the Empress Marya's Institutions,[14] or even in the customs—but it had to carry with it a salary of five thousand rubles and be in a ministry other than that in which they had failed to appreciate him.

And this quest of Ivan Ilych's was crowned with remarkable and unexpected success. At Kursk an acquaintance of his, F. I. Ilyin, got into the first-class carriage, sat down beside Ivan Ilych, and told him of a telegram just received by the Governor of Kursk announcing that a change was about to take place in the ministry: Peter Ivanovich was to be superseded by Ivan Semenovich.

The proposed change, apart from its significance for Russia, had a special significance for Ivan Ilych, because by bringing forward a new man, Peter Petrovich, and consequently his friend Zachar Ivanovich, it was highly favourable for Ivan Ilych, since Zachar Ivanovich was a friend and colleague of his.

In Moscow this news was confirmed, and on reaching Petersburg Ivan Ilych found Zachar Ivanovich and received a definite promise of an appointment in his former department of Justice.

A week later he telegraphed his wife: "Zachar in Miller's place. I shall receive appointment on presentation of report."

Thanks to this change of personnel, Ivan Ilych had unexpectedly obtained an appointment in his former ministry which placed him two stages above his former colleagues besides giving him five thousand rubles salary and three thousand five hundred rubles for expenses connected with his removal. All his ill humour towards his former enemies and the whole department vanished, and Ivan Ilych was completely happy.

He returned to the country more cheerful and contented than he had been for a long time. Praskovya Fedorovna also cheered up and a truce was arranged between them. Ivan Ilych told of how he had been fêted by everybody in Petersburg, how all those who had been his enemies were put to shame and now fawned on him, how envious they were of his appointment, and how much everybody in Petersburg had liked him.

Praskovya Fedorovna listened to all this and appeared to believe it. She did not contradict anything, but only made plans for their life in the town to which they were going. Ivan Ilych saw with delight that these plans were his plans, that he and his wife agreed, and that, after a stumble, his life was regaining its due and natural character of pleasant lightheartedness and decorum.

Ivan Ilych had come back for a short time only, for he had to take up his new duties on the 10th of September. Moreover, he needed time to settle into the new place, to move all his belongings from the province, and to buy and order many additional things: in a word, to make such arrangements as he had resolved on, which were almost exactly what Praskovya Fedorovna too had decided on.

Now that everything had happened so fortunately, and that he and his wife were at one in their aims and moreover saw so little of one another, they got on together better than they had done since the first years of marriage. Ivan Ilych had thought of taking his family away with him at once, but the insistence of his wife's brother and her sister-in-law, who had suddenly become particularly amiable and friendly to him and his family, induced him to depart alone.

So he departed, and the cheerful state of mind induced by his success and by the harmony between his wife and himself, the one intensifying the other, did not leave him. He found a delightful house, just the thing both he and his wife had dreamt of. Spacious, lofty reception rooms in the old style, a convenient and

[14] Charities founded by Empress Marya Feodorovna (1759–1828), the wife of Czar Paul I.

dignified study, rooms for his wife and daughter, a study for his son—it might have been specially built for them. Ivan Ilych himself superintended the arrangements, chose the wallpapers, supplemented the furniture (preferably with antiques which he considered particularly *comme il faut*), and supervised the upholstering. Everything progressed and progressed and approached the ideal he had set himself: even when things were only half completed they exceeded his expectations. He saw what a refined and elegant character, free from vulgarity, it would all have when it was ready. On falling asleep he pictured to himself how the reception-room would look. Looking at the yet unfinished drawing-room he could see the fireplace, the screen, the what-not, the little chairs dotted here and there, the dishes and plates on the walls, and the bronzes, as they would be when everything was in place. He was pleased by the thought of how his wife and daughter, who shared his taste in this matter, would be impressed by it. They were certainly not expecting as much. He had been particularly successful in finding, and buying cheaply, antiques which gave a particularly aristocratic character to the whole place. But in his letters he intentionally understated everything in order to be able to surprise them. All this so absorbed him that his new duties—though he liked his official work—interested him less than he expected. Sometimes he even had moments of absent-mindedness during the Court Sessions, and would consider whether he should have straight or curved cornices for his curtains. He was so interested in it all that he often did things himself, rearranging the furniture, or rehanging the curtains. Once when mounting a stepladder to show the upholsterer, who did not understand, how he wanted the hangings draped, he made a false step and slipped, but being a strong and agile man he clung on and only knocked his side against the knob of the window frame. The bruised place was painful but the pain soon passed, and he felt particularly bright and well just then. He wrote: "I feel fifteen years younger." He thought he would have everything ready by September, but it dragged on till mid-October. But the result was charming not only in his eyes but to everyone who saw it.

In reality it was just what is usually seen in the houses of people of moderate means who want to appear rich, and therefore succeed only in resembling others like themselves: there were damasks, dark wood, plants, rugs, and dull and polished bronzes—all the things people of a certain class have in order to resemble other people of that class. His house was so like the others that it would never have been noticed, but to him it all seemed to be quite exceptional. He was very happy when he met his family at the station and brought them to the newly furnished house all lit up, where a footman in a white tie opened the door into the hall decorated with plants, and when they went on into the drawing-room and the study uttering exclamations of delight. He conducted them everywhere, drank in their praises eagerly, and beamed with pleasure. At tea that evening, when Praskovya Fedorovna among other things asked him about his fall, he laughed, and showed them how he had gone flying and had frightened the upholsterer.

"It's a good thing I'm a bit of an athlete. Another man might have been killed, but I merely knocked myself, just here; it hurts when it's touched, but it's passing off already—it's only a bruise."

So they began living in their new home—in which, as always happens, when they got thoroughly settled in they found they were just one room short—and with the increased income, which as always was just a little (some five hundred rubles) too little, but it was all very nice.

Things went particularly well at first, before everything was finally arranged and while something had still to be done: this thing bought, that thing ordered, another thing moved, and something else adjusted. Though there were some disputes between husband and wife, they were both so well satisfied and had so much to do that it all passed off without any serious quarrels. When nothing was left to arrange it became rather dull and something seemed to be lacking, but they were then making acquaintances, forming habits, and life was growing fuller.

Ivan Ilych spent his mornings at the law court and came home to dinner, and at first he was generally in a good humour, though he occasionally became irritable just on account of his house. (Every spot on the tablecloth or the upholstery, and every broken window-blind string, irritated him. He had devoted so much trouble to arranging it all that every disturbance of it distressed him.) But on the whole his life ran its course as he believed life should do: easily, pleasantly, and decorously.

He got up at nine, drank his coffee, read the paper, and then put on his undress uniform and went to the law courts. There the harness in which he worked had already been stretched to fit him and he donned it without a hitch: petitioners, inquiries at the chancery, the chancery itself, and the sittings public and administrative. In all this the thing was to exclude everything fresh and vital, which always disturbs the regular course of official business, and to admit only official relations with people, and then only on official grounds. A man would come, for instance, wanting some information. Ivan Ilych, as one in whose sphere the matter did not lie, would have nothing to do with him: but if the man had some business with him in his official capacity, something that could be expressed on officially stamped paper, he would do everything, positively everything he could within the limits of such relations, and in doing so would maintain the semblance of friendly human relations, that is, would observe the courtesies of life. As soon as the official relations ended, so did everything else. Ivan Ilych possessed this capacity to separate his real life from the official side of affairs and not mix the two, in the highest degree, and by long practice and natural aptitude had brought it to such a pitch that sometimes, in the manner of a virtuoso, he would even allow himself to let the human and official relations mingle. He let himself do this just because he felt that he could at any time he chose resume the strictly official attitude again and drop the human relation. And he did it all easily, pleasantly, correctly, and even artistically. In the intervals between the sessions he smoked, drank tea, chatted a little about politics, a little about general topics, a little about cards, but most of all about official appointments. Tired, but with the feelings of a virtuoso— one of the first violins who had played his part in an orchestra with precision—he would return home to find that his wife and daughter had been out paying calls, or had a visitor, and that his son had been to school, had done his homework with his tutor, and was duly learning what is taught at High Schools. Everything was as it should be. After dinner, if they had no visitors, Ivan Ilych sometimes read a book that was being much discussed at the time, and in the evening settled down to work, that is, read official papers, compared the depositions of witnesses, and noted paragraphs of the Code applying to them. This was neither dull nor amusing. It was dull when he might have been playing bridge, but if no bridge was available it was at any rate better than doing nothing or sitting with his wife. Ivan Ilych's chief pleasure was giving little dinners to which he invited men and women of good social position, and just as his drawing-room resembled all other drawing-rooms so did his enjoyable little parties resemble all other such parties.

Once they even gave a dance. Ivan Ilych enjoyed it and everything went off well, except that it led to a violent quarrel with his wife about the cakes and sweets. Praskovya Fedorovna had made her own plans, but Ivan Ilych insisted on getting everything from an expensive confectioner and ordered too many cakes, and the quarrel occurred because some of those cakes were left over and the confectioner's bill came to forty-five rubles. It was a great and disagreeable quarrel. Praskovya Fedorovna called him "a fool and an imbecile," and he clutched at his head and made angry allusions to divorce.

But the dance itself had been enjoyable. The best people were there, and Ivan Ilych had danced with Princess Trufonova, a sister of the distinguished founder of the Society "Bear my Burden."

The pleasures connected with his work were pleasures of ambition; his social pleasures were those of vanity; but Ivan Ilych's greatest pleasure was playing bridge. He acknowledged that whatever disagreeable incident happened in his life, the pleasure that beamed like a ray of light above everything else was to sit down to bridge with good players, not noisy partners, and of course to four-handed bridge (with five players it was annoying to have to stand out, though one pretended not to mind), to play a clever and serious game (when the cards allowed it) and then to have supper and drink a glass of wine. After a game of bridge, especially if he had won a little (to win a large sum was unpleasant), Ivan Ilych went to bed in specially good humour.

So they lived. They formed a circle of acquaintances among the best people and were visited by people of importance and by young folk. In their views as to their acquaintances, husband and wife and daughter were entirely agreed, and tacitly and unanimously kept at arm's length and shook off the various shabby friends and relations who, with much show of affection, gushed into the drawing-room with its Japanese plates on the walls. Soon these shabby friends ceased to obtrude themselves and only the best people remained in the Golovins' set.

Young men made up to Lisa, and Petrischhev, an examining magistrate and Dmitri Ivanovich Petrischev's son and sole heir, began to be so attentive to her that Ivan Ilych had already spoken to Praskovya Fedorovna about it, and considered whether they should not arrange a party for them, or get up some private theatricals.

So they lived, and all went well, without change, and life flowed pleasantly.

IV

They were all in good health. It could not be called ill health if Ivan Ilych sometimes said that he had a queer taste in his mouth and felt some discomfort in his left side.

But this discomfort increased and, though not exactly painful, grew into a sense of pressure in his side accompanied by ill humour. And his irritability became worse and worse and began to mar the agreeable, easy, and correct life that had established itself in the Golovin family. Quarrels between husband and wife became more and more frequent, and soon the ease and amenity disappeared and even the decorum was barely maintained. Scenes again became frequent, and very few of those islets remained on which husband and wife could meet without an explosion. Praskovya Fedorovna now had good reason to say that her husband's temper was trying. With characteristic exaggeration she said he had always had a dreadful temper, and that it had needed all her good nature to put up with it for twenty years. It was true that now the quarrels were started by him. His bursts of temper always came just before dinner, often just as he began to eat his soup. Sometimes he noticed that a plate or dish was chipped, or the food was not right, or his son put his elbow on the table, or his daughter's hair was not done as he liked it, and for all this he blamed Praskovya Fedorovna. At first she retorted and said disagreeable things to him, but once or twice he fell into such a rage at the beginning of dinner that she realized it was due to some physical derangement brought on by taking food, and so she restrained herself and did not answer, but only hurried to get the dinner over. She regarded this self-restraint as highly praiseworthy. Having come to the conclusion that her husband had a dreadful temper and made her life miserable, she began to feel sorry for herself, and the more she pitied herself the more she hated her husband. She began to wish he would die; yet she did not want him to die because then his salary would cease. And this irritated her against him still more. She considered herself dreadfully unhappy just because not even his death could save her, and though she concealed her exasperation, that hidden exasperation of hers increased his irritation also.

After one scene in which Ivan Ilych had been particularly unfair and after which he had said in explanation that he certainly was irritable but that it was due to his not being well, she said that if he was ill it should be attended to, and insisted on his going to see a celebrated doctor.

He went. Everything took place as he had expected and as it always does. There was the usual waiting and the important air assumed by the doctor, with which he was so familiar (resembling that which he himself assumed in court), and the sounding and listening, and the questions which called for answers that were foregone conclusions and were evidently unnecessary, and the look of importance which implied that "if only you put yourself in our hands we will arrange everything—we know indubitably how it has to be done, always in the same way for everybody alike." It was all just as it was in the law courts. The doctor put on just the same air towards him as he himself put on towards an accused person.

The doctor said that so-and-so indicated that there was so-and-so inside the patient, but if the investigation of so-and-so did not confirm this, then he must assume that and that. If he assumed that and that, then . . . and so on. To Ivan Ilych only one question was important: was his case serious or not? But the doctor ignored that inappropriate question. From his point of view it was not the one under consideration, the real question was to decide between a floating kidney, chronic catarrh, or appendicitis. It was not a question of Ivan Ilych's life or death, but one between a floating kidney and appendicitis. And that question the doctor solved brilliantly, as it seemed to Ivan Ilych, in favour of the appendix, with the reservation that should an examination of the urine give fresh indications the matter would be reconsidered. All this was just what Ivan Ilych had himself brilliantly accomplished a thousand times in dealing with men on trial. The doctor summed up just as brilliantly, looking over his spectacles triumphantly and even gaily at the accused. From the doctor's summing up Ivan Ilych concluded that things were bad, but that for the doctor, and perhaps for everybody else, it was a matter of indifference, though for him it was bad. And this conclusion struck him painfully, arousing in him a great feeling of pity for himself and of bitterness towards the doctor's indifference to a matter of such importance.

He said nothing of this, but rose, placed the doctor's fee on the table, and remarked with a sigh: "We sick people probably often put inappropriate questions. But tell me, in general, is this complaint dangerous, or not? . . ."

The doctor looked at him sternly over his spectacles with one eye, as if to say: "Prisoner, if you will not keep to the questions put to you, I shall be obliged to have you removed from the court."

"I have already told you what I consider necessary and proper. The analysis may show something more." And the doctor bowed.

Ivan Ilych went out slowly, seated himself disconsolately on his sledge, and drove home. All the way home he was going over what the doctor had said, trying to translate those complicated, obscure, scientific phrases into plain language and find in them an answer to the question: "Is my condition bad? Is it very bad? Or is there as yet nothing much wrong?" And it seemed to him that the meaning of what the doctor had said was that it was very bad. Everything in the streets seemed depressing. The cabmen, the houses, the passers-by, and the shops, were dismal. His ache, this dull gnawing ache that never ceased for a moment, seemed to have acquired a new and more serious significance from the doctor's dubious remarks. Ivan Ilych now watched it with a new and oppressive feeling.

He reached home and began to tell his wife about it. She listened, but in the middle of his account his daughter came in with her hat on, ready to go out with her mother. She sat down reluctantly to listen to this tedious story, but could not stand it long, and her mother too did not hear him to the end.

"Well, I am very glad," she said. "Mind now to take your medicine regularly. Give me the prescription and I'll send Gerasim to the chemist's." And she went to get ready to go out.

While she was in the room Ivan Ilych had hardly taken time to breathe, but he sighed deeply when she left it.

"Well," he thought, "perhaps it isn't so bad after all."

He began taking his medicine and following the doctor's directions, which had been altered after the examination of the urine. But then it happened that there was a contradiction between the indications drawn from the examination of the urine and the symptoms that showed themselves. It turned out that what was happening differed from what the doctor had told him, and that he had either forgotten, or blundered, or hidden something from him. He could not, however, be blamed for that, and Ivan Ilych still obeyed his orders implicitly and at first derived some comfort from doing so.

From the time of his visit to the doctor, Ivan Ilych's chief occupation was the exact fulfilment of the doctor's instructions regarding hygiene and the taking of medicine, and the observation of his pain and his excretions. His chief interests came to be people's ailments and people's health. When sickness, deaths, or recoveries, were mentioned in his presence, especially when the illness resembled his own, he listened with agitation which he tried to hide, asked questions, and applied what he heard to his own case.

The pain did not grow less, but Ivan Ilych made efforts to force himself to think that he was better. And he could do this so long as nothing agitated him. But as soon as he had any unpleasantness with his wife, any lack of success in his official work, or held bad cards at bridge, he was at once acutely sensible of his disease. He had formerly borne such mischances, hoping soon to adjust what was wrong, to master it and attain success, or make a grand slam. But now every mischance upset him and plunged him into despair. He would say to himself: "There now, just as I was beginning to get better and the medicine had begun to take effect, comes this accursed misfortune, or unpleasantness . . ." And he was furious with the mishap, or with the people who were causing the unpleasantness and killing him, for he felt that this fury was killing him but could not restrain it. One would have thought that it should have been clear to him that this exasperation with circumstances and people aggravated his illness, and that he ought therefore to ignore unpleasant occurrences. But he drew the very opposite conclusion: he said that he needed peace, and he watched for everything that might disturb it and became irritable at the slightest infringement of it. His condition was rendered worse by the fact that he read medical books and consulted doctors. The progress of his disease was so gradual that he could deceive himself when comparing one day with another—the difference was so slight. But when he consulted the doctors it seemed to him that he was getting worse, and even very rapidly. Yet despite this he was continually consulting them.

That month he went to see another celebrity, who told him almost the same as the first had done but put his questions rather differently, and the interview with this celebrity only increased Ivan Ilych's doubts and fears. A friend of a friend of his, a very good doctor, diagnosed his illness again quite differently from the others, and though he predicted recovery, his questions and suppositions bewildered Ivan Ilych still more and increased his doubts. A homeopathist[15] diagnosed the disease in yet another way, and prescribed medicine which Ivan Ilych took secretly for a week. But after a week, not feeling any improvement and having lost confidence both in the former doctor's treatment and in this one's, he became still more despondent. One day a lady acquaintance mentioned a cure effected by a wonder-working icon. Ivan Ilych caught himself listening attentively and beginning to believe that it had oc-curred. This incident alarmed him. "Has my mind really weakened to such an extent?" he asked himself. "Nonsense! It's all rubbish. I mustn't give way to nervous fears but having chosen a doctor must keep strictly to his treatment. That is what I will do. Now it's all settled. I won't think about it, but will follow the treatment seriously till summer, and then we shall see. From now there must be no more of this wavering!" This was easy to say but impossible to carry out. The pain in his side oppressed him and seemed to grow worse and more incessant, while the taste in his mouth grew stranger and stranger. It seemed to him that his breath had a disgusting smell, and he was conscious of a loss of appetite and strength. There was no deceiving himself: something terrible, new, and more important than anything before in his life, was taking place within him of which he alone was aware. Those about him did not understand or would not understand it, but thought everything in the world was going on as usual. That tormented Ivan Ilych more than anything. He saw that his household, especially his wife and daughter who were in a perfect whirl of visiting, did not understand anything of it and were annoyed that he was so depressed and exacting, as if he were to blame for it. Though they tried to disguise it he saw that he was an obstacle in their path, and that his wife had adopted a definite line in regard to his illness and kept to it regardless of anything he said or did. Her attitude was this: "You know," she would say to her friends, "Ivan Ilych can't do as other people do, and keep to the treatment prescribed for him. One day he'll take his drops and keep strictly to his diet and go to bed in good time, but the next day unless I watch him he'll suddenly forget his medicine, eat sturgeon—which is forbidden—and sit up playing cards until one o'clock in the morning."

"Oh, come, when was that?" Ivan Ilych would ask in vexation. "Only once at Peter Ivanovich's."

"And yesterday with Shebek."

"Well, even if I hadn't stayed up, this pain would have kept me awake."

"Be that as it may you'll never get well like that, but will always make us wretched."

Praskovya Fedorovna's attitude to Ivan Ilych's illness, as she expressed it both to others and to him, was that it was his own fault and was another of the annoyances he caused her. Ivan Ilych felt that this opinion escaped her involuntarily—but that did not make it easier for him.

At the law courts too, Ivan Ilych noticed, or thought he noticed, a strange

---

[15] A medical practitioner who treated disease with drugs.

attitude towards himself. It sometimes seemed to him that people were watching him inquisitively as a man whose place might soon be vacant. Then again, his friends would suddenly begin to chaff him in a friendly way about his low spirits, as if the awful, horrible, and unheard-of thing that was going on within him, incessantly gnawing at him and irresistibly drawing him away, was a very agreeable subject for jests. Schwartz in particular irritated him by his jocularity, vivacity, and *savoir-faire*, which reminded him of what he himself had been ten years ago.

Friends came to make up a set and they sat down to cards. They dealt, bending the new cards to soften them, and he sorted the diamonds in his hand and found he had seven. His partner said "No trumps" and supported him with two diamonds. What more could be wished for? It ought to be jolly and lively. They would make a grand slam. But suddenly Ivan Ilych was conscious of that gnawing pain, that taste in his mouth, and it seemed ridiculous that in such circumstances he should be pleased to make a grand slam.

He looked at his partner Mikhail Mikhaylovich, who rapped the table with his strong hand and instead of snatching up the tricks pushed the cards courteously and indulgently towards Ivan Ilych that he might have the pleasure of gathering them up without the trouble of stretching out his hand for them. "Does he think I am too weak to stretch out my arm?" thought Ivan Ilych, and forgetting what he was doing he over-trumped his partner, missing the grand slam by three tricks. And what was most awful of all was that he saw how upset Mikhail Mikhaylovich was about it but did not himself care. And it was dreadful to realize why he did not care.

They all saw that he was suffering, and said: "We can stop if you are tired. Take a rest." Lie down? No, he was not at all tired, and he finished the rubber. All were gloomy and silent. Ivan Ilych felt that he had diffused this gloom over them and could not dispel it. They had supper and went away, and Ivan Ilych was left alone with the consciousness that his life was poisoned and was poisoning the lives of others, and that this poison did not weaken but penetrated more and more deeply into his whole being.

With this consciousness, and with physical pain besides the terror, he must go to bed, often to lie awake the greater part of the night. Next morning he had to get up again, dress, go to the law courts, speak, and write; or if he did not go out, spend at home those twenty-four hours a day each of which was a torture. And he had to live thus all alone on the brink of an abyss, with no one who understood or pitied him.

V

So one month passed and then another. Just before the New Year his brother-in-law came to town and stayed at their house. Ivan Ilych was at the law courts and Praskovya Fedorovna had gone shopping. When Ivan Ilych came home and entered his study he found his brother-in-law there—a healthy, florid man—unpacking his portmanteau himself. He raised his head on hearing Ivan Ilych's footsteps and looked up at him for a moment without a word. That stare told Ivan Ilych everything. His brother-in-law opened his mouth to utter an exclamation of surprise but checked himself, and that action confirmed all.

"I have changed, eh?"

"Yes, there is a change."

And after that, try as he would to get his brother-in-law to return to the subject of his looks, the latter would say nothing about it. Praskovya Fedorovna came home and her brother went out to her. Ivan Ilych locked the door and began to examine himself in the glass, first full face, then in profile. He took up a portrait of himself taken with his wife, and compared it with what he saw in the glass. The change in him was immense. Then he bared his arms to the elbow, looked at them, drew the sleeves down again, sat down on an ottoman, and grew blacker than night.

"No, no, this won't do!" he said to himself, and jumped up, went to the table, took up some law papers and began to read them, but could not continue. He unlocked the door and went into the reception-room. The door leading to the drawing-room was shut. He approached it on tiptoe and listened.

"No, you are exaggerating!" Praskovya Fedorovna was saying.

"Exaggerating! Don't you see it? Why, he's a dead man! Look at his eyes—there's no light in them. But what is it that is wrong with him?"

"No one knows. Nikolaevich (that was another doctor) said something, but I don't know what. And Leschetitsky (this was the celebrated specialist) said quite the contrary . . ."

Ivan Ilych walked away, went to his own room, lay down, and began musing: "The kidney, a floating kidney." He recalled all the doctors had told him of how it detached itself and swayed about. And by an effort of imagination he tried to catch that kidney and arrest it and support it. So little was needed for this, it seemed to him. "No, I'll go to see Peter Ivanovich again." (That was the friend whose friend was a doctor.) He rang, ordered the carriage, and got ready to go.

"Where are you going, Jean?" asked his wife, with a specially sad and exceptionally kind look.

This exceptionally kind look irritated him. He looked morosely at her.

"I must go to see Peter Ivanovich."

He went to see Peter Ivanovich, and together they went to see his friend, the doctor. He was in, and Ivan Ilych had a long talk with him.

Reviewing the anatomical and psychological details of what in the doctor's opinion was going on inside him, he understood it all.

There was something, a small thing, in the vermiform appendix. It might all come right. Only stimulate the energy of the organ and check the activity of another, then absorption would take place and everything would come right. He got home rather late for dinner, ate his dinner, and conversed cheerfully, but could not for a long time bring himself to go back to work in his room. At last, however, he went to his study and did what was necessary, but the consciousness that he had put something aside—an important, intimate matter which he would revert to when his work was done—never left him. When he had finished his work he remembered that this intimate matter was the thought of his vermiform appendix. But he did not give himself up to it, and went to the drawing-room for tea. There were callers there, including the examining magistrate who was a desirable match for his daughter, and they were conversing, playing the piano and singing. Ivan Ilych, as Praskovya Fedorovna remarked, spent that evening more cheerfully than usual, but he never for a moment forgot that he had postponed the important matter of the appendix. At eleven o'clock he said good-night and went to his bedroom. Since his illness he had slept in a small room next to his study. He undressed and took up a novel by Zola,[16] but instead of reading it he fell into thought, and in his imagination that desired improvement in the vermiform appendix occurred. There was the absorption and evacuation and the reestablishment of normal activity. "Yes, that's it!" he said to himself. "One need only

---

[16] Émile Zola (1840–1902), the French novelist; "father" of the naturalistic novel.

assist nature, that's all." He remembered his medicine, rose, took it, and lay down on his back watching for the beneficient action of the medicine and for it to lessen the pain. "I need only take it regularly and avoid all injurious influences. I am already feeling better, much better." He began touching his side: it was not painful to the touch. "There, I really don't feel it. It's much better already." He put out the light and turned on his side ... "The appendix is getting better, absorption is occurring." Suddenly he felt the old, familiar, dull, gnawing pain, stubborn and serious. There was the same familiar loathsome taste in his mouth. His heart sank and he felt dazed. "My God! My God!" he muttered. "Again, again! And it will never cease." And suddenly the matter presented itself in a quite different aspect. "Vermiform appendix! Kidney!" he said to himself. "It's not a question of appendix or kidney, but of life and ... death. Yes, life was there and now it is going, going and I cannot stop it. Yes. Why deceive myself? Isn't it obvious to everyone but me that I'm dying, and that it's only a question of weeks, days ... it may happen this moment. There was light and now there is darkness. I was here and now I'm going there! Where?" A chill came over him, his breathing ceased, and he felt only the throbbing of his heart.

"When I am not, what will there be? There will be nothing. Then where shall I be when I am no more? Can this be dying? No, I don't want to!" He jumped up and tried to light the candle, felt for it with trembling hands, dropped candle and candlestick on the floor, and fell back on his pillow.

"What's the use? It makes no difference," he said to himself, staring with wide-open eyes into the darkness. "Death. Yes, death. And none of them know or wish to know it, and they have no pity for me. Now they are playing." (He heard through the door the distant sound of a song and its accompaniment.) "It's all the same to them, but they will die too! Fools! I first, and they later, but it will be the same for them. And now they are merry ... the beasts!"

Anger choked him and he was agonizingly, unbearably miserable. "It is impossible that all men have been doomed to suffer this awful horror!" He raised himself.

"Something must be wrong. I must calm myself—must think it all over from the beginning." And he again began thinking. "Yes, the beginning of my illness: I knocked my side, but I was still quite well that day and the next. It hurt a little, then rather more. I saw the doctors, then followed despondency and anguish, more doctors, and I drew nearer to the abyss. My strength grew less and I kept coming nearer and nearer, and now I have wasted away and there is no light in my eyes. I think of the appendix—but this is death! I think of mending the appendix, and all the while here is death! Can it really be death?" Again terror seized him and he gasped for breath. He leant down and began feeling for the matches, pressing with his elbow on the stand beside the bed. It was in his way and hurt him, he grew furious with it, pressed on it still harder, and upset it. Breathless and in despair he fell on his back, expecting death to come immediately.

Meanwhile the visitors were leaving. Praskovya Fedorovna was seeing them off. She heard something fall and came in.

"What has happened?"

"Nothing. I knocked it over accidentally."

She went out and returned with a candle. He lay there panting heavily, like a man who has run a thousand yards, and stared upwards at her with a fixed look.

"What is it, Jean?"

"No ... o ... thing. I upset it." ("Why speak of it? She won't understand," he thought.)

And in truth she did not understand. She picked up the stand, lit the candle, and hurried away to see another visitor off. When she came back he still lay on his back, looking upwards.

"What is it? Do you feel worse?"

"Yes."

She shook her head and sat down.

"Do you know, Jean, I think we must ask Leshchetitsky to come and see you here."

This meant calling in the famous specialist, regardless of expense. He smiled malignantly and said "No." She remained a little longer and then went up to him and kissed his forehead.

While she was kissing him he hated her from the bottom of his soul and with difficulty refrained from pushing her away.

"Good-night. Please God you'll sleep."

"Yes."

VI

Ivan Ilych saw that he was dying, and he was in continual despair.

In the depth of his heart he knew he was dying, but not only was he not accustomed to the thought, he simply did not and could not grasp it.

The syllogism he had learnt from Kiezewetter's Logic:[17] "Caius is a man, men are mortal, therefore Caius is mortal," had always seemed to him correct as applied to Caius, but certainly not as applied to himself. That Caius—man in the abstract—was mortal, was perfectly correct, but he was not Caius, not an abstract man, but a creature quite, quite separate from all others. He had been little Vanya, with a mamma and a papa, with Mitya and Volodya, with the toys, a coachman and a nurse, afterwards with Katenka and with all the joys, griefs, and delights of childhood, boyhood, and youth. What did Caius know of the smell of that striped leather ball Vanya had been so fond of? Had Caius kissed his mother's hand like that, and did the silk of her dress rustle so for Caius? Had he rioted like that at school when the pastry was bad? Had Caius been in love like that? Could Caius preside at a session as he did? "Caius really was mortal, and it was right for him to die; but for me, little Vanya, Ivan Ilych, with all my thoughts and emotions, it's altogether a different matter. It cannot be that I ought to die. That would be too terrible."

Such was his feeling.

"If I had to die like Caius I should have known it was so. An inner voice would have told me so, but there was nothing of the sort in me and I and all my friends felt that our case was quite different from that of Caius. And now here it is!" he said to himself. "It can't be. It's impossible! But here it is. How is this? How is one to understand it?"

He could not understand it, and tried to drive this false, incorrect, morbid thought away and to replace it by other proper and healthy thoughts. But that thought, and not the thought only but the reality itself, seemed to come and confront him.

And to replace that thought he called up a succession of others, hoping to find in them some support. He tried to get back into the former current of thoughts

---

[17] Karl Kiezewetter (1766–1819), the German philosopher who authored a widely used text on logic (1796).

that had once screened the thought of death from him. But strange to say, all that had formerly shut off, hidden, and destroyed his consciousness of death, no longer had that effect. Ivan Ilych now spent most of his time in attempting to re-establish that old current. He would say to himself: "I will take up my duties again—after all I used to live by them." And banishing all doubts he would go to the law courts, enter into conversation with his colleagues, and sit carelessly as was his wont, scanning the crowd with a thoughtful look and leaning both his emaciated arms on the arms of his oak chair; bending over as usual to a colleague and drawing his papers nearer he would interchange whispers with him, and then suddenly raising his eyes and sitting erect would pronounce certain words and open the proceedings. But suddenly in the midst of those proceedings the pain in his side, regardless of the stage the proceedings had reached, would begin its own gnawing work. Ivan Ilych would turn his attention to it and try to drive the thought of it away, but without success. *It* would come and stand before him and look at him, and he would be petrified and the light would die out of his eyes, and he would again begin asking himself whether *It* alone was true. And his colleagues and subordinates would see with surprise and distress that he, the brilliant and subtle judge, was becoming confused and making mistakes. He would shake himself, try to pull himself together, manage somehow to bring the sitting to a close, and return home with the sorrowful consciousness that his judicial labours could not as formerly hide from him what he wanted them to hide, and could not deliver him from *It*. And what was worst of all was that *It* drew his attention to itself not in order to make him take some action but only that he should look at *It*, look it straight in the face: look at it and without doing anything, suffer inexpressibly.

And to save himself from this condition Ivan Ilych looked for consolations— new screens—and new screens were found and for a while seemed to save him, but then they immediately fell to pieces or rather became transparent, as if *It* penetrated them and nothing could veil *It*.

In these latter days he would go into the drawing-room he had arranged—that drawing-room where he had fallen and for the sake of which (how bitterly ridiculous it seemed) he had sacrificed his life—for he knew that his illness originated with that knock. He would enter and see that something had scratched the polished table. He would look for the cause of this and find that it was the bronze ornamentation of an album, that had got bent. He would take up the expensive album which he had lovingly arranged, and feel vexed with his daughter and her friends for their untidiness—for the album was torn here and there and some of the photographs turned upside down. He would put it carefully in order and bend the ornamentation back into position. Then it would occur to him to place all those things in another corner of the room, near the plants. He would call the footman, but his daughter or wife would come to help him. They would not agree, and his wife would contradict him, and he would dispute and grow angry. But that was all right, for then he did not think about *It*. *It* was invisible.

But then, when he was moving something himself, his wife would say: "Let the servants do it. You will hurt yourself again." And suddenly *It* would flash through the screen and he would see it. It was just a flash, and he hoped it would disappear, but he would involuntarily pay attention to his side. "It sits there as before, gnawing just the same!" And he could no longer forget *It*, but could distinctly see it looking at him from behind the flowers. "What is it all for?"

"It really is so! I lost my life over that curtain as I might have done when storming a fort. Is that possible? How terrible and how stupid. It can't be true! It can't, but it is."

He would go to his study, lie down, and again be alone with *It:* face to face with *It*. And nothing could be done with *It* except to look at it and shudder.

VII

How it happened it is impossible to say because it came about step by step, unnoticed, but in the third month of Ivan Ilych's illness, his wife, his daughter, his son, his acquaintances, the doctors, the servants, and above all he himself, were aware that the whole interest he had for other people was whether he would soon vacate his place, and at last release the living from the discomfort caused by his presence and be himself released from his sufferings.

He slept less and less. He was given opium and hypodermic injections or morphine, but this did not relieve him. The dull depression he experienced in a somnolent condition at first gave him a little relief, but only as something new, afterwards it became as distressing as the pain itself or even more so.

Special foods were prepared for him by the doctors' orders, but all those foods became increasingly distasteful and disgusting to him.

For his excretions also special arrangements had to be made, and this was a torment to him every time—a torment from the uncleanliness, the unseemliness, and the smell, and from knowing that another person had to take part in it.

But just through this most unpleasant matter Ivan Ilych obtained comfort. Gerasim, the butler's young assistant, always came in to carry the things out. Gerasim was a clean, fresh peasant lad, grown stout on town food and always cheerful and bright. At first the sight of him, in his clean Russian peasant costume, engaged on that disgusting task embarrassed Ivan Ilych.

Once when he got up from the commode too weak to draw up his trousers, he dropped into a soft armchair and looked with horror at his bare, enfeebled thighs with the muscles so sharply marked on them.

Gerasim with a firm light tread, his heavy boots emitting a pleasant smell of tar and fresh winter air, came in wearing a clean Hessian apron, the sleeves of his print shirt tucked up over his strong bare young arms and refraining from looking at his sick master out of consideration for his feelings, and restraining the joy of life that beamed from his face, he went up to the commode.

"Gerasim!" said Ivan Ilych in a weak voice.

Gerasim started, evidently afraid he might have committed some blunder, and with a rapid movement turned his fresh, kind, simple young face which just showed the first downy signs of a beard.

"Yes, sir?"

"That must be very unpleasant for you. You must forgive me. I am helpless."

"Oh, why, sir," and Gerasim's eyes beamed and he showed his glistening white teeth, "what's a little trouble? It's a case of illness with you, sir."

And his deft strong hands did their accustomed task, and he went out of the room stepping lightly. Five minutes later he as lightly returned.

Ivan Ilych was still sitting in the same position in the armchair.

"Gerasim," he said when the latter had replaced the freshly-washed utensil. "Please come here and help me." Gerasim went up to him. "Lift me up. It is hard for me to get up, and I have sent Dmitri away."

Gerasim went up to him, grasped his master with his strong arms deftly but gently, in the same way that he stepped—lifted him, supported him with one hand, and with the other drew up his trousers and would have set him down again, but Ivan Ilych asked to be led to the sofa. Gerasim, without an effort and without apparent pressure, led him, almost lifting him, to the sofa and placed him on it.

"Thank you. How easily and well you do it all!"

Gerasim smiled again and turned to leave the room. But Ivan Ilych felt his presence such a comfort that he did not want to let him go.

"One thing more, please move up that chair. No, the other one—under my feet. It is easier for me when my feet are raised."

Gerasim brought the chair, set it down gently in place, and raised Ivan Ilych's legs on to it. It seemed to Ivan Ilych that he felt better while Gerasim was holding up his legs.

"It's better when my legs are higher," he said. "Place that cushion under them."

Gerasim did so. He again lifted the legs and placed them, and again Ivan Ilych felt better while Gerasim held his legs. When he set them down Ivan Ilych fancied he felt worse.

"Gerasim," he said. "Are you busy now?"

"Not at all, sir," said Gerasim, who had learnt from the townfolk how to speak to gentlefolk.

"What have you still to do?"

"What have I to do? I've done everything except chopping the logs for tomorrow."

"Then hold my legs up a bit higher, can you?"

"Of course I can. Why not?" And Gerasim raised his master's legs higher and Ivan Ilych thought that in that position he did not feel any pain at all.

"And how about the logs?"

"Don't trouble about that, sir. There's plenty of time."

Ivan Ilych told Gerasim to sit down and hold his legs, and began to talk to him. And strange to say it seemed to him that he felt better while Gerasim held his legs up.

After that Ivan Ilych would sometimes call Gerasim and get him to hold his legs on his shoulders, and he liked talking to him. Gerasim did it all easily, willingly, simply, and with a good nature that touched Ivan Ilych. Health, strength, and vitality in other people were offensive to him, but Gerasim's strength and vitality did not mortify but soothed him.

What tormented Ivan Ilych most was the deception, the lie, which for some reason they all accepted, that he was not dying but was simply ill, and that he only need keep quiet and undergo a treatment and then something very good would result. He however knew that do what they would nothing would come of it, only still more agonizing suffering and death. This deception tortured him—their not wishing to admit what they all knew and what he knew, but wanting to lie to him concerning his terrible condition, and wishing and forcing him to participate in that lie. Those lies—lies enacted over him on the eve of his death and destined to degrade this awful, solemn act to the level of their visitings, their curtains, their sturgeon for dinner—were a terrible agony for Ivan Ilych. And strangely enough, many times when they were going through their antics over him he had been within a hairbreadth of calling out to them: "Stop lying! You know and I know that I am dying. Then at least stop lying about it!" But he had never had the spirit to do it. The awful terrible act of his dying was, he could see, reduced by those about him to the level of a casual, unpleasant, and almost indecorous incident (as if someone entered a drawing-room diffusing an unpleasant odor) and this was done by that very decorum which he had served all his life long. He saw that no one felt for him, because no one even wished to grasp his position. Only Gerasim recognized it and pitied him. And so Ivan Ilych felt at ease only with him. He felt comforted when Gerasim supported his legs (sometimes all night long) and refused to go to bed, saying: "Don't you worry, Ivan Ilych. I'll get sleep enough later on," or when he suddenly became familiar and exclaimed: "If you weren't sick it would be another matter, but as it is, why should I grudge a little trouble?" Gerasim alone did not lie; everything showed that he alone understood the facts of the case and did not consider it necessary to disguise them, but simply felt sorry for his emaciated and enfeebled master. Once when Ivan Ilych was sending him away he even said straight out: "We shall all of us die, so why should I grudge a little trouble?"—expressing the fact that he did not think his work burdensome, because he was doing it for a dying man and hoped someone would do the same for him when his time came.

Apart from this lying, or because of it, what most tormented Ivan Ilych was that no one pitied him as he wished to be pitied. At certain moments after prolonged suffering he wished most of all (though he would have been ashamed to confess it) for someone to pity him as a sick child is pitied. He longed to be petted and comforted. He knew he was an important functionary, that he had a beard turning grey, and that therefore what he longed for was impossible, but still he longed for it. And in Gerasim's attitude toward him there was something akin to what he wished for, and so that attitude comforted him. Ivan Ilych wanted to be petted and cried over, and then his colleague Shebek would come, and instead of weeping and being petted, Ivan Ilych would assume a serious, severe, and profound air, and by force of habit would express his opinion on a decision of the Court of Cassation[18] and would stubbornly insist on that view. This falsity around him and within him did more than anything else to poison his last days.

VIII

It was morning. He knew it was morning because Gerasim had gone, and Peter the footman had come and put out the candles, drawn back one of the curtains, and began quietly to tidy up. Whether it was morning or evening, Friday or Sunday, made no difference, it was all just the same: the gnawing, unmitigated, agonizing pain, never ceasing for an instant, the consciousness of life inexorably waning but not yet extinguished, the approach of that ever dreaded and hateful Death which was the only reality, and always the same falsity. What were days, weeks, hours, in such a case?

"Will you have some tea, sir?"

"He wants things to be regular, and wishes the gentlefolk to drink tea in the morning," thought Ivan Ilych, and only said "No."

"Wouldn't you like to move onto the sofa, sir?"

"He wants to tidy up the room, and I'm in the way. I am uncleanliness and disorder," he thought, and said only:

"No, leave me alone."

The man went on bustling about. Ivan Ilych stretched out his hand. Peter came up, ready to help.

"What is it, sir?"

"My watch."

Peter took the watch which was close at hand and gave it to his master.

"Half-past eight. Are they up?"

[18] The court of high appeals.

"No sir, except Vladimir Ivanich" (the son) "who has gone to school. Praskovya Fedorovna ordered me to wake her if you asked for her. Shall I do so?"

"No, there's no need to." "Perhaps I'd better have some tea," he thought, and added aloud: "Yes, bring me some tea."

Peter went out. Left alone Ivan Ilych dreaded being left alone. "How can I keep him here? Oh yes, my medicine." "Peter, give me my medicine." "Why not? Perhaps it may still do me some good." He took a spoonful and swallowed it. "No, it won't help. It's all tomfoolery, all deception," he decided as soon as he became aware of the familiar, sickly, hopeless taste. "No, I can't believe in it any longer. But the pain, why this pain? If it would only cease just for a moment!" And he moaned. Peter turned towards him. "It's all right. Go and fetch me some tea."

Peter went out. Left alone Ivan Ilych groaned not so much with pain, terrible though that was, as from mental anguish. Always and for ever the same, always these endless days and nights. If only it would come quicker! If only *what* would come quicker? Death, darkness? . . . No, no! Anything rather than death!

When Peter returned with the tea on a tray, Ivan Ilych stared at him for a time in perplexity, not realizing who and what he was. Peter was disconcerted by that look and his embarrassment brought Ivan Ilych to himself.

"Oh, tea! All right, put it down. Only help me to wash and put on a clean shirt."

And Ivan Ilych began to wash. With pauses for rest, he washed his hands and then his face, cleaned his teeth, brushed his hair, and looked in the glass. He was terrified by what he saw, especially by the limp way in which his hair clung to his pallid forehead.

While his shirt was being changed he knew that he would be still more frightened at the sight of his body, so he avoided looking at it. Finally he was ready. He drew on a dressing-gown, wrapped himself in a plaid, and sat down in the armchair to take his tea. For a moment he felt refreshed, but as soon as he began to drink the tea he was again aware of the same taste, and the pain also returned. He finished it with an effort, and then lay down stretching out his legs, and dismissed Peter.

Always the same. Now a spark of hope flashes up, then a sea of despair rages, and always pain; always pain, always despair, and always the same. When alone he had a dreadful and distressing desire to call someone, but he knew beforehand that with others present it would be still worse. "Another dose of morphine—to lose consciousness. I will tell him, the doctor, that he must think of something else. It's impossible, impossible, to go on like this."

An hour and another pass like that. But now there is a ring at the door bell. Perhaps it's the doctor? It is. He comes in fresh, hearty, plump, and cheerful, with that look on his face that seems to say: "There now, you're in a panic about something, but we'll arrange it all for you directly!" The doctor knows this expression is out of place here, but he has put it on once for all and can't take it off—like a man who has put on a frock-coat in the morning to pay a round of calls.

The doctor rubs his hands vigorously and reassuringly.

"Brr! How cold it is! There's such a sharp frost; just let me warm myself!" he says, as if it were only a matter of waiting till he was warm, and then he would put everything right.

"Well now, how are you?"

Ivan Ilych feels that the doctor would like to say: "Well, how are our affairs?" but that even he feels that this would not do, and says instead: "What sort of a night have you had?"

Ivan Ilych looks at him as much as to say: "Are you really never ashamed of lying?'' But the doctor does not wish to understand this question, and Ivan Ilych says: "Just as terrible as ever. The pain never leaves me and never subsides. If only something . . ."

"Yes, you sick people are always like that. . . . There, now I think I am warm enough. Even Praskovya Fedorovna, who is so particular, could find no fault with my temperature. Well, now I can say good-morning," and the doctor presses his patient's hand.

Then, dropping his former playfulness, he begins with a most serious face to examine the patient, feeling his pulse and taking his temperature, and then begins the sounding and auscultation.

Ivan Ilych knows quite well and definitely that all this is nonsense and pure deception, but when the doctor, getting down on his knee, leans over him, putting his ear first higher then lower, and performs various gymnastic movements over him with a significant expression on his face, Ivan Ilych submits to it all as he used to submit to the speeches of the lawyers, though he knew very well that they were all lying and why they were lying.

The doctor, kneeling on the sofa, is still sounding him when Praskovya Fedorovna's silk dress rustles at the door and she is heard scolding Peter for not having let her know of the doctor's arrival.

She comes in, kisses her husband, and at once proceeds to prove that she has been up a long time already, and only owing to a misunderstanding failed to be there when the doctor arrived.

Ivan Ilych looks at her, scans her all over, sets against her the whiteness and plumpness and cleanness of her hands and neck, the gloss of her hair, and the sparkle of her vivacious eyes. He hates her with his whole soul. And the thrill of hatred he feels for her makes him suffer from her touch.

Her attitude towards him and his disease is still the same. Just as the doctor had adopted a certain relation to his patient which he could not abandon, so had she formed one towards him—that he was not doing something he ought to do and was himself to blame, and that she reproached him lovingly for this—and she could not now change that attitude.

"You see he doesn't listen to me and doesn't take his medicine at the proper time. And above all he lies in a position that is no doubt bad for him—with his legs up."

She described how he made Gerasim hold his legs up.

The doctor smiled with a contemptuous affability that said: "What's to be done? These sick people do have foolish fancies of that kind, but we must forgive them."

When the examination was over the doctor looked at his watch, and then Praskovya Fedorovna announced to Ivan Ilych that it was of course as he pleased, but she had sent to-day for a celebrated specialist who would examine him and have a consultation with Michael Danilovich (their regular doctor).

"Please don't raise any objections. I am doing this for my own sake," she said ironically, letting it be felt that she was doing it all for his sake and only said this to leave him no right to refuse. He remained silent, knitting his brows. He felt that he was so surrounded and involved in a mesh of falsity that it was hard to unravel anything.

Everything she did for him was entirely for her own sake, and she told him she was doing for herself what she actually was doing for herself, as if that was so incredible that he must understand the opposite.

At half-past eleven the celebrated specialist arrived. Again the sounding began and the significant conversations in his presence and in another room, about the kidneys and the appendix, and the questions and answers, with such an air of importance that again, instead of the real question of life and death which now alone confronted him, the question arose of the kidney and appendix which were not behaving as they ought to and would now be attacked by Michael Danilovich and the specialist and forced to amend their ways.

The celebrated specialist took leave of him with a serious though not hopeless look, and in reply to the timid question Ivan Ilych, with eyes glistening with fear and hope, put to him as to whether there was a chance of recovery, said that he could not vouch for it but there was a possibility. The look of hope with which Ivan Ilych watched the doctor out was so pathetic that Praskovya Fedorovna, seeing it, even wept as she left the room to hand the doctor his fee.

The gleam of hope kindled by the doctor's encouragement did not last long. The same room, the same pictures, curtains, wall-paper, medicine bottles, were all there, and the same aching suffering body, and Ivan Ilych began to moan. They gave him a subcutaneous injection and he sank into oblivion.

It was twilight when he came to. They brought his dinner and he swallowed some beef tea with difficulty, and then everything was the same again and night was coming on.

After dinner, at seven o'clock, Praskovya Fedorovna came into the room in evening dress, her full bosom pushed up by her corset, and with traces of powder on her face. She had reminded him in the morning that they were going to the theatre. Sarah Bernhardt[19] was visiting the town and they had a box, which he had insisted on their taking. Now he had forgotten about it and her toilet offended him, but he concealed his vexation when he remembered that he had himself insisted on their securing a box and going because it would be an instructive and aesthetic pleasure for the children.

Praskovya Fedorovna came in, self-satisfied but yet with a rather guilty air. She sat down and asked how he was but, as he saw, only for the sake of asking and not in order to learn about it, knowing that there was nothing to learn—and then went on to what she really wanted to say: that she would not on any account have gone but that the box had been taken and Helen and their daughter were going, as well as Petrishchev (the examining magistrate, their daughter's fiancé) and that it was out of the question to let them go alone; but that she would have much preferred to sit with him for a while; and he must be sure to follow the doctor's orders while she was away.

"Oh, and Fedor Petrovich" (the fiancé) "would like to come in. May he? And Lisa?"

"All right."

Their daughter came in in full evening dress, her fresh young flesh exposed (making a show of that very flesh which in his own case caused so much suffering), strong, healthy, evidently in love, and impatient with illness, suffering, and death, because they interfered with her happiness.

Fedor Petrovich came in too, in evening dress, his hair curled *à la Capoul*,[20] a tight stiff collar round his long sinewy neck, an enormous white shirt-front and narrow black trousers tightly stretched over his strong thighs. He had one white glove tightly drawn on, and was holding his opera hat in his hand.

Following him the schoolboy crept in unnoticed, in a new uniform, poor little fellow, and wearing gloves. Terribly dark shadows showed under his eyes, the meaning of which Ivan Ilych knew well.

[19] Sarah Bernhardt (1844–1923), the famous French actress; she appeared in St. Petersburg in 1882.
[20] A popular contemporary hair style named after the French tenor Victor Capoul (1839–1924).

His son had always seemed pathetic to him, and now it was dreadful to see the boy's frightened look of pity. It seemed to Ivan Ilych that Vasya was the only one besides Gerasim who understood and pitied him.

They all sat down and again asked how he was. A silence followed. Lisa asked her mother about the opera-glasses, and there was an altercation between mother and daughter as to who had taken them and where they had been put. This occasioned some unpleasantness.

Fedor Petrovich inquired of Ivan Ilych whether he had ever seen Sarah Bernhardt. Ivan Ilych did not at first catch the question, but then replied: "No, have you seen her before?"

"Yes, in *Adrienne Lecouvreur.*"[21]

Praskovya Fedorovna mentioned some rôles in which Sarah Bernhardt was particularly good. Her daughter disagreed. Conversation sprang up as to the elegance and realism of her acting—the sort of conversation that is always repeated and is always the same.

In the midst of the conversation Fedor Petrovich glanced at Ivan Ilych and became silent. The others also looked at him and grew silent. Ivan Ilych was staring with glittering eyes straight before him, evidently indignant with them. This had to be rectified, but it was impossible to do so. The silence had to be broken, but for a time no one dared to break it and they all became afraid that the conventional deception would suddenly become obvious and the truth become plain to all. Lisa was the first to pluck up courage and break that silence, but by trying to hide what everybody was feeling, she betrayed it.

"Well, if we are going it's time to start," she said, looking at her watch, a present from her father, and with a faint and significant smile at Fedor Petrovich relating to something known only to them. She got up with a rustle of her dress.

They all rose, said good-night, and went away.

When they had gone it seemed to Ivan Ilych that he felt better; the falsity had gone with them. But the pain remained—that same pain and that same fear that made everything monotonously alike, nothing harder and nothing easier. Everything was worse.

Again minute followed minute and hour followed hour. Everything remained the same and there was no cessation. And the inevitable end of it all became more and more terrible.

"Yes, send Gerasim here," he replied to a question Peter asked.

IX

His wife returned late at night. She came in on tiptoe, but he heard her, opened his eyes, and made haste to close them again. She wished to send Gerasim away and to sit with him herself, but he opened his eyes and said: "No, go away."

"Are you in great pain?"

"Always the same."

"Take some opium."

He agreed and took some. She went away.

Till about three in the morning he was in a state of stupefied misery. It seemed to him that he and his pain were being thrust into a narrow, deep black sack, but though they were pushed further and further in they could not be pushed to the bottom. And this, terrible enough in itself, was accompanied by suffering. He was frightened yet wanted to fall through the sack, he struggled but yet co-operated.

[21] The play written by French dramatist Eugène Scribe (1791–1861).

And suddenly he broke through, fell, and regained consciousness. Gerasim was sitting at the foot of the bed dozing quietly and patiently, while he himself lay with his emaciated stockinged legs resting on Gerasim's shoulders; the same shaded candle was there and the same unceasing pain.

"Go away, Gerasim," he whispered.

"It's all right, sir. I'll stay a while."

"No. Go away."

He removed his legs from Gerasim's shoulders, turned sideways onto his arm, and felt sorry for himself. He only waited till Gerasim had gone into the next room and then restrained himself no longer but wept like a child. He wept on account of his helplessness, his terrible loneliness, the cruelty of man, the cruelty of God, and the absence of God.

"Why hast Thou done all this? Why hast Thou brought me here? Why, why dost Thou torment me so terribly?"

He did not expect an answer and yet wept because there was no answer and could be none. The pain again grew more acute, but he did not stir and did not call. He said to himself: "Go on! Strike me! But what is it for? What have I done to Thee? What is it for?"

Then he grew quiet and not only ceased weeping but even held his breath and became all attention. It was as though he were listening not to an audible voice but to the voice of his soul, to the current of thoughts arising within him.

"What is it you want?" was the first clear conception capable of expression in words, that he heard.

"What do you want? What do you want?" he repeated to himself.

"What do I want? To live and not to suffer," he answered.

And again he listened with such concentrated attention that even his pain did not distract him.

"To live? How?" asked his inner voice.

"Why, to live as I used to—well and pleasantly."

"As you lived before, well and pleasantly?" the voice repeated.

And in imagination he began to recall the best moments of his pleasant life. But strange to say none of those best moments of his pleasant life now seemed at all what they had then seemed—none of them except the first recollections of childhood. There, in childhood, there had been something really pleasant with which it would be possible to live if it could return. But the child who had experienced that happiness existed no longer, it was like a reminiscence of somebody else.

As soon as the period began which had produced the present Ivan Ilych, all that had then seemed joys now melted before his sight and turned into something trivial and often nasty.

And the further he departed from childhood and the nearer he came to the present the more worthless and doubtful were the joys. This began with the School of Law. A little that was really good was still found there—there was light-heartedness, friendship, and hope. But in the upper classes there had already been fewer of such good moments. Then during the first years of his official career, when he was in the service of the Governor, some pleasant moments again occurred: they were the memories of love for a woman. Then all became confused and there was still less of what was good; later on again there was still less that was good, and the further he went the less there was. His marriage, a mere accident, then the disenchantment that followed it, his wife's bad breath and the sensuality and hypocrisy: then that deadly official life and those preoccupations about money, a year of it, and two, and ten, and twenty, and always the same thing. And the longer it lasted the more deadly it became. "It is as if I had been going downhill while I imagined I was going up. And that is really what it was. I was going up in public opinion, but to the same extent life was ebbing away from me. And now it is all done and there is only death.''

"Then what does it mean? Why? It can't be that life is so senseless and horrible. But if it really has been so horrible and senseless, why must I die and die in agony? There is something wrong!''

"Maybe I did not live as I ought to have done,'' it suddenly occurred to him. "But how could that be, when I did everything properly?'' he replied, and immediately dismissed from his mind this, the sole solution of all the riddles of life and death, as something quite impossible.

"Then what do you want now? To live? Live how? Live as you lived in the law courts when the usher proclaimed "The Judge is coming!' The judge is coming, the judge!'' he repeated to himself. "Here he is, the judge. But I am not guilty!'' he exclaimed angrily. "What is it for?'' And he ceased crying, but turning his face to the wall continued to ponder on the same question: Why, and for what purpose, is there all this horror? But however much he pondered he found no answer. And whenever the thought occurred to him, as it often did, that it all resulted from his not having lived as he ought to have done, he at once recalled the correctness of his whole life and dismissed so strange an idea.

X

Another fortnight passed. Ivan Ilych now no longer left his sofa. He would not lie in bed but lay on the sofa, facing the wall nearly all the time. He suffered ever the same unceasing agonies and in his loneliness pondered always on the same insoluble question: "What is this? Can it be that it is Death?'' And the inner voice answered: "Yes, it is Death.''

"Why these sufferings?'' And the voice answered, "For no reason—they just are so.'' Beyond and besides this there was nothing.

From the very beginning of his illness, ever since he had first been to see the doctor, Ivan Ilych's life had been divided between two contrary and alternating moods: now it was despair and the expectation of this uncomprehended and terrible death, and now hope and an intently interested observation of the functioning of his organs. Now before his eyes there was only a kidney or an intestine that temporarily evaded its duty, and now only that incomprehensible and dreadful death from which it was impossible to escape.

These two states of mind had alternated from the very beginning of his illness, but the further it progressed the more doubtful and fantastic became the conception of the kidney, and the more real the sense of impending death.

He had but to call to mind what he had been three months before and what he was now, to call to mind with what regularity he had been going downhill, for every possibility of hope to be shattered.

Latterly during that loneliness in which he found himself as he lay facing the back of the sofa, a loneliness in the midst of a populous town and surrounded by numerous acquaintances and relations but that yet could not have been more complete anywhere—either at the bottom of the sea or under the earth—during that terrible loneliness Ivan Ilych had lived only in memories of the past. Pictures of his past rose before him one after another. They always began with what was nearest in time and then went back to what was most remote—to his childhood—and rested there. If he thought of the stewed prunes that had been offered him that day, his mind went back to the raw shrivelled French plums of his childhood, their peculiar flavour and the flow of saliva when he sucked their stones, and along with the memory of that taste came a whole series of memories of those days: his nurse, his brother, and their toys. "No, I mustn't think of that. . . . It is too painful," Ivan Ilych said to himself, and brought himself back to the present—to the button on the back of the sofa and the creases in its morocco. "Morocco is expensive, but it does not wear well: there had been a quarrel about it. It was a different kind of quarrel and a different kind of morocco that time when we tore father's portfolio and were punished, and mamma brought us some tarts. . . ." And again his thoughts dwelt on his childhood, and again it was painful and he tried to banish them and fix his mind on something else.

Then again together with that chain of memories another series passed through his mind—of how his illness had progressed and grown worse. There also the further back he looked the more life there had been. There had been more of what was good in life and more of life itself. The two merged together. "Just as the pain went on getting worse and worse so my life grew worse and worse," he thought. "There is one bright spot there at the back, at the beginning of life, and afterwards all becomes blacker and blacker and proceeds more and more rapidly—in inverse ratio to the square of the distance from death," thought Ivan Ilych. And the example of a stone falling downwards with increasing velocity entered his mind. Life, a series of increasing sufferings, flies further and further towards its end—the most terrible suffering. "I am flying. . . ." He shuddered, shifted himself, and tried to resist, but was already aware that resistance was impossible, and again with eyes weary of gazing but unable to cease seeing what was before them, he stared at the back of the sofa and waited—awaiting that dreadful fall and shock and destruction.

"Resistance is impossible!" he said to himself. "If I could only understand what it is all for! But that too is impossible. An explanation would be possible if it could be said that I have not lived as I ought to. But it is impossible to say that," and he remembered all the legality, correctitude, and propriety of his life. "That at any rate can certainly not be admitted," he thought, and his lips smiled ironically as if someone could see that smile and be taken in by it. "There is no explanation! Agony, death. . . . What for?"

XI

Another two weeks went by in this way and during that fortnight an event occured that Ivan Ilych and his wife had desired. Petrishchev formally proposed. It happened in the evening. The next day Praskovya Fedorovna came into her husband's room considering how best to inform him of it, but that very night there had been a fresh change for the worse in his condition. She found him still lying on the sofa but in a different position. He lay on his back, groaning and staring fixedly straight in front of him.

She began to remind him of his medicines, but he turned his eyes towards her with such a look that she did not finish what she was saying; so great an animosity, to her in particular, did that look express.

"For Christ's sake let me die in peace!" he said.

She would have gone away, but just then their daughter came in and went up to say good morning. He looked at her as he had done at his wife, and in reply to her inquiry about his health said dryly that he would soon free them all of himself. They were both silent and after sitting with him for a while went away.

"Is it our fault?" Lisa said to her mother. "It's as if we were to blame! I am sorry for papa, but why should we be tortured?"

The doctor came at his usual time. Ivan Ilych answered "Yes" and "No," never taking his angry eyes from him, and at last said: "You know you can do nothing for me, so leave me alone."

"We can ease your sufferings."

"You can't even do that. Let me be."

The doctor went into the drawing-room and told Praskovya Fedorovna that the case was very serious and that the only resource left was opium to allay her husband's sufferings, which must be terrible.

It was true, as the doctor said, that Ivan Ilych's physical sufferings were terrible, but worse than the physical sufferings were his mental sufferings which were his chief torture.

His mental sufferings were due to the fact that that night, as he looked at Gerasim's sleepy, good-natured face with its prominent cheek-bones, the question suddenly occurred to him: "What if my whole life has really been wrong?"

It occurred to him that what had appeared perfectly impossible before, namely that he had not spent his life as he should have done, might after all be true. It occurred to him that his scarcely perceptible attempts to struggle against what was considered good by the most highly placed people, those scarcely noticeable impulses which he had immediately suppressed, might have been the real thing, and all the rest false. And his professional duties and the whole arrangement of his life and of his family, and all his social and official interests, might all have been false. He tried to defend all those things to himself and suddenly felt the weakness of what he was defending. There was nothing to defend.

"But if that is so," he said to himself, "and I am leaving this life with the consciousness that I have lost all that was given me and it is impossible to rectify it—what then?"

He lay on his back and began to pass his life in review in quite a new way. In the morning when he saw first his footman, then his wife, then his daughter, and then the doctor, their every word and movement confirmed to him the awful truth that had been revealed to him during the night. In them he saw himself—all that for which he had lived and saw clearly that it was not real at all, but a terrible and huge deception which had hidden both life and death. This consciousness intensified his physical suffering tenfold. He groaned and tossed about, and pulled at his clothing which choked and stifled him. And he hated them on that account.

He was given a large dose of opium and became unconscious, but at noon his sufferings began again. He drove everybody away and tossed from side to side.

His wife came to him and said:

"Jean, my dear, do this for me. It can't do any harm and often helps. Healthy people often do it."

He opened his eyes wide.

"What? Take communion? Why? It's unnecessary! However. . . ."

She began to cry.

"Yes, do, my dear. I'll send for our priest. He is such a nice man."

"All right. Very well," he muttered.

When the priest came and heard his confession, Ivan Ilych was softened and seemed to feel a relief from his doubts and consequently from his sufferings, and for a moment there came a ray of hope. He again began to think of the vermiform appendix and the possibility of correcting it. He received the sacrament with tears in his eyes.

When they laid him down again afterwards he felt a moment's ease, and the hope that he might live awoke in him again. He began to think of the operation that had been suggested to him. "To live! I want to live!" he said to himself.

His wife came in to congratulate him after his communion, and when uttering the usual conventional words she added:

"You feel better, don't you?"

Without looking at her he said "Yes."

Her dress, her figure, the expression of her face, the tone of her voice, all revealed the same thing. "This is wrong, it is not as it should be. All you have lived for and still live for is falsehood and deception, hiding life and death from you." And as soon as he admitted that thought, his hatred and his agonizing physical suffering again sprang up, and with that suffering a consciousness of the unavoidable, approaching end. And to this was added a new sensation of grinding shooting pain and a feeling of suffocation.

The expression of his face when he uttered that "yes" was dreadful. Having uttered it, he looked her straight in the eyes, turned on his face with a rapidity extraordinary in his weak state and shouted:

"Go away! Go away and leave me alone!"

XII

From that moment the screaming began that continued for three days, and was so terrible that one could not hear it through two closed doors without horror. At the moment he answered his wife he realized that he was lost, that there was no return, that the end had come, the very end, and his doubts were still unsolved and remained doubts.

"Oh! Oh! Oh!" he cried in various intonations. He had begun by screaming "I won't!" and continued screaming on the letter "o."

For three whole days, during which time did not exist for him, he struggled in that black sack into which he was being thrust by an invisible, resistless force. He struggled as a man condemned to death struggles in the hands of the executioner, knowing that he cannot save himself. And every moment he felt that despite all his efforts he was drawing nearer and nearer to what terrified him. He felt that his agony was due to his being thrust into that black hole and still more to his not being able to get right into it. He was hindered from getting into it by his conviction that his life had been a good one. That very justification of his life held him fast and prevented his moving forward, and it caused him most torment of all.

Suddenly some force struck him in the chest and side, making it still harder to breathe, and he fell through the hole and there at the bottom was a light. What had happened to him was like the sensation one sometimes experiences in a railway carriage when one thinks one is going backwards while one is really going forwards and suddenly becomes aware of the real direction.

"Yes, it was all not the right thing," he said to himself, "but that's no matter. It can be done. But what *is* the right thing?" he asked himself, and suddenly grew quiet.

This occurred at the end of the third day, two hours before his death. Just then his schoolboy son had crept softly in and gone up to the bedside. The dying man was still screaming desperately and waving his arms. His hand fell on the boy's head, and the boy caught it, pressed it to his lips, and began to cry.

At that very moment Ivan Ilych fell through and caught sight of the light, and it was revealed to him that though his life had not been what it should have been, this could still be rectified. He asked himself, "What *is* the right thing?" and grew still, listening. Then he felt that someone was kissing his hand. He opened his eyes, looked at his son, and felt sorry for him. His wife came up to him and he glanced at her. She was gazing at him open-mouthed, with undried tears on her nose and cheek and a despairing look on her face. He felt sorry for her too.

"Yes, I am making them wretched," he thought. "They are sorry, but it will be better for them when I die." He wished to say this but had not the strength to utter it. "Besides, why speak? I must act," he thought. With a look at his wife he indicated his son and said: "Take him away . . . sorry for him . . . sorry for you too. . . ." He tried to add, "forgive me," but said "forego" and waved his hand, knowing that He whose understanding mattered would understand.

And suddenly it grew clear to him that what had been oppressing him and would not leave him was all dropping away at once from two sides, from ten sides, and from all sides. He was sorry for them, he must act so as not to hurt them: release them and free himself from these sufferings. "How good and how simple!" he thought. "And the pain?" he asked himself. "What has become of it? Where are you, pain?"

He turned his attention to it.

"Yes, here it is. Well, what of it? Let the pain be."

"And death . . . where is it?"

He sought his former accustomed fear of death and did not find it. "Where is it? What death?" There was no fear because there was no death.

In place of death there was light.

"So that's what it is!" he suddenly exclaimed aloud. "What joy!"

To him all this happened in a single instant, and the meaning of that instant did not change. For those present his agony continued for another two hours. Something rattled in his throat, his emaciated body twitched, then the gasping and rattle became less and less frequent.

"It is finished!" said someone near him.

He heard these words and repeated them in his soul.

"Death is finished," he said to himself. "It is no more!"

He drew in a breath, stopped in the midst of a sigh, stretched out, and died.

[1886]

Sarah Orne Jewett   *1849–1909*

A WHITE HERON

I

The woods were already filled with shadows one June evening, just before eight o'clock, though a bright sunset still glimmered faintly among the trunks of the trees. A little girl was driving home her cow, a plodding, dilatory, provoking creature in her behavior, but a valued companion for all that. They were going away from the western light, and striking deep into the dark woods, but their feet were familiar with the path, and it was no matter whether their eyes could see it or not.

There was hardly a night the summer through when the old cow could be found waiting at the pasture bars; on the contrary, it was her greatest pleasure to hide herself away among the high huckleberry bushes, and though she wore a loud bell she had made the discovery that if one stood perfectly still it would not ring. So Sylvia had to hunt for her until she found her, and call Co'! Co'! with never an answering Moo, until her childish patience was quite spent. If the creature had not given good milk and plenty of it, the case would have seemed very different to her owners. Besides, Sylvia had all the time there was, and very little use to make of it. Sometimes in pleasant weather it was a consolation to look upon the cow's pranks as an intelligent attempt to play hide and seek, and as the child had no playmates she lent herself to this amusement with a good deal of zest. Though this chase had been so long that the wary animal herself had given an unusual signal of her whereabouts, Sylvia had only laughed when she came upon Mistress Moolly at the swampside, and urged her affectionately homeward with a twig of birch leaves. The old cow was not inclined to wander farther, she even turned in the right direction for once as they left the pasture, and stepped along the road at a good pace. She was quite ready to be milked now, and seldom stopped to browse. Sylvia wondered what her grandmother would say because they were so late. It was a great while since she had left home at half past five o'clock, but everybody knew the difficulty of making this errand a short one. Mrs. Tilley had chased the horned torment too many summer evenings herself to blame any one else for lingering, and was only thankful as she waited that she had Sylvia, nowadays, to give such valuable assistance. The good woman suspected that Sylvia loitered occasionally on her own account; there never was such a child for straying about out-of-doors since the world was made! Everybody said that it was a good change for a little maid who had tried to grow for eight years in a crowded manufacturing town, but, as for Sylvia herself, it seemed as if she never had been alive at all before she came to live at the farm. She thought often with wistful compassion of a wretched dry geranium that belonged to a town neighbor.

" 'Afraid of folks,' " old Mrs. Tilley said to herself, with a smile, after she had made the unlikely choice of Sylvia from her daughter's houseful of children, and was returning to the farm. " 'Afraid of folks,' they said! I guess she won't be troubled no great with 'em up to the old place!" When they reached the door of the lonely house and stopped to unlock it, and the cat came to purr loudly, and rub against them, a deserted pussy, indeed, but fat with young robins, Sylvia whispered that this was a beautiful place to live in, and she never should wish to go home.

The companions followed the shady woodroad, the cow taking slow steps, and the child very fast ones. The cow stopped long at the brook to drink, as if the pasture were not half a swamp, and Sylvia stood still and waited, letting her bare feet cool themselves in the shoal[1] water, while the great twilight moths struck softly against her. She waded on through the brook as the cow moved away, and listened to the thrushes with a heart that beat fast with pleasure. There was a stirring in the great boughs overhead. They were full of little birds and beasts that seemed to be wide-awake, and going about their world, or else saying goodnight to each other in sleepy twitters. Sylvia herself felt sleepy as she walked along. However, it was not much farther to the house, and the air was soft and sweet. She was not often in the woods so late as this, and it made her feel as if she were a part of the gray shadows and the moving leaves. She was just thinking how long it seemed since she first came to the farm a year ago, and wondering if everything went on in the noisy town just the same as when she was there; the thought of the great red-faced boy who used to chase and frighten her made her hurry along the path to escape from the shadow of the trees.

Suddenly this little woods-girl is horrorstricken to hear a clear whistle not very far away. Not a bird's whistle, which would have a sort of friendliness, but a boy's whistle, determined, and somewhat aggressive. Sylvia left the cow to whatever sad fate might await her, and stepped discretely aside into the bushes, but she was just too late. The enemy had discovered her, and called out in a very cheerful and persuasive tone, "Halloa, little girl, how far is it to the road?" and trembling Sylvia answered almost inaudibly, "A good ways."

She did not dare to look boldly at the tall young man, who carried a gun over his shoulder, but she came out of her bush and again followed the cow, while he walked alongside.

"I have been hunting for some birds," the stranger said kindly, "and I have lost my way, and need a friend very much. Don't be afraid," he added gallantly. "Speak up and tell me what your name is, and whether you think I can spend the night at your house, and go out gunning early in the morning."

Sylvia was more alarmed than before. Would not her grandmother consider her much to blame? But who could have foreseen such an accident as this? It did not appear to be her fault, and she hung her head as if the stem of it were broken, but managed to answer "Sylvy," with much effort when her companion again asked her name.

Mrs. Tilley was standing in the doorway when the trio came into view. The cow gave a loud moo by way of explanation.

"Yes, you'd better speak up for yourself, you old trial! Where'd she tucked herself away this time, Sylvy?" Sylvia kept an awed silence; she knew by instinct that her grandmother did not comprehend the gravity of the situation. She must be mistaking the stranger for one of the farmer-lads of the region.

The young man stood his gun beside the door, and dropped a heavy gamebag beside it; then he bade Mrs. Tilley good-evening, and repeated his wayfarer's story, and asked if he could have a night's lodging.

"Put me anywhere you like," he said. "I must be off early in the morning,

---

[1] Shallow.

before day; but I am very hungry, indeed. You can give me some milk at any rate, that's plain.''

''Dear sakes, yes,'' responded the hostess, whose long slumbering hospitality seemed to be easily awakened. ''You might fare better if you went out on the main road a mile or so, but you're welcome to what we've got. I'll milk right off, and you make yourself at home. You can sleep on husks or feathers,'' she proffered graciously. ''I raised them all myself. There's good pasturing for geese just below here towards the ma'sh. Now step round and set a plate for the gentleman, Sylvy!'' And Sylvia promptly stepped. She was glad to have something to do, and she was hungry herself.

It was a surprise to find so clean and comfortable a little dwelling in this New England wilderness. The young man had known the horrors of its most primitive housekeeping, and the dreary squalor of that level of society which does not rebel at the companionship of hens. This was the best thrift of an old-fashioned farmstead, though on such a small scale that it seemed like a hermitage. He listened eagerly to the old woman's quaint talk, he watched Sylvia's pale face and shining gray eyes with ever growing enthusiasm, and insisted that this was the best supper he had eaten for a month; then, afterward, the new-made friends sat down in the doorway together while the moon came up.

Soon it would be berry-time, and Sylvia was a great help at picking. The cow was a good milker, though a plaguy[2] thing to keep track of, the hostess gossiped frankly, adding presently that she had buried four children, so that Sylvia's mother and a son (who might be dead) in California were all the children she had left. ''Dan, my boy, was a great hand to go gunning,'' she explained sadly. ''I never wanted for pa'tridges or gray squer'ls while he was to home. He's been a great wand'rer, I expect, and he's no hand to write letters. There, I don't blame him, I'd ha' seen the world myself if it had been so I could.

''Sylvia takes after him,'' the grandmother continued affectionately, after a minute's pause. ''There ain't a foot o' ground she don't know her way over, and the wild creatur's counts her one o' themselves. Squer'ls she'll tame to come an' feed right out o' her hands, and all sorts o' birds. Last winter she got the jay-birds to bangeing here, and I believe she'd 'a' scanted herself of her own meals to have plenty to throw out amongst 'em, if I had n't kep' watch. Anything but crows, I tell her, I'm willin' to help support,—though Dan he went an' tamed one o' them that did seem to have reason same as folks. It was round here a good spell after he went away. Dan an' his father they did n't hitch,—but he never held up his head ag'in after Dan had dared him an' gone off.''

The guest did not notice this hint of family sorrows in his eager interest in something else.

''So Sylvy knows all about birds, does she?'' he exclaimed, as he looked round at the little girl who sat, very demure but increasingly sleepy, in the moonlight. ''I am making a collection of birds myself. I have been at it ever since I was a boy.'' (Mrs. Tilley smiled.) ''There are two or three very rare ones I have been hunting for these five years. I mean to get them on my own ground if they can be found.''

''Do you cage 'em up?'' asked Mrs. Tilley doubtfully, in response to this enthusiastic announcement.

''Oh, no, they're stuffed and preserved, dozens and dozens of them,'' said the ornithologist, ''and I have shot or snared every one myself. I caught a glimpse of a white heron three miles from here on Saturday, and I have followed it in this

---

[2] Bothersome, annoying.

direction. They have never been found in this district at all. The little white heron, it is," and he turned again to look at Sylvia with the hope of discovering that the rare bird was one of her acquaintances.

But Sylvia was watching a hop-toad in the narrow footpath.

"You would know the heron if you saw it," the stranger continued eagerly. "A queer tall white bird with soft feathers and long thin legs. And it would have a nest perhaps in the top of a high tree, made of sticks, something like a hawk's nest."

Sylvia's heart gave a wild beat; she knew that strange white bird, and had once stolen softly near where it stood in some bright green swamp grass, away over at the other side of the woods. There was an open place where the sunshine always seemed strangely yellow and hot, where tall, nodding rushes grew, and her grand-mother had warned her that she might sink in the soft black mud underneath and never be heard of more. Not far beyond were the salt marshes and beyond those was the sea, the sea which Sylvia wondered and dreamed about, but never had looked upon, though its great voice could often be heard above the noise of the woods on stormy nights.

"I can't think of anything I should like so much as to find that heron's nest," the handsome stranger was saying. "I would give ten dollars to anybody who could show it to me," he added desperately, "and I mean to spend my whole vacation hunting for it if need be. Perhaps it was only migrating, or had been chased out of its own region by some bird of prey."

Mrs. Tilley gave amazed attention to all this, but Sylvia still watched the toad, not divining, as she might have done at some calmer time, that the creature wished to get to its hole under the doorstep, and was much hindered by the unusual spectators at that hour of the evening. No amount of thought, that night, could decide how many wished-for treasures the ten dollars, so lightly spoken of, would buy.

The next day the young sportsman hovered about the woods, and Sylvia kept him company, having lost her first fear of the friendly lad, who proved to be most kind and sympathetic. He told her many things about the birds and what they knew and where they lived and what they did with themselves. And he gave her a jackknife, which she thought as great a treasure as if she were a desert-islander. All day long he did not once make her troubled or afraid except when he brought down some unsuspecting singing creature from its bough. Sylvia would have liked him vastly better without his gun; she could not understand why he killed the very birds he seemed to like so much. But as the day waned, Sylvia still watched the young man with loving admiration. She had never seen anybody so charming and delightful; the woman's heart, asleep in the child, was vaguely thrilled by a dream of love. Some premonition of that great power stirred and swayed these young foresters who traversed the solemn woodlands with soft-footed silent care. They stopped to listen to a bird's song; they pressed forward again eagerly, parting the branches,—speaking to each other rarely and in whispers; the young man going first and Sylvia following, fascinated, a few steps behind, with her gray eyes dark with excitement.

She grieved because the longed-for white heron was elusive, but she did not lead the guest, she only followed, and there was no such thing as speaking first. The sound of her own unquestioned voice would have terrified her,—it was hard enough to answer yes or no when there was need of that. At last evening began to fall, and they drove the cow home together, and Sylvia smiled with pleasure when they came to the place where she heard the whistle and was afraid only the night before.

II

Half a mile from home, at the farther edge of the woods, where the land was highest, a great pine-tree stood, the last of its generation. Whether it was left for a boundary mark, or for what reason, no one could say; the woodchoppers who had felled its mates were dead and gone long ago, and a whole forest of sturdy trees, pines and oaks and maples, had grown again. But the stately head of this old pine towered above them all and made a landmark for sea and shore miles and miles away. Sylvia knew it well. She had always believed that whoever climbed to the top of it could see the ocean; and the little girl had often laid her hand on the great rough trunk and looked up wistfully at those dark boughs that the wind always stirred, no matter how hot and still the air might be below. Now she thought of the tree with a new excitement, for why, if one climbed it at break of day, could not one see all the world, and easily discover whence the white heron flew, and mark the place, and find the hidden nest?

What a spirit of adventure, what wild ambition! What fancied triumph and delight and glory for the later morning when she could make known the secret! It was almost too real and too great for the childish heart to bear.

All night the door of the little house stood open, and the whippoorwills came and sang upon the very step. The young sportsman and his old hostess were sound asleep, but Sylvia's great design kept her broad awake and watching. She forgot to think of sleep. The short summer night seemed as long as the winter darkness, and at last when the whippoorwills ceased, and she was afraid the morning would after all come too soon, she stole out of the house and followed the pasture path through the woods, hastening toward the open ground beyond, listening with a sense of comfort and companionship to the drowsy twitter of a half-awakened bird, whose perch she had jarred in passing. Alas, if the great wave of human interest which flooded for the first time this dull little life should sweep away the satisfactions of an existence heart to heart with nature and the dumb life of the forest!

There was the huge tree asleep yet in the paling moonlight, and small and hopeful Sylvia began with utmost bravery to mount to the top of it, with tingling, eager blood coursing the channels of her whole frame, with her bare feet and fingers, that pinched and held like bird's claws to the monstrous ladder reaching up, up almost to the sky itself. First she must mount the white oak tree that grew alongside, where she was almost lost among the dark branches and the green leaves heavy and wet with dew; a bird fluttered off its nest, and a red squirrel ran to and fro and scolded pettishly at the harmless housebreaker. Sylvia felt her way easily. She had often climbed there, and knew that higher still one of the oak's upper branches chafed against the pine trunk, just where its lower boughs were set close together. There, when she made the dangerous pass from one tree to the other, the great enterprise would really begin.

She crept out along the swaying oak limb at last, and took the daring step across into the old pine-tree. The way was harder than she thought; she must reach far and hold fast, the sharp dry twigs caught and held her and scratched her like angry talons, the pitch[3] made her thin little fingers clumsy and stiff as she went round and round the tree's great stem, higher and higher upward. The sparrows and robins in the woods below were beginning to wake and twitter to the dawn, yet it seemed much lighter there aloft in the pine-tree, and the child knew that she must hurry if her project were to be of any use.

---

[3] Pine resin.

The tree seemed to lengthen itself out as she went up, and to reach farther and farther upward. It was like a great main-mast to the voyaging earth; it must truly have been amazed that morning through all its ponderous frame as it felt this determined spark of human spirit creeping and climbing from higher branch to branch. Who knows how steadily the least twigs held themselves to advantage this light, weak creature on her way! The old pine must have loved his new dependent. More than all the hawks, and bats, and moths, and even the sweet-voiced thrushes, was the brave, beating heart of the solitary gray-eyed child. And the tree stood still and held away the winds that June morning while the dawn grew bright in the east.

Sylvia's face was like a pale star, if one had seen it from the ground, when the last thorny bough was past, and she stood trembling and tired but wholly triumphant, high in the tree-top. Yes, there was the sea with the dawning sun making a golden dazzle over it, and toward that glorious east flew two hawks with slow-moving pinions. How low they looked in the air from that height when before one had only seen them far up, and dark against the blue sky. Their gray feathers were as soft as moths; they seemed only a little way from the tree, and Sylvia felt as if she too could go flying away among the clouds. Westward, the woodlands and farms reached miles and miles into the distance; here and there were church steeples, and white villages; truly it was a vast and awesome world.

The birds sang louder and louder. At last the sun came up bewilderingly bright. Sylvia could see the white sails of ships out at sea, and the clouds that were purple and rose-colored and yellow at first began to fade away. Where was the white heron's nest in the sea of green branches, and was this wonderful sight and pageant of the world the only reward for having climbed to such a giddy height? Now look down again, Sylvia, where the green marsh is set among the shining birches and dark hemlocks; there where you saw the white heron once you will see him again; look, look! a white spot of him like a single floating feather comes up from the dead hemlock and grows larger, and rises, and comes close at last, and goes by the landmark pine with steady sweep of wing and outstretched slender neck and crested head. And wait! wait! do not move a foot or a finger, little girl, do not send an arrow of light and consciousness from your two eager eyes, for the heron has perched on a pine bough not far beyond yours, and cries back to his mate on the nest, and plumes his feathers for the new day!

The child gives a long sigh a minute later when a company of shouting catbirds comes also to the tree, and vexed by their fluttering and lawlessness the solemn heron goes away. She knows his secret now, the wild, light, slender bird that floats and wavers, and goes back like an arrow presently to his home in the green world beneath. Then Sylvia, well satisfied, makes her perilous way down again, not daring to look far below the branch she stands on, ready to cry sometimes because her fingers ache and her lamed feet slip. Wondering over and over again what the stranger would say to her, and what he would think when she told him how to find his way straight to the heron's nest.

"Sylvy, Sylvy!" called the busy old grandmother again and again, but nobody answered, and the small husk bed was empty, and Sylvia had disappeared.

The guest waked from a dream, and remembering his day's pleasure hurried to dress himself that it might sooner begin. He was sure from the way the shy little girl looked once or twice yesterday that she had at least seen the white heron, and now she must really be persuaded to tell. Here she comes now, paler than ever, and her worn old frock is torn and tattered, and smeared with pine pitch. The grandmother and the sportsman stand in the door together and question her, and the splendid moment has come to speak of the dead hemlock-tree by the green marsh.

But Sylvia does not speak after all, though the old grandmother fretfully rebukes her, and the young man's kind appealing eyes are looking straight in her own. He can make them rich with money; he has promised it, and they are poor now. He is so well worth making happy, and he waits to hear the story she can tell.

No, she must keep silence! What is it that suddenly forbids her and makes her dumb? Has she been nine years growing, and now, when the great world for the first time puts out a hand to her, must she thrust it aside for a bird's sake? The murmur of the pine's green branches in her ears, she remembers how the white heron came flying through the golden air and how they watched the sea and the morning together, and Sylvia cannot speak; she cannot tell the heron's secret and give its life away.

Dear loyalty, that suffered a sharp pang as the guest went away disappointed later in the day, that could have served and followed him and loved him as a dog loves! Many a night Sylvia heard the echo of his whistle haunting the pasture path as she came home with the loitering cow. She forgot even her sorrow at the sharp report of his gun and the piteous sight of thrushes and sparrows dropping silent to the ground, their songs hushed and their pretty feathers stained and wet with blood. Were the birds better friends than their hunter might have been,—who can tell? Whatever treasures were lost to her, woodlands and summer-time, remember! Bring your gifts and graces and tell your secrets to this lonely country child!

[1886]

Arthur Conan Doyle   *1859–1930*

A SCANDAL IN BOHEMIA

To Sherlock Holmes she is always *the* woman. I have seldom heard him mention her under any other name. In his eyes she eclipses and predominates the whole of her sex. It was not that he felt any emotion akin to love for Irene Adler. All emotions, and that one particularly, were abhorrent to his cold, precise but admirably balanced mind. He was, I take it, the most perfect reasoning and observing machine that the world has seen, but as a lover he would have placed himself in a false position. He never spoke of the softer passions, save with a gibe and a sneer. They were admirable things for the observer—excellent for drawing the veil from men's motives and actions. But for the trained reasoner to admit such intrusions into his own delicate and finely adjusted temperament was to introduce a distracting factor which might throw a doubt upon all his mental results. Grit in a sensitive instrument, or a crack in one of his own high-power lenses, would not be more disturbing than a strong emotion in a nature such as his. And yet there was but one woman to him, and that woman was the late Irene Adler, of dubious and questionable memory.

I had seen little of Holmes lately. My marriage had drifted us away from each other. My own complete happiness, and the home-centered interests which rise up around the man who first finds himself master of his own establishment, were sufficient to absorb all my attention, while Holmes, who loathed every form of society with his whole Bohemian[1] soul, remained in our lodgings in Baker Street, buried among his old books, and alternating from week to week between cocaine and ambition, the drowsiness of the drug, and the fierce energy of his own keen nature. He was still, as ever, deeply attracted by the study of crime, and occupied his immense faculties and extraordinary powers of observation in following out those clues, and clearing up those mysteries which had been abandoned as hopeless by the official police. From time to time I heard some vague account of his doings: of his summons to Odessa[2] in the case of the Trepoff murder, of his clearing up of the singular tragedy of the Atkinson brothers at Trincomalee,[3] and finally of the mission which he had accomplished so delicately and successfully for the reigning family of Holland. Beyond these signs of his activity, however, which I merely shared with all the readers of the daily press, I knew little of my former friend and companion.

One night—it was on the twentieth of March, 1888—I was returning from a journey to a patient (for I had now returned to civil practice), when my way led me through Baker Street. As I passed the well-remembered door, which must always be associated in my mind with my wooing, and with the dark incidents of the *Study in Scarlet*,[4] I was seized with a keen desire to see Holmes again, and to know how he was employing his extraordinary powers. His rooms were brilliantly lit, and, even as I looked up, I saw his tall, spare figure pass twice in a dark

---

[1] Bohemia, where Holmes' client comes from, was once a kingdom of Europe and is now a province of western Czechoslovakia. It is also a term for a community of individuals of artistic or literary tastes whose members adopt manners or standards of behavior that differ from those around them. Used in this latter sense, it simply means unconventional or unorthodox.

[2] A city in southern Russia, on the Black Sea.

[3] A city on the island of Sri Lanka (then Ceylon), off the southeast coast of India.

[4] The first of the Sherlock Holmes stories, published in 1887.

silhouette against the blind. He was pacing the room swiftly, eagerly, with his head sunk upon his chest and his hands clasped behind him. To me, who knew his every mood and habit, his attitude and manner told their own story. He was at work again. He had risen out of his drug-created dreams and was hot upon the scent of some new problem. I rang the bell and was shown up to the chamber which had formerly been in part my own.

His manner was not effusive. It seldom was; but he was glad, I think, to see me. With hardly a word spoken, but with a kindly eye, he waved me to an armchair, threw across his case of cigars, and indicated a spirit case and a gasogene[5] in the corner. Then he stood before the fire and looked me over in his singular introspective fashion.

"Wedlock suits you," he remarked. "I think, Watson, that you have put on seven and a half pounds since I saw you."

"Seven!" I answered.

"Indeed, I should have thought a little more. Just a trifle more, I fancy, Watson. And in practice again, I observe. You did not tell me that you intended to go into harness."

"Then, how do you know?"

"I see it, I deduce it. How do I know that you have been getting yourself very wet lately, and that you have a most clumsy and careless servant girl?"

"My dear Holmes," said I, "this is too much. You would certainly have been burned, had you lived a few centuries ago. It is true that I had a country walk on Thursday and came home in a dreadful mess, but as I have changed my clothes I can't imagine how you deduce it. As to Mary Jane, she is incorrigible, and my wife has given her notice; but there, again, I fail to see how you work it out."

He chuckled to himself and rubbed his long, nervous hands together.

"It is simplicity itself," said he; "my eyes tell me that on the inside of your left shoe, just where the firelight strikes it, the leather is scored by six almost parallel cuts. Obviously they have been caused by someone who has very carelessly scraped round the edges of the sole in order to remove crusted mud from it. Hence, you see, my double deduction that you had been out in vile weather, and that you had a particularly malignant boot-slitting specimen of the London slavey.[6] As to your practice, if a gentleman walks into my rooms smelling of iodoform,[7] with a black mark of nitrate of silver upon his right forefinger, and a bulge on the right side of his top hat to show where he has secreted his stethoscope, I must be dull, indeed, if I do not pronounce him to be an active member of the medical profession."

I could not help laughing at the ease with which he explained his process of deduction. "When I hear you give your reasons," I remarked, "the thing always appears to me to be so ridiculously simple that I could easily do it myself, though at each successive instance of your reasoning I am baffled until you explain your process. And yet I believe that my eyes are as good as yours."

"Quite so," he answered, lighting a cigarette, and throwing himself down into an armchair. "You see, but you do not observe. The distinction is clear. For example, you have frequently seen the steps which lead up from the hall to this room."

"Frequently."

"How often?"

---

[5] A device for making soda water—to go with the spirits.
[6] A bootblack.   [7] An antiseptic.

"Well, some hundreds of times."

"Then how many are there?"

"How many? I don't know."

"Quite so! You have not observed. And yet you have seen. That is just my point. Now, I know that there are seventeen steps, because I have both seen and observed. By the way, since you are interested in these little problems, and since you are good enough to chronicle one or two of my trifling experiences, you may be interested in this." He threw over a sheet of thick, pink-tinted notepaper which had been lying open upon the table. "It came by the last post,"[8] said he. "Read it aloud."

The note was undated, and without either signature or address.

"There will call upon you tonight, at a quarter to eight o'clock (it said), a gentleman who desires to consult you upon a matter of the very deepest moment. Your recent services to one of the royal houses of Europe have shown that you are one who may safely be trusted with matters which are of an importance which can hardly be exaggerated. This account of you we have from all quarters received. Be in your chamber then at that hour, and do not take it amiss if your visitor wear a mask.

"This is indeed a mystery," I remarked. "What do you imagine that it means?"

"I have no data yet. It is a capital mistake to theorize before one has data. Insensibly one begins to twist facts to suit theories, instead of theories to suit facts. But the note itself. What do you deduce from it?"

I carefully examined the writing, and the paper upon which it was written.

"The man who wrote it was presumably well to do," I remarked, endeavouring to imitate my companion's processes. "Such paper could not be bought under half a crown[9] a packet. It is peculiarly strong and stiff."

"Peculiar—that is the very word," said Holmes. "It is not an English paper at all. Hold it up to the light."

I did so, and saw a large "E" with a small "g," a "P," and a large "G" with a small "t" woven into the texture of the paper.

"What do you make of that?" asked Holmes.

"The name of the maker, no doubt; or his monogram, rather."

"Not at all. The 'G' with the small 't' stands for 'Gesellschaft,' which is the German for "Company.' It is a customary contraction like our 'Co.' 'P,' of course, stands-for 'Papier.' Now for the 'Eg.' Let us glance at our Continental Gazetteer." He took down a heavy brown volume from his shelves. "Eglow, Eglonitz—here we are, Egria. It is in a German-speaking country—in Bohemia, not far from Carlsbad. 'Remarkable as being the scene of the death of Wallenstein,[10] and for its numerous glass-factories and paper-mills.' Ha, ha, my boy, what do you make of that?" His eyes sparkled, and he sent up a great blue triumphant cloud from his cigarette.

"The paper was made in Bohemia," I said.

"Precisely. And the man who wrote the note is a German. Do you note the peculiar construction of the sentence—'This account of you we have from all quarters received.' A Frenchman or Russian could not have written that. It is the

---

[8] At the time of the story, the mail was delivered six times a day in the Baker Street area.

[9] An English coin worth two and a half shillings.

[10] A duke assassinated in 1634; later made the subject of a tragedy by Schiller.

German who is uncourteous to his verbs. It only remains, therefore, to discover what is wanted by this German who writes upon Bohemian paper and prefers wearing a mask to showing his face. And here he comes, if I am not mistaken, to resolve all our doubts.''

As he spoke there was the sharp sound of horses' hoofs and grating wheels against the curb, followed by a sharp pull at the bell. Holmes whistled.

"A pair, by the sound," said he. "Yes," he continued, glancing out of the window. "A nice little brougham[11] and a pair of beauties. A hundred and fifty guineas[12] apiece. There's money in this case, Watson, if there is nothing else.''

"I think that I had better go, Holmes.''

"Not a bit, Doctor. Stay where you are. I am lost without my Boswell.[13] And this promises to be interesting. It would be a pity to miss it.''

"But your client—''

"Never mind him. I may want your help, and so may he. Here he comes. Sit down in that armchair, Doctor, and give us your best attention.''

A slow and heavy step, which had been heard upon the stairs and in the passage, paused immediately outside the door. Then there was a loud and authoritative tap.

"Come in!" said Holmes.

A man entered who could hardly have been less than six feet six inches in height, with the chest and limbs of a Hercules.[14] His dress was rich with a richness which would, in England, be looked upon as akin to bad taste. Heavy bands of astrakhan[15] were slashed across the sleeves and fronts of his double-breasted coat, while the deep blue cloak which was thrown over his shoulders was lined with flame-coloured silk and secured at the neck with a brooch which consisted of a single flaming beryl.[16] Boots which extended halfway up his calves, and which were trimmed at the top with rich brown fur, completed the impression of barbaric opulence which was suggested by his whole appearance. He carried a broad-brimmed hat in his hand, while he wore across the upper part of his face, extending down past the cheekbones, a black vizard mask,[17] which he had apparently adjusted that very moment, for his hand was still raised to it as he entered. From the lower part of the face he appeared to be a man of strong character, with a thick, hanging lip, and a long, straight chin suggestive of resolution pushed to the length of obstinacy.

"You had my note?" he asked with a deep harsh voice and a strongly marked German accent. "I told you that I would call." He looked from one to the other of us, as if uncertain which to address.

"Pray take a seat," said Holmes. "This is my friend and colleague, Dr. Watson, who is occasionally good enough to help me in my cases. Whom have I the honour to address?''

"You may address me as the Count Von Kramm, a Bohemian nobleman. I understand that this gentleman, your friend, is a man of honour and discretion, whom I may trust with a matter of the most extreme importance. If not, I should much prefer to communicate with you alone.''

[11] A closed four-wheel carriage.

[12] A guinea is an English gold coin worth twenty-one shillings (one pound and one shilling).

[13] James Boswell (1740–1795) was the biographer of Samuel Johnson (1709–1784), the famous English critic, author, and conversationalist.

[14] The son of Zeus, and a hero of extraordinary strength and courage.

[15] Fur made from the skin of young lambs from the Astrakhan region of Russia.

[16] Bluish green, prism-shaped mineral.   [17] A mask covering eyes, nose, and forehead.

I rose to go, but Holmes caught me by the wrist and pushed me back into my chair. "It is both, or none," said he. "You may say before this gentleman anything which you may say to me."

The Count shrugged his broad shoulders. "Then I must begin," said he, "by binding you both to absolute secrecy for two years; at the end of that time the matter will be of no importance. At present it is not too much to say that it is of such weight it may have an influence upon European history."

"I promise," said Holmes.

"And I."

"You will excuse this mask," continued our strange visitor. "The august person who employs me wishes his agent to be unknown to you, and I may confess at once that the title by which I have just called myself is not exactly my own."

"I was aware of it," said Holmes drily.

"The circumstances are of great delicacy, and every precaution has to be taken to quench what might grow to be an immense scandal and seriously compromise one of the reigning families of Europe. To speak plainly, the matter implicates the great House of Ormstein, hereditary kings of Bohemia."

"I was also aware of that," murmured Holmes, setting himself down in his armchair and closing his eyes.

Our visitor glanced with some apparent surprise at the languid, lounging figure of the man who had been no doubt depicted to him as the most incisive reasoner and most energetic agent in Europe. Holmes slowly reopened his eyes and looked impatiently at his gigantic client.

"If your Majesty would condescend to state your case," he remarked, "I should be better able to advise you."

The man sprang from his chair and paced up and down the room in uncontrollable agitation. Then, with a gesture of desperation, he tore the mask from his face and hurled it upon the ground. "You are right," he cried; "I am the King. Why should I attempt to conceal it?"

"Why, indeed?" murmured Holmes. "Your Majesty had not spoken before I was aware that I was addressing Wilhelm Gottsriech Sigismond von Ormstein, Grand Duke of Cassel-Felstein, and hereditary King of Bohemia."

"But you can understand," said our strange visitor, sitting down once more and passing his hand over his high white forehead, "you can understand that I am not accustomed to doing such business in my own person. Yet the matter was so delicate that I could not confide it to an agent without putting myself in his power. I have come incognito[18] from Prague for the purpose of consulting you."

"Then, pray consult," said Holmes, shutting his eyes once more.

"The facts are briefly these: Some five years ago, during a lengthy visit to Warsaw, I made the acquaintance of the well-known adventuress, Irene Adler. The name is no doubt familiar to you."

"Kindly look her up in my index, Doctor," murmured Holmes without opening his eyes. For many years he had adopted a system of docketing[19] all paragraphs concerning men and things, so that it was difficult to name a subject or a person on which he could not at once furnish information. In this case I found her biography sandwiched in between that of a Hebrew rabbi and that of a staff commander who had written a monograph upon the deep-sea fishes.

---

[18] Italian: under an assumed name or title.   [19] Briefly summarizing.

"Let me see!" said Holmes. "Hum! Born in New Jersey in the year 1858. Contralto—hum! La Scala,[20] hum! Prima donna[21] Imperial Opera of Warsaw— yes! Retired from operatic stage—ha! Living in London—quite so! Your Majesty, as I understand, became entangled with this young person, wrote her some compromising letters, and is now desirous of getting those letters back."

"Precisely so. But how—"

"Was there a secret marriage?"

"None."

"No legal papers or certificates?"

"None."

"Then I fail to follow your Majesty. If this young person should produce her letters for blackmailing or other purposes, how is she to prove their authenticity?"

"There is the writing."

"Pooh, pooh! Forgery."

"My private notepaper."

"Stolen."

"My own seal."

"Imitated."

"My photograph."

"Bought."

"We were both in the photograph."

"Oh, dear! That is very bad! Your Majesty has indeed committed an indiscretion."

"I was mad—insane."

"You have compromised yourself seriously."

"I was only Crown Prince then. I was young. I am but thirty now."

"It must be recovered."

"We have tried and failed."

"Your Majesty must pay. It must be bought."

"She will not sell."

"Stolen, then."

"Five attempts have been made. Twice burglars in my pay ransacked her house. Once we diverted her luggage when she traveled. Twice she has been waylaid. There has been no result."

"No sign of it?"

"Absolutely none."

Holmes laughed. "It is quite a pretty little problem," said he.

"But a very serious one to me," returned the King reproachfully.

"Very, indeed. And what does she propose to do with the photograph?"

"To ruin me."

"But how?"

"I am about to be married."

"So I have heard."

"To Clotilde Lothman von Saxe-Meningen, second daughter of the King of Scandinavia. You may know the strict principles of her family. She is herself the very soul of delicacy. A shadow of a doubt as to my conduct would bring the matter to an end."

"And Irene Adler?"

---

[20] The most famous opera house in Italy, located in Milan.
[21] Italian: the leading female soloist in an opera company.

"Threatens to send them the photograph. And she will do it. I know that she will do it. You do not know her, but she has a soul of steel. She has the face of the most beautiful of women, and the mind of the most resolute of men. Rather than I should marry another woman, there are no lengths to which she would not go—none."

"You are sure that she has not sent it yet?"

"I am sure."

"And why?"

"Because she has said that she would send it on the day when the betrothal was publicly proclaimed. That will be next Monday."

"Oh, then we have three days yet," said Holmes with a yawn. "That is very fortunate, as I have one or two matters of importance to look into just at present. Your Majesty will, of course, stay in London for the present?"

"Certainly. You will find me at the Langham[22] under the name of the Count Von Kramm."

"Then I shall drop you a line to let you know how we progress."

"Pray do so. I shall be all anxiety."

"Then, as to money?"

"You have carte blanche."[23]

"Absolutely?"

"I tell you that I would give one of the provinces of my kingdom to have that photograph."

"And for present expenses?"

The King took a heavy chamois[24] leather bag from under his cloak and laid it on the table.

"There are three hundred pounds in gold and seven hundred in notes," he said.

Holmes scribbled a receipt upon a sheet of his notebook and handed it to him.

"And Mademoiselle's address?" he asked.

"Is Briony Lodge, Serpentine Avenue, St. John's Wood."[25]

Holmes took a note of it. "One other question," said he. "Was the photograph a cabinet?"[26]

"It was."

"Then, goodnight, your Majesty, and I trust that we shall soon have some good news for you. And goodnight, Watson," he added, as the wheels of the royal brougham rolled down the street. "If you will be good enough to call tomorrow afternoon at three o'clock I should like to chat this little matter over with you."

2

At three o'clock precisely I was at Baker Street, but Holmes had not yet returned. The landlady informed me that he had left the house shortly after eight o'clock in the morning. I sat down beside the fire, however, with the intention of awaiting him, however long he might be. I was already deeply interested in his inquiry, for, though it was surrounded by none of the grim and strange features

---

[22] One of London's grand hotels of the period.   [23] Unconditional authority or permission.

[24] The chamois is a small, deerlike animal.

[25] A desirable residential area of Italian-type villas in northwest London.

[26] That is, a photograph approximately $4'' \times 5\frac{1}{2}''$.

which were associated with the two crimes which I have already recorded,[27]still, the nature of the case and the exalted station of his client gave it a character of its own. Indeed, apart from the nature of the investigation which my friend had on hand, there was something in his masterly grasp of a situation, and his keen, incisive reasoning, which made it a pleasure to me to study his system of work, and to follow the quick, subtle methods by which he disentangled the most inextricable mysteries. So accustomed was I to his invariable success that the very possibility of his failing had ceased to enter into my head.

It was close upon four before the door opened, and a drunken-looking groom, ill-kempt and side-whiskered, with an inflamed face and disreputable clothes, walked into the room. Accustomed as I was to my friend's amazing powers in the use of disguises, I had to look three times before I was certain that it was indeed he. With a nod he vanished into the bedroom, whence he emerged in five minutes tweed-suited and respectable, as of old. Putting his hands into his pockets, he stretched out his legs in front of the fire and laughed heartily for some minutes.

"Well, really!" he cried, and then he choked and laughed again until he was obliged to lie back, limp and helpless, in the chair.

"What is it?"

"It's quite too funny. I am sure you could never guess how I employed my morning, or what I ended by doing."

"I can't imagine. I suppose that you have been watching the habits, and perhaps the house, of Miss Irene Adler."

"Quite so; but the sequel was rather unusual. I will tell you, however. I left the house a little after eight o'clock this morning in the character of a groom out of work. There is a wonderful sympathy and freemasonry[28] among horsy men. Be one of them, and you will know all that there is to know. I soon found Briony Lodge. It is a *bijou*[29] villa, with a garden at the back, but built out in front right up to the road, two stories. Chubb lock[30]to the door. Large sitting room on the right side, well furnished, with long windows almost to the floor, and those preposterous English window fasteners which a child could open. Behind there was nothing remarkable, save that the passage window could be reached from the top of the coach house. I walked round it and examined it closely from every point of view, but without noting anything else of interest.

"I then lounged down the street and found, as I expected, that there was a mews[31] in a lane which runs down by one wall of the garden. I lent the ostlers[32] a hand in rubbing down their horses, and received in exchange twopence, a glass of half and half, two fills of shag tobacco, and as much information as I could desire about Miss Adler, to say nothing of half a dozen other people in the neighbourhood in whom I was not in the least interested, but whose biographies I was compelled to listen to."

"And what of Irene Adler?" I asked.

"Oh, she has turned all the men's heads down in that part. She is the daintiest thing under a bonnet on this planet. So say the Serpentine-mews, to a man. She lives quietly, sings at concerts, drives out at five every day, and returns at seven sharp for dinner. Seldom goes out at other times, except when she sings. Has only

---

[27] "A Scandal in Bohemia" was the third published Sherlock Holmes adventure; the first two were "A Study in Scarlet" (1887) and "The Sign of the Four" (1890).
[28] The Masons were and are a Protestant fraternal organization.
[29] French: charming.   [30] A particular make of English lock with tumblers.
[31] A small street behind a house, containing stables.   [32] Stablemen.

one male visitor, but a good deal of him. He is dark, handsome, and dashing, never calls less than once a day, and often twice. He is a Mr. Godfrey Norton, of the Inner Temple.[33] See the advantages of a cabman as a confidant. They had driven him home a dozen times from Serpentine-mews, and knew all about him. When I had listened to all they had to tell, I began to walk up and down near Briony Lodge once more, and to think over my plan of campaign.

"This Godfrey Norton was evidently an important factor in the matter. He was a lawyer. That sounded ominous. What was the relation between them, and what the object of his repeated visits? Was she his client, his friend, or his mistress? If the former, she had probably transferred the photograph to his keeping. If the latter, it was less likely. On the issue of this question depended whether I should continue my work at Briony Lodge, or turn my attention to the gentleman's chambers in the Temple. It was a delicate point, and it widened the field of my inquiry. I fear that I bore you with these details, but I have to let you see my little difficulties, if you are to understand the situation."

"I am following you closely," I answered.

"I was still balancing the matter in my mind when a hansom cab drove up to Briony Lodge, and a gentleman sprang out. He was a remarkably handsome man, dark, aquiline, and moustached—evidently the man of whom I had heard. He appeared to be in a great hurry, shouted to the cabman to wait, and brushed past the maid who opened the door with the air of a man who was thoroughly at home.

"He was in the house about half an hour, and I could catch glimpses of him in the windows of the sitting room, pacing up and down, talking excitedly, and waving his arms. Of her I could see nothing. Presently he emerged, looking even more flurried than before. As he stepped up to the cab, he pulled a gold watch from his pocket and looked at it earnestly. 'Drive like the devil,' he shouted, 'first to Gross & Hankey's in Regent Street,[34] and then to the Church of St. Monica in the Edgeware Road. Half a guinea if you do it in twenty minutes!'

"Away they went, and I was just wondering whether I should not do well to follow them when up the lane came a neat little landau,[35] the coachman with his coat only half-buttoned, and his tie under his ear, while all the tags of his harness were sticking out of the buckles. It hadn't pulled up before she shot out of the hall door and into it. I only caught a glimpse of her at the moment, but she was a lovely woman, with a face that a man might die for.

"'The Church of St. Monica, John,' she cried, 'and half a sovereign[36] if you reach it in twenty minutes.'

"This was quite too good to lose, Watson. I was just balancing whether I should run for it, or whether I should perch behind her landau when a cab came through the street. The driver looked twice at such a shabby fare, but I jumped in before he could object. 'The Church of St. Monica,' said I, 'and half a sovereign if you reach it in twenty minutes.' It was twenty-five minutes to twelve, and of course it was clear enough what was in the wind.

"My cabby drove fast. I don't think I ever drove faster, but the others were there before us. The cab and the landau with their steaming horses were in front of the door when I arrived. I paid the man and hurried into the church. There was not a soul there save the two whom I had followed and a surpliced clergyman, who seemed to be expostulating with them. They were all three standing in a knot in

---

[33] A legal society whose building of the same name is occupied by lawyers and law students.
[34] Presumably a jeweler's, located in fashionable Regent Street.
[35] A two-seated, four-wheeled, light carriage.   [36] An English gold coin worth a pound.

front of the altar. I lounged up the side aisle like any other idler who has dropped into a church. Suddenly, to my surprise, the three at the altar faced round to me, and Godfrey Norton came running as hard as he could towards me.

" 'Thank God,' he cried. "You'll do. Come! Come!'

" 'What then?' I asked.

" 'Come, man, come, only three minutes, or it won't be legal.'

"I was half-dragged up to the altar, and before I knew where I was I found myself mumbling responses which were whispered in my ear, and vouching for things of which I knew nothing, and generally assisting in the secure tying up of Irene Adler, spinster, to Godfrey Norton, bachelor. It was all done in an instant, and there was the gentleman thanking me on the one side and the lady on the other, while the clergyman beamed on me in front. It was the most preposterous position in which I ever found myself in my life, and it was the thought of it that started me laughing just now. It seems that there had been some informality about their license, that the clergyman absolutely refused to marry them without a witness of some sort, and that my lucky appearance saved the bridegroom from having to sally out into the streets in search of a best man. The bride gave me a sovereign, and I mean to wear it on my watchchain in memory of the occasion."

"This is a very unexpected turn of affairs," said I; "and what then?"

"Well, I found my plans very seriously menaced. It looked as if the pair might take an immediate departure, and so necessitate very prompt and energetic measures on my part. At the church door, however, they separated, he driving back to the Temple, and she to her own house. 'I shall drive out in the park[37] at five as usual,' she said as she left him. I heard no more. They drove away in different directions, and I went off to make my own arrangements."

"Which are?"

"Some cold beef and a glass of beer," he answered, ringing the bell. "I have been too busy to think of food, and I am likely to be busier still this evening. By the way, Doctor, I shall want your cooperation."

"I shall be delighted."

"You don't mind breaking the law?"

"Not in the least."

"Nor running a chance of arrest?"

"Not in a good cause."

"Oh, the cause is excellent!"

"Then I am your man."

"I was sure that I might rely on you."

"But what is it you wish?"

"When Mrs. Turner[38] has brought in the tray I will make it clear to you. Now," he said as he turned hungrily on the simple fare that our landlady had provided, "I must discuss it while I eat, for I have not much time. It is nearly five now. In two hours we must be on the scene of action. Miss Irene, or Madame, rather, returns from her drive at seven. We must be at Briony Lodge to meet her."

"And what then?"

"You must leave that to me. I have already arranged what is to occur. There is only one point on which I must insist. You must not interfere, come what may. You understand?"

[37] Probably Regent's Park.

[38] In every other Sherlock Holmes story the landlady is identified as Mrs. Hudson. This discrepancy, and how to account for it, has bothered Sherlockians greatly.

"I am to be neutral?"

"To do nothing whatever. There will probably be some small unpleasantness. Do not join in it. It will end in my being conveyed into the house. Four or five minutes afterwards the sitting room window will open. You are to station yourself close to that open window."

"Yes."

"You are to watch me, for I will be visible to you."

"Yes."

"And when I raise my hand—so—you will throw into the room what I give you to throw, and will, at the same time, raise the cry of fire. You quite follow me?"

"Entirely."

"It is nothing very formidable," he said, taking a long cigar-shaped roll from his pocket. "It is an ordinary plumber's smoke-rocket,[39] fitted with a cap at either end to make it self-lighting. Your task is confined to that. When you raise your cry of fire, it will be taken up by quite a number of people. You may then walk to the end of the street, and I will rejoin you in ten minutes. I hope that I have made myself clear?"

"I am to remain neutral, to get near the window, to watch you, and at the signal to throw in this object, then to raise the cry of fire, and to await you at the corner of the street."

"Precisely."

"Then you may entirely rely on me."

"That is excellent. I think, perhaps, it is almost time that I prepare for the new role I have to play."

He disappeared into his bedroom and returned in a few minutes in the character of an amiable and simple-minded Nonconformist clergyman. His broad black hat, his baggy trousers, his white tie, his sympathetic smile, and general look of peering and benevolent curiosity were such as Mr. John Hare[40] alone could have equaled. It was not merely that Holmes changed his costume. His expression, his manner, his very soul seemed to vary with every fresh part that he assumed. The stage lost a fine actor, even as science lost an acute reasoner, when he became a specialist in crime.

It was a quarter past six when we left Baker Street, and it still wanted ten minutes to the hour when we found ourselves in Serpentine Avenue. It was already dusk, and the lamps were just being lighted as we paced up and down in front of Briony Lodge, waiting for the coming of its occupant. The house was just such as I had pictured it from Sherlock Holmes's succinct description, but the locality appeared to be less private than I expected. On the contrary, for a small street in a quiet neighbourhood, it was remarkably animated. There was a group of shabbily dressed men smoking and laughing in a corner, a scissors-grinder with his wheel, two guardsmen who were flirting with a nurse-girl, and several well-dressed young men who were lounging up and down with cigars in their mouths.

"You see," remarked Holmes, as we paced to and fro in front of the house, "this marriage rather simplifies matters. The photograph becomes a double-edged weapon now. The chances are that she would be as averse to its being seen by Mr. Godfrey Norton, as our client is to its coming to the eyes of his princess. Now the question is, Where are we to find the photograph?"

"Where, indeed?"

---

[39] A device used by plumbers to detect leaks in drains.
[40] John Hare (1844–1921) was a well-known actor of the day.

"It is most unlikely that she carries it about with her. It is cabinet size. Too large for easy concealment about a woman's dress. She knows that the King is capable of having her waylaid and searched. Two attempts of the sort have already been made. We may take it, then, that she does not carry it about with her."

"Where, then?"

"Her banker or her lawyer. There is that double possibility. But I am inclined to think neither. Women are naturally secretive, and they like to do their own secreting. Why should she hand it over to anyone else? She could trust her own guardianship, but she could not tell what indirect or political influence might be brought to bear upon a businessman. Besides, remember that she had resolved to use it within a few days. It must be where she can lay her hands upon it. It must be in her own house."

"But it has twice been burgled."

"Pshaw! They did not know how to look."

"But how will you look?"

"I will not look."

"What then?"

"I will get her to show me."

"But she will refuse."

"She will not be able to. But I hear the rumble of wheels. It is her carriage. Now carry out my orders to the letter."

As he spoke the gleam of the side-lights of a carriage came round the curve of the avenue. It was a smart little landau which rattled up to the door of Briony Lodge. As it pulled up, one of the loafing men at the corner dashed forward to open the door in the hope of earning a copper,[41] but was elbowed away by another loafer, who had rushed up with the same intention. A fierce quarrel broke out, which was increased by the two guardsmen, who took sides with one of the loungers, and by the scissors-grinder, who was equally hot upon the other side. A blow was struck, and in an instant the lady, who had stepped from her carriage, was the center of a little knot of flushed and struggling men, who struck savagely at each other with their fists and sticks. Holmes dashed into the crowd to protect the lady; but just as he reached her he gave a cry and dropped to the ground, with the blood running freely down his face. At his fall the guardsmen took to their heels in one direction and the loungers in the other, while a number of better dressed people, who had watched the scuffle without taking part in it, crowded in to help the lady and to attend to the injured man. Irene Adler, as I will still call her, had hurried up the steps; but she stood at the top with her superb figure outlined against the lights of the hall, looking back into the street.

"Is the poor gentleman much hurt?" she asked.

"He is dead," cried several voices.

"No, no, there's life in him!" shouted another. "But he'll be gone before you can get him to hospital."

"He's a brave fellow," said a woman. "They would have had the lady's purse and watch if it hadn't been for him. They were a gang, and a rough one, too. Ah, he's breathing now."

"He can't lie in the street. May we bring him in, marm?"

"Surely. Bring him into the sitting room. There is a comfortable sofa. This way, please!"

Slowly and solemnly he was borne into Briony Lodge and laid out in the prin-

---

[41] A copper coin.

cipal room, while I still observed the proceedings from my post by the window. The lamps had been lit, but the blinds had not been drawn, so that I could see Holmes as he lay upon the couch. I do not know whether he was seized with compunction at that moment for the part he was playing, but I know that I never felt more heartily ashamed of myself in my life than when I saw the beautiful creature against whom I was conspiring, or the grace and kindliness with which she waited upon the injured man. And yet it would be the blackest treachery to Holmes to draw back now from the part which he had intrusted to me. I hardened my heart, and took the smoke-rocket from under my ulster.[42] After all, I thought, we are not injuring her. We are but preventing her from injuring another.

Holmes had sat up upon the couch, and I saw him motion like a man who is in need of air. A maid rushed across and threw open the window. At the same instant I saw him raise his hand, and at the signal I tossed my rocket into the room with a cry of "Fire!" The word was no sooner out of my mouth than the whole crowd of spectators, well dressed and ill—gentlemen, ostlers, and servant-maids—joined in a general shriek of "Fire!" Thick clouds of smoke curled through the room and out at the open window. I caught a glimpse of rushing figures, and a moment later the voice of Holmes from within assuring them that it was a false alarm. Slipping through the shouting crowd I made my way to the corner of the street, and in ten minutes was rejoined to find my friend's arm in mine, and to get away from the scene of uproar. He walked swiftly and in silence for some few minutes until we had turned down one of the quiet streets which lead towards the Edgeware Road.

"You did it very nicely, Doctor," he remarked. "Nothing could have been better. It is all right."

"You have the photograph?"

"I know where it is."

"And how did you find out?"

"She showed me, as I told you she would."

"I am still in the dark."

"I do not wish to make a mystery," said he, laughing. "The matter was perfectly simple. You, of course, saw that everyone in the street was an accomplice. They were all engaged for the evening."

"I guessed as much."

"Then, when the row broke out, I had a little moist red paint in the palm of my hand. I rushed forward, fell down, clapped my hand to my face, and became a piteous spectacle. It is an old trick."

"That also I could fathom."

"Then they carried me in. She was bound to have me in. What else could she do? And into her sitting room, which was the very room which I suspected. It lay between that and her bedroom, and I was determined to see which. They laid me on a couch, I motioned for air, they were compelled to open the window, and you had your chance."

"How did that help you?"

"It was all-important. When a woman thinks that her house is on fire, her instinct is at once to rush to the thing which she values most. It is a perfectly overpowering impulse, and I have more than once taken advantage of it. In the case of the Darlington substitution scandal it was of use to me, and also in the Arnsworth Castle business. A married woman grabs at her baby; an unmarried one reaches for her jewel-box. Now it was clear to me that our lady of today had

---

[42] A long, loose overcoat.

nothing in the house more precious to her than what we are in quest of. She would rush to secure it. The alarm of fire was admirably done. The smoke and shouting were enough to shake nerves of steel. She responded beautifully. The photograph is in a recess behind a sliding panel just above the right bell-pull. She was there in an instant, and I caught a glimpse of it as she half drew it out. When I cried out that it was a false alarm, she replaced it, glanced at the rocket, rushed from the room, and I have not seen her since. I rose, and, making my excuses, escaped from the house. I hesitated whether to attempt to secure the photograph at once; but the coachman had come in, and as he was watching me narrowly it seemed safer to wait. A little over-precipitance may ruin all.''

''And now?'' I asked.

''Our quest is practically finished. I shall call with the King tomorrow, and with you, if you care to come with us. We will be shown into the sitting room to wait for the lady, but it is probable that when she comes she may find neither us nor the photograph. It might be a satisfaction to his Majesty to regain it with his own hands.''

''And when will you call?''

''At eight in the morning. She will not be up, so that we shall have a clear field. Besides, we must be prompt, for this marriage may mean a complete change in her life and habits. I must wire to the King without delay.''

We had reached Baker Street and had stopped at the door. He was searching his pockets for the key when someone passing said:

''Good-night, Mister Sherlock Holmes.''

There were several people on the pavement at the time, but the greeting appeared to come from a slim youth in an ulster who had hurried by.

''I've heard that voice before,'' said Holmes, staring down the dimly lit street. ''Now, I wonder who the deuce that could have been.''

3

I slept at Baker Street that night, and we were engaged upon our toast and coffee in the morning when the King of Bohemia rushed into the room.

''You have really got it!'' he cried, grasping Sherlock Holmes by either shoulder and looking eagerly into his face.

''Not yet.''

''But you have hopes?''

''I have hopes.''

''Then, come. I am all impatient to be gone.''

''We must have a cab.''

''No, my brougham is waiting.''

''Then that will simplify matters.'' We descended and started off once more for Briony Lodge.

''Irene Adler is married,'' remarked Holmes.

''Married! When?''

''Yesterday.''

''But to whom?''

''To an English lawyer named Norton.''

''But she could not love him.''

''I am in hopes that she does.''

''And why in hopes?''

''Because it would spare your Majesty all fear of future annoyance. If the lady loves her husband, she does not love your Majesty. If she does not love your Majesty, there is no reason why she should interfere with your Majesty's plan."

"It is true. And yet—Well! I wish she had been of my own station! What a queen she would have made!" he relapsed into a moody silence, which was not broken until we drew up in Serpentine Avenue.

The door of Briony Lodge was open, and an elderly woman stood upon the steps. She watched us with a sardonic eye as we stepped from the brougham.

"Mr. Sherlock Holmes, I believe?" said she.

"I am Mr. Holmes," answered my companion, looking at her with a questioning and rather startled gaze.

"Indeed! My mistress told me that you were likely to call. She left this morning with her husband by the 5:15 train from Charing Cross for the Continent."

"What!" Sherlock Holmes staggered back, white with chagrin and surprise. "Do you mean that she has left England?"

"Never to return."

"And the papers?" asked the King hoarsely. "All is lost."

"We shall see." He pushed past the servant and rushed into the drawing room, followed by the King and myself. The furniture was scattered about in every direction, with dismantled shelves and open drawers, as if the lady had hurriedly ransacked them before her flight. Holmes rushed at the bellpull, tore back a small sliding shutter, and, plunging in his hand, pulled out a photograph and a letter. The photograph was of Irene Adler herself in evening dress, the letter was superscribed to "Sherlock Holmes, Esq. To be left till called for." My friend tore it open, and we all three read it together. It was dated at midnight of the preceding night and ran in this way:

My Dear Mr. Sherlock Holmes:

You really did it very well. You took me in completely. Until after the alarm of fire, I had not a suspicion. But then, when I found how I had betrayed myself, I began to think. I had been warned against you months ago. I had been told that if the King employed an agent it would certainly be you. And your address had been given me. Yet, with all this, you made me reveal what you wanted to know. Even after I became suspicious, I found it hard to think evil of such a dear, kind old clergyman. But, you know, I have been trained as an actress myself. Male costume is nothing new to me. I often take advantage of the freedom which it gives. I sent John, the coachman, to watch you, ran upstairs, got into my walking clothes, as I call them, and came down just as you departed.

Well, I followed you to your door, and so made sure that I was really an object of interest to the celebrated Mr. Sherlock Holmes. Then I, rather imprudently, wished you goodnight, and started for the Temple to see my husband.

We both thought the best resource was flight, when pursued by so formidable an antagonist; so you will find the nest empty when you call tomorrow. As to the photograph, your client may rest in peace. I love and am loved by a better man than he. The King may do what he will without hindrance from one whom he has cruelly wronged. I keep it only to safeguard myself, and to preserve a weapon which will always secure me from any steps which he might take in the future. I leave a photograph which he might care to possess; and I remain, dear Mr. Sherlock Holmes,

Irene Norton, *nee* Adler.

"What a woman—oh, what a woman!" cried the King of Bohemia, when we had all three read this epistle. "Did I not tell you how quick and resolute she was? Would she not have made an admirable queen? Is it not a pity that she was not on my level?"

"From what I have seen of the lady she seems indeed to be on a very different level to your Majesty," said Holmes coldly. "I am sorry that I have not been able to bring your Majesty's business to a more successful conclusion."

"On the contrary, my dear sir," cried the King; "nothing could be more successful. I know that her word is inviolate. The photograph is now as safe as if it were in the fire."

"I am glad to hear your Majesty say so."

"I am immensely indebted to you. Pray tell me in what way I can reward you. This ring—" He slipped an emerald snake ring from his finger and held it out upon the palm of his hand.

"Your Majesty has something which I should value even more highly," said Holmes.

"You have but to name it."

"This photograph!"

The King stared at him in amazement.

"Irene's photograph!" he cried. "Certainly, if you wish it."

"I thank your Majesty. Then there is no more to be done in the matter. I have the honour to wish you a very good morning." He bowed, and, turning away without observing the hand which the King had stretched out to him, he set off in my company for his chambers.

And that was how a great scandal threatened to affect the kingdom of Bohemia, and how the best plans of Mr. Sherlock Holmes were beaten by a woman's wit. He used to make merry over the cleverness of women, but I have not heard him do it of late. And when he speaks of Irene Adler, or when he refers to her photograph, it is always under the honourable title of *the* woman.

(1891)

Charlotte Perkins Gilman *1860–1935*

THE YELLOW WALL-PAPER

It is very seldom that mere ordinary people like John and myself secure ancestral halls for the summer.

A colonial mansion, a hereditary estate, I would say a haunted house, and reach the height of romantic felicity—but that would be asking too much of fate!

Still I will proudly declare that there is something queer about it.

Else, why should it be let so cheaply? And why have stood so long untenanted?

John laughs at me, of course, but one expects that in marriage.

John is practical in the extreme. He has no patience with faith, an intense horror of superstition, and he scoffs openly at any talk of things not to be felt and seen and put down in figures.

John is a physician, and *perhaps*—(I would not say it to a living soul, of course, but this is dead paper and a great relief to my mind—) *perhaps* that is one reason I do not get well faster.

You see he does not believe I am sick!

And what can one do?

If a physician of high standing, and one's own husband, assures friends and relatives that there is really nothing the matter with one but temporary nervous depression—a slight hysterical tendency—what is one to do?

My brother is also a physician, and also of high standing, and he says the same thing.

So I take phosphates or phosphites—whichever it is, and tonics, and journeys, and air, and exercise, and am absolutely forbidden to "work" until I am well again.

Personally, I disagree with their ideas.

Personally, I believe that congenial work, with excitement and change, would do me good.

But what is one to do?

I did write for a while in spite of them; but it *does* exhaust me a good deal—having to be so sly about it, or else meet with heavy opposition.

I sometimes fancy that in my condition if I had less opposition and more society and stimulus—but John says the very worst thing I can do is to think about my condition, and I confess it always makes me feel bad.

So I will let it alone and talk about the house.

The most beautiful place! It is quite alone, standing well back from the road, quite three miles from the village. It makes me think of English places that you read about, for there are hedges and walls and gates that lock, and lots of separate little houses for the gardeners and people.

There is a *delicious* garden! I never saw such a garden—large and shady, full of box-bordered paths, and lined with long grape-covered arbors with seats under them.

There were greenhouses, too, but they are all broken now.

There was some legal trouble, I believe, something about the heirs and coheirs; anyhow, the place has been empty for years.

That spoils my ghostliness, I am afraid, but I don't care—there is something strange about the house—I can feel it.

I even said so to John one moonlight evening, but he said what I felt was a *draught,* and shut the window.

I get unreasonably angry with John sometimes. I'm sure I never used to be so sensitive. I think it is due to this nervous condition.

But John says if I feel so, I shall neglect proper self-control; so I take pains to control myself—before him, at least, and that makes me very tired.

I don't like our room a bit. I wanted one downstairs that opened on the piazza and had roses all over the window, and such pretty old-fashioned chintz hangings! but John would not hear of it.

He said there was only one window and not room for two beds, and no near room for him if he took another.

He is very careful and loving, and hardly lets me stir without special direction.

I have a schedule prescription for each hour in the day; he takes all care from me, and so I feel basely ungrateful not to value it more.

He said we came here solely on my account, that I was to have perfect rest and all the air I could get. "Your exercise depends on your strength, my dear," said he, "and your food somewhat on your appetite; but air you can absorb all the time." So we took the nursery at the top of the house.

It is a big, airy room, the whole floor nearly, with windows that look all ways, and air and sunshine galore. It was nursery first and then playroom and gymnasium, I should judge; for the windows are barred for little children, and there are rings and things in the walls.

The paint and paper look as if a boys' school had used it. It is stripped off—the paper—in great patches all around the head of my bed, about as far as I can reach, and in a great place on the other side of the room low down. I never saw a worse paper in my life.

One of those sprawling flamboyant patterns committing every artistic sin.

It is dull enough to confuse the eye in following, pronounced enough to constantly irritate and provoke study, and when you follow the lame uncertain curves for a little distance they suddenly commit suicide—plunge off at outrageous angles, destroy themselves in unheard of contradictions.

The color is repellent, almost revolting; a smouldering unclean yellow, strangely faded by the slow-turning sunlight.

It is a dull yet lurid orange in some places, a sickly sulphur tint in others.

No wonder the children hated it! I should hate it myself if I had to live in this room long.

There comes John, and I must put this away,—he hates to have me write a word.

*

We have been here two weeks, and I haven't felt like writing before, since that first day.

I am sitting by the window now, up in this atrocious nursery, and there is nothing to hinder my writing as much as I please, save lack of strength.

John is away all day, and even some nights when his cases are serious.

I am glad my case is not serious!

But these nervous troubles are dreadfully depressing.

John does not know how much I really suffer. He knows there is no *reason* to suffer, and that satisfies him.

Of course it is only nervousness. It does weigh on me so not to do my duty in any way!

I meant to be such a help to John, such a real rest and comfort, and here I am a comparative burden already!

Nobody would believe what an effort it is to do what little I am able,—to dress and entertain, and order things.

It is fortunate Mary is so good with the baby. Such a dear baby!

And yet I *cannot* be with him, it makes me so nervous.

I suppose John never was nervous in his life. He laughs at me so about this wall-paper!

At first he meant to repaper the room, but afterwards he said that I was letting it get the better of me, and that nothing was worse for a nervous patient than to give way to such fancies.

He said that after the wall-paper was changed it would be the heavy bedstead, and then the barred windows, and then that gate at the head of the stairs, and so on.

"You know the place is doing you good," he said, "and really, dear, I don't care to renovate the house just for a three months' rental."

"Then do let us go downstairs," I said, "there are such pretty rooms there."

Then he took me in his arms and called me a blessed little goose, and said he would go down cellar, if I wished, and have it whitewashed into the bargain.

But he is right enough about the beds and windows and things.

It is an airy and comfortable room as any one need wish, and, of course, I would not be so silly as to make him uncomfortable just for a whim.

I'm really getting quite fond of the big room, all but that horrid paper.

Out of one window I can see the garden, those mysterious deep-shaded arbors, the riotous old-fashioned flowers, and bushes and gnarly trees.

Out of another I get a lovely view of the bay and a little private wharf belonging to the estate. There is a beautiful shaded lane that runs down there from the house. I always fancy I see people walking in these numerous paths and arbors, but John has cautioned me not to give way to fancy in the least. He says that with my imaginative power and habit of story-making, a nervous weakness like mine is sure to lead to all manner of excited fancies, and that I ought to use my will and good sense to check the tendency. So I try.

I think sometimes that if I were only well enough to write a little it would relieve the press of ideas and rest me.

But I find I get pretty tired when I try.

It is so discouraging not to have any advice and companionship about my work. When I get really well, John says we will ask Cousin Henry and Julia down for a long visit; but he says he would as soon put fireworks in my pillowcase as to let me have those stimulating people about now.

I wish I could get well faster.

But I must not think about that. This paper looks to me as if it *knew* what a vicious influence it had!

There is a recurrent spot where the pattern lolls like a broken neck and two bulbous eyes stare at you upside down.

I get positively angry with the impertinence of it and the everlastingness. Up and down and sideways they crawl, and those absurd, unblinking eyes are everywhere. There is one place where two breadths didn't match, and the eyes go all up and down the line, one a little higher than the other.

I never saw so much expression in an inanimate thing before, and we all know how much expression they have! I used to lie awake as a child and get more entertainment and terror out of blank walls and plain furniture than most children could find in a toy-store.

I remember what a kindly wink the knobs of our big, old bureau used to have, and there was one chair that always seemed like a strong friend.

I used to feel that if any of the other things looked too fierce I could always hop into that chair and be safe.

The furniture in this room is no worse than inharmonious, however, for we had to bring it all from downstairs. I suppose when this was used as a playroom they had to take the nursery things out, and no wonder! I never saw such ravages as the children have made here.

The wall-paper, as I said before, is torn off in spots, and it sticketh closer than a brother—they must have had perseverance as well as hatred.

Then the floor is scratched and gouged and splintered, the plaster itself is dug out here and there, and this great heavy bed which is all we found in the room, looks as if it had been through the wars.

But I don't mind it a bit—only the paper.

There comes John's sister. Such a dear girl as she is, and so careful of me! I must not let her find me writing.

She is a perfect and enthusiastic housekeeper, and hopes for no better profession. I verily believe she thinks it is the writing which made me sick!

But I can write when she is out, and see her a long way off from these windows.

There is one that commands the road, a lovely shaded winding road, and one that just looks off over the country. A lovely country, too, full of great elms and velvet meadows.

This wall-paper has a kind of subpattern in a different shade, a particularly irritating one, for you can only see it in certain lights, and not clearly then.

But in the places where it isn't faded and where the sun is just so—I can see a strange, provoking, formless sort of figure, that seems to skulk about behind that silly and conspicuous front design.

There's sister on the stairs!

*

Well, the Fourth of July is over! The people are all gone and I am tired out. John thought it might do me good to see a little company, so we just had mother and Nellie and the children down for a week.

Of course I didn't do a thing. Jennie sees to everything now.

But it tired me all the same.

John says if I don't pick up faster he shall send me to Weir Mitchell[1] in the fall.

But I don't want to go there at all. I had a friend who was in his hands once, and she says he is just like John and my brother, only more so!

Besides, it is such an undertaking to go so far.

I don't feel as if it was worth while to turn my hand over for anything, and I'm getting dreadfully fretful and querulous.

I cry at nothing, and cry most of the time.

Of course I don't when John is here, or anybody else, but when I am alone.

And I am alone a good deal just now. John is kept in town very often by serious cases, and Jennie is good and lets me alone when I want her to.

So I walk a little in the garden or down that lovely lane, sit on the porch under the roses, and lie down up here a good deal.

I'm getting really fond of the room in spite of the wall-paper. Perhaps *because* of the wall-paper.

---

[1] Silas Weir Mitchell (1829–1914), the Philadelphia neurologist-psychologist who introduced "rest cure" for nervous diseases. His medical books include *Diseases of the Nervous System, Especially of Woman* (1881).

It dwells in my mind so!

I lie here on this great immovable bed—it is nailed down, I believe—and follow that pattern about by the hour. It is as good as gymnastics, I assure you. I start, we'll say, at the bottom, down in the corner over there where it has not been touched, and I determine for the thousandth time that I *will* follow that pointless pattern to some sort of a conclusion.

I know a little of the principle of design, and I know this thing was not arranged on any laws of radiation, or alternation, or repetition, or symmetry, or anything else that I ever heard of.

It is repeated, of course, by the breadths, but not otherwise.

Looked at in one way each breadth stands alone, the bloated curves and flour-ishes—a kind of "debased Romanesque" with *delirium tremens*[2] go waddling up and down in isolated columns of fatuity.

But, on the other hand, they connect diagonally, and the sprawling outlines run off in great slanting waves of optic horror, like a lot of wallowing seaweeds in full chase.

The whole thing goes horizontally, too, at least it seems so, and I exhaust myself in trying to distinguish the order of its going in that direction.

They have used a horizontal breadth for a frieze, and that adds wonderfully to the confusion.

There is one end of the room where it is almost intact, and there, when the crosslights fade and the low sun shines directly upon it, I can almost fancy radi-ation after all, the interminable grotesques seem to form around a common centre and rush off in headlong plunges of equal distraction.

It makes me tired to follow it. I will take a nap I guess.

*

I don't know why I should write this.

I don't want to.

I don't feel able.

And I know John would think it absurd. But I *must* say what I feel and think in some way—it is such a relief!

But the effort is getting to be greater than the relief.

Half the time now I am awfully lazy, and lie down ever so much.

John says I mustn't lose my strength, and has me take cod liver oil and lots of tonics and things, to say nothing of ale and wine and rare meat.

Dear John! He loves me very dearly, and hates to have me sick. I tried to have a real earnest reasonable talk with him the other day, and tell him how I wish he would let me go and make a visit to Cousin Henry and Julia.

But he said I wasn't able to go, nor able to stand it after I got there; and I did not make out a very good case for myself, for I was crying before I had finished.

It is getting to be a great effort for me to think straight. Just this nervous weakness I suppose.

And dear John gathered me up in his arms, and just carried me upstairs and laid me on the bed, and sat by me and read to me till it tired my head.

He said I was his darling and his comfort and all he had, and that I must take care of myself for his sake, and keep well.

[2] Mental disorientation caused by excessive use of alcohol and characterized by physical tremors.

He says no one but myself can help me out of it, that I must use my will and self-control and not let any silly fancies run away with me.

There's one comfort, the baby is well and happy, and does not have to occupy this nursery with the horrid wall-paper.

If we had not used it, that blessed child would have! What a fortunate escape! Why, I wouldn't have a child of mine, an impressionable little thing, live in such a room for worlds.

I never thought of it before, but it is lucky that John kept me here after all, I can stand it so much easier than a baby, you see.

Of course I never mention it to them any more—I am too wise,—but I keep watch of it all the same.

There are things in that paper that nobody knows but me, or ever will.

Behind that outside pattern the dim shapes get clearer every day.

It is always the same shape, only very numerous.

And it is like a woman stooping down and creeping about behind that pattern. I don't like it a bit. I wonder—I begin to think—I wish John would take me away from here!

*

It is so hard to talk with John about my case, because he is so wise, and because he loves me so.

But I tried it last night.

It was moonlight. The moon shines in all around just as the sun does.

I hate to see it sometimes, it creeps so slowly, and always comes in by one window or another.

John was asleep and I hated to waken him, so I kept still and watched the moonlight on that undulating wall-paper till I felt creepy.

The faint figure behind seemed to shake the pattern, just as if she wanted to get out.

I got up softly and went to feel and see if the paper *did* move, and when I came back John was awake.

"What is it, little girl?" he said. "Don't go walking about like that—you'll get cold."

I thought it was a good time to talk, so I told him that I really was not gaining here, and that I wished he would take me away.

"Why, darling!" said he, "our lease will be up in three weeks, and I can't see how to leave before."

"The repairs are not done at home, and I cannot possibly leave town just now. Of course if you were in any danger, I could and would, but you really are better, dear, whether you can see it or not. I am a doctor, dear, and I know. You are gaining flesh and color, your appetite is better, I feel really much easier about you."

"I don't weigh a bit more," said I, "nor as much; and my appetite may be better in the evening when you are here, but it is worse in the morning when you are away!"

"Bless her little heart!" said he with a big hug, "she shall be as sick as she pleases! But now let's improve the shining hours by going to sleep, and talk about it in the morning!"

"And you won't go away?" I asked gloomily.

"Why, how can I, dear? It is only three weeks more and then we will take a nice little trip of a few days while Jennie is getting the house ready. Really dear you are better!"

"Better in body perhaps—" I began, and stopped short, for he sat up straight and looked at me with such a stern, reproachful look that I could not say another word.

"My darling," said he, "I beg of you, for my sake and for our child's sake, as well as for your own, that you will never for one instant let that idea enter your mind! There is nothing so dangerous, so fascinating, to a temperament like yours. It is a false and foolish fancy. Can you not trust me as a physician when I tell you so?"

So of course I said no more on that score, and we went to sleep before long. He thought I was asleep first, but I wasn't, and lay there for hours trying to decide whether that front pattern and the back pattern really did move together or separately.

*

On a pattern like this, by daylight, there is a lack of sequence, a defiance of law, that is a constant irritant to a normal mind.

The color is hideous enough, and unreliable enough, and infuriating enough, but the pattern is torturing.

You think you have mastered it, but just as you get well underway in following, it turns a back-somersault and there you are. It slaps you in the face, knocks you down, and tramples upon you. It is like a bad dream.

The outside pattern is a florid arabesque, reminding one of a fungus. If you can imagine a toadstool in joints, an interminable string of toadstools, budding and sprouting in endless convolutions—why, that is something like it.

That is, sometimes!

There is one marked peculiarity about this paper, a thing nobody seems to notice but myself, and that is that it changes as the light changes.

When the sun shoots in through the east windows—I always watch for that first long, straight ray—it changes so quickly that I never can quite believe it.

That is why I watch it always.

By moonlight—the moon shines in all night when there is a moon—I wouldn't know it was the same paper.

At night in any kind of light, in twilight, candlelight, lamplight, and worst of all by moonlight, it becomes bars! The outside pattern I mean, and the woman behind it is as plain as can be.

I didn't realize for a long time what the thing was that showed behind, that dim sub-pattern, but now I am quite sure it is a woman.

By daylight she is subdued, quiet. I fancy it is the pattern that keeps her so still. It is so puzzling. It keeps me quiet by the hour.

I lie down ever so much now. John says it is good for me, and to sleep all I can.

Indeed he started the habit by making me lie down for an hour after each meal.

It is a very bad habit I am convinced, for you see I don't sleep.

And that cultivates deceit, for I don't tell them I'm awake—O no!

The fact is I am getting a little afraid of John.

He seems very queer sometimes, and even Jennie has an inexplicable look.

It strikes me occasionally, just as a scientific hypothesis,—that perhaps it is the paper!

I have watched John when he did not know I was looking, and come into the room suddenly on the most innocent excuses, and I've caught him several times *looking at the paper!* And Jennie too. I caught Jennie with her hand on it once.

She didn't know I was in the room, and when I asked her in a quiet, a very quiet voice, with the most restrained manner possible, what she was doing with the paper—she turned around as if she had been caught stealing, and looked quite angry—asked me why I should frighten her so!

Then she said that the paper stained everything it touched, that she had found yellow smooches on all my clothes and John's, and she wished we would be more careful!

Did not that sound innocent? But I know she was studying that pattern, and I am determined that nobody shall find it out but myself!

*

Life is very much more exciting now than it used to be. You see I have something more to expect, to look forward to, to watch. I really do eat better, and am more quiet than I was.

John is so pleased to see me improve! He laughed a little the other day, and said I seemed to be flourishing in spite of my wall-paper.

I turned it off with a laugh. I had no intention of telling him it was *because* of the wall-paper—he would make fun of me. He might even want to take me away.

I don't want to leave now until I have found it out. There is a week more, and I think that will be enough.

*

I'm feeling ever so much better! I don't sleep much at night, for it is so interesting to watch developments; but I sleep a good deal in the daytime.

In the daytime it is tiresome and perplexing.

There are always new shoots on the fungus, and new shades of yellow all over it. I cannot keep count of them, though I have tried conscientiously.

It is the strangest yellow, that wallpaper! It makes me think of all the yellow things I ever saw—not beautiful ones like buttercups, but old foul, bad yellow things.

But there is something else about that paper—the smell! I noticed it the moment we came into the room, but with so much air and sun it was not bad. Now we have had a week of fog and rain, and whether the windows are open or not, the smell is here.

It creeps all over the house.

I find it hovering in the dining-room, skulking in the parlor, hiding in the hall, lying in wait for me on the stairs.

It gets into my hair.

Even when I go to ride, if I turn my head suddenly and surprise it—there is that smell!

Such a peculiar odor, too! I have spent hours in trying to analyze it, to find what it smelled like.

It is not bad—at first, and very gentle, but quite the subtlest, most enduring odor I ever met.

In this damp weather it is awful, I wake up in the night and find it hanging over me.

It used to disturb me at first. I thought seriously of burning the house—to reach the smell.

But now I am used to it. The only thing I can think of that it is like is the *color* of the paper! A yellow smell.

There is a very funny mark on this wall, low down, near the mopboard. A streak that runs round the room. It goes behind every piece of furniture, except the bed, a long, straight, even *smooch*, as if it had been rubbed over and over.

I wonder how it was done and who did it, and what they did it for. Round and round and round—round and round and round!—it makes me dizzy!

*

I really have discovered something at last.

Through watching so much at night when it changes so, I have finally found out.

The front pattern *does* move—and no wonder! The woman behind shakes it!

Sometimes I think there are a great many women behind, and sometimes only one, and she crawls around fast, and her crawling shakes it all over.

Then in the very bright spots she keeps still, and in the very shady spots she just takes hold of the bars and shakes them hard.

And she is all the time trying to climb through. But nobody could climb through that pattern—it strangles so; I think that is why it has so many heads.

They get through, and then the pattern strangles them off and turns them upside down, and makes their eyes white!

If those heads were covered or taken off it would not be half so bad.

*

I think that woman gets out in the daytime!

And I'll tell you why—privately—I've seen her!

I can see her out of every one of my windows!

It is the same woman, I know, for she is always creeping, and most women do not creep by daylight.

I see her in that long shaded lane, creeping up and down. I see her in those dark grape arbors, creeping all around the garden.

I see her on that long road under the trees, creeping along, and when a carriage comes she hides under the blackberry vines.

I don't blame her a bit. It must be very humiliating to be caught creeping by daylight!

I always lock the door when I creep by daylight. I can't do it at night, for I know John would suspect something at once.

And John is so queer now, that I don't want to irritate him. I wish he would take another room! Besides, I don't want anybody to get that woman out at night but myself.

I often wonder if I could see her out of all the windows at once.

But, turn as fast as I can, I can only see out of one at one time.

And though I always see her, she *may* be able to creep faster than I can turn!

I have watched her sometimes away off in the open country, creeping as fast as a cloud shadow in a high wind.

*

If only that top pattern could be gotten off from the under one! I mean to try it, little by little.

I have found out another funny thing, but I shan't tell it this time! It does not do to trust people too much.

There are only two more days to get this paper off, and I believe John is beginning to notice. I don't like the look in his eyes.

And I heard him ask Jennie a lot of professional questions about me. She had a very good report to give.

She said I slept a good deal in the daytime.

John knows I don't sleep very well at night, for all I'm so quiet!

He asked me all sorts of questions, too, and pretended to be very loving and kind.

As if I couldn't see through him!

Still, I don't wonder he acts so, sleeping under this paper for three months.

It only interests me, but I feel sure John and Jennie are secretly affected by it.

*

Hurrah! This is the last day, but it is enough. John to stay in town over night, and won't be out until this evening.

Jennie wanted to sleep with me—the sly thing! but I told her I should undoubtedly rest better for a night all alone.

That was clever, for really I wasn't alone a bit! As soon as it was moonlight and that poor thing began to crawl and shake the pattern, I got up and ran to help her.

I pulled and she shook, I shook and she pulled, and before morning we had peeled off yards of that paper.

A strip about as high as my head and half around the room.

And then when the sun came and that awful pattern began to laugh at me, I declared I would finish it to-day!

We go away to-morrow, and they are moving all my furniture down again to leave things as they were before.

Jennie looked at the wall in amazement, but I told her merrily that I did it out of pure spite at the vicious thing.

She laughed and said she wouldn't mind doing it herself, but I must not get tired.

How she betrayed herself that time!

But I am here, and no person touches this paper but me,—not *alive!*

She tried to get me out of the room—it was too patent! But I said it was so quiet and empty and clean now that I believed I would lie down again and sleep all I could; and not to wake me even for dinner—I would call when I woke.

So now she is gone, and the servants are gone, and the things are gone, and there is nothing left but that great bedstead nailed down, with the canvas mattress we found on it.

We shall sleep downstairs to-night, and take the boat home to-morrow.

I quite enjoy the room, now it is bare again.

How those children did tear about here!

This bedstead is fairly gnawed!

But I must get to work.

I have locked the door and thrown the key down into the front path.

I don't want to go out, and I don't want to have anybody come in, till John comes.

I want to astonish him.

I've got a rope up here that even Jennie did not find. If that woman does get out, and tries to get away, I can tie her!

But I forgot I could not reach far without anything to stand on!

This bed will *not* move!

I tried to lift and push it until I was lame, and then I got so angry I bit off a little piece at one corner—but it hurt my teeth.

Then I peeled off all the paper I could reach standing on the floor. It sticks horribly and the pattern just enjoys it! All those strangled heads and bulbous eyes and waddling fungus growths just shriek with derision!

I am getting angry enough to do something desperate. To jump out of the window would be admirable exercise, but the bars are too strong even to try.

Besides I wouldn't do it. Of course not. I know well enough that a step like that is improper and might be misconstrued.

I don't like to *look* out of the windows even—there are so many of those creeping women, and they creep so fast.

I wonder if they all come out of that wall-paper as I did?

But I am securely fastened now by my well-hidden rope—you don't get *me* out in the road there!

I suppose I shall have to get back behind the pattern when it comes night, and that is hard!

It is so pleasant to be out in this great room and creep around as I please!

I don't want to go outside. I won't, even if Jennie asks me to.

For outside you have to creep on the ground, and everything is green instead of yellow.

But here I can creep smoothly on the floor, and my shoulder just fits in that long smooch around the wall, so I cannot lose my way.

Why there's John at the door!

It is no use, young man, you can't open it!

How he does call and pound!

Now he's crying for an axe.

It would be a shame to break down that beautiful door!

"John dear!" said I in the gentlest voice, "the key is down by the front steps, under a plaintain leaf!"

That silenced him for a few moments.

Then he said—very quietly indeed, "Open the door, my darling!"

"I can't," said I. "The key is down by the front door under a plaintain leaf!"

And then I said it again, several times, very gently and slowly, and said it so often that he had to go and see, and he got it of course, and came in. He stopped short by the door.

"What is the matter?" he cried. "For God's sake, what are you doing!"

I kept on creeping just the same, but I looked at him over my shoulder.

"I've got out at last," said I, "in spite of you and Jane! And I've pulled off most of the paper, so you can't put me back!"

Now why should that man have fainted? But he did, and right across my path by the wall, so that I had to creep over him every time!

[1892]

Kate Chopin *1851–1904*

THE STORM

I

The leaves were so still that even Bibi thought it was going to rain. Bobinôt, who was accustomed to converse on terms of perfect equality with his little son, called the child's attention to certain somber clouds that were rolling with sinister intention from the west, accompanied by a sullen, threatening roar. They were at Friedheimer's store and decided to remain there till the storm had passed. They sat within the door on two empty kegs: Bibi was four years old and looked very wise.

"Mama'll be 'fraid, yes," he suggested with blinking eyes.

"She'll shut the house. Maybe she got Sylvie helpin' her this evenin'," Bobinôt responded reassuringly.

"No; she ent got Sylvie. Sylvie was helpin' her yistiday," piped Bibi.

Bobinôt arose and going across to the counter purchased a can of shrimps, of which Calixta was very fond. Then he returned to his perch on the keg and sat stolidly holding the can of shrimps while the storm burst. It shook the wooden store and seemed to be ripping great furrows in the distant field. Bibi laid his little hand on his father's knee and was not afraid.

II

Calixta, at home, felt no uneasiness for their safety. She sat at a side window sewing furiously on a sewing machine. She was greatly occupied and did not notice the approaching storm. But she felt very warm and often stopped to mop her face on which the perspiration gathered in beads. She unfastened her white sacque[1] at the throat. It began to grow dark, and suddenly realizing the situation she got up hurriedly and went about closing windows and doors.

Out on the small front gallery she had hung Bobinôt's Sunday clothes to air and she hastened out to gather them before the rain fell. As she stepped outside, Alcée Laballière rode in at the gate. She had not seen him very often since her marriage, and never alone. She stood there with Bobinôt's coat in her hands, and the big rain drops began to fall. Alcée rode his horse under the shelter of a side projection where the chickens had huddled and there were plows and a harrow piled up in the corner.

"May I come and wait on your gallery till the storm is over, Calixta?" he asked.

"Come 'long in, M'sieur Alcée."

His voice and her own startled her as if from a trance, and she seized Bobinôt's vest. Alcée, mounting to the porch, grabbed the trousers and snatched Bibi's braided jacket that was about to be carried away by a sudden gust of wind. He expressed an intention to remain outside, but it was soon apparent that he might as well have been out in the open: the water beat in upon the boards in driving sheets, and he went inside, closing the door after him. It was even necessary to put something beneath the door to keep the water out.

[1] A short jacket that buttons at the neck.

"My! what a rain! It's good two years sence it rain' like that," exclaimed Calixta as she rolled up a piece of bagging and Alcée helped her to thrust it beneath the crack.

She was a little fuller of figure than five years before when she married; but she had lost nothing of her vivacity. Her blue eyes still retained their melting quality; and her yellow hair, dishevelled by the wind and rain, kinked more stubbornly than ever about her ears and temples.

The rain beat upon the low, shingled roof with a force and clatter that threatened to break an entrance and deluge them there. They were in the dining room—the sitting room—the general utility room. Adjoining was her bed room, with Bibi's couch along side her own. The door stood open, and the room with its white, monumental bed, its closed shutters, looked dim and mysterious.

Alcée flung himself into a rocker and Calixta nervously began to gather up from the floor the lengths of a cotton sheet which she had been sewing.

"If this keeps up, *Dieu sait*[2] if the levees goin' to stan' it!" she exclaimed.

"What have you got to do with the levees?"

"I got enough to do! An' there's Bobinôt with Bibi out in that storm—if he only didn' left Friedheimer's!"

"Let us hope, Calixta, that Bobinôt's got sense enough to come in out of a cyclone."

She went and stood at the window with a greatly disturbed look on her face. She wiped the frame that was clouded with moisture. It was stiflingly hot. Alcée got up and joined her at the window, looking over her shoulder. The rain was coming down in sheets obscuring the view of far-off cabins and enveloping the distant wood in a gray mist. The playing of the lightning was incessant. A bolt struck a tall chinaberry tree at the edge of the field. It filled all visible space with a blinding glare and the crash seemed to invade the very boards they stood upon.

Calixta put her hands to her eyes, and with a cry, staggered backward. Alcée's arm encircled her, and for an instant he drew her close and spasmodically to him.

"*Bonte!*"[3] she cried, releasing herself from his encircling arm and retreating from the window, "the house'll go next! If I only knew w'ere Bibi was!" She would not compose herself; she would not be seated. Alcée clasped her shoulders and looked into her face. The contact of her warm, palpitating body when he had unthinkingly drawn her into his arms, had aroused all the old-time infatuation and desire for her flesh.

"Calixta," he said, "don't be frightened. Nothing can happen. The house is too low to be struck, with so many tall trees standing about. There! aren't you going to be quiet? say, aren't you?" He pushed her hair back from her face that was warm and steaming. Her lips were as red and moist as pomegranate seed. Her white neck and a glimpse of her full, firm bosom disturbed him powerfully. As she glanced up at him the fear in her liquid blue eyes had given place to a drowsy gleam that unconsciously betrayed a sensuous desire. He looked down into her eyes and there was nothing for him to do but to gather her lips in a kiss. It reminded him of Assumption.[4]

"Do you remember—in Assumption, Calixta?" he asked in a low voice broken by passion. Oh! she remembered; for in Assumption he had kissed her and kissed

[2] "God only knows."   [3] "Heavens!"

[4] Assumption Parish (or County), near the coastal parishes of southern Louisiana. It was there that Calixta had gone in an earlier Chopin story, "At the 'Cadian Ball" (1892), and first met Alcée Laballière.

and kissed her; until his senses would well nigh fail, and to save her he would resort to a desperate flight. If she was not an immaculate dove in those days, she was still inviolate; a passionate creature whose very defenselessness had made her defense, against which his honor forbade him to prevail. Now—well, now—her lips seemed in a manner free to be tasted, as well as her round, white throat and her whiter breasts.

They did not heed the crashing torrents, and the roar of the elements made her laugh as she lay in his arms. She was a revelation in that dim, mysterious chamber; as white as the couch she lay upon. Her firm, elastic flesh that was knowing for the first time its birthright, was like a creamy lily that the sun invites to contribute its breath and perfume to the undying life of the world.

The generous abundance of her passion, without guile or trickery, was like a white flame which penetrated and found response in depths of his own sensuous nature that had never yet been reached.

When he touched her breasts they gave themselves up in quivering ecstasy, inviting his lips. Her mouth was a fountain of delight. And when he possessed her, they seemed to swoon together at the very borderland of life's mystery.

He stayed cushioned upon her, breathless, dazed, enervated, with his heart beating like a hammer upon her. With one hand she clasped his head, her lips lightly touching his forehead. The other hand stroked with a soothing rhythm his muscular shoulders.

The growl of the thunder was distant and passing away. The rain beat softly upon the shingles, inviting them to drowsiness and sleep. But they dared not yield.

The rain was over; and the sun was turning the glistening green world into a palace of gems. Calixta, on the gallery, watched Alcée ride away. He turned and smiled at her with a beaming face; and she lifted her pretty chin in the air and laughed aloud.

III

Bobinôt and Bibi, trudging home, stopped without at the cistern to make themselves presentable.

"My! Bibi, w'at will yo' mama say! You ought to be ashame'. You oughtn' put on those good pants. Look at 'em! An' that mud on yo' collar! How you got that mud on yo' collar, Bibi? I never saw such a boy!'' Bibi was the picture of pathetic resignation. Bobinôt was the embodiment of serious solicitude as he strove to remove from his own person and his son's the signs of their tramp over heavy roads and through wet fields. He scraped the mud off Bibi's bare legs and feet with a stick and carefully removed all traces from his heavy brogans. Then, prepared for the worst—the meeting with an over-scrupulous housewife, they entered cautiously at the back door.

Calixta was preparing supper. She had set the table and was dripping coffee at the hearth. She sprang up as they came in.

"Oh, Bobinôt! You back! My! but I was uneasy. W'ere you been during the rain? An' Bibi? he ain't wet? he ain't hurt?'' She had clasped Bibi and was kissing him effusively. Bobinôt's explanations and apologies which he had been composing all along the way, died on his lips as Calixta felt him to see if he were dry, and seemed to express nothing but satisfaction at their safe return.

"I brought you some shrimps, Calixta,'' offered Bobinôt, hauling the can from his ample side pocket and laying it on the table.

"Shrimps! Oh, Bobinôt! you too good fo' anything!" and she gave him a smacking kiss on the cheek that resounded. "*J'vous reponds,*[5] we'll have a feas' to night! umph-umph!"

Bobinôt and Bibi began to relax and enjoy themselves, and when the three seated themselves at table they laughed much and so loud that anyone might have heard them as far away as Laballière's.

IV

Alcée Laballière wrote to his wife, Clarisse, that night. It was a loving letter, full of tender solicitude. He told her not to hurry back, but if she and the babies liked it at Biloxi, to stay a month longer. He was getting on nicely; and though he missed them, he was willing to bear the separation a while longer—realizing that their health and pleasure were the first things to be considered.

V

As for Clarisse, she was charmed upon receiving her husband's letter. She and the babies were doing well. The society was agreeable; many of her old friends and acquaintances were at the bay. And the first free breath since her marriage seemed to restore the pleasant liberty of her maiden days. Devoted as she was to her husband, their intimate conjugal life was something which she was more than willing to forego for a while.

So the storm passed and everyone was happy.

[1898]

---

[5] "I tell you."

Stephen Crane   *1871–1900*

THE BLUE HOTEL

I

The Palace Hotel at Fort Romper was painted a light blue, a shade that is on the legs of a kind of heron, causing the bird to declare its position against any background. The Palace Hotel, then, was always screaming and howling in a way that made the dazzling winter landscape of Nebraska seem only a grey swampish hush. It stood alone on the prairie, and when the snow was falling the town two hundred yards away was not visible. But when the traveller alighted at the railway station he was obliged to pass the Palace Hotel before he could come upon the company of low clapboard houses which composed Fort Romper, and it was not to be thought that any traveller could pass the Palace Hotel without looking at it. Pat Scully, the proprietor, had proved himself a master of strategy when he chose his paints. It is true that on clear days, when the great transcontinental expresses, long lines of swaying Pullmans, swept through Fort Romper, passengers were overcome at the sight, and the cult that knows the brown-reds and the subdivisions of the dark greens of the East expressed shame, pity, horror, in a laugh. But to the citizens of this prairie town and to the people who would naturally stop there, Pat Scully had performed a feat. With this opulence and splendour, these creeds, classes, egotisms, that streamed through Romper on the rails day after day, they had no colour in common.

As if the displayed delights of such a blue hotel were not sufficiently enticing, it was Scully's habit to go every morning and evening to meet the leisurely trains that stopped at Romper and work his seductions upon any man that he might see wavering, gripsack in hand.

One morning, when a snow-crusted engine dragged its long string of freight cars and its one passenger coach to the station, Scully performed the marvel of catching three men. One was a shaky and quick-eyed Swede, with a great shining cheap valise; one was a tall bronzed cowboy, who was on his way to a ranch near the Dakota line; one was a little silent man from the East, who didn't look it, and didn't announce it. Scully practically made them prisoners. He was so nimble and merry and kindly that each probably felt it would be the height of brutality to try to escape. They trudged off over the creaking board sidewalks in the wake of the eager little Irishman. He wore a heavy fur cap squeezed tightly down on his head. It caused his two red ears to stick out stiffly, as if they were made of tin.

At last, Scully, elaborately, with boisterous hospitality, conducted them through the portals of the blue hotel. The room which they entered was small. It seemed to be merely a proper temple for an enormous stove, which, in the centre, was humming with godlike violence. At various points on its surface the iron had become luminous and glowed yellow from the heat. Beside the stove Scully's son Johnnie was playing High-Five[1] with an old farmer who had whiskers both grey and sandy. They were quarrelling. Frequently the old farmer turned his face toward a box of sawdust—coloured brown from tobacco juice—that was behind the stove, and spat with an air of great impatience and irritation. With a loud flourish of words Scully destroyed the game of cards, and bustled his son upstairs

---

[1] A popular card game, the forerunner of modern contract bridge; also called Cinch or Pedro.

with part of the baggage of the new guests. He himself conducted them to three basins of the coldest water in the world. The cowboy and the Easterner burnished themselves fiery red with this water, until it seemed to be some kind of metal-polish. The Swede, however, merely dipped his fingers gingerly and with trepidation. It was notable that throughout this series of small ceremonies the three travellers were made to feel that Scully was very benevolent. He was conferring great favours upon them. He handed the towel from one to another with an air of philanthropic impulse.

Afterward they went to the first room, and, sitting about the stove, listened to Scully's officious clamour at his daughters, who were preparing the midday meal. They reflected in the silence of experienced men who tread carefully amid new people. Nevertheless, the old farmer, stationary, invincible in his chair near the warmest part of the stove, turned his face from the sawdust-box frequently and addressed a glowing commonplace to the strangers. Usually he was answered in short but adequate sentences by either the cowboy or the Easterner. The Swede said nothing. He seemed to be occupied in making furtive estimates of each man in the room. One might have thought that he had the sense of silly suspicion which comes to guilt. He resembled a badly frightened man.

Later, at dinner, he spoke a little, addressing his conversation entirely to Scully. He volunteered that he had come from New York, where for ten years he had worked as a tailor. These facts seemed to strike Scully as fascinating, and afterward he volunteered that he had lived at Romper for fourteen years. The Swede asked about the crops and the price of labour. He seemed barely to listen to Scully's extended replies. His eyes continued to rove from man to man.

Finally, with a laugh and a wink, he said that some of these Western communities were very dangerous; and after his statement he straightened his legs under the table, tilted his head, and laughed again, loudly. It was plain that the demonstration had no meaning to the others. They looked at him wondering and in silence.

II

As the men trooped heavily back into the front room, the two little windows presented views of a turmoiling sea of snow. The huge arms of the wind were making attempts—mighty, circular, futile—to embrace the flakes as they sped. A gate-post like a still man with a blanched face stood aghast amid this profligate fury. In a hearty voice Scully announced the presence of a blizzard. The guests of the blue hotel, lighting their pipes, assented with grunts of lazy masculine contentment. No island of the sea could be exempt in the degree of this little room with its humming stove. Johnnie, son of Scully, in a tone which defined his opinion of his ability as a card-player, challenged the old farmer of both grey and sandy whiskers to a game of High-Five. The farmer agreed with a contemptuous and bitter scoff. They sat close to the stove, and squared their knees under a wide board. The cowboy and the Easterner watched the game with interest. The Swede remained near the window, aloof, but with a countenance that showed signs of an inexplicable excitement.

The play of Johnnie and the grey-beard was suddenly ended by another quarrel. The old man arose while casting a look of heated scorn at his adversary. He slowly buttoned his coat, and then stalked with fabulous dignity from the room. In the discreet silence of all other men the Swede laughed. His laughter rang somehow childish. Men by this time had begun to look at him askance, as if they wished to inquire what ailed him.

A new game was formed jocosely. The cowboy volunteered to become the partner of Johnnie, and they all then turned to ask the Swede to throw in his lot with the little Easterner. He asked some questions about the game, and, learning that it wore many names, and that he had played it when it was under an alias, he accepted the invitation. He strode toward the men nervously, as if he expected to be assaulted. Finally, seated, he gazed from face to face and laughed shrilly. This laugh was so strange that the Easterner looked up quickly, the cowboy sat intent and with his mouth open, and Johnnie paused, holding the cards with still fingers.

Afterward there was a short silence. Then Johnnie said, "Well, let's get at it. Come on now!" They pulled their chairs forward until their knees were bunched under the board. They began to play, and their interest in the game caused the others to forget the manner of the Swede.

The cowboy was a board-whacker. Each time that he held superior cards he whanged them, one by one, with exceeding force, down upon the improvised table, and took the tricks with a glowing air of prowess and pride that sent thrills of indignation into the hearts of his opponents. A game with a board-whacker in it is sure to become intense. The countenances of the Easterner and the Swede were miserable whenever the cowboy thundered down his aces and kings, while Johnnie, his eyes gleaming with joy, chuckled and chuckled.

Because of the absorbing play none considered the strange ways of the Swede. They paid strict heed to the game. Finally, during a lull caused by a new deal, the Swede suddenly addressed Johnnie: "I suppose there have been a good many men killed in this room." The jaws of the others dropped and they looked at him.

"What in hell are you talking about?" said Johnnie.

The Swede laughed again his blatant laugh, full of a kind of false courage and defiance. "Oh, you know what I mean all right," he answered.

"I'm a liar if I do!" Johnnie protested. The card was halted, and the men stared at the Swede. Johnnie evidently felt that as the son of the proprietor he should make a direct inquiry. "Now, what might you be drivin' at, mister?" he asked. The Swede winked at him. It was a wink full of cunning. His fingers shook on the edge of the board. "Oh, maybe you think I have been to nowheres. Maybe you think I'm a tenderfoot?"

"I don't know nothin' about you," answered Johnnie, "and I don't give a damn where you've been. All I got to say is that I don't know what you're driving at. There hain't never been nobody killed in this room."

The cowboy, who had been steadily gazing at the Swede, then spoke: "What's wrong with you, mister?"

Apparently it seemed to the Swede that he was formidably menaced. He shivered and turned white near the corners of his mouth. He sent an appealing glance in the direction of the little Easterner. During these moments he did not forget to wear his air of advanced pot-valour.[2] "They say they don't know what I mean," he remarked mockingly to the Easterner.

The latter answered after prolonged and cautious reflection. "I don't understand you," he said, impassively.

The Swede made a movement then which announced that he thought he had encountered treachery from the only quarter where he had expected sympathy, if not help. "Oh, I see you are all against me. I see——"

The cowboy was in a state of deep stupefaction. "Say," he cried, as he tumbled the deck violently down upon the board, "say, what are you gittin' at, hey?"

---

[2] Drunken bravado.

The Swede sprang up with the celerity of a man escaping from a snake on the floor. "I don't want to fight!" he shouted. "I don't want to fight!"

The cowboy stretched his long legs indolently and deliberately. His hands were in his pockets. He spat into the sawdust-box. "Well, who the hell thought you did?" he inquired.

The Swede backed rapidly toward a corner of the room. His hands were out protectingly in front of his chest, but he was making an obvious struggle to control his fright. "Gentlemen," he quavered, "I suppose I am going to be killed before I can leave this house! I suppose I am going to be killed before I can leave this house!" In his eyes was the dying-swan look. Through the windows could be seen the snow turning blue in the shadow of dusk. The wind tore at the house, and some loose thing beat regularly against the clapboards like a spirit tapping.

A door opened, and Scully himself entered. He paused in surprise as he noted the tragic attitude of the Swede. Then he said, "What's the matter here?"

The Swede answered him swiftly and eagerly: "These men are going to kill me."

"Kill you!" ejaculated Scully. "Kill you! What are you talkin'?"

The Swede made the gesture of a martyr.

Scully wheeled sternly upon his son. "What is this, Johnnie?"

The lad had grown sullen. "Damned if I know," he answered. "I can't make no sense to it." He began to shuffle the cards, fluttering them together with an angry snap. "He says a good many men have been killed in this room, or something like that. And he says he's goin' to be killed here too. I don't know what ails him. He's crazy, I shouldn't wonder."

Scully then looked for explanation to the cowboy, but the cowboy simply shrugged his shoulders.

"Kill you?" said Scully again to the Swede. "Kill you? Man, you're off your nut."

"Oh, I know," burst out the Swede. "I know what will happen. Yes, I'm crazy—yes. Yes, of course, I'm crazy—yes. But I know one thing—" There was a sort of sweat of misery and terror upon his face. "I know I won't get out of here alive."

The cowboy drew a deep breath, as if his mind was passing into the last stages of dissolution. "Well, I'm doggoned," he whispered to himself.

Scully wheeled suddenly and faced his son. "You've been troublin' this man!"

Johnnie's voice was loud with its burden of grievance. "Why, good Gawd, I ain't done nothin' to 'im."

The Swede broke in. "Gentlemen, do not disturb yourselves. I will leave this house. I will go away, because"—he accused them dramatically with his glance—"because I do not want to be killed."

Scully was furious with his son. "Will you tell me what is the matter, you young divil? What's the matter, anyhow? Speak out!"

"Blame it!" cried Johnnie in despair, "don't I tell you I don't know? He—he says we want to kill him, and that's all I know. I can't tell what ails him."

The Swede continued to repeat: "Never mind, Mr. Scully; never mind. I will leave this house. I will go away, because I do not wish to be killed. Yes, of course, I am crazy—yes. But I know one thing! I will go away. I will leave this house. Never mind, Mr. Scully; never mind. I will go away."

"You will not go 'way," said Scully. "You will not go 'way until I hear the reason of this business. If anybody has troubled you I will take care of him. This is my house. You are under my roof, and I will not allow any peaceable man to be troubled here." He cast a terrible eye upon Johnnie, the cowboy, and the Easterner.

"Never mind, Mr. Scully; never mind. I will go away. I do not wish to be killed."
The Swede moved toward the door which opened upon the stairs. It was evidently
his intention to go at once for his baggage.

"No, no," shouted Scully peremptorily; but the white-faced man slid by him
and disappeared. "Now," said Scully severely, "what does this mane?"

Johnnie and the cowboy cried together: "Why, we didn't do nothin' to 'im!"

Scully's eyes were cold. "No," he said, "you didn't?"

Johnnie swore a deep oath. "Why, this is the wildest loon I ever see. We didn't
do nothin' at all. We were just sittin' here playin' cards, and he——"

The father suddenly spoke to the Easterner. "Mr. Blanc," he asked, "what has
these boys been doin'?"

The Easterner reflected again. "I didn't see anything wrong at all," he said at
last, slowly.

Scully began to howl. "But what does it mane?" He stared ferociously at his son.
"I have a mind to lather you for this, me boy."

Johnnie was frantic. "Well, what have I done?" he bawled at his father.

III

"I think you are tongue-tied," said Scully finally to his son, the cowboy, and the
Easterner; and at the end of this scornful sentence he left the room.

Upstairs the Swede was swifly fastening the straps of his great valise. Once his
back happened to be half turned toward the door, and, hearing a noise there, he
wheeled and sprang up, uttering a loud cry. Scully's wrinkled visage showed grimly
in the light of the small lamp he carried. This yellow effulgence, streaming upward, coloured only his prominent features, and left his eyes, for instance, in
mysterious shadow. He resembled a murderer.

"Man! man!" he exclaimed, "have you gone daffy?"

"Oh, no! Oh, no!" rejoined the other. "There are people in this world who
know pretty nearly as much as you do—understand?"

For a moment they stood gazing at each other. Upon the Swede's deathly pale
cheeks were two spots brightly crimson and sharply edged, as if they had been
carefully painted. Scully placed the light on the table and sat himself on the edge
of the bed. He spoke ruminatively. "By cracky, I never heard of such a thing in my
life. It's a complete muddle. I can't, for the soul of me, think how you ever got this
idea into your head." Presently he lifted his eyes and asked: "And did you sure
think they were going to kill you?"

The Swede scanned the old man as if he wished to see into his mind. "I did,"
he said at last. He obviously suspected that this answer might precipitate an
outbreak. As he pulled on a strap his whole arm shook, the elbow wavering like a
bit of paper.

Scully banged his hand impressively on the footboard of the bed. "Why, man,
we're goin' to have a line of ilictric street-cars in this town next spring."

" 'A line of electric street-cars,' " repeated the Swede, stupidly.

"And," said Scully, "there's a new railroad goin' to be built down from Broken
Arm to here. Not to mintion the four churches and the smashin' big brick school-
house. Then there's the big factory, too. Why, in two years Romper'll be a met-
tro-*pol*-is."

Having finished the preparation of his baggage, the Swede straightened himself. "Mr. Scully," he said, with sudden hardihood, "how much do I owe you?"

"You don't owe me anythin'," said the old man, angrily.

"Yes, I do," retorted the Swede. He took seventy-five cents from his pocket and tendered it to Scully; but the latter snapped his fingers in disdainful refusal. However, it happened that they both stood gazing in a strange fashion at three silver pieces on the Swede's open palm.

"I'll not take your money," said Scully at last. "Not after what's been goin' on here." Then a plan seemed to strike him. "Here," he cried, picking up his lamp and moving toward the door. "Here! Come with me a minute."

"No," said the Swede, in overwhelming alarm.

"Yes," urged the old man. "Come on! I want you to come and see a picter—just across the hall—in my room."

The Swede must have concluded that his hour was come. His jaw dropped and his teeth showed like a dead man's. He ultimately followed Scully across the corridor, but he had the step of one hung in chains.

Scully flashed the light high on the wall of his own chamber. There was revealed a ridiculous photograph of a little girl. She was leaning against a balustrade of gorgeous decoration, and the formidable bang to her hair was prominent. The figure was as graceful as an upright sled-stake, and, withal, it was of the hue of lead. "There," said Scully, tenderly, "that's the picter of my little girl that died. Her name was Carrie. She had the purtiest hair you ever saw! I was that fond of her, she——"

Turning then, he saw that the Swede was not contemplating the picture at all, but, instead, was keeping keen watch on the gloom in the rear.

"Look, man!" cried Scully, heartily. "That's the picter of my little gal that died. Her name was Carrie. And then here's the picter of my oldest boy, Michael. He's a lawyer in Lincoln, an' doin' well. I gave that boy a grand eddication, and I'm glad for it now. He's a fine boy. Look at 'im now. Ain't he bold as blazes, him there in Lincoln, an honoured an' respicted gintleman! An honoured and respicted gintleman," concluded Scully with a flourish. And, so saying, he smote the Swede jovially on the back.

The Swede faintly smiled.

"Now," said the old man, "there's only one more thing." He dropped suddenly to the floor and thrust his head beneath the bed. The Swede could hear his muffled voice. "I'd keep it under me piller if it wasn't for that boy Johnnie. Then there's the old woman——Where is it now? I never put it twice in the same place. Ah, now come out with you!"

Presently he backed clumsily from under the bed, dragging with him an old coat rolled into a bundle. "I've fetched him," he muttered. Kneeling on the floor, he unrolled the coat and extracted from its heart a large yellow-brown whisky-bottle.

His first maneuver was to hold the bottle up to the light. Reassured, apparently, that nobody had been tampering with it, he thrust it with a generous movement toward the Swede.

The weak-kneed Swede was about to eagerly clutch this element of strength, but he suddenly jerked his hand away and cast a look of horror upon Scully.

"Drink," said the old man affectionately. He had risen to his feet, and now stood facing the Swede.

There was a silence. Then again Scully said: "Drink!"

The Swede laughed wildly. He grabbed the bottle, put it to his mouth; and as his lips curled absurdly around the opening and his throat worked, he kept his glance, burning with hatred, upon the old man's face.

IV

After the departure of Scully the three men, with the card-board still upon their knees, preserved for a long time an astounded silence. Then Johnnie said: "That's the dod-dangedest Swede I ever see."

"He ain't no Swede," said the cowboy, scornfully.

"Well, what is he then?" cried Johnnie. "What is he then?"

"It's my opinion," replied the cowboy deliberately, "he's some kind of a Dutchman." It was a venerable custom of the country to entitle as Swedes all light-haired men who spoke with a heavy tongue. In consequence the idea of the cowboy was not without its daring. "Yes, sir," he repeated. "It's my opinion this feller is some kind of a Dutchman."

"Well, he says he's a Swede, anyhow," muttered Johnnie, sulkily. He turned to the Easterner: "What do you think, Mr. Blanc?"

"Oh, I don't know," replied the Easterner.

"Well, what do you think makes him act that way?" asked the cowboy.

"Why, he's frightened." The Easterner knocked his pipe against a rim of the stove. "He's clear frightened out of his boots."

"What at?" cried Johnnie and the cowboy together.

The Easterner reflected over his answer.

"What at?" cried the others again.

"Oh, I don't know, but it seems to me this man has been reading dime novels, and he thinks he's right out in the middle of it—the shootin' and stabbin' and all."

"But," said the cowboy, deeply scandalized, "this ain't Wyoming, ner none of them places. This is Nebrasker."

"Yes," added Johnnie, "an' why don't he wait till he gits *out West?*"

The travelled Easterner laughed. "It isn't different there even—not in these days. But he thinks he's right in the middle of hell."

Johnnie and the cowboy mused long.

"It's awful funny," remarked Johnnie at last.

"Yes," said the cowboy. "This is a queer game. I hope we don't git snowed in, because then we'd have to stand this here man bein' around with us all the time. That wouldn't be no good."

"I wish pop would throw him out," said Johnnie.

Presently they heard a loud stamping on the stairs, accompanied by ringing jokes in the voice of old Scully, and laughter, evidently from the Swede. The men around the stove stared vacantly at each other. "Gosh!" said the cowboy. The door flew open, and old Scully, flushed and anecdotal, came into the room. He was jabbering at the Swede, who followed him, laughing bravely. It was the entry of two roisterers from a banquet hall.

"Come now," said Scully sharply to the three seated men, "move up and give us a chance at the stove." The cowboy and the Easterner obediently sidled their chairs to make room for the new-comers. Johnnie, however, simply arranged himself in a more indolent attitude, and then remained motionless.

"Come! Git over, there," said Scully.

"Plenty of room on the other side of the stove," said Johnnie.

"Do you think we want to sit in the draught?" roared the father.

But the Swede here interposed with a grandeur of confidence. "No, no. Let the boy sit where he likes," he cried in a bullying voice to the father.

"All right! All right!" said Scully, deferentially. The cowboy and the Easterner exchanged glances of wonder.

The five chairs were formed in a crescent about one side of the stove. The Swede began to talk; he talked arrogantly, profanely, angrily. Johnnie, the cowboy, and the Easterner maintained a morose silence, while old Scully appeared to be receptive and eager, breaking in constantly with sympathetic ejaculations.

Finally the Swede announced that he was thirsty. He moved in his chair, and said that he would go for a drink of water.

"I'll git it for you," cried Scully at once.

"No," said the Swede, contemptuously. "I'll get it for myself." He arose and stalked with the air of an owner off into the executive parts of the hotel.

As soon as the Swede was out of hearing Scully sprang to his feet and whispered intensely to the others: "Upstairs he thought I was tryin' to poison 'im."

"Say," said Johnnie, "this makes me sick. Why don't you throw 'im out in the snow?"

"Why, he's all right now," declared Scully. "It was only that he was from the East, and he thought this was a tough place. That's all. He's all right now."

The cowboy looked with admiration upon the Easterner. "You were straight," he said. "You were on to that there Dutchman."

"Well," said Johnnie to his father, "he may be all right now, but I don't see it. Other time he was scared, but now he's too fresh."

Scully's speech was always a combination of Irish brogue and idiom, Western twang and idiom, and scraps of curiously formal diction taken from the story-books and newspapers. He now hurled a strange mass of language at the head of his son. "What do I keep? What do I keep? What do I keep?" he demanded, in a voice of thunder. He slapped his knee impressively, to indicate that he himself was going to make reply, and that all should heed. "I keep a hotel," he shouted. "A hotel, do you mind? A guest under my roof has sacred privileges. He is to be intimidated by none. Not one word shall he hear that would prijudice him in favour of goin' away. I'll not have it. There's no place in this here town where they can say they iver took in a guest of mine because he was afraid to stay here." He wheeled suddenly upon the cowboy and the Easterner. "Am I right?"

"Yes, Mr. Scully," said the cowboy, "I think you're right."

"Yes, Mr. Scully," said the Easterner, "I think you're right."

V

At six-o'clock supper, the Swede fizzed like a fire-wheel. He sometimes seemed on the point of bursting into riotous song, and in all his madness he was encouraged by old Scully. The Easterner was encased in reserve; the cowboy sat in wide-mouthed amazement, forgetting to eat, while Johnnie wrathily demolished great plates of food. The daughters of the house, when they were obliged to replenish the biscuits, approached as warily as Indians, and, having succeeded in their purpose, fled with ill-concealed trepidation. The Swede domineered the whole feast, and he gave it the appearance of a cruel bacchanal. He seemed to have grown suddenly taller; he gazed, brutally disdainful, into every face. His voice rang through the room. Once when he jabbed out harpoon-fashion with his fork to pinion a biscuit, the weapon nearly impaled the hand of the Easterner, which had been stretched quietly out for the same biscuit.

After supper, as the men filed toward the other room, the Swede smote Scully ruthlessly on the shoulder. "Well, old boy, that was a good, square meal." Johnnie looked hopefully at his father; he knew that shoulder was tender from an old fall; and, indeed, it appeared for a moment as if Scully was going to flame out over the matter, but in the end he smiled a sickly smile and remained silent. The others understood from his manner that he was admitting his responsibility for the Swede's new view-point.

Johnnie, however, addressed his parent in an aside. "Why don't you license somebody to kick you downstairs?" Scully scowled darkly by way of reply.

When they were gathered about the stove, the Swede insisted on another game of High-Five. Scully gently deprecated the plan at first, but the Swede turned a wolfish glare upon him. The old man subsided, and the Swede canvassed the others. In his tone there was always a great threat. The cowboy and the Easterner both remarked indifferently that they would play. Scully said that he would presently have to go to meet the 6.58 train, and so the Swede turned menacingly upon Johnnie. For a moment their glances crossed like blades, and then Johnnie smiled and said, "Yes, I'll play."

They formed a square, with the little board on their knees. The Easterner and the Swede were again partners. As the play went on, it was noticeable that the cowboy was not board-whacking as usual. Meanwhile, Scully, near the lamp, had put on his spectacles and, with an appearance curiously like an old priest, was reading a newspaper. In time he went out to meet the 6.58 train, and, despite his precautions, a gust of polar wind whirled into the room as he opened the door. Besides scattering the cards, it chilled the players to the marrow. The Swede cursed frightfully. When Scully returned, his entrance disturbed a cosy and friendly scene. The Swede again cursed. But presently they were once more intent, their heads bent forward and their hands moving swiftly. The Swede had adopted the fashion of board-whacking.

Scully took up his paper and for a long time remained immersed in matters which were extraordinarily remote from him. The lamp burned badly, and once he stopped to adjust the wick. The newspaper, as he turned from page to page, rustled with a slow and comfortable sound. Then suddenly he heard three terrible words: "You are cheatin'!"

Such scenes often prove that there can be little of dramatic import in environment. Any room can present a tragic front; any room can be comic. This little den was now hideous as a torture-chamber. The new faces of the men themselves had changed it upon the instant. The Swede held a huge fist in front of Johnnie's face, while the latter looked steadily over it into the blazing orbs of his accuser. The Easterner had grown pallid; the cowboy's jaw had dropped in that expression of bovine amazement which was one of his important mannerisms. After the three words, the first sound in the room was made by Scully's paper as it floated forgotten to his feet. His spectacles had also fallen from his nose, but by a clutch he had saved them in air. His hand, grasping the spectacles, now remained poised awkwardly and near his shoulder. He stared at the card-players.

Probably the silence was while a second elapsed. Then, if the floor had been suddenly twitched out from under the men they could not have moved quicker. The five had projected themselves headlong toward a common point. It happened that Johnnie, in rising to hurl himself upon the Swede, had stumbled slightly because of his curiously instinctive care for the cards and the board. The loss of the moment allowed time for the arrival of Scully, and also allowed the cowboy time to give the Swede a great push which sent him staggering back. The men found tongue together, and hoarse shouts of rage, appeal, or fear burst from every throat. The cowboy pushed and jostled feverishly at the Swede, and the Easterner and Scully clung wildly to Johnnie; but through the smoky air, above the swaying bodies of the peace-compellers, the eyes of the two warriors ever sought each other in glances of challenge that were at once hot and steely.

Of course the board had been overturned, and now the whole company of cards was scattered over the floor, where the boots of the men trampled the fat and painted kings and queens as they gazed with their silly eyes at the war that was waging above them.

Scully's voice was dominating the yells. "Stop now! Stop, I say! Stop, now——"

Johnnie, as he struggled to burst through the rank formed by Scully and the Easterner, was crying, "Well, he says I cheated! He says I cheated! I won't allow no man to say I cheated! If he says I cheated, he's a —— ——!"

The cowboy was telling the Swede, "Quit, now! Quit, d'ye hear——"

The screams of the Swede never ceased: "He did cheat! I saw him! I saw him——"

As for the Easterner, he was importuning in a voice that was not heeded: "Wait a moment, can't you? Oh, wait a moment. What's the good of a fight over a game of cards? Wait a moment——"

In this tumult no complete sentences were clear. "Cheat"—"Quit"—"He says"—these fragments pierced the uproar and rang out sharply. It was remarkable that, whereas Scully undoubtedly made the most noise, he was the least heard of any of the riotous band.

Then suddenly there was a great cessation. It was as if each man had paused for breath; and although the room was still lighted with the anger of men, it could be seen that there was no danger of immediate conflict, and at once Johnnie, shouldering his way forward, almost succeeded in confronting the Swede. "What did you say I cheated for? What did you say I cheated for? I don't cheat, and I won't let no man say I do!"

The Swede said, "I saw you! I saw you!"

"Well," cried Johnnie, "I'll fight any man what says I cheat!"

"No, you won't," said the cowboy. "Not here."

"Ah, be still, can't you?" said Scully, coming between them.

The quiet was sufficient to allow the Easterner's voice to be heard. He was repeating, "Oh, wait a moment, can't you? What's the good of a fight over a game of cards? Wait a moment!"

Johnnie, his red face appearing above his father's shoulder, hailed the Swede again. "Did you say I cheated?"

The Swede showed his teeth. "Yes."

"Then," said Johnnie, "we must fight."

"Yes, fight," roared the Swede. He was like a demoniac. "Yes, fight! I'll show you what kind of a man I am! I'll show you who you want to fight! Maybe you think I can't fight! Maybe you think I can't! I'll show you, you skin, you card-sharp! Yes, you cheated! You cheated! You cheated!"

"Well, let's go at it, then, mister," said Johnnie, coolly.

The cowboy's brow was beaded with sweat from his efforts in intercepting all sorts of raids. He turned in despair to Scully. "What are you goin' to do now?"

A change had come over the Celtic visage of the old man. He now seemed all eagerness; his eyes glowed.

"We'll let them fight," he answered, stalwartly. "I can't put up with it any longer. I've stood this damned Swede till I'm sick. We'll let them fight."

VI

The men prepared to go out of doors. The Easterner was so nervous that he had great difficulty in getting his arms into the sleeves of his new leather coat. As the cowboy drew his fur cap down over his ears his hands trembled. In fact, Johnnie and old Scully were the only ones who displayed no agitation. These preliminaries were conducted without words.

Scully threw open the door. "Well, come on," he said. Instantly a terrific wind caused the flame of the lamp to struggle at its wick, while a puff of black smoke sprang from the chimney-top. The stove was in mid-current of the blast, and its voice swelled to equal the roar of the storm. Some of the scarred and bedabbled cards were caught up from the floor and dashed helplessly against the farther wall. The men lowered their heads and plunged into the tempest as into a sea.

No snow was falling, but great whirls and clouds of flakes, swept up from the ground by the frantic winds, were streaming southward with the speed of bullets. The covered land was blue with the sheen of an unearthly satin, and there was no other hue save where, at the low, black railway station—which seemed incredibly distant—one light gleamed like a tiny jewel. As the men floundered into a thigh-deep drift, it was known that the Swede was bawling out something. Scully went to him, put a hand on his shoulder, and projected an ear. "What's that you say?" he shouted.

"I say," bawled the Swede again, "I won't stand much show against this gang. I know you'll all pitch on me."

Scully smote him reproachfully on the arm. "Tut, man!" he yelled. The wind tore the words from Scully's lips and scattered them far alee.

"You are all a gang of——" boomed the Swede, but the storm also seized the remainder of this sentence.

Immediately turning their backs upon the wind, the men had swung around a corner to the sheltered side of the hotel. It was the function of the little house to preserve here, amid this great devastation of snow, an irregular V-shape of heavily encrusted grass, which crackled beneath the feet. One could imagine the great drifts piled against the windward side. When the party reached the comparative peace of this spot it was found that the Swede was still bellowing.

"Oh, I know what kind of a thing this is! I know you'll all pitch on me. I can't lick you all!"

Scully turned upon him panther-fashion. "You'll not have to whip all of us. You'll have to whip my son Johnnie. An' the man what troubles you durin' that time will have me to dale with."

The arrangements were swiftly made. The two men faced each other, obedient to the harsh commands of Scully, whose face, in the subtly luminous gloom, could be seen set in the austere impersonal lines that are pictured on the countenances of the Roman veterans. The Easterner's teeth were chattering, and he was hopping up and down like a mechanical toy. The cowboy stood rock-like.

The contestants had not stripped off any clothing. Each was in his ordinary attire. Their fists were up, and they eyed each other in a calm that had the elements of leonine cruelty in it.

During this pause, the Easterner's mind, like a film, took lasting impressions of three men—the iron-nerved master of the ceremony; the Swede, pale, motionless, terrible; and Johnnie, serene yet ferocious, brutish yet heroic. The entire prelude had in it a tragedy greater than the tragedy of action, and this aspect was accentuated by the long, mellow cry of the blizzard, as it sped the tumbling and wailing flakes into the black abyss of the south.

"Now!" said Scully.

The two combatants leaped forward and crashed together like bullocks. There was heard the cushioned sound of blows, and of a curse squeezing out from between the tight teeth of one.

As for the spectators, the Easterner's pent-up breath exploded from him with a pop of relief, absolute relief from the tension of the preliminaries. The cowboy bounded into the air with a yowl. Scully was immovable as from supreme amazement and fear at the fury of the fight which he himself had permitted and arranged.

For a time the encounter in the darkness was such a perplexity of flying arms that it presented no more detail than would a swiftly revolving wheel. Occasionally a face, as if illumined by a flash of light, would shine out, ghastly and marked with pink spots. A moment later, the men might have been known as shadows, if it were not for the involuntary utterance of oaths that came from them in whispers.

Suddenly a holocaust of warlike desire caught the cowboy, and he bolted forward with the speed of a broncho. "Go it, Johnnie! go it! Kill him! Kill him!"

Scully confronted him. "Kape back," he said; and by his glance the cowboy could tell that this man was Johnnie's father.

To the Easterner there was a monotony of unchangeable fighting that was an abomination. This confused mingling was eternal to his sense, which was concentrated in a longing for the end, the priceless end. Once the fighters lurched near him, and as he scrambled hastily backward he heard them breathe like men on the rack.

"Kill him, Johnnie! Kill him! Kill him! Kill him!" The cowboy's face was contorted like one of those agony masks in museums.

"Keep still," said Scully, icily.

Then there was a sudden loud grunt, incomplete, cut short, and Johnnie's body swung away from Swede and fell with sickening heaviness to the grass. The cowboy was barely in time to prevent the mad Swede from flinging himself upon his prone adversary. "No, you don't," said the cowboy, interposing an arm. "Wait a second."

Scully was at his son's side. "Johnnie! Johnnie, me boy!" His voice had a quality of melancholy tenderness. "Johnnie! Can you go on with it?" He looked anxiously down into the bloody, pulpy face of his son.

There was a moment of silence, and then Johnnie answered in his ordinary voice, "Yes, I—it—yes."

Assisted by his father he struggled to his feet. "Wait a bit now till you git your wind," said the old man.

A few paces away the cowboy was lecturing the Swede. "No, you don't! Wait a second!"

The Easterner was plucking at Scully's sleeve. "Oh, this is enough," he pleaded. "This is enough! Let it go as it stands. This is enough!"

"Bill," said Scully, "git out of the road." The cowboy stepped aside. "Now." The combatants were actuated by a new caution as they advanced toward collision. They glared at each other, and then the Swede aimed a lightning blow that carried with it his entire weight. Johnnie was evidently half stupid from weakness, but he miraculously dodged, and his fist sent the over-balanced Swede sprawling.

The cowboy, Scully, and the Easterner burst into a cheer that was like a chorus of triumphant soldiery, but before its conclusion the Swede had scuffed agilely to his feet and come in berserk abandon at his foe. There was another perplexity of flying arms, and Johnnie's body again swung away and fell, even as a bundle might fall from a roof. The Swede instantly staggered to a little wind-waved tree and leaned upon it, breathing like an engine, while his savage and flamelit eyes roamed from face to face as the men bent over Johnnie. There was a splendour of isolation in his situation at this time which the East-erner felt once when, lifting his eyes from the man on the ground, he beheld that mysterious and lonely figure, waiting.

"Are you any good yet, Johnnie?" asked Scully in a broken voice.

The son gasped and opened his eyes languidly. After a moment he answered, "No—I ain't—any good—any—more." Then, from shame and bodily ill, he began to weep, the tears furrowing down through the blood-stains on his face. "He was too—too—too heavy for me."

Scully straightened and addressed the waiting figure.

"Stranger," he said, evenly, "it's all up with our side." Then his voice changed into that vibrant huskiness which is commonly the tone of the most simple and deadly announcements. "Johnnie is whipped."

Without replying, the victor moved off on the route to the front door of the hotel.

The cowboy was formulating new and unspellable blasphemies. The Easterner was startled to find that they were out in a wind that seemed to come direct from the shadowed arctic floes. He heard again the wail of the snow as it was flung to its grave in the south. He knew now that all this time the cold had been sinking into him deeper and deeper, and he wondered that he had not perished. He felt indifferent to the condition of the vanquished man.

"Johnnie, can you walk?" asked Scully.

"Did I hurt—hurt him any?" asked the son.

"Can you walk, boy? Can you walk?"

Johnnie's voice was suddenly strong. There was a robust impatience in it. "I asked you whether I hurt him any!"

"Yes, yes, Johnnie," answered the cowboy, consolingly; "he's hurt a good deal."

They raised him from the ground, and as soon as he was on his feet he went tottering off, rebuffing all attempts at assistance. When the party rounded the corner they were fairly blinded by the pelting of the snow. It burned their faces like fire. The cowboy carried Johnnie through the drift to the door. As they entered, some cards again rose from the floor and beat against the wall.

The Easterner rushed to the stove. He was so profoundly chilled that he almost dared to embrace the glowing iron. The Swede was not in the room. Johnnie sank into a chair and, folding his arms on his knees, buried his face in them. Scully, warming one foot and then the other at a rim of the stove, muttered to himself with Celtic mournfulness. The cowboy had removed his fur cap, and with a dazed and rueful air he was running one hand through his tousled locks. From overhead they could hear the creaking of boards, as the Swede tramped here and there in his room.

The sad quiet was broken by the sudden flinging open of a door that led toward the kitchen. It was instantly followed by an inrush of women. They precipitated themselves upon Johnnie amid a chorus of lamentation. Before they carried their prey off to the kitchen, there to be bathed and harangued with that mixture of sympathy and abuse which is a feat of their sex, the mother straightened herself and fixed old Scully with an eye of stern reproach, "Shame be upon you, Patrick Scully!" she cried. "Your own son, too. Shame be upon you!"

"There, now! Be quiet, now!" said the old man, weakly.

"Shame be upon you, Patrick Scully!" The girls, rallying to this slogan, sniffed disdainfully in the direction of those trembling accomplices, the cowboy and the Easterner. Presently they bore Johnnie away, and left the three men to dismal reflection.

VII

"I'd like to fight this here Dutchman myself," said the cowboy, breaking a long silence.

Scully wagged his head sadly. "No, that wouldn't do. It wouldn't be right. It wouldn't be right."

"Well, why wouldn't it?" argued the cowboy. "I don't see no harm in it."

"No," answered Scully, with mournful heroism. "It wouldn't be right. It was Johnnie's fight, and now we mustn't whip the man just because he whipped Johnnie."

"Yes, that's true enough," said the cowboy; "but—he better not get fresh with me, because I couldn't stand no more of it."

"You'll not say a word to him," commanded Scully, and even then they heard the tread of the Swede on the stairs. His entrance was made theatric. He swept the door back with a bang and swaggered to the middle of the room. No one looked at him. "Well," he cried, insolently, at Scully, "I s'pose you'll tell me now how much I owe you?"

The old man remained stolid. "You don't owe me nothin'."

"Huh!" said the Swede, "huh! Don't owe 'im nothin'."

The cowboy addressed the Swede. "Stranger, I don't see how you come to be so gay around here."

Old Scully was instantly alert. "Stop!" he shouted, holding his hand forth, fingers upward. "Bill, you shut up!"

The cowboy spat carelessly into the sawdust-box. "I didn't say a word, did I?" he asked.

"Mr. Scully," called the Swede, "how much do I owe you?" It was seen that he was attired for departure, and that he had his valise in his hand.

"You don't owe me nothin'," repeated Scully in the same imperturbable way.

"Huh!" said the Swede. "I guess you're right. I guess if it was any way at all, you'd owe me somethin'. That's what I guess." He turned to the cowboy. "'Kill him! Kill him! Kill him!'" he mimicked, and then guffawed victoriously. "'Kill him!'" He was convulsed with ironical humour.

But he might have been jeering the dead. The three men were immovable and silent, staring with glassy eyes at the stove.

The Swede opened the door and passed into the storm, giving one derisive glance backward at the still group.

As soon as the door was closed, Scully and the cowboy leaped to their feet and began to curse. They trampled to and fro, waving their arms and smashing into the air with their fists. "Oh, but that was a hard minute!" wailed Scully. "That was a hard minute! Him there leerin' and scoffin'! One bang at his nose was worth forty dollars to me that minute! How did you stand it, Bill?"

"How did I stand it?" cried the cowboy in a quivering voice. "How did I stand it? Oh!"

The old man burst into sudden brogue. "I'd loike to take that Swade," he wailed, "and hould 'im down on a shtone flure and bate 'im to a jelly wid a shtick!"

The cowboy groaned in sympathy. "I'd like to git him by the neck and ha-ammer him"—he brought his hand down on a chair with a noise like a pistol-shot—"hammer that there Dutchman until he couldn't tell himself from a dead coyote!"

"I'd bate 'im until he——"

"I'd show *him* some things——"

And then together they raised a yearning, fanatic cry "Oh-o-oh! if we only could——"

"Yes!"

"Yes!"

"And then I'd——"

"O-o-oh!"

VIII

The Swede, tightly gripping his valise, tacked across the face of the storm as if he carried sails. He was following a line of little naked, gasping trees which, he knew, must mark the way of the road. His face, fresh from the pounding of Johnnie's fists, felt more pleasure than pain in the wind and the driving snow. A number of square shapes loomed upon him finally, and he knew them as the houses of the main body of the town. He found a street and made travel along it, leaning heavily upon the wind whenever, at a corner, a terrific blast caught him.

He might have been in a deserted village. We picture the world as thick with conquering and elate humanity, but here, with the bugles of the tempest pealing, it was hard to imagine a peopled earth. One viewed the existence of man then as a marvel, and conceded a glamour of wonder to these lice which were caused to cling to a whirling, fire-smitten, ice-locked, disease-stricken, space-lost bulb. The conceit of man was explained by this storm to be the very engine of life. One was a coxcomb not to die in it. However, the Swede found a saloon.

In front of it an indomitable red light was burning, and the snowflakes were made blood-colour as they flew through the circumscribed territory of the lamp's shining. The Swede pushed open the door of the saloon and entered. A sanded expanse was before him, and at the end of it four men sat about a table drinking. Down one side of the room extended a radiant bar, and its guardian was leaning upon his elbows listening to the talk of the men at the table. The Swede dropped his valise upon the floor and, smiling fraternally upon the barkeeper, said, "Gimme some whisky, will you?" The man placed a bottle, a whisky-glass, and a glass of ice-thick water upon the bar. The Swede poured himself an abnormal portion of whisky and drank it in three gulps. "Pretty bad night," remarked the bartender, indifferently. He was making the pretension of blindness which is usually a distinction of his class; but it could have been seen that he was furtively studying the half-erased blood-stains on the face of the Swede. "Bad night," he said again.

"Oh, it's good enough for me," replied the Swede, hardily, as he poured himself some more whisky. The barkeeper took his coin and manoeuvred it through its reception by the highly nickelled cash-machine. A bell rang; a card labelled "20 cts." had appeared.

"No," continued the Swede, "this isn't too bad weather. It's good enough for me."

"So?" murmured the barkeeper, languidly.

The copious drams made the Swede's eyes swim, and he breathed a trifle heavier. "Yes, I like this weather. I like it. It suits me." It was apparently his design to impart a deep significance to these words.

"So?" murmured the bartender again. He turned to gaze dreamily at the scroll-like birds and bird-like scrolls which had been drawn with soap upon the mirrors in back of the bar.

"Well, I guess I'll take another drink," said the Swede, presently. "Have something?"

"No, thanks; I'm not drinkin'," answered the bartender. Afterward he asked, "How did you hurt your face?"

The Swede immediately began to boast loudly. "Why, in a fight. I thumped the soul out of a man down here at Scully's hotel."

The interest of the four men at the table was at last aroused.

"Who was it?" said one.

"Johnnie Scully," blustered the Swede. "Son of the man what runs it. He will be pretty near dead for some weeks, I can tell you. I made a nice thing of him, I did. He couldn't get up. They carried him in the house. Have a drink?"

Instantly the men in some subtle way encased themselves in reserve. "No, thanks," said one. The group was of curious formation. Two were prominent local business men; one was the district attorney; and one was a professional gambler of the kind known as "square." But a scrutiny of the group would not have enabled an observer to pick the gambler from the men of more reputable pursuits. He was, in fact, a man so delicate in manner, when among people of fair class, and so judicious in his choice of victims, that in the strictly masculine part of the town's life he had come to be explicitly trusted and admired. People called him a thoroughbred. The fear and contempt with which his craft was regarded were undoubtedly the reason why his quiet dignity shone conspicuous above the quiet dignity of men who might be merely hatters, billiard-markers, or grocery clerks. Beyond an occasional unwary traveller who came by rail, this gambler was supposed to prey solely upon reckless and senile farmers, who, when flush with good crops, drove into town in all the pride and confidence of an absolutely invulnerable stupidity. Hearing at times in circuitous fashion of the despoilment of such a farmer, the important men of Romper invariably laughed in contempt of the victim, and if they thought of the wolf at all, it was with a kind of pride at the knowledge that he would never dare think of attacking their wisdom and courage. Besides, it was popular that this gambler had a real wife and two real children in a neat cottage in a suburb, where he led an exemplary home life; and when any one even suggested a discrepancy in his character, the crowd immediately vociferated descriptions of this virtuous family circle. Then men who led exemplary home lives, and men who did not lead exemplary home lives, all subsided in a bunch, remarking that there was nothing more to be said.

However, when a restriction was placed upon him—as, for instance, when a strong clique of members of the new Pollywog Club refused to permit him, even as a spectator, to appear in the rooms of the organization—the candour and gentleness with which he accepted the judgment disarmed many of his foes and made his friends more desperately partisan. He invariably distinguished between himself and a respectable Romper man so quickly and frankly that his manner actually appeared to be a continual broadcast compliment.

And one must not forget to declare the fundamental fact of his entire position in Romper. It is irrefutable that in all affairs outside his business, in all matters that occur eternally and commonly between man and man, this thieving card-player was so generous, so just, so moral, that, in a contest, he could have put to flight the consciences of nine tenths of the citizens of Romper.

And so it happened that he was seated in this saloon with the two prominent local merchants and the district attorney.

The Swede continued to drink raw whisky, meanwhile babbling at the barkeeper and trying to induce him to indulge in potations. "Come on. Have a drink. Come on. What—no? Well, have a little one, then. By gawd, I've whipped a man to-night, and I want to celebrate. I whipped him good, too. Gentlemen," the Swede cried to the men at the table, "have a drink?"

"Ssh!" said the barkeeper.

The group at the table, although furtively attentive, had been pretending to be deep in talk, but now a man lifted his eyes toward the Swede and said, shortly, "Thanks. We don't want any more."

At this reply the Swede ruffled out his chest like a rooster. "Well," he exploded, "it seems I can't get anybody to drink with me in this town. Seems so, don't it? Well!"

"Ssh!" said the barkeeper.

"Say," snarled the Swede, "don't you try to shut me up. I won't have it. I'm a gentleman, and I want people to drink with me. And I want 'em to drink with me now. *Now*—do you understand?" He rapped the bar with his knuckles.

Years of experience had calloused the bartender. He merely grew sulky. "I hear you," he answered.

"Well," cried the Swede, "listen hard then. See those men over there? Well, they're going to drink with me, and don't you forget it. Now you watch."

"Hi!" yelled the barkeeper, "this won't do!"

"Why won't it?" demanded the Swede. He stalked over to the table, and by chance laid his hand upon the shoulder of the gambler. "How about this?" he asked wrathfully. "I asked you to drink with me."

The gambler simply twisted his head and spoke over his shoulder. "My friend, I don't know you."

"Oh, hell!" answered the Swede, "come and have a drink."

"Now, my boy," advised the gambler, kindly, "take your hand off my shoulder and go 'way and mind your own business." He was a little, slim man, and it seemed strange to hear him use this tone of heroic patronage to the burly Swede. The other men at the table said nothing.

"What! You won't drink with me, you little dude? I'll make you, then! I'll make you!" The Swede had grasped the gambler frenziedly at the throat, and was dragging him from his chair. The other men sprang up. The barkeeper dashed around the corner of his bar. There was a great tumult, and then was seen a long blade in the hand of the gambler. It shot forward, and a human body, this citadel of virtue, wisdom, power, was pierced as easily as if it had been a melon. The Swede fell with a cry of supreme astonishment.

The prominent merchants and the district attorney must have at once tumbled out of the place backward. The bartender found himself hanging limply to the arm of a chair and gazing into the eyes of a murderer.

"Henry," said the latter, as he wiped his knife on one of the towels that hung beneath the bar rail, "you tell 'em where to find me. I'll be home, waiting for 'em.'' Then he vanished. A moment afterward the barkeeper was in the street dinning through the storm for help and, moreover, companionship.

The corpse of the Swede, alone in the saloon, had its eyes fixed upon a dreadful legend that dwelt atop of the cash-machine: "This registers the amount of your purchase.''

IX

Months later, the cowboy was frying pork over the stove of a little ranch near the Dakota line, when there was a quick thud of hoofs outside, and presently the Easterner entered with the letters and the papers.

"Well,'' said the Easterner at once, "the chap that killed the Swede has got three years. Wasn't much, was it?''

"He has? Three years?'' The cowboy poised his pan of pork, while he ruminated upon the news. "Three years. That ain't much.''

"No. It was a light sentence,'' replied the Easterner as he unbuckled his spurs. "Seems there was a good deal of sympathy for him in Romper.''

"If the bartender had been any good,'' observed the cowboy, thoughtfully, "he would have gone in and cracked that there Dutchman on the head with a bottle in the beginnin' of it and stopped all this here murderin'.''

"Yes, a thousand things might have happened,'' said the Easterner, tartly.

The cowboy returned his pan of pork to the fire, but his philosophy continued. "It's funny, ain't it? If he hadn't said Johnnie was cheatin' he'd be alive this minute. He was an awful fool. Game played for fun, too. Not for money. I believe he was crazy.''

"I feel sorry for that gambler,'' said the Easterner.

"Oh, so do I,'' said the cowboy. "He don't deserve none of it for killin' who he did.''

"The Swede might not have been killed if everything had been square.''

"Might not have been killed?'' exclaimed the cowboy. "Everythin' square? Why, when he said that Johnnie was cheatin' and acted like such a jackass? And then in the saloon he fairly walked up to git hurt?'' With these arguments the cowboy browbeat the Easterner and reduced him to rage.

"You're a fool!'' cried the Easterner, viciously. "You're a bigger jackass than the Swede by a million majority. Now let me tell you one thing. Let me tell you something. Listen! Johnnie *was* cheating!''

" 'Johnnie,' '' said the cowboy, blankly. There was a minute of silence, and then he said, robustly, "Why, no. The game was only for fun.''

"Fun or not,'' said the Easterner, "Johnnie was cheating. I saw him. I know it. I saw him. And I refused to stand up and be a man. I let the Swede fight it out alone. And you—you were simply puffing around the place wanting to fight. And then old Scully himself! We are all in it! This poor gambler isn't even a noun. He is kind of an adverb. Every sin is the result of a collaboration. We, five of us, have collaborated in the murder of this Swede. Usually there are from a dozen to forty women really involved in every murder, but in this case it seems to be only five men—you, I, Johnnie, old Scully; and that fool of an unfortunate gambler came merely as a culmination, the apex of a human movement, and gets all the punishment.''

The cowboy, injured and rebellious, cried out blindly into this fog of mysterious theory: "Well, I didn't do anythin', did I?''

[1898]

Anton Chekhov   *1860–1904*

THE DARLING*

Olenka, the daughter of the retired collegiate assessor, Plemyanniakov, was sitting in her back porch, lost in thought. It was hot, the flies were persistent and teasing, and it was pleasant to reflect that it would soon be evening. Dark rain-clouds were gathering from the east, and bringing from time to time a breath of moisture in the air.

Kukin, who was the manager of an open-air theatre called the Tivoli, and who lived in the lodge, was standing in the middle of the garden looking at the sky.

"Again!" he observed despairingly. "It's going to rain again! Rain every day, as though to spite me. I might as well hang myself! It's ruin! Fearful losses every day."

He flung up his hands, and went on, addressing Olenka:

"There! that's the life we lead, Olga Semyonovna. It's enough to make one cry. One works and does one's utmost; one wears oneself out, getting no sleep at night, and racks one's brain what to do for the best. And then what happens? To begin with, one's public is ignorant, boorish. I give them the very best operetta, a dainty masque, first rate music-hall artists. But do you suppose that's what they want! They don't understand anything of that sort. They want a clown; what they ask for is vulgarity. And then look at the weather! Almost every evening it rains. It started on the tenth of May, and it's kept it up all May and June. It's simply awful! The public doesn't come, but I've to pay the rent just the same, and pay the artists."

The next evening the clouds would gather again, and Kukin would say with an hysterical laugh:

"Well, rain away, then! Flood the garden, drown me! Damn my luck in this world and the next! Let the artists have me up! Send me to prison!—to Siberia!—the scaffold! Ha, ha, ha!"

And next day the same thing.

Olenka listened to Kukin with silent gravity, and sometimes tears came into her eyes. In the end his misfortunes touched her; she grew to love him. He was a small thin man, with a yellow face, and curls combed forward on his forehead. He spoke in a thin tenor; as he talked his mouth worked on one side, and there was always an expression of despair on his face; yet he aroused a deep and genuine affection in her. She was always fond of some one, and could not exist without loving. In earlier days she had loved her papa, who now sat in a dark-ened room, breathing with difficulty; she had loved her aunt who used to come every other year from Bryansk;[1] and before that, when she was at school, she had loved her French master. She was a gentle, soft-hearted, compassionate girl, with mild, tender eyes and very good health. At the sight of her full rosy cheeks, her soft white neck with a little dark mole on it, and the kind, naive smile, which came into her face when she listened to anything pleasant, men thought, "Yes, not half bad," and smiled too, while lady visitors could not refrain from seizing her hand in the middle of a conversation, exclaiming in a gush of de-light, "You darling!"

The house in which she had lived from her birth upwards, and which was left

---

* *Translated by Constance Garnett.*
[1] A city southwest of Moscow.

her in her father's will, was at the extreme end of the town, not far from the Tivoli. In the evenings and at night she could hear the band playing, and the crackling and banging of fireworks, and it seemed to her that it was Kukin struggling with his destiny, storming the entrenchments of his chief foe, the indifferent public; there was a sweet thrill at her heart, she had no desire to sleep, and when he returned home at daybreak, she tapped softly at her bedroom window, and showing him only her face and one shoulder through the curtain, she gave him a friendly smile....

He proposed to her, and they were married. And when he had a closer view of her neck and her plump, fine shoulders, he threw up his hands, and said:

"You darling!"

He was happy, but as it rained on the day and night of his wedding, his face still retained an expression of despair.

They got on very well together. She used to sit in his office, to look after things in the Tivoli, to put down the accounts and pay the wages. And her rosy cheeks, her sweet, naïve, radiant smile, were to be seen now at the office window, now in the refreshment bar or behind the scenes of the theatre. And already she used to say to her acquaintances that the theatre was the chief and most important thing in life, and that it was only through the drama that one could derive true enjoyment and become cultivated and humane.

"But do you suppose the public understands that?" she used to say. "What they want is a clown. Yesterday we gave 'Faust Inside Out,' and almost all the boxes were empty; but if Vanitchka and I had been producing some vulgar thing, I assure you the theatre would have been packed. Tomorrow Vanitchka and I are doing 'Orpheus in Hell.'[2] Do come."

And what Kukin said about the theatre and the actors she repeated. Like him she despised the public for their ignorance and their indifference to art; she took part in the rehearsals, she corrected the actors, she kept an eye on the behaviour of the musicians, and when there was an unfavourable notice in the local paper, she shed tears, and then went to the editor's office to set things right.

The actors were fond of her and used to call her "Vanitchka and I," and "the darling"; she was sorry for them and used to lend them small sums of money, and if they deceived her, she used to shed a few tears in private, but did not complain to her husband.

They got on well in the winter too. They took the theatre in the town for the whole winter, and let it for short terms to a Little Russian company, or to a conjurer, or to a local dramatic society. Olenka grew stouter, and was always beaming with satisfaction, while Kukin grew thinner and yellower, and continually complained of their terrible losses, although he had not done badly all the winter. He used to cough at night, and she used to give him hot raspberry tea or lime-flower water, to rub him with eau-de-Cologne and to wrap him in her warm shawls.

"You're such a sweet pet!" she used to say with perfect sincerity, stroking his hair. "You're such a pretty dear!"

Towards Lent he went to Moscow to collect a new troupe, and without him she could not sleep, but sat all night at her window, looking at the stars, and she compared herself with the hens, who are awake all night and uneasy when the cock is not in the hen-house. Kukin was detained in Moscow, and wrote that he would be back at Easter, adding some instructions about the Tivoli. But on the Sunday

[2] Two nineteenth-century plays, the first a "travesty" (1888), the second a musical (1858).

before Easter, late in the evening, came a sudden ominous knock at the gate; some one was hammering on the gate as though on a barrel—boom, boom, boom! The drowsy cook went flopping with her bare feet through the puddles, as she ran to open the gate.

"Please open," said some one outside in a thick bass. "There is a telegram for you."

Olenka had received telegrams from her husband before, but this time for some reason she felt numb with terror. With shaking hands she opened the telegram and read as follows:

IVAN PETROVITCH DIED SUDDENLY TO-DAY. AWAITING
IMMATE INSTRUCTIONS FUFUNERAL TUESDAY.

That was how it was written in the telegram—"fufuneral," and the utterly incomprehensible word "immate." It was signed by the stage manager of the operatic company.

"My darling!" sobbed Olenka. "Vanitchka, my precious, my darling! Why did I ever meet you! Why did I know you and love you! Your poor heartbroken Olenka is all alone without you!"

Kukin's funeral took place on Tuesday in Moscow, Olenka returned home on Wednesday, and as soon as she got indoors she threw herself on her bed and sobbed so loudly that it could be heard next door, and in the street.

"Poor darling!" the neighbours said, as they crossed themselves. "Olga Semyonovna, poor darling! How she does take on!"

Three months later Olenka was coming home from mass, melancholy and in deep mourning. It happened that one of her neighbours, Vassily Andreitch Pustovalov, returning home from church, walked back beside her. He was the manager at Babakayev's, the timber merchant's. He wore a straw hat, a white waistcoat, and a gold watch-chain, and looked more like a country gentleman than a man in trade.

"Everything happens as it is ordained, Olga Semyonovna," he said gravely, with a sympathetic note in his voice; "and if any of our dear ones die, it must be because it is the will of God, so we ought to have fortitude and bear it submissively."

After seeing Olenka to her gate, he said good-bye and went on. All day afterwards she heard his sedately dignified voice, and whenever she shut her eyes she saw his dark beard. She liked him very much. And apparently she had made an impression on him, too, for not long afterwards an elderly lady, with whom she was only slightly acquainted, came to drink coffee with her, and as soon as she was seated at table began to talk about Pustovalov, saying that he was an excellent man whom one could thoroughly depend upon, and that any girl would be glad to marry him. Three days later Pustovalov came himself. He did not stay long, only about ten minutes, and he did not say much, but when he left, Olenka loved him—loved him so much that she lay awake all night in a perfect fever, and in the morning she sent for the elderly lady. The match was quickly arranged, and then came the wedding.

Pustovalov and Olenka got on very well together when they were married.

Usually he sat in the office till dinner-time, then he went out on business, while Olenka took his place, and sat in the office till evening, making up accounts and booking orders.

"Timber gets dearer every year; the price rises twenty per cent," she would say to her customers and friends. "Only fancy we used to sell local timber, and now Vassitchka always has to go for wood to the Mogilev district.[3] And the freight!" she would add, covering her cheeks with her hands in horror. "The freight!"

It seemed to her that she had been in the timber trade for ages and ages, and that the most important and necessary thing in life was timber; and there was something intimate and touching to her in the very sound of words such as "baulk," "post," "beam," "pole," "scantling," "batten," "lath," "plank," etc.

At night when she was asleep she dreamed of perfect mountains of planks and boards, and long strings of wagons, carting timber somewhere far away. She dreamed that a whole regiment of six-inch beams forty feet high, standing on end, was marching upon the timber-yard; that logs, beams, and boards knocked together with the resounding crash of dry wood, kept falling and getting up again, piling themselves on each other. Olenka cried out in her sleep, and Pustovalov said to her tenderly: "Olenka, what's the matter, darling? Cross yourself!"

Her husband's ideas were hers. If he thought the room was too hot, or that business was slack, she thought the same. Her husband did not care for entertainments, and on holidays he stayed at home. She did likewise.

"You are always at home or in the office," her friends said to her. "You should go to the theatre, darling, or to the circus."

"Vassitchka and I have no time to go to theatres," she would answer sedately. "We have no time for nonsense. What's the use of these theatres?"

On Saturdays Pustovalov and she used to go to the evening service; on holidays to early mass, and they walked side by side with softened faces as they came home from church. There was a pleasant fragrance about them both, and her silk dress rustled agreeably. At home they drank tea, with fancy bread and jams of various kinds, and afterwards they ate pie. Every day at twelve o'clock there was a savoury smell of beet-root soup and of mutton or duck in their yard, and on fast-days of fish, and no one could pass the gate without feeling hungry. In the office the samovar[4] was always boiling, and customers were regaled with tea and cracknels.[5] Once a week the couple went to the baths and returned side by side, both red in the face.

"Yes, we have nothing to complain of, thank God," Olenka used to say to her acquaintances. "I wish every one were as well off as Vassitchka and I."

When Pustovalov went away to buy wood in the Mogilev district, she missed him dreadfully, lay awake and cried. A young veterinary surgeon in the army, called Smirnin, to whom they had let their lodge, used sometimes to come in in the evening. He used to talk to her and play cards with her, and this entertained her in her husband's absence. She was particularly interested in what he told her of his home life. He was married and had a little boy, but was separated from his wife because she had been unfaithful to him, and now he hated her and used to send her forty roubles a month for the maintenance of their son. And hearing of all this, Olenka sighed and shook her head. She was sorry for him.

"Well, God keep you," she used to say to him at parting, as she lighted him down the stairs with a candle. "Thank you for coming to cheer me up, and may the Mother of God give you health."

And she always expressed herself with the same sedateness and dignity, the same reasonableness, in imitation of her husband. As the veterinary surgeon was disappearing behind the door below, she would say,

"You know, Vladimir Platonitch, you'd better make it up with your wife. You

---

[3] A city on the Dnieper River west of Moscow.   [4] An urn used to boil water.
[5] Hard brittle biscuits.

should forgive her for the sake of your son. You may be sure the little fellow understands.''

And when Pustovalov came back, she told him in a low voice about the veterinary surgeon and his unhappy home life, and both sighed and shook their heads and talked about the boy, who, no doubt, missed his father, and by some strange connection of ideas, they went up to the holy ikons,[6] bowed to the ground before them and prayed that God would give them children.

And so the Pustovalovs lived for six years quietly and peaceably in love and complete harmony.

But behold! one winter day after drinking hot tea in the office, Vassily Andreitch went out into the yard without his cap on to see about sending off some timber, caught cold and was taken ill. He had the best doctors, but he grew worse and died after four months' illness. And Olenka was a widow once more.

"I've nobody, now you've left me, my darling," she sobbed, after her husband's funeral. "How can I live without you, in wretchedness and misery! Pity me, good people, all alone in the world!"

She went about dressed in black with long "weepers,"[7] and gave up wearing hat and gloves for good. She hardly ever went out, except to church, or to her husband's grave, and led the life of a nun. It was not till six months later that she took off the weepers and opened the shutters of the windows. She was sometimes seen in the mornings, going with her cook to market for provisions, but what went on in her house and how she lived now could only be surmised. People guessed, from seeing her drinking tea in her garden with the veterinary surgeon, who read the newspaper aloud to her, and from the fact that, meeting a lady she knew at the post-office, she said to her:

"There is no proper veterinary inspection in our town, and that's the cause of all sorts of epidemics. One is always hearing of people's getting infection from the milk supply, or catching diseases from horses and cows. The health of domestic animals ought to be as well cared for as the health of human beings."

She repeated the veterinary surgeon's words, and was of the same opinion as he about everything. It was evident that she could not live a year without some attachment, and had found new happiness in the lodge. In any one else this would have been censured, but no one could think ill of Olenka; everything she did was so natural. Neither she nor the veterinary surgeon said anything to other people of the change in their relations, and tried, indeed, to conceal it, but without success, for Olenka could not keep a secret. When he had visitors, men serving in his regiment, and she poured out tea or served the supper, she would begin talking of the cattle plague, of the foot and mouth disease, and of the municipal slaughter-houses. He was dreadfully embarrassed, and when the guests had gone, he would seize her by the hand and hiss angrily:

"I've asked you before not to talk about what you don't understand. When we veterinary surgeons are talking among ourselves, please don't put your word in. It's really annoying."

And she would look at him with astonishment and dismay, and ask him in alarm: "But, Voloditchka, what *am* I to talk about?"

And with tears in her eyes she would embrace him, begging him not to be angry, and they were both happy.

But this happiness did not last long. The veterinary surgeon departed, departed for ever with his regiment, when it was transferred to a distant place—to Siberia, it may be. And Olenka was left alone.

---

[6] Religious images.   [7] Mourning bands.

Now she was absolutely alone. Her father had long been dead, and his armchair lay in the attic, covered with dust and lame of one leg. She got thinner and plainer, and when people met her in the street they did not look at her as they used to, and did not smile to her; evidently her best years were over and left behind, and now a new sort of life had begun for her, which did not bear thinking about. In the evening Olenka sat in the porch, and heard the band playing and the fireworks popping in the Tivoli, but now the sound stirred no response. She looked into her yard without interest, thought of nothing, wished for nothing, and afterwards, when night came on she went to bed and dreamed of her empty yard. She ate and drank as it were unwillingly.

And what was worst of all, she had no opinions of any sort. She saw the objects about her and understood what she saw, but could not form any opinion about them, and did not know what to talk about. And how awful it is not to have any opinions! One sees a bottle, for instance, or the rain, or a peasant driving in his cart, but what the bottle is for, or the rain, or the peasant, and what is the meaning of it, one can't say, and could not even for a thousand roubles. When she had Kukin, or Pustovalov, or the veterinary surgeon, Olenka could explain everything, and give her opinion about anything you like, but now there was the same emptiness in her brain and in her heart as there was in her yard outside. And it was as harsh and as bitter as wormwood in the mouth.

Little by little the town grew in all directions. The road became a street, and where the Tivoli and the timber-yard had been, there were new turnings and houses. How rapidly time passes! Olenka's house grew dingy, the roof got rusty, the shed sank on one side, and the whole yard was overgrown with docks and stinging-nettles.[8] Olenka herself had grown plain and elderly; in summer she sat in the porch, and her soul, as before, was empty and dreary and full of bitterness. In winter she sat at her window and looked at the snow. When she caught the scent of spring, or heard the chime of the church bells, a sudden rush of memories from the past came over her, there was a tender ache in her heart, and her eyes brimmed over with tears; but this was only for a minute, and then came emptiness again and the sense of the futility of life. The black kitten, Briska, rubbed against her and purred softly, but Olenka was not touched by these feline caresses. That was not what she needed. She wanted a love that would absorb her whole being, her whole soul and reason—that would give her ideas and an object in life, and would warm her old blood. And she would shake the kitten off her skirt and say with vexation:

"Get along; I don't want you!"

And so it was, day after day and year after year, and no joy, and no opinions. Whatever Mavra, the cook, said she accepted.

One hot July day, towards evening, just as the cattle were being driven away, and the whole yard was full of dust, some one suddenly knocked at the gate. Olenka went to open it herself and was dumbfounded when she looked out: she saw Smirnin, the veterinary surgeon, grey-headed, and dressed as a civilian. She suddenly remembered everything. She could not help crying and letting her head fall on his breast without uttering a word, and in the violence of her feeling she did not notice how they both walked into the house and sat down to tea.

"My dear Vladimir Platonitch! What fate has brought you?" she muttered, trembling with joy.

"I want to settle here for good, Olga Semyonovna," he told her. "I have resigned my post, and have come to settle down and try my luck on my own

8 Weedy and prickly plants.

account. Besides, it's time for my boy to go to school. He's a big boy. I am reconciled with my wife, you know.''

"Where is she?'' asked Olenka.

"She's at the hotel with the boy, and I'm looking for lodgings.''

"Good gracious, my dear soul! Lodgings? Why not have my house? Why shouldn't that suit you? Why, my goodness, I wouldn't take any rent!'' cried Olenka in a flutter, beginning to cry again. "You live here, and the lodge will do nicely for me. Oh dear! how glad I am!''

Next day the roof was painted and the walls were whitewashed, and Olenka, with her arms akimbo, walked about the yard giving directions. Her face was beaming with her old smile, and she was brisk and alert as though she had waked from a long sleep. The veterinary's wife arrived—a thin, plain lady, with short hair and a peevish expression. With her was her little Sasha, a boy of ten, small for his age, blue-eyed, chubby, with dimples in his cheeks. And scarcely had the boy walked into the yard when he ran after the cat, and at once there was the sound of his gay joyous laugh.

"Is that your puss, auntie?'' he asked Olenka. "When she has little ones, do give us a kitten. Mamma is awfully afraid of mice.''

Olenka talked to him, and gave him tea. Her heart warmed and there was a sweet ache in her bosom, as though the boy had been her own child. And when he sat at the table in the evening, going over his lessons, she looked at him with deep tenderness and pity as she murmured to herself:

"You pretty pet! . . . my precious! . . . Such a fair little thing, and so clever.''

" 'An island is a piece of land which is entirely surrounded by water,' '' he read aloud.

"An island is a piece of land,'' she repeated, and this was the first opinion to which she gave utterance with positive conviction after so many years of silence and dearth of ideas.

Now she had opinions of her own, and at supper she talked to Sasha's parents, saying how difficult the lessons were at the high schools, but that yet the high-school was better than a commercial one, since with a high-school education all careers were open to one, such as being a doctor or an engineer.

Sasha began going to the high school. His mother departed to Harkov to her sister's and did not return; his father used to go off every day to inspect cattle, and would often be away from home for three days together, and it seemed to Olenka as though Sasha was entirely abandoned, that he was not wanted at home, that he was being starved, and she carried him off to her lodge and gave him a little room there.

And for six months Sasha had lived in the lodge with her. Every morning Olenka came into his bedroom and found him fast asleep, sleeping noiselessly with his hand under his cheek. She was sorry to wake him.

"Sashenka,'' she would say mournfully, "get up, darling. It's time for school.''

He would get up, dress and say his prayers, and then sit down to breakfast, drink three glasses of tea, and eat two large cracknels and half a buttered roll. All this time he was hardly awake and a little ill-humoured in consequence.

"You don't quite know your fable, Sashenka,'' Olenka would say, looking at him as though he were about to set off on a long journey. "What a lot of trouble I have with you! You must work and do your best, darling, and obey your teachers.''

"Oh, do leave me alone!'' Sasha would say.

Then he would go down the street to school, a little figure, wearing a big cap and carrying a satchel on his shoulder. Olenka would follow him noiselessly.

"Sashenka!" she would call after him, and she would pop into his hand a date or a caramel. When he reached the street where the school was, he would feel ashamed of being followed by a tall, stout woman; he would turn round and say:

"You'd better go home, auntie. I can go the rest of the way alone."

She would stand still and look after him fixedly till he had disappeared at the school-gate.

Ah, how she loved him! Of her former attachments not one had been so deep; never had her soul surrendered to any feeling so spontaneously, so disinterestedly, and so joyously as now that her maternal instincts were aroused. For this little boy with the dimple in his cheek and the big school cap, she would have given her whole life, she would have given it with joy and tears of tenderness. Why? Who can tell why?

When she had seen the last of Sasha, she returned home, contented and serene, brimming over with love; her face, which had grown younger during the last six months, smiled and beamed; people meeting her looked at her with pleasure.

"Good-morning, Olga Semyonovna, darling. How are you, darling?"

"The lessons at the high school are very difficult now," she would relate at the market. "It's too much; in the first class yesterday they gave him a fable to learn by heart, and a Latin translation and a problem. You know it's too much for a little chap."

And she would begin talking about the teachers, the lessons, and the school books, saying just what Sasha said.

At three o'clock they had dinner together: in the evening they learned their lessons together and cried. When she put him to bed, she would stay a long time making the Cross over him and murmuring a prayer; then she would go to bed and dream of that far-away misty future when Sasha would finish his studies and become a doctor or an engineer, would have a big house of his own with horses and a carriage, would get married and have children. . . . She would fall asleep still thinking of the same thing, and tears would run down her cheeks from her closed eyes, while the black cat lay purring beside her: "Mrr, mrr, mrr."

Suddenly there would come a loud knock at the gate.

Olenka would wake up breathless with alarm, her heart throbbing. Half a minute later would come another knock.

"It must be a telegram from Harkov," she would think, beginning to tremble from head to foot. "Sasha's mother is sending for him from Harkov. . . . Oh, mercy on us!"

She was in despair. Her head, her hands, and her feet would turn chill, and she would feel that she was the most unhappy woman in the world. But another minute would pass, voices would be heard: it would turn out to be the veterinary surgeon coming home from the club.

"Well, thank God!" she would think.

And gradually the load in her heart would pass off, and she would feel at ease. She would go back to bed thinking of Sasha, who lay sound asleep in the next room, sometimes crying out in his sleep:

"I'll give it you! Get away! Shut up!"

[1899]

Joseph Conrad   *1857–1924*

THE SECRET SHARER

I

On my right hand there were lines of fishing-stakes resembling a mysterious system of half-submerged bamboo fences, incomprehensible in its division of the domain of tropical fishes, and crazy[1] of aspect as if abandoned for ever by some nomad tribe of fishermen now gone to the other end of the ocean; for there was no sign of human habitation as far as the eye could reach. To the left a group of barren islets, suggesting ruins of stone walls, towers, and blockhouses, had its foundations set in a blue sea that itself looked solid, so still and stable did it lie below my feet; even the track of light from the westering sun shone smoothly, without that animated glitter which tells of an imperceptible ripple. And when I turned my head to take a parting glance at the tug which had just left us anchored outside the bar, I saw the straight line of the flat shore joined to the stable sea, edge to edge, with a perfect and unmarked closeness, in one levelled floor half brown, half blue under the enormous dome of the sky. Corresponding in their insignificance to the islets of the sea, two small clumps of trees, one on each side of the only fault in the impeccable joint, marked the mouth of the river Meinam[2] we had just left on the first preparatory stage of our homeward journey; and, far back on the inland level, a larger and loftier mass, the grove surrounding the great Paknam pagoda,[3] was the only thing on which the eye could rest from the vain task of exploring the monotonous sweep of the horizon. Here and there gleams as of a few scattered pieces of silver marked the windings of the great river; and on the nearest of them, just within the bar, the tug steaming right into the land became lost to my sight, hull and funnel and masts, as though the impassive earth had swallowed her up without an effort, without a tremor. My eye followed the light cloud of her smoke, now here, now there, above the plain, according to the devious curves of the stream, but always fainter and farther away, till I lost it at last behind the mitre-shaped hill of the great pagoda. And then I was left alone with my ship, anchored at the head of the Gulf of Siam.

She floated at the starting-point of a long journey, very still in an immense stillness, the shadows of her spars flung far to the eastward by the setting sun. At that moment I was alone on her decks. There was not a sound in her—and around us nothing moved, nothing lived, not a canoe on the water, not a bird in the air, not a cloud in the sky. In this breathless pause at the threshold of a long passage we seemed to be measuring our fitness for a long and arduous enterprise, the appointed task of both our existences to be carried out, far from all human eyes, with only sky and sea for spectators and for judges.

There must have been some glare in the air to interfere with one's sight, because it was only just before the sun left us that my roaming eyes made out beyond the highest ridge of the principal islet of the group something which did away with the solemnity of perfect solitude. The tide of darkness flowed on swiftly;

---

[1] Irregular, crooked.

[2] The Meinam River (Chao Phraya) flows southward through the city of Bangkok and enters the Gulf of Thailand (Gulf of Siam).

[3] The Paknam Pagoda sits at the mouth of the river.

and with tropical suddenness a swarm of stars came out above the shadowy earth, while I lingered yet, my hand resting lightly on my ship's rail as if on the shoulder of a trusted friend. But, with all that multitude of celestial bodies staring down at one, the comfort of quiet communion with her was gone for good. And there were also disturbing sounds by this time—voices, footsteps forward; the steward flitted along the main-deck, a busily ministering spirit; a hand-bell tinkled urgently under the poop-deck. . . .

I found my two officers waiting for me near the supper table, in the lighted cuddy. We sat down at once, and as I helped the chief mate, I said:

"Are you aware that there is a ship anchored inside the islands? I saw her mastheads above the ridge as the sun went down."

He raised sharply his simple face, overcharged by a terrible growth of whisker, and emitted his usual ejaculations: "Bless my soul, sir! You don't say so!"

My second mate was a round-cheeked, silent young man, grave beyond his years, I thought; but as our eyes happened to meet I detected a slight quiver on his lips. I looked down at once. It was not my part to encourage sneering on board my ship. It must be said, too, that I knew very little of my officers. In consequence of certain events of no particular significance, except to myself, I had been appointed to the command only a fortnight before. Neither did I know much of the hands forward. All these people had been together for eighteen months or so, and my position was that of the only stranger on board. I mention this because it has some bearing on what is to follow. But what I felt most was my being a stranger to the ship; and if all the truth must be told, I was somewhat of a stranger to myself. The youngest man on board (barring the second mate), and untried as yet by a position of the fullest responsibility, I was willing to take the adequacy of the others for granted. They had simply to be equal to their tasks; but I wondered how far I should turn out faithful to that ideal conception of one's own personality every man sets up for himself secretly.

Meantime the chief mate, with an almost visible effect of collaboration on the part of his round eyes and frightful whiskers, was trying to evolve a theory of the anchored ship. His dominant trait was to take all things into earnest consideration. He was of a painstaking turn of mind. As he used to say, he "liked to account to himself" for practically everything that came in his way, down to a miserable scorpion he had found in his cabin a week before. The why and the wherefore of that scorpion—how it got on board and came to select his room rather than the pantry (which was a dark place and more what a scorpion would be partial to), and how on earth it managed to drown itself in the inkwell of his writing-desk—had exercised him infinitely. The ship within the islands was much more easily accounted for; and just as we were about to rise from table he made his pronouncement. She was, he doubted not, a ship from home lately arrived. Probably she drew too much water to cross the bar except at the top of spring tides. Therefore she went into that natural harbor to wait for a few days in preference to remaining in an open roadstead.[4]

"That's so," confirmed the second mate, suddenly, in his slightly hoarse voice. "She draws over twenty feet. She's the Liverpool ship *Sephora* with a cargo of coal. Hundred and twenty-three days from *Cardiff*."[5]

---

[4] A sheltered offshore anchorage.

[5] Liverpool is a port city of the River Mersey in northwest England; Cardiff is a port city in Wales to the south.

We looked at him in surprise.

"The tugboat skipper told me when he came on board for your letters, sir," explained the young man. "He expects to take her up the river the day after tomorrow."

After thus overwhelming us with the extent of his information he slipped out of the cabin. The mate observed regretfully that he "could not account for that young fellow's whims." What prevented him telling us all about it at once, he wanted to know.

I detained him as he was making a move. For the last two days the crew had had plenty of hard work, and the night before they had very little sleep. I felt painfully that I—a stranger—was doing something unusual when I directed him to let all hands turn in without setting an anchor-watch. I proposed to keep on deck myself till one o'clock or thereabouts. I would get the second mate to relieve me at that hour.

"He will turn out the cook and the steward at four," I concluded, "and then give you a call. Of course at the slightest sign of any sort of wind we'll have the hands up and make a start at once."

He concealed his astonishment. "Very well, sir." Outside the cuddy[6] he put his head in the second mate's door to inform him of my unheard-of caprice to take a five hours' anchor-watch[7] on myself. I heard the other raise his voice incredulously—"What? The Captain himself?" Then a few more murmurs, a door closed, then another. A few moments later I went on deck.

My strangeness, which had made me sleepless, had prompted that unconventional arrangement, as if I had expected in those solitary hours of the night to get on terms with the ship of which I knew nothing, manned by men of whom I knew very little more. Fast alongside a wharf, littered like any ship in port with a tangle of unrelated things, invaded by unrelated shore people, I had hardly seen her yet properly. Now, as she lay cleared for sea, the stretch of her main-deck seemed to me very fine under the stars. Very fine, very roomy for her size, and very inviting. I descended the poop[8] and paced the waist, my mind picturing to myself the coming passage through the Malay Archipelago,[9] down the Indian Ocean, and up the Atlantic. All its phases were familiar enough to me, every characteristic, all the alternatives which were likely to face me on the high seas—everything! . . . except the novel responsibility of command. But I took heart from the reasonable thought that the ship was like other ships, the men like other men, and that the sea was not likely to keep any special surprises expressly for my discomfiture.

Arrived at that comforting conclusion, I bethought myself of a cigar and went below to get it. All was still down there. Everybody at the after end of the ship was sleeping profoundly. I came out again on the quarter-deck, agreeably at ease in my sleeping-suit on that warm breathless night, barefooted, a glowing cigar in my teeth, and, going forward, I was met by the profound silence of the fore end of the ship. Only as I passed the door of the forecastle I heard a deep, quiet, trustful sigh of some sleeper inside. And suddenly I rejoiced in the great security of the sea as compared with the unrest of the land, in my choice of that untempted life presenting no disquieting problems, invested with an elementary moral beauty by the

---

[6] A small cabin.

[7] The tour of duty (or watch) while a ship rides at anchor.

[8] The stern or rear of the ship.

[9] A group of islands in the Indian and Pacific oceans that includes Sumatra, Java, Borneo, and the Philippines.

absolute straightforwardness of its appeal and by the singleness of its purpose.

The riding-light[10] in the fore-rigging burned with a clear, untroubled, as if symbolic, flame, confident and bright in the mysterious shades of the night. Passing on my way aft along the other side of the ship, I observed that the rope sideladder, put over, no doubt, for the master of the tug when he came to fetch away our letters, had not been hauled in as it should have been. I became annoyed at this, for exactitude in small matters is the very soul of discipline. Then I reflected that I had myself peremptorily dismissed my officers from duty, and by my own act had prevented the anchor-watch being formally set and things properly attended to. I asked myself whether it was wise ever to interfere with the established routine of duties even from the kindest of motives. My action might have made me appear eccentric. Goodness only knew how that absurdly whiskered mate would "account" for my conduct, and what the whole ship thought of that informality of their new captain. I was vexed with myself.

Not from compunction certainly, but, as it were mechanically, I proceeded to get the ladder in myself. Now a sideladder of that sort is a light affair and comes in easily, yet my vigorous tug, which should have brought it flying on board, merely recoiled upon my body in a totally unexpected jerk. What the devil! . . . I was so astounded by the immovableness of that ladder that I remained stockstill, trying to account for it to myself like that imbecile mate of mine. In the end, of course, I put my head over the rail.

The side of the ship made an opaque belt of shadow on the darkling glassy shimmer of the sea. But I saw at once something elongated and pale floating very close to the ladder. Before I could form a guess a faint flash of phosphorescent light, which seemed to issue suddenly from the naked body of man, flickered in the sleeping water with the elusive, silent play of summer lightning in a night sky. With a gasp I saw revealed to my stare a pair of feet, the long legs, a broad livid back immersed right up to the neck in a greenish cadaverous glow. One hand, awash, clutched the bottom rung of the ladder. He was complete but for the head. A headless corpse! The cigar dropped out of my gaping mouth with a tiny plop and a short hiss quite audible in the absolute stillness of all things under heaven. At that I suppose he raised up his face, a dimly pale oval in the shadow of the ship's side. But even then I could only barely make out down there the shape of his black-haired head. However, it was enough for the horrid, frost-bound sensation which had gripped me about the chest to pass off. The moment of vain exclamations was past, too. I only climbed on the spare spar and leaned over the rail as far as I could, to bring my eyes nearer to that mystery floating alongside.

As he hung by the ladder, like a resting swimmer, the sea-lightning played about his limbs at every stir; and he appeared in it ghastly, silvery, fish-like. He remained as mute as a fish, too. He made no motion to get out of the water, either. It was inconceivable that he should not attempt to come on board, and strangely troubling to suspect that perhaps he did not want to. And my first words were prompted by just that troubled incertitude.

"What's the matter?" I asked in my ordinary tone, speaking down to the face upturned exactly under mine.

"Cramp," it answered, no louder. Then slightly anxious, "I say, no need to call any one."

"I was not going to," I said.

"Are you alone on deck?"

---

[10] A light displayed on deck while a ship is "riding" at anchor.

"Yes."

I had somehow the impression that he was on the point of letting go the ladder to swim away beyond my ken[11]—mysterious as he came. But, for the moment, this being appearing as if he had risen from the bottom of the sea (it was certainly the nearest land to the ship) wanted only to know the time. I told him. And he, down there, tentatively:

"I suppose your captain's turned in?"

"I am sure he isn't," I said.

He seemed to struggle with himself, for I heard something like the low, bitter murmur of doubt. "What's the good?" His next words came out with a hesitating effort.

"Look here, my man. Could you call him out quietly?"

I thought the time had come to declare myself.

"*I* am the captain."

I heard a "By Jove!" whispered at the level of the water. The phosphorescence flashed in the swirl of the water all about his limbs, his other hand seized the ladder.

"My name's Leggatt."

The voice was calm and resolute. A good voice. The self-possession of that man had somehow induced a corresponding state in myself. It was very quietly that I remarked:

"You must be a good swimmer."

"Yes. I've been in the water practically since nine o'clock. The question for me now is whether I am to let go this ladder and go on swimming till I sink from exhaustion, or—to come on board here."

I felt this was no mere formula of desperate speech, but a real alternative in the view of a strong soul. I should have gathered from this that he was young; indeed, it is only the young who are ever confronted by such clear issues. But at the time it was pure intuition on my part. A mysterious communication was established already between us two—in the face of that silent, darkened tropical sea. I was young, too; young enough to make no comment. The man in the water began suddenly to climb up the ladder, and I hastened away from the rail to fetch some clothes.

Before entering the cabin I stood still, listening in the lobby at the foot of the stairs.[12] A faint snore came through the closed door of the chief mate's room. The second mate's door was on the hook, but the darkness in there was absolutely soundless. He, too, was young and could sleep like a stone. Remained the steward, but he was not likely to wake up before he was called. I got a sleeping-suit out of my room and, coming back on deck, saw the naked man from the sea sitting on the main-hatch, glimmering white in the darkness, his elbows on his knees and his head in his hands. In a moment he had concealed his damp body in a sleeping-suit of the same grey-stripe pattern as the one I was wearing and followed me like my double on the poop. Together we moved right aft, barefooted, silent.

"What is it?" I asked in a deadened voice, taking the lighted lamp out of the binnacle, and raising it to his face.

"An ugly business."

He had rather regular features; a good mouth; light eyes under somewhat heavy, dark eyebrows; a smooth, square forehead; no growth on his cheeks; a

---

[11] View or sight.
[12] Hallway, corridor.

small, brown moustache, and a well-shaped, round chin. His expression was concentrated, meditative, under the inspecting light of the lamp I held up to his face; such as a man thinking hard in solitude might wear. My sleeping-suit was just right for his size. A well-knit young fellow of twenty-five at most. He caught his lower lip with the edge of white, even teeth.

"Yes," I said, replacing the lamp in the binnacle. The warm, heavy tropical night closed upon his head again.

"There's a ship over there," he murmured.

"Yes, I know. The *Sephora*. Did you know of us?"

"Hadn't the slightest idea. I am the mate of her ——" He paused and corrected himself. "I should say I *was*."

"Aha! Something wrong?"

"Yes. Very wrong indeed. I've killed a man."

"What do you mean? Just now?"

"No, on the passage. Weeks ago. Thirty-nine south. When I say a man ——"

"Fit of temper," I suggested, confidently.

The shadowy, dark head, like mine, seemed to nod imperceptibly above the ghostly grey of my sleeping-suit. It was, in the night, as though I had been faced by my own reflection in the depths of a sombre and immense mirror.

"A pretty thing to have to own up to for a Conway boy," murmured my double, distinctly.

"You're a Conway boy?"[13]

"I am," he said, as if startled. . . . Then, slowly "Perhaps you too ——"

It was so; but being a couple of years older I had left before he joined. After a quick interchange of dates a silence fell; and I thought suddenly of my absurd mate with his terrific whiskers and the "Bless my soul—you don't say so" type of intellect. My double gave me an inkling of his thoughts by saying: "My father's a parson in Norfolk.[14] Do you see me before a judge and jury on that charge? For myself I can't see the necessity. There are fellows that an angel from heaven——And I am not that. He was one of those creatures that are just simmering all the time with a silly sort of wickedness. Miserable devils that have no business to live at all. He wouldn't do his duty and wouldn't let anybody else do theirs. But what's the good of talking! You know well enough the son of ill-conditioned snarling cur——"

He appealed to me as if our experiences had been as identical as our clothes. And I knew well enough the pestiferous danger of such a character where there are no means of legal repression. And I knew well enough also that my double there was no homicidal ruffian. I did not think of asking him for details, and he told me the story roughly in brusque, disconnected sentences. I needed no more. I saw it all going on as though I were myself inside that other sleeping-suit.

"It happened while we were setting a reefed foresail, at dusk. Reefed foresail! You understand the sort of weather. The only sail we had left to keep the ship running; so you may guess what it had been like for days. Anxious sort of job, that. He gave me some of his cursed insolence at the sheet.[15] I tell you I was overdone with this terrific weather that seemed to have no end to it. Terrific, I tell you—and

---

[13] The *Conway* was a training vessel used to prepare officers for both the British Royal Navy and the British merchant service.

[14] A county in eastern England bordering the North Sea.

[15] A rope or chain attached to the lower corner of a sail for shortening or slacking it.

a deep ship. I believe the fellow himself was half crazed with funk.[16] It was no time for gentlemanly reproof, so I turned round and felled him like an ox. He up and at me. We closed just as an awful sea made for the ship. All hands saw it coming and took to the rigging, but I had him by the throat, and went on shaking him like a rat, the men above us yelling. 'Look out! look out!' Then a crash as if the sky had fallen on my head. They say that for over ten minutes hardly anything was to be seen of the ship—just the three masts and a bit of the forecastle[17] head and of the poop all awash driving along in a smother of foam. It was a miracle that they found us, jammed together behind the forebits. It's clear that I meant business, because I was holding him by the throat still when they picked us up. He was black in the face. It was too much for them. It seems they rushed us aft together, gripped as we were, screaming 'Murder!' like a lot of lunatics, and broke into the cuddy. And the ship running for her life, touch and go all the time, any minute her last in a sea fit to turn your hair grey only a-looking at it. I understand that the skipper, too, started raving like the rest of them. The man had been deprived of sleep for more than a week, and to have this sprung on him at the height of a furious gale nearly drove him out of his mind. I wonder they didn't fling me overboard after getting the carcass of their precious ship-mate out of my fingers. They had rather a job to separate us, I've been told. A sufficiently fierce story to make an old judge and a respectable jury sit up a bit. The first thing I heard when I came to myself was the maddening howling of that endless gale, and on that the voice of the old man. He was hanging on to my bunk, staring into my face out of his sou'wester.

" 'Mr. Leggatt, you have killed a man. You can act no longer as chief mate of this ship.' "

His care to subdue his voice made it sound monotonous. He rested a hand on the end of the skylight to steady himself with, and all that time did not stir a limb, so far as I could see. "Nice little tale for a quiet tea-party," he concluded in the same tone.

One of my hands, too, rested on the end of the skylight; neither did I stir a limb, so far as I knew. We stood less than a foot from each other. It occurred to me that if old "Bless my soul—you don't say so" were to put his head up the companion and catch sight of us, he would think he was seeing double, or imagine himself come upon a scene of weird witchcraft; the strange captain having a quiet confabulation by the wheel with his own grey ghost. I became very much concerned to prevent anything of the sort. I heard the other's soothing undertone.

"My father's a parson in Norfolk," it said. Evidently he had forgotten he had told me this important fact before. Truly a nice little tale.

"You had better slip down into my stateroom now," I said, moving off stealthily. My double followed my movements; our bare feet made no sound; I let him in, closed the door with care, and, after giving a call to the second mate, returned on deck for my relief.

"Not much sign of any wind yet," I remarked when he approached.

"No, sir. Not much," he assented, sleepily, in his hoarse voice, with just enough deference, no more, and barely suppressing a yawn.

"Well, that's all you have to look out for. You have got your orders."

"Yes, sir."

I paced a turn or two on the poop and saw him take up his position face forward with his elbow in the ratlines of the mizzen-rigging before I went below. The

---

[16] Fear.

[17] The area at the bow of a ship where the crew is housed.

mate's faint snoring was still going on peacefully. The cuddy lamp was burning over the table on which stood a vase with flowers, a polite attention from the ship's provision merchant—the last flowers we should see for the next three months at the very least. Two bunches of bananas hung from the beam symmetrically, one on each side of the rudder-casing. Everything was as before in the ship—except that two of her captain's sleeping-suits were simultaneously in use, one motionless in the cuddy, the other keeping very still in the captain's stateroom.

It must be explained here that my cabin had the form of the capital letter L the door being within the angle and opening into the short part of the letter. A couch was to the left, the bed-place to the right; my writing-desk and the chronometers' table[18] faced the door. But any one opening it, unless he stepped right inside, had no view of what I call the long (or vertical) part of the letter. It contained some lockers surmounted by a bookcase; and a few clothes, a thick jacket or two, caps, oilskin coat, and such like, hung on hooks. There was at the bottom of that part a door opening into my bath-room, which could be entered also directly from the saloon.[19] But that way was never used.

The mysterious arrival had discovered the advantage of this particular shape. Entering my room, lighted strongly by a big bulkhead lamp swung on gimbals[20] above my writing-desk, I did not see him anywhere till he stepped out quietly from behind the coats hung in the recessed part.

"I heard somebody moving about, and went in there at once," he whispered.

I, too, spoke under my breath.

"Nobody is likely to come in here without knocking and getting permission."

He nodded. His face was thin and the sunburn faded, as though he had been ill. And no wonder. He had been, I heard presently, kept under arrest in his cabin for nearly seven weeks. But there was nothing sickly in his eyes or in his expression. He was not a bit like me, really; yet, as we stood leaning over my bed-place, whispering side by side, with our dark heads together and our backs to the door, anybody bold enough to open it stealthily would have been treated to the uncanny sight of a double captain busy talking in whispers with his other self.

"But all this doesn't tell me how you came to hang on to our side-ladder," I inquired, in the hardly audible murmurs we used, after he had told me something more of the proceedings on board the *Sephora* once the bad weather was over.

"When we sighted Java Head[21] I had had time to think all those matters out several times over. I had six weeks of doing nothing else, and with only an hour or so every evening for a tramp on the quarterdeck."

He whispered, his arms folded on the side of my bed-place, staring through the open port. And I could imagine perfectly the manner of this thinking out—a stubborn if not a steadfast operation; something of which I should have been perfectly incapable.

"I reckoned it would be dark before we closed with the land," he continued, so low that I had to strain my hearing, near as we were to each other, shoulder touching shoulder almost. "So I asked to speak to the old man. He always seemed very sick when he came to see me—as if he could not look me in the face. You know, that foresail saved the ship. She was too deep to have run long under bare

---

[18] A chronometer is an instrument used for determining longitude at sea.
[19] The officers' dining room.
[20] A device which allows a light or compass to remain suspended horizontally regardless of the motion of the ship.
[21] A famous landmark at the western tip of the island of Java at the southern entrance to the Sunda Straits, a channel between Java and Sumatra.

poles. And it was I that managed to set it for him. Anyway, he came. When I had him in my cabin—he stood by the door looking at me as if I had the halter round my neck already—I asked him right away to leave my cabin door unlocked at night while the ship was going through Sunda Straits. There would be the Java coast within two or three miles, off Angier Point. I wanted nothing more. I've had a prize for swimming my second year in the Conway."

"I can believe it," I breathed out.

"God only knows why they locked me in every night. To see some of their faces you'd have thought they were afraid I'd go about at night strangling people. Am I a murdering brute? Do I look it? By Jove! if I had been he wouldn't have trusted himself like that into my room. You'll say I might have chucked him aside and bolted out, there and then—it was dark already. Well, no. And for the same reason I wouldn't think of trying to smash the door. There would have been a rush to stop me at the noise, and I did not mean to get into a confounded scrimmage. Somebody else might have got killed—for I would not have broken out only to get chucked back, and I did not want any more of that work. He refused, looking more sick than ever. He was afraid of the men, and also of that old second mate of his who had been sailing with him for years—a grey-headed old humbug; and his steward, too, had been with him devil knows how long—seventeen years or more—a dogmatic sort of loafer who hated me like poison, just because I was the chief mate. No chief mate ever made more than one voyage in the *Sephora*, you know. Those two old chaps ran the ship. Devil only knows what the skipper wasn't afraid of (all his nerve went to pieces altogether in that hellish spell of bad weather we had)—of what the law would do to him—of his wife, perhaps. Oh, yes! she's on board. Though I don't think she would have meddled. She would have been only too glad to have me out of the ship in any way. The 'brand of Cain'[22] business, don't you see. That's all right. I was ready enough to go off wandering on the face of the earth—and that was price enough to pay for an Abel of that son. Anyhow, he wouldn't listen to me. 'This thing must take its course. I represent the law here.' He was shaking like a leaf. 'So you won't?' 'No!' 'Then I hope you will be able to sleep on that,' I said, and turned my back on him. 'I wonder that *you* can,' cries he, and locks the door.

"Well, after that, I couldn't. Not very well. That was three weeks ago. We have had a slow passage through the Java Sea;[23] drifted about Carimata[24] for ten days. When we anchored here they thought, I suppose, it was all right. The nearest land (and that's five miles) is the ship's destination; the consul would soon set about catching me; and there would have been no object in bolting to these islets there. I don't suppose there's a drop of water on them. I don't know how it was, but tonight that steward, after bringing me my supper, went out to let me eat it, and left the door unlocked. And I ate it—all there was, too. After I had finished I strolled out on the quarter-deck. I don't know that I meant to do anything. A breath of fresh air was all I wanted, I believe. Then a sudden temptation came over me. I kicked off my slippers and was in the water before I had made up my mind fairly. Somebody heard the splash and they raised an awful hullabaloo. 'He's gone! Lower the boats! He's committed suicide! No, he's swimming.' Certainly I

---

[22] Cain, the eldest son of Adam and Eve, slew his brother Abel out of jealousy (Genesis 4). God not only punished Cain by making him a fugitive and outcast but, to assure his punishment, "put a mark on Cain, lest any who came upon him should kill him."

[23] That part of the Pacific Ocean lying between the islands of Java and Borneo.

[24] The Karimata Strait lies to the north between Borneo and Sumatra.

was swimming. It's not so easy for a swimmer like me to commit suicide by drowning. I landed on the nearest islet before the boat left the ship's side. I heard them pulling about in the dark, hailing, and so on, but after a bit they gave up. Everything quieted down and the anchorage became as still as death. I sat down on a stone and began to think. I felt certain they would start searching for me at daylight. There was no place to hide on those stony things—and if there had been, what would have been the good? But now I was clear of that ship, I was not going back. So after a while I took off all my clothes, tied them up in a bundle with a stone inside, and dropped them in the deep water on the outer side of that islet. That was suicide enough for me. Let them think what they liked, but I didn't mean to drown myself. I meant to swim till I sank—but that's not the same thing. I struck out for another of these little islands, and it was from that one that I first saw your riding-light. Something to swim for. I went on easily, and on the way I came upon a flat rock a foot or two above the water. In the daytime, I dare say, you might make it out with a glass from your poop. I scrambled up on it and rested myself for a bit. Then I made another start. That last spell must have been over a mile."

His whisper was getting fainter and fainter, and all the time he stared straight out through the port-hole, in which there was not even a star to be seen. I had not interrupted him. There was something that made comment impossible in his narrative, or perhaps in himself; a sort of feeling, a quality, which I can't find a name for. And when he ceased, all I found was a futile whisper: "So you swam for our light?"

"Yes—straight for it. It was something to swim for. I couldn't see any stars low down because the coast was in the way, and I couldn't see the land, either. The water was like glass. One might have been swimming in a confounded thousand-feet deep cistern with no place for scrambling out anywhere; but what I didn't like was the notion of swimming round and round like a crazed bullock before I gave out; and as I didn't mean to go back . . . No. Do you see me being hauled back, stark naked, off one of these little islands by the scruff of the neck and fighting like a wild beast? Somebody would have got killed for certain, and I did not want any of that. So I went on. Then your ladder——"

"Why didn't you hail the ship?" I asked, a little louder.

He touched my shoulder lightly. Lazy footsteps came right over our heads and stopped. The second mate had crossed from the other side of the poop and might have been hanging over the rail for all we knew.

"He couldn't hear us talking—could he?" My double breathed into my very ear, anxiously.

His anxiety was an answer, a sufficient answer, to the question I had put to him. An answer containing all the difficulty of that situation. I closed the porthole quietly, to make sure. A louder word might have been overheard.

"Who's that?" he whispered then.

"My second mate. But I don't know much more of the fellow than you do."

And I told him a little about myself. I had been appointed to take charge while I least expected anything of the sort, not quite a fortnight ago. I didn't know either the ship or the people. Hadn't had the time in port to look about me or size anybody up. And as to the crew, all they knew was that I was appointed to take the ship home. For the rest, I was almost as much of a stranger on board as himself, I said. And at the moment I felt it most acutely. I felt that it would take very little to make me a suspect person in the eyes of the ship's company.

He had turned about meantime; and we, the two strangers in the ship, faced each other in identical attitudes.

"Your ladder——" he murmured, after a silence. "Who'd have thought of finding a ladder hanging over at night in a ship anchored out here! I felt just then a very unpleasant faintness. After the life I've been leading for nine weeks, anybody would have got out of condition. I wasn't capable of swimming round as far as your rudder-chains. And, lo and behold! there was a ladder to get hold of. After I gripped it I said to myself, 'What's the good?' When I saw a man's head looking over I thought I would swim away presently and leave him shouting—in whatever language it was. I didn't mind being looked at. I—I liked it. And then you speaking to me so quietly—as if you had expected me—made me hold on a little longer. It had been a confounded lonely time—I don't mean while swimming. I was glad to talk a little to somebody that didn't belong to the *Sephora*. As to asking for the captain, that was a mere impulse. It could have been no use, with all the ship knowing about me and the other people pretty certain to be round here in the morning. I don't know—I wanted to be seen, to talk with somebody, before I went on. I don't know what I would have said. . . . 'Fine night, isn't it?' or something of the sort."

"Do you think they will be round here presently?" I asked with some incredulity. "Quite likely," he said, faintly.

He looked extremely haggard all of a sudden. His head rolled on his shoulders.

"H'm. We shall see then. Meantime get into that bed," I whispered. "Want help? There."

It was a rather high bed-place with a set of drawers underneath. This amazing swimmer really needed the lift I gave him by seizing his leg. He tumbled in, rolled over on his back, and flung one arm across his eyes. And then, with his face nearly hidden, he must have looked exactly as I used to look in that bed. I gazed upon my other self for a while before drawing across carefully the two green serge curtains which ran on a brass rod. I thought for a moment of pinning them together for greater safety, but I sat down on the couch, and once there I felt unwilling to rise and hunt for a pin. I would do it in a moment. I was extremely tired, in a peculiarly intimate way, by the strain of stealthiness, by the effort of whispering and the general secrecy of his excitement. It was three o'clock by now and I had been on my feet since nine, but I was not sleepy; I could not have gone to sleep. I sat there, fagged out, looking at the curtains, trying to clear my mind of the confused sensation of being in two places at once, and greatly bothered by an exasperating knocking in my head. It was a relief to discover suddenly that it was not in my head at all, but on the outside of the door. Before I could collect myself the words "Come in" were out of my mouth, and the steward entered with a tray, bringing in my morning coffee. I had slept, after all, and I was so frightened that I shouted, "This way! I am here, steward," as though he had been miles away. He put down the tray on the table next the couch and only then said, very quietly, "I can see you are here, sir." I felt him give me a keen look, but I dared not meet his eyes just then. He must have wondered why I had drawn the curtains of my bed before going to sleep on the couch. He went out, hooking the door open as usual.

I heard the crew washing decks above me. I knew I would have been told at once if there had been any wind. Calm, I thought, and I was doubly vexed. Indeed, I felt dual more than ever. The steward reappeared suddenly in the doorway. I jumped up from the couch so quickly that he gave a start.

"What do you want here?"

"Close your port, sir—they are washing decks."

"It is closed," I said, reddening.

"Very well, sir." But he did not move from the doorway and returned my stare in an extraordinary, equivocal manner for a time. Then his eyes wavered, all his expression changed, and in a voice unusually gentle, almost coaxingly:

"May I come in to take the empty cup away, sir?"

"Of course!" I turned my back on him while he popped in and out. Then I unhooked and closed the door and even pushed the bolt. This sort of thing could not go on very long. The cabin was as hot as an oven, too. I took a peep at my double, and discovered that he had not moved, his arm was still over his eyes; but his chest heaved; his hair was wet; his chin glistened with perspiration. I reached over him and opened the port.

"I must show myself on deck," I reflected.

Of course, theoretically, I could do what I liked, with no one to say nay to me within the whole circle of the horizon; but to lock my cabin door and take the key away I did not dare. Directly I put my head out of the companion I saw the group of my two officers, the second mate barefooted, the chief mate in long indian-rubber boots, near the break of the poop, and the steward half-way down the poop-ladder talking to them eagerly. He happened to catch sight of me and dived, the second ran down on the main-deck shouting some order or other, and the chief mate came to meet me, touching his cap.

There was a sort of curiosity in his eye that I did not like. I don't know whether the steward had told them that I was "queer" only, or downright drunk, but I know the man meant to have a good look at me. I watched him coming with a smile which, as he got into point-blank range, took effect and froze his very whiskers. I did not give him time to open his lips.

"Square the yards by lifts and braces[25] before the hands go to breakfast."

It was the first particular order I had given on board that ship; and I stayed on deck to see it executed, too. I had felt the need of asserting myself without loss of time. That sneering young cub got taken down a peg or two on that occasion, and I also seized the opportunity of having a good look at the face of every foremast man as they filed past me to go to the after braces. At breakfast time, eating nothing myself, I presided with such frigid dignity that the two mates were only too glad to escape from the cabin as soon as decency permitted; and all the time the dual working of my mind distracted me almost to the point of insanity. I was constantly watching myself, my secret self, as dependent on my actions as my own personality, sleeping in that bed, behind that door which faced me as I sat at the head of the table. It was very much like being mad, only it was worse because one was aware of it.

I had to shake him for a solid minute, but when at last he opened his eyes it was in the full possession of his senses, with an inquiring look.

"All's well so far," I whispered. "Now you must vanish into the bath-room."

He did so, as noiseless as a ghost, and then I rang for the steward, and facing him boldly, directed him to tidy up my stateroom while I was having my bath—"and be quick about it." As my tone admitted of no excuses, he said, "Yes, sir," and ran off to fetch his dust-pan and brushes. I took a bath and did most of my dressing, splashing, and whistling softly for the steward's edification, while the secret sharer of my life stood drawn up bolt upright in that little space, his face looking very sunken in daylight, his eyelids lowered under the stern, dark line of his eyebrows drawn together by a slight frown.

When I left him there to go back to my room the steward was finishing dusting. I sent for the mate and engaged him in some insignificant conversation. It was, as

[25] The command is to square the yards in order to sail before the wind.

it were, trifling with the terrific character of his whiskers; but my object was to give him an opportunity for a good look at my cabin. And then I could at last shut, with a clear conscience, the door of my stateroom and get my double back into the recessed part. There was nothing else for it. He had to sit still on a small folding stool, half smothered by the heavy coats hanging there. We listened to the steward going into the bath-room out of the saloon, filling the water-bottles there, scrubbing the bath, setting things to rights, whisk, bang, clatter—out again into the saloon—turn the key—click. Such was my scheme for keeping my second self invisible. Nothing better could be contrived under the circumstances. And there we sat; I at my writing-desk ready to appear busy with some papers, he behind me out of sight of the door. It would not have been prudent to talk in daytime; and I could not have stood the excitement of that queer sense of whispering to myself. Now and then, glancing over my shoulder, I saw him far back there, sitting rigidly on the low stool, his bare feet close together, his arms folded, his head hanging on his breast—and perfectly still. Anybody would have taken him for me.

I was fascinated by it myself. Every moment I had to glance over my shoulder. I was looking at him when a voice outside the door said:

"Beg pardon, sir."

"Well!" . . . I kept my eyes on him, and so when the voice outside the door announced, "There's a ship's boat coming our way, sir," I saw him give a start—the first movement he had made for hours. But he did not raise his bowed head.

"All right. Get the ladder over."

I hesitated. Should I whisper something to him? But what? His immobility seemed to have been never disturbed. What could I tell him he did not know already? . . . Finally I went on deck.

II

The skipper of the *Sephora* had a thin red whisker all round his face, and the sort of complexion that goes with hair of that colour; also the particular, rather smeary shade of blue in the eyes. He was not exactly a showy figure; his shoulders were high, his stature but middling—one leg slightly more bandy[26] than the other. He shook hands, looking vaguely around. A spiritless tenacity was his main characteristic, I judged. I behaved with a politeness which seemed to disconcert him. Perhaps he was shy. He mumbled to me as if he were ashamed of what he was saying; gave his name (it was something like Archbold—but at this distance of years I hardly am sure), his ship's name, and a few other particulars of that sort, in the manner of a criminal making a reluctant and doleful confession. He had had terrible weather on the passage out—terrible—terrible—wife aboard, too.

By this time we were seated in the cabin and the steward brought in a tray with a bottle and glasses. "Thanks! No." Never took liquor. Would have some water, though. He drank two tumblerfuls. Terrible thirsty work. Ever since daylight had been exploring the islands round his ship.

"What was that for—fun?" I asked, with an appearance of polite interest.

"No!" He sighed. "Painful duty."

As he persisted in his mumbling and I wanted my double to hear every word, I hit upon the notion of informing him that I regretted to say I was hard of hearing.

"Such a young man, too!" he nodded, keeping his smeary blue, unintelligent eyes fastened upon me. What was the cause of it—some disease? he inquired,

[26] Bent.

without the least sympathy and as if he thought that, if so, I'd got no more than I deserved.

"Yes; disease," I admitted in a cheerful tone which seemed to shock him. But my point was gained, because he had to raise his voice to give me his tale. It is not worth while to record that version. It was just over two months since all this had happened, and he had thought so much about it that he seemed completely muddled as to its bearings, but still immensely impressed.

"What would you think of such a thing happening on board your own ship? I've had the *Sephora* for these fifteen years. I am a well-known shipmaster."

He was densely distressed—and perhaps I should have sympathized with him if I had been able to detach my mental vision from the unsuspected sharer of my cabin as though he were my second self. There he was on the other side of the bulkhead,[27] four or five feet from us, no more, as we sat in the saloon. I looked politely at Captain Archbold (if that was his name), but it was the other I saw; in a grey sleeping-suit, seated on a low stool, his bare feet close together, his arms folded, and every word said between us falling into the ears of his dark head bowed on his chest.

"I have been at sea now, man and boy, for seven-and-thirty years, and I've never heard of such a thing happening in an English ship. And that it should be my ship. Wife on board, too."

I was hardly listening to him.

"Don't you think," I said, "that the heavy sea which, you told me, came aboard just then might have killed the man? I have seen the sheer weight of a sea kill a man very neatly, by simply breaking his neck."

"Good God!" he uttered, impressively, fixing his smeary blue eyes on me. "The sea! No man killed by the sea ever looked like that." He seemed positively scandalized at my suggestion. And as I gazed at him, certainly not prepared for anything original on his part, he advanced his head close to mine and thrust his tongue out at me so suddenly that I couldn't help starting back.

After scoring over my calmness in this graphic way he nodded wisely. If I had seen the sight, he assured me, I would never forget it as long as I lived. The weather was too bad to give the corpse a proper sea burial. So next day at dawn they took it up on the poop, covering its face with a bit of bunting;[28] he read a short prayer, and then, just as it was, in its oilskins and long boots, they launched it amongst those mountainous seas that seemed ready every moment to swallow up the ship herself and the terrified lives on board of her.

"That reefed foresail saved you," I threw in.

"Under God—it did," he exclaimed fervently. "It was by a special mercy, I firmly believe, that it stood some of those hurricane squalls."

"It was the setting of that sail which——" I began.

"God's own hand in it," he interrupted me. "Nothing less could have done it. I don't mind telling you that I hardly dared give the order. It seemed impossible that we could touch anything without losing it, and then our last hope would have been gone."

The terror of that gale was on him yet. I let him go on for a bit, then said, casually—as if returning to a minor subject:

"You were very anxious to give up your mate to the shore people, I believe?"

He was. To the law. His obscure tenacity on that point had in it something

---

[27] A partition which divides a ship into compartments.
[28] Light cloth used for making flags.

incomprehensible and a little awful; something, as it were, mystical, quite apart from his anxiety that he should not be suspected of "countenancing any doings of that sort." Seven-and-thirty virtuous years at sea, of which over twenty of immaculate command, and the last fifteen in the *Sephora*, seemed to have laid him under some pitiless obligation.

"And you know," he went on, groping shamefacedly amongst his feelings, "I did not engage that young fellow. His people had some interest with my owners. I was in a way forced to take him on. He looked very smart, very gentlemanly, and all that. But do you know—I never liked him, somehow. I am a plain man. You see, he wasn't exactly the sort for the chief mate of a ship like the *Sephora*."

I had become so connected in thoughts and impressions with the secret sharer of my cabin that I felt as if I, personally, were being given to understand that I, too, was not the sort that would have done for the chief mate of a ship like the *Sephora*. I had no doubt of it in my mind.

"Not at all the syle of man. You understand," he insisted, superfluously, looking hard at me.

I smiled urbanely. He seemed at a loss for a while.

"I suppose I must report a suicide."

"Beg pardon?"

"Sui-cide! That's what I'll have to write to my owners directly I get in."

"Unless you manage to recover him before to-morrow," I assented, dispassionately. . . . "I mean, alive."

He mumbled something which I really did not catch, and I turned my ear to him in a puzzled manner. He fairly bawled:

"The land—I say, the mainland is at least seven miles off my anchorage."

"About that."

My lack of excitement, of curiosity, of surprise, of any sort of pronounced interest, began to arouse his distrust. But except for the felicitous pretence of deafness I had not tried to pretend anything. I had felt utterly incapable of playing the part of ignorance properly, and therefore was afraid to try. It is also certain that he had brought some ready-made suspicions with him, and that he viewed my politeness as a strange and unnatural phenomenon. And yet how else could I have received him? Not heartily! That was impossible for psychological reasons, which I need not state here. My only object was to keep off his inquiries. Surlily? Yes, but surliness might have provoked a point-blank question. From its novelty to him and from its nature, punctilious courtesy was the manner best calculated to restrain the man. But there was the danger of his breaking through my defense bluntly. I could not, I think, have met him by a direct lie, also for psychological (not moral) reasons. If he had only known how afraid I was of his putting my feeling of identity with the other to the test! But, strangely enough—(I thought of it only afterwards)—I believe that he was not a little disconcerted by the reverse side of that weird situation, by something in me that reminded him of the man he was seeking—suggested a mysterious similitude to the young fellow he had distrusted and disliked from the first.

However that might have been, the silence was not very prolonged. He took another oblique step.

"I reckon I had no more than a two-mile pull to your ship. Not a bit more."

"And quite enough, too, in this awful heat," I said.

Another pause full of mistrust followed. Necessity, they say, is mother of invention, but fear, too, is not barren of ingenious suggestions. And I was afraid he would ask me point-blank for news of my other self.

"Nice little saloon, isn't it?" I remarked, as if noticing for the first time the way his eyes roamed from one closed door to the other. "And very well fitted out, too. Here, for instance," I continued, reaching over the back of my seat negligently and flinging the door open, "is my bath-room."

He made an eager movement, but hardly gave it a glance. I got up, shut the door of the bath-room, and invited him to have a look round, as if I were very proud of my accommodation. He had to rise and be shown round, but he went through the business without any raptures whatever.

"And now we'll have a look at my stateroom," I declared, in a voice as loud as I dared to make it, crossing the cabin to the starboard[29] side with purposely heavy steps.

He followed me in and gazed around. My intelligent double had vanished. I played my part.

"Very convenient—isn't it?"

"Very nice. Very comf . . ." He didn't finish and went out brusquely as if to escape from some unrighteous wiles of mine. But it was not to be. I had been too frightened not to feel vengeful; I felt I had him on the run, and I meant to keep him on the run. My polite insistence must have had something menacing in it, because he gave in suddenly. And I did not let him off a single item; mate's room, pantry, storerooms, the very sail-locker which was also under the poop—he had to look into them all. When at last I showed him out on the quarter-deck he drew a long, spiritless sigh, and mumbled dismally that he must really be going back to his ship now. I desired my mate, who had joined us, to see to the captain's boat.

The man of whiskers gave a blast on the whistle which he used to wear hanging round his neck, and yelled, "*Sephora*'s away!" My double down there in my cabin must have heard, and certainly could not feel more relieved than I. Four fellows came running out from somewhere forward and went over the side, while my own men, appearing on deck too, lined the rail. I escorted my visitor to the gangway ceremoniously, and nearly overdid it. He was a tenacious beast. On the very ladder he lingered, and in that unique, guiltily conscientious manner of sticking to the point:

"I say . . . you . . . you don't think that—"

I covered his voice loudly:

"Certainly not. . . . I am delighted. Good-bye."

I had an idea of what he meant to say, and just saved myself by the privilege of defective hearing. He was too shaken generally to insist, but my mate, close witness of that parting, looked mystified and his face took on a thoughtful cast. As I did not want to appear as if I wished to avoid all communication with my officers, he had the opportunity to address me.

"Seems a very nice man. His boat's crew told our chaps a very extraordinary story, if what I am told by the steward is true. I suppose you had it from the captain, sir?"

"Yes. I had a story from the captain."

"A very horrible affair—isn't it, sir?"

"It is."

"Beats all these tales we hear about murders in Yankee ships."

"I don't think it beats them. I don't think it resembles them in the least."

"Bless my soul—you don't say so! But of course I've no acquaintance whatever with American ships, not I, so I couldn't go against your knowledge. It's horrible

---

[29] Right hand.

enough for me. . . . But the queerest part is that those fellows seemed to have some idea the man was hidden aboard here. They had really. Did you ever hear of such a thing?''

"Preposterous—isn't it?"

We were walking to and fro athwart the quarter-deck. No one of the crew forward could be seen (the day was Sunday), and the mate pursued:

"There was some little dispute about it. Our chaps took offence. 'As if we would harbor a thing like that,' they said. 'Wouldn't you like to look for him in our coalhole?' Quite a tiff. But they made it up in the end. I suppose he did drown himself. Don't you, sir?''

"I don't suppose anything."

"You have no doubt in the matter, sir?"

"None whatever."

I left him suddenly. I felt I was producing a bad impression, but with my double down there it was most trying to be on deck. And it was almost as trying to be below. Altogether a nerve-trying situation. But on the whole I felt less torn in two when I was with him. There was no one in the whole ship whom I dared take into my confidence. Since the hands had got to know his story, it would have been impossible to pass him off for any one else, and an accidental discovery was to be dreaded now more than ever. . . .

The steward being engaged in laying the table for dinner, we could talk only with our eyes when I first went down. Later in the afternoon we had a cautious try at whispering. The Sunday quietness of the ship was against us; the stillness of air and water around her was against us; the elements, the men were against us— everything was against us in our secret partnership; time itself—for this could not go on forever. The very trust in Providence was, I suppose, denied to his guilt. Shall I confess that this thought cast me down very much? And as to the chapter of accidents which counts for so much in the book of success, I could only hope that it was closed. For what favorable accident could be expected?

"Did you hear everything?'' were my first words as soon as we took up our position side by side, leaning over my bed-place.

He had. And the proof of it was his earnest whisper, "The man told you he hardly dared to give the order."

I understood the reference to be to that saving foresail.

"Yes. He was afraid of it being lost in the setting."

"I assure you he never gave the order. He may think he did, but he never gave it. He stood there with me on the break[30] of the poop after the maintopsail blew away, and whimpered about our last hope—positively whimpered about it and nothing else—and the night coming on! To hear one's skipper go on like that in such weather was enough to drive any fellow out of his mind. It worked me up into a sort of desperation. I just took it into my own hands and went away from him, boiling, and——But what's the use telling you? *You* know! . . . Do you think that if I had not been pretty fierce with them I should have got the men to do any-thing? Not it! The bo's'n[31] perhaps? Perhaps! It wasn't a heavy sea—it was a sea gone mad! I suppose the end of the world will be something like that; and a man may have the heart to see it coming once and be done with it—but to have to face it day after day——I don't blame anybody. I was precious little better than the rest. Only—I was an officer of that old coal-wagon, anyhow——''

[30] Elevated section.

[31] Bosun (boatswain): the officer in charge of the ship's deck crew, rigging, and anchors.

"I quite understand," I conveyed that sincere assurance into his ear. He was out of breath with whispering; I could hear him pant slightly. It was all very simple. The same strung-up force which had given twenty-four men a chance, at least, for their lives, had, in a sort of recoil, crushed an unworthy mutinous existence.

But I had no leisure to weigh the merits of the matter—footsteps in the saloon, a heavy knock. "There's enough wind to get under way with, sir." Here was the call of a new claim upon my thoughts and even upon my feelings.

"Turn the hands up," I cried through the door. "I'll be on deck directly."

I was going out to make the acquaintance of my ship. Before I left the cabin our eyes met—the eyes of the only two strangers on board. I pointed to the recessed part where the little camp-stool awaited him and laid my finger on my lips. He made a gesture—somewhat vague—a little mysterious, accompanied by a faint smile, as if of regret.

This is not the place to enlarge upon the sensations of a man who feels for the first time a ship move under his feet to his own independent word. In my case they were not unalloyed. I was not wholly alone with my command; for there was that stranger in my cabin. Or rather, I was not completely and wholly with her. Part of me was absent. That mental feeling of being in two places at once affected me physically as if the mood of secrecy had penetrated my very soul. Before an hour had elapsed since the ship had begun to move, having occasion to ask the mate (he stood by my side) to take a compass bearing of the Pagoda, I caught myself reaching up to his ear in whispers. I say I caught myself, but enough had escaped to startle the man. I can't describe it otherwise than by saying that he shied. A grave, preoccupied manner, as though he were in possession of some perplexing intelligence, did not leave him henceforth. A little later I moved away from the rail to look at the compass with such a stealthy gait that the helmsman noticed it—and I could not help noticing the unusual roundness of his eyes. These are trifling instances, though it's to no commander's advantage to be suspected of ludicrous eccentricities. But I was also more seriously affected. There are to a seaman certain words, gestures, that should in given conditions come as naturally, as instinctively as the winking of a menaced eye. A certain order should spring on to his lips without thinking; a certain sign should get itself made, so to speak, without reflection. But all unconscious alertness had abandoned me. I had to make an effort of will to recall myself back (from the cabin) to the conditions of the moment. I felt that I was appearing an irresolute commander to those people who were watching me more or less critically.

And, besides, there were the scares. On the second day out, for instance, coming off the deck in the afternoon (I had straw slippers on my bare feet) I stopped at the open pantry door and spoke to the steward. He was doing something there with his back to me. At the sound of my voice he nearly jumped out of his skin, as the saying is, and incidentally broke a cup.

"What on earth's the matter with you?" I asked, astonished.

He was extremely confused. "Beg your pardon, sir. I made sure you were in your cabin."

"You see I wasn't."

"No, sir. I could have sworn I had heard you moving in there not a moment ago. It's most extraordinary . . . very sorry, sir."

I passed on with an inward shudder. I was so identified with my secret double that I did not even mention the fact in those scanty, fearful whispers we exchanged. I suppose he had made some slight noise of some kind or other. It would have been miraculous if he hadn't at one time or another. And yet, haggard as he appeared, he looked always perfectly self-controlled, more than calm—almost invulnerable. On my suggestion he remained almost entirely in the bath-room, which, upon the whole, was the safest place. There could be really no shadow of an excuse for any one ever wanting to go in there, once the steward had done with it. It was a very tiny place. Sometimes he reclined on the floor, his legs bent, his head sustained on one elbow. At others I would find him on the camp-stool, sitting in his grey sleeping-suit and with his cropped dark hair like a patient, unmoved convict. At night I would smuggle him into my bed-place, and we would whisper together, with the regular footfalls of the officer of the watch passing and repassing over our heads. It was an infinitely miserable time. It was lucky that some tins of fine preserves were stowed in a locker in my stateroom; hard bread I could always get hold of; and so he lived on stewed chicken, paté de foie gras,[32] asparagus, cooked oysters, sardines—on all sorts of abominable sham delicacies out of tins. My early morning coffee he always drank; and it was all I dared do for him in that respect.

Every day there was the horrible maneuvering to go through so that my room and then the bath-room should be done in the usual way. I came to hate the sight of the steward, to abhor the voice of that harmless man. I felt that it was he who would bring on the disaster of discovery. It hung like a sword over our heads.

The fourth day out, I think (we were then working down the east side of the Gulf of Siam, tack for tack,[33] in light winds and smooth water)—the fourth day, I say, of this miserable juggling with the unavoidable, as we sat at our evening meal, that man, whose slightest movement I dreaded, after putting down the dishes ran up on deck busily. This could not be dangerous. Presently he came down again; and then it appeared that he remembered a coat of mine which I had thrown over a rail to dry after having been wetted in a shower which had passed over the ship in the afternoon. Sitting stolidly at the head of the table I became terrified at the sight of the garment on his arm. Of course he made for my door. There was no time to lose.

"Steward," I thundered. My nerves were so shaken that I could not govern my voice and conceal my agitation. This was the sort of thing that made my terrifically whiskered mate tap his forehead with his forefinger. I had detected him using that gesture while talking on deck with a confidential air to the carpenter. It was too far to hear a word, but I had no doubt that this pantomime could only refer to the strange new captain.

"Yes, sir," the pale-faced steward turned resignedly to me. It was this maddening course of being shouted at, checked without rhyme or reason, arbitrarily chased out of my cabin, suddenly called into it, sent flying out of his pantry on incomprehensible errands, that accounted for the growing wretchedness of his expression.

"Where are you going with that coat?"

"To your room, sir."

"Is there another shower coming?"

"I'm sure I don't know, sir. Shall I go up again and see, sir?"

"No! never mind."

My object was attained, as of course my other self in there would have heard everything that passed. During this interlude my two officers never raised their

---

[32] Paste made of goose liver.

[33] A series of sailing maneuvers.

eyes off their respective plates; but the lip of that confounded cub, the second mate, quivered visibly.

I expected the steward to hook my coat on and come out at once. He was very slow about it; but I dominated my nervousness sufficiently not to shout after him. Suddenly I became aware (it could be heard plainly enough) that the fellow for some reason or other was opening the door of the bath-room. It was the end. The place was literally not big enough to swing a cat[34] in. My voice died in my throat and I went stony all over. I expected to hear a yell of surprise and terror, and made a movement, but had not the strength to get on my legs. Everything remained still. Had my second self taken the poor wretch by the throat? I don't know what I could have done next moment if I had not seen the steward come out of my room, close the door, and then stand quietly by the sideboard.

"Saved," I thought. "But, no! Lost! Gone! He was gone!"

I laid my knife and fork down and leaned back in my chair. My head swam. After a while, when sufficiently recovered to speak in a steady voice, I instructed my mate to put the ship round at eight o'clock himself.

"I won't come on deck," I went on. "I think I'll turn in, and unless the wind shifts I don't want to be disturbed before midnight. I feel a bit seedy."

"You did look middling bad a little while ago," the chief mate remarked without showing any great concern.

They both went out, and I stared at the steward clearing the table. There was nothing to be read on that wretched man's face. But why did he avoid my eyes I asked myself. Then I thought I should like to hear the sound of his voice.

"Steward!"

"Sir!" Startled as usual.

"Where did you hang up that coat?"

"In the bath-room, sir." The usual anxious tone. "It's not quite dry yet, sir."

For some time longer I sat in the cuddy. Had my double vanished as he had come? But of his coming there was an explanation, whereas his disappearance would be inexplicable. . . . I went slowly into my dark room, shut the door, lighted the lamp, and for a time dared not turn round. When at last I did I saw him standing bolt-upright in the narrow recessed part. It would not be true to say I had a shock, but an irresistible doubt of his bodily existence flitted through my mind. Can it be, I asked myself, that he is not visible to other eyes than mine? It was like being haunted. Motionless, with a grave face, he raised his hands slightly at me in a gesture which meant clearly, "Heavens! what a narrow escape!" Narrow indeed. I think I had come creeping quietly as near insanity as any man who has not actually gone over the border. That gesture restrained me, so to speak.

The mate with the terrific whiskers was now putting the ship on the other tack. In the moment of profound silence which follows upon the hands going to their stations I heard on the poop his raised voice: "Hard alee!"[35] and the distant shout of the order repeated on the maindeck. The sails, in that light breeze, made but a faint fluttering noise. It ceased. The ship was coming round slowly; I held my breath in the renewed stillness of expectation; one wouldn't have thought that there was a single living soul on her decks. A sudden brisk shout, "Mainsail haul!" broke the spell, and in the noisy cries and rush overhead of the men running away with the main-brace we two, down in my cabin, came together in our usual position by the bed-place.

---

[34] Cat-o-nine-tails: a short whip made of knotted chords fastened to a handle, used in discipline.
[35] Push hard on the tiller in order to turn the ship in the direction in which the wind is blowing.

He did not wait for my question. "I heard him fumbling here and just managed to squat myself down in the bath," he whispered to me. "The fellow only opened the door and put his arm in to hang the coat up. All the same———"

"I never thought of that," I whispered back, even more appalled than before at the closeness of the shave, and marvelling at that something unyielding in his character which was carrying him through so finely. There was no agitation in his whisper. Whoever was being driven distracted, it was not he. He was sane. And the proof of his sanity was continued when he took up the whispering again.

"It would never do for me to come to life again."

It was something that a ghost might have said. But what he was alluding to was his old captain's reluctant admission of the theory of suicide. It would obviously serve his turn—if I had understood at all the view which seemed to govern the unalterable purpose of his action.

"You must maroon me as soon as ever you can get amongst these islands off the Cambodje[36] shore," he went on.

"Maroon you! We are not living in a boy's adventure tale," I protested. His scornful whispering took me up.

"We aren't indeed! There's nothing of a boy's tale in this. But there's nothing else for it. I want no more. You don't suppose I am afraid of what can be done to me? Prison or gallows or whatever they may please. But you don't see me coming back to explain such things to an old fellow in a wig and twelve respectable tradesmen, do you? What can they know whether I am guilty or not—or of *what* I am guilty, either? That's my affair. What does the Bible say? 'Driven off the face of the earth.'[37] Very well. I am off the face of the earth now. As I came at night so I shall go."

"Impossible!" I murmured. "You can't."

"Can't? . . . Not naked like a soul on the Day of Judgment. I shall freeze on to this sleeping-suit. The Last Day is not yet—and . . . you have understood thoroughly. Didn't you?"

I felt suddenly ashamed of myself. I may say truly that I understood—and my hesitation in letting that man swim away from my ship's side had been a mere sham sentiment, a sort of cowardice.

"It can't be done now till next night," I breathed out. "The ship is on the offshore tack and the wind may fail us."

"As long as I know that you understand," he whispered. "But of course you do. It's a great satisfaction to have got somebody to understand. You seem to have been there on purpose." And in the same whisper, as if we two whenever we talked had to say things to each other which were not fit for the world to hear, he added, "It's very wonderful."

We remained side by side talking in our secret way—but sometimes silent or just exchanging a whispered word or two at long intervals. And as usual he stared through the port. A breath of wind came now and again into our faces. The ship might have been moored in dock, so gently and on an even keel she slipped through the water, that did not murmur even at our passage, shadowy and silent like a phantom sea.

At midnight I went on deck, and to my mate's great surprise put the ship round on the other tack. His terrible whiskers flitted round me in silent criticism. I certainly should not have done it if it had been only a question of getting out of

---

[36] Cambodian.

[37] Another allusion to the biblical story of Cain. The line quoted is from Genesis 4:14 (see note 22).

that sleepy gulf as quickly as possible. I believe he told the second mate, who relieved him, that it was a great want of judgment. The other only yawned. That intolerable cub shuffled about so sleepily and lolled against the rails in such a slack, improper fashion that I came down on him sharply.

"Aren't you properly awake yet?"

"Yes, sir! I am awake."

"Well, then, be good enough to hold yourself as if you were. And keep a lookout. If there's any current we'll be closing with some islands before daylight."

The east side of the gulf is fringed with islands, some solitary, others in groups. On the blue background of the high coast they seem to float on silvery patches of calm water, arid and grey, or dark green and rounded like clumps of evergreen bushes, with the larger ones, a mile or two long, showing the outlines of ridges, ribs of grey rock under the dank mantle of matted leafage. Unknown to trade, to travel, almost to geography, the manner of life they harbor is an unsolved secret. There must be villages—settlements of fishermen at least—on the largest of them, and some communication with the world is probably kept up by native craft.

But all that forenoon, as we headed for them, fanned along by the faintest of breezes, I saw no sign of man or canoe in the field of the telescope I kept on pointing at the scattered group.

At noon I gave no orders for a change of course, and the mate's whiskers became much concerned and seemed to be offering themselves unduly to my notice. At last I said:

"I am going to stand right in. Quite in—as far as I can take her."

The stare of extreme surprise imparted an air of ferocity also to his eyes, and he looked truly terrific for a moment.

"We're not doing well in the middle of the gulf," I continued, casually. "I am going to look for the land breezes tonight."

"Bless my soul! Do you mean, sir, in the dark amongst the lot of all them islands and reefs and shoals?"

"Well—if there are any regular land breezes at all on this coast one must get close inshore to find them, mustn't one?"

"Bless my soul!" he exclaimed again under his breath. All that afternoon he wore a dreamy, contemplative appearance which in him was a mark of perplexity. After dinner I went into my stateroom as if I meant to take some rest. There we two bent our dark heads over a half-unrolled chart lying on my bed.

"There," I said. "It's got to be Koh-ring.[38] I've been looking at it ever since sunrise. It has got two hills and a low point. It must be inhabited. And on the coast opposite there is what looks like the mouth of a biggish river—with some town, no doubt, not far up. It's the best chance for you that I can see."

"Anything. Koh-ring let it be."

He looked thoughtfully at the chart as if surveying chances and distances from a lofty height—and following with his eyes his own figure wandering on the blank land of Cochin-China,[39] and then passing off that piece of paper clean out of sight into uncharted regions. And it was as if the ship had two captains to plan her course for her. I had been so worried and restless running up and down that I had not had the patience to dress that day. I had remained in my sleeping-suit, with straw slippers and a soft floppy hat. The closeness of the heat in the gulf had been

[38] Koh means island, though no island of this name can be identified at the head of the Gulf of Siam (or Gulf of Thailand as it is now known).

[39] French Indochina (now Vietnam) lying between the Gulf of Siam and the South China Sea.

most oppressive, and the crew were used to see me wandering in that airy attire.

"She will clear the south point as she heads now," I whispered into his ear. "Goodness only knows when, though, but certainly after dark. I'll edge her in to half a mile, as far as I may be able to judge in the dark——"

"Be careful," he murmured, warningly—and I realized suddenly that all my future, the only future for which I was fit, would perhaps go irretrievably to pieces in any mishap to my first command.

I could not stop a moment longer in the room. I motioned him to get out of sight and made my way on the poop. That unplayful cub had the watch. I walked up and down for a while thinking things out, then beckoned him over.

"Send a couple of hands to open the two quarter-deck ports," I said, mildly.

He actually had the impudence, or else so forgot himself in his wonder at such an incomprehensible order, as to repeat:

"Open the quarter-deck ports! What for, sir?"

"The only reason you need concern yourself about is because I tell you to do so. Have them open wide and fastened properly."

He reddened and went off, but I believe made some jeering remark to the carpenter as to the sensible practice of ventilating a ship's quarter-deck. I know he popped into the mate's cabin to impart the fact to him because the whiskers came on deck, as it were by chance, and stole glances at me from below—for signs of lunacy or drunkenness, I suppose.

A little before supper, feeling more restless than ever, I rejoined, for a moment, my second self. And to find him sitting so quietly was surprising, like something against nature, inhuman.

I developed my plan in a hurried whisper.

"I shall stand in as close as I dare and then put her round. I will presently find means to smuggle you out of here into the sail-locker, which communicates with the lobby. But there is an opening, a sort of square for hauling the sails out, which gives straight on the quarter-deck and which is never closed in fine weather, so as to give air to the sails. When the ship's way is deadened in stays[40] and all the hands are aft at the main-braces you will have a clear road to slip out and get overboard through the open quarter-deck port. I've had them both fastened up. Use a rope's end to lower yourself into the water so as to avoid a splash—you know. It could be heard and cause some beastly complication."

He kept silent for a while, then whispered, "I understand."

"I won't be there to see you go," I began with an effort. "The rest . . . I only hope I have understood, too."

"You have. From first to last"—and for the first time there seemed to be a faltering, something strained in his whisper. He caught hold of my arm, but the ringing of the supper bell made me start. He didn't, though; he only released his grip.

After supper I didn't come below again till well past eight o'clock. The faint, steady breeze was loaded with dew; and the wet, darkened sails held all there was of propelling power in it. The night, clear and starry, sparkled darkly, and the opaque, lightless patches shifting slowly against the low stars were the drifting islets. On the port bow there was a big one more distant and shadowily imposing by the great space of sky it eclipsed.

On opening the door I had a back view of my very own self looking at a chart. He had come out of the recess and was standing near the table.

---

[40] Slow down or come to a halt.

"Quite dark enough," I whispered.

He stepped back and leaned against my bed with a level, quiet glance. I sat on the couch. We had nothing to say to each other. Over our heads the officer of the watch moved here and there. Then I heard him move quickly. I knew what that meant. He was making for the companion; and presently his voice was outside my door.

"We are drawing in pretty fast, sir. Land looks rather close."

"Very well," I answered. "I am coming on deck directly."

I waited till he was gone out of the cuddy, then rose. My double moved too. The time had come to exchange our last whispers, for neither of us was ever to hear each other's natural voice.

"Look here!" I opened a drawer and took out three sovereigns.[41] "Take this anyhow. I've got six and I'd give you the lot, only I must keep a little money to buy some fruit and vegetables for the crew from native boats as we go through Sunda Straits."

He shook his head.

"Take it," I urged him, whispering desperately. "No one can tell what——"

He smiled and slapped meaningly the only pocket of the sleeping-jacket. It was not safe, certainly. But I produced a large old silk handkerchief of mine, and tying the three pieces of gold in a corner, pressed it on him. He was touched, I suppose, because he took it at last and tied it quickly round his waist under the jacket, on his bare skin.

Our eyes met; several seconds elapsed, till, our glances still mingled, I extended my hand and turned the lamp out. Then I passed through the cuddy, leaving the door of my room wide open. . . . "Steward!"

He was still lingering in the pantry in the greatness of his zeal, giving a rub-up to a plated cruet stand the last thing before going to bed. Being careful not to wake up the mate, whose room was opposite, I spoke in an undertone.

He looked round anxiously. "Sir!"

"Can you get me a little hot water from the galley?"

"I am afraid, sir, the galley fire's been out for some time now."

"Go and see."

He flew up the stairs.

"Now," I whispered, loudly, into the saloon—too loudly, perhaps, but I was afraid I couldn't make a sound. He was by my side in an instant—the double captain slipped past the stairs—through a tiny dark passage . . . a sliding door. We were in the sail-locker, scrambling on our knees over the sails. A sudden thought struck me. I saw myself wandering bare-footed, bareheaded, the sun beating on my dark poll. I snatched off my floppy hat and tried hurriedly in the dark to ram it on my other self. He dodged and fended off silently. I wonder what he thought had come to me before he understood and suddenly desisted. Our hands met gropingly, lingered united in a steady, motionless clasp for a second. . . . No word was breathed by either of us when they separated.

I was standing quietly by the pantry door when the steward returned.

"Sorry, sir. Kettle barely warm. Shall I light the spirit-lamp?"[42]

"Never mind."

I came out on deck slowly. It was now a matter of conscience to shave the land as close as possible—for now he must go overboard whenever the ship was put in

[41] English gold coins worth a pound.
[42] A lamp which burns a liquid fuel used for heating.

stays. Must! There could be no going back for him. After a moment I walked over to leeward and my heart flew into my mouth at the nearness of the land on the bow. Under any other circumstances I would not have held on a minute longer. The second mate had followed me anxiously.

I looked on till I felt I could command my voice.

"She may weather,"[43] I said then in a quiet tone.

"Are you going to try that, sir?" he stammered out incredulously.

I took no notice of him and raised my tone just enough to be heard by the helmsman.

"Keep her good full."[44]

"Good full, sir."

The wind fanned my cheek, the sails slept, the world was silent. The strain of watching the dark loom of the land grow bigger and denser was too much for me. I had shut my eyes—because the ship must go closer. She must! The stillness was intolerable. Were we standing still?

When I opened my eyes the second view started my heart with a thump. The black southern hill of Koh-ring seemed to hang right over the ship like a towering fragment of the everlasting night. On that enormous mass of blackness there was not a gleam to be seen, not a sound to be heard. It was gliding irresistibly towards us and yet seemed already within reach of the hand. I saw the vague figures of the watch grouped in the waist, gazing in awed silence.

"Are you going on, sir?" inquired an unsteady voice at my elbow.

I ignored it. I had to go on.

"Keep her full. Don't check her way. That won't do now," I said, warningly.

"I can't see the sails very well," the helmsman answered me, in strange, quavering tones.

Was she close enough? Already she was, I won't say in the shadow of the land, but in the very blackness of it, already swallowed up as it were, gone too close to be recalled, gone from me altogether.

"Give the mate a call," I said to the young man who stood at my elbow as still as death. "And turn all hands up."

My tone had a borrowed loudness reverberated from the height of the land. Several voices cried out together: "We are all on deck, sir."

Then stillness again, with the great shadow gliding closer, towering higher, without a light, without a sound. Such a hush had fallen on the ship that she might have been a bark of the dead floating in slowly under the very gate of Erebus.[45]

"My God! Where are we?"

It was the mate moaning at my elbow. He was thunderstruck, and as it were deprived of the moral support of his whiskers. He clapped his hands and absolutely cried out, "Lost!"

"Be quiet," I said, sternly.

He lowered his tone, but I saw the shadowy gesture of his despair. "What are we doing here?"

"Looking for the land wind."

He made as if to tear his hair, and addressed me recklessly.

"She will never get out. You have done it, sir. I knew it'd end in something like

---

[43] Pass safely.
[44] Keep the sails filled with wind.
[45] In Greek mythology the dark region through which dead souls must pass on their way to Hades.

this. She will never weather, and you are too close now to stay. She'll drift ashore before she's round. O my God!''

I caught his arm as he was raising it to batter his poor devoted head, and shook it violently.

"She's ashore already," he wailed, trying to tear himself away.

"Is she? . . . Keep good full there!"

"Good full, sir," cried the helmsman in a frightened, thin, child-like voice.

I hadn't let go the mate's arm and went on shaking it. "Ready about,[46] do you hear? You go forward"—shake—"and stop there"—shake—"and hold your noise"—shake—"and see these headsheets properly overhauled"—shake, shake—shake.

And all the time I dared not look towards the land lest my heart should fail me. I released my grip at last and he ran forward as if fleeing for dear life.

I wondered what my double there in the sail-locker thought of this commotion. He was able to hear everything—and perhaps he was able to understand why, on my conscience, it had to be thus close—no less. My first order "Hard alee!" re-echoed ominously under the towering shadow of Koh-ring as if I had shouted in a mountain gorge. And then I watched the land intently. In that smooth water and light wind it was impossible to feel the ship coming-to.[47] No! I could not feel her. And my second self was making now ready to slip out and lower himself overboard. Perhaps he was gone already . . . ?

The great black mass brooding over our very mastheads began to pivot away from the ship's side silently. And now I forgot the secret stranger ready to depart, and remembered only that I was a total stranger to the ship. I did not know her. Would she do it? How was she to be handled?

I swung the mainyard and waited helplessly. She was perhaps stopped, and her very fate hung in the balance, with the black mass of Koh-ring like the gate of the everlasting night towering over her taffrail. What would she do now? Had she way on her yet? I stepped to the side swiftly, and on the shadowy water I could see nothing except a faint phosphorescent flash revealing the glassy smoothness of the sleeping surface. It was impossible to tell—and I had not learned yet the feel of my ship. Was she moving? What I needed was something easily seen, a piece of paper, which I could throw overboard and watch. I had nothing on me. To run down for it I didn't dare. There was no time. All at once my strained, yearning stare distinguished a white object floating within a yard of the ship's side. White on the black water. A phosphorescent flash passed under it. What was that thing? . . . I recognized my own floppy hat. It must have fallen off his head . . . and he didn't bother. Now I had what I wanted—the saving mark for my eyes. But I hardly thought of my other self, now gone from the ship, to be hidden for ever from all friendly faces, to be a fugitive and a vagabond on the earth, with no brand of the curse on his sane forehead to stay a slaying hand . . . too proud to explain.

And I watched the hat—the expression of my sudden pity for his mere flesh. It had been meant to save his homeless head from the dangers of the sun. And now—behold—it was saving the ship, by serving me for a mark to help out the ignorance of my strangeness. Ha! It was drifting forward, warning me just in time that the ship had gathered sternway.

"Shift the helm," I said in a low voice to the seaman standing still like a statue.

---

[46] Be prepared to shift the sails (to tack).
[47] Coming to a halt.

The man's eyes glistened wildly in the binnacle light[48] as he jumped round to the other side and spun round the wheel.

I walked to the break of the poop. On the overshadowed deck all hands stood by the forebraces waiting for my order. The stars ahead seemed to be gliding from right to left. And all was so still in the world that I heard the quiet remark "She's round," passed in a tone of intense relief between two seamen.

"Let go and haul."

The foreyards ran round with a great noise, amidst cheery cries. And now the frightful whiskers made themselves heard giving various orders. Already the ship was drawing ahead. And I was alone with her. Nothing! no one in the world should stand now between us, throwing a shadow on the way of silent knowledge and mute affection, the perfect communion of a seaman with his first command.

Walking to the taffrail,[49] I was in time to make out, on the very edge of a darkness thrown by a towering black mass like the very gateway of Erebus—yes, I was in time to catch an evanescent glimpse of my white hat left behind to mark the spot where the secret sharer of my cabin and of my thoughts, as though he were my second self, had lowered himself into the water to take his punishment: a free man, a proud swimmer striking out for a new destiny.

[1910]

---

[48] A light over the ship's compass.
[49] The rail around the ship's stern.

James Joyce *1882–1941*

ARABY

North Richmond Street, being blind, was a quiet street except at the hour when the Christian Brothers' School[1] set the boys free. An uninhabited house of two storeys stood at the blind end, detached from its neighbours in a square ground. The other houses of the street, conscious of decent lives within them, gazed at one another with brown imperturbable faces.

The former tenant of our house, a priest, had died in the back drawing-room. Air, musty from having been long enclosed, hung in all the rooms, and the waste room behind the kitchen was littered with old useless papers. Among these I found a few paper-covered books, the pages of which were curled and damp: *The Abbot*, by Walter Scott, *The Devout Communicant* and *The Memoirs of Vidocq*.[2] I liked the last best because its leaves were yellow. The wild garden behind the house contained a central apple-tree and a few straggling bushes under one of which I found the late tenant's rusty bicycle-pump. He had been a very charitable priest; in his will he had left all his money to institutions and the furniture of his house to his sister.

When the short days of winter came dusk fell before we had well eaten our dinners. When we met in the street the houses had grown sombre. The space of sky above us was the colour of ever-changing violet and towards it the lamps of the street lifted their feeble lanterns. The cold air stung us and we played till our bodies glowed. Our shouts echoed in the silent street. The career of our play brought us through the dark muddy lanes behind the houses where we ran the gauntlet of the rough tribes from the cottages, to the back doors of the dark dripping gardens where odours arose from the ashpits, to the dark odorous stables where a coachman smoothed and combed the horse or shook music from the buckled harness. When we returned to the street light from the kitchen windows had filled the areas. If my uncle was seen turning the corner we hid in the shadow until we had seen him safely housed. Or if Mangan's sister came out on the doorstep to call her brother in to his tea we watched her from our shadow peer up and down the street. We waited to see whether she would remain or go in and, if she remained, we left our shadow and walked up to Mangan's steps resignedly. She was waiting for us, her figure defined by the light from the half-opened door. Her brother always teased her before he obeyed and I stood by the railings looking at her. Her dress swung as she moved her body and the soft rope of her hair tossed from side to side.

Every morning I lay on the floor in the front parlour watching her door. The blind was pulled down to within an inch of the sash so that I could not be seen. When she came out on the doorstep my heart leaped. I ran to the hall, seized my books and followed her. I kept her brown figure always in my eye and, when we came near the point at which our ways diverged, I quickened my pace and passed her. This happened morning after morning. I had never spoken to her,

[1] A famous Catholic day school in Dublin.
[2] *The Abbot* (1820) by Sir Walter Scott (1771–1832) is an historical romance about Mary Queen of Scots; *The Devout Communicant* (1813) is a Catholic guide to "pious meditations" by Friar Pacificus Baker (1695–1774); *The Memoirs of Vidocq* (1829) traces the career of François-Jules Vidocq (1775–1857), a French criminal-turned-detective.

except for a few casual words, and yet her name was like a summons to all my foolish blood.

Her image accompanied me even in places the most hostile to romance. On Saturday evenings when my aunt went marketing I had to go to carry some of the parcels. We walked through the flaring streets, jostled by drunken men and bargaining women, amid the curses of labourers, the shrill litanies of shop-boys who stood on guard by the barrels of pigs' cheeks, the nasal chanting of street-singers, who sang a *come-all-you*[3] about O'Donovan Rossa,[4] or a ballad about the troubles in our native land. These noises converged in a single sensation of life for me: I imagined that I bore my chalice safely through a throng of foes. Her name sprang to my lips at moments in strange prayers and praises which I myself did not understand. My eyes were often full of tears (I could not tell why) and at times a flood from my heart seemed to pour itself out into my bosom. I thought little of the future. I did not know whether I would ever speak to her or not or, if I spoke to her, how I could tell her of my confused adoration. But my body was like a harp and her words and gestures were like fingers running upon the wires.

One evening I went into the back drawing-room in which the priest had died. It was a dark rainy evening and there was no sound in the house. Through one of the broken panes I heard the rain impinge upon the earth, the fine incessant needles of water playing in the sodden beds. Some distant lamp or lighted window gleamed below me. I was thankful that I could see so little. All my senses seemed to desire to veil themselves and, feeling that I was about to slip from them, I pressed the palms of my hands together until they trembled, murmuring: *"O love! O love!"* many times.

At last she spoke to me. When she addressed the first words to me I was so confused that I did not know what to answer. She asked me was I going to *Araby*. I forgot whether I answered yes or no. It would be a splendid bazaar, she said she would love to go.

"And why can't you?" I asked.

While she spoke she turned a silver bracelet round and round her wrist. She could not go, she said, because there would be a retreat that week in her convent. Her brother and two other boys were fighting for their caps and I was alone at the railings. She held one of the spikes, bowing her head towards me. The light from the lamp opposite our door caught the white curve of her neck, lit up her hair that rested there and, falling, lit up the hand upon the railing. It fell over one side of her dress and caught the white border of a petticoat, just visible as she stood at ease.

"It's well for you," she said.

"If I go," I said, "I will bring you something."

What innumerable follies laid waste my waking and sleeping thoughts after that evening! I wished to annihilate the tedious intervening days. I chafed against the work of school. At night in my bedroom and by day in the classroom her image came between me and the page I strove to read. The syllables of the word *Araby* were called to me through the silence in which my soul luxuriated and cast an Eastern enchantment over me. I asked for leave to go to the bazaar on Saturday night. My aunt was surprised and hoped it was not some Freemason[5] affair. I

---

[3] One of any number of popular street songs on a topical subject beginning "Come all you . . . ."
[4] Refers to Jeremiah O'Donovan (1831–1915), a leader in Ireland's struggle for independence, whose activities earned him the nickname "Dynamite Rossa."
[5] A Protestant fraternal organization.

answered few questions in class. I watched my master's face pass from amiability to sternness; he hoped I was not beginning to idle. I could not call my wandering thoughts together. I had hardly any patience with the serious work of life which, now that it stood between me and my desire, seemed to me child's play, ugly monotonous child's play.

On Saturday morning I reminded my uncle that I wished to go to the bazaar in the evening. He was fussing at the hallstand, looking for the hat-brush, and answered me curtly:

"Yes, boy, I know."

As he was in the hall I could not go into the front parlour and lie at the window. I left the house in bad humour and walked slowly towards the school. The air was pitilessly raw and already my heart misgave me.

When I came home to dinner my uncle had not yet been home. Still it was early. I sat staring at the clock for some time and, when its ticking began to irritate me, I left the room. I mounted the staircase and gained the upper part of the house. The high cold empty gloomy rooms liberated me and I went from room to room singing. From the front window I saw my companions playing below in the street. Their cries reached me weakened and indistinct and, leaning my forehead against the cool glass, I looked over at the dark house where she lived. I may have stood there for an hour, seeing nothing but the brown-clad figure cast by my imagination, touched discreetly by the lamplight at the curved neck, at the hand upon the railings and at the border below the dress.

When I came downstairs again I found Mrs. Mercer sitting at the fire. She was an old garrulous woman, a pawnbroker's widow, who collected used stamps for some pious purpose. I had to endure the gossip of the tea-table. The meal was prolonged beyond an hour and still my uncle did not come. Mrs. Mercer stood up to go: she was sorry she couldn't wait any longer, but it was after eight o'clock and she did not like to be out late, as the night air was bad for her. When she had gone I began to walk up and down the room, clenching my fists. My aunt said:

"I'm afraid you may put off your bazaar for this night of Our Lord."

At nine o'clock I heard my uncle's latchkey in the halldoor. I heard him talking to himself and heard the hallstand rocking when it had received the weight of his overcoat. I could interpret these signs. When he was midway through his dinner I asked him to give me the money to go to the bazaar. He had forgotten.

"The people are in bed and after their first sleep now," he said.

I did not smile. My aunt said to him energetically:

"Can't you give him the money and let him go? You've kept him late enough as it is."

My uncle said he was very sorry he had forgotten. He said he believed in the old saying: "All work and no play makes Jack a dull boy." He asked me where I was going and, when I had told him a second time he asked me did I know *The Arab's Farewell to his Steed*.[6] When I left the kitchen he was about to recite the opening lines of the piece to my aunt.

I held a florin[7] tightly in my hand as I strode down Buckingham Street towards the station. The sight of the streets thronged with buyers and glaring with gas recalled to me the purpose of my journey. I took my seat in a third-class carriage of a deserted train. After an intolerable delay the train moved out of the station slowly. It crept onward among ruinous houses and over the twinkling river. At

[6] A poem by the English poet-novelist Caroline Norton (1808–1877).
[7] Two shillings; a shilling was until recently one-twentieth of a British pound.

Westland Row Station a crowd of people pressed to the carriage doors; but the porters moved them back, saying that it was a special train for the bazaar. I remained alone in the bare carriage. In a few minutes the train drew up beside an improvised wooden platform. I passed out on to the road and saw by the lighted dial of a clock that it was ten minutes to ten. In front of me was a large building which displayed the magical name.

I could not find any sixpenny entrance and, fearing that the bazaar would be closed, I passed in quickly through a turnstile, handing a shilling to a weary-looking man. I found myself in a big hall girdled at half its height by a gallery. Nearly all the stalls were closed and the greater part of the hall was in darkness. I recognised a silence like that which pervades a church after a service. I walked into the centre of the bazaar timidly. A few people were gathered about the stalls which were still open. Before a curtain, over which the words *Café Chantant*[8] were written in coloured lamps, two men were counting money on a salver. I listened to the fall of the coins.

Remembering with difficulty why I had come I went over to one of the stalls and examined porcelain vases and flowered tea-sets. At the door of the stall a young lady was talking and laughing with two young gentlemen. I remarked their English accents and listened vaguely to their conversation.

"O, I never said such a thing!"

"O, but you did!"

"O, but I didn't!"

"Didn't she say that?"

"Yes. I heard her."

"O, there's a . . . fib!"

Observing me the young lady came over and asked me did I wish to buy anything. The tone of her voice was not encouraging; she seemed to have spoken to me out of a sense of duty. I looked humbly at the great jars that stood like eastern guards at either side of the dark entrance to the stall and murmured:

"No, thank you."

The young lady changed the position of one of the vases and went back to the two young men. They began to talk of the same subject. Once or twice the young lady glanced at me over her shoulder.

I lingered before her stall, though I knew my stay was useless, to make my interest in her wares seem the more real. Then I turned away slowly and walked down the middle of the bazaar. I allowed the two pennies to fall against the sixpence in my pocket. I heard a voice call from one end of the gallery that the light was out. The upper part of the hall was now completely dark.

Gazing up into the darkness I saw myself as a creature driven and derided by vanity; and my eyes burned with anguish and anger.

[1914]

[8] Concert coffee house.

James Joyce   *1882–1941*

THE DEAD

Lily, the caretaker's daughter, was literally run off her feet. Hardly had she brought one gentleman into the little pantry behind the office on the ground floor and helped him off with his overcoat than the wheezy hall-door bell clanged again and she had to scamper along the bare hallway to let in another guest. It was well for her she had not to attend to the ladies also. But Miss Kate and Miss Julia had thought of that and had converted the bathroom upstairs into a ladies' dressing-room. Miss Kate and Miss Julia were there, gossiping and laughing and fussing, walking after each other to the head of the stairs, peering down over the banisters and calling down to Lily to ask her who had come.

It was always a great affair, the Misses Morkan's annual dance. Everybody who knew them came to it, members of the family, old friends of the family, the members of Julia's choir, any of Kate's pupils that were grown up enough, and even some of Mary Jane's pupils too. Never once had it fallen flat. For years and years it had gone off in splendid style, as long as anyone could remember; ever since Kate and Julia, after the death of their brother Pat, had left the house in Stoney Batter[1] and taken Mary Jane, their only niece, to live with them in the dark, gaunt house on Usher's Island,[2] the upper part of which they had rented from Mr. Fulham, the corn-factor[3] on the ground floor. That was a good thirty years ago if it was a day. Mary Jane, who was then a little girl in short clothes, was now the main prop of the household, for she had the organ in Haddington Road.[4] She had been through the Academy[5] and gave a pupils' concert every year in the upper room of the Antient Concert Rooms.[6] Many of her pupils belonged to the better-class families on the Kingstown and Dalkey line.[7] Old as they were, her aunts also did their share. Julia, though she was quite grey, was still the leading soprano in Adam and Eve's,[8] and Kate, being too feeble to go about much, gave music lessons to beginners on the old square piano in the back room. Lily, the caretaker's daughter, did housemaid's work for them. Though their life was modest, they believed in eating well; the best of everything: diamond-bone sirloins, three-shilling tea and the best bottled stout.[9] But Lily seldom made a mistake in the orders, so that she got on well with her three mistresses. They were fussy, that was all. But the only thing they would not stand was back answers.

Of course, they had good reason to be fussy on such a night. And then it was long after ten o'clock and yet there was no sign of Gabriel and his wife. Besides they were dreadfully afraid that Freddy Malins might turn up screwed.[10] They would not wish for worlds that any of Mary Jane's pupils should see him under the influence; and when he was like that it was sometimes very hard to manage him.

[1] An area in northwest Dublin.
[2] A section of the Quay (the stone embankment used for the loading and unloading of ships) on the south bank of the River Liffey in central Dublin.
[3] Corn merchant or broker, usually working on a commission basis.
[4] Mary Jane is organist at a church located at the southeastern edge of metropolitan Dublin.
[5] The Royal Academy of Music, located in Merrion Square in southeastern Dublin.
[6] A concert hall, located not far from the Academy.
[7] A fashionable suburban area southeast of Dublin.
[8] The popular name for the Franciscan Church of St. Francis of Assissi near Usher's Island.
[9] A type of strong beer.   [10] Drunk.

Freddy Malins always came late, but they wondered what could be keeping Gabriel: and that was what brought them every two minutes to the banisters to ask Lily had Gabriel or Freddy come.

"O, Mr. Conroy," said Lily to Gabriel when she opened the door for him, "Miss Kate and Miss Julia thought you were never coming. Good-night, Mrs. Conroy."

"I'll engage they did," said Gabriel, "but they forget that my wife here takes three mortal hours to dress herself."

He stood on the mat, scraping the snow from his goloshes, while Lily led his wife to the foot of the stairs and called out:

"Miss Kate, here's Mrs. Conroy."

Kate and Julia came toddling down the dark stairs at once. Both of them kissed Gabriel's wife, said she must be perished alive, and asked was Gabriel with her.

"Here I am as right as the mail, Aunt Kate! Go on up. I'll follow," called out Gabriel from the dark.

He continued scraping his feet vigorously while the three women went upstairs, laughing, to the ladies' dressing-room. A light fringe of snow lay like a cape on the shoulders of his overcoat and like toecaps on the toes of his goloshes; and, as the buttons of his overcoat slipped with a squeaking noise through the snow-stiffened frieze,[11] a cold fragrant air from out-of-doors escaped from crevices and folds.

"Is it snowing again, Mr. Conroy?" asked Lily.

She had preceded him into the pantry to help him off with his overcoat. Gabriel smiled at the three syllables she had given his surname and glanced at her. She was a slim, growing girl, pale in complexion and with hay-coloured hair. The gas in the pantry made her look still paler. Gabriel had known her when she was a child and used to sit on the lowest step nursing a rag doll.

"Yes, Lily," he answered, "and I think we're in for a night of it."

He looked up at the pantry ceiling, which was shaking with the stamping and shuffling of feet on the floor above, listened for a moment to the piano and then glanced at the girl, who was folding his overcoat carefully at the end of a shelf.

"Tell me, Lily," he said in a friendly tone, "do you still go to school?"

"O no, sir," she answered. "I'm done schooling this year and more."

"O, then," said Gabriel gaily, "I suppose we'll be going to your wedding one of these fine days with your young man, eh?"

The girl glanced back at him over her shoulder and said with great bitterness:

"The men that is now is only all palaver and what they can get out of you."

Gabriel coloured, as if he felt he had made a mistake and, without looking at her, kicked off his goloshes and flicked actively with his muffler at his patent-leather shoes.

He was a stout, tallish young man. The high colour of his cheeks pushed upwards even to his forehead, where it scattered itself in a few formless patches of pale red; and on his hairless face there scintillated restlessly the polished lenses and the bright gilt rims of the glasses which screened his delicate and restless eyes. His glossy black hair was parted in the middle and brushed in a long curve behind his ears where it curled slightly beneath the groove left by his hat.

When he had flicked lustre into his shoes he stood up and pulled his waistcoat down more tightly on his plump body. Then he took a coin rapidly from his pocket.

"O Lily," he said, thrusting it into her hands, "it's Christmas-time, isn't it? Just . . . here's a little. . . ."

---

[11] Cloth.

He walked rapidly towards the door.

"O no, sir!" cried the girl, following him. "Really, sir, I wouldn't take it."

"Christmas-time! Christmas-time!" said Gabriel, almost trotting to the stairs and waving his hand to her in deprecation.

The girl, seeing that he had gained the stairs, called out after him:

"Well, thank you, sir."

He waited outside the drawing-room door until the waltz should finish, listening to the skirts that swept against it and to the shuffling of feet. He was still discomposed by the girl's bitter and sudden retort. It had cast a gloom over him which he tried to dispel by arranging his cuffs and the bows of his tie. He then took from his waistcoat[12] pocket a little paper and glanced at the headings he had made for his speech. He was undecided about the lines from Robert Browning,[13] for he feared they would be above the heads of his hearers. Some quotation that they would recognise from Shakespeare or from the Melodies[14] would be better. The indelicate clacking of the men's heels and the shuffling of their soles reminded him that their grade of culture differed from his. He would only make himself ridiculous by quoting poetry to them which they could not understand. They would think that he was airing his superior education. He would fail with them just as he had failed with the girl in the pantry. He had taken up a wrong tone. His whole speech was a mistake from first to last, an utter failure.

Just then his aunts and his wife came out of the ladies' dressing-room. His aunts were two small, plainly dressed old women. Aunt Julia was an inch or so the taller. Her hair, drawn low over the tops of her ears, was grey; and grey also, with darker shadows, was her large flaccid face. Though she was stout in build and stood erect, her slow eyes and parted lips gave her the appearance of a woman who did not know where she was or where she was going. Aunt Kate was more vivacious. Her face, healthier than her sister's, was all puckers and creases, like a shrivelled red apple, and her hair, braided in the same old-fashioned way, had not lost its ripe nut colour.

They both kissed Gabriel frankly. He was their favourite nephew, the son of their dead elder sister, Ellen, who had married T. J. Conroy of the Port and Docks.[15]

"Gretta tells me you're not going to take a cab back to Monkstown[16] tonight, Gabriel," said Aunt Kate.

"No," said Gabriel, turning to his wife, "we had quite enough of that last year, hadn't we? Don't you remember, Aunt Kate, what a cold Gretta got out of it? Cab windows rattling all the way, and the east wind blowing in after we passed Merrion.[17] Very jolly it was. Gretta caught a dreadful cold."

Aunt Kate frowned severely and nodded her head at every word.

"Quite right, Gabriel, quite right," she said. "You can't be too careful."

"But as for Gretta there," said Gabriel, "she'd walk home in the snow if she were let."

Mrs. Conroy laughed.

---

[12] Vest.   [13] Robert Browning (1812–1889), the British Victorian poet.

[14] The *Irish Melodies*, an enormously popular collection of patriotic and sentimental songs, with accompanying music, by Thomas Moore (1779–1852), the son of a Dublin grocer, published in installments between 1807 and 1834.

[15] The board responsible for managing the Port of Dublin.

[16] A village on Dublin Bay, south of the city.

[17] A village on Dublin Bay between Monkstown and the city.

"Don't mind him, Aunt Kate," she said. "He's really an awful bother, what with green shades for Tom's eyes at night and making him do the dumb-bells, and forcing Eva to eat the stir-about.[18] The poor child! And she simply hates the sight of it! . . . O, but you'll never guess what he makes me wear now!"

She broke out into a peal of laughter and glanced at her husband, whose admiring and happy eyes had been wandering from her dress to her face and hair. The two aunts laughed heartily, too, for Gabriel's solicitude was a standing joke with them.

"Goloshes!" said Mrs. Conroy. "That's the latest. Whenever it's wet underfoot I must put on my goloshes. Tonight even, he wanted me to put them on, but I wouldn't. The next thing he'll buy me will be a diving suit."

Gabriel laughed nervously and patted his tie reassuringly, while Aunt Kate nearly doubled herself, so heartily did she enjoy the joke. The smile soon faded from Aunt Julia's face and her mirthless eyes were directed towards her nephew's face. After a pause she asked:

"And what are goloshes, Gabriel?"

"Goloshes, Julia!" exclaimed her sister. "Goodness me, don't you know what goloshes are? You wear them over your . . . over your boots, Gretta, isn't it?"

"Yes," said Mrs. Conroy. "Guttapercha[19] things. We both have a pair now. Gabriel says everyone wears them on the Continent."[20]

"O, on the Continent," murmured Aunt Julia, nodding her head slowly.

Gabriel knitted his brows and said, as if he were slightly angered:

"It's nothing very wonderful, but Gretta thinks it very funny because she says the word reminds her of Christy Minstrels."[21]

"But tell me, Gabriel," said Aunt Kate, with brisk tact. "Of course, you've seen about the room. Gretta was saying . . ."

"O the room is all right," replied Gabriel. "I've taken one in the Gresham."

"To be sure," said Aunt Kate, "by far the best thing to do. And the children, Gretta, you're not anxious about them?"

"O, for one night," said Mrs. Conroy. "Besides, Bessie will look after them."

"To be sure," said Aunt Kate again. "What a comfort it is to have a girl like that, one you can depend on! There's that Lily, I'm sure I don't know what has come over her lately. She's not the girl she was at all."

Gabriel was about to ask his aunt some questions on this point, but she broke off suddenly to gaze after her sister, who had wandered down the stairs and was craning her neck over the banisters.

"Now, I ask you," she said almost testily, "where is Julia going? Julia! Julia! Where are you going?"

Julia, who had gone half way down one flight, came back and announced blandly:

"Here's Freddy."

At the same moment a clapping of hands and a final flourish of the pianist told that the waltz had ended. The drawing-room door was opened from within and some couples came out. Aunt Kate drew Gabriel aside hurriedly and whispered into his ear:

[18] Porridge.
[19] Gutta-percha is an elastic, rubber-like material (made from the gum of the percha tree found in southeast Asia) used for water protection.
[20] The continent of Europe.
[21] The popular American minstrel group which performed widely during the late nineteenth century.

"Slip down, Gabriel, like a good fellow and see if he's all right, and don't let him up if he's screwed. I'm sure he's screwed. I'm sure he is."

Gabriel went to the stairs and listened over the banisters. He could hear two persons talking in the pantry. Then he recognised Freddy Malins' laugh. He went down the stairs noisily.

"It's such a relief," said Aunt Kate to Mrs. Conroy, "that Gabriel is here. I always feel easier in my mind when he's here. . . . Julia, there's Miss Daly and Miss Power will take some refreshment. Thanks for your beautiful waltz, Miss Daly. It made lovely time."

A tall wizen-faced man, with a stiff grizzled moustache and swarthy skin, who was passing out with his partner, said:

"And may we have some refreshment, too, Miss Morkan?"

"Julia," said Aunt Kate summarily, "and here's Mr. Browne and Miss Furlong. Take them in, Julia, with Miss Daly and Miss Power."

"I'm the man for the ladies," said Mr. Browne, pursing his lips until his moustache bristled and smiling in all his wrinkles. "You know, Miss Morkan, the reason they are so fond of me is——"

He did not finish his sentence, but, seeing that Aunt Kate was out of earshot, at once led the three young ladies into the back room. The middle of the room was occupied by two square tables placed end to end, and on these Aunt Julia and the caretaker were straightening and smoothing a large cloth. On the sideboard were arrayed dishes and plates, and glasses and bundles of knives and forks and spoons. The top of the closed square piano served also as a sideboard for viands[22] and sweets. At a smaller sideboard in one corner two young men were standing, drinking hop-bitters.[23]

Mr. Browne led his charges thither and invited them all, in jest, to some ladies' punch, hot, strong and sweet. As they said they never took anything strong, he opened three bottles of lemonade for them. Then he asked one of the young men to move aside, and, taking hold of the decanter, filled out for himself a goodly measure of whisky. The young men eyed him respectfully while he took a trial sip.

"God help me," he said, smiling, "it's the doctor's orders."

His wizened face broke into a broader smile, and the three young ladies laughed in musical echo to his pleasantry, swaying their bodies to and fro, with nervous jerks of their shoulders. The boldest said:

"O, now, Mr. Browne, I'm sure the doctor never ordered anything of the kind."

Mr. Browne took another sip of his whisky and said, with sidling mimicry:

"Well, you see, I'm like the famous Mrs. Cassidy, who is reported to have said: 'Now, Mary Grimes,[24] if I don't take it, make me take it, for I feel I want it.' "

His hot face had leaned forward a little too confidentially and he had assumed a very low Dublin accent so that the young ladies, with one instinct, received his speech in silence. Miss Furlong, who was one of Mary Jane's pupils, asked Miss Daly what was the name of the pretty waltz she had played; and Mr. Browne, seeing that he was ignored, turned promptly to the two young men who were more appreciative.

A red-faced young woman, dressed in pansy, came into the room, excitedly clapping her hands and crying:

"Quadrilles! Quadrilles!"[25]

---

[22] Choice and tasty dishes.   [23] A kind of dry ale.
[24] As in the case of Mrs. Cassidy, the intended allusion is unclear.
[25] A square dance for four couples.

Close on her heels came Aunt Kate, crying:

"Two gentlemen and three ladies, Mary Jane!"

"O, here's Mr. Bergin and Mr. Kerrigan," said Mary Jane. "Mr. Kerrigan, will you take Miss Power? Miss Furlong, may I get you a partner, Mr. Bergin. O, that'll just do now."

"Three ladies, Mary Jane," said Aunt Kate.

The two young gentlemen asked the ladies if they might have the pleasure, and Mary Jane turned to Miss Daly.

"O, Miss Daly, you're really awfully good, after playing for the last two dances, but really we're so short of ladies tonight."

"I don't mind in the least, Miss Morkan."

"But I've a nice partner for you, Mr. Bartell D'Arcy, the tenor. I'll get him to sing later on. All Dublin is raving about him."

"Lovely voice, lovely voice!" said Aunt Kate.

As the piano had twice begun the prelude to the first figure Mary Jane led her recruits quickly from the room. They had hardly gone when Aunt Julia wandered slowly into the room, looking behind her at something.

"What is the matter, Julia?" asked Aunt Kate anxiously. "Who is it?"

Julia, who was carrying in a column of table-napkins, turned to her sister and said, simply, as if the question had surprised her:

"It's only Freddy, Kate, and Gabriel with him."

In fact right behind her Gabriel could be seen piloting Freddy Malins across the landing. The latter, a young man of about forty, was of Gabriel's size and build, with very round shoulders. His face was fleshy and pallid, touched with colour only at the thick hanging lobes of his ears and at the wide wings of his nose. He had coarse features, a blunt nose, a convex and receding brow, tumid and protruded lips. His heavy-lidded eyes and the disorder of his scanty hair made him look sleepy. He was laughing heartily in a high key at a story which he had been telling Gabriel on the stairs and at the same time rubbing the knuckles of his left fist backwards and forwards into his left eye.

"Good-evening, Freddy," said Aunt Julia.

Freddy Malins bade the Misses Morkan good-evening in what seemed an off-hand fashion by reason of the habitual catch in his voice and then, seeing that Mr. Browne was grinning at him from the sideboard, crossed the room on rather shaky legs and began to repeat in an undertone the story he had just told to Gabriel.

"He's not so bad, is he?" said Aunt Kate to Gabriel.

Gabriel's brows were dark but he raised them quickly and answered:

"O, no, hardly noticeable."

"Now, isn't he a terrible fellow!" she said. "And his poor mother made him take the pledge[26] on New Year's Eve. But come on, Gabriel, into the drawing-room."

Before leaving the room with Gabriel she signalled to Mr. Browne by frowning and shaking her forefinger in warning to and fro. Mr. Browne nodded in answer and, when she had gone, said to Freddy Malins:

"Now, then, Teddy, I'm going to fill you out a good glass of lemonade just to buck you up."

Freddy Malins, who was nearing the climax of his story, waved the offer aside impatiently but Mr. Browne, having first called Freddy Malins' attention to a disarray in his dress, filled out and handed him a full glass of lemonade. Freddy

[26] To stop drinking.

Malins' left hand accepted the glass mechanically, his right hand being engaged in the mechanical readjustment of his dress. Mr. Browne, whose face was once more wrinkling with mirth, poured out for himself a glass of whisky while Freddy Malins exploded, before he had well reached the climax of his story, in a kink of high-pitched bronchitic[27] laughter and, setting down his untasted and overflowing glass, began to rub the knuckles of his left fist backwards and forwards into his left eye, repeating words of his last phrase as well as his fit of laughter would allow him.

Gabriel could not listen while Mary Jane was playing her Academy piece, full of runs and difficult passages, to the hushed drawing-room. He liked music but the piece she was playing had no melody for him and he doubted whether it had any melody for the other listeners, though they had begged Mary Jane to play something. Four young men, who had come from the refreshment-room to stand in the doorway at the sound of the piano, had gone away quietly in couples after a few minutes. The only persons who seemed to follow the music were Mary Jane herself, her hands racing along the key-board or lifted from it at the pauses like those of a priestess in momentary imprecation, and Aunt Kate standing at her elbow to turn the page.

Gabriel's eyes, irritated by the floor, which glittered with beeswax under the heavy chandelier, wandered to the wall above the piano. A picture of the balcony scene in *Romeo and Juliet*[28] hung there and beside it was a picture of the two murdered princes in the Tower[29] which Aunt Julia had worked in red, blue and brown wools when she was a girl. Probably in the school they had gone to as girls that kind of work had been taught for one year. His mother had worked for him as a birthday present a waistcoat of purple tabinet,[30] with little foxes' heads upon it, lined with brown satin and having round mulberry buttons. It was strange that his mother had had no musical talent though Aunt Kate used to call her the brains carrier of the Morkan family. Both she and Julia had always seemed a little proud of their serious and matronly sister. Her photograph stood before the pierglass.[31] She held an open book on her knees and was pointing out something in it to Constantine who, dressed in a man-o'-war suit,[32] lay at her feet. It was she who had chosen the name of her sons for she was very sensible of the dignity of family life.[33] Thanks to her, Constantine was now senior curate[34] in Balbriggan[35] and, thanks to her, Gabriel himself had taken his degree in the Royal University.[36] A shadow passed over his face as he remembered her sullen opposition to his marriage. Some slighting phrases she had used still rankled in his memory; she had once spoken of Gretta as being country cute and that was not true of Gretta at all. It was Gretta who had nursed her during all her last long illness in their house at Monkstown.

He knew that Mary Jane must be near the end of her piece for she was playing

---

[27] Wheezing or squeaking sound caused by a cold in the bronchial tubes leading to the lungs.

[28] The allusion is, of course, to the famous scene between the two lovers in the second act of Shakespeare's tragedy in 1595, with Juliet on the balcony above and Romeo in the garden below.

[29] According to tradition Richard III of England (1453–1485) ordered his two small nephews murdered in the Tower of London in order to protect his claim to the throne.

[30] A poplin-like fabric.   [31] A large mirror.   [32] A sailor suit.

[33] Constantine the Great (280?–337) was the first Roman emperor to sanction and protect Christianity and to become a Christian.

[34] Clergyman.   [35] A town located on the Irish Sea, some twenty miles north of Dublin.

[36] The Royal University, organized by legislative act in 1879, offered no courses, but rather established and administered examinations in a variety of academic subjects and granted degrees to those who performed satisfactorily.

again the opening melody with runs of scales after every bar and while he waited for the end the resentment died down in his heart. The piece ended with a trill of octaves in the treble and a final deep octave in the bass. Great applause greeted Mary Jane as, blushing and rolling up her music nervously, she escaped from the room. The most vigorous clapping came from the four young men in the doorway who had gone away to the refreshment-room at the beginning of the piece but had come back when the piano had stopped.

Lancers[37] were arranged. Gabriel found himself partnered with Miss Ivors. She was a frank-mannered talkative young lady, with a freckled face and prominent brown eyes. She did not wear a low-cut bodice and the large brooch which was fixed in the front of her collar bore on it an Irish device[38] and motto.

When they had taken their places she said abruptly:

"I have a crow to pluck with you."

"With me?" said Gabriel.

She nodded her head gravely.

"What is it?" asked Gabriel, smiling at her solemn manner.

"Who is G. C.?" answered Miss Ivors, turning her eyes upon him.

Gabriel coloured and was about to knit his brows, as if he did not understand, when she said bluntly:

"O, innocent Amy! I have found out that you write for *The Daily Express.*[39] Now, aren't you ashamed of yourself?"

"Why should I be ashamed of myself?" asked Gabriel, blinking his eyes and trying to smile.

"Well, I'm ashamed of you," said Miss Ivors frankly. "To say you'd write for a paper like that. I didn't think you were a West Briton."[40]

A look of perplexity appeared on Gabriel's face. It was true that he wrote a literary column every Wednesday in *The Daily Express,* for which he was paid fifteen shillings. But that did not make him a West Briton surely. The books he received for review were almost more welcome than the paltry cheque. He loved to feel the covers and turn over the pages of newly printed books. Nearly every day when his teaching in the college was ended he used to wander down the quays to the second-hand booksellers, to Hickey's on Bachelor's Walk, to Web's or Massey's on Aston's Quay, or to O'Clohissey's in the by-street.[41] He did not know how to meet her charge. He wanted to say that literature was above politics. But they were friends of many years' standing and their careers had been parallel, first at the University[42] and then as teachers: he could not risk a grandiose phrase with her. He continued blinking his eyes and trying to smile and murmured lamely that he saw nothing political in writing reviews of books.

When their turn to cross had come he was still perplexed and inattentive. Miss Ivors promptly took his hand in a warm grasp and said in a soft friendly tone:

"Of course, I was only joking. Come, we cross now."

[37] A type of quadrille; see note 25.
[38] An emblem or design.
[39] A Dublin newspaper with a nationalistic editorial policy.
[40] The term, as used, is derogatory. It refers to an Irishman whose views and attitudes on matters political and cultural are more British than Irish and who tends to regard Ireland itself as a province "West of Briton."
[41] All are well-known Dublin bookselling establishments of the period.
[42] Presumably Gabriel attended University College, Dublin at the same time Miss Ivors was attending an institution for women, since University College at the time was closed to women.

When they were together again she spoke of the University question[43] and Gabriel felt more at ease. A friend of hers had shown her his review of Browning's poems. That was how she had found out the secret: but she liked the review immensely. Then she said suddenly:

"O, Mr. Conroy, will you come for an excursion to the Aran Isles[44] this summer? We're going to stay there a whole month. It will be splendid out in the Atlantic. You ought to come. Mr. Clancy is coming, and Mr. Kilkelly and Kathleen Kearney. It would be splendid for Gretta too if she'd come. She's from Connacht,[45] isn't she?"

"Her people are," said Gabriel shortly.

"But you will come, won't you?" said Miss Ivors, laying her warm hand eagerly on his arm.

"The fact is," said Gabriel, "I have just arranged to go——"

"Go where?" asked Miss Ivors.

"Well, you know, every year I go for a cycling tour with some fellows and so——"

"But where?" asked Miss Ivors.

"Well, we usually go to France or Belgium or perhaps Germany," said Gabriel awkwardly.

"And why do you go to France and Belgium," said Miss Ivors, "instead of visiting your own land?"

"Well," said Gabriel, "it's partly to keep in touch with the languages and partly for a change."

"And haven't you your own language to keep in touch with—Irish?" asked Miss Ivors.

"Well," said Gabriel, "if it comes to that, you know, Irish is not my language."

Their neighbors had turned to listen to the cross-examination. Gabriel glanced right and left nervously and tried to keep his good humour under the ordeal which was making a blush invade his forehead.

"And haven't you your own land to visit," continued Miss Ivors, "that you know nothing of, your own people, and your own country?"

"O, to tell you the truth," retorted Gabriel suddenly, "I'm sick of my own country, sick of it!"

"Why?" asked Miss Ivors.

Gabriel did not answer for his retort had heated him.

"Why?" repeated Miss Ivors.

They had to go visiting together and, as he had not answered her, Miss Ivors said warmly:

"Of course, you've no answer."

Gabriel tried to cover his agitation by taking part in the dance with great energy. He avoided her eyes for he had seen a sour expression on her face. But when they met in the long chain he was surprised to feel his hand firmly pressed. She looked at him from under her brows for a moment quizzically until he smiled. Then, just as the chain was about to start again, she stood on tiptoe and whispered into his ear:

[43] A reference to the long and protracted Anglo-Irish debate dating from the 1840s over what kind of universities Ireland was to have. The "question" had yet to be resolved to the satisfaction of the Irish educators at the time of Joyce's story.
[44] Islands off Galway on the west coast of Ireland, celebrated for their old-fashioned "Irish" character.
[45] A province in northwest Ireland.

"West Briton!"

When the lancers were over Gabriel went away to a remote corner of the room where Freddy Malins' mother was sitting. She was a stout feeble old woman with white hair. Her voice had a catch in it like her son's and she stuttered slightly. She had been told that Freddy had come and that he was nearly all right. Gabriel asked her whether she had had a good crossing. She lived with her married daughter in Glasgow[46] and came to Dublin on a visit once a year. She answered placidly that she had had a beautiful crossing and that the captain had been most attentive to her. She spoke also of the beautiful house her daughter kept in Glasgow, and of all the friends they had there. While her tongue rambled on Gabriel tried to banish from his mind all memory of the unpleasant incident with Miss Ivors. Of course the girl or woman, or whatever she was, was an enthusiast but there was a time for all things. Perhaps he ought not to have answered her like that. But she had no right to call him a West Briton before people, even in joke. She had tried to make him ridiculous before people, heckling him and staring at him with her rabbit's eyes.

He saw his wife making her way towards him through the waltzing couples. When she reached him she said into his ear:

"Gabriel, Aunt Kate wants to know won't you carve the goose as usual. Miss Daly will carve the ham and I'll do the pudding."

"All right," said Gabriel.

"She's sending in the younger ones first as soon as this waltz is over so that we'll have the table to ourselves."

"Were you dancing?" asked Gabriel.

"Of course I was. Didn't you see me? What row had you with Molly Ivors?"

"No row. Why? Did she say so?"

"Something like that. I'm trying to get that Mr. D'Arcy to sing. He's full of conceit, I think."

"There was no row," said Gabriel moodily, "only she wanted me to go for a trip to the west of Ireland and I said I wouldn't."

His wife clasped her hands excitedly and gave a little jump.

"O, do go, Gabriel," she said. "I'd love to see Galway again."

"You can go if you like," said Gabriel coldly.

She looked at him for a moment, then turned to Mrs. Malins and said:

"There's a nice husband for you, Mrs. Malins."

While she was threading her way back across the room Mrs. Malins, without adverting to the interruption, went on to tell Gabriel what beautiful places there were in Scotland and beautiful scenery. Her son-in-law brought them every year to the lakes and they used to go fishing. Her son-in-law was a splendid fisher. One day he caught a beautiful big fish and the man in the hotel cooked it for their dinner.

Gabriel hardly heard what she said. Now that supper was coming near he began to think again about his speech and about the quotation. When he saw Freddy Malins coming across the room to visit his mother Gabriel left the chair free for him and retired into the embrasure of the window. The room had already cleared and from the back room came the clatter of plates and knives. Those who still remained in the drawing-room seemed tired of dancing and were conversing quietly in little groups. Gabriel's warm trembling fingers tapped the cold pane of the window. How cool it must be outside! How pleasant it would be to walk out

---

[46] Port city in southwest Scotland.

alone, first along by the river and then through the park![47] The snow would be lying on the branches of the trees and forming a bright cap on the top of the Wellington Monument.[48] How much more pleasant it would be there than at the supper-table!

He ran over the headings of his speech: Irish hospitality, sad memories, the Three Graces,[49] Paris,[50] the quotation from Browning. He repeated to himself a phrase he had written in his review: "One feels that one is listening to a thought-tormented music." Miss Ivors had praised the review. Was she sincere? Had she really any life of her own behind all her propagandism? There had never been any ill-feeling between them until that night. It unnerved him to think that she would be at the supper-table, looking up at him while he spoke with her critical quizzing eyes. Perhaps she would not be sorry to see him fail in his speech. An idea came into his mind and gave him courage. He would say, alluding to Aunt Kate and Aunt Julia: "Ladies and Gentlemen, the generation which is now on the wane among us may have had its faults but for my part I think it had certain qualities of hospitality, of humour, of humanity, which the new and very serious and hyper-educated generation that is growing up around us seems to me to lack." Very good: that was one for Miss Ivors. What did he care that his aunts were only two ignorant old women?

A murmur in the room attracted his attention. Mr. Browne was advancing from the door, gallantly escorting Aunt Julia, who leaned upon his arm, smiling and hanging her head. An irregular musketry of applause escorted her also as far as the piano and then, as Mary Jane seated herself on the stool, and Aunt Julia, no longer smiling, half turned so as to pitch her voice fairly into the room, gradually ceased. Gabriel recognised the prelude. It was that of an old song of Aunt Julia's— *Arrayed for the Bridal.*[51] Her voice, strong and clear in tone, attacked with great spirit the runs which embellish the air and though she sang very rapidly she did not miss even the smallest of the grace notes. To follow the voice, without looking at the singer's face, was to feel and share the excitement of swift and secure flight. Gabriel applauded loudly with all the others at the close of the song and loud applause was borne in from the invisible supper-table. It sounded so genuine that a little colour struggled into Aunt Julia's face as she bent to replace in the music-stand the old leather-bound songbook that had her initials on the cover. Freddy Malins, who had listened with his head perched sideways to hear her better, was still applauding when everyone else had ceased and talking animatedly to his mother who nodded her head gravely and slowly in acquiescence. At last, when he could clap no more, he stood up suddenly and hurried across the room to Aunt Julia whose hand he seized and held in both his hands, shaking it when words failed him or the catch in his voice proved too much for him.

"I was just telling my mother," he said, "I never heard you sing so well, never.

---

[47] Phoenix Park, across the River Liffey and not too far to the west of Usher's Island.

[48] An obelisk in Phoenix Park to Arthur Wellesley, the Duke of Wellington (1769–1852), who defeated Napoleon at Waterloo in 1815 and served as British Prime Minister from 1828 to 1830. Though born in Dublin, the "Iron Duke," as he was called, adopted a conservative "English" posture toward the nationalistic aspirations of his native country.

[49] The three daughters of Zeus in Greek mythology—Aglaia, Euphrosyne, and Thalia—who dispensed and inspired beauty and charm.

[50] The son of Priam, King of Troy. In Greek mythology Paris awarded the title of "fairest" to Aphrodite in a beauty contest and she in return helped him carry off Helen—an act that precipitated the Trojan War.

[51] A sentimental song written by Englishman George Linley (1798–1865) to music taken from Vicenzo Bellini's opera of 1835, *I Puritani* (*The Puritans*).

No, I never heard your voice so good as it is tonight. Now! Would you believe that now? That's the truth. Upon my word and honour that's the truth. I never heard your voice sound so fresh and so . . . so clear and fresh, never.''

Aunt Julia smiled broadly and murmured something about compliments as she released her hand from his grasp. Mr. Browne extended his open hand towards her and said to those who were near him in the manner of a showman introducing a prodigy to an audience:

"Miss Julia Morkan, my latest discovery!"

He was laughing very heartily at this himself when Freddy Malins turned to him and said:

"Well, Browne, if you're serious you might make a worse discovery. All I can say is I never heard her sing half so well as long as I am coming here. And that's the honest truth."

"Neither did I," said Mr. Browne. "I think her voice has greatly improved."

Aunt Julia shrugged her shoulders and said with meek pride:

"Thirty years ago I hadn't a bad voice as voices go."

"I often told Julia," said Aunt Kate emphatically, "that she was simply thrown away in that choir. But she never would be said[52] by me."

She turned as if to appeal to the good sense of the others against a refractory child while Aunt Julia gazed in front of her, a vague smile of reminiscence playing on her face.

"No," continued Aunt Kate, "she wouldn't be said or led by anyone, slaving there in that choir night and day, night and day. Six o'clock on Christmas morning! And all for what?"

"Well, isn't it for the honour of God, Aunt Kate?" asked Mary Jane, twisting round on the piano-stool and smiling.

Aunt Kate turned fiercely on her niece and said:

"I know all about the honour of God, Mary Jane, but I think it's not at all honourable for the pope to turn out the women out of the choirs[53] that have slaved there all their lives and put little whipper-snappers of boys over their heads. I suppose it is for the good of the Church if the pope does it. But it's not just, Mary Jane, and it's not right."

She had worked herself into a passion and would have continued in defence of her sister for it was a sore subject with her but Mary Jane, seeing that all the dancers had come back, intervened pacifically:

"Now, Aunt Kate, you're giving scandal to Mr. Browne who is of the other persuasion."

Aunt Kate turned to Mr. Browne, who was grinning at this allusion to his religion, and said hastily:

"O, I don't question the pope's being right. I'm only a stupid old woman and I wouldn't presume to do such a thing. But there's such a thing as common everyday politeness and gratitude. And if I were in Julia's place I'd tell that Father Healey straight up to his face . . ."

"And besides, Aunt Kate," said Mary Jane, "we really are all hungry and when we are hungry we are all very quarrelsome."

"And when we are thirsty we are also quarrelsome," added Mr. Browne.

[52] Advised.
[53] Pope Pius X, who served as pope from 1903 to 1914, decreed in 1903 that women were no longer to be permitted to be part of the church choir.

"So that we had better go to supper," said Mary Jane, "and finish the discussion afterwards."

On the landing outside the drawing-room Gabriel found his wife and Mary Jane trying to persuade Miss Ivors to stay for supper. But Miss Ivors, who had put on her hat and was buttoning her cloak, would not stay. She did not feel in the least hungry and she had already overstayed her time.

"But only for ten minutes, Molly," said Mrs. Conroy. "That won't delay you."

"To take a pick itself,"[54] said Mary Jane, "after all your dancing."

"I really couldn't," said Miss Ivors.

"I am afraid you didn't enjoy yourself at all," said Mary Jane hopelessly.

"Ever so much, I assure you," said Miss Ivors, "but you really must let me run off now."

"But how can you get home?" asked Mrs. Conroy.

"O, it's only two steps up the quay."

Gabriel hesitated a moment and said:

"If you will allow me, Miss Ivors, I'll see you home if you are really obliged to go."

But Miss Ivors broke away from them.

"I won't hear it," she cried. "For goodness' sake go in to your suppers and don't mind me. I'm quite well able to take care of myself."

"Well, you're the comical girl, Molly," said Mrs. Conroy frankly.

"*Beannacht libh*,"[55] cried Miss Ivors, with a laugh, as she ran down the staircase.

Mary Jane gazed after her, a moody puzzled expression on her face, while Mrs. Conroy leaned over the banisters to listen for the hall-door. Gabriel asked himself was he the cause of her abrupt departure. But she did not seem to be in ill humour: she had gone away laughing. He stared blankly down the staircase.

At the moment Aunt Kate came toddling out of the supper-room, almost wringing her hands in despair.

"Where is Gabriel?" she cried. "Where on earth is Gabriel? There's everyone waiting in there, stage to let,[56] and nobody to carve the goose!"

"Here I am, Aunt Kate!" cried Gabriel, with sudden animation, "ready to carve a flock of geese, if necessary."

A fat brown goose lay at one end of the table and at the other end, on a bed of creased paper strewn with sprigs of parsley, lay a great ham, stripped of its outer skin and peppered over with crust crumbs, a neat paper frill round its shin and beside this was a round of spiced beef. Between these rival ends ran parallel lines of side-dishes: two little minsters of jelly, red and yellow; a shallow dish full of blocks of blancmange[57] and red jam, a large green leaf-shaped dish with a stalk-shaped handle, on which lay bunches of purple raisins and peeled almonds, a companion dish on which lay a solid rectangle of Smyrna figs, a dish of custard topped with grated nutmeg, a small bowl full of chocolates and sweets wrapped in gold and silver papers and a glass vase in which stood some tall celery stalks. In the centre of the table there stood, as sentries to a fruit-stand which upheld a pyramid of oranges and American apples, two squat old-fashioned decanters of cut glass, one containing port and the other dark sherry. On the closed square piano a pudding in a huge yellow dish lay in waiting and behind it were three squads of bottles of stout and ale and minerals, drawn up according to the colours of their

[54] To have a little bite.   [55] An Irish saying: Farewell, my blessings go with you.
[56] Ready to go.   [57] A type of gelatin dessert shaped in a mold.

uniforms, the first two black, with brown and red labels, the third and smallest squad white, with transverse green sashes.

Gabriel took his seat boldly at the head of the table and, having looked to the edge of the carver, plunged his fork firmly into the goose. He felt quite at ease now for he was an expert carver and liked nothing better than to find himself at the head of a well-laden table.

"Miss Furlong, what shall I send you?" he asked. "A wing or a slice of the breast?"

"Just a small slice of the breast."

"Miss Higgins, what for you?"

"O, anything at all, Mr. Conroy."

While Gabriel and Miss Daly exchanged plates of goose and plates of ham and spiced beef Lily went from guest to guest with a dish of hot floury potatoes wrapped in a white napkin. This was Mary Jane's idea and she had also suggested apple sauce for the goose but Aunt Kate had said that plain roast goose without any apple sauce had always been good enough for her and she hoped she might never eat worse. Mary Jane waited on her pupils and saw that they got the best slices and Aunt Kate and Aunt Julia opened and carried across from the piano bottles of stout and ale for the gentlemen and bottles of minerals for the ladies. There was a great deal of confusion and laughter and noise, the noise of orders and counter-orders, of knives and forks, of corks and glass-stoppers. Gabriel began to carve second helpings as soon as he had finished the first round without serving himself. Everyone protested loudly so that he compromised by taking a long draught of stout for he had found the carving hot work. Mary Jane settled down quietly to her supper but Aunt Kate and Aunt Julia were still toddling round the table, walking on each other's heels, getting in each other's way and giving each other unheeded orders. Mr. Browne begged of them to sit down and eat their suppers and so did Gabriel but they said there was time enough, so that, at last Freddy Malins stood up and, capturing Aunt Kate, plumped her down on her chair amid general laughter.

When everyone had been well served Gabriel said, smiling:

"Now, if anyone wants a little more of what vulgar people call stuffing let him or her speak."

A chorus of voices invited him to begin his own supper and Lily came forward with three potatoes which she had reserved for him.

"Very well," said Gabriel amiably, as he took another preparatory draught, "kindly forget my existence, ladies and gentlemen, for a few minutes."

He set to his supper and took no part in the conversation with which the table covered Lily's removal of the plates. The subject of talk was the opera company which was then at the Theatre Royal.[58] Mr. Bartell D'Arcy, the tenor, a dark-complexioned young man with a smart moustache, praised very highly the leading contralto of the company but Miss Furlong thought she had a rather vulgar style of production. Freddy Malins said there was a Negro chieftain singing in the second part of the Gaiety pantomime who had one of the finest tenor voices he had ever heard.

"Have you heard him?" he asked Mr. Bartell D'Arcy across the table.

"No," answered Mr. Bartell D'Arcy carelessly.

[58] Together with the Gaiety, below, the Theatre Royal was one of Dublin's major turn of the century theaters.

"Because," Freddy Malins explained, "now I'd be curious to hear your opinion of him. I think he has a grand voice."

"It takes Teddy to find out the really good things," said Mr. Browne familiarly to the table.

"And why couldn't he have a voice too?" asked Freddy Malins sharply. "Is it because he's only a black?"

Nobody answered this question and Mary Jane led the table back to the legitimate opera. One of her pupils had given her a pass for *Mignon*.[59] Of course it was very fine, she said, but it made her think of poor Georgina Burns.[60] Mr. Browne could go back farther still, to the old Italian companies that used to come to Dublin—Tietjens, Ilma de Murzka, Campanini, the great Trebelli, Giuglini, Ravelli, Aramburo.[61] Those were the days, he said, when there was something like singing to be heard in Dublin. He told too of how the top gallery of the old Royal[62] used to be packed night after night, of how one night an Italian tenor had sung five encores to Let me like a Soldier fall,[63] introducing a high C every time, and of how the gallery boys would sometimes in their enthusiasm unyoke the horses from the carriage of some great prima donna[64] and pull her themselves through the streets to her hotel. Why did they never play the grand old operas now, he asked, *Dinorah*,[65] *Lucrezia Borgia*?[66] Because they could not get the voices to sing them: that was why.

"Oh, well," said Mr. Bartell D'Arcy, "I presume there are as good singers today as there were then."

"Where are they?" asked Mr. Browne defiantly.

"In London, Paris, Milan," said Mr. Bartell D'Arcy warmly. "I suppose Caruso,[67] for example, is quite as good, if not better than any of the men you have mentioned."

"Maybe so," said Mr. Browne. "But I may tell you I doubt it strongly."

"O, I'd give anything to hear Caruso sing," said Mary Jane.

"For me," said Aunt Kate, who had been picking a bone, "there was only one tenor. To please me, I mean. But I suppose none of you ever heard of him."

"Who was he, Miss Morkan?" asked Mr. Bartell D'Arcy politely.

"His name," said Aunt Kate, "was Parkinson.[68] I heard him when he was in his prime and I think he had then the purest tenor voice that was ever put into a man's throat."

"Strange," said Mr. Bartell D'Arcy. "I never even heard of him."

"Yes, yes, Miss Morkan is right," said Mr. Browne. "I remember hearing of old Parkinson but he's too far back for me."

"A beautiful, pure, sweet, mellow English tenor," said Aunt Kate with enthusiasm.

---

[59] A French opera, written in 1886 by Ambroise Thomas (1811–1896).

[60] The allusion is unclear.

[61] All those named were popular nineteenth-century opera stars.

[62] The "old" Theatre Royal was destroyed by fire in 1880; it was replaced by the new Theatre Royal.

[63] From the opera Maritana (1845) by Irish composer William Wallace (1812–1865).

[64] An opera company's leading female soloist.

[65] A French opera by Giacomo Meyerbeer (1791–1864) that premiered in 1859.

[66] An Italian opera by Gaetano Donizetti (1797–1848) that premiered in 1833.

[67] Enrico Caruso (1874–1921), generally regarded as the greatest Italian tenor of all time, was the idol of the opera world during the early twentieth century.

[68] The allusion is unclear.

Gabriel having finished, the huge pudding was transferred to the table. The clatter of forks and spoons began again. Gabriel's wife served out spoonfuls of the pudding and passed the plates down the table. Midway down they were held up by Mary Jane, who replenished them with raspberry or orange jelly or with blanc-mange and jam. The pudding was of Aunt Julia's making and she received praises for it from all quarters. She herself said that it was not quite brown enough.

"Well, I hope, Miss Morkan," said Mr. Browne, "that I'm brown enough for you because, you know, I'm all brown."

All the gentlemen, except Gabriel, ate some of the pudding out of compliment to Aunt Julia. As Gabriel never ate sweets the celery had been left for him. Freddy Malins also took a stalk of celery and ate it with his pudding. He had been told that celery was a capital thing for the blood and he was just then under doctor's care. Mrs. Malins, who had been silent all through the supper, said that her son was going down to Mount Melleray[69] in a week or so. The table then spoke of Mount Melleray, how bracing the air was down there, how hospitable the monks were and how they never asked for a penny-piece from their guests.

"And do you mean to say," asked Mr. Browne incredulously, "that a chap can go down there and put up there as if it were a hotel and live on the fat of the land and then come away without paying anything?"

"O, most people give some donation to the monastery when they leave," said Mary Jane.

"I wish we had an institution like that in our Church," said Mr. Browne candidly.

He was astonished to hear that the monks never spoke, got up at two in the morning and slept in their coffins. He asked what they did it for.

"That's the rule of the order," said Aunt Kate firmly.

"Yes, but why?" asked Mr. Browne.

Aunt Kate repeated that it was the rule that was all. Mr. Browne still seemed not to understand. Freddy Malins explained to him, as best he could, that the monks were trying to make up for the sins committed by all the sinners in the outside world. The explanation was not very clear for Mr. Browne grinned and said:

"I like that idea very much but wouldn't a comfortable spring bed do them as well as a coffin?"

"The coffin," said Mary Jane, "is to remind them of their last end."

As the subject had grown lugubrious it was buried in a silence of the table during which Mrs. Malins could be heard saying to her neighbour in an indistinct undertone:

"They are very good men, the monks, very pious men."

The raisins and almonds and figs and apples and oranges and chocolates and sweets were now passed about the table and Aunt Julia invited all the guests to have either port or sherry. At first Mr. Bartell D'Arcy refused to take either but one of his neighbours nudged him and whispered something to him upon which he allowed his glass to be filled. Gradually as the last glasses were being filled the conversation ceased. A pause followed, broken only by the noise of the wine and by unsettlings of chairs. The Misses Morkan, all three, looked down at the table-cloth. Someone coughed once or twice and then a few gentlemen patted the table gently as a signal for silence. The silence came and Gabriel pushed back his chair and stood up.

---

[69] Mount Melleray, located in County Waterford in southeastern Ireland. It is the site of a Trappist monastery founded in 1822, whose guest house received alcoholics seeking a cure.

The patting at once grew louder in encouragement and then ceased altogether. Gabriel leaned his ten trembling fingers on the tablecloth and smiled nervously at the company. Meeting a row of upturned faces he raised his eyes to the chandelier. The piano was playing a waltz tune and he could hear the skirts sweeping against the drawing-room door. People, perhaps, were standing in the snow on the quay outside, gazing up at the lighted windows and listening to the waltz music. The air was pure there. In the distance lay the park where the trees were weighted with snow. The Wellington Monument wore a gleaming cap of snow that flashed westward over the white field of Fifteen Acres.[70]

He began:

"Ladies and Gentlemen,

"It has fallen to my lot this evening, as in years past, to perform a very pleasing task but a task for which I am afraid my poor powers as a speaker are all too inadequate."

"No, no!" said Mr. Browne.

"But, however that may be, I can only ask you tonight to take the will for the deed and to lend me your attention for a few moments while I endeavour to express to you in words what my feelings are on this occasion.

"Ladies and Gentlemen, it is not the first time that we have gathered together under this hospitable roof, around this hospitable board. It is not the first time that we have been the recipients—or perhaps, I had better say, the victims—of the hospitality of certain good ladies."

He made a circle in the air with his arm and paused. Everyone laughed or smiled at Aunt Kate and Aunt Julia and Mary Jane who all turned crimson with pleasure. Gabriel went on more boldly:

"I feel more strongly with every recurring year that our country has no tradition which does it so much honour and which it should guard so jealously as that of its hospitality. It is a tradition that is unique as far as my experience goes (and I have visited not a few places abroad) among the modern nations. Some would say, perhaps, that with us it is rather a failing than anything to be boasted of. But granted even that, it is, to my mind, a princely failing, and one that I trust will long be cultivated among us. Of one thing, at least, I am sure. As long as this one roof shelters the good ladies aforesaid—and I wish from my heart it may do so for many and many a long year to come—the tradition of genuine warm-hearted courteous Irish hospitality, which our forefathers have handed down to us and which we in turn must hand down to our descendants, is still alive among us."

A hearty murmur of assent ran round the table. It shot through Gabriel's mind that Miss Ivors was not there and that she had gone away discourteously: and he said with confidence in himself:

"Ladies and Gentlemen,

A new generation is growing up in our midst, a generation actuated by new ideas and new principles. It is serious and enthusiastic for these new ideas and its enthusiasm, even when it is misdirected, is, I believe, in the main sincere. But we are living in a sceptical and, if I may use the phrase, a thought-tormented age: and sometimes I fear that this new generation, educated or hyper-educated as it is, will lack those qualities of humanity, of hospitality, of kindly humour which belonged to an older day. Listening tonight to the names of all those great singers of the past it seemed to me, I must confess, that we were living in a less spacious age. Those days might, without exaggeration, be called spacious days: and if they are

[70] An open field in Phoenix Park, often used as a parade ground and for other public events.

gone beyond recall let us hope, at least, that in gatherings such as this we shall still speak of them with pride and affection, still cherish in our hearts the memory of those dead and gone great ones whose fame the world will not willingly let die."

"Hear, hear!" said Mr. Browne loudly.

"But yet," continued Gabriel, his voice falling into a softer inflection, "there are always in gatherings such as this sadder thoughts that will recur to our minds: thoughts of the past, of youth, of changes, of absent faces that we miss here tonight. Our path through life is strewn with many such sad memories: and were we to brood upon them always we could not find the heart to go on bravely with our work among the living. We have all of us living duties and living affections which claim, and rightly claim, our strenuous endeavours.

"Therefore, I will not linger on the past. I will not let any gloomy moralising intrude upon us here tonight. Here we are gathered together for a brief moment from the bustle and rush of our everyday routine. We are met here as friends, in the spirit of good-fellowship, as colleagues, also to a certain extent, in the true spirit of *camaraderie*, and as the guests of—what shall I call them—the Three Graces of the Dublin musical world."

The table burst into applause and laughter at this allusion. Aunt Julia vainly asked each of her neighbours in turn to tell her what Gabriel had said.

"He says we are the Three Graces, Aunt Julia," said Mary Jane.

Aunt Julia did not understand but she looked up, smiling, at Gabriel, who continued in the same vein:

"Ladies and Gentlemen,

"I will not attempt to play tonight the part that Paris played on another occasion. I will not attempt to choose between them. The task would be an invidious one and one beyond my poor powers. For when I view them in turn, whether it be our chief hostess herself, whose good heart, whose too good heart, has become a byword with all who know her, or her sister, who seems to be gifted with perennial youth and whose singing must have been a surprise and a revelation to us all tonight, or, last but not least, when I consider our youngest hostess, talented, cheerful, hard-working and the best of nieces, I confess, Ladies and Gentlemen, that I do not know to which of them I should award the prize."

Gabriel glanced down at his aunts and, seeing the large smile on Aunt Julia's face and the tears which had risen to Aunt Kate's eyes, hastened to his close. He raised his glass of port gallantly, while every member of the company fingered a glass expectantly, and said loudly:

"Let us toast them all three together. Let us drink to their health, wealth, long life, happiness and prosperity and may they long continue to hold the proud and self-won position which they hold in their profession and the position of honour and affection which they hold in our hearts."

All the guests stood up, glass in hand, and turning towards the three seated ladies, sang in unison, with Mr. Browne as leader:

> For they are jolly gay fellows,
> For they are jolly gay fellows,
> For they are jolly gay fellows,
> Which nobody can deny.

Aunt Kate was making frank use of her handkerchief and even Aunt Julia seemed moved. Freddy Malins beat time with his pudding-fork and the singers turned towards one another, as if in melodious conference, while they sang with emphasis:

> Unless he tells a lie,
> Unless he tells a lie,

Then, turning once more towards their hostesses, they sang:

> For they are jolly gay fellows,
> For they are jolly gay fellows,
> For they are jolly gay fellows,
> Which nobody can deny.

The acclamation which followed was taken up beyond the door of the supper-room by many of the other guests and renewed time after time, Freddy Malins acting as officer with his fork on high.

The piercing morning air came into the hall where they were standing so that Aunt Kate said:

"Close the door, somebody. Mrs. Malins will get her death of cold."

"Browne is out there, Aunt Kate," said Mary Jane.

"Browne is everywhere," said Aunt Kate, lowering her voice.

Mary Jane laughed at her tone.

"Really," she said archly, "he is very attentive."

"He has been laid on[71] here like the gas," said Aunt Kate in the same tone, "all during the Christmas."

She laughed herself this time good humouredly and then added quickly:

"But tell him to come in, Mary Jane, and close the door. I hope to goodness he didn't hear me."

At that moment the hall-door was opened and Mr. Browne came in from the doorstep, laughing as if his heart would break. He was dressed in a long green overcoat with mock astrakhan[72] cuffs and collar and wore on his head an oval fur cap. He pointed down the snow-covered quay from where the sound of shrill prolonged whistling was borne in.

"Teddy will have all the cabs in Dublin out," he said.

Gabriel advanced from the little pantry behind the office, struggling into his overcoat and, looking round the hall, said:

"Gretta not down yet?"

"She's getting on her things, Gabriel," said Aunt Kate.

"Who's playing up there?" asked Gabriel.

"Nobody. They're all gone."

"O no, Aunt Kate," said Mary Jane. "Bartell D'Arcy and Miss O'Callaghan aren't gone yet."

"Someone is fooling at the piano anyhow," said Gabriel.

Mary Jane glanced at Gabriel and Mr. Browne and said with a shiver:

"It makes me feel cold to look at you two gentlemen muffled up like that. I wouldn't like to face your journey home at this hour."

"I'd like nothing better this minute," said Mr. Browne stoutly, "than a rattling fine walk in the country or a fast drive with a good spanking goer between the shafts."

---

[71] Supplied.

[72] Fur, in this case fake, made from the skins of young lambs from the Astrakhan region of Russia.

"We used to have a very good horse and trap[73] at home," said Aunt Julia sadly.

"The never-to-be-forgotten Johnny," said Mary Jane, laughing.

Aunt Kate and Gabriel laughed too.

"Why, what was wonderful about Johnny?" asked Mr. Browne.

"The late lamented Patrick Morkan, our grandfather, that is," explained Gabriel, "commonly known in his later years as the old gentleman, was a glue-boiler."

"O, now, Gabriel," said Aunt Kate, laughing, "he had a starch mill."

"Well, glue or starch," said Gabriel, "the old gentleman had a horse by the name of Johnny. And Johnny used to work in the old gentleman's mill, walking round and round in order to drive the mill. That was all very well; but now comes the tragic part about Johnny. One fine day the old gentleman thought he'd like to drive out with the quality to a military review in the park."

"The Lord have mercy on his soul," said Aunt Kate compassionately.

"Amen," said Gabriel. "So the old gentleman, as I said, harnessed Johnny and put on his very best tall hat and his very best stock collar and drove out in grand style from his ancestral mansion somewhere near Back Lane,[74] I think."

Everyone laughed, even Mrs. Malins, at Gabriel's manner and Aunt Kate said:

"O, now, Gabriel, he didn't live in Back Lane, really. Only the mill was there."

"Out from the mansion of his forefathers," continued Gabriel, "he drove with Johnny. And everything went on beautifully until Johnny came in sight of King Billy's statue:[75] and whether he fell in love with the horse King Billy sits on or whether he thought he was back again in the mill, anyhow he began to walk round the statue."

Gabriel paced in a circle round the hall in his goloshes amid the laughter of the others.

"Round and round he went," said Gabriel, "and the old gentleman, who was a very pompous old gentleman, was highly indignant. 'Go on, sir! What do you mean, sir? Johnny! Johnny! Most extraordinary conduct! Can't understand the horse!' "

The peal of laughter which followed Gabriel's imitation of the incident was interrupted by a resounding knock at the hall door. Mary Jane ran to open it and let in Freddy Malins. Freddy Malins, with his hat well back on his head and his shoulders humped with cold, was puffing and steaming after his exertions.

"I could only get one cab," he said.

"O, we'll find another along the quay," said Gabriel.

"Yes," said Aunt Kate, "Better not keep Mrs. Malins standing in the draught."

Mrs. Malins was helped down the front steps by her son and Mr. Browne and, after many manoeuvres, hoisted into the cab. Freddy Malins clambered in after her and spent a long time settling her on the seat, Mr. Browne helping him with advice. At last she was settled comfortably and Freddy Malins invited Mr. Browne into the cab. There was a good deal of confused talk, and then Mr. Browne got into the cab. The cabman settled his rug over his knees, and bent down for the address. The confusion grew greater and the cabman was directed differently by Freddy Malins and Mr. Browne, each of whom had his head out through a window

---

[73] A light carriage.   [74] A street in a rundown area of central Dublin.

[75] William of Orange (1650–1702), who reigned as King of England from 1689 to 1702, defeated the Irish at the Battle of the Boyne in 1690 and went on to bring Ireland effectively under British control. His equestrian statue stood in front of Trinity College in central Dublin not far to the east of Usher's Island.

of the cab. The difficulty was to know where to drop Mr. Browne along the route, and Aunt Kate, Aunt Julia and Mary Jane helped the discussion from the doorstep with cross directions and contradictions and abundance of laughter. As for Freddy Malins he was speechless with laughter. He popped his head in and out of the window every moment to the great danger of his hat, and told his mother how the discussion was progressing, till at last Mr. Browne shouted to the bewildered cabman above the din of everybody's laughter:

"Do you know Trinity College?"

"Yes, sir," said the cabman.

"Well, drive bang up against Trinity College gates," said Mr. Browne, "and then we'll tell you where to go. You understand now?"

"Yes, sir," said the cabman.

"Make like a bird for Trinity College."

"Right, sir," said the cabman.

The horse was whipped up and the cab rattled off along the quay amid a chorus of laughter and adieus.

Gabriel had not gone to the door with the others. He was in a dark part of the hall gazing up the staircase. A woman was standing near the top of the first flight, in the shadow also. He could not see her face but he could see the terra-cotta[76] and salmon-pink panels of her skirt which the shadow made appear black and white. It was his wife. She was leaning on the banisters, listening to something. Gabriel was surprised at her stillness and strained his ear to listen also. But he could hear little save the noise of laughter and dispute on the front steps, a few chords struck on the piano and a few notes of a man's voice singing.

He stood still in the gloom of the hall, trying to catch the air that the voice was singing and gazing up at his wife. There was grace and mystery in her attitude as if she were a symbol of something. He asked himself what is a woman standing on the stairs in the shadow, listening to distant music, a symbol of. If he were a painter he would paint her in that attitude. Her blue felt hat would show off the bronze of her hair against the darkness and the dark panels of her skirt would show off the light ones. Distant Music he would call the picture if he were a painter.

The hall-door was closed; and Aunt Kate, Aunt Julia and Mary Jane came down the hall, still laughing.

"Well, isn't Freddy terrible?" said Mary Jane. "He's really terrible."

Gabriel said nothing but pointed up the stairs towards where his wife was standing. Now that the hall-door was closed the voice and the piano could be heard more clearly. Gabriel held up his hand for them to be silent. The song seemed to be in the old Irish tonality[77] and the singer seemed uncertain both of his words and of his voice. The voice, made plaintive by distance and by the singer's hoarseness, faintly illuminated the cadence of the air with words expressing grief:

> O, the rain falls on my heavy locks
> And the dew wets my skin,
> My babe lies cold . . .[78]

---

[76] Grayish or reddish orange.

[77] The five-tone scale of early Irish music.

[78] From "The Lass of Aughrim," an old Irish ballad that tells the story of a seduced and rejected girl who drowns at sea with her babe in her arms.

"O," exclaimed Mary Jane. "It's Bartell D'Arcy singing and he wouldn't sing all the night. O, I'll get him to sing a song before he goes."

"O, do, Mary Jane," said Aunt Kate.

Mary Jane brushed past the others and ran to the staircase, but before she reached it the singing stopped and the piano was closed abruptly.

"O, what a pity!" she cried. "Is he coming down, Gretta?"

Gabriel heard his wife answer yes and saw her come down towards them. A few steps behind her were Mr. Bartell D'Arcy and Miss O'Callaghan.

"O, Mr. D'Arcy," cried Mary Jane, "it's downright mean of you to break off like that when we were all in raptures listening to you."

"I have been at him all the evening," said Miss O'Callaghan, "and Mrs. Conroy, too, and he told us he had a dreadful cold and couldn't sing."

"O, Mr. D'Arcy," said Aunt Kate, "now that was a great fib to tell."

"Can't you see that I'm as hoarse as a crow?" said Mr. D'Arcy roughly.

He went into the pantry hastily and put on his overcoat. The others, taken aback by his rude speech, could find nothing to say. Aunt Kate wrinkled her brows and made signs to the others to drop the subject. Mr. D'Arcy stood swathing his neck carefully and frowning.

"It's the weather," said Aunt Julia, after a pause.

"Yes, everybody has colds," said Aunt Kate readily, "everybody."

"They say," said Mary Jane, "we haven't had snow like it for thirty years; and I read this morning in the newspapers that the snow is general all over Ireland."

"I love the look of snow," said Aunt Julia sadly.

"So do I," said Miss O'Callaghan. "I think Christmas is never really Christmas unless we have the snow on the ground."

"But poor Mr. D'Arcy doesn't like the snow," said Aunt Kate, smiling.

Mr. D'Arcy came from the pantry, fully swathed and buttoned, and in a repentant tone told them the history of his cold. Everyone gave him advice and said it was a great pity and urged him to be very careful of his throat in the night air. Gabriel watched his wife, who did not join in the conversation. She was standing right under the dusty fanlight and the flame of the gas lit up the rich bronze of her hair, which he had seen her drying at the fire a few days before. She was in the same attitude and seemed unaware of the talk about her. At last she turned towards them and Gabriel saw that there was colour on her cheeks and that her eyes were shining. A sudden tide of joy went leaping out of his heart.

"Mr. D'Arcy," she said, "what is the name of that song you were singing?"

"It's called *The Lass of Aughrim*," said Mr. D'Arcy, "but I couldn't remember it properly. Why? Do you know it?"

"*The Lass of Aughrim,*" she repeated. "I couldn't think of the name."

"It's a very nice air," said Mary Jane. "I'm sorry you were not in voice tonight."

"Now, Mary Jane," said Aunt Kate, "don't annoy Mr. D'Arcy. I won't have him annoyed."

Seeing that all were ready to start she shepherded them to the door, where goodnight was said:

"Well, good-night, Aunt Kate, and thanks for the pleasant evening."

"Good-night, Gabriel. Good-night, Gretta!"

"Good-night, Aunt Kate, and thanks ever so much. Good-night, Aunt Julia."

"O, good-night, Gretta, I didn't see you."

"Good-night, Mr. D'Arcy. Good-night, Miss O'Callaghan."

"Good-night, Miss Morkan."

"Good-night, again."

"Good-night, all. Safe home."

"Good-night. Good night."

The morning was still dark. A dull, yellow light brooded over the houses and the river; and the sky seemed to be descending. It was slushy underfoot; and only streaks and patches of snow lay on the roofs, on the parapets[79] of the quay and on the area railings. The lamps were still burning redly in the murky air and, across the river, the palace of the Four Courts[80] stood out menacingly against the heavy sky.

She was walking on before him with Mr. Bartell D'Arcy, her shoes in a brown parcel tucked under one arm and her hands holding her skirt up from the slush. She had no longer any grace of attitude, but Gabriel's eyes were still bright with happiness. The blood went bounding along his veins; and the thoughts went rioting through his brain, proud, joyful, tender, valorous.

She was walking on before him so lightly and so erect that he longed to run after her noiselessly, catch her by the shoulders and say something foolish and affectionate into her ear. She seemed to him so frail that he longed to defend her against something and then to be alone with her. Moments of their secret life together burst like stars upon his memory. A heliotrope[81] envelope was lying beside his breakfast-cup and he was caressing it with his hand. Birds were twittering in the ivy and the sunny web of the curtain was shimmering along the floor: he could not eat for happiness. They were standing on the crowded platform and he was placing a ticket inside the warm palm of her glove. He was standing with her in the cold, looking in through a grated window at a man making bottles in a roaring furnace. It was very cold. Her face, fragrant in the cold air, was quite close to his; and suddenly he called out to the man at the furnace:

"Is the fire hot, sir?"

But the man could not hear with the noise of the furnace. It was just as well. He might have answered rudely.

A wave of yet more tender joy escaped from his heart and went coursing in warm flood along his arteries. Like the tender fire of stars moments of their life together, that no one knew of or would ever know of, broke upon and illumined his memory. He longed to recall to her those moments, to make her forget the years of their dull existence together and remember only their moments of ecstasy. For the years, he felt, had not quenched his soul or hers. Their children, his writing, her household cares had not quenched all their souls' tender fire. In one letter that he had written to her then he had said: "Why is it that words like these seem to me so dull and cold? Is it because there is no word tender enough to be your name?"

Like distant music these words that he had written years before were borne towards him from the past. He longed to be alone with her. When the others had gone away, when he and she were in the room in the hotel, then they would be alone together. He would call her softly:

"Gretta!"

Perhaps she would not hear at once: she would be undressing. Then something in his voice would strike her. She would turn and look at him. . . .

At the corner of Winetavern Street[82] they met a cab. He was glad of its rattling

---

[79] Walls.

[80] A building housing the courts of Ireland on the north bank of the River Liffey.

[81] Purple.

[82] Gabriel and Gretta have walked about three hundred yards from Usher's Island.

noise as it saved him from conversation. She was looking out of the window and seemed tired. The others spoke only a few words, pointing out some building or street. The horse galloped along wearily under the murky morning sky, dragging his old rattling box after his heels, and Gabriel was again in a cab with her, galloping to catch the boat, galloping to their honeymoon.

As the cab drove across O'Connell Bridge[83] Miss O'Callaghan said:

"They say you never cross O'Connell Bridge without seeing a white horse."

"I see a white man this time," said Gabriel.

"Where?" asked Mr. Bartell D'Arcy.

Gabriel pointed to the statue, on which lay patches of snow. Then he nodded familiarly to it and waved his hand.

"Good-night, Dan," he said gaily.

When the cab drew up before the hotel, Gabriel jumped out and, in spite of Mr. Bartell D'Arcy's protest, paid the driver. He gave the man a shilling over his fare. The man saluted and said:

"A prosperous New Year to you, sir."

"The same to you," said Gabriel cordially.

She leaned for a moment on his arm in getting out of the cab and while standing at the curbstone, bidding the others good-night. She leaned lightly on his arm, as lightly as when she had danced with him a few hours before. He had felt proud and happy then, happy that she was his, proud of her grace and wifely carriage. But now, after the kindling again of so many memories, the first touch of her body, musical and strange and perfumed, sent through him a keen pang of lust. Under cover of her silence he pressed her arm closely to his side; and, as they stood at the hotel door, he felt that they had escaped from their lives and duties, escaped from home and friends and run away together with wild and radiant hearts to a new adventure.

An old man was dozing in a great hooded chair in the hall. He lit a candle in the office and went before them to the stairs. They followed him in silence, their feet falling in soft thuds on the thickly carpeted stairs. She mounted the stairs behind the porter,[84] her head bowed in the ascent, her frail shoulders curved as with a burden, her skirt girt tightly about her. He could have flung his arms about her hips and held her still, for his arms were trembling with desire to seize her and only the stress of his nails against the palms of his hands held the wild impulse of his body in check. The porter halted on the stairs to settle his guttering candle. They halted, too, on the steps below him. In the silence Gabriel could hear the falling of the molten wax into the tray and the thumping of his own heart against his ribs.

The porter led them along a corridor and opened a door. Then he set his unstable candle down on a toilet-table and asked at what hour they were to be called in the morning.

"Eight," said Gabriel.

The porter pointed to the tap of the electric-light and began a muttered apology, but Gabriel cut him short.

"We don't want any light. We have light enough from the street. And I say," he

---

[83] The bridge over the River Liffey named for Daniel O'Connell (1775–1847), the Irish moderate political leader who led a campaign to regain religious and political freedoms from the British. His statue is at the northern end of the bridge.
[84] Doorman.

added, pointing to the candle, "You might remove that handsome article, like a good man."

The porter took up his candle again, but slowly, for he was surprised by such a novel idea. Then he mumbled good-night and went out. Gabriel shot the lock to.

A ghastly light from the street lamp lay in a long shaft from one window to the door. Gabriel threw his overcoat and hat on a couch and crossed the room towards the window. He looked down into the street in order that his emotion might calm a little. Then he turned and leaned against a chest of drawers with his back to the light. She had taken off her hat and cloak and was standing before a large swinging mirror, unhooking her waist. Gabriel paused for a few moments, watching her, and then said:

"Gretta!"

She turned away from the mirror slowly and walked along the shaft of light towards him. Her face looked so serious and weary that the words would not pass Gabriel's lips. No, it was not the moment yet.

"You looked tired," he said.

"I am a little," she answered.

"You don't feel ill or weak?"

"No, tired: that's all."

She went on to the window and stood there, looking out. Gabriel waited again and then, fearing that diffidence was about to conquer him, he said abruptly:

"By the way, Gretta!"

"What is it?"

"You know that poor fellow Malins?" he said quickly.

"Yes. What about him?"

"Well, poor fellow, he's a decent sort of chap, after all," continued Gabriel in a false voice. "He gave me back that sovereign[85] I lent him, and I didn't expect it, really. It's a pity he wouldn't keep away from that Browne, because he's not a bad fellow, really."

He was trembling now with annoyance. Why did she seem so abstracted? He did not know how he could begin. Was she annoyed, too, about something? If she would only turn to him or come to him of her own accord! To take her as she was would be brutal. No, he must see some ardour in her eyes first. He longed to be master of her strange mood.

"When did you lend him the pound?" she asked, after a pause.

Gabriel strove to restrain himself from breaking out into brutal language about the sottish Malins and his pound. He longed to cry to her from his soul, to crush her body against his, to overmaster her. But he said:

"O, at Christmas, when he opened that little Christmas-card shop in Henry Street."[86]

He was in such a fever of rage and desire that he did not hear her come from the window. She stood before him for an instant, looking at him strangely. Then, suddenly raising herself on tiptoe and resting her hands lightly on his shoulders, she kissed him.

"You are a very generous person, Gabriel," she said.

Gabriel, trembling with delight at her sudden kiss and at the quaintness of her

---

[85] English gold coin.

[86] In Britain and Ireland Christmas cards were traditionally sold in special shops opened during the holiday season for that purpose, with the profits often going to charity.

phrase, put his hands on her hair and began smoothing it back, scarcely touching it with his fingers. The washing had made it fine and brilliant. His heart was brimming over with happiness. Just when he was wishing for it she had come to him of her own accord. Perhaps her thoughts had been running with his. Perhaps she had felt the impetuous desire that was in him, and then the yielding mood had come upon her. Now that she had fallen to him so easily, he wondered why he had been so diffident.

He stood, holding her head between his hands. Then, slipping one arm swiftly about her body and drawing her towards him, he said softly:

"Gretta, dear, what are you thinking about?"

She did not answer nor yield wholly to his arm. He said again, softly:

"Tell me what it is, Gretta. I think I know what is the matter. Do I know?"

She did not answer at once. Then she said in an outburst of tears:

"O, I am thinking about that song, *The Lass of Aughrim.*"

She broke loose from him and ran to the bed and, throwing her arms across the bed-rail, hid her face. Gabriel stood stock-still for a moment in astonishment and then followed her. As he passed in the way of the cheval-glass[87] he caught sight of himself in full length, his broad, well-filled shirt-front, the face whose expression always puzzled him when he saw it in a mirror, and his glimmering gilt rimmed eyeglasses. He halted a few paces from her and said:

"What about the song? Why does that make you cry?"

She raised her head from her arms and dried her eyes with the back of her hand like a child. A kinder note than he had intended went into his voice.

"Why, Gretta?" he asked.

"I am thinking about a person long ago who used to sing that song."

"And who was the person long ago?" asked Gabriel, smiling.

"It was a person I used to know in Galway when I was living with my grandmother," she said.

The smile passed away from Gabriel's face. A dull anger began to gather again at the back of his mind and the dull fires of his lust began to glow angrily in his veins.

"Someone you were in love with?" he asked ironically.

"It was a young boy I used to know," she answered, "named Michael Furey. He used to sing that song, *The Lass of Aughrim.* He was very delicate."

Gabriel was silent. He did not wish her to think that he was interested in this delicate boy.

"I can see him so plainly," she said, after a moment. "Such eyes as he had: big, dark eyes! And such an expression in them—an expression!"

"O, then, you are in love with him?" said Gabriel.

"I used to go out walking[88] with him," she said, "when I was in Galway."

A thought flew across Gabriel's mind.

"Perhaps that was why you wanted to go to Galway with that Ivors girl?" he said coldly.

She looked at him and asked in surprise:

"What for?"

Her eyes made Gabriel feel awkward. He shrugged his shoulders and said:

"How do I know? To see him, perhaps.

She looked away from him along the shaft of light towards the window in silence.

[87] A long mirror mounted on swivels in a frame.   [88] Dating.

"He is dead," she said at length. "He died when he was only seventeen. Isn't it a terrible thing to die so young as that?"

"What was he?" asked Gabriel, still ironically.

"He was in the gasworks,"[89] she said.

Gabriel felt humiliated by the failure of his irony and by the evocation of this figure from the dead, a boy in the gasworks. While he had been full of memories of their secret life together, full of tenderness and joy and desire, she had been comparing him in her mind with another. A shameful consciousness of his own person assailed him. He saw himself as a ludicrous figure, acting as a pennyboy[90] for his aunts, a nervous, well-meaning sentimentalist, orating to vulgarians and idealising his own clownish lusts, the pitiable fatuous fellow he had caught a glimpse of in the mirror. Instinctively he turned his back more to the light lest she might see the shame that burned upon his forehead.

He tried to keep up his tone of cold interrogation, but his voice when he spoke was humble and indifferent.

"I suppose you were in love with this Michael Furey, Gretta," he said.

"I was great[91] with him at that time," she said.

Her voice was veiled and sad. Gabriel, feeling now how vain it would be to try to lead her whither he had purposed, caressed one of her hands and said, also sadly:

"And what did he die of so young, Gretta? Consumption,[92] was it?"

"I think he died for me," she answered.

A vague terror seized Gabriel at this answer, as if, at that hour when he had hoped to triumph, some impalpable and vindictive being was coming against him, gathering forces against him in its vague world. But he shook himself free of it with an effort of reason and continued to caress her hand. He did not question her again, for he felt that she would tell him of herself. Her hand was warm and moist: it did not respond to his touch, but he continued to caress it just as he had caressed her first letter to him that spring morning.

"It was in the winter," she said, "about the beginning of the winter when I was going to leave my grandmother's and come up here to the convent. And he was ill at the time in his lodgings in Galway and wouldn't be let out, and his people in Oughterard[93] were written to. He was in decline, they said, or something like that. I never knew rightly."

She paused for a moment and sighed.

"Poor fellow," she said. "He was very fond of me and he was such a gentle boy. We used to go out together, walking, you know, Gabriel, like the way they do in the country. He was going to study singing only for his health. He had a very good voice, poor Michael Furey."

"Well; and then?" asked Gabriel.

"And then when it came to the time for me to leave Galway and come up to the convent he was much worse and I wouldn't be let see him so I wrote him a letter saying I was going up to Dublin and would be back in the summer, and hoping he would be better then."

She paused for a moment to get her voice under control, and then went on:

"Then the night before I left, I was in my grandmother's house in Nuns'

---

[89] A utility plant manufacturing gas from coal to be used for lighting and heating.
[90] Someone engaged in cheap or inferior work.   [91] Close or intimate friends.
[92] Tuberculosis.   [93] A village northwest of Galway.

Island,[94] packing up, and I heard gravel thrown up against the window. The window was so wet I couldn't see, so I ran downstairs as I was and slipped out the back into the garden and there was the poor fellow at the end of the garden, shivering.''

"And did you not tell him to go back?" asked Gabriel.

"I implored of him to go home at once and told him he would get his death in the rain. But he said he did not want to live. I can see his eyes as well as well! He was standing at the end of the wall where there was a tree.''

"And did he go home?" asked Gabriel.

"Yes, he went home. And when I was only a week in the convent he died and he was buried in Oughterard, where his people came from. O, the day I heard that, that he was dead!''

She stopped, choking with sobs, and, overcome by emotion, flung herself face downward on the bed, sobbing in the quilt. Gabriel held her hand for a moment longer, irresolutely, and then, shy of intruding on her grief, let it fall gently and walked to the window.

She was fast asleep.

Gabriel, leaning on his elbow, looked for a few moments unresentfully on her tangled hair and half-open mouth, listening to her deep-drawn breath. So she had had that romance in her life: a man had died for her sake. It hardly pained him now to think how poor a part he, her husband, had played in her life. He watched her while she slept, as though he and she had never lived together as man and wife. His curious eyes rested long upon her face and on her hair: and, as he thought of what she must have been then, in that time of her first girlish beauty, a strange, friendly pity for her entered his soul. He did not like to say even to himself that her face was no longer beautiful, but he knew that it was no longer the face for which Michael Furey had braved death.

Perhaps she had not told him all the story. His eyes moved to the chair over which she had thrown some of her clothes. A petticoat string dangled to the floor. One boot stood upright, its limp upper fallen down: the fellow of it lay upon its side. He wondered at his riot of emotions of an hour before. From what had it proceeded? From his aunt's supper, from his own foolish speech, from the wine and dancing, the merry-making when saying good-night in the hall, the pleasure of the walk along the river in the snow. Poor Aunt Julia! She, too, would soon be a shade with the shade of Patrick Morkan and his horse. He had caught that haggard look upon her face for a moment when she was singing *Arrayed for the Bridal.* Soon, perhaps, he would be sitting in that same drawing-room, dressed in black, his silk hat on his knees. The blinds would be drawn down and Aunt Kate would be sitting beside him, crying and blowing her nose and telling him how Julia had died. He would cast about in his mind for some words that might console her, and would find only lame and useless ones. Yes, yes: that would happen very soon.

The air of the room chilled his shoulders. He stretched himself cautiously along under the sheets and lay down beside his wife. One by one, they were all becoming shades. Better pass boldly into that other world, in the full glory of some passion, than fade and wither dismally with age. He thought of how she who lay beside him had locked in her head for so many years that image of her lover's eyes when he had told her that he did not wish to live.

---

[94] An island in the Galway River, where it flows through the city of Galway, and named after a convent located there.

Generous tears filled Gabriel's eyes. He had never felt like that himself towards any woman, but he knew that such a feeling must be love. The tears gathered more thickly in his eyes and in the partial darkness he imagined he saw the form of a young man standing under a dripping tree. Other forms were near. His soul had approached that region where dwell the vast hosts of the dead. He was conscious of, but could not apprehend, their wayward and flickering existence. His own identity was fading out into a grey impalpable world: the solid world itself, which these dead had one time reared and lived in, was dissolving and dwindling.

A few light taps upon the pane made him turn to the window. It had begun to snow again. He watched sleepily the flakes, silver and dark, falling obliquely against the lamplight. The time had come for him to set out on his journey westward. Yes, the newspapers were right: snow was general all over Ireland. It was falling on every part of the dark central plain, on the treeless hills, falling softly upon the Bog of Allen[95] and, farther westward, softly falling into the dark mutinous Shannon waves.[96] It was falling, too, upon every part of the lonely churchyard on the hill where Michael Furey lay buried. It lay thickly drifted on the crooked crosses and headstones, on the spears of the little gate, on the barren thorns. His soul swooned slowly as he heard the snow falling faintly through the universe and faintly falling, like the descent of their last end, upon all the living and the dead.

[1914]

---

[95] An area of wet marshy ground some twenty-five miles southwest of Dublin.
[96] The Shannon River, west of Dublin, flows southwest across Ireland to the sea.

Susan Glaspell   *1882–1948*

A JURY OF HER PEERS

When Martha Hale opened the storm-door and got a cut of the north wind, she ran back for her big woolen scarf. As she hurriedly wound that round her head her eye made a scandalized sweep of her kitchen. It was no ordinary thing that called her away—it was probably farther from ordinary than anything that had ever happened in Dickson County. But what her eye took in was that her kitchen was in no shape for leaving: her bread all ready for mixing, half the flour sifted and half unsifted.

She hated to see things half done; but she had been at that when the team from town stopped to get Mr. Hale, and then the sheriff came running in to say his wife wished Mrs. Hale would come too—adding, with a grin, that he guessed she was getting scarey and wanted another woman along. So she had dropped everything right where it was.

"Martha!" now came her husband's impatient voice. "Don't keep folks waiting out here in the cold."

She again opened the storm-door, and this time joined the three men and the one woman waiting for her in the big two-seated buggy.

After she had the robes tucked around her she took another look at the woman who sat beside her on the back seat. She had met Mrs. Peters the year before at the county fair, and the thing she remembered about her was that she didn't seem like a sheriff's wife. She was small and thin and didn't have a strong voice. Mrs. Gorman, sheriff's wife before Gorman went out and Peters came in, had a voice that somehow seemed to be backing up the law with every word. But if Mrs. Peters didn't look like a sheriff's wife, Peters made it up in looking like a sheriff. He was to a dot the kind of man who could get himself elected sheriff—a heavy man with a big voice, who was particularly genial with the law-abiding, as if to make it plain that he knew the difference between criminals and non-criminals. And right there it came into Mrs. Hale's mind, with a stab, that this man who was so pleasant and lively with all of them was going to the Wrights' now as a sheriff.

"The country's not very pleasant this time of year," Mrs. Peters at last ventured, as if she felt they ought to be talking as well as the men.

Mrs. Hale scarcely finished her reply, for they had gone up a little hill and could see the Wright place now, and seeing it did not make her feel like talking. It looked very lonesome this cold March morning. It had always been a lonesome-looking place. It was down in a hollow, and the poplar trees around it were lonesome-looking trees. The men were looking at it and talking about what had happened. The county attorney was bending to one side of the buggy, and kept looking steadily at the place as they drew up to it.

"I'm glad you came with me," Mrs. Peters said nervously, as the two women were about to follow the men in through the kitchen door.

Even after she had her foot on the door-step, her hand on the knob, Martha Hale had a moment of feeling she could not cross that threshold. And the reason it seemed she couldn't cross it now was simply because she hadn't crossed it before. Time and time again it had been in her mind, "I ought to go over and see Minnie Foster"—she still thought of her as Minnie Foster, though for twenty years she had been Mrs. Wright. And then there was always something to do and Minnie Foster would go from her mind. But *now* she could come.

The men went over to the stove. The women stood close together by the door. Young Henderson, the county attorney, turned around and said, "Come up to the fire, ladies."

Mrs. Peters took a step forward, then stopped. "I'm not—cold," she said.

And so the two women stood by the door, at first not even so much as looking around the kitchen.

The men talked for a minute about what a good thing it was the sheriff had sent his deputy out that morning to make a fire for them, and then Sheriff Peters stepped back from the stove, unbuttoned his outer coat, and leaned his hands on the kitchen table in a way that seemed to mark the beginning of official business. "Now, Mr. Hale," he said in a sort of semi-official voice, "before we move things about, you tell Mr. Henderson just what it was you saw when you came here yesterday morning."

The county attorney was looking around the kitchen.

"By the way," he said, "has anything been moved?" He turned to the sheriff. "Are things just as you left them yesterday?"

Peters looked from cupboard to sink; from that to a small worn rocker a little to one side of the kitchen table.

"It's just the same."

"Somebody should have been left here yesterday," said the county attorney.

"Oh—yesterday," returned the sheriff, with a little gesture as of yesterday having been more than he could bear to think of. "When I had to send Frank to Morris Center for that man who went crazy—let me tell you, I had my hands full *yesterday*. I knew you could get back from Omaha by to-day, George, and as long as I went over everything here myself—"

"Well, Mr. Hale," said the county attorney, in a way of letting what was past and gone go, "tell just what happened when you came here yesterday morning."

Mrs. Hale, still leaning against the door, had that sinking feeling of the mother whose child is about to speak a piece. Lewis often wandered along and got things mixed up in a story. She hoped he would tell this straight and plain, and not say unnecessary things that would just make things harder for Minnie Foster. He didn't begin at once, and she noticed that he looked queer—as if standing in that kitchen and having to tell what he had seen there yesterday morning made him almost sick.

"Yes, Mr. Hale?" the county attorney reminded.

"Harry and I had started to town with a load of potatoes," Mrs. Hale's husband began.

Harry was Mrs. Hale's oldest boy. He wasn't with them now, for the very good reason that those potatoes never got to town yesterday and he was taking them this morning, so he hadn't been home when the sheriff stopped to say he wanted Mr. Hale to come over to the Wright place and tell the county attorney his story there, where he could point it all out. With all Mrs. Hale's other emotions came the fear that maybe Harry wasn't dressed warm enough—they hadn't any of them realized how that north wind did bite.

"We come along this road," Hale was going on, with a motion of his hand to the road over which they had just come, "and as we got in sight of the house I says to Harry, 'I'm goin' to see if I can't get John Wright to take a telephone.' You see," he explained to Henderson, "unless I can get somebody to go in with me they won't come out this branch road except for a price *I* can't pay. I'd spoke to Wright about it once before; but he put me off, saying folks talked too much anyway, and all he asked was peace and quiet—guess you know about how much he talked himself. But I thought maybe if I went to the house and talked about it before his wife, and said all the women-folks liked the telephones, and that in this lonesome stretch of road it would be a good thing—well, I said to Harry that that was what I was going to say—though I said at the same time that I didn't know as what his wife wanted made much difference to John—"

Now, there he was!—saying things he didn't need to say. Mrs. Hale tried to catch her husband's eye, but fortunately the county attorney interrupted with:

"Let's talk about that a little later, Mr. Hale. I do want to talk about that, but I'm anxious now to get along to just what happened when you got here."

When he began this time, it was very deliberately and carefully:

"I didn't see or hear anything. I knocked at the door. And still it was all quiet inside. I knew they must be up—it was past eight o'clock. So I knocked again, louder, and I thought I heard somebody say 'Come in.' I wasn't sure—I'm not sure yet. But I opened the door—this door," jerking a hand toward the door by which the two women stood, "and there, in that rocker"—pointing to it—"sat Mrs. Wright."

Every one in the kitchen looked at the rocker. It came into Mrs. Hale's mind that that rocker didn't look in the least like Minnie Foster—the Minnie Foster of twenty years before. It was a dingy red, with wooden rungs up the back and the middle rung was gone, and the chair sagged to one side.

"How did she—look?" the county attorney was inquiring.

"Well," said Hale, "she looked—queer."

"How do you mean—queer?"

As he asked it he took out a note-book and pencil. Mrs. Hale did not like the sight of that pencil. She kept her eye fixed on her husband, as if to keep him from saying unnecessary things that would go into that note-book and make trouble.

Hale did speak guardedly, as if the pencil had affected him too.

"Well, as if she didn't know what she was going to do next. And kind of—done up."

"How did she seem to feel about your coming?"

"Why, I don't think she minded—one way or other. She didn't pay much attention. I said, 'Ho' do, Mrs. Wright? It's cold, ain't it?' And she said, 'Is it?'—and went on pleatin' at her apron.

"Well, I was surprised. She didn't ask me to come up to the stove, or to sit down, but just set there, not even lookin' at me. And so I said: 'I want to see John.'

"And then she—laughed. I guess you would call it a laugh.

"I thought of Harry and the team outside, so I said, a little sharp, 'Can I see John?' 'No,' says she—kind of dull like. "Ain't he home?' says I. Then she looked at me. 'Yes,' says she, 'he's home.' 'Then why can't I see him?' I asked her, out of patience with her now. 'Cause he's dead,' says she, just as quiet and dull—and fell to pleatin' her apron. 'Dead?' says I, like you do when you can't take in what you've heard.

"She just nodded her head, not getting a bit excited, but rockin' back and forth.

"'Why—where is he?' says I, not knowing *what* to say.

"She just pointed upstairs—like this"—pointing to the room above.

"I got up, with the idea of going up there myself. By this time I—didn't know what to do. I walked from there to here; then I says: 'Why, what did he die of?'

"'He died of a rope around his neck,' says she; and just went on pleatin' at her apron."

Hale stopped speaking, and stood staring at the rocker, as if he were still seeing the woman who had sat there the morning before. Nobody spoke; it was as if every one were seeing the woman who had sat there the morning before.

"And what did you do then?" the county attorney at last broke the silence.

"I went out and called Harry. I thought I might—need help. I got Harry in, and we went upstairs." His voice fell almost to a whisper. "There he was—lying over the—"

"I think I'd rather have you go into that upstairs," the county attorney interrupted, "where you can point it all out. Just go on now with the rest of the story."

"Well, my first thought was to get that rope off. It looked—"

He stopped, his face twitching.

"But Harry, he went up to him, and he said, 'No, he's dead all right, and we'd better not touch anything.' So we went downstairs.

"She was still sitting that same way. 'Has anybody been notified?' I asked. 'No,' says she, unconcerned.

"'Who did this, Mrs. Wright?' said Harry. He said it business-like, and she stopped pleatin' at her apron. 'I don't know,' she says. "You don't *know*?' says Harry. 'Weren't you sleepin' in the bed with him?' 'Yes,' says she, 'but I was on the inside.' 'Somebody slipped a rope around his neck and strangled him, and you didn't wake up?' says Harry. 'I didn't wake up,' she said after him.

"We may have looked as if we didn't see how that could be, for after a minute she said, 'I sleep sound.'

"Harry was going to ask her more questions, but I said maybe that weren't our business; maybe we ought to let her tell her story first to the coroner or the sheriff. So Harry went fast as he could over to High Road—the Rivers' place, where there's a telephone."

"And what did she do when she knew you had gone for the coroner?" The attorney got his pencil in his hand all ready for writing.

"She moved from that chair to this one over here"—Hale pointed to a small chair in the corner—"and just sat there with her hands held together and looking down. I got a feeling that I ought to make some conversation, so I said I had come in to see if John wanted to put in a telephone; and at that she started to laugh, and then she stopped and looked at me—scared."

At the sound of a moving pencil the man who was telling the story looked up.

"I dunno—maybe it wasn't scared," he hastened; "I wouldn't like to say it was. Soon Harry got back, and then Dr. Lloyd came, and you, Mr. Peters, and so I guess that's all I know that you don't."

He said that last with relief, and moved a little, as if relaxing. Every one moved a little. The county attorney walked toward the stair door.

"I guess we'll go upstairs first—then out to the barn and around there."

He paused and looked around the kitchen.

"You're convinced there was nothing important here?" he asked the sheriff. "Nothing that would—point to any motive?"

The sheriff too looked all around, as if to re-convince himself.

"Nothing here but kitchen things," he said, with a little laugh for the insignificance of kitchen things.

The county attorney was looking at the cupboard—a peculiar, ungainly structure, half closet and half cupboard, the upper part of it being built in the wall, and the lower part just the old-fashioned kitchen cupboard. As if its queerness attracted him, he got a chair and opened the upper part and looked in. After a moment he drew his hand away sticky.

"Here's a nice mess," he said resentfully.

The two women had drawn nearer, and now the sheriff's wife spoke.

"Oh—her fruit," she said, looking to Mrs. Hale for sympathetic understanding. She turned back to the county attorney and explained: "She worried about that when it turned so cold last night. She said the fire would go out and her jars might burst."

Mrs. Peters' husband broke into a laugh.

"Well, can you beat the women! Held for murder, and worrying about her preserves!"

The young attorney set his lips.

"I guess before we're through with her she may have something more serious than preserves to worry about."

"Oh, well," said Mrs. Hale's husband, with good-natured superiority, "women are used to worrying over trifles."

The two women moved a little closer together. Neither of them spoke. The county attorney seemed suddenly to remember his manners—and think of his future.

"And yet," said he, with the gallantry of a young politician, "for all their worries, what would we do without the ladies?"

The women did not speak, did not unbend. He went to the sink and began washing his hands. He turned to wipe them on the roller towel—whirled it for a cleaner place.

"Dirty towels! Not much of a housekeeper, would you say, ladies?"

He kicked his foot against some dirty pans under the sink.

"There's a great deal of work to be done on a farm," said Mrs. Hale stiffly.

"To be sure. And yet"—with a little bow to her—"I know there are some Dickson County farm-houses that do not have such roller towels." He gave it a pull to expose its full length again.

"Those towels get dirty awful quick. Men's hands aren't always as clean as they might be."

"Ah, loyal to your sex, I see," he laughed. He stopped and gave her a keen look. "But you and Mrs. Wright were neighbors. I suppose you were friends, too."

Martha Hale shook her head.

"I've seen little enough of her of late years. I've not been in this house—it's more than a year."

"And why was that? You didn't like her?"

"I liked her well enough," she replied with spirit. "Farmers' wives have their hands full, Mr. Henderson. And then"—She looked around the kitchen.

"Yes?" he encouraged.

"It never seemed a very cheerful place," said she, more to herself than to him.

"No," he agreed; "I don't think any one would call it cheerful. I shouldn't say she had the home-making instinct."

"Well, I don't know as Wright had, either," she muttered.

"You mean they didn't get on very well?" he was quick to ask.

"No; I don't mean anything," she answered, with decision. As she turned a little away from him, she added: "But I don't think a place would be any the cheerfuler for John Wright's bein' in it."

"I'd like to talk to you about that a little later, Mrs. Hale," he said. "I'm anxious to get the lay of things upstairs now."

He moved toward the stair door, followed by the two men.

"I suppose anything Mrs. Peters does'll be all right?" the sheriff inquired. "She was to take in some clothes for her, you know—and a few little things. We left in such a hurry yesterday.''

The county attorney looked at the two women whom they were leaving alone there among the kitchen things.

"Yes—Mrs. Peters," he said, his glance resting on the woman who was not Mrs. Peters, the big farmer woman who stood behind the sheriff's wife. "Of course Mrs. Peters is one of us," he said, in a manner of entrusting responsibility. "And keep your eye out, Mrs. Peters, for anything that might be of use. No telling; you women might come upon a clue to the motive—and that's the thing we need."

Mr. Hale rubbed his face after the fashion of a show man getting ready for a pleasantry.

"But would the women know a clue if they did come upon it?" he said; and, having delivered himself of this, he followed the others through the stair door.

The women stood motionless and silent, listening to the footsteps, first upon the stairs, then in the room above them.

Then, as if releasing herself from something strange, Mrs. Hale began to arrange the dirty pans under the sink, which the county attorney's disdainful push of the foot had deranged.

"I'd hate to have men comin' into my kitchen," she said testily—"snoopin' round and criticizin'."

"Of course it's no more than their duty," said the sheriff's wife, in her manner of timid acquiescence.

"Duty's all right," replied Mrs. Hale bluffly; "but I guess that deputy sheriff that come out to make the fire might have got a little of this on." She gave the roller towel a pull. "Wish I'd thought of that sooner! Seems mean to talk about her for not having things slicked up, when she had to come away in such a hurry."

She looked around the kitchen. Certainly it was not "slicked up." Her eye was held by a bucket of sugar on a low shelf. The cover was off the wooden bucket, and beside it was a paper bag—half full.

Mrs. Hale moved toward it.

"She was putting this in there," she said to herself—slowly.

She thought of the flour in her kitchen at home—half sifted, half not sifted. She had been interrupted and had left things half done. What had interrupted Minnie Foster? Why had that work been left half done? She made a move as if to finish it,—unfinished things always bothered her,—and then she glanced around and saw that Mrs. Peters was watching her—and she didn't want Mrs. Peters to get that feeling she had got of work begun and then—for some reason—not finished.

"It's a shame about her fruit," she said, and walked toward the cupboard that the county attorney had opened, and got on the chair, murmuring: "I wonder if it's all gone."

It was a sorry enough looking sight, but "Here's one that's all right," she said at last. She held it toward the light. "This is cherries, too." She looked again. "I declare I believe that's the only one."

With a sigh, she got down from the chair, went to the sink, and wiped off the bottle.

She'll feel awful bad, after all her hard work in the hot weather. I remember the afternoon I put up my cherries last summer."

She set the bottle on the table, and, with another sigh, started to sit down in the rocker. But she did not sit down. Something kept her from sitting down in that chair. She straightened—stepped back, and, half turned away, stood looking at it, seeing the woman who sat there "pleatin' at her apron."

The thin voice of the sheriff's wife broke in upon her: "I must be getting those things from the front room closet." She opened the door into the other room, started in, stepped back. "You coming with me, Mrs. Hale?" she asked nervously. "You—you could help me get them."

They were soon back—the stark coldness of that shut-up room was not a thing to linger in.

"My!" said Mrs Peters, dropping the things on the table and hurrying to the stove.

Mrs. Hale stood examining the clothes the woman who was being detained in town had said she wanted.

"Wright was close!" she exclaimed, holding up a shabby black skirt that bore the marks of much making over. "I think maybe that's why she kept so much to herself. I s'pose she felt she couldn't do her part; and then, you don't enjoy things when you feel shabby. She used to wear pretty clothes and be lively—when she was Minnie Foster, one of the town girls, singing in the choir. But that—oh, that was twenty years ago."

With a carefulness in which there was something tender, she folded the shabby clothes and piled them at one corner of the table. She looked at Mrs. Peters, and there was something in the other woman's look that irritated her.

"She don't care," she said to herself. "Much difference it makes to her whether Minnie Foster had pretty clothes when she was a girl."

Then she looked again, and she wasn't so sure; in fact, she hadn't at any time been perfectly sure about Mrs. Peters. She had that shrinking manner, and yet her eyes looked as if they could see a long way into things.

"This all you was to take in?" asked Mrs. Hale.

"No," said the sheriff's wife; "she said she wanted an apron. Funny thing to want," she ventured in her nervous little way, "for there's not much to get you dirty in jail, goodness knows. But I suppose just to make her feel more natural. If you're used to wearing an apron—. She said they were in the bottom drawer of this cupboard. Yes—here they are. And then her little shawl that always hung on the stair door."

She took the small gray shawl from behind the door leading upstairs, and stood a minute looking at it.

Suddenly Mrs. Hale took a quick step toward the other woman.

"Mrs. Peters!"

"Yes, Mrs. Hale?"

"Do you think she—did it?"

A frightened look blurred the other things in Mrs. Peters' eyes.

"Oh, I don't know," she said, in a voice that seemed to shrink away from the subject.

"Well, I don't think she did," affirmed Mrs. Hale stoutly. "Asking for an apron, and her little shawl. Worryin' about her fruit."

"Mr. Peters says—" Footsteps were heard in the room above; she stopped, looked up, then went on in a lowered voice: "Mr. Peters says—it looks bad for her. Mr. Henderson is awful sarcastic in a speech, and he's going to make fun of her saying she didn't—wake up."

For a moment Mrs. Hale had no answer. Then, "Well, I guess John Wright didn't wake up—when they was slippin' that rope under his neck," she muttered.

"No, it's *strange*," breathed Mrs. Peters. "They think it was such a—funny way to kill a man."

She began to laugh; at sound of the laugh, abruptly stopped.

"That's just what Mr. Hale said," said Mrs. Hale, in a resolutely natural voice. "There was a gun in the house. He says that's what he can't understand."

"Mr. Henderson said, coming out, that what was needed for the case was a motive. Something to show anger—or sudden feeling."

"Well, I don't see any signs of anger around here," said Mrs. Hale. "I don't—"

She stopped. It was as if her mind tripped on something. Her eye was caught by a dish-towel in the middle of the kitchen table. Slowly she moved toward the table. One half of it was wiped clean, the other half messy. Her eyes made a slow, almost unwilling turn to the bucket of sugar and the half empty bag beside it. Things begun—and not finished.

After a moment she stepped back, and said, in that manner of releasing herself:

"Wonder how they're finding things upstairs? I hope she had it a little more red up there. You know,"—she paused, and feeling gathered,—"it seems kind of *sneaking*; locking her up in town and coming out here to get her own house to turn against her!"

"But, Mrs. Hale," said the sheriff's wife, "the law is the law."

"I s'pose 'tis," answered Mrs. Hale shortly.

She turned to the stove, saying something about that fire not being much to brag of. She worked with it a minute, and when she straightened up she said aggressively:

"The law is the law—and a bad stove is a bad stove. How'd you like to cook on this?"—pointing with the poker to the broken lining. She opened the oven door and started to express her opinion of the oven; but she was swept into her own thoughts, thinking of what it would mean, year after year, to have that stove to wrestle with. The thought of Minnie Foster trying to bake in that oven—and the thought of her never going over to see Minnie Foster—.

She was startled by hearing Mrs. Peters say: "A person gets discouraged—and loses heart."

The sheriff's wife had looked from the stove to the sink—to the pail of water which had been carried in from outside. The two women stood there silent, above them the footsteps of the men who were looking for evidence against the woman who had worked in that kitchen. That look of seeing into things, of seeing through a thing to something else, was in the eyes of the sheriff's wife now. When Mrs. Hale next spoke to her, it was gently:

"Better loosen up your things, Mrs. Peters. We'll not feel them when we go out."

Mrs. Peters went to the back of the room to hang up the fur tippet[1] she was wearing. A moment later she exclaimed, "Why, she was piecing a quilt," and held up a large sewing basket piled high with quilt pieces.

Mrs. Hale spread some of the blocks on the table.

"It's log-cabin pattern," she said, putting several of them together. "Pretty, isn't it?"

They were so engaged with the quilt that they did not hear the footsteps on the stairs. Just as the stair door opened Mrs. Hale was saying:

"Do you suppose she was going to quilt it or just knot it?"

The sheriff threw up his hands.

"They wonder whether she was going to quilt it or just knot it!"

There was a laugh for the ways of women, a warming of hands over the stove, and then the county attorney said briskly:

[1] Cape.

"Well, let's go right out to the barn and get that cleared up."

"I don't see as there's anything so strange," Mrs. Hale said resentfully, after the outside door had closed on the three men—"our taking up our time with little things while we're waiting for them to get the evidence. I don't see as it's anything to laugh about."

"Of course they've got awful important things on their minds," said the sheriff's wife apologetically.

They returned to an inspection of the blocks for the quilt. Mrs. Hale was looking at the fine, even sewing, and preoccupied with thoughts of the woman who had done that sewing, when she heard the sheriff's wife say, in a queer tone:

"Why, look at this one."

She turned to take the block held out to her.

"The sewing," said Mrs. Peters, in a troubled way. "All the rest of them have been so nice and even—but—this one. Why, it looks as if she didn't know what she was about!"

Their eyes met—something flashed to life, passed between them; then, as if with an effort, they seemed to pull away from each other. A moment Mrs. Hale sat there, her hands folded over that sewing which was so unlike all the rest of the sewing. Then she had pulled a knot and drawn the threads.

"Oh, what are you doing, Mrs. Hale?" asked the sheriff's wife, startled.

"Just pulling out a stitch or two that's not sewed very good," said Mrs. Hale mildly.

"I don't think we ought to touch things," Mrs. Peters said, a little helplessly.

"I'd just finish up this end," answered Mrs. Hale, still in that mild, matter-of-fact fashion.

She threaded a needle and started to replace bad sewing with good. For a little while she sewed in silence. Then, in that thin, timid voice, she heard:

"Mrs. Hale!"

"Yes, Mrs. Peters?"

"What do you suppose she was so—nervous about?"

"Oh, *I* don't know," said Mrs. Hale, as if dismissing a thing not important enough to spend much time on. "I don't know as she was—nervous. I sew awful queer sometimes when I'm just tired."

She cut a thread, and out of the corner of her eye looked up at Mrs. Peters. The small, lean face of the sheriff's wife seemed to have tightened up. Her eyes had that look of peering into something. But the next moment she moved, and said in her thin, indecisive way:

"Well, I must get those clothes wrapped. They may be through sooner than we think. I wonder where I could find a piece of paper—and string."

"In that cupboard, maybe," suggested Mrs. Hale, after a glance around.

One piece of the crazy sewing remained unripped. Mrs. Peters' back turned, Martha Hale now scrutinized that piece, compared it with the dainty, accurate sewing of the other blocks. The difference was startling. Holding this block made her feel queer, as if the distracted thoughts of the woman who had perhaps turned to it to try and quiet herself were communicating themselves to her.

Mrs. Peters' voice roused her.

"Here's a bird-cage," she said. "Did she have a bird, Mrs. Hale?"

"Why, I don't know whether she did or not." She turned to look at the cage Mrs. Peters was holding up. "I've not been here in so long." She sighed. "There was a man round last year selling canaries cheap—but I don't know as she took one. Maybe she did. She used to sing real pretty herself."

Mrs. Peters looked around the kitchen.

"Seems kind of funny to think of a bird here." She half laughed—an attempt to put up a barrier. "But she must have had one—or why would she have a cage? I wonder what happened to it."

"I suppose maybe the cat got it," suggested Mrs. Hale, resuming her sewing.

"No; she didn't have a cat. She's got that feeling some people have about cats—being afraid of them. When they brought her to our house yesterday, my cat got in the room, and she was real upset and asked me to take it out."

"My sister Bessie was like that," laughed Mrs. Hale.

The sheriff's wife did not reply. The silence made Mrs. Hale turn round. Mrs. Peters was examining the bird-cage.

"Look at this door," she said slowly. "It's broke. One hinge has been pulled apart."

Mrs. Hale came nearer.

"Looks as if some one must have been—rough with it."

Again their eyes met—startled, questioning, apprehensive. For a moment neither spoke nor stirred. Then Mrs. Hale, turning away, said brusquely:

"If they're going to find any evidence, I wish they'd be about it. I don't like this place."

"But I'm awful glad you came with me, Mrs. Hale." Mrs. Peters put the bird-cage on the table and sat down. "It would be lonesome for me—sitting here alone."

"Yes, it would, wouldn't it?" agreed Mrs. Hale, a certain determined naturalness in her voice. She picked up the sewing, but now it dropped in her lap, and she murmured in a different voice: "But I tell you what I *do* wish, Mrs. Peters. I wish I had come over sometimes when she was here. I wish—I had."

"But of course you were awful busy, Mrs. Hale. Your house—and your children."

"I could've come," retorted Mrs. Hale shortly. "I stayed away because it weren't cheerful—and that's why I ought to have come. I"—she looked around —"I've never liked this place. Maybe because it's down in a hollow and you don't see the road. I don't know what it is, but it's a lonesome place, and always was. I wish I had come over to see Minnie Foster sometimes. I can see now—" She did not put it into words.

"Well, you mustn't reproach yourself," counseled Mrs. Peters. "Somehow, we just don't see how it is with other folks till—something comes up."

"Not having children makes less work," mused Mrs. Hale, after a silence, "but it makes a quiet house—and Wright out to work all day—and no company when he did come in. Did you know John Wright, Mrs. Peters?"

"Not to know him. I've seen him in town. They say he was a good man."

"Yes—good," conceded John Wright's neighbor grimly. "He didn't drink, and kept his word as well as most, I guess, and paid his debts. But he was a hard man, Mrs. Peters. Just to pass the time of day with him—." She stopped, shivered a little. "Like a raw wind that gets to the bone." Her eye fell upon the cage on the table before her, and she added, almost bitterly: "I should think she would've wanted a bird!"

Suddenly she leaned forward, looking intently at the cage. "But what do you s'pose went wrong with it?"

"I don't know," returned Mrs. Peters; "unless it got sick and died."

But after she said it she reached over and swung the broken door. Both women watched it as if somehow held by it.

"You didn't know—her?" Mrs. Hale asked, a gentler note in her voice.

"Not till they brought her yesterday," said the sheriff's wife.

"She—come to think of it, she was kind of like a bird herself. Real sweet and pretty, but kind of timid and—fluttery. How—she—did—change."

That held her for a long time. Finally, as if struck with a happy thought and relieved to get back to everyday things, she exclaimed:

"Tell you what, Mrs. Peters, why don't you take the quilt in with you? It might take up her mind."

"Why, I think that's a real nice idea, Mrs. Hale," agreed the sheriff's wife, as if she too were glad to come into the atmosphere of a simple kindness. "There couldn't possibly be any objection to that, could there? Now, just what will I take? I wonder if her patches are in here—and her things."

They turned to the sewing basket.

"Here's some red," said Mrs. Hale, bringing out a roll of cloth. Underneath that was a box. "Here, maybe her scissors are in here—and her things." She held it up. "What a pretty box! I'll warrant that was something she had a long time ago—when she was a girl."

She held it in her hand a moment; then, with a little sigh, opened it.

Instantly her hand went to her nose.

"Why—!"

Mrs. Peters drew nearer—then turned away.

"There's something wrapped up in this piece of silk," faltered Mrs. Hale.

"This isn't her scissors," said Mrs. Peters in a shrinking voice.

Her hand not steady, Mrs. Hale raised the piece of silk. "Oh, Mrs. Peters!" she cried. "It's—"

Mrs. Peters bent closer.

"It's the bird," she whispered.

"But, Mrs. Peters!" cried Mrs. Hale. "*Look* at it! Its neck—look at its neck! It's all—other side *to.*"

She held the box away from her.

The sheriff's wife again bent closer.

"Somebody wrung its neck," said she, in a voice that was slow and deep.

And then again the eyes of the two women met—this time clung together in a look of dawning comprehension, of growing horror. Mrs. Peters looked from the dead bird to the broken door of the cage. Again their eyes met. And just then there was a sound at the outside door.

Mrs. Hale slipped the box under the quilt pieces in the basket, and sank into the chair before it. Mrs. Peters stood holding to the table. The county attorney and the sheriff came in from outside.

"Well, ladies," said the county attorney, as one turning from serious things to little pleasantries, "have you decided whether she was going to quilt it or knot it?"

"We think," began the sheriff's wife in a flurried voice, "that she was going to—knot it."

He was too preoccupied to notice the change that came in her voice on that last.

"Well, that's very interesting, I'm sure," he said tolerantly. He caught sight of the bird-cage. "Has the bird flown?"

"We think the cat got it," said Mrs. Hale in a voice curiously even.

He was walking up and down, as if thinking something out.

"Is there a cat?" he asked absently.

Mrs. Hale shot a look up at the sheriff's wife.

"Well, not *now*," said Mrs. Peters. "They're superstitious, you know; they leave."

She sank into her chair.

The county attorney did not heed her. "No sign at all of any one having come in from the outside," he said to Peters, in the manner of continuing an interrupted conversation. "Their own rope. Now let's go upstairs again and go over it, piece by piece. It would have to have been some one who knew just the—"

The stair door closed behind them and their voices were lost.

The two women sat motionless, not looking at each other, but as if peering into something and at the same time holding back. When they spoke now it was as if they were afraid of what they were saying, but as if they could not help saying it.

"She liked that bird," said Martha Hale, low and slowly. "She was going to bury it in that pretty box."

"When I was a girl," said Mrs. Peters, under her breath, "my kitten—there was a boy took a hatchet, and before my eyes—before I could get there—" She covered her face an instant. "If they hadn't held me back I would have"—she caught herself, looked upstairs where footsteps were heard, and finished weakly—"hurt him."

Then they sat without speaking or moving.

"I wonder how it would seem," Mrs. Hale at last began, as if feeling her way over strange ground—"never to have had any children around?" Her eyes made a slow sweep of the kitchen, as if seeing what that kitchen had meant through all the years. "No, Wright wouldn't like the bird," she said after that—"a thing that sang. She used to sing. He killed that too." Her voice tightened.

Mrs. Peters moved uneasily.

"Of course we don't know who killed the bird."

"I knew John Wright," was Mrs. Hale's answer.

"It was an awful thing was done in this house that night, Mrs. Hale," said the sheriff's wife. "Killing a man while he slept—slipping a thing round his neck that choked the life out of him."

Mrs. Hale's hand went out to the bird-cage.

"His neck. Choked the life out of him."

"We don't *know* who killed him," whispered Mrs. Peters wildly. "We don't *know*."

Mrs. Hale had not moved. "If there had been years and years of—nothing, then a bird to sing to you, it would be awful—still—after the bird was still."

It was as if something within her not herself had spoken, and it found in Mrs. Peters something she did not know as herself.

"I know what stillness is," she said, in a queer, monotonous voice. "When we homesteaded in Dakota, and my first baby died—after he was two years old—and me with no other then—"

Mrs. Hale stirred.

"How soon do you suppose they'll be through looking for evidence?"

"I know what stillness is," repeated Mrs. Peters, in just the same way. Then she too pulled back. "The law has got to punish crime, Mrs. Hale," she said in her tight little way.

"I wish you'd seen Minnie Foster," was the answer, "when she wore a white dress with blue ribbons, and stood up there in the choir and sang."

The picture of that girl, the fact that she had lived neighbor to that girl for twenty years, and had let her die for lack of life, was suddenly more than she could bear.

"Oh, I *wish* I'd come over here once in a while!" she cried. "That was a crime! That was a crime! Who's going to punish that?"

"We mustn't take on," said Mrs. Peters, with a frightened look toward the stairs.

"I might 'a' *known* she needed help! I tell you, It's *queer*, Mrs. Peters. We live close together, and we live far apart. We all go through the same things—it's all just a different kind of the same thing! If it weren't—why do you and I *understand*? Why do we *know*—what we know this minute?"

She dashed her hand across her eyes. Then, seeing the jar of fruit on the table, she reached out for it and choked out:

"If I was you I wouldn't *tell* her her fruit was gone! Tell her it *ain't*. Tell her it's all right—all of it. Here—take this in to prove it to her! She—she may never know whether it was broke or not."

She turned away.

Mrs. Peters reached out for the bottle of fruit as if she were glad to take it—as if touching a familiar thing, having something to do, could keep her from something else. She got up, looked about for something to wrap the fruit in, took a petticoat from the pile of clothes she had brought from the front room, and nervously started winding that round the bottle.

"My!" she began, in a high, false voice, "it's a good thing the men couldn't hear us! Getting all stirred up over a little thing like a—dead canary." She hurried over that. "As if that could have anything to do with—with—My, wouldn't they *laugh*?"

Footsteps were heard on the stairs.

"Maybe they would," muttered Mrs. Hale—"maybe they wouldn't."

"No, Peters," said the county attorney incisively; "it's all perfectly clear, except the reason for doing it. But you know juries when it comes to women. If there was some definite thing—something to show. Something to make a story about. A thing that would connect up with this clumsy way of doing it."

In a covert way Mrs. Hale looked at Mrs. Peters. Mrs. Peters was looking at her. Quickly they looked away from each other. The outer door opened and Mr. Hale came in.

"I've got the team round now," he said. "Pretty cold out there."

"I'm going to stay here awhile by myself," the county attorney suddenly announced. "You can send Frank out for me, can't you?" he asked the sheriff. "I want to go over everything. I'm not satisfied we can't do better."

Again, for one brief moment, the two women's eyes found one another.

The sheriff came up to the table.

"Did you want to see what Mrs. Peters was going to take in?"

The county attorney picked up the apron. He laughed.

"Oh, I guess they're not very dangerous things the ladies have picked out."

Mrs. Hale's hand was on the sewing basket in which the box was concealed. She felt that she ought to take her hand off the basket. She did not seem able to. He picked up one of the quilt blocks which she had piled on to cover the box. Her eyes felt like fire. She had a feeling that if he took up the basket she would snatch it from him.

But he did not take it up. With another little laugh, he turned away, saying:

"No; Mrs. Peters doesn't need supervising. For that matter, a sheriff's wife is married to the law. Ever think of it that way, Mrs. Peters?"

Mrs. Peters was standing beside the table. Mrs. Hale shot a look up at her; but she could not see her face. Mrs. Peters had turned away. When she spoke, her voice was muffled.

"Not—just that way," she said.

"Married to the law!" chuckled Mrs. Peters' husband. He moved toward the door into the front room, and said to the county attorney:

"I just want you to come in here a minute, George. We ought to take a look at these windows.

"Oh—windows," said the county attorney scoffingly.

"We'll be right out, Mr. Hale," said the sheriff to the farmer, who was still waiting by the door.

Hale went to look after the horses. The sheriff followed the county attorney into the other room. Again—for one moment—the two women were alone in that kitchen.

Martha Hale sprang up, her hands tight together, looking at that other woman, with whom it rested. At first she could not see her eyes, for the sheriff's wife had not turned back, since she turned away at that suggestion of being married to the law. But now Mrs. Hale made her turn back. Her eyes made her turn back. Slowly, unwillingly, Mrs. Peters turned her head until her eyes met the eyes of the other woman. There was a moment when they held each other in a steady, burning look in which there was no evasion nor flinching. Then Martha Hale's eyes pointed the way to the basket in which was hidden the thing that would make certain the conviction of the other woman—that woman who was not there and yet who had been there with them all through the hour.

For a moment Mrs. Peters did not move. And then she did it. With a rush forward, she threw back the quilt pieces, got the box, tried to put it in her handbag. It was too big. Desperately she opened it, started to take the bird out. But there she broke—she could not touch the bird. She stood helpless, foolish.

There was the sound of a knob turning in the inner door. Martha Hale snatched the box from the sheriff's wife, and got it in the pocket of her big coat just as the sheriff and the county attorney came back into the kitchen.

"Well, Henry," said the county attorney facetiously, "at least we found out that she was not going to quilt it. She was going to—what is it you call it, ladies?"

Mrs. Hale's hand was against the pocket of her coat.

"We call it—knot it, Mr. Henderson."

[1917]

Franz Kafka   *1883–1924*

A HUNGER ARTIST*

During these last decades the interest in professional fasting has markedly diminished. It used to pay very well to stage such great performances under one's own management, but today that is quite impossible. We live in a different world now. At one time the whole town took a lively interest in the hunger artist; from day to day of his fast the excitement mounted; everybody wanted to see him at least once a day; there were people who bought season tickets for the last few days and sat from morning till night in front of his small barred cage; even in the nighttime there were visiting hours, when the whole effect was heightened by torch flares; on fine days the cage was set out in the open air, and then it was the children's special treat to see the hunger artist; for their elders he was often just a joke that happened to be in fashion, but the children stood openmouthed, holding each other's hands for greater security, marveling at him as he sat there pallid in black tights, with his ribs sticking out so prominently, not even on a seat but down among straw on the ground, sometimes giving a courteous nod, answering questions with a constrained smile, or perhaps stretching an arm through the bars so that one might feel how thin it was, and then again withdrawing deep into himself, paying no attention to anyone or anything, not even to the all-important striking of the clock that was the only piece of furniture in his cage, but merely staring into vacancy with half-shut eyes, now and then taking a sip from a tiny glass of water to moisten his lips.

Besides casual onlookers there were also relays of permanent watchers selected by the public, usually butchers, strangely enough, and it was their task to watch the hunger artist day and night, three of them at a time, in case he should have some secret recourse to nourishment. This was nothing but a formality, instituted to reassure the masses, for the initiates knew well enough that during his fast the artist would never in any circumstances, not even under forcible compulsion, swallow the smallest morsel of food; the honor of his profession forbade it. Not every watcher, of course, was capable of understanding this; there were often groups of night watchers who were very lax in carrying out their duties and deliberately huddled together in a retired corner to play cards with great absorption, obviously intending to give the hunger artist the chance of a little refreshment, which they supposed he could draw from some private hoard. Nothing annoyed the artist more than such watchers; they made him miserable; they made his fast seem unendurable; sometimes he mastered his feebleness sufficiently to sing during their watch for as long as he could keep going, to show them how unjust their suspicions were. But that was of little use; they only wondered at his cleverness in being able to fill his mouth even while singing. Much more to his taste were the watchers who sat close up to the bars, who were not content with the dim night lighting of the hall but focused him in the full glare of the electric pocket torch given them by the impresario. The harsh light did not trouble him at all, in any case he could never sleep properly, and he could always drowse a little, whatever the light, at any hour, even when the hall was thronged with noisy onlookers. He was quite happy at the prospect of spending a sleepless night with such watchers; he was ready to exchange jokes with them, to tell them stories out

* Translated by Willa and Edwin Muir.

of his nomadic life, anything at all to keep them awake and demonstrate to them again that he had no eatables in his cage and that he was fasting as not one of them could fast. But his happiest moment was when the morning came and an enormous breakfast was brought them, at his expense, on which they flung themselves with the keen appetite of healthy men after a weary night of wakefulness. Of course there were people who argued that this breakfast was an unfair attempt to bribe the watchers, but that was going rather too far, and when they were invited to take on a night's vigil without a breakfast, merely for the sake of the cause, they made themselves scarce, although they stuck stubbornly to their suspicions.

Such suspicions, anyhow, were a necessary accompaniment to the profession of fasting. No one could possibly watch the hunger artist continuously, day and night, and so no one could produce first-hand evidence that the fast had really been rigorous and continuous; only the artist himself could know that, he was therefore bound to be the sole completely satisfied spectator of his own fast. Yet for other reasons he was never satisfied; it was not perhaps mere fasting that had brought him to such skeleton thinness that many people had regretfully to keep away from his exhibitions, because the sight of him was too much for them, perhaps it was dissatisfaction with himself that had worn him down. For he alone knew, what no other initiate knew, how easy it was to fast. It was the easiest thing in the world. He made no secret of this, yet people did not believe him; at the best they set him down as modest; most of them, however, thought he was out for publicity or else was some kind of cheat who found it easy to fast because he had discovered a way of making it easy, and then had the impudence to admit the fact, more or less. He had to put up with all that, and in the course of time had got used to it, but his inner dissatisfaction always rankled, and never yet, after any term of fasting—this must be granted to his credit—had he left the cage of his own free will. The longest period of fasting was fixed by his impresario at forty days, beyond that term he was not allowed to go, not even in great cities, and there was good reason for it, too. Experience had proved that for about forty days the interest of the public could be stimulated by a steadily increasing pressure of advertisement, but after that the town began to lose interest, sympathetic support began notably to fall off; there were of course local variations as between one town and another or one country and another, but as a general rule forty days marked the limit. So on the fortieth day the flower-bedecked cage was opened, enthusiastic spectators filled the hall, a military band played, two doctors entered the cage to measure the results of the fast, which were announced through a megaphone, and finally two young ladies appeared, blissful at having been selected for the honor, to help the hunger artist down the few steps leading to a small table on which was spread a carefully chosen invalid repast. And at this very moment the artist always turned stubborn. True, he would entrust his bony arms to the outstretched helping hands of the ladies bending over him, but stand up he would not. Why stop fasting at this particular moment, after forty days of it? He had held out for a long time, an illimitably long time; why stop now, when he was in his best fasting form, or rather, not yet quite in his best fasting form? Why should he be cheated of the fame he would get for fasting longer, for being not only the record hunger artist of all time, which presumably he was already, but for beating his own record by a performance beyond human imagination, since he felt that there were no limits to his capacity for fasting? His public pretended to admire him so much, why should it have so little patience with him; if he could endure fasting longer, why shouldn't the public endure it? Besides, he was tired, he was comfortable sitting in the straw, and now he was supposed to lift himself to his full height and go down to a meal the very thought of which gave him a nausea that only the presence of the ladies kept him from betraying, and even that with an effort. And he looked up into the eyes of the ladies who were apparently so friendly and in reality so cruel, and shook his head, which felt too heavy on its strengthless neck. But then there happened yet again what always happened. The impresario came forward, without a word— for the band made speech impossible—lifted his arms in the air above the artist, as if inviting Heaven to look down upon its creature here in the straw, this suffering martyr, which indeed he was, although in quite another sense; grasped him around the emaciated waist, with exaggerated caution, so that the frail condition he was in might be appreciated; and committed him to the care of the blenching ladies, not without secretly giving him a shaking so that his legs and body tottered and swayed. The artist now submitted completely; his head lolled on his breast as if it had landed there by chance; his body was hollowed out; his legs in a spasm of self-preservation clung close to each other at the knees, yet scraped on the ground as if it were not really solid ground, as if they were only trying to find solid ground; and the whole weight of his body, a featherweight after all, relapsed onto one of the ladies, who, looking around for help and panting a little—this post of honor was not at all what she had expected it to be—first stretched her neck as far as she could to keep her face at least free from contact with the artist, then finding this impossible, and her more fortunate companion not coming to her aid but merely holding extended in her own trembling hand the little bunch of knucklebones that was the artist's, to the great delight of the spectators burst into tears and had to be replaced by an attendant who had long been stationed in readiness. Then came the food, a little of which the impresario managed to get between the artist's lips, while he sat in a kind of half-fainting trance, to the accompaniment of cheerful patter designed to distract the public's attention from the artist's condition; after that, a toast was drunk to the public, supposedly prompted by a whisper from the artist in the impresario's ear; the band confirmed it with a mighty flourish, the spectators melted away, and no one had any cause to be dissatisfied with the proceedings, no one except the hunger artist himself, he only, as always.

So he lived for many years, with small regular intervals of recuperation, in visible glory, honored by the world, yet in spite of that troubled in spirit, and all the more troubled because no one would take his trouble seriously. What comfort could he possibly need? What more could he possibly wish for? And if some good-natured person, feeling sorry for him, tried to console him by pointing out that his melancholy was probably caused by fasting, it could happen, especially when he had been fasting for some time, that he reacted with an outburst of fury and to the general alarm began to shake the bars of his cage like a wild animal. Yet the impresario had a way of punishing these outbreaks which he rather enjoyed putting into operation. He would apologize publicly for the artist's behavior, which was only to be excused, he admitted, because of the irritability caused by fasting; a condition hardly to be understood by well-fed people; then by natural transition he went on to mention the artist's equally incomprehensible boast that he could fast for much longer than he was doing; he praised the high ambition, the good will, the great self-denial undoubtedly implicit in such a statement; and then quite simply countered it by bringing out photographs, which were also on sale to the public, showing the artist on the fortieth day of a fast lying in bed almost dead from exhaustion. This perversion of the truth, familiar to the artist though it was, always unnerved him afresh and proved too much for him. What was a consequence of the premature ending of his fast was here presented as the cause of it! To fight against this lack of understanding, against a whole world of nonunderstanding, was impossible. Time and again in good faith he stood by the bars listening to the impresario, but as soon as the photographs appeared he always let go and sank with a groan back onto his straw, and the reassured public could once more come close and gaze at him.

A few years later when the witnesses of such scenes called them to mind, they often failed to understand themselves at all. For meanwhile the aforementioned change in public interest had set in; it seemed to happen almost overnight; there may have been profound causes for it, but who was going to bother about that; at any rate the pampered hunger artist suddenly found himself deserted one fine day by the amusement-seekers, who went streaming past him to other more-favored attractions. For the last time the impresario hurried him over half Europe to discover whether the old interest might still survive here and there; all in vain; everywhere, as if by secret agreement, a positive revulsion from professional fasting was in evidence. Of course it could not really have sprung up so suddenly as all that, and many premonitory symptoms which had not been sufficiently re-marked or suppressed during the rush and glitter of success now came retrospectively to mind, but it was now too late to take any countermeasures. Fasting would surely come into fashion again at some future date, yet that was no comfort for those living in the present. What, then, was the hunger artist to do? He had been applauded by thousands in his time and could hardly come down to showing himself in a street booth at village fairs, and as for adopting another profession, he was not only too old for that but too fanatically devoted to fasting. So he took leave of the impresario, his partner in an unparalleled career, and hired himself to a large circus; in order to spare his own feelings he avoided reading the conditions of his contract.

A large circus with its enormous traffic in replacing and recruiting men, ani-mals, and apparatus can always find a use for people at any time, even for a hunger artist, provided of course that he does not ask too much, and in this particular case anyhow it was not only the artist who was taken on but his famous and long-known name as well, indeed considering the peculiar nature of his performance, which was not impaired by advancing age, it could not be objected that here was an artist past his prime, no longer at the height of his professional skill, seeking a refuge in some quiet corner of a circus; on the contrary, the hunger artist averred that he could fast as well as ever, which was entirely credible, he even alleged that if he were allowed to fast as he liked, and this was at once promised him without more ado, he could astound the world by establishing a record never yet achieved, a statement that certainly provoked a smile among the other professionals, since it left out of account the change in public opinion, which the hunger artist in his zeal conveniently forgot.

He had not, however, actually lost his sense of the real situation and took it as a matter of course that he and his cage should be stationed, not in the middle of the ring as a main attraction, but outside, near the animal cages, on a site that was after all easily accessible. Large and gaily painted placards made a frame for the cage and announced what was to be seen inside it. When the public came throng-ing out in the intervals to see the animals, they could hardly avoid passing the hunger artist's cage and stopping there for a moment, perhaps they might even have stayed longer had not those pressing behind them in the narrow gangway, who did not understand why they should be held up on their way toward the excitements of the menagerie, made it impossible for anyone to stand gazing quietly for any length of time. And that was the reason why the hunger artist, who had of course been looking forward to these visiting hours as the main achievement of his life, began instead to shrink from them. At first he could hardly wait for the intervals; it was exhilarating to watch the crowds come streaming his way, until only too soon—not even the most obstinate self-deception, clung to almost consciously, could hold out against the fact—the conviction was borne in upon him that these people, most of them, to judge from their actions, again and again, without exception, were all on their way to the menagerie. And the first sight of them from the distance remained the best. For when they reached his cage he was at once deafened by the storm of shouting and abuse that arose from the two contending factions, which renewed themselves continuously, of those who wanted to stop and stare at him—he soon began to dislike them more than the others—not out of real interest but only out of obstinate self-assertiveness, and those who wanted to go straight on to the animals. When the first great rush was past, the stragglers came along, and these, whom nothing could have prevented from stopping to look at him as long as they had breath, raced past with long strides, hardly even glancing at him, in their haste to get to the menagerie in time. And all too rarely did it happen that he had a stroke of luck, when some father of a family fetched up before him with his children, pointed a finger at the hunger artist, and explained at length what the phenomenon meant, telling stories of earlier years when he himself had watched similar but much more thrilling performances, and the children, still rather uncomprehending, since neither inside nor outside school had they been sufficiently prepared for this lesson—what did they care about fasting?—yet showed by the brightness of their intent eyes that new and better times might be coming. Perhaps, said the hunger artist to himself many a time, things would be a little better if his cage were set not quite so near the menagerie. That made it too easy for people to make their choice, to say nothing of what he suffered from the stench of the menagerie, the animals' restlessness by night, the carrying past of raw lumps of flesh for the beasts of prey, the roaring at feeding times, which depressed him continually. But he did not dare to lodge a complaint with the management; after all, he had the animals to thank for the troops of people who passed his cage, among whom there might always be one here and there to take an interest in him, and who could tell where they might seclude him if he called attention to his existence and thereby to the fact that, strictly speaking, he was only an impediment on the way to the menagerie.

A small impediment, to be sure, one that grew steadily less. People grew familiar with the strange idea that they could be expected, in times like these, to take an interest in a hunger artist, and with this familiarity the verdict went out against him. He might fast as much as he could, and he did so; but nothing could save him now, people passed him by. Just try to explain to anyone the art of fasting! Anyone who has no feeling for it cannot be made to understand it. The fine placards grew dirty and illegible, they were torn down; the little notice board telling the number of fast days achieved, which at first was changed carefully every day, had long stayed at the same figure, for after the first few weeks even this small task seemed pointless to the staff; and so the artist simply fasted on and on, as he had once dreamed of doing, and it was no trouble to him, just as he had always foretold, but no one counted the days, no one, not even the artist himself, knew what records he was already breaking, and his heart grew heavy. And when once in a while some leisurely passer-by stopped, made merry over the old figure on the board, and spoke of swindling, that was in its way the stupidest lie ever invented by indifference and inborn malice, since it was not the hunger artist who was cheating, he was working honestly, but the world was cheating him of his reward.

Many more days went by, however, and that too came to an end. An overseer's eye fell on the cage one day and he asked the attendants why this perfectly good cage should be left standing there unused with dirty straw inside it; nobody knew, until one man, helped out by the notice board, remembered about the hunger artist. They poked into the straw with sticks and found him in it. "Are you still fasting?" asked the overseer, "when on earth do you mean to stop?" "Forgive me, everybody," whispered the hunger artist; only the overseer, who had his ear to the bars, understood him. "Of course," said the overseer, and tapped his forehead with a finger to let the attendants know what state the man was in, "we forgive you." "I always wanted you to admire my fasting," said the hunger artist. "We do admire it," said the overseer, affably. "But you shouldn't admire it," said the hunger artist. "Well then we don't admire it," said the overseer, "but why shouldn't we admire it?" "Because I have to fast, I can't help it," said the hunger artist. "What a fellow you are," said the overseer, "and why can't you help it?" "Because," said the hunger artist, lifting his head a little and speaking, with his lips pursed, as if for a kiss, right into the overseer's ear, so that no syllable might be lost, "because I couldn't find the food I liked. If I had found it, believe me, I should have made no fuss and stuffed myself like you or anyone else." These were his last words, but in his dimming eyes remained the firm though no longer proud persuasion that he was still continuing to fast.

"Well, clear this out now!" said the overseer, and they buried the hunger artist, straw and all. Into the cage they put a young panther. Even the most insensitive felt it refreshing to see this wild creature leaping around the cage that had so long been dreary. The panther was all right. The food he liked was brought him without hesitation by the attendants; he seemed not even to miss his freedom; his noble body, furnished almost to the bursting point with all that it needed, seemed to carry freedom around with it too; somewhere in his jaws it seemed to lurk; and the joy of life streamed with such ardent passion from his throat that for the onlookers it was not easy to stand the shock of it. But they braced themselves, crowded around the cage, and did not want ever to move away.

[1922]

Katherine Mansfield   *1888–1923*

THE FLY

"Y'are very snug in here," piped old Mr. Woodifield, and he peered out of the great, green leather armchair by his friend the boss's desk as a baby peers out of its pram. His talk was over; it was time for him to be off. But he did not want to go. Since he had retired, since his . . . stroke, the wife and the girls kept him boxed up in the house every day of the week except Tuesday. On Tuesday he was dressed up and brushed and allowed to cut back to the City for the day. Though what he did there the wife and girls couldn't imagine. Made a nuisance of himself to his friends, they supposed. . . . Well, perhaps so. All the same, we cling to our last pleasures as the tree clings to its last leaves. So there sat old Woodifield, smoking a cigar and staring almost greedily at the boss, who rolled in his office chair, stout, rosy, five years older than he, and still going strong, still at the helm. It did one good to see him.

Wistfully, admiringly, the old voice added, "It's snug in here, upon my word!"

"Yes, it's comfortable enough," agreed the boss, and he flipped the *Financial Times* with a paper-knife. As a matter of fact he was proud of his room; he liked to have it admired, especially by old Woodifield. It gave him a feeling of deep, solid satisfaction to be planted there in the midst of it in full view of that frail old figure in the muffler.

"I've had it done up lately," he explained, as he had explained for the past how many?—weeks. "New carpet," and he pointed to the bright red carpet with a pattern of large white rings. "New furniture," and he nodded towards the massive bookcase and the table with legs like twisted treacle. "Electric heating!" He waved almost exultantly towards the five transparent, pearly sausages glowing so softly in the tilted copper pan.

But he did not draw old Woodifield's attention to the photograph over the table of a grave-looking boy in uniform standing in one of those spectral photographers' parks with photographers' storm-clouds behind him. It was not new. It had been there for over six years.

"There was something I wanted to tell you," said old Woodifield, and his eyes grew dim remembering. "Now what was it? I had it in my mind when I started out this morning." His hands began to tremble, and patches of red showed above his beard.

Poor old chap, he's on his last pins, thought the boss. And, feeling kindly, he winked at the old man, and said jokingly, "I tell you what. I've got a little drop of something here that'll do you good before you go out into the cold again. It's beautiful stuff. It wouldn't hurt a child." He took a key off his watch-chain, unlocked a cupboard below his desk, and drew forth a dark, squat bottle. "That's the medicine," said he. "And the man from whom I got it told me on the strict Q.T. it came from the cellars at Windsor Cassel."[1]

Old Woodifield's mouth fell open at the sight. He couldn't have looked more surprised if the boss had produced a rabbit.

"It's whisky, ain't it?" he piped, feebly.

The boss turned the bottle and lovingly showed him the label. Whisky it was.

"D'you know," said he, peering up at the boss wonderingly, "they won't let me touch it at home." And he looked as though he was going to cry.

---

[1] Windsor Castle, west of London; the residence of the British royal family.

"Ah, that's where we know a bit more than the ladies," cried the boss, swooping across for two tumblers that stood on the table with the water-bottle, and pouring a generous finger into each. "Drink it down. It'll do you good. And don't put any water with it. It's sacrilege to tamper with stuff like this. Ah!" He tossed off his, pulled out his handkerchief, hastily wiped his moustaches, and cocked an eye at old Woodifield, who was rolling his in his chaps.

The old man swallowed, was silent a moment, and then said faintly, "It's nutty!" But it warmed him; it crept into his chill old brain—he remembered.

"That was it," he said, heaving himself out of his chair. "I thought you'd like to know. The girls were in Belgium last week having a look at poor Reggie's grave,[2] and they happened to come across your boy's. They're quite near each other, it seems."

Old Woodifield paused, but the boss made no reply. Only a quiver in his eyelids showed that he heard.

"The girls were delighted with the way the place is kept," piped the old voice. "Beautifully looked after. Couldn't be better if they were at home. You've not been across, have yer?"

"No, no!" For various reasons the boss had not been across.

"There's miles of it," quavered old Woodifield, "and it's all as neat as a garden. Flowers growing on all the graves. Nice broad paths." It was plain from his voice how much he liked a nice broad path.

The pause came again. Then the old man brightened wonderfully.

"D'you know what the hotel made the girls pay for a pot of jam?" he piped. "Ten francs! Robbery, I call it. It was a little pot, so Gertrude says, no bigger than a half-crown. And she hadn't taken more than a spoonful when they charged her ten francs. Gertrude brought the pot away with her to teach 'em a lesson. Quite right, too; it's trading on our feelings. They think because we're over there having a look around we're ready to pay anything. That's what it is." And he turned towards the door.

"Quite right, quite right!" cried the boss, though what was quite right he hadn't the least idea. He came round by his desk, followed the shuffling footsteps to the door, and saw the old fellow out. Woodifield was gone.

For a long moment the boss stayed, staring at nothing, while the grey-haired office messenger, watching him, dodged in and out of his cubbyhole like a dog that expects to be taken for a run. Then: "I'll see nobody for half an hour, Macey," said the boss. "Understand? Nobody at all."

"Very good, sir."

The door shut, the firm heavy steps recrossed the bright carpet, the fat body plumped down in the spring chair, and leaning forward, the boss covered his face with his hands. He wanted, he intended, he had arranged to weep. . . .

It had been a terrible shock to him when old Woodifield sprang that remark upon him about the boy's grave. It was exactly as though the earth had opened and he had seen the boy lying there with Woodifield's girls staring down at him. For it was strange. Although over six years had passed away, the boss never thought of the boy except as lying unchanged, unblemished in his uniform, asleep for ever. "My son!" groaned the boss. But no tears came yet. In the past, in the first months and even years after the boy's death, he had only to say those words to be overcome by such grief that nothing short of a violent fit of weeping could relieve him. Time, he had declared then, he had told everybody, could make no differ-

---

[2] The reference is to one of a number of World War I British military cemeteries in Belgium.

ence. Other men perhaps might recover, might live their loss down, but not he. How was it possible? His boy was an only son. Ever since his birth the boss had worked at building up this business for him; it had no other meaning if it was not for the boy. Life itself had come to have no other meaning. How on earth could he have slaved, denied himself, kept going all those years without the promise for ever before him of the boy's stepping into his shoes and carrying on where he left off?

And that promise had been so near being fulfilled. The boy had been in the office learning the ropes for a year before the war. Every morning they had started off together; they had come back by the same train. And what congratulations he had received as the boy's father! No wonder; he had taken to it marvellously. As to his popularity with the staff, every man jack of them down to old Macey couldn't make enough of the boy. And he wasn't in the least spoilt. No, he was just his bright, natural self, with the right word for everybody, with that boyish look and his habit of saying, "Simply splendid!"

But all that was over and done with as though it never had been. The day had come when Macey had handed him the telegram that brought the whole place crashing about his head. "Deeply regret to inform you . . ." And he had left the office a broken man, with his life in ruins.

Six years ago, six years . . . How quickly time passed! It might have happened yesterday. The boss took his hands from his face; he was puzzled. Something seemed to be wrong with him. He wasn't feeling as he wanted to feel. He decided to get up and have a look at the boy's photograph. But it wasn't a favorite photograph of his; the expression was unnatural. It was cold, even stern looking. The boy had never looked like that.

At that moment the boss noticed that a fly had fallen into his broad inkpot, and was trying feebly but desperately to clamber out again. Help! help! said those struggling legs. But the sides of the inkpot were wet and slippery; it fell back again and began to swim. The boss took up a pen, picked the fly out of the ink, and shook it on to a piece of blotting-paper. For a fraction of a second it lay still on the dark patch that oozed round it. Then the front legs waved, took hold, and, pulling its small sodden body up it began the immense task of cleaning the ink from its wings. Over and under, over and under, went a leg along a wing, as the stone goes over and under the scythe. Then there was a pause, while the fly, seeming to stand on the tips of its toes, tried to expand first one wing and then the other. It succeeded at last, and, sitting down, it began, like a minute cat, to clean its face. Now one could imagine that the little front legs rubbed against each other lightly, joyfully. The horrible danger was over; it had escaped; it was ready for life again.

But just then the boss had an idea. He plunged his pen back into the ink, leaned his thick wrist on the blotting paper, and as the fly tried its wings down came a great heavy blot. What would it make of that? What indeed! The little beggar seemed absolutely cowed, stunned, and afraid to move because of what would happen next. But then, as if painfully, it dragged itself forward. The front legs waved, caught hold, and, more slowly this time, the task began from the beginning.

He's a plucky little devil, thought the boss, and he felt a real admiration for the fly's courage. That was the way to tackle things; that was the right spirit. Never say die; it was only a question of . . . But the fly had again finished its laborious task, and the boss had just time to refill his pen, to shake fair and square on the new-cleaned body yet another dark drop. What about it this time? A painful moment of suspense followed. But behold, the front legs were again waving; the boss felt a rush of relief. He leaned over the fly and said to it tenderly, "You artful little b . . ." And he actually had the brilliant notion of breathing on it to help the drying process. All the same, there was something timid and weak about its efforts now, and the boss decided that this time should be the last, as he dipped the pen into the inkpot.

It was. The last blot on the soaked blotting-paper, and the draggled fly lay in it and did not stir. The back legs were stuck to the body; the front legs were not to be seen.

"Come on," said the boss. "Look sharp!" And he stirred it with his pen—in vain. Nothing happened or was likely to happen. The fly was dead.

The boss lifted the corpse on the end of the paper-knife and flung it into the waste-paper basket. But such a grinding feeling of wretchedness seized him that he felt positively frightened. He started forward and pressed the bell for Macey.

"Bring me some fresh blotting-paper," he said, sternly, "and look sharp about it." And while the old dog padded away he fell to wondering what it was he had been thinking about before. What was it? It was . . . He took out his handkerchief and passed it inside his collar. For the life of him he could not remember.

[1922]

Agatha Christie *1890–1976*

THE WITNESS FOR THE PROSECUTION

Mr. Mayherne adjusted his pince-nez[1] and cleared his throat with a little dry-as-dust cough that was wholly typical of him. Then he looked again at the man opposite him, the man charged with willful murder.

Mr. Mayherne was a small man, precise in manner, neatly, not to say foppishly dressed, with a pair of very shrewd and piercing gray eyes. By no means a fool. Indeed, as a solicitor,[2] Mr. Mayherne's reputation stood very high. His voice, when he spoke to his client, was dry but not unsympathetic.

"I must impress upon you again that you are in very grave danger, and that the utmost frankness is necessary."

Leonard Vole, who had been staring in a dazed fashion at the blank wall in front of him, transferred his glance to the solicitor.

"I know," he said hopelessly. "You keep telling me so. But I can't seem to realize yet that I'm charged with murder—*murder*. And such a dastardly crime, too."

Mr. Mayherne was practical, not emotional. He coughed again, took off his pince-nez, polished them carefully, and replaced them on his nose. Then he said:

"Yes, yes, yes. Now, my dear Mr. Vole, we're going to make a determined effort to get you off—and we shall succeed—we shall succeed. But I must have all the facts. I must know just how damaging the case against you is likely to be. Then we can fix upon the best line of defense."

Still the young man looked at him in the same dazed, hopeless fashion. To Mr. Mayherne the case had seemed black enough, and the guilt of the prisoner assured. Now, for the first time, he felt a doubt.

"You think I'm guilty," said Leonard Vole, in a low voice. "But, by God, I swear I'm not! It looks pretty black against me, I know that. I'm like a man caught in a net—the meshes of it all round me, entangling me whichever way I turn. But I didn't do it, Mr. Mayherne, I didn't do it!"

In such a position a man was bound to protest his innocence. Mr. Mayherne knew that. Yet, in spite of himself, he was impressed. It might be, after all, that Leonard Vole was innocent.

"You are right, Mr. Vole," he said gravely. "The case does look very black against you. Nevertheless, I accept your assurance. Now, let us get to facts. I want you to tell me in your own words exactly how you came to make the acquaintance of Miss Emily French."

"It was one day in Oxford Street.[3] I saw an elderly lady crossing the road. She was carrying a lot of parcels. In the middle of the street she dropped them, tried to recover them, found a bus was almost on top of her, and just managed to reach the curb safely, dazed and bewildered by people having shouted at her. I recovered her parcels, wiped the mud off them as best I could, retied the string of one, and returned them to her."

"There was no question of your having saved her life?"

"Oh, dear me, no! All I did was to perform a common act of courtesy. She was

---

[1] Eyeglasses clipped to the bridge of the nose.
[2] A legal counsel who prepares cases for senior lawyers (or barristers) to plead in a British court.
[3] A fashionable street in central London.

extremely grateful, thanked me warmly, and said something about my manners not being those of most of the younger generation—I can't remember the exact words. Then I lifted my hat and went on. I never expected to see her again. But life is full of coincidences. That very evening I came across her at a party at a friend's house. She recognized me at once and asked that I should be introduced to her. I then found out that she was a Miss Emily French and that she lived at Cricklewood. I talked to her for some time. She was, I imagine, an old lady who took sudden and violent fancies to people. She took one to me on the strength of a perfectly simple action which anyone might have performed. On leaving, she shook me warmly by the hand and asked me to come and see her. I replied, of course, that I should be very pleased to do so, and she then urged me to name a day. I did not want particularly to go, but it would have seemed churlish to refuse, so I fixed on the following Saturday. After she had gone, I learned something about her from my friends. That she was rich, eccentric, lived alone with one maid and owned no less than eight cats."

"I see," said Mr. Mayherne. "The question of her being well off came up as early as that?"

"If you mean that I inquired—" began Leonard Vole hotly, but Mr. Mayherne stilled him with a gesture.

"I have to look at the case as it will be presented by the other side. An ordinary observer would not have supposed Miss French to be a lady of means. She lived poorly, almost humbly. Unless you had been told the contrary, you would in all probability have considered her to be in poor circumstances—at any rate to begin with. Who was it exactly who told you that she was well off?"

"My friend, George Harvey, at whose house the party took place."

"Is he likely to remember having done so?"

"I really don't know. Of course it is some time ago now."

"Quite so, Mr. Vole. You see, the first aim of the prosecution will be to establish that you were in low water financially—that is true, is it not?

Leonard Vole flushed.

"Yes," he said, in a low voice. "I'd been having a run of infernal bad luck just then."

"Quite so," said Mr. Mayherne again. "That being, as I say, in low water financially, you met this rich old lady and cultivated her acquaintance assiduously. Now if we are in a position to say that you had no idea she was well off, and that you visited her out of pure kindness of heart—"

"Which is the case."

"I dare say. I am not disputing the point. I am looking at it from the outside point of view. A great deal depends on the memory of Mr. Harvey. Is he likely to remember that conversation or is he not? Could he be confused by counsel into believing that it took place later?"

Leonard Vole reflected for some minutes. Then he said steadily enough, but with a rather paler face:

"I do not think that that line would be successful, Mr. Mayherne. Several of those present heard his remark, and one or two of them chaffed me about my conquest of a rich old lady."

The solicitor endeavored to hide his disappointment with a wave of the hand.

"Unfortunate," he said. "But I congratulate you upon your plain speaking, Mr. Vole. It is to you I look to guide me. Your judgment is quite right. To persist in the line I spoke of would have been disastrous. We must leave that point. You made the acquaintance of Miss French, you called upon her, the acquaintanceship progressed. We want a clear reason for all this. Why did you, a young man of thirty-three, good-looking, fond of sport, popular with your friends, devote so much of your time to an elderly woman with whom you could hardly have anything in common?"

Leonard Vole flung out his hands in a nervous gesture.

"I can't tell you—I really can't tell you. After the first visit she pressed me to come again, spoke of being lonely and unhappy. She made it difficult for me to refuse. She showed so plainly her fondness and affection for me that I was placed in an awkward position. You see, Mr. Mayherne, I've got a weak nature—I drift— I'm one of those people who can't say 'No.' And believe me or not, as you like, after the third or fourth visit I paid her, I found myself getting genuinely fond of the old thing. My mother died when I was young, an aunt brought me up, and she, too, died before I was fifteen. If I told you that I genuinely enjoyed being mothered and pampered, I dare say you'd only laugh."

Mr. Mayherne did not laugh. Instead he took off his pince-nez again and polished them, a sign with him that he was thinking deeply.

"I accept your explanation, Mr. Vole," he said at last. "I believe it to be psychologically probable. Whether a jury would take that view of it is another matter. Please continue your narrative. When was it that Miss French first asked you to look into her business affairs?"

"After my third or fourth visit to her. She understood very little of money matters, and was worried about some investments."

Mr. Mayherne looked up sharply.

"Be careful, Mr. Vole. The maid, Janet Mackenzie, declares that her mistress was a good woman of business and transacted all her own affairs, and this is borne out by the testimony of her bankers."

"I can't help that," said Vole earnestly. "That's what she said to me."

Mr. Mayherne looked at him for a moment or two in silence. Though he had no intention of saying so, his belief in Leonard Vole's innocence was at that moment strengthened. He knew something of the mentality of elderly ladies. He saw Miss French, infatuated with the good-looking young man, hunting about for pretexts that would bring him to the house. What more likely than that she should plead ignorance of business, and beg him to help her with her money affairs? She was enough of a woman of the world to realize that any man is slightly flattered by such an admission of his superiority. Leonard Vole had been flattered. Perhaps, too, she had not been averse to letting this young man know that she was wealthy. Emily French had been a strong-willed old woman, willing to pay her price for what she wanted. All this passed rapidly through Mr. Mayherne's mind, but he gave no indication of it, and asked instead a further question.

"And you did handle her affairs for her at her request?"

"I did."

"Mr. Vole," said the solicitor, "I am going to ask you a very serious question, and one to which it is vital I should have a truthful answer. You were in low water financially. You had the handling of an old lady's affairs—an old lady who, according to her own statement, knew little or nothing of business. Did you at any time, or in any manner, convert to your own use the securities which you handled? Did you engage in any transaction for your own pecuniary advantage which will not bear the light of day?" He quelled the other's response. "Wait a minute before you answer. There are two courses open to us. Either we can make a feature of your probity and honesty in conducting her affairs whilst pointing out how unlikely it is that you would commit murder to obtain money which you might have obtained by such infinitely easier means. If, on the other hand, there is anything in your dealings which the prosecution will get hold of—if, to put it baldly, it can be proved that you swindled the old lady in any way, we must take the line that you had no motive for murder, since she was already a profitable source of income to you. You perceive the distinction. Now, I beg of you, take your time before you reply."

But Leonard Vole took no time at all.

"My dealings with Miss French's affairs were all perfectly fair and above board. I acted for her interests to the very best of my ability, as anyone will find who looks into the matter."

"Thank you," said Mr. Mayherne. "You relieve my mind very much. I pay you the compliment of believing that you are far too clever to lie to me over such an important matter."

"Surely," said Vole eagerly, "the strongest point in my favor is the lack of motive. Granted that I cultivated the acquaintanceship of a rich old lady in the hopes of getting money out of her—that, I gather, is the substance of what you have been saying—surely her death frustrates all my hopes?"

The solicitor looked at him steadily. Then, very deliberately, he repeated his unconscious trick with his pince-nez. It was not until they were firmly replaced on his nose that he spoke.

"Are you not aware, Mr. Vole, that Miss French left a will under which you are the principal beneficiary?"

"What?" The prisoner sprang to his feet. His dismay was obvious and unforced. "My God! What are you saying? She left her money to me?"

Mr. Mayherne nodded slowly. Vole sank down again, his head in his hands. "You pretend you know nothing of this will?"

"Pretend? There's no pretense about it. I knew nothing about it."

"What would you say if I told you that the maid, Janet Mackenzie, swears that you *did* know? That her mistress told her distinctly that she had consulted you in the matter, and told you of her intentions?"

"Say? That she's lying! No, I go too fast. Janet is an elderly woman. She was a faithful watchdog to her mistress, and she didn't like me. She was jealous and suspicious. I should say that Miss French confided her intentions to Janet, and that Janet either mistook something she said, or else was convinced in her own mind that I had persuaded the old lady into doing it. I dare say that she herself believes now that Miss French actually told her so."

"You don't think she dislikes you enough to lie deliberately about the matter?"

Leonard Vole looked shocked and startled.

"No, indeed! Why should she?"

"I don't know," said Mr. Mayherne thoughtfully. "But she's very bitter against you."

The wretched young man groaned again.

"I'm beginning to see," he muttered. "It's frightful. I made up to her, that's what they'll say, I got her to make a will leaving her money to me, and then I go there that night, and there's nobody in the house—they find her the next day— oh! my God, it's awful!"

"You are wrong about there being nobody in the house," said Mr. Mayherne. "Janet, as you remember, was to go out for the evening. She went, but about half past nine she returned to fetch the pattern of a blouse sleeve which she had promised her friend. She let herself in by the back door, went upstairs and fetched it, and went out again. She heard voices in the sitting room, though she could not distinguish what they said, but she will swear that one of them was Miss French's and one was a man's."

"At half past nine," said Leonard Vole. "At half past nine . . ." He sprang to his feet. "But then I'm saved—saved—"

"What do you mean, saved?" cried Mr. Mayherne, astonished.

"By half past nine I was at home again! My wife can prove that. I left Miss French about five minutes to nine. I arrived home about twenty past nine. My wife was there waiting for me. Oh, thank God—thank God! And bless Janet Mackenzie's sleeve pattern."

In his exuberance, he hardly noticed that the grave expression on the solicitor's face had not altered. But the latter's words brought him down to earth with a bump.

"Who, then, in your opinion, murdered Miss French?"

"Why, a burglar, of course, as was thought at first. The window was forced, you remember. She was killed with a heavy blow from a crowbar, and the crowbar was found lying on the floor beside the body. And several articles were missing. But for Janet's absurd suspicions and dislike of me, the police would never have swerved from the right track."

"That will hardly do, Mr. Vole," said the solicitor. "The things that were missing were mere trifles of no value, taken as a blind. And the marks on the window were not at all conclusive. Besides, think for yourself. You say you were no longer in the house by half past nine. Who, then, was the man Janet heard talking to Miss French in the sitting room? She would hardly be having an amicable conversation with a burglar?"

"No," said Vole. "No—" He looked puzzled and discouraged. "But, anyway," he added with reviving spirit, "it lets me out. I've got an alibi. You must see Romaine—my wife—at once."

"Certainly," acquiesced the lawyer. "I should already have seen Mrs. Vole but for her being absent when you were arrested. I wired to Scotland at once, and I understand that she arrives back tonight. I am going to call upon her immediately I leave here."

Vole nodded, a great expression of satisfaction settling down over his face.

"Yes, Romaine will tell you. My God! It's a lucky chance, that."

"Excuse me, Mr. Vole, but you are very fond of your wife?"

"Of course."

"And she of you?"

"Romaine is devoted to me. She'd do anything in the world for me."

He spoke enthusiastically, but the solicitor's heart sank a little lower. The testimony of a devoted wife—would it gain credence?

"Was there anyone else who saw you return at nine-twenty? A maid, for instance?"

"We have no maid."

"Did you meet anyone in the street on the way back?"

"Nobody I know. I rode part of the way in a bus. The conductor might remember."

Mr. Mayherne shook his head doubtfully.

"There is no one, then, who can confirm your wife's testimony?"

"No. But it isn't necessary, surely?"

"I dare say not. I dare say not," said Mr. Mayherne hastily. "Now there's just one thing more. Did Miss French know that you were a married man?"

"Oh, yes."

"Yet you never took your wife to see her. Why was that?"

For the first time, Leonard Vole's answer came halting and uncertain.

"Well—I don't know."

"Are you aware that Janet Mackenzie says her mistress believed you to be single and contemplated marrying you in the future?"

Vole laughed.

"Absurd! There was forty years' difference in age between us."

"It has been done," said the solicitor dryly. "The fact remains. Your wife never met Miss French?"

"No—" Again the constraint.

"You will permit me to say," said the lawyer, "that I hardly understand your attitude in the matter."

Vole flushed, hesitated, and then spoke.

"I'll make a clean breast of it. I was hard up, as you know. I hoped that Miss French might lend me some money. She was fond of me, but she wasn't at all interested in the struggles of a young couple. Early on, I found that she had taken it for granted that my wife and I didn't get on—were living apart. Mr. Mayherne—I wanted the money—for Romaine's sake. I said nothing and allowed the old lady to think what she chose. She spoke of my being an adopted son to her. There was never any question of marriage—that must be just Janet's imagination."

"And that is all?"

"Yes—that is all."

Was there just a shade of hesitation in the words? The lawyer fancied so. He rose and held out his hand.

"Good-by, Mr. Vole." He looked into the haggard young face and spoke with an unusual impulse. "I believe in your innocence in spite of the multitude of facts arrayed against you. I hope to prove it and vindicate you completely."

Vole smiled back at him.

"You'll find the alibi is all right," he said cheerfully.

Again he hardly noticed that the other did not respond.

"The whole thing hinges a good deal on the testimony of Janet Mackenzie," said Mr. Mayherne. "She hates you. That much is clear."

"She can hardly hate me," protested the young man.

The solicitor shook his head as he went out.

"Now for Mrs. Vole," he said to himself.

He was seriously disturbed by the way the thing was shaping.

The Voles lived in a small shabby house near Paddington Green.[4] It was to this house that Mr. Mayherne went.

In answer to his ring, a big slatternly woman, obviously a charwoman, answered the door.

"Mrs. Vole? Has she returned yet?"

"Got back an hour ago. But I dunno if you can see her."

"If you will take my card to her," said Mr. Mayherne quietly, "I am quite sure that she will do so."

The woman looked at him doubtfully, wiped her hand on her apron and took the card. Then she closed the door in his face and left him on the step outside.

In a few minutes, however, she returned with a slightly altered manner.

"Come inside, please."

[4] Paddington is a district in western London.

She ushered him into a tiny drawing room. Mr. Mayherne, examining a drawing on the wall, started up suddenly to face a tall, pale woman who had entered so quietly that he had not heard her.

"Mr. Mayherne? You are my husband's solicitor, are you not? You have come from him? Will you please sit down?"

Until she spoke, he had not realized that she was not English. Now, observing her more closely, he noticed the high cheekbones, the dense blue-black of the hair, and an occasional very slight movement of the hands that was distinctly foreign. A strange woman, very quiet. So quiet as to make one uneasy. From the very first Mr. Mayherne was conscious that he was up against something that he did not understand.

"Now, my dear Mrs. Vole," he began, "you must not give way—"

He stopped. It was so very obvious that Romaine Vole had not the slightest intention of giving way. She was perfectly calm and composed.

"Will you please tell me about it?" she said. "I must know everything. Do not think to spare me. I want to know the worst." She hesitated, then repeated in a lower tone, with a curious emphasis which the lawyer did not understand: "I want to know the worst."

Mr. Mayherne went over his interview with Leonard Vole. She listened attentively, nodding her head now and then.

"I see," she said, when he had finished. "He wants me to say that he came in at twenty minutes past nine that night?"

"He did come in at that time?" said Mr. Mayherne sharply.

"That is not the point," she said coldly. "Will my saying so acquit him? Will they believe me?"

Mr. Mayherne was taken aback. She had gone so quickly to the core of the matter.

"That is what I want to know," she said. "Will it be enough? Is there anyone else who can support my evidence?"

There was a suppressed eagerness in her manner that made him vaguely uneasy.

"So far there is no one else," he said reluctantly.

"I see," said Romaine Vole.

She sat for minute or two perfectly still. A little smile played over her lips.

The lawyer's feeling of alarm grew stronger and stronger.

"Mrs. Vole—" he began. "I know what you must feel—"

"Do you?" she asked. "I wonder."

"In the circumstances—"

"In the circumstances—I intend to play a lone hand."

He looked at her in dismay.

"But, my dear Mrs. Vole—you are overwrought. Being so devoted to your husband—"

"I beg your pardon?"

The sharpness of her voice made him start. He repeated in a hesitating manner: "Being so devoted to your husband—"

Romaine Vole nodded slowly, the same strange smile on her lips.

"Did he tell you that I was devoted to him?" she asked softly. "Ah! yes, I can see he did. How stupid men are! Stupid—stupid—stupid—"

She rose suddenly to her feet. All the intense emotion that the lawyer had been conscious of in the atmosphere was now concentrated in her tone.

"I hate him, I tell you! I hate him. I hate him. I hate him! I would like to see him hanged by the neck till he is dead."

The lawyer recoiled before her and the smoldering passion in her eyes.

She advanced a step nearer and continued vehemently:

"Perhaps I shall see it. Supposing I tell you that he did not come in that night at twenty past nine, but at twenty past ten? You say that he tells you he knew nothing about the money coming to him. Supposing I tell you he knew all about it, and counted on it, and committed murder to get it? Supposing I tell you that he admitted to me that night when he came in what he had done? That there was blood on his coat? What then? Supposing that I stand up in court and say all these things?"

Her eyes seemed to challenge him. With an effort, he concealed his growing dismay and endeavored to speak in a rational tone.

"You cannot be asked to give evidence against your husband—"

"He is not my husband!"

The words came out so quickly that he fancied he had misunderstood her.

"I beg your pardon? I—"

"He is not my husband."

The silence was so intense that you could have heard a pin drop.

"I was an actress in Vienna. My husband is alive but in a madhouse. So we could not marry. I am glad now."

She nodded defiantly.

"I should like you to tell me one thing," said Mr. Mayherne. He contrived to appear as cool and unemotional as ever. "Why are you so bitter against Leonard Vole?"

She shook her head, smiling a little.

"Yes, you would like to know. But I shall not tell you. I will keep my secret. . . ."

Mr. Mayherne gave his dry little cough and rose.

"There seems no point in prolonging this interview," he remarked. "You will hear from me again after I have communicated with my client."

She came closer to him, looking into his eyes with her own wonderful dark ones.

"Tell me," she said, "did you believe—honestly—that he was innocent when you came here today?"

"I did," said Mr. Mayherne.

"You poor little man," she laughed.

"And I believe so still," finished the lawyer. "Good evening, madam."

He went out of the room, taking with him the memory of her startled face.

"This is going to be the devil of a business," said Mr. Mayherne to himself as he strode along the street.

Extraordinary, the whole thing. An extraordinary woman. A very dangerous woman. Women were the devil when they got their knife into you.

What was to be done? That wretched young man hadn't a leg to stand upon. Of course, possibly he did commit the crime. . . .

"No," said Mr. Mayherne to himself. "No—there's almost too much evidence against him. I don't believe this woman. She was trumping up the whole story. But she'll never bring it into court."

He wished he felt more conviction on the point.

The police court proceedings were brief and dramatic. The principal witnesses for the prosecution were Janet Mackenzie, maid to the dead woman, and Romaine Heilger, Austrian subject, the mistress of the prisoner.

Mr. Mayherne sat in court and listened to the damning story that the latter told. It was on the lines she had indicated to him in their interview.

The prisoner reserved his defense and was committed for trial.

Mr. Mayherne was at his wit's end. The case against Leonard Vole was black beyond words. Even the famous K.C.[5] who was engaged for the defense held out little hope.

"If we can shake that Austrian woman's testimony, we might do something," he said dubiously. "But it's a bad business."

Mr. Mayherne had concentrated his energies on one single point. Assuming Leonard Vole to be speaking the truth, and to have left the murdered woman's house at nine o'clock, who was the man Janet heard talking to Miss French at half past nine?

The only ray of light was in the shape of a scapegrace nephew who had in bygone days cajoled and threatened his aunt out of various sums of money. Janet Mackenzie, the solicitor learned, had always been attached to this young man, and had never ceased urging his claims upon her mistress. It certainly seemed possible that it was this nephew who had been with Miss French after Leonard Vole left, especially as he was not to be found in any of his old haunts.

In all other directions, the lawyer's researches had been negative in their result. No one had seen Leonard Vole entering his own house or leaving that of Miss French. No one had seen any other man enter or leave the house in Cricklewood. All inquiries drew blank.

It was the eve of the trial when Mr. Mayherne received the letter which was to lead his thoughts in an entirely new direction.

It came by the six o'clock post. An illiterate scrawl, written on common paper and enclosed in a dirty envelope with the stamp stuck on crooked.

Mr. Mayherne read it through once or twice before he grasped its meaning.

"Dear Mister:
"Youre the lawyer chap wot acts for the young feller. If you want that painted foreign hussy showd up for wot she is an her pack of lies you come to 16 Shaw's Rents Stepney tonight It ull cawst you 2 hundred quid[6] Arsk for Missis Mogson."

The solicitor read and reread this strange epistle. It might, of course, be a hoax, but when he thought it over, he became increasingly convinced that it was genuine, and also convinced that it was the one hope for the prisoner. The evidence of Romaine Heilger damned him completely, and the line the defense meant to pursue, the line that the evidence of a woman who had admittedly lived an immoral life was not to be trusted, was at best a weak one.

Mr. Mayherne's mind was made up. It was his duty to save his client at all costs. He must go to Shaw's Rents.

He had some difficulty in finding the place, a ramshackle building in an evil-smelling slum, but at last he did so, and on inquiry for Mrs. Mogson was sent up to a room on the third floor. On this door he knocked, and getting no answer, knocked again.

At this second knock, he heard a shuffling sound inside, and presently the door was opened cautiously half an inch and a bent figure peered out.

[5] King's Counsel, one of a select number of eminent barristers chosen to represent the British Crown in court.
[6] Quid is the slang term for pound sterling, the basic monetary unit of Great Britain.

Suddenly the woman, for it was a woman, gave a chuckle and opened the door wider.

"So it's you, dearie," she said, in a wheezy voice. "Nobody with you, is there? No playing tricks? That's right. You can come in—you can come in."

With some reluctance the lawyer stepped across the threshold into the small dirty room, with its flickering gas jet. There was an untidy unmade bed in a corner, a plain deal table and two rickety chairs. For the first time Mr. Mayherne had a full view of the tenant of this unsavory apartment. She was a woman of middle age, bent in figure, with a mass of untidy gray hair and a scarf wound tightly round her face. She saw him looking at this and laughed again, the same curious toneless chuckle.

"Wondering why I hide my beauty, dear? He, he, he. Afraid it may tempt you, eh? But you shall see—you shall see."

She drew aside the scarf and the lawyer recoiled involuntarily before the almost formless blur of scarlet. She replaced the scarf again.

"So you're not wanting to kiss me, dearie? He, he, I don't wonder. And yet I was a pretty girl once—not so long ago as you'd think, either. Vitriol,[7] dearie, vitriol— that's what did that. Ah! but I'll be even with 'em—"

She burst into a hideous torrent of profanity which Mr. Mayherne tried vainly to quell. She fell silent at last, her hands clenching and unclenching themselves nervously.

"Enough of that," said the lawyer sternly. "I've come here because I have reason to believe you can give me information which will clear my client, Leonard Vole. Is that the case?"

Her eyes leered at him cunningly.

"What about the money, dearie?" she wheezed. "Two hundred quid, you re- member."

"It is your duty to give evidence, and you can be called upon to do so."

"That won't do, dearie. I'm an old woman, and I know nothing. But you give me two hundred quid, and perhaps I can give you a hint or two. See?"

"What kind of hint?"

"What should you say to a letter? A letter from *her.* Never mind how I got hold of it. That's my business. It'll do the trick. But I want my two hundred quid."

Mr. Mayherne looked at her coldly and made up his mind.

"I'll give you ten pounds, nothing more. And only that if this letter is what you say it is."

"Ten pounds?" She screamed and raved at him.

"Twenty," said Mr. Mayherne, "and that's my last word."

He rose as if to go. Then, watching her closely, he drew out a pocketbook and counted out twenty one-pound notes.

"You see," he said. "That is all I have with me. You can take it or leave it."

But already he knew that the sight of the money was too much for her. She cursed and raved impotently, but at last she gave in. Going over to the bed, she drew something out from beneath the tattered mattress.

"Here you are, damn you!" she snarled. "It's the top one you want."

It was a bundle of letters that she threw to him, and Mr. Mayherne untied them and scanned them in his usual cool, methodical manner. The woman, watching him eagerly, could gain no clue from his impassive face.

[7] Sulfuric acid.

He read each letter through, then returned again to the top one and read it a second time. Then he tied the whole bundle up again carefully.

They were love letters, written by Romaine Heilger, and the man they were written to was not Leonard Vole. The top letter was dated the day of the latter's arrest.

"I spoke true, dearie, didn't I?" whined the woman. "It'll do for her, that letter?"

Mr. Mayherne put the letters in his pocket, then he asked a question.

"How did you get hold of this correspondence?"

"That's telling," she said with a leer. "But I know something more. I heard in court what that hussy said. Find out where she was at twenty past ten, the time she says she was at home. Ask at the Lion Road Cinema. They'll remember—a fine upstanding girl like that—curse her!"

"Who is the man?" asked Mr. Mayherne. "There's only a Christian name here."

The other's voice grew thick and hoarse, her hands clenched and unclenched. Finally she lifted one to her face.

"He's the man that did this to me. Many years ago now. She took him away from me—a chit[8] of a girl she was then. And when I went after him—and went for him, too—he threw the cursed stuff at me! And she laughed—damn her! I've had it in for her for years. Followed her, I have, spied upon her. And now I've got her! She'll suffer for this, won't she, Mr. Lawyer? She'll suffer?"

"She will probably be sentenced to a term of imprisonment for perjury," said Mr. Mayherne quietly.

"Shut away—that's what I want. You're going, are you? Where's my money? Where's that good money?"

Without a word, Mr. Mayherne put down the notes on the table. Then, drawing in a deep breath, he turned and left the squalid room. Looking back, he saw the old woman crooning over the money.

He wasted no time. He found the cinema in Lion Road easily enough, and, shown a photograph of Romaine Heilger, the commissionaire[9] recognized her at once. She had arrived at the cinema with a man some time after ten o'clock on the evening in question. He had not noticed her escort particularly, but he remembered the lady who had spoken to him about the picture that was showing. They stayed until the end, about an hour later.

Mr. Mayherne was satisfied. Romaine Heilger's evidence was a tissue of lies from beginning to end. She had evolved it out of her passionate hatred. The lawyer wondered whether he would ever know what lay behind that hatred. What had Leonard Vole done to her? He had seemed dumfounded when the solicitor had reported her attitude to him. He had declared earnestly that such a thing was incredible—yet it had seemed to Mr. Mayherne that after the first astonishment his protests had lacked sincerity.

He did know. Mr. Mayherne was convinced of it. He knew, but he had no intention of revealing the fact. The secret between those two remained a secret. Mr. Mayherne wondered if someday he should come to learn what it was.

The solicitor glanced at his watch. It was late, but time was everything. He hailed a taxi and gave an address.

"Sir Charles must know of this at once," he murmured to himself as he got in.

                                        *   *   *

_____
[8] A pert or precocious young girl or woman.   [9] Doorman or janitor.

The trial of Leonard Vole for the murder of Emily French aroused widespread interest. In the first place the prisoner was young and good-looking, then he was accused of a particularly dastardly crime, and there was the further interest of Romaine Heilger, the principal witness for the prosecution. There had been pictures of her in many papers, and several fictitious stories as to her origin and history.

The proceedings opened quietly enough. Various technical evidence came first. Then Janet Mackenzie was called. She told substantially the same story as before. In cross-examination, counsel for the defense succeeded in getting her to contradict herself once or twice over her account of Vole's association with Miss French; he emphasized the fact that though she had heard a man's voice in the sitting room that night, there was nothing to show that it was Vole who was there, and he managed to drive home a feeling that jealousy and dislike of the prisoner were at the bottom of a good deal of her evidence.

Then the next witness was called.

"Your name is Romaine Heilger?"

"Yes."

"You are an Austrian subject?"

"Yes."

"For the last three years you have lived with the prisoner and passed yourself off as his wife?"

Just for a moment Romaine Heilger's eyes met those of the man in the dock. Her expression held something curious and unfathomable.

"Yes."

The questions went on. Word by word the damning facts came out. On the night in question the prisoner had taken out a crowbar with him. He had returned at twenty minutes past ten, and had confessed to having killed the old lady. His cuffs had been stained with blood, and he had burned them in the kitchen stove. He had terrorized her into silence by means of threats.

As the story proceeded, the feeling of the court which had, to begin with, been slightly favorable to the prisoner, now set dead against him. He himself sat with downcast head and moody air, as though he knew he were doomed.

Yet it might have been noted that her own counsel sought to restrain Romaine's animosity. He would have preferred her to be more unbiased.

Formidable and ponderous, counsel for the defense arose.

He put it to her that her story was a malicious fabrication from start to finish, that she had not even been in her own house at the time in question, that she was in love with another man and was deliberately seeking to send Vole to his death for a crime he did not commit.

Romaine denied these allegations with superb insolence.

Then came the surprising denouement,[10] the production of the letter. It was read aloud in court in the midst of a breathless stillness.

"Max, beloved, the Fates have delivered him into our hands! He has been arrested for murder—but, yes, the murder of an old lady! Leonard, who would not hurt a fly! At last I shall have my revenge. The poor chicken! I shall say that he came in that night with blood upon him—that he confessed to me. I shall hang him, Max—and when he hangs, he will know and realize that it was

[10] Unravelling.

Romaine who sent him to his death. And then—happiness, Beloved! Happiness at last!"

There were experts present ready to swear that the handwriting was that of Romaine Heilger, but they were not needed. Confronted with the letter, Romaine broke down utterly and confessed everything. Leonard Vole had returned to the house at the time he said, twenty past nine. She had invented the whole story to ruin him.

With the collapse of Romaine Heilger, the case for the Crown[11] collapsed also. Sir Charles called his few witnesses, the prisoner himself went into the box and told his story in a manly, straightforward manner, unshaken by cross-examination.

The prosecution endeavored to rally, but without great success. The judge's summing up was not wholly favorable to the prisoner, but a reaction had set in and the jury needed little time to consider their verdict.

"We find the prisoner not guilty."

Leonard Vole was free!

Little Mr. Mayherne hurried from his seat. He must congratulate his client.

He found himself polishing his pince-nez vigorously and checked himself. His wife had told him only the night before that he was getting a habit of it. Curious things, habits. People themselves never knew they had them.

An interesting case—a very interesting case. That woman, now, Romaine Heilger.

The case was dominated for him still by the exotic figure of Romaine Heilger. She had seemed a pale, quiet woman in the house at Paddington, but in court she had flamed out against the sober background, flaunting herself like a tropical flower.

If he closed his eyes, he could see her now, tall and vehement, her exquisite body bent forward a little, her right hand clenching and unclenching itself unconsciously all the time.

Curious things, habits. That gesture of hers with the hand was her habit, he supposed. Yet he had seen someone else do it quite lately. Who was it, now? Quite lately—

He drew in his breath with a gasp as it came back to him. The woman in Shaw's Rents. . . .

He stood still, his head whirling. It was impossible—Yet, Romaine Heilger was an actress.

The K.C. came up behind him and clapped him on the shoulder.

"Congratulated our man yet? He's had a narrow shave, you know. Come along and see him."

But the little lawyer shook off the other's hand.

He wanted one thing only—to see Romaine Heilger face to face.

He did not see her until some time later, and the place of their meeting is not relevant.

"So you guessed," she said, when he had told her all that was in his mind. "The face? Oh! that was easy enough, and the light of that gas jet was too bad for you to see the make-up."

"But why—why—"

"Why did I play a lone hand?" She smiled a little, remembering the last time she had used the words.

[11] The state or government.

"Such an elaborate comedy!"

"My friend—I had to save him. The evidence of a woman devoted to him would not have been enough—you hinted as much yourself. But I know something of the psychology of crowds. Let my evidence be wrung from me, as an admission, damning me in the eyes of the law, and a reaction in favor of the prisoner would immediately set in."

"And the bundle of letters?"

"One alone, the vital one, might have seemed like a—what do you call it?—put-up job."

"Then the man called Max?"

"Never existed, my friend."

"I still think," said Mr. Mayherne, in an aggrieved manner, "that we could have got him off by the—er—normal procedure."

"I dared not risk it. You see you thought he was innocent—"

"And you knew it? I see," said little Mr. Mayherne.

"My dear Mr. Mayherne," said Romaine, "you do not see at all. I knew—he was guilty!"

> For the most part, laws are but like spiders' webs,
> taking the small gnats, or perhaps sometimes the
> fat flesh flies, but hornets that have sharp stings
> and greater strength, break through them.
>
> Sir John Harington, *Orlando Furioso*[12]

[1924]

---

[12] The *Orlando Furioso*, published in 1516, is an Italian Renaissance epic written by the poet Ludovico Ariosto (1474–1533). Harington (1561–1612) translated it into English in 1591.

Ernest Hemingway 1898–1961

HILLS LIKE WHITE ELEPHANTS

The hills across the valley of the Ebro were long and white. On this side there was no shade and no trees and the station was between two lines of rails in the sun. Close against the side of the station there was the warm shadow of the building and a curtain, made of strings of bamboo beads, hung across the open door into the bar, to keep out flies. The American and the girl with him sat at a table in the shade, outside the building. It was very hot and the express from Barcelona would come in forty minutes. It stopped at this junction for two minutes and went on to Madrid.[1]

"What should we drink?" the girl asked. She had taken off her hat and put it on the table.

"It's pretty hot," the man said.

"Let's drink beer."

"Dos cervezas," the man said into the curtain.

"Big ones?" a woman asked from the doorway.

"Yes. Two big ones."

The woman brought two glasses of beer and two felt pads. She put the felt pads and the beer glasses on the table and looked at the man and the girl. The girl was looking off at the line of hills. They were white in the sun and the country was brown and dry.

"They look like white elephants," she said.

"I've never seen one," the man drank his beer.

"No, you wouldn't have."

"I might have," the man said. "Just because you say I wouldn't have doesn't prove anything."

The girl looked at the bead curtain. "They've painted something on it," she said. "What does it say?"

"Anis del Toro. It's a drink."

"Could we try it?"

The man called "Listen" through the curtain. The woman came out from the bar.

"Four reales."[2]

"We want two Anis del Toro."

"With water?"

"Do you want it with water?"

"I don't know," the girl said. "Is it good with water?"

"It's all right."

"You want them with water?" asked the woman.

"Yes, with water."

"It tastes like licorice," the girl said and put the glass down.

"That's the way with everything."

"Yes," said the girl. "Everything tastes of licorice. Especially all the things you've waited so long for, like absinthe."

"Oh, cut it out."

[1] The references to the Ebro River and the cities of Barcelona and Madrid identify the setting as Spain.
[2] Spanish coins.

"You started it," the girl said. "I was being amused. I was having a fine time."

"Well, let's try and have a fine time."

"All right. I was trying. I said the mountains looked like white elephants. Wasn't that bright?"

"That was bright."

"I wanted to try this new drink. That's all we do, isn't it—look at things and try new drinks?"

"I guess so."

The girl looked across at the hills.

"They're lovely hills," she said. "They don't really look like white elephants. I just meant the coloring of their skin through the trees."

"Should we have another drink?"

"All right."

The warm wind blew the bead curtain against the table.

"The beer's nice and cool," the man said.

"It's lovely," the girl said.

"It's really an awfully simple operation, Jig," the man said. "It's not really an operation at all."

The girl looked at the ground the table legs rested on.

"I know you wouldn't mind it, Jig. It's really not anything. It's just to let the air in."

The girl did not say anything.

"I'll go with you and I'll stay with you all the time. They just let the air in and then it's all perfectly natural."

"Then what will we do afterward?"

"We'll be fine afterward. Just like we were before."

"What makes you think so?"

"That's the only thing that bothers us. It's the only thing that's made us unhappy."

The girl looked at the bead curtain, put her hand out and took hold of two of the strings of beads.

"And you think then we'll be all right and be happy."

"I know we will. You don't have to be afraid. I've known lots of people that have done it."

"So have I," said the girl. "And afterward they were all so happy."

"Well," the man said, "if you don't want to you don't have to. I wouldn't have you do it if you didn't want to. But I know it's perfectly simple."

"And you really want to?"

"I think it's the best thing to do. But I don't want you to do it if you don't really want to."

"And if I do it you'll be happy and things will be like they were and you'll love me?"

"I love you now. You know I love you."

"I know. But if I do it, then it will be nice again if I say things are like white elephants, and you'll like it?"

"I'll love it. I love it now but I just can't think about it. You know how I get when I worry."

"If I do it you won't ever worry?"

"I won't worry about that because it's perfectly simple."

"Then I'll do it. Because I don't care about me."

"What do you mean?"

"I don't care about me."

"Well, I care about you."

"Oh, yes. But I don't care about me. And I'll do it and then everything will be fine."

"I don't want you to do it if you feel that way."

The girl stood up and walked to the end of the station. Across, on the other side, were fields of grain and trees along the banks of the Ebro. Far away, beyond the river, were mountains. The shadow of a cloud moved across the field of grain and she saw the river through the trees.

"And we could have all this," she said. "And we could have everything and every day we make it more impossible."

"What did you say?"

"I said we could have everything."

"We can have everything."

"No, we can't."

"We can have the whole world."

"No, we can't."

"We can go everywhere."

"No, we can't. It isn't ours any more."

"It's ours."

"No, it isn't. And once they take it away, you never get it back."

"But they haven't taken it away."

"We'll wait and see."

"Come on back in the shade," he said. "You mustn't feel that way."

"I don't feel any way," the girl said. "I just know things."

"I don't want you to do anything that you don't want to do——"

"Nor that isn't good for me," she said. "I know. Could we have another beer?"

"All right. But you've got to realize——"

"I realize," the girl said. "Can't we maybe stop talking?"

They sat down at the table and the girl looked across at the hills on the dry side of the valley and the man looked at her and at the table.

"You've got to realize," he said, "that I don't want you to do it if you don't want to. I'm perfectly willing to go through with it if it means anything to you."

"Doesn't it mean anything to you? We could get along."

"Of course it does. But I don't want anybody but you. I don't want any one else. And I know it's perfectly simple."

"Yes, you know it's perfectly simple."

"It's all right for you to say that, but I do know it."

"Would you do something for me now?"

"I'd do anything for you."

"Would you please please please please please please please stop talking?"

He did not say anything but looked at the bags against the wall of the station. There were labels on them from all the hotels where they had spent nights.

"But I don't want you to," he said, "I don't care anything about it."

"I'll scream," the girl said.

The woman came out through the curtains with two glasses of beer and put them down on the damp felt pads. "The train comes in five minutes," she said.

"What did she say?" asked the girl.

"That the train is coming in five minutes."

The girl smiled brightly at the woman, to thank her.

"I'd better take the bags over to the other side of the station," the man said. She smiled at him.

"All right. Then come back and we'll finish the beer."

He picked up the two heavy bags and carried them around the station to the other tracks. He looked up the tracks but could not see the train. Coming back, he walked through the barroom, where people waiting for the train were drinking. He drank an Anis at the bar and looked at the people. They were all waiting reasonably for the train. He went out through the bead curtain. She was sitting at the table and smiled at him.

"Do you feel better?" he asked.

"I feel fine," she said. "There's nothing wrong with me. I feel fine."

[1927]

William Faulkner   *1897–1962*

A ROSE FOR EMILY

I

When Miss Emily Grierson died, our whole town went to her funeral: the men through a sort of respectful affection for a fallen monument, the women mostly out of curiosity to see the inside of her house, which no one save an old manservant—a combined gardener and cook—had seen in at least ten years.

It was a big, squarish frame house that had once been white, decorated with cupolas and spires and scrolled balconies in the heavily lightsome style of the seventies, set on what had once been our most select street. But garages and cotton gins had encroached and obliterated even the august names of that neighborhood; only Miss Emily's house was left, lifting its stubborn and coquettish decay above the cotton wagons and the gasoline pumps—an eyesore among eyesores. And now Miss Emily had gone to join the representatives of those august names where they lay in the cedar-bemused cemetery among the ranked and anonymous graves of Union and Confederate soldiers who fell at the battle of Jefferson.

Alive, Miss Emily had been a tradition, a duty, and a care; a sort of hereditary obligation upon the town, dating from that day in 1894 when Colonel Sartoris, the mayor—he who fathered the edict that no Negro woman should appear on the streets without an apron—remitted her taxes, the dispensation dating from the death of her father on into perpetuity. Not that Miss Emily would have accepted charity. Colonel Sartoris invented an involved tale to the effect that Miss Emily's father had loaned money to the town, which the town, as a matter of business, preferred this way of repaying. Only a man of Colonel Sartoris' generation and thought could have invented it, and only a woman could have believed it.

When the next generation, with its more modern ideas, became mayors and aldermen, this arrangement created some little dissatisfaction. On the first of the year they mailed her a tax notice. February came, and there was no reply. They wrote her a formal letter, asking her to call at the sheriff's office at her convenience. A week later the mayor wrote her himself, offering to call or to send his car for her, and received in reply a note on paper of an archaic shape, in a thin, flowing calligraphy in faded ink, to the effect that she no longer went out at all. The tax notice was also enclosed, without comment.

They called a special meeting of the Board of Aldermen. A deputation waited upon her, knocked at the door through which no visitor had passed since she ceased giving china-painting lessons eight or ten years earlier. They were admitted by the old Negro into a dim hall from which a stairway mounted into still more shadow. It smelled of dust and disuse—a close, dank smell. The Negro led them into the parlor. It was furnished in heavy, leather-covered furniture. When the Negro opened the blinds of one window, they could see that the leather was cracked; and when they sat down, a faint dust rose sluggishly about their thighs, spinning with slow motes in the single sun-ray. On a tarnished gilt easel before the fireplace stood a crayon portrait of Miss Emily's father.

They rose when she entered—a small, fat woman in black, with a thin gold chain descending to her waist and vanishing into her belt, leaning on an ebony cane with a tarnished gold head. Her skeleton was small and spare; perhaps that was why what would have been merely plumpness in another was obesity in her. She looked bloated, like a body long submerged in motionless water, and of that pallid hue. Her eyes, lost in the fatty ridges of her face, looked like two small pieces of coal pressed into a lump of dough as they moved from one face to another while the visitors stated their errand.

She did not ask them to sit. She just stood in the door and listened quietly until the spokesman came to a stumbling halt. Then they could hear the invisible watch ticking at the end of the gold chain.

Her voice was dry and cold. "I have no taxes in Jefferson. Colonel Sartoris explained it to me. Perhaps one of you can gain access to the city records and satisfy yourselves."

"But we have. We are the city authorities, Miss Emily. Didn't you get a notice from the sheriff, signed by him?"

"I received a paper, yes," Miss Emily said. "Perhaps he considers himself the sheriff . . . I have no taxes in Jefferson."

"But there is nothing on the books to show that, you see. We must go by the—"

"See Colonel Sartoris. I have no taxes in Jefferson."

"But, Miss Emily—"

"See Colonel Sartoris." (Colonel Sartoris had been dead almost ten years.) "I have no taxes in Jefferson. Tobe!" The Negro appeared. "Show these gentlemen out."

II

So she vanquished them, horse and foot, just as she had vanquished their fathers thirty years before about the smell. That was two years after her father's death and a short time after her sweetheart—the one we believed would marry her—had deserted her. After her father's death she went out very little; after her sweetheart went away, people hardly saw her at all. A few of the ladies had the temerity to call, but were not received, and the only sign of life about the place was the Negro man—a young man then—going in and out with a market basket.

"Just as if a man—any man—could keep a kitchen properly," the ladies said; so they were not surprised when the smell developed. It was another link between the gross, teeming world and the high and mighty Griersons.

A neighbor, a woman, complained to the mayor, Judge Stevens, eighty years old.

"But what will you have me do about it, madam?" he said.

"Why, send her word to stop it," the woman said. "Isn't there a law?"

"I'm sure that won't be necessary," Judge Stevens said. "It's probably just a snake or a rat that nigger of hers killed in the yard. I'll speak to him about it."

The next day he received two more complaints, one from a man who came in diffident deprecation. "We really must do something about it, Judge. I'd be the last one in the world to bother Miss Emily, but we've got to do something." That night the Board of Aldermen met—three graybeards and one younger man, a member of the rising generation.

"It's simple enough," he said. "Send her word to have her place cleaned up. Give her a certain time to do it in, and if she don't . . ."

"Dammit, sir," Judge Stevens said, "will you accuse a lady to her face of smelling bad?"

So the next night, after midnight, four men crossed Miss Emily's lawn and slunk about the house like burglars, sniffing along the base of the brickwork and at the cellar openings while one of them performed a regular sowing motion with his hand out of a sack slung from his shoulder. They broke open the cellar door and sprinkled lime there, and in all the outbuildings. As they recrossed the lawn, a window that had been dark was lighted and Miss Emily sat in it, the light behind her, and her upright torso motionless as that of an idol. They crept quietly across the lawn and into the shadow of the locusts that lined the street. After a week or two the smell went away.

That was when people had begun to feel really sorry for her. People in our town, remembering how old lady Wyatt, her great-aunt, had gone completely crazy at last, believed that the Griersons held themselves a little too high for what they really were. None of the young men were quite good enough for Miss Emily and such. We had long thought of them as a tableau, Miss Emily a slender figure in white in the background, her father a spraddled silhouette in the foreground, his back to her and clutching a horsewhip, the two of them framed by the back-flung front door. So when she got to be thirty and was still single, we were not pleased exactly, but vindicated; even with insanity in the family she wouldn't have turned down all of her chances if they had really materialized.

When her father died, it got about that the house was all that was left to her; and in a way, people were glad. At last they could pity Miss Emily. Being left alone, and a pauper, she had become humanized. Now she too would know the old thrill and the old despair of a penny more or less.

The day after his death all the ladies prepared to call at the house and offer condolence and aid, as is our custom. Miss Emily met them at the door, dressed as usual and with no trace of grief on her face. She told them that her father was not dead. She did that for three days, with the ministers calling on her, and the doctors, trying to persuade her to let them dispose of the body. Just as they were about to resort to law and force, she broke down, and they buried her father quickly.

We did not say she was crazy then. We believed she had to do that. We remembered all the young men her father had driven away, and we knew that with nothing left, she would have to cling to that which had robbed her, as people will.

III

She was sick for a long time. When we saw her again, her hair was cut short, making her look like a girl, with a vague resemblance to those angels in colored church windows—sort of tragic and serene.

The town had just let the contracts for paving the sidewalks, and in the summer after her father's death they began the work. The construction company came with niggers and mules and machinery, and a foreman named Homer Barron, a Yankee—a big, dark, ready man, with a big voice and eyes lighter than his face. The little boys would follow in groups to hear him cuss the niggers, and the niggers singing in time to the rise and fall of picks. Pretty soon he knew everybody in town. Whenever you heard a lot of laughing anywhere about the square, Homer Barron would be in the center of the group. Presently we began to see him and Miss Emily on Sunday afternoons driving in the yellow-wheeled buggy and the matched team of bays from the livery stable.

At first we were glad that Miss Emily would have an interest, because the ladies all said, "Of course a Grierson would not think seriously of a Northerner, a day laborer." But there were still others, older people, who said that even grief could not cause a real lady to forget *noblesse oblige*—without calling it *noblesse oblige*. They just said, "Poor Emily. Her kinsfolk should come to her." She had some kin in Alabama; but years ago her father had fallen out with them over the estate of old lady Wyatt, the crazy woman, and there was no communication between the two families. They had not even been represented at the funeral.

And as soon as the old people said, "Poor Emily," the whispering began. "Do you suppose it's really so?" they said to one another. "Of course it is. What else could . . ." This behind their hands; rustling of craned silk and satin behind jalousies closed upon the sun of Sunday afternoon as the thin, swift clop-clop-clop of the matched team passed: "Poor Emily."

She carried her head high enough—even when we believed that she was fallen. It was as if she demanded more than ever the recognition of her dignity as the last Grierson; as if it had wanted that touch of earthiness to reaffirm her impervious-ness. Like when she bought the rat poison, the arsenic. That was over a year after they had begun to say "Poor Emily," and while the two female cousins were visiting her.

"I want some poison," she said to the druggist. She was over thirty then, still a slight woman, though thinner than usual, with cold, haughty black eyes in a face the flesh of which was strained across the temples and about the eyesockets as you imagine a lighthouse-keeper's face ought to look. "I want some poison," she said.

"Yes, Miss Emily. What kind? For rats and such? I'd recom—"

"I want the best you have. I don't care what kind."

The druggist named several. "They'll kill anything up to an elephant. But what you want is—"

"Arsenic," Miss Emily said. "Is that a good one?"

"Is . . . arsenic? Yes, ma'am. But what you want—"

"I want arsenic."

The druggist looked down at her. She looked back at him, erect, her face like a strained flag. "Why, of course," the druggist said. "If that's what you want. But the law requires you to tell what you are going to use it for."

Miss Emily just stared at him, her head tilted back in order to look him eye for eye, until he looked away and went and got the arsenic and wrapped it up. The Negro delivery boy brought her the package; the druggist didn't come back. When she opened the package at home there was written on the box, under the skull and bones: "For rats."

IV

So the next day we all said, "She will kill herself"; and we said it would be the best thing. When she had first begun to be seen with Homer Barron, we had said, "She will marry him." Then we said, "She will persuade him yet," because Homer himself had remarked—he liked men, and it was known that he drank with the younger men in the Elks' Club—that he was not a marrying man. Later we said, "Poor Emily" behind the jalousies as they passed on Sunday afternoon in the glittering buggy, Miss Emily with her head high and Homer Barron with his hat cocked and a cigar in his teeth, reins and whip in a yellow glove.

Then some of the ladies began to say that it was a disgrace to the town and a bad example to the young people. The men did not want to interfere, but at last the ladies forced the Baptist minister—Miss Emily's people were Episcopal—to call upon her. He would never divulge what happened during that interview, but he refused to go back again. The next Sunday they again drove about the streets, and the following day the minister's wife wrote to Miss Emily's relations in Alabama.

So she had blood-kin under her roof again and we sat back to watch developments. At first nothing happened. Then we were sure that they were to be married. We learned that Miss Emily had been to the jeweler's and ordered a man's toilet set in silver, with the letters H. B. on each piece. Two days later we learned that she had bought a complete outfit of men's clothing, including a nightshirt, and we said, "They are married." We were really glad. We were glad because the two female cousins were even more Grierson than Miss Emily had ever been.

So we were not surprised when Homer Barron—the streets had been finished some time since—was gone. We were a little disappointed that there was not a public blowing-off, but we believed that he had gone on to prepare for Miss Emily's coming, or to give her a chance to get rid of the cousins. (By that time it was a cabal, and we were all Miss Emily's allies to help circumvent the cousins.) Sure enough, after another week they departed. And, as we had expected all along, within three days Homer Barron was back in town. A neighbor saw the Negro man admit him at the kitchen door at dusk one evening.

And that was the last we saw of Homer Barron. And of Miss Emily for some time. The Negro man went in and out with the market basket, but the front door remained closed. Now and then we would see her at a window for a moment, as the men did that night when they sprinkled the lime, but for almost six months she did not appear on the streets. Then we knew that this was to be expected too; as if that quality of her father which had thwarted her woman's life so many times had been too virulent and too furious to die.

When we next saw Miss Emily, she had grown fat and her hair was turning gray. During the next few years it grew grayer and grayer until it attained an even pepper-and-salt iron-gray, when it ceased turning. Up to the day of her death at seventy-four it was still that vigorous iron-gray, like the hair of an active man.

From that time on her front door remained closed, save for a period of six or seven years, when she was about forty, during which she gave lessons in china-painting. She fitted up a studio in one of the downstairs rooms, where the daughters and granddaughters of Colonel Sartoris' contemporaries were sent to her with the same regularity and in the same spirit that they were sent to church on Sundays with a twenty-five cent piece for the collection plate. Meanwhile her taxes had been remitted.

Then the newer generation became the backbone and the spirit of the town, and the painting pupils grew up and fell away and did not send their children to her with boxes of color and tedious brushes and pictures cut from the ladies' magazines. The front door closed upon the last one and remained closed for good. When the town got free postal delivery, Miss Emily alone refused to let them fasten the metal numbers above her door and attach a mailbox to it. She would not listen to them.

Daily, monthly, yearly we watched the Negro grow grayer and more stooped, going in and out with the market basket. Each December we sent her a tax notice, which would be returned by the post office a week later, unclaimed. Now and then we would see her in one of the downstairs windows—she had evidently shut up the top floor of the house like the carven torso of an idol in a niche, looking or not looking at us, we could never tell which. Thus she passed from generation to generation—dear, inescapable, impervious, tranquil, and perverse.

And so she died. Fell ill in the house filled with dust and shadows, with only a doddering Negro man to wait on her. We did not even know she was sick; we had long since given up trying to get any information from the Negro. He talked to no one, probably not even to her, for his voice had grown harsh and rusty, as if from disuse.

She died in one of the downstairs rooms, in a heavy walnut bed with a curtain, her gray head propped on a pillow yellow and moldy with age and lack of sunlight.

V

The Negro met the first of the ladies at the front door and let them in, with their hushed, sibilant voices and their quick, curious glances, and then he disappeared. He walked right through the house and out the back and was not seen again.

The two female cousins came at once. They held the funeral on the second day, with the town coming to look at Miss Emily beneath a mass of bought flowers, with the crayon face of her father musing profoundly above the bier and the ladies sibilant and macabre; and the very old men—some in their brushed Confederate uniforms—on the porch and the lawn, talking of Miss Emily as if she had been a contemporary of theirs, believing that they had danced with her and courted her perhaps, confusing time with its mathematical progression, as the old do, to whom all the past is not a diminishing road but, instead, a huge meadow which no winter ever quite touches, divided from them now by the narrow bottle-neck of the most recent decade of years.

Already we knew that there was one room in that region above stairs which no one had seen in forty years, and which would have to be forced. They waited until Miss Emily was decently in the ground before they opened it.

The violence of breaking down the door seemed to fill this room with pervading dust. A thin, acrid pall as of the tomb seemed to lie everywhere upon this room decked and furnished as for a bridal: upon the valance curtains of faded rose color, upon the rose-shaded lights, upon the dressing table, upon the delicate array of crystal and the man's toilet things backed with tarnished silver, silver so tarnished that the monogram was obscured. Among them lay a collar and tie, as if they had just been removed, which, lifted, left upon the surface a pale crescent in the dust. Upon a chair hung the suit, carefully folded; beneath it the two mute shoes and the discarded socks.

The man himself lay in the bed.

For a long while we just stood there, looking down at the profound and fleshless grin. The body had apparently once lain in the attitude of an embrace, but now the long sleep that outlasts love, that conquers even the grimace of love, had cuckolded him. What was left of him, rotten beneath what was left of the nightshirt, had become inextricable from the bed in which he lay; and upon him and upon the pillow beside him lay that even coating of the patient and biding dust.

Then we noticed that in the second pillow was the indentation of a head. One of us lifted something from it, and leaning forward, that faint and invisible dust dry and acrid in the nostrils, we saw a long strand of iron-gray hair.

[1930]

William Faulkner   *1897–1962*

BARN BURNING

The store in which the Justice of the Peace's court was sitting smelled of cheese. The boy, crouched on his nail keg at the back of the crowded room, knew he smelled cheese, and more: from where he sat he could see the ranked shelves close-packed with the solid, squat, dynamic shapes of tin cans whose labels his stomach read, not from the lettering which meant nothing to his mind but from the scarlet devils and the silver curve of fish—this, the cheese which he knew he smelled and the hermetic meat[1] which his intestines believed he smelled coming in intermittent gusts momentary and brief between the other constant one, the smell and sense just a little of fear because mostly of despair and grief, the old fierce pull of blood. He could not see the table where the Justice sat and before which his father and his father's enemy (*our enemy* he thought in that despair; *ourn! mine and hisn both! He's my father!*) stood, but he could hear them, the two of them that is, because his father had said no word yet:

"But what proof have you, Mr. Harris?"

"I told you. The hog got into my corn. I caught it up and sent it back to him. He had no fence that would hold it. I told him so, warned him. The next time I put the hog in my pen. When he came to get it I gave him enough wire to patch up his pen. The next time I put the hog up and kept it. I rode down to his house and saw the wire I gave him still rolled on to the spool in his yard. I told him he could have the hog when he paid me a dollar pound fee. That evening a nigger came with the dollar and got the hog. He was a strange nigger. He said, 'He say to tell you wood and hay kin burn.' I said, 'What?' 'That whut he say to tell you,' the nigger said. 'Wood and hay kin burn.' That night my barn burned. I got the stock out but I lost the barn."

"Where is the nigger? Have you got him?"

"He was a strange nigger, I tell you. I don't know what became of him."

"But that's not proof. Don't you see that's not proof?"

"Get that boy up here. He knows." For a moment the boy thought too that the man meant his older brother until Harris said, "Not him. The little one. The boy," and, crouching, small for his age, small and wiry like his father, in patched and faded jeans even too small for him, with straight, uncombed, brown hair and eyes gray and wild as storm scud, he saw the men between himself and the table part and become a lane of grim faces, at the end of which he saw the Justice, a shabby, collarless, graying man in spectacles, beckoning him. He felt no floor under his bare feet; he seemed to walk beneath the palpable weight of the grim turning faces. His father, stiff in his black Sunday coat donned not for the trial but for the moving, did not even look at him. *He aims for me to lie,* he thought, again with that frantic grief and despair. *And I will have to do hit.*

"What's your name, boy?" the Justice said.

"Colonel Sartoris Snopes,"[2] the boy whispered.

---

[1] Canned meat.

[2] The shrewd, ambitious, and largely amoral Snopes family appear in many of Faulkner's works. Their social and economic rise is the subject of the so-called "Snopes Trilogy" of novels: *The Hamlet* (1940), for which the present story was originally intended, *The Town* (1957), and *The Mansion* (1959). The boy is named for Colonel John Sartoris (1823–1876), Faulkner's larger-than-life plantation owner and Civil War hero.

"Hey?" the Justice said. "Talk louder. Colonel Sartoris? I reckon anybody named for Colonel Sartoris in this country can't help but tell the truth, can they?" The boy said nothing. *Enemy! Enemy!* he thought; for a moment he could not even see, could not see that the Justice's face was kindly nor discern that his voice was troubled when he spoke to the man named Harris: "Do you want me to question this boy?" But he could hear, and during those subsequent long seconds while there was absolutely no sound in the crowded little room save that of quiet and intent breathing it was as if he had swung outward at the end of a grape vine, over a ravine, and at the top of the swing had been caught in a prolonged instant of mesmerized gravity, weightless in time.

"No!" Harris said violently, explosively. "Damnation! Send him out of here!" Now time, the fluid world, rushed beneath him again, the voices coming to him again through the smell of cheese and sealed meat, the fear and despair and the old grief of blood:

"This case is closed. I can't find against you, Snopes, but I can give you advice. Leave this country and don't come back to it."

His father spoke for the first time, his voice cold and harsh, level, with out emphasis: "I aim to. I don't figure to stay in a country among people who . . ." he said something unprintable and vile, addressed to no one.

"That'll do," the Justice said. "Take your wagon and get out of this country before dark. Case dismissed."

His father turned, and he followed the stiff black coat, the wiry figure walking a little stiffly from where a Confederate provost's man's[3] musket ball had taken him in the heel on a stolen horse thirty years ago, followed the two backs now, since his older brother had appeared from somewhere in the crowd, no taller than the father but thicker, chewing tobacco steadily, between the two lines of grim-faced men and out of the store and across the worn gallery and down the sagging steps and among the dogs and half-grown boys in the mild May dust, where as he passed a voice hissed:

"Barn burner!"

Again he could not see, whirling; there was a face in a red haze, moonlike, bigger than the full moon, the owner of it half again his size, he leaping in the red haze toward the face, feeling no blow, feeling no shock when his head struck the earth, scrabbling up and leaping again, feeling no blow this time either and tasting no blood, scrabbling up to see the other boy in full flight and himself already leaping into pursuit as his father's hand jerked him back, the harsh, cold voice speaking above him: "Go get in the wagon."

It stood in a grove of locusts and mulberries across the road. His two hulking sisters in their Sunday dresses and his mother and her sister in calico and sunbonnets were already in it, sitting on and among the sorry residue of the dozen and more movings which even the boy could remember—the battered stove, the broken beds and chairs, the clock inlaid with mother-of-pearl, which would not run, stopped at some fourteen minutes past two o'clock of a dead and forgotten day and time, which had been his mother's dowry. She was crying, though when she saw him she drew her sleeve across her face and began to descend from the wagon. "Get back," the father said.

"He's hurt. I got to get some water and wash his . . ."

"Get back in the wagon," his father said. He got in too, over the tail-gate. His father mounted to the seat where the older brother already sat and struck the gaunt mules two savage blows with the peeled willow, but without heat. It was not

[3] Military policeman.

even sadistic; it was exactly that same quality which in later years would cause his descendants to over-run the engine before putting a motor car into motion, striking and reining back in the same movement. The wagon went on, the store with its quiet crowd of grimly watching men dropped behind; a curve in the road hid it. *Forever* he thought. *Maybe he's done satisfied now, now that he has* . . . stopping himself, not to say it aloud even to himself. His mother's hand touched his shoulder.

"Does hit hurt?" she said.

"Naw," he said. "Hit don't hurt. Lemme be."

"Can't you wipe some of the blood off before hit dries?"

"I'll wash to-night," he said. "Lemme be, I tell you."

The wagon went on. He did not know where they were going. None of them ever did or ever asked, because it was always somewhere, always a house of sorts waiting for them a day or two days or even three days away. Likely his father had already arranged to make a crop on another farm before he . . . Again he had to stop himself. He (the father) always did. There was something about his wolflike independence and even courage when the advantage was at least neutral which impressed strangers, as if they got from his latent ravening ferocity not so much a sense of dependability as a feeling that his ferocious conviction in the rightness of his own actions would be of advantage to all whose interest lay with his.

That night they camped, in a grove of oaks and beeches where a spring ran. The nights were still cool and they had a fire against it, of a rail lifted from a nearby fence and cut into lengths—a small fire, neat, niggard almost, a shrewd fire; such fires were his father's habit and custom always, even in freezing weather. Older, the boy might have remarked this and wondered why not a big one; why should not a man who had not only seen the waste and extravagance of war, but who had in his blood an inherent voracious prodigality with material not his own, have burned everything in sight? Then he might have gone a step farther and thought that that was the reason: that niggard blaze was the living fruit of nights passed during those four years in the woods hiding from all men, blue or gray, with his strings of horses (captured horses, he called them). And older still, he might have divined the true reason: that the element of fire spoke to some deep mainspring of his father's being, as the element of steel or of powder spoke to other men, as the one weapon for the preservation of integrity, else breath were not worth the breathing, and hence to be regarded with respect and used with discretion.

But he did not think this now and he had seen those same niggard blazes all his life. He merely ate his supper beside it and was already half asleep over his iron plate when his father called him, and once more he followed the stiff back, the stiff and ruthless limp, up the slope and on to the starlit road where, turning, he could see his father against the stars but without face or depth—a shape black, flat, and bloodless as though cut from tin in the iron folds of the frockcoat which had not been made for him, the voice harsh like tin and without heat like tin:

"You were fixing to tell them. You would have told him." He didn't answer. His father struck him with the flat of his hand on the side of the head, hard but without heat, exactly as he had struck the two mules at the store, exactly as he would strike either of them with any stick in order to kill a horse fly, his voice still without heat or anger: "You're getting to be a man. You got to learn. You got to learn to stick to your own blood or you ain't going to have any blood to stick to you. Do you think either of them, any man there this morning, would? Don't you know all they wanted was a chance to get at me because they knew I had them beat? Eh?" Later, twenty years later, he was to tell himself, "If I had said they wanted only truth, justice, he would have hit me again." But now he said nothing. He was not crying. He just stood there. "Answer me," his father said.

"Yes," he whispered. His father turned.

"Get on to bed. We'll be there tomorrow."

To-morrow they were there. In the early afternoon the wagon stopped before a paintless two-room house identical almost with the dozen others it had stopped before even in the boy's ten years, and again, as on the other dozen occasions, his mother and aunt got down and began to unload the wagon, although his two sisters and his father and brother had not moved.

"Likely hit ain't fitten for hawgs," one of the sisters said.

"Nevertheless, fit it will and you'll hog it and like it," his father said. "Get out of them chairs and help your Ma unload."

The two sisters got down, big, bovine, in a flutter of cheap ribbons; one of them drew from the jumbled wagon bed a battered lantern, the other a worn broom. His father handed the reins to the older son and began to climb stiffly over the wheel. "When they get unloaded, take the team to the barn and feed them." Then he said, and at first the boy thought he was still speaking to his brother: "Come with me."

"Me?" he said.

"Yes," his father said. "You."

"Abner," his mother said. His father paused and looked back—the harsh level stare beneath the shaggy, graying, irascible brows.

"I reckon I'll have a word with the man that aims to begin to-morrow owning me body and soul for the next eight months."

They went back up the road. A week ago—or before last night, that is—he would have asked where they were going, but not now. His father had struck him before last night but never before had he paused afterward to explain why; it was as if the blow and the following calm, outrageous voice still rang, repercussed, divulging nothing to him save the terrible handicap of being young, the light weight of his few years, just heavy enough to prevent his soaring free of the world as it seemed to be ordered but not heavy enough to keep him footed solid in it, to resist it and try to change the course of its events.

Presently he could see the grove of oaks and cedars and the other flowering trees and shrubs where the house would be, though not the house yet. They walked beside a fence massed with honeysuckle and Cherokee roses and came to a gate swinging open between two brick pillars, and now, beyond a sweep of drive, he saw the house for the first time and at that instant he forgot his father and the terror and despair both, and even when he remembered his father again (who had not stopped) the terror and despair did not return. Because, for all the twelve movings, they had sojourned until now in a poor country, a land of small farms and fields and houses, and he had never seen a house like this before. *Hit's big as a courthouse* he thought quietly, with a surge of peace and joy whose reason he could not have thought into words, being too young for that: *They are safe from him. People whose lives are a part of this peace and dignity are beyond his touch, he no more to them than a buzzing wasp: capable of stinging for a little moment but that's all; the spell of this peace and dignity rendering even the barns and stable and cribs which belong to it impervious to the puny flames he might contrive* . . . this, the peace and joy, ebbing for an instant as he looked again at the stiff black back, the stiff and implacable limp of the figure which was not dwarfed by the house, for the reason that it had never looked big anywhere and which now, against the serene columned backdrop, had more than ever that impervious quality of something cut ruthlessly from tin, depthless, as though, sidewise to the sun, it would cast no shadow. Watching him, the boy remarked the absolutely undeviating course which his father held and saw the stiff foot come squarely down in a pile of fresh droppings where a horse had stood in the drive and which his father could have avoided by a simple change of stride. But it ebbed only for a moment, though he could not have thought this into words either, walking on in the spell of the house, which he could even want but without envy, without sorrow, certainly never with that ravening and jealous rage which unknown to him walked in the ironlike black coat before him: *Maybe he will feel it too. Maybe it will even change him now from what maybe he couldn't help but be.*

They crossed the portico. Now he could hear his father's stiff foot as it came down on the boards with clocklike finality, a sound out of all proportion to the displacement of the body it bore and which was not dwarfed either by the white door before it, as though it had attained to a sort of vicious and ravening minimum not to be dwarfed by anything—the flat, wide, black hat, the formal coat of broadcloth which had once been black but which had now that friction-glazed greenish cast of the bodies of old house flies, the lifted sleeve which was too large, the lifted hand like a curled claw. The door opened so promptly that the boy knew the Negro must have been watching them all the time, an old man with neat grizzled hair, in a linen jacket, who stood barring the door with his body, saying, "Wipe yo foots, white man, fo you come in here. Major ain't home nohow."

"Get out of my way, nigger," his father said, without heat too, flinging the door back and the Negro also and entering, his hat still on his head. And now the boy saw the prints of the stiff foot on the doorjamb and saw them appear on the pale rug behind the machinelike deliberation of the foot which seemed to bear (or transmit) twice the weight which the body compassed. The Negro was shouting "Miss Lula! Miss Lula!" somewhere behind them, then the boy, deluged as though by a warm wave by a suave turn of carpeted stair and a pendant glitter of chandeliers and a mute gleam of gold frames, heard the swift feet and saw her too, a lady—perhaps he had never seen her like before either—in a gray, smooth gown with lace at the throat and an apron tied at the waist and the sleeves turned back, wiping cake or biscuit dough from her hands with a towel as she came up the hall, looking not at his father at all but at the tracks on the blond rug with an expression of incredulous amazement.

"I tried," the Negro cried. "I tole him to . . ."

"Will you please go away?" she said in a shaking voice. "Major de Spain is not at home. Will you please go away?"

His father had not spoken again. He did not speak again. He did not even look at her. He just stood stiff in the center of the rug, in his hat, the shaggy iron-gray brows twitching slightly above the pebble-colored eyes as he appeared to examine the house with brief deliberation. Then with the same deliberation he turned; the boy watched him pivot on the good leg and saw the stiff foot drag round the arc of the turning, leaving a final long and fading smear. His father never looked at it, he never once looked down at the rug. The Negro held the door. It closed behind them, upon the hysteric and indistinguishable woman-wail. His father stopped at the top of the steps and scraped his boot clean on the edge of it. At the gate he stopped again. He stood for a moment, planted stiffly on the stiff foot, looking back at the house. "Pretty and white, ain't it?" he said. "That's sweat. Nigger sweat. Maybe it ain't white enough yet to suit him. Maybe he wants to mix some white sweat with it."

Two hours later the boy was chopping wood behind the house within which his mother and aunt and the two sisters (the mother and aunt, not the two girls, he knew that; even at this distance and muffled by walls the flat loud voices of the two girls emanated an incorrigible idle inertia) were setting up the stove to prepare a meal, when he heard the hooves and saw the linen-clad man on a fine sorrel mare, whom he recognized even before he saw the rolled rug in front of the Negro youth following on a fat bay carriage horse—a suffused, angry face vanishing, still at full gallop, beyond the corner of the house where his father and brother were sitting in the two tilted chairs; and a moment later, almost before he could have put the axe down, he heard the hooves again and watched the sorrel mare go back out of the yard, already galloping again. Then his father began to shout one of the sisters' names, who presently emerged backward from the kitchen door dragging the rolled rug along the ground by one end while the other ·sister walked behind it.

"If you ain't going to tote, go on and set up the wash pot," the first said.

"You, Sarty!" the second shouted. "Set up the wash pot!" His father appeared at the door, framed against that shabbiness, as he had been against that other bland perfection, impervious to either, the mother's anxious face at his shoulder.

"Go on," the father said. "Pick it up." The two sisters stooped, broad, lethargic; stooping, they presented an incredible expanse of pale cloth and a flutter of tawdry ribbons.

"If I thought enough of a rug to have to git hit all the way from France I wouldn't keep hit where folks coming in would have to tromp on hit," the first said. They raised the rug.

"Abner," the mother said. "Let me do it."

"You go back and git dinner," his father said. "I'll tend to this."

From the woodpile through the rest of the afternoon the boy watched them, the rug spread flat in the dust beside the bubbling wash-pot, the two sisters stooping over it with that profound and lethargic reluctance, while the father stood over them in turn, implacable and grim, driving them though never raising his voice again. He could smell the harsh homemade lye[4] they were using; he saw his mother come to the door once and look toward them with an expression not anxious now but very like despair; he saw his father turn, and he fell to with the axe and saw from the corner of his eye his father raise from the ground a flattish fragment of field stone and examine it and return to the pot, and this time his mother actually spoke: "Abner. Abner. Please don't. Please, Abner."

Then he was done too. It was dusk; the whippoorwills had already begun. He could smell coffee from the room where they would presently eat the cold food remaining from the mid-afternoon meal, though when he entered the house he realized they were having coffee again probably because there was a fire on the hearth, before which the rug now lay spread over the backs of the two chairs. The tracks of his father's foot were gone. Where they had been were now long, water-cloudy scoriations resembling the sporadic course of a Lilliputian[5] mowing machine.

It still hung there while they ate the cold food and then went to bed, scattered without order or claim up and down the two rooms, his mother in one bed, where his father would later lie, the older brother in the other, himself, the aunt, and the two sisters on pallets on the floor. But his father was not in bed yet. The last thing the boy remembered was the depthless, harsh silhouette of the hat and coat

[4] A caustic, alkaline solution.
[5] Lilliputians are the six-inch tall inhabitants of the island of Lilliput in Jonathan Swift's *Gulliver's Travels* (1726).

bending over the rug and it seemed to him that he had not even closed his eyes when the silhouette was standing over him, the fire almost dead behind it, the stiff foot prodding him awake. "Catch up the mule," his father said.

When he returned with the mule his father was standing in the black door, the rolled rug over his shoulder. "Ain't you going to ride?" he said.

"No. Give me your foot."

He bent his knee into his father's hand, the wiry, surprising power flowed smoothly, rising, he rising with it, on to the mule's bare back (they had owned a saddle once; the boy could remember it though not when or where) and with the same effortlessness his father swung the rug up in front of him. Now in the starlight they retraced the afternoon's path, up the dusty road rife with honey-suckle, through the gate and up the black tunnel of the drive to the lightless house, where he sat on the mule and felt the rough warp of the rug drag across his thighs and vanish.

"Don't you want me to help?" he whispered. His father did not answer and now he heard again that stiff foot striking the hollow portico with that wooden and clocklike deliberation, that outrageous overstatement of the weight it carried. The rug, hunched, not flung (the boy could tell that even in the darkness) from his father's shoulder struck the angle of wall and floor with a sound unbelievably loud, thunderous, then the foot again, unhurried and enormous; a light came on in the house and the boy sat, tense, breathing steadily and quietly and just a little fast, though the foot itself did not increase its beat at all, descending the steps now; now the boy could see him.

"Don't you want to ride now?" he whispered. "We kin both ride now," the light within the house altering now, flaring up and sinking. *He's coming down the stairs now,* he thought. He had already ridden the mule up beside the horse block; presently his father was up behind him and he doubled the reins over and slashed the mule across the neck, but before the animal could begin to trot the hard, thin arm came round him, the hard, knotted hand jerking the mule back to a walk.

In the first red rays of the sun they were in the lot, putting plow gear on the mules. This time the sorrel mare was in the lot before he heard it at all, the rider collarless and even bareheaded, trembling, speaking in a shaking voice as the woman in the house had done, his father merely looking up once before stooping again to the hame[6] he was buckling, so that the man on the mare spoke to his stooping back:

"You must realize you have ruined that rug. Wasn't there anybody here, any of your women . . ." he ceased, shaking, the boy watching him, the older brother leaning now in the stable door, chewing, blinking slowly and steadily at nothing apparently. "It cost a hundred dollars. But you never had a hundred dollars. You never will. So I'm going to charge you twenty bushels of corn against your crop. I'll add it in your contract and when you come to the commissary you can sign it. That won't keep Mrs. de Spain quiet but maybe it will teach you to wipe your feet off before you enter her house again."

Then he was gone. The boy looked at his father, who still had not spoken or even looked up again, who was now adjusting the logger-head[7] in the hame.

"Pap," he said. His father looked at him—the inscrutable face, the shaggy brows beneath which the gray eyes glinted coldly. Suddenly the boy went toward him, fast, stopping as suddenly. "You done the best you could!" he cried. "If he wanted hit done different why didn't he wait and tell you how? He won't git no

[6] Part of a harness.   [7] See Footnote 6.

twenty bushels! He won't git none! We'll gether hit and hide hit! I kin watch . . ."

"Did you put the cutter back in that straight stock[8] like I told you?"

"No, sir," he said.

"Then go do it."

That was Wednesday. During the rest of that week he worked steadily, at what was within his scope and some which was beyond it, with an industry that did not need to be driven nor even commanded twice; he had this from his mother, with the difference that some at least of what he did he liked to do, such as splitting wood with the half-size axe which his mother and aunt had earned, or saved money somehow, to present him with at Christmas. In company with the two older women (and on one afternoon, even one of the sisters), he built pens for the shoat[9] and the cow which were a part of his father's contract with the landlord, and one afternoon, his father being absent, gone somewhere on one of the mules, he went to the field.

They were running a middle buster[10] now, his brother holding the plow straight while he handled the reins, and walking beside the straining mule, the rich black soil shearing cool and damp against his bare ankles, he thought *Maybe this is the end of it. Maybe even that twenty bushels that seems hard to have to pay for just a rug will be a cheap price for him to stop forever and always from being what he used to be;* thinking, dreaming now, so that his brother had to speak sharply to him to mind the mule: *Maybe he even won't collect the twenty bushels. Maybe it will all add up and balance and vanish—corn, rug, fire; the terror and grief, the being pulled two ways like between two teams of horses—gone, done with for ever and ever.*

Then it was Saturday; he looked up from beneath the mule he was harnessing and saw his father in the black coat and hat. "Not that," his father said. "The wagon gear." And then, two hours later, sitting in the wagon bed behind his father and brother on the seat, the wagon accomplished a final curve, and he saw the weathered paintless store with its tattered tobacco- and patent-medicine posters and the tethered wagons and saddle animals below the gallery. He mounted the gnawed steps behind his father and brother, and there again was the lane of quiet, watching faces for the three of them to walk through. He saw the man in spectacles sitting at the plank table and he did not need to be told this was a Justice of the Peace; he sent one glare of fierce, exultant, partisan defiance at the man in collar and cravat now, whom he had seen but twice before in his life, and that on a galloping horse, who now wore on his face an expression not of rage but of amazed unbelief which the boy could not have known was at the incredible circumstance of being sued by one of his own tenants, and came and stood against his father and cried at the Justice: "He ain't done it! He ain't burnt . . ."

"Go back to the wagon," his father said.

"Burnt?" the Justice said. "Do I understand this rug was burned too?"

"Does anybody here claim it was?" his father said. "Go back to the wagon." But he did not, he merely retreated to the rear of the room, crowded as that other had been, but not to sit down this time, instead, to stand pressing among the motionless bodies, listening to the voices:

"And you claim twenty bushels of corn is too high for the damage you did to the rug?"

"He brought the rug to me and said he wanted the tracks washed out of it. I washed the tracks out and took the rug back to him."

---

[8] The reference is to a plow.   [9] A young pig.   [10] A kind of plow.

"But you didn't carry the rug back to him in the same condition it was in before you made the tracks on it."

His father did not answer, and now for perhaps half a minute there was no sound at all save that of breathing, the faint, steady suspiration[11] of complete and intent listening.

"You decline to answer that, Mr. Snopes?" Again his father did not answer. "I'm going to find against you, Mr. Snopes. I'm going to find that you were responsible for the injury to Major de Spain's rug and hold you liable for it. But twenty bushels of corn seems a little high for a man in your circumstances to have to pay. Major de Spain claims it cost a hundred dollars. October corn will be worth about fifty cents. I figure that if Major de Spain can stand a ninety-five dollar loss on something he paid cash for, you can stand a five-dollar loss you haven't earned yet. I hold you in damages to Major de Spain to the amount of ten bushels of corn over and above your contract with him, to be paid to him out of your crop at gathering time. Court adjourned."

It had taken no time hardly, the morning was but half begun. He thought they would return home and perhaps back to the field, since they were late, far behind all other farmers. But instead his father passed on behind the wagon, merely indicating with his hand for the older brother to follow with it, and crossed the road toward the blacksmith shop opposite, pressing on after his father, overtaking him, speaking, whispering up at the harsh, calm face beneath the weathered hat: "He won't git no ten bushels neither. He won't git one. We'll . . ." until his father glanced for an instant down at him, the face absolutely calm, the grizzled eyebrows tangled above the cold eyes, the voice almost pleasant, almost gentle:

"You think so? Well, we'll wait till October anyway."

The matter of the wagon—the setting of a spoke or two and the tightening of the tires—did not take long either, the business of the tires accomplished by driving the wagon into the spring branch behind the shop and letting it stand there, the mules nuzzling into the water from time to time, and the boy on the seat with the idle reins, looking up the slope and through the sooty tunnel of the shed where the slow hammer rang and where his father sat on an upended cypress bolt,[12] easily, either talking or listening, still sitting there when the boy brought the dripping wagon up out of the branch and halted it before the door.

"Take them on to the shade and hitch," his father said. He did so and returned. His father and the smith and a third man squatting on his heels inside the door were talking, about crops and animals; the boy, squatting too in the ammoniac dust and hoof-parings and scales of rust, heard his father tell a long and unhurried story out of the time before the birth of the older brother even when he had been a professional horsetrader. And then his father came up beside him where he stood before a tattered last year's circus poster on the other side of the store, gazing rapt and quiet at the scarlet horses, the incredible poisings and convolutions of tulle[13] and tights and the painted leers of comedians, and said, "It's time to eat."

But not at home. Squatting beside his brother against the front wall, he watched his father emerge from the store and produce from a paper sack a segment of cheese and divide it carefully and deliberately into three with his pocket knife and produce crackers from the same sack. They all three squatted on the gallery and ate, slowly, without talking; then in the store again, they drank from a tin dipper tepid water smelling of the cedar bucket and of living beech trees. And still they

---

[11] Sighing, breathing out.   [12] The bar of a gate.   [13] Silk dress.

did not go home. It was a horse lot this time, a tall rail fence upon and along which men stood and sat and out of which one by one horses were led, to be walked and trotted and then cantered back and forth along the road while the slow swapping and buying went on and the sun began to slant westward, they—the three of them— watching and listening, the older brother with his muddy eyes and his steady, inevitable tobacco, the father commenting now and then on certain of the animals, to no one in particular.

It was after sundown when they reached home. They ate supper by lamplight, then, sitting on the doorstep, the boy watched the night fully accomplish, listening to the whippoorwills and the frogs, when he heard his mother's voice: "Abner! No! No! Oh, God. Oh, God. Abner!" and he rose, whirled, and saw the altered light through the door where a candle stub now burned in a bottle neck on the table and his father, still in the hat and coat, at once formal and burlesque as though dressed carefully for some shabby and ceremonial violence, emptying the reservoir of the lamp back into the five-gallon kerosene can from which it had been filled, while the mother tugged at his arm until he shifted the lamp to the other hand and flung her back, not savagely or viciously, just hard, into the wall, her hands flung out against the wall for balance, her mouth open and in her face the same quality of hopeless despair as had been in her voice. Then his father saw him standing in the door.

"Go to the barn and get that can of oil we were oiling the wagon with," he said. The boy did not move. Then he could speak.

"What . . ." he cried. "What are you . . ."

"Go get that oil," his father said. "Go."

Then he was moving, running, outside the house, toward the stable: this the old habit, the old blood which he had not been permitted to choose for himself, which had been bequeathed him willy nilly and which had run for so long (and who knew where, battening on what of outrage and savagery and lust) before it came to him. *I could keep on,* he thought. *I could run on and on and never look back, never need to see his face again. Only I can't. I can't,* the rusted can in his hand now, the liquid sploshing in it as he ran back to the house and into it, into the sound of his mother's weeping in the next room, and handed the can to his father.

"Ain't you going to even send a nigger?" he cried. "At least you sent a nigger before!"

This time his father didn't strike him. The hand came even faster than the blow had, the same hand which had set the can on the table with almost excruciating care flashing from the can toward him too quick for him to follow it, gripping him by the back of his shirt and on to tiptoe before he had seen it quit the can, the face stooping at him in breathless and frozen ferocity, the cold, dead voice speaking over him to the older brother who leaned against the table, chewing with that steady, curious, sidewise motion of cows:

"Empty the can into the big one and go on. I'll catch up with you."

"Better tie him up to the bedpost," the brother said.

"Do like I told you," the father said. Then the boy was moving, his bunched shirt and the hard, bony hand between his shoulder-blades, his toes just touching the floor, across the room and into the other one, past the sisters sitting with spread heavy thighs in the two chairs over the cold hearth, and to where his mother and aunt sat side by side on the bed, the aunt's arms about his mother's shoulders.

"Hold him," the father said. The aunt made a startled movement. "Not you," the father said. "Lennie. Take hold of him. I want to see you do it." His mother took him by the wrist. "You'll hold him better than that. If he gets loose don't you know what he is going to do? He will go up yonder." He jerked his head toward the road. "Maybe I'd better tie him."

"I'll hold him," his mother whispered.

"See you do then." Then his father was gone, the stiff foot heavy and measured upon the boards, ceasing at last.

Then he began to struggle. His mother caught him in both arms, he jerking and wrenching at them. He would be stronger in the end, he knew that. But he had no time to wait for it. "Lemme go!" he cried. "I don't want to have to hit you!"

"Let him go!" the aunt said. "If he don't go, before God, I am going up there myself!"

"Don't you see I can't?" his mother cried. "Sarty! Sarty! No! No! Help me, Lizzie!"

Then he was free. His aunt grasped at him but it was too late. He whirled, running, his mother stumbled forward on to her knees behind him, crying to the nearer sister: "Catch him, Net! Catch him!" But that was too late too, the sister (the sisters were twins, born at the same time, yet either of them now gave the impression of being, encompassing as much living meat and volume and weight as any other two of the family) not yet having begun to rise from the chair, her head, face, alone merely turned, presenting to him in the flying instant an astonishing expanse of young female features untroubled by any surprise even, wearing only an expression of bovine interest. Then he was out of the room, out of the house, in the mild dust of the starlit road and the heavy rifeness[14] of honeysuckle, the pale ribbon unspooling with terrific slowness under his running feet, reaching the gate at last and turning in, running, his heart and lungs drumming, on up the drive toward the lighted house, the lighted door. He did not knock, he burst in, sobbing for breath, incapable for the moment of speech; he saw the astonished face of the Negro in the linen jacket without knowing when the Negro had appeared.

"De Spain!" he cried, panted. "Where's . . ." then he saw the white man too emerging from a white door down the hall. "Barn!" he cried. "Barn!"

"What?" the white man said. "Barn?"

"Yes!" the boy cried. "Barn!"

"Catch him!" the white man shouted.

But it was too late this time too. The Negro grasped his shirt, but the entire sleeve, rotten with washing, carried away, and he was out that door too and in the drive again, and had actually never ceased to run even while he was screaming into the white man's face.

Behind him the white man was shouting. "My horse! Fetch my horse!" and he thought for an instant of cutting across the park and climbing the fence into the road, but he did not know the park nor how high the vine-massed fence might be and he dared not risk it. So he ran on down the drive, blood and breath roaring; presently he was in the road again though he could not see it. He could not hear either: the galloping mare was almost upon him before he heard her, and even then he held his course, as if the very urgency of his wild grief and need must in a moment more find him wings, waiting until the ultimate instant to hurl himself aside and into the weed-choked roadside ditch as the horse thundered past and on, for an instant in furious silhouette against the stars, the tranquil early summer night sky which, even before the shape of the horse and rider vanished, stained

---

[14] Fullness, abundance.

abruptly and violently upward: a long, swirling roar incredible and soundless, blotting the stars, and he springing up and into the road again, running again, knowing it was too late yet still running even after he heard the shot and, an instant later, two shots, pausing now without knowing he had ceased to run, crying "Pap! Pap!", running again before he knew he had begun to run, stumbling, tripping over something and scrabbling up again without ceasing to run, looking backward over his shoulder at the glare as he got up, running on among the invisible trees, panting, sobbing, "Father! Father!"

At midnight he was sitting on the crest of a hill. He did not know it was midnight and he did not know how far he had come. But there was no glare behind him now and he sat now, his back toward what he had called home for four days anyhow, his face toward the dark woods which he would enter when breath was strong again, small, shaking steadily in the chill darkness, hugging himself into the remainder of his thin, rotten shirt, the grief and despair now no longer terror and fear but just grief and despair. *Father. My father,* he thought. "He was brave!" he cried suddenly, aloud but not loud, no more than a whisper: "He was! He was in the war! He was in Colonel Sartoris' cav'ry!" not knowing that his father had gone to that war a private in the fine old European sense, wearing no uniform, admitting the authority of and giving fidelity to no man or army or flag, going to war as Malbrouck[15] himself did: for booty—it meant nothing and less than nothing to him if it were enemy booty or his own.

The slow constellations wheeled on. It would be dawn and then sun-up after a while and he would be hungry. But that would be to-morrow and now he was only cold, and walking would cure that. His breathing was easier now and he decided to get up and go on, and then he found that he had been asleep because he knew it was almost dawn, the night almost over. He could tell that from the whippoor-wills. They were everywhere now among the dark trees below him, constant and inflectioned and ceaseless, so that, as the instant for giving over to the day birds drew nearer and nearer, there was no interval at all between them. He got up. He was a little stiff, but walking would cure that too as it would the cold, and soon there would be the sun. He went on down the hill, toward the dark woods within which the liquid silver voices of the birds called unceasing—the rapid and urgent beating of the urgent and quiring heart of the late spring night. He did not look back.

[1939]

---

[15] *"Malbrouck s'en va-t-en guerre"* ("Malbrouck is off to war") is the first line of a popular eighteenth-century French nursery rhyme about a warrior hero.

D. H. Lawrence 1885–1930

THE ROCKING-HORSE WINNER

There was a woman who was beautiful, who started with all the advantages, yet she had no luck. She married for love, and the love turned to dust. She had bonny children, yet she felt they had been thrust upon her, and she could not love them. They looked at her coldly, as if they were finding fault with her. And hurriedly she felt she must cover up some fault in herself. Yet what it was that she must cover up she never knew. Nevertheless, when her children were present, she always felt the centre of her heart go hard. This troubled her, and in her manner she was all the more gentle and anxious for her children, as if she loved them very much. Only she herself knew that at the centre of her heart was a hard little place that could not feel love, no, not for anybody. Everybody else said of her: "She is such a good mother. She adores her children." Only she herself, and her children themselves, knew it was not so. They read it in each other's eyes.

There were a boy and two little girls. They lived in a pleasant house, with a garden, and they had discreet servants, and felt themselves superior to anyone in the neighbourhood.

Although they lived in style, they felt always an anxiety in the house. There was never enough money. The mother had a small income, and the father had a small income, but not nearly enough for the social position which they had to keep up. The father went into town to some office. But though he had good prospects, these prospects never materialized. There was always the grinding sense of the shortage of money, though the style was always kept up.

At last the mother said: "I will see if *I* can't make something." But she did not know where to begin. She racked her brains, and tried this thing and the other, but could not find anything successful. The failure made deep lines come into her face. Her children were growing up, they would have to go to school. There must be more money, there must be more money. The father, who was always very handsome and expensive in his tastes, seemed as if he never *would* be able to do anything worth doing. And the mother, who had a great belief in herself, did not succeed any better, and her tastes were just as expensive.

And so the house came to be haunted by the unspoken phrase: *There must be more money! There must be more money!* The children could hear it all the time, though nobody said it aloud. They heard it at Christmas, when the expensive and splendid toys filled the nursery. Behind the shining modern rocking-horse, behind the smart doll's house, a voice would start whispering: "There *must* be more money! There *must* be more money!" And the children would stop playing, to listen for a moment. They would look into each other's eyes, to see if they had all heard. And each one saw in the eyes of the other two that they too had heard. "There *must* be more money! There *must* be more money!"

It came whispering from the springs of the still-swaying rocking-horse, and even the horse, bending his wooden, champing head, heard it. The big doll, sitting so pink and smirking in her new pram, could hear it quite plainly, and seemed to be smirking all the more self-consciously because of it. The foolish puppy, too, that took the place of the teddybear, he was looking so extraordinarily foolish for no other reason but that he heard the secret whisper all over the house: "There *must* be more money!"

Yet nobody ever said it aloud. The whisper was everywhere, and therefore no one spoke it. Just as no one ever says: "We are breathing!" in spite of the fact that breath is coming and going all the time.

"Mother," said the boy Paul one day, "why don't we keep a car of our own? Why do we always use uncle's, or else a taxi?"

"Because we're the poor members of the family," said the mother.

"But why *are* we, mother?"

"Well—I suppose," she said slowly and bitterly, "it's because your father has no luck."

The boy was silent for some time.

"Is luck money, mother?" he asked, rather timidly.

"No, Paul. Not quite. It's what causes you to have money."

"Oh!" said Paul vaguely. "I thought when Uncle Oscar said *filthy lucker,* it meant money."

"*Filthy lucre* does mean money," said the mother. "But it's lucre, not luck."

"Oh!" said the boy. "Then what *is* luck, mother?"

"It's what causes you to have money. If you're lucky you have money. That's why it's better to be born lucky than rich. If you're rich, you may lose your money. But if you're lucky, you will always get more money."

"Oh! Will you? And is father not lucky?"

"Very unlucky, I should say," she said bitterly.

The boy watched her with unsure eyes.

"Why?" he asked.

"I don't know. Nobody ever knows why one person is lucky and another unlucky."

"Don't they? Nobody at all? Does *nobody* know?"

"Perhaps God. But He never tells."

"He ought to, then. And aren't you lucky either, mother?"

"I can't be, if I married an unlucky husband."

"But by yourself, aren't you?"

"I used to think I was, before I married. Now I think I am very unlucky indeed."

"Why?"

"Well—never mind! Perhaps I'm not really," she said.

The child looked at her to see if she meant it. But he saw, by the lines of her mouth, that she was only trying to hide something from him.

"Well, anyhow," he said stoutly, "I'm a lucky person."

"Why?" said his mother, with a sudden laugh.

He stared at her. He didn't even know why he had said it.

"God told me," he asserted, brazening it out.

"I hope He did, dear!" she said, again with a laugh, but rather bitter.

"He did, mother!"

"Excellent!" said the mother, using one of her husband's exclamations.

The boy saw she did not believe him; or rather, that she paid no attention to his assertion. This angered him somewhat, and made him want to compel her attention.

He went off by himself, vaguely, in a childish way, seeking for the clue to 'luck.' Absorbed, taking no heed of other people, he went about with a sort of stealth, seeking inwardly for luck. He wanted luck, he wanted it, he wanted it. When the two girls were playing dolls in the nursery, he would sit on his big rocking-horse, charging madly into space, with a frenzy that made the little girls peer at him uneasily. Wildly the horse careered, the waving dark hair of the boy tossed, his eyes had a strange glare in them. The little girls dared not speak to him.

When he had ridden to the end of his mad little journey, he climbed down and stood in front of his rocking-horse, staring fixedly into its lower face. Its red mouth was slightly open, its big eye was wide and glassy-bright.

"Now!" he would silently command the snorting steed. "Now, take me to where there is luck! Now take me!"

And he would slash the horse on the neck with the little whip he had asked Uncle Oscar for. He *knew* the horse could take him to where there was luck, if only he forced it. So he would mount again and start on his furious ride, hoping at last to get there. He knew he could get there.

"You'll break your horse, Paul!" said the nurse.

"He's always riding like that! I wish he'd leave off!" said his elder sister Joan.

But he only glared down on them in silence. Nurse gave him up. She could make nothing of him. Anyhow, he was growing beyond her.

One day his mother and his Uncle Oscar came in when he was on one of his furious rides. He did not speak to them.

"Hallo, you young jockey! Riding a winner?" said his uncle.

"Aren't you growing too big for a rocking-horse? You're not a very little boy any longer, you know," said his mother.

But Paul only gave a blue glare from his big, rather close-set eyes. He would speak to nobody when he was in full tilt. His mother watched him with an anxious expression on her face.

At last he suddenly stopped forcing his horse into the mechanical gallop and slid down.

"Well, I got there!" he announced fiercely, his blue eyes still flaring, and his sturdy long legs straddling apart.

"Where did you get to?" asked his mother.

"Where I wanted to go," he flared back at her.

"That's right, son!" said Uncle Oscar. "Don't you stop till you get there. What's the horse's name?"

"He doesn't have a name," said the boy.

"Gets on without all right?" asked the uncle.

"Well, he has different names. He was called Sansovino last week."

"Sansovino, eh? Won the Ascot.[1] How did you know this name?"

"He always talks about horse-races with Bassett," said Joan.

The uncle was delighted to find that his small nephew was posted with all the racing news. Bassett, the young gardener, who had been wounded in the left foot in the war and had got his present job through Oscar Cresswell, whose batman he had been, was a perfect blade of the 'turf.' He lived in the racing events, and the small boy lived with him.

Oscar Cresswell got it all from Bassett.

"Master Paul comes and asks me, so I can't do more than tell him, sir," said Bassett, his face terribly serious, as if he were speaking of religious matters.

"And does he ever put anything on a horse he fancies?"

"Well—I don't want to give him away—he's a young sport, a fine sport, sir. Would you mind asking him himself? He sort of takes a pleasure in it, and perhaps he'd feel I was giving him away, sir, if you don't mind."

Bassett was serious as a church.

The uncle went back to his nephew and took him off for a ride in the car.

"Say, Paul, old man, do you ever put anything on a horse?" the uncle asked.

[1] The famous horse race run at the Ascot Heath racetrack near Ascot, England.

The boy watched the handsome man closely.

"Why, do you think I oughtn't to?" he parried.

"Not a bit of it! I thought perhaps you might give me a tip for the Lincoln."[2]

The car sped on into the country, going down to Uncle Oscar's place in Hampshire.

"Honour bright?" said the nephew.

"Honour bright, son!" said the uncle.

"Well, then, Daffodil."

"Daffodil! I doubt it, sonny. What about Mirza?"

"I only know the winner," said the boy. "That's Daffodil."

"Daffodil, eh?"

There was a pause. Daffodil was an obscure horse comparatively.

"Uncle!"

"Yes, son?"

"You won't let it go any further, will you? I promised Bassett."

"Bassett be damned, old man! What's he got to do with it?"

"We're partners. We've been partners from the first. Uncle, he lent me my first five shillings, which I lost. I promised him, honour bright, it was only between me and him; only you gave me that ten-shilling note I started winning with, so I thought you were lucky. You won't let it go any further, will you?"

The boy gazed at his uncle from those big, hot, blue eyes, set rather close together. The uncle stirred and laughed uneasily.

"Right you are, son! I'll keep your tip private. Daffodil, eh? How much are you putting on him?"

"All except twenty pounds," said the boy. "I keep that in reserve."

The uncle thought it a good joke.

"You keep twenty pounds in reserve, do you, you young romancer? What are you betting then?"

"I'm betting three hundred," said the boy gravely. "But it's between you and me, Uncle Oscar! Honour bright?"

The uncle burst into a roar of laughter.

"It's between you and me all right, you young Nat Gould,"[3] he said, laughing. "But where's your three hundred?"

"Bassett keeps it for me. We're partners."

"You are, are you! And what is Bassett putting on Daffodil?"

"He won't go quite as high as I do, I expect. Perhaps he'll go a hundred and fifty."

"What, pennies?" laughed the uncle.

"Pounds," said the child, with a surprised look at his uncle. "Bassett keeps a bigger reserve than I do."

Between wonder and amusement Uncle Oscar was silent. He pursued the matter no further, but he determined to take his nephew with him to the Lincoln races.

"Now, son," he said, "I'm putting twenty on Mirza, and I'll put five on for you on any horse you fancy. What's your pick?"

"Daffodil, uncle."

"No, not the fiver on Daffodil!"

---

[2] The Lincolnshire Handicap run at Lincoln Downs.

[3] Nathaniel Gould (1857–1919), a well-known writer who used horse racing as the subject for his journalism and fiction.

"I should if it was my own fiver," said the child.

"Good! Good! Right you are! A fiver for me and a fiver for you on Daffodil."

The child had never been to a racemeeting before, and his eyes were blue fire. He pursed his mouth tight and watched. A Frenchman just in front had put his money on Lancelot. Wild with excitement, he flayed his arms up and down, yelling *"Lancelot! Lancelot!"* in his French accent.

Daffodil came in first, Lancelot second, Mirza third. The child, flushed and with eyes blazing, was curiously serene. His uncle brought him four five-pound notes, four to one.

"What am I to do with these?" he cried, waving them before the boy's eyes.

"I suppose we'll talk to Bassett," said the boy. "I expect I have fifteen hundred now; and twenty in reserve; and this twenty."

His uncle studied him for some moments.

"Look here, son!" he said. "You're not serious about Bassett and that fifteen hundred, are you?"

"Yes, I am. But it's between you and me, uncle. Honour bright?"

"Honour bright all right, son! But I must talk to Bassett."

"If you'd like to be a partner, uncle, with Bassett and me, we could all be partners. Only, you'd have to promise, honour bright, uncle, not to let it go beyond us three. Bassett and I are lucky, and you must be lucky, because it was your ten shillings I started winning with. . . ."

Uncle Oscar took both Bassett and Paul into Richmond Park for an afternoon, and there they talked.

"It's like this, you see, sir," Bassett said. "Master Paul would get me talking about racing events, spinning yarns, you know, sir. And he was always keen on knowing if I'd made or if I'd lost. It's about a year since, now, that I put five shillings on Blush of Dawn for him: and we lost. Then the luck turned, with that ten shillings he had from you: that we put on Singhalese. And since that time, it's been pretty steady, all things considering. What do you say, Master Paul?"

"We're all right when we're sure," said Paul. "It's when we're not quite sure that we go down."

"Oh, but we're careful then," said Bassett.

"But when are you *sure?*" smiled Uncle Oscar.

"It's Master Paul, sir," said Bassett in a secret, religious voice. "It's as if he had it from heaven. Like Daffodil, now, for the Lincoln. That was as sure as eggs."

"Did you put anything on Daffodil?" asked Oscar Cresswell.

"Yes, sir. I made my bit."

"And my nephew?"

Bassett was obstinately silent, looking at Paul.

"I made twelve hundred, didn't I, Bassett? I told uncle I was putting three hundred on Daffodil."

"That's right," said Bassett, nodding.

"But where's the money?" asked the uncle.

"I keep it safe locked up, sir. Master Paul he can have it any minute he likes to ask for it."

"What, fifteen hundred pounds?"

"And twenty! And *forty,* that is, with the twenty he made on the course."

"It's amazing!" said the uncle.

"If Master Paul offers you to be partners, sir, I would, if I were you: if you'll excuse me," said Bassett.

Oscar Cresswell thought about it.

"I'll see the money," he said.

They drove home again, and, sure enough, Bassett came round to the garden-house with fifteen hundred pounds in notes. The twenty pounds reserve was left with Joe Glee, in the Turf Commission deposit.

"You see, it's all right, uncle, when I'm *sure!* Then we go strong, for all we're worth. Don't we, Bassett?"

"We do that, Master Paul."

"And when are you sure?" said the uncle, laughing.

"Oh, well, sometimes I'm *absolutely* sure, like about Daffodil," said the boy; "and sometimes I have an idea; and sometimes I haven't even an idea, have I, Bassett? Then we're careful, because we mostly go down."

"You do, do you! And when you're sure, like about Daffodil, what makes you sure, sonny?"

"Oh, well, I don't know," said the boy uneasily. "I'm sure, you know, uncle; that's all."

"It's as if he had it from heaven, sir," Bassett reiterated.

"I should say so!" said the uncle.

But he became a partner. And when the Leger[4] was coming on Paul was "sure" about Lively Spark, which was a quite inconsiderable horse. The boy insisted on putting a thousand on the horse, Bassett went for five hundred, and Oscar Cresswell two hundred. Lively Spark came in first, and the betting had been ten to one against him. Paul had made ten thousand.

"You see," he said, "I was absolutely sure of him."

Even Oscar Cresswell had cleared two thousand.

"Look here, son," he said, "this sort of thing makes me nervous."

"It needn't, uncle! Perhaps I shan't be sure again for a long time."

"But what are you going to do with your money?" asked the uncle.

"Of course," said the boy, "I started it for mother. She said she had no luck, because father is unlucky, so I thought if *I* was lucky, it might stop whispering."

"What might stop whispering?"

"Our house. I *hate* our house for whispering."

"What does it whisper?"

"Why—why"—the boy fidgeted—"why, I don't know. But it's always short of money, you know, uncle."

"I know it, son, I know it."

"You know people send mother writs,[5] don't you uncle?"

"I'm afraid I do," said the uncle.

"And then the house whispers, like people laughing at you behind your back. It's awful, that is! I thought if I was lucky————"

"You might stop it," added the uncle.

The boy watched him with big blue eyes, that had an uncanny cold fire in them, and he said never a word.

"Well, then!" said the uncle. "What are we doing?"

"I shouldn't like mother to know I was lucky," said the boy.

"Why not, son?"

"She'd stop me."

"I don't think she would."

"Oh!"—and the boy writhed in an odd way—"I *don't* want her to know, uncle."

"All right, son! We'll manage it without her knowing."

---

[4] The St. Leger Stakes run at Doncaster.   [5] Presumably, dunning letters from creditors.

They managed it very easily. Paul, at the other's suggestion, handed over five thousand pounds to his uncle, who deposited it with the family lawyer, who was then to inform Paul's mother that a relative had put five thousand pounds into his hands, which sum was to be paid out a thousand pounds at a time, on the mother's birthday, for the next five years.

"So she'll have a birthday present of a thousand pounds for five successive years," said Uncle Oscar. "I hope it won't make it all the harder for her later."

Paul's mother had her birthday in November. The house had been 'whispering' worse than ever lately, and, even in spite of his luck, Paul could not bear up against it. He was very anxious to see the effect of the birthday letter, telling his mother about the thousand pounds.

When there were no visitors, Paul now took his meals with his parents, as he was beyond the nursery control. His mother went into town nearly every day. She had discovered that she had an odd knack of sketching furs and dress materials, so she worked secretly in the studio of a friend who was the chief 'artist' for the leading drapers. She drew the figures of ladies in furs and ladies in silk and sequins for the newspaper advertisements. This young woman artist earned several thousand pounds a year, but Paul's mother only made several hundreds, and she was again dissatisfied. She so wanted to be first in something, and she did not succeed, even in making sketches for drapery advertisements.

She was down to breakfast on the morning of her birthday. Paul watched her face as she read her letters. He knew the lawyer's letter. As his mother read it, her face hardened and became more expressionless. Then a cold, determined look came on her mouth. She hid the letter under the pile of others, and said not a word about it.

"Didn't you have anything nice in the post for your birthday, mother?" said Paul.

"Quite moderately nice," she said, her voice cold and absent.

She went away to town without saying more.

But in the afternoon Uncle Oscar appeared. He said Paul's mother had had a long interview with the lawyer, asking if the whole five thousand could not be advanced at once, as she was in debt.

"What do you think, uncle?" asked the boy.

"I leave it to you, son."

"Oh, let her have it, then! We can get some more with the other," said the boy.

"A bird in the hand is worth two in the bush, laddie!" said Uncle Oscar.

"But I'm sure to *know* for the Grand National; or the Lincolnshire; or else the Derby.[6] I'm sure to know for *one* of them," said Paul.

So Uncle Oscar signed the agreement, and Paul's mother touched the whole five thousand. Then something very curious happened. The voices in the house suddenly went mad, like a chorus of frogs on a spring evening. There were certain new furnishings, and Paul had a tutor. He was *really* going to Eton, his father's school, in the following autumn. There were flowers in the winter, and a blossoming of the luxury Paul's mother had been used to. And yet the voices in the house, behind the sprays of mimosa and almond-blossom, and from under the piles of iridescent cushions, simply trilled and screamed in a sort of ecstasy: "There *must* be more money! Oh-h-h; there *must* be more money. Oh, now, now-w! Now-w-w—there *must* be more money!—more than ever! More than ever!"

___

[6] Well-known British horse races: the Grand National run at Aintree, the Lincolnshire run at Lincoln Downs, and the Derby run at Epsom Downs.

It frightened Paul terribly. He studied away at his Latin and Greek with his tutor. But his intense hours were spent with Bassett. The Grand National had gone by: he had not 'known,' and had lost a hundred pounds. Summer was at hand. He was in agony for the Lincoln. But even for the Lincoln he didn't 'know,' and he lost fifty pounds. He became wild-eyed and strange, as if something were going to explode in him.

"Let it alone, son! Don't you bother about it!" urged Uncle Oscar. But it was as if the boy couldn't really hear what his uncle was saying.

"I've got to know for the Derby! I've got to know for the Derby!" the child reiterated, his big blue eyes with a sort of madness.

His mother noticed how overwrought he was.

"You'd better go to the seaside. Wouldn't you like to go now to the seaside, instead of waiting? I think you'd better," she said, looking down at him anxiously, her heart curiously heavy because of him.

But the child lifted his uncanny blue eyes.

"I couldn't possibly go before the Derby, mother!" he said. "I couldn't possibly!"

"Why not?" she said, her voice becoming heavy when she was opposed. "Why not? You can still go from the seaside to see the Derby with your Uncle Oscar, if that's what you wish. No need for you to wait here. Besides, I think you care too much about these races. It's a bad sign. My family has been a gambling family, and you won't know till you grow up how much damage it has done. But it has done damage. I shall have to send Bassett away, and ask Uncle Oscar not to talk racing to you, unless you promise to be reasonable about it: go away to the seaside and forget it. You're all nerves!"

"I'll do what you like, mother, so long as you don't send me away till after the Derby," the boy said.

"Send you away from where? Just from this house?"

"Yes," he said, gazing at her.

"Why, you curious child, what makes you care about this house so much, suddenly? I never knew you loved it."

He gazed at her without speaking. He had a secret within a secret, something he had not divulged, even to Bassett or to his Uncle Oscar.

But his mother, after standing undecided and a little bit sullen for some moments, said:

"Very well, then! Don't go to the seaside till after the Derby, if you don't wish it. But promise me you won't let your nerves go to pieces. Promise you won't think so much about horse-racing and *events*, as you call them!"

"Oh no," said the boy casually. "I won't think much about them, mother. You needn't worry. I wouldn't worry, mother, if I were you."

"If you were me and I were you," said his mother, "I wonder what we *should* do!"

"But you know you needn't worry, mother, don't you?" the boy repeated.

"I should be awfully glad to know it," she said wearily.

"Oh, well, you *can*, you know. I mean, you *ought* to know you needn't worry," he insisted.

"Ought I? Then I'll see about it," she said.

Paul's secret of secrets was his wooden horse, that which had no name. Since he was emancipated from a nurse and a nursery-governess, he had had his rocking-horse removed to his own bedroom at the top of the house.

"Surely you're too big for a rocking-horse!" his mother had remonstrated.

"Well, you see, mother, till I can have a *real* horse, I like to have *some* sort of animal about," had been his quaint answer.

"Do you feel he keeps you company?" she laughed.

"Oh yes! He's very good, he always keeps me company, when I'm there," said Paul.

So the horse, rather shabby, stood in an arrested prance in the boy's bedroom.

The Derby was drawing near, and the boy grew more and more tense. He hardly heard what was spoken to him, he was very frail, and his eyes were really uncanny. His mother had sudden strange seizures of uneasiness about him. Sometimes, for half an hour, she would feel a sudden anxiety about him that was almost anguish. She wanted to rush to him at once, and know he was safe.

Two nights before the Derby, she was at a big party in town, when one of her rushes of anxiety about her boy, her firstborn, gripped her heart till she could hardly speak. She fought with the feeling, might and main, for she believed in common sense. But it was too strong. She had to leave the dance and go down-stairs to telephone to the country. The children's nursery-governess was terribly surprised and startled at being rung up in the night.

"Are the children all right, Miss Wilmot?"

"Oh yes, they are quite all right."

"Master Paul? Is he all right?"

"He went up to bed as right as a trivet. Shall I run up and look at him?"

"No," said Paul's mother reluctantly. "No! Don't trouble. It's all right. Don't sit up. We shall be home fairly soon." She did not want her son's privacy intruded upon.

"Very good," said the governess.

It was about one o'clock when Paul's mother and father drove up to their house. All was still. Paul's mother went to her room and slipped off her white fur cloak. She had told her maid not to wait up for her. She heard her husband downstairs, mixing a whisky and soda.

And then, because of the strange anxiety at her heart, she stole upstairs to her son's room. Noiselessly she went along the upper corridor. Was there a faint noise? What was it?

She stood, with arrested muscles, outside his door, listening. There was a strange, heavy, and yet not loud noise. Her heart stood still. It was a soundless noise, yet rushing and powerful. Something huge, in violent, hushed motion. What was it? What in God's name was it? She ought to know. She felt that she knew the noise. She knew what it was.

Yet she could not place it. She couldn't say what it was. And on and on it went, like a madness.

Softly, frozen with anxiety and fear, she turned the door-handle.

The room was dark. Yet in the space near the window, she heard and saw something plunging to and fro. She gazed in fear and amazement.

Then suddenly she switched on the light, and saw her son, in his green pyjamas, madly surging on the rocking-horse. The blaze of light suddenly lit him up, as he urged the wooden horse, and lit her up, as she stood, blonde, in her dress of pale green and crystal, in the doorway.

"Paul!" she cried. "Whatever are you doing?"

"It's Malabar!" he screamed in a powerful, strange voice. "It's Malabar!"

His eyes blazed at her for one strange and senseless second, as he ceased urging his wooden horse. Then he fell with a crash to the ground, and she, all her tormented motherhood flooding upon her, rushed to gather him up.

But he was unconscious, and unconscious he remained, with some brain-fever. He talked and tossed, and his mother sat stonily by his side.

"Malabar! It's Malabar! Bassett, Bassett, I *know!* it's Malabar!"

So the child cried, trying to get up and urge the rocking-horse that gave him his inspiration.

"What does he mean by Malabar?" asked the heart-frozen mother.

"I don't know," said the father stonily.

"What does he mean by Malabar?" she asked her brother Oscar.

"It's one of the horses running for the Derby," was the answer.

And, in spite of himself, Oscar Cresswell spoke to Bassett, and himself put a thousand on Malabar: at fourteen to one.

The third day of the illness was critical: they were waiting for a change. The boy, with his rather long, curly hair, was tossing ceaselessly on the pillow. He neither slept nor regained consciousness, and his eyes were like blue stones. His mother sat, feeling her heart had gone, turned actually into a stone.

In the evening, Oscar Cresswell did not come, but Bassett sent a message, saying could he come up for one moment, just one moment? Paul's mother was very angry at the intrusion, but on second thought she agreed. The boy was the same. Perhaps Bassett might bring him to consciousness.

The gardener, a shortish fellow with a little brown moustache and sharp little brown eyes, tiptoed into the room, touched his imaginary cap to Paul's mother, and stole to the bedside, staring with glittering, smallish eyes at the tossing, dying child.

"Master Paul!" he whispered. "Master Paul! Malabar came in first all right, a clean win. I did as you told me. You've made over seventy thousand pounds, you have; you've got over eighty thousand. Malabar came in all right, Master Paul."

"Malabar! Malabar! Did I say Malabar, mother? Did I say Malabar? Do you think I'm lucky, mother? I knew Malabar, didn't I? Over eighty thousand pounds! I call that lucky, don't you, mother? Over eighty thousand pounds! I knew, didn't I know I knew? Malabar came in all right. If I ride my horse till I'm sure, then I tell you, Bassett, you can go as high as you like. Did you go for all you were worth, Bassett?"

"I went a thousand on it, Master Paul."

"I never told you, mother, that if I can ride my horse, and *get there*, then I'm absolutely sure—oh, absolutely! Mother, did I ever tell you? I *am* lucky!"

"No, you never did," said his mother.

But the boy died in the night.

And even as he lay dead, his mother heard her brother's voice saying to her: "My God, Hester, you're eighty-odd thousand to the good, and a poor devil of a son to the bad. But, poor devil, poor devil, he's best gone out of a life where he rides his rocking-horse to find a winner."

[1933]

Kay Boyle   *1903–1992*

ASTRONOMER'S WIFE

There is an evil moment on awakening when all things seem to pause. But for women, they only falter and may be set in action by a single move: a lifted hand and the pendulum will swing, or the voice raised and through every room the pulse takes up its beating. The astronomer's wife felt the interval gaping and at once filled it to the brim. She fetched up her gentle voice and sent it warily down the stairs for coffee, swung her feet out upon the oval mat, and hailed the morning with her bare arms' quivering flesh drawn taut in rhythmic exercise: left, left, left my wife and fourteen children, right, right, right in the middle of the dusty road.

The day would proceed from this, beat by beat, without reflection, like every other day. The astronomer was still asleep, or feigning it, and she, once out of bed, had come into her own possession. Although scarcely ever out of sight of the impenetrable silence of his brow, she would be absent from him all the day in being clean, busy, kind. He was a man of other things, a dreamer. At times he lay still for hours, at others he sat upon the roof behind his telescope, or wandered down the pathway to the road and out across the mountains. This day, like any other, would go on from the removal of the spot left there from dinner on the astronomer's vest to the severe thrashing of the mayonnaise for lunch. That man might be each time the new arching wave, and woman the undertow that sucked him back, were things she had been told by his silence were so.

In spite of the earliness of the hour, the girl had heard her mistress's voice and was coming up the stairs. At the threshold of the bedroom she paused, and said: "Madame, the plumber is here."

The astronomer's wife put on her white and scarlet smock very quickly and buttoned it at the neck. Then she stepped carefully around the motionless spread of water in the hall.

"Tell him to come right up," she said. She laid her hands on the bannisters and stood looking down the wooden stairway. "Ah, I am Mrs. Ames," she said softly as she saw him mounting. "I am Mrs. Ames," she said softly, softly down the flight of stairs. "I am Mrs. Ames," spoken soft as a willow weeping. "The professor is still sleeping. Just step this way."

The plumber himself looked up and saw Mrs. Ames with her voice hushed, speaking to him. She was a youngish woman, but this she had forgotten. The mystery and silence of her husband's mind lay like a chiding finger on her lips. Her eyes were gray, for the light had been extinguished in them. The strange dim halo of her yellow hair was still uncombed and sideways on her head.

For all of his heavy boots, the plumber quieted the sound of his feet, and together they went down the hall, picking their way around the still lake of water that spread as far as the landing and lay docile there. The plumber was a tough, hardy man; but he took off his hat when he spoke to her and looked her fully, almost insolently in the eye.

"Does it come from the wash-basin," he said, "or from the other . . . ?"

"Oh, from the other," said Mrs. Ames without hesitation.

In this place the villas were scattered out few and primitive, and although beauty lay without there was no reflection of her face within. Here all was awkward and unfit; a sense of wrestling with uncouth forces gave everything an austere countenance. Even the plumber, dealing as does a woman with matters under hand, was grave and stately. The mountains round about seemed to have cast them into the shadow of great dignity.

Mrs. Ames began speaking of their arrival that summer in the little villa, mourning each event as it followed on the other.

"Then, just before going to bed last night," she said, "I noticed something was unusual."

The plumber cast down a folded square of sackcloth on the brimming floor and laid his leather apron on it. Then he stepped boldly onto the heart of the island it shaped and looked long into the overflowing bowl.

"The water should be stopped from the meter in the garden," he said at last.

"Oh, I did that," said Mrs. Ames, "the very first thing last night. I turned it off at once, in my nightgown, as soon as I saw what was happening. But all this had already run in."

The plumber looked for a moment at her red kid slippers. She was standing just at the edge of the clear, pure-seeming tide.

"It's no doubt the soil lines," he said severely. "It may be that something has stopped them, but my opinion is that the water seals aren't working. That's the trouble often enough in such cases. If you had a valve you wouldn't be caught like this."

Mrs. Ames did not know how to meet this rebuke. She stood, swaying a little, looking into the plumber's blue relentless eye.

"I'm sorry—I'm sorry that my husband," she said, "is still—resting and cannot go into this with you. I'm sure it must be very interesting. . . ."

"You'll probably have to have the traps sealed," said the plumber grimly, and at the sound of this Mrs. Ames' hand flew in dismay to the side of her face. The plumber made no move, but the set of his mouth as he looked at her seemed to soften. "Anyway, I'll have a look from the garden end," he said.

"Oh, do," said the astronomer's wife in relief. Here was a man who spoke of action and object as simply as women did! But however hushed her voice had been, it carried clearly to Professor Ames who lay, dreaming and solitary, upon his bed. He heard their footsteps come down the hall, pause, and skip across the pool of overflow.

"Katherine!" said the astronomer in a ringing tone. "There's a problem worthy of your mettle!"

Mrs. Ames did not turn her head, but led the plumber swiftly down the stairs. When the sun in the garden struck her face, he saw there was a wave of color in it, but this may have been anything but shame.

"You see how it is," said the plumber, as if leading her mind away. "The drains run from these houses right down the hill, big enough for a man to stand upright in them, and clean as a whistle too." There they stood in the garden with the vegetation flowering in disorder all about. The plumber looked at the astronomer's wife. "They come out at the torrent[1] on the other side of the forest beyond there," he said.

But the words the astronomer had spoken still sounded in her in despair. The mind of man, she knew, made steep and sprightly flights, pursued illusion, took foothold in the nameless things that cannot pass between the thumb and finger. But whenever the astronomer gave voice to the thoughts that soared within him,

---

[1] Stream.

she returned in gratitude to the long expanses of his silence. Desert-like they stretched behind and before the articulation of his scorn.

Life, life is an open sea, she sought to explain it in sorrow, and to survive women cling to the floating débris on the tide. But the plumber had suddenly fallen upon his knees in the grass and had crooked his fingers through the ring of the drains' trap-door. When she looked down she saw that he was looking up into her face, and she saw too that his hair was as light as gold.

"Perhaps Mr. Ames," he said rather bitterly, "would like to come down with me and have a look around?"

"Down?" said Mrs. Ames in wonder.

"Into the drains," said the plumber brutally. "They're a study for a man who likes to know what's what."

"Oh, Mr. Ames," said Mrs. Ames in confusion. "He's still—still in bed, you see."

The plumber lifted his strong, weathered face and looked curiously at her. Surely it seemed to him strange for a man to linger in bed, with the sun pouring yellow as wine all over the place. The astronomer's wife saw his lean cheeks, his high, rugged bones, and the deep seams in his brow. His flesh was as firm and clean as wood, stained richly tan with the climate's rigor. His fingers were blunt, but comprehensible to her, gripped in the ring and holding the iron door wide. The backs of his hands were bound round and round with ripe blue veins of blood.

"At any rate," said the astronomer's wife, and the thought of it moved her lips to smile a little, "Mr. Ames would never go down there alive. He likes going up," she said. And she, in her turn, pointed, but impudently, towards the heavens. "On the roof. Or on the mountains. He's been up on the tops of them many times."

"It's matter of habit," said the plumber, and suddenly he went down the trap. Mrs. Ames saw a bright little piece of his hair still shining, like a star, long after the rest of him had gone. Out of the depths, his voice, hollow and dark with foreboding, returned to her. "I think something has stopped the elbow," was what he said.

This was speech that touched her flesh and bone and made her wonder. When her husband spoke of height, having no sense of it, she could not picture it nor hear. Depth or magic passed her by unless a name were given. But madness in a daily shape, as elbow stopped, she saw clearly and well. She sat down on the grasses, bewildered that it should be a man who had spoken to her so.

She saw the weeds springing up, and she did not move to tear them up from life. She sat powerless, her senses veiled, with no action taking shape beneath her hands. In this way some men sat for hours on end, she knew, tracking a single thought back to its origin. The mind of man could balance and divide, weed out, destroy. She sat on the full, burdened grasses, seeking to think, and dimly waiting for the plumber to return.

Whereas her husband had always gone up, as the dead go, she knew now that there were others who went down, like the corporeal being of the dead. That men were then divided into two bodies now seemed clear to Mrs. Ames. This knowledge stunned her with its simplicity and took the uneasy motion from her limbs. She could not stir, but sat facing the mountains' rocky flanks, and harking in silence to lucidity. Her husband was the mind, this other man the meat, of all mankind.

After a little, the plumber emerged from the earth: first the light top of his head, then the burnt brow, and then the blue eyes fringed with whitest lash. He braced his thick hands flat on the pavings of the garden-path and swung himself completely from the pit.

"It's the soil lines," he said pleasantly. "The gases," he said as he looked down upon her lifted face, "are backing up the drains."

"What in the world are we going to do?" said the astronomer's wife softly. There was a young and strange delight in putting questions to which true answers would be given. Everything the astronomer had ever said to her was a continuous query to which there could be no response.

"Ah, come, now," said the plumber, looking down and smiling. "There's a remedy for every ill, you know. Sometimes it may be that," he said as if speaking to a child, "or sometimes the other thing. But there's always a help for everything a-miss."

Things come out of herbs and make you young again, he might have been saying to her; or the first good rain will quench any drought; or time of itself will put a broken bone together.

"I'm going to follow the ground pipe out right to the torrent," the plumber was saying. "The trouble's between here and there and I'll find it on the way. There's nothing at all that can't be done over for the caring," he was saying, and his eyes were fastened on her face in insolence, or gentleness, or love.

The astronomer's wife stood up, fixed a pin in her hair, and turned around towards the kitchen. Even while she was calling the servant's name, the plumber began speaking again.

"I once had a cow that lost her cud," the plumber was saying. The girl came out on the kitchen-step and Mrs. Ames stood smiling at her in the sun.

"The trouble is very serious, very serious," she said across the garden. "When Mr. Ames gets up, please tell him I've gone down."

She pointed briefly to the open door in the pathway, and the plumber hoisted his kit on his arm and put out his hand to help her down.

"But I made her another in no time," he was saying, "out of flowers and things and what-not."

"Oh," said the astronomer's wife in wonder as she stepped into the heart of the earth. She took his arm, knowing that what he said was true.

[1936]

Richard Wright   *1908–1960*

THE MAN WHO WAS ALMOST A MAN

Dave struck out across the fields, looking homeward through paling light. Whut's the use talkin wid em niggers in the field? Anyhow, his mother was putting supper on the table. Them niggers can't understan nothing. One of these days he was going to get a gun and practice shooting, then they couldn't talk to him as though he were a little boy. He slowed, looking at the ground. Shucks, Ah ain scareda them even ef they are biggern me! Aw, Ah know whut Ahma do. Ahm going by ol Joe's sto n git that Sears Roebuck catlog n look at them guns. Mebbe Ma will lemme buy one when she gits mah pay from ol man Hawkins. Ahma beg her t gimme some money. Ahm ol ernough to hava gun. Ahm seventeen. Almost a man. He strode, feeling his long loose-jointed limbs. Shucks, a man oughta hava little gun aftah he done worked hard all day.

He came in sight of Joe's store. A yellow lantern glowed on the front porch. He mounted steps and went through the screen door, hearing it bang behind him. There was a strong smell of coal oil and mackerel fish. He felt very confident until he saw fat Joe walk in through the rear door, then his courage began to ooze.

"Howdy, Dave! Whutcha want?"

"How yuh, Mistah Joe? Aw, Ah don wanna buy nothing. Ah jus wanted t see ef yuhd lemme look at tha catlog erwhile."

"Sure! You wanna see it here?"

"Nawsuh. Ah wans t take it home wid me. Ah'll bring it back termorrow when Ah come in from the fiels."

"You plannin on buying something?"

"Yessuh."

"Your ma lettin you have your own money now?"

"Shucks. Mistah Joe, Ahm gittin t be a man like anybody else!"

Joe laughed and wiped his greasy white face with a red bandanna.

"Whut you plannin on buyin?"

Dave looked at the floor, scratched his head, scratched his thigh, and smiled. Then he looked up shyly.

"Ah'll tell yuh, Mistah Joe, ef yuh promise yuh won't tell."

"I promise."

"Waal, Ahma buy a gun."

"A gun? Whut you want with a gun?"

"Ah wanna keep it."

"You ain't nothing but a boy. You don't need a gun."

"Aw, lemme have the catlog, Mistah Joe. Ah'll bring it back."

Joe walked through the rear door. Dave was elated. He looked around at barrels of sugar and flour. He heard Joe coming back. He craned his neck to see if he were bringing the book. Yeah, he's got it. Gawddog, he's got it!

"Here, but be sure you bring it back. It's the only one I got."

"Sho, Mistah Joe."

"Say, if you wanna buy a gun, why don't you buy one from me? I gotta gun to sell."

"Will it shoot?"

410

"Sure it'll shoot."

"Whut kind is it?"

"Oh, it's kinda old . . . a left-hand Wheeler. A pistol. A big one."

"Is it got bullets in it?"

"It's loaded."

"Kin Ah see it?"

"Where's your money?"

"Whut yuh wan fer it?"

"I'll let you have it for two dollars."

"Just two dollahs? Shuck, Ah could buy tha when Ah git mah pay."

"I'll have it here when you want it."

"Awright, suh. Ah be in fer it."

He went through the door, hearing it slam again behind him. Ahma git some money from Ma n buy me a gun! Only two dollahs! He tucked the thick catalogue under his arm and hurried.

"Where yuh been, boy?" His mother held a steaming dish of black-eyed peas.

"Aw, Ma, Ah jus stopped down the road t talk wid the boys."

"Yuh know bettah t keep suppah waitin."

He sat down, resting the catalogue on the edge of the table.

"Yuh git up from there and git to the well n wash yosef! Ah ain feedin no hogs in mah house!"

She grabbed his shoulder and pushed him. He stumbled out of the room, then came back to get the catalogue.

"Whut this?"

"Aw, Ma, it's jusa catlog."

"Who yuh git it from?"

"From Joe, down at the sto."

"Waal, thas good. We kin use it in the outhouse."

"Naw, Ma." He grabbed for it. "Gimme ma catlog, Ma."

She held onto it and glared at him.

"Quit hollerin at me! Whut's wrong wid yuh? Yuh crazy?"

"But Ma, please. It ain mine! It's Joe's! He tol me t bring it back t im termorrow."

She gave up the book. He stumbled down the back steps, hugging the thick book under his arm. When he had splashed water on his face and hands, he groped back to the kitchen and fumbled in a corner for the towel. He bumped into a chair; it clattered to the floor. The catalogue sprawled at his feet. When he had dried his eyes he snatched up the book and held it again under his arm. His mother stood watching him.

"Now, ef yuh gonna act a fool over that ol book, Ah'll take it n burn it up."

"Nah, Ma, please."

"Waal, set down n be still!"

He sat down and drew the oil lamp close. He thumbed page after page, unaware of the food his mother set on the table. His father came in. Then his smaller brother.

"Whutcha got there, Dave?" his father asked.

"Jusa catlog," he answered, not looking up.

"Yeah, here they is!" His eyes glowed at blue-and-black revolvers. He glanced up, feeling sudden guilt. His father was watching him. He eased the book under the table and rested it on his knees. After the blessing was asked, he ate. He scooped up peas and swallowed fat meat without chewing. Buttermilk helped to wash it down. He did not want to mention money before his father. He would do much better by cornering his mother when she was alone. He looked at his father uneasily out of the edge of his eye.

"Boy, how come yuh don quit foolin wid tha book n eat yo suppah?"

"Yessuh."

"How you n ol man Hawkins gitten erlong?"

"Suh?"

"Can't yuh hear? Why don yuh lissen? Ah ast yu how wuz yuh n ol man Hawkins gittin erlong?"

"Oh, swell, Pa. Ah plows mo lan than anybody over there."

"Waal, yuh oughta keep yo mind on whut yuh doin."

"Yessuh."

He poured his plate full of molasses and sopped it up slowly with a chunk of cornbread. When his father and brother had left the kitchen, he still sat and looked again at the guns in the catalogue, longing to muster courage enough to present his case to his mother. Lawd, ef Ah only had tha pretty one! He could almost feel the slickness of the weapon with his fingers. If he had a gun like that he would polish it and keep it shining so it would never rust. N Ah'd keep it loaded, by Gawd!

"Ma?" His voice was hesitant.

"Hunh?"

"Ol man Hawkins give yuh mah money yit?"

"Yeah, but ain no use yuh thinking bout throwin nona it erway. Ahm keepin tha money sos yuh kin have cloes t go to school this winter."

He rose and went to her side with the open catalogue in his palms. She was washing dishes, her head bent low over a pan. Shyly he raised the book. When he spoke, his voice was husky, faint.

"Ma, Gawd knows Ah wans one of these."

"One of whut?" she asked, not raising her eyes.

"One of these," he said again, not daring even to point. She glanced up at the page, then at him with wide eyes.

"Nigger, is yuh gone plumb crazy?"

"Aw, Ma—"

"Git outta here! Don yuh talk t me bout no gun! Yuh a fool!"

"Ma, Ah kin buy one fer two dollahs."

"Not ef Ah knows it, yuh ain!"

"But yuh promised me one—"

"Ah don care whut Ah promised! Yuh ain nothing but a boy yit!"

"Ma, ef yuh lemme buy one Ah'll *never* ast yuh fer nothing no mo."

"Ah tol yuh t git outta here! Yuh ain gonna toucha penny of tha money fer no gun! Thas how come Ah has Mistah Hawkins t pay yo wages t me, cause Ah knows yuh ain got no sense."

"But, Ma, we needa gun. Pa ain got no gun. We needa gun in the house. Yuh kin never tell whut might happen."

"Now don yuh try to maka fool outta me, boy! Ef we did hava gun, yuh wouldn't have it!"

He laid the catalogue down and slipped his arm around her waist.

"Aw, Ma, Ah done worked hard alla summer n ain ast yuh fer nothin, is Ah, now?"

"Thas whut yuh spose t do!"

"But Ma, Ah wans a gun. Yuh kin lemme have two dollahs outta mah money. Please, Ma. I kin give it to Pa . . . Please, Ma! Ah loves yuh, Ma."

When she spoke her voice came soft and low.

"Whut yu wan wida gun, Dave? Yuh don need no gun. Yuh'll git in trouble. N ef yo pa jus thought Ah let yuh have money t buy a gun he'd hava fit."

"Ah'll hide it, Ma. It ain but two dollahs."

"Lawd, chil, whut's wrong wid yuh?"

"Ain nothin wrong, Ma. Ahm almos a man now. Ah wans a gun."

"Who gonna sell yuh a gun?"

"Ol Joe at the sto."

"N it don cos but two dollahs?"

"Thas all, Ma. Jus two dollahs. Please, Ma."

She was stacking the plates away; her hands moved slowly, reflectively. Dave kept an anxious silence. Finally, she turned to him.

"Ah'll let yuh git tha gun ef yuh promise me one thing."

"Whut's tha, Ma?"

"Yuh bring it straight back t me, yuh hear? It be fer Pa."

"Yessum! Lemme go now, Ma."

She stooped, turned slightly to one side, raised the hem of her dress, rolled down the top of her stocking, and came up with a slender wad of bills.

"Here," she said. "Lawd knows yuh don need no gun. But yer pa does. Yuh bring it right back t me, yuh hear? Ahma put it up. Now ef yuh don, Ahma have yuh pa lick yuh so hard yuh won fergit it."

"Yessum."

He took the money, ran down the steps, and across the yard.

"Dave! Yuuuuuh Daaaaave!"

He heard, but he was not going to stop now. "Naw, Lawd!"

The first movement he made the following morning was to reach under his pillow for the gun. In the gray light of dawn he held it loosely, feeling a sense of power. Could kill a man with a gun like this. Kill anybody, black or white. And if he were holding his gun in his hand, nobody could run over him; they would have to respect him. It was a big gun, with a long barrel and a heavy handle. He raised and lowered it in his hand, marveling at its weight.

He had not come straight home with it as his mother had asked; instead he had stayed out in the fields, holding the weapon in his hand, aiming it now and then at some imaginary foe. But he had not fired it; he had been afraid that his father might hear. Also he was not sure he knew how to fire it.

To avoid surrendering the pistol he had not come into the house until he knew that they were all asleep. When his mother had tiptoed to his bedside late that night and demanded the gun, he had first played possum; then he had told her that the gun was hidden outdoors, that he would bring it to her in the morning. Now he lay turning it slowly in his hands. He broke it, took out the cartridges, felt them, and then put them back.

He slid out of bed, got a long strip of old flannel from a trunk, wrapped the gun in it, and tied it to his naked thigh while it was still loaded. He did not go in to breakfast. Even though it was not yet daylight, he started for Jim Hawkins' plantation. Just as the sun was rising he reached the barns where the mules and plows were kept.

"Hey! That you Dave?"

He turned. Jim Hawkins stood eying him suspiciously.

"What're yuh doing here so early?"

"Ah didn't know Ah wuz gittin up so early, Mistah Hawkins. Ah wuz fixin t hitch up ol Jenny n take her t the fiels."

"Good. Since you're so early, how about plowing that stretch down by the woods?"

"Suits me, Mistah Hawkins."

"O.K. Go to it!"

He hitched Jenny to a plow and started across the fields. Hot dog! This was just what he wanted. If he could get down by the woods, he could shoot his gun and nobody would hear. He walked behind the plow, hearing the traces creaking, feeling the gun tied tight to his thigh.

When he reached the woods, he plowed two whole rows before he decided to take out the gun. Finally, he stopped, looked in all directions, then untied the gun and held it in his hand. He turned to the mule and smiled.

"Know whut this is, Jenny? Naw, yuh wouldn know! Yuhs jusa ol mule! Anyhow, this is a gun, n it kin shoot, by Gawd!"

He held the gun at arm's length. Whut t hell, Ahma shoot this thing! He looked at Jenny again.

"Lissen here, Jenny! When Ah pull this ol trigger, Ah don wan yuh t run n acka fool now!"

Jenny stood with head down, her short ears pricked straight. Dave walked off about twenty feet, held the gun far out from him at arm's length, and turned his head. Hell, he told himself, Ah ain afraid. The gun felt loose in his fingers; he waved it wildly for a moment. Then he shut his eyes and tightened his forefinger. Bloom! A report half deafened him and he thought his right hand was torn from his arm. He heard Jenny whinnying and galloping over the field, and he found himself on his knees, squeezing his fingers hard between his legs. His hand was numb, he jammed it into his mouth, trying to warm it, trying to stop the pain. The gun lay at his feet. He did not quite know what had happened. He stood up and stared at the gun as though it were a living thing. He gritted his teeth and kicked the gun. Yuh almos broke mah arm! He turned to look for Jenny; she was far over the fields, tossing her head and kicking wildly.

"Hol on there, ol mule!"

When he caught up with her she stood trembling, walling her big white eyes at him. The plow was far away; the traces had broken. Then Dave stopped short, looking, not believing. Jenny was bleeding. Her left side was red and wet with blood. He went closer. Lawd, have mercy! Wondah did Ah shoot this mule? He grabbed for Jenny's mane. She flinched, snorted, whirled, tossing her head.

"Hol on now! Hol on."

Then he saw the hole in Jenny's side, right between the ribs. It was round, wet, red. A crimson stream streaked down the front leg, flowing fast. Good Gawd! Ah wuzn't shootin at tha mule. He felt panic. He knew he had to stop that blood, or Jenny would bleed to death. He had never seen so much blood in all his life. He chased the mule for half a mile, trying to catch her. Finally she stopped, breathing hard, stumpy tail half arched. He caught her mane and led her back to where the plow and gun lay. Then he stooped and grabbed handfuls of damp black earth and tried to plug the bullet hole. Jenny shuddered, whinnied, and broke from him.

"Hol on! Hol on now!"

He tried to plug it again, but blood came anyhow. His fingers were hot and sticky. He rubbed dirt into his palms, trying to dry them. Then again he attempted to plug the bullet hole, but Jenny shied away, kicking her heels high. He stood helpless. He had to do something. He ran at Jenny; she dodged him. He watched a red stream of blood flow down Jenny's leg and form a bright pool at her feet.

"Jenny . . . Jenny," he called weakly.

His lips trembled. She's bleeding t death! He looked in the direction of home, wanting to go back, wanting to get help. But he saw the pistol lying in the damp black clay. He had a queer feeling that if he only did something, this would not be; Jenny would not be there bleeding to death.

When he went to her this time, she did not move. She stood with sleepy, dreamy eyes; and when he touched her she gave a low-pitched whinny and knelt to the ground, her front knees slopping in blood.

"Jenny . . . Jenny . . ." he whispered.

For a long time she held her neck erect; then her head sank, slowly. Her ribs swelled with a mighty heave and she went over.

Dave's stomach felt empty, very empty. He picked up the gun and held it gingerly between his thumb and forefinger. He buried it at the foot of a tree. He took a stick and tried to cover the pool of blood with dirt but what was the use? There was Jenny lying with her mouth open and her eyes walled and glassy. He could not tell Jim Hawkins he had shot his mule. But he had to tell something. Yeah, Ah'll tell em Jenny started gittin wil n fell on the joint of the plow. . . . But that would hardly happen to a mule. He walked across the field slowly, head down.

It was sunset. Two of Jim Hawkins' men were over near the edge of the woods digging a hole in which to bury Jenny. Dave was surrounded by a knot of people, all of whom were looking down at the dead mule.

"I don't see how in the world it happened," said Jim Hawkins for the tenth time.

The crowd parted and Dave's mother, father, and small brother pushed into the center.

"Where Dave?" his mother called.

"There he is," said Jim Hawkins.

His mother grabbed him.

"Whut happened, Dave? Whut yuh done?"

"Nothin."

"C mon, boy, talk," his father said.

Dave took a deep breath and told the story he knew nobody believed. "Waal," he drawled. "Ah brung ol Jenny down here sos Ah could do mah plowin. Ah plowed bout two rows, just like yuh see." He stopped and pointed at the long rows of upturned earth. "Then somethin musta been wrong wid ol Jenny. She wouldn ack right a-tall. She started snortin n kickin her heels. Ah tried t hol her, but she pulled erway, rearin n goin in. Then when the point of the plow was stickin up in the air, she swung erroun n twisted herself back on it . . . She stuck herself n started t bleed. N fo Ah could do anything, she wuz dead."

"Did you ever hear of anything like that in all your life?" asked Jim Hawkins.

There were white and black standing in the crowd. They murmured. Dave's mother came close to him and looked hard into his face. "Tell the truth, Dave," she said.

"Looks like a bullet hole to me," said one man.

"Dave, whut yuh do wid the gun?" his mother asked.

The crowd surged in, looking at him. He jammed his hands into his pockets, shook his head slowly from left to right, and backed away. His eyes were wide and painful.

"Did he hava gun?" asked Jim Hawkins.

"By Gawd, Ah tol yuh tha wuz a gun wound," said a man, slapping his thigh.

His father caught his shoulders and shook him till his teeth rattled.

"Tell whut happened, yuh rascal! Tell whut . . ."

Dave looked at Jenny's stiff legs and began to cry.

"Whut yuh do wid tha gun?" his mother asked.

"Whut wuz he doin wida gun?" his father asked.

"Come on and tell the truth," said Hawkins. "Ain't nobody going to hurt you . . ."

His mother crowded close to him.

"Did yuh shoot tha mule, Dave?"

Dave cried, seeing blurred white and black faces.

"Ahh ddinn gggo tt sshooot hher . . . Ah ssswear ffo Gawd Ahh ddin. . . . Ah wuz a-trying to sssee ef the old gggun would sshoot—"

"Where yuh git the gun from?" his father asked.

"Ah got it from Joe, at the sto."

"Where yuh git the money?"

"Ma give it t me."

"He kept worryin me, Bob. Ah had t. Ah tol im t bring the gun right back t me . . . It was fer yuh, the gun."

"But how yuh happen to shoot that mule?" asked Jim Hawkins.

"Ah wuzn shootin at the mule, Mistah Hawkins. The gun jumped when Ah pulled the trigger . . . N fo Ah knowed anythin Jenny was there a-bleedin."

Somebody in the crowd laughed. Jim Hawkins walked close to Dave and looked into his face.

"Well, looks like you have bought you a mule, Dave."

"Ah swear fo Gawd, Ah didn go t kill the mule, Mistah Hawkins!"

"But you killed her!"

All the crowd was laughing now. They stood on tiptoe and poked heads over one another's shoulders.

"Well, boy, looks like yuh done bought a dead mule! Hahaha!"

"Ain tha ershame."

"Hohohohoho."

Dave stood, head down, twisting his feet in the dirt.

"Well, you needn't worry about it, Bob," said Jim Hawkins to Dave's father. "Just let the boy keep on working and pay me two dollars a month."

"What yuh wan fer yo mule, Mistah Hawkins?"

Jim Hawkins screwed up his eyes.

"Fifty dollars."

"Whut yuh do wid tha gun?" Dave's father demanded.

David said nothing.

"Yuh wan me t take a tree n beat yuh till yuh talk!"

"Nawsuh!"

"What yuh do wid it?"

"Ah throwed it erway."

"Where?"

"Ah . . . Ah throwed it in the creek."

"Waal, c mon home. N firs thing in the mawnin git to tha creek n fin tha gun."

"Yessuh."

"Whut yuh pay fer it?"

"Two dollahs."

"Take tha gun n git yo money back n carry it t Mistah Hawkins, yuh hear? N don fergit Ahma lam you black bottom good fer this! Now march yosef on home, suh!"

Dave turned and walked slowly. He heard people laughing. Dave glared, his eyes welling with tears. Hot anger bubbled in him. Then he swallowed and stumbled on.

That night Dave did not sleep. He was glad that he had gotten out of killing the mule so easily, but he was hurt. Something hot seemed to turn over inside him each time he remembered how they had laughed. He tossed on his bed, feeling his hard pillow. N Pa says he's gonna beat me . . . He remembered other beatings, and his back quivered. Naw, naw, Ah sho don wan im t beat me tha way no mo. Dam em all! Nobody ever gave him anything. All he did was work. They treat me like a mule, n then they beat me. He gritted his teeth. N Ma had t tell on me.

Well, if he had to, he would take old man Hawkins that two dollars. But that meant selling the gun. And he wanted to keep that gun. Fifty dollars for a dead mule.

He turned over, thinking how he had fired the gun. He had an itch to fire it again. Ef other men kin shoota gun, by Gawd, Ah kin! He was still, listening. Mebbe they all sleepin now. The house was still. He heard the soft breathing of his brother. Yes, now! He would go down and get that gun and see if he could fire it! He eased out of bed and slipped into overalls.

The moon was bright. He ran almost all the way to the edge of the woods. He stumbled over the ground, looking for the spot where he had buried the gun. Yeah, here it is. Like a hungry dog scratching for a bone, he pawed it up. He puffed his black cheeks and blew dirt from the trigger and barrel. He broke it and found four cartridges unshot. He looked around; the fields were filled with silence and moonlight. He clutched the gun stiff and hard in his fingers. But, as soon as he wanted to pull the trigger, he shut his eyes and turned his head. Naw, Ah can't shoot wid mah eyes closed n mah head turned. With effort he held his eyes open; then he squeezed. *Blooooom!* He was stiff, not breathing. The gun was still in his hands. Dammit, he'd done it! He fired again, *Blooooom!* He smiled. *Blooooom! Blooooom! Click, click.* There! It was empty. If anybody could shoot a gun, he could. He put the gun into his hip pocket and started across the fields.

When he reached the top of a ridge he stood straight and proud in the moonlight, looking at Jim Hawkins' big white house, feeling the gun sagging in his pocket. Lawd, ef Ah had just one mo bullet Ah'd taka shot at tha house. Ah'd like t scare ol man Hawkins jusa little . . . Jusa enough t let im know Dave Saunders is a man.

To his left the road curved, running to the tracks of the Illinois Central. He jerked his head, listening. From far off came a faint *hoooof-hoooof; hoooof-hoooof; hoooof-hoooof.* . . . He stood rigid. Two dollahs a mont. Les see now . . . Tha means it'll take bout two years. Shucks! Ah'll be dam!

He started down the road, toward the tracks. Yeah, here she comes! He stood beside the track and held himself stiffly. Here she comes, erroun the ben . . . C mon, yuh slow poke! C mon! He had his hand on his gun; something quivered in his stomach. Then the train thundered past, the gray and brown box cars rumbling and clinking. He gripped the gun tightly; then he jerked his hand out of his pocket. Ah betcha Bill wouldn't do it! Ah betcha . . . The cars slid past, steel grinding upon steel. Ahm ridin yuh ternight, so hep me Gawd! He was hot all over. He hesitated just a moment; then he grabbed, pulled atop of a car, and lay flat. He felt his pocket; the gun was still there. Ahead the long rails were glinting in the moonlight, stretching away, away to somewhere, somewhere where he could be a man . . .

[1940]

Eudora Welty *1909–*

WHY I LIVE AT THE P.O.

I was getting along fine with Mama, Papa-Daddy and Uncle Rondo until my sister Stella-Rondo just separated from her husband and came back home again. Mr. Whitaker! Of course I went with Mr. Whitaker first, when he first appeared here in China Grove, taking "Pose Yourself" photos, and Stella-Rondo broke us up. Told him I was one-sided. Bigger on one side than the other, which is a deliberate, calculated falsehood: I'm the same. Stella-Rondo is exactly twelve months to the day younger than I am and for that reason she's spoiled.

She's always had anything in the world she wanted and then she'd throw it away. Papa-Daddy gave her this gorgeous Add-a-Pearl necklace when she was eight years old and she threw it away playing baseball when she was nine, with only two pearls.

So as soon as she got married and moved away from home the first thing she did was separate! From Mr. Whitaker! This photographer with the popeyes she said she trusted. Came home from one of those towns up in Illinois and to our complete surprise brought this child of two.

Mama said she like to made her drop dead for a second. "Here you had this marvelous blonde child and never so much as wrote your mother a word about it," says Mama. "I'm thoroughly ashamed of you." But of course she wasn't.

Stella-Rondo just calmly takes off this *hat*, I wish you could see it. She says, "Why, Mama, Shirley-T.'s adopted, I can prove it."

"How?" says Mama, but all I says was, "H'm!" There I was over the hot stove, trying to stretch two chickens over five people and a completely unexpected child into the bargain, without one moment's notice.

"What do you mean—"H'm!?" says Stella-Rondo, and Mama says, "I heard that, Sister."

I said that oh, I didn't mean a thing, only that whoever Shirley-T. was, she was the spit-image of Papa-Daddy if he'd cut off his beard, which of course he'd never do in the world. Papa-Daddy's Mama's papa and sulks.

Stella-Rondo got furious! She said, "Sister, I don't need to tell you you got a lot of nerve and always did have and I'll thank you to make no future reference to my adopted child whatsoever."

"Very well," I said. "Very well, very well. Of course I noticed at once she looks like Mr. Whitaker's side too. That frown. She looks like a cross between Mr. Whitaker and Papa-Daddy."

"Well, all I can say is she isn't."

"She looks exactly like Shirley Temple[1] to me," says Mama, but Shirley-T. just ran away from her.

So the first thing Stella-Rondo did at the table was turn Papa-Daddy against me.

"Papa-Daddy," she says. He was trying to cut up his meat. "Papa-Daddy!" I was taken completely by surprise. Papa-Daddy is about a million years old and's got this long-long beard. "Papa-Daddy, Sister says she fails to understand why you don't cut off your beard."

So Papa-Daddy l-a-y-s down his knife and fork! He's real rich. Mama says he is, he says he isn't. So he says, "Have I heard correctly? You don't understand why I don't cut off my beard?"

---

[1] Shirley Temple (1928–   ), the most popular child movie star of the 1930s.

"Why," I says, "Papa-Daddy, of course I understand, I did not say any such of a thing, the idea!"

He says, "Hussy!"

I says, "Papa-Daddy, you know I wouldn't any more want you to cut off your beard than the man in the moon. It was the farthest thing from my mind! Stella-Rondo sat there and made that up while she was eating breast of chicken."

But he says, "So the postmistress fails to understand why I don't cut off my beard. Which job I got you through my influence with the government. 'Bird's nest'—is that what you call it?"

Not that it isn't the next to smallest P.O. in the entire state of Mississippi.

I says, "Oh, Papa-Daddy," I says, "I didn't say any such of a thing, I never dreamed it was a bird's nest, I have always been grateful though this is the next to smallest P.O. in the state of Mississippi, and I do not enjoy being referred to as a hussy by my own grandfather."

But Stella-Rondo says, "Yes, you did say it too. Anybody in the world could of heard you, that had ears."

"Stop right there," says Mama, looking at *me*.

So I pulled my napkin straight back through the napkin ring and left the table.

As soon as I was out of the room Mama says, "Call her back, or she'll starve to death," but Papa-Daddy says, "This is the beard I started growing on the Coast when I was fifteen years old." He would of gone on till nightfall if Shirley-T. hadn't lost the Milky Way she ate in Cairo.[2]

So Papa-Daddy says, "I am going out and lie in the hammock, and you can all sit here and remember my words: I'll never cut off my beard as long as I live, even one inch, and I don't appreciate it in you at all." Passed right by me in the hall and went straight out and got in the hammock.

It would be a holiday. It wasn't five minutes before Uncle Rondo suddenly appeared in the hall in one of Stella-Rondo's flesh-colored kimonos, all cut on the bias, like something Mr. Whitaker probably thought was gorgeous.

"Uncle Rondo!" I says. "I didn't know who that was! Where are you going?"

"Sister," he says, "get out of my way, I'm poisoned."

"If you're poisoned stay away from Papa-Daddy," I says. "Keep out of the hammock. Papa-Daddy will certainly beat you on the head if you come within forty miles of him. He thinks I deliberately said he ought to cut off his beard after he got me the P.O., and I've told him and told him and told him, and he acts like he just don't hear me. Papa-Daddy must of gone stone deaf."

"He picked a fine day to do it then," says Uncle Rondo, and before you could say "Jack Robinson" flew out in the yard.

What he'd really done, he'd drunk another bottle of that prescription. He does it every single Fourth of July as sure as shooting, and it's horribly expensive. Then he falls over in the hammock and snores. So he insisted on zigzagging right on out to the hammock, looking like a half-wit.

Papa-Daddy woke up with this horrible yell and right there without moving an inch he tried to turn Uncle Rondo against me. I heard every word he said. Oh, he told Uncle Rondo I didn't learn to read till I was eight years old and he didn't see how in the world I ever got the mail put up at the P.O., much less read it all, and he said if Uncle Rondo could only fathom the lengths he had gone to to get me that job! And he said on the other hand he thought Stella-Rondo had a brilliant mind and deserved credit for getting out of town. All the time he was just lying

[2] Cairo, Illinois.

there swinging as pretty as you please and looping out his beard, and poor Uncle Rondo was *pleading* with him to slow down the hammock, it was making him as dizzy as a witch to watch it. But that's what Papa-Daddy likes about a hammock. So Uncle Rondo was too dizzy to get turned against me for the time being. He's Mama's only brother and is a good case of a one-track mind. Ask anybody. A certified pharmacist.

Just then I heard Stella-Rondo raising the upstairs window. While she was married she got this peculiar idea that it's cooler with the windows shut and locked. So she has to raise the window before she can make a soul hear her outdoors.

So she raises the window and says, *"Oh!"* You would have thought she was mortally wounded.

Uncle Rondo and Papa-Daddy didn't even look up, but kept right on with what they were doing. I had to laugh.

I flew up the stairs and threw the door open! I says, "What in the wide world's the matter, Stella-Rondo? You mortally wounded?"

"No," she says, "I am not mortally wounded but I wish you would do me the favor of looking out that window there and telling me what you see."

So I shade my eyes and look out the window.

"I see the front yard," I says.

"Don't you see any human beings?" she says.

"I see Uncle Rondo trying to run Papa-Daddy out of the hammock," I says. "Nothing more. Naturally, it's so suffocating-hot in the house, with all the windows shut and locked, everybody who cares to stay in their right mind will have to go out and get in the hammock before the Fourth of July is over."

"Don't you notice anything different about Uncle Rondo?" asks Stella-Rondo.

"Why, no, except he's got on some terrible-looking flesh-colored contraption I wouldn't be found dead in, is all I can see," I says.

"Never mind, you won't be found dead in it, because it happens to be part of my trousseau, and Mr. Whitaker took several dozen photographs of me in it," says Stella-Rondo. "What on earth could Uncle Rondo *mean* by wearing part of my trousseau out in the broad open daylight without saying so much as 'Kiss my foot,' *knowing* I only got home this morning after my separation and hung my negligee up on the bathroom door, just as nervous as I could be?"

"I'm sure I don't know, and what do you expect me to do about it?" I says. "Jump out the window?"

"No, I expect nothing of the kind. I simply declare that Uncle Rondo looks like a fool in it, that's all," she says. "It makes me sick to my stomach."

"Well, he looks as good as he can," I says. "As good as anybody in reason could." I stood up for Uncle Rondo, please remember. And I said to Stella-Rondo, "I think I would do well not to criticize so freely if I were you and came home with a two-year-old child I had never said a word about, and no explanation whatever about my separation."

"I asked you the instant I entered this house not to refer one more time to my adopted child, and you gave me your word of honor you would not," was all Stella-Rondo would say, and started pulling out every one of her eyebrows with some cheap Kress[3] tweezers.

So I merely slammed the door behind me and went down and made some green-tomato pickle. Somebody had to do it. Of course Mama had turned both the niggers loose; she always said no earthly power could hold one anyway on the

[3] S. S. Kresge Company, a chain of variety stores.

Fourth of July, so she wouldn't even try. It turned out that Jaypan fell in the lake and came within a very narrow limit of drowning.

So Mama trots in. Lifts up the lid and says, "H'm! Not very good for your Uncle Rondo in his precarious condition, I must say. Or poor little adopted Shirley-T. Shame on you!"

That made me tired. I says, "Well, Stella-Rondo had better thank her lucky stars it was her instead of me came trotting in with that very peculiar-looking child. Now if it had been me that trotted in from Illinois and brought a peculiar-looking child of two, I shudder to think of the reception I'd of got, much less controlled the diet of an entire family."

"But you must remember, Sister, that you were never married to Mr. Whitaker in the first place and didn't go up to Illinois to live," says Mama, shaking a spoon in my face. "If you had I would of been just as overjoyed to see you and your little adopted girl as I was to see Stella-Rondo, when you wound up with your separation and came on back home."

"You would not," I says.

"Don't contradict me, I would," says Mama.

But I said she couldn't convince me though she talked till she was blue in the face. Then I said, "Besides, you know as well as I do that that child is not adopted."

"She most certainly is adopted," says Mama, stiff as a poker.

I says, "Why, Mama, Stella-Rondo had her just as sure as anything in this world, and just too stuck up to admit it."

"Why, Sister," said Mama. "Here I thought we were going to have a pleasant Fourth of July, and you start right out not believing a word your own baby sister tells you!"

"Just like Cousin Annie Flo. Went to her grave denying the facts of life," I remind Mama.

"I told you if you ever mentioned Annie Flo's name I'd slap your face," says Mama, and slaps my face.

"All right, you wait and see," I says.

"I," says Mama, "I prefer to take my children's word for anything when it's humanly possible." You ought to see Mama, she weighs two hundred pounds and has real tiny feet.

Just then something perfectly horrible occurred to me.

"Mama," I says, "can that child talk?" I simply had to whisper! "Mama, I wonder if that child can be—you know—in any way? Do you realize," I says, "that she hasn't spoken one single, solitary word to a human being up to this minute? This is the way she looks," I says, and I looked like this.

Well, Mama and I just stood there and stared at each other. It was horrible!

"I remember well that Joe Whitaker frequently drank like a fish," says Mama. "I believed to my soul he drank *chemicals.*" And without another word she marches to the foot of the stairs and calls Stella-Rondo.

"Stella-Rondo? O-o-o-o-o! Stella-Rondo!"

"What?" says Stella-Rondo from upstairs. Not even the grace to get up off the bed.

"Can that child of yours talk?" asks Mama.

Stella-Rondo says, "Can she what?"

"Talk! Talk!" says Mama. "Burdyburdyburdyburdy!"

So Stella-Rondo yells back, "Who says she can't talk?"

"Sister says so," says Mama.

"You didn't have to tell me, I know whose word of honor don't mean a thing in this house," says Stella-Rondo.

And in a minute the loudest Yankee voice I ever heard in my life yells out, "OE'm Pop-OE the Sailor-r-r-r Ma-a-an!"[4] and then somebody jumps up and down in the upstairs hall. In another second the house would of fallen down.

"Not only talks, she can tap-dance!" calls Stella-Rondo. "Which is more than some people I won't name can do."

"Why, the little precious darling thing!" Mama says, so surprised. "Just as smart as she can be!" Starts talking baby talk right there. Then she turns on me. "Sister, you ought to be thoroughly ashamed! Run upstairs this instant and apologize to Stella-Rondo and Shirley-T."

"Apologize for what?" I says. "I merely wondered if the child was normal, that's all. Now that she's proved she is, why, I have nothing further to say."

But Mama just turned on her heel and flew out, furious. She ran right upstairs and hugged the baby. She believed it was adopted. Stella-Rondo hadn't done a thing but turn her against me from upstairs while I stood there helpless over the hot stove. So that made Mama, Papa-Daddy and the baby all on Stella-Rondo's side.

Next, Uncle Rondo.

I must say that Uncle Rondo has been marvelous to me at various times in the past and I was completely unprepared to be made to jump out of my skin, the way it turned out. Once Stella-Rondo did something perfectly horrible to him—broke a chain letter from Flanders Field[5] and he took the radio back he had given her and gave it to me. Stella-Rondo was furious! For six months we all had to call her Stella instead of Stella-Rondo, or she wouldn't answer. I always thought Uncle Rondo had all the brains of the entire family. Another time he sent me to Mammoth Cave,[6] with all expenses paid.

But this would be the day he was drinking that prescription, the Fourth of July.

So at supper Stella-Rondo speaks up and says she thinks Uncle Rondo ought to try to eat a little something. So finally Uncle Rondo said he would try a little cold biscuits and ketchup, but that was all. So *she* brought it to him.

"Do you think it wise to disport with ketchup in Stella-Rondo's flesh-colored kimono?" I says. Trying to be considerate! If Stella-Rondo couldn't watch out for her trousseau, somebody had to.

"Any objections?" asks Uncle Rondo, just about to pour out all the ketchup.

"Don't mind what she says, Uncle Rondo," says Stella-Rondo. "Sister has been devoting this solid afternoon to sneering out my bedroom window at the way you look."

"What's that?" says Uncle Rondo. Uncle Rondo has got the most terrible temper in the world. Anything is liable to make him tear the house down if it comes at the wrong time.

So Stella-Rondo says, "Sister says, 'Uncle Rondo certainly does look like a fool in that pink kimono!' "

Do you remember who it was really said that?

Uncle Rondo spills out all the ketchup and jumps out of his chair and tears off

[4] "I'm Popeye the Sailor Man," a line from a popular song, *ca.* 1940.
[5] The famous American military cemetery in Belgium containing World War I dead.
[6] Mammoth Cave, Kentucky, the world's largest known system of natural underground caverns.

the kimono and throws it down on the dirty floor and puts his foot on it. It had to be sent all the way to Jackson to the cleaners and re-pleated.

"So that's your opinion of your Uncle Rondo, is it?" he says. "I look like a fool, do I? Well, that's the last straw. A whole day in this house with nothing to do, and then to hear you come out with a remark like that behind my back!"

"I didn't say any such of a thing, Uncle Rondo," I says, "and I'm not saying who did, either. Why, I think you look all right. Just try to take care of yourself and not talk and eat at the same time," I says. "I think you better go lie down."

"Lie down my foot," says Uncle Rondo. I ought to of known by that he was fixing to do something perfectly horrible.

So he didn't do anything that night in the precarious state he was in—just played Casino with Mama and Stella-Rondo and Shirley-T. and gave Shirley-T. a nickel with a head on both sides. It tickled her nearly to death, and she called him "Papa." But at 6:30 A.M. the next morning, he threw a whole five-cent package of some unsold one-inch firecrackers from the store as hard as he could into my bedroom and they every one went off. Not one bad one in the string. Anybody else, there'd be one that wouldn't go off.

Well, I'm just terribly susceptible to noise of any kind, the doctor has always told me I was the most sensitive person he had ever seen in his whole life, and I was simply prostrated. I couldn't eat! People tell me they heard it as far as the cemetery, and old Aunt Jep Patterson, that had been holding her own so good, thought it was Judgment Day and she was going to meet her whole family. It's usually so quiet here.

And I'll tell you it didn't take me any longer than a minute to make up my mind what to do. There I was with the whole entire house on Stella-Rondo's side and turned against me. If I have anything at all I have pride.

So I just decided I'd go straight down to the P.O. There's plenty of room there in the back, I says to myself.

Well! I made no bones about letting the family catch on to what I was up to. I didn't try to conceal it.

The first thing they knew, I marched in where they were all playing Old Maid and pulled the electric oscillating fan out by the plug, and everything got real hot. Next I snatched the pillow I'd done the needlepoint on right off the davenport from behind Papa-Daddy. He went "Ugh!" I beat Stella-Rondo up the stairs and finally found my charm bracelet in her bureau drawer under a picture of Nelson Eddy.[7]

"So that's the way the land lies," says Uncle Rondo. There he was, piecing on the ham. "Well, Sister, I'll be glad to donate my army cot if you got any place to set it up, providing you'll leave right this minute and let me get some peace." Uncle Rondo was in France.

"Thank you kindly for the cot and 'peace' is hardly the word I would select if I had to resort to firecrackers at 6:30 A.M. in a young girl's bedroom," I says back to him. "And as to where I intend to go, you seem to forget my position as postmistress of China Grove, Mississippi," I says. "I've always got the P.O."

Well, that made them all sit up and take notice.

I went out front and started digging up some four-o'clocks[8] to plant around the P.O.

"Ah-ah-ah!" says Mama, raising the window. "Those happen to be my four-

[7] Nelson Eddy (1901–1967), a popular singer, appeared in many musical films of the 1930s.
[8] A common variety of garden plants.

o'clocks. Everything planted in that star is mine. I've never known you to make anything grow in your life."

"Very well," I says. "But I take the fern. Even you, Mama, can't stand there and deny that I'm the one watered that fern. And I happen to know where I can send in a box top and get a packet of one thousand mixed seeds, no two the same kind, free."

"Oh, where?" Mama wants to know.

But I says, "Too late. You 'tend to your house, and I'll 'tend to mine. You hear things like that all the time if you know how to listen to the radio. Perfectly marvelous offers. Get anything you want free."

So I hope to tell you I marched in and got that radio, and they could of all bit a nail in two, especially Stella-Rondo, that it used to belong to, and she well knew she couldn't get it back, I'd sue for it like a shot. And I very politely took the sewing-machine motor I helped pay the most on to give Mama for Christmas back in 1929, and a good big calendar, with the first-aid remedies on it. The thermometer and the Hawaiian ukulele certainly were rightfully mine, and I stood on the step-ladder and got all my watermelon-rind preserves and every fruit and vegetable I'd put up, every jar. Then I began to pull the tacks out of the bluebird wall vases on the archway to the dining room.

"Who told you you could have those, Miss Priss?" says Mama, fanning as hard as she could.

"I bought 'em and I'll keep track of 'em," I says. "I'll tack 'em up one on each side the post-office window, and you can see 'em when you come to ask me for your mail, if you're so dead to see 'em."

"Not I! I'll never darken the door to that post office again if I live to be a hundred," Mama says. "Ungrateful child! After all the money we spent on you at the Normal."[9]

"Me either," says Stella-Rondo. "You can just let my mail lie there and *rot,* for all I care. I'll never come and relieve you of a single, solitary piece."

"I should worry," I says. "And who you think's going to sit down and write you all those big fat letters and postcards, by the way? Mr. Whitaker? Just because he was the only man ever dropped down in China Grove and you got him— unfairly—is he going to sit down and write you a lengthy correspondence after you come home giving no rhyme nor reason whatsoever for your separation and no explanation for the presence of that child? I may not have your brilliant mind, but I fail to see it."

So Mama says, "Sister, I've told you a thousand times that Stella-Rondo simply got homesick, and this child is far too big to be hers," and she says, "Now, why don't you all just sit down and play Casino?"

Then Shirley-T. sticks out her tongue at me in this perfectly horrible way. She has no more manners than the man in the moon. I told her she was going to cross her eyes like that some day and they'd stick.

"It's too late to stop me now," I says. "You should have tried that yesterday. I'm going to the P.O. and the only way you can possibly see me is to visit me there."

So Papa-Daddy says, "You'll never catch me setting foot in that post office, even if I should take a notion into my head to write a letter some place." He says, "I won't have you reachin' out of that little old window with a pair of shears and cuttin' off any beard of mine. I'm too smart for you!"

"We all are," says Stella-Rondo.

[9] Normal school: a two-year school for preparing teachers.

But I said, "If you're so smart, where's Mr. Whitaker?"

So then Uncle Rondo says, "I'll thank you from now on to stop reading all the orders I get on postcards and telling everybody in China Grove what you think is the matter with them," but I says, "I draw my own conclusions and will continue in the future to draw them." I says, "If people want to write their inmost secrets on penny postcards, there's nothing in the wide world you can do about it, Uncle Rondo."

"And if you think we'll ever *write* another postcard you're sadly mistaken," says Mama.

"Cutting off your nose to spite your face then," I says. "But if you're all determined to have no more to do with the U.S. mail, think of this: What will Stella-Rondo do now, if she wants to tell Mr. Whitaker to come after her?"

"Wah!" says Stella-Rondo. I knew she'd cry. She had a conniption fit right there in the kitchen.

"It will be interesting to see how long she holds out," I says. "And now—I am leaving."

"Good-bye," says Uncle Rondo.

"Oh, I declare," says Mama, "to think that a family of mine should quarrel on the Fourth of July, or the day after, over Stella-Rondo leaving old Mr. Whitaker and having the sweetest little adopted child! It looks like we'd all be glad!"

"Wah!" says Stella-Rondo, and has a fresh conniption fit.

"*He* left *her*—you mark my words," I says.

"That's Mr. Whitaker. I know Mr. Whitaker. After all, I knew him first. I said from the beginning he'd up and leave her. I foretold every single thing that's happened."

"Where did he go?" asks Mama.

"Probably to the North Pole, if he knows what's good for him," I says.

But Stella-Rondo just bawled and wouldn't say another word. She flew to her room and slammed the door.

"Now look what you've gone and done, Sister," says Mama. "You go apologize."

"I haven't got time, I'm leaving," I says.

"Well, what are you waiting around for?" asks Uncle Rondo.

So I just picked up the kitchen clock and marched off, without saying "Kiss my foot" or anything, and never did tell Stella-Rondo good-bye.

There was a nigger girl going along on a little wagon right in front.

"Nigger girl," I says, "come help me haul these things down the hill, I'm going to live in the post office."

Took her nine trips in her express wagon. Uncle Rondo came out on the porch and threw her a nickel.

And that's the last I've laid eyes on any of my family or my family laid eyes on me for five solid days and nights. Stella-Rondo may be telling the most horrible tales in the world about Mr. Whitaker, but I haven't heard them. As I tell everybody, I draw my own conclusions.

But oh, I like it here. It's ideal, as I've been saying. You see, I've got everything cater-cornered, the way I like it. Hear the radio? All the war news. Radio, sewing machine, book ends, ironing board and that great big piano lamp—peace, that's what I like. Butter-bean vines planted all along the front where the strings are.

Of course, there's not much mail. My family are naturally the main people in China Grove, and if they prefer to vanish from the face of the earth, for all the mail they get or the mail they write, why, I'm not going to open my mouth. Some of the folks here in town are taking up for me and some turned against me. I know which is which. There are always people who will quit buying stamps just to get on the right side of Papa-Daddy.

But here I am, and here I'll stay. I want the world to know I'm happy.

And if Stella-Rondo should come to me this minute, on bended knees, and *attempt* to explain the incidents of her life with Mr. Whitaker, I'd simply put my fingers in both my ears and refuse to listen.

[1941]

Katherine Anne Porter   *1890–1980*

THE GRAVE

The grandfather, dead for more than thirty years, had been twice disturbed in his long repose by the constancy and possessiveness of his widow. She removed his bones first to Louisiana and then to Texas as if she had set out to find her own burial place, knowing well she would never return to the places she had left. In Texas she set up a small cemetery in a corner of her first farm, and as the family connection grew, and oddments of relations came over from Kentucky to settle, it contained at last about twenty graves. After the grandmother's death, part of her land was to be sold for the benefit of certain of her children, and the cemetery happened to lie in the part set aside for sale. It was necessary to take up the bodies and bury them again in the family plot in the big new public cemetery, where the grandmother had been buried. At last her husband was to lie beside her for eternity, as she had planned.

The family cemetery had been a pleasant small neglected garden of tangled rose bushes and ragged cedar trees and cypress, the simple flat stones rising out of uncropped sweet-smelling wild grass. The graves were lying open and empty one burning day when Miranda and her brother Paul, who often went together to hunt rabbits and doves, propped their twenty-two Winchester rifles carefully against the rail fence, climbed over and explored among the graves. She was nine years old and he was twelve.

They peered into the pits all shaped alike with such purposeful accuracy, and looking at each other with pleased adventurous eyes, they said in solemn tones: "These were graves!" trying by words to shape a special, suitable emotion in their minds, but they felt nothing except an agreeable thrill of wonder: they were seeing a new sight, doing something they had not done before. In them both there was also a small disappointment at the entire commonplaceness of the actual spectacle. Even if it had once contained a coffin for years upon years, when the coffin was gone a grave was just a hole in the ground. Miranda leaped into the pit that had held her grandfather's bones. Scratching around aimlessly and pleasurably as any young animal, she scooped up a lump of earth and weighed it in her palm. It had a pleasantly sweet, corrupt smell, being mixed with cedar needles and small leaves, and as the crumbs fell apart, she saw a silver dove no larger than a hazel nut, with spread wings and a neat fan-shaped tail. The breast had a deep round hollow in it. Turning it up to the fierce sunlight, she saw that the inside of the hollow was cut in little whorls. She scrambled out, over the pile of loose earth that had fallen back into one end of the grave, calling to Paul that she had found something, he must guess what . . . His head appeared smiling over the rim of another grave. He waved a closed hand at her. "I've got something too!" They ran to compare treasures, making a game of it, so many guesses each, all wrong, and a final showdown with opened palms. Paul had found a thin wide gold ring carved with intricate flowers and leaves. Miranda was smitten at the sight of the ring and wished to have it. Paul seemed more impressed by the dove. They made a trade, with some little bickering. After he had got the dove in his hand, Paul said, "Don't you know what this is? This is a screw head for a *coffin!* . . . I'll bet nobody else in the world has one like this!"

Miranda glanced at it without covetousness. She had the gold ring on her thumb; it fitted perfectly. "Maybe we ought to go now," she said, "maybe one of the niggers 'll see us and tell somebody." They knew the land had been sold, the cemetery was no longer theirs, and they felt like trespassers. They climbed back over the fence, slung their rifles loosely under their arms—they had been shooting at targets with various kinds of firearms since they were seven years old—and set out to look for the rabbits and doves or whatever small game might happen along. On these expeditions Miranda always followed at Paul's heels along the path, obeying instructions about handling her gun when going through fences; learning how to stand it up properly so it would not slip and fire unexpectedly; how to wait her time for a shot and not just bang away in the air without looking, spoiling shots for Paul, who really could hit things if given a chance. Now and then, in her excitement at seeing birds whizz up suddenly before her face, or a rabbit leap across her very toes, she lost her head, and almost without sighting she flung her rifle up and pulled the trigger. She hardly ever hit any sort of mark. She had no proper sense of hunting at all. Her brother would be often completely disgusted with her. "You don't care whether you get your bird or not," he said. "That's no way to hunt." Miranda could not understand his indignation. She had seen him smash his hat and yell with fury when he had missed his aim. "What I like about shooting," said Miranda, with exasperating inconsequence, "is pulling the trigger and hearing the noise."

"Then, by golly," said Paul, "whyn't you go back to the range and shoot at bulls-eyes?"

"I'd just as soon," said Miranda, "only like this, we walk around more."

"Well, you just stay behind and stop spoiling my shots," said Paul, who, when he made a kill, wanted to be certain he had made it. Miranda, who alone brought down a bird once in twenty rounds, always claimed as her own any game they got when they fired at the same moment. It was tiresome and unfair and her brother was sick of it.

"Now, the first dove we see, or the first rabbit, is mine," he told her. "And the next will be yours. Remember that and don't get smarty."

"What about snakes?" asked Miranda idly. "Can I have the first snake?"

Waving her thumb gently and watching her gold ring glitter, Miranda lost interest in shooting. She was wearing her summer roughing outfit: dark blue overalls, a light blue shirt, a hired-man's straw hat, and thick brown sandals. Her brother had the same outfit except his was a sober hickory-nut color. Ordinarily Miranda preferred her overalls to any other dress, though it was making rather a scandal in the countryside, for the year was 1903, and in the back country the law of female decorum had teeth in it. Her father had been criticized for letting his girls dress like boys and go careering around astride barebacked horses. Big sister Maria, the really independent and fearless one, in spite of her rather affected ways, rode at a dead run with only a rope knotted around her horse's nose. It was said the motherless family was running down, with the Grandmother no longer there to hold it together. It was known that she had discriminated against her son Harry in her will, and that he was in straits about money. Some of his old neighbors reflected with vicious satisfaction that now he would probably not be so stiffnecked, nor have any more high-stepping horses either. Miranda knew this, though she could not say how. She had met along the road old women of the kind who smoked corn-cob pipes, who had treated her grandmother with most sincere respect. They slanted their gummy old eyes side-ways at the granddaughter and said, "Ain't you ashamed of yoself, Missy? It's aginst the Scriptures to dress like that. Whut yo Pappy thinkin about?" Miranda, with her powerful social sense, which was like a fine set of antennae radiating from every pore of her skin, would feel ashamed because she knew well it was rude and ill-bred to shock anybody, even bad-tempered old crones, though she had faith in her father's judgment and was perfectly comfortable in the clothes. Her father had said, "They're just what you need, and they'll save your dresses for school . . ." This sounded quite simple and natural to her. She had been brought up in rigorous economy. Wastefulness was vulgar. It was also a sin. These were truths; she had heard them repeated many times and never once disputed.

Now the ring, shining with the serene purity of fine gold on her rather grubby thumb, turned her feelings against her overalls and sockless feet, toes sticking through the thick brown leather straps. She wanted to go back to the farmhouse, take a good cold bath, dust herself with plenty of Maria's violet talcum powder— provided Maria was not present to object, of course—put on the thinnest, most becoming dress she owned, with a big sash, and sit in a wicker chair under the trees . . . These things were not all she wanted, of course; she had vague stirrings of desire for luxury and a grand way of living which could not take precise form in her imagination but were founded on family legend of past wealth and leisure. These immediate comforts were what she could have, and she wanted them at once. She lagged rather far behind Paul, and once she thought of just turning back without a word and going home. She stopped, thinking that Paul would never do that to her, and so she would have to tell him. When a rabbit leaped, she let Paul have it without dispute. He killed it with one shot.

When she came up with him, he was already kneeling, examining the wound, the rabbit trailing from his hands. "Right through the head," he said complacently, as if he had aimed for it. He took out his sharp, competent bowie knife and started to skin the body. He did it very cleanly and quickly. Uncle Jimbilly knew how to prepare the skins so that Miranda always had fur coats for her dolls, for though she never cared much for her dolls she liked seeing them in fur coats. The children knelt facing each other over the dead animal. Miranda watched admiringly while her brother stripped the skin away as if he were taking off a glove. The flayed flesh emerged dark scarlet, sleek, firm; Miranda with thumb and finger felt the long fine muscles with the silvery flat strips binding them to the joints. Brother lifted the oddly bloated belly. "Look," he said, in a low amazed voice. "It was going to have young ones."

Very carefully he slit the thin flesh from the center ribs to the flanks, and a scarlet bag appeared. He slit again and pulled the bag open, and there lay a bundle of tiny rabbits, each wrapped in a thin scarlet veil. The brother pulled these off and there they were, dark gray, their sleek wet down lying in minute even ripples, like a baby's head just washed, their unbelievably small delicate ears folded close, their little blind faces almost featureless.

Miranda said, "Oh, I want to *see*," under her breath. She looked and looked— excited but not frightened, for she was accustomed to the sight of animals killed in hunting—filled with pity and astonishment and a kind of shocked delight in the wonderful little creatures for their own sakes, they were so pretty. She touched one of them ever so carefully, "Ah, there's blood running over them," she said and began to tremble without knowing why. Yet she wanted most deeply to see and to know. Having seen, she felt at once as if she had known all along. The very memory of her former ignorance faded, she had always known just this. No one had ever told her anything out right, she had been rather unobservant of the animal life around her because she was so accustomed to animals. They seemed simply disorderly and unaccountably rude in their habits, but altogether natural and not very interesting. Her brother had spoken as if he had known about everything all along. He may have seen all this before. He had never said a word to her, but she knew now a part at least of what he knew. She understood a little of the secret, formless intuitions in her own mind and body, which had been clearing up, taking form, so gradually and so steadily she had not realized that she was learning what she had to know. Paul said cautiously, as if he were talking about something forbidden: "They were just about ready to be born." His voice dropped on the last word. "I know," said Miranda, "like kittens. I know, like babies." She was quietly and terribly agitated, standing again with her rifle under her arm, looking down at the bloody heap. "I don't want the skin," she said, "I won't have it." Paul buried the young rabbits again in their mother's body, wrapped the skin around her, carried her to a clump of sage bushes, and hid her away. He came out again at once and said to Miranda, with an eager friendliness, a confidential tone quite unusual in him, as if he were taking her into an important secret on equal terms: "Listen now. Now you listen to me, and don't ever forget. Don't you ever tell a living soul that you saw this. Don't tell a soul. Don't tell Dad because I'll get into trouble. He'll say I'm leading you into things you ought not to do. He's always saying that. So now don't you go and forget and blab out sometime the way you're always doing . . . Now, that's a secret. Don't you tell."

Miranda never told, she did not wish to tell anybody. She thought about the whole worrisome affair with confused unhappiness for a few days. Then it sank quietly into her mind and was heaped over by accumulated thousands of impressions, for nearly twenty years. One day she was picking her path among the puddles and crushed refuse of a market street in a strange city of a strange country, when without warning, plain and clear in its true colors as if she looked through a frame upon a scene that had not stirred nor changed since the moment it happened, the episode of that far-off day leaped from its burial place before her mind's eye. She was so reasonlessly horrified she halted suddenly staring, the scene before her eyes dimmed by the vision back of them. An Indian vendor had held up before her a tray of dyed sugar sweets, in the shapes of all kinds of small creatures: birds, baby chicks, baby rabbits, lambs, baby pigs. They were in gay colors and smelled of vanilla, maybe. . . . It was a very hot day and the smell in the market, with its piles of raw flesh and wilting flowers, was like the mingled sweetness and corruption she had smelled that other day in the empty cemetery at home: the day she had remembered always until now vaguely as the time she and her brother had found treasure in the opened graves. Instantly upon this thought the dreadful vision faded, and she saw clearly her brother, whose childhood face she had forgotten, standing again in the blazing sunshine, again twelve years old, a pleased sober smile in his eyes, turning the silver dove over and over in his hands.

[1944]

Ralph Ellison   *1914–*

KING OF THE BINGO GAME

The woman in front of him was eating roasted peanuts that smelled so good that he could barely contain his hunger. He could not even sleep and wished they'd hurry and begin the bingo game. There, on his right, two fellows were drinking wine out of a bottle wrapped in a paper bag, and he could hear soft gurgling in the dark. His stomach gave a low, gnawing growl. "If this was down South," he thought, "all I'd have to do is lean over and say, 'Lady, gimme a few of those peanuts, please ma'am,' and she'd pass me the bag and never think nothing of it." Or he could ask the fellows for a drink in the same way. Folks down South stuck together that way; they didn't even have to know you. But up here it was different. Ask somebody for something, and they'd think you were crazy. Well, I ain't crazy. I'm just broke, 'cause I got no birth certificate to get a job, and Laura 'bout to die 'cause we got no money for a doctor. But I ain't crazy. And yet a pinpoint of doubt was focused in his mind as he glanced toward the screen and saw the hero stealthily entering a dark room and sending the beam of a flashlight along a wall of bookcases. This is where he finds the trapdoor, he remembered. The man would pass abruptly through the wall and find the girl tied to a bed, her legs and arms spread wide, and her clothing torn to rags. He laughed softly to himself. He had seen the picture three times, and this was one of the best scenes.

On his right the fellow whispered wide-eyed to his companion, "Man, look a-yonder!"

"Damn!"

"Wouldn't I like to have her tied up like that . . ."

"Hey! That fool's letting her loose!"

"Aw, man, he loves her."

"Love or no love!"

The man moved impatiently beside him, and he tried to involve himself in the scene. But Laura was on his mind. Tiring quickly of watching the picture he looked back to where the white beam filtered from the projection room above the balcony. It started small and grew large, specks of dust dancing in its whiteness as it reached the screen. It was strange how the beam always landed right on the screen and didn't mess up and fall somewhere else. But they had it all fixed. Everything was fixed. Now suppose when they showed that girl with her dress torn the girl started taking off the rest of her clothes, and when the guy came in he didn't untie her but kept her there and went to taking off his own clothes? *That* would be something to see. If a picture got out of hand like that those guys up there would go nuts. Yeah, and there'd be so many folks in here you couldn't find a seat for nine months! A strange sensation played over his skin. He shuddered. Yesterday he'd seen a bedbug on a woman's neck as they walked out into the bright street. But exploring his thigh through a hole in his pocket he found only goose pimples and old scars.

The bottle gurgled again. He closed his eyes. Now a dreamy music was accompanying the film and train whistles were sounding in the distance, and he was a boy again walking along a railroad trestle down South, and seeing the train coming, and running back as fast as he could go, and hearing the whistle blowing, and getting off the trestle to solid ground just in time, with the earth trembling beneath his feet, and feeling relieved as he ran down the cinder-strewn embankment onto the highway, and looking back and seeing with terror that the train had left the track and was following him right down the middle of the street, and all the white people laughing as he ran screaming . . .

"Wake up there, buddy! What the hell do you mean hollering like that? Can't you see we trying to enjoy this here picture?"

He stared at the man with gratitude.

"I'm sorry, old man," he said. "I musta been dreaming."

"Well, here, have a drink. And don't be making no noise like that, damn!"

His hands trembled as he tilted his head. It was not wine, but whiskey. Cold rye whiskey. He took a deep swoller, decided it was better not to take another, and handed the bottle back to its owner.

"Thanks, old man," he said.

Now he felt the cold whiskey breaking a warm path straight through the middle of him, growing hotter and sharper as it moved. He had not eaten all day, and it made him light-headed. The smell of the peanuts stabbed him like a knife, and he got up and found a seat in the middle aisle. But no sooner did he sit than he saw a row of intense-faced young girls, and got up again, thinking, "You chicks musta been Lindy-hopping somewhere." He found a seat several rows ahead as the lights came on, and he saw the screen disappear behind a heavy red and gold curtain; then the curtain rising, and the man with the microphone and a uniformed attendant coming on the stage.

He felt for his bingo cards, smiling. The guy at the door wouldn't like it if he knew about his having *five* cards. Well, not everyone played the bingo game; and even with five cards he didn't have much of a chance. For Laura, though, he had to have faith. He studied the cards, each with its different numerals, punching the free center hole in each and spreading them neatly across his lap; and when the lights faded he sat slouched in his seat so that he could look from his cards to the bingo wheel with but a quick shifting of his eyes.

Ahead, at the end of the darkness, the man with the microphone was pressing a button attached to a long cord and spinning the bingo wheel and calling out the number each time the wheel came to rest. And each time the voice rang out his finger raced over the cards for the number. With five cards he had to move fast. He became nervous; there were too many cards, and the man went too fast with his grating voice. Perhaps he should just select one and throw the others away. But he was afraid. He became warm. Wonder how much Laura's doctor would cost? Damn that, watch the cards! And with despair he heard the man call three in a row which he missed on all five cards. This way he'd never win . . .

When he saw the row of holes punched across the third card, he sat paralyzed and heard the man call three more numbers before he stumbled forward, screaming.

"Bingo! Bingo!"

"Let that fool up there," someone called.

"Get up there, man!"

He stumbled down the aisle and up the steps to the stage into a light so sharp and bright that for a moment it blinded him, and he felt that he had moved into the spell of some strange, mysterious power. Yet it was as familiar as the sun, and he knew it was the perfectly familiar bingo.

The man with the microphone was saying something to the audience as he held out his card. A cold light flashed from the man's finger as the card left his hand. His knees trembled. The man stepped closer, checking the card against the numbers chalked on the board. Suppose he had made a mistake? The pomade on the man's hair made him feel faint, and he backed away. But the man was checking the card over the microphone now, and he had to stay. He stood tense, listening.

"Under the O, forty-four," the man chanted. "Under the I, seven. Under the G, three. Under the B, ninety-six. Under the N, thirteen!"

His breath came easier as the man smiled at the audience.

"Yessir, ladies and gentlemen, he's one of the chosen people!"

The audience rippled with laughter and applause.

"Step right up to the front of the stage."

He moved slowly forward, wishing that the light was not so bright.

"To win to-night's jackpot of $36.90 the wheel must stop between the double zero, understand?"

He nodded, knowing the ritual from the many days and nights he had watched the winners march across the stage to press the button that controlled the spinning wheel and receive the prizes. And now he followed the instructions as though he'd crossed the slippery stage a million prize-winning times.

The man was making some kind of a joke, and he nodded vacantly. So tense had he become that he felt a sudden desire to cry and shook it away. He felt vaguely that his whole life was determined by the bingo wheel; not only that which would happen now that he was at last before it, but all that had gone before, since his birth, and his mother's birth and the birth of his father. It had always been there, even though he had not been aware of it, handing out the unlucky cards and numbers of his days. The feeling persisted, and he started quickly away. I better get down from here before I make a fool of myself, he thought.

"Here, boy," the man called. "You haven't started yet."

Someone laughed as he went hesitantly back.

"Are you all reet?"

He grinned at the man's jive talk, but no words would come, and he knew it was not a convincing grin. For suddenly he knew that he stood on the slippery brink of some terrible embarrassment.

"Where are you from, boy?" the man asked.

"Down South."

"He's from down South, ladies and gentlemen," the man said. "Where from? Speak right into the mike."

"Rocky Mont," he said. "Rock' Mont, North Car'lina."

"So you decided to come down off that mountain to the U.S.," the man laughed. He felt that the man was making a fool of him, but then something cold was placed in his hand, and the lights were no longer behind him.

Standing before the wheel he felt alone, but that was somehow right, and he remembered his plan. He would give the wheel a short quick twirl. Just a touch of the button. He had watched it many times, and always it came close to double zero when it was short and quick. He steeled himself; the fear had left, and he felt a profound sense of promise, as though he were about to be repaid for all the things he'd suffered all his life. Trembling, he pressed the button. There was a whirl of lights, and in a second he realized with finality that though he wanted to, he could not stop. It was as though he held a high-powered line in his naked hand. His nerves tightened. As the wheel increased its speed it seemed to draw him more and more into its power, as though it held his fate; and with it came a deep need to submit, to whirl, to lose himself in its swirl of color. He could not stop it now. So let it be.

The button rested snugly in his palm where the man had placed it. And now he became aware of the man beside him, advising him through the microphone, while behind the shadowy audience hummed with noisy voices. He shifted his feet. There was still that feeling of helplessness within him, making part of him desire to turn back, even now that the jackpot was right in his hand. He squeezed the button until his fist ached. Then, like the sudden shriek of a subway whistle, a doubt tore through his head. Suppose he did not spin the wheel long enough? What could he do, and how could he tell? And then he knew, even as he wondered, that as long as he pressed the button, he could control the jackpot. He and only he could determine whether or not it was to be his. Not even the man with the microphone could do anything about it now. He felt drunk. Then, as though he had come down from a high hill into a valley of people, he heard the audience yelling.

"Come down from there, you jerk!"

"Let somebody else have a chance . . ."

"Ole Jack thinks he done found the end of the rainbow . . ."

The last voice was not unfriendly, and he turned and smiled dreamily into the yelling mouths. Then he turned his back squarely on them.

"Don't take too long, boy," a voice said.

He nodded. They were yelling behind him. Those folks did not understand what had happened to him. They had been playing the bingo game day in and night out for years, trying to win rent money or hamburger change. But not one of those wise guys had discovered this wonderful thing. He watched the wheel whirling past the numbers and experienced a burst of exaltation: This is God! This is the really truly God! He said it aloud, "This is God!"

He said it with such absolute conviction that he feared he would fall fainting into the footlights. But the crowd yelled so loud that they could not hear. Those fools, he thought. I'm here trying to tell them the most wonderful secret in the world, and they're yelling like they gone crazy. A hand fell upon his shoulder.

"You'll have to make a choice now, boy. You've taken too long."

He brushed the hand violently away.

"Leave me alone, man. I know what I'm doing!"

The man looked surprised and held on to the microphone for support. And because he did not wish to hurt the man's feelings he smiled, realizing with a sudden pang that there was no way of explaining to the man just why he had to stand there pressing the button forever.

"Come here," he called tiredly.

The man approached, rolling the heavy microphone across the stage.

"Anybody can play this bingo game, right?" he said.

"Sure, but . . ."

He smiled, feeling inclined to be patient with this slick looking white man with his blue shirt and his sharp gabardine suit.

"That's what I thought," he said. "Anybody can win the jackpot as long as they get the lucky number, right?"

"That's the rule, but after all . . ."

"That's what I thought," he said. "And the big prize goes to the man who knows how to win it?"

The man nodded speechlessly.

"Well then, go on over there and watch me win like I want to. I ain't going to hurt nobody," he said, "and I'll show you how to win. I mean to show the whole world how it's got to be done."

And because he understood, he smiled again to let the man know that he held nothing against him for being white and impatient. Then he refused to see the man any longer and stood pressing the button, the voices of the crowd reaching him like sounds in distant streets. Let them yell. All the Negroes down there were just ashamed because he was black like them. He smiled inwardly, knowing how it was. Most of the time he was ashamed of what Negroes did himself. Well, let them be ashamed for something this time. Like him. He was like a long thin black wire that was being stretched and wound upon the bingo wheel; wound until he wanted to scream; wound, but this time himself controlling the winding and the sadness and the shame, and because he did, Laura would be all right. Suddenly the lights flickered. He staggered backwards. Had something gone wrong? All this noise. Didn't they know that although he controlled the wheel, it also controlled him, and unless he pressed the button forever and forever and ever it would stop, leaving him high and dry, dry and high on this hard high slippery hill and Laura dead? There was only one chance; he had to do whatever the wheel demanded. And gripping the button in despair, he discovered with surprise that it imparted a nervous energy. His spine tingled. He felt a certain power.

Now he faced the raging crowd with defiance, its screams penetrating his ear-drums like trumpets shrieking from a juke-box. The vague faces glowing in the bingo lights gave him a sense of himself that he had never known before. He was running the show, by God! They had to react to him, for he was their luck. This is me, he thought. Let the bastards yell. Then someone was laughing inside him, and he realized that somehow he had forgotten his own name. It was a sad, lost feeling to lose your name, and a crazy thing to do. That name had been given him by the white man who had owned his grandfather a long lost time ago down South. But maybe those wise guys knew his name.

"Who am I?" he screamed.

"Hurry up and bingo, you jerk!"

They didn't know either, he thought sadly. They didn't even know their own names, they were all poor nameless bastards. Well, he didn't need that old name; he was reborn. For as long as he pressed the button he was The-man-who-pressed-the-button-who-held-the-prize-who-was-the-King-of-Bingo. That was the way it was, and he'd have to press the button even if nobody understood, even though Laura did not understand.

"Live!" he shouted.

The audience quieted like the dying of a huge fan.

"Live, Laura, baby. I got holt of it now, sugar. Live!"

He screamed it, tears streaming down his face. "I got nobody but YOU!"

The screams tore from his very guts. He felt as though the rush of blood to his head would burst out in baseball seams of small red droplets, like a head beaten by police clubs. Bending over he saw a trickle of blood splashing the toe of his shoe. With his free hand he searched his head. It was his nose. God, suppose something has gone wrong? He felt that the whole audience had somehow en-tered him and was stamping its feet in his stomach and he was unable to throw them out. They wanted the prize, that was it. They wanted the secret for them-selves. But they'd never get it; he would keep the bingo wheel whirling forever, and Laura would be safe in the wheel. But would she? It had to be, because if she were not safe the wheel would cease to turn; it could not go on. He had to get away, *vomit* all, and his mind formed an image of himself running with Laura in his arms down the tracks of the subway just ahead of an A train, running desper-ately *vomit* with people screaming for him to come out but knowing no way of leaving the tracks because to stop would bring the train crushing down upon him and to attempt to leave across the other tracks would mean to run into a hot third rail as high as his waist which threw blue sparks that blinded his eyes until he could hardly see.

He heard singing and the audience was clapping its hands.

> Shoot the liquor to him, Jim, boy!
> Clap-clap-clap
> Well a-calla the cop
> He's blowing his top!
> Shoot the liquor to him, Jim, boy!

Bitter anger grew within him at the singing. They think I'm crazy. Well let 'em laugh. I'll do what I got to do.

He was standing in an attitude of intense listening when he saw that they were watching something on the stage behind him. He felt weak. But when he turned he saw no one. If only his thumb did not ache so. Now they were applauding. And for a moment he thought that the wheel had stopped. But that was impossible, his thumb still pressed the button. Then he saw them. Two men in uniform beckoned from the end of the stage. They were coming toward him, walking in step, slowly, like a tap-dance team returning for a third encore. But their shoulders shot forward, and he backed away, looking wildly about. There was nothing to fight them with. He had only the long black cord which led to a plug somewhere back stage, and he couldn't use that because it operated the bingo wheel. He backed slowly, fixing the men with his eyes as his lips stretched over his teeth in a tight, fixed grin; moved toward the end of the stage and realizing that he couldn't go much further, for suddenly the cord became taut and he couldn't afford to break the cord. But he had to do something. The audience was howling. Suddenly he stopped dead, seeing the men halt, their legs lifted as in an interrupted step of a slow-motion dance. There was nothing to do but run in the other direction and he dashed forward, slipping and sliding. The men fell back, surprised. He struck out violently going past.

"Grab him!"

He ran, but all too quickly the cord tightened, resistingly, and he turned and ran back again. This time he slipped them, and discovered by running in a circle before the wheel he could keep the cord from tightening. But this way he had to flail his arms to keep the men away. Why couldn't they leave a man alone? He ran, circling.

"Ring down the curtain," someone yelled. But they couldn't do that. If they did the wheel flashing from the projection room would be cut off. But they had him before he could tell them so, trying to pry open his fist, and he was wrestling and trying to bring his knees into the fight and holding on to the button, for it was his life. And now he was down, seeing a foot coming down, crushing his wrist cruelly, down, as he saw the wheel whirling serenely above.

"I can't give it up," he screamed. Then quietly, in a confidential tone, "Boys, I really can't give it up."

It landed hard against his head. And in the blank moment they had it away from him, completely now. He fought them trying to pull him up from the stage as he watched the wheel spin slowly to a stop. Without surprise he saw it rest at double zero.

"You see," he pointed bitterly.

"Sure, boy, sure, it's O. K.," one of the men said, smiling.

And seeing the man bow his head to someone he could not see, he felt very, very happy; he would receive what all the winners received.

But as he warmed in the justice of the man's tight smile he did not see the man's slow wink, nor see the bow-legged man behind him step clear of the swiftly descending curtain and set himself for a blow. He only felt the dull pain exploding in his skull, and he knew even as it slipped out of him that his luck had run out on the stage.

[1944]

Shirley Jackson   *1919–1965*

THE LOTTERY

The morning of June 27th was clear and sunny, with the fresh warmth of a full-summer day; the flowers were blossoming profusely and the grass was richly green. The people of the village began to gather in the square, between the post office and the bank, around ten o'clock; in some towns there were so many people that the lottery took two days and had to be started on June 26th, but in this village, where there were only about three hundred people, the whole lottery took less than two hours, so it could begin at ten o'clock in the morning and still be through in time to allow the villagers to get home for noon dinner.

The children assembled first, of course. School was recently over for the summer, and the feeling of liberty sat uneasily on most of them; they tended to gather together quietly for a while before they broke into boisterous play, and their talk was still of the classroom and the teacher, of books and reprimands. Bobby Martin had already stuffed his pockets full of stones, and the other boys soon followed his example, selecting the smoothest and roundest stones; Bobby and Harry Jones and Dickie Delacroix—the villagers pronounced this name "Delacroy"—eventually made a great pile of stones in one corner of the square and guarded it against the raids of the other boys. The girls stood aside, talking among themselves, looking over their shoulders at the boys, and the very small children rolled in the dust or clung to the hands of their older brothers or sisters.

Soon the men began to gather, surveying their own children, speaking of planting and rain, tractors and taxes. They stood together, away from the pile of stones in the corner, and their jokes were quiet and they smiled rather than laughed. The women, wearing faded house dresses and sweaters, came shortly after their menfolk. They greeted one another and exchanged bits of gossip as they went to join their husbands. Soon the women, standing by their husbands, began to call to their children, and the children came reluctantly, having to be called four or five times. Bobby Martin ducked under his mother's grasping hand and ran, laughing, back to the pile of stones. His father spoke up sharply, and Bobby came quickly and took his place between his father and his oldest brother.

The lottery was conducted—as were the square dances, the teen-age club, the Halloween program—by Mr. Summers, who had time and energy to devote to civic activities. He was a round-faced, jovial man and he ran the coal business, and people were sorry for him, because he had no children and his wife was a scold. When he arrived in the square, carrying the black wooden box, there was a murmur of conversation among the villagers, and he waved and called, "Little late today, folks." The postmaster, Mr. Graves, followed him, carrying a three-legged stool, and the stool was put in the center of the square and Mr. Summers set the black box down on it. The villagers kept their distance, leaving a space between themselves and the stool, and when Mr. Summers said, "Some of you fellows want to give me a hand?" there was a hesitation before two men, Mr. Martin and his oldest son, Baxter, came forward to hold the box steady on the stool while Mr. Summers stirred up the papers inside it.

The original paraphernalia for the lottery had been lost long ago, and the black box now resting on the stool had been put into use even before Old Man Warner, the oldest man in town, was born. Mr. Summers spoke frequently to the villagers about making a new box, but no one liked to upset even as much tradition as was represented by the black box. There was a story that the present box had been made with some pieces of the box that had preceded it, the one that had been constructed when the first people settled down to make a village here. Every year, after the lottery, Mr. Summers began talking again about a new box, but every year the subject was allowed to fade off without anything's being done. The black box grew shabbier each year; by now it was no longer completely black but splintered badly along one side to show the original wood color, and in some places faded or stained.

Mr. Martin and his oldest son, Baxter, held the black box securely on the stool until Mr. Summers had stirred the papers thoroughly with his hand. Because so much of the ritual had been forgotten or discarded, Mr. Summers had been successful in having slips of paper substituted for the chips of wood that had been used for generations. Chips of wood, Mr. Summers had argued, had been all very well when the village was tiny, but now that the population was more than three hundred and likely to keep on growing, it was necessary to use something that would fit more easily into the black box. The night before the lottery, Mr. Summers and Mr. Graves made up the slips of paper and put them in the box, and it was then taken to the safe of Mr. Summers' coal company and locked up until Mr. Summers was ready to take it to the square next morning. The rest of the year, the box was put away, sometimes one place, sometimes another; it had spent one year in Mr. Graves's barn and another year underfoot in the post office, and sometimes it was set on a shelf in the Martin grocery and left there.

There was a great deal of fussing to be done before Mr. Summers declared the lottery open. There were the lists to make up—of heads of families, heads of households in each family, members of each household in each family. There was the proper swearing-in of Mr. Summers by the postmaster, as the official of the lottery; at one time, some people remembered, there had been a recital of some sort, performed by the official of the lottery, a perfunctory, tuneless chant that had been rattled off duly each year; some people believed that the official of the lottery used to stand just so when he said or sang it, others believed that he was supposed to walk among the people, but years and years ago this part of the ritual had been allowed to lapse. There had been, also, a ritual salute, which the official of the lottery had had to use in addressing each person who came up to draw from the box, but this also had changed with time, until now it was felt necessary only for the official to speak to each person approaching. Mr. Summers was very good at all this; in his clean white shirt and blue jeans, with one hand resting carelessly on the black box, he seemed very proper and important as he talked interminably to Mr. Graves and the Martins.

Just as Mr. Summers finally left off talking and turned to the assembled villagers, Mrs. Hutchinson came hurriedly along the path to the square, her sweater thrown over her shoulders, and slid into place in the back of the crowd. "Clean forgot what day it was," she said to Mrs. Delacroix, who stood next to her, and they both laughed softly. "Thought my old man was out back stacking wood," Mrs. Hutchinson went on, "and then I looked out the window and the kids was gone, and then I remembered it was the twenty-seventh and came a-running." She dried her hands on her apron, and Mrs. Delacroix said, "You're in time, though. They're still talking away up there."

Mrs. Hutchinson craned her neck to see through the crowd and found her husband and children standing near the front. She tapped Mrs. Delacroix on the arm as a farewell and began to make her way through the crowd. The people separated good-humoredly to let her through; two or three people said, in voices just loud enough to be heard across the crowd, "Here comes your Missus, Hutchinson," and "Bill, she made it after all." Mrs. Hutchinson reached her husband, and Mr. Summers, who had been waiting, said cheerfully, "Thought we were going to have to get on without you, Tessie." Mrs. Hutchinson said, grinning, "Wouldn't have me leave m'dishes in the sink, now, would you, Joe?," and soft laughter ran through the crowd as the people stirred back into position after Mrs. Hutchinson's arrival.

"Well, now," Mr. Summers said soberly, "guess we better get started, get this over with, so's we can go back to work. Anybody ain't here?"

"Dunbar," several people said. "Dunbar, Dunbar."

Mr. Summers consulted his list. "Clyde Dunbar," he said. "That's right. He's broke his leg hasn't he? Who's drawing for him?"

"Me, I guess," a woman said, and Mr. Summers turned to look at her. "Wife draws for her husband," Mr. Summers said. "Don't you have a grown boy to do it for you, Janey?" Although Mr. Summers and everyone else in the village knew the answer perfectly well, it was the business of the official of the lottery to ask such questions formally. Mr. Summers waited with an expression of polite interest while Mrs. Dunbar answered.

"Horace's not but sixteen yet," Mrs. Dunbar said regretfully. "Guess I gotta fill in for the old man this year."

"Right," Mr. Summers said. He made a note on the list he was holding. Then he asked, "Watson boy drawing this year?"

A tall boy in the crowd raised his hand. "Here," he said. "I'm drawing for m'mother and me." He blinked his eyes nervously and ducked his head as several voices in the crowd said things like "Good fellow, Jack," and "Glad to see your mother's got a man to do it."

"Well," Mr. Summers said, "guess that's everyone. Old Man Warner make it?"

"Here," a voice said, and Mr. Summers nodded.

A sudden hush fell on the crowd as Mr. Summers cleared his throat and looked at the list. "All ready?" he called. "Now, I'll read the names—heads of families first—and the men come up and take a paper out of the box. Keep the paper folded in your hand without looking at it until everyone has had a turn. Everything clear?"

The people had done it so many times that they only half listened to the directions; most of them were quiet, wetting their lips, not looking around. Then Mr. Summers raised one hand high and said, "Adams." A man disengaged himself from the crowd and came forward. "Hi, Steve," Mr. Summers said, and Mr. Adams said, "Hi, Joe." They grinned at one another humorlessly and nervously. Then Mr. Adams reached into the black box and took out a folded paper. He held it firmly by one corner as he turned and went hastily back to his place in the crowd, where he stood a little apart from his family, not looking down at his hand.

"Allen," Mr. Summers said. "Anderson. . . . Bentham."

"Seems like there's no time at all between lotteries any more," Mrs. Delacroix said to Mrs. Graves in the back row. "Seems like we got through with the last one only last week."

"Time sure goes fast," Mrs. Graves said.

"Clark. . . . Delacroix."

"There goes my old man," Mrs. Delacroix said. She held her breath while her husband went forward.

"Dunbar," Mr. Summers said, and Mrs. Dunbar went steadily to the box while one of the women said, "Go on, Janey," and another said, "There she goes."

"We're next," Mrs. Graves said. She watched while Mr. Graves came around from the side of the box, greeted Mr. Summers gravely, and selected a slip of paper from the box. By now, all through the crowd there were men holding the small folded papers in their large hands, turning them over and over nervously. Mrs. Dunbar and her two sons stood together, Mrs. Dunbar holding the slip of paper.

"Harburt. . . . Hutchinson."

"Get up, there, Bill," Mrs. Hutchinson said, and the people near her laughed.

"Jones."

"They do say," Mr. Adams said to Old Man Warner, who stood next to him, "that over in the north village they're talking of giving up the lottery."

Old Man Warner snorted. "Pack of crazy fools," he said. "Listening to the young folks, nothing's good enough for *them*. Next thing you know, they'll be wanting to go back to living in caves, nobody work any more, live *that* way for a while. Used to be a saying about 'Lottery in June, Corn be heavy soon.' First thing you know, we'd all be eating stewed chickweed and acorns. There's *always* been a lottery," he added petulantly. "Bad enough to see young Joe Summers up there joking with everybody."

"Some places have already quit lotteries," Mrs. Adams said.

"Nothing but trouble in *that*," Old Man Warner said stoutly. "Pack of young fools."

"Martin." And Bobby Martin watched his father go forward. "Overdyke. . . . Percy."

"I wish they'd hurry," Mrs. Dunbar said to her older son. "I wish they'd hurry."

"They're almost through," her son said.

"You get ready to run tell Dad," Mrs. Dunbar said.

Mr. Summers called his own name and then stepped forward precisely and selected a slip from the box. Then he called, "Warner."

"Seventy-seventh year I been in the lottery," Old Man Warner said as he went through the crowd. "Seventy-seventh time."

"Watson." The tall boy came awkwardly through the crowd. Someone said, "Don't be nervous, Jack," and Mr. Summers said, "Take your time, son."

"Zanini."

After that, there was a long pause, a breathless pause, until Mr. Summers, holding his slip of paper in the air, said, "All right, fellows." For a minute, no one moved, and then all the slips of paper were opened. Suddenly, all the women began to speak at once, saying, "Who is it?," "Who's got it?," "Is it the Dunbars?," "Is it the Watsons?" Then the voices began to say, "It's Hutchinson. It's Bill," "Bill Hutchinson's got it."

"Go tell your father," Mrs. Dunbar said to her older son.

People began to look around to see the Hutchinsons. Bill Hutchinson was standing quiet, staring down at the paper in his hand. Suddenly, Tessie Hutchinson shouted to Mr. Summers, "You didn't give him time enough to take any paper he wanted. I saw you. It wasn't fair!"

"Be a good sport, Tessie," Mrs. Delacroix called, and Mrs. Graves said, "All of us took the same chance."

"Shut up, Tessie," Bill Hutchinson said.

"Well, everyone," Mr. Summers said, "that was done pretty fast, and now we've got to be hurrying a little more to get done in time." He consulted his next list.

"Bill," he said, "you draw for the Hutchinson family. You got any other house-holds in the Hutchinsons?"

"There's Don and Eva," Mrs. Hutchinson yelled. "Make *them* take their chance!"

"Daughters draw with their husbands' families, Tessie," Mr. Summers said gently. "You know that as well as anyone else."

"It wasn't *fair*," Tessie said.

"I guess not, Joe," Bill Hutchinson said regretfully. "My daughter draws with her husband's family, that's only fair. And I've got no other family except the kids."

"Then, as far as drawing for families is concerned, it's you," Mr. Summers said in explanation, "and as far as drawing for households is concerned, that's you, too. Right?"

"Right," Bill Hutchinson said.

"How many kids, Bill?" Mr. Summers asked formally.

"Three," Bill Hutchinson said. "There's Bill, Jr., and Nancy, and little Dave. And Tessie and me."

"All right, then," Mr. Summers said. "Harry, you got their tickets back?"

Mr. Graves nodded and held up the slips of paper. "Put them in the box, then," Mr. Summers directed. "Take Bill's and put it in."

"I think we ought to start over," Mrs. Hutchinson said, as quietly as she could. "I tell you it wasn't *fair*. You didn't give him time enough to choose. *Every*body saw that."

Mr. Graves had selected the five slips and put them in the box, and he dropped all the papers but those onto the ground, where the breeze caught them and lifted them off.

"Listen, everybody," Mrs. Hutchinson was saying to the people around her.

"Ready, Bill?" Mr. Summers asked, and Bill Hutchinson, with one quick glance around at his wife and children, nodded.

"Remember," Mr. Summers said, "take the slips and keep them folded until each person has taken one. Harry, you help little Dave." Mr. Graves took the hand of the little boy, who came willingly with him up to the box. "Take a paper out of the box, Davy," Mr. Summers said. Davy put his hand into the box and laughed. "Take just *one* paper," Mr. Summers said. "Harry, you hold it for him." Mr. Graves took the child's hand and removed the folded paper from the tight fist and held it while little Dave stood next to him and looked up at him wonderingly.

"Nancy next," Mr. Summers said. Nancy was twelve, and her school friends breathed heavily as she went forward, switching her skirt, and took a slip daintily from the box. "Bill, Jr.," Mr. Summers said, and Billy, his face red and his feet overlarge, nearly knocked the box over as he got a paper out. "Tessie," Mr. Summers said. She hesitated for a minute, looking around defiantly, and then set her lips and went up to the box. She snatched a paper out and held it behind her.

"Bill," Mr. Summers said, and Bill Hutchinson reached into the box and felt around, bringing his hand out at last with the slip of paper in it.

The crowd was quiet. A girl whispered, "I hope it's not Nancy," and the sound of the whisper reached the edges of the crowd.

"It's not the way it used to be," Old Man Warner said clearly. "People ain't the way they used to be."

"All right," Mr. Summers said. "Open the papers. Harry, you open little Dave's."

Mr. Graves opened the slip of paper and there was a general sigh through the crowd as he held it up and everyone could see that it was blank. Nancy and Bill, Jr., opened theirs at the same time, and both beamed and laughed, turning around to the crowd and holding their slips of paper above their heads.

"Tessie," Mr. Summers said. There was a pause, and then Mr. Summers looked at Bill Hutchinson, and Bill unfolded his paper and showed it. It was blank.

"It's Tessie," Mr. Summers said, and his voice was hushed. "Show us her paper, Bill."

Bill Hutchinson went over to his wife and forced the slip of paper out of her hand. It had a black spot on it, the black spot Mr. Summers had made the night before with the heavy pencil in the coal-company office. Bill Hutchinson held it up, and there was a stir in the crowd.

"All right, folks," Mr. Summers said. "Let's finish quickly."

Although the villagers had forgotten the ritual and lost the original black box, they still remembered to use stones. The pile of stones the boys had made earlier was ready; there were stones on the ground with the blowing scraps of paper that had come out of the box. Mrs. Delacroix selected a stone so large she had to pick it up with both hands and turned to Mrs. Dunbar. "Come on," she said. "Hurry up."

Mrs. Dunbar had small stones in both hands, and she said, gasping for breath, "I can't run at all. You'll have to go ahead and I'll catch up with you."

The children had stones already, and someone gave little Davy Hutchinson a few pebbles.

Tessie Hutchinson was in the center of a cleared space by now, and she held her hands out desperately as the villagers moved in on her. "It isn't fair," she said. A stone hit her on the side of the head.

Old Man Warner was saying, "Come on, come on, everyone." Steve Adams was in the front of the crowd of villagers, with Mrs. Graves beside him.

"It isn't fair, it isn't right," Mrs. Hutchinson screamed, and then they were upon her.

[1948]

Flannery O'Connor   *1925–1964*

A GOOD MAN IS HARD TO FIND

The grandmother didn't want to go to Florida. She wanted to visit some of her connnections in east Tennessee and she was seizing at every chance to change Bailey's mind. Bailey was the son she lived with, her only boy. He was sitting on the edge of his chair at the table, bent over the orange sports section of the *Journal*. "Now look here, Bailey," she said, "see here, read this," and she stood with one hand on her thin hip and the other rattling the newspaper at his bald head. "Here this fellow that calls himself The Misfit is aloose from the Federal Pen and headed toward Florida and you read here what it says he did to these people. Just you read it. I wouldn't take my children in any direction with a criminal like that aloose in it. I couldn't answer to my conscience if I did."

Bailey didn't look up from his reading so she wheeled around then and faced the children's mother, a young woman in slacks, whose face was as broad and innocent as a cabbage and was tied around with a green head-kerchief that had two points on the top like rabbit's ears. She was sitting on the sofa, feeding the baby his apricots out of a jar. "The children have been to Florida before," the old lady said. "You all ought to take them somewhere else for a change so they would see different parts of the world and be broad. They never have been to east Tennessee."

The children's mother didn't seem to hear her but the eight-year-old boy, John Wesley, a stocky child with glasses, said, "If you don't want to go to Florida, why dontcha stay at home?" He and the little girl, June Star, were reading the funny papers on the floor.

"She wouldn't stay at home to be queen for a day," June Star said without raising her yellow head.

"Yes and what would you do if this fellow, The Misfit, caught you?" the grandmother asked.

"I'd smack his face," John Wesley said.

"She wouldn't stay at home for a million bucks," June Star said. "Afraid she'd miss something. She has to go everywhere we go."

"All right, Miss," the grandmother said. "Just remember that the next time you want me to curl your hair."

June Star said her hair was naturally curly.

The next morning the grandmother was the first one in the car, ready to go. She had her big black valise that looked like the head of a hippopotamus in one corner, and underneath it she was hiding a basket with Pitty Sing,[1] the cat, in it. She didn't intend for the cat to be left alone in the house for three days because he would miss her too much and she was afraid he might brush against one of the gas burners and accidentally asphyxiate himself. Her son, Bailey, didn't like to arrive at a motel with a cat.

She sat in the middle of the back seat with John Wesley and June Star on either side of her. Bailey and the children's mother and the baby sat in front and they left Atlanta at eight forty-five with the mileage on the car at 55890. The grandmother wrote this down because she thought it would be interesting to say how

---

[1] The name of one of the "three little maids from school" in Gilbert and Sullivan's operetta *The Mikado* (1885).

many miles they had been when they got back. It took them twenty minutes to reach the outskirts of the city.

The old lady settled herself comfortably, removing her white cotton gloves and putting them up with her purse on the shelf in front of the back window. The children's mother still had on slacks and still had her head tied up in a green kerchief, but the grandmother had on a navy blue straw sailor hat with a bunch of white violets on the brim and a navy blue dress with a small white dot in the print. Her collars and cuffs were white organdy trimmed with lace and at her neckline she had pinned a purple spray of cloth violets containing a sachet. In case of an accident, anyone seeing her dead on the highway would know at once that she was a lady.

She said she thought it was going to be a good day for driving, neither too hot nor too cold, and she cautioned Bailey that the speed limit was fifty-five miles an hour and that the patrolmen hid themselves behind billboards and small clumps of trees and sped out after you before you had a chance to slow down. She pointed out interesting details of the scenery: Stone Mountain;[2] the blue granite that in some places came up to both sides of the highway; the brilliant red clay banks slightly streaked with purple; and the various crops that made rows of green lace-work on the ground. The trees were full of silver-white sunlight and the meanest of them sparkled. The children were reading comic magazines and their mother had gone back to sleep.

"Let's go through Georgia fast so we won't have to look at it much," John Wesley said.

"If I were a little boy," said the grandmother, "I wouldn't talk about my native state that way. Tennessee has the mountains and Georgia has the hills."

"Tennessee is just a hillbilly dumping ground," John Wesley said, "and Georgia is a lousy state too."

"You said it," June Star said.

"In my time," said the grandmother, folding her thin veined fingers, "children were more respectful of their native states and their parents and everything else. People did right then. Oh look at the cute little pickaninny!" she said and pointed to a Negro child standing in the door of a shack. "Wouldn't that make a picture, now?" she asked and they all turned and looked at the little Negro out of the back window. He waved.

"He didn't have any britches on," June Star said.

"He probably didn't have any," the grandmother explained. "Little niggers in the country don't have things like we do. If I could paint, I'd paint that picture," she said.

The children exchanged comic books.

The grandmother offered to hold the baby and the children's mother passed him over the front seat to her. She set him on her knee and bounced him and told him about the things they were passing. She rolled her eyes and screwed up her mouth and stuck her leathery thin face into his smooth bland one. Occasionally he gave her a faraway smile. They passed a large cotton field with five or six graves fenced in the middle of it, like a small island. "Look at the graveyard!" the grandmother said, pointing it out. "That was the old family burying ground. That belonged to the plantation."

---

[2] Stone Mountain, Georgia, some sixteen miles east of Atlanta, at over 700 feet is the largest stone mountain in North America. Sculpted into its side are the figures of Civil War heroes Jefferson Davis, Robert E. Lee, and Stonewall Jackson, further making Stone Mountain a tourist attraction.

"Where's the plantation?" John Wesley asked.

"Gone With the Wind,"[3] said the grandmother. "Ha. Ha."

When the children finished all the comic books they had brought, they opened the lunch and ate it. The grandmother ate a peanut butter sandwich and an olive and would not let the children throw the box and the paper napkins out the window. When there was nothing else to do they played a game by choosing a cloud and making the other two guess what shape it suggested. John Wesley took one the shape of a cow and June Star guessed a cow and John Wesley said, no, an automobile, and June Star said he didn't play fair, and they began to slap each other over the grandmother.

The grandmother said she would tell them a story if they would keep quiet. When she told a story, she rolled her eyes and waved her head and was very dramatic. She said once when she was a maiden lady she had been courted by a Mr. Edgar Atkins Teagarden from Jasper, Georgia. She said he was a very good-looking man and a gentleman and that he brought her a watermelon every Saturday afternoon with his initials cut in it, E. A. T. Well, one Saturday, she said, Mr. Teagarden brought the watermelon and there was nobody at home and he left it on the front porch and returned in his buggy to Jasper, but she never got the watermelon, she said, because a nigger boy ate it when he saw the initials, E. A. T.! This story tickled John Wesley's funny bone and he giggled and giggled but June Star didn't think it was any good. She said she wouldn't marry a man that just brought her a watermelon on Saturday. The grandmother said she would have done well to marry Mr. Teagarden because he was a gentleman and had bought Coca-Cola stock when it first came out and that he had died only a few years ago, a very wealthy man.

They stopped at The Tower for barbecued sandwiches. The Tower was a part stucco and part wood filling station and dance hall set in a clearing outside of Timothy. A fat man named Red Sammy Butts ran it and there were signs stuck here and there on the building and for miles up and down the highway saying, TRY RED SAMMY'S FAMOUS BARBECUE. NONE LIKE FAMOUS RED SAMMY'S! RED SAM! THE FAT BOY WITH THE HAPPY LAUGH, A VETERAN! RED SAMMY'S YOUR MAN!

Red Sammy was lying on the bare ground outside The Tower with his head under a truck while a gray monkey about a foot high, chained to a small china-berry tree, chattered nearby. The monkey sprang back into the tree and got on the highest limb as soon as he saw the children jump out of the car and run toward him.

Inside, The Tower was a long dark room with a counter at one end and tables at the other and dancing space in the middle. They all sat down at a board table next to the nickelodeon[4] and Red Sam's wife, a tall burnt-brown woman with hair and eyes lighter than her skin, came and took their order. The children's mother put a dime in the machine and played "The Tennessee Waltz," and the grandmother said that tune always made her want to dance. She asked Bailey if he would like to dance but he only glared at her. He didn't have a naturally sunny disposition like she did and trips made him nervous. The grandmother's brown eyes were very bright. She swayed her head from side to side and pretended she was dancing in her chair. June Star said play something she could tap to so the

---

[3] *Gone With the Wind,* Margaret Mitchell's novel of 1936 about the Civil War South, made into the now-classic motion picture of 1939 starring Clark Gable and Vivien Leigh.

[4] Juke box.

children's mother put in another dime and played a fast number and June Star stepped out onto the dance floor and did her tap routine.

"Ain't she cute?" Red Sam's wife said, leaning over the counter. "Would you like to come be my little girl?"

"No I certainly wouldn't," June Star said. "I wouldn't live in a broken-down place like this for a million bucks!" and she ran back to the table.

"Ain't she cute?" the woman repeated, stretching her mouth politely.

"Arn't you ashamed?" hissed the grandmother.

Red Sam came in and told his wife to quit lounging on the counter and hurry up with these people's order. His khaki trousers reached just to his hip bones and his stomach hung over them like a sack of meal swaying under his shirt. He came over and sat down at a table nearby and let out a combination sigh and yodel. "You can't win," he said. "You can't win," and he wiped his sweating red face off with a gray handkerchief. "These days you don't know who to trust," he said. "Ain't that the truth?"

"People are certainly not nice like they used to be," said the grandmother.

"Two fellers come in here last week," Red Sammy said, "driving a Chrysler. It was a old beat-up car but it was a good one and these boys looked all right to me. Said they worked at the mill and you know I let them fellers charge the gas they bought? Now why did I do that?"

"Because you're a good man!" the grandmother said at once.

"Yes'm, I suppose so," Red Sam said as if he were struck with this answer.

His wife brought the orders, carrying the five plates all at once without a tray, two in each hand and one balanced on her arm. "It isn't a soul in this green world of God's that you can trust," she said. "And I don't count nobody out of that, not nobody," she repeated, looking at Red Sammy.

"Did you read about that criminal, The Misfit, that's escaped?" asked the grandmother.

"I wouldn't be a bit surprised if he didn't attack this place right here," said the woman. "If he hears about it being here, I wouldn't be none surprised to see him. If he hears it's two cent in the cash register, I wouldn't be a tall surprised if he . . ."

"That'll do," Red Sam said. "Go bring these people their Co'-Colas," and the woman went off to get the rest of the order.

"A good man is hard to find," Red Sammy said. "Everything is getting terrible. I remember the day you could go off and leave your screen door unlatched. Not no more."

He and the grandmother discussed better times. The old lady said that in her opinion Europe was entirely to blame for the way things were now. She said the way Europe acted you would think we were made of money and Red Sam said it was no use talking about it, she was exactly right. The children ran outside into the white sunlight and looked at the monkey in the lacy chinaberry tree. He was busy catching fleas on himself and biting each one carefully between his teeth as if it were a delicacy.

They drove off again into the hot afternoon. The grandmother took cat naps and woke up every few minutes with her own snoring. Outside of Toomsboro[5] she woke up and recalled an old plantation that she had visited in this neighborhood once when she was a young lady. She said the house had six white columns across the front and that there was an avenue of oaks leading up to it and two little

---

[5] Georgia town, southeast of Atlanta.

wooden trellis arbors on either side in front where you sat down with your suitor after a stroll in the garden. She recalled exactly which road to turn off to get to it. She knew that Bailey would not be willing to lose any time looking at an old house, but the more she talked about it, the more she wanted to see it once again and find out if the little twin arbors were still standing. "There was a secret panel in this house," she said craftily, not telling the truth but wishing that she were, "and the story went that all the family silver was hidden in it when Sherman came through[6] but it was never found . . ."

"Hey!" John Wesley said. "Let's go see it! We'll find it! We'll poke all the woodwork and find it! Who lives there? Where do you turn off at? Hey Pop, can't we turn off there?"

"We never have seen a house with a secret panel!" June Star shrieked. "Let's go to the house with the secret panel! Hey Pop, can't we go see the house with the secret panel!"

"It's not far from here, I know," the grandmother said. "It wouldn't take over twenty minutes."

Bailey was looking straight ahead. His jaw was as rigid as a horsehoe. "No," he said.

The children began to yell and scream that they wanted to see the house with the secret panel. John Wesley kicked the back of the front seat and June Star hung over her mother's shoulder and whined desperately into her ear that they never had any fun even on their vacation, that they could never do what THEY wanted to do. The baby began to scream and John Wesley kicked the back of the seat so hard that his father could feel the blows in his kidney.

"All right!" he shouted and drew the car to a stop at the side of the road. "Will you all shut up? Will you all just shut up for one second? If you don't shut up, we won't go anywhere."

"It would be very educational for them," the grandmother murmured.

"All right," Bailey said, "but get this: this is the only time we're going to stop for anything like this. This is the one and only time."

"The dirt road that you have to turn down is about a mile back," the grand-mother directed. "I marked it when we passed."

"A dirt road," Bailey groaned.

After they had turned around and were headed toward the dirt road, the grandmother recalled other points about the house, the beautiful glass over the front doorway and the candle-lamp in the hall. John Wesley said that the secret panel was probably in the fireplace.

"You can't go inside this house," Bailey said. "You don't know who lives there."

"While you all talk to the people in front, I'll run around behind and get in a window," John Wesley suggested.

"We'll all stay in the car," his mother said.

They turned onto the dirt road and the car raced roughly along in a swirl of pink dust. The grandmother recalled the times when there were no paved roads and thirty miles was a day's journey. The dirt road was hilly and there were sudden washes in it and sharp curves on dangerous embankments. All at once they would

---

[6] A Union army led by General William Tecumseh Sherman (1820–1891) conducted its famous march through Georgia "from Atlanta to the sea" in November and December of 1864, creating widespread devastation in its path as it deliberately sought to destroy the economic underpinnings of a declining Confederacy.

be on a hill, looking down over the blue tops of trees for miles around, then the next minute, they would be in a red depression with the dust-coated trees looking down on them.

"This place had better turn up in a minute," Bailey said, "or I'm going to turn around."

The road looked as if no one had traveled on it in months.

"It's not much farther," the grandmother said and just as she said it, a horrible thought came to her. The thought was so embarrassing that she turned red in the face and her eyes dilated and her feet jumped up, upsetting her valise in the corner. The instant the valise moved, the newspaper top she had over the basket under it rose with a snarl and Pitty Sing, the cat, sprang onto Bailey's shoulder.

The children were thrown to the floor and their mother, clutching the baby, was thrown out the door onto the ground; the old lady was thrown into the front seat. The car turned over once and landed right-side-up in a gulch off the side of the road. Bailey remained in the driver's seat with the cat—gray-striped with a broad white face and an orange nose—clinging to his neck like a caterpillar.

As soon as the children saw they could move their arms and legs, they scrambled out of the car, shouting, "We've had an ACCIDENT!" The grandmother was curled up under the dashboard, hoping she was injured so that Bailey's wrath would not come down on her all at once. The horrible thought she had had before the accident was that the house she had remembered so vividly was not in Georgia but in Tennessee.

Bailey removed the cat from his neck with both hands and flung it out the window against the side of a pine tree. Then he got out of the car and started looking for the children's mother. She was sitting against the side of the red gutted ditch, holding the screaming baby, but she only had a cut down her face and a broken shoulder. "We've had an ACCIDENT!" the children screamed in a frenzy of delight.

"But nobody's killed," June Star said with disappointment as the grandmother limped out of the car, her hat still pinned to her head but the broken front brim standing up at a jaunty angle and the violet spray hanging off the side. They all sat down in the ditch, except the children, to recover from the shock. They were all shaking.

"Maybe a car will come along," said the children's mother hoarsely.

"I believe I have injured an organ," said the grandmother, pressing her side, but no one answered her. Bailey's teeth were clattering. He had on a yellow sport shirt with bright blue parrots designed in it and his face was as yellow as the shirt. The grandmother decided that she would not mention that the house was in Tennessee.

The road was about ten feet above and they could see only the tops of the trees on the other side of it. Behind the ditch they were sitting in there were more woods, tall and dark and deep. In a few minutes they saw a car some distance away on top of a hill, coming slowly as if the occupants were watching them. The grandmother stood up and waved both arms dramatically to attract their attention. The car continued to come on slowly, disappeared around a bend and appeared again, moving even slower, on top of the hill they had gone over. It was a big black battered hearse-like automobile. There were three men in it.

It came to a stop just over them and for some minutes, the driver looked down with a steady expressionless gaze to where they were sitting, and didn't speak. Then he turned his head and muttered something to the other two and they got out. One was a fat boy in black trousers and a red sweat shirt with a silver stallion embossed on the front of it. He moved around on the right side of them and stood staring, his mouth partly open in a kind of loose grin. The other had on khaki pants and a blue striped coat and a gray hat pulled down very low, hiding most of his face. He came around slowly on the left side. Neither spoke.

The driver got out of the car and stood by the side of it, looking down at them. He was an older man than the other two. His hair was just beginning to gray and he wore silver-rimmed spectacles that gave him a scholarly look. He had a long creased face and didn't have on any shirt or undershirt. He had on blue jeans that were too tight for him and was holding a black hat and a gun. The two boys also had guns.

"We've had an ACCIDENT!" the children screamed.

The grandmother had the peculiar feeling that the bespectacled man was some-one she knew. His face was as familiar to her as if she had known him all her life but she could not recall who he was. He moved away from the car and began to come down the embankment, placing his feet carefully so that he wouldn't slip. He had on tan and white shoes and no socks, and his ankles were red and thin. "Good afternoon," he said. "I see you all had you a little spill."

"We turned over twice!" said the grandmother.

"Oncet," he corrected. "We seen it happen. Try their car and see will it run, Hiram," he said quietly to the boy with the gray hat.

"What you got that gun for?" John Wesley asked. "Whatcha gonna do with that gun?"

"Lady," the man said to the children's mother, "would you mind calling them children to sit down by you? Children make me nervous. I want all you all to sit down right together there where you're at."

"What are you telling US what to do for?" June Star asked.

Behind them the line of woods gaped like a dark open mouth. "Come here," said their mother.

"Look here now," Bailey began suddenly, "we're in a predicament! We're in . . ."

The grandmother shrieked. She scrambled to her feet and stood staring. "You're The Misfit!" she said. "I recognized you at once!"

"Yes'm," the man said, smiling slightly as if he were pleased in spite of himself to be known, "but it would have been better for all of you, lady, if you hadn't of reckernized me."

Bailey turned his head sharply and said something to his mother that shocked even the children. The old lady began to cry and The Misfit reddened.

"Lady," he said, "don't you get upset. Sometimes a man says things he don't mean. I don't reckon he meant to talk to you thataway."

"You wouldn't shoot a lady, would you?" the grandmother said and removed a clean hankerchief from her cuff and began to slap at her eyes with it.

The Misfit pointed the toe of his shoe into the ground and made a little hole and then covered it up again. "I would hate to have to," he said.

"Listen," the grandmother almost screamed, "I know you're a good man. You don't look a bit like you have common blood. I know you must come from nice people!"

"Yes mam," he said, "finest people in the world." When he smiled he showed a row of strong white teeth. "God never made a finer woman than my mother and my daddy's heart was pure gold," he said. The boy with the red sweat shirt had come around behind them and was standing with his gun at his hip. The Misfit squatted down on the ground. "Watch them children, Bobby Lee," he said. "You know they make me nervous.'' He looked at the six of them huddled together in front of him and he seemed to be embarrassed as if he couldn't think of anything to say. "Ain't a cloud in the sky," he remarked, looking up at it. "Don't see no sun but don't see no cloud neither."

"Yes, it's a beautiful day," said the grandmother. "Listen," she said, "you shouldn't call yourself The Misfit because I know you're a good man at heart. I can just look at you and tell."

"Hush!" Bailey yelled. "Hush! Everybody shut up and let me handle this!" He was squatting in the position of a runner about to sprint forward but he didn't move.

"I pre-chate that, lady," The Misfit said and drew a little circle in the ground with the butt of his gun.

"It'll take a half a hour to fix this here car," Hiram called, looking over the raised hood of it.

"Well, first you and Bobby Lee get him and that little boy to step over yonder with you," The Misfit said, pointing to Bailey and John Wesley. "The boys want to ast you something," he said to Bailey. "Would you mind stepping back in them woods there with them?"

"Listen," Bailey began, "we're in a terrible predicament! Nobody realizes what this is," and his voice cracked. His eyes were as blue and intense as the parrots in his shirt and he remained perfectly still.

The grandmother reached up to adjust her hat brim as if she were going to the woods with him but it came off in her hand. She stood staring at it and after a second she let it fall on the ground. Hiram pulled Bailey up by the arm as if he were assisting an old man. John Wesley caught hold of his father's hand and Bobby Lee followed. They went off toward the woods and just as they reached the dark edge, Bailey turned and supporting himself against a gray naked pine trunk, he shouted, "I'll be back in a minute, Mamma, wait on me!"

"Come back this instant!" his mother shrilled but they all disappeared into the woods.

"Bailey Boy!" the grandmother called in a tragic voice but she found she was looking at The Misfit squatting on the ground in front of her. "I just know you're a good man," she said desperately. "You're not a bit common!"

"Nome, I ain't a good man," The Misfit said after a second, as if he had considered her statement carefully, "but I ain't the worst in the world neither. My daddy said I was a different breed of dog from my brothers and sisters. 'You know,' Daddy said, 'it's some that can live their whole life out without asking about it and it's others has to know why it is, and this boy is one of the latters. He's going to be into everything!' '' He put on his black hat and looked up suddenly and then away deep into the woods as if he were embarrassed again. "I'm sorry I don't have on a shirt before you ladies," he said, hunching his shoulders slightly. "We buried our clothes that we had on when we escaped and we're just making do until we can get better. We borrowed these from some folks we met," he explained.

"That's perfectly all right," the grandmother said. "Maybe Bailey has an extra shirt in his suitcase."

"I'll look and see terrectly," The Misfit said.

"Where are they taking him?" the children's mother screamed.

"Daddy was a card himself," The Misfit said. "You couldn't put anything over on him. He never got in trouble with the Authorities though. Just had the knack of handling them."

"You could be honest too if you'd only try," said the grandmother. "Think how wonderful it would be to settle down and live a comfortable life and not have to think about somebody chasing you all the time."

The Misfit kept scratching in the ground with the butt of his gun as if he were thinking about it. "Yes'm, somebody is always after you," he murmured.

The grandmother noticed how thin his shoulder blades were just behind his hat because she was standing up looking down on him. "Do you ever pray?" she asked.

He shook his head. All she saw was the black hat wiggle between his shoulder blades. "Nome," he said.

There was a pistol shot from the woods, followed closely by another. Then silence. The old lady's head jerked around. She could hear the wind move through the tree tops like a long satisfied insuck of breath. "Bailey Boy!" she called.

"I was a gospel singer for a while," The Misfit said. "I been most everything. Been in the arm service, both land and sea, at home and abroad, been twict married, been an undertaker, been with the railroads, plowed Mother Earth, been in a tornado, seen a man burnt alive oncet," and he looked up at the children's mother and the little girl who were sitting close together, their faces white and their eyes glassy; "I even seen a woman flogged," he said.

"Pray, pray," the grandmother began, "pray, pray . . ."

"I never was a bad boy that I remember of," The Misfit said in an almost dreamy voice, "but somewheres along the line I done something wrong and got sent to the penitentiary. I was buried alive," and he looked up and held her attention to him by a steady stare.

"That's when you should have started to pray," she said. "What did you do to get sent to the penitentiary that first time?"

"Turn to the right, it was a wall," The Misfit said, looking up again at the cloudless sky. "Turn to the left, it was a wall. Look up it was a ceiling, look down it was a floor. I forget what I done, lady. I set there and set there, trying to remember what it was I done and I ain't recalled it to this day. Oncet in a while, I would think it was coming to me, but it never come."

"Maybe they put you in by mistake," the old lady said vaguely.

"Nome," he said. "It wasn't no mistake. They had the papers on me."

"You must have stolen something," she said.

The Misfit sneered slightly. "Nobody had nothing I wanted," he said. "It was a head-doctor at the penitentiary said what I had done was kill my daddy but I known that for a lie. My daddy died in nineteen ought nineteen of the epidemic flu[7] and I never had a thing to do with it. He was buried in the Mount Hopewell Baptist churchyard and you can go there and see for yourself."

"If you would pray," the old lady said, "Jesus would help you."

"That's right," The Misfit said.

"Well then, why don't you pray?" she asked trembling with delight suddenly.

"I don't want no hep," he said. "I'm doing all right by myself."

Bobby Lee and Hiram came ambling back from the woods. Bobby Lee was dragging a yellow shirt with bright blue parrots in it.

"Thow me that shirt, Bobby Lee," The Misfit said. The shirt came flying at him and landed on his shoulder and he put it on. The grandmother couldn't name what the shirt reminded her of. "No, lady," The Misfit said while he was buttoning

[7] The global influenza epidemic of 1918–1919 took the lives of more than half a million Americans.

it up, "I found out the crime don't matter. You can do one thing or you can do another, kill a man or take a tire off his car, because sooner or later you're going to forget what it was you done and just be punished for it."

The children's mother had begun to make heaving noises as if she couldn't get her breath. "Lady," he asked, "would you and that little girl like to step off yonder with Bobby Lee and Hiram and join your husband?"

"Yes, thank you," the mother said faintly. Her left arm dangled helplessly and she was holding the baby, who had gone to sleep, in the other. "Hep that lady up, Hiram," The Misfit said as she struggled to climb out of the ditch, "and Bobby Lee, you hold onto that little girl's hand."

"I don't want to hold hands with him," June Star said. "He reminds me of a pig."

The fat boy blushed and laughed and caught her by the arm and pulled her off into the woods after Hiram and her mother.

Alone with The Misfit, the grandmother found that she had lost her voice. There was not a cloud in the sky nor any sun. There was nothing around her but woods. She wanted to tell him that he must pray. She opened and closed her mouth several times before anything came out. Finally she found herself saying, "Jesus. Jesus," meaning, Jesus will help you, but the way she was saying it, it sounded as if she might be cursing.

"Yes'm," The Misfit said as if he agreed. "Jesus thown everything off balance. It was the same case with Him as with me except He hadn't committed any crime and they could prove I had committed one because they had the papers on me. Of course," he said, "they never shown me my papers. That's why I sign myself now. I said long ago, you get you a signature and sign everything you do and keep a copy of it. Then you'll know what you done and you can hold up the crime to the punishment and see do they match and in the end you'll have something to prove you ain't been treated right. I call myself The Misfit," he said, "because I can't make what all I done wrong fit what all I gone through in punishment."

There was a piercing scream from the woods, followed closely by a pistol report. "Does it seem right to you, lady, that one is punished a heap and another ain't punished at all?"

"Jesus!" the old lady cried. "You've got good blood! I know you wouldn't shoot a lady! I know you come from nice people! Pray! Jesus, you ought not to shoot a lady. I'll give you all the money I've got!"

"Lady," The Misfit said, looking beyond her far into the woods, "there never was a body that give the undertaker a tip."

There were two more pistol reports and the grandmother raised her head like a parched old turkey hen crying for water and called, "Bailey Boy, Bailey Boy!" as if her heart would break.

"Jesus was the only One that ever raised the dead," The Misfit continued, "and He shouldn't have done it. He thown everything off balance. If He did what He said, then it's nothing for you to do but thow away everything and follow Him, and if He didn't then it's nothing for you to do but enjoy the few minutes you got left the best way you can—by killing somebody or burning down his house or doing some other meanness to him. No pleasure but meanness," he said and his voice had become almost a snarl.

"Maybe He didn't raise the dead," the old lady mumbled, not knowing what she was saying and feeling so dizzy that she sank down in the ditch with her legs twisted under her.

"I wasn't there so I can't say He didn't," The Misfit said. "I wisht I had of been there," he said, hitting the ground with his fist. "It ain't right I wasn't there because if I had of been there I would of known. Listen lady," he said in a high voice, "if I had of been there I would of known and I wouldn't be like I am now." His voice seemed about to crack and the grandmother's head cleared for an instant. She saw the man's face twisted close to her own as if he were going to cry and she murmured, "Why you're one of my babies. You're one of my own children!" She reached out and touched him on the shoulder. The Misfit sprang back as if a snake had bitten him and shot her three times through the chest. Then he put his gun down on the ground and took off his glasses and began to clean them.

Hiram and Bobby Lee returned from the woods and stood over the ditch, looking down at the grandmother who half sat and half lay in a puddle of blood with her legs crossed under her like a child's and her face smiling up at the cloudless sky.

Without his glasses, The Misfit's eyes were red-rimmed and pale and defenseless-looking. "Take her off and thow her where you thown the others," he said, picking up the cat that was rubbing itself against his leg.

"She was a talker, wasn't she?" Bobby Lee said, sliding down the ditch with a yodel.

"She would of been a good woman," The Misfit said, "if it had been somebody there to shoot her every minute of her life."

"Some fun!" Bobby Lee said.

"Shut up, Bobby Lee," The Misfit said. "It's no real pleasure in life."

[1953]

John Cheever   *1912–1982*

O YOUTH AND BEAUTY!

At the tag end of nearly every long, large Saturday-night party in the suburb of Shady Hill, when almost everybody who was going to play golf or tennis in the morning had gone home hours ago and the ten or twelve people remaining seemed powerless to bring the evening to an end although the gin and whiskey were running low, and here and there a woman who was sitting out her husband would have begun to drink milk; when everybody had lost track of time, and the baby-sitters who were waiting at home for these diehards would have long since stretched out on the sofa and fallen into a deep sleep, to dream about cooking-contest prizes, ocean voyages, and romance; when the bellicose drunk, the crap-shooter, the pianist, and the woman faced with the expiration of her hopes had all expressed themselves; when every proposal—to go to the Farquarsons' for breakfast, to go swimming, to go and wake up the Townsends, to go here and go there—died as soon as it was made, then Trace Bearden would begin to chide Cash Bentley about his age and thinning hair. The chiding was preliminary to moving the living-room furniture. Trace and Cash moved the tables and the chairs, the sofas and the fire screen, the woodbox and the footstool; and when they had finished, you wouldn't know the place. Then if the host had a revolver, he would be asked to produce it. Cash would take off his shoes and assume a starting crouch behind a sofa. Trace would fire the weapon out of an open window, and if you were new to the community and had not understood what the preparations were about, you would then realize that you were watching a hurdle race. Over the sofa went Cash, over the tables, over the fire screen and the woodbox. It was not exactly a race, since Cash ran it alone, but it was extraordinary to see this man of forty surmount so many obstacles so gracefully. There was not a piece of furniture in Shady Hill that Cash could not take in his stride. The race ended with cheers, and presently the party would break up.

Cash was, of course, an old track star, but he was never aggressive or tiresome about his brilliant past. The college where he had spent his youth had offered him a paying job on the alumni council, but he had refused it, realizing that that part of his life was ended. Cash and his wife, Louise, had two children, and they lived in a medium-cost ranch house on Alewives Lane. They belonged to the country club, although they could not afford it, but in the case of the Bentleys nobody ever pointed this out, and Cash was one of the best-liked men in Shady Hill. He was still slender—he was careful about his weight—and he walked to the train in the morning with a light and vigorous step that marked him as an athlete. His hair was thin, and there were mornings when his eyes looked bloodshot, but this did not detract much from a charming quality of stubborn youthfulness.

In business Cash had suffered reverses and disappointments, and the Bentleys had many money worries. They were always late with their tax payments and their mortgage payments, and the drawer of the hall table was stuffed with unpaid bills; it was always touch and go with the Bentleys and the bank. Louise looked pretty enough on Saturday night, but her life was exacting and monotonous. In the pockets of her suits, coats, and dresses there were little wads and scraps of paper on which was written: "Oleomargarine, frozen spinach, Kleenex, dog biscuit, hamburger, pepper, lard . . ." When she was still half awake in the morning, she was putting on the water for coffee and diluting the frozen orange juice. Then she

456

would be wanted by the children. She would crawl under the bureau on her hands and knees to find a sock for Toby. She would lie flat on her belly and wiggle under the bed (getting dust up her nose) to find a shoe for Rachel. Then there were the housework, the laundry, and the cooking, as well as the demands of the children. There always seemed to be shoes to put on and shoes to take off, snowsuits to be zipped and unzipped, bottoms to be wiped, tears to be dried, and when the sun went down (she saw it set from the kitchen window) there was the supper to be cooked, the baths, the bedtime story, and the Lord's Prayer. With the sonorous words of the Our Father in a darkened room the children's day was over, but the day was far from over for Louise Bentley. There were the darning, the mending, and some ironing to do, and after sixteen years of housework she did not seem able to escape her chores even while she slept. Snowsuits, shoes, baths, and groceries seemed to have permeated her subconscious. Now and then she would speak in her sleep—so loudly that she woke her husband. "I can't *afford* veal cutlets," she said one night. Then she sighed uneasily and was quiet again.

By the standards of Shady Hill, the Bentleys were a happily married couple, but they had their ups and downs. Cash could be very touchy at times. When he came home after a bad day at the office and found that Louise, for some good reason, had not started supper, he would be ugly. "Oh, for Christ sake!" he would say, and go into the kitchen and heat up some frozen food. He drank some whiskey to relax himself during this ordeal, but it never seemed to relax him, and he usually burned the bottom out of a pan, and when they sat down for supper the dining space would be full of smoke. It was only a question of time before they were plunged into a bitter quarrel. Louise would run upstairs, throw herself onto the bed and sob. Cash would grab the whiskey bottle and dose himself. These rows, in spite of the vigor with which Cash and Louise entered into them, were the source of a great deal of pain for both of them. Cash would sleep downstairs on the sofa, but sleep never repaired the damage, once the trouble had begun, and if they met in the morning, they would be at one another's throats in a second. Then Cash would leave for the train, and, as soon as the children had been taken to nursery school, Louise would put on her coat and cross the grass to the Beardens' house. She would cry into a cup of warmed-up coffee and tell Lucy Bearden her troubles. What was the meaning of marriage? What was the meaning of love? Lucy always suggested that Louise get a job. It would give her emotional and financial independence, and that, Lucy said, was what she needed.

The next night, things would get worse. Cash would not come home for dinner at all, but would stumble in at about eleven, and the whole sordid wrangle would be repeated, with Louise going to bed in tears upstairs and Cash again stretching out on the living-room sofa. After a few days and nights of this, Louise would decide that she was at the end of her rope. She would decide to go and stay with her married sister in Mamaroneck.[1] She usually chose a Saturday, when Cash would be at home, for her departure. She would pack a suitcase and get her War Bonds from the desk. Then she would take a bath and put on her best slip. Cash, passing the bedroom door, would see her. Her slip was transparent, and suddenly he was all repentance, tenderness, charm, wisdom, and love. "Oh, my darling!" he would groan, and when they went downstairs to get a bite to eat about an hour later, they would be sighing and making cow eyes at one another; they would be the happiest married couple in the whole eastern United States. It was usually at about this time that Lucy Bearden turned up with the good news that she had

---

[1] A fashionable bedroom community in Westchester County, north of New York City.

found a job for Louise. Lucy would ring the doorbell, and Cash, wearing a bath-robe, would let her in. She would be brief with Cash, naturally, and hurry into the dining room to tell poor Louise the good news. "Well, that's very nice of you to have looked," Louise would say wanly, "but I don't think that I want a job any more. I don't think that Cash wants me to work, do you, sweetheart?" Then she would turn her big dark eyes on Cash, and you could practically smell smoke. Lucy would excuse herself hurriedly from this scene of depravity, but never left with any hard feelings, because she had been married for nineteen years herself and she knew that every union has its ups and downs. She didn't seem to leave any wiser, either; the next time the Bentleys quarreled, she would be just as intent as ever on getting Louise a job. But these quarrels and reunions, like the hurdle race, didn't seem to lose their interest through repetition.

On a Saturday night in the spring, the Farquarsons gave the Bentleys an anni-versary party. It was their seventeenth anniversary. Saturday afternoon, Louise Bentley put herself through preparations nearly as arduous as the Monday wash. She rested for an hour, by the clock, with her feet high in the air, her chin in a sling, and her eyes bathed in some astringent solution. The clay packs, the too tight girdle, and the plucking and curling and painting that went on were all aimed at rejuvenation. Feeling in the end that she had not been entirely success-ful, she tied a piece of veiling over her eyes—but she was a lovely woman, and all the cosmetics that she had struggled with seemed, like her veil, to be drawn transparently over a face where mature beauty and a capacity for wit and passion were undisguisable. The Farquarsons' party was nifty, and the Bentleys had a wonderful time. The only person who drank too much was Trace Bearden. Late in the party, he began to chide Cash about his thinning hair and Cash good-naturedly began to move the furniture around. Harry Farquarson had a pistol, and Trace went out onto the terrace to fire it up at the sky. Over the sofa went Cash, over the end table, over the arms of the wing chair and the fire screen. It was a piece of carving on a chest that brought him down, and down he came like a ton of bricks.

Louise screamed and ran to where he lay. He had cut a gash in his forehead, and someone made a bandage to stop the flow of blood. When he tried to get up, he stumbled and fell again, and his face turned a terrible green. Harry telephoned Dr. Parminter, Dr. Hopewell, Dr. Altman, and Dr. Barnstable, but it was two in the morning and none of them answered. Finally, a Dr. Yerkes—a total stranger—agreed to come. Yerkes was a young man—he did not seem old enough to be a doctor—and he looked around at the disordered room and the anxious company as if there was something weird about the scene. He got off on the wrong foot with Cash. "What seems to be the matter, old-timer?" he asked.

Cash's leg was broken. The doctor put a splint on it, and Harry and Trace carried the injured man out to the doctor's car. Louise followed them in her own car to the hospital, where Cash was bedded down in a ward. The doctor gave Cash a sedative, and Louise kissed him and drove home in the dawn.

Cash was in the hospital for two weeks, and when he came home he walked with a crutch and his broken leg was in a heavy cast. It was another ten days before he could limp to the morning train. "I won't be able to run the hurdle race any more, sweetheart," he told Louise sadly. She said that it didn't matter, but while it didn't matter to her, it seemed to matter to Cash. He had lost weight in the hospital. His spirits were low. He seemed discontented. He did not himself understand what had happened. He, or everything around him, seemed subtly to have changed for the worse. Even his senses seemed to conspire to damage the ingenuous world that he had enjoyed for so many years. He went into the kitchen late one night to make himself a sandwich, and when he opened the icebox door he noticed a rank smell. He dumped the spoiled meat into the garbage, but the smell clung to his nostrils. A few days later he was in the attic, looking for his varsity sweater. There were no windows in the attic and his flashlight was dim. Kneeling on the floor to unlock a trunk, he broke a spider web with his lips. The frail web covered his mouth as if a hand had been put over it. He wiped it impatiently, but also with the feeling of having been gagged. A few nights later, he was walking down a New York side street in the rain and saw an old whore standing in a doorway. She was so sluttish and ugly that she looked like a cartoon of Death, but before he could appraise her—the instant his eyes took an impression of her crooked figure—his lips swelled, his breathing quickened, and he experienced all the other symptoms of erotic excitement. A few nights later, while he was reading *Time* in the living room, he noticed that the faded roses Louise had brought in from the garden smelled more of earth than of anything else. It was a putrid, compelling smell. He dropped the roses into a wastebasket, but not before they had reminded him of the spoiled meat, the whore, and the spider web.

He had started going to parties again, but without the hurdle race to run, the parties of his friends and neighbors seemed to him interminable and stale. He listened to their dirty jokes with an irritability that was hard for him to conceal. Even their countenances discouraged him, and, slumped in a chair, he would regard their skin and their teeth narrowly, as if he were himself a much younger man.

The brunt of his irritability fell on Louise, and it seemed to her that Cash, in losing the hurdle race, had lost the thing that had preserved his equilibrium. He was rude to his friends when they stopped in for a drink. He was rude and gloomy when he and Louise went out. When Louise asked him what was the matter, he only murmured, "Nothing, nothing, nothing," and poured himself some bourbon. May and June passed, and then the first part of July, without his showing any improvement.

Then it is a summer night, a wonderful summer night. The passengers on the eight-fifteen see Shady Hill—if they notice it at all—in a bath of placid golden light. The noise of the train is muffled in the heavy foliage, and the long car windows look like a string of lighted aquarium tanks before they flicker out of sight. Up on the hill, the ladies say to one another, "Smell the grass! Smell the trees!" The Farquarsons are giving another party, and Harry has hung a sign, WHISKEY GULCH, from the rose arbor, and is wearing a chef's white hat and an apron. His guests are still drinking, and the smoke from his meat fire rises, on this windless evening, straight up into the trees.

In the clubhouse on the hill, the first of the formal dances for the young people begins around nine. On Alewives Lane sprinklers continue to play after dark. You can smell the water. The air seems as fragrant as it is dark—it is a delicious element to walk through—and most of the windows on Alewives Lane are open to it. You can see Mr. and Mrs. Bearden, as you pass, looking at their television. Joe Lockwood, the young lawyer who lives on the corner, is practicing a speech to the jury before his wife. "I intend to show you," he says, "that a man of probity, a man whose reputation for honesty and reliability . . ." He waves his bare arms as he speaks. His wife goes on knitting. Mrs. Carver—Harry Farquarson's mother-in-law—glances up at the sky and asks, *"Where* did all the stars come from?" She is old and foolish, and yet she is right: Last night's stars seem to have drawn to themselves a new range of galaxies, and the night sky is not dark at all, except where there is a tear in the membrane of light. In the unsold house lots near the track a hermit thrush is singing.

The Bentleys are at home. Poor Cash has been so rude and gloomy that the Farquarsons have not asked him to their party. He sits on the sofa beside Louise, who is sewing elastic into the children's underpants. Through the open window he can hear the pleasant sounds of the summer night. There is another party, in the Rogerses' garden, behind the Bentleys'. The music from the dance drifts down the hill. The band is sketchy—saxophone, drums, and piano—and all the selections are twenty years old. The band plays "Valencia," and Cash looks tenderly toward Louise, but Louise, tonight, is a discouraging figure. The lamp picks out the gray in her hair. Her apron is stained. Her face seems colorless and drawn. Suddenly, Cash begins frenziedly to beat his feet in time to the music. He sings some gibberish—Jabajabajabajaba—to the distant saxophone. He sighs and goes into the kitchen.

Here a faint, stale smell of cooking clings to the dark. From the kitchen window Cash can see the lights and figures of the Rogerses' party. It is a young people's party. The Rogers girl has asked some friends in for dinner before the dance, and now they seem to be leaving. Cars are driving away. "I'm covered with grass stains," a girl says. "I hope the old man remembered to buy gasoline," a boy says, and a girl laughs. There is nothing on their minds but the passing summer nights. Taxes and the elastic in underpants—all the unbeautiful facts of life that threaten to crush the breath out of Cash—have not touched a single figure in this garden. Then jealousy seizes him—such savage and bitter jealousy that he feels ill.

He does not understand what separates him from these children in the garden next door. He has been a young man. He has been a hero. He has been adored and happy and full of animal spirits, and now he stands in a dark kitchen, deprived of his athletic prowess, his impetuousness, his good looks—of everything that means anything to him. He feels as if the figures in the next yard are the specters from some party in that past where all his tastes and desires lie, and from which he has been cruelly removed. He feels like a ghost of the summer evening. He is sick with longing. Then he hears voices in the front of the house. Louise turns on the kitchen light. "Oh, here you are," she says. "The Beardens stopped in. I think they'd like a drink."

Cash went to the front of the house to greet the Beardens. They wanted to go up to the club, for one dance. They saw, at a glance, that Cash was at loose ends, and they urged the Bentleys to come. Louise got someone to stay with the children and then went upstairs to change.

When they got to the club, they found a few friends of their age hanging around the bar, but Cash did not stay in the bar. He seemed restless and perhaps drunk. He banged into a table on his way through the lounge to the ballroom. He cut in on a young girl. He seized her too vehemently and jigged her off in an ancient two-step. She signaled openly for help to a boy in the stag line, and Cash was cut out. He walked angrily off the dance floor onto the terrace. Some young couples there withdrew from one another's arms as he pushed open the screen door. He walked to the end of the terrace, where he hoped to be alone, but here he surprised another young couple, who got up from the lawn, where they seemed to have been lying, and walked off in the dark toward the pool.

Louise remained in the bar with the Beardens. "Poor Cash is tight," she said.

And then, "He told me this afternoon that he was going to paint the storm windows," she said. "Well, he mixed the paint and washed the brushes and put on some old fatigues and went into the cellar. There was a telephone call for him at around five, and when I went down to tell him, do you know what he was doing? He was just sitting there in the dark with a cocktail shaker. He hadn't touched the storm windows. He was just sitting there in the dark, drinking Martinis."

"Poor Cash," Trace said.

"You ought to get a job," Lucy said. "That would give you emotional and financial independence." As she spoke, they all heard the noise of furniture being moved around in the lounge.

"Oh, my God!" Louise said. "He's going to run the race. Stop him, Trace, stop him! He'll hurt himself. He'll kill himself!"

They all went to the door of the lounge. Louise again asked Trace to interfere, but she could see by Cash's face that he was way beyond remonstrating with. A few couples left the dance floor and stood watching the preparations. Trace didn't try to stop Cash—he helped him. There was no pistol, so he slammed a couple of books together for the start.

Over the sofa went Cash, over the coffee table, the lamp table, the fire screen, and the hassock. All his grace and strength seemed to have returned to him. He cleared the big sofa at the end of the room and instead of stopping there, he turned and started back over the course. His face was strained. His mouth hung open. The tendons of his neck protruded hideously. He made the hassock, the fire screen, the lamp table, and the coffee table. People held their breath when he approached the final sofa, but he cleared it and landed on his feet. There was some applause. Then he groaned and fell. Louise ran to his side. His clothes were soaked with sweat and he gasped for breath. She knelt down beside him and took his head in her lap and stroked his thin hair.

Cash had a terrible hangover on Sunday, and Louise let him sleep until it was nearly time for church. The family went off to Christ Church together at eleven, as they always did. Cash sang, prayed, and got to his knees, but the most he ever felt in church was that he stood outside the realm of God's infinite mercy, and, to tell the truth, he no more believed in the Father, the Son, and the Holy Ghost than does my bull terrier. They returned home at one to eat the overcooked meat and stony potatoes that were their customary Sunday lunch. At around five, the Parminters called up and asked them over for a drink. Louise didn't want to go, so Cash went alone. (Oh, those suburban Sunday nights, those Sunday-night blues! Those departing weekend guests, those stale cocktails, those half-dead flowers, those trips to Harmon to catch the Century,[2] those postmortems and pickup suppers!) It was sultry and overcast. The dog days were beginning. He drank gin with the Parminters for an hour or two and then went over to the Townsends' for a drink. The Farquarsons called up the Townsends and asked them to come over and bring Cash with them, and at the Farquarsons' they had some more drinks and ate the leftover party food. The Farquarsons' were glad to see that Cash seemed like himself again. It was half past ten or eleven when he got home. Louise was upstairs, cutting out of the current copy of *Life* those scenes of

---

[2] Harmon, on the east bank of the Hudson River north of Ossining, was where the Twentieth-Century Limited, America's most famous passenger train, stopped to switch its locomotive from electric to steam before making the sixteen-hour overnight run from New York City to Chicago. It was thus a convenient point of departure for residents of Westchester County and nearby Connecticut.

mayhem, disaster, and violent death that she felt might corrupt her children. She always did this. Cash came upstairs and spoke to her and then went down again. In a little while, she heard him moving the living-room furniture around. Then he called to her, and when she went down, he was standing at the foot of the stairs in his stocking feet, holding the pistol out to her. She had never fired it before, and the directions he gave her were not much help.

"Hurry up," he said, "I can't wait all night."

He had forgotten to tell her about the safety, and when she pulled the trigger nothing happened.

"It's that little lever," he said. "Press that little lever." Then, in his impatience, he hurdled the sofa anyhow.

The pistol went off and Louise got him in midair. She shot him dead.

[1954]

Doris Lessing *1919–*

WINE

A man and woman walked towards the boulevard from a little hotel in a side street.

The trees were still leafless, black, cold; but the fine twigs were swelling towards spring, so that looking upward it was with an expectation of the first glimmering greenness. Yet everything was calm, and the sky was a calm, classic blue.

The couple drifted slowly along. Effort, after days of laziness, seemed impossible; and almost at once they turned into a cafe and sank down, as if exhausted, in the glass-walled space that was thrust forward into the street.

The place was empty. People were seeking the midday meal in the restaurants. Not all: that morning crowds had been demonstrating, a procession had just passed, and its straggling end could still be seen. The sounds of violence, shouted slogans and singing, no longer absorbed the din of Paris traffic; but it was these sounds that had roused the couple from sleep.

A waiter leaned at the door, looking after the crowds, and he reluctantly took an order for coffee.

The man yawned; the woman caught the infection; and they laughed with an affectation of guilt and exchanged glances before their eyes, without regret, parted. When the coffee came, it remained untouched. Neither spoke. After some time the woman yawned again; and this time the man turned and looked at her critically, and she looked back. Desire asleep, they looked. This remained: that while everything which drove them slept, they accepted from each other a sad irony; they could look at each other without illusion, steady-eyed.

And then, inevitably, the sadness deepened in her till she consciously resisted it; and into him came the flicker of cruelty.

"Your nose needs powdering," he said.

"You need a whipping boy."

But always he refused to feel sad. She shrugged, and, leaving him to it, turned to look out. So did he. At the far end of the boulevard there was a faint agitation, like stirred ants, and she heard him mutter, "Yes, and it still goes on. . . ."

Mocking, she said, "Nothing changes, everything always the same. . . ."

But he had flushed. "I remember," he began, in a different voice. He stopped, and she did not press him, for he was gazing at the distant demonstrators with a bitterly nostalgic face.

Outside drifted the lovers, the married couples, the students, the old people. There the stark trees; there the blue, quiet sky. In a month the trees would be vivid green; the sun would pour down heat; the people would be brown, laughing, bare-limbed. No, no, she said to herself, at this vision of activity. Better the static sadness. And, all at once, unhappiness welled up in her, catching her throat, and she was back fifteen years in another country. She stood in blazing tropical moonlight, stretching her arms to a landscape that offered her nothing but silence; and then she was running down a path where small stones glinted sharp underfoot, till at last she fell spent in a swath of glistening grass. Fifteen years.

It was at this moment that the man turned abruptly and called the waiter and ordered wine.

"What," she said humorously, "already?"

"Why not?"

For the moment she loved him completely and maternally, till she suppressed the counterfeit and watched him wait, fidgeting, for the wine, pour it, and then set the two glasses before them beside the still-brimming coffee cups. But she was again remembering that night, envying the girl ecstatic with moonlight, who ran crazily through the trees in an unsharable desire for—but what was the point.

"What are you thinking of?" he asked, still a little cruel.

"Ohhh," she protested humorously.

"That's the trouble, that's the trouble." He lifted his glass, glanced at her, and set it down. "Don't you want to drink?"

"Not yet."

He left his glass untouched and began to smoke.

These movements demanded some kind of gesture—something slight, even casual, but still an acknowledgement of the separateness of those two people in each of them; the one seen, perhaps, as a soft-staring never-closing eye, observing, always observing, with a tired compassion; the other, a shape of violence that struggled on in the cycle of desire and rest, creation and achievement.

He gave it to her. Again their eyes met in the grave irony, before he turned away, flicking his fingers irritably against the table; and she turned also, to note the black branches where the sap was tingling.

"I remember," he began; and again she said, in protest, "Ohhh!"

He checked himself. "Darling," he said dryly, "you're the only woman I've ever loved." They laughed.

"It must have been this street. Perhaps this cafe—only they change so. When I went back yesterday to see the place where I came every summer, it was a *pâtisserie*,[1] and the woman had forgotten me. There was a whole crowd of us—we used to go around together—and I met a girl here, I think, for the first time. There were recognized places for contacts; people coming from Vienna or Prague, or wherever it was, knew the places—it couldn't be this cafe, unless they've smartened it up. We didn't have the money for all this leather and chromium."

"Well, go on."

"I keep remembering her, for some reason. Haven't thought of her for years. She was about sixteen, I suppose. Very pretty—no, you're quite wrong. We used to study together. She used to bring her books to my room. I liked her, but I had my own girl, only she was studying something else, I forget what." He paused again, and again his face was twisted with nostalgia, and involuntarily she glanced over her shoulder down the street. The procession had completely disappeared; not even the sounds of singing and shouting remained.

"I remember her because . . ." And after a preoccupied silence: "Perhaps it is always the fate of the virgin who comes and offers herself, naked, to be refused."

"What!" she exclaimed, startled. Also, anger stirred in her. She noted it, and sighed. "Go on."

"I never made love to her. We studied together all that summer. Then, one weekend, we all went off in a bunch. None of us had any money, of course, and we used to stand on the pavements and beg lifts, and meet up again in some village. I was with my own girl, but that night we were helping the farmer get in his fruit, in payment for using his barn to sleep in, and I found this girl Marie was beside me. It was moonlight, a lovely night, and we were all singing and making love. I kissed her, but that was all. That night she came to me. I was sleeping up

[1] A bakery specializing in pastry.

in the loft with another lad. He was asleep. I sent her back down to the others. They were all together down in the hay. I told her she was too young. But she was no younger than my own girl." He stopped; and after all these years his face was rueful and puzzled. "I don't know," he said. "I don't know why I sent her back." Then he laughed. "Not that it matters, I suppose."

"Shameless hussy," she said. The anger was strong now. "You had kissed her, hadn't you?"

He shrugged. "But we were all playing the fool. It was a glorious night— gathering apples, the farmer shouting and swearing at us because we were making love more than working, and singing and drinking wine. Besides, it was that time: the youth movement. We regarded faithfulness and jealousy and all that sort of thing as remnants of bourgeois morality." He laughed again, rather painfully. "I kissed her. There she was, beside me, and she knew my girl was with me that weekend."

"You kissed her," she said accusingly.

He fingered the stem of his wine glass, looking over at her and grinning. "Yes, darling," he almost crooned at her. "I kissed her."

She snapped over into anger. "There's a girl all ready for love. You make use of her for working. Then you kiss her. You know quite well . . ."

"What do I know quite well?"

"It was a cruel thing to do."

"I was a kid myself. . . ."

"Doesn't matter." She noted, with discomfort, that she was almost crying. "Working with her! Working with a girl of sixteen, all summer!"

"But we all studied very seriously. She was a doctor afterwards, in Vienna. She managed to get out when the Nazis came in, but . . ."

She said impatiently, "Then you kiss her, on *that* night. Imagine her, waiting till the others were asleep, then she climbed up the ladder to the loft, terrified the other man might wake up, then she stood watching you sleep, and she slowly took off her dress and . . ."

"Oh, I wasn't asleep. I pretended to be. She came up dressed. Shorts and sweater—our girls didn't wear dresses and lipstick—more bourgeois morality. I watched her strip. The loft was full of moonlight. She put her hand over my mouth and came down beside me." Again, his face was filled with rueful amazement. "God knows, I can't understand it myself. She was a beautiful creature. I don't know why I remember it. It's been coming into my mind the last few days." After a pause, slowly twirling the wine glass: "I've been a failure in many things, but not with . . ." He quickly lifted her hand, kissed it, and said sincerely: "I don't know why I remember it now, when . . ." Their eyes met, and they sighed.

She said slowly, her hand lying in his: "And so you turned her away."

He laughed. "Next morning she wouldn't speak to me. She started a love affair with my best friend—a man who'd been beside me that night in the loft, as a matter of fact. She hated my guts, and I suppose she was right."

"Think of her. Think of her at that moment. She picked up her clothes, hardly daring to look at you. . . ."

"As a matter of fact, she was furious. She called me all the names she could think of; I had to keep telling her to shut up, she'd wake the whole crowd."

"She climbed down the ladder and dressed again, in the dark. Then she went out of the barn, unable to go back to the others. She went into the orchard. It was still brilliant moonlight. Everything was silent and deserted, and she remembered how you'd all been singing and laughing and making love. She went to the tree where you'd kissed her. The moon was shining on the apples. She'll never forget it, never, never!''

He looked at her curiously. The tears were pouring down her face.

"It's terrible," she said. "Terrible. Nothing could ever make up to her for that. Nothing, as long as she lived. Just when everything was most perfect, all her life, she'd suddenly remember that night, standing alone, not a soul anywhere, miles of damned empty moonlight. . . ."

He looked at her shrewdly. Then, with a sort of humorous, deprecating grimace, he bent over and kissed her and said: "Darling, it's not my fault; it just isn't my fault."

"No," she said.

He put the wine glass into her hands; and she lifted it, looked at the small crimson globule of warming liquid, and drank with him.

[1957]

James Baldwin   *1924–1987*

SONNY'S BLUES

I read about it in the paper, in the subway, on my way to work. I read it, and I couldn't believe it, and I read it again. Then perhaps I just stared at it, at the newsprint spelling out his name, spelling out the story. I stared at it in the swinging lights of the subway car, and in the faces and bodies of the people, and in my own face, trapped in the darkness which roared outside.

It was not to be believed and I kept telling myself that, as I walked from the subway station to the high school. And at the same time I couldn't doubt it. I was scared, scared for Sonny. He became real to me again. A great block of ice got settled in my belly and kept melting there slowly all day long, while I taught my classes algebra. It was a special kind of ice. It kept melting, sending trickles of ice water all up and down my veins, but it never got less. Sometimes it hardened and seemed to expand until I felt my guts were going to come spilling out or that I was going to choke or scream. This would always be at a moment when I was remembering some specific thing Sonny had once said or done.

When he was about as old as the boys in my classes his face had been bright and open, there was a lot of copper in it; and he'd had wonderfully direct brown eyes, and great gentleness and privacy. I wondered what he looked like now. He had been picked up, the evening before, in a raid on an apartment downtown, for peddling and using heroin.

I couldn't believe it: but what I mean by that is that I couldn't find any room for it anywhere inside me. I had kept it outside me for a long time. I hadn't wanted to know. I had had suspicions, but I didn't name them, I kept putting them away. I told myself that Sonny was wild, but he wasn't crazy. And he'd always been a good boy, he hadn't ever turned hard or evil or disrespectful the way kids can, so quick, so quick, especially in Harlem.[1] I didn't want to believe that I'd ever see my brother going down, coming to nothing, all that light in his face gone out, in the condition I'd already seen so many others. Yet it had happened and here I was, talking about algebra to a lot of boys who might, every one of them for all I knew, be popping off needles every time they went to the head.[2] Maybe it did more for them than algebra could.

I was sure that the first time Sonny had ever had horse,[3] he couldn't have been much older than these boys were now. These boys, now, were living as we'd been living them, they were growing up with a rush and their heads bumped abruptly against the low ceiling of their actual possibilities. They were filled with rage. All they really knew were two darknesses, the darkness of their lives, which was now closing in on them, and the darkness of the movies, which had blinded them to that other darkness, and in which they now, vindictively, dreamed, at once more together than they were at any other time, and more alone.

When the last bell rang, the last class ended, I let out my breath. It seemed I'd been holding it for all that time. My clothes were wet—I may have looked as though I'd been sitting in a steam bath, all dressed up, all afternoon. I sat alone in the classroom a long time. I listened to the boys outside, downstairs, shouting and cursing and laughing. Their laughter struck me for perhaps the first time. It

---

[1] The famous black community along the Harlem and East Rivers on Manhattan's Upper East Side.
[2] Slang for bathroom or toilet.   [3] Heroin.

was not the joyous laughter which—God knows why—one associates with children. It was mocking and insular, its intent was to denigrate. It was disenchanted, and in this, also, lay the authority of their curses. Perhaps I was listening to them because I was thinking about my brother and in them I heard my brother. And myself.

One boy was whistling a tune, at once very complicated and very simple, it seemed to be pouring out of him as though he were a bird, and it sounded very cool and moving through all that harsh, bright air, only just holding its own through all those other sounds.

I stood up and walked over to the window and looked down into the courtyard. It was the beginning of the spring and the sap was rising in the boys. A teacher passed through them every now and again, quickly, as though he or she couldn't wait to get out of that courtyard, to get those boys out of their sight and off their minds. I started collecting my stuff. I thought I'd better get home and talk to Isabel.

The courtyard was almost deserted by the time I got downstairs. I saw this boy standing in the shadow of a doorway, looking just like Sonny. I almost called his name. Then I saw that it wasn't Sonny, but somebody we used to know, a boy from around our block. He'd been Sonny's friend. He'd never been mine, having been too young for me, and, anyway, I'd never liked him. And now, even though he was a grown-up man, he still hung around that block, still spent hours on the street corners, was always high and raggy. I used to run into him from time to time and he'd often work around to asking me for a quarter or fifty cents. He always had some real good excuse, too, and I always gave it to him, I don't know why.

But now, abruptly, I hated him. I couldn't stand the way he looked at me, partly like a dog, partly like a cunning child. I wanted to ask him what the hell he was doing in the school courtyard.

He sort of shuffled over to me, and he said, "I see you got the papers. So you already know about it."

"You mean about Sonny? Yes, I already know about it. How come they didn't get you?"

He grinned. It made him repulsive and it also brought to mind what he'd looked like as a kid. "I wasn't there. I stay away from them people."

"Good for you." I offered him a cigarette and I watched him through the smoke. "You come all the way down here just to tell me about Sonny?"

"That's right." He was sort of shaking his head and his eyes looked strange, as though they were about to cross. The bright sun deadened his damp dark brown skin and it made his eyes look yellow and showed up the dirt in his kinked hair. He smelled funky.[4] I moved a little away from him and I said, "Well, thanks. But I already know about it and I got to get home."

"I'll walk you a little ways," he said. We started walking. There were a couple of kids still loitering in the courtyard and one of them said goodnight to me and looked strangely at the boy beside me.

"What're you going to do?" he asked me. "I mean, about Sonny?"

"Look. I haven't seen Sonny for over a year, I'm not sure I'm going to do anything. Anyway, what the hell *can* I do?"

"That's right," he said quickly, "ain't nothing you can do. Can't much help old Sonny no more, I guess."

It was what I was thinking and so it seemed to me he had no right to say it.

---

[4] Unpleasant or offensive.

"I'm surprised at Sonny, though," he went on—he had a funny way of talking, he looked straight ahead as though he were talking to himself—"I thought Sonny was a smart boy, I thought he was too smart to get hung."

"I guess he thought so too," I said sharply, "and that's how he got hung. And how about you? You're pretty goddamn smart, I bet."

Then he looked directly at me, just for a minute. "I ain't smart," he said. "If I was smart, I'd have reached for a pistol a long time ago."

"Look. Don't tell *me* your sad story, if it was up to me, I'd give you one." Then I felt guilty—guilty, probably, for never having supposed that the poor bastard *had* a story of his own, much less a sad one, and I asked, quickly, "What's going to happen to him now?"

He didn't answer this. He was off by himself some place. "Funny thing," he said, and from his tone we might have been discussing the quickest way to get to Brooklyn, "when I saw the papers this morning, the first thing I asked myself was if I had anything to do with it. I felt sort of responsible."

I began to listen more carefully. The subway station was on the corner, just before us, and I stopped. He stopped, too. We were in front of a bar and he ducked slightly, peering in, but whoever he was looking for didn't seem to be there. The juke box was blasting away with something black and bouncy and I half watched the barmaid as she danced her way from the juke box to her place behind the bar. And I watched her face as she laughingly responded to something someone said to her, still keeping time to the music. When she smiled one saw the little girl, one sensed the doomed, still-struggling woman beneath the battered face of the semi-whore.

"I never *give* Sonny nothing," the boy said finally, "but a long time ago I come to school high and Sonny asked me how it felt." He paused, I couldn't bear to watch him, I watched the barmaid, and I listened to the music which seemed to be causing the pavement to shake. "I told him it felt great." The music stopped, the barmaid paused and watched the juke box until the music began again. "It did."

All this was carrying me some place I didn't want to go. I certainly didn't want to know how it felt. It filled everything, the people, the houses, the music, the dark, quicksilver barmaid, with menace; and this menace was their reality.

"What's going to happen to him now?" I asked again.

"They'll send him away some place and they'll try to cure him." He shook his head. "Maybe he'll even think he's kicked the habit. Then they'll let him loose"—he gestured, throwing his cigarette into the gutter. "That's all."

"What do you mean, that's *all*?"

But I knew what he meant.

"I *mean*, that's *all*." He turned his head and looked at me, pulling down the corners of his mouth. "Don't you know what I mean?" he asked, softly.

"How the hell *would* I know what you mean?" I almost whispered it, I don't know why.

"That's right," he said to the air, "how would *he* know what I mean?" He turned toward me again, patient and calm, and yet I somehow felt him shaking, shaking as though he were going to fall apart. I felt that ice in my guts again, the dread I'd felt all afternoon; and again I watched the barmaid, moving about the bar, washing glasses, and singing. "Listen. They'll let him out and then it'll just start all over again. That's what I mean."

"You mean—they'll let him out. And then he'll just start working his way back in again. You mean he'll never kick the habit. Is that what you mean?"

"That's right," he said, cheerfully. "*You* see what I mean."

"Tell me," I said at last, "why does he want to die? He must want to die, he's killing himself, why does he want to die?"

He looked at me in surprise. He licked his lips. "He don't want to die. He wants to live. Don't nobody want to die, ever."

Then I wanted to ask him—too many things. He could not have answered, or if he had, I could not have borne the answers. I started walking. "Well, I guess it's none of my business."

"It's going to be rough on old Sonny," he said. We reached the subway station. "This is your station?" he asked. I nodded. I took one step down. "Damn!" he said, suddenly. I looked up at him. He grinned again. "Damn it if I didn't leave all my money home. You ain't got a dollar on you, have you? Just for a couple of days, is all."

All at once something inside gave and threatened to come pouring out of me. I didn't hate him any more. I felt that in another moment I'd start crying like a child.

"Sure," I said. "Don't sweat." I looked in my wallet and didn't have a dollar, I only had a five. "Here," I said. "That hold you?"

He didn't look at it—he didn't want to look at it. A terrible, closed look came over his face, as though he were keeping the number on the bill a secret from him and me. "Thanks," he said, and now he was dying to see me go. "Don't worry about Sonny. Maybe I'll write him or something."

"Sure," I said. "You do that. So long."

"Be seeing you," he said. I went on down the steps.

And I didn't write Sonny or send him anything for a long time. When I finally did, it was just after my little girl died, he wrote me back a letter which made me feel like a bastard.

Here's what he said:

Dear brother,

You don't know how much I needed to hear from you. I wanted to write you many a time but I dug how much I must have hurt you and so I didn't write. But now I feel like a man who's been trying to climb up out of some deep, real deep and funky hole and just saw the sun up there, outside. I got to get outside.

I can't tell you much about how I got here. I mean I don't know how to tell you. I guess I was afraid of something or I was trying to escape from something and you know I have never been very strong in the head (smile). I'm glad Mama and Daddy are dead and can't see what's happened to their son and I swear if I'd known what I was doing I would never have hurt you so, you and a lot of other fine people who were nice to me and who believed in me.

I don't want you to think it had anything to do with me being a musician. It's more than that. Or maybe less than that. I can't get anything straight in my head down here and I try not to think about what's going to happen to me when I get outside again. Sometime I think I'm going to flip and *never* get outside and sometime I think I'll come straight back. I tell you one thing, though, I'd rather blow my brains out than go through this again. But that's what they all say, so they tell me. If I tell you when I'm coming to New York and if you could meet me, I sure would appreciate it. Give my love to Isabel and the kids and I was sure sorry to hear about little Gracie. I wish I could be like Mama and say the Lord's will be done, but I don't know it seems to me that trouble is the one thing that never does get stopped and I don't know what good it does to blame it on the Lord. But maybe it does some good if you believe it.

Your brother,
Sonny

Then I kept in constant touch with him and I sent him whatever I could and I went to meet him when he came back to New York. When I saw him many things I thought I had forgotten came flooding back to me. This was because I had begun, finally, to wonder about Sonny, about the life that Sonny lived inside. This life, whatever it was, had made him older and thinner and it had deepened the distant stillness in which he had always moved. He looked very unlike my baby brother. Yet, when he smiled, when we shook hands, the baby brother I'd never known looked out from the depths of his private life, like an animal waiting to be coaxed into the light.

"How you been keeping?" he asked me.

"All right. And you?"

"Just fine." He was smiling all over his face. "It's good to see you again."

"It's good to see you."

The seven years' difference in our ages lay between us like a chasm: I wondered if these years would ever operate between us as a bridge. I was remembering, and it made it hard to catch my breath, that I had been there when he was born; and I had heard the first words he had ever spoken. When he started to walk, he walked from our mother straight to me. I caught him just before he fell when he took the first steps he ever took in this world.

"How's Isabel?"

"Just fine. She's dying to see you."

"And the boys?"

"They're fine, too. They're anxious to see their uncle."

"Oh, come on. You know they don't remember me."

"Are you kidding? Of course they remember you."

He grinned again. We got into a taxi. We had a lot to say to each other, far too much to know how to begin.

As the taxi began to move, I asked, "You still want to go to India?"

He laughed. "You still remember that. Hell, no. This place is Indian enough for me."

"It used to belong to them," I said.

And he laughed again. "They damn sure knew what they were doing when they got rid of it."

Years ago, when he was around fourteen, he'd been all hipped on the idea of going to India. He read books about people sitting on rocks, naked, in all kinds of weather, but mostly bad, naturally, and walking barefoot through hot coals and arriving at wisdom. I used to say that it sounded to me as though they were getting away from wisdom as fast as they could. I think he sort of looked down on me for that.

"Do you mind," he asked, "if we have the driver drive alongside the park? On the west side—I haven't seen the city in so long."

"Of course not," I said. I was afraid that I might sound as though I were humoring him, but I hoped he wouldn't take it that way.

So we drove along, between the green of the park and the stony, lifeless elegance of hotels and apartment buildings, toward the vivid, killing streets of our
childhood. These streets hadn't changed, though housing projects jutted up out
of them now like rocks in the middle of a boiling sea. Most of the houses in which
we had grown up had vanished, as had the stores from which we had stolen, the
basements in which we had first tried sex, the rooftops from which we had hurled
tin cans and bricks. But houses exactly like the houses of our past yet dominated
the landscape, boys exactly like the boys we once had been found themselves
smothering in these houses, came down into the streets for light and air and
found themselves encircled by disaster. Some escaped the trap, most didn't. Those
who got out always left something of themselves behind, as some animals ampu-
tate a leg and leave it in the trap. It might be said, perhaps, that I had escaped,
after all, I was a school teacher; or that Sonny had, he hadn't lived in Harlem for
years. Yet, as the cab moved uptown through streets which seemed, with a rush, to
darken with dark people, and as I covertly studied Sonny's face, it came to me that
what we both were seeking through our separate cab windows was that part of
ourselves which had been left behind. It's always at the hour of trouble and
confrontation that the missing member aches.

We hit 110th Street and started rolling up Lenox Avenue. And I'd known this
avenue all my life, but it seemed to me again, as it had seemed on the day I'd first
heard about Sonny's trouble, filled with a hidden menace which was its very
breath of life.

"We almost there," said Sonny.

"Almost." We were both too nervous to say anything more.

We live in a housing project. It hasn't been up long. A few days after it was up
it seemed uninhabitably new, now, of course, it's already rundown. It looks like a
parody of the good, clean, faceless life—God knows the people who live in it do
their best to make it a parody. The beat-looking grass lying around isn't enough
to make their lives green, the hedges will never hold out the streets, and they know
it. The big windows fool no one, they aren't big enough to make space out of no
space. They don't bother with the windows, they watch the TV screen instead. The
playground is most popular with the children who don't play at jacks, or skip rope,
or roller skate, or swing, and they can be found in it after dark. We moved in partly
because it's not too far from where I teach, and partly for the kids; but it's really
just like the houses in which Sonny and I grew up. The same things happen, they'll
have the same things to remember. The moment Sonny and I started into the
house I had the feeling that I was simply bringing him back into the danger he
had almost died trying to escape.

Sonny has never been talkative. So I don't know why I was sure he'd be dying
to talk to me when supper was over the first night. Everything went fine, the oldest
boy remembered him, and the youngest boy liked him, and Sonny had remembered to bring something for each of them; and Isabel, who is really much nicer
than I am, more open and giving, had gone to a lot of trouble about dinner and
was genuinely glad to see him. And she's always been able to tease Sonny in a way
that I haven't. It was nice to see her face so vivid again and to hear her laugh and
watch her make Sonny laugh. She wasn't, or, anyway, she didn't seem to be, at all
uneasy or embarrassed. She chatted as though there were no subject which had to
be avoided and she got Sonny past his first, faint stiffness. And thank God she was
there, for I was filled with that icy dread again. Everything I did seemed awkward
to me, and everything I said sounded freighted with hidden meaning. I was trying
to remember everything I'd heard about dope addiction and I couldn't help

watching Sonny for signs. I wasn't doing it out of malice. I was trying to find out something about my brother. I was dying to hear him tell me he was safe.

"Safe!" my father grunted, whenever Mama suggested trying to move to a neighborhood which might be safer for children. "Safe, hell! Ain't no place safe for kids, nor nobody."

He always went on like this, but he wasn't, ever, really as bad as he sounded, not even on weekends, when he got drunk. As a matter of fact, he was always on the lookout for "something a little better," but he died before he found it. He died suddenly, during a drunken weekend in the middle of the war, when Sonny was fifteen. He and Sonny hadn't ever got on too well. And this was partly because Sonny was the apple of his father's eye. It was because he loved Sonny so much and was frightened for him, that he was always fighting with him. It doesn't do any good to fight with Sonny. Sonny just moves back, inside himself, where he can't be reached. But the principal reason that they never hit it off is that they were so much alike. Daddy was big and rough and loud-talking, just the opposite of Sonny, but they both had—that same privacy.

Mama tried to tell me something about this, just after Daddy died. I was home on leave from the army.

This was the last time I ever saw my mother alive. Just the same, this picture gets all mixed up in my mind with pictures I had of her when she was younger. The way I always see her is the way she used to be on a Sunday afternoon, say, when the old folks were talking after the big Sunday dinner. I always see her wearing pale blue. She'd be sitting on the sofa. And my father would be sitting in the easy chair, not far from her. And the living room would be full of church folks and relatives. There they sit, in chairs all around the living room, and the night is creeping up outside, but nobody knows it yet. You can see the darkness growing against the windowpanes and you hear the street noises every now and again, or maybe the jangling beat of a tambourine from one of the churches close by, but it's real quiet in the room. For a moment nobody's talking, but every face looks darkening, like the sky outside. And my mother rocks a little from the waist, and my father's eyes are closed. Everyone is looking at something a child can't see. For a minute they've forgotten the children. Maybe a kid is lying on the rug, half asleep. Maybe somebody's got a kid in his lap and is absent-mindedly stroking the kid's head. Maybe there's a kid, quiet and big-eyed, curled up in a big chair in the corner. The silence, the darkness coming, and the darkness in the faces frightens the child obscurely. He hopes that the hand which strokes his forehead will never stop—will never die. He hopes that there will never come a time when the old folks won't be sitting around the living room, talking about where they've come from, and what they've seen, and what's happened to them and their kinfolk.

But something deep and watchful in the child knows that this is bound to end, is already ending. In a moment someone will get up and turn on the light. Then the old folks will remember the children and they won't talk any more that day. And when light fills the room, the child is filled with darkness. He knows that every time this happens he's moved just a little closer to that darkness outside. The darkness outside is what the old folks have been talking about. It's what they've come from. It's what they endure. The child knows that they won't talk any more because if he knows too much about what's happened to *them*, he'll know too much too soon, about what's going to happen to *him*.

The last time I talked to my mother, I remember I was restless. I wanted to get out and see Isabel. We weren't married then and we had a lot to straighten out between us.

There Mama sat, in black, by the window. She was humming an old church song, *Lord, you brought me from a long ways off.* Sonny was out somewhere. Mama kept watching the streets.

"I don't know," she said, "if I'll ever see you again, after you go off from here. But I hope you'll remember the things I tried to teach you."

"Don't talk like that," I said, and smiled. "You'll be here a long time yet."

She smiled, too, but she said nothing. She was quiet for a long time. And I said, "Mama, don't you worry about nothing. I'll be writing all the time, and you be getting the checks. . . ."

"I want to talk to you about your brother," she said, suddenly. "If anything happens to me he ain't going to have nobody to look out for him."

"Mama," I said, "ain't nothing going to happen to you *or* Sonny. Sonny's all right. He's a good boy and he's got good sense."

"It ain't a question of his being a good boy," Mama said, "nor of his having good sense. It ain't only the bad ones, nor yet the dumb ones that get sucked under." She stopped, looking at me. "Your Daddy once had a brother," she said, and she smiled in a way that made me feel she was in pain. "You didn't never know that, did you?"

"No," I said, "I never knew that," and I watched her face.

"Oh, yes," she said, "your Daddy had a brother." She looked out of the window again. "I know you never saw your Daddy cry. But *I* did—many a time, through all these years."

I asked her, "What happened to his brother? How come nobody's ever talked about him?"

This was the first time I ever saw my mother look old.

"His brother got killed," she said, "when he was just a little younger than you are now. I knew him. He was a fine boy. He was maybe a little full of the devil, but he didn't mean nobody no harm."

Then she stopped and the room was silent, exactly as it had sometimes been on those Sunday afternoons. Mama kept looking out into the streets.

"He used to have a job in the mill," she said, "and, like all young folks, he just liked to perform on Saturday nights. Saturday nights, him and your father would drift around to different places, go to dances and things like that, or just sit around with people they knew, and your father's brother would sing, he had a fine voice, and play along with himself on his guitar. Well, this particular Saturday night, him and your father was coming home from some place, and they were both a little drunk and there was a moon that night, it was bright like day. Your father's brother was feeling kind of good, and he was whistling to himself, and he had his guitar slung over his shoulder. They was coming down a hill and beneath them was a road that turned off from the highway. Well, your father's brother, being always kind of frisky, decided to run down this hill, and he did, with that guitar banging and clanging behind him, and he ran across the road, and he was making water behind a tree. And your father was sort of amused at him and he was still coming down the hill, kind of slow. Then he heard a car motor and that same minute his brother stepped from behind the tree, into the road, in the moonlight. And he started to cross the road. And your father started to run down the hill, he says he don't know why. This car was full of white men. They was all drunk, and when they seen your father's brother they let out a great whoop and holler and they aimed the car straight at him. They was having fun, they just wanted to scare him, the way they do sometimes, you know. But they was drunk. And I guess the boy, being drunk, too, and scared, kind of lost his head. By the time he jumped it was too late. Your father says he heard his brother scream when the car rolled over him, and he heard the wood of that guitar when it give, and he heard them strings go flying, and he heard them white men shouting, and the car kept on a-going and it ain't stopped till this day. And, time your father got down the hill, his brother weren't nothing but blood and pulp.''

Tears were gleaming on my mother's face. There wasn't anything I could say.

"He never mentioned it," she said, "because I never let him mention it before you children. Your Daddy was like a crazy man that night and for many a night thereafter. He says he never in his life seen anything as dark as that road after the lights of that car had gone away. Weren't nothing, weren't nobody on that road, just your Daddy and his brother and that busted guitar. Oh, yes. Your Daddy never did really get right again. Till the day he died he weren't but that every white man he saw was the man that killed his brother.''

She stopped and took out her handkerchief and dried her eyes and looked at me.

"I ain't telling you all this," she said, "to make you scared or bitter or to make you hate nobody. I'm telling you this because you got a brother. And the world ain't changed.''

I guess I didn't want to believe this. I guess she saw this in my face. She turned away from me, toward the window again, searching those streets.

"But I praise my Redeemer," she said at last, "that He called your Daddy home before me. I ain't saying it to throw no flowers at myself, but, I declare, it keeps me from feeling too cast down to know I helped your father get safely through this world. Your father always acted like he was the roughest, strongest man on earth. And everybody took him to be like that. But if he hadn't had *me* there—to see his tears!''

She was crying again. Still, I couldn't move. I said, "Lord, Lord, Mama, I didn't know it was like that.''

"Oh, honey," she said, "there's a lot that you don't know. But you are going to find it out." She stood up from the window and came over to me. "You got to hold on to your brother," she said, "and don't let him fall, no matter what it looks like is happening to him and no matter how evil you gets with him. You going to be evil with him many a time. But don't you forget what I told you, you hear?''

"I won't forget," I said. "Don't you worry, I won't forget. I won't let nothing happen to Sonny.''

My mother smiled as though she were amused at something she saw in my face. Then, "You may not be able to stop nothing from happening. But you got to let him know you's *there.*''

Two days later I was married, and then I was gone. And I had a lot of things on my mind and I pretty well forgot my promise to Mama until I got shipped home on a special furlough for her funeral.

And, after the funeral, with just Sonny and me alone in the empty kitchen, I tried to find out something about him.

"What do you want to do?" I asked him.

"I'm going to be a musician," he said.

For he had graduated, in the time I had been away, from dancing to the juke box to finding out who was playing what, and what they were doing with it, and he had bought himself a set of drums.

"You mean, you want to be a drummer?" I somehow had the feeling that being a drummer might be all right for other people but not for my brother Sonny.

"I don't think," he said, looking at me very gravely, "that I'll ever be a good drummer. But I think I can play a piano."

I frowned. I'd never played the role of the older brother quite so seriously before, had scarcely ever, in fact, *asked* Sonny a damn thing. I sensed myself in the presence of something I didn't really know how to handle, didn't understand. So I made my frown a little deeper as I asked: "What kind of musician do you want to be?"

He grinned. "How many kinds do you think there are?"

"Be *serious*," I said.

He laughed, throwing his head back, and then looked at me. "I *am* serious."

"Well, then, for Christ's sake, stop kidding around and answer a serious question. I mean, do you want to be a concert pianist, you want to play classical music and all that, or—or what?" Long before I finished he was laughing again. "For Christ's *sake*, Sonny!"

He sobered, but with difficulty. "I'm sorry. But you sound so—*scared!*" and he was off again.

"Well, you may think it's funny now, baby, but it's not going to be so funny when you have to make your living at it, let me tell you *that*." I was furious because I knew he was laughing at me and I didn't know why.

"No," he said, very sober now, and afraid, perhaps, that he'd hurt me, "I don't want to be a classical pianist. That isn't what interests me. I mean"—he paused, looking hard at me, as though his eyes would help me to understand, and then gestured helplessly, as though perhaps his hand would help—"I mean, I'll have a lot of studying to do, and I'll have to study *everything*, but, I mean, I want to play *with*—jazz musicians." He stopped. "I want to play jazz," he said.

Well, the word had never before sounded as heavy, as real, as it sounded that afternoon in Sonny's mouth. I just looked at him and I was probably frowning a real frown by this time. I simply couldn't see why on earth he'd want to spend his time hanging around nightclubs, clowning around on bandstands, while people pushed each other around a dance floor. It seemed—beneath him, somehow. I had never thought about it before, had never been forced to, but I suppose I had always put jazz musicians in a class with what Daddy called "good-time people."

"Are you *serious*?"

"Hell, *yes*, I'm serious."

He looked more helpless than ever, and annoyed, and deeply hurt.

I suggested, helpfully: "You mean—like Louis Armstrong?"[5]

His face closed as though I'd struck him. "No. I'm not talking about none of that old-time, down home crap."

"Well, look, Sonny, I'm sorry, don't get mad. I just don't altogether get it, that's all. Name somebody—you know, a jazz musician you admire."

"Bird."

"Who?"

"Bird! Charlie Parker![6] Don't they teach you nothing in the goddamn army?"

I lit a cigarette. I was surprised and then a little amused to discover that I was

---

[5] Louis ("Satchmo") Armstrong (1900–1971), the famous black jazz trumpeter. Associated with traditional New Orleans-style jazz.

[6] Charles ("Bird") Parker (1920–1950), an experimental and innovative jazz saxophonist. Together with Dizzy Gillespie (1917–1993), Parker was responsible for the rise of "bebop" jazz of the 1940s. He was addicted to heroin for most of his life.

trembling. "I've been out of touch," I said. "You'll have to be patient with me. Now. Who's this Parker character?"

"He's just one of the greatest jazz musicians alive," said Sonny, sullenly, his hands in his pockets, his back to me. "Maybe *the* greatest," he added, bitterly, "that's probably why *you* never heard of him."

"All right," I said, "I'm ignorant. I'm sorry. I'll go out and buy all the cat's records right away, all right?"

"It don't," said Sonny, with dignity, "make any difference to me. I don't care what you listen to. Don't do me no favors."

I was beginning to realize that I'd never seen him so upset before. With another part of my mind I was thinking that this would probably turn out to be one of those things kids go through and that I shouldn't make it seem important by pushing it too hard. Still, I didn't think it would do any harm to ask: "Doesn't all this take a lot of time? Can you make a living at it?"

He turned back to me and half leaned, half sat, on the kitchen table. "Everything takes time," he said, "and—well, yes, sure, I can make a living at it. But what I don't seem to be able to make you understand is that it's the only thing I want to do."

"Well, Sonny," I said, gently, "you know people can't always do exactly what they *want* to do—"

"*No*, I don't know that," said Sonny, surprising me. "I think people *ought* to do what they want to do, what else are they alive for?"

"You getting to be a big boy," I said desperately, "it's time you started thinking about your future."

"I'm thinking about my future," said Sonny, grimly. "I think about it all the time."

I gave up. I decided, if he didn't change his mind, that we could always talk about it later. "In the meantime," I said, "you got to finish school." We had already decided that he'd have to move in with Isabel and her folks. I knew this wasn't the ideal arrangement because Isabel's folks are inclined to be dicty and they hadn't especially wanted Isabel to marry me. But I didn't know what else to do. "And we have to get you fixed up at Isabel's."

There was a long silence. He moved from the kitchen table to the window. "That's a terrible idea. You know it yourself."

"Do you have a *better* idea?"

He just walked up and down the kitchen for a minute. He was as tall as I was. He had started to shave. I suddenly had the feeling that I didn't know him at all.

He stopped at the kitchen table and picked up my cigarettes. Looking at me with a kind of mocking, amused defiance, he put one between his lips. "You mind?"

"You smoking already?"

He lit the cigarette and nodded, watching me through the smoke. "I just wanted to see if I'd have the courage to smoke in front of you." He grinned and blew a great cloud of smoke to the ceiling. "It was easy." He looked at my face. "Come on, now. I bet you was smoking at my age, tell the truth."

I didn't say anything but the truth was on my face, and he laughed. But now there was something very strained in his laugh. "Sure. And I bet that ain't all you was doing."

He was frightening me a little. "Cut the crap," I said. "We already decided that you was going to go and live at Isabel's. Now what's got into you all of a sudden?"

"*You* decided it," he pointed out. "*I* didn't decide nothing." He stopped in front of me, leaning against the stove, arms loosely folded. "Look, brother. I don't want to stay in Harlem no more, I really don't." He was very earnest. He looked at me, then over toward the kitchen window. There was something in his eyes I'd never seen before, some thoughtfulness, some worry all his own. He rubbed the muscle of one arm. "It's time I was getting out of here."

"Where do you want to *go*, Sonny?"

"I want to join the army. Or the navy, I don't care. If I say I'm old enough, they'll believe me."

Then I got mad. It was because I was so scared. "You must be crazy. You goddamn fool, what the hell do you want to go and join the *army* for?"

"I just told you. To get out of Harlem."

"Sonny, you haven't even finished *school*. And if you really want to be a musician, how do you expect to study if you're in the *army*?"

He looked at me, trapped, and in anguish. "There's ways. I might be able to work out some kind of deal. Anyway, I'll have the G.I. Bill[7] when I come out."

"*If* you come out." We stared at each other. "Sonny, please. Be reasonable. I know the setup is far from perfect. But we got to do the best we can."

"I ain't learning nothing in school," he said. "Even when I go." He turned away from me and opened the window and threw his cigarette out into the narrow alley. I watched his back. "At least, I ain't learning nothing you'd want me to learn." He slammed the window so hard I thought the glass would fly out, and turned back to me. "And I'm sick of the stink of these garbage cans!"

"Sonny," I said, "I know how you feel. But if you don't finish school now, you're going to be sorry later that you didn't." I grabbed him by the shoulders. "And you only got another year. It ain't so bad. And I'll come back and I swear I'll help you do *whatever* you want to do. Just try to put up with it till I come back. Will you please do that? For me?"

He didn't answer and he wouldn't look at me.

"Sonny. You hear me?"

He pulled away. "I hear you. But you never hear anything *I* say."

I didn't know what to say to that. He looked out of the window and then back at me. "OK," he said, and sighed. "I'll try."

Then I said, trying to cheer him up a little, "They got a piano at Isabel's. You can practice on it."

And as a matter of fact, it did cheer him up for a minute. "That's right," he said to himself. "I forgot that." His face relaxed a little. But the worry, the thoughtfulness, played on it still, the way shadows play on a face which is staring into the fire.

But I thought I'd never hear the end of that piano. At first, Isabel would write me, saying how nice it was that Sonny was so serious about his music and how, as soon as he came in from school, or wherever he had been when he was supposed to be at school, he went straight to that piano and stayed there until suppertime. And, after supper, he went back to that piano and stayed there until everybody went to bed. He was at the piano all day Saturday and all day Sunday. Then he bought a record player and started playing records. He'd play one record over and

---

[7] The popular name for the government program providing educational and financial benefits to military veterans.

over again, all day long sometimes, and he'd improvise along with it on the piano. Or he'd play one section of the record, one chord, one change, one progression, then he'd do it on the piano. Then back to the record. Then back to the piano.

Well, I really don't know how they stood it. Isabel finally confessed that it wasn't like living with a person at all, it was like living with sound. And the sound didn't make any sense to her, didn't make any sense to any of them—naturally. They began, in a way, to be afflicted by this presence that was living in their home. It was as though Sonny were some sort of god, or monster. He moved in an atmosphere which wasn't like theirs at all. They fed him and he ate, he washed himself, he walked in and out of their door; he certainly wasn't nasty or unpleasant or rude, Sonny isn't any of those things; but it was as though he were all wrapped up in some cloud, some fire, some vision all his own; and there wasn't any way to reach him.

At the same time, he wasn't really a man yet, he was still a child, and they had to watch out for him in all kinds of ways. They certainly couldn't throw him out. Neither did they dare to make a great scene about that piano because even they dimly sensed, as I sensed, from so many thousands of miles away, that Sonny was at that piano playing for his life.

But he hadn't been going to school. One day a letter came from the school board and Isabel's mother got it—there had, apparently, been other letters but Sonny had torn them up. This day, when Sonny came in, Isabel's mother showed him the letter and asked where he'd been spending his time. And she finally got it out of him that he'd been down in Greenwich Village[8] with musicians and other characters, in a white girl's apartment. And this scared her and she started to scream at him and what came up, once she began—though she denies it to this day—was what sacrifices they were making to give Sonny a decent home and how little he appreciated it.

Sonny didn't play the piano that day. By evening, Isabel's mother had calmed down but then there was the old man to deal with, and Isabel herself. Isabel says she did her best to be calm but she broke down and started crying. She says she just watched Sonny's face. She could tell, by watching him, what was happening with him. And what was happening was that they penetrated his cloud, they had reached him. Even if their fingers had been a thousand times more gentle than human fingers ever are, he could hardly help feeling that they had stripped him naked and were spitting on that nakedness. For he also had to see that his presence, that music, which was life or death to him, had been torture for them and that they had endured it, not at all for his sake, but only for mine. And Sonny couldn't take that. He can take it a little better today than he could then but he's still not very good at it and, frankly, I don't know anybody who is.

The silence of the next few days must have been louder than the sound of all the music ever played since time began. One morning, before she went to work, Isabel was in his room for something and she suddenly realized that all of his records were gone. And she knew for certain that he was gone. And he was. He went as far as the navy would carry him. He finally sent me a postcard from some place in Greece and that was the first I knew that Sonny was still alive. I didn't see him any more until we were both back in New York and the war had long been over.

He was a man by then, of course, but I wasn't willing to see it. He came by the house from time to time, but we fought almost every time we met. I didn't like the

---

[8] The area of Manhattan's Lower East Side which has traditionally been the center of New York's avant-garde cultural life.

way he carried himself, loose and dreamlike all the time, and I didn't like his friends, and his music seemed to be merely an excuse for the life he led. It sounded just that weird and disordered.

Then we had a fight, a pretty awful fight, and I didn't see him for months. By and by I looked him up, where he was living, in a furnished room in the Village, and I tried to make it up. But there were lots of other people in the room and Sonny just lay on his bed, and he wouldn't come downstairs with me, and he treated these other people as though they were his family and I weren't. So I got mad and then he got mad, and then I told him that he might just as well be dead as live the way he was living. Then he stood up and he told me not to worry about him any more in life, that he *was* dead as far as I was concerned. Then he pushed me to the door and the other people looked on as though nothing were happening, and he slammed the door behind me. I stood in the hallway, staring at the door. I heard somebody laugh in the room and then the tears came to my eyes. I started down the steps, whistling to keep from crying, I kept whistling to myself, *You going to need me, baby, one of these cold, rainy days.*

I read about Sonny's trouble in the spring. Little Grace died in the fall. She was a beautiful little girl. But she only lived a little over two years. She died of polio and she suffered. She had a slight fever for a couple of days, but it didn't seem like anything and we just kept her in bed. And we would certainly have called the doctor, but the fever dropped, she seemed to be all right. So we thought it had just been a cold. Then, one day, she was up, playing, Isabel was in the kitchen fixing lunch for the two boys when they'd come in from school, and she heard Grace fall down in the living room. When you have a lot of children you don't always start running when one of them falls, unless they start screaming or something. And, this time, Grace was quiet. Yet, Isabel says that when she heard that *thump* and then that silence, something happened in her to make her afraid. And she ran to the living room and there was little Grace on the floor, all twisted up, and the reason she hadn't screamed was that she couldn't get her breath. And when she did scream, it was the worst sound, Isabel says, that she'd ever heard in all her life, and she still hears it sometimes in her dreams. Isabel will sometimes wake me up with a low, moaning, strangled sound and I have to be quick to awaken her and hold her to me and where Isabel is weeping against me seems a mortal wound.

I think I may have written Sonny the very day that little Grace was buried. I was sitting in the living room in the dark, by myself, and I suddenly thought of Sonny. My trouble made his real.

One Saturday afternoon, when Sonny had been living with us, or, anyway, been in our house, for nearly two weeks, I found myself wandering aimlessly about the living room, drinking from a can of beer, and trying to work up the courage to search Sonny's room. He was out, he was usually out whenever I was home, and Isabel had taken the children to see their grandparents. Suddenly I was standing still in front of the living room window, watching Seventh Avenue. The idea of searching Sonny's room made me still. I scarcely dared to admit to myself what I'd be searching for. I didn't know what I'd do if I found it. Or if I didn't.

On the sidewalk across from me, near the entrance to a barbecue joint, some people were holding an old-fashioned revival meeting. The barbecue cook, wearing a dirty white apron, his conked[9] hair reddish and metallic in the pale sun, and

[9] Straightened and greased.

a cigarette between his lips, stood in the doorway, watching them. Kids and older people paused in their errands and stood there, along with some older men and a couple of very tough-looking women who watched everything that happened on the avenue, as though they owned it, or were maybe owned by it. Well, they were watching this, too. The revival was being carried on by three sisters in black, and a brother. All they had were their voices and their Bibles and a tambourine. The brother was testifying[10] and while he testified two of the sisters stood together, seeming to say, amen, and the third sister walked around with the tambourine outstretched and a couple of people dropped coins into it. Then the brother's testimony ended and the sister who had been taking up the collection dumped the coins into her palm and transferred them to the pocket of her long black robe. Then she raised both hands, striking the tambourine against the air, and then against one hand, and she started to sing. And the two other sisters and the brother joined in.

It was strange, suddenly, to watch, though I had been seeing these street meetings all my life. So, of course, had everybody else down there. Yet, they paused and watched and listened and I stood still at the window. "*'Tis the old ship of Zion,*" they sang, and the sister with the tambourine kept a steady, jangling beat, "*it has rescued many a thousand!*" Not a soul under the sound of their voices was hearing this song for the first time, not one of them had been rescued. Nor had they seen much in the way of rescue work being done around them. Neither did they especially believe in the holiness of the three sisters and the brother, they knew too much about them, knew where they lived, and how. The woman with the tambourine, whose voice dominated the air, whose face was bright with joy, was divided by very little from the woman who stood watching her, a cigarette between her heavy, chapped lips, her hair a cuckoo's nest, her face scarred and swollen from many beatings, and her black eyes glittering like coal. Perhaps they both knew this, which was why, when, as rarely, they addressed each other, they addressed each other as Sister. As the singing filled the air the watching, listening faces underwent a change, the eyes focusing on something within; the music seemed to soothe a poison out of them; and time seemed, nearly, to fall away from the sullen, belligerent, battered faces, as though they were fleeing back to their first condition, while dreaming of their last. The barbecue cook half shook his head and smiled, and dropped his cigarette and disappeared into his joint. A man fumbled in his pockets for change and stood holding it in his hand impatiently, as though he had just remembered a pressing appointment further up the avenue. He looked furious. Then I saw Sonny, standing on the edge of the crowd. He was carrying a wide, flat notebook with a green cover, and it made him look, from where I was standing, almost like a schoolboy. The coppery sun brought out the copper in his skin, he was very faintly smiling, standing very still. Then the singing stopped, the tambourine turned into a collection plate again. The furious man dropped in his coins and vanished, so did a couple of the women, and Sonny dropped some change in the plate, looking directly at the woman with a little smile. He started across the avenue, toward the house. He has a slow, loping walk, something like the way Harlem hipsters walk, only he's imposed on this his own half-beat. I had never really noticed it before.

I stayed at the window, both relieved and apprehensive. As Sonny disappeared from my sight, they began singing again. And they were still singing when his key turned in the lock.

[10] Publicly professing his religious faith.

"Hey," he said.

"Hey, yourself. You want some beer?"

"No. Well, maybe." But he came up to the window and stood beside me, looking out. "What a warm voice," he said.

They were singing *If I could only hear my mother pray again!*

"Yes," I said, "and she can sure beat that tambourine."

"But what a terrible song," he said, and laughed. He dropped his notebook on the sofa and disappeared into the kitchen. "Where's Isabel and the kids?"

"I think they went to see their grandparents. You hungry?"

"No." He came back into the living room with his can of beer. "You want to come some place with me tonight?"

I sensed, I don't know how, that I couldn't possibly say no. "Sure. Where?"

He sat down on the sofa and picked up his notebook and started leafing through it. "I'm going to sit in with some fellows in a joint in the Village."

"You mean, you're going to play, tonight?"

"That's right." He took a swallow of his beer and moved back to the window. He gave me a sidelong look. "If you can stand it."

"I'll try," I said.

He smiled to himself and we both watched as the meeting across the way broke up. The three sisters and the brother, heads bowed, were singing *God be with you till we meet again.* The faces around them were very quiet. Then the song ended. The small crowd dispersed. We watched the three women and the lone man walk slowly up the avenue.

"When she was singing before," said Sonny, abruptly, "her voice reminded me for a minute of what heroin feels like sometimes—when it's in your veins. It makes you feel sort of warm and cool at the same time. And distant. And—and sure." He sipped his beer, very deliberately not looking at me. I watched his face. "It makes you feel—in control. Sometimes you've got to have that feeling."

"Do you?" I sat down slowly in the easy chair.

"Sometimes." He went to the sofa and picked up his notebook again. "Some people do."

"In order," I asked, "to play?" And my voice was very ugly, full of contempt and anger.

"Well"—he looked at me with great, troubled eyes, as though, in fact, he hoped his eyes would tell me things he could never otherwise say—"they *think* so. And *if* they think so—!"

"And what do *you* think?" I asked.

He sat on the sofa and put his can of beer on the floor. "I don't know," he said, and I couldn't be sure if he were answering my question or pursuing his thoughts. His face didn't tell me. "It's not so much to *play*. It's to *stand* it, to be able to make it at all. On any level." He frowned and smiled: "In order to keep from shaking to pieces."

"But these friends of yours," I said, "they seem to shake themselves to pieces pretty goddamn fast."

"Maybe." He played with the notebook. And something told me that I should curb my tongue, that Sonny was doing his best to talk, that I should listen. "But of course you only know the ones that've gone to pieces. Some don't—or at least they haven't *yet* and that's just about all *any* of us can say." He paused. "And then there are some who just live, really, in hell, and they know it and they see what's happening and they go right on. I don't know." He sighed, dropped the notebook, folded his arms. "Some guys, you can tell from the way they play, they on something *all* the time. And you can see that, well, it makes something real for them. But of course," he picked up his beer from the floor and sipped it and put the can down again, "they *want* to, too, you've got to see that. Even some of them that say they don't—*some*, not all."

"And what about you?" I asked—I couldn't help it. "What about you? Do *you* want to?"

He stood up and walked to the window and remained silent for a long time. Then he sighed. "Me," he said. Then: "While I was downstairs before, on my way here, listening to that woman sing, it struck me all of a sudden how much suffering she must have had to go through—to sing like that. It's *repulsive* to think you have to suffer that much."

I said: "But there's no way not to suffer—is there, Sonny?"

"I believe not," he said and smiled, "but that's never stopped anyone from trying." He looked at me. "Has it?" I realized, with this mocking look, that there stood between us, forever, beyond the power of time or forgiveness, the fact that I had held silence—so long!—when he had needed human speech to help him. He turned back to the window. "No, there's no way not to suffer. But you try all kinds of ways to keep from drowning in it, to keep on top of it, and to make it seem—well, like *you.* Like you did something, all right, and now you're suffering for it. You know?" I said nothing. "Well you know," he said, impatiently, "why *do* people suffer? Maybe it's better to do something to give it a reason, *any* reason."

"But we just agreed," I said, "that there's no way not to suffer. Isn't it better, then, just to—take it?"

"But nobody just takes it," Sonny cried, "that's what I'm telling you! *Everybody* tries not to. You're just hung up on the *way* some people try—it's not *your* way!"

The hair on my face began to itch, my face felt wet. "That's not true," I said, "that's not true. I don't give a damn what other people do, I don't even care how they suffer. I just care how *you* suffer." And he looked at me. "Please believe me," I said, "I don't want to see you—die—trying not to suffer."

"I won't," he said, flatly, "die trying not to suffer. At least, not any faster than anybody else."

"But there's no need," I said, trying to laugh, "is there? in killing yourself."

I wanted to say more, but I couldn't. I wanted to talk about will power and how life could be—well, beautiful. I wanted to say that it was all within; but was it? or, rather, wasn't that exactly the trouble? And I wanted to promise that I would never fail him again. But it would all have sounded—empty words and lies.

So I made the promise to myself and prayed that I would keep it.

"It's terrible sometimes, inside," he said, "that's what's the trouble. You walk these streets, black and funky and cold, and there's not really a living ass to talk to, and there's nothing shaking, and there's no way of getting it out—that storm inside. You can't talk it and you can't make love with it, and when you finally try to get with it and play it, you realize *nobody's* listening. So *you've* got to listen. You got to find a way to listen."

And then he walked away from the window and sat on the sofa again, as though all the wind had suddenly been knocked out of him. "Sometimes you'll do *any-thing* to play, even cut your mother's throat." He laughed and looked at me. "Or your brother's." Then he sobered. "Or your own." Then: "Don't worry. I'm all right now and I think I'll *be* all right. But I can't forget—where I've been. I don't mean just the physical place I've been, I mean where I've *been.* And *what* I've been."

"What have you been, Sonny?" I asked.

He smiled—but sat sideways on the sofa, his elbow resting on the back, his fingers playing with his mouth and chin, not looking at me. "I've been something I didn't recognize, didn't know I could be. Didn't know anybody could be." He stopped, looking inward, looking helplessly young, looking old. "I'm not talking about it now because I feel *guilty* or anything like that—maybe it would be better if I did, I don't know. Anyway, I can't really talk about it. Not to you, not to anybody," and now he turned and faced me. "Sometimes, you know, and it was actually when I was most *out* of the world, I felt that I was in it, that I was *with* it, really, and I could play or I didn't really have to *play*, it just came out of me, it was there. And I don't know how I played, thinking about it now, but I know I did awful things, those times, sometimes, to people. Or it wasn't that I *did* anything to them—it was that they weren't real." He picked up the beer can; it was empty; he rolled it between his palms: "And other times—well, I needed a fix, I needed to find a place to lean, I needed to clear a space to *listen*—and I couldn't find it, and I—went crazy, I did terrible things to *me*, I was terrible *for* me." He began pressing the beer can between his hands, I watched the metal begin to give. It glittered, as he played with it, like a knife, and I was afraid he would cut himself, but I said nothing. "Oh well. I can never tell you. I was all by myself at the bottom of something, stinking and sweating and crying and shaking, and I smelled it, you know? *my* stink, and I thought I'd die if I couldn't get away from it and yet, all the same, I knew that everything I was doing was just locking me in with it. And I didn't know," he paused, still flattening the beer can, "I didn't know, I still *don't* know, something kept telling me that maybe it was good to smell your own stink, but I didn't think that *that* was what I'd been trying to do—and—who can stand it?" and he abruptly dropped the ruined beer can, looking at me with a small, still smile, and then rose, walking to the window as though it were the lodestone rock. I watched his face, he watched the avenue. "I couldn't tell you when Mama died—but the reason I wanted to leave Harlem so bad was to get away from drugs. And then, when I ran away, that's what I was running from—really. When I came back, nothing had changed, *I* hadn't changed, I was just—older." And he stopped, drumming with his fingers on the windowpane. The sun had vanished, soon darkness would fall. I watched his face. "It can come again," he said, almost as though speaking to himself. Then he turned to me. "It can come again," he repeated. "I just want you to know that."

"All right," I said, at last. "So it can come again. All right."

He smiled, but the smile was sorrowful. "I had to try to tell you," he said.

"Yes," I said. "I understand that."

"You're my brother," he said, looking straight at me, and not smiling at all.

"Yes," I repeated, "yes. I understand that."

He turned back to the window, looking out. "All that hatred down there," he said, "all that hatred and misery and love. It's a wonder it doesn't blow the avenue apart."

We went to the only nightclub on a short, dark street, downtown. We squeezed through the narrow, chattering, jam-packed bar to the entrance of the big room, where the bandstand was. And we stood there for a moment, for the lights were very dim in this room and we couldn't see. Then, "Hello, boy," said a voice and an enormous black man, much older than Sonny or myself, erupted out of all that atmospheric lighting and put an arm around Sonny's shoulder. "I been sitting right here," he said, "waiting for you."

He had a big voice, too, and heads in the darkness turned toward us.

Sonny grinned and pulled a little away, and said, "Creole, this is my brother. I told you about him."

Creole shook my hand. "I'm glad to meet you, son," he said, and it was clear that he was glad to meet me *there*, for Sonny's sake. And he smiled, "You got a real musician in *your* family," and he took his arm from Sonny's shoulder and slapped him, lightly, affectionately, with the back of his hand.

"Well. Now I've heard it all," said a voice behind us. This was another musician, and a friend of Sonny's, a coal-black, cheerful-looking man, built close to the ground. He immediately began confiding to me, at the top of his lungs, the most terrible things about Sonny, his teeth gleaming like a lighthouse and his laugh coming up out of him like the beginning of an earthquake. And it turned out that everyone at the bar knew Sonny, or almost everyone; some were musicians, working there, or nearby, or not working, some were simply hangers-on, and some were there to hear Sonny play. I was introduced to all of them and they were all very polite to me. Yet, it was clear that, for them, I was only Sonny's brother. Here, I was in Sonny's world. Or, rather: his kingdom. Here, it was not even a question that his veins bore royal blood.

They were going to play soon and Creole installed me, by myself, at a table in a dark corner. Then I watched them, Creole, and the little black man, and Sonny, and the others, while they horsed around, standing just below the bandstand. The light from the bandstand spilled just a little short of them and, watching them laughing and gesturing and moving about, I had the feeling that they, nevertheless, were being most careful not to step into that circle of light too suddenly: that if they moved into the light too suddenly, without thinking, they would perish in flame. Then, while I watched, one of them, the small, black man, moved into the light and crossed the bandstand and started fooling around with his drums. Then—being funny and being, also, extremely ceremonious—Creole took Sonny by the arm and led him to the piano. A woman's voice called Sonny's name and a few hands started clapping. And Sonny, also being funny and being ceremonious, and so touched, I think, that he could have cried, but neither hiding it nor showing it, riding it like a man, grinned, and put both hands to his heart and bowed from the waist.

Creole then went to the bass fiddle and a lean, very bright-skinned brown man jumped up on the bandstand and picked up his horn. So there they were, and the atmosphere on the bandstand and in the room began to change and tighten. Someone stepped up to the microphone and announced them. Then there were all kinds of murmurs. Some people at the bar shushed others. The waitress ran around, frantically getting in the last orders, guys and chicks got closer to each other, and the lights on the bandstand, on the quartet, turned to a kind of indigo. Then they all looked different there. Creole looked about him for the last time, as though he were making certain that all his chickens were in the coop, and then he—jumped and struck the fiddle. And there they were.

All I know about music is that not many people ever really hear it. And even then, on the rare occasions when something opens within, and the music enters, what we mainly hear, or hear corroborated, are personal, private, vanishing evocations. But the man who creates the music is hearing something else, is dealing with the roar rising from the void and imposing order on it as it hits the air. What is evoked in him, then, is of another order, more terrible because it has no words, and triumphant, too, for that same reason. And his triumph, when he triumphs, is ours. I just watched Sonny's face. His face was troubled, he was working hard, but he wasn't with it. And I had the feeling that, in a way, everyone on the bandstand was waiting for him, both waiting for him and pushing him along. But as I began to watch Creole, I realized that it was Creole who held them all back. He had them on a short rein. Up there, keeping the beat with his whole body, wailing on the fiddle, with his eyes half closed, he was listening to everything, but he was listening to Sonny. He was having a dialogue with Sonny. He wanted Sonny to leave the shoreline and strike out for the deep water. He was Sonny's witness that deep water and drowning were not the same thing—he had been there, and he knew. And he wanted Sonny to know. He was waiting for Sonny to do the things on the keys which would let Creole know that Sonny was in the water.

And, while Creole listened, Sonny moved, deep within, exactly like someone in torment. I had never before thought of how awful the relationship must be between the musician and his instrument. He has to fill it, this instrument, with the breath of life, his own. He has to make it do what he wants it to do. And a piano is just a piano. It's made out of so much wood and wires and little hammers and big ones, and ivory. While there's only so much you can do with it, the only way to find this out is to try; to try and make it do everything.

And Sonny hadn't been near a piano for over a year. And he wasn't on much better terms with his life, not the life that stretched before him now. He and the piano stammered, started one way, got scared, stopped; started another way, panicked, marked time, started again; then seemed to have found a direction, panicked again, got stuck. And the face I saw on Sonny I'd never seen before. Everything had been burned out of it, and, at the same time, things usually hidden were being burned in, by the fire and fury of the battle which was occurring in him up there.

Yet, watching Creole's face as they neared the end of the first set, I had the feeling that something had happened, something I hadn't heard. Then they finished, there was scattered applause, and then, without an instant's warning, Creole started into something else, it was almost sardonic, it was Am I Blue.[11] And, as though he commanded, Sonny began to play. Something began to happen. And Creole let out the reins. The dry, low, black man said something awful on the drums, Creole answered, and the drums talked back. Then the horn insisted, sweet and high, slightly detached perhaps, and Creole listened, commenting now and then, dry, and driving, beautiful and calm and old. Then they all came together again, and Sonny was part of the family again. I could tell this from his face. He seemed to have found, right there beneath his fingers, a damn brand-new piano. It seemed that he couldn't get over it. Then, for awhile, just being happy with Sonny, they seemed to be agreeing with him that brand-new pianos certainly were a gas.

Then Creole stepped forward to remind them that what they were playing was the blues. He hit something in all of them, he hit something in me, myself, and the music tightened and deepened, apprehension began to beat the air. Creole began to tell us what the blues were all about. They were not about anything very new. He and his boys up there were keeping it new, at the risk of ruin, destruction, madness, and death, in order to find new ways to make us listen. For, while the tale of how we suffer, and how we are delighted, and how we may triumph is never new, it always must be heard. There isn't any other tale to tell, it's the only light we've got in all this darkness.

And this tale, according to that face, that body, those strong hands on those

---

[11] Blues song, written by Grant Clark and Harry Akst and recorded by famous blues singer Billie Holiday.

strings, has another aspect in every country, and a new depth in every generation. Listen, Creole seemed to be saying, listen. Now these are Sonny's blues. He made the little black man on the drums know it, and the bright, brown man on the horn. Creole wasn't trying any longer to get Sonny in the water. He was wishing him Godspeed. Then he stepped back, very slowly, filling the air with the immense suggestion that Sonny speak for himself.

Then they all gathered around Sonny and Sonny played. Every now and again one of them seemed to say, amen. Sonny's fingers filled the air with life, his life. But that life contained so many others. And Sonny went all the way back, he really began with the spare, flat statement of the opening phrase of the song. Then he began to make it his. It was very beautiful because it wasn't hurried and it was no longer a lament. I seemed to hear with what burning he had made it his, with what burning we had yet to make it ours, how we could cease lamenting. Freedom lurked around us and I understood, at last, that he could help us to be free if we would listen, that he would never be free until we did. Yet, there was no battle in his face now. I heard what he had gone through, and would continue to go through until he came to rest in earth. He had made it his: that long line, of which we knew only Mama and Daddy. And he was giving it back, as everything must be given back, so that, passing through death, it can live forever. I saw my mother's face again, and felt, for the first time, how the stones of the road she had walked on must have bruised her feet. I saw the moonlit road where my father's brother died. And it brought something else back to me, and carried me past it, I saw my little girl again and felt Isabel's tears again, and I felt my own tears begin to rise. And I was yet aware that this was only a moment, that the world waited outside, as hungry as a tiger, and that trouble stretched above us, longer than the sky.

Then it was over. Creole and Sonny let out their breath, both soaking wet, and grinning. There was a lot of applause and some of it was real. In the dark, the girl came by and I asked her to take drinks to the bandstand. There was a long pause, while they talked up there in the indigo light and after awhile I saw the girl put a Scotch and milk on top of the piano for Sonny. He didn't seem to notice it, but just before they started playing again, he sipped from it and looked toward me, and nodded. Then he put it back on top of the piano. For me, then, as they began to play again, it glowed and shook above my brother's head like the very cup of trembling.[12]

[1957]

---

[12] See Isaiah 51:17–23.

Tillie Olsen   *1913–*

I STAND HERE IRONING

I stand here ironing, and what you asked me moves tormented back and forth with the iron.

"I wish you would manage the time to come in and talk with me about your daughter. I'm sure you can help me understand her. She's a youngster who needs help and whom I'm deeply interested in helping."

"Who needs help.". . . Even if I came, what good would it do? You think because I am her mother I have a key, or that in some way you could use me as a key? She has lived for nineteen years. There is all that life that has happened outside of me, beyond me.

And when is there time to remember, to sift, to weigh, to estimate, to total? I will start and there will be an interruption and I will have to gather it all together again. Or I will become engulfed with all I did or did not do, with what should have been and what cannot be helped.

She was a beautiful baby. The first and only one of our five that was beautiful at birth. You do not guess how new and uneasy her tenancy in her now-loveliness. You did not know her all those years she was thought homely, or see her poring over her baby pictures, making me tell her over and over how beautiful she had been—and would be, I would tell her—and was now, to the seeing eye. But the seeing eyes were few or non-existent. Including mine.

I nursed her. They feel that's important nowadays. I nursed all the children, but with her, with all the fierce rigidity of first motherhood, I did like the books then said. Though her cries battered me to trembling and my breasts ached with swollenness, I waited till the clock decreed.

Why do I put that first? I do not even know if it matters, or if it explains anything.

She was a beautiful baby. She blew shining bubbles of sound. She loved motion, loved light, loved color and music and textures. She would lie on the floor in her blue overalls patting the surface so hard in ecstasy her hands and feet would blur. She was a miracle to me, but when she was eight months old I had to leave her daytimes with the woman downstairs to whom she was no miracle at all, for I worked or looked for work and for Emily's father, who "could no longer endure" (he wrote in his good-bye note) "sharing want with us."

I was nineteen. It was the pre-relief, pre-WPA[1] world of the depression. I would start running as soon as I got off the streetcar, running up the stairs, the place smelling sour, and awake or asleep to startle awake, when she saw me she would break into a clogged weeping that could not be comforted, a weeping I can hear yet.

After a while I found a job hashing at night so I could be with her days, and it was better. But it came to where I had to bring her to his family and leave her.

It took a long time to raise the money for her fare back. Then she got chicken pox and I had to wait longer. When she finally came, I hardly knew her, walking quick and nervous like her father, looking like her father, thin, and dressed in a

---

[1] The Works Progress Administration (WPA) was created by President Franklin D. Roosevelt in June 1933 to create jobs during the Great Depression.

shoddy red that yellowed her skin and glared at the pockmarks. All the baby loveliness gone.

She was two. Old enough for nursery school they said, and I did not know then what I know now—the fatigue of the long day, and the lacerations of group life in the kinds of nurseries that are only parking places for children.

Except that it would have made no difference if I had known. It was the only place there was. It was the only way we could be together, the only way I could hold a job.

And even without knowing, I knew. I knew the teacher that was evil because all these years it has curdled into my memory, the little boy hunched in the corner, her rasp, "why aren't you outside, because Alvin hits you? that's no reason, go out, scaredy." I knew Emily hated it even if she did not clutch and implore "don't go Mommy" like the other children, mornings.

She always had a reason why we should stay home. Momma, you look sick, Momma. I feel sick, Momma, the teachers aren't there today, they're sick. Momma, we can't go, there was a fire there last night. Momma, it's a holiday today, no school, they told me.

But never a direct protest, never rebellion. I think of our others in their three-, four-year-oldness—the explosions, the tempers, the denunciations, the demands —and I feel suddenly ill. I put the iron down. What in me demanded that goodness in her? And what was the cost, the cost to her of such goodness?

The old man living in the back once said in his gentle way: "You should smile at Emily more when you look at her." What *was* in my face when I looked at her? I loved her. There were all the acts of love.

It was only with the others I remembered what he said, and it was the face of joy, and not of care or tightness or worry I turned to them—too late for Emily. She does not smile easily, let alone almost always as her brothers and sisters do. Her face is closed and sombre, but when she wants, how fluid. You must have seen it in her pantomimes, you spoke of her rare gift for comedy on the stage that rouses a laughter out of the audience so dear they applaud and applaud and do not want to let her go.

Where does it come from, that comedy? There was none of it in her when she came back to me that second time, after I had had to send her away again. She had a new daddy now to learn to love, and I think perhaps it was a better time.

Except when we left her alone nights, telling ourselves she was old enough. "Can't you go some other time, Mommy, like tomorrow?" she would ask. "Will it be just a little while you'll be gone? Do you promise?"

The time we came back, the front door open, the clock on the floor in the hall. She rigid awake. "It wasn't just a little while. I didn't cry. Three times I called you, just three times, and then I ran downstairs to open the door so you could come faster. The clock talked loud. I threw it away, it scared me what it talked."

She said the clock talked loud again that night I went to the hospital to have Susan. She was delirious with the fever that comes before red measles, but she was fully conscious all the week I was gone and the week after we were home when she could not come near the new baby or me.

She did not get well. She stayed skeleton thin, not wanting to eat, and night after night she had nightmares. She would call for me, and I would rouse from exhaustion to sleepily call back: "You're all right, darling, go to sleep, it's just a dream," and if she still called, in a sterner voice, "now go to sleep, Emily, there's nothing to hurt you." Twice, only twice, when I had to get up for Susan anyhow, I went in to sit with her.

Now when it is too late (as if she would let me hold and comfort her like I do the others) I get up and go to her at once at her moan or restless stirring. "Are you awake, Emily? Can I get you something?" And the answer is always the same: "No, I'm all right, go back to sleep, Mother."

They persuaded me at the clinic to send her away to a convalescent home in the country where "she can have the kind of food and care you can't manage for her, and you'll be free to concentrate on the new baby." They still send children to that place. I see pictures on the society page of sleek young women planning affairs to raise money for it, or dancing at the affairs, or decorating Easter eggs or filling Christmas stockings for the children.

They never have a picture of the children so I do not know if the girls still wear those gigantic red bows and the ravaged looks on the every other Sunday when parents can come to visit "unless otherwise notified"—as we were notified the first six weeks.

Oh it is a handsome place, green lawns and tall trees and fluted flower beds. High up on the balconies of each cottage the children stand, the girls in their red bows and white dresses, the boys in white suits and giant red ties. The parents stand below shrieking up to be heard and the children shriek down to be heard, and between them the invisible wall "Not To Be Contaminated by Parental Germs or Physical Affection."

There was a tiny girl who always stood hand in hand with Emily. Her parents never came. One visit she was gone. "They moved her to Rose College," Emily shouted in explanation. "They don't like you to love anybody here."

She wrote once a week, the labored writing of a seven-year-old. "I am fine. How is the baby. If I write my leter nicly I will have a star. Love." There never was a star. We wrote every other day, letters she could never hold or keep but only hear read—once. "We simply do not have room for children to keep any personal possessions," they patiently explained when we pieced one Sunday's shrieking together to plead how much it would mean to Emily, who loved so to keep things, to be allowed to keep her letters and cards.

Each visit she looked frailer. "She isn't eating," they told us.

(They had runny eggs for breakfast or mush with lumps, Emily said later, I'd hold it in my mouth and not swallow. Nothing ever tasted good, just when they had chicken.)

It took us eight months to get her released home, and only the fact that she gained back so little of her seven lost pounds convinced the social worker.

I used to try to hold and love her after she came back, but her body would stay stiff, and after a while she'd push away. She ate little. Food sickened her, and I think much of life too. Oh she had physical lightness and brightness, twinkling by on skates, bouncing like a ball up and down up and down over the jump rope, skimming over the hill; but these were momentary.

She fretted about her appearance, thin and dark and foreign-looking at a time when every little girl was supposed to look or thought she should look a chubby blonde replica of Shirley Temple[2]. The doorbell sometimes rang for her, but no one seemed to come and play in the house or be a best friend. Maybe because we moved so much.

There was a boy she loved painfully through two school semesters. Months later she told me how she had taken pennies from my purse to buy him candy. "Licorice was his favorite and I brought him some every day, but he still liked Jennifer

[2] Shirley Temple (1928–   ) was the most popular child actress of the 1930s.

better'n me. Why, Mommy?'' The kind of question for which there is no answer.

School was a worry to her. She was not glib or quick in a world where glibness and quickness were easily confused with ability to learn. To her overworked and exasperated teachers she was an overconscientious "slow learner" who kept trying to catch up and was absent entirely too often.

I let her be absent, though sometimes the illness was imaginary. How different from my now-strictness about attendance with the others. I wasn't working. We had a new baby, I was home anyhow. Sometimes, after Susan grew old enough, I would keep her home from school, too, to have them all together.

Mostly Emily had asthma, and her breathing, harsh and labored, would fill the house with a curiously tranquil sound. I would bring the two old dresser mirrors and her boxes of collections to her bed. She would select beads and single earrings, bottle tops and shells, dried flowers and pebbles, old postcards and scraps, all sorts of oddments; then she and Susan would play Kingdom, setting up landscapes and furniture, peopling them with action.

Those were the only times of peaceful companionship between her and Susan. I have edged away from it, that poisonous feeling between them, that terrible balancing of hurts and needs I had to do between the two, and did so badly, those earlier years.

Oh there are conflicts between the others too, each one human, needing, demanding, hurting, taking—but only between Emily and Susan, no, Emily toward Susan that corroding resentment. It seems so obvious on the surface, yet it is not obvious. Susan, the second child, Susan, golden- and curly-haired and chubby, quick and articulate and assured, everything in appearance and manner Emily was not; Susan, not able to resist Emily's precious things, losing or sometimes clumsily breaking them; Susan telling jokes and riddles to company for applause while Emily sat silent (to say to me later: that was *my* riddle, Mother, I told it to Susan); Susan, who for all the five years' difference in age was just a year behind Emily in developing physically.

I am glad for that slow physical development that widened the difference between her and her contemporaries, though she suffered over it. She was too vulnerable for that terrible world of youthful competition, of preening and parading, of constant measuring of yourself against every other, of envy, "If I had that copper hair," "If I had that skin. . . ." She tormented herself enough about not looking like the others, there was enough of the unsureness, the having to be conscious of words before you speak, the constant caring—what are they thinking of me? without having it all magnified by the merciless physical drives.

Ronnie is calling. He is wet and I change him. It is rare there is such a cry now. That time of motherhood is almost behind me when the ear is not one's own but must always be racked and listening for the child cry, the child call. We sit for a while and I hold him, looking out over the city spread in charcoal with its soft aisles of light. "*Shoogily,*" he breathes and curls closer. I carry him back to bed, asleep. *Shoogily.* A funny word, a family word, inherited from Emily, invented by her to say: *comfort.*

In this and other ways she leaves her seal, I say aloud. And startle at my saying it. What do I mean? What did I start to gather together, to try and make coherent? I was at the terrible, growing years. War years. I do not remember them well. I was working, there were four smaller ones now, there was not time for her. She had to help be a mother, and housekeeper, and shopper. She had to set her seal. Mornings of crisis and near hysteria trying to get lunches packed, hair combed, coats and shoes found, everyone to school or Child Care on time, the baby ready for transportation. And always the paper scribbled on by a smaller one, the book looked at by Susan then mislaid, the homeowrk not done. Running out to that huge school where she was one, she was lost, she was a drop, suffering over the unpreparedness, stammering and unsure in her classes.

There was so little time left at night after the kids were bedded down. She would struggle over books, always eating (it was in those years she developed her enormous appetite that is legendary in our family) and I would be ironing, or preparing food for the next day, or writing V-mail[3] to Bill, or tending the baby. Sometimes, to make me laugh, or out of despair, she would imitate happenings or types at school.

I think I said once: "Why don't you do something like this in the school amateur show?" One morning she phoned me at work, hardly understandable through the weeping: "Mother, I did it. I won, I won; they gave me first prize; they clapped and clapped and wouldn't let me go."

Now suddenly she was Somebody, and as imprisoned in her difference as she had been in anonymity.

She began to be asked to perform at other high schools, even in colleges, then at city and statewide affairs. The first one we went to, I only recognized her that first moment when thin, shy, she almost drowned herself into the curtains. Then: Was this Emily? The control, the command, the convulsing and deadly clowning, the spell, then the roaring, stamping audience, unwilling to let this rare and precious laughter out of their lives.

Afterwards: You ought to do something about her with a gift like that—but without money or knowing how, what does one do? We have left it all to her, and the gift has as often eddied inside, clogged and clotted, as been used and growing.

She is coming. She runs up the stairs two at a time with her light graceful step, and I know she is happy tonight. Whatever it was that occasioned your call did not happen today.

"Aren't you ever going to finish the ironing, Mother? Whistler painted his mother in a rocker.[4] I'd have to paint mine standing over an ironing board." This is one of her communicative nights and she tells me everything and nothing as she fixes herself a plate of food out of the icebox.

She is so lovely. Why did you want me to come in at all? Why were you concerned? She will find her way.

She starts up the stairs to bed. "Don't get me up with the rest in the morning." "But I thought you were having midterms." "Oh, those," she comes back in, kisses me, and says quite lightly, "in a couple of years when we'll all be atom-dead they won't matter a bit."

She has said it before. She *believes* it. But because I have been dredging the past, and all that compounds a human being is so heavy and meaningful in me, I cannot endure it tonight.

I will never total it all. I will never come in to say: She was a child seldom smiled at. Her father left me before she was a year old. I had to work her first six years when there was work, or I sent her home and to his relatives. There were years she had care she hated. She was dark and thin and foreign-looking in a world where the prestige went to blondness and curly hair and dimples, she was slow where glibness was prized. She was a child of anxious, not proud, love. We were poor and

---

[3] Mail sent to American servicemen overseas during World War II.
[4] An allusion to the famous portrait that James McNeill Whistler (1834–1903) painted of his mother in 1872.

could not afford for her the soil of easy growth. I was a young mother, I was a
distracted mother. There were the other children pushing up, demanding. Her
younger sister seemed all that she was not. There were years she did not want me
to touch her. She kept too much in herself, her life was such she had to keep too
much in herself. My wisdom came too late. She has much to her and probably
little will come of it. She is a child of her age, of depression, of war, of fear.

   Let her be. So all that is in her will not bloom—but in how many does it? There
is still enough left to live by. Only help her to know—help make it so there is cause
for her to know—that she is more than this dress on the ironing board, helpless
before the iron.

                                                                            [1961]

Alice Munro   *1931–*

THE OFFICE

The solution to my life occurred to me one evening while I was ironing a shirt. It was simple but audacious. I went into the living room where my husband was watching television and I said, "I think I ought to have an office."

It sounded fantastic, even to me. What do I want an office for? I have a house; it is pleasant and roomy and has a view of the sea; it provides appropriate places for eating and sleeping, and having baths and conversations with one's friends. Also I have a garden; there is no lack of space.

No. But here comes the disclosure which is not easy for me: I am a writer. That does not sound right. Too presumptuous; phony, or at least unconvincing. Try again. I write. Is that better? I *try* to write. That makes it worse. Hypocritical humility. Well then?

It doesn't matter. However I put it, the words create their space of silence, the delicate moment of exposure. But people are kind, the silence is quickly absorbed by the solicitude of friendly voices, crying variously, how wonderful, and good for *you*, and well, that *is* intriguing. And what do you write, they inquire with spirit. Fiction, I reply, bearing my humiliation by this time with ease, even a suggestion of flippancy, which was not always mine, and again, again, the perceptible circles of dismay are smoothed out by such ready and tactful voices—which have however exhausted their stock of consolatory phrases, and can say only, *"Ah!"*

So this is what I want an office for (I said to my husband): to write in. I was at once aware that it sounded like a finicky requirement, a piece of rare self-indulgence. To write, as everyone knows, you need a typewriter, or at least a pencil, some paper, a table and chair; I have all these things in a corner of my bedroom. But now I want an office as well.

And I was not even sure that I was going to write in it, if we come down to that. Maybe I would sit and stare at the wall; even that prospect was not unpleasant to me. It was really the sound of the word "office" that I liked, its sound of dignity and peace. And purposefulness and importance. But I did not care to mention this to my husband, so I launched instead into a high-flown explanation which went, as I remember, like this:

A house is all right for a man to work in. He brings his work into the house, a place is cleared for it; the house rearranges itself as best it can around him. Everybody recognizes that his work *exists*. He is not expected to answer the telephone, to find things that are lost, to see why the children are crying, or feed the cat. He can shut his door. Imagine (I said) a mother shutting her door, and the children knowing she is behind it; why, the very thought of it is outrageous to them. A woman who sits staring into space, into a country that is not her husband's or her children's is likewise known to be an offence against nature. So a house is not the same for a woman. She is not someone who walks into the house, to make use of it, and will walk out again. She *is* the house; there is no separation possible.

(And this is true, though as usual when arguing for something I am afraid I do not deserve, I put it in too emphatic and emotional terms. At certain times, perhaps on long spring evenings, still rainy and sad, with the cold bulbs in bloom and a light too mild for promise drifting over the sea, I have opened the windows and felt the house shrink into wood and plaster and those humble elements of

494

which it is made, and the life in it subside, leaving me exposed, empty-handed, but feeling a fierce and lawless quiver of freedom, of loneliness too harsh and perfect for me now to bear. Then I know how the rest of the time I am sheltered and encumbered, how insistently I am warmed and bound.)

"Go ahead, if you can find one cheap enough," is all my husband had to say to this. He is not like me, he does not really want explanations. That the heart of another person is a closed book, is something you will hear him say frequently, and without regret.

Even then I did not think it was something that could be accomplished. Perhaps at bottom it seemed to me too improper a wish to be granted. I could almost more easily have wished for a mink coat, for a diamond necklace; these are things women do obtain. The children, learning of my plans, greeted them with the most dashing skepticism and unconcern. Nevertheless I went down to the shopping centre which is two blocks from where I live; there I had noticed for several months, and without thinking how they could pertain to me, a couple of For Rent signs in the upstairs windows of a building that housed a drugstore and a beauty parlour. As I went up the stairs I had a feeling of complete unreality; surely renting was a complicated business, in the case of offices; you did not simply knock on the door of the vacant premises and wait to be admitted; it would have to be done through channels. Also, they would want too much money.

As it turned out, I did not even have to knock. A woman came out of one of the empty offices, dragging a vacuum cleaner, and pushing it with her foot, towards the open door across the hall, which evidently led to an apartment in the rear of the building. She and her husband lived in this apartment; their name was Malley; and it was indeed they who owned the building and rented out the offices. The rooms she had just been vacuuming were, she told me, fitted out for a dentist's office, and so would not interest me, but she would show me the other place. She invited me into her apartment while she put away the vacuum and got her key. Her husband, she said with a sigh I could not interpret, was not at home.

Mrs. Malley was a black-haired, delicate-looking woman, perhaps in her early forties, slatternly but still faintly appealing, with such arbitrary touches of femininity as the thin line of bright lipstick, the pink feather slippers on obviously tender and swollen feet. She had the swaying passivity, the air of exhaustion and muted apprehension, that speaks of a life spent in close attention on a man who is by turns vigorous, crotchety and dependent. How much of this I saw at first, how much decided on later is of course impossible to tell. But I did think that she would have no children, the stress of her life, whatever it was, did not allow it, and in this I was not mistaken.

The room where I waited was evidently a combination living room and office. The first things I noticed were models of ships—galleons, clippers, Queen Marys—sitting on the tables, the window sills, the television. Where there were no ships there were potted plants and a clutter of what are sometimes called "masculine" ornaments—china deer heads, bronze horses, huge ashtrays of heavy, veined, shiny material. On the walls were framed photographs and what might have been diplomas. One photo showed a poodle and a bulldog, dressed in masculine and feminine clothing, and assuming with dismal embarrassment a pose of affection. Written across it was "Old Friends." But the room was really dominated by a portrait, with its own light and a gilded frame; it was of a good-looking, fair-haired man in middle age, sitting behind a desk, wearing a business suit and looking pre-eminently prosperous, rosy and agreeable. Here again, it is probably hindsight on my part that points out that in the portrait there is evident also some uneasiness, some lack of faith the man has in this role, a tendency he has to spread himself too bountifully and insistently, which for all anyone knows may lead to disaster.

Never mind the Malleys. As soon as I saw that office, I wanted it. It was larger than I needed, being divided in such a way that it would be suitable for a doctor's office. (We had a chiropractor in here but he left, says Mrs. Malley in her regretful but uninformative way.) The walls were cold and bare, white with a little grey, to cut the glare for the eyes. Since there were no doctors in evidence, nor had been, as Mrs. Malley freely told me, for some time, I offered twenty-five dollars a month. She said she would have to speak to her husband.

The next time I came my offer was agreed upon, and I met Mr. Malley in the flesh. I explained, as I had already done to his wife, that I did not want to make use of my office during regular business hours, but during the weekends and sometimes in the evening. He asked me what I would use it for, and I told him, not without wondering first whether I ought to say I did stenography.

He absorbed the information with good humour, "Ah, you're a writer."

"Well yes. I write."

"Then we'll do our best to see you're comfortable here," he said expansively. "I'm a great man for hobbies myself. All these ship-models, I do them in my spare time, they're a blessing for the nerves. People need an occupation for their nerves. I daresay you're the same."

"Something the same," I said, resolutely agreeable, even relieved that he saw my behaviour in this hazy and tolerant light. At least he did not ask me, as I half-expected, who was looking after the children, and did my husband approve? Ten years, maybe fifteen, had greatly softened, spread and defeated the man in the picture. His hips and thighs had now a startling accumulation of fat, causing him to move with a sigh, a cushiony settling of flesh, a ponderous matriarchal discomfort. His hair and eyes had faded, his features blurred, and the affable, predatory expression had collapsed into one of troubling humility and chronic mistrust. I did not look at him. I had not planned, in taking an office, to take on the responsibility of knowing any more human beings.

On the weekend I moved in, without the help of my family, who would have been kind. I brought my typewriter and a card table and chair, also a little wooden table on which I set a hot plate, a kettle, a jar of instant coffee, a spoon and a yellow mug. That was all. I brooded with satisfaction on the bareness of my walls, the cheap dignity of my essential furnishings, the remarkable lack of things to dust, wash or polish.

The sight was not so pleasing to Mr. Malley. He knocked on my door soon after I was settled and said that he wanted to explain a few things to me—about unscrewing the light in the outer room, which I would not need, about the radiator and how to work the awning outside the window. He looked around at everything with gloom and mystification and said it was an awfully uncomfortable place for a lady.

"Its perfectly all right for me," I said, not as discouragingly as I would have liked to, because I always have a tendency to placate people whom I dislike for no good reason, or simply do not want to know. I make elaborate offerings of courtesy sometimes, in the foolish hope that they will go away and leave me alone.

"What you want is a nice easy chair to sit in, while you're waiting for inspiration to hit. I've got a chair down in the basement, all kinds of stuff down there since my mother passed on last year. There's a bit of carpet rolled up in a corner down there, it isn't doing anybody any good. We could get this place fixed up so's it'd be a lot more homelike for you."

But really, I said, but really I like it as it is.

"If you wanted to run up some curtains, I'd pay you for the material. Place needs a touch of colour, I'm afraid you'll get morbid sitting in here."

Oh, no, I said, and laughed, I'm sure I won't.

"It'd be a different story if you was a man. A woman wants things a bit cosier."

So I got up and went to the window and looked down into the empty Sunday street through the slats of the Venetian blind, to avoid the accusing vulnerability of his fat face and I tried out a cold voice that is to be heard frequently in my thoughts but has great difficulty getting out of my cowardly mouth. "Mr. Malley, please don't bother me about this any more. I said it suits me. I have everything I want. Thanks for showing me about the light."

The effect was devastating enough to shame me. "I certainly wouldn't dream of bothering you," he said, with precision of speech and aloof sadness. "I merely made these suggestions for your comfort. Had I realized I was in your way, I would of left some time ago." When he had gone I felt better, even a little exhilarated at my victory though still ashamed of how easy it had been. I told myself that he would have had to be discouraged sooner or later, it was better to have it over with at the beginning.

The following weekend he knocked on my door. His expression of humility was exaggerated, almost enough so to seem mocking, yet in another sense it was real and I felt unsure of myself.

"I won't take up a minute of your time," he said. "I never meant to be a nuisance. I just wanted to tell you I'm sorry I offended you last time and I apologize. Here's a little present if you will accept."

He was carrying a plant whose name I did not know; it had thick, glossy leaves and grew out of a pot wrapped lavishly in pink and silver foil.

"There," he said, arranging this plant in a corner of my room. "I don't want any bad feelings with you and me. I'll take the blame. And I thought, maybe she won't accept furnishings, but what's the matter with a nice little plant, that'll brighten things up for you."

It was not possible for me, at this moment, to tell him that I did not want a plant. I hate house plants. He told me how to take care of it, how often to water it and so on; I thanked him. There was nothing else I could do, and I had the unpleasant feeling that beneath his offering of apologies and gifts he was well aware of this and in some way gratified by it. He kept on talking, using the words *bad feelings, offended, apologize.* I tried once to interrupt, with the idea of explaining that I had made provision for an area in my life where good feelings, or bad, did not enter in, that between him and me, in fact, it was not necessary that there be any feelings at all; but this struck me as a hopeless task. How could I confront, in the open, this craving for intimacy? Besides, the plant in its shiny paper had confused me.

"How's the writing progressing?" he said, with an air of putting all our unfortunate differences behind him.

"Oh, about as usual."

"Well if you ever run out of things to write about, I got a barrelful." Pause. "But I guess I'm just eatin' into your time here," he said with a kind of painful buoyancy. This was a test, and I did not pass it. I smiled, my eyes held by that magnificent plant; I said it was all right.

"I was just thinking about the fellow was in here before you. Chiropractor. You could of wrote a book about him."

I assumed a listening position, my hands no longer hovering over the keys. If cowardice and insincerity are big vices of mine, curiosity is certainly another.

"He had a good practice built up here. The only trouble was, he gave more adjustments than was listed in the book of chiropractory. Oh, he was adjusting right and left. I came in here after he moved out, and what do you think I found? Soundproofing! This whole room was soundproofed, to enable him to make his adjustments without disturbing anybody. This very room you're sitting writing your stories in.

"First we knew of it was a lady knocked on my door one day, wanted me to provide her with a passkey to his office. He'd locked his door against her.

"I guess he just got tired of treating her particular case. I guess he figured he'd been knocking away at it long enough. Lady well on in years, you know, and him just a young man. He had a nice young wife too and a couple of the prettiest children you ever would want to see. Filthy some of the things that go on in this world."

It took me some time to realize that he told this story not simply as a piece of gossip, but as something a writer would be particularly interested to hear. Writing and lewdness had a vague delicious connection in his mind. Even this notion, however, seemed so wistful, so infantile, that it struck me as a waste of energy to attack it. I knew now I must avoid hurting him for my own sake, not for his. It had been a great mistake to think that a little roughness would settle things.

The next present was a teapot. I insisted that I drank only coffee and told him to give it to his wife. He said that tea was better for the nerves and that he had known right away I was a nervous person, like himself. The teapot was covered with gilt and roses and I knew that it was not cheap, in spite of its extreme hideousness. I kept it on my table. I also continued to care for the plant, which thrived obscenely in the corner of my room. I could not decide what else to do. He bought me a wastebasket, a fancy one with Chinese mandarins on all eight sides; he got a foam rubber cushion for my chair. I despised myself for submitting to this blackmail. I did not even really pity him; it was just that I could not turn away, I could not turn away from that obsequious hunger. And he knew himself my tolerance was bought; in a way he must have hated me for it.

When he lingered in my office now he told me stories of himself. It occurred to me that he was revealing his life to me in the hope that I would write it down. Of course he had probably revealed it to plenty of people for no particular reason, but in my case there seemed to be a special, even desperate necessity. His life was a series of calamities, as people's lives often are; he had been let down by people he had trusted, refused help by those he had depended on, betrayed by the very friends to whom he had given kindness and material help. Other people, mere strangers and passersby, had taken time to torment him gratuitously, in novel and inventive ways. On occasion, his very life had been threatened. Moreover his wife was a difficulty, her health being poor and her temperament unstable; what was he to do? You see how it is, he said, lifting his hands, but I live. He looked to me to say yes.

I took to coming up the stairs on tiptoe, trying to turn my key without making a noise; this was foolish of course because I could not muffle my typewriter. I actually considered writing in longhand, and wished repeatedly for the evil chiropractor's soundproofing. I told my husband my problem and he said it was not a problem at all. Tell him you're busy, he said. As a matter of fact I did tell him; every time he came to my door, always armed with a little gift or an errand, he asked me how I was and I said that today I was busy. Ah, then, he said, as he eased himself through the door, he would not keep me a minute. And all the time, as I have said, he knew what was going on in my mind, how I weakly longed to be rid of him. He knew but could not afford to care.

One evening after I had gone home I discovered that I had left at the office a letter I had intended to post, and so I went back to get it. I saw from the street that the light was on in the room where I worked. Then I saw him bending over the card table. Of course, he came in at night and read what I had written! He heard me at the door, and when I came in he was picking up my wastebasket, saying he thought he would just tidy things up for me. He went out at once. I did not say anything, but found myself trembling with anger and gratification. To have found a just cause was a wonder, an unbearable relief.

Next time he came to my door I had locked it on the inside. I knew his step, his chummy cajoling knock. I continued typing loudly, but not uninterruptedly, so he would know I heard. He called my name, as if I was playing a trick; I bit my lips together not to answer. Unreasonably as ever, guilt assailed me but I typed on. That day I saw the earth was dry around the roots of the plant; I let it alone.

I was not prepared for what happened next. I found a note taped to my door, which said that Mr. Malley would be obliged if I would step into his office. I went at once to get it over with. He sat at his desk surrounded by obscure evidences of his authority; he looked at me from a distance, as one who was now compelled to see me in a new and sadly unfavourable light; the embarrassment which he showed seemed not for himself, but me. He started off by saying, with a rather stagey reluctance, that he had known of course when he took me in that I was a writer.

"I didn't let that worry me, though I have heard things about writers and artists and that type of person that didn't strike me as very encouraging. You know the sort of thing I mean."

This was something new; I could not think what it might lead to.

"Now you came to me and said, Mr. Malley, I want a place to write in. I believed you. I gave it to you. I didn't ask any questions. That's the kind of person I am. But you know the more I think about it, well, the more I am inclined to wonder."

"Wonder what?" I said.

"And your own attitude, that hasn't helped to put my mind at ease. Locking yourself in and refusing to answer your door. That's not a normal way for a person to behave. Not if they got nothing to hide. No more than it's normal for a young woman, says she has a husband and kids, to spend her time rattling away on a typewriter."

"But I don't think that—"

He lifted his hand, a forgiving gesture. "Now all I ask is, that you be open and aboveboard with me, I think I deserve that much, and if you are using that office for any other purpose, or at any other times than you let on, and having your friends or whoever they are up to see you—"

"I don't know what you mean."

"And another thing, you claim to be a writer. Well I read quite a bit of material, and I never have seen your name in print. Now maybe you write under some other name?"

"No," I said.

"Well I don't doubt there are writers whose names I haven't heard," he said genially. "We'll let that pass. Just you give me your word of honour there won't be any more deceptions, or any carryings-on, et cetera, in that office you occupy—"

My anger was delayed somehow, blocked off by a stupid incredulity. I only knew enough to get up and walk down the hall, his voice trailing after me, and lock the door. I thought—I must go. But after I had sat down in my own room, my work in front of me, I thought again how much I liked this room, how well I worked in it, and I decided not to be forced out. After all, I felt, the struggle between us had reached a deadlock. I could refuse to open the door, refuse to look at his notes, refuse to speak to him when we met. My rent was paid in advance and if I left now it was unlikely that I would get any refund. I resolved not to care. I had been taking my manuscript home every night, to prevent his reading it, and now it seemed that even this precaution was beneath me. What did it matter if he read it, any more than if the mice scampered over it in the dark? Several times after this I found notes on my door. I intended not to read them, but I always did. His accusations grew more specific. He had heard voices in my room. My behaviour was disturbing his wife when she tried to take her afternoon nap. (I never came in the afternoons, except on weekends.) He had found a whisky bottle in the garbage.

I wondered a good deal about that chiropractor. It was not comfortable to see how the legends of Mr. Malley's life were built up.

As the notes grew more virulent our personal encounters ceased. Once or twice I saw his stooped, sweatered back disappearing as I came into the hall. Gradually our relationship passed into something that was entirely fantasy. He accused me now, by note, of being intimate with people from *Numero Cinq*. This was a coffee-house in the neighbourhood, which I imagine he invoked for symbolic purposes. I felt that nothing much more would happen now, the notes would go on, their contents becoming possibly more grotesque and so less likely to affect me.

He knocked on my door on a Sunday morning, about eleven o'clock. I had just come in and taken my coat off and put my kettle on the hot plate.

This time it was another face, remote and transfigured, that shone with the cold light of intense joy at discovering the proofs of sin.

"I wonder," he said with emotion, "if you would mind following me down the hall?"

I followed him. The light was on in the washroom. This washroom was mine and no one else used it, but he had not given me a key for it and it was always open. He stopped in front of it, pushed back the door and stood with his eyes cast down, expelling his breath discreetly.

"Now who done that?" he said, in a voice of pure sorrow.

The walls above the toilet and above the washbasin were covered with drawings and comments of the sort you see sometimes in public washrooms on the beach, and in town hall lavatories in the little decaying towns where I grew up. They were done with a lipstick, as they usually are. Someone must have got up here the night before, I thought, possibly some of the gang who always loafed and cruised around the shopping centre on Saturday nights.

"It should have been locked," I said, coolly and firmly as if thus to remove myself from the scene. "It's quite a mess."

"It sure is. It's pretty filthy language, in my book. Maybe it's just a joke to your friends, but it isn't to me. Not to mention the art work. That's a nice thing to see when you open a door on your own premises in the morning."

I said, "I believe lipstick will wash off."

"I'm just glad I didn't have my wife see a thing like this. Upsets a woman that's had a nice bringing up. Now why don't you ask your friends up here to have a party with their pails and brushes? I'd like to have a look at the people with that kind of a sense of humour."

I turned to walk away and he moved heavily in front of me.

"I don't think there's any question how these decorations found their way onto my walls."

"If you're trying to say I had anything to do with it," I said, quite flatly and wearily, "you must be crazy."

"How did they get there then? Whose lavatory is this? Eh, whose?"

"There isn't any key to it. Anybody can come up here and walk in. Maybe some kids off the street came up here and did it last night after I went home, how do I know?"

"It's a shame the way the kids gets blamed for everything, when it's the elders that corrupts them. That's a thing you might do some thinking about, you know. There's laws. Obscenity laws. Applies to this sort of thing and literature too as I believe."

This is the first time I ever remember taking deep breaths, consciously, for purposes of self-control. I really wanted to murder him. I remember how soft and loathsome his face looked, with the eyes almost closed, nostrils extended to the soothing odour of righteousness, the odour of triumph. If this stupid thing had not happened, he would never have won. But he had. Perhaps he saw something in my face that unnerved him, even in this victorious moment, for he drew back to the wall, and began to say that actually, as a matter of fact, he had not really felt it was the sort of thing I personally would do, more the sort of thing that perhaps certain friends of mine—I got into my own room, shut the door.

The kettle was making a fearful noise, having almost boiled dry. I snatched it off the hot plate, pulled out the plug and stood for a moment choking on rage. This spasm passed and I did what I had to do. I put my typewriter and paper on the chair and folded the card table. I screwed the top tightly on the instant coffee and put it and the yellow mug and the teaspoon into the bag in which I had brought them; it was still lying folded on the shelf. I wished childishly to take some vengeance on the potted plant, which sat in the corner with the flowery teapot, the wastebasket, the cushion, and—I forgot—a little plastic pencil sharpener behind it.

When I was taking things down to the car Mrs. Malley came. I had seen little of her since the first day. She did not seem upset, but practical and resigned.

"He is lying down," she said. "He is not himself."

She carried the bag with the coffee and the mug in it. She was so still I felt my anger leave me, to be replaced by an absorbing depression.

I have not yet found another office. I think that I will try again some day, but not yet. I have to wait at least until that picture fades that I see so clearly in my mind, though I never saw it in reality—Mr. Malley with his rags and brushes and a pail of soapy water, scrubbing in his clumsy way, his deliberately clumsy way, at the toilet walls, stooping with difficulty, breathing sorrowfully, arranging in his mind the bizarre but somehow never quite satisfactory narrative of yet another betrayal of trust. While I arrange words, and think it is my right to be rid of him.

[1962]

Alice Munro   *1931–*

MENESETEUNG

I

Columbine, bloodroot,
And wild bergamot,
Gathering armfuls,
Giddily we go.

Offerings, the book is called. Gold lettering on a dull-blue cover. The author's full name underneath: Almeda Joynt Roth. The local paper, the *Vidette*, referred to her as "our poetess." There seems to be a mixture of respect and contempt, both for her calling and for her sex—or for their predictable conjuncture. In the front of the book is a photograph, with the photographer's name in one corner, and the date: 1865. The book was published later, in 1873.

The poetess has a long face; a rather long nose; full, somber dark eyes, which seem ready to roll down her cheeks like giant tears; a lot of dark hair gathered around her face in droopy rolls and curtains. A streak of gray hair plain to see, although she is, in this picture, only twenty-five. Not a pretty girl but the sort of woman who may age well, who probably won't get fat. She wears a tucked and braid-trimmed dark dress or jacket, with a lacy, floppy arrangement of white material—frills or a bow—filling the deep V at the neck. She also wears a hat, which might be made of velvet, in a dark color to match the dress. It's the untrimmed, shapeless hat, something like a soft beret, that makes me see artistic intentions, or at least a shy and stubborn eccentricity, in this young woman, whose long neck and forward-inclining head indicate as well that she is tall and slender and somewhat awkward. From the waist up, she looks like a young nobleman of another century. But perhaps it was the fashion.

"In 1854," she writes in the preface to her book, "my father brought us—my mother, my sister Catherine, my brother William, and me—to the wilds of Canada West (as it then was). My father was a harness-maker by trade, but a cultivated man who could quote by heart from the Bible, Shakespeare, and the writings of Edmund Burke.[1] He prospered in this newly opened land and was able to set up a harness and leather-goods store, and after a year to build the comfortable house in which I live (alone) today. I was fourteen years old, the eldest of the children, when we came into this country from Kingston,[2] a town whose handsome streets I have not seen again but often remember. My sister was eleven and my brother nine. The third summer that we lived here, my brother and sister were taken ill of a prevalent fever and died within a few days of each other. My dear mother did not regain her spirits after this blow to our family. Her health declined, and after another three years she died. I then became housekeeper to my father and was happy to make his home for twelve years, until he died suddenly one morning at his shop.

[1] William Shakespeare (1564–1616), the British dramatist and poet, and Edmund Burke (1729–1797), the British parliamentary leader, statesman, and orator.
[2] Kingston, Ontario, is located on the northeast shore of Lake Ontario near the head of the St. Lawrence River.

"From my earliest years I have delighted in verse and I have occupied myself—
and sometimes allayed my griefs, which have been no more, I know, than any
sojourner on earth must encounter—with many floundering efforts at its composition. My fingers, indeed, were always too clumsy for crochetwork, and those
dazzling productions of embroidery which one sees often today—the overflowing
fruit and flower baskets, the little Dutch boys, the bonneted maidens with their
watering cans—have likewise proved to be beyond my skill. So I offer instead, as
the product of my leisure hours, these rude posies, these ballads, couplets, reflections."

Titles of some of the poems: "Children at Their Games," "The Gypsy Fair," "A
Visit to My Family," "Angels in the Snow," "Champlain[3] at the Mouth of the
Meneseteung," "The Passing of the Old Forest," and "A Garden Medley." There
are some other, shorter, poems, about birds and wildflowers and snowstorms.
There is some comically intentioned doggerel about what people are thinking
about as they listen to the sermon in church.

"Children at Their Games": The writer, a child, is playing with her brother and
sister—one of those games in which children on different sides try to entice and
catch each other. She plays on in the deepening twilight, until she realizes that she
is alone, and much older. Still she hears the (ghostly) voices of her brother and
sister calling. *Come over, come over, let Meda come over.* (Perhaps Almeda was called
Meda in the family, or perhaps she shortened her name to fit the poem.)

"The Gypsy Fair": The Gypsies have an encampment near the town, a "fair,"
where they sell cloth and trinkets, and the writer as a child is afraid that she may
be stolen by them, taken away from her family. Instead, her family has been taken
away from her, stolen by Gypsies she can't locate or bargain with.

"A Visit to My Family": A visit to the cemetery, a one-sided conversation.

"Angels in the Snow": The writer once taught her brother and sister to make
"angels" by lying down in the snow and moving their arms to create wing shapes.
Her brother always jumped up carelessly, leaving an angel with a crippled wing.
Will this be made perfect in Heaven, or will he be flying with his own makeshift,
in circles?

"Champlain at the Mouth of the Meneseteung": This poem celebrates the
popular, untrue belief that the explorer sailed down the eastern shore of Lake
Huron[4] and landed at the mouth of the major river.

"The Passing of the Old Forest": A list of all the trees—their names, appearance, and uses—that were cut down in the original forest, with a general description of the bears, wolves, eagles, deer, waterfowl.

"A Garden Medley": Perhaps planned as a companion to the forest poem.
Catalogue of plants brought from European countries, with bits of history and
legend attached, and final Canadianness resulting from this mixture.

The poems are written in quatrains or couplets. There are a couple of attempts
at sonnets, but mostly the rhyme scheme is simple—*abab* or *abcb*. The rhyme used
is what was once called "masculine" ("shore"/"before"), though once in a while
it is "feminine" ("quiver"/"river"). Are those terms familiar anymore? No poem
is unrhymed.

---

[3] Samuel de Champlain (1567–1635), the French explorer who made eleven voyages to Canada,
founded Quebec, the first permanent French colony in America, and explored much of the area in
which the story is set.
[4] The second largest of the Great Lakes, bounded on the north and east by the Canadian province of
Ontario.

II

White roses cold as snow
Bloom where those "angels" lie.
Do they but rest below
Or, in God's wonder, fly?

In 1879, Almeda Roth was still living in the house at the corner of Pearl and Dufferin streets, the house her father had built for his family. The house is there today: the manager of the liquor store lives in it. It's covered with aluminum siding; a closed-in porch has replaced the veranda. The woodshed, the fence, the gates, the privy, the barn—all these are gone. A photograph taken in the eighteen-eighties shows them all in place. The house and fence look a little shabby, in need of paint, but perhaps that is just because of the bleached-out look of the brownish photograph. The lace-curtained windows look like white eyes. No big shade tree is in sight, and, in fact, the tall elms that overshadowed the town until the nineteen-fifties, as well as the maples that shade it now, are skinny young trees with rough fences around them to protect them from the cows. Without the shelter of those trees, there is a great exposure—back yards, clotheslines, woodpiles, patchy sheds and barns and privies—all bare, exposed, provisional looking. Few houses would have anything like a lawn, just a patch of plantains[5] and anthills and raked dirt. Perhaps petunias growing on top of a stump, in a round box. Only the main street is graveled; the other streets are dirt roads, muddy or dusty according to season. Yards must be fenced to keep animals out. Cows are tethered in vacant lots or pastured in back yards, but sometimes they get loose. Pigs get loose, too, and dogs roam free or nap in a lordly way on the boardwalks. The town has taken root, it's not going to vanish, yet it still has some of the look of an encampment. And, like an encampment, it's busy all the time—full of people, who, within the town, usually walk wherever they're going; full of animals, which leave horse buns, cowpats, dog turds, that ladies have to hitch up their skirts for; full of the noise of building and of drivers shouting at their horses and of the trains that come in several times a day.

I read about that life in the *Vidette*.

The population is younger than it is now, than it will ever be again. People past fifty usually don't come to a raw, new place. There are quite a few people in the cemetery already, but most of them died young, in accidents or childbirth or epidemics. It's youth that's in evidence in town. Children—boys—rove through the streets in gangs. School is compulsory for only four months a year, and there are lots of occasional jobs that even a child of eight or nine can do—pulling flax, holding horses, delivering groceries, sweeping the boardwalk in front of stores. A good deal of time they spend looking for adventures. One day they follow an old woman, a drunk nicknamed Queen Aggie. They get her into a wheelbarrow and trundle her all over town, then dump her into a ditch to sober her up. They also spend a lot of time around the railway station. They jump on shunting cars and dart between them and dare each other to take chances, which once in a while result in their getting maimed or killed. And they keep an eye out for any strangers coming into town. They follow them, offer to carry their bags, and direct them (for a five-cent piece) to a hotel. Strangers who don't look so prosperous are taunted and tormented. Speculation surrounds all of them—it's like a cloud of flies. Are they coming to town to start up a new business, to persuade people to

---

[5] Low, short-stemmed herbs.

invest in some scheme, to sell cures or gimmicks, to preach on the street corners? All these things are possible any day of the week. Be on your guard, the *Vidette* tells people. These are times of opportunity and danger. Tramps, confidence men, hucksters, shysters, plain thieves, are traveling the roads, and particularly the railroads. Thefts are announced: money invested and never seen again, a pair of trousers taken from the clothesline, wood from the woodpile, eggs from the henhouse. Such incidents increase in the hot weather.

Hot weather brings accidents, too. More horses run wild then, upsetting buggies. Hands caught in the wringer while doing the washing, a man lopped in two at the sawmill, a leaping boy killed in a fall of lumber at the lumberyard. Nobody sleeps well. Babies wither with summer complaint, and fat people can't catch their breath. Bodies must be buried in a hurry. One day a man goes through the streets ringing a cowbell and calling "Repent! Repent!" It's not a stranger this time, it's a young man who works at the butcher shop. Take him home, wrap him in cold wet cloths, give him some nerve medicine, keep him in bed, pray for his wits. If he doesn't recover, he must go to the asylum.

Almeda Roth's house faces on Dufferin Street, which is a street of considerable respectability. On this street merchants, a mill owner, an operator of salt wells, have their houses. But Pearl Street, which her back windows overlook and her back gate opens onto, is another story. Workmen's houses are adjacent to hers. Small but decent row houses—that is all right. Things deteriorate toward the end of the block, and the next, last one becomes dismal. Nobody but the poorest people, the unrespectable and undeserving poor, would live there at the edge of a boghole (drained since then), called the Pearl Street Swamp. Bushy and luxuriant weeds grow there, makeshift shacks have been put up, there are piles of refuse and debris and crowds of runty children, slops are flung from doorways. The town tries to compel these people to build privies, but they would just as soon go in the bushes. If a gang of boys goes down there in search of adventure, it's likely they'll get more than they bargained for. It is said that even the town constable won't go down Pearl Street on a Saturday night. Almeda Roth has never walked past the row housing. In one of those houses lives the young girl Annie, who helps her with her housecleaning. That young girl herself, being a decent girl, has never walked down to the last block or the swamp. No decent woman ever would.

But that same swamp, lying to the east of Almeda Roth's house, presents a fine sight at dawn. Almeda sleeps at the back of the house. She keeps to the same bedroom she once shared with her sister Catherine—she would not think of moving to the larger front bedroom, where her mother used to lie in bed all day, and which was later the solitary domain of her father. From her window she can see the sun rising, the swamp mist filling with light, the bulky, nearest trees floating against that mist and the trees behind turning transparent. Swamp oaks, soft maples, tamarack, bitternut.

III

> Here where the river meets the inland sea,
> Spreading her blue skirts from the solemn wood,
> I think of birds and beasts and vanished men,
> Whose pointed dwellings on these pale sands stood.

One of the strangers who arrived at the railway station a few years ago was Jarvis Poulter, who now occupies the house next to Almeda Roth's—separated from hers by a vacant lot, which he has bought, on Dufferin Street. The house is plainer than the Roth house and has no fruit trees or flowers planted around it. It is understood that this is a natural result of Jarvis Poulter's being a widower and living alone. A man may keep his house decent, but he will never—if he is a proper man—do much to decorate it. Marriage forces him to live with more ornament as well as sentiment, and it protects him, also, from the extremities of his own nature—from a frigid parsimony or a luxuriant sloth, from squalor, and from excessive sleeping, drinking, smoking, or freethinking.

In the interests of economy, it is believed, a certain estimable gentleman of our town persists in fetching water from the public tap and supplementing his fuel supply by picking up the loose coal along the railway track. Does he think to repay the town or the railway company with a supply of free salt?

This is the Vidette, full of shy jokes, innuendo, plain accusation, that no newspaper would get away with today. It's Jarvis Poulter they're talking about—though in other passages he is spoken of with great respect, as a civil magistrate, an employer, a churchman. He is close, that's all. An eccentric, to a degree. All of which may be a result of his single condition, his widower's life. Even carrying his water from the town tap and filling his coal pail along the railway track. This is a decent citizen, prosperous: a tall—slightly paunchy?—man in a dark suit with polished boots. A beard? Black hair streaked with gray. A severe and self-possessed air, and a large pale wart among the bushy hairs of one eyebrow? People talk about a young, pretty, beloved wife, dead in childbirth or some horrible accident, like a house fire or a railway disaster. There is no ground for this, but it adds interest. All he has told them is that his wife is dead.

He came to this part of the country looking for oil. The first oil well in the world was sunk in Lambton County,[6] south of here, in the eighteen-fifties. Drilling for oil, Jarvis Poulter discovered salt. He set to work to make the most of that. When he walks home from church with Almeda Roth, he tells her about his salt wells. They are twelve hundred feet deep. Heated water is pumped down into them, and that dissolves the salt. Then the brine is pumped to the surface. It is poured into great evaporator pans over slow, steady fires, so that the water is steamed off and the pure, excellent salt remains. A commodity for which the demand will never fail.

"The salt of the earth," Almeda says.

"Yes," he says, frowning. He may think this disrespectful. She did not intend it so. He speaks of competitors in other towns who are following his lead and trying to hog the market. Fortunately, their wells are not drilled so deep, or their evaporating is not done so efficiently. There is salt everywhere under this land, but it is not so easy to come by as some people think.

Does that not mean, Almeda says, that there was once a great sea?

Very likely, Jarvis Poulter says. Very likely. He goes on to tell her about other enterprises of his—a brickyard, a lime kiln. And he explains to her how this operates, and where the good clay is found. He also owns two farms, whose woodlots supply the fuel for his operations.

Among the couples strolling home from church on a recent, sunny Sabbath morning we noted a certain salty gentleman and literary lady, not perhaps in their first youth but by no means blighted by the frosts of age. May we surmise?

[6] Located in the southeastern part of the province of Ontario.

This kind of thing pops up in the *Vidette* all the time.

May they surmise, and is this courting? Almeda Roth has a bit of money, which her father left her, and she has her house. She is not too old to have a couple of children. She is a good enough housekeeper, with the tendency toward fancy iced cakes and decorated tarts which is seen fairly often in old maids. (Honorable mention at the Fall Fair.) There is nothing wrong with her looks, and naturally she is in better shape than most married women of her age, not having been loaded down with work and children. But why was she passed over in her earlier, more marriageable years, in a place that needs women to be partnered and fruitful? She was a rather gloomy girl—that may have been the trouble. The deaths of her brother and sister and then of her mother, who lost her reason, in fact, a year before she died, and lay in her bed talking nonsense—those weighed on her, so she was not lively company. And all that reading and poetry—it seemed more of a drawback, a barrier, an obsession, in the young girl than in the middle-aged woman, who needed something, after all, to fill her time. Anyway, it's five years since her book was published, so perhaps she has got over that. Perhaps it was the proud, bookish father, encouraging her?

Everyone takes it for granted that Almeda Roth is thinking of Jarvis Poulter as a husband and would say yes if he asked her. And she is thinking of him. She doesn't want to get her hopes up too much, she doesn't want to make a fool of herself. She would like a signal. If he attended church on Sunday evenings, there would be a chance, during some months of the year, to walk home after dark. He would carry a lantern. (There is as yet no street lighting in town.) He would swing the lantern to light the way in front of the lady's feet and observe their narrow and delicate shape. He might catch her arm as they step off the boardwalk. But he does not go to church at night.

Nor does he call for her, and walk with her *to* church on Sunday mornings. That would be a declaration. He walks her home, past his gate as far as hers; he lifts his hat then and leaves her. She does not invite him to come in—a woman living alone could never do such a thing. As soon as a man and woman of almost any age are alone together within four walls, it is assumed that anything may happen. Spontaneous combustion, instant fornication, an attack of passion. Brute instinct, triumph of the senses. What possibilities men and women must see in each other to infer such dangers. Or, believing in the dangers, how often they must think about the possibilities.

When they walk side by side she can smell his shaving soap, the barber's oil, his pipe tobacco, the wool and linen and leather smell of his manly clothes. The correct, orderly, heavy clothes are like those she used to brush and starch and iron for her father. She misses that job—her father's appreciation, his dark, kind authority. Jarvis Poulter's garments, his smell, his movement, all cause the skin on the side of her body next to him to tingle hopefully, and a meek shiver raises the hairs on her arms. Is this to be taken as a sign of love? She thinks of him coming into her—*their*—bedroom in his long underwear and his hat. She knows this outfit is ridiculous, but in her mind he does not look so; he has the solemn effrontery of a figure in a dream. He comes into the room and lies down on the bed beside her, preparing to take her in his arms. Surely he removes his hat? She doesn't know, for at this point a fit of welcome and submission overtakes her, a buried gasp. He would be her husband.

One thing she has noticed about married women, and that is how many of them have to go about creating their husbands. They have to start ascribing preferences, opinions, dictatorial ways. Oh, yes, they say, my husband is very particular. He won't touch turnips. He won't eat fried meat. (Or he will only eat fried meat.) He likes me to wear blue (brown) all the time. He can't stand organ music. He hates to see a woman go out bareheaded. He would kill me if I took one puff of tobacco. This way, bewildered, sidelong-looking men are made over, made into husbands, heads of households. Almeda Roth cannot imagine herself doing that. She wants a man who doesn't have to be made, who is form already and determined and mysterious to her. She does not look for companionship. Men—except for her father—seem to her deprived in some way, incurious. No doubt that is necessary, so that they will do what they have to do. Would she herself, knowing that there was salt in the earth, discover how to get it out and sell it? Not likely. She would be thinking about the ancient sea. That kind of speculation is what Jarvis Poulter has, quite properly, no time for.

Instead of calling for her and walking her to church, Jarvis Poulter might make another, more venturesome declaration. He could hire a horse and take her for a drive out to the country. If he did this, she would be both glad and sorry. Glad to be beside him, driven by him, receiving this attention from him in front of the world. And sorry to have the countryside removed for her—filmed over, in a way, by his talk and preoccupations. The countryside that she has written about in her poems actually takes diligence and determination to see. Some things must be disregarded. Manure piles, of course, and boggy fields full of high, charred stumps, and great heaps of brush waiting for a good day for burning. The meandering creeks have been straightened, turned into ditches with high, muddy banks. Some of the crop fields and pasture fields are fenced with big, clumsy uprooted stumps, others are held in a crude stitchery of rail fences. The trees have all been cleared back to the woodlots. And the woodlots are all second growth. No trees along the roads or lanes or around the farmhouses, except a few that are newly planted, young and weedy looking. Clusters of log barns—the grand barns that are to dominate the countryside for the next hundred years are just beginning to be built—and mean-looking log houses, and every four or five miles a ragged little settlement with a church and school and store and a blacksmith shop. A raw countryside just wrenched from the forest, but swarming with people. Every hundred acres is a farm, every farm has a family, most families have ten or twelve children. (This is the country that will send them—to northern Ontario and the West.) It's true that you can gather wildflowers in spring in the woodlots, but you'd have to walk through herds of horned cows to get to them.

IV

> The Gypsies have departed.
> Their camping-ground is bare.
> Oh, boldly would I bargain now
> At the Gypsy Fair.

Almeda suffers a good deal from sleeplessness, and the doctor has given her bromides[7] and nerve medicine. She takes the bromides, but the drops gave her dreams that were too vivid and disturbing, so she has put the bottle by for an emergency. She told the doctor her eyeballs felt dry, like hot glass, and her joints ached. Don't read so much, he said, don't study; get yourself good and tired out

---

[7] Sedatives.

with housework, take exercise. He believes that her troubles would clear up if she got married. He believes this in spite of the fact that most of his nerve medicine is prescribed for married women.

So Almeda cleans house and helps clean the church, she lends a hand to friends who are wallpapering or getting ready for a wedding, she bakes one of her famous cakes for the Sunday-school picnic. On a hot Saturday in August she decides to make some grape jelly. Little jars of grape jelly will make fine Christmas presents, or offerings to the sick. But she started late in the day and the jelly is not made by nightfall. In fact, the hot pulp has just been dumped into the cheesecloth bag, to strain out the juice. Almeda drinks some tea and eats a slice of cake with butter (a childish indulgence of hers), and that's all she wants for supper. She washes her hair at the sink and sponges off her body, to be clean for Sunday. She doesn't light a lamp. She lies down on the bed with the window wide open and a sheet just up to her waist, and she does feel wonderfully tired. She can even feel a little breeze.

When she wakes up, the night seems fiery hot and full of threats. She lies sweating on her bed, and she has the impression that the noises she hears are knives and saws and axes—all angry implements chopping and jabbing and boring within her head. But it isn't true. As she comes further awake she recognizes the sounds that she has heard sometimes before—the fracas of a summer Saturday night on Pearl Street. Usually the noise centers on a fight. People are drunk, there is a lot of protest and encouragement concerning the fight, somebody will scream "Murder!" Once, there was a murder. But it didn't happen in a fight. An old man was stabbed to death in his shack, perhaps for a few dollars he kept in the mattress.

She gets out of bed and goes to the window. The night sky is clear, with no moon and with bright stars. Pegasus hangs straight ahead, over the swamp. Her father taught her that constellation—automatically, she counts its stars. Now she can make out distinct voices, individual contributions to the row. Some people, like herself, have evidently been wakened from sleep. "Shut up!" they are yelling. "Shut up that caterwauling or I'm going to come down and tan the arse off yez!"

But nobody shuts up. It's as if there were a ball of fire rolling up Pearl Street, shooting off sparks—only the fire is noise, it's yells and laughter and shrieks and curses, and the sparks are voices that shoot off alone. Two voices gradually distinguish themselves—a rising and falling howling cry and a steady throbbing, low-pitched stream of abuse that contains all those words which Almeda associates with danger and depravity and foul smells and disgusting sights. Someone—the person crying out, "Kill me! Kill me now!"—is being beaten. A woman is being beaten. She keeps crying, "Kill me! Kill me!" and sometimes her mouth seems choked with blood. Yet there is something taunting and triumphant about her cry. There is something theatrical about it. And the people around are calling out, "Stop it! Stop that!" or "Kill her! Kill her!" in a frenzy, as if at the theater or a sporting match or a prizefight. Yes, thinks Almeda, she has noticed that before—it is always partly a charade with these people; there is a clumsy sort of parody, an exaggeration, a missed connection. As if anything they did—even a murder—might be something they didn't quite believe but were powerless to stop.

Now there is the sound of something thrown—a chair, a plank?—and of a woodpile or part of a fence giving way. A lot of newly surprised cries, the sound of running, people getting out of the way, and the commotion has come much closer. Almeda can see a figure in a light dress, bent over and running. That will be the woman. She has got hold of something like a stick of wood or a shingle, and she turns and flings it at the darker figure running after her.

"Ah, go get her!" the voices cry. "Go baste her one!"

Many fall back now; just the two figures come on and grapple, and break loose again, and finally fall down against Almeda's fence. The sound they make becomes very confused—gagging, vomiting, grunting, pounding. Then a long, vibrating, choking sound of pain and self-abasement, self-abandonment, which could come from either or both of them.

Almeda has backed away from the window and sat down on the bed. Is that the sound of murder she has heard? What is to be done, what is she to do? She must light a lantern, she must go downstairs and light a lantern—she must go out into the yard, she must go downstairs. Into the yard. The lantern. She falls over on her bed and pulls the pillow to her face. In a minute. The stairs, the lantern. She sees herself already down there, in the back hall, drawing the bolt of the back door. She falls asleep.

She wakes, startled, in the early light. She thinks there is a big crow sitting on her windowsill, talking in a disapproving but unsurprised way about the events of the night before. "Wake up and move the wheelbarrow!" it says to her, scolding, and she understands that it means something else by "wheelbarrow"—something foul and sorrowful. Then she is awake and sees that there is no such bird. She gets up at once and looks out the window.

Down against her fence there is a pale lump pressed—a body.

Wheelbarrow.

She puts a wrapper over her nightdress and goes downstairs. The front rooms are still shadowy, the blinds down in the kitchen. Something goes *plop, plup,* in a leisurely, censorious way, reminding her of the conversation of the crow. It's just the grape juice, straining overnight. She pulls the bolt and goes out the back door. Spiders have draped their webs over the doorway in the night, and the hollyhocks are drooping, heavy with drew. By the fence, she parts the sticky hollyhocks and looks down and she can see.

A woman's body heaped up there, turned on her side with her face squashed down into the earth. Almeda can't see her face. But there is a bare breast let loose, brown nipple pulled long like a cow's teat, and a bare haunch and leg, the haunch bearing a bruise as big as a sunflower. The unbruised skin is grayish, like a plucked, raw drumstick. Some kind of nightgown or all-purpose dress she has on. Smelling of vomit. Urine, drink, vomit.

Barefoot, in her nightgown and flimsy wrapper, Almeda runs away. She runs around the side of her house between the apple trees and the veranda; she opens the front gate and flees down Dufferin Street to Jarvis Poulter's house, which is the nearest to hers. She slaps the flat of her hand many times against the door.

"There is the body of a woman," she says when Jarvis Poulter appears at last. He is in his dark trousers, held up with braces, and his shirt is half unbuttoned, his face unshaven, his hair standing up on his head. "Mr. Poulter, excuse me. A body of a woman. At my back gate."

He looks at her fiercely. "Is she dead?"

His breath is dank, his face creased, his eyes bloodshot.

"Yes. I think murdered," says Almeda. She can see a little of his cheerless front hall. His hat on a chair. "In the night I woke up. I heard a racket down on Pearl Street," she says, struggling to keep her voice low and sensible. "I could hear this—pair. I could hear a man and a woman fighting."

He picks up his hat and puts it on his head. He closes and locks the front door, and puts the key in his pocket. They walk along the boardwalk and she sees that she is in her bare feet. She holds back what she feels a need to say next—that she is responsible, she could have run out with a lantern, she could have screamed (but who needed more screams?), she could have beat the man off. She could have run for help then, not now.

They turn down Pearl Street, instead of entering the Roth yard. Of course the body is still there. Hunched up, half bare, the same as before.

Jarvis Poulter doesn't hurry or halt. He walks straight over to the body and looks down at it, nudges the leg with the toe of his boot, just as you'd nudge a dog or a sow.

"You," he says, not too loudly but firmly, and nudges again.

Almeda tastes bile at the back of her throat.

"Alive," says Jarvis Poulter, and the woman confirms this. She stirs, she grunts weakly.

Almeda says, "I will get the doctor." If she had touched the woman, if she had forced herself to touch her, she would not have made such a mistake.

"Wait," says Jarvis Poulter. "Wait. Let's see if she can get up."

"Get up, now," he says to the woman. "Come on. Up, now. Up."

Now a startling thing happens. The body heaves itself onto all fours, the head is lifted—the hair all matted with blood and vomit—and the woman begins to bang this head, hard and rhythmically, against Almeda Roth's picket fence. As she bangs her head she finds her voice, and lets out an open-mouthed yowl, full of strength and what sounds like an anguished pleasure.

"Far from dead," says Jarvis Poulter. "And I wouldn't bother the doctor."

"There's blood," says Almeda as the woman turns her smeared face.

"From her nose," he says. "Not fresh." He bends down and catches the horrid hair close to the scalp to stop the head banging.

"You stop that now," he says. "Stop it. Gwan home now. Gwan home, where you belong." The sound coming out of the woman's mouth has stopped. He shakes her head slightly, warning her, before he lets go of her hair. "Gwan home!"

Released, the woman lunges forward, pulls herself to her feet. She can walk. She weaves and stumbles down the street, making intermittent, cautious noises of protest. Jarvis Poulter watches her for a moment to make sure that she's on her way. Then he finds a large burdock leaf,[8] on which he wipes his hand. He says, "There goes your dead body!"

The back gate being locked, they walk around to the front. The front gate stands open. Almeda still feels sick. Her abdomen is bloated; she is hot and dizzy.

"The front door is locked," she says faintly. "I came out by the kitchen." If only he would leave her, she could go straight to the privy. But he follows. He follows her as far as the back door and into the back hall. He speaks to her in a tone of harsh joviality that she had never before heard from him. "No need for alarm," he says. "It's only the consequences of drink. A lady oughtn't to be living alone so close to a bad neighborhood." He takes hold of her arm just above the elbow. She can't open her mouth to speak to him, to say thank you. If she opened her mouth she would retch.

What Jarvis Poulter feels for Almeda Roth at this moment is just what he has not felt during all those circumspect walks and all his own solitary calculations of her probable worth, undoubted respectability, adequate comeliness. He has not been able to imagine her as a wife. Now that is possible. He is sufficiently stirred by her loosened hair—prematurely gray but thick and soft—her flushed face, her light

---

[8] A coarse, prickly herb.

clothing, which nobody but a husband should see. And by her indiscretion, her agitation, her foolishness, her need?

"I will call on you later," he says to her. "I will walk with you to church."

At the corner of Pearl and Dufferin streets last Sunday morning there was discovered, by a lady resident there, the body of a certain woman of Pearl Street, thought to be dead but only, as it turned out, dead drunk. She was roused from her heavenly—or otherwise—stupor by the firm persuasion of Mr. Poulter, a neighbour and a Civil Magistrate, who had been summoned by the lady resident. Incidents of this sort, unseemly, troublesome, and disgraceful to our town, have of late become all too common.

V

I sit at the bottom of sleep,
As on the floor of the sea.
And fanciful Citizens of the Deep.
Are graciously greeting me.

As soon as Jarvis Poulter has gone and she has heard her front gate close, Almeda rushes to the privy. Her relief is not complete, however, and she realizes that the pain and fullness in her lower body come from an accumulation of menstrual blood that has not yet started to flow. She closes and locks the back door. Then, remembering Jarvis Poulter's words about church, she writes on a piece of paper, "I am not well, and wish to rest today." She sticks this firmly into the outside frame of the little window in the front door. She locks that door, too. She is trembling, as if from a great shock or danger. But she builds a fire, so that she can make tea. She boils water, measures the tea leaves, makes a large pot of tea, whose steam and smell sicken her further. She pours out a cup while the tea is still quite weak and adds to it several dark drops of nerve medicine. She sits to drink it without raising the kitchen blind. There, in the middle of the floor, is the cheesecloth bag hanging on its broom handle between the two chair backs. The grape pulp and juice has stained the swollen cloth a dark purple. *Plop, plup* into the basin beneath. She can't sit and look at such a thing. She takes her cup, the teapot, and the bottle of medicine into the dining room.

She is still sitting there when the horses start to go by on the way to church, stirring up clouds of dust. The roads will be getting hot as ashes. She is there when the gate is opened and a man's confident steps sound on her veranda. Her hearing is so sharp she seems to hear the paper taken out of the frame and unfolded—she can almost hear him reading it, hear the words in his mind. Then the footsteps go the other way, down the steps. The gate closes. An image comes to her of tombstones—it makes her laugh. Tombstones are marching down the street on their little booted feet, their long bodies inclined forward, their expressions preoccupied and severe. The church bells are ringing.

Then the clock in the hall strikes twelve and an hour has passed.

The house is getting hot. She drinks more tea and adds more medicine. She knows that the medicine is affecting her. It is responsible for her extraordinary languor, her perfect immobility, her unresisting surrender to her surroundings. That is all right. It seems necessary.

Her surroundings—some of her surroudnings—in the dining room are these:

walls covered with dark green garlanded wallpaper, lace curtains and mulberry velvet curtains on the windows, a table with a crocheted cloth and a bowl of wax fruit, a pinkish-gray carpet with nosegays[9] of blue and pink roses, a sideboard spread with embroidered runners and holding various patterned plates and jugs and the silver tea things. A lot of things to watch. For every one of these patterns, decorations, seems charged with life, ready to move and flow and alter. Or possibly to explode. Almeda Roth's occupation throughout the day is to keep an eye on them. Not to prevent their alteration so much as to catch them at it—to understand it, to be a part of it. So much is going on in this room that there is no need to leave it. There is not even the thought of leaving it.

Of course, Almeda in her observations cannot escape words. She may think she can, but she can't. Soon this glowing and swelling begins to suggest words—not specific words but a flow of words somewhere, just about ready to make themselves known to her. Poems, even. Yes, again, poems. Or one poem. Isn't that the idea —one very great poem that will contain everything and, oh, that will make all the other poems, the poems she has written, inconsequential, mere trial and error, mere rags? Stars and flowers and birds and trees and angels in the snow and dead children at twilight—that is not the half of it. You have to get in the obscene racket on Pearl Street and the polished toe of Jarvis Poulter's boot and the plucked-chicken haunch with its blue-black flower. Almeda is a long way now from human sympathies or fears or cozy household considerations. She doesn't think about what could be done for that woman or about keeping Jarvis Poulter's dinner warm and hanging his long underwear on the line. The basin of grape juice has overflowed and is running over her kitchen floor, staining the boards of the floor, and the stain will never come out.

She has to think of so many things at once—Champlain and the naked Indians and the salt deep in the earth but as well as the salt the money, the money-making intent brewing forever in heads like Jarvis Poulter's. Also, the brutal storms of winter and the clumsy and benighted deeds on Pearl Street. The changes of climate are often violent, and if you think about it there is no peace even in the stars. All this can be borne only if it is channeled into a poem, and the word "channeled" is appropriate, because the name of the poem will be—it *is*—"The Meneseteung." The name of the poem is the name of the river. No, in fact it is the river, the Meneseteung, that is the poem—with its deep holes and rapids and blissful pools under the summer trees and its grinding blocks of ice thrown up at the end of winter and its desolating spring floods. Almeda looks deep, deep into the river of her mind and into the tablecloth, and she sees the crocheted roses floating. They look bunchy and foolish, her mother's crocheted roses—they don't look much like real flowers. But their effort, their floating independence, their pleasure in their silly selves, does seem to her so admirable. A hopeful sign. *Meneseteung.*

She doesn't leave the room until dusk, when she goes out to the privy again and discovers that she is bleeding, her flow has started. She will have to get a towel, strap it on, bandage herself up. Never before, in health, has she passed a whole day in her nightdress. She doesn't feel any particular anxiety about this. On her way through the kitchen she walks through the pool of grape juice. She knows that she will have to mop it up, but not yet, and she walks upstairs leaving purple footprints and smelling her escaping blood and the sweat of her body that has sat all day in the closed hot room.

[9] Small bunches of flowers.

No need for alarm.

For she hasn't thought that crocheted roses could float away or that tombstones could hurry down the street. She doesn't mistake that for reality, and neither does she mistake anything else for reality, and that is how she knows that she is sane.

VI

> I dream of you by night,
> I visit you by day.
> Father, Mother,
> Sister, Brother,
> Have you no word to say?

April 22, 1903. At her residence, on Tuesday last, between three and four o'clock in the afternoon, there passed away a lady of talent and refinement whose pen, in days gone by, enriched our local literature with a volume of sensitive, eloquent verse. It is a sad misfortune that in later years the mind of this fine person had become somewhat clouded and her behaviour, in consequence, somewhat rash and unusual. Her attention to decorum and to the care and adornment of her person had suffered, to the degree that she had become, in the eyes of those unmindful of her former pride and daintiness, a familiar eccentric, or even, sadly, a figure of fun. But now all such lapses pass from memory and what is recalled is her excellent published verse, her labours in former days in the Sunday school, her dutiful care of her parents, her noble womanly nature, charitable concerns, and unfailing religious faith. Her last illness was of mercifully short duration. She caught cold, after having become thoroughly wet from a ramble in the Pearl Street bog. (It has been said that some urchins chased her into the water, and such is the boldness and cruelty of some of our youth, and their observed persecution of this lady, that the tale cannot be entirely discounted.) The cold developed into pneumonia, and she died, attended at the last by a former neighbour, Mrs. Bert (Annie) Friels, who witnessed her calm and faithful end.

January, 1904. One of the founders of our community, an early maker and shaker of this town, was abruptly removed from our midst on Monday morning last, whilst attending to his correspondence in the office of his company. Mr. Jarvis Poulter possessed a keen and lively commercial spirit, which was instrumental in the creation of not one but several local enterprises, bringing the benefits of industry, productivity, and employment to our town.

I looked for Almeda Roth in the graveyard. I found the family stone. There was just one name on it—Roth. Then I noticed two flat stones in the ground, a distance of a few feet—six feet?—from the upright stone. One of these said "Papa," the other "Mama." Farther out from these I found two other flat stones, with the names William and Catherine on them. I had to clear away some overgrowing grass and dirt to see the full name of Catherine. No birth or death dates for anybody, nothing about being dearly beloved. It was a private sort of memorializing, not for the world. There were no roses, either—no sign of a rosebush. But perhaps it was taken out. The grounds keeper doesn't like such things, they are a nuisance to the lawnmower, and if there is nobody left to object he will pull them out.

I thought that Almeda must have been buried somewhere else. When this plot was bought—at the time of the two children's deaths—she would still have been expected to marry, and to lie finally beside her husband. They might not have left room for her here. Then I saw that the stones in the ground fanned out from the upright stone. First the two for the parents, then the two for the children, but these were placed in such a way that there was room for a third, to complete the fan. I paced out from "Catherine" the same number of steps that it took to get from "Catherine" to "William," and at this spot I began pulling grass and scrabbling in the dirt with my bare hands. Soon I felt the stone and knew that I was right. I worked away and got the whole stone clear and I read the name "Meda." There it was with the others, staring at the sky.

I made sure I had got to the edge of the stone. That was all the name there was—Meda. So it was true that she was called by that name in the family. Not just in the poem. Or perhaps she chose her name from the poem, to be written on her stone.

I thought that there wasn't anybody alive in the world but me who would know this, who would make the connection. And I would be the last person to do so. But perhaps this isn't so. People are curious. A few people are. They will be driven to find things out, even trivial things. They will put things together, knowing all along that they may be mistaken. You see them going around with notebooks, scraping the dirt off gravestones, reading microfilm, just in the hope of seeing this trickle in time, making a connection, rescuing one thing from the rubbish.

[1988]

John Updike   *1932–*

A & P

In walks these three girls in nothing but bathing suits. I'm in the third checkout slot, with my back to the door, so I don't see them until they're over by the bread. The one that caught my eye first was the one in the plaid green two-piece. She was a chunky kid, with a good tan and a sweet broad soft-looking can with those two crescents of white just under it, where the sun never seems to hit, at the top of the backs of her legs. I stood there with my hand on a box of HiHo crackers trying to remember if I rang it up or not. I ring it up again and the customer starts giving me hell. She's one of these cash-register-watchers, a witch about fifty with rouge on her cheekbones and no eyebrows, and I know it made her day to trip me up. She'd been watching cash registers for fifty years and probably never seen a mistake before.

By the time I got her feathers smoothed and her goodies into a bag—she gives me a little snort in passing, if she'd been born at the right time they would have burned her over in Salem—by the time I get her on her way the girls had circled around the bread and were coming back, without a pushcart, back my way along the counters, in the aisle between the checkouts and the Special bins. They didn't even have shoes on. There was this chunky one, with the two-piece—it was bright green and the seams on the bra were still sharp and her belly was still pretty pale so I guessed she just got it (the suit)—there was this one, with one of those chubby berry-faces, the lips all bunched together under her nose, this one, and a tall one, with black hair that hadn't quite frizzed right, and one of these sunburns right across under the eyes, and a chin that was too long—you know, the kind of girl other girls think is very "striking" and "attractive" but never quite makes it, as they very well know, which is why they like her so much—and then the third one, that wasn't quite so tall. She was the queen. She kind of led them, the other two peeking around and making their shoulders round. She didn't look around, not this queen, she just walked straight on slowly, on these long white prima-donna legs. She came down a little hard on her heels, as if she didn't walk in her bare feet that much, putting down her heels and then letting the weight move along to her toes as if she was testing the floor with every step, putting a little deliberate extra action into it. You never know for sure how girls' minds work (do you really think it's a mind in there or just a little buzz like a bee in a glass jar?) but you got the idea she had talked the other two into coming in here with her, and now she was showing them how to do it, walk slow and hold yourself straight.

She had on a kind of dirty-pink—beige maybe, I don't know— bathing suit with a little nubble all over it and, what got me, the straps were down. They were off her shoulders looped loose around the cool tops of her arms, and I guess as a result the suit had slipped a little on her, so all around the top of the cloth there was this shining rim. If it hadn't been there you wouldn't have known there could have been anything whiter than those shoulders. With the straps pushed off, there was nothing between the top of the suit and the top of her head except just *her*, this clean bare plane of the top of her chest down from the shoulder bones like a dented sheet of metal tilted in the light. I mean, it was more than pretty.

She had sort of oaky hair that the sun and salt had bleached, done up in a bun that was unravelling, and a kind of prim face. Walking into the A & P with your straps down, I suppose it's the only kind of face you *can* have. She held her head so high her neck, coming up out of those white shoulders, looked kind of stretched, but I didn't mind. The longer her neck was, the more of her there was.

She must have felt in the corner of her eye me and over my shoulder Stokesie in the second slot watching, but she didn't tip. Not this queen. She kept her eyes moving across the racks, and stopped, and turned so slow it made my stomach rub the inside of my apron, and buzzed to the other two, who kind of huddled against her for relief, and then they all three of them went up the cat-and-dog-food-breakfast-cereal-macaroni-rice-raisins-seasonings-spreads-spaghetti-soft-drinks-crackers-and-cookies aisle. From the third slot I look straight up this aisle to the meat counter, and I watched them all the way. The fat one with the tan sort of fumbled with the cookies, but on second thought she put the package back. The sheep pushing their carts down the aisle—the girls were walking against the usual traffic (not that we have one-way signs or anything)—were pretty hilarious. You could see them, when Queenie's white shoulders dawned on them, kind of jerk, or hop, or hiccup, but their eyes snapped back to their own baskets and on they pushed. I bet you could set off dynamite in an A & P and the people would by and large keep reaching and checking oatmeal off their lists and muttering "Let me see, there was a third thing, began with A, asparagus, no, ah, yes, applesauce!" or whatever it is they do mutter. But there was no doubt, this jiggled them. A few house-slaves in pin curlers even looked around after pushing their carts past to make sure what they had seen was correct.

You know, it's one thing to have a girl in a bathing suit down on the beach, where what with the glare nobody can look at each other much anyway, and another thing in the cool of the A & P, under the fluorescent lights, against all those stacked packages, with her feet paddling along naked over our checker-board green-and-cream rubber-tile floor.

"Oh Daddy," Stokesie said beside me. "I feel so faint."

"Darling," I said. "Hold me tight." Stokesie's married, with two babies chalked up on his fuselage already, but as far as I can tell that's the only difference. He's twenty-two, and I was nineteen this April.

"Is it done?" he asks, the responsible married man finding his voice. I forgot to say he thinks he's going to be manager some sunny day, maybe in 1990 when it's called the Great Alexandrov and Petrooshki Tea Company or something.

What he meant was, our town is five miles from a beach, with a big summer colony out on the Point, but we're right in the middle of town, and the women generally put on a shirt or shorts or something before they get out of the car into the street. And anyway these are usually women with six children and varicose veins mapping their legs and nobody, including them, could care less. As I say, we're right in the middle of town, and if you stand at our front doors you can see two banks and the Congregational church and the newspaper store and three real-estate offices and about twenty-seven old freeloaders tearing up Central Street because the sewer broke again. It's not as if we're on the Cape; we're north of Boston and there's people in this town haven't seen the ocean for twenty years.

The girls had reached the meat counter and were asking McMahon something. He pointed, they pointed, and they shuffled out of sight behind a pyramid of Diet Delight peaches. All that was left for us to see was old McMahon patting his mouth and looking after them sizing up their joints. Poor kids, I began to feel sorry for them, they couldn't help it.

. . .

Now here comes the sad part of the story, at least my family says it's sad, but I don't think it's so sad myself. The store's pretty empty, it being Thursday afternoon, so there was nothing much to do except lean on the register and wait for the girls to show up again. The whole store was like a pinball machine and I didn't know which tunnel they'd come out of. After a while they come around out of the far aisle, around the light bulbs, records at discount of the Caribbean Six or Tony Martin Sings or some such gunk you wonder they waste the wax on, sixpacks of candy bars, and plastic toys done up in cellophane that fall apart when a kid looks at them anyway. Around they come, Queenie still leading the way, and holding a little gray jar in her hand. Slots Three through Seven are unmanned and I could see her wondering between Stokes and me, but Stokesie with his usual luck draws an old party in baggy gray pants who stumbles up with four giant cans of pineapple juice (what do these bums *do* with all that pineapple juice? I've often asked myself) so the girls come to me. Queenie puts down the jar and I take it into my fingers icy cold. Kingfish Fancy Herring Snacks in Pure Sour Cream: 49¢. Now her hands are empty, not a ring or a bracelet, bare as God made them, and I wonder where the money's coming from. Still with that prim look she lifts a folded dollar bill out of the hollow at the center of her nubbled pink top. The jar went heavy in my hand. Really, I thought that was so cute.

Then everybody's luck begins to run out. Lengel comes in from haggling with a truck full of cabbages on the lot and is about to scuttle into that door marked MANAGER behind which he hides all day when the girls touch his eye. Lengel's pretty dreary, teaches Sunday school and the rest, but he doesn't miss that much. He comes over and says, "Girls, this isn't the beach."

Queenie blushes, though maybe it's just a brush of sunburn I was noticing for the first time, now that she was so close. "My mother asked me to pick up a jar of herring snacks." Her voice kind of startled me, the way voices do when you see the people first, coming out so flat and dumb yet kind of tony, too, the way it ticked over "pick up" and "snacks." All of a sudden I slid right down her voice into her living room. Her father and the other men were standing around in ice-cream coats and bow ties and the women were in sandals picking up herring snacks on toothpicks off a big glass plate and they were all holding drinks the color of water with olives and sprigs of mint in them. When my parents have somebody over they get lemonade and if it's a real racy affair Schlitz in tall glasses with "They'll Do It Every Time" cartoons stencilled on.

"That's all right," Lengel said. "But this isn't the beach." His repeating this struck me as funny, as if it had just occurred to him, and he had been thinking all these years the A & P was a great big dune and he was the head lifeguard. He didn't like my smiling—as I say he doesn't miss much—but he concentrates on giving the girls that sad Sunday-school-superintendent stare.

Queenie's blush is no sunburn now, and the plump one in plaid, that I liked better from the back—a really sweet can—pipes up, "We weren't doing any shopping. We just came in for the one thing."

"That makes no difference," Lengel tells her, and I could see from the way his eyes went that he hadn't noticed she was wearing a two-piece before. "We want you decently dressed when you come in here."

"We *are* decent," Queenie says suddenly, her lower lip pushing, getting sore now that she remembers her place, a place from which the crowd that runs the A & P must look pretty crummy. Fancy Herring Snacks flashed in her very blue eyes.

"Girls, I don't want to argue with you. After this come in here with your shoulders covered. It's our policy." He turns his back. That's policy for you. Policy is what the kingpins want. What the others want is juvenile delinquency.

All this while, the customers had been showing up with their carts but, you know, sheep, seeing a scene, they had all bunched up on Stokesie, who shook open a paper bag as gently as peeling a peach, not wanting to miss a word. I could feel in the silence everybody getting nervous, most of all Lengel, who asks me, "Sammy, have you rung up their purchase?"

I thought and said "No" but it wasn't about that I was thinking. I go through the punches, 4, 9, GROC, TOT—it's more complicated than you think, and after you do it often enough, it begins to make a little song, that you hear words to, in my case " Hello (*bing*) there, you (*gung*) hap-py *pee*-pul (*splat*)!"—the *splat* being the drawer flying out. I uncrease the bill, tenderly as you may imagine, it just having come from between the two smoothest scoops of vanilla I had ever known were there, and pass a half and a penny into her narrow pink palm, and nestle the herrings in a bag and twist its neck and hand it over, all the time thinking.

The girls, and who'd blame them, are in a hurry to get out, so I say "I quit" to Lengel quick enough for them to hear, hoping they'll stop and watch me, their unsuspected hero. They keep right on going, into the electric eye; the door flies open and they flicker across the lot to their car, Queenie and Plaid and Big Tall Goony-Goony (not that as raw material she was so bad), leaving me with Lengel and a kink in his eyebrow.

"Did you say something, Sammy?"

"I said I quit."

"I thought you did."

"You didn't have to embarrass them."

"It was they who were embarrassing us."

I started to say something that came out "Fiddle-de-doo." It's a saying of my grandmother's, and I know she would have been pleased.

"I don't think you know what you're saying," Lengel said.

"I know you don't," I said. "But I do." I pull the bow at the back of my apron and start shrugging it off my shoulders. A couple customers that had been heading for my slot begin to knock against each other, like scared pigs in a chute.

Lengel sighs and begins to look very patient and old and gray. He's been a friend of my parents for years. "Sammy, you don't want to do this to your Mom and Dad," he tells me. It's true, I don't. But it seems to me that once you begin a gesture it's fatal not to go through with it. I fold the apron, "Sammy" stitched in red on the pocket, and put it on the counter, and drop the bow tie on top of it. The bow tie is theirs, if you've ever wondered. "You'll feel this for the rest of your life," Lengel says, and I know that's true, too, but remembering how he made that pretty girl blush makes me so scrunchy inside I punch the No Sale tab and the machine whirs "pee-pul" and the drawer splats out. One advantage to this scene taking place in summer, I can follow this up with a clean exit, there's no fumbling around getting your coat and galoshes, I just saunter into the electric eye in my white shirt that my mother ironed the night before, and the door heaves itself open, and outside the sunshine is skating around on the asphalt.

I looked around for my girls, but they're gone, of course. There wasn't anybody but some young married screaming with her children about some candy they didn't get by the door of a powder-blue Falcon station wagon. Looking back in the big windows, over the bags of peat moss and aluminum lawn furniture stacked on the pavement, I could see Lengel in my place in the slot, checking the sheep through. His face was dark gray and his back stiff, as if he'd just had an injection of iron, and my stomach kind of fell as I felt how hard the world was going to be to me hereafter.

[1962]

Joyce Carol Oates   *1938–*

WHERE ARE YOU GOING, WHERE HAVE YOU BEEN?

For Bob Dylan[1]

Her name was Connie. She was fifteen and she had a quick, nervous giggling habit of craning her neck to glance into mirrors or checking other people's faces to make sure her own was all right. Her mother, who noticed everything and knew everything and who hadn't much reason any longer to look at her own face, always scolded Connie about it. "Stop gawking at yourself. Who are you? You think you're so pretty?" she would say. Connie would raise her eyebrows at these familiar old complaints and look right through her mother, into a shadowy vision of herself as she was right at that moment: she knew she was pretty and that was everything. Her mother had been pretty once too, if you could believe those old snapshots in the album, but now her looks were gone and that was why she was always after Connie.

"Why don't you keep your room clean like your sister? How've you got your hair fixed—what the hell stinks? Hair spray? You don't see your sister using that junk."

Her sister June was twenty-four and still lived at home. She was a secretary in the high school Connie attended, and if that wasn't bad enough—with her in the same building—she was so plain and chunky and steady that Connie had to hear her praised all the time by her mother and her mother's sisters. June did this, June did that, she saved money and helped clean the house and cooked and Connie couldn't do a thing, her mind was all filled with trashy daydreams. Their father was away at work most of the time and when he came home he wanted supper and he read the newspaper at supper and after supper he went to bed. He didn't bother talking much to them, but around his bent head Connie's mother kept picking at her until Connie wished her mother was dead and she herself was dead and it was all over. "She makes me want to throw up sometimes," she complained to her friends. She had a high, breathless, amused voice that made everything she said sound a little forced, whether it was sincere or not.

There was one good thing: June went places with girl friends of hers, girls who were just as plain and steady as she, and so when Connie wanted to do that her mother had no objections. The father of Connie's best friend drove the girls the three miles to town and left them at a shopping plaza so they could walk through the stores or go to a movie, and when he came to pick them up at eleven he never bothered to ask what they had done.

They must have been familiar sights, walking around the shopping plaza in their shorts and flat ballerina slippers that always scuffed the sidewalk, with charm bracelets jingling on their thin wrists; they would lean together to whisper and laugh secretly if someone passed who amused or interested them. Connie had long dark blond hair that drew everyone's eye to it, and she wore part of it pulled up on her head and puffed out and the rest of it she let fall down her back. She wore a pull-over jersey blouse that looked one way when she was at home and another way when she was away from home. Everything about her had two sides to it, one for home and one for anywhere that was not home: her walk, which

---

[1] Bob Dylan (1941–   ) is the composer, author, and singer who devised and popularized folk-rock during the 1960s. Joyce Carol Oates has said that Dylan's song "It's All Over Now, Baby Blue" was on her mind at the time she wrote the story.

could be childlike and bobbing, or languid enough to make anyone think she was hearing music in her head; her mouth, which was pale and smirking most of the time, but bright and pink on these evenings out; her laugh, which was cynical and drawling at home—"Ha, ha, very funny,"—but high-pitched and nervous anywhere else, like the jingling of the charms on her bracelet.

Sometimes they did go shopping or to a movie, but sometimes they went across the highway, ducking fast across the busy road, to a drive-in restaurant where older kids hung out. The restaurant was shaped like a big bottle, though squatter than a real bottle, and on its cap was a revolving figure of a grinning boy holding a hamburger aloft. One night in midsummer they ran across, breathless with daring, and right away someone leaned out a car window and invited them over, but it was just a boy from high school they didn't like. It made them feel good to be able to ignore him. They went up through the maze of parked and cruising cars to the bright-lit, fly-infested restaurant, their faces pleased and expectant as if they were entering a sacred building that loomed up out of the night to give them what haven and blessing they yearned for. They sat at the counter and crossed their legs at the ankles, their thin shoulders rigid with excitement, and listened to the music that made everything so good: the music was always in the background, like music at a church service; it was something to depend upon.

A boy named Eddie came in to talk with them. He sat backwards on his stool, turning himself jerkily around in semicircles and then stopping and turning back again, and after a while he asked Connie if she would like something to eat. She said she would and so she tapped her friend's arm on the way out—her friend pulled her face up into a brave, droll look—and Connie said she would meet her at eleven, across the way. "I just hate to leave her like that," Connie said earnestly, but the boy said that she wouldn't be alone for long. So they went out to his car, and on the way Connie couldn't help but let her eyes wander over the windshields and faces all around her, her face gleaming with a joy that had nothing to do with Eddie or even this place; it might have been the music. She drew her shoulders up and sucked in her breath with the pure pleasure of being alive, and just at that moment she happened to glance at a face just a few feet from hers. It was a boy with shaggy black hair, in a convertible jalopy painted gold. He stared at her and then his lips widened into a grin. Connie slit her eyes at him and turned away, but she couldn't help glancing back and there he was, still watching her. He wagged a finger and laughed and said, "Gonna get you, baby," and Connie turned away again without Eddie noticing anything.

She spent three hours with him, at the restaurant where they ate hamburgers and drank Cokes in wax cups that were always sweating, and then down an alley a mile or so away, and when he left her off at five to eleven only the movie house was still open at the plaza. Her girl friend was there, talking with a boy. When Connie came up, the two girls smiled at each other and Connie said, "How was the movie?" and the girl said "*You* should know." They rode off with the girl's father, sleepy and pleased, and Connie couldn't help but look back at the darkened shopping plaza with its big empty parking lot and its signs that were faded and ghostly now, and over at the drive-in restaurant where cars were still circling tirelessly. She couldn't hear the music at this distance.

Next morning June asked her how the movie was and Connie said, "So-so."

She and that girl and occasionally another girl went out several times a week, and the rest of the time Connie spent around the house—it was summer vacation—getting in her mother's way and thinking, dreaming about the boys she met. But all the boys fell back and dissolved into a single face that was not even a face but an idea, a feeling, mixed up with the urgent insistent pounding of the music and the humid night air of July. Connie's mother kept dragging her back to the daylight by finding things for her to do or saying suddenly, "What's this about the Pettinger girl?"

And Connie would say nervously, "Oh, her. That dope." She always drew thick clear lines between herself and such girls, and her mother was simple and kind enough to believe it. Her mother was so simple, Connie thought, that it was maybe cruel to fool her so much. Her mother went scuffling around the house in old bedroom slippers and complained over the telephone to one sister about the other, then the other called up and the two of them complained about the third one. If June's name was mentioned her mother's tone was approving, and if Connie's name was mentioned it was disapproving. This did not really mean she disliked Connie, and actually Connie thought that her mother preferred her to June just because she was prettier, but the two of them kept up a pretense of exasperation, a sense that they were tugging and struggling over something of little value to either of them. Sometimes, over coffee, they were almost friends, but something would come up—some vexation that was like a fly buzzing suddenly around their heads—and their faces went hard with contempt.

One Sunday Connie got up at eleven—none of them bothered with church—and washed her hair so it could dry all day long in the sun. Her parents and sister were going to a barbecue at an aunt's house and Connie said no, she wasn't interested, rolling her eyes to let her mother know just what she thought of it. "Stay home alone then," her mother said sharply. Connie sat out back in a lawn chair and watched them drive away, her father quiet and bald, hunched around so that he could back the car out, her mother with a look that was still angry and not at all softened through the windshield, and in the back seat poor old June, all dressed up as if she didn't know what a barbecue was, with all the running yelling kids and the flies. Connie sat with her eyes closed in the sun, dreaming and dazed with the warmth about her as if this were a kind of love, the caresses of love, and her mind slipped over onto thoughts of the boy she had been with the night before and how nice he had been, how sweet it always was, not the way someone like June would suppose but sweet, gentle, the way it was in movies and promised in songs; and when she opened her eyes she hardly knew where she was, the back yard ran off into weeds and a fence-like line of trees and behind it the sky was perfectly blue and still. The asbestos "ranch house" that was now three years old startled her—it looked small. She shook her head as if to get awake.

It was too hot. She went inside the house and turned on the radio to drown out the quiet. She sat on the edge of her bed, barefoot, and listened for an hour and a half to a program called XYZ Sunday Jamboree, record after record of hard, fast, shrieking songs she sang along with, interspersed by exclamations from "Bobby King": "An' look here, you girls at Napoleon's—Son and Charley want you to pay real close attention to this song coming up!"

And Connie paid close attention herself, bathed in a glow of slow-pulsed joy that seemed to rise mysteriously out of the music itself and lay languidly about the airless little room, breathed in and breathed out with each gentle rise and fall of her chest.

After a while she heard a car coming up the drive. She sat up at once, startled, because it couldn't be her father so soon. The gravel kept crunching all the way in from the road—the driveway was long—and Connie ran to the window. It was a car she didn't know. It was an open jalopy, painted a bright gold that caught the sunlight opaquely. Her heart began to pound and her fingers snatched at her hair, checking it, and she whispered, "Christ. Christ," wondering how bad she looked. The car came to a stop at the side door and the horn sounded four short taps, as if this were a signal Connie knew.

She went into the kitchen and approached the door slowly, then hung out the screen door, her bare toes curling off the step. There were two boys in the car and now she recognized the driver: he had shaggy, shabby black hair that looked crazy as a wig and he was grinning at her.

"I ain't late, am I?" he said.

"Who the hell do you think you are?" Connie said.

"Toldja I'd be out, didn't I?"

"I don't even know who you are."

She spoke sullenly, careful to show no interest or pleasure, and he spoke in a fast, bright monotone. Connie looked past him to the other boy, taking her time. He had fair brown hair, with a lock that fell onto his forehead. His sideburns gave him a fierce, embarrassed look, but so far he hadn't even bothered to glance at her. Both boys wore sunglasses. The driver's glasses were metallic and mirrored everything in miniature.

"You wanta come for a ride?" he said.

Connie smirked and let her hair fall loose over one shoulder.

"Don'tcha like my car? New paint job," he said. "Hey."

"What?"

"You're cute."

She pretended to fidget, chasing flies away from the door.

"Don'tcha believe me, or what?" he said.

"Look, I don't even know who you are," Connie said in disgust.

"Hey, Ellie's got a radio, see. Mine broke down." He lifted his friend's arm and showed her the little transistor radio the boy was holding, and now Connie began to hear the music. It was the same program that was playing inside the house. "Bobby King?" she said.

"I listen to him all the time. I think he's great."

"He's kind of great," Connie said reluctantly.

"Listen, that guy's *great*. He knows where the action is."

Connie blushed a little, because the glasses made it impossible for her to see just what this boy was looking at. She couldn't decide if she liked him or if he was just a jerk, and so she dawdled in the doorway and wouldn't come down or go back inside. She said, "What's all that stuff painted on your car?"

"Can'tcha read it?" He opened the door very carefully, as if he were afraid it might fall off. He slid out just as carefully, planting his feet firmly on the ground, the tiny metallic world in his glasses slowing down like gelatine hardening, and in the midst of it Connie's bright green blouse. "This here is my name, to begin with," he said. ARNOLD FRIEND was written in tarlike black letters on the side, with a drawing of a round, grinning face that reminded Connie of a pumpkin, except it wore sunglasses. "I wanta introduce myself, I'm Arnold Friend and that's my real name and I'm gonna be your friend, honey, and inside the car's Ellie Oscar, he's kinda shy." Ellie brought his transistor radio up to his shoulder and balanced it there. "Now, these numbers are a secret code, honey," Arnold Friend explained. He read off the numbers 33, 19, 17 and raised his eyebrows at her to see what she thought of that, but she didn't think much of it. The left rear fender had been smashed and around it was written, on the gleaming gold background: DONE BY

CRAZY WOMAN DRIVER. Connie had to laugh at that. Arnold Friend was pleased at her laughter and looked up at her. "Around the other side's a lot more—you wanta come and see them?"

"No."

"Why not?"

"Why should I?"

"Don'tcha wanta see what's on the car? Don'tcha wanta go for a ride?"

"I don't know."

"Why not?"

"I got things to do."

"Like what?"

"Things."

He laughed as if she had said something funny. He slapped his thighs. He was standing in a strange way, leaning back against the car as if he were balancing himself. He wasn't tall, only an inch or so taller than she would be if she came down to him. Connie liked the way he was dressed, which was the way all of them dressed: tight faded jeans stuffed into black, scuffed boots, a belt that pulled his waist in and showed how lean he was, and a white pullover shirt that was a little soiled and showed the hard small muscles of his arms and shoulders. He looked as if he probably did hard work, lifting and carrying things. Even his neck looked muscular. And his face was a familiar face, somehow: the jaw and chin and cheeks slightly darkened because he hadn't shaved for a day or two, and the nose long and hawklike, sniffing as if she were a treat and he was going to gobble up and it was all a joke.

"Connie, you ain't telling the truth. This is your day set aside for a ride with me and you know it," he said, still laughing. The way he straightened and recovered from his fit of laughing showed that it had been all fake.

"How do you know what my name is?" she said suspiciously.

"It's Connie."

"Maybe and maybe not."

"I know my Connie," he said, wagging his finger. Now she remembered him even better, back at the restaurant, and her cheeks warmed at the thought of how she had sucked in her breath just at the moment she passed him—how she must have looked to him. And he had remembered her. "Ellie and I come out here especially for you," he said. "Ellie can sit in back. How about it?"

"Where?"

"Where what?"

"Where're we going?"

He looked at her. He took off the sunglasses and she saw how pale the skin around his eyes was, like holes that were not in shadow but instead in light. His eyes were like chips of broken glass that catch the light in an amiable way. He smiled. It was as if the idea of going for a ride somewhere, to someplace, was a new idea to him.

"Just for a ride, Connie sweetheart."

"I never said my name was Connie," she said.

"But I know what it is. I know your name and all about you, lots of things," Arnold Friend said. He had not moved yet but stood still leaning back against the side of his jalopy. "I took a special interest in you, such a pretty girl, and found out all about you—like I know your parents and sister are gone somewheres and I know where and how long they're going to be gone, and I know who you were with last night, and your best girl friend's name is Betty. Right?"

He spoke in a simple lilting voice, exactly as if he were reciting the words to a song. His smile assured her that everything was fine. In the car Ellie turned up the volume on his radio and did not bother to look around at them.

"Ellie can sit in the back seat," Arnold Friend said. He indicated his friend with a casual jerk of his chin, as if Ellie did not count and she should not bother with him.

"How'd you find out all that stuff?" Connie said.

"Listen: Betty Schultz and Tony Fitch and Jimmy Pettinger and Nancy Pettinger," he said in a chant. "Raymond Stanley and Bob Hunter—"

"Do you know all those kids?"

"I know everybody."

"Look, you're kidding. You're not from around here."

"Sure."

"But—how come we never saw you before?"

"Sure you saw me before," he said. He looked down at his boots, as if he were a little offended. "You just don't remember."

"I guess I'd remember you," Connie said.

"Yeah?" He looked up at this, beaming. He was pleased. He began to mark time with the music from Ellie's radio, tapping his fists lightly together. Connie looked away from his smile to the car, which was painted so bright it almost hurt her eyes to look at it. She looked at the name, ARNOLD FRIEND. And up at the front fender was an expression that was familiar—MAN THE FLYING SAUCERS. It was an expression kids had used the year before but didn't use this year. She looked at it for a while as if the words meant something to her that she did not yet know.

"What're you thinking about? Huh?" Arnold Friend demanded. "Not worried about your hair blowing around in the car, are you?"

"No."

"Think I maybe can't drive good?"

"How do I know?"

"You're a hard girl to handle. How come?" he said. "Don't you know I'm your friend? Didn't you see me put my sign in the air when you walked by?"

"What sign?"

"My sign." And he drew an X in the air, leaning out toward her. They were maybe ten feet apart. After his hand fell back to his side the X was still in the air, almost visible. Connie let the screen door close and stood perfectly still inside it, listening to the music from her radio and the boy's blended together. She stared at Arnold Friend. He stood there so stiffly relaxed, pretending to be relaxed, with one hand idly on the door handle as if he were keeping himself up that way and had no intention of ever moving again. She recognized most things about him, the tight jeans that showed his thighs and buttocks and the greasy leather boots and the tight shirt, and even that slippery friendly smile of his, that sleepy dreamy smile that all the boys used to get across ideas they didn't want to put into words. She recognized all this and also the singsong way he talked, slightly mocking, kidding, but serious and a little melancholy, and she recognized the way he tapped one fist against the other in homage to the perpetual music behind him. But all these things did not come together.

She said suddenly, "Hey, how old are you?"

His smile faded. She could see then that he wasn't a kid, he was much older—thirty, maybe more. At this knowledge her heart began to pound faster.

"That's a crazy thing to ask. Can'tcha see I'm your own age?"

"Like hell you are."

"Or maybe a coupla years older. I'm eighteen."

"Eighteen?" she said doubtfully.

He grinned to reassure her and lines appeared at the corners of his mouth. His teeth were big and white. He grinned so broadly his eyes became slits and she saw how thick the lashes were, thick and black as if painted with a black tarlike material. Then, abruptly, he seemed to become embarrassed and looked over his shoulder at Ellie. "*Him*, he's crazy," he said. "Ain't he a riot? He's a nut, a real character." Ellie was still listening to the music. His sunglasses told nothing about what he was thinking. He wore a bright orange shirt unbuttoned halfway to show his chest, which was a pale, bluish chest and not muscular like Arnold Friend's. His shirt collar was turned up all around and the very tips of the collar pointed out past his chin as if they were protecting him. He was pressing the transistor radio up against his ear and sat there in a kind of daze, right in the sun.

"He's kinda strange," Connie said.

"Hey, she says you're kinda strange! Kinda strange!" Arnold Friend cried. He pounded on the car to get Ellie's attention. Ellie turned for the first time and Connie saw with shock that he wasn't a kid either—he had a fair, hairless face, cheeks reddened slightly as if the veins grew too close to the surface of his skin, the face of a forty-year-old baby. Connie felt a wave of dizziness rise in her at this sight and she stared at him as if waiting for something to change the shock of the moment, make it all right again. Ellie's lips kept shaping words, mumbling along with the words blasting in his ear.

"Maybe you two better go away," Connie said faintly.

"What? How come?" Arnold Friend cried. "We come out here to take you for a ride. It's Sunday." He had the voice of the man on the radio now. It was the same voice, Connie thought. "Don'tcha know it's Sunday all day? And honey, no matter who you were with last night, today you're with Arnold Friend and don't you forget it! Maybe you better step out here," he said, and this last was in a different voice. It was a little flatter, as if the heat was finally getting to him.

"No. I got things to do."

"Hey."

"You two better leave."

"We ain't leaving until you come with us."

"Like hell I am—"

"Connie, don't fool around with me. I mean—I mean, don't fool *around*," he said, shaking his head. He laughed incredulously. He placed his sunglasses on top of his head, carefully, as if he were indeed wearing a wig, and brought the stems down behind his ears. Connie stared at him, another wave of dizziness and fear rising in her so that for a moment he wasn't even in focus but was just a blur standing there against his gold car, and she had the idea that he had driven up the driveway all right but had come from nowhere before that and belonged nowhere and that everything about him and even about the music that was so familiar to her was only half real.

"If my father comes and sees you—"

"He ain't coming. He's at a barbecue."

"How do you know that?"

"Aunt Tillie's. Right now they're—uh—they're drinking. Sitting around," he said vaguely, squinting as if he were staring all the way to town and over to Aunt Tillie's back yard. Then the vision seemed to get clear and he nodded energetically. "Yeah. Sitting around. There's your sister in a blue dress, huh? And high heels, the poor sad bitch—nothing like you, sweetheart! And your mother's helping some fat woman with the corn, they're cleaning the corn—husking the corn—"

"What fat woman?" Connie cried.

"How do I know what fat woman, I don't know every goddamn fat woman in the world!" Arnold Friend laughed.

"Oh, that's Mrs. Hornsby. . . . Who invited her?" Connie said. She felt a little lightheaded. Her breath was coming quickly.

"She's too fat. I don't like them fat. I like them the way you are, honey," he said, smiling sleepily at her. They stared at each other for a while through the screen door. He said softly, "Now, what you're going to do is this: you're going to come out that door. You're going to sit up front with me and Ellie's going to sit in the back, the hell with Ellie, right? This isn't Ellie's date. You're my date. I'm your lover, honey."

"What? You're crazy—"

"Yes, I'm your lover. You don't know what that is but you will," he said. "I know that too. I know all about you. But look: it's real nice and you couldn't ask for nobody better than me, or more polite. I always keep my word. I'll tell you how it is, I'm always nice at first, the first time. I'll hold you so tight you won't think you have to try to get away or pretend anything because you'll know you can't. And I'll come inside you where it's all secret and you'll give in to me and you'll love me—"

"Shut up! You're crazy!" Connie said. She backed away from the door. She put her hands up against her ears as if she'd heard something terrible, something not meant for her. "People don't talk like that, you're crazy," she muttered. Her heart was almost too big now for her chest and its pumping made sweat break out all over her. She looked out to see Arnold Friend pause and then take a step toward the porch, lurching. He almost fell. But, like a clever drunken man, he managed to catch his balance. He wobbled in his high boots and grabbed hold of one of the porch posts.

"Honey?" he said. "You still listening?"

"Get the hell out of here!"

"Be nice, honey. Listen."

"I'm going to call the police—"

He wobbled again and out of the side of his mouth came a fast spat curse, an aside not meant for her to hear. But even this "Christ!" sounded forced. Then he began to smile again. She watched this smile come, awkward as if he were smiling from inside a mask. His whole face was a mask, she thought wildly, tanned down to his throat but then running out as if he had plastered make-up on his face but had forgotten about his throat.

"Honey—? Listen, here's how it is. I always tell the truth and I promise you this: I ain't coming in that house after you."

"You better not! I'm going to call the police if you—if you don't—"

"Honey," he said, talking right through her voice, "honey, I'm not coming in there but you are coming out here. You know why?"

She was panting. The kitchen looked like a place she had never seen before, some room she had run inside but that wasn't good enough, wasn't going to help her. The kitchen window had never had a curtain, after three years, and there were dishes in the sink for her to do—probably—and if you ran your hand across the table you'd probably feel something sticky there.

"You listening, honey? Hey?"

"—going to call the police—"

"Soon as you touch the phone I don't need to keep my promise and can come inside. You won't want that."

She rushed forward and tried to lock the door. Her fingers were shaking. "But why lock it," Arnold Friend said gently, talking right into her face. "It's just a screen door. It's just nothing." One of his boots was at a strange angle, as if his foot wasn't in it. It pointed out to the left, bent at the ankle. "I mean, anybody can break through a screen door and glass and wood and iron or anything else if he needs to, anybody at all, and specially Arnold Friend. If the place got lit up with a fire, honey, you'd come runnin' out into my arms, right into my arms an' safe at home—like you knew I was your lover and'd stopped fooling around. I don't mind a nice shy girl but I don't like no fooling around." Part of those words were spoken with a slight rhythmic lilt, and Connie somehow recognized them—the echo of a song from last year, about a girl rushing into her boy friend's arms and coming home again—

Connie stood barefoot on the linoleum floor, staring at him. "What do you want?" she whispered.

"I want you," he said.

"What?"

"Seen you that night and thought, that's the one, yes sir. I never needed to look anymore."

"But my father's coming back. He's coming to get me. I had to wash my hair first—" She spoke in a dry, rapid voice, hardly raising it for him to hear.

"No, your daddy is not coming and yes, you had to wash your hair and you washed it for me. It's nice and shining and all for me. I thank you sweetheart," he said with a mock bow, but again he almost lost his balance. He had to bend and adjust his boots. Evidently his feet did not go all the way down; the boots must have been stuffed with something so that he would seem taller. Connie stared out at him and behind him at Ellie in the car, who seemed to be looking off toward Connie's right, into nothing. This Ellie said, pulling the words out of the air one after another as if he were just discovering them, "You want me to pull out the phone?"

"Shut your mouth and keep it shut," Arnold Friend said, his face red from bending over or maybe from embarrassment because Connie had seen his boots. "This ain't none of your business."

"What—what are you doing? What do you want?" Connie said. "If I call the police they'll get you, they'll arrest you—"

"Promise was not to come in unless you touch that phone, and I'll keep that promise," he said. He resumed his erect position and tried to force his shoulders back. He sounded like a hero in a movie, declaring something important. But he spoke too loudly and it was as if he were speaking to someone behind Connie. "I ain't made plans for coming in that house where I don't belong but just for you to come out to me, the way you should. Don't you know who I am?"

"You're crazy," she whispered. She backed away from the door but did not want to go into another part of the house, as if this would give him permission to come through the door. "What do you . . . you're crazy, you. . . ."

"Huh? What're you saying, honey?"

Her eyes darted everywhere in the kitchen. She could not remember what it was, this room.

"This is how it is, honey: you come out and we'll drive away, have a nice ride.

But if you don't come out we're gonna wait till your people come home and then they're all going to get it."

"You want that telephone pulled out?" Ellie said. He held the radio away from his ear and grimaced, as if without the radio the air was too much for him.

"I toldja shut up, Ellie," Arnold Friend said, "you're deaf, get a hearing aid, right? Fix yourself up. This little girl's no trouble and's gonna be nice to me, so Ellie keep to yourself, this ain't your date—right? Don't hem in on me, don't hog, don't crush, don't bird dog, don't trail me," he said in a rapid, meaningless voice, as if he were running through all the expressions he'd learned but was no longer sure which of them was in style, then rushing on to new ones, making them up with his eyes closed. "Don't crawl under my fence, don't squeeze in my chipmunk hole, don't sniff my glue, suck my popsicle, keep your own greasy fingers on yourself!" He shaded his eyes and peered in at Connie, who was backed against the kitchen table. "Don't mind him, honey, he's just a creep. He's a dope. Right? I'm the boy for you and like I said, you come out here nice like a lady and give me your hand, and nobody else gets hurt, I mean, your nice old bald-headed daddy and your mummy and your sister in her high heels. Because listen: why bring them in this?"

"Leave me alone," Connie whispered.

"Hey, you know that old woman down the road, the one with the chickens and stuff—you know her?"

"She's dead!"

"Dead? What? You know her?" Arnold Friend said.

"She's dead—"

"Don't you like her?"

"She's dead—she's—she isn't here any more—"

"But don't you like her, I mean, you got something against her? Some grudge or something?" Then his voice dipped as if he were conscious of a rudeness. He touched the sunglasses perched up on top of his head as if to make sure they were still there. "Now, you be a good girl."

"What are you going to do?"

"Just two things, or maybe three," Arnold Friend said. "But I promise it won't last long and you'll like me the way you get to like people you're close to. You will. It's all over for you here, so come on out. You don't want your people in any trouble, do you?"

She turned and bumped against a chair or something, hurting her leg, but she ran into the back room and picked up the telephone. Something roared in her ear, a tiny roaring, and she was so sick with fear that she could do nothing but listen to it—the telephone was clammy and very heavy and her fingers groped down to the dial but were too weak to touch it. She began to scream into the phone, into the roaring. She cried out, she cried for her mother, she felt her breath start jerking back and forth in her lungs as if it were something Arnold Friend was stabbing her with again and again with no tenderness. A noisy sorrowful wailing rose all about her and she was locked inside it the way she was locked inside this house.

After a while she could hear again. She was sitting on the floor with her wet back against the wall.

Arnold Friend was saying from the door, "That's a good girl. Put the phone back."

She kicked the phone away from her.

"No, honey. Pick it up. Put it back right."

She picked it up and put it back. The dial tone stopped.

"That's a good girl. Now, you come outside."

She was hollow with what had been fear but what was now just an emptiness. All that screaming had blasted it out of her. She sat, one leg cramped under her, and deep inside her brain was something like a pinpoint of light that kept going and would not let her relax. She thought, I'm not going to see my mother again. She thought, I'm not going to sleep in my bed again. Her bright green blouse was all wet.

Arnold Friend said, in a gentle-loud voice that was like a stage voice, "The place where you came from ain't there any more, and where you had in mind to go is cancelled out. This place you are now—inside your daddy's house—is nothing but a cardboard box I can knock down any time. You know that and always did know it. You hear me?"

She thought, I have got to think. I have got to know what to do.

"We'll go out to a nice field, out in the country here where it smells so nice and it's sunny," Arnold Friend said. "I'll have my arms tight around you so you won't need to try to get away and I'll show you what love is like, what it does. The hell with this house! It looks solid all right," he said. He ran a fingernail down the screen and the noise did not make Connie shiver, as it would have the day before. "Now, put your hand on your heart, honey. Feel that? That feels solid too but we know better. Be nice to me, be sweet like you can because what else is there for a girl like you but to be sweet and pretty and give in?—and get away before her people come back?

She felt her pounding heart. Her hand seemed to enclose it. She thought for the first time in her life that it was nothing that was hers, that belonged to her, but just a pounding, living thing inside this body that wasn't really hers either.

"You don't want them to get hurt," Arnold Friend went on. "Now, get up, honey. Get up all by yourself."

She stood.

"Now, turn this way. That's right. Come over here to me.—Ellie, put that away, didn't I tell you? You dope. You miserable creepy dope," Arnold Friend said. His words were not angry but only part of an incantation. The incantation was kindly. "Now, come out through the kitchen to me, honey, and let's see a smile, try it, you're a brave, sweet little girl and now they're eating corn and hot dogs cooked to bursting over an outdoor fire, and they don't know one thing about you and never did and honey, you're better than them because not one of them would have done this for you."

Connie felt the linoleum under her feet; it was cool. She brushed her hair back out of her eyes. Arnold Friend let go of the post tentatively and opened his arms for her, his elbows pointing in toward each other and his wrists limp, to show that this was an embarrassed embrace and a little mocking, he didn't want to make her self-conscious.

She put her hand against the screen. She watched herself push the door slowly open as if she were back safe somewhere in the other doorway, watching this body and this head of long hair moving out into the sunlight where Arnold Friend waited.

"My sweet little blue-eyed girl," he said in a half-sung sigh that had nothing to do with her brown eyes but was taken up just the same by the vast, sunlit reaches of the land behind him and on all sides of him—so much land that Connie had never seen before and did not recognize except to know that she was going to it.

[1966]

Joyce Carol Oates   *1938–*

FOUR SUMMERS

I

It is some kind of special day. "Where's Sissie?" Ma says. Her face gets sharp, she is frightened. When I run around her chair she laughs and hugs me. She is pretty when she laughs. Her hair is long and pretty.

We are sitting at the best table of all, out near the water. The sun is warm and the air smells nice. Daddy is coming back from the building with some glasses of beer, held in his arms. He makes a grunting noise when he sits down.

"Is the lake deep?" I ask them.

They don't hear me, they're talking. A woman and a man are sitting with us. The man marched in the parade we saw just awhile ago; he is a volunteer fireman and is wearing a uniform. Now his shirt is pulled open because it is hot. I can see the dark curly hair way up by his throat; it looks hot and prickly.

A man in a soldier's uniform comes over to us. They are all friends, but I can't remember him. We used to live around here, Ma told me, and then we moved away. The men are laughing. The man in the uniform leans back against the railing, laughing, and I am afraid it will break and he will fall into the water.

"Can we go out in a boat, Dad?" says Jerry.

He and Frank keep running back and forth. I don't want to go with them, I want to stay by Ma. She smells nice. Frank's face is dirty with sweat. "Dad," he says, whining, "can't we go out in a boat? Them kids are going out."

A big lake is behind the building and the open part where we are sitting. Some people are rowing on it. This tavern is noisy and everyone is laughing; it is too noisy for Dad to think about what Frank said.

"Harry," says Ma, "the kids want a boat ride. Why don't you leave off drinking and take them?"

"What?" says Dad.

He looks up from laughing with the men. His face is damp with sweat and he is happy. "Yeah, sure, in a few minutes. Go over there and play and I'll take you out in a few minutes."

The boys run out back by the rowboats, and I run after them. I have a bag of potato chips.

An old man with a white hat pulled down over his forehead is sitting by the boats, smoking. "You kids be careful," he says.

Frank is leaning over and looking at one of the boats. "This here is the best one," he says.

"Why's this one got water in it?" says Jerry.

"You kids watch out. Where's your father?" the man says.

"He's gonna take us for a ride," says Frank.

"Where is he?"

The boys run along, looking at the boats that are tied up. They don't bother with me. The boats are all painted dark green, but the paint is peeling off some of them in little pieces. There is water inside some of them. We watch two people come in, a man and a woman, The woman is giggling. She has on a pink dress and she leans over to trail one finger in the water. "What's all this filthy stuff by the

531

shore?'' she says. There is some scum in the water. It is colored a light brown, and there are little seeds and twigs and leaves in it.

The man helps the woman out of the boat. They laugh together. Around their rowboat little waves are still moving; they make a churning noise that I like.

"Where's Dad?" Frank says.

"He ain't coming," says Jerry.

They are tossing pebbles out into the water. Frank throws his sideways, twisting his body. He is ten and very big. "I bet he ain't coming," Jerry says, wiping his nose with the back of his hand.

After awhile we go back to the table. Behind the table is the white railing, and then the water, and then the bank curves out so that the weeping willow trees droop over the water. More men in uniforms, from the parade, are walking by.

"Dad," says Frank, "can't we go out? Can't we? There's a real nice boat there—"

"For Christ's sake, get them off me," Dad says. He is angry with Ma. "Why don't you take them out?"

"Honey, I can't row."

"Should we take out a boat, us two?" the other woman says. She has very short, wet-looking hair. It is curled in tiny little curls close to her head and is very bright. "We'll show them, Lenore. Come on, let's give your kids a ride. Show these guys how strong we are."

"That's all you need, to sink a boat," her husband says.

They all laugh.

The table is filled with brown beer bottles and wrappers of things. I can feel how happy they all are together, drawn together by the round table. I lean against Ma's warm leg and she pats me without looking down. She lunges forward and I can tell even before she says something that she is going to be loud.

"You guys're just jealous! Afraid we'll meet some soldiers!" she says.

"Can't we go out, Dad? Please?" Frank says. "We won't fight. . . ."

"Go and play over there. What're those kids doing—over there?" Dad says, frowning. His face is damp and loose, the way it is sometimes when he drinks. "In a little while, okay? Ask your mother."

"She can't do it," Frank says.

"They're just jealous," Ma says to the other woman, giggling. "They're afraid we might meet somebody somewhere."

"Just who's gonna meet this one here?" the other man says, nodding with his head at his wife.

Frank and Jerry walk away. I stay by Ma. My eyes burn and I want to sleep, but they won't be leaving for a long time. It is still daylight. When we go home from places like this it is always dark and getting chilly and the grass by our house is wet.

"Duane Dorsey's in jail," Dad says. "You guys heard about that?"

"Duane? Yeah, really?"

"It was in the newspaper. His mother-in-law or somebody called the police, he was breaking windows in her house."

"That Duane was always a nut!"

"Is he out now, or what?"

"I don't know, I don't see him these days. We had a fight," Dad says.

The woman with the short hair looks at me. "She's a real cute little thing," she says, stretching her mouth. "She drink beer, Lenore?"

"I don't know."

"Want some of mine?"

She leans toward me and holds the glass by my mouth. I can smell the beer and the warm stale smell of perfume. There are pink lipstick smudges on the glass.

"Hey, what the hell are you doing?" her husband says.

When he talks rough like that I remember him: we were with him once before.

"Are you swearing at me?" the woman says.

"Leave off the kid, you want to make her a drunk like yourself?"

"It don't hurt, one little sip. . . ."

"It's okay," Ma says. She puts her arm around my shoulders and pulls me closer to the table.

"Let's play cards. Who wants to?" Dad says.

"Sissie wants a little sip, don't you?" the woman says. She is smiling at me and I can see that her teeth are darkish, not nice like Ma's.

"Sure, go ahead," says Ma.

"I said leave off that, Sue, for Christ's sake," the man says. He jerks the table. He is a big man with a thick neck; he is bigger than Dad. His eyebrows are blond, lighter than his hair, and are thick and tufted. Dad is staring at something out on the lake without seeing it. "Harry, look, my goddam wife is trying to make your kid drink beer."

"Who's getting hurt?" Ma says angrily.

Pa looks at me all at once and smiles. "Do you want it, baby?"

I have to say yes. The woman grins and holds the glass down to me, and it clicks against my teeth. They laugh. I stop swallowing right away because it is ugly, and some of the beer drips down on me. "Honey, you're so clumsy," Ma says, wiping me with a napkin.

"She's a real cute girl," the woman says, sitting back in her chair. "I wish I had a nice little girl like that."

"Lay off that," says her husband.

"Hey, did you bring any cards?" Dad says to the soldier.

"They got some inside."

"Look, I'm sick of cards," Ma says.

"Yeah, why don't we all go for a boat ride?" says the woman. "Be real nice, something new. Every time we get together we play cards. How's about a boat ride?"

"It better be a big boat, with you in it," her husband says. He is pleased when everyone laughs, even the woman. The soldier lights a cigarette and laughs. "How come your cousin here's so skinny and you're so fat?"

"She isn't fat," says Ma. "What the hell do you want? Look at yourself."

"Yes, the best days of my life are behind me," the man says. He wipes his face and then presses a beer bottle against it. "Harry, you're lucky you moved out. It's all going downhill, back in the neighborhood."

"You should talk, you let our house look like hell," the woman says. Her face is blotched now, some parts pale and some red. "Harry don't sit out in his back yard all weekend drinking. He gets something done."

"Harry's younger than me."

Ma reaches over and touches Dad's arm. "Harry, why don't you take the kids out? Before it gets dark."

Dad lifts his glass and finishes his beer. "Who else wants more?" he says.

"I'll get them, you went last time," the soldier says.

"Get a chair for yourself," says Dad. "We can play poker."

"I don't want to play poker, I want to play rummy," the woman says.

"At church this morning Father Reilly was real mad," says Ma. "He said some kids or somebody was out in the cemetery and left some beer bottles. Isn't that awful?"

"Duane Dorsey used to do worse than that," the man says, winking.

"Hey, who's that over there?"

"You mean that fat guy?"

"Isn't that the guy at the lumberyard that owes all that money?"

Dad turns around. His chair wobbles and he almost falls; he is angry.

"This goddamn place is too crowded," he says.

"This is a real nice place," the woman says. She is taking something out of her purse. "I always liked it, didn't you, Lenore?"

"Sue and me used to come here a lot," says Ma. "And not just with you two, either."

"Yeah, we're real jealous," the man says.

"You should be," says the woman.

The soldier comes back. Now I can see that he is really a boy. He runs to the table with the beer before he drops anything. He laughs.

"Jimmy, your ma wouldn't like to see you drinking!" the woman says happily.

"Well, she ain't here."

"Are they still living out in the country?" Ma says to the woman.

"Sure. No electricity, no running water, no bathroom—same old thing. What can you do with people like that?"

"She always talks about going back to the Old Country," the soldier says. "Thinks she can save up money and go back."

"Poor old bastards don't know there was a war," Dad says. He looks as if something tasted bad in his mouth. "My old man died thinking he could go back in a year or two. Stupid old bastards!"

"Your father was real nice. . . ." Ma says.

"Yeah, real nice," says Dad. "Better off dead."

Everybody is quiet.

"June Dieter's mother's got the same thing," the woman says in a low voice to Ma. "She's had it a year now and don't weigh a hundred pounds—you remember how big she used to be."

"She was big, all right," Ma says.

"Remember how she ran after June and slapped her? We were there—some guys were driving us home."

"Yeah. So she's got it too."

"Hey," says Dad, "why don't you get a chair, Jimmy? Sit down here."

The soldier looks around. His face is raw in spots, broken out. But his eyes are nice. He never looks at me.

"Get a chair from that table," Dad says.

"Those people might want it."

"Hell, just take it. Nobody's sitting on it."

"They might—"

Dad reaches around and yanks the chair over. The people look at him but don't say anything. Dad is breathing hard. "Here, sit here," he says. The soldier sits down.

Frank and Jerry come back. They stand by Dad, watching him, "Can we go out now?" Frank says.

"What?"

"Out for a boat ride."

"What? No, next week. Do it next week. We're going to play cards."

"You said—"

"Shut up, we'll do it next week." Dad looks up and shades his eyes. "The lake don't look right anyway."

"Lot's of people are out there—"

"I said shut up."

"Honey," Ma whispers, "let him alone. Go and play by yourselves."

"Can we sit in the car?"

"Okay, but don't honk the horn."

"Ma, can't we go for a ride?"

"Go and play by yourselves, stop bothering us," she says. "Hey, will you take Sissie?"

They look at me. They don't like me, I can see it, but they take me with them. We run through the crowd and somebody spills a drink—he yells at us. "Oops, got to watch it!" Frank giggles.

We run along the walk by the boat. A woman in a yellow dress is carrying a baby. She looks at us like she doesn't like us.

Down at the far end some kids are standing together.

"Hey, lookit that," Frank says.

A blackbird is caught in the scum, by one of the boats. It can't fly up. One of the kids, a long-legged girl in a dirty dress, is poking at it with a stick.

The bird's wings keep fluttering but it can't get out. If it could get free it would fly and be safe, but the scum holds it down.

One of the kids throws a stone at it. "Stupid old goddamn bird," somebody says. Frank throws a stone. They are all throwing stones. The bird doesn't know enough to turn away. Its feathers are all wet and dirty. One of the stones hits the bird's head.

"Take that!" Frank says, throwing a rock. The water splashes up and some of the girls scream.

I watch them throwing stones. I am standing at the side. If the bird dies, then everything can die, I think. Inside the tavern there is music from the jukebox.

II

We are at the boathouse tavern again. It is a mild day, a Sunday afternoon. Dad is talking with some men; Jerry and I are waiting by the boats. Mommy is at home with the new baby. Frank has gone off with some friends of his, to a stock-car race. There are some people here, sitting out at the tables, but they don't notice us.

"Why doesn't he hurry up?" Jerry says.

Jerry is twelve now. He has pimples on his forehead and chin.

He pushes one of the rowboats with his foot. He is wearing sneakers that are dirty. I wish I could get in that boat and sit down, but I am afraid. A boy not much older than Jerry is squatting on the boardwalk, smoking. You can tell he is in charge of the boats.

"Daddy, come on. Come on," Jerry says, whining. Daddy can't hear him.

I have mosquito bites on my arms and legs. There are mosquitoes and flies around here; the flies crawl around the sticky mess left on tables. A car over in the parking lot has its radio on loud. You can hear the music all this way. "He's coming," I tell Jerry so he won't be mad. Jerry is like Dad, the way his eyes look.

"Oh, that fat guy keeps talking to him," Jerry says.

The fat man is one of the bartenders; he has on a dirty white apron. All these men are familiar. We have been seeing them for years. He punches Dad's arm, up by the shoulder, and Dad pushes him. They are laughing, though. Nobody is mad.

"I'd sooner let a nigger—" the bartender says. We can't hear anything more, but the men laugh again.

"All he does is drink," Jerry says. "I hate him."

At school, up on the sixth-grade floor, Jerry got in trouble last month. The principal slapped him. I am afraid to look at Jerry when he's mad.

"I hate him, I wish he'd die," Jerry says.

Dad is trying to come to us, but every time he takes a step backward and gets ready to turn, one of the men says something. There are three men beside him. Their stomachs are big, but Dad's isn't. He is wearing dark pants and a white shirt; his tie is in the car. He wears a tie to church, then takes it off. He has his shirt sleeves rolled up and you can see how strong his arms must be.

Two women cross over from the parking lot. They are wearing high-heeled shoes and hats and bright dresses—orange and yellow—and when they walk past the men look at them. They go into the tavern. The men laugh about something. The way they laugh makes my eyes focus on something away from them—a bird flying in the sky—and it is hard for me to look anywhere else. I feel as if I'm falling asleep.

"Here he comes!" Jerry says.

Dad walks over to us, with his big steps. He is smiling and carrying a bottle of beer, "Hey, kid," he says to the boy squatting on the walk, "how's about a boat?"

"This one is the best," Jerry says.

"The best, huh? Great." Dad grins at us. "Okay, Sissie, let's get you in. Be careful now." He picks me up even though I am too heavy for it, and sets me in the boat. It hurts a little where he held me, under the arms, but I don't care.

Jerry climbs in. Dad steps and something happens—he almost slips, but he catches himself. With the wet oar he pushes us off from the boardwalk.

Dad can row fast. The sunlight is gleaming on the water. I sit very still, facing him, afraid to move. The boat goes fast, and Dad is leaning back and forth and pulling on the oars, breathing hard, doing everything fast like he always does. He is always in a hurry to get things done. He has set the bottle of beer down by his leg, pressed against the side of the boat so it won't fall.

"There's the guys we saw go out before," Jerry says. Coming around the island is a boat with three boys in it, older than Jerry. "They went on the island. Can we go there too?"

"Sure," says Dad. His eyes squint in the sun. He is suntanned, and there are freckles on his forehead. I am sitting close to him, facing him, and it surprises me what he looks like—he is like a stranger, with his eyes narrowed. The water beneath the boat makes me feel funny. It keeps us up now, but if I fell over the side I would sink and drown.

"Nice out here, huh?" Dad says. He is breathing hard.

"We should go over that way to get on the island," Jerry says.

"This goddamn oar has splinters in it," Dad says. He hooks the oar up and lets us glide. He reaches down to get the bottle of beer. Though the lake and some trees and the buildings back on shore are in front of me, what makes me look at it is my father's throat, the way it bobs when he swallows. He wipes his forehead. "Want to row, Sissie?" he says.

"Can I?"

"Let me do it," says Jerry.

"Naw, I was just kidding," Dad says.

"I can do it. It ain't hard."

"Stay where you are," Dad says.

He starts rowing again, faster. Why does he go so fast? His face is getting red, the way it does at home when he has trouble with Frank. He clears his throat and spits over the side; I don't like to see that but I can't help but watch. The other boat glides past us, heading for shore. The boys don't look over at us.

Jerry and I look to see if anyone else is on the island, but no one is. The island is very small. You can see around it.

"Are you going to land on it, Dad?" Jerry says.

"Sure okay." Dad's face is flushed and looks angry.

The boat scrapes bottom and bumps. "Jump out and pull it in," Dad says. Jerry jumps out. His shoes and socks are wet now, but Dad doesn't notice. The boat bumps; it hurts me. I am afraid. But then we're up on the land and Dad is out and lifting me. "Nice ride, sugar?" he says.

Jerry and I run around the island. It is different from what we thought, but we don't know why. There are some trees on it, some wild grass, and then bare caked mud that goes down to the water. The water looks dark and deep on the other side, but when we get there it's shallow. Lily pads grow there; everything is thick and tangled. Jerry wades in the water and gets his pants legs wet. "There might be money in the water," he says.

Some napkins and beer cans are nearby. There is part of a hotdog bun, with flies buzzing around it.

When we got back by Dad, we see him squatting over the water doing something. His back jerks. Then I see that he is being sick. He is throwing up in the water and making a noise like coughing.

Jerry turns around right away and runs back. I follow him, afraid. On the other side we can look back at the boathouse and wish we were there.

III

Marian and Betty went to the show, but I couldn't. She made me come along here with them. "And cut out that snippy face," Ma said, to let me know she's watching. I have to help her take care of Linda—poor fat Linda, with her runny nose! So here we are inside the tavern. There's too much smoke, I hate smoke. Dad is smoking a cigar. I won't drink any more root beer, it's flat, and I'm sick of potato chips. Inside me there is something that wants to run away, that hates them. How loud they are, my parents! My mother spilled something on the front of her dress, but does she notice? And my aunt Lucy and uncle Joe, they're here. Try to avoid them. Lucy has false teeth that make everyone stare at her. I know that everyone is staring at us. I could hide my head in my arms and turn away, I'm so tired and my legs hurt from sunburn and I can't stand them any more.

"So did you ever hear from them? That letter you wrote?" Ma says to Lucy.

"I'm still waiting. Somebody said you got to have connections to get on the show. But I don't believe it. That Howie Masterson that's the emcee, he's a real nice guy. I can tell."

"It's all crap," Dad says. "You women believe anything."

"I don't believe it," I say.

"Phony as hell," says my uncle.

"You do too believe it, Sissie," says my mother. "Sissie thinks he's cute. I know she does."

"I hate that guy!" I tell her, but she and my aunt are laughing. "I said I hate him! He's greasy."

"All that stuff is phony as hell," says my Uncle Joe. He is tired all the time, and right now he sits with his head bowed. I hate his bald head with the little fringe of gray hair on it. At least my father is still handsome. His jaws sag and there are lines in his neck—edged with dirt, I can see, embarrassed—and his stomach is bulging a little against the table, but still he is a handsome man. In a place like this women look at him. What's he see in *her*? they think. My mother had her hair cut too short last time; she looks queer. There is a photograph taken of her when she was young, standing by someone's motorcycle, with her hair long. In the photograph she was pretty, almost beautiful, but I don't believe it. Not really. I can't believe it, and I hate her. Her forehead gathers itself up in little wrinkles whenever she glances down at Linda, as if she can't remember who Linda is.

"Well, nobody wanted you, kid," she once said to Linda. Linda was a baby then, one year old. Ma was furious, standing in the kitchen where she was washing the floor, screaming: "Nobody wanted you, it was a goddamn accident! An accident!" That surprised me so I didn't know what to think, and I didn't know if I hated Ma or not; but I kept it all a secret . . . only my girl friends know, and I won't tell the priest either. Nobody can make me tell. I narrow my eyes and watch my mother leaning forward to say something—it's like she's going to toss something out on the table—and think that maybe she isn't my mother after all, and she isn't that pretty girl in the photograph, but someone else.

"A woman was on the show last night that lost two kids in a fire. Her house burned down," my aunt says loudly. "And she answered the questions right off and got a lot of money and the audience went wild. You could see she was a real lady. I love that guy, Howie Masterson. He's real sweet."

"He's a bastard," Dad says.

"Harry, what the hell? You never even seen him," Ma says.

"I sure as hell never did. Got better things to do at night." Dad turns to my uncle and his voice changes. "I'm on the night shift, now."

"Yeah, I hate that, I—"

"I can sleep during the day. What's the difference?"

"I hate those night shifts."

"What's there to do during the day?" Dad says flatly. His eyes scan us at the table as if he doesn't see anything, then they seem to fall off me and go behind me, looking at nothing.

"Not much," says my uncle, and I can see his white scalp beneath his hair. Both men are silent.

Dad pours beer into his glass and spills some of it. I wish I could look away. I love him, I think, but I hate to be here. Where would I rather be? With Marian and Betty at the movies, or in my room, lying on the bed and staring at the photographs of movie stars on my walls—those beautiful people that never say anything—while out in the kitchen my mother is waiting for my father to come home so they can continue their quarrel. It never stops, that quarrel. Sometimes they laugh together, kid around, they kiss. Then the quarrel starts up again in a few minutes.

"Ma, can I go outside and wait in the car?" I say. "Linda's asleep."

"What's so hot about the car?" she says, looking at me.

"I'm tired. My sunburn hurts."

Linda is sleeping in Ma's lap, with her mouth open and drooling on the front of her dress. "Okay, go on," Ma says. "But we're not going to hurry just for you."

When she has drunk too much there is a struggle in her between being angry and being affectionate; she fights both of them, as if standing with her legs apart and her hands on her hips, bracing a strong wind.

When I cross through the crowded tavern I'm conscious of people looking at me. My hair lost its curl because it was so humid today, my legs are too thin, my figure is flat and not nice like Marian's—I want to hide somewhere, hide my face from them. I hate this noisy place and these people. Even the music is ugly because it belongs to them. Then, when I'm outside, the music gets faint right away and it doesn't sound so bad. It's cooler out here. No one is around. Out back, the old rowboats are tied up. Nobody's on the lake. There's no moon, the sky is overcast, it was raining earlier.

When I turn around, a man is standing by the door watching me.

"What're you doing?" he says.

"Nothing."

He has dark hair and a tanned face, I think, but everything is confused because the light from the door is pinkish—there's a neon sign there. My heart starts to pound. The man leans forward to stare at me. "Oh, I thought you were somebody else," he says.

I want to show him I'm not afraid. "Yeah, really? Who did you think I was?" When we ride on the school bus we smile out the windows at strange men, just for fun. We do that all the time. I'm not afraid of any of them.

"You're not her," he says.

Some people come out the door and he has to step out of their way. I say to him, "Maybe you seen me around here before. We come here pretty often."

"Who do you come with?" He is smiling as if he thinks I'm funny. "Anybody I know?"

"That's my business."

It's a game. I'm not afraid. When I think of my mother and father inside, something makes me want to step closer to this man—why should I be afraid? I could be wild like some of the other girls. Nothing surprises me.

We keep on talking. At first I can tell he wants me to come inside the tavern with him, but then he forgets about it; he keeps talking. I don't know what we say, but we talk in drawling voices, smiling at each other but in a secret, knowing way, as if each one of us knew more than the other. My cheeks start to burn. I could be wild like Betty is sometimes—like some of the other girls. Why not? Once before I talked with a man like this, on the bus. We were both sitting in the back. I wasn't afraid. This man and I keep talking and we talk about nothing, he wants to know how old I am, but it makes my heart pound so hard that I want to touch my chest to calm it. We are walking along the old boardwalk and I say: "Somebody took me out rowing once here."

"Is that so?" he says. "You want me to take you out?"

He has a hard, handsome face. I like that face. Why is he alone? When he smiles I know he's laughing at me, and this makes me stand taller, walk with my shoulders raised.

"Hey, are you with somebody inside there?" he says.

"I left them."

"Have a fight?"

"A fight, yes."

He looks at me quickly. "How old are you anyway?"

"That's none of your business."

"Girls your age are all alike."

"We're not all alike!" I arch my back and look at him in a way I must have learned somewhere—where?—with my lips not smiling but ready to smile, and my eyes narrowed. One leg is turned as if I'm ready to jump from him. He sees all this. He smiles.

"Say, you're real cute."

We're walking over by the parking lot now. He touches my arm. Right away my heart trips, but I say nothing, I keep walking. High above us the tree branches are moving in the wind. It's cold for June. It's late—after eleven. The man is wearing a jacket, but I have on a sleeveless dress and there are goose-pimples on my arms.

"Cold, huh?" he says.

He takes hold of my shoulders and leans toward me. This is to show me he's no kid, he's grown-up, this is how they do things; when he kisses me his grip on my shoulders gets tighter. "I better go back," I say to him. My voice is queer.

"What?" he says.

I am wearing a face like one of those faces pinned up in my room, and what if I lose it? This is not my face. I try to turn away from him.

He kisses me again. His breath smells like beer, maybe, it's like my father's breath, and my mind is empty; I can't think what to do. Why am I here? My legs feel numb, my fingers are cold. The man rubs my arms and says, "You should have a sweater or something. . . ."

He is waiting for me to say something, to keep on the way I was before. But I have forgotten how to do it. Before, I was Marian or one of the older girls; now I am just myself. I am fourteen. I think of Linda sleeping in my mother's lap, and something frightens me.

"Hey, what's wrong?" the man says.

He sees I'm afraid but pretends he doesn't. He comes to me again and embraces me, his mouth presses against my neck and shoulder, I feel as if I'm suffocating. "My car's over here," he says, trying to catch his breath. I can't move. Something dazzling and icy rises up in me, an awful fear, but I can't move and can't say anything. He is touching me with his hands. His mouth is soft but wants too much from me. I think, What is he doing? Do they all do this? Do I have to have it done to me too?

"You cut that out," I tell him.

He steps away. His chest is heaving and his eyes look like a dog's eyes, surprised and betrayed. The last thing I see of him is those eyes, before I turn and run back to the tavern.

IV

Jesse says, "Let's stop at this place. I been here a few times before."

It's the Lakeside Bar. That big old building with the grubby siding, and a big pink neon sign in front, and the cinder driveway that's so bumpy. Yes, everything the same. But different too—smaller, dirtier. There is a custard stand nearby with a glaring orange roof, and people are crowded around it. That's new. I haven't been here for years.

"I feel like a beer," he says.

He smiles at me and caresses my arm. He treats me as if I were something that might break; in my cheap linen maternity dress I feel ugly and heavy. My flesh is so soft and thick that nothing could hurt it.

"Sure, honey. Pa used to stop in here too."

We cross through the parking lot to the tavern. Wild grass grows along the sidewalk and in the cracks of the sidewalk. Why is this place so ugly to me? I feel as if a hand were pressing against my chest, shutting off my breath. Is there some secret here? Why am I afraid?

I catch sight of myself in a dusty window as we pass. My hair is long, down to my shoulders. I am pretty, but my secret is that I am pretty like everyone is. My husband loves me for this but doesn't know it. I have a pink mouth and plucked darkened eyebrows and soft bangs over my forehead; I know everything, I have no need to learn from anyone else now. I am one of those girls younger girls study closely, to learn from. On buses, in five-and-tens, thirteen-year-old girls must look at me solemnly, learning, memorizing.

"Pretty Sissie!" my mother likes to say when we visit, though I told her how I hate that name. She is proud of me for being pretty, but thinks I'm too thin. "You'll fill out nice, after the baby," she says. Herself, she is fat and veins have begun to darken on her legs; she scuffs around the house in bedroom slippers. Who is my mother? When I think of her I can't think of anything—do I love her or hate her, or is there nothing there?

Jesse forgets and walks ahead of me, I have to walk fast to catch up. I'm wearing pastel-blue high heels—that must be because I am proud of my legs. I have little else. Then he remembers and turns to put out his hand for me, smiling to show he is sorry. Jesse is the kind of young man thirteen-year-old girls stare at secretly; he is not a man, not old enough, but not a boy either. He is a year older than I am, twenty. When I met him he was wearing a navy uniform and he was with a girl friend of mine.

Just a few people sitting outside at the tables. They're afraid of rain—the sky doesn't look good. And how bumpy the ground is here, bare spots and little holes and patches of crab grass, and everywhere napkins and junk. Too many flies outside. Has this place changed hands? The screens at the window don't fit right; you can see why flies get inside. Jesse opens the door for me and I go in. All bars smell alike. There is a damp, dark odor of beer and something indefinable—spilled soft drinks, pretzels getting stale? This bar is just like any other. Before we were married we went to places like this, Jesse and me and other couples. We had to spend a certain amount of time doing things like that—and going to movies, playing miniature golf, bowling, dancing, swimming—then we got married, now we're going to have a baby. I think of the baby all the time, because my life will be changed then; everything will be different. Four months from now. I should be frightened, but a calm laziness has come over me. It was so easy for my mother. . . . But it will be different with me because my life will be changed by it, and nothing every changed my mother. You couldn't change her! Why should I think? Why should I be afraid? My body is filled with love for this baby, and I will never be the same again.

We sit down at a table near the bar. Jesse is in a good mood. My father would have liked him, I think; when he laughs Jesse reminds me of him. Why is a certain kind of simple, healthy, honest man always destined to lose everything? Their souls are as clean and smooth as the muscular line of their arms. At night I hold Jesse, thinking of my father and what happened to him—all that drinking, then the accident at the factory—and I pray that Jesse will be different. I hope that his quick, open, loud way of talking is just a disguise, that really he is someone else—slower and calculating. That kind of man grows old without jerks and spasms. Why did I marry Jesse?

Someone at the bar turns around, and it's a man I think I know—I have known. Yes. That man outside, the man I met outside. I stare at him, my heart pounding, and he doesn't see me. He is dark, his hair is neatly combed but is thinner than before; he is wearing a cheap gray suit. But is it the same man? He is standing with a friend and looking around, as if he doesn't like what he sees. He is tired too. He has grown years older.

Our eyes meet. He glances away. He doesn't remember—that frightened girl he held in his arms.

I am tempted to put my hand on Jesse's arm and tell him about that man, but how can I? Jesse is talking about trading in our car for a new one. . . . I can't move, my mind seems to be coming to a stop. Is that the man I kissed, or someone else? A feeling of angry loss comes over me. Why should I lose everything? Everything? Is it the same man, and would he remember? My heart bothers me, it's stupid to be like this: here I sit, powdered and sweet, a girl safely married, pregnant and secured to the earth, with my husband beside me. He still loves me. Our love keeps on. Like my parents' love, it will subside someday, but nothing surprises me because I have learned everything.

The man turns away, talking to his friend. They are weary, tired of something. He isn't married yet, I think, and that pleases me. Good. But why are these men always tired? Is it the jobs they hold, the kind of men who stop in at this tavern? Why do they flash their teeth when they smile, but stop smiling so quickly? Why do their children cringe from them sometimes—an innocent upraised arm a frightening thing? Why do they grow old so quickly, sitting at kitchen tables with bottles of beer? They are everywhere, in every house. All the houses in this neighborhood and all neighborhoods around here. Jesse is young, but the outline of what he will be is already in his face; do you think I can't see it? Their lives are like hands dealt out to them in their innumerable card games. You pick up the sticky cards, and there it is: there it is. Can't change anything, all you can do is switch some cards around, stick one in here, one over here . . . pretend there is some sense, a secret scheme.

The man at the bar tosses some coins down and turns to go. I want to cry out to him, "Wait, wait!" But I cannot. I sit helplessly and watch him leave. Is it the same man? If he leaves I will be caught here, what can I do? I can almost hear my mother's shrill laughter coming in from outside, and some drawling remark of my father's—lifting for a moment above the music. Those little explosions of laughter, the slap of someone's hand on the damp table in anger, the clink of bottles accidentally touching—and there, there, my drunken aunt's voice, what is she saying? I am terrified at being left with them. I watch the man at the door and think that I could have loved him. I know it.

He has left, he and his friend. He is nothing to me, but suddenly I feel tears in my eyes. What's wrong with me? I hate everything that springs upon me and seems to draw itself down and oppress me in a way I could never explain to anyone. . . . I am crying because I am pregnant, but not with that man's child. It could have been his child, I could have gone with him to his car; but I did nothing, I ran away, I was afraid, and now I'm sitting here with Jesse, who is picking the label off his beer bottle with his thick squarish fingernails. I did nothing. I was afraid. Now he has left me here and what can I do?

I let my hand fall onto my stomach to remind myself that I am in love: with this baby, with Jesse, with everything. I am in love with our house and our life and the future and even this moment—right now—that I am struggling to live through.

[1967]

Alice Walker *1944–*

TO HELL WITH DYING

"To hell with dying," my father would say. "These children want Mr. Sweet!"

Mr. Sweet was a diabetic and an alcoholic and a guitar player and lived down the road from us on a neglected cotton farm. My older brothers and sisters got the most benefit from Mr. Sweet, for when they were growing up he had quite a few years ahead of him and so was capable of being called back from the brink of death any number of times—whenever the voice of my father reached him as he lay expiring. "To hell with dying, man," my father would say, pushing the wife away from the bedside (in tears although she knew the death was not necessarily the last one unless Mr. Sweet really wanted it to be). "These children want Mr. Sweet!" And they did want him, for at a signal from Father they would come crowding around the bed and throw themselves on the covers, and whoever was the smallest at the time would kiss him all over his wrinkled brown face and tickle him so that he would laugh all down in his stomach, and his mustache, which was long and sort of straggly, would shake like Spanish moss and was also that color.

Mr. Sweet had been ambitious as a boy, wanted to be a doctor or lawyer or sailor, only to find that black men fare better if they are not. Since he could become none of these things he turned to fishing as his only earnest career and playing the guitar as his only claim to doing anything extraordinarily well. His son, the only one that he and his wife, Miss Mary, had, was shiftless as the day is long and spent money as if he were trying to see the bottom of the mint, which Mr. Sweet would tell him was the clean brown palm of his hand. Miss Mary loved her "baby," however, and worked hard to get him the "li'l necessaries" of life, which turned out mostly to be women.

Mr. Sweet was a tall, thinnish man with thick kinky hair going dead white. He was dark brown, his eyes were squinty and sort of bluish, and he chewed Brown Mule tobacco. He was constantly on the verge of being blind drunk, for he brewed his own liquor and was not in the least a stingy sort of man, and was always very melancholy and sad, though frequently when he was "feelin' good" he'd dance around the yard with us, usually keeling over just as my mother came to see what the commotion was.

Toward all of us children he was very kind, and had the grace to be shy with us, which is unusual in grown-ups. He had great respect for my mother for she never held his drunkenness against him and would let us play with him even when he was about to fall in the fireplace from drink. Although Mr. Sweet would sometimes lose complete or nearly complete control of his head and neck so that he would loll in his chair, his mind remained strangely acute and his speech not too affected. His ability to be drunk and sober at the same time made him an ideal playmate, for he was as weak as we were and we could usually best him in wrestling, all the while keeping a fairly coherent conversation going.

We never felt anything of Mr. Sweet's age when we played with him. We loved his wrinkles and would draw some on our brows to be like him, and his white hair was my special treasure and he knew it and would never come to visit us just after he had had his hair cut off at the barbershop. Once he came to our house for something, probably to see my father about fertilizer for his crops because, although he never paid the slightest attention to his crops, he liked to know what things would be best to use on them if he ever did. Anyhow, he had not come with his hair since he had just had it shaved off at the barbershop. He wore a huge straw hat to keep off the sun and also to keep his head away from me. But as soon as I saw him I ran up and demanded that he take me up and kiss me with his funny beard which smelled so strongly of tobacco. Looking forward to burying my small fingers into his woolly hair, I threw away his hat only to find he had done something to his hair, that it was no longer there! I let out a squall which made my mother think that Mr. Sweet had finally dropped me in the well or something and from that day I've been wary of men in hats. However, not long after, Mr. Sweet showed up with his hair grown out and just as white and kinky and impenetrable as it ever was.

Mr. Sweet used to call me his princess, and I believed it. He made me feel pretty at five and six, and simply outrageously devastating at the blazing age of eight and a half. When he came to our house with his guitar the whole family would stop whatever they were doing to sit around him and listen to him play. He liked to play "Sweet Georgia Brown," that was what he called me sometimes, and also he liked to play "Caldonia" and all sorts of sweet, sad, wonderful songs which he sometimes made up. It was from one of these songs that I heard that he had had to marry Miss Mary when he had in fact loved somebody else (now living in Chi-ca-go, or De-stroy, Michigan). He was not sure that Joe Lee, her "baby," was also his baby. Sometimes he would cry and that was an indication that he was about to die again. And so we would all get prepared, for we were sure to be called upon.

I was seven the first time I remember actually participating in one of Mr. Sweet's "revivals"—my parents told me I had participated before, I had been the one chosen to kiss him and tickle him long before I knew the rite of Mr. Sweet's rehabilitation. He had come to our house, it was a few years after his wife's death, and was very sad, and also, typically, very drunk. He sat on the floor next to me and my older brother, the rest of the children were grown up and lived elsewhere, and began to play his guitar and cry. I held his woolly head in my arms and wished I could have been old enough to have been the woman he loved so much and that I had not been lost years and years ago.

When he was leaving, my mother said to us that we'd better sleep light that night for we'd probably have to go over to Mr. Sweet's before daylight. And we did. For soon after we had gone to bed one of the neighbors knocked on our door and called my father and said that Mr. Sweet was sinking fast and if he wanted to get in a word before the crossover he'd better shake a leg and get over to Mr. Sweet's house. All the neighbors knew to come to our house if something was wrong with Mr. Sweet, but they did not know how we always managed to make him well, or at least stop him from dying, when he was so often near death. As soon as we heard the cry we got up, my brother and I and my mother and father, and put on our clothes. We hurried out of the house and down the road for we were always afraid that we might someday be too late and Mr. Sweet would get tired of dallying.

When we got to the house, a very poor shack really, we found the front room full of neighbors and relatives and someone met us at the door and said it was all very sad that old Mr. Sweet Little (for Little was his family name, although we mostly ignored it) was about to kick the bucket. My parents were advised not to take my brother and me into the "death room," seeing we were so young and all, but we were so much more accustomed to the death room than he that we ignored him and dashed in without giving his warning a second thought. I was almost in tears, for these deaths upset me fearfully, and the thought of how much depended on me and my brother (who was such a ham most of the time) made me very nervous.

The doctor was bending over the bed and turned back to tell us for at least the tenth time in the history of my family that, alas, old Mr. Sweet Little was dying and that the children had best not see the face of implacable death (I didn't know what "implacable" was, but whatever it was, Mr. Sweet was not!). My father pushed him rather abruptly out of the way saying, as he always did and very loudly for he was saying it to Mr. Sweet, "To hell with dying, man, these children want Mr. Sweet"—which was my cue to throw myself upon the bed and kiss Mr. Sweet all around the whiskers and under the eyes and around the collar of his nightshirt where he smelled so strongly of all sorts of things, mostly liniment.

I was very good at bringing him around, for as soon as I saw that he was struggling to open his eyes I knew he was going to be all right, and so could finish my revival sure of success. As soon as his eyes were open he would begin to smile and that way I knew that I had surely won. Once, though, I got a tremendous scare, for he could not open his eyes and later I learned that he had had a stroke and that one side of his face was stiff and hard to get into motion. When he began to smile I could tickle him in earnest because I was sure that nothing would get in the way of his laughter, although once he began to cough so hard that he almost threw me off his stomach, but that was when I was very small, little more than a baby, and my bushy hair had gotten in his nose.

When we were sure he would listen to us we would ask him why he was in bed and when he was coming to see us again and could we play his guitar, which more than likely would be leaning against the bed. His eyes would get all misty and he would sometimes cry out loud, but we never let it embarrass us, for he knew that we loved him and that we sometimes cried too for no reason. My parents would leave the room to just the three of us; Mr. Sweet, by that time, would be propped up in bed with a number of pillows behind his head and with me sitting and lying on his shoulder and along his chest. Even when he had trouble breathing he would not ask me to get down. Looking into my eyes he would shake his white head and run a scratchy old finger all around my hairline, which was rather low down, nearly to my eyebrows, and made some people say I looked like a baby monkey.

My brother was very generous in all this, he let me do all the revivaling—he had done it for years before I was born and so was glad to be able to pass it on to someone new. What he would do while I talked to Mr. Sweet was pretend to play the guitar, in fact pretend that he was a young version of Mr. Sweet, and it always made Mr. Sweet glad to think that someone wanted to be like him—of course, we did not know this then, we played the thing by ear, and whatever he seemed to like, we did. We were desperately afraid that he was just going to take off one day and leave us.

It did not occur to us that we were doing anything special; we had not learned that death was final when it did come. We thought nothing of triumphing over it so many times, and in fact became a trifle contemptuous of people who let themselves be carried away. It did not occur to us that if our father had been dying we could not have stopped it, that Mr. Sweet was the only person over whom we had power.

When Mr. Sweet was in his eighties I was studying in the university many miles from home. I saw him whenever I went home, but he was never on the verge of dying that I could tell and I began to feel that my anxiety for his health and psychological well-being was unnecessary. By this time he not only had a mustache but a long flowing snow-white beard, which I loved and combed and braided for hours. He was very peaceful, fragile, gentle, and the only jarring note about him was his old steel guitar, which he still played in the old sad, sweet, down-home blues way.

On Mr. Sweet's ninetieth birthday I was finishing my doctorate in Massachusetts and I had been making arrangements to go home for several weeks' rest. That morning I got a telegram telling me that Mr. Sweet was dying again and could I please drop everything and come home. Of course I could. My dissertation could wait and my teachers would understand when I explained to them when I got back. I ran to the phone, called the airport, and within four hours I was speeding along the dusty road to Mr. Sweet's.

The house was more dilapidated than when I was last there, barely a shack, but it was overgrown with yellow roses which my family had planted many years ago. The air was heavy and sweet and very peaceful. I felt strange walking through the gate and up the old rickety steps. But the strangeness left me as I caught sight of the long white beard I loved so well flowing down the thin body over the familiar quilt coverlet. Mr. Sweet!

His eyes were closed tight and his hands, crossed over his stomach, were thin and delicate, no longer scratchy. I remembered how always before I had run and jumped up on him just anywhere; now I knew he would not be able to support my weight. I looked around at my parents, and was surprised to see that my father and mother also looked old and frail. My father, his own hair very gray, leaned over the quietly sleeping old man, who, incidentally, smelled still of wine and tobacco, and said, as he'd done so many times, "To hell with dying, man! My daughter is home to see Mr. Sweet!" My brother had not been able to come as he was in the war in Asia. I bent down and gently stroked the closed eyes and gradually they began to open. The closed, wine-stained lips twitched a little, then parted in a warm, slightly embarrassed smile. Mr. Sweet could see me and he recognized me and his eyes looked very spry and twinkly for a moment. I put my head down on the pillow next to his and we just looked at each other for a long time. Then he began to trace my peculiar hairline with a thin, smooth finger. I closed my eyes when his finger halted above my ear (he used to rejoice at the dirt in my ears when I was little), his hand stayed cupped around my cheek. When I opened my eyes, sure that I had reached him in time, his were closed.

Even at twenty-four how could I believe that I had failed? that Mr. Sweet was really gone? He had never gone before. But when I looked at my parents I saw that they were holding back tears. They had loved him dearly. He was like a piece of rare and delicate china which was always being saved from breaking and which finally fell. I looked long at the old face, the wrinkled forehead, the red lips, the hands that still reached out to me. Soon I felt my father pushing something cool into my hands. It was Mr. Sweet's guitar. He had asked them months before to give it to me; he had known that even if I came next time he would not be able to respond in the old way. He did not want me to feel that my trip had been for nothing.

The old guitar! I plucked the strings, hummed "Sweet Georgia Brown." The magic of Mr. Sweet lingered still in the cool steel box. Through the window I could catch the fragrant delicate scent of tender yellow roses. The man on the high old-fashioned bed with the quilt coverlet and the flowing white beard had been my first love.

[1967]

Alice Walker   *1944–*

NINETEEN FIFTY-FIVE

1955

The car is a brand new red Thunderbird convertible, and it's passed the house more than once. It slows down real slow now, and stops at the curb. An older gentleman dressed like a Baptist deacon gets out on the side near the house, and a young fellow who looks about sixteen gets out on the driver's side. They are white, and I wonder what in the world they are doing in this neighborhood.

Well, I say to J. T., put your shirt on, anyway, and let me clean these glasses offa the table.

We had been watching the ballgame on TV. I wasn't actually watching, I was sort of daydreaming, with my foots up in J. T.'s lap.

I seen 'em coming on up the walk, brisk, like they coming to sell something, and then they rung the bell, and J. T. declined to put on a shirt but instead disappeared into the bedroom where the other television is. I turned down the one in the living room; I figured I'd be rid of these two double quick and J. T. could come back out again.

Are you Gracie Mae Still? asked the old guy, when I opened the door and put my hand on the lock inside the screen.

And I don't need to buy a thing, said I.

What makes you think we're sellin'? he asks, in that hearty Southern way that makes my eyeballs ache.

Well, one way or another and they're inside the house and the first thing the young fellow does is raise the TV a couple of decibels. He's about five feet nine, sort of womanish looking, with real dark white skin and a red pouting mouth. His hair is black and curly and he looks like a Loosianna creole.[1]

About one of your songs, says the deacon. He is maybe sixty, with white hair and beard, white silk shirt, black linen suit, black tie and black shoes. His cold gray eyes look like they're sweating.

One of my songs?

Traynor here just *loves* your songs. Don't you, Traynor? He nudges Traynor with his elbow. Traynor blinks, says something I can't catch in a pitch I don't register.

The boy learned to sing and dance livin' round you people out in the country. Practically cut his teeth on you.

Traynor looks up at me and bites his thumbnail.

I laugh.

Well, one way or another they leave with my agreement that they can record one of my songs. The deacon writes me a check for five hundred dollars, the boy grunts his awareness of the transaction, and I am laughing all over myself by the time I rejoin J. T.

Just as I am snuggling down beside him though I hear the front door bell going off again.

Forgit his hat? asks J. T.

---

[1] A descendant of Louisiana's original French settlers.

I hope not, I say.

The deacon stands there leaning on the door frame and once again I'm thinking of those sweaty-looking eyeballs of his. I wonder if sweat makes your eyeballs pink because his are sure pink. Pink and gray and it strikes me that nobody I'd care to know is behind them.

I forgot one little thing, he says pleasantly. I forgot to tell you Traynor and I would like to buy up all of those records you made of the song. I tell you we sure do love it.

Well, love it or not, I'm not so stupid as to let them do that without making 'em pay. So I says, Well, that's gonna cost you. Because, really, that song never did sell all that good, so I was glad they was going to buy it up. But on the other hand, them two listening to my song by themselves, and nobody else getting to hear me sing it, give me a pause.

Well, one way or another the deacon showed me where I would come out ahead on any deal he had proposed so far. Didn't I give you five hundred dollars? he asked. What white man—and don't even need to mention colored—would give you more? We buy up all your records of that particular song: first, you git royalties. Let me ask you, how much you sell that song for in the first place? Fifty dollars? A hundred, I say. And no royalties from it yet, right? Right. Well, when we buy up all of them records you gonna git royalties. And that's gonna make all them race record shops sit up and take notice of Gracie Mae Still. And they gonna push all them other records of yourn they got. And you no doubt will become one of the big name colored recording artists. And then we can offer you another five hundred dollars for letting us do all this for you. And by God you'll be sittin' pretty! You can go out and buy you the kind of outfit a star should have. Plenty sequins and yards of red satin.

I had done unlocked the screen when I saw I could get some more money out of him. Now I held it wide open while he squeezed through the opening between me and the door. He whipped out another piece of paper and I signed it.

He sort of trotted out to the car and slid in beside Traynor, whose head was back against the seat. They swung around in a u-turn in front of the house and then they was gone.

J. T. was putting his shirt on when I got back to the bedroom. Yankees beat the Orioles 10-6, he said. I believe I'll drive out to Paschal's pond and go fishing. Wanta go?

While I was putting on my pants J. T. was holding the two checks.

I'm real proud of a woman that can make cash money without leavin' home, he said. And I said *Umph.* Because we met on the road with me singing in first one little low-life jook after another, making ten dollars a night for myself if I was lucky, and sometimes bringin' home nothing but my life. And J. T. just loved them times. The way I was fast and flashy and always on the go from one town to another. He loved the way my singin' made the dirt farmers cry like babies and the womens shout Honey, hush! But that's mens. They loves any style to which you can get 'em accustomed.

1956

My little grandbaby called me one night on the phone: Little Mama, Little Mama, there's a white man on the television singing one of your songs! Turn on channel 5.

Lord, if it wasn't Traynor. Still looking half asleep from the neck up, but kind of awake in a nasty way from the waist down. He wasn't doing too bad with my song either, but it wasn't just the song the people in the audience was screeching and screaming over, it was that nasty little jerk he was doing from the waist down.

Well, Lord have mercy, I said, listening to him. If I'da closed my eyes, it could have been me. He had followed every turning of my voice, side streets, avenues, red lights, train crossings and all. It give me a chill.

Everywhere I went I heard Traynor singing my song, and all the little white girls just eating it up. I never had so many ponytails switched across my line of vision in my life. They was so *proud.* He was a *genius.*

Well, all that year I was trying to lose weight anyway and that and high blood pressure and sugar kept me pretty well occupied. Traynor had made a smash from a song of mine, I still had seven hundred dollars of the original one thousand dollars in the bank, and I felt if I could just bring my weight down, life would be sweet.

1957

I lost ten pounds in 1956. That's what I give myself for Christmas. And J. T. and me and the children and their friends and grandkids of all description had just finished dinner—over which I had put on nine and a half of my lost ten—when who should appear at the front door but Traynor. Little Mama, Little Mama! It's that white man who sings —— —— ——. The children didn't call it my song anymore. Nobody did. It was funny how that happened. Traynor and the deacon had bought up all my records, true, but on his record he had put "written by Gracie Mae Still." But that was just another name on the label, like "produced by Apex Records."

On the TV he was inclined to dress like the deacon told him. But now he looked presentable.

Merry Christmas, said he.

And same to you, Son.

I don't know why I called him Son. Well, one way or another they're all our sons. The only requirement is that they be younger than us. But then again, Traynor seemed to be aging by the minute.

You looks tired, I said. Come on in and have a glass of Christmas cheer.

J. T. ain't never in his life been able to act decent to a white man he wasn't working for, but he poured Traynor a glass of bourbon and water, then he took all the children and grandkids and friends and whatnot out to the den. After while I heard Traynor's voice singing the song, coming from the stereo console. It was just the kind of Christmas present my kids would consider cute.

I looked at Traynor, complicit. But he looked like it was the last thing in the world he wanted to hear. His head was pitched forward over his lap, his hands holding his glass and his elbows on his knees.

I done sung that song seem like a million times this year, he said. I sung it on the Grand Ole Opry, I sung it on the Ed Sullivan show. I sung it on Mike Douglas,[2]

---

[2] The Grand Ole Opry is America's most famous country-western radio (later television) show; originating from Nashville; Ed Sullivan (1902–1974) emceed the "Ed Sullivan Show" on CBS Television from 1948–1971; Mike Douglas (1925–   ) has hosted a number of talk-variety programs on both radio and television.

I sung it at the Cotton Bowl, the Orange Bowl. I sung it at Festivals. I sung it at Fairs. I sung it overseas in Rome, Italy, and once in a submarine *underseas*. I've sung it and sung it, and I'm making forty thousand dollars a day offa it, and you know what, I don't have the faintest notion what that song means.

Whatchumean, what do it mean? It mean what it says. All I could think was: These suckers is making forty thousand a *day* offa my song and now they gonna come back and try to swindle me out of the original thousand.

It's just a song, I said. Cagey. When you fool around with a lot of no count mens you sing a bunch of 'em. I shrugged.

Oh, he said. Well. He started brightening up. I just come by to tell you I think you are a great singer.

He didn't blush, saying that. Just said it straight out.

And I brought you a little Christmas present too. Now you take this little box and you hold it until I drive off. Then you take it outside under that first streetlight back up the street aways in front of that green house. Then you open the box and see . . . Well, just *see*.

What had come over this boy, I wondered, holding the box. I looked out the window in time to see another white man come up and get in the car with him and then two more cars full of white mens start out behind him. They was all in long black cars that looked like a funeral procession.

Little Mama, Little Mama, what it is? One of my grandkids come running up and started pulling at the box. It was wrapped in gay Christmas paper—the thick, rich kind that it's hard to picture folks making just to throw away.

J. T. and the rest of the crowd followed me out the house, up the street to the streetlight and in front of the green house. Nothing was there but somebody's gold-grilled white Cadillac. Brandnew and most distracting. We got to looking at it so till I almost forgot the little box in my hand. While the others were busy making 'miration I carefully took off the paper and ribbon and folded them up and put them in my pants pocket. What should I see but a pair of genuine solid gold caddy keys.

Dangling the keys in front of everybody's nose, I unlocked the caddy, mo tioned for J. T. to git in on the other side, and us didn't come back home for two days.

1960

Well, the boy was sure nuff famous by now. He was still a mite shy of twenty but already they was calling him the Emperor of Rock and Roll.

Then what should happen but the draft.

Well, says J. T. There goes all this Emperor of Rock and Roll business.

But even in the army the womens was on him like white on rice. We watched it on the News.

Dear Gracie Mae (he wrote from Germany),

How you? Fine I hope as this leaves me doing real well. Before I come in the army I was gaining a lot of weight and gitting jittery from making all them dumb movies. But now I exercise and eat right and get plenty of rest. I'm more awake than I been in ten years.

I wonder if you are writing any more songs?

Sincerely,
Traynor

I wrote him back:

> *Dear Son,*
>
> *We is all fine in the Lord's good grace and hope this finds you the same. J. T. and me be out all times of the day and night in that car you give me—which you know you didn't have to do. Oh, and I do appreciate the mink and the new self-cleaning oven. But if you send anymore stuff to eat from Germany I'm going to have to open up a store in the neighborhood just to get rid of it. Really, we have more than enough of everything. The Lord is good to us and we don't know Want.*
>
> *Glad to here you is well and gitting your right rest. There ain't nothing like exercising to help that along. J. T. and me work some part of every day that we don't go fishing in the garden.*
>
> *Well, so long Soldier.*
>
> *Sincerely,*
> *Gracie Mae*

He wrote:

> *Dear Gracie Mae,*
>
> *I hope you and J. T. like that automatic power tiller I had one of the stores back home send you. I went through a mountain of catalogs looking for it—I wanted something that even a woman could use.*
>
> *I've been thinking about writing some songs of my own but every time I finish one it don't seem to be about nothing I've actually lived myself. My agent keeps sending me other people's songs but they just sound mooney. I can hardly git through 'em without gagging.*
>
> *Everybody still loves that song of yours. They ask me all the time what do I think it means, really. I mean, they want to know just what I want to know. Where out of your life did it come from?*
>
> *Sincerely,*
> *Traynor*

1968

I didn't see the boy for seven years. No. Eight. Because just about everybody was dead when I saw him again. Malcolm X, King, the president and his brother,[3] and even J. T. J. T. died of a head cold. It just settled in his head like a block of ice, he said, and nothing we did moved it until one day he just leaned out the bed and died.

His good friend Horace helped me put him away, and then about a year later Horace and me started going together. We was sitting out on the front porch swing one summer night, dusk-dark, and I saw this great procession of lights winding to a stop.

---

[3] The allusions, of course, are to Malcolm X (1925–1965), the Black Muslim leader; Martin Luther King, Jr. (1929–1968), the civil rights leader; President John F. Kennedy (1917–1963), and his brother Robert Kennedy (1925–1968), the Attorney General—all of whom were assassinated.

Holy Toledo! said Horace. (He's got a real sexy voice like Ray Charles.)[4] Look *at* it. He meant the long line of flashy cars and the white men in white summer suits jumping out on the drivers' sides and standing at attention. With wings they could pass for angels, with hoods they could be the Klan.

Traynor comes waddling up the walk.

And suddenly I know what it is he could pass for. An Arab like the ones you see in storybooks. Plump and soft and with never a care about weight. Because with so much money, who cares? Traynor is almost dressed like someone from a storybook too. He has on, I swear, about ten necklaces. Two sets of bracelets on his arms, at least one ring on every finger, and some kind of shining buckles on his shoes, so that when he walks you get quite a few twinkling lights.

Gracie Mae, he says, coming up to give me a hug. J. T.

I explain that J. T. passed. That this is Horace.

Horace, he says, puzzled but polite, sort of rocking back on his heels, Horace. That's it for Horace. He goes in the house and don't come back.

Looks like you and me is gained a few, I say.

He laughs. The first time I ever heard him laugh. It don't sound much like a laugh and I can't swear that it's better than no laugh a'tall.

He's gitting fat for sure, but he's still slim compared to me. I'll never see three hundred pounds again and I've just about said (excuse me) fuck it. I got to thinking about it one day an' I thought: aside from the fact that they say it's unhealthy, my fat ain't never been no trouble. Mens always have loved me. My kids ain't never complained. Plus they's fat. And fat like I is I looks distinguished. You see me coming and you know somebody's *there*.

Gracie Mae, he says, I've come with a personal invitation to you to my house tomorrow for dinner. He laughed. What did it sound like? I couldn't place it. See them men out there? he asked me. I'm sick and tired of eating with them. They don't never have nothing to talk about. That's why I eat so much. But if you come to dinner tomorrow we can talk about the old days. You can tell me about that farm I bought you.

I sold it, I said.

You did?

Yeah, I said, I did. Just cause I said I liked to exercise by working in a garden didn't mean I wanted five hundred acres! Anyhow, I'm a city girl now. Raised in the country it's true. Dirt poor—the whole bit—but that's all behind me now.

Oh well, he said, I didn't mean to offend you.

We sat a few minutes listening to the crickets.

Then he said: You wrote that song while you was still on the farm, didn't you, or was it right after you left?

You had somebody spying on me? I asked.

You and Bessie Smith[5] got into a fight over it once, he said.

You *is* been spying on me!

But I don't know what the fight was about, he said. Just like I don't know what happened to your second husband. Your first one died in the Texas electric chair. Did you know that? Your third one beat you up, stole your touring costumes and your car and retired with a chorine[6] to Tuskegee. He laughed. He's still there.

I had been mad, but suddenly I calmed down. Traynor was talking very dream-

[4] Ray Charles (1930–   ), the blues singer.
[5] Bessie Smith (1898–1937), one of America's most famous early blues singers.
[6] Slang: a chorus girl.

ily. It was dark but seems like I could tell his eyes weren't right. It was like some*thing* was sitting there talking to me but not necessarily with a person behind it.

You gave up on marrying and seem happier for it. He laughed again. I married but it never went like it was supposed to. I never could squeeze any of my own life either into it or out of it. It was like singing somebody else's record. I copied the way it was sposed to be *exactly* but I never had a clue what marriage meant.

I bought her a diamond ring as big as your fist. I bought her clothes. I built her a mansion. But right away she didn't want the boys to stay there. Said they smoked up the bottom floor. Hell, there were *five* floors.

No need to grieve, I said. No need to. Plenty more where she come from.

He perked up. That's part of what that song means, ain't it? No need to grieve. Whatever it is, there's plenty more down the line.

I never really believed that way back when I wrote that song, I said. It was all bluffing then. The trick is to live long enough to put your young bluffs to use. Now if I was to sing that song today, I'd tear it up. 'Cause I done lived long enough to know it's *true*. Them words could hold me up.

I ain't lived that long, he said.

Look like you on your way, I said. I don't know why, but the boy seemed to need some encouraging. And I don't know, seem like one way or another you talk to rich white folks and you end up reassuring *them*. But what the hell, by now I feel something for the boy. I wouldn't be in his bed all alone in the middle of the night for nothing. Couldn't be nothing worse than being famous the world over for something you don't even understand. That's what I tried to tell Bessie. She wanted the same song. Overheard me practicing it one day, said, with her hands on her hips: Gracie Mae, I'ma sing your song tonight. I *likes* it.

Your lips be too swole to sing, I said. She was mean and she was strong, but I trounced her.

Ain't you famous enough with your own stuff? I said. Leave mine alone. Later on, she thanked me. By then she was Miss Bessie Smith to the World, and I was still Miss Gracie Mae Nobody from Notasulga.

The next day all these limousines arrived to pick me up. Five cars and twelve bodyguards. Horace picked that morning to start painting the kitchen.

Don't paint the kitchen, fool, I said. The only reason that dumb boy of ours is going to show me his mansion is because he intends to present us with a new house.

What you gonna do with it? he asked me, standing there in his shirtsleeves stirring the paint.

Sell it. Give it to the children. Live in it on weekends. It don't matter what I do. He sure don't care.

Horace just stood there shaking his head. Mama you sure looks *good,* he says. Wake me up when you git back.

Fool, I say, and pat my wig in front of the mirror.

The boy's house is something else. First you come to this mountain, and then you commence to drive and drive up this road that's lined with magnolias. Do magnolias grow on mountains? I was wondering. And you come to lakes and you come to ponds and you come to deer and you come up on some sheep. And I figure these two is sposed to represent England and Wales. Or something out of Europe. And you just keep on coming to stuff. And it's all pretty. Only the man driving my car don't look at nothing but the road. Fool. And then *finally,* after all this time, you begin to go up the driveway. And there's more magnolias—only they're not in such good shape. It's sort of cool up this high and I don't think they're gonna make it. And then I see this building that looks like if it had a name it woud be The Tara Hotel.[7] Columns and steps and outdoor chandeliers and rocking chairs. Rocking chairs? Well, and there's the boy on the steps dressed in a dark green satin jacket like you see folks wearing on TV late at night, and he looks sort of like a fat dracula[8] with all that house rising behind him, and standing beside him there's this little white vision of loveliness that he introduces as his wife.

He's nervous when he introduces us and he says to her: This is Gracie Mae Still, I want you to know me. I mean . . . and she gives him a look that would fry meat.

Won't you come in, Gracie Mae, she says, and that's the last I see of her.

He fishes around for something to say or do and decides to escort me to the kitchen. We go through the entry and the parlor and the breakfast room and the dining room and the servants' passage and finally get there. The first thing I notice is that, altogether, there are five stoves. He looks about to introduce me to one.

Wait a minute, I say. Kitchens don't do nothing for me. Let's go sit on the front porch.

Well, we hike back and we sit in the rocking chairs rocking until dinner.

Gracie Mae, he says down the table, taking a piece of fried chicken from the woman standing over him, I got a little surprise for you.

It's a house, ain't it? I ask, spearing a chitlin.[9]

You're getting *spoiled,* he says. And the way he says *spoiled* sounds funny. He slurs it. It sounds like his tongue is too thick for his mouth. Just that quick he's finished the chicken and is now eating chitlins *and* a pork chop. *Me* spoiled, I'm thinking.

I already got a house. Horace is right this minute painting the kitchen. I bought that house. My kids feel comfortable in that house.

But this one I bought you is just like mine. Only a little smaller.

I still don't need no house. And anyway who would clean it?

He looked surprised.

Really, I think, some peoples advance *so* slowly.

I hadn't thought of that. But what the hell, I'll get you somebody to live in.

I don't want other folks living 'round me. Makes me nervous.

You *don't?* It *do?*

What I want to wake up and see folks I don't even know for?

He just sits there downtable staring at me. Some of that feeling is in the song, ain't it? Not the words, the *feeling.* What I want to wake up and see folks I don't even know for? But I see twenty folks a day I don't even know, including my wife.

This food wouldn't be bad to wake up to though, I said. The boy had found the genius of corn bread.

He looked at me real hard. He laughed. Short. They want what you got but they don't want you. They want what I got only it ain't mine. That's what makes 'em so hungry for me when I sing. They getting the flavor of something but they

---

[7] Tara is the name of Scarlett O'Hara's Georgia plantation in Margaret Mitchell's Civil War romance *Gone With the Wind* (1936).
[8] The vampire "hero" of Bram Stoker's famous novel of 1897.
[9] A food made from cooked hog intestines.

ain't getting the thing itself. They like a pack of hound dogs trying to gobble up a scent.

You talking 'bout your fans?

Right. Right. He says.

Don't worry 'bout your fans. I say. They don't know their asses from a hole in the ground. I doubt there's a honest one in the bunch.

That's the point. Dammit, that's the point! He hits the table with his fist. It's so solid it don't even quiver. You need a honest audience! You can't have folks that's just gonna lie right back to you.

Yeah, I say, it was small compared to yours, but I had one. It would have been worth my life to try to sing 'em somebody else's stuff that I didn't know nothing about.

He must have pressed a buzzer under the table. One of his flunkies zombies up.

Git Johnny Carson,[10] he says.

On the phone? asks the zombie.

On the phone, says Traynor, what you think I mean, git him offa the front porch? Move your ass.

So two weeks later we's on the Johnny Carson show.

Traynor is all corseted down nice and looks a little bit fat but mostly good. And all the women that grew up on him and my song squeal and squeal. Traynor says: The lady who wrote my first hit record is here with us tonight, and she's agreed to sing it for all of us, just like she sung it forty-five years ago. Ladies and Gentlemen, the great Gracie Mae Still!

Well, I had tried to lose a couple of pounds my own self, but failing that I had me a very big dress made. So I sort of rolls over next to Traynor, who is dwarfed by me, so that when he puts his arm around back of me to try to hug me it looks funny to the audience and they laugh.

I can see this pisses him off. But I smile out there at 'em. Imagine squealing for twenty years and not knowing why you're squealing? No more sense of endings and beginnings than hogs.

It don't matter, Son, I say. Don't fret none over me.

I commence to sing. And I sound——wonderful. Being able to sing good ain't all about having a good singing voice a'tall. A good singing voice helps. But when you come up in the Hard Shell Baptist church like I did you understand early that the fellow that sings is the singer. Them that waits for programs and arrangements and letters from home is just good voices occupying body space.

So there I am singing my own song, my own way. And I give it all I got and enjoy every minute of it. When I finish Traynor is standing up clapping and clapping and beaming at first me and then the audience like I'm his mama for true. The audience claps politely for about two seconds.

Traynor looks disgusted.

He comes over and tries to hug me again. The audience laughs.

Johnny Carson looks at us like we both weird.

Traynor is mad as hell. He's supposed to sing something called a love ballad. But instead he takes the mike, turns to me and says: Now see if my imitation still holds up. He goes into the same song, *our* song, I think, looking out at his flaky audience. And he sings it just the way he always did. My voice, my tone, my

---

[10] Johnny Carson (1925–   ), the host of NBC's "Tonight" television show from 1962 to 1992.

inflection, everything. But he forgets a couple of lines. Even before he's finished the matronly squeals begin.

He sits down next to me looking whipped.

It don't matter, Son, I say, patting his hand. You don't even know those people. Try to make the people you know happy.

Is that in the song? he asks.

Maybe. I say.

1977

For a few years I hear from him, then nothing. But trying to lose weight takes all the attention I got to spare. I finally faced up to the fact that my fat is the hurt I don't admit, not even to myself, and that I been trying to bury it from the day I was born. But also when you git real old, to tell the truth, it ain't as pleasant. It gits lumpy and slack. Yuck. So one day I said to Horace, I'ma git this shit offa me.

And he fell in with the program like he always try to do and Lord such a procession of salads and cottage cheese and fruit juice!

One night I dreamed Traynor had split up with his fifteenth wife. He said: *You meet 'em for no reason. You date 'em for no reason. You marry 'em for no reason. I do it all but I swear it's just like somebody else doing it. I feel like I can't remember Life.*

The boy's in trouble, I said to Horace.

You've always said that, he said.

I have?

Yeah. You always said he looked asleep. You can't sleep through life if you wants to live it.

You not such a fool after all, I said, pushing myself up with my cane and hobbling over to where he was. Let me sit down on your lap, I said, while this salad I ate takes effect.

In the morning we heard Traynor was dead. Some said fat, some said heart, some said alcohol, some said drugs. One of the children called from Detroit. Them dumb fans of his is on a crying rampage, she said. You just ought to turn on the t.v.

But I didn't want to see 'em. They was crying and crying and didn't even know what they was crying for. One day this is going to be a pitiful country, I thought.

[1981]

Gabriel García Márquez   1928–

A Very Old Man with Enormous Wings*

A Tale for Children

On the third day of rain they had killed so many crabs inside the house that Pelayo had to cross his drenched courtyard and throw them into the sea, because the newborn child had a temperature all night and they thought it was due to the stench. The world had been sad since Tuesday. Sea and sky were a single ash-gray thing and the sands of the beach, which on March nights glimmered like pow-dered light, had become a stew of mud and rotten shellfish. The light was so weak at noon that when Pelayo was coming back to the house after throwing away the crabs, it was hard for him to see what it was that was moving and groaning in the rear of the courtyard. He had to go very close to see that it was an old man, a very old man, lying face down in the mud, who, in spite of his tremendous efforts, couldn't get up, impeded by his enormous wings.

Frightened by that nightmare, Pelayo ran to get Elisenda, his wife, who was putting compresses on the sick child, and he took her to the rear of the courtyard. They both looked at the fallen body with mute stupor. He was dressed like a ragpicker. There were only a few faded hairs left on his bald skull and very few teeth in his mouth, and his pitiful condition of a drenched great-grandfather had taken away any sense of grandeur he might have had. His huge buzzard wings, dirty and half-plucked, were forever entangled in the mud. They looked at him so long and so closely that Pelayo and Elisenda very soon overcame their surprise and in the end found him familiar. Then they dared speak to him, and he answered in an incomprehensible dialect with a strong sailor's voice. That was how they skipped over the inconvenience of the wings and quite intelligently concluded that he was a lonely castaway from some foreign ship wrecked by the storm. And yet, they called in a neighbor woman who knew everything about life and death to see him, and all she needed was one look to show them their mistake.

"He's an angel," she told them. "He must have been coming for the child, but the poor fellow is so old that the rain knocked him down."

On the following day everyone knew that a flesh-and-blood angel was held captive in Pelayo's house. Against the judgment of the wise neighbor woman, for whom angels in those times were the fugitive survivors of a celestial conspiracy, they did not have the heart to club him to death. Pelayo watched over him all afternoon from the kitchen, armed with his bailiff's[1] club, and before going to bed he dragged him out of the mud and locked him up with the hens in the wire chicken coop. In the middle of the night, when the rain stopped, Pelayo and Elisenda were still killing crabs. A short time afterward the child woke up without a fever and with a desire to eat. Then they felt magnanimous and decided to put the angel on a raft with fresh water and provisions for three days and leave him to his fate on the high seas. But when they went out into the courtyard with the first light of dawn, they found the whole neighborhood in front of the chicken coop having fun with the angel, with-out the slightest reverence, tossing him things to eat through the openings in the wire as if he weren't a supernatural creature but a circus animal.

* Translated by Gregory Rabassa.
[1] A bailiff is a government official who serves writs and makes arrests.

Father Gonzaga arrived before seven o'clock, alarmed at the strange news. By that time onlookers less frivolous than those at dawn had already arrived and they were making all kinds of conjectures concerning the captive's future. The simplest among them thought that he should be named mayor of the world. Others of sterner mind felt that he should be promoted to the rank of five-star general in order to win all wars. Some visionaries hoped that he could be put to stud in order to implant on earth a race of winged wise men who could take charge of the universe. But Father Gonzaga, before becoming a priest, had been a robust wood-cutter. Standing by the wire, he reviewed his catechism in an instant and asked them to open the door so that he could take a close look at that pitiful man who looked more like a huge decrepit hen among the fascinated chickens. He was lying in a corner drying his open wings in the sunlight among the fruit peels and breakfast leftovers that the early risers had thrown him. Alien to the impertinences of the world, he only lifted his antiquarian eyes and murmured something in his dialect when Father Gonzaga went into the chicken coop and said good morning to him in Latin. The parish priest had his first suspicion of an impostor when he saw that he did not understand the language of God or know how to greet His ministers. Then he noticed that seen close up he was much too human: he had an unbearable smell of the outdoors, the back side of his wings was strewn with parasites and his main feathers had been mistreated by terrestrial winds, and nothing about him measured up to the proud dignity of angels. Then he came out of the chicken coop and in a brief sermon warned the curious against the risks of being ingenuous. He reminded them that the devil had the bad habit of making use of carnival tricks in order to confuse the unwary. He argued that if wings were not the essential element in determining the difference between a hawk and an airplane, they were even less so in the recognition of angels. Nevertheless, he promised to write a letter to his bishop so that the latter would write to his primate so that the latter would write to the Supreme Pontiff [2] in order to get the final verdict from the highest courts.

His prudence fell on sterile hearts. The news of the captive angel spread with such rapidity that after a few hours the courtyard had the bustle of a marketplace and they had to call in troops with fixed bayonets to disperse the mob that was about to knock the house down. Elisenda, her spine all twisted from sweeping up so much marketplace trash, then got the idea of fencing in the yard and charging five cents admission to see the angel.

The curious came from far away. A traveling carnival arrived with a flying acrobat who buzzed over the crowd several times, but no one paid any attention to him because his wings were not those of an angel but, rather, those of a sidereal [3] bat. The most unfortunate invalids on earth came in search of health: a poor woman who since childhood had been counting her heartbeats and had run out of numbers; a Portuguese man who couldn't sleep because the noise of the stars disturbed him; a sleepwalker who got up at night to undo the things he had done while awake; and many others with less serious ailments. In the midst of that shipwreck disorder that made the earth tremble, Pelayo and Elisenda were happy with fatigue, for in less than a week they had crammed their rooms with money and the line of pilgrims waiting their turn to enter still reached beyond the horizon.

The angel was the only one who took no part in his own act. He spent his time

---

[2] I.e., the Pope.
[3] Sidereal means, literally, pertaining to the stars, star-like.

trying to get comfortable in his borrowed nest, befuddled by the hellish heat of the oil lamps and sacramental candles that had been placed along the wire. At first they tried to make him eat some mothballs, which, according to the wisdom of the wise neighbor woman, were the food prescribed for angels. But he turned them down, just as he turned down the papal lunches[4] that the penitents brought him, and they never found out whether it was because he was an angel or because he was an old man that in the end he ate nothing but eggplant mush. His only supernatural virtue seemed to be patience. Especially during the first days, when the hens pecked at him, searching for the stellar parasites that proliferated in his wings, and the cripples pulled out feathers to touch their defective parts with, and even the most merciful threw stones at him, trying to get him to rise so they could see him standing. The only time they succeeded in arousing him was when they burned his side with an iron for branding steers, for he had been motionless for so many hours that they thought he was dead. He awoke with a start, ranting in his hermetic[5] language and with tears in his eyes, and he flapped his wings a couple of times, which brought on a whirlwind of chicken dung and lunar dust and a gale of panic that did not seem to be of this world. Although many thought that his reaction had been one not of rage but of pain, from then on they were careful not to annoy him, because the majority understood that his passivity was not that of a hero taking his ease but that of a cataclysm in repose.

Father Gonzaga held back the crowd's frivolity with formulas of maidservant inspiration while awaiting the arrival of a final judgment on the nature of the captive. But the mail from Rome showed no sense of urgency. They spent their time finding out if the prisoner had a navel, if his dialect had any connection with Aramaic,[6] how many times he could fit on the head of a pin, or whether he wasn't just a Norwegian with wings. Those meager letters might have come and gone until the end of time if a providential event had not put an end to the priest's tribulations.

It so happened that during those days, among so many other carnival attractions, there arrived in town the traveling show of the woman who had been changed into a spider for having disobeyed her parents. The admission to see her was not only less than the admission to see the angel, but people were permitted to ask her all manner of questions about her absurd state and to examine her up and down so that no one would ever doubt the truth of her horror. She was a frightful tarantula the size of a ram and with the head of a sad maiden. What was most heartrending, however, was not her outlandish shape but the sincere affliction with which she recounted the details of her misfortune. While still practically a child she had sneaked out of her parents' house to go to a dance, and while she was coming back through the woods after having danced all night without permission, a fearful thunderclap rent the sky in two and through the crack came the lightning bolt of brimstone that changed her into a spider. Her only nourishment came from the meatballs that charitable souls chose to toss into her mouth. A spectacle like that, full of so much human truth and with such a fearful lesson, was bound to defeat without even trying that of a haughty angel who scarcely deigned to look at mortals. Besides, the few miracles attributed to the angel showed a certain mental disorder, like the blind man who didn't recover his sight but grew three new teeth, or the paralytic who didn't get to walk but almost won the lottery,

[4] Expensive and lavish meals.   [5] I.e., unintelligible.
[6] An all-but-extinct Semitic language, which originated in ninth-century Syria and at one time was one of the most important and widespread languages of the ancient world.

and the leper whose sores sprouted sunflowers. Those consolation miracles, which
were more like mocking fun, had already ruined the angel's reputation when the
woman who had been changed into a spider finally crushed him completely. That
was how Father Gonzaga was cured forever of his insomnia and Pelayo's courtyard
went back to being as empty as during the time it had rained for three days and
crabs walked through the bedrooms.

The owners of the house had no reason to lament. With the money they saved
they built a two-story mansion with balconies and gardens and high netting so that
crabs wouldn't get in during the winter, and with iron bars on the windows so that
angels wouldn't get in. Pelayo also set up a rabbit warren close to town and gave
up his job as bailiff for good, and Elisenda bought some satin pumps with high
heels and many dresses of iridescent silk, the kind worn on Sunday by the most
desirable women in those times. The chicken coop was the only thing that didn't
receive any attention. If they washed it down with creolin[7] and burned tears of
myrrh[8] inside it every so often, it was not in homage to the angel but to drive away
the dungheap stench that still hung everywhere like a ghost and was turning the
new house into an old one. At first, when the child learned to walk, they were
careful that he not get too close to the chicken coop. But then they began to lose
their fears and got used to the smell, and before the child got his second teeth
he'd gone inside the chicken coop to play, where the wires were falling apart. The
angel was no less standoffish with him than with other mortals, but he tolerated
the most ingenious infamies with the patience of a dog who had no illusions. They
both came down with chicken pox at the same time. The doctor who took care of
the child couldn't resist the temptation to listen to the angel's heart, and he found
so much whistling in the heart and so many sounds in his kidneys that it seemed
impossible for him to be alive. What surprised him most, however, was the logic
of his wings. They seemed so natural on that completely human organism that he
couldn't understand why other men didn't have them too.

When the child began school it had been some time since the sun and rain had
caused the collapse of the chicken coop. The angel went dragging himself about
here and there like a stray dying man. They would drive him out of the bedroom
with a broom and a moment later find him in the kitchen. He seemed to be in so
many places at the same time that they grew to think that he'd been duplicated,
that he was reproducing himself all through the house, and the exasperated and
unhinged Elisenda shouted that it was awful living in that hell full of angels. He
could scarcely eat and his antiquarian eyes had also become so foggy that he went
about bumping into posts. All he had left were the bare cannulae[9] of his last
feathers. Pelayo threw a blanket over him and extended him the charity of letting
him sleep in the shed, and only then did they notice that he had a temperature
at night, and was delirious with the tongue twisters of an old Norwegian. That was
one of the few times they became alarmed, for they thought he was going to die
and not even the wise neighbor woman had been able to tell them what to do with
dead angels.

And yet he not only survived his worst winter, but seemed improved with the
first sunny days. He remained motionless for several days in the farthest corner of
the courtyard, where no one would see him, and at the beginning of December
some large, stiff feathers began to grow on his wings, the feathers of a scarecrow,
which looked more like another misfortune of decrepitude. But he must have
known the reason for those changes, for he was quite careful that no one should

---

[7] Disinfectant.   [8] Incense.   [9] Horny shafts.

notice them, that no one should hear the sea chanteys that he sometimes sang under the stars. One morning Elisenda was cutting some bunches of onions for lunch when a wind that seemed to come from the high seas blew into the kitchen. Then she went to the window and caught the angel in his first attempts at flight. They were so clumsy that his fingernails opened a furrow in the vegetable patch and he was on the point of knocking the shed down with the ungainly flapping that slipped on the light and couldn't get a grip on the air. But he did manage to gain altitude. Elisenda let out a sigh of relief, for herself and for him, when she saw him pass over the last houses, holding himself up in some way with the risky flapping of a senile vulture. She kept watching him even when she was through cutting the onions and she kept on watching until it was no longer possible for her to see him, because then he was no longer an annoyance in her life but an imaginary dot on the horizon of the sea.

[1968]

Leslie Silko   1948–

YELLOW WOMAN

I

My thigh clung to his with dampness, and I watched the sun rising up through the tamaracks and willows. The small brown water birds came to the river and hopped across the mud, leaving brown scratches in the alkali-white crust. They bathed in the river silently. I could hear the water, almost at our feet where the narrow fast channel bubbled and washed green ragged moss and fern leaves. I looked at him beside me, rolled in the red blanket on the white river sand. I cleaned the sand out of the cracks between my toes, squinting because the sun was above the willow trees. I looked at him for the last time, sleeping on the white river sand.

I felt hungry and followed the river south the way we had come the afternoon before, following our footprints that were already blurred by lizard tracks and bug trails. The horses were still lying down, and the black one whinnied when he saw me but he did not get up—maybe it was because the corral was made out of thick cedar branches and the horses had not yet felt the sun like I had. I tried to look beyond the pale red mesas to the pueblo. I knew it was there, even if I could not see it, on the sandrock hill above the river, the same river that moved past me now and had reflected the moon last night.

The horse felt warm underneath me. He shook his head and pawed the sand. The bay whinnied and leaned against the gate trying to follow, and I remembered him asleep in the red blanket beside the river. I slid off the horse and tied him close to the other horse. I walked north with the river again, and the white sand broke loose in footprints over footprints.

"Wake up."

He moved in the blanket and turned his face to me with his eyes still closed. I knelt down to touch him.

"I'm leaving."

He smiled now, eyes still closed. "You are coming with me, remember?" He sat up now with his bare dark chest and belly in the sun.

"Where?"

"To my place."

"And will I come back?"

He pulled his pants on. I walked away from him, feeling him behind me and smelling the willows.

"Yellow Woman," he said.

I turned to face him. "Who are you?" I asked.

He laughed and knelt on the low, sandy bank, washing his face in the river. "Last night you guessed my name, and you knew why I had come."

I stared past him at the shallow moving water and tried to remember the night, but I could only see the moon in the water and remember his warmth around me.

"But I only said that you were him and that I was Yellow Woman—I'm not really her–I have my own name and I come from the pueblo on the other side of the mesa. Your name is Silva and you are a stranger I met by the river yesterday afternoon."

He laughed softly. "What happened yesterday has nothing to do with what you will do today, Yellow Woman."

"I know—that's what I'm saying—the old stories about the ka'tsina spirit[1] and Yellow Woman can't mean us."

My old grandpa liked to tell those stories best. There is one about Badger and Coyote who went hunting and were gone all day, and when the sun was going down they found a house. There was a girl living there alone, and she had light hair and eyes and she told them that they could sleep with her. Coyote wanted to be with her all night so he sent Badger into a prairie-dog hole, telling him he thought he saw something in it. As soon as Badger crawled in, Coyote blocked up the entrance with rocks and hurried back to Yellow Woman.

"Come here," he said gently.

He touched my neck and I moved close to him to feel his breathing and to hear his heart. I was wondering if Yellow Woman had known who she was—if she knew that she would become part of the stories. Maybe she'd had another name that her husband and relatives called her so that only the ka'tsina from the north and the storytellers would know her as Yellow Woman. But I didn't go on; I felt him all around me, pushing me down into the white river sand.

Yellow Woman went away with the spirit from the north and lived with him and his relatives. She was gone for a long time, but then one day she came back and she brought twin boys.

"Do you know the story?"

"What story?" He smiled and pulled me close to him as he said this. I was afraid lying there on the red blanket. All I could know was the way he felt, warm, damp, his body beside me. This is the way it happens in the stories, I was thinking, with no thought beyond the moment she meets the ka'tsina spirit and they go.

"I don't have to go. What they tell in stories was real only then, back in time immemorial, like they say."

He stood up and pointed at my clothes tangled in the blanket. "Let's go," he said.

I walked beside him, breathing hard because he walked fast, his hand around my wrist. I had stopped trying to pull away from him, because his hand felt cool and the sun was high, drying the river bed into alkali. I will see someone, eventually I will see someone, and then I will be certain that he is only a man—some man from nearby—and I will be sure that I am not Yellow Woman. Because she is from out of time past and I live now and I've been to school and there are highways and pickup trucks that Yellow Woman never saw.

It was an easy ride north on horseback. I watched the change from the cottonwood trees along the river to the junipers that brushed past us in the foothills, and finally there were only piñons,[2] and when I looked up at the rim of the mountain plateau I could see pine trees growing on the edge. Once I stopped to look down, but the pale sandstone had disappeared and the river was gone and the dark lava hills were all around. He touched my hand, not speaking, but always singing softly a mountain song and looking into my eyes.

I felt hungry and wondered what they were doing at home now— my mother, my grandmother, my husband, and the baby. Cooking breakfast, saying, "Where

[1] A supernatural spirit believed by the Indians to inhabit 11,000-foot Mt. Taylor near the Laguna Pueblo reservation.
[2] A type of pine tree.

did she go?—maybe kidnapped," and Al going to the tribal police with the details: "She went walking along the river."

The house was made with black lava rock and red mud. It was high above the spreading miles of arroyos and long mesas. I smelled a mountain smell of pitch and buck brush. I stood there beside the black horse, looking down on the small, dim country we had passed, and I shivered.

"Yellow Woman, come inside where it's warm."

II

He lit a fire in the stove. It was an old stove with a round belly and an enamel coffeepot on top. There was only the stove, some faded Navajo blankets, and a bedroll and cardboard box. The floor was made of smooth adobe plaster, and there was one small window facing east. He pointed at the box.

"There's some potatoes and the frying pan." He sat on the floor with his arms around his knees pulling them close to his chest and he watched me fry the potatoes. I didn't mind him watching me because he was always watching me—he had been watching me since I came upon him sitting on the river bank trimming leaves from a willow twig with his knife. We ate from the pan and he wiped the grease from his fingers on his Levis.

"Have you brought women here before?" He smiled and kept chewing, so I said, "Do you always use the same tricks?"

"What tricks?" He looked at me like he didn't understand.

"The story about being a ka'tsina from the mountains. The story about Yellow Woman."

Silva was silent; his face was calm.

"I don't believe it. Those stories couldn't happen now," I said.

He shook his head and said softly, "But someday they will talk about us, and they will say, "Those two lived long ago when things like that happened.' "

He stood up and went out. I ate the rest of the potatoes and thought about things—about the noise the stove was making and the sound of the mountain wind outside. I remembered yesterday and the day before, and then I went outside.

I walked past the corral to the edge where the narrow trail cut through the black rim rock. I was standing in the sky with nothing around me but the wind that came down from the blue mountain peak behind me. I could see faint mountain images in the distance miles across the vast spread of mesas and valleys and plains. I wondered who was over there to feel the mountain wind on those sheer blue edges—who walks on the pine needles in those blue mountains.

"Can you see the pueblo?" Silva was standing behind me.

I shook my head. "We're too far away."

"From here I can see the world." He stepped out on the edge. "The Navajo reservation begins over there." He pointed to the east. "The Pueblo boundaries are over here." He looked below us to the south, where the narrow trail seemed to come from. "The Texans have their ranches over there, starting with that valley, the Concho Valley. The Mexicans run some cattle over there too."

"Do you ever work for them?"

"I steal from them," Silva answered. The sun was dropping behind us and the shadows were filling the land below. I turned away from the edge that dropped forever into the valleys below.

"I'm cold," I said; "I'm going inside." I started wondering about this man who could speak the Pueblo language so well but who lived on a mountain and rustled cattle. I decided that this man Silva must be Navajo, because Pueblo men didn't do things like that.

"You must be a Navajo."

Silva shook his head gently. "Little Yellow Woman," he said, "you never give up, do you? I have told you who I am. The Navajo people know me, too." He knelt down and unrolled the bedroll and spread the extra blankets out on a piece of canvas. The sun was down, and the only light in the house came from outside— the dim orange light from sundown.

I stood there and waited for him to crawl under the blankets.

"What are you waiting for?" he said, and I lay down beside him. He undressed me slowly like the night before beside the river—kissing my face gently and running his hands up and down my belly and legs. He took off my pants and then he laughed.

"Why are you laughing?"

"You are breathing so hard."

I pulled away from him and turned my back to him.

He pulled me around and pinned me down with his arms and chest. "You don't understand, do you, little Yellow Woman? You will do what I want."

And again he was all around me with his skin slippery against mine, and I was afraid because I understood that his strength could hurt me. I lay underneath him and I knew that he could destroy me. But later, while he slept beside me, I touched his face and I had a feeling—the kind of feeling for him that overcame me that morning along the river. I kissed him on the forehead and he reached out for me.

When I woke up in the morning he was gone. It gave me a strange feeling because for a long time I sat there on the blankets and looked around the little house for some object of his—some proof that he had been there or maybe that he was coming back. Only the blankets and the cardboard box remained. The .30-30[3] that had been leaning in the corner was gone, and so was the knife I had used the night before. He was gone, and I had my chance to go now. But first I had to eat, because I knew it would be a long walk home.

I found some dried apricots in the cardboard box, and I sat down on a rock at the edge of the plateau rim. There was no wind and the sun warmed me. I was surrounded by silence. I drowsed with apricots in my mouth, and I didn't believe that there were highways or railroads or cattle to steal.

When I woke up, I stared down at my feet in the black mountain dirt. Little black ants were swarming over the pine needles around my foot. They must have smelled the apricots. I thought about my family far below me. They would be wondering about me, because this had never happened to me before. The tribal police would file a report. But if old Grandpa weren't dead he would tell them what happened—he would laugh and say, "Stolen by a ka'tsina, a mountain spirit. She'll come home—they usually do." There are enough of them to handle things. My mother and grandmother will raise the baby like they raised me. Al will find someone else, and they will go on like before, except that there will be a story about the day I disappeared while I was walking along the river. Silva had come for me; he said he had. I did not decide to go. I just went. Moonflowers blossom in

[3] Rifle.

the sand hills before dawn, just as I followed him. That's what I was thinking as I wandered along the trail through the pine trees.

It was noon when I got back. When I saw the stone house I remembered that I had meant to go home. But that didn't seem important any more, maybe because there were little blue flowers growing in the meadow behind the stone house and the gray squirrels were playing in the pines next to the house. The horses were standing in the corral, and there was a beef carcass hanging on the shady side of a big pine in front of the house. Flies buzzed around the clotted blood that hung from the carcass. Silva was washing his hands in a bucket full of water. He must have heard me coming because he spoke to me without turning to face me.

"I've been waiting for you."

"I went walking in the big pine trees."

I looked into the bucket full of bloody water with brown-and-white animal hairs floating in it. Silva stood there letting his hand drip, examining me intently.

"Are you coming with me?"

"Where?" I asked him.

"To sell the meat in Marquez."

"If you're sure it's O.K."

"I wouldn't ask you if it wasn't," he answered.

He sloshed the water around in the bucket before he dumped it out and set the bucket upside down near the door. I followed him to the corral and watched him saddle the horses. Even beside the horses he looked tall, and I asked him again if he wasn't Navajo. He didn't say anything; he just shook his head and kept cinching up the saddle.

"But Navajos are tall."

"Get on the horse," he said, "and let's go."

The last thing he did before we started down the steep trail was to grab the .30-30 from the corner. He slid the rifle into the scabbard that hung from his saddle.

"Do they ever try to catch you?" I asked.

"They don't know who I am."

"Then why did you bring the rifle?"

"Because we are going to Marquez where the Mexicans live."

III

The trail leveled out on a narrow ridge that was steep on both sides like an animal spine. On one side I could see where the trail went around the rocky gray hills and disappeared into the southeast where the pale sandrock mesas stood in the distance near my home. On the other side was a trail that went west, and as I looked far into the distance I thought I saw the little town. But Silva said no, that I was looking in the wrong place, that I just thought I saw houses. After that I quit looking off into the distance; it was hot and the wildflowers were closing up their deep-yellow petals. Only the waxy cactus flowers bloomed in the bright sun, and I saw every color that a cactus blossom can be; the white ones and the red ones were still buds, but the purple and the yellow were blossoms, open full and the most beautiful of all.

Silva saw him before I did. The white man was riding a big gray horse, coming up the trail toward us. He was traveling fast and the gray horse's feet sent rocks rolling off the trail into the dry tumbleweeds. Silva motioned for me to stop and we watched the white man. He didn't see us right away, but finally his horse whinnied at our horses and he stopped. He looked at us briefly before he loped the gray horse across the three hundred yards that separated us. He stopped his horse in front of Silva, and his young fat face was shadowed by the brim of his hat. He didn't look mad, but his small, pale eyes moved from the blood-soaked gunny sacks hanging from my saddle to Silva's face and then back to my face.

"Where did you get the fresh meat?" the white man asked.

"I've been hunting," Silva said, and when he shifted his weight in the saddle the leather creaked.

"The hell you have, Indian. You've been rustling cattle. We've been looking for the thief for a long time."

The rancher was fat, and sweat began to soak through his white cowboy shirt and the wet cloth stuck to the thick rolls of belly fat. He almost seemed to be panting from the exertion of talking, and he smelled rancid, maybe because Silva scared him.

Silva turned to me and smiled. "Go back up the mountain, Yellow Woman."

The white man got angry when he heard Silva speak in a language he couldn't understand. "Don't try anything, Indian. Just keep riding to Marquez. We'll call the state police from there."

The rancher must have been unarmed because he was very frightened and if he had a gun he would have pulled it out then. I turned my horse around and the rancher yelled, "Stop!" I looked at Silva for an instant and there was something ancient and dark—something I could feel in my stomach— in his eyes, and when I glanced at his hand I saw his finger on the trigger of the .30-30 that was still in the saddle scabbard. I slapped my horse across the flank and the sacks of raw meat swung against my knees as the horse leaped up the trail. It was hard to keep my balance, and once I thought I felt the saddle slipping backward; it was because of this that I could not look back.

I didn't stop until I reached the ridge where the trail forked. The horse was breathing deep gasps and there was a dark film of sweat on its neck. I looked down in the direction I had come from, but I couldn't see the place. I waited. The wind came up and pushed warm air past me. I looked up at the sky, pale blue and full of thin clouds and fading vapor trails left by jets.

I think four shots were fired—I remember hearing four hollow explosions that reminded me of deer hunting. There could have been more shots after that, but I couldn't have heard them because my horse was running again and the loose rocks were making too much noise as they scattered around his feet.

Horses have a hard time running downhill, but I went that way instead of uphill to the mountain because I thought it was safer. I felt better with the horse running southeast past the round gray hills that were covered with cedar trees and black lava rock. When I got to the plain in the distance I could see the dark green patches of tamaracks that grew along the river; and beyond the river I could see the beginning of the pale sandrock mesas. I stopped the horse and looked back to see if anyone was coming; then I got off the horse and turned the horse around, wondering if it would go back to its corral under the pines on the mountain. It looked back at me for a moment and then plucked a mouthful of green tumbleweeds before it trotted back up the trail with its ears pointed forward, carrying its head daintily to one side to avoid stepping on the dragging reins. When the horse disappeared over the last hill, the gunny sacks full of meat were still swinging and bouncing.

IV

I walked toward the river on a wood-hauler's road that I knew would eventually lead to the paved road. I was thinking about waiting beside the road for someone to drive by, but by the time I got to the pavement I had decided it wasn't very far to walk if I followed the river back the way Silva and I had come.

The river water tasted good, and I sat in the shade under a cluster of silvery willows. I thought about Silva, and I felt sad at leaving him; still, there was something strange about him, and I tried to figure it out all the way back home.

I came back to the place on the river bank where he had been sitting the first time I saw him. The green willow leaves that he had trimmed from the branch were still lying there, wilted in the sand. I saw the leaves and I wanted to go back to him—to kiss him and to touch him—but the mountains were too far away now. And I told myself, because I believe it, he will come back sometime and be waiting again by the river.

I followed the path up from the river into the village. The sun was getting low, and I could smell supper cooking when I got to the screen door of my house. I could hear their voices inside—my mother was telling my grandmother how to fix the Jell-O and my husband, Al, was playing with the baby. I decided to tell them that some Navajo had kidnaped me, but I was sorry that old Grandpa wasn't alive to hear my story because it was the Yellow Woman stories he liked to tell best.

[1974]

Patricia Zelver   *1923–*

LOVE LETTERS

My sister, Jean, has sent a fifteenth birthday card to my daughter, Rebecca. On it, she writes, "It seems I have among my effects your mother's love letters. Am sending them on."

"I can hardly wait," says Rebecca.

"What makes you think you are going to read *my* love letters?"

"They'll be rated Family Entertainment. Hot Stuff."

"You're quite right not to get your expectations up. The fact is—I can't imagine what they are. I was never much of a letter writer, and your father and I met in graduate school, so we never corresponded."

"Maybe you had a flaming passion for some pimply kid in the fifth grade."

"Maybe."

My husband—I shall call him "Richard"—is a well-known Social Scientist with a well-known Foundation on the San Francisco Peninsula. He is an authority on Urban-Suburban Problems and, particularly, the modern "nuclear" family. He has written many books and papers, including a Best-Seller, which, for a time, was a topic of much discussion among bright young people who are now middle-aged. It dissected and analyzed the sort of existence we lead here in Vista Verde, a subdivision of homes on wooded three-acre lots. For this reason, I know what is wrong. The big thing that is wrong, of course, is that there is no Focus, no Foundation. All the old mainstays—to which we once turned for guidance and comfort—no longer work. Church. Patriotism. The Family. The Boy Scouts. Pride in Craftsmanship. Excellence in Plumbing and Termite Inspection, et cetera. I am not, I hope, diminishing my husband's accomplishments by pointing out that others have foreseen the Apocalypse. "Things fall apart; the center cannot hold." W. B Yeats.[1] To mention one. The question is, what to do about it? Poets are no more helpful here than Social Scientists.

When Richard hears about my love letters he asks me if I know that, according to a recent study, 65 percent of married women who had premarital affairs with not more than two other partners other than their husbands had happier marriages than those who had more than two premarital affairs or those who had no premarital affairs.

I asked him how you measured happiness?

"You set up certain criteria and select a control group. There was a similar study done with rats—"

"Do rats get married?" I say.

"You're not being serious," he says sorrowfully. He is a nice man and enjoys sharing his ideas with me. I cannot tell him how deadly serious I am.

"Anyhow, my only premarital affair was with you," I say. "What does that make me?"

"We're not talking about you," he says. "As far as I'm concerned, everything to do with you is dandy. But we're talking about the Norm."

"I don't care about the Norm," I say. "I just care about me."

*   *   *

[1] The quotation is from William Butler Yeats's (1865–1939) poem "The Second Coming" (1921).

My two sons, Adam and Andrew, are tall and blond. This year they look like sheriffs. They have drooping mustaches, wear cowboy hats, heavy metal belt buckles, and boots that scar our hardwood floors when they visit. They walk with a lazy grace, talk without moving their lips, and have quaint, courtly manners. They are both utterly lovely. Yet, as they grow older and nicer, they become less real. Did I give birth to them, or are they some kind of changelings? I know, now, all the mistakes I made bringing them up, but they aren't on hard drugs, have spent no time in jail, and people tell me I am lucky because we "communicate." Is this fair of them to have remained untouched, pure in heart, despite my blunders? Perhaps, casting no shadow, I am the one who is unreal. When we "communicate" they seem to be gazing through me as if I am transparent. I feel spurned, rejected.

When they hear about my love letters, their lips twitch in an almost-grin. How can a phantom have had love letters? Still, their reaction is suitable to the occasion and makes me feel comfortable. It is Rebecca who makes me uneasy; scornful as she is about the contents of the letters, I suspect she harbors some vestige of hope, and that, as usual, I shall disappoint her.

Rebecca has had all the advantages of a third child, of my experience as a mother. But, again—I feel the lack of any influence; she isn't nice at all. She uses a platinum rinse on her hair and frizzles it with an electric curling iron. It smells of chemicals and singe. Her lips are scarlet; there are tubercular-looking patches of rouge on each powdered cheek. Sickly colored "frocks" from an antique-dress boutique have replaced her jeans. She has scarcely been out of doors all summer. She sits on the living-room couch, the curtains drawn, plucking her eyebrows to a fine line, watching TV or listening to bad reissues of songs from the Roaring Twenties, the Nostalgic Thirties, the Swinging Forties. She is waiting for something to happen. So far, nothing has. There is the implication that I am to blame.

Life is not wholly dull; there are constant surprises. Last year, our best friends, Libby and Jack Coleman, were divorced. We had considered them the most devoted couple we knew. We don't see the Thompsons anymore, or is it that the Thompsons don't see us? This needs to be analyzed, explained. When Rebecca grows up (perhaps I should say "comes of age"), should we move to the Country or the City, or is it too late for a change?

"Remember this song?" says Rebecca.
"I've heard it, I guess."
"Did you shimmy[2] to it?"
"I didn't shimmy."
"You were a Vamp,[3] weren't you?"
"That was before my time."
I have taken up French and Yoga to escape her. Proper breathing, my Yoga teacher says, is the Answer to Everything.

Our street, La Floresta, has changed since we moved here twenty years ago. It is filled with strange little kids. When I drive down the block I toot my horn; they jeer and don't move. There is a fat boy who throws pebbles at my windshield.

*   *   *

[2] A very energetic vibrational dancing style popular during the 1920s.
[3] A sexually aggressive young woman associated with the Roaring Twenties.

"Remember this one?" says Rebecca.

"Sort of."

"You were a Flapper.[4] Right?"

"You seem to have a feeling for history, but you lack the facts."

"Well, you had to be *something*!"

"It was wartime," I say. "Most of the boys were gone. I was just a healthy American girl. I helped my mother and kept my room clean and studied hard and excelled in outdoor sports." My voice is priggish, to cover up my deficiencies. Still, I cling to some integrity. I refuse to provide her with a labeled and packaged Past, complete with period costumes, period slang, the names of "classic cars," scraps of old songs to which I fell passionately in love. Maybe some people had a Past like that, but it does not represent mine. My past seems as unreal to me as the present has begun to feel. I am not going to pass out bonbons. I am uncompromising.

"You were a Wimp. I thought so," says Rebecca.

Our friends, the Abbotts, have bought a twenty-five-year supply of dried food in case of disaster. A millionaire acquaintance of theirs is putting all his money into Swiss banks. The chic young couple across the street are getting rid of their possessions. They have put their stuffed eagle, their collection of old cigar labels, and an Art Deco[5] statuette of a nude girl into the pickup bin in front of their driveway. The fat boy has run off with the eagle.

"Have you ever considered cosmetic surgery?" asks Rebecca.

"I intend to age gracefully," I tell her.

"You could just have your eyes done. And those little lines above your mouth. Nothing ages a woman so much as those mouth lines."

"Americans," I say (quoting Richard), "put too much emphasis on youth."

"Well, you're not an Italian or an Arab," she says.

I look into the mirror. It is true that the Warp of Gravity has had its effect. I decide to buy a pair of those new tinted glasses and some scarves to hide my neck. I shall age—ungracefully.

Adam and Andrew drop in. They cannot bear to look at their sister. Their pure sheriff hearts are dismayed by her. I want to apologize for the aberration on the couch, which I am harboring, but it would only embarrass them. They have come to tell me they are moving to Oregon, before the Oregonians seal off the borders. They will live in a commune modeled after the Early Christian communities and support themselves by organic farming. They hope, they say, with a compassionate look at me, to avoid the Rat Race.

"Do you need money?" I ask them.

They look shocked, but accept a hundred dollars as a donation to the farm.

Richard is in Chicago, at the Airport Hilton. He is attending a conference on Urban Life. I would go with him were it not for Rebecca. She is too old for a sitter, but how can I leave our home in charge of her? Cigarette ash might smolder under the sofa cushions, burst into flame in the night. The house plants would

---

[4] A fashionable young woman of the 1920s.

[5] A decorative art style of the 1920s and 1930s, originally Parisian.

wither; the dog, starve. Burglars could ransack the premises, and she would not notice.

The paper Richard will deliver at the Conference is called "Urbanity as Differentiated from Modern Urban Living." One of the things that he points out in this paper is the lack of street life in Suburbia; there are few places where all types of people, of all ages, can meet on a casual friendly basis, such as, for example, a neighborhood Pub. All the entertainment on the Peninsula is done in homes in a grand archaic manner as if "there were still a servant class." Gourmet cooking is much admired. If someone did want to open a neighborhood Pub in Vista Verde, the Vista Verde Neighborhood Association would fight the application; it would not be considered a good influence for young people and would attract doubtful elements. Would Richard and I fight the Association on this issue? Who knows, we may still decide to move, and there is no question—given the present climate of opinion—that a Pub would lower property values.

Rebecca has changed her name to Maxine.
"Could it be that you are having an Identification Problem?" I ask her. It would not do to reveal the fact that I am suffering from the same malaise. Perhaps daughters inherit this disease from mothers.

Richard is still gone, and I miss him. I mix myself a martini before dinner. (Rebecca-Maxine does not eat meals; she nibbles like a rabbit all day long. The sight of a full plate fills her with revulsion.)
It is dusk. The view from our picture window is of the hills. One would never guess, from the careful way we oriented our house, that there are other homes around.

Older, single women, or widowed, [wrote Richard in his Best-Seller] are often ostracized from mixed, middle-class society. This problem was handled in various ways at various times in different cultures. At one time, in Europe, single gentlewomen were sent into convents, not to take religious orders, but to assure them of protection. In India, a woman of a certain caste was expected to throw herself on her husband's funeral prye. . . .

I think of calling up Libby Coleman, but it is too late. She has a drinking problem and turns mean after five o'clock.

"Why do you wear dark glasses indoors?" says the woman who sits next to me in my Yoga class.
"They're not dark glasses. They are specially tinted," I say.

"Didja ever see *The Great Gatsby*?"[6] says Rebecca-Maxine.
"I read the book."
"It was a book?"
"A very good one."
"Didja carry a flask in Prohibition times?"[7]

[6] F. Scott Fitzgerald's (1896–1940) novel published in 1925 and set in the 1920s.
[7] The Prohibition Amendment of 1919, which outlawed the manufacture, sale, and transportation of intoxicating liquor, went into effect in January 1920 and lasted until December 1933.

"I was too young to drink then."
Rebecca-Maxine looks at me with disgust.

A letter from Richard. He has heard an interesting paper on the Marital Problems of ex-priests and nuns. A Woman's Liberation group is picketing their conference, demanding more women in the Social Sciences. A colleague of his was hit by a tomato. Police were called. He is sympathetic to the women's causes; something, of course, needs to be done. But he was also, he has to admit, a bit frightened by their faces. "Their faces," he writes, "looked like the Furies,[8] contorted with rage and a lust for revenge." He hopes all is well at home.

I am doing poorly in French Conversation. I am unable to make the right sounds. "Stick out your lips until they touch mine," says Madame Cozier. I assume this is just a figure of speech. Just the same, I become stiff, numb, paralyzed by the inhibitions of my linguistic background. Americans do not do things like that with their lips. Madame Cozier is impatient with me. She is at least ten years older than I; her vitality and confidence oppresses me.

I return from Yoga. Rebecca-Maxine is, as usual, on the living-room couch. But, instead of lying down, chewing on the yellowed-ivory cigarette holder she picked up at St. Vincent de Paul's,[9] she is sitting up! The curtains are open; the living room has less of the hothouse atmosphere surrounding a kept woman waiting for her lover. I detect a sparkle in her eyes, a new vibrancy in her voice.
"Your love letters have come!"
No use asking her if she has opened them; letters and envelopes are scattered about on the cushions; the manila envelope in which they arrived is on the floor.
"You could have told me," she says accusingly.
"Told you—what?"
"Well, about—everything." She is looking at me with a new look—one of grudging admiration. "I thought you were just a Wimp," she says.
"Wasn't I?" I try to sound indifferent to hide my curiosity.
"You never said you were a Glamour Girl. Sweetheart of the Ninety-first Division. Miss Pinup of 1943."
"Rebecca—what on earth? Maybe Jean made a mistake. Are you sure they're *my* letters?"
"Lissen to this—It's from—wait a sec—Private First Class John 'Skipper' Schneider, Army Air Force Flexible Gunnery School, Las Vegas Army Air Field. Who was he?"
I try to remember. "Rebecca, there was an army camp near my college. Whole divisions were trained there. Men came and went—"
"You're telling me!"

Sweetheart of the 91st Division, Miss Emily Abbot
My dear Miss Abbott:
Was it real? Time: A summer's Saturday night. Scene: The USO. Song: *As Time Goes By.*[10] Characters: A brand new Private; gauche; awkward; speechless. The Prettiest Girl in the World. An Honest-to-God Glamour Girl. [I shudder.]

[8] The avenging deities of Greek mythology.   [9] A Catholic charitable organization.
[10] A song made famous by Rudy Vallee in the 1930s and then revived in Humphrey Bogart's classic film *Casablanca* in 1942.

Mood: Sexy. Seriously, Emily dear, when I think of you, it makes this ol' War almost seem worthwhile. . . .

"What does 'Flexible Gunnery' mean?" says Rebecca.

"I don't know. Something awful." I think of Adam, of Andrew. Pvt. John "Skipper" Schneider was probably Andrew's age.

In the meantime, *Please* write. A letter from you would mean more than I can tell you.

"Did you write?" says Rebecca-Maxine.

"I'm sure I must have. It was our patriotic duty."

"Was he cute?"

"I . . . of course."

"I guess he'd have to be, you were so popular. There are *lots* more."

Ensign R. E. Lidwick, USNR
USS *Todd.* AKA 71
c/o FPO
San Francisco

"Oh, Ricky Lidwick. He went to high school with me. He married . . . let's see . . . Esther Smith."

"Must have been on the rebound, judging from this:

Emily, will you reserve what time you can spare in the Christmas holidays for a love-sick sailor, who . . .

"It's all cut out, here," says Rebecca-Maxine.

"Censored, probably. He was going to tell the position of his ship or their destination."

Rebecca looks puzzled. Then, "Oh, yes, like on TV," she says.

Captain F. R. Browne
MP School, IRTC
Camp Robinson, Ark.

Emily Dearest—

My leave seems more like a dream than reality. Well, it was certainly worth the trip across the continent to see a certain girl (initials E. A.). I know your picture is hanging over bunks in both Theaters of War, but do you think you could manage to send me one, too? Make a real effort, huh? Until my next leave, if there is one—I think of you constantly.

All my love,
Frank

"Here's 'Skipper' Schneider, again," says Rebecca-Maxine. "This one's kind of a joke, I guess."

War Department Directive 3 67/8 L.
Army Air Force Flexible Gunnery School
Las Vegas Army Air Field

To Miss Emily Abbott;
Subject: Wanted, a date during furlough over Christmas holiday by Army
Gunner 319134006.

My Dear Miss Abbott:
The War Department requests that you contribute your part to victory by
making one of the Army's new aerial gunners happy over the holidays by going
out with him for several dates while he is home on furlough—Hoping you will
comply with our direct order,

we remain

G 2 Staff
Skipper Schneider
by Private Schneider

The afternoon wears on. I should be starting dinner. Instead, I sit, transfixed—
and listen.

First Lt. Jimmy Olson, on maneuvers with the 11th Armored Division, would
prefer to be looking into a fine Pi Phi[11] fire with me—to the music of Jan Garber,
Alvino Ray, the King Sisters. (The Pi Phis, he adds, could use a few new records.
A little Benny Goodman, or some Artie Shaw.)[12] Anyhow, it was great seeing me,
especially since there will undoubtedly be a *slight interlude* before he gets up to the
University again. His morale is low, so—let the Infantryman hear about the good
old life—and especially Miss Emily Abbott.

Midshipman Carl "Buddy" Grant can't decide what to do when he gets out of
the Navy. Should he run a hand laundry? Be a scrubwoman? Clean toilets? He
signs off "Love and all those Indoor Sports."

Ensign Harry Long, of Yale University, is still at Staten Island on a "cruise." On
his one liberty he went to Brooklyn and watched the Dodgers play the Cardinals.
He doesn't know if this has any interest for a pretty Pi Phi, he doesn't want to bore
her, so he'll stop. But I did say I would write and I had promised to send a
picture . . .

Rebecca-Maxine shuffles through the letters. "No, that's not the one," she says.
"I wanted Private Schneider again."
"Oh, yes, how is Private Schneider?" I say.
"Well not so hot. Here it is."

We are doing the following things—firing rifles, jumping with life jackets,
rowing whaleboats, going through gas chambers, studying torpedoes, mine

[11] Pi Beta Phi, a national sorority.
[12] Musicians and singers associated with the so-called Swing Era of jazz, when big bands such as those
led by Benny Goodman (1909–1986) and Artie Shaw (1910–) were in vogue. It began in the
mid-1930s and lasted through World War II.

cutters, types of ships, etc. You'd think we were in the Navy or something. Oh, and we had a little lecture on sharks. That was enchanting. Soon—the Big Pond. Still waiting for a letter and that photograph. I think of you constantly.

He says, "Love." Then, there's an arrow, pointing to *Love* and a balloon, like in the Funny Papers, and inside the balloon it says, "Convention." Then, there's another arrow, and another balloon, and inside that balloon, it says, "I hope *you're* conventional—a little."

"What does the 'Big Pond' mean?"

"I suppose he was shipping out soon."

"Yeah, he was. Here's a telegram from him."

NO WORD FROM YOU BUT SHIPPING
TOMORROW LOTS OF LUCK SKIPPER.

"Were you all broken up when he was killed?"

"Killed!"

"Lissen—"

If anything happened to him, he wanted me to send you this ID bracelet. He thought you might like it as a momento from someone whose memory he carried into battle. Sorry to be the one who breaks the news, but the official word, of course, goes to his family. He spoke of you often, and died bravely in the service of his country.

Rebecca-Maxine sighs. It is a wistful, dreamy sigh. She is filled with respect, with awe—for me! I am no longer a Wimp. I have lived! Dimly, ever so dimly, I recall that someone whom I dated—once? twice?—died in the War. Yes, I think I recall something like that.

"He carried your memory . . . into battle," she says.

"It didn't mean a thing," I say.

Rebecca-Maxine doesn't listen.

How can I explain. I go over the words in my mind . . . I was not a Glamour Girl. I was not Miss Pinup. I was not the Sweetheart of the Ninety-first. It was all in their heads. Private Schneider was just a lonely kid, facing death. I was . . . Miss Fantasy. A phantom of his imagination. Just a Phantom!

"If it didn't mean a thing, why are you crying?" says Rebecca-Maxine. She answers the question for me. "Probably you blotted out the memory on account of it was basically too painful, right?"

Am I crying? If I am, it's certainly for the wrong reason. Oh, weep for Private Schneider, he is dead. Was he blond? Brunette? Tall? Short? Did he have a sense of humor? Was he a good dancer? A clumsy one? If I'm crying, it's because I *don't* remember him. Aerial Gunner "Skipper" Schneider. Transparent. Casting no shadow. A Phantom, like myself.

I brush my hand across my eyes. My hand is wet. Real tears! Do phantoms weep? This is a puzzling question, worthy of investigation. Something is out of key. An illogical *something*.

"I've decided to change my name to 'Emily' says Rebecca-Maxine. "It sounds neat in the letters."

"You can't do that!" My voice is fierce, almost savage. It startles me as much as it does her.

"Why not?"

"Because it's *my* name, not yours! What's more, they're *my* love letters, too! Listen," I say to her, "you listen to me. Wipe off that corpselike makeup and get up off that couch and go get your own love letters," I say.

[1980]

Raymond Carver   1939–1988

CATHEDRAL

This blind man, an old friend of my wife's, he was on his way to spend the night. His wife had died. So he was visiting the dead wife's relatives in Connecticut. He called my wife from his in-laws'. Arrangements were made. He would come by train, a five-hour trip, and my wife would meet him at the station. She hadn't seen him since she worked for him one summer in Seattle ten years ago. But she and the blind man had kept in touch. They made tapes and mailed them back and forth. I wasn't enthusiastic about his visit. He was no one I knew. And his being blind bothered me. My idea of blindness came from the movies. In the movies, the blind moved slowly and never laughed. Sometimes they were led by seeing-eye dogs. A blind man in my house was not something I looked forward to.

That summer in Seattle she had needed a job. She didn't have any money. The man she was going to marry at the end of the summer was in officers' training school. He didn't have any money, either. But she was in love with the guy, and he was in love with her, etc. She'd seen something in the paper: HELP WANTED— *Reading to Blind Man*, and a telephone number. She phoned and went over, was hired on the spot. She'd worked with this blind man all summer. She read stuff to him, case studies, reports, that sort of thing. She helped him organize his little office in the county social-service department. They'd become good friends, my wife and the blind man. How do I know these things? She told me. And she told me something else. On her last day in the office, the blind man asked if he could touch her face. She agreed to this. She told me he touched his fingers to every part of her face, her nose—even her neck! She never forgot it. She even tried to write a poem about it. She was always trying to write a poem. She wrote a poem or two every year, usually after something really important had happened to her.

When we first started going out together, she showed me the poem. In the poem, she recalled his fingers and the way they had moved around over her face. In the poem, she talked about what she had felt at the time, about what went through her mind when the blind man touched her nose and lips. I can remember I didn't think much of the poem. Of course, I didn't tell her that. Maybe I just don't understand poetry. I admit it's not the first thing I reach for when I pick up something to read.

Anyway, this man who'd first enjoyed her favors, the officer-to-be, he'd been her childhood sweetheart. So okay. I'm saying that at the end of the summer she let the blind man run his hands over her face, said goodbye to him, married her childhood etc., who was now a commissioned officer, and she moved away from Seattle. But they'd kept in touch, she and the blind man. She made the first contact after a year or so. She called him up one night from an Air Force base in Alabama. She wanted to talk. They talked. He asked her to send him a tape and tell him about her life. She did this. She sent the tape. On the tape, she told the blind man about her husband and about their life together in the military. She told the blind man she loved her husband but she didn't like it where they lived and she didn't like it that he was a part of the military-industrial thing. She told the blind man she'd written a poem and he was in it. She told him that she was writing a poem about what it was like to be an Air Force officer's wife. The poem wasn't finished yet. She was still writing it. The blind man made a tape. He sent her the tape. She made a tape. This went on for years. My wife's officer was posted to one base and then another. She sent tapes from Moody AFB, McGuire, Mc-Connell, and finally Travis, near Sacramento,[1] where one night she got to feeling lonely and cut off from people she kept losing in that moving-around life. She got to feeling she couldn't go it another step. She went in and swallowed all the pills and capsules in the medicine chest and washed them down with a bottle of gin. Then she got into a hot bath and passed out.

But instead of dying, she got sick. She threw up. Her officer— why should he have a name? he was the childhood sweetheart, and what more does he want?— came home from somewhere, found her, and called the ambulance. In time, she put it all on a tape and sent the tape to the blind man. Over the years, she put all kinds of stuff on tapes and sent the tapes off lickety-split. Next to writing a poem every year, I think it was her chief means of recreation. On one tape, she told the blind man she'd decided to live away from her officer for a time. On another tape, she told him about her divorce. She and I began going out, and of course she told her blind man about it. She told him everything, or so it seemed to me. Once she asked me if I'd like to hear the latest tape from the blind man. This was a year ago. I was on the tape, she said. So I said okay, I'd listen to it. I got us drinks and we settled down in the living room. We made ready to listen. First she inserted the tape into the player and adjusted a couple of dials. Then she pushed a lever. The tape squeaked and someone began to talk in this loud voice. She lowered the volume. After a few minutes of harmless chitchat, I heard my own name in the mouth of this stranger, this blind man I didn't even know! And then this: "From all you've said about him, I can only conclude—" But we were interrupted, a knock at the door, something, and we didn't ever get back to the tape. Maybe it was just as well. I'd heard all I wanted to.

Now this same blind man was coming to sleep in my house.

"Maybe I could take him bowling," I said to my wife. She was at the draining board doing scalloped potatoes. She put down the knife she was using and turned around.

"If you love me," she said, "you can do this for me. If you don't love me, okay. But if you had a friend, any friend, and the friend came to visit, I'd make him feel comfortable." She wiped her hands with the dish towel.

"I don't have any blind friends," I said.

"You don't have *any* friends," she said. "Period. Besides," she said, "goddamn it, his wife's just died! Don't you understand that? The man's lost his wife!"

I didn't answer. She'd told me a little about the blind man's wife. Her name was Beulah, Beulah! That's a name for a colored woman.

"Was his wife a Negro?" I asked.

"Are you crazy?" my wife said. "Have you just flipped or something?" She picked up a potato. I saw it hit the floor, then roll under the stove. "What's wrong with you?" she said. "Are you drunk?"

"I'm just asking," I said.

Right then my wife filled me in with more detail than I cared to know. I made a drink and sat at the kitchen table to listen. Pieces of the story began to fall into place.

Beulah had gone to work for the blind man the summer after my wife had stopped working for him. Pretty soon Beulah and the blind man had themselves a church wedding. It was a little wedding—who'd want to go to such a wedding in the first place?— just the two of them, plus the minister and the minister's wife. But it was a church wedding just the same. It was what Beulah had wanted, he'd

---

[1] Airforce bases in Georgia, New Jersey, Kansas, and California respectively.

said. But even then Beulah must have been carrying the cancer in her glands. After they had been inseparable for eight years—my wife's word, *inseparable*—Beulah's health went into a rapid decline. She died in a Seattle hospital room, the blind man sitting beside the bed and holding on to her hand. They'd married, lived and worked together, slept together—had sex, sure—and then the blind man had to bury her. All this without his having ever seen what the goddamned woman looked like. It was beyond my understanding. Hearing this, I felt sorry for the blind man for a little bit. And then I found myself thinking what a pitiful life this woman must have led. Imagine a woman who could never see herself as she was seen in the eyes of her loved one. A woman who could go on day after day and never receive the smallest compliment from her beloved. A woman whose husband could never read the expression on her face, be it misery or something better. Someone who could wear makeup or not—what difference to him? She could, if she wanted, wear green eye-shadow around one eye, a straight pin in her nostril, yellow slacks and purple shoes, no matter. And then to slip off into death, the blind man's hand on her hand, his blind eyes streaming tears—I'm imagining now—her last thought maybe this: that he never even knew what she looked like, and she on an express to the grave. Robert was left with a small insurance policy and half of a twenty-peso Mexican coin. The other half of the coin went into the box with her. Pathetic.

So when the time rolled around, my wife went to the depot to pick him up. With nothing to do but wait—sure, I blamed him for that—I was having a drink and watching the TV when I heard the car pull into the drive. I got up from the sofa with my drink and went to the window to have a look.

I saw my wife laughing as she parked the car. I saw her get out of the car and shut the door. She was still wearing a smile. Just amazing. She went around to the other side of the car to where the blind man was already starting to get out. This blind man, feature this, he was wearing a full beard! A beard on a blind man! Too much, I say. The blind man reached into the back seat and dragged out a suitcase. My wife took his arm, shut the car door, and, talking all the way, moved him down the drive and then up the steps to the front porch. I turned off the TV. I finished my drink, rinsed the glass, dried my hands. Then I went to the door.

My wife said, "I want you to meet Robert. Robert, this is my husband. I've told you all about him." She was beaming. She had this blind man by his coat sleeve.

The blind man let go of his suitcase and up came his hand.

I took it. He squeezed hard, held my hand, and then he let it go.

"I feel like we've already met," he boomed.

"Likewise," I said. I didn't know what else to say. Then I said, "Welcome. I've heard a lot about you." We began to move then, a little group, from the porch into the living room, my wife guiding him by the arm. The blind man was carrying his suitcase in his other hand. My wife said things like, "To your left here, Robert. That's right. Now watch it, there's a chair. That's it. Sit down right here. This is the sofa. We just bought this sofa two weeks ago."

I started to say something about the old sofa. I'd liked that old sofa. But I didn't say anything. Then I wanted to say something else, small-talk, about the scenic ride along the Hudson. How going *to* New York, you should sit on the right-hand side of the train, and coming *from* New York, the left-hand side.

"Did you have a good train ride?" I said. "Which side of the train did you sit on, by the way?"

"What a question, which side!" my wife said. "What's it matter which side?" she said.

"I just asked," I said.

"Right side," the blind man said. "I hadn't been on a train in nearly forty years. Not since I was a kid. With my folks. That's been a long time. I'd nearly forgotten the sensation. I have winter in my beard now," he said. "So I've been told, anyway. Do I look distinguished, my dear?" the blind man said to my wife.

"You look distinguished, Robert," she said. "Robert," she said. "Robert, it's just so good to see you."

My wife finally took her eyes off the blind man and looked at me. I had the feeling she didn't like what she saw. I shrugged.

I've never met, or personally known, anyone who was blind. This blind man was late forties, a heavy-set, balding man with stooped shoulders, as if he carried great weight there. He wore brown slacks, brown shoes, a light-brown shirt, a tie, a sports coat. Spiffy. He also had this full beard. But he didn't use a cane and he didn't wear dark glasses. I'd always thought dark glasses were a must for the blind. Fact was, I wished he had a pair. At first glance, his eyes looked like anyone else's eyes. But if you looked close, there was something different about them. Too much white in the iris, for one thing, and the pupils seemed to move around in the sockets without his knowing it or being able to stop it. Creepy. As I stared at his face, I saw the left pupil turn in toward his nose while the other made an effort to keep in one place. But it was only an effort, for that eye was on the roam without his knowing it or wanting it to be.

I said, "Let me get you a drink. What's your pleasure? We have a little of everything. It's one of our pastimes."

"Bub, I'm a Scotch man myself," he said fast enough in this big voice.

"Right," I said. Bub! "Sure you are. I knew it."

He let his fingers touch his suitcase, which was sitting alongside the sofa. He was taking his bearings. I didn't blame him for that.

"I'll move that up to your room," my wife said.

"No, that's fine," the blind man said loudly. "It can go up when I go up."

"A little water with the Scotch?" I said.

"Very little," he said.

"I knew it," I said.

He said, "Just a tad. The Irish actor, Barry Fitzgerald?[2] I'm like that fellow. When I drink water, Fitzgerald said, I drink water. When I drink whiskey, I drink whiskey." My wife laughed. The blind man brought his hand up under his beard. He lifted his beard slowly and let it drop.

I did the drinks, three big glasses of Scotch with a splash of water in each. Then we made ourselves comfortable and talked about Robert's travels. First the long flight from the West Coast to Connecticut, we covered that. Then from Connecticut up here by train. We had another drink concerning that leg of the trip.

I remembered having read somewhere that the blind didn't smoke because, as speculation had it, they couldn't see the smoke they exhaled. I thought I knew that much and that much only about blind people. But this blind man smoked his cigarette down to the nubbin[3] and then lit another one. This blind man filled his ashtray and my wife emptied it.

When we sat down at the table for dinner, we had another drink. My wife

[2] Barry Fitzgerald (1888–1961), the Irish-born character actor of both stage and film, was noted for his lovable if cantankerous personality.
[3] Butt or end.

heaped Robert's plate with cube steak, scalloped potatoes, green beans. I buttered him up two slices of bread. I said, "Here's bread and butter for you." I swallowed some of my drink. "Now let us pray," I said, and the blind man lowered his head. My wife looked at me, her mouth agape. "Pray the phone won't ring and the food doesn't get cold," I said.

We dug in. We ate everything there was to eat on the table. We ate like there was no tomorrow. We didn't talk. We ate. We scarfed.[4] We grazed that table. We were into serious eating. The blind man had right away located his foods, he knew just where everything was on his plate. I watched with admiration as he used his knife and fork on the meat. He'd cut two pieces of meat, fork the meat into his mouth, and then go all out for the scalloped potatoes, the beans next, and then he'd tear off a hunk of buttered bread and eat that. He'd follow this up with a big drink of milk. It didn't seem to bother him to use his fingers once in a while, either.

We finished everything, including half a strawberry pie. For a few moments, we sat as if stunned. Sweat beaded on our faces. Finally, we got up from the table and left the dirty plates. We didn't look back. We took ourselves into the living room and sank into our places again. Robert and my wife sat on the sofa. I took the big chair. We had us two or three more drinks while they talked about the major things that had come to pass for them in the past ten years. For the most part, I just listened. Now and then I joined in. I didn't want him to think I'd left the room, and I didn't want her to think I was feeling left out. They talked of things that had happened to them—to them!—these past ten years. I waited in vain to hear my name on my wife's sweet lips: "And then my dear husband came into my life"—something like that. But I heard nothing of the sort. More talk of Robert. Robert had done a little of everything, it seemed, a regular blind jack-of-all-trades. But most recently he and his wife had had an Amway[5] distributorship, from which, I gathered, they'd earned their living, such as it was. The blind man was also a ham radio operator. He talked in his loud voice about conversations he'd had with fellow operators in Guam, in the Philippines, in Alaska, and even in Tahiti. He said he'd have a lot of friends there if he ever wanted to go visit those places. From time to time, he'd turn his blind face toward me, put his hand under his beard, ask me something. How long had I been in my present position? (Three years.) Did I like my work? (I didn't.) Was I going to stay with it? (What were the options?) Finally, when I thought he was beginning to run down, I got up and turned on the TV.

My wife looked at me with irritation. She was heading toward a boil. Then she looked at the blind man and said, "Robert, do you have a TV?"

The blind man said, "My dear, I have two TVs. I have a color set and a black-and-white thing, an old relic. It's funny, but if I turn the TV on, and I'm always turning it on, I turn on the color set. It's funny, don't you think?"

I didn't know what to say to that. I had absolutely nothing to say to that. No opinion. So I watched the news program and tried to listen to what the announcer was saying.

"This is a color TV," the blind man said. "Don't ask me how, but I can tell."

"We traded up a while ago," I said.

The blind man had another taste of his drink. He lifted his beard, sniffed it, and let it fall. He leaned forward on the sofa. He positioned his ashtray on the coffee table, then put the lighter to his cigarette. He leaned back on the sofa and crossed his legs at the ankles.

---

[4] Stuffed ourselves.   [5] Amway specializes in cleaning products.

My wife covered her mouth, and then she yawned. She stretched. She said, "I think I'll go upstairs and put on my robe. I think I'll change into something else. Robert, you make yourself comfortable," she said.

"I'm comfortable," the blind man said.

"I want you to feel comfortable in this house," she said.

"I am comfortable," the blind man said.

After she'd left the room, he and I listened to the weather report and then to the sports roundup. By that time, she'd been gone so long I didn't know if she was going to come back. I thought she might have gone to bed. I wished she'd come back downstairs. I didn't want to be left alone with a blind man. I asked him if he wanted another drink, and he said sure. Then I asked if he wanted to smoke some dope with me. I said I'd just rolled a number. I hadn't, but I planned to do so in about two shakes.

"I'll try some with you," he said.

"Damn right," I said. "That's the stuff."

I got our drinks and sat down on the sofa with him. Then I rolled us two fat numbers. I lit one and passed it. I brought it to his fingers. He took it and inhaled.

"Hold it as long as you can," I said. I could tell he didn't know the first thing.

My wife came back downstairs wearing her pink robe and her pink slippers.

"What do I smell?" she said.

"We thought we'd have us some cannabis,"[6] I said.

My wife gave me a savage look. Then she looked at the blind man and said, "Robert, I didn't know you smoked."

He said, "I do now, my dear. There's a first time for everything. But I don't feel anything yet."

"This stuff is pretty mellow," I said. "This stuff is mild. It's dope you can reason with," I said. "It doesn't mess you up."

"Not much it doesn't, bub," he said, and laughed.

My wife sat on the sofa between the blind man and me. I passed her the number. She took it and toked[7] and then passed it back to me. "Which way is this going?" she said. Then she said, "I shouldn't be smoking this. I can hardly keep my eyes open as it is. That dinner did me in. I shouldn't have eaten so much."

"It was the strawberry pie," the blind man said. "That's what did it," he said, and he laughed his big laugh. Then he shook his head.

"There's more strawberry pie," I said.

"Do you want some more, Robert?" my wife said.

"Maybe in a little while," he said.

We gave our attention to the TV. My wife yawned again. She said, "Your bed is made up when you feel like going to bed, Robert. I know you must have had a long day. When you're ready to go to bed, say so." She pulled his arm. "Robert?"

He came to and said, "I've had a real nice time. This beats tapes, doesn't it?"

I said, "Coming at you," and I put the number between his fingers. He inhaled, held the smoke, and then let it go. It was like he'd been doing it since he was nine years old.

"Thanks, bub," he said. "But I think this is all for me. I think I'm beginning to feel it," he said. He held the burning roach[8] out for my wife.

"Same here," she said. "Ditto. Me, too." She took the roach and passed it to

---

[6] Marijuana.   [7] Inhaled.

[8] A nearly consumed marijuana cigarette.

me. "I may just sit here for a while between you two guys with my eyes closed. But don't let me bother you, okay? Either one of you. If it bothers you, say so. Otherwise, I may just sit here with my eyes closed until you're ready to go to bed," she said. "Your bed's made up, Robert, when you're ready. It's right next to our room at the top of the stairs. We'll show you up when you're ready. You wake me up now, you guys, if I fall asleep." She said that and then she closed her eyes and went to sleep.

The news program ended. I got up and changed the channel. I sat back down on the sofa. I wished my wife hadn't pooped out. Her head lay across the back of the sofa, her mouth open. She'd turned so that her robe had slipped away from her legs, exposing a juicy thigh. I reached to draw her robe back over her, and it was then that I glanced at the blind man. What the hell! I flipped the robe open again.

"You say when you want some strawberry pie," I said.

"I will," he said.

I said, "Are you tired? Do you want me to take you up to your bed? Are you ready to hit the hay?"

"Not yet," he said. "No, I'll stay up with you, bub. If that's all right. I'll stay up until you're ready to turn in. We haven't had a chance to talk. Know what I mean? I feel like me and her monopolized the evening." He lifted his beard and he let it fall. He picked up his cigarettes and his lighter.

"That's all right," I said. Then I said, "I'm glad for the company."

And I guess I was. Every night I smoked dope and stayed up as long as I could before I fell asleep. My wife and I hardly ever went to bed at the same time. When I did go to sleep, I had these dreams. Sometimes I'd wake up from one of them, my heart going crazy.

Something about the church and the Middle Ages was on the TV. Not your run-of-the-mill TV fare. I wanted to watch something else. I turned to the other channels. But there was nothing on them, either. So I turned back to the first channel and apologized.

"Bub, it's all right," the blind man said. "It's fine with me. Whatever you want to watch is okay. I'm always learning something. Learning never ends. It won't hurt me to learn something tonight. I got ears," he said.

We didn't say anything for a time. He was leaning forward with his head turned at me, his right ear aimed in the direction of the set. Very disconcerting. Now and then his eyelids drooped and then they snapped open again. Now and then he put his fingers into his beard and tugged, like he was thinking about something he was hearing on the television.

On the screen, a group of men wearing cowls was being set upon and tormented by men dressed in skeleton costumes and men dressed as devils. The men dressed as devils wore devil masks, horns, and long tails. This pageant was part of a procession. The Englishman who was narrating the thing said it took place in Spain once a year. I tried to explain to the blind man what was happening.

"Skeletons," he said. "I know about skeletons," he said, and he nodded.

The TV showed this one cathedral. Then there was a long, slow look at another one. Finally, the picture switched to the famous one in Paris, with its flying buttresses and its spires reaching up to the clouds. The camera pulled away to show the whole of the cathedral rising above the skyline.

There were times when the Englishman who was telling the thing would shut up, would simply let the camera move around over the cathedrals. Or else the camera would tour the countryside, men in fields walking behind oxen. I waited as long as I could. Then I felt I had to say something. I said, "They're showing the outside of this cathedral now. Gargoyles. Little statues carved to look like monsters. Now I guess they're in Italy. Yeah, they're in Italy. There's paintings on the walls of this one church."

"Are those fresco paintings, bub?" he asked, and he sipped from his drink.

I reached for my glass. But it was empty. I tried to remember what I could remember. "You're asking me are those frescoes?" I said. "That's a good question. I don't know."

The camera moved to a cathedral outside Lisbon. The differences in the Portuguese cathedral compared with the French and Italian were not that great. But they were there. Mostly the interior stuff. Then something occurred to me, and I said, "Something has occurred to me. Do you have any idea what a cathedral is? What they look like, that is? Do you follow me? If somebody says cathedral to you, do you have any notion what they're talking about? Do you know the difference between that and a Baptist church, say?"

He let the smoke dribble from his mouth. "I know they took hundreds of workers fifty or a hundred years to build," he said. "I just heard the man say that, of course. I know generations of the same families worked on a cathedral. I heard him say that, too. The men who began their life's work on them, they never lived to see the completion of their work. In that wise, bub, they're no different from the rest of us, right?" He laughed. Then his eyelids drooped again. His head nodded. He seemed to be snoozing. Maybe he was imagining himself in Portugal. The TV was showing another cathedral now. This one was in Germany. The Englishman's voice droned on. "Cathedrals," the blind man said. He sat up and rolled his head back and forth. "If you want the truth, bub, that's about all I know. What I just said. What I heard him say. But maybe you could describe one to me? I wish you'd do it. I'd like that. If you want to know, I really don't have a good idea."

I stared hard at the shot of the cathedral on the TV. How could I even begin to describe it? But say my life depended on it. Say my life was being threatened by an insane guy who said I had to do it or else.

I stared some more at the cathedral before the picture flipped off into the countryside. There was no use. I turned to the blind man and said, "To begin with, they're very tall." I was looking around the room for clues. "They reach way up. Up and up. Toward the sky. They're so big, some of them, they have to have these supports. To help hold them up, so to speak. These supports are called buttresses. They remind me of viaducts, for some reason. But maybe you don't know viaducts, either? Sometimes the cathedrals have devils and such carved into the front. Sometimes lords and ladies. Don't ask me why this is," I said.

He was nodding. The whole upper part of his body seemed to be moving back and forth.

"I'm not doing so good, am I?" I said.

He stopped nodding and leaned forward on the edge of the sofa. As he listened to me, he was running his fingers through his beard. I wasn't getting through to him, I could see that. But he waited for me to go on just the same. He nodded, like he was trying to encourage me. I tried to think what else to say. "They're really big," I said. "They're massive. They're built of stone. Marble, too, sometimes. In those olden days, when they built cathedrals, men wanted to be close to God. In

FICTION

those olden days, God was an important part of everyone's life. You could tell this from their cathedral-building. I'm sorry," I said, "but it looks like that's the best I can do for you. I'm just no good at it."

"That's all right, bub," the blind man said. "Hey, listen. I hope you don't mind my asking you: Can I ask you something? Let me ask you a simple question, yes or no. I'm just curious and there's no offense. You're my host. But let me ask if you are in any way religious? You don't mind my asking?"

I shook my head. He couldn't see that, though. A wink is the same as a nod to a blind man. "I guess I don't believe in it. In anything. Sometimes it's hard. You know what I'm saying?"

"Sure, I do," he said.

"Right," I said.

The Englishman was still holding forth. My wife sighed in her sleep. She drew a long breath and went on with her sleeping.

"You'll have to forgive me," I said. "But I can't tell you what a cathedral looks like. It just isn't in me to do it. I can't do any more than I've done."

The blind man sat very still, his head down, as he listened to me.

I said, "The truth is, cathedrals don't mean anything special to me. Nothing. Cathedrals. They're something to look at on late-night TV. That's all they are."

It was then that the blind man cleared his throat. He brought something up. He took a handkerchief from his back pocket. Then he said, "I get it, bub. It's okay. It happens. Don't worry about it," he said. "Hey, listen to me. Will you do me a favor? I got an idea. Why don't you find us some heavy paper? And a pen. We'll do something. We'll draw one together. Get us a pen and some heavy paper. Go on, bub, get the stuff," he said.

So I went upstairs. My legs felt like they didn't have any strength in them. They felt like they did after I'd done some running. In my wife's room, I looked around. I found some ballpoints in a little basket on her table. And then I tried to think where to look for the kind of paper he was talking about.

Downstairs, in the kitchen, I found a shopping bag with onion skins in the bottom of the bag. I emptied the bag and shook it. I brought it into the living room and sat down with it near his legs. I moved some things, smoothed the wrinkles from the bag, spread it out on the coffee table.

The blind man got down from the sofa and sat next to me on the carpet.

He ran his fingers over the paper. He went up and down the sides of the paper. The edges, even the edges. He fingered the corners.

"All right," he said. "All right, let's do her."

He found my hand, the hand with the pen. He closed his hand over my hand. "Go ahead, bub, draw," he said. "Draw. You'll see. I'll follow along with you. It'll be okay. Just begin now like I'm telling you. You'll see. Draw," the blind man said.

So I began. First I drew a box that looked like a house. It could have been the house I lived in. Then I put a roof on it. At either end of the roof, I drew spires. Crazy.

"Swell," he said. "Terrific. You're doing fine," he said. "Never thought anything like this could happen in your lifetime, did you, bub? Well, it's a strange life, we all know that. Go on now. Keep it up."

I put in windows with arches. I drew flying buttresses. I hung great doors. I couldn't stop. The TV station went off the air. I put down the pen and closed and opened my fingers. The blind man felt around over the paper. He moved the tips of his fingers over the paper, all over what I had drawn, and he nodded.

"Doing fine," the blind man said.

I took up the pen again, and he found my hand. I kept at it. I'm no artist. But I kept drawing just the same.

My wife opened up her eyes and gazed at us. She sat up on the sofa, her robe hanging open. She said, "What are you doing? Tell me, I want to know."

I didn't answer her.

The blind man said, "We're drawing a cathedral. Me and him are working on it. Press hard," he said to me. "That's right. That's good," he said. "Sure. You got it, bub. I can tell. You didn't think you could. But you can, can't you? You're cooking with gas now. You know what I'm saying? We're going to really have us something here in a minute. How's the old arm?" he said. "Put some people in there now. What's a cathedral without people?"

My wife said "What's going on? Robert, what are you doing? What's going on?"

"It's all right," he said to her. "Close your eyes now," the blind man said to me. I did it. I closed them just like he said.

"Are they closed?" he said. "Don't fudge."

"They're closed," I said.

"Keep them that way," he said. He said, "Don't stop now. Draw."

So we kept on with it. His fingers rode my fingers as my hand went over the paper. It was like nothing else in my life up to now.

Then he said, "I think that's it. I think you got it," he said. "Take a look. What do you think?"

But I had my eyes closed. I thought I'd keep them that way for a little longer. I thought it was something I ought to do.

"Well?" he said. "Are you looking?"

My eyes were still closed. I was in my house. I knew that. But I didn't feel like I was inside anything.

"It's really something," I said.

[1981]

Garrison Keillor   *1942–*

THE TIP-TOP CLUB

The idea of pouring warm soapy water into overshoes and wearing them around the house to give yourself a relaxing footbath while you work is one that all fans of WLT's "The Tip-Top Club" seem to have remembered over the years, along with the idea that if you're depressed you should sit down and write a letter to yourself praising all of your good qualities, and the idea of puffing cigarette smoke at violets to prevent aphids.

Every evening, Sunday through Thursday, at 10:00 P.M. ("and now ... direct from the Tip-Top studio in downtown Minneapolis ..."), WLT played the Tip-Top theme song—

> Whenever you feel blue, think of something nice to do;
> That's the motto of the Tip-Top crew.
> Don't let it get you down, wear a smile and not a frown,
> And you'll be feeling tip-top too.

—and Bud Swenson came on the air with his friendly greeting: "Good evening, Tip-Toppers, and welcome to *your* show. This is your faithful recording secretary, chief cook and bottle-washer, Bud Swenson, calling the Club to order and waiting to hear from you." And of the hundreds of calls that came in on the Tip-Top line (847-8677, or T-I-P-T-O-P-S), and of the fifty or sixty that actually got on the air, many were from listeners who simply wanted Bud to know they were doing fine, feeling good, and enjoying the show. "And—oh, yes," they might add, "we got our boots on," referring to overshoes.

Every night, Bud got at least one request for a copy of the poem a woman had written about writing a letter to yourself. It was called "Dear Me," it was a hundred and eight lines long, WLT mailed out 18,000 copies of it in the six months after it was written (May 18, 1956), and it began:

> When I look around these days
> And hear blame instead of praise
> (For to bless is so much harder than to damn),
> It makes me feel much better
> To write myself a letter
> And tell myself how good I really am.
>
> Dear Me, Sorry it's been
> So long since I took pen
> In hand and scribbled off a word or two.
> I'm busy with my work and such,
> But I need to keep in touch
> Cause the very closest friend I have is you.
>
> Through times of strife and toil,
> You've always remained loyal
> And stuck with me when other friends were far,
> And because we are so close,
> I think of you the most
> And of just how near and dear to me you are.

As for puffing smoke at violets, it touched off a debate that lasted for years. For months after it was suggested by an elderly woman, Bud got call after call from listeners who said that smoke-puffing would *not* discourage aphids; that even if it would, there are *better* ways to discourage aphids; and, worse, that it might encourage young people to take up smoking.

The pro-puffers replied hotly that: (1) you don't have to *inhale* in order to *puff* on a plant; (2) the treatment should be given only once a week or so; and (3) anyone who wants to smoke probably will go ahead and do it *anyway*, violets or *no* violets.

As time passed, the issue became confused in the minds of some Tip-Toppers, who came to think that Bud himself was a smoker (he was not). To the very end (November 26, 1969), he got calls from listeners wanting to know if he didn't agree with them that smoking is a filthy habit. (He did.)

At Bud's retirement party, Roy Elmore, Jr., president of WLT, presented him with twenty-five potted violet plants, one for each year of service.

Controversy was the very thing that distinguished "The Tip-Top Club." It had none. Edgar Elmore, the founder of WLT, abhorred controversy, and the terms of his will bound his heir, Roy Jr., to abhor it also. Though Edgar never heard Bud's show, having died in 1940, eleven years before the Club was formed, he certainly would have enjoyed it very much, as Roy Jr. told Bud frequently. No conversation about religion or politics was permitted, nor were callers allowed to be pessimistic or moody on the air. If a person started in to be moody, he or she was told firmly and politely to hang up and *listen* to the show and it would cheer him or her up. Few had to be told.

Vacations and pets were favorite Tip-Top topics, along with household hints, children, gardening, memories of long ago, favorite foods, great persons, good health and how to keep it, and of course the weather. Even when the weather was bad, even in times of national crisis, the Tip-Toppers always came up with cheerful things to talk about.

One reason for the show's cheery quality and the almost complete absence of crank calls was Bud's phone policy. After the first year he never divulged the Tip-Top phone number over the air (nor, for that matter, over the phone). In fact, it was an unlisted number, and one could obtain it only from another Tip-Topper. This tended to limit participation to those who understood the rules and accepted them.

The main reason for the show's cheery quality was Bud himself and his radio personality. His voice wasn't deep but his style of speaking was warm and reassuring, and he always tried to look on the bright side, even as host of "The Ten o'Clock News" (starting July 1, 1944). On the newscast, Bud played up features and human-interest stories and he skimmed over what he called "the grim stuff." He might devote fifteen seconds to a major earthquake and three minutes to a story about a chimpanzee whose finger paintings had been exhibited at a New York gallery and fooled all the critics. His approach offended a few listeners ("the *New York Times* crowd," he called them), but most people liked it. Bud pulled in fifty or sixty fan letters a week, more than all other WLT newscasters combined.

After reading a few headlines, he'd say, "Oh, here's something you might be interested in," and he'd tell about a dog that had actually learned to sing and sing on key, or read a story about the world's largest known tomato, or about a three-year-old kid who was a whiz at chess; and then he'd talk about a dog that *he* knew, or a kid *he* knew, or a tomato *he* had seen, and then he'd say, "Well, I don't know. Let me know what *you* think."

At first, some letters said, "What happened to the news?" but they quickly dwindled. ("Anger doesn't last," Roy Jr. said. "Only love is lasting. Angry people spout off once and then get over it. The people who love you are loyal to the end.") Most of the letters were about a story Bud had read: the letter writer described a similar experience that *he* had had, or quoted a poem or a saying that the story had reminded *her* of—and Bud made sure to read every one of those letters on the air. One day in the winter of 1950, Roy Jr. said, "It's time to close down the News. You need a new shingle."

According to Bud, the Tip-Top Club was the idea of a woman in St. Paul. "We love your show," she wrote in January 1951, "and feel that truly it is our show too. When I listen, as I do every night, I feel as if I am among friends and we are all members of a club that gathers around our radios. We share ideas and experiences, we inspire each other with beautiful thoughts, and I only wish I could meet personally every one of the wonderful people who also write to you, for when they write to you, they are truly writing to me also."

Bud read her letter on the air, and listeners responded favorably to the idea of a club. (Since he had often referred to his stories as "News-Toppers," Bud suggested the name Tip-Top Club and it stuck.)

Nobody at WLT quite remembers who came up with the phone idea. WLT had been doing remote broadcasts over telephone lines for years, starting with the "WLT Barn Dance and Bean Feed" in 1938; all that needed to be done to put a telephone signal on the air was wrap the bare end of one wire around the bare end of another. One night, Bud's engineer, Harlan, did just that, and a woman's voice came on describing dark thunderstorm clouds moving east toward Minneapolis.

"Is it raining there yet?" asked Bud.

"No," she said, "but it will be, any minute now. But I've got my boots on!"

Roy Jr. was leery of the phone idea from the start. "Every foulmouth in town will be slobbering into his telephone for the chance to get on the air," he told Bud. "Every creep who writes on toilet walls, every dummy, every drunken son-of-a-bitch from hell to breakfast. We'll be running a nuthouse. We'll lose our license in a week."

Then Harlan came forward with his tape loop. Harlan was one who seldom cracked a smile, but when WLT bought its first tape recorders, two big Ampexes, in 1949, he was like a boy with a new toy. He recorded everything on tape, and he played around with it, and his favorite game was to play around with Bud's voice. At first, he got a kick out of playing Bud's voice at a faster speed so he sounded like a hysterical woman; then backward, which sounded like Russian; then slower, so Bud sounded drunk; and then Harlan became fascinated with editing Bud. With a razor blade in hand, Harlan went through thousands of feet of Bud tape, finding a word here and a word there, and a vowel sound here and a consonant there, making new words, and snipping and splicing hundreds of little bits of tape to form a few sentences spoken in Bud's own voice, in which Bud spoke, in his own warm and reassuring tones, about having carnal relations with dogs, cats, tomatoes, small boys, chimpanzees, overshoes, fruit jars, lawn mowers. It was disgusting, and also an amazing feat of patience. In two years, Harlan assembled just three minutes of Bud.

Harlan solved the problem of loonies by the simple trick of threading a continuous loop of tape through two machines sitting side by side. Bud and his telephone caller could be recorded on the first machine, which fed the tape to the second machine, which played it back on the air three seconds later. If the caller said something not befitting the show, Harlan, listening to the first machine, would have three seconds in which to turn off the second. "Can't beat it," said Harlan. "I hit the button and they die like rats."

Nevertheless, Roy Jr. was on hand for the first taped show and supervised the Stop button personally. "I trust you," he told Harlan, "but the way you talk, you might not notice profanity until it is too late." Bud explained the tape loop on the air and invited calls as Roy Jr. hunched over the machine, his finger in position, like a ship's gunner waiting for incoming aircraft. The first caller was a man who wanted to know more about the loop and if it might have useful applications in the home. He got flustered in mid-call and stopped. On his radio at home, he heard his own voice, delayed by tape, saying what he had said three seconds before. "Please turn your radio down," Bud said. It was a line that he was to repeat thousands of times in the next eighteen years.

"This has been an historic event," Roy Jr. said proudly when the show was over. He had cut off just two calls, the first one after the words "What in hell——" and the second at the mention of the Pope ("Probably nothing, but I wasn't about to take chances," he explained to Harlan).

Most of the calls were about the tape loop, with all callers favoring its use, howbeit with some trepidation that a mechanical failure or employee carelessness might lead to tragedy. Several were worried that certain persons might try to fool Bud, opening their calls with a few innocuous remarks and then slipping in a fast one. ("Thanks for the tip," said Bud. "I'm confident we can handle them.")

Communists, people agreed, might be particularly adept at subverting the tape loop. Communists, one man reported, learned these techniques at special schools, including how to insinuate their beliefs into a conversation without anyone being the wiser. ("Appreciate your concern, sir, and, believe me, we'll be on guard.")

It was three weeks before Roy Jr. turned over the guard duty to Harlan and Alice the switchboard girl. Alice was to screen all callers: no kids, no foreign accents, and nobody who seemed unusually intense or determined to get on the air. Harlan was the second line of defense. Roy Jr. instructed him to listen carefully to each call and try to anticipate what the caller was driving at; and if the conversation should drift toward deep waters—hit the button. No politics. No religion except for general belief in the Almighty, thankfulness for His gifts, wonder at His creation, etc. No criticism of others, not even the caller's kith and kin. Roy Jr. didn't want them to get dragged into family squabbles and maybe have to give equal time to a miffed husband or mother-in-law giving *their* side of it. No promotion of products, services, clubs, fund drives, or events.

"What's left to talk about?" Harlan wondered. "Not a goddamn helluva lot."

And, at first, the Tip-Toppers seemed unsure of what to talk about too. "Just thought I'd call and say hi," one would say. "Great. What are you doing tonight?" Bud would ask. "Oh, not much," the caller would reply. "Just sitting here listening to the show."

Gradually, though, they loosened up, and when Bud said to a caller, "Tell me about yourself," the caller generally did. Most Tip-Toppers seemed to be older persons leading quiet lives and keeping busy with hobbies and children and grandchildren, and, judging from the interest in household hints, their homes were neat as a pin and in good repair. They were unfailingly courteous ("The distinguished gentleman who spoke earlier on cats was very well-informed on most points, but I feel he may have overlooked the fact that cats will not shed if brushed regularly"), and soon Harlan was taking his finger off the button and relaxing in the control room and even leaving for a smoke now and then. The few nuts who called in Alice soon recognized by voice—she enjoyed talking with them, and after a few conversations they always asked for her and not for Bud. They sent her gifts, usually pamphlets or books but occasionally a box of cookies or a cake, which, on Harlan's advice, she did not eat. Three months went by, and not a single nut got past the loop; Roy Jr. raised Bud's salary and even gave him a contract—six months with an option of renewing for three more.

"It is so pleasant in this day and age when we are subjected to so much dissension and mud-slinging to take a rest and listen to a show that follows the old adage 'If you can't say something nice, don't say anything at all,' " a woman wrote to Bud. "I am a faithful listener-in and now have a telephone in my bedroom so that I can participate after turning in. I go to sleep listening to the show, and I believe I sleep better knowing it is there."

Sleep was a major item on the Tip-Top agenda: how much is needed? how to get it? what position is best? Many scorned the eight-hour quota as wasteful and self-indulgent and said four or five is enough for any adult. "The secret of longevity is to stay out of bed," said one oldster.

Most members disagreed; they felt they needed more sleep, and one call asking for a cure for insomnia would set off an avalanche of sleep tips—warm milk, a hot bath, a brisk walk, a brief prayer, a mild barbiturate—each of which had gotten the caller through some difficult nights. A doctor (he called in often, usually to settle somebody's hash on the value of vitamins, chiropractic medicine, and vegetarian diets) offered the opinion that worry causes 95 percent of all sleeplessness. He suggested that Tip-Toppers who go to bed with restless thoughts should fill their minds instead with pleasant memories and plans for vacations.

As for vacations, there were strong voices in the Club who argued that a Minnesotan's vacation money should be kept at home, not spent abroad. The rest of the world, it was said, could be seen perfectly well in the pages of the *National Geographic*. There was general agreement, however, that the purpose of a vacation is to rest and enjoy yourself and not necessarily to visit family members or to catch up on work around the house.

Housework was important, though, a sure antidote for grief and worry and feeling sorry for yourself. To scrub a floor or paint a wall or make a pie was better than going to a psychiatrist. At the same time, there was no use taking more time than necessary to get the job done, and every job had its shortcuts. "What's a quick way to get bubblegum out of hair?" a woman would ask, and minutes later, a legion of women who had faced that very problem would rally to her side. Give the Club a problem, and in short order the Club solved it, whether it be a wobbly table, a grape-juice stain, or a treacherous stair tread, and then it suggested two or three things you could do in the time you had saved, such as making lovely and useful gifts from egg cartons, Popsicle sticks, and bottle caps.

And then there were hobbies. Bud often asked callers, particularly the shyer ones, to talk about their hobbies. He *never* asked about their occupations, not after the first few times: the answers were always apologetic-sounding—"Oh, I'm just a truck driver," or "Oh, I just work for the Post Office." But ask someone what he did in his spare time and the answer might be good for five or ten minutes.

Club members tended to be collectors. It seemed as if every object of which there was more than one sort, type, shape, brand, color, or configuration was the object of some collector's affection. "I have matchbook covers from more than thirty-five countries." "Some of my fruit jars have been appraised at ten dollars and more." "I hope someday to open a license-plate museum." "I plan to donate my nails to the historical society."

Bird-watching, a sort of collecting, was also popular, and Bud had to put a damper on the bird people, they were so fanatical. One might call in and say, "I wonder if anyone out there can help me identify a bird I heard this morning. Its call sounded something like this—" and then whistle, "*twee-twee, twee-twee,*" and suddenly Alice was swamped with calls, some identifying the bird, some saying they had heard it too and didn't know what it was either, and others wondering if the bird's call perhaps wasn't more of a "*twee-it, twee-it.*"

Five nights a week, from 10:00 P.M. to sign-off, Bud sat in Studio B behind a table, the earphones clamped on, and scribbled notes on a pad as one Tip-Topper after another poured it out. After the first few months of the tape loop, he quit reading news stories, and after the Club had hit full stride, telephonically speaking, he himself said very little, aside from an occasional question. He became a listener. For eighteen years, from 1951 to 1969, he sat in the same chair, in the same position (slightly hunched, head down and supported with one hand, the other hand writing, feet on the floor), and heard the same stuff, until he seemed to lose whatever personality he had in the beginning. He became neutral. "A goddamn ghost," Harlan said. "When he comes in, I don't even see him anymore. He don't really exist, except on the air."

At the age of sixty-five, he quietly retired. He didn't mention his retirement on "The Tip-Top Club." Tip-Toppers didn't know he was gone until they tuned in one night and heard Wayne Bargy. Wayne was the only WLT announcer willing to take the show. Others had subbed for Bud before when he took vacations and they noted a certain snideness, a meanness, among the Tip-Toppers, who implied in their conversations that the new man, while adequate, was certainly no Bud. "Bud would *know* that," a caller might say. "Bud wouldn't have said that." "Maybe I'll talk to Bud about it. When is Bud coming back?"

So one night out of the clear blue it was "The Tip-Top Club with Wayne Bargy," and one can only imagine the shock that Bud's fans felt to hear a new theme song (Simon and Garfunkel's "Sounds of Silence") instead of the old Tip-Top song, and then Wayne Bargy delivering a tribute to Bud as if Bud were dead. He called him "an innovator" and "a genius" and "a man who was totally concerned about others." "I loved him," said Wayne. "He was a totally understanding, giving type of man. He was someone I could always talk to about my problems.

"Friends, I know you're as disappointed as I am that Bud won't be here with us anymore, and let me tell you, I'd give anything if he were, and I want to be honest with you and admit that I've never done this type of show before and I don't know how good I am at talking with people, and maybe some of you will even wonder what I'm doing in the radio business and I have to admit that you may have a point there, but I would rather be honest about this than sit here and pretend that I'm somebody that I'm not, because I think that honesty has a place in radio, I don't think a radio personality has to be some sort of star or an idol or anything, I think he can be a real person, and even if I should fail and would quit this show tomorrow, I'd still be satisfied knowing I had done it my way and not tried to be like somebody else."

The Tip-Toppers heard him out; there was a minute or so of lull at the switchboard (perhaps they were too dazed to dial, or else they were composing carefully what they would say); and then the first wave struck. Even Harlan was surprised by the abuse Wayne got.

First call: "Why wait until tomorrow? Why not quit tonight?" (Wayne: "Thanks for calling.") A man said, "Oh, don't worry that we'll consider you a star, Wayne. Don't worry about that for one minute!" (Wayne: "Okay, I won't.") A woman said it was the worst night of her life. (Wayne: "It's hard for all of us.") "You make me absolutely sick. You're the biggest mistake they've made down there!" ("I appreciate your honesty, sir. I don't necessarily agree with that statement, but I think it's important that you feel you can be honest with me.")

By midnight, Wayne had logged almost a hundred calls, most of them quite brief and most cut off by Harlan. The longest exchange was with a woman who wanted to know where Bud was. Wayne said that Bud had retired.

SHE: Then I'd like his number.

HE: I'm sorry?

SHE: I want Bud's phone number.

HE: I—ma'am, I wish I could give you that but I can't, it's against company policy. We don't give out announcers' home numbers to the general public.

SHE: Well, *I'm* not the general public. I'm Grace Ritter and he knows me even if you don't.

HE: I'm sorry, but—

SHE: And this is his show, and I think he has a right to know what you're doing to it! (CLICK)

During the midnight newscast, Roy Jr. called and told Wayne he was doing great. "I knew it'd be tough sledding the first night," he said, "but you stick in there. They're sore about Bud, but in three weeks they'll get tired and give up and all you'll get is flowers."

It didn't work that way. For one thing, Wayne had little interest in the old Tip-Top topics. He was divorced and lived in an efficientcy apartment (no lawn to keep up, no maintenance responsibilities) and had no pets or children. His major interest was psychology. "People fascinate me," he said. ("You don't fascinate *me*," someone said.) He read psychology books and talked about them on the air. He said that he was undergoing therapy, and it had helped him to understand himself better. ("What's to understand?")

His other interests were eating out in foreign restaurants, attending films, and planning a trip to the Far East. ("How about leaving tomorrow?") Occasionally, he got a friendly caller who also liked Szechuan[1] cuisine or Carl Rogers or Woody Allen[2] movies, and he reached out and hung onto that call for dear life. Those calls would last for fifteen, twenty minutes, as if the caller were an old college chum he hadn't heard from in ages, but when he hung up, the Tip-Toppers were waiting, more determined than ever.

THEM: This show is so boring. You talk about stuff that nobody but you is interested in.

HIM: I really think you're mistaken about that, at least I hope you are, but more importantly, I think that I would have no business being here if I *didn't* talk

---

[1] A type of Chinese cooking noted for its spiciness.
[2] Carl Rogers (1902–1987), the American psychotherapist and author; Woody Allen (1935–), the American movie actor and director, author, and comedian.

about things that interest me, because, when all is said and done, I do have to be myself.

THEM: That's the problem, Wayne. Yourself. You're dull.

HIM: Well, I grant you I'm not slick or polished, and I'm not a comedian, but that's not my job. Basically, I'm a communicator, and whatever my faults or failures in relating to people, I do try to be positive.

THEM: You're positively boring.

HIM: Well, let's talk about that. Define your terms. What do you mean by "boring"?

What they meant was Wayne Bargy. For all he said about keeping an open mind ("You got a hole in your head, Wayne!") and not condemning others but trying to understand people who may be different from ourselves ("You're different from everybody, Wayne! You're a different species!"), the Club kept a united front against him.

One night, Wayne casually mentioned that it was his first anniversary hosting the show. The switchboard sizzled. One man said it was time for Club members to take action, and before Harlan could cut him off he announced a time and a place for the meeting.

Word came back that the Tip-Toppers had elected officers and were putting together a mailing list for a monthly newsletter. It was said the Club was assigning members to "listening squads" with each squad assigned two hours of "Wayne duty" a week. The squad members were responsible for listening to the show and calling in frequently. The newsletter printed a list of things to say.

It was harder on Harlan than on Wayne. Harlan had started to assemble a special Wayne Bargy tape, but he had no time to work on it. What with Wayne giving out the phone number every fifteen minutes, the show was attracting oddballs, in addition to the legions of Tip-Toppers, and Harlan was cutting calls off the air by the dozens. One night, after Wayne had talked about his divorce (he said that he and his wife didn't "relate to each other sexually"), there passed a long half hour during which no call was fit to broadcast. "I was slapping them down like barnyard flies. We were up to our ears in crazies," said Harlan. "Finally, my fingers got sore, and Alice pulled the plug on the switchboard and her and me sat down and had a cup of coffee and left that poor dumb SOB sit and die by himself."

Wayne talked a long time that night. He said he'd had a typical middle-class upbringing until he went to college, which opened his mind up to new possibilities. He said he had gone into radio because it had tremendous possibilities for creative communication. This show was a tremendous opportunity to get people to open up their minds. He viewed himself as an educator of sorts.

"I'll be honest," he said. "The past year has been rough. There's a lot of anger and violence out there—and I don't say people shouldn't feel that way, but I do feel people should be willing to change. Life is change. We all change. I've changed. Frankly, when I started doing this show, I didn't come off very well. I didn't communicate well. I had a hard time relating to working-class people. I think I've improved. I'm learning. I've put my feelings on the line, and I've benefited from it. I'm going to keep on trying."

He did keep on trying, and the Tip-Toppers kept calling—"We won't go away, Wayne!" they said, and he said, "I don't want you to go away. I want you to stay and let's get to know each other." That summer WLT did a survey that showed that most of the Tip-Top Club audience was over forty (72 percent), the least desirable age group to advertisers, and in July the station switched the Tip-Top slot to what it called "a modified middle-of-the-road pop-rock format" with a disc jockey who never talked except to give time, temperature, and commercials. His name was Michael Keske, but he never said it on the air.

[1981]

Bobbie Ann Mason *1940–*

SHILOH

Leroy Moffitt's wife, Norma Jean, is working on her pectorals. She lifts three-pound dumbbells to warm up, then progresses to a twenty-pound barbell. Standing with her legs apart, she reminds Leroy of Wonder Woman.

"I'd give anything if I could just get these muscles to where they're real hard," says Norma Jean. "Feel this arm. It's not as hard as the other one."

"That's 'cause you're right-handed," says Leroy, dodging as she swings the barbell in an arc.

"Do you think so?"

"Sure."

Leroy is a truckdriver. He injured his leg in a highway accident four months ago, and his physical therapy, which involves weights and a pulley, prompted Norma Jean to try building herself up. Now she is attending a body-building class. Leroy has been collecting temporary disability since his tractor-trailer jackknifed in Missouri, badly twisting his left leg in its socket. He has a steel pin in his hip. He will probably not be able to drive his rig again. It sits in the backyard, like a gigantic bird that has flown home to roost. Leroy has been home in Kentucky for three months, and his leg is almost healed, but the accident frightened him and he does not want to drive any more long hauls. He is not sure what to do next. In the meantime, he makes things from craft kits. He started by building a miniature log cabin from notched Popsicle sticks. He varnished it and placed it on the TV set, where it remains. It reminds him of a rustic Nativity scene. Then he tried string art (sailing ships on black velvet), a macrame owl kit, a snap-together B-17 Flying Fortress,[1] and a lamp made out of a model truck, with a light fixture screwed in the top of the cab. At first the kits were diversions, something to kill time, but now he is thinking about building a full-scale log house from a kit. It would be considerably cheaper than building a regular house, and besides, Leroy has grown to appreciate how things are put together. He has begun to realize that in all the years he was on the road he never took time to examine anything. He was always flying past scenery.

"They won't let you build a log cabin in any of the new subdivisions," Norma Jean tells him.

"They will if I tell them it's for you," he says, teasing her. Ever since they were married, he has promised Norma Jean he would build her a new home one day. They have always rented, and the house they live in is small and nondescript. It does not even feel like a home, Leroy realizes now.

Norma Jean works at the Rexall drugstore, and she has acquired an amazing amount of information about cosmetics. When she explains to Leroy the three stages of complexion care, involving creams, toners, and moisturizers, he thinks happily of other petroleum products—axle grease, diesel fuel. This is a connection between him and Norma Jean. Since he has been home, he has felt unusually tender about his wife and guilty over his long absences. But he can't tell what she feels about him. Norma Jean has never complained about his traveling; she has never made hurt remarks, like calling his truck a "widow-maker." He is reasonably certain she has been faithful to him, but he wishes she would celebrate his per-

---

[1] A type of bomber, which was the mainstay of the U.S. World War II airforce.

manent homecoming more happily. Norma Jean is often startled to find Leroy at home, and he thinks she seems a little disappointed about it. Perhaps he reminds her too much of the early days of their marriage, before he went on the road. They had a child who died as an infant, years ago. They never speak about their memories of Randy, which have almost faded, but now that Leroy is home all the time, they sometimes feel awkward around each other, and Leroy wonders if one of them should mention the child. He has the feeling that they are waking up out of a dream together—that they must create a new marriage, start afresh. They are lucky they are still married. Leroy had read that for most people losing a child destroys the marriage—or else he heard this on *Donahue.* He can't always remember where he learns things anymore.

At Christmas, Leroy bought an electric organ for Norma Jean. She used to play the piano when she was in high school. "It don't leave you," she told him once. "It's like riding a bicycle."

The new instrument had so many keys and buttons that she was bewildered by it at first. She touched the keys tentatively, pushed some buttons, then pecked out "Chopsticks." It came out as an amplified fox-trot rhythm, with marimba sounds.

"It's an orchestra!" she cried.

The organ had a pecan-look finish and eighteen preset chords, with optional flute, violin, trumpet, clarinet, and banjo accompaniments. Norma Jean mastered the organ almost immediately. At first she played Christmas songs. Then she bought *The Sixties Songbook* and learned every tune in it, adding variations to each with the rows of brightly colored buttons.

"I didn't like these old songs back then," she said. "But I have this crazy feeling I missed something."

"You didn't miss a thing," said Leroy.

Leroy likes to lie on the couch and smoke a joint and listen to Norma Jean play "Can't Take My Eyes Off You" and "I'll Be Back." He is back again. After fifteen years on the road, he is finally settling down with the woman he loves. She is still pretty. Her skin is flawless. Her frosted curls resemble pencil trimmings.

Now that Leroy has come home to stay, he notices how much the town has changed. Subdivisions are spreading across western Kentucky like an oil slick. The sign at the edge of town says "Pop: 11,500"—only seven hundred more than it said twenty years before. Leroy can't figure out who is living in all the new houses. The farmers who used to gather around the courthouse square on Saturday afternoons to play checkers and spit tobacco juice have gone. It has been years since Leroy has thought about the farmers, and they have disappeared without his noticing.

Leroy meets a kid named Stevie Hamilton in the parking lot at the new shopping center. While they pretend to be strangers meeting over a stalled car, Stevie tosses an ounce of marijuana under the front seat of Leroy's car. Stevie is wearing orange jogging shoes and a T-shirt that says CHATTAHOOCHEE SUPER-RAT. His father is a prominent doctor who lives in one of the expensive subdivisions in a new white-columned brick house that looks like a funeral parlor. In the phone book under his name there is a separate number, with the listing "Teenagers."

"Where do you get this stuff?" asks Leroy. "From your pappy?"

"That's for me to know and you to find out," Stevie says. He is slit-eyed and skinny.

"What else you got?"

"What you interested in?"

"Nothing special. Just wondered."

Leroy used to take speed on the road. Now he has to go slowly. He needs to be mellow. He leans back against the car and says, "I'm aiming to build me a log house, soon as I get time. My wife, though, I don't think she likes the idea."

"Well, let me know when you want me again," Stevie says. He has a cigarette in his cupped palm, as though sheltering it from the wind. He takes a long drag, then stomps it on the asphalt and slouches away.

Stevie's father was two years ahead of Leroy in high school. Leroy is thirty-four. He married Norma Jean when they were both eighteen, and their child Randy was born a few months later, but he died at the age of four months and three days. He would be about Stevie's age now. Norma Jean and Leroy were at the drive-in, watching a double feature (*Dr. Strangelove* and *Lover Come Back*), and the baby was sleeping in the back seat. When the first movie ended, the baby was dead. It was the sudden infant death syndrome. Leroy remembers handing Randy to a nurse at the emergency room, as though he were offering her a large doll as a present. A dead baby feels like a sack of flour. "It just happens sometimes," said the doctor, in what Leroy always recalls as a nonchalant tone. Leroy can hardly remember the child anymore, but he still sees vividly a scene from *Dr. Strangelove* in which the President of the United States was talking in a folksy voice on the hot line to the Soviet premier about the bomber accidentally headed toward Russia. He was in the War Room, and the world map was lit up. Leroy remembers Norma Jean standing catatonically beside him in the hospital and himself thinking: Who is this strange girl? He had forgotten who she was. Now scientists are saying that crib death is caused by a virus. Nobody knows anything, Leroy thinks. The answers are always changing.

When Leroy gets home from the shopping center, Norma Jean's mother, Mabel Beasley, is there. Until this year, Leroy has not realized how much time she spends with Norma Jean. When she visits, she inspects the closets and then the plants, informing Norma Jean when a plant is droopy or yellow. Mabel calls the plants "flowers," although there are never any blooms. She always notices if Norma Jean's laundry is piling up. Mabel is a short, overweight woman whose tight, brown-dyed curls look more like a wig than the actual wig she sometimes wears. Today she has brought Norma Jean an off-white dust ruffle she made for the bed; Mabel works in a custom-upholstery shop.

"This is the tenth one I made this year," Mabel says. "I got started and couldn't stop."

"It's real pretty," says Norma Jean.

"Now we can hide things under the bed," says Leroy, who gets along with his mother-in-law primarily by joking with her. Mabel has never really forgiven him for disgracing her by getting Norma Jean pregnant. When the baby died, she said that fate was mocking her.

"What's that thing?" Mabel says to Leroy in a loud voice, pointing to a tangle of yarn on a piece of canvas.

Leroy holds it up for Mabel to see. "It's my needlepoint," he explains. "This is a *Star Trek* pillow cover."

"That's what a woman would do," says Mabel. "Great day in the morning!"

"All the big football players on TV do it," he says.

"Why, Leroy, you're always trying to fool me. I don't believe you for one minute. You don't know what to do with yourself—that's the whole trouble. Sewing!"

"I'm aiming to build us a log house," says Leroy. "Soon as my plans come."

"Like *heck* you are," says Norma Jean. She takes Leroy's needlepoint and shoves it into a drawer. "You have to find a job first. Nobody can afford to build now anyway."

Mabel straightens her girdle and says, "I still think before you get tied down y'all ought to take a little run to Shiloh."

"One of these days, Mama," Norma Jean says impatiently.

Mabel is talking about Shiloh, Tennessee. For the past few years, she has been urging Leroy and Norma Jean to visit the Civil War battleground there.[2] Mabel went there on her honeymoon—the only real trip she ever took. Her husband died of a perforated ulcer when Norma Jean was ten, but Mabel, who was accepted into the United Daughters of the Confederacy in 1975, is still preoccupied with going back to Shiloh.

"I've been to kingdom come and back in that truck out yonder," Leroy says to Mabel, "but we never yet set foot in that battleground. Ain't that something? How did I miss it?"

"It's not even that far," Mabel says.

After Mabel leaves, Norma Jean reads to Leroy from a list she has made. "Things you could do," she announces. "You could get a job as a guard at Union Carbide, where they'd let you set on a stool. You could get on at the lumberyard. You could do a little carpenter work, if you want to build so bad. You could—"

"I can't do something where I'd have to stand up all day."

"You ought to try standing up all day behind a cosmetics counter. It's amazing that I have strong feet, coming from two parents that never had strong feet at all." At the moment Norma Jean is holding on to the kitchen counter, raising her knees one at a time as she talks. She is wearing two-pound ankle weights.

"Don't worry," says Leroy. "I'll do something."

"You could truck calves to slaughter for somebody. You wouldn't have to drive any big old truck for that."

"I'm going to build you this house," says Leroy. "I want to make you a real home."

"I don't want to live in any log cabin."

"It's not a cabin. It's a house."

"I don't care. It looks like a cabin."

"You and me together could lift those logs. It's just like lifting weights."

Norma Jean doesn't answer. Under her breath, she is counting. Now she is marching through the kitchen. She is doing goose steps.

Before his accident, when Leroy came home he used to stay in the house with Norma Jean, watching TV in bed and playing cards. She would cook fried chicken, picnic ham, chocolate pie—all his favorites. Now he is home alone much of the time. In the mornings, Norma Jean disappears, leaving a cooling place in the bed. She eats a cereal called Body Buddies, and she leaves the bowl on the table, with the soggy tan balls floating in a milk puddle. He sees things about Norma Jean that he never realized before. When she chops onions, she stares off into a corner, as if she can't bear to look. She puts on her house slippers almost precisely at nine o'clock every evening and nudges her jogging shoes under the couch. She saves

[2] "Bloody Shiloh," a battle noted for its carnage and for the poor generalship on both sides, ended on April 7, 1862, with a victory by the Union forces under the command of Ulysses S. Grant (1822–1885), who is mentioned below. In its aftermath the Confederates withdrew to Corinth, Mississippi.

bread heels for the birds. Leroy watches the birds at the feeder. He notices the peculiar way goldfinches fly past the window. They close their wings, then fall, then spread their wings to catch and lift themselves. He wonders if they close their eyes when they fall. Norma Jean closes her eyes when they are in bed. She wants the lights turned out. Even then, he is sure she closes her eyes.

He goes for long drives around town. He tends to drive a car rather carelessly. Power steering and an automatic shift make a car feel so small and inconsequential that his body is hardly involved in the driving process. His injured leg stretches out comfortably. Once or twice he has almost hit something, but even the prospect of an accident seems minor in a car. He cruises the new subdivisions, feeling like a criminal rehearsing for a robbery. Norma Jean is probably right about a log house being inappropriate here in the new subdivisions. All the houses look grand and complicated. They depress him.

One day when Leroy comes home from a drive he finds Norma Jean in tears. She is in the kitchen making a potato and mushroom-soup casserole, with grated-cheese topping. She is crying because her mother caught her smoking.

"I didn't hear her coming. I was standing here puffing away pretty as you please," Norma Jean says, wiping her eyes.

"I knew it would happen sooner or later," says Leroy, putting his arm around her.

"She don't know the meaning of the word 'knock,' " says Norma Jean. "It's a wonder she hadn't caught me years ago."

"Think of it this way," Leroy says. "What if she caught me with a joint?"

"You better not let her!" Norma Jean shrieks. "I'm warning you, Leroy Moffitt!"

"I'm just kidding. Here, play me a tune. That'll help you relax."

Norma Jean puts the casserole in the oven and sets the timer. Then she plays a ragtime tune, with horns and banjo, as Leroy lights up a joint and lies on the couch, laughing to himself about Mabel's catching him at it. He thinks of Stevie Hamilton—a doctor's son pushing grass. Everything is funny. The whole town seems crazy and small. He is reminded of Virgil Mathis, a boastful policeman Leroy used to shoot pool with. Virgil recently led a drug bust in a back room at a bowling alley, where he seized ten thousand dollars' worth of marijuana. The newspaper had a picture of him holding up the bags of grass and grinning widely. Right now, Leroy can imagine Virgil breaking down the door and arresting him with a lungful of smoke. Virgil would probably have been alerted to the scene because of all the racket Norma Jean is making. Now she sounds like a hard-rock band. Norma Jean is terrific. When she switches to a Latin-rhythm version of "Sunshine Superman," Leroy hums along. Norma Jean's foot goes up and down, up and down.

"Well, what do you think?" Leroy says, when Norma Jean pauses to search through her music.

"What do I think about what?"

His mind has gone blank. Then he says, "I'll sell my rig and build us a house." That wasn't what he wanted to say. He wanted to know what she thought—what she *really* thought—about them.

"Don't start in on that again," says Norma Jean. She begins playing "Who'll Be the Next in Line?"

Leroy used to tell hitchhikers his whole life story—about his travels, his hometown, the baby. He would end with a question: "Well, what do you think?" It was just a rhetorical question. In time, he had the feeling that he'd been telling the same story over and over to the same hitchhikers. He quit talking to hitchhikers when he realized how his voice sounded—whining and self-pitying, like some teenage-tragedy song. Now Leroy has the sudden impulse to tell Norma Jean about himself, as if he had just met her. They have known each other so long they have forgotten a lot about each other. They could become reacquainted. But when the oven timer goes off and she runs to the kitchen, he forgets why he wants to do this.

The next day, Mabel drops by. It is Saturday and Norma Jean is cleaning. Leroy is studying the plans of his log house, which have finally come in the mail. He has them spread out on the table—big sheets of stiff blue paper, with diagrams and numbers printed in white. While Norma Jean runs the vacuum, Mabel drinks coffee. She sets her coffee cup on a blueprint.

"I'm just waiting for time to pass," she says to Leroy, drumming her fingers on the table.

As soon as Norma Jean switches off the vacuum, Mabel says in a loud voice, "Did you hear about the datsun dog that killed the baby?"

Norma Jean says, "The word is 'dachshund.'"

"They put the dog on trial. It chewed the baby's legs off. The mother was in the next room all the time." She raises her voice. "They thought it was neglect."

Norma Jean is holding her ears. Leroy manages to open the refrigerator and get some Diet Pepsi to offer Mabel. Mabel still has some coffee and she waves away the Pepsi.

"Datsuns are like that," Mabel says. "They're jealous dogs. They'll tear a place to pieces if you don't keep an eye on them."

"You better watch out what you're saying, Mabel," says Leroy.

"Well, facts is facts."

Leroy looks out the window at his rig. It is like a huge piece of furniture gathering dust in the backyard. Pretty soon it will be an antique. He hears the vacuum cleaner. Norma Jean seems to be cleaning the living room rug again.

Later, she says to Leroy, "She just said that about the baby because she caught me smoking. She's trying to pay me back."

"What are you talking about?" Leroy says, nervously shuffling blueprints.

"You know good and well," Norma Jean says. She is sitting in a kitchen chair with her feet up and her arms wrapped around her knees. She looks small and helpless. She says, "The very idea, her bringing up a subject like that! Saying it was neglect."

"She didn't mean that," Leroy says.

"She might not have *thought* she meant it. She always says things like that. You don't know how she goes on."

"But she didn't really mean it. She was just talking."

Leroy opens a king-sized bottle of beer and pours it into two glasses, dividing it carefully. He hands a glass to Norma Jean and she takes it from him mechanically. For a long time, they sit by the kitchen window watching the birds at the feeder.

Something is happening. Norma Jean is going to night school. She has graduated from her six-week body-building course and now she is taking an adult-education course in composition at Paducah Community College. She spends her evenings outlining paragraphs.

"First you have a topic sentence," she explains to Leroy. "Then you divide it up. Your secondary topic has to be connected to your primary topic."

To Leroy, this sounds intimidating. "I never was any good in English," he says.

"It makes a lot of sense."

"What are you doing this for, anyhow?"

She shrugs. "It's something to do." She stands up and lifts her dumbbells a few times.

"Driving a rig, nobody ever cared about my English."

"I'm not criticizing your English."

Norma Jean used to say, "If I lose ten minutes' sleep, I just drag all day." Now she stays up late, writing compositions. She got a B on her first paper—a how-to theme on soup-based casseroles. Recently Norma Jean has been cooking unusual foods—tacos, lasagna, Bombay chicken. She doesn't play the organ anymore, though her second paper was called "Why Music Is Important to Me." She sits at the kitchen table, concentrating on her outlines, while Leroy plays with his log house plans, practicing with a set of Lincoln Logs. The thought of getting a truckload of notched, numbered logs scares him, and he wants to be prepared. As he and Norma Jean work together at the kitchen table, Leroy has the hopeful thought that they are sharing something, but he knows he is a fool to think this. Norma Jean is miles away. He knows he is going to lose her. Like Mabel, he is just waiting for time to pass.

One day, Mabel is there before Norma Jean gets home from work, and Leroy finds himself confiding in her. Mabel, he realizes, must know Norma Jean better than he does.

"I don't know what's got into that girl," Mabel says. "She used to go to bed with the chickens. Now you say she's up all hours. Plus her a-smoking. I like to died."

"I want to make her this beautiful home," Leroy says, indicating the Lincoln Logs. "I don't think she even wants it. Maybe she was happier with me gone."

"She don't know what to make of you, coming home like this."

"Is that it?"

Mabel takes the roof off his Lincoln Log cabin. "You couldn't get *me* in a log cabin," she says. "I was raised in one. It's no picnic, let me tell you."

"They're different now," says Leroy.

"I tell you what," Mabel says, smiling oddly at Leroy.

"What?"

"Take her on down to Shiloh. Y'all need to get out together, stir a little. Her brain's all balled up over them books."

Leroy can see traces of Norma Jean's features in her mother's face. Mabel's worn face has the texture of crinkled cotton, but suddenly she looks pretty. It occurs to Leroy that Mabel has been hinting all along that she wants them to take her with them to Shiloh.

"Let's all go to Shiloh," he says. "You and me and her. Come Sunday."

Mabel throws up her hands in protest. "Oh, no, not me. Young folks want to be by themselves."

When Norma Jean comes in with groceries, Leroy says excitedly, "Your mama here's been dying to go to Shiloh for thirty-five years. It's about time we went, don't you think?"

"I'm not going to butt in on anybody's second honeymoon," Mabel says.

"Who's going on a honeymoon, for Christ's sake?" Norma Jean says loudly.

"I never raised no daughter of mine to talk that-a-way," Mabel says.

"You ain't seen nothing yet," says Norma Jean. She starts putting away boxes and cans, slamming cabinet doors.

"There's a log cabin at Shiloh," Mabel says. "It was there during the battle. There's bullet holes in it."

"When are you going to *shut up* about Shiloh, Mama?" asks Norma Jean.

"I always thought Shiloh was the prettiest place, so full of history," Mabel goes on. "I just hoped y'all could see it once before I die, so you could tell me about it." Later, she whispers to Leroy, "You do what I said. A little change is what she needs."

"Your name means "the king,' " Norma Jean says to Leroy that evening. He is trying to get her to go to Shiloh, and she is reading a book about another century.

"Well, I reckon I ought to be right proud."

"I guess so."

"Am I still king around here?"

Norma Jean flexes her biceps and feels them for hardness. "I'm not fooling around with anybody, if that's what you mean," she says.

"Would you tell me if you were?"

"I don't know."

"What does *your* name mean?"

"It was Marilyn Monroe's real name."[3]

"No kidding!"

"Norma comes from the Normans. They were invaders," she says. She closes her book and looks hard at Leroy. "I'll go to Shiloh with you if you'll stop staring at me."

On Sunday, Norma Jean packs a picnic and they go to Shiloh. To Leroy's relief, Mabel says she does not want to come with them. Norma Jean drives, and Leroy, sitting beside her, feels like some boring hitchhiker she has picked up. He tries some conversation, but she answers him in monosyllables. At Shiloh, she drives aimlessly through the park, past bluffs and trails and steep ravines. Shiloh is an immense place, and Leroy cannot see it as a battleground. It is not what he expected. He thought it would look like a golf course. Monuments are everywhere, showing through the thick clusters of trees. Norma Jean passes the log cabin Mabel mentioned. It is surrounded by tourists looking for bullet holes.

"That's not the kind of log house I've got in mind," says Leroy apologetically.

"I know *that.*"

"This is a pretty place. Your mama was right."

"It's O.K.," says Norma Jean. "Well, we've seen it. I hope she's satisfied."

They burst out laughing together.

At the park museum, a movie on Shiloh is shown every half hour, but they decide that they don't want to see it. They buy a souvenir Confederate flag for Mabel, and then they find a picnic spot near the cemetery. Norma Jean has brought a picnic cooler, with pimiento sandwiches, soft drinks, and Yodels. Leroy eats a sandwich and then smokes a joint, hiding it behind the picnic cooler. Norma Jean has quit smoking altogether. She is picking cake crumbs from the cellophane wrapper, like a fussy bird.

Leroy says, "So the boys in gray ended up in Corinth. The Union soldiers zapped 'em finally. April 7, 1862."

They both know that he doesn't know any history. He is just talking about some of the historical plaques they have read. He feels awkward, like a boy on a date with an older girl. They are still just making conversation.

---

[3] The real name of American motion-picture actress Marilyn Monroe (1926–1962) was either Norma Jean Baker or Norma Jean Mortenson.

"Corinth is where Mama eloped to," says Norma Jean.

They sit in silence and stare at the cemetery for the Union dead and, beyond, at a tall cluster of trees. Campers are parked nearby, bumper to bumper, and small children in bright clothing are cavorting and squealing. Norma Jean wads up the cake wrapper and squeezes it tightly in her hand. Without looking at Leroy, she says, "I want to leave you."

Leroy takes a bottle of Coke out of the cooler and flips off the cap. He holds the bottle poised near his mouth but cannot remember to take a drink. Finally he says, "No, you don't."

"Yes, I do."

"I won't let you."

"You can't stop me."

"Don't do me that way."

Leroy knows Norma Jean will have her own way. "Didn't I promise to be home from now on?" he says.

"In some ways, a woman prefers a man who wanders," says Norma Jean. "That sounds crazy, I know."

"You're not crazy."

Leroy remembers to drink from his Coke. Then he says, "Yes, you *are* crazy. You and me could start all over again. Right back at the beginning."

"We *have* started all over again," says Norma Jean. "And this is how it turned out."

"What did I do wrong?"

"Nothing."

"Is this one of those women's lib things?" Leroy asks.

"Don't be funny."

The cemetery, a green slope dotted with white markers, looks like a subdivision site. Leroy is trying to comprehend that his marriage is breaking up, but for some reason he is wondering about white slabs in a graveyard.

"Everything was fine till Mama caught me smoking," says Norma Jean, standing up. "That set something off."

"What are you talking about?"

"She won't leave me alone—*you* won't leave me alone." Norma Jean seems to be crying, but she is looking away from him. "I feel eighteen again. I can't face that all over again." She starts walking away. "No, it *wasn't* fine. I don't know what I'm saying. Forget it."

Leroy takes a lungful of smoke and closes his eyes as Norma Jean's words sink in. He tries to focus on the fact that thirty-five hundred soldiers died on the grounds around him. He can only think of that war as a board game with plastic soldiers. Leroy almost smiles, as he compares the Confederates' daring attack on the Union camps and Virgil Mathis's raid on the bowling alley. General Grant, drunk and furious, shoved the Southerners back to Corinth, where Mabel and Jet Beasley were married years later, when Mabel was still thin and good-looking. The next day, Mabel and Jet visited the battleground, and then Norma Jean was born, and then she married Leroy and they had a baby, which they lost, and now Leroy and Norma Jean are here at the same battleground. Leroy knows he is leaving out a lot. He is leaving out the insides of history. History was always just names and dates to him. It occurs to him that building a house out of logs is similarly empty—too simple. And the real inner workings of a marriage, like most of history, have escaped him. Now he sees that building a log house is the dumbest idea he could have had. It was clumsy of him to think Norma Jean would want a log house. It was a crazy idea. He'll have to think of something else, quickly. He will wad the blueprints into tight balls, and fling them into the lake. Then he'll get moving again. He opens his eyes. Norma Jean has moved away and is walking through the cemetery, following a serpentine brick path.

Leroy gets up to follow his wife, but his good leg is asleep and his bad leg still hurts him. Norma Jean is far away, walking rapidly toward the bluff by the river, and he tries to hobble toward her. Some children run past him, screaming noisily. Norma Jean has reached the bluff, and she is looking out over the Tennessee River. Now she turns toward Leroy and waves her arms. Is she beckoning to him? She seems to be doing an exercise for her chest muscles. The sky is unusually pale—the color of the dust ruffle Mabel made for their bed.

[1982]

Susan Minot   *1956–*

LUST

Leo was from a long time ago, the first one I ever saw nude. In the spring before the Hellmans filled their pool, we'd go down there in the deep end, with baby oil, and like that. I met him the first month away at boarding school. He had a halo from the campus light behind him. I flipped.

Roger was fast. In his illegal car, we drove to the reservoir, the radio blaring, talking fast, fast, fast. He was always going for my zipper. He got kicked out sophomore year.

By the time the band got around to playing "Wild Horses," I had tasted Bruce's tongue. We were clicking in the shadows on the other side of the amplifier, out of Mrs. Donovan's line of vision. It tasted like salt, with my neck bent back, because we had been dancing so hard before.

Tim's line: "I'd like to see you in a bathing suit." I knew it was his line when he said the exact same thing to Annie Hines.

You'd go on walks to get off campus. It was raining like hell, my sweater as sopped as a wet sheep. Tim pinned me to a tree, the woods light brown and dark brown, a white house half hidden with the lights already on. The water was as loud as a crowd hissing. He made certain comments about my forehead, about my cheeks.

We started off sitting at one end of the couch and then our feet were squished against the armrest and then he went over to turn off the TV and came back after he had taken off his shirt and then we slid onto the floor and he got up again to close the door, then came back to me, a body waiting on the rug.

You'd try to wipe off the table or to do the dishes and Willie would untuck your shirt and get his hands up under in front, standing behind you, making puffy noises in your ear.

*

He likes it when I wash my hair. He covers his face with it and if I start to say something, he goes, "Shush."

For a long time, I had Philip on the brain. The less they noticed you, the more you got them on the brain.

My parents had no idea. Parents never really know what's going on, especially when you're away at school most of the time. If she met them, my mother might say, "Oliver seems nice" or "I like that one" without much of an opinion. If she didn't like them, "He's a funny fellow, isn't he?" or "Johnny's perfectly nice but

607

a drink of water." My father was too shy to talk to them at all unless they played sports and he'd ask them about that.

The sand was almost cold underneath because the sun was long gone. Eben piled a mound over my feet, patting around my ankles, the ghostly surf rumbling behind him in the dark. He was the first person I ever knew who died, later that summer, in a car crash. I thought about it for a long time.

"Come here," he says on the porch.
I go over to the hammock and he takes my wrist with two fingers.
"What?"
He kisses my palm then directs my hand to his fly.

Songs went with whichever boy it was. "Sugar Magnolia" was Tim, with the line "Rolling in the rushes / down by the riverside." With "Darkness Darkness," I'd picture Philip with his long hair. Hearing "Under My Thumb" there'd be the smell of Jamie's suede jacket.

We hid in the listening rooms during study hall. With a record cover over the door's window, the teacher on duty couldn't look in. I came out flushed and heady and back at the dorm was surprised how red my lips were in the mirror.

One weekend at Simon's brother's, we stayed inside all day with the shades down, in bed, then went out to Store 24 to get some ice cream. He stood at the magazine rack and read through *MAD* while I got butterscotch sauce, craving something sweet.

I could do some things well. Some things I was good at, like math or painting or even sports, but the second a boy put his arm around me, I forgot about wanting to do anything else, which felt like a relief at first until it became like sinking into a muck.

*

It was different for a girl.

When we were little, the brothers next door tied up our ankles. They held the door of the goat house and wouldn't let us out till we showed them our underpants. Then they'd forget about being after us and when we played whiffle ball, I'd be just as good as they were.

Then it got to be different. Just because you have on a short skirt, they yell from the cars, slowing down for a while, and if you don't look, they screech off and call you a bitch.

"What's the matter with me?" they say, point-blank.
Or else, "Why won't you go out with me? I'm not asking you to get married," about to get mad.
Or it'd be, trying to be reasonable, in a regular voice, "Listen, I just want to have a good time."

So I'd go because I couldn't think of something to say back that wouldn't be obvious, and if you go out with them, you sort of have to do something.

I sat between Mack and Eddie in the front seat of the pickup. They were having a fight about something. I've a feeling about me.

Certain nights you'd feel a certain surrender, maybe if you'd had wine. The surrender would be forgetting yourself and you'd put your nose to his neck and feel like a squirrel, safe, at rest, in a restful dream. But then you'd start to slip from that and the dark would come in and there'd be a cave. You make out the dim shape of the windows and feel yourself become a cave, filled absolutely with air, or with a sadness that wouldn't stop.

Teenage years. You know just what you're doing and don't see the things that start to get in the way.

Lots of boys, but never two at the same time. One was plenty to keep you in a state. You'd start to see a boy and something would rush over you like a fast storm cloud and you couldn't possibly think of anyone else. Boys took it differently. Their eyes perked up at any little number that walked by. You'd act like you weren't noticing.

The joke was that the school doctor gave out the pill like aspirin. He didn't ask you anything. I was fifteen. We had a picture of him in assembly, holding up an IUD shaped like a T. Most girls were on the pill, if anything, because they couldn't handle a diaphragm. I kept the dial in my top drawer like my mother and thought of her each time I tipped out the yellow tablets in the morning before chapel.

If they were too shy, I'd be more so. Andrew was nervous. We stayed up with his family album, sharing a pack of Old Golds. Before it got light, we turned on the TV. A man was explaining how to plant seedlings. His mouth jerked to the side in a tic. Andrew thought it was a riot and kept imitating him. I laughed to be polite. When we finally dozed off, he dared to put his arm around me, but that was it.

You wait till they come to you. With half fright, half swagger, they stand one step down. They dare to touch the button on your coat then lose their nerve and quickly drop their hand so you—you'd do anything for them. You touch their cheek.

The girls sit around in the common room and talk about boys, smoking their heads off.
"What are you complaining about?" says Jill to me when we talk about problems.
"Yeah," says Giddy. "You always have a boyfriend."
I look at them and think, As if.

I thought the worst thing anyone could call you was a cock-teaser. So, if you flirted, you had to be prepared to go through with it. Sleeping with someone was perfectly normal once you had done it. You didn't really worry about it. But there were other problems. The problems had to do with something else entirely.

*

Mack was during the hottest summer ever recorded. We were renting a house on an island with all sorts of other people. No one slept during the heat wave, walking around the house with nothing on which we were used to because of the nude beach. In the living room, Eddie lay on top of a coffee table to cool off. Mack and I, with the bedroom door open for air, sweated and sweated all night.

"I can't take this," he said at three A.M. "I'm going for a swim." He and some guys down the hall went to the beach. The heat put me on edge. I sat on a cracked chest by the open window and smoked and smoked till I felt even worse, waiting for something—I guess for him to get back.

One was on a camping trip in Colorado. We zipped our sleeping bags together, the coyotes' hysterical chatter far away. Other couples murmured in other tents. Paul was up before sunrise, starting a fire for breakfast. He wasn't much of a talker in the daytime. At night, his hand leafed about in the hair at my neck.

There'd be times when you overdid it. You'd get carried away. All the next day, you'd be in a total fog, delirious, absent-minded, crossing the street and nearly getting run over.

The more girls a boy has, the better. He has a bright look, having reaped fruits, blooming. He stalks around, sure-shouldered, and you have the feeling he's got more in him, a fatter heart, more stories to tell. For a girl, with each boy it's as though a petal gets plucked each time.

Then you start to get tired. You begin to feel diluted, like watered-down stew.

Oliver came skiing with us. We lolled by the fire after everyone had gone to bed. Each creak you'd think was someone coming downstairs. The silver loop bracelet he gave me had been a present from his girlfriend before.

On vacations, we went skiing, or you'd go south if someone invited you. Some people had apartments in New York that their families hardly ever used. Or summer houses, or older sisters. We always managed to find someplace to go.

We made the plan at coffee hour. Simon snuck out and met me at Main Gate after lights-out. We crept to the chapel and spent the night in the balcony. He tasted like onions from a submarine sandwich.

The boys are one of two ways: either they can't sit still or they don't move. In front of the TV, they won't budge. On weekends they play touch football while we sit on the sidelines, picking blades of grass to chew on, and watch. We're always watching them run around. We shiver in the stands, knocking our boots together to keep our toes warm, and they whizz across the ice, chopping their sticks around the puck. When they're in the rink, they refuse to look at you, only eyeing each other beneath low helmets. You cheer for them but they don't look up, even if it's a face-off when nothing's happening, even if they're doing drills before any game has started at all.

Dancing under the pink tent, he bent down and whispered in my ear. We slipped away to the lawn on the other side of the hedge. Much later, as he was leaving the buffet with two plates of eggs and sausage, I saw the grass stains on the knees of his white pants.

Tim's was shaped like a banana, with a graceful curve to it. They're all different. Willie's like a bunch of walnuts when nothing was happening, another's as thin as a thin hot dog. But it's like faces; you're never really surprised.

Still, you're not sure what to expect.

I look into his face and he looks back. I look into his eyes and they look back at mine. Then they look down at my mouth so I look at his mouth, then back to his eyes then, backing up, at his whole face. I think, Who? Who are you? His head tilts to one side.
I say, "Who are you?"
"What do you mean?"
"Nothing."
I look at his eyes again, deeper. Can't tell who he is, what he thinks.
"What?" he says. I look at his mouth.
"I'm just wondering," I say and go wandering across his face. Study the chin line. It's shaped like a persimmon.
"Who are you? What are you thinking?"
He says, "What the hell are you talking about?"

Then they get mad after, when you say enough is enough. After, when it's easier to explain that you don't want to. You wouldn't dream of saying that maybe you weren't really ready to in the first place.

Gentle Eddie. We waded into the sea, the waves round and plowing in, buffalo-headed, slapping our thighs. I put my arms around his freckled shoulders and he held me up, buoyed by the water, and rocked me like a sea shell.

I had no idea whose party it was, the apartment jam-packed, stepping over people in the hallway. The room with the music was practically empty, the bare floor, me in red shoes. This fellow slides onto one knee and takes me around the waist and we rock to jazzy tunes, with my toes pointing heavenward, and waltz and spin and dip to "Smoke Gets in Your Eyes" or "I'll Love You Just for Now." He puts his head to my chest, runs a sweeping hand down my inside thigh and we go loose-limbed and sultry and as smooth as silk and I stamp my red heels and he takes me into a swoon. I never saw him again after that but I thought, I could have loved that one.

You wonder how long you can keep it up. You begin to feel as if you're showing through, like a bathroom window that only lets in grey light, the kind you can't see out of.

They keep coming around. Johnny drives up at Easter vacation from Baltimore and I let him in the kitchen with everyone sound asleep. He has friends waiting in the car.

"What are you, crazy? It's pouring out there," I say.

"It's okay," he says. "They understand."

So he gets some long kisses from me, against the refrigerator, before he goes because I hate those girls who push away a boy's face as if she were made out of Ivory soap, as if she's that much greater than he is.

The note on my cubby told me to see the headmaster. I had no idea for what. He had received complaints about my amorous displays on the town green. It was Willie that spring. The headmaster told me he didn't care what I did but that Casey Academy had a reputation to uphold in the town. He lowered his glasses on his nose. "We've got twenty acres of woods on this campus," he said. "If you want to smooch with your boyfriend, there are twenty acres for you to do it out of the public eye. You read me?"

Everybody'd get weekend permissions for different places, then we'd all go to someone's house whose parents were away. Usually there'd be more boys than girls. We raided the liquor closet and smoked pot at the kitchen table and you'd never know who would end up where, or with whom. There were always disasters. Ceci got bombed and cracked her head open on the banister and needed stitches. Then there was the time Wendel Blair walked through the picture window at the Lowes' and got slashed to ribbons.

He scared me. In bed, I didn't dare look at him. I lay back with my eyes closed, luxuriating because he knew all sorts of expert angles, his hands never fumbling, going over my whole body, pressing the hair up and off the back of my head, giving an extra hip shove, as if to say *There.* I parted my eyes slightly, keeping the screen of my lashes low because it was too much to look at him, his mouth loose and pink and parted, his eyes looking through my forehead, or kneeling up, looking through my throat. I was ashamed but couldn't look him in the eye.

You wonder about things feeling a little off-kilter. You begin to feel like a piece of pounded veal.

At boarding school, everyone gets depressed. We go in and see the house-mother, Mrs. Gunther. She got married when she was eighteen. Mr. Gunther was her high school sweetheart, the only boyfriend she ever had.

"And you knew you wanted to marry him right off?" we ask her.

She smiles and says, "Yes."

"They always want something from you," says Jill, complaining about her boy-friend.

"Yeah," says Giddy. "You always feel like you have to deliver something."

"You do," says Mrs. Gunther. "Babies."

After sex, you curl up like a shrimp, something deep inside you ruined, slammed in a place that sickens at slamming, and slowly you fill up with an overwhelming sadness, an elusive gaping worry. You don't try to explain it, filled with the knowledge that it's nothing after all, everything filling up finally and absolutely with death. After the briskness of loving, loving stops. And you roll over with death stretched out alongside you like a feather boa, or a snake, light as air, and you . . . you don't even ask for anything or try to say something to him because it's obviously your own damn fault. You haven't been able to—to what? To open your heart. You open your legs but can't, or don't dare anymore, to open your heart.

It starts this way:
You stare into their eyes. They flash like all the stars are out. They look at you seriously, their eyes at a low burn and their hands no matter what starting off shy and with such a gentle touch that the only thing you can do is take that tenderness and let yourself be swept away. When, with one attentive finger they tuck the hair behind your ear, you—
You do everything they want.
Then comes after. After when they don't look at you. They scratch their balls, stare at the ceiling. Or if they do turn, their gaze is altogether changed. They are surprised. They turn casually to look at you, distracted, and get a mild distracted surprise. You're gone. Their blank look tells you that the girl they were fucking is not there anymore. You seem to have disappeared.

[1984]

Donald Barthelme *1933–1989*

BASIL FROM HER GARDEN

A—In the dream, my father was playing the piano, a Beethoven[1] something, in a large concert hall that was filled with people. I was in the audience and I was reading a book. I suddenly realized that this was the wrong thing to do when my father was performing, so I sat up and paid attention. He was playing very well, I thought. Suddenly the conductor stopped the performance and began to sing a passage for my father, a passage that my father had evidently botched. My father listened attentively, smiling at the conductor.

Q—Does your father play? In actuality?

A—Not a note.

Q—Did the conductor resemble anyone you know?

A—He looked a bit like Althea. The same cheekbones and the same chin.

Q—Who is Althea?

A—Someone I know.

Q—What do you do, after work, in the evenings or on weekends?

A—Just ordinary things.

Q—No special interests?

A—I'm very interested in bow-hunting. These new boys they have now, what they call a compound bow. Also, I'm a member of the Galapagos Society,[2] we work for the environment, it's really a very effective—

Q—And what else?

A—Well, adultery. I would say that that's how I spend most of my free time. In adultery.

Q—You mean regular adultery.

A—Yes. Sleeping with people to whom one is not legally bound.

Q—These are women.

A—Invariably.

Q—And so that's what you do, in the evenings or on weekends.

A—I had this kind of strange experience. Today is Saturday, right? I called up this haircutter that I go to, her name is Ruth, and asked for an appointment. I needed a haircut. So she says she has openings at ten, ten-thirty, eleven, eleven-thirty, twelve, twelve-thirty—On a Saturday. Do you think the world knows something I don't know?

Q—It's possible.

A—What if she stabs me in the ear with the scissors?

Q—Unlikely, I would think.

A—Well, she's a good soul. She's had several husbands. They've all been master sergeants, in the Army. She seems to gravitate toward NCO Clubs.[3] Have you noticed all these little black bugs flying around here? I don't know where they come from.

Q—They're very small, they're like gnats.

A—They come in clouds, then they go away.

[1] Ludwig van Beethoven (1770–1827), the German composer.
[2] The Galapagos Islands, a group of islands belonging to Ecuador, some 650 miles west of the mainland, are home to many rare and endangered birds and animals, including the famed Galapagos Tortoise, hence the society's name.
[3] Clubs for noncommissioned officers.

*   *   *

A—I sometimes think of myself as a person who, you know what I mean, could have done something else, it doesn't matter what particularly. Just something else. I saw an ad in the Sunday paper for the CIA,[4] a recruiting ad, maybe a quarter of a page, and I suddenly thought, It might be interesting to do that. Even though I've always been opposed to the CIA, when they were trying to bring Cuba down, the stuff with Lumumba in Africa,[5] the stuff in Central America. . . . Then here is this ad, perfectly straightforward, "where your career is America's strength" or something like that, "aptitude for learning a foreign language is a plus" or something like that. I've always been good at languages, and I'm sitting there thinking about how my résumé might look to them, starting completely over in something completely new, changing the very sort of person I am, and there was an attraction, a definite attraction. Of course the maximum age was thirty-five. I guess they want them more malleable.

Q—So, in the evenings or on weekends—

A—Not every night or every weekend. I mean, this depends on the circumstances. Sometimes my wife and I go to dinner with people, or watch television—

Q—But in the main—

A—It's not that often. It's once in a while.

Q—Adultery is a sin.

A—It is classified as a sin, yes. Absolutely.

Q—The Seventh Commandment says—

A—I know what it says. I was raised on the Seventh Commandment. But.

Q—But what?

A—The Seventh Commandment is wrong.

Q—It's wrong?

A—Some outfits call it the Sixth and others the Seventh. It's wrong.

Q—The whole Commandment?

A—I don't know how it happened, whether it's a mistranslation from the Aramaic or whatever, it may not even have been Aramaic,[6] I don't know, I certainly do not pretend to scholarship in this area, but my sense of the matter is that the Seventh Commandment is an error.

Q—Well if that was true it would change quite a lot of things, wouldn't it?

A—Take the pressure off, a bit.

Q—Have you told your wife?

A—Yes, Grete knows.

Q—How'd she take it?

A—Well, she *liked* the Seventh Commandment. You could reason that it was in her interest to support the Seventh Commandment for the preservation of the family unit and this sort of thing but to reason that way is, I would say, to take an extremely narrow view of Grete, of what she thinks. She's not predictable. She once told me that she didn't want me, she wanted a suite of husbands, ten or twenty—

Q—What did you say?

---

[4] The Central Intelligence Agency gathers military and political information for U.S. government agencies.

[5] Patrice Lumumba (1925–1961), the African nationalist who became the first premier of the Republic of the Congo and died following a coup d'état.

[6] The ancient Semitic language spoken throughout the Near East from 700 B.C. to A.D. 700.

A—I said, Go to it.

Q—Well, how does it make you feel? Adultery.

A—There's a certain amount of guilt attached. I feel guilty. But I feel guilty even without adultery. I exist in a morass of guilt. There's maybe a little additional wallop of guilt but I already feel so guilty that I hardly notice it.

Q—Where does all this guilt come from? The extra-adulterous guilt?

A—I keep wondering if, say, there is intelligent life on other planets, the scientists argue that something like two percent of the other planets have the conditions, the physical conditions, to support life in the way it happened here, did Christ visit each and every planet, go through the same routine, the Agony in the Garden, the Crucifixion, and so on. . . . And these guys on these other planets, these life forms, maybe they look like boll weevils or something, on a much larger scale of course, were they told that they shouldn't go to bed with other attractive six-foot boll weevils arrayed in silver and gold and with little squirts of Opium behind the ears? Doesn't make sense. But of course our human understanding is imperfect.

Q—You haven't answered me. This general guilt—

A—Yes, that's the interesting thing. I hazard that it is not guilt so much as it is inadequacy. I feel that everything is being nibbled away, because I can't *get it right*—

Q—Would you like to be able to fly?

A—It's crossed my mind.

Q—Myself, I think about being just sort of a regular person, one who worries about cancer a lot, every little thing a prediction of cancer, no I don't want to go for my every-two-years checkup because what if they find something? I wonder what will kill me and when it will happen and how it will happen, and I wonder about my parents, who are still alive, and what will happen to them. This seems to me to be a proper set of things to worry about. Last things.

A—I don't think God gives a snap about adultery. This is just an opinion, of course.

Q—So how do you, how shall I put it, pursue—

A—You think about this staggering concept, the mind of God, and then you think He's sitting around worrying about this guy and this woman at the Beechut TraveLodge? I think not.

Q—Well, He doesn't have to think about every particular instance, He just sort of laid out the general principles—

A—He also created creatures who, with a single powerful glance—

Q—The eyes burn.

A—They do.

Q—The heart leaps.

A—Like a terrapin.

Q—Stupid youth returns.

A—Like hockey sticks falling out of a long-shut closet.

Q—Do you play?

A—I did. Many years ago.

Q—Who is Althea?

A—Someone I know.

Q—We're basically talking about Althea.

A—Yes. I thought you understood that.

Q—We're not talking about wholesale—

A—Oh Lord no. Who has the strength?

Q—What's she like?

A—She's I guess you'd say a little on the boring side. To the innocent eye.

Q—She appears to be a contained, controlled person, free of raging internal fires.

A—But my eye is not innocent. To the already corrupted eye, she's—

Q—I don't want to question you too closely on this. I don't want to strain your powers of—

A—Well, no, I don't mind talking about it. It fell on me like a ton of bricks. I was walking in the park one day.

Q—Which park?

A—That big park over by—

Q—Yeah, I know the one.

A—This woman was sitting there.

Q—They sit in parks a lot, I've noticed that. Especially when they're angry. The solitary bench. Shoulders raised, legs kicking—

A—I've crossed both major oceans by ship—the Pacific twice, on troopships, the Atlantic once, on a passenger liner. You stand out there, at the rail, at dusk, and the sea is limitless, water in every direction, never-ending, you think *water forever*, the movement of the ship seems slow but also seems inexplorable, you feel you will be moving this way forever, the Pacific is about seventy million square miles, about one-third of the earth's surface, the ship might be making twenty knots, I'm eating oranges because that's all I can keep down, twelve days of it with thousands of young soldiers all around, half of them seasick—On the Queen Mary,[7] in tourist class, we got rather good food, there was a guy assigned to our table who had known Paderewski, the great pianist who was also Prime Minister of Poland,[8] he talked about Paderewski for four days, an ocean of anecdotes—

Q—When I was first married, when I was twenty, I didn't know where the clitoris was. I didn't know there was such a thing. Shouldn't somebody have told me?

A—Perhaps your wife?

Q—Of course, she was too shy. In those days people didn't go around saying, This is the clitoris and this is what its proper function is and this is what you can do to help out. I finally found it. In a book.

A—German?

Q—Dutch.

A—A dead bear in a blue dress, face down on the kitchen floor. I trip over it, in the dark, when I get up at 2 A.M. to see if there's anything to eat in the refrigerator. It's an architectural problem, marriage. If we could live in separate houses, and visit each other when we felt particularly gay—It would be expensive, yes. But as it is she has to endure me in all my worst manifestations, early in the morning and late at night and in the nutsy obssessed noontimes. When I wake up from my nap you don't *get* the laughing cavalier, you get a rank pigfooted belching blunderer. I knew this one guy who built a wall down the middle of his

---

[7] One of the great British ocean liners built during the 1930s; since 1967 it has been permanently docked at Long Beach, California.

[8] Jan Paderewski (1860–1914), as the text suggests, was an accomplished pianist as well as a skillful Polish political statesman.

apartment. An impenetrable wall. He had a very big apartment. It worked out very well. Concrete block, basically, with fibre-glass insulation on top of that and sheet-rock on top of that—

Q—What about coveting your neighbor's wife?

A—Well on one side there are no wives, strictly speaking, there are two floors and two male couples, all very nice people. On the other side, Bill and Rachel have the whole house. I like Rachel but I don't covet her. I could covet her, she's covetable, quite lovely and spirited, but in point of fact our relationship is that of neighborliness. I jump-start her car when her battery is dead, she gives me basil from her garden, she's got acres of basil, not literally acres but—Anyhow, I don't think that's much of a problem, coveting your neighbor's wife. Just speaking administratively, I don't see why there's an entire Commandment devoted to it. It's a mental exercise, coveting. To covet is not necessarily to take action.

Q—I covet my neighbor's leaf blower. It has this neat Vari-Flo deal that lets you—

A—I can see that.

Q—I am feverishly interested in these questions.

Q—Ethics has always been where my heart is.

Q—Moral precepting stings the dull mind into attentiveness.

Q—I'm only a bit depressed, only a bit.

Q—A new arrangement of ideas, based upon the best thinking, would produce a more humane moral order, which we need.

Q—Apple honey, disposed upon the sexual parts, is not an index of decadence. Decadence itself is not as bad as it's been painted.

Q—That he watched his father play the piano when his father could not play the piano and that he was reading a book while his father played the piano in a very large hall before a very large audience only means that he finds his roots, as it were, untrustworthy. The father imagined as a root. That's not unusual.

Q—As for myself, I am content with too little, I know this about myself and I do not commend myself for it and perhaps one day I shall be able to change myself into a hungrier being. Probably not.

Q—The leaf blower, for example.

A—I see Althea now and then, not often enough. We sigh together in a particular bar, it's almost always empty. She tells me about her kids and I tell her about my kids. I obey the Commandments, the sensible ones. Where they don't know what they're talking about I ignore them. I keep thinking about the story of the two old women in church listening to the priest discoursing on the dynamics of the married state. At the end of the sermon one turns to the other and says, "I wish I knew as little about it as he does."

Q—He critiques us, we critique Him. Does Grete also engage in dalliance?

A—How quaint you are. I think she has friends whom she sees now and then.

Q—How does that make you feel?

A—I wish her well.

Q—What's in your wallet?

A—The usual. Credit cards, pictures of children, driver's license, forty dollars in cash, Amex[9] receipts—

_____
[9] American Express credit card.

Q—I sometimes imagine that I am in Pest Control. I have a small white truck with a red diamond-shaped emblem on the door and a white jumpsuit with the same emblem on the breast pocket. I park the truck in front of a subscriber's neat three-hundred-thousand-dollar home, extract the silver cannister of deadly pest killer from the back of the truck, and walk up the brick sidewalk to the house's front door. Chimes ring, the door swings open, a young wife in jeans and a pink flannel shirt worn outside the jeans is standing there. "Pest Control," I say. She smiles at me, I smile back and move past her into the house, into the handsomely appointed kitchen. The cannister is suspended by a sling from my right shoulder, and, pumping the mechanism occasionally with my right hand, I point the nozzle of the hose at the baseboards and begin to spray. I spray alongside the refrigerator, alongside the gas range, under the sink, and behind the kitchen table. Next, I move to the bathrooms, pumping and spraying. The young wife is in another room, waiting for me to finish. I walk into the main sitting room and spray discreetly behind the largest pieces of furniture, an oak sideboard, a red plush Victorian couch, and along the inside of the fireplace. I do the study, spraying the Columbia Encyclopedia, he's been looking up the Seven Years' War, 1756–63,[10] yellow highlighting there, and behind the forty-five-inch RCA television. The master bedroom requires just touches, short bursts in her closet which must avoid the two dozen pairs of shoes there and in his closet which contains six to eight long guns in canvas cases. Finally I spray the laundry room with its big white washer and dryer, and behind the folding table stacked with sheets and towels already folded. Who folds? I surmise that she folds. Unless one of the older children, pressed into service, folds. In my experience they are unlikely to fold. Maybe the au pair. Finished, I tear a properly made out receipt from my receipt book and present it to the young wife. She scribbles her name in the appropriate space and hands it back to me. The house now stinks quite palpably but I know and she knows that the stench will dissipate in two to four hours. The young wife escorts me to the door, and, in parting, pins a silver medal on my chest and kisses me on both cheeks. Pest Control!

A—Yes, one could fit in in that way. It's finally a matter, perhaps, of fit. Appropriateness. Fit in a stately or sometimes hectic dance with nonfit. What we have to worry about.

Q—It seems to me that we have quite a great deal to worry about. Does the radish worry about itself in this way? Yet the radish is a living thing. Until it's cooked.

A—Grete is mad for radishes, can't get enough. I like frozen Mexican dinners, Patio, I have them for breakfast, the freezer is stacked with them—

Q—Transcendence is possible.

A—Yes.

Q—Is it possible?

A—Not out of the question.

Q—Is it really possible?

A—Yes, Believe me.

[1985]

---

[10] The European war that pitted Britain and Prussia against France and Austria; its phase in North America is known as the "French and Indian War."

Ann Beattie   *1947–*

JANUS[1]

The bowl was perfect. Perhaps it was not what you'd select if you faced a shelf of bowls, and not the sort of thing that would inevitably attract a lot of attention at a crafts fair, yet it had real presence. It was as predictably admired as a mutt who has no reason to suspect he might be funny. Just such a dog, in fact, was often brought out (and in) along with the bowl.

Andrea was a real-estate agent, and when she thought that some prospective buyers might be dog-lovers, she would drop off her dog at the same time she placed the bowl in the house that was up for sale. She would put a dish of water in the kitchen for Mondo, take his squeaking plastic frog out of her purse and drop it on the floor. He would pounce delightedly, just as he did every day at home, batting around his favorite toy. The bowl usually sat on a coffee table, though recently she had displayed it on top of a pine blanket chest and on a lacquered table. It was once placed on a cherry table beneath a Bonnard[2] still-life, where it held its own.

Everyone who has purchased a house or who has wanted to sell a house must be familiar with some of the tricks used to convince a buyer that the house is quite special: a fire in the fireplace in early evening; jonquils in a pitcher on the kitchen counter, where no one ordinarily has space to put flowers; perhaps the slight aroma of spring, made by a single drop of scent vaporizing from a lamp bulb.

The wonderful thing about the bowl, Andrea thought, was that it was both subtle and noticeable—a paradox of a bowl. Its glaze was the color of cream and seemed to glow no matter what light it was placed in. There were a few bits of color in it—tiny geometric flashes—and some of these were tinged with flecks of silver. They were as mysterious as cells seen under a microscope; it was difficult not to study them, because they shimmered, flashing for a split second, and then resumed their shape. Something about the colors and their random placement suggested motion. People who liked country furniture always commented on the bowl, but then it turned out that people who felt comfortable with Biedermeier[3] loved it just as much. But the bowl was not at all ostentatious, or even so noticeable that anyone would suspect that it had been put in place deliberately. They might notice the height of the ceiling on first entering a room, and only when their eye moved down from that, or away from the refraction of sunlight on a pale wall, would they see the bowl. Then they would go immediately to it and comment. Yet they always faltered when they tried to say something. Perhaps it was because they were in the house for a serious reason, not to notice some object.

Once, Andrea got a call from a woman who had not put in an offer on a house she had shown her. That bowl, she said—would it be possible to find out where the owners had bought that beautiful bowl? Andrea pretended that she did not know what the woman was referring to. A bowl, somewhere in the house? Oh, on a table under the window. Yes, she would ask, of course. She let a couple of days

[1] The Roman god, the spirit of all beginnings, who is identified with doors, gates, and other places of passage. Janus is usually artistically represented as a figure with two faces, looking in opposite directions.

[2] Pierre Bonnard (1867–1947), a French painter known for intimate family and domestic scenes painted in brilliant hues.

[3] A style of nineteenth-century German middle-class furniture which became increasingly ornate.

pass, then called back to say that the bowl had been a present and the people did not know where it had been purchased.

When the bowl was not being taken from house to house, it sat on Andrea's coffee table at home. She didn't keep it carefully wrapped (although she transported it that way, in a box); she kept it on the table, because she liked to see it. It was large enough so that it didn't seem fragile, or particularly vulnerable if anyone sideswiped the table or Mondo blundered into it at play. She had asked her husband to please not drop his house key in it. It was meant to be empty.

When her husband first noticed the bowl, he had peered into it and smiled briefly. He always urged her to buy things she liked. In recent years, both of them had acquired many things to make up for all the lean years when they were graduate students, but now that they had been comfortable for quite a while, the pleasure of new possessions dwindled. Her husband had pronounced the bowl "pretty," and he had turned away without picking it up to examine it. He had no more interest in the bowl than she had in his new Leica.[4]

She was sure that the bowl brought her luck. Bids were often put in on houses where she had displayed the bowl. Sometimes the owners, who were always asked to be away or to step outside when the house was being shown, didn't even know that the bowl had been in their house. Once—she could not imagine how—she left it behind, and then she was so afraid that something might have happened to it that she rushed back to the house and sighed with relief when the woman owner opened the door. The bowl, Andrea explained—she had purchased a bowl and set it on the chest for safekeeping while she toured the house with the prospective buyers, and she . . . She felt like rushing past the frowning woman and seizing her bowl. The owner stepped aside, and it was only when Andrea ran to the chest that the lady glanced at her a little strangely. In the few seconds before Andrea picked up the bowl, she realized that the owner must have just seen that it had been perfectly placed, that the sunlight struck the bluer part of it. Her pitcher had been moved to the far side of the chest, and the bowl predominated. All the way home, Andrea wondered how she could have left the bowl behind. It was like leaving a friend at an outing—just walking off. Sometimes there were stories in the paper about families forgetting a child somewhere and driving to the next city. Andrea had only gone a mile down the road before she remembered.

In time, she dreamed of the bowl. Twice, in a waking dream—early in the morning, between sleep and a last nap before rising—she had a clear vision of it. It came into sharp focus and startled her for a moment—the same bowl she looked at every day.

She had a very profitable year selling real estate. Word spread, and she had more clients than she felt comfortable with. She had the foolish thought that if only the bowl were an animate object she could thank it. There were times when she wanted to talk to her husband about the bowl. He was a stockbroker, and sometimes told people that he was fortunate to be married to a woman who had such a fine aesthetic sense and yet could also function in the real world. They were a lot alike, really—they had agreed on that. They were both quiet people—reflective, slow to make value judgments, but almost intractable once they had come to a conclusion. They both liked details, but while ironies attracted her, he was more impatient and dismissive when matters became many-sided or unclear. But they both knew this; it was the kind of thing they could talk about when they

[4] A fine German-made brand of camera.

were alone in the car together, coming home from a party or after a weekend with friends. But she never talked to him about the bowl. When they were at dinner, exchanging their news of the day, or while they lay in bed at night listening to the stereo and murmuring sleepy disconnections, she was often tempted to come right out and say that she thought that the bowl in the living room, the cream-colored bowl, was responsible for her success. But she didn't say it. She couldn't begin to explain it. Sometimes in the morning, she would look at him and feel guilty that she had such a constant secret.

Could it be that she had some deeper connection with the bowl—a relationship of some kind? She corrected her thinking: how could she imagine such a thing, when she was a human being and it was a bowl? It was ridiculous. Just think of how people lived together and loved each other . . . But was that always so clear, always a relationship? She was confused by these thoughts, but they remained in her mind. There was something within her now, something real, that she never talked about.

The bowl was a mystery, even to her. It was frustrating, because her involvement with the bowl contained a steady sense of unrequited good fortune; it would have been easier to respond if some sort of demand were made in return. But that only happened in fairy tales. The bowl was just a bowl. She did not believe that for one second. What she believed was that it was something she loved.

In the past, she had sometimes talked to her husband about a new property she was about to buy or sell—confiding some clever strategy she had devised to persuade owners who seemed ready to sell. Now she stopped doing that, for all her strategies involved the bowl. She became more deliberate with the bowl, and more possessive. She put it in houses only when no one was there, and removed it when she left the house. Instead of just moving a pitcher or a dish, she would remove all the other objects from a table. She had to force herself to handle them carefully, because she didn't really care about them. She just wanted them out of sight.

She wondered how the situation would end. As with a lover, there was no exact scenario of how matters would come to a close. Anxiety became the operative force. It would be irrelevant if the lover rushed into someone else's arms, or wrote her a note and departed to another city. The horror was the possibility of the disappearance. That was what mattered.

She would get up at night and look at the bowl. It never occurred to her that she might break it. She washed and dried it without anxiety, and she moved it often, from coffee table to mahogany corner table or wherever, without fearing an accident. It was clear that she would not be the one who would do anything to the bowl. The bowl was only handled by her, set safely on one surface or another; it was not very likely that anyone would break it. A bowl was a poor conductor of electricity: it would not be hit by lightning. Yet the idea of damage persisted. She did not think beyond that—to what her life would be without the bowl. She only continued to fear that some accident would happen. Why not, in a world where people set plants where they did not belong, so that visitors touring a house would be fooled into thinking that dark corners got sunlight—a world full of tricks?

She had first seen the bowl several years earlier, at a crafts fair she had visited half in secret, with her lover. He had urged her to buy the bowl. She didn't *need* any more things, she told him. But she had been drawn to the bowl, and they had lingered near it. Then she went on to the next booth, and he came up behind her, tapping the rim against her shoulder as she ran her fingers over a wood carving. "You're still insisting that I buy that?" she said. "No," he said. "I bought it for you." He had bought her other things before this—things she liked more, at first—the child's ebony-and-turquoise ring that fitted her little finger; the wooden box, long and thin, beautifully dovetailed, that she used to hold paper clips; the soft gray sweater with a pouch pocket. It was his idea that when he could not be there to hold her hand she could hold her own—clasp her hands inside the lone pocket that stretched across the front. But in time she became more attached to the bowl than to any of his other presents. She tried to talk herself out of it. She owned other things that were more striking or valuable. It wasn't an object whose beauty jumped out at you; a lot of people must have passed it by before the two of them saw it that day.

Her lover had said that she was always too slow to know what she really loved. Why continue with her life the way it was? Why be two-faced, he asked her. He had made the first move toward her. When she would not decide in his favor, would not change her life and come to him, he asked her what made her think she could have it both ways. And then he made the last move and left. It was a decision meant to break her will, to shatter her intransigent ideas about honoring previous commitments.

Time passed. Alone in the living room at night, she often looked at the bowl sitting on the table, still and safe, unilluminated. In its way, it was perfect: the world cut in half, deep and smoothly empty. Near the rim, even in dim light, the eye moved toward one small flash of blue, a vanishing point on the horizon.

[1985]

Ursula K. Le Guin   *1929–*

HORSE CAMP

All the other Seniors were over at the street side of the parking lot, but Sal stayed with her sister Norah while they waited for the bus drivers. "Maybe you'll be in the creek cabin," Sal said, quiet and serious. "I had it second year. It's the best one. Number Five."

"How do they—when do you, like, find out what cabin?" asked Norah.

"They better remember we're in the same cabin," Ev said, sounding shrill. Norah did not look at her. She and Ev had planned for months and known for weeks that they were to be cabinmates, but what good was that if they never found their cabin, and also Sal was not looking at Ev, only at Norah. Sal was cool, a tower of ivory.

"They show you around as soon as you get there," she said, her quiet voice speaking directly to Norah's dream last night of never finding the room where she had to take a test she was late for and looking among endless thatched barracks in a forest of thin black trees growing very close together, like hair under a hand lens. Norah had told no one the dream, and now remembered and forgot it. "Then you have dinner, and First Campfire," Sal said. "Kimmy's going to be a counsellor again. She's really neat. Listen, you tell old Meredy . . ."

Norah drew breath. In all the histories of Horse Camp which she had asked for and heard over and over for three years—the thunderstorm story, the horse-thief story, the wonderful Stevens Mountain stories—in all of them Meredy the handler had been: Meredy said, Meredy did, Meredy knew . . .

"Tell him I said hi," Sal said, with a shadowy smile, looking across the parking lot at the far, insubstantial towers of downtown. Behind them the doors of the Junior Girls bus gasped open. One after another the engines of the four buses roared and spewed. Across the asphalt, in the hot morning light, small figures were lining up and climbing into the Junior Boys bus. High, rough, faint voices bawled. "O.K., hey, have fun," Sal said. She hugged Norah and then, keeping a hand on her arm, looked down at her intently for a moment from the tower of ivory. She turned away. Norah watched her walk, light-foot and buxom, across the black gap to the others of her kind, who enclosed her, greeting her, "Sal! Hey, Sal!"

Ev was twitching and nickering, "Come on, Nor, come on. We'll have to sit way at the back. Come on!" Side by side, they pressed into the line below the gaping doorway of the bus.

In Number Five cabin, four iron cots, thin-mattressed, gray-blanketed, stood strewn with bottles of insect repellent and styling mousse, T-shirts lettered "UCSD" and "I ♥ Teddy Bears," a flashlight, an apple, a comb with hair caught in it, a paperback book open face down: "The Black Colt of Pirate Island." Over the shingle roof huge second-growth redwoods cast deep shade, and a few feet below the porch the creek ran out into sunlight over brown stones streaming bright-green weed. Behind the cabin Jim Meredith, the horse-handler, a short man of fifty who had ridden as a jockey in his teens, walked along the well-beaten path, quick and a bit bowlegged. Meredith's lips were pressed firmly together. His eyes, narrow and darting, glanced from cabin to cabin, from side to side. Far through the trees high voices cried.

The counsellors know what is to be known. Red Ginger, blond Kimmy, and beautiful black Sue: they know the vices of Pal, and how to keep Trigger from putting her head down and drinking for ten minutes from every creek. They strike the great shoulders smartly: "Aw, get over, you big lunk!" They know how to swim underwater, how to sing in harmony, how to get seconds, and when a shoe is loose. They know where they are. They know where the rest of Horse Camp is. "Home Creek runs into Little River here," Kimmy says, drawing lines in the soft dust with a redwood twig that breaks. "Senior Girls here, Senior Boys across there, Junior Birdmen about here."

"Who needs 'em?" says Sue, yawning. "Come on, who's going to help me walk the mares?"

They were all around the campfire on Quartz Meadow after the long first day of the First Overnight. The counsellors were still singing, but very soft, so soft you almost couldn't hear them, lying in the sleeping bag listening to One Spot stamp and Trigger snort and the shifting at the pickets, standing in the fine, cool alpine grass listening to the soft voices and the sleepers shifting and, later, one coyote down the mountain singing all alone.

"Nothing wrong with you. Get up!" said Meredy, and slapped her hip. Turning her long, delicate head to him with a deprecating gaze, Philly got to her feet. She stood a moment, shuddering the reddish silk of her flank as if to dislodge flies, tested her left foreleg with caution, and then walked on, step by step. Step by step, watching, Norah went with her. Inside her body there was still a deep trembling. As she passed him, the handler just nodded. "You're all right," he meant. She was all right.

Freedom, the freedom to run, freedom is to run. Freedom is galloping. What else can it be? Only other ways to run, imitations of galloping across great highlands with the wind. Oh, Philly, sweet Philly, my love! If Ev and Trigger couldn't keep up she'd slow down and come round in a while, after a while, over there, across the long, long field of grass, once she had learned this by heart and knew it forever, the purity, the pure joy.

"Right leg, Nor," said Meredy. And passed on to Cass and Tammy.

You have to start with the right fore. Everything else is all right. Freedom depends on this, that you start with the right fore, that long leg well balanced on its elegant pastern, that you set down that tiptoe middle fingernail, so hard and round, and spurn the dirt. High-stepping, trot past old Meredy, who always hides his smile.

Shoulder to shoulder, she and Ev, in the long heat of afternoon, in a trance of light, across the home creek in the dry wild oats and cow parsley of the Long Pasture. I was afraid before I came here, thinks Norah, incredulous, remembering childhood. She leans her head against Ev's firm and silken side. The sting of small flies awakens, the swish of long tails sends to sleep. Down by the creek, in a patch of coarse grass, Philly grazes and dozes. Sue comes striding by, winks wordless, beautiful as a burning coal, lazy and purposeful, bound for the shade of the willows. Is it worth getting up to go down to get your feet in the cool water? Next year Sal will be too old for a camper, but can come back as a counsellor, come back here. Norah will come back a second-year camper, Sal a counsellor. They will be here. This is what freedom is, what goes on—the sun in summer, the wild grass, coming back each year.

Coming back from the long pack trip to Stevens Mountain, weary and dirty, thirsty and in bliss, coming down from the high places, in line, Sue jogging just in front of her and Ev half asleep behind her—some sound or motion caught and turned Norah's head to look across the alpine field. On the far side, under dark firs, a line of horses, mounted and with packs: "Look!"

Ev snorted. Sue flicked her ears and stopped. Norah halted in line behind her, stretching her neck to see. She saw her sister going first in the distant line, the small head proudly borne. She was walking light-foot and easy, fresh, just starting up the high passes of the mountain. On her back a young man sat erect, his fine, fair head turned a little aside, to the forest. One hand was on his thigh, the other on the reins, guiding her. Norah called out and then broke from the line, going to Sal, calling out to her. "No, no, no, no!" she called. Behind her, Ev and then Sue called to her, "Nor! Nor!"

Sal did not hear or heed. Going straight ahead, the color of ivory, distant in the clear, dry light, she stepped into the shadow of the trees. The others and their riders followed, jogging one after the other till the last was gone.

Norah had stopped in the middle of the meadow, and stood in grass in sunlight. Flies hummed.

She tossed her head, turned, and trotted back to the line. She went along it from one to the next, teasing, chivying, Kimmy yelling at her to get back in line, till Sue broke out of line to chase her and she ran, and then Ev began to run, whinnying shrilly, and then Cass and Philly and all the rest, the whole bunch, cantering first and then running flat out, running wild, racing, heading for Horse Camp and the Long Pasture, for Meredy and the long evening standing in the fenced field, in the sweet dry grass, in the fetlock-shallow water of the home creek.

[1986]

Norman Lavers   *1935–*

THE TELEGRAPH RELAY STATION

Three days beyond the fort on the stage, following the line of telegraph poles like a spider slowly clambering its web. The dry grass prairie is sere and burned looking, like brown skin with a worn ghost of hair on it, the buffalo far to the south at this time of year—Thanksgiven day—but packs of white wolves standing and looking at us curiously. What can they find to eat? All morning long we look forward to seeing the telegraph relay station, mainly because there is utterly nothing else to see. That is the place where I will depart from my two fellow passengers, and wait for the stage that comes through from the north, and will take me south to my destination.

There 't is! Curly hollers back down to us, and we bump each other to be first to crane our heads out the window, squinting our eyes into the dust and bits of broke-off dry grass. It's a low cabin of adobe, the same color of the bare dirt, but a steep peaked roof to shrug off the winter snows, no trees or bushes about it.

When we get closer, we see extra poles at the front, where the telegraph wire we are following goes into the building, then comes back out on the other side and rejoins the line of poles continuing straight ahead. But it is a crossroads, and the wire from the line of poles coming down from the north also enters the building, then reemerges and continues south, following the southern road.

Well before we reach it, a man has emerged from the front door, a fur cap with ear flaps, buttoning his coat as he runs and stumbles towards us. He reaches us, shouting happily up at Curly, then walks alongside, directly in our dust, escorting us to the station. He is looking in the window at us, face gawped in grin, waving to us repeatedly, so that we must answer his wave half a dozen times. I see that tears are streaming his joyful face.

We crawl out, patting the trip dust off our coats, out of our beards, beating our hats against our legs, unkinking our stiff backs, stamping our frozen feet on the hard ground. He ushers us in to the welcome of a hot stove, takes our coats from us, thrusts steaming tin cups of coffee at us, burning our hands and our lips on the metal, the whole room filled with the savory smell of fresh buffalo steaks cooking. Thanksgiven, he says. He sits us at the rough table, neatly set, and while we eat he stands and watches us, thrilled, like a child looking at his new Christmas presents, though the only gift we have for him is our brief human presence, before we carry on in our different directions.

I bid Curly, and my two fellow passengers—friends now, after two weeks of travel—adieu, and the coach, which seemed to roll so slowly when we were in it, is out of sight and hearing within minutes, and there is no sound but the steady wind whistling in the overhead wires. I turn to my host—I will be staying overnight, my connecting coach arriving the next day noon—and he is not looking down the now empty road. He is frankly staring at me, a smile hovering about his mouth, with something of the expectancy of a new groom regarding his fresh bride. I feel a little stirring of alarm, though I am certain the man is quite harmless.

Will you have more to eat? he asks eagerly.

I couldn't force in another bite, thank you very much.

My pleasure, my pleasure. No need to thank me. More coffee, then?

Yes, that would be lovely, I say (I am already sloshing).

We sit across from each other at the table. With his bulky cap and coat off, my host is a small slight mostly bald man. He watches me for any least chance to serve me, leaps to the stove to set a straw ablaze to light my cigar.

He cannot seem to stop talking.

O it's lonely lonely here, he says, then bursts out laughing.

I can well imagine.

You can't. No no I didn't mean that to sound so short and dismissing. I am sure you are a compassionate, deep imagining man, I can see it in the kindness of your eyes. But you simply can't. Nothing here to see, day in day out. The stages come by once or twice a week while the roads are open, but in winter—O, it's too terrible. Nothing, my friend, nothing. The howling wind. The endless blizzards. There is a strong rope that leads to the outhouse, though it is only fifty paces from here. It looks ridiculous now, but in another month, when the snows come, it will be dire necessity. You cling to it all the way out, and cling to it all the way back. Take your hand off it in a white-out blizzard and at once you lose direction. You can't see even your feet and you lose sense of up and down, so that you topple over. O it's too—ridiculous! Again he bursts out laughing.

I have my mouth open to say, How do you keep your sanity? but thinking better of it, say, Have you no partner here?

Ha, that is a story indeed. I had a partner when I first came here. In fact, he taught me everything. I could no more send or receive a wire than talk to the man in the moon, but he taught me. I came in, just like you, on the stage one day. Well, I had no job, no real prospects, so he convinced me to stay. In our very first winter together, he went out one night for a call of nature, and I never saw hide nor hair again. I suspect he wandered off on purpose, the skunk, just so's not to face it anymore. Anyway, I found out next spring he made it to an Indian village, where he spent the winter. But nothing could ever drag him back here again. Me, I went through the rest of that endless winter—I remember it as almost always night-time—completely alone. All that kept mind together was the messages coming in for me to transmit onwards, and the answers returning. That world of ticking sounds under my finger became like my family. I became like a blind man with only my sense of touch and hearing to connect me to the outside. But a wonderful sort of blind man who could be in all places at once, hear everybody talking everywhere. The next summer I got me an Indian woman to stay here, not very bright or very good looking, but a sweet enough soul. But in the winter when I needed her most, she up and died on me, and I was alone again. The summers are not so bad, because sometimes, like now, I get a soul to talk to—And say! What a treat you are!—but the winters! O! O! O!—and here is another one sprang upon us. Wait! Here's a call coming in.

I hear the loud tickety-tack. He rushes to his desk, takes the stub of pencil off his ear, and begins writing down characters on his notepad. Then he is tappity-tapping on his own big finger key. He waits, more tickety-tack, more writing, then he turns to me, a broad smile on his face.

It was for you, he says. They got a heavy snow up north—early this year—and your coach will be delayed a couple of days till they can dig out. Cross your fingers. If they get more snow and can't get through, there won't be no more runs till next spring.

The bitter smell of coffee awakes me. He is shoving the tin cup into my face. There is a candle lit on the table, and the fire is roaring, though he must have built it up quiet as a mouse to keep from disturbing me. It is still crisp in the room, and the sun is not up so it should be pitch dark out, but instead there is a sort of curious luminescence from the windows, a cold glowing. The wind has stopped and it is utterly still.

You'd better come have a look at this, my host says. He still has that smile playing about his mouth, the bride-groom eagerness. I struggle into my trousers, my bare feet on the frozen floor, and come with him to the window and look out.

Immense soft white flakes are curving down swiftly. They are already four inches deep on the railing outside. The sky is brightening, but there is absolutely nothing to see except sheet after sheet of swirling flakes until all is lost in an amorphous whiteness.

By noon it is a foot of snow with no surcease, by sunset two feet, and the flakes are falling even faster as I make another trip to the outhouse, my boots going clear to the ground through the soft wet snow at every step. I spend the day pacing the four corners of the tiny cabin, trying to stifle my panic. I have already read twenty times till I have memorized it the stage schedule, which seems to be the only reading matter in the building. How could I have been so stupid, so improvident? How can I even contemplate six months in this worse than a penitentiary? My host watches me eagerly, rushing to serve me any way he can. That old expression, "keeping body and soul together," has suddenly a problematical cast.

I toss and turn all night thinking: This early freak of storm will melt off in a day or two and I can still escape, but each time I sneak over to the window, it is still pouring out of the heavens. By morning it is four feet deep, and though there was little to see before in the wide empty plain, now there is nothing whatever, a mere blank and formless white clear to the extent of vision. I sit by the fire in stunned despair, refusing breakfast, and then dinner, only drinking coffee, and gnawing at a piece of biskett to save gnawing at my own knuckle.

My host is busy. Calls are coming in constantly for him to relay north or south, east or west, people stranded in the sudden storm, connections missed, meetings aborted, a wedding cancelled.

I am a reading man, I say in agony, is there nothing whatever in this cabin to read?

His eyes light up, and he goes at once to his cedar chest, rummages frantically, throwing out clothing in all directions, comes up with a large cloth package, unties the strings fastening it, reaches in and comes up with his treasure—and a true treasure it seems when I realize what it is. It is an immense family Bible. A whole great nation's compendium of wisdom and philosophy and morality which, such is the state of my spiritual nature, I had never been able to read past the begats. Here indeed is hope I could spend some of my time profitably. He pulls the table over by the fire, pulls up the most comfortable chair to it, and sets the great heavy tome flat on the table, and brings the lanthorn up by it.

I am in no hurry. I mean to savor every word, mull it over, draw from it its full substance, chew it and digest it. I open to the title page, where it is inscribed with his family name, and with the date of purchase, going back to a time before we were the United States. And there, one after the other, the names of various of his antecedents, all on the male side, and later on, to judge by the dates, brothers of his, and finally his own name some three or four times, and after each signature, the date, and a solemn pledge never again to imbibe in spiritous liquors.

I turn to page one, and read: In the beginning God created the heav'n & the earth. & the earth was without form, & voyde; & darkness was upon the face of the deep. & the Spirit of God moved upon the face of the waters.

*   *   *

It stops snowing for a few days, but it does not melt. Only, the four feet settles into one foot, and develops sufficient crust that it will support our snowshoes and we can tramp about with a gun looking for game, though there is none. Then it snows more feet, then settles, and so on. Each morning one or other of us digs out the back door and the path to the outhouse. There is a covered porch that leads to the barn with our food supplies and fuel (dried buffalo chips). The front door is blocked by drifted snow which comes half way up the windows, reducing what little light there is from outside.

I am once more bogged down in the begats. My host knows from his experience that it is best for us to pursue our separate occupations, only coming together to talk at meals, and after supper at night when we sit together about the fire. He is surprisingly busy relaying messages during the day. In quiet moments he rolls and smokes cigarettes and sits by the partially occluded window. I scribble notes in my notebooks, try to plow forward in the Bible. We make shift to pass the day, he much better at it than I. At meals now he is serene and I am the one who cannot stop talking. We have told each other every last wrinkle of our life histories. He seems tranquilly happy at the unexpected boon of my company. For my own part I feel, at moments, a scream starting from somewhere deep in my bowels. I think, if I hear one more tapity tap from his tinny machine I will launch my head through each of his window panes in turn. I envision lifting up the stove and shaking its burning faggots out on the floor. I daydream artillery barrages.

He is sensitive to my moods, watching me from the tail of his eye. I stand up with the idea of taking the shotgun outside and merely firing it off. He rises too, with a smile, and says, Come here, you might as well learn how this operates.

I am told about inventor Samuel F.B. Morse[1] and his ingenious international code based on long and short sounds electrically transmitted down hundreds of miles of wire. At each point where resistance in the wire begins to slow and weaken the signal, there is a relay station where an operator "reads" the message, then sends it off fresh on a new wire to continue its journey. In this way virtually instantaneous communication can connect thousands of square miles of territory, in time our entire nation.

He takes a page of my notebook, and with his pencil writes down the code for me. A . __ ; B __ . . . ; C __ . __ . ; and so on. I have a quick memory and study it all day until I have it by heart. Now I listen with new interest to the tickety tack, but it is too fast, I can't catch the rhythm, I can't break in to see where it starts and stops. He laughs at my frustration—I was the same, he says. In a quiet moment he says: get your pad and take this—and with his pencil he taps a message on the wood of the table, slowly and carefully. He has to repeat it several times before I get it all.

W-H-A-T-H-A-T-H-G-O-D-W-R-O-U-G-H-T

Then I try, and, haltingly, referring back to my notebook, I send the same message back to him, then again, doing it swifter.

The next morning there is a purpose to get up. I sit at the desk beside him, taking down the messages on my own notepad, then comparing with him. At first I only get a letter or a word here and there, but then more and more. Finally I get an entire message perfectly. He jumps to his feet, I jump to my feet, and we embrace.

---

[1] Samuel F.B. Morse (1791–1872) developed the electric telegraph (beginning in 1832) and the "Morse Code" system for the transmission of messages.

You've got the calling, he says. Those with the calling catch on at once, the others never.

We send messages back and forth by pencil tapping, and finally he says I am ready to transmit a message. The first is a botch, I am so frightened and tentative on the big electric key, and he has to come in after me and re-send it. But then I get the touch—he's right, I do have a gift—and I am able to send slowly and accurately, then faster, not so fast as him by a long-shot, but tolerable.

One day he says, you're my partner now. I'm not afraid to obey a call of nature, or take a snooze, or go out scouting for game, because I know you are here to back me.

To prove it he leaves me for an hour to ramble around on his snow shoes, and messages start coming in at once, and a couple of times I have to ask for repeats, and a couple of times I have to apologize and make a second transmission, and at first I am sweating profusely—but by the time he gets back I feel competent and professional.

Nevertheless it is a long time before I am relaxed enough to begin paying attention to the messages themselves. At first they are mere alphabetical counters I am receiving and relaying on, and that takes every ounce of my concentration. But little by little they begin to flesh out into words, become voices that I hear in my head almost as I hear spoken voices. The speakers begin to take on human form in my mind. And—since we have no sense of the passage of time here, and our minds seem to sleep between transmissions—even though answers come a day or several days after an original message, in our senses, suspended in our memories, the replies seem to come close after, as if we were overhearing actual conversations.

TO ED WOBURN AT FT CLAPTON HAPPY BIRTHDAY THIS DAY YOUR FOND BROS TOM MOSE JOSIAH WALTER

TO ANYONE INDIAN TERRITORY WORD OF MY HUSBAND JIM THOMPSON REWARD ELIZ THOMPSON

TO ANYONE FT CLAPTON AREA OR SOUTH WIDOW 38 HARD WORKER SAVINGS LOOK ALRIGHT PLUMP SEEK MAN W LAND PURP MATRIMONY FLO BUSKIRK

TO RICK CRUM AT PAWNY CORNERS CANT GET THRO SNOW SEE YOU NEXT YR BIG DRINKING PARTY THEN SAM

TO FLO BUSKIRK AT FT LEAVENWORTH[2] AM 33 HAVE 138 ACR SOME CATTLE HORSES PROSPECTS GOOD SLIGHT LIMP FT CLAPTON AREA ED WOBURN

TO FLO BUSKIRK AT FT LEAVENWORTH HAVE 5000 ACR MANY CAT-TLE HORSES TANNERY MILL GOOD WATER FT CLAPTON AREA AM 73 CY MCCLINTOCK

TO FLO BUSKIRK AT FT LEAVENWORTH AM 21 GOOD LOOKING PAWNY CORNERS AREA BUY LAND W YR SAVINGS RICK CRUM

Wait, my host says. Don't send those last three on.

What do you mean?

We've got to think about them first. If you sent her the one of that probably

[2] Fort Leavenworth on the Missouri in northeast Kansas was constructed in 1827 to guard the Oregon Trail. The town of Leavenworth, a freighting center for the West, developed nearby.

worthless flighty pup Rick Crum, think what will happen. She's newly widowed. I
know what that's like when your mate is suddenly gone. You're no longer getting
what your body is used to, your blood is up in you. She might make a terrible
mistake.

I start laughing. So—what?—do we only send on the one from the well-heeled
Cy McClintock?

No. That's no good either. After her loss, she may be down, she may have lost
confidence in the future, she might make a cautious choice for the old geezer,
and get trapped into a marriage with no tenderness in it.. She's still relatively
young. It's got to be Ed Woburn. He's a good man. See how much his brothers
like him. Just send that one on.

You can't be serious! We don't know any of this. "Slight limp" may mean
wooden leg. We can't take this kind of responsibility for someone else's life. We
just have to send the offers on and let her make her own choice. People have to
be free to make their own mistakes. That's what life's about.

You don't know this place as well as I do. That's not how we work things here.
This is my relay station.

TO JAY CHALMERS AT COTTONWOOD GROVE DADDY SO GLAD TO
HEAR YOU ARE ALIVE AND WELL WHEN CAN YOU RETURN ALWAYS
LOVE YR DTR CLEMINTINE

Don't send that one either.
Why, for goodness' sake?
I'll answer it from here, he says. And while I watch stupified he taps out:

TO CLEMINTINE CHALMERS IN ST. LOUIS CANT COME THIS YR MY
DEAR CAUGHT BY EARLY SNOW NEXT SPRING FOR SURE FONDLY
DADDY.

He looks at me sheepishly. She's been sending inquiries for her Dad for a year.
He's dead out there somewhere, or abandoned her. I couldn't stand her waiting
so piteously for him, so I—well I manufactured some answers from him.

What're you going to do if he really answers sometime?

That already happened on another case, a woman looking for her husband.
What a nightmare.

Do you mean you do this all the time?

Do you think I've probably made a mistake? he asks.

I sure do, I say, then wish I hadn't answered so quick when I see his face wince
with pain and fear, and then slowly sort of cave in.

I didn't intend it to be that way. (To my astonishment he is blubbering, in
tears.) I just wanted to help, to be encouraging, to do something to ward off the
god-awful loneliness and isolation. Now I've got dozens of them, whole families
I've invented and put into contact, marriages that are going forward or being
restored when one or other probably don't exist. I'm in so deep I can't get out of
it anymore, I have to keep inventing more and more people in a big web and
somehow keep them all separated from each other, and separated in my own
mind. Once I caught myself making up a reply to another person I had made up.
O me, what have I done.

He drops his head into his hands and looks so desolated I reach around and pat
his shoulder.

Then he throws his head back up.

You were absolutely right, he says, I should have left them free in the first place. What do you figure I should do now?

Well, for a start, don't do any new ones. And for the others—and the whole great complex mess of it suddenly comes present to me, and I cannot stop a groan, which my host, who has been hanging eagerly to my words, matches, and sinks his head back down on the table again—For the others, I go on, I guess you can't say anything now, but you'll just have to start disengaging 'em. Kill off this one, marry off that one.

O that's so easy to say, he moans, but how can I really do it? These are human beings I have got myself involved with, how can I let them down so brutally?

You've just got to, I say. We'll work on it together. I'll stand by you, and we'll think of something case by case.

I've got a call of nature, he says, and heads for the door.

Your coat and hat, I say. (The blizzard has been blowing nonstop for two days.)

O. Yes, he says, and puts them on.

He pulls the door open, snow swirling in and scattering across the floor, then closes it carefully behind him.

As soon as he is gone, calls start coming in.

TO FLO BUSKIRK AT FT LEAVENWORTH AM 41 WIDOWER HAVE LAND W WATER CATTLE SOME WHEAT AT CEDAR SPRS NR CLAPTON AREA HARD WORK BUT GOOD LIFE WE HAVE BOTH BEEN HURT BUT WE CAN START AGAIN PLEASE COME JIM THOMPSON

That one sounds so good I am sure my host would have no objection to it, so I relay it forward. I had not yet sent the other three proposals, and I catch myself thinking, there will be no harm waiting a bit longer, till she has had a chance to respond to this good one. But I realize I am falling into the same trap my host fell into, and so I send those three as well, giving her all four to make up her own mind about. But I admit to myself I am pulling for Jim Thompson.

More calls come in.

TO ANYONE INDIAN TERRITORY WORD OF MY HUSBAND JIM THOMPSON REWARD ELIZ THOMPSON

I have relayed it forward before the import strikes me like a blow to the head. That son of a bitch conniving bigamist Jim Thompson! Where is my host now? We've got to discuss this one.

But he does not come in. It's been a hour.

He wouldn't! That's not funny.

I put on my coat and hood and wrap my muffler about my face, leaving only the tiniest slit for my eyes. I pull open the door. New snow has already drifted in deep. The pathway is already nearly filled in, with almost no trace of his footsteps. The wind is blowing hard pellets of snow-ice directly into me, striking me like gravel. I get the door closed and plough my way forward, clinging to the lifeline with one mitten. Close to my eyes I can see the flurrying movement of the driving pellets, but farther than a foot from my eyes I can see nothing. It is mid-day, but it might as well be mid-night, except that instead of pitch dark it is snow white. I lose my vertical equilibrium and fall to the side, for a terrifying instant almost losing contact with the line, but my fingers get a death grip on it, and I pull myself back up, though up has little meaning for me. I flounder on. I am gasping, and every time my breath rushes out, it builds a little deeper mask of ice on the wool material of my muffler right before my nose and lips—and in my rising panic, that I seek to push back down, I wonder if I am slowly walling myself into a cage of my own frozen breath. I feel I have gone a mile forward, though I know the line is scarce thirty yards. I want very much to turn back, but that will answer nothing, so I continue doggedly forward, until my head strikes with a bump against the door of the outhouse. I have to dig with my hands now to clear a little space to drag the door open. I feel about inside even putting my hand the length of my arm down the hole itself. Empty. Empty. The scream is inside me like a bubble moving about in my body for an opening out of which to discharge itself.

My own path has already filled in, but it is easier returning to the cabin with the wind behind me. I have to brush away the snow that has blown inside the door before I have room to shut it fast. I hear the tickety tacking as I pull off my stiff coat and throw it to the floor. I am already taking it down in my head before I get to my pad of paper and begin writing it.

> TO JIM THOMPSON AT CEDAR SPRS HAVE 1000 FROM LIFE INS YES I HAVE BEEN HURT BUT I HEAR KINDNESS IN YR VOICE HOPING FLO BUSKIRK

Grimly, I relay the message on, but every instinct tells me I should not have.

The answer when it comes is so cynical I cannot force my fingers onto the key, cannot enter into complicity with him in that way, so at least for the time being I set the message aside:

> TO FLO BUSKIRK AT FT LEAVENWORTH 1ST BREAK IN SNOW I COME TO FT LEAVENWORTH IF I SUIT WE CAN MARRY TRANSFER FUNDS ETC I HEAR YR BEAUTIFUL SOUL YR JIM

I hear a scratching at the wall, my heart leaps and I race to the door, but it is not my host returned, it is a rat trying to scratch his way in. The walls and the ceiling are filled with them. We hear them all night trying to get in when we are trying to sleep. And when the wind stops for a moment, the wolves commence howling in the most hideous manner. We see nothing outside anymore, the snow drifted above the tops of the windows.

I come back and look at Jim Thompson's diabolically clever hypocritical messages to that trusting woman, I brood over his treatment of both those trusting women, his deserted wife still seeking him, fearing he is in trouble. Anger flares up in me, and I take action.

> TO ELIZ THOMPSON IN ST LOUIS REGRET INFORM HUSBAND JIM THOMPSON DIED HERO SAVING CHILDREN FROM INDIANS LAST WORDS I LOVE YOU ELIZ PLEASE START NEW LIFE A FRIEND JOHN RINDO
> TO FLO BUSKIRK AT FT LEAVENWORTH YOU FAT COW 1000 NOT ENOUGH WIRE WHEN YOU HAVE 10000 JIM THOMPSON

I am thinking, How could my host be so selfish? I need him here. I need to talk to him.

> TO JOHN RINDO AT PLAINS CROSSING YOU SOUND NICE CAN I COME TO YOU IN SPRING FOR ADVICE RE STARTING NEW LIFE YR NEW FRIEND ELIZ THOMPSON

Hm, that was a short period of mourning. Perhaps there was more equality in that marriage than I suspected.

Then a message comes down from the far north, with a notation that it has already been forwarded down from farther north from the Athabasca.[3]

> TO ELIZ THOMPSON DEAREST AM ALIVE AND WELL CDNT WRITE WHILE A FAILURE BUT NOW IVE HIT IT LEAD AND SILVER WE ARE ON EASY STREET DID IT ALL FOR YOU COMING BACK TO MY DARLING IN THE SPRING ALWAYS FAITHFUL LOVE JIM

I pace round and round the four corners of the single room. It is abundantly clear that Jim Thompson cannot send messages to widow Buskirk from nearby Cedar Springs, and at the same time send messages to his wife Elizabeth from up in the high Athabasca, and be one and the same person. He could however send both these messages if he was in fact two unrelated, and perhaps quite decent and honorable people who happen to share, by coincidence, the same name.

This comes next:

> TO FLO BUSKIRK AT FT LEAVENWORTH WHY HAVEN'T YOU REPLIED ALL I HAVE I WANT TO SHARE W YOU EAGERLY JIM

Now how do I send that one on? Especially when this comes:

> TO CY MCCLINTOCK AT FT CLAPTON AM SERIOUSLY CONSIDERING YR PROPOSAL PLEASE SEND MORE DETAILS LAND AND HOLDINGS RESPECTFULLY FLO BUSKIRK

I try this:

> TO ELIZ THOMPSON REGRET TERRIBLE MISTAKE BUT HAPPY OUT-COME YR HUSBAND ALIVE AND WELL DIFFERENT JIM THOMPSON KILLED YOU WILL HEAR FROM TRUE HUSBAND SHORTLY WITH GOOD NEWS SINCERELY JOHN RINDO

The rats scratch at the walls, the ceiling, under the floor, trying to get in. The tickety tacking starts up again.

> TO JOHN RINDO AT PLAINS CROSSING YOU STILL SOUND NICE HUS-BAND ALWAYS A FAILURE CRAMPS MY STYLE MUST SEE YOU SOONEST DEAR BOY THINKING OF MY NEW LIFE FONDLY ELIZ THOMPSON

I do not feel very happy about it, but it is time to send forward his news of lead and silver and easy street. I do so. The next message is not long in coming, and not unexpected.

[3] A lake and river in the Rocky Mountains of Alberta, Canada.

TO JOHN RINDO AT PLAINS CROSSING FORGET ALL FORMER COR-
RESPONDENCE MY WONDERFUL HUSBAND RETURNING I AM SO
HAPPY RESPECTFULLY ELIZ THOMPSON

Is what I create worse than what I leave alone? Should I never have started?
Should I refuse to go on? Around about is the white whirling chaos of the void, the
bitter cold of non-being. Is that better, as my host evidently came to believe? My
host frozen into whiteness himself, unless he made it to the Indians. The small
gnawing animals scurry in the walls and chew chew chew to breach the thin
envelope into my warm room.

The tickety tack is going again.

TO JAY CHALMERS AT COTTONWOOD GROVE DADDY LIFE IS SO
HARD PLEASE MY FATHER SPEAK TO ME ELSE HOW CAN I KNOW YOU
EXIST ALWAYS LOVE YR DTR CLEMINTINE

[1991]

Louise Erdrich *1954–*

MAUSER

You had to know Travis Houpart not to like him, that was the thing. When people first encountered him, women especially, they thought they'd met a man worth meeting. The mustache was so trim, that reassuring dark brown, then the Christlike eyes, clear as scorched butter. The whole of him was so regular-featured and even-toned that the voice was no surprise, warm and crisp as a newscaster's, telling mild jokes and deflecting any question you might ask.

He bought me a drink on a night I needed one, a night I was down.

"You shouldn't be alone." And there he was. He wore a clean white shirt, short-sleeved. His forearms were tanned and muscular, the left one a darker brown from poking out the truck window.

"Hi, Travis."

"Where's your boyfriend?"

I told him, although he knew.

"The guy's crazy." Travis's defense of me was so blunt and sincere I sort of believed in it, or at least appreciated that someone cared enough to put on the act. I'd been dropped for a woman who also worked for the firm. Travis had followed me into the bar to present himself as the consolation prize, except that he was pure liability. I pushed the drink away.

"I'm not going to do anything stupid, I swear," he said. He lifted one hand, looked at me, all solemn.

"I'm not going to do anything stupid either."

He put down his hand and ducked his head, craned toward me as if he was looking into a small, dark room.

"To be honest . . ." He rubbbed his eyes, as if to adjust his vision, and then put his fingers to his brow. "I was kind of hoping that you would."

"You're getting a couple of gray hairs here." I touched above my ear. "Distinguished."

"My wife says so, too."

That meant the bullshit was behind us. From talking to other women, I knew that once Travis mentioned his wife the conversation got more realistic.

"I do appreciate you coming over," I said. "Really, the drink and all. But, anyway, what's new with you? With Mauser?"

All of a sudden Travis looked depressed. His shirt wrinkled as his shoulders slumped. The expression on his face sagged. The lines along his mouth deepened and his mouth pinched; a sour indignation formed.

"You might say I'd like to kill the guy," he offered. "I just can't stand the type. My dad was like that. Military-minded. Do this. Do that."

"Well, he is your boss," I pointed out.

Travis looked at me, all puzzled, like what did that have to do with it?

Mauser and Travis had reached a kind of stalemate. Their horns were locked, and as they stared into each other's eyes they pawed themselves deeper into the earth. Mauser had the edge some days, and Travis's purchase on their turf improved on others. From the outside, the match seemed hardly even; you had to know the background. The firm itself, general road improvement and construction, belonged to Jack Mauser, a huge, flat-stomached Welsh-German. Dressing down employees on the work site, he combined the drama of a Richard Burton[1] delivery with raw Teutonic[2] rage. His angers were explosive and foul, much feared, although his good favor was avidly sought as well.

Mauser was a fair-minded man, but he had a streak of irrational vulnerability: he adored his one sister in the world, Rhonda, pampered her as though she made up for the wife and children that he didn't have. She'd married Travis, a laid-back good-time boy with high-school basketball trophies rusting on top of the TV, and girlfriends, lots of those. Rhonda worshipped him nonetheless, and she had to be protected. At least Travis worked where Mauser could keep an eye on him; there was no question of firing the man. And so Travis became as much a part of things as anyone, even though his only job was to haul gravel, asphalt, sand, whatever was needed. Travis worked with false eagerness, expending a lot of visible energy, jumping in and out of the cab, kicking tires, talking long and hard. But by the end of the day, without fail, he had always hauled by many tons the least amount. He would not have lasted a week anywhere but at Jack Mauser's. His brother-in-law knew this fact, and hated it.

The candy-apple-red Cadillac that was, besides Rhonda, the only thing in this world that Mauser truly loved raised a gray plume of dust that hung in the air and turned a ruddy pink, reflecting the morning sky. Sunrises in the dry autumn west of Sioux Falls[3] were spectacular. We saw them all. At Mauser's, everybody, even the payroll clerks, started work at 7 A.M. and went until whenever. The push was on. There was so much to do before snow and the first hard frost. It was the best time of the year in many ways for Jack Mauser, who forced his Caddie to feats of quick driving and exhorted, managed, raged from site to site, screaming at what was yet to be done as contract deadlines approached. For Travis, of course, this time of year was the worst. No one around him had time to shoot the shit. There was an overriding panic in the air, an aura of strain. No one had time to sit and smoke or to drink a Pepsi from the cooler on the passenger's side of Travis's truck. People kept their ears cocked, their heads turned. Mauser could spin out of nowhere, at any time, a streak of dire color. Charges had been brought against him two years ago—assault and battery on an employee over a minor slipup in the gravel-to-sand mixture. It was not just the drama of his rage people feared; it was the actuality of Jack Mauser's temper, the rock of his fists, the pleasure that anger gave him.

I did my job well, so I never ran foul of him. He and Travis could kill each other and be done with it, for all that I cared at the time.

My office was at the far end of a trailer. I practically had my own bathroom, and nobody bothered me past nine, which is when I shut my door to drink a cup of tea with honey and stare into the screen of my computer. It was maybe noon, a day I was far into the payroll, when the trailer bounced on its concrete blocks and Travis walked into my room.

"Can I be straight with you?" he asked.

"Not if you want your paycheck."

"I don't care about that. Here."

He took a short chain from his pocket, bent forward, took my wrist, and snapped it on. There was a charm attached to the bracelet, a little silver bird. I looked at the thing as it rested on my wrist. It was the kind of gesture that just stops you. In

---

[1] Richard Burton (1925–1984), the British actor.   [2] Germanic.
[3] A small city of 80,000 in southeastern South Dakota.

the moment of my hesitation Travis leaned over and put his lips right where a doctor takes your pulse. I spread my fingers wide and pushed his face away.

"Get out of here," I said.

But I kept the charm. Remember, I'd just been burned by a man without any. It helped to have Travis, so attractive on the outside, turn his attentions to me. People don't change, I told myself, so don't expect more. If he's flirting behind his wife's back, he will do the same to you.

"This thing was stamped like a million others from a piece of tin," I told myself that night when I took it off. The next morning, before work, I put it back on. I am not kidding when I say my former boyfriends had not been all that attractive. I go for the unusual in men, and people with good looks get generalized early in life, too well defined to have any character of interest. I need character. You see, I am a person you cannot tell had surgery. Had teeth fixed. Worked very hard at looking nice. It sharpens you, growing up as the last person anyone ever noticed in a classroom. I guess I looked down on pretty people, and I know that I was right about that if Travis was an example.

Look how empty: he was living off his wife's brother's good will. At the same time he was making moves on me. Look how vain: when he knew Mauser wasn't anywhere in range he would kill the engine of his truck, get out, stretch. He always did this in front of my window in the accounts trailer. He made sure to stand within a woman's gaze, because it magnified him, warmed him. He fed, like a bee on syrup, on female admiration.

Given all that, why did I find myself thinking about Travis? Why, the day before Mauser came around to check the weights and measurements and sign the pay-checks, did I protect Travis? Without letting him know, I changed his tonnage. I made him look useful. It was a kind of insurance that he would be kept on. I did this even though I knew that the yellow copy of the unchanged original was already over in the files in Sioux Falls. Files that sat around in cardboard boxes or served as coffee tables, true, but files that were accurate records.

It got bad. I would wake up in the middle of the night, hungry. I had two rooms. I would walk into the other and open the refrigerator and stare into the cold, bright box, thinking of Travis Houpart. Those deep-brown eyes, sad, but of course I would light them up. Those smooth arms taut with muscle. How did he get strong? He never lifted anything.

I was reaching for the milk one night, a glass to calm me down and put me back to sleep, when the phone rang.

I let it ring. But it sounded so loud, so unreal, that I picked it up and held the receiver carefully to my ear.

"Please, I've got to see you."

"Fine," I said. "Tomorrow."

My voice shook as I put the receiver down. I waited. It rang again.

"No," said Travis. "I want to see you now."

Was it like I thought it would be? Worse—it was better. For me, those nights were like floating before you've learned how to swim. As long as I held my breath and stretched out my arms and legs, I stayed up. But when I needed to breathe I sank in a swirl of panic.

"I'm not the kind of person who can afford to get hurt," I told Travis.

He murmured, turned toward me in a sleep I thought was fake. I leaned over him and pinned his arm down and spoke into his face.

"Don't hurt me."

"What the hell do you mean? You're hurting *me*."

Did I visualize Travis ditching Rhonda, and him and me joining till death did us part? Did I pretend this role was satisfying? Did I need so little? Maybe I just wanted the chance to leave somebody first for once, to have the pleasure and not the illusions. They were there all the same, though; somehow I'd got it into my head that I meant something to this guy. Because it can happen. Clichés in love songs. Roses, violets, little tin birds. Sometimes you can't think fast enough to keep them from getting to you.

I was in my office around ten, waiting for the boss. I heard the steps, the door opened, but it was Travis with a can of cold soda pop in his hand.

"What do you want?"

I was nervous, shut the door behind him.

Travis put the can on my desk and then came around the side to pick me up. He wanted to put me on the desk top, too. But I can make myself heavier than I look, and I slumped down, unwilling. He tried to pull me up, to push me, but it was lots of trouble, and he started to pant with the effort.

"Come on. Help," he said.

I laughed, then I heard the set of steps that for sure were Mauser's, and I twisted sideways. "Let go."

He didn't. He held me in front of him and put his hands on me, looking over my shoulder in expectation, and that was when I saw he had decided on the spur of the moment to use me to get to Mauser. I was a prop, a plastic blow-up companion, a partner easily disposed of. His real relationship was not with me, or maybe any woman, but with Mauser. Like a dad to him. Like a brick wall.

The door opened. I punched my fists against Travis so hard he grinned. Then I kicked. At once, Travis fell away, doubled over in the corner of the room. I whirled around, but the door had shut, and already I could hear the red Cadillac accelerating. I didn't look at Travis. I sat down at my desk and rubbed my arms. They felt bruised and sore, and I was tired, so very tired. A wave of sleep washed over me, the sudden urge to sink against the desk, and it was all I could do to keep sitting upright.

"Come on." Travis stood behind me. "It was a joke."

He put his hands on my shoulders, began to knead the muscles of my back. He leaned over, put his hand on the desk for balance. I stapled it. Or I mean I tried to, because of course I was too awkward to really get his hand under the black handle of the instrument. He backed off.

"That was a joke, too," I said.

Jack Mauser fired me fair and square, I'll give him that. Two days went by and I thought perhaps he had been able to accept what only became true at the last possible moment: that I was resisting advances. He went back through the files, however, and found the figures that I'd falsified in Travis's favor. The notice was on my desk on Thursday morning: "Be gone by one." I left at eleven. I was on the road leading from the site when I saw Travis's truck approaching. I could see it clearly. The cab was yellow and green—crop colors, garish.

I have a small car, a compact, but I moved into the middle of the road. I'm not so different from Mauser. When I love someone, that's it. You can drive me past a limit, too. This feeling had been building in me for the past two days, a wild fever that made me throw things at the wall and slam the door of my refrigerator so hard the seal popped. Now everything felt right. This was the moment, I decided. Travis had had things too easy in life so far. I jammed my foot on the gas, and kept going. The colors of his truck blurred. The road went by. Fields. Then we were too close. The grille of the truck loomed and Travis laid on the horn. I kept my hands steady on the wheel, locked my ankle, and Travis took the ditch with a full load of gravel.

He hung up on the far incline. I saw this once I'd stopped and remembered to breathe. I got out and walked back. He'd been travelling slow enough to negotiate the declivity, but the ground was soft where water had collected a month ago, and at once his back wheels sank into the hard muck just enough to keep him where he was, so that he could not escape from Mauser's Cadillac, spinning its plume out at a distance and approaching fast.

Travis got out and we looked at each other across the ditch. There was plenty of time to talk, but not enough to think of what to say. We saw Mauser screaming from his open window, and then, at the crossroad, he drove down into the shallow ditch. He rode its dry edges carefully, straddling the bottom until he got to Travis's truck and swung right up beside it on the driver's side. He jumped out with a crowbar in his fist.

"Gun it out, fuckhead."

You see a thunderhead building in the sky, a blistering rose color. You see boot-camp sergeants in bad movies. Mauser's rage was a combination. It was a natural disaster mixed with dumb old saws. It was dangerous. His voice popped and sang in three pitches. His face went purple and his neck bulged from the collar of his shirt. He puffed up like a bullfrog. Then he snapped.

Travis jumped into the cab and restarted the engine, but his wheels spun the ruts deeper. He tried rocking backward, but he was too heavy. He tried forward, but the nose of the truck was at too steep a pitch. And as he worked, Mauser swung the bar in the air, stamped his feet, and yelled so hard it looked like he'd split in half. I edged back to my car. I leaned against the rear window, and stayed, so I saw it all clearly. I saw the thought enter Travis's desperate head. I saw him think that he was simply too heavy. I saw him start the dump. The dump bed went up, but the tailgate had banged shut and did not release, so that the load, instead of flooding out the back, collected there. And slowly—I could see it happen—the weight began to lift the front wheels right up off the ground.

Mauser hopped in the air, shrieked like the noon whistle, but the loud whine of the hydraulic dump in Travis's ears seemed to hypnotize him. Up, up the truck went, until the gravel began to course over the rim of the sides, and then it was too late for everything. We all saw it at the same moment, I suppose, though only Mauser moved. He leaped to the passenger's-side door of the truck, and lifted his bar to break the window, but couldn't balance right as the truck settled back on its haunches and in slow motion listed sideways, groaning. Its shadow began to edge over the Cadillac parked snug against it. Then the truck went with its own weight and toppled the rest of the way, crushing the car.

Suddenly Mauser stood on top of the door, which was a solid floor beneath his feet. He looked down. Through the glass he must have seen Travis, looking back up at him, and beneath him the buckled roof of clear red. Things gave deep in the Cadillac's interior, perhaps the wheel or the glove-leather seats. There was a thud, a series of smaller thunks, gentler sounds than that first awful noise of metal crumpling. I guess it was the smallness of the sound that stopped Mauser. He stood on the pile of truck and man caught inside and flattened car underneath. Then he straightened up and looked around, as though he'd climbed there just to get the view. He squinted at the horizon, which was empty and quiet beyond the edge of the field. When Travis began to thrash around below him, pounding to get out, Mauser bent over with the crowbar. I thought he was going to pull his brother-in-law out, save him if only to beat him up. But instead of breaking in the window, Mauser pried the handle off the door. Then he climbed down off the cab of the truck and walked toward me.

Halfway to where I waited, he threw the iron bar down in the yellow grass. He kept the door handle in his hand, though, as if something would attach to it, and when we stood across from one another he extended the handle to me, as if it was up to me to make sense of what had happened.

"Is he O.K.?" I asked.

He took the door handle back, then nodded his big, rough head.

"Not a scratch."

He walked around to the passenger's side of my car. We both got in at the same time, and I began to drive away from the accident. When we stopped at the four-way light in town, I looked at Mauser for directions, and he looked back at me, giving none. So we idled there. One car and then another went around us, honking, and still we looked at each other for a clue.

"You feel sorry for him? Think I should go back?"

"No," I said. "Of course not. He was a mistake."

"O.K. Pull over there. I'm hungry."

He pointed to a seafood quick-stop. Obedient, I switched lanes and pulled in. About that time, I must have gotten tired of them all, because when the drive-up intercom wasn't working right I said to Mauser, "You get out. You give the order. You're the voice of authority."

He was a man of solid worth and deep attachments, Mauser. He had a temper, but I didn't have to fear it anymore. I just drove off. I was beginning to like this new habit of leaving men in odd positions. Last I saw, he was talking earnestly to a square of beige plastic under a sign that advertised the fried things you could eat that were trawled from the sea.

[1991]

II

POETRY

II

POETRY

4

❧❧❧❧❧❧❧

What Is Poetry?

What is poetry? One modern poet, perhaps a little vexed by this question, replied that poetry, unlike prose, is a form of writing in which few lines run to the edge of the page. Although this half-facetious response may have been intended to force the questioner to formulate his or her own definition of poetry, it also expresses how difficult it is to distinguish between poetry and prose on any grounds other than their appearance on the printed page. All imaginative literature—whether poetry, prose, or drama—is primarily concerned with human feelings and attitudes. This is why literature is one of the humanities. And nearly all great literature tries to recreate human experiences that involve the reader emotionally and intellectually. What then makes poetry unique and important? What *is* poetry?

Let us begin our study of poetry by considering a sentence in prose: "So much depends upon a red wheelbarrow, glazed with rain water, beside the white chickens." After a brief puzzled frown, few readers would give that sentence a second thought. It is certainly not a poem. Or is it? When the words are arranged somewhat differently on paper, they do take on the appearance of poetry:

THE RED WHEELBARROW

so much depends
upon

a red wheel
barrow

glazed with rain
water

beside the white
chickens.

645

In fact, this is a very well-known poem, written by William Carlos Williams and published in 1923.

Only two things have changed: we now know that the words were written by a well-known poet, and their arrangement on paper is different. Perhaps in principle we should not be influenced by our knowledge of the author's name. After all, a good poem should be able to stand on its own merits. In practice, however, we *do* look more closely at words—even apparently ordinary words—if we know that they were written by a famous poet. Hence Robert Frost once contended that "poetry is the kind of thing poets write."

If "The Red Wheelbarrow" *is* a poem, then its poetic nature must somehow grow out of the interplay between the meaning of the words and their arrangement on paper. It turns out, in fact, that this relationship between form and content is one of the key characteristics of poetry. But how does the arrangement of these words—their *form*, if you will—relate to meaning in this particular case? First, we might notice that Williams's rearrangement of the words creates an intriguing visual pun. The first line, "so much depends," stands out all alone on the page. The rest of the poem quite literally "depends" on that line, in the original sense of *hanging down* from it. Note, too, how the first two lines constitute a *stanza*, a group of lines separated by white space from the other stanzas in the poem. That first stanza does not itself contain any imagery. The content of the poem—however "much" that is—all "depends" upon the first stanza both visually, grammatically, and logically.

Once we begin thinking about form, we might go on to note that there is a pleasing pattern of repetition in the lines. There are four stanzas. In each stanza the first line contains three words while the second line contains only one. Furthermore, Williams continues to play with visual effects. By breaking up the word *wheelbarrow* in the second stanza, Williams arrests the eye. As soon as we form the picture of a "red wheel" in our minds in line 3, line 4 instructs us to transform it into a "red wheel / barrow." The same sort of thing happens as the rain in line 5 becomes rain water in line 6. Throughout the poem in fact, the first line of each stanza depends upon the second to expand, complement, or even alter the meaning. Thus the form of the poem helps to communicate its message that all things in life are interdependent.

Obviously, "The Red Wheelbarrow" is not a typical poem, but surely any adequate definition of poetry must allow its inclusion. Hence, we can reach one conclusion about part of the definition of poetry: **a poem is a composition that makes you think about words and their arrangement.**

Furthermore, if "The Red Wheelbarrow" is a poem, we can reach five other conclusions about what poetry is not.

1.   Poetry is not always rhymed. "The Red Wheelbarrow" is unrhymed. Most of the great poetic passages in the plays of Shakespeare are unrhymed. Milton's *Paradise Lost* is unrhymed. So much of the poetry of the twentieth century is unrhymed that the return to traditional forms (including rhyme) by contemporary poets is seen as a surprising new trend.

2.   Poetry is not always metrical. While we have noted a pattern in the structure of "The Red Wheelbarrow," the lines do not sustain any particular rhythm. Despite Edgar Allan Poe's contention that "poetry is the rhythmical creation of beauty," formal rhythmic patterns, or meters, are no more necessary than rhyme in great poetry. A composition in meter and rhyme is entitled to be called verse, but not necessarily poetry. Nursery rhymes like "Jack and Jill" or "Twinkle, Twinkle Little Star" are not poetry; nor are the facile verses on greeting cards. Poetry is *often* metrical, but it need not always be.

3. Poetry is not always concerned with beauty. William Carlos Williams's lines on the red wheelbarrow may strike readers as funny, or pretentious, or simply matter-of-fact, but it is a rare reader who would cry out at the beauty of this description. Generally, the goal of a poet is to recreate human experience as vividly, powerfully, and originally as possible. Sometimes the poet seeks to make the words beautiful, as Edgar Allan Poe does in "Annabel Lee" (1850) or as John Keats does in his "Ode to a Nightingale" (1819). But often the subject of the poem itself is distinctly unbeautiful and the poem, in keeping with its subject, sounds harsh, grating, or downright ugly. How else could Wilfred Owen write about a mustard gas attack during World War I in "Dulce et Decorum Est" (1920)? How else could Jonathan Swift describe a grimy eighteenth-century street in "A Description of the Morning" (1709)?

4. Poetry is not always high-toned and moral. In "The Red Wheelbarrow" Williams makes what some may consider a pompous pronouncement about rain water and white chickens, but the moral significance of the lines—if indeed they have any—is certainly not apparent. Since great poetry always involves human perceptions and human experiences, there is perhaps always a moral and ethical dimension to poetry. Yet good poetry is rarely preachy. When Robert Browning, for example, describes a bizarre sexual strangulation in "Porphyria's Lover" (1836), or a cruel, tyrannical duke in "My Last Duchess" (1842), or a petty, spiteful monk in "Soliloquy of the Spanish Cloister" (1842), he lets the characters speak for themselves, and he lets the readers reach whatever moral conclusions they wish.

5. Poetry is not always profound. William Carlos Williams wrote only sixteen words in "The Red Wheelbarrow." Although most of us accept that poetry is more concentrated than ordinary speech, we expect too much if we expect great profundity from only sixteen words. Nevertheless, Williams does challenge us to think for ourselves about the significance of the wheelbarrow, the rain water, and the chickens. When we do so, we may well conclude with Thomas Dilworth that these three images "suggest the major components of agrarian life—which may, in turn, suggest all civilized life in its practical aspect. The wheelbarrow represents human labor and ingenuity; the chickens represent animals bred for human nourishment; and the rain represents the life-giving natural elements. The interrelationship of these components makes possible civilized life."[1] While some may object that Dilworth's analysis is fabricating symbols in order to make the poem seem more significant than it is, we are probably all willing to grant that Williams's poem is capable of stimulating us to think about the interdependence of life. If the poem itself is not profound, it may nonetheless cause us to think about life a bit more deeply.

So far our quest to define poetry leaves us in much the same predicament first described by the great eighteenth-century critic and lexicographer Samuel Johnson. When asked for a definition of poetry, he replied, "Why, sir, it is much easier to say what it is not. We all know what light is; but it is not easy to *tell* what it is." Two hundred years later we are not really much closer to an answer. Indeed,

---

[1] "Williams's "The Red Wheelbarrow,'" *The Explicator*, 40 (Summer 1982): 40–41.

poets themselves have often struggled to define poetry without, perhaps, shedding much light—or at least without providing definitive answers. Nevertheless, here are a handful of poems about poetry (or the experience of reading it) that may help you develop a better feel for the meaning of the word.

Five Poems on Poetry

SOUND AND SENSE

(From *An Essay on Criticism,* part 2)

True ease in writing comes from art, not chance,
As those move easiest who have learned to dance.
'Tis not enough no harshness gives offence,
365 The sound must seem an echo to the sense.
Soft is the strain when Zephyr° gently blows,   *the west wind*
And the smooth stream in smoother numbers flows;
But when loud surges lash the sounding shore,
The hoarse, rough verse should like the torrent roar.
370 When Ajax² strives, some rock's vast weight to throw,
The line too labours, and the words move slow;
Not so, when swift Camilla³ scours the plain,
Flies o'er the unbending corn, and skims along the main.
Hear how Timotheus'⁴ varied lays surprise,
375 And bid alternate passions fall and rise!
While, at each change, the son of Libyan Jove⁵
Now burns with glory, and then melts with love;
Now his fierce eyes with sparkling fury glow;
Now sighs steal out, and tears begin to flow:
380 Persians and Greeks like turns° of nature° found,   *changes / mood*
And the world's victor stood subdued by sound!
The power of music all our hearts allow,
And what Timotheus was, is Dryden now.

—Alexander Pope [1711]

❧ QUESTIONS ❧

1. How accurate is the analogy between writing good poetry and dancing well?

2. What does Pope do to make the sound of his lines echo their sense in lines 366–373?

² A hero in the *Iliad* celebrated for his strength.
³ A heroine in the *Aeneid.*
⁴ The illusion is to John Dryden's "Alexander's Feast" (1697).
⁵ Alexander the Great.

3. What is the effect of the brief references to Zephyr, Ajax, Camilla, Timotheus, Jove, and Dryden?

4. Do you agree that in good poetry "The sound must seem an echo to the sense"?

ON FIRST LOOKING INTO CHAPMAN'S HOMER

Much have I travell'd in the realms of gold,
And many goodly states and kingdoms seen:
Round many western islands have I been
Which bards in fealty to Apollo° hold.   *the god of poetry*
5   Oft of one wide expanse had I been told
That deep-browed Homer ruled as his demesne;°   *domain*
Yet did I never breathe its pure serene
Till I heard Chapman speak out loud and bold:
Then felt I like some watcher of the skies
10 When a new planet swims into his ken;
Or like stout Cortez[6] when with eagle eyes
He stared at the Pacific—and all his men
Looked at each other with a wild surmise—
Silent, upon a peak in Darien.

—John Keats [1816]

❧ QUESTIONS ❧

1. What does Keats mean by "the realms of gold"?

2. What is the effect of the brief references to Apollo, Homer, Chapman, and Cortez?

3. Examine the imagery in the poem. What are its ranges in the sweep of time and space?

4. What general situation does Keats describe in the first eight lines?

5. What new sensation does he describe in the last six lines? What has caused that new sensation?

6. How effective is the analogy with Cortez in describing the emotions you feel upon reading a poem that truly moves you? How effective is the analogy with an astronomer discovering a new planet?

7. Does it make a difference that this poem records an actual experience of Keats? When Keats was twenty-one, his former teacher Cowden Clarke showed him a copy of George Chapman's vigorous translations of Homer's *Iliad* and *Odyssey*. Keats and Clarke stayed up all night in rapture reading and discussing the poems. After returning home at dawn, Keats immediately composed this famous sonnet and sent it to Clarke as an expression of thanks.

---

[6] Hernando Cortés (1485–1547) conquered the Aztecs in Mexico, but he did not discover the Pacific Ocean. Vasco Núñez de Balboa did that in 1513. Darien is in eastern Panama.

ARS POETICA

A poem should be palpable and mute
As a globed fruit,

Dumb
As old medallions to the thumb,

5   Silent as the sleeve-worn stone
Of casement ledges where the moss has grown—

A poem should be wordless
As the flight of birds.

                *

A poem should be motionless in time
10   As the moon climbs,

Leaving, as the moon releases
Twig by twig the night-entangled trees,

Leaving, as the moon behind the winter leaves,
Memory by memory the mind—

15 A poem should be motionless in time
As the moon climbs.

                *

A poem should be equal to:
Not true.

For all the history of grief
20 An empty doorway and a maple leaf.

For love
The leaning grasses and two lights above the sea—

A poem should not mean
But be.

—Archibald MacLeish [1926]

❧ QUESTIONS ❧

1. This poem is divided into three parts, with the divisions indicated by an asterisk. What is the subject of each separate division? Can you put into your own words the statement about poetry made in each of the three sections?

2. This poem uses many comparisons (similes and metaphors). Which comparisons do you especially like? Are there any you think are inappropriate in defining the nature of poetry? Explain your views.

3. To what extent does MacLeish's own poem live up to his definition of poetry?

WORD

The word bites like a fish.
Shall I throw it back free
   Arrowing to that sea
Where thoughts lash tail and fin?
   Or shall I pull it in
To rhyme upon a dish?

—Stephen Spender [1949]

❧ QUESTIONS ❧

1. In what sense does a good word, a poetic word, bite like a fish? Try to explain what you think Spender means.

2. What does Spender seem to be saying about the differences between free verse and rhymed verse?

3. Judging from this poem, what kind of verse does Spender himself prefer?

AMERICAN POETRY

Whatever it is, it must have
A stomach that can digest
Rubber, coal, uranium, moons, poems.

Like the shark, it contains a shoe.
It must swim for miles through the desert
Uttering cries that are almost human.

—Louis Simpson [1963]

❧ QUESTIONS ❧

1. What is the effect of opening this poem on American poetry with the words "Whatever it is . . ."?

2. What kind of stomach is capable of digesting "Rubber, coal, uranium, moons, poems"? Is there anything particularly American about that list of indigestibles?

3. Do you think that poetry is anything like a shark? Explain your opinion.

4. How can a shark (or a poem) "swim for miles through the desert"? Is this paradox appropriate in a description of poetry or the task of an American poet?

5. Why are the cries of the poet (or the poem) "almost human"?

As the previous examples illustrate, poets throughout the ages have differed in their assumptions about the genre, and it is unrealistic to expect a single definition of poetry to serve equally well for all periods in literary history. If we stand outside the spectrum of history, we can see how one view dominates an age only to give way to another. So long as poetry remains a vital form of human expression, we can expect that its techniques and purposes will continue to change.

What *is* poetry? We ask again. Although we may be unable to answer this question for all time, we *can* summarize those elements in the definition of poetry that have remained nearly constant throughout the ages.

Poetry, like all literature, attempts to communicate an author's emotional and intellectual responses to his or her own existence and to the surrounding world. It is an expression of what is thought and felt, rather than what is known as fact. It depends on observation, just as science does, but poetry draws comparisons between phenomena that science might find distant and unrelated. When Keats wishes to share his emotions upon first reading Chapman's translation of Homer's poetry, he finds an apt metaphor in the conquistador's silent wonder at the vast Pacific Ocean. When MacLeish wishes to describe the unity and concreteness of poetry, he uses a vivid comparison: "A poem should be palpable and mute / As a globed fruit." Such comparisons require a bold leap of imagination in both the poet and the reader. When they are effective, they reproduce emotions in the reader similar to those actually experienced by the author. Thus, **poetry is fundamentally metaphoric and is capable of communicating in very few words thoughts and emotions of great complexity.**

Prose literature, of course, is capable of achieving everything suggested in the preceding paragraph. As a result of modern experiments with free verse and the increasing literary artistry of short story writers and novelists, the distinctions between poetry and prose are often slight and sometimes blurred. Hence, all of the techniques of poetry can, on occasion, be properly considered in the critical explication of fiction and drama. However, poetry ordinarily does differ from prose in several significant ways. First, **poetry provides a traditionally accepted format (in ballads, lyrics, odes, and sonnets) for the publication of short but independent pieces of narration, description, or reflection.** Second, **"poetic license" permits verse to depart on occasion from the standard rules of logic and grammar governing ordinary prose.** Third, **poetry tends to make more use than prose of symbolism, imagery, and figures of speech.** And finally, **poetry relies more heavily than prose on the sound and rhythm of speech and hence often employs both rhyme and meter.**

The formal patterns of meter and rhyme, which continue to dominate poetry despite modern experiments with free verse, place obvious restrictions on the poet's choice of words. The poet must write carefully and reflectively in order to find words that not only fulfill the demands of meter and rhyme, but also express the meaning in a manner that complements the imagery and tone of the rest of the poem. This careful use of language is the most significant difference between ordinary prose and poetry. The ordinary prose writer neatly builds an argument using words the way a mason builds a house using bricks; the poet is an artisan who creates a fieldstone hearth—each stone or each word is turned over, examined, and often laid aside until it can be placed where its shape, weight, and color will contribute to the strength and beauty of the whole. **Prose, according to Samuel Taylor Coleridge, is "words in their best order," and poetry is "the best words in their best order."**

Very little of the poetry of any age comes up to the high standards set in the previous paragraph. Even great poets write relatively few great poems, and our disappointment in the inferior works of notable poets is often greater than it is in the secondary works of great novelists. This, too, points out a difference between prose and poetry. Mediocre prose is often enjoyable in much the same way that a walk in the city can be enjoyable even though it is not so fresh and invigorating as a hike through the wilderness. But if prose is like walking, then poetry is like riding. Either the rider *or* the mount will have control over the rhythm, the pace, and the direction of the journey. When the horse is in command—that is, when the meter and rhyme govern the poet—the ride will be uneven, misdirected, unintelligible, and sometimes fearsome. When the rider is in control—that is, when the poet fully controls the rhythm and sound—the gait will be swift, smooth, graceful, and elegant.

In the preceding paragraphs we have compared the poet with an artisan and an equestrian. Both comparisons convey something about the essential quality of poetry. Perhaps, however, they emphasize too strongly the skill of the poet and not strongly enough the skills that are necessary in an appreciative reader. Poetry shares with all other literary genres the fact that it is a form of communication between the author and the reader. It depends as much on the goodwill, intelligence, and experience of the latter as on the genius of the former. Robert Frost once said that writing free verse is like playing tennis with the net down. Regardless of whether we agree with Frost's implied criticism of free verse, his remark underscores the fact that poetry is a game played according to established rules between poet and form and also between poet and reader. In order to play the game, in order to understand poetry, one must first learn the rules.

5

Denotation and Connotation

Words are the building-blocks of poetry. By the time students enter college, they have heard at least 100 million words in school; spoken 30 million words in school and out; and read, in spite of television, some 10 million words. During the years of formal schooling, language is so ingrained in us that we cannot imagine an existence without words; our most private thoughts often take the form of an inner dialogue and even our dreams incorporate words. In short, we become so sophisticated in language, and at such an early age, that we seldom realize the complexity of the language we read, speak, and hear.

Our understanding of language, whether as listeners or as readers, depends almost entirely on two factors: our knowledge of the meaning of individual words and our recognition of various cues (syntax, punctuation, and structure in reading; syntax, emphasis, and vocal pauses in listening) which direct our attention to the relationships among the words.[1] When we read a poem, our first concern is with the meaning of individual words, but it soon becomes clear that meaning is largely determined by context and by the interrelationships of words in a sentence. Several of the elements of poetry, however, are occasionally independent of context: particularly denotation and connotation. **A word's *denotation* is its dictionary definition; its *connotation* is that set of associations and emotional overtones carried by the word.** Each word in a language is distinguished from every other word by its unique combination of denotations and connotations; there are no perfect synonyms. Poetry is the form of writing that takes greatest advantage of the personalities of words; it welcomes their eccentricities. **No word in great**

---

[1] Literary critics have not sufficiently emphasized the fact that poetry gives—through rhythm, rhyme, and verse form—more cues about meaning than prose. This was even more obvious in the Middle Ages than it is now. Our elaborate gradations of punctuation are relatively recent inventions; medieval scribes used only the slash and the period. Consequently, medieval manuscripts are much easier to read in verse than in prose and, perhaps as a result, verse was often preferred for any composition of lasting value.

poetry can be moved or replaced without changing and perhaps harming the whole. An understanding of the meaning of individual words, therefore, is essential in understanding poetry.

DENOTATION

"When I use a word," Humpty Dumpty said in rather a scornful tone, "it means just what I choose it to mean—neither more nor less."

"The question is," said Alice, "whether you *can* make words mean so many different things."

"The question is," said Humpty Dumpty, "which is to be Master—that's all."

Alice was too much puzzled to say anything, so after a minute Humpty Dumpty began again. "They've a temper, some of them—particularly verbs, they're the proudest—adjectives you can do anything with, but not verbs— however, *I* can manage the whole lot of them! Impenetrability! That's what *I* say!"

—From *Through the Looking Glass,* Lewis Carroll [1871]

As is often the case, Lewis Carroll's humor is far from absurd. In fact, the quotation points to an interesting paradox about words: **A word is only an accurate tool of communication if it conveys the same idea to both the speaker and the listener; yet the meanings of words continually change and, despite the existence of dictionaries, words can only be said to mean what people *think* they mean.** New words are continually entering the language and old words dropping out or changing their implications. Furthermore, the same word can mean different things to different people or different things in different contexts. If, for example, we say of someone, "He's a bit red," we may mean that he is embarrassed, sunburned, or attracted to Communism, depending on the context. Similarly, if a man living in the fifteenth century introduced a woman as John Smith's "mistress," he would have been praising her as an honest wife of noble blood. Today, such an introduction might openly suggest the lack of a marriage license.

If we object to using words that carry the clutter of variant definitions based on history, location, and context . . . well, we can turn to *new* words, freshly minted to meet their creators' needs. Lewis Carroll was remarkably adept at coining such words. We are indebted to him for the *boojum* (which is now the name of a species of tree found in Baja California), the *snark* (now used as the trade name of a small sailboat), and the Cheshire Cat's smile. To Joseph Heller, we owe the expression *Catch-22*, and to Harriet Beecher Stowe, we owe *Uncle Tom*. The military's fondness for acronyms has produced *radar* (radio detection and ranging) and *snafu* (situation normal all fouled up).[2] The list goes on.

The various meanings of the words we have been discussing so far are all *denotations*—that is, they are listed as definitions in nearly any good dictionary. Most of us, when asked the meaning of any particular word, reply with a single, rather loose, definition. But **we know that nearly every word has many definitions and that its denotation in a particular instance will depend largely on the context.** These multiple meanings make the whole issue of a word's denotation much more

---

[2] Not all acronyms are felicitous or dignified. Richard Nixon's ill-fated Committee to Re-elect the President was known as CREEP, the device used by NASA to blow up misguided missiles is called EGADS (Electronic Ground Automatic Destruct System), and the policy governing our nuclear defense strategy used to be known as MAD (Mutual Assured Destruction).

complex and much less clear-cut than it may seem at first. It is an indication of the complexity of this issue that the most authoritative dictionary in the language, *The Oxford English Dictionary* (1933), is 16,464 pages long. In it one finds, for example, more than eighteen pages (with three columns of print to the page) defining the verb *set,* which is capable of taking on 154 separate senses with nearly a thousand minor subdivisions of meaning.

The first task in understanding a poem, then, is to understand thoroughly each word in it. Often, the best clues to the meaning of an unfamiliar word are to be found within the poem itself. Suppose, for example, that one wishes to know the meaning of "heal-all" in the following sonnet by Robert Frost:

DESIGN

I found a dimpled spider, fat and white,
On a white heal-all, holding up a moth
Like a white piece of rigid satin cloth—
Assorted characters of death and blight
5   Mixed ready to begin the morning right,
Like the ingredients of a witches' broth—
A snow-drop spider, a flower like a froth,
And dead wings carried like a paper kite.
What had that flower to do with being white,
10 The wayside blue and innocent heal-all?
What brought the kindred spider to that height,
Then steered the white moth thither in the night?
What but the design of darkness to appall?—
If design govern in a thing so small.

                                                        —Robert Frost [1936]

A dictionary only tells us that a "heal-all" is either a panacea of some kind or one of a number of plants (*Rhodiola rosea, Valeriana officinalis, Prunella vulgaris,* and *Collinsonia canadensis*) that are thought to have medicinal value. Although accurate, this definition is no real help. If we don't know what a "heal-all" is in the first place, we certainly aren't going to know anything about a *Rhodiola rosea* or any of the other species listed. If we turn to a book on horticulture for help, we will learn where these plants grow, how large they get, how many stamens and pistils the flowers have, and so on. We may even find pictures of each of the four plants, but without referring to the poem we won't learn anything telling us which of the four Frost meant or what emotions he hoped to evoke in the reader through the name. In comparison, look at the information about the word contained in the poem itself. There we learn that a heal-all is a blue flower (lines 9 and 10) of substantial height and size. It is large enough to support a fat spider and tall enough so that Frost is surprised to see the spider on it. We learn that it grows by the wayside and that it is innocent; if it doesn't heal everything, as its name suggests, it is not ordinarily poisonous either. But the particular heal-all in the poem is unusual and almost an object of horror. It is blighted and white, a deformed member of its species. Thus, Frost sees its frothlike flowers as a fitting element in a witches' brew—and a fitting element in a poem that raises the possibility of malevolent destiny.

In the course of the poem, Frost has defined what he means by a heal-all. He has told us about the flower and, more importantly, he has told us about himself and the destiny he thinks governs existence. We learn what the word *heal-all* means and also what it symbolizes for Frost. The risk involved in defining a word from its context is, of course, that we are often unable to differentiate between the general denotative meaning of the word and its special significance for the poet. For this reason it is wise to check any definitions derived from context with those given in the dictionary.

Any ample dictionary will answer most of the needs of the student-critic. Yet one should keep in mind that **the meaning of words changes with time,** and dictionaries of only one volume seldom trace historical change. As a result of the civil rights movement of the 1960s, for example, the verb *discriminate* has come to mean "to make a decision based on prejudice." In the *Oxford English Dictionary,* however, the history of the word reveals that prior to about 1880 the verb meant only "to distinguish, differentiate, or exercise discernment." According to these early meanings of the word, an intelligent person should always be discriminating; today, we hope to avoid discriminating. Such changes in language are so common that we can expect to find some archaism in virtually every poem written before the beginning of the eighteenth century.

CONNOTATION

As we have seen, denotation refers to the dictionary meaning of a word. Connotation, on the other hand, is determined by the ideas associated with or suggested by the word. **Denotation is the meaning a word gives *to* a sentence; connotation is the verbal coloring a word takes on *from* those sentences in which it is commonly used.** When a word like *discriminate* is uniformly employed in a narrow set of circumstances (in this case, involving some form of prejudice), its connotations may eventually be incorporated into the definition of the word itself. This is the principal process by which the definitions of words change. Thus, a word's connotations may be compared to the living, growing bark of a tree, and its denotations, like the rings in the tree's core, are the permanent record of its past growth. To change the simile slightly, the denotations of a word are visible, like a tree's branches and leaves; the connotations are the roots, which go deeply into the subsoil of our experience creating invisible ties between contexts and associations and drawing up nourishment for a continuing growth above ground.

Most of us manipulate the connotations of words every day. The person described scornfully as "my old man" during a "rap session" in the dormitory is apt to become "Dad" during the weekly "chat" on the phone about the high costs at college and finally to become "my father" during a formal "interview" with the financial aid officer. In each set of examples, the denotative meanings remain essentially unchanged—the father remains a father and the conversation remains a conversation—but the connotations change dramatically. As these examples demonstrate, **speakers and writers manipulate connotations in an almost instinctive effort to set a tone**—whether it be the laid back informality of the "rap session" or painful formality of an "interview."

Many words have multiple and even conflicting connotations. For example, in the sonnet by Frost on page 656 the spider, the moth, and the flower are all white. Most of the time we associate the adjective *white* with innocence, purity, and cleanliness. A young bride is customarily married in a white gown and angels are depicted wearing white robes. In other contexts, however, this color can also signify pallor, illness, blight, or even death. Frost is probably drawing on both sets of connotations in his poem. The white moth fluttering toward its destruction in the darkness is harmless and innocent; the white flower that attracts it is blighted and unusual; and the fat white spider is a ghastly object of poison and death. Frost expects us to react—perhaps even shudder—at this departure from the normal and expected. Indeed, Frost's own attitude changes. In the last six lines he moves from questioning to despair—("What had . . . ? What brought . . . ? What but . . . ?")—as his conviction grows that such an evil distortion of "whiteness" can only be brought about by "the design of darkness to appall." This evolution is summarized in that final word "appall," the original denotation of which is "to make pale" or even (considering the many uses of "white" in the poem) "to make white." Thus, Frost creates an ironic pun based on the denotation of "appall," but in this instance the burden of the word's meaning is carried by its connotation. In ordinary usage the word "appall" inevitably carries connotations of horror—so much so that "horrify" is usually listed as one of its definitions in modern dictionaries— and indeed Frost *is* horrified by this design of darkness and hopes through his poem to make us share his horror.

A word's connotations, like its denotations, may change over time. A humorous example of change in a word's connotations occurs in Samuel Taylor Coleridge's "Sonnet to the Reverend W. L. Bowles" (1796). Coleridge claims that the verses of Reverend Bowles were capable of soothing a tumultuous mind:

> As the great Spirit erst with plastic sweep
> Mov'd on the darkness of the unform'd deep.

Coleridge here uses *plastic* to mean having the superhuman "power of molding or shaping formless material"—a meaning of the word that the dictionary still lists. Most modern readers, however, think of cheap merchandise when they hear the word *plastic* and think of brooms when they hear the word *sweep*. Thus, because of these changes in connotation, we may mistakenly picture the Holy Spirit pushing a cheap plastic broom when we first read Coleridge's lines.

Poems for Further Study

THE NAKED AND THE NUDE

For me, the naked and the nude
(By lexicographers[3] construed
As synonyms that should express
The same deficiency of dress
5   Or shelter) stand as wide apart
As love from lies, or truth from art.

Lovers without reproach will gaze
On bodies naked and ablaze;
The Hippocratic[4] eye will see
10   In nakedness, anatomy;

---

[3] Those who make dictionaries.
[4] Hippocrates (c. 460–377 B.C.) was the Greek physician generally thought to have founded medical science.

And naked shines the Goddess when
She mounts her lion among men.

The nude are bold, the nude are sly
To hold each treasonable eye.
15 While draping by a showman's trick
Their dishabille[5] in rhetoric,
They grin a mock-religious grin
Of scorn at those of naked skin.

The naked, therefore, who compete
20 Against the nude may know defeat;
Yet when they both together tread
The briary pastures of the dead,
By Gorgons[6] with long whips pursued,
How naked go the sometime nude!

—Robert Graves [1957]

🌿 QUESTIONS 🌿

1. Use a dictionary to check the denotations of the words *naked* and *nude*. Is Graves correct in calling them synonyms?

2. What does Graves mean when he says that for him "the naked and the nude . . . stand as wide apart / As love from lies, or truth from art." How far do you think that Graves wishes to carry his simile? Does Graves equate the nude with love or lies? Truth or art? (Look for the answers to these questions in stanzas 2 and 3.)

3. What are the differences in connotations of the words *naked* and *nude*? How successfully does Graves develop the implications of these differing connotations?

4. What is the denotation of the word *dishabille* in the third stanza? What are its connotations? Why are both the denotation and connotation of the word useful to Graves?

5. What is a "mock-religious grin"? Why would the nude stare in that way at the naked? Why does Graves choose the word *grin* instead of *smile*?

6. Explain the meaning of the poem's final line.

CARGOES

Quinquireme of Nineveh from distant Ophir,
Rowing home to haven in sunny Palestine,
With a cargo of ivory,

---

[5] State of being undressed.
[6] Hideous, terrifying women of Greek mythology—the mere sight of whom turns men to stone.

And apes and peacocks,
5   Sandalwood, cedarwood, and sweet white wine.

Stately Spanish galleon coming from the Isthmus
Dipping through the Tropics by the palm-green shores,
With a cargo of diamonds,
Emeralds, amethysts,
10   Topazes, and cinnamon, and gold moidores.°   *Portuguese coins*

Dirty British coaster with a salt-caked smoke stack,
Burning through the Channel in the mad March days,
With a cargo of Tyne coal,
Road-rails, pig-lead,
15   Firewood, iron-ware, and cheap tin trays.

                                             —John Masefield [1902]

❧ QUESTIONS ❧

1.   This poem is divided into three stanzas. What is the subject of each
stanza? What are the similarities between the stanzas? What are the differences—especially in the third stanza?

2.   Discuss the connotations of the names of the various cargo ships. Discuss
the connotations of the ports the ships service and of the cargo in each ship.

3.   What thematic point about the British empire does Masefield make
through his manipulations of connotations?

6

※⅍※⅍⁰⅍※⅍

Allusion

When the English peasants marched against London in their ill-fated revolt of 1381, it is said that they rallied their spirits by chanting this brief ditty:

> When Adam dalf°   *delved, farmed*
> And Eve span°   *spun (yarn)*
> Who was then the gentleman?

The peasants wanted to throw off their serfdom and assume the rights of free-born citizens. Their argument, at least in the chant, depended on a Biblical allusion: in Genesis, when God created humankind, he made Adam and Eve, not nobles and serfs—how then is serfdom justified?

A literary *allusion* **is a brief reference to a person, place, phrase, or event drawn from history or literature. Allusions are effective not because of the meaning of the words themselves but because of the associations or connotations that allusive words carry for the informed reader. The use of allusion allows poets to reinforce an argument by illustration, to compress complex ideas into brief phrases, and to suggest thoughts they may not wish to state directly.** In the case at hand, the peasants' allusive chant allowed them to request their freedom without putting it in the form of a rebellious demand and to support their position with the authority of the Bible.

Names, as in the example just cited, **are the most common forms of allusion** and the easiest to identify. As another example of names used allusively, let us look at a stanza from Lord Byron's *Don Juan:*

> When amatory poets sing their loves
>   In liquid lines mellifluously bland,
> And pair their rhymes as Venus yokes her doves,
>   They little think what mischief is in hand;

661

> The greater their success the worse it proves,
>   As Ovid's verse may give to understand;
> Even Petrarch's self, if judged with due severity,
>   Is the Platonic pimp of all posterity.
>
> —From *Don Juan*, Lord Byron [1821]

Byron uses four allusions in eight lines. The first is almost self-explanatory: a poet's rhymes are paired in the same way as the doves that draw Venus's chariot through the heavens are yoked into pairs. The allusion is intended less to send the reader stumbling off to consult a copy of Ovid's *Metamorphoses* than to imitate the similes of conventional love poetry; it requires only that the reader remember that Venus is the goddess of love. Byron then goes on to argue that the more successful poets are in writing about love, the worse it is for public morality, "As Ovid's verse may give to understand." Although Byron only expects from his reader the general knowledge that Ovid is renowned as the most seductive of all love poets, he may also be alluding to the rumor that Ovid was banished from Rome because his verse had tempted the daughter of Emperor Caesar Augustus into having an illicit love affair. The reference to Petrarch in line 7 assumes that the reader will know that this fourteenth-century Italian poet (who wrote 227 sonnets about his unrequited love for Laura living and another 90 about his love for Laura dead) has inspired many seductive sonnet cycles. A final allusion is contained in the incongruous expression "Platonic pimp." Byron's point here is that Petrarch's verse may well have been spiritual or Platonic in fact, but it was erotic and seductive in effect. The brief allusion to *Platonic love,* which denotes "spiritual love" to literate readers, serves to emphasize that allusion, like denotation and connotation, is one of the factors in determining the meaning of words.

Allusion through literary name-dropping is generally less effective than allusion through quotation or imitation of an author's works. Historically important and well-stated words have an emotional impact that transcends their denotative meaning. **A literary allusion that is created through quotation draws on our reaction to the quoted work, the circumstances under which the work was written, and the whole range of our attitudes toward the author.** We respond with patriotism to the idealism of the *Declaration of Independence* ("We hold these truths to be self-evident . . ."); with mystical piety to the Gospel according to St. John ("In the beginning was the Word, and the Word was with God, and the Word was God"); and with a shiver to the opening of Edgar Allan Poe's "The Raven" ("Once upon a midnight dreary . . ."). When Keats wrote of "deep-browed Homer" (see p. 649), he was imitating Homer's penchant for such epithets as his often repeated "rosy-fingered Dawn." When Coleridge, in his sonnet to Reverend Bowles, compared the calming of his mind to the calming of waves after the great Spirit "Mov'd on the darkness of the unform'd deep," he was alluding to Genesis, Chapter 1, verse 2:

> And the earth was without form, and void; and darkness was upon the face of the deep. And the Spirit of God moved upon the face of the waters.

Such examples of allusion all refer to *famous* people, events, or words, because **an allusion is only effective if it is understood and appreciated by the reader. But poets themselves often gain considerable notoriety as public figures, so that allusions to events in their personal lives come to be widely understood.** For instance, Byron alludes to events in his own life when he writes in the first canto of *Don Juan,*

> 'Tis pity learned virgins ever wed
>   With persons of no sort of education.
> Or gentlemen, who, though well born and bred,
>   Grow tired of scientific conversation:
> I don't choose to say much on this head.
>   I'm a plain man, and in a single station,
> But—Oh! ye lords of ladies intellectual,
> Inform us truly, have they not hen-peck'd you all?
>
> —From *Don Juan*, Lord Byron [1819]

The irony in the stanza may elude us if we fail to recognize that Byron's wife Annabella had been a "learned virgin," that he often called her the "Princess of Parallelograms" and "a walking calculation," and that their separation proceedings provided scandal enough to delight gossips throughout England *and* Europe. Similarly, when Laurence Sterne, the eighteenth-century novelist and clergyman, was married, he wryly made reference to this event in his personal life by taking as his keynote for the following day's sermon this passage from Luke 5:5: "We have toiled all the night and taken nothing."

Poems for Further Study

THE GARDEN OF LOVE

I went to the Garden of Love,
And saw what I never had seen:
A Chapel was built in the midst,
Where I used to play on the green.°   lawn

5   And the gates of this Chapel were shut,
And "Thou shalt not" writ over the door;
So I turned to the Garden of Love
That so many sweet flowers bore;

And I saw it was filled with graves,
10   And tombstones where flowers should be;
And priests in black gowns were walking their rounds,
And binding with briars my joys and desires.

—William Blake [1794]

🐝 QUESTIONS 🐝

1. The speaker in this poem describes the "Garden of Love" as he remembers it from his innocent youth and as it appears to him now. What was the garden like in the past? How has it changed? How does the speaker feel about these changes?

2. To what is Blake alluding when he says that "Thou shalt not" was written

over the door of the chapel. (There are two fairly obvious possibilities. See if you can identify them both.)

3.   Why does Blake capitalize the words *Garden* and *Love*? Is he merely creating a proper name (like the Rose Garden at the White House)? Or does he want us to concentrate on the garden? What other garden is associated with religion, love, the loss of innocence, and the unwelcome presence of death? How does the discovery of this allusion affect your interpretation of the poem?

4.   Explain the allusion in the last line of the poem.

5.   To what extent does this poem portray each individual's experiences in growing to maturity? To what extent does the poem synopsize the historical development of the Christian church? How do you think Blake feels about the organized church and the "mature" adult?

MYTH

```
     Long afterward, Oedipus, old and blinded, walked the
     roads.      He smelled a familiar smell.      It was
     the Sphinx.      Oedipus said, "I want to ask one question.
     Why didn't I recognize my mother?"      "You gave the
5    wrong answer," said the Sphinx.      "But that was what
     made everything possible," said Oedipus.      "No," she said.
     "When I asked, What walks on four legs in the morning,
     two at noon, and three in the evening, you answered,
     Man.      You didn't say anything about woman."
10   "When you say Man," said Oedipus, "you include women
     too. Everyone knows that."      She said, "That's what
     you think."
```

—Muriel Rukeyser [1973]

❧ QUESTIONS ❧

1.   To what is Rukeyser alluding when she begins her poem with the words "long afterward"? Long after what? (If you are not familiar with the story of Oedipus, read *King Oedipus* in the drama section of this anthology—or consult a standard encyclopedia.)

2.   In what sense does "man" walk on four legs in the morning, two at noon, and three in the evening? What do morning, noon, and evening symbolize?

3.   What is the point of Rukeyser's poem? (To what extent does Rukeyser link Oedipus's failure to include women in answering the Sphinx's riddle with his later failure to recognize his own mother?)

7

꽃꽃꽃꽃꽃꽃꽃

Repetition and Ambiguity

Thus far, we have been examining elements in the meaning of words that are nearly independent of their context in a poem. It is the poetic context, however, that now requires attention because context alone allows us to distinguish among the competing possibilities offered by a word's denotations and connotations. **A word will rarely mean exactly the same thing in two different contexts, even within the same poem.**

The *repetition* **of a word or phrase in itself tends to change the emphasis and to make prominent what otherwise might be overlooked.** This is Robert Frost's intention in repeating the last line in the final stanza of the following well-known poem:

STOPPING BY WOODS ON A SNOWY EVENING

Whose woods these are I think I know.
His house is in the village though;
He will not see me stopping here
To watch his woods fill up with snow.

5   My little horse must think it queer
To stop without a farmhouse near
Between the woods and frozen lake
The darkest evening of the year.

He gives his harness bells a shake
10   To ask if there is some mistake.
The only other sound's the sweep
Of easy wind and downy flake.

The woods are lovely, dark and deep,
But I have promises to keep,

15   And miles to go before I sleep,
                And miles to go before I sleep.
                        —Robert Frost [1923]

At first we are inclined to take the last line literally: the narrator must not linger because his trip home is a long one, and presumably he is already late. But, when repeated, the line attains an emphasis that makes this literal interpretation unsatisfactory. We may then ask ourselves a number of questions: What "promises" might go unkept because of this sojourn in the woods? What have the dark woods to do with "sleep?" And, finally, what kind of sleep is the poet talking about? The literal interpretation of the lines seems too mundane to accept the emphasis that Frost's repetition suggests, and we are tempted to look for additional meaning. The "promises to keep" perhaps suggest the whole burden of life's obligations, while the dark woods may be a bittersweet symbol of escape from these responsibilities into fantasy, fairyland, or premature death. And the final word "sleep," when repeated, assumes a greater finality because we know that our final sleep is death itself. The simple repetition of a line thus encourages us to change our interpretation of the entire poem, affecting both its denotation and symbolism.

Frost achieves a different transformation of meaning by repeating the word "white" in the first three lines of his sonnet "Design":

> I found a dimpled spider, fat and white,
> On a white heal-all, holding up a moth
> Like a white piece of rigid satin cloth—

By repeating the word "white" he focuses our attention on it. Nothing obliged Frost to repeat himself; adjectives like *pallid, bleached, sallow, wan, hoary,* and *pale* are roughly synonymous and could have introduced the variety in style and imagery that ordinarily is desirable in a poem. But each of these alternatives suggests a slightly different shade of white and each carries a slightly different connotation. Only by repeating the *same* word can Frost make the point that the colors are identical. The blighted flower has perfectly concealed the hideous albino spider, and the single white flower in a field of blue has, presumably, enticed the moth into the trap. The incident is remarkable because of its improbability and suggests to the poet that this eerie nighttime rendezvous may have been foreordained. The repetition of "white," a color associated with both innocence and death, builds in the reader a foreboding of evil design, a bleak and blighted destiny in which even the purest of colors can serve the purposes of darkness.

In stanzaic poetry and ballads, repetition is often introduced in the form of a *refrain*, or chorus. The refrain generally occurs at the close of a stanza, where it helps to establish meter, influence mood, or add emphasis. A refrain may be identical in each stanza or it may vary in subtle but important ways during the course of the poem. An example of the effective use of a refrain is found in Rudyard Kipling's "Recessional":

RECESSIONAL
God of our fathers, known of old,
Lord of our far-flung battle-line,
Beneath whose awful Hand we hold
Dominion over palm and pine—

5   Lord God of Hosts, be with us yet,
      Lest we forget lest we forget!

      The tumult and the shouting dies;
          The captains and the kings depart:
      Still stands Thine ancient sacrifice,
10   An humble and a contrite heart.
      Lord God of Hosts, be with us yet,
      Lest we forget—lest we forget!

      Far-called, our navies melt away;
          On dune and headland sinks the fire:
15   Lo, all our pomp of yesterday
          Is one with Nineveh and Tyre![1]
      Judge of nations, spare us yet,
      Lest we forget—lest we forget!

      If, drunk with sight of power, we loose
20   Wild tongues that have not Thee in awe,
      Such boastings as the Gentiles[2] use,
          Or lesser breeds without the Law—
      Lord God of Hosts, be with us yet,
      Lest we forget—lest we forget!

25   For heathen heart that puts her trust
          In reeking tube and iron shard,
      All valiant dust that builds on dust,
          And guarding, calls not Thee to guard,
      For frantic boast and foolish word—
30   Thy mercy on Thy people, Lord!
                              —Rudyard Kipling [1897]

A recessional is a hymn sung at the end of a religious service to signal the stately withdrawal of the priest and choir. Kipling's "Recessional," however, was not intended as a contribution to Anglican church music. It was written at the end of the festivities commemorating Queen Victoria's Diamond Jubilee, in her sixtieth year on the throne of England, and it reflects Kipling's emotions as he contemplates the end of an era. In 1897 Great Britain still governed an extensive empire, but her colonial power had already been challenged by the Sepoy rebellion in India and the Boer War in South Africa. Kipling was born in India and had sympathy for the native population, even though he endorsed the ideals of English colonial government. As we will see, Kipling's poem expresses the complexity of his attitudes and, in doing so, draws on many of the literary devices we have discussed earlier. Behind the celebration of the Diamond Jubilee—behind even Kipling's expression of faith in God—we sense in the poem a prophetic lament for the decline of a once glorious empire.

Three of the poem's five stanzas contain an identical two-line refrain:

      Lord God of Hosts, be with us yet,
      Lest we forget—lest we forget!

[1] Nineveh and Tyre: Prosperous Old Testament cities destroyed by God because of their impiety.
[2] Gentiles: Any persons who are not Jewish. Here used to mean anyone who does not believe in the true faith as, for example, the inhabitants of Nineveh and Tyre.

The contribution of this refrain to the meaning of the poem depends in part on its literary allusions, in part on the meaning of the words themselves, and in part on repetition. The phrase "Lord God of Hosts" or "Lord of Hosts" occurs frequently in the Bible, especially in the passages describing the destruction of Nineveh by heathen hordes and God's subsequent warnings against impiety. The analogy with the British empire is obvious. Apart from these Biblical allusions, Kipling's two-line refrain combines both a prayer and a warning: a prayer for God's continuing presence in the hearts of the English people and an implicit warning about the consequences of neglecting Him. The repetition of "lest we forget" in the second line of the refrain makes this warning all the more solemn. Thus, the refrain and the repetition within it not only add an air of solemnity and piety to the mood of the poem, but also underscore the slight differences in the refrain of the third stanza and the radical differences in the last stanza. As it happens, these stanzas present us with important clues to the meaning of the poem, clues best discussed in the context of *ambiguity*.

The use of a word or phrase in such a way as to give it two or more competing meanings is called *ambiguity*. In many instances, ambiguity is both a stylistic flaw and an annoyance because it creates confusion. In fact, the famous "Charge of the Light Brigade," immortalized in verse by Alfred Lord Tennyson, would never have taken place were it not for an ambiguity in Lord Raglan's orders to the commander in the field, Lord Lucan: "Lord Raglan wishes the cavalry to advance rapidly to the front, and try to prevent the enemy carrying away the guns." Unfortunately, as Tennyson pointed out, there were cannon to the right of them, cannon to the left of them, and cannon straight ahead. When the baffled Lord Lucan asked *which* guns were meant, the officer who had delivered the order frowned, pointed vaguely into the valley, and said sharply, "There, my Lord, is your enemy. There are your guns." With more courage than common sense, the Light Brigade charged the most distant guns—into the pages of history. As a result of ambiguity in the initial orders, of the 673 horsemen who entered the valley, only 195 returned.

As was the case in Lord Raglan's order, **ambiguity is often a result of imprecise wording. Other forms of ambiguity involve a play on the dual meanings of a particular word or a particular syntactic structure.** As an example of the former, let us say that you are driving a friend home for the first time. As you approach an intersection, you ask, "Which way? Left?"

"Right!" your companion replies.

No exercise of logic can tell you whether the word *Right* here means "That is correct, turn left!" or "No! Turn right!" Only more information can clarify your friend's meaning.

Most cases of ambiguity involve a similar play on the meanings of a particular word, but it is also possible to have syntactic ambiguity—that is, ambiguity caused by the ordering of words. For example, there is a story that when Pyrrhus, the king of Epirus, consulted the oracle at Delphi before going into battle, he was encouraged by the prophesy that "Pyrrhus the Romans shall conquer," which he interpreted as meaning that he, Pyrrhus, would prove victorious. The Romans, however, were also encouraged because the sentence seemed to them equivalent to "The Romans shall conquer Pyrrhus." The actual battle demonstrated that the ambiguity of the oracle was appropriate. Although Pyrrhus won the field, he did so at such a cost that he was recorded as saying, "Another such victory, and we are lost." This battle, by the way, gave rise to the phrase *Pyrrhic victory*, which in itself incorporates the paradox (a form of ambiguity) of a costly and thus undesirable victory.

As the preceding example illustrates, **ambiguity can be used by a careful writer to increase the subtlety, impact, and concision of an expression. It can conceal truths that are only superficially contradictory** (as in the oracle's prophesy), **display an honest ambivalence, expand poetic meaning, or create humor or shock.**

Ambivalence and expanded meaning are both revealed in Kipling's "Recessional." Here the ambiguity is not created by a single word with contradictory meanings, but rather by the dual interpretations that the poem as a whole invites. Each stanza is appropriate to the occasion of Victoria's Diamond Jubilee, at the end of which the captains and the kings depart, the naval vessels return to their normal duties, the celebratory bonfires die into embers, and the satisfied English masses boast of the national might. But at the same time each stanza can also be interpreted as a comment on the future of the empire, and it is precisely this prophetic element that makes the poem so memorable.

This duality of meaning is not forced on us until the third stanza. If by the lines, "Far-called, our navies melt away;/ On dune and headland sinks the fire," Kipling is referring to the dispersal of ships after the naval display on the Thames and to the fading of bonfires, then surely he is exaggerating when he says, "Lo, all our pomp of yesterday/ Is one with Nineveh and Tyre." The end of a celebration is scarcely like the annihilation of these two biblical cities and their civilizations. And surely his prayer, "Judge of Nations, spare us yet,/ Lest we forget—lest we forget!" is nonsensical because nothing about the close of the Jubilee directly suggests the fall of the British empire.

In order to make sense of the stanza we must interpret it *figuratively,* paying as much attention to connotation as to denotation. It is true that the bonfires of the Jubilee were set on England's "dune and headland," but these words are equally applicable to the extremities of the empire—Egypt, India, and Africa. In discussions of empires, a "fire" or conflagration may be used to describe a minor uprising, such as the Indian Mutiny of 1857, the first Boer War in 1881, or the British defeat at Khartoum in 1885. All of these well-publicized "fires" along the outskirts of the British empire occurred during the years preceding Victoria's Diamond Jubilee. Furthermore, in primitive regions, the campfire is the symbol of civilization, which staves off encroaching savagery. The sinking fire, when accompanied by allusions to the fall of Nineveh and Tyre, thus suggests unrest and upheaval along the fringes of the empire. The same suggestion is included in the preceding line, "Far-called, our navies melt away"—especially because melting (as with ice) is ordinarily an irreversible process. By implication, the strength of a navy that melts away is permanently diminished. Furthermore, "far-called" is not quite the same as "widely deployed." Kipling's term suggests that the navy has been called into action rather than merely reassigned to simple peace-keeping missions.

After Kipling has drawn our attention to his intentional ambiguity in this third stanza, we may turn with renewed interest to the earlier stanzas. If we pursue Kipling's allusions to Nineveh and Tyre by reading in the Bible Chapters 26–28 of Ezekiel and Chapters 1–3 of Nahum, we discover that Nineveh, like England, had "multiplied [her] merchants above the stars of heaven" and that her "crowned are as the locusts, and [her] captains as the great grasshoppers, which camp in the hedges in the cold day, but when the sun ariseth they flee away." Suddenly Kipling's simple statement that "the captains and the kings depart" takes on ominous connotations. No longer is this just a reference to their return to other duties after the Diamond Jubilee; now it has become a prophesy of their unreliability during future upheavals in the empire.

Similarly, the expression "Lord God of Hosts" becomes ambiguous as the poem progresses and as we begin to track down Kipling's Biblical allusions. In the first stanza it seems obvious that God is on England's side. He is, after all, "Lord of our far-flung battle-line." His "Hosts" are the hordes of British soldiers and loyal Indian sepoys who have long and successfully defended the empire. But again, after reading the Bible, we discover that the "Lord of Hosts" destroys Tyre by raising up in revolt "the terrible of nations." Like England, Tyre had been a great sea power but eventually had begun to boast, "I am a God, and I sit in the midst of the seas." These boasts, like those Kipling admonishes in the fourth and fifth stanzas, were made by men "drunk with sight of power" who put their trust in "reeking tube and iron shard" (guns and bullets) instead of in God. Their fate was to be swallowed up by the "lesser breeds without the law" and this is exactly what Kipling fears may happen to England. Thus, in commemorating Queen Victoria's Diamond Jubilee, Kipling has written what he fears may prove to be the empire's dirge. He is obviously ambivalent—torn between his pride in the "far-flung battle-line" and his shame in the "reeking tube and iron shard" that maintain it. This ambivalence laps at his consciousness like the waves of a rising tide through the repetitions of the word "lest," meaning "for fear that . . . for fear that!" Eventually his fears predominate and he bursts out with the concluding prayer:

> For frantic boast and foolish word—
> Thy mercy on thy people, Lord!

Poems for Further Study

DESERT PLACES

Snow falling and night falling fast, oh, fast
In a field I looked into going past,
And the ground almost covered smooth in snow,
But a few weeds and stubble showing last.

5   The woods around it have it—it is theirs.
All animals are smothered in their lairs.
I am too absent-spirited to count;
The loneliness includes me unawares.

And lonely as it is that loneliness
10   Will be more lonely ere it will be less—
A blanker whiteness of benighted[3] snow
With no expression, nothing to express.

---

[3] Overtaken by darkness or night.

They cannot scare me with their empty spaces
Between stars—on stars where no human race is.
15 I have it in me so much nearer home
To scare myself with my own desert places.

—Robert Frost [1936]

_____ ❧ QUESTIONS ❧ _____

1.   As in "Stopping by Woods on a Snowy Evening" (page 665), the solitary speaker pauses near nightfall to watch the woods fill up with snow. How is the speaker's situation and attitude different in "Desert Places"?

2.   Why is the field emphasized in this poem and why are the woods emphasized in the other?

3.   What difference does it make that the speaker is absolutely alone in this poem and accompanied by a horse in the other?

4.   In "Stopping by Woods on a Snowy Evening" Frost continually suggests interactions between the speaker and the owner of the land, between the speaker and his horse, and between the speaker and those to whom he has made promises. Are there any interactions in "Desert Places"? Indeed, are there any people, animals, or objects with which the speaker can interact?

5.   Why does Frost describe the animals as "smothered in their lairs" (l. 6)? Why does he not provide antecedents for any of the *it*'s in line 5—"The woods around it have it—it is theirs"? Why does he not provide an antecedent for *they* in line 13—"They cannot scare me with their empty spaces"?

6.   Lines 11–12 suggest that the snow will have "no expression, nothing to express." Would one expect snow to have something to express? Could the speaker now be describing his own loneliness?

7.   Where are the speaker's "own desert places"? What is he afraid of? How can he—indeed how does he—combat his fear?

8.   Frost uses repetition frequently in this poem—particularly in lines 1, 5, 8 through 10, and 12. Analyze the effects of the repetition in each of these instances.

BOTH SIDES NOW

Bows and flows of angel hair,
And ice cream castles in the air,
And feather canyons ev'rywhere,
I've looked at clouds that way.
5 But now they only block the sun,
They rain and snow on ev'ryone.
So many things I would have done.
But clouds got in my way.
I've looked at clouds from both sides now,
10 From up and down and still somehow

It's cloud illusions I recall;
I really don't know clouds
At all.

Moons and Junes and ferris wheels,
15 The dizzy dancing way you feel,
As ev'ry fairy tale comes real,
I've looked at love that way.
But now it's just another show,
You leave 'em laughing when you go.
20 And if you care, don't let them know,
Don't give yourself away.
I've looked at love from both sides now,
From give and take and still somehow
It's love's illusions I recall;
25 I really don't know love
At all.

Tears and fears and feeling proud,
To say "I love you" right out loud,
Dreams and schemes and circus crowds,
30 I've looked at life that way.
But now old friends are acting strange,
They shake their heads, they say I've changed.
But something's lost but something's gained,
In living ev'ry day.
35 I've looked at life from both sides now,
From win and lose and still somehow
It's life's illusions I recall;
I really don't know life
At all.

—Joni Mitchell [1967]

❧ QUESTIONS ❧

1.   Mitchell's song is divided into three stanzas. What is the subject of each
stanza? Consider the development from one stanza to another. What is implied about the changes in the speaker's age and point of view as the poem
unfolds?

2.   Consider the structure of each stanza. What three divisions of thought
are repeated in each stanza? What do these sections within each stanza tell us
about the growth and development of the speaker?

3.   Each stanza includes a refrain, but the refrains are not all identical. What
does the refrain contribute to the meaning of each stanza and how do the
slight changes in the refrain help to develop Mitchell's theme? What major
statement do you think she wishes to make about life and illusions?

8

❀❀❀❀❀❀❀

Puns and Paradoxes

THE PUN

An ambiguous statement that is intended to be humorous is called a *pun*. Puns almost invariably attain their effect by using one of the thousands of word pairs in English (called homonyms) that are identical in sound and spelling but differ in meaning. If, for example, a woman tells us she knows nothing of labor, she has either never borne children or never held down a job, depending on whether she is using *labor* to mean "the pains and efforts of childbirth" or "employment." **A pun that is risqué or sexually suggestive is called *double entendre* (a French phrase meaning "to understand in two ways").**

Shakespeare uses *double entendre* with exuberance in the final couplet of Sonnet CXLIII:

CXLIII

Lo, as a careful housewife runs to catch
One of her feathered creatures broke away,
Sets down her babe, and makes all swift dispatch
In pursuit of the thing she would have stay;
5   Whilst her neglected child holds her in chase,
Cries to catch her whose busy care is bent
To follow that which flies before her face,
Not prizing her poor infant's discontent:
So runn'st thou after that which flies from thee,
10   Whilst I thy babe chase thee afar behind;
But if thou catch thy hope, turn back to me,
And play the mother's part, kiss me, be kind;
So will I pray that thou mayst have thy "Will,"
If thou turn back and my loud crying still.
               —William Shakespeare [ca. 1600]

673

If we have read Shakespeare's other sonnets (particularly, numbers CXXXIII, CXXXIV, CXLII, and CXLIV), we know that this one is addressed to the famous "woman colour'd ill," with whom he is in love; we also know that she is in love with Shakespeare's friend, "a man right fair." The first twelve lines of the poem carefully prepare us for the concluding couplet. The dark lady is compared with a housewife who chases after a "feathered" creature (presumably a cock or hen, but possibly also a fashionable, "feathered" courtier),[1] while her "neglected child" (Shakespeare) chases after her. Thus, the phrase "have thy 'Will' " may mean:

> So I will pray that thou mayst recapture the hen
> If thou turn back and my loud crying still.

But the original phrase "have thy will," when applied to relations between the sexes, may also mean to "satisfy one's lust"; and finally, to "have thy 'Will' " may mean—rather shockingly—that "Will" Shakespeare is prepared to tolerate his mistress's sexual infidelities so long as she returns to him afterward. In effect, Shakespeare has created a *triple entendre!*

THE PARADOX

Just as a pun is a form of ambiguity that plays on words, a paradox plays on ideas. When Mark Twain wrote, for example, that soap and education are less sudden than a massacre but more deadly in the long run, he was using a paradox. He expected his readers to recognize that, although the analogy is literally untrue, it would pass for truth with anyone who has seen the anguish of a schoolboy forced to wash or sit still. The paradox turns on the difference between physical death and the "deadly fear" of soap or the "deadly boredom" of school, and it alludes to the death of imagination that sometimes results from the "civilizing" influence of soap and education. Thus, **a *paradox* is a statement that is true in some sense, even though at first it appears self-contradictory and absurd. When a paradox is expressed in only two words (living death, wise fool, etc.) it is called an *oxymoron*.**

Paradoxes are used in poetry for at least three reasons. First, they invariably startle the reader. They are unexpected and, initially, inexplicable. Next, paradoxes involve the reader in an effort at understanding. And finally, if that effort is successful, each paradox delights the reader with a personal sense of discovery. **Like allegory and metaphor, a paradox requires the reader to participate intellectually in the creation of literary meaning.** Without this active participation, a paradox is simply incomprehensible.

In the sonnet "Design" (p. 656) Frost builds toward a paradox by lulling us into complacency with his fluid and unanswerable rhetorical questions:

> What had that flower to do with being white,
> The wayside blue and innocent heal-all?
> What brought the kindred spider to that height,
> Then steered the white moth thither in the night?

Then, just as we are beginning to reassure ourselves that such incidents may be the result of pure happenstance, Frost startles us by suggesting a paradoxical solution:

---

[1] The phrase *"feathered creatures"* is, therefore, *ambiguous* and can serve as one more example of that rhetorical device.

What but design of darkness to appall?—
If design govern in a thing so small.

According to Frost, the appalling congruence of whites in the poem is the "design of darkness." At first, perhaps, our intellects rebel against the paradox that darkness controls these three white objects—it is, after all, a little nonsensical. But Frost's intention is to hint at the possibility that malevolence or evil lurks beneath the otherwise orderly surface of the natural world. By creating the paradox of a darkness that transforms the purest of whites into "assorted characters of death and blight," he makes us question our faith in the eventual triumph of good over evil.

In general, a paradox involves a contradiction between the physical or material meaning of words and their spiritual, emotional, or supernatural connotation, as in the case of Frost's poem. Such contradictory connotations also govern Mark Twain's lighthearted paradox, for soap and education are emotionally, but not physically, painful. Because paradoxes are capable of playing on the contrasts between earthly and spiritual truths, they are particularly common in religious revelations. In the ancient *Upanishads* of India (the chief theological documents of Hinduism), we learn, for instance, that "the gods love the obscure and hate the obvious." And the *Katha Upanishad* contains a number of paradoxes that raise questions about the interrelationship among mind, matter, and reality:

> If the slayer thinks he slays,
> If the slain thinks he is slain,
> Both these do not understand:
> He slays not, is not slain.
> —From the *Katha Upanishad*
> [700–600 B.C.]

Similarly, Taoism, a Chinese religion that dates back more than 2,000 years, teaches that

> One may know the world without going out of doors.
> One may see the Way of Heaven without looking through the windows.
> The further one goes, the less one knows.
> Therefore the sage knows without going about,
> Understands without seeing,
> And accomplishes without any action.
> —From *The Way of Lao-tzu* [600–200 B.C.]

Later, in the Gospel according to St. John, 11:25–6, we find Jesus saying,

I am the resurrection, and the life: he that believeth in me, though he were dead, yet shall he live:
And whosoever liveth and believeth in me shall never die.
> —From the *New Testament* [first century A.D.]

In each case the paradox is initially disconcerting, or at least difficult to understand; however, each ultimately extends to us the principal consolation of religion: the faith in an existence that is more permanent and more attractive than the nasty, brutish, and short life sometimes said to be allotted to ordinary human beings.

Pure paradoxes, involving wholly contradictory ideas, are relatively uncommon in poetry. However, *incongruity,* a similar rhetorical device, is plentiful. **A word, a phrase, or an idea is said to be incongruous when it is out of keeping, inconsistent, or inappropriate in its particular surroundings.** As was the case with ambiguity, incongruity is sometimes a stylistic flaw—a sign of sloppy thinking or imprecise writing—but when used carefully, it can subtly change the meaning of the surrounding words. When Byron wrote about amatory poets who "sing their loves/ In liquid lines mellifluously bland," he relied on the incongruity of the word "bland" to indicate his satiric disapproval of most love poetry. Byron knew very well that bland writing, like bland food, is usually dull or tasteless—the very opposite of the spicy passion one would expect to find in love poetry. This startling word choice hits us like a slap in the face when we have been expecting a gentle goodnight kiss and effectively conveys Byron's distaste for conventional love poetry.

Poems for Further Study

"WHOSO LIST TO HUNT, I KNOW WHERE IS AN HIND!"[2]

Whoso list° to hunt, I know where is an hind!	*wishes*
But as for me, helas!° I may no more!	*alas*
The vain travail° hath wearied me so sore,	*labor*
I am of them that furthest come behind!	

5 Yet may I, by no means, my wearied mind
    Draw from the deer! but as she fleeth afore,
    Fainting I follow. I leave off therefore,
Since in a net I seek to hold the wind!
Who list her hunt, I put him out of doubt,
10   As well as I, may spend his time in vain!
    And graven with diamonds, in letters plain,
There is written, her fair neck round about,
    'Noli me tangere!'[3] *for CÆSAR's I am;*
    And wild for to hold, though I seem tame.'

—Sir Thomas Wyatt [posthumous, 1557]

🌿 QUESTIONS 🌿

1.   What is the literal situation described in the poem? What has the speaker been hunting? Why is he wearied? What advice does he give to the reader?

2.   How does Wyatt's pun involving the word *deer* give to the poem a second—and more scandalous—meaning? How do the various elements in the

---

[2] Adapted from Petrarch, *Rime,* sonnet 190.
[3] "Touch me not!" Wyatt's sonnet is thought to refer to the situation of Anne Boleyn (1507–1536) in whom Wyatt took an interest both before and after her liaison with Henry VIII (1491–1547).

poem (the hunt, the hind, the vain travail, the diamond necklace, the reference to Caesar, and the final warning) all fit this second reading?

3.   How do the connotations of the hunt serve to characterize both the speaker and the woman he pursues?

4.   What do you make of the paradox of seeking to hold the wind in a net? How well does that paradox describe the situation of a man on the verge of abandoning his pursuit of a fleet-footed deer? How well does it fit the situation of one who is despairing of success in an illicit love affair with a married woman?

THE MAN HE KILLED

"Had he and I but met
   By some old ancient inn,
We should have sat us down to wet
   Right many a nipperkin![4]

5 "But ranged as infantry,
      And staring face to face,
   I shot at him as he at me,
      And killed him in his place.

   "I shot him dead because—
10   Because he was my foe,
   Just so: my foe of course he was;
      That's clear enough; although

   "He thought he'd 'list, perhaps,
      Off-hand like—just as I—
15 Was out of work—had sold his traps—
      No other reason why.

   "Yes; quaint and curious war is!
      You shoot a fellow down
   You'd treat if met where any bar is,
20   Or help to half-a-crown."

                              —Thomas Hardy [1909]

❧ QUESTIONS ❧

1.   What paradox about warfare is at the heart of this poem? Does Hardy explain and resolve the paradox or simply bring it to your attention?

2.   How does the repetition in the third stanza affect the poem's tone?

---

[4] Half-pint of beer or ale.

3. The speaker in this poem is a common soldier. What were his motives for enlisting? What is his attitude toward "the enemy"?

4. Why does Hardy avoid any mention of the reasons for the warfare? Do you think he is being fair or merely manipulating the reader? Explain your position.

9

Irony

The term *irony* refers to a contrast or discrepancy between appearance and reality. This discrepancy can take on a number of different forms.

In *dramatic irony* the state of affairs known to the audience (or reader) is the reverse of what its participants suppose it to be. This is the form of irony used in *King Oedipus*. When the action of the play begins, Oedipus believes that, by fleeing his homeland as a youth, he has evaded the prophesy that he will murder his father and marry his mother. The audience knows, however, that he has already committed these crimes. (The audience's knowledge derives in part from the fact that Sophocles was writing about a widely known Theban legend and in part from the prophecies made by the oracle Tiresias early in the play.) Thus, the tragic impact of *King Oedipus* depends largely on our fascination with the plight of a man who is unaware of his own past, unable to avoid his own destiny, and driven remorselessly toward his fate by his very efforts to avoid it.

In *situational irony* a set of circumstances turns out to be the reverse of what is appropriate or expected. Richard Cory, the "hero" of Edwin Arlington Robinson's poem, is widely envied and admired because of his wealth, his charm, and his apparently agreeable life. Everything about him leads the "people on the pavement"—and the reader as well—to assume that he must be happy. He is "a gentleman from sole to crown," "clean favored," "quietly arrayed," and "richer than a king." In a world polarized between rich and poor, beautiful and plain, dignified and common, "them" and "us," Richard Cory seems without question to be "one of them," until the last lines of the poem show us otherwise:

RICHARD CORY

Whenever Richard Cory went down town,
We people on the pavement looked at him:
He was a gentleman from sole to crown,
Clean favored, and imperially slim.

5   And he was always quietly arrayed,
         And he was always human when he talked;
         But still he fluttered pulses when he said;
         "Good-morning," and he glittered when he walked.

         And he was rich—yes, richer than a king—
10   And admirably schooled in every grace:
         In fine, we thought that he was everything
         To make us wish that we were in his place.

         So on we worked, and waited for the light,
         And went without the meat, and cursed the bread;
15   And Richard Cory, one calm summer night,
         Went home and put a bullet through his head.
                                    —Edwin Arlington Robinson [1897]

Henry David Thoreau once wrote that "the mass of men lead lives of quiet desperation." Ironically, Richard Cory's suicide suggests that he was, after all, "one of us."

The most common form of irony, *verbal irony*, involves a contrast between what is literally said and what is actually meant. Lord Byron wittily uses this figure of speech to satirize religious hypocrisy in explaining that a serious illness has made him pious—presumably because of the usual fear of dying unrepentant:

         The first attack at once proved the Divinity
            (But that I never doubted, nor the Devil);
         The next, the Virgin's mystical virginity;
            The third, the usual Origin of Evil;
         The fourth at once established the whole Trinity
            On so uncontrovertible a level
         That I devoutly wished the three were four,
         On purpose to believe so much the more.
                                    —From *Don Juan,* Lord Byron [1823]

Verbal irony always requires the reader to detect the discrepancy between the denotative meaning of the words and the author's intention in using them—in this case, between Byron's *claim* that he wished the three persons of the Trinity were four and his *purpose* in satirizing death-bed piety. Thus, verbal irony is the riskiest of all poetic devices because there is always the possibility that the author's intentions will go unrecognized. In 1702, for example, Daniel Defoe, who was himself a Puritan "dissenter," anonymously wrote an essay called "The Shortest Way with the Dissenters," in which he tried to satirize the excessive zeal of his Anglican opponents by ironically contending that Puritan ministers should be hanged and all members of their congregations banished. To his surprise, no one perceived the irony: the Anglican establishment fully endorsed his proposals. Public unrest followed, the government intervened, and Defoe was fined, pilloried, and imprisoned—all because his irony was so badly misunderstood.

Jonathan Swift, Defoe's contemporary, escaped a similar misunderstanding by making his ironic exaggerations so extreme that no one could miss the point and take them seriously. In 1729, when he wanted to draw the attention of the Anglican government to the plight of starving Catholic children, he published *A Modest Proposal for Preventing the Children of Poor People in Ireland from Being a Burden to Their Parents or Country, and for Making Them Beneficial to the Public.* In this pamphlet he suggested that they be fattened, slaughtered, and sold as a delicacy like veal:

A child will make two dishes at an entertainment for friends; and when the family dines alone, the fore or hind quarter will make a reasonable dish, and seasoned with a little pepper or salt will be very good boiled on the fourth day, especially in winter.

—From *A Modest Proposal,* Jonathan Swift [1729]

In using such overstatement to ridicule the government's disregard of the suffer-. ings of the Irish Catholics, Swift hoped to force a change in British policy. Just as a surgeon's blade cuts so that it may cure, Swift's language is corrosive so that it may be corrective. **Writing** such as this, **which holds up persons, ideas, or things to varying degrees of ridicule or contempt in order to bring about some desirable change, is known as** *satire.*

Swift, Defoe, and Byron all sought to underscore and identify their ironies through exaggeration or *overstatement* (sometimes called *hyperbole*). Each hoped that the reader would perceive the exaggeration and therefore interpret the text as meaning the opposite of what it appeared to say. Swift really recommended Christian charity, not infanticide; Defoe really endorsed Christian tolerance, not narrow bigotry; and Byron really advocated Deism or agnosticism, not hypocritical piety.

The other principal means by which poets signal irony is *understatement*—as when J. Alfred Prufrock, the protagonist of T. S. Eliot's famous poem, sadly reflects in a moment of self-disparagement that he has "measured out [his] life with coffee spoons." Just as overstatement is too emphatic, too exuberant, or too harsh, an understatement is too mild or too reserved. In both cases the reader's attention is arrested and his or her sensitivity to potential irony heightened because the poet's words are literally unbelievable.

Understated irony is often sarcastic. Unlike satire, *sarcasm* **(from the Greek word** *sarkazein* **meaning "to tear flesh") is intended to hurt, not heal.** Prufrock's bitter reflections about his life are often sarcastic. For a more modern and clearer example of sarcasm, consider Sir Winston Churchill's characterization of his political rival, Clement Atlee (Prime Minister of England, 1949–1951): "a very modest man—and with reason." Sarcasm, however, is not always so understated. Oscar Wilde, the nineteenth-century English novelist and dramatist, for example, was obviously exaggerating when he sarcastically claimed that "there are two ways of disliking poetry: one way is to dislike it, the other is to read Pope."

Although we have suggested that both overstatement and understatement often signal irony, it is wise to remember that they are not invariably ironic. Overstatement is especially susceptible to use and abuse in everyday speech by those who hope to be vivacious and enthusiastic. It is the linguistic equivalent of a facile smile. Thus, we sometimes exclaim, "How time flies!" when we mean, "it's getting late"; or, when we meet someone for the first time, we may say, "I'm delighted to meet you!" when we mean only, "Hello." Sometimes poets also overstate the truth as a means of showing enthusiasm; but, they, of course, find fresh and original ways of revitalizing tired hyperbolic formulas. Andrew Marvell expresses the idea of time flying by writing in "To His Coy Mistress" (1681),

> But ever at my back I hear
> Time's winged chariot hurrying near.

And Dr. Faustus, in Christopher Marlowe's play of that name (1589), greets Helen of Troy, not with a lame "pleased to meet you," but with a rhetorical question that combines metonymy and overstatement in an expression of sheer rapture:

> Was this the face that launched a thousand ships,
> And burnt the topless towers of Ilium?

Indeed, it may be that exuberance and a delight in words are the fundamental qualities of poetry. Poetry, it has been said, is what is lost in translation. The poet's use of ambiguity, irony, puns, and paradoxes depends almost entirely on the fact that certain words have multiple meanings. A skilled poet is almost by definition sensitive to the specific denotations and connotations of each word at his or her command. A poet knows that any change in word choice is a change in poetic meaning; that any attempt to translate, paraphrase, or summarize a poem is also an attempt to rewrite it—an act that inevitably damages its essence. Even the gentlest touch can be destructive. One cannot, even in admiration, stretch out the wings of the monarch butterfly without brushing the gold from their tips.

But if, in criticism as in entomology, we murder to dissect, what we murder through literary criticism is imperishable. After we have learned all we can from dissection, we have only to turn away from the battered specimen on the critic's pages—we have only to turn back to the poem itself—in order to find our monarch butterfly both alive and made more beautiful by understanding.

Poems for Further Study

OZYMANDIAS[1]

I met a traveller from an antique land
Who said: "Two vast and trunkless legs of stone
Stand in the desert. Near them, on the sand,
Half sunk, a shattered visage lies, whose frown,
5   And wrinkled lip, and sneer of cold command,
Tell that its sculptor well those passions read
Which yet survive, stamped on these lifeless things,
The hand that mocked them and the heart that fed.[2]
And on the pedestal these words appear—
10   "My name is Ozymandias, king of kings:
Look on my works, ye mighty, and despair!'
Nothing beside remains. Round the decay
Of that colossal wreck, boundless and bare
The lone and level sands stretch far away."

—Percy Bysshe Shelley [1818]

---

[1] The Greek name for Ramses II, a king of Egypt in the thirteenth century B.C.
[2] "Hand" and "heart" are the direct objects of the verb "survive." The sneering passions shown in the sculpture have outlived the hand of the artist and the heart of Ozymandias.

❦ QUESTIONS ❦

1.   What can you tell about the personality of Ozymandias from the expression on his sculpted face and from the size of the sculpture? What can you tell about the sculptor?

2.   What forms of irony are used in this poem? What conclusion about the durability of human achievements do you think Shelley wishes us to reach?

3.   What attitude toward kings is implicitly conveyed in this poem? (If possible, do some background reading about Shelley himself and the times in which he lived.)

4.   Consider the structure of the poem. What is the main subject of the first eight lines? How is that subject slightly changed and developed in the last six lines?

"IS MY TEAM PLOUGHING"

"Is my team ploughing,
    That I was used to drive
And hear the harness jingle
    When I was man alive?"

5 Ay, the horses trample,
    The harness jingles now;
No change though you lie under
    The land you used to plough.

"Is football playing
10   Along the river shore,
With lads to chase the leather,
    Now I stand up no more?"

Ay, the ball is flying,
    The lads play heart and soul;
15 The goal stands up, the keeper
    Stands up to keep the goal.

"Is my girl happy,
    That I thought hard to leave,
And has she tired of weeping
20   As she lies down at eve?"

Ay, she lies down lightly,
    She lies not down to weep:
Your girl is well contented.
    Be still, my lad, and sleep.

25   "Is my friend hearty,
        Now I am thin and pine,
     And has he found to sleep in
        A better bed than mine?"

     Yes, lad, I lie easy,
30   I lie as lads would choose;
     I cheer a dead man's sweetheart,
        Never ask me whose.

                    —A. E. Housman [1896]

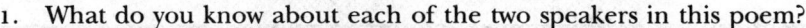

🌿 QUESTIONS 🌿

1. What do you know about each of the two speakers in this poem?

2. What reassurance does the first speaker seem to desire and receive?

3. Discuss the use of ambiguity and *double entendre* in the living friend's responses during the second half of the poem. How are these responses ironic?

4. In answer to each of the dead man's questions about changes in the world, the living friend says in essence, "Everything remains as it was before you died; nothing has changed." Is he telling the truth?

5. Housman is often seen as a cynical poet. How and where does his cynicism show up in this poem?

10

⁂⁂⁂

Imagery

Words that call upon our senses are referred to as *images*. Images may appeal to any of our five senses and may be expressed in a single word, a phrase, a sentence, or even several sentences. Poets use imagery, for example, to paint a verbal picture of a calm mountain lake, to capture a fleeting birdsong, or to recall the odor of dead fish, the taste of champagne, or the feel of a wool sweater on bare skin. Notice how William Shakespeare uses imagery to capture the essence of spring and winter in the following poems from *Love's Labour's Lost* (1594):

[SPRING]

	When daisies pied,° and violets blue,	*many-colored*
	And lady-smocks all silver white,	
	And cuckoo-buds, of yellow hue,	
	Do paint the meadows with delight,	
5	The cuckoo then on ev'ry tree	
	Mocks married men, for thus sings he;	
	Cuckoo!	
	Cuckoo! cuckoo!—O word of fear,	
	Unpleasing to a married ear!	
10	When shepherds pipe on oaten straws,°	*reed pipes*
	And merry larks are ploughmen's clocks,	
	When turtles tread° and rooks and daws,	*turtledoves mate*
	And maidens bleach their summer smocks;	
	The cuckoo then on every tree	
15	Mocks married men, for thus sings he;	

685

Cuckoo!
Cuckoo! Cuckoo!—O word of fear,
Unpleasing to a married ear!

—William Shakespeare [1594]

❧ QUESTIONS ❧

1.   What is the predominant mood in the first four lines of each stanza?
Where does the delight in spring seem to lead one and why is spring a season
to be feared by married men?

2.   Paraphrase line 4. Why is Shakespeare's highly figurative language more
effective than an explicit, literal statement about the many-colored meadows?

3.   What note of discord enters the poem in lines 5-9? How does this unexpected shift in the poem's direction reflect the poet's awareness both of the
natural changes caused by spring and of the emotional changes that spring
encourages? What connotations are suggested by the cuckoo's cry? Does this
incongruity in the various ideas connoted by spring make the poem better or
worse? Why?

4.   Examine the poem's imagery. How much does the combination of visual
and aural imagery contribute to its effectiveness? How much is added by the
range of images (springtime flowers, birds, and people)?

5.   What conventions of pastoral poetry play a part in the second stanza? Is
the cuckoo's "word of fear" a part of the pastoral tradition or does it add a
note of realism?

6.   Why does Shakespeare break his metrical pattern in lines 7 and 16?

[WINTER]

When icicles hang by the wall,
   And Dick the shepherd blows his nail,
And Tom bears logs into the hall,
   And milk comes frozen home in pail;
5   When blood is nipt, and ways be foul,
   Then nightly sings the staring owl,
           Tu-whoo!
Tu-whit! tu-whoo! a merry note,
While greasy Joan doth keel° the pot.   *stir*

10   When all aloud the wind doth blow,
   And coughing drowns the parson's saw,°   *proverb*
And birds sit brooding in the snow,
   And Marian's nose looks red and raw;
When roasted crabs° hiss in the bowl,   *crabapples*
15   Then nightly sings the staring owl,
           Tu-whoo!

Tu-whit! tu-whoo! a merry note,
While greasy Joan doth keel the pot.

—William Shakespeare [1594]

❧ QUESTIONS ❧

1. Compare this poem with "Spring." What similarities do you find in meter, rhyme scheme, and organization?

2. Why does Shakespeare use specific names—Dick, Tom, Joan, and Marian—in this poem, while he did not in "Spring"? What emotions and activities does Shakespeare wish you to see as being nearly universal in the spring? Are there any emotions or activities that he wishes you to believe are equally widespread in the winter?

3. Is the owl's cry really "a merry note"? What are the connotations of the owl's hooting? Why does Shakespeare use irony here?

4. Compare the imagery in "Winter" and "Spring." Which poem evokes a wider range of senses?

As Shakespeare's poems suggest, everything we know about the seasons of the year (not to mention the seasons in our lives and the phenomena of nature) is a result of what we have seen, heard, smelled, tasted, touched, and felt internally. Our senses provide the link between our minds and external reality. Sensations alone create for us the familiar world of men and women, mountains and valleys, lakes and rivers, physical pleasure and physical pain. So, too, with poetry. Poems without imagery are like a people without vision or hearing. Both exist in darkness and in silence, struggling for understanding in a world of inexpressible abstractions.

One of the achievements of mankind, of course, is the development of languages and systems of thought that allow us to intellectualize our experiences. When we read a poem we are actually declaring ourselves independent of the sensations of the moment. We call forth from our memories various sensual experiences or images. We rearrange those memories in the patterns suggested by the poet—patterns that often do not correspond with any of our actual experiences. In so doing, we participate in vicarious experiences. Images, therefore, are the windows through which we see (or imagine) how other men and women live, and love, and die. They enable us to make discoveries about ourselves, about others, and about the world in which we live.

To some extent, all words create images. The most abstract terms, as well as the most precise verbal pictures, require us to find meaning *in the words* by recollecting, however vaguely, experiences of our own in which we have read, heard, or used those words. Words such as *dragonfly, hollow,* and *heft* summon up fairly specific sensual responses based on sight, sound, and muscular exertion. We see mentally the bulbous eyes, the quivering wings, and the slim, hovering body of the dragonfly. We hear mentally the "hollow" sound of a voice in an empty room. We feel mentally a muscular play in the forearm and shoulder at the "heft" of a nine-iron, a favorite tennis racquet, or a crammed suitcase. But if we replace these imagistic words with scientific or generic terms—if, that is, *dragonfly* becomes *insect, hollow* becomes *void,* and *heft* becomes *specific gravity*—suddenly our mental images are deflated, like limp balloons, because the new terms are mere abstractions divorced from physical sensation.

A good poet always searches for an exact image—an image with its own spicy taste, aroma, and appearance—in preference to the trite and overly general words or combinations of words served up like a tasteless pasta in sentimental verse. The difference between concrete, original imagery and imprecise, overworked banality can be illustrated by comparing the first stanza of George Meredith's *Modern Love* with three stanzas on the same subject (the discovery of infidelity) in "Lady Byron's Reply to Lord Byron's 'Fare Thee Well' ":

> By this he knew she wept with waking eyes:
> That, at his hand's light quiver by her head,
> The strange low sobs that shook their common bed,
> Were called into her with a sharp surprise,
> And strangled mute, like little gaping snakes,
> Dreadfully venomous to him. She lay
> Stone-still, and the long darkness flowed away
> With muffled pulses. Then, as midnight makes
> Her giant heart of Memory and Tears
> Drink the pale drug of silence, and so beat
> Sleep's heavy measure, they from head to feet
> Were moveless, looking through their dead black years,
> By vain regret scrawled over the blank wall.
> Like sculptured effigies, they might be seen
> Upon their marriage-tomb, the sword between;
> Each wishing for the sword that severs all.
> —From *Modern Love,* George Meredith [1862]

> Yes, farewell, farewell forever,
>   Thou thyself hast fix'd our doom,
> Bade hope's sweetest blossoms wither,
>   Never more for me to bloom.
>   . . .
> Wrapt in dreams of joy abiding
>   On thy breast my head hath lain,
> In thy love and truth confiding,
>   Bliss I cannot know again.
>
> When thy heart by me "glanc'd over"
>   First displayed the guilty stain,
> Would these eyes had closed forever,
>   Ne'er to weep thy crimes again.
>   —From "Lady Byron's Reply,"
>   Anonymous

Both poets describe their feelings of betrayal, but "Lady Byron's" hack work is entirely devoid of real action and imagery. It is made up of sentimental commonplaces whose only virtue is that we can understand them without bothering to think. Each line from "Yes, farewell, farewell forever" to "Ne'er to weep thy crimes again" deserves, and most likely gets, nothing more than an exasperated groan from readers who recognize that this "poet" has nothing new to say, nothing original to describe, no actions to represent, no knowledge of the world, and no understanding of poetic style beyond that which allows her to pull at the "throbbing heart-strings" of the most sentimental and imperceptive readers.

In contrast, Meredith's poetry is packed with specific sensory experiences. It is true that throughout the stanza the unhappy marriage partners lie almost motionless. But Meredith allows us to see the wife as she weeps with "waking eyes," to watch her reaction at "his hand's light quiver by her head," to hear and feel "the strange low sobs that shook their common bed," and perhaps even to taste the bitterness of "the pale drug of silence." Furthermore, a series of vivid phrases builds a sense of muscular tension: the wife's sobs were *"strangled mute";* she *"lay stone still";* together they looked back on "dead black years,/ By vain regret *scrawled* over the blank wall."

Few poets find ways to call into play as many different senses as Meredith has in this stanza. Only the sense of smell is missing; and, as if to make up for the deficiency, Meredith manages to work an image of smell into his second stanza, where the wife's beauty sickens the husband, "as at breath of poison flowers." No doubt this exhaustive catalogue of sensory imagery is intentional. Meredith's purpose is to show that the subtle change in the relationship between the former lovers has uprooted their lives and left them unable to engage in any human experience without seeing it anew and finding in it signs of their own emotional distress.

Thus, Meredith makes a thematic point by showing that every sensation the couple feels is altered by their present unhappiness. The use of poetic imagery does far more than simply add vigor to his writing; and what is true of Meredith's poem is true of poetry in general. **Poets often choose their imagery according to some *principle of selection* and develop it with some meaningful pattern in mind.** In Meredith's case, the principle of selection is an attempt to convey the fact that all of the husband's senses have been altered by the discovery of his wife's infidelity. A second principle of selection is at work in Meredith's preoccupation throughout the poem with images of death. The first stanza alone makes reference to snakes, venoms, pale drugs, dead black years, sculptured effigies, and marriage tombs. At no point in the stanza does Meredith *tell* us that he is describing the death of love; however, his images allow us to determine that this must be his theme—that the wife's slight stiffening at her husband's touch is a sign of marital *rigor mortis.*

We should also be aware of the *pattern of development* in the imagery of the stanza. Initially, the focus is on the woman's waking eyes and the quivering hand beside her head. Then Meredith expands our vision to take in the bed, the surrounding darkness, and finally midnight's "giant heart of Memory and Tears." The effect is like that achieved by "zooming out" while filming a movie. It puts the marriage partners at the center of a universe that resonates "with muffled pulses" to their sufferings. Having established this broad perspective, Meredith uses imagery that closes in again—first to the memories scrawled across the blank walls and then to the marriage-tomb and the imaginary sword between the man and wife. This cyclical pattern in the development of the imagery is one of several devices Meredith uses to make each stanza a self-contained and satisfying "sonnet."[1] It contributes to our impression that *Modern Love* is an autobiographical

---

[1] The stanza is not technically a sonnet because it is formed entirely of quatrains and contains sixteen lines to the sonnet's fourteen. Nevertheless, critics from Swinburne to Trevelyan have recognized the independence of each stanza by using the term *sonnet.*

series of journal entries chronicling the failure of an actual marriage. This poetic illusion, derived in large part from the pattern in the development of Meredith's imagery, makes *Modern Love* seem contemporary and realistic to each new generation of readers. It is one of the major stylistic features of the poem.

On rare occasions the principle of selection or pattern of development in imagery is more than simply a stylistic feature. It may provide a key to the entire poem or even to the poet's entire personality. In the poetry of Percy Bysshe Shelley, for example, we find repeated images involving sunsets, the wind and waves, moonlight, fountains, veiled women, and shadows. The very fact that Shelley returns so frequently to the same images suggests that he is giving voice to a philosophical preoccupation—namely, that the reality of life lies beneath its surface features and that everything we think to be real is in fact the product of unseen forces. As a result, Shelley's images are often indirect: the colors of the sunset proceed from the unseen sun; the waves are driven by the unseen wind, and the wind itself is caused by unknown forces; moonlight is reflected indirectly from the sun; fountains pulse as a result of unseen pressures; veils conceal feminine beauty; and shadows are indirect images. In each image there is a veil of some kind that conceals the true source of beauty, for Shelley was a strong believer in Platonic idealism.[2] Here, for example, is a brief poem by Shelley that reveals his typical concern for the reality that transcends appearances:

TO——

> Music, when soft voices die,
> Vibrates in the memory;
> Odors, when sweet violets sicken,
> Live within the sense they quicken.
>
> 5   Rose leaves, when the rose is dead,
> Are heaped for the belovèd's bed;
> And so thy thoughts, when thou art gone,
> Love itself shall slumber on.

> —Percy Bysshe Shelley
> [posthumous, 1824]

🌿 QUESTIONS 🌿

1. Examine the imagery in the poem. What different senses does Shelley call into play?

2. What are the similarities between the various images in the poem?

3. What thematic statements about beauty, love, departure, and death grow out of the poem?

---

[2] In Plato's allegory of the cave in *The Republic,* human beings are chained in such a way that they see only shadows cast on the wall of the cave and hear voices echoing from that wall. Naturally, they mistake the shadows and echoes for reality.

4. Examine the syntactic ambiguity in the final two lines. Does Shelley mean that the memories of the beloved will become the bed of love? Does he mean that Love itself will continue to dream about ("slumber on") the loved one ("thy thoughts")? Could he mean both at once?

We have seen that images make writing tangible, and we have seen that the manipulation of imagery is implicit in creative thought. In general, the more exact and evocative the imagery in a poem, the more interested and entertained the reader will remain. Imagery is as indispensable to an exciting poem as action and emotion are to an exciting life. Furthermore, **the poet's choice and arrangement of images may provide important clues to thematic and artistic purposes in philosophical poetry.** Shelley's belief in the Platonic ideal of intellectual beauty was abstract in the extreme, and it was a continual challenge to his poetic capabilities to find a way to write about the themes that interested him without allowing his poetry to degenerate into images that the reader would be unable to comprehend intellectually or emotionally.

Even themes less abstract than Shelley's are necessarily difficult to express imagistically. Although Meredith examines the effect on the human spirit of disappointments in love, he finds no direct way to tell us that this is his theme. To cope with the difficulty of discussing abstract ideas in imagistic language, poets normally turn to poetic comparisons, the subject of our next chapter.

11

Comparisons

In one poem Margaret Atwood refers to a landcrab as a "mouth on stilts." In another Sylvia Plath listens to her new-born child's "moth-breath." Elsewhere John Updike describes an ex-basketball player named Flick Webb whose "hands were like wild birds." In Sonnet 129 Shakespeare describes lust as "a swallowed bait,/ On purpose laid to make the taker mad." And in Sonnet 116 he describes love as "an ever-fixèd mark,/ That looks on tempests, and is never shaken." Each of these examples involves the use of a poetic comparison. **Poetic comparisons may take a variety of forms: *simile, metaphor, conceit, synecdoche, metonymy,* and *juxtaposition*.** Each form of comparison, however, serves the same basic set of purposes. **Poets generally use comparisons to express abstract ideas in imagistic language,** thereby stimulating the reader's imagination, providing additional information, and opening up endless opportunities for entertainment and persuasion. Consider, for example, the following poem in which the speaker tries to seduce a young woman by comparing the consequences of their lovemaking with those of an insignificant flea-bite.

THE FLEA

> Mark but this flea, and mark in this,
> How little that, which thou deny'st me, is;
> Me it sucked first, and now sucks thee,
> And in this flea our two bloods mingled be;
> Confess it. This cannot be said
> A sin, or shame, or loss of maidenhead,
> Yet this enjoys, before it woo,

5

And pampered swells with one blood made of two,
And this, alas! is more than we would do.

10   Oh stay, three lives in one flea spare,
Where we almost, nay more than married are.
This flea is you and I, and this
Our marriage bed and marriage temple is;
Though parents grudge, and you, we are met,
15   And cloistered in these living walls of jet.
Though use° make you apt° to kill me,   *custom / inclined*
Let not to that, self-murder added be,
And sacrilege, three sins in killing three.

Cruel and sudden, hast thou since
20   Purpled thy nail in blood of innocence?
Wherein could this flea guilty be,
Except in that drop, which it sucked from thee?
Yet thou triumph'st, and say'st that thou
Find'st not thyself nor me the weaker now;
25   'Tis true; then learn how false fears be:
Just so much honor, when thou yield'st to me,
Will waste, as this flea's death took life from thee.

—John Donne [1633]

❧ QUESTIONS ❧

1.   What similarities between the flea-bite and lovemaking does the speaker develop in the first stanza?

2.   What is the young woman about to do in the second stanza? How are the speaker's arguments that she should spare the flea related to his efforts to seduce her?

3.   What has the woman done by the beginning of the third stanza? Why has she done so? How does the speaker turn her action into one more argument that she should give herself to him?

4.   How convincing do you find the speaker's arguments? How ingenious are they? What do you think would be their effect upon the woman—that is, what do you think will be the consequences of this attempt at seduction? Why?

In developing this analogy at such length, Donne is creating an ***extended comparison or conceit.*** He uses the flea as one argument to illustrate that the physical relationship he desires is not in itself a significant event: a very similar union has already taken place within the flea without "sin, nor shame, nor loss of maidenhead." Thus, in "The Flea," as in shopping or voting, a comparison identifies and illustrates some of the issues involved in making a decision.

As we have noted, poetic comparisons may take a variety of forms. This variety is well represented by the five comparisons in the first two stanzas of John Donne's "Valediction: Forbidding Mourning" (1633):

> As virtuous men pass mildly away,
>   And whisper to their souls, to go,
> Whilst some of their sad friends do say,
>   The breath goes now, and some say, no:
>
> So let us melt, and make no noise,
>   No tear-floods, nor sigh-tempests move,
> 'Twere profanation of our joys
>   To tell the laity our love.

The first of the comparisons runs through four and one-half lines and says, in essence, "Let us be just as calm in separating as virtuous men are in dying." **Comparisons** such as this, **which formally develop a similarity between two things using** *as, as when, like, than,* **or other equivalent constructions, are known as** *similes* **(similes assert similarity). However, when a poet asserts that two terms are identical instead of merely similar he creates a** *metaphor.* In Donne's lines here, the hyphenated terms ("tear-floods" and "sigh-tempests"), although exaggerations, are good examples of metaphors; the speaker in the poem condemns those separating lovers who shed tears in a flood and sigh like a windy tempest. Most metaphors are expressed somewhat more fully than Donne's, using a form of the verb "to be," as in Shakespeare's assertion that "All the world's a stage."

Both similes and metaphors are common in everyday speech. We say somebody is "sharp as a tack" or "as slow as molasses"; a brand-new car may be either a "lemon" or a "peach." Such similes and metaphors may once have been original and exciting, but they have become overused. Indeed, a shiny new comparison, like the latest model from Detroit, may emerge from the factory with a built-in obsolescence. Even though the comparison may originally have been a very good one, constant repetition may eventually cause us to react with insensitivity, indifference, or even hostility. The better the metaphor is, the more miles are put on it and the more rapidly it is worn out. Good poets, like all good writers, know this and as a result seek constantly to manufacture new analogies.

All similes and metaphors contain two parts, or terms. The *principal* or *primary term* is the one that conveys the literal statement made in the poem. In Donne's metaphors of "tear-floods" and "sigh-tempests," the literal statement concerns tears and sighs—hence, these are his principal terms. The *secondary term* in a metaphor is used figuratively to add color, connotations, and specificity to the more abstract primary term. Thus, Donne's "floods" and "tempests" are his secondary terms. Some literary critics call the primary term in a metaphor its *tenor* and the secondary term its *vehicle.*

An analogy in which one or both of these terms is implied but not stated may properly be called a metaphor, but we prefer the term *implied comparison* **as being clearer and more accurate.** When, for example, Donne writes, " 'Twere profanation of our joys/ To tell the laity our love," he is using one form of implied comparison. What he means is that their love is holy and spiritual like a secret religious ceremony, but only the primary term of the simile ("our love") is actually expressed. The idea that this love is analogous to a religious rite is implicit in the use of the words "profanation" and "laity," but this similarity is left unstated.

On rare occasions, both terms in a comparison may be implied, as in Donne's phrase, "So let us melt." Here he is comparing the separation of spiritual lovers with the gentle natural process that transforms ice to water; however, he relies on the reader to reconstruct mentally this comparison from the single clue he provides in the verb "melt."

While metaphors, similes, and implied comparisons are useful to poets primarily because they offer a mechanism for stating abstract truths through specific images, they also contribute intellectual stimulation, emotional connotations, and conciseness. In the two stanzas just examined, Donne has been struggling to put into words his conception of the relationship between himself and his lover and of how their separation can best reveal the depth of their love. Donne wisely avoids any generalized statement of his intentions, choosing instead to express himself entirely through images of a dying man, of melting, of floods and tempests, and of clergy and laity. In addition to making his writing vivid and concrete, these images are intellectually stimulating, imaginative, and even a little audacious. The gist of Donne's argument is that true love is not wholly physical. It is capable of going through a change in state from physical to spiritual (as the soul does in death), or from fixed to formless (as hard ice becomes fluid water). By confronting, in the beginning, the exaggerated fear that separation foreshadows death, Donne is able to transform that fear into a religious consolation in which the secret joys of the lovers become sacramental experiences. In one bold and inherently sacrilegious sentence, Donne manages to tie together an awe-inspiring image of human mortality, a fundamental law of physics, the stormy forces of nature, and the powerful attraction of love. All of this imagery is permeated with emotional overtones (sorrow, resignation, fear, piety) that might have been lost in any direct statement about spiritual love, self-restraint, and patience. Finally, Donne's comparisons allow him to express all of this in only fifty-five words. Comparisons, in short, give to poetry both density and conciseness. They link the human senses with human psychology without acknowledging the stages in logic and analysis that underlie this union.

Several other forms of implied comparison may occasionally be encountered in poetry. **In *synecdoche*, a part of something is used to suggest the *whole* thing.** George Meredith includes synecdoche when he uses the phrase "she wept with waking eyes" (p. 688). Obviously the woman is awake—not just her "waking eyes." **In *metonymy* (meaning "change of name"), something associated with an object or idea replaces what is actually meant.** Shakespeare uses metonymy when he writes that "the poet's pen/ ... gives to airy nothing/ A local habitation and a name," since the poet, and not his pen, is clearly responsible for imaginative creation. Both synecdoche and metonymy are frequently found in slang. A "redneck" is a working man whose neck has been toughened by years in the wind and sun; an "old hand" means an experienced worker; and the "heavy" in a movie is a villain whose enormous size and aggressive behavior have become conventional.

One final form of implied comparison is created through juxtaposition. **In *juxtaposition*, two items are merely placed side by side. The author makes no overt comparison between these items and draws no inferences.** The reader is free to make of them what he or she will. An interesting example of juxtaposition occurs in Henry Reed's post–World War II poem entitled "Lessons of the War: Naming of Parts." Each of the five stanzas in the poem describes a stage in the military exercise of breaking down and naming the parts of an army rifle;

and then, in juxtaposition to this, Reed "names" some of the parts of spring-time.

NAMING OF PARTS

Today we have naming of parts. Yesterday,
We had daily cleaning. And tomorrow morning,
We shall have what to do after firing. But today,
Today we have naming of parts. Japonica
5   Glistens like coral in all of the neighboring gardens,
       And today we have naming of parts.

This is the lower sling swivel. And this
Is the upper sling swivel, whose use you will see,
when you are given your slings. And this is the piling swivel,
10   Which in your case you have not got. The branches
Hold in the gardens their silent, eloquent gestures,
       Which in our case we have not got.

This is the safety-catch, which is always released
With an easy flick of the thumb. And please do not let me
15   See anyone using his finger. You can do it quite easy
If you have any strength in your thumb. The blossoms
Are fragile and motionless, never letting anyone see
       Any of them using their finger.

And this you can see is the bolt. The purpose of this
20   Is to open the breech, as you see. We can slide it
Rapidly backwards and forwards: we call this
Easing the spring. And rapidly backwards and forwards
The early bees are assaulting and fumbling the flowers:
       They call it easing the Spring.

25   They call it easing the Spring: it is perfectly easy
If you have any strength in your thumb: like the bolt,
And the breech, and the cocking-piece, and the point of balance,
Which in our case we have not got; and the almond-blossom
Silent in all of the gardens and the bees going backwards and
       forwards,
30   For today we have naming of parts.
                                                        —Henry Reed [1947]

The first stanza is representative of the technique followed throughout the poem. The first four sentences of the stanza are mechanical, denotative, and dull, whereas the first clause in the next sentence ("Japonica/ Glistens like coral in all of the neighboring gardens") is naturalistic, figurative, imagistic, and apprecia-tive. We see the author's mind at play just as it had been at rather dull work in the preceding lines. We see him transform himself from a military automaton to a sensually aware human being. We see him in an act of mental rebellion against a numbing, mechanical, and inhumane routine. At the same time that his hands and arms go through the rituals of slaughter, his eyes and intellect follow the processes of natural rebirth. From a strictly logical point of view, the two parts of Reed's stanza are incompatible, but he unites them by his repetition of the final phrase, "today we have naming of parts." And in that repetition Reed is implicitly asserting his ability to metamorphose his army experiences in a triumph of human feeling over inhumane behavior.

Juxtaposition is rarely used with as great a dramatic effect as in "Naming of Parts," but it is frequently important in creating the impression of fate or inevitability. When Edwin Arlington Robinson wrote that "Richard Cory, one calm summer night,/ Went home and put a bullet through his head," he was juxtaposing the calm, warm weather and the cold, irrational act of suicide in order to prod us into pondering possible reasons for Richard Cory's death. And when Robert Frost found "a dimpled spider, fat and white,/ On a white heal-all, holding up a moth," the juxtaposition of those symbols of death, blight, and innocence became ominous and profound.

Poems for Further Study

MORNING SONG

Love set you going like a fat gold watch.
The midwife slapped your footsoles, and your bald cry
Took its place among the elements.

Our voices echo, magnifying your arrival. New statue.
5   In a drafty museum, your nakedness
Shadows our safety. We stand round blankly as walls.

I'm no more your mother
Than the cloud that distils a mirror to reflect its own slow
Effacement at the wind's hand.

10   All night your moth-breath
Flickers among the flat pink roses. I wake to listen:
A far sea moves in my ear.

One cry, and I stumble from bed, cow-heavy and floral
In my Victorian nightgown.
15   Your mouth opens clean as a cat's. The window square

Whitens and swallows its dull stars. And now you try
Your handful of notes;
The clear vowels rise like balloons.

—Sylvia Plath [1961]

❧ QUESTIONS ❧

1. Who is Plath addressing in this poem? In what sense is it a "Morning Song"?

2. What similes and metaphors can you find in this poem? What emotions
of a new mother do these comparisons help Plath to express?

3. What do you think of Plath's reactions to motherhood? Do you find her
reactions expected or unexpected? Are they believable? Are they uniformly
commendable? Are they honest?

LANDCRAB

A lie, that we come from water.
The truth is we were born
from stones, dragons, the sea's
teeth, as you testify,
5   with your crust and jagged scissors.

Hermit, hard socket
for a timid eye,
you're a soft gut scuttling
sideways, a blue skull,
10   round bone on the prowl,
Wolf of treeroots and gravelly holes,
a mouth on stilts,
the husk of a small demon.

Attack, voracious
15   eating, and flight:
it's a sound routine
for staying alive on edges.
Then there's the tide, and that dance
you do for the moon
20   on wet sand, claws raised
to fend off your mate,
your coupling a quick
dry clatter of rocks.
For mammals
25   with their lobes and bulbs,
scruples and warm milk,
you've nothing but contempt.

Here you are, a frozen scowl
targeted in flashlight,
30   then gone: a piece of what
we are, not all,
my stunted child, my momentary
face in the mirror,
my tiny nightmare.

—Margaret Atwood [1981]

❧ QUESTIONS ❧

1.   Why does Atwood contend that we were "born from stones, dragons, the sea's / teeth"? What does such a contention imply about human beings?

2.   Examine the similes and metaphors used in describing the landcrab. What emotional responses do those comparisons evoke?

3.   What characteristics are necessary for "staying alive on edges"? How are these characteristics reflected in the landcrab's lovemaking and its attitude toward mammals?

4.   Why does Atwood conclude her poem with a series of implied comparisons that show her kinship (and ours) with the landcrab?

12

❧❧❧❧❧❧

Personification, Apostrophe, and Animism

The portrayal of an idea, object, or animal as having human traits is called **personification**. Storms and ships, for example, have traditionally been personified by being given human names. **Personification constitutes a form of implied comparison and allows the poet to describe with energy and vitality what might otherwise have remained inanimate or lackluster.** Notice how Edward FitzGerald's personification of an earthen wine bowl enlivens the following lines and makes his message about enjoying life clearer and more forceful:

> Then to this earthen Bowl did I adjourn
> My Lip the secret Well of Life to learn:
> And Lip to Lip it murmur'd—"While you live
> Drink! for once dead you never shall return."
>
> —From *The Rubáiyát of Omar Khayyám,*
> Edward FitzGerald [1859]

❧ QUESTIONS ❧

1. Explain the pun (involving the word *lip*) in line 3. How does it contribute to the personification?

2. Consider the connotations of an "earthen" bowl—especially in the context of a discussion of death.

3. The advice, "While you live / Drink!" is in one sense quite straightforward, but in another sense it is profoundly ambiguous. Drink what? What are

the possibilities? (In answering this question, you may wish to read additional selections from the *Rubáiyát*, printed elsewhere in this anthology. See the *Index* for page numbers.)

Apostrophe, a limited form of personification, occurs when a poet or one of his or her characters addresses a speech to someone absent or something nonhuman. Although apostrophe is often ineffective in poetry, Geoffrey Chaucer uses it throughout his humorous "Complaint to His Empty Purse" (1399), which begins:

> To you, my purse, and to non other wight°   *person*
> Complayne I, for ye be my lady dere!

and Shakespeare uses apostrophe during King Lear's ragings on the heath:

> Blow, winds, and crack your cheeks! Rage! Blow!
> You cataracts and hurricanoes, spout
> Till you have drench'd our steeples, drown'd the cocks!°   *weathervanes*
> You sulph'rous and thought-executing fires,
> Vaunt-couriers° of oak-cleaving thunderbolts,   *fore-runners*
> Singe my white head! And thou, all-shaking thunder,
> Strike flat the thick rotundity o' th' world!
> Crack nature's mold, all germens° spill at once   *germs, seeds*
> That makes ingrateful man!

> —From *King Lear,* William Shakespeare [1605]

However, Chaucer's address to his purse is but a playful piece of foolishness and Lear's address to the storm is but a symptom of his madness. In neither case does the poet expect us to see any utility in talking to wallet and wind. If apostrophe were *always* used ironically, as in both of these examples, or comically, as in Robert Burns's poems "To a Mouse" and "To a Louse," then inept poets would undoubtedly have developed some other means of debasing the English language. As things are, however, too many second-rate poems are packed with silly and sentimental apostrophes to Truth, Beauty, Love, and a host of other capitalized abstractions. Weak poets, having worked themselves or their characters up to a stage of violent emotions, often degenerate into what John Ruskin called the "pathetic fallacy" of facile and unimaginative personification. The trite and insipid tribute of Anna Laetitia Barbauld to "Life" is a typical example of the worst form of apostrophe:

> Life! We've been long together,
> Through pleasant and through cloudy weather;
> 'Tis hard to part when friends are dear—
> Perhaps 'twill cost a sigh, a tear.
> —From "Life," Anna Laetitia Barbauld [1811]

Excessive personification or apostrophe is not the only way to ruin a poem, but it may be the most reliable.

A poet may also describe an idea or inanimate object as though it were living, without attributing human traits to it. Before the development of the motion picture, this device could be called animation, but because that term is now best confined to cartoons, **we will use the term** *animism* **for poetic comparisons that give life to inanimate objects.** Carl Sandburg employs animism to good effect in his brief poem "Fog":

FOG

> The fog comes
> on little cat feet
> It sits looking
> over harbor and city
> on silent haunches
> and then moves on.
> —Carl Sandburg [1916]

Similarly, Robert Burns uses an animistic simile when he compares the high spirits of love with the appearance of a newly sprung rose:

> O, my luve is like a red red rose
> That's newly sprung in June
> O, my luve is like the melodie
> That's sweetly played in tune.
> —From "A Red, Red Rose,"
> Robert Burns [1796]

Of course, Burns is also comparing the woman he loves (as well as the emotion of love) with a red rose—young, fresh, fragrant, and beautiful. All depends on whether "my luve" is taken as meaning "my feeling when in love" or "my loved one." In the former, a feeling or idea is animated by comparison with the rose; in the latter, the appearance and personality of the maiden are described. Because both interpretations are compatible, this pleasant ambiguity is best left unresolved; however, we should at least mention that the second reading suggests yet another form of comparison. This technique of speaking about a person in terms that are more applicable to a plant, animal, or machine is just the opposite of personification, and yet, oddly, it has no commonly accepted name other than simile or metaphor. T. S. Eliot used this form of comparison in "The Love Song of J. Alfred Prufrock" (1917) to add to the narrator's scorn for his own insignificance:

> I should have been a pair of ragged claws
> Scuttling across the floors of silent seas.

Theodore Roethke, in his "Elegy to Jane," described the "sidelong pickerel smile" of one of his former students, whom he also compared to a wren, a sparrow, and a skittery pigeon. And early blues musicians, whose roots were in the soil of the Mississippi Delta, compared themselves to a variety of country creatures in such songs as "The Bull Frog Blues" (Willie Harris), "The Crawling Kingsnake Blues" (John Lee Hooker), and "The Milk Cow's Calf Blues" (Robert Johnson) in describing their passions and sorrows.

Poems for Further Study

"APPARENTLY WITH NO SURPRISE"

Apparently with no surprise
To any happy Flower
The Frost beheads it at its play—
In accidental power—
5   The blonde Assassin passes on—
The Sun proceeds unmoved
To measure off another Day
For an Approving God.

—Emily Dickinson
[posthumous, 1890]

❧ QUESTIONS ❧

1. To what extent are the Flower and the Frost personified in this poem? What words are applied to them that are more typically used in discussions of human beings? How accurate is the poem as a literal description of the effect of frost on flowers?

2. What attitude toward God is expressed in this poem? How much design does Dickinson see in the forces of nature?

EX-BASKETBALL PLAYER

Pearl Avenue runs past the high-school lot,
Bends with the trolley tracks, and stops, cut off
Before it has a chance to go two blocks,
At Colonel McComsky Plaza. Berth's Garage
5   Is on the corner facing west, and there,
Most days, you'll find Flick Webb, who helps Berth out.

Flick stands tall among the idiot pumps—
Five on a side, the old bubble-head style,
Their rubber elbows hanging loose and low.
10   One's nostrils are two S's, and his eyes
An E and O. And one is squat, without
A head at all—more of a football type.

Once Flick played for the high-school team, the Wizards.
He was good: in fact, the best. In '46
15   He bucketed three hundred ninety points,
A county record still. The ball loved Flick.
I saw him rack up thirty-eight or forty
In one home game. His hands were like wild birds.

He never learned a trade, he just sells gas,
20   Checks oil, and changes flats. Once in a while,
As a gag, he dribbles an inner tube,
But most of us remember anyway.
His hands are fine and nervous on the lug wrench.
It makes no difference to the lug wrench, though.

25   Off work, he hangs around Mae's luncheonette.
Grease-gray and kind of coiled, he plays pinball,
Smokes those thin cigars, nurses lemon phosphates.
Flick seldom says a word to Mae, just nods
Beyond her face toward bright applauding tiers
30   Of Necco Wafers, Nibs, and Juju Beads.

—John Updike [1957]

❧ QUESTIONS ❧

1.   Where does Flick Webb work? On what kind of street? Doing what kind of job?

2.   How and why does Updike personify the gasoline pumps at Berth's Garage?

3.   How does Flick put to use the skills he learned as a basketball player? Describe the "crowd" that now observes and applauds his prowess.

4.   How fulfilling is Flick's life after high school? What comment about high school athletics is implicit in this poem?

13

❧❧❧❧❧❧

Symbol and Allegory

As we noted in our discussion of fiction, **a *symbol* is something that stands for something else, and an *allegory* is a narrative that uses a system of implied comparisons—often including symbols—to develop two or more simultaneous levels of meaning.** Both devices occur naturally in literature to expand the suggestiveness and significance of literature.

Normally, a *symbol* is an image that has an overt literal function in a poem, but it also evokes a range of additional meanings. Like the physical universe, a symbol is finite but unbounded: finite in the sense that the symbol itself is specific and imagistic, but unbounded in the sense that the limits on the possible interpretations of the symbol are often difficult to define. For example, in Robert Frost's well-known poem, "The Road Not Taken," the road itself is vividly described. As readers, we easily imagine the yellow wood, the branching, grassy paths, the "leaves no step had trodden black," and the minor dilemma of the speaker as he pauses before making his choice. Thus far, the road is simply a road and the poem very pleasantly describes a woodland walk early in the morning. However, Frost puts greater emphasis on this choice of paths than the simple incident itself would seem to merit. If this choice really only involves two roads in a yellow wood, why should the speaker "be telling this with a sigh/ Somewhere ages and ages hence"? Surely no ordinary choice between woodland paths is so memorable and so important. And why should he repeat the fact that the roads fork and that he chose the "one less travelled by"? And finally, how could such a choice really make "all the difference"? Clearly, the poem has started out as a description of a simple incident, but somewhere along the way that incident has become a symbol of the more significant decisions in life that all of us are inevitably called upon to make. To be sure, the exact nature of those decisions remains unclear. We cannot say with absolute certainty that it is a poem about the choice of a career, for it could just as easily refer to any choice between two attractive options—the choice between two hobbies, the choice between two weekend dates, the choice between two churches, or any number of other possibilities. All we can say with certainty is that the poem is about the choice between two roads in a yellow wood, but that it is *also* about other choices in life that may be taken casually and seem unimportant at the time, while ultimately making "all the difference."

As in the case of this poem by Frost, **a symbol is an image that expands in meaning through the friction of emphasis until it inflames the imagination. A symbol remains what it is as an image, but it also takes on new and tenuous meanings that cast a flickering, magical glow over the work as a whole.**

A symbol may be *private* **(its meaning known only to one person),** *original* **(its meaning defined by its context in a particular work), or** *traditional* **(its meaning defined by our common culture and heritage).** At its most complex, a symbol may be all three as, for example, in "The Whale," a poem that occurs in the ninth chapter of Herman Melville's *Moby Dick:*

THE WHALE

The ribs and terrors in the whale,
        Arched over me a dismal gloom,
While all God's sun-lit waves rolled by,
        And left me deepening down to doom.

5   I saw the opening maw° of hell,   *jaws*
        With endless pains and sorrows there;
Which none but they that feel can tell—
        Oh, I was plunging to despair.

        In black distress, I called my God,
10   When I could scarce believe him mine,
He bowed his ear to my complaints—
        No more the whale did me confine.

        With speed he flew to my relief,
            As on a radiant dolphin borne;
15   Awful, yet bright, as lightning shone
        The face of my Deliverer God.

        My song for ever shall record
            That terrible, that joyful hour;
I give the glory to my God,
20   His all the mercy and the power.
                        —Herman Melville [1851]

Here, and throughout *Moby Dick,* the whale is a private symbol, in the sense that it emerges from Melville's own whaling experiences. Melville once wrote, "If, at my death my executors (or more properly, my creditors) find any precious manuscripts in my desk, then I prospectively ascribe all the honor and glory to whaling; for a whale-ship was my Yale and Harvard." But actual experience with whales may have been responsible for only part of the private symbolism in the poem. The battle with the whale may also have served as a metaphor for confrontation with Melville's own despair and may also reflect the "dismal gloom" of his failure to make a living as a bank clerk, a teacher, a surveyor, a seaman, and finally an author. When he completed *Moby Dick,* Melville was in debt to his publisher and to his friends, and he saw little hope of attaining solvency.

No one, of course, can truly gauge the extent to which a poem symbolizes an author's personal turmoil, but there can be no doubt that the whale in *Moby Dick* is an original, powerful, and fully developed symbol within the novel. Even in this brief poem it is clear that the whale is an object of horror, a force of evil, and an embodiment of the darkest spiritual despair. These symbolic associations arise out of the poem itself and require of the reader only a sensitivity to the meaning of words.

The poem, however, also suggests the traditional *parable* (**an instructive moral story**) of Jonah, who was thrown to the whale because of a lack of faith in God, confined to the whale's belly in black distress, and finally resurrected after calling upon God for assistance. In this sense, the whale is an *archetype* (**a basic and repeated element of plot, character, or theme**) that symbolizes separation from God and even death; its symbolic associations are traditional—that is, common to all readers who share the Judeo-Christian heritage.

Symbols are not, however, always this complex. In one sense, symbolism is the most common of all linguistic devices. After all, a word is nothing but a sound that symbolizes a particular image or concept. No word has meaning unless our human ability to symbolize makes it so. There is no necessary connection, for example, between the word *dog* and the familiar four-legged animal we associate with that word; after all, people of other nations have developed the same symbolic associations with other sounds: *chien* in French, *Hund* in German, *canis* in Latin, and so on.

Even **literary symbols are often quite simple.** Winter, for example, often is a symbol of old age, spring of youth, summer of maturity, and autumn of decline. Similarly, a lamb may be a symbol of innocence, a lion of courage, a fire of vitality, and a rock of firmness. In each case, an implied comparison is drawn between a vivid image and an abstract quality.

The one-to-one correspondences set up by these symbols are akin to those established in simple *allegories* like the medieval morality play, *Everyman*. The hero, Everyman, is accompanied on his journey to the grave by characters whose actions and even names symbolize his Good-Deeds, Five Wits, Strength, Discretion, Beauty, and Knowledge. *Everyman* is known as an allegory because its simple symbols are systematically used to emphasize the moral point that only our good deeds are of lasting value both in life and after death. **An *allegory* is a type of narrative that attempts to reinforce its thesis by making its characters (and sometimes its events and setting as well) represent specific abstract ideas. The systems of symbols used in allegories often tend toward didacticism and overt moral instruction.** Such blatancy is a major reason why allegory is no longer a popular literary mode.

It is incorrect, however, to say that allegory no longer has a place in literature. Just as symbolism is a universal element of language, allegory is a universal element of fictional narration. Any literary (as opposed to journalistic) presentation of characters or events invariably prompts the reader to inquire, "What does it mean? What is the author's point?" And such questions represent the first step toward uncovering an allegorical purpose. Graham Hough, an important contemporary scholar, has developed a useful example of the process:

We read some report of, say, treachery, sexual misadventure, and violence in the newspapers, and it is there only to record the fact that such events took place. We read of the same sequence of events in a novel or a short story, and we can hardly escape the feeling that it is there to say something to us about human passions and motives in general.

From there it is only a step to seeing the characters as types of Treachery, Violence and Lust. . . .[1]

If the actions of fictional characters are highly idiosyncratic and suggest no universal traits of humanity, we will probably be reluctant to identify them as allegorical "types"; but if the thematic element in the story is strong— that is, if the story seems to be making a general comment about humanity—it must to some extent suggest allegorical possibilities.

The problem facing the student of literature is not, then, whether a given story, poem, or play includes symbolism and allegory, but whether these nearly universal elements of literature are so important in the specific work that they need to be isolated, discussed, and evaluated. We can best resolve this problem by asking ourselves two questions. First, does the author put unusual emphasis on a particular image or series of images? Second, does the poem or story fail to make literal sense *unless* we interpret the images symbolically or allegorically? An affirmative answer to either or both questions should make us suspect that the author may be using images as symbols—perhaps, but not necessarily, in an allegory.

Discussions of symbolic or allegorical meanings in literature should always be pursued with caution. Because all words are in some sense symbolic and because every theme is in some sense allegorical, inexperienced critics (and even some experienced ones) are too easily tempted to "read things into" the works they study. Even at its best, symbol-hunting is an attempt at mind reading. We can all easily identify the images an author uses, but we often get into trouble when we begin to speculate about what the author intended in choosing them. Unless we can find strong evidence in the poem to support our symbolic interpretations, there is a very high probability that the only mind we are reading is our own. When authors think their symbols are important, we can be quite confident that the authors will hint at their meaning in one or more places. When no authorial interpretation (or even acknowledgment) of the symbols can be found, the wise critic will think carefully before insisting on a symbolic interpretation. Like Hawthorne's Ethan Brand, who looked throughout the world for the Unpardonable Sin—before finding it in himself—we may find that the symbolic meanings we seek in the works of others exist only in the smithy of our own souls.

Poems for Further Study

"WHAT IS OUR LIFE? A PLAY OF PASSION"

What is our life? A play of passion,
Our mirth the music of division;
Our mothers' wombs the tiring-houses° be   *dressing rooms*
Where we are dressed for this short comedy;
5   Heaven the judicious, sharp spectator is
That sits and marks still who doth act amiss;

[1] *An Essay on Criticism* (London: Duckworth, 1966) 121.

Our graves that hide us from the searching sun
Are like drawn curtains when the play is done:
Thus march we, playing, to our latest° rest,   *last*
10   Only we die in earnest, that's no jest.

—Sir Walter Raleigh [1612]

❧ QUESTIONS ❧

1. A "play of passion" (now usually called a passion play) was a medieval or renaissance drama presenting the stages in the suffering and death of Jesus Christ. What allegorical relationships between such a play and human life are presented in this poem?

2. How long does the music last in the divisions between acts in a play? How much of human life is given over to mirth?

3. What does Raleigh mean when he speaks of life as "this short comedy"? Is he being ironic? Bitter? Cynical?

4. How does Raleigh portray God and humans' relationship with God?

5. What is the effect of the final couplet upon the interpretation of the whole poem?

CROSSING THE BAR

Sunset and evening star,
    And one clear call for me!
And may there be no moaning of the bar,[2]
    When I put out to sea,

5 But such a tide as moving seems asleep,
    Too full for sound and foam,
When that which drew from out the boundless deep
    Turns again home.

Twilight and evening bell,
10   And after that the dark!
And may there be no sadness of farewell,
    When I embark;

For tho' from out our bourne° of Time and Place   *limits*
    The flood may bear me far,
15 I hope to see my Pilot face to face
    When I have crossed the bar.

—Alfred, Lord Tennyson [1889]

---

[2] The sound of surf washing over a very shallow sand bar at the mouth of a river.

❧ QUESTIONS ❧

1. This poem is usually given an allegorical interpretation. In the first stanza, what are the allegorical referents of the "sunset," the "one clear call," the "moaning of the bar," and the putting out to sea?

2. In stanza two, why does the speaker wish to be carried on a tide that "moving seems asleep" and is too deep for "sound and foam"? And what is the force that "drew from out the boundless deep"?

3. How is the first line of the third stanza different from the first line of stanza one? What does "the dark" represent? And in what sense does the speaker embark?

4. Why does the speaker refer to escaping "our bourne of Time and Place" in stanza four? Who is meant by the Pilot?

5. How well does the title "Crossing the Bar" summarize the poem both as a statement on dying and on setting sail?

THE ROAD NOT TAKEN

Two roads diverged in a yellow wood,
And sorry I could not travel both
And be one traveler, long I stood
And looked down one as far as I could
5   To where it bent in the undergrowth;

Then took the other, as just as fair,
And having perhaps the better claim,
Because it was grassy and wanted wear;
Though as for that the passing there
10   Had worn them really about the same,

And both that morning equally lay
In leaves no step had trodden black.
Oh, I kept the first for another day!
Yet knowing how way leads on to way,
15   I doubted if I should ever come back.

I shall be telling this with a sigh
Somewhere ages and ages hence:
Two roads diverged in a wood, and I—
I took the one less traveled by,
20   And that has made all the difference.

—Robert Frost [1916]

❧ QUESTIONS ❧

1.   How does Frost prod us into reading this poem symbolically? Specifically, how does the last stanza change the significance of this simple incident?

2.   Can you speculate about the decisions in Frost's life (or anyone else's) which could have been made in this light-hearted way and yet could have "made all the difference"?

3.   Laurence Perrine sees the poem as "an expression of regret that one's ability to explore different life possibilities is so sharply limited. It comes from a man who loves life and thirsts after more of it." What details in the poem support such an interpretation?

14

✕✕✕✕✕✕✕

The Plain Sense
of Poetry

As I. A. Richards noted more than half a century ago in his seminal book *Practical Criticism* (1929), the chief problem faced by the student of poetry is "the difficulty of making out (the poem's) plain sense." In the preceding pages we have identified some of the sources of this difficulty by demonstrating that poets often use unfamiliar denotations, connotations, or allusions and may change the meaning of words through repetition, ambiguity, puns, paradoxes, and irony. Furthermore, poetic comparisons, although often vivid and delightful, may also be suggestive, symbolic, or ambiguous. Finally, poetry is, as a general rule, much more densely packed with meaning than prose. The author of a sonnet has, after all, only fourteen lines in which to make a point—a restriction that requires either making a very minor point or making every word count. A sonnetlike density is traditionally expected in poetry, even when the actual length of the poem is not limited by any formal strictures. In spite of these difficulties, the simple prose meaning of most poetry can be determined by using common sense and our accumulated knowledge of how poetry works.

As you study the poems in this text, you should sketch out mentally (or better yet record in your notebook) provisional responses to each of the seven steps in seeking the plain sense of poetry:

1. **List Denotations and Connotations.** As we have already shown, many words have multiple meanings, and poets often intentionally play on this multiplicity. We need to be cautious, of course, about assuming that an author is always—or even generally—toying with multiple denotations. In poetry, as in prose, an author normally intends to make a clear and forceful point, and ambiguity, by its very nature, must always interfere with the clarity of a statement. But even if the poet avoids ambiguity, he or she is almost certainly cognizant of the connotations of each word and may use them to modify the meaning. Thus, in studying a poem for the first time, the reader should look up in the dictionary any difficult or

unfamiliar words and jot down their definitions and connotations. Let us see how we can apply this first recommendation to the analysis of the following well-known lyric:

UPON JULIA'S CLOTHES

Whenas in silks my Julia goes
Then, then (methinks) how sweetly flows
That liquefaction of her clothes.

Next, when I cast mine eyes and see
5   That brave vibration each way free;
O how that glittering taketh me!
—Robert Herrick [1648]

Like most poetry written in an age and in circumstances quite different from our own, these six lines present several problems in denotation. After more than three hundred years, we have naturally changed some of the ways in which we use words, and Herrick's vocabulary, although not archaic, is uncommon and distinctive. To be on the safe side, we might look up a half-dozen words with the following results:

> *whenas:* whenever
> *goes:* moves about, leaves
> *methinks:* it seems to me
> *liquefaction:* fluidity
> *cast:* turn, direct, throw
> *brave:* courageous, showy, colorful

In moving from denotation to connotation and commentary, we find more to interest a literary critic:

silks: Silken clothing is thin, expensive, lustrous, and sensuous. Although Herrick is presumably referring to a silken dress, "silks" may also connote silk stockings or a silk nightgown. Thus, the connotations of the word are luxuriant and slightly sensual.

my Julia: The use of the possessive adjective "my" suggests that Julia may be Herrick's possession, his mistress—both confirming and compounding the sensuous connotations of "silks."

goes: This is a curious word choice. Clearly, when Julia "goes," she is walking. Perhaps Herrick thought that walking was too common an activity and perhaps, too, he was trying to be precise, for a woman in a long, full skirt may seem to glide about—or "go"— without seeming to walk at all. Possibly Herrick wanted to suggest that Julia was leaving, "going away." If so, "whenas" reminds us that this is something that she does frequently, and we may be tempted to assume that Herrick is describing her as she leaves after a lovers' tryst. In addition, the choice of "goes" was in part dictated by Herrick's need for a word to rhyme with "flows" and "clothes."

liquefaction: Here sound connotations come into play. The word itself is equivalent to "liquid action," but it rolls off the tongue more smoothly and thus is most appropriate.

cast mine eyes: The phrase is vigorous and active. Because Herrick had been watching Julia in the first three lines, these words must mean something more than
that he simply continued to look at her. If indeed Julia had been leaving in the
first sentence, then in "casting" his eyes, Herrick is probably turning his head
to watch her receding figure. The phrase shows Herrick's strong attraction to
Julia.

brave: We have already had something to say about the denotations of the adjective "brave." Undoubtedly, Herrick is using the archaic definitions, "showy" or
"colorful"; however, those were secondary definitions even in Herrick's day,
and therefore the connotations of "boldness" and "courage" cannot be escaped.

vibration: In the twentieth century we are apt to associate this word with very rapid
oscillations—especially with the vibrations of automobiles, trains, and planes
moving at high speed. In the seventeenth century, however, the word was most
often used to describe the slow swing of a pendulum. In this poem, therefore,
"that brave vibration each way free" suggests the gentle side-to-side swishing of
a woman's skirts. And, in fact, the bravado and freedom of these oscillations
may indicate that Julia's swaying motion is a trifle wanton.

2. Analyze the Syntax. If the meaning of a particular sentence is unclear,
analyze its syntax by identifying the subject, the verb, the object, and the function
of the major clauses. We have just as much right to expect syntactic clarity in verse
as in prose, and no poet who habitually disregards the rules of English grammar
can earn the respect of literate readers unless his or her verse has remarkable
compensatory elements. Of course, good poets sometimes, by design, use syntax
ambiguously to suggest competing interpretations (remember the Delphic oracle's "Pyrrhus the Romans shall conquer"?); however, this possibility merely underscores the need to understand fully the syntactic relationships among words.

Herrick's brief poem "Upon Julia's Clothes" is constructed of two parallel
sentences. Each consists of a subordinate clause followed by an exclamation.
Because the two sentences are similar in so many respects, the slight differences
between them are all the more pronounced. The first sentence is introspective
("methinks") and intransitive ("how sweetly flows/ That liquefaction of her
clothes"). In contrast, the second sentence is active ("I cast mine eyes") and
transitive ("O how that glittering taketh me"). In the first sentence, Herrick is a
reflective observer; in the second, he is acting and being acted upon. The two
sentences combine to suggest that he is prey to a passion that intensifies as he
watches the rustling of his mistress's clothing. Even in the choice of his syntactic
subjects, we find him moving from water ("liquefaction") to fire ("glittering")
and thus from tranquility to excitement.

3. Identify the Figures of Speech. By definition, figurative language is not
meant to be taken literally. Poetic language differs from ordinary language to
point the way toward meaningful emotional truths. When Herrick exclaims,
"Then, then (methinks) how sweetly flows/ That liquefaction of her clothes," he
certainly does not mean that Julia's dress dribbles down into a soggy pool at her
feet—although that is the image we may get if we try to interpret his lines literally.
Actually, Herrick is drawing an implied comparison between the soft, shiny movements of Julia's silken dress and the gentle, rippling flow of a stream.

This is the only figure of speech used in Herrick's brief poem, and we should
not ordinarily expect to find more in such short poetic passages. Figurative lan-

guage is like champagne: the first glass or two raises the spirits, but too much of it befuddles and bewilders the brain. Whenever an author *does* use numerous figures of speech, it becomes absolutely essential to identify the various types being used (whether allusion, ambiguity, irony, paradox, pun, or one of the various forms of comparison), and it is often useful as well to recast those figures, at least temporarily, into language that is not poetic. Allusions, ironies, paradoxes, and puns should be explained; metaphors and implied comparisons should be rewritten as similes; and symbols should be identified. To do so without greatly distorting the poem, we must be sensitive to the connotations of words and to the uses of ambiguity.

  4. **Paraphrase the Poem.** The purpose of a paraphrase is to help us understand the prose sense of a poem by changing the poetic language of difficult passages into language that we can easily comprehend. This process is the most direct means of making sure that we understand what a poem says—quite apart from how well it is said.

  Having enumerated denotations and connotations, analyzed syntax, and identified figures of speech, it should not be difficult to write down a full prose statement of the poem's content. Thus, ''Upon Julia's Clothes'' might be paraphrased as follows:

Whenever my Julia walks in silks, then (it seems to me) that the sounds made by the movement of her clothing are as lovely as the rippling of a stream. Next, when I look at the colorful swaying of her skirts, O how their glittering attracts me!

  Any paraphrase, as long as it is reasonable, helps us to check our understanding of a poem's literal meaning by expressing it in slightly different words. The process itself, however, is fraught with risks. We may be tempted to substitute our own prose statement for the poem itself, which may obscure our appreciation of the poem's style and feeling. Or, we may persuade ourselves that the poem means exactly what we say it means and nothing else—a conclusion that glosses over the questionable decisions about denotation and connotation that must be made in attempting to paraphrase any poem. For example, by changing only a few words in our paraphrase of ''Upon Julia's Clothes'' we can begin to interpret the poem more sensuously:

Whenever my mistress Julia comes toward me dressed in silks, then (it seems to me) that her clothes flow about her body as smoothly and beautifully as water in a stream. Next, when I turn my eyes and see the saucy and free swing in her walk as she passes, O how the sparkle of her skirts enamours me!

  It would be difficult to determine a rational reason for preferring one of these paraphrases over the other. The first moves from the *sound* of Julia's dress to the *sight* of it, whereas the second implies that Herrick watches Julia as she walks by—admiring her figure from front and rear. The first paraphrase is a little too staid; the second a little too steamy. The poem itself contains something of both; it manages to be suggestive without the slightest trace of immorality. This elusiveness is, of course, exactly what makes poetry more interesting than common prose. Stripping the nuances from a poem is like skimming the cream from milk: it takes away the richness and taste. In each case, what remains is thin, watery, and almost denatured. The language of poetry is *not* static or technical or purely denotative; it is rich and complex, and no paraphrase can fully do it justice. Yet, the risks of leaving the poem's prose meaning unstated are even greater, for then the ambiguities of poetic diction may entice the reader into believing that his or her own preoccupations and fantasies are somehow mirrored in each line. If anything, the temptation to read something into the poem that its actual content will not justify implies a greater disrespect for the written word than the opposite risk of relying too heavily on the paraphrase. The latter may be nothing more than a shadow of the true poetic substance, but the former is too often the product of an overstimulated imagination, having little relationship to the poem.

5. Visualize and Summarize the Imagery and Actions. The preceding steps have all been analytical. They require us to look up definitions, to examine verbal structures, to reword sentences: to act, to think, and to write. In doing so, however, we have omitted what is certainly the most important process of all: to enjoy. When we relax and allow the poet's imagery to carry us into the world of imagination, we are most in harmony with the true poetic impulse. But more than that, visualizing the events in the poem and attempting to recreate imaginatively everything that the poet describes can often be indispensable to careful critical judgment. Careless writers sometimes juxtapose incongruous and even ludicrous images because they themselves fail to see clearly what they ask their readers to envision: for example, "In the game of life it's sink or swim, and you need to hang in there by your toenails, swinging for the bleachers whenever opportunity knocks." The use of such incongruous comparisons is called *mixed metaphor*.

Once we have tried to visualize everything that the poet describes for us, we will find it easier to summarize the action and circumstances in the poem. In so doing, we will generally wish to identify the speaker (who may or may not be the poet), the setting, and the circumstances. A summary of "Upon Julia's Clothes" will not add much to our understanding of the poem because the poem itself is so short and uncomplicated. However, Frost's sonnet "Design," which is only slightly longer, can snap into focus if we first visualize it and then summarize our vision in something like the following manner:

The poet, on a morning walk along a roadside, sees a white moth within the grasp of a white spider perched on a white and blighted wildflower. This strange and incongruous combination leads him to reflect about the role of fate in the events of the world.

A line-by-line paraphrase of "Design" might isolate and clarify problems in the interpretation of specific words and phrases, but it would also equal or exceed the length of the original fourteen-line poem. A simple three-line summary, such as the one proposed here, has an advantage: it allows us to think of the poem as a totality—to get a single image of it—and that image, if well formed, can serve as a starting point for further explanation, analysis, and understanding.

6.   Evaluate the Poem's Tone. The tone of a poem is created by the author's overall attitude toward the subject or audience. It helps to determine the choice of words and rhetorical devices. Thus, when we wish to evaluate a poem's tone, we do so by examining the emotional effects of its words, images, and figures of speech (particularly overstatement, understatement, irony, paradox, and ambiguity). In any collection of poetry, we will find some poems in which the tone is obvious; others in which it is complex; and still others in which it changes as the poet develops his or her thoughts.

In many cases, the author's tone is unmistakable. "Upon Julia's Clothes," for example, clearly reflects Herrick's passionate preoccupation with Julia. His attitude is expressed directly by his exclamations, "how sweetly flows/ That liquefaction of her clothes" and "O how that glittering taketh me!" And it is expressed indirectly by the fact that the poet's excitement is stimulated so easily. We recognize that he must indeed be deeply in love if so small a thing as the rustle of Julia's skirts drives him to such poetic expression. Herrick's tone, then, is enraptured, loving, and excited.

The analysis of tone becomes more difficult when the author uses irony, paradox, or ambiguity because conflicting meanings and, hence, conflicting attitudes toward the subject are implied by those devices. When, for example, Byron writes that a serious illness made him so devoutly religious that he wished the three persons of the Trinity were four "On purpose to believe so much the more," we will wholly misunderstand his tone and meaning unless we recognize that he is being ironic. The literal sense of the words is at odds with their real intention, and Byron's tone is sceptical, instead of pious, and playful, instead of serious.

The determination of tone becomes even more complex when, as in the case of Frost's "Design," the poet's attitude seems to change as he reflects more and more deeply on the significance of the events he describes. The first eight lines of Frost's poem are largely descriptive. The tone is observing, meticulous, and perhaps a little eerie. We see the flower, the moth, and the spider close up, as if through a magnifying glass; and the preoccupation with death and blight, along with the analogy to a witches' broth, is chilling. The next six lines present three rhetorical questions and a final conditional clause. Here Frost begins to inquire into the meaning of what he has just described. The first two questions merely underscore the unusual combination of events that brought together the blighted flower, the albino spider, and the innocent white moth. Frost's tone is inquisitive and concerned, but still fairly neutral and objective. In the last question, however, the tone suddenly becomes fearful. What else, Frost asks, can this incident be "but the design of darkness to appall?" Then Frost moves in a direction that at first appears reassuring when he doubts, almost as an afterthought, "If design govern in a thing so small." Yet the line also opens up the unsettling possibility that there is no design at all and the world is governed by chance. If there is any reassurance in these thoughts, that reassurance ought to be thoroughly undermined by the fearful realization that the scene *has* seemed fated. The designs of darkness *have* seemed to operate—even at the insignificant level of the moth, the spider, and the innocent heal-all! This sobering and somewhat horrifying possibility ultimately summarizes the direction toward which the poem—both in tone and in meaning—has been moving all along.

7. **Identify the Theme. A literary *theme*, as we use the term in this text, is the central idea or insight that unifies and controls the total work. It is the main point an author wishes to make about his or her subject.** As such, identifying a poem's theme involves two steps: finding the poem's subject and formulating the poet's main statement about that subject.

It is easy to determine the subject of most poems: often it is named or suggested by the title, and, of course, it is the focus of the whole poem. Herrick's title, "Upon Julia's Clothes," clearly names his subject—although we might add that the only significance of the clothes is that Julia is wearing them. At heart, the poem is an expression of Herrick's love for Julia. And this more general statement of the subject carries us far toward understanding the poem's theme, which— broadly stated—is that everything associated with the woman one loves becomes as beautiful and enchanting as she is.

The title of Frost's sonnet, "Design," reflects both the poem's subject and its theme. The subject is the possibility of design in the convergence of the white flower, the white moth, and the white spider. The theme—as nearly as one can state what Frost leaves only as a question—is that perhaps the designs of darkness control even the trivial and insignificant events in nature.

Stating a poem's theme in one sentence can be useful in summarizing its purpose and importance, but it also can be a coarse and misleading approach to poetry. If Herrick or Frost had wished to develop only those themes that we have assigned to their poems, then they could easily have stated their purposes more directly. In the case of Herrick's poem, we have probably looked too hard for the significance of his simple imagistic description. Herrick himself probably realized that a poem of six lines cannot state abstract truths without sounding pompous and grandiose. A brief description may suggest those truths, but it ought not insist on them. The scope of Herrick's poem is wisely confined to the movement of Julia's clothes; it does not actually describe her clothing nor does it describe her person, for these subjects, presumably, would require a much more lavish treatment. The poem does not mention Herrick's love for Julia, nor does it assert Julia's beauty—everything, therefore, that we have said about the poem's theme is deduced without any direct support from a text that is imagistic rather than judgmental or argumentative.

The attempt to determine the plain sense of a poem by following the seven steps outlined in this chapter will give you a much clearer understanding of the literal meaning of the poem and of the issues in it that are worthy of explication and analysis. However, a written explication or analysis will not necessarily include each of those seven steps as an explicit portion of the essay. Moreover, a formal explication will normally go on to examine the matters of versification and form discussed in the next two chapters. You should use the seven steps outlined and the section on "Questions to Ask About Poetry" (pp. 776–777) to discover the ideas that you may wish to include in an essay. For advice on how to write your explication or analysis, see the section on "Writing About Literature" (pp. 5–27).

Poems for Further Study

DELIGHT IN DISORDER

A sweet disorder in the dress
Kindles in clothes a wantonness:
A lawn° about the shoulders thrown   *fine linen shawl*
Into a fine distraction:
5 An erring lace, which here and there
Enthrals the crimson stomacher.[1]
A cuff neglectful, and thereby
Ribbands° to flow confusedly: *ribbons*
A winning wave, deserving note,
10 In the tempestuous petticoat:

[1] A separate piece of cloth held in place by laces and covering a woman's bosom.

A careless shoe-string, in whose tie
I see a wild civility:
Do more bewitch me than when art
Is too precise in every part.

—Robert Herrick [1648]

❦ QUESTIONS ❦

1. What is Herrick's principle of selection in choosing the imagery?

2. What words in the poem give some indication of the speaker's response to the woman and his assumptions about her personality?

3. How is the poem's imagery organized? Is there a pattern of development?

4. Consider the poem's rhyme scheme and rhythm. Is Herrick's own verse "too precise in every part," or does it, like the lady's "sweet disorder in the dress," demonstrate "a wide civility"?

ANTHEM FOR DOOMED YOUTH

What passing-bells for these who die as cattle?
  Only the monstrous anger of the guns.
  Only the stuttering rifles' rapid rattle
Can patter out their hasty orisons.°   *prayers*
5 No mockeries for them from prayers or bells,
  Nor any voice of mourning save the choirs,—
The shrill, demented choirs of wailing shells;
  And bugles calling for them from sad shires.

What candles may be held to speed them all?
10   Not in the hands of boys, but in their eyes
Shall shine the holy glimmers of good-byes.
  The pallor of girls' brows shall be their pall;
Their flowers the tenderness of silent minds,
And each slow dusk a drawing-down of blinds.

—Wilfred Owen [posthumous, 1920]

❦ QUESTIONS ❦

1. What is an anthem? Does this poem meet the definition of an anthem?

2. Who are the doomed youths in the poem? (Consider the date of publication in answering this question.)

3. According to Owen, what passing bells, prayers, choirs, candles, pall, and flowers are accorded to the youths he is describing?

4. How would you describe the speaker's tone and his attitude toward warfare?

5. Is Owen successful in making the sound of this poem echo its sense? Explain your answer.

NOT WAVING BUT DROWNING

Nobody heard him, the dead man,
But still he lay moaning:
I was much further out than you thought
And not waving but drowning.

5   Poor chap, he always loved larking
And now he's dead
It must have been too cold for him his heart gave way,
They said.

Oh, no no no, it was too cold always
10   (Still the dead one lay moaning)
I was much too far out all my life
And not waving but drowning.

—Stevie Smith [1957]

❧ QUESTIONS ❧

1. How many speakers are there in this poem? Do you think that the words are actually spoken—or are they the words that would have been or should have been spoken?

2. If the drowned man lies "moaning" (line 2), how can he be "dead" (line 1)?

3. Why did no one attempt to rescue the drowning man? Why does no one hear his moaning? How do the people on the beach misunderstand the dead man's personality and motives?

4. In what sense did the dead man's heart give way?

5. What is the effect of the repetition in the poem? What symbolic or allegorical interpretation of the events does it encourage?

15

❧❧❧❧❧❧❧❧

Rhythm and Meter

If you hold a conch shell to your ear, you will seem to hear within it the rhythmic rush and retreat of the sea surf. Although children find deep fascination and mystery in this audible reminder of the ocean, science explains away that magic meter as an echo of the blood throbbing in the listener's own inner ear. But in this case, as indeed in many others, the scientific explanation does less to erase our wonder than to transpose it and intellectualize it. The rhythm of the conch— the crashing of the sea—is also in the beat of our blood, the core of our very being. We are, it seems, rhythm-making creatures. When we listen to the monotone ticking of a wristwatch, we hear it as a rhythmic tic-tock. The rattle of a moving train is heard as a rhythmic clickety-clack. We hear the drumming of a horse's hooves as clip-clop. We make something rhythmic out of even the most dull and invariable experiences.

This affection for rhythm has never been fully explained, but it is probably the result of the natural rhythms of human life. In addition to the systolic and diastolic beat of the heart, there are similar rhythms in our breathing, in our movements as bipeds, and in a great variety of our habitual activities. Generations of farmers, pressing one ear to a cow's churning and drum-tight belly, have rhythmically squeezed her milk into a pail. Generations of farm men have raised and dropped a hoe or slung and recoiled a scythe. Generations of farm women have rhythmically kneaded dough or scrubbed at a washboard. Generations of children have grown up loving chants, nursery rhymes, and jingles.

It should come as no surprise then that both prose and poetry are rhythmic. According to the nineteenth-century French poet Charles Baudelaire, "rhythm and rhyme answer in man to the immortal needs of monotony, symmetry, and surprise." Furthermore, **strong emotions tend to find memorable expression through strong rhythms.** This is obviously true of music, dance, and poetry; but it can also be true of prose. Julius Caesar's pride in conquering Gaul shone through the rhythms of his message to the Roman senate, "Veni, vidi, vici!" ("*I came*, I *saw*,

721

I *conquered!"*) Patrick Henry's belief in the cause of American independence was passionately expressed through the strong, rhythmical patterns in his speech to the Virginia Convention on March 23, 1775:

The gentlemen may cry, Peace, Peace! but there is no peace. The war is actually begun! The next gale that sweeps from the north shall bring to our ears the clash of resounding arms! . . . Is life so dear or peace so sweet as to be purchased at the price of chains and slavery? Forbid it, Almighty God. I know not what course others may take, but as for me, give me liberty or give me death!

Abraham Lincoln's firm belief in the need for reconciliation following the Civil War was beautifully embodied in the cadence of his second inaugural address of 1865:

With malice toward none, with charity for all, with firmness in the right as God gives us to see the right, let us bind up the Nation's wounds.

As we have just seen, poets have no monopoly on rhythm; it is also true that the correct use of meter does not make a poet, any more than the correct use of grammar makes a novelist or the correct use of chewing tobacco makes a baseball player. As Ralph Waldo Emerson observed in 1844, **"it is not meters, but a meter-making argument that makes a poem—a thought so passionate and alive that like the spirit of a plant or an animal it has an architecture of its own and adorns nature with a new thing."** Just as our hearts beat vigorously at moments of violent emotion, so, too, our words begin to beat more forcefully while we express those emotions—and the rhythms of poetic words often re-create in a careful reader the same sense of breathless excitement that possessed the poet.

Although we respond as readily to the rhythms of prose as poetry, the fact remains that most poetry (and little prose) is cast into formal metrical patterns. Perhaps the reason for this, as we have already suggested, is that the metrical patterns of verse help to create a more direct relationship to natural human rhythms than is possible in prose. When the alternating accents of iambic verse are read aloud, they almost inevitably match the 72 beats per minute of our pulse. Moreover, when we speak aloud, our words are naturally grouped in response to our breathing. After giving voice to eight or ten syllables, most speakers must pause for another breath. English verse makes the speaker's breathing easier by being written in lines of roughly equal length. The two most common measures in our language, tetrameter and pentameter, normally contain eight and ten syllables, respectively. Lines longer than pentameter are uncommon because they can be difficult to recite. Shorter lines, like trimeter which has six syllables, by encouraging rapid breathing, give the illusion of haste or excitement. Thus, verse itself is both a response to human physiology and an influence on it. **Like a natural force, verse sets up a pattern of expectations that we recognize intuitively and to which we respond both physically and emotionally.** The study of metrics allows us to name and to analyze the prevailing rhythms of most poems.

Meter is basically a system for helping the reader reproduce the rhythm intended by the author. The word *meter* comes from the Greek "metron," meaning "measure." These words, *meter* and *measure,* are used interchangeably in describing poetic rhythms. The units with which we measure verse are the syllable, the foot, the line, and sometimes the stanza and the canto. **A *syllable,* which is the smallest unit in metrics, is any word or part of a word produced in speech by a**

single pulse of breath. It is a simple link in the chain of sounds. Between sixty and eighty percent of the words in English poetry are monosyllables—words like *root, tree, leaf, fruit, man, child, boy, girl, a, an,* and *the.* The remaining words are polysyllabic and are divided by dictionaries into their individual links of sound: *re-main-ing, pol-y-syl-lab-ic, di-vi-ded,* etc. **The basic rhythmic unit in verse is called a *foot* and is composed of an established number of stressed (emphasized) and unstressed syllables. An established number of feet makes up a *line* and an established number of lines often makes up a *stanza.* The number of lines or stanzas in a *canto* (a unit or section of a long poem) is rarely fixed in advance.**

SCANSION

The process by which we discover the dominant rhythm in a poem is called *scansion.* **The basic steps in scanning a poem are quite simple and entail (1) finding the number of syllables in a typical line, (2) marking the stressed or accented syllables in each line and (3) identifying the prevailing foot and the number of feet per line.** It should be noted that the entire process focuses on the number of syllables and stresses in a given line of poetry. For this reason, English verse is said to be written in syllabic-stress meters.

Now let us go through each step in the scansion process for a representative poem, "On First Looking into Chapman's Homer" by John Keats:

ON FIRST LOOKING INTO CHAPMAN'S HOMER

1 Much have I travell'd in the realms of gold
2 And many goodly states and kingdoms seen,
3 Round many western islands have I been
4 Which bards in fealty to Apollo hold.
5 Oft of one wide expanse had I been told
6 That deep-browed Homer ruled as his demesne:
7 Yet did I never breathe its pure serene
8 Till I heard Chapman speak out loud and bold.
9 Then felt I like some watcher of the skies
10 When a new planet swims into his ken;
11 Or like stout Cortez when with eagle eyes
12 He stared at the Pacific—and all his men
13 Look'd at each other with a wild surmise—
14 Silent upon a peak in Darien.

—John Keats [1816]

1. **Find the number of syllables in a typical line.** Inspection of the poem shows that the typical line contains ten syllables, but lines 4, 6, 12, and 14 present minor problems in syllabification. The word "fealty" in line 4 is usually divided into three syllables, "fe/al/ty," but because this would give the line a total of eleven, we may feel more comfortable eliding "fe/al" into one syllable which sounds like the word *feel.* There are, in fact, an unusual number of words in our language that are divided differently on different occasions: for example, *unusual* (un-use-yul, un-use-u-al), *our* (are, ow-er), *different* (diff-er-ent, diff-rent), *occasions* (o-cay-zhuns, o-cay-zhi-ens). Moreover, the syllabification of certain words has changed over the centuries—notably in the pronunciation of the *ed* forms of verbs: *bathed* was once *bath-ed, in-spired* was once *in-spi-red, changed* was once *chang-*

ed, and even now *aged* may be pronounced *age-ed.* Archaic forms are, of course, common in medieval verse, but they are sometimes deliberately used in more contemporary poetry where the unanticipated accents are generally marked *(changéd).* Keats, however, so often required his readers to pronounce the final *ed* of verbs that in the first line of "On First Looking into Chapman's Homer," he used the contraction "travell'd" to show that the end of the verb was *not* to be sounded.

Alternate pronunciations and archaisms are only two of the problems of syllabification. Many of us are unfamiliar with the pronunciation of some words used in poetry. In line 6, for example, the word *demesne* appears to have three syllables, but we learn from the dictionary that it may be pronounced to rhyme with *serene,* in line 7:

> *de • mesne* (di-mān′, -ēn′) .... 3. any territory or domain.

Thus, line 6, like most of the others, contains the expected ten syllables. In line 14 we might again turn to a dictionary to reassure ourselves that "Darien" does indeed have the three syllables (Da/ri/en) required by the meter.

No reading of line 12, however, can produce any fewer than eleven syllables, and therefore we are forced to describe that one line as slightly irregular. **The expectation of a predictable number of syllables in a line is *only* an expectation. Slight variations are normal and even desirable when they serve some rhythmic function.** But in order to discuss a poem's rhythm, we must learn to identify the pattern of stressed and unstressed syllables.

2. **Mark the stressed or accented syllables in each line.** The problem of determining where the stresses fall in poetry is more complex than counting the syllables, but with a good ear and the guidance of a few simple rules, most readers can produce satisfactory results.

The first rule is that **a poem's meter should not change the normal pronunciation of a polysyllabic word.** In all words of two syllables or more, the accentuation is marked in most dictionaries.[1] Thus, in lines 3 and 4, for example, we can immediately mark several stressed syllables. The dictionary tells us that the accent falls on the middle syllable of "A • pól • lo" and on the first syllables of "mán •y," "wés • tern," "iś • lands," and "feál • ty." If we place a straight line over the accented syllables, the preliminary scansion of the lines looks like this:

> Round mānȳ wēstern īslands have I been
> Which bards in feālty to Apōllo hold.

The second rule is that **monosyllabic words have no inherent stress; they take on stresses to fit the metrical pattern of the poem and the rhetorical rhythm of a particular sentence.** In other words, monosyllables may be either stressed or unstressed. In general, however, the emphasis should fall where it would in a normal prose reading of the lines. **Usually, the stresses will fall on the most important words—especially nouns and verbs.** Less important words, like articles, prepositions and conjunctions, are rarely stressed. In addition, in normal English prose,

---

[1] One should note, however, that not all dictionaries mark the secondary accents in polysyllabic words, and sometimes the same word can be pronounced in different ways. E.g., *infinitive* and *infínitive.*

stressed and unstressed syllables tend to alternate. When we read Keats's lines aloud we find that weak, but still noticeable, stresses fall on "have" and "been," while more pronounced emphasis is placed on "bards" and "hold." If we now mark each of these as an accented syllable and mark the remaining unaccented syllables with a cup (˘), we will have produced a complete metrical picture of the lines:

> Round many western islands have I been
> Which bards in fealty to Apollo hold.

1. Identify the prevailing foot and the number of feet per line. Having scanned the lines, we now need only name the specific meter being used. **In the syllabic-stress system there are only five commonly used feet: iambic, anapestic, trochaic, dactylic, and spondaic.**

TABLE OF METRICAL FEET

Name	Example
Dactyl	"Much have I
Trochee	travell'd
Anapest	in the realms
Iamb	of gold."
Spondee	John Keats.

Of these, the iamb is by far the most popular and versatile. It is the principal foot used in such narrative and dramatic verse as Chaucer's *Canterbury Tales,* Shakespeare's plays, Milton's *Paradise Lost,* Wordsworth's *Prelude,* Byron's *Don Juan,* and most other substantial poems written in English. The iambic foot is equally popular in lyric verse and ballads and is required in sonnets. It is, therefore, used in Keats's sonnet, "On First Looking into Chapman's Homer," and the two lines that we have just scanned can be shown to have five iambic feet to the line:

> Round man/y wes/tern is/lands have/ I been
> Which bards/ in feal/ty to/ Apol/ lo hold.

We use a vertical slash (/) to mark the divisions between the feet. These divisions are helpful in counting the feet, but they do not signal pauses in speech; they may fall either between words or between the syllables of a word.

In critical analysis we generally replace the wordy and awkward phrase "five feet to the line" with the term *pentameter.* The technical term for each of the possible lines in English poetry is provided in the following list:

> *monometer:* one foot per line
> *dimeter:* two feet per line
> *trimeter:* three feet per line
> *tetrameter:* four feet per line
> *pentameter:* five feet per line
> *hexameter:* six feet per line

heptameter: seven feet per line
octameter: eight feet per line

Of these, pentameter and tetrameter are the most commonly used.

Once chosen, the dominant metrical foot normally remains fixed throughout a given poem. Thus, for example, iambic rhythm prevails in Donne's "A Valediction: Forbidding Mourning" (p. 821), whereas trochaic rhythm prevails in Blake's "The Tyger" (p. 855) and anapestic rhythm dominates Poe's "Annabel Lee" (p. 738). **Although the principal metrical foot almost invariably remains unchanged throughout a poem, the length of the lines often varies according to a pre-established pattern.** "A Valediction: Forbidding Mourning" and "The Tyger" are tetrameter throughout, but in "Annabel Lee" tetrameter alternates with trimeter.

Thus, in choosing iambic pentameter for "Chapman's Homer," Keats commits himself to creating the possibility of a scansion that includes five metrical feet in each line, and he has to work within the expectation that each line will follow an iambic rhythm. We use the words *possibility* and *expectation* because the metrical pattern of a poem is not intended to be a straitjacket that restricts all movement and permits scant room to breathe. Rather, the pattern should be cut like a well-tailored dress that complements both the shape and the movement of the human form it adorns. Deviations from the expected metrical pattern create surprise, emphasis, and often delight.

Anapestic, dactylic, trochaic, and spondaic feet are all used more frequently to provide variety in iambic verse than to set the rhythm of an entire poem. As the examples in our Table of Metrical Feet show, each of these (except the spondee) is used in the first line of Keats's sonnet:

>   *dactyl*   *trochee*   *anapest*   *iamb*
> Much have Ĭ/ travell'd/ in the realms/ of gold . . .

Keats's first line is, therefore, highly irregular, and two questions now confront us: What purposes are served by variations from an established meter? And how do different rhythms affect our emotional response to poetry?

A partial answer to the first question was proposed by Samuel Johnson when he wrote, in his "Life of Dryden" (1781), that "the essence of verse is regularity and its ornament is variety." This implies that **a poem should be regular enough to establish a pattern and varied enough to banish monotony.** It is a corollary to the familiar rule endorsing moderation in all things, and in recent years it has become almost commonplace to condemn poets whose meters are too regular.

There is, however, little value in a more detailed attempt to state a general principle about regularity and variety in meter. Such esthetic judgments can only be made within the context of a particular poem's meaning. What *can* be said, however, is that **rhythm and any deviations from rhythm should contribute to the overall effect sought in the poem.** According to the well-known modern critic Cleanth Brooks, **"What is wanted is neither a dead mechanical beat nor a jumble of patternless incoherence, but the rich expressiveness of a verse that is alive with the tension of living speech."**[2]

"The tension of living speech" is an apt expression for the effect of metrical

---

[2] Cleanth Brooks and Robert Penn Warren, *Understanding Poetry*, 4th ed. (New York: Holt, Rinehart and Winston, 1976) 503.

variation in "On First Looking into Chapman's Homer." If we look again at its first line, we see that, although it has ten syllables and can conceivably be read as iambic pentameter,

Mŭch HĀVE/ Ĭ TRĀ/vell'd ĬN/ the REĀLMS/ ŏf GŌLD,

such a reading distorts the rhythms of living speech. But if we read the line naturally,

MŪCH hăve Ĭ/ TRĀvell'd/ in the REĀLMS/ ŏf GŌLD,

we find neither a metrical pattern—indeed, each foot is different—nor the five feet we expect in pentameter. Clearly, Keats is creating a tension between living speech and our expectations of a sonnet. The line has fewer accents and more unstressed syllables than we expect; and because unstressed syllables roll rapidly from the tongue, the pace of the line is more rapid than in standard iambic pentameter. This can be stated as a general principle of metrics: **unaccented syllables in anapests and dactyls accelerate the pace; heavily accented syllables in spondees slow the pace.**

Furthermore, Keats has arranged the unstressed syllables so that nearly all of them pour forth in two rolling clusters. Thus, the poem begins with a sense of surprise and breathless excitement. As we continue reading, we learn that this tone is exactly right for the story Keats has to tell. Reading Chapman's translation of Homer was a new and exciting experience for Keats. It showed him that poetry could unexpectedly "speak out loud and bold"; it did not need to be a syrupy concoction of unvaried sweetness. The rhythm in the first line of the sonnet helps to capture and communicate Keats's emotions.

One line in a sonnet is, of course, insufficient to set the tone for the rest of the poem, but the rhythm of this first line is repeated again and again. The dactyl-trochee combination, which helps to make these first syllables forceful and rugged, occurs at the beginning of lines 5, 7, 9, 13, and 14:

1	Mūch hăve Ĭ / tră vell'd/ ...
5	Ōft ŏf ŏne/ wĭde ĕx/panse ...
7	Yĕt dĭd Ĭ/ nĕver/ ...
9	Thĕn fĕlt Ĭ/ lĭke sŏme/ ...
13	Lŏok'd ăt ĕach/ ŏther / ...
14	Sĭlent ŭp/on ă / ...

The tension between regular iambic pentameter and Keats's startling irregularity is especially noticeable in the final verses, both because these lines occur at the poem's climax and because two irregular patterns occur in immediate succession. Keats achieves a perfect blending of sound and sense when he says of Cortez:

12	Hĕ stared/ ăt thĕ Pă /cĭfĭc//—ănd all / hĭs mĕn
13	Lŏok'd ăt ĕach/ ŏther// wĭth ă wĭld/ sŭrmise—
14	Sĭlent// ŭpŏn/ ă peak / ĭn Dă/rĭen.

In describing the metrical effects in this combination of lines, we will find it useful to define three more terms: *end-stopped verse, enjambment,* and the *caesura.* **An end-stopped line,** like line 13 in Keats's sonnet, **is simply one that concludes with a pause.** A strongly end-stopped verse ends with some mark of punctuation—a comma, semicolon, colon, dash, question mark, exclamation point, or period. The punctuation tells the reader to pause for breath and emphasis. Although a lightly end-stopped verse may have no formal punctuation, it must still mark a pause between phrases or clauses. Lines 1, 3, 5, 7, and 11 are all lightly end-stopped. *Enjambment* **(or "striding over"),** as in line 12 of Keats's sonnet, **is the running on of one line into the next without a grammatical pause.** End-stopping tends to reinforce the metrical structure of a poem, whereas enjambment tends to minimize the difference between the sound of verse and that of prose. **A** *caesura* **(marked with a double slash, //) is a pause that occurs near the middle of most verses.** This pause may be indicated by punctuation, as in line 12; or it may fall between phrases, as in line 13. If a line has an even number of feet, the caesura tends to bisect it, as in line 13. One advantage of iambic pentameter is that its five accents can never be divided evenly. This ensures a certain amount of variety in even the most regular pentameters and opens up the possibility of a caesural pause as late as the fourth foot or as early as the first (line 14).

How do end-stopping, enjambment, and the caesural pause contribute to the impact of Keats's poem? It is quite apparent that a dramatic pause is signaled by the dash at the end of line 13. The effect of this pause is to emphasize the "wild surmise" and to encourage us to determine *what* is surmised. These men have discovered an entirely new ocean and are briefly struck dumb with wonder. They pause, just as Keats's punctuation forces us to pause. The content of these lines is in absolute harmony with their end-stopped rhythm.

The contribution of the enjambment from line 12 to 13 is also important, but it is atypical of the general effect of that device. If we examine Keats's poem as a whole, we find that exactly half of the lines are run-on or very lightly end-stopped. Thus, the poem has the typographical appearance of verse, but because strongly end-stopped lines are avoided, it has a fluid movement resembling that of melodious prose. In this respect, Keats's style is unusually mature for a poet who had not yet reached the age of legal majority. Most other great poets from Chaucer and Shakespeare to Byron and Wordsworth passed through a period of strong end-stopping before evolving at last to a more flexible style. But the enjambment at line 12 is grammatical only. In prose we do not ordinarily pause between a subject and verb. We use but one breath to say, "and all his men looked at each other." But when these words are put into a sonnet and scanned, a substantial pause before "Look'd" is almost obligatory for several reasons. In the first place most readers of poetry inevitably pause slightly at the end of a line of verse—even when such a pause is not syntactic. The end-line pause is one of our expectations in verse. Furthermore, in this particular case, the last syllable of line 12 ("mēn") is accented, as is the first syllable of line 13 ("Lŏok'd"). As we mentioned before, strong accents in juxtaposition always slow the pace of poetry, here augmenting the natural end-line pause. And finally, it makes dramatic sense to pause before "Look'd." The pause helps to create suspense and emphasis. It informs us that this is a penetrating look, a look of rapture and astonishment. Hence, the grammatical enjambment between lines 12 and 13 is offset by a combination of poetic effects, and once again we have "verse that is alive with the tension of living speech."

The caesural pauses in lines 12 and 13 merit no special analysis—the one in line

12 is plainly grammatical and the one in line 13 falls at the exact midpoint of the line and between two prepositional phrases, each of which independently modifies the verb. We might, however, be tempted to omit the caesura we placed after the first foot in line 14,

$$\text{Sĭlĕnt// ŭpŏn/ ă pēak/ ĭn Dā/riĕn.}$$

It certainly could not be placed later in the line because it would then either divide words within a prepositional phrase or separate two phrases closely linked both in logic and in grammar. And in placing a caesura after "Silent," we disrupt the rhythm of the dactyl-trochee combination that has characterized the poem. But if we wish to protect that rhythm, we must omit the caesura altogether and scan the line in a way that produces an unusual monosyllabic foot:

$$\text{Sĭlĕnt ŭp/ ŏn ă/ pēak/ ĭn Dā/riĕn.}^3$$

Of the two options, the former is clearly preferable. It is closer to regular iambic pentameter; it includes the expected caesura at a grammatically acceptable place; and, most importantly, it helps the sound of the poem to echo its sense. A momentary silence *should* follow the word—as if in recognition of its meaning.

In summary, the goal of a metrical analysis is to clarify how the rhythm of language contributes to its poetic meaning. In order to assist in this process, the full scansion of a poem or passage should identify the underlying metrical pattern; analyze the important deviations from that pattern; and consider the effects of end-stopping, enjambment, and placement of the caesura. An analysis of rhythmic effects that is not based on scansion is likely to be imprecise and unintelligible; however, scansion that does not include analysis and interpretation is mechanical and meaningless.

Poems for Further Study

MY HEART LEAPS UP

My heart leaps up when I behold
A rainbow in the sky:
So was it when my life began;
So is it now I am a man;
So be it when I shall grow old,
    Or let me die!
The Child is father of the Man;
And I could wish my days to be
Bound each to each by natural piety.

—William Wordsworth [1807]

---

[3] Note that the placement of the caesura marks the only audible difference in the two possibilities in scansion. It makes no difference in the rhythm whether the feet are scanned as a trochee and four iambs or as a dactyl, a trochee, a monosyllable, and two iambs. Both scansions should be read in precisely the same manner.

❧ QUESTIONS ❧

1. How does the personification in line 1 help Wordsworth to communicate his emotional response to the rainbow?

2. What connotations—both biblical and otherwise—are associated with the rainbow?

3. How does the parallelism of lines 3-6 ("So was it . . . So is it . . . So be it . . .") increase the forcefulness of the entreaty? Why does Wordsworth wish to emphasize his enduring pleasure in natural beauty?

4. What truth is there in the paradox of line 7? What does Wordsworth mean by this paradox?

5. Scan the poem. What is the dominant rhythm? What meter prevails? What is the rhetorical effect of the shortened lines (lines 2 and 6)? Why does Wordsworth include an extra foot in the last line?

LA BELLE DAME SANS MERCI[4]

"O what can ail thee, knight-at-arms,
    Alone and palely loitering?
The sedge° is withered from the lake,   *coarse, clumped grass*
    And no birds sing.

5   "O what can ail thee, knight-at-arms,
    So haggard and so woe-begone?
The squirrel's granary is full,
    And the harvest's done.

"I see a lily on thy brow
10   With anguish moist and fever dew;
And on thy cheek a fading rose
    Fast withereth too."

"I met a lady in the meads,°   *meadows*
    Full beautiful—a faery's child,
15   Her hair was long, her foot was light,
    And her eyes were wild.

"I made a garland for her head,
    And bracelets too, and fragrant zone;°   *girdle (belt)*
She looked at me as she did love,
20   And made sweet moan.

"I set her on my pacing steed
    And nothing else saw all day long,
For sideways would she lean, and sing
    A faery's song.

---

[4] The title, which means "The Beautiful Lady Without Mercy," is borrowed from a medieval French poem by Alain Chartier.

25   "She found me roots of relish sweet,
            And honey wild and manna[5] dew,
        And sure in language strange she said,
                'I love thee true!'

        "She took me to her elfin grot,
30   And there she wept and sighed full sore;
        And there I shut her wild, wild eyes
                With kisses four.

        "And there she lullèd me asleep,
            And there I dreamed—Ah! woe betide!
35   The latest dream I ever dreamed
                On the cold hill's side.

        "I saw pale kings and princes too,
            Pale warriors, death-pale were they all;
        Who cried—'La belle dame sans merci
40   Hath thee in thrall!'

        "I saw their starved lips in the gloom°   *twilight*
            With horrid warning gapèd wide,
        And I awoke and found me here
                On the cold hill's side.

45   "And this is why I sojourn here
            Alone and palely loitering,
        Though the sedge is withered from the lake,
                And no birds sing."

                                        —John Keats [1820]

 QUESTIONS

1. How many speakers are in the poem and what are their situations?

2. What evidence suggests that the knight-at-arms is dying? What is the cause of his suffering?

3. What does the setting contribute to the effect of the poem?

4. Is the "lady in the meads" just "a faery's child," or is she a demon-lover who enchants men and then leaves them to die of love-longing? What details in lines 13–33 make her seem especially enchanting?

5. Does the knight's dream in lines 37–44 do him any good? Why does the knight lose his lady? Why does the knight remain where the lady left him?

6. Scan the poem. What is the dominant rhythm and what meters are used? How does the short, heavily accented line that ends each stanza contribute to the mood of the poem?

---

[5] Miraculous and sustaining. See the Bible, Exodus 16:14–36.

"I TASTE A LIQUOR NEVER BREWED"

I taste a liquor never brewed—
From Tankards scooped in Pearl—
Not all the Vats upon the Rhine
Yield such an Alcohol!

5   Inebriate of Air—am I—
And Debauchee of Dew—
Reeling—thro endless summer days—
From inns of Molten Blue—

When "Landlords" turn the drunken Bee
10   Out of the Foxglove's door—
When Butterflies—renounce their "drams"—
I shall but drink the more!

Till Seraphs° swing their snowy Hats—   *angels*
And Saints—to windows run—
15   To see the little Tippler
Leaning against the—Sun—

—Emily Dickinson [1861]

❧ QUESTIONS ❧

1. What conceit dominates the poem and serves as its controlling metaphor? How do the various images in the poem—the "Inebriate of Air," the "Debauchee of Dew," the "inns of Molten Blue," and so on—contribute to the development of the conceit?

2. How does the speaker characterize herself? What is her condition? What is her tone?

3. Consider Dickinson's punctuation. Does it contribute to the creation of tone and meaning—or does it merely interfere with clarity?

4. Scan the poem. What is the dominant rhythm? What is the meter? Dickinson's speaker is a somewhat reeling "Inebriate of Air." Does she ever manipulate the rhythm to make the sound of the poem stagger along with its speaker?

16

✻✻✻✻✻

Rhythm and Meter
Part 2

Although the iambic pentameter of Keats's sonnet on "Chapman's Homer" is the most common of English meters, it is by no means the only possible rhythm. Nor is the syllabic-stress system the only possible approach to writing and scanning verse. Before closing our discussion of rhythm and meter, let us briefly survey the variety of poetic meters, the limitations of syllabic-stress scansion, and the other possible systems of scanning English verse.

VARIETY OF METERS. While trochees, anapests, and dactyls are most frequently used to provide variety within an iambic rhythm, each can also establish the underlying meter of a poem, and each creates a very different rhythmic effect. The rhythm of a poem does not, of course, dictate its tone. Rhythm is at best a contributing factor that can be used by able poets to complement the mood created through the denotations and connotations of words. There are, however, differences among the four basic meters of English poetry, and these differences can easily be heard, even though their effects cannot be perfectly described.

The *trochee* (*travell'd*) **is the mirror image of the iamb and is perhaps even more common than the iamb in everyday speech.** The plurals of many monosyllabic words become trochaic (*fĭshĕs, hoŭsĕs, āxĕs,* etc.) and a great many two-syllable words are natural trochees (*pōĕt, wātĕr, āblĕ,* etc.).

Trochaic and iambic meters do not differ greatly in their effects. In fact, trochaic pentameter can be described as iambic pentameter with a defective first foot and an extra syllable at the end.

trochaic ´˘ | ´˘ | ´˘ | ´˘ | ´˘

iambic ˘ | ˘´ | ˘´ | ˘´ | ˘´

Because the first syllable in a trochaic line is accented, poems in this meter often sound assertive and vigorous. But the use of trochees makes end rhyme difficult

733

because rhyme words are usually stressed. Thus, some poems that start out with a trochaic rhythm end up iambic, as in the catalectic (meaning "incomplete") trochaic tetrameter of John Donne's "Song":

SONG

Go, and catch a falling star,
    Get with child a mandrake root,[1]
Tell me where all past years are,
    Or who cleft the Devil's foot.
5   Teach me to hear mermaids singing,
    Or to keep off envy's stinging,
        And find,
        What wind
Serves to advance an honest mind.

10   If thou be'st born to strange sights,
    Things invisible to see,
Ride ten thousand days and nights,
    Till age snow white hairs on thee,
Thou, when thou return'st, wilt tell me
15   All strange wonders, that befell thee,
        And swear,
        No where
Lives a woman true and fair.

If thou find'st one, let me know,
20   Such a pilgrimage were sweet;
Yet do not, I would not go,
    Though at next door we might meet.
Though she were true when you met her,
And last, till you write your letter,
25   Yet she
        Will be
False, ere I come, to two or three.

—John Donne [posthumous, 1633]

❧ QUESTIONS ❧

1. To whom is the poem addressed? What is the speaker's tone? What is his opinion about the constancy of women?

2. Donne lists seven impossibilities in his first nine lines. What eighth impossibility does he have in mind throughout this stanza?

3. Where and with what effect does Donne use overstatement in this poem?

4. Scan the poem. Where does Donne manipulate the rhythm to create rhetorical effects? How do the two short lines (monometers) in each stanza

---

[1] The root of the mandrake resembles a human torso and legs.

affect the rhythm of the poem? What is the advantage of slowing up the movement of the poem before the final line in each stanza? Where is this advantage most obvious and most effective?

Incantations are often trochaic, possibly because the strong accents that begin each trochaic line complement a chanting rhythm:

> Double/, double// toil and/ trouble;
> Fire/ burn and// cauldron/ bubble.

> —From *Macbeth*,
> William Shakespeare [ca. 1607]

Very probably, this hint of the supernatural in trochaic rhythms guided Edgar Allan Poe in choosing the meter for "The Raven" (1845):

> Once up/on a/ midnight/ dreary,// while I/ pondered/ weak and/ weary,
> Over/ many a/ quaint and/ curious// volume/ of for/gotten/ lore—

A *dactyl* (Much have I) is a trochee with an extra unstressed syllable. Because unstressed syllables are pronounced easily, poems in dactylic meter move with a rapid, waltzing beat (dum-dee-dee, dum-dee-dee). The dactylic dimeter of Ralph Hodgson's "Eve" provides a good example of the lyrical but unsettling possibilities in the rhythm:

EVE

> Eve, with her basket, was
> Deep in the bells and grass,
> Wading in bells and grass
> Up to her knees,
> 5 Picking a dish of sweet
> Berries and plums to eat,
> Down in the bells and grass
> Under the trees.
>
> Mute as a mouse in a
> 10 Corner the cobra lay,
> Curled round a bough of the
> Cinnamon tall. . . .
> Now to get even and
> Humble proud Heaven and
> 15 Now was the moment or
> Never at all.
>
> "Eva!" Each syllable
> Light as a flower fell,
> "Eva!" he whispered the
> 20 Wondering maid,
> Soft as a bubble sung
> Out of a linnet's° lung,   *a small songbird*

Soft and most silverly
"Eva!" he said.

25 Picture that orchard sprite,
Eve, with her body white,
Supple and smooth to her
Slim finger tips,
Wondering, listening,
30 Listening, wondering,
Eve with a berry
Half-way to her lips.

Oh had our simple Eve
Seen through the make-believe!
35 Had she but known the
Pretender he was!
Out of the boughs he came,
Whispering still her name,
Tumbling in twenty rings
40 Into the grass.

Here was the strangest pair
In the world anywhere,
Eve in the bells and grass
Kneeling, and he
45 Telling his story low. . . .
Singing birds saw them go
Down the dark path to
The Blasphemous Tree.

Oh what a clatter when
50 Titmouse° and Jenny Wren   *a chickadee*
Saw him successful and
Taking his leave!
How the birds rated him,
How they all hated him!
55 How they all pitied
Poor motherless Eve!

Picture her crying
Outside in the lane,
Eve, with no dish of sweet
60 Berries and plums to eat,
Haunting the gate of the
Orchard in vain. . . .
Picture the lewd delight
Under the hill tonight—
65 "Eva!" the toast goes round,
"Eva!" again.

—Ralph Hodgson [1913]

❧ QUESTIONS ❧

1. Compare the story of Eve in this poem with the account in Genesis. What details does Hodgson add to the story? What is the effect of those details in creating setting, mood, motive, and character?

2. Examine the last stanza of the poem very carefully. How has the setting changed both in time and in space? Why does Hodgson change the setting?

3. Scan the poem (or at least several stanzas). What are the effects of the rhythm and meter? How do they contribute to the poem?

The dactyl is a rapid meter. Examine how Alfred Tennyson takes advantage of the strength and speed of dactyls to imitate the drumming of galloping horses in his famous "Charge of the Light Brigade":

> Half a league,/ half a league
> Half a league/ onward,
> All in the/ Valley of/ Death
> Rode the six/ hundred
> "Forward the/ Light Brigade!
> Charge for the/ guns!" he said:
> Into the/ Valley of/ Death
> Rode the six/ hundred.
>
> —From "The Charge of the Light Brigade,"
> Alfred, Lord Tennyson [1854]

And Longfellow also uses the unfamiliar sound of the dactylic line to accentuate the primitive, pagan mood at the beginning of "Evangeline" (1847):

> This is the/ forest prim/eval.// The/ murmuring/ pines and the/ hemlocks/ . . .
> Stand like/ Druids of/ old.

The *anapest* (in the realms), like the dactyl, is a rapid meter, but in proceeding from unstressed syllables to stressed ones, it also parallels the iamb. Hence, it has none of the strangeness of the dactyl or trochee. It works well in rapidly paced poems:

> The Assyr/ian came/ down// like the wolf/ on the fold,
> And his co/horts were gleam/ing in pur/ple and gold;
> And the sheen/ of their spears// was like stars/ on the sea,
> When the Blue/ wave rolls night/ly on deep/ Galilee.
>
> —From "The Destruction of Sennacherib,"
> Lord Byron [1815]

And it also pleases in very mellifluous ones:

ANNABEL LEE

It was many and many a year ago.
　　In a kingdom by the sea
That a maiden there lived whom you may know
　　By the name of Annabel Lee;—
5　　And this maiden she lived with no other thought
　　　　Than to love and be loved by me.

She was a child and *I* was a child,
　　In this kingdom by the sea,
But we loved with a love that was more than love—
10　　　I and my Annabel Lee—
With a love that the wingèd seraphs° of Heaven　　　　　　　　*angels*
　　Coveted her and me.

And this was the reason that, long ago,
　　In this kingdom by the sea,
15　　A wind blew out of a cloud by night
　　　Chilling my Annabel Lee;
So that her highborn kinsmen came
　　And bore her away from me,
To shut her up in a sepulchre
20　　　In this kingdom by the sea.

The angels, not half so happy in Heaven,
　　　Went envying her and me:—
Yes! that was the reason (as all men know,
　　In this kingdom by the sea)
25　That the wind came out of the cloud, chilling
　　　And killing my Annabel Lee.

But our love it was stronger by far than the love
　　Of those who were older than we—
　　Of many far wiser than we—
30　And neither the angels in Heaven above
　　　Nor the demons down under the sea,
Can ever dissever my soul from the soul
　　　Of the beautiful Annabel Lee:—

For the moon never beams without bringing me dreams
35　　Of the beautiful Annabel Lee;
And the stars never rise but I see the bright eyes
　　Of the beautiful Annabel Lee;
And so, all the night-tide, I lie down by the side
Of my darling, my darling, my life and my bride,
40　　In her sepulchre there by the sea—
　　　In her tomb by the side of the sea.

—Edgar Allan Poe [posthumous, 1850]

❧ QUESTIONS ❧

1. What was the speaker's relationship with Annabel Lee? What claims does the speaker make about their love?

2. Throughout the poem, Poe frequently repeats the phrase "kingdom by the sea." What is the effect of that repetition? What, if anything, does the sea come to symbolize? What does the sky symbolize? What does the land symbolize?

3. What does the speaker mean when he says that "we loved with a love that was more than love"? Why does he emphasize that *"She* was a child and *I* was a child"?

4. How does the speaker explain the cause of Annabel Lee's death?

5. How does the speaker console himself in the final stanza?

6. Scan the poem. How do the rhythm and meter contribute to the mood of the poem?

Someone once argued that a long poem in anapests, like a long ride on a roller coaster, is apt to cause nausea, but there can be little doubt that this rolling meter is exquisitely suited to many brief pieces.

The *spondee* (John Keats) is never the dominant meter in a whole poem, but one or two spondees will tend to dominate a line. This is well illustrated in Alexander Pope's lines on the role of sound and rhythm in poetry:

> True ease in writing comes from art, not chance,
> As those move easiest who have learned to dance.
> 'Tis not enough no harshness gives offense,
> The sound must seem an echo to the sense:
> Soft is the strain when Zephyr gently blows,
> And the smooth stream in smoother numbers flows;
>
> But when/ loud sur/ges lash// the sound/ing shore,
> The hoarse,/ rough verse// should like/ the tor/rent roar;
> When A/jax strives// some rock's/ vast weight/ to throw,
> The line/ too/ labors,/ and the words/ move slow.

> —From "An Essay on Criticism," Alexander Pope [1711]

There is at least one spondee in each of the last four lines, and each time a spondee occurs three stressed syllables line up in front of us like hard blocks of granite that our voices must surmount. **Stressed syllables require more effort from the speaker and they take longer to pronounce than unstressed syllables. As a result, spondees always slow down the pace of a poem.** They can be especially useful when an author wishes to express anger or violence, as in King Lear's line:

> Blow, winds,/ and crack/ your cheeks!// Rage! Blow!

In addition to the four principal rhythms (iambic, trochaic, anapestic, and dactylic) and that of the slow spondee, there are a great many feet with unpronounceable Greek names that pop up occasionally to vary the dominant rhythm of a poem: *pyrrhic* (˘˘), *bacchius* (˘ ‾‾), *antibacchius* (‾‾ ˘), *amphimacer* (‾ ˘ ‾), *amphibrach* (˘ ‾ ˘), and so on. Although there is no need to remember these names, their existence demonstrates that, within the framework of a dominant rhythm, a poet may proceed almost as he or she pleases. The poet has what is called the "poetic license" to take liberties with meter, syntax, and even diction, *providing* the result is a more forceful, unified, and distinctive poem.

THE LIMITATIONS OF SYLLABIC STRESS SCANSION. The rules of scansion are loose, and nearly every line of verse can be marked in a number of ways. We have, for example, scanned King Lear's line as two spondees and two iambs:

> Blow, winds,/ and crack/ your cheeks!// Rage!/Blow!

But because the line occurs in a passage that is predominantly iambic pentameter, we might choose to give it the required five feet by marking with a caret (ˆ) the pauses that would naturally fall after the two exclamation points:

> Blow, winds,/ and crack/ your cheeks!// Rage! Blow!

Similarly, we have scanned the first line of "On First Looking into Chapman's Homer" as a dactyl, trochee, anapest, and iamb.

> Much have I/ travell'd// in the realms/ of gold.

It could also be a trochee, iamb, pyrrhic, and two iambs:

> Much have/ I tra/vell'd in/ the realms/ of gold.

Such changes in scansion are cosmetic only and indicate no significant difference in the way each line *should be* read.

There is, however, considerable room for actual changes in the way a line *can* be read. Different readers rarely use stresses and pauses in precisely the same places, as anyone can testify after hearing one of Hamlet's soliloquies spoken by actors so different as Laurence Olivier, Richard Burton, Richard Chamberlain, and Mel Gibson. Sometimes we do not agree on the syllables that should be stressed or on the relative amount of stress on each. **Scansion is,** after all, **a system of simplifying and visually presenting the complex rhythm in a line. It is not an exact science.** Even if a precise system were possible, it would be too complicated to be useful in pointing out the simple, recurring rhythms of poetry. There must be a certain amount of flexibility in the scansion of any poem.

Although we must accept the limitations of our system and recognize that there will rarely be only one "right" way of scanning a poem, we must also recognize that this loosely constructed system is of considerable usefulness to both poets and readers. Because syllabic-stress meters are common in English poetry and their scansion is well understood, poets can confidently expect that readers will pick up most of the clues to rhythm that the meter conveys and therefore will read the lines with an emphasis closely approximating what was intended. Conversely, readers can easily determine a poem's underlying meter and then decide how they wish to read each line. The decisions made should be based, where possible, on the poem's content, its prose emphases, and its basic meter. The commonly accepted terminology of scansion allows us to explain more easily the decisions about the rhythm that we have made and how these decisions reflect and reinforce the meaning of the poem. Finally, the prevalence of syllabic-stress meters allows great poets to create a tension between the rhythm of ordinary speech and the heartbeat of the poetic line. The discovery of new possibilities in poetic rhythm in a poem like "Chapman's Homer" is one of the pleasures of travel in the realms of gold.

ALTERNATE SYSTEMS OF SCANSION. The syllabic stress system of metrics slowly came to dominate English poetry between the twelfth and sixteenth centuries because it proved better suited to the evolving English language than any of the competing systems: *accentual-alliterative meters, purely syllabic meters, quantitative meters,* and *free verse.* Nonetheless, each of these has left its mark on English poetry.

Alliterative, accentual, or *strong-stress* **verse was the metrical system native to our Anglo-Saxon forebears.** An impressive amount of alliterative poetry survived the Middle Ages, but only two medieval poems in this meter are encountered frequently enough to deserve mention here. *Beowulf,* the earliest surviving poem in a European language, was composed about A.D. 725; it describes the epic adventures of Beowulf in defeating the male monster Grendel and then Grendel's dam before Beowulf himself succumbs to a fire-breathing dragon. The poem is written in Old English, which is so different from modern English that it must be learned just like a foreign language. **Each line in standard alliterative tetrameter has a variable number of unaccented syllables and four strong stresses, three of which are usually emphasized by alliteration. The line is bisected by a caesural pause.**

The same alliterative meter is used in the Middle English Arthurian romance, *Sir Gawain and the Green Knight.* The following lines, which describe Gawain's sufferings during his winter quest for the Green Knight, provide an example of the original appearance of the meter. Note where the accents are in the following lines:

> For werre wrathed hym not so much,// that wynter was wors,
>
> When the colde cler water// from the clouds schadde,
>
> And fries er hit falle mygth// to the fale erthe.
>
> Ner slayn wyth the slete// he sleped in his yrnes
>
> Mo nyghtes then innoghe// in naked rokkes,
>
> Ther as claterande fro the crest// the colde borne rennes,
>
> And henged heghe// over his hede in hard ysse-ikkles.[2]

—From *Sir Gawain and the Green Knight,* anonymous [ca. 1375]

Of the poems considered in this text, "Eve" (p. 735) is perhaps classifiable as strong-stress dimeter rather than as dactylic dimeter. Each line has only two strong stresses, while the number of unstressed syllables varies from two to four. "Fog," by Carl Sandburg (p. 702), is also best classified as strong-stress dimeter. Each line

[2] Translation: For fighting troubled him not so much, that winter was worse,/ When the cold clear water from the clouds fell,/ And froze ere it might fall to the faded earth./ Near slain with sleet he slept in his irons (armor)/ More nights than enough in naked rocks,/ There where clattering from the crest the cold stream ran,/ And hung high over his head in hard icicles.

has two major stresses that are surrounded, in no particular pattern, by weakly stressed or unstressed syllables. In addition, Gerard Manley Hopkins adopted a strong-stress system, which he called *sprung rhythm* and used in most of his poems; W. S. Merwin in "Leviathan" (p. 1020) directly imitated Old English verse forms. In general, the strong-stress system requires alliteration if it is to sound poetic, and the required alliteration is too limiting and too repetitive to appeal to most modern poets. When strong-stress verse is used without alliteration, as in Sandburg's "Fog," it has the appearance and sound of free verse. Here is a good example of an alliterative strong-stress poem that directly imitates the patterns of Old and Middle English verse:

ANGLOSAXON STREET

Dawndrizzle ended   dampness streams from
blotching brick and   blank plasterwaste
Faded housepatterns   hoary and finicky
unfold stuttering   stick like a phonograph

5   Here is a ghetto   gotten for goyim°   *non-Jews*
O with care denuded of   nigger and kike
No coonsmell rankles   reeks only cellarrot
attar° of carexhaust   catcorpse and cookinggrease   *fragrance*
Imperial hearts   heave in this haven

10   Cracks across windows   are welded with slogans
There'll Always Be An England   enhances geraniums
and V's for a Victory   vanquish the housefly

Ho! with climbing sun   march the bleached beldames
festooned with shopping bags   farded° flatarched   *made-up*
15   bigthewed Saxonwives   stepping over buttrivers
waddling back wienerladen   to suckle smallfry

Hoy! with sunslope   shrieking over hydrants
flood from learninghall   the lean fingerlings
Nordic nobblecheeked   not all clean of nose
20   leaping Commandowise   into leprous lanes

What! after whistleblow!   spewed from wheelboat
after daylong doughtiness   dire handplay
in sewertrench or sandpit   come Saxonthegns[3]
Junebrown Jutekings   jawslack for meat

25   Sit after supper   on smeared doorsteps
not humbly swearing   hatedeeds on Huns
profiteers politicians   pacifists Jews

Then by twobit magic   to muse in movie
unlock picturehoard   or lope to alehall

---

[3] Among the early Anglo-Saxons *thegns* or *thanes* were freemen who held land in return for military service. In the context of this poem, however, "Saxonthegns" (and "Jutekings") appear to be ironic descriptions of ordinary Englishmen—many of whom have Saxon or Jutish ancestry.

30   soaking bleakly   in beer skittleless[4]
        Home again to hotbox   and humid husbandhood
        in slumbertrough adding   sleepily to Angelkin

        Alongside in lanenooks   carling° and leman°   *peasant girl / lover*
        caterwaul and clip   careless of Saxonry
35   with moonglow and haste   and a higher heartbeat

        Slumbers now slumtrack   unstinks cooling
        waiting brief for milkmaid   mornstar and worldrise

                                    —Earle Birney [1942]

❧ QUESTIONS ❧

1.   The first three stanzas give an overview of the Anglosaxon street—perhaps at dawn. In what nation and in what time period is the poem set?

2.   Is this a racist poem? If not, why does Birney use offensive racial epithets in the second stanza?

3.   What organizational pattern dominates the poem from the fourth stanza on? What different residents of the street come into prominence at different times of the day? How kindly does Birney treat these residents?

4.   Why do you think that Birney imitates Old and Middle English alliterative verse in writing the poem? Mark off the stresses and the alliterating syllables in a few lines of the poem. What is the effect of using this rather archaic and primitive verse form?

Purely *syllabic meters*, which are based solely on the number of syllables per line, represent another alternative to the syllabic-stress system. Some modern languages, notably French, make little use of stress in speech. Each syllable is given roughly the same weight. As a result, French poetry is based almost entirely on syllable count.

After the French-speaking Normans conquered the Saxons at Hastings in 1066, our modern English language began to emerge as a hybrid between Old English and Old French; at the same time, modern syllabic-stress meters began to emerge, as the alliterative tradition of Old English poetry met with the syllabic tradition of French verse.

In the absence of other musical devices (rhyme, alliteration, etc.), *syllabic verse* is often indistinguishable from prose, as we see in the following poem:

VOX HUMANA[5]

        Being without quality
        I appear to you at first

[4] Skittles is a form of bowling, and the expression "all beer and skittles" is commonly used to mean *pure pleasure and enjoyment.* Apparently, there is little real enjoyment in the lives of those besotted by "beer skittleless."

[5] The human voice.

as an unkempt smudge, a blur,
an indefinite haze, mere-
5   ly pricking the eyes, almost
nothing. Yet you perceive me.

I have been always most close
when you had least resistance,
falling asleep, or in bars;
10 during the unscheduled hours,
though strangely without substance,
I hang, there and ominous.

Aha, sooner or later
you will have to name me, and,
15 as you name, I shall focus,
I shall become more precise.
O Master (for you command
in naming me, you prefer)!

I was, for Alexander,[6]
20 the certain victory; I
was hemlock for Socrates;[7]
and, in the dry night, Brutus
waking before Philippi
stopped me, crying out, "Caesar!"[8]

25 Or if you call me the blur
that in fact I am, you shall
yourself remain blurred, hanging
like smoke indoors. For you bring,
to what you define now, all
30 there is, ever, of future.

—Thom Gunn [1957]

❧ QUESTIONS ❧

1.   What is the subject of this poem? In other words, what is that concept or
feeling or thing "without quality" that Gunn sets out to describe?

2.   Explain the apparent paradox that this concept without quality has been
"always most close / when you had least resistance"?

3.   Why does naming this concept bring it into focus?

---

[6] Alexander the Great (356–323 B.C.) helped through his conquests to spread Greek culture through
Egypt and the East.
[7] The Greek philosopher Socrates (c. 470–399 B.C.) engaged in his most important and influential
dialogues as a result of his trial, imprisonment, and condemnation for impiety and corrupting the
youth of Athens.
[8] In Shakespeare's play, Brutus, who had earlier helped to murder Caesar, sees Caesar's ghost on the
night before his defeat at Philippi.

4. What is the effect of the allusions in the fourth stanza? What are the similarities between Alexander's "certain victory," Socrates's hemlock, and Brutus's vision of Caesar?

5. What structure does this poem have, and how does Gunn's choice of pure syllabic meter contribute to the poem's theme?

Although Gunn's lines can be defended because their formlessness is in harmony with the poem's theme, they are still open to the criticism that anyone with the mental capacity to count on his or her fingers can write as poetically as this. Under the circumstances, it is no surprise that few English poems are written in purely syllabic verse.

A third alternative to syllabic-stress verse is made possible by the differences in the amount of time it takes to pronounce various syllables. The word *truths,* for example, takes longer to say than *lies*—even though each is monosyllabic. *Quantitative meter* is based on the length (in units of time) of various syllables, instead of on the relative degree of their stress.

Greek and Latin poetry was based on quantitative metrics, and therefore the few English poems in quantitative verse have usually been written by poets who were heavily influenced by the classics. During the late sixteenth century, at the height of the English revival of Greek and Latin learning, such poets as Spenser and Sidney experimented briefly with quantity in verse before concluding that most English syllables take up about the same amount of time in pronunciation and that few readers are able to perceive the slight differences that do exist.

It is, however, possible to demonstrate some quantitative differences in English pronunciation. The first line of the following couplet reads much more rapidly than the second, even though both have an identical number of syllables:

> By slight syllables we show
> Those truths whose worth you now know.

But there is a great difference between this theoretical possibility and its application in fluent poetry. The most that can be said is that quantitative factors sometimes play a secondary role in the impact of normal syllabic-stress verse. When, for example, Alexander Pope wrote about the effects of sound in poetry, he skillfully used lengthy vowel sounds (ow, oar, ough, ur) to slow down the movement of his lines:

> But when loud surges lash the sounding shore.
> The hoarse, rough verse should like the torrent roar.

Free verse, the final alternative to syllabic-stress meter, is not a meter at all. In free verse, the poet does not attempt to produce a formal pattern of metrical feet, quantitative feet, or syllable count, but instead allows the poem to develop "freely" in any manner that contributes to the overall rhythm and effect of the words. The only real distinctions between free verse and the rhythmical prose of Thomas Paine or Abraham Lincoln are that (1) free verse uses variable line length as a unit in rhythm, (2) free verse may use rhyme more frequently than would be acceptable in prose, and (3) free verse is less restrained than prose by the rules of logic and grammar. Free verse is sometimes also said to be written in **open form,**

meaning that the poet's choice of form is unconstricted by the fixed patterns of rhythm and rhyme.

In Elizabeth Bishop's free verse poem "Sandpiper," for example, the number of syllables per line ranges from 6 to 13, the number of stresses ranges from three to six, and the metrical pattern remains irregular throughout the poem:

SANDPIPER

The roaring alongside he takes for granted,
and that every so often the world is bound to shake.
He runs, he runs to the south, finical, awkward,
in a state of controlled panic, a student of Blake.

5   The beach hisses like fat. On his left, a sheet
of interrupting water comes and goes
and glazes over his dark and brittle feet.
He runs, he runs straight through it, watching his toes.

—Watching, rather, the spaces of sand between them,
10   where (no detail too small) the Atlantic drains
rapidly backwards and downwards. As he runs,
he stares at the dragging grains.

The world is a mist. And then the world is
minute and vast and clear. The tide
15   is higher or lower. He couldn't tell you which.
His beak is focussed; he is preoccupied,

looking for something, something, something.
Poor bird, he is obsessed!
The millions of grains are black, white, tan, and gray,
20   mixed with quartz grains, rose and amethyst.
—Elizabeth Bishop [1947]

It would be inaccurate, however, to say that Bishop's free verse lacks form. The poem is broken up into four-line units, or stanzas, in which the second line always rhymes with the fourth. Thus, the poem has the visual appearance and sound of verse, while its rhythm remains as hectic and irregular as the darting motion of the sandpiper itself. The poem begins with two flowing and forceful lines describing the surf; then it continues with brief, erratic, and repetitious phrases that help to characterize the bird's mindless panic: "He runs, he runs . . . watching . . . watching . . . he runs, he stares . . . focussed . . . preoccupied,/ looking for something, something, something./ Poor bird, he is obsessed!"

The central portion of the poem is a descriptive tour de force, but it shows only the bleak and monotonous aspects of the sandpiper's existence. In the final lines, however, the point of view shifts. After being told *about* a bird "looking for something, something, something," we now see *with* him that the millions of grains of sand that slip through his toes are "black, white, tan, and gray,/ mixed with quartz grains, rose and amethyst." The existence that had seemed so futile and repetitious a moment earlier is now varied, and even beautiful. The endless patterns of sliding sand, like those in a child's kaleidoscope, offer their own delightful rewards. And suddenly, too, the poem achieves an unexpected unity. We may at first have chuckled at Bishop's description of the sandpiper as "finical, awkward,/ in a state of controlled panic, a student of Blake." The implied comparison makes fun of the often fanatical followers of the famous Romantic poet, William Blake, whose preoccupation with his own visionary experiences was so great that his wife once complained, "I have very little of Mr. Blake's company. He is always in Paradise." But by the end of the poem we learn to view the sandpiper and all "students of Blake" more sympathetically. Certainly they see something the rest of us do not; and perhaps in their preoccupation they see many things more closely, more clearly, and more perceptively than we. (It was Blake himself, after all, who remarked that one could see the world in a grain of sand.)

Free verse is no longer experimental or even new. Although it is an established and popular alternative to syllabic-stress meters, it does not appear that free verse will ever entirely supplant conventional metrics, for there are many advantages to meter. In the first place, poets use meter because it is traditional. It allies them with Chaucer, Shakespeare, Milton, Wordsworth, Byron, Tennyson, Frost, and scores of other distinguished literary men and women. A poem that breaks with this long tradition risks an unsympathetic response from an audience that is accustomed to meter in poetry. Second, the use of meter demonstrates that the author took at least some care in writing, and this implies that he or she considered the content of the poem important. Few authors are likely to bother versifying ideas they think are trivial. (It is true, of course, that prose and free verse may be every bit as carefully crafted as metrical poetry, but the latter signals its importance through its form.) Third, a regular rhythm is inherently musical. It lays down a beat that appeals to us not only in poetry, but also in the sonatas of Beethoven and the songs of The Beach Boys. Fourth, regular rhythms arise out of strong emotions and enhance them in an auditor. They seem to be tied in with the rhythms of our human body. And fifth, meter creates an opportunity for interaction between the sound and sense of language. The tension between the expected and the actual rhythm of a particular line makes it easier for a poet to establish a tone—to speed up the rhythm where the illusion of speed, excitement, or fluidity is wanted, and to slow it down where the content demands emphasis and sobriety.

Meter, then, is useful, but it cannot make an otherwise weak poem strong. Meter is only one of many ingredients in verse, although it is a catalytic ingredient, as Coleridge noted in comparing it to yeast, "worthless or disagreeable by itself, but giving vivacity and spirit to the liquor with which it is proportionally combined." Dame Edith Sitwell may have been even closer to the truth, however, when she argued that rhythm is "to the world of sound, what light is to the world of sight." It is, finally, the rhythm of a poem, and not its meter, that should be the focus of commentary.

17

🌿🌿🌿🌿🌿🌿🌿

Rhyme and Other Manipulations of Sound

Two words *rhyme* when they end with the same sound. In *perfect rhyme*, the final vowel and any succeeding consonant sounds are identical, and the preceding consonant sounds are different. Although words in perfect rhyme may be similar in spelling, they need not be. Thus, *ripe* and *tripe* rhyme to the eye and to the ear, but *rhyme* and *sublime* or *enough* and *snuff* rely entirely on aural similarity.

Rhyme is the most unnatural, the most noticeable, the most controversial, and possibly the most common of all poetic devices. Almost as soon as critics began to examine the elements of poetry, they also began to bicker about the merits of rhyme. Milton, for example, claimed, in 1668, that rhyme is "the invention of a barbarous age" and appeals only to "vulgar readers," to which Edward Young added the observation, a century later (1759), that rhyme, "in epic poetry is a sore disease, in the tragic absolute death. . . . but our lesser poetry stands in need of a toleration for it; it raises that, but sinks the great, as spangles adorn children, but expose men." Interestingly enough, it is harder to find defenders of rhyme, although John Dryden, writing in 1664, felt that the device has so many advantages "that it were lost time to name them," and in 1702, Edward Bysshe called rhyme "the chief ornament of versification in any of the modern languages." On the whole, rhyme's detractors seem to make a more vigorous and impassioned argument; yet the great majority of all anthologized poetry in every period (including our own) is rhymed. Evidently, rhyme adds something to poetry. The question is, what?

Rhyme contributes to the effect of poetry in at least six ways:

1. **Rhyme rings an audible end to each line.** This is important because the rhythm of iambic verse is so similar to that of prose that without the aid of rhyme the sense of hearing poetry can easily be lost. Rhyme helps us to recognize aurally where one line ends and the next begins and thus reinforces the rhythmic pattern of the poem.

748

2. **Rhyme makes words memorable.** Of course, it cannot in itself make words *worthy* of being remembered; the content of the poem must do that. But rhyme has always been used to make things *easier* to remember. Wandering medieval minstrels, whose livelihood depended on their ability to delight a crowd with the lengthy adventures of Sir Gawain or King Arthur, used a tale's rhyming pattern as a prod to memory in the same way that we still use rhyming chants in daily life ("Thirty days hath September").

3. **Rhyme is pleasing because it is inherently musical.** Verse appeals to small children long before they understand the full meaning of the words they chant, and rhyme is almost always used in popular songs.

4. **Rhyme can be used to affect the pace and tone of poetry, as well.** In the following stanza from "The Rime of the Ancient Mariner," for example, Coleridge uses the first four rhyme words ("prow," "blow," "shadow," and "foe") at the eighth, sixteenth, twenty-first, and twenty-fourth syllables to enhance the illusion of a chasing (and gaining!) storm:

> With sloping masts and dipping prow,
> As who pursued with yell and blow
> Still treads the shadow of his foe,
> And forward bends his head,
> The ship drove fast, loud roared the blast,
> And southward aye we fled.
> —From "The Rime of the Ancient Mariner,"
> Samuel Taylor Coleridge [1798]

5. **Well-managed rhymes are a sign of skill.** Much of the fun in reading a poem like Byron's *Don Juan* is to observe how the poet wriggles out of the tight spots created by words that seem impossible to rhyme. When, for example, he ends the first line of the following quatrain with "annuities," we may think him trapped, only to watch him scamper gleefully through the rhyme without the slightest apparent strain:

> 'Tis said that persons living on annuities
> Are longer lived than others,— God knows why,
> Unless to plague the grantors,—yet so true it is,
> That some, I really think, do never die.
> —From *Don Juan*, Lord Byron [1819]

Conversely, poorly managed rhymes are a sign of clumsiness, as Pope made clear in "An Essay on Criticism":

> Where'er you find 'the cooling western breeze,'
> In the next line it 'whispers through the trees';
> If crystal streams 'with pleasing murmurs creep,'
> The reader's threatened (not in vain) with 'sleep.'
> —From "An Essay on Criticism,"
> Alexander Pope [1711]

6. **Because worn rhymes are so tiring and because interesting ones are difficult to find, a good rhyme facilitates witticism.** Rhyme used in comic or satiric poetry tends to sharpen a well-honed phrase, as, for example, in the "Epitaph Intended for his Wife," attributed to John Dryden:

> Here lies my wife: here let her lie!
> Now she's at rest, and so am I.

and in Hilaire Belloc's sardonic "Lines for a Christmas Card":

> May all my enemies go to Hell.
> Noel, Noel, Noel, Noel.

One has only to rewrite these lines without rhyme (substituting *dwell* for Dryden's "lie" and *Amen* for Belloc's "Noel") to recognize that, with the change of words, the humor is lost.

In summary, rhyme in poetry is like salt in cooking. It adds almost nothing to nutrition, but it appeals to our taste. A poem that is unseasoned by rhyme may be as dull as a saltless diet, whereas too much rhyme, like too much salt, may spoil the dish.

Rhyme ordinarily falls on an accented syllable at the end of a line, in which case it is called *masculine end rhyme.* **In** *feminine (or double) rhyme,* **the final two syllables in a line rhyme, and the final syllable is unaccented. In** *triple rhyme,* **three syllables rhyme.** Both double and triple rhyme are generally used to create a comic effect. In the following stanza, lines 1, 3, and 5 are masculine end rhymes, lines 4 and 6 are feminine end rhymes, and lines 7 and 8 are triple rhymes.

> 'Tis pity learned virgins ever wed
>   With persons of no sort of education,
> Or gentlemen, who, though well born and bred,
>   Grow tired of scientific conversation:
> I don't choose to say much on this head,
>   I'm a plain man, and in a simple station,
> But Oh! ye lords of ladies intellectual,
> Inform us truly have they not hen-peck'd you all?
> —From *Don Juan,* Lord Byron [1819]

Not all rhymes fall at the end of a line. *Internal rhyme* **occurs within a line of poetry.** Often the word preceding the caesura rhymes with the last word in the line, as in Poe's "The Raven":

> Once upon a midnight *dreary,* while I pondered weak and *weary*

But internal rhyme may occur anywhere within a line or even between lines:

> And the silken, sad, *uncertain* rustling of each purple *curtain*
> *Thrilled* me—*filled* me with fantastic terrors never felt before
> So that now, to still the *beating* of my heart I stood *repeating*
> " 'Tis some visiter *entreating* entrance at my chamber door."
> —From "The Raven," Edgar Allan Poe [1845]

In *imperfect rhyme* **the sound of two words is similar but it is not as close as is required in** *true* **or** *perfect rhyme.* In the lines just quoted, "silken" and "uncertain" are imperfect rhymes, as are "filled," "felt," and "still." Ogden Nash combines imperfect rhyme with an ingenious play on words in the following anecdote on a happy marriage:

> I believe a little incompatibility is
> the spice of life, particularly if he has
> income and she is pattable.

**Imperfectly rhymed words generally contain identical vowels or identical conso-
nants, but not both.** Imperfect rhyme is also referred to as approximate rhyme, or
as half-rhyme, near rhyme, oblique rhyme, off-rhyme, or slant rhyme.

False rhyme **pairs the sounds of accented with unaccented syllables.** In the lines
we quoted from "The Rime of the Ancient Mariner," "sha̅do̅w" is a false internal
rhyme with "hĭs foe:"

> With sloping masts and dipping prow,
> As who pursued with yell and blow
> Still treads the *shadow* of *his foe* . . .

And at the same time, "prow" and "blow" are known as *visual rhymes*. These
words—and such others as "rough-bough" and "love-prove"— rhyme to the eye,
but not to the ear. Their spellings are similar, but their pronunciations are different.

Finally, *repetition* is occasionally used as an alternative to true rhyme. It provides
the recurrence of sound expected in rhyme, but not the difference in meaning
and initial consonants that makes rhyme delightful.

Modern poets have, on the whole, set themselves apart from much traditional
poetry by replacing true rhymes with one or more of the alternatives, and so
retaining some sense of music without rhyme's characteristic chime. Let us examine how W. H. Auden uses rhyme in describing the surf-washed shore of an
island:

LOOK, STRANGER

> Look, stranger, at this island now
> The leaping light for your delight discovers,
> Stand stable here
> And silent be,
> 5   That through the channels of the ear
> May wander like a river
> The swaying sound of the sea.
>
> Here at the small field's ending pause
> Where the chalk wall falls to the foam, and its tall ledges
> 10   Oppose the pluck
> And knock of the tide,
> And the shingle scrambles after the suck-
> ing surf, and the gull lodges
> A moment on its sheer side.
>
> 15   Far off like floating seeds the ships
> Diverge on urgent voluntary errands;
> And the full view
> Indeed may enter
> And move in memory as now these clouds do,
> 20   That pass the harbor mirror
> And all the summer through the water saunter.
>
> —W. H. Auden [1936]

Although the words are musical, the poem is not arranged in any of the easily
recognizable patterns of verse. The meter is loosely based on the strong-stress
system, and the rhyme scheme is unconventional. The first line in each stanza is

unrhymed. The second and sixth lines are imperfect rhymes. The third line rhymes perfectly with the fifth, as does the fourth line with the seventh. **We can simplify our description of the rhyme scheme in "Look, Stranger" (or any other poem) by representing each new rhyme sound by a different letter of the alphabet, with capital letters reserved for perfect rhymes and lower-case letters for imperfect, false, or visual rhymes, and by representing unrhymed lines with an X.** Thus, each of Auden's stanzas rhymes according to the scheme XaBCBaC. Identifying the *rhyme scheme* in this way is an important stage in cataloguing the manipulations of rhythm and rhyme within a specific poem. Although some critics prefer to ignore the various forms of partial rhyme, the system we have outlined allows us to indicate the subtle presence of imperfect, false, and visual rhymes without unduly complicating our representation of the total rhyme pattern. The rhyme schemes of most poems, of course, can be fully described using only the capital letters and the X for unrhymed lines.

Schematizing the rhyme in this way leads us to two important observations about the effect of Auden's verse. First, although six out of these seven lines rhyme, each of the first four lines ends with a different and unrelated sound. (In the first stanza the actual words are "now," "discovers," "here," and "be.") This means that each stanza is more than half complete before Auden begins to give it the sound of rhyming verse. Second, Auden never establishes a strong and repeated interval between rhymes. In most poetry, the rhymes recur predictably— every ten syllables in Pope's iambic pentameter couplets (p. 648), every twelve syllables in the anapestic tetrameter couplets of Byron's "The Destruction of Sennacherib" (p. 870), and so on. Almost immediately, we subconsciously pick up the rhyme pattern and begin to *expect* rhymes at the proper intervals. Auden makes it difficult for us to have any such expectations because he varies the interval between his rhymes. "Here" (line 3) is separated by twelve syllables from its rhyming partner "ear" (line 5), while "be" (line 4) is separated by twenty-two syllables from "sea" (line 7) and "discovers" (line 2) is separated by twenty-three syllables from its approximate rhyme with "river" (line 6). Although the second and third stanzas follow the same rhyme scheme, the number of syllables separating the rhyme words may vary because lines of strong-stress meter often differ in number of syllables. "Look, Stranger" is in fact rhyme-dense (for example, it has a total of six rhyming words in the forty-nine syllables of the first stanza, whereas a comparable number of rhymes in Pope's iambic pentameter would require sixty syllables). But we scarcely even perceive the rhyme in reading Auden's verse, whereas it is unmistakable in Pope's.

By declining to use a conventional, repetitive rhyme scheme, Auden willingly risks alienating those readers who feel his writing is "just not poetry" in order to capture that subtle sense of beauty and harmony that is the poem's theme. Auden is, indeed, attempting to describe the chalk cliffs, the surf-driven pebbles (or shingle), the perched gull, the urgent ships, and the drifting clouds, but he is even more interested in the process by which he and presumably all of us take such scenes of natural beauty to heart until "the full view/ Indeed may enter/ And move in memory as now these clouds do." Auden, no doubt, knows that a poet cannot hope to match the visual representation of the seaside in a photograph, a painter's landscape, or a film. But he knows as well that these visual media are not as effective as words in conveying the effects of rhythmic and natural movement on a human observer. Thus, his description of the setting is filled with activity: the "leaping light," "the pluck and knock of the tide," the "sucking surf," and even the memory of the whole scene that, like the drifting clouds, will "all the summer through the water saunter." And yet the actions he describes are not the purposeful and goal-oriented actions of hectic human life; they are sedate, rhythmic, and inherent in nature. Even the ships, which Auden knows "diverge on urgent voluntary errands," appear to him from the cliffs "like floating seeds."

What Auden wants, then, is not the methodical chime of repeated rhyme and not the businesslike stolidity of prose, but a more natural harmony that "through the channels of the ear/ May wander like a river" re-creating "the swaying sound of the sea." Auden's idiosyncratic use of rhyme is but one of the musical devices that help him to do so. **The similarity of vowel or consonant sounds, which we call** *imperfect rhyme* **when it occurs at the ends of lines, may also occur within lines where it is known more specifically as** *alliteration, assonance,* **or** *consonance.*

Alliteration **is the repetition in two or more nearby words of initial consonant sounds** ("Where the chalk wall *f*alls to the *f*oam," line 9). *Assonance* **is the repetition in two or more nearby words of similar vowel sounds** ("ch*a*lk w*a*ll f*a*lls"). **And** *consonance* **is the repetition in two or more nearby words of similar consonant sounds preceded by different accented vowels** ("cha*lk*," "plu*ck*," "kno*ck*"). Each of these devices is melodious although less so than rhyme itself. For this reason, each is particularly appropriate in developing Auden's description of a natural and harmonious setting. Virtually every line reverberates with the subtle music of one or more of these three devices, and in some lines several musical effects are interwoven. Take, for example, the second stanza. The *aw* sound in "small" is repeated in "pause," and then in the next line this assonance is compounded by consonance and internal rhyme in the series "chalk wall falls." The *f* of "falls" alliterates with "foam," and the *all* sound is picked up again in "tall." In the third line, the *p*'s of "oppose" are reiterated in "pluck." (This hybrid of consonance and alliteration is one of many musical effects in verse with no formal name.) The fourth line has consonance ("pluck/ knock"); the fifth has alliteration and assonance, which carry over into the sixth ("*sh*ingle *s*crambles after the *s*uck-/ ing *s*urf" and "*s*ucking s*u*rf and the g*u*ll"); and the seventh line combines alliteration ("*sh*eer *s*ide") with the repetition of the *m* sounds in "*m*o*m*ent." This high concentration of musical effects is repeated in both of the other stanzas.

As if all this were not enough, Auden also uses the emotional overtones of the various vowels and consonants to further heighten the beauty of his description. **In general, those vowels that are produced through pursed and rounded lips tend to be soothing and** *euphonious*—although sometimes somber. We say "Oooh," "Ahh," and "Oh" in spontaneous expressions of pleasure and surprise. Conversely, those vowels that are produced with widely stretched lips tend to convey excitement, astonishment, or fright. Scared people "SHRIEEEK" and unhappy children "whine" and "wail." Such **grating and unpleasant sounds are said to be** *cacophonous.* Consonants, too, tend to divide into euphonious and cacophonous groups. Among the former we should list the liquid sounds of *r* and *l*, the nasal sounds of *m* and *n*, and such gentle sounds as *f, v, th,* and *sh.* Auden uses these soft consonants in "Look, Stranger" when he is describing the static appearance of the ships,

> Far off like floating seeds the ships,
> Diverge on urgent voluntary errands;

He also uses them to reinforce the idea that the very harmony of the scene makes it memorable:

        And the full view
        Indeed may enter
        And move in memory as now these clouds do.

Other consonants, called explosives—*p, b, d, k, t,* and hard *g*—create harsh, cacophonous effects. Auden uses these in his second stanza to describe the crash of the surf against the shore:

            . . . its tall ledges
        Oppose the pluck
        And knock of the tide,
        And the shingle scrambles after the suck-
        ing surf and the gull lodges
        A moment on its sheer side.

In fact, in "Look, Stranger" the meaning of the words may be less important than their rhythm and sound. To be sure, Auden describes the setting clearly, but it is a scene that, in one form or another, has been experienced by all. We are impressed not so much by what Auden has to say, as by the way he says it.

   In our analysis of Auden's poem perhaps we have emphasized too heavily the emotional overtones implicit in verbal sounds. If we examine any significant number of successful poems, we will find examples of harsh sounds used to create beauty or smooth sounds used with force and vigor. Few poets have ever been more conscious of the effects of sound than Pope in his lines on sound and sense in poetry (p. 648). It is indeed easy to applaud the liquid consonants (*f, r, n, m, th*) and melodious vowels ("s*o*ft," "bl*o*ws," "sm*oo*th") in his couplet on the sound of smooth verse:

        Soft is the strain when Zephyr gently blows,
        And the smooth stream in smoother numbers flows.

In the next couplet, the sibilants *(s, sh)* and guttural vowels ("h*oa*rse, ro*ugh* v*e*rse") help to complement the stormy theme:

        But when loud surges lash the sounding shore
        The hoarse, rough verse should like the torrent roar.

And in the third couplet, a series of awkward consonantal combinations ("Aja*x* st*r*ives some ro*ck's* v*ast w*eight") helps to slow the pace of the labored lines:

        When Ajax strives some rock's vast weight to throw,
        The line too labors, and the verse moves slow.

   Yet Pope's lines also show us the dangers of generalization about the emotional effects of vowel and consonant sounds. The "hoarse, rough verse" in the second couplet is packed with liquid and nasal consonants, "whe*n l*oud su*r*ges *l*ash the sou*nd*ing sh*o*re," and the same is true in the third couplet where "*the l*i*ne* too *l*abors, a*nd the* ve*r*se m*o*ves sl*o*w." In these lines the liquid sounds have little moderating effect on the prevailing harshness of the verse. Obviously, **the mean-**

ing of words can be more important than their sound in determining emotional connotations. Softness of vowels and consonants cannot make "foulness" fair or "murder" musical. **With the exception of a few truly *onomatopoetic* words—for example, words like *moo*, *hiss*, and *clang*, whose sounds suggest their meanings—it is doubtful that the sounds of individual words often echo their senses.** When "loud surges lash the sounding shore" in Pope's verse, the words *sound* harsh and forceful because of their denotations. And although the *l*- and *s*-alliteration may in fact be pleasing to the ear, it does less to create a liquid beauty than to increase our sense of harshness by emphasizing the important words.

In the final analysis, the manipulations of sound that we have examined in this section are characteristic of all good writing. Authors base their word choice in large part on what "sounds" best. Theoretically, then, every piece of prose or poetry could be examined for the effect of sound on sense, but the problem is that our techniques of analysis are coarse and many of the decisions that authors make are complex, delicate, and even subconscious. We are like chemists struggling to determine a molecular weight using a physician's scale. In such circumstances one must concentrate on the macroscopic, cumulative effect of many microscopic interactions, for it is out of such interactions that the sounds of poetry are created.

Poems for Further Study

JABBERWOCKY[1]

'T was brillig, and the slithy toves
Did gyre and gimble in the wabe;
All mimsy were the borogoves,
And the mome raths outgrabe.

5   "Beware the Jabberwock, my son!
The jaws that bite, the claws that catch!
Beware the Jubjub bird, and shun
The frumious Bandersnatch!"

He took his vorpal sword in hand:
10   Long time the manxome foe he sought—
So rested he by the Tumtum tree,
And stood awhile in thought.

And as in uffish thought he stood,
The Jabberwock, with eyes of flame,
15   Came whiffling through the tulgey wood,
And burbled as it came!

One, two! One, two! And through and through
The vorpal blade went snicker-snack!
He left it dead, and with its head
20   He went galumphing back.

[1] From *Through the Looking Glass*. In Chapter 6 Humpty Dumpty attempts to explain the poem.

"And hast thou slain the Jabberwock?
Come to my arms, my beamish boy!
O frabjous day! Callooh! Callay!"
He chortled in his joy.

25   'T was brillig, and the slithy toves
Did gyre and gimble in the wabe;
All mimsy were the borogoves,
And the mome raths outgrabe.

—Lewis Carroll [1872]

🌿 QUESTIONS 🌿

1. This poem is filled with newly created words, but it is nonetheless possible to summarize the story told in it. Do so.

2. Make up your own brief definitions of the following words: *brillig, slithy, toves, gyre, gimble, wabe, mimsy, borogoves, mome, raths, outgrabe, Jabberwock, Jubjub bird, frumious, Bandersnatch, vorpal, manxome, Tumtum tree, uffish, wiffling, tulgey, galumphing, frabjous.*

3. Explain some of the effects of alliteration, consonance, and assonance in the poem. How do those sound devices help you to determine the meaning of the fabricated words?

WINTER REMEMBERED

Two evils, monstrous either one apart,
Possessed me, and were long and loath at going:
A cry of Absence, Absence, in the heart,
And in the wood the furious winter blowing.

5   Think not, when fire was bright upon my bricks,
And past the tight boards hardly a wind could enter,
I glowed like them, the simple burning sticks,
Far from my cause, my proper heat and center.

Better to walk forth in the frozen air
10   And wash my wound in the snows; that would be healing;
Because my heart would throb less painful there,
Being caked with cold, and past the smart of feeling.

And where I walked, the murderous winter blast
Would have this body bowed, these eyeballs streaming,
15   And though I think this heart's blood froze not fast
It ran too small to spare one drop for dreaming.

Dear love, these fingers that had known your touch,
And tied our separate forces first together,
Were ten poor idiot fingers not worth much,
20   Ten frozen parsnips hanging in the weather.

                         —John Crowe Ransom [1924]

❧ QUESTIONS ❧

1.   What are the two evils that possessed the speaker? Does the speaker choose the word "Possessed" with a full awareness of its connotations in demonology?

2.   What does the speaker mean when he says he remained cold, "Far from my cause, my proper heat and center" (line 8)?

3.   Why does he prefer being out in the cold (lines 9–16)?

4.   Describe the poem's rhyme scheme. What makes it unusual? Does the poem's rhyme scheme complement its predominantly melancholy mood?

5.   What is the predominant rhythm of the poem? What are the effects of the deviations from the prevalent rhythm in lines 15 and 19?

6.   The poem develops an extended comparison linking the effects of separation and of winter. How well does the last stanza bring both sides of the comparison to a climax? What do you make of the final image of "Ten frozen parsnips hanging in the weather"?

7.   How effectively does Ransom use alliteration, assonance, and consonance in the poem? Explain your answer by citing examples.

DULCE ET DECORUM EST

Bent double, like old beggars under sacks,
Knock-kneed, coughing like hags, we cursed through sludge,
Till on the haunting flares we turned our backs,
And towards our distant rest began to trudge.
5   Men marched asleep. Many had lost their boots,
But limped on, blood-shod. All went lame, all blind;
Drunk with fatigue; deaf even to the hoots
Of gas-shells dropping softly behind.

Gas, GAS! Quick boys!—An ecstasy of fumbling,
10   Fitting the clumsy helmets just in time,
But someone still was yelling out and stumbling
And floundering like a man in fire or lime.—
Dim through the misty panes and thick green light,
As under a green sea, I saw him drowning.

15   In all my dreams before my helpless sight
He plunges at me, guttering, choking, drowning.

If in some smothering dreams, you too could pace
Behind the wagon that we flung him in,
And watch the white eyes writhing in his face,
20   His hanging face, like a devil's sick of sin;
If you could hear, at every jolt, the blood
Come gargling from the froth-corrupted lungs,
Bitter as the cud
Of vile, incurable sores on innocent tongues,—
25   My friend, you would not tell with such high zest
To children ardent for some desperate glory,
The old Lie: Dulce et decorum est
Pro patria mori.[2]

—Wilfred Owen [posthumous, 1920]

🌿 QUESTIONS 🌿

1. What can you tell about the speaker from this poem? What effects have the events described in the poem had upon him? What is his attitude toward war and toward the supposed glory of dying for one's country?

2. Owen uses many comparisons in the poem. Pinpoint as many of these comparisons as you can and discuss their effects.

3. Owen makes frequent use of alliteration, assonance, and consonance. Identify and analyze what you consider to be the most effective instances of these sound devices.

4. Analyze the metrics in the poem. What is the dominant rhythm? What is the prevailing meter? Where does Owen manipulate the rhythm particularly effectively?

[2] A line by the Roman poet Horace (65–8 B.C.) meaning, "It is sweet and fitting to die for your country."

18

❧❧❧❧❧❧❧

Structure and Form in Poetry

Nearly all writing combines the narrative, dramatic, descriptive, and expository modes of expression. We rarely find any of these in a pure form in literature because an author's goal of creating interest and variety ordinarily requires that the modes be mixed. For the purpose of illustration, however, we can compose examples of how the same situation might be treated in each of the four modes:

Narrative: The boys crossed the street and entered the store.
Dramatic: "Look! There's a candy store." "Let's cross over and buy some taffy."
Descriptive: On one side of the street stood the two boys, jingling the coins in their pockets; on the other side were the large-paned windows of the store front, advertising in antique letters: DAN'S OLD-FASHIONED CANDIES.
Expository: The boys wanted to cross the street to buy some candy.

A narrative approach concentrates on action. In its pure form, it uses only nouns and transitive verbs, but such writing usually lacks appeal to the senses and to the intellect. As a result, narration does not necessarily predominate in narrative poetry; rather, the impulse to tell a story remains uppermost in the narrative poet's mind as he or she interweaves narration, description, dialogue, and explanation.

The principal forms of narrative poetry are the *epic*, which tells the book-length adventures of the founders of a nation or a culture (for example, *The Iliad, Paradise Lost*); **the *romance*, which often resembles the epic in length and adventurousness but puts greater emphasis on love and supernatural events** (*The Odyssey*, Tennyson's *Idylls of the King*); **the *poetic tale* or short story in verse** (Chaucer's *Miller's Tale*, Rosetti's *Goblin Market*); **and the *ballad*, a short narrative song** (see p. 763). The structure of narrative poetry closely resembles that of fiction: it proceeds from an exposition of the setting, circumstances, and characters, through a period of complication (rising action), to a crisis and subsequent resolution.

The dramatic approach focuses on dialogue. Action and setting are conveyed through the spoken comments of the characters rather than through direct authorial description. Because poetry makes use of the aural qualities of language, most plays written before the twentieth century were composed in verse. Verse is, however, an artificial form of speech, and therefore twentieth-century realistic drama has mainly been written in prose, although the continuing popularity of musicals serves to remind us that poetic effects do appeal to theatrical audiences.

The *dramatic monologue*, which is the chief format for dramatic poetry, is a fairly long speech by a fictional narrator that is usually addressed to a second, silent character. During such monologues as Robert Browning's "My Last Duchess" or Tennyson's "Ulysses," the narrator reveals both his character and his motives at some crucial moment in his life. Because a monologue is basically reflective, the structure of a dramatic monologue rarely follows that of the conventional short story. It is likely to be digressive, argumentative, and analytic rather than strictly narrative.

A poem that is primarily descriptive or expository is called a *lyric*. Lyric poems range widely in subject, theme, and scope of treatment, but they are alike in their preoccupation with ideas, emotions, and the poet's state of mind. Although a narrative element is sometimes present, the lyric poet never concentrates on the story.

Many of the poems in this anthology are lyrics, and by briefly examining a few of them, we can only begin to suggest the dozens of possible structures for lyric verse. A description may, for example, move from nearby objects to far-off ones, as in the second and third stanzas of Auden's "Look, Stranger" (p. 751). Or description may be followed by inquiry and analysis, as in Frost's "Design" (p. 656). Frequently a specific incident leads up to a more general conclusion, as when Shakespeare (see p. 673) describes the emotions of an infant crawling after its mother as a symbol of his own passion for his mistress. The presentation may be chronological, like Herrick's in "Upon Julia's Clothes" (p. 713); may increase in emotional intensity, like Kipling's "Recessional" (p. 666); or may be analogical, like Donne's "A Valediction: Forbidding Mourning" (p. 821). In addition, descriptions can conceivably be organized according to the various senses or emotions evoked, and an argument can use comparison and contrast, order of importance, or parallelism to give structure to the whole. No exhaustive list of organizational structures is either possible or desirable.

In each of its formats—narrative, dramatic, and lyric—poetry varies more in length and content than either fiction or drama. Hence, the only useful generalizations about poetic structure are the broad ones that every element in a well-structured poem should have an identifiable function, and that the poem itself should build to a unified effect or series of effects.

STANDARD VERSE FORMS

In prose fiction, form is almost entirely subservient to meaning, but in poetry the verse form provides guidelines to the development of ideas. Verse is, as we argued earlier, a game played between the poet and the form. As in other games, the rules are essentially arbitrary. Why must a baseball cross the plate to be called a strike? What practical purpose is served by hitting a tennis ball over a mesh net and into a rectangular court? Why can a pawn not move backward or a bishop sideways? Why must a sonnet have just fourteen lines? The answer in each case is that the rules of the game help to provide a structure within which we can act and a standard against which we can measure our skills and the skills of others. A poet is challenged by the verse form to write as well as possible within certain restrictions. These restrictions do make the writing more difficult, but they also add to the achievement; and by forcing the poet to experiment with different means of expressing thoughts, they often help better to define what the poet really wants to say and how it can best be said.

Blank Verse

As we have seen, verse can be either rhymed or unrhymed. **Unrhymed iambic pentameter is called *blank verse*.** English blank verse was first written in 1557 by Henry Howard, the Earl of Surrey, in his translation of Virgil's *Aeneid*. It was then adapted to use in drama by Sackville and Norton in *Gorboduc* (1565); however, not until Marlowe and Shakespeare took up the line in the 1580s did its strength, sonority, and variety become evident, as illustrated in Shakespeare's famous characterization of Julius Caesar:

> Why, man he doth bestride the narrow world
> Like a colossus, and we petty men
> Walk under his huge legs and peep about
> To find ourselves dishonorable graves
> —From *Julius Caesar*,
> William Shakespeare [ca. 1600]

In 1664 Milton extended the uses of blank verse to the epic in his *Paradise Lost*. Although little blank verse was written in the eighteenth century, it has been used extensively since.

Stanzaic Verse

Although blank verse is normally organized, like prose, into paragraphs of variable length, rhymed verse is usually cast into units called stanzas. Often, the meter, rhyme scheme, and number of lines are identical in each stanza of a given poem (as in Donne's "The Flea," p. 692). Occasionally, particularly in odes, the structure may vary from stanza to stanza, but no poem really deserves to be called stanzaic unless it regularly uses rhyme or a refrain. Individual stanzas must contain at least two lines and rarely exceed nine.

A *couplet*, formed of a single pair of rhymed lines, is the smallest possible stanzaic unit. When many of the couplets in a poem express a complete thought in two rhetorically balanced lines (as in Pope's lines on sound and sense, p. 648), the poet is said to use the *closed couplet*. The mere use of closed couplets does not, however, constitute a stanzaic structure. Pope's couplets are not visually separate from one another, nor are they always syntactically separate. Individual sentences frequently carry over into a third or fourth line. These run-on verses limit the utility of the couplet as an element of logical structure, and as a result Pope uses paragraphs instead of stanzas as his organizational units.

A few poems, however, are cast into stanzaic couplets. One of the most impressive is Gwendolyn Brooks's short study of young, inner city pool players:

WE REAL COOL

The Pool Players
Seven at the Golden Shovel

We real cool. We
Left school. We

Lurk late. We
Strike straight. We

Sing sin. We
Thin gin. We

Jazz June. We
Die soon.
                    —Gwendolyn Brooks [1960]

Brooks's use of couplets, the simplest of all stanzaic structures, is only one of the ways in which she demonstrates the simplistic thinking of her speakers. Each word in the poem is a monosyllable, and each sentence but three words long. Although the speakers—apparently chanting in unison—may demonstrate how "cool" they are through their use of alliteration, assonance, consonance, and rhyme, they also demonstrate how uneducated they are through their limited vocabularies and their dialectical English. They are fully characterized by their short words, short sentences, short stanzas, short list of achievements, and short lives. In this case at least, the couplet is the perfect choice of stanza for the poem's purpose and content.

If couplets have rarely been used as independent stanzas, they have nevertheless been popular as complete poems. Most two-line poems are epigrams. **An *epigram* is a concentrated witticism that can be written in either verse or prose—although the couplet is the dominant choice. Whatever its form, an epigram must be short, sharp, and swift—as startling as a wasp and as quick to sting.** Both Belloc's "Lines for a Christmas Card" and Dryden's "Epitaph on His Wife" (p. 750) are epigrammatic. For a third example of an epigram, consider Coleridge's definition of the form:

> What is an epigram? A dwarfish whole;
> Its body brevity, and wit its soul.

Many epigrams are buried within longer poems. All of Pope's poems are packed with this form of wit (for example, the first two lines on sound and sense, p. 648); and the final couplets in many of the stanzas in Byron's *Don Juan* are epigrammatic (see pp. 661 and 663), as are the concluding couplets of many of Shakespeare's sonnets.

A three-line stanza is called a *tercet*. A *triplet* is a tercet in which all three lines rhyme together. Herrick's "Upon Julia's Clothes" (p. 713) is an example of a poem using this stanza. ***Terza rima*, a form of three-line stanza popularized by the thirteenth-century Italian poet Dante, establishes an interlocking rhyme scheme in the following pattern: ABA BCB CDC, etc. The closing stanza is either a quatrain or a couplet.** Of the comparatively few famous English poems written in *terza rima*, perhaps the best known is Shelley's "Ode to the West Wind" (p. 878).

A unit of four lines, a *quatrain,* is the most common stanzaic form in English poetry. Although many different rhyme schemes have been used in quatrains, the most often used is *crossed rhyme,* in which the first line rhymes with the third and the second with the fourth, ABAB. Usually the first and third lines are tetrameter, the second and fourth trimeter. This is the pattern of Donne's "Valediction: Forbidding Mourning" (p. 821), Wordsworth's "She Dwelt Among the Untrodden Ways" (p. 864) and Poe's "Annabel Lee" (p. 738).

An iambic pentameter quatrain in which the first two lines rhyme with the last (AAXA) is known as a *rubais* because it was popularized in the *Rubáiyát of Omar Khayyám* (1859) by Edward FitzGerald. The stanza is particularly useful in epigrams because it is similar to a closed couplet, although it develops its point in four lines instead of just two. The first two lines in the quatrain are metrically identical to a closed couplet, but the next two lines, instead of developing a separate idea, extend and complement the first two. Thus, the entire quatrain is like a single couplet in which each line has twenty syllables and the first line contains an internal rhyme:

> *Couplet 1*————Come, fill the Cup, and in the Fire of Spring
> ╱————Your Winter-garment of Repentance fling:
> ╱   The Bird of Time has but a little way
> *Couplet 2*————To flutter—and the Bird is on the Wing.
> —From *The Rubáiyát of Omar Khayyám,*
> Edward FitzGerald (1859)

In short, the *rubais* combines the unity and wit of a couplet with the freedom and scope of a quatrain.

Other quatrains use rhyme schemes based on a single rhyme (AAAA), a pair of couplets (AABB), or an "envelope" (ABBA), but the most important quatrain of all is the stanza used in traditional folk ballads—a stanza composed of alternating lines of iambic tetrameter and iambic trimeter rhyming (XAXA).

A *ballad* is a short narrative poem telling of a single dramatic incident. The *traditional ballad* is part of our oral heritage, and one basic story may evolve into dozens of variant forms as it is recited or sung at different times to different audiences. "Bonny Barbara Allan" is certainly one of the most widely known and frequently altered of all ballads. It has gone through so many different versions over the years that one critic has observed wryly, "Barbara Allan's ninety-two progeny are something of a record achievement, certainly for a lady who, according to the ballad, scorned her lover. One is thankful that she did not encourage him!"[1] The version we reprint is the one sung so beautifully by Joan Baez on her *Ballad Book, Volume 2* (Vanguard, VMS-73115):

BONNY BARBARA ALLAN

> Twas in the merry month of May
> When green buds all were swellin'
> Sweet William on his death bed lay
> For the love of Barbary Allan.
>
> 5   He sent his servant to the town
> To the place where she was dwellin'

---

[1] Arthur Kyle Davis, Jr., *Traditional Ballads of Virginia.* (Cambridge, Mass.: Harvard UP, 1929) 302.

Saying, "You must come to my master dear
If your name be Barbary Allan."

So slowly, slowly she got up,
10   And slowly she drew nigh him,
And the only word to him did say,
"Young man I think you're dying."

He turned his face unto the wall,
And death was in him wellin',
15   "Goodbye, goodbye, to my friends all.
Be good to Barbary Allan."

When he was dead and laid in grave,
She heard the death bells knellin',
And every stroke to her did say,
20   "Hard-hearted Barbary Allan."

"Oh mother, oh mother, go dig my grave.
Make it both long and narrow.
Sweet William died of love for me,
And I will die of sorrow.

25   "And father, oh father, go dig my grave.
Make it both long and narrow.
Sweet William died on yesterday,
And I will die tomorrow."

Barbary Allen was buried in the old churchyard.
30   Sweet William was buried beside her.
Out of Sweet William's heart there grew a rose;
Out of Barbary Allan's a briar.

They grew and grew in the old churchyard
Till they could grow no higher.
35   At the end they formed a true lovers' knot,
And the rose grew round the briar.
                                        —Anonymous

  **Because traditional ballads (also referred to as *folk* or *popular ballads*) were
composed for an oral presentation before an audience, they tell simple, direct
stories using dialogue, repetition, and refrains in an effort to capture the interest
and attention of an audience that may, after all, be hearing the story for the first
time. Ballads tend to be objective, abrupt, and concise. The first few lines catch
our interest with a question or a tense situation. Thereafter, the characters spring
to life, acting and speaking with relatively little external commentary by the author. Some ballads use the refrain for the purpose of advancing or commenting
on the narrative. The themes of ballads are those of continuing popular interest:
unhappy love, feats of war or bravado, shipwrecks, murder, and domestic quarrels.**
  After the end of the Middle Ages and after the development of the printing
press, concern for originality in composition naturally increased, and the circulation and communal creation of folk ballads declined. The ballad stanza has,
however, remained popular, particularly in the former slave states of the South,

where Negro spirituals and blues evolved with the same format and vitality as in the traditional ballad. Furthermore, professional poets and songwriters ranging from Rudyard Kipling *(Barrack-Room Ballads)* to Bob Dylan ("The Ballad of the Thin Man," etc.) have composed delightful literary ballads that prove both the adaptability and the continuing popularity of the form.

Stanzas of five lines, or *quintets*, **are infrequently found in English poetry and none of the many possible rhyme schemes has emerged as particularly prevalent.** It says something about the unpopularity of this stanza that two of the best-known of the poems that employ it are such slight lyrics as Robert Herrick's "The Night-Piece: To Julia" (rhyming AABBA) and Edmund Waller's "Go, Lovely Rose" (rhyming ABABB). The two poems together total only forty lines.

A six line stanza is called a *sestet.* **The most common pattern for sestets is the one Shakespeare always used for the last six lines (or sestet) in his sonnets. It is composed of a crossed rhyme quatrain followed by a couplet (ABABCC), all in iambic pentameter.** Shakespeare first used this sestet in his innovative and popular erotic tale, *Venus and Adonis* (1593), in which his handling of the stanza is light, humorous, and witty; he normally describes the action in the quatrain and cleverly summarizes it or introduces a new and incongruous image in the succeeding, epigrammatic couplet. In the following lines Venus has just seen Adonis and courted him with breathless, burning phrases:

> With this she seizeth on his sweating palm,
> The precedent of pith and livelihood,
> And, trembling in her passion, calls it balm,
> Earth's sovereign salve to do a goddess good.
> > Being so enrag'd, desire doth lend her force
> > Courageously to pluck him from his horse.

> Over one arm the lusty courser's rein,
> Under the other was the tender boy,
> Who blush'd and pouted in a dull disdain,
> With leaden appetite, unapt to toy;
> > She red and hot as coals of glowing fire,
> > He red for shame, but frosty in desire.
> > > —From *Venus and Adonis,*
> > > William Shakespeare [1593]

Here, the concluding couplets emphasize the comic reversal of roles in the poem: Venus manfully plucks Adonis from his horse in the first stanza, and in the second she is flushed with dissolute passion while Adonis blushes in virginal shame.

The *septet*, **or seven-line stanza, is normally cast into the pattern known as** *rhyme royal* **because it was used in the only long poem written by an English-speaking king,** *The King's Quhair* **by James I of Scotland (ca. 1425).** The rhyme scheme differs from that of the Shakespearean sestet by the addition of another B-rhyme at the end of the quatrain (ABABBCC); the line remains iambic pentameter.

Rhyme royal was first used in English poetry by Chaucer, who felt that the stanza was appropriate for the themes of "The Prioress's Tale," *Troilus and Criseyde,* and other serious poems. When Shakespeare came to write the "graver labour" that he had promised in the dedication to *Venus and Adonis,* he chose to use rhyme royal, and the result was the tragic and melodramatic *Rape of Lucrece* (1594). There is, however, nothing necessarily serious about poems written in this stanza. If anything, its closely packed rhymes and paired couplets may be most appropriate in witty verse, as in W. H. Auden's rambling and comic "Letter to Lord Byron."

The most important *octet* or eight-line stanza is *ottava rima,* which is like a stretched Shakespearean sestet: eight lines of iambic pentameter rhyming (ABA-BABCC). Lord Byron stamped this stanza with the witty, satiric, and exuberant characteristics of his own personality by using it in his epic comedy, *Don Juan* (p. 871).

One of the most intricate stanzaic patterns is the nine-line *Spenserian stanza.* First used in 1590 by Edmund Spenser in *The Faerie Queene* (p. 807), this stanza is made up of eight lines of iambic pentameter rhyming ABABBCBC and a final C-rhyme of iambic hexameter (called an Alexandrine). The stanza has often been praised for its majesty and effectiveness in poems with serious themes. To a large extent, this praise is only a recognition that Spenser made majestic and effective use of the stanza in *The Faerie Queene.* Because the stanza inevitably recalls Spenser's poem, later poets have generally used it to create a Spenserian sense of romance, morality, and heroism. So, too, *ottava rima* connotes Byron's witty hedonism, and the Shakespearean sestet connotes the light eroticism of *Venus and Adonis.* The impact of each form on the tone and mood of poetry is often less a product of the stanza itself, than of one unforgettable use of the stanza. Unlike most other stanzas, however, the Spenserian is capable of great variety. Depending on how the poet breaks up his or her thoughts, the stanza can either produce the sound of two couplets (ABA BB CB CC), of a modified *terza rima* (ABA BB CBC C), or of many variations of couplets, tercets, quatrains, and quintets. Spenser frequently molds his stanza into two clear quatrains and a final stark Alexandrine, as in the following description of a knight who has lost his honor and his chastity in a luxurious "Bower of Bliss":

> His warlike armes, the idle instruments
> Of sleeping praise, were hong upon a tree,
> And his brave shield, full of old moniments,
> Was fowly ra'st, that none the signes might see;
> Ne for them, ne for honour cared hee,
> Ne ought, that did to his advancement tend,
> But in lewd loves, and wastefull luxuree,
> His dayes, his goods, his bodie he did spend:
> O horrible enchantment, that him so did blend.
>
> —From *The Faerie Queene,* Book II, Canto XII,
> Edmund Spenser (1590)

By avoiding a monotonous pattern, poets using Spenserian stanzas can vary the effect of their rhymes in much the same way that musicians create variations of a melody. This variety of sound patterns may explain why the Spenserian is the only complex stanza that has been repeatedly used in long poems. In addition to *The Faerie Queene,* it is the stanza of Robert Burns's *Cotter's Saturday Night,* Shelley's *Adonais,* Keats's *Eve of St. Agnes,* and Byron's *Childe Harold.*

The Spenserian is the longest of the well-known stanzas, and it includes in itself many of the lyrical possibilities of shorter stanzas. As such it reconfirms a number of general observations about the nature and function of stanzaic verse itself. **First, stanzaic verse gives the poet an opportunity to impose something akin to the order and structure of prose (for stanzas have many of the virtues of paragraphs) without unduly restricting or sacrificing internally the peculiar expressiveness of** poetry. Second, the type of stanza the poet chooses is important. Certain stanzaic patterns inevitably carry with them traditional associations which neither poet nor reader can ignore. The heroic couplet, for example, is unavoidably associated with Pope's satiric wit, in much the same way that ottava rima calls to mind Byron's risqué and exuberant humor. Finally, the less dense the rhymes in a particular stanza, the more frequently it is used in developing serious plots and themes; conversely, the more dense the rhyme, the less serious the subject matter and the greater the probability of a witty, satiric, or comic treatment.

Not all stanzaic poems are constructed out of regular and repeating structural units. *Odes* are particularly likely to be idiosyncratic, with each stanza differing from others in the same poem both in rhyme scheme and in length of line. This freedom is limited only by a common understanding that an ode must be a long lyric poem that is serious and dignified in subject, tone, and style. It strives to create a mood of meditative sublimity. Some of the more notable free-form odes in English include Wordsworth's "Intimations of Immortality," Coleridge's "Dejection," and Allen Tate's "Ode to the Confederate Dead."

Historically, odes were not always as free in form as they usually are today. In ancient Greece they were strictly organized choral songs that sometimes were written to signal the division between scenes in a play and at other times to celebrate an event or individual. These *Pindaric odes,* named after the Greek poet Pindar (518–438 B.C.), develop through sequences of three different stanzas: *strophe, antistrophe,* and *epode.* The metrical pattern of each strophe remains the same throughout the ode, as does the pattern of each antistrophe and epode. Originally, the strophe was sung and danced by one half of the chorus, after which antistrophe was performed by the other half of the chorus using the same steps of the strophe in reverse. The epode was then performed by the combined chorus. Regular Pindaric odes are quite uncommon in English, the best known being Thomas Gray's "The Bard" and "The Progress of Poetry."

Horatian odes, patterned after those of the Roman poet Horace (65–8 B.C.), retain one stanzaic structure throughout—that is, they are regular stanzaic poems dealing with lofty, lyrical subjects. Some of the better-known Horatian odes are Keats's "Ode on a Nightingale" (p. 881), "To Autumn" (p. 884), "Ode on a Grecian Urn" (p. 883), and "Ode on Melancholy" (p. 885).

Fixed Poetic Forms

The stanzaic patterns we have described are only one way in which poets attempt to create a recognizable tune analogous to a song-writer's melody. The other way is to use one of the fixed poetic forms—the haiku, sonnet, ballade, villanelle, rondeau, sestina, limerick, and so on. Of these, the haiku, the limerick, and the sonnet have achieved a significant place in English poetry; however, all are alike in two respects: all are brief, and all create their moods through the combined effects of a fixed verse pattern and the traditional connotations associated with that pattern. The haiku, for example, is generally associated with brief suggestive images, the limerick with light humor, and the sonnet with love.

A *haiku* is a form of poetry that originated in Japan during the thirteenth century. It consists of three lines of five, seven, and five syllables, respectively. Because of the brevity of the form there is little room for anything more than the presentation of a single concentrated image or emotion. Thus, haiku poems, like these examples by Moritake and Basho, tend to be allusive and suggestive:

THE FALLING FLOWER

What I thought to be
Flowers soaring to their boughs
Were bright butterflies.

—Moritake [1452–1540]

LIGHTNING IN THE SKY

Lightning in the sky!
In the deeper dark is heard
A night-heron's cry.

—Matsuo Basho [1644–1694]

The influence of the Japanese haiku on the twentieth-century Imagist movement has been profound and is reflected in such familiar anthology pieces as Ezra Pound's "In a Station of the Metro" and William Carlos Williams's "The Red Wheelbarrow."

A *limerick* **is a form of light verse. Its five lines rhyme AABBA. The A-rhymed lines are in anapestic trimeter; the others are in dimeter.** Surprisingly, many serious authors have tried their hand at this little form—among them Edward Lear (who wrote over two hundred limericks), Robert Louis Stevenson, Rudyard Kipling, and Oliver Wendell Holmes. The following pun attributed to Holmes on the name "Henry Ward Beecher" helps to create one of the best of the printable limericks:

> The Reverend Henry Ward Beecher
> Called a hen a most elegant creature.
> The hen, pleased with that,
> Laid an egg in his hat.
> And thus did the hen reward Beecher.
>
> —Anonymous

More typical, is the slightly off-color humor of the following:

> I sat next the Duchess at tea.
> It was just as I feared it would be.
> Her rumblings abdominal
> Were simply abominable,
> And everyone thought it was me!
>
> —Anonymous

In comparison with the haiku and the limerick, the *sonnet* is a more distinguished and inspiring form. Indeed, poets often become so enamored of the "little song" (the literal meaning of *sonnet*) that some have written nothing else and a few—including William Wordsworth and Dante Gabriel Rossetti—have composed rapturous sonnets on sonnetry.

Technically, **a sonnet is a lyric poem of fourteen iambic pentameter lines, usually following one of two established models: the Italian form or the English form. The** *Italian sonnet* **(or** *Petrarchan sonnet,* **named after the Italian Renaissance poet Petrarch) consists of an eight-line octave, rhyming ABBAABBA, followed by a six-line sestet, rhyming variously CDECDE, CDCDCD, etc. Normally, the octave presents a situation or issue, and the sestet explores or resolves it.** Both "On First Looking into Chapman's Homer" (p. 649) and "Design" (p. 656) are Petrarchan sonnets. Keats's octave relates what he had heard about Homer before reading his poetry, while the sestet examines Keats's emotions after discovering the beauties of Homer through Chapman's translation. Frost uses his octave to describe the three objects he encounters on his morning walk; his sestet raises questions about their origin and meaning.

The *English sonnet* (or *Shakespearean sonnet*) consists of three quatrains and a concluding couplet, rhyming ABAB CDCD EFEF GG. A variant of the English sonnet, the *Spenserian sonnet*, links its quatrains by employing the rhyme scheme ABAB BCBC CDCD EE. Although the English sonnet may describe an issue and its resolution using the same octave-sestet structure as in the Italian form, the three quatrains of the Shakespearean sonnet often present three successive images, actions, or arguments, which are then summed up in a final, epigrammatic couplet. A typical Shakespearean sonnet (number CXLIII) is quoted on page 673. Note that in this case the sonnet does take the form of an octave, presenting a hypothesis ("as a careful housewife"), and a sestet, presenting a conclusion ("So runn'st thou"). But the sonnet also breaks into three quatrains and a couplet. The first quatrain describes a housewife in pursuit of a stray cock or hen; the second tells how her neglected child chases after her; and the third explains that Shakespeare is in a situation like that of the child, whereas his mistress (who is presumably running after another man) is like the housewife. Finally, the concluding couplet summarizes and resolves the situation with a pun on William Shakespeare's first name:

> So I will pray that thou mayst have thy "Will,"
> If thou turn back and my loud crying still.

The sonnet became popular in England during the sixteenth century largely because of translations and imitations of Petrarch's passionate cycle of sonnets addressed to his mistress Laura. Similar sonnet sequences were written by Sir Philip Sidney (*Astrophel and Stella*, 1580), Samuel Daniel (*Delia*, 1592), Michael Drayton (*Idea*, 1593), Edmund Spenser (*Amoretti* and *Epithalamion*, 1595), and William Shakespeare (*Sonnets*, 1609). This deluge of amorous sonnets helped to establish the belief that the sonnet itself must always deal with love—a presumption that is still widespread. As early as 1631, Milton challenged this popular notion by writing sonnets of personal reflection, moral criticism, and political comment. The sonnets by Shakespeare, Keats, and Frost, quoted earlier in this text, demonstrate that Milton was correct and that the sonnet can be used in themes ranging from Shakespeare's barnyard humor to Keats's pleasure in reading to Frost's brooding about "the design of darkness to appall." It is this adaptability that makes the sonnet so much more important in literary history than other fixed forms, such as the haiku and the limerick.

VISUAL FORMS

All verse makes some appeal to the eye. We see where the lines begin and end, and from that information we can often tell something about the poetic emphasis and meaning. For some poets, however, this limited visual element is not enough. William Blake, for example, printed his poems himself so that he would be sure that both the calligraphy and the marginal illustrations would contribute to the overall effect. Thus, when we read the poems from his *Songs of Innocence* (1789) and *Songs of Experience* (1794), we must at the very least remember that the words only convey part of his intention. Few other poets have shared Blake's broad interests in both literature and graphic art, but many have experimented with three methods of expanding poetic meaning through visual form.

Typographical Analogies

Throughout history writers have underscored the content of their work by manipulating the way that words appear on the page. Capital letters convey urgency and loudness: STOP! HELP! COME HERE! Lower-case letters, particularly in names, suggest humility or timidity (but paradoxically also attract attention): *e.e. cummings, archie and mehitabel,* and so on. Additional letters or spaces in a line can suggest stuttering (*c-c-cold*), reverberation (*shockkk*), delay (*s l o w l y*), and distance (*l o n g*). Conversely, deleted letters or spaces indicate speed (*quickasawink*) and compactness (*huddld*). Misspellings, like *X-mass* and *Amerikkka,* make a visual statement by reminding us respectively of the cross borne by Christ and of the role played by the Ku Klux Klan during certain periods of American history. Furthermore, certain typesetting techniques allow the appearance of words to mirror their meanings: o^{ver}, un_{der}, cramped, or ^{tail}ing. e. e. cummings popularized the use of typographical analogies in modern poetry (see "Buffalo Bill's," p. 968). Although these devices sometimes become contrived and gimmicky, other contemporary poets such as Allen Ginsberg and Howard Nemerov have occasionally introduced tricks of typography into their poems.

Picture Poems

By careful word choice and clever typesetting, poets can sometimes create a visual image of the object or idea they are describing. Although picture poems have never been numerous, they are by no means new. One finds them in ancient Greek literature, as well as in the recent movement toward *concretism* (the concern with a poem's visual appearance rather than with its words). In most cases, visual poems tend to be lighthearted, as in Lewis Carroll's *Alice in Wonderland,* where the tale the Mouse tells Alice takes the form of a long, serpentine "tail" that wanders down half a page. The ingenious seventeenth-century poet George Herbert proved, however, that visual effects are not always frivolous. He formed his religious meditation on the altar of the human heart into the shape of an altar in the following poem:

THE ALTAR

A   broken   ALTAR,   Lord,   thy   servant   rears,
Made   of   a   heart,   and   cemented   with   tears:
Whose   parts   are   as   thy   hand   did   frame;
No   workman's   tool   hath   touched   the   same.
5   A   HEART   alone
Is   such   a   stone,
As   nothing   but
Thy   power   doth   cut.
Wherefore   each   part
10   Of   my   hard   heart
Meets   in   this   frame,
To   praise   thy   Name:
That,   if   I   chance   to   hold   my   peace,
These   stones   to   praise   thee   may   not   cease.
15   O   let   thy   blessed   SACRIFICE   be   mine,
And   sanctify   this   ALTAR   to   be   thine.
—George Herbert [1633]

Acrostics

An *acrostic* is a poem in which certain letters (ordinarily the first in each line) spell out a word when read from top to bottom or bottom to top. The best-known acrostics in English literature are those by John Davies in praise of Queen Elizabeth I. Every poem in his volume of *Hymns of Astraea* (1599) spells out the words *Elisabetha Regina*—Elizabeth, the Queen.

TO THE SPRING

E   arth now is green and heaven is blue,
L   ively spring which makes all new,
I   olly spring, doth enter;
S   weet young sun-beams do subdue
A   ngry, aged winter.
B   lasts are mild and seas are calm,
E   very meadow flows with balm,
T   he earth wears all her riches;
H   armonious birds sing such a psalm
A   s ear and heart bewitches.

R   eserve, sweet spring, this nymph of ours
E   ternal garlands of thy flowers;
G   reen garlands never wasting;
I   n her shall last our fair spring
N   ow and forever flourishing
A   s long as heaven is lasting.

—John Davies [1599]

All of these visual effects may occasionally play a useful role in good poetry, but they are more often signs of weakness—superficial and relatively easy techniques used by poets who are content to be ingenious. In the final analysis, the words of poetry and the energy, intellect, and feeling communicated by those words are of far more importance to truly great writing than even the most meticulous adherence to the external requirements of verse form.

Poems for Further Study

DREAM VARIATIONS

To fling my arms wide
In some place of the sun,
To whirl and to dance
Till the white day is done.
Then rest at cool evening
Beneath a tall tree
While night comes on gently,
    Dark like me—
That is my dream!

5

10   To fling my arms wide
      In the face of the sun,
      Dance! Whirl! Whirl!
      Till the quick day is done.
      Rest at pale evening . . .
15   A tall, slim tree . . .
      Night coming tenderly
            Black like me.

                    —Langston Hughes [1924]

❧ QUESTIONS ❧

1.   Compare the two stanzas in this poem. How are the two dream variations alike? What are the differences? (Pay particular attention to changes in the connotations of words.)

2.   What rhythm and meter are used in the poem? How does Hughes manipulate the rhythm to create mood and meaning?

3.   Is this poem merely about dancing or does each stanza present a somewhat different symbolic presentation of racial relations? How does Hughes encourage us to read the poem symbolically?

"THEY FLEE FROM ME, THAT SOMETIME DID ME SEEK"[2]

      They flee from me, that sometime did me seek,
          With naked foot, stalking in my chamber.
      I have seen them gentle, tame, and meek;
          That now are wild, and do not remember
5   That sometime they put themselves in danger
             To take bread at my hand: and now they range,
             Busily seeking, with a continual change.

      Thanked be fortune! it hath been otherwise
          Twenty times better! But once, in special,
10   In thin array, after a pleasant guise,
          When her loose gown from her shoulders did fall,
          And she me caught in her arms long and small,
             Therewithal sweetly did me kiss;
             And softly said, "Dear heart! how like you this?"

15   It was no dream! I lay broad waking!
             But all is turned, thorough my gentleness,

---

[2] The first published version of this poem in Richard Tottel's miscellany, *Songs and Sonnets* (1557), imposes the title "The Lover Showeth How He Is Forsaken of Such as He Sometimes Enjoyed." No title is supplied in the authoritative *Egerton Ms. 2711.*

> Into a strange fashion of forsaking;
> And I have leave to go, of her goodèness!
> And she also, to use newfangleness!
20 But since that I so kindèly am served,
> I would fain know what she hath deserved?

—Sir Thomas Wyatt [posthumous, 1557]

❧ QUESTIONS ❧

1. What comparison dominates the first stanza? What words in this stanza are appropriate in describing women? What change has taken place in those who once sought the speaker's chamber?

2. The second stanza examines one instance when "it hath been otherwise." How do Wyatt's details in this stanza move from general to specific and contribute to the vividness and intensity of the scene he recalls? How does the double pun in the words "dear heart" contribute to the pattern of the poem's imagery?

3. The third stanza restates the situation of the forsaken speaker. What has been the reward for his "gentleness"? Does the speaker really believe he has been treated "kindèly"? The word "kindely" may mean "according to kind" or "according to nature" in addition to "nicely." Do you think that Wyatt intended the word "kindely" to create an ironic pun? What is the speaker's attitude toward the woman who formerly sought his company?

4. What stanzaic form does Wyatt use? What is the relationship between Wyatt's use of stanzas and the organization and development of his ideas?

"SINCE THERE'S NO HELP, COME LET US KISS AND PART"

> Since there's no help, come let us kiss and part;
> Nay, I have done, you get no more of me;
> And I am glad, yea, glad with all my heart,
> That thus so cleanly I myself can free.
5 Shake hands for ever, cancel all our vows,
> And when we meet at any time again,
> Be it not seen in either of our brows
> That we one jot of former love retain.
> Now at the last gasp of love's latest breath,
10 When, his pulse failing, passion speechless lies,
> When faith is kneeling by his bed of death,
> And innocence is closing up his eyes,
> —Now if thou wouldst, when all have given him over,
> From death to life thou might'st him yet recover.

—Michael Drayton [1619]

🌿 QUESTIONS 🌿

1. What situation is described in this poem and what dramatic interactions may be presumed to occur between the speaking and nonspeaking participants in the drama?

2. Why does Drayton personify love, passion, faith, and innocence in lines 6–14? What is the relationship between these personifications and the two separating lovers?

3. Can you deduce the reason(s) why the speaker insists upon breaking up with the woman? What must she do if their love is not to expire?

4. How does Drayton use the structure of sonnet in developing this episode?

THE WAKING

I wake to sleep, and take my waking slow.
I feel my fate in what I cannot fear.
I learn by going where I have to go.

5   We think by feeling. What is there to know?
I hear my being dance from ear to ear.
I wake to sleep, and take my waking slow.

Of those so close beside me, which are you?
God bless the Ground! I shall walk softly there,
And learn by going where I have to go.

10   Light takes the Tree; but who can tell us how?
The lowly worm climbs up a winding stair;
I wake to sleep, and take my waking slow.

Great Nature has another thing to do
To you and me; so take the lively air,
15   And, lovely, learn by going where to go.

This shaking keeps me steady. I should know.
What falls away is always. And is near.
I wake to sleep, and take my waking slow.
I learn by going where I have to go.

                                        —Theodore Roethke [1953]

🌿 QUESTIONS 🌿

1. What is the subject of Roethke's poem and how is his attitude toward that subject revealed in the poem's first stanza?

2. What is Roethke's attitude toward thinking and feeling in stanza 2? How are thought and feeling related to waking and sleeping?

3.   Stanzas 3 to 5 develop insights on life, death, and nature. How are the insights relevant to the poem's concern with waking and sleeping?

4.   How does the poem's form (see **villanelle** in the *Handbook*) add to its effectiveness?

EASTER WINGS

Lord, who createdst man in wealth and store,°   *plenty*
Though foolishly he lost the same,
Decaying more and more
Till he became
5   Most poor:
With thee
O let me rise
As larks, harmoniously,
And sing this day thy victories:
10   Then shall the fall further the flight in me.

My tender age in sorrow did begin:
And still with sicknesses and shame
Thou didst so punish sin,
That I became
15   Most thin.
With thee
Let me combine,
And feel this day thy victory;
For, if I imp[3] my wing on thine,
20   Affliction shall advance the flight in me.

—George Herbert [1633]

 QUESTIONS

1.   This is a picture poem. What does the shape of each stanza depict?

2.   How does the shape of each stanza both complement and reveal Herbert's ideas?

3.   What religious insights does Herbert develop? Why is the title "Easter Wings" appropriate to both the poem's form and content?

---

[3] A term from falconry meaning to graft feathers into a wing to restore the ability to fly.

19

Questions to Ask About Poetry

In the preceding pages we have discussed the formal elements of poetry. What follows is a set of questions that will draw upon your accumulated knowledge. These questions should clarify your response and help you to begin the interpretation of a poem that you are studying for the first time.

Before listing the questions, we should, however, add a few words of caution. First, poems differ greatly in their emphases. Not all of the questions that follow will be equally applicable to the analysis of every poem; therefore, you need to follow to some extent your intuition in order to understand what makes a particular poem vital and appealing. Second, although analysis of an author's success in manipulating the elements of poetry can add to an appreciation and understanding of any poem, you should not assume that poems that *require* extensive explication to be understood are necessarily better than those that do not. Explication is one means—and generally the most important means—of coming to understand why an author has written what he or she has. Some poems require much explication and some little. But great poetry should be a pleasure to read, not a punishment. We can expect this pleasure to grow as analysis and mature reflection increase our understanding, but the enjoyment of poetry is, and should remain, visceral as well as intellectual.

QUESTIONS TO ASK AND ANSWER

First, read the poem carefully (aloud at least once), making sure that you understand the *denotative meaning* of each word. (Be sure to use both your dictionary and the editor's notes, if any.)

1. Who is the speaker? What kind of person does he or she seem to be? To whom is he or she speaking and what are his or her point of view and relation to the

subject? What is the general mood or *tone* of the poem? Is it consistent throughout, or is there a shift?

2. What is the situation or occasion of the poem? What is the setting in time and space?

3. Does the poet manipulate the meanings of words using any of the following devices: *connotation, allusion, repetition, ambiguity, punning, paradox, irony*? How does the use of these devices add to the resonance and significance of the denotative meaning?

4. Examine the poem's *imagery*. Are any images repeated or otherwise emphasized? Does the imagery in the poem develop according to a logical pattern? Can you determine why the poet uses the images that he or she does?

5. What forms of poetic comparison (*metaphor, simile,* etc.) are used and what do they add to the poem's imagery and meaning?

6. Does the poem make use of *symbol* or *allegory*?

7. *Paraphrase* and *summarize* the poem. What is the poem's *theme,* argument, or central idea and how is it developed? (Be alert to repeated images, the stanzaic pattern, rhetorical devices, etc.)

8. What are the *meter* and *rhyme scheme* of the poem? What other significant repetitions of sounds (*alliteration, assonance, consonance*) occur in the poem? How do they contribute to the effect of the poem? What is the form of the poem (*sonnet, ode, lyric, dramatic monologue,* etc.)? Are the meter, rhyme scheme, and form appropriate?

9. *Criticize* and *evaluate.* How well do you think the poet has achieved a total integration of the materials? What is *your* reaction to the poem? Do you like the poem? If so, why? If not, why not?

20

꧁꧂꧁꧂꧁꧂

Poems

꧁ **EARLY POPULAR SONGS AND BALLADS[1]** ꧂

"SUMER IS ICUMEN IN"[2]

Sumer is icumen in!
Lhude sing, cuccu!
Groweth sed and bloweth med,
And springth the wood nu.
5   Sing, cuccu!

Awe bleteth after lomb,
Lhouth after clave cu.
Bulluc sterteth, bucke verteth.
Murie sing, cuccu!

---

[1] The seven anonymous poems that follow (two lyrics and five ballads) originated in England during the Middle Ages and, in a variety of versions, became part of our oral heritage in poetry. In each case we have selected the version of the poem that seems to us to have the greatest poetic value.

[2] This famous song from a monk's commonplace book of the mid-thirteenth century is a good example (using our modern alphabet) of the early English language. It may be translated as follows: "Summer is a-coming in! / Loudly sing, cuckoo! / Groweth seed and flowereth mead, / And springeth the wood now. / Sing, cuckoo! / Ewe bleateth after lamb, / Loweth after calf cow. / Bullock starteth, buck farteth. / Merry sing, cuckoo! / Cuckoo! cuckoo! / Well singest thou, cuckoo! / Nor cease thou never now. / REFRAIN / Sing cuckoo, now! Sing cuckoo! / (*One repeats this as many times as necessary, pausing at the end.*) / Sing cuckoo now! Sing cuckoo! / (*Another says this, pausing in the middle and not at the end, but immediately repeating the beginning.*)

10   Cuccu! cuccu!
        Wel singes thu, cuccu.
        Ne swik thu naver nu.

       REFRAIN
        Sing cuccu! Sing cuccu!
[*Hoc repetit unus quociens opus est, faciens pausacionem in fine.*]
15   Sing cuccu nu! Sing cuccu!
[*Hoc dicit alius, pausans in medio et no in fine, set immediate repetens principium.*]

"O WESTERN WIND"

   O western° wind, when wilt thou blow   *I.e., spring*
    That the small rain down can rain?
  Christ, that my love were in my arms
    And I in my bed again!

LORD RANDAL

 "O where hae ye been, Lord Randal, my son?
 O where hae ye been, my handsome young man?"
 "I hae been to the wild wood; mother, make my bed soon,
 For I'm weary wi' hunting, and fain wald lie down."

5 "Where gat ye your dinner, Lord Randal, my son?
 Where gat ye your dinner, my handsome young man?"
 "I dined wi' my true-love; mother, make my bed soon,
 For I'm weary wi' hunting, and fain wald lie down."

 "What gat ye to your dinner, Lord Randal, my son?
10 What gat ye to your dinner, my handsome young man?"
 "I gat eels boiled in broo;° mother, make my bed soon,   *broth*
 For I'm weary wi' hunting, and fain wald lie down."

 "What became of your bloodhounds, Lord Randal, my son?
 What became of your bloodhounds, my handsome young man?"
15 "O they swelled and they died; mother, make my bed soon,
 For I'm weary wi' hunting, and fain wald lie down."

 "O I fear ye are poisoned, Lord Randal, my son!
 O I fear ye are poisoned, my handsome young man!"
 "O yes! I am poisoned; mother, make my bed soon,
20 For I'm sick at the heart, and I fain wald lie down."

GET UP AND BAR THE DOOR

   It fell about the Martinmas time,°   *Nov. 11*
    And a gay time it was then,
  When our good wife got puddings to make,
    And she's boiled them in the pan.

5   The wind sae cauld° blew south and north,   *So cold*
      And blew into the floor;
    Quoth our goodman to our goodwife,
      "Gae° out and bar the door."   *Go*

    "My hand is in my hussyfskap,°   *housework*
10   Goodman, as ye may see;
    An° it shoud nae be barred this hundred year,   *If*
      It's no be° barred for° me."   *not going to be / by*

    They made a paction° tween them twa,°   *pact / two*
      They made it firm and sure,
15   That the first word whaeer° shoud speak,   *whoever*
      Shoud rise and bar the door.

    Then by there came two gentlemen,
      At twelve o'clock at night,
    And they could neither see house nor hall,
20   Nor coal nor candle-light.

    "Now whether is this a rich man's house,
      Or whether is it a poor?"
    But neer a word wad ane° o them speak,   *either*
      For barring of the door.

25   And first they ate the white puddings,
      And then they ate the black;
    Tho muckle° thought the goodwife to herself,   *much*
      Yet neer a word she spake.

    Then said the one unto the other,
30   "Here, man, tak ye my knife;
    Do ye tak aff the auld man's beard,
      And I'll kiss the goodwife."

    "But there 's nae water in the house,
      And what shall we do than?"
35   "What ails ye at the pudding-broo,°   *broth of the pudding*
      That boils into the pan?"

    O up then started our goodman,
      An angry man was he:
    "Will ye kiss my wife before my een,
40   And scad° me wi pudding-bree?"   *scald*

    Then up and started our goodwife,
      Gied three skips on the floor:
    "Goodman, you've spoken the foremost word,
      Get up and bar the door."

SIR PATRICK SPENS

The king sits in Dumferling town,
    Drinking the blude-reid° wine: *blood-red*
"O whar will I get guid° sailor,   *good*
    To sail this ship of mine?"

5   Up and spak an eldern° knicht,   *elderly*
    Sat at the king's richt knee:
"Sir Patrick Spens is the best sailor
    That sails upon the sea."

The king has written a braid° letter   *broad*
10   And signed it wi' his hand,
And sent it to Sir Patrick Spens,
    Was walking on the sand.

The first line that Sir Patrick read,
    A loud lauch° lauched he;   *laugh*
15   The next line that Sir Patrick read,
    The tear blinded his ee.°   *eye*

"O wha° is this has done this deed,   *who*
    This ill deed done to me,
To send me out this time o' the year,
20   To sail upon the sea?

"Mak haste, mak haste, my mirry men all,
    Our guid ship sails the morn."
"O say na° sae,° my master dear,   *not / so*
    For I fear a deadly storm.

25   Late, late yestre'en I saw the new moon
    Wi' the auld moon in her arm,
And I fear, I fear, my dear master,
    That we will come to harm."

O our Scots nobles were richt° laith°   *right / loath*
30   To weet° their cork-heeled shoon,°   *wet / shoes*
Bot lang° or° a' the play were played   *long / ere*
    Their hats they swam aboon.°   *above*

O lang, lang may their ladies sit,
    Wi' their fans into their hand,
35   Or ere they see Sir Patrick Spens
    Come sailing to the land.

O lang, lang may the ladies stand
    Wi' their gold kems° in their hair,   *combs*
Waiting for their ain° dear lords,   *own*
40   For they'll see them na mair.

Half o'er,° half o'er to Aberdour   *over*
   It's fifty fadom° deep,   *fathoms*
And there lies guid Sir Patrick Spens
   Wi' the Scots lords at his feet.

MARY HAMILTON

Word is to the kitchen gone
And word is to the hall
And word is up to madam the queen
And that's the worst of all,
5   That Mary Hamilton's born a babe
To the highest steward of all.

"Arise, arise, Mary Hamilton.
Arise and tell to me
What thou hast done with thy wee babe
10   I saw and heard weep by thee."

"I put him in a tiny boat
And cast him out to sea
That he might sink or he might swim
But he'd never come back to me."

15   "Arise, arise, Mary Hamilton.
Arise and come with me.
There is a wedding in Glascow town
This night we'll go and see."

She put not on her robes of black
20   Nor her robes of brown.
She put on her robes of white
To ride into Glascow Town.

As she rode into Glascow Town
The city for to see
25   The bailiff's wife and the provost's wife
Cried, "Out and alas for thee."

"Ah ye need not weep for me,"
She cried, "Ye need not weep for me.
For had I not slain my own sweet babe
30   This death I would not need.

"Ah, little did my mother think
When first she cradled me
The lands I was to travel in
And the death I was to die.

35   "Last night I washed the queen's feet
        And put the gold in her hair,
        And the only reward I find for this
        The gallows to be my share.

        "Cast off, cast off my gown," she cried.
40   "But let my petticoat be
        And tie a necking round my face
        The gallows I would not see."

        Then by them come the king himself.
        And looked up with a pitiful eye.
45   "Come down, come down, Mary Hamilton;
        Tonight you'll dine with me."

        "Ah, hold your tongue my sovereign liege
        And let your folly be,
        For if you'd a mind to save my life,
50   You'd never have shamed me.

        "Last night there were four Marys.
        Tonight there'll be but three.
        There was Mary Eaton and Mary Seaton
        And Mary Carmichael and me."

MATTY GROVES

        High ho, high ho, holiday!
        The best day of the year!
        Little Matty Groves to church did go
        Some holy words to hear,
5   Some holy words to hear.

        He spied three ladies dressed in black
        As they came into view.
        Lord Ireland's wife was gaily clad,
        A flower among the few,
10   A flower among the few.

        She tripped up to Matty Groves,
        Her eyes so low cast down,
        Saying, "Pray, oh pray, come with me stay
        As you pass through the town,
15   As you pass through the town."

        "I cannot go, I dare not go.
        I fear 'twould cost my life
        For I see by the little ring you wear
        You are Lord Ireland's wife,
20   You're the great Lord Ireland's wife."

"This may be false, this may be true.
I can't deny it all.
Lord Ireland's gone to consecrate
King Henry at Whitehall,
25   King Henry at Whitehall.

"Oh pray, oh pray, come with me stay.
I'll hide thee out of sight.
I'll serve you there beyond compare
And sleep with you the night,
30   And sleep with you the night."

Her little page did listen well
To all that they did say
And ere the sun could rise again
He quickly sped away,
35   He quickly sped away.

And he did run the king's highway.
He swam across the tide.
He ne'er did stop till that he came
To the great Lord Ireland's side,
40   To the great Lord Ireland's side.

"What news, what news, my bully boy?
What news brings you to me?
My castle burned, my tenants robbed,
My lady with baby?
45   My lady with baby?"

"No harm is come to your house and land,"
The little page did say.
"But Matty Groves is bedded up
With your fair lady gay,
50   With your fair lady gay."

Lord Ireland called his merry men.
He bade them with him go.
He bade them ne'er a word to speak
And ne'er a horn to blow,
55   And ne'er a horn to blow.

But among Lord Ireland's merry men
Was one who wished no ill.
And the bravest lad in all the crew
Blew his horn so loud and shrill,
60   Blew his horn so loud and shrill.

"What's this, what's this?" cried Matty Groves.
"What's this that I do hear?

It must be Lord Ireland's merry men,
The ones that I do fear,
The ones that I do fear."

"Lie down, lie down, little Matty Groves
And keep my back from cold.
It's only Lord Ireland's merry men
A calling the sheep to fold,
A calling the sheep to fold."

Little Matty Groves he did lie down.
He took a nap asleep.
And when he woke Lord Ireland was
A standing at his feet,
A standing at his feet.

"How now, how now, my bully boy?
Ah, how do you like my sheets?
And how do you like my fair young bride
Who lies in your arms asleep,
Who lies in your arms asleep?"

"Ah, it's very well I like your bed
And it's fine I like your sheets,
But it's best I like your fair young bride
Who lies in my arms asleep,
Who lies in my arms asleep."

"Rise up, rise up, little Matty Groves,
As fast as ere you can.
In England it shall ne'er be said
I slew a sleeping man,
I slew a sleeping man."

And the first stroke little Matty struck
He hurt Lord Ireland sore
But the next stroke Lord Ireland struck.
Little Matty struck no more,
Little Matty struck no more.

"Rise up, rise up, my gay young bride.
Draw on your pretty clothes.
Now tell me do you like me best
Or do you like your Matty Groves,
Or the darling Matty Groves."

She picked up Matty's dying head.
She kissed him from cheek to chin,
Said, "It's Matty Groves I'd rather have
Than Ireland and all his kin,
Than Ireland and all his kin.

"Ah, woe is me and woe is thee,
Why stayed ye not your hand?
For you have killed the fairest lad
In all of England,
In all of England."

110

❦ MEDIEVAL POETRY ❦

Geoffrey Chaucer   *1342?–1400*

THE CANTERBURY TALES

FROM *"General Prologue"*

Whan that Aprille with his shoures sote°	*sweet*
The droghte of Marche hath perced to the rote,	
And bathed every veyne in swich licour,	
Of which vertu° engendered is the flour;°	*power / flower*
5 Whan Zephirus° eek° with his swete breeth	*the west wind / also*
Inspired hath in every holt° and heeth°	*woods / heath*
The tendre croppes, and the yonge sonne	
Hath in the Ram his halfe cours y-ronne,[1]	
And smale fowles maken melodye,	
10 That slepen al the night with open yë;°	*eye*
(So priketh° hem nature in hir corages):°	*pricks / hearts*
Than longen folk to goon on pilgrimages	
(And palmers° for to seken straunge strondes)°	*pilgrims / lands*
To ferne halwes, couthe in sondry londes;[2]	
15 And specially, from every shires ende	
Of Engelond, to Caunterbury[3] they wende,°	*go*
The holy blisful martir for to seke,	
That hem hath holpen,° whan that they were	*helped*
seke.°	*sick*
Bifel° that, in that seson on a day,	*It happened*
20 In Southwerk at the Tabard[4] as I lay	
Redy to wenden° on my pilgrimage	*go*
To Caunterbury with ful devout corage,	
At night was come in-to that hostelrye°	*inn*
Wel nyne and twenty in a companye,	
25 Of sondry folk, by aventure° y-falle	*chance*
In felawshipe, and pilgrims were they alle,	
That toward Caunterbury wolden° ryde;	*wished to*
The chambres and the stables weren wyde,	
And wel we weren esed atte beste.[5]	
30 And shortly, whan the sonne was to reste,	
So hadde I spoken with hem everichon,°	*every one*
That I was of hir felawshipe anon,°	*at once*
And made forward° erly for to ryse,	*a pact*

[1] The sun is young because it is only half-way through the Ram, or Aries (March 21 to April 20), the first sign in the medieval zodiac.

[2] I.e., to foreign shrines well-known in sundry lands.

[3] Canterbury, a cathedral city in England, where St. Thomas à Becket became a martyr ("the holy blisful martir," line 17) in 1170.

[4] The Tabard, an inn in Southwark, then a suburb of London.

[5] I.e., accommodated in the best manner.

To take our wey, ther as I yow devyse.°   *describe*
35   But natheles, whyl I have tyme and space,
Er that I ferther in this tale pace,
Me thinketh it acordaunt° to resoun,   *according*
To telle yow al the condicioun
Of ech of hem, so as it semed me,
40   And whiche they weren, and of what degree;°   *status*
And eek in what array° that they were inne: *clothing*

MILLER

545   The Miller was a stout carl,° for the nones   *churl*
Ful big he was of braun, and eek of bones;
That proved° wel, for over-al ther° he cam,   *was proven / wherever*
At wrastling he wolde have alwey the ram.[1]
He was short-sholdred, brood,° a thikke   *broad*
        knarre,°   *head*
550   Ther nas no dore that he nolde° heve of harre,°   *could not / off hinge*
Or breke it, at a renning,° with his heed.   *running*
His berd° as any sowe or fox was reed,   *beard*
And ther-to brood, as though it were a spade.
Up-on the cop° right of his nose he hade   *top*
555   A werte,° and ther-on stood a tuft of heres,°   *wart / hairs*
Reed as the bristles of a sowes eres;°   *ears*
His nose-thirles° blake° were and wyde.   *nostrils / black*
A swerd and bokeler° bar° he by his syde;   *shield / bore*
His mouth as greet was as a greet forneys.°   *furnace*
560   He was a janglere° and a goliardeys,°   *loudmouth / lewd joker*
And that was most of sinne and harlotryes.°   *ribaldry*
Wel coude he stelen corn, and tollen thryes;[2]
And yet he hadde a thombe of gold,[3] pardee.°   *by God*
A whyt cote° and a blew hood wered° he.   *coat / wore*
565   A baggepype wel coude he blowe and sowne,
And ther-with-al he broghte us out of towne.

REEVE

        The Reve° was a sclendre colerik man,   *overseer*
His berd was shave as ny° as ever he can.   *close*
His heer was by his eres round y-shorn.
590   His top was dokked° lyk a preest biforn.   *cut short, tonsured*
Ful longe were his legges, and ful lene,
Y-lyk° a staf, ther was no calf y-sene.°   *like / visible*
Wel coude he kepe° a gerner° and a binne,°   *guard / granary / chest*
Ther was noon auditour coude on him winne.°   *get the better of him*
595   Wel wiste° he, by the droghte, and by the reyn,   *knew*

[1] The ram, first prize in medieval wrestling matches.
[2] I.e., take thrice his proper fee for grinding corn.
[3] Proverbially, "an honest miller has a thumb of gold."

The yelding of his seed, and of his greyn.

His lordes sheep, his neet,° his dayerye,   *cattle*

His swyn, his hors, his stoor,° and his pultyre,   *stock*

Was hoolly in this reves governing,

600 And by his covenaunt° yaf° the rekening,   *agreement / gave*

Sin that his lord was twenty yeer of age;

Ther coude no man bringe him in arrerage.°   *arrears*

Ther nas baillif, ne herde,° ne other hyne.°   *herdsman / farmhand*

That he ne knew his sleighte and his covyne,°   *deceit*

605 They were adrad° of him, as of the deeth.°   *afraid / the plague*

His woning° was ful fair up-on an heeth,   *dwelling*

With grene treës shadwed was his place.

He coude bettre than his lord purchace.

Ful riche he was astored prively,°   *stocked secretly*

610 His lord wel coude he plesen subtilly,

To yeve° and lene° him of his owne good,°   *give / lend / goods*

And have a thank, and yet a cote and hood.

In youthe he lerned hadde a good mister;°   *occupation*

He was a wel good wrighte,° a carpenter.   *workman*

615 This reve sat up-on a full good stot,°   *horse*

That was al pomely° grey, and highte° Scot.   *dappled / named*

A long surcote° of pers° up-on he hade,   *overcoat / blue*

And by his syde he bar a rusty blade.

Of Northfolk was this reve, of which I telle,

620 Bisyde a toun men clepen Baldeswelle.

Tukked[1] he was, as is a frere, aboute,

And ever he rood the hindreste of our route.

THE MILLER'S PROLOGUE

Here folwen the wordes bitwene the Host and the Millere.

Whan that the Knight had thus his tale y-told,

3110 In al the route° nas ther yong ne old   *company*

That he ne seyde it was a noble storie,

And worthy for to drawn to memorie;

And namely the gentils° everichoon.   *well bred folks*

Our Hoste lough and swoor, "so moot° I goon,°   *might / go (walk)*

3115 This gooth aright; unbokeled is the male;°   *pack*

Lat see now who shal telle another tale:

For trewely, the game is wel bigonne.

Now telleth ye, sir Monk, if that ye conne,°   *can*

Sumwhat, to quyte° with the Knightes tale."   *requite*

3120 The Miller, that for-dronken° was al pale,   *because of drink*

So that unnethe° up-on his hors he sat,   *scarcely*

He nolde avalen° neither hood ne hat,   *take off*

Ne abyde no man for his curteisye,

---

[1] He wore his cloak tucked up.

But in Pilates vois[1] he gan to crye,

3125   And swoor by armes and by blood and bones,

"I can° a noble tale for the nones,   *know*

With which I wol now quyte the Knightes tale."

Our Hoste saugh° that he was dronke of ale,   *saw*

And seyde: "abyd, Robin, my leve° brother,   *dear*

3130   Som bettre man shal telle us first another:

Abyd, and lat us werken thriftily."°   *sensibly*

"By goddes soul," quod he, "that wol nat I;

For I wol speke, or elles go my wey."

Our Hoste answerde: "tel on, a devel wey!°   *in the devil's name*

3135   Thou art a fool, thy wit is overcome."

      "Now herkneth,"° quod the Miller, "alle and   *listen*
         some!

But first I make a protestacioun

That I am dronke, I knowe it by my soun;

And therfore, if that I misspeke or seye,

3140   Wyte° it the ale of Southwerk, I yow preye;   *think*

For I wol telle a legende and a lyf

Bothe of a Carpenter, and of his wyf,

How that a clerk hath set the wrightes cappe."[2]

      The Reve answerde and seyde, "stint thy clappe,°   *chatter*

3145   Lat be thy lewed dronken harlotrye.

It is a sinne and eek a greet folye

To apeiren° any man, or him diffame,   *injure*

And eek to bringen wyves in swich fame.

Thou mayst y-nogh of othere thinges seyn."

3150   This dronken Miller spak ful sone ageyn,

And seyde, "leve brother Osewold,

Who hath no wyf, he is no cokewold.°   *cuckold*

But I sey nat therfore that thou art oon;

Ther been ful gode wyves many oon,

3155   And ever a thousand gode ayeyns° oon badde,   *against*

That knowestow wel thy-self, but-if° thou madde.°   *unless / are mad*

Why artow angry with my tale now?

I have a wyf, pardee,° as well as thou,   *by god*

Yet nolde° I, for the oxen in my plogh,   *would not*

3160   Taken up-on me more than y-nogh,

As demen° of my-self that I were oon;   *deeming*

I wol beleve wel that I am noon.

An housbond shal nat been inquisitif

Of goddes privetee,° nor of his wyf.   *private matters*

3165   So° he may finde goddes foyson° there,   *so long as / plenty*

Of the remenant nedeth nat enquere."°   *inquire*

      What sholde I more seyn, but this Millere

He nolde his wordes for no man forbere,

But tolde his cherles tale in his manere;

---

[1] In the medieval mystery plays Pontius Pilate, the governor of Judea when Christ was crucified, spoke loudly and harshly.

[2] I.e., how a clerk got the better of the carpenter.

3170 Me thinketh that I shal reherce° it here.   *retell*
And ther-fore every gentil wight° I preye,   *genteel person*
For goddes love, demeth nat° that I seye   *do not think*
Of evel entente, but that I moot reherce
Hir tales alle, be they bettre or werse,
3175 Or elles falsen° som of my matere.   *falsify*
And therfore, who-so list it nat y-here,
Turne over the leef, and chese another tale;
For he shal finde y-nowe, grete and smale,
Of storial° thing that toucheth gentillesse,   *historical*
3180 And eek moralitee and holinesse;
Blameth nat me if that ye chese amis.
The Miller is a cherl, ye knowe wel this;
So was the Reve, and othere many mo,
And harlotrye they tolden bothe two.
3185 Avyseth yow° and putte me out of blame;   *be advised*
And eek men shal nat make ernest of game.

Here endeth the prologe.

THE MILLERES TALE

Here biginneth the Millere his tale.

Whylom° ther was dwellinge at Oxenford   *once*
A riche gnof,° that gestes° heeld to bord,°   *knave / guests / board*
And of his craft he was a Carpenter.
3190 With him ther was dwellinge a povre° scoler,   *poor*
Had lerned art, but al his fantasye
Was turned for to lerne astrologye,
And coude a certeyn of conclusiouns
To demen by interrogaciouns,[1]
3195 If that men axed° him in certain houres,   *asked*
Whan that men sholde have droghte or elles
    shoures,
Or if men axed him what sholde bifalle
Of every thing, I may nat rekene hem alle.
This clerk was cleped° hende° Nicholas;   *named / courteous*
3200 Of derne° love he coude° and of solas;°   *secret / knew / pleasure*
And ther-to he was sleigh and ful privee,°   *secretive*
And lyk a mayden meke for to see.
A chambre hadde he in that hostelrye
Allone, with-outen any companye,
3205 Ful fetisly° y-dight° with herbes swote,°   *fitly / furnished / sweet*
And he him-self as swete as is the rote
Of licorys, or any cetewale.°   *setwall (a spice)*
His Almageste[2] and bokes grete and smale,

---

[1] I.e., and knew how to reach a certain number of conclusions through interrogations.
[2] A treatise on astrology.

His astrelabie,° longinge for° his art, — *astrolabe / belonging to*
3210 His augrim-stones° layen faire a-part — *counting stones*
On shelves couched° at his beddes heed: — *placed*
His presse° y-covered with a falding° reed. — *cupboard / woolen cloth*
And al above ther lay a gay sautrye,[3]
On which he made a nightes melodye
3215 So swetely, that al the chambre rong;
And *Angelus ad virginem*[4] he song;
And after that he song the kinges note,° — *tune*
Ful often blessed was his mery throte.
And thus this swete clerk his tyme spente
3220 After his freendes finding° and his rente.° — *presents / regular income*
   This Carpenter had wedded newe° a wyf — *recently*
Which that he lovede more than his lyf;
Of eightetene yeer she was of age.
Jalous he was, and heeld hir narwe° in cage, — *closely*
3225 For she was wilde and yong, and he was old,
And demed him-self ben lyk a cokewold.° — *cuckold*
He new nat Catoun,[5] for his wit was rude,
That bad° man sholde wedde his similitude. — *bade*
Men sholde wedden after° hir estaat,° — *according to / state*
3230 For youthe and elde° is often at debaat. — *old age*
But sith that he was fallen in the snare,
He moste endure, as other folk, his care.
   Fair was this yonge wyf, and ther-with-al
As any wesele° hir body gent° and smal. — *weasel / graceful*
3235 A ceynt° she werede barred° al of silk, — *belt / striped*
A barmclooth° eek as whyt as morne milk — *apron*
Up-on hir lendes,° ful of many a gore.° — *loins / pleat*
Whyt was hir smok° and brouded° al bifore — *smock / embroidered*
And eek bihinde, on hir coler° aboute, — *collar*
3240 Of col-blak silk, with-inne and eek with-oute.
The tapes° of hir whyte voluper° — *ribbons / cap*
Were of the same suyte of° hir coler; — *material as*
Hir filet° brood° of silk, and set ful hye: — *headband / broad*
And sikerly° she hadde a likerous° yë. — *certainly / lecherous*
3245 Ful smale° y-pulled° were hir browes two, — *finely / plucked*
And tho were bent, and blake as any sloo.° — *sloe (a plum)*
She was ful more blisful on to see
Than is the newe pere-jonette° tree; — *pear*
And softer than the wolle is of a wether.° — *sheep*
3250 And by hir girdel heeng a purs of lether
Tasseld with silk, and perled° with latoun.° — *studded / brass*
In al this world, to seken up and doun,
There nis no man so wys, that coude thenche° — *think of*
So gay a popelote,° or swich° a wenche. — *doll / such*

---

[3] A psaltery, an ancient stringed instrument.
[4] "The Angel to the Virgin"
[5] Dionysius Cato (fourth-century A.D. Roman author) in whose *Distichs* occurs the maxim cited by the Miller.

3255	Ful brighter was the shyning of hir hewe°	*complexion*
	Than in the tour° the noble° y-forged newe.	*tower / gold coin*
	But of hir song, it was as loude and yerne°	*lively*
	As any swalwe° sittinge on a berne.	*swallow*
	Ther-to she coude skippe and make game,	
3260	As any kide or calf folwinge his dame.	
	Hir mouth was swete as bragot° or the meeth,°	*bragget / mead*
	Or hord of apples leyd in hey or heeth.°	*heather*
	Winsinge° she was, as is a joly colt,	*skittish*
	Long as a mast, and upright as a bolt.°	*arrow*
3265	A brooch she baar up-on hir lowe coler,	
	As brood as is the bos° of a bocler.°	*boss / shield*
	Hir shoes were laced on hir legges hye;	
	She was a prymerole,° a pigges-nye°	*primrose / sweetie*
	For any lord to leggen° in his bedde,	*lay*
3270	Or yet for any good yeman° to wedde.	*yeoman*
	Now sire, and eft° sire, so bifel the cas,	*again*
	That on a day this hende Nicholas	
	Fil° with this yonge wyf to rage° and pleye,	*happened / romp*
	Whyl that hir housbond was at Oseneye,[6]	
3275	As clerkes ben ful subtile and ful queynte;°	*clever*
	And prively he caughte hir by the queynte,°	*crotch*
	And seyde, "y-wis,° but if ich° have my wille,	*truly / I*
	For derne° love of thee, lemman,° I spille."°	*secret / lover / die*
	And heeld hir harde by the haunche-bones,°	*hip bones*
3280	And seyde, "lemman, love me al at-ones,°	*at once*
	Or I wol dyen, also° god me save!"	*so*
	And she sprong as a colt doth in the trave,[7]	
	And with hir heed she wryed° faste awey,	*wriggled*
	And seyde, "I wol nat kisse thee, by my fey,	
3285	Why, lat be," quod she, "lat be, Nicholas,	
	Or I wol crye out harrow° and allas.	*help*
	Do wey° your handes for your curteisye!"	*take away*
	This Nicholas gan mercy for to crye,	
	And spak so faire, and profred hir° so faste,	*propositioned her*
3290	That she hir love him graunted atte laste,	
	And swoor hir ooth, by seint Thomas of Kent,[8]	
	That she wol been at his comandement,	
	Whan that she may hir leyser° wel espye.	*leisure*
	"Myn housbond is so ful of jalousye,	
3295	That but ye wayte wel and been privee,°	*secretive*
	I woot right wel I nam but deed," quod she.	
	"Ye moste been ful derne, as in this cas."	
	"Nay ther-of care thee noght," quod Nicholas,	
	"A clerk had litherly° biset° his whyle,°	*ill / used / time*
3300	But-if he coude a carpenter bigyle."	
	And thus they been acorded and y-sworn	

[6] Oseney, near Oxford.
[7] A frame used in shoeing a restive horse.
[8] St. Thomas à Becket, who was slain in Canterbury Cathedral in Kent in 1170.

To wayte a tyme, as I have told biforn.
Whan Nicholas had doon thus everydeel,
And thakked° hir aboute the lendes° weel,   *stroked / loins*
3305   He kist hir swete, and taketh his sautrye,
And pleyeth faste, and maketh melodye.
Than fil° it thus, that to the parish-chirche,   *befell*
Cristes owne werkes for to wirche,
This gode wyf wente on an haliday;°   *holy day*
3310   Hir forheed shoon as bright as any day,
So was it wasshen whan she leet° hir werk.   *left*
    Now was ther of that chirche a parish-clerk,
The which that was y-cleped° Absolon.   *called*
Crul° was his heer, and as the gold it shoon,   *curly*
3315   And strouted° as a fanne large and brode;   *spread out*
Ful streight and even lay his joly shode.°   *part*
His rode° was reed, his eyen greye as goos;°   *complexion / goose*
With Powles window corven on his shoos,[9]
In hoses° rede he wente fetisly.°   *stockings / fashionably*
3320   Y-clad he was ful smal° and proprely,   *finely*
Al in a kirtel° of a light wachet;°   *tunic / blue*
Ful faire and thikke been the poyntes° set.   *laces*
And ther-up-on he hadde a gay surplys°   *surplice*
As whyt as is the blosme up-on the rys.°   *bough*
3325   A mery child he was, so god me save,
Wel coude he laten° blood and clippe and shave,   *let*
And make a chartre° of lond or acquitaunce.   *title*
In twenty manere coude he trippe and daunce
After the scole of Oxenforde tho,
3330   And with his legges casten° to and fro,   *leap*
And pleyen songes on a small rubible;°   *fiddle*
Ther-to he song som-tyme a loud quinible;°   *falsetto*
And as wel coude he pleye on his giterne.°   *guitar*
In al the toun nas brewhous ne taverne
3335   That he ne visited with his solas,°   *entertainment*
Ther any gaylard° tappestere° was.   *flirtatious / barmaid*
But sooth to seyn, he was somdel squaymous°   *squeamish*
Of farting, and of speche daungerous.°   *fastidious*
    This Absolon, that jolif was and gay,
3340   Gooth with a sencer° on the haliday,   *censer*
Sensinge the wyves of the parish faste;
And many a lovely look on hem he caste,
And namely on this carpenteres wyf.
To loke on hir him thoughte a mery lyf,
3345   She was so propre and swete and likerous.°   *voluptuous*
I dar wel seyn, if she had been a mous,
And he a cat, he wolde hir hente° anon.   *seize*
    This parish-clerk, this joly Absolon,
Hath in his herte swich a love-longinge,
3350   That of no wyf ne took he noon offringe;

---

[9] Absolon's fashionable shoes were latticed like the windows of St. Paul's Cathedral in London.

For curteisye, he seyde, he wolde noon.
The mone, whan it was night, ful brighte shoon,
And Absolon his giterne hath y-take,
For paramours, he thoghte for to wake.
3355 And forth he gooth, jolif and amorous,
Till he cam to the carpenteres hous
A litel after cokkes hadde y-crowe;
And dressed him up by a shot-windowe°   *shuttered window*
That was up-on the carpenteres wal.
3360 He singeth in his vois gentil and smal,
"Now, dere lady, if thy wille be,
I preye yow that ye wol rewe° on me,"   *have pity*
Ful wel acordaunt° to his giterninge.°   *pitched / guitar-playing*
This carpenter awook, and herde him singe,
3365 And spak un-to his wyf, and seyde anon,
"What! Alison! herestow nat Absolon
That chaunteth thus under our boures° wal?"   *bedroom*
And she answerde hir housbond ther-with-al,
"Yis, god wot, John, I here it every-del."
3370   This passeth forth; what wol ye bet° than wel?   *better*
Fro day to day this joly Absolon
So woweth° hir, that him is wo bigon.   *woos*
He waketh al the night and al the day;
He kempte° hise lokkes brode, and made him   *combed*
    gay;
3375 He woweth hir by menes° and brocage,°   *go-betweens / mediation*
And swoor he wolde been hir owne page;
He singeth, brokkinge° as a nightingale;   *quavering*
He sente hir piment,° meeth,° and spyced ale,   *spiced wine / mead*
And wafres,° pyping hote out of the glede;°   *pastries / coals*
3380 And for she was of toune, he profred mede.°   *payment*
For som folk wol ben wonnen for richesse,
And som for strokes, and som for gentillesse.
    Somtyme, to shewe his lightnesse and
        maistrye,°   *virtuosity*
He pleyeth Herodes on a scaffold hye.[10]
3385 But what availleth him as in this cas?
She loveth so this hende Nicholas,
That Absolon may blowe the bukkes horn,[11]
He ne hadde for his labour but a scorn;
And thus she maketh Absolon hir ape,
3390 And al his ernest turneth til a jape.°   *joke*
Ful sooth is this proverbe, it is no lye,
Men seyn right thus, "alwey the nye slye
Maketh the ferre leve to be looth."[12]
For though that Absolon be wood° or wrooth,°   *mad / wrathful*
3395 By-cause that he fer was from hir sighte,

[10] He acted the part of Herod in a nativity play staged on a high platform.
[11] I.e., Absolon will go unrewarded.
[12] "Always the nigh, sly man makes the far-away lover loathed."

This nye° Nicholas stood in his lighte.   *nearby*
  Now bere thee wel, thou hende Nicholas!
For Absolon may waille and singe "allas."
And so bifel it on a Saterday,
3400 This carpenter was goon til° Osenay;   *to*
And hende Nicholas and Alisoun
Acorded been to this conclusioun,
That Nicholas shal shapen him a wyle
This sely° jalous housbond to bigyle;   *naïve*
3405 And if so be the game wente aright,
She sholde slepen in his arm al night,
For this was his desyr and hir also.
And right anon, with-outen wordes mo,
This Nicholas no lenger wolde tarie,
3410 But doth ful softe un-to his chambre carie
Bothe mete and drinke for a day or tweye,°   *two*
And to hir housbonde bad hir for to seye,
If that he axed after Nicholas,
She sholde seye she niste° where he was,   *knew not*
3415 Of al that day she saugh him nat with ye;
She trowed° that he was in maladye,   *believed*
For, for no cry, hir mayde coude him calle;
He nolde answere, for no-thing that mighte falle.
  This passeth forth al thilke° Saterday,   *that*
3420 That Nicholas stille in his chambre lay,
And eet and sleep, or dide what him leste,°   *pleased*
Til Sonday, that the sonne gooth to reste.
  This sely carpenter hath greet merveyle
Of Nicholas, or what thing mighte him eyle,°   *ail*
3425 And seyde, "I am adrad,° by seint Thomas,   *afraid*
It stondeth nat aright with Nicholas.
God shilde° that he deyde sodeynly!   *forbid*
This world is now ful tikel,° sikerly;   *unstable*
I saugh to-day a cors° y-born to chirche   *corpse*
3430 That now, on Monday last, I saugh him wirche.°   *work*
  Go up," quod he un-to his knave anoon,
"Clepe° at his dore, or knokke with a stoon,   *call*
Loke how it is, and tel me boldely."
  This knave gooth him up ful sturdily,
3435 And at the chambre-dore, whyl that he stood,
He cryde and knokked as that he were wood:°   *insane*
"What! how! what do ye, maister Nicholay?
How may ye slepen al the longe day?"
  But al for noght, he herde nat a word;
3440 An hole he fond, ful lowe up-on a bord,
Ther as° the cat was wont in for to crepe;   *where*
And at that hole he looked in ful depe,
And at the laste he hadde of him a sighte.
This Nicholas sat gaping over up-righte,
3445 As he had kyked° on the newe mone.   *gazed*
Adoun he gooth, and tolde his maister sone

In what array he saugh this ilke man.
This carpenter to blessen him bigan,
And seyde, "help us, seinte Frideswyde!"[13]
3450   A man woot° litel what him shal bityde.   *knows*
This man is falle, with his astromye,
In som woodnesse° or in som agonye;   *madness*
I thoghte ay wel how that it sholde be!
Men sholde nat knowe of goddes privetee.°   *secrets*
3455   Ye, blessed be alwey a lewed° man,   *ignorant*
That noght but only his bileve° can!°   *faith / knows*
So ferde° another clerk with astromye;   *fared*
He walked in the feeldes for to prye
Up-on the sterres, what ther sholde bifalle,
3460   Til he was in a marle-pit y-falle;
He saugh nat that. But yet, by seint Thomas,
Me reweth° sore° of hende Nicholas.   *sorrow / greatly*
He shal be rated of° his studying,   *berated for*
If that I may, by Jesus, hevene king!
3465   Get me a staf, that I may underspore,°   *pry up*
Whyl that thou, Robin, hevest up the dore.
He shal out of his studying, as I gesse"—
And to the chambre-dore he gan him dresse.°   *address*
His knave was a strong carl° for the nones,°   *fellow / task*
3470   And by the haspe he haf° it up atones,°   *heaved / at once*
In-to the floor the dore fil anon.
This Nicholas sat ay as stille as stoon,
And ever gaped upward in-to the eir.
This carpenter wende° he were in despeir,   *thought*
3475   And hente° him by the sholdres mightily,   *grasped*
And shook him harde, and cryde spitously,°   *harshly*
"What! Nicholay! what, how! what! loke adoun!
Awake, and thenk on Cristes passioun;
I crouche° thee from elves and fro wightes!"°   *exorcise / creatures*
3480   Ther-with the night-spel seyde he anon-rightes°   *immediately*
On foure halves° of the hous aboute,   *sides*
And on the threshfold of the dore withoute:—
     "Jesu Crist, and sëynt Benedight,°   *St. Benedict*
Blesse this hous from every wikked wight,
3485   For nightes verye,[14] the white *paternoster!*°   *Lord's prayer*
Where wentestow, seynt Petres soster?°   *sister*
And atte laste this hende Nicholas
Gan for to syke° sore, and seyde, "allas!   *sigh*
Shal al the world be lost eftsones° now?"   *again*
3490   This carpenter answerde, "what seystow?
What! thenk on god, as we don, men that
     swinke."°   *work*
This Nicholas answerde, "fecche me drinke;

---

[13] The patron saint of Oxford.
[14] Possibly a contraction of *venerye* meaning "hanky-panky," or else a variant of *werye* meaning "worry"—hence, *for night's worry*.

And after wol I speke in privetee
Of certeyn thing that toucheth me and thee;
3495   I wol telle it non other man, certeyn.''
    This carpenter goth doun, and comth ageyn,
And broghte of mighty ale a large quart;
And whan that each of hem had dronke his part,
This Nicholas his dore faste shette,
3500   And doun the carpenter by him he sette.
    He seyde, ''John, myn hoste lief° and dere,   *beloved*
Thou shalt up-on thy trouthe° swere me here,   *word of honor*
That to no wight thou shalt this conseil° wreye;°   *advice / betray*
For it is Cristes conseil that I seye,
3505   And if thou telle it man,° thou are forlore,°   *to anyone / lost*
For this vengaunce thou shalt han° therfore,   *have*
That if thou wreye me, thou shalt be wood!''
''Nay, Crist forbede it, for his holy blood!''
Quod tho° this sely man, ''I nam no labbe,°   *then / blabber*
3510   Ne, though I seye, I name nat lief° to gabbe.   *likely*
Sey what thou wolt, I shal it never telle
To child ne wyf, by him that harwed° helle!''[15]   *harrowed*
''Now John,'' quod Nicholas, ''I wol nat lye;
I have y-founde in myn astrologye,
3515   As I have loked in the mone bright,
That now, a Monday next, at quarter-night,°   *nearly dawn*
Shal falle a reyn and that so wilde and wood,
That half so greet was never Noës° flood.   *Noah's*
This world,'' he seyde, ''in lasse than in an hour
3520   Shal al be dreynt,° so hidous is the shour;   *drowned*
Thus shal mankynde drenche° and lese° hir lyf.''   *drown / lose*
    This carpenter answerde, ''allas, my wyf!
And shal she drenche? allas! myn Alisoun!''
For sorwe of this he fil almost adoun,
3425   And seyde, ''is ther no remedie in this cas?''
''Why, yis, for gode,'' quod hende Nicholas,
''If thou wolt werken after lore° and reed;°   *learning / advice*
Thou mayst nat werken after thyn owene heed.°   *head*
For thus seith Salomon, that was ful trewe,
3530   ''Work al by conseil, and thou shalt nat rewe.'°   *repent*
And if thou werken wolt by good conseil,
I undertake, with-outen mast and seyl,°   *sail*
Yet shal I saven hir and thee and me.
Hastow nat herd how saved was Noë,
3535   Whan that our lord had warned him biforn
That al the world with water sholde be lorn?''°   *lost*
    ''Yis,'' quod this carpenter, ''ful yore ago.''
    ''Hastow nat herd,'' quod Nicholas, ''also
The sorwe of Noë with his felawshipe,
3540   Er that he mighte gete his wyf to shipe?
Him had be lever,° I dar wel undertake,   *more happy*

---

[15] Many Christians believe that Christ descended into Hell between his crucifixion and his resurrection to bring the just out of Limbo.

At thilke tyme, than alle hise wetheres° blake,   *rams*
That she hadde had a ship hir-self allone.
And ther-fore, wostou° what is best to done?   *do you know*
3545   This asketh haste, and of an hastif° thing   *urgent*
Men may nat preche or maken tarying.
   Anon go gete us faste in-to this in°   *inn*
A kneding-trogh, or elles a kimelin,°   *tub*
For ech of us, but loke that they be large,
3550   In whiche we mowe° swimme° as in a barge,   *may / float*
And han ther-inne vitaille° suffisant   *victuals*
But for a day; fy on the remenant!
The water shal aslake° and goon away   *abate*
Aboute pryme° up-on the nexte day.   *daybreak*
3555   But Robin may nat wite° of this, thy knave,   *know*
Ne eek° thy mayde Gille I may nat save;   *also*
Axe nat why, for though thou aske me,
I wol nat tellen goddes privetee.
Suffiseth thee, but if° thy wittes madde,°   *unless / go mad*
3560   To han° as greet° a grace as Noë hadde.   *have / great*
Thy wyf shal I wel saven, out of doute,
Go now thy wey, and speed thee heeraboute.
   But whan thou hast, for hir and thee and me,
Y-geten us thise kneding-tubbes three,
3565   Than shaltow hange hem in the roof ful hye,
That no man of our purveyaunce° spye.   *preparations*
And whan thou thus hast doon as I have seyd,
And hast our vitaille faire in hem y-leyd,
And eek an ax, to smyte the corde atwo
3570   When that the water comth, that we may go,
And broke an hole an heigh,° up-on the gable,   *on high*
Unto the gardin-ward,° over the stable,   *garden-side*
That we may frely passen forth our way
Whan that the grete shour is goon away—
3575   Than shaltow swimme as myrie, I undertake,
As doth the whyte doke° after hir drake.   *duck*
Than wol I clepe, "how! Alison! how! John!
Be myrie, for the flood wol passe anon.'
And thou wolt seyn, "hayl, maister Nicholay!
3580   Good morwe, I se thee wel, for it is day.'
And than shul we be lordes al our lyf
Of al the world, as Noë and his wyf.
   But of o thyng I warne thee ful right,
Be wel avysed, on that ilke night
3585   That we ben entred in-to shippes bord,
That noon of us ne speke nat a word,
Ne clepe, ne crye, but been in his preyere;
For it is goddes owne heste dere.°   *dear behest*
   Thy wyf and thou mote hange fer a-twinne,°   *apart*
3590   For that bitwixe yow shal be no sinne
No more in looking than ther shal in dede;
This ordinance is seyd, go, god thee spede!
Tomorwe at night, whan men ben alle aslepe,

In-to our kneding-tubbes wol we crepe,
3595 And sitten ther, abyding goddes grace.
Go now thy wey, I have no lenger space
To make of this no lenger sermoning.
Men seyn thus, "send the wyse, and sey no-thing;"[16]
Thou art so wys, it nedeth thee nat teche;
3600 Go, save our lyf, and that I thee biseche."
      This sely carpenter goth forth his wey.
Ful ofte he seith "allas" and "weylawey,"
And to his wyf he tolde his privetee;°   *secret*
And she was war,° and knew it bet° than he,   *aware / better*
3605 What al this queynte cast° was for to seye.   *device*
But nathelees she ferde° as she wolde deye,   *pretended*
And seyde, "allas! go forth thy wey anon,
Help us to scape,° or we ben lost echon;°   *escape / each one*
I am thy trewe verray wedded wyf;
3610 Go, dere spouse, and help to save our lyf."
      Lo! which a greet thyng is affeccioun!°   *emotion*
Men may dye of imaginacioun,
So depe may impressioun be take.
This sely carpenter biginneth quake;
3615 Him thinketh verraily that he may see
Noës flood come walwing° as the see   *tumbling*
To drenchen Alisoun, his hony dere.
He wepeth, weyleth, maketh sory chere,
He syketh with ful many a sory swogh.°   *sound*
3620 He gooth and geteth him a kneding-trogh,
And after that a tubbe and a kimelin,
And prively he sente hem to his in,°   *house*
And heng hem in the roof in privetee.
His owne hand he made laddres three,
3625 To climben by the ronges and the stalkes°   *uprights*
Un-to the tubbes hanginge in the balkes,°   *beams*
And hem vitailled,° bothe trogh and tubbe,   *stocked*
With breed and chese, and good ale in a jubbe,°   *jug*
Suffysinge right y-nogh as for a day.
3630 But er° that he had maad al this array,°   *before / arrangements*
He sente his knave, and eek his wenche also,
Up-on his nede° to London for to go.   *need or business*
And on the Monday, whan it drow to night,
He shette his dore with-oute candel-light,
3635 And dressed° al thing as it sholde be,   *set up*
And shortly, up they clomben alle three;
They sitten stille wel a furlong-way.[17]
      "Now, *Pater-noster,* clom!"° seyde Nicholay,   *clam up*
And "clom," quod John, and "clom," seyde
            Alisoun.
3640 This carpenter seyde his devocioun,°   *prayers*
And stille he sit, and biddeth his preyere,

---

[16] "A word to the wise is enough."
[17] The time it takes to walk a furlong (1/8 mile).

Awaytinge on the reyn, if he it here.
The dede sleep, for wery bisinesse,
Fil° on this carpenter right, as I gesse,   *Fell*
3645   Aboute corfew-tyme,° or litel more;   *curfew time (dusk)*
For travail° of his goost° he groneth sore,   *suffering / spirit*
And eft° he routeth,° for his heed mislay.   *later / snores*
Doun of the laddre stalketh Nicholay.
And Alisoun, ful softe adoun she spedde;
3650   With-outen wordes mo, they goon to bedde
Ther-as the carpenter is wont to lye.
Ther was the revel and the melodye;
And thus lyth Alison and Nicholas,
In bisinesse of mirthe and of solas,°   *pleasure*
3655   Til that the belle of laudes° gan to ringe,   *lauds (before dawn)*
And freres in the chauncel° gonne singe.   *chancel*
This parish-clerk, this amorous Absolon,
That is for love alwey so wo bigon,
Up-on the Monday was at Oseneye
3660   With companye, him to disporte and pleye,
And axed up-on cas° a cloisterer   *chance*
Ful prively after John the carpenter;
And he drough him a-part out of the chirche,
And seyde, "I noot,° I saugh him here   *know not*
    nat wirche
3665   Sin Saterday; I trow that he be went
For timber, ther our abbot hath him sent;
For he is wont for timber for to go,
And dwellen at the grange° a day or two;   *farm*
Or elles he is at his house, certeyn;
3670   Wher that he be, I can nat sothly° seyn."   *truthfully*
This Absolon ful joly was and light,
And thoghte, "now is tyme wake° al night;   *to wake*
For sikirly° I saugh him nat stiringe   *certainly*
Aboute his dore sin day bigan to springe.
3675   So moot I thryve, I shal, at cokkes crowe,
Ful prively knokken at his windowe
That stant ful lowe up-on his boures wal.°   *bedroom wall*
To Alison now wol I tellen al
My love-longing, for yet I shal nat misse
3680   That at the leste wey I shal hir kisse.
Som maner confort shal I have, parfay,°   *in faith*
My mouth hath icched° al this longe day;   *itched*
That is a signe of kissing atte leste.
Al night me mette° eek, I was at a feste.   *dreamed*
3685   Therfor I wol gon slepe an houre or tweye.
And al the night than wol I wake and pleye."
Whan that the firste cok hath crowe, anon
Up rist° this joly lover Absolon,   *rised*
And him arrayeth gay, at point-devys.°   *meticulously*
3690   But first he cheweth greyn[18] and lycorys,

---

[18] Grain of Paradise, a spice.

To smellen swete, er he had kembd° his heer.   *combed*
Under his tonge a trewe love° he beer,   *a four-leafed herb*
For ther-by wende° he to ben gracious.°   *supposed / attractive*
He rometh to the carpenteres hous,

3695   And stille he stant under the shot-windowe;
Un-to his brest it raughte,° it was so lowe;   *reached*
And softe he cogheth with a semi-soun°—   *low voice*
"What do ye, honey-comb, swete Alisoun?
My faire brid, my swete cinamome,°   *cinnamon*

3700   Awaketh, lemman myn,° and speketh to me!   *my love*
Wel litel thenken ye up-on my wo,
That for your love I swete° ther I go.   *sweat*
No wonder is thogh that I swelte° and swete;   *swelter*
I moorne as doth a lamb after the tete.°   *teat*

3705   Y-wis, lemman, I have swich love-longinge,
That lyk a turtel° trewe is my moorninge;   *turtledove*
I may nat ete na more than a mayde."
    "Go fro the window, Jakke fool," she sayde,
"As help me god, it wol nat be "com ba° me,'   *kiss*

3710   I love another, and elles I were to blame,
Wel bet than thee, by Jesu, Absolon!
Go forth thy wey, or I wol caste a ston,
And lat me slepe, a twenty devel wey!"
    "Allas," quod Absolon, "and weylawey!

3715   That trewe love was ever so yvel° biset!   *evilly*
Than kisse me, sin° it may be no bet,   *since*
For Jesus love and for the love of me."
    "Wiltow than go thy wey ther-with?" quod she.
    "Ye, certes, lemman," quod this Absolon.

3720   "Thanne make thee redy," quod she, "I come
        anon;"
And un-to Nicholas she seyde stille,°   *softly*
"Now hust,° and thou shalt laughen al thy fille."   *hush*
This Absolon doun sette him on his knees,
And seyde, "I am a lord at all degrees;°   *accounts*

3725   For after this I hope ther cometh more!
Lemman, thy grace, and swete brid, thyn ore!"
    The window she undoth, and that in haste,
"Have do," quod she, "com of, and speed thee
        faste,
Lest that our neighebores thee espye."

3730   This Absolon gan wype his mouth ful drye;
Derk was the night as pich, or as the cole,
And at the window out she putte hir hole,
And Absolon, him fil no bet no wers,
But with his mouth he kiste hir naked ers°   *ass*

3735   Ful savourly,° er he was war° of this.   *savorily / aware*
Abak he sterte,° and thoghte it was amis,   *started*
For wel he wiste a womman hath no berd;
He felte a thing al rough and long y-herd,°   *haired*
And seyde, "fy! allas! what have I do?"

3740	"Tehee!" quod she, and clapte the window to;	
	And Absolon goth forth a sory pas.°	*at a sad pace*
	"A berd, a berd!" quod hende Nicholas.	
	"By goddes *corpus*,° this goth faire and weel!"	*body*
	This sely Absolon herde every deel,°	*bit*
3745	And on his lippe he gan for anger byte;	
	And to him-self he seyde, "I shal thee quyte!"°	*requite*
	Who rubbeth now, who froteth° now his	*scrubs*
	lippes	
	With dust, with sond, with straw, with clooth,	
	with chippes,	
	But Absolon, that seith ful ofte, "allas!	
3750	My soule bitake° I un-to Sathanas,°	*commend / Satan*
	But me wer lever° than al this toun," quod he,	*more eager*
	"Of this despyt awroken° for to be!	*avenged*
	Allas!" quod he, "allas! I ne hadde y-bleynt!"[19]	
	His hote love was cold and al y-queynt;°	*quenched*
3755	For fro that tyme that he had kiste hir ers,	
	Of paramours he sette° nat a kers,°	*cared / cress*
	For he was heled° of his maladye;	*healed*
	Ful ofte paramours he gan deffye,	
	And weep as dooth a child that is y-bete.°	*beaten*
3760	A softe paas° he wente over the strete	*quietly*
	Un-til a smith men cleped daun° Gerveys,	*master*
	That in his forge smithed plough-harneys,°	*plough fittings*
	He sharpeth shaar° and culter° bisily.	*plowshare / coulter*
	This Absolon knokketh al esily,°	*softly*
3765	And seyde, "undo, Gerveys, and that anon."	
	"What, who artow?" "It am I, Absolon."	
	"What, Absolon! for Cristes swete tree,°	*cross*
	Why ryse ye so rathe,° ey, *ben'cite!*°	*early / bless me*
	What eyleth yow? som gay gerl, god it woot,	
3770	Hath broght yow thus up-on the viritoot;	
	By sëynt Note,[20] ye woot wel what I mene."	
	This Absolon ne roghte° nat a bene°	*cared / bean*
	Of al his pley, no word agayn he yaf;	
	He hadde more tow on his distaf[21]	
3775	Than Gerveys knew, and seyde, "freend so dere,	
	That hote culter° in the chimenee here,	*hot iron plow-blade*
	As lene° it me, I have ther-with to done,	*Please loan*
	And I wol bringe it thee agayn ful sone."	
	Gerveys answered, "certes, were it gold,	
3780	Or in a poke nobles° alle untold,	*coins in a poke (bag)*
	Thou sholdest have, as I am trewe smith;	
	Ey, Cristes foo! what wol ye do ther-with?"	
	"Ther-of," quod Absolon, "be as be may;	
	I shal wel telle it thee to-morwe day"—	

[19] I.e., Alas, that I had not turned aside!
[20] St. Neot, who lived during the ninth century A.D.
[21] More tow on his distaff—hence, more on his mind.

3785 And caughte the culter by the colde stele.
Ful softe out at the dore he gan to stele,
And wente un-to the carpenteres wal.
He cogheth first, and knokketh ther-with-al
Upon the windowe, right as he dide er.
3790   This Alison answerde, "Who is ther
That knokketh so? I warante° it a theef."   *bet*
   "Why, nay," quod he, "god woot, my swete
      leef,°   *beloved*
I am thyn Absolon, my dereling!
Of gold," quod he, "I have thee broght a ring;
3795 My moder yaf it me, so god me save,
Ful fyn it is, and ther-to wel y-grave;°   *engraved*
This wol I yeve thee, if thou me kisse!"
   This Nicholas was risen for to pisse,
And thoghte he wolde amenden° al the jape,°   *improve / joke*
3800 He sholde kisse his ers er that he scape.
And up the windowe dide he hastily,
And out his ers he putteth prively
Over the buttok, to the haunche-bon;°   *thigh-bone*
And ther-with spak this clerk, this Absolon,
3805 "Spek, swete brid, I noot nat wher thou art."
   This Nicholas anon leet flee° a fart,   *fly*
As greet as it had been a thonder-dent,°   *thunderclap*
That with the strook he was almost y-blent;°   *blinded*
And he was redy with his iren hoot,
3810 And Nicholas amidde the ers he smoot.°   *smote*
   Of gooth° the skin an hande-brede° aboute, *off goes / handsbreadth*
The hote culter brende so his toute,°   *rump*
And for the smert he wende for° to dye.   *hoped*
As he were wood,° for wo he gan to crye— *out of his mind*
3815 "Help! water! water! help, for goddes herte!"
   This carpenter out of his slomber sterte,
And herde oon cryen "water" as he were wood,
And thoghte, "Allas! now comth Nowélis flood!"
He sit him up with-outen wordes mo,
3820 And with his ax he smoot the corde a-two,
And doun goth al; he fond neither to selle,
Ne breed ne ale, til he cam to the selle
Up-on the floor;[22] and ther aswowne° he lay.   *unconscious*
   Up sterte hir Alison, and Nicholay,
3825 And cryden "out" and "harrow" in the strete.
The neighebores, bothe smale and grete,
In ronnen, for to gauren° on this man,   *stare*
That yet aswowne he lay, bothe pale and wan;
For with the fal he brosten° hadde his arm;   *broken*
3830 But stonde he moste un-to his owne harm.
For whan he spak, he was anon° bore doun° *at once / borne down*
With hende Nicholas and Alisoun.

---

[22] He found time to sell neither bread nor ale until he hit the floor.

They tolden every man that he was wood,
He was agast so of "Nowélis flood"
3835   Thurgh fantasye, that of his vanitee
He hadde y-boght him kneding-tubbes three.
And hadde hem hanged in the roof above;
And that he preyed hem, for goddes love,
To sitten in the roof, *par companye.*°   *for company*
3840   The folk gan laughen at his fantasye;
In-to the roof they kyken° and they gape,   *gaze*
And turned al his harm un-to a jape.
For what so that this carpenter answerde,
It was for noght, no man his reson herde;
3845   With othes° grete he was so sworn adoun,   *oaths, curses*
That he was holden wood in al the toun;
For every clerk anon-right heeld with other.
They seyde, "the man is wood, my leve brother;"
And every wight gan laughen of this stryf.°   *strife*
3850   Thus swyved° was the carpenteres wyf,   *seduced*
For al his keping and his jalousye;
And Absolon hath kist hir nether° ye;   *bottom*
And Nicholas is scalded in the toute.°   *rump*
This tale is doon, and god save al the route!°   *company*

                        [ca. 1390]

❧ RENAISSANCE POETRY ❧

Sir Thomas Wyatt   *1503–1542*

"MY GALLEY, CHARGÈD WITH FORGETFULNESS"[1]

My galley, chargèd with forgetfulness,
  Through sharp seas, in winter nights, doth pass
'Tween rock and rock; and eke° mine enemy, alas,   *also*
That is my lord, steereth with cruelness.
5 And, every oar, a thought in readiness,
  As though that death were light in such a case.
  An endless wind doth tear the sail apace,
Of forcèd sighs, and trusty fearfulness.
A rain of tears, a cloud of dark disdain,
10 Hath done the wearied cords great hinderance,
  Wreathèd with error, and eke with ignorance.
The stars be hid, that led me to this pain.
Drownèd is reason, that should me comfort;[2]
And I remain, despairing of the port.

                  [posthumous, 1557]

Elizabeth I, Queen of England   *1533–1603*

ON MONSIEUR'S DEPARTURE

I grieve and dare not show my discontent,
I love and yet am forced to seem to hate,
I do, yet dare not say I ever meant,
I seem stark mute but inwardly do prate.
5 I am and not, I freeze and yet am burned,
  Since from myself another self I turned.

My care is like my shadow in the sun,
Follows me flying, flies when I pursue it,
Stands and lies by me, doth what I have done.
10 His too familiar care doth make me rue it.
  No means I find to rid him from my breast,
  Till by the end of things it be suppressed.

Some gentler passion slide into my mind,
For I am soft and made of melting snow;
15 Or be more cuel, love, and so be kind.

---

[1] In Richard Tottel's *Songs and Sonnets* (1557) this poem is given the title "The Lover Compareth His State to a Ship in Perilous Storm Tossed on the Sea."
[2] Some versions of the poem read "consort" for "comfort."

Let me or float or sink, be high or low.
Or let me live with some more sweet content,
Or die and so forget what love ere meant.

[ca. 1600]

Edmund Spenser *1552–1599*

THE FAERIE QUEENE

FROM *Book I, Canto I*

A Gentle Knight was pricking° on the plaine, *spurring*
Y cladd in mightie armes and silver shielde,
Wherein old dints of deepe wounds did remaine,
The cruell markes of many a bloudy fielde;
5 Yet armes till that time did he never wield:
His angry steede did chide his foming bitt,
As much disdayning to the curbe to yield:
Full jolly° knight he seemd, and faire did sitt, *handsome*
As one for knightly giusts° and fierce encounters fitt. *jousts*

10 But on his brest a bloudie Crosse he bore,
The deare remembrance of his dying Lord,
For whose sweete sake that glorious badge he wore,
And dead as living ever him ador'd:
Upon his shield the like was also scor'd,
15 For soveraine° hope, which in his helpe he had: *powerful*
Right faithful true he was in deede and word,
But of his cheere° did seeme too solemne sad; *expression*
Yet nothing did he dread, but ever was ydrad.° *dreaded*

Upon a great adventure he was bond,° *bound*
20 That greatest *Gloriana* to him gave,
That greatest Glorious Queene of *Faerie* lond,
To winne him worship, and her grace to have,
Which of all earthly things he most did crave;
And ever as he rode, his hart did earne° *yearn*
25 To prove his puissance° in battell brave *might*
Upon his foe, and his new force to learne;
Upon his foe, a Dragon horrible and stearne.

A lovely Ladie rode him faire beside,
Upon a lowly Asse more white then snow,
30 Yet she much whiter, but the same did hide
Under a vele,° that wimpled° was full low, *veil / folded*
And over all a blacke stole she did throw,
As one that inly mournd: so was she sad,

And heavie sat upon her palfrey° slow: *a gentle horse*
35   Seemed in heart some hidden care she had,
And by her in a line° a milke white lambe she lad.°   *leash / led*

So pure an innocent, as that same lambe,
She was in life and every vertuous lore,
And by descent from Royall lynage came
40   Of ancient Kings and Queenes, that had of yore
Their scepters stretcht from East to Westerne shore,
And all the world in their subjection held;
Till that infernal feend with foule uprore
Forwasted° all their land, and them expeld: *destroyed*
45   Whom to avenge, she had this Knight from far
compeld.°   *summoned*

Behind her farre away a Dwarfe did lag,
That lasie seemd in being ever last,
Or wearièd with bearing of her bag
Of needments at his backe. Thus as they past,
50   The day with cloudes was suddeine overcast,
And angry *Jove* an hideous storme of raine
Did poure into his Lemans lap° so fast,   *lover's lap (earth)*
That every wight° to shrowd° it did constrain,   *creature / shelter*
And this faire couple eke° to shroud themselves were   *also*
fain.°   *eager*

55   Enforst° to seeke some covert° nigh at hand,   *Forced / cover*
A shadie grove not far away they spide,
That promist ayde the tempest to withstand:
Whose loftie trees yclad with sommers pride,
Did spred so broad, that heavens light did hide,
60   Not perceable° with power of any starre: *pierceable*
And all within were pathes and alleies wide,
With footing worne, and leading inward farre:
Faire harbour that them seems; so in they entred arre.

And foorth they passe, with pleasure forward led,
65   Joying to heare the birdes sweete harmony,
Which therein shrouded from the tempest dred,
Seemd in their song to scorne the cruell sky.
Much can° they prayse the trees so straight and hy,   *did*
The sayling Pine, the Cedar proud and tall,
70   The vine-prop Elme, the Poplar never dry,
The builder Oake, sole king of forrests all,
The Aspine good for staves, the Cypresse funerall.

The Laurell, meed° of mightie Conquerors   *reward*
And Poets sage, the Firre that weepeth still,°   *always*
75   The Willow worne of forlorne Paramours,
The Eugh° obedient to the benders will,   *yew*
The Birch for shaftes, the Sallow° for the mill,   *goat willow*

   The Mirrhe sweete bleeding in the bitter wound,[1]
    The warlike Beech, the Ash for nothing ill,
80   The fruitfull Olive, and the Platane° round,   *plane tree*
   The carver Holme,° the Maple seeldom inward sound.   *holm oak*

   Led with delight, they thus beguile the way,
    Untill the blustring storme is overblowne;
    When weening° to returne, whence they did stray,   *thinking*
85   They cannot finde that path, which first was showne,
    But wander too and fro in wayes unknowne,
    Furthest from end then, when they neerest weene,° *think themselves*
    That makes them doubt, their wits be not their owne:
    So many pathes, so many turnings seene,
90   That which of them to take, in diverse doubt they been.

   At last resolving forward still to fare,
    Till that some end they finde or° in or out,   *either*
    That path they take, that beaten seemd most bare,
    And like to lead the labyrinth about;°   *without*
95   Which when by tract° they hunted had throughout, *lapse of time*
    At length it brought them to a hollow cave,
    Amid the thickest woods. The Champion stout
    Eftsoones° dismounted from his courser brave,   *Then*
  And to the Dwarfe a while his needlesse spere he gave.

100 Be well aware, quoth then that Ladie milde,
    Least suddaine mischiefe ye too rash provoke:
    The danger hid, the place unknowne and wilde,
    Breedes dreadfull doubts: Oft fire is without smoke,
    And perill without show: therefore your stroke
105   Sir knight with-hold, till further triall made.
    Ah Ladie (said he) shame were to revoke
    The forward footing for° an hidden shade: *on account of*
  Vertue gives her selfe light, through darkenesse for to
    wade.

   Yea but (quoth she) the perill of this place
110   I better wot° then you, though now too late   *know*
    To wish you backe returne with foule disgrace,
    Yet wisedome warnes, whilest foot is in the gate,
    To stay the steppe, ere forcèd to retrate.°   *retreat*
    This is the wandring wood, this *Errours den,*
115   A monster vile, whom God and man does hate:
    Therefore I read° beware. Fly fly (quoth then   *advise*
  The fearefull Dwarfe:) this is no place for living men.

   But full of fire and greedy hardiment,
    The youthfull knight could not for ought be staide,

[1] Myrrh is obtained from cuts ("wounds") in the tree's bark.

120 But forth unto the darksome hole he went,
     And lookèd in: his glistring armor made
     A litle glooming light, much like a shade,
     By which he saw the ugly monster plaine,
     Halfe like a serpent horribly displaide,
125   But th'other halfe did womans shape retaine,
     Most lothsom, filthie, foule, and full of vile disdaine.

     And as she lay upon the durtie ground,
     Her huge long taile her den all overspred,
     Yet was in knots and many boughtes° upwound,   *coils*
130 Pointed with mortall sting. Of her there bred
     A thousand yong ones, which she dayly fed,
     Sucking upon her poisonous dugs, eachone
     Of sundry shapes, yet all ill favorèd:
     Soone as that uncouth° light upon them shone,   *unfamiliar*
135 Into her mouth they crept, and suddain all were gone.

     Their dam upstart, out of her den effraide,°   *frightened*
     And rushed forth, hurling her hideous taile
     About her cursèd head, whose folds displaid
     Were stretcht now forth at length without entraile.°   *windings*
140 She lookt about, and seeing one in mayle
     Armèd to point,° sought back to turne againe;   *to the teeth*
     For light she hated as the deadly bale,°   *harm*
     Ay° wont in desert darknesse to remaine,   *Always*
     Where plaine none might her see, nor she see any
         plaine.

145 Which when the valiant Elfe° perceiv'd, he lept   *fairy knight*
     As Lyon fierce upon the flying pray,
     And with his trenchand° blade her boldly kept   *sharp*
     From turning backe, and forcèd her to stay:
     Therewith enrag'd she loudly gan to bray,
150 And turning fierce, her speckled taile advaunst,
     Threatning her angry sting, him to dismay:
     Who nought aghast, his mightie hand enhaunst:°   *lifted*
     The stroke down from her head unto her shoulder
         glaunst.°   *glanced*

     Much daunted with that dint,° her sence was dazd,   *stroke*
155 Yet kindling rage, her selfe she gathered round,
     And all attonce her beastly body raizd
     With doubled forces high above the ground:
     Tho° wrapping up her wrethèd sterne° arownd,   *Then / tail*
     Lept fierce upon his shield, and her huge traine°   *tail*
160 All suddenly about his body wound,
     That hand or foot to stirre he strove in vaine:
     God helpe the man so wrapt in *Errours* endlesse traine.°   *course*

His Lady sad to see his sore constraint,
    Cride out, Now now Sir knight, shew what ye bee,
165   Add faith unto your force, and be not faint:
    Strangle her, else she sure will strangle thee.
    That when he heard, in great perplexitie,
    His gall did grate for griefe° and high disdaine,   *wrath*
    And knitting all his force got one hand free,
170   Wherewith he grypt her gorge with so great paine,
That soone to loose her wicked bands did her
      constraine.

Therewith she spewd out of her filthy maw°   *gut*
    A floud of poyson horrible and blacke,
    Full of great lumpes of flesh and gobbets° raw,   *fragments*
175   Which stunck so vildly,° that it forst him slacke   *vilely*
    His grasping hold, and from her turne him backe:
    Her vomit full of bookes and papers was,
    With loathly frogs and toades, which eyes did lacke,
    And creeping sought way in the weedy gras:
180 Her filthy parbreake° all the place defilèd has.   *vomit*

As when old father *Nilus* gins to swell
    With timely pride above the *Aegyptian* vale,
    His fattie° waves do fertile slime outwell,   *greasy*
    And overflow each plaine and lowly dale:
185   But when his later spring° gins to avale,°   *flood / abate*
    Huge heapes of mudd he leaves, wherein there
      breed
    Ten thousand kindes of creatures, partly male
    And partly female of his fruitfull seed;
Such ugly monstrous shapes elsewhere may no man
    reed.°   *see*

190 The same so sore annoyèd has the knight,
    That welnigh chokèd with the deadly stinke,
    His forces faile, ne° can no longer fight.   *nor*
    Whose corage when the feend perceiv'd to shrinke,
195   She pourèd forth out of her hellish sinke
    Her fruitfull cursèd spawne of serpents small,
    Deformèd monsters, fowle, and blacke as inke,
    Which swarming all about his legs did crall,
And him encombred sore, but could not hurt at all.

As gentle Shepheard in sweete even-tide,
200   When ruddy *Phoebus* gins to welke° in west,   *sink*
    High on an hill, his flocke to vewen° wide,   *view*
    Markes which do byte their hasty supper best;
    A cloud of combrous gnattes do him molest,
    All striving to infixe their feeble stings,
205   That from their noyance° he no where can rest,   *annoyance*

But with his clownish hands their tender wings
He brusheth oft, and oft doth mar their murmurings.

Thus ill bestedd,° and fearefull more of shame,   *situated*
   Then of the certaine perill he stood in,
210   Halfe furious° unto his foe he came,   *mad*
   Resolv'd in minde all suddenly to win,
   Or soone to lose, before he once would lin;°   *cease*
   And strooke at her with more than manly force,
   That from her body full of filthie sin
215   He raft° her hatefull head without remorse;   *cut off*
A streame of cole bloud forth gushed from her corse.°   *corpse*

Her scattred brood, soone as their Parent deare
   They saw so rudely falling to the ground,
   Groning full deadly, all with troublous feare,
220   Gathred themselves about her body round,
   Weening their wonted entrance to have found
   At her wide mouth: but being there withstood
   They flockèd all about her bleeding wound,
   And suckèd up their dying mothers blood,
225   Making her death their life, and eke her hurt their
      good.

That detestable sight him much amazde,
   To see th'unkindly Impes° of heaven accurst,   *young demons*
   Devoure their dam;° on whom while so he gazd,   *mother*
   Having all satisfide their bloudy thurst,
230   Their bellies swolne he saw with fulnesse burst,
   And bowels gushing forth: well worthy end
   Of such as drunke her life, the which them nurst;
   Now needeth him no lenger labour spend,
His foes have slaine themselves, with whom he should
      contend.

235   His Ladie seeing all, that chaunst, from farre
   Approcht in hast to greet his victorie,
   And said, Faire knight, borne under happy starre,
   Who see your vanquisht foes before you lye;
   Well worthy be you of that Armorie,°   *coat of arms*
240   Wherein ye have great glory wonne this day,
   And proov'd your strength on a strong enimie,
   Your first adventure: many such I pray,
And henceforth ever wish, that like succeed it may.

                            [1590]

"ONE DAY I WROTE HER NAME UPON THE STRAND"

One day I wrote her name upon the strand,°   *beach*
But came the waves and washed it away:
Again I wrote it with a second hand,
But came the tide and made my pains his prey.
5   "Vain man," said she, "that doest in vain assay,
A mortal thing so to immortalize,
For I myself shall like to this decay,
And eek° my name be wiped out likewise."   *also*
"Not so," quod° I, "let baser things devise   *said*
10   To die in dust, but you shall live by fame:
My verse your virtues rare shall eternize,
And in the heavens write your glorious name.
Where whenas death shall all the world subdue,
Our love shall live, and later life renew."

[1595]

Sir Walter Raleigh   *1552–1618*

[THE NYMPH'S REPLY TO THE SHEPHERD][1]

If all the world and love were young,
And truth in every shepherd's tongue,
These pretty pleasures might me move
To live with thee and be thy love.

5   Time drives flocks from field to fold;
When rivers rage and rocks grow cold;
And Philomel[2] becometh dumb;
The rest complain of cares to come.

The flowers do fade, and wanton fields
10   To wayward winter reckoning yields:
A honey tongue, a heart of gall,
Is fancy's spring, but sorrow's fall.

Thy gowns, thy shoes, thy beds of roses,
Thy cap, thy kirtle,° and thy posies,   *dress*

[1] This poem was written in answer to Christopher Marlowe's "The Passionate Shepherd to His Love" (1599).
[2] One of the myths in Ovid's *Metamorphoses* (ca. 8 A.D.) relates that Philomel's tongue was cut out by her brother-in-law Tereus, who wished to silence her complaints and keep her from revealing that he had raped her.

15   Soon break, soon wither, soon forgotten:
               In folly ripe, in reason rotten.

               Thy belt of straw and ivy-buds,
               Thy coral clasps and amber studs,
               All these in me no means can move
20   To come to thee and be thy love.

               But could youth last, and love still breed,
               Had joys no date, nor age no need,
               Then these delights my mind might move
               To live with thee and be thy love.
                                  [1600]

[EPITAPH]

               Even such is time, that takes in trust
               Our youth, our joys, our all we have,
               And pays us but with earth and dust;
                  Who in the dark and silent grave,
5   When we have wandered all our ways,
               Shuts up the story of our days;
               But from this earth, this grave, this dust,
               My God shall raise me up, I trust.
                           [posthumous, 1628]

Sir Philip Sidney   *1554–1586*

"THOU BLIND MAN'S MARK"

     Thou blind man's mark, thou fool's self-chosen snare,
     Fond fancy's scum, and dregs of scattered thought;
     Band of all evils, cradle of causeless care;
     Thou web of will, whose end is never wrought;
5   Desire, desire! I have too dearly bought,
     With price of mangled mind, thy worthless ware;
     Too long, too long, asleep thou hast me brought,
     Who should my mind to higher things prepare.
     But yet in vain thou hast my ruin sought;
10   In vain thou madest me to vain things aspire;
     In vain thou kindlest all thy smoky fire;
     For virtue hath this better lesson taught,
     Within myself to seek my only hire,
     Desiring nought but how to kill desire.
                             [posthumous, 1598]

Chidiock Tichborne   *1558?–1586*

TICHBORNE'S ELEGY, WRITTEN WITH HIS OWN HAND IN THE TOWER BEFORE HIS EXECUTION[1]

My prime of youth is but a frost of cares,
My feast of joy is but a dish of pain,
My crop of corn° is but a field of tares,°   *wheat / weeds*
And all my good is but vain hope of gain;
5   The day is past, and yet I saw no sun,
And now I live, and now my life is done.

My tale was heard and yet it was not told,
My fruit is fallen, yet my leaves are green,
My youth is spent and yet I am not old,
10   I saw the world and yet I was not seen;
My thread is cut and yet it is not spun,
And now I live, and now my life is done.

I sought my death and found it in my womb,
I looked for life and saw it was a shade,
15   I trod the earth and knew it was my tomb,
And now I die, and now I was but made;
My glass is full, and now my glass is run,
And now I live, and now my life is done.

                                                            [1586]

Christopher Marlowe   *1564–1593*

THE PASSIONATE SHEPHERD TO HIS LOVE

Come live with me and be my love;
And we will all the pleasures prove°   *test*
That hills and valleys, dales and fields,
Or woods or steepy mountain yields.

5   And we will sit upon the rocks,
And see the shepherds feed their flocks
By shallow rivers, to whose falls
Melodious birds sing madrigals.°   *songs*

And I will make thee beds of roses
10   And a thousand fragrant posies;
A cap of flowers, and a kirtle°   *dress*
Embroidered all with leaves of myrtle.

---

[1] On September 20, 1586, Tichborne was hanged and then "disemboweled before life was extinct" for participating in a plot to murder Queen Elizabeth I.

A gown made of the finest wool
Which from our pretty lambs we pull;
15   Fair-linèd slippers for the cold,
With buckles of the purest gold.

A belt of straw and ivy-buds
With coral clasps and amber studs:
And if these pleasures may thee move,
20   Come live with me and be my love.

The shepherd swains shall dance and sing
For thy delight each May morning:
If these delights thy mind may move,
Then live with me and be my love.

                     [posthumous, 1599]

William Shakespeare *1564–1616*

"IF I PROFANE WITH MY UNWORTHIEST HAND"

[*A Sonnet from* Romeo and Juliet]

ROMEO. *(To Juliet)* If I profane with my unworthiest hand
This holy shrine,° the gentle sin is this;   *i.e., Juliet's hand*
My lips, two blushing pilgrims,° ready stand   *travelers to a shrine*
To smooth that rough touch with a tender kiss.
5   JULIET. Good pilgrim, you do wrong your hand too
      much,
Which mannerly° devotion shows in this;   *well bred*
For saints have hands that pilgrims' hands do
      touch,
And palm to palm is holy palmer's° kiss.   *pilgrim's*
ROMEO. Have not saints lips, and holy palmers too?
10   JULIET. Ay, pilgrim, lips that they must use in prayer.
ROMEO. O! then, dear saint, let lips do what hands do;
They pray. Grant thou, lest faith turn to despair.
JULIET. Saints do not move, though grant for
      prayer's sake.
ROMEO. Then move not, while my prayers' effect I take.
             [*Kisses her*]
                       [1596]

SONNET XVIII

Shall I compare thee to a summer's day?
Thou art more lovely and more temperate:
Rough winds do shake the darling buds of May,
And summer's lease hath all too short a date:

5   Sometime too hot the eye of heaven shines,
And often is his gold complexion dimmed;
And every fair° from fair sometime declines,   *fair woman*
By chance, or nature's changing course,
    untrimmed;°   *stripped of trimmings*
But thy eternal summer shall not fade,
10   Nor lose possession of that fair thou owest;°   *ownest*
Nor shall death brag thou wander'st in his
    shade,
When in eternal lines to time thou growest:
So long as men can breathe, or eyes can see,
So long lives this, and this gives life to thee.
                            [1609]

SONNET LV

Not marble, nor the gilded monuments
Of princes, shall outlive this powerful rhyme;
But you shall shine more bright in these contents
Than unswept stone, besmeared with sluttish time.
5   When wasteful war shall statues overturn,
And broils root out the works of masonry;
Nor Mars his sword[1] nor war's quick fire shall burn
The living record of your memory.
'Gainst death and all-oblivious enmity
10   Shall you pace forth; your praise shall still find
    room,
Even in the eyes of all posterity
That wear this world out to the ending doom.°   *Judgment Day*
So till the judgment that yourself arise,
You live in this, and dwell in lovers' eyes.
                            [1609]

SONNET LXV

Since brass, nor stone, nor earth, nor boundless sea,
But sad mortality o'er-sways their power,
How with this rage shall beauty hold a plea,°   *defense in law*
Whose action° is no stronger than a flower?   *legal action*
5   O how shall summer's honey breath hold out
Against the wreckful siege of battering days,
When rocks impregnable are not so stout,
Nor gates of steel so strong, but time decays?
O fearful meditation! where, alack!
10   Shall time's best jewel from time's chest lie hid?
Or what strong hand can hold his swift foot back?
Or who his spoil of beauty can forbid?

---

[1] Mars' sword. Mars is the Roman god of war.

O none, unless this miracle have might,
That in black ink my love may still shine bright.
                                                             [1609]

SONNET CXVI

Let me not to the marriage of true minds
Admit impediments.[1] Love is not love
Which alters when it alteration finds,
Or bends with the remover to remove:
5   O no! it is an ever-fixèd mark,
That looks on tempests, and is never shaken;
It is the star to every wandering bark,°   *ship*
Whose worth's unknown, although his height° be taken.   *altitude*
Love's not time's fool, though rosy lips and cheeks
10   Within his bending sickle's compass° come;   *reach*
Love alters not with his brief hours and weeks,
But bears° it out even to the edge of doom.   *lasts*
If this be error, and upon me proved,
I never writ, nor no man ever loved.
                                                             [1609]

SONNET CXXIX

The expense° of spirit in a waste° of shame   *draining / wasteland*
Is lust in action; and till action, lust
Is perjured, murderous, bloody, full of blame,
Savage, extreme, rude, cruel, not to trust;
5   Enjoyed no sooner, but despisèd straight;
Past reason hunted; and no sooner had,
Past reason hated, as a swallowed bait,
On purpose laid to make the taker mad:
Mad in pursuit, and in possession so;
10   Had, having, and in quest to have, extreme;
A bliss in proof,°—and proved, a very woe;   *the act (of coition)*
Before, a joy proposed; behind, a dream:
All this the world well knows; yet none
        knows well
To shun the heaven that leads men to this hell.
                                                             [1609]

SONNET CXXX

My mistress' eyes are nothing like the sun;
Coral is far more red than her lips' red:
If snow be white, why then her breasts are dun;°   *dull brown*

---

[1] Hindrances. Shakespeare is alluding to the words used in the Anglican marriage service.

blush-colored

5
If hairs be wires, black wires grow on her head.
I have seen roses damasked,° red and white,
But no such roses see I in her cheeks;
And in some perfumes is there more delight
Than in the breath that from my mistress reeks.
I love to hear her speak,—yet well I know

10
That music hath a far more pleasing sound;
I grant I never saw a goddess go,°—
My mistress, when she walks, treads on the ground;
And yet, by heaven, I think my love as rare
As any she bely'd° with false compare.

walk

proved false

[1609]

"FEAR NO MORE THE HEAT O' TH' SUN"

[*A Song in* Cymbeline]

Fear no more the heat o' th' sun,
  Nor the furious winter's rages;
Thou thy worldly task hast done,
  Home art gone, and ta'en thy wages:
5
Golden lads and girls all must,
As chimney-sweepers, come to dust.

Fear no more the frown o' th' great,
  Thou art past the tyrant's stroke;
Care no more to clothe and eat,
10
  To thee the reed is as the oak.
The sceptre, learning, physic, must
All follow this, and come to dust.

Fear no more the lightning-flash,
  Nor th' all-dreaded thunder stone;[1]
15
Fear not slander, censure rash,
  Thou hast finished joy and moan.
All lovers young, all lovers must
Consign° to thee, and come to dust.

deliver (themselves)

No exorciser harm thee!
20
  Nor no witchcraft charm thee!
Ghost unlaid forbear thee!
  Nothing ill come near thee!
Quiet consummation have,
And renownèd be thy grave!

[1610]

---

[1] Falling stones were believed to cause the sound of thunder.

"FULL FATHOM FIVE"

[*A Song in* The Tempest]

Full fathom five thy father lies;
  Of his bones are coral made;
Those are pearls that were his eyes:
  Nothing of him that doth fade,
But doth suffer a sea change
Into something rich and strange.
Sea nymphs hourly ring his knell:
  Ding-dong.
Hark! now I hear them—Ding-dong, bell.

[1612]

SEVENTEENTH-CENTURY POETRY

John Donne *1572–1631*

THE GOOD-MORROW

I wonder by my troth, what thou and I
  Did, till we loved? Were we not weaned till then,
But sucked on country pleasures, childishly?
  Or snorted we in the seven sleepers' den?[1]
'Twas so; but this,° all pleasures fancies be. *except for love*
If ever any beauty I did see,
Which I desired, and got, 'twas but a dream of thee.

And now good morrow to our waking souls,
  Which watch not one another out of fear;
For love, all love of other sights controls,
  And makes one little room, an everywhere.
Let sea-discoverers to new worlds have gone,
Let maps to others, worlds on worlds have shown,
Let us possess one world; each hath one, and is one.

My face in thine eye, thine in mine appears,
  And true plain hearts do in the faces rest;
Where can we find two better hemispheres
  Without sharp° north, without declining west? *cold*
Whatever dies, was not mixed equally;[2]
  If our two loves be one, or, thou and I
Love so alike that none do slacken, none can die.

[posthumous, 1633]

A VALEDICTION: FORBIDDING MOURNING

As virtuous men pass mildly away,
And whisper to their souls to go,
Whilst some of their sad friends do say,
"The breath goes now," and some say, "No,"

So let us melt and make no noise,
No tear-floods, nor sigh-tempests move;
'Twere profanation of our joys
To tell the laity our love.

[1] Seven young Christians supposedly slept for 187 years after being walled up in a cave in A.D. 249 during the reign of the Roman emperor Decius.
[2] In medieval philosophy death was a result of an imperfect mixture of elements; when the elements are perfectly balanced, immortality should be possible.

Moving of th' earth brings harm and fears;
10   Men reckon what it did and meant.
But trepidation of the spheres,
Though greater far, is innocent.

Dull sublunary lovers' love
(Whose soul is sense) cannot admit
15   Absence, because it doth remove
Those things which elemented it.

But we by a love so much refined
That ourselves know not what it is,
Inter-assurèd of the mind,
20   Care less eyes, lips, and hands to miss.

Our two souls, therefore, which are one,
Though I must go, endure not yet
A breach, but an expansion,
Like gold to airy thinness beat.

25   If they be two, they are two so
As stiff twin compasses are two;
Thy soul, the fixed foot, makes no show
To move, but doth if th' other do.

And though it in the center sit,
30   Yet when the other far doth roam,
It leans and hearkens after it,
And grows erect as that comes home.

Such wilt thou be to me, who must,
Like th' other foot, obliquely run;
35   Thy firmness makes my circle just,
And makes me end where I begun.

                         [posthumous, 1633]

THE SUN RISING

Busy old fool, unruly sun,
    Why dost thou thus,
Through windows, and through curtains call on us?
Must to thy motions lovers' seasons run?
5   Saucy pedantic wretch, go chide
       Late school-boys, and sour prentices.°   *apprentices*
Go tell court-huntsmen that the King will ride.
Call country ants to harvest offices;
Love, all alike, no season knows, nor clime,
10   Nor hours, days, months, which are the rags of time.

Thy beams, so reverend and strong
Why shouldst thou think?
I could eclipse and cloud them with a wink,
But that I would not lose her sight so long:
15   If her eyes have not blinded thine,
    Look, and tomorrow late, tell me
Whether both the Indias[1] of spice and mine
Be where thou left'st them, or lie here with me.
Ask for those kings whom thou saw'st yesterday,
20 And thou shalt hear, All here in one bed lay.

    She is all states, and all princes, I,
    Nothing else is.
Princes do but play us; compared to this,
All honor's mimic;° all wealth alchemy.[2]   *mimicry*
25   Thou, sun, art half as happy as we,
    In that the world's contracted thus;
Thine age asks ease, and since thy duties be
To warm the world, that's done in warming us.
Shine here to us, and thou art everywhere;
30 This bed thy center is, these walls, thy sphere.

                [posthumous, 1633]

THE CANONIZATION

For God's sake hold your tongue, and let me love,
    Or chide my palsy, or my gout,
My five grey hairs, or ruined fortunes flout;
With wealth your state, your mind with arts
        improve,
5   Take you a course,° get you a place,°   *direction / appointment*
    Observe His Honor or his Grace,
Or the king's real or his stamped face°   *i.e., on a coin*
    Contemplate; what you will, approve,°   *try out*
    So you will let me love.

10   Alas, alas! who's injured by my love?
    What merchant's ships have my sighs drowned?
Who says my tears have overflowed his ground?
When did my colds a forward spring remove?
    When did the heats, which my veins fill,
15   Add one more to the plaguy bill?[1]
Soldiers find wars, and lawyers find out still
    Litigious men, which quarrels move,
    Though she and I do love.

---

[1] The East Indies were noted for spices; the West Indies for gold and silver mines.
[2] The pseudo-science of turning base metal into gold—hence, in this context, "fraudulent" or "phoney."
[1] Deaths from the plague were recorded in a weekly bill or list.

Call us what you will, we are made such by love;
20   Call her one, me another fly;
We are tapers too, and at our own cost die;
And we in us find th' eagle and the dove;
        The phoenix riddle hath more wit
        By us; we two being one, are it:²
25 So to one neutral thing both sexes fit.
        We die and rise the same, and prove
            Mysterious by this love.

We can die by it, if not live by love.
        And if unfit for tomb and hearse
30 Our legend be, it will be fit for verse;
And if no piece of chronicle we prove,
        We'll build in sonnets pretty rooms.
        As well a well-wrought urn becomes
The greatest ashes, as half-acre tombs;
35   And by these hymns all shall approve°   *certify*
            Us canonized for love:

And thus invoke° us: "You whom reverend love   *pray to*
        Made one another's hermitage;
You to whom love was peace, that now is rage,
40 Who did the whole world's soul contract, and
            drove
        Into the glasses° of your eyes,   *reflecting surfaces*
        (So made such mirrors, and such spies,
That they did all to you epitomize)³
        Countries, towns, courts: beg from above
45   A pattern of your love."⁴
                                        [posthumous, 1633]

THE RELIQUE

When my grave is broke up again
Some second guest to entertain,
(For graves have learned that woman-head,°   *female trait*
To be to more than one a bed)
5   And he that digs it, spies
A bracelet of bright hair about the bone,
        Will he not let us alone,
And think that there a loving couple lies

---

² The mythological phoenix lights its own funeral pyre, is consumed by the fire, and then is resurrected
  from its own ashes. Donne's lovers repeat this cycle through their desire, gratification, sexual exhaustion, and renewed desire.
³ Donne's lovers see reflected in each other's eyes not only themselves, but also (more figuratively than
  literally) a background of countries, towns, and courts; therefore they have found in each other an
  epitome of the whole world.
⁴ I.e., Donne and his mistress, as saints of love, should beg God to send to earth a model of their love.

Who thought that this device might be some way
10   To make their souls, at the last busy day,
Meet at this grave, and make a little stay?

If this fall in a time, or land,
Where mis-devotion° doth command,   *idolatry*
Then he that digs us up will bring
15   Us to the bishop, and the king,
To make us reliques; then
Thou shalt be a Mary Magdalen, and I
A something else thereby;
All women shall adore us, and some men;
20   And since at such time miracles are sought,
I would have that age by this paper taught
What miracles we harmless lovers wrought.

First we loved well and faithfully,
Yet knew not what we loved, nor why;
25   Diff'rence of sex no more we knew,
Than our guardian angels do;
Coming and going we
Perchance might kiss, but not between those meals;
Our hands ne'er touched the seals,
30   Which Nature, injured by late law, set free:
These miracles we did; but now, alas!
All measure and all language I should pass,
Should I tell what a miracle she was.
[posthumous, 1633]

"DEATH BE NOT PROUD"

Death, be not proud, though some have called thee
Mighty and dreadful, for thou art not so;
For those, whom thou think'st thou dost overthrow,
Die not, poor death; nor yet canst thou kill me.
5   From rest and sleep, which but thy picture° be,   *image, representation*
Much pleasure; then from thee much more must flow:
And soonest our best men with thee do go,
Rest of their bones, and soul's delivery.
Thou art slave to fate, chance, kings, and desperate
men,
10   And dost with poison, war, and sickness dwell,
And poppy° or charms can make us sleep as well,   *opium*
And better than thy stroke. Why swell'st thou then?
One short sleep past, we wake eternally;
And death shall be no more; Death, thou shalt die.
[posthumous, 1633]

"BATTER MY HEART, THREE-PERSONED GOD"

Batter my heart, three-personed God; for you
As yet but knock, breathe, shine, and seek to mend;
That I may rise and stand, o'erthrow me and bend
Your force, to break, blow, burn, and make me new.
5   I, like an usurped° town to another due,   *seized*
Labor to admit you, but oh, to no end;
Reason, your viceroy° in me, me should defend,   *deputy*
But is captived, and proves weak or untrue;
Yet dearly I love you, and would be loved fain,°   *gladly*
10   But am betrothed unto your enemy:
Divorce me, untie, or break that knot again,
Take me to you, imprison me; for I,
Except you enthrall me, never shall be free;
Nor ever chaste, except you ravish me.
                          [posthumous, 1633]

Ben Jonson   *1572–1637*

SONG: TO CELIA

Drink to me only with thine eyes,
    And I will pledge° with mine;   *toast you*
Or leave a kiss but in the cup,
    And I'll not look for wine.
5 The thirst, that from the soul doth rise,
    Doth ask a drink divine:
But might I of Jove's nectar sup,
    I would not change for thine.

I sent thee, late, a rosy wreath,
10   Not so much honoring thee,
As giving it a hope, that there
    It could not withered be.
But thou thereon did'st only breathe,
    And sent'st it back to me:
15 Since when, it grows, and smells, I swear,
    Not of itself, but thee.
                          [1616]

Robert Herrick   *1591–1674*

TO THE VIRGINS, TO MAKE MUCH OF TIME

Gather ye rosebuds while ye may,
    Old Time is still a-flying:
And this same flower that smiles today
    Tomorrow will be dying.

5   The glorious lamp of heaven, the sun,
               The higher he's a-getting,
           The sooner will his race be run,
               And nearer he's to setting.

           That age is best which is the first,
10   When youth and blood are warmer;
           But being spent, the worse, and worst
               Times still succeed the former.

           Then be not coy, but use your time,
               And while ye may, go marry:
15   For having lost but once your prime,
               You may for ever tarry.

                            [1648]

THE NIGHT-PIECE: TO JULIA

           Her eyes the glow-worm° lend thee,   *larva of the firefly*
           The shooting stars attend thee;
               And the elves also,
               Whose little eyes glow
5   Like the sparks of fire, befriend thee.

           No Will-o'-the-wisp° mislight thee,   *swamp fire*
           Nor snake or slow-worm° bite thee;   *lizard*
               But on, on thy way,
               Not making a stay,
10   Since ghost there's none to affright thee.

           Let not the dark thee cumber:°   *encumber*
           What though the moon does slumber?
               The stars of the night
               Will lend thee their light
15   Like tapers clear without number.

           Then, Julia, let me woo thee,
           Thus, thus to come unto me;
               And when I shall meet
               Thy silv'ry feet,
20   My soul I'll pour into thee.

                            [1648]

THE RESURRECTION POSSIBLE AND PROBABLE

           For each one body that i' th' earth is sown
           There's an uprising but of one for one,
           But for each grain° that in the ground is thrown   *head of wheat*

Threescore or fourscore spring up thence for one;
5   So that the wonder is not half so great
Of ours, as is the rising of the wheat.

[1648]

UPON JULIA'S VOICE

So smooth, so sweet, so silvery is thy voice,
As, could they hear, the Damned would make no noise,
But listen to thee (walking in thy chamber)
Melting melodious words to Lutes of Amber.

[1648]

George Herbert   *1593–1633*

THE PULLEY

When God at first made man,
Having a glass of blessings standing by—
"Let us," said He, "pour on him all we can;
Let the world's riches, which dispersèd lie,
5   Contract into a span."°   *a handspan*

So strength first made a way,
Then beauty flowed, then wisdom, honor, pleasure:
When almost all was out, God made a stay,
Perceiving that, alone of all his treasure,
10   Rest in the bottom lay.

"For if I should," said He,
"Bestow this jewel also on my creature,
He would adore my gifts instead of me,
And rest in nature, not the God of nature;
15   So both should losers be.

"Yet let him keep the rest,
But keep them with repining restlessness;
Let him be rich and weary, that at least,
If goodness lead him not, yet weariness
20   May toss him to my breast."

[1633]

LOVE

Love bade me welcome: yet my soul drew back,
    Guilty of dust and sin.
But quick-eyed Love, observing me grow slack
    From my first entrance in,
5 Drew nearer to me, sweetly questioning
    If I lacked anything.

"A guest," I answered, "worthy to be here:"
    Love said, "You shall be he."
"I, the unkind, ungrateful? Ah, my dear,
10   I cannot look on thee."
Love took my hand and smiling did reply,
    "Who made the eyes but I?"

"Truth, Lord; but I have marred them; let my shame
    Go where it doth deserve."
15   "And know you not," says Love, "who bore the blame?"
    "My dear, then I will serve."
"You must sit down," says Love, "and taste my meat."
    So I did sit and eat.

                   [1633]

Edmund Waller   *1606–1687*

ON A GIRDLE

That which her slender waist confined
Shall now my joyful temples bind;
No monarch but would give his crown,
His arms might do what this had done.

5   It was my heaven's extremest sphere,
The pale° which held that lovely deer: *encircling fence*
My joy, my grief, my hope, my love,
Did all within this circle move.

A narrow compass! and yet there
10 Dwelt all that's good, and all that's fair!
Give me but what this ribband° bound,   *ribbon*
Take all the rest the sun goes round!

                   [1686]

John Milton   *1608–1674*

"WHEN I CONSIDER HOW MY LIGHT IS SPENT"

When I consider how my light is spent[1]
  Ere half my days, in this dark world and wide,
  And that one talent° which is death to hide,   *i.e., writing*
  Lodged with me useless, though my soul more bent
5 To serve therewith my maker, and present
  My true account, lest he returning chide.
  "Doth God exact day-labor, light denied?"
  I fondly° ask; but patience, to prevent   *foolishly*

---

[1] Milton gradually lost his vision between 1644 and 1652.

That murmur, soon replies, "God doth not need
10   Either man's work, or his own gifts; who best
        Bear his mild yoke, they serve him best: his state
Is kingly; thousands at his bidding speed,
        And post o'er land and ocean without rest;
        They also serve who only stand and wait."

[1673]

ON THE LATE MASSACRE IN PIEDMONT[2]

Avenge, O Lord, thy slaughtered saints, whose bones
        Lie scattered on the Alpine mountains cold;
        Even them who kept thy truth so pure of old,
        When all our fathers worshipped stocks and
            stones,°   *graven images*
5   Forget not: in thy book record their groans
        Who were thy sheep, and in their ancient fold
        Slain by the bloody Piemontese that rolled
        Mother with infant down the rocks. Their moans
The vales° redoubled to the hills, and they   *valleys*
10   To Heaven. Their martyred blood and ashes sow
        O'er all the Italian fields, where still doth sway
The triple tyrant;° that from these may grow   *the Pope*
        A hundred fold, who having learned thy way
        Early may fly the Babylonian woe.[3]

[1673]

Sir John Suckling   *1609–1642*

[THE CONSTANT LOVER]

Out upon it! I have loved
    Three whole days together!
And am like to love three more,
    If it prove fair weather.

5   Time shall moult away his wings
    Ere he shall discover
In the whole wide world again
    Such a constant lover.

But the spite° on 't is, no praise   *chagrin*
10   Is due at all to me:
Love with me had made no stays,
    Had it any been but she.

___

[2] On April 24, 1655, the Protestants living in the Alpine villages of the Piedmont (northern Italy and
southern France) were slaughtered by the Catholic soldiers of neighboring Savoy.
[3] Milton and other Puritans often associated the Catholic Church with the "whore of Babylon"
(Revelations 17).

Had it any been but she,
And that very face,
There had been at least ere this
A dozen dozen in her place.

[posthumous, 1659]

Richard Lovelace *1618–1657*

TO LUCASTA, GOING TO THE WARS

Tell me not, sweet, I am unkind,
That from the nunnery
Of thy chaste breast and quiet mind
To war and arms I fly.

True, a new mistress now I chase,
The first foe in the field;
And with a stronger faith embrace
A sword, a horse, a shield.

Yet this inconstancy is such
As thou too shalt adore;
I could not love thee, dear, so much,
Loved I not honor more.

[1649]

TO ALTHEA, FROM PRISON

When Love with unconfinèd wings
Hovers within my gates,
And my divine Althea brings
To whisper at the grates;
When I lie tangled in her hair
And fettered to her eye,
The birds that wanton in the air
Know no such liberty.

When flowing cups run swiftly round
With no allaying Thames,[1]
Our careless heads with roses bound,
Our hearts with loyal flames;
When thirsty grief in wine we steep,
When healths and draughts go free—
Fishes that tipple in the deep
Know no such liberty.

[1] I.e., undiluted with water.

When, like committed° linnets,° I   *caged / songbirds*
   With shriller throat shall sing
The sweetness, mercy, majesty,
   And glories of my King;
When I shall voice aloud how good
   He is, how great should be,
Enlargèd winds, that curl the flood,
   Know no such liberty.

Stone walls do not a prison make,
   Nor iron bars a cage;
Minds innocent and quiet take
   That for an hermitage;
If I have freedom in my love
   And in my soul am free,
Angels alone, that soar above,
   Enjoy such liberty.

[1649]

TO AMARANTHA, THAT SHE WOULD DISHEVEL HER HAIR

Amarantha sweet and fair,
Ah, braid no more that shining hair!
As my curious hand or eye
Hovering round thee, let it fly!

Let it fly as unconfined
As its calm ravisher the wind,
Who hath left his darling, th' East,
To wanton o'er that spicy nest.

Every tress must be confest,
But neatly tangled at the best;
Like a clew° of golden thread   *ball*
Most excellently ravellèd.

Do not then wind up that light
In ribbands, and o'ercloud in night,
Like the Sun in 's early ray;
But shake your head, and scatter day!

See, 'tis broke! Within this grove,
The bower and the walks of love,
Weary lie we down and rest
And fan each other's panting breast.

Here we'll strip and cool our fire
In cream below, in milk-baths higher;
And when all wells are drawn dry,
I'll drink a tear out of thine eye,

25   Which our very joys shall leave,
              That sorrows thus we can deceive;
              Or our very sorrows weep,
              That joys so ripe so little keep.

                               [1649]

Andrew Marvell   *1621–1678*

TO HIS COY MISTRESS

          Had we but world enough, and time,
          This coyness, lady, were no crime
          We would sit down and think which way
          To walk, and pass our long love's day.
5   Thou by the Indian Ganges' side
          Shouldst rubies find: I by the tide
          Of Humber[1] would complain. I would
          Love you ten years before the Flood,
          And you should, if you please, refuse
10   Till the conversion of the Jews.[2]
          My vegetable love should grow
          Vaster than empires, and more slow;
          An hundred years should go to praise
          Thine eyes and on thy forehead gaze;
15   Two hundred to adore each breast,
          But thirty thousand to the rest;
          An age at least to every part,
          And the last age should show your heart.
          For, lady, you deserve this state,[3]
20   Nor would I love at lower rate.
            But at my back I always hear
          Time's wingèd chariot hurrying near;
          And yonder all before us lie
          Deserts of vast eternity.
25   Thy beauty shall no more be found,
          Nor, in thy marble vault, shall sound
          My echoing song: then worms shall try
          That long preserved virginity,
          And your quaint honor turn to dust,
30   And into ashes all my lust:
          The grave's a fine and private place,
          But none, I think, do there embrace.
            Now therefore, while the youthful hue
          Sits on thy skin like morning dew,
35   And while thy willing soul transpires

[1] The Humber River flowing past Hull, a city in the North of England, where Marvell lived.
[2] According to traditional Christian beliefs, this is to take place just before the Last Judgment.
[3] Stateliness.

At every pore with instant fires,[4]
Now let us sport us while we may,
And now, like amorous birds of prey,
Rather at once our time devour
40 Than languish in his slow-chapt[5] power.
Let us roll all our strength and all
Our sweetness up into one ball,
And tear our pleasures with rough strife
Thorough the iron gates of life:
45 Thus, though we cannot make our sun
Stand still, yet we will make him run.

[posthumous, 1681]

THE DEFINITION OF LOVE

My love is of a birth as rare
As 'tis, for object, strange and high;
It was begotten by despair,
Upon impossibility.

5 Magnanimous despair alone
Could show me so divine a thing,
Where feeble hope could ne'er have flown,
But vainly flapped its tinsel wing.

And yet I quickly might arrive
10 Where my extended soul is fixed;[1]
But fate does iron wedges drive,
And always crowds itself betwixt.

For fate with jealous eye does see
Two perfect loves, nor lets them close,[2]
15 Their union would her ruin be,
And her tyrannic power depose.

And therefore her decrees of steel
Us as the distant poles have placed,
(Though Love's whole world on us doth wheel)
20 Not by themselves to be embraced,

Unless the giddy heaven fall,
And earth some new convulsion tear,
And, us to join, the world should all
Be cramped into a planisphere.[3]

---

[4] I.e., while your willing soul reveals itself through your blushes ("instant fires").
[5] Slow-jawed—hence, slowly destroying.
[1] Marvell imagines his soul extending out and fixed upon his mistress.
[2] Come together.
[3] A sphere flattened so that the north and south poles touch.

25 As lines, so loves oblique may well
Themselves in every angle greet:[4]
But ours, so truly parallel,
Though infinite, can never meet.

Therefore the love which us doth bind,
30 But fate so enviously debars,
Is the conjunction of the mind,
And opposition of the stars.

[posthumous, 1681]

Katherine Philips *1631–1664*

AGAINST LOVE

Hence, Cupid! with your cheating toys.
Your real Griefs, and painted Joys,
Your Pleasure which itself destroys.
Lovers like men in fevers burn and rave,
5 And only what will injure them do crave.
Men's weakness makes Love so severe,
They give him power by their fear,
And make the shackles which they wear.
Who to another does his heart submit;
10 Makes his own Idol, and then worships it.
Him whose heart is all his own,
Peace and liberty does crown;
He apprehends no killing frown.
He feels no raptures which are joys diseased,
15 And is not much transported, but still pleased.

[1664]

John Dryden *1631–1700*

RONDELAY

Chloe found *Amyntas* lying,
    All in tears, upon the plain,
Sighing to himself, and crying,
    Wretched I, to love in vain!
5   Kiss me, dear, before my dying;
        Kiss me once, and ease my pain.

---

[4] Oblique or non-parallel lines eventually intersect, just as imperfect, sinful lovers do.

Sighing to himself, and crying,
    Wretched I, to love in vain!
Ever scorning, and denying
10   To reward your faithful swain;
Kiss me, dear, before my dying;
    Kiss me once, and ease my pain!

Ever scorning, and denying
    To reward your faithful swain.
15   *Chloe*, laughing at his crying,
    Told him, that he lov'd in vain:
Kiss me, dear, before my dying;
    Kiss me once, and ease my pain!

    Chloe, laughing at his crying,
20   Told him that he lov'd in vain;
But repenting, and complying,
    When he kiss'd, she kiss'd again:
Kiss'd him up, before his dying;
    Kiss'd him up, and eas'd his pain.
                             [1693]

SONG

Sylvia the fair, in the bloom of fifteen
Felt an innocent warmth, as she lay on the green;
She had heard of a pleasure, and something she
    guessed
By the towzing[1] and tumbling and touching her
    breast:
5 She saw the men eager, but was at a loss,
What they meant by their sighing and kissing so
    close;
    By their praying and whining,
    And clasping and twining,
    And panting and wishing,
10   And sighing and kissing,
    And sighing and kissing so close.

"Ah," she cried, "ah for a languishing Maid
In a country of Christians to die without aid!
Not a Whig, or a Tory, or Trimmer at least,[2]
15 Or a Protestant parson or Catholick priest,
To instruct a young virgin that is at a loss
What they meant by their sighing and kissing so
    close;

---

[1] Rough fondling.
[2] Traditionally, Whigs are members of the liberal political party in Great Britain; Tories are politically
  conservative; and Trimmers are those who change (or trim) their political views to suit the times.

By their praying and whining,
And clasping and twining,
20   And panting and wishing,
And sighing and kissing,
And sighing and kissing so close."

Cupid in shape of a swain[3] did appear,
He saw the sad wound, and in pity drew near,
25   Then show'd her his arrow, and bid her not fear,
For the pain was no more than a maiden may bear;
When the balm was infus'd, she was not at a loss
What they meant by their sighing and kissing so
close;
By their praying and whining,
30   And clasping and twining,
And panting and wishing,
And sighing and kissing,
And sighing and kissing so close.

[1685]

Aphra Behn   *1640–1689*

TO THE FAIR CLARINDA, WHO MADE LOVE TO ME, IMAGINED MORE THAN WOMAN[1]

Fair lovely maid, or if that title be
Too weak, too feminine for nobler thee,
Permit a name that more approaches truth:
And let me call thee lovely charming youth.
5   This last will justify my soft complaint,[2]
While that may serve to lessen my constraint;
And without blushes I the youth pursue,
When so much beauteous woman is in view.
Against thy charms we struggle but in vain;
10   With thy deluding form thou givest us pain,
While the bright nymph betrays us to the swain.
In pity to our sex sure thou wert sent,
That we might love and yet be innocent:
For sure no crime with thee we can commit;
15   Or if we should—thy form excuses it.
For who that gathers fairest flowers believes
A snake lies hid beneath the fragrant leaves.

---

[3] A young rustic lover.
[1] I.e., imagined as a hermaphrodite, endowed with the characteristics of both sexes.
[2] "This last" name of masculine "youth" justifies the sexual desire in her "soft complaint," "while that" earlier name of "fair lovely maid" makes that desire seem innocent.

Thou beauteous wonder of a different kind,
Soft Cloris with the dear Alexis joined;
Whene'er the manly part of thee would plead
Thou tempts us with the image of the maid,
While we the noblest passions do extend
The love to Hermes, Aphrodite the friend.

[1688]

❧ EIGHTEENTH-CENTURY POETRY ❧

Matthew Prior   *1664–1721*

AN EPITAPH

Interred beneath this marble stone
Lie sauntering Jack and idle Joan.
While rolling threescore years and one
Did round this globe their courses run;
5   If human things went ill or well;
If changing empires rose or fell;
The morning passed, the evening came,
And found this couple still the same.
They walked and ate, good folks: what then?
10   Why then they walked and ate again.
They soundly slept the night away;
They did just nothing all the day;
And having buried children four,
Would not take pains to try for more.
15   Nor sister either had, nor brother:
They seemed just tallied° for each other.   *fit*
    Their moral° and economy°   *morals / parsimony*
Most perfectly they made agree:
Each virtue kept its proper bound,
20   Nor trespassed on the other's ground.
Nor fame, nor censure they regarded:
They neither punished, nor rewarded.
He cared not what the footmen did;
Her maids she neither praised, nor chid:°   *scolded*
25   So every servant took his course;
And bad at first, they all grew worse.
Slothful disorder filled his stable,
And sluttish plenty decked her table.
Their beer was strong; their wine was port;
30   Their meal was large; their grace was short.
They gave the poor the remnant-meat
Just when it grew not fit to eat.
    They paid the church and parish rate,°   *tax*
And took, but read not the receipt;
35   For which they claimed their Sunday's due
Of slumbering in an upper pew.
    No man's defects sought they to know,
So never made themselves a foe.
No man's good deeds did they commend,
40   So never raised themselves a friend.

Nor cherished they relations poor:
That might decrease their present store;
Not barn nor house did they repair:
That might oblige their future heir.
45   They neither added, nor confounded.°   *squandered*
They neither wanted, nor abounded.
Each Christmas they accompts° did clear;   *accounts*
And wound their bottom round the year.[1]
Nor tear nor smile did they employ
50   At news of public grief or joy.
When bells were rung and bonfires made,
If asked, they ne'er denied their aid:
Their jug was to the ringers carried,
Whoever either died, or married.
55   Their billet° at the fire was found,   *firewood*
Whoever was deposed, or crowned.
    Nor good, nor bad, nor fools, nor wise;
They would not learn, nor could advise;
Without love, hatred, joy, or fear,
60   They led—a kind of—as it were;
Nor wished, nor cared, nor laughed, nor cried:
And so they lived; and so they died.
                         [1718]

Jonathan Swift *1667–1745*

A DESCRIPTION OF THE MORNING

Now hardly here and there a hackney-coach°   *carriage for hire*
Appearing, showed the ruddy morn's approach.
Now Betty from her master's bed had flown,
And softly stole to discompose her own;
5   The slip-shod 'prentice from his master's door
Had pared° the dirt and sprinkled° round the   *diminished / moistened*
    floor.
Now Moll had whirled her mop with dext'rous airs,
Prepared to scrub the entry and the stairs.
The youth with broomy stumps began to trace°   *search for old nails*
10   The kennel-edge,° where wheels had worn the place.   *gutter*
The small-coal man° was heard with cadence deep,   *charcoal vendor*
Till drowned in shriller notes of chimney-sweep:
Duns° at his lordship's gate began to meet;   *bill collectors*
And brickdust Moll had screamed through half
    the street.[2]
15   The turnkey now his flock returning sees,
Duly let out a-nights to steal for fees:[3]

---

[1] I.e., continued to unwind the thread of their lives throughout the year.
[2] Moll sells brick dust for use as a scouring powder.
[3] The jailer lets his prisoners out to steal during the night and then collects a fee from them as they
return in the morning.

The watchful bailiffs take their silent stands,
And schoolboys lag with satchels in their hands.

[1709]

John Gay   *1685–1732*

MY OWN EPITAPH

Life is a jest; and all things show it.
I thought so once; but now I know it.

[1720]

THE MAN AND THE FLEA

Whether on earth, in air, or main,°   open sea
Sure every thing alive is vain!
  Does not the hawk all fowls survey,
As destined only for his prey?
And do not tyrants, prouder things,   5
Think men were born for slaves to kings?
  When the crab views the pearly strands,°   beaches
Or Tagus,[1] bright with golden sands,
Or crawls beside the coral grove,
And hears the ocean roll above;   10
"Nature is too profuse," says he,
"Who gave all these to pleasure me!"
  When bord'ring pinks and roses bloom,
And every garden breathes perfume,
When peaches glow with sunny dyes,   15
Like Laura's cheek, when blushes rise;
When with huge figs the branches bend;
When clusters from the vine depend;
The snail looks round on flower and tree,
And cries, "All these were made for me!"   20
  "What dignity's in human nature,"
Says Man, the most conceited creature,
As from a cliff he cast his eye,
And viewed the sea and arched sky!
The sun was sunk beneath the main,   25
The moon, and all the starry train
Hung the vast vault of heaven. The Man
His contemplation thus began.
  "When I behold this glorious show,
And the wide watry world below,   30
The scaly people of the main,
The beasts that range the wood or plain,
The winged inhabitants of air,
The day, the night, the various year,

---

[1] The Tagus River flows through central Spain and Portugal to the Atlantic.

35   And know all these by heaven designed
     As gifts to pleasure human kind,
     I cannot raise my worth too high;
     Of what vast consequence am I!"
        "Not of th' importance you suppose,"
40   Replies a Flea upon his nose:
     "Be humble, learn thyself to scan;°   *analyze*
     Know, pride was never made for man.
     'Tis vanity that swells thy mind.
     What, heaven and earth for thee designed!
45   For thee! Made only for our need;
     That more important Fleas might feed."
                                    [1727]

Alexander Pope   *1688–1744*

AN ESSAY ON CRITICISM

FROM *Part 2*

     A little learning is a dangerous thing;
     Drink deep, or taste not the Pierian spring.[1]
     There shallow draughts intoxicate the brain,
     And drinking largely sobers us again.
     Fired at first sight with what the Muse imparts,
220 In fearless youth we tempt the heights of arts,
     While from the bounded level of our mind,
     Short views we take, nor see the lengths behind,
     But more advanced, behold with strange surprise
     New, distant scenes of endless science° rise!   *knowledge*
225 So pleased at first, the towering Alps we try,   .
     Mount o'er the vales, and seem to tread the sky;
     The eternal snows appear already past,
     And the first clouds and mountains seem the last:
     But those attained, we tremble to survey
230 The growing labors of the lengthened way,
     The increasing prospect tires our wandering eyes,
     Hills peep o'er hills, and Alps on Alps arise!
                                    [1711]

AN ESSAY ON MAN

FROM *Epistle II*

     I. Know then thyself, presume not God to scan;°   *scrutinize*
     The proper study of mankind is Man.
     Placed on this isthmus of a middle state,

---

[1] A spring sacred to the Muses.

A being darkly wise, and rudely° great;   *crudely*
5   With too much knowledge for the Sceptic side,
With too much weakness for the Stoic's pride,
He hangs between; in doubt to act, or rest,
In doubt to deem himself a god, or beast;
In doubt his mind or body to prefer,
10   Born but to die, and reasoning but to err;
Alike in ignorance, his reason such,
Whether he thinks too little, or too much:
Chaos of thought and passion, all confused;
Still by himself abused, or disabused;
15   Created half to rise, and half to fall;
Great lord of all things, yet a prey to all;
Sole judge of truth, in endless error hurled:
The glory, jest, and riddle of the world!

[1733]

Thomas Gray   *1716–1771*

ELEGY WRITTEN IN A COUNTRY CHURCHYARD

The curfew tolls the knell of parting day,
The lowing herd wind slowly o'er the lea,°   *meadow*
The plowman homeward plods his weary way,
And leaves the world to darkness and to me.

5   Now fades the glimmering landscape on the sight,
And all the air a solemn stillness holds,
Save where the beetle wheels his droning flight,
And drowsy tinklings lull the distant folds;

Save that from yonder ivy-mantled tower
10   The moping owl does to the moon complain
Of such as, wand'ring near her secret bower,
Molest her ancient solitary reign.

Beneath those rugged elms, the yew-tree's shade,
Where heaves the turf in many a mould'ring heap,
15   Each in his narrow cell for ever laid,
The rude° forefathers of the hamlet sleep.   *rugged*

The breezy call of incense-breathing Morn,
The swallow twitt'ring from the straw-built shed,
The cock's shrill clarion, or the echoing horn,
20   No more shall rouse them from their lowly bed.

For them no more the blazing hearth shall burn,
Or busy housewife ply her evening care:
No children run to lisp their sire's return,
Or climb his knees the envied kiss to share.

25   Oft did the harvest to their sickle yield,
            Their furrow oft the stubborn glebe° has broke: *field*
        How jocund did they drive their team afield!
            How bowed the woods beneath their sturdy stroke!

        Let not Ambition mock their useful toil,
30   Their homely joys, and destiny obscure;
        Nor Grandeur hear with a disdainful smile
            The short and simple annals of the poor.

        The boast of heraldry, the pomp of power,
            And all that beauty, all that wealth e'er gave,
35   Awaits alike th' inevitable hour:
            The paths of glory lead but to the grave.

        Nor you, ye proud, impute to these the fault,
            If Memory o'er their tomb no trophies° rise,   *monuments*
        Where through the long-drawn aisle and fretted° vault   *decorated*
40   The pealing anthem swells the note of praise.

        Can storied urn or animated° bust   *lifelike*
            Back to its mansion call the fleeting breath?
        Can Honor's voice provoke° the silent dust,   *arouse*
            Or Flatt'ry soothe the dull cold ear of death?

45   Perhaps in this neglected spot is laid
            Some heart once pregnant with celestial fire;
        Hands, that the rod of empire might have swayed,
            Or waked to ecstasy the living lyre.

        But Knowledge to their eyes her ample page
50   Rich with the spoils of time did ne'er unroll;
        Chill Penury° repressed their noble rage,   *poverty*
            And froze the genial current of the soul.

        Full many a gem of purest ray serene
            The dark unfathomed caves of ocean bear:
55   Full many a flower is born to blush unseen,
            And waste its sweetness on the desert air.

        Some village Hampden[1] that with dauntless breast
            The little tyrant of his fields withstood,
        Some mute inglorious Milton here may rest,
60   Some Cromwell guiltless of his country's blood.

---

[1] John Hampden (1594–1643), a member of the English House of Commons, forcefully opposed
Charles I. John Milton (1608–1674), the author of *Paradise Lost*, wrote vigorously against the divine
right of kings to rule and became Cromwell's spokesman. Oliver Cromwell (1599–1658) led the
forces that deposed Charles I; he subsequently became the Puritan dictator of England.

Th' applause of list'ning senates to command,
　The threats of pain and ruin to despise,
To scatter plenty o'er a smiling land,
　And read their history in a nation's eyes,

65　Their lot forbade; nor circumscribed alone
　Their growing virtues, but their crimes confined;
Forbade to wade through slaughter to a throne.
　And shut the gates of mercy on mankind,

The struggling pangs of conscious truth to hide,
70　To quench the blushes of ingenuous shame,
Or heap the shrine of Luxury and Pride
　With incense kindled at the Muse's flame.

Far from the madding° crowd's ignoble strife　　　　　*raving*
　Their sober wishes never learned to stray;
75　Along the cool sequestered vale of life
　They kept the noiseless tenor of their way.

Yet even these bones from insult to protect
　Some frail memorial still erected nigh,
With uncouth rhymes and shapeless sculpture decked,°　*decorated*
80　Implores the passing tribute of a sigh.

Their name, their years, spelt by th' unlettered muse,
　The place of fame and elegy supply:
And many a holy text around she strews,
　That teach the rustic moralist to die.

85　For who, to dumb Forgetfulness a prey,
　This pleasing anxious being e'er resigned,
Left the warm precincts of the cheerful day,
　Nor cast one longing lingering look behind?

On some fond breast the parting soul relies,
90　Some pious drops the closing eye requires;
E'en from the tomb the voice of Nature cries,
　E'en in our ashes live their wonted fires.

For thee, who, mindful of th' unhonored dead,
　Dost in these lines their artless tale relate;
95　If chance, by lonely contemplation led,
　Some kindred spirit shall inquire thy fate,

Haply some hoary-headed° swain may say,　　　　　*gray-haired*
　"Oft have we seen him at the peep of dawn
Brushing with hasty steps the dews away
100　To meet the sun upon the upland lawn.

"There at the foot of yonder nodding beech
    That wreathes its old fantastic roots so high,
His listless length at noontide would he stretch,
    And pore upon the brook that babbles by.

105   "Hard by yon wood, now smiling as in scorn,
    Mutt'ring his wayward fancies he would rove,
Now drooping, woeful wan, like one forlorn,
    Or crazed with care, or crossed in hopeless love.

"One morn I missed him on the customed hill,
110   Along the heath and near his fav'rite tree;
Another came; nor yet beside the rill,
    Nor up the lawn, nor at the wood was he;

"The next with dirges due in sad array
    Slow through the church-way path we saw him
        borne.
115 Approach and read (for thou canst read) the lay
    Graved on the stone beneath yon agèd thorn:"

The Epitaph

Here rests his head upon the lap of Earth
    A youth to Fortune and to Fame unknown.
Fair Science° frowned not on his humble birth,   *knowledge*
120   *And Melancholy marked him for her own.*

Large was his bounty, and his soul sincere,
    Heaven did a recompense as largely send:
He gave to Mis'ry all he had, a tear,
    He gained from Heaven ('twas all he wished) a friend.

125 *No farther seek his merits to disclose,*
    Or draw his frailties from their dread abode
(There they alike in trembling hope repose),
    The bosom of his Father and his God.

                               [1751]

George Crabbe   *1754–1832*

PROCRASTINATION

Love will expire—the gay, the happy dream
Will turn to scorn, indiff'rence, or esteem:
Some favour'd pairs, in this exchange, are bless'd,
Nor sigh for raptures in a state of rest;
5 Others, ill match'd, with minds unpair'd, repent
At once the deed, and know no more content;
From joy to anguish they, in haste, decline,

And with their fondness, their esteem resign;
More luckless still their fate, who are the prey
10   Of long-protracted hope and dull delay;
'Mid plans of bliss the heavy hours pass on,
Till love is wither'd, and till joy is gone.
    This gentle flame two youthful hearts possess'd,
The sweet disturber of unenvied rest:
15   The prudent Dinah was the maid beloved,
And the kind Rupert was the swain approved:
A wealthy aunt her gentle niece sustain'd,
He, with a father, at his desk, remain'd;
The youthful couple, to their vows sincere,
20   Thus loved expectant; year succeeding year,
With pleasant views and hopes, but not a prospect near.
Rupert some comfort in his station saw,
But the poor virgin lived in dread and awe;
Upon her anxious looks the widow smiled,
25   And bade her wait, "for she was yet a child."
She for her neighbour had a due respect,
Nor would his son encourage or reject;
And thus the pair, with expectations vain,
Beheld the seasons change and change again:
30   Meantime the nymph her tender tales perused,
Where cruel aunts impatient girls refused;
While hers, though teasing, boasted to be kind,
And she, resenting, to be all resign'd.
    The dame was sick, and the youth applied
35   For her consent, she groan'd, and cough'd, and cried:
Talk'd of departing, and again her breath
Drew hard, and cough'd, and talk'd again of death:
"Here you may live, my Dinah! here the boy
And you together my estate enjoy;"
40   Thus to the lovers was her mind express'd,
Till they forbore to urge the fond request.
    Servant, and nurse, and comforter, and friend,
Dinah had still some duty to attend;
But yet their walk, when Rupert's evening call
45   Obtain'd an hour, made sweet amends for all;
So long they now each other's thoughts had known,
That nothing seem'd exclusively their own;
But with the common wish, the mutual fear,
They now had travell'd to their thirtieth year.
50   At length a prospect open'd—but, alas!
Long time must yet, before the union, pass;
Rupert was call'd in other clime, t'increase
Another's wealth, and toil for future peace;
Loth were the lovers; but the aunt declared
55   'Twas fortune's call, and they must be prepared;
"You now are young, and for this brief delay,
And Dinah's care, what I bequeath will pay;
All will be yours; nay, love, suppress that sigh;

The kind must suffer, and the best must die."
60   Then came the cough, and strong the signs it gave
Of holding long contention with the grave.
   The lovers parted with a gloomy view,
And little comfort but that both were true;
He for uncertain duties doom'd to steer,
65   While hers remain'd too certain and severe.
   Letters arrived, and Rupert fairly told
"His cares were many, and his hopes were cold;
The view more clouded, that was never fair,
And love alone preserved him from despair:"
70   In other letters brighter hopes he drew,
"His friends were kind, and he believed them true."
   When the sage widow Dinah's grief descried,
She wonder'd much why one so happy sigh'd:
Then bade her see how her poor aunt sustain'd.
75   The ills of life, nor murmur'd nor complain'd.
To vary pleasures, from the lady's chest
Were drawn the pearly string and tabby vest;
Beads, jewels, laces, all their value shown,
With the kind notice—"They will be your own."
80   This hope, these comforts cherish'd day by day,
To Dinah's bosom made a gradual way;
Till love of treasure had as large a part,
As love of Rupert, in the virgin's heart.
Whether it be that tender passions fail,
85   From their own nature, while the strong prevail;
Or whether av'rice, like the poison-tree,
Kills all beside it, and alone will be;
Whatever cause prevail'd, the pleasure grew
In Dinah's soul,—she loved the hoards to view;
90   With lively joy those comforts she survey'd,
And love grew languid in the careful maid.
   Now the grave niece partook the widow's cares,
Look'd to the great and ruled the small affairs;
Saw clean'd the plate, arranged the china show,
95   And felt her passion for a shilling grow:
Th' indulgent aunt increased the maid's delight,
By placing tokens of her wealth in sight;
She loved the value of her bonds to tell,
And spake of stocks, and how they rose and fell.
100   This passion grew, and gain'd at length such sway,
That other passions shrank to make it way;
Romantic notions now the heart forsook,
She read but seldom, and she changed her book;
And for the verses she was wont to send,
105   Short was her prose, and she was Rupert's friend.
Seldom she wrote, and then the widow's cough,
And constant call, excused her breaking off;
Who, now oppress'd, no longer took the air,
But sate and dozed upon an easy chair.

110   The cautious doctor saw the case was clear,
       But judged it best to have companions near;
       They came, they reason'd, they prescribed—at last,
       Like honest men, they said their hopes were past;
       Then came a priest—'tis comfort to reflect,
115   When all is over, there was no neglect;
       And all was over—by her husband's bones,
       The widow rests beneath the sculptured stones,
       That yet record their fondness and their fame,
       While all they left the virgin's care became;
120   Stock, bonds, and buildings;—it disturb'd her rest,
       To think what load of troubles she possess'd:
       Yet, if a trouble, she resolved to take
       Th' important duty, for the donor's sake;
       She too was heiress to the widow's taste,
125   Her love of hoarding, and her dread of waste.
           Sometimes the past would on her mind intrude,
       And then a conflict full of care ensued;
       The thoughts of Rupert on her mind would press,
       His worth she knew, but doubted his success;
130   Of old she saw him heedless; what the boy
       Forbore to save, the man would not enjoy;
       Oft had he lost the chance that care would seize,
       Willing to live, but more to live at ease:
       Yet could she not a broken vow defend,
135   And Heav'n, perhaps, might yet enrich her friend.
           Month after month was pass'd, and all were spent
       In quiet comfort and in rich content:
       Miseries there were, and woes the world around,
       But these had not her pleasant dwelling found;
140   She knew that mothers grieved, and widows wept,
       And she was sorry, said her prayers, and slept:
       Thus pass'd the seasons, and to Dinah's board
       Gave what the seasons to the rich afford;
       For she indulged, nor was her heart so small,
145   That one strong passion should engross it all.
           A love of splendour now with av'rice strove,
       And oft appear'd to be the stronger love:
       A secret pleasure fill'd the widow's breast,
       When she reflected on the hoards possess'd;
150   But livelier joy inspired th' ambitious maid,
       When she the purchase of those hoards display'd:
       In small but splendid room she loved to see
       That all was placed in view and harmony;
       There, as with eager glance she look'd around,
155   She much delight in every object found;
       While books devout were near her—to destroy,
       Should it arise, an overflow of joy.
           Within that fair apartment, guests might see
       The comforts cull'd for wealth by vanity:
160   Around the room an Indian paper blazed,

With lively tint and figures boldly raised;
Silky and soft upon the floor below,
Th' elastic carpet rose with crimson glow;
All things around implied both cost and care,
165 What met the eye was elegant or rare:
Some curious trifles round the room were laid,
By hope presented to the wealthy maid:
Within a costly case of varnish'd wood,
In level rows, her polish'd volumes stood;
170 Shown as a favour to a chosen few,
To prove what beauty for a book could do:
A silver urn with curious work was fraught;
A silver lamp from Grecian pattern wrought:
Above her head, all gorgeous to behold,
175 A time-piece stood on feet of burnish'd gold;
A stag's-head crest adorn'd the pictured case,
Through the pure crystal shone th' enamell'd face;
And while on brilliants moved the hands of steel,
It click'd from pray'r to pray'r, from meal to meal.
180   Here as the lady sate, a friendly pair
Stept in t' admire the view, and took their chair:
They then related how the young and gay
Were thoughtless wandering in the broad highway;
How tender damsels sail'd in tilted boats,
185 And laugh'd with wicked men in scarlet coats;
And how we live in such degen'rate times,
That men conceal their wants, and show their crimes;
While vicious deeds are screen'd by fashion's name,
And what was once our pride is now our shame.
190   Dinah was musing, as her friends discoursed,
When these last words a sudden entrance forced
Upon her mind, and what was once her pride
And now her shame, some painful views supplied;
Thoughts of the past within her bosom press'd,
195 And there a change was felt, and was confess'd:
While thus the virgin strove with secret pain,
Her mind was wandering o'er the troubled main;
Still she was silent, nothing seem'd to see,
But sate and sigh'd in pensive reverie.
200   The friends prepared new subjects to begin,
When tall Susannah, maiden starch, stalk'd in;
Not in her ancient mode, sedate and slow,
As when she came, the mind she knew, to know;
Nor as, when list'ning half an hour before,
205 She twice or thrice tapp'd gently at the door;
But, all decorum cast in wrath aside,
"I think the devil's in the man!" she cried;
"A huge sailor, with his tawny cheek,
And pitted face, will with my lady speak;
210 He grinn'd an ugly smile, and said he knew,
Please you, my lady, 'twould be joy to you;

What must I answer?"—Trembling and distress'd
Sank the pale Dinah by her fears oppress'd;
When thus alarm'd, and brooking no delay,
215   Swift to her room the stranger made his way.
    "Revive, my love!" said he, "I've done thee harm,
Give me thy pardon," and he look'd alarm:
Meantime the prudent Dinah had contrived
Her soul to question, and she then revived.
220   "See! my good friend," and then she raised her head,
"The bloom of life, the strength of youth is fled;
Living we die; to us the world is dead;
We parted bless'd with health, and I am now
Age-struck and feeble, so I find art thou;
225   Thine eye is sunken, furrow'd is thy face,
And downward look'st thou—so we run our race;
And happier they, whose race is nearly run,
Their troubles over, and their duties done."
    "True, lady, true, we are not girl and boy;
230   But time has left us something to enjoy."
    "What! thou hast learn'd my fortune?—yes, I live
To feel how poor the comforts wealth can give;
Thou too perhaps art wealthy; but our fate
Still mocks our wishes, wealth is come too late."
235   "To me nor late nor early; I am come
Poor as I left thee to my native home:
Nor yet," said Rupert, "will I grieve; 'tis mine
To share thy comforts, and the glory thine;
For thou wilt gladly take that generous part
240   That both exalts and gratifies the heart;
While mine rejoices."—"Heavens!" return'd the maid,
"This talk to one so wither'd and decay'd?
No! all my care is now to fit my mind
For other spousal, and to die resign'd:
245   As friend and neighbour, I shall hope to see
These noble views, this pious love in thee;
That we together may the change await,
Guides and spectators in each other's fate;
When fellow-pilgrims, we shall daily crave
250   The mutual prayer that arms us for the grave."
    Half angry, half in doubt, the lover gazed
On the meek maiden, by her speech amazed;
"Dinah," said he, "dost thou respect thy vows?
What spousal mean'st thou?—thou art Rupert's spouse;
255   The chance is mine to take, and thine to give;
But, trifling this, if we together live:
Can I believe, that, after all the past,
Our vows, our loves, thou wilt be false at last?
Something thou hast—I know not what—in view;
260   I find thee pious—let me find thee true."
    "Ah! cruel this; but do, my friend, depart;
And to its feelings leave my wounded heart."

"Nay, speak at once; and Dinah, let me know,
Mean'st thou to take me, now I'm wreck'd, in tow?
265 Be fair; nor longer keep me in the dark;
Am I forsaken for a trimmer spark?[1]
Heav'n's spouse thou art not; nor can I believe
That God accepts her who will man deceive:
True I am shatter'd, I have service seen,
270 And service done, and have in trouble been;
My cheek (it shames me not) has lost its red,
And the brown buff is o'er my features spread;
Perchance my speech is rude; for I among
Th' untamed have been, in temper and in tongue;
275 Have been trepann'd,[2] have lived in toil and care,
And wrought for wealth I was not doom'd to share;
It touch'd me deeply, for I felt a pride
In gaining riches for my destined bride:
Speak then my fate; for these my sorrows past,
280 Time lost, youth fled, hope wearied, and at last
This doubt of thee—a childish thing to tell,
But certain truth—my very throat they swell;
They stop the breath, and but for shame could I
Give way to weakness, and with passion cry;
285 These are unmanly struggles, but I feel
This hour must end them, and perhaps will heal."—
    Here Dinah sigh'd as if afraid to speak—
And then repeated—"They were frail and weak;
His soul she loved, and hoped he had the grace
290 To fix his thoughts upon a better place."
    She ceased;—with steady glance, as if to see
The very root of this hypocrisy,—
He her small fingers moulded in his hard
And bronzed broad hand; then told her his regard,
295 His best respect were gone, but love had still
Hold in his heart, and govern'd yet the will—
Or he would curse her:—saying this, he threw
The hand in scorn away, and bade adieu
To every lingering hope, with every care in view.
300 Proud and indignant, suffering, sick, and poor,
He grieved unseen; and spoke of love no more—
Till all he felt in indignation died,
As hers had sunk in avarice and pride.
    In health declining, as in mind distress'd,
305 To some in power his troubles he confess'd,
And shares a parish-gift;—at prayers he sees
The pious Dinah dropp'd upon her knees;
Thence as she walks the street with stately air,
As chance directs, oft meet the parted pair:
310 When he, with thickset coat of badge-man's blue,
Moves near her shaded silk of changeful hue;

---

[1] A slimmer suitor.
[2] Tricked.

When his thin locks of grey approach her braid,
A costly purchase made in beauty's aid;
When his frank air, and his unstudied pace,
315 Are seen with her soft manner, air, and grace,
And his plain artless look with her sharp meaning face;
It might some wonder in a stranger move,
How these together could have talk'd of love.
  Behold them now!—see there a tradesman stands,
320 And humbly hearkens to some fresh commands;
He moves to speak, she interrupts him—"Stay,"
Her air expresses—"Hark! to what I say:"
Ten paces off, poor Rupert on a seat
Has taken refuge from the noon-day heat,
325 His eyes on her intent, as if to find
What were the movements of that subtle mind:
How still!—how earnest is he!—it appears
His thoughts are wand'ring through his earlier years;
Through years of fruitless labour, to the day
330 When all his earthly prospects died away:
"Had I," he thinks, "been wealthier of the two,
Would she have found me so unkind, untrue?
Or knows not man when poor, what man when rich will do?
Yes, yes! I feel that I had faithful proved,
335 And should have soothed and raised her, bless'd and loved."
  But Dinah moves—she had observed before
The pensive Rupert at an humble door:
Some thoughts of pity raised by his distress,
Some feeling touch of ancient tenderness;
340 Religion, duty urged the maid to speak
In terms of kindness to a man so weak:
But pride forbad, and to return would prove
She felt the shame of his neglected love;
Nor wrapp'd in silence could she pass, afraid
345 Each eye should see her, and each heart upbraid;
One way remain'd—the way the Levite took,
Who without mercy could on misery look;
(A way perceived by craft, approved by pride),
She cross'd, and pass'd him on the other side.

[1812]

William Blake   *1757–1827*

FROM *Songs of Innocence*

THE LITTLE BLACK BOY

My mother bore me in the southern wild,
  And I am black, but O, my soul is white!
White as an angel is the English child,
  But I am black, as if bereaved° of light.   robbed

⁵ My mother taught me underneath a tree,
　　And, sitting down before the heat of day,
She took me on her lap and kissèd me,
　　And, pointing to the east, began to say:

"Look at the rising sun: there God does live,
¹⁰　　And gives his light, and gives his heat away,
And flowers and trees and beasts and men receive
　　Comfort in morning, joy in the noonday.

"And we are put on earth a little space,
　　That we may learn to bear the beams of love;
¹⁵ And these black bodies and this sunburnt face
　　Are but a cloud, and like a shady grove.

"For when our souls have learned the heat to bear,
　　The cloud will vanish, we shall hear his voice,
Saying, 'Come out from the grove, my love and care,
²⁰　　And round my golden tent like lambs rejoice.' "

Thus did my mother say, and kissèd me,
　　And thus I say to little English boy.
When I from black and he from white cloud free,
　　And round the tent of God like lambs we joy,

²⁵ I'll shade him from the heat till he can bear
　　To lean in joy upon our Father's knee;
And then I'll stand and stroke his silver hair,
　　And be like him, and he will then love me.

[1789]

THE CHIMNEY SWEEPER

When my mother died I was very young,
And my father sold me while yet my tongue
Could scarcely cry " 'weep! 'weep! 'weep! 'weep!"
So your chimneys I sweep and in soot I sleep.

⁵ There's little Tom Dacre, who cried when his head
That curled like a lamb's back, was shaved, so I said,
"Hush, Tom! never mind it, for when your head's bare,
You know that the soot cannot spoil your white hair."

And so he was quiet, and that very night,
¹⁰ As Tom was a-sleeping he had such a sight!
That thousands of sweepers, Dick, Joe, Ned, and Jack,
Were all of them locked up in coffins of black;

And by came an angel who had a bright key,
And he opened the coffins and set them all free;
¹⁵ Then down a green plain, leaping, laughing they run,
And wash in a river and shine in the sun;

Then naked and white, all their bags left behind,
They rise upon clouds and sport in the wind.
And the angel told Tom, if he'd be a good boy,
20   He'd have God for his father and never want joy.

And so Tom awoke; and we rose in the dark
And got with our bags and our brushes to work.
Tho' the morning was cold, Tom was happy and warm;
So if all do their duty, they need not fear harm.

[1789]

FROM *Songs of Experience*

THE CHIMNEY SWEEPER

A little black thing among the snow:
Crying weep, weep, in notes of woe!
Where are thy father and mother? Say?
They are both gone up to the church to pray.

5   Because I was happy upon the heath,
And smiled among the winter's snow:
They clothed me in the clothes of death,
And taught me to sing the notes of woe.

And because I am happy, and dance and sing,
10   They think they have done me no injury:
And are gone to praise God and his priest and king
Who make up a heaven of our misery.

[1794]

THE SICK ROSE

O Rose thou art sick.
The invisible worm,
That flies in the night
In the howling storm:

5   Has found out thy bed
Of crimson joy:
And his dark secret love
Does thy life destroy.

[1794]

THE TYGER

Tyger, Tyger, burning bright
In the forests of the night,
What immortal hand or eye
Could frame thy fearful symmetry?

5   In what distant deeps or skies
    Burnt the fire of thine eyes?
    On what wings dare he aspire?
    What the hand dare seize the fire?

    And what shoulder and what art
10 Could twist the sinews of thy heart?
    And, when thy heart began to beat,
    What dread hand and what dread feet?

    What the hammer? What the chain?
    In what furnace was thy brain?
15 What the anvil? What dread grasp
    Dare its deadly terrors clasp?

    When the stars threw down their spears,
    And watered heaven with their tears,
    Did He smile his work to see?
20 Did He who made the lamb make thee?

    Tyger, Tyger, burning bright
    In the forests of the night,
    What immortal hand or eye
    Dare frame thy fearful symmetry?
                                    [1794]

LONDON

    I wander thro' each chartered street,
    Near where the chartered° Thames does flow,   *bound*
    And mark in every face I meet
    Marks of weakness, marks of woe.

5   In every cry of every man,
    In every infant's cry of fear,
    In every voice, in every ban,
    The mind-forged manacles I hear.

    How the chimney-sweeper's cry
10 Every black'ning church appalls,
    And the hapless soldier's sigh,
    Runs in blood down palace walls.

    But most thro' midnight streets I hear
    How the youthful harlot's curse
15 Blasts the new-born infant's tear
    And blights with plagues the marriage hearse.
                                    [1794]

THE CLOD AND THE PEBBLE

"Love seeketh not Itself to please,
Nor for itself hath any care,
But for another gives its ease,
And builds a Heaven in Hell's despair."

5   So sung a little Clod of Clay
Trodden with the cattle's feet,
But a Pebble of the brook
Warbled out these metres meet:

"Love seeketh only Self to please,
10   To bind another to Its delight,
Joys in another's loss of ease,
And builds a Hell in Heaven's despite."

                                    [1794]

A POISON TREE

I was angry with my friend:
I told my wrath, my wrath did end.
I was angry with my foe:
I told it not, my wrath did grow.

5   And I water'd it in fears,
Night & morning with my tears;
And I sunned it with smiles,
And with soft deceitful wiles.

And it grew both day and night,
10   Till it bore an apple bright;
And my foe beheld it shine,
And he knew that it was mine,

And into my garden stole
When the night had veil'd the pole:
15   In the morning glad I see
My foe outstretch'd beneath the tree.

                                    [1794]

Robert Burns *1759–1796*

"I ONCE WAS A MAID"

I once was a maid, tho' I cannot tell when,
An' still my delight is in proper young men;
Some one of a troop of dragoons° was my daddie,   *cavalrymen*
No wonder I'm fond of a sodger°-laddie.   *soldier*

5 The first of my loves was a swaggering blade,
To rattle the thundering drum was his trade;
His leg was so tight, and his cheek was so ruddy,
Transported I was with my sodger laddie.

10 But the godly old chaplain left him in the lurch,
The sword I forsook for the sake of the church,
He ventured the soul, and I risk'd the body,
T'was then I proved false to my sodger laddie.

Full soon I grew sick of my sanctified sot.
The regiment at large for a husband I got;
15 From the gilded spontoon[1] to the life I was ready,
I asked no more but a sodger laddie.

But the peace it reduced me to beg in despair,
Till I met my old boy at a Cunningham fair;
His rags regimental they fluttered so gaudy,
20 My heart it rejoiced at my sodger laddie.

An' now I have lived—I know not how long,
An' still I can join in a cup or a song;
But whilst with both hands I can hold the glass steady,
Here's to thee, my hero, my sodger laddie.

[1785]

TO A MOUSE, ON TURNING HER UP IN HER NEST WITH THE PLOUGH, NOVEMBER, 1785

Wee, sleekit,° cow'rin', tim'rous beastie,	*sleek*
O what a panic's in thy breastie!	
Thou need na start awa sae hasty,	
Wi' bickering brattle!°	*scamper*
5 I wad be laith to rin an' chase thee	
Wi' murd'ring pattle!°	*small spade*
I'm truly sorry man's dominion	
Has broken Nature's social union,	
An' justifies that ill opinion	
10 Which makes thee startle	
At me, thy poor earth-born companion,	
An' fellow-mortal!	
I doubt na, whiles,° but thou may thieve;	*at times*
What then? poor beastie, thou maun live!	
15 A daimen-icker° in a thrave°	*odd ear / thousand*
'S a sma' request:	
I'll get a blessin' wi' the lave,°	*remnant*
And never miss 't!	

[1] A half-pike or halberd carried by infantry officers.

20

Thy wee bit housie, too, in ruin!
Its silly wa's° the win's are strewin'!   *walls*
An' naething, now, to big° a new ane,   *build*
       O' foggage° green!   *foliage*
An' bleak December's winds ensuin',
       Baith snell° an' keen!   *bitter*

25

Thou saw the fields laid bare and waste.
An' weary winter comin' fast,
An' cozie here, beneath the blast,
       Thou thought to dwell,
30 Till crash! the cruel coulter° past   *plow*
       Out-thro' thy cell.

That wee bit heap o' leaves an' stibble
Has cost thee mony a weary nibble!
Now thou's turn'd out, for a' thy trouble,
       But° house or hald,°   *Without / hold*
35 To thole° the winter's sleety dribble,   *suffer*
       An' cranreuch° cauld!   *frozen dew*

But, Mousie, thou art no thy lane,°   *not alone*
In proving foresight may be vain:
The best laid schemes o' mice an' men
40   Gang aft a-gley,°   *awry*
An' lea'e us nought but grief an' pain
       For promis'd joy.

Still thou art blest compar'd wi' me!
The present only toucheth thee:
45 But oh! I backward cast my e'e
       On prospects drear!
An' forward tho' I canna see,
       I guess an' fear!
                 [1786]

A RED, RED ROSE

O, my luve is like a red, red rose
    That's newly sprung in June:
O, my luve is like the melodie
    That's sweetly play'd in tune.

5

So fair art thou, my bonnie lass,
    So deep in luve am I:
And I will luve thee still, my dear,
    Till a' the seas gang dry.

Till a' the seas gang dry, my dear,
10   And the rocks melt wi' the sun:
And I will luve thee still, my dear,
    While the sands o' life shall run.

And fair thee weel, my only luve,
    And fair thee weel awhile!
15 And I will come again, my luve,
    Tho' it were ten thousand mile.

[1796]

FOR A' THAT AND A' THAT

Is there, for honest poverty,
    That hings his head, and a' that;
The coward-slave, we pass him by,
    We dare be poor for a' that!
5   For a' that, and a' that,
            Our toils obscure, and a' that,
        The rank is but the guinea's stamp,
            The man's the gowd° for a' that.   *gold*

What though on hamely fare we dine,
10   Wear hoddin-grey,° and a' that;   *coarse, undyed wool*
Gie fools their silks, and knaves their wine,
    A man's a man for a' that.
            For a' that, and a' that,
            Their tinsel show, and a' that;
15   The honest man, tho' e'er sae poor,
            Is king o' men for a' that.

Ye see yon birkie,° ca'd a lord,   *young fellow*
    Wha struts, and stares, and a' that;
Tho' hundreds worship at his word,
20   He's but a coof° for a' that.   *numbskull*
            For a' that, and a' that,
            His ribband, star,° and a' that,   *star of knighthood*
        The man of independent mind,
            He looks and laughs at a' that.

25 A prince can mak a belted knight,
    A marquis, duke, and a' that;
But an honest man's aboon° his might,   *above*
    Guid faith, he mauna fa'° that!   *mustn't claim*
            For a' that, and a' that,
30   Their dignities, and a' that,
        The pith o' sense, and pride o' worth,
            Are higher rank than a' that.

Then let us pray that come it may,
    As come it will for a' that,
35 That sense and worth, o'er a' the earth,
    Shall bear the gree,° and a' that.   *prize*
            For a' that and a' that,
            It's coming yet, for a' that,
        That man to man, the warld o'er,
40   Shall brothers be for a' that.

[1795]

❦ NINETEENTH-CENTURY POETRY ❦

William Wordsworth   *1770–1850*

LINES

Composed a Few Miles Above Tintern Abbey on Revisiting the Banks of the Wye During a Tour. July 13, 1798

Five years have passed; five summers, with the length
Of five long winters! and again I hear
These waters, rolling from their mountain-springs
With a soft inland murmur.—Once again
5 Do I behold these steep and lofty cliffs,
That on a wild secluded scene impress
Thoughts of more deep seclusion; and connect
The landscape with the quiet of the sky.
The day is come when I again repose
10 Here, under this dark sycamore, and view
These plots of cottage-ground, these orchard-tufts,
Which at this season, with their unripe fruits,
Are clad in one green hue, and lose themselves
'Mid groves and copses. Once again I see
15 These hedge-rows, hardly hedge-rows, little lines
Of sportive wood run wild: these pastoral farms,
Green to the very door; and wreaths of smoke
Sent up, in silence, from among the trees!
With some uncertain notice, as might seem
20 Of vagrant dwellers in the houseless woods,
Or of some hermit's cave, where by his fire
The hermit sits alone.   These beauteous forms,
Through a long absence, have not been to me
As is a landscape to a blind man's eye:
25 But oft, in lonely rooms, and 'mid the din
Of towns and cities, I have owed to them
In hours of weariness, sensations sweet,
Felt in the blood, and felt along the heart;
And passing even into my purer mind,
30 With tranquil restoration:°—feelings too   *recollection*
Of unremembered pleasure: such, perhaps,
As have no slight or trivial influence
On that best portion of a good man's life,
His little, nameless, unremembered, acts
35 Of kindness and of love. Nor less, I trust,
To them I may have owed another gift,

861

Of aspect more sublime; that blessed mood
In which the burthen of the mystery,
In which the heavy and the weary weight
40 Of all this unintelligible world,
Is lightened:—that serene and blessed mood,
In which the affections gently lead us on,—
Until, the breath of this corporeal frame
And even the motion of our human blood
45 Almost suspended, we are laid asleep
In body, and become a living soul:
While with an eye made quiet by the power
Of harmony, and the deep power of joy,
We see into the life of things.
                                     If this
50 Be but a vain belief, yet, oh! how oft—
In darkness and amid the many shapes
Of joyless daylight; when the fretful stir
Unprofitable, and the fever of the world,
Have hung upon the beatings of my heart—
55 How oft, in spirit, have I turned to thee,
O sylvan Wye! thou wanderer through the woods,
How often has my spirit turned to thee!

And now, with gleams of half-extinguished thought,
With many recognitions dim and faint,
60 And somewhat of a sad perplexity,
The picture of the mind revives again:
While here I stand, not only with the sense
Of present pleasure, but with pleasing thoughts
That in this moment there is life and food
65 For future years. And so I dare to hope,
Though changed, no doubt, from what I was when
      first
I came along these hills; when like a roe°   *a small deer*
I bounded o'er the mountains, by the sides
Of the deep rivers, and the lonely streams,
70 Wherever nature led: more like a man
Flying from something that he dreads than one
Who sought the thing he loved. For nature then
(The coarser pleasures of my boyish days,
And their glad animal movements all gone by)
75 To me was all in all.—I cannot paint
What then I was. The sounding cataract°   *waterfall*
Haunted me like a passion: the tall rock,
The mountain, and the deep and gloomy wood,
Their colors and their forms, were then to me
80 An appetite; a feeling and a love,
That had no need of a remoter charm,
By thought supplied, nor any interest
Unborrowed from the eye.—That time is past,
And all its aching joys are now no more,
85 And all its dizzy raptures. Not for this

Faint I, nor mourn nor murmur; other gifts
Have followed; for such loss, I would believe,
Abundant recompense. For I have learned
To look on nature, not as in the hour
90   Of thoughtless youth; but hearing oftentimes
The still, sad music of humanity,
Nor harsh nor grating, though of ample power
To chasten and subdue. And I have felt
A presence that disturbs me with the joy
95   Of elevated thoughts; a sense sublime
Of something far more deeply interfused,
Whose dwelling is the light of setting suns,
And the round ocean and the living air,
And the blue sky, and in the mind of man:
100   A motion and a spirit, that impels
All thinking things, all objects of all thought,
And rolls through all things. Therefore am I still
A lover of the meadows and the woods,
And mountains; and of all that we behold
105   From this green earth; of all the mighty world
Of eye, and ear,—both what they half create,
And what perceive; well pleased to recognize
In nature and the language of the sense
The anchor of my purest thoughts, the nurse,
110   The guide, the guardian of my heart, and soul
Of all my moral being.
                Nor perchance,
If I were not thus taught, should I the more
Suffer my genial spirits° to decay: *creative powers*
For thou art with me here upon the banks
115   Of this fair river; thou my dearest Friend,°   *his sister Dorothy*
My dear, dear Friend; and in thy voice I catch
The language of my former heart, and read
My former pleasures in the shooting lights
Of thy wild eyes. Oh! yet a little while
120   May I behold in thee what I was once,
My dear, dear Sister! and this prayer I make,
Knowing that Nature never did betray
The heart that loved her; 'tis her privilege,
Through all the years of this our life, to lead
125   From joy to joy: for she can so inform
The mind that is within us, so impress
With quietness and beauty, and so feed
With lofty thoughts, that neither evil tongues,
Rash judgments, nor the sneers of selfish men,
130   Nor greetings where no kindness is, nor all
The dreary intercourse of daily life,
Shall e'er prevail against us, or disturb
Our cheerful faith, that all which we behold
Is full of blessings. Therefore let the moon
135   Shine on thee in thy solitary walk;
And let the misty mountain-winds be free

To blow against thee: and, in after years,
When these wild ecstasies shall be matured
Into a sober pleasure; when thy mind
140   Shall be a mansion for all lovely forms,
Thy memory be as a dwelling-place
For all sweet sounds and harmonies; oh! then,
If solitude, or fear, or pain, or grief,
Should be thy portion, with what healing thoughts
145   Of tender joy wilt thou remember me,
And these my exhortations! Nor, perchance—
If I should be where I no more can hear
Thy voice, nor catch from thy wild eyes these gleams
Of past existence—wilt thou then forget
150   That on the banks of this delightful stream
We stood together; and that I, so long
A worshipper of Nature, hither came
Unwearied in that service: rather say
With warmer love—oh! with far deeper zeal
155   Of holier love. Nor wilt thou then forget,
That after many wanderings, many years
Of absence, these steep woods and lofty cliffs,
And this green pastoral landscape, were to me
More dear, both for themselves and for thy sake!

[1798]

"SHE DWELT AMONG THE UNTRODDEN WAYS"

She dwelt among the untrodden ways
    Beside the springs of Dove,
A maid whom there were none to praise
    And very few to love:

5   A violet by a mossy stone
    Half hidden from the eye!
Fair as a star, when only one
    Is shining in the sky.

She lived unknown, and few could know
10   When Lucy ceased to be;
But she is in her grave, and oh,
    The difference to me!

[1800]

I WANDERED LONELY AS A CLOUD

I wandered lonely as a cloud
    That floats on high o'er vales and hills,
When all at once I saw a crowd,
    A host, of golden daffodils;
5   Beside the lake, beneath the trees,
Fluttering and dancing in the breeze.

Continuous as the stars that shine
  And twinkle on the Milky Way,
They stretched in never-ending line
  Along the margin of a bay:
10   Ten thousand saw I at a glance,
Tossing their heads in sprightly dance.

The waves beside them danced, but they
  Out-did the sparkling waves in glee:
15   A poet could not but be gay,
  In such a jocund company:
I gazed—and gazed—but little thought
What wealth the show to me had brought:

For oft, when on my couch I lie
20   In vacant or in pensive mood,
They flash upon that inward eye
  Which is the bliss of solitude;
And then my heart with pleasure fills,
And dances with the daffodils.

[1807]

"SHE WAS A PHANTOM OF DELIGHT"

She was a phantom of delight
When first she gleamed upon my sight;
A lovely apparition, sent
To be a moment's ornament;
5   Her eyes as stars of twilight fair;
Like twilight's, too, her dusky hair;
But all things else about her drawn
From May-time and the cheerful dawn;
A dancing shape, an image gay,
10   To haunt, to startle, and waylay.

I saw her upon nearer view,
A spirit, yet a woman too!
Her household motions light and free,
And steps of virgin liberty;
15   A countenance in which did meet
Sweet records, promises as sweet;
A creature not too bright or good
For human nature's daily food;
For transient sorrows, simple wiles,
20   Praise, blame, love, kisses, tears, and smiles.

And now I see with eye serene
The very pulse of the machine;
A being breathing thoughtful breath,
A traveller between life and death;
25   The reason firm, the temperate will,
Endurance, foresight, strength, and skill;

A perfect woman, nobly planned,
To warn, to comfort, and command;
And yet a spirit still, and bright
30   With something of angelic light.

[1807]

LONDON, 1802

Milton! thou shouldst be living at this hour:
England hath need of thee: she is a fen
Of stagnant waters: altar, sword, and pen,
Fireside, the heroic wealth of hall and bower,
5   Have forfeited their ancient English dower
Of inward happiness. We are selfish men;
Oh! raise us up, return to us again;
And give us manners, virtue, freedom, power.
Thy soul was like a Star, and dwelt apart;
10   Thou hadst a voice whose sound was like the sea:
Pure as the naked heavens, majestic, free,
So didst thou travel on life's common way,
In cheerful godliness; and yet thy heart
The lowliest duties on herself did lay.

[1807]

COMPOSED UPON WESTMINSTER BRIDGE, SEPTEMBER 3, 1802

Earth has not anything to show more fair:
    Dull would he be of soul who could pass by
    A sight so touching in its majesty:
This city now doth like a garment wear
5   The beauty of the morning; silent, bare,
    Ships, towers, domes, theaters, and temples lie
    Open unto the fields, and to the sky;
All bright and glittering in the smokeless air.
Never did sun more beautifully steep
10   In his first splendor, valley, rock, or hill;
Ne'er saw I, never felt, a calm so deep!
    The river glideth at his own sweet will:
Dear God! the very houses seem asleep;
    And all that mighty heart is lying still!

[1807]

"THE WORLD IS TOO MUCH WITH US"

The world is too much with us; late and soon,
    Getting and spending, we lay waste our powers:
    Little we see in Nature that is ours;
We have given our hearts away, a sordid boon:
5   This sea that bares her bosom to the moon;

The winds that will be howling at all hours,
And are up-gathered now like sleeping flowers;
For this, for everything, we are out of tune;
It moves us not.—Great God! I'd rather be
10   A pagan suckled in a creed outworn;
So might I, standing on this pleasant lea,°   *meadow*
Have glimpses that would make me less forlorn;
Have sight of Proteus[1] rising from the sea;
Or hear old Triton[2] blow his wreathèd horn.

[1807]

Samuel Taylor Coleridge *1772–1834*

KUBLA KHAN

In Xanadu did Kubla Khan
A stately pleasure-dome decree:
Where Alph, the sacred river, ran
Through caverns measureless to man
5   Down to a sunless sea.
So twice five miles of fertile ground
With walls and towers were girdled round:
And there were gardens bright with sinuous rills
Where blossomed many an incense-bearing tree;
10   And here were forests ancient as the hills,
Enfolding sunny spots of greenery.

But O, that deep romantic chasm which slanted
Down the green hill athwart a cedarn cover!°   *across a cedar woods*
A savage place! as holy and enchanted
15   As e'er beneath a waning moon was haunted
By woman wailing for her demon-lover!
And from this chasm, with ceaseless turmoil
          seething
As if this earth in fast thick pants were
          breathing,
A mighty fountain momently° was forced;   *every moment*
20   Amid whose swift half-intermitted burst
Huge fragments vaulted like rebounding hail,
Or chaffy grain beneath the thresher's flail:
And 'mid these dancing rocks at once and ever
It flung up momently the sacred river.
25   Five miles meandering with a mazy motion
Through wood and dale the sacred river ran,
Then reached the caverns measureless to man,
And sank in tumult to a lifeless ocean:
And 'mid this tumult Kubla heard from far

[1] A Greek sea god capable of changing shapes at will.
[2] A Greek sea god often depicted with a conch-shell trumpet.

30 Ancestral voices prophesying war!
  The shadow of the dome of pleasure
   Floated midway on the waves;
  Where was heard the mingled measure
  From the fountain and the caves.
35 It was a miracle of rare device,
A sunny pleasure-dome with caves of ice!

  A damsel with a dulcimer
   In a vision once I saw:
  It was an Abyssinian maid,
40   And on her dulcimer she played,
  Singing of Mount Abora.
  Could I revive within me,
   Her symphony and song,
To such a deep delight 'twould win me,
45 That with music loud and long,
I would build that dome in air,
That sunny dome! those caves of ice!
And all who heard should see them there,
And all should cry, Beware! Beware!
50 His flashing eyes, his floating hair!
Weave a circle round him thrice,
  And close your eyes with holy dread,
  For he on honey-dew hath fed,
And drunk the milk of Paradise.

            [1816]

WORK WITHOUT HOPE

[*Lines Composed* 21st February 1825]

All Nature seems at work. Slugs leave their lair—
The bees are stirring—birds are on the wing—
And Winter, slumbering in the open air,
Wears on his smiling face a dream of Spring!
5 And I, the while, the sole unbusy thing,
Nor honey make, nor pair, nor build, nor sing.

Yet well I ken° the banks where amaranths[1] blow,   *know*
Have traced the fount whence streams of nectar flow.
Bloom, O ye amaranths! bloom for whom ye may,
10 For me ye bloom not! Glide, rich streams, away!
With lips unbrightened, wreathless brow, I stroll:
And would you learn the spells that drowse my soul?
Work without hope draws nectar in a sieve,
And hope without an object cannot live.

            [1828]

---

[1] Mythical ever-blooming flowers.

ON DONNE'S POETRY

With Donne, whose muse on dromedary° trots,   *camel*
Wreathe iron pokers into truelove knots;
Rhyme's sturdy cripple, fancy's maze and clue,
Wit's forge and fire-blast, meaning's press and screw.

[posthumous, 1836]

Leigh Hunt *1784–1859*

RONDEAU

Jenny kissed me when we met,
   Jumping from the chair she sat in;
Time, you thief, who love to get
   Sweets into your list, put that in!
5 Say I'm weary, say I'm sad,
   Say that health and wealth have missed me,
Say I'm growing old, but add,
   Jenny kissed me.

[1838]

George Gordon, Lord Byron *1788–1824*

LINES INSCRIBED UPON A CUP[1] FORMED FROM A SKULL

Start not—nor deem my spirit fled;
   In me behold the only skull,
From which, unlike a living head,
   Whatever flows is never dull.

5 I lived, I loved, I quaff'd, like thee:
   I died: let earth my bones resign;
Fill up—thou canst not injure me;
   The worm hath fouler lips than thine.

Better to hold the sparkling grape,
10   Than nurse the earth-worm's slimy brood:
And circle in the goblet's shape
   The drink of gods, than reptile's food.

Where once my wit, perchance, hath shone,
   In aid of others' let me shine;
15 And when, alas! our brains are gone,
   What nobler substitute than wine?

---

[1] The cup still exists at Newstead Abbey. The base is made of solid silver and the bowl is highly polished and, in Byron's words, "of a mottled colour like a tortoise-shell."

Quaff while thou canst: another race,
  When thou and thine, like me, are sped,
May rescue thee from earth's embrace,
  And rhyme and revel with the dead.

Why not? since through life's little day
  Our heads such sad effects produce;
Redeem'd from worms and wasting clay,
  This chance is theirs, to be of use.

                                        [1808]

SHE WALKS IN BEAUTY

She walks in Beauty, like the night
  Of cloudless climes and starry skies;
And all that's best of dark and bright
  Meet in her aspect and her eyes;
Thus mellowed to that tender light
  Which Heaven to gaudy day denies.

One shade the more, one ray the less,
  Had half impaired the nameless grace
Which waves in every raven tress,
  Or softly lightens o'er her face;
Where thoughts serenely sweet express,
  How pure, how dear their dwelling-place.

And on that cheek, and o'er that brow,
  So soft, so calm, yet eloquent,
The smiles that win, the tints that glow,
  But tell of days in goodness spent,
A mind at peace with all below,
  A heart whose love is innocent!

                                        [1815]

THE DESTRUCTION OF SENNACHERIB[1]

The Assyrian came down like the wolf on the fold,
And his cohorts were gleaming in purple and gold;
And the sheen of their spears was like stars on the sea,
When the blue wave rolls nightly on deep Galilee.

Like the leaves of the forest when summer is green,
That host with their banners at sunset were seen:
Like the leaves of the forest when autumn hath blown,
That host on the morrow lay withered and strown.

---

[1] King of Assyria. See II Kings 19.

For the Angel of Death spread his wings on the blast,
10　And breathed in the face of the foe as he passed;
And the eyes of the sleepers waxed deadly and chill,
And their hearts but once heaved, and for ever grew still!

And there lay the steed with his nostril all wide,
But through it there rolled not the breath of his pride;
15　And the foam of his gasping lay white on the turf,
And cold as the spray of the rock-beating surf.

And there lay the rider distorted and pale,
With the dew on his brow and the rust on his mail;
And the tents were all silent, the banners alone,
20　The lances unlifted, the trumpet unblown.

And the widows of Ashur° are loud in their wail,　　　　　　　*Assyria*
And the idols are broke in the temple of Baal;°　　　　　　　*a sun god*
And the might of the Gentile,° unsmote by the sword,　　　　*non-Jew*
Hath melted like snow in the glance of the Lord!

[1815]

DON JUAN

Fragment on the back of the Poet's MS. of Canto 1

I would to heaven that I were so much clay,
　As I am blood, bone, marrow, passion, feeling—
Because at least the past were passed away—
　And for the future—(but I write this reeling,
5　Having got drunk exceedingly today,
　So that I seem to stand upon the ceiling)
I say—the future is a serious matter—
And so—for God's sake—hock° and soda-water!　　　　　　*a white wine*

FROM *Canto 1*

CCXVIII

What is the end of Fame? 'tis but to fill
　A certain portion of uncertain paper:
Some liken it to climbing up a hill,
　Whose summit, like all hills, is lost in vapor;
5　For this men write, speak, preach, and heroes kill,
　And bards burn what they call their "midnight
　　　taper,"
To have, when the original is dust,
A name, a wretched picture, and worse bust.

[1819]

FROM *Canto 2*

CLXXIX

Man, being reasonable, must get drunk;
    The best of life is but intoxication:
Glory, the grape, love, gold, in these are sunk
    The hopes of all men, and of every nation;
5   Without their sap, how branchless were the trunk
    Of life's strange tree, so fruitful on occasion:
But to return Get very drunk: and when
You wake with headache, you shall see what then.

        . . . .

CXCVI

An infant when it gazes on a light,
    A child the moment when it drains the breast,
A devotee when soars the Host° in sight,   *Eucharist*
    An Arab with a stranger for a guest,
5   A sailor when the prize has struck° in fight,   *surrendered*
    A miser filling his most hoarded chest,
Feel rapture; but not such true joy are reaping
As they who watch o'er what they love while sleeping.

CXCVII

For there it lies so tranquil, so beloved,
10   All that it hath of life with us is living;
So gentle, stirless, helpless, and unmoved,
    And all unconscious of the joy 'tis giving;
All it hath felt, inflicted, passed, and proved,
    Hushed into depths beyond the watcher's diving;
15 There lies the thing we love with all its errors
And all its charms, like death without its terrors.

                                 [1819]

FROM *Canto 3*

V

'Tis melancholy, and a fearful sign
    Of human frailty, folly, also crime,
That love and marriage rarely can combine,
    Although they both are born in the same clime;
5   Marriage from love, like vinegar from wine
    A sad, sour, sober beverage by time
Is sharpened from its high celestial flavor
Down to a very homely household savor.

VI

There's something of antipathy, as 'twere,
10   Between their present and their future state;
A kind of flattery that's hardly fair
    Is used until the truth arrives too late—

Yet what can people do, except despair?
  The same things change their names at such a rate;
15 For instance—passion in a lover's glorious,
  But in a husband is pronounced uxorious.°   *too fond*

VII
Men grow ashamed of being so very fond;
  They sometimes also get a little tired
  (But that, of course, is rare), and then despond:
20   The same things cannot always be admired,
Yet 'tis "so nominated in the bond,"[1]
  That both are tied till one shall have expired.
Sad thought! to lose the spouse that was adorning
Our days, and put one's servants into mourning.

VIII
25 There's doubtless something in domestic doings
  Which forms, in fact, true love's antithesis;
Romances paint at full length people's wooings,
  But only give a bust of marriages;
For no one cares for matrimonial cooings,
30   There's nothing wrong in a connubial° kiss: *marital*
Think you, if Laura had been Petrarch's wife,
He would have written sonnets all his life?[2]

IX
All tragedies are finished by a death,
  All comedies are ended by a marriage;
35 The future states of both are left to faith,
  For authors fear description might disparage
The worlds to come of both, or fall beneath,
  And then both worlds would punish their miscarriage;
So leaving each their priest and prayer-book ready,
40 They say no more of Death or of the Lady.

    . . . .

LXXXVIII
But words are things, and a small drop of ink,
  Falling like dew, upon a thought, produces
That which makes thousands, perhaps millions, think;
  'Tis strange, the shortest letter which man uses
5 Instead of speech, may form a lasting link
  Of ages; to what straits old Time reduces
Frail man, when paper—even a rag like this,
Survives himself, his tomb, and all that's his.

                  [1821]

---

[1] The bond of marriage. See Shakespeare's *The Merchant of Venice*, Act 4, Scene 1.
[2] The Italian poet Petrarch (1304–1374) wrote a famous cycle of sonnets to Laura. In his manuscript
Byron gave a more risqué twist to these lines:
  Had Petrarch's passion led to Petrarch's wedding,
  How many sonnets had ensued the bedding?

FROM *Canto 11*

I

When Bishop Berkeley[1] said "there was no matter"
   And proved it—'twas no matter what he said:
They say his system 'tis in vain to batter,
   Too subtle for the airiest human head;
5 And yet who can believe it? I would shatter
   Gladly all matters down to stone or lead,
Or adamant, to find the world a spirit,
And wear my head, denying that I wear it.

                            [1823]

FROM *Canto 14*

I

If from great nature's or our own abyss
   Of thought we could but snatch a certainty,
Perhaps mankind might find the path they miss—
   But then 'twould spoil much good philosophy.
5 One system eats another up, and this
   Much as old Saturn ate his progeny;[2]
For when his pious consort gave him stones
In lieu of sons, of these he made no bones.

II

But System doth reverse the Titan's breakfast,
10   And eats her parents, albeit the digestion
Is difficult: Pray tell me, can you make fast,
   After due search, your faith to any question?
Look back o'er ages, ere unto the stake fast
   You bind yourself, and call some mode the best one.
15 Nothing more true than *not* to trust your senses;
And yet what are your other evidences?

III

For me, I know nought; nothing I deny,
   Admit, reject, contemn;° and what know *you*,   *scorn*
Except perhaps that you were born to die?
20   And both may after all turn out untrue.
An age may come, Font° of Eternity,   *beginning*
   When nothing shall be either old or new.
Death, so called, is a thing which makes men weep,
And yet a third of life is passed in sleep.

---

[1] Bishop George Berkeley (1685–1753) was an Irish philosopher who argued that physical objects exist only in the mind of the perceiver and in the mind of God.
[2] Saturn is the Roman name for Cronus, a Titan who was warned that he would be destroyed by his own children. Therefore he ate each of his offspring at birth until one, Zeus, was concealed from him and later forced his father to vomit forth the other gods.

IV

A sleep without dreams, after a rough day
25   Of toil, is what we covet most; and yet
How clay shrinks back from more quiescent clay!
    The very Suicide that pays his debt
At once without instalments (an old way
30   Of paying debts, which creditors regret)
Lets out impatiently his rushing breath,
    Less from disgust of life than dread of death.

[1823]

Percy Bysshe Shelley *1792–1822*

MONT BLANC[1]

Lines Written in the Vale of Chamouni

I

The everlasting universe of things
Flows through the mind, and rolls its rapid waves,
Now dark, now glittering, now reflecting gloom,
Now lending splendor, where from secret springs
5 The source of human thought its tribute brings
Of waters,—with a sound but half its own,
Such as a feeble brook will oft assume
In the wild woods, among the mountains lone,
Where waterfalls around it leap forever,
10 Where woods and winds contend, and a vast river
Over its rocks ceaselessly bursts and raves.

II

Thus thou, Ravine of Arve—dark, deep Ravine—
Thou many-colored, many-voicèd vale,
Over whose pines, and crags, and caverns sail
15 Fast cloud-shadows, and sunbeams! awful scene,
Where Power in likeness of the Arve comes down
From the ice-gulfs that grid his secret throne
Bursting through these dark mountains like the flame
Of lightning through the tempest! thou dost lie,—
20 Thy giant brood of pines around thee clinging,
Children of elder time, in whose devotion
The chainless winds still come and ever came
To drink their odors, and their mighty swinging

[1] "The poem was composed under the immediate impression of the deep and powerful feelings excited by the objects which it attempts to describe; and, as an undisciplined overflowing of the soul, rests its claim to approbation on an attempt to imitate the untamable wildness and inaccessible solemnity from which those feelings sprang." (Shelley's note.)

   The "objects" were Mont Blanc (the highest mountain in Europe) and the river Arve that descends from the mountain's inaccessible glaciers through the valley of Chamonix in southeastern France.

To hear—an old and solemn harmony;
25 Thine earthly rainbows stretched across the sweep
Of the ethereal waterfall, whose veil
Robes some unsculptured image; the strange sleep
Which when the voices of the desert fail
Wraps all in its own deep eternity;
30 Thy caverns echoing to the Arve's commotion—
A loud, lone sound no other sound can tame.
Thou art pervaded with that ceaseless motion,
Thou art the path of that unresting sound,
Dizzy Ravine! and when I gaze on thee,
35 I seem as in a trance sublime and strange
To muse on my own separate fantasy,
My own, my human mind, which passively
Now renders and receives fast influencings,
Holding an unremitting interchange
40 With the clear universe of things around;
One legion of wild thoughts, whose wandering wings
Now float above thy darkness, and now rest,
Where that or thou art no unbidden guest,
In the still cave of the witch Poesy,
45 Seeking among the shadows that pass by—
Ghosts of all things that are—some shade of thee,
Some phantom, some faint image; till the breast
From which they fled recalls them, thou art there!

III

Some say that gleams of a remoter world
50 Visit the soul in sleep,—that death is slumber,
And that its shapes the busy thoughts outnumber
Of those who wake and live. I look on high;
Has some unknown Omnipotence unfurled
The veil of life and death? or do I lie
55 In dream, and does the mightier world of sleep
Spread far around and inaccessibly
Its circles? For the very spirit fails,
Driven like a homeless cloud from steep to steep
That vanishes among the viewless gales!
60 Far, far above, piercing the infinite sky,
Mont Blanc appears,—still, snowy and serene—
Its subject mountains their unearthly forms
Pile around it, ice and rock; broad vales between
Of frozen floods, unfathomable deeps,
65 Blue as the overhanging heaven, that spread
And wind among the accumulated steeps;
A desert peopled by the storms alone,
Save when the eagle brings some hunter's bone,
And the wolf tracks her there. How hideously
70 Its shapes are heaped around! rude, bare and high,
Ghastly, and scarred, and riven.—Is this the scene
Where the old Earthquake-dæmon taught her young

Ruin? Were these their toys? or did a sea
Of fire envelop once this silent snow?
75 None can reply—all seems eternal now.
The wilderness has a mysterious tongue
Which teaches awful doubt, or faith so mild,
So solemn, so serene, that man may be
But for such faith with Nature reconciled;[2]
80 Thou hast a voice, great Mountain, to repeal
Large codes of fraud and woe;[3] not understood
By all, but which the wise, and great, and good,
Interpret, or make felt, or deeply feel.

IV

The fields, the lakes, the forests and the streams,
85 Ocean, and all the living things that dwell
Within the dædal° earth; lightning, and rain,   *varied*
Earthquake, and fiery flood, and hurricane,
The torpor of the year when feeble dreams
Visit the hidden buds or dreamless sleep
90 Holds every future leaf and flower, the bound
With which from that detested trance they leap,
The works and ways of man, their death and birth,
And that of him and all that his may be,—
All things that move and breathe with toil and sound
95 Are born and die, revolve, subside and swell;
Power dwells apart in its tranquillity,
Remote, serene, and inaccessible;—
And *this,* the naked countenance of earth
On which I gaze, even these primeval mountains,
100 Teach the adverting° mind. The glaciers creep,   *observing*
Like snakes that watch their prey, from their far fountains,
Slow rolling on; there many a precipice
Frost and the sun in scorn of mortal power
Have piled—dome, pyramid and pinnacle,
105 A city of death, distinct with many a tower
And wall impregnable of beaming ice;
Yet not a city, but a flood of ruin
Is there, that from the boundaries of the sky
Rolls its perpetual stream; vast pines are strewing
110 Its destined path, or in the mangled soil
Branchless and shattered stand; the rocks, drawn down
From yon remotest waste, have overthrown
The limits of the dead and living world,
Never to be reclaimed. The dwelling-place
115 Of insects, beasts and birds, becomes its spoil,
Their food and their retreat forever gone;

---

[2] The wilderness teaches either scepticism about the existence of God or (less acceptable to Shelley) a simple, Wordsworthian faith "that all which we behold / Is full of blessings" (*Tintern Abbey,* lines 133–134).
[3] The "voice" of the mountain contradicts the commonly held social and religious codes.

So much of life and joy is lost. The race
Of man flies far in dread; his work and dwelling
Vanish, like smoke before the tempest's stream,
120 And their place is not known. Below, vast caves
Shine in the rushing torrents' restless gleam,
Which from those secret chasms in tumult welling
Meet in the vale; and one majestic river,
The breath and blood of distant lands, forever
125 Rolls its loud waters to the ocean waves,
Breathes its swift vapors to the circling air.

V

Mont Blanc yet gleams on high: the power is there,
The still and solemn power of many sights
And many sounds, and much of life and death.
130 In the calm darkness of the moonless nights,
In the lone glare of day, the snows descend
Upon that mountain; none beholds them there,
Nor when the flakes burn in the sinking sun,
Or the star-beams dart through them; winds contend
135 Silently there, and heap the snow, with breath
Rapid and strong, but silently! Its home
The voiceless lightning in these solitudes
Keeps innocently, and like vapor broods
Over the snow. The secret strength of things,
140 Which governs thought, and to the infinite dome
Of heaven is as a law, inhabits thee!
And what were thou, and earth, and stars, and sea,
If to the human mind's imaginings
Silence and solitude were vacancy?[4]

[1817]

ODE TO THE WEST WIND[1]

I

O wild west wind, thou breath of autumn's being,
Thou, from whose unseen presence the leaves dead
Are driven, like ghosts from an enchanter fleeing,

---

[4] Shelley concludes by asking what importance the silent and solitary power of Mont Blanc would have if the human mind were incapable of imagination.

[1] "This poem was conceived and chiefly written in a wood that skirts the Arno, near Florence, and on a day when that tempestuous wind, whose temperature is at once mild and animating, was collecting the vapors which pour down the autumnal rains. They began, as I foresaw, at sunset with a violent tempest of hail and rain, attended by that magnificent thunder and lightning peculiar to the Cisalpine regions.

"The phenomenon alluded to at the conclusion of the third stanza is well known to naturalists. The vegetation at the bottom of the sea, of rivers, and of lakes, sympathizes with that of the land in the change of seasons, and is consequently influenced by the winds which announce it." [Shelley's note.]

Yellow, and black, and pale, and hectic red
5   Pestilence-stricken multitudes: O thou,
Who chariotest to their dark wintry bed

The wingèd seeds, where they lie cold and low,
Each like a corpse within its grave, until
Thine azure sister of the spring shall blow

10   Her clarion o'er the dreaming earth, and fill
(Driving sweet buds like flocks to feed in air)
With living hues and odors plain and hill:

Wild Spirit, which art moving everywhere;
Destroyer and preserver; hear, oh, hear!

II

15   Thou on whose stream, mid the steep sky's commotion,
Loose clouds like earth's decaying leaves are shed,
Shook from the tangled boughs of heaven and ocean,

Angels of rain and lightning: there are spread
On the blue surface of thine airy surge,
20   Like the bright hair uplifted from the head

Of some fierce Mænad,[2] even from the dim verge
Of the horizon to the zenith's height,
The locks of the approaching storm. Thou dirge

Of the dying year, to which this closing night
25   Will be the dome of a vast sepulchre,
Vaulted with all thy congregated might

Of vapors, from whose solid atmosphere
Black rain, and fire, and hail will burst: oh, hear!

III

Thou who didst waken from his summer dreams
30   The blue Mediterranean, where he lay,
Lulled by the coil of his crystalline streams,

Beside a pumice isle[3] in Baiæ's bay,[4]
And saw in sleep old palaces and towers
Quivering within the wave's intenser day,

35   All overgrown with azure moss and flowers
So sweet the sense faints picturing them! Thou
For whose path the Atlantic's level powers

[2] A frenzied female follower of Bacchus, the Greek god of wine.
[3] An island of volcanic stone.   [4] Near Naples.

Cleave themselves into chasms, while far below
The sea-blooms and the oozy woods which wear
40   The sapless foliage of the ocean know

Thy voice, and suddenly grow gray with fear,
And tremble and despoil themselves: oh, hear!

IV

If I were a dead leaf thou mightest bear;
If I were a swift cloud to fly with thee;
45   A wave to pant beneath thy power, and share

The impulse of thy strength, only less free
Than thou, O uncontrollable! If even
I were as in my boyhood, and could be

The comrade of thy wanderings over heaven,
50   As then, when to outstrip thy skyey speed
Scarce seemed a vision; I would ne'er have striven

As thus with thee in prayer in my sore need.
Oh, lift me as a wave, a leaf, a cloud!
I fall upon the thorns of life! I bleed!

55   A heavy weight of hours has chained and bowed
One too like thee: tameless, and swift, and proud.

V

Make me thy lyre, even as the forest is:
What if my leaves are falling like its own!
The tumult of thy mighty harmonies

60   Will take from both a deep, autumnal tone,
Sweet though in sadness. Be thou, Spirit fierce,
My spirit! Be thou me, impetuous one!

Drive my dead thoughts over the universe
Like withered leaves to quicken a new birth!
65   And, by the incantation of this verse,

Scatter, as from an unextinguished hearth
Ashes and sparks, my words among mankind!
Be through my lips to unawakened earth

The trumpet of a prophecy! O Wind,
70   If winter comes, can spring be far behind?

                                                      [1820]

SONNET

Lift not the painted veil which those who live
Call Life: though unreal shapes be pictured there,
And it but mimic all we would believe
With colors idly spread—behind, lurk Fear
5   And Hope, twin Destinies; who ever weave
Their shadows, o'er the chasm, sightless and drear.
I knew one who had lifted it—he sought,
For his lost heart was tender, things to love,
But found them not, alas! nor was there aught
10   The world contains, the which he could approve.
Through the unheeding many he did move,
A splendor among shadows, a bright blot
Upon this gloomy scene, a Spirit that strove
For truth, and like the Preacher found it not.

[1824]

John Keats *1795–1821*

ODE TO A NIGHTINGALE

I

My heart aches, and a drowsy numbness pains
My sense, as though of hemlock I had drunk,
Or emptied some dull opiate to the drains
One minute past, and Lethe-wards[1] had sunk:
5   'T is not through envy of thy happy lot,
But being too happy in thine happiness,—
That thou, light-wingèd Dryad[2] of the trees,
In some melodious plot
Of beechen green, and shadows numberless,
10   Singest of summer in full-throated ease.

II

O for a draught of vintage! that hath been
Cooled a long age in the deep-delved earth,
Tasting of Flora[3] and the country-green,
Dance, and Provençal song,[4] and sunburnt mirth!
15   O for a beaker full of the warm South,
Full of the true, the blushful Hippocrene,[5]
With beaded bubbles winking at the brim,
And purple-stainèd mouth;
That I might drink, and leave the world unseen,
20   And with thee fade away into the forest dim:

[1] Toward Lethe, the river of forgetfulness in the Underworld.
[2] Wood nymph.   [3] The goddess of flowers.
[4] The medieval troubadors of Provence in southern France were famous for their songs.
[5] A mythological fountain whose waters bring poetic inspiration.

III

Fade far away, dissolve, and quite forget
 What thou among the leaves hast never known,
The weariness, the fever, and the fret
 Here, where men sit and hear each other groan;
Where palsy shakes a few, sad, last gray hairs,
 Where youth grows pale, and spectre-thin, and dies;
  Where but to think is to be full of sorrow
   And leaden-eyed despairs,
Where Beauty cannot keep her lustrous eyes,
 Or new Love pine at them beyond tomorrow.

IV

Away! away! for I will fly to thee,
 Not charioted by Bacchus and his pards,[6]
But on the viewless wings of Poesy,
 Though the dull brain perplexes and retards:
Already with thee! tender is the night,
 And haply the Queen-Moon is on her throne,
  Clustered around by all her starry Fays;°   *fairies*
   But here there is no light,
Save what from heaven is with the breezes blown
 Through verdurous glooms and winding mossy
   ways.

V

I cannot see what flowers are at my feet,
 Nor what soft incense hangs upon the boughs,
But, in embalmèd° darkness, guess each sweet   *sweet smelling*
 Wherewith the seasonable month endows
The grass, the thicket, and the fruit-tree wild;
 White hawthorn, and the pastoral eglantine;
  Fast fading violets covered up in leaves;
   And mid-May's eldest child,
The coming musk-rose, full of dewy wine,
 The murmurous haunt of flies on summer eves.

VI

Darkling[7] I listen; and, for many a time
 I have been half in love with easeful Death,
Called him soft names in many a musèd rhyme,
 To take into the air my quiet breath;
Now more than ever seems it rich to die,
 To cease upon the midnight with no pain,
  While thou art pouring forth thy soul abroad
   In such an ecstasy!
Still wouldst thou sing, and I have ears in vain—
 To thy high requiem become a sod.

[6] Bacchus, the god of wine, rode in a chariot drawn by leopards. [7] In the dark.

VII

Thou wast not born for death, immortal Bird!
No hungry generations tread thee down;
The voice I hear this passing night was heard
In ancient days by emperor and clown:
65   Perhaps the self-same song that found a path
Through the sad heart of Ruth,[8] when, sick for home,
She stood in tears amid the alien corn;
The same that oft-times hath
Charmed magic casements, opening on the foam
70   Of perilous seas, in faery lands forlorn.

VIII

Forlorn! the very word is like a bell
To toll me back from thee to my sole self!
Adieu! the fancy cannot cheat so well
As she is famed to do, deceiving elf.
75   Adieu! adieu! thy plaintive anthem fades
Past the near meadows, over the still stream,
Up the hill-side; and now 't is buried deep
In the next valley-glades:
Was it a vision, or a waking dream?
80   Fled is that music:—do I wake or sleep?

[1819]

ODE ON A GRECIAN URN

I

Thou still unravished bride of quietness,
Thou foster-child of Silence and slow Time,
Sylvan historian, who canst thus express
A flowery tale more sweetly than our rhyme:
5   What leaf-fringed legend haunts about thy shape
Of deities or mortals, or of both,
In Tempe[1] or the dales of Arcady?[2]
What men or gods are these? What maidens loth?
What mad pursuit? What struggle to escape?
10   What pipes and timbrels? What wild ecstasy?

II

Heard melodies are sweet, but those unheard
Are sweeter; therefore, ye soft pipes, play on;
Not to the sensual ear, but, more endeared
Pipe to the spirit ditties of no tone:
15   Fair youth, beneath the trees, thou canst not leave
Thy song, nor ever can those trees be bare;
Bold lover, never, never canst thou kiss,
Though winning near the goal—yet, do not grieve;
She cannot fade, though thou hast not thy bliss,
20   For ever wilt thou love, and she be fair!

---

[8] A young widow in the Bible, Ruth 2.   [1] A valley in Greece famous for its beauty.
[2] Arcadia, a region in ancient Greece, often used to represent the perfect pastoral environment.

III

Ah, happy, happy boughs! that cannot shed
   Your leaves, nor ever bid the spring adieu;
And, happy melodist, unwearièd,
   For ever piping songs for ever new;
25 More happy love! more happy, happy love!
   For ever warm and still to be enjoyed,
     For ever panting, and for ever young;
All breathing human passion far above,
   That leaves a heart high-sorrowful and cloyed,
30   A burning forehead, and a parching tongue.

IV

Who are these coming to the sacrifice?
   To what green altar, O mysterious priest,
Lead'st thou that heifer lowing at the skies,
   And all her silken flanks with garlands drest?
35 What little town by river or sea shore,
   Or mountain-built with peaceful citadel,
     Is emptied of this folk, this pious morn?
And, little town, thy streets for evermore
   Will silent be; and not a soul to tell
40   Why thou art desolate, can e'er return.

V

O Attic shape! Fair attitude! with brede°   *ornamentation*
   Of marble men and maidens overwrought,
With forest branches and the trodden weed;
   Thou, silent form, dost tease us out of thought
45 As doth eternity: Cold pastoral!
   When old age shall this generation waste,
     Thou shalt remain, in midst of other woe
   Than ours, a friend to man, to whom thou say'st,
"Beauty is truth, truth beauty,"—that is all
50   Ye know on earth, and all ye need to know.
                       [1820]

TO AUTUMN

I

Season of mists and mellow fruitfulness,
   Close bosom-friend of the maturing sun;
Conspiring with him how to load and bless
   With fruit the vines that round the thatch-eaves run;
5 To bend with apples the mossed cottage-trees,
   And fill all fruit with ripeness to the core;
     To swell the gourd, and plump the hazel shells
   With a sweet kernel; to set budding more,
And still more, later flowers for the bees,
10 Until they think warm days will never cease,
     For summer has o'er-brimmed their clammy cells.

II

Who hath not seen thee oft amid thy store?
　Sometimes whoever seeks abroad may find
Thee sitting careless on a granary floor,
15　　Thy hair soft-lifted by the winnowing wind;
Or on a half-reaped furrow sound asleep,
　Drowsed with the fume of poppies, while thy hook
　　Spares the next swath and all its twinèd flowers:
And sometimes like a gleaner thou dost keep
20　　Steady thy laden head across a brook;
　Or by a cider-press, with patient look,
　　Thou watchest the last oozings hours by hours.

III

Where are the songs of spring? Ay, where are they?
　Think not of them, thou hast thy music too,—
25　While barred clouds bloom the soft-dying day,
　And touch the stubble-plains with rosy hue;
Then in a wailful choir the small gnats mourn
　Among the river sallows,° borne aloft　　　　　　　　　　　　*willows*
　　Or sinking as the light wind lives or dies;
30　And full-grown lambs loud bleat from hilly bourn;°　　　　　*territory*
　Hedge-crickets sing; and now with treble soft
　The redbreast whistles from a garden-croft,°　　　　　*a garden plot*
　　And gathering swallows twitter in the skies.

[1820]

ODE ON MELANCHOLY

I

No, no! go not to Lethe,[1] neither twist
　Wolf's-bane, tight-rooted, for its poisonous wine;
Nor suffer thy pale forehead to be kissed
　By nightshade, ruby grape of Proserpine,[2]
5　Make not your rosary of yew-berries,
　Nor let the beetle, or the death-moth be
　　Your mournful Psyche, nor the downy owl
A partner in your sorrow's mysteries;
　For shade to shade will come too drowsily,
10　　And drown the wakeful anguish of the soul.

II

But when the melancholy fit shall fall
Sudden from heaven like a weeping cloud,
That fosters the droop-headed flowers all,

---

[1] The river of forgetfulness in the Underworld.

[2] In Roman mythology Proserpine is the queen of the Underworld. Wolf's-bane (line 2) and night-shade (line 4) are poisonous plants. Yew-berries (line 5), the beetle (line 6), and the death-moth (line 6) are all associated with death. Psyche (line 7), or the butterfly, personifies the soul in Greek mythology.

And hides the green hills in an April shroud;
15   Then glut thy sorrow on a morning rose,
        Or on the rainbow of the salt-sand wave,
        Or on the wealth of globèd peonies;
    Or if thy mistress some rich anger shows,
        Emprison her soft hand, and let her rave,
20   And feed deep, deep upon her peerless eyes.

III

    She dwells with Beauty—Beauty that must die;
        And Joy, whose hand is ever at his lips
    Bidding adieu; and aching Pleasure nigh,
        Turning to poison while the bee-mouth sips:
25   Aye, in the very temple of Delight
        Veiled Melancholy has her sovran shrine,
            Though seen of none save him whose strenuous tongue
    Can burst Joy's grape against his palate fine;
    His soul shall taste the sadness of her might,
30   And be among her cloudy trophies hung.

                                                        [1820]

"BRIGHT STAR, WOULD I WERE STEADFAST AS THOU ART!"

    Bright star, would I were steadfast as thou art!
        Not in lone splendor hung aloft the night,
    And watching, with eternal lids apart,
        Like Nature's patient sleepless Eremite,°   *hermit*
5   The moving waters at their priestlike task
        Of pure ablution° round earth's human   *washing, purifying*
          shores
    Or gazing on the new soft fallen mask
        Of snow upon the mountains and the moors:
    No—yet still steadfast, still unchangeable,
10   Pillowed upon my fair love's ripening breast,
    To feel for ever its soft fall and swell,
        Awake for ever in a sweet unrest,
    Still, still to hear her tender-taken breath,
    And so live ever—or else swoon to death.

                                                        [posthumous, 1838]

"IF BY DULL RHYMES OUR ENGLISH MUST BE CHAINED"

    If by dull rhymes our English must be chained,
        And, like Andromeda,[1] the sonnet sweet
    Fettered, in spite of pained loveliness;
    Let us find out, if we must be constrained,
5   Sandals more interwoven and complete

---

[1] Chained to a rock as a sacrifice to a sea monster, Andromeda in Greek mythology was saved at the last moment by Perseus.

To fit the naked foot of poesy;
Let us inspect the lyre, and weigh the stress
Of every chord, and see what may be gained
     By ear industrious, and attention meet;
10   Misers of sound and syllable, no less
Than Midas[2] of his coinage, let us be
     Jealous of dead leaves in the bay-wreath crown:
So, if we may not let the Muse be free,
     She will be bound with garlands of her own.

[posthumous, 1848]

"WHEN I HAVE FEARS THAT I MAY CEASE TO BE"

When I have fears that I may cease to be
     Before my pen has gleaned my teeming brain,
Before high pilèd books, in charactry,°   *letters*
     Hold like rich garners° the full-ripened grain;   *granaries*
5   When I behold, upon the night's starred face,
     Huge cloudy symbols of a high romance,
And think that I may never live to trace
     Their shadows, with the magic hand of chance;
And when I feel, fair creature of an hour!
10   That I shall never look upon thee more,
Never have relish in the faery power
     Of unreflecting love;—then on the shore
Of the wide world I stand alone, and think
Till love and fame to nothingness do sink.

[posthumous, 1848]

Ralph Waldo Emerson   *1803–1882*

EACH AND ALL

Little thinks, in the field, yon red-cloaked clown[1]
Of thee from the hill-top looking down;
The heifer that lows in the upland farm,
Far-heard, lows not thine ear to charm;
5   The sexton, tolling his bell at noon,
Deems not that great Napoleon
Stops his horse, and lists with delight,
Whilst his files sweep round yon Alpine height;
Nor knowest thou what argument
10   Thy life to thy neighbor's creed has lent.
All are needed by each one;
Nothing is fair or good alone.

---

[2] The miserly King Midas is a character in Greek mythology who was granted his wish that everything he touched should turn to gold.
[1] A farmer or peasant.

    I thought the sparrow's note from heaven,
    Singing at dawn on the alder bough;
15   I brought him home, in his nest, at even;
    He sings the song, but it cheers not now,
    For I did not bring home the river and sky;—
    He sang to my ear,—they sang to my eye.
    The delicate shells lay on the shore;
20   The bubbles of the latest wave
    Fresh pearls to their enamel gave,
    And the bellowing of the savage sea
    Greeted their safe escape to me.
    I wiped away the weeds and foam,
25   I fetched my sea-born treasures home;
    But the poor, unsightly, noisome things
    Had left their beauty on the shore
    With the sun and the sand and the wild uproar.
    The lover watched his graceful maid,
30   As 'mid the virgin train she strayed,
    Nor knew her beauty's best attire
    Was woven still by the snow-white choir.
    At last she came to his hermitage,
    Like the bird from the woodlands to the cage;—
35   The gay enchantment was undone,
    A gentle wife, but fairy none.
    Then I said, "I covet truth;
    Beauty is unripe childhood's cheat;
    I leave it behind with the games of youth:"—
40   As I spoke, beneath my feet
    The ground-pine curled its pretty wreath,
    Running over the club-moss burrs;
    I inhaled the violet's breath;
    Around me stood the oaks and firs;
45   Pine-cones and acorns lay on the ground;
    Over me soared the eternal sky,
    Full of light and of deity;
    Again I saw, again I heard,
    The rolling river, the morning bird;—
50   Beauty through my senses stole;
    I yielded myself to the perfect whole.

                     [1839]

THE SNOW-STORM

    Announced by all the trumpets of the sky,
    Arrives the snow, and, driving o'er the fields,
    Seems nowhere to alight: the whited air
    Hides hills and woods, the river, and the heaven,
5   And veils the farm-house at the garden's end.
    The sled and traveller stopped, the courier's feet
    Delayed, all friends shut out, the housemates sit
    Around the radiant fireplace, enclosed
    In a tumultuous privacy of storm.

10 Come see the north wind's masonry.
Out of an unseen quarry evermore
Furnished with tile, the fierce artificer
Curves his white bastions with projected roof
Round every windward stake, or tree, or door.
15 Speeding, the myriad-handed, his wild work
So fanciful, so savage, nought cares he
For number or proportion. Mockingly,
On coop or kennel he hangs Parian[1] wreaths;
A swan-like form invests the hidden thorn;
20 Fills up the farmer's lane from wall to wall,
Maugre° the farmer's sighs; and at the gate   *Despite*
A tapering turret overtops the work.
And when his hours are numbered, and the world
Is all his own, retiring, as he were not,
25 Leaves, when the sun appears, astonished Art
To mimic in slow structures, stone by stone,
Built in an age, the mad wind's night-work,
The frolic architecture of the snow.

[1841]

DAYS

Daughters of Time, the hypocritic Days,
Muffled and dumb like barefoot dervishes,[2]
And marching single in an endless file,
Bring diadems° and fagots° in their hands.   *crowns / bundles of sticks*
5 To each they offer gifts after his will,
Bread, kingdoms, stars, and sky that holds
   them all.
I, in my pleached garden,[3] watched the pomp,
Forgot my morning wishes, hastily
Took a few herbs and apples, and the Day
10 Turned and departed silent. I, too late,
Under her solemn fillet° saw the scorn.   *headband*

[1857]

Elizabeth Barrett Browning   *1806–1861*

FINITE AND INFINITE

The wind sounds only in opposing straits,
The sea beside the shore; man's spirit rends
Its quiet only up against the ends
Of wants and oppositions, loves and hates,
5 Where, worked and worn by passionate debates,

---

[1] A famous type of white marble from the Greek islands of Paros.
[2] Moslem ascetics who achieve ecstasy by performing whirling dances.
[3] A type of formal garden in which the trees and bushes have been interlaced.

And losing by the loss it apprehends,
The flesh rocks round, and every breath it sends
Is ravelled to a sigh. All tortured states
Suppose a straitened place. Jehovah, Lord,
10   Make room for rest, around me! out of sight
Now float me, of the vexing land abhorred,
Till, in deep calms of space, my soul may right
Her nature, shoot large sail on lengthening cord,
And rush exultant on the Infinite.

[1850]

Henry Wadsworth Longfellow   *1807–1882*

MEZZO CAMMIN[1]

Written at Boppard on the Rhine, August 25, 1842
Just Before Leaving for Home

Half of my life is gone, and I have let
   The years slip from me and have not fulfilled
   The aspiration of my youth, to build
   Some tower of song with lofty parapet.
5   Not indolence, nor pleasure, nor the fret
   Of restless passions that would not be stilled,
   But sorrow, and a care that almost killed,[2]
   Kept me from what I may accomplish yet;

Though, half-way up the hill, I see the Past
10   Lying beneath me with its sounds and sights,—
   A city in the twilight dim and vast,
With smoking roofs, soft bells, and gleaming lights,—
   And hear above me on the autumnal blast
   The cataract of Death far thundering from the heights.

[1846]

SNOW-FLAKES

Out of the bosom of the Air,
   Out of the cloud-folds of her garments shaken,
Over the woodlands brown and bare,
   Over the harvest-fields forsaken,
5   Silent, and soft, and slow
      Descends the snow.

---

[1] The title (meaning "midway along the journey") is taken from the first line of Dante's *Divine Comedy* (completed in 1321); when he wrote this poem in 1842 at age 35, Longfellow had reached the midpoint of the Biblical "three-score years and ten."
[2] The poet's first wife had died in 1835.

Even as our cloudy fancies take
  Suddenly shape in some divine expression,
Even as the troubled heart doth make
10   In the white countenance confession,
    The troubled sky reveals
    The grief it feels.

This is the poem of the air,
  Slowly in silent syllables recorded;
15 This is the secret of despair
  Long in its cloudy bosom hoarded,
    Now whispered and revealed
    To wood and field.

           [1863]

THE TIDE RISES, THE TIDE FALLS

The tide rises, the tide falls,
The twilight darkens, the curlew° calls;   *shore bird*
Along the sea-sands damp and brown
The traveller hastens toward the town,
5   And the tide rises, the tide falls.

Darkness settles on roofs and walls,
But the sea, the sea in the darkness calls;
The little waves, with their soft, white hands,
Efface the footprints in the sands,
10   And the tide rises, the tide falls.

The morning breaks; the steeds in their stalls
Stamp and neigh, as the hostler° calls;   *stableman*
The day returns, but nevermore
Returns the traveller to the shore,
15   And the tide rises, the tide falls.

           [1880]

Edgar Allan Poe   *1809–1849*

TO HELEN

Helen, thy beauty is to me
  Like those Nicéan[1] barks of yore,
That gently, o'er a perfumed sea,
  The weary, way-worn wanderer bore
5   To his own native shore.

---

[1] The allusion is unclear.

On desperate seas long wont to roam,
  Thy hyacinth[2] hair, thy classic face,
Thy Naiad[3] airs have brought me home
  To the glory that was Greece
10   And the grandeur that was Rome.

Lo! in yon brilliant window-niche
  How statue-like I see thee stand,
The agate lamp within thy hand!
Ah, Psyche[4] from the regions which
15   Are Holy Land!
                                        [1831]

ELDORADO[1]

    Gaily bedight,
    A gallant knight,
In sunshine and in shadow,
Had journeyed long,
5   Singing a song,
In search of Eldorado.

But he grew old—
This knight so bold—
And o'er his heart a shadow
10   Fell as he found
No spot of ground
That looked like Eldorado.

And, as his strength
Failed him at length,
15 He met a pilgrim shadow—
"Shadow," said he,
"Where can it be—
This land of Eldorado?"

"Over the Mountains
20   Of the Moon,
Down the Valley of the Shadow,
Ride, boldly ride,"
The shade replied,—
"If you seek for Eldorado!"
                                [posthumous, 1850]

[2] Curly or wavy.   [3] Nymphs of Greek mythology associated with lakes, rivers, and fountains.
[4] The Greek word for "soul," personified in Greek mythology as a beautiful maiden loved by Cupid.
[1] The legendary kingdom of gold sought after by early Spanish explorers. By Poe's time Eldorado had
become synonymous with any elusive land of untold wealth.

Edward FitzGerald   *1809–1883*

from THE RUBÁIYÁT OF OMAR KHAYYÁM[1]

Come, fill the Cup, and in the fire of Spring
Your Winter-garment of Repentance fling:
   The Bird of Time has but a little way
To flutter—and the Bird is on the Wing.

5   Whether at Naishápúr or Babylon,
Whether the Cup with sweet or bitter run,
   The Wine of Life keeps oozing drop by drop,
The Leaves of Life keep falling one by one.

A Book of Verses underneath the Bough,
10 A Jug of wine, a Loaf of Bread—and Thou
   Beside me singing in the Wilderness—
Oh, Wilderness were Paradise enow!

Some for the Glories of This World; and some
Sigh for the Prophet's Paradise to come;
15   Ah, take the Cash, and let the Credit go,
Nor heed the rumble of a distant Drum!

The Worldly Hope men set their Hearts upon
Turns Ashes—or it prospers; and anon,
   Like Snow upon the Desert's dusty Face,
20 Lighting a little hour or two—is gone.

Why, all the Saints and Sages who discussed
Of the Two Worlds so wisely—they are thrust
   Like foolish Prophets forth; their Words to Scorn
Are scattered, and their Mouths are stopt with Dust.

25   Myself when young did eagerly frequent
Doctor and Saint, and heard great argument
   About it and about: but evermore
Came out by the same Door where in I went.

With them the seed of Wisdom did I sow,
30 And with mine own hand wrought to make it grow;
   And this was all the Harvest that I reaped—
"I came like Water, and like Wind I go."

[1] The 17 quatrains reprinted here are selected from the 97 quatrains in FitzGerald's fourth edition of the *Rubáiyát*. Each quatrain (or *rubais*) is an independent poem—though occasionally (as in lines 21–32) a series of *rubais* may develop related ideas. Omar Khayyám was a Persian poet (ca. 1048–1122) whose *rubais* were translated and adapted by FitzGerald.

Perplext no more with Human or Divine,
Tomorrow's tangle to the winds resign,
    And lose your fingers in the tresses of
35   The Cypress-slender Minister of Wine.

You know, my Friends, with what a brave Carouse
I made a Second Marriage in my house;
    Divorced old barren Reason from my Bed,
40   And took the Daughter of the Vine to Spouse.

For "Is" and "Is-not" though with Rule and Line
And "Up-and-down" by Logic I define,
    Of all that one should care to fathom, I
Was never deep in anything but—Wine.

45   O threats of Hell and Hopes of Paradise!
One thing at least is certain—*This* Life flies;
    One thing is certain and the rest is Lies,
The Flower that once has blown for ever dies.

But helpless Pieces of the Game He plays
50   Upon this Chequer-board of Nights and Days;
    Hither and thither moves, and checks, and slays,
And one by one back in the Closet lays.

The Moving Finger writes; and, having writ,
Moves on: nor all your Piety nor Wit
55   Shall lure it back to cancel half a Line,
Nor all your Tears wash out a Word of it.

Yesterday *This* Day's Madness did prepare;
Tomorrow's Silence, Triumph, or Despair:
    Drink! for you know not whence you came, nor why:
60   Drink! for you know not why you go, nor where.

And much as Wine has played the Infidel,
And robbed me of my Robe of Honor—Well,
    I wonder often what the Vintners buy
One half so precious as the stuff they sell.

65   Ah Love! could you and I with Him conspire
To grasp this sorry Scheme of Things entire,
    Would not we shatter it to bits—and then
Remould it nearer to the Heart's Desire!

                                               [1859]

Alfred, Lord Tennyson   *1809–1892*

ULYSSES[1]

It little profits that an idle king,
By this still hearth, among these barren crags,
Matched with an aged wife, I mete° and dole°   *allot / give sparingly*
Unequal laws unto a savage race,
5   That hoard, and sleep, and feed, and know not me.
I cannot rest from travel: I will drink
Life to the lees:° all times I have enjoyed   *dregs*
Greatly, have suffered greatly, both with those
That loved me, and alone; on shore, and when
10   Thro' scudding drifts° the rainy Hyades°   *spray / a constellation*
Vexed the dim sea. I am become a name;
For always roaming with a hungry heart
Much have I seen and known: cities of men
And manners, climates, councils, governments,
15   Myself not least, but honored of them all;
And drunk delight of battle with my peers,
Far on the ringing plains of windy Troy.
I am a part of all that I have met;
Yet all experience is an arch wherethro'
20   Gleams that untravelled world, whose margin fades
For ever and for ever when I move.
How dull it is to pause, to make an end,
To rust unburnished, not to shine in use!
As tho' to breathe were life. Life piled on life
25   Were all too little, and of one to me
Little remains: but every hour is saved
From that eternal silence, something more,
A bringer of new things; and vile it were
For some three suns° to store and hoard myself,   *years*
30   And this gray spirit yearning in desire
To follow knowledge like a sinking star,
Beyond the utmost bound of human thought.
      This is my son, mine own Telemachus,
To whom I leave the sceptre and the isle—
35   Well-loved of me, discerning to fulfil
This labor, by slow prudence to make mild
A rugged people, and thro' soft degees
Subdue them to the useful and the good.
Most blameless is he, centered in the sphere
40   Of common duties, decent not to fail
In offices of tenderness, and pay

---

[1] The poem takes place after Ulysses' return from the Trojan War and after he has had time to grow bored with peace, Penelope, and politics. Ulysses is, of course, the Roman name for Odysseus, the hero of Homer's *Odyssey*.

Meet adoration to my household gods,
When I am gone. He works his work, I mine.
   There lies the port; the vessel puffs her sail:
45   There gloom the dark broad seas. My mariners,
Souls that have toiled, and wrought, and thought with me—
That ever with a frolic welcome took
The thunder and the sunshine, and opposed
Free hearts, free foreheads—you and I are old;
50   Old age hath yet his honor and his toil;
Death closes all; but something ere the end,
Some work of noble note, may yet be done,
Not unbecoming men that strove with Gods.
The lights begin to twinkle from the rocks:
55   The long day wanes: the slow moon climbs: the deep
Moans round with many voices. Come, my friends,
'T is not too late to seek a newer world.
Push off, and sitting well in order smite
The sounding furrows; for my purpose holds
60   To sail beyond the sunset, and the baths
Of all the western stars, until I die.
It may be that the gulfs will wash us down:
It may be we shall touch the Happy Isles,°   *Elysium or Paradise*
And see the great Achilles,° whom we knew.   *a Greek hero*
65   Tho' much is taken, much abides; and tho'
We are not now that strength which in old days
Moved earth and heaven, that which we are, we are:
One equal temper of heroic hearts,
Made weak by time and fate, but strong in will
70   To strive, to seek, to find, and not to yield.
                             [1842]

"BREAK, BREAK, BREAK"

Break, break, break,
   On thy cold gray stones, O Sea!
And I would that my tongue could utter
   The thoughts that arise in me.

5   O well for the fisherman's boy,
   That he shouts with his sister at play!
O well for the sailor lad,
   That he sings in his boat on the bay!

And the stately ships go on
10   To their haven under the hill;
But O for the touch of a vanished hand,
   And the sound of a voice that is still!

Break, break, break,
   At the foot of thy crags, O Sea!
15 But the tender grace of a day that is dead
   Will never come back to me.

                  [1842]

THE EAGLE: A FRAGMENT

He clasps the crag with crooked hands;
Close to the sun in lonely lands,
Ringed with the azure world, he stands.

The wrinkled sea beneath him crawls:
5 He watches from his mountain walls,
And like a thunderbolt he falls.

                  [1851]

"FLOWER IN THE CRANNIED WALL"

Flower in the crannied wall,
I pluck you out of the crannies,
I hold you here, root and all, in my hand.
Little flower—but *if* I could understand
5 What you are, root and all, and all in all,
I should know what God and man is.

                  [1869]

Robert Browning   *1812–1889*

PORPHYRIA'S LOVER

The rain set early in to-night,
   The sullen wind was soon awake,
It tore the elm-tops down for spite,
   And did its worst to vex the lake:
5   I listened with heart fit to break;
When glided in Porphyria; straight
   She shut the cold out and the storm,
And kneeled and made the cheerless grate
   Blaze up, and all the cottage warm;
10   Which done, she rose, and from her form
Withdrew the dripping cloak and shawl,
   And laid her soiled gloves by, untied
Her hat, and let the damp hair fall,
   And, last, she sat down by my side
15   And called me. When no voice replied,
She put my arm about her waist,

And made her smooth white shoulder bare,
And all her yellow hair displaced,
    And, stooping, made my cheek lie there,
    And spread, o'er all, her yellow hair,
Murmuring how she loved me—she
    Too weak, for all her heart's endeavor,
To set its struggling passion free
    From pride, and vainer ties dissever,
    And give herself to me forever.
But passion sometimes would prevail,
    Nor could tonight's gay feast restrain
A sudden thought of one so pale
    For love of her, and all in vain:
    So, she was come through wind and rain.
Be sure I looked up at her eyes
    Happy and proud; at last I knew
Porphyria worshipped me; surprise
    Made my heart swell, and still it grew
    While I debated what to do.
That moment she was mine, mine, fair,
    Perfectly pure and good: I found
A thing to do, and all her hair
    In one long yellow string I wound
    Three times her little throat around,
And strangled her. No pain felt she;
    I am quite sure she felt no pain.
As a shut bud that holds a bee,
    I warily oped her lids: again
    Laughed the blue eyes without a stain.
And I untightened next the tress
    About her neck; her cheek once more
Blushed bright beneath my burning kiss:
    I propped her head up as before,
    Only, this time my shoulder bore
Her head, which droops upon it still:
    The smiling rosy little head,
So glad it has its utmost will,
    That all it scorned at once is fled,
    And I, its love, am gained instead!
Porphyria's love: she guessed not how
    Her darling one wish would be heard.
And thus we sit together now,
    And all night long we have not stirred,
    And yet God has not said a word!

                                    [1836]

20

25

30

35

40

45

50

55

60

MY LAST DUCHESS[1]

Ferrara

That's my last Duchess painted on the wall,
Looking as if she were alive. I call
That piece a wonder, now: Frà Pandolf's hands
Worked busily a day, and there she stands.
Will 't please you sit and look at her? I said
"Frà Pandolf" by design: for never read
Strangers like you that pictured countenance,
The depth and passion of its earnest glance,
But to myself they turned (since none puts by
The curtain I have drawn for you, but I)
And seemed as they would ask me, if they durst,
How such a glance came there; so, not the first
Are you to turn and ask thus. Sir, 't was not
Her husband's presence only, called that spot
Of joy into the Duchess' cheek: perhaps
Frà Pandolf chanced to say "Her mantle laps
Over my lady's wrist too much," or "Paint
Must never hope to reproduce the faint
Half-flush that dies along her throat:" such stuff
Was courtesy, she thought, and cause enough
For calling up that spot of joy. She had
A heart—how shall I say?—too soon made glad,
Too easily impressed; she liked whate'er
She looked on, and her looks went everywhere.
Sir, 't was all one! My favor at her breast,
The dropping of the daylight in the West,
The bough of cherries some officious fool
Broke in the orchard for her, the white mule
She rode with round the terrace—all and each
Would draw from her alike the approving speech,
Or blush, at least. She thanked men,—good! but thanked
Somehow—I know not how—as if she ranked
My gift of a nine-hundred-years-old name
With anybody's gift. Who'd stoop to blame
This sort of trifling? Even had you skill
In speech—(which I have not)—to make your will
Quite clear to such an one, and say, "Just this
Or that in you disgusts me; here you miss,
Or there exceed the mark"—and if she let
Herself be lessoned so, nor plainly set
Her wits to yours, forsooth, and made excuse,
—E'en then would be some stooping; and I choose
Never to stoop. Oh sir, she smiled, no doubt,
Whene'er I passed her; but who passed without

---

[1] In 1564 Alphonso II, Duke of Ferrara, actually did negotiate a second marriage after the death (under suspicious circumstances) of his first wife, Lucrezia, at the age of seventeen.

45 Much the same smile? This grew; I gave commands;
Then all smiles stopped together. There she stands
As if alive. Will 't please you rise? We'll meet
The company below, then. I repeat,
The Count your master's known munificence
50 Is ample warrant that no just pretence
Of mine for dowry will be disallowed;
Though his fair daughter's self, as I avowed
At starting, is my object. Nay, we'll go
Together down, sir. Notice Neptune, though,
55 Taming a sea-horse, thought a rarity,
Which Claus of Innsbruck cast in bronze for me?

[1842]

MEETING AT NIGHT

The gray sea and the long black land;
And the low yellow half-moon large and low:
And the startled little waves that leap
In fiery ringlets from their sleep,
5 As I gain the cove with pushing prow,
And quench its speed i' the slushy sand.

Then a mile of warm sea-scented beach;
Three fields to cross till a farm appears;
A tap at the pane, the quick sharp scratch
10 And blue spurt of a lighted match,
And a voice less loud, through joys and fears,
Than the two hearts beating each to each!

[1845]

PARTING AT MORNING

Round the cape of a sudden came the sea,
And the sun looked over the mountain's rim:
And straight was a path of gold for him,°   *the sun*
And the need of a world of men for me.

[1845]

SOLILOQUY OF THE SPANISH CLOISTER

I

Gr-rr—there go, my heart's abhorrence!
   Water your damned flower-pots, do!
If hate killed men, Brother Lawrence,
   God's blood, would not mine kill you!
5 What? your myrtle-bush wants trimming?
   Oh, that rose has prior claims—
Needs its leaden vase filled brimming?
   Hell dry you up with its flames!

II

At the meal we sit together:
    Salve tibi!° I must hear   *Hail to thee!*
Wise talk of the kind of weather,
    Sort of season, time of year:
Not a plenteous cork-crop: scarcely
    Dare we hope oak-galls,[1] *I doubt:*
What's the Latin name for "parsley"?
    What's the Greek name for Swine's Snout?

III

Whew! We'll have our platter burnished,
    Laid with care on our own shelf!
With a fire-new spoon we're furnished,
    And a goblet for ourself,
Rinsed like something sacrificial
    Ere 'tis fit to touch our chaps°—   *lips*
Marked with L. for our initial!
    (He-he! There his lily snaps!)

IV

Saint, forsooth! While brown Dolores
    Squats outside the Covent bank
With Sanchicha, telling stories,
    Steeping tresses in the tank,
Blue-black, lustrous, thick like horsehairs,
    —Can't I see his dead eye glow,
Bright as 'twere a Barbary corsair's?°   *pirate's*
    (That is, if he'd let it show!)

V

When he finishes refection,°   *refreshment*
    Knife and fork he never lays
Cross-wise, to my recollection,
    As do I, in Jesu's praise.
I the Trinity illustrate,
    Drinking watered orange-pulp—
In three sips the Arian[2] frustrate;
    While he drains his at one gulp.

VI

Oh, those melons? If he's able
    We're to have a feast! so nice!
One goes to the Abbot's table,
    All of us get each a slice.
How go on your flowers? None double?
    Not one fruit-sort can you spy?
Strange!—And I, too, at such trouble,
    Keep them close-nipped on the sly!

[1] Diseased oak shoots, used in tanning.
[2] The Arian heresy (after Arius, A.D. 256–336) was to deny the doctrine of the Trinity.

VII

There's a great text in Galatians,[3]
50   Once you trip on it, entails
Twenty-nine distinct damnations,
      One sure, if another fails:
If I trip him just a-dying,
      Sure of heaven as sure can be,
55   Spin him round and send him flying
      Off to hell, a Manichee?[4]

VIII

Or, my scrofulous° French novel   *degenerate*
      On grey paper with blunt type!
Simply glance at it, you grovel
60   Hand and foot in Belial's gripe:°   *the Devil's grip*
If I double down its pages
      At the woeful sixteenth print,
When he gathers his greengages,°   *plums*
      Ope a sieve and slip it in't?

IX

65   Or, there's Satan! one might venture
      Pledge one's soul to him, yet leave
Such a flaw in the indenture
      As he'd miss till, past retrieve,
Blasted lay that rose-acacia
70   We're so proud of! *Hy, Zy, Hine* . . .
'St, there's Vespers!° *Plena gratiâ*   *evening prayers*
Ave, Virgo![5] Gr-r-r you swine!

                                 [1842]

Walt Whitman *1819–1892*

WHEN I HEARD THE LEARNED ASTRONOMER

When I heard the learned astronomer,
When the proofs, the figures, were ranged in columns before me,
When I was shown the charts and diagrams, to add, divide,
    and measure them,
When I sitting heard the astronomer where he lectured with much
    applause in the lecture-room,
5   How soon unaccountable I became tired and sick,
Till rising and gliding out I wandered off by myself,
In the mystical moist night-air, and from time to time,
Looked up in perfect silence at the stars.

                                   [1865]

---

[3] See the Bible, Galatians 5:15–23.
[4] A follower of Manes, a third-century Persian philosopher who held that the world was governed by
contending principles of light and darkness.
[5] Hail, Virgin, full of grace.

A NOISELESS PATIENT SPIDER

A noiseless patient spider,
I marked where on a little promontory it stood isolated,
Marked how to explore the vacant vast surrounding,
It launched forth filament, filament, filament, out of itself,
5 Ever unreeling them, ever tirelessly speeding them.

And you O my soul where you stand,
Surrounded, detached, in measureless oceans of space,
Ceaselessly musing, venturing, throwing, seeking the spheres to connect
   them,
Till the bridge you will need be formed, till the ductile anchor hold,
10 Till the gossamer thread you fling catch somewhere, O my soul.

                                                    [1871]

CAVALRY CROSSING A FORD

A line in long array where they wind betwixt green islands,
They take a serpentine course, their arms flash in the sun—hark to the
   musical clank,
Behold the silvery river; in it the splashing horses loitering stop to drink,
Behold the brown-faced men, each group, each person a picture, the
   negligent rest on the saddles,
5 Some emerge on the opposite bank, others are just entering the ford—
   while,
Scarlet and blue and snowy white,
The guidon flags flutter gayly in the wind.

                                                    [1865]

THE DALLIANCE OF THE EAGLES

Skirting the river road, (my forenoon walk, my rest,)
Skyward in air a sudden muffled sound, the dalliance of the eagles,
The rushing amorous contact high in space together,
The clinching interlocking claws, a living, fierce, gyrating wheel,
5 Four beating wings, two beaks, a swirling mass tight grappling,
In tumbling turning clustering loops, straight downward falling,
Till o'er the river pois'd, the twain yet one, a moment's lull,
A motionless still balance in the air, then parting, talons loosing,
Upward again on slow-firm pinions slanting, their separate diverse
   flight,
10 She hers, he his, pursuing.

                                                    [1880]

TO A LOCOMOTIVE IN WINTER

Thee for my recitative,
Thee in the driving storm even as now, the snow, the
  winter-day declining,
Thee in thy panoply, thy measur'd dual throbbing and thy
  beat convulsive,
Thy black cylindric body, golden brass and silvery steel,
5 Thy ponderous side-bars, parallel and connecting rods,
  gyrating, shuttling at thy sides,
Thy metrical, now swelling pant and roar, now tapering in
  the distance,
Thy great protruding head-light fix'd in front,
Thy long, pale, floating vapor-pennants, tinged with
  delicate purple,
The dense and murky clouds out-belching from thy
  smoke-stack,
10 Thy knitted frame, thy springs and valves, the tremulous
  twinkle of thy wheels,
Thy train of cars, behind, obedient, merrily following,
Through gale or calm, now swift, now slack, yet steadily
  careering;
Type of the modern—emblem of motion and power—pulse
  of the continent,
For once come serve the Muse and merge in verse, even as
  here I see thee,
15 With storm and buffeting gusts of wind and falling snow,
By day thy warning ringing bell to sound its notes,
By night thy silent signal lamps to swing.
Fierce-throated beauty!
Roll through my chant with all thy lawless music, thy
  swinging lamps at night,
20 Thy madly-whistled laughter, echoing, rumbling like an
  earthquake, rousing all,
Law of thyself complete, thine own track firmly holding,
(No sweetness debonair of tearful harp or glib piano thine,)
Thy trills of shrieks by rocks and hills return'd,
Launch'd o'er the prairies wide, across the lakes,
25 To the free skies unpent° and glad and strong.   *unlimited*

[1876]

Matthew Arnold   *1822–1888*

DOVER BEACH

The sea is calm to-night.
The tide is full, the moon lies fair
Upon the straits;—on the French coast the light
Gleams and is gone; the cliffs of England stand,
5 Glimmering and vast, out in the tranquil bay.

Come to the window, sweet is the night-air!
Only, from the long line of spray
Where the sea meets the moon-blanched sand,
Listen! you hear the grating roar
10 Of pebbles which the waves draw back, and fling,
At their return, up the high strand,°   shore
Begin, and cease, and then again begin,
With tremulous cadence slow, and bring
The eternal note of sadness in.

15   Sophocles long ago
Heard it on the Aegæan, and it brought
Into his mind the turbid ebb and flow
Of human misery; we
Find also in the sound a thought,
20   Hearing it by this distant northern sea.

The sea of faith
Was once, too, at the full, and round earth's shore
Lay like the folds of a bright girdle furled.
But now I only hear
25 Its melancholy, long, withdrawing roar,
Retreating, to the breath
Of the night-wind, down the vast edges drear
And naked shingles° of the world.   *gravelly beaches*

Ah, love, let us be true
30 To one another! for the world, which seems
To lie before us like a land of dreams,
So various, so beautiful, so new,
Hath really neither joy, nor love, nor light,
Nor certitude, nor peace, nor help for pain;
35 And we are here as on a darkling° plain   *darkening*
Swept with confused alarms of struggle and flight,
Where ignorant armies clash by night.

[1867]

Emily Dickinson *1830–1886*

"SUCCESS IS COUNTED SWEETEST"

Success is counted sweetest
By those who ne'er succeed.
To comprehend a nectar
Requires sorest need.

5   Not one of all the purple Host
Who took the Flag today
Can tell the definition
So clear of Victory

As he defeated—dying—
10   On whose forbidden ear
The distant strains of triumph
Burst agonized and clear!

[1878]

"THE SOUL SELECTS HER OWN SOCIETY"

The Soul selects her own Society—
Then—shuts the Door—
To her divine Majority—
Present no more—

5 Unmoved—she notes the Chariots—pausing—
At her low Gate—
Unmoved—an Emperor be kneeling
Upon her Mat—

I've known her—from an ample nation—
10 Choose One—
Then—close the Valves of her attention—
Like Stone—

[posthumous, 1890]

"A BIRD CAME DOWN THE WALK"

A Bird came down the Walk—
He did not know I saw—
He bit an Angleworm in halves
And ate the fellow, raw,

5 And then he drank a Dew
From a convenient Grass—
And then hopped sidewise to the Wall
To let a Beetle pass—

He glanced with rapid eyes
10 That hurried all around—
They looked like frightened Beads, I thought—
He stirred his Velvet Head

Like one in danger, Cautious,
I offered him a Crumb
15 And he unrolled his feathers
And rowed him softer home—

Than Oars divide the Ocean,
Too silver for a seam—
Or Butterflies, off Banks of Noon
20 Leap, plashless as they swim.

[posthumous, 1891]

"AFTER GREAT PAIN, A FORMAL FEELING COMES"

After great pain, a formal feeling comes—
The Nerves sit ceremonious, like Tombs—
The stiff Heart questions was it He, that bore,
And Yesterday, or Centuries before?

5   The Feet, mechanical, go round—
Of Ground, or Air, or Ought—
A Wooden way
Regardless grown,
A Quartz contentment, like a stone—

10   This is the Hour of Lead—
Remembered, if outlived,
As Freezing persons, recollect the Snow—
First—Chill—then Stupor—then the letting go—
[posthumous, 1929]

"I HEARD A FLY BUZZ—WHEN I DIED"

I heard a Fly buzz—when I died—
The Stillness in the Room
Was like the Stillness in the Air—
Between the Heaves of Storm—

5   The Eyes around—had wrung them dry—
And Breaths were gathering firm
For that last Onset—when the King
Be witnessed—in the Room—

I willed my Keepsakes—Signed away
10 What portion of me be
Assignable—and then it was
There interposed a Fly—

With Blue—uncertain stumbling Buzz—
Between the light—and me—
15 And then the Windows failed—and then
I could not see to see—
[posthumous, 1896]

"I LIKE TO SEE IT LAP THE MILES"

I like to see it lap the Miles—
And lick the Valleys up—
And stop to feed itself at Tanks—
And then—prodigious step

5 Around a Pile of Mountains—
   And supercilious peer
   In Shanties—by the sides of Roads—
   And then a Quarry pare

   To fit its Ribs
10 And crawl between
   Complaining all the while
   In horrid—hooting stanza—
   Then chase itself down Hill—

   And neigh like Boanerges[1]—
15 Then—punctual as a Star
   Stop—docile and omnipotent
   At its own stable door—
                              [posthumous, 1891]

"BECAUSE I COULD NOT STOP FOR DEATH"

   Because I could not stop for Death—
   He kindly stopped for me—
   The Carriage held but just Ourselves—
   And Immortality.

5 We slowly drove—He knew no haste
   And I had put away
   My labor and my leisure too,
   For His Civility—

   We passed the School, where Children strove
10 At Recess—in the Ring—
   We passed the Fields of Gazing Grain—
   We passed the Setting Sun—

   Or rather—He passed Us—
   The Dews drew quivering and chill—
15 For only Gossamer, my Gown—
   My Tippet°—only Tulle°—   *shawl / silk gauze*

   We paused before a House that seemed
   A Swelling of the Ground—
   The Roof was scarcely visible—
20 The Cornice—in the Ground—

   Since then—'tis Centuries—and yet
   Feels shorter than the Day
   I first surmised the Horses' Heads
   Were toward Eternity—
                              [posthumous, 1890]

[1] A loud preacher or orator, from two Hebrew words meaning "sons of thunder."

Christina Rossetti *1830–1894*

IN AN ARTIST'S STUDIO

One face looks out from all his canvases,
   One selfsame figure sits or walks or leans:
   We found her hidden just behind those screens,
That mirror gave back all her loveliness.
5 A queen in opal or in ruby dress,
   A nameless girl in freshest summer-greens,
   A saint, an angel—every canvas means
The same one meaning, neither more nor less.
He feeds upon her face by day and night,
10   And she with true kind eyes looks back on him,
Fair as the moon and joyful as the light:
   Not wan with waiting, not with sorrow dim;
Not as she is, but was when hope shone bright;
   Not as she is, but as she fills his dream.

                         [1861]

A BIRTHDAY

My heart is like a singing bird
   Whose nest is in a watered shoot:
My heart is like an apple-tree
   Whose boughs are bent with thickset fruit;
5 My heart is like a rainbow shell
   That paddles in a halcyon° sea;   *calm*
My heart is gladder than all these
   Because my love is come to me.

Raise me a dais° of silk and down;   *throne*
10   Hang it with vair° and purple dyes;   *fur*
Carve it in doves and pomegranates,
   And peacocks with a hundred eyes;
Work it in gold and silver grapes,
   In leaves and silver fleurs-de-lys;°   *lily-shaped emblems*
15 Because the birthday of my life
   Is come, my love is come to me.

                         [1862]

GOBLIN MARKET

Morning and evening
Maids heard the goblins cry,
"Come buy our orchard fruits,
Come buy, come buy:
5 Apples and quinces,
Lemons and oranges,

Plump unpecked cherries,
Melons and raspberries,
Bloom-down-cheeked peaches,
10   Swart-headed mulberries,
Wild free-born cranberries,
Crab-apples, dewberries,
Pineapples, blackberries,
Apricots, strawberries—
15   All ripe together
In summer weather—
Morns that pass by,
Fair eves that fly;
Come buy, come buy:
20   Our grapes fresh from the vine,
Pomegranates full and fine,
Dates and sharp bullaces,[1]
Rare pears and greengages,[2]
Damsons and bilberries,[3]
25   Taste them and try:
Currants and gooseberries,
Bright-fire-like barberries,
Figs to fill your mouth,
Citrons from the South,
30   Sweet to tongue and sound to eye;
Come buy, come buy."

Evening by evening
Among the brook-side rushes,
Laura bowed her head to hear,
35   Lizzie veiled her blushes;
Crouching close together
In the cooling weather,
With clasping arms and cautioning lips,
With tingling cheeks and finger tips.
40   "Lie close," Laura said,
Pricking up her golden head.
"We must not look at goblin men,
We must not buy their fruits;
Who knows upon what soil they fed
45   Their hungry thirsty roots?"
"Come buy," call the goblins
Hobbling down the glen.
"Oh," cried Lizzie, "Laura, Laura,
You should not peep at goblin men."
50   Lizzie covered up her eyes,
Covered close lest they should look;
Laura reared her glossy head,
And whispered like the restless brook:
"Look, Lizzie, look, Lizzie,

[1] Wild plums.   [2] Another variety of plum.   [3] A small blue-black berry.

55   Down the glen tramp little men.
      One hauls a basket,
      One bears a plate,
      One lugs a golden dish
      Of many pounds' weight.
60   How fair the vine must grow
      Whose grapes are so luscious!
      How warm the wind must blow
      Through those fruit bushes!"
      "No," said Lizzie, "No, no, no;
65   Their offers should not charm us,
      Their evil gifts would harm us."
      She thrust a dimpled finger
      In each ear, shut eyes and ran.
      Curious Laura chose to linger,
70   Wondering at each merchant man.
      One had a cat's face,
      One whisked a tail,
      One tramped at a rat's pace,
      One crawled like a snail,
75   One like a wombat prowled obtuse and furry,
      One like a ratel[4] tumbled hurry-skurry.
      She heard a voice like voice of doves
      Cooing all together;
      They sounded kind and full of loves
80   In the pleasant weather.

      Laura stretched her gleaming neck
      Like a rush-imbedded swan,
      Like a lily from the beck,[5]
      Like a moonlit poplar branch,
85   Like a vessel at the launch
      When its last restraint is gone.

      Backward up the mossy glen
      Turned and trooped the goblin men,
      With their shrill repeated cry,
90   "Come buy, come buy."
      When they reached where Laura was
      They stood stock still upon the moss,
      Leering at each other,
      Brother with queer brother;
95   Signaling each other,
      Brother with sly brother.
      One set his basket down,
      One reared his plate;
      One began to weave a crown
100   Of tendrils, leaves, and rough nuts brown
      (Men sell not such in any town);

[4] An animal like a badger.   [5] Rocky stream.

One heaved the golden weight
Of dish and fruit to offer her:
"Come buy, come buy," was still their cry.
105 Laura stared but did not stir,
Longed but had no money.
The whisk-tailed merchant bade her taste
In tones as smooth as honey,
The cat-faced purred,
110 The rat-paced spoke a word
Of welcome, and the snail-paced even was heard;
One parrot-voiced and jolly
Cried, "Pretty Goblin" still for "Pretty Polly";
One whistled like a bird.

115 But sweet-tooth Laura spoke in haste:
"Good folk, I have no coin;
To take were to purloin.
I have no copper in my purse,
I have no silver either,
120 And all my gold is on the furze[6]
That shakes in windy weather
Above the rusty heather.[7]"
"You have much gold upon your head,"
They answered all together:
125 "Buy from us with a golden curl."
She clipped a precious golden lock,
She dropped a tear more rare than pearl,
Then sucked their fruit globes fair or red.
Sweeter than honey from the rock,
130 Stronger than man-rejoicing wine,
Clearer than water flowed that juice;
She never tasted such before,
How should it cloy with length of use?
She sucked and sucked and sucked the more
135 Fruits which that unknown orchard bore;
She sucked until her lips were sore;
Then flung the emptied rinds away,
But gathered up one kernel stone,
And knew not was it night or day
140 As she turned home alone.

Lizzie met her at the gate,
Full of wise upbraidings:
"Dear, you should not stay so late,
Twilight is not good for maidens;
145 Should not loiter in the glen
In the haunts of goblin men.
Do you not remember Jeanie,
How she met them in the moonlight,

---

[6] A prickly evergreen shrub with yellow flowers.   [7] A low-growing plant of the heath family.

Took their gifts both choice and many,
150 Ate their fruits and wore their flowers
Plucked from bowers
Where summer ripens at all hours?
But ever in the moonlight
She pined and pined away;
155 Sought them by night and day,
Found them no more, but dwindled and grew gray;
Then fell with the first snow,
While to this day no grass will grow
Where she lies low;
160 I planted daisies there a year ago
That never blow.[8]
You should not loiter so."
"Nay, hush," said Laura;
"Nay, hush, my sister.
165 I ate and ate my fill,
Yet my mouth waters still.
Tomorrow night I will
Buy more"; and kissed her.
"Have done with sorrow;
170 I'll bring you plums tomorrow
Fresh on their mother twigs,
Cherries worth getting;
You cannot think what figs
My teeth have met in,
175 What melons icy-cold
Piled on a dish of gold
Too huge for me to hold,
What peaches with a velvet nap,
Pellucid grapes without one seed.
180 Odorous indeed must be the mead
Whereon they grow, and pure the wave they drink
With lilies at the brink,
And sugar-sweet their sap."

Golden head by golden head,
185 Like two pigeons in one nest
Folded in each other's wings,
They lay down in their curtained bed;
Like two blossoms on one stem,
Like two flakes of new-fall'n snow,
190 Like two wands of ivory
Tipped with gold for awful kings.
Moon and stars gazed in at them,
Wind sang to them lullaby,
Lumbering owls forebore to fly,
195 Not a bat flapped to and fro
Round their nest;

[8] Blossom.

Cheek to cheek and breast to breast
Locked together in one nest.

Early in the morning
200   When the first cock crowed his warning,
Neat like bees, as sweet and busy,
Laura rose with Lizzie;
Fetched in honey, milked the cows,
Aired and set to rights the house,
205   Kneaded cakes of whitest wheat,
Cakes for dainty mouths to eat,
Next churned butter, whipped up cream,
Fed their poultry, sat and sewed;
Talked as modest maidens should—
210   Lizzie with an open heart,
Laura in an absent dream,
One content, one sick in part;
One warbling for the mere bright day's delight,
One longing for the night.

215   At length slow evening came.
They went with pitchers to the reedy brook;
Lizzie most placid in her look,
Laura most like a leaping flame.
They drew the gurgling water from its deep.
220   Lizzie plucked purple and rich golden flags,
Then turning homeward said: "The sunset flushes
Those furthest loftiest crags;
Come, Laura, not another maiden lags.
No willful squirrel wags;
225   The beasts and birds are fast asleep."

But Laura loitered still among the rushes,
And said the bank was steep,
And said the hour was early still,
The dew not fall'n, the wind not chill;
230   Listening ever, but not catching
The customary cry,
"Come buy, come buy,"
With its iterated jingle
Of sugar-baited words;
235   Not for all her watching
Once discerning even one goblin
Racing, whisking, tumbling, hobbling—
Let alone the herds
That used to tramp along the glen,
240   In groups or single,
Of brisk fruit-merchant men.

Till Lizzie urged, "O Laura, come;
I hear the fruit-call, but I dare not look.

245　　You should not loiter longer at this brook;
　　　Come with me home.
　　　The stars rise, the moon bends her arc,
　　　Each glowworm winks her spark.
　　　Let us get home before the night grows dark,
　　　For clouds may gather
250　　Though this is summer weather,
　　　Put out the lights and drench us through;
　　　Then if we lost our way what should we do?"

　　　Laura turned cold as stone
　　　To find her sister heard that cry alone,
255　　That goblin cry,
　　　"Come buy our fruits, come buy."
　　　Must she then buy no more such dainty fruit?
　　　Must she no more such succous[9] pasture find,
　　　Gone deaf and blind?
260　　Her tree of life drooped from the root;
　　　She said not one word in her heart's sore ache;
　　　But peering through the dimness, naught discerning,
　　　Trudged home, her pitcher dripping all the way;
　　　So crept to bed, and lay
265　　Silent till Lizzie slept;
　　　Then sat up in a passionate yearning,
　　　And gnashed her teeth for balked desire, and wept
　　　As if her heart would break.

　　　Day after day, night after night,
270　　Laura kept watch in vain
　　　In sullen silence of exceeding pain.
　　　She never caught again the goblin cry,
　　　"Come buy, come buy";
　　　She never spied the goblin men
275　　Hawking their fruits along the glen.
　　　But when the noon waxed bright
　　　Her hair grew thin and gray;
　　　She dwindled, as the fair full moon doth turn
　　　To swift decay and burn
280　　Her fire away.

　　　One day, remembering her kernel-stone,
　　　She set it by a wall that faced the south;
　　　Dewed it with tears, hoped for a root,
　　　Watched for a waxing shoot,
285　　But there came none.
　　　It never saw the sun,
　　　It never felt the trickling moisture run;
　　　While with sunk eyes and faded mouth
　　　She dreamed of melons, as a traveler sees

[9] Succulent, juicy.

290   False waves in desert drouth
        With shade of leaf-crowned trees,
        And burns the thirstier in the sandful breeze.

        She no more swept the house,
        Tended the fowls or cows,
295   Fetched honey, kneaded cakes of wheat,
        Brought water from the brook;
        But sat down listless in the chimney-nook
        And would not eat.

        Tender Lizzie could not bear
300   To watch her sister's cankerous care,
        Yet not to share.
        She night and morning
        Caught the goblin's cry:
        "Come buy our orchard fruits,
305   Come buy, come buy."
        Beside the brook, along the glen,
        She heard the tramp of goblin men,
        The voice and stir
        Poor Laura could not hear;
310   Longed to buy fruit to comfort her,
        But feared to pay too dear.
        She thought of Jeanie in her grave,
        Who should have been a bride;
        But who for joys brides hope to have
315   Fell sick and died
        In her gay prime,
        In earliest winter time,
        With the first glazing time,[10]
        With the first snow-fall of crisp winter time.

320   Till Laura dwindling
        Seemed knocking at Death's door.
        Then Lizzie weighed no more
        Better and worse;
        But put a silver penny in her purse,
325   Kissed Laura, crossed the heath with clumps of furze
        At twilight, halted by the brook,
        And for the first time in her life
        Began to listen and look.

        Laughed every goblin
330   When they spied her peeping;
        Came toward her hobbling,
        Flying, running, leaping,
        Puffing and blowing,
        Chuckling, clapping, crowing,

[10] Frost.

335   Clucking and gobbling,
        Mopping and mowing,
        Full of airs and graces,
        Pulling wry faces,
        Demure grimaces,
340   Cat-like and rat-like,
        Ratel- and wombat-like,
        Snail-paced in a hurry,
        Parrot-voiced and whistler,
        Helter-skelter, hurry-skurry,
345   Chattering like magpies,
        Fluttering like pigeons,
        Gliding like fishes—
        Hugged her and kissed her,
        Squeezed and caressed her,
350   Stretched up their dishes,
        Panniers,[11] and plates:
        "Look at our apples
        Russet and dun,
        Bob at our cherries,
355   Bite at our peaches,
        Citrons and dates,
        Grapes for the asking,
        Pears red with basking
        Out in the sun,
360   Plums on their twigs;
        Pluck them and suck them—
        Pomegranates, figs."

        "Good folk," said Lizzie,
        Mindful of Jeanie,
365   "Give me much and many";
        Held out her apron,
        Tossed them her penny.
        "Nay, take a seat with us,
        Honor and eat with us,"
370   They answered, grinning:
        "Our feast is but beginning.
        Night yet is early,
        Warm and dew-pearly,
        Wakeful and starry.
375   Such fruits as these
        No man can carry;
        Half their bloom would fly,
        Half their dew would dry,
        Half their flavor would pass by.
380   Sit down and feast with us,
        Be welcome guest with us,
        Cheer you and rest with us."—

[11] Baskets.

"Thank you," said Lizzie, "but one waits
At home alone for me;
385 So without further parleying,
If you will not sell me any
Of your fruits though much and many,
Give me back my silver penny
I tossed you for a fee."—
390 They began to scratch their pates,
No longer wagging, purring,
But visibly demurring,
Grunting and snarling.
One called her proud,
395 Cross-grained, uncivil;
Their tones waxed loud,
Their looks were evil.
Lashing their tails,
They trod and hustled her,
400 Elbowed and jostled her,
Clawed with their nails,
Barking, mewing, hissing, mocking,
Tore her gown and soiled her stocking,
Twitched her hair out by the roots,
405 Stamped upon her tender feet,
Held her hands and squeezed their fruits
Against her mouth to make her eat.

White and golden Lizzie stood,
Like a lily in a flood—
410 Like a rock of blue-veined stone
Lashed by tides obstreperously—
Like a beacon left alone
In a hoary, roaring sea,
Sending up a golden fire—
415 Like a fruit-crowned orange-tree
White with blossoms honey-sweet
Sore beset by wasp and bee—
Like a royal virgin town
Topped with gilded dome and spire
420 Close beleaguered by a fleet
Mad to tug her standard down.

One may lead a horse to water;
Twenty cannot make him drink.
Though the goblins cuffed and caught her,
425 Coaxed and fought her,
Bullied and besought her,
Scratched her, pinched her black as ink,
Kicked and knocked her,
Mauled and mocked her,
430 Lizzie uttered not a word;
Would not open lip from lip

Lest they should cram a mouthful in;
But laughed in heart to feel the drip
Of juice that siruped all her face,
435   And lodged in dimples of her chin,
And streaked her neck which quaked like curd.
At last the evil people,
Worn out by resistance,
Flung back her penny, kicked their fruit
440   Along whichever road they took,
Not leaving root or stone or shoot;
Some writhed into the ground,
Some dived into the brook
With ring and ripple,
445   Some scudded on the gale without a sound,
Some vanished in the distance.

In a smart, ache, tingle,
Lizzie went her way;
Knew not was it night or day;
450   Sprang up the bank, tore through the furze,
Threaded copse and dingle,
And heard her penny jingle
Bouncing in her purse—
Its bounce was music to her ear.
455   She ran and ran
As if she feared some goblin man
Dogged her with gibe or curse
Or something worse;
But not one goblin skurried after,
460   Nor was she pricked by fear;
The kind heart made her windy-paced
That urged her home quite out of breath with haste
And inward laughter.

She cried, "Laura," up the garden,
465   "Did you miss me?
Come and kiss me.
Never mind my bruises.
Hug me, kiss me, suck my juices
Squeezed from goblin fruits for you,
470   Goblin pulp and goblin dew.
Eat me, drink me, love me;
Laura, make much of me;
For your sake I have braved the glen
And had to do with goblin merchant men."

475   Laura started from her chair,
Flung her arms up in the air,
Clutched her hair:
"Lizzie, Lizzie, have you tasted
For my sake the fruit forbidden?

480 Must your light like mine be hidden,
Your young life like mine be wasted,
Undone in mine undoing,
And ruined in my ruin,
Thirsty, cankered, goblin-ridden?"—
485 She clung about her sister,
Kissed and kissed and kissed her;
Tears once again
Refreshed her shrunken eyes,
Dropping like rain
490 After long sultry drouth;
Shaking with anguish, fear, and pain,
She kissed and kissed her with a hungry mouth.
Her lips began to scorch,
That juice was wormwood to her tongue,
495 She loathed the feast.
Writhing as one possessed, she leaped and sung,
Rent all her robe, and wrung
Her hands in lamentable haste,
And beat her breast.
500 Her locks streamed like the torch
Borne by a racer at full speed,
Or like the mane of horses in their flight,
Or like an eagle when she stems the light
Straight toward the sun,
505 Or like a caged thing freed,
Or like a flying flag when armies run.

Swift fire spread through her veins, knocked at her heart,
Met the fire smoldering there
And overbore its lesser flame;
510 She gorged on bitterness without a name—
Ah, fool, to choose such part
Of soul-consuming care!
Sense failed in the mortal strife;
Like the watch-tower of a town
515 Which an earthquake shatters down,
Like a lightning-stricken mast,
Like a wind-uprooted tree
Spun about,
Like a foam-topped waterspout
520 Cast down headlong in the sea,
She fell at last;
Pleasure past and anguish past,
Is it death or is it life?

Life out of death.
525 That night long Lizzie watched by her,
Counted her pulse's flagging stir,
Felt for her breath,
Held water to her lips, and cooled her face

With tears and fanning leaves.
530 But when the first birds chirped about their eaves,
And early reapers plodded to the place
Of golden sheaves,
And dew-wet grass
Bowed in the morning winds so brisk to pass,
535 And new buds with new day
Opened of cup-like lilies on the stream,
Laura awoke as from a dream,
Laughed in the innocent old way,
Hugged Lizzie but not twice or thrice;
540 Her gleaming locks showed not one thread of gray,
Her breath was sweet as May,
And light danced in her eyes.

Days, weeks, months, years
Afterwards, when both were wives
545 With children of their own;
Their mother-hearts beset with fears,
Their lives bound up in tender lives;
Laura would call the little ones
And tell them of her early prime,
550 Those pleasant days long gone
Of not-returning time,
Would talk about the haunted glen,
The wicked quaint fruit-merchant men,
Their fruits like honey to the throat
555 But poison in the blood
(Men sell not such in any town);
Would tell them how her sister stood
In deadly peril to do her good,
And win the fiery antidote:
560 Then joining hands to little hands
Would bid them cling together—
"For there is no friend like a sister
In calm or stormy weather;
To cheer one on the tedious way,
565 To fetch one if one goes astray,
To lift one if one totters down,
To strengthen whilst one stands."

[1862]

❧ MODERN POETRY ❧

Thomas Hardy *1840–1928*

NEUTRAL TONES

We stood by a pond that winter day,
And the sun was white, as though chidden of God,
And a few leaves lay on the starving sod;
   —They had fallen from an ash, and were gray.

5   Your eyes on me were as eyes that rove
Over tedious riddles of years ago;
And some words played between us to and fro
   On which lost the more by our love.

The smile on your mouth was the deadest thing
10   Alive enough to have strength to die;
And a grin of bitterness swept thereby
   Like an ominous bird a-wing. . . .

Since then, keen lessons that love deceives,
And wrings with wrong, have shaped to me
15   Your face, and the God-curst sun, and a tree,
   And a pond edged with grayish leaves.

                       [1898]

THE DARKLING[1] THRUSH

I leant upon a coppice gate[2]
   When Frost was spectre-gray,
And Winter's dregs made desolate
   The weakening eye of day.
5   The tangled bine-stems[3] scored the sky
   Like strings of broken lyres,
And all mankind that haunted nigh
   Had sought their household fires.

The land's sharp features seemed to be
10   The Century's corpse[4] outleant,
His crypt the cloudy canopy,
   The wind his death-lament.

[1] In the dark.   [2] The gate to a small thicket.
[3] Twining stems of shrubbery.   [4] The poem was composed on December 31, 1900.

The ancient pulse of germ and birth
    Was shrunken hard and dry,
15   And every spirit upon earth
    Seemed fervorless as I.

At once a voice arose among
    The bleak twigs overhead
In a full-hearted evensong
20   Of joy illimited;
An aged thrush, frail, gaunt, and small,
    In blast-beruffled plume,
Had chosen thus to fling his soul
    Upon the growing gloom.

25   So little cause for carolings
    Of such ecstatic sound
Was written on terrestrial things
    Afar or nigh around,
That I could think there trembled through
30   His happy good-night air
Some blessed Hope, whereof he knew
    And I was unaware.

             [1902]

THE CONVERGENCE OF THE TWAIN

(*Lines on the loss of the 'Titanic'*[1])

I

In a solitude of the sea
Deep from human vanity,
And the Pride of Life that planned her, stilly couches she.

II

5   Steel chambers, late the pyres
   Of her salamandrine[2] fires,
Cold currents thrid,° and turn to rhythmic tidal lyres.   *thread*

III

Over the mirrors meant
To glass the opulent
The sea-worm crawls—grotesque, slimed, dumb, indifferent.

IV

10   Jewels in joy designed
   To ravish the sensuous mind
Lie lightless, all their sparkles bleared and black and blind.

---

[1] The "unsinkable" luxury liner that sank with enormous loss of life after striking an iceberg on April 15, 1912.
[2] An allusion to mythological reptiles supposed to be able to live in fire or, possibly, an allusion to the elemental spirit living in fire in the natural philosophy of Paracelsus (c. 1493–1541).

V

Dim moon-eyed fishes near
Gaze at the gilded gear
15   And query: "What does this vaingloriousness down here?" ...

VI

Well: while was fashioning
This creature of cleaving wing,
The Immanent Will that stirs and urges everything

VII

Prepared a sinister mate
20   For her—so gaily great—
A Shape of Ice, for the time far and dissociate.

VIII

And as the smart ship grew
In stature, grace, and hue,
In shadowy silent distance grew the Iceberg too.

IX

25   Alien they seemed to be:
No mortal eye could see
The intimate welding of their later history,

X

Or sign that they were bent
By paths coincident
30   On being anon twin halves of one august event,

XI

Till the Spinner of the Years
Said "Now!" And each one hears,
And consummation comes, and jars two hemispheres.

[1912]

CHANNEL FIRING[1]

That night your great guns, unawares,
Shook all our coffins as we lay,
And broke the chancel[2] window-squares,
We thought it was the Judgment-day

5   And sat upright. While drearisome
Arose the howl of wakened hounds:
The mouse let fall the altar-crumb,
The worms drew back into the mounds,

[1] The title refers to gunnery practice in the English Channel shortly before the commencement of World War I.
[2] The part of a church around the altar.

The glebe cow[3] drooled. Till God called, "No;
10 It's gunnery practice out at sea
Just as before you went below;
The world is as it used to be:

"All nations striving strong to make
Red war yet redder. Mad as hatters
15 They do no more for Christès sake
Than you who are helpless in such matters.

"That this is not the judgment-hour
For some of them's a blessed thing,
For if it were they'd have to scour
20 Hell's floor for so much threatening. . . .

"Ha, ha. It will be warmer when
I blow the trumpet (if indeed
I ever do; for you are men,
And rest eternal sorely need)."

25 So down we lay again. "I wonder,
Will the world ever saner be,"
Said one, "than when He sent us under
In our indifferent century!"

And many a skeleton shook his head.
30 "Instead of preaching forty year,"
My neighbour Parson Thirdly said,
"I wish I had stuck to pipes and beer."

Again the guns disturbed the hour,
Roaring their readiness to avenge,
35 As far inland as Stourton Tower,[4]
And Camelot, and starlit Stonehenge.

[1914]

Gerard Manley Hopkins   *1844–1889*

GOD'S GRANDEUR

The world is charged with the grandeur of God.
    It will flame out, like shining from shook foil;°   *gold foil*
    It gathers to a greatness, like the ooze of oil
Crushed. Why do men then now not reck° his rod?   *take heed of*
5 Generations have trod, have trod, have trod;
    And all is seared with trade; bleared, smeared with toil;
    And wears man's smudge and shares man's smell: the soil
Is bare now, nor can foot feel, being shod.

---

[3] The cow of the parsonage.
[4] Stourton Tower commemorates King Alfred's victory over the invading Danes in 879. Camelot was the location of King Arthur's court (supposedly in the sixth century A.D.). The massive stones at Stonehenge were used in the mysterious Druidic rites of prehistoric England.

And for all this, nature is never spent;
10   There lives the dearest freshness deep down things;
And though the last lights off the black West went
     Oh, morning, at the brown brink eastward, springs—
Because the Holy Ghost over the bent
     World broods with warm breast and with ah! bright
         wings.

                                        [posthumous, 1918]

HEAVEN—HAVEN

A Nun Takes the Veil

          I have desired to go
               Where springs not fail,
     To fields where flies no sharp and sided hail
          And a few lilies blow.

5   And I have asked to be
               Where no storms come,
     Where the green swell is in the havens dumb,
          And out of the swing of the sea.

                                        [posthumous, 1918]

PIED BEAUTY

     Glory be to God for dappled things—
          For skies of couple-color as a brinded° cow;   *spotted*
               For rose-moles all in stipple° upon trout that swim;   *dots*
     Fresh-firecoal chestnut-falls; finches' wings;
5   Landscape plotted and pieced—fold, fallow, and plough;
               And áll trádes, their gear and tackle and trim.°   *equipment*

     All things counter, original, spare, strange;
          Whatever is fickle, freckled (who knows how?)
               With swift, slow; sweet, sour; adazzle, dim;
10   He fathers-forth whose beauty is past change:
                    Praise him.

                                        [posthumous, 1918]

THE WINDHOVER:[1]

To Christ our Lord

     I caught this morning morning's minion,° kingdom of   *favorite*
          daylight's dauphin,° dapple° -dawn-drawn Falcon, in   *heir / mottled*
          his riding
     Of the rolling level underneath him steady air, and
          striding

---
[1] The sparrowhawk, which seems to hover in a headwind.

High there, how he rung° upon the rein of a wimpling°   *circled / rippling*
   wing
5   In his ecstasy! then off, off forth on swing,
      As a skate's heel sweeps smooth on a bow-bend: the
         hurl and gliding
      Rebuffed the big wind. My heart in hiding
   Stirred for a bird,—the achieve of, the mastery of the
         thing!

   Brute beauty and valor and act, oh, air, pride, plume, here
10   Buckle! AND the fire that breaks from thee then, a billion
   Times told lovelier, more dangerous, O my chevalier!

   No wonder of it: shéer plód makes plough down sillion[2]
   Shine, and blue-bleak embers, ah my dear,
      Fall, gall° themselves, and gash gold-vermilion.   *chafe*

[posthumous, 1918]

SPRING AND FALL:

To a Young Child

   Márgarét, áre you gríeving
   Over Goldengrove unleaving?
   Leáves, like the things of man, you
   With your fresh thoughts care for, can you?
5   Áh! ás the heart grows older
   It will come to such sights colder
   By and by, nor spare a sigh
   Though worlds of wanwood leafmeal[1] lie;
   And yet you *will* weep and know why.
10   Now no matter, child, the name:
   Sórrow's spríngs áre the same.
   Nor mouth had, no nor mind, expressed
   What heart heard of, ghost° guessed: *spirit*
   It ís the blight man was born for,
15   It is Margaret you mourn for.

[posthumous, 1918]

A. E. Housman   *1859–1936*

"WHEN I WAS ONE-AND-TWENTY"

   When I was one-and-twenty
      I heard a wise man say,
   "Give crowns and pounds and guineas
      But not your heart away;

---

[2] An archaic word meaning "a ridge between furrows."
[1] Hopkins has created the words *wanwood* and *leafmeal. Leafmeal* is probably a noun meaning "a mulch of leaves." *Wanwood* would then be an adjective meaning "dark-woods."

5   Give pearls away and rubies
          But keep your fancy free."
       But I was one-and-twenty,
          No use to talk to me.

       When I was one-and-twenty
10   I heard him say again,
       "The heart out of the bosom
          Was never given in vain;
       'Tis paid with sighs a plenty
          And sold for endless rue."
15   And I am two-and-twenty,
          And oh, 'tis true, 'tis true.

                                        [1896]

"WITH RUE MY HEART IS LADEN"

       With rue my heart is laden
          For golden friends I had,
       For many a rose-lipt maiden
          And many a lightfoot lad.

5   By brooks too broad for leaping
          The lightfoot boys are laid;
       The rose-lipt girls are sleeping
          In fields where roses fade.

                                        [1896]

TO AN ATHLETE DYING YOUNG

       The time you won your town the race
       We chaired you through the market-place;
       Man and boy stood cheering by,
       And home we brought you shoulder-high.

5   Today, the road all runners come,
       Shoulder-high we bring you home,
       And set you at your threshold down,
       Townsman of a stiller town.

       Smart lad, to slip betimes away
10   From fields where glory does not stay
       And early though the laurel grows
       It withers quicker than the rose.

       Eyes the shady night has shut
       Cannot see the record cut,
15   And silence sounds no worse than cheers
       After earth has stopped the ears:

Now you will not swell the rout
Of lads that wore their honors out,
Runners whom renown outran
20   And the name died before the man.

So set, before its echoes fade,
The fleet foot on the sill of shade,
And hold to the low lintel up
The still-defended challenge-cup.

25   And round that early-laurelled head
Will flock to gaze the strengthless dead,
And find unwithered on its curls
The garland briefer than a girl's.

[1896]

"TERENCE, THIS IS STUPID STUFF"

"Terence, this[1] is stupid stuff:
You eat your victuals fast enough;
There can't be much amiss, 'tis clear,
To see the rate you drink your beer.
5   But oh, good Lord, the verse you make,
It gives a chap the belly-ache.
The cow, the old cow, she is dead;
It sleeps well, the hornèd head:
We poor lads, 'tis our turn now
10   To hear such tunes as killed the cow.
Pretty friendship 'tis to rhyme
Your friends to death before their time
Moping melancholy mad:
Come, pipe a tune to dance to, lad."

15   Why, if 'tis dancing you would be,
There's brisker pipes than poetry.
Say, for what were hop-yards meant,
Or why was Burton built on Trent?[2]
Oh many a peer of England brews
20   Livelier liquor than the Muse,
And malt does more than Milton can
To justify God's ways to man.[3]
Ale, man, ale's the stuff to drink
For fellows whom it hurts to think:
25   Look into the pewter pot
To see the world as the world's not.

---

[1] This poetry.   [2] Burton-on-Trent is an English city famous for its breweries.
[3] An allusion to the opening of Milton's *Paradise Lost* (1667).

And faith, 'tis pleasant till 'tis past:
The mischief is that 'twill not last.
Oh I have been to Ludlow[4] fair
30   And left my necktie God knows where,
And carried halfway home, or near,
Pints and quarts of Ludlow beer:
Then the world seemed none so bad,
And I myself a sterling lad;
35   And down in lovely muck I've lain,
Happy till I woke again.
Then I saw the morning sky:
Heigho, the tale was all a lie;
The world, it was the old world yet,
40   I was I, my things were wet,
And nothing now remained to do
But begin the game anew.

        Therefore, since the world has still
Much good, but much less good than ill,
45   And while the sun and moon endure
Luck's a chance, but trouble's sure,
I'd face it as a wise man would,
And train for ill and not for good.
'Tis true, the stuff I bring for sale
50   Is not so brisk a brew as ale:
Out of a stem that scored[5] the hand
I wrung it in a weary land.
But take it: if the smack is sour,
The better for the embittered hour;
55   It should do good to heart and head
When your soul is in my soul's stead;
And I will friend you, if I may,
In the dark and cloudy day.

        There was a king reigned in the East:
60   There, when kings will sit to feast,
They get their fill before they think
With poisoned meat and poisoned drink.
He gathered all that springs to birth
From the many-venomed earth;
65   First a little, thence to more,
He sampled all her killing store;
And easy, smiling, seasoned sound,
Sate the king when healths went round.
They put arsenic in his meat
70   And stared aghast to watch him eat;
They poured strychnine in his cup
And shook to see him drink it up:

---

[4] A town in Shropshire.   [5] Cut.

They shook, they stared as white's their shirt:
Them it was their poison hurt.
75 —I tell the tale that I heard told.
Mithridates,[6] he died old.

[1896]

"ON WENLOCK EDGE"

On Wenlock Edge[1] the wood's in trouble;
His forest fleece the Wrekin[2] heaves;
The gale, it plies the saplings double,
And thick on Severn[3] snow the leaves.

5 'Twould blow like this through holt and hanger[4]
When Uricon[5] the city stood:
'Tis the old wind in the old anger,
But then it threshed another wood.

Then, 'twas before my time, the Roman
10 At yonder heaving hill would stare:
The blood that warms an English yeoman,
The thoughts that hurt him, they were there.

There, like the wind through woods in riot,
Through him the gale of life blew high;
15 The tree of man was never quiet:
Then 'twas the Roman, now 'tis I.

The gale, it plies the saplings double,
It blows so hard, 'twill soon be gone:
Today the Roman and his trouble
20 Are ashes under Uricon.

[1896]

"LOVELIEST OF TREES"

Loveliest of trees, the cherry now
Is hung with bloom along the bough,
And stands about the woodland ride
Wearing white for Eastertide.

5 Now, of my threescore years and ten,
Twenty will not come again,
And take from seventy springs a score,
It only leaves me fifty more.

[6] In his *Natural History* the Roman writer Pliny (A.D. 23–79) tells this story of Mithridates VI, King of Pontus (ca. 133 B.C.–63 B.C.).
[1] Ridge.   [2] Wrekin Hill.   [3] The Severn River.   [4] Woods and shed.
[5] A Roman city once located near Shrewsbury, England.

10
And since to look at things in bloom
Fifty springs are little room,
About the woodlands I will go
To see the cherry hung with snow.

[1896]

EIGHT O'CLOCK

He stood, and heard the steeple
  Sprinkle the quarters on the morning town.
One, two, three, four, to market-place and people
  It tossed them down.

5
Strapped, noosed, nighing his hour,
  He stood and counted them and cursed his luck;
And then the clock collected in the tower
  Its strength, and struck.

[1922]

William Butler Yeats   *1865–1939*

THE LAKE ISLE OF INNISFREE

I will arise and go now, and go to Innisfree,
And a small cabin build there, of clay and wattles° made: *woven limbs*
Nine bean-rows will I have there, a hive for the honeybee,
And live alone in the bee-loud glade.

5
And I shall have some peace there, for peace comes
    dropping slow,
Dropping from the veils of the morning to where the cricket
    sings;
There midnight's all a glimmer, and noon a purple glow,
And evening full of the linnet's° wings.   *a songbird*

10
I will arise and go now, for always night and day
I hear lake water lapping with low sounds by the shore;
While I stand on the roadway, or on the pavements grey,
I hear it in the deep heart's core.

[1892]

THE WILD SWANS AT COOLE[1]

The trees are in their autumn beauty,
The woodland paths are dry,
Under the October twilight the water
Mirrors a still sky;
5 Upon the brimming water among the stones
Are nine-and-fifty swans.

The nineteenth autumn has come upon me
Since I first made my count;
I saw, before I had well finished,
10 All suddenly mount
And scatter wheeling in great broken rings
Upon their clamorous wings.

I have looked upon those brilliant creatures,
And now my heart is sore.
15 All's changed since I, hearing at twilight,
The first time on this shore,
The bell-beat of their wings above my head,
Trod with a lighter tread.

Unwearied still, lover by lover,
20 They paddle in the cold
Companionable streams or climb the air;
Their hearts have not grown old;
Passion or conquest, wander where they will,
Attend upon them still.

25 But now they drift on the still water,
Mysterious, beautiful;
Among what rushes will they build,
By what lake's edge or pool
Delight men's eyes when I awake some day
30 To find they have flown away?

[1917]

THE SECOND COMING[1]

Turning and turning in the widening gyre[2]
The falcon cannot hear the falconer;
Things fall apart; the center cannot hold;
Mere anarchy is loosed upon the world,

---

[1] Between 1897 and 1916 (when this poem was written), Yeats had often been a guest at Coole Park, his friend Lady Gregory's country estate.
[1] The title alludes to the Second Coming of Christ predicted in Matthew 24, but also symbolizes the end of one age and the commencement of another.
[2] The widening spiral flown by the falcon takes it so far out that it no longer hears its master. Yeats uses the gyre or spiral as a symbol of extension and dissolution in the cycle of our civilization.

5   The blood-dimmed tide is loosed, and everywhere
The ceremony of innocence is drowned;
The best lack all conviction, while the worst
Are full of passionate intensity.

Surely some revelation is at hand;
10   Surely the Second Coming is at hand.
The Second Coming! Hardly are those words out
When a vast image out of *Spiritus Mundi*[3]
Troubles my sight: somewhere in sands of the desert
A shape with lion body and the head of a man,[4]
15   A gaze blank and pitiless as the sun,
Is moving its slow thighs, while all about it
Reel shadows of the indignant desert birds.
The darkness drops again; but now I know
That twenty centuries of stony sleep
20   Were vexed to nightmare by a rocking cradle,[5]
And what rough beast, its hour come round at last,
Slouches toward Bethlehem to be born?

                              [1921]

LEDA AND THE SWAN[1]

A sudden blow: the great wings beating still
Above the staggering girl, her thighs caressed
By the dark webs, her nape caught in his bill,
He holds her helpless breast upon his breast.

5   How can those terrified vague fingers push
The feathered glory from her loosening thighs?
And how can body, laid in that white rush,
But feel the strange heart beating where it lies?

A shudder in the loins engenders there
10   The broken wall, the burning roof and tower
And Agamemnon dead.
                  Being so caught up,
So mastered by the brute blood of the air,
Did she put on his knowledge with his power
Before the indifferent beak could let her drop?

                              [1924]

---

[3] The spirit of the world, a form of universal subconscious serving as a storehouse of images.
[4] A Sphinx-like creature.
[5] Yeats's idea is, perhaps, that the rocking of Christ's cradle produced, after twenty centuries, the awakening Sphinx.
[1] In Greek mythology Leda was raped by Zeus in the form of a swan; she subsequently gave birth to Helen, who caused the destruction of Troy, and Clytemnestra, who murdered her husband Agamemnon upon his return from Troy.

SAILING TO BYZANTIUM

I

That is no country for old men. The young
In one another's arms, birds in the trees
—Those dying generations—at their song,
The salmon-falls, the mackerel-crowded seas,
5 Fish, flesh, or fowl, commend all summer long
Whatever is begotten, born, and dies.
Caught in that sensual music all neglect
Monuments of unageing intellect.

II

An aged man is but a paltry thing,
10 A tattered coat upon a stick, unless
Soul clap its hands and sing, and louder sing
For every tatter in its mortal dress,
Nor is there singing school but studying
Monuments of its own magnificence;
15 And therefore I have sailed the seas and come
To the holy city of Byzantium.[1]

III

O sages standing in God's holy fire
As in the gold mosaic of a wall,
Come from the holy fire, perne in a gyre,[2]
20 And be the singing-masters of my soul.
Consume my heart away; sick with desire
And fastened to a dying animal
It knows not what it is; and gather me
Into the artifice of eternity.

IV

25 Once out of nature I shall never take
My bodily form from any natural thing,
But such a form as Grecian goldsmiths make
Of hammered gold and gold enamelling
To keep a drowsy Emperor awake;
30 Or set upon a golden bough to sing
To lords and ladies of Byzantium
Of what is past, or passing, or to come.

[1927]

---

[1] Yeats contrasts the sensuality and mortality of the modern world with the permanence and artifice
found in medieval Byzantium (the site of modern Istanbul, Turkey). In *A Vision* (1937) he wrote: "I
think that in early Byzantium, maybe never before or since in recorded history, religious, aesthetic
and practical life were one, that architect and artificer . . . spoke to the multitude and the few alike.
The painter, the mosaic worker, the worker in gold and silver, the illuminator of sacred books, were
almost impersonal, almost perhaps without the consciousness of individual design, absorbed in their
subject-matter and that the vision of a whole people."
[2] Spiral down.

Bert Leston Taylor ("B.L.T.")   *1866–1921*

UPON JULIA'S ARCTICS

Whenas galoshed my Julia goes,
Unbuckled all from top to toes,
How swift the poem becometh prose!
And when I cast mine eyes and see
5   Those arctics flopping each way free,
Oh, how that flopping floppeth me!

Edwin Arlington Robinson   *1869–1935*

REUBEN BRIGHT

Because he was a butcher and thereby
Did earn an honest living (and did right),
I would not have you think that Reuben Bright
Was any more a brute than you or I;
5   For when they told him that his wife must die,
He stared at them, and shook with grief and fright,
And cried like a great baby half that night,
And made the women cry to see him cry.

And after she was dead, and he had paid
10   The singers and the sexton and the rest,
He packed a lot of things that she had made
Most mournfully away in an old chest
Of hers, and put some chopped-up cedar boughs
In with them, and tore down the slaughter-house.

[1897]

MINIVER CHEEVY

Miniver Cheevy, child of scorn,
   Grew lean while he assailed the seasons;
He wept that he was ever born,
   And he had reasons.

5   Miniver loved the days of old
   When swords were bright and steeds were prancing;
The vision of a warrior bold
   Would set him dancing.

Miniver sighed for what was not,
    And dreamed, and rested from his labors;
He dreamed of Thebes and Camelot,
    And Priam's neighbors.[1]

Miniver mourned the ripe renown
    That made so many a name so fragrant;
He mourned Romance, now on the town,
    And Art, a vagrant.

Miniver loved the Medici,[2]
    Albeit he had never seen one;
He would have sinned incessantly
    Could he have been one.

Miniver cursed the commonplace
    And eyed a khaki suit with loathing;
He missed the medieval grace
    Of iron clothing.

Miniver scorned the gold he sought,
    But sore annoyed was he without it;
Miniver thought, and thought, and thought,
    And thought about it.

Miniver Cheevy, born too late,
    Scratched his head and kept on thinking;
Miniver coughed, and called it fate,
    And kept on drinking.

                                    [1910]

NEW ENGLAND

Here where the wind is always north-north-east
And children learn to walk on frozen toes,
Wonder begets an envy of all those
Who boil elsewhere with such a lyric yeast
Of love that you will hear them at a feast
Where demons would appeal for some repose,
Still clamoring where the chalice overflows
And crying wildest who have drunk the least.

[1] Thebes was an ancient Greek city, famous as the setting of numerous legends—including stories involving Cadmus, Niobe, Oedipus, and Bacchus. Camelot was the legendary site of King Arthur's court. Priam was the king of Troy during the Trojan War.

[2] An Italian banking family that ruled Florence and Tuscany from the fifteenth to the eighteenth centuries, the Medicis were famous for their love of the arts and their unscrupulous pursuit of political power.

Passion is here a soilure of the wits,
10   We're told, and Love a cross for them to bear;
Joy shivers in the corner where she knits
And Conscience always has the rocking-chair,
Cheerful as when she tortured into fits
The first cat that was ever killed by Care.

[1923]

Paul Laurence Dunbar   *1872–1906*

WE WEAR THE MASK

We wear the mask that grins and lies,
It hides our cheeks and shades our eyes—
This debt we pay to human guile;
With torn and bleeding hearts we smile,
5   And mouth with myriad subtleties.

Why should the world be over-wise,
In counting all our tears and sighs?
Nay, let them only see us, while
    We wear the mask.

10   We smile, but, O great Christ, our cries
To thee from tortured souls arise.
We sing, but oh the clay is vile
Beneath our feet, and long the mile;
But let the world dream otherwise,
15   We wear the mask!

[1896]

SYMPATHY

I know what the caged bird feels, alas!
    When the sun is bright on the upland slopes;
When the wind stirs soft through the springing grass,
And the river flows like a stream of glass;
5   When the first bird sings and the first bud opes,
And the faint perfume from its chalice steals—
I know what the caged bird feels!

I know why the caged bird beats his wing
    Till its blood is red on the cruel bars;
10   For he must fly back to his perch and cling
When he fain would be on the bough a-swing;
    And a pain still throbs in the old, old scars
And they pulse again with a keener sting—
I know why he beats his wing!

15   I know why the caged bird sings, ah me,
            When his wing is bruised and his bosom sore,—
        When he beats his bars and he would be free;
        It is not a carol of joy or glee,
            But a prayer that he sends from his heart's deep core,
20   But a plea, that upward to Heaven he flings—
        I know why the caged bird sings!

                                                                                 [1899]

Leonora Speyer   *1872–1956*

THE LADDER

        I had a sudden vision in the night,
        I did not sleep, I dare not say I dreamed,
        Beside my bed a curious ladder gleamed
        And lifted upward toward the sky's dim height;
5   And every rung shone luminous and white,
        And every rung a woman's body seemed
        Out-stretched, and down the sides her long hair streamed:
        And you, you climbed that ladder of delight.

        You climbed sure-footed, naked rung by rung,
10   Clasped them and trod them, called them by their name,
        And my name too, I heard you speak at last;
        You stood upon my breast the while and flung
        A hand up to the next—and then, oh shame,
        I kissed the foot that bruised me as it passed.

                                                                                 [1931]

Amy Lowell   *1874–1925*

THE TAXI

        When I go away from you
        The world beats dead
        Like a slackened drum.
        I call out for you against the jutted stars
5   And shout into the ridges of the wind.
        Streets coming fast,
        One after the other,
        Wedge you away from me,
        And the lamps of the city prick my eyes
10   So that I can no longer see your face.
        Why should I leave you,
        To wound myself upon the sharp edges of the night?

                                                                                 [1914]

PATTERNS

I walk down the garden paths,
And all the daffodils
Are blowing, and the bright blue squills.
I walk down the patterned garden-paths
5   In my stiff, brocaded gown.
With my powdered hair and jewelled fan,
I too am a rare
Pattern. As I wander down
The garden paths.

10   My dress is richly figured,
And the train
Makes a pink and silver stain
On the gravel, and the thrift
Of the borders.
15   Just a plate of current fashion,
Tripping by in high-heeled, ribboned shoes.
Not a softness anywhere about me,
Only whalebone and brocade.
And I sink on a seat in the shade
20   Of a lime tree. For my passion
Wars against the stiff brocade.
The daffodils and squills
Flutter in the breeze
As they please.
25   And I weep;
For the lime-tree is in blossom
And one small flower has dropped upon my bosom.

And the plashing of waterdrops
In the marble fountain
30   Comes down the garden-paths.
The dripping never stops.
Underneath my stiffened gown
Is the softness of a woman bathing in a marble basin,
A basin in the midst of hedges grown
35   So thick, she cannot see her lover hiding,
But she guesses he is near,
And the sliding of the water
Seems the stroking of a dear
Hand upon her.
40   What is Summer in a fine brocaded gown!
I should like to see it lying in a heap upon the ground.
All the pink and silver crumpled up on the ground.

I would be the pink and silver as I ran along the paths,
And he would stumble after,
45   Bewildered by my laughter.
I should see the sun flashing from his sword-hilt and the buckles
   on his shoes.

I would choose
To lead him in a maze along the patterned paths,
A bright and laughing maze for my heavy-booted lover.
50 Till he caught me in the shade,
And the buttons of his waistcoat bruised my body as he clasped me,
Aching, melting, unafraid.
With the shadows of the leaves and the sundrops
And the plopping of the waterdrops,
55 All about us in the open afternoon—
I am very like to swoon
With the weight of this brocade,
For the sun sifts through the shade.

Underneath the fallen blossom
60 In my bosom,
Is a letter I have hid.
It was brought to me this morning by a rider from the Duke.
"Madam, we regret to inform you that Lord Hartwell
Died in action Thursday se'nnight."[1]
65 As I read it in the white, morning sunlight,
The letters squirmed like snakes.
"Any answer, Madam?" said my footman.
"No," I told him.
"See that the messenger takes some refreshment.
70 No, no answer."
And I walked into the garden,
Up and down the patterned paths,
In my stiff, correct brocade.
The blue and yellow flowers stood up proudly in the sun,
75 Each one.
I stood upright too,
Held rigid to the pattern
By the stiffness of my gown.
Up and down I walked,
80 Up and down.

In a month he would have been my husband.
In a month, here, underneath this lime,
We would have broken the pattern;
He for me, and I for him,
85 He as Colonel, I as Lady,
On this shady seat.
He had a whim
That sunlight carried blessing.
And I answered, "It shall be as you have said."
90 Now he is dead.

In Summer and in Winter I shall walk
Up and down
The patterned garden-paths

[1] Seven days and nights, a week.

In my stiff, brocaded gown.
95   The squills and daffodils
Will give place to pillared roses, and to asters, and to snow.
I shall go
Up and down,
In my gown.
100   Gorgeously arrayed,
Boned and stayed.
And the softness of my body will be guarded from embrace
By each button, hook, and lace.
For the man who should loose me is dead,
105   Fighting with the Duke in Flanders,
In a pattern called a war.
Christ! What are patterns *for?*

[1915]

Robert Frost   *1874–1963*

AFTER APPLE-PICKING

My long two-pointed ladder's sticking through a tree
Toward heaven still,
And there's a barrel that I didn't fill
Beside it, and there may be two or three
5   Apples I didn't pick upon some bough.
But I am done with apple-picking now.
Essence of winter sleep is on the night,
The scent of apples: I am drowsing off.
I cannot rub the strangeness from my sight
10   I got from looking through a pane of glass
I skimmed this morning from the drinking trough
And held against the world of hoary grass.
It melted, and I let it fall and break.
But I was well
15   Upon my way to sleep before it fell,
And I could tell
What form my dreaming was about to take.
Magnified apples appear and disappear,
Stem end and blossom end,
20   And every fleck of russet showing clear.
My instep arch not only keeps the ache,
It keeps the pressure of a ladder-round.
I feel the ladder sway as the boughs bend.
And I keep hearing from the cellar bin
25   The rumbling sound
Of load on load of apples coming in.
For I have had too much

Of apple-picking: I am overtired
Of the great harvest I myself desired.
30   There were ten thousand thousand fruit to touch,
Cherish in hand, lift down, and not let fall.
For all
That struck the earth,
No matter if not bruised or spiked with stubble,
35   Went surely to the cider-apple heap
As of no worth.
One can see what will trouble
This sleep of mine, whatever sleep it is.
Were he not gone,
40   The woodchuck could say whether it's like his
Long sleep, as I describe its coming on,
Or just some human sleep.

[1914]

BIRCHES

When I see birches bend to left and right
Across the lines of straighter darker trees,
I like to think some boy's been swinging them.
But swinging doesn't bend them down to stay
5   As ice-storms do. Often you must have seen them
Loaded with ice a sunny winter morning
After a rain. They click upon themselves
As the breeze rises, and turn many-colored
As the stir cracks and crazes their enamel.
10   Soon the sun's warmth makes them shed crystal shells
Shattering and avalanching on the snow-crust—
Such heaps of broken glass to sweep away
You'd think the inner dome of heaven had fallen.
They are dragged to the withered bracken° by the load,   *coarse ferns*
15   And they seem not to break; though once they are bowed
So low for long, they never right themselves:
You may see their trunks arching in the woods
Years afterwards, trailing their leaves on the ground
Like girls on hands and knees that throw their hair
20   Before them over their heads to dry in the sun.
But I was going to say when Truth broke in
With all her matter-of-fact about the ice-storm
I should prefer to have some boy bend them
As he went out and in to fetch the cows—
25   Some boy too far from town to learn baseball,
Whose only play was what he found himself,
Summer or winter, and could play alone.
One by one he subdued his father's trees
By riding them down over and over again
30   Until he took the stiffness out of them,

And not one but hung limp, not one was left
For him to conquer. He learned all there was
To learn about not launching out too soon
And so not carrying the tree away
35 Clear to the ground. He always kept his poise
To the top branches, climbing carefully
With the same pains you use to fill a cup
Up to the brim, and even above the brim.
Then he flung outward, feet first, with a swish,
40 Kicking his way down through the air to the ground.
So was I once myself a swinger of birches.
And so I dream of going back to be.
It's when I'm weary of considerations,
And life is too much like a pathless wood
45 Where your face burns and tickles with the cobwebs
Broken across it, and one eye is weeping
From a twig's having lashed across it open.
I'd like to get away from earth awhile
And then come back to it and begin over.
50 May no fate willfully misunderstand me
And half grant what I wish and snatch me away
Not to return. Earth's the right place for love:
I don't know where it's likely to go better.
I'd like to go by climbing a birch tree,
55 And climb black branches up a snow-white trunk
Toward heaven, till the tree could bear no more,
But dipped its top and set me down again.
That would be good both going and coming back.
One could do worse than be a swinger of birches.

[1916]

THE OVEN BIRD[1]

There is a singer everyone has heard,
Loud, a mid-summer and a mid-wood bird,
Who makes the solid tree trunks sound again.
He says that leaves are old and that for flowers
5 Mid-summer is to spring as one to ten.
He says the early petal-fall is past
When pear and cherry bloom went down in showers
On sunny days a moment overcast;
And comes that other fall we name the fall.
10 He says the highway dust is over all.
The bird would cease and be as other birds
But that he knows in singing not to sing.
The question that he frames in all but words
Is what to make of a diminished thing.

[1916]

[1] An American warbler noted for its shrill call and for the dome-shaped oven-like nests which it builds on the ground.

DUST OF SNOW

The way a crow
Shook down on me
The dust of snow
From a hemlock tree

5   Has given my heart
A change of mood
And saved some part
Of a day I had rued.

[1923]

FIRE AND ICE

Some say the world will end in fire,
Some say in ice.
From what I've tasted of desire
I hold with those who favor fire.
5   But if it had to perish twice,
I think I know enough of hate
To say that for destruction ice
Is also great
And would suffice.

[1923]

NOTHING GOLD CAN STAY

Nature's first green is gold,
Her hardest hue to hold.
Her early leaf's a flower;
But only so an hour.

5   Then leaf subsides to leaf.
So Eden sank to grief,
So dawn goes down to day.
Nothing gold can stay.

[1923]

ACQUAINTED WITH THE NIGHT

I have been one acquainted with the night.
I have walked out in rain—and back in rain.
I have outwalked the furthest city light.

I have looked down the saddest city lane.
5   I have passed by the watchman on his beat
And dropped my eyes, unwilling to explain.

I have stood still and stopped the sound of feet
When far away an interrupted cry
Came over houses from another street,

10   But not to call me back or say good-by;
And further still at an unearthly height,
One luminary clock against the sky

Proclaimed the time was neither wrong nor right.
I have been one acquainted with the night.

[1928]

NEITHER OUT FAR NOR IN DEEP

The people along the sand
All turn and look one way.
They turn their back on the land.
They look at the sea all day.

5   As long as it takes to pass
A ship keeps raising its hull;
The wetter ground like glass
Reflects a standing gull.

The land may vary more;
10   But wherever the truth may be—
The water comes ashore,
And the people look at the sea.

They cannot look out far.
They cannot look in deep.
15   But when was that ever a bar
To any watch they keep?

[1936]

COME IN

As I came to the edge of the woods,
Thrush music—hark!
Now if it was dusk outside,
Inside it was dark.

5   Too dark in the woods for a bird
By sleight of wing
To better its perch for the night,
Though it still could sing.

The last of the light of the sun
10   That had died in the west
Still lived for one song more
In a thrush's breast.

Far in the pillared dark
Thrush music went—
15 Almost like a call to come in
To the dark and lament.

But no, I was out for stars:
I would not come in.
I meant not even if asked,
20 And I hadn't been.

[1942]

DIRECTIVE

Back out of all this now too much for us,
Back in a time made simple by the loss
Of detail, burned, dissolved, and broken off
Like graveyard marble sculpture in the weather,
5 There is a house that is no more a house
Upon a farm that is no more a farm
And in a town that is no more a town.
The road there, if you'll let a guide direct you
Who only has at heart your getting lost,
10 May seem as if it should have been a quarry—
Great monolithic knees the former town
Long since gave up pretence of keeping covered.
And there's a story in a book about it:
Besides the wear of iron wagon wheels
15 The ledges show lines ruled southeast northwest,
The chisel work of an enormous Glacier
That braced his feet against the Arctic Pole.
You must not mind a certain coolness from him
Still said to haunt this side of Panther Mountain.
20 Nor need you mind the serial ordeal
Of being watched from forty cellar holes
As if by eye pairs out of forty firkins.[1]
As for the woods' excitement over you
That sends light rustle rushes to their leaves,
25 Charge that to upstart inexperience.
Where were they all not twenty years ago?
They think too much of having shaded out
A few old pecker-fretted apple trees.
Make yourself up a cheering song of how
30 Someone's road home from work this once was,
Who may be just ahead of you on foot
Or creaking with a buggy load of grain.
The height of the adventure is the height
Of country where two village cultures faded
35 Into each other. Both of them are lost.
And if you're lost enough to find yourself

[1] Small wooden casks.

By now, pull in your ladder road behind you
And put a sign up CLOSED to all but me.
Then make yourself at home. The only field
40   Now left's no bigger than a harness gall.[2]
First there's the children's house of make believe,
Some shattered dishes underneath a pine,
The playthings in the playhouse of the children.
Weep for what little things could make them glad.
45   Then for the house that is no more a house,
But only a belilaced cellar hole,
Now slowly closing like a dent in dough.
This was no playhouse but a house in earnest.
Your destination and your destiny's
50   A brook that was the water of the house,
Cold as a spring as yet so near its source,
Too lofty and original to rage.
(We know the valley streams that when aroused
Will leave their tatters hung on barb and thorn.)
55   I have kept hidden in the instep arch
Of an old cedar at the waterside
A broken drinking goblet like the Grail[3]
Under a spell so the wrong ones can't find it,
So can't get saved, as Saint Mark says they mustn't.[4]
60   (I stole the goblet from the children's playhouse.)
Here are your waters and your watering place.
Drink and be whole again beyond confusion.

                                                                     [1947]

Carl Sandburg   *1878–1967*

CHICAGO

Hog Butcher for the World,
Tool Maker, Stacker of Wheat,
Player with Railroads and the Nation's Freight Handler;
Stormy, husky, brawling,
5   City of the Big Shoulders:
They tell me you are wicked and I believe them, for I have seen
    your painted women under the gas lamps luring the farm boys.
And they tell me you are crooked and I answer: Yes, it is true I
    have seen the gunman kill and go free to kill again.
And they tell me you are brutal and my reply is: On the faces of
    women and children I have seen the marks of wanton hunger.

---

[2] An abrasion or sore on a horse caused by the rubbing of the harness.
[3] The cup or chalice which Jesus drank from during the Last Supper, which subsequently became the object of many medieval quests in Arthurian romance, including those by "wrong ones" who were unworthy of its pursuit.
[4] See Mark 4:11–12.

And having answered so I turn once more to those who sneer at this
    my city, and I give them back the sneer and say to them:
10   Come and show me another city with lifted head singing so proud
    to be alive and coarse and strong and cunning.
Flinging magnetic curses amid the toil of piling job on job, here is a tall
    bold slugger set vivid against the little soft cities;
Fierce as a dog with tongue lapping for action, cunning as a savage
    pitted against the wilderness,
        Bareheaded,
        Shoveling,
15   Wrecking,
        Planning,
        Building, breaking, rebuilding,
Under the smoke, dust all over his mouth, laughing with white teeth,
Under the terrible burden of destiny laughing as a young man
    laughs,
20   Laughing even as an ignorant fighter laughs who has never lost a
    battle,
Bragging and laughing that under his wrist is the pulse, and under his
    ribs the heart of the people,
        Laughing!
Laughing the stormy, husky, brawling laughter of Youth, half-naked,
    sweating, proud to be Hog Butcher, Tool Maker, Stacker of
    Wheat, Player with railroads and Freight Handler to the Nation.

                                                        [1916]

Wallace Stevens   *1879–1955*

DISILLUSIONMENT OF TEN O'CLOCK

    The houses are haunted
    By white night-gowns.
    None are green,
    Or purple with green rings,
5   Or green with yellow rings,
    Or yellow with blue rings.
    None of them are strange,
    With socks of lace
    And beaded ceintures.°   *sashes or belts*
10   People are not going
    To dream of baboons and periwinkles.°   *edible snails*
    Only, here and there, an old sailor,
    Drunk and asleep in his boots,
    Catches tigers
15   In red weather.

                          [1915]

PETER QUINCE AT THE CLAVIER[1]

I

Just as my fingers on these keys
Make music, so the selfsame sounds
On my spirit make a music, too.

Music is feeling, then, not sound;
And thus it is that what I feel,
Here in this room, desiring you,

Thinking of your blue-shadowed silk,
Is music. It is like the strain
Waked in the elders by Susanna.[2]

Of a green evening, clear and warm,
She bathed in her still garden, while
The red-eyed elders watching, felt

The basses of their beings throb
In witching chords, and their thin blood
Pulse pizzicati[3] of Hosanna.[4]

II

In the green water, clear and warm,
Susanna lay.
She searched
The touch of springs,
And found
Concealed imaginings.
She sighed,
For so much melody.

Upon the bank, she stood
In the cool
Of spent emotions.
She felt, among the leaves,
The dew
Of old devotions.

She walked upon the grass,
Still quavering.
The winds were like her maids,
On timid feet,
Fetching her woven scarves,
Yet wavering.

---

[1] A keyboard; presumably the keyboard of a harmonium or reed organ. *Harmonium* (1923) was the title of Stevens's first volume of collected poems.

[2] The virtuous wife in "The History of Susanna" in the Old Testament Apocrypha, falsely accused of adultery by two Hebrew elders whose advances she had rejected. Their charge was exposed by Daniel who had the two men put to death.

[3] Musical notes produced by plucking a stringed instrument.

[4] An exclamation of praise or adoration to God.

A breath upon her hand
Muted the night,
She turned—
A cymbal crashed,
40 And roaring horns.

III

Soon, with a noise like tambourines,
Came her attendant Byzantines.[5]

They wondered why Susanna cried
Against the elders by her side;

45 And as they whispered, the refrain
Was like a willow swept by rain.

Anon, their lamps' uplifted flame
Revealed Susanna and her shame.

And then, the simpering Byzantines
50 Fled, with a noise like tambourines.

IV

Beauty is momentary in the mind—
The fitful tracing of a portal;
But in the flesh it is immortal.

The body dies; the body's beauty lives.
55 So evenings die, in their green going,
A wave, interminably flowing.
So gardens die, their meek breath scenting
The cowl of winter, done repenting.
So maidens die, to the auroral°   *dawn*
60 Celebration of a maiden's choral.

Susanna's music touched the bawdy strings
Of those white elders; but, escaping,
Left only Death's ironic scraping.
Now, in its immortality, it plays
65 On the clear viol of her memory,
And makes a constant sacrament of praise.

[1923]

ANECDOTE OF THE JAR

I placed a jar in Tennessee,
And round it was, upon a hill.
It made the slovenly wilderness
Surround that hill.

[5] Natives of the Greek city of Byzantium, now Istanbul in Turkey.

5   The wilderness rose up to it,
     And sprawled around, no longer wild.
     The jar was round upon the ground
     And tall and of a port in air.

10   It took dominion everywhere.
     The jar was gray and bare.
     It did not give of bird or bush,
     Like nothing else in Tennessee.

                                          [1923]

THE EMPEROR OF ICE-CREAM

     Call the roller of big cigars,
     The muscular one, and bid him whip
     In kitchen cups concupiscent curds.
     Let the wenches dawdle in such dress
5   As they are used to wear, and let the boys
     Bring flowers in last month's newspapers.
     Let be be finale of seem.
     The only emperor is the emperor of ice-cream.

     Take from the dresser of deal,°   *pine*
10   Lacking the three glass knobs, that sheet
     On which she embroidered fantails once
     And spread it so as to cover her face.
     If her horny feet protrude, they come
     To show how cold she is, and dumb.
15   Let the lamp affix its beam.
     The only emperor is the emperor of ice-cream.
                                          [1923]

William Carlos Williams   *1883–1963*

QUEEN-ANN'S-LACE

     Her body is not so white as
     anemone petals nor so smooth—nor
     so remote a thing. It is a field
     of the wild carrot[1] taking
5   the field by force; the grass
     does not raise above it.
     Here is no question of whiteness,
     white as can be, with a purple mole
     at the center of each flower.
10   Each flower is a hand's span

[1] Queen Anne's Lace, or wild carrot, is a plant with numerous tiny white blossoms clustered around
a single purple one, or mole.

of her whiteness. Wherever
his hand has lain there is
a tiny purple blemish. Each part
is a blossom under his touch
15   to which the fibres of her being
stem one by one, each to its end,
until the whole field is a
white desire, empty, a single stem,
a cluster, flower by flower,
20   a pious wish to whiteness gone over—
or nothing.

                  [1921]

THIS IS JUST TO SAY

I have eaten
the plums
that were in
the icebox

5   and which
you were probably
saving
for breakfast

Forgive me
10   they were delicious
so sweet
and so cold

           [1934]

THE DANCE

In Breughel's great picture, The Kermess,[1]
the dancers go round, they go round and
around, the squeal and the blare and the
tweedle of bagpipes, a bugle and fiddles
5   tipping their bellies (round as the thick-
sided glasses whose wash they impound)
their hips and their bellies off balance
to turn them. Kicking and rolling about
the Fair Grounds, swinging their butts, those
10   shanks must be sound to bear up under such
rollicking measures, prance as they dance
in Breughel's great picture, The Kermess.

           [1944]

[1] The picture by Flemish painter Peter Breughel (c. 1525–1569) depicts the annual outdoor festival or fair (the kermess) celebrated in the Low Countries (the Netherlands, Belgium, and Luxembourg).

LANDSCAPE WITH THE FALL OF ICARUS[1]

According to Brueghel
when Icarus fell
it was spring

a farmer was ploughing
his field
the whole pageantry

of the year was
awake tingling
near

the edge of the sea
concerned
with itself

sweating in the sun
that melted
the wings' wax

unsignificantly
off the coast
there was

a splash quite unnoticed
this was
Icarus drowning
                    [1960]

5

10

15

20

Sara Teasdale   *1884–1933*

BARTER

Life has loveliness to sell—
    All beautiful and splendid things,
Blue waves whitened on a cliff,
    Climbing fire that sways and sings,
And children's faces looking up
Holding wonder like a cup.

5

[1] The title of a painting by Peter Breughel (ca. 1525–1569). It depicts the myth of Icarus, a young Greek, who, in escaping with his father from the island of Crete by means of wings held together by wax, flew too near the sun; the wax melted and Icarus fell to his death in the sea. Compare this poem with W. H. Auden's "Musée des Beaux Arts," p. 981.

Life has loveliness to sell—
　　Music like a curve of gold,
Scent of pine trees in the rain,
　　Eyes that love you, arms that hold,
And for your spirit's still delight,
Holy thoughts that star the night.

Spend all you have for loveliness,
　　Buy it and never count the cost,
For one white singing hour of peace
　　Count many a year of strife well lost,
And for a breath of ecstasy
Give all you have been or could be.

[1917]

Ezra Pound *1885–1972*

IN A STATION OF THE METRO°   *The Paris subway*

The apparition of these faces in the crowd;
Petals on a wet, black bough.

[1916]

ANCIENT MUSIC[1]

Winter is icumen in,
Lhude sing Goddamm,
Raineth drop and staineth slop,
And how the wind doth ramm!
　　　　Sing: Goddamm.
Skiddeth bus and sloppeth us,
An ague hath my ham.
Freezeth river, turneth liver,
　　　　Damn you, sing: Goddamm.
Goddamm, Goddamm, 'tis why I am, Goddamm,
　　　　So 'gainst the winter's balm.
Sing goddamm, damm, sing Goddamm,
Sing goddamm, sing goddamm, DAMM.

[1926]

---

[1] Compare Pound's poem with the medieval lyric he is parodying, "Sumer Is Icumen In," p. 778.

Robinson Jeffers   *1887–1962*

HURT HAWKS

I

The broken pillar of the wing jags from the clotted shoulder,
The wing trails like a banner in defeat,
No more to use the sky forever but live with famine
And pain a few days: cat nor coyote
5   Will shorten the week of waiting for death, there is game without
      talons.
He stands under the oak-bush and waits
The lame feet of salvation; at night he remembers freedom
And flies in a dream, the dawns ruin it.
He is strong and pain is worse to the strong, incapacity is worse.
10   The curs of the day come and torment him
At distance, no one but death the redeemer will humble that head,
The intrepid readiness, the terrible eyes.
The wild God of the world is sometimes merciful to those
That ask mercy, not often to the arrogant.
15   You do not know him, you communal people, or you have forgotten
      him;
Intemperate and savage, the hawk remembers him;
Beautiful and wild, the hawks, and men that are dying, remember
      him.

II

I'd sooner, except the penalties, kill a man than a hawk; but the
      great redtail
Had nothing left but unable misery
20   From the bone too shattered for mending, the wing that trailed
      under his talons when he moved.
We had fed him six weeks, I gave him freedom,
He wandered over the foreland hill and returned in the evening,
      asking for death,
Not like a beggar, still eyed with the old
Implacable arrogance. I gave him the lead gift in the twilight. What fell
      was relaxed,
25   Owl-downy, soft feminine feathers; but what
Soared: the fierce rush: the night-herons by the flooded river cried
      fear at its rising
Before it was quite unsheathed from reality.

[1928]

Marianne Moore   *1887–1972*

POETRY

I, too, dislike it: there are things that are important beyond
      all this fiddle.
  Reading it, however, with a perfect contempt for it, one
      discovers in
5   it after all, a place for the genuine.
      Hands that can grasp, eyes
      that can dilate, hair that can rise
        if it must, these things are important not because a

high-sounding interpretation can be put upon them but be-
10   cause they are
  useful. When they become so derivative as to become
      unintelligible,
  the same thing may be said for all of us, that we
      do not admire what
15   we cannot understand: the bat
        holding on upside down or in quest of something to

eat, elephants pushing, a wild horse taking a roll, a tireless
      wolf under
  a tree, the immovable critic twitching his skin like a horse
20   that feels a flea, the base-
  ball fan, the statistician—
      nor is it valid
      to discriminate against "business documents and

school-books"; all these phenomena are important. One
25   must make a distinction
  however: when dragged into prominence by half poets,
      the result is not poetry,
  nor till the poets among us can be
      "literalists of
30   the imagination"—above
      insolence and triviality and can present

for inspection, "imaginary gardens with real toads in them,"
      shall we have
  it. In the meantime, if you demand on the one hand,
35   the raw material of poetry in
      all its rawness and
      that which is on the other hand
      genuine, you are interested in poetry.

[1921]

T. S. Eliot   *1888–1965*

THE LOVE SONG OF J. ALFRED PRUFROCK

S'io credesse che mia risposta fosse
A persona che mai tornasse al mondo,
Questa fiamma staria senza piu scosse.
Ma perciocche giammai di questo fondo
Non torno vivo alcun, s'i'odo il vero,
Senza tema d'infamia ti rispondo.[1]

Let us go then, you and I,
When the evening is spread out against the sky
Like a patient etherised upon a table;
Let us go, through certain half-deserted streets,
5   The muttering retreats
Of restless nights in one-night cheap hotels
And sawdust restaurants with oyster-shells:
Streets that follow like a tedious argument
Of insidious intent
10   To lead you to an overwhelming question. . .
Oh, do not ask, "What is it?"
Let us go and make our visit.

In the room the women come and go
Talking of Michelangelo.[2]

15   The yellow fog that rubs its back upon the window-panes,
The yellow smoke that rubs its muzzle on the window-panes
Licked its tongue into the corners of the evening,
Lingered upon the pools that stand in drains,
Let fall upon its back the soot that falls from chimneys,
20   Slipped by the terrace, made a sudden leap,
And seeing that it was a soft October night,
Curled once about the house, and fell asleep.

And indeed there will be time
For the yellow smoke that slides along the street,
25   Rubbing its back upon the window-panes;
There will be time, there will be time
To prepare a face to meet the faces that you meet;
There will be time to murder and create,
And time for all the works and days[3] of hands
30   That lift and drop a question on your plate;

[1] The statement introducing the confession of the poet Guido da Montefeltro in Dante's *Inferno* (1321), canto xxvii, 61–66: "If I thought that I was speaking/ to someone who would go back to the world,/ this flame would shake no more. / But since nobody has ever gone back alive from this place, if what I hear is true,/ I answer you without fear of infamy."
[2] Michelangelo (1474–1564), the most famous artist of the Italian Renaissance.
[3] Possibly an allusion to *Works and Days,* a poem giving practical advice on farming by the Greek poet Hesiod (8th century B.C.).

Time for you and time for me,
And time yet for a hundred indecisions,
And for a hundred visions and revisions,
Before the taking of a toast and tea.

35   In the room the women come and go
        Talking of Michelangelo.

        And indeed there will be time
        To wonder, "Do I dare?" and, "Do I dare?"
        Time to turn back and descend the stair,
40   With a bald spot in the middle of my hair—
        [They will say: "How his hair is growing thin!"]
        My morning coat, my collar mounting firmly to the chin,
        My necktie rich and modest, but asserted by a simple pin—
        [They will say: "But how his arms and legs are thin!"]
45   Do I dare
        Disturb the universe?
        In a minute there is time
        For decisions and revisions which a minute will reverse.

        For I have known them all already, known them all:—
50   Have known the evenings, mornings, afternoons,
        I have measured out my life with coffee spoons;
        I know the voices dying with a dying fall[4]
        Beneath the music from a farther room.
            So how should I presume?

55   And I have known the eyes already, known them all—
        The eyes that fix you in a formulated phrase,
        And when I am formulated, sprawling on a pin,
        When I am pinned and wriggling on the wall,
        Then how should I begin
60   To spit out all the butt-ends of my days and ways?
            And how should I presume?

        And I have known the arms already, known them all—
        Arms that are braceleted and white and bare
        [But in the lamplight, downed with light brown hair!]
65   Is it perfume from a dress
        That makes me so digress?
        Arms that lie along a table, or wrap about a shawl.
            And should I then presume?
            And how should I begin?

70   Shall I say, I have gone at dusk through narrow streets
        And watched the smoke that rises from the pipes
        Of lonely men in shirt-sleeves, leaning out of windows? . . .

[4] See Shakespeare's *Twelfth Night* (1623), Act 1, Scene 1, 1–4.

I should have been a pair of ragged claws
Scuttling across the floors of silent seas.

. . . . . .

75 And the afternoon, the evening, sleeps so peacefully!
Smoothed by long fingers,
Asleep . . . tired . . . or it malingers,
Stretched on the floor, here beside you and me.
Should I, after tea and cakes and ices,
80 Have the strength to force the moment to its crisis?
But though I have wept and fasted, wept and prayed,
Though I have seen my head [grown slightly bald] brought in
          upon a platter,[5]
I am no prophet—and here's no great matter;
I have seen the moment of my greatness flicker,
85 And I have seen the eternal Footman hold my coat, and snicker,
And in short, I was afraid.

And would it have been worth it, after all,
After the cups, the marmalade, the tea,
Among the porcelain, among some talk of you and me,
90 Would it have been worth while,
To have bitten off the matter with a smile,
To have squeezed the universe into a ball[6]
To roll it toward some overwhelming question,
To say: "I am Lazarus,[7] come from the dead,
95 Come back to tell you all, I shall tell you all"—
If one, settling a pillow by her head,
     Should say: "That is not what I meant at all.
     That is not it, at all."

And would it have been worth it, after all,
100 Would it have been worth while,
After the sunsets and the dooryards and the sprinkled streets,
After the novels, after the teacups, after the skirts that trail along
          the floor—
And this, and so much more?—
It is impossible to say just what I mean!
105 But as if a magic lantern threw the nerves in patterns on a
          screen:
Would it have been worth while
If one, settling a pillow or throwing off a shawl,
And turning toward the window, should say:
     "That is not it at all,
110 That is not what I meant, at all."

[5] An allusion to John the Baptist, the New Testament prophet, whose head was presented to Queen Herodias on a charger. Matthew 14:3–11.
[6] See Andrew Marvell's "To His Coy Mistress" (1681), lines 41–42, p. 833.
[7] The man raised by Jesus from the dead, John 11:1–44.

No! I am not Prince Hamlet,[8] nor was meant to be;
Am an attendant lord, one that will do
To swell a progress,[9] start a scene or two,
Advise the prince; no doubt, an easy tool,
115   Deferential, glad to be of use,
Politic, cautious, and meticulous;
Full of high sentence[10] but a bit obtuse;
At times, indeed, almost ridiculous—
Almost, at times, the Fool.

120   I grow old ... I grow old ...
        I shall wear the bottoms of my trousers rolled.

        Shall I part my hair behind? Do I dare to eat a peach?
        I shall wear white flannel trousers, and walk upon the beach.
        I have heard the mermaids singing, each to each.

125   I do not think that they will sing to me.

        I have seen them riding seaward on the waves
Combing the white hair of the waves blown back
When the wind blows the water white and black.

        We have lingered in the chambers of the sea
130   By sea-girls wreathed with seaweed red and brown
Till human voices wake us, and we drown.

[1917]

JOURNEY OF THE MAGI[1]

    "A cold coming we had of it,
Just the worst time of the year
For a journey, and such a long journey:
The ways deep and the weather sharp,
5   The very dead of winter."
And the camels galled,[2] sore-footed, refractory,
Lying down in the melting snow.
There were times we regretted
The summer palaces on slopes, the terraces,
10   And the silken girls bringing sherbet.
Then the camel men cursing and grumbling

---

[8] The hero of Shakespeare's tragedy (1603); the "attendant lord" may refer to Polonius, the sententious courtier in the same play.
[9] A formal state journey by a king through his realm.   [10] Sententiousness.
[1] The wise men from the East who journeyed to Bethlehem to pay homage to the baby Jesus (Matthew 2:1–12).
[2] Sores caused by the friction of a saddle.

And running away, and wanting their liquor and women,
And the night-fires going out, and the lack of shelters,
And the cities hostile and the towns unfriendly
15   And the villages dirty and charging high prices:
A hard time we had of it.
At the end we preferred to travel all night,
Sleeping in snatches,
With the voices singing in our ears, saying
20   That this was all folly.

All this was a long time ago, I remember,
And I would do it again, but set down
This set down
35   This: were we led all that way for
Birth or Death? There was a Birth, certainly,
We had evidence and no doubt. I had seen birth and death,
But had thought they were different; this Birth was
Hard and bitter agony for us, like Death, our death.
40   We returned to our places, these Kingdoms,
But no longer at ease here, in the old dispensation,
With an alien people clutching their gods.
I should be glad of another death.

Then at dawn we came down to a temperate valley,
Wet, below the snow line, smelling of vegetation;
With a running stream and a water-mill beating the darkness,
And three trees on the low sky,
25   And an old white horse galloped away in the meadow.
Then we came to a tavern with vine-leaves over the lintel,
Six hands at an open door dicing for pieces of silver,
And feet kicking the empty wine-skins.
But there was no information, and so we continued
30   And arrived at evening, not a moment too soon
Finding the place; it was (you may say) satisfactory.

[1927]

John Crowe Ransom   *1888–1974*

BELLS FOR JOHN WHITESIDE'S DAUGHTER

There was such speed in her little body,
And such lightness in her footfall,
It is no wonder her brown study
Astonishes us all.

5   Her wars were bruited in our high window.
We looked among orchard trees and beyond
Where she took arms against her shadow,
Or harried unto the pond

10 The lazy geese, like a snow cloud
Dripping their snow on the green grass,
Tricking and stopping, sleepy and proud,
Who cried in goose, Alas,

For the tireless heart within the little
Lady with rod that made them rise
15 From their noon apple-dreams and scuttle
Goose-fashion under the skies!

But now go the bells, and we are ready,
In one house we are sternly stopped
To say we are vexed at her brown study,
20 Lying so primly propped.

[1924]

PIAZZA PIECE

—I am a gentleman in a dustcoat trying
To make you hear. Your ears are soft and small
And listen to an old man not at all,
They want the young men's whispering and sighing.
5 But see the roses on your trellis dying
And hear the spectral singing of the moon;
For I must have my lovely lady soon,
I am a gentleman in a dustcoat trying.

—I am a lady young in beauty waiting
10 Until my truelove comes, and then we kiss.
But what grey man among the vines is this
Whose words are dry and faint as in a dream?
Back from my trellis, Sir, before I scream!
I am a lady young in beauty waiting.

[1927]

Claude McKay *1890–1948*

THE HARLEM DANCER

Applauding youths laughed with young prostitutes
And watched her perfect, half-clothed body sway;
Her voice was like the sound of blended flutes
Blown by black players upon a picnic day.
5 She sang and danced on gracefully and calm,
The light gauze hanging loose about her form;
To me she seemed a proudly-swaying palm
Grown lovelier for passing through a storm.
Upon her swarthy neck black shiny curls
10 Luxuriant fell; and tossing coins in praise,

The wine-flushed, bold-eyed boys, and even the girls,
Devoured her shape with eager, passionate gaze;
But looking at her falsely-smiling face,
I knew her self was not in that strange place.

[1922]

IF WE MUST DIE

If we must die, let it not be like hogs
Hunted and penned in an inglorious spot,
While round us bark the mad and hungry dogs,
Making their mock at our accurséd lot.
5 If we must die, O let us nobly die,
So that our precious blood may not be shed
In vain; then even the monsters we defy
Shall be constrained to honor us though dead!
O kinsmen! We must meet the common foe!
10 Though far outnumbered let us show us brave,
And for their thousand blows deal one deathblow!
What though before us lies the open grave?
Like men we'll face the murderous, cowardly pack,
Pressed to the wall, dying, but fighting back!

[1922]

Edna St. Vincent Millay   *1892–1950*

"TIME DOES NOT BRING RELIEF"

Time does not bring relief; you all have lied
    Who told me time would ease me of my pain!
    I miss him in the weeping of the rain;
I want him at the shrinking of the tide;
5 The old snows melt from every mountain-side,
    And last year's leaves are smoke in every lane;
    But last year's bitter loving must remain
Heaped on my heart, and my old thoughts abide!

There are a hundred places where I fear
10   To go,—so with his memory they brim!
And entering with relief some quiet place
Where never fell his foot or shone his face
I say, "There is no memory of him here!"
    And so stand stricken, so remembering him!

[1917]

WITCH-WIFE

She is neither pink nor pale,
    And she never will be all mine;
She learned her hands in a fairy-tale,
    And her mouth on a valentine.

5 She has more hair than she needs;
    In the sun 'tis a woe to me!
And her voice is a string of colored beads,
    Or steps leading into the sea.

She loves me all that she can,
10 And her ways to my ways resign;
But she was not made for any man,
    And she never will be all mine.

                [1917]

AFTERNOON ON A HILL

I will be the gladdest thing
    Under the sun!
I will touch a hundred flowers
    And not pick one.

5 I will look at cliffs and clouds
    With quiet eyes,
Watch the wind bow down the grass,
    And the grass rise.

And when lights begin to show
10   Up from the town,
I will mark which must be mine,
    And then start down!

                [1917]

"LOVE IS NOT ALL"

Love is not all: it is not meat nor drink
Nor slumber nor a roof against the rain;
Nor yet a floating spar to men that sink
And rise and sink and rise and sink again;
5 Love can not fill the thickened lung with breath,
Nor clean the blood, nor set the fractured bone;
Yet many a man is making friends with death
Even as I speak, for lack of love alone.
It well may be that in a difficult hour,
10 Pinned down by pain and moaning for release,
Or nagged by want past resolution's power,

I might be driven to sell your love for peace,
Or trade the memory of this night for food.
It well may be. I do not think I would.

[1931]

Archibald MacLeish   *1892–1982*

YOU, ANDREW MARVELL[1]

And here face down beneath the sun
And here upon earth's noonward height
To feel the always coming on
The always rising of the night:

5   To feel creep up the curving east
The earthly chill of dusk and slow
Upon those under lands the vast
And ever climbing shadow grow

And strange at Ecbatan[2] the trees
10   Take leaf by leaf the evening strange
The flooding dark about their knees
The mountains over Persia change

And now at Kermanshah the gate
Dark empty and the withered grass
15   And through the twilight now the late
Few travelers in the westward pass

And Baghdad darken and the bridge
Across the silent river gone
And through Arabia the edge
20   Of evening widen and steal on

And deepen on Palmyra's street
The wheel rut in the ruined stone
And Lebanon fade out and Crete
High through the clouds and overblown

25   And over Sicily the air
Still flashing with the landward gulls
And loom and slowly disappear
The sails above the shadowy hulls

---

[1] The allusion is to English seventeenth-century poet Andrew Marvell (1621–1678), and specifically to lines 21–22 of his "To His Coy Mistress" (1681); see p. 833.

[2] A city in ancient Persia; the cities that follow, Kermanshah in Iran, Baghdad in Iraq, and Palmyra in Syria, are all associated with ancient civilizations.

30 And Spain go under and the shore
Of Africa the gilded sand
And evening vanish and no more
The low pale light across that land

Nor now the long light on the sea:
And here face downward in the sun
35 To feel how swiftly how secretly
The shadow of the night comes on ...
    [1930]

Dorothy Parker *1893–1967*

RÉSUMÉ

Razors pain you;
Rivers are damp;
Acids stain you;
And drugs cause cramp.
5 Guns aren't lawful;
Nooses give;
Gas smells awful;
You might as well live.
    [1926]

Morris Bishop *1893–1973*

$E = mc^2$

What was our trust, we trust not,
 What was our faith, we doubt;
Whether we must or must not
 We may debate about.
5 The soul perhaps is a gust of gas
 And wrong is a form of right—
But we know that Energy equals Mass
 By the Square of the Speed of Light.

What we have known, we know not,
10 What we have proved, abjure.
Life is a tangled bow-knot,
 But one thing still is sure.
Come, little lad; come, little lass,
 Your docile creed recite:
15 "We know that Energy equals Mass
 By the Square of the Speed of light."
    [1954]

e. e. cummings   *1894–1962*

"BUFFALO BILL'S"

Buffalo Bill's[1]
defunct
    who used to
    ride a watersmooth-silver
5   stallion
and break onetwothreefourfive pigeonsjustlikethat
                         Jesus

he was a handsome man
              and what i want to know is
10 how do you like your blueeyed boy
Mister Death

                                  [1923]

"IN JUST-"

in Just-
spring   when the world is mud-
luscious the little
lame balloonman

5 whistles   far   and wee

and eddieandbill come
running from marbles and
piracies and it's
spring

10 when the world is puddle-wonderful

the queer
old balloonman whistles
far   and   wee
and bettyandisbel come dancing

15 from hop-scotch and jump-rope and

it's
spring
and
    the

20   goat-footed

balloonMan   whistles
far
and
wee
                  [1923]

---

[1] The nickname of William F. Cody (1846–1917), a famous American Indian fighter and frontier
scout and an impresario of the wild west show.

"NOBODY LOSES ALL THE TIME"

nobody loses all the time

    i had an uncle named
    Sol who was a born failure and
    nearly everybody said he should have gone
5   into vaudeville perhaps because my Uncle Sol could
    sing McCann He Was A Diver on Xmas Eve like Hell Itself which
    may or may not account for the fact that my Uncle

    Sol indulged in that possibly most inexcusable
    of all to use a highfalootin phrase
10   luxuries that is or to
    wit farming and be
    it needlessly
    added

    my Uncle Sol's farm
15   failed because the chickens
    ate the vegetables so
    my Uncle Sol had a
    chicken farm till the
    skunks ate the chickens when

20   my Uncle Sol
    had a skunk farm but
    the skunks caught cold and
    died and so
    my Uncle Sol imitated the
25   skunks in a subtle manner

    or by drowning himself in the watertank
    but somebody who'd given my Uncle Sol a Victor
    Victrola and records while he lived presented to
    him upon the auspicious occasion of his decease a
30   scrumptious not to mention splendiferous funeral with
    tall boys in black gloves and flowers and everything and

    i remember we all cried like the Missouri
    when my Uncle Sol's coffin lurched because
    somebody pressed a button
35   (and down went
    my Uncle
    Sol

    and started a worm farm)

[1923]

"NEXT TO OF COURSE GOD AMERICA I"

"next to of course god america i
love you land of the pilgrims' and so forth oh
say can you see by the dawn's early my
country 'tis of centuries come and go
5 and are no more what of it we should worry
in every language even deafanddumb
thy sons acclaim your glorious name by gorry
by jingo by gee by gosh by gum
why talk of beauty what could be more beaut-
10 iful than these heroic happy dead
who rushed like lions to the roaring slaughter
they did not stop to think they died instead
then shall the voice of liberty be mute?"

He spoke. And drank rapidly a glass of water
                                                              [1926]

"MY SWEET OLD ETCETERA"

my sweet old etcetera
aunt lucy during the recent

war could and what
is more did tell you just
5 what everybody was fighting

for,
my sister
isabel created hundreds
(and
10 hundreds)of socks not to
mention shirts fleaproof earwarmers

etcetera wristers etcetera, my
mother hoped that

i would die etcetera
15 bravely of course my father used
to become hoarse talking about how it was
a privilege and if only he
could meanwhile my

self etcetera lay quietly
20 in the deep mud et

cetera
(dreaming,
et
    cetera, of
25 Your smile
eyes knees and of your Etcetera)
                                                              [1926]

"ANYONE LIVED IN A PRETTY HOW TOWN"

anyone lived in a pretty how town
(with up so floating many bells down)
spring summer autumn winter
he sang his didn't he danced his did.

5 Women and men (both little and small)
cared for anyone not at all
they sowed their isn't they reaped their same
sun moon stars rain

children guessed (but only a few
10 and down they forgot as up they grew
autumn winter spring summer)
that noone loved him more by more

when by now and tree by leaf
she laughed his joy she cried his grief
15 bird by snow and stir by still
anyone's any was all to her

someone married their everyones
laughed their cryings and did their dance
(sleep wake hope and then) they
20 said their nevers they slept their dream

stars rain sun moon
(and only the snow can begin to explain
how children are apt to forget to remember
with up so floating many bells down)

25 one day anyone died i guess
(and noone stooped to kiss his face)
busy folk buried them side by side
little by little and was by was

all by all and deep by deep
30 and more by more they dream their sleep
noone and anyone earth by april
wish by spirit and if by yes.

Women and men (both dong and ding)
summer autumn winter spring
35 reaped their sowing and went their came
sun moon stars rain

[1940]

"PITY THIS BUSY MONSTER,MANUNKIND,"

pity this busy monster,manunkind,

not. Progress is a comfortable disease:
your victim(death and life safely beyond)

plays with the bigness of his littleness
5   —electrons deify one razorblade
into a mountainrange;lenses extend

unwish through curving wherewhen till unwish
returns on its unself.
                              A world of made
10   is not a world of born—pity poor flesh

and trees,poor stars and stones,but never this
fine specimen of hypermagical

ultraomnipotence. We doctors know

a hopeless case if—listen:there's a hell
15   of a good universe next door;let's go
                                                        [1943]

Jean Toomer   *1894–1967*

REAPERS

Black reapers with the sound of steel on stones
Are sharpening scythes. I see them place the hones
In their hip-pockets as a thing that's done,
And start their silent swinging, one by one.
5   Black horses drive a mower through the weeds,
And there, a field rat, startled, squealing bleeds,
His belly close to ground. I see the blade,
Blood-stained, continue cutting weeds and shade.
                                                        [1923]

Louise Bogan   *1897–1970*

WOMEN

Women have no wilderness in them,
They are provident instead,
Content in the tight hot cell of their hearts
To eat dusty bread.

5   They do not see cattle cropping red winter grass,
They do not hear
Snow water going down under culverts
Shallow and clear.

They wait, when they should turn to journeys.
10   They stiffen, when they should bend.
They use against themselves that benevolence
To which no man is friend.

They cannot think of so many crops to a field
Or of clean wood cleft by an axe.
15   Their love is an eager meaninglessness
Too tense, or too lax.

They hear in every whisper that speaks to them
A shout and a cry.
As like as not, when they take life over their door-sills
20   They should let it go by.

[1966]

Hart Crane   *1899–1932*

BLACK TAMBOURINE

The interests of a black man in a cellar
Mark tardy judgment on the world's closed door.
Gnats toss in the shadow of a bottle,
And a roach spans a crevice in the floor.

5   Aesop,[1] driven to pondering, found
Heaven with the tortoise and the hare;
Fox brush and sow ear top his grave
And mingling incantations on the air.

The black man, forlorn in the cellar,
10   Wanders in some mid-kingdom, dark, that lies,
Between his tambourine, stuck on the wall,
And, in Africa, a carcass quick with flies.

[1926]

---

[1] The sixth-century B.C. slave to whom is attributed the famous collection of beast fables.

Langston Hughes *1902–1967*

THE NEGRO SPEAKS OF RIVERS

I've known rivers:
I've known rivers ancient as the world and older than the
    flow of human blood in human veins.

My soul has grown deep like the rivers.

5   I bathed in the Euphrates[1] when dawns were young.
I built my hut near the Congo and it lulled me to sleep.
I looked upon the Nile and raised the pyramids above it.
I heard the singing of the Mississippi when Abe Lincoln
    went down to New Orleans, and I've seen its muddy
10   bosom turn all golden in the sunset.

I've known rivers:
Ancient, dusky rivers.

My soul has grown deep like the rivers.

[1926]

HARLEM[2]

What happens to a dream deferred?
    Does it dry up
    like a raisin in the sun?
    Or fester like a sore—
5   And then run?

    Does it stink like rotten meat?
    Or crust and sugar over—
    like a syrupy sweet?

    Maybe it just sags
10   like a heavy load.

    Or does it explode?

[1951]

---

[1] The Euphrates, flowing from Turkey into Syria and Iraq, and the Nile, flowing through Egypt, helped
to nurture the ancient Babylonian and Egyptian civilizations. The Congo flows through central Africa
to the Atlantic, while the Mississippi cuts through the heartland of the United States on its way to New
Orleans and the Gulf of Mexico.
[2] Traditionally black section of New York City.

THEME FOR ENGLISH B

The instructor said,

> *Go home and write*
> *a page tonight.*
> *And let that page come out of you—*
> *Then, it will be true.*

I wonder if it's that simple?
I am twenty-two, colored, born in Winston-Salem.
I went to school there, then Durham,[1] then here
to this college[2] on the hill above Harlem.
I am the only colored student in my class.

The steps from the hill lead down into Harlem,
through a park, then I cross St. Nicholas,[3]
Eighth Avenue, Seventh, and I come to the Y,
the Harlem Branch Y, where I take the elevator
up to my room, sit down, and write this page:

It's not easy to know what is true for you or me
at twenty-two, my age. But I guess I'm what
I feel and see and hear, Harlem, I hear you:
hear you, hear me—we two—you, me, talk on this page,
(I hear New York, too.) Me—who?

Well, I like to eat, sleep, drink, and be in love.
I like to work, read, learn, and understand life.
I like a pipe for a Christmas present,
or records—Bessie,[4] bop, or Bach.[5]
I guess being colored doesn't make me *not* like
the same things other folks like who are other races.
So will my page be colored that I write?

Being me, it will not be white.
But it will be
a part of you, instructor.
You are white—
yet a part of me, as I am a part of you.
That's American.
Sometimes perhaps you don't want to be a part of me.
Nor do I often want to be a part of you.
But we are, that's true!
As I learn from you,
I guess you learn from me—

[1] Cities in North Carolina.   [2] Columbia University.   [3] Avenue in Harlem.
[4] Bessie Smith (1898?–1937), the famous American blues singer.
[5] Johann Sebastian Bach (1685–1750), the German composer.

      although you're older—and white—
40   and somewhat more free.

      This is my page for English B.

                                    [1951]

                          ADVICE

              Folks, I'm telling you,
              birthing is hard
              and dying is mean—
              so get yourself
5   a little loving
              in between.

                                    [1946]

                Ogden Nash *1902–1971*

                  VERY LIKE A WHALE

   One thing that literature would be greatly the better for
   Would be a more restricted employment by authors of simile and
        metaphor.
   Authors of all races, be they Greeks, Romans, Teutons or Celts,
   Can't seem just to say that anything is the thing it is but have to go out
        of their way to say that it is like something else.
5 What does it mean when we are told
   That the Assyrian came down like a wolf on the fold?[1]
   In the first place, George Gordon Byron had had enough experience
   To know that it probably wasn't just one Assyrian, it was a lot of
        Assyrians.
   However, as too many arguments are apt to induce apoplexy and thus
        hinder longevity,
10 We'll let it pass as one Assyrian for the sake of brevity.
   Now then, this particular Assyrian, the one whose cohorts were gleaming
        in purple and gold,
   Just what does the poet mean when he says he came down like a wolf on
        the fold?
   In heaven and earth more than is dreamed of in our philosophy there
        are a great many things.
   But I don't imagine that among them there is a wolf with purple and
        gold cohorts or purple and gold anythings.
15 No, no, Lord Byron, before I'll believe that this Assyrian was actually like
        a wolf I must have some kind of proof;
   Did he run on all fours and did he have a hairy tail and a big red mouth
        and big white teeth and did he say Woof woof?

---

[1] The first line of "The Destruction of Sennacherib" (1815) by Lord Byron (1788–1824); see p. 870.
(Assyria was an ancient culture of the Near East.)

Frankly I think it very unlikely, and all you were entitled to say, at the
    very most,
Was that the Assyrian cohorts came down like a lot of Assyrian cohorts
    about to destroy the Hebrew host.
But that wasn't fancy enough for Lord Byron, oh dear me no, he had to
    invent a lot of figures of speech and then interpolate them.
20 With the result that whenever you mention Old Testament soldiers to
    people they say Oh yes, they're the ones that a lot of wolves dressed
    up in gold and purple ate them.
That's the kind of thing that's being done all the time by poets, from
    Homer to Tennyson;
They're always comparing ladies to lilies and veal to venison.
And they always say things like that the snow is a white blanket after a
    winter storm.
Oh it is, is it, all right then, you sleep under a six-inch blanket of snow
    and I'll sleep under a half-inch blanket of unpoetical blanket material
    and we'll see which one keeps warm.
25 And after that maybe you'll begin to comprehend dimly
What I mean by too much metaphor and simile.

[1935]

Countee Cullen *1903–1946*

FOR A LADY I KNOW

She even thinks that up in heaven
    Her class lies late and snores,
While poor black cherubs rise at seven
    To do celestial chores.

[1924]

YET DO I MARVEL

I doubt not God is good, well-meaning, kind,
And did He stoop to quibble could tell why
The little buried mole continues blind,
Why flesh that mirrors Him must some day die,
5 Make plain the reason tortured Tantalus
Is baited by the fickle fruit, declare
If merely brute caprice dooms Sisyphus
To struggle up a never-ending stair.
Inscrutable His ways are, and immune
10 To catechism by a mind too strewn
With petty cares to slightly understand
What awful brain compels His awful hand.
Yet do I marvel at this curious thing:
To make a poet black, and bid him sing!

[1925]

INCIDENT

(For Eric Walrond)

Once riding in old Baltimore,
 Heart-filled, head-filled with glee,
I saw a Baltimorean
 Keep looking straight at me.

5 Now I was eight and very small,
 And he was no whit bigger,
And so I smiled, but he poked out
 His tongue, and called me, "Nigger."

I saw the whole of Baltimore
10 From May until December;
Of all the things that happened there
 That's all that I remember.

        [1925]

Phyllis McGinley *1905–1978*

THE 5:32

She said, If tomorrow my world were torn in two,
Blacked out, dissolved, I think I would remember
(As if transfixed in unsurrendering amber)
This hour best of all the hours I knew:
5 When cars came backing into the shabby station,
Children scuffing the seats, and the women driving
With ribbons around their hair, and the trains arriving,
And the men getting off with tired but practiced motion.

Yes, I would remember my life like this, she said:
10 Autumn, the platform red with Virginia creeper,
And a man coming toward me, smiling, the evening paper
Under his arm, and his hat pushed back on his head;
And wood smoke lying like haze on the quiet town,
And dinner waiting, and the sun not yet gone down.

        [1932]

REFLECTIONS OUTSIDE OF A GYMNASIUM

The belles of the eighties were soft,
 They were ribboned and ruffled and gored,
With bustles built proudly aloft
 And Bosoms worn dashingly for'rd.
5 So, doting on bosoms and bustles,
 By fashion and circumstance pent,

They languished, neglecting their muscles,
    Growing flabby and plump and content.
Their most strenuous sport
10   A game of croquet
On a neat little court
    In the cool of the day,
Or dipping with ladylike motions,
Fully clothed, into decorous oceans.

15 The eighties surveyed with alarm
    A figure long-legged and thinnish;
And they had not discovered the charm
    Of a solid-mahogany finish.
Of suns that could darken or speckle
20   Their delicate skins they were wary.
They found it distasteful to freckle
    Or brown like a nut or a berry.
So they sat in the shade
    Or they put on a hat
25 And frequently stayed
    Fairly healthy at that
(And never lay nightlong awake
For sunburn and loveliness' sake).

When ladies rode forth, it was news,
30   Though sidewise ensconced on the saddle.
And when they embarked in canoes
    A gentleman wielded the paddle.
They never felt urged to compete
    With persons excessively agile.
35 Their slippers were small on their feet
    And they thought it no shame to be fragile.
Could they swim? They could not.
Did they dive? They forbore it.
And nobody thought
40   The less of them for it.

No, none pointed out how their course was absurd,
Though their tennis was feeble, their golf but a word.
When breezes were chilly, they wrapped up in flannels,
They couldn't turn cartwheels, they didn't swim channels,
45 They seldom climbed mountains, and, what was more shocking,
Historians doubt that they even went walking.
If unenergetic,
    A demoiselle dared to
Be no more athletic
50   Then ever she cared to.
Oh, strenuous comrades and maties,
How pleasant was life in the eighties!

[1936]

PORTRAIT OF GIRL
WITH COMIC BOOK

Thirteen's no age at all. Thirteen is nothing.
It is not wit, or powder on the face,
Or Wednesday matinees, or misses' clothing,
Or intellect, or grace.
5   Twelve has its tribal customs. But thirteen
Is neither boys in battered cars nor dolls,
Not *Sara Crewe*, or movie magazine,
Or pennants on the walls.

Thirteen keeps diaries and tropical fish
10 (A month, at most); scorns jumpropes in the spring;
Could not, would fortune grant it, name its wish;
Wants nothing, everything;
Has secrets from itself, friends it despises;
Admits none to the terrors that it feels;
15 Owns half a hundred masks but no disguises;
And walks upon its heels.

Thirteen's anomalous—not that, not this:
Not folded bud, or wave that laps a shore,
Or moth proverbial from the chrysalis.
20 Is the one age defeats the metaphor.
Is not a town, like childhood, strongly walled
But easily surrounded; is no city.
Nor, quitted once, can it be quite recalled—
Not even with pity.

[1952]

THE CONQUERORS

It seems vainglorious and proud
Of Atom-man to boast aloud
     His prowess homicidal
When one remembers how for years,
5   With their rude stones and humble spears,
Our sires, at wiping out their peers,
     Were almost never idle.

Despite his under-fissioned art
The Hittite[1] made a splendid start
10   Toward smiting lesser nations;
While Tamerlane,[2] it's widely known,
Without a bomb to call his own
     Destroyed whole populations.

---

[1] Ancient peoples of Asia Minor and Syria from about 2000–700 B.C.
[2] Tamerlane (1336–1405) was a brutal and ferocious Mongol leader whose forces conquered vast
territories stretching from the Black Sea to the Persian Gulf.

15 Nor did the ancient Persian need
Uranium to kill his Mede,[3]
The Viking earl, his foeman.
The Greeks got excellent results
With swords and engined catapults.
A chariot served the Roman.

20 Mere cannon garnered quite a yield
On Waterloo's[4] tempestuous field.
At Hastings[5] and at Flodden[6]
Stout countrymen, with just a bow
And arrow, laid their thousands low.
25 And Gettysburg[7] was sodden.

Though doubtless now our shrewd machines
Can blow the world to smithereens
More tidily and so on,
Let's give our ancestors their due.
30 Their ways were coarse, their weapons few.
But ah! how wondrously they slew
With what they had to go on.

[1959]

W. H. Auden *1907–1973*

MUSÉE DES BEAUX ARTS[1]

About suffering they were never wrong,
The Old Masters: how well they understood
Its human position; how it takes place
While someone else is eating or opening a window or just walking
dully along;
5 How, when the aged are reverently, passionately waiting
For the miraculous birth, there always must be
Children who did not specially want it to happen, skating
On a pond at the edge of the wood:
They never forgot
10 That even the dreadful martyrdom must run its course

---

[3] An inhabitant of ancient Media in what is now northwest Iran. McGinley is probably alluding to the victory in 549 B.C. of the Persian Emperor Cyrus II (also known as Cyrus the Great) over Astyages, the king of the Medes.

[4] In the Battle of Waterloo (culminating on June 18, 1815), the French Emperor Napoleon was decisively defeated by the allied British and Prussian forces.

[5] The Normans, led by William the Conqueror, defeated the Saxon King Harold at the Battle of Hastings in 1066, leading to the Norman conquest of England.

[6] In 1513 at the Battle of Flodden Field in Northumberland, King James IV of Scotland was defeated by the English.

[7] At the Battle of Gettysburg (July 1–3, 1863), the Union forces led by General George Meade stopped Confederate General Robert E. Lee's invasion of Pennsylvania with great loss of life on both sides.

[1] Museum of Fine Arts. Compare Auden's poem with William Carlos Williams's "Landscape with the Fall of Icarus," p. 954.

Anyhow in a corner, some untidy spot
Where the dogs go on with their doggy life and the torturer's horse
Scratches its innocent behind on a tree.

In Brueghel's *Icarus*,[2] for instance: how everything turns away
15   Quite leisurely from the disaster; the ploughman may
Have heard the splash, the forsaken cry,
But for him it was not an important failure; the sun shone
As it had to on the white legs disappearing into the green
Water; and the expensive delicate ship that must have seen
20   Something amazing, a boy falling out of the sky,
Had somewhere to get to and sailed calmly on.

[1940]

THE UNKNOWN CITIZEN

(To JS/ 07/M/ 378
This Marble Monument
Is Erected by the State)

He was found by the Bureau of Statistics to be
One against whom there was no official complaint,
And all the reports on his conduct agree
That, in the modern sense of an old-fashioned word, he was a saint,
5   For in everything he did he served the Greater Community.
Except for the War till the day he retired
He worked in a factory and never got fired,
But satisfied his employers, Fudge Motors Inc.
Yet he wasn't a scab or odd in his views,
10   For his Union reports that he paid his dues,
(Our report on his Union shows it was sound)
And our Social Psychology workers found
That he was popular with his mates and liked a drink.
The Press are convinced that he bought a paper every day
15   And that his reactions to advertisements were normal in every way.
Policies taken out in his name prove that he was fully insured,
And his Health-card shows he was once in hospital but left it cured.
Both Producers Research and High-Grade Living declare
He was fully sensible to the advantages of the Instalment Plan
20   And had everything necessary to the Modern Man,
A phonograph, a radio, a car and a frigidaire.
Our researchers into Public Opinion are content
That he held the proper opinions for the time of year;
When there was peace, he was for peace; when there was war, he
went.
25   He was married and added five children to the population,

[2] *Icarus* by the Flemish painter Pieter Brueghel (c. 1520–1569) depicts the fall of Icarus, who, in Greek
mythology, had flown too close to the sun on man-made wings of feathers and wax.

Which our Eugenist says was the right number for a parent of his
    generation,
And our teachers report that he never interfered with their education.
Was he free? Was he happy? The question is absurd:
Had anything been wrong, we should certainly have heard.

[1939]

Theodore Roethke   *1908–1963*

DOLOR

I have known the inexorable sadness of pencils,
Neat in their boxes, dolor of pad and paper-weight,
All the misery of manilla folders and mucilage,
Desolation in immaculate public places,
5 Lonely reception room, lavatory, switchboard,
The unalterable pathos of basin and pitcher,
Ritual of multigraph, paper-clip, comma,
Endless duplication of lives and objects.
And I have seen dust from the walls of institutions,
10 Finer than flour, alive, more dangerous than silica,
Sift, almost invisible, through long afternoons of tedium,
Dropping a fine film on nails and delicate eyebrows,
Glazing the pale hair, the duplicate grey standard faces.

[1948]

ELEGY FOR JANE

My Student, Thrown by a Horse

I remember the neckcurls, limp and damp as tendrils;
And her quick look, a sidelong pickerel smile;
And how, once startled into talk, the light syllables leaped for her,
And she balanced in the delight of her thought,
5 A wren, happy, tail into the wind,
Her song trembling the twigs and small branches.
The shade sang with her;
The leaves, their whispers turned to kissing;
And the mold sang in the bleached valleys under the rose.

10 Oh, when she was sad, she cast herself down into such a pure depth,
Even a father could not find her:
Scraping her cheek against straw;
Stirring the clearest water.

My sparrow, you are not here,
15 Waiting like a fern, making a spiny shadow.
The sides of wet stones cannot console me,
Nor the moss, wound with the last light.

If only I could nudge you from this sleep,
My maimed darling, my skittery pigeon.

20 Over this damp grave I speak the words of my love:
I, with no rights in this matter,
Neither father nor lover.

[1953]

I KNEW A WOMAN

I knew a woman, lovely in her bones,
When small birds sighed, she would sigh back at them;
Ah, when she moved, she moved more ways than one:
The shapes a bright container can contain!

5   Of her choice virtues only gods should speak,
Or English poets who grew up on Greek
(I'd have them sing in chorus, cheek to cheek).

How well her wishes went! She stroked my chin,
She taught me Turn, and Counter-turn, and Stand;

10 She taught me Touch, that undulant white skin;
I nibbled meekly from her proffered hand;
She was the sickle; I, poor I, the rake,
Coming behind her for her pretty sake
(But what prodigious mowing we did make).

15 Love likes a gander, and adores a goose:
Her full lips pursed, the errant note to seize;
She played it quick, she played it light and loose;
My eyes, they dazzled at her flowing knees;
Her several parts could keep a pure repose,

20 Or one hip quiver with a mobile nose
(She moved in circles, and those circles moved).

Let seed be grass, and grass turn into hay:
I'm martyr to a motion not my own;
What's freedom for? To know eternity.

25 I swear she cast a shadow white as stone.
But who would count eternity in days?
These old bones live to learn her wanton ways:
(I measure time by how a body sways).

[1958]

ROOT CELLAR

Nothing would sleep in that cellar, dank as a ditch,
Bulbs broke out of boxes hunting for chinks in the dark,
Shoots dangled and drooped,
Lolling obscenely from mildewed crates,

5   Hung down long yellow evil necks, like tropical snakes.
And what a congress of stinks!—

Roots ripe as old bait,
Pulpy stems, rank, silo-rich,
Leaf-mold, manure, lime, piled against slippery planks.
10   Nothing would give up life:
Even the dirt kept breathing a small breath.

[1948]

Elizabeth Bishop   *1911–1979*

THE ARMADILLO

For Robert Lowell

This is the time of year
When almost every night
the frail, illegal fire balloons appear.
Climbing the mountain height,

5   rising toward a saint
still honored in these parts,
the paper chambers flush and fill with light
that comes and goes, like hearts.

Once up against the sky it's hard
10   to tell them from the stars—
planets, that is—the tinted ones:
Venus going down, or Mars,

or the pale green one. With a wind,
they flare and falter, wobble and toss;
15   but if it's still they steer between
the kite sticks of the Southern Cross,

receding, dwindling, solemnly
and steadily forsaking us,
or, in the downdraft from a peak,
20   suddenly turning dangerous.

Last night another big one fell.
It splattered like an egg of fire
against the cliff behind the house.
The flame ran down. We saw the pair

25   of owls who nest there flying up
and up, their whirling black-and-white
stained bright pink underneath, until
they shrieked up out of sight.

The ancient owls' nest must have burned.
30   Hastily, all alone,

a glistening armadillo left the scene,
rose-flecked, head down, tail down,

and then a baby rabbit jumped out,
short-eared, to our surprise.
35   So soft!—a handful of intangible ash
with fixed, ignited eyes.

Too pretty, dreamlike mimicry!
O falling fire and piercing cry
and panic, and a weak mailed fist
40   *clenched ignorant against the sky!*

[1965]

Josephine Miles   *1911–1985*

REASON

Said, Pull her up a bit will you, Mac, I want to unload there.
Said, Pull her up my rear end, first come first serve.
Said, Give her the gun, Bud, he needs a taste of his own bumper.
Then the usher came out and got into the act:
5   Said, Pull her up, pull her up a bit, we need this space, sir.
Said, For God's sake, is this still a free country or what?
You go back and take care of Gary Cooper's horse
And leave me handle my own car.

Saw them unloading the lame old lady,
10   Ducked out under the wheel and gave her an elbow,
Said, All you needed to do was just explain;
Reason, Reason is my middle name.

[1955]

Robert Hayden   *1913–1980*

THOSE WINTER SUNDAYS

Sundays too my father got up early
and put his clothes on in the blueblack cold,
then with cracked hands that ached
from labor in the weekday weather made
5   banked fires blaze. No one ever thanked him.

I'd wake and hear the cold splintering, breaking.
When the rooms were warm, he'd call,
and slowly I would rise and dress,
fearing the chronic angers of that house,

10   Speaking indifferently to him,
who had driven out the cold

and polished my good shoes as well.
What did I know, what did I know
of love's austere and lonely offices?

[1962]

Karl Shapiro *1913–*

DRUG STORE

I do remember an apothecary,
And hereabouts 'a dwells[1]

It baffles the foreigner like an idiom,
And he is right to adopt it as a form
Less serious than the living-room or bar;
    For it disestablishes the cafe,
5 Is a collective, and on basic country.

Not that it praises hygiene and corrupts
The ice-cream parlor and the tobacconist's
Is it a center; but that the attractive symbols
    Watch over puberty and leer
10 Like rubber bottles waiting for sick-use.

Youth comes to jingle nickels and crack wise;
The baseball scores are his, the magazines
Devoted to lust, the jazz, the Coca-Cola,
    The lending-library of love's latest.
15 He is the customer; he is heroized.

And every nook and cranny of the flesh
Is spoken to by packages with wiles.
"Buy me, buy me," they whimper and cajole;
    The hectic range of lipsticks pouts,
20 Revealing the wicked and the simple mouth.

With scarcely any evasion in their eye
They smoke, undress their girls, exact a stance;
But only for a moment. The clock goes round;
    Crude fellowships are made and lost;
25 They slump on booths like rags, not even drunk.

[1942]

AUTO WRECK

Its quick soft silver bell beating, beating,
And down the dark one ruby flare
Pulsing out red light like an artery,

---

[1] The quotation is from William Shakespeare's *Romeo and Juliet* (1597), Act 5, Scene 1.

The ambulance at top speed floating down
Past beacons and illuminated clocks
Wings in a heavy curve, dips down,
And brakes speed, entering the crowd.
The doors leap open, emptying light;
Stretchers are laid out, the mangled lifted
And stowed into the little hospital.
Then the bell, breaking the hush, tolls once,
And the ambulance with its terrible cargo
Rocking, slightly rocking, moves away,
As the doors, an afterthought, are closed.

We are deranged, walking among the cops
Who sweep glass and are large and composed.
One is still making notes under the light.
One with a bucket douches ponds of blood
Into the street and gutter.
One hangs lanterns on the wrecks that cling,
Empty husks of locusts, to iron poles.

Our throats were tight as tourniquets,
Our feet were bound with splints, but now,
Like convalescents intimate and gauche,
We speak through sickly smiles and warn
With the stubborn saw of common sense,
The grim joke and the banal resolution.
The traffic moves around with care,
But we remain, touching a wound
That opens to our richest horror.
Already old, the question Who shall die?
Becomes unspoken Who is innocent?
For death in war is done by hands;
Suicide has cause and stillbirth, logic;
And cancer, simple as a flower, blooms.
But this invites the occult mind,
Cancels our physics with a sneer,
And spatters all we knew of denouement
Across the expedient and wicked stones.

[1942]

Dylan Thomas *1914–1953*

THE FORCE THAT THROUGH THE GREEN FUSE DRIVES THE FLOWER

The force that through the green fuse drives the flower
Drives my green age; that blasts the roots of trees
Is my destroyer.
And I am dumb to tell the crooked rose
My youth is bent by the same wintry fever.

The force that drives the water through the rocks
Drives my red blood; that dries the mouthing streams
Turns mine to wax.
And I am dumb to mouth unto my veins
10   How at the mountain spring the same mouth sucks.

The hand that whirls the water in the pool
Stirs the quicksand; that ropes the blowing wind
Hauls my shroud sail.
And I am dumb to tell the hanging man
15   How of my clay is made the hangman's lime.

The lips of time leech to the fountain head;
Love drips and gathers, but the fallen blood
Shall calm her sores.
And I am dumb to tell a weather's wind
20   How time has ticked a heaven round the stars.

And I am dumb to tell the lover's tomb
How at my sheet goes the same crooked worm.

[1934]

FERN HILL[1]

Now as I was young and easy under the apple boughs
About the lilting house and happy as the grass was green,
    The night above the dingle° starry,   *wooded dale*
      Time let me hail and climb
5   Golden in the heydays of his eyes,
And honoured among wagons I was prince of the apple
    towns
And once below a time I lordly had the trees and leaves
        Trail with daisies and barley
      Down the rivers of the windfall light.

10 And as I was green and carefree, famous among the barns
About the happy yard and singing as the farm was home,
      In the sun that is young once only,
        Time let me play and be
      Golden in the mercy of his means,
15 And green and golden I was huntsman and herdsman, the
    calves
Sang to my horn, the foxes on the hills barked clear and
    cold,
        And the sabbath rang slowly
      In the pebbles of the holy streams.

All the sun long it was running, it was lovely, the hay
20 Fields high as the house, the tunes from the chimneys,

[1] A farm owned by Thomas's aunt.

it was air
    And playing, lovely and watery
      And fire green as grass.
    And nightly under the simple stars
As I rode to sleep the owls were bearing the farm away,

25   All the moon long I heard, blessed among stables, the
      night-jars°   *nighthawks*
        Flying with the ricks,° and the horses   *haystacks*
        Flashing into the dark.

And then to awake, and the farm, like a wanderer white
With the dew, come back, the cock on his shoulder: it was
    all
30   Shining, it was Adam and maiden,
        The sky gathered again
    And the sun grew round that very day.
So it must have been after the birth of the simple light
In the first, spinning place, the spellbound horses walking
    warm
35   Out of the whinnying green stable
        On to the fields of praise.

And honoured among foxes and pheasants by the gay house
Under the new made clouds and happy as the heart was
    long,
        In the sun born over and over,
40   I ran my heedless ways,
        My wishes raced through the house high hay
And nothing I cared, at my sky blue trades, that time allows
In all his tuneful turning so few and such morning songs
        Before the children green and golden
45   Follow him out of grace.

Nothing I cared, in the lamb white days, that time would
    take me
Up to the swallow thronged loft by the shadow of my hand,
        In the moon that is always rising,
        Nor that riding to sleep
50   I should hear him fly with the high fields
And wake to the farm forever fled from the childless land.
Oh as I was young and easy in the mercy of his means,
        Time held me green and dying
        Though I sang in my chains like the sea.
                              [1946]

DO NOT GO GENTLE INTO THAT GOOD NIGHT

    Do not go gentle into that good night,
    Old age should burn and rave at close of day;
    Rage, rage against the dying of the light.

Though wise men at their end know dark is right,
Because their words had forked no lightning they
Do not go gentle into that good night.

Good men, the last wave by, crying how bright
Their frail deeds might have danced in a green bay,
Rage, rage against the dying of the light.

Wild men who caught and sang the sun in flight,
And learn, too late, they grieved it on its way,
Do not go gentle into that good night.

Grave men, near death, who see with blinding sight
Blind eyes could blaze like meteors and be gay,
Rage, rage against the dying of the light.

And you, my father, there on the sad height,
Curse, bless, me now with your fierce tears, I pray.
Do not go gentle into that good night.
Rage, rage against the dying of the light.

[1952]

Randall Jarrell   *1914–1965*

THE DEATH OF THE BALL TURRET GUNNER[1]

From my mother's sleep I fell into the State,
And I hunched in its belly till my wet fur froze.
Six miles from earth, loosed from its dream of life,
I woke to black flak and the nightmare fighters.
When I died they washed me out of the turret with a hose.

[1945]

EIGHTH AIR FORCE

If, in an odd angle of the hutment,°   *encampment*
A puppy laps the water from a can
Of flowers, and the drunk sergeant shaving
Whistles *O Paradiso!*[2]—shall I say that man
Is not as men have said: a wolf to man?

The other murderers troop in yawning;
Three of them play Pitch,° one sleeps, and one   *a card game*
Lies counting missions, lies there sweating

[1] "A ball turret was a plexiglass sphere set into the belly of a B-17 or B-24, and inhabited by two .50 caliber machine guns and one man, a short small man." (Jarrell's note)
[2] Aria from Giacomo Meyerbeer's opera *L'Africaine* (1865).

10   Till even his heart beats: One; One; One.
     O murderers! . . . Still, this is how it's done:

     This is a war. . . . But since these play, before they die,
     Like puppies with their puppy; since, a man,
     I did as these have done, but did not die—
     I will content the people as I can
15   And give up these to them: Behold the man!³

     I have suffered, in a dream, because of him,
     Many things;⁴ for this last savior, man,
     I have lied as I lie now. But what is lying?
     Men wash their hands, in blood, as best they can:
20   I find no fault in this just man.

                                                              [1948]

William Stafford   *1914–*

FOR THE GRAVE OF DANIEL BOONE¹

     The farther he went the farther home grew.
     Kentucky became another room;
     the mansion arched over the Mississippi;
     flowers were spread all over the floor.
5   He traced ahead a deepening home,
     and better, with goldenrod:

     Leaving the snakeskin of place after place,
     going on—after the trees
     the grass, a bird flying after a song.
10   Rifle so level, sighting so well
     his picture freezes down to now,
     a story-picture for children.

     They go over the velvet falls
     into the tapestry of his time,
15   heirs to the landscape, feeling no jar:
     it is like evening; they are the quail
     surrounding his fire, coming in for the kill;
     their little feet move sacred sand.

     Children, we live in a barbwire time
20   but like to follow the old hands back—
     the ring in the light, the knuckle, the palm,

---

³ See John 19:4–5.   ⁴ See Matthew 27:19.
¹ Daniel Boone (1734–1820), the American pathfinder whose early explorations led to the settlement of Kentucky. In 1775, it was Boone, at the head of a party of woodsmen, who blazed the famous Wilderness Road through the Appalachians, which opened up the American West. In 1799, at the age of 65, Boone again moved westward, "over the Mississippi" into Missouri, because, according to legend, "I want more elbow-room." Boone died in Missouri at the age of 86; in 1845 his remains and those of his wife were moved to Frankfort, Kentucky.

　　　　all the way to Daniel Boone,
　　　　hunting our own kind of deepening home.
　　　　From the land that was his I heft this rock.

25　　　Here on his grave I put it down.

　　　　　　　　　　　　　　　　　　[1957]

AT THE BOMB TESTING SITE

　　　　At noon in the desert a panting lizard
　　　　waited for history, its elbows tense,
　　　　watching the curve of a particular road
　　　　as if something might happen.

5　　　It was looking at something farther off
　　　　than people could see, an important scene
　　　　acted in stone for little selves
　　　　at the flute end of consequences.

　　　　There was just a continent without much on it
10　　　under a sky that never cared less.
　　　　Ready for a change, the elbows waited.
　　　　The hands gripped hard on the desert.
　　　　　　　　　　　　　　　　　[1966]

TRAVELING THROUGH THE DARK

Traveling through the dark I found a deer
dead on the edge of the Wilson River road.
It is usually best to roll them into the canyon:
that road is narrow; to swerve might make more dead.

5　　By glow of the tail-light I stumbled back of the car
and stood by the heap, a doe, a recent killing;
she had stiffened already, almost cold.
I dragged her off; she was large in the belly.

My fingers touching her side brought me the reason—
10　　her side was warm; her fawn lay there waiting,
alive, still, never to be born.
Beside that mountain road I hesitated.

The car aimed ahead its lowered parking lights;
under the hood purred the steady engine.
15　　I stood in the glare of the warm exhaust turning red;
around our group I could hear the wilderness listen.

I thought hard for us all—my only swerving—
then pushed her over the edge into the river.
　　　　　　　　　　　　　　　　[1962]

Robert Lowell   1917–1977

SKUNK HOUR

(For Elizabeth Bishop)[1]

Nautilus Island's[2] hermit
heiress still lives through winter in her Spartan cottage;
her sheep still graze above the sea.
Her son's a bishop. Her farmer
5   is first selectman[3] in our village;
she's in her dotage.

Thirsting for
the hierarchic privacy
of Queen Victoria's century,[4]
10   she buys up all
the eyesores facing her shore,
and lets them fall.

The season's ill—
we've lost our summer millionaire,
15   who seemed to leap from an L. L. Bean[5]
catalogue. His nine-knot yawl[6]
was auctioned off to lobstermen.
A red fox stain covers Blue Hill.[7]

And now our fairy
20   decorator brightens his shop for fall;
his fishnet's filled with orange cork,
orange, his cobbler's bench and awl;
there is no money in his work,
he'd rather marry.

25   One dark night,
my Tudor Ford[8] climbed the hill's skull;
I watched for love-cars. Lights turned down,
they lay together, hull to hull,

---

[1] Elizabeth Bishop (1911–1979), the American poet. Lowell has indicated in one of his essays that his poem is modeled on her poem "The Armadillo": both poems "use short line stanzas, start with drifting description and end with a single animal."

[2] The poem is set in the vicinity of Castine, Maine, on Penobscot Bay, where Lowell had a summer home.

[3] An elected New England town official.

[4] Queen Victoria ruled Great Britain from 1837 to 1901.

[5] The famous mail-order house in Freeport, Maine, specializing in sporting goods and camping equipment.

[6] A sailboat capable of doing nine nautical miles an hour.

[7] According to Lowell: "the rusty reddish color of autumn on Blue Hill near (Bangor, Maine) where we were living."

[8] The name given by the Ford Motor Company to its two-door model.

where the graveyard shelves on the town. . . .
30 My mind's not right.

A car radio bleats,
"Love, O careless Love. . . ."[9] I hear
my ill-spirit sob in each blood cell,
as if my hand were at its throat. . . .
35 I myself am hell;[10]
nobody's here—

only skunks, that search
in the moonlight for a bite to eat.
They march on their soles up Main Street:
40 white stripes, moonstruck eyes' red fire
under the chalk-dry and spar spire
of the Trinitarian Church.[11]

I stand on top
of our back steps and breathe the rich air—
45 a mother skunk with her column of kittens swills the garbage pail.
She jabs her wedge-head in a cup
of sour cream, drops her ostrich tail,
and will not scare.

[1959]

THE MOUTH OF THE HUDSON[1]

(For Esther Brooks)

A single man stands like a bird-watcher,
and scuffles the pepper and salt snow
from a discarded, gray
Westinghouse Electric cable drum.
5 He cannot discover America by counting
the chains of condemned freight-trains
from thirty states. They jolt and jar
and junk in the siding below him.
He has trouble with his balance.
10 His eyes drop,
and he drifts with the wild ice
ticking seaward down the Hudson,
like the blank sides of a jig-saw puzzle.

The ice ticks seaward like a clock.
15 A Negro toasts

[9] Words from a well-known folksong.
[10] An allusion to Milton's *Paradise Lost*, IV, 75, where Satan says: "Which way I fly is hell; myself am hell."
[11] A church which subscribes to a belief in the doctrine of the Trinity, the theological union of Father, Son, and Holy Ghost, in one godhead.
[1] The Hudson River flows into New York Bay.

wheat-seeds over the coke-fumes
of a punctured barrel.
Chemical air
sweeps in from New Jersey,
20   and smells of coffee.

Across the river,
ledges of suburban factories tan
in the sulphur-yellow sun
of the unforgivable landscape.

[1964]

Gwendolyn Brooks   *1917–*

SADIE AND MAUD

Maud went to college.
Sadie stayed at home.
Sadie scraped life
With a fine-tooth comb.

5   She didn't leave a tangle in.
Her comb found every strand.
Sadie was one of the livingest chits[1]
In all the land.

Sadie bore two babies
10   Under her maiden name.
Maud and Ma and Papa
Nearly died of shame.
Every one but Sadie
Nearly died of shame.

15   When Sadie said her last so-long
Her girls struck out from home.
(Sadie had left as heritage
Her fine-tooth comb.)

Maud, who went to college,
20   Is a thin brown mouse.
She is living all alone
In this old house.

[1945]

THE MOTHER

Abortions will not let you forget.
You remember the children you got that you did not get,

---

[1] Pert young women.

The damp small pulps with a little or with no hair,
The singers and workers that never handled the air.
5 You will never neglect or beat
Them, or silence or buy with a sweet.
You will never wind up the sucking-thumb
Or scuttle off ghosts that come.
You will never leave them, controlling your luscious sigh,
10 Return for a snack of them, with gobbling mother-eye.

I have heard in the voices of the wind the voices of my dim
        killed children.
I have contracted. I have eased
My dim dears at the breasts they could never suck.
I have said, Sweets, if I sinned, if I seized
15 Your luck
And your lives from your unfinished reach,
If I stole your births and your names,
Your straight baby tears and your games,
Your stilted or lovely loves, your tumults, your marriages, aches,
        and your deaths,
20 If I poisoned the beginnings of your breaths,
Believe that even in my deliberateness I was not deliberate.
Though why should I whine,
Whine that the crime was other than mine?—
Since anyhow you are dead.
25 Or rather, or instead,
You were never made.
But that too, I am afraid,
Is faulty: oh, what shall I say, how is the truth to be said?
You were born, you had body, you died.
30 It is just that you never giggled or planned or cried.

Believe me, I loved you all.
Believe me, I knew you, though faintly, and I loved, I loved you
All.

                                                    [1945]

"FIRST FIGHT. THEN FIDDLE"

First fight. Then fiddle. Ply the slipping string
With feathery sorcery; muzzle the note
With hurting love; the music that they wrote
Bewitch, bewilder. Qualify to sing
5 Threadwise. Devise no salt, no hempen thing
For the dear instrument to bear. Devote
The bow to silks and honey. Be remote
A while from malice and from murdering.
But first to arms, to armor. Carry hate
10 In front of you and harmony behind.
Be deaf to music and to beauty blind.

Win war. Rise bloody, maybe not too late
For having first to civilize a space
Wherein to play your violin with grace.

[1949]

THE LOVERS OF THE POOR

      arrive. The Ladies from the Ladies' Betterment
  League
Arrive in the afternoon, the late light slanting
In diluted gold bars across the boulevard brag
Of proud, seamed faces with mercy and murder hinting
5   Here, there, interrupting, all deep and debonair,
The pink paint on the innocence of fear;
Walk in a gingerly manner up the hall.
Cutting with knives served by their softest care,
Served by their love, so barbarously fair.
10   Whose mothers taught: You'd better not be cruel!
You had better not throw stones upon the wrens!
Herein they kiss and coddle and assault
Anew and dearly in the innocence
With which they baffle nature. Who are full,
15   Sleek, tender-clad, fit, fiftyish, a-glow, all
Sweetly abortive, hinting at fat fruit,
Judge it high time that fiftyish fingers felt
Beneath the lovelier planes of enterprise.
To resurrect. To moisten with milky chill.
20   To be a random hitching post or plush.
To be, for wet eyes, random and handy hem.
      Their guild is giving money to the poor.
The worthy poor. The very very worthy.
And beautiful poor. Perhaps just not too swarthy?
25   Perhaps just not too dirty nor too dim
Nor—passionate. In truth, what they could wish
Is—something less than derelict or dull.
Not staunch enough to stab, though, gaze for gaze!
God shield them sharply from the beggar-bold!
30   The noxious needy ones whose battle's bald
Nonetheless for being voiceless, hits one down.
      But it's all so bad! and entirely too much for them.
The stench; the urine, cabbage, and dead beans,
Dead porridges of assorted dusty grains,
35   The old smoke, *heavy* diapers, and, they're told,
Something called chitterlings. The darkness. Drawn
Darkness, or dirty light. The soil that stirs.
The soil that looks the soil of centuries.
And for that matter the *general* oldness. Old
40   Wood. Old marble. Old tile. Old old old.

Not homekind Oldness! Not Lake Forest, Glencoe.[1]
Nothing is sturdy, nothing is majestic,
There is no quiet drama, no rubbed glaze, no
Unkillable infirmity of such
45   A tasteful turn as lately they have left,
Glencoe, Lake Forest, and to which their cars
Must presently restore them. When they're done
With dullards and distortions of this fistic
Patience of the poor and put-upon.
50   They've never seen such a make-do-ness as
Newspaper rugs before! In this, this "flat,"
Their hostess is gathering up the oozed, the rich
Rugs of the morning (tattered! the bespattered . . .),
Readies to spread clean rugs for afternoon.
55   Here is a scene for you. The Ladies look,
In horror, behind a substantial citizeness
Whose trains clank out across her swollen heart.
Who, arms akimbo, almost fills a door.
All tumbling children, quilts dragged to the floor
60   And tortured thereover, potato peelings, soft-
Eyed kitten, hunched-up, haggard, to-be-hurt.
        Their League is allotting largesse to the Lost.
But to put their clean, their pretty money, to put
Their money collected from delicate rose-fingers
65   Tipped with their hundred flawless rose-nails seems . . .
        They own Spode, Lowestoft, candelabra,
Mantels, and hostess gowns, and sunburst clocks,
Turtle soup, Chippendale, red satin "hangings,"
Aubussons and Hattie Carnegie. They Winter
70   In Palm Beach; cross the Water in June; attend,
When suitable, the nice Art Institute;
Buy the right books in the best bindings; saunter
On Michigan,[2] Easter mornings, in sun or wind.
Oh Squalor! This sick four-story hulk, this fibre
75   With fissures everywhere! Why, what are bringings
Of loathe-love largesse? What shall peril hungers
So old old, what shall flatter the desolate?
Tin can, blocked fire escape and chitterling
And swaggering seeking youth and the puzzled wreckage
80   Of the middle passage, and urine and stale shames
And, again, the porridges of the underslung
And children children children. Heavens! That
Was a rat, surely, off there, in the shadows? Long
And long-tailed? Gray? The Ladies from the Ladies'
85   Betterment League agree it will be better
To achieve the outer air that rights and steadies,
To hie to a house that does not holler, to ring

---

[1] Wealthy suburbs north of Chicago.
[2] Michigan Avenue in Chicago is lined with up-scale shops.

Bells elsetime, better presently to cater
To no more Possibilities, to get
90   Away. Perhaps the money can be posted.
Perhaps they two may choose another Slum!
Some serious sooty half-unhappy home!—
Where loathe-love likelier may be invested.
                    Keeping their scented bodies in the center
95   Of the hall as they walk down the hysterical hall,
They allow their lovely skirts to graze no wall,
Are off at what they manage of a canter,
And, resuming all the clues of what they were,
Try to avoid inhaling the laden air.

                                                        [1959]

THE BEAN EATERS

They eat beans mostly, this old yellow pair.
Dinner is a casual affair.
Plain chipware on a plain and creaking wood,
Tin flatware.

5   Two who are Mostly Good.
Two who have lived their day,
But keep on putting on their clothes
And putting things away.

And remembering . . .
10   Remembering, with twinklings and twinges,
As they lean over the beans in their rented back room
        that is full of beads and receipts and dolls and cloths,
        tobacco crumbs, vases and fringes.

                                                        [1959]

ULYSSES[1]

RELIGION

At home we pray every morning, we
get down on our knees in a circle,
holding hands, holding Love,
and we sing Hallelujah.

5   Then we go into the World.

Daddy *speeds*, to break bread with his Girl Friend.
Mommy's a Boss. And a lesbian.
(She too has a nice Girl Friend.)

---

[1] The poem that follows is a dramatic monologue spoken by a child named Ulysses.

My brothers and sisters and I come to school.
10 We bring knives pistols bottles, little boxes, and cans.

We talk to the man who's cool at the playground gate.
Nobody Sees us, nobody stops our sin.

Our teachers feed us geography.
We spit it out in a hurry.

15 Now we are coming home.

At home, we pray every evening, we
get down on our knees in a circle,
holding hands, holding Love.

And we sing Hallelujah.

[1991]

MERLE[1]

UNCLE SEAGRAM

My uncle likes me too much.

I am five and a half years old, and in kindergarten.
In kindergarten everything is clean.

My uncle is six feet tall with seven bumps on his chin.
5 My uncle is six feet tall, and he stumbles.
He stumbles because of his Wonderful Medicine
packed in his pocket all times.

Family is ma and pa and my uncle,
three brothers, three sisters, and me.

10 Every night at my house we play checkers and dominoes.
My uncle sits *close.*
There aren't any shoes or socks on his feet.
Under the table a big toe tickles my ankle.
Under the oilcloth his thin knee beats into mine.
15 And mashes. And mashes.

When we look at TV
my uncle picks *me* to sit on his lap.
As I sit, he gets hard in the middle.
I squirm, but he keeps me, and kisses my ear.

20 I am not even a girl.

Once, when I went to the bathroom,
My uncle noticed, came in, shut the door,

---

[1] The poem that follows is spoken by a child named Merle.

put his long white tongue in my ear,
and whispered "We're Best Friends, and Family,
25   and we know how to keep Secrets."

My uncle likes me too much. I am worried.

I do not like my uncle anymore.

[1991]

Lawrence Ferlinghetti   *1919–*

CONSTANTLY RISKING ABSURDITY

Constantly risking absurdity
                          and death
        whenever he performs
                      above the heads
5   of his audience
        the poet like an acrobat
                    climbs on rime
                        to a high wire of his own making
    and balancing on eyebeams
10   above a sea of faces
            paces his way
                        to the other side of day
    performing entrechats
                    and sleight-of-foot tricks
15   and other high theatrics
                        and all without mistaking
            any thing
                    for what it may not be

        For he's the super realist
20   who must perforce perceive
            taut truth
                    before the taking of each stance or step
        in his supposed advance
                            toward that still higher perch
25   where Beauty stands and waits
                        with gravity
                            to start her death-defying leap

    And he
        a little charleychaplin man
30   who may or may not catch
            her fair eternal form
                        spreadeagled in the empty air
            of existence
                                        [1958]

May Swenson *1919–1989*

WOMEN

Women	Or they
should be	should be
pedestals	little horses
moving	those wooden
pedestals	sweet
moving	oldfashioned
to the	painted
motions	rocking
of men	horses

the gladdest things in the toyroom

The	feelingly
pegs	and then
of their	unfeelingly
ears	To be
so familiar	joyfully
and dear	ridden
to the trusting	rockingly
fists	ridden until
To be chafed	the restored

egos dismount and the legs stride away

Immobile	willing
sweetlipped	to be set
sturdy	into motion
and smiling	Women
women	should be
should always	pedestals
be waiting	to men

[1970]

Richard Wilbur *1921–*

A SIMILE FOR HER SMILE

Your smiling, or the hope, the thought of it,
Makes in my mind such pause and abrupt ease
As when the highway bridgegates fall,
Balking the hasty traffic, which must sit
On each side massed and staring, while
Deliberately the drawbridge starts to rise:

Then horns are hushed, the oilsmoke rarifies,
Above the idling motors one can tell
The packet's smooth approach, the slip,
10   Slip of the silken river past the sides,
The ringing of clear bells, the dip
And slow cascading of the paddle wheel.

[1950]

MUSEUM PIECE

The good gray guardians of art
Patrol the halls on spongy shoes,
Impartially protective, though
Perhaps suspicious of Toulouse.[1]

5   Here dozes one against the wall,
Disposed upon a funeral chair.
A Degas dancer pirouettes[2]
Upon the parting of his hair.

See how she spins! The grace is there,
10   But strain as well is plain to see.
Degas loved the two together:
Beauty joined to energy.

Edgar Degas purchased once
A fine El Greco,[3] which he kept
15   Against the wall beside his bed
To hang his pants on while he slept.

[1950]

SLEEPLESS AT CROWN POINT

All night, this headland
Lunges into the rumpling
Capework of the wind

[1976]

THE STAR SYSTEM

While you're a white-hot youth, emit the rays
Which, now unmarked, shall dazzle future days.
Burn for the joy of it, and waste no juice
On hopes of prompt discovery. Produce!
5   Then, white with years, live wisely and survive.

---

[1] Henri de Toulouse-Lautrec (1864–1901), a French painter and lithographer.
[2] Edgar Degas (1834–1917), a French painter noted for his pictures of ballet dancers.
[3] El Greco (1548?–1614?), a Spanish painter.

Thus you may be on hand when you arrive,
And, like Antares, rosily dilate,
And for a time be gaseous and great.

Philip Larkin   *1922–1985*

CHURCH GOING

Once I am sure there's nothing going on
I step inside, letting the door thud shut.
Another church: matting, seats, and stone,
And little books; sprawlings of flowers, cut
5   For Sunday, brownish now; some brass and stuff
Up at the holy end; the small neat organ;
And a tense, musty, unignorable silence,
Brewed God knows how long. Hatless, I take off
My cycle-clips in awkward reverence,

10   Move forward, run my hand around the font.
From where I stand, the roof looks almost new—
Cleaned, or restored? Someone would know: I don't.
Mounting the lectern, I peruse a few
Hectoring large-scale verses, and pronounce
15   "Here endeth" much more loudly than I'd meant.
The echoes snigger briefly. Back at the door
I sign the book, donate an Irish sixpence,
Reflect the place was not worth stopping for.

Yet stop I did: in fact I often do,
20   And always end much at a loss like this,
Wondering what to look for; wondering, too,
When churches fall completely out of use
What we shall turn them into, if we shall keep
A few cathedrals chronically on show,
25   Their parchment, plate and pyx[1] in locked cases,
And let the rest rent-free to rain and sheep.
Shall we avoid them as unlucky places?

Or, after dark, will dubious women come
To make their children touch a particular stone;
30   Pick simples[2] for a cancer; or on some
Advised night see walking a dead one?
Power of some sort or other will go on
In games, in riddles, seemingly at random;
But superstition, like belief, must die,

---

[1] A container in which the Communion wafers are kept.
[2] Plants or herbs with real or reputed medicinal powers.

35 And what remains when disbelief has gone?
Grass, weedy pavement, brambles, buttress,³ sky,

A shape less recognisable each week,
A purpose more obscure. I wonder who
Will be the last, the very last, to seek
40 This place for what it was; one of the crew
That tap and jot and know what rood-lofts⁴ were?
Some ruin-bibber,⁵ randy⁶ for antique,
Or Christmas-addict, counting on a whiff
Of gown-and-bands and organ-pipes and myrrh?⁷
45 Or will he be my representative,

Bored, uninformed, knowing the ghostly silt
Dispersed, yet tending to this cross of ground
Through suburb scrub because it held unspilt
So long and equably what since is found
50 Only in separation—marriage, and birth,
And death, and thoughts of these—for whom was built
This special shell? For, though I've no idea
What this accoutred frowsty⁸ barn is worth,
It pleases me to stand in silence here;

55 A serious house on serious earth it is,
In whose blent air all our compulsions meet,
Are recognized, and robed as destinies.
And that much never can be obsolete,
Since someone will forever be surprising
60 A hunger in himself to be more serious,
And gravitating with it to this ground,
Which, he once heard, was proper to grow wise in,
If only that so many dead lie round.

[1955]

Mari Evans

I AM A BLACK WOMAN

I am a black woman
the music of my song
some sweet arpeggio¹ of tears
is written in a minor key
5 and I
can be heard humming in the night
Can be heard
                humming
in the night

³ A structure, often of stone, lending support to a wall.
⁴ Lofts or galleries within a church.   ⁵ An habitué of ruins.
⁶ Literally, lecherous.   ⁷ Incense.   ⁸ Must.
¹ A musical chord in which the notes are played quickly and singly.

10   I saw my mate leap screaming to the sea
        and I / with these hands / cupped the lifebreath
        from my issue in the canebrake
        I lost Nat's[2] swinging body in a rain of tears
        and heard my son scream all the way from Anzio[3]
15   for Peace he never knew. . . . I
        learned Da Nang[4] and Pork Chop Hill[5]
        in anguish

        Now my nostrils know the gas
        and these trigger tire / d fingers
20   seek the softness in my warrior's beard

        I
        am a black woman
        tall as a cypress
        strong
25   beyond all definition still
        defying place
        and time
        and circumstance
            assailed
30   impervious
                    indestructible
        Look
            on me and be
        renewed
                                    [1970]

Alan Dugan   *1923–*

LOVE SONG: I AND THOU

        Nothing is plumb, level or square:
            the studs are bowed, the joists
        are shaky by nature, no piece fits
            any other piece without a gap
5   or pinch, and bent nails
            dance all over the surfacing
        like maggots. By Christ
            I am no carpenter. I built
        the roof for myself, the walls
10   for myself, the floors

---

[2] Nat Turner (1800–1831) was hanged after leading a slave revolt in Southampton County, Virginia,
    during which 85 whites were killed.
[3] A coastal town in Italy, the site of a major (and very bloody) Allied landing during World War II.
[4] The site of many battles for control of a large U.S. military base during the Vietnam War.
[5] A hill that was repeatedly captured and recaptured by the Chinese and American forces during the
    Korean War.

for myself, and got
    hung up in it myself. I
danced with a purple thumb
    at this house-warming, drunk
15 with my prime whiskey: rage.
    Oh I spat rage's nails
into the frame-up of my work:
    it held. It settled plumb,
level, solid, square and true
20   for that great moment. Then
it screamed and went on through,
    skewing as wrong the other way.
God damned it. This is hell,
    but I planned it, I sawed it,
25 I nailed it, and I
    will live in it until it kills me.
I can nail my left palm
    to the left-hand cross-piece but
I can't do everything myself.
30   I need a hand to nail the right,
a help, a love, a you, a wife.
                  [1961]

Anthony Hecht   *1923–*

"MORE LIGHT! MORE LIGHT!"[1]

For Heinrich Blücher and Hannah Arendt[2]

Composed in the Tower before his execution
These moving verses, and being brought at that time
Painfully to the stake, submitted, declaring thus:
"I implore my God to witness that I have made no crime."

5 Nor was he forsaken of courage, but the death was horrible,
The sack of gunpowder failing to ignite.
His legs were blistered sticks on which the black sap
Bubbled and burst as he howled for the Kindly Light.

And that was but one, and by no means one of the worst;
10 Permitted at least his pitiful dignity;
And such as were by made prayers in the name of Christ,
That shall judge all men, for his soul's tranquility.

---

[1] Supposedly the final words of Johann Wolfgang von Goethe (1749–1832), a German whose accomplishments as a poet, novelist, playwright, scientist, and philosopher made him one of the intellectual giants of his age.
[2] Hannah Arendt (1906–1975), the author of the classic *Origins of Totalitarianism* (1951), who came to the United States from Germany in 1941 with her husband Heinrich Blücher, a professor of philosophy.

We move now to outside a German wood
Three men are there commanded to dig a hole
15 In which the two Jews are ordered to lie down
And be buried alive by the third, who is a Pole.

Not light from the shrine at Weimar[3] beyond the hill
Nor light from heaven appeared. But he did refuse.
A Lüger[4] settled back deeply in its glove.
20 He was ordered to change places with the Jews.

Much casual death had drained away their souls.
The thick dirt mounted toward the quivering chin.
When only the head was exposed the order came
To dig him out again and to get back in.

25 No light, no light in the blue Polish eye.
When he finished a riding boot packed down the earth.
The Lüger hovered lightly in its glove.
He was shot in the belly and in three hours bled to death.

No prayers or incense rose up in those hours
30 Which grew to be years, and every day came mute
Ghosts from the ovens, sifting through crisp air,
And settled upon his eyes in a black soot.

[1967]

THE DOVER BITCH

A Criticism of Life

So there stood Matthew Arnold and this girl
With the cliffs of England crumbling away behind them,
And he said to her, "Try to be true to me,
And I'll do the same for you, for things are bad
5 All over, etc., etc."
Well now, I knew this girl. It's true she had read
Sophocles in a fairly good translation
And caught that bitter allusion to the sea,
But all the time he was talking she had in mind
10 The notion of what his whiskers would feel like
On the back of her neck. She told me later on
That after a while she got to looking out
At the lights across the channel, and really felt sad,
Thinking of all the wine and enormous beds
15 And blandishments in French and the perfumes.
And then she got really angry. To have been brought
All the way down from London, and then be addressed

---

[3] A city in Germany, once the home of Goethe; nearby stood Buchenwald, the infamous Nazi concentration camp.
[4] A German make of pistol.

As sort of a mournful cosmic last resort
Is really tough on a girl, and she was pretty.
20 Anyway, she watched him pace the room
And finger his watch-chain and seem to sweat a bit,
And then she said one or two unprintable things.
But you mustn't judge her by that. What I mean to say is,
She's really all right. I still see her once in a while
25 And she always treats me right. We have a drink
And I give her a good time, and perhaps it's a year
Before I see her again, but there she is,
Running to fat, but dependable as they come,
And sometimes I bring her a bottle of *Nuit d'Amour*.

[1968]

Denise Levertov   *1923–*

AT THE EDGE

How much I should like to begin
a poem with And—presupposing
the hardest said—
the moss cleared off the stone,
5   the letters plain.
How the round moon
would shine into all the corners
of such a poem and show
the words! Moths and dazzled
10 awakened birds
would freeze in its light!
The lines would be
an outbreak of bells
and I swinging on the rope!

15 Yet, not desiring apocrypha[1]
but true revelation,
what use to pretend the stone discovered,
anything visible?
That poem indeed
20 may not be carved there, may lie
—the quick of mystery—
in animal eyes gazing
from the thicket,
a creature of unknown size,
25 fierce, terrified, having teeth or
no defense, but whom
no And may approach suddenly.

[1959]

---

[1] Books of the Bible that are of questionable authority or authenticity as opposed to those which have the sanction of "true revelation."

Louis Simpson   *1923–*

SUMMER STORM

In that so sudden summer storm they tried
Each bed, couch, closet, carpet, car-seat, table,
Both river banks, five fields, a mountain side,
Covering as much ground as they were able.

5   A lady, coming on them in the dark
In a white fixture, wrote to the newspapers
Complaining of the statues in the park.
By Cupid, but they cut some pretty capers!

The envious oxen in still rings would stand
10   Ruminating. Their sweet incessant plows
I think had changed the contours of the land
And made two modest conies° move their house.   *rabbits*

God rest them well, and firmly shut the door.
Now they are married Nature breathes once more.

                                                            [1949]

Lisel Mueller   *1924–*

FIRST SNOW IN LAKE COUNTY

All night it fell around us
as if the sky had been sheared,
its fleece dropping forever
past our windows, until our room
5   was as chaste and sheltered
as Ursula's, where she lay
and dreamed herself in heaven:
and in the morning we saw
that the vision had held, looked out
10   on such a sight as we wish for
all our lives:
a thing, place, time
untouched and uncorrupted,
the world before we were here.

15   Even the wind held its peace.

And already, as our eyes
hung on, hung on, we longed
to make that patience bear
our tracks, already our daughter
20   put on her boots and screamed,

and the dog jumped with the joy
of splashing the white with yellow
and digging through the snow
to the scents and sounds below.

[1965]

Maxine Kumin   *1925–*

TOGETHER

The water closing
over us and the
going down is all.
Gills are given.
5   We convert in a
town of broken hulls
and green doubloons.
O you dead pirates
hear us! There is
10   no salvage. All
you know is the color
of warm caramel. All
is salt. See how
our eyes have migrated
15   to the uphill side?
Now we are new round
mouths and no spines
letting the water cover.
It happens over
20   and over, me in
your body and you
in mine.

[1970]

WOODCHUCKS

Gassing the woodchucks didn't turn out right.
The knockout bomb from the Feed and Grain Exchange
was featured as merciful, quick at the bone
and the case we had against them was airtight
5   both exits shoehorned shut with puddingstone,°   *cement*
but they had a sub-sub-basement out of range.

Next morning they turned up again, no worse
for the cyanide than we for our cigarettes
and state-store Scotch, all of us up to scratch.
10   They brought down the marigolds as a matter of course
and then took over the vegetable patch
nipping the broccoli shoots, beheading the carrots.

The food from our mouths, I said, righteously thrilling
to the feel of the .22, the bullets' neat noses.
15 I, a lapsed pacifist fallen from grace
puffed with Darwinian pieties for killing,
now drew a bead on the littlest woodchuck's face.
He died down in the everbearing roses.

Ten minutes later I dropped the mother. She
20 flipflopped in the air and fell, her needle teeth
still hooked in a leaf of early Swiss chard.
Another baby next. O one-two-three
the murderer inside me rose up hard,
the hawkeye killer came on stage forthwith.

25 There's one chuck left. Old wily fellow, he keeps
me cocked and ready day after day after day.
All night I hunt his humped-up form. I dream
I sight along the barrel in my sleep.
If only they'd all consented to die unseen
30 gassed underground the quiet Nazi way.

[1972]

Carolyn Kizer *1925–*

BITCH

Now, when he and I meet, after all these years,
I say to the bitch inside me, don't start growling.
He isn't a trespasser anymore,
Just an old acquaintance tipping his hat.
5 My voice says, "Nice to see you,"
As the bitch starts to bark hysterically.
He isn't an enemy now,
Where are your manners, I say, as I say,
"How are the children? They must be growing up."
10 At a kind word from him, a look like the old days,
The bitch changes her tone: she begins to whimper.
She wants to snuggle up to him, to cringe.
Down, girl! Keep your distance
Or I'll give you a taste of the choke-chain.
15 "Fine, I'm just fine," I tell him.
She slobbers and grovels.
After all, I am her mistress. She is basically loyal.
It's just that she remembers how she came running
Each evening, when she heard his step;
20 How she lay at his feet and looked up adoringly
Though he was absorbed in his paper;
Or, bored with her devotion, ordered her to the kitchen
Until he was ready to play.
But the small careless kindnesses

25 When he'd had a good day, or a couple of drinks,
Come back to her now, seem more important
Than the casual cruelties, the ultimate dismissal.
"It's nice to know you are doing so well," I say.
He couldn't have taken you with him;
30 You were too demonstrative, too clumsy,
Not like the well-groomed pets of his new friends.
"Give my regards to your wife," I say. You gag
As I drag you off by the scruff,
Saying, "Goodbye! Goodbye! Nice to have seen you again."

[1984]

Robert Creeley   *1926–*

I KNOW A MAN

As I sd to my
friend, because I am
always talking,—John, I

5 sd, which was not his
name, the darkness sur-
rounds us, what

can we do against
it, or else, shall we &
why not, buy a goddamn big car,

10 drive, he sd, for
christ's sake, look
out where yr going.

[1962]

Alastair Reid   *1926–*

CURIOSITY

may have killed the cat; more likely
the cat was just unlucky, or else curious
to see what death was like, having no cause
to go on licking paws, or fathering
5 litter on litter of kittens, predictably.

Nevertheless, to be curious
is dangerous enough. To distrust
what is always said, what seems,
to ask odd questions, interfere in dreams,
10 leave home, smell rats, have hunches,
cannot endear them to those doggy circles

where well-smelt baskets, suitable wives, good lunches
are the order of things, and where prevails
much wagging of incurious heads and tails.

15   Face it. Curiosity
will not cause him to die—
only lack of it will.
Never to want to see
the other side of the hill
20   or some improbable country
where living is an idyll
(although a probable hell)
would kill us all.
only the curious
25   have, if they live, a tale
worth telling at all.

    Dogs say cats love too much, are irresponsible,
are changeable, marry too many wives,
desert their children, chill all dinner tables
30   with tales of their nine lives.
Well, they are lucky. Let them be
nine-lived and contradictory,
curious enough to change, prepared to pay
the cat-price, which is to die
35   and die again and again,
each time with no less pain.
A cat minority of one
is all that can be counted on
to tell the truth. And what cats have to tell
40   on each return from hell
is this: that dying is what the living do,
that dying is what the loving do,
and that dead dogs are those who never know
that dying is what, to live, each has to do.

[1959]

W. D. Snodgrass *1926–*

APRIL INVENTORY

The green catalpa tree has turned
All white; the cherry blooms once more.
In one whole year I haven't learned
A blessed thing they pay you for.
5   The blossoms snow down in my hair;
The trees and I will soon be bare.

The trees have more than I to spare.
The sleek, expensive girls I teach,
Younger and pinker every year,

10   Bloom gradually out of reach.
      The pear tree lets its petals drop
      Like dandruff on a tabletop.

      The girls have grown so girlish now
      I have to nudge myself to stare.
15   This year they smile and mind me how
      My teeth are falling with my hair.
      In thirty years I may not get
      Younger, shrewder, or out of debt.

      The tenth time, just a year ago,
20   I made myself a little list
      Of all the things I'd ought to know,
      Then told my parents, analyst,
      And everyone who's trusted me
      I'd be substantial, presently.

25   I haven't read one book about
      A book or memorized one plot.
      Or found a mind I did not doubt.
      I learned one date. And then forgot.
      And one by one the solid scholars
30   Get the degrees, the jobs, the dollars.

      And smile above their starchy collars.
      I taught my classes Whitehead's[1] notions;
      One lovely girl, a song of Mahler's.[2]
      Lacking a source book and promotions,
35   I taught one child the colors of
      A luna moth and how to love.

      I taught myself to name my name,
      To bark back, loosen love and crying;
      To ease my woman so she came,
40   To ease an old man who was dying.
      I have not learned how often I
      Can win, can love, but choose to die.

      I have not learned there is a lie
      Love shall be blonder, slimmer, younger;
45   That my equivocating eye
      Loves only by my body's hunger;
      That I have forces, true to feel,
      Or that the lovely world is real.

      While scholars speak authority
50   And wear their ulcers on their sleeves,

[1] Alfred North Whitehead (1861–1947), an English philosopher and mathematician.
[2] Gustav Mahler (1860–1911), an Austrian composer and conductor.

My eyes in spectacles shall see
These trees procure and spend their leaves.
There is a value underneath
The gold and silver in my teeth.

55 Though trees turn bare and girls turn wives,
We shall afford our costly seasons;
There is a gentleness survives
That will outspeak and has its reasons.
There is a loveliness exists,
60 Preserves us; not for specialists.

[1959]

David Wagoner   *1926–*

MEETING A BEAR

If you haven't made noise enough to warn him, singing, shouting,
Or thumping sticks against trees as you walk in the woods,
Giving him time to vanish
(As he wants to) quietly sideways through the nearest thicket,
5   You may wind up standing face to face with a bear.
Your near future,
Even your distant future, may depend on how he feels
Looking at you, on what he makes of you
And your upright posture
10 Which, in his world, like a down-swayed head and humped shoulders,
Is a standing offer to fight for territory
And a mate to go with it.
Gaping and staring directly are as risky as running:
To try for dominance or moral authority
15 Is an empty gesture,
And taking to your heels is an invitation to a dance
Which, from your point of view, will be no circus.
He won't enjoy your smell
Or anything else about you, including your ancestors
20 Or the shape of your snout. If the feeling's mutual,
It's still out of balance:
He doesn't *care* what you think or calculate; your disapproval
Leaves him as cold as the opinions of salmon.
He may feel free
25 To act out all his own displeasures with a vengeance:
You would do well to try your meekest behavior,
Standing still
As long as you're not mauled or hugged, your eyes downcast.
But if you must make a stir, do everything sidelong,
30 Gently and naturally,
Vaguely oblique. Withdraw without turning and start saying
Softly, monotonously, whatever comes to mind
Without special pleading:

Nothing hurt or reproachful to appeal to his better feelings.
35 He has none, only a harder life than yours.
There's no use singing
National anthems or battle hymns or alma maters[1]
Or any other charming or beastly music.
Use only the dullest,
40 Blandest, most colorless, undemonstrative speech you can think of,
Bears, for good reason, find it embarrassing
Or at least disarming
And will forget their claws and cover their eyeteeth as an answer.
Meanwhile, move off, yielding the forest floor
45 As carefully as your honor.

[1975]

WALKING IN A SWAMP

When you first feel the ground under your feet
Going soft and uncertain,
It's best to start running as fast as you can slog
Even though falling
5 Forward on your knees and lunging like a cripple.
You may escape completely
Being bogged down in those few scampering seconds.
But if you're caught standing
In deep mud, unable to walk or stagger,
10 It's time to reconsider
Your favorite postures, textures, and means of moving,
Coming to even terms
With the kind of dirt that won't take no for an answer.
You must lie down now,
15 Like it or not: if you're in it up to your thighs,
Be seated gently,
Lie back, open your arms, and dream of floating
In a sweet backwater.
Slowly your sunken feet will rise together,
20 And you may slither
Spread-ottered casually backwards out of trouble.
If you stay vertical
And, worse, imagine you're in a fearful struggle,
Trying to swivel
25 One stuck leg at a time, keeping your body
Above it all,
Immaculate, you'll sink in even deeper,
Becoming an object lesson
For those who wallow after you through the mire,
30 In which case you should know
For near-future reference: muck is one part water,
One part what-have-you,

---

[1] School or college songs.

Including yourself, now in it over your head,
As upright as ever.

[1975]

James Wright   *1927–1980*

A BLESSING

Just off the highway to Rochester, Minnesota,
Twilight bounds softly forth on the grass.
And the eyes of those two Indian ponies
Darken with kindness.
5   They have come gladly out of the willows
To welcome my friend and me.
We step over the barbed wire into the pasture
Where they have been grazing all day, alone.
They ripple tensely, they can hardly contain their happiness
10 That we have come.
They bow shyly as wet swans. They love each other.
There is no loneliness like theirs.
At home once more,
They begin munching the young tufts of spring in the darkness.
15 I would like to hold the slenderer one in my arms,
For she has walked over to me
And nuzzled my left hand.
She is black and white.
Her mane falls wild on her forehead,
20 And the light breeze moves me to caress her long ear
That is delicate as the skin over a girl's wrist.
Suddenly I realize
That if I stepped out of my body I would break
Into blossom.

[1963]

AUTUMN BEGINS IN MARTINS FERRY, OHIO[1]

In the Shreve High football stadium,
I think of Polacks nursing long beers in Tiltonsville,
And gray faces of Negroes in the blast furnace at Benwood,
And the ruptured night watchman of Wheeling Steel,
5   Dreaming of heroes.

All the proud fathers are ashamed to go home.
Their women cluck like starved pullets,
Dying for love.

---

[1] Martins Ferry and Tiltonsville, Ohio, and Benwood and Wheeling, West Virginia, are all steel towns lying along the banks of the Ohio River that serves as the border between the two states.

Therefore,
10   Their sons grow suicidally beautiful
At the beginning of October,
And gallop terribly against each other's bodies.

[1963]

LYING IN A HAMMOCK AT WILLIAM DUFFY'S FARM IN PINE ISLAND, MINNESOTA

Over my head, I see the bronze butterfly,
Asleep on the black trunk,
Blowing like a leaf in green shadow.
Down the ravine behind the empty house,
5   The cowbells follow one another
Into the distances of the afternoon.
To my right,
In a field of sunlight between two pines,
The droppings of last year's horses
10   Blaze up into golden stones.
I lean back, as the evening darkens and comes on.
A chicken hawk floats over, looking for home.
I have wasted my life.

[1961]

Galway Kinnell *1927–*

BLACKBERRY EATING

I love to go out in late September
among the fat, overripe, icy, black blackberries
to eat blackberries for breakfast,
the stalks very prickly, a penalty
5   they earn for knowing the black art
of blackberry-making; and as I stand among them
lifting the stalks to my mouth, the ripest berries
fall almost unbidden to my tongue,
as words sometimes do, certain peculiar words
10   like *strengths* or *squinched,*
many-lettered, one-syllabled lumps,
which I squeeze, squinch open, and splurge well
in the silent, startled, icy, black language
of blackberry-eating in late September.

[1980]

W. S. Merwin *1927–*

LEVIATHAN[1]

This is the black sea-brute bulling through wave-wrack,
Ancient as ocean's shifting hills, who in sea-toils

---

[1] Literally, any large creature; usually associated with the whale.

Travelling, who furrowing the salt acres
Heavily, his wake hoary behind him,[2]
5   Shoulder spouting, the fist of his forehead
Over wastes gray-green crashing, among horses unbroken
From bellowing fields, past bone-wreck of vessels,
Tide-ruin, wash of lost bodies bobbing
No longer sought for, and islands of ice gleaming,
10 Who ravening the rank flood, wave-marshalling,
Overmastering the dark sea-marches, finds home
And harvest. Frightening to foolhardiest
Mariners, his size were difficult to describe:
The hulk of him is like hills heaving,
15 Dark, yet as crags of drift-ice, crowns cracking in thunder,
Like land's self by night black-looming, surf churning and trailing
Along his shores' rushing, shoal-water boding
About the dark of his jaws; and who should moor at his edge
And fare on afoot would find gates of no gardens,
20 But the hill of dark underfoot diving,
Closing overhead, the cold deep, and drowning.
He is called Leviathan, and named for rolling,
First created he was of all creatures,[3]
He has held Jonah[4] three days and nights,
25 He is that curling serpent that in ocean is,[5]
Sea-fright he is, and the shadow under the earth.
Days there are, nonetheless, when he lies
Like an angel, although a lost angel
On the waste's unease, no eye of man moving,
30 Bird hovering, fish flashing, creature whatever
Who after him came to herit earth's emptiness.
Froth at flanks seething soothes to stillness,
Waits; with one eye he watches
Dark of night sinking last, with one eye dayrise
35 As at first over foaming pastures. He makes no cry
Though that light is a breath. The sea curling,
Star-climbed, wind-combed, cumbered with itself still
As at first it was, is the hand not yet contented
Of the Creator. And he waits for the world to begin.

                                                                    [1956]

THE DRUNK IN THE FURNACE

For a good decade
The furnace stood in the naked gully, fireless
And vacant as any hat. Then when it was
No more to them than a hulking black fossil
5   To erode unnoticed with the rest of the junk-hill
By the poisonous creek, and rapidly to be added
        To their ignorance,

---

[2] See Job 41:32.   [3] See Genesis 1:21.
[4] The Old Testament prophet who was swallowed by a "great fish." See the Book of Jonah.
[5] See Isaiah 27:1.

They were afterwards astonished
To confirm, one morning, a twist of smoke like a pale
10   Resurrection, staggering out of its chewed hole,
And to remark then other tokens that someone,
Cosily bolted behind the eye-holed iron
Door of the drafty burner, had there established
      His bad castle.

15   Where he gets his spirits
It's a mystery. But the stuff keeps him musical:
Hammer-and-anvilling with poker and bottle
To his jugged bellowings, till the last groaning clang
As he collapses onto the rioting
20   Springs of a litter of car-seats ranged on the grates,
      To sleep like an iron pig.

      In their tar-paper church
On a text about stoke-holes that are sated never
Their Reverend lingers. They nod and hate trespassers.
25   When the furnace wakes, though, all afternoon
Their witless offspring flock like piped rats to its siren
Crescendo, and agape on the crumbling ridge
      Stand in a row and learn.

                    [1960]

Anne Sexton   *1928–1974*

LULLABY

It is a summer evening.
The yellow moths sag
against the locked screens
and the faded curtains
5   suck over the window sills
and from another building
a goat calls in his dreams.
This is the TV parlour
in the best ward at Bedlam[1]
10   The night nurse is passing
out the evening pills.
She walks on two erasers,
padding by us one by one.

My sleeping pill is white.
15   It is a splendid pearl;
it floats me out of myself,
my stung skin as alien
as a loose bolt of cloth.

---

[1] A lunatic asylum or madhouse; originally the popular name for the Hospital of St. Mary of Bethlehem
in London, an early asylum for the insane.

20

I will ignore the bed.
I am linen on a shelf.
Let the others moan in secret;
let each lost butterfly
go home. Old woollen head,
take me like a yellow moth

25

while the goat calls hush-
a-bye.

[1960]

HER KIND

I have gone out, a possessed witch,
haunting the black air, braver at night;
dreaming evil, I have done my hitch
over the plain houses, light by light:

5

lonely thing, twelve-fingered, out of mind.
A woman like that is not a woman, quite.
I have been her kind.

I have found the warm caves in the woods,
filled them with skillets, carvings, shelves,

10

closets, silks, innumerable goods;
fixed the suppers for the worms and the elves:
whining, rearranging the disaligned.
A woman like that is misunderstood.
I have been her kind.

15

I have ridden in your cart, driver,
waved my nude arms at villages going by,
learning the last bright routes, survivor
where your flames still bite my thigh
and my ribs crack where your wheels wind.

20

A woman like that is not ashamed to die.
I have been her kind.

[1960]

THE TRUTH THE DEAD KNOW

*For My Mother, Born March 1902, Died March 1959
and My Father, Born February 1900, Died June 1959*

Gone, I say and walk from church,
refusing the stiff procession to the grave,
letting the dead ride alone in the hearse.
It is June. I am tired of being brave.

5

We drive to the Cape.[1] I cultivate
myself where the sun gutters from the sky,

---

[1] Cape Cod, Massachusetts.

where the sea swings in like an iron gate
and we touch. In another country people die.

My darling, the wind falls in like stones
10   from the whitehearted water and when we touch
we enter touch entirely. No one's alone.
Men kill for this, or for as much.

And what of the dead? They lie without shoes
in their stone boats. They are more like stone
15   than the sea would be if it stopped. They refuse
to be blessed, throat, eye and knucklebone.

[1962]

Maya Angelou   *1928–*

MY ARKANSAS

There is a deep brooding
In Arkansas.
Old crimes like moss pend
from poplar trees.
5   The sullen earth
is much too
red for comfort.

Sunrise seems to hesitate
and in that second
10   lose its
incandescent aim, and
dusk no more shadows
than the noon.
The past is brighter yet.

15   Old hates and
ante-bellum lace, are rent
but not discarded.
Today is yet to come
in Arkansas.
20   It writhes. It writhes in awful
waves of brooding.

[1978]

THE HEALTH-FOOD DINER

No sprouted wheat and soya shoots
And Brussels in a cake,
Carrot straw and spinach raw,
(Today, I need a steak).

5   Not thick brown rice and rice pilau
                         Or mushrooms creamed on toast,
                         Turnips mashed and parsnips hashed,
                         (I'm dreaming of a roast).

                         Health-food folks around the world
10   Are thinned by anxious zeal,
                         They look for help in seafood kelp
                         (I count on breaded veal).

                         No Smoking signs, raw mustard greens,
                         Zucchini by the ton,
15   Uncooked kale and bodies frail
                         Are sure to make me run
                                     to

                         Loins of pork and chicken thighs
                         And standing rib, so prime,
                         Pork chops brown and fresh ground round
20   (I crave them all the time).

                         Irish stews and boiled corned beef
                         and hot dogs by the scores,
                         or any place that saves a space
                         For smoking carnivores.

                                   [1983]

ON THE PULSE OF MORNING

    A Rock, A River, A Tree
    Hosts to species long since departed,
    Marked the mastodon,
    The dinosaur, who left dried tokens
5   Of their sojourn here
    On our planet floor,
    Any broad alarm of their hastening doom
    Is lost in the gloom of dust and ages.

    But today, the Rock cries out to us, clearly, forcefully,
10 Come, you may stand upon my
    Back and face your distant destiny,
    But seek no haven in my shadow.
    I will give you no hiding place down here.

    You, created only a little lower than
15 The angels, have crouched too long in
    The bruising darkness
    Have lain too long
    Face down in ignorance.
    Your mouths spilling words

20   Armed for slaughter.
The Rock cries out to us today, you may stand upon me,
But do not hide your face.

Across the wall of the world,
A River sings a beautiful song. It says,
25   Come, rest here by my side.

Each of you, a bordered country,
Delicate and strangely made proud,
Ye thrusting perpetually under siege.
Your armed struggles for profit
30   Have left collars of waste upon
My shore, currents of debris upon my breast.
Yet today I call you to my riverside,
If you will study war no more. Come,
Clad in peace, and I will sing the songs
35   The Creator gave to me when I and the
Tree and the rock were one.
Before cynicism was a bloody sear across your
Brow and when you yet knew you still knew nothing.
The River sang and sings on.

40   There is a true yearning to respond to
The singing River and the wise Rock.
So say the Asian, the Hispanic, the Jew
The African, the Native American, the Sioux,
The Catholic, the Muslim, the French, the Greek
45   The Irish, the Rabbi, the Priest, the Sheik,
The Gay, the Straight, the Preacher,
The privileged, the homeless, the Teacher.

They hear. They all hear.
The speaking of the Tree.

50   They hear the first and last of every Tree
Speak to humankind today. Come to me,
here beside the River.
Plant yourself beside the River.

Each of you, descendant of some passed
55   On traveller, has been paid for.
You, who gave me my first name, you
Pawnee, Apache, Seneca, you
Cherokee Nation, who rested with me, then
Forced on bloody feet, left me to the employment of
60   Other seekers—desperate for gain, starving for gold.
You, the Turk, the Arab, the Swede, the German, the Es-
    kimo, the Scot,
You the Ashanti, the Yoruba, the Kru, bought,
Sold, stolen, arriving on a nightmare
Praying for a dream.

65   Here, root yourselves beside me.
      I am that Tree planted by the River,
      Which will not be moved.
      I, the Rock, I, the River, I, the Tree
      I am yours—your passages have been paid.
70   Lift up your faces, you have a piercing need
      For this bright morning dawning for you.
      History, despite its wrenching pain,
      Cannot be unlived, but if faced
      With courage, need not be lived again.

75   Lift up your eyes upon
      This day breaking for you.
      Give birth again
      To the dream.

      Women, children, men,
80   Take it into the palms of your hands,
      Mold it into the shape of your most
      Private need. Sculpt it into
      The image of your most public self.
      Lift up your hearts
85   Each new hour holds new chances
      For a new beginning.
      Do not be wedded forever
      To fear, yoked eternally
      To brutishness.

90   The horizon leans forward,
      Offering you space to place new steps of change.
      Here, on the pulse of this fine day
      You may have the courage
      To look up and out and upon me, the
95   Rock, the River, the Tree, your country.
      No less to Midas than the mendicant.
      No less to you now than the mastodon then.

      Here, on the pulse of this new day
      You may have the grace to look up and out
100   And into your sister's eyes, and into
      Your brother's face, your country
      And say simply
      Very simply
      With hope—
105   Good morning.

                                                    [1993]

Cynthia Macdonald   *1928–*

TWO BROTHERS IN A FIELD OF ABSENCE

Because as they cut it was that special green, they decided
To make a woman of the fresh hay. They wished to lie in green, to wrap

Themselves in it, light but not pale, silvered but not grey.
Green and ample, big enough so both of them could shelter together
5   In any of her crevices, the armpit, the join
Of hip and groin. They—who knew what there was to know, about baling
The modern way with hay so you rolled it up like a carpet,
Rather than those loose stacks—they packed the green body tight
So she wouldn't fray. Each day they moulted her to keep her
10 Green and soft. Only her hair was allowed to ripen into yellow tousle.

The next weeks whenever they stopped cutting they lay with her.
She was always there, waiting, reliable, their green woman.
She gathered them in, yes she did,
Into the folds of herself, like the mother they hadn't had.
15 Like the women they had had, only more pliant, more graceful,
Welcoming in a way you never just found.
They not only had the awe of taking her,
But the awe of having made her. They drank beer
Leaning against the pillow of her belly
20 And one would tell the other, "Like two Adams creating."
And they marveled as they placed
The cans at her ankles, at her neck, at her wrists so she
Glittered gold and silver. They adorned what they'd made.
After harrowing they'd come to her, drawing
25 The fountains of the Plains, the long line
Of irrigating spray and moisten her up.
And lean against her tight, green thighs to watch buzzards
Circle black against the pink stain of the sunset.
What time she began to smolder they never knew—
30 Sometime between night when they'd left her
And evening when they returned. Wet, green hay
Can go a long time smoldering before you notice. It has a way
Of catching itself, of asserting that
There is no dominion over it but the air. And it flares suddenly
35 Like a red head losing her temper, and allows its long bright hair
To tangle in the air, letting you know again
That what shelters you can turn incendiary in a flash.
And then there is only the space of what has been,
An absence in the field, memory in the shape of a woman.

                                                                                                [1991]

Richard Howard   *1929*–

OYSTERING

"Messieurs, l'huitre étoit bonne. Adieu. Vivez en paix."
                                        —*Boileau*[1]

Secret they are, sealed, annealed, and brainless
And solitary as Dickens[2] said, but

---

[1] The quotation is from the French poet Nicholas Boileau (1636–1711): "Sirs, the oyster was good. Farewell. Live in peace."
[2] Charles Dickens (1812–1870), the British novelist.

They have something to say: that there is more
Than one way to yield. The first—and the hardest,
5 The most nearly hindered—is when you pull
Them off the rocks, a stinking, sawing sedge
Sucking them back under the black mud, full
Of hermit crabs and their borrowed snailshells,
Minnows scattering like superstitions,
10 The surf dragging, and every power
Life permits them holding out, holding on
For dear life. Sometimes the stones give way first,
Before *they* will, but still we gather them,
Even if our hands are bloody as meat,
15 For a lunch Queen Victoria preferred:
"A barrel of Wellfleet oysters, points down"
Could last across the ocean, all the way
To Windsor, wakening a widow's taste.
We ate them this afternoon, out of their
20 Armor that was formidably grooved, though
It proved our own reversal wiser still:
Keep the bones and stones inside, or never
Leave the sea. "He was a brave man," Swift[3] said,
"Who first eat one." Even now, precedent
25 Of centuries is not always enough.
Driving the knife into muscles that mould
The valves so close to being impartial,
Surrender, when it comes—and it must come:
Lavish after that first grudging release
30 Back there in the sea, the giving over
Of despair, this time—makes me speculate.
Like Oscar and oysters, I feel "always
Slightly immortal when in the sea": what
Happens now we are out? Is the risk worth
35 While for a potential pearl? No, what we're
Really after is the moment of release,
The turn and tear of the blade that tightens,
Tortures, ultimately tells. When you spread
The shells, something always sticks to the wrong
40 One, and a few drops of liquor dribble
Into the sand. Scrape it off: in the full
Half, as well as a Fautrier, a Zen
Garden, and the smell of herring brine that
Ferenczi said we remember from the womb,
45 Lunch is served, in shiny stoneware sockets,
Blue milk in the sea's filthiest cup. More
Easily an emblem for the inner man
Than dinner, sundered, for the stomach. We
Take them queasily, wonder as we gulp
50 When it is—then, now, tomorrow—they're dead.

[1967]

---

[3] Jonathan Swift (1667–1745), Irish satirist and poet.

Thom Gunn   *1929–*

BLACK JACKETS

In the silence that prolongs the span
Rawly of music when the record ends,
   The red-haired boy who drove a van
In weekday overalls but, like his friends,

5   Wore cycle boots and jacket here
To suit the Sunday hangout he was in,
   Heard, as he stretched back from his beer,
Leather creak softly round his neck and chin.

      Before him, on a coal-black sleeve
10   Remote exertion had lined, scratched, and burned
   Insignia that could not revive
The heroic fall or climb where they were earned.

      On the other drinkers bent together,
Concocting selves for their impervious kit,
15   He saw it as no more than leather
Which, taut across the shoulders grown to it,

      Sent through the dimness of a bar
As sudden and anonymous hints of light
   As those that shipping give, that are
20   Now flickers in the Bay, now lost in night.

He stretched out like a cat, and rolled
The bitterish taste of beer upon his tongue,
   And listened to a joke being told:
The present was the things he stayed among.

25   If it was only loss he wore,
He wore it to assert, with fierce devotion,
   Complicity and nothing more.
He recollected his initiation,

      And one especially of the rites.
30   For on his shoulders they had put tattoos:
   The group's name on the left, The Knights,
And on the right the slogan Born To Lose.

[1973]

X. J. Kennedy   *1929–*

CROSS TIES

Out walking ties left over from a track
Where nothing travels now but rust and grass,

I could take stock in something that would pass
Bearing down Hell-bent from behind my back:
5 A thing to sidestep or go down before,
Far-off, indifferent as that curfew's wail
The evening wind flings like a sack of mail
Or close up as the moon whose headbeam stirs
A flock of cloud to make tracks. Down to strafe
10 The bristled grass a hawk falls—there's a screech
Like steel wrenched taut till severed. Out of reach
Or else beneath desiring, I go safe,
Walk on, tensed for a leap, unreconciled
To a dark void all kindness.
                                    When I spill
15 The salt I throw the Devil some and, still,
I let them sprinkle water on my child.

                                                 [1969]

Adrienne Rich   *1929–*

AUNT JENNIFER'S TIGERS

Aunt Jennifer's tigers prance across a screen,
Bright topaz denizens of a world of green.
They do not fear the men beneath the tree;
They pace in sleek chivalric certainty.

5 Aunt Jennifer's fingers fluttering through her wool
Find even the ivory needle hard to pull.
The massive weight of Uncle's wedding band
Sits heavily upon Aunt Jennifer's hand.

When Aunt is dead, her terrified hands will lie
10 Still ringed with ordeals she was mastered by.
The tigers in the panel that she made
Will go on prancing, proud and unafriad.

                                                 [1951]

STORM WARNINGS

The glass° has been falling all the afternoon,   *barometer*
And knowing better than the instrument
What winds are walking overhead, what zone
Of gray unrest is moving across the land,
5 I leave the book upon a pillowed chair
And walk from window to closed window, watching
Boughs strain against the sky

And think again, as often when the air
Moves inward toward a silent core of waiting,

10   How with a single purpose time has traveled
        By secret currents of the undiscerned
        Into this polar realm. Weather abroad
        And weather in the heart alike come on
        Regardless of prediction.

15   Between foreseeing and averting change
        Lies all the mastery of elements
        Which clocks and weatherglasses cannot alter.
        Time in the hand is not control of time,
        Nor shattered fragments of an instrument
20   A proof against the wind; the wind will rise,
        We can only close the shutters.

        I draw the curtains as the sky goes black
        And set a match to candles sheathed in glass
        Against the keyhole draught, the insistent whine
25   Of weather through the unsealed aperture.
        This is our sole defense against the season;
        These are the things that we have learned to do
        Who live in troubled regions.

                                          [1951]

THE KNIGHT

        A knight rides into the noon,
        and his helmet points to the sun,
        and a thousand splintered suns
        are the gaiety of his mail.
5   The soles of his feet glitter
        and his palms flash in reply,
        and under his crackling banner
        he rides like a ship in sail.

        A knight rides into the noon,
10   and only his eye is living,
        a lump of bitter jelly
        set in a metal mask,
        betraying rags and tatters
        that cling to the flesh beneath
15   and wear his nerves to ribbons
        under the radiant casque.

        Who will unhorse this rider
        and free him from between
        the walls of iron, the emblems
20   crushing his chest with their weight?
        Will they defeat him gently,
        or leave him hurled on the green,

his rags and wounds still hidden
under the great breastplate?

[1957]

Ted Hughes   *1930–*

PIKE

Pike, three inches long, perfect
Pike in all parts, green tigering the gold.
Killers from the egg: the malevolent aged grin.
They dance on the surface among the flies.

5   Or move, stunned by their own grandeur,
Over a bed of emerald, silhouette
Of submarine delicacy and horror.
A hundred feet long in their world.

In ponds, under the heat-struck lily pads—
10   Gloom of their stillness:
Logged on last year's black leaves, watching upwards.
Or hung in an amber cavern of weeds

The jaw's hooked clamp and fangs
Not to be changed at this date;
15   A life subdued to its instrument;
The gills kneading quietly, and the pectorals.

Three we kept behind glass,
Jungled in weed: three inches, four,
And four and a half: fed fry to them—
20   Suddenly there were two. Finally one

With a sag belly and the grin it was born with.
And indeed they spare nobody.
Two, six pounds each, over two feet long,
High and dry and dead in the willow-herb—

25   One jammed past its gills down the other's gullet:
The outside eye stared: as a vice locks—
The same iron in this eye
Though its film shrank in death.

A pond I fished, fifty yards across,
30   Whose lilies and muscular tench[1]
Had outlasted every visible stone
Of the monastery that planted them—

[1] Fish similar to carp.

Stilled legendary depth:
It was as deep as England. It held
35   Pike too immense to stir, so immense and old
That past nightfall I dared not cast

But silently cast and fished
With the hair frozen on my head
For what might move, for what eye might move.
40   The still splashes on the dark pond,

Owls hushing the floating woods
Frail on my ear against the dream
Darkness beneath night's darkness had freed,
That rose slowly towards me, watching.

[1959]

AN OTTER

I

Underwater eyes, an eel's
Oil of water body, neither fish nor beast is the otter:
Four-legged yet water-gifted, to outfish fish;
With webbed feet and long ruddering tail
5   And a round head like an old tomcat.

Brings the legend of himself
From before wars or burials, in spite of hounds and vermin-poles;
Does not take root like the badger. Wanders, cries;
Gallops along land he no longer belongs to;
10   Re-enters the water by melting.

Of neither water nor land. Seeking
Some world lost when first he dived, that he cannot come at since,
Takes his changed body into the holes of lakes;
As if blind, cleaves the stream's push till he licks
15   The pebbles of the source; from sea

To sea crosses in three nights
Like a king in hiding. Crying to the old shape of the starlit land,
Over sunken farms where the bats go round,
Without answer. Till light and birdsong come
20   Walloping up roads with the milk wagon.

II

The hunt's lost him. Pads on mud,
Among sedges, nostrils a surface bead,
The otter remains, hours. The air,
Circling the globe, tainted and necessary,

25 Mingling tobacco-smoke, hounds and parsley,
Comes carefully to the sunk lungs.
So the self under the eye lies,
Attendant and withdrawn. The otter belongs

In double robbery and concealment—
30 From water that nourishes and drowns, and from land
That gave him his length and the mouth of the hound.
He keeps fat in the limpid integument

Reflections live on. The heart beats thick,
Big trout muscle out of the dead cold;
35 Blood is the belly of logic; he will lick
The fishbone bare. And can take stolen hold

On a bitch otter in a field full
Of nervous horses, but linger nowhere.
Yanked above hounds, reverts to nothing at all,
40 To this long pelt over the back of a chair.

[1960]

Ruth Fainlight   *1931–*

FLOWER FEET

(SILK SHOES IN THE WHITWORTH ART GALLERY, MANCHESTER, ENGLAND)

Real women's feet wore these objects
that look like toys or spectacle cases stitched
from bands of coral, jade, and apricot silk
embroidered with twined sprays of flowers.
5 Those hearts, tongues, crescents, and disks, leather
shapes an inch across, are the soles of shoes
no wider or longer than the span of my ankle.
If the feet had been cut off and the raw stumps
thrust inside the openings, surely
10 it could not hurt more than broken toes, twisted
back and bandaged tight. An old woman,
leaning on a cane outside her door
in a Chinese village, smiled to tell how
she fought and cried, how when she stood on points
15 of pain that gnawed like fire, nurse and mother
praised her tottering walk on flower feet.
Her friends nodded, glad the times had changed.
Otherwise, they would have crippled their daughters.

[1989]

George Starbuck   *1931–*

MARGARET ARE YOU DRUG[1]

Cool it Mag.
Sure it's a drag
With all that green flaked out.
Next thing you know they'll be changing the color of bread.

5   But look, Chick,
Why panic?
Sevennyeighty years, we'll *all* be dead.

Roll with it, Kid,
I did.
10   Give it the old benefit of the doubt.

I mean leaves
Schmeaves.
You sure you aint just feeling sorry for yourself?

[1966]

Sylvia Plath   *1932–1963*

METAPHORS

I'm a riddle in nine syllables,
An elephant, a ponderous house,
A melon strolling on two tendrils.
O red fruit, ivory, fine timbers!
5   This loaf's big with its yeasty rising.
Money's new-minted in this fat purse.
I'm a means, a stage, a cow in calf.
I've eaten a bag of green apples,
Boarded the train there's no getting off.

[1960]

MEDALLION

By the gate with star and moon
Worked into the peeled orange wood
The bronze snake lay in the sun

Inert as a shoelace; dead
5   But pliable still, his jaw
Unhinged and his grin crooked,

---

[1] This is one of Starbuck's "Translations from the English." Compare it with its source poem, Gerard Manley Hopkins's "Spring and Fall" (p. 927).

Tongue a rose-colored arrow.
Over my hand I hung him.
His little vermilion eye

10 Ignited with a glassed flame
As I turned him in the light;
When I split a rock one time

The garnet bits burned like that.
Dust dulled his back to ochre
15 The way sun ruins a trout.

Yet his belly kept its fire
Going under the chainmail,
The old jewels smoldering there

In each opaque belly-scale:
20 Sunset looked at through milk glass.
And I saw white maggots coil

Thin as pins in the dark bruise
Where his innards bulged as if
He were digesting a mouse.

25 Knifelike, he was chaste enough,
Pure death's metal. The yardman's
Flung brick perfected his laugh.

[1962]

MIRROR

I am silver and exact. I have no preconceptions.
Whatever I see I swallow immediately
Just as it is, unmisted by love or dislike.
I am not cruel, only truthful—
5 The eye of a little god, four-cornered.
Most of the time I meditate on the opposite wall.
It is pink, with speckles. I have looked at it so long
I think it is a part of my heart. But it flickers.
Faces and darkness separate us over and over.

10 Now I am a lake. A woman bends over me,
Searching my reaches for what she really is.
Then she turns to those liars, the candles or the moon.
I see her back, and reflect it faithfully.
She rewards me with tears and an agitation of hands.
15 I am important to her. She comes and goes.
Each morning it is her face that replaces the darkness.
In me she has drowned a young girl, and in me an old woman
Rises toward her day after day, like a terrible fish.

[1963]

Peter Meinke   *1932–*

ADVICE TO MY SON

The trick is, to live your days
as if each one may be your last
(for they go fast, and young men lose their lives
in strange and unimaginable ways)
but at the same time, plan long range
(for they go slow: if you survive
the shattered windshield and the bursting shell
you will arrive
at our approximation here below
of heaven or hell).

To be specific, between the peony and the rose
plant squash and spinach, turnips and tomatoes;
beauty is nectar
and nectar, in a desert, saves—
but the stomach craves stronger sustenance
than the honied vine.

Therefore, marry a pretty girl
after seeing her mother;
speak truth to one man,
work with another;
and always serve bread with your wine.

But, son
always serve wine.

[1965]

Linda Pastan   *1932–*

JUMP CABLING

When our cars   touched
When you lifted the hood   of mine
To see the intimate workings   underneath,
When we were bound   together
By a pulse of pure   energy,
When my car like the   princess
In the tale woke with a   start,
I thought why not ride the rest of the way together?

[1984]

ETHICS

In ethics class so many years ago
our teacher asked this question every fall:
if there were a fire in a museum
which would you save, a Rembrandt[1] painting
5   or an old woman who hadn't many
years left anyhow? Restless on hard chairs
caring little for pictures or old age
we'd opt one year for life, the next for art
and always half-heartedly. Sometimes
10   the woman borrowed my grandmother's face
leaving her usual kitchen to wander
some drafty, half-imagined museum.
One year, feeling clever, I replied
why not let the woman decide herself?
15   Linda, the teacher would report, eschews
the burdens of responsibility.
This fall in a real museum I stand
before a real Rembrandt, old woman,
or nearly so, myself. The colors
20   within this frame are darker than autumn,
darker even than winter—the browns of earth,
though earth's most radiant elements burn
through the canvas. I know now that woman
and painting and season are almost one
25   and all beyond saving by children.

[1978]

MARKS

My husband gives me an A
for last night's supper,
an incomplete for my ironing,
a B plus in bed.
5   My son says I am average,
an average mother, but if
I put my mind to it
I could improve.
My daughter believes
10   in Pass/Fail and tells me
I pass. Wait 'til they learn
I'm dropping out.

[1978]

---

[1] Rembrandt van Rijn (1606–1669) was a Dutch painter and graphic artist of enormous fame and influence.

Felix Mnthali   *1933*–

THE STRANGLEHOLD OF ENGLISH LIT

(For Molara Ogundipe-Leslie)

Those questions, sister,
Those questions
      stand
      stab
5   jab
    and gore
too close to the centre!

For if we had asked
why Jane Austen's people[1]
10 carouse all day
and do no work

would Europe in Africa
have stood
the test of time?
15 and would she still maul
the flower of our youth
in the south?
Would she?

Your elegance of deceit,
20 Jane Austen,
lulled the sons and daughters
of the dispossessed
into a calf-love
with irony and satire
25 around imaginary people.

While history went on mocking
the victims of branding irons
and sugar-plantations
that made Jane Austen's people
30 wealthy beyond compare!

Eng. Lit., my sister,
was more than a cruel joke—
it was the heart
of alien conquest.

35 How could questions be asked
at Makerere and Ibadan,

---

[1] Jane Austen (1775–1817) wrote a series of famous novels about the life of the gentry in early nineteenth-century England.

Dakar and Ford Hare—
with Jane Austen
at the centre?
40   How could they be answered?
[1961]

Wole Soyinka   *1934–*

TELEPHONE CONVERSATION

The price seemed reasonable, location
Indifferent. The landlady swore she lived
Off premises. Nothing remained
But self-confession. "Madam," I warned,
5   "I hate a wasted journey—I am African."
Silence. Silenced transmission of
Pressurized good-breeding. Voice, when it came,
Lipstick coated, long gold-rolled
Cigarette-holder pipped. Caught I was, foully.
10   "HOW DARK?" . . . I had not misheard. . . . "ARE YOU LIGHT
OR VERY DARK?" Button B. Button A. Stench
Of rancid breath of public hide-and-speak.
Red booth. Red pillar-box. Red double-tiered
Omnibus squelching tar. It *was* real! Shamed
15   By ill-mannered silence, surrender
Pushed dumbfoundment to beg simplification.
Considerate she was, varying the emphasis—
"ARE YOU DARK? OR VERY LIGHT?" Revelation came.
"You mean—like plain or milk chocolate?"
20   Her assent was clinical, crushing in its light
Impersonality. Rapidly, wave-length adjusted.
I chose. "West African sepia"—and as afterthought,
"Down in my passport." Silence for spectroscopic
Flight of fancy, till truthfulness clanged her accent
25   Hard on the mouthpiece. "WHAT'S THAT?" conceding
"DON'T KNOW WHAT THAT IS." "Like brunette."
"THAT'S DARK, ISN'T IT?" "Not altogether.
Facially, I am brunette, but madam, you should see
The rest of me. Palm of my hand, soles of my feet
30   Are a peroxide blonde. Friction, caused—
Foolishly madam—by sitting down, has turned
My bottom raven black—One moment madam!"—sensing
Her receiver rearing on the thunderclap
About my ears—"Madam," I pleaded, "wouldn't you rather
35   See for yourself?"
[1960]

Marge Piercy   *1936–*

TO BE OF USE

The people I love the best
jump into work head first
without dallying in the shallows
and swim off with sure strokes almost out of sight.
5   They seem to become natives of that element,
the black sleek heads of seals
bouncing like half-submerged balls.

I love people who harness themselves, an ox to a heavy cart,
who pull like water buffalo, with massive patience,
10   who strain in the mud and the muck to move things forward,
who do what has to be done, again and again.

I want to be with people who submerge
in the task, who go into the fields to harvest
and work in a row and pass the bags along,
15   who stand in the line and haul in their places,
who are not parlor generals and field deserters
but move in a common rhythm
when the food must come in or the fire be put out.

The work of the world is common as mud.
20   Botched, it smears the hands, crumbles to dust.
But the thing worth doing well done
has a shape that satisfies, clean and evident.
Greek amphoras for wine or oil,
Hopi[1] vases that held corn, are put in museums
25   but you know they were made to be used.
The pitcher cries for water to carry
and a person for work that is real.

                                                                                    [1973]

A WORK OF ARTIFICE

The bonsai tree
in the attractive pot
could have grown eighty feet tall
on the side of a mountain
5   till split by lightning.
But a gardener
carefully pruned it.
It is nine inches high.
Every day as he

---

[1] A tribe of Pueblo Indians living in northeastern Arizona and known for the beauty of their pottery; the name *Hopi* means "the peaceful ones."

10   whittles back the branches
      the gardener croons,
      It is your nature
      to be small and cozy,
      domestic and weak;
15   how lucky, little tree,
      to have a pot to grow in.
      With living creatures
      one must begin very early
      to dwarf their growth:
20   the bound feet,
      the crippled brain,
      the hair in curlers,
      the hands you
      love to touch.

                                    [1973]

THE WOMAN IN THE ORDINARY

      The woman in the
      ordinary pudgy graduate student girl
      is crouching with eyes and muscles clenched.
      Round and smooth as a pebble
5   you efface yourself
      under ripples of conversation and debate.
      The woman in the block of ivory soap
      has massive thighs that neigh
      and great breasts and strong arms that blare and trumpet.
10   The woman of the golden fleece
      laughs from the belly uproariously
      inside the girl who imitates
      a Christmas card virgin with glued hands.
      It is time to bust out of girlscout camp.
15   It is time to stop running
      for most popular sweetheart of Campbell Soup.
      You are still searching for yourself in others' eyes
      and creeping so you wont be punished.
      In you bottled up is a woman peppery as curry,
20   a yam of a woman of butter and brass,
      compounded of acid and sweet like a pineapple,
      like a handgrenade set to explode,
      like goldenrod ready to bloom.

                                    [1971]

Blanche Farley   *1937–*

THE LOVER NOT TAKEN

      Committed to one, she wanted both
      And, mulling it over, long she stood,

Alone on the road, loath
To leave, wanting to hide in the undergrowth.
5   This new guy, smooth as a yellow wood

Really turned her on. She liked his hair,
His smile. But the other, Jack, had a claim
On her already and she had to admit, he did wear
Well. In fact, to be perfectly fair,
10 He understood her. His long, lithe frame

Beside hers in the evening tenderly lay.
Still, if this blond guy dropped by someday,
Couldn't way just lead on to way?
No. For if way led on and Jack
15 Found out, she doubted if he would ever come back.

Oh, she turned with a sigh.
Somewhere ages and ages hence,
She might be telling this. "And I—"
She would say, "stood faithfully by."
20 But by then who would know the difference?

With that in mind, she took the fast way home,
The road by the pond, and phoned the blond.
                                        [1984]

Amy Jo Schoonover   *1937–*

RONDEAU:[1] AN UN-LOVE SONG

Among the other things that do not matter
I hear you boasting your unending love.
That trap, at least, I know to rise above
As quicksand lie or envy's brittle patter.

5   While dreams decay and lifetime idols shatter
What in the world can you be thinking of?
Among the other things that do not matter
I hear you boasting your unending love.

I watch the rosy petals fall and scatter
10 And listen for the melancholy dove:
He does not mourn his poor rejected love!

---

[1] In a letter to the editors, Ms. Schoonover has pointed out that this is "a Rondeau in the style of Charles d'Orleans." A brief definition of a rondeau may be found in the glossary at the back of this book.

You mimic now the squirrel's antic chatter
Among the other things that do not matter.
[1978]

Robert Phillips *1938–*

MIDDLE AGE: A NOCTURNE

The silver tea service
assembles, stands at attention
when you walk by.
Like some lost regiment,
it wears tarnished coats.

The grand piano bares
yellowed teeth as you
give it the brushoff.
You no longer tickle its fancy.
The feeling is mutual.

The liquor cabinet chokes
on dusty bottles. You're forbidden.
In the wines, sediment
settles like sentiment,
like expectations.

You visit your children's rooms.
In their sleep they breathe
heavily. In their waking
they bear new adulthood
easily. They don't need you.

In her dreams your wife sheds
responsibilities like cellulite,
acquires a new habit.
A gaunt nun of the old order,
she bends to a mystical flame.

All the pictures have been
looked at, all the books read.
Your former black mistress,
the telephone, hangs around;
there's no one you want to call.

But early this morning,
in the upper field—
seven young deer
grazing in the rain!
[1966]

Margaret Atwood   *1939–*

YOU FIT INTO ME

you fit into me
like a hook into an eye

a fish hook
an open eye

[1971]

Pattiann Rogers   *1940–*

PORTRAIT

This is a picture of you
Reading this poem. Concentrate
On the finite movement
Of your eyes as they travel
5   At this moment across
The page, your fingers
Maintaining the stability
Of the sheet. Focus on the particular
Fall of your hair, the scent
10   Of your hands, the placement of your
Feet now as they acknowledge
Their name.

Simultaneously with these words, be aware
Of your tongue against
15   Your teeth, the aura
Of heat at your neckline
And wrists, the sense
Of your breath inside its own hollows.

Imagine yourself
20   Ten feet away and look back
At your body positioned
Here with this book. Picture
The perspective, the attitude
Of your shoulders and hips,
25   The bend of your head as you
Read of yourself.

Watch how you turn back as you
Remember the sounds surrounding you now,
As you recall the odors
30   Of wood fibers in this place
Or the lack of them.

And take note of this part
Of your portrait—the actual
Mechanism by which you are perceiving
35   The picture, the fixed
Expression on your face as you
Arrange these words at this moment
Into their proper circles, as you
Straighten out the aspects
40   Of the page, the linguistics of the sight
And color of light on the paper.

This is the printed
Form of you watching
Yourself now as you consider
45   Your person. This portrait is
Finished when you raise
Your eyes.

[1978]

Sharon Olds   *1942*–

SEX WITHOUT LOVE

How do they do it, the ones who make love
without love? Beautiful as dancers,
gliding over each other like ice-skaters
over the ice, fingers hooked
5   inside each other's bodies, faces
red as steak, wine, wet as the
children at birth whose mothers are going to
give them away. How do they come to the
come to the   come to the   God   come to the
10   still waters, and not love
the one who came there with them, light
rising slowly as steam off their joined
skin? These are the true religious,
the purists, the pros, the ones who will not
15   accept a false Messiah, love the
priest instead of the God. They do not
mistake the lover for their own pleasure,
they are like great runners: they know they are alone
with the road surface, the cold, the wind,
20   the fit of their shoes, their over-all cardio-
vascular health—just factors, like the partner
in the bed, and not the truth, which is the
single body alone in the universe
against its own best time.

[1984]

Nikki Giovanni   *1943–*

POETRY

poetry is motion graceful
as a fawn
gentle as a teardrop
strong like the eye
5 finding peace in a crowded room
we poets tend to think
our words are golden
though emotion speaks too
loudly to be defined
10 by silence

sometimes after midnight or just before
the dawn
we sit typewriter in hand
pulling loneliness around us
15 forgetting our lovers or children
who are sleeping
ignoring the weary wariness
of our own logic
to compose a poem
20   no one understands it
it never says "love me" for poets are
beyond love
it never says "accept me" for poems seek not
acceptance but controversy
25 it only says "i am" and therefore
i concede that you are too

a poem is pure energy
horizontally contained
between the mind
30 of the poet and the ear of the reader
if it does not sing discard the ear
for poetry is song
if it does not delight discard
the heart for poetry is joy
35 if it does not inform then close
off the brain for it is dead
if it cannot heed the insistent message
that life is precious

which is all we poets
40 wrapped in our loneliness
are trying to say

[1975]

Wendy Rose   *1948–*

LOO-WIT[1]

The way they do
this old woman
no longer cares
what others think
5   but spits her black tobacco
any which way
stretching full length
from her bumpy bed.
Finally up
10   she sprinkles ash on the snow,
cold and rocky buttes
that promise nothing
but winter is going at last.
Centuries of cedar
15   have bound her to earth,
huckleberry ropes
lay prickly about her neck.
Her children play games
(no sense of tomorrow);
20   her eyes are covered
with bark and she wakes
at night, fears
she is blind.
Nothing but tricks
25   left in this world,
nothing to keep
an old woman home.
Around her
machinery growls,
30   snarls and ploughs
great patches of her skin.
She crouches
in the north,
the source
35   of her trembling—
dawn appearing
with the shudder
of her slopes.
Blackberries unravel,
40   stones dislodge;
it's not as if
they weren't warned.

---

[1] A Native American word meaning "lady of fire" and referring to Mt. St. Helens, the volcano in Washington that erupted explosively on May 18, 1980.

She was sleeping
but she heard the boot scrape,
45 the creaking floor;
felt the pull of the blanket
from her thin shoulder.
With one free hand
she finds her weapons
50 and raises them high;
clearing the twigs from her throat
she sings, she sings,
shaking the sky like a blanket about her
Loo-wit sings and sings and sings!

[1983]

Michael Blumenthal *1949–*

BACK FROM THE WORD PROCESSING COURSE, I SAY TO MY OLD TYPEWRITER

Old friend, you
who were once in the avant-garde,
you of the thick cord
and the battered plug,
5 the slow and deliberate characters
proportionally spaced, shall we
go on together as before?
Shall we remain married
out of the cold dittos of conviction
10 and habit? Or should we move on
to some new technology of ease
and embellishment—Should I run off
with her, so much like you when
you were young, my aged Puella
15 of the battered keys, so lovely
in that bleached light of the first morning?

Old horse,
what will it be like
when the next young filly
20 comes along? How will I love you,
crate of my practised strokes,
when she cries out: *new new*
and asks me to dance again?
Oh plow for now, old boat,
25 through these familiar waters,
make the tides come in
once more! Concubined love,
take me again into your easy arms,
make this page wild once more
30 like a lustful sheet! Be wet,
sweet toy, with your old ink:

vibrate those aging hips again
beneath these trembling hands.

[1984]

Edward Hirsch   *1950–*

DANCE OF THE MOON

She means nothing to me
Familiar old crone, spoiled Latin bitch
With her rumpled palms and swampy breasts
Fattening nightly, offering herself to strangers.

5   What does it matter to me
If she bares her bosom to the trees
Like a spayed cat, or an aged whore
Promising a tourist his fortune?

Each day she wastes herself in sleep;
10 Each night she douses herself in perfume
And buries her body in layers of cloth,
In red petticoats and white slips

Until finally, at the end of each month
She emerges, dancing from the clouds
15 Naked, leaving her wet clothes
In a puddle of branches!

Let her dance all night if she
Wants to, let her dance on the lake
Or in the folds of the red curtains,
20 But keep her away from me

With her drowsy lips and warm mouth,
With her tongue pressed against the glass.
Each night I tell myself that she's only
A pomegranate, or at best, the skull of a cabbage,

25 And yet she continues to haunt me,
To keep me awake with her sensual dancing;
And turning away from the window
I can hear her calling to me

With my voice, nuzzling under my arm,
30 Singing to me from the moisture of my lungs;
That staggering old bitch, my heart,
Flaming up in a chest of branches!

[1981]

Rick Lott   *1950–*

EXILE

A shrivelled leaf pirouettes
at the end of a spider's broken thread.

Again no rain today and the green tongues
of corn wither to silence
5 in the dusty light.

Water has withdrawn its grace
from the sand of riverbeds,
and trout crowd the pools, slim bodies
pale as the hands of praying monks.

10 The frontier of summer shimmers
on the horizon, and along
the roads bees skim the tiny flames
of clover, grains of ash clinging
to back legs, lost honey never
15 to sting our tongues to life.

In the early dark that flickers
with heat lightning, we wait
for the stirring wings of the storm,

watch bats
20 swoop for insects, startled flight
faithful to echoes from an unseen world.
                                                          [1991]

Cathy Song   *1955–*

THE WHITE PORCH

I wrap the blue towel
after washing,
around the damp
weight of hair, bulky
5 as a sleeping cat,
and sit out on the porch.
Still dripping water,
it'll be dry by supper,
by the time the dust
10 settles off your shoes,
though it's only five
past noon. Think
of the luxury: how to use
the afternoon like the stretch

15   of lawn spread before me.
There's the laundry,
sun-warm clothes at twilight,
and the mountain of beans
in my lap. Each one,
20   I'll break and snap
thoughtfully in half.

But there is this slow arousal.
The small buttons
of my cotton blouse
25   are pulling away from my body.
I feel the strain of threads,
the swollen magnolias
heavy as a flock of birds
in the tree. Already,
30   the orange sponge cake
is rising in the oven.
I know you'll say it makes
your mouth dry
and I'll watch you
35   drench your slice of it
in canned peaches
and lick the plate clean.

So much hair, my mother
used to say, grabbing
40   the thick braided rope
in her hands while we washed
the breakfast dishes, discussing
dresses and pastries.
My mind often elsewhere
45   as we did the morning chores together.
Sometimes, a few strands
would catch in her gold ring.
I worked hard then,
anticipating the hour
50   when I would let the rope down
at night, strips of sheets,
knotted and tied,
while she slept in tight blankets.
My hair, freshly washed
55   like a measure of wealth,
like a bridal veil.
Crouching in the grass,
you would wait for the signal,
for the movement of curtains
60   before releasing yourself
from the shadow of moths.
Cloth, hair and hands,
smuggling you in.

[1983]

Leslie Adrienne Miller   *1956–*

DEER HARVEST

Mole, mouse, squirrel, rabbit,
none have I known,
but the hunter I know.
I am married to him by blood.
5   He is my cousin, my uncle, my grandfather,
farmers all. I have loved
his language of grunts and twangs,
the marks of weather in his face,
the hard large hand that holds
10   the lamb, the pig, the white pine door
of the modest church.

I would not have seen the flight
of deer across his east field
in a morning still bitten by hard frost,
15   had he not stopped his truck,
lifted that wide hand to show a bounty
of flying white tails,
airborne beauty really, or so
it seemed to a girl
20   who never lived from the land.

Now as I watch the head of a dead doe
lolling from a tailgate on the 10 o'clock news,
four hooves, shiny as glazed clay,
taken out from under her
25   by a bullet I might have examined
in the hand of my cousin,
I think not of her shudder,
her young waiting for days
where she left them in the brush,
30   but of the kick of the rifle
against the shoulder of a man
who watched his corn twist and dwarf
in a field of August heat,
who watched the breath of his cattle
35   raise the shadow of dust on sparse grass,
whose sons watch the shimmer
of heat on an empty silo,
chewing weeds for all they're worth.

I swallow my love
40   for the light-footed travel,
the elegant thin face
nudging the birch, the fawn.
This beauty is food as surely
as the juice burst tomato
45   that never came to this year's vine.

[1990]

III

DRAMA

III

DRAMA

21

What Is Drama?

The word *drama* comes from the Greek verb *dran,* meaning "to perform." When we speak of a drama, we mean a story in dialogue performed by actors, on a stage, before an audience—in other words, a *play.* We also use the term *drama* in a more general sense to refer to the literary genre that encompasses all written plays and to the profession of writing, producing, and performing plays.

Because drama presupposes performance, it is not a purely literary genre. It combines the use of language with representational arts involving scenery, costuming, and the actors' physical appearance. It also makes use of vocal emphasis and tone of voice, along with such nonverbal forms of expression as physical gesture, facial expression, and sometimes music and dance. Thus, a drama only becomes a complete work of art when it is seen on the stage, and the written text of a play is only its skeletal frame—lacking flesh, blood, and a life of its own. This skeletal script is, however, the only permanent part of a play. The rest is ephemeral: it changes to some degree with each night's performance and, to a considerable extent, with each new production. Presentations of Greek tragedy, for example, have ranged from stately, historically accurate productions to loose, avant-garde adaptations. In one production of Euripides's *The Bacchae* (ca. 405 B.C.) we watch "larger than life" actors struggle to speak clearly while costumed in oversized masks, padded clothing, and sandals with thick platform soles. And in another production of the same play (renamed *Dionysus in 69*), we find naked women splashing their way through oceans of stage blood, engaging in simulated sex, and writhing through a savage "birth ritual."

Such extremes serve to remind us that the script is the only part of the play over which the author has complete control; the rest is the collaborative creation of many different artists, some of whom may misunderstand and therefore misrepresent what the author intended. Because we can never know exactly how Sophocles, Shakespeare, Molière, and other early dramatists staged their plays, we can never reproduce exactly the work of art they intended. But in reading the words of the play, we *can* share in the imaginative experience that—even more than success on the stage—is responsible for the survival and enduring popularity of great drama. We know, for example, that the plays of Euripides (ca. 480–407 B.C.) were not popular with the audience when first presented in ancient Greece. Yet Euripides' plays have survived through the ages, and those of his more popular contemporaries are all but forgotten. Apparently, Euripides' intense, introverted style and penetrating character analyses appealed to the readers who commissioned and preserved manuscripts of his plays. In contrast, the record for the longest continuous run for a single play is held by Agatha Christie's *The Mousetrap*, which, whatever its merit as drama, as of 1992 had been on stage for 40 years and more than 16,650 performances. Christie's play will not, of course, continue its run forever. Someday the show will close, and thereafter its survival will depend on readers. Only if the demand by the play-reading public is sufficient to keep a play in print, and only if the play in its written form appeals to a succession of producers and directors, can we expect that it will truly become a stage classic.

This is precisely what has happened in the case of Euripides, Shakespeare, and other great classic and modern dramatists, whose readers have almost always outnumbered their viewers. Even today, when the average citizen has an unparalleled opportunity to see outstanding theater on stage (or in adaptations for television or film), copies of printed scripts continue to be sold in ever-increasing numbers. Although most lovers of the theater insist upon *seeing* great drama performed, they insist equally upon owning, reading, and studying the plays they love.

The reason for this phenomenon is clear enough: when we study drama as literature—that is, when we study the text of the play, apart from its staging—we may not see the entire work intended by the author, but we do see the words exactly as the playwright wrote them, or as they have been translated, without any cutting, rearranging, or rewriting by the director and without the interpretive assistance (or hindrance) of the actors. The written script may be skeletal compared to a stage presentation, but that limitation can help us to concentrate on the play's structure and on those elements of drama that fall directly under the author's control.

DRAMA AND POETRY

As soon as we think of drama as a form of literature, we begin to notice that a play shares many similarities with a long narrative poem. In fact, from the days of ancient Greece through the first half of the nineteenth century, most plays were written in verse. The dramatic works of Aeschylus, Sophocles, Euripides, Aristophanes, Marlowe, Shakespeare, Jonson, Molière, Racine, Corneille, and many others are largely or entirely poetic. Even Ibsen, who probably did more than any other dramatist to make prose acceptable in tragedy, wrote two of his most famous plays, *Brand* (1866) and *Peer Gynt* (1867), in verse.

The reasons for the historical predominance of verse in drama are not difficult to discover. Drama, like poetry, is meant to be heard. As a result, like poetry, it sometimes makes use of the aural qualities of rhythm and rhyme. Furthermore, because Greek drama originally grew out of choral songs, it was only natural that the musical elements in the songs should be preserved in the plays; and because Greek drama served as a model for most subsequent generations, verse remained an integral part of most playwriting until a growing preoccupation with realism near the end of the nineteenth century made the contrivance of dialogue in verse undesirable. Finally, many of the stages used for drama were relatively barren, and the playwright was forced to evoke through poetic language any characteristics of the setting that he or she wished the audience to envision. Thus, poetic diction, imagery, and techniques of versification became thoroughly integrated into the drama.

One cannot conclude, however, that drama is inevitably a form of poetry. Indeed, in the last century new poetic dramas have rarely been successful on the stage. Popular taste has changed, and audiences now demand realism instead of poetic flourishes. Of course, many of these realistic plays—especially those of Tennessee Williams and Eugene O'Neill—are written in prose which is so imagistic and suggestive that it may be studied as a form of free verse, but even if we confine this discussion to plays more obviously written in verse, we will find some differences between poetry and drama. In the first place, a poem is usually meant for only one speaker; a play for two or more. Similarly, a poem can be written in virtually any verse form, while a play (in English) is limited by tradition to blank verse, heroic couplets, or prose. Finally, most poems are quite short, while most plays are comparatively long. When we speak of the poetry in Shakespeare's plays, we ordinarily refer to only a few well-known passages: the descriptions of Cleopatra's barge or her death in *Antony and Cleopatra,* Marc Antony's oration in *Julius Caesar,* Portia's speech on mercy in *The Merchant of Venice,* Othello's last words, Hamlet's soliloquies, and so on. Such passages, and others like them, are memorized and anthologized almost as if they were separate poems, while the rest of each play, whether it is truly poetic or not, is read, performed, and analyzed in much the same way as if it were prose. Shakespeare, after all, was human and like other men was apt to put in an occasional dull day at his desk. Take, for example, the following brief scene from *Othello:*

SCENE 2: *A room in the castle. Enter* OTHELLO, IAGO, *and* GENTLEMEN.

OTHELLO. These letters give, Iago, to the pilot,
And by him do my duties to the Senate.
That done, I will be walking on the works.
Repair there to me.
IAGO. Well, my good lord, I'll do 't.
OTHELLO. This fortification, gentlemen, shall we see 't?
GENTLEMEN. We'll wait upon your lordship.
[*Exeunt.*]

—From *Othello,* act 3, scene 2,
William Shakespeare [1604]

Even if this scene of only six lines served some dramatic function, it would be uninspired writing. Othello's letters to the Senate have no further significance, nor does his inspection of the fortifications. The scene is an encounter of no substance that serves only to waste a little stage time, allowing Cassio to begin the interview with Desdemona that was promised in the preceding scene and that we join in progress in the subsequent one.

The same kind of mechanical drama is even more common in the works of lesser dramatists. The quantity of true poetry in a play is always slight when compared with the larger body of dialogue that is necessary to move the characters around and push the action forward. Indeed, the preponderance of prosaic and merely competent lines in a play helps to make the poetic moments stand out more clearly, so that they seem (to quote Shakespeare) "as the spots of heaven, / More fiery by the night's blackness."

DRAMA AND FICTION

If we take it as axiomatic that the best of a play approaches the level of poetry while the bulk of it remains prosaic, then it follows that most drama is closer to fiction than to poetry. Plays are fictitious both in the literal sense that their plots are generally untrue and in the figurative sense that they intend to convey general truths. Like a novel, a play always tells a story. It cannot be purely lyric, descriptive, or argumentative—although each of these modes of expression has a place in drama. Instead, a play begins like a typical short story with an introduction to the characters, the situation, and the setting. It rapidly develops some conflict among the characters that typically reaches a crisis in the fourth act and finds its resolution in the fifth. And in presenting its action, a play manipulates many of the elements found in a short story. Aristotle, the first theoretician of drama, identified six basic elements in the genre: setting, character, plot, language, theme, and music. All but the last are also elements of fiction, and music is no longer requisite or even common in modern drama.

Despite these similarities, a play clearly differs from a short story and drama differs from fiction. Some of the main differences between the genres emerge in the handling of point of view, time, and structure. Unlike a short story, which can present the action from many different points of view, a play is obliged to present its story dramatically. The characters speak directly to one another, and the audience observes their actions without the assistance of a narrator to fill in background information, draw conclusions, and generally serve as a guide to the significance of unfolding events.[1] The playwright cannot pry into the minds of the characters as an omniscient narrator might, and the audience can have no knowledge of a character's thoughts, emotions, or past unless these emerge through dialogue, physical action, or the use of soliloquy.

Because of its dramatic point of view, a play takes place in the perpetual present tense. Where the short story or the novel always implicitly begins, "Once upon a time . . . ," a play both begins and proceeds with "now . . . now . . . now!" The audience always knows what the characters *are doing* while they are onstage, but the playwright has no unobtrusive means of showing what they *have done* either before the curtain rises or while they are offstage. The confidant, who is made privy to another's past, and the messenger, who reports offstage activities, are obvious and sometimes inadequate substitutes for fictional omniscience. Indeed, the author's desire to supply characters with a past helps us to understand why many plays focus on heroes whose exploits are already known to the audience through history or legend.

Another way of stating the difference between fiction and drama is to observe that **a play is structured around a succession of *scenes*. A new scene is needed**

---

[1] *Our Town* (1938) by Thornton Wilder, *The Glass Menagerie* (1944) by Tennessee Williams, *After the Fall* (1964) by Arthur Miller, and a number of other modern plays use a narrator to introduce and control the action, but even in these plays the narrator must eventually step aside and allow the events to unfold objectively and dramatically.

whenever there is a change of setting or time. (In many French and a few English dramas, a new scene also begins with the entrance or exit of any major character.) **The scenes are often then grouped into *acts*, which indicate the major units in the development of the plot.** The formal division of plays into acts and scenes represents a major difference between the structure of drama and that of fiction. In the latter, the plot *may* unfold as a chronological series of scenes, but there is nothing to keep an author from reminiscing within a scene. Thus, fiction may present a convoluted series of stories within stories—*The Arabian Nights* provides many examples—but drama is obliged to present only those plots that can be developed continuously and chronologically.[2]

In the following pages, as we examine the influence of the actors, the audience, and the stage, we will discover other ways in which drama differs from poetry and fiction; it should now be clear, however, that the major elements of drama are also the major elements of poetry and fiction. Our present task is not to describe new literary elements, but rather to explain how the special conditions of dramatic presentation influence the playwight's handling of fictional and poetic devices.

THE ACTORS

Because drama is primarily designed for performance, we can expect that the greatest plays will encourage and successfully incorporate the creative potential of the actors. A dramatist writes with the knowledge that the play will be presented on stage in a way that emphasizes tonal implications and fulfills the incidents suggested by the dialogue. But while a professional playwright seeks to encourage the actors to interpret their lines creatively, he or she may wish to be sure that the larger thematic impact of the play remains unchanged by different acting styles. By writing their plays for specific stage companies, some dramatists are able to retain a greater measure of control over the initial stage production. Not only can these dramatists conceive the play and write the first draft with the strengths and limitations of key actors and actresses already in mind, but they can also supervise the rehearsals and revise the parts of the play that seem ill-suited to the actors. In many cases, therefore, the text of the play that emerges is the result of some form of collaboration between the playwright and the actors.

Because a playwright must assume that the roles in the script will be played by real people, with real idiosyncrasies in personality and appearance, there is no need to describe any character's external appearance. The audience can see for itself what Ibsen's Hedda Gabler looks like, and a description of Hedda's appearance, such as one might find in a novel, becomes redundant and unnecessary in the dialogue of a play. Of course, the author's parenthetic stage directions sometimes do include a description of the characters. Hedda, for example, is introduced as

a woman of nine-and-twenty. Her face and figure show refinement and distinction. Her complexion is pale and opaque. Her steel-gray eyes express a cold, unruffled repose. Her hair is of an agreeable medium brown but not particularly abundant. She is dressed in a tasteful, somewhat loose-fitting morning gown.

—From *Hedda Gabler*, act 1, Henrik Ibsen [1890]

[2] There are, to be sure, exceptions, as usual. In *Our Town*, to cite Wilder's play again, the action returns to the past in the last act.

But such comments are directed at readers, not viewers. They underscore the fact that a playwright often writes simultaneously for two audiences: one in the theater and the other in the armchair.

In writing for the theater, the dramatist has in the actors a great advantage over the novelist, for the characters in a play *are* real. They live and breathe, stand up and sit down, sigh and smile, enter and exit—all with greater realism than even the most competent novelist can create. The actions and expressions of several characters can be conveyed on stage in a matter of seconds, whereas a novelist might have to devote several pages to a description of the same incidents. As a result, drama has an immediate impact that fiction and poetry can never equal. The illusion of reality in some plays or films is as close as art can ever come to bringing its fictional incidents to life.

But although the playwright is relieved from describing the physical appearance or actions of the characters at length, he or she *cannot* analyze their personalities and motives directly and concisely. An omniscient inquiry into how and why a character speaks, moves, and thinks as he or she does is both desirable and entertaining in a novel by Dickens, but it is not easy to present through dialogue on a stage. Instead, a dramatist individualizes the characters by giving them distinctive habits or quirks of speech and by allowing them to express their personalities through action. Soon after Hedda Gabler first appears on stage, for example, we see her impatience with any references to her femininity or possible pregnancy:

TESMAN. . . . Auntie, take a good look at Hedda before you go! See how handsome she is!

MISS TESMAN. Oh, my dear boy, there's nothing new in that. Hedda was always lovely. [*She nods and goes toward the right.*]

TESMAN [*following*]. Yes, but have you noticed what splendid condition she is in? How she has filled out on the journey?

HEDDA [*crossing the room*]. Oh, do be quiet!

MISS TESMAN [*who has stopped and turned*]. Filled out?

TESMAN. Of course you don't notice it so much now that she has that dress on. But I, who can see—

HEDDA [*at the glass door, impatient*]. Oh, you can't see anything.

TESMAN. It must be the mountain air in the Tyrol—

HEDDA [*curtly interrupting*]. I am exactly as I was when I started.

TESMAN. So you insist, but I'm quite certain you are not. Don't you agree with me, Auntie?

MISS TESMAN [*who has been gazing at her with folded hands*]. Hedda is lovely—lovely—lovely. [*Goes up to her, takes her head between both hands, draws it downward and kisses her hair.*] God bless and preserve Hedda Tesman—for George's sake.

HEDDA [*gently freeing herself*]. Oh! Let me go.

MISS TESMAN [*in quiet emotion*]. I shall not let a day pass without coming to see you.

TESMAN. No, you won't, will you, Auntie? Eh?

MISS TESMAN. Good-by—good-by! [*She goes out by the hall door.* TESMAN *accompanies her. The door remains half open.* TESMAN *can be heard repeating his message to Aunt Rina and his thanks for the slippers. In the meantime* HEDDA *walks about the room raising her arms and clenching her hands as if in desperation. Then she flings back the curtains from the glass door and stands there looking out.*]

—From *Hedda Gabler*, act 1, Henrik Ibsen [1890]

Even here the superiority of fictional omniscience in describing motives and emotions is obvious. Ibsen's parenthetic stage directions succinctly and unambiguously inform the reader about the attitudes of the characters. Where these describe actions ("She nods and goes toward the right"), there is no problem presenting them on stage. Where they describe a tone of voice ("HEDDA [at the glass door, impatient]") they can be a challenge to acting skills but are still likely to be understood by the audience. When, however, they indicate a state of mind more than a tone of voice, the reader is apt to fare very much better than the viewer. How, for example, is Miss Tesman's "quiet emotion" to be conveyed in her final comment to Hedda?

Usually, Ibsen avoids vague instructions about an actor's tone of voice and strives instead to bring out his characters' attitudes through their words and actions. Hedda, for example, is frustrated by the timid and retiring role that nineteenth-century women were expected to play. Like many other women of the day, she feels imprisoned by the one-sided decorum imposed by her male-dominated society. To dramatize this, Ibsen never allows her to leave her own constricting household during the play's four acts. Through her conversations with Eilert Lövborg and Judge Brack, we discover that she wishes she could participate in the excitement and dissipations of masculine life, but is hindered by a dread of scandal. Thus, although she tries to satisfy her adventurous urges by manipulating the lives of others—particularly Tesman and Eilert—her repressed passions continually break out. These aspects of her personality are given dramatic form by her actions in the brief scene quoted here. She grows irritated at the allusions to her pregnancy, clenches her fists, restlessly paces to and from the windows of the parlor, and a few moments later begins to toy with guns. Using these and other dramatic indications of Hedda's underlying turmoil, Ibsen is able to expose the hidden core of her personality without access to the novelist's omniscient narration.

While writing into the script words and actions that help to define the characters, a playwright must also allow some room for the actors' interpretation and self-expression. In other words, a successful play will stimulate and inspire the actors to use their talents creatively in presenting the play before an audience. In practice, the meaning of the play and the vital intellectual substance that animates each character should be suggested in the script but not rigidly imposed on it. Thus, Ibsen wisely leaves it unclear whether Hedda truly wishes she were a man or is simply rebelling against the traditionally subdued role of her sex. Part of the pleasure of the theater for habitual playgoers derives from this artistic ambiguity. In successive productions of established classics, those who follow the theater closely are able to see how different actresses and actors interpret their roles and are able to compare those interpretations with perceptions based on a study of the text.

But while a dramatist must allow some flexibility in the characterizations to accommodate the actors' differences in physical appearance as well as their need for creative self-expression, he or she must not allow these freedoms to get out of hand. A play, like most other literary works, ordinarily presents an ethical point or some thematic statement about the world and our place in it that the playwright feels to be both relevant and significant. Because drama is a collaborative art—drawing on the talents of the actors, director, musicians, stagehands, scenic artists, and others—a playwright must learn to sketch theme and plot in simple, vigorous, and bold strokes, to be certain that the "message" will come through to the audience. Good drama implies the successive unfolding of the implications of one overarching idea: Hedda's desire to control a human destiny, Tartuffe's hypocrisy, Othello's jealousy, Oedipus's false pride. In each case the central idea is traced by the course of seemingly inevitable events. It is not in the power of the actors to change the concept of the play, just as it is not in the power of an engineer to change the downhill flow of a river. The natural path may be momentarily blocked, but its ultimate course cannot be stopped or stayed.

A careful and single-minded plot development is but one means by which playwrights sometimes seek to control the influence of the cast on the impact of a play. As already noted, many dramatists have composed their plays with the specific abilities of specific actors in mind in an effort to minimize the risk of parts being misplayed. The parts in Shakespeare's plays, for example, were often carefully tailored to suit his fellow members of the Lord Chamberlain's Men (later the King's Men), a professional acting company with which Shakespeare was associated throughout his career. Thus, we find that while Will Kempe was with the company, Shakespeare wrote into his plays a part for a boisterous and farcical clown; but when Kempe was replaced by Robert Armin, the role of the clown became more subtle and witty. Similarly, Shakespeare could confidently create the demanding roles of Hamlet, Lear, and Othello because he knew that in Richard Burbage the company had an actor capable of playing such diverse parts. One of the many contemporary tributes to Burbage's skill describes him as follows:

> His stature small, but every thought and mood
> Might thoroughly from the face be understood
> And his whole action he could change with ease
> From ancient Lear to youthful Pericles.

Shakespeare himself is said to have specialized in playing old men—the old servant Adam in *As You Like It,* the ghost in *Hamlet,* and so on.

In addition to writing specific roles for specific actors, Shakespeare and other Renaissance playwrights had to write all the female parts in such a way that they could be played by preadolescent boys. (Up until about 1660, acting was considered a profession too depraved for women. Men played all the women's parts, even in ancient Greece and Rome.) Naturally, the nude scenes that now abound in films and on the stage would have been out of the question in Shakespeare's day—for reasons other than moral decorum. Indeed, demonstrations of physical passion are comparatively rare in Shakespearean drama because too much kissing and clutching between characters whom the audience knows full well to be a man and a boy might break down the dramatic illusion and become either ludicrous or offensive. In all of *Othello,* a play about sexual conduct and misconduct, there are only four kisses. Three are mere courtesy kisses given to Desdemona in public by Cassio and Othello after she has survived a fierce storm at sea. The only kiss in private is the one Othello gives the sleeping Desdemona just before he suffocates her. Similarly, the height of the balcony in *Romeo and Juliet* keeps the lovers apart during their most passionate moments, and in *Antony and Cleopatra* there is but one embrace before the death scene.

The influence of the actors on the script of a play is not unique to Shakespearean drama. All playwrights must work within the limitations imposed by the medium. Dramatists are, for example, obviously limited in the number of characters they can use. Even though Aristophanes in *Lysistrata* (411 B.C.) wanted to show the effects of a sex strike by the entire female population of Greece, he actually used only three Athenians and one Spartan in speaking roles—with perhaps a score of nonspeaking women to stand for all the rest. Apart from the fact that only a limited number of actors can fit on a stage, the number of speaking roles in a play must be few enough so that the director can round up (and pay) enough accomplished actors and few enough so that the audience can remember who they all are. By convention, as well as by economic and practical necessity, Greek dramatists limited themselves to three speakers and a chorus. This does not mean that there were only three parts in a play, but rather that only three speaking characters could be on stage at any one time. Because the same actors might play several roles (changing masks and costumes offstage), the number of speaking roles could range anywhere from two to twenty, but the dramatist had at all times to balance the requirements of his story with the practical concerns of allowing the actors sufficient time to change costume and of matching the physical and vocal demands of the roles to those of the actors available to play them. It would not do, for example, to send an actor playing a husky, deep-voiced king offstage and then to bring him back as a petite princess. The same character would be physically unable to play both parts. These restrictions are less stringent in plays written after the golden age of Greek drama (ca. 480–380 B.C.), but accomplished playwrights have always manipulated their plots to allow some doubling up of parts and have always been aware that the physical size of the stage itself does not allow them to portray the assembled masses of contending armies. Hence, in the prologue to *Henry the Fifth*, Shakespeare asks the audience to

> Suppose within the girdle of these walls
> Are now confined two mighty monarchies,
>
> . . . .
>
> Into a thousand parts divide one man;
> And make imaginary puissance;
> Think, when we talk of horses, that you see them
> Printing their proud hoofs i' th' receiving earth.
> For 'tis your thoughts that now must deck our kings.
>
> —From *Henry the Fifth*, "Prologue,"
> William Shakespeare [1599]

One final way in which the actors influence the drama deserves mention: plays are sometimes conceived, and often revised, as a result of the advice of the actors and the director. Indeed, contemporary plays normally open "out of town" to allow time for revision before risking an expensive production—and facing the critics—in the heart of New York. A similar process has operated throughout the history of the theater, and Shakespeare's plays, in this sense at least, are probably much the better for having remained unpublished until long experience on the stage had taught the members of his company which lines played well and which were in need of revision.

THE AUDIENCE

A few plays are intended only to be read and therefore are known as **closet dramas** (*Samson Agonistes* by Milton, *Cain* by Byron, and *Prometheus Unbound* by Shelley are notable examples); but most plays make an effort to please an audience massed in a theater. Playwrights who compose for the stage have learned by experience the truth of Samuel Johnson's eighteenth-century dictum that

> The drama's laws the drama's patrons give,
> And we who live to please, must please to live.

The goal of a playwright is to fill the theater and to keep on filling it for as long as possible. A play must have popular appeal, and the quest for it naturally influences the choice and treatment of dramatic subjects.

Alexander Dumas (the elder) once claimed that all he needed for success on the stage was "four boards, two actors, and a passion." Dumas knew, as all of us now do, that the ingredients for a popular play (and certainly for popular TV) usually include sex and violence—the two principal motives for passionate dialogue. As the tragedian in Tom Stoppard's *Rosencrantz and Guildenstern Are Dead* put it, well-liked plays are of the "blood, love, and rhetoric school":

> ... I can do you blood and love without the rhetoric, and I can do you blood and rhetoric without the love, and I can do you all three concurrent or consecutive, but I can't do you love and rhetoric without the blood. Blood is compulsory—they're all blood [in tragedy], you see.
>
> —From *Rosencrantz and Guildenstern Are Dead*, act 1, Tom Stoppard [1967]

The plots of most plays do in fact focus on one of the violent passions (anger, jealousy, revenge, lust, treachery) or on some form of love (love of woman, love of home, love of country, love of justice). Aristophanes' *Lysistrata*, for example, cleverly combines love of woman, love of country, and simple lust; *Othello* builds on jealousy; and much of the plot of *Hedda Gabler* revolves on Hedda's envy of Thea. Other plays examine the effects of less violent, but still powerful, passions: pride in *King Oedipus*, zealotry in *Tartuffe*, and prudery in *Mrs. Warren's Profession*.

Plays do differ, however, as John Dryden once observed, because of the historical differences in the play-going audience:

> They who have best succeeded on the stage
> Have still conformed their genius to the age.

Greek dramas were presented before huge audiences drawn from all levels of society, from poor to rich and from illiterate to sophisticated. Attendance was viewed as a religious duty. As a result, the tragedies dealt with simple and well-known stories that all members of the audience could understand; but they did have to deal with the play's subject in a way that underscored the necessity of reverence for the gods and their decrees. Elizabethan dramas were also aimed at an audience drawn from all levels of society, but by then the connection of the theater with religion had been severed. Thus, Shakespeare's plays contained enough blood and love to keep the illiterate mob in the pit entertained and enough lofty rhetoric to please the lords and ladies in the box seats, but they did not seek to inculcate any particular religious or philosophic views.

By the late nineteenth century, the price of a theater ticket exceeded the means of the laboring classes, and therefore plays like *Hedda Gabler* (1890) portray the problems and conditions of life in the upper and middle classes. There is occasionally a bit of genteel poverty in the plays of this period, but the degrading and impoverished conditions of factory labor are almost entirely ignored. More recently, the technological revolution of the twentieth century has meant that people can often find their entertainment at home on television or at the local movie theater. Most of the people who attend plays today do so because they want to combine culture with entertainment. As a result, much contemporary drama tends to be intellectual and allusive, as in the witty manipulations of *Hamlet* in

Tom Stoppard's *Rosencrantz and Guildenstern Are Dead* (1967) or in the parody of Agatha Christie's *Mousetrap* in Stoppard's *The Real Inspector Hound* (1967).

Even in modern drama, however, the plot usually makes an appeal to mass psychology. The playwright must cling first to those elemental passions and emotions common to all humanity and only secondarily, if at all, stimulate the qualities of intellect, in which people differ. The audience in a theater is, after all, a crowd and therefore "less intellectual and more emotional than the individuals that compose it. It is less reasonable, less judicious, less disinterested, more credulous, more primitive, more partisan."[3] In a theater, the sophisticated responses of the few are outnumbered by the instinctive responses of the many. As a result, the dramatist writes for a live audience that is spontaneous and unreflective in both its approval and disapproval.

Because most members of the audience can be expected to see the play once and only once, a successful play must be clearly plotted, easy to understand, and both familiar and acceptable in its theme. Playwrights satisfy the tastes of the times, but they rarely guide them. A novel may survive, even if its initial acclaim is slight, so long as those who first read and understand it are able to influence subsequent intellectual and literary thinking. But a play that fails in its first performance is unlikely to be published at all. Even if a few enthusiasts keep it from sinking immediately into oblivion, one costly failure on Broadway is usually sufficient to scare away future producers. The financial risks in producing plays are more clear-cut than those in publishing novels. If a new play proves to be unpopular, the initial costs involved in scenery, costuming, and rehearsal are not recouped, and the debts mount every day that actors play before a half-filled house. In contrast, if a new novel at first seems unpopular, the cost of storing a few thousand copies will scarcely distress the publisher as long as the demand is constant and seems likely to grow. Thus, a play, unlike a novel, must please upon first acquaintance; and if it is to have durable literary value, it must continue to please during successive viewings or readings. The challenge in writing drama is, thus, to be at once popular *and* intellectually stimulating. Comparatively few playwrights have succeeded at being both.

There are a number of good reasons for the frequent failures in the theater. Even if a playwright chooses a popular subject and develops the plot with simplicity and grace, he or she cannot be confident of pleasing an audience unless the structure of the play is carefully crafted to meet the physical needs of spectators: the duration of scenes and the mixture of dialogue and action, for example, must be adapted to the audience's attention span. A play, like other forms of literature, is principally composed of words, but too much talk and too little action may produce a result about as exciting as a town council meeting. Conversely, actions that remain uninterpreted by dialogue quickly become chaotic. A sword fight on stage may show the physical agility of the actors and the conflict between characters; but if it is continued too long, it threatens to turn the drama into a gladiatorial exhibition, in which most of the interest is drained by the recognition that the swords are wooden, the blood is artificial, and each thrust or parry has been carefully choreographed in advance.

In some ways, of course, the playwright has a tremendous amount of control. Once the theater is darkened and the play begins, the audience is captive: the

---

[3] Clayton Hamilton, as quoted by Brander Matthews, *A Study of the Drama* (New York: Houghton Mifflin, 1910) 88.

seats all face the stage, the only well lit part of the theater. When the curtain rises, any lingering conversations are "shushed." The closely packed patrons watch and listen attentively because they have paid to do so, because there is little else they *can* do in a dark theater, and because the seating arrangement makes it difficult to leave before the intermission.

These theatrical conditions directly influence the structure of the play. As much as dramatists may lust after the novelist's right to a leisurely introduction, they must resign themselves to the bald fact that, because no audience can sit still for more than an hour at a time, the play must be at its intriguing best by the intermission. Similarly, a play that begins at 8:00 P.M. must certainly end by 11:00 P.M., lest all the teenagers with curfews, all the parents with babysitters, and all the young couples with romantic plans leave *en masse* before the final curtain.

THE THEATER

In writing a play, a dramatist is always aware of the physical conditions of the theater. These conditions often govern the actions and settings that can be presented, as well as the way in which the scenes are developed. The size of the theater, the proximity of the audience to the stage, and the characteristics of the stage itself influence the scenery, the costuming, and the actors' methods.

As we will see, the conditions for staging Greek drama were unlike those for Elizabethan drama, Elizabethan unlike neoclassical, and neoclassical unlike modern. Nonetheless, each stage provides an arena within which the words and actions of the performers are observed by an audience of substantial size. It follows that some actions are too minute and others too grand to be staged effectively. In Shakespeare's *Othello*, for example, Desdemona's handkerchief is a vital element in the plot, but this piece of cloth, which is too small to bind Othello's forehead, is also too small to be seen clearly by the most distant members of the audience. Thus, Shakespeare takes care to identify it in the dialogue whenever he introduces it on stage. For example, when Bianca flings the handkerchief back to Cassio in act 4, scene 1, Othello, who is watching from a distance, says, "By heaven, that should be my handkerchief!" And then, to clear up any possible confusion, Iago, who has had a closer vantage point, drives home the identification:

IAGO. And did you see the handkerchief?
OTHELLO. Was that mine?
IAGO. Yours, by this hand. And to see how he prizes the foolish woman your wife! She gave it him, and he hath given it his whore.

Large events can be even more difficult to present on stage. In the second act of *Othello*, Shakespeare wishes to describe the arrival at Cyprus of Cassio, Desdemona, and Othello after they have been separated by a storm at sea. Naturally it is difficult to depict either the turbulent sea or the arrival of the shattered flotilla. Instead Shakespeare introduces three minor characters whose primary function is to help us imagine the setting and events offstage:

SCENE 1: *A seaport in Cyprus. An open place near the wharf.*
Enter MONTANO *and* TWO GENTLEMEN.

MONTANO. What from the cape can you discern at sea?
FIRST GENTLEMAN. Nothing at all. It is a high-wrought flood.

I cannot 'twixt the heaven and the main
Descry° a sail.																			*see*
    MONTANO.   Methinks the wind hath spoke aloud at land,
A fuller blast ne'er shook our battlements.
If it hath ruffianed° so upon the sea														*raged*
What ribs of oak, when mountains melt on them,
Can hold the mortise? What shall we hear of this?
    SECOND GENTLEMAN. A segration° of the Turkish fleet.							*dispersal*
For do but stand upon the foaming shore,
The chidden billow seems to pelt the clouds;
The wind-shaked surge, with high and monstrous mane,
Seems to cast water on the burning bear,°											*a constellation*
And quench the guards of the ever-fixed pole.
I never did like molestation° view														*disruption*
On the enchafed flood.°																	*raging sea*
    MONTANO.   If that the Turkish fleet
Be not ensheltered and embayed, they are drowned.
It is impossible to bear it out.
[*Enter a* THIRD GENTLEMAN.]
    THIRD GENTLEMAN.   News, lads! Our wars are done.
The desperate tempest hath so banged the Turks
That their designment° halts. A noble ship of Venice										*plan*
Hath seen a grievous wreck and sufferance°											*suffering*
On most part of their fleet.
    MONTANO.   How! Is this true?
    THIRD GENTLEMAN.   The ship is here put in,
A Veronesa. Michael Cassio,
Lieutenant to the warlike Moor Othello,
Is come on shore, the Moor himself at sea,
And is in full commission here for Cyprus.

—From *Othello*, act 2, scene 1, William Shakespeare [1604]

Presumably the first gentleman is standing at one edge of the stage looking into the distance as though out to sea. He shouts back to the others that he sees nothing but enormous waves. The second gentleman, who has recently stood on the shore, gives a fuller and more poetic account of the storm. Then the third gentleman, having just come from the wharf, brings news of the destruction of the Turkish fleet and the arrival of Cassio's ship. Thus, events that Shakespeare would have had difficulty portraying on stage are made vivid and convincing through the dramatic accounts of three different reporters.

Just as the actions in a drama are limited by the size of the stage and its distance from the audience, so, too, the settings are influenced by the practical problems associated with a visual presentation. Some scenes are next to impossible to stage. Act 2 of Lord Byron's *Cain* (1822), for example, opens in "the Abyss of Space" and a stage direction in act 3 (which is set outside of Eden) reads: "The fire upon the altar of Abel kindles into a column of the brightest flame, and ascends to heaven; while a whirlwind throws down the altar of Cain, and scatters the fruits abroad upon the earth."

As a closet drama, Byron's play was never intended to be staged, but similar difficulties sometimes present themselves in conventional plays. Shortly after Byron's death, in fact, his poem "Mazeppa" was dramatized. We can only pity the poor director who was asked in one scene to show the hero "strapped to the back of a wild horse, while birds peck at his eyes, lightning destroys a tree on stage, and wolves pursue the horse."

During the late nineteenth century, in response to a demand for greater realism, playwrights began to specify the arrangement of furniture in a room, the number of pictures on the walls, and sometimes even the thickness of the butter on a piece of stage toast. Here is the first stage direction in Ibsen's *Hedda Gabler:*

SCENE: *A spacious, handsome and tastefully furnished drawing room, decorated in dark colors. In the back a wide doorway with curtains drawn back, leading into a smaller room decorated in the same style as the drawing room. In the right-hand wall of the front room a folding door leading out to the hall. In the opposite wall, on the left, a glass door, also with curtains drawn back. Through the panes can be seen part of a veranda outside and trees covered with autumn foliage. An oval table, with a cover on it and surrounded by chairs, stands well forward. In front, by the wall on the right, a wide stove of dark porcelain, a high-backed armchair, a cushioned footrest and two footstools. A settee with a small round table in front of it fills the upper right-hand corner. In front, on the left, a little way from the wall, a sofa. Further back than the glass door a piano. On either side of the doorway at the back a whatnot with terra-cotta and majolica ornaments. Against the back wall of the inner room a sofa, with a table, and one or two chairs. Over the sofa hangs the portrait of a handsome elderly man in a general's uniform. Over the table, a hanging lamp with an opal glass shade. A number of bouquets are arranged about the drawing room in vases and glasses. Others lie upon the tables. The floors in both rooms are covered with thick carpets. Morning light. The sun shines in through the glass door.*

—From *Hedda Gabler,* act 1, Henrik Ibsen [1890]

Clearly, a setting as complex as this cannot be changed for every new scene. As it happens, all of the action in *Hedda Gabler* takes place in the same two rooms. Similarly, the entire action of *King Oedipus* takes place in front of the royal palace at Thebes, that of *Lysistrata* before the Acropolis, and that of *Tartuffe* in Orgon's house. In a fair number of plays, however, the scene changes with every act, and in a few, like *Othello*, it changes for virtually every scene. Yet, even in *Othello,* a stage with half-dozen different acting areas and a few movable props can be made to convey the whole range of settings.

Unlike the novelist or the film-maker, the playwright cannot allow the plot to flow freely across unlimited fields of action. If the scenery is to be at all realistic, very few settings can be used unless the playwright is prepared to have the work produced only in the few modern theaters with "revolving stages," on which several realistic sets can be erected and alternately used. Even if the scenery is only suggestive, the playwright is much more limited by the genre than other narrative artists. In general, the action of a play takes place in only one or two locales. These may be quite narrowly and specifically defined in realistic drama (Hedda's drawing room, for example) or broadly conceived in more imaginative works (Venice and Cyprus in *Othello*), but a play that uses too many settings risks confusing the audience and consequently failing in the theater. Shakespeare's *Antony and Cleopatra,* for example, is a poetic masterpiece, but it has rarely been successful on the stage because its forty-two scenes skip bewilderingly around the Roman Empire, and the action spans years rather than days. Ordinarily, it is only through the devices of a film-maker or a novelist that such action can be presented clearly and convincingly.

Thus far, we have been discussing the general effects of any theater on the scenes and actions of drama, but different theaters in different historical periods have had quite different impacts on the drama. A play like *Othello* is written for the intimate Elizabethan stage. The subtle and insinuating facial expressions necessary for a convincing portrayal of Iago's manipulation of Othello would have been lost in the vast amphitheaters of ancient Greece. Similarly, the stark plots and grand rhetoric of Greek tragedy might seem histrionic and ridiculous in the confines of a small modern theater. In order to understand a play, in short, we must know something about the stage for which it was written. In the past, most masterpieces of the drama have been produced in one of four basic theaters: the classical Greek theater, the Elizabethan theater, the neoclassical French theater, and the realistic "box set." Modern drama, however, has moved toward a more flexible theater that can easily be adapted to suit the specific needs of each new play.

The Classical Greek Theater (ca. 480–380 B.C.)

Greek Drama grew out of the primitive rituals performed in conjunction with the three annual festivals dedicated to Dionysus (or Bacchus), the god of fertility, regeneration, and wine. Indeed, the very names for the three forms of Greek drama—tragedy, comedy, and satyr play—derive from the worship of Dionysus. The word *tragedy* means "goat song," probably referring to the goat-skinned satyrs; the derivation of the term *satyr play* is obvious; and the word *comedy* comes from *comos,* Greek for "revelry." In time, such rituals evolved into the drama of Aeschylus, Euripides, Sophocles, and Aristophanes as the uninhibited revels of Dionysus were exchanged for more dignified role playing within a formal theatrical setting. Nonetheless, the classic drama of the ancient Greeks retained, however loosely, its original ties with religion. It continued to be performed only three times a year and then in massive doses of four or five plays a day—circumstances that had an important impact on the audience, the content, and the structure of Greek drama.

In the first place, the audience in a Greek theater was enormous. Everyone who wanted to see a play had only a few opportunities each year to do so, and the idea of attending was all the more attractive because of the sporting element inherent in the prizes awarded for the best tragedies and comedies. The theater of Dionysus at Athens (see Figures 1 and 2), which was used in the first productions of all the great fifth-century Greek plays, probably seated about 17,000. The theater at Epidaurus, built a century later, seated 20,000; and the theater at Ephesus held more than 50,000. Because no existing building was large enough to accommodate so vast a crowd, the plays were performed outdoors in the natural basin formed where two hills met.

During the life of Sophocles (495–406 B.C.) the audience sat on wooden benches that ascended the hillside, more than half encircling an *orchestra* or "dancing place" some 78 feet in diameter. A wooden building called the *skene* (from which we derive the term *scene*) closed off the second half of the amphitheater. It served as an acoustical wall (reflecting the voices of the actors back into the audience), a scenic background (representing any building central to the action), and a convenient place for the three principal actors to change masks and costumes. The narrow space between the *skene* and the *orchestra* was known as the *proskenion* and served as the main acting area.[4] **The *proscenium*, in modern stage-**

---

[4] There is much confusion over what the Greeks actually meant by the term *proskenion*. Some scholars think that it referred to the wall of the *skene;* others that it referred to a row of columns that supported the roof of a porch extending out from the *skene;* and still others agree with our interpretation. Literally, the word means "before" (*pro-*) "the skene" (*skenion*).

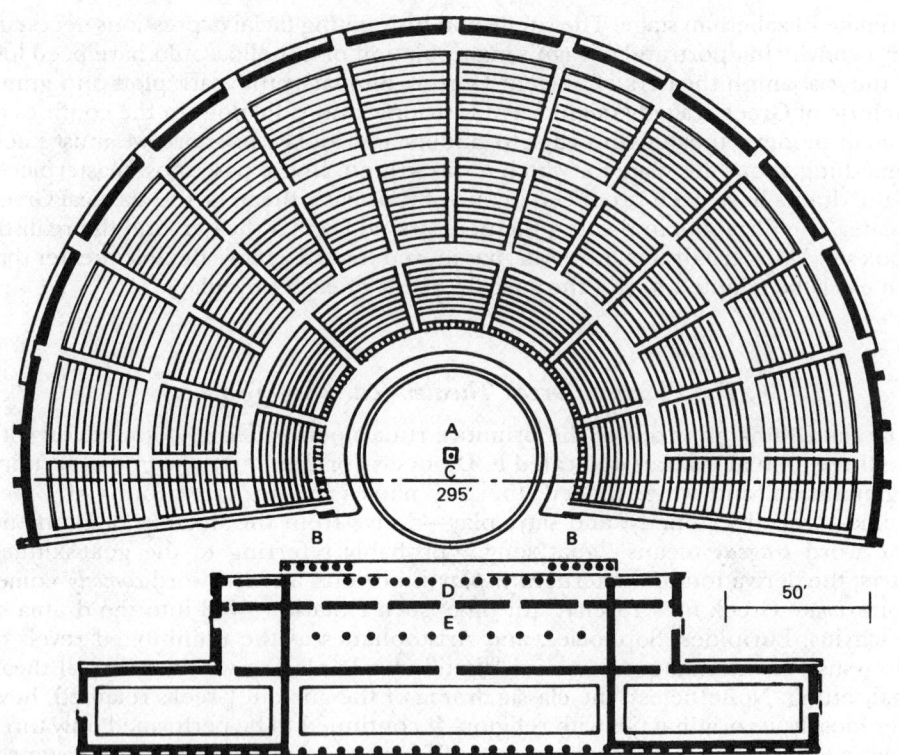

FIGURE 1.   Plan of the Theater of Dionysus at Athens. *A. orchestra; B. chorus entrance; C. altar to Dionysus; D. proskenion; E. skene.*

craft, is the forward part of the stage between the curtain and the orchestra. The arch from which the curtain hangs is the *proscenium arch.*

The chorus normally remained in the *orchestra,* while the major characters moved from the *proskenion* to the *orchestra* and back again, according to the script. The chorus and any processions entered and exited along the edge of the stands to the far right or left of the *skene.* Although the major characters used these aisles when the plot called for an outside entrance, at times they also emerged from, or retreated into, one of the three doors of the *skene* as if from a temple, palace, or some other building. Action on a balcony or a cliff could be staged on top of the *skene,* and when the gods appeared, as they sometimes did to interfere directly in the affairs of men, they were lowered from the top of the *skene* by a crane. **The term *deus ex machina* (meaning "the god from the machine") is sometimes used to describe (and often deride) such divine interventions.**

This massive open-air arena naturally imposed special conditions on the plays performed in it. First of all, there was no curtain to rise at the beginning, fall at the end, and separate the various scenes. As a result, the chorus had to march on stage early in the play (the *parados*) and off stage at the end (the *exodos*). The continuous presence of the chorus during the intervening period encouraged a constant setting throughout the play and a close correspondence between the period of time covered by the play and the amount of real time that elapsed during the actual on-stage presence of the chorus. As a result, Greek drama

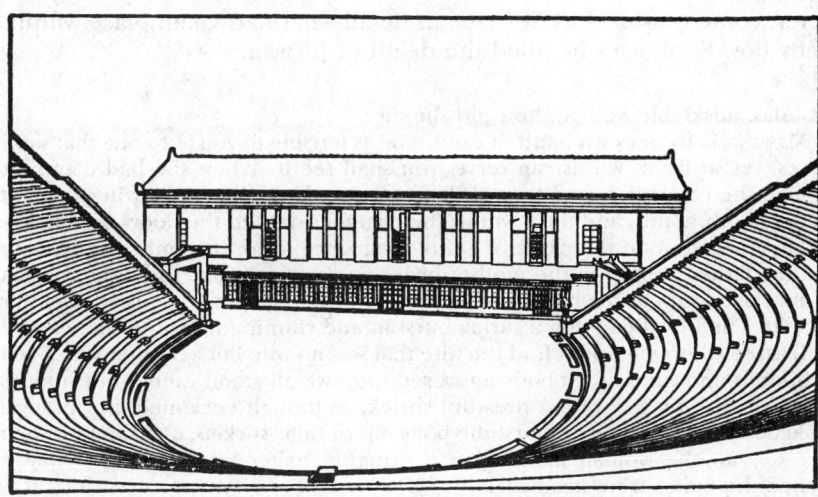

FIGURE 2.   A Reconstruction of a Classical Greek Theater. Note the large "dancing place" or *orchestra*, the encircling tiers of benches, and the scene building or *skene* at the rear. In this case the *skene* includes a raised platform stage. (From Ernst Robert Fiechter's *Die Baugeschichtliche Entwicklung des Antiken Theaters.*)

tended to concentrate on a single complex situation.[5] The typical Greek tragedy begins only a matter of hours before its catastrophe is to occur. The characters stand on the brink of disaster, and the playwright swiftly tells us how they got there, using a formal prologue or a series of interviews with messengers, nurses, and other minor characters. In the first moments of *King Oedipus*, for example, we learn that a plague afflicts Thebes because the murderer of the former king, Laius, has not been punished. Oedipus immediately vows to find the killer and drive him from the land. The remainder of the play works out the consequences of this impetuous vow by revealing that Oedipus himself is the killer, that Laius was his father, and therefore that Laius's wife, Jocasta, is actually Oedipus's mother as well as his wife and the mother of his children.

The four scenes, or *episodes,* during which Oedipus discovers the tragedy of his past are separated from one another not by the fall of a curtain but by a series of choral interludes called odes. Each *ode* (or *stasimon*) was accompanied by music and the choreographed dancing of the chorus. During these odes the chorus was able to provide essential background information, reflect on past actions, or anticipate future ones. Often, too, the responses of the chorus represent those of an ideal audience or provide a lyric respite from the intense emotions of the episodes. In addition these interludes may symbolize the passage of time necessary to send for a character or accomplish some other offstage action.

Because the theater was unenclosed and the plays were performed during the daytime, the action of Greek drama normally also took place during the daytime, out-of-doors. However, some events in Greek drama did require an interior set-ting—Jocasta's suicide is an example—and, accordingly, Greeks were forced to improvise. One frequently used technique was to have a messenger, or some other

---

[5] The unity of place, time, and action demanded in the neoclassical drama of the seventeenth and eighteenth centuries was an outgrowth of these tendencies. Greek playwrights did not, however, formally require adherence to these three unities.

character, come outside and describe in detail what had taken place within. This is exactly how Sophocles handled the death of Jocasta:

CHORUS. Alas, miserable woman, how did she die?

SECOND MESSENGER. By her own hand. It cannot be as terrible to you as to one that saw it with his eyes, yet so far as words can serve, you shall see it. When she had come into the vestibule, she ran half crazed towards her marriage-bed, clutching at her hair with the fingers of both hands, and once within the chamber dashed the doors together behind her. Then called upon the name of Laius, long since dead, remembering that son who killed the father and upon the mother begot an accursed race. And wailed because of that marriage wherein she had borne a two-fold race—husband by husband, children by her child. Then Oedipus with a shriek burst in and running here and there asked for a sword, asked where he would find the wife that was no wife but a mother who had borne his children and himself. Nobody answered him, we all stood dumb; but supernatural power helped him, for, with a dreadful shriek, as though beckoned, he sprang at the double doors, drove them in, burst the bolts out of their sockets, and ran into the room. There we saw the woman hanging in a swinging halter, and with a terrible cry he loosened the halter from her neck.

—From *King Oedipus*, Sophocles [430 B.C.]

A second possibility was simply to throw open the doors of the *skene* and allow the audience to peer inside. Although this technique later worked in the smaller Elizabethan theater, the size of the Greek theater and the unavoidable obscurity of the interior of the *skene* rendered this approach unsatisfactory. To overcome this obstacle, the Greeks constructed a platform on wheels (the *eccyclema*) that could be rolled out of the *skene* as required. This device became the accepted convention for portraying an interior scene or tableau.

The size of the Greek theater had still other effects on the nature of Greek drama. The actors wore large masks, padded clothing, and platform sandals in order to increase their stature and expressiveness for the viewers at the rear of the amphitheater. Although those costumes must have significantly restricted mobility and made physical actions awkward, the masks were designed to function like primitive megaphones and improved the carrying power of the actors' voices. As such, it is little wonder that Greek drama came to be made up of words rather than actions. This verbal emphasis complements the Greek dramatist's preoccupation with motive and character rather than plot, for the state of mind and feelings of an individual can only be fully explained and analyzed using words. The excellence of Greek tragedy came about in part because it was a drama of the mind and not the body.

Then, as now, the audience exerted its influence on both the structure and the content of the plays presented. Because Greek audiences remained in the theater all day, lapses of attention, and periods of jostling, munching, joking, and dozing were inevitable. It was nevertheless essential that all the members of the audience understand the key turning points of the action if the play were to succeed at all; as a result, playwrights preferred to present bold, simple stories that were either familiar to the audience (for example, the story of Oedipus) or, in the case of comedy, predicated on a simple, straightforward hypothesis (in *Lysistrata* that sexual denial can put an end to war). Not surprisingly, given the religious traditions associated with drama and the stylization imposed by the use of masks, many tragic plots were drawn from mythology. The comedies, on the other hand, sought a similar ease of understanding by burlesquing contemporary personalities and events.

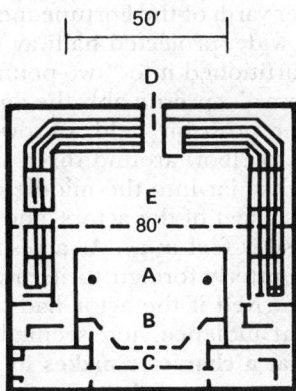

FIGURE 3.   Plan of the Fortune Theater, London. *A. front stage; B. back stage; C. inner stage; D. entrance; E. courtyard.*

The Elizabethan Theater (ca. 1550–1620)

The decline of the Roman Empire brought an end to the Greek theater, and for nearly a thousand years Europe produced little drama of significant literary merit. It is true that the Catholic church, in about the tenth century, began to encourage the production of plays filled with moral or religious instruction, but these anonymous creations are more important as historical curiosities than as dramatic achievements. As a result, when the rediscovery of Greek and Roman literature first spread through Europe to England, few people had any idea what a theater ought to look like. Plays were put on wherever a stage could be erected or a crowd could gather. Amateur groups performing at a university and professionals performing at an inn found that the courtyard provided a ready-made theater. A fairly large stage could be easily set up at one end, and the audience could watch the play from the surrounding yard or balconies. The balcony immediately above the stage, in turn, could be conveniently used by the actors for playing scenes that called for a hill, a cliff, an upstairs window, or any other high place.

No doubt innkeepers found that an afternoon play stimulated business. Those standing in the courtyard watching the play could take their minds off their aching feet by calling for more beer, and the surrounding bedchambers encouraged other forms of trade—so much so that the municipal officials of London (who were staunch puritans) soon began to regulate the production of plays, denouncing the "evil practices of incontinency in great Inns having chambers and secret places adjoining to their open stages and galleries, inveigling and allurement of maidens." As a result of these regulations, several of the theatrical companies decided to build their own playhouses just outside of the city limits. It is hardly surprising that when they did so, beginning in about 1576, they patterned their theaters on the very courtyards to which they had become accustomed.

The existing evidence about the size, shape, and structure of the Elizabethan stage and theater is scanty, but it does allow us to state some facts positively and to make other educated guesses. From a contract for the construction of the Fortune Theater (see Figures 3 and 4) we know that the building was square and relatively small, measuring 80 feet on each side. (The Globe Theater, where Shakespeare's plays were performed, was about the same size, but octagonal or even round.) The pit, or inner yard, of the Fortune measured 55 feet per side, and the stage, which was 43 feet wide, projected halfway (exactly 27½ feet) into the yard. Three galleries were partitioned into "two-penny rooms" and "convenient divisions for gentlemen's rooms"—presumably the equivalent of box seats. When filled to capacity, the theater probably held a crowd of about 1500, with the common folk pressed elbow to elbow around three sides of the stage.

Because the stage intruded so far into the middle of the audience, most spectators sat or stood within thirty feet of the actors, and even the distant corners of the third balcony were but sixty feet away. As a result, the Elizabethan theater fostered a sense of intimacy utterly foreign to its predecessor. *Asides* and *soliloquies,* which would seem contrived if the actor had to strain visibly to make his stage whisper carry to a distant audience, here seemed natural and unaffected. **An aside is a brief comment, that a character makes in the presence of others, intending only some of them—or none of them—to hear it. A *soliloquy* is a speech delivered by a character alone on stage.** Because of the intimacy of the Elizabethan theater, Elizabethan plays came to be filled with lines intended for the audience alone. In the third act of *Othello,* where Iago comes **downstage** toward the audience with Desdemona's handkerchief in his hand, he is so near the audience that his low reflections are delivered almost conspiratorially into their ears:

> I will in Cassio's lodging lose this napkin,
> And let him find it. Trifles light as air
> Are to the jealous confirmations strong
> As proofs of Holy Writ. This may do something.
> The Moor already changes with my poison.

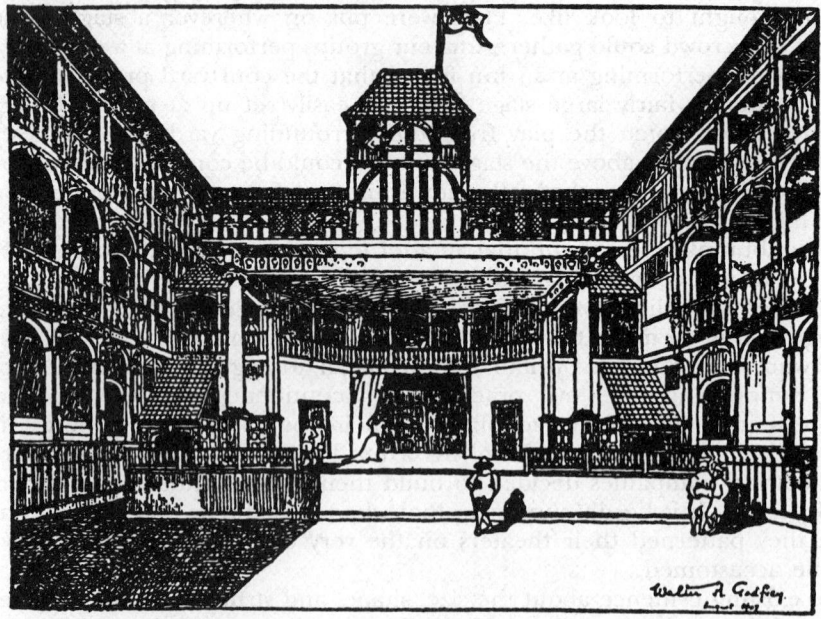

FIGURE 4.   A Reconstruction of the Fortune Theater by Walter H. Godfrey. Note the platform stage projecting into the "pit," the curtained inner stage, the two side entrances, the balcony, the "crow's nest," and the three rows of galleries for spectators. (From *Shakespeare's Theatre* by Ashley H. Thorndike.)

> Dangerous conceits are in their natures poisons,
> Which at the first are scarce found to distaste,
> But with a little act upon the blood
> Burn like the mines of sulphur.
>
> —From *Othello*, act 3, scene 3,
> William Shakespeare [1604]

When Othello subsequently enters *upstage,* he is some forty to fifty feet away from Iago; consequently, Iago can comment on Othello's visible agitation without fear of being overheard. He sees that, in fact, jealousy does "burn like the mines of sulphur" within Othello's breast, and he addresses the spectators directly: "I did say so. / Look where he comes!" **The terms *downstage* and *upstage* derive from the period when the stage was raked, or tilted, toward the audience. When actors moved toward the audience they literally moved down the stage, and in moving away they climbed slightly up.**

In addition to intimacy, the Elizabethan stage also had versatility. It probably contained at least three different acting areas (see Figure 4). The main one was, of course, the 27½- by 43-foot platform. In this large neutral area, characters could meet and interact without raising any question in the minds of an Elizabethan audience about the exact setting. In the original text of *Othello*, for example, there are only three directions for setting, and all of them are quite indefinite: two call for the use of an inner chamber or curtained area and one for an upstairs window. If, for some reason, a specific setting *was* important, the characters themselves would describe it, as in the seaport scene quoted earlier (p. 1068).

An inner stage behind the main platform may have been used to represent the interior of a council chamber, a bedroom, a tent, a tomb, a throne room, and so on. Act 1, scene 3 of *Othello* seems to require that this inner stage be screened by curtains that can be drawn to reveal "the Duke and Senators set at a table." Similarly, act 5, scene 2 opens on "Desdemona in bed." Because every other scene in the play calls for each character to enter, speak his lines, and then exit, only these two scenes need to be staged in the curtained chamber.

According to the records available to us, some form of upper stage or balcony apparently extended above the inner stage. In act 1, scene 1 of *Othello*, Roderigo and Iago converse in the street before calling up to Brabantio who "appears above, at a window." Similarly, Juliet appears at a window in her first balcony scene. Such stage directions, together with the "convenient windows" called for in the contract for the Fortune Theater, imply that these areas were either shuttered or curtained so that the characters could suddenly "appear." But the balcony must also on occasion have provided a fairly large area in which several characters could meet, as indicated by such stage directions as "Enter Cleopatra and her maids aloft."

Although there may also have been an even higher balcony for the musicians (or for action taking place in a tower or in the crow's nest of a ship), few scenes—none in *Othello*—were staged very far above the crowd assembled in the yard. In fact, the vast majority of the scenes in Elizabethan drama were presented on the main stage, so that the audience was able to see and hear clearly.

Because the audience stood around three sides of the main stage, it was impossible to use a curtain to separate scenes. And because the public theaters were unenclosed and plays were performed during the daytime, it was impossible to throw the stage into darkness during a change of scene. Hence, a scene would start with the entrance of one or more characters, and the locale would remain the same until all of the characters left the stage—or were carted off, if dead ("Exeunt severally; Hamlet dragging in [i.e., offstage] Polonius"). Action in a new locale would then commence with a new set of entrances. We know that at least two doors could be used for entrances and exits because of such stage directions as the following: ("Enter Pompey at one door, with drum and trumpet: at another, Caesar, Lepidus, Antony, Maecenas, Agrippa, with soldiers marching").

The different settings in an Elizabethan play were rarely indicated by any change in props or scenery. *Othello* contains fifteen different scenes, and if the suggested stage directions of modern editions are followed, a production would require at least eleven different settings. Obviously, such changes were impossible on an open stage. Indeed, if the list of properties owned by the Fortune Theater is indicative of the period, scenery was used mainly to adorn the inner stage and even there only sparingly. Among the bulkiest were:

> i rock, i cage, i tomb, i Hell mouth.
> i tomb of Guido, i tomb of Dido, i bedstead.
> viii lances, i pair of stairs for Phaeton.
> i golden fleece; ii rackets; i bay tree.
> Iris head, & rainbow; i little altar.
> ii fanes of feathers; Bellendon stable; i tree of golden
>   apples; Tantalus' tree; ix iron targets.
> i copper target, & xvii foils.
> i wheel and frame in the Siege of London.
> i cauldron for the Jew.

For the most part, Elizabethans relied on words rather than props to give a sense of locale.

All of this means that the Elizabethan theater, with its multiple acting areas and its imaginary settings, was well suited to plays with rapidly shifting scenes and continuous action. It gave rise to a form of drama entirely unlike that of ancient Greece. Instead of the play starting a few fictional hours before the crisis (as in *Oedipus*), the Renaissance play starts at the beginning of a story and skips from time to time and place to place until the crisis is reached. Act 1 of *Othello,* for example, begins in Venice on the night of Othello and Desdemona's marriage. Then act 2 skips more than a week ahead to a period when all of the principals arrive in Cyprus, and there the action requires two more nights and a day. Because Elizabethan plays range freely in time and setting, all of the most dramatic moments in a story are presented on stage. Thus, if *King Oedipus* had been written by Shakespeare, the audience might have seen and heard events that Sophocles included only as reminiscences—particularly, the original prophecies of the oracle to Oedipus, Oedipus's flight from Corinth, and his murder of Laius at the place where three roads meet. Scenes of violence, which occur offstage in Greek tragedy (like the death of Jocasta) were physically enacted before the Elizabethan audience. *Othello* includes several sword fights, three murders, and a suicide—all on stage. And this carnage is only moderate by Renaissance standards. (Note that despite its general paucity of props, the Fortune Theater inventoried *seventeen* foils!) The audience standing in the yard demanded action, and the versatile Elizabethan stage made this demand easy to fulfill.

The Neoclassical French Theater (ca. 1660–1800)

The early acting companies of France, like those of England, toured the countryside, playing wherever they could. As luck would have it, tennis had been popular in France during the fifteenth century, and many noblemen had erected indoor tennis courts, some of which were transformed during the next two centuries into primitive theaters. A temporary stage would be erected on one half of the court; ordinary folk would stand or sit on wooden benches in the other half, and the nobles would be seated in the galleries overlooking the playing area. It was in such converted quarters that Corneille and Molière, two of the greatest of the neoclassical playwrights, saw their first plays produced.

Thus, early French theaters evolved in a direction that differed radically from their Elizabethan counterparts. The single most significant change was the increased separation of the actors from the audience. Whereas the Elizabethan audience had nearly encircled the actors, the seventeenth-century French audience sat along one side of the stage and looked in on the action, as if peering through an invisible wall (see Figures 5 and 6). This arrangement eventually led to the use of a front curtain to conceal the stage between acts and made possible elaborate changes of scenery.

Because all members of the audience watched the play from a similar vantage point, **the setting could be vividly depicted on huge flat canvases, using the devices of perspective developed by the painters of the Italian Renaissance** (see Figure 6). **These *flats* could easily be replaced, providing the opportunity for changes in setting.** The curtain concealed the scene before the start of the play, but thereafter any changes in scenery were made mechanically in full view of the audience, as a form of special effect. In his prologues Molière himself was not beyond using fountains, aerial chariots, the descent of a god in a cloud, or a maiden emerging from a sea shell to bring the crowd to its feet and to delight the king.

It is almost axiomatic in theater that whenever innovations in staging begin to turn drama into spectacle, the quality of the writing in plays declines. However, at least three factors kept seventeenth-century French drama from degenerating into exhibitionistic extravaganzas. First, **neoclassical scholars and critics imposed their standards on the age by requiring that every play fulfill the three unities: *unity of***

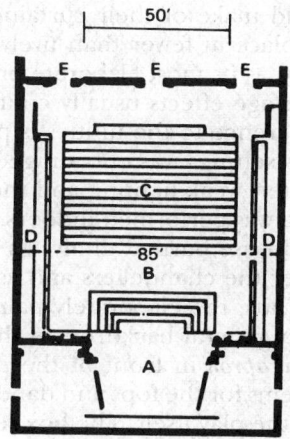

FIGURE 5. Plan of the Richelieu-Molière Theater, Paris. *A. stage; B. parterre; C. seats; D. galleries; E. entrances.*

FIGURE 6.   A Neoclassical Theater in Strasburg (1655). Note the flat wings representing rows of buildings, the painted backdrop showing the continuation of the street, and the actors at the forefront of the stage beneath the chandeliers. (From *Wiener Szenische Kunst* by Joseph Gregor.)

time mandated that the play's action should be confined to a single day; *unity of action* forbade subplots and irrelevant or incongruous episodes; and *unity of place* required that all of the action take place in a single setting or vicinity. The exclusion of digressions and the limitation on settings greatly constricted the use that French playwrights could make of their curtained stage. Molière's *Tartuffe* (1664), for example, takes place in fewer than twelve hours, in a single setting that has a simple dinner table as its most elaborate prop. Those plays by Molière that do include spectacular stage effects usually confine them to a prologue or epilogue, so that formal adherence to the unities is preserved.

The simplicity of Molière's settings was encouraged by two physical characteristics of the neoclassical theater: weak lighting and the presence of spectators on the stage itself. French drama was performed indoors, often under artificial light, and the tallow candles then in use burned dimly. As a result, most of the acting took place immediately under the chandeliers and as far downstage (as close to the audience) as possible. Thus, the elaborately painted flats served less as the setting for the play than as a general backdrop to the action, which often took place on the narrow strip or **apron** in front of the proscenium arch. The dark interior also presented problems for the fops and dandies who came to the theater as much to be seen as to see the play itself. The box seats were likely to remain in the shadows, and because many of those vain creatures were wealthy patrons, the theater owners accommodated them with seats (sometimes as many as two hundred) on the stage. Naturally, such seating cut down the available acting area and limited the ability of stagehands to move bulky properties around.

As a result of the seating, the lighting, and the neoclassical rules of composition, most of the plays in this period were set in a single place of general resort—a courtyard, a street, a drawing room. The plots developed scenes of emotional intensity, but because decorum and probability were required by unity of action, they rarely erupted into the violent activity that so often left the Elizabethan stage littered with bodies. The drama of the period is witty, intellectual, and refined. Characteristically, it depicts highly idealized and artificial conversations among men and women (female parts were now actually performed by women) representing broad human types—classical heroes or gods in tragedy, contemporary scoundrels or buffoons in comedy. It is an intentionally stylized drama based on the premise that fixed rules of structure are necessary in refined literature.

The Development of the Box Set (ca. 1830–1920)

In 1642 Oliver Cromwell and his Puritan followers closed down all the playhouses in England, and by the time they were reopened in 1660, the Elizabethan theater was dead. Not surprisingly, given the predilection of Charles II and his court for all things French, the English drama that succeeded the Restoration was heavily influenced by the neoclassical conventions of the French theater—an influence that persisted throughout most of the eighteenth century. In the nineteenth century, however, the situation changed. A series of important technical innovations encouraged dramatists to abandon neoclassicism in favor of a drama characterized by realistic (mimetic) plots performed within equally realistic settings.

The first of these changes was the introduction, between 1820 and 1840, of gas lighting. Not only were gas lights brighter than the candles and oil lamps that had hitherto served, but now all the lights in the house could be controlled from a single instrument panel. For the first time, a director could focus the audience's attention on the lighted stage by leaving the rest of the auditorium in total darkness; this increased control over stage lights allowed playwrights to switch their scenes from day to night without recourse to cumbersome passages of dialogue calling attention to the fact. The improved lighting also allowed the actors to move more or less freely about the setting, instead of forcing them to remain out in front of the proscenium arch. Such maneuverability naturally called greater attention to the setting, which could now become a functional, rather than simply an ornamental, feature of the play. As a consequence, directors began to eliminate the backdrops and the artificial perspective of movable flats.

Soon after 1830, the *box set* was introduced in England. In its ultimate development, the box set is identical to a real room with one wall removed. Even though the audience can peer through this "invisible" fourth wall to eavesdrop on the action taking place within, the actors pretend that the invisible wall exists. Thus, asides directed to the audience can no longer occur and soliloquies must be strictly limited to those emotional moments during which a character might logically be overheard talking to himself. Nineteenth-century producers understandably relished these innovations and some went so far as to boast in their advertisements of having sets with real ceilings, real doors, and working locks. The description of the set for *Hedda Gabler* is a typical example of the meticulous care with which late nineteenth-century playwrights envisioned the locale of their plays.

At about the same time that candlelight was being replaced by gas, directors also discovered ways to focus spotlights on single characters. This was first achieved by burning small chunks of lime and reflecting the light off of curved mirrors onto the leading man or leading lady (who was then, quite literally, "in the limelight"). Most directors, understandably, became enamored with the technique, and throughout the nineteenth century talented actors and actresses often held to the limelight to the detriment of the play as a whole. A particularly fine speech by Edmund Kean or Sarah Kemble Siddons, for example, might bring the audience to its feet in midscene. And if the applause were long and loud enough, Kean or Siddons would simply recite the speech again as an encore. The inevitable effect of such an emphasis was to encourage dramatists to concentrate on writing good parts for the leading roles without giving equal attention to plot, structure, and theme.

A further development in nineteenth-century stagecraft was the increasing use made of the curtain spanning the proscenium arch. Until about 1875, the curtain was used only to screen the stage before the start of the play; once raised, it did not fall again until the end of the last act. The intention, of course, was to startle and delight the spectators when the curtain first rose on the fanciful world of the theater and then to entertain them by magically transforming that world before their eyes. So long as the scenery was mainly composed of paintings on flats that could be slid off stage mechanically and replaced by others, such changes of scene could occur swiftly and smoothly. But the advent of the realistic box set inevitably brought with it an increasing number of unwieldy props. The stage became cluttered with footstools, sofas, armchairs, end tables, vases, and portraits that stagehands were required to cart off or rearrange during any change of scene. The whole process soon became more frantic than magical and more distracting than entertaining. Furthermore, to effect such changes before the eyes of the audience only served to break down the illusion of reality. In order to sustain the illusion, directors and playwrights began to use the curtain between acts and even between scenes.

This had an immediate and important influence on the text of plays written in the final quarter of the nineteenth century. Before then a scene or an act necessarily began with a set of entrances and concluded with some pretext calling for the characters to exit—usually a variant of "Come! Let's be off to dine [or drink, or dance, or what have you]." The increased use of the curtain freed the dramatist from such constrictions. The emphasis changed from finding a way of getting the characters offstage to finding a way of building dramatic tension and emphasizing basic themes at the end of acts or scenes. The resulting *curtain line* **(a moment of high drama at the very end of an act or scene)** is perhaps the most distinctive feature of modern drama. Ibsen was among the first to employ the curtain line, and in *Hedda Gabler* he honed it to perfection. Each act ends on a note of high drama, but for the purpose of illustration, we will look at the conclusion to the third act:

LÖVBORG. Good-by, Mrs. Tesman. And give George Tesman my love. [*He is on the point of going.*]

HEDDA. No, wait! I must give you a memento to take with you. [*She goes to the writing table and opens the drawer and the pistol case, then returns to* LÖVBORG *with one of the pistols.*]

LÖVBORG [*looks at her*]. This? Is this the memento?

HEDDA [*nodding slowly*]. Do you recognize it? It was aimed at you once.
LÖVBORG. You should have used it then.
HEDDA. Take it—and do you use it now.
LÖVBORG [*puts the pistol in his breast pocket*]. Thanks!
HEDDA. And beautifully, Eilert Lövborg. Promise me that!
LÖVBORG. Good-by, Hedda Gabler. [*He goes out by the hall door.*]

[HEDDA *listens for a moment at the door. Then she goes up to the writing table, takes out the packet of manuscript, peeps under the cover, draws a few of the sheets half out and looks at them. Next she goes over and seats herself in the armchair beside the stove, with the packet in her lap. Presently she opens the stove door and then the packet.*]

HEDDA [*throws one of the quires into the fire and whispers to herself*]. Now I am burning your child, Thea! Burning it, curlylocks! [*Throwing one or two more quires into the stove.*] Your child and Eilert Lövborg's. [*Throws the rest in.*] I am burning—I am burning your child.

—From *Hedda Gabler*, act 3, Henrik Ibsen [1890]

With growing horror, we realize not only that Hedda is encouraging Eilert to kill himself, but also that she could have prevented his death by returning the manuscript. She burns the only copy of Eilert's book because she is insanely jealous that Thea, "that pretty little fool" as Hedda thinks of her, should after all have had "her fingers in a man's destiny." The curtain drops just as Hedda reaches her deepest and most chilling insight into her own actions: "I am burning—I am burning your child."

The Modern Theater

Twentieth-century stagecraft has been characterized by flexibility. An improved understanding of the past has allowed us to stage the plays of Sophocles, Shakespeare, Molière, and others with greater fidelity to the original intentions of the author. Furthermore, modern critical principles encourage playwrights and directors to put aside their *a priori* notions about staging and recognize that each play requires and deserves a separate approach. Continuing technical developments in the twentieth century have facilitated this flexibility both through further refinements in lighting and through machinery that can easily manipulate the sets and sometimes even the seating arrangement in the theater.

Although most modern theaters retain the proscenium arch and a clear division between the audience and the actors, many small theaters (especially temporary ones) have experimented with other structures. The most innovative of these have tried to recreate the intimacy and versatility of the Elizabethan stage either in small semicircular amphitheaters or in arena theaters. **Arena staging or theater-in-the-round has emerged as the most distinctive twentieth-century contribution to stagecraft. The audience totally surrounds the stage and is therefore as close to the action of the play as is physically possible. Entrances and exits are made through the aisles normally used by the spectators and in some cases these become secondary acting areas, as well.** Inevitably, however, the actors cannot simultaneously face all members of the audience. So long as the play focuses on the conflict between at least two characters, this presents no problem. When the two square off, all members of the audience will have at least a frontal view of one character or a profile of both. When the dramatic interest is focused totally on one character, however, as it is in the final moments of *Othello,* one fourth of the audience is apt to feel frustrated at being unable to see his face and hear his climactic speech clearly. For this reason, arena staging is less successful than other approaches for plays with one dominant role.

Most of the major playhouses in America were built long before arena staging became widely accepted, but they, too, have adapted to the twentieth-century demand for flexibility. Modern set designs have been transformed by a consensus that their primary purpose is to provide three-dimensional areas for acting. The movable flats that were used well into the twentieth century to create perspective in outdoor settings have now been all but eliminated. Playwrights and directors seem to agree that everything depicted on stage should be functional and esthetically pleasing but not necessarily realistic. The sets should draw no attention to themselves or away from the acting. The general trend has been toward a simple, almost architectural stage, with platforms at various levels linked by stairways and ramps. The modern set strives to be suggestive and intellectually stimulating instead of purely pictorial, and this aim is facilitated by modern electrical lighting, which can actually create moods by "drawing" on the stage with shadows and prismatic colors to transform a single set into a constantly changing environment.

The trends in the modern theater have imposed no new conditions on playwrights; instead, they have been freed from many of the old limitations of the stage. This flexibility is best illustrated by the range of settings used in the classics of modern drama. Eugene O'Neill's *Desire Under the Elms* (1924), for example, takes place in, and immediately outside of, the Cabot farmhouse. O'Neill's own sketches show the exterior of the farmhouse, with various sections of the wall removed as the action shifts from one room to another. In effect, it is a stage with multiple box sets. Arthur Miller's *Death of a Salesman* (1949) also calls for the interior of a house, but in this case all of the walls are invisible and the house itself becomes a large, skeletal structure of various platforms for acting and observing actions. Finally, Tom Stoppard's *Rosencrantz and Guildenstern Are Dead* (1967) is set on a barren stage, "a place without any visible character"; it requires only a platform with two different levels and a few simple properties.

The causes of the modern trend toward flexibility, suggestivity, and simplicity of setting are complex, but certainly television and the movies have had something to do with it. Before films became popular, there had been an ever-increasing trend toward spectacle in the theater. Although crowds once flocked to playhouses to see a theatrical railroad engine steaming along toward the bound heroine or baying bloodhounds pursuing the bleeding hero, they soon found that the movies—through close-ups, cuts, and editing—could present those thrills more realistically while indulging in the additional expensive luxuries of having the train explode or the hero slog through miles of snake-infested swamp. Within a few years, therefore, playhouses ceased to stage spectacular extravaganzas, and drama once again became the verbal and intellectual experience previously enjoyed by the Elizabethans and the Greeks.

22

The Elements of Drama

For the most part, the elements of drama are identical to those of fiction and poetry. Plays have plots, themes, characters, and settings and make use of the many devices of poetic diction. Thus, many of the steps in the analysis of a play should parallel those used for a poem or a short story. At the same time, however, drama is a different literary genre and it imposes its own constraints on the playwright's use of certain elements of literature. These unique aspects of dramatic writing are our present concern.

Every play unfolds a story through the dialogue and actions of its characters. An understanding of these four elements—story, dialogue, action, and character—is therefore crucial to the appreciation of drama.

DIALOGUE

Tom Stoppard's *Rosencrantz and Guildenstern Are Dead* has no story apart from that already told in *Hamlet;* its principal characters are notable mainly because no one can distinguish between them; and the most significant action in the play is prolonged waiting. Part of the fun of Stoppard's work is that he has nearly stripped drama to its one indispensible element, dialogue.

A theatrical production without dialogue can be a mime or a ballet, but it is never a play. As Stoppard himself might have put it: a play can give you talk and characters without much action. And a play can give you talk and action without strong characters. But a play cannot give you characters and action without talk. It is all talk in drama.

Dramatic dialogue, however, is very different from the kind of dialogue that makes up so much of our ordinary lives. Actual conversation is full of hesitations, pauses, fragments, misunderstandings, and repetitions. The communication itself is often as much a product of inflections, gestures, and facial expressions as it is of the spoken word. It depends so much on innuendo and allusions to previous conversations that an outsider is often unable to determine the exact meaning of a discussion heard out of context. This in fact was Richard Nixon's contention when he protested in July and August 1973 against the release of the transcripts of his conversations about the Watergate break-in. The following selection from the Nixon tapes may have been one of the most important moments in the history of the United States presidency; its release shocked the nation and eventually led to Nixon's resignation in August 1974. As we will see, however, it is far from being good drama:

THE SETTING. *March 21, 1973, 10:12 A.M. The Oval Office*

THE PARTICIPANTS. *Richard Nixon and John Dean*

THE SITUATION. *Dean has just reviewed the history of the Watergate cover-up, calling it a "cancer" close to the presidency. Having described the continual demands for hush money by the Watergate burglars, he continues:*

DEAN. . . . It will cost money. It is dangerous. People around here are not pros at this sort of thing. This is the sort of thing Mafia people can do: washing money, getting clean money, and things like that. We just don't know about those things, because we are not criminals and not used to dealing in that business.

NIXON. That's right.

DEAN. It is a tough thing to know how to do.

NIXON. Maybe it takes a gang to do that.

DEAN. That's right. There is a real problem as to whether we could even do it. Plus there is a real problem in raising money. Mitchell has been working on raising some money. He is one of the ones with the most to lose. But there is no denying the fact that the White House, in Ehrlichman, Haldeman, and Dean, are involved in some of the early money decisions.

NIXON. How much money do you need?

DEAN. I would say these people are going to cost a million dollars over the next two years.

NIXON. We could get that. On the money, if you need the money you could get that. You could get a million dollars. You could get it in cash. I know where it could be gotten. It is not easy, but it could be done. But the question is who the hell would handle it? Any ideas on that?

DEAN. That's right. Well, I think that is something that Mitchell ought to be charged with.

NIXON. I would think so too.

DEAN. And get some pros to help him.

—From *Submission of Recorded Presidential Conversations,* April 30, 1974

It is clear enough that the president and his chief counsel are discussing obstruction of justice, acquiescence in blackmail, and involvement with professional criminals. The very topics of conversation are momentous and appalling. Yet the passage is stylistically weak and grammatically inept. The conversation redundantly returns to the difficulty of raising the money and the need for "pros" to handle the payoffs; and when Dean digresses into a discussion of the White House involvement, the president brings him back to the point by asking, "How much money do you need?" The sentences are choppy and inelegant, and the participants do not come to a clear decision until many exchanges later. Even then the discussion does not end. It meanders along for at least another hour, with the participants drifting away from the central issue and then darting back to it like minnows chasing a spinner.

In contrast, important conversations in drama slash past trivial details and strike the lure with vigor and directness. A play necessarily packs a story of significance into two or three hours of stage time. As a result, each sentence is hard and muscular—made up of concrete nouns and active verbs. The dialogue continuously and clearly builds toward its point, eliminating irrelevancies and unnecessary repetitions. When trimmed to its dramatic core, a real conversation, like the one between Richard Nixon and John Dean, might well be cut by half.

Dramatic dialogue ordinarily carries with it still another burden: it must include sufficient background information to fix the time, place, and circumstances of the action firmly in the mind of the audience. Nixon and Dean, after all, knew each other well and also knew the circumstances surrounding the issues described in their conversation; the playwright, however, must introduce the characters and provide background information before the audience can really understand what is going on. Although some playwrights prefer to have a narrator set the scene in a formal prologue—as, for example, in Tennessee Williams's *The Glass Menagerie* or Thornton Wilder's *Our Town*—most try to bring out the background information gradually during the play's first act. Ibsen was a master of the gradual introduction, as illustrated in the first few moments of *Hedda Gabler:*

MISS JULIANA TESMAN, *with her bonnet on and carrying a parasol, comes in from the hall, followed by* BERTA, *who carries a bouquet wrapped in paper.* MISS TESMAN *is a comely and pleasant-looking lady of about sixty-five. She is nicely but simply dressed in a gray walking costume.* BERTA *is a middle-aged woman of plain and rather countrified appearance.*

MISS TESMAN [*stops close to the door, listens and says softly*]. Upon my word, I don't believe they are stirring yet!

BERTA [*also softly*]. I told you so, miss. Remember how late the steamboat got in last night. And then, when they got home!—good lord, what a lot the young mistress had to unpack before she could get to bed.

MISS TESMAN. Well, well—let them have their sleep out. But let us see that they get a good breath of the fresh morning air when they do appear. [*She goes to the glass door and throws it open.*]

BERTA [*beside table, at a loss what to do with the bouquet in her hand*]. I declare, there isn't a bit of room left. I think I'll put it down here, miss. [*She places it on the piano.*]

MISS TESMAN. So you've got a new mistress now, my dear Berta. Heaven knows it was a wrench to me to part with you.

BERTA [*on the point of weeping*]. And do you think it wasn't hard for me too, miss? After all the blessed years I've been with you and Miss Rina.

MISS TESMAN. We must make the best of it, Berta. There was nothing else to be done. George can't do without you, you see—he absolutely can't. He has had you to look after him ever since he was a little boy.

BERTA. Ah, but, Miss Julia, I can't help thinking of Miss Rina lying helpless at home there, poor thing. And with only that new girl too! She'll never learn to take proper care of an invalid.

MISS TESMAN. Oh, I shall manage to train her. And of course, you know, I shall take most of it upon myself. You needn't be uneasy about my poor sister, my dear Berta.

BERTA. Well, but there's another thing, miss. I'm so mortally afraid I shan't be able to suit the young mistress.

MISS TESMAN. Oh well—just at first there may be one or two things—

BERTA. Most like she'll be terrible grand in her ways.

MISS TESMAN. Well, you can't wonder at that—General Gabler's daughter! Think of the sort of life she was accustomed to in her father's time. Don't you remember how we used to see her riding down the road along with the general? In that long black habit—and with feathers in her hat?

BERTA. Yes, indeed—I remember well enough! But, good lord, I should never have dreamt in those days that she and Master George would make a match of it.

MISS TESMAN. Nor I. But by-the-bye, Berta—while I think of it: in future you mustn't say Master George. You must say Doctor Tesman.

BERTA. Yes, the young mistress spoke of that too—last night—the moment they set foot in the house. Is it true then, miss?

MISS TESMAN. Yes, indeed it is. Only think, Berta—some foreign university has made him a doctor—while he has been abroad, you understand. I hadn't heard a word about it until he told me himself upon the pier.

BERTA. Well, well, he's clever enough for anything, he is. But I didn't think he'd have gone in for doctoring people too.

MISS TESMAN. No, no, it's not that sort of doctor he is. [*Nods significantly.*] But let me tell you, we may have to call him something still grander before long.

BERTA. You don't say so! What can that be, miss?

MISS TESMAN [*smiling*]. H'm—wouldn't you like to know!

—From *Hedda Gabler*, Henrik Ibsen [1890]

Everything in this conversation is natural and unstrained, yet it tells us all that we immediately need to know about the main characters and their relationships with one another. We learn that George Tesman and his new wife have just returned from their honeymoon, that no one had ever dreamt the two would wed, that prior to his marriage George had lived with his two aunts and the maid Berta, and that George had recently been awarded a doctorate by "some foreign university." These few facts give us our bearings and prepare us for the entrance of George and Hedda. They also hint at Hedda's romantic past and George's professional ambitions, thus preparing us for the entrance of Eilert Lövborg, who is about to compete for George's academic position as he had once competed for Hedda's affections.

But we learn even more. Ibsen is so economical a craftsman that these few lines of dialogue also contribute to the characterization of George, Hedda, and Aunt Julia. We learn, for example, that George is helpless and relies on others to provide him with the comforts of life. When Aunt Julia must choose whether Berta should stay with Aunt Rina or go with George, she decides that her invalid sister is more self-sufficient than her nephew. We also learn that George is not the elegant sort of man one would expect to marry a general's daughter, although his aunts and Berta are genuinely fond of him. Thus, when we first see Tesman on stage we have been prepared, subtly, for his kindly, methodical, sentimental, and slightly incompetent approach to life.

Hedda, on the other hand, is a far more formidable character. She is mentioned by Berta and Julia with anxiety. Because Hedda is so "grand in her ways," Berta fears that she "shan't be able to suit the young mistress" and Aunt Julia agrees that "at first there may be one or two things." Aunt Julia's reminiscences about how Hedda used to ride in a long black habit with feathers in her hat prepare us for a woman of aristocratic and romantic disposition. And Hedda's insistence that her husband be called Doctor Tesman hints at her desire for a dignified and proper place in society. These few introductory remarks, then, indicate that Hedda is likely to be emotionally unsuited to a drab life with Tesman and suggest that her romantic predilections may eventually come into conflict with her equally strong desire for propriety.

Finally, the lines indirectly characterize Aunt Julia. She is a fussy, meddling, and kindly woman who habitually thinks of others first. She listens carefully to find out if the newlyweds are stirring, throws open the glass door to give them plenty of air, and gives up her own maid to be sure they will be well served. Berta's mistaken assumption that George has become a medical doctor apparently triggers one of the preoccupations of Aunt Julia's prying mind. The allusion to a medial doctor in the context of George's marriage evidently arouses her hope that the household may soon need an obstetrical physician and that George will become a father as well as a doctor of philosophy. She nods significantly and says mysteriously, "we may have to call him something still grander [than doctor] before long."

Yet another function of the dialogue in this introductory scene is to foreshadow themes of later importance. The oblique allusion to Hedda's possible pregnancy is but one such example. In a more overt and pragmatic way, the opening dialogue and accompanying actions often help to initiate events that are further developed as the play progresses. The bouquet that is in Berta's hand as the play opens carries a card promising a visit from Thea Elvsted, a visit that will develop into a competition between Hedda and Thea for control over Eilert Lövborg. Similarly, Aunt Julia's well-intentioned opening of the glass doors will later irritate Hedda, who prefers a "softer light" and complains, "Oh—there the servant has gone and opened the veranda door and let in a whole flood of sunshine." From that point on, Hedda maliciously seeks opportunities to goad Aunt Julia and to prevent any attempt to create a tight family circle that will include George's aunts. As the play unfolds, the expressed anxieties of Aunt Julia and Berta that "there may be one or two" points of conflict between them and Hedda are amply confirmed.

In summary, the dialogue in Ibsen's plays, as in most other plays, serves many simultaneous functions. It is used to provide necessary factual information, to reminisce, to characterize, to speculate, and to foreshadow. Such dialogue may take the form of discussion (as in the quoted scene), argument, or inquiry. It may accompany and clarify actions or simply reveal attitudes and opinions. In short, good dialogue is a very flexible narrative tool.

Dialogue is not, however, an easy tool to use. A playwright, unlike a novelist, cannot simply halt proceedings to introduce formal character sketches or to set a scene; nor can a playwright exert the same direct control over the "story." A fictional "yarn" is spun out of a voice that the author, as narrator, can fully control. But the dramatist has no voice of his or her own. When the curtain rises, the fabric of the plot must emerge naturally from interwoven and independent threads of conversation.

When we argue that the plot of a play must emerge naturally from its dialogue, we do not mean that the dialogue itself must inevitably be "natural" or "realistic." As the Watergate tapes demonstrate, the real words of real people often seem awkward and unnatural in transcript. But art is not life. We hold art to a higher standard of probability, eloquence, and organization; therefore, nearly all dramatic dialogue is more rhetorical—more poetic, if you will—than real dialogue. Even so, however, there is an enormous range between the dialogue of *Hedda Gabler,* for example, and that of *Othello.* Part of the difference results from the fact that the former is written in prose, the latter in verse; and verse is almost always much richer than prose in sound, rhythm, and imagery.

There is, however, also the matter of level of style. The language of *Othello* is often lofty and formal; the language of *Hedda Gabler,* by contrast, is colloquial and informal. Listen to the reflections of Othello as he looks upon Desdemona by candlelight before mercilessly slaying her:

> If I quench thee, thou flaming minister,
> I can thy former light restore,
> Should I repent me: but once put out thy light,
> Thou cunning'st pattern of excelling nature,
> I know not where is that Promethean heat
> That can thy light relume. When I have plucked the rose,
> I cannot give it vital growth again,
> It must needs wither: I'll smell it on the tree.
>   [*Kissing her.*]
> Ah, balmy breath, that dost almost persuade
> Justice to break her sword! One more, one more.
> Be thus when thou art dead, and I will kill thee,
> And love thee after.
>
> —From *Othello,* act 5, scene 2,
> William Shakespeare [1604]

Even in this moment of aroused emotion Othello's thoughts roll forth in grammatically complete and relatively complex sentences. His fevered and fertile imagination leads him to express himself through a series of poetic devices. First he compares snuffing a candle with snuffing Desdemona's life; then he alludes to the Greek myth of Prometheus, a Titan who originally gave fire to mankind; next he compares the beauty of Desdemona with that of the rose that "must needs wither" when plucked; and finally, after bending to "smell it on the tree," he uses personification in claiming that Desdemona's "balmy breath" could "almost persuade / Justice to break her sword." Plays like *Othello,* which make use of careful syntax and copious poetic devices, are said to be written in the **high style.**

The language of *Hedda Gabler* is, of course, far different. Notice, for example, the casual and conversational tone. Phrases are inserted to capture the flavor of everyday speech ("upon my word," "good lord," "well, well," "I declare"[1]). Grammatical relationships, too, are informal: the dialogue is sprinkled with dashes to indicate incomplete thoughts or sudden changes in direction. And Ibsen makes no attempt to use poetical devices. Playwrights occasionally carry this colloquial **low style** even further and use ungrammatical and dialectical speech as a tool of characterization. The back-country accents and diction of the Cabots, for example, help Eugene O'Neill explore crude and elemental passions in *Desire Under the Elms.* Similarly, Stanley Kowalski's inarticulate speech in Tennessee Williams's *A Streetcar Named Desire* underscores his assertive, uneducated, and violent character. And even in *Othello* Iago's worldly and profane speech helps to identify him as a villain.

Dramatic theory during the classical and neoclassical periods held that tragedy should be written in the high style and that the colloquial, or low, style was appropriate only to comedy. In practice, however, as the plays of Shakespeare amply demonstrate, such a distinction need not be rigidly observed, and in more modern times it has been all but abandoned. Most drama is mixed in style, rising to eloquence or falling to informality according to the inherent demands of the dramatic situation.

---

[1] If these expressions seem too stilted to qualify as "everyday speech," remember that *Hedda Gabler* was written more than 100 years ago and has been translated into English from the original Norwegian. It is always well to bear such factors in mind when considering the language of a play.

STORY

People come to the theater because they wish to be entertained. Although they may be willing to admire fine writing or to tolerate moral instruction, they demand an engrossing story. An audience is, after all, a crowd, and the principal desire of a crowd is to find out "what happens next." Drama, however, would emphasize story even if it were not demanded by the audience, for the dramatic point of view necessitates a fundamentally chronological development of action. Reminiscences can be, and often are, used to precipitate the action, but once the play has begun, the events on the stage inevitably unfold according to the simple time sequence of a story.

Dramatic actions as they unfold upon the stage do not, of course, simply "happen"; they are premeditated and artistically arranged by the playwright to yield a dramatic plot. The ability to understand the story (the "what happens") may satisfy our basic desire as theatergoers to be entertained, but as literary critics we also need to understand not only "what happens" but "why"—a question that invariably forces us to consider the dynamics of plot.

Like a typical short story, the plot of nearly every play contains five structural elements: *exposition, complication, crisis, falling action,* **and** *resolution.* The principal difference between fictional and dramatic plots is that the latter are more regular in their use of these five elements, as is illustrated in the following paragraphs.

Exposition

The *exposition* **provides essential background information, introduces the cast, begins the characterization, and initiates the action.** Some exposition is always provided in the first scene, and all of the essential background material is usually provided by the end of the first act. Sometimes a formal prologue or introduction by a narrator helps to set the scene, but more often there is no sharp division between the exposition and the complication that follows. In fact, **most plays begin** *in medias res* **(in the middle of things), just after some event has taken place that will eventually lead to the crisis.**

EXAMPLES OF THE SITUATION AT THE COMMENCEMENT OF DRAMATIC ACTION

King Oedipus. A plague afflicts Thebes because the murderer of King Laius has never been punished.

Othello. Othello and Desdemona have secretly married; and Cassio, rather than Iago, has been made Othello's lieutenant.

Tartuffe. To be nearer to his religious adviser, Orgon has installed Tartuffe in his home.

Hedda Gabler. After their honeymoon, Hedda and George have returned to town, as has Eilert Lövborg, who is seeking to publish a new book. Rumor has it that George's faculty appointment must await the outcome of a competition with Eilert.

The situation at the outset of a play usually gives us important clues to its direction and meaning. We do not, for example, see Oedipus at his moment of early triumph over the Sphinx; instead we first see him as he proudly promises that he will discover Laius's killer just as he once discovered the meaning of the

Sphinx's riddle. The play explores the consequences of this rash promise. Similarly, *Othello* does not begin with a scene showing Othello's wedding ceremony, but rather with the conspiracy between Roderigo and Iago, in order to focus the audience's attention immediately on Iago's thirst for revenge.

Complication

The *complication* introduces and develops the conflict. It commences when one or more of the main characters first become aware of an impending difficulty or when their relationships first begin to change.

EXAMPLES OF INITIAL COMPLICATION

King Oedipus. Tiresias alleges that Oedipus has murdered Laius.
Othello. Iago recognizes that Cassio's courteous attentions to Desdemona can be used to make Othello jealous (act 2, scene 2).
Tartuffe. Orgon reveals his decision that Mariane must marry Tartuffe instead of Valère, whom she loves (act 2, scene 1).
Hedda Gabler. Thea informs Hedda that Eilert Lövborg is in town and that he is still preoccupied by the memory of an unknown woman (act 1).

It is not always possible to identify the precise point at which the complication of the plot begins. The plot of *Othello,* for example, obviously turns on Iago's ability to make Othello suspect Desdemona of infidelity. But how does this suspicion originate? Does it begin as a scheme in Iago's brain when, having seen Cassio take Desdemona by the hand (act 2, scene 2), he whispers slyly, "With as little a web as this will I ensnare as great a fly as Cassio"? Or does it begin somewhat later (act 3, scene 3), when (as Cassio parts from Desdemona) Iago says to Othello, "Ha! I like not that"? Or did Othello's jealousy start as early as act 1, scene 3, when Brabantio exclaimed, "Look to her, Moor, if thou has eyes to see. She has deceived her father, and may thee"? In a sense it begins at each place. It was foreshadowed in act 1, scene 3; first plotted by Iago in act 2, scene 2; and first felt by Othello in act 3, scene 3. From relatively small beginnings, Othello's jealousy grows until it dominates his entire personality. Much of the impact of the play results from the fact that the tragedy that ultimately destroys Othello has its roots in such small and indefinite beginnings.

In other plays, however, the conflict and its thematic significance are immediately clear. Oedipus's pride and impetuosity are implicit in his very first speech, but they only take on the aspect of tragic flaws when he refuses to check the accuracy of the prophesies reported by Tiresias and rashly concludes that the priest has joined with Creon in conspiring to usurp his throne. Similarly, Orgon's excessive faith in Tartuffe is clear throughout the first act, but only becomes dangerous and destructive when it leads him to break his promise that Valère shall marry Mariane. In both plays, the tensions that dramatically affect the protagonist's subsequent conduct are implicit in the opening scenes.

Crisis

The *crisis*, or turning point of the play, occurs at the moment of peak emotional intensity and usually involves a decision, a decisive action, or an open conflict

between the protagonist and antagonist. It is often called the *obligatory scene* because the audience demands to *see* such moments acted out on stage.

EXAMPLES OF THE CRISIS

King Oedipus. The shepherd's information about Oedipus's birth finally convinces the king that he has murdered his father and married his mother. Meanwhile Jocasta has gone into the palace to kill herself.

Othello. Through the machinations of Iago, Othello sees Desdemona's handkerchief in the hand of Cassio and concludes that she must die for her infidelity (act 4, scene 1).

Tartuffe. While hidden under a table, Orgon hears Tartuffe trying to seduce his wife and finally recognizes Tartuffe's hypocrisy for what it is (act 4, scene 5).

Hedda Gabler. Instead of returning Eilert's manuscript, Hedda encourages him to believe it is lost and gives him a pistol with which to commit suicide. After he has left, she burns the manuscript (act 3).

Just as it is sometimes difficult to determine where the conflict originates, it is sometimes also difficult to determine when the crisis takes place. Once Othello has seen Cassio with Desdemona's handkerchief, he is convinced of her guilt and the tragic conclusion of the play is foreordained. The scene, then, marks an important turning point in the characterization of Othello. But the dramatic tension continues to mount until the confrontation between Othello and Desdemona in her bed chamber (act 5, scene 2). We do not *know* that Othello will actually kill Desdemona until he does so. And only when he does so in spite of Desdemona's moving pleas and his own obvious reluctance, do we recognize the extent to which his jealousy has blinded him. Clearly, this scene, too, is a crisis in the plot and another turning point in the characterization of Othello. A hundred lines further into the scene we find yet another crisis and another turning point when Emilia tells Othello that Desdemona could not have given the handkerchief to Cassio for she, Emilia, had found it and given it to Iago. This revelation is the turning point in Iago's fortunes; it finally shows Othello how mistaken he has been all along. In the few remaining moments of the play, Othello rises again to the dignity and nobility that had first characterized him.

It is a mistake, therefore, in plays like *Othello* always to seek the crisis within a single moment of emotional intensity. Great literature is never bound by formula. Instead, as critics we must learn to look carefully at each moment of high drama in an effort to determine what we can learn from it about the play, its characters, and their relationship to the playwright's overall intention.

Falling Action and Resolution

As the consequences of the crisis accumulate, events develop a momentum of their own. Especially in tragedy, the *falling action* of the play results from the protagonist's loss of control and a final catastrophe often appears inevitable. The plot of a comedy, however, frequently includes some unexpected twist (for example, the intervention of the king or the revelation of the hero's true parents). This twist cuts sharply through all difficulties and allows the play to end on a happy note. In both tragedy and comedy, the *resolution* brings to an end the conflict that has been implicit (or explicit) since the play's opening scenes. When the curtain falls, the relationships among the characters have once more stabilized.

EXAMPLES OF THE FALLING ACTION AND RESOLUTION

King Oedipus. Oedipus blinds himself in sorrow and then is banished by the new king, Creon.

Othello. After smothering Desdemona, Othello learns of her innocence and slays himself.

Tartuffe. Using a deed that Orgon had foolishly signed, Tartuffe attempts to expel Orgon and his family from their own home. At the last moment, Tartuffe is arrested and imprisoned by order of the king.

Hedda Gabler. After Eilert's death, George and Thea set to work reproducing the lost manuscript. Hedda, whom George has commended to Judge Brack's attention, finds herself in Brack's power when he threatens to reveal information that would involve her in scandal. Rather than become Brack's mistress or tolerate scandal, Hedda shoots herself.

The resolution, or *dénouement*, merits special attention because it is the author's last chance to get the point across. Thus, it is not surprising that the resolution often contains a clear statement (or restatement) of the theme and a full revelation of character. In the last lines of *Hedda Gabler,* for example, Hedda realizes that Thea will indeed inspire Tesman just as she had Eilert Lövborg, while she, Hedda, can do "nothing in the world to help them." And Othello, in his last lines, begs that, when relating his story, Lodovico and Gratiano will speak

> Of one that loved not wisely but too well,
> Of one not easily jealous, but, being wrought,
> Perplexed in the extreme, of one whose hand,
> Like the base Indian, threw a pearl away
> Richer than all his tribe—of one whose subdued eyes,
> Albeit unused to the melting mood,
> Drop tears as fast as the Arabian trees
> Their medicinal gum.
>
> —From *Othello*, act 5, scene 2,
> William Shakespeare [1604]

In the last lines of *Tartuffe*, the officer presents Molière's conception of the ideal man:

We live under a king who is an enemy to fraud, a king whose eyes look into the depths of all hearts, and who cannot be deceived by the most artful imposter. Gifted with a fine discernment, his lofty soul at all times sees things in the right light. He is never betrayed into exaggeration, and his sound judgment never falls into any excess. He confers an everlasting glory upon men of worth; but this zeal does not radiate blindly: his esteem for the sincere does not close his heart to the horror aroused by those who are treacherous.

> —From *Tartuffe*, act 5, scene 7,
> Molière [1664]

And finally, the chorus pronounces a telling judgment upon Oedipus, as that play closes:

Chorus. Make way for Oedipus. All people said,
"That is a fortunate man;"
And now what storms are beating on his head!

"That is a fortunate man,"
Call no man fortunate that is not dead.
The dead are free from pain.

—From *King Oedipus,* Sophocles [430 B.C.]

In each case the lines are so crucial and so clearly a summary of what the author finds most important that literary critics often use them as keys to unlock the riches of each play.

Although virtually all plays include an exposition, complication, crisis, falling action, and resolution, and most take approximately the same amount of time to perform, they differ drastically in the amount of fictional time covered by the action shown on stage. In plays like *King Oedipus, Tartuffe,* and *Hedda Gabler,* the action begins just a few hours before the crisis. This allows the drama to unfold before the spectators' eyes, much as if they were looking in on real events. But because nearly any plot of significance builds to a crisis that caps a series of events dating back months or years, these *unfolding plots* necessarily make use of reminiscences introduced via the testimony of elderly step-parents, conversations between friends and servants, or other similar strategies. The manipulation of these reminiscences requires considerable ingenuity in order to avoid a sense of obvious contrivance. One alternative is to present the action episodically, skipping weeks, months, or years between scenes as the chief events leading up to the crisis are acted out on stage. *Othello* and most other Elizabethan plays employ such *episodic plots.*

Whether a plot is unfolding or episodic, it ought to be tightly structured and pruned of unnecessary characters, actions, speeches, and scenes. The term *well-made play,* or *"pièce bien faite,"* was coined by Eugène Scribe, a French playwright (1791–1861), to describe such plots—especially when they proceed logically from cause to effect in building toward a climatic scene in which the hero triumphs by revealing some adeptly foreshadowed secret. Although the formula prescribed by Scribe is now out-of-date, the craftsmanship he advocated will never be. It is, and always has been, an unmistakable sign of good drama. The first truly well-made plays were not written by Scribe or Ibsen, but by Aeschylus and Sophocles. And the latter's *King Oedipus* probably conforms more closely than any later drama to the description of the well-made play first given in Aristotle's *Poetics:*

The plot, being an imitation of an action must imitate one action and that a whole, the structural union of the parts being such that, if any one of them is displaced or removed, the whole will be disjointed and disturbed.[2]

CHARACTER

For many of us, an interest in literature is an outgrowth of our interest in people and their personalities. Drama is particularly satisfying in this respect, for plays are inevitably and immediately concerned with the human beings who are impersonated by live actors and actresses on the stage. The terms used to describe characters in drama are, for the most part, the same as those used for fiction. In fact, some of these terms were originally borrowed from drama to describe fictional

[2] *The Poetics of Aristotle,* 3rd ed., trans. by S. H. Butcher (New York: Macmillan Publishing Company, 1902) 35.

qualities. **The *dramatis personae* (or characters) of a play usually include a *protagonist* (the play's central character) and an opposing *antagonist* or an antagonistic force. (The protagonist in a tragedy, however, is often called the *tragic hero*.)** Othello and Oedipus are clearly protagonists; Iago is Othello's antagonist; and the will of the gods is the antagonistic force opposing Oedipus. **A great many plays also include a *confidant* (*confidante* if female) to whom a major character "confides" his or her most private thoughts and feelings.** Emilia, for example, serves as Desdemona's confidante in *Othello,* just as Dorine is Mariane's confidante in *Tartuffe.* **A *foil* is a minor figure whose contrasting personality in some ways clarifies that of a major character,** as Cléante's moderation serves as a foil for Orgon's zealotry in *Tartuffe* and as Shakespeare's Laertes becomes a foil for Hamlet while both are seeking to revenge their fathers' deaths. **A *caricature* is a character with a habit or trait that is carried to a ridiculous extreme.** In *Hedda Gabler* George Tesman, who has spent his honeymoon researching a book on "the domestic industries of Brabant during the Middle Ages" is a caricature of the scholarly temperament. And nearly everyone in *Tartuffe* is a caricature of some aspect of seventeenth-century French society.

This terminology underscores the obvious difference between ***major* and *minor* characters. The parts of the protagonist and antagonist are major, whereas those of the confidant and foil are often (but not always) minor.** Because it is only reasonable to assume that most of a playwright's attention will be focused on his major characters, one of our first steps in the analysis of a play should be to identify the characters who have leading roles. The most obvious clue is the number of lines spoken by each character: major characters have many, and minor characters few. But more importantly, major characters are usually individualized and given both complex motives and a past, while minor characters often have no past at all and sometimes represent no more than a common character type. One has said nearly all that need be said about the characters of the messenger and the shepherd in *King Oedipus* as soon as their titles are mentioned. They have few individual traits and serve primarily to convey information to Oedipus and the audience. Similarly, Judge Brack in *Hedda Gabler* is a middle-aged rake whose single motive is to establish a comfortable triangular friendship in which Hedda becomes his mistress while George remains his friend. No such simple statements, however, can accurately describe the personalities of major characters like Oedipus, Othello, and Hedda. In order to understand these individuals, we must look carefully at the various means of characterization used to bring them to life.

Characterizing details in drama come to us from many different sources. We immediately learn something from the *name and physical appearance* of each character—although this information is often unreliable. The characters in *Othello,* for example, so often use the adjective *honest* when they refer to Iago that it seems (ironically) a part of his name, and they mistakenly take his coarse manner and military bearing as signs of simplicity and firmness. A second method of characterization is through an individual's *patterns of action* over the course of the play. Hedda Gabler's pacing, for example, is an indication of her sense of suffocating confinement in her role as a woman. Much characterization, however, is accomplished through dialogue in one of four ways. A character can reveal his or her personality and motives, as Iago often does, through *asides and soliloquies.* There may also be self-revelation in *the way a character speaks* because dialect, word choice, and grammar all provide clues to a person's background and intelligence. Othello's "perfect soul" is partially revealed through his eloquence, while Iago's idiomatic slang marks him as a "profane wretch" (according to Brabantio) in the very first scene of the play. *The way a character responds to others* is also important. Adversity seems at first only to make Othello more self-confident. When swords on both sides are drawn as Brabantio seeks to arrest Othello, the latter averts a crisis with composure: "Good signior, you shall more command with years / Than with your weapons." Yet the violent temper of this eminent soldier eventually surfaces, and he himself recognizes that he is one not easily made jealous or moved to anger, "but, being wrought,/ Perplexed in the extreme." Finally, *what others say about a character* can help us to understand him or her. As we have seen, the conversation between Aunt Julia and Berta is packed with observations, speculations, reminiscences, and judgments about Hedda and Tesman. These characterizing details come at us in fragmentary glimpses during the normal ebb and flow of the conversation. Occasionally, however, an author may provide a more concentrated sketch of a character's actions or personality—usually in the form of such *hidden narration* as the messenger's account of Oedipus's rage after learning his true parentage (see p. 1074).

The process of understanding drama is very closely linked to our ability to understand the personalities and motives of the major characters. As we read and study a play, we inevitably raise a host of questions: Why does Iago dedicate himself to tormenting Othello? Why is Othello so susceptible to Iago's manipulations? What makes the lost handkerchief so important to Othello? Why does Desdemona lie about the handkerchief? What stops Othello and Desdemona from talking about their misunderstanding openly and fully? Is Othello thoroughly noble or is his character seriously flawed in some way? These questions, and others like them, are concerned with fundamental character traits and express our expectation that the actions of the characters should be plausible, consistent, and adequately motivated. In attempting to answer them, we continually compare what is said by or about a character with the way in which that character acts on stage, searching for the thread of unity that creates a convincing personality.

At the same time, however, characters who are too consistent generally seem unrealistic. Conventional wisdom tells us that real people are full of surprises and so, in literature, we tend to demand characters who are capable of surprising us in a convincing way. Their motives should be complex and even competing, as Othello's obvious love for Desdemona competes with his injured pride when he thinks that she has been unfaithful to him. Moreover, those characters who most interest us usually undergo a process of growth and change during the course of the play. Othello fascinates us as he sinks from his initial nobility to an all-consuming jealousy, before rising again in the tragic self-knowledge of his last speech. Similarly, Oedipus's blind complacency and self-satisfaction break down as the unfolding events force him to see the criminal actions of his past. At the end of the play, this banished and self-blinded man realizes that, although his eyes once were clear, he has had "neither sight nor knowledge."

We must be careful, however, not to push too far the demand for growth and change in character. Many fine plays, including *Tartuffe* and *Hedda Gabler,* present personalities or dilemmas without even hinting at the possibility of moral improvement or permanent solutions. Apparently Molière felt that a man like Tartuffe can be imprisoned but rarely improved, and that Orgon is as naturally impetuous in desiring Tartuffe's punishment as he had earlier been in praising him. Similarly, *Hedda Gabler* is a bleak study of a fundamentally pathological personality. The value of such drama is not that it creates characters just like our next-door neighbors, but rather that it shows how only slight distortions in personality can destabilize the whole structure of ordinary social relationships.

ACTION

John Wilmot, the Earl of Rochester, once criticized Charles II as a king who "never said a foolish thing / Nor ever did a wise one." Many a dramatist, after seeing his plays poorly acted, must have sympathized with the response of Charles II: "This is very true: for my words are my own, and my actions are my ministers'." The playwright must live with the parallel and sometimes melancholy realization that, while his words are his own, his actions are the actors'. Fortunately for the play-going public, actors are much more successful at putting the words of a play into action than bureaucrats are at implementing those of heads of government.

Although the actions in a play may sometimes be indicated or suggested in the script, they are just as often the inevitable by-products of the performance. When Berta and Aunt Julia are talking in the first scene of *Hedda Gabler* (see p. 1087), we should not assume that they face each other motionlessly throughout their conversation. Ibsen himself directs them to perform a few actions—close the front door, open the door to the veranda, put down the bouquet, and so on—but twelve consecutive exchanges take place without a single stage direction. What do these women do with their hands during these exchanges? Do they remain motionless or move about the room? Do they face each other, the audience, or neither? Ibsen doesn't say, but surely some actions must take place—if only an averted glance here and a penetrating look there. Although the lines must be spoken, the director is free to present them as he wishes, and this presentation will affect both the characterization of the speakers and the degree of dramatic emphasis given to their words.

As readers of drama, we may attempt to be our own director, moving the characters about an imaginary stage and endowing them with gestures and expressions suitable to the dialogue. Most of us, however, are content to concentrate on the words in the play and leave the accompanying actions vague, except where they are demanded by the script. In either approach, however, we must be very sensitive to actions implied in the dialogue. This is especially true when we read plays written before the middle of the nineteenth century. Thereafter the techniques of the novel began to infiltrate drama and the playwright's stage directions became more frequent and more detailed. But early playwrights kept their stage directions to an absolute minimum. Here, for example, is part of a scene from Shakespeare's *Othello* as it was published in the famous *First Folio* (1623):

> [*Enter* LODOVICO, DESDEMONA, *and* ATTENDANTS]
> LODOVICO. Save you worthy General!
> OTHELLO. With all my heart, sir.
> LODOVICO. The Duke and Senators of Venice greet you.
> OTHELLO. I kiss the instrument of their pleasures.
> DESDEMONA. And what's the news, good Cousin Lodovico?
> IAGO. I am very glad to see you, signior.
>   Welcome to Cyprus.
> LODOVICO. I thank you. How does Lieutenant Cassio?
> IAGO. Lives, sir.

DESDEMONA. Cousin, there's fall'n between him and my lord
   An unkind breach, but you shall make all well.
OTHELLO. Are you sure of that?
DESDEMONA. My lord?
OTHELLO. "This fail you not to do, as you will—"
LODOVICO. He did not call, he's busy in the paper.
   Is there division 'twixt my lord and Cassio?
DESDEMONA. A most unhappy one. I would do much
   To atone them, for the love I bear to Cassio.
OTHELLO. Fire and brimstone!
DESDEMONA. My lord?
OTHELLO. Are you wise?
DESDEMONA. What, is he angry?
LODOVICO. Maybe the letter moved him,
   For, as I think, they do command him home,
   Deputing Cassio in his government.
DESDEMONA. By my troth, I am glad on 't.
OTHELLO. Indeed!
DESDEMONA. My lord?
OTHELLO. I am glad to see you mad.
DESDEMONA. Why, sweet Othello?
OTHELLO. Devil!
DESDEMONA. I have not deserved this.
LODOVICO. My lord, this would not be believed in Venice.
   Though I should swear I saw 't. 'Tis very much.
   Make her amends, she weeps.
OTHELLO. O devil, devil!
   If that the earth could teem with a woman's tears,
   Each drop she falls would prove a crocodile.
   Out of my sight!
DESDEMONA. I will not stay to offend you.
LODOVICO. Truly, an obedient lady.
   I do beseech your lordship, call her back.

                              —From *Othello*, act 4, scene 1,
                              William Shakespeare [1604]

   The only stage direction is that calling for the entrance of Lodovico, Desdemona, and attendants. But if we read the lines with care, we realize that Lodovico
has brought a letter from Venice that he gives to Othello at line 3, and that
Othello refers to this letter when he says, "I kiss the instrument of their pleasures." Presumably, Othello does kiss the letter, and he must open it before line
14, when he pretends to be deeply engrossed in his reading. We can also conclude
that Othello slaps Desdemona when he calls her a devil in line 31, for Lodovico
later exclaims to Iago, "What, strike his wife!" And we know that Desdemona must
start to leave the stage after saying, "I will not stay to offend you" (line 40),
because Lodovico asks Othello to call her back in line 42.
   All of these actions are implicit in the dialogue, and most modern texts of the
play formally incorporate them into editorial stage directions. Even so, however,
the questions, counterquestions, exclamations, and asides in the rapid exchanges
between lines 8 and 31 presume many additional actions and interactions. As
readers we may not pause to speculate on the exact nature of this interplay, but
we should realize that here, as in all drama, the script itself is only a partial guide
to the dramatic action, as any glance at a director's prompt book would quickly

prove. Both the formal stage directions and the creative contributions of the actors and director are designed either to emphasize the themes and character traits introduced in the dialogue or to stimulate further dialogue. The relationship between dialogue and dramatic action is like that between a diamond and its setting in a ring: in both cases the latter enhances and emphasizes the value and clarity of the former.

23

❋❋❋❋❋❋

The Classifications
of Drama

No one denies that *tragedy* and *comedy* are the major subgenres of drama, but the debate over their precise meaning has persisted through at least one hundred generations of philosophers and literary critics. Can this immense investment of intellectual energy have been worthwhile? The ability to classify plays may not help us in any important way to understand what a playwright has done, why he or she has done it, or what makes the play interesting. Yet these are the questions with which we must always deal in order to understand literature. Moreover, making a simple distinction between tragedy and comedy is about as easy as determining whether we more often sorrow or smile in reading or viewing a particular play. It is only when we demand precision in defining the kinds of plot, character, and action that create tragic or comic emotions that the issue becomes complex and irresolvable.

Most playwrights have been indifferent to these matters of classification, preferring simply to write their plays and let others worry about categorizing them. Plato tells us that Socrates once cornered Agathon, a respected tragic playwright, and Aristophanes, the greatest comic playwright, at the end of a party in Athens. In his enthusiasm for philosophy, Socrates began to lecture them on his theory that the genius of comedy is the same as that of tragedy. Being drowsy and half drunk, both poets agreed, shared another cup of wine, and promptly dozed off, leaving Socrates to peddle his theory elsewhere.

If the responses of Agathon and Aristophanes were universal, we would not need to discuss tragedy and comedy any further. However, some playwrights do write plays according to some theory of the formal principles for each subgenre, and therefore we need to have at least rudimentary knowledge of the theories behind tragedy and comedy.

TRAGEDY

The first, and most influential, literary theorist was Aristotle (384–322 B.C.) whose famous definition of tragedy remains the cornerstone upon which all discussions of the subject must build. *Tragedy,* Aristotle contended,

is an imitation of an action of high importance, complete and of some amplitude; in language enhanced by distinct and varying beauties; acted not narrated; by means of pity and fear effecting its purgation of these emotions.[1]

This definition puts much of its emphasis on the tragic action, or story, which Aristotle thought should be serious, complex, and tightly structured. Tragedy does not need to show events that have happened, but only those that would happen, given a certain set of circumstances. The events must be arranged in a causal progression, so that no action in the play can be eliminated or displaced without damaging the whole structure. Ideally the plot should include both irony and a surprising disclosure, each evolving naturally out of the story. In *King Oedipus*, for example, the arrival of the messenger is ironic because the news of Polybus's death might be expected to release Oedipus from any fear of murdering his father, but instead it leads directly to the disclosure of his incest and parricide. Thus, the plot interweaves the irony with the fatal disclosure.

The requirement that the action of a tragedy be of "high importance" led Aristotle to demand that the protagonist be nobly born and more admirable than ordinary men. He cannot, however, be morally perfect because the best plots arise when his downfall is the inevitable consequence of some defect in character (or *tragic flaw*). The spectacle of a good man dragged to destruction by a single error arouses in the audience both pity and fear, leading to a *catharsis*, a psychological state through which those emotions are purged; the audience leaves the theater relieved, or even exalted, rather than depressed.

This Aristotelian definition accurately reflects the goal of most Greek, Roman, and neoclassical tragedy, but it is too narrow to include many serious and important plays written during other periods. Richard III, Macbeth, and Hedda Gabler, for example, are certainly *less* virtuous than ordinary men and women; it is debatable whether Romeo, Juliet, Hamlet, and Othello have tragic flaws; and very few of the characters in modern drama are nobly born. A definition of tragedy that excludes most of the work of Shakespeare and all of Ibsen—not to mention that of more recent playwrights—cannot be complete.

A more modern view is that there are at least three variations of the tragic situation or tragic emotion.[2] **Some plays ask us to look on the sufferings of the tragic hero as a human sacrifice that is necessary to cleanse society.** The fall of Oedipus, for example, is necessary to purge Thebes of hidden crime and to free the city from a plague imposed by the gods. Similarly, Richard III, Iago, and Macbeth can all be viewed as warped personalities who must perish before ordinary and stable social relationships can reassert themselves. As these examples suggest, the plots of sacrificial tragedies take one of two forms. The tragic hero suffers either through the will of the gods (like Oedipus) or through a rejection by society (like Macbeth). And in either form the protagonist may merit his

---

[1] Aristotle on *The Art of Fiction*, trans. by L. J. Potts (Cambridge, England: Cambridge University Press, 1962) 24.

[2] See E. M. W. Tillyard, *Shakespeare's Problem Plays* (Toronto: University of Toronto Press, 1949) 14–17.

suffering, as Oedipus and Macbeth do, or he may be an innocent victim of forces beyond his control, as are Romeo and Juliet.

A second tragic pattern arises from the paradox of the fortunate fall. As plots of this kind unfold, we realize that the hero's destruction is necessary if he is to rise to a higher level of personal awareness and development. Othello, for example, must be brought to recognize his responsibility for Desdemona's death if he is to change from a man who once spoke smugly of his "perfect soul" into a tragic figure who accepts himself as one who "Like the base Indian, threw away a pearl / Richer than all his tribe." Oedipus must be blinded before he can truly see. And King Lear must be stripped of his regal pride and forced to "hovel . . . with swine and rogues forlorn in short and musty straw" before he can find his humanity. Tragedies of this second kind reaffirm our human capacity to learn from our experiences; they extend to us the reassurance that even in defeat we can rise above our limitations to an immortal grandeur.

A third tragic pattern involves the simple spectacle of sufferings that greatly exceed normal bounds. The tragic characters struggle helplessly to survive in an environment weighted against them. Like small insects entangled in a web, their futile flutterings express their surprise, regret, and bewilderment at the difference between their own fate and that of other men. Such plays usually include an inquiry by the characters and the playwright into the purpose (or futility) of the tragic individual's sufferings and the role of all human suffering in the scheme of the universe. If Tom Stoppard's *Rosencrantz and Guildenstern Are Dead* is a tragedy at all, it is a tragedy of inexplicable suffering. From the first scene to the last, the characters question the reasons for their involvement in the action and the nature of the world into which they are unwillingly cast. Ultimately their plight becomes a symbol of our plight, and Stoppard persuades us that the death they experience is not simply a variant of the tragedian's phoney "deaths for all ages and occasions," but rather, like real death, "the endless time of never coming back . . . a gap you can't see, and when the wind blows through it, it makes no sound. . . ."

Should we, however, define *Rosencrantz and Guildenstern Are Dead* as a tragedy? It is tragic in the sense that the main characters are victims of forces beyond their control; it is tragic in the sense that the protagonists are destroyed; and, moreover, it is tragic in the sense that the plot deals with issues of high importance, such as reality, fate, and death. But from start to finish, the dialogue is hilarious. If comedy has anything to do with humor, then surely this play qualifies as comic. The situation of Stoppard's characters, and by extension that of all human beings, is absurd—both macabre and wildly funny. It is senseless, silly, and sobering, all at the same time. In contemporary theater, we call this mixture of tragedy and comedy the **theater of the absurd;** its very existence reminds us that there need be no sharp distinction between the frowning mask of tragedy and the smiling mask of comedy.

COMEDY

Horace Walpole, the eighteenth-century man of letters, once observed that "the world is a comedy to those that think, a tragedy to those who feel." Walpole's comparison is as good a guide as any to the key differences between these two modes of drama. The tragic hero is closely examined and portrayed as an individual; the comic character is viewed intellectually from a distance and represents a broad human "type"—a young lover, a hypocrite, an elegant fop, and so on.

The tragic mode asks us to sympathize with the hero and imagine ourselves in his position; the comic mode suggests that we step back from life and look with amusement on the humorous predicament of others. The subject matter of comedy is often as serious as that of tragedy, but the comic playwright consciously distorts events and personalities in order to remind the audience that the play deals with fantasy and not fact. The plots of comedy are usually convoluted exercises in authorial imagination; the plots of tragedy are sobering relevations of our emotional and psychological core.

A lighthearted but intellectual approach to comedy has prevailed from the very beginning. The extant plays of Aristophanes (called **Old Comedy**) are carefully structured explorations of a bizarre intellectual hypothesis. What would happen, he asks in *Lysistrata* (411 B.C.), if all Greek women refused to participate in sexual relations until the Peloponnesian War was brought to an end? Suppose (in *The Birds*) that one could found an empire in the air and starve the gods by intercepting the smoke from earthly sacrifices. Imagine (in *The Clouds*) that a farmer attends the school of Socrates in hopes of learning how to avoid paying his debts. In each case the idea and background of the situation are presented in the prologue. The merits and deficiencies of the hypothesis are then formally explored in an *agon*, or debate. The application of the debate is then illustrated in a series of episodes that concludes with a final song and a scene of merriment. In addition, each play contains a number of elements that apparently were required by convention: the entrance of a wildly costumed chorus, an elaborately structured song (*parabasis*) in which the playwright lectures the audience and satirizes the society, and a host of meticulous rules ranging from a required form of *agon* to the necessity of reciting the *pignos* or "choking song" in only one breath.

Within this highly structured form, Aristophanes continually sought to satirize the society at large and its most prominent individuals. He repeatedly attacked the Peloponnesian War and decadent innovations in religion, education, and poetry. He created ridiculous caricatures of Socrates, Euripides, Aeschylus, the politicians of Athens, and even the Greek gods. And throughout it all he continually explored and distorted the implications of his initial intellectual hypothesis.

Few modern comedies have been influenced by the Aristophanic tradition because the hypothetical postulate with which Old Comedy begins tends to favor a rather limiting form of social satire. The plays of Aristophanes are so filled with topical and personal allusions that many parts of them are now unintelligible. In order to survive as a literary form, comedy had to begin using plots and characters that could be universally understood and enjoyed.

By the time Aristophanes wrote his last comedy, *Plutus*, in 388 B.C., he had already evolved beyond the conventions of Old Comedy. The **New Comedy** that ensued has proven to be remarkably durable. Even today most comedies continue to follow the same plot structure:

What normally happens is that a young man wants a young woman, that his desire is resisted by some opposition, usually paternal, and that near the end of the play some twist in the plot enables the hero to have his will. . . . The movement of comedy is usually a movement from one kind of society to another. At the beginning of the play the obstructing characters are in charge of the play's society, and the audience recognizes that they are usurpers. At the end of the play the device in the plot that brings the hero and heroine together causes a new society to crystallize around the hero. . . .

The appearance of this new society is frequently signalized by some kind of party or festive ritual, which either appears at the end of the play or is assumed to take place immediately afterward.[3]

Northrop Frye, the critic cited here, has also identified most of the other conventional elements of comedy. He argues that the form appeals most directly to the young men and women in the audience, who identify with the hero and heroine precisely because these protagonists are unindividualized representatives of youth in whom each member of the audience can find his or her own traits. The antagonist who blocks the hero's wishes is either a father or a father-figure and is often made ridiculous by the exaggeration of a single character trait. Molière's Tartuffe and Orgon are typical blocking figures, just as Mariane and Valère are the nondescript protagonists. The plot itself usually overflows with complications that place all of the characters in ticklish situations, and these complications are often resolved by an unexpected twist in the plot, such as the miraculous intervention of the king at the end of *Tartuffe*. At the beginning of *Tartuffe*, hypocrisy dominates the play's society, but by the end a more sensible and honest social structure has emerged that will be celebrated through the marriage of Valère and Mariane.

When the main sources of humor in a play are the ludicrous complications of love, the play is called a *romantic comedy*. **When the emphasis is on the ridiculous foibles or characteristics of the blocking figures, it is called a** *comedy of humours*. (This term derives from the medieval physiological theory of the "four humours," four identifiable elements believed to determine and control individual temperament and personality; an imbalance was thought to result in a lopsided, eccentric personality who became a natural object for comic treatment.) **When the play makes fun of the affectations, manners, and conventions of human behavior, it is called a** *comedy of manners*. And **when it achieves its effects through buffoonery, horseplay, and crude jokes, it is called a** *farce*.

Minute subcategories such as those defined in the preceding paragraph can be compounded almost indefinitely by considering that broad middle ground between tragedy and comedy. The players who performed before the court in *Hamlet* were supposed to be capable of acting "tragedy, comedy, history, pastoral, pastoral-comical, historical-pastoral, tragical-historical, tragical-comical-historical-pastoral, scene individable, or poem unlimited." Shakespeare's mockery of such generic hair splitting is implicit in the exaggerations of the list and in his satire of Polonius, who utters it. Contemporary drama criticism may have moved away from pastoral, historical, and the various hyphenated couplings, but it has developed a myriad of other terms to describe minor classifications of the tone and structure of drama. The most significant of these (*domestic tragedy, melodrama, naturalism, realism, revenge tragedy, thesis play*, etc.) are defined in the *Handbook* appended to this text.

[3] Northrop Frye, *Anatomy of Criticism: Four Essays* (Princeton: Princeton University Press, 1957) 163.

24

❈❈❈❈❈

Analyzing and Evaluating Drama

Although all plays differ from one another, at times radically, certain fundamental questions can be asked of virtually every play as an aid in identifying and understanding its major features. As noted in our discussion of drama, plays inevitably share many elements with both fiction and poetry; as a result, a number of the questions that follow assume a general familiarity with the two earlier sections of this book.

QUESTIONS TO ASK AND ANSWER

Plot

1. Describe the plot in terms of its *exposition, complication, crisis, falling action,* and *conclusion.* Is the plot unified? Do the individual acts and scenes seem logically related to each other? Are there any scenes that seem to be unnecessary?
2. What is the essential problem or conflict on which the plot turns? Where does the turning point seem to occur? How is the plot resolved? Does the resolution seem to be an appropriate and satisfactory one?
3. Compare the end of the play with its beginning. What are the major changes that have taken place?
4. Describe the function of each act and scene. Do certain scenes seem to be linked in some way in order to contrast with or reinforce one another? Do any of the scenes seem to present a microcosm, condensation, or metaphor of the play as a whole?
5. In what ways does the opening act or scene serve the purpose of exposition, and how is this exposition achieved? What important events have taken place before the play opens? In what ways does the exposition serve to introduce or *foreshadow* the major problems or conflicts of the plot?

1106

6. Does the play contain one or more *subplots*? If so, what is their relationship to the main plot of the play? Are they, for example, intended to reinforce, contrast, or parody the main action?

Character

1. Who is the *protagonist* of the play, and who is the *antagonist*?
2. What is the function of the play's other major characters? What is their relationship to the protagonist and antagonist and to each other?
3. What is the function of the play's minor characters? Is their role mainly one of exposition or interpretation, or are they used as *foils* to oppose, contrast, or caricature certain of the major characters?
4. What methods does the playwright employ to establish and reveal the characters?
5. Are the actions of the characters properly motivated, consistent, and plausible?
6. Do any of the characters serve *symbolic* or *allegorical* functions?
7. To what extent does the playwright rely on the reader's or audience's prior knowledge of one or more of the characters? (Remember that many of the major figures of Greek tragedy were well known in advance to their audiences.)

Dialogue

1. Is the dialogue written in *high style, low style,* or some combination of the two?
2. How does the dialogue of the characters differ? How do such differences serve as an aid in characterization?
3. What stylistic devices contribute most to the play's dialogue? (Consider, for example, the use the playwright makes of patterns of poetic rhythm and sound, repetition, puns or word play, comparison, allusion, imagery, irony, symbolism, etc.)
4. Does the playwright make use of certain key words or phrases that gain a cumulative effect and added significance through repetition in a succession of contexts?

Setting

1. What is the play's setting in time and space?
2. To what extent does the setting functionally serve to aid in characterization, establish and sustain atmosphere, and/or influence plot?
3. What is the relationship of the setting to the play's action? Does it serve to reinforce the action, or is the relationship one of contrast?
4. Does the setting have symbolic overtones?

Theme

1. What is the play's theme or controlling idea?
2. How is the theme presented? Is it explicitly stated by one or more of the characters or is it merely implied by the action? What specific passages of dialogue or action contribute most clearly to the revelation or presentation of theme? To what extent do such moments occur at or near the ends of acts or scenes as a way of building dramatic tension?

3. What is the value or significance of the play's theme? Is it topical or universal in its application?

Other Aspects of Drama

1. *Title.* Consider the play's title. What clues does it provide, if any, in identifying the playwright's emphasis?
2. *Dramatic conventions.* To what extent does the playwright make use of such dramatic conventions as *asides, soliloquies,* a *chorus,* or the *three unities* of time, place, and action? What function or functions do these conventions serve? To what extent do these conventions reflect the kind of theater in which the play was originally staged?
3. *Actions and stage directions.* Identify the major physical actions of the play and explain their significance.
4. What help, if any, do the author's stage directions provide in helping the reader to understand the play?
5. *Classification.* Is the play a *tragedy,* a *comedy,* or some hybrid of two or more types? (Be prepared to explain your answer by making reference to the discussion in the text.)
6. *Audience appeal.* To what extent is the appeal of the play topical (that is, to what extent does it contain certain elements that reflect the manners, customs, attitudes, and beliefs of the society for which it was originally written)? To what extent is its appeal permanent and universal?

Evaluating the Whole

1. How well do you think the playwright has managed to achieve a total integration of his or her materials?
2. What is *your* reaction to the play? Do you like the play? If so, why? If not, why not?

25

❧❧❧❧❧❧❧❧

Plays

Sophocles   *ca. 496–406* B.C.

KING OEDIPUS

Translated by William Butler Yeats

PERSONS IN THE PLAY

OEDIPUS, *King of Thebes*
JOCASTA, *wife of Oedipus*
ANTIGONE, *daughter of Oediupus*
ISMENE, *daughter of Oedipus*
CREON, *brother-in-law of Oedipus*

TIRESIAS, *a seer*
A PRIEST
MESSENGERS
A HERDSMAN

CHORUS

SCENE
The Palace of King Oedipus at Thebes

OEDIPUS. Children, descendants of old Cadmus,[1] why do you come before me, why do you carry the branches of suppliants, while the city smokes with incense and murmurs with prayer and lamentation? I would not learn from any mouth but yours, old man, therefore I question you myself. Do you know of anything that I can do and have not done? How can I, being the man I am, being King Oedipus, do other than all I know? I were indeed hard of heart did I not pity such suppliants.

PRIEST. Oedipus, King of my country, we who stand before your door are of all ages, some too young to have walked so many miles, some—priests of Zeus such as I—too old. Among us stand the pick of the young men, and behind in the market-places the people throng, carrying suppliant branches.[2] We all stand here because the city stumbles towards death, hardly able to raise up

---

[1] Cadmus was the legendary founder of ancient Thebes, a city located about 30 miles northwest of Athens, Greece.
[2] Before praying for help, the Greeks often laid laurel boughs at the temples of the gods.

its head. A blight has fallen upon the fruitful blossoms of the land, a blight upon flock and field and upon the bed of marriage—plague ravages the city. Oedipus, King, not God but foremost of living men, seeing that when you first came to this town of Thebes you freed us from that harsh singer, the riddling Sphinx,[3] we beseech you, all we suppliants, to find some help; whether you find it by your power as a man, or because, being near the Gods, a God has whispered you. Uplift our State; think upon your fame; your coming brought us luck, be lucky to us still; remember that it is better to rule over men than over a waste place, since neither walled town nor ship is anything if it be empty and no man within it.

OEDIPUS. My unhappy children! I know well what need has brought you, what suffering you endure; yet, sufferers though you be, there is not a single one whose suffering is as mine—each mourns himself, but my soul mourns the city, myself, and you. It is not therefore as if you came to arouse a sleeping man. No! Be certain that I have wept many tears and searched hither and thither for some remedy. I have already done the only thing that came into my head for all my search. I have sent the son of Menoeceus, Creon, my own wife's brother, to the Pythian House of Phoebus,[4] to hear if deed or word of mine may yet deliver this town. I am troubled, for he is a long time away—a longer time than should be—but when he comes I shall not be an honest man unless I do whatever the God commands.

PRIEST. You have spoken at the right time. They have just signalled to us that Creon has arrived.

OEDIPUS. O King Apollo, may he bring brighter fortune, for his face is shining!

PRIEST. He brings good news, for he is crowned with bay.

OEDIPUS. We shall know soon. Brother-in-law, Menoeceus' son, what news from the God?

CREON. Good news; for pain turns to pleasure when we have set the crooked straight.

OEDIPUS. But what is the oracle?—so far the news is neither good nor bad.

CREON. If you would hear it with all these about you, I am ready to speak. Or do we go within?

OEDIPUS. Speak before all. The sorrow I endure is less for my own life than these.

CREON. Then, with your leave, I speak. Our lord Phoebus bids us drive out a defiling thing that has been cherished in this land.

OEDIPUS. By what purification?[5]

---

[3] The Sphinx, a monster half female and half lion, terrorized Thebes by slaying every traveller who failed to solve her riddle: "What goes on four feet in the morning, two at noon, and three in the evening?" When Oedipus answered "Man" (who crawls in infancy, walks erect in maturity, and leans on a cane in senility), the Sphinx leaped in despair from the side of a cliff.

[4] The priests of Phoebus Apollo (the god of the Sun, prophecy, truth, poetry, and music) were reputed to see into the future, though often expressing their knowledge in ambiguous quotations or riddles. Their golden house was called "Pythian" in honor of Apollo's victory over the serpent Python.

[5] In drafting this modernized version of the play, Yeats, who was himself a playwright of considerable reputation, frequently omitted portions of the original text that he found either redundant or dramatically inadvisable. Here, and in subsequent footnotes we have supplied the most significant of the omitted passages using the translation by Richard C. Jebb consulted by Yeats himself. Thus, Jebb's translation continues:

> CREON. By banishing a man, or by bloodshed in quittance of bloodshed, since it is that blood which brings the tempest on our city.
> OEDIPUS. And who is the man whose fate he thus reveals?

CREON. King Laius was our King before you came to pilot us.

OEDIPUS. I know—but not of my own knowledge, for I never saw him.

CREON. He was killed; and the God now bids us revenge it on his murderers, whoever they be.

OEDIPUS. Where shall we come upon their track after all these years? Did he meet his death in house or field, at home or in some foreign land?

CREON. In a foreign land: he was journeying to Delphi.

OEDIPUS. Did no fellow-traveller see the deed? Was there none there who could be questioned?

CREON. All perished but one man who fled in terror and could tell for certain but one thing of all he had seen.

OEDIPUS. One thing might be a clue to many things.

CREON. He said that they were fallen upon by a great troop of robbers.

OEDIPUS. What robbers would be so daring unless bribed from here?

CREON. Such things were indeed guessed at, but Laius once dead no avenger arose. We were amid our troubles.

OEDIPUS. But when royalty had fallen what troubles could have hindered search?

CREON. The riddling Sphinx put those dark things out of our thoughts—we thought of what had come to our own doors.

OEDIPUS. But I will start afresh and make the dark things plain. In doing right by Laius I protect myself, for whoever slew Laius might turn a hand against me. Come, my children, rise up from the altar steps; lift up these suppliant boughs and let all the children of Cadmus be called thither that I may search out everything and find for all happiness or misery as God wills.

PRIEST. May Phoebus, sender of the oracle, come with it and be our saviour and deliverer!

The CHORUS *enter.*

Chorus

What message comes to famous Thebes from the Golden House?
What message of disaster from that sweet-throated Zeus?
What monstrous thing our fathers saw do the seasons bring?
Or what that no man ever saw, what new monstrous thing?
Trembling in every limb I raise my loud importunate cry,
And in a sacred terror wait the Delian God's[6] reply.

Apollo chase the God of Death that leads no shouting men,
Bears no rattling shield and yet consumes this form with pain.
Famine takes what the plague spares, and all the crops are lost;
No new life fills the empty place—ghost flits after ghost
To that God-trodden western shore, as flit benighted birds.
Sorrow speaks to sorrow, but no comfort finds in words.

Hurry him from the land of Thebes with a fair wind behind
Out on to that formless deep where not a man can find
Hold for an anchor-fluke, for all is world-enfolding sea;
Master of the thunder-cloud, set the lightning free,

---

[6] Apollo was supposedly born on Delos, an island about 90 miles east-southeast of Athens.

And add the thunder-stone to that and fling them on his head,
For death is all the fashion now, till even Death be dead.

We call against the pallid face of this God-hated God
The springing heel of Artemis[7] in the hunting sandal shod,
The tousle-headed Maenads,[8] blown torch and drunken sound,
The stately Lysian king[9] himself with golden fillet crowned,
And in his hands the golden bow and the stretched golden string,
And Bacchus' wine-ensanguined face that all the Maenads sing.

OEDIPUS. You are praying, and it may be that your prayer will be answered; that if
    you hear my words and do my bidding you may find help out of all your trouble.
    This is my proclamation, children of Cadmus. Whoever among you knows by
    what man Laius, son of Labdacus, was killed, must tell all he knows. If he fear
    for himself and being guilty denounce himself, he shall be in the less danger,
    suffering no worse thing than banishment. If on the other hand there be one
    that knows that a foreigner did the deed, let him speak, and I shall give him a
    reward and my thanks: but if any man keep silent from fear or to screen a
    friend, hear all what I will do to that man. No one in this land shall speak to
    him, nor offer sacrifice beside him; but he shall be driven from their homes as
    if he himself had done the deed. And in this I am the ally of the Pythian God
    and of the murdered man, and I pray that the murderer's life may, should he
    be so hidden and screened, drop from him and perish away, whoever he may
    be, whether he did the deed with others or by himself alone:[10] and on you I lay
    it to make—so far as man may—these words good, for my sake, and for the
    God's sake, and for the sake of this land. And even if the God had not spurred
    us to it, it were a wrong to leave the guilt unpurged, when one so noble, and he
    your King, had perished; and all have sinned that could have searched it out
    and did not: and now since it is I who hold the power which he held once, and
    have his wife for wife—she who would have borne him heirs had he but lived—I
    take up this cause even as I would were it that of my own father. And if there be
    any who do not obey me in it, I pray that the Gods send them neither harvest
    of the earth nor fruit of the womb; but let them be wasted by his plague, or by
    one more dreadful still. But may all be blessed for ever who hear my words and
    do my will!
CHORUS. We do not know the murderer, and it were indeed more fitting that
    Phoebus, who laid the task upon us, should name the man.
OEDIPUS. No man can make the Gods speak against their will.
CHORUS. Then I will say what seems the next best thing.
OEDIPUS. If there is a third course, show it.
CHORUS. I know that our lord Tiresias is the seer most like to our lord Phoebus, and
    through him we may unravel all.
OEDIPUS. So I was advised by Creon, and twice already have I sent to bring him.
CHORUS. If we lack his help we have nothing but vague and ancient rumours.
OEDIPUS. What rumours are they? I would examine every story.

---

[7] Artemis (or Diana) was a goddess associated with chastity, hunting, and the moon.
[8] The Maenads were female followers of Bacchus (or Dionysus), the god of wine and revelry.
[9] Apollo.
[10] Jebb's translation continues: "And for myself I pray that if, with my privity, he should become an
    inmate of my house, I may suffer the same things which even now I called down upon others."

CHORUS. Certain wayfarers were said to have killed the King.

OEDIPUS. I know, I know. But who was there that saw it?

CHORUS. If there is such a man, and terror can move him, he will not keep silence when they have told him of your curses.

OEDIPUS. He that such a deed did not terrify will not be terrified because of a word.

CHORUS. But there is one who shall convict him. For the blind prophet comes at last—in whom alone of all men the truth lives.

Enter TIRESIAS, *led by a boy.*

OEDIPUS. Tiresias, mast of all knowledge, whatever may be spoken, whatever is unspeakable, whatever omens of earth and sky reveal, the plague is among us, and from that plague, Great Prophet, protect us and save us. Phoebus in answer to our question says that it will not leave us till we have found the murderers of Laius, and driven them into exile or put them to death. Do you therefore neglect neither the voice of birds, nor any other sort of wisdom, but rescue yourself, rescue the State, rescue me, rescue all that are defiled by the deed. For we are in your hands, and what greater task falls to a man than to help other men with all he knows and has?

TIRESIAS. Aye, and what worse task than to be wise and suffer for it? I know this well; it slipped out of mind, or I would never have come.

OEDIPUS. What now?

TIRESIAS. Let me go home. You will bear your burden to the end more easily, and I bear mine—if you but give me leave for that.

OEDIPUS. Your words are strange and unkind to the State that bred you.

TIRESIAS. I see that you, on your part, keep your lips tight shut, and therefore I have shut mine that I may come to no misfortune.

OEDIPUS. For God's love do not turn away—if you have knowledge. We suppliants implore you on our knees.

TIRESIAS. You are fools—I will bring misfortune neither upon you nor upon myself.

OEDIPUS. What is this? You know all and will say nothing? You are minded to betray me and Thebes?

TIRESIAS. Why do you ask these things? You will not learn them from me.

OEDIPUS. What! Basest of the base! You would enrage the very stones. Will you never speak out? Cannot anything touch you?

TIRESIAS. The future will come of itself though I keep silent.

OEDIPUS. Then seeing that come it must, you had best speak out.

TIRESIAS. I will speak no further. Rage if you have a mind to; bring out all the fierceness that is in your heart.

OEDIPUS. That will I. I will not spare to speak my thoughts. Listen to what I have to say. It seems to me that you have helped to plot the deed; and, short of doing it with your own hands, have done the deed yourself. Had you eyesight I would declare that you alone had done it.

TIRESIAS. So that is what you say? I charge you to obey the decree that you yourself have made, and from this day out to speak neither to these nor to me. You are the defiler of this land.

OEDIPUS. So brazen in your impudence? How do you hope to escape punishment?

TIRESIAS. I have escaped; my strength is in my truth.

OEDIPUS. Who taught you this? You never got it by your art.

TIRESIAS. You, because you have spurred me to speech against my will.

OEDIPUS. What speech? Speak it again that I may learn it better.

TIRESIAS. You are but tempting me—you understood me well enough.

OEDIPUS. No; not so that I can say I know it; speak it again.

TIRESIAS. I say that you are yourself the murderer that you seek.

OEDIPUS. You shall rue it for having spoken twice such outrageous words.

TIRESIAS. Would you that I say more that you may be still angrier?

OEDIPUS. Say what you will. I will not let it move me.

TIRESIAS. I say that you are living with your next of kin in unimagined shame.

OEDIPUS. Do you think you can say such things and never smart for it?

TIRESIAS. Yes, if there be strength in truth.

OEDIPUS. There is; yes—for everyone but you. But not for you that are maimed in ear and in eye and in wit.

TIRESIAS. You are but a poor wretch flinging taunts that in a little while everyone shall fling at you.

OEDIPUS. Night, endless night has covered you up so that you can neither hurt me nor any man that looks upon the sun.

TIRESIAS. Your doom is not to fall by me. Apollo is enough: it is his business to work out your doom.

OEDIPUS. Was it Creon that planned this or you yourself?

TIRESIAS. Creon is not your enemy; you are your own enemy.

OEDIPUS. Power, ability, position, you bear all burdens, and yet what envy you create! Great must that envy be if envy of my power in this town—a power put into my hands unsought—has made trusty Creon, my old friend Creon, secretly long to take that power from me; if he has suborned this scheming juggler, this quack and trickster, this man with eyes for his gains and blindness in his art. Come, come, where did you prove yourself a seer? Why did you say nothing to set the townsmen free when the riddling Sphinx was here? Yet that riddle was not for the first-comer to read; it needed the skill of a seer. And none such had you! Neither found by help of birds, nor straight from any God. No, I came; I silenced her, I the ignorant Oedipus, it was I that found the answer in my mother-wit, untaught by any birds. And it is I that you would pluck out of my place, thinking to stand close to Creon's throne. But you and the plotter of all this shall mourn despite your zeal to purge the land. Were you not an old man, you had already learnt how bold you are and learnt it to your cost.

CHORUS. Both this man's words and yours, Oedipus, have been said in anger. Such words cannot help us here, nor any but those that teach us to obey the oracle.

TIRESIAS. King though you are, the right to answer when attacked belongs to both alike. I am not subject to you, but to Loxias;[11] and therefore I shall never be Creon's subject. And I tell you, since you have taunted me with blindness, that though you have your sight, you cannot see in what misery you stand, nor where you are living, nor with whom, unknowing what you do—for you do not know the stock you come of—you have been your own kin's enemy be they living or be they dead. And one day a mother's curse and father's curse alike shall drive you from this land in dreadful haste with darkness upon those eyes.[12] Therefore, heap your scorn on Creon and on my message if you have a mind to; for no one of living men shall be crushed as you shall be crushed.

---

[11] Another name for Apollo.

[12] Jebb's translation continues: "And what place shall not be harbour to thy shriek, what of all Cithaeron shall not ring with it soon when thou hast learnt the meaning of the nuptials in which, within that house, thou didst find a fatal haven, after a voyage so fair? And a throng of other ills thou guessest not, which shall make thee level with thy true self and with thine own brood."

OEDIPUS. Begone this instant! Away, away! Get you from these doors!

TIRESIAS. I had never come but that you sent for me.

OEDIPUS. I did not know you were mad.

TIRESIAS. I may seem mad to you, but your parents thought me sane.

OEDIPUS. My parents! Stop! Who was my father?

TIRESIAS. This day shall you know your birth; and it will ruin you.

OEDIPUS. What dark words you always speak!

TIRESIAS. But are you not most skilful in the unravelling of dark words?

OEDIPUS. You mock me for that which made me great?

TIRESIAS. It was that fortune that undid you.

OEDIPUS. What do I care? For I delivered all this town.

TIRESIAS. Then I will go: boy, lead me out of this.

OEDIPUS. Yes, let him lead you. You take vexation with you.

TIRESIAS. I will go: but first I will do my errand. For frown though you may you cannot destroy me. The man for whom you look, the man you have been threatening in all the proclamations about the death of Laius, the man is here. He seems, so far as looks go, an alien; yet he shall be found a native Theban and shall nowise be glad of that fortune. A blind man, though now he has his sight; a beggar, though now he is most rich; he shall go forth feeling the ground before him with his stick;[13] so you go in and think on that, and if you find I am in fault say that I have no skill in prophecy. [TIRESIAS *is led out by the boy.* OEDIPUS *enters the palace.*]

Chorus

The Delphian rock has spoken out, now must a wicked mind,
Planner of things I dare not speak and of this bloody wrack,
Pray for feet that are as fast as the four hoofs of the wind:
Cloudy Parnassus[14] and the Fates thunder at his back.
That sacred crossing-place of lines upon Parnassus' head,
Lines that have run through North and South, and run through
     West and East,
That navel of the world[15] bids all men search the mountain wood,
The solitary cavern, till they have found that infamous beast.

CREON *enters from the house.*

CREON. Fellow-citizens, having heard that King Oedipus accuses me of dreadful things, I come in my indignation. Does he think that he has suffered wrong from me in these present troubles, or anything that could lead to wrong, whether in word or deed? How can I live under blame like that? What life would be worth having if by you here, and by my nearest friends, called a traitor through the town?

CHORUS. He said it in anger, and not from his heart out.

---

[13] Jebb's tanslation continues: "And he shall be found at once brother and father of the children with whom he consorts; son and husband of the woman who bore him; heir to his father's bed, shedder of his father's blood."

[14] A mountain near Delphi, sacred to Apollo; hence, through metonymy, another name for Apollo himself.

[15] The "navel of the world" and the "sacred crossing place of lines" is Delphi.

CREON. He said it was I put up the seer to speak those falsehoods.
CHORUS. Such things were said.
CREON. And had he his right mind saying it?
CHORUS. I do not know—I do not know what my masters do.

OEDIPUS *enters.*

OEDIPUS. What brought you here? Have you a face so brazen that you come to my house—you, the proved assassin of its master—the certain robber of my crown? Come, tell me in the face of the Gods what cowardice, or folly, did you discover in me that you plotted this? Did you think that I would not see what you were at till you had crept upon me, or seeing it would not ward it off? What madness to seek a throne, having neither friends nor followers!
CREON. Now, listen, hear my answer, and then you may with knowledge judge between us.
OEDIPUS. You are plausible, but waste words now that I know you.
CREON. Hear what I have to say. I can explain it all.
OEDIPUS. One thing you will not explain away—that you are my enemy.
CREON. You are a fool to imagine that senseless stubbornness sits well upon you.
OEDIPUS. And you to imagine that you can wrong a kinsman and escape the penalty.
CREON. That is justly said, I grant you; but what is this wrong that you complain of?
OEDIPUS. Did you advise, or not, that I should send for that notorious prophet?
CREON. And I am of the same mind still.
OEDIPUS. How long is it, then, since Laius—
CREON. What, what about him?
OEDIPUS. Since Laius was killed by an unknown hand?
CREON. That was many years ago.
OEDIPUS. Was this prophet at his trade in those days?
CREON. Yes; skilled as now and in equal honour.
OEDIPUS. Did he ever speak of me?
CREON. Never certainly when I was within earshot.
OEDIPUS. And did you enquire into the murder?
CREON. We did enquire but learnt nothing.
OEDIPUS. And why did he not tell out his story then?
CREON. I do not know. When I know nothing I say nothing.
OEDIPUS. This much at least you know and can say out.
CREON. What is that? If I know it I will say it.
OEDIPUS. That if he had not consulted you he would never have said that it was I who killed Laius.
CREON. You know best what he said; but now, question for question.
OEDIPUS. Question your fill—I cannot be proved guilty of that blood.
CREON. Answer me then. Are you not married to my sister?
OEDIPUS. That cannot be denied.
CREON. And do you not rule as she does? And with a like power?
OEDIPUS. I give her all she asks for.
CREON. And am not I the equal of you both?
OEDIPUS. Yes: and that is why you are so false a friend.
CREON. Not so; reason this out as I reason it, and first weigh this: who would prefer to lie awake amid terrors rather than to sleep in peace, granting that his power

is equal in both cases? Neither I nor any sober-minded man. You give me what I ask and let me do what I want, but were I King I would have to do things I did not want to do. Is not influence and no trouble with it better than any throne, am I such a fool as to hunger after unprofitable honours? Now all are glad to see me, every one wishes me well, all that want a favour from you ask speech of me—finding in that their hope. Why should I give up these things and take those? No wise mind is treacherous. I am no contriver of plots, and if another took to them he would not come to me for help. And in proof of this go to the Pythian Oracle, and ask if I have truly told what the Gods said: and after that, if you have found that I have plotted with the Soothsayer, take me and kill me; not by the sentence of one mouth only—but of two mouths, yours and my own. But do not condemn me in a corner, upon some fancy and without proof. What right have you to declare a good man bad or a bad good? It is as bad a thing to cast off a true friend as it is for a man to cast away his own life—but you will learn these things with certainty when the time comes; for time alone shows a just man; though a day can show a knave.

CHORUS. King! He has spoken well, he gives himself time to think; a headlong talker does not know what he is saying.

OEDIPUS. The plotter is at his work, and I must counterplot headlong, or he will get his ends and I miss mine.

CREON. What will you do then? Drive me from the land?

OEDIPUS. Not so; I do not desire your banishment—but your death.

CREON. You are not sane.

OEDIPUS. I am sane at least in my own interest.

CREON. You should be in mine also.

OEDIPUS. No, for you are false.

CREON. But if you understand nothing?

OEDIPUS. Yet I must rule.

CREON. Not if you rule badly.

OEDIPUS. Hear him, O Thebes!

CREON. Thebes is for me also, not for you alone.

CHORUS. Cease, princes: I see Jocasta coming out of the house; she comes just in time to quench the quarrel.

JOCASTA *enters.*

JOCASTA. Unhappy men! Why have you made this crazy uproar? Are you not ashamed to quarrel about your own affairs when the whole country is in trouble? Go back into the palace, Oedipus, and you, Creon, to your own house. Stop making all this noise about some petty thing.

CREON. Your husband is about to kill me—or to drive me from the land of my fathers.

OEDIPUS. Yes: for I have convicted him of treachery against me.

CREON. Now may I perish accursed if I have done such a thing!

JOCASTA. For God's love believe it, Oedipus. First, for the sake of his oath, and then for my sake, and for the sake of these people here.

CHORUS [*all*]. King, do what she asks.

OEDIPUS. What would you have me do?

CHORUS. Not to make a dishonourable charge, with no more evidence than rumour, against a friend who has bound himself with an oath.

OEDIPUS. Do you desire my exile or my death?

CHORUS. No, by Helios,[16] by the first of all the Gods, may I die abandoned by Heaven and earth if I have that thought! What breaks my heart is that our public griefs should be increased by your quarrels.

OEDIPUS. Then let him go, though I am doomed thereby to death or to be thrust dishonoured from the land; it is your lips, not his, that move me to compassion; wherever he goes my hatred follows him.

CREON. You are as sullen in yielding as you were vehement in anger, but such natures are their own heaviest burden.

OEDIPUS. Why will you not leave me in peace and begone?

CREON. I will go away; what is your hatred to me? In the eyes of all here I am a just man. [*He goes.*]

CHORUS. Lady, why do you not take your man in to the house?

JOCASTA. I will do so when I have learned what has happened.

CHORUS. The half of it was blind suspicion bred of talk; the rest the wounds left by injustice.

JOCASTA. It was on both sides?

CHORUS. Yes.

JOCASTA. What was it?

CHORUS. Our land is vexed enough. Let the thing alone now that it is over. [Exit leader of CHORUS.]

JOCASTA. In the name of the Gods, King, what put you in this anger?

OEDIPUS. I will tell you; for I honour you more than these men do. The cause is Creon and his plots against me.

JOCASTA. Speak on, if you can tell clearly how this quarrel arose.

OEDIPUS. He says that I am guilty of the blood of Laius.

JOCASTA. On his own knowledge, or on hearsay?

OEDIPUS. He has made a rascal of a seer his mouthpiece.

JOCASTA. Do not fear that there is truth in what he says. Listen to me, and learn to your comfort that nothing born of woman can know what is to come. I will give you proof of that. An oracle came to Laius once, I will not say from Phoebus, but from his ministers, that he was doomed to die by the hand of his own child sprung from him and me. When his child was but three days old, Laius bound its feet together and had it thrown by sure hands upon a trackless mountain; and when Laius was murdered at the place where three highways meet, it was, or so at least the rumour says, by foreign robbers. So Apollo did not bring it about that the child should kill its father, nor did Laius die in the dreadful way he feared by his child's hand. Yet that was how the message of the seers mapped out the future. Pay no attention to such things. What the God would show he will need no help to show it, but bring it to light himself.

OEDIPUS. What restlessness of soul, lady, has come upon me since I heard you speak, what a tumult of the mind!

JOCASTA. What is this new anxiety? What has startled you?

OEDIPUS. You said that Laius was killed where three highways meet.

JOCASTA. Yes: that was the story.

OEDIPUS. And where is the place?

JOCASTA. In Phocis where the road divides branching off to Delphi and to Daulia.

OEDIPUS. And when did it happen? How many years ago?

JOCASTA. News was published in this town just before you came into power.

[16] Apollo.

Oedipus. O Zeus! What have you planned to do unto me?

Jocasta. He was tall; the silver had just come into his hair; and in shape not greatly unlike to you.

Oedipus. Unhappy that I am! It seems that I have laid a dreadful curse upon myself, and did not know it.

Jocasta. What do you say? I tremble when I look on you, my King.

Oedipus. And I have a misgiving that the seer can see indeed. But I will know it all more clearly, if you tell me one thing more.

Jocasta. Indeed, though I tremble I will answer whatever you ask.

Oedipus. Had he but a small troop with him; or did he travel like a great man with many followers?

Jocasta. There were but five in all—one of them a herald; and there was one carriage with Laius in it.

Oedipus. Alas! It is now clear indeed. Who was it brought the news, lady?

Jocasta. A servant—the one survivor.

Oedipus. Is he by chance in the house now?

Jocasta. No; for when he found you reigning instead of Laius he besought me, his hand clasped in mine, to send him to the fields among the cattle that he might be far from the sight of this town; and I sent him. He was a worthy man for a slave and might have asked a bigger thing.

Oedipus. I would have him return to us without delay.

Jocasta. Oedipus, it is easy. But why do you ask this?

Oedipus. I fear that I have said too much, and therefore I would question him.

Jocasta. He shall come, but I too have a right to know what lies so heavy upon your heart, my King.

Oedipus. Yes: and it shall not be kept from you now that my fear has grown so heavy. Nobody is more to me than you, nobody has the same right to learn my good or evil luck. My father was Polybus of Corinth, my mother the Dorian Merope, and I was held the foremost man in all that town until a thing happened—a thing to startle a man, though not to make him angry as it made me. We were sitting at the table, and a man who had drunk too much cried out that I was not my father's son—and I, though angry, restrained my anger for that day; but the next day went to my father and my mother and questioned them. They were indignant at the taunt and that comforted me—and yet the man's words rankled, for they had spread a rumour through the town. Without consulting my father or my mother I went to Delphi, but Phoebus told me nothing of the thing for which I came, but much of other things—things of sorrow and of terror: that I should live in incest with my mother, and beget a brood that men would shudder to look upon; that I should be my father's murderer. Hearing those words I fled out of Corinth, and from that day have but known where it lies when I have found its direction by the stars. I sought where I might escape those infamous things—the doom that was laid upon me. I came in my flight to that very spot where you tell me this king perished. Now, lady, I will tell you the truth. When I had come close up to those three roads, I came upon a herald, and a man like him you have described seated in a carriage. The man who held the reins and the old man himself would not give me room, but thought to force me from the path, and I struck the driver in my anger. The old man, seeing what I had done, waited till I was passing him and then struck me upon the head. I paid him back in full, for I knocked him out of the carriage with a blow of my stick. He rolled on his back, and after that I killed them all. If this stranger were indeed Laius, is there a more miserable man in the world than the man before you? Is there a man more hated of Heaven? No stranger, no citizen, may receive him into his house, not a soul may speak to him, and no mouth but my own mouth has laid this curse upon me. Am I not wretched? May I be swept from this world before I have endured this doom!

CHORUS. These things, O King, fill us with terror; yet hope till you speak with him that saw the deed, and have learnt all.

OEDIPUS. Till I have learnt all, I may hope. I await the man that is coming from the pastures.

JOCASTA. What is it that you hope to learn?

OEDIPUS. I will tell you. If his tale agrees with yours, then I am clear.

JOCASTA. What tale of mine?

OEDIPUS. He told you that Laius met his death from robbers; if he keeps to that tale now and speaks of several slayers, I am not the slayer. But if he says one lonely wayfarer, then beyond a doubt the scale dips to me.

JOCASTA. Be certain of this much at least, his first tale was of robbers. He cannot revoke that tale—the city heard it and not I alone. Yet, if he should somewhat change his story, King, at least he cannot make the murder of Laius square with prophecy; for Loxias plainly said of Laius that he would die by the hand of my child. That poor innocent did not kill him, for it died before him. Therefore from this out I would not, for all divination can do, so much as look to my right hand or to my left hand, or fear at all.

OEDIPUS. You have judged well; and yet for all that, send and bring this peasant to me.

JOCASTA. I will send without delay. I will do all that you would have of me—but let us come in to the house. [*They go in to the house.*]

Chorus

For this one thing above all I would be praised as a man,
That in my words and my deeds I have kept those laws in mind
Olympian Zeus, and that high clear Empyrean,[17]
Fashioned, and not some man or people of mankind,
Even those sacred laws nor age nor sleep can blind.

A man becomes a tyrant out of insolence,
He climbs and climbs, until all people call him great,
He seems upon the summit, and God flings him thence;
Yet an ambitious man may lift up a whole State,
And in his death be blessed, in his life fortunate.

And all men honour such; but should a man forget
The holy images, the Delphian Sibyl's trance,[18]
And the world's navel-stone, and not be punished for it
And seem most fortunate, or even blessed perchance,
Why should we honour the Gods, or join the sacred dance?

---

[17] Zeus, the most powerful of the Greek gods, was said to live on Mt. Olympus, the highest mountain in Greece. The Empyrean is the highest heaven.

[18] The Sibyl, a female soothsayer, fell into a trance while telling fortunes.

JOCASTA *enters from the palace.*

JOCASTA. It has come into my head, citizens of Thebes, to visit every altar of the Gods, a wreath in my hand and a dish of incense. For all manner of alarms trouble the soul of Oedipus, who instead of weighing new oracles by old, like a man of sense, is at the mercy of every mouth that speaks terror. Seeing that my words are nothing to him, I cry to you, Lysian Apollo, whose altar is the first I meet: I come, a suppliant, bearing symbols of prayer; O, make us clean, for now we are all afraid, seeing him afraid, even as they who see the helmsman afraid.

Enter MESSENGER.

MESSENGER. May I learn from you, strangers, where is the home of King Oedipus? Or better still, tell me where he himself is, if you know.

CHORUS. This is his house, and he himself, stranger, is within it, and this lady is the mother of his children.

MESSENGER. Then I call a blessing upon her, seeing what man she has married.

JOCASTA. May God reward those words with a like blessing, stranger! But what have you come to seek or to tell?

MESSENGER. Good news for your house, lady, and for your husband.

JOCASTA. What news? From whence have you come?

MESSENGER. From Corinth, and you will rejoice at the message I am about to give you; yet, maybe, it will grieve you.

JOCASTA. What is it? How can it have this double power?

MESSENGER. The people of Corinth, they say, will take him for king.

JOCASTA. How then? Is old Polybus no longer on the throne?

MESSENGER. No. He is in his tomb.

JOCASTA. What do you say? Is Polybus dead, old man?

MESSENGER. May I drop dead if it is not the truth.

JOCASTA. Away! Hurry to your master with this news. O oracle of the Gods, where are you now? This is the man whom Oedipus feared and shunned lest he should murder him, and now this man has died a natural death, and not by the hand of Oedipus.

Enter OEDIPUS.

OEDIPUS. Jocasta, dearest wife, why have you called me from the house?

JOCASTA. Listen to this man, and judge to what the oracles of the Gods have come.

OEDIPUS. And he—who may he be? And what news has he?

JOCASTA. He has come from Corinth to tell you that your father, Polybus, is dead.

OEDIPUS. How, stranger? Let me have it from your own mouth.

MESSENGER. If I am to tell the story, the first thing is that he is dead and gone.

OEDIPUS. By some sickness or by treachery?

MESSENGER. A little thing can bring the aged to their rest.

OEDIPUS. Ah! He died, it seems, from sickness?

MESSENGER. Yes; and of old age.

OEDIPUS. Alas! Alas! Why, indeed, my wife, should one look to that Pythian seer, or to the birds that scream above our heads? For they would have it that I was doomed to kill my father. And now he is dead—hid already beneath the earth. And here am I—who had no part in it, unless indeed he died from longing for me. If that were so, I may have caused his death; but Polybus has carried the

oracles with him into Hades—the oracles as men have understood them—and
they are worth nothing.

JOCASTA. Did I not tell you so, long since?

OEDIPUS. You did, but fear misled me.

JOCASTA. Put this trouble from you.[19]

OEDIPUS. Those bold words would sound better, were not my mother living. But as
it is—I have some grounds for fear; yet you have said well.

JOCASTA. Yet your father's death is a sign that all is well.

OEDIPUS. I know that: but I fear because of her who lives.

MESSENGER. Who is this woman who makes you afraid?

OEDIPUS. Merope, old man, the wife of Polybus.

MESSENGER. What is there in her to make you afraid?

OEDIPUS. A dreadful oracle sent from Heaven, stranger.

MESSENGER. Is it a secret, or can you speak it out?

OEDIPUS. Loxias said that I was doomed to marry my own mother, and to shed my
father's blood. For that reason I fled from my house in Corinth; and I did right,
though there is great comfort in familiar faces.

MESSENGER. Was it indeed for that reason that you went into exile?

OEDIPUS. I did not wish, old man, to shed my father's blood.

MESSENGER. King, have I not freed you from that fear?

OEDIPUS. You shall be fittingly rewarded.

MESSENGER. Indeed, to tell the truth, it was for that I came; to bring you home and
be the better for it——

OEDIPUS. No! I will never go to my parents' home.

MESSENGER. Oh, my son, it is plain enough, you do not know what you do.

OEDIPUS. How, old man? For God's love, tell me.

MESSENGER. If for these reasons you shrink from going home.

OEDIPUS. I am afraid lest Phoebus has spoken true.

MESSENGER. You are afraid of being made guilty through Merope?

OEDIPUS. That is my constant fear.

MESSENGER. A vain fear.

OEDIPUS. How so, if I was born of that father and mother?

MESSENGER. Because they were nothing to you in blood.

OEDIPUS. What do you say? Was Polybus not my father?

MESSENGER. No more nor less than myself.

OEDIPUS. How can my father be no more to me than you who are nothing to me?

MESSENGER. He did not beget you any more than I.

OEDIPUS. No? Then why did he call me his son?

MESSENGER. He took you as a gift from these hands of mine.

OEDIPUS. How could he love so dearly what came from another's hands?

MESSENGER. He had been childless.

OEDIPUS. If I am not your son, where did you get me?

MESSENGER. In a wooded valley of Cithaeron.

OEDIPUS. What brought you wandering there?

---

[19] Jebb's translation continues:

> OEDIPUS. But surely I must needs fear my mother's bed?
>
> JOCASTA. Nay, what should mortal fear, for whom the decrees of fortune are supreme, and who hath
> clear foresight of nothing? 'Tis best to live at random, as one may. But fear not thou touching
> wedlock with thy mother. Many men ere now have so fared in dreams also: but he to whom
> these things are as nought bears his life most easily.

MESSENGER. I was in charge of mountain sheep.

OEDIPUS. A shepherd—a wandering, hired man.

MESSENGER. A hired man who came just in time.

OEDIPUS. Just in time—had it come to that?

MESSENGER. Have not the cords left their marks upon your ankles?

OEDIPUS. Yes, that is an old trouble.

MESSENGER. I took your feet out of the spancel.[20]

OEDIPUS. I have had those marks from the cradle.

MESSENGER. They have given you the name you bear.[21]

OEDIPUS. Tell me, for God's sake, was that deed my mother's or my father's?

MESSENGER. I do not know—he who gave you to me knows more of that than I.

OEDIPUS. What? You had me from another? You did not chance on me yourself?

MESSENGER. No. Another shepherd gave you to me.

OEDIPUS. Who was he? Can you tell me who he was?

MESSENGER. I think that he was said to be of Laius' household.

OEDIPUS. The king who ruled this country long ago?

MESSENGER. The same—the man was herdsman in his service.

OEDIPUS. Is he alive, that I might speak with him?

MESSENGER. You people of this country should know that.

OEDIPUS. Is there any one here present who knows the herd he speaks of? Any one who has seen him in the town pastures? The hour has come when all must be made clear.

CHORUS. I think he is the very herd you sent for but now; Jocasta can tell you better than I.

JOCASTA. Why ask about that man? Why think about him? Why waste a thought on what this man has said? What he has said is of no account.

OEDIPUS. What, with a clue like that in my hands and fail to find out my birth?

JOCASTA. For God's sake, if you set any value upon your life, give up this search—my misery is enough.

OEDIPUS. Though I be proved the son of a slave, yes, even of three generations of slaves, you cannot be made base-born.

JOCASTA. Yet, hear me, I implore you. Give up this search.

OEDIPUS. I will not hear of anything but searching the whole thing out.

JOCASTA. I am only thinking of your good—I have advised you for the best.

OEDIPUS. Your advice makes me impatient.

JOCASTA. May you never come to know who you are, unhappy man!

OEDIPUS. Go, some one, bring the herdsman here—and let that woman glory in her noble blood.

JOCASTA. Alas, alas, miserable man! Miserable! That is all that I can call you now or for ever. [*She goes out.*]

CHORUS. Why has the lady gone, Oedipus, in such a transport of despair? Out of this silence will burst a storm of sorrows.

OEDIPUS. Let come what will. However lowly my origin I will discover it. That woman, with all a woman's pride, grows red with shame at my base birth. I think myself the child of Good Luck, and that the years are my foster-brothers. Sometimes they have set me up, and sometimes thrown me down, but he that has Good Luck for mother can suffer no dishonour. That is my origin, nothing can change it, so why should I renounce this search into my birth?

---

[20] A noose for tethering animals.   [21] Oedipus means "swollen-feet."

Chorus

Oedipus' nurse, mountain of many a hidden glen,
Be honoured among men;
A famous man, deep-thoughted, and his body strong;
Be honoured in dance and song.
Who met in the hidden glen? Who let his fancy run
Upon nymph of Helicon?[22]
Lord Pan or Lord Apollo or the mountain Lord
By the Bacchantes adored?

OEDIPUS. If I, who have never met the man, may venture to say so, I think that the
   herdsman we await approaches; his venerable age matches with this stranger's,
   and I recognize as servants of mine those who bring him. But you, if you have
   seen the man before, will know the man better than I.
CHORUS. Yes, I know the man who is coming; he was indeed in Laius' service, and
   is still the most trusted of the herdsmen.
OEDIPUS. I ask you first, Corinthian stranger, is this the man you mean?
MESSENGER. He is the very man.
OEDIPUS. Look at me, old man! Answer my questions. Were you once in Laius'
   service?
HERDSMAN. I was: not a bought slave, but reared up in the house.
OEDIPUS. What was your work—your manner of life?
HERDSMAN. For the best part of my life I have tended flocks.
OEDIPUS. Where, mainly?
HERDSMAN. Cithaeron or its neighbourhood.
OEDIPUS. Do you remember meeting with this man there?
HERDSMAN. What man do you mean?
OEDIPUS. This man. Did you ever meet him?
HERDSMAN. I cannot recall him to mind.
MESSENGER. No wonder in that, master; but I will bring back his memory. He and
   I lived side by side upon Cithaeron. I had but one flock and he had two. Three
   full half-years we lived there, from spring to autumn, and every winter I drove
   my flock to my own fold, while he drove his to the fold of Laius. Is that right?
   Was it not so?
HERDSMAN. True enough; though it was long ago.
MESSENGER. Come, tell me now—do you remember giving me a boy to rear as my
   own foster-son?
HERDSMAN. What are you saying? Why do you ask me that?
MESSENGER. Look at that man, my friend, he is the child you gave me.
HERDSMAN. A plague upon you! Cannot you hold your tongue?
OEDIPUS. Do not blame him, old man; your own words are more blameable.
HERDSMAN. And how have I offended, master?
OEDIPUS. In not telling of that boy he asks of.
HERDSMAN. He speaks from ignorance, and does not know what he is saying.
OEDIPUS. If you will not speak with a good grace you shall be made to speak.

---

[22] The Chorus speculates that perhaps Oedipus's mother was a Greek nymph seduced by Pan (a
   playful god of the fields and forests), or Apollo, or Dionysus (the god of wine and revelry, worshipped by his female followers, the Bacchantes).

HERDSMAN. Do not hurt me for the love of God, I am an old man.

OEDIPUS. Some one there, tie his hands behind his back.

HERDSMAN. Alas! Wherefore! What more would you learn?

OEDIPUS. Did you give this man the child he speaks of?

HERDSMAN. I did: would I had died that day!

OEDIPUS. Well, you may come to that unless you speak the truth.

HERDSMAN. Much more am I lost if I speak it.

OEDIPUS. What! Would the fellow make more delay?

HERDSMAN. No, no. I said before that I gave it to him.

OEDIPUS. Where did you come by it? Your own child, or another?

HERDSMAN. It was not my own child—I had it from another.

OEDIPUS. From any of those here? From what house?

HERDSMAN. Do not ask any more, master; for the love of God do not ask.

OEDIPUS. You are lost if I have to question you again.

HERDSMAN. It was a child from the house of Laius.

OEDIPUS. A slave? Or one of his own race?

HERDSMAN. Alas! I am on the edge of dreadful words.

OEDIPUS. And I of hearing: yet hear I must.

HERDSMAN. It was said to have been his own child. But your lady within can tell you of these things best.

OEDIPUS. How? It was she who gave it to you?

HERDSMAN. Yes, King.

OEDIPUS. To what end?

HERDSMAN. That I should make away with it.

OEDIPUS. Her own child?

HERDSMAN. Yes: from fear of evil prophecies.

OEDIPUS. What prophecies?

HERDSMAN. That he should kill his father.

OEDIPUS. Why, then, did you give him up to this old man?

HERDSMAN. Through pity, master, believing that he would carry him to whatever land he had himself come from—but he saved him for dreadful misery; for if you are what this man says, you are the most miserable of all men.

OEDIPUS. O! O! All brought to pass! All truth! Now, O light, may I look my last upon you, having been found accursed in bloodshed, accursed in marriage, and in my coming into the world accursed! (*He rushes into the palace.*)

Chorus

What can the shadow-like generations of man attain
But build up a dazzling mockery of delight that under their touch
 dissolves again?
Oedipus seemed blessed, but there is no man blessed amongst men.

Oedipus overcame the woman-breasted Fate;[23]
He seemed like a strong tower against Death and first among the
 fortunate;
He sat upon the ancient throne of Thebes, and all men called him
 great.

[23] I.e., the Sphinx, whose riddle Oedipus solved.

But, looking for a marriage-bed, he found the bed of his birth,
Tilled the field his father had tilled, cast seed into the same abound-
    ing earth;
Entered through the door that had sent him wailing forth.

Begetter and begot as one! How could that be hid?
What darkness cover up that marriage-bed? Time watches, he is
    eagle-eyed,
And all the works of man are known and every soul is tried.

Would you had never come to Thebes, nor to this house,
Nor riddled with the woman-breasted Fate, beaten off Death and
    succoured us,
That I had never raised this song, heartbroken Oedipus!

SECOND MESSENGER [*coming from the house*]. Friends and kinsmen of this house! What
    deeds must you look upon, what burden of sorrow bear, if true to race you still
    love the House of Labdacus. For not Ister nor Phasis[24] could wash this house
    clean, so many misfortunes have been brought upon it, so many has it brought
    upon itself, and those misfortunes are always the worst that a man brings upon
    himself.
CHORUS. Great already are the misfortunes of this house, and you bring us a new
    tale.
SECOND MESSENGER. A short tale in the telling: Jocasta, our Queen, is dead.
CHORUS. Alas, miserable woman, how did she die?
SECOND MESSENGER. By her own hand. It cannot be as terrible to you as to one that
    saw it with his eyes, yet so far as words can serve, you shall see it. When she had
    come into the vestibule, she ran half crazed towards her marriage-bed, clutch-
    ing at her hair with the fingers of both hands, and once within the chamber
    dashed the doors together behind her. Then called upon the name of Laius,
    long since dead, remembering that son who killed the father and upon the
    mother begot an accursed race. And wailed because of that marriage wherein
    she had borne a two-fold race—husband by husband, children by her child.
    Then Oedipus with a shriek burst in and running here and there asked for a
    sword, asked where he would find the wife that was no wife but a mother who
    had borne his children and himself. Nobody answered him, we all stood dumb;
    but supernatural power helped him, for, with a dreadful shriek, as though
    beckoned, he sprang at the double doors, drove them in, burst the bolts out of
    their sockets, and ran into the room. There we saw the woman hanging in a
    swinging halter, and with a terrible cry he loosened the halter from her neck.
    When that unhappiest woman lay stretched upon the ground, we saw another
    dreadful sight. He dragged the golden brooches from her dress and lifting
    them struck them upon his eyeballs, crying out, "You have looked enough upon
    those you ought never to have looked upon, failed long enough to know those
    that you should have known; henceforth you shall be dark.' He struck his eyes,
    not once, but many times, lifting his hands and speaking such or like words. The
    blood poured down and not with a few slow drops, but all at once over his beard
    in a dark shower as it were hail. [*The* CHORUS *wails and he steps further on to the
    stage.*] Such evils have come forth from the deeds of those two and fallen not on

---

[24] Two large rivers.

one alone but upon husband and wife. They inherited much happiness, much good fortune; but to-day, ruin, shame, death, and loud crying, all evils that can be counted up, all, all are theirs.

CHORUS. Is he any quieter?

SECOND MESSENGER. He cries for someone to unbar the gates and to show to all the men of Thebes his father's murderer, his mother's—the unholy word must not be spoken. It is his purpose to cast himself out of the land that he may not bring all this house under his curse. But he has not the strength to do it. He must be supported and led away. The curtain is parting; you are going to look upon a sight which even those who shudder must pity.

Enter OEDIPUS.

OEDIPUS. Woe, woe is me! Miserable, miserable that I am! Where am I? Where am I going? Where am I cast away? Who hears my words?

CHORUS. Cast away indeed, dreadful to the sight of the eye, dreadful to the ear.

OEDIPUS. Ah, friend, the only friend left to me, friend still faithful to the blind man! I know that you are there; blind though I am, I recognise your voice.

CHORUS. Where did you get the courage to put out your eyes? What unearthly power drove you to that?

OEDIPUS. Apollo, friends, Apollo, but it was my own hand alone, wretched that I am, that quenched these eyes.

CHORUS. You were better dead than blind.

OEDIPUS. No, it is better to be blind. What sight is there that could give me joy? How could I have looked into the face of my father when I came among the dead, aye, or on my miserable mother, since against them both I sinned such things that no halter can punish? And what to me this spectacle, town, statue, wall, and what to me this people, since I, thrice wretched, I, noblest of Theban men, have doomed myself to banishment, doomed myself when I commanded all to thrust out the unclean thing?

CHORUS. It had indeed been better if that herdsman had never taken your feet out of the spancel or brought you back to life.

OEDIPUS. O three roads, O secret glen; O coppice[25] and narrow way where three roads met; you that drank up the blood I spilt, the blood that was my own, my father's blood: remember what deeds I wrought for you to look upon, and then, when I had come hither, the new deeds that I wrought. O marriage-bed that gave me birth and after that gave children to your child, creating an incestuous kindred of fathers, brothers, sons, wives, and mothers. Yes, all the shame and the uncleanness that I have wrought among men.

CHORUS. For all my pity I shudder and turn away.

OEDIPUS. Come near, condescend to lay your hands upon a wretched man; listen, do not fear. My plague can touch no man but me. Hide me somewhere out of this land for God's sake, or kill me, or throw me into the sea where you shall never look upon me more.

Enter CREON *and attendants.*

CHORUS. Here Creon comes at a fit moment; you can ask of him what you will, help or counsel, for he is now in your place. He is King.

---

[25] A thicket of small trees.

OEDIPUS. What can I say to him? What can I claim, having been altogether unjust to him.

CREON. I have not come in mockery, Oedipus, nor to reproach you. Lead him in to the house as quickly as you can. Do not let him display his misery before strangers.

OEDIPUS. I must obey, but first, since you have come in so noble a spirit, you will hear me.

CREON. Say what you will.

OEDIPUS. I know that you will give her that lies within such a tomb as befits your own blood, but there is something more, Creon. My sons are men and can take care of themselves, but my daughters, my two unhappy daughters, that have ever eaten at my own table and shared my food, watch over my daughters, Creon. If it is lawful, let me touch them with my hands. Grant it, Prince, grant it, noble heart. I would believe, could I touch them, that I still saw them. [ISMENE *and* ANTIGONE *are led in by attendants.*] But do I hear them sobbing? Has Creon pitied me and sent my children, my darlings? Has he done this?

CREON. Yes, I ordered it, for I know how greatly you have always loved them.

OEDIPUS. Then may you be blessed, and may Heaven be kinder to you than it has been to me! My children, where are you? Come hither—hither—come to the hands of him whose mother was your mother; the hands that put out your father's eyes, eyes once as bright as your own; his who, understanding nothing, seeing nothing, became your father by her that bore him. I weep when I think of the bitter life that men will make you live, and the days that are to come. Into what company dare you go, to what festival, but that you shall return home from it not sharing in the joys, but bathed in tears? When you are old enough to be married, what man dare face the reproach that must cling to you and to your children? What misery is there lacking? Your father killed his father, he begat you at the spring of his own being, offspring of her that bore him. That is the taunt that would be cast upon you and on the man that you should marry. That man is not alive; my children, you must wither away in barrenness. Ah, son of Menoeceus,[26] listen. Seeing that you are the only father now left to them, for we their parents are lost, both of us lost, do not let them wander in beggary—are they not your own kindred?—do not let them sink down into my misery. No, pity them, seeing them utterly wretched in helpless childhood if you do not protect them. Show me that you promise, generous man, by touching me with your hand. [CREON *touches him.*] My children, there is much advice that I would give you were you but old enough to understand, but all I can do now is bid you pray that you may live wherever you are let live, and that your life be happier than your father's.

CREON. Enough of tears. Pass into the house.

OEDIPUS. I will obey, though upon conditions.

CREON. Conditions?

OEDIPUS. Banish me from this country. I know that nothing can destroy me, for I wait some incredible fate; yet cast me upon Cithaeron, chosen by my father and my mother for my tomb.

CREON. Only the Gods can say yes or no to that.

OEDIPUS. No, for I am hateful to the Gods.

CREON. If that be so you will get your wish the quicker. They will banish that which they hate.

[26] Creon.

OEDIPUS. Are you certain of that?
CREON. I would not say it if I did not mean it.
OEDIPUS. Then it is time to lead me within.
CREON. Come, but let your children go.
OEDIPUS. No, do not take them from me.
CREON. Do not seek to be master; you won the mastery but could not keep it to the
 end. [*He leads Oedipus into the palace, followed by Ismene, Antigone, and attendants.*]

Chorus

Make way for Oedipus. All people said,
"That is a fortunate man";
And now what storms are beating on his head!
"That is a fortunate man,"
Call no man fortunate that is not dead.
The dead are free from pain.

THE END

[ca. 429 B.C.]

Aristophanes   ca. 450–385 B.C.

LYSISTRATA

Translated by Douglass Parker

CHARACTERS OF THE PLAY

LYSISTRATA⎫
KLEONIKE ⎬ *Athenian women*
MYRRHINE ⎭
LAMPITO, *a Spartan woman*
ISMENIA, *a Boiotian girl*
KORNTHIAN GIRL
POLICEWOMAN
KORYPHAIOS OF THE MEN
CHORUS OF OLD MEN *of Athens*
KORYPHAIOS OF THE WOMEN
CHORUS OF OLD WOMEN *of Athens*
COMMISSIONER OF PUBLIC SAFETY

FOUR POLICEMEN
KINESIAS, *Myrrhine's husband*
CHILD *of Kinesias and Myrrhine*
SLAVE
SPARTAN HERALD
SPARTAN AMBASSADOR
FLUTE-PLAYER
ATHENIAN WOMEN
PELOPONNESIAN WOMEN
PELOPONNESIAN MEN
ATHENIAN MEN

SCENE

A street in Athens. In the background, the Akropolis; center, its gateway, the Propylaia. The time is early morning. LYSISTRATA *is discovered alone, pacing back and forth in furious impatience.*

LYSISTRATA.
  Women!
  Announce a debauch in honor of Bacchos,
  a spree for Pan,[1] some footling fertility fieldday,
  and traffic stops—the streets are absolutely clogged
  with frantic females banging on tambourines. No urging
  for an orgy!
              But *today*—there's not one woman here.
[*Enter* KLEONIKE].
  Correction: one. Here comes my next door neighbor.
  —Hello, Kleonike.
KLEONIKE.
              Hello to *you*, Lysistrata.
  —But what's the fuss? Don't look so barbarous, baby;
  knitted brows just aren't your style.
LYSISTRATA.
              It doesn't
  matter, Kleonike—I'm on fire right down to the bone.
  I'm positively ashamed to be a woman—a member

---

[1] Bacchos (or Bacchus) is the Greek god of wine and revelry. Pan, the god of the fields and forests, is usually depicted as a lecherous satyr with the head and torso of a man but the horns and shaggy hindquarters of a goat.

of a sex which can't even live up to male slanders!
To hear our husbands talk, we're *sly:* deceitful,
always plotting, monsters of intrigue. . . .

KLEONIKE. [*Proudly.*]

That's us!

LYSISTRATA.
And so we agreed to meet today and plot
an intrigue that really deserves the name of monstrous . . .
and WHERE are the women?

Slyly asleep at home—
they won't get up for anything!

KLEONIKE.

Relax, honey.
They'll be here. You know a woman's way is hard—
mainly the way out of the house: fuss over hubby,
wake the maid up, put the baby down, bathe him,
feed him . . .

LYSISTRATA.

Trivia. They have more fundamental business to engage in.

KLEONIKE.

Incidentally, Lysistrata, just why are
you calling this meeting? Nothing teeny, I trust?

LYSISTRATA.
Immense.

KLEONIKE.

Hmmm. And pressing?

LYSISTRATA.

Unthinkably tense.

KLEONIKE.
Then where IS everybody?

LYSISTRATA.

Nothing like that. If it were,
we'd already be in session. Seconding motions.
—No, *this* came to hand some time ago. I've spent
my nights kneading it, mulling it, filing it down. . . .

KLEONIKE.
Too bad. There can't be very much left.

LYSISTRATA.

Only this:
the hope and salvation of Hellas lies with the WOMEN!

KLEONIKE.
Lies with the women? Now *there's* a last resort.

LYSISTRATA.
It lies with us to decide affairs of state
and foreign policy.

The Spartan Question:[2] Peace
or Extirpation?

---

[2] "The Spartan Question" is a reference to the Peloponnesian War (431–404 B.C.) which was dominating Athenian life at the time this play was written (411 B.C.). The war was fought between Sparta and Athens, the most powerful of the city-states in Greece (also called Hellas). The various women in the play gather from all parts of Greece and represent the contending factions and their allies.

KLEONIKE.
                                           How *fun!*
                                   I cast an Aye for Extirpation
LYSISTRATA.
The Utter Annihilation of every last Boiotian?
KLEONIKE.
AYE!—I mean Nay. Clemency, please, for those
scrumptious eels.[3]
LYSISTRATA.
          And as for Athens . . . I'd rather not put
the thought into words. Just fill in the blanks, if you will.
—To the point: if we can meet and reach agreement
here and now with the girls from Thebes and the Peloponnese,
we'll form an alliance and save the States of Greece!
KLEONIKE.
Us? Be practical. Wisdom from women? There's nothing
cosmic about cosmetics—and Glamor is our only talent.
All we can do is *sit,* primped and painted,
     made up and dressed up,
[*Getting carried away in spite of her argument.*]
                                   ravishing in saffron wrappers,
peekaboo peignoirs, exquisite negligees, those chic,
expensive little slippers that come from the East . . .
LYSISTRATA.
Exactly. You've hit it. I see our way to salvation
in just such ornamentation—in slippers and slips, rouge
and perfumes, negligees and decolletage. . . .
KLEONIKE.
                                           How so?
LYSISTRATA.
So effectively that not one husband will take up his spear
against another . . .
KLEONIKE.
                                   Peachy!
                          I'll have that kimono
dyed . . .
LYSISTRATA.
          . . . or shoulder his shield . . .
KLEONIKE.
                                                   . . . squeeze into that
daring negligee . . .
LYSISTRATA.
          . . . or unsheathe his sword!
KLEONIKE.
                                           . . . and buy those
slippers!
LYSISTRATA.
Well, now. Don't you think the girls should be here?

---

[3] Eels from Lake Kopais in Boiotia were considered a delicacy.

KLEONIKE.

Be here? Ages ago—they should have flown! [*She stops.*]
But no. You'll find out. These are authentic Athenians:
no matter what they do, they do it late.

LYSISTRATA.

But what about the out-of-town delegations? There isn't
a woman here from the Shore; none from Salamis . . .

KLEONIKE.

That's quite a trip. They usually get on board
at sunup. Probably riding at anchor now.

LYSISTRATA.

I thought the girls from Acharnai would be here first.
I'm especially counting on them. And they're not here.

KLEONIKE.

I think Theogenes' wife is under way.
When I went by, she was hoisting her sandals . . . [*Looking off right.*]

But look!

Some of the girls are coming!

Women enter from the right. LYSISTRATA *looks off to the left
where more—a ragged lot—are straggling in.*

LYSISTRATA.

And more over here!

KLEONIKE.

Where did you find *that* group?

LYSISTRATA.

They're from the outskirts.

KLEONIKE.

Well, that's something. If you haven't done anything
else, you've really ruffled up the outskirts.

[MYRRHINE *enters guiltily from the right.*]

MYRRHINE.

Oh, Lysistrata,
we aren't late, are we?

Well, *are* we?

Speak to me!

LYSISTRATA.

What is it, Myrrhine? Do you want a medal for tardiness?
Honestly, such behavior, with so much at stake . . .

MYRRHINE.

I'm sorry. I couldn't find my girdle in the dark.
And anyway, we're here now. So tell us all about it,
whatever it is.

KLEONIKE.

No, wait a minute. Don't
begin just yet. Let's wait for those girls from Thebes
and the Peloponnese.

LYSISTRATA.

Now *there* speaks the proper attitude.

[LAMPITO, *a strapping Spartan woman, enters left, leading
a pretty Boiotian girl* (ISMENIA) *and a huge, steatopygous*[4]
KORINTHIAN.]
And here's our lovely Spartan.
Hello, Lampito
dear. Why darling, you're simply ravishing! Such
a blemishless complexion—so clean, so out-of-doors!
And will you look at that figure—the pink of perfection!
KLEONIKE.
I'll bet you could strangle a bull.
LAMPITO.
I calklate so.
Hit's fitness whut done it, fitness and dancin'. You know
the step?
[*Demonstrating.*]
Foot it out back'ards an' toe yore twitchet. [The women crowd around
LAMPITO.]
KLEONIKE.
What unbelievably beautiful bosoms!
LAMPITO.
Shuckins,
whut fer you tweedlin' me up so? I feel like a heifer
come fair-time.
LYSISTRATA. [*Turning to* ISMENIA.]
And who is this young lady here?
LAMPITO.
Her kin's purt-near the bluebloodiest folk in Thebes—
the First Fam'lies of Boiotia.
LYSISTRATA. [*As they inspect* ISMENIA.]
Ah, picturesque Boiotia:
her verdant meadows, her fruited plain . . .
KLEONIKE. [*Peering more closely.*]
Her sunken
garden where no grass grows. A cultivated country.
LYSISTRATA. [*Gaping at the gawking* KORINTHIAN.]
And who is *this*—er—little thing?
LAMPITO.
She hails
from over by Korinth, but her kinfolk's quality—mighty
big back there.
KLEONIKE. [*On her tour of inspection.*]
She's mighty big back *here*.
LAMPITO.
The womenfolk's all assemblied. Who-all's notion
was this-hyer confabulation?
LYSISTRATA.
Mine.
LAMPITO.
Git on with the give-out.
I'm hankerin' to hear.

---

[4] Big-buttocked.

MYRRHINE.

                    Me, too! I can't imagine
what could be so important. Tell us about it!

LYSISTRATA.

    Right away.
           —But first, a question. It's not
an involved one. Answer yes or no. [*A pause.*]

MYRRHINE.

                          Well, ASK it!

LYSISTRATA.

    It concerns the fathers of your children—your husbands,
absent on active service. I know you all have men
abroad.
        —Wouldn't you like to have them home?

KLEONIKE.

    My husband's been gone for the last five months! Way up
to Thrace, watchdogging military waste. It's horrible!

MYRRHINE.

    Mine's been posted to Pylos for seven whole months!

LAMPITO.

    My man's no sooner rotated out of the line
than he's plugged back in. Hain't no discharge in this war!

KLEONIKE.

    And lovers can't be had for love or money,
not even synthetics. Why, since those beastly Milesians
revolted and cut off the leather trade, that handy
do-it-yourself kit's *vanished* from the open market!

LYSISTRATA.

    If I can devise a scheme for ending the war,
I gather I have your support?

KLEONIKE.

                    You can count on me!
If you need money, I'll pawn the shift off my back—[*Aside.*] and drink up the
cash before the sun goes down.

MYRRHINE.

    Me, too! I'm ready to split myself right up
the middle like a mackerel, and give you half!

LAMPITO.

    Me, too! I'd climb Taygetos Mountain plumb
to the top to git the leastes' peek at Peace!

LYSISTRATA.

    Very well, I'll tell you. No reason to keep a secret. [*Importantly, as the women
cluster around her.*]
We can force our husbands to negotiate Peace,
Ladies, by exercising steadfast Self-Control—
By Total Abstinence . . . [*A pause.*]

KLEONIKE.

              From WHAT?

MYRRHINE.

                    Yes, what?

LYSISTRATA.

                        You'll do it?

KLEONIKE.
Of course we'll do it! We'd even *die!*
LYSISTRATA.
                                              Very well,
then here's the program:
                                    Total Abstinence
                                              from SEX!
[*The cluster of women dissolves.*]
—Why are you turning away? Where are you going?
[*Moving among the women.*]
—What's this? Such stricken expressions! Such gloomy gestures!
—Why so pale?
                    —Whence these tears?
                                              —What IS this?
Will you do it or won't you?
                                    Cat got your tongue?
KLEONIKE.
Afraid I can't make it. Sorry.
                              On with the War!
MYRRHINE.
Me neither. Sorry.
                        On with the War!
LYSISTRATA.
                                        This from
my little mackerel? The girl who was ready, a minute
ago, to split herself right up the middle?
KLEONIKE. [*Breaking in between* LYSISTRATA *and* MYRRHINE.]
Try something else. Try anything. If you say so,
I'm willing to walk through fire barefoot.
                                        But not
to give up SEX—there's nothing like it, Lysistrata!
LYSISTRATA. [*To* MYRRHINE.]
And you?
MYRRHINE.
            Me, too! I'll walk through fire.
LYSISTRATA.
                                        Women!
Utter sluts, the entire sex! Will-power,
nil. We're perfect raw material for Tragedy,
the stuff of heroic lays. "Go to bed with a god
and then get rid of the baby"—that sums us up! [*Turning to* LAMPITO.]
—Oh, Spartan, be a dear. If *you* stick by me,
just you, we still may have a chance to win.
Give me your vote.
LAMPITO.
                        Hit's right onsettlin' fer gals
to sleep all lonely-like, withouten no humpin'.
But I'm on yore side. We shore need Peace, too.
LYSISTRATA.
You're a darling—the only woman here
worthy of the name!

KLEONIKE.

> Well, just suppose we *did*,
> as much as possible, abstain from . . . what you said,
> you know—not that we *would*—could something like
> that bring Peace any sooner?

LYSISTRATA.

> Certainly. Here's how it works:
> We'll paint, powder, and pluck ourselves to the last
> detail, and stay inside, wearing those filmy
> tunics that set off everything we *have*—
>
> and then
> slink up to the men. They'll snap to attention, go
> absolutely *mad* to love us—
>
> but we won't let them. We'll Abstain.
> —I imagine they'll conclude a treaty rather quickly.

LAMPITO. [*Nodding.*]

> Menelaos he tuck one squint at Helen's bubbies
> all nekkid, and plumb throwed up. [*Pause for thought.*]
>
> Throwed up his sword.

KLEONIKE.

> Suppose the men just leave us flat?

LYSISTRATA.

> In that case,
> we'll have to take things into our own hands.

KLEONIKE.

> There simply isn't any reasonable facsimile!
> —Suppose they take us by force and drag us off
> to the bedroom against our wills?

LYSISTRATA.

> Hang on to the door.

KLEONIKE.

> Suppose they beat us?

LYSISTRATA.

> Give in——but be bad sports.
> Be nasty about it—they don't enjoy these forced
> affairs. So make them suffer.
>
> Don't worry; they'll stop
> soon enough. A married man wants harmony—
> cooperation, not rape.

KLEONIKE.

> Well, I suppose so. . . .
> [*Looking from* LYSISTRATA *to* LAMPITO.]
> If *both* of you approve this, then so do we.

LAMPITO.

> Hain't worried over our menfolk none. We'll bring 'em
> round to makin' a fair, straightfor'ard Peace
> withouten no nonsense about it. But take this rackety
> passel in Athens: I misdoubt no one could make 'em
> give over thet blabber of theirn.

LYSISTRATA.
                              They're our concern.
Don't worry. We'll bring them around.
LAMPITO.
                                    Not likely.
Not long as they got ships kin still sail straight,
an' thet fountain of money up thar in Athene's temple.[5]
LYSISTRATA.
That point is quite well covered:
                              We're taking over
The Akropolis, including Athene's temple, today.
It's set: Our oldest women have their orders.
They're up there now, pretending to sacrifice, waiting
for us to reach an agreement. As soon as we do,
they seize the Akropolis.
LAMPITO.
                    The way you put them thengs,
I swear I can't see how we kin possibly lose!
LYSISTRATA.
Well, now that it's settled, Lampito, let's not lose
any time. Let's take the Oath to make this binding.
LAMPITO.
Just trot out thet-thar Oath. We'll swear it.
LYSISTRATA.
                                  Excellent.
—Where's a policewoman? [*A huge girl, dressed as a Skythian archer (the Athenian
police) with bow and circular shield, lumbers up and gawks.*]
                                    —What are *you* looking for?
[*Pointing to a spot in front of* the women.] Put your shield down here.
[*The girl obeys.*]
                    No, hollow *up!* [*The girl reverses the shield.* LYSISTRATA *looks about
                    brightly.*]
—Someone give me the entrails. [*A dubious silence.*]
KLEONIKE.
                          Lysistrata, what kind
of an Oath are we supposed to swear?
LYSISTRATA.
                              The Standard.
Aischylos[6] used it in a play, they say—the one where
you slaughter a sheep and swear on a shield.
KLEONIKE.
                                  Lysistrata,
you *do not* swear an Oath for *Peace* on a *shield!*
LYSISTRATA.
What Oath do you want? [*Exasperated.*]
                    Something bizarre and expensive?
A fancier victim—"Take one white horse and
disembowel"?

[5] The Athenians kept a reserve fund of one thousand silver coins in the back of Athene's temple,
   located on a hill called the Akropolis.
[6] Aeschylus (525–456 B.C.) was the earliest of the great Greek playwrights.

KLEONIKE.

White horse: The symbolism's too obscure.

LYSISTRATA.

Then how

do we swear this oath?

KLEONIKE.

Oh, *I* can tell you

that, if you'll let me.

First, we put an enormous

black cup right here—hollow up, of course.

Next, into the cup we slaughter a jar of Thasian

wine, and swear a mighty Oath that we won't . . .

dilute it with water.

LAMPITO. [*To* KLEONIKE.]

Let me corngratulate you—

that were the beatenes' Oath I ever heerd on!

LYSISTRATA. [*Calling inside.*] Bring out a cup and a jug of wine!

[*Two women emerge, the first staggering under the weight of a huge black cup, the second even more burdened with a tremendous wine jar.* KLEONIKE *addresses them.*]

KLEONIKE.

You darlings!

What a tremendous display of pottery! [*Fingering the cup.*]

A girl

could get a glow just *holding* a cup like this! [*She grabs it away from the first woman, who exits.*]

LYSISTRATA. [*Taking the wine jar from the second serving woman (who exits), she barks at* KLEONIKE.] Put that down and help me butcher this boar! [KLEONIKE *puts down the cup, over which she and* LYSISTRATA *together hold the jar of wine (the "boar").* LYSISTRATA *prays.*]

O Mistress Persuasion,

O Cup of Devotion,

Attend our invocation:

Accept this oblation,

Grant our petition,

Favor our mission.

[LYSISTRATA *and* KLEONIKE *tip up the jar and pour the gurgling wine into the cup.* MYRRHINE, LAMPITO, *and the others watch closely.*]

MYRRHINE.

Such an attractive shade of blood. And the spurt—

pure Art!

LAMPITO.

Hit shore do smell mighty purty!

[LYSISTRATA *and* KLEONIKE *put down the empty wine jar.*]

KLEONIKE.

Girls, let me be the first [*Launching herself at the cup.*] to take the Oath!

LYSISTRATA. [*Hauling* KLEONIKE *back.*]

You'll have to wait your turn like everyone else.

—Lampito, how do we manage with this mob?

Cumbersome.

—Everyone place her right hand on the cup. [*The women surround the cup and obey.*]

I need a spokeswoman. One of you to take
the Oath in behalf of the rest. [*The women edge away from* KLEONIKE, *who reluctantly
finds herself elected.*]
                                                    The rite will conclude
with a General Pledge of Assent by all of you, thus
confirming the Oath. Understood? [*Nods from the women.* LYSISTRATA *addresses*
KLEONIKE.]
                                                                        Repeat after me:

LYSISTRATA.
I will withhold all rights of access or entrance
KLEONIKE.
I will withhold all rights of access or entrance
LYSISTRATA.
From every husband, lover, or casual acquaintance
KLEONIKE.
from every husband, lover, or casual acquaintance
LYSISTRATA.
Who moves in my direction in erection.
                                                                —Go on
KLEONIKE.
who m-moves in my direction in erection.
                                                        Ohhhhh!
—Lysistrata, my knees are shaky. Maybe I'd better . . .
LYSISTRATA.
I will create, imperforate in cloistered chastity,
KLEONIKE.
I will create, imperforate in cloistered chastity,
LYSISTRATA.
A newer, more glamorous, supremely seductive me
KLEONIKE.
a newer, more glamorous, supremely seductive me
LYSISTRATA.
And fire my husband's desire with my molten allure—
KLEONIKE.
and fire my husband's desire with my molten allure—
LYSISTRATA.
But remain, to his panting advances, icily pure.
KLEONIKE.
but remain, to his panting advances, icily pure.
LYSISTRATA.
If he should force me to share the connubial couch,
KLEONIKE.
If he should force me to share the connubial couch,
LYSISTRATA.
I refuse to return his stroke with the teeniest twitch.
KLEONIKE.
I refuse to return his stroke with the teeniest twitch.
LYSISTRATA.
I will not lift my slippers to touch the thatch
KLEONIKE.
I will not lift my slippers to touch the thatch

LYSISTRATA.
Or submit sloping prone in a hangdog crouch.
KLEONIKE.
or submit sloping prone in a hangdog crouch.
LYSISTRATA.

**If I this oath maintain,
may I drink this glorious wine.**

KLEONIKE.

If I this oath maintain,
may I drink this glorious wine.

LYSISTRATA.

**But if I slip or falter,
let me drink water.**

KLEONIKE.

But if I slip or falter,
let me drink water.

LYSISTRATA.
—And now the General Pledge of Assent:
WOMEN.

A-MEN!

LYSISTRATA.
Good. I'll dedicate the oblation. [*She drinks deeply.*]
KLEONIKE.

Not too much,
darling. You know how anxious we are to become
allies and friends.

Not to mention *staying* friends.
[*She pushes* LYSISTRATA *away and drinks. As the women take their turns at the cup, loud
cries and alarums are heard offstage.*]
LAMPITO.
What-all's that bodacious ruckus?
LYSISTRATA.

Just what I told you:
It means the women have taken the Akropolis. Athene's
Citadel is ours!

It's time for you to go,
Lampito, and set your affairs in order in Sparta. [*Indicating the other women in*
LAMPITO's *group.*]
Leave these girls here as hostages.
[LAMPITO *exits left.* LYSISTRATA *turns to the others.*]

Let's hurry inside
the Akropolis and help the others shoot the bolts.
KLEONIKE.
Don't you think the men will send reinforcements
against us as soon as they can?
LYSISTRATA.

So where's the worry?
The men can't burn their way in or frighten us out.
The Gates are ours—they're proof against fire and fear—
and they open only on our conditions.

KLEONIKE.

                                                      Yes!
That's the spirit—let's deserve our reputations: [*As the women hurry off into the Akropolis.*]
UP THE SLUTS!

WAY FOR THE OLD IMPREGNABLES!

The door shuts behind the women, and the stage is empty. A pause, and the CHORUS OF MEN *shuffles on from the left in two groups, led by their* KORYPHAIOS.[7] *They are incredibly aged Athenians; though they may acquire spryness later in the play, at this point they are sheer decrepitude. Their normally shaky progress is impeded by their burdens: each man not only staggers under a load of wood across his shoulders, but has his hands full as well—in one, an earthen pot containing fire (which is in constant danger of going out); in the other, a dried vinewood torch, not yet lit. Their progress toward the Akropolis is very slow.*

KORYPHAIOS OF MEN. [*To the right guide of the* FIRST SEMICHORUS, *who is stumbling along in mild agony.*]
Forward, Swifty, keep 'em in step! Forget your shoulder.
I know these logs are green and heavy—but duty, boy, duty!
SWIFTY. [*Somewhat inspired, he quavers into slow song to set a pace for his group.*]
                    I'm never surprised. At my age, life
                    is just one damned thing after another.
                    And yet, I never thought my wife
                    was anything more than a home-grown bother.
                            But now, dadblast her,
                            she's a National Disaster!
FIRST SEMICHORUS OF MEN.
                            What a catastrophe—
                                    MATRIARCHY!
                    They've brought Athene's statue[8] to heel,
                    they've put the Akropolis under a seal,
                    they've copped the whole damned commonweal . . .
                    What is there left for them to steal?
KORYPHAIOS OF MEN. [*To the right guide of the* SECOND SEMICHORUS *a slower soul, if possible, than* SWIFTY.]
                    Now, Chipper, speed's the word. The Akropolis, on the double!
                    Once we're there, we'll pile these logs around them, and convene
                    a circuit court for a truncated trial. Strictly impartial:
                    With a show of hands, we'll light a spark of justice under
                    every woman who brewed this scheme. We'll burn them all
                    on the first ballot—and the first to go is Ly . . .
[*Pause for thought.*]
                                                      is Ly . . .
[*Remembering and pointing at a spot in the audience.*]
                    is *Lykon's* wife—and there she is, right over there![9]

---

[7] A term for the leader of the chorus.
[8] A wooden statue thought of as the guardian of the city.
[9] "Rhodia, wife of the demagogue Lykon, was a real person, frequently lampooned for her morality. In a not unusual breaking of the dramatic illusion, her name occurs here as a surprise for the expected 'Lysistrata.' " (Translator's note.)

CHIPPER. [*Taking up the song again.*]
> I won't be twitted, I won't be guyed,
> I'll teach these women not to trouble us!
> Kleomenes the Spartan tried
> expropriating our Akropolis[10]
>> some time ago—
>> ninety-five years or so—

SECOND SEMICHORUS OF MEN.
> but he suffered damaging losses
>> when he ran across US!
> He breathed defiance—and more as well:
> No bath for six years—you could tell.
> We fished him out of the Citadel
> and quelled his spirit—but not his smell.

KORYPHAIOS OF MEN.
> That's how I took him. A savage siege:
>> Seventeen ranks
> of shields were massed at that gate, with blanket infantry cover.
> I slept like a baby.
>> So when mere women (who gall the gods
> and make Euripides[11] sick) try the same trick, should I
> sit idly by?
>> Then demolish the monument I won at Marathon![12]

FIRST SEMICHORUS OF MEN. [*Singly.*]
>> —The last lap of our journey!
>> —I greet it with some dismay.
>> —The danger doesn't deter me,
>>> —but
> it's uphill
>> —all the way.
> —Please, somebody,
>> —find a jackass
>>> to drag these logs
>>>> to the top.
>> —I ache to join the fracas,
>>> —but
> my shoulder's aching
>>>> —to stop.

SWIFTY.
> Backward there's no turning.
> Upward and onward, men!
> And keep those firepots burning, or
> we make this trip again.

CHORUS OF MEN. [*Blowing into their firepots, which promptly send forth clouds of smoke.*]
> With a puff (pfffff)....

---

[10] "Kleomenes' occupation of the Akropolis in 508, high point of his unsuccessful bid to help establish the Athenian aristocrats, lasted rather less than the six years which the Chorus seems to remember. The actual time was two days." (Translator's note.)

[11] A Greek playwright (ca. 480–407 B.C.).

[12] The site of a famous Greek victory over the Persians in 490 B.C.

and a cough (hhhhhh). . . .
The smoke! I'll choke! Turn it off!

SECOND SEMICHORUS OF MEN. [*Singly.*]
—Damned embers.
—Should be muzzled.
—There oughta be a law.
—They jumped me
—when I whistled
—and then
they gnawed my eyeballs
— raw.
—There's lava in my lashes.
—My lids are oxidized.
—My brows are braised.
—These ashes are
volcanoes
—in disguise.

CHIPPER.
This way, men. And remember,
The Goddess needs our aid.
So don't be stopped by cinders. Let's
press on to the stockade!

CHORUS OF MEN. [*Blowing again into their firepots, which erupt as before.*]
With a huff (hfffff). . . .
and a chuff (chffff). . . .
Drat that smoke. Enough is enough!

KORYPHAIOS OF MEN. [*Signalling the* CHORUS, *which has now tottered into position before the Akropolis gate, to stop, and peering into his firepot.*]
Praise be to the gods, it's awake. There's fire in the old fire yet.
—Now the directions. See how they strike you:
First, we deposit
these logs at the entrance and light our torches. Next, we crash
the gate. When that doesn't work, we request admission. Politely.
When *that* doesn't work, we burn the damned door down, and smoke
these women into submission,
That seem acceptable? Good.
Down with the load . . . ouch, that smoke! Sonofabitch!
[*A horrible tangle results as the* CHORUS *attempts to deposit the logs. The* KORYPHAIOS *turns to the audience.*]
Is there a general in the house? We have a logistical
problem. . . .
[*No answer. He shrugs.*] Same old story. Still at loggerheads over in Samos.[13]
[*With great confusion, the logs are placed somehow.*] That's better. The pressure's off.
I've got my backbone back. [*To his firepot.*]
What, pot? You forgot your part in the plot?
Urge that smudge.
to be hot on the dot and scorch my torch.
Got it, pot?

---

[13] After the annihilation of the Athenian forces sent to the island of Sicily in 415 B.C., most of the remaining generals were sent to Samos (a Greek island off Asia Minor) in an effort to shore up the allegiance and prepare an attack against those city states that had defected to Sparta.

[*Praying.*]

Queen Athene, let these strumpets
crumple before our attack.
Grant us victory, male supremacy . . .
and a testimonial plaque.

The men plunge their torches into firepots and arrange themselves purposefully before the gate. Engaged in their preparations, they do not see the sudden entrance, from the right, of the Chorus of Women, *led by their* Koryphaios. *These wear long cloaks and carry pitchers of water. They are very old—though not so old as the men—but quite spry. In their turn, they do not perceive the* Chorus of Men.

Koryphaios of Women. [*Stopping suddenly.*]
What's this—soot? And smoke as well? I may be all wet,
but this might mean fire. Things look dark, girls; we'll
have to dash. [*They move ahead, at a considerably faster pace than the men.*]
First Semichorus of Women.
[*Singly.*]

Speed! Celerity!	Save our sorority
from arson. Combustion.	And heat exhaustion.
Don't let our sisterhood	shrivel to blisterhood.

Fanned into slag by hoary typhoons.
By flatulent, nasty, gusty baboons.
We're late! Run!
The girls might be done

[*Tutte.*[14]]

Filling my pitcher	was absolute torture:
The fountains in town	are so *crowded* at dawn,
glutted with masses	of the lower classes
blatting and battering,	shoving, and shattering
jugs. But I juggled	my burden, and wriggled
away to extinguish	the igneous anguish

of neighbor, and sister, and daughter—
Here's Water!
Second Semichorus of Women.
[*Singly.*]

Get wind of the news?	The gaffers are loose.
The blowhards are off	with fuel enough
to furnish a bathhouse.	But the finish is pathos:

They're scaling the heights with a horrid proposal.
They're threatening women with rubbish disposal!
How ghastly—how gauche![15]
burned up with the trash!

[*Tutte.*]

Preserve me, Athene,	from gazing on any
matron or maid	auto-da-fé'd.[16]
Cover with grace	these redeemers of Greece
from battles, insanity,	Man's inhumanity.
Gold-browed goddess,	hither to aid us!
Fight as our ally,	join in our sally

[14] All together.   [15] Awkward, graceless.   [16] Burned at the stake.

against pyromaniac slaughter—
　　　　Haul Water!

KORYPHAIOS OF WOMEN. [*Noticing for the first time the* CHORUS OF MEN, *still busy at their firepots, she cuts off a member of her* CHORUS *who seems about to continue the song.*]
Hold it. What have we here? You don't catch true-blue
patriots red-handed. These are authentic degenerates,
male, taken *in flagrante.*[17]

KORYPHAIOS OF MEN.
　　　　　　Oops. Female troops. This could be upsetting.
I didn't expect such a flood of reserves.

KORYPHAIOS OF WOMEN.
　　　　　　　　　　　　　　Merely a spearhead.
If our numbers stun you, watch that yellow streak
spread. We represent just one percent of one percent of
This Woman's Army.

KORYPHAIOS OF MEN.
Never been confronted with such backtalk. Can't allow
it. Somebody pick up a log and pulverize that brass.
　　　　　　　　　　　　　　Any volunteers?

[*There are none among the male chorus.*]

KORYPHAIOS OF WOMEN.
Put down the pitchers, girls. If they start waving that lumber,
we don't want to be encumbered.

KORYPHAIOS OF MEN.
　　　　　　　Look, men, a few sharp jabs
will stop that jawing. It never fails.
　　　　　　　　　　　　　The poet Hipponax
swears by it.[18]

[*Still no volunteers. The* KORYPHAIOS OF WOMEN *advances.*]

KORYPHAIOS OF WOMEN.
　　　　　　Then step right up. Have a jab at me.
Free shot.

KORYPHAIOS OF MEN. [*Advancing reluctantly to meet her.*]
　　　　　　Shut up! I'll peel your pelt. I'll pit your pod.

KORYPHAIOS OF WOMEN.
The name is Stratyllis. I dare you to lay one finger on me.

KORYPHAIOS OF MEN.
I'll lay on you with a fistful. Er—any specific threats?

KORYPHAIOS OF WOMEN. [*Earnestly.*]
I'll crop your lungs and reap your bowels, bite by bite,
and leave no balls on the body for other bitches to
gnaw.

KORYPHAIOS OF MEN. [*Retreating hurriedly.*]
Can't beat Euripides for insight. And I quote:
　　　　　　　　　　　　No creature's found

---

[17] In the act.
[18] The Greek refers to Boupalos, a sculptor, who was frequently mocked by Hipponax: e.g., "Hold my clothes; I'll sock Boupalos in the jaw."

so lost to shame as Woman.

Talk about realist playwrights!

KORYPHAIOS OF WOMEN.

Up with the water, ladies. Pitchers at the ready, place!

KORYPHAIOS OF MEN.

Why the water, you sink of iniquity? More sedition?

KORYPHAIOS OF WOMEN.

Why the fire, you walking boneyard? Self-cremation?

KORYPHAIOS OF MEN.

I brought this fire to ignite a pyre and fricassee your friends.

KORYPHAIOS OF WOMEN.

I brought this water to douse your pyre. Tit for tat.

KORYPHAIOS OF MEN.

You'll douse my fire? Nonsense!

KORYPHAIOS OF WOMEN.

You'll see, when the facts soak in.

KORYPHAIOS OF MEN.

I have the torch right here. Perhaps I should barbecue *you.*

KORYPHAIOS OF WOMEN.

If you have any soap, I could give you a bath.

KORYPHAIOS OF MEN.

A bath from those polluted hands?

KORYPHAIOS OF WOMEN.

Pure enough for a blushing young bridegroom.

KORYPHAIOS OF MEN.

Enough of that insolent lip.

KORYPHAIOS OF WOMEN.

It's merely freedom of speech.

KORYPHAIOS OF MEN.

I'll stop that screeching!

KORYPHAIOS OF WOMEN.

You're helpless outside the jury-box.

KORYPHAIOS OF MEN. [*Urging his men, torches at the ready, into a charge.*]

Burn, fire, burn!

KORYPHAIOS OF WOMEN. [*As the women empty their pitchers over the men.*]

And cauldron bubble.

KORYPHAIOS OF MEN.   [*Like this troops, soaked and routed.*]

Arrgh!

KORYPHAIOS OF WOMEN.

Goodness.

What seems to be the trouble? Too hot?

KORYPHAIOS OF MEN.

Hot, hell! Stop it!

What do you think you're doing?

KORYPHAIOS OF WOMEN.

If you must know, I'm gardening.

Perhaps you'll bloom.

KORYPHAIOS OF MEN.
                            Perhaps I'll fall right off the vine!
I'm withered, frozen, shaking . . .
KORYPHAIOS OF WOMEN.
                                    Of course. But, providentially,
you brought along your smudgepot.
                            The sap should rise eventually.
[*Shivering, the* CHORUS OF MEN *retreats in utter defeat.*]

A COMMISSIONER OF PUBLIC SAFETY *enters from the left, followed quite reluctantly by a squad of police—our Skythian archers. He surveys the situation with disapproval.*

COMMISSIONER.
Fire, eh? Females again—spontaneous combustion
of lust. Suspected as much.
                            Rubadubdubbing, incessant
incontinent keening for wine, damnable funeral
foofaraw for Adonis resounding from roof to roof—
heard it all before . . .[19] [*Savagely, as the* KORYPHAIOS OF MEN *tries to interpose a remark.*]
                            and WHERE?
                            The ASSEMBLY!
Recall, if you can, the debate on the Sicilian Question:
That bullbrained demagogue Demostratos (who will rot, I trust)
rose to propose a naval task force.
                            His wife,
writhing with religion on a handy roof, bleated
a dirge:
"BEREFT! OH WOE OH WOE FOR ADONIS!"
And so of course Demostratos, taking his cue,
outblatted her:
                    "A DRAFT! ENROLL THE WHOLE OF
    ZAKYNTHOS!"
His wife, a smidgin stewed, renewed her yowling:
"OH GNASH YOUR TEETH AND BEAT YOUR
BREASTS FOR ADONIS!"
And so of course Demostratos (that god-detested blot,
that foul-lunged son of an ulcer) gnashed tooth and nail
and voice, and bashed and rammed his program through.
And THERE is the Gift of Women:
                            MORAL CHAOS!
KORYPHAIOS OF MEN.
Save your breath for actual felonies, Commissioner;
see what's happened to us! Insolence, insults,

---

[19] In mythology Adonis was adored by Aphrodite, the goddess of love, but he was killed while hunting a boar after disregarding a warning from Aphrodite. His death was mourned by the Greek women in annual religious festivals. During one of the festivals of Adonis the ill-fated Sicilian expedition was debated in the Athenian assembly. In the following lines the Commissioner recalls the arguments in favor of sending out a naval task force and manning it with troops drafted on the island of Zakynthos.

these we pass over, but not lèse-majesté.[20]
                                                                                      We're flooded
with indignity from those bitches' pitchers—like a bunch
of weak-bladdered brats. Our cloaks are sopped. We'll sue!
COMMISSIONER.
Useless. Your suit won't hold water. Right's on their side.
For female depravity, gentlemen, WE stand guilty—
we, their teachers, preceptors of prurience, accomplices
before the fact of fornication. We sowed them in sexual
license, and now we reap rebellion.
                                                                      The proof?
Consider. Off we trip to the goldsmith's to leave
an order:
        "That bangle you fashioned last spring for my wife
    is sprung. She was thrashing around last night, and the prong
    popped out of the bracket. I'll be tied up all day—I'm
    boarding the ferry right now—but my wife'll be home.
    If you get the time, please stop by the house in a bit
    and see if you can't do something—anything—to fit
    a new prong into the bracket of her bangle."
                                                                      And bang.
Another one ups to a cobbler—young, but no apprentice,
full kit of tools, ready to give his awl—
and delivers this gem:
                            "My wife's new sandals are tight.
    The cinch pinches her pinkie right where she's sensitive.
    Drop in at noon with something to stretch her cinch
    and give it a little play."
                                                      And a cinch it is.
Such hanky-panky we have to thank for today's
Utter Anarchy: I, a Commissioner of Public
Safety, duly invested with extraordinary powers
to protect the State in the Present Emergency, have secured
a source of timber to outfit our fleet and solve
the shortage of oarage. I need the money immediately . . .
and WOMEN, no less, have locked me out of the Treasury! [*Pulling himself
together.*]
—Well, no profit in standing around. [*To one of the archers.*]
                                                                      Bring
the crowbars. I'll jack these women back on their
pedestals!
        —WELL, you slack-jawed jackass? What's the
attraction? Wipe that thirst off your face. I said *crow*bar,
not saloon!—all right, men, all together. Shove those
bars underneath the gate and HEAVE! [*Grabbing up a crowbar.*]
                                                      I'll take this side.
And now let's root them out, men, ROOT them out.
One, Two . . .

[20] Treason.

The gates to the Akropolis burst open suddenly, disclosing LYSISTRATA. *She is perfectly composed and bears a large spindle. The* COMMISSIONER *and the* POLICE *fall back in consternation.*

LYSISTRATA.
                    Why the moving equipment?
I'm quite well motivated, thank you, and here I am.
Frankly, you don't need crowbars nearly so much as
brains.
COMMISSIONER.
    Brains? O name of infamy! Where's a policeman?
[*He grabs wildly for the* FIRST ARCHER *and shoves him toward* LYSISTRATA.]
    Arrest that woman!
                    Better tie her hands behind her.
LYSISTRATA.
    By Artemis, goddess of the hunt, if he lays a finger
    on me, he'll rue the day he joined the force!
[*She jabs the spindle viciously at the* FIRST ARCHER, *who leaps, terrified, back to his comrades.*]
COMMISSIONER.
    What's this—retreat? never! Take her on the flank.
[*The* FIRST ARCHER *hangs back. The* COMMISSIONER *grabs the* SECOND ARCHER.]
    —Help him.
                    —Will the two of you kindly TIE HER UP?
[*He shoves them toward* LYSISTRATA. KLEONIKE, *carrying a large chamber pot, springs out of the entrance and advances on the* SECOND ARCHER.]

KLEONIKE.
    By Artemis, goddess of the dew, if you so much
    as touch her, I'll stomp the shit right out of you!
[*The two Archers run back to their group.*]
COMMISSIONER.
    Shit? Shameless! Where's another policeman? [*He grabs the* THIRD ARCHER *and propels him toward* KLEONIKE.]
    Handcuff *her* first. Can't stand a foul-mouthed female.

MYRRHINE, *carrying a large, blazing lamp, appears at the entrance and advances on the* THIRD ARCHER.

MYRRHINE.
    By Artemis, bringer of light, if you lay a finger
    on her, you won't be able to stop the swelling!
[*The* THIRD ARCHER *dodges her swing and runs back to the group.*]
COMMISSIONER.
    Now what? Where's an officer? [*Pushing the* FOURTH ARCHER *toward* MYRRHINE.]
                    Apprehend that woman!
    I'll see that *somebody* stays to take the blame!

ISMENIA THE BOIOTIAN, *carrying a huge pair of pincers, appears at the entrance and advances on the* FOURTH ARCHER.

ISMENIA.

By Artemis, goddess of Tauris, if you go near
that girl, I'll rip the hair right out of your head!
[*The* FOURTH ARCHER *retreats hurriedly.*]

COMMISSIONER.

What a colossal mess: Athens' Finest—
finished! [*Arranging the* ARCHERS.]
      Now, men, a little *esprit de corps.*[21] Worsted
by women? Drubbed by drabs?
                    Never!
                        Regroup,
reform that thin red line.
                  Ready?
                      CHARGE!
[*He pushes them ahead of him.*]

LYSISTRATA.

I warn you. We have four battalions behind us—
full-armed combat infantrywomen, trained
from the cradle . . .

COMMISSIONER.

            Disarm them, Officers! Go for the hands!

LYSISTRATA. [*Calling inside the Akropolis.*]

MOBILIZE THE RESERVES!
[*A horde of women, armed with household articles, begins to pour from the Akropolis.*]
                Onward, you ladies from hell!
Forward, you market militia, you battle-hardened
bargain hunters, old sales compaigners, grocery
grenadiers, veterans never bested by an overcharge!
You troops of the breadline, doughgirls—
                  INTO THE FRAY!
Show them no mercy!
            Push!
                Jostle!
                  Shove!
Call them nasty names!
            Don't be ladylike.
[*The women charge and rout the Archers in short order.*]
Fall back—don't strip the enemy! The day is ours!
[*The women obey, and the* ARCHERS *run off left. The* COMMISSIONER, *dazed, is left muttering to himself.*]

COMMISSIONER.

Gross ineptitude. A sorry day for the Force.

LYSISTRATA.

Of course. What did you expect? We're not slaves;
we're freeborn Women, and when we're scorned, we're
full of fury. Never Underestimate the Power of a Woman.

COMMISSIONER.

Power? You mean Capacity. I should have remembered
the proverb: *The lower the tavern, the higher the dudgeon.*

---

[21] Group spirit.

KORYPHAIOS OF MEN.
   Why cast your pearls before swine, Commissioner? I know you're a civil
servant, but don't overdo it. Have you forgotten the bath
they gave us—in public,
                              fully dressed,
                                             totally soapless?
   Keep rational discourse for *people!*
[*He aims a blow at the* KORYPHAIOS OF WOMEN, *who dodges and raises her pitcher.*]
KORYPHAIOS OF WOMEN.
                              I might point out that lifting
one's hand against a neighbor is scarcely civilized
behavior—and entails, for the lifter, a black eye.
                              I'm really peaceful by nature,
compulsively inoffensive—a perfect doll. My ideal is a
well-bred repose that doesn't even stir up dust . . . [*Swinging at the* KORYPHAIOS OF
MEN *with the pitcher.*]
                              unless some no-good lowlife
tries to rifle my hive and gets my dander up!
[*The* KORYPHAIOS OF MEN *backs hurriedly away, and the* CHORUS OF MEN *goes into a worried
dance.*]
CHORUS OF MEN.
[*Singly.*]
                    O Zeus, what's the use of this constant abuse?
                    How do we deal with this female zoo?
                    Is there no solution to Total Immersion?
                        What can a poor man DO?
[*Tutti.*]
                    Query the Adversary!
                    Ferret out their story!
                    What end did they have in view,
                    to seize the city's sanctuary,
                    snatch its legendary eyrie,[22]
                    snare an area so very
                        terribly taboo?
KORYPHAIOS OF MEN. [*To the* COMMISSIONER.]
   Scrutinize those women! Scour their depositions—assess their rebuttals!
   Masculine honor demands this affair be probed to the bottom!
COMMISSIONER. [*Turning to the women from the Akropolis.*]
   All right, you. Kindly inform me, dammit, in your own words:
   What possible object could you have had in blockading the Treasury?
LYSISTRATA.
   We thought we'd deposit the money in escrow and withdraw you men
   from the war.
COMMISSIONER.
                    The money's the cause of the war?
LYSISTRATA.
                              And all our internal
disorders—the Body Politic's chronic bellyaches: What
causes Peisandros' frantic rantings, or the raucous cau-

---

[22] Eagle's nest—hence, the Acropolis, a stronghold on a hill overlooking the rest of Athens.

cuses of the Friends of Oligarchy?[23] The chance for graft.
                              But now, with the money up there,
they can't upset the City's equilibrium—or lower its
balance.
COMMISSIONER.
And what's your next step?
LYSISTRATA.
                    Stupid question. We'll budget the money.
COMMISSIONER.
You'll budget the money?
LYSISTRATA.
                    Why should you find that so shocking?
We budget the household accounts, and you don't object
at all.
COMMISSIONER.
That's different.
LYSISTRATA.
                    Different? How?
COMMISSIONER.
                              The War Effort needs this money!
LYSISTRATA.
Who needs the War Effort?
COMMISSIONER.
                         Every patriot who pulses to save
all that Athens holds near and dear . . .
LYSISTRATA.
                                   Oh, *that.* Don't worry.
We'll save you.
COMMISSIONER.
              You will save us?
LYSISTRATA.
                              Who else?
COMMISSIONER.
                    But this is unscrupulous!
LYSISTRATA.
We'll save you. You can't deter us.
COMMISSIONER.
                                   Scurrilous!
LYSISTRATA.
                              You seem disturbed.
This makes it difficult. But, still—we'll save you.
COMMISSIONER.
                              Doubtless illegal!
LYSISTRATA.
We deem it a duty. For friendship's sake.
COMMISSIONER.
                         Well, forsake this friend:
I DO NOT WANT TO BE SAVED, DAMMIT!
LYSISTRATA.
                    All the more reason.
It's not only Sparta; now we'll have to save you from
you.

---

[23] One of the political clubs in Athens that sought public offices for their members.

COMMISSIONER.
　Might I ask where you women conceived this concern
　about War and Peace?
LYSISTRATA. [*Loftily.*]
　　　　　　　　　　　　We shall explain.
COMMISSIONER. [*Making a fist.*]
　　　　　　　　　　　　Hurry up, and you won't
　get hurt.
LYSISTRATA.
　　　　　Then *listen*. And do try to keep your hands to
　yourself.
COMMISSIONER. [*Moving threateningly toward her.*]
　I can't. Righteous anger forbids restraint, and decrees . . .
KLEONIKE. [*Brandishing her chamber pot.*]
　Multiple fractures?
COMMISSIONER. [*Retreating.*]
　　　　　Keep those croaks for yourself, you old crow!
[*To* LYSISTRATA.]
　All right, lady, I'm ready. Speak.
LYSISTRATA.
　　　　　　　　　　　　I shall proceed:
　When the War began, like the prudent, dutiful wives that
　we are, we tolerated you men, and endured your actions
　　in silence. (Small wonder—
　you wouldn't let us say boo.)
　　　　　　　　　　　You were not precisely the answer
　to a matron's prayer—we knew you too well, and found out more.
　Too many times, as we sat in the house, we'd hear that
　you'd done it again—manhandled another affair of
　state with your usual staggering incompetence. Then,
　masking our worry with a nervous laugh,
　we'd ask you, brightly, "How was the Assembly today, dear? Anything
　in the minutes about Peace?" And my husband would give his stock reply.
　"What's that to you? Shut up!" And I did.
KLEONIKE. [*Proudly.*]
　　　　　　　　　　　　I never shut up!
COMMISSIONER.
　I trust you were shut up. Soundly.
LYSISTRATA.
　　　　　　　　　　　Regardless, *I* shut up.
　And then we'd learn that you'd passed another decree,
　fouler than the first, and we'd ask again: "Darling, how
　did you manage anything so idiotic?" And my
　husband, with his customary glare, would tell me to spin
　my thread, or else get a clout on the head.
　And of course he'd quote from Homer:
　　　　　　　Ye menne must husband ye warre.[24]
COMMISSIONER.
　Apt and irrefutably right.

[24] From the *Iliad*, Book 6, line 492.

LYSISTRATA.

Right, you miserable misfit?
To keep us from giving advice while you fumbled the
City away in the Senate? Right, indeed!
                    But this time was really too much:
Wherever we went, we'd hear you engaged in the same conversation:
"What Athens needs is a Man."
                    "But there isn't a Man in the country."
"You can say that again."
                    There was obviously no time to lose.
We women met in immediate convention and passed a
unanimous resolution: To work in concert for safety and
Peace in Greece. We have valuable advice to impart,
and if you can possibly deign to emulate our silence,
and take your turn as audience, we'll rectify you—
we'll straighten you out and set you right.

COMMISSIONER.

You'll set *us* right? You go too far. I cannot permit
such a statement to . . .

LYSISTRATA.

                    Shush.

COMMISSIONER.

                    I categorically decline to shush
for some confounded woman, who wears—as a constant
reminder of congenital inferiority, an injunction to
public silence—a veil!
Death before such dishonor!

LYSISTRATA. [*Removing her veil.*]

                    If that's the only obstacle . . .
I feel you need a new panache,
so take the veil, my dear Commissioner, and drape it thus—

                    and SHUSH!

[*As she winds the veil around the startled* COMMISSIONER'S *head,* KLEONIKE *and* MYRRHINE, *with carding-comb and wool-basket, rush forward and assist in transforming him into a woman.*]

KLEONIKE.

                    Accept, I pray, this humble comb.

MYRRHINE.

                    Receive this basket of fleece as well.

LYSISTRATA.

                    Hike up your skirts, and card your wool,
                    and gnaw your beans—and stay at home!
                    While we rewrite Homer:
                    Y^e WOMEN must WIVE ye warre!

[*To the* CHORUS OF WOMEN, *as the* COMMISSIONER *struggles to remove his new outfit.*]
Women, weaker vessels, arise!

                    Put down your pitchers.
It's our turn, now. Let's supply our friends with some
moral support.

[*The* CHORUS OF WOMEN *dances to the same tune as the* MEN, *but with much more confidence.*]

CHORUS OF WOMEN.
[*Singly.*]

> Oh, yes! I'll dance to bless their success.
> Fatigue won't weaken my will. Or my knees.
> I'm ready to join in any jeopardy.
> > with girls as good as *these!*

[*Tutte.*]

> A tally of their talents
> convinces me they're giants
> of excellence. To commence:
> there's Beauty, Duty, Prudence, Science,
> Self-Reliance, Compliance, Defiance,
> and Love of Athens in balanced alliance
> with Common Sense!

KORYPHAIOS OF WOMEN. [*To the women from the Akropolis.*]
Autochthonous[25] daughters of Attika, sprung from the
soil that bore your mothers, the spiniest, spikiest
nettles known to man, prove your mettle and attack!
Now is no time to dilute your anger. You're
running ahead of the wind!

LYSISTRATA.

> We'll wait for the wind
from heaven. The gentle breath of Love and his Kyprian
mother[26] will imbue our bodies with desire, and raise a
storm to tense and tauten these blasted men until they
crack. And soon we'll be on every tongue in
Greece—the *Pacifiers.*

COMMISSIONER.

> That's quite
a mouthful. How will you win it?

LYSISTRATA.

> First, we intend to withdraw
that crazy Army of Occupation from the downtown
shopping section.

KLEONIKE.
Aphrodite be praised!

LYSISTRATA.

> The pottery shop and the grocery stall
are overstocked with soldiers, clanking around like
those maniac Korybants,[27]
armed to the teeth for a battle.

COMMISSIONER.

> A Hero is Always Prepared!

LYSISTRATA.
I suppose he is. But it does look silly to shop for sardines
from behind a shield.

---

[25] Native.
[26] Aphrodite; Kyprian because she was said to have been born from the sea near Cyprus.
[27] Armed priests of Cybele, the goddess of Nature.

KLEONIKE.

I'll second that. I saw
a cavalry captain buy vegetable soup on horseback. He
carried the whole mess home in his helmet.

And then that fellow from Thrace,
shaking his buckler and spear—a menace straight from the stage.
The saleslady was stiff with fright. He was hogging her ripe figs—free.

COMMISSIONER.

I admit, for the moment, that Hellas' affairs are in one
hell of a snarl. But how can you set them straight?

LYSISTRATA.

Simplicity itself.

COMMISSIONER.

Pray demonstrate.

LYSISTRATA.

It's rather like yarn. When a hank's in a tangle,
we lift it—*so*—and work out the snarls by winding it up
on spindles, now this way, now that way.

That's how we'll wind up the War,
if allowed: We'll work out the snarls by sending Special Commissions—
back and forth, now this way, now that way—to ravel
these tense international kinks.

COMMISSIONER.

I lost your thread, but I know there's a hitch.
Spruce up the world's disasters with spindles—typically
woolly female logic.

LYSISTRATA.

If *you* had a scrap of logic, you'd adopt
our wool as a master plan for Athens.

COMMISSIONER.

What course of action
does the wool advise?

LYSISTRATA.

Consider the City as fleece, recently
shorn. The first step is Cleansing: Scrub it in a public
bath, and remove all corruption, offal, and sheepdip.

Next, to the couch
for Scutching and Plucking: Cudgel the leeches and
similar vermin loose with a club, then pick the prickles
and cockleburs out. As for the clots—those lumps
that clump and cluster in knots and snarls to snag
important posts—you comb these out,
twist off their heads, and discard.

Next, to raise the City's
nap, you card the citizens together in a single basket
of common weal and general welfare. Fold in our loyal
Resident Aliens, all Foreigners of proven and tested
friendship, and any Disenfranchised Debtors. Combine
these closely with the rest.
Lastly, cull the colonies settled by our own people:
these are nothing but flocks of wool from the City's
fleece, scattered throughout the world. So gather home

these far-flung flocks, amalgamate them with the others.
      Then, drawing this blend
of stable fibers into one fine staple, you spin a mighty
bobbin of yarn—and weave, without bias or seam, a
cloak to clothe the City of Athens!

COMMISSIONER.
                             This is too much! The City's
died in the wool, worsted by the distaff side—by women
who bore no share in the War. . . .

LYSISTRATA.
                     None, you hopeless hypocrite?
The quota we bear is double. First, we delivered our
sons to fill out the front lines in Sicily . . .

COMMISSIONER.
                    Don't tax me with that memory.

LYSISTRATA.
Next, the best years of our lives were levied. Top-level
strategy attached our joy, and we sleep alone.
                  But it's not the matrons
like us who matter. I mourn for the virgins, bedded in
single blessedness, with nothing to do but grow old.

COMMISSIONER.
                    Men *have* been known
to age, as well as women.

LYSISTRATA.
                No, not as well as—better.
A man, an absolute antique, comes back from the war, and he's barely
doddered into town before he's married the veriest nymphet.
But a woman's season is brief; it slips, and she'll have
no husband, but sit out her life groping at omens—and finding no men.

COMMISSIONER.
Lamentable state of affairs. Perhaps we can rectify matters:
[*To the audience.*]
    TO EVERY MAN JACK, A CHALLENGE:
                    ARISE!
Provided you can . . .

LYSISTRATA.
Instead, Commissioner, why not simply curl up and *die*?
           Just buy a coffin; here's the place.
[*Banging him on the head with her spindle.*]
           I'll knead you a cake for the wake—and *these*
[*Winding the threads from the spindle around him.*]
           make excellent wreaths. So Rest In Peace.

KLEONIKE. [*Emptying the chamber pot over him.*]
           Accept these tokens of deepest grief.

MYRRHINE. [*Breaking her lamp over his head.*]
           A final garland for the dear deceased.

LYSISTRATA.
           May I supply any last request?
           Then run along. You're due at the wharf:

Charon's[28] anxious to sail—
you're holding up the boat for Hell!

COMMISSIONER.

This is monstrous—maltreatment of a public official—
maltreatment of ME!
                    I must repair directly
to the Board of Commissioners, and present my
colleagues concrete evidence of the sorry specifics of
this shocking attack!

[*He staggers off left.* LYSISTRATA *calls after him.*]

LYSISTRATA.

You won't haul us into court on a charge of neglecting
the dead, will you? (How like a man to insist
on his rights—even his last ones.) Two days between
death and funeral, that's the rule.
                              Come back here early
day after tomorrow, Commissioner:
                        We'll lay you out.

[LYSISTRATA *and her women re-enter the Akropolis. The* KORYPHAIOS OF MEN *advances to address the audience.*]

KORYPHAIOS OF MEN.

Wake up, Athenians! Preserve your freedom—the time
is Now! [*To the* CHORUS OF MEN.]
   Strip for action, men. Let's cope with the current mess.

[*The men put off their long mantles, disclosing short tunics underneath, and advance toward the audience.*]

CHORUS OF MEN.

This trouble may be terminal; it has a loaded odor,
   an ominous aroma of constitutional rot.
My nose gives a prognosis of radical disorder—
   it's just the first installment of an absolutist plot!
         The Spartans are behind it:
         they must have masterminded
some morbid local contacts (engineered by Kleisthenes).[29]
         Predictably infected,
         the women straightway acted
to commandeer the City's cash. They're feverish to freeze
         my be-all,
         my end-all . . .
         my *payroll!*

KORYPHAIOS OF MEN.

The symptoms are clear. Our birthright's already nibbled. And oh, so
daintily: WOMEN ticking off troops for improper etiquette.
WOMEN propounding their featherweight views on the fashionable use
and abuse of the shield. And (if any more proof were needed) WOMEN
nagging us to trust the Nice Spartan, and put our heads

---

28 The boatman who ferries dead souls across the river Styx.
29 Kleisthenes was a notoriously effeminate contemporary of Aristophanes'—hence, suspected of
being in league with the women.

in his toothy maw—to make a dessert and call it Peace.
They've woven the City a seamless shroud, bedecked with the legend
DICTATORSHIP.
      But I won't be hemmed in. I'll use
their weapon against them, and uphold the right by sneakiness
        With knyf under cloke,
gauntlet in glove, sword in olivebranch, [*Slipping slowly toward the* KORYPHAIOS OF
WOMEN.]
          I'll take up my post
in Statuary Row, beside our honored National Heroes,
the natural foes of tyranny: Harmodios,
        Aristogeiton,
          and Me.[30]

[*Next to her.*]
 Striking an epic pose, so, with the full approval
of the immortal gods,
      I'll bash this loathesome hag in the jaw!
[*He does, and runs cackling back to the* MEN. *She shakes a fist after him.*]
KORYPHAIOS OF WOMEN.
 Mama won't know her little boy when he gets home!
[*To the* WOMEN, *who are eager to launch a full-scale attack.*]
 Let's not be hasty, fellow . . . hags. Cloaks off first.

The WOMEN *remove their mantles, disclosing tunics very like those of the* MEN, *and advance
toward the audience.*

CHORUS OF WOMEN.
 We'll address you, citizens, in beneficial, candid,
  patriotic accents, as our breeding says we must,
since, from the age of seven, Athens graced me with a
  splendid string of civic triumphs to signalize her
   trust:
    I was Relic-Girl quite early,
     then advanced to Maid of Barley;
in Artemis' "Pageant of the Bear" I played the lead.
    To cap this proud progression,
    I led the whole procession
at Athene's Celebration, certified and pedigreed
     —that cachet[31]
    so distingué[32] —
    a *Lady!*
KORYPHAIOS OF WOMEN. [*To the audience.*]
 I trust this establishes my qualifications. I may, I take it,
address the City to its profit? Thank you.
       I admit to being a woman—
but don't sell my contribution short on that account.
It's better than the present panic. And my word is as
good as my bond, because I hold stock in Athens—
stock I paid for in sons.

---

[30] Statues of the heroes Harmodios and Aristogeiton were carved by the sculptor Kritios.
[31] Official seal. [32] Distinguished.

[*To the* CHORUS OF MEN.]

—But you, you doddering bankrupts, where are your
   shares in the State?
[*Slipping slowly toward the* KORYPHAIOS OF MEN.]
   Your grandfathers willed you the Mutual Funds from
      the Persian War—
   and where are they?[33]
[*Nearer.*]
                        You dipped into capital, then lost interest . . .
and now a pool of your assets won't fill a hole in the ground.
All that remains is one last potential killing—Athens.
   Is there any rebuttal?
[*The* KORYPHAIOS OF MEN *gestures menacingly. She ducks down, as if to ward off a blow,
and removes a slipper.*]

                        Force is a footling resort. I'll take
   my very sensible shoe, and paste you in the jaw!
[*She does so, and runs back to the women.*]
CHORUS OF MEN.
                  Their native respect for our manhood is small,
                  and keeps getting smaller. Let's bottle their gall.
                  The man who won't battle has no balls at all!
KORYPHAIOS OF MEN.
   All right, men, skin out of the skivvies. Let's give them
   a whiff of Man, full strength. No point in muffling
   the essential Us. [*The men remove their tunics.*]
CHORUS OF MEN.
                  A century back, we soared to the Heights[34]
                     and beat down Tyranny there.
                  Now's the time to shed our moults
                     and fledge our wings once more,
                  to rise to the skies in our reborn force,
                     and beat back Tyranny here!
KORYPHAIOS OF MEN.
   No fancy grappling with these grannies; straightforward strength. The tiniest
   toehold, and those nimble, fiddling fingers will have their
   foot in the door, and we're done for.
                        No amount of know-how can lick
   a woman's knack.
                        They'll want to build ships . . . next thing we know,
   we're all at sea, fending off female boarding parties.
   (Artemisia fought us at Salamis. Tell me, has anyone
   caught her yet?)

---

[33] "This money originally made up the treasury of the Delian League, an alliance of Greek states
against Persia formed by the Athenian Aristeides in 477; following its transfer, for safety's sake,
from the island of Delos to Athens in 454, it became for all practical purposes Athenian property,
supported by tribute from the Allies. Athens' heavy expenses in Sicily, followed by the Allies'
nonpayment and defection, made this question all too pointed in early 411." (Translator's
note.)

[34] The men of the family of Pericles held out in the mountains north of Athens during their first
attempt to overthrow the tyrant Hippias in 513 B.C.

But we're *really* sunk if they take up horses. Scratch
the Cavalry:
>A woman is an easy rider with a natural seat.
Take her over the jumps bareback, and she'll never slip
her mount. (That's how the Amazons nearly took Athens. On horseback.
Check on Mikon's mural down in the Stoa.)
>>Anyway,
the solution is obvious. Put every woman in her place—
stick her in the stocks.
>To do this, first snare your woman around the neck.

[*He attempts to demonstrate on the* KORYPHAIOS OF WOMEN. *After a brief tussle, she works loose and chases him back to the* MEN.]

CHORUS OF WOMEN.
>The beast in me's eager and fit for a brawl.
>Just rile me a bit and she'll kick down the wall.
>You'll bawl to your friends that you've no balls at all.

KORYPHAIOS OF WOMEN.
All right, ladies, strip for action. Let's give them a whiff
of *Femme Enragée* piercing and pungent, but not at
all tart. [*The* WOMEN *remove their tunics.*]

CHORUS OF WOMEN.
>We're angry. The brainless bird who tangles
>>with *us* has gummed his last mush.
>In fact, the coot who even heckles
>>is being daringly rash.
>So look to your nests, you reclaimed eagles—
>>whatever you lay, we'll squash!

KORYPHAIOS OF WOMEN.
Frankly, you don't faze me. *With* me, I have my friends—
Lampito from Sparta; that genteel girl from Thebes, Ismenia—
committed to me forever. *Against* me, you—permanently
out of commission. So do your damnedest.
>>Pass a law.
Pass seven. Continue the winning ways that have made
your name a short and ugly household word.
>>Like yesterday:
I was giving a little party, nothing fussy, to honor
the goddess Hekate. Simply to please my daughters,
I'd invited a sweet little thing from the neighborhood—flawless pedigree,
>perfect
taste, a credit to any gathering—a Boiotian eel.
But she had to decline. Couldn't pass the border. You'd passed a law.
Not that you care for my party. You'll overwork your right of passage
till your august body is overturned,
>>and you break your silly neck!

[*She deftly grabs the* KORYPHAIOS OF MEN *by the ankle and upsets him. He scuttles back to the* MEN, *who retire in confusion.*]

LYSISTRATA *emerges from the citadel, obviously distraught.*

KORYPHAIOS OF WOMEN. [*Mock-tragic.*]
> *Mistress, queen of this our subtle scheme*
> *why burst you from the hall with brangled brow?*

LYSISTRATA.
> *Oh, wickedness of woman! The female mind*
> *does sap my soul and set my wits a-totter.*

KORYPHAIOS OF WOMEN.
> *What drear accents are these?*

LYSISTRATA.
>   *The merest truth.*

KORYPHAIOS OF WOMEN.
> *Be nothing loath to tell the tale to friends.*

LYSISTRATA.
> *'Twere shame to utter, pain to hold unsaid.*

KORYPHAIOS OF WOMEN.
> *Hide not from me affliction which we share.*

LYSISTRATA.
> *In briefest compass,*
[*Dropping the paratragedy.*]
>   we want to get laid.

KORYPHAIOS OF WOMEN.
>   By Zeus!

LYSISTRATA.
>   No, no, not HIM!
>   Well, that's the way things are.
> I've lost my grip on the girls—they're mad for men!
> But sly—they slip out in droves.
>   A minute ago,
> I caught one scooping out the little hole
> that breaks through just below Pan's grotto.[35]
>   One
> had jerry-rigged some block-and-tackle business
> and was wriggling away on a rope.
>   Another just flat
> deserted.
>   Last night I spied one mounting a sparrow,
> all set to take off for the nearest bawdyhouse. I hauled
> her back by the hair.
>   And excuses, pretexts for overnight
> passes? I've heard them all.
>   Here comes one. Watch.

[*To the* FIRST WOMAN, *as she runs out of the Akropolis.*]
> —You, there! What's your hurry?

FIRST WOMAN.
>   I have to get home.
> I've got all this lovely Milesian wool in the house,
> and the moths will simply batter it to bits!

---

[35] A cave on the Acropolis.

LYSISTRATA.

                                          I'll bet.

Get back inside.

FIRST WOMAN.

              I swear I'll hurry right back!
—Just time enough to spread it out on the couch?

LYSISTRATA.

    Your wool will stay unspread. And you'll stay here.

FIRST WOMAN.

    Do I have to let my piecework *rot?*

LYSISTRATA.

                                          Possibly.

The SECOND WOMAN *runs on.*

SECOND WOMAN.

    Oh dear, oh goodness, what shall I do—my flax!
    I left and forgot to peel it!

LYSISTRATA.

                              Another one.
    She suffers from unpeeled flax.
                                    —Get back inside!

SECOND WOMAN.

    I'll be right back. I just have to pluck the fibers.

LYSISTRATA.

    No. No plucking. You start it, and everyone else
    will want to go and do their plucking, too.

The THIRD WOMAN, *swelling conspicuously, hurries on, praying loudly.*

THIRD WOMAN.

    O Goddess of Childbirth, grant that I not deliver
    until I get me from out this sacred precinct!

LYSISTRATA.

    What sort of nonsense is *this?*

THIRD WOMAN.

                                    I'm due—any second!

LYSISTRATA.

    You weren't pregnant yesterday.

THIRD WOMAN.

                                    Today I am—
    a miracle!
                    Let me go home for a midwife, *please!*
    I may not make it!

LYSISTRATA.

[*Restraining her.*]
                    You can do better than that.
[*Tapping the woman's stomach and receiving a metallic clang.*]
    What's this? It's hard.

THIRD WOMAN.

                            I'm going to have a boy.

LYSISTRATA.
Not unless he's made of bronze. Let's see.
[*She throws open the* THIRD WOMAN'S *cloak, exposing a huge bronze helmet.*]
Of all the brazen . . . You've stolen the helmet from
Athene's statue! Pregnant, indeed!
THIRD WOMAN.
I am *so* pregnant!
LYSISTRATA.
Then why the helmet?
THIRD WOMAN.
I thought my time might come
while I was still on forbidden ground. If it did,
I could climb inside Athene's helmet and have
my baby there.
The pigeons do it all the time.
LYSISTRATA.
Nothing but excuses! [*Taking the helmet.*]
This is your baby. I'm afraid
you'll have to stay until we give it a name.
THIRD WOMAN.
But the Akropolis is *awful.* I can't even sleep! I saw
the snake that guards the temple.
LYSISTRATA.
That snake's a fabrication.
THIRD WOMAN.
I don't care *what* kind it is—I'm *scared!*
[*The other women, who have emerged from the citadel, crowd around.*]
KLEONIKE.
And those goddamned holy owls; All night long,
tu-wit; tu-wu—they're hooting me into my grave!
LYSISTRATA.
Darlings, let's call a halt to this hocus-pocus.
You miss your men—now isn't that the trouble?
[*Shamefaced nods from the group.*]
Don't you think they miss you just as much?
I can assure you, their nights are every bit
as hard as yours. So be good girls; endure!
Persist a few days more, and Victory is ours.
It's fated: a current prophecy declares that the men
will go down to defeat before us, provided that *we*
maintain a United Front. [*Producing a scroll.*]
I happen to have
a copy of the prophecy.
KLEONIKE.
Read it!
LYSISTRATA.
Silence, *please:*
[*Reading from the scroll.*]
**But when the swallows, in flight from the
hoopoes, have flocked to a hole
on high, and stoutly eschew their**

accustomed perch on the pole,
yea, then shall Thunderer Zeus to
    their suff'ring establish a stop,
by making the lower the upper . . .

KLEONIKE.
    Then *we'll* be lying on top?

LYSISTRATA.
    But should these swallows, indulging their
        lust for the perch, lose heart,
    dissolve their flocks in winged dissension,
        and singly depart
    the sacred stronghold, breaking the
        bands that bind them together—
    then know them as lewd, the pervertedest
        birds that ever wore feather.

KLEONIKE.
    There's nothing obscure about *that* oracle. Ye gods!

LYSISTRATA.
    Sorely beset as we are, we must not flag
    or falter. So back to the citadel!

[*As the women troop inside.*]
                                    And if we fail
    that oracle, darlings, our image is absolutely *mud!*
[*She follows them in. A pause, and the Choruses assemble.*]

CHORUS OF MEN.
                        I have a simple
                        tale to relate you,
                        a sterling example
                        of masculine virtue:

                The huntsman bold Melanion
                    was once a harried quarry.
                The women in town tracked him down
                    and badgered him to marry.

                Melanion knew the cornered male
                    eventually cohabits.
                Assessing the odds, he took to the woods
                    and lived by trapping rabbits.

                He stuck to the virgin stand, sustained
                    by rabbit meat and hate,
                and never returned, but ever remained
                    an alfresco[36] celibate.

                Melanion is our ideal;
                    his loathing makes us free.

---

[36] Outdoor.

                    Our dearest aim is the gemlike flame
                        of his misogyny.[37]
OLD MAN.

                    Let me kiss that wizened cheek. . . .
OLD WOMAN.
[*Threatening with a fist.*]
                    A wish too rash for that withered flesh.
OLD MAN.

                    and lay you low with a highflying kick.
    [*He tries one and misses.*]
OLD WOMAN.
                    Exposing an overgrown underbrush.
OLD MAN.
    A hairy behind, historically, means
        masculine force: Myronides
    harassed the foe with his mighty mane,
        and furry Phormion swept the seas
            of enemy ships, never meeting his match
            such was the nature of his thatch.[38]
CHORUS OF WOMEN.
                    I offer an anecdote
                    for your opinion,
                    an adequate antidote
                    for your Melanion:

                    Timon, the noted local grouch,
                    put rusticating hermits
            out of style by building his wilds
                    inside the city limits

                    He shooed away society
                    with natural battlements:
            his tongue was edged; his shoulder, frigid;
                    his beard, a picket fence

                    When random contacts overtaxed him,
                    he didn't stop to pack,
            but loaded curses on the male of the species,
                    left town, and never came back.

                    Timon, you see, was a misanthrope
                    in a properly narrow sense:
            his spleen was vented only on men . . .
                    we were his dearest friends.
OLD WOMAN. [*Making a fist.*]
            Enjoy a chop to that juiceless chin?

---

[37] Hatred of women.

[38] Myronides, an Athenian general, and Phormion, an Athenian admiral, won important military battles many years before the action in the play.

OLD MAN. [*Backing away.*]
> I'm jolted already. Thank you, no.

OLD WOMAN.
> Perhaps a trip from a well-turned shin?

[*She tries a kick and misses.*]

OLD MAN.
> Brazenly baring the mantrap below.

OLD WOMAN.
> At least it's *neat*. I'm not too sorry
>   to have you see my daintiness.
> My habits are still depilatory;
>   age hasn't made me a bristly mess.
>   Secure in my smoothness, I'm never in doubt—
>   though even down is out.

[LYSISTRATA *mounts the platform and scans the horizon. When her gaze reaches the left, she stops suddenly.*]

LYSISTRATA.
> Ladies, attention! Battle stations, please!
> And quickly!

[*A general rush of women to the battlements.*]

KLEONIKE.
>   What is it?

MYRRHINE.
>   What's all the shouting for?

LYSISTRATA.
> A MAN!
> [*Consternation.*]
>   Yes, it's a man. And he's coming this way!
> Hmm. Seems to have suffered a seizure. Broken out
> with a nasty attack of love.
> [*Prayer, aside.*]
>   O Aphrodite,
>   Mistress all-victorious,
>   mysterious, voluptuous,
>   you who make the crooked straight . . .
>   don't let this happen to US!

KLEONIKE.
> I don't care who he is—*where is he?*

LYSISTRATA. [*Pointing.*]
>   Down there—
> just flanking that temple—Demeter the Fruitful.

KLEONIKE.
>   My.
> Definitely a man.

MYRRHINE. [*Craning for a look.*]
>   I wonder who it can be?

LYSISTRATA.
> See for yourselves.—Can anyone identify him?

MYRRHINE.
> Oh lord, I can.
>   *That* is my husband—Kinesias.

LYSISTRATA. [*To* MYRRHINE.]
Your duty is clear.
Pop him on the griddle, twist
the spit, braize him, baste him, stew him in his own
juice, do him to a turn. Sear him with kisses,
coyness, caresses, *everything*—
but stop where Our Oath
begins.
MYRRHINE.
Relax. I can take care of this.
LYSISTRATA.
Of course
you can, dear. Still, a little help can't hurt, now
can it? I'll just stay around for a bit
and—er—poke up the fire.
—Everyone else inside!

Exit all the women but LYSISTRATA, *on the platform, and* MYRRHINE, *who stands near the Akropolis entrance, hidden from her husband's view.* KINESIAS *staggers on, in erection and considerable pain, followed by a male slave who carries a baby boy.*

KINESIAS.
OUCH!!
Omigod.
Hypertension, twinges. . . . I can't hold out much more.
I'd rather be dismembered.
How long, ye gods, how long?
LYSISTRATA.
[*Officially.*]
WHO GOES THERE?
WHO PENETRATES OUR POSITIONS?
KINESIAS.
Me.
LYSISTRATA.
—A Man?
KINESIAS.
Every inch.
LYSISTRATA.
Then inch yourself out
of here. Off Limits to Men.
KINESIAS.
This *is* the limit.
Just who are *you* to throw me out?
LYSISTRATA.
The Lookout.
KINESIAS.
Well, look here, Lookout. I'd like to see Myrrhine.
How's the outlook?
LYSISTRATA.
Unlikely. Bring Myrrhine

to you? The idea!
                              Just by the by, who are you?
KINESIAS.
    A private citizen. Her husband, Kinesias.
LYSISTRATA.
                                                          No!
    Meeting you—I'm overcome!
                                      Your name, you know,
    is not without its fame among us girls.
    [*Aside.*]
    —Matter of fact, we have a name for *it.*—
    I swear, you're never out of Myrrhine's mouth.
    She won't even nibble a quince, or swallow an egg,
    without reciting, "Here's to Kinesias!"
KINESIAS.
                                      For god's sake,
    will you . . .
LYSISTRATA. [*Sweeping on over his agony.*]
                  Word of honor, it's true. Why, when
    we discuss our husbands (you know how women are),
    Myrrhine refuses to argue. She simply insists:
    "Compared with Kinesias, the rest have *nothing!*"
    Imagine!
KINESIAS.
    Bring her out here!
LYSISTRATA.
                  Really? And what would I
    get out of this?
KINESIAS.
                  You see my situation. I'll raise
    whatever I can. This can all be yours.
LYSISTRATA.
                                      Goodness.
    It's really her place. I'll go and get her.
[*She descends from the platform and moves to* MYRRHINE, *out of* KINESIAS' *sight.*]
KINESIAS.
                                      Speed!
    —Life is a husk. She left our home, and happiness
    went with her. Now pain is the tenant. Oh, to enter
    that wifeless house, to sense that awful emptiness,
    to eat that tasteless, joyless food—it makes
    it hard, I tell you.
                  Harder all the time.
MYRRHINE. [*Still out of his sight, in a voice to be overheard.*]
    Oh, I *do* love him! I'm mad about him! But he
    doesn't want my love. Please don't make me see him.
KINESIAS.
    Myrrhine darling, why do you *act* this way?
    Come down here!
MYRRHINE. [*Appearing at the wall.*)
                  Down there? Certainly not!

KINESIAS.
It's me, Myrrhine. I'm begging you. Please come down.
MYRRHINE.
I don't see why you're begging me. You don't need me.
KINESIAS.
I don't need you? I'm at the end of my rope!
MYRRHINE.
I'm leaving. [*She turns.* KINESIAS *grabs the boy from the slave.*]
KINESIAS.
  No! Wait! At least you'll have to listen
to the voice of your child.
[*To the boy, in a fierce undertone.*]
    —(Call your mother!)
[*Silence.*]
    . . . to the voice
of your very own child . . .
    —(Call your mother, brat!)
CHILD.
MOMMYMOMMYMOMMY!
KINESIAS.
Where's your maternal instinct? He hasn't been washed
or fed for a week. How can you be so pitiless?
MYRRHINE.
Him I pity. Of all the pitiful excuses
for a father. . . .
KINESIAS.
  Come down here, dear. For the baby's sake.
MYRRHINE.
Motherhood! I'll have to come. I've got no choice.
KINESIAS. [*Soliloquizing as she descends.*]
It may be me, but I'll swear she looks years younger—
and gentler—her eyes caress me. And then they flash:
that anger, that verve, that high-and-mighty air!
She's fire, she's ice—and I'm stuck right in the middle.
MYRRHINE. [*Taking the baby.*]
Sweet babykins with such a nasty daddy!
Here, let Mummy kissums. Mummy's little darling.
KINESIAS. [*The injured husband.*]
You should be ashamed of yourself, letting those women
lead you around. Why do you DO these things?
You only make me suffer and hurt your poor,
sweet self.
MYRRHINE.
  Keep your hands away from me!
KINESIAS.
But the house, the furniture, everything we own—you're
letting it go to hell!
MYRRHINE.
  Frankly, I couldn't care less.
KINESIAS.
But your weaving's unraveled—the loom is full of
chickens! You couldn't care less about *that*?

MYRRHINE.

I certainly couldn't.

KINESIAS.

And the holy rites of Aphrodite? Think how long
that's been.

Come on, darling, let's go home.

MYRRHINE.

I absolutely refuse!

Unless you agree to a truce

to stop the war.

KINESIAS.

Well, then, if that's your decision,
we'll STOP the war!

MYRRHINE.

Well, then, if that's your decision,
I'll come back—*after* it's done.

But, for the present,

I've sworn off.

KINESIAS.

At least lie down for a minute.

We'll talk.

MYRRHINE.

I know what you're up to—NO!
—And yet. . . . I really can't say I don't love you . . .

KINESIAS.

You love me?

So what's the trouble? *Lie down.*

MYRRHINE.

Don't be disgusting.

In front of the baby?

KINESIAS.

Er . . . no. Heaven Forefend.

[*Taking the baby and pushing it at the slave.*]
—Take this home.

[*The slave obeys.*]

—Well, darling, we're rid of the kid . . .

let's go to bed?

MYRRHINE.

Poor dear.

But where does one do

this sort of thing?

KINESIAS.

Where? All we need is a little
nook. . . . We'll try Pan's grotto. Excellent spot.

MYRRHINE.

[*With a nod at the Akropolis.*]

I'll have to be pure to get back in *there.* How can I
expunge my pollution?

KINESIAS.

Sponge off in the pool next door.

MYRRHINE.
I did swear an Oath. I'm supposed to purjure myself?
KINESIAS.
Bother the Oath. Forget it—I'll take the blame. [*A pause.*]
MYRRHINE.
Now I'll go get us a cot.
KINESIAS.
No! Not a cot!
The ground's enough for us.
MYRRHINE.
I'll get the cot.
For all your faults, I refuse to put you to bed
in the dirt. [*She exits into the Akropolis.*]
KINESIAS.
She certainly loves me. That's nice to know.
MYRRHINE. [*Returning with a rope-tied cot.*]
Here. You hurry to bed while I undress.
[KINESIAS *lies down.*]
Gracious me—I forgot. We need a mattress.
KINESIAS.
Who wants a mattress? Not me!
MYRRHINE.
Oh, yes, you do.
It's perfectly squalid on the ropes.
KINESIAS.
Well, give me a kiss
to tide me over.
MYRRHINE.
Voilà.
[*She pecks at him and leaves.*]
KINESIAS.
OoolaLAlala!
—Make it a quick trip, dear.
MYRRHINE.
[*Entering with the mattress, she waves* KINESIAS *off the cot and lays the mattress on it.*]
Here we are.
Our mattress. Now hurry to bed while I undress. [KINESIAS *lies down again.*]
Gracious me—I forgot. You don't have a pillow.
KINESIAS.
I do *not* need a pillow
MYRRHINE.
I know, but *I* do.
[*She leaves.*]
KINESIAS.
What a lovefeast! Only the table gets laid.
MYRRHINE. [*Returning with a pillow.*]
Rise and shine!
[KINESIAS *jumps up. She places the pillow.*]
And now I have everything I need.
KINESIAS. [*Lying down again.*]

You certainly do.
                          Come here, my little jewelbox!
MYRRHINE.
   Just taking off my bra.
                          Don't break your promise:
   no cheating about the Peace.
KINESIAS.
                                    I swear to god,
   I'll die first!
MYRRHINE.
   [*Coming to him.*]
                          Just look. You don't have a blanket.
KINESIAS.
   I didn't plan to go camping—I want to make love!
MYRRHINE.
   Relax. You'll get your love. I'll be right back. [*She leaves.*]
KINESIAS.
   Relax? I'm dying a slow death by dry goods!
MYRRHINE. [*Returning with the blanket.*]
                                                  Get up!
KINESIAS. [*Getting out of bed.*]
   I've been up for hours. I was up before I was up.
[MYRRHINE *spreads the blanket on the mattress, and he lies down again.*]
MYRRHINE.
   I presume you want perfume?
KINESIAS.
                          Positively NO!
MYRRHINE.
   Absolutely *yes*—whether you want it or not. [*She leaves.*]
KINESIAS.
   Dear Zeus, I don't ask for much—but please let her
       spill it.
MYRRHINE. [*Returning with a bottle.*]
   Hold out your hand like a good boy.
                                      Now rub it in.
KINESIAS. [*Obeying and sniffing.*]
   This is to quicken desire? Too strong. It grabs
   your nose and bawls out: *Try again tomorrow.*
MYRRHINE.
   I'm *awful!* I brought you that rancid Rhodian brand. [*She starts off with the bottle.*]
KINESIAS.
   This is just *lovely*. Leave it, woman!
MYRRHINE.
                          Silly!
[*She leaves.*]
KINESIAS.
   God damn the clod who first concocted perfume!
MYRRHINE. [*Returning with another bottle.*]
   Here, try this flask.
KINESIAS.
                  Thanks—but you try mine.

Come to bed, you witch—
and please stop bringing
things!
MYRRHINE.
That is exactly what I'll do.
There go my shoes.
Incidentally, darling, you *will*
remember to vote for the truce?
KINESIAS.
I'LL THINK IT OVER!

[MYRRHINE *runs off for good.*]
That woman's laid me waste—destroyed me, root
and branch!
I'm scuttled,
gutted,
up the spout!
And Myrrhine's gone!
[*In a parody of a tragic kommos.*[39]]
Out upon't! But how? But where?
Now I have lost the fairest fair,
how screw my courage to yet another
sticking-place? Aye, there's the rub—
And yet, this wagging, wanton babe
must soon be laid to rest, or else . . .
Ho, Pandar!
Pandar!
I'd hire a nurse.
KORYPHAIOS OF MEN.
Grievous your bereavement, cruel
the slow tabescence[40] of your soul.
I bid my liquid pity mingle.

Oh, where the soul, and where, alack!
the cod to stand the taut attack
of swollen prides, the scorching tensions
that ravine up the lumbar regions?
His morning lay
has gone astray.
KINESIAS. [*In agony.*]
O Zeus, reduce the throbs, the throes!
KORYPHAIOS OF MEN.
I turn my tongue to curse the cause
of your affliction—that jade, that slut,
that hag, that ogress . . .
KINESIAS.
No! Slight not
my light-o'-love, my dove, my sweet!

---

[39] A lyric performed by the actor and chorus together.
[40] Wasting away.

KORYPHAIOS OF MEN.

>Sweet!
>   O Zeus who rul'st the sky,
>snatch that slattern up on high,
>crack thy winds, unleash thy thunder,
>tumble her over, trundle her under,
>juggle her from hand to hand;
>twirl her ever near the ground—
>drop her in a well-aimed fall
>on our comrade's tool! That's all.

KINESIAS *exits left.*

A SPARTAN HERALD *enters from the right, holding his cloak together in a futile attempt to conceal his condition.*

HERALD.
>This Athens? Where-all kin I find the Council of Elders
>or else the Executive Board? I brung some news.

The COMMISSIONER, *swathed in his cloak, enters from the left.*

COMMISSIONER.
>And what are you—a man? a signpost? a joint-stock
>company?

HERALD.
>   A herald, sonny, a honest-to-Kastor[41]
>herald. I come to chat 'bout thet-there truce.

COMMISSIONER.
>. . . carrying a concealed weapon? Pretty underhanded.

HERALD.
>[*Twisting to avoid the* COMMISSIONER'*s direct gaze.*]
>Hain't done no sech a thang!

COMMISSIONER.
>   Very well, stand still.
>Your cloak's out of crease—hernia? Are the roads that bad?

HERALD.
>I swear this feller's plumb tetched in the haid!

COMMISSIONER. [*Throwing open the Spartan's cloak, exposing the phallus.*]
>   You clown,
>you've got an erection!

HERALD. [*Wildly embarrassed.*]
>   Hain't got no sech a thang!
>You stop this-hyer foolishment!

COMMISSIONER.
>   What *have* you got there, then?

---

[41] The twin gods, Castor and Pollux, were especially revered by the Spartans.

HERALD.
Thet-thur's a Spartan *epistle.*[42] In code.
COMMISSIONER.

I have the key.

[*Throwing open his cloak.*]
Behold another Spartan *epistle.* In code.
[*Tiring of teasing.*]
Let's get down to cases. I know the score,
so tell me the truth.

How are things with you in Sparta?
HERALD.
Thangs is up in the air. The whole Alliance
is purt-near 'bout to explode. We-uns'll need barrels,
'stead of women.
COMMISSIONER.

What was the cause of this outburst?
The great god Pan?
HERALD.

Nope. I'll lay 'twere Lampito,
most likely. She begun, and then they was off
and runnin' at the post in a bunch, every last little gal
in Sparta, drivin' their menfolk away from the winner's
circle.
COMMISSIONER.

How are you taking this?
HERALD.

Painful-like.
Everyone's doubled up worse as a midget nursin'
a wick in a midnight wind come moon-dark time.
Cain't even tetch them little old gals on the moosey
without we all agree to a Greece-wide Peace.
COMMISSIONER.
Of course!

A universal female plot—all Hellas
risen in rebellion—I should have known!

Return
to Sparta with this request:

Have them despatch us
A Plenipotentiary Commission, fully empowered
to conclude an armistice. I have full confidence
that I can persuade our Senate to do the same,
without extending myself. The evidence is at hand.
HERALD.
I'm a-flyin', Sir! I hev never heered your equal!
[*Exeunt hurriedly, the* COMMISSIONER *to the left, the* HERALD *to the right.*]

---

[42] A rod used in sending coded messages. The original message was written on a strip of paper spiralled around the rod. Once unwrapped it could only be deciphered if wrapped around an identical rod.

KORYPHAIOS OF MEN.
>The most unnerving work of nature,
>the pride of applied immortality,
>is the common female human.
>No fire can match, no beast can best her.
>O Unsurmountability,
>thy name—worse luck—is Woman.

KORYPHAIOS OF WOMEN.
>After such knowledge, why persist
>in wearing out this feckless
>war between the sexes?
>When can I apply for the post
>of ally, partner, and general friend?

KORYPHAIOS OF MEN.
>I won't be ployed to revise, re-do,
>amend, extend, or bring to an end
>my irreversible credo:
>*Misogyny Forever!*
>—The answer's never.

KORYPHAIOS OF WOMEN.
>All right. Whenever you choose.
>But, for the present, I refuse
>to let you look your absolute worst,
>parading around like an unfrocked freak:
>I'm coming over and get you dressed.

She dresses him in his tunic, an action (like others in this scene) imitated by the members of the CHORUS OF WOMEN *toward their opposite numbers in the* CHORUS OF MEN.

KORYPHAIOS OF MEN.
>This seems sincere. It's not a trick.
>Recalling the rancor with which I stripped,
>I'm overlaid with chagrin.

KORYPHAIOS OF WOMEN.
>Now you resemble a man,
>not some ghastly practical joke.
>And if you show me a little respect
>(and promise not to kick), I'll extract
>the beast in you.

KORYPHAIOS OF MEN. [*Searching himself.*]
>   What beast in me?

KORYPHAIOS OF WOMEN.
>That insect. There. The bug that's stuck
>in your eye.

KORYPHAIOS OF MEN. [*Playing along dubiously.*]
>This gnat?

KORYPHAIOS OF WOMEN.
>Yes, nitwit!

KORYPHAIOS OF MEN.
>Of course.

That steady, festering agony.....
You've put your finger on the source
of all my lousy troubles. Please
roll back the lid and scoop it out.
I'd like to see it.

KORYPHAIOS OF WOMEN.
All right, I'll do it.

[*Removing the imaginary insect.*]
Although, of all the impossible cranks....
Do you sleep in a swamp? Just look at this.
I've never seen a bigger chigger.

KORYPHAIOS OF MEN.
Thanks.
Your kindness touches me deeply. For years,
that thing's been sinking wells in my eye.
Now you've unplugged me. Here come the tears.

KORYPHAIOS OF WOMEN.
I'll dry your tears, though I can't say why.

[*Wiping away the tears.*]
Of all the irresponsible boys....
And I'll kiss you.

KORYPHAIOS OF MEN.
Don't you kiss me!

KORYPHAIOS OF WOMEN.
What made you think you had a choice? [*She kisses him.*]

KORYPHAIOS OF MEN.
All right, damn you, that's enough of that ingrained palaver.
I can't disput e the truth or logic of the pithy old proverb:

> *Life with women is hell.*
> *Life without women is hell, too.*

And so we conclude a truce with you, on the following terms:
in future, a mutual moratorium on mischief in all its forms.
Agreed?—Let's make a single chorus and start our song.

[*The two Choruses unite and face the audience.*]

CHORUS OF MEN.
We're not about to introduce
the standard personal abuse—
    the Choral Smear
Of Present Persons (usually,
in every well-made comedy,
    inserted here).
Instead, in deed and utterance, we
shall now indulge in philanthropy
    because we feel
that members of the audience
endure, in the course of current events,
    sufficient hell.
Therefore, friends, be rich! Be flush!
Apply to us, and borrow cash
    in large amounts.

The Treasury stands behind us—there—
and we can personally take care
        of small accounts.
Drop up today. Your credit's good.
Your loan won't have to be repaid
        in full until
the war is over. And then, your debt
is only the money you actually get—
        nothing at all.

CHORUS OF WOMEN.

Just when we meant to entertain
some madcap gourmets from out of town
        —such flawless taste!—
the present unpleasantness intervened,
and now we fear the feast we planned
        will go to waste.
The soup is waiting, rich and thick;
I've sacrificed a suckling pig
        —the *pièce de résistance*[43]—
whose toothsome cracklings should amaze
the most fastidious gourmets—
        you, for instance.
To everybody here, I say
take potluck at my house today
        with me and mine.
Bathe and change as fast as you can,
bring the children, hurry down,
        and walk right in.
Don't bother to knock. No need at all.
My house is yours. Liberty Hall.
        What are friends for?
Act self-possessed when you come over;
it may help out when you discover
        I've locked the door.

A delegation of Spartans enters from the right, with difficulty. They have removed their cloaks, but hold them before themselves in an effort to conceal their condition.

KORYPHAIOS OF MEN.
  What's this? Behold the Spartan ambassadors,
      dragging their beards,
  pussy-footing along. It appears they've developed
      a hitch in the crotch.
[*Advancing to greet them.*]
  Men of Sparta, I bid you welcome!
                                      And now
  to the point: What predicament brings you among us?
SPARTAN.
  We-uns is up a stump. Hain't fit fer chatter.

---

[43] Main dish.

[Flipping aside his cloak.]
Here's our predicament. Take a look for yourselfs.
KORYPHAIOS OF MEN.
Well, I'll be damned—a regular disaster area.
Inflamed. I imagine the temperature's rather intense?
SPARTAN.
Hit ain't the heat, hit's the tumidity.

But words
won't help what ails us. We-uns come after Peace.
Peace from any person, at any price.

[Enter the Athenian delegation from the left, led by KINESIAS. *They are wearing cloaks, but are obviously in as much travail as the Spartans.*

KORYPHAIOS OF MEN.
Behold our local Sons of the Soil, stretching
their garments away from their groins, like wrestlers.
Grappling with their plight. Some sort of athlete's disease, no doubt.
An outbreak of epic proportions.

Athlete's foot?
No. Could it be athlete's . . . ?
KINESIAS. *[Breaking in.]*

Who can tell us
how to get hold of Lysistrata? We've come as delegates
to the Sexual Congress.
[Opening his cloak.]

Here are our credentials.
KORYPHAIOS OF MEN.
[Ever the scientist, looking from the Athenians to the Spartans and back again.]
The words are different, but the malady seems the same.
[To KINESIAS.]Dreadful disease. When the crisis reaches its height,
what do you take for it?
KINESIAS.

Whatever comes to hand.
But now we've reached the bitter end. It's Peace
or we fall back on Kleisthenes.

And he's got a waiting list.
KORYPHAIOS OF MEN. *[To the Spartans.]*
Take my advice and put your clothes on. If someone
from that self-appointed Purity League comes by, you
may be docked. They do it to the statues of Hermes,
they'll do it to you.[44]
KINESIAS. *[Since he has not yet noticed the Spartans, he interprets the warning as meant for him, and hurriedly pulls his cloak together, as do the other Athenians.]*
Excellent advice.
SPARTAN.

Hit shorely is.
Hain't nothing to argue after. Let's git dressed.

[44] In 415 B.C. the Athenian statues of Hermes, the god of messengers and thieves, were mutilated by vandals.

[*As they put on their cloaks, the Spartans are finally noticed by* KINESIAS.]
KINESIAS.
   Welcome, men of Sparta! This is a shameful
   disgrace to masculine honor.
SPARTAN.
                              Hit could be worser.
   Ef them Herm-choppers seed us all fired up,
   they'd *really* take us down a peg or two.
KINESIAS.
   Gentlemen, let's descend to details. Specifically,
   why are you here?
SPARTAN.
                              Ambassadors. We come to dicker
   'bout thet-thur Peace.
KINESIAS.
                              Perfect! Precisely our purpose.
   Let's send for Lysistrata. Only she can reconcile
   our differences. There'll be no Peace for us without her.
SPARTAN.
   We-uns ain't fussy. Call Lysistratos, too, if you want.

The gates to the Akropolis open, and LYSISTRATA *emerges, accompanied by her handmaid,*
PEACE —*a beautiful girl without a stitch on.* PEACE *remains out of sight by the gates until*
summoned.

KORYPHAIOS OF MEN.
   Hail, most virile of women! Summon up all your experience:
   Be terrible and tender,
                              lofty and lowbrow,
                                                severe and demure.
   Here stand the Leaders of Greece, enthralled by your charm.
   They yield the floor to you and submit their claims for your arbitration.
LYSISTRATA.
   Really, it shouldn't be difficult, if I can catch them
   all bothered, before they start to solicit each other.
   I'll find out soon enough. Where's Peace?
                                          —Come here.
[PEACE *moves from her place by the gates to* LYSISTRATA. *The delegations goggle at her.*]
   Now, dear, first get those Spartans and bring them to me.
   Take them by the hand, but don't be pushy about it,
   not like our husbands (no savoir-faire[45] at all!).
   Be a lady, be proper, do just what you'd do at home:
   if hands are refused, conduct them by the handle.
[PEACE *leads the Spartans to a position near* LYSISTRATA.)
   And now a hand to the Athenians—it doesn't matter
   where; accept any offer—and bring *them* over.
[PEACE *conducts the Athenians to a position near* LYSISTRATA, *opposite the Spartans.*]
   You Spartans move up closer—right *here*—
[*To the Athenians.*]

---

[45] Knowledge of the gracious way to do things.

and *you*
stand over *here.*
                     —And now attend my speech.
[*This the delegations do with some difficulty, because of the conflicting attractions of* PEACE,
who is standing beside her mistress.]
   I am a woman—but not without some wisdom:
   my native wit is not completely negligible,
   and I've listened long and hard to the discourse of my
   elders—my education is not entirely despicable.
                                          Well,
   now that I've got you, I intend to give you hell,
   and I'm perfectly right. Consider your actions:
                                 At festivals,
   in Pan-Hellenic harmony, like true blood-brothers, you share
   the selfsame basin of holy water, and sprinkle
   altars all over Greece—Olympia, Delphoi,
   Thermopylai . . . (I could go on and on, if length
   were my only object.)
                     But now, when the Persians sit by
   and wait, in the very presence of your enemies, you fight
   each other, destroy *Greek* men, destroy *Greek* cities!
   —Point One of my address is now concluded.
KINESIAS. [*Gazing at* PEACE.]
   I'm destroyed, if this is drawn out much longer!
LYSISTRATA. [*Serenely unconscious of the interruption.*]
   —Men of Sparta, I direct these remarks to you.
   Have you forgotten that a Spartan suppliant once came
   to beg assistance from Athens? Recall Perikleidas:
   Fifty years ago, he clung to our altar,
   his face dead-white above his crimson robe, and pleaded
   for an army. Messene was pressing you hard in revolt,
   and to this upheaval, Poseidon, the Earthshaker, added
   another.
                     But Kimon took four thousand troops
   from Athens—an army which saved the state of Sparta.
   Such treatment have you received at the hands of Athens,
   you who devastate the country that came to your aid!
KINESIAS. [*Stoutly; the condemnation of his enemy has made him forget the girl momentarily.*]
   You're right, Lysistrata. The Spartans are clearly in the wrong!
SPARTAN. [*Guiltily backing away from* PEACE, *whom he has attempted to pat.*]
   Hit's wrong, I reckon, but that's the purtiest behind . . .
LYSISTRATA. [*Turning to the Athenians.*]
   —Men of Athens, do you think I'll let *you* off?
   Have you forgotten the Tyrant's days,[46] when you wore
   the smock of slavery, when the Spartans turned to the
   spear, cut down the pride of Thessaly, despatched the

---

[46] "The reign of Hippias, expelled by Athenians in 510 with the aid of Kleomenes and his Spartans,
who defeated the tyrant's Thessalian allies." (Translator's note.)

friends of tyranny, and dispossessed your oppressors?

Recall:

On that great day, your only allies were Spartans;
your liberty came at their hands, which stripped away
your servile garb and clothed you again in Freedom!

SPARTAN. [*Indicating* LYSISTRATA.]
Hain't never seed no higher type of woman.

KINESIAS. [*Indicating* PEACE.]
Never saw one I wanted so much to top.

LYSISTRATA. [*Oblivious to the byplay, addressing both groups.*]
With such a history of mutual benefits conferred
and received, why are you fighting? Stop this wickedness!
Come to terms with each other! What prevents you?

SPARTAN.
We'd a heap sight druther make Peace, if we was
indemnified with a plumb strategic location.

[*Pointing at* PEACE'S REAR.]

We'll take thet butte.[47]

LYSISTRATA.
Butte?

SPARTAN.
The Promontory of Pylos—Sparta's Back Door.
We've missed it fer a turrible spell. [*Reaching.*]

Hev to keep our
hand in.

KINESIAS. [*Pushing him away.*]
The price is too high—you'll never take that!

LYSISTRATA.
Oh, let them have it.

KINESIAS.
What room will we have left
for maneuvers?

LYSISTRATA.
Demand another spot in exchange.

KINESIAS. [*Surveying* PEACE *like a map as he addresses the* SPARTAN.]
Then you hand over to us—uh, let me see—
let's try Thessaly[48] [*Indicating the relevant portions of* PEACE.]
First of all, Easy Mountain . . .
then the Maniac Gulf behind it . . .

and down to Megara
for the legs . . .

---

[47] In the lines that follow, the discussion of the terms for peace is packed with *double entendre*. "That butte" is both a prominent part of the female anatomy and a reference to the promontory of Pylos, a region in Greece that the Spartans longed to control.

[48] Puns on proper names, particularly geographical ones, rarely transfer well, as the following bits of sexual cartography will show. "Easy Mountain": an impossible pun on Mt. Oita, replacing the Greek's *Echinous,* a town in Thessaly whose name recalls *echinos* "hedgehog"—slang for the female genitalia. "Maniac Gulf": for Maliac Gulf, with less dimension than the Greek's *Mêlia kolpon,* which puns both on bosom and pudendum. The "legs of Megara" are the walls that connected that city with her seaport, Nisaia. (Translator's note.)

SPARTAN.

You cain't take all of thet! Yore plumb
out of yore mind!

LYSISTRATA. [*To* KINESIAS.]

Don't argue. Let the legs go.

[KINESIAS *nods. A pause. General smiles of agreement.*]

KINESIAS. [*Doffing his cloak.*]

I feel an urgent desire to plow a few furrows.

SPARTAN. [*Doffing his cloak.*]

Hit's time to work a few loads of fertilizer in.

LYSISTRATA.

Conclude the treaty and the simple life is yours.
If such is your decision convene your councils,
and then deliberate the matter with your allies.

KINESIAS.

Deliberate? Allies?

We're over-extended already!
Wouldn't every ally approve our position—
Union Now?

SPARTAN.

I know I kin speak for ourn.

KINESIAS.

And I for ours.

They're just a bunch of gigolos.

LYSISTRATA.

I heartily approve.

Now first attend to your purification,
then we, the women, will welcome you to the Citadel
and treat you to all the delights of a home-cooked
banquet. Then you'll exchange your oaths and pledge
your faith, and every man of you will take his wife and
depart for home. [LYSISTRATA *and* PEACE *enter the Akropolis.*]

KINESIAS.

Let's hurry!

SPARTAN.

Lead on, everwhich
way's yore pleasure.

KINESIAS.

This way, then—and HURRY!

[*The delegations exeunt at a run.*]

CHORUS OF WOMEN.

I'd never stint on anybody.
And now I include, in my boundless bounty,
    the younger set.
Attention, you parents of teenage girls
about to debut in the social whirl.
    Here's what you get:
Embroidered linens, lush brocades,
a huge assortment of ready-mades,
    from mantles to shifts;

plus bracelets and bangles of solid gold—
every item my wardrobe holds—
    absolute gifts!
Don't miss this offer. Come to my place,
barge right in, and make your choice.
    You can't refuse.
Everything there must go today.
Finders keepers—cart it away!
    How can you lose?
Don't spare me. Open all the locks.
Break every seal. Empty every box.
    Keep ferreting—
And your sight's considerably better than mine
if you should possibly chance to find
    a single thing.

CHORUS OF MEN.
    Troubles, friend? Too many mouths
to feed, and not a scrap in the house
    to see you through?
Faced with starvation? Don't give it a thought.
Pay attention; I'll tell you what
    I'm gonna do.
I overbought. I'm overstocked.
Every room in my house is clogged
    with flour (best ever),
glutted with luscious loaves whose size
you wouldn't believe. I need the space;
    do me a favor:
Bring gripsacks, knapsacks, duffle bags,
pitchers, cisterns, buckets, and kegs
    around to me.
A courteous servant will see to your needs;
he'll fill them up with A-1 wheat—
    and all for free!
—Oh. Just one final word before
you turn your steps to my front door:
    I happen to own
a dog. Tremendous animal.
Can't stand a leash. And bites like hell—
    better stay home.

[*The united* CHORUS *flocks to the door of the Akropolis.*]
KORYPHAIOS OF MEN. [*Banging at the door.*]
  Hey, open up in there!

The door opens, and the COMMISSIONER *appears. He wears a wreath, carries a torch, and is slightly drunk. He addresses the* KORYPHAIOS.

COMMISSIONER.
                You know the Regulations.
  Move along!
[*He sees the entire* CHORUS.]

                    —And why are YOU lounging around?
I'll wield my trusty torch and scorch the lot!

[*The* CHORUS *backs away in mock horror. He stops and looks at his torch.*]
—*This* is the bottom of the barrel. A cheap burlesque bit.
I refuse to do it. I have my pride.
[*With a start, he looks at the audience, as though hearing a protest. He shrugs and addresses the audience.*]

                              —No choice, eh?
Well, if that's the way it is, we'll take the trouble.
Anything to keep you happy.
[*The* CHORUS *advances eagerly.*]
KORYPHAIOS OF MEN.
                         Don't forget us!
We're in this too. Your trouble is ours!
COMMISSIONER. [*Resuming his character and jabbing with his torch at the Chorus.*]
                         Keep moving!
Last man out of the way goes home without hair!
Don't block the exit. Give the Spartans some room.
They've dined in comfort; let them go home in peace.

The CHORUS *shrinks back from the door.* KINESIAS, *wreathed and quite drunk, appears at the door. He speaks his first speech in Spartan.*

KINESIAS.
Hain't never seed sech a spread! Hit were splendiferous!
COMMISSIONER.
I gather the Spartans won friends and influenced people?
KINESIAS.
And *we've* never been so brilliant. It was the wine.
COMMISSIONER.
Precisely.
           The reason? A sober Athenian is just
non compos.[49] If I can carry a little proposal
I have in mind, our Foreign Service will flourish,
guided by this rational rule:
                         No Ambassador
Without a Skinful.
                 Reflect on our past performance:
Down to a Spartan parley we troop, in a state
of disgusting sobriety, looking for trouble. It muddles
our senses: we read between the lines; we hear,
not what the Spartans say, but what we suspect
they might have been about to be going to say.
We bring back paranoid reports—cheap fiction, the fruit
of temperance. Cold-water diplomacy, pah!
                              Contrast
this evening's total pleasure, the free-and-easy

[49] *Non compos mentis*, not of sound mind.

give-and-take of friendship: If we were singing,

> *Just Kleitagora and me,*
> *Alone in Thessaly,*

and someone missed his cue and cut in loudly,

> *Ajax, son of Telamon,*
> *He was one hell of a man*

no one took it amiss, or started a war;
we clapped him on the back and gave three cheers.
[*During this recital, the* CHORUS *has sidled up to the door.*]
—Dammit, are you back here again?
[*Waving his torch.*]

Scatter!

Get out of the road! Gangway, you gallowsbait!
KINESIAS.
Yes, everyone out of the way. They're coming out.

Through the door emerge the Spartan delegation, a flutist, the Athenian delegation, LYSI-
STRATA, KLEONIKE, MYRRHINE, *and the rest of the women from the citadel, both Athenian and
Peloponnesian. The* CHORUS *splits into its male and female components and draws to the
sides to give the procession room.*

SPARTAN. [*To the* FLUIST.]
Friend and kinsman, take up them pipes a yourn.
I'd like fer to shuffle a bit and sing a right sweet
song in honor of Athens and us'uns, too.
COMMISSIONER. [*To the* FLUIST.]
Marvelous, marvelous—come, take up your pipes!
[*To the* SPARTAN.]
I certainly love to see you Spartans dance.
[*The* FLUIST *plays, and the* SPARTAN *begins a slow dance.*]
SPARTAN.

> Memory,
> send me
> your Muse,
> who knows
> our glory,
> knows Athens'—
> Tell the story:
> At Artemision
> like gods, they stampeded
> the hulks of the Medes, and
> beat them.[50]
>
> And Leonidas
> leading us—

---

[50] Near Artemision in 480 B.C. the Athenian navy defeated the navy of the Persians (or Medes).
Meanwhile Leonidas with 300 Spartans held the pass at Thermopylae against the entire Persian
army.

the wild boars
whetting their tusks.
And the foam flowered,
flowered and flowed,
down our cheeks
to our knees below.
The Persians there
like the sands of the sea—

Hither, huntress,
virgin, goddess,
tracker, slayer,
to our truce!
Hold us ever
fast together;
bring our pledges
love and increase;
wean us from the
fox's wiles—
Hither, huntress!
Virgin, hither!

LYSISTRATA. [*Surveying the assemblage with a proprietary air.*]
  Well, the preliminaries are over—very nicely, too.
  So, Spartans,
[*Indicating the Peloponnesian women who have been hostages.*]
          take these girls back home. And *you*
[*To the Athenian delegation, indicating the women from the Akropolis.*]
  take *these* girls. Each man stand by his wife, each wife
  by her husband. Dance to the gods' glory, and thank
  them for the happy ending. And, from now on, please be
  careful. Let's not make the same mistakes again.
[*The delegations obey; the men and women of the* CHORUS *join again for a rapid ode.*]
CHORUS.[51]

          Start the chorus dancing,
          Summon all the Graces,
      Send a shout to Artemis in invocation.
          Call upon her brother,
          healer, chorus master,
      Call the blazing Bacchus, with his maddened muster.

          Call the flashing, fiery Zeus, and
          call his mighty, blessed spouse, and
          call the gods, call all the gods,
          to witness now and not forget
          our gentle, blissful Peace—the gift,

---

[51] The Athenian chorus concludes with a song invoking many of the Greek gods: Artemis, the goddess
of chastity; her brother Apollo, the god of medicine and music; Bacchus, the god of wine and
revelry; Zeus, the leader of the gods; and Hera, the wife of Zeus. Fittingly, the song concludes with
an appeal to Aphrodite, the goddess of love—for love, as stimulated by the sex-strike and the nude
figure of Peace, has brought an end to the war.

the deed of Aphrodite.
                    Ai!
          Alalai!   Paion!
          Leap you! Paion!
          Victory! Alalai!
          Hail!   Hail!   Hail!

LYSISTRATA.
     Spartan, let's have another song from you, a new one.
SPARTAN.[52]

                    Leave darlin' Taygetos,
                    Spartan Muse! Come to us
               once more, flyin'
               and glorifyin'
               Spartan themes:
               the god at Amyklai,
               bronze-house Athene,
               Tyndaros' twins,
               the valiant ones,
          playin' still by Eurotas' streams.

                    Up! Advance!
                    Leap to the dance!

                    Help us hymn Sparta,
               lover of dancin',
               lover of foot-pats,
               where girls go prancin'
          like fillies along Eurotas' banks,
          whirlin' the dust, twinklin' their shanks,
                    shakin' their hair
                    like Maenads playin'
                    and jugglin' the thyrsis,
                    in frenzy obeyin'
          Leda's daughter, the fair, the pure
          Helen, the mistress of the choir.

                    Here, Muse, here!
                    Bind up your hair!

          Stamp like a deer! Pound your feet!
          Clap your hands! Give us a beat!

                    Sing the greatest,
                    sing the mightiest,

---

[52] The Spartan's song celebrates Apollo, worshipped in the Spartan town of Amyklai; Athene, whose temple in Sparta was bronze-plated; Kastor and Pollux, the twin sons of Tyndaros, who were supposedly born by the Eurotas River in Sparta; and Helen, wife of the Spartan king Menelaos and the indirect cause of the Trojan War. Fittingly, the Spartan's song concludes with the praises of Athene, the patroness of Athens—thus reaffirming the peace between Sparta and Athens.

sing the conqueror,
sing to honor her—

Athene of the Bronze House!
Sing Athene!

[*Exeunt omnes, dancing and singing.*]

[411 B.C.]

William Shakespeare (1564–1616)

A MIDSUMMER NIGHT'S DREAM

CHARACTERS

THESEUS, *Duke of Athens*
EGEUS, *Father to* HERMIA
LYSANDER
DEMETRIUS } *in love with* HERMIA.
PHILOSTRATE, *Master of the Revels to*
   THESEUS
QUINCE, *a Carpenter*
SNUG, *a Joiner*
BOTTOM, *a Weaver*
FLUTE, *a Bellows-mender*
SNOUT, *a Tinker*
STARVELING, *a Tailor*
HIPPOLYTA, *Queen of the Amazons,*
   betrothed to THESEUS
HERMIA, *in love with* LYSANDER
HELENA, *in love with* DEMETRIUS

OBERON, *King of the Fairies*
TITANIA, *Queen of the Fairies*
PUCK *or* ROBIN-GOODFELLOW
PEAS-BLOSSOM
COBWEB
MOTH } *Fairies*
MUSTARD-SEED
PYRAMUS
THISBE   *Characters in the*
WALL   *Interlude performed by*
MOONSHINE *the "rude mechanicals"*
LION
Other Fairies attending their Queen and
   King
Attendants on THESEUS *and* HIPPOLYTA

SCENE:
Athens; and a Wood near it.

ACT I

SCENE I
ATHENS. *A Room in the Palace of* THESEUS.

Enter THESEUS, HIPPOLYTA, PHILOSTRATE, *and* Attendants.

THESEUS. Now, fair Hippolyta, our nuptial hour
  Draws on apace; four happy days bring in
  Another moon: but, oh, methinks, how slow
  This old moon wanes! she lingers° my desires,   *delays*
  Like to a step-dame, or a dowager,
  Long withering out a young man's revenue.[1]
HIPPOLYTA. Four days will quickly steep themselves in°   *be swallowed up in*
    nights;
  Four nights will quickly dream away the time;
  And then the moon, like to a silver bow
  New bent in heaven, shall behold the night
  Of our solemnities.
THESEUS.   Go, Philostrate,

---

[1] The allusion is to a stepmother or a widow who draws upon her deceased husband's estate, thus depleting the son's inheritance.

Stir up the Athenian youth to merriments;
Awake the pert° and nimble spirit of mirth: *lively*
Turn melancholy forth to funerals,—
The pale companion is not for our pomp.°   *celebration*
[*Exit* PHILOSTRATE.]
Hippolyta, I woo'd thee with my sword,
And won thy love, doing thee injuries;
But I will wed thee in another key,
With pomp, with triumph,° and with revelling.   *festive entertainment*

[*Enter* EGEUS, HERMIA, LYSANDER, *and* DEMETRIUS.]

EGEUS. Happy be Theseus, our renownèd duke!
THESEUS. Thanks, good Egeus: what's the news with thee?
EGEUS. Full of vexation come I, with complaint
　　Against my child, my daughter Hermia.—
　　Stand forth, Demetrius.—My noble lord,
　　This man hath my consent to marry her.—
　　Stand forth, Lysander:—and, my gracious duke,
　　This man hath bewitch'd the bosom of my child:—
　　Thou, thou, Lysander, thou hast given her rhymes,
　　And interchang'd love-tokens with my child:
　　Thou hast by moon-light at her window sung,
　　With feigning voice, verses of feigning love;
　　And stol'n th' impression of her fantasy
　　With bracelets of thy hair, rings, gawds,° conceits,°   *bits of finery / fancy articles*
　　Knacks,° trifles, nosegays, sweet-meats (messengers   *knick knacks*
　　Of strong prevailment° in unharden'd youth):   *influence*
　　With cunning hast thou filch'd my daughter's heart;
　　Turn'd her obedience, which is due to me,
　　To stubborn harshness:—and, my gracious duke,
　　Be it so she will not here before your grace
　　Consent to marry with Demetrius,
　　I beg the ancient privilege of Athens,—
　　As she is mine, I may dispose of her:
　　Which shall be either to this gentleman,
　　Or to her death, according to our law
　　Immediately provided° in that case.   *expressly stipulated*
THESEUS. What say you, Hermia? be advis'd, fair maid:
　　To you your father should be as a god;
　　One that compos'd your beauties; yea, and one
　　To whom you are but as a form in wax,
　　By him imprinted, and within his power
　　To leave the figure, or disfigure° it.   *destroy*
　　Demetrius is a worthy gentleman.
HERMIA. So is Lysander.
THESEUS. 　　　　　　　　In himself he is;
　　But, in this kind, wanting your father's voice,
　　The other must be held the worthier.
HERMIA. I would my father look'd but with my eyes.
THESEUS. Rather, your eyes must with his judgment look.

HERMIA. I do entreat your grace to pardon me.
   I know not by what power I am made bold,
   Nor how it may concern° my modesty,   *befit*
   In such a presence here, to plead my thoughts;
   But I beseech your grace, that I may know
   The worst that may befall me in this case,
   If I refuse to wed Demetrius.
THESEUS. Either to die the death,° or to abjure   *be put to death*
   For ever the society of men.
   Therefore, fair Hermia, question your desires;
   Know of your youth, examine well your blood,°   *feelings*
   Whether, if you yield not to your father's choice,
   You can endure the livery° of a nun;   *habit*
   For aye to be in shady cloister mew'd,°   *shut up, confined*
   To live a barren sister all your life,
   Chanting faint hymns to the cold fruitless moon.
   Thrice blessèd they, that master so their blood,
   To undergo such maiden pilgrimage;
   But earthlier happy is the rose distill'd,°   *reduced to its essence*
   Than that which, withering on the virgin thorn
   Grows, lives, and dies, in single blessedness.
HERMIA. So will I grow, so live, so die, my lord,
   Ere I will yield my virgin patent° up   *right to my virginity*
   Unto his lordship, whose unwishèd yoke
   My soul consents not to give sovereignty.
THESEUS. Take time to pause; and, by the next new moon,—
   The sealing-day betwixt my love and me
   For everlasting bond of fellowship,—
   Upon that day either prepare to die
   For disobedience to your father's will,
   Or else to wed Demetrius, as he would;
   Or on Diana's altar to protest,°   *vow*
   For aye, austerity° and single life.   *abstinence*
DEMETRIUS. Relent, sweet Hermia:—and, Lysander, yield
   Thy crazèd° title to my certain right.   *unsound*
LYSANDER. You have her father's love, Demetrius;
   Let me have Hermia's: do you marry him.
EGEUS. Scornful Lysander! true, he hath my love,—
   And what is mine my love shall render him;
   And she is mine, and all my right of her
   I do estate unto° Demetrius.   *bestow upon*
LYSANDER. I am, my lord, as well deriv'd° as he,   *as of good an ancestry*
   As well possess'd;° my love is more than his;   *endowed*
   My fortunes every way as fairly rank'd
   (If not with vantage,°) as Demetrius';   *indeed better*
   And, which is more than all these boasts can be,
   I am belov'd of beauteous Hermia:
   Why should not I, then, prosecute my right?
   Demetrius, I'll avouch it to his head,°   *to his face*
   Made love to Nedar's daughter, Helena,
   And won her soul; and she, sweet lady, dotes,

Devoutly dotes, dotes in idolatry,
Upon this spotted° and inconstant man.   *blemished*
THESEUS. I must confess that I have heard so much,
  And with Demetrius thought to have spoke thereof;
  But, being over-full of self-affairs,°   *my own concerns*
  My mind did lose it.—But, Demetrius, come;
  And come, Egeus: you shall go with me,
  I have some private schooling for you both.—
  For you, fair Hermia, look you arm° yourself   *ready*
  To fit your fancies to your father's will;
  Or else the law of Athens yields you up
  (Which by no means we may extenuate)°   *mitigate*
  To death, or to a vow of single life.—
  Come, my Hippolyta: what cheer, my love?—
  Demetrius, and Egeus, go along:
  I must employ you in some business
  Against° our nuptial; and confer with you   *in preparation for*
  Of something nearly° that concerns yourselves.   *closely*
EGEUS. With duty and desire we follow you.
  [*Exeunt* THESEUS, HIPPOLYTA, EGEUS, DEMETRIUS, *and train.*]
LYSANDER. How now, my love! Why is your cheek so pale?
  How chance the roses there do fade so fast?
HERMIA. Belike,° for want of rain, which I could well   *probably*
  Beteem° them from the tempest of mine eyes.   *grant*
LYSANDER. Ah me! for aught that ever I could read,
  Could ever hear by tale or history,
  The course of true love never did run smooth:
  But, either it was different in blood,°—   *parentage*
HERMIA. O cross! too high to be enthrall'd to low!
LYSANDER. Or else misgraffèd° in respect of years,—   *badly matched*
HERMIA. O spite! too old to be engag'd to young!
LYSANDER. Or else it stood upon the choice of friends,—
HERMIA. O hell! to choose love by another's eye!
LYSANDER. Or, if there were a sympathy° in choice,   *agreement*
  War, death, or sickness, did lay siege to it,
  Making it momentany° as a sound,   *momentary*
  Swift as a shadow, short as any dream;
  Brief as the lightning in the collied° night,   *black*
  That, in a spleen,° unfolds both heaven and earth,   *fit of passion*
  And ere a man hath power to say,—Behold!
  The jaws of darkness do devour it up:
  So quick bright things come to confusion.
HERMIA. If, then true lovers have been ever cross'd,°   *thwarted*
  It stands as an edict in destiny:
  Then let us teach our trial patience,
  Because it is a customary cross,
  As due to love as thoughts, and dreams, and sighs,
  Wishes, and tears, poor fancy's° followers.   *love's*
LYSANDER. A good persuasion:° therefore, hear me, Hermia.   *belief, doctrine*
  I have a widow aunt, a dowager
  Of great revènue, and she hath no child:

From Athens is her house remote seven leagues;
And she respects° me as her only son.   *regards, looks upon*
There, gentle Hermia, may I marry thee:
And to that place the sharp Athenian law
Cannot pursue us. If thou lov'st me, then,
Steal forth thy father's house to-morrow night;
And in the wood, a league without° the town,   *outside*
Where I did meet thee once with Helena,
To do observance to a morn of May,
There will I stay for thee.
HERMIA. My good Lysander!
I swear to thee, by Cupid's strongest bow;
By his best arrow with the golden head;
By the simplicity of Venus' doves;
By that which knitteth souls and prospers loves,
And by that fire which burn'd the Carthage queen,
When the false Trojan under sail was seen;[2]
By all the vows that ever men have broke,
In number more than ever women spoke;—
In that same place thou hast appointed me,
To-morrow truly will I meet with thee.
LYSANDER. Keep promise, love. Look, here comes Helena.

Enter HELENA.

HERMIA. God speed fair Helena! Whither away?
HELENA. Call you me fair? that fair again unsay.
Demetrius loves your fair°: O happy fair!   *beauty*
Your eyes are lode-stars°; and your tongue's sweet air   *guiding stars*
More tuneable° than lark to shepherd's ear,   *tuneful*
When wheat is green, when hawthorn buds appear.
Sickness is catching: O, were favour° so,   *beauty*
Yours would I catch, fair Hermia! ere I go,
My ear should catch your voice, my eye your eye,
My tongue should catch your tongue's sweet melody.
Were the world mine, Demetrius being bated,°   *excepted*
The rest I'll give to be to you translated.°   *transformed*
O, teach me how you look; and with what art
You sway the motion of Demetrius' heart!
HERMIA. I frown upon him, yet he loves me still.
HELENA. O that your frowns would teach my smiles such skill.
HERMIA. I give him curses, yet he gives me love.
HELENA. O that my prayers could such affection move!
HERMIA. The more I hate, the more he follows me.
HELENA. The more I love, the more he hateth me.
HERMIA. His folly, Helena, is no fault of mine.
HELENA. None, but your beauty: would that fault were mine!

[2] The allusion is to Dido, Queen and founder of Carthage, who, according to Virgil's *Aeneid*, watched her Trojan lover, Aeneas, sail away and then committed suicide by throwing herself upon her own funeral pyre.

HERMIA. Take comfort: he no more shall see my face;
   Lysander and myself will fly this place.—
   Before the time I did Lysander see,
   Seem'd Athens as a paradise to me:
   O, then, what graces in my love do dwell,
   That he hath turn'd a heaven unto a hell!
LYSANDER. Helen, to you our minds we will unfold:
   To-morrow night, when Phoebe³ doth behold
   Her silver visage in the wat'ry glass,
   Decking with liquid pearl the bladed grass,
   (A time that lovers' flights doth still° conceal,)   *always*
   Through Athens' gates have we devis'd to steal.
HERMIA. And in the wood, where often you and I
   Upon faint° primrose-beds were wont to lie,   *pale*
   Emptying our bosoms of their counsel sweet,
   There my Lysander and myself shall meet;
   And thence from Athens turn away our eyes,
   To seek new friends and stranger companies.⁴
   Farewell, sweet playfellow; pray thou for us;
   And good luck grant thee thy Demetrius!—
   Keep word, Lysander: we must starve our sight
   From lovers' food till morrow deep midnight.
LYSANDER. I will, my Hermia—[*Exit* HERMIA.] Helena, adieu:
   As you on him, Demetrius dote on you! [*Exit.*]
HELENA. How happy some, o'er other some° can be!   *some others*
   Through Athens I am thought as fair as she:
   But what of that? Demetrius thinks not so;
   He will not know, what all but he do know;
   And as he errs, doting on Hermia's eyes,
   So I, admiring of his qualities.
   Things base and vile, holding no quantity,
   Love can transpose to form and dignity:
   Love looks not with the eyes, but with the mind;
   And therefore is wing'd Cupid painted blind:
   Nor hath Love's mind of any judgment taste;
   Wings, and no eyes, figure° unheedy haste: *symbolize*
   And therefore is Love said to be a child,
   Because in choice he is so oft beguil'd.
   As waggish° boys in game° themselves forswear,   *mischievous/jest, sport*
   So the boy Love is perjur'd every where:
   For ere Demetrius look'd on Hermia's eyne,°   *eyes*
   He hail'd down oaths that he was only mine;
   And when this hail some heat from Hermia felt,
   So he dissolv'd, and showers of oaths did melt.
   I will go tell him of fair Hermia's flight:
   Then to the wood will he, to-morrow night,
   Pursue her; and for this intelligence°   *information*
   If I have thanks it is a dear expense:°   *a great sacrifice*

³ Another name for Diana, the goddess of the moon.
⁴ That is, the company or fellowship of strangers.

But herein mean I to enrich my pain,
To have his sight thither and back again. [*Exit.*]

SCENE II

ATHENS. *A room in* QUINCE's *House.*

Enter QUINCE, SNUG, BOTTOM, FLUTE, SNOUT, *and* STARVELING.

QUINCE. Is all our company here?

BOTTOM. You were best to call them generally, man by man,
  according to the scrip.°   *written paper*

QUINCE. Here is the scroll of every man's name, which is
  thought fit, through all Athens, to play in our interlude°   *play*
  before the duke and the duchess on his wedding-day at
  night.

BOTTOM. First, good Peter Quince, say what the play treats on;
  then read the names of the actors; and so grow to a
  point.°   *bring to a conclusion*

QUINCE. Marry,[5] our play is—The most lamentable comedy,
  and most cruel death of Pyramus and Thisby.

BOTTOM. A very good piece of work, I assure you, and a merry.—Now, good Peter Quince, call forth your actors by the
  scroll.—Masters, spread yourselves.

QUINCE. Answer, as I call you.—Nick Bottom, the weaver.

BOTTOM. Ready. Name what part I am for, and proceed.

QUINCE. You, Nick Bottom, are set down for Pyramus.

BOTTOM. What is Pyramus? a lover, or a tyrant?

QUINCE. A lover, that kills himself most gallantly for love.

BOTTOM. That will ask some tears in the true performing of it:
  if I do it, let the audience look to their eyes; I will move
  storms, I will condole° in some measure. To the rest:—   *lament*
  yet my chief humour is for a tyrant: I could play Ercles°   *Hercules*
  rarely, or a part to tear a cat° in, to make all split.   *rant and rave*

        "The raging rocks
        And shivering shocks
        Shall break the locks
            Of prison-gates;

        And Phibbus' car[6]
        Shall shine from far,
        And make and mar
            The foolish fates."

This was lofty!—Now name the rest of the players.—This is
Ercles' vein, a tyrant's vein;—a lover is more condoling.

QUINCE. Francis Flute, the bellows-mender.

FLUTE. Here, Peter Quince.

QUINCE. You must take Thisby on you.

---

[5] A mild oath, from the Virgin Mary.
[6] The chariot of Phoebus, the sun god.

FLUTE. What is Thisby? a wandering knight?

QUINCE. It is the lady that Pyramus must love.

FLUTE. Nay, faith, let not me play a woman; I have a beard
coming.

QUINCE. That's all one: you shall play it in a mask, and you
may speak as small as you will.

BOTTOM. An° I may hide my face, let me play this Thisby too: *if*
I'll speak in a monstrous little voice;—"Thisne, Thisne"—
"Ah, Pyramus, my lover dear! thy Thisby dear, and lady
dear!"

QUINCE. No, no; you must play Pyramus:—and, Flute, you
Thisby.

BOTTOM. Well, proceed.

QUINCE. Robin Starveling, the tailor.

STARVELING. Here, Peter Quince.

QUINCE. Robin Starveling, you must play Thisby's mother.—
Tom Snout, the tinker.

SNOUT. Here, Peter Quince.

QUINCE. You, Pyramus's father;—myself, Thisby's father;—
Snug, the joiner, you, the lion's part:—and, I hope, here is
a play fitted.

SNUG. Have you the lion's part written? pray you, if it be, give
it me, for I am slow of study.

QUINCE. You may do it extempore, for it is nothing but roaring.

BOTTOM. Let me play the lion too: I will roar, that I will do any
man's heart good to hear me; I will roar, that I will make
the duke say, "Let him roar again, let him roar again."

QUINCE. An° you should do it too terribly, you would fright   *if*
the duchess and the ladies, that they would shriek; and that
were enough to hang us all.

ALL. That would hang us, every mother's son.

BOTTOM. I grant you, friends, if that you should fright the
ladies out of their wits, they would have no more
discretion° but to hang us: but I will aggravate° my voice   *choice/moderate*
so, that I will roar you as gently as any sucking dove; I will
roar you an 'twere° any nightingale.   *as if it were*

QUINCE. You can play no part but Pyramus; for Pyramus is a
sweet-faced man; a proper° man, as one shall see in a sum-   *handsome*
mer's day; a most lovely, gentlemanlike man: therefore,
you must needs play Pyramus.

BOTTOM. Well, I will undertake it. What beard were I best to
play it in?

QUINCE. Why, what you will.

BOTTOM. I will discharge° it in either your straw-colour beard,   *perform*
your orange-tawny beard, your purple-in-grain° beard, or   *purple*
your French-crown-colour° beard, your perfect yellow.   *the color of a French*
     gold coin
QUINCE. Some of your French crowns have no hair at all, and
then you will play bare-faced.—But masters, here are your
parts: and I am to entreat you, request you, and desire you,
to con° them by to-morrow night; and meet me in the palace   *learn*

wood, a mile without the town, by moon-light; there will we
rehearse,—for if we meet in the city, we shall be dogged with
company, and our devices known. In the meantime, I will
draw a bill° of properties, such as our play wants. I pray you,   *draw up a list*
fail me not.

BOTTOM. We will meet; and there we may rehearse more obscenely, and courageously. Take pains; be perfect; adieu.

QUINCE. At the duke's oak we meet.

BOTTOM. Enough; hold, or cut bow-strings.⁷   [*Exeunt.*]

ACT II

SCENE I
A Wood near ATHENS.

Enter a FAIRY *and* PUCK, *from opposite sides.*

PUCK. How now, spirit! whither wander you?
FAIRY.   Over hill, over dale,
                    Thorough bush, thorough° brier,   *through*
                Over park, over pale,°   *fence*
                    Thorough flood, thorough fire,
                I do wander every where,
                Swifter than the moon's sphere;⁸
                And I serve the fairy queen,
                To dew her orbs upon the green;⁹
                The cowslips tall her pensioners° be;   *retinue, guards*
                In their gold coats spots you see;
                Those be rubies, fairy favours,
                In those freckles live their savours°   *fragrances*
                I must go seek some dew-drops here,
                And hang a pearl in every cowslip's ear.
                Farewell, thou lob° of spirits; I'll be gone: *bumpkin*
                Our queen and all her elves come here anon.°   *presently*
PUCK. The king doth keep his revels here to-night:
    Take heed the queen come not within his sight;
    For Oberon is passing fell and wrath,°   *exceedingly angry*
    Because that she, as her attendant, hath
    A lovely boy, stol'n from an Indian king;
    She never had so sweet a changeling:¹⁰
    And jealous Oberon would have the child
    Knight of his train, to trace° the forests wild;   *traverse, range over*
    But she, perforce, withholds the loved boy,

---

⁷ Apparently a proverbial expression derived from archery.
⁸ According to the Ptolemaic astronomy of Shakespeare's day, the sun, moon, and stars revolved
  around the earth in spheres.
⁹ Dark, circular rings of grass thought in Shakespeare's time to be the work of fairies.
¹⁰ Changelings were the children (often ugly or stupid) whom the fairies substituted for those they
  stole. Here, however, the reference is to the child stolen.

Crowns him with flowers, and makes him all her joy:
And now they never meet in grove or green,
By fountain clear, or spangled star-light sheen,°   *bright*
But they do square°; that° all their elves, for fear,   *quarrel/so that*
Creep into acorn cups, and hide them there.

FAIRY. Either I mistake your shape and making quite,
Or else you are that shrewd° and knavish sprite,   *mischievous*
Call'd Robin Good-fellow: are you not he
That frights the maidens of the villagery;
Skims milk,[11] and sometimes labours in the quern,[12]
And bootless° makes the breathless housewife churn;   *fruitlessly*
And sometime makes the drink to bear no barm°;   *froth or head*
Misleads night-wanderers, laughing at their harm?
Those that Hobgoblin call you, and sweet Puck,
You do their work, and they shall have good luck:
Are not you he?

PUCK.   Thou speak'st aright
I am that merry wanderer of the night.
I jest to Oberon, and make him smile,
When I a fat and bean-fed° horse beguile,   *well-fed*
Neighing in likeness of a filly foal:
And sometime lurk I in a gossip's bowl,[13]
In very likeness of a roasted crab;°   *crabapple*
And, when she drinks, against her lips I bob,
And on her wither'd dew-lap[14] pour the ale.
The wisest aunt, telling the saddest° tale,   *most serious*
Sometime for three-foot stool mistaketh me;
Then slip I from her bum, down topples she,
And "tailor"[15] cries, and falls into a cough;
And then the whole quire° hold their hips, and loffe;   *company*
And waxen° in their mirth, and neeze,° and swear   *increase/sneeze*
A merrier hour was never wasted there.—
But, room,° Fairy! here comes Oberon.   *give room, stand aside*

FAIRY. And here my mistress—Would that he were gone!

SCENE II

The same.

Enter OBERON *from one side, with his train; and* TITANIA
from the other, with hers.

OBERON. Ill met by moon-light, proud Titania.
TITANIA. What, jealous Oberon! Fairies, skip hence:
I have forsworn his bed and company.
OBERON. Tarry, rash wanton:° am not I thy lord?   *rebel*
TITANIA. Then, I must be thy lady: but I know
When thou hast stol'n away from fairy land,

---

[11] Steals the cream.   [12] A hand-mill used for grinding grain.
[13] A popular drink made of ale, nutmeg, sugar, and roasted crabapples.
[14] The pendulous folds of flesh hanging from the throat.   [15] The reference is unclear.

And in the shape of Corin[16] sat all day,
Playing on pipes of corn, and versing love°   *composing love poetry*
To amorous Phillida. Why art thou here,
Come from the farthest steep° of India,   *mountain range*
But that, forsooth, the bouncing Amazon,
Your buskin'd° mistress and your warrior love,   *wearing hunter's boots*
To Theseus must be wedded? and you come
To give their bed joy and prosperity.

OBERON. How canst thou thus, for shame, Titania,
Glance° at my credit with Hippolyta,   *hint critically*
Knowing I know thy love to Theseus?
Didst thou not lead him through the glimmering night
From Perigenia,[17] whom he ravishèd?
And make him with fair Æglé break his faith,
With Ariadne, and Antiopa?

TITANIA. These are the forgeries° of jealousy: *inventions*
And never, since the middle summer's spring,°   *beginning*
Met we on hill, in dale, forest, or mead,
By pavèd° fountain, or by rushy brook,   *pebbled*
Or on the beachèd margent° of the sea,   *margin*
To dance our ringlets° to the whistling wind,   *circular dances*
But with thy brawls° thou hast disturb'd our sport.   *noisiness*
Therefore the winds, piping to us in vain,
As in revenge, have suck'd up from the sea
Contagious° fogs; which, falling in the land,   *noxious*
Have every pelting° river made so proud,   *paltry, insignificant*
That they have overborne their continents:°   *banks*
The ox hath therefore stretch'd his yoke in vain,
The ploughman lost his sweat; and the green corn
Hath rotted ere his youth attain'd a beard:
The fold stands empty in the drownèd field,
And crows are fatted with the murrain° flock   *diseased*
The nine-men's morris[18] is fill'd up with mud;
And the quaint mazes in the wanton green,°   *lush grass*
For lack of tread are undistinguishable:
The human mortals want their winter here;
No night is now with hymn or carol blest:—
Therefore the moon, the governess of floods,
Pale in her anger, washes all the air,
That rheumatic° diseases do abound: *cold-like*
And thorough this distemperature° we see   *disorder*
The seasons alter: hoary-headed frosts
Fall in the fresh lap of the crimson rose;
And on old Hyem's° chin, and icy crown,   *winter's*
An odorous chaplet of sweet summer buds

---

[16] Corin, like Phillida (see later), were common names in pastoral poetry for a shepherd and a
shepherdess.
[17] Scholars believe that Shakespeare found this name, like those of Aegle, Ariadne, and Antiopa, in a
contemporary translation of Plutarch's *Life of Theseus*.
[18] A game played out of doors on a kind of chessboard laid out in the grass.

Is, as in mockery, set. The spring, the summer,
The childing° autumn, angry winter, change   *fruitful*
Their wonted° liveries; and the 'mazèd° world,   *usual/bewildered*
By their increase,° now knows not which is which: *produce*
And this same progeny of evils comes
From our debate,° from our dissension;   *quarrel*
We are their parents and original.

OBERON. Do you amend it, then; it lies in you:
Why should Titania cross her Oberon?
I do but beg a little changeling boy,
To be my henchman.°   *page boy*

TITANIA.   Set your heart at rest:
The fairy land buys not the child of me.
His mother was a votaress° of my order: *woman who has taken vows*
And, in the spicèd Indian air, by night,
Full often hath she gossip'd by my side;
And sat with me on Neptune's¹⁹ yellow sands,
Marking th' embarkèd traders° on the flood;   *trading ship*
When we have laugh'd to see the sails conceive,
And grow big-bellied, with the wanton wind;
Which she, with pretty and with swimming gait°   *regular motion*
Following,° (her womb then rich with my young squire)   *resembling*
Would imitate, and sail upon the land,
To fetch me trifles, and return again,
As from a voyage, rich with merchandize.
But she, being mortal, of that boy did die;
And for her sake I do rear up her boy;
And for her sake I will not part with him.

OBERON. How long within this wood intend you stay?

TITANIA. Perchance till after Theseus' wedding-day.
If you will patiently dance in our round,
And see our moonlight revels, go with us;
If not, shun me, and I will spare° your haunts.   *avoid*

OBERON. Give me that boy, and I will go with thee.

TITANIA. Not for thy fairy kingdom.—Fairies, away!
We shall chide° downright, if I longer stay.   *quarrel*
[*Exit* TITANIA, *with her train.*]

OBERON. Well, go thy way: thou shalt not from this grove,
Till I torment thee for this injury.—
My gentle Puck, come hither. Thou remember'st
Since° once I sat upon a promontory,   *when*
And heard a mermaid, on a dolphin's back,
Uttering such dulcet and harmonious breath,
That the rude° sea grew civil at her song,   *rough*
And certain stars shot madly from their spheres,
To hear the sea-maid's music.

PUCK.   I remember.

OBERON. That very time I saw (but thou couldst not),
Flying between the cold moon and the earth,

---

¹⁹ The Roman god of the sea.

Cupid all arm'd: a certain aim he took
At a fair vestal thronèd by° the west,   *in the region of*
And loos'd his love-shaft smartly from his bow,
As it should pierce a hundred thousand hearts:
But I might see young Cupid's fiery shaft
Quench'd in the chaste beams of the wat'ry moon,
And the imperial vot'ress passèd on,
In maiden meditation, fancy-free.
Yet mark'd I where the bolt of Cupid fell
It fell upon a little western flower,
Before milk-white, now purple with love's wound,
And maidens call it, love-in-idleness.°   *the pansy*
Fetch me that flower; the herb I show'd thee once:
The juice of it on sleeping eyelids laid,
Will make or man or woman madly dote
Upon the next live creature that it sees.
Fetch me this herb; and be thou here again,
Ere the leviathan° can swim a league.   *sea monster, whale*
PUCK. I'll put a girdle round about the earth
    In forty minutes. [*Exit.*]
OBERON.   Having once this juice,
I'll watch Titania when she is asleep,
And drop the liquor of it in her eyes.
The next thing then she waking looks upon.
(Be it on lion, bear, or wolf, or bull,
On meddling monkey, or on busy ape,)
She shall pursue it with the soul° of love: *single-minded devotion*
And ere I take this charm off from her sight,
(As I can take it with another herb)
I'll make her render up her page to me.
But who comes here? I am invisible;
And I will over-hear their conference.

Enter DEMETRIUS, HELENA *following him.*

DEMETRIUS. I love thee not, therefore pursue me not.
    Where is Lysander, and fair Hermia?
    The one I'll slay, the other slayeth me.
    Thou told'st me they were stol'n into this wood;
    And here am I, and wood° within this wood,   *frantic, mad*
    Because I cannot meet my Hermia.
    Hence! get thee gone, and follow me no more.
HELENA. You draw me, you hard-hearted adamant;[20]
    But yet you draw not iron, for my heart
    Is true as steel: leave you° your power to draw,   *give up*
    And I shall have no power to follow you.
DEMETRIUS. Do I entice you? Do I speak you fair?

---

[20] A stone of impenetrable hardness and magnetic properties.

Or, rather, do I not in plainest truth
Tell you, I do not nor I cannot love you?
Helena. And even for that do I love you the more.
I am your spaniel; and, Demetrius,
The more you beat me, I will fawn on you:
Use me but as your spaniel, spurn me, strike me,
Neglect me, lose me; only give me leave,
Unworthy as I am, to follow you.
What worser place can I beg in your love,
(And yet a place of high respect with me,)
Than to be usèd as you use your dog?
Demetrius. Tempt not too much the hatred of my spirit;
For I am sick when I do look on thee.
Helena. And I am sick when I look not on you.
Demetrius. You do impeach° your modesty too much,   *challenge, call in question*
To leave the city, and commit yourself
Into the hands of one that loves you not;
To trust the opportunity of night,
And the ill counsel of a desert place,
With the rich worth of your virginity.
Helena. Your virtue is my privilege for that.°   *because*
It is not night when I do see your face,
Therefore I think I am not in the night;
Nor doth this wood lack worlds of company,
For you, in my respect,° are all the world: *regard, estimation*
Then how can it be said I am alone,
When all the world is here to look on me?
Demetrius. I'll run from thee and hide me in the brakes,°   *thickets*
And leave thee to the mercy of wild beasts.
Helena. The wildest hath not such a heart as you.
Run when you will, the story shall be chang'd,—
Apollo flies, and Daphne holds the chase;[21]
The dove pursues the griffin[22]; the mild hind°   *doe*
Makes speed to catch the tiger,—bootless° speed,   *useless*
When cowardice pursues, and valour flies!
Demetrius. I will not stay thy° questions; let me go: *stay for, listen to*
Or, if thou follow me, do not believe
But I shall do thee mischief in the wood.
Helena. Ay, in the temple, in the town, the field,
You do me mischief. Fie, Demetrius!
Your wrongs do set a scandal on my sex:
We cannot fight for love, as men may do;
We should be woo'd, and were not made to woo.
I'll follow thee, and make a heaven of hell,
To die upon° the hand I love so well.   *by means of*
[*Exeunt* Demetrius *and* Helena.]

---

[21] The allusion is to the nymph Daphne, who, fleeing the embraces of Apollo, became changed into a laurel tree.
[22] A mythological creature, half lion and half eagle.

OBERON. Fare thee well, nymph: ere he do leave this grove,
Thou shalt fly him, and he shall seek thy love.—

Re-enter PUCK.

Hast thou the flower there? Welcome, wanderer.
PUCK. Ay, there it is.
OBERON.   I pray thee, give it me.
I know a bank where the wild thyme blows,
Where ox-lips, and the nodding violet grows;
Quite over-canopied with luscious woodbine,
With sweet musk-roses, and with eglantine:
Where sleeps Titania some time° of the night,   *at some time or another*
Lull'd in these flowers with dances and delight,
And there the snake throws her enamel'd skin,
Weed° wide enough to wrap a fairy in.   *garment*
And with the juice of this I'll streak° her eyes,   *mark*
And make her full of hateful fantasies.
Take thou some of it, and seek through this grove:
A sweet Athenian lady is in love
With a disdainful youth: anoint his eyes;
But do it, when the next thing he espies
May be the lady. Thou shalt know the man
By the Athenian garments he hath on.
Effect it with some care, that he may prove
More fond on her, than she upon her love:
And look thou meet me ere the first cock crow.
PUCK. Fear not, my lord, your servant shall do so. [*Exit.*]

SCENE III
Another part of the Wood.

Enter TITANIA, *with her train.*

TITANIA. Come, now a roundel,° and a fairy song;   *a dance in a ring or circle*
Then, for the third part of a minute, hence;—
Some, to kill cankers° in the musk-rose buds;   *caterpillars*
Some, war with rear-mice° for their leathern wings,   *bats*
To make my small elves coats; and some, keep back
The clamorous owl, that nightly hoots, and wonders
At our quaint° spirits. Sing me now asleep;   *dainty*
Then to your offices,° and let me rest.   *duties*

SONG

1 FAIRY. Ye spotted snakes, with double° tongue,   *forked*
          Thorny hedge-hogs, be not seen;
          Newts, and blind-worms,[23] do no wrong;
          Come not near our fairy queen:

---

[23] Both were at one time thought to be venomous.

CHORUS. Philomel,° with melody,   *the nightingale*
    Sing in our sweet lullaby;
    Lulla, lulla, lullaby; lulla, lulla, lullaby:
    Never harm,
    Nor spell nor charm,
    Come our lovely lady nigh;
    So, good night, with lullaby.

2 FAIRY. Weaving spiders, come not here;
    Hence, you long legg'd spinners, hence!
    Beetles black, approach not near;
    Worm, nor snail, do no offence.°   *harm*

CHORUS. Philomel, with melody, &c.

1 FAIRY. Hence, away! now all is well.
    One, aloof, stand sentinel.

[*Exeunt* FAIRIES. TITANIA *sleeps.*]

Enter OBERON.

OBERON [*Squeezes the flower on* TITANIA*'s eye-lids*]. What thou
      seest when thou dost wake,
    Do it for thy true love take;
    Love, and languish for his sake:
    Be it ounce,° or cat,° or bear,   *lynx/wildcat*
    Pard,° or boar with bristled hair,   *leopard*
    In thy eye that shall appear
    When thou wak'st, it is thy dear.
    Wake when some vile thing is near. [*Exit.*]

Enter LYSANDER *and* HERMIA.

LYSANDER. Fair love, you faint with wandering in the wood;
    And to speak troth,° I have forgot our way: *truth*
    We'll rest us, Hermia, if you think it good,
    And tarry for the comfort of the day.
HERMIA. Be it so, Lysander: find you out a bed;
    For I upon this bank will rest my head.
LYSANDER. One turf shall serve as pillow for us both;
    One heart, one bed, two bosoms, and one troth.
HERMIA. Nay, good Lysander; for my sake, my dear,
    Lie farther off yet; do not lie so near.
LYSANDER. O, take the sense, sweet, of my innocence!
    Love takes the meaning in love's conference.
    I mean, that my heart unto yours is knit,
    So that but one heart we can make of it:
    Two bosoms interchainèd with an oath;
    So then, two bosoms, and a single troth.
    Then, by your side no bed-room me deny;
    For, lying so, Hermia, I do not lie.

HERMIA. Lysander riddles very prettily:—
    Now much beshrew° my manners and my pride,   *curse upon*
    If Hermia meant to say, Lysander lied.
    But, gentle friend, for love and courtesy
    Lie farther off; in human modesty,
    Such separation as may well be said
    Becomes a virtuous bachelor and a maid,—
    So far be distant; and, good night, sweet friend.
    Thy love ne'er alter till thy sweet life end!
LYSANDER. Amen, amen, to that fair prayer, say I;
    And then end life, when I end loyalty!
    Here is my bed: sleep give thee all his rest!
HERMIA. With half that wish the wisher's eyes be press'd!
    [*They sleep.*]

Enter PUCK.

PUCK. Through the forest have I gone,
    But Athenian found I none,
    On whose eyes I might approve°   *put to the test*
    This flower's force in stirring love.
    Night and silence! who is here?
    Weeds of Athens he doth wear:
    This is he, my master said,
    Despisèd the Athenian maid;
    And here the maiden, sleeping sound,
    On the dank and dirty ground:—
    Pretty soul! she durst not lie
    Near this lack-love, this kill-courtesy,
        [*Squeezes the flower on* LYSANDER*'s eyelids.*]
    Churl, upon thy eyes I throw
    All the power this charm doth owe.°   *possess*
    When thou wak'st, let love forbid
    Sleep his seat on thy eyelid:
    So awake when I am gone,
    For I must now to Oberon.   [*Exit.*]

Enter DEMETRIUS *and* HELENA, *running.*

HELENA. Stay, though thou kill me, sweet Demetrius.
DEMETRIUS. I charge thee, hence; and do not haunt me thus.
HELENA. O, wilt thou darkling° leave me? do not so.   *in the dark*
DEMETRIUS. Stay, on thy peril: I alone will go.
    [*Exit* DEMETRIUS.]
HELENA. O, I am out of breath in this fond° chase!   *foolish*
    The more my prayer, the lesser is my grace.°   *luck, fortune*
    Happy is Hermia, wheresoe'er she lies;
    For she hath blessèd and attractive eyes.
    How came her eyes so bright? Not with salt tears:
    If so, my eyes are oftener wash'd than hers.
    No, no, I am as ugly as a bear;
    For beasts that meet me, run away for fear:

Therefore no marvel though Demetrius
Do, as a monster, fly my presence thus.
What wicked and dissembling glass of mine
Made me compare with Hermia's sphery eyne?°— *starry eyes*
But who is here?—Lysander!—on the ground!
Dead? or asleep?—I see no blood, no wound.—
Lysander, if you live, good Sir, awake.

LYSANDER [*Awaking*]. And run through fire I will, for thy sweet
       sake.
Transparent Helena! Nature here shows art,
That through thy bosom makes me see thy heart.
Where is Demetrius? O, how fit a word
Is that vile name to perish on my sword!

HELENA. Do not say so, Lysander; say not so.
What though he love your Hermia? Lord, what though?
Yet Hermia still loves you: then be content.

LYSANDER. Content with Hermia! No; I do repent
The tedious minutes I with her spent.
Not Hermia, but Helena I love:
Who will not change a raven for a dove?
The will of man is by his reason sway'd;
And reason says you are the worthier maid.
Things growing are not ripe until their season:
So I, being young, till now ripe not to reason;
And touching now the point° of human skill, *highest point*
Reason becomes the marshal to my will,
And leads me to your eyes; where I o'erlook° *read*
Love's stories, written in love's richest book.

HELENA. Wherefore was I to this keen mockery born?
When, at your hands, did I deserve this scorn?
Is't not enough, is't not enough, young man,
That I did never, no, nor never can,
Deserve a sweet look from Demetrius' eye,
But you must flout my insufficiency?
Good troth, you do me wrong,—good sooth,° you do,— *truly*
In such disdainful manner me to woo.
But fare you well: perforce I must confess,
I thought you lord of more true gentleness.° *gentility*
O, that a lady, of one man refus'd,
Should of another therefore be abus'd! [*Exit.*]

LYSANDER. She sees not Hermia.—Hermia, sleep thou there:
And never may'st thou come Lysander near!
For, as a surfeit of the sweetest things
The deepest loathing to the stomach brings;
Or, as the heresies, that men do leave,
Are hated most of those they did deceive;
So thou, my surfeit and my heresy,
Of all be hated, but the most of me!
And, all my powers, address° your love and might *apply*
To honour Helen, and to be her knight. [*Exit.*]

HERMIA [*Awaking*]. Help me, Lysander, help me! do thy best

To pluck this crawling serpent from my breast!
Ah me, for pity!—what a dream was here!
Lysander, look how I do quake with fear:
Methought a serpent eat my heart away,
And you sat smiling at his cruel prey.°—   *preying*
Lysander!—What, remov'd?—Lysander! lord!—
What, out of hearing? gone? no sound, no word?
Alack! where are you? speak, an if you hear;
Speak, of all loves! I swoon almost with fear.
No?—then I well perceive you are not nigh:
Either death, or you, I'll find immediately.   [*Exit.*]

ACT III

SCENE I

The Wood. TITANIA *lying asleep.*
Enter QUINCE, SNUG, BOTTOM, FLUTE, SNOUT, *and* STARVELING.

BOTTOM. Are we all met?
QUINCE. Pat, pat°; and here's a marvellous convenient place   *on the dot*
  for our rehearsal. This green plot shall be our stage, this
  hawthorn brake our 'tiring-house° and we will do it in ac-   *dressing room*
  tion, as we will do it before the duke.
BOTTOM. Peter Quince,—
QUINCE. What say'st thou, bully° Bottom?   *worthy*
BOTTOM. There are things in this comedy of "Pyramus and
  Thisby," that will never please. First, Pyramus must draw a
  sword to kill himself; which the ladies cannot abide. How
  answer you that?
SNOUT. By'rlakin,[24] a parlous° fear.   *perilous*
STARVELING. I believe we must leave the killing out, when all is
  done.
BOTTOM. Not a whit: I have a device to make all well. Write me
  a prologue; and let the prologue seem to say, we will do no
  harm with our swords, and that Pyramus is not killed indeed; and, for the more better assurance, that I, Pyramus,
  am not Pyramus, but Bottom the weaver. This will put
  them out of fear.
QUINCE. Well, we will have such a prologue; and it shall be
  written in eight and six.[25]
BOTTOM. No, make it two more; let it be written in eight and
  eight.
SNOUT. Will not the ladies be afeard of the lion?
STARVELING. I fear it, I promise you.
BOTTOM. Masters, you ought to consider with yourselves: to
  bring in, —God shield us!—a lion among ladies, is a most
  dreadful thing; for there is not a more fearful wild-fowl
  than your lion, living; and we ought to look to it.

---

[24] An oath, "By Our Lady."
[25] In alternating lines of eight and six syllables, the meter of traditional ballads.

Snout. Therefore, another prologue must tell he is not a lion.

Bottom. Nay, you must name his name, and half his face must be seen through the lion's neck, and he himself must speak through, saying thus, or to the same defect,—"Ladies,— or, fair ladies,—I would wish you,—or, I would request you,—or, I would entreat you, —not to fear, not to tremble: my life for yours. If you think I come hither as a lion, it were pity of my life: no, I am no such thing; I am a man as other men are:"—and there, indeed, let him name his name, and tell them plainly, he is Snug, the joiner.

Quince. Well, it shall be so. But there is two hard things,— that is, to bring the moonlight into a chamber, for, you know, Pyramus and Thisby meet by moonlight.

Snug. Doth the moon shine that night we play our play?

Bottom. A calendar, a calendar! look in the almanack; find out moonshine, find out moonshine.

Quince. Yes, it doth shine that night.

Bottom. Why, then may you leave a casement of the great chamber window, where we play, open; and the moon may shine in at the casement.

Quince. Ay; or else one must come in with a bush of thorns[26] and a lanthorn,° and say he comes to disfigure, or to present, the person of moonshine. Then, there is another thing: we must have a wall in the great chamber; for Pyramus and Thisby, says the story, did talk through the chink of a wall.   *lantern*

Snug. You can never bring in a wall.—What say you, Bottom?

Bottom. Some man or other must present wall: and let him have some plaster, or some loam, or some rough-cast[27] about him, to signify wall; and let him hold his fingers thus, and through that cranny shall Pyramus and Thisby whisper.

Quince. If that may be, then all is well. Come, sit down, every mother's son, and rehearse your parts. Pyramus, you begin. When you have spoken your speech, enter into that brake;— and so every one according to his cue.

Enter Puck *behind.*

Puck. What hempen home-spuns° have we swaggering here,   *rustics*
So near the cradle of the fairy queen?
What, a play toward!° I'll be an auditor;   *in preparation*
An actor too, perhaps if I see cause.

Quince. Speak, Pyramus.—Thisby, stand forth.

Pyramus. "Thisby, the flowers of odious savours sweet,"—

Quince. "Odours," "odours."

Pyramus. —"odours savours sweet:

---

[26] According to a popular legend then current, the moon was often characterized as a man with a bundle of sticks (or thorns) on his back.

[27] A mixture of lime and gravel used for plastering the outside of walls.

So hath thy breath, my dearest Thisby, dear.—
But hark, a voice! stay thou but here a while,
    And by and by I will to thee appear."   [*Exit.*]
PUCK [*Aside*]. A stranger Pyramus than e'er play'd here!
    [*Exit.*]
THISBE. Must I speak now?
QUINCE. Ay, marry, must you; for you must understand he
    goes but to see a noise that he heard, and is to come again.
THISBE. "Most radiant Pyramus, most lily-white of hue,
    Of colour like the red rose on triumphant° brier,   *magnified*
Most brisky juvenal,° and eke° most lovely Jew,²⁸   *lively youth/also*
    As true as truest horse, that yet would never tire,
I'll meet thee, Pyramus, at Ninny's tomb."
QUINCE. "Ninus' tomb," man. Why, you must not speak that
    yet; that you answer to Pyramus: you speak all your part at
    once, cues and all.—Pyramus, enter: your cue is past; it is,
    "never tire."
THISBE. O,—"As true as truest horse, that yet would never
    tire."

Re-enter PUCK, *and* BOTTOM *with an ass's head.*

PYRAMUS. "If I were, fair Thisby, I were only thine:"—
QUINCE. O monstrous! O strange! we are haunted.—
    Pray, masters! fly, masters!—Help!
    [*Exit, with* SNUG, FLUTE, SNOUT, *and* STARVELING.]
PUCK. I'll follow you, I'll lead you about a round,°   *roundabout way*
    Through bog, through bush, through brake, through
        brier;
    Sometime a horse I'll be, sometime a hound,
        A hog, a headless bear, sometime a fire;
    And neigh, and bark, and grunt, and roar, and burn,
    Like horse, hound, hog, bear, fire, at every turn. [*Exit.*]
BOTTOM. Why do they run away? this is a knavery of them, to
    make me afeard.

Re-enter SNOUT.

SNOUT. O Bottom! thou art changed! what do I see on thee?
BOTTOM. What do you see? you see an ass's head of your own,
    do you?   [*Exit* SNOUT.]

Re-enter QUINCE.

QUINCE. Bless thee, Bottom! bless thee! thou art translated.°   *transformed*
    [*Exit.*]
BOTTOM. I see their knavery: this is to make an ass of me, to
    fright me, if they could. But I will not stir from this place,
    do what they can: I will walk up and down here, and I will
    sing, that they shall hear I am not afraid.   [*Sings.*]

---

²⁸ Jewel? The exact meaning of the word is unclear.

> The ousel-cock°, so black of hue,   *blackbird*
>   With orange-tawny bill,
> The throstle° with his note so true,   *thrush*
>   The wren with little quill:°—   *song*

TITANIA [*Awaking*]. What angel wakes me from my flowery
  bed?
BOTTOM [*Sings*].

> The finch, the sparrow, and the lark,
>   The plain-song cuckoo gray,
> Whose note full many a man doth mark,
>   And dares not answer, nay;—

for, indeed, who would set his wit to so foolish a bird? who
would give a bird the lie, though he cry "cuckoo" never
so?
TITANIA. I pray thee, gentle mortal, sing again:
  Mine ear is much enamour'd of thy note
  So is mine eye enthrallèd to thy shape;
  And thy fair virtue's force, perforce doth move me,
  On the first view, to say, to swear, I love thee.
BOTTOM. Methinks, mistress, you should have little reason for
  that: and yet, to say the truth, reason and love keep little
  company together now-a-days;—the more the pity, that
  some honest neighbours will not make them friends. Nay,
  I can gleek° upon occasion.   *joke*
TITANIA. Thou art as wise as thou art beautiful.
BOTTOM. Not so, neither: but if I had wit enough to get out of
  this wood, I have enough to serve mine own turn.
TITANIA. Out of this wood do not desire to go:
  Thou shalt remain here, whether thou wilt or no.
  I am a spirit of no common rate,°—   *estimation*
  The summer still doth tend upon my state;
  And I do love thee: therefore go with me;
  I'll give thee fairies to attend on thee;
  And they shall fetch thee jewels from the deep,
  And sing, while thou on pressèd flowers dost sleep:
  And I will purge thy mortal grossness so,
  That thou shalt like an airy spirit go.—
  Peas-blossom! Cobweb! Moth! and Mustard-seed!

Enter PEAS-BLOSSOM, COBWEB, MOTH, *and* MUSTARD-SEED.

PEAS-BLOSSOM. Ready.
COBWEB.   And I.
MOTH.   And I.
MUSTARD-SEED.   And I.
ALL FOUR.   Where shall we go?
TITANIA. Be kind and courteous to this gentleman:

Hop in his walks, and gambol in his eyes;
Feed him with apricocks,° and dewberries,°   *apricots / blackberries*
With purple grapes, green figs, and mulberries;
The honey-bags steal from the humble-bees,
And for night tapers crop their waxen thighs,
And light them at the fiery glow-worm's eyes,
To have my love to bed, and to arise;
And pluck the wings from painted butterflies,
To fan the moon-beams from his sleeping eyes:
Nod to him, elves, and do him courtesies.

PEAS-BLOSSOM. Hail, mortal!

COBWEB. Hail!

MOTH. Hail!

MUSTARD-SEED. Hail!

BOTTOM. I cry° your worships' mercy,° heartily.—I beseech   *beg / pardon*
  your worship's name.

COBWEB. Cobweb.

BOTTOM. I shall desire you of more acquaintance, good master Cobweb: if I cut my finger, I shall make bold with
  you.[29]—Your name, honest gentleman?

PEAS-BLOSSOM. Peas-blossom.

BOTTOM. I pray you, commend me to mistress Squash,[30] your
  mother, and to master Peascod, your father. Good master
  Peas-blossom, I shall desire you of more acquaintance
  too.—Your name, I beseech you, Sir?

MUSTARD-SEED. Mustard-seed.

BOTTOM. Good master Mustard-seed, I know your patience
  well: that same cowardly, giant-like ox-beef, hath devoured
  many a gentleman of your house: I promise you, your kindred hath made my eyes water ere now. I desire you of
  more acquaintance, good master Mustard-seed.

TITANIA. Come, wait upon him; lead him to my bower.
  The moon, methinks, looks with a wat'ry eye,
  And when she weeps, weeps every little flower,
  Lamenting some enforcèd° chastity.   *violated*
  Tie up my love's tongue, bring him silently. [*Exeunt.*]

SCENE II
Another part of the Wood.

[*Enter* OBERON.]

OBERON. I wonder if Titania be awak'd;
  Then, what it was that next came in her eye,
  Which she must dote on in extremity.—
  Here comes my messenger.—[*Enter* PUCK.] How now, mad
    spirit!

---

[29] In Shakespeare's time cobwebs were applied to stop bleeding.
[30] The name of the unripe pod of a pea (or peascod).

What night-rule° now about this haunted grove?   *diversions or disorders*
PUCK. My mistress with a monster is in love.   *of the night*
  Near to her close° and consecrated bower,   *secret*
  While she was in her dull and sleeping hour,
  A crew of patches,° rude mechanicals,°   *clowns/working men*
  That work for bread upon Athenian stalls,
  Were met together to rehearse a play,
  Intended for great Theseus' nuptial day.
  The shallowest thick-skin of that barren sort,°   *dull company*
  Who Pyramus presented, in their sport
  Forsook his scene, and enter'd in a brake.
  When I did him at this advantage take,
  An ass's nowl° I fixèd on his head: *head*
  Anon his Thisbe must be answerèd,
  And forth my mimic° comes. When they him spy,   *comic actor*
  As wild geese that the creeping fowler eye,
  Or russet-pated choughs,° many in sort,   *grey-headed jackdaws*
  Rising and cawing at the gun's report,
  Sever themselves,° and madly sweep the sky;   *scatter*
  So, at his sight, away his fellows fly;
  And, at our stamp, here o'er and o'er one falls;
  He murder cries, and help from Athens calls.
  Their sense thus weak, lost with their fears thus strong,
  Made senseless things begin to do them wrong,
  For briers and thorns at their apparel snatch;
  Some, sleeves,—some, hats,—from yielders all things catch.
  I led them on in this distracted fear,
  And left sweet Pyramus translated° there.   *transformed*
  When in that moment (so it came to pass,)
  Titania wak'd, and straightway lov'd an ass.
OBERON. This falls out better than I could devise.
  But hast thou yet latch'd° the Athenian's eyes   *captured*
  With the love-juice, as I did bid thee do?
PUCK. I took him sleeping, (that is finish'd too,)
  And the Athenian woman by his side;
  That, when he wak'd, of force° she must be ey'd.   *necessity*

Enter DEMETRIUS *and* HERMIA.

OBERON. Stand close: this is the same Athenian.
PUCK. This is the woman; but not this the man.
DEMETRIUS. O, why rebuke you him that loves you so?
  Lay breath so bitter on your bitter foe.
HERMIA. Now I but chide; but I should use thee worse,
  For thou, I fear, hast given me cause to curse.
  If thou hast slain Lysander in his sleep,
  Being o'er shoes in° blood, plunge in the deep,   *waded in*
  And kill me too.
  The sun was not so true unto the day,

As he to me: would he have stol'n away
From sleeping Hermia? I'll believe as soon,
This whole earth may be bor'd; and that the moon
May through the centre creep, and so displease
Her brother's noon-tide with th' Antipodes.
It cannot be but thou hast murder'd him;
So should a murderer look,—so dead°, so grim.   deadly
DEMETRIUS. So should the murder'd look; and so should I,
Pierc'd through the heart with your stern cruelty:
Yet you, the murderer, look as bright, as clear,
As yonder Venus[31] in her glimmering sphere.
HERMIA. What's this to my Lysander? where is he?
Ah, good Demetrius, wilt thou give him me?
DEMETRIUS. I had rather give his carcase to my hounds.
HERMIA. Out, dog! out, cur! thou driv'st me past the bounds
Of maiden's patience. Hast thou slain him, then?
Henceforth be never number'd among men!
O, once° tell true, tell true, e'en for my sake!   once for all
Durst thou have look'd upon him being awake,
And hast thou kill'd him sleeping? O brave touch°!   deed
Could not a worm,° an adder, do so much?   snake
An adder did it; for with doubler° tongue   more deceitful
Than thine, thou serpent, never adder stung.
DEMETRIUS. You spend your passion on a mispris'd mood°:   mistaken anger
I am not guilty of Lysander's blood;
Nor is he dead, for aught that I can tell.
HERMIA. I pray thee, tell me, then, that he is well.
DEMETRIUS. An if I could, what should I get therefore?
HERMIA. A privilege, never to see me more:—
And from thy hated presence part I so:
See me no more, whether he be dead or no.   [Exit.]
DEMETRIUS. There is no following her in this fierce vein:
Here therefore, for a while I will remain.
So sorrow's heaviness doth heavier grow
For debt that bankrupt sleep doth sorrow owe;
Which now in some slight measure it will pay,
If for his tender° here I make some stay.   [Lies down and   offer
sleeps.]
OBERON. What hast thou done? thou hast mistaken quite,
And laid the love-juice on some true-love's sight:
Of thy misprison° must perforce ensue   mistake
Some true-love turn'd, and not a false turn'd true.
PUCK. Then fate o'er-rules; that, one man holding troth,
A million fail, confounding oath on oath.
OBERON. About the wood go swifter than the wind,
And Helena of Athens look thou find:
All fancy-sick° she is, and pale of cheer°   love-sick/face

---

[31] Venus, the evening star, is also the goddess of love.

With sighs of love, that cost the fresh blood dear:[32]
By some illusion see thou bring her here:
I'll charm his eyes against° she do appear,　　　　　　　　　*in expectation of when*
PUCK. I go, I go; look how I go,—
　　Swifter than arrow from the Tartar's[33] bow.　　　　[*Exit.*]
OBERON. Flower of this purple die,
　　　Hit with Cupid's archery,
　　[*Squeezes the flower on DEMETRIUS's eyelids.*]
　　　　Sink in apple° of his eye!　　　　　　　　　　　　　*pupil*
　　　　When his love he doth espy,
　　　　Let her shine as gloriously
　　　　As the Venus of the sky.—
　　　　When thou wak'st, if she be by,
　　　　Beg of her for remedy.

Re-enter PUCK.

PUCK. Captain of our fairy band,
　　　Helena is here at hand;
　　　And the youth, mistook by me,
　　　Pleading for a lover's fee.°　　　　　　　　　　　　*reward*
　　　Shall we their fond pageant° see?　　　　　　　　　*foolish spectacle*
　　　Lord, what fools these mortals be!
OBERON. Stand aside: the noise they make
　　　Will cause Demetrius to awake.
PUCK. Then will two at once woo one,—
　　　That must needs be sport alone°;　　　　　　　　　*unique*
　　　And those things do best please me,
　　　That befall preposterously.

Enter LYSANDER *and* HELENA.

LYSANDER. Why should you think that I should woo in scorn?
　　Scorn and derision never come in tears:
　　Look, when I vow, I weep, and vows so born,
　　　In their nativity all truth appears.[34]
　　How can these things in me seem scorn to you,
　　Bearing the badge of faith,° to prove them true?　　*i.e., his tears*
HELENA. You do advance your cunning more and more.
　　When truth kills truth, O devilish-holy fray!
　　These vows are Hermia's: will you give her o'er?
　　Weigh oath with oath, and you will nothing weigh:
　　Your vows to her and me, put in two scales,
　　Will even weigh; and both as light as tales.
LYSANDER. I had no judgment when to her I swore.
HELENA. Nor none, in my mind, now you give her o'er.

---

[32] An allusion to the popular belief that a sigh causes the loss of a drop of blood.
[33] The Tartars were savage tribesmen from central Asia.
[34] That is, vows born in weeping are truthful ones.

LYSANDER. Demetrius loves her, and he loves not you.

DEMETRIUS [*Awaking*]. O Helen, goddess, nymph, perfect, divine!

To what, my love, shall I compare thine eyne?
Crystal is muddy. O, how ripe in show
Thy lips, those kissing cherries, tempting grow!
That pure congealèd white, high Taurus[35] snow,
Fann'd with the eastern wind, turns to a crow
When thou hold'st up thy hand: O, let me kiss
This princess of pure white, this seal of bliss!

HELENA. O spite! O hell! I see you all are bent
To set against me, for your merriment:
If you were civil, and knew courtesy,
You would not do me thus much injury.
Can you not hate me, as I know you do,
But you must join in souls[36] to mock me too?
If you were men, as men you are in show,
You would not use a gentle lady so;
To vow, and swear, and superpraise my parts,°   qualities
When I am sure you hate me with your hearts.
You both are rivals, and love Hermia;
And now both rivals, to mock Helena:
A trim° exploit, a manly enterprise,   fine
To conjure tears up in a poor maid's eyes
With your derision! none of noble sort
Would so offend a virgin, and extort
A poor soul's patience, all to make you sport.

LYSANDER. You are unkind, Demetrius; be not so;
For you love Hermia;—this you know I know:
And here, with all good-will, with all my heart,
In Hermia's love I yield you up my part;
And yours of Helena to me bequeath,
Whom I do love, and will do to my death.

HELENA. Never did mockers waste more idle breath.

DEMETRIUS. Lysander, keep thy Hermia; I will none:[37]
If e'er I lov'd her, all that love is gone.
My heart to her but as guest-wise sojourn'd,
And now to Helen is it home return'd,
There to remain.

LYSANDER.   Helen, it is not so.

DEMETRIUS. Disparage not the faith thou dost not know,
Lest, to thy peril, thou aby it dear.°—   pay dearly for it
Look, where thy love comes; yonder is thy dear.

Re-enter HERMIA.

HERMIA. Dark night, that from the eye his function takes,

---

[35] A high mountain range in Turkey.
[36] Heart and soul, with your whole being.
[37] I want no part of her.

The ear more quick of apprehension makes;
Wherein it doth impair the seeing sense,
It pays the hearing double recompense.—
Thou art not by mine eye, Lysander, found;
Mine ear, I thank it, brought me to thy sound.
But why unkindly didst thou leave me so?

LYSANDER. Why should he stay, whom love doth press to go?

HERMIA. What love could press Lysander from my side?

LYSANDER. Lysander's love, that would not let him bide,—
Fair Helena; who more engilds the night
Than all yon fiery oes and eyes° of light.   *stars*
Why seek'st thou me? could not this make thee know,
The hate I bear thee made me leave thee so?

HERMIA. You speak not as you think: it cannot be.

HELENA. Lo, she is one of this confederacy!
Now I perceive they have conjoin'd, all three,
To fashion this false sport in spite° of me.   *contempt*
Injurious° Hermia! most ungrateful maid!   *insulting*
Have you conspir'd, have you with these contriv'd
To bait me with this foul derision?
Is all the counsel that we two have shar'd,
The sisters' vows, the hours that we have spent,
When we have chid the hasty-footed time
For parting us,—O! is all forgot?
All school-days' friendship, childhood innocence?
We, Hermia, like two artificial° gods,   *highly skilled in art*
Have with our needls° created both one flower,   *needles*
Both on one sampler, sitting on one cushion,
Both warbling of one song, both in one key;
As if our hands, our sides, voices, and minds,
Had been incorporate. So we grew together,
Like to a double cherry, seeming parted;
But yet a union in partition,
Two lovely berries moulded on one stem;
So, with two seeming bodies, but one heart;
Two of the first, like coats in heraldry,
Due to one, and crownèd with one crest.
And will you rent° our ancient love asunder,   *rend*
To join with men in scorning your poor friend?
It is not friendly, 'tis not maidenly:
Our sex, as well as I, may chide you for it,
Though I alone do feel the injury.

HERMIA. I am amazèd at your passionate words.
I scorn you not: it seems that you scorn me.

HELENA. Have you not set Lysander, as in scorn,
To follow me, and praise my eyes and face?
And made your other love, Demetrius,
(Who even but now did spurn me with his foot,)
To call me goddess, nymph, divine, and rare,
Precious, celestial? Wherefore speaks he this
To her he hates? and wherefore doth Lysander

Deny your love, so rich within his soul,
And tender me, forsooth, affection,
But by your setting on, by your consent?
What though I be not so in grace as you,
So hung upon with love, so fortunate;
But miserable most to love unlov'd?
This you should pity, rather than despise.

HERMIA. I understand not what you mean by this.

HELENA. Ay, do, persèver, counterfeit sad° looks,   *serious*
Make mouths upon me when I turn my back;
Wink each at other; hold° the sweet jest up: *keep*
This sport, well carried, shall be chronicled.
If you have any pity, grace, or manners,
You would not make me such an argument.°   *subject of merriment*
But, fare ye well: 'tis partly mine own fault;
Which death, or absence, soon shall remedy.

LYSANDER. Stay, gentle Helena; hear my excuse:
My love, my life, my soul, fair Helena!

HELENA. O excellent!

HERMIA.   Sweet, do not scorn her so.

DEMETRIUS. If she cannot entreat, I can compel.

LYSANDER. Thou canst compel no more than she entreat:
Thy threats have no more strength than her weak
   prayers.—
Helen, I love thee; by my life, I do:
I swear by that which I will lose for thee,
To prove him false that says I love thee not.

DEMETRIUS. I say I love thee more than he can do.

LYSANDER. If thou say so, withdraw, and prove it too.

DEMETRIUS. Quick, come!

HERMIA.   Lysander, whereto tends all this?

LYSANDER. Away, you Ethiop!°   *Ethiopian*

DEMETRIUS.   No, no, Sir:—
Seem to break loose, take on, as[38] you would follow;
But yet come not: you are a tame man, go!

LYSANDER [to HERMIA]. Hang off, thou cat, thou burr! vile thing,
   let loose,
Or I will shake thee from me like a serpent!

HERMIA. Why are you grown so rude? what change is this,
Sweet love?

LYSANDER.   Thy love? out, tawny Tartar, out!
Out, loathèd medìcine! O hated potion, hence!

HERMIA. Do you not jest?

HELENA.   Yes, 'sooth; and so do you.

LYSANDER. Demetrius, I will keep my word with thee.

DEMETRIUS. I would I had your bond, for I perceive
A weak bond holds you: I'll not trust your word.

LYSANDER. What, should I hurt her, strike her, kill her dead?
Although I hate her, I'll not harm her so.

---

[38] Make a commotion as if.

HERMIA. What, can you do me greater harm than hate?
    Hate me! wherefore? O me! what news, my love?
    Am not I Hermia? Are not you Lysander?
    I am as fair now, as I was erewhile.
    Since night, you lov'd me; yet, since night you left me:
    Why, then you left me (O, the gods forbid!)
    In earnest, shall I say?
LYSANDER.   Ay, by my life;
    And never did desire to see thee more.
    Therefore be out of hope, of question, of doubt:
    Be certain, nothing truer; 'tis no jest,
    That I do hate thee, and love Helena.
HERMIA. O me!—you juggler!° you canker-blossom!°   *trickster/blighted blossom*
    You thief of love! what, have you come by night,
    And stol'n my love's heart from him?
HELENA.   Fine, i' faith!
    Have you no modesty, no maiden shame,
    No touch of bashfulness? What, will you tear
    Impatient answers from my gentle tongue?
    Fie, fie! you counterfeit,° you puppet you!   *cheat*
HERMIA. Puppet! why, so: ay, that way goes the game.
    Now I perceive that she hath made compare
    Between our statures; she hath urg'd her height;
    And with her personage,° her tall personage,   *figure*
    Her height, forsooth, she hath prevail'd with him.—
    And are you grown so high in his esteem,
    Because I am so dwarfish and so low?
    How low am I, thou painted maypole? speak;
    How low am I? I am not yet so low,
    But that my nails can reach unto thine eyes.
HELENA. I pray you, though you mock me, gentlemen,
    Let her not hurt me. I was never curst;°   *fierce*
    I have no gift at all in shrewishness;
    I am a right° maid for my cowardice: *real*
    Let her not strike me. You perhaps may think,
    Because she is something° lower than myself,   *somewhat*
    That I can match her.
HERMIA.   Lower! hark, again.
HELENA. Good Hermia, do not be so bitter with me.
    I evermore did love you, Hermia,
    Did ever keep your counsels, never wrong'd you;
    Save that, in love unto Demetrius,
    I told him of your stealth° unto this wood.   *stealing away*
    He follow'd you, for love, I follow'd him;
    But he hath chid me hence, and threaten'd me
    To strike me, spurn me, nay, to kill me too:
    And now, so you will let me quiet go,
    To Athens will I bear my folly back,
    And follow you no farther: let me go:
    You see how simple and how fond° I am.   *tender*
HERMIA. Why, get you gone: who is't that hinders you?

HELENA. A foolish heart, that I leave here behind.
HERMIA. What, with Lysander?
HELENA.   With Demetrius.
LYSANDER. Be not afraid; she shall not harm thee, Helena.
DEMETRIUS. No, Sir, she shall not, though you take her part.
HELENA. O, when she is angry, she is keen and shrewd!
   She was a vixen when she went to school;
   And though she be but little, she is fierce.
HERMIA. Little again! nothing but low and little!—
   Why will you suffer her to flout me thus?
   Let me come to her.
LYSANDER.   Get you gone, you dwarf!
   You minimus,° of hindering knot-grass[39] made;   *insignificant creature*
   You bead, you acorn!
DEMETRIUS.   You are too officious
   In her behalf that scorns your services.
   Let her alone: speak not of Helena;
   Take not her part; for, if thou dost intend
   Never so little show of love to her,
   Thou shalt aby° it,   *pay for*
LYSANDER.   Now she holds me not;
   Now follow, if thou dar'st, to try whose right,—
   Or thine or mine,—is most in Helena.
DEMETRIUS. Follow? nay, I'll go with thee, cheek by jole.°   *jowl*
   [*Exeunt* LYSANDER *and* DEMETRIUS.]
HERMIA. You, mistress, all this coil° is 'long of° you: *turmoil/because*
   Nay, go not back.
HELENA.   I will not trust you, I,
   Nor longer stay in your curst company.
   Your hands, than mine, are quicker for a fray;
   My legs are longer though, to run away.   [*Exit.*]
HERMIA. I am amaz'd, and know not what to say.   [*Exit.*]
OBERON. This is thy negligence: still thou mistak'st,
   Or else commit'st thy knaveries wilfully.
PUCK. Believe me, king of shadows, I mistook.
   Did not you tell me I should know the man
   By the Athenian garments he had on?
   And so far blameless proves my enterprise,
   That I have 'nointed an Athenian's eyes;
   And so far am I glad it so did sort,°   *turn out*
   As this their jangling I esteem a sport.
OBERON. Thou seest, these lovers seek a place to fight:
   Hie° therefore, Robin, overcast the night;   *hasten*
   The starry welkin° cover thou anon   *sky*
   With drooping fog, as black as Acheron;[40]
   And lead these testy rivals so astray,
   As° one come not within another's way.   *that*

[39] A tough weed.
[40] Acheron is one of the four rivers of Hades, the underworld.

Like to Lysander sometime frame thy tongue,
Then stir Demetrius up with bitter wrong;° *insult*
And sometime rail thou like Demetrius;
And from each other look thou lead them thus,
Till o'er their brows death-counterfeiting sleep
With leaden legs and batty° wings doth creep: *bat-like*
Then crush this herb into Lysander's eye;
Whose liquor hath this virtuous° property, *powerful*
To take from thence all error with his might,
And make his eye-balls roll with wonted sight.
When they next wake, all this derision
Shall seem a dream, and fruitless vision;
And back to Athens shall the lovers wend,
With league, whose date° till death shall never end. *duration*
Whiles I in this affair do thee employ,
I'll to my queen, and beg her Indian boy;
And then I will her charmèd eye release
From monster's view, and all things shall be peace.
PUCK. My fairy lord, this must be done with haste,
For night's swift dragons[41] cut the clouds full fast,
And yonder shines Aurora's harbinger;[42]
At whose approach, ghosts, wandering here and there,
Troop home to church-yards: damnèd spirits all,
That in cross-ways and floods have burial,
Already to their wormy beds are gone;
For fear lest day should look their shames upon,
They wilfully themselves exile from light,
And must for aye consort with black-brow'd night.
OBERON. But we are spirits of another sort:
I with the morning's love have oft made sport;
And, like a forester, the groves may tread,
Even till the eastern gate, all fiery-red,
Opening on Neptune[43] with fair blessèd beams,
Turns into yellow gold his salt green streams.
But, notwithstanding, haste; make no delay:
We may effect this business yet ere day. [*Exit* OBERON.]
PUCK. Up and down, up and down,
I will lead them up and down:
I am fear'd in field and town:
Goblin, lead them up and down.
Here comes one.

Re-enter LYSANDER.

LYSANDER. Where art thou, proud Demetrius? speak thou now.
PUCK. Here, villain! drawn° and ready. Where art thou? *with sword drawn*
LYSANDER. I will be with thee straight.

[41] The chariot of Cynthia, the Roman goddess of moon, was said to be pulled across the sky by dragons.
[42] Aurora is the Roman goddess of the dawn; her harbinger is Venus, the morning star.
[43] The Roman god of waters.

PUCK.   Follow me, then,
   To plainer° ground. [*Exit* LYSANDER *as following the voice.*]   *more level or open*

Re-enter DEMETRIUS.

DEMETRIUS.   Lysander! speak again.
   Thou runaway, thou coward, art thou fled?
   Speak! In some bush? Where dost thou hide thy head?
PUCK. Thou coward! art thou bragging to the stars,
   Telling the bushes that thou look'st for wars,
   And wilt not come? Come, recreant; come, thou child;
   I'll whip thee with a rod: he is defil'd
   That draws a sword on thee.
DEMETRIUS.   Yea, art thou there?
PUCK. Follow my voice: we'll try no manhood here.
   [*Exeunt.*]

Re-enter LYSANDER.

LYSANDER. He goes before me, and still dares me on:
   When I come where he calls, then he is gone.
   The villain is much lighter-heel'd than I:
   I follow'd fast, but faster he did fly;
   That fallen am I in dark uneven way,
   And here will rest me. [*Lies down.*] Come, thou gentle day!
   For if but once thou show me thy grey light,
   I'll find Demetrius, and revenge this spite.   [*Sleeps.*]

Re-enter PUCK *and* DEMETRIUS.

PUCK. Ho! ho! ho! Coward, why com'st thou not?
DEMETRIUS. Abide° me, if thou dar'st; for well I wot°   *face/know*
   Thou runn'st before me, shifting every place,
   And dar'st not stand, nor look me in the face.
   Where art thou now?
PUCK.   Come hither: I am here.
DEMETRIUS. Nay, then, thou mock'st me. Thou shalt 'by this
      dear,
   If ever I thy face by day-light see
   Now, go thy way. Faintness constraineth me
   To measure out my length on this cold bed.
   By day's approach look to be visited.   [*Lies down and
   sleeps.*]

Re-enter HELENA.

HELENA. O weary night! O long and tedious night!
      Abate° thy hours: shine, comforts, from the east,   *shorten*
   That I may back to Athens, by day-light,
      From these that my poor company detest:
   And sleep, that sometimes shuts up sorrow's eye,

Steal me a while from mine own company.
[*Lies down and sleeps.*]
PUCK. Yet but three? Come one more;
    Two of both kinds make up four.
    Here she comes, curst° and sad:—   *short tempered*
    Cupid is a knavish lad,
    Thus to make poor females mad.

Re-enter HERMIA.

HERMIA. Never so weary, never so in woe;
    Bedabbled with the dew, and torn with briers;
    I can no farther crawl, no farther go;
    My legs can keep no pace with my desires.
    Here will I rest me till the break of day.
    Heavens shield Lysander, if they mean a fray!
[*Lies down and sleeps.*]
PUCK. On the ground sleep sound:
    I'll apply to your eye,
    Gentle lover, remedy.
[*Squeezing the herb on* LYSANDER's *eyelids.*]
    When thou wak'st, thou tak'st
    True delight in the sight
    Of thy former lady's eye:
    And the country proverb known,
    That every man should take his own,
    In your waking shall be shown:
        Jack shall have Jill;
        Naught shall go ill;
    The man shall have his mare again,
    And all shall be well.   [*Exit.*]

ACT IV

SCENE I
The Wood.

[*Enter* TITANIA *and* BOTTOM; LYSANDER, DEMETRIUS, HERMIA, *and* HELENA, *still lying asleep.* PEAS-BLOSSOM, COBWEB, MOTH, MUSTARD-SEED, *and other* FAIRIES *attending;* OBERON *behind unseen.*]

TITANIA. Come, sit thee down upon this flowery bed,
    While I thy amiable° cheeks do coy,°   *lovely/caress*
    And stick musk-roses in thy sleek smooth head,
    And kiss thy fair large ears, my gentle joy.
BOTTOM. Where's Peas-blossom?
PEAS-BLOSSOM. Ready.
BOTTOM. Scratch my head, Peas-blossom.—Where's monsieur
    Cobweb?

COBWEB. Ready.

BOTTOM. Monsieur Cobweb, good monsieur, get your weapons in your hand, and kill me a red-hipped humble-bee on
the top of a thistle; and, good monsieur, bring me the
honey-bag. Do not fret yourself too much in the action,
monsieur; and, good monsieur, have a care the honey-bag
break not; I would be loath to have you overflown with a
honey-bag, signior.—Where's monsieur Mustard-seed?

MUSTARD-SEED. Ready.

BOTTOM. Give me your neif,° monsieur Mustard-seed. Pray   *fist*
you, leave your courtesy,° good monsieur.   *omit formality*

MUSTARD-SEED. What's your will?

BOTTOM. Nothing, good monsieur, but to help cavalery° Cob-   *cavalier*
web to scratch. I must to the barber's, monsieur; for methinks I am marvellous hairy about the face; and I am such
a tender ass, if my hair do but tickle me, I must scratch.

TITANIA. What, wilt thou hear some music, my sweet love?

BOTTOM. I have a reasonable good ear in music: let us have
the tongs and the bones.°   *crude musical instruments*

TITANIA. Or say, sweet love, what thou desir'st to eat:

BOTTOM. Truly, a peck of provender: I could munch your
good dry oats. Methinks I have a great desire to a bottle°   *bundle*
of hay: good hay, sweet hay, hath no fellow.

TITANIA. I have a venturous fairy that shall seek
The squirrel's hoard, and fetch thee new nuts.

BOTTOM. I had rather have a handful or two of dried peas.
But, I pray you, let none of your people stir me: I have an
exposition of sleep come upon me.

TITANIA. Sleep thou, and I will wind thee in my arms.—
Fairies, be gone, and be all ways° away.— [*Exeunt* FAIRIES.]   *in every direction*
So doth the woodbine the sweet honeysuckle
Gently entwist: the female ivy so
Enrings the barky fingers of the elm.
O, how I love thee, how I dote on thee!   [*They sleep.*]

Enter PUCK.

OBERON [*Advancing*]. Welcome, good Robin. Seest thou this
sweet sight?
Her dotage now I do begin to pity:
For, meeting her of late behind the wood,
Seeking sweet favours° for this hateful fool,   *gifts of flowers*
I did upbraid her, and fall out with her;
For she his hairy temples then had rounded
With coronet of fresh and fragrant flowers;
And that same dew, which sometime on the buds
Was wont to swell, like round and orient° pearls,   *lustrous*
Stood now within the pretty flow'rets' eyes,
Like tears, that did their own disgrace bewail.
When I had at my pleasure taunted her,

And she in mild terms begg'd my patience,
I then did ask of her her changeling child;
Which straight she gave me; and her fairies sent
To bear him to my bower in fairy land.
And now I have the boy, I will undo
This hateful imperfection of her eyes:
And, gentle Puck, take this transformèd scalp
From off the head of this Athenian swain;
That he, awaking when the other° do,   *others*
May all to Athens back again repair,°   *return*
And think no more of this night's accidents,
But as the fierce vexation of a dream.
But first I will release the fairy queen.
[*Touching her eyes with a herb.*]
    Be, as thou wast wont to be;
    See, as thou wast wont to see:
    Dian's bud o'er Cupid's flower°   *the pansy*
    Hath such force and blessèd power.
Now, my Titania; wake you, my sweet queen.
TITANIA. My Oberon! what visions have I seen!
Methought I was enamour'd of an ass.
OBERON. There lies your love.
TITANIA.   How came these things to pass?
O, how mine eyes do loathe this visage now!
OBERON. Silence, awhile.—Robin, take off this head.—
Titania, music call; and strike more dead
Than common sleep, of all these five the sense.
TITANIA. Music, ho! music! such as charmeth sleep.
[*Still music.*]
PUCK. Now, when thou wak'st, with thine own fool's eyes peep.
OBERON. Sound, music! Come, my queen, take hands with
    me,
And rock the ground whereon these sleepers be.
Now thou and I are new in amity,
And will to-morrow midnight solemnly
Dance in Duke Theseus' house triumphantly,
And bless it to all fair prosperity.
There shall the pairs of faithful lovers be
Wedded, with Theseus, all in jollity.
PUCK.   Fairy king, attend, and mark:
    I do hear the morning lark.
OBERON. Then, my queen, in silence sad,
    Trip we after the night's shade:
    We the globe can compass soon,
    Swifter than the wandering moon.
TITANIA. Come, my lord; and in our flight,
    Tell me how it came this night,
    That I sleeping here was found
    With these mortals on the ground.
    [*Exeunt. Horns sound within.*]

Enter THESEUS, HIPPOLYTA, EGEUS, *and train.*

THESEUS. Go, one of you, find out the forester;
    For now our observation° is perform'd;   *the observance of May Day rites*
    And since we have the vaward° of the day,   *early part*
    My love shall hear the music of my hounds;
    Uncouple° in the western valley; let them go: *unleash*
    Despatch, I say, and find the forester.—
    [*Exit an* Attendant.]
    We will, fair queen, up to mountain's top,
    And mark the musical confusion
    Of hounds and echo in conjunction.
HIPPOLYTA. I was with Hercules and Cadmus once,
    When in a wood of Crete they bay'd° the bear   *brought to bay*
    With hounds of Sparta:⁴⁴ never did I hear
    Such gallant chiding°; for, besides the groves,   *noise*
    The skies, the fountains, every region near
    Seem'd all one mutual cry: I never heard
    So musical a discord, such sweet thunder.
THESEUS. My hounds are bred out of the Spartan kind,
    So flew'd,° so sanded°; and their heads are hung   *with large chaps/sandy-colored*
    With ears that sweep away the morning dew;
    Crook-knee'd, and dew-lapp'd like Thessalian bulls;
    Slow in pursuit, but match'd in mouth like bells,
    Each under each. A cry more tuneable°   *melodious*
    Was never holla'd to, nor cheer'd with horn,
    In Crete, in Sparta, nor in Thessaly:
    Judge, when you hear.—But, soft!° what nymphs are these?   *stop*
EGEUS. My lord, this is my daughter here asleep;
    And this, Lysander; this Demetrius is;
    This Helena, old Nedar's Helena:
    I wonder of their being here together.
THESEUS. No doubt they rose up early to observe
    The rite of May; and, hearing our intent,
    Came here in grace of° our solemnity.—   *to grace*
    But speak, Egeus; is not this the day
    That Hermia should give answer of her choice?
EGEUS. It is, my lord.
THESEUS. Go, bid the huntsmen wake them with their horns.
    [*Exit an* Attendant. *Horns, and shout within.* LYSANDER, DE-
    METRIUS, HERMIA, *and* HELENA, *awake and start up.*]
    Good-morrow, friends. Saint Valentine° is past: *Saint Valentine's Day*
    Begin these wood-birds but to couple now?
LYSANDER. Pardon, my lord.
    [*He and the rest kneel.*]
THESEUS.   I pray you all, stand up.
    I know you two are rival enemies:
    How comes this gentle concord in the world,

---

⁴⁴ Hercules and Cadmus (though unrelated) were figures of classical antiquity; Crete and Sparta were
   both famous for their hounds.

That hatred is so far from jealousy,°   *suspicion, mistrust*
To sleep by hate, and fear no enmity?
LYSANDER. My lord, I shall reply amazedly,
  Half sleep, half waking: but as yet, I swear,
  I cannot truly say how I came here;
  But, as I think, (for truly would I speak,—
  And now I do bethink me, so it is)
  I came with Hermia hither: our intent
  Was to be gone from Athens, where we might,
  Without° the peril of the Athenian law—   *beyond*
EGEUS. Enough, enough, my lord; you have enough
  I beg the law, the law, upon his head.—
  They would have stol'n away; they would, Demetrius,
  Thereby to have defeated° you and me,   *cheated*
  You of your wife, and me of my consent,—
  Of my consent that she should be your wife.
DEMETRIUS. My lord, fair Helen told me of their stealth,
  Of this their purpose hither to this wood;
  And I in fury hither follow'd them,
  Fair Helena in fancy following me.
  But, my good lord, I wot° not by what power,   *know*
  (But by some power it is,) my love to Hermia,
  Melted as the snow, seems to me now
  As the remembrance of an idle gawd,°   *worthless toy*
  Which in my childhood I did dote upon;
  And all the faith, the virtue of my heart,
  The object, and the pleasure of mine eye,
  Is only Helena. To her, my lord,
  Was I betroth'd ere I saw Hermia:
  But, like in sickness, did I loathe this food;
  But, as in health, come to my natural taste,
  Now do I wish it, love it, long for it.
  And will for evermore be true to it.
THESEUS. Fair lovers, you are fortunately met:
  Of this discourse we more will hear anon.—
  Egeus, I will overbear your will;
  For in the temple, by and by, with us,
  These couples shall eternally be knit.
  And, for the morning now is something worn,
  Our purpos'd hunting shall be set aside.
  Away, with us, to Athens: three and three,
  We'll hold a feast in great solemnity.°—   *celebration*
  Come, Hippolyta.
  [*Exeunt* THESEUS, HIPPOLYTA, EGEUS, *and train.*]
DEMETRIUS. These things seem small and undistinguishable,
  Like far-off mountains turnèd into clouds.
HERMIA. Methinks I see these things with parted eye,°   *eyes out of focus*
  When every thing seems double.
HELENA.   So methinks:
  And I have found Demetrius, like a jewel,
  Mine own, and not mine own.

DEMETRIUS.   Are you sure
  That we are awake? It seems to me
  That yet we sleep, we dream.—Do not you think
  The duke was here, and bid us follow him?
HERMIA. Yea; and my father.
HELENA.   And Hippolyta.
LYSANDER. And he did bid us follow to the temple.
DEMETRIUS. Why then, we are awake: let's follow him;
  And by the way let us recount our dreams.
  [*Exeunt* LYSANDER, DEMETRIUS, HERMIA, *and* HELENA.]
BOTTOM [*Awaking*]. When my cue comes, call me, and I will
  answer: —my next is, "Most fair Pyramus."—Hey, ho!—
  Peter Quince! Flute, the bellows-mender! Snout, the
  tinker! Starveling!—God's my life! stolen hence, and left
  me asleep! I have had a most rare vision. I have had a
  dream,—past the wit of man to say what dream it was: man
  is but an ass, if he go about to expound this dream. Methought I was—there is no man can tell what. Methought
  I was, and methought I had,—but man is but a patched°   *motley*
  fool, if he will offer to say what methought I had. The eye
  of man hath not heard, the ear of man hath not seen,
  man's hand is not able to taste, his tongue to conceive, nor
  his heart to report, what my dream was. I will get Peter
  Quince to write a ballad of this dream: it shall be called
  Bottom's Dream, because it hath no bottom; and, I will
  sing it in the latter end of a play, before the duke: perad-
  venture, to make it the more gracious,° I shall sing it at her   *appealing*
  death.
  [*Exit.*]

SCENE II
ATHENS. *A Room in* QUINCE'S *House.*

Enter QUINCE, FLUTE, SNOUT, *and* STARVELING.

QUINCE. Have you sent to Bottom's house? is he come home
  yet?
STARVELING. He cannot be heard of. Out of doubt, he is
  transported.°   *carried away*
FLUTE. If he come not, then the play is marred: it goes not
  forward, doth it?
QUINCE. It is not possible: you have not a man in all Athens
  able to discharge° Pyramus but he.   *act*
FLUTE. No, he hath simply the best wit° of any handycraft   *mind*
  man in Athens.
QUINCE. Yea, and the best person° too; and he is a very   *appearance*
  paramour for a sweet voice.
FLUTE. You must say, paragon: a paramour is, God bless us! a
  thing of naught.°   *something wicked*

Enter SNUG.

SNUG. Masters, the duke is coming from the temple, and
  there is two or three lords and ladies more married: if our
  sport had gone forward, we had all been made men.[45]
FLUTE. O sweet bully Bottom! Thus hath he lost sixpence
  a-day during his life; he could not have 'scaped sixpence
  a-day: an° the duke had not given him sixpence a-day for   *if*
  playing Pyramus, I'll be hanged; he would have deserved it:
  sixpence a-day in Pyramus, or nothing.

Enter BOTTOM.

BOTTOM. Where are these lads? where are these hearts?°   *good fellows*
QUINCE. Bottom!—O most courageous day! O most happy
  hour!
BOTTOM. Masters, I am to discourse wonders: but ask me not
  what; for if I tell you, I am no true Athenian. I will tell you
  every thing, right as it fell out.
QUINCE. Let us hear, sweet Bottom.
BOTTOM. Not a word of me. All that I will tell you is, that the
  duke hath dined. Get your apparel together, good strings
  to your beards, new ribbons to your pumps°; meet pres-   *shoes*
  ently at the palace; every man look o'er his part; for the
  short and the long is, our play is preferred.° In any case,   *recommended*
  let Thisby have clean linen; and let not him that plays the
  lion pare his nails, for they shall hang out for the lion's
  claws. And, most dear actors, eat no onions nor garlick, for
  we are to utter sweet breath; and I do not doubt but to hear
  them say, it is a sweet comedy. No more words: away! go;
  away!
[*Exeunt.*]

ACT V

SCENE I
ATHENS. *An Apartment in the Palace of* THESEUS.

Enter THESEUS, HIPPOLYTA, PHILOSTRATE, Lords, *and* Attendants.

HIPPOLYTA. 'Tis strange, my Theseus, that these lovers speak
  of.
THESEUS. More strange than true: I never may believe
  These antique° fables, nor these fairy toys.°   *fantastic / idle tales*
  Lovers and madmen have such seething brains,
  Such shaping fantasies, that apprehend
  More than cool reason ever comprehends.
  The lunatic, the lover, and the poet,

[45] Our fortunes would have been made.

Are of imagination all compact:°—   *composed*
One sees more devils than vast hell can hold,—
That is, the madman, the lover, all as frantic,
Sees Helen's beauty[46] in a brow of Egypt.°   *gypsy's face*
The poet's eye, in a fine frenzy rolling,
Doth glance from heaven to earth, from earth to heaven;
And, as imagination bodies forth
The forms of things unknown, the poet's pen
Turns them to shapes, and gives to airy nothing
A local habitation and a name.
Such tricks hath strong imagination,
That, if it would but apprehend some joy,
It comprehends some bringer of that joy,
Or in the night, imagining some fear,
How easy is a bush suppos'd a bear!
HIPPOLYTA. But all the story of the night told over,
And all their minds transfigur'd so together,
More witnesseth than fancy's images,
And grows to something of great constancy;°   *consistency*
But, howsoever, strange and admirable.°   *to be wondered at*
THESEUS. Here come the lovers, full of joy and mirth.

Enter LYSANDER, DEMETRIUS, HERMIA, *and* HELENA.

Joy, gentle friends! joy, and fresh days of love,
Accompany your hearts!
LYSANDER.   More than to us
Wait in your royal walks, your board, your bed!
THESEUS. Come now; what masks,[47] what dances shall we have,
To wear away this long age of three hours,
Between our after-supper,° and bed-time?   *dessert*
Where is our usual manager of mirth?
What revels are in hand? Is there no play,
To ease the anguish of a torturing hour?
Call Philostrate.
PHILOSTRATE.   Here, mighty Theseus.
THESEUS. Say, what abridgment° have you for this evening?   *pastime*
What mask? what music? How shall we beguile
The lazy time, if not with some delight?
PHILOSTRATE. There is a brief° how many sports are ripe: *summary*
Make choice of which your highness will see first.
                                         [*Giving a paper.*]
THESEUS [*Reads*]. "The battle with the Centaurs,[48] to be sung
By an Athenian eunuch to the harp."—
We'll none of that: that have I told my love,
In glory of my kinsman Hercules.—
[*Reads.*] "The riot of the tipsy Bacchanals,

---

[46] The allusion is to Helen of Troy, famous for her beauty.
[47] Entertainments, or masques, featuring masked dancers.
[48] A race of men, half-human and half-horse.

Tearing the Thracian singer[49] in their rage."—

That is an old device;° and it was play'd   *entertainment*

When I from Thebes came last a conqueror.—

[*Reads.*] "The thrice three Muses mourning for the death

    Of learning, late deceas'd in beggary."—

That is some satire, keen and critical,

Not sorting° with a nuptial ceremony.—   *appropriate to*

[*Reads.*] "A tedious brief scene of young Pyramus,

    And his love Thisbe; very tragical mirth."—

Merry and tragical! Tedious and brief!

That is, hot ice and wondrous strange snow.

How shall we find the concord of this discord?

PHILOSTRATE. A play there is, my lord, some ten words long,

  Which is as brief as I have known a play;

  But by ten words, my lord, it is too long,

  Which makes it tedious; for in all the play

  There is not one word apt, one player fitted:

  And tragical, my noble lord, it is;

  For Pyramus therein doth kill himself.

  Which, when I saw rehears'd, I must confess,

  Made mine eyes water; but more merry tears

  The passion of loud laughter never shed.

THESEUS. What are they that do play it?

PHILOSTRATE. Hard-handed men, that work in Athens here,

  Which never labour'd in their minds till now;

  And now have toil'd their unbreath'd° memories   *unpracticed*

  With this same play, against your nuptial.

THESEUS. And we will hear it.

PHILOSTRATE.   No, my noble lord;

  It is not for you: I have heard it over,

  And it is nothing, nothing in the world;

  Unless you can find sport in their intents,

  Extremely stretch'd and conn'd° with cruel pain,   *strained and pored over*

  To do you service.

THESEUS.   I will hear that play;

  For never any thing can be amiss,

  When simpleness and duty tender it.

  Go, bring them in:—and take your places, ladies.

  [*Exit* PHILOSTRATE.]

HIPPOLYTA. I love not to see wretchedness o'ercharg'd,°   *overburdened*

  And duty in his service perishing.

THESEUS. Why, gentle sweet, you shall see no such thing.

HIPPOLYTA. He says they can do nothing in this kind.

THESEUS. The kinder we, to give them thanks for nothing.

  Our sport shall be to take what they mistake:

  And what poor duty cannot do,

  Noble respect takes it in might, not merit.

  Where I have come, great clerks° have purposèd   *scholars*

---

[49] The allusion is to Orpheus, the son of Apollo, who played the lyre with great sweetness. According to the legend referred to here, Apollo was torn apart by followers of the god Bacchus.

To greet me with premeditated welcomes;
Where I have seen them shiver and look pale,
Make periods in the midst of sentences,
Throttle their practis'd accent in their fears,
And, in conclusion, dumbly have broke off,
Not paying me a welcome. Trust me, sweet,
Out of this silence, yet, I pick'd a welcome;
And in the modesty° of fearful° duty   *deference/timid*
I read as much, as from the rattling tongue
Of saucy and audacious eloquence.
Love, therefore, and tongue-tied simplicity,
In least speak most, to my capacity.°   *understanding*

Enter PHILOSTRATE.

PHILOSTRATE. So please your grace, the prologue is addrest.°   *ready*
THESEUS. Let him approach.   [*Flourish of trumpets.*]

Enter PROLOGUE.

PROLOGUE. "If we offend, it is with our good will.
    That you should think, we come not to offend,
But with good-will.   To show our simple skill,
    That is the true beginning of our end.
Consider, then, we come but in despite.°   *in ill-will to spite you*
    We do not come as minding to content you,
Our true intent is.   All for your delight,
    We are not here.   That you should here repent
      you,
The actors are at hand; and, by their show,
You shall know all, that you are like to know."
THESEUS. This fellow doth not stand upon points.
LYSANDER. He hath rid his prologue like a rough colt; he knows
    not the stop. A good moral, my lord: it is not enough to
    speak, but to speak true.
HIPPOLYTA. Indeed, he hath played on his prologue,
    like a child on a recorder°; a sound, but not in   *flute-like instrument*
    government.°   *under control*
THESEUS. His speech was like a tangled chain; nothing im-
    paired, but all disordered. Who is next?

Enter PYRAMUS *and* THISBE, WALL, MOONSHINE, *and* LION, *as in dumb show.*

PROLOGUE. "Gentles, perchance you wonder at this show;
    But wonder on, till truth make all things plain.
This man is Pyramus, if you would know;
    This beauteous lady Thisby is, certain.
This man, with lime and rough-cast, doth present
    Wall, that vile Wall which did these lovers sunder;
And through Wall's chink, poor souls, they are con-
    tent

To whisper; at the which let no man wonder.
This man, with lantern, dog, and bush of thorn,
   Presenteth Moonshine; for, if you will know,
By moonshine did these lovers think no scorn
   To meet at Ninus' tomb, there, there to woo.
This grisly beast, which Lion hight° by name,   *is called*
The trusty Thisby, coming first by night,
Did scare away, or rather did affright;
And, as she fled, her mantle she did fall,°   *let fall*
   Which Lion vile with bloody mouth did stain.
Anon comes Pyramus, sweet youth and tall,°   *valiant*
   And finds his trusty Thisby's mantle slain:
Whereat, with blade, with bloody blameful blade,
   He bravely broach'd° his boiling bloody breast: *stabbed*
And Thisby, tarrying in mulberry shade,
   His dagger drew, and died. For all the rest,
Let Lion, Moonshine, Wall, and lovers twain,
At large discourse, while here they do remain."
[*Exeunt* PROLOGUE, THISBE, LION, *and* MOONSHINE.]
THESEUS. I wonder, if the lion be to speak.
DEMETRIUS. No wonder, my lord:
   One lion may, when many asses do.
WALL. "In this same interlude it doth befall,
   That I, one Snout by name, present a wall;
And such a wall, as I would have you think,
That had in it a cranny'd hole or chink,
Through which the lovers, Pyramus and Thisby,
Did whisper often very secretly.
This lime, this rough-cast, and this stone, doth show
That I am that same wall; the truth is so:
And this the cranny is, right and sinister,°   *left*
Through which the fearful lovers are to whisper."
THESEUS. Would you desire lime and hair to speak better?
DEMETRIUS. It is the wittiest° partition that ever I heard   *cleverest*
   discourse, my lord.
THESEUS. Pyramus draws near the wall: silence!

Enter PYRAMUS.

PYRAMUS. "O grim-look'd night! O night with hue so black!
   O night, which ever art when day is not!
O night, O night! alack, alack, alack!
   I fear my Thisby's promise is forgot!—
And thou, O wall, O sweet, O lovely wall,
   That stand'st between her father's ground and
      mine;
Thou wall, O wall, O sweet, and lovely wall,
   Show me thy chink to blink through with mine
      eyne!
[*Wall holds up his fingers.*]
   Thanks, courteous wall: Jove shield thee well for
      this!

But what see I? No Thisby do I see.
O wicked wall, through whom I see no bliss!
Curst be thy stones for thus deceiving me!"

THESEUS. The wall, methinks, being sensible,° should   *capable of*
curse again.   *emotion or feeling*

PYRAMUS. No, in truth, Sir, he should not. "Deceiving me," is
Thisby's cue: she is to enter now, and I am to spy her
through the wall. You shall see, it will fall° pat as I told   *occur*
you.—Yonder she comes.

[*Enter* THISBE.]

THISBE. "O wall, full often hast thou heard my moans,
For parting my fair Pyramus and me!
My cherry lips have often kiss'd thy stones,
Thy stones with lime and hair knit up in thee."

PYRAMUS. "I see a voice: now will I to the chink,
To spy an I can hear my Thisby's face.—Thisby!"

THISBE. "My love! thou art my love, I think."

PYRAMUS. "Think what thou wilt, I am thy lover's grace°;   *i.e., your grace*
And, like Limander, am I trusty still."

THISBE. "And I like Helen,⁵⁰ till the fates me kill."

PYRAMUS. "Not Shafalus to Procrus was so true."

THISBE. "As Shafalus to Procrus,⁵¹ I to you."

PYRAMUS. "O! kiss me through the hole of this vile wall!"

THISBE. "I kiss the wall's hole, not your lips at all."

PYRAMUS. "Wilt thou at Ninny's tomb meet me straightway?"

THISBE. "'Tide° life, 'tide death, I come without delay."   *come*
[*Exeunt* PYRAMUS *and* THISBE.]

WALL. "Thus have I, wall, my part dischargèd so;
And, being done, thus wall away doth go."   [*Exit.*]

THESEUS. Now is the mural° down between the two neigh-   *wall*
bours.

DEMETRIUS. No remedy, my lord, when walls are so wilful to
hear without warning.

HIPPOLYTA. This is the silliest stuff that ever I heard.

THESEUS. The best in this kind are but shadows; and the worst
are no worse, if imagination amend them.

HIPPOLYTA. It must be your imagination then, and not theirs.

THESEUS. If we imagine no worse of them than they of themselves, they may pass for excellent men.—Here come two
noble beasts in, a moon and a lion.

Enter LION *and* MOONSHINE.

---

⁵⁰ Limander and Helen are errors for what should be Leander and Hero, two famous classical lovers.
Leander nightly swam across the Hellespont to be with his beloved. One night he drowned. Hero,
overcome by grief, then drowned herself by leaping into the sea.

⁵¹ Again errors, for Cephalus and his faithful wife, Procris, whom he accidently killed with a javelin.

LION. "You, ladies, you, whose gentle hearts do fear
    The smallest monstrous mouse that creeps on floor,
    May now perchance both quake and tremble here,
    When lion rough in wildest rage doth roar.
    Then know that I, one Snug the joiner, am
    No lion fell,° nor else no lion's dam;   *lion's skin*
    For, if I should as lion come in strife
    Into this place, 'twere pity of my life."
THESEUS. A very gentle beast, and of a good conscience.
DEMETRIUS. The very best at a beast, my lord, that e'er I saw.
LYSANDER. This lion is a very fox for his valour.
THESEUS. True; and a goose for his discretion.
DEMETRIUS. Not so, my lord; for his valour cannot carry his
    discretion; and the fox carries the goose.
THESEUS. His discretion, I am sure, cannot carry his valour; for
    the goose carries not the fox. It is well: leave it to his
    discretion, and let us listen to the moon.
MOONSHINE. "This lantern doth the horned moon present;"—
DEMETRIUS. He should have worn the horns on his head.[52]
THESEUS. He is no crescent,° and his horns are invisible   *new or waxing moon*
    within the circumference.
MOONSHINE. "This lantern doth the horned moon present;
    Myself the man i' the moon do seem to be."
THESEUS. This is the greatest error of all the rest: the man
    should be put into the lantern. How is it else the man i' the
    moon?
DEMETRIUS. He dares not come there for° the candle; for, you   *because of*
    see, it is already in snuff.°   *anger*
HIPPOLYTA. I am aweary of this moon: would he would change!
THESEUS. It appears, by his small light of discretion, that he is
    in the wane; but yet, in courtesy, in all reason, we must
    stay° the time.   *await*
LYSANDER. Proceed, moon.
MOONSHINE. All that I have to say, is, to tell you that the lan-
    tern is the moon; I, the man in the moon; this thorn-bush,
    my thorn-bush; and this dog, my dog.
DEMETRIUS. Why, all these should be in the lantern; for all
    these are in the moon. But, silence! here comes Thisbe.

Enter THISBE.

THISBE. "This is old Ninny's tomb. Where is my love?"
LION [*Roaring*]. "Oh—."   [THISBE *runs off.*]
DEMETRIUS. Well roared, lion.
THESEUS. Well run, Thisbe.
HIPPOLYTA. Well shone, moon.—Truly, the moon shines with
    a good grace.   [*The* Lion *tears* THISBE *'s mantle, and exit.*]
THESEUS. Well moused,° lion.   *torn*
DEMETRIUS. And then came Pyramus.

[52] The allusion is to the horns of a cuckold.

LYSANDER. And so the lion vanished.

Enter PYRAMUS.

PYRAMUS. "Sweet moon, I thank thee for thy sunny beams
   I thank thee, moon, for shining now so bright;
   For, by thy gracious, golden, glittering streams,
   I trust to taste of truest Thisbe's sight.
     But stay,—O spite!—
     But mark, poor knight,
   What dreadful dole° is here!   <i>cause for grief</i>
     Eyes, do you see?
     How can it be?
   O dainty duck! O dear!
     Thy mantle good,
     What, stain'd with blood?
   Approach, ye furies fell!
     O fates,[53] come, come,
     Cut thread and thrum[54];
   Quail,° crush, conclude, and quell°!"   <i>overpower/kill</i>
THESEUS. This passion,°and the death of a dear friend, would <i>suffering</i>
 go near to make a man look sad.
HIPPOLYTA. Beshrew my heart, but I pity the man.
PYRAMUS. "O wherefore, nature, didst thou lions frame?
   Since lion vile hath here deflower'd my dear:
  Which is—no, no—which was the fairest dame
   That liv'd, that lov'd, that lik'd, that look'd with
    cheer.
     Come, tears, confound;
     Out, sword, and wound
   The pap of Pyramus,—
     Ay, that left pap,
     Where heart doth hop:—   [<i>Stabs himself.</i>]
   Thus die I, thus, thus, thus!
     Now am I dead,
     Now am I fled;
   My soul is in the sky:
     Tongue, lose thy light!
     Moon, take thy flight! [<i>Exit</i> MOONSHINE.]
   Now die, die, die, die, die." [<i>Dies.</i>]
DEMETRIUS. No die, but an ace, for him; for he is but one.
LYSANDER. Less than an ace, man; for he is dead; he is nothing.
THESEUS. With the help of a surgeon, he might yet recover,
 and prove an ass.
HIPPOLYTA. How chance moonshine is gone, before Thisbe
 comes back and finds her lover?

---

[53] The Roman goddesses of vengeance. The Fates were the three goddesses who spun, drew out, and
 then cut the thread of human life.
[54] The warp and weft of the loom; here used as a synonym for everything together.

THESEUS. She will find him by starlight.—Here she comes; and
 her passion ends the play.

Re-enter THISBE.

HIPPOLYTA. Methinks she should not use a long one for such
 a Pyramus: I hope she will be brief.
DEMETRIUS. A mote° will turn the balance, which°   *small particle/whether*
 Pyramus, which° Thisbe, is the better; he for a man, God   *or*
 warrant° us,—she for a woman, God bless us.   *defend*
LYSANDER. She hath spied him already with those sweet eyes.
DEMETRIUS. And thus she moans, *videlicet:*—
THISBE.   "Asleep, my love?
          What, dead, my dove?
      O Pyramus, arise!
          Speak, speak. Quite dumb?
          Dead, dead? A tomb
      Must cover thy sweet eyes.
          These lily lips,
          This cherry nose,
      These yellow cowslip cheeks,
          Are gone, are gone:
          Lovers, make moan:
      His eyes were green as leeks.
          O, sisters three,[55]
          Come, come to me,
      With hands as pale as milk;
          Lay them in gore,
          Since you have shore°   *shorn*
      With shears his thread of silk.
          Tongue, not a word:
          Come, trusty sword;
      Come, blade, my breast imbrue:°   *stain with blood*
[*Stabs herself.*]
          And farewell, friends,—
          Thus Thisby ends,—
      Adieu, adieu, adieu."   [*Dies.*]
THESEUS. Moonshine and Lion are left to bury the dead.
DEMETRIUS. Ay, and Wall too.
BOTTOM. No, I assure you; the wall is down that parted their
 fathers. Will it please you to see the epilogue, or to hear a
 Bergomask[56] dance between two of our company?
THESEUS. No epilogue, I pray you; for your play needs no
 excuse. Never excuse; for when the players are all dead,
 there need none to be blamed. Marry, if he that writ it, had
 play'd Pyramus, and hanged himself in Thisbe's garter, it
 would have been a fine tragedy: and so it is, truly; and very

[55] The Fates, see Note 53.
[56] A rustic dance that originated in northern Italy among the people of Bergamo.

notably discharged. But come, your Bergomask: let your
epilogue alone.   [*A dance.*]

The iron tongue° of midnight hath told twelve:—   *of a bell*
Lovers, to bed; 'tis almost fairy time.
I fear we shall out-sleep the coming morn,
As much as we this night have overwatch'd.°   *kept watch over*
This palpable gross° play hath well beguil'd   *stupid*
The heavy gait of night.—Sweet friends, to bed.—
A fortnight hold we this solemnity,
In nightly revels, and new jollity.   [*Exeunt.*]

SCENE II

Enter PUCK.

PUCK. Now the hungry lion roars,
     And the wolf behowls the moon;
Whilst the heavy ploughman snores,
     All with weary task fordone.°   *exhausted*
Now the wasted° brands do glow,   *burned out*
     Whilst the screech-owl, screeching loud,
Puts the wretch that lies in woe,
     In remembrance of a shroud.
Now it is the time of night,
     That the graves, all gaping wide,
Every one lets forth his sprite,
     In the church-way paths to glide:
And we fairies, that do run
     By the triple Hecate's team,[57]
From the presence of the sun,
     Following darkness like a dream,
Now are frolic°: not a mouse   *merry*
Shall disturb this hallow'd house:
I am sent, with broom, before,
To sweep the dust behind the door.

Enter OBERON *and* TITANIA, *with their train.*

OBERON. Through the house give glimmering light,
     By the dead and drowsy fire:
Every elf, and fairy sprite,
     Hop as light as bird from brier;
And this ditty, after me,
     Sing, and dance it trippingly.
TITANIA. First, rehearse your song by rote,
     To each word a warbling note:
Hand in hand, with fairy grace,
     Will we sing, and bless this place.   [*Song and dance.*]

[57] Hecate is the goddess of the moon; her team is her chariot.

OBERON. Now, until the break of day,
  Through this house each fairy stray.
  To the best bride-bed will we,
  Which by us shall blessèd be;
  And the issue there create°   *created*
  Ever shall be fortunate.
  So shall all the couples three
  Ever true in loving be;
  And the blots of nature's hand
  Shall not in their issue stand;
  Never mole, hare-lip, nor scar,
  Nor mark prodigious,° such as are   *birthmark*
  Despisèd in nativity,
  Shall upon their children be.
  With this field-dew consecrate,°   *consecrated*
  Every fairy take his gait;°   *way*
  And each several° chamber bless,   *separate*
  Through this palace, with sweet peace:
  Ever shall in safety rest,
  And the owner of it blest.
  Trip away; make no stay;
  Meet me all by break of day.
  [*Exeunt* OBERON, TITANIA, *and train.*]
PUCK. If we shadows have offended,
  Think but this, (and all is mended,)
  That you have but slumber'd here,
  While these visions did appear.
  And this weak and idle theme,
  No more yielding but a dream,
  Gentles,° do not reprehend: *gentle folk*
  If you pardon, we will mend.°   *improve*
  And, as I'm an honest Puck,
  If we have unearnèd luck
  Now to 'scape the serpent's tongue,°   *hisses*
  We will make amends ere long;
  Else the Puck a liar call:
  So, good night unto you all.
  Give me your hands,° if we be friends,   *applause*
  And Robin shall restore amends.°   [*Exit.*]   *return satisfaction*

[1595–1596]

William Shakespeare *(1564–1616)*

OTHELLO, THE MOOR OF VENICE

CHARACTERS

DUKE OF VENICE
BRABANTIO, *a senator, Desdemona's father*
OTHER SENATORS
GRATIANO, *brother to Brabantio*
LODOVICO, *kinsman to Brabantio*
OTHELLO, *a noble Moor in the service of the Venetian state*
CASSIO, *his lieutenant*

IAGO, *his ancient*
RODERIGO, *a Venetian gentleman*
MONTANO, *Othello's predecessor in the government of Cyprus*
CLOWN, *servant to Othello*
DESDEMONA, *daughter to Brabantio and wife to Othello*
EMILIA, *wife to Iago*
BIANCA, *mistress to Cassio*

SAILOR, MESSENGER, HERALD, OFFICERS, GENTLEMEN, MUSICIANS, AND ATTENDANTS

SCENE:
Venice: a seaport in Cyprus.

ACT I

SCENE I
Venice. A street.

Enter RODERIGO *and* IAGO.

RODERIGO. Tush, never tell me; I take it much unkindly
  That thou, Iago, who hast had my purse
  As if the strings were thine, shouldst know of this.
IAGO. 'Sblood, but you will not hear me.
  If ever I did dream of such a matter,
  Abhor me.
RODERIGO. Thou told'st me thou didst hold him in thy hate.
IAGO. Despise me, if I do not. Three great ones of the city,
  In personal suit to make me his lieutenant,
  Off-caped° to him: and, by the faith of man,   *doffed caps*
  I know my price, I am worth no worse a place:
  But he, as loving his own pride and purposes,
  Evades them, with a bombast circumstance°   *pompous speech*
  Horribly stuffed with epithets of war;
  And, in conclusion,
  Nonsuits° my mediators; for, "Certes,"° says he,   *rejects / to be sure*
  "I have already chose my officer."
  And what was he?
  Forsooth, a great arithmetician,°   *theorist*
  One Michael Cassio, a Florentine,
  A fellow almost damned in a fair wife;[1]

---

[1] Iago's meaning is unclear since Cassio is unmarried. However, in the source used by Shakespeare, Cassio was married and this reference to his fair wife is probably just a careless carryover.

That never set a squadron in the field,
Nor the division of a battle knows
More than a spinster; unless the bookish theoric,
Wherein the togèd° consuls can propose,   *toga-wearing*
As masterly as he: mere prattle without practice
Is all his soldiership. But he, sir, had the election:
And I, of whom his eyes had seen the proof
At Rhodes, at Cyprus and on other grounds
Christian and heathen, must be be-lee'd and calmed°   *becalmed*
By debitor and creditor: this counter-caster,°   *bookkeeper*
He, in good time, must his lieutenant be,
And I—God bless the mark!—his Moorship's ancient.°   *standard-bearer*
RODERIGO. By heaven, I rather would have been his hangman.
IAGO. Why, there's no remedy; 'tis the curse of service,
Preferment goes by letter° and affection,   *references*
And not by old gradation,° where each second   *seniority*
Stood heir to the first. Now, sir, be judge yourself
Whether I in any just term am affined°   *bound*
To love the Moor.
RODERIGO.   I would not follow him then.
IAGO. O, sir, content you;
I follow him to serve my turn upon him:
We cannot all be masters, nor all masters
Cannot be truly followed. You shall mark
Many a duteous and knee-crooking knave,
That doting on his own obsequious bondage
Wears out his time, much like his master's ass,
For nought but provender,° and when he's old, cashiered:° *food / fired*
Whip me such honest knaves. Others there are
Who, trimmed° in forms and visages of duty,   *dressed*
Keep yet their hearts attending on themselves,
And throwing but shows of service on their lords
Do well thrive by them, and when they have lined their
    coats
Do themselves homage:° these fellows have some soul,   *serve*
And such a one do I profess myself.
For, sir,
It is as sure as you are Roderigo,
Were I the Moor, I would not be Iago:
In following him, I follow but myself;
Heaven is my judge, not I for love and duty,
But seeming so, for my peculiar° end: *personal*
For when my outward action doth demonstrate
The native act and figure of my heart
In compliment extern,° 'tis not long after   *external appearance*
But I will wear my heart upon my sleeve
For daws° to peck at: I am not what I am.   *crows*
RODERIGO. What a full fortune does the thick-lips° owe,°   *Othello / own*
If he can carry't° thus!   *handle it*
IAGO.   Call up her father,
Rouse him: make after him, poison his delight,
Proclaim him in the streets; incense her kinsmen,

And, though he in a fertile climate dwell,
Plague him with flies: though that his joy be joy,
Yet throw such changes of vexation on't
As it may lose some color.

RODERIGO. Here is her father's house; I'll call aloud.

IAGO. Do; with like timorous° accent and dire yell   *terrifying*
As when, by night and negligence, the fire
Is spied in populous cities.

RODERIGO. What, ho, Brabantio! Signior Brabantio, ho!

IAGO. Awake! what, ho, Brabantio! thieves! thieves! thieves!
Look to your house, your daughter and your bags!
Thieves! thieves!

BRABANTIO *appears above, at a window.*

BRABANTIO. What is the reason of this terrible summons?
What is the matter there?

RODERIGO. Signior, is all your family within?

IAGO. Are your doors locked?

BRABANTIO.   Why, wherefore ask you this?

IAGO. 'Zounds,° sir, you're robbed; for shame, put on   *by God's wounds*
your gown;
Your heart is burst, you have lost half your soul;
Even now, now, very now, an old black ram
Is tupping° your white ewe. Arise, arise;   *coupling with*
Awake the snorting° citizens with the bell,   *snoring*
Or else the devil will make a grandsire of you:
Arise, I say.

BRABANTIO.   What, have you lost your wits?

RODERIGO. Most reverend signior, do you know my voice?

BRABANTIO. Not I: what are you?

RODERIGO. My name is Roderigo.

BRABANTIO.   The worser welcome:
I have charged thee not to haunt about my doors:
In honest plainness thou hast heard me say
My daughter is not for thee; and now, in madness,
Being full of supper and distempering draughts,°   *befuddling drinks*
Upon malicious bravery,° dost thou come   *bravado*
To start° my quiet.   *disturb*

RODERIGO. Sir, sir, sir,—

BRABANTIO.   But thou must needs be sure
My spirit and my place have in them power
To make this bitter to thee.

RODERIGO.   Patience, good sir.

BRABANTIO. What tell'st thou me of robbing? This is Venice;
My house is not a grange.°   *farm*

RODERIGO.   Most grave Brabantio,
In simple and pure soul I come to you.

IAGO. 'Zounds, sir, you are one of those that will not
serve God, if the devil bid you. Because we come to do
you service and you think we are ruffians, you'll have your

daughter covered with a Barbary° horse; you'll have your   *North African*
nephews° neigh to you; you'll have coursers° for cousins,   *grandsons / horses*
and gennets° for germans.°   *Spanish horses / kinfolk*

BRABANTIO. What profane wretch art thou?

IAGO. I am one, sir, that comes to tell you your daughter
and the Moor are now making the beast with two backs.

BRABANTIO. Thou art a villain.

IAGO.   You are—a senator.

BRABANTIO. This thou shalt answer; I know thee, Roderigo.

RODERIGO. Sir, I will answer any thing. But, I beseech you,
  If 't be your pleasure and most wise consent,
  As partly I find it is, that your fair daughter,
  At this odd-even° and dull watch o' the night,   *wee hour*
  Transported with no worse nor better guard
  But with a knave of common hire, a gondolier,
  To the gross clasps of a lascivious Moor,—
  If this be known to you, and your allowance,°   *permission*
  We then have done you bold and saucy° wrongs;   *impudent*
  But if you know not this, my manners tell me
  We have your wrong rebuke. Do not believe
  That, from° the sense of all civility,   *contrary to*
  I thus would play and trifle with your reverence:
  Your daughter, if you have not given her leave,
  I say again, hath made a gross revolt,
  Tying her duty, beauty, wit and fortunes,
  In an extravagant and wheeling° stranger   *roving*
  Of here and everywhere. Straight satisfy yourself:
  If she be in her chamber or your house,
  Let loose on me the justice of the state
  For thus deluding you.

BRABANTIO.   Strike on the tinder, ho!
  Give me a taper!° call up all my people!   *candle*
  This accident° is not unlike my dream: *event*
  Belief of it oppresses me already.
  Light, I say! light! [*Exit above.*]

IAGO.   Farewell; for I must leave you:
  It seems not meet, nor wholesome to my place,
  To be produced—as, if I stay, I shall—
  Against the Moor: for I do know, the state,
  However this may gall him with some check,°   *reprimand*
  Cannot with safety cast° him; for he's embarked   *dismiss*
  With such loud reason to the Cyprus wars,
  Which even now stand in act,° that, for their souls,   *have begun*
  Another of his fathom° they have none   *capability*
  To lead their business: in which regard,
  Though I do hate him as I do hell-pains,
  Yet for necessity of present life,
  I must show out a flag and sign of love,
  Which is indeed but sign. That you shall surely find him,
  Lead to the Sagittary° the raised search;   *an inn*
  And there will I be with him. So farewell. [*Exit.*]

Enter, below, BRABANTIO, *in his night-gown, and* SERVANTS *with torches.*

BRABANTIO. It is too true an evil: gone she is;
    And what's to come of my despisèd time
    Is nought but bitterness. Now, Roderigo,
    Where didst thou see her? O unhappy girl!
    With the Moor, say'st thou? Who would be a father!
    How didst thou know 'twas she? O, she deceives me
    Past thought! What said she to you? Get more tapers.
    Raise all my kindred. Are they married, think you?
RODERIGO. Truly, I think they are.
BRABANTIO. O heaven! How got she out? O treason of the
    blood!
    Fathers, from hence trust not your daughters' minds
    By what you see them act. Is there not charms
    By which the property° of youth and maidhood   *true nature*
    May be abused? Have you not read, Roderigo,
    Of some such thing?
RODERIGO.   Yes, sir, I have indeed.
BRABANTIO. Call up my brother. O, would you had had her!
    Some one way, some another. Do you know
    Where we may apprehend her and the Moor?
RODERIGO. I think I can discover him, if you please
    To get good guard and go along with me.
BRABANTIO. Pray you, lead on. At every house I'll call;
    I may command at most. Get weapons, ho!
    And raise some special officers of night.
    On, good Roderigo; I'll deserve° your pains. [*Exeunt.*]   *reward*

SCENE II
Another street.

Enter OTHELLO, IAGO, *and* ATTENDANTS *with torches.*

IAGO. Though in the trade of war I have slain men,
    Yet do I hold it very stuff o' the conscience
    To do no contrived murder: I lack iniquity
    Sometimes to do me service: nine or ten times
    I had thought to have yerked° him here under the ribs.   *stabbed*
OTHELLO. 'Tis better as it is.
IAGO.   Nay, but he prated
    And spoke such scurvy and provoking terms
    Against your honor,
    That, with the little godliness I have,
    I did full hard forbear° him. But I pray you, sir,   *with difficulty spare*
    Are you fast married? Be assured of this,
    That the magnifico° is much beloved,   *nobleman*
    And hath in his effect a voice potential
    As double° as the duke's: he will divorce you,   *strong*
    Or put upon you what restraint and grievance

The law, with all his might to enforce it on,
Will give him cable.° *scope*
OTHELLO.   Let him do his spite:
My services, which I have done for signiory,° *government*
Shall out-tongue° his complaints. 'Tis yet to know— *speak louder than*
Which, when I know that boasting is an honor,
I shall promulgate—I fetch my life and being
From men of royal siege,° and my demerits° *rank / merits*
May speak unbonneted° to as proud a fortune *proudly*
As this that I have reached: for know, Iago,
But that I love the gentle Desdemona,
I would not my unhoused free condition
Put into circumscription and confine° *i.e., marriage*
For the sea's worth. But, look! what lights come yond?
IAGO. Those are the raisèd father and his friends:
You were best go in.
OTHELLO.   Not I; I must be found:
My parts,° my title and my perfect soul, *qualities*
Shall manifest me rightly. Is it they?
IAGO. By Janus, I think no.

Enter CASSIO, *and certain* OFFICERS *with torches.*

OTHELLO. The servants of the duke, and my lieutenant.
The goodness of the night upon you, friends!
What is the news?
CASSIO.   The duke does greet you, general,
And he requires your haste-post-haste appearance,
Even on the instant.
OTHELLO.   What is the matter, think you?
CASSIO. Something from Cyprus, as I may divine:° *speculate*
It is a business of some heat:° the galleys *urgency*
Have sent a dozen sequent° messengers *successive*
This very night at one another's heels;
And many of the consuls, raised and met,
Are at the duke's already: you have been hotly called for;
When, being not at your lodging to be found,
The senate hath sent about three several° quests *separate*
To search you out.
OTHELLO.   'Tis well I am found by you.
I will but spend a word here in the house,
And go with you. [*Exit.*]
CASSIO.   Ancient,° what makes he here? *Ensign*
IAGO. Faith, he tonight hath boarded a land carack:[2]
If it prove lawful prize, he's made for ever.
CASSIO. I do not understand.
IAGO.   He's married.
CASSIO.   To who?

[2] A trading ship with a high stern; a treasure ship.

Re-enter OTHELLO.

IAGO. Marry, to—Come, captain, will you go?
OTHELLO.   Have with you.
CASSIO. Here comes another troop to seek for you.
IAGO. It is Brabantio: general, be advised;
　　He comes to bad intent.

Enter BRABANTIO, RODERIGO, *and* OFFICERS *with torches and weapons.*

OTHELLO.   Holla! stand there!
RODERIGO. Signior, it is the Moor.
BRABANTIO.   Down with him, thief!
　　[*They draw on both sides.*]
IAGO. You, Roderigo! come, sir, I am for you.
OTHELLO. Keep up your bright swords, for the dew will rust
　　them.
　　Good signior, you shall more command with years
　　Than with your weapons.
BRABANTIO. O thou foul thief, where hast thou stowed my
　　daughter?
　　Damned as thou art, thou hast enchanted her;
　　For I'll refer me to all things of sense,°   *common sense*
　　If she in chains of magic were not bound,
　　Whether a maid so tender, fair and happy,
　　So opposite to marriage that she shunned
　　The wealthy curled° darlings of our nation,   *i.e., coiffured*
　　Would ever have, to incur a general mock,
　　Run from her guardage° to the sooty bosom   *legal home*
　　Of such a thing as thou, to fear, not to delight.
　　Judge me the world, if 'tis not gross° in sense   *obvious*
　　That thou hast prasticed on her with foul charms,
　　Abused her delicate youth with drugs or minerals
　　That weaken motion: I'll have't disputed on;
　　'Tis probable, and palpable to thinking.
　　I therefore apprehend and do attach° thee   *arrest*
　　For an abuser of the world, a practiser
　　Of arts inhibited° and out of warrant.°   *prohibited / unlawful*
　　Lay hold upon him: if he do resist,
　　Subdue him at his peril.
OTHELLO.   Hold your hands,
　　Both you of my inclining and the rest:
　　Were it my cue to fight, I should have known it
　　Without a prompter. Where will you that I go
　　To answer this your charge?
BRABANTIO.   To prison, till fit time
　　Of law and course of direct session
　　Call thee to answer.
OTHELLO.   What if I do obey?
　　How may the duke be therewith satisfied,
　　Whose messengers are here about my side,

Upon some present business of the state
To bring me to him?
FIRST OFFICER.   'Tis true, most worthy signior;
The duke's in council, and your noble self,
I am sure, is sent for,
BRABANTIO.   How! the duke in council!
In this time of the night! Bring him away:
Mine's not an idle cause: the duke himself,
Or any of my brothers of the state,
Cannot but feel this wrong as 'twere their own;
For if such actions may have passage free,
Bond-slaves and pagans shall our statesmen be. [*Exeunt.*]

SCENE III
A council-chamber.

The DUKE *and* SENATORS *sitting at a table;* OFFICERS *attending.*

DUKE. There is no composition° in these news   *consistency*
That gives them credit.
FIRST SENATOR.   Indeed they are disproportioned;
My letters say a hundred and seven galleys.
DUKE. And mine, a hundred and forty.
SECOND SENATOR.   And mine, two hundred:
But though they jump° not on a just° account,—   *settle / precise*
As in these cases, where the aim° reports,   *trend*
'Tis oft with difference,—yet do they all confirm
A Turkish fleet, and bearing up to Cyprus.
DUKE. Nay, it is possible enough to judgement:
I do not so secure me in° the error,   *take such assurance from*
But° the main article I do approve°   *But that / believe*
In fearful sense.
SAILOR [*Within*]. What, ho! what, ho! what, ho!
FIRST OFFICER. A messenger from the galleys.

Enter SAILOR.

DUKE.   Now, what's the business?
SAILOR. The Turkish preparation makes for Rhodes;
So was I bid report here to the state
By Signior Angelo.
DUKE. How say you by this change!
FIRST SENATOR.   This cannot be,
By no assay° of reason: 'tis a pageant°   *test / ploy*
To keep us in false gaze. When we consider
The importancy of Cyprus to the Turk,
And let ourselves again but understand
That as it more concerns the Turk than Rhodes,
So may he with more facile question° bear° it,   *battle / capture*
For that it stands not in such warlike brace,°   *condition*
But altogether lacks the abilities°   *strengths*

That Rhodes is dressed in: if we make thought of this,
We must not think the Turk is so unskilful
To leave that latest which concerns him first,
Neglecting an attempt of ease and gain,
To wake and wage° a danger profitless.   *risk*
DUKE. Nay, in all confidence, he's not for Rhodes.
FIRST OFFICER. Here is more news.

Enter a MESSENGER.

MESSENGER. The Ottomites,° reverend and gracious,   *Turks*
   Steering with due course toward the isle of Rhodes,
   Have there injointed° them with an after° fleet.   *combined / following*
FIRST SENATOR. Ay, so I thought. How many, as you guess?
MESSENGER. Of thirty sail: and now they do re-stem°   *turn about to*
   Their backward course, bearing with frank appearance
   Their purposes toward Cyprus. Signior Montano,
   Your trusty and most valiant servitor,
   With his free duty recommends° you thus,   *informs*
   And prays you to believe him.
DUKE. 'Tis certain then for Cyprus.
   Marcus Luccicos, is not he in town?
FIRST SENATOR. He's now in Florence.
DUKE. Write from us to him; post-post-haste dispatch.
FIRST SENATOR. Here comes Brabantio and the valiant Moor.

Enter BRABANTIO, OTHELLO, IAGO, RODERIGO, *and* OFFICERS.

DUKE. Valiant Othello, we must straight employ you
   Against the general enemy Ottoman.
   [*To Brabantio*]. I did not see you; welcome, gentle signior;
   We lacked your counsel and your help tonight.
BRABANTIO. So did I yours. Good your grace, pardon me;
   Neither my place nor aught I heard of business
   Hath raised me from my bed, nor doth the general care
   Take hold on me; for my particular grief
   Is of so flood-gate° and o'erbearing nature   *overflowing*
   That it engluts° and swallows other sorrows,   *engulfs*
   And it is still itself.
DUKE.   Why, what's the matter?
BRABANTIO. My daughter! O, my daughter!
ALL.   Dead?
BRABANTIO.   Ay, to me;
   She is abused, stol'n from me and corrupted
   By spells and medicines bought of mountebanks;°   *quacks*
   For nature so preposterously to err,
   Being not deficient, blind, or lame of sense,
   Sans° witchcraft could not.   *without*
DUKE. Who'er he be that in this foul proceeding
   Hath thus beguiled your daughter of herself

And you of her, the bloody book of law
You shall yourself read in the bitter letter
After your own sense, yea, though our proper° son   own
Stood in your action.°   court action
BRABANTIO.   Humbly I thank your grace.
Here is the man, this Moor; whom now, it seems,
Your special mandate for the state-affairs
Hath hither brought.
ALL.   We are very sorry for't.
DUKE [*To* OTHELLO]. What in your own part can you say to
    this?
BRABANTIO. Nothing, but this is so.
OTHELLO. Most potent, grave, and reverend signiors,
My very noble and approved good masters,
That I have ta'en away this old man's daughter,
It is most true; true, I have married her:
The very head and front of my offending
Hath this extent, no more. Rude am I in my speech,
And little blest with the soft phrase of peace;
For since these arms of mine had seven years' pith°,   strength
Till now some nine moons wasted, they have used
Their dearest° action in the tented field;   most important
And little of this great world can I speak,
More than pertains to feats of broil and battle;
And therefore little shall I grace my cause
In speaking for myself. Yet, by your gracious patience,
I will a round unvarnished tale deliver
Of my whole course of love; what drugs, what charms,
What conjuration and what mighty magic—
For such proceeding I am charged withal—
I won his daughter.
BRABANTIO.   A maiden never bold;
Of spirit so still and quiet that her motion°   soul
Blushed at herself; and she—in spite of nature,
Of years, of country, credit, everything—
To fall in love with what she feared to look on!
It is a judgement maimed and most imperfect
That will confess perfection so could err
Against all rules of nature; and must be driven
To find out practices of cunning hell,
Why this should be. I therefore vouch again,
That with some mixtures powerful o'er the blood,
Or with some dram conjured to this effect,
He wrought upon her.
DUKE.   To vouch° this, is no proof,   assert
Without more certain and more overt test
Than these thin habits° and poor likelihoods   dressings
Of modern° seeming do prefer against him.   ordinary
FIRST SENATOR. But, Othello, speak:
Did you by indirect and forced courses

Subdue and poison this young maid's affections?
Or came it by request, and such fair question
As soul to soul affordeth?

OTHELLO.   I do beseech you,
Send for the lady to the Sagittary,
And let her speak of me before her father:
If you do find me foul in her report,
The trust, the office I do hold of you,
Not only take away, but let your sentence
Even fall upon my life.

DUKE.   Fetch Desdemona hither.

OTHELLO. Ancient, conduct them; you best know the place.
  [*Exeunt* IAGO *and* ATTENDANTS.]
And till she come, as truly as to heaven
I do confess that vices of my blood,
So justly to your grave ears I'll present
How I did thrive in this fair lady's love
And she in mine.

DUKE. Say it, Othello.

OTHELLO. Her father loved me, oft invited me,
Still questioned me the story of my life
From year to year, the battles, sieges, fortunes,
That I have passed.
I ran it through, even from my boyish days
To the very moment that he bade me tell it:
Wherein I spake of most disastrous chances,
Of moving accidents by flood and field,
Of hair-breadth 'scapes i' the imminent deadly breach,
Of being taken by the insolent foe,
And sold to slavery, of my redemption thence,
And portance° in my travels' history: *deportment*
Wherein of antres° vast and deserts idle,   *caves*
Rough quarries, rocks, and hills whose heads touch
    heaven,
It was my hint to speak,—such was the process;
And of the Cannibals that each other eat,
The Anthropophagi,° and men whose heads   *man-eaters*
Do grow beneath their shoulders. This to hear
Would Desdemona seriously incline:
But still the house-affairs would draw her thence;
Which ever as she could with haste dispatch,
She'd come again, and with a greedy ear
Devour up my discourse: which I observing,
Took once a pliant° hour, and found good means   *convenient*
To draw from her a prayer of earnest heart
That I would all my pilgrimage dilate.°   *relate*
Whereof my parcels she had something heard,
But not intentively:° I did consent,   *attentively*
And often did beguile her of her tears
When I did speak of some distressful stroke
That my youth suffered. My story being done,

She gave me for my pains a world of sighs:
She swore, in faith, 'twas strange, 'twas passing strange;
'Twas pitiful, 'twas wondrous pitiful:
She wished she had not heard it, yet she wished
That heaven had made her such a man: she thanked me,
And bade me, if I had a friend that loved her,
I should but teach him how to tell my story,
And that would woo her. Upon this hint I spake:
She loved me for the dangers I had passed,
And I loved her that she did pity them.
This only is the witchcraft I have used.
Here comes the lady; let her witness it.

Enter DESDEMONA, IAGO, *and* ATTENDANTS.

DUKE. I think this tale would win my daughter too.
    Good Brabantio,
    Take up this mangled matter at the best:
    Men do their broken weapons rather use
    Than their bare hands.
BRABANTIO.   I pray you, hear her speak:
    If she confess that she was half the wooer,
    Destruction on my head, if my bad blame
    Light on the man! Come hither, gentle mistress:
    Do you perceive in all this noble company
    Where most you owe obedience?
DESDEMONA.   My noble father,
    I do perceive here a divided duty:
    To you I am bound for life and education;
    My life and education both do learn me
    How to respect you; you are the lord of duty,
    I am hitherto your daughter: but here's my husband,
    And so much duty as my mother showed
    To you, preferring you before her father,
    So much I challenge° that I may profess   *assert*
    Due to the Moor my lord.
BRABANTIO.   God be with you! I have done.
    Please it your grace, on to the state-affairs:
    I had rather to adopt a child than get° it.   *beget*
    Come hither, Moor:
    I here do give thee that with all my heart,
    Which, but thou hast already, with all my heart
    I would keep from thee. For your sake, jewel,
    I am glad at soul I have no other child;
    For thy escape would teach me tyranny,
    To hang clogs° on them. I have done, my lord.   *weights*
DUKE. Let me speak like yourself, and lay a sentence
    Which, as a grise° or step, may help these lovers   *degree*
    Into your favor.
    When remedies are past, the griefs are ended
    By seeing the worst, which late° on hopes depended.   *until lately*

To mourn a mischief that is past and gone
Is the next way to draw new mischief on.
What cannot be preserved when fortune takes,
Patience her injury a mockery makes.
The robbed that smiles steals something from the thief;
He robs himself that spends a bootless° grief.   *useless*
BRABANTIO. So let the Turk of Cyprus us beguile;
We lose it not so long as we can smile.
He bears the sentence well, that nothing bears
But the free comfort which from thence he hears;
But he bears both the sentence and the sorrow,
That, to pay grief, must of poor patience borrow.
These sentences, to sugar or to gall,
Being strong on both sides, are equivocal:
But words are words; I never yet did hear
That the bruised heart was piercèd° through the ear.   *relieved (lanced)*
I humbly beseech you, proceed to the affairs of state.
DUKE. The Turk with a most mighty preparation makes for
Cyprus. Othello, the fortitude of the place is best known to
you; and though we have there a substitute of most al-
lowed° sufficiency, yet opinion, a sovereign mistress of ef-   *acknowledged*
fects, throws a more safer voice on you: you must therefore
be content to slubber° the gloss of your new fortunes with   *sully*
this more stubborn and boisterous expedition.
OTHELLO. The tyrant custom, most grave senators,
Hath made the flinty and steel couch of war
My thrice-driven° bed of down: I do agnize°   *thrice-sifted / recognize*
A natural and prompt alacrity
I find in hardness; and do undertake
These present wars against the Ottomites.
Most humbly therefore bending to your state,
I crave fit disposition° for my wife,   *provision*
Due reference° of place and exhibition,°   *assignment / funds*
With such accommodation and besort°   *company*
As levels with her breeding.
DUKE.   If you please,
Be 't at her father's.
BRABANTIO.   I'll not have it so.
OTHELLO. Nor I.
DESDEMONA.   Nor I, I would not there reside,
To put my father in impatient thoughts
By being in his eye. Most gracious duke,
To my unfolding lend your prosperous ear,
And let me find a charter° in your voice   *permission*
To assist my simpleness.
DUKE. What would you, Desdemona?
DESDEMONA. That I did love the Moor to live with him,
My downright violence and storm of fortunes
May trumpet to the world: my heart's subdued
Even to the very quality° of my lord: *appearance*
I saw Othello's visage in his mind,

And to his honor and his valiant parts
Did I my soul and fortunes consecrate.
So that, dear lords, if I be left behind,
A moth of peace, and he go to the war,
The rites for which I love him are bereft me,
And I a heavy interim shall support
By his dear absence. Let me go with him.
OTHELLO. Let her have your voices.
    Vouch with me, heaven, I therefore beg it not,
To please the palate of my appetite;
Nor to comply with heat°—the young affects°   *lust / youthful passions*
In me defunct—and proper° satisfaction;   *personal*
But to be free and bounteous to her mind:
And heaven defend° your good souls, that you think   *forbid*
I will your serious and great business scant
For° she is with me. No, when light-winged toys   *Because*
Of feathered Cupid seel° with wanton dullness   *blind*
My speculative and officed instruments,[3]
That my disports° corrupt and taint my business,   *diversions*
Let housewives make a skillet of my helm,°   *helmet*
And all indign° and base adversities   *unworthy*
Make head against my estimation!°   *reputation*
DUKE. Be it as you shall privately determine,
Either for her stay or going: the affair cries haste,
And speed must answer 't; you must hence tonight.
DESDEMONA. Tonight, my lord?
DUKE.   This night.
OTHELLO.   With all my heart.
DUKE. At nine i' the morning here we'll meet again.
Othello, leave some officer behind,
And he shall our commission bring to you;
With such things else of quality and respect
As doth import° you.   *matter to*
OTHELLO.   So please your grace, my ancient;
A man he is of honesty and trust:
To his conveyance I assign my wife,
With what else needful your good grace shall think
To be sent after me.
DUKE.   Let it be so.
    Good night to every one. [*To* BRABANTIO] And, noble sig-
      nior,
If virtue no delighted° beauty lack,   *delightful*
Your son-in-law is far more fair than black.
FIRST SENATOR. Adieu, brave Moor; use Desdemona well.
BRABANTIO. Look to her, Moor, if thou has eyes to see:
She has deceived her father, and may thee.
    [*Exeunt* DUKE, SENATORS, OFFICERS, &c.]
OTHELLO. My life upon her faith! Honest Iago,
My Desdemona must I leave to thee:

---

[3] My clear-sighted and properly functioning faculties.

I prithee, let thy wife attend on her;
And bring them after in the best advantage.°   *opportunity*
Come, Desdemona; I have but an hour
Of love, of worldly matters and direction,
To spend with thee: we must obey the time.
[*Exeunt* OTHELLO *and* DESDEMONA.]
RODERIGO. Iago!
IAGO. What say'st thou, noble heart?
RODERIGO. What will I do, thinkest thou?
IAGO. Why, go to bed and sleep.
RODERIGO. I will incontinently° drown myself.   *immediately*
IAGO. If thou dost, I shall never love thee after. Why, thou silly
     gentleman!
RODERIGO. It is silliness to live when to live is torment; and
     then have we a prescription to die when death is our phy-
     sician.
IAGO. O villanous! I have looked upon the world for four
     times seven years; and since I could distinguish betwixt a
     benefit and an injury, I never found man that knew how to
     love himself. Ere I would say I would drown myself for the
     love of a guinea-hen,° I would change my humanity with a   *whore*
     baboon.
RODERIGO. What should I do? I confess it is my shame to be so
     fond; but it is not in my virtue to amend it.
IAGO. Virtue! a fig! 'tis in ourselves that we are thus or thus.
     Our bodies are gardens; to the which our wills are garden-
     ers: so that if we will plant nettles° or sow lettuce, set hys-   *weeds*
     sop° and weed up thyme, supply it with one gender of   *a mint*
     herbs or distract it with many, either to have it sterile with
     idleness or manured with industry, why, the power and
     corrigible° authority of this lies in our wills. If the bal-   *corrective*
     ance of our lives had not one scale of reason to poise°   *counterweight*
     another of sensuality, the blood and baseness of our na-
     tures would conduct us to most preposterous conclusions:
     but we have reason to cool our raging motions, our carnal
     stings, our unbitted° lusts; whereof I take this, that you   *unbridled*
     call love, to be a sect° or scion.°   *cutting / graft*
RODERIGO. It cannot be.
IAGO. It is merely a lust of the blood and a permission of
     the will. Come, be a man: drown thyself! drown cats and
     blind puppies. I have professed me thy friend, and I con-
     fess me knit to thy deserving with cables of perdurable°   *everlasting*
     toughness: I could never better stead° thee than now.   *assist*
     Put money in thypurse; follow thou the wars; defeat° thy   *disguise*
     favor° within an usurped° beard; I say, put money in thy   *face / false*
     purse. It cannot be that Desdemona should long continue
     her love to the Moor—put money in thy purse—nor he his
     to her: it was a violent commencement, and thou shalt see
     an answerable sequestration;° put but money in thy purse.   *similar separation*
     These Moors are changeable in their wills:—fill thy purse
     with money. The food that to him now is as luscious as

locusts, shall be to him shortly as bitter as coloquintida.°   *bitter apple*
She must change for youth: when she is sated with his
body, she will find the error of her choice: she must have
change, she must: therefore put money in thy purse. If
thou wilt needs damn thyself, do it a more delicate way
than drowning. Make all the money thou canst: if sancti-
mony and a frail vow betwixt an erring barbarian and a
supersubtle Venetian be not too hard for my wits and all
the tribe of hell, thou shalt enjoy her; therefore make
money. A pox of drowning thyself! it is clean out of the
way: seek thou rather to be hanged in compassing° thy joy   *attaining*
than to be drowned and go without her.

RODERIGO. Wilt thou be fast° to my hopes, if I depend on the   *true*
    issue?

IAGO. Thou art sure of me: go, make money: I have told thee
    often, and I retell thee again and again, I hate the Moor:
    my cause is hearted;° thine hath no less reason. Let us be   *heart-felt*
    conjunctive° in our revenge against him: if thou canst   *joined*
    cuckold him, thou dost thyself a pleasure, me a sport.
    There are many events in the womb of time, which will be
    delivered. Traverse; go; provide thy money. We will have
    more of this tomorrow. Adieu.

RODERIGO. Where shall we meet 'i the morning?

IAGO. At my lodging.

RODERIGO. I'll be with thee betimes.°   *early*

IAGO. Go to; farewell. Do you hear, Roderigo?

RODERIGO. What say you?

IAGO. No more of drowning, do you hear?

RODERIGO. I am changed: I'll go sell all my land. [*Exit.*]

IAGO. Thus do I ever make my fool my purse;
    For I mine own gained knowledge should profane,
    If I would time expend with such a snipe°   *fool*
    But for my sport and profit. I hate the Moor;
    And it is thought abroad that 'twixt my sheets
    He has done my office: I know not if 't be true;
    But I for mere suspicion in that kind
    Will do as if for surety.° He holds me well;   *certainty*
    The better shall my purpose work on him.
    Cassio's a proper° man: let me see now;   *handsome*
    To get his place, and to plume up° my will   *satisfy*
    In double knavery—How, how?—Let's see:—
    After some time, to abuse Othello's ear
    That he is too familiar with his wife.
    He hath a person and a smooth dispose°   *disposition*
    To be suspected; framed to make women false.
    The Moor is of a free and open nature,
    That thinks men honest that but seem to be so;
    And will as tenderly be led by the nose
    As asses are.
    I haven't. It is engendered. Hell and night
    Must bring this monstrous birth to the world's light. [*Exit.*]

ACT II

SCENE I

A seaport in Cyprus. An open place near the quay.

Enter MONTANO *and two* GENTLEMEN.

MONTANO. What from the cape can you discern at sea?
FIRST GENTLEMAN. Nothing at all: it is a high-wrought flood;
  I cannot, 'twixt the heaven and the main,
  Descry° a sail.   *See*
MONTANO. Methinks the wind hath spoke aloud at land;
  A fuller blast ne'er shook our battlements:
  If it hath ruffianed° so upon the sea,   *raged*
  What ribs of oak, when mountains melt on them,
  Can hold the mortise?[4] What shall we hear of this?
SECOND GENTLEMAN. A segregation° of the Turkish fleet: *dispersal*
  For do but stand upon the foaming shore,
  The chidden° billow seems to pelt the clouds;   *driven*
  The wind-shaked surge, with high and monstrous mane,
  Seems to cast water on the burning bear,°   *a constellation*
  And quench the guards[5] of the ever-fixèd pole:
  I never did like molestation° view   *disruption*
  On the enchafèd flood.°   *raging sea*
MONTANO.   If that the Turkish fleet
  Be not ensheltered and embayed, they are drowned;
  It is impossible to bear it out.

Enter a third GENTLEMAN.

THIRD GENTLEMAN. News, lads! Our wars are done.
  The desperate tempest hath so banged the Turks,
  That their designment° halts: a noble ship of Venice   *plan*
  Hath seen a grievous wreck and sufferance°   *suffering*
  On most part of their fleet.
MONTANO. How! Is this true?
THIRD GENTLEMAN.   The ship is here put in,
  A Veronesa; Michael Cassio,
  Lieutenant to the warlike Moor Othello,
  Is come on shore: the Moor himself at sea,
  And is in full commission here for Cyprus.
MONTANO. I am glad on't; 'tis a worthy governor.
THIRD GENTLEMAN. But this same Cassio, though he speak of
    comfort
  Touching the Turkish loss, yet he looks sadly
  And prays the Moor be safe; for they were parted
  With foul and violent tempest.

[4] The slot into which the ribs of the ship are fitted.
[5] The stars near (or guarding) the North Star.

MONTANO.   Pray heavens he be;
  For I have served him, and the man commands
  Like a full soldier. Let's to the seaside, ho!
  As well to see the vessel that's come in
  As to throw out our eyes for brave Othello,
  Even till we make the main and the aerial blue
  An indistinct regard.°   *view (horizon)*
THIRD GENTLEMAN.   Come, let's do so;
  For every minute is expectancy
  Of more arrivance.

Enter CASSIO.

CASSIO. Thanks, you the valiant of this warlike isle,
  That so approve the Moor! O, let the heavens
  Give him defence against the elements,
  For I have lost him on a dangerous sea.
MONTANO. Is he well shipped?
CASSIO. His bark is stoutly timbered, and his pilot
  Of very expert and approved allowance;°   *acclaim*
  Therefore my hopes, not surfeited to death,°   *not excessive*
  Stand in bold cure.° [*A cry within:* "A sail, a sail, a sail!"]   *in good stead*

Enter a fourth GENTLEMAN.

CASSIO. What noise?
FOURTH GENTLEMAN. The town is empty; on the brow o' the sea
  Stand ranks of people, and then cry "A sail!"
CASSIO. My hopes do shape him for the governor.
[*Guns heard.*]
SECOND GENTLEMEN. They do discharge their shot of courtesy:
  Our friends at least.
CASSIO.   I pray you, sir, go forth,
  And give us truth who 'tis that is arrived.
SECOND GENTLEMAN. I shall.   [*Exit.*]
MONTANO. But, good lieutenant, is your general wived?
CASSIO. Most fortunately: he hath achieved a maid
  That paragons° description and wild fame;   *tops*
  One that excels the quirks of blazoning° pens,   *praising*
  And in the essential vesture° of creation   *clothing*
  Does tire the ingener.°   *creator of the praise*

Re-enter second GENTLEMAN.

                         How now! who has put in?
SECOND GENTLEMAN. 'Tis one Iago, ancient to the general.
CASSIO. He has had most favorable and happy speed:
  Tempests themselves, high seas, and howling winds,
  The guttered° rocks, and congregated sands,   *jagged*
  Traitors ensteeped° to clog° the guiltless keel,   *submerged / obstruct*

As having sense of beauty, do omit°   *neglect*
Their mortal° natures, letting go safely by   *deadly*
The divine Desdemona.
MONTANO.   What is she?
CASSIO. She that I spake of, our great captain's captain,
Left in the conduct of the bold Iago;
Whose footing° here anticipates our thoughts   *setting foot*
A se'nnight's° speed. Great Jove, Othello guard,   *week's*
And swell his sail with thine own powerful breath,
That he may bless this bay with his tall ship,
Make love's quick pants in Desdemona's arms,
Give renewed fire to our extincted spirits,
And bring all Cyprus comfort.

Enter DESDEMONA, EMILIA, IAGO, RODERIGO, *and* ATTENDANTS.

                                        O, behold,
The riches of the ship is come on shore!
Ye men of Cyprus, let her have your knees.
Hail to thee, lady! and the grace of heaven,
Before, behind thee, and on every hand,
Enwheel° thee round!   *Encircle*

DESDEMONA.   I thank you, valiant Cassio.
What tidings can you tell me of my lord?
CASSIO. He is not yet arrived: nor know I aught
But that he's well and will be shortly here.
DESDEMONA. O, but I fear—How lost you company?
CASSIO. The great contention of the sea and skies
Parted our fellowship—But, hark! a sail.
[*A cry within:* "A sail, a sail!" *Guns heard.*]
SECOND GENTLEMAN. They give their greeting to the citadel:
This likewise is a friend.
CASSIO.   See for the news.
[*Exit* GENTLEMAN.]
Good ancient, you are welcome. [*To* EMILIA.] Welcome,
    mistress:
Let it not gall your patience, good Iago,
That I extend° my manners; 'tis my breeding   *show*
That gives me this bold show of courtesy. [*Kissing her.*]
IAGO. Sir, would she give you so much of her lips
As of her tongue she oft bestows on me,
You'ld have enough.
DESDEMONA.   Alas, she has no speech.
IAGO. In faith, too much;
I find it still when I have list° to sleep: *desire*
Marry, before your ladyship, I grant,
She puts her tongue a little in her heart
And chides with thinking.
EMILIA. You have little cause to say so.

IAGO. Come on, come on; you are pictures out of doors,
    Bells in your parlors, wild-cats in your kitchens,
    Saints in your injuries, devils being offended,
    Players in your housewifery, and housewives° in your beds,   *i.e., hard working*
DESDEMONA. O, fie upon thee, slanderer!
IAGO. Nay, it is true, or else I am a Turk:
    You rise to play, and go to bed to work.
EMILIA. You shall not write my praise.
IAGO.   No, let me not.
DESDEMONA. What wouldst thou write of me, if thou shouldst
    praise me?
IAGO. O gentle lady, do not put me to't;
    For I am nothing if not critical.
DESDEMONA. Come on, assay°—There's one gone to the   *try*
    harbor?
IAGO. Ay, madam.
DESDEMONA. I am not merry; but I do beguile°   *divert attention from*
    The thing I am by seeming otherwise.
    Come, how wouldst thou praise me?
IAGO. I am about it; but indeed my invention
    Comes from my pate as birdlime does from frize;[6]
    It plucks out brains and all: but my Muse labors,
    And thus she is delivered.
    If she be fair° and wise, fairness and wit,   *blonde, pretty*
    The one's for use, the other useth it.
DESDEMONA. Well praised! How if she be black° and witty?   *brunette, ugly*
IAGO. If she be black, and thereto have a wit,
    She'll find a white° that shall her blackness fit.   *fair person*
DESDEMONA. Worse and worse.
EMILIA. How if fair and foolish?
IAGO. She never yet was foolish that was fair;
    For even her folly helped her to an heir.
DESDEMONA. These are old fond° paradoxes to make fools   *foolish*
    laugh i' the alehouse. What miserable praise hast thou for
    her that's foul and foolish?
IAGO. There's none so foul, and foolish thereunto,
    But does foul pranks which fair and wise ones do.
DESDEMONA. O heavy ignorance! thou praisest the worst best.
    But what praise couldst thou bestow on a deserving woman
    indeed, one that in the authority of her merit did justly
    put on° the vouch° of very malice itself?   *claim / praise*
IAGO. She that was ever fair and never proud,
    Had tongue at will and yet was never loud,
    Never lacked gold and yet went never gay,°   *gaily dressed*
    Fled from her wish and yet said "Now I may;"
    She that, being angered, her revenge being nigh,
    Bade her wrong stay and her displeasure fly;

---

[6] I.e., but indeed my ideas come from my brain as unwillingly as tar comes unstuck from coarse cloth.

She that in wisdom never was so frail
To change the cod's head for the salmon's tail;[7]
She that could think and ne'er disclose her mind,
See suitors following and not look behind;
She was a wight,° if ever such wight were,—   *person*
DESDEMONA. To do what?
IAGO. To suckle fools and chronicle small beer.°   *keep trivial accounts*
DESDEMONA. O most lame and impotent conclusion! Do not
learn of him, Emilia, though he be thy husband. How say
you, Cassio? Is he not a most profane and liberal° coun-   *lewd*
sellor?
CASSIO. He speaks home,° madam: you may relish him more   *pointedly*
in the soldier than in the scholar.
IAGO [*aside*]. He takes her by the palm: ay, well said, whisper:
with as little a web as this will I ensnare as great a fly as
Cassio. Ay, smile upon her, do; I will gyve° thee in thine   *fetter*
own courtship. You say true; 'tis so, indeed: if such tricks
as these strip you out of your lieutenantry, it had been
better you had not kissed your three fingers so oft, which
now again you are most apt to play the sir° in. Very good;   *gentleman*
well kissed! an excellent courtesy! 'tis so, indeed. Yet again
your fingers to your lips? Would they were clyster-pipes°   *enema tubes*
for your sake! [*Trumpet within.*] The Moor! I know his trumpet.
CASSIO. 'Tis truly so.
DESDEMONA. Let's meet him and receive him.
CASSIO. Lo, where he comes!

Enter OTHELLO *and* ATTENDANTS.

OTHELLO. O my fair warrior!
DESDEMONA.   My dear Othello!
OTHELLO. It gives me wonder great as my content
To see you here before me. O my soul's joy!
If after every tempest come such calms,
May the winds blow till they have wakened death!
And let the laboring bark climb hills of seas
Olympus-high and duck again as low
As hell's from heaven! If it were now to die,
'Twere now to be most happy; for I fear,
My soul hath her content so absolute
That not another comfort like to this
Succeeds in unknown fate.
DESDEMONA.   The heavens forbid
But that our loves and comforts should increase,
Even as our days do grow!
OTHELLO.   Amen to that, sweet powers!

---

[7] The cod, a common edible fish, is often said to be all head. The salmon is a delicacy, but its tail would
be inedible.

I cannot speak enough of this content;
It stops me here; it is too much of joy:
And this, and this, the greatest discords be [*Kissing her.*]
That e'er our hearts shall make!

Iago.   [*Aside*] O, you are well tuned now!
But I'll set down the pegs that make this music
As honest as I am.[8]

Othello.   Come, let us to the castle.
News, friends; our wars are done, the Turks are drowned.
How does my old acquaintance of this isle?
Honey, you shall be well desired in Cyprus;
I have found great love amongst them. O my sweet,
I prattle out of fashion, and I dote
In mine own comforts. I prithee, good Iago,
Go to the bay, and disembark my coffers:°   *chests*
Bring thou the master to the citadel;
He is a good one, and his worthiness
Does challenge° much respect. Come, Desdemona,   *lay claim to*
Once more well met at Cyprus.
[*Exeunt all but* Iago *and* Roderigo.]

Iago. Do thou meet me presently at the harbor. Come hither.
If thou be'st valiant—as, they say, base men being in love
have then a nobility in their natures more than is native to
them—list° me. The lieutenant tonight watches on the   *hear*
court of guard. First, I must tell thee this: Desdemona is
directly in love with him.

Rod. With him! why, 'tis not possible.

Iago. Lay thy finger thus,° and let thy soul be instructed.   *on your lips*
Mark me with what violence she first loved the Moor, but
for bragging and telling her fantastical lies: and will she
love him still for prating? Let not thy discreet heart think
it. Her eye must be fed; and what delight shall she have
to look on the devil? When the blood is made dull with
the act of sport, there should be, again to inflame it and
to give satiety a fresh appetite, loveliness in favor,° sym-   *face*
pathy in years, manners and beauties; all which the Moor
is defective in: now, for want of these required conveniences, her delicate tenderness will find itself abused,
begin to heave the gorge,° disrelish and abhor the Moor;   *vomit*
very nature will instruct her in it and compel her to some
second choice. Now, sir, this granted—as it is a most preg-
nant° and unforced position—who stands so eminently in   *well conceived*
the degree of this fortune as Cassio does? A knave very vol-
uble; no further conscionable than in putting on the mere
form of civil and humane seeming, for the better compass-
ing of his salt° and most hidden loose affection? Why,   *salty, lustful*
none; why, none: a slipper° and subtle knave; a finder out   *slippery*

---

[8] I.e., Iago will untune the heartstrings of Othello and Desdemona until their loving music is no more
honest (harmonious) than he is.

of occasions that has an eye can stamp and counterfeit advantages, though true advantage never present itself: a devilish knave! Besides, the knave is handsome, young, and hath all those requisites in him that folly and green minds look after: a pestilent complete knave; and the woman hath found him already.

RODERIGO. I cannot believe that in her; she's full of most blest condition.

IAGO. Blest fig's-end! The wine she drinks is made of grapes: if she had been blest, she would never have loved the Moor: blest pudding! Didst thou not see her paddle° with the palm of his hand? Didst not mark that?   *toy*

RODERIGO. Yes, that I did; but that was but courtesy.

IAGO. Lechery, by this hand; an index and obscure prologue to the history of lust and foul thoughts. They met so near with their lips that their breaths embraced together. Villanous thoughts, Roderigo! When these mutualities so marshal the way, hard at hand comes the master and main exercise, the incorporate° conclusion: pish! But, sir, be you ruled by me: I have brought you from Venice. Watch you tonight; for the command, I'll lay't upon you: Cassio knows you not: I'll not be far from you: do you find some occasion to anger Cassio, either by speaking too loud or tainting° his discipline, or from what other course you please, which the time shall more favorably minister.   *carnal*   *discrediting*

RODERIGO. Well.

IAGO. Sir, he is rash and very sudden in choler,° and haply may strike at you: provoke him, that he may; for even out of that will I cause these of Cyprus to mutiny; whose qualification° shall come into no true taste again but by the displanting of Cassio. So shall you have a shorter journey to your desires by the means I shall then have to prefer° them, and the impediment most profitably removed, without the which there were no expectation of our prosperity.   *anger*   *equanimity*   *advance*

RODERIGO. I will do this, if I can bring it to any opportunity.

IAGO. I warrant° thee. Meet me by and by at the citadel: I must fetch his necessaries ashore. Farewell.   *promise*

RODERIGO. Adieu. [*Exit.*]

IAGO. That Cassio loves her, I do well believe it;
That she loves him, 'tis apt° and of great credit:°   *possible / credibility*
The Moor, howbeit that I endure him not,
Is of a constant, loving, noble nature;
And I dare think he'll prove to Desdemona
A most dear husband. Now, I do love her too,
Not out of absolute lust, though peradventure°   *perhaps*
I stand accountant for as great a sin,
But partly led to diet° my revenge,   *feed*
For that I do suspect the lusty Moor
Hath leaped into my seat;° the thought whereof   *i.e., cuckolded me*
Doth like a poisonous mineral gnaw my inwards;

And nothing can or shall content my soul
Till I am evened with him, wife for wife;
Or failing so, yet that I put the Moor
At least into a jealousy so strong
That judgement cannot cure. Which thing to do,
If this poor trash of Venice, whom I trash°   *restrain*
For his quick hunting, stand the putting on,°   *on (the scent)*
I'll have our Michael Cassio on the hip,°   *i.e., the ground*
Abuse him to the Moor in the rank garb;°   *insinuating style*
For I fear Cassio with my night-cap° too;   *wife*
Make the Moor thank me, love me and reward me,
For making him egregiously an ass
And practising upon his peace and quiet
Even to madness. 'Tis here, but yet confused:
Knavery's plain face is never seen till used. [*Exit.*]

SCENE II
A street.

Enter a HERALD *with a proclamation;* PEOPLE *following.*

HERALD. It is Othello's pleasure, our noble and valiant general, that upon certain tidings now arrived, importing the
mere perdition° of the Turkish fleet, every man put him-   *total loss*
self into triumph; some to dance, some to make bonfires,
each man to what sport and revels his addiction° leads   *inclination*
him: for, besides these beneficial news, it is the celebration
of his nuptial. So much was his pleasure should be pro-
claimed. All offices° are open, and there is full liberty of   *mess-halls*
feasting from this present hour of five till the bell have told
eleven. Heaven bless the isle of Cyprus and our noble general Othello! [*Exeunt.*]

SCENE III
A hall in the castle.

Enter OTHELLO, DESDEMONA, CASSIO *and* ATTENDANTS.

OTHELLO. Good Michael, look you to the guard tonight:
Let's teach ourselves that honorable stop,°   *self-restraint*
Not to outsport discretion.
CASSIO. Iago hath direction what to do;
But notwithstanding with my personal eye
Will I look to't.
OTHELLO.   Iago is most honest.
Michael, good night: tomorrow with your earliest
Let me have speech with you. Come, my dear love,
The purchase made, the fruits are to ensue;

That profit's yet to come 'tween me and you.
Good night. [*Exeunt* OTHELLO, DESDEMONA, *and* ATTENDANTS.]

Enter IAGO.

CASSIO. Welcome, Iago; we must to the watch.
IAGO. Not this hour, lieutenant; 'tis not yet ten 'o the
    clock. Our general cast° us thus early for the love of his   *dismissed*
    Desdemona; who let us not therefore blame: he hath not
    yet made wanton the night with her, and she is sport for
    Jove.
CASSIO. She's a most exquisite lady.
IAGO. And, I'll warrant her, full of game.
CASSIO. Indeed she's a most fresh and delicate creature.
IAGO. What an eye she has! Methinks it sounds° a parley°   *signals / conference*
    to provocation.°   *sexual excitement*
CASSIO. An inviting eye; and yet methinks right modest.
IAGO. And when she speaks, is it not an alarum° to love?   *call*
CASSIO. She is indeed perfection.
IAGO. Well, happiness to their sheets! Come, lieutenant, I
    have a stoup° of wine; and here without are a brace° of   *half-gallon / pair*
    Cyprus gallants that would fain have a measure to the
    health of black Othello.
CASSIO. Not tonight, good Iago: I have very poor and unhappy
    brains for drinking: I could well wish courtesy would invent
    some other custom of entertainment.
IAGO. O, they are our friends; but one cup: I'll drink for you.
CASSIO. I have drunk but one cup tonight, and that was
    craftily qualified° too, and behold what innovation° it   *diluted / change*
    makes here: I am unfortunate in the infirmity and dare not
    task my weakness with any more.
IAGO. What, man! 'Tis a night of revels: the gallants desire it.
CASSIO. Where are they?
IAGO. Here at the door; I pray you, call them in.
CASSIO. I'll do 't; but it dislikes me. [*Exit.*]
IAGO. If I can fasten but one cup upon him,
    With that which he hath drunk tonight already,
    He'll be as full of quarrel and offence
    As my young mistress' dog. Now my sick fool Roderigo,
    Whom love hath turned almost the wrong side out,
    To Desdemona hath tonight caroused
    Potations pottle-deep;° and he's to watch: *by the potful*
    Three lads of Cyprus, noble swelling spirits,
    That hold their honors in a wary distance,°   *touchily*
    The very elements of this warlike isle,
    Have I tonight flustered with flowing cups,
    And they watch too. Now, 'mongst this flock of drunkards,
    Am I to put our Cassio in some action
    That may offend the isle. But here they come:
    If consequence° do but approve° my dream,   *events / confirm*
    My boat sails freely, both with wind and stream.

Re-enter CASSIO; *with him* MONTANO *and* GENTLEMEN;
SERVANTS *following with wine.*

CASSIO. 'Fore God, they have given me a rouse° already. drink
MONTANO. Good faith, a little one; not past a pint, as I am a
soldier.
IAGO. Some wine, ho!
    [*Sings.*] And let me the canakin° clink, clink; little pot
        And let me the canakin clink:
            A soldier's a man;
            A life's but a span;
        Why then let a soldier drink.
    Some wine, boys!
CASSIO. 'Fore God, an excellent song.
IAGO. I learned it in England, where indeed they are most
    potent in potting:° your Dane, your German, and your swag- draining pots
    bellied Hollander,—Drink, ho!—are nothing to your En-
    glish.
CASSIO. Is your Englishman so expert in his drinking?
IAGO. Why, he drinks you with facility your Dane dead drunk;
    he sweats not to overthrow your Almain;° he gives your German
    Hollander a vomit ere the next pottle° can be filled. pot
CASSIO. To the health of our general!
MONTANO. I am for it, lieutenant, and I'll do you justice.° equal you
IAGO. O sweet England!

    [*Sings.*] King Stephen was a worthy peer,
        His breeches cost him but a crown;
        He held them sixpence all too dear,
            With that he called the tailor lown.° rascal

        He was a wight of high renown,
            And thou are but of low degree:
        'Tis pride that pulls the country down;
            Then take thine auld° cloak about thee. old

    Some wine, ho!
CASSIO. Why, this is a more exquisite song than the other.
IAGO. Will you hear't again?
CASSIO. No; for I hold him to be unworthy of his place that
    does those things. Well: God's above all; and there be souls
    must be saved, and there be souls must not be saved.
IAGO. It's true, good lieutenant.
CASSIO. For mine own part—no offence to the general, nor
    any man of quality—I hope to be saved.
IAGO. And so do I too, lieutenant.
CASSIO. Ay, but, by your leave, not before me; the lieutenant
    is to be saved before the ancient. Let's have no more of
    this; let's to our affairs. God forgive us our sins! Gentlemen,
    let's look to our business. Do not think, gentlemen, I am
    drunk: this is my ancient: this is my right hand, and
    this is my left. I am not drunk now; I can stand well enough,
    and speak well enough.

ALL. Excellent well.

CASSIO. Why, very well then; you must not think then that I am
  drunk. [*Exit.*]

MONTANO. To the platform, masters; come, let's set the watch.

IAGO. You see this fellow that is gone before;
  He is a soldier fit to stand by Caesar
  And give direction: and do but see his vice;
  'Tis to his virtue a just equinox,°   *an exact equal*
  The one as long as the other: 'tis pity of him.
  I fear the trust Othello puts him in
  On some odd time of his infirmity
  Will shake this island.

MONTANO.   But is he often thus?

IAGO. 'Tis evermore the prologue to his sleep:
  He'll watch the horologe° a double set,°   *clock / twice around*
  If drink rock not his cradle.

MONTANO.   It were well
  The general were put in mind of it.
  Perhaps he sees it not, or his good nature
  Prizes the virtue that appears in Cassio
  And looks not on his evils: is not this true?

Enter RODERIGO.

IAGO [*Aside to him*]. How now, Roderigo!
  I pray you, after the lieutenant; go. [*Exit* RODERIGO.]

MONTANO. And 'tis great pity that the noble Moor
  Should hazard such a place as his own second
  With one of an ingraft° infirmity: *ingrained*
  It were an honest action to say
  So to the Moor.

IAGO.   Not I, for this fair island:
  I do love Cassio well, and would do much
  To cure him of this evil:—But, hark! what noise?
  [*A cry within:* "Help! help!"]

Re-enter CASSIO, *driving in* RODERIGO.

CASSIO. 'Zounds! you rogue! you rascal!

MONTANO. What's the matter, lieutenant?

CASSIO. A knave teach me my duty! But I'll beat the knave into
  a wicker bottle.

RODERIGO. Beat me!

CASSIO. Dost thou prate, rogue? [*Striking* RODERIGO.]

MONTANO. Nay, good lieutenant; I pray, you, sir, hold your
  hand.

CASSIO. Let me go, sir, or I'll knock you o'er the mazzard.°   *head*

MONTANO. Come, come, you're drunk.

CASSIO. Drunk! [*They fight.*]

IAGO [*Aside to* RODERIGO]. Away, I say; go out, and cry a mutiny.
  [*Exit* RODERIGO.]

Nay, good lieutenant! God's will, gentlemen!
Help, ho!—Lieutenant,—sir,—Montano—sir;—
Help, masters!—Here's a goodly watch indeed!
[*A bell rings.*]
Who's that that rings the bell?—Diablo,° ho!   *The devil*
The town will rise: God's will, lieutenant, hold;
You will be shamed forever.

Re-enter OTHELLO *and* ATTENDANTS.

OTHELLO.   What is the matter here?
MONTANO. 'Zounds, I bleed still; I am hurt to the death.
  [*Faints.*]
OTHELLO. Hold, for your lives!
IAGO. Hold, ho! Lieutenant,—sir,—Montano,—Gentlemen,—
  Have you forgot all sense of place and duty?
  Hold! the general speaks to you; hold, hold, for shame!
OTHELLO. Why, how now, ho! from whence ariseth this?
  Are we turned Turks, and to ourselves do that
  Which heaven hath forbid the Ottomites?
  For Christian shame, put by this barbarous brawl;
  He that stirs next to carve for his own rage
  Holds his soul light; he dies upon his motion.
  Silence that dreadful bell! It frights the isle
  From her propriety. What is the matter, masters?
  Honest Iago, that look'st dead with grieving,
  Speak, who began this? On thy love, I charge thee.
IAGO. I do not know: friends all but now, even now,
  In quarter,° and in terms like bride and groom   *on watch*
  Devesting° them for bed; and then, but now,   *disrobing*
  As if some planet had unwitted men,
  Swords out, and tilting one at other's breast,
  In opposition bloody. I cannot speak
  Any beginning to this peevish odds;°   *fight*
  And would in action glorious I had lost
  Those legs that brought me to a part of it!
OTHELLO. How comes it, Michael, you are thus forgot?
CASSIO. I pray you, pardon me; I cannot speak.
OTHELLO. Worthy Montano, you were wont be civil;
  The gravity and stillness of your youth
  The world hath noted, and your name is great
  In mouths of wisest censure:° what's the matter,   *opinion*
  That you unlace your reputation thus,
  And spend your rich opinion for the name
  Of a night-brawler? Give me answer to it.
MONTANO. Worthy Othello, I am hurt to danger:
  Your officer, Iago, can inform you—
  While I spare speech, which something now offends° me—   *pains*
  Of all that I do know: nor know I aught
  By me that's said or done amiss this night;
  Unless self-charity be sometimes a vice,

And to defend ourselves it be a sin
When violence assails us.

OTHELLO.   Now, by heaven,
My blood begins my safer guides to rule,
And passion, having my best judgement collied,°   *blackened*
Assays° to lead the way: if I once stir,   *attempts*
Or do but lift this arm, the best of you
Shall sink in my rebuke. Give me to know
How this foul route began, who set it on,
And he that is approved° in this offence,   *convicted*
Though he had twinned with me, both at a birth,
Shall lose me. What! in a town of war,
Yet wild, the people's hearts brimful of fear,
To manage private and domestic quarrel,
In night, and on the court and guard of safety!
'Tis monstrous. Iago, who began 't?

MONTANO. If partially affined,° or leagued in office,   *obligated*
Thou dost deliver more or less than truth,
Thou art no soldier.

IAGO.   Touch me not so near:
I had rather have this tongue cut from my mouth
Than it should do offence to Michael Cassio;
Yet, I persuade myself, to speak the truth
Shall nothing wrong him. Thus it is, general.
Montano and myself being in speech,
There comes a fellow crying out for help,
And Cassio following him with determined sword,
To execute upon him. Sir, this gentleman
Steps in to Cassio and entreats his pause:
Myself the crying fellow did pursue,
Lest by his clamor—as it so fell out—
The town might fall in fright: he, swift of foot,
Outran my purpose; and I returned the rather
For that I heard the clink and fall of swords,
And Cassio high in oath; which till tonight
I ne'er might say before. When I came back—
For this was brief—I found them close together,
At blow and thrust; even as again they were
When you yourself did part them.
More of this matter cannot I report:
But men are men; the best sometimes forget:
Though Cassio did some little wrong to him,
As men in rage strike those that wish them best,
Yet surely Cassio, I believe, received
From him that fled some strange indignity,
Which patience could not pass.

OTHELLO.   I know, Iago,
Thy honesty and love doth mince this matter,
Making it light to Cassio. Cassio, I love thee;
But never more be officer of mine.

Re-enter DESDEMONA, *attended.*

Look, if my gentle love be not raised up!
I'll make thee an example.
DESDEMONA.   What's the matter?
OTHELLO. All's well now, sweeting; come away to bed.
Sir, for your hurts, myself will be your surgeon:
Lead him off. [*To* MONTANO, *who is led off.*]
Iago, look with care about the town,
And silence those whom this vile brawl distracted.
Come, Desdemona: 'tis the soldiers' life
To have their balmy slumbers waked with strife.
[*Exeunt all but* IAGO *and* CASSIO.]
IAGO. What, are you hurt, lieutenant?
CASSIO. Ay, past all surgery.
IAGO. Marry, heaven forbid!
CASSIO. Reputation, reputation, reputation! O, I have lost my
reputation! I have lost the immortal part of myself, and
what remains is bestial. My reputation, Iago, my reputa-
tion!
IAGO. As I am an honest man, I thought you had received some
bodily wound; there is more sense in that than in reputa-
tion. Reputation is an idle and most false imposition;° oft   *covering*
got without merit and lost without deserving: you have lost
no reputation at all, unless you repute yourself such a loser.
What, man! there are ways to recover the general again: you
are but now cast° in his mood,° a punishment   more   in   *dismissed / anger*
policy than in malice; even so as one would beat his offence-
less dog to affright an imperious lion: sue to him again, and
he's yours.
CASSIO. I will rather sue to be despised than to deceive so good
a commander with so slight, so drunken, and so indis-
creet an officer. Drunk? and speak parrot?° and squab-   *i.e., like a parrot*
ble? swagger? swear? and discourse fustian° with one's own   *poppycock*
shadow? O thou invisible spirit of wine, if thou hast no
name to be known by, let us call thee devil!
IAGO. What was he that you followed with your sword?
What had he done to you?
CASSIO. I know not.
IAGO. Is't possible?
CASSIO. I remember a mass of things, but nothing distinctly, a
quarrel, but nothing wherefore. O God, that men should
put an enemy in their mouths to steal away their brains!
that we should, with joy, pleasance, revel and applause,
transform ourselves into beasts!
IAGO. Why, but you are now well enough: how came you thus
recovered?
CASSIO. It hath pleased the devil drunkenness to give place to
the devil wrath: one unperfectness shows me another, to
make me frankly despise myself.
IAGO. Come, you are too severe a moraler: as the time, the

place, and the condition of this country stands, I could
heartily wish this had not befallen; but since it is as it is,
mend it for your own good.

CASSIO. I will ask him for my place again; he shall tell me I am
a drunkard! Had I as many mouths as Hydra,[9] such an
answer would stop them all. To be now a sensible man, by
and by a fool, and presently a beast! O strange! Every
inordinate cup is unblest, and the ingredient is a devil.

IAGO. Come, come, good wine is a good familiar creature, if
it be well used: exclaim no more against it. And, good
lieutenant, I think you think I love you.

CASSIO. I have well approved° it, sir. I drunk!   demonstrated

IAGO. You or any man living may be drunk at some time, man.
I'll tell you what you shall do. Our general's wife is now the
general. I may say so in this respect, for that he hath devoted and given up himself to the contemplation, mark
and denotement° of her parts and graces: confess yourself   notation
freely to her; importune her help to put you in your place
again: she is of so free,° so kind, so apt, so blessed a dis-   generous
position, she holds it a vice in her goodness not to do more
than she is requested: this broken joint between you and
her husband entreat her to splinter;° and, my fortunes   splint, repair
against any lay° worth naming, this crack of your love shall   wager
grow stronger than it was before.

CASSIO. You advise me well.

IAGO. I protest, in the sincerity of love and honest kindness.

CASSIO. I think it freely; and betimes° in the morning I will   early
beseech the virtuous Desdemona to undertake for me: I
am desperate of my fortunes if they check me here.

IAGO. You are in the right. Good night, lieutenant; I must to
the watch.

CASSIO. Good night, honest Iago. [Exit.]

IAGO. And what's he then that says I play the villain?
When this advice is free I give and honest,
Probal° to thinking, and indeed the course   probable
To win the Moor again? For 'tis most easy
The inclining Desdemona to subdue°   win over
In any honest suit. She's framed as fruitful
As the free elements. And then for her
To win the Moor—were't to renounce his baptism,
All seals and symbols of redeemèd sin—
His soul is so enfettered to her love,
That she may make, unmake, do what she list,°   likes
Even as her appetite shall play the god
With his weak function.° How am I then a villain   (as commander)
To counsel Cassio to this parallel course,
Directly to his good? Divinity of hell!
When devils will the blackest sins put on,
They do suggest at first with heavenly shows,
As I do now: for whiles this honest fool

---

[9] A mythical monster with nine heads.

Plies Desdemona to repair his fortunes,
And she for him pleads strongly to the Moor.
I'll pour this pestilence into his ear,
That she repeals° him for her body's lust: *appeals for*
And by how much she strives to do him good,
She shall undo her credit with the Moor.
So will I turn her virtue into pitch;
And out of her own goodness make the net
That shall enmesh them all.

Enter Roderigo.

How now, Roderigo!
Roderigo. I do follow here in the chase, not like a hound that
    hunts, but one that fills up the cry.° My money is almost   *pack*
    spent; I have been tonight exceedingly well cudgelled;° and   *beaten*
    I think the issue will be, I shall have so much experience
    for my pains; and so, with no money at all and a little more
    wit, return again to Venice.
Iago. How poor are they that have not patience!
    What wound did ever heal but by degrees?
    Thou know'st we work by wit and not by witchcraft,
    And wit depends on dilatory time.
    Does't not go well? Cassio hath beaten thee,
    And thou by that small hurt hast cashiered Cassio:
    Though other things grow fair against the sun,
    Yet fruits that blossom first will first be ripe:
    Content thyself awhile. By the mass, 'tis morning;
    Pleasure and action make the hours seem short.
    Retire thee; go where thou art billeted:
    Away, I say; thou shalt know more hereafter:
    Nay, get thee gone. [*Exit* Roderigo.] Two things are to be
      done:
    My wife must move° for Cassio to her mistress: *plead*
    I'll set her on;
    Myself the while to draw the Moor apart,
    And bring him jump° when he may Cassio find   *just*
    Soliciting his wife: ay, that's the way;
    Dull not device by coldness and delay. [*Exit.*]

ACT III

SCENE I
Before the castle.

Enter Cassio *and some* Musicians.

Cassio. Masters, play here; I will content° your pains; Some-   *reward*
    thing that's brief; and bid "Good morrow, general."
    [*Music.*]

Enter Clown.

CLOWN. Why, masters, have your instruments been in Naples,
  that they speak i' the nose thus?[10]
FIRST MUSICIAN. How, sir, how!
CLOWN. Are these, I pray you, wind-instruments?
FIRST MUSICIAN. Ay, marry, are they, sir.
CLOWN. O, thereby hangs a tail.
FIRST MUSICIAN. Whereby hangs a tale, sir?
CLOWN. Marry, sir, by many a wind-instrument that I know.
  But, masters, here's money for you: and the general so
  likes your music, that he desires you, for love's sake, to
  make no more noise with it.
FIRST MUSICIAN. Well, sir, we will not.
CLOWN. If you have any music that may not be heard, to 't
  again: but, as they say, to hear music the general does not
  greatly care.
FIRST MUSICIAN. We have none such, sir.
CLOWN. Then put up your pipes in your bag, for I'll away: go;
  vanish into air; away! [*Exeunt* MUSICIANS.]
CASSIO. Dost thou hear, my honest friend?
CLOWN. No, I hear not your honest friend; I hear you.
CASSIO. Prithee, keep up thy quillets.° There's a poor piece   *quibbles*
  of gold for thee: if the gentlewoman that attends the gen-
  eral's wife be stirring, tell her there's one Cassio entreats
  her a little favor of speech: wilt thou do this?
CLOWN. She is stirring, sir; if she will stir hither, I shall seem
  to notify unto her.
CASSIO. Do, good my friend. [*Exit* CLOWN.]

Enter IAGO.

                    In happy time, Iago.
IAGO. You have not been a-bed, then?
CASSIO. Why, no; the day had broke
  Before we parted. I have made bold, Iago.
  To send in to your wife: my suit to her
  Is, that she will to virtuous Desdemona
  Procure me some access.
IAGO.   I'll send her to you presently;
  And I'll devise a mean to draw the Moor
  Out of the way, that your converse and business
  May be more free.
CASSIO. I humbly thank you for't. [*Exit* IAGO.] I never knew
  A Florentine more kind and honest.

Enter EMILIA.

EMILIA. Good morrow, good lieutenant: I am sorry
  For your displeasure; but all will sure be well.

---

[10] A reference to the nasal Neapolitan accent but also to the free-wheeling reputation and endemic
  syphilis (damaging the nose in advanced stages) of this sailors' town.

The general and his wife are talking of it,
And speaks for you stoutly: the Moor replies,
That he you hurt is of great fame in Cyprus
And great affinity,° and that in wholesome wisdom   *family*
He might not but refuse you; but he protests he loves you,
And needs no other suitor but his likings
To take the safest occasion by the front°   *forelock*
To bring you in again.

CASSIO.   Yet, I beseech you,
If you think fit, or that it may be done,
Give me advantage of some brief discourse
With Desdemona alone.

EMILIA.   Pray you, come in:
I will bestow you where you shall have time
To speak your bosom freely.

CASSIO.   I am much bound to you. [*Exeunt.*]

SCENE II
A room in the castle.

Enter OTHELLO, IAGO, *and* GENTLEMEN.

OTHELLO. These letters give, Iago, to the pilot;
And by him do my duties to the senate:
That done, I will be walking on the works;°   *fortifications*
Repair there to me.

IAGO.   Well, my good lord, I'll do 't.

OTHELLO. This fortification, gentlemen, shall we see 't?

GENTLEMAN. We'll wait upon your lordship. [*Exeunt.*]

SCENE III
The garden of the castle.

Enter DESDEMONA, CASSIO, *and* EMILIA.

DESDEMONA. Be thou assured, good Cassio, I will do
All my abilities in thy behalf.

EMILIA. Good madam, do: I warrant it grieves my husband
As if the case were his.

DESDEMONA. O, that's an honest fellow. Do not doubt, Cassio,
But I will have my lord and you again
As friendly as you were.

CASSIO.   Bounteous madam,
Whatever shall become of Michael Cassio,
He's never any thing but your true servant.

DESDEMONA. I know 't: I thank you. You do love my lord:
You have known him long; and be you well assured
He shall in strangeness° stand no farther off   *estrangement*
Than in a politic° distance.   *diplomatic*

CASSIO.   Ay, but, lady,
That policy may either last so long,

Or feed upon such nice and waterish diet,
Or breed itself so out of circumstance,
That, I being absent and my place supplied,
My general will forget my love and service.

DESDEMONA. Do not doubt° that; before Emilia here   *fear*
I give thee warrant of thy place: assure thee,
If I do vow a friendship, I'll perform it
To the last article: my lord shall never rest;
I'll watch him tame[11] and talk him out of patience;
His bed shall seem a school, his board a shrift;°   *confessional*
I'll intermingle every thing he does
With Cassio's suit: therefore be merry, Cassio;
For thy solicitor shall rather die
Than give thy cause away.

Enter OTHELLO *and* IAGO, *at a distance.*

EMILIA. Madam, here comes my lord.
CASSIO. Madam, I'll take my leave.
DESDEMONA. Nay, stay and hear me speak.
CASSIO. Madam, not now: I am very ill at ease,
    Unfit for mine own purposes.
DESDEMONA. Well, do your discretion. [*Exit* CASSIO.]
IAGO. Ha! I like not that.
OTHELLO. What dost thou say?
IAGO. Nothing, my lord: or if—I know not what.
OTHELLO. Was not that Cassio parted from my wife?
IAGO. Cassio, my lord! No, sure, I cannot think it,
    That he would steal away so guilty-like,
    Seeing you coming.
OTHELLO.   I do believe 'twas he.
DESDEMONA. How now, my lord!
    I have been talking with a suitor here,
    A man that languishes in your displeasure.
OTHELLO. Who is't you mean?
DESDEMONA. Why, your lieutenant, Cassio. Good my lord,
    If I have any grace or power to move you,
    His present reconciliation take;
    For if he be not one that truly loves you,
    That errs in ignorance and not in cunning,
    I have no judgement in an honest face:
    I prithee, call him back.
OTHELLO.   Went he hence now?
DESDEMONA. Ay, sooth;° so humbled,   *true*
    That he hath left part of his grief with me,
    To suffer with him. Good love, call him back.
OTHELLO. Not now, sweet Desdemona; some other time.
DESDEMONA. But shall't be shortly?
OTHELLO.   The sooner, sweet, for you.

[11] Hawks are sometimes kept awake until tamed.

DESDEMONA. Shall't be tonight at supper?
OTHELLO. No, not tonight.
DESDEMONA. Tomorrow dinner then?
OTHELLO. I shall not dine at home;
  I meet the captains at the citadel.
DESDEMONA. Why then tomorrow night; or Tuesday morn;
  On Tuesday noon, or night; on Wednesday morn:
  I prithee, name the time; but let it not
  Exceed three days: in faith, he's penitent;
  And yet his trespass, in our common reason—
  Save that, they say, the wars must make examples
  Out of their best—is not almost a fault
  To incur a private check.° When shall he come?   *rebuke*
  Tell me, Othello: I wonder in my soul,
  What you would ask me, that I should deny,
  Or stand so mammering° on. What! Michael Cassio,   *hesitant*
  That came a-wooing with you, and so many a time
  When I have spoke of you dispraisingly
  Hath ta'en your part; to have so much to do
  To bring him in! Trust me, I could do much—
OTHELLO. Prithee, no more: let him come when he will;
  I will deny thee nothing.
DESDEMONA. Why, this is not a boon;°   *gift*
  'Tis as I should entreat you wear your gloves,
  Or feed on nourishing dishes, or keep you warm,
  Or sue to you to do a peculiar profit
  To your own person: nay, when I have a suit
  Wherein I mean to touch your love indeed,
  It shall be full of poise° and difficult weight,   *matter*
  And fearful to be granted.
OTHELLO. I will deny thee nothing:
  Whereon, I do beseech thee, grant me this,
  To leave me but a little to myself.
DESDEMONA. Shall I deny you? No: farewell, my lord.
OTHELLO. Farewell, my Desdemona: I'll come to thee straight.
DESDEMONA. Emilia, come. Be as your fancies teach you;
  Whate'er you be, I am obedient.
  [*Exeunt* DESDEMONA *and* EMILIA.]
OTHELLO. Excellent wretch! Perdition catch my soul,
  But I do love thee! And when I love thee not,
  Chaos is come again.
IAGO. My noble lord,—
OTHELLO. What dost thou say, Iago?
IAGO. Did Michael Cassio, when you wooed my lady,
  Know of your love?
OTHELLO. He did, from first to last: why dost thou ask?
IAGO. But for a satisfaction of my thought;
  No further harm.
OTHELLO. Why of thy thought, Iago?
IAGO. I did not think he had been acquainted with her.
OTHELLO. O, yes, and went between us very oft.

IAGO. Indeed!

OTHELLO. Indeed! ay, indeed: discern'st thou aught in that?
   Is he not honest?

IAGO. Honest, my lord!

OTHELLO. Honest! ay, honest.

IAGO. My lord, for aught I know.

OTHELLO. What dost thou think?

IAGO. Think, my lord!

OTHELLO. Think, my lord! By heaven, he echoes me,
   As if there were some monster in his thought
   Too hideous to be shown. Thou dost mean something:
   I heard thee say even now, thou likedst not that,
   When Cassio left my wife: what didst not like?
   And when I told thee he was of my counsel
   In my whole course of wooing, thou criedst 'Indeed!'
   And didst contract and purse thy brow together,
   As if thou then hadst shut up in thy brain
   Some horrible conceit:° if thou dost love me,   *idea*
   Show me thy thought.

IAGO. My lord, you know I love you.

OTHELLO.   I think thou dost;
   And for I know thou'rt full of love and honesty
   And weigh'st thy words before thou givest them breath,
   Therefore these stops of thine fright me the more:
   For such things in a false disloyal knave
   Are tricks of custom; but in a man that's just
   They're close delations,° working from the heart,   *secret charges*
   That passion cannot rule.

IAGO.   For Michael Cassio,
   I dare be sworn I think that he is honest.

OTHELLO. I think so too.

IAGO.   Men should be what they seem;
   Or those that be not, would they might seem none!

OTHELLO. Certain, men should be what they seem.

IAGO. Why then I think Cassio's an honest man.

OTHELLO. Nay, yet there's more in this:
   I prithee, speak to me as to thy thinkings,
   As thou dost ruminate, and give thy worst of thoughts
   The worst of words.

IAGO.   Good my lord, pardon me:
   Though I am bound to every act of duty,
   I am not bound to that all slaves are free to.
   Utter my thoughts? Why, say they are vile and false;
   As where's that palace whereinto foul things
   Sometimes intrude not? Who has a breast so pure,
   But some uncleanly apprehensions
   Keep leets° and law-days, and in session sit   *courts*
   With meditations lawful?

OTHELLO. Thou dost conspire against thy friend, Iago,
   If thou but think'st him wronged and makest his ear
   A stranger to thy thoughts.

IAGO.   I do beseech you—

Though I perchance am vicious in my guess,
As, I confess, it is my nature's plague
To spy into abuses, and oft my jealousy
Shapes faults that are not—that your wisdom yet,
From one that so imperfectly conceits,°   *speculates*
Would take no notice, nor build yourself a trouble
Out of his scattering and unsure observance.
It were not for your quiet nor your good,
Nor for my manhood, honesty, or wisdom,
To let you know my thoughts.
OTHELLO.   What dost thou mean?
IAGO. Good name in man and woman, dear my lord,
Is the immediate jewel of their souls:
Who steals my purse steals trash; 'tis something, nothing;
'Twas mine, 'tis his, and has been slave to thousands;
But he that filches from me my good name
Robs me of that which not enriches him
And makes me poor indeed.
OTHELLO. By heaven, I'll know thy thoughts.
IAGO. You cannot, if my heart were in your hand;
Nor shall not, whilst 'tis in my custody.
OTHELLO. Ha!
IAGO.   O, beware, my lord, of jealousy;
It is the green-eyed monster, which doth mock°   *torment*
The meat it feeds on: that cuckold lives in bliss
Who, certain of his fate, loves not his wronger;
But, O, what damnèd minutes tells he o'er
Who dotes, yet doubts, suspects, yet strongly loves!
OTHELLO. O misery!
IAGO. Poor and content is rich, and rich enough;
But riches fineless° is as poor as winter   *without end*
To him that ever fears he shall be poor:
Good heaven, the souls of all my tribe defend
From jealousy!
OTHELLO.   Why, why is this?
Think'st thou I'ld make a life of jealousy,
To follow still the changes of the moon
With fresh suspicions? No; to be once in doubt
Is once to be resolved: exchange me for a goat,
When I shall turn the business of my soul
To such exsufflicate° and blown° surmises,   *puffed up / swollen*
Matching thy inference. 'Tis not to make me jealous
To say my wife is fair, feeds well, loves company,
Is free of speech, sings, plays and dances well;
Where virtue is, these are more virtuous:
Nor from mine own weak merits will I draw
The smallest fear or doubt of her revolt;
For she had eyes, and chose me. No, Iago;
I'll see before I doubt; when I doubt, prove;
And on the proof, there is no more but this,
Away at once with love or jealousy!
IAGO. I am glad of it; for now I shall have reason

To show the love and duty that I bear you
With franker spirit: therefore, as I am bound,
Receive it from me. I speak not yet of proof.
Look to your wife; observe her well with Cassio;
Wear your eye thus, not jealous nor secure:
I would not have your free and noble nature
Out of self-bounty° be abused; look to 't: *your own kindness*
I know our country disposition well;
In Venice they do let heaven see the pranks
They dare not show their husbands; their best conscience
Is not to leave 't undone, but keep 't unknown.

OTHELLO. Dost thou say so?

IAGO. She did deceive her father, marrying you;
And when she seemed to shake and fear your looks,
She loved them most.

OTHELLO.   And so she did.

IAGO.   Why, go to° then;   *go on*
She that so young could give out such a seeming,
To seel° her father's eyes up close as oak—   *sew*
He thought 'twas witchcraft—but I am much to blame;
I humbly do beseech you of your pardon
For too much loving you.

OTHELLO.   I am bound to thee for ever.

IAGO. I see this hath a little dashed your spirits.

OTHELLO. Not a jot,° not a jot.   *bit*

IAGO.   I' faith, I fear it has.
I hope you will consider what is spoke
Comes from my love; but I do see you're moved:
I am to pray you not to strain my speech
To grosser issues nor to larger reach
Than to suspicion.

OTHELLO. I will not.

IAGO.   Should you do so, my lord,
My speech should fall into such vile success
As my thoughts aim not at. Cassio's my worthy friend—
My lord, I see you're moved.

OTHELLO.   No, not much moved:
I do not think but Desdemona's honest.°   *chaste*

IAGO. Long live she so! and long live you to think so!

OTHELLO. And yet, how nature erring from itself—

IAGO. Ay, there's the point: as—to be bold with you—
Not to affect° many proposèd matches   *like*
Of her own clime, complexion and degree,
Whereto we see in all things nature tends—
Foh! one may smell in such a will° most rank,   *lust*
Foul disproportion, thoughts unnatural.
But pardon me: I do not in position°   *hypothesis*
Distinctly speak of her; though I may fear
Her will, recoiling to her better judgement,
May fall° to match you with her country forms,°   *happen / countrymen*
And happily° repent.   *perhaps*

OTHELLO.   Farewell, farewell:
 If more thou dost perceive, let me know more;
 Set on thy wife to observe: leave me, Iago.
IAGO [*Going*]. My lord, I take my leave.
OTHELLO. Why did I marry? This honest creature doubtless
 Sees and knows more, much more, than he unfolds.
IAGO [*Returning*]. My lord, I would I might entreat your honor
 To scan° this thing no further; leave it to time: *analyze*
 Though it be fit that Cassio have his place,
 For sure he fills it up with great ability,
 Yet, if you please to hold him off awhile,
 You shall by that perceive him and his means:
 Note if your lady strain° his entertainment°   *urge / employment*
 With any strong or vehement importunity;
 Much will be seen in that. In the mean time,
 Let me be thought too busy in my fears—
 As worthy cause I have to fear I am—
 And hold her free,° I do beseech your honor.   *guiltless*
OTHELLO. Fear not my government.°   *self-control*
IAGO. I once more take my leave. [*Exit.*]
OTHELLO. This fellow's of exceeding honesty,
 And knows all qualities,° with a learnèd spirit,   *natures*
 Of human dealings. If I do prove her haggard,°   *a strayed hawk*
 Though that her jesses° were my dear heart-strings, *restraining straps*
 I'ld whistle her off and let her down° the wind   *fly down*
 To prey° at fortune.° Haply, for I am black   *hunt / random*
 And have not those soft parts of conversation
 That chamberers° have, or for I am declined   *womanizers*
 Into the vale of years,—yet that's not much—
 She's gone; I am abused, and my relief
 Must be to loathe her. O curse of marriage,
 That we can call these delicate creatures ours,
 And not their appetites! I had rather be a toad,
 And live upon the vapor of a dungeon,
 Than keep a corner in the thing I love
 For others' uses. Yet, 'tis the plague of great ones;
 Prerogatived are they less than the base;
 'Tis destiny unshunnable, like death:
 Even then this forkèd plague° is fated to us   *cuckoldry*
 When we do quicken.° Desdemona comes: *are conceived*

Re-enter DESDEMONA *and* EMILIA.

 If she be false, O, then heaven mocks itself!
 I'll not believe 't.
DESDEMONA.   How now, my dear Othello!
 Your dinner, and the generous islanders
 By you invited, do attend your presence.
OTHELLO. I am to blame.
DESDEMONA.   Why do you speak so faintly?
 Are you not well?
OTHELLO. I have a pain upon my forehead here.

DESDEMONA. Faith, that's with watching; 'twill away again:
    Let me but bind it hard, within this hour
    It will be well.
OTHELLO.   Your napkin is too little;
    [*He puts the handkerchief from him; and she drops it.*]
    Let it alone. Come, I'll go in with you.
DESDEMONA. I am very sorry that you are not well.
    [*Exeunt* OTHELLO *and* DESDEMONA.]
EMILIA. I am glad I have found this napkin:
    This was her first remembrance from the Moor:
    My wayward husband hath a hundred times
    Woo'd me to steal it; but she so loves the token,
    For he conjured her she should ever keep it,
    That she reserves it evermore about her
    To kiss and talk to. I'll have the work ta'en out,°   copied
    And give 't Iago: what he will do with it
    Heaven knows, not I;
    I nothing but to please his fantasy.°   whim

                            Re-enter IAGO.

IAGO. How now! What do you here alone?
EMILIA. Do not you chide; I have a thing for you.
IAGO. A thing for me? It is a common thing—
EMILIA. Ha!
IAGO. To have a foolish wife.
EMILIA. O, is that all? What will you give me now
    For that same handkerchief?
IAGO.   What handkerchief?
EMILIA. What handkerchief!
    Why, that the Moor first gave to Desdemona;
    That which so often you did bid me steal.
IAGO. Hast stol'n it from her?
EMILIA. No, faith; she let it drop by negligence,
    And, to the advantage, I being here took 't up.
    Look, here it is.
IAGO.   A good wench; give it me.
EMILIA. What will you do with 't, that you have been so earnest
    To have me filch it?
IAGO   [*Snatching it*]. Why, what's that to you?
EMILIA. If 't be not for some purpose of import,°   importance
    Give 't me again: poor lady, she'll run mad
    When she shall lack it.
IAGO. Be not acknown on 't;° I have use for it.   knowledgeable about it
    Go, leave me. [*Exit* EMILIA.]
    I will in Cassio's lodging lose this napkin,
    And let him find it. Trifles light as air
    Are to the jealous confirmations strong
    As proofs of holy writ: this may do something.
    The Moor already changes with my poison:
    Dangerous conceits are in their natures poisons,

Which at the first are scarce found to distaste,
But with a little act upon the blood
Burn like the mines of sulphur. I did say so:
Look, where he comes!

Re-enter OTHELLO.

Not poppy, nor mandragora,°   *a narcotic*
Nor all the drowsy syrups of the world,
Shall ever medicine thee to that sweet sleep
Which thou owedst° yesterday.   *owned*
OTHELLO.   Ha! ha! false to me?
IAGO. Why, how now, general! no more of that.
OTHELLO. Avaunt! Be gone! thou hast set me on the rack:
I swear 'tis better to be much abused
Than but to know't a little.
IAGO.   How now, my lord!
OTHELLO. What sense had I of her stol'n hours of lust?
I saw't not, thought it not, it harmed not me:
I slept the next night well, was free and merry;
I found not Cassio's kisses on her lips:
He that is robbed, not wanting what is stol'n,
Let him not know't and he's not robbed at all.
IAGO. I am sorry to hear this.
OTHELLO. I had been happy, if the general camp,
Pioners° and all, had tasted her sweet body,   *Privates*
So I had nothing known. O, now forever
Farewell the tranquil mind! farewell content!
Farewell the plumèd troop and the big wars
That make ambition virtue! O, farewell,
Farewell the neighing steed and the shrill trump,
The spirit-stirring drum, the ear-piercing fife,
The royal banner and all quality,
Pride, pomp and circumstances° of glorious war!   *pageantry*
And, O you mortal engines,° whose rude throats   *cannons*
The immortal Jove's dread clamors counterfeit,
Farewell! Othello's occupation's gone!
IAGO. Is't possible, my lord?
OTHELLO. Villain, be sure thou prove my love a whore;
Be sure of it; give me the <u>ocular proof;</u>
Or, by the worth of man's eternal soul,
Thou hadst been better have been born a dog
Than answer my waked wrath!
IAGO.   Is't come to this?
OTHELLO. Make me to see't; or at the least so prove it,
That the probation° bear no hinge nor loop   *proof*
To hang a doubt on; or woe upon thy life!
IAGO. My noble lord,—
OTHELLO. If thou dost slander her and torture me,
Never pray more; abandon all remorse;
On horror's head horrors accumulate;

Do deeds to make heaven weep, all earth amazed;
For nothing canst thou to damnation add
Greater than that.
IAGO.   O grace! O heaven defend me!
Are you a man? Have you a soul or sense?
God be wi' you; take mine office. O wretched fool,
That livest to make thine honesty a vice!
O monstrous world! Take note, take note, O world,
To be direct and honest is not safe.
I thank you for this profit,° and from hence   *gain (in wisdom)*
I'll love no friend sith° love breeds such offence.   *since*
OTHELLO. Nay, stay: thou shouldst be honest.
IAGO. I should be wise; for honesty's a fool,
And loses that it works for.
OTHELLO.   By the world,
I think my wife be honest, and think she is not;
I think that thou are just, and think thou are not:
I'll have some proof. Her name, that was as fresh
As Dian's° visage, is now begrimed and black   *goddess of chastity*
As mine own face. If there be cords, or knives,
Poison, or fire, or suffocating streams,
I'll not endure it. Would I were satisfied!
IAGO. I see, sir, you are eaten up with passion:
I do repent me that I put it to you.
You would be satisfied?
OTHELLO.   Would! nay, I will.
IAGO. And may: but, how? How satisfied, my lord?
Would you, the supervisor, grossly gape on?
Behold her topped?
OTHELLO.   Death and damnation! O!
IAGO. It were a tedious difficulty, I think,
To bring them to that prospect: damn them then,
If ever mortal eyes do see them bolster°   *sleep together*
More than their own! What then? How then?
What shall I say? Where's satisfaction?
It is impossible you should see this,
Were they as prime° as goats, as hot as monkeys,   *lustful*
As salt° as wolves in pride,° and fools as gross   *desirous / heat*
As ignorance made drunk. But yet, I say,
If imputation and strong circumstances,
Which lead directly to the door of truth,
Will give you satisfaction, you may have't.
OTHELLO. Give me a living reason she's disloyal.
IAGO. I do not like the office:
But sith I am entered in this cause so far,
Pricked° to 't by foolish honesty and love,   *Driven*
I will go on. I lay with Cassio lately,
And being troubled with a raging tooth,
I could not sleep.
There are a kind of men so loose of soul,
That in their sleeps will mutter their affairs:

One of this kind is Cassio:
In sleep I heard him say "Sweet Desdemona,
Let us be wary, let us hide our loves";
And then, sir, would he gripe° and wring my hand,   *grip*
Cry "O sweet creature!" and then kiss me hard,
As if he plucked up kisses by the roots,
That grew upon my lips: then laid his leg
Over my thigh, and sighed and kissed, and then
Cried "Cursed fate that gave thee to the Moor!"
OTHELLO. O monstrous! monstrous!
IAGO.   Nay, this was but his dream.
OTHELLO. But this denoted a foregone conclusion:
'Tis a shrewd doubt,° though it be but a dream.   *astute suspicion*
IAGO. And this may help to thicken other proofs
That do demonstrate thinly.
OTHELLO.   I'll tear her all to pieces.
IAGO. Nay, but be wise: yet we see nothing done;
She may be honest yet. Tell me but this;
Have you not sometimes seen a handkerchief
Spotted with strawberries in your wife's hand?
OTHELLO. I gave her such a one; 'twas my first gift.
IAGO. I know not that: but such a handkerchief—
I am sure it was your wife's—did I today
See Cassio wipe his beard with.
OTHELLO.   If it be that,—
IAGO. If it be that, or any that was hers,
It speaks against her with the other proofs.
OTHELLO. O, that the slave had forty thousand lives!
One is too poor, too weak for my revenge.
Now do I see 'tis true. Look here, Iago;
All my fond love thus do I blow to heaven:
'Tis gone.
Arise, black vengeance, from thy hollow cell!
Yield up, O love, thy crown and hearted throne
To tyrannous hate! Swell, bosom, with thy fraught,°   *freight*
For 'tis of aspics' tongues!
IAGO.   Yet be content.
OTHELLO. O, blood, blood, blood!
IAGO. Patience, I say; your mind perhaps may change.
OTHELLO. Never, Iago. Like to the Pontic sea,°   *Black Sea*
Whose icy current and compulsive course
Ne'er feels retiring ebb, but keeps due on
To the Propontic and the Hellespont;[12]
Even so my bloody thoughts, with violent pace,
Shall ne'er look back, ne'er ebb to humble love,
Till that a capable° and wide revenge   *capacious*
Swallow them up. Now, by yond marble heaven,

---

[12] The "Propontic" is another name for the Sea of Marmara; the "Hellespont" is an ancient name for the Dardanelles through which Sea of Marmara drains into the Mediterranean Sea.

In the due reverence of a sacred vow [*Kneels.*]
I here engage my words.
IAGO.   Do not rise yet [*Kneels.*]
Witness, you ever-burning lights above,
You elements that clip° us round about,   *encircle*
Witness that here Iago doth give up
The execution° of his wit, hands, heart,   *action*
To wronged Othello's service! Let him command,
And to obey shall be in me remorse,°   *an act of pity*
What bloody business ever.
OTHELLO.   I greet thy love,
Not with vain thanks, but with acceptance bounteous,
And will upon the instant put thee to 't:
Within these three days let me hear thee say
That Cassio's not alive.
IAGO. My friend is dead; 'tis done at your request:
But let her live.
OTHELLO.   Damn her, lewd minx! O, damn her!
Come, go with me apart: I will withdraw,
To furnish me with some swift means of death
For the fair devil. Now art thou my lieutenant.
IAGO. I am your own for ever. [*Exeunt.*]

SCENE IV
Before the castle.

Enter DESDEMONA, EMILIA, *and* CLOWN.

DESDEMONA. Do you know, sirrah, where Lieutenant Cassio
   lies?
CLOWN. I dare not say he lies any where.
DESDEMONA. Why, man?
CLOWN. He's a soldier; and for one to say a soldier lies,
   is° stabbing.   *i.e., is cause for*
DESDEMONA. Go to: where lodges he?
CLOWN. To tell you where he lodges, is to tell you where I lie.
DESDEMONA. Can any thing be made of this?
CLOWN. I know not where he lodges; and for me to devise
   a lodging, and say he lies here or he lies there, were to lie
   in mine own throat.
DESDEMONA. Can you inquire him out and be edified by re-
   port?
CLOWN. I will catechize the world for him; that is, make ques-
   tions and by them answer.
DESDEMONA. Seek him, bid him come hither: tell him I have
   moved my lord on his behalf and hope all will be well.
CLOWN. To do this is within the compass of man's wit, and
   therefore I will attempt the doing it. [*Exit.*]
DESDEMONA. Where should I lose that handkerchief, Emilia?
EMILIA. I know not, madam.
DESDEMONA. Believe me, I had rather have lost my purse
   Full of crusadoes:° and, but my noble Moor   *gold coins*

Is true of mind and made of no such baseness
As jealous creatures are, it were enough
To put him to ill thinking.
EMILIA.   Is he not jealous?
DESDEMONA. Who, he? I think the sun where he was born
Drew all such humors° from him.   *feelings*
EMILIA.   Look, where he comes.
DESDEMONA. I will not leave him now till Cassio
Be called to him.

Enter OTHELLO.

How is 't with you, my lord?
OTHELLO. Well, my good lady. [*Aside*] O, hardness to dissemble!
How do you, Desdemona?
DESDEMONA.   Well, my good lord.
OTHELLO. Give me your hand: this hand is moist, my lady.
DESDEMONA. It yet has felt no age nor known no sorrow.
OTHELLO. This argues fruitfulness and liberal heart:
Hot, hot, and moist: this hand of yours requires
A sequester° from liberty, fasting and prayer,   *separation*
Much castigation, exercise devout;
For here's a young and sweating devil here,
That commonly rebels. 'Tis a good hand,
A frank one.
DESDEMONA.   You may, indeed, say so;
For 'twas that hand that gave away my heart.
OTHELLO. A liberal hand: the hearts of old gave hands;
But our new heraldry is hands, not hearts.
DESDEMONA. I cannot speak of this. Come now, your promise.
OTHELLO. What promise, chuck?°   *dear*
DESDEMONA. I have sent to bid Cassio come speak with you.
OTHELLO. I have a salt and sorry rheum° offends me;   *cold*
Lend me thy handkerchief.
DESDEMONA. Here, my lord.
OTHELLO. That which I gave you.
DESDEMONA. I have it not about me.
OTHELLO. Not?
DESDEMONA. No, indeed, my lord.
OTHELLO. That's a fault. That handkerchief
Did an Egyptian to my mother give;
She was a charmer,° and could almost read   *magician*
The thoughts of people: she told her, while she kept it
'Twould make her amiable and subdue my father
Entirely to her love, but if she lost it
Or made a gift of it, my father's eye
Should hold her loathed and his spirits should hunt
After new fancies: she dying gave it me,
And bid me, when my fate would have me wive,
To give it her. I did so: and take heed on 't;
Make it a darling like your precious eye;

To lose 't or give 't away were such perdition
As nothing else could match,
DESDEMONA.   Is't possible?
OTHELLO. 'Tis true: there's magic in the web of it:
  A sibyl,° that had numbered in the world   *prophetess*
  The sun to course two hundred compasses,
  In her prophetic fury sewed the work;
  The worms were hallowed that did breed the silk;
  And it was dyed in mummy° which the skillful   *fluid from mummies*
  Conserved of maidens' hearts.
DESDEMONA.   Indeed! is't true?
OTHELLO. Most veritable; therefore look to 't well.
DESDEMONA. Then would to God that I had never seen 't!
OTHELLO. Ha! wherefore?
DESDEMONA. Why do you speak so startingly and rash?
OTHELLO. Is 't lost? Is 't gone? Speak, is it out 'o the way?
DESDEMONA. Heaven bless us!
OTHELLO. Say you?
DESDEMONA. It is not lost; but what an if it were?
OTHELLO. How!
DESDEMONA. I say, it is not lost.
OTHELLO. Fetch 't, let me see it.
DESDEMONA. Why, so I can, sir, but I will not now.
  This is a trick to put me from my suit:
  Pray you, let Cassio be received again.
OTHELLO. Fetch me the handkerchief: my mind misgives.
DESDEMONA. Come, come;
  You'll never meet a more sufficient° man.   *able*
OTHELLO. The handkerchief!
DESDEMONA.   I pray, talk me of Cassio.
OTHELLO. The handkerchief!
DESDEMONA.   A man that all his time
  Hath founded his good fortunes on your love,
  Shared dangers with you,—
OTHELLO. The handkerchief!
DESDEMONA. In sooth, you are to blame.
OTHELLO. Away! [*Exit.*]
EMILIA. Is not this man jealous?
DESDEMONA. I ne'er saw this before.
  Sure there's some wonder in this handkerchief:
  I am most unhappy in the loss of it.
EMILIA. 'Tis not a year or two shows us a man:
  They are all but stomachs and we all but food;
  They eat us hungerly, and when they are full
  They belch us. Look you, Cassio and my husband.

Enter CASSIO *and* IAGO.

IAGO. There is no other way; 'tis she must do 't:
  And, lo, the happiness!° Go and importune her.   *luck*
DESDEMONA. How now, good Cassio! What's the news with you?

CASSIO. Madam, my former suit: I do beseech you
   That by your virtuous means I may again
   Exist, and be a member of his love
   Whom I with all the office° of my heart   *service*
   Entirely honor: I would not be delayed.
   If my offence be of such moral kind
   That nor my service past nor present sorrows
   Nor purposed merit in futurity
   Can ransom me into his love again,
   But to know so must be my benefit;
   So shall I clothe me in a forced content
   And shut myself up in some other course
   To fortune's alms.
DESDEMONA.   Alas, thrice-gentle Cassio!
   My advocation° is not now in tune;   *advocacy*
   My lord is not my lord, nor should I know him
   Were he in favor° as in humor altered.   *appearance*
   So help me every spirit sanctified,
   As I have spoken for you all my best
   And stood within the blank° of his displeasure   *center*
   For my free speech! You must awhile be patient:
   What I can do I will; and more I will
   Than for myself I dare: let that suffice you.
IAGO. Is my lord angry?
EMILIA.   He went hence but now,
   And certainly in strange unquietness.
IAGO. Can he be angry? I have seen the cannon,
   When it hath blown his ranks into the air,
   And, like the devil, from his very arm
   Puffed his own brother; and can he be angry?
   Something of moment then: I will go meet him:
   That's matter in't indeed if he be angry.
DESDEMONA. I prithee, do so. [*Exit* IAGO.]
                   Something sure of state,
   Either from Venice or some unhatched practice°   *uncovered plot*
   Made demonstrable here in Cyprus to him,
   Hath puddled° his clear spirit; and in such cases   *muddied*
   Men's natures wrangle with inferior things,
   Though great ones are their object. 'Tis even so;
   For let our finger ache, and it indues°   *brings*
   Our other healthful members even to that sense
   Of pain: nay, we must think men are not gods,
   Nor of them look for such observancy°   *observances*
   As fits the bridal. Beshrew° me much, Emilia,   *Curse*
   I was, unhandsome° warrior as I am,   *unfitting*
   Arraigning his unkindness with my soul;
   But now I find I had suborned° the witness,   *induced to perjury*
   And he's indicted falsely.
EMILIA. Pray heaven it be state-matters, as you think,
   And no conception nor no jealous toy
   Concerning you.

DESDEMONA. Alas the day, I never gave him cause!
EMILIA. But jealous souls will not be answered so;
   They are not ever jealous for the cause,
   But jealous for they are jealous: 'tis a monster
   Begot upon itself, born on itself.
DESDEMONA. Heaven keep that monster from Othello's mind!
EMILIA. Lady, amen.
DESDEMONA. I will go seek him. Cassio, walk hereabout:
   If I do find him fit, I'll move your suit,
   And seek to effect it to my uttermost.
CASSIO. I humbly thank your ladyship.
   [*Exeunt* DESDEMONA *and* EMILIA.]

                       Enter BIANCA.

BIANCA. Save you, friend Cassio!
CASSIO.   What make you from home?
   How is it with you, my most fair Bianca?
   I' faith, sweet love, I was coming to your house.
BIANCA. And I was going to your lodging, Cassio.
   What, keep a week away? Seven days and nights?
   Eight score eight hours? And lovers' absent hours,
   More tedious than the dial° eight score times?   *whole day*
   O weary reckoning!
CASSIO.   Pardon me, Bianca:
   I have this while with leaden thoughts been pressed;
   But I shall in a more continuate° time   *uninterrupted*
   Strike off this score° of absence. Sweet Bianca,   *account*
   [*Giving her* DESDEMONA'S *handkerchief.*]
   Take me this work out.
BIANCA.   O Cassio, whence came this?
   This is some token from a newer friend:
   To the felt absence now I feel a cause:
   Is 't come to this? Well, well.
CASSIO.   Go to, woman!
   Throw your vile guesses in the devil's teeth,
   From whence you have them. You are jealous now
   That this is from some mistress, some remembrance:
   No, by my faith, Bianca.
BIANCA.   Why, whose is it?
CASSIO. I know not, sweet: I found it in my chamber.
   I like the work well: ere it be demanded—
   As like enough it will—I'ld have it copied:
   Take it, and do 't; and leave me for this time.
BIANCA. Leave you! Wherefore?
CASSIO. I do attend here on the general;
   And think it no addition, nor my wish,
   To have him see me womaned.°   *with a woman*
BIANCA.   Why, I pray you?
CASSIO. Not that I love you not.
BIANCA.   But that you do not love me.

I pray you, bring me on the way a little;
And say if I shall see you soon at night.
Cassio. 'Tis but a little way that I can bring you;
For I attend here: but I'll see you soon.
Bianca. 'Tis very good; I must be circumstanced.°   *ruled by circumstances*
[*Exeunt.*]

ACT IV

SCENE I

Cyprus. Before the castle.

Enter Othello *and* Iago.

Iago. Will you think so?
Othello.   Think so, Iago!
Iago.   What,
To kiss in private?
Othello.   An unauthorized kiss.
Iago. Or to be naked with her friend in bed
An hour or more, not meaning any harm?
Othello. Naked in bed, Iago, and not mean harm!
It is hypocrisy against the devil:
They that mean virtuously and yet do so,
The devil their virtue tempts and they tempt heaven.
Iago. So they do nothing, 'tis a venial slip:
But if I give my wife a handkerchief—
Othello. What then?
Iago. Why, then, 'tis hers, my lord; and being hers,
She may, I think, bestow 't on any man.
Othello. She is protectress of her honor too:
May she give that?
Iago. Her honor is an essence that's not seen;
They have it very oft that have it not:
But for the handkerchief—
Othello. By heaven, I would most gladly have forgot it:
Thou said'st—O, it comes o'er my memory,
As doth the raven° o'er the infected house,   (*emblem of death*)
Boding to all—he had my handkerchief.
Iago. Ay, what of that?
Othello.   That's not so good now.
Iago.   What
If I had said I had seen him do you wrong?
Or heard him say—as knaves be such abroad,
Who having, by their own importunate suit
Or voluntary dotage of° some mistress,   *doting on*
Convincèd° or supplied° them, cannot choose   *seduced / met the desires of*
But they must blab—
Othello.   Hath he said anything?
Iago. He hath, my lord; but be you well assured,
No more than he'll unswear.

OTHELLO.   What hath he said?

IAGO. Faith, that he did—I know not what he did.

OTHELLO. What? What?

IAGO. Lie—

OTHELLO.   With her?

IAGO.   With her, on her; what you will.

OTHELLO. Lie with her! lie on her!—We say lie on her, when
they belie her.—Lie with her! 'Zounds, that's fulsome!°   *disgusting*
Handkerchief—confessions—handkerchief!—To confess,
and be hanged for his labor; first, to be hanged, and then
to confess. I tremble at it. Nature would not invest herself
in such shadowing passion without some instruction.[13] It is
not words that shakes me thus. Pish! Noses, ears and lips.
Is 't possible?—Confess?—Handkerchief?—O devil!
[*Falls in a trance.*]

IAGO. Work on,
My medicine, work! Thus credulous fools are caught;
And many worthy and chaste dames even thus,
All guiltless, meet reproach. What, ho! my lord!
My lord, I say! Othello!

Enter CASSIO.

How now, Cassio!

CASSIO. What's the matter?

IAGO. My lord is fall'n into an epilepsy:
This is his second fit; he had one yesterday.

CASSIO. Rub him about the temples.

IAGO.   No, forbear;
The lethargy° must have his quiet course: *stupor*
If not, he foams at mouth, and by and by
Breaks out to savage madness. Look, he stirs:
Do you withdraw yourself a little while,
He will recover straight: when he is gone,
I would on great occasion° speak with you. [*Exit* CASSIO.]   *important matters*
How is it, general? Have you not hurt your head?

OTHELLO. Dost thou mock me?

IAGO.   I mock you! No, by heaven.
Would you would bear your fortune like a man!

OTHELLO. A hornèd° man's a monster and a beast.   *cuckolded*

IAGO. There's many a beast then in a populous city,
And many a civil monster.

OTHELLO. Did he confess it?

IAGO.   Good sir, be a man;
Think every bearded fellow that's but yoked°   *married*
May draw with you: there's millions now alive
That nightly lie in those unproper° beds   *unchaste*
Which they dare swear peculiar:° your case is better.   *theirs alone*
O, 'tis the spite of hell, the fiend's arch-mock,

---

[13] I.e., my nature would not be so darkened with passion unless there were some cause.

To lip° a wanton in a secure couch.   *kiss*
And to suppose her chaste! No, let me know;
And knowing what I am, I know what she shall be.
OTHELLO. O, thou art wise; 'tis certain.
IAGO.   Stand you awhile apart;
Confine yourself but in a patient list.°   *mood*
Whilst you were here o'erwhelmed with your grief—
A passion most unsuiting such a man—
Cassio came hither: I shifted him away,
And laid good 'scuse upon your ecstasy;°   *trance*
Bade him anon return and here speak with me;
The which he promised. Do but encave° yourself,   *conceal*
And mark the fleers,° the gibes and notable scorns,   *sneers*
That dwell in every region of his face;
For I will make him tell the tale anew,
Where, how, how oft, how long ago and when
He hath and is again to cope° your wife: *cover*
I say, but mark his gesture. Marry,° patience;   *Indeed*
Or I shall say you are all in all in spleen,°   *passion*
And nothing of a man.
OTHELLO.   Dost thou hear, Iago?
I will be found most cunning in my patience;
But—dost thou hear?—most bloody.
IAGO.   That's not amiss;
But yet keep time in all. Will you withdraw?
[OTHELLO *retires.*]
Now will I question Cassio of Bianca,
A housewife that by selling her desires
Buys herself bread and clothes: it is a creature
That dotes on Cassio; as 'tis the strumpet's plague
To beguile many and be beguiled by one.
He, when he hears of her, cannot refrain
From the excess of laughter. Here he comes.

Re-enter CASSIO.

As he shall smile, Othello shall go mad;
And his unbookish° jealousy must construe   *ignorant*
Poor Cassio's smiles, gestures and light behavior,
Quite in the wrong. How do you now, lieutenant?
CASSIO. The worser that you give me the addition°   *additional title*
Whose want even kills me.
IAGO. Ply Desdemona well, and you are sure on 't.
Now, if this suit lay in Bianca's power,
How quickly should you speed!
CASSIO.   Alas, poor caitiff!°   *wretch*
OTHELLO. Look, how he laughs already!
IAGO. I never knew a woman love man so.
CASSIO. Alas, poor rogue! I think, i' faith, she loves me.
OTHELLO. Now he denies it faintly and laughs it out.
IAGO. Do you hear, Cassio?

OTHELLO.   Now he importunes him
   To tell it o'er: go to; well said, well said.
IAGO. She gives it out that you shall marry her.
   Do you intend it?
CASSIO. Ha, ha, ha!
OTHELLO. Do you triumph, Roman? Do you triumph?
CASSIO. I marry her! what, a customer!° I prithee, bear some   *prostitute*
   charity to my wit; do not think it so unwholesome. Ha, ha,
   ha!
OTHELLO. So, so, so, so: they laugh that win.
IAGO. Faith, the cry goes that you shall marry her.
CASSIO. Prithee, say true.
IAGO. I am a very villain else.
OTHELLO. Have you scored me?° Well.   *paid me back*
CASSIO. This is the monkey's own giving out: she is persuaded
   I will marry her, out of her own love and flattery, not out
   of my promise.
OTHELLO. Iago beckons me; now he begins the story.
CASSIO. She was here even now; she haunts me in every place.
   I was the other day talking on the sea-bank with certain
   Venetians; and thither comes the bauble,° and, by this   *plaything*
   hand, she falls me thus about my neck—
OTHELLO. Crying "O dear Cassio!" as it were: his gesture
   imports it.
CASSIO. So hangs and lolls and weeps upon me; so hales°   *drags*
   and pulls me: ha, ha, ha!
OTHELLO. Now he tells how she plucked him to my chamber.
   O, I see that nose of yours, but not that dog I shall throw
   it to.
CASSIO. Well, I must leave her company.
IAGO. Before me! Look, where she comes.
CASSIO. 'Tis such another fitchew!° Marry, a perfumed one.   *polecat, harlot*

Enter BIANCA.

What do you mean by this haunting of me?
BIANCA. Let the devil and his dam haunt you! What did you
   mean by that same handkerchief you gave me even now?
   I was a fine fool to take it. I must take out the work? A
   likely piece of work, that you should find it in your chamber, and not know who left it there! This is some minx's
   token, and I must take out the work? There; give it your
   hobby-horse:° wheresoever you had it, I'll take out no work   *rocking horse, whore*
   on 't.
CASSIO. How now, my sweet Bianca! How now! How now!
OTHELLO. By heaven, that should be my handkerchief!
BIANCA. An you'll come to supper tonight, you may; an
   you will not, come when you are next prepared for. [*Exit.*]
IAGO. After her, after her.
CASSIO. Faith, I must; she'll rail i' the street else.

IAGO. Will you sup there?

CASSIO. Faith, I intend so.

IAGO. Well, I may chance to see you; for I would very
fain speak with you.

CASSIO. Prithee, come; will you?

IAGO. Go to; say no more. [*Exit* CASSIO.]

OTHELLO [*Advancing*]. How shall I murder him, Iago?

IAGO. Did you perceive how he laughed at his vice?

OTHELLO. O Iago!

IAGO. And did you see the handkerchief?

OTHELLO. Was that mine?

IAGO. Yours, by this hand: and to see how he prizes the foolish
woman your wife! She gave it him, and he hath given it his
whore.

OTHELLO. I would have him nine years a-killing. A fine woman!
a fair woman! a sweet woman!

IAGO. Nay, you must forget that.

OTHELLO. Ay, let her rot, and perish, and be damned tonight;
for she shall not live: no, my heart is turned to stone; I
strike it, and it hurts my hand. O, the world hath not a
sweeter creature: she might lie by an emperor's side, and
command him tasks.

IAGO. Nay, that's not your way.

OTHELLO. Hang her! I do but say what she is: so delicate with
her needle: an admirable musician: O, she will sing the
savageness out of a bear: of so high and plenteous wit and
invention:—

IAGO. She's the worse for all this.

OTHELLO. O, a thousand thousand times: and then, of so
gentle a condition!°   *nature*

IAGO. Aye, too gentle.°   *generous*

OTHELLO. Nay, that's certain: but yet the pity of it, Iago! O
Iago, the pity of it, Iago!

IAGO. If you are so fond over her iniquity, give her patent° to   *permission*
offend; for, if it touch not you, it comes near nobody.

OTHELLO. I will chop her into messes.° Cuckold me!   *porridge*

IAGO. O, 'tis foul in her.

OTHELLO. With mine officer!

IAGO. That 's fouler.

OTHELLO. Get me some poison, Iago; this night. I'll not ex-
postulate with her, lest her body and beauty unprovide°   *unsettle*
my mind again: this night, Iago.

IAGO. Do it not with poison, strangle her in her bed,
even the bed she hath contaminated.

OTHELLO. Good, good: the justice of it pleases: very good.

IAGO. And for Cassio, let me be his undertaker: you shall
hear more by midnight.

OTHELLO. Excellent good. [*A trumpet within.*] What trumpet
is that same?

IAGO. Something from Venice, sure. 'Tis Lodovico come
from the duke: and, see, your wife is with him.

Enter LODOVICO, DESDEMONA, *and* ATTENDANTS.

LODOVICO. God save the worthy general!

OTHELLO.   With all my heart, sir.

LODOVICO. The duke and senators of Venice greet you.

    [*Gives him a letter.*]

OTHELLO. I kiss the instrument of their pleasures.

    [*Opens the letter, and reads.*]

DESDEMONA. And what's the news, good cousin Lodovico?

IAGO. I am very glad to see you, signior;

    Welcome to Cyprus.

LODOVICO. I thank you. How does Lieutenant Cassio?

IAGO. Lives, sir.

DESDEMONA. Cousin, there's fall'n between him and my lord

    An unkind breach: but you shall make all well.

OTHELLO. Are you sure of that?

DESDEMONA. My lord?

OTHELLO [*Reads*]. "This fail you not to do, as you will—"

LODOVICO. He did not call; he's busy in the paper.

    Is there division 'twixt my lord and Cassio?

DESDEMONA. A most unhappy one: I would do much

    To atone° them, for the love I bear to Cassio.   reunite

OTHELLO. Fire and brimstone!

DESDEMONA. My lord?

OTHELLO. Are you wise?

DESDEMONA. What, is he angry?

LODOVICO.   May be the letter moved him;

    For, as I think, they do command him home,

    Deputing° Cassio in his government.°   substituting / office

DESDEMONA. By my troth, I am glad on 't.

OTHELLO.   Indeed!

DESDEMONA.   My lord?

OTHELLO. I am glad to see you mad.

DESDEMONA.   Why, sweet Othello?

OTHELLO. Devil! [*Striking her.*]

DESDEMONA. I have not deserved this.

LODOVICO. My lord, this would not be believed in Venice,

    Though I should swear I saw 't: 'tis very much:

    Make her amends; she weeps.

OTHELLO.   O devil, devil!

    If that the earth could teem° with woman's tears,   bear offspring

    Each drop she falls would prove a crocodile.[14]

    Out of my sight!

DESDEMONA.   I will not stay to offend you. [*Going.*]

LODOVICO. Truly, an obedient lady:

    I do beseech your lordship, call her back.

OTHELLO. Mistress!

DESDEMONA. My lord?

---

[14] The crocodile was thought to shed false tears over its victims.

OTHELLO. What would you with her, sir?
LODOVICO.   Who, I, my lord?
OTHELLO. Ay; you did wish that I would make her turn:
　Sir, she can turn and turn, and yet go on,
　And turn again; and she can weep, sir, weep;
　And she's obedient, as you say, obedient,
　Very obedient. Proceed you in your tears.
　Concerning this, sir,—O well-painted passion!—
　I am commanded home. Get you away;
　I'll send for you anon. Sir, I obey the mandate,
　And will return to Venice. Hence, avaunt!°   *be gone*
　[*Exit* DESDEMONA.]
　Cassio shall have my place. And, sir, tonight,
　I do entreat that we may sup together:
　You are welcome, sir, to Cyprus. Goats and monkeys!
　[*Exit.*]
LODOVICO. Is this the noble Moor whom our full senate
　Call all in all sufficient? This the nature
　Whom passion could not shake? whose solid virtue
　The shot of accident nor dart of chance
　Could neither graze nor pierce?
IAGO.   He is much changed.
LODOVICO. Are his wits safe? Is he not light of brain?
IAGO. He's that he is: I may not breathe my censure°   *adverse opinion*
　What he might be: if what he might he is not,
　I would to heaven he were!
LODOVICO.   What, strike his wife!
IAGO. Faith, that was not so well; yet would I knew
　That stroke would prove the worst!
LODOVICO.   Is it his use?°   *habit*
　Or did the letters work upon his blood,
　And new create this fault?
IAGO.   Alas, alas!
　It is not honesty in me to speak
　What I have seen and known. You shall observe him,
　And his own courses will denote him so
　That I may save my speech: do but go after,
　And mark how he continues.
LODOVICO. I am sorry that I am deceived in him. [*Exeunt.*]

SCENE II
A room in the castle.

Enter OTHELLO *and* EMILIA.

OTHELLO. You have seen nothing, then?
EMILIA. Nor ever heard, nor ever did suspect.
OTHELLO. Yes, you have seen Cassio and she together.
EMILIA. But then I saw no harm, and then I heard
　Each syllable that breath made up between them.
OTHELLO. What, did they never whisper?

EMILIA.   Never, my lord.

OTHELLO. Nor send you out o' the way?

EMILIA. Never.

OTHELLO. To fetch her fan, her gloves, her mask, nor
    nothing?

EMILIA. Never, my lord.

OTHELLO. That's strange.

EMILIA. I durst, my lord, to wager she is honest,°   *chaste*
    Lay down my soul at stake:° if you think other,   *as wager*
    Remove your thought; it doth abuse your bosom.
    If any wretch have put this in your head,
    Let heaven requite it with the serpent's curse!
    For if she be not honest, chaste and true,
    There's no man happy; the purest of their wives
    Is foul as slander.

OTHELLO.   Bid her come hither: go. [*Exit* EMILIA.]
    She says enough: yet she's a simple bawd
    That cannot say as much. This is a subtle whore,
    A closet lock and key of villanous secrets:
    And yet she'll kneel and pray; I have seen her do 't.

Enter DESDEMONA *with* EMILIA.

DESDEMONA. My lord, what is your will?

OTHELLO.   Pray, chuck, come
    hither.

DESDEMONA. What is your pleasure?

OTHELLO.   Let me see your eyes;
    Look in my face.

DESDEMONA.   What horrible fancy's this?

OTHELLO [*To* EMILIA]. Some of your function,[15] mistress;
    Leave procreants° alone and shut the door;   *fornicators*
    Cough, or cry hem, if anybody come:
    Your mystery,° your mystery: nay, dispatch. [*Exit* EMILIA.]   *trade*

DESDEMONA. Upon my knees, what doth your speech import?
    I understand a fury in your words,
    But not the words.

OTHELLO. Why, what are thou?

DESDEMONA. Your wife, my lord; your true and loyal wife.

OTHELLO. Come, swear it, damn thyself;
    Lest, being like one of heaven, the devils themselves
    Should fear to seize thee: therefore be double-damned;
    Swear thou art honest.

DESDEMONA.   Heaven doth truly know it.

OTHELLO. Heaven truly knows that thou art false as hell.

DESDEMONA. To whom, my lord? With whom? How am I false?

OTHELLO. O Desdemona! Away! away! away!

DESDEMONA. Alas the heavy day! Why do you weep?
    Am I the motive of these tears, my lord?

---

[15] I.e., perform your function as madam of the brothel.

If haply° you my father do suspect   *perhaps*
An instrument of this your calling back,
Lay not your blame on me: if you have lost him,
Why, I have lost him too.

OTHELLO.   Had it pleased heaven
To try me with affliction; had they rained
All kinds of sores and shames on my bare head,
Steeped me in poverty to the very lips,
Given to captivity me and my utmost hopes,
I should have found in some place of my soul
A drop of patience: but, alas, to make me
A fixèd figure for the time of scorn
To point his slow unmoving finger at!
Yet could I bear that too; well, very well:
But there, where I have garnered° up my heart,   *stored*
Where either I must live or bear no life,
The fountain from the which my current runs,
Or else dries up; to be discarded thence!
Or keep it as a cistern for foul toads
To knot and gender° in! Turn thy complexion° there,   *mate / Turn pale*
Patience, thou young and rose-lipped cherubin,—
Ay, there, look grim as hell!

DESDEMONA. I hope my noble lord esteems me honest.

OTHELLO. O, ay; as summer flies are in the shambles,°   *butcher shop*
That quicken even with blowing.[16] O thou weed,
Who art so lovely fair and smell'st so sweet
That the sense aches at thee, would thou hadst ne'er been
    born!

DESDEMONA. Alas, what ignorant° sin have I committed?   *unwitting*

OTHELLO. Was this fair paper, this most goodly book,
Made to write "whore" upon? What committed!
Committed! O thou public commoner!°   *whore*
I should make very forges of my cheeks,
That would to cinders burn up modesty,
Did I but speak thy deeds. What committed!
Heaven stops the nose at it, and the moon winks;
The bawdy wind, that kisses all it meets,
Is hushed within the hollow mine of earth,
And will not hear it. What committed!
Impudent strumpet!

DESDEMONA.   By heaven, you do me wrong.

OTHELLO. Are not you a strumpet!

DESDEMONA.   No, as I am a Christian:
If to preserve this vessel for my lord
From any other foul unlawful touch
Be not to be a strumpet, I am none.

OTHELLO. What, not a whore?

DESDEMONA.   No, as I shall be saved.

OTHELLO. Is 't possible?

---

[16] That are impregnated even the moment after giving birth.

DESDEMONA. O, heaven forgive us!
OTHELLO.   I cry you mercy then:
  I took you for that cunning whore of Venice
  That married with Othello. [*Raising his voice*] You, mistress,
  That have the office opposite to Saint Peter,
  And keep the gate of hell!

Re-enter EMILIA.

             You, you, ay, you!
  We have done our course;° there's money for your pains: *sexual encounter*
  I pray you, turn the key, and keep our counsel. [*Exit.*]
EMILIA. Alas, what does this gentleman conceive?
  How do you, madam? How do you, my good lady?
DESDEMONA. Faith, half asleep.
EMILIA. Good madam, what's the matter with my lord?
DESDEMONA. With who?
EMILIA. Why, with my lord, madam.
DESDEMONA. Who is thy lord?
EMILIA.   He that is yours, sweet lady.
DESDEMONA. I have none: do not talk to me, Emilia;
  I cannot weep, nor answer have I none
  But what should go by water.° Prithee, tonight   *tears*
  Lay on my bed my wedding sheets: remember;
  And call thy husband hither.
EMILIA.   Here's a change indeed! [*Exit.*]
DESDEMONA. 'Tis meet I should be used so, very meet.
  How have I been behaved, that he might stick°   *put*
  The small'st opinion° on my least misuse?°   *suspicion / error*

Re-enter EMILIA with IAGO.

IAGO. What is your pleasure, madam? How is't with you?
DESDEMONA. I cannot tell. Those that do teach young babes
  Do it with gentle means and easy tasks:
  He might have chid me so; for, in good faith,
  I am a child to chiding.
IAGO.   What's the matter, lady?
EMILIA. Alas, Iago, my lord hath so bewhored her,
  Thrown such despite° and heavy terms upon her,   *scorn*
  As true hearts cannot bear.
DESDEMONA. Am I that name, Iago?
IAGO.   What name, fair lady?
DESDEMONA. Such as she says my lord did say I was.
EMILIA. He called her whore: a beggar in his drink
  Could not have laid such terms upon his callat.°   *slut*
IAGO. Why did he so?
DESDEMONA. I do not know; I am sure I am none such.
IAGO. Do not weep, do not weep. Alas the day!
EMILIA. Hath she forsook so many noble matches,

Her father and her country and her friends,
To be called whore? Would it not make one weep?
DESDEMONA. It is my wretched fortune.
IAGO.   Beshrew° him for't!   *Evil befall*
How comes this trick° upon him?   *foolishness*
DESDEMONA.   Nay, heaven doth know.
EMILIA. I will be hanged, if some eternal villain,
    Some busy and insinuating rogue,
    Some cogging,° cozening° slave, to get some office.   *cheating / deceiving*
    Have not devised this slander; I'll be hanged else.
IAGO. Fie, there is no such man; it is impossible.
DESDEMONA. If any such there be, heaven pardon him!
EMILIA. A halter pardon him! And hell gnaw his bones!
    Why should he call her whore? Who keeps her company?
    What place? What time? What form? What likelihood?
    The Moor's abused by some most villanous knave,
    Some base notorious knave, some scurvy fellow,
    O heaven, that such companions thou'ldst unfold,°   *expose*
    And put in every honest hand a whip
    To lash the rascals naked through the world
    Even from the east to the west!
IAGO.   Speak within door.°   *quietly*
EMILIA. O, fie upon them! Some such squire he was
    That turned your wit the seamy side without,
    And made you to suspect me with the Moor.
IAGO. You are a fool; go to.
DESDEMONA.   O good Iago,
    What shall I do to win my lord again?
    Good friend, go to him; for, by this light of heaven,
    I know not how I lost him. Here I kneel:
    If e'er my will did trespass 'gainst his love
    Either in discourse of thought or actual deed,
    Or that mine eyes, mine ears, or any sense,
    Delighted them in any other form,
    Or that I do not yet, and ever did,
    And ever will, though he do shake me off
    To beggarly divorcement, love him dearly,
    Comfort forswear° me! Unkindness may do much;   *forsake*
    And his unkindness may defeat my life,
    But never taint my love. I cannot say "whore":
    It doth abhor me now I speak the word;
    To do the act that might the addition° earn   *name*
    Not the world's mass of vanity could make me.
IAGO. I pray you, be content; 'tis but his humor;
    The business of the state does him offense,
    And he does chide with you.
DESDEMONA. If 'twere no other,—
IAGO. 'Tis but so, I warrant. [*Trumpet within.*]
    Hark, how these instruments summon to supper!
    The messengers of Venice stay° the meat: *await*

Go in, and weep not; all things shall be well.
[*Exeunt* DESDEMONA *and* EMILIA.]

Enter RODERIGO.

How now, Roderigo!

RODERIGO. I do not find that thou dealest justly with me.

IAGO. What in the contrary.

RODERIGO. Every day thou daffest me° with some device,   *turn me aside*
Iago; and rather, as it seems to me now, keepest from me
all conveniency° than suppliest me with the least advantage   *opportunity*
of hope. I will indeed no longer endure it; nor am I yet
persuaded to put up in peace what already I have foolishly
suffered.

IAGO. Will you hear me, Roderigo?

RODERIGO. Faith, I have heard too much; for your words and
performances are no kin together.

IAGO. You charge me most unjustly.

RODERIGO. With nought but truth. I have wasted myself out
of my means. The jewels you have had from me to deliver
to Desdemona would half have corrupted a votarist:° you   *nun*
have told me she hath received them and returned me
expectations and comforts of sudden° respect and acquain-   *immediate*
quaintance; but I find none.

IAGO. Well; go to; very well.

RODERIGO. Very well! Go to! I cannot go to, man; nor 'tis not
very well: by this hand, I say 'tis very scurvy, and begin to
find myself fopped° in it.   *made foolish*

IAGO. Very well.

RODERIGO. I tell you 'tis not very well. I will make myself known
to Desdemona: if she will return me my jewels, I will give
over my suit and repent my unlawful solicitation; if not,
assure yourself I will seek satisfaction of you.

IAGO. You have said now?

RODERIGO. Ay, and said nothing but what I protest intendment°   *intention*
of doing.

IAGO. Why, now I see there's mettle° in thee; and even from   *spirit*
this instant do build on thee a better opinion than ever
before. Give me thy hand, Roderigo: thou hast taken
against me a most just exception; but yet, I protest, I have
dealt most directly in thy affair.

RODERIGO. It hath not appeared.

IAGO. I grant indeed it hath not appeared, and your suspicion
is not without wit and judgement. But, Roderigo, if thou
hast that in thee indeed, which I have greater reason to believe now than ever, I mean purpose, courage and valor, this
night show it; if thou the next night following enjoy not Desdemona, take me from this world with treachery and devise
engines° for my life.   *instruments of torture*

RODERIGO. Well, what is it? Is it within reason and compass?° reach
IAGO. Sir, there is especial commission come from Venice to
depute Cassio in Othello's place.
RODERIGO. Is that true? Why then Othello and Desdemona
return again to Venice.
IAGO. O, no; he goes into Mauritania, and takes away with him
the fair Desdemona, unless his abode be lingered here by
some accident: wherein none can be so determinate°   as   *convincing*
the removing of Cassio.
RODERIGO. How do you mean, removing of him?
IAGO. Why, by making him uncapable of Othello's place;
knocking out his brains.
RODERIGO. And that you would have me to do?
IAGO. Ay, if you dare do yourself a profit and a right. He
sups tonight with a harlotry, and thither will I go to him:
he knows not yet of his honorable fortune. If you will
watch his going thence, which I will fashion to fall out
between twelve and one, you may take him at your pleasure: I will be near to second your attempt, and he shall
fall between us. Come, stand not amazed at it, but go
along with me; I will show you such a necessity in his
death that you shall think yourself bound to put it on
him. It is now high supper-time, and the night grows to
waste: about it.
RODERIGO. I will hear further reason for this.
IAGO. And you shall be satisfied. [*Exeunt.*]

SCENE III
Another room in the castle.

Enter OTHELLO, LODOVICO, DESDEMONA, EMILIA, *and* ATTENDANTS.

LODOVICO. I do beseech you, sir, trouble yourself no further.
OTHELLO. O, pardon me; 'twill do me good to walk.
LODOVICO. Madam, good night; I humbly thank your ladyship.
DESDEMONA. Your honor is most welcome.
OTHELLO.   Will you walk sir?
O,—Desdemona,—
DESDEMONA. My lord?
OTHELLO. Get you to bed on the instant; I will be returned
forthwith: dismiss your attendant there: look it be done.
DESDEMONA. I will, my lord.
[*Exeunt* OTHELLO, LODOVICO, *and* ATTENDANTS.]
EMILIA. How goes it now? He looks gentler than he did.
DESDEMONA. He says he will return incontinent:°   *immediately*
He hath commanded me to go to bed,
And bade me to dismiss you.
EMILIA.   Dismiss me!

DESDEMONA. It was his bidding; therefore, good Emilia,
  Give me my nightly wearing, and adieu:
  We must not now displease him.
EMILIA. I would you had never seen him!
DESDEMONA. So would not I: my love doth so approve him,
  That even his stubbornness, his checks,° his frowns,—   *rebukes*
  Prithee, unpin me,—have grace and favor in them.
EMILIA. I have laid those sheets you bade me on the bed.
DESDEMONA. All's one. Good faith, how foolish are our minds!
  If I do die before thee, prithee, shroud me
  In one of those same sheets.
EMILIA.   Come, come, you talk.
DESDEMONA. My mother had a maid called Barbara:
  She was in love; and he she loved proved mad
  And did forsake her: she had a song of "willow";
  An old thing 'twas, but it expressed her fortune,
  And she died singing it: that song tonight
  Will not go from my mind; I have much to do
  But to go hang my head all at one side
  And sing it like poor Barbara. Prithee, dispatch.
EMILIA. Shall I go fetch your nightgown.
DESDEMONA.   No, unpin me here.
  This Lodovico is a proper man.
EMILIA. A very handsome man.
DESDEMONA. He speaks well.
EMILIA. I know a lady in Venice would have walked
  barefoot to Palestine for a touch of his nether° lip.   *lower*
DESDEMONA [*Singing*]. "The poor soul sat sighing by a
      sycamore tree,
    Sing all a green willow;
  Her hand on her bosom, her head on her knee,
    Sing willow, willow, willow:
  The fresh streams ran by her, and murmured her moans;
    Sing willow, willow, willow;
  Her salt tears fell from her, and softened the stones"—
  Lay by these:—
  [*Singing*.] "Sing willow, willow, willow."
  Prithee, hie° thee; he'll come anon:°—   *hasten / soon*
  [*Singing*.] "Sing all a green willow must be my garland.
    Let nobody blame him; his scorn I approve"—
  Nay, that's not next. Hark! who is't that knocks?
EMILIA. It's the wind.
DESDEMONA [*Singing*]. "I called my love false love; but what
      said he then?
    Sing willow, willow, willow:
  If I court moe° women, you'll couch with moe men."   *more*
  So get thee gone; good night. Mine eyes do itch;
  Doth that bode weeping?
EMILIA.   'Tis neither here nor there.

DESDEMONA. I have heard it said so. O, these men, these men!
  Dost thou in conscience think,—tell me, Emilia,—
  That there be women do abuse their husbands
  In such gross kind?
EMILIA.   There be some such, no question.
DESDEMONA. Wouldst thou do such a deed for all the world?
EMILIA. Why, would not you?
DESDEMONA.   No, by this heavenly light!
EMILIA. Nor I neither by this heavenly light; I might do 't
  as well i' the dark.
DESDEMONA. Wouldst thou do such a deed for all the world?
EMILIA. The world's a huge thing: it is a great price
  For a small vice.
DESDEMONA.   In troth, I think thou wouldst not.
EMILIA. In troth, I think I should; and undo 't when I had done.
  Marry, I would not do such a thing for a joint-ring,° nor   *cheap ring*
  for measures of lawn,° nor for gowns, petticoats, nor caps,   *fine linen*
  nor any petty exhibition; but, for the whole world,—why,
  who would not make her husband a cuckold to make him
  a monarch? I should venture purgatory for 't.
DESDEMONA. Beshrew me, if I would do such a wrong
  For the whole world.
EMILIA. Why, the wrong is but a wrong i' the world; and having
  the world for your labor, 'tis a wrong in your own world,
  and you might quickly make it right.
DESDEMONA. I do not think there is any such woman.
EMILIA. Yes, a dozen; and as many to the
  Vantage° as would store° the world they played for.   *to boot / people*
  But I do think it is their husbands' faults
  If wives do fall: say that they slack their duties
  And pour our treasures into foreign laps,
  Or else break out in peevish jealousies,
  Throwing restraint upon us, or say they strike us,
  Or scant° our former having° in despite,   *reduce / allowance*
  Why, we have galls,° and though we have some grace,   *tempers*
  Yet have we some revenge. Let husbands know
  Their wives have sense like them: they see and smell
  And have their palates both for sweet and sour,
  As husbands have. What is it that they do
  When they change us for others? Is it sport?
  I think it is: and doth affection breed it?
  I think it doth: is 't frailty that thus errs?
  It is so too: and have not we affections,
  Desires for sport, and frailty, as men have?
  Then let them use us well: else let them know,
  The ills we do, their ills instruct us so.
DESDEMONA. Good night, good night: heaven me such uses°
  send,   *habits*
  Not to pick bad from bad, but by bad mend! [*Exeunt.*]

ACT V

SCENE I
Cyprus. A street.

Enter IAGO *and* RODERIGO.

IAGO. Here, stand behind this bulk;° straight will he come: *framework*
  Wear thy good rapier bare, and put it home:
  Quick, quick; fear nothing; I'll be at thy elbow:
  It makes us, or it mars us; think on that,
  And fix most firm thy resolution.
RODERIGO. Be near at hand; I may miscarry in 't.
IAGO. Here, at thy hand: be bold, and take thy stand.
  [*Retires.*]
RODERIGO. I have no great devotion to the deed;
  And yet he hath given me satisfying reasons:
  'Tis but a man gone. Forth, my sword: he dies.
IAGO. I have rubbed this young quat° almost to the sense,°   *pimple / quick*
  And he grows angry. Now, whether he kill Cassio,
  Or Cassio him, or each do kill the other,
  Every way makes my gain: live Roderigo,
  He calls me to a restitution large
  Of gold and jewels that I bobbed° from him,   *filched*
  As gifts to Desdemona:
  It must not be: if Cassio do remain,
  He hath a daily beauty in his life
  That makes me ugly; and besides, the Moor
  May unfold° me to him; there stand I in much peril: *expose*
  No, he must die. Be 't so. I hear him coming.

[*Enter* CASSIO.]

RODERIGO. I know his gait; 'tis he. Villain, thou diest!
  [*Makes a pass at* CASSIO.]
CASSIO. That thrust had been mine enemy indeed,
  But that my coat is better than thou know'st:
  I will make proof of thine. [*Draws, and wounds* RODERIGO.]
RODERIGO.   O, I am slain!
  [IAGO *from behind wounds* CASSIO *in the leg, and exit.*]
CASSIO. I am maimed forever. Help, ho! murder! murder!
  [*Falls.*]

[*Enter* OTHELLO.]

OTHELLO. The voice of Cassio: Iago keeps his word.
RODERIGO. O, villain that I am!
OTHELLO.   It is even so.
CASSIO. O, help, ho! light! a surgeon!

OTHELLO. 'Tis he. O brave Iago, honest and just,
   That hast such noble sense of thy friend's wrong!
   Thou teachest me. Minion,° your dear lies dead,   *Mistress*
   And your unblest fate hies:° strumpet, I come!   *hastens*
   Forth of my heart those charms, thine eyes, are blotted;
   Thy bed lust-stained shall with lust's blood be spotted.
   [*Exit.*]

Enter LODOVICO *and* GRATIANO.

CASSIO. What, ho! No watch?° No passage?° Murder!   *sentries / passersby*
   Murder!
GRATIANO. 'Tis some mischance;° the cry is very direful.   *mishap*
CASSIO. O, help!
LODOVICO. Hark!
RODERIGO. O wretched villain!
LODOVICO. Two or three groan: it is a heavy night:
   These may be counterfeits: let's think 't unsafe
   To come in to the cry without more help.
RODERIGO. Nobody come? Then shall I bleed to death.
LODOVICO. Hark!

Re-enter IAGO, *with a light.*

GRATIANO. Here's one comes in his shirt, with light and weap-
   ons.
IAGO. Who's there? Whose noise is this that cries on murder?
LODOVICO. We do not know.
IAGO.   Did not you hear a cry?
CASSIO. Here, here! For heaven's sake, help me!
IAGO.   What's the matter?
GRATIANO. This is Othello's ancient, as I take it.
LODOVICO. The same indeed; a very valiant fellow.
IAGO. What are you here that cry so grievously?
CASSIO. Iago? O, I am spoiled, undone by villains!
   Give me some help.
IAGO. O me, lieutenant! What villains have done this?
CASSIO. I think that one of them is hereabout,
   And cannot make away.
IAGO.   O treacherous villains!
   What are you there? Come in and give some help.
   [*To* LODOVICO *and* GRATIANO.]
RODERIGO. O, help me here!
CASSIO. That's one of them.
IAGO.   O murderous slave! O villain!
   [*Stabs* RODERIGO.]
RODERIGO. O damned Iago! O inhuman dog!
IAGO. Kill men i' the dark! Where be these bloody thieves?
   How silent is this town! Ho! murder! murder!
   What may you be? Are you of good or evil!
LODOVICO. As you shall prove us, praise us.

IAGO. Signior Lodovico?

LODOVICO. He, sir.

IAGO. I cry you mercy. Here's Cassio hurt by villains.

GRATIANO. Cassio!

IAGO. How is 't, brother?

CASSIO. My leg is cut in two.

IAGO.   Marry, heaven forbid!
    Light, gentlemen: I'll bind it with my shirt.

                    [*Enter* BIANCA.]

BIANCA. What is the matter, ho? Who is't that cried?

IAGO. Who is't that cried!

BIANCA. O my dear Cassio! My sweet Cassio! O Cassio, Cassio,
    Cassio!

IAGO. O notable strumpet! Cassio, may you suspect
    Who they should be that have thus mangled you?

CASSIO. No.

GRATIANO. I am sorry to find you thus: I have been to seek you.

IAGO. Lend me a garter. So. O, for a chair.
    To bear him easily hence!

BIANCA. Alas, he faints! O Cassio, Cassio, Cassio!

IAGO. Gentlemen all, I do suspect this trash
    To be a party in this injury,
    Patience awhile, good Cassio. Come, come;
    Lend me a light. Know we this face or no?
    Alas, my friend and my dear countryman
    Roderigo? No:—yes, sure: O heaven! Roderigo.

GRATIANO. What, of Venice?

IAGO. Even he sir. Did you know him?

GRATIANO.   Know him! Ay.

IAGO. Signior Gratiano? I cry you gentle pardon;
    These bloody accidents must excuse my manners,
    That so neglected you.

GRATIANO.   I am glad to see you.

IAGO. How do you, Cassio? O, a chair, a chair!

GRATIANO. Roderigo!

IAGO. He, he, 'tis he. [*A chair brought in.*] O, that's well
    said; the chair:
    Some good man bear him carefully from hence;
    I'll fetch the general's surgeon. [*To* BIANCA.] For you, mis-
    tress,
    Save you your labor. He that lies slain here, Cassio,
    Was my dear friend. What malice was between you?

CASSIO. None in the world; nor do I know the man.

IAGO [*to* BIANCA]. What, look you pale? O, bear him out
    o' the air.

[CASSIO *and* RODERIGO *are borne off.*]
    Stay you, good gentlemen. Look you pale, mistress?
    Do you perceive the gastness° of her eye?   ghastliness
    Nay, if you stare, we shall hear more anon.

Behold her well; I pray you, look upon her.
Do you see, gentlemen? Nay, guiltiness will speak,
Though tongues were out of use.

Enter EMILIA.

EMILIA. 'Las, what's the matter? What's the matter, husband?
IAGO. Cassio hath here been set on in the dark
   By Roderigo, and fellows that are 'scaped:
   He's almost slain, and Roderigo dead.
EMILIA. Alas, good gentleman! Alas, good Cassio!
IAGO. This is the fruit of whoring. Prithee, Emilia,
   Go know of Cassio where he supped tonight.
   What, do you shake at that?
BIANCA. He supped at my house: but I therefore shake not.
IAGO. O, did he so? I charge you, go with me.
EMILIA. Fie, fie upon thee, strumpet!
BIANCA. I am no strumpet; but of life as honest
   As you that thus abuse me.
EMILIA.   As I! Foh! Fie upon thee!
IAGO. Kind gentlemen, let's go see poor Cassio dressed.°   *bandaged*
   Come, mistress, you must tell's another tale.
   Emilia, run you to the citadel,
   And tell my lord and lady what hath happed!
   Will you go on? I pray. [*Aside*] This is the night
   That either makes me or fordoes° me quite. [*Exeunt.*]   *undoes*

SCENE II
A bedchamber in the castle: DESDEMONA *in bed asleep; a light burning.*

Enter OTHELLO.

OTHELLO. It is the cause, it is the cause, my soul:
   Let me not name it to you, you chaste stars!
   It is the cause. Yet I'll not shed her blood,
   Nor scar that whiter skin of hers than snow
   And smooth as monumental alabaster.
   Yet she must die, else she'll betray more men.
   Put out the light, and then put out the light:
   If I quench thee, thou flaming minister,
   I can again thy former light restore,
   Should I repent me: but once put out thy light,
   Thou cunning'st pattern of excelling nature,
   I know not where is that Promethean[17] heat
   That can thy light relume.° When I have plucked the rose,   *restore*
   I cannot give it vital growth again,
   It must needs wither. I'll smell it on the tree.
   [*Kissing her.*]
   Ah, balmy breath, that dost almost persuade

[17] In Greek mythology Prometheus stole fire from the gods and gave it to man.

Justice to break her sword! One more, one more:
Be thus when thou art dead, and I will kill thee,
And love thee after. One more, and this the last.
So sweet was ne'er so fatal. I must weep,
But they are cruel tears. This sorrow's heavenly;
It strikes where it doth love. She wakes.

DESDEMONA. Who's there? Othello?

OTHELLO.   Ay, Desdemona.

DESDEMONA. Will you come to bed, my lord?

OTHELLO. Have you prayed tonight, Desdemona?

DESDEMONA.   Ay, my lord.

OTHELLO. If you bethink yourself of any crime
  Unreconciled as yet to heaven and grace,
  Solicit for it straight.

DESDEMONA. Alas, my lord, what may you mean by that?

OTHELLO. Well, do it, and be brief: I will walk by.
  I would not kill thy unpreparèd spirit.
  No, heaven forfend!° I would not kill thy soul.   *forbid*

DESDEMONA. Talk you of killing?

OTHELLO. Ay, I do.

DESDEMONA. Then heaven have mercy on me!

OTHELLO. Amen, with all my heart!

DESDEMONA. If you say so, I hope you will not kill me.

OTHELLO. Hum!

DESDEMONA. And yet I fear you; for you are fatal then
  When your eyes roll so. Why I should fear I know not.
  Since guiltiness I know not; but yet I feel I fear.

OTHELLO. Think on thy sins.

DESDEMONA.   They are loves I bear to you.

OTHELLO. Ay, and for that thou diest.

DESDEMONA. That death's unnatural that kills for loving.
  Alas, why gnaw you so your nether° lip?   *lower*
  Some bloody passion shakes your very frame:
  These are portents;° but yet I hope, I hope,   *omens*
  They do not point on me.

OTHELLO.   Peace, and be still!

DESDEMONA. I will so. What's the matter?

OTHELLO. That handkerchief which I so loved and gave thee
  Thou gavest to Cassio.

DESDEMONA.   No, by my life and soul!
  Send for the man, and ask him.

OTHELLO.   Sweet soul, take heed,
  Take heed of perjury; thou art on thy deathbed.

DESDEMONA. Ay, but not yet to die.

OTHELLO.   Yes, presently:
  Therefore confess thee freely of thy sin;
  For to deny each article with oath
  Cannot remove nor choke° the strong conception°   *stifle / belief*
  That I do groan withal. Thou art to die.

DESDEMONA. Then Lord have mercy on me!

OTHELLO.   I say, amen.
DESDEMONA. And have you mercy too! I never did
   Offend you in my life; never loved Cassio
   But with such general warranty of heaven
   As I might love. I never gave him token.
OTHELLO. By heaven, I saw my handkerchief in 's hand.
   O perjured woman! Thou dost stone° my heart,   *harden*
   And makest me call what I intend to do
   A murder, which I thought a sacrifice.
   I saw the handkerchief.
DESDEMONA.   He found it then;
   I never gave it him. Send for him hither;
   Let him confess a truth.
OTHELLO.   He hath confessed.
DESDEMONA. What, my lord?
OTHELLO. That he hath used thee.
DESDEMONA.   How? Unlawfully?
OTHELLO. Ay.
DESDEMONA.   He will not say so.
OTHELLO.   No, his mouth is stopped;
   Honest Iago hath ta'en order for't.
DESDEMONA. O, my fear interprets!° What, is he dead?   *explains (itself)*
OTHELLO. Had all his hairs been lives, my great revenge
   Had stomach° for them all.   *appetite*
DESDEMONA. Alas, he is betrayed, and I undone!
OTHELLO. Out, strumpet! Weep'st thou for him to my face?
DESDEMONA. O, banish me, my lord, but kill me not!
OTHELLO. Down, strumpet!
DESDEMONA. Kill me tomorrow; let me live tonight!
OTHELLO. Nay, if you strive,—
DESDEMONA. But half an hour!
OTHELLO.   Being done, there is no pause.
DESDEMONA. But while I say one prayer!
OTHELLO.   It is too late. [*He stifles her.*]
EMILIA [*Within*]. My lord, my lord! What, ho! My lord, my
   lord!
OTHELLO. What noise is this? Not dead? Not yet quite dead?
   I that am cruel am yet merciful;
   I would not have thee linger in thy pain.
   So, so.
EMILIA [*Within*]. What, ho! My lord, my lord!
OTHELLO.   Who's there?
EMILIA [*Within*]. O, good my lord, I would speak a word with
   you!
OTHELLO. Yes: 'tis Emilia. By and by. She's dead.
   'Tis like she comes to speak of Cassio's death.
   The noise was here. Ha! No more moving?
   Still as the grave. Shall she come in? Were 't good?
   I think she stirs again. No. What's best to do?
   If she come in, she'll sure speak to my wife.

My wife! My wife! What wife? I have no wife.
O, insupportable! O heavy hour!
Methinks it should be now a huge eclipse
Of sun and moon, and that the affrighted globe
Should yawn° at alteration.   *i.e., in earthquake*
EMILIA [*within*].   I do beseech you
   That I may speak with you, O, good my lord!
OTHELLO. I had forgot thee. O, come in, Emilia.
   Soft;° by and by. Let me the curtains draw.   *Quietly*
   Where art thou? [*Unlocks the door.*]

Enter EMILIA.

        What's the matter with thee now?
EMILIA. O, my good lord, yonder's foul murders done!
OTHELLO. What, now?
EMILIA. But now, my lord.
OTHELLO. It is the very error of the moon;
   She comes more nearer earth than she was wont
   And makes men mad.
EMILIA. Cassio, my lord, hath killed a young Venetian
   Called Roderigo.
OTHELLO.   Roderigo killed!
   And Cassio killed!
EMILIA.   No, Cassio is not killed.
OTHELLO. Not Cassio killed! Then murder's out of tune,
   And sweet revenge grows harsh.
DESDEMONA. O, falsely, falsely murdered!
EMILIA.   Alas, what cry is that?
OTHELLO. That! What?
EMILIA. Out; and alas! That was my lady's voice.
   Help! Help, ho! Help! O lady, speak again!
   Sweet Desdemona! O sweet mistress, speak!
DESDEMONA. A guiltless death I die.
EMILIA. O, who hath done this deed?
DESDEMONA. Nobody; I myself. Farewell.
   Commend me to my kind lord. O, farewell! [*Dies.*]
OTHELLO. Why, how should she be murdered?
EMILIA.   Alas, who knows?
OTHELLO. You heard her say herself, it was not I.
EMILIA. She said so. I must needs report the truth.
OTHELLO. She's like a liar gone to burning hell.
   'Twas I that killed her.
EMILIA.   O, the more angel she,
   And you the blacker devil!
OTHELLO. She turned to folly and she was a whore.
EMILIA. Thou dost belie her and thou art a devil.
OTHELLO. She was false as water.
EMILIA.   Thou art rash as fire, to say
   That she was false. O, she was heavenly true!
OTHELLO. Cassio did top her; ask thy husband else.

O, I were damned beneath all depth in hell,
But that I did proceed upon just grounds
To this extremity. Thy husband knew it all.

EMILIA. My husband!

OTHELLO. Thy husband.

EMILIA. That she was false to wedlock?

OTHELLO. Ay, with Cassio. Nay, had she been true,
If heaven would make me such another world
Of one entire and perfect chrysolite,°   *topaz*
I'ld not have sold her for it.

EMILIA. My husband!

OTHELLO.   Ay, 'twas he that told me first.
An honest man he is, and hates the slime
That sticks on filthy deeds.

EMILIA.   My husband!

OTHELLO. What needs this iteration, woman? I say thy husband.

EMILIA. O mistress, villany hath made mocks with° love!   *a mockery of*
My husband say that she was false!

OTHELLO.   He, woman;
I say thy husband. Dost understand the word?
My friend, thy husband, honest, honest Iago.

EMILIA. If he say so, may his pernicious soul
Rot half a grain a day! He lies to the heart.
She was too fond of her most filthy bargain.

OTHELLO. Ha!

EMILIA. Do thy worst:
This deed of thine is no more worthy heaven
Than thou wast worthy her.

OTHELLO.   Peace, you were best.

EMILIA. Thou hast not half that power to do me harm
As I have to be hurt. O gull!° O dolt!   *simpleton*
As ignorant as dirt! Thou hast done a deed—
I care not for thy sword; I'll make thee known,
Though I lost twenty lives. Help! Help! ho! Help!
The Moor hath killed my mistress! Murder! Murder!

Enter MONTANO, GRATIANO, IAGO, *and others.*

MONTANO. What is the matter? How now, general!

EMILIA. O, are you come, Iago? You have done well,
That men must lay their murders on your neck.

GRATIANO. What is the matter?

EMILIA. Disprove this villain, if thou be'st a man.
He says thou told'st him that his wife was false.
I know thou didst not, thou'rt not such a villain.
Speak, for my heart is full.

IAGO. I told him what I thought, and told no more
Than what he found himself was apt and true.

EMILIA. But did you ever tell him she was false?

IAGO. I did.

EMILIA. You told a lie, an odious, damnèd lie;
   Upon my soul, a lie, a wicked lie!
   She false with Cassio! Did you say with Cassio?
IAGO. With Cassio, mistress. Go to, charm° your tongue.   *control*
EMILIA. I will not charm my tongue; I am bound to speak:
   My mistress here lies murdered in her bed,—
ALL. O heavens forfend!
EMILIA. And your reports have set the murder on.
OTHELLO. Nay, stare not, masters. It is true indeed.
GRATIANO. 'Tis a strange truth.
MONTANO. O monstrous act!
EMILIA.   Villany, villany, villany!
   I think upon't. I think. I smell't. O villany!
   I thought so then. I'll kill myself for grief,
   O villany, villany!
IAGO. What, are you mad? I charge you, get you home.
EMILIA. Good gentlemen, let me have leave to speak.
   'Tis proper I obey him, but not now.
   Perchance, Iago, I will ne'er go home.
OTHELLO. O! O! O! [*Falling on the bed.*]
EMILIA.   Nay, lay thee down and roar;
   For thou hast killed the sweetest innocent
   That e'er did lift up eye.
OTHELLO [*Rising*].   O, she was foul!
   I scarce did know you, uncle. There lies your niece,
   Whose breath indeed these hands have newly stopped.
   I know this act shows° horrible and grim.   *looks*
GRATIANO. Poor Desdemona! I am glad thy father's dead.
   Thy match was mortal to him, and pure grief
   Shore his old thread in twain. Did he live now,
   This sight would make him do a desperate turn;°   *deed*
   Yea, curse his better angel from his side,
   And fall to reprobation.°   *damnation*
OTHELLO. 'Tis pitiful; but yet Iago knows
   That she with Cassio hath the act of shame
   A thousand times committed; Cassio confessed it.
   And she did gratify his amorous works
   With that recognizance and pledge of love
   Which I first gave her; I saw it in his hand.
   It was a handkerchief, an antique token
   My father gave my mother.
EMILIA. O heaven! O heavenly powers!
IAGO. 'Zounds! Hold your peace.
EMILIA.   'Twill out, 'twill out. I peace!
   No, I will speak as liberal° as the north.°   *freely, coldly / north wind*
   Let heaven and men and devils let them all,
   All, all, cry shame against me, yet I'll speak.
IAGO. Be wise, and get you home.
EMILIA.   I will not.
   [IAGO *offers to stab* EMILIA.]
GRATIANO.   Fie!
   Your sword upon a woman!

EMILIA. O thou dull Moor! That handkerchief thou speak'st of
  I found by fortune and did give my husband;
  For often with a solemn earnestness,
  More than indeed belonged to such a trifle,
  He begged of me to steal it.
IAGO.   Villanous whore!
EMILIA. She give it Cassio! No, alas, I found it,
  And I did give't my husband.
IAGO.   Filth, thou liest!
EMILIA. By heaven, I do not, I do not, gentlemen.
  O murderous coxcomb!° What should such a fool   *dunce*
  Do with so good a wife!
OTHELLO.   Are there no stones in heaven
  But what serve for the thunder?[18] Precious villain!
  [*He runs at* IAGO. IAGO, *from behind, stabs* EMILIA, *and exit.*]
GRATIANO. The woman falls; sure, he hath killed his wife.
EMILIA. Ay, ay. O, lay me by my mistress' side.
GRATIANO. He's gone, but his wife's killed.
MONTANO. 'Tis a notorious villain. Take you this weapon,
  Which I have here recovered from the Moor.
  Come, guard the door without; let him not pass,
  But kill him rather. I'll after that same villain,
  For 'tis a damned slave.
  [*Exeunt all but* OTHELLO *and* EMILIA.]
OTHELLO.   I am not valiant neither,
  But every puny whipster° gets my sword.   *whipping boy*
  But why should honor outlive honesty?
  Let it go all.
EMILIA.   What did thy song bode, lady?
  Hark, canst thou hear me? I will play the swan,
  And die in music. [*Singing.*] Willow, willow, willow.
  Moor, she was chaste; she loved thee, cruel Moor;
  So come my soul to bliss, as I speak true;
  So speaking as I think, I die, I die. [*Dies.*]
OTHELLO. I have another weapon in this chamber;
  It is a sword of Spain, the ice-brook's temper.°—   *i.e., tempered in ice-water*
  O, here it is. Uncle, I must come forth.
GRATIANO [*within*]. If thou attempt it, it will cost thee dear.
  Thou hast no weapon, and perforce must suffer.
OTHELLO. Look in upon me then, and speak with me,
  Or, naked as I am, I will assault thee.

Re-enter GRATIANO.

GRATIANO. What is the matter?
OTHELLO.   Behold, I have a weapon;
  A better never did itself sustain
  Upon a soldier's thigh. I have seen the day

---

[18] Thunder was thought by some Elizabethans to be caused by huge boulders falling from the sky and bouncing along the ground.

That with this little arm and this good sword
I have made my way through more impediments
Than twenty times your stop.° But, O vain boast!   opposition
Who can control his fate? 'Tis not so now.
Be not afraid, though you do see me weaponed;
Here is my journey's end, here is my butt°   target
And very sea-mark° of my utmost° sail.   marker / farthest
Do you go back dismayed? 'Tis a lost fear:
Man but a rush° against Othello's breast,   reed
And he retires. Where should Othello go?
Now, how dost thou look now? O ill-starred wench!
Pale as thy smock! When we shall meet at compt,°   Judgment
This look of thine will hurl my soul from heaven,
And fiends will snatch at it. Cold, cold, my girl!
Even like thy chastity. O cursed slave!
Whip me, ye devils,
From the possession of this heavenly sight!
Blow me about in winds! Roast me in sulphur!
Wash me in steep-down gulfs of liquid fire!
O Desdemona! Desdemona! Dead!
Oh! Oh! Oh!

Enter LODOVICO, MONTANO, CASSIO *carried in a chair,*
and OFFICERS *with* IAGO, *prisoner.*

LODOVICO. Where is this rash and most unfortunate man?
OTHELLO. That's he that was Othello. Here I am.
LODOVICO. Where is that viper? Bring the villain forth.
OTHELLO. I look down towards his feet; but that's a fable.
   If that thou be'st a devil,° I cannot kill thee. [*Wounds* IAGO.]   *i.e., with cloven feet*
LODOVICO. Wrench his sword from him.
IAGO.   I bleed, sir, but not killed.
OTHELLO. I am not sorry neither. I'ld have thee live;
   For, in my case, 'tis happiness to die.
LODOVICO. O thou Othello, that wert once so good,
   Fall'n in the practice° of a damnèd slave,   scheming
   What shall be said to thee?
OTHELLO.   Why, any thing.
   An honorable murderer, if you will;
   For nought did I in hate, but all in honor.
LODOVICO. This wretch hath part confessed his villany.
   Did you and he consent in Cassio's death?
OTHELLO. Ay.
CASSIO. Dear general, I never gave you cause.
OTHELLO. I do believe it, and I ask your pardon.
   Will you, I pray, demand that demi-devil
   Why he hath thus ensnared my soul and body?
IAGO. Demand me nothing; what you know, you know.
   From this time forth I never will speak word.
LODOVICO. What, not to pray?
GRATIANO.   Torments will ope your lips.

OTHELLO. Well, thou dost best.
LODOVICO. Sir, you shall understand what hath befall'n,
    Which, as I think, you know not. Here is a letter
    Found in the pocket of the slain Roderigo,
    And here another. The one of them imports
    The death of Cassio to be undertook
    By Roderigo.
OTHELLO. O villain!
CASSIO.   Most heathenish and most gross!
LODOVICO. Now here's another discontented paper,
    Found in his pocket too; and this, it seems,
    Roderigo meant to have sent this damned villain;
    But that, belike, Iago in the interim
    Came in and satisfied him.
OTHELLO.   O the pernicious caitiff!°   *villain*
    How came you, Cassio, by that handkerchief
    That was my wife's?
CASSIO.   I found it in my chamber.
    And he himself confessed but even now
    That there he dropped it for a special purpose
    Which wrought to his desire.
OTHELLO.   O fool! fool! fool!
CASSIO. There is besides in Roderigo's letter,
    How he upbraids Iago, that he made him
    Brave° me upon the watch; whereon it came   *Defy*
    That I was cast,° and even but now he spake   *dismissed*
    After long seeming dead, Iago hurt him,
    Iago set him on.
LODOVICO. You must forsake this room, and go with us.
    Your power and your command is taken off,
    And Cassio rules in Cyprus. For this slave,
    If there be any cunning cruelty
    That can torment him much and hold him long,
    It shall be his. You shall close prisoner rest,
    Till that the nature of your fault be known
    To the Venetian state. Come, bring away.
OTHELLO. Soft you; a word or two before you go.
    I have done the state some service, and they know't.
    No more of that. I pray you, in your letters,
    When you shall these unlucky deeds relate,
    Speak of me as I am; nothing extenuate,
    Nor set down aught in malice. Then must you speak
    Of one that loved not wisely but too well;
    Of one not easily jealous but, being wrought,
    Perplexed in the extreme; of one whose hand,
    Like the base Indian, threw a pearl away
    Richer than all his tribe; of one whose subdued eyes,
    Albeit unused to the melting mood,
    Drop tears as fast as the Arabian trees
    Their medicinal gum. Set you down this;
    And say besides, that in Aleppo once,

Where a malignant and a turbaned Turk
Beat a Venetian and traduced° the state,   slandered
I took by the throat the circumcisèd dog
And smote him, thus. [*Stabs himself.*]
LODOVICO. O bloody period!
GRATIANO.   All that's spoke is marred.
OTHELLO. I kissed thee ere I killed thee. No way but this,
Killing myself, to die upon a kiss.
[*Falls on the bed, and dies.*]
CASSIO. This did I fear, but thought he had no weapon;
For he was great of heart.
LODOVICO [*to* IAGO].   O Spartan[19] dog,
More fell° than anguish, hunger, or the sea!   cruel
Look on the tragic loading of this bed;
This is thy work. The object poisons sight;
Let it be hid. Gratiano, keep the house,
And seize upon the fortunes of the Moor,
For they succeed on you. To you, lord governor,
Remains the censure of this hellish villain,
The time, the place, the torture: O, enforce it!
Myself will straight aboard, and to the state
This heavy act with heavy heart relate. [*Exeunt.*]

[1604]

---

[19] The Spartans were famous for ferocity.

Molière (Jean-Baptiste Poquelin) *1622–1673*

TARTUFFE
OR
THE HYPOCRITE
(L'Imposteur)

A Comedy

Translated by A. R. Waller

CHARACTERS

MME. PERNELLE, *Orgon's mother*

ORGON, *Elmire's husband*

ELMIRE, *Orgon's wife*

DAMIS, *Orgon's son, Elmire's stepson*

MARIANE, *Orgon's daughter, Elmire's stepdaughter, and Valère's lover*

VALÈRE, *Mariane's lover*

CLÉANTE, *Orgon's brother-in-law*

TARTUFFE, *a hypocrite*

DORINE, *Mariane's maid*

M. LOYAL, *a bailiff*

POLICE OFFICER

FLIPOTE, *Mme. Pernelle's servant*

LAURENT, *Tartuffe's servant*

SCENE
Paris

ACT I

SCENE I

MADAME PERNELLE *and* FLIPOTE, *her servant*, ELMIRE,
MARIANE, DORINE, DAMIS, CLÉANTE

MME. PERNELLE. Come along, Flipote, come along; let me get away from them.

ELMIRE. You walk so fast that I can scarcely keep up with you.

MME. PERNELLE. You need not come any further, child. I can dispense with such ceremony.

ELMIRE. We only give what is due to you. But, mother, why are you in such a hurry to leave us?

MME. PERNELLE. Because I cannot bear to see such goings on and no one takes any pains to meet my wishes. Yes, I leave your house not very well pleased: you ignore all my advice, you do not show any respect for anything, everyone says what he likes, and it is just like the Court of King Pétaud.[1]

DORINE. If . . .

MME. PERNELLE. You are far too free with your tongue for your position, my lass, and too saucy. You offer your advice about everything.

DAMIS. But . . .

MME. PERNELLE. You are a fool thrice over, my boy, though it is your own grandmother who says it. I have told your father a hundred times that you will become a ne'er-do-well, and will cause him nothing but trouble.

MARIANE. I think . . .

---

[1] A court without order where every man is his own master.

MME. PERNELLE. As for you, his sister, you put on such a demure air that it is difficult to catch you tripping. But, as the saying is, still waters are the most dangerous, and I hate your underhand ways.

ELMIRE. But, mother . . .

MME. PERNELLE. Let me tell you, daughter, that your whole conduct is entirely wrong. You ought to set them a good example: their late mother did much better. You are extravagant: I am shocked to see you decked out like a princess. If a woman wishes to please her husband only, she has no need for so much finery, my child.

CLÉANTE. But, madam, after all . . .

MME. PERNELLE. As for you, sir, who are her brother, I think very highly of you, and I both love and respect you, but, at the same time, if I were my son, her husband, I should request you not to enter our house. You are always laying down rules of conduct which respectable people should not follow. I speak rather frankly to you, but that is my nature: I do not mince matters when I have anything on my mind.

DAMIS. Your Mr. Tartuffe is, no doubt, an excellent person . . .

MME. PERNELLE. He is a very worthy man, one who should be listened to; and it makes me very angry to hear him sneered at by a fool like you.

DAMIS. What! Am I to permit a censorious bigot to exercise a tyrannical influence in the family; and are we not to be allowed any pleasures unless this good gentleman condescends to give his consent?

DORINE. Were we to listen to him and to put faith in his maxims, we should look upon all our acts as criminal, for the zealous critic finds fault with everything.

MME. PERNELLE. And whatever he finds fault with deserves censure. He wants to lead you to Heaven, and it is my son's duty to teach you to value him.

DAMIS. No; look here, grandmother, neither my father nor anyone else shall ever induce me to think well of him: I should be false to myself were I to speak otherwise. His ways irritate me constantly. I can see what the consequence will be: that underbred fellow and I will soon quarrel.

DORINE. Surely it is a scandalous thing to see a stranger exercise such authority in this house: to see a beggar, who, when he came, had not shoes on his feet, and whose whole clothing may have been worth twopence, so far forget himself as to interfere with everything, and play the master.

MME. PERNELLE. Ah! mercy on me! it would be much better if everything were done in accordance with his good rules.

DORINE. He is a saint in your opinion, but, in mine, he is a hypocrite.

MME. PERNELLE. What language!

DORINE. I should not like to trust myself either with him or with his man Laurent, without good security.

MME. PERNELLE. I do not know what the servant may be at heart, but I will swear the master is a worthy man. You all hate and flout him because he tells you unpleasant truths. His anger is directed against sin, and his only desire is to further the cause of Heaven.

DORINE. Yes; but why, especially for some time past, can he not bear any one to come to the house? Why is a polite call so offensive to Heaven that he needs make noise enough about it to split our heads? Between ourselves I will tell you what I think. Upon my word, I believe that he is jealous of Madame.

MME. PERNELLE. Hold your tongue, and take care what you say. He is not the only person who blames these visits. The whole neighborhood is annoyed by the bustle of the people you receive, their carriages always waiting before the door, and the noisy crowd of servants. I am willing to believe that there is no actual harm done, but people will talk, and it is better not to give them cause.

CLÉANTE. Ah! madam, how can you stop people talking? It would be a sorry thing if in this world we had to give up our best friends, because of idle chatter aimed at us. And even if we could bring ourselves to do so, do you think it would stop people's tongues? There is not any protection against slander. Do not let us pay any attention to foolish gossip, but endeavour to live honestly and leave the scandal-mongers to say what they will.

DORINE. Probably our neighbor Daphné, and her little husband, are at the bottom of all this slander. Those who are the most ridiculous in their own conduct are always the first to libel others. They are quick to get hold of the slightest rumor of a love-affair, to spread it abroad with high glee, giving the story just what twist they like. They paint the actions of others in their own colors, thinking thereby to justify their own conduct to the world; and in the vain hope of a resemblance they try to give their intrigues some show of innocence, or else to shift to other shoulders a part of that blame with which they themselves are overburdened.

MME. PERNELLE. All these arguments have nothing to do with the matter. Everybody knows that Orante leads an exemplary life, and that all her thoughts are towards heaven. Well, I have been told that she strongly disapproves of the company who visit here.

DORINE. The example is admirable, and the lady is beyond reproach! It is true that she lives an austere life, but age is responsible for her fervent zeal, and people know that she is a prude because she cannot help it. She made the most of all her advantages while she had the power of attracting attention. But now that her eyes have lost their luster she renounces the world which renounces her, and hides under the pompous cloak of prudence the decay of her worn-out charms. Such is the last shift of a modern coquette. Mortified to see their lovers fall away from them, their gloomy despair sees nothing for it, when thus forsaken, but the rôle of prudery; and in their strictness these good women censure everything and pardon nothing. They loudly condemn the actions of others, not from principles of charity, but out of envy, since they cannot bear to see another taste those pleasures for which age has taken away their appetite.

MME. PERNELLE. These are idle tales told to please you. I have to be silent in your house, my child, for madam, by gossiping, holds the dice the whole day.[2] Still, I mean to have my say in my turn. I tell you that my son never did a wiser act than when he received this good man into his family; Heaven mercifully sent him into your house to convert your erring thoughts. You ought to hear him for your soul's sake, since he censures nothing but that which deserves censure. All these visits, these balls, these tales, are inventions of the evil one. Not one good word is heard at them, nothing but idle gossip, songs and chatter. Often enough the neighbor comes in for his share, and there is scandal right and left. Indeed the heads of sensible people are quite turned by the distraction of these gatherings. A thousand ill-natured stories are spread abroad in no time; and, as a certain doctor very truly said the other day, it is a perfect tower of Babylon, for every one babbles as long as he likes. And to tell the story which brought this up . . . Here is this gentleman giggling already! Go and find the fools who make you laugh, and unless . . . Good-bye, my child. I'll say no more. My regard for your house has fallen by one-half, and it will be a very long time before I set foot in it again. [*Slapping* Flipote's *face.*] Come along, you, don't stand there dreaming and gaping. Good Lord! I'll warm your ears for you, come on, hussy, come on.

---

[2] I.e., she dominates the conversation.

SCENE II
CLÉANTE, DORINE

CLÉANTE. I will not follow her lest she should begin scolding me again. How that old woman . . .

DORINE. Ah! truly it is a pity that she does not hear you use such language. She would soon tell you *your* age, and that *she* is not yet old enough to deserve that title.

CLÉANTE. What a passion she got into with us about nothing, and how infatuated she seems with her Tartuffe!

DORINE. Oh! indeed, her infatuation is nothing in comparison with her son's, and if you could see him you would say he was far worse! During our civil troubles he gained a reputation for sense, and showed some courage in serving his prince, but he has become an idiot since his head has been full of Tartuffe. He calls him brother, and in his heart loves him a hundred times more than he loves mother, son, daughter, and wife. He makes him the sole confidant of all his secrets, and the sage adviser of all his actions. He caresses him, kisses him, and I do not think he could show more affection to a mistress. He will have him seated at the head of the table, and is delighted to see him eat as much as half-a-dozen other people. All the choice morsels are given to him, and if he chance to hiccup he says to him, "God bless you!" In short, he is crazy about him; he is his all, his hero; he admires him at all points, quotes him on all occasions; he considers that his most trifling actions are miracles, and every word he utters an oracle. Tartuffe, who understands his dupe, and wishes to make the most profit out of him, is clever enough to impose upon him in a hundred different shams. He constantly extorts money from him by his cant, and takes upon himself the right to find fault with us all. Even that puppy of a footboy of his has the cheek to lecture us; he preaches at us with indignant looks, and throws away our ribbons, rouge, and patches.[3] Only the other day the wretch tore a handkerchief to pieces which he found in a 'Flower of the Saints,' saying that it was an abominable sin to put the devil's trappings side by side with holy things.

SCENE III
ELMIRE, MARIANE, DAMIS, CLÉANTE, DORINE

ELMIRE. You are very lucky to have missed the sermon she gave us at the door. But I have just seen my husband, and as he did not see me I shall go and wait upstairs for him.

CLÉANTE. I will wait for him here for a little longer, only to bid him "Good-morning."

DAMIS. Sound him a little about my sister's marriage. I suspect that Tartuffe opposes it, because he puts my father up to so many evasions; and you know what a great interest I take in it. If the same passion influences my sister and Valère, his sister is, as you know, dear to me, and if it were necessary . . .

DORINE. Here he is.

---

[3] It was the fashion at the time for women to wear small black patches to cover up blemishes (or scars from smallpox) on their faces.

SCENE IV
ORGON, CLÉANTE, DORINE

ORGON. Ah! good-morning, brother.

CLÉANTE. I am glad to see you back. I was just going away. The country is not very attractive just now.

ORGON. Dorine . . . Just one moment, brother, I beg. You will, I know, let me relieve my mind by asking how things have gone here. Has all been well during the last two days? What has happened? How are they all?

DORINE. The day before yesterday Madam was feverish from morning to night, with a splitting headache.

ORGON. And Tartuffe?

DORINE. Tartuffe? He is in excellent health, stout and fat, with a fresh complexion and ruddy lips.

ORGON. Poor man!

DORINE. In the evening she felt very sick, and her head ached so violently she could not touch anything at supper.

ORGON. And Tartuffe?

DORINE. He took his supper, in her presence, and very devoutly ate a brace of partridges and half a leg of mutton hashed.

ORGON. Poor man!

DORINE. She passed the whole night without closing her eyes for a moment, kept from sleeping by her feverishness, and we were obliged to sit up with her until morning.

ORGON. And Tartuffe?

DORINE. Comfortably drowsy when he got up from the table, he went to his bedroom and quickly tumbled into his warmed bed, where he slept undisturbed till the morning.

ORGON. Poor man!

DORINE. At length we prevailed upon her to be bled,[4] and immediately she felt relieved.

ORGON. And Tartuffe?

DORINE. He took heart again, as was only right, and to fortify himself against all ills, and to make up for the blood which Madam had lost, he drank four large bumpers of wine at breakfast.

ORGON. Poor man!

DORINE. Both are now well again, and I will go and tell Madam how pleased you are at her recovery.

SCENE V
ORGON, CLÉANTE

CLÉANTE. She is making game of you, brother, to your face, and, without wishing to vex you, I tell you frankly there is good reason for it. Who ever heard of such a whim? How can you be so infatuated with a man at this time of day as to forget everything else for him? And, after having saved him from want by taking him into your own house you should go so far as . . .

ORGON. Stop there, brother, you do not know the man of whom you speak.

---

[4] Doctors in Molière's day frequently opened a vein in a patient's arm in an effort to drain off the tainted blood thought to cause illness.

CLÉANTE. I do not know him then, if you like; but, after all, to know what sort of a man he is . . .

ORGON. Brother, you would be only too glad to know him, and your astonishment would be boundless. He is a man . . . who . . . ha! . . . a man . . . in fact, a man. He who follows attentively his precepts enjoys a profound peace, and looks upon the rest of the world as so much dross. Yes, I am quite another man since I conversed with him. He teaches me that I must not set my affections upon anything; he detaches my heart from all ties; and I could see my brother, children, mother and wife die without caring as much as a snap of the fingers.

CLÉANTE. Humane feelings these, brother!

ORGON. Oh! had you but seen him as I first saw him, you would have for him the same affection that I have. Every day he would come to church, and with mild looks kneel down in front of me. He drew upon himself the attention of the whole congregation by the fervor of his prayers to Heaven; he sighed deeply in his saintly raptures and kissed the ground humbly every moment, and when I came out he would steal quickly before me to the door to offer me holy water. Having learnt who he was, and that he was poor—through his footboy—who copies everything he does—I gave him presents, but he always modestly wished to return me some part of them. "It is too much, too much by half," he would say, "I do not deserve your pity." And when I refused to take it back he distributed it to the poor before my eyes. At last Heaven moved me to take him into my house, and since then everything has seemed to prosper here. He reproves everything, and, with a view to my honor, he shows an extreme solicitude even towards my wife. He tells me of those who cast sweet looks her way, and he is six times more jealous of her than I am. You would never guess how far he carries his zeal: he accuses himself of sin over the slightest trifle; a mere nothing is enough to shock him; he even accused himself the other day for having killed a flea too angrily which he caught whilst saying his prayers.

CLÉANTE. Really, brother, I think you must be crazy. Are you joking at my expense with this nonsense? How can you pretend that all this foolery . . . ?

ORGON. Brother, your talk savors of free thought: you are somewhat tainted with it; and, as I have repeatedly told you, you will draw down some heavy judgment upon your head.

CLÉANTE. That is the usual style of talking among your set; they want everyone to be as blind as themselves. To be clear-sighted is to be a free-thinker, and he who does not bow down to idle affectations has neither respect for nor faith in sacred things. I tell you none of your sermons frighten me: I know what I say, and Heaven sees my heart. We are not ruled by your formalists. There are pretenders to devotion as to courage; and even as those who are truly brave when honor calls are not those who make the most noise, so the good and truly pious, in whose footsteps we ought to follow, are not those who make so many grimaces. What? will you not make any distinction between hypocrisy and sincerity? Will you speak of them in the same words, and render the same homage to the mask as to the face, put artifice on a level with sincerity, confound the appearance with the reality, value the shadow as much as the substance and false coin as good? Men, truly, are strange beings! They are never seen in their proper nature; reason's boundaries are too limited for them; in every character they overact the part; and they often mar that which is most noble by too much exaggeration and by wilful extremes. But this, brother, is by the way.

ORGON. Yes, you are doubtless a doctor, revered by all; all the learning of the ages is concentrated in you; you alone are wise, enlightened, an oracle, a Cato[5] for the present age; and compared with you, all men are fools.

CLÉANTE. No, brother, I am not a revered teacher, nor do I possess all wisdom; my learning is simply the knowledge of how to tell the false from the true. And since I do not know any character more admirable than the truly devout, nor anything in the world more noble and more beautiful than the righteous fervor of a sincere piety, neither do I know anything more odious than the whited sepulchre of a specious zeal; than these barefaced hypocrites, these hireling bigots, whose sacrilegious and deceitful mouthings impose on people with impunity, who jest as they please with all that men hold most holy and sacred; these slaves of self-interest who barter religion and make a trade of it, and who would purchase honor and reputation with a false uplifting of the eyes and affected groans. These men, I say, whom we see possessed of such uncommon ardor, make their fortunes in this world by way of the next; themselves asking each day some new favor, they preach solitude in the midst of the Court, burning with zeal and great in prayer. They know how to reconcile their profession with their vices, are passionate, revengeful, faithless, full of deceit, and, in order to ruin a man, insolently cover their fierce resentment with the cloak of Heaven's interests. They are doubly dangerous in their bitter wrath for they use against us the weapons we revere; and their anger, for which they are commended, prompts them to kill us with a consecrated blade. There are too many of these false characters; the truly devout are easily recognised. Our age, brother, has shown us some who should serve us as glorious examples: look at Ariston, look at Périandre, Oronte, Alcidamas, Polydore, Clitandre[6]—no one denies their title. These are not boasters of virtue; unbearable ostentation is not seen in them; their piety is human, is reasonable; they do not condemn all our actions: they think there is too much arrogance in these censures; and, leaving haughty words to others, they reprove our actions by their own. They do not build upon the appearances of evil, and their minds are inclined to think well of others. No spirit of cabal is found in them; they have no intrigues to scent out; their sole care is to live rightly. They do not persecute a sinner; it is only the sin itself they hate. Neither do they desire to vindicate the interests of Heaven with a keener zeal than Heaven itself shows. These are the people I admire; that is the right way to live; there is, in short, the example to be followed. Your man, to speak truly, is not of this mold: you applaud his piety in good faith, but I believe you are dazzled by a false glitter.

ORGON. Have you said your say, my dear brother?

CLÉANTE. Yes.

ORGON. I am your humble servant. [*Going.*]

CLÉANTE. One word, brother, I pray. Let us drop this discussion. You know you promised Valère he should become your son-in-law?

ORGON. Yes.

CLÉANTE. And that you had fixed the happy day.

ORGON. True.

CLÉANTE. Why, then, defer the ceremony?

---

[5] Marcus Porcius Cato (234–149 B.C.), a Roman consul renowned for devotion to virtue; or his great-grandson, Marcus Porcius Cato, the Younger (95–46 B.C.), a philosopher.
[6] Fictitious, not historical, persons.

ORGON. I do not know.

CLÉANTE. Have you another design in view?

ORGON. Perhaps.

CLÉANTE. You will break your word?

ORGON. I do not say that.

CLÉANTE. No obstacle, I believe, can prevent you fulfilling your promises.

ORGON. That depends.

CLÉANTE. Why so much circumspection about a word? Valère sent me to see you on this matter.

ORGON. Heaven be praised!

CLÉANTE. But what shall I tell him?

ORGON. What you please.

CLÉANTE. But it is necessary to know your intentions. What, then, are they?

ORGON. To perform the will of Heaven.

CLÉANTE. Come, speak to the point. Valère has your word. Will you keep it or not?

ORGON. Good-bye.

CLÉANTE. I am afraid his love will not run smooth, and I ought to tell him what is going on.

END OF THE FIRST ACT

ACT II

SCENE I
ORGON, MARIANE

ORGON. Mariane.

MARIANE. Yes, father.

ORGON. Come here, I have something to say to you privately.

MARIANE. What are you looking for?

ORGON. [*looking into a small side-room.*] I am looking to see whether anyone is there who might overhear us; this is a most likely little place for such a purpose. Now, we are all right. Mariane, I have always found you very good-natured, and you have always been dear to me.

MARIANE. I am very grateful for your fatherly love.

ORGON. That is well said, my child, and in order to deserve it your chief care ought to be to please me.

MARIANE. It is my dearest wish.

ORGON. Very well. What do you think of our guest Tartuffe?

MARIANE. Who, I?

ORGON. You. Think well before you answer.

MARIANE. Oh, dear! I will say anything you like.

ORGON. That is sensibly spoken. Tell me, then, my child, that he is a man whose virtues shine forth, that you love him, and that it would make you very happy were I to choose him for your husband. Eh?

MARIANE. [*draws back, surprised.*] Eh?

ORGON. What is the matter?

MARIANE. What did you say?

ORGON. What?

MARIANE. Am I mistaken?

ORGON. Why?

MARIANE. Whom do you wish me to say I love, father? Whom do I wish you to choose as my husband?

ORGON. Tartuffe.

MARIANE. I don't wish anything of the kind, father, I assure you. Why would you make me tell such a lie?

ORGON. But I wish it to be the truth, and it is enough for you that I have made up my mind on the subject.

MARIANE. What, father, would you . . . ?

ORGON. Yes, my child, I intend to unite Tartuffe to my family by your marriage. I have decided that he shall be your husband, and since you have promised, I . . .

SCENE II
DORINE, ORGON, MARIANE

ORGON. What are you doing here? Your curiosity must be very great, my girl, to urge you to come and listen to us in this way.

DORINE. Indeed, I don't know whether the report is conjecture or simply chance words, but I have just heard some news about this marriage and I treated it as a mere jest.

ORGON. Why? Is the thing incredible?

DORINE. So much so that I could not believe it from your lips, Monsieur.

ORGON. I know how to make you believe it, though.

DORINE. Yes, yes, you tell us a pretty story.

ORGON. I tell you what you will see happen very shortly.

DORINE. Nonsense!

ORGON. I am not jesting, my child.

DORINE. Come, do not believe your father, he is joking.

ORGON. I tell you . . .

DORINE. No, you may say what you like, and no one will believe you.

ORGON. My anger will very soon . . .

DORINE. Very well, we will believe you, but so much the worse for you. What, is it possible, Monsieur, with that air of wisdom and your well-bearded face, that you would be silly enough to want . . .

ORGON. Now listen: you have taken certain liberties in this house, my girl, which I do not like.

DORINE. Let us talk without becoming angry, Monsieur, I beg. Are you making game of everybody by means of this scheme? Your daughter will never do for a bigot: he has other things to think about. Besides, what good will such an alliance be to you? Why, with all your wealth, do you choose a beggar for a son-in-law?

ORGON. Be quiet. If he has nothing he ought to be the more esteemed. His poverty is, without doubt, a noble poverty; it should raise him above all worldly greatness since he has allowed himself to be deprived of his wealth by caring too little for earthly affairs, and by his ardent attachment to things eternal. My help may be the means of getting him out of his troubles and of restoring his property to him: his estates are well known in his native place, but even as he is he is a gentleman.

DORINE. Well, he says he is, but this vanity, Monsieur, does not agree well with his piety. He who embraces the simplicity of a holy life should not boast of his name and lineage: the humble ways of goodness have nothing in common with the glare of ambition. Why such pride? But what I say vexes you: let us speak of himself and leave his quality. Can you have the heart to bestow such a daughter as yours upon a man of his stamp? Ought you not to have some regard for propriety and foresee the consequences of this union? You must know the girl's virtue is not safe when she is married against her inclinations, that her living virtuously depends upon the qualities of the husband who is given to her, and that those who have the finger of scorn pointed at them make their wives what we see they are. It is truly no easy task to be faithful to certain husbands; and he who gives his daughter to a man she hates is responsible to heaven for the sins she commits. Consider, then, to what perils your design exposes you.

ORGON. I see I shall have to learn from her how to live.

DORINE. You could not do better than follow my advice.

ORGON. Do not let us waste time, my child, with this silly talk. I am your father, and I know what is good for you. I had betrothed you to Valère, but I hear he is inclined to gambling, and I also suspect he is a free-thinker, for I never see him at church.

DORINE. Would you like him to go there at stated times like those who go to be seen?

ORGON. I don't ask your advice upon the matter. Tartuffe is on the best possible terms with heaven, and that is a treasure second to none. This union will crown your wishes with every blessing. It will be full of pleasure and joy. You will live together in faithful love like two young children, like turtledoves, there will not be any miserable disputes between you, and you will make anything you like of him.

DORINE. She? Why, I am sure she will never make anything of him but a fool.

ORGON. Good gracious! what language!

DORINE. I tell you he looks it all over, and his destiny, Monsieur, will be stronger than your daughter's virtue.

ORGON. Don't interrupt me. Try to hold your tongue without poking your nose into what does not concern you.

DORINE. I only speak for your good, Monsieur. [*She interrupts him every time he turns to speak to his daughter.*]

ORGON. You are too good! Be quiet, will you?

DORINE. If I did not like you . . .

ORGON. I do not need affection.

DORINE. But I will care for you, Monsieur, in spite of yourself.

ORGON. Ah!

DORINE. Your honor is dear to me, and I cannot bear that you should be jeered at by every one.

ORGON. Will you be silent?

DORINE. It is a shame to let you make such an alliance.

ORGON. Will you hold your peace, you viper, whose brazen face . . .

DORINE. What! you a religious man and you give way to anger?

ORGON. Yes, my choler is roused to fury by your nonsense. I insist upon your holding your tongue.

DORINE. Very well. But if I cannot speak I shall think all the more.

ORGON. Think, if you like, but take care not to tell your thoughts to me, or . . . beware. [*Turning towards his daughter.*] I have deliberately weighed everything as a prudent man should.

DORINE. It makes me furious not to be allowed to speak. [*She is silent when he looks towards her.*]

ORGON. Without being a fop Tartuffe's looks are such . . .

DORINE. Yes, he has a fine mug.

ORGON. That even if you do not appreciate his other qualities . . . [*He turns towards her, and looks at her, his arms folded.*]

DORINE. There's a fine bargain! If I were in her place, depend upon it no man should marry me against my will with impunity. I would soon let him see, after the wedding-day, that a woman has always her vengeance in her own hands.

ORGON. Then you do not mean to take any notice of what I say?

DORINE. What are you complaining about? I was not speaking to you.

ORGON. What were you doing then?

DORINE. I was speaking to myself.

ORGON. All right. I must give her the back of my hand for her unbearable insolence. [*He prepares to slap* DORINE'S *face; and* DORINE *stands silent and erect each time he looks at her.*] You ought to approve of my plan, my child . . . and have faith in the husband . . . I have chosen for you . . . Why do you not speak to yourself?

DORINE. Because I have no more to say to myself.

ORGON. Only a little word.

DORINE. It does not suit me.

ORGON. I was waiting for you.

DORINE. I am not such a fool.

ORGON. In short, my girl, you must obey, and show all deference to my choice.

DORINE. [*running away.*] I would take care I would not marry such a husband.

ORGON. [*He tries to slap* DORINE'S *face and misses her.*] You have a pestilent hussy there, my child, with whom I cannot live without forgetting myself. I feel I am not fit now to continue the conversation. Such insolent speeches have put me in so great a passion that I must have a breath of air to compose myself.

SCENE III
DORINE, MARIANE

DORINE. Tell me, have you lost your tongue; must I play your part in this matter? To think you allow such an absurd proposal to be made to you without your saying a word against it!

MARIANE. What would you have me do against a tyrannical father?

DORINE. Anything to ward off such a fate.

MARIANE. But what?

DORINE. Tell him a heart cannot love at the bidding of another, that you marry to please yourself not him, that, as the matter concerns you alone it is you, not him, whom the husband must please, and that, since he is so charmed with his Tartuffe, he can marry him himself without any hindrance.

MARIANE. A father has such authority over us that I admit I have not had the courage to say anything.

DORINE. Let us talk it all over. Valère has proposed to you: do you love him, pray, or do you not?

MARIANE. Oh! Dorine, you are very unjust to me. How can you ask me such a question? Have I not opened my heart to you a hundred times on this subject? Do you not know how much I love him?

DORINE. How do I know your lips have spoken what your heart felt and that you really care for this lover?

MARIANE. You wrong me greatly, Dorine, to doubt it. Surely my real feelings have shown themselves only too plainly.

DORINE. Then you love him?

MARIANE. Yes, passionately.

DORINE. And apparently he loves you just as ardently.

MARIANE. I believe so.

DORINE. And you both are eager to be married.

MARIANE. Most certainly.

DORINE. What do you mean to do, then, about this other match?

MARIANE. To kill myself if I am forced into it.

DORINE. Good! I had not thought of that way out of the difficulty; you have but to die to be rid of troubles; what an excellent remedy! It puts me out of all patience to hear such talk.

MARIANE. Good heavens! what a temper you are in, Dorine. You have no sympathy for people in their troubles.

DORINE. I have no pity for those who talk nonsense and give way at the critical moment as you do.

MARIANE. But what can I do? I am afraid.

DORINE. Love asks for courage.

MARIANE. Have I wavered in my love of Valère? Is it not his place to win me from my father?

DORINE. What if your father is a downright lunatic, who has gone clean crazy over his Tartuffe, and who does not keep his promise about this marriage: is your lover to be blamed for that?

MARIANE. But am I, by haughty refusal and contemptuous disdain, to let everyone see my own heart is too deeply smitten? However much I desire Valère, am I to cast aside for him my womanly modesty and my filial duty? And would you have me show my heart to the whole world . . . ?

DORINE. No, no! I won't ask you to do anything. I see you wish to belong to Monsieur Tartuffe; and I should do wrong, now I come to think of it, were I to dissuade you from such a marriage. What excuse have I for opposing your wishes? The match in itself is very advantageous. Monsieur Tartuffe! oh! oh! is it nothing that is proposed? Indeed, Monsieur Tartuffe, to look at the thing in the right light, is not a man to be trifled with by any means, and it is not a piece of bad luck to be his better half. The world has already crowned him with glory; he passes for an aristocrat in his own parish, well set up in person, with his red ears and his florid complexion. How very happy you will be with such a husband!

MARIANE. Oh! dear . . .

DORINE. What delight you will experience when you become the wife of such a bridegroom!

MARIANE. Oh! stop such talk, I beg you, and show me the way to avoid this marriage. Let us make an end of it. I give in, and am ready to do anything.

DORINE. A daughter should obey her father even if he wished her to marry an ape. Yours is an enviable fate; of what do you complain? You will go in the coach to his native town and find yourself rich in uncles and cousins whom it will delight you exceedingly to entertain. You will soon be introduced into the best society; you will begin by visits to the magistrate's wife and the tax-surveyor's lady, who will honor you with a folding-stool. At carnival time you may hope for a ball there, the grand local band, consisting of two bagpipes, in attendance, and possibly the learned ape will be present and marionettes, only, if your husband . . .

MARIANE. Oh! you are enough to kill me. Help me rather with your advice.

DORINE. I am your servant.

MARIANE. Ah! Dorine, for pity's sake . . .

DORINE. This matter ought to go through in order to punish you.

MARIANE. My dear girl!

DORINE. No.

MARIANE. If my declared vows . . .

DORINE. No. Tartuffe is your man, and you must have him.

MARIANE. You know I have always trusted in you. Help me . . .

DORINE. No, upon my word you shall be tartuffed.

MARIANE. Very well, since my fate fails to move you, leave me alone henceforth with my despair: my heart shall borrow help from that, and I know there is one unfailing remedy for my misery. [*She turns to go.*]

DORINE. Here! stop, stop, come back. I won't be angry any longer. It seems I must take pity on you, in spite of everything.

MARIANE. Dorine, you may be sure if they force me to endure this cruel martyrdom I shall surely die.

DORINE. Do not worry yourself. We will be too clever for them, and prevent . . . But here comes your lover Valère.

SCENE IV
VALÈRE, MARIANE, DORINE

VALÈRE. I have just been told a very pretty piece of news which I did not know.

MARIANE. What is it?

VALÈRE. That you are to marry Tartuffe.

MARIANE. It is true my father has this design in his head.

VALÈRE. Your father, Madam . . .

MARIANE. Has changed his mind: he has just proposed this thing to me.

VALÈRE. What, seriously?

MARIANE. Yes, seriously. He has declared himself openly for the match.

VALÈRE. And what is your own decision in the matter, Madam.

MARIANE. I do not know.

VALÈRE. A candid answer. You do not know?

MARIANE. No.

VALÈRE. No?

MARIANE. What do you advise me?

VALÈRE. I? I advise you to accept this husband.

MARIANE. You advise me that?

VALÈRE. Yes.

MARIANE. In earnest?

VALÈRE. Without doubt: the choice is excellent and well worth considering.

MARIANE. Very well, then, sir, I will act on the advice.

VALÈRE. That will not be very disagreeable, I imagine.

MARIANE. Not more painful than for you to give it.

VALÈRE. I? I gave it to please you, Madam.

MARIANE. And I? I shall follow it to please you.

DORINE. Let us see what will come of this.

VALÈRE. This, then, is your affection? And it was deception when you . . .

MARIANE. Pray do not let us talk any more of that. You told me plainly I ought to accept the husband selected for me: and I declare I intend to do so, since you have given me that salutary advice.

VALÈRE. Do not make my advice your excuse. You had already made up your mind, and you seized a frivolous pretext to justify the breaking of your word.

MARIANE. Very true, and well put.

VALÈRE. No doubt; and you never really loved me.

MARIANE. Alas! think so if you please.

VALÈRE. Yes, yes, if I please; but my slighted love may perchance forestall you in a similar design; and I know where to offer both my heart and my hand.

MARIANE. Ah! I do not doubt it. The love which merit can command . . .

VALÈRE. For Heaven's sake, let us leave merit out of the question: there is but little of it in me, no doubt, and you have given proof of it. But I have great hopes of the kindness another woman will have for me, and I know whose heart will not be ashamed to consent to make up for my loss when I am free.

MARIANE. The loss is not great; and you will be consoled easily enough by this exchange.

VALÈRE. I shall do my best, you may depend. To be forgotten wounds self-love; every endeavor must be used to forget also; and if one does not succeed, one must at least pretend to do so; for it is an unpardonable weakness to appear loving when forsaken.

MARIANE. Truly, what noble and praiseworthy sentiments.

VALÈRE. Most certainly; and they should be approved by everyone. What? Would you have me for ever cherish in my heart the warmth of my passion for you? Am I to see you throw yourself into the arms of another before my face, and not elsewhere bestow the heart you no longer want?

MARIANE. On the contrary: I confess that is exactly what I desire. I wish the thing were done already.

VALÈRE. You wish it?

MARIANE. Yes.

VALÈRE. You insult me, Madam. I will go at once to satisfy you. [*He turns to go but keeps on coming back.*]

MARIANE. Very well.

VALÈRE. Recollect at least that it is you yourself who drive me to this extremity.

MARIANE. Yes.

VALÈRE. And that the design I have in my mind is but to follow your example.

MARIANE. My example let it be.

VALÈRE. Be it so: you will be served just as you wish.

MARIANE. I am very glad.

VALÈRE. You see me for the last time in your life.

MARIANE. That is all right.

VALÈRE. Eh? [*He goes; and when he is near the door he returns.*]

MARIANE. What?

VALÈRE. Did you call me?

MARIANE. I? You are dreaming.

VALÈRE. Ah! well, I will go my way then. Farewell, Madam.

MARIANE. Farewell, Monsieur.

DORINE. I think you are mad to talk such nonsense; I have left you to quarrel all this time to see how far you would go. Stop there, seigneur Valère! [*She takes hold of his arm to stop him, and he makes a great show of resistance.*]

VALÈRE. Well, what do you want, Dorine?

DORINE. Come here.

VALÈRE. No, no, I am too indignant. Do not turn me away from doing her will.

DORINE. Stop.

VALÈRE. No, do you not see my mind is made up?

DORINE. Ah!

MARIANE. He cannot bear to see me, my presence drives him away. I had much better give up the place to him.

DORINE. [*She leaves* VALÈRE *and runs to* MARIANE.] Here goes another. Where are you running off to?

MARIANE. Let me go.

DORINE. You must come back.

MARIANE. No, no, Dorine, it is in vain for you to try to keep me.

VALÈRE. I see plainly the sight of me annoys her, and doubtless I had better rid her of my presence.

DORINE. [*She leaves* MARIANE *and runs to* VALÈRE.] Again? Deuce take you if I wish it! Stop this fooling and come here, both of you. [*She seizes hold of them both.*]

VALÈRE. What do you want?

MARIANE. What are you going to do?

DORINE. To bring you together again, and set things straight. Are you mad to wrangle like this?

VALÈRE. Did you not hear how she spoke to me?

DORINE. Are you an idiot to have got into such a passion?

MARIANE. Did you not see how it all happened, and how he treated me?

DORINE. Folly on both sides. She has no other wish than to remain yours; I can vouch for it. He loves you only, and desires nothing else than to be your husband; I will answer for it with my life.

MARIANE. Why, then, did you give me such advice?

VALÈRE. Why did you ask for it on such a subject?

DORINE. What a couple of fools you are. Come, now, give me your hands here.

VALÈRE. [*giving his hand to* DORINE.] What is the good of my hand?

DORINE. Ah! now, then, yours.

MARIANE. [*also giving her hand.*] What is the good of my hand?

DORINE. Goodness! be quick, come on. You both are fonder of each other than you think.

VALÈRE. Don't do things with such a bad grace, then, but give a man a civil look. [MARIANE *turns her eyes on* VALÈRE *and smiles a little.*]

DORINE. What silly creatures lovers are, to be sure!

VALÈRE. But still, have I not cause to complain of you? And, to say the least, were you not unkind to utter such cruel things to me?

MARIANE. But you, are you not also the most ungrateful man . . . ?

DORINE. Let us leave all this talk for another time, and consider how we can avert this wretched marriage.

MARIANE. Tell us, then, what plans we must prepare.

DORINE. We will try every means. Your father is only jesting, and it is mere talk; but as for you, you had better pretend to humor his whim dutifully, so that in case of alarm it would be easier for you to put the wedding off indefinitely. In gaining time, we remedy everything. Sometimes you will give sudden illness as an excuse, and so cause delays; at other times you will bring forward some ill-omen: you had the ill-luck to meet a corpse, broke a mirror, or dreamt of muddy water. But the best of all is that they cannot marry you either to others or to him unless you say "yes." However, the best way to succeed, I think, is for you two not to be seen talking together. [*To* VALÈRE.] Go away at once, and without delay employ your friends to make her father keep his promise to you. We will enlist the efforts of his brother and the interest of the step-mother on our side. Good-bye.

VALÈRE. [*To* MARIANE.] Whatever efforts we all make my greatest hope is really in you.

MARIANE. [*To* VALÈRE.] I cannot answer for the will of a father, but I will not belong
　　to any one but Valère.

VALÈRE. Oh! how happy you make me. And whatever they may attempt . . .

DORINE. Ah! lovers never weary of chattering. Be off, I tell you.

VALÈRE. [*He goes a step and returns.*] In short . . .

DORINE. What a cackle you make! You take yourself off that way; and you, the other.
　　[*Pushing each by the shoulder.*]

END OF THE SECOND ACT

ACT III

SCENE I
DAMIS, DORINE

DAMIS. May I be struck down by lightning this very moment, may everybody look
　　upon me as the greatest of scamps, if there is any respect or power to stop me
　　from doing something rash!

DORINE. For heaven's sake control your temper: your father merely mentioned the
　　matter. People do not carry out all they propose: there is many a slip 'twixt the
　　cup and the lip.

DAMIS. I must put a stop to this fellow's intrigues and whisper a few words in his ear.

DORINE. Gently, gently, let your stepmother manage him, and your father as well.
　　She has some influence over Tartuffe; he agrees with all she says, and very likely
　　he has a tender feeling for her. Would to heaven it were true! That would be a
　　fine thing! Indeed, she has thought it best to send for him in your interest: she
　　wants to sound him about the marriage which makes you so furious, to find out
　　his feelings, and to let him know what unhappy contentions it would cause were
　　he to entertain the least hope of realising this scheme. His man told me he was
　　at his prayers so I could not see him; but he said he was just coming down;
　　therefore, pray be gone and leave me to wait for him.

DAMIS. I want to be present throughout this interview.

DORINE. Certainly not: they must be alone.

DAMIS. I will not say anything to him.

DORINE. You deceive yourself: we know what rages you get into, and that would be
　　the surest way to spoil everything. Go away.

DAMIS. No; I will look on, without losing my temper.

DORINE. How tiresome you are! Here he comes. Do go away.

SCENE II
TARTUFFE, LAURENT, DORINE

TARTUFFE. [*Perceiving* DORINE.] Laurent, lock up my hairshirt and my scourge, and
　　pray heaven ever to enlighten you. If any one comes to see me, say I have gone
　　to the prisoners to distribute the alms I have received.

DORINE. What affectation and boasting!

TARTUFFE. What do you want?

DORINE. To tell you . . .

TARTUFFE. [*He takes a handkerchief out of his pocket.*] Ah! for the sake of heaven, pray
　　take this handkerchief before you speak to me.

DORINE. What for?

TARTUFFE. To cover that bosom which I cannot bear to see. Such a sight is injurious to the soul and gives birth to sinful thoughts.

DORINE. You are mightily susceptible, then, to temptation, and the flesh seems to make a great impression on your senses. Truly, I do not know why you should take fire so quickly: as for me, my passions are not so easily roused, were I to see you unclothed from top to toe your hide would not tempt me.

TARTUFFE. Be a little more modest in your conversation, or I shall leave you at once.

DORINE. No, no, I am going to leave you in peace, and I have only two words to say to you. Madame is coming down into this room, and wishes the favor of a few moments' talk with you.

TARTUFFE. Alas! most willingly.

DORINE. [*To herself.*] How sweet we are! Upon my word, I still stick to what I said about it.

TARTUFFE. Will she soon be here?

DORINE. I think I hear her. Yes, here she is. I will leave you together.

SCENE III
ELMIRE, TARTUFFE

TARTUFFE. May a supremely bountiful heaven ever bestow upon you health of body and of soul, and bless your days as abundantly as the humblest of its servants can desire.

ELMIRE. I am much obliged for this pious wish. But let us sit down, to be a little more at our ease.

TARTUFFE. Have you quite recovered from your indisposition?

ELMIRE. Quite: the fever soon left me.

TARTUFFE. My prayers are not worthy to have drawn down such favor from heaven; but I have not offered up a single pious aspiration which has not had your recovery for its object.

ELMIRE. You are too solicitous in my behalf.

TARTUFFE. It is impossible to be too anxious concerning your precious health; I would have sacrificed my own to re-establish yours.

ELMIRE. You carry Christian charity to an extreme; I am much indebted to you for all this kindness.

TARTUFFE. I do much less for you than you deserve.

ELMIRE. I wished to speak privately to you on a certain matter. I am very glad no one is watching us.

TARTUFFE. I am equally delighted, and it is indeed very pleasant, Madame, to find myself quite alone with you. I have often implored heaven to grant me this favor, but until now it has been denied me.

ELMIRE. I too wish a few words with you; I hope you will speak openly to me and not hide anything from me.

TARTUFFE. I have but the wish, in return for this singular favor, to lay bare my whole soul to you, and to swear to you that the reports which I have spread abroad concerning the visits paid here to your charms do not spring from any hatred towards you, but rather from a passionate zeal which carries me away, and from a pure motive . . .

ELMIRE. I quite understand, I feel sure the pains you take are for my welfare.

TARTUFFE. [*He presses the end of her fingers.*] Yes, Madame, you are right, and such is my devotion . . .

ELMIRE. Oh! you squeeze me too hard.

TARTUFFE. It is from excess of zeal. I never had any intention of doing you any other ill; I would much sooner . . . [*He places his hand on her knee.*]

ELMIRE. Why do you put your hand there?

TARTUFFE. I am feeling your dress: the stuff is very soft.

ELMIRE. Oh! please, leave off, I am very ticklish. [*She pushes back her chair, and* TARTUFFE *draws his nearer.*]

TARTUFFE. Heavens! how marvellous is the workmanship of this lace! Work nowadays is wonderfully skilful; one could not imagine anything more beautifully made.

ELMIRE. It is true. But let us talk a little about our business. They say my husband wishes to break his word and give you his daughter. Tell me, is it true?

TARTUFFE. He did just mention it; but, Madame, to tell you the truth, that is not the happiness for which I sigh; I see elsewhere the perfect attractions of that bliss which is the end of all my desires.

ELMIRE. That is because you have no love for the things of the earth.

TARTUFFE. My breast does not contain a heart of flint.

ELMIRE. I quite believe all your sighs tend heavenwards, and that nothing here below satisfies your desires.

TARTUFFE. Our love for the beauty which is eternal does not stifle in us the love for things fleeting; our senses can easily be charmed with the perfect works which heaven has created. Its reflected loveliness shines forth in such as are like you; but in you yourself it displays its choicest wonders. It has lavished on your face a beauty which dazzles the eyes and transports the heart, and I am unable to gaze on you, you perfect creature, without adoring in you the author of nature, and without feeling my heart seized with a passionate love for the most beautiful of the portraits in which he has delineated himself. At first I feared lest this secret tenderness might be but an artful assault of the evil one; and my heart even resolved to flee from your eyes, fearing you might be a stumbling-block in the way of my salvation. But at last I learnt, ah! most entrancing beauty, that this passion need not be a guilty one, that I could reconcile it with modesty, and so I have let my heart give way to it. It is, I own, a very great presumption in me to dare to offer you this heart; but my love expects everything from your kindness, and nothing from the vain efforts of my weakness. In you is my hope, my happiness, my peace, on you depends my torment or my bliss; in truth, I shall be happy if you will it, or unhappy if such be your pleasure: you are the sole arbitress.

ELMIRE. The declaration is most gallant, but it is certainly a little surprising. I think you ought to have guarded your heart more carefully, and have reflected a little upon such a design. A pious man like you, whose name is in every one's mouth . . .

TARTUFFE. Ah! I may be pious, but I am none the less a man; and when your heavenly charms are seen the heart surrenders without reasoning. I know such language from me must seem strange; but, after all, Madame, I am not an angel, and, if you condemn my avowal, you must lay the blame on your captivating attractions. You became the queen of my heart the moment your ethereal beauty first shone upon me; the ineffable sweetness of your divine looks broke down the resistance of my obstinate heart; it overcame everything—fasting, prayers, tears, and diverted all my thoughts to the consideration of your charms. My looks and my sighs have declared this to you a thousand times, and to make it still clearer I now add my voice. If it should happen that you would look upon the sufferings of your unworthy slave a little kindly, if you would only of your bounty take compassion upon me and deign to stoop even to my insignificance, I should ever have for you, ah! miracle of grace, a devotion beyond comparison. With me your reputation is not in danger, and you need not fear any disgrace from me. All those court gallants upon whom women dote are noisy in their doings and boastful in their talk, ceaselessly bragging of their successes; they do not receive any favors which they do not divulge, and their indiscreet tongues, in which people believe, dishonor the altar where their hearts worship. But people like ourselves love more discreetly, and our secrets are always safely kept. The care which we take of our reputation is a sufficient safeguard to the woman loved, who finds, in accepting our devotion, love without scandal and pleasure without fear.

ELMIRE. I have listened to what you say, and your eloquence expresses itself to me in sufficiently strong terms. Are you not afraid I may be disposed to tell my husband of this ardent devotion, and that the sudden knowledge of such a feeling may well cause him to change his friendship for you?

TARTUFFE. I know you are too gracious, and that you will forgive my boldness; you will excuse, in consideration of human frailty, the passionate raptures of a love which offends you, and you will consider, when you look in your mirror, that people are not blind, and that a man is of the flesh.

ELMIRE. Others may perhaps take all this in a different way, but I will exercise discretion. I will not speak to my husband about the matter, but I want one thing from you in return: and that is, to forward honestly and openly the union of Valère and Mariane, and to renounce the unjust power which would enrich you with what belongs to another, and . . .

SCENE IV
DAMIS, ELMIRE, TARTUFFE

DAMIS. [*Coming out of the little room in which he had been hiding.*] No, Madame, no; this ought to be made public. I have been in here, where I have overheard everything; and heaven in its goodness seems to have directed me here to confound the pride of a traitor who wrongs me, to point out a way to take vengeance on his hypocrisy and his insolence, to undeceive my father and to show him plainly the heart of the scoundrel who speaks to you of love.

ELMIRE. No, Damis: it is sufficient that he promises to amend and tries to deserve the forgiveness to which I have committed myself. Since I have promised it, do not make me break my word. I have no mind to cause a scandal: a woman laughs at such follies, and never troubles her husband's ears with them.

DAMIS. You have your reasons for acting thus and I have mine also for dealing otherwise. It is a mockery to wish to spare him; the insolent pride of his bigotry has lorded it over my just anger but too often, and he has caused too many troubles in our house. The knave has governed my father too long, and he has thwarted my love as well as Valère's. It is necessary my father should have his eyes opened to this treachery, and Providence has offered me for that an easy opportunity for which I am thankful. It is too favorable to be neglected: and were I not to use it whilst I have it in my hands, I should deserve to have it snatched away from me.

ELMIRE. Damis . . .

DAMIS. No, by your leave, I must take my own counsel. My heart is now overjoyed: it is in vain for you to try to persuade me to give up the pleasure of revenging myself. I shall disclose the affair without delay, and here is just the very opportunity I want.

SCENE V

ORGON, DAMIS, TARTUFFE, ELMIRE

DAMIS. Come, father, we will enliven your arrival with an altogether novel and very surprising piece of news. You are well rewarded for all your caresses; this gentleman amply recompenses your kindness. His great zeal for you has just revealed itself: it aims at nothing less than to dishonor you. I have here overheard him make shameful avowal of a guilty passion. She, being too prudent and good-natured, insisted at all hazards upon keeping the matter secret; but I cannot countenance such impudence, and I should wrong you were I to keep silence.

ELMIRE. Yes, I hold that it is better never to disturb the peace of mind of one's husband by such silly nonsense. Honor does not depend on the confession of attacks upon it, and it is enough for us that we know how to protect ourselves. These are my own sentiments. You would not have said anything, Damis, if I had had more influence over you.

SCENE VI

ORGON, DAMIS, TARTUFFE

ORGON. What do I hear? Good heavens, is it possible?

TARTUFFE. Yes, brother, I am a wicked, miserable and guilty sinner, full of iniquity, the greatest wretch who ever lived. Every moment of my life is weighed down with pollution; it is nothing but a mass of crime and corruption, and I see that heaven, for my punishment, intends to mortify me on this occasion. I throw away the pride of self-defence no matter what great crime I may be accused of. Believe what they tell you, let your wrath take up arms and drive me, like a criminal, from your house. I deserve even greater shame than I shall have in being turned away.

ORGON. [To his son.] Ah! you villain, how dare you try to sully the purity of his virtue by such falsehoods?

DAMIS. What? Does the feigned meekness of this hypocrite make you give the lie to . . . ?

ORGON. Be quiet, you accursed plague.

TARTUFFE. Oh! let him speak: you chide him wrongfully and you had much better believe his story. Why be favorable to me in the face of such an assertion? Are you aware, after all, of what I am capable? Why trust in my bearing, brother? Why believe me good because of my outward professions? No, no; you suffer yourself to be deceived by appearances, and I am, alas! just what these people think. The world takes me for a worthy man; but the simple truth is that I am worthless. [Addressing DAMIS.] Yes, my dear boy, speak: accuse me of treachery, infamy, theft, murder; overwhelm me with still more despicable names. I do not deny them, I have deserved them; on my knees I will bear the shameful ignominy due to the sins of my life.

ORGON. [To TARTUFFE.] This is too much, my brother. [To his son.] Wretch, does not your heart relent?

DAMIS. What? can his words so far deceive you . . . ?

ORGON. Hold your tongue, rascal. [*To* TARTUFFE.] Oh! rise, my brother, I beseech
you. [*To his son.*] Infamous scoundrel!

DAMIS. He can . . .

ORGON. Be quiet.

DAMIS. Intolerable! What? I am taken for . . .

ORGON. If you say another word I will break every bone.

TARTUFFE. Control yourself, my brother, in heaven's name. I would rather suffer
the greatest injury than that he should receive the slightest hurt on my account.

ORGON. [*To his son.*] Ungrateful wretch!

TARTUFFE. Leave him alone. If I must on my knees ask you to forgive him . . .

ORGON. [*To Tartuffe.*] Oh! you jest? [*To his son.*] Rascal! See how good he is.

DAMIS. Then . . .

ORGON. Cease.

DAMIS. What? I . . .

ORGON. Cease, I say. I know well the motive which makes you accuse him. You all
hate him; and I now see my wife, children and servants all incensed against him.
You try every impudent trick to drive this saintly person away from me. But the
more you strive to send him away, the greater efforts I shall make to keep him
here longer, and I will haste my daughter's marriage to him to crush the pride
of the whole family.

DAMIS. You mean to force her to take him?

ORGON. Yes, scoundrel, this very night, to confound you all. Ah! I defy the whole
household. I will let you know I am the master and must be obeyed. You wretch,
come and retract what you have said, and throw yourself instantly at his feet to
beg his pardon.

DAMIS. Who, I? Of this villain who, by his impostures . . .

ORGON. Ah! you refuse, you scamp, and abuse him besides? A stick! A stick! [*To*
TARTUFFE.] Do not prevent me. [*To his son.*] Begone this instant out of my sight,
and never have the face to set foot in my house again.

DAMIS. Yes, I will go; but . . .

ORGON. Quick, leave the place. I disinherit you, you hangdog, and curse you, as
well.

SCENE VII
ORGON, TARTUFFE

ORGON. To affront a holy person in such a manner!

TARTUFFE. Oh Heaven! forgive him the pain he causes me. [*To* ORGON.] If you only
knew with what anguish I see them endeavor to blacken my character in the
eyes of my brother . . .

ORGON. Alas!

TARTUFFE. The very thought of such ingratitude is so great a torture to me that . . .
The horror I feel . . . My heart is too full to speak, and I believe I shall die.

ORGON. [*He runs in tears to the door through which he had driven his son.*] Villain! How
I regret I held my hand and that I did not instantly make an end of you on the
spot. Compose yourself, brother, and do not grieve.

TARTUFFE. Let us put an end to these miserable disputes. I see what great friction
I cause in this house, and I feel sure it is needful, my brother, that I should go
away.

ORGON. What? You are not in earnest?

TARTUFFE. They hate me, and I see they will seek to rouse suspicions in you as to my integrity.

ORGON. What does it matter? Do you think I pay any attention to what they say?

TARTUFFE. They will not fail to continue, never fear, and the same stories which now you reject you may at another time credit.

ORGON. No, brother, never.

TARTUFFE. Oh! my brother, a wife can very easily influence the mind of her husband.

ORGON. No, no.

TARTUFFE. Let me leave here at once and thus remove all occasion for their attacks.

ORGON. No, you shall stay: my life is at stake.

TARTUFFE. Ah! well, then I must mortify myself. Nevertheless, if you would . . .

ORGON. Ah!

TARTUFFE. Be it so: let us not say anything more about it. But I know how I must act in the future. Honor is a delicate matter, and friendship enjoins me to prevent reports and not to give cause for suspicion. I will shun your wife, and you shall not see me . . .

ORGON. No, You shall see her frequently in spite of everyone. I desire nothing more than to jolt society, and I wish her to be seen in your company at all hours. Nor is this all: the better to defy them all you shall be my sole heir, and I will go forthwith to arrange in due form that the whole of my property shall be made yours. A good and faithful friend, whom I take for son-in-law, is far dearer to me than son, wife, or kindred. Will you not accept my offer?

TARTUFFE. The will of heaven be done in all things!

ORGON. Poor man! Let us go quickly to draw up the deed: then may envy itself burst with spite.

END OF THE THIRD ACT

ACT IV

SCENE I
CLÉANTE, TARTUFFE

CLÉANTE. Indeed, you may believe me, everybody is talking about it. The scandal which this rumor makes is not to your credit. I have met you, Monsieur, very seasonably, and I can tell you plainly my view of the matter, in two words. I do not sift these reports to the bottom; I pass them by and admit the worst view of the case. Let us grant that Damis has not acted wisely, and it may be you have been accused in error: does it not become a Christian to forgive the offence and to extinguish in him every desire for vengeance? And, because of your quarrel, ought you to suffer a father to drive a son out of his house? I repeat it, and I tell you candidly, high and low are scandalised by it. If you take my advice, you will make peace and not push matters to extremes. Make an offering to God of all your resentment, and restore the son to the father's favor.

TARTUFFE. Alas! So far as I am concerned I would do so with all my heart. I do not bear him any ill-will, Monsieur, I forgive him everything. I do not blame him for anything. I would serve him to the best of my power. But the interests of heaven cannot consent to it; and if he returns home I must go away. After his unparalleled behavior intercourse between us would give rise to scandal. Heaven knows what every one would think of it at once! They would impute it to sheer policy on my part, and it would be said everywhere that, knowing myself to be guilty, I affect a charitable zeal for my accuser; that I am afraid of him; and that I wish to conciliate him in order to bribe him in an underhand manner to silence.

CLÉANTE. You are putting us off, Monsieur, with sham excuses. All your arguments are too far-fetched. Why do you take upon yourself the interests of heaven? Cannot it punish sinners without our help? Leave vengeance to it, leave vengeance to it, and remember only the forgiveness which it directs towards offences. Do not trouble yourself about men's judgments when you follow the sovereign edicts of heaven. What? Shall the paltry fear of men's opinion prevent the accomplishment of a good deed? No, no; let us always do what heaven commands, and not trouble our minds with any other care.

TARTUFFE. I have already told you, Monsieur, that I forgive him as heaven enjoins. But, after the scandal and insult of today, heaven does not ordain that I should live with him.

CLÉANTE. And does it require you, Monsieur, to lend your ears to what a mere whim dictates to his father, and to accept the gift which is made you of a property to which in justice you cannot pretend to have any claim?

TARTUFFE. Those who know me will not think I act from interested motives. All the riches of this world have few attractions for me. I am not dazzled by their false glitter. If I bring myself to take this gift which the father wishes to make to me, it is merely because I fear all this wealth will fall into wicked hands, and that it will be shared only by those who will put it here to bad uses, and not employ it, as I propose to do, for the glory of heaven and the well-being of my fellow-men.

CLÉANTE. Ah! Monsieur, do not entertain these delicate scruples, which may give ground of complaint to a rightful heir. Allow him, without giving yourself any anxiety, to enjoy his rights at his own peril; and consider that it is far better for him to make a bad use of it than that people should accuse you of defrauding him of it. I only wonder you could have suffered unblushingly such a proposal to be made you. For, in truth, do we find among the maxims of true piety one which teaches how to plunder a lawful heir? And, if it is a fact that heaven has put in your heart an invincible obstacle against your living with Damis, would it not be better for you, as a discreet person, honorably to retire from this house, rather than to allow the son of the house to be turned out of it, against all reason, on your account? Believe me, Monsieur, it would give a proof of your probity . . .

TARTUFFE. Monsieur, it is half-past three: a certain religious exercise calls me upstairs; pray excuse me for leaving you so soon.

CLÉANTE. Ah!

SCENE II
ELMIRE, MARIANE, DORINE, CLÉANTE

DORINE. For pity's sake join us in all we do for her, Monsieur. She is suffering great misery, and the agreement which her father has concluded for tonight drives her every moment to despair. Here he comes. Let us unite our efforts, I beseech you, to try, either by force or by skill to frustrate this unhappy design which causes us all this trouble.

SCENE III

ORGON, ELMIRE, MARIANE, CLÉANTE, DORINE

ORGON. Ah! I am delighted to find you all here. [*To* MARIANE.] I have something in this document which will please you: you know already what I mean.

MARIANE. [*On her knees.*] Father, in the name of that heaven which knows my grief, in the name of everything that can move your heart, forego a little of a father's rights and do not exact this obedience from me. Do not compel me, by this harsh command, to reproach heaven with my duty to you; do not, oh my father, render most miserable the life which, alas! you gave me. If, contrary to the sweet hopes I had cherished, you forbid me to belong to the one whom I have dared to love, I implore you on my knees at least, of your goodness, to spare me the horror of belonging to one whom I abhor. Do not drive me to despair by exerting all your authority over me.

ORGON. [*Feeling himself soften.*] Be firm, my heart; none of this human weakness.

MARIANE. I do not feel aggrieved at your tenderness for him; indulge in it, give him your wealth, and, if that is not enough, add all mine to it: I consent with all my heart and give it to you. But, at least, do not go so far as to include my person, let me wear out in the hardships of a convent the rest of the sad days that heaven has allotted to me.

ORGON. Ah! girls always wish to become nuns when a father crosses their love-sick inclinations. Get up: the more your heart recoils from accepting the offer, the greater will be your merit. Mortify your senses by this marriage, and do not trouble me any further.

DORINE. But what . . . ?

ORGON. You hold your tongue: mind your own business. I absolutely forbid you to dare to say a single word.

CLÉANTE. If you will allow me to speak and advise . . .

ORGON. Brother, your advice is the best in the world, and I value it highly: you will permit me, however, not to take it.

ELMIRE. [*To* ORGON.] In the face of all this I do not know I can say more than that I am astonished at your blindness. You must be quite bewitched with the man and altogether prejudiced in his favor, to deny the truth of what we tell you took place today.

ORGON. I am your humble servant, but I judge by appearances. I know how lenient you are towards my rascal of a son, and you were afraid to disown the trick which he wished to play on the poor fellow. In fact, you took it too calmly to be believed. You should have been a little more disturbed.

ELMIRE. Is it necessary one's honor should take up arms so furiously at a simple declaration of tender feelings? Is it not possible to give a fitting answer without anger in the eyes and invective on the lips? For myself, I simply laugh at such talk; it does not please me to make a noise about it. I prefer to show that prudence can be accompanied by gentleness. I am not at all like the savage prudes who defend their honor with tooth and nail, and who are ready, at the slightest word, to tear a man's eyes out. Heaven preserve me from such discretion! I prefer a virtue that has nothing of the tigress about it, and I believe a quiet and cold rebuff is not less efficient in repelling an advance.

ORGON. Nevertheless, I understand the whole affair and I will not be imposed upon.

ELMIRE. Once more, I wonder at this strange weakness: but what answer would your incredulity give me, if I made you see we have told you the truth?

ORGON. See?

ELMIRE. Yes.

ORGON. Nonsense.

ELMIRE. Never mind! Suppose I found a way of convincing you irresistibly?

ORGON. Moonshine.

ELMIRE. What a man you are! At least, answer me. I do not ask you to believe us, but, look here, suppose we found a place where you could plainly see and hear everything, what would you say then of your good man?

ORGON. In that case I should say . . . I should not say anything, for such a thing could not be.

ELMIRE. Your delusion has lasted too long, and you have taxed us too much with imposture. You must, to satisfy me, and without going any further, be a witness of all that has been told you.

ORGON. Be it so. I take you at your word. We will see your cleverness and how you can carry out this undertaking.

ELMIRE. Make him come here.

DORINE. He is very crafty and perhaps it will be difficult to catch him.

ELMIRE. No; people are easily duped by those whom they love. Self-love leads the way to self-deceit. [*Speaking to* CLÉANTE *and to* MARIANE.] Tell him to come down to me. And you, withdraw.

SCENE IV

ELMIRE, ORGON

ELMIRE. Let us bring this table nearer and you go under it.

ORGON. Why?

ELMIRE. It is necessary you should be well concealed.

ORGON. Why under this table?

ELMIRE. Oh! good heavens, never mind; I have thought out my plan, and you shall judge of it. Go under there, I tell you; and, when you are there, take care you are neither seen nor heard.

ORGON. I must say my complaisance in this matter is great, but I will see you through with your scheme.

ELMIRE. You will not have anything with which to reproach me, that I swear. [*To her husband, under the table.*] Now mind! I am going to speak on a strange subject and you must not be shocked in any way. As I have undertaken to convince you, I must be allowed to say whatever I choose. Since I am compelled to it, I shall flatter this hypocrite until he lets fall his mask: I shall encourage the impudent desires of his love, and give free scope to his audacity. As I am going to pretend to yield to his wishes for your sake alone, and the better to confound him, things need not go any further than you like, and I will cease as soon as you are convinced. I leave it to you to stop his mad passion when you think matters have gone far enough, to spare your wife, and not to expose me longer than is necessary to disabuse you. This is your concern, you must decide, and . . . Here he comes. Keep still, and do not show yourself.

SCENE V

TARTUFFE, ELMIRE, ORGON

TARTUFFE. They tell me you wish to speak to me here.

ELMIRE. Yes. I have some secrets to reveal to you. But shut the door before I begin to tell them to you. Look everywhere, lest we should be surprised. We must certainly not have such an affair here as we had a little while ago. I was never so surprised. Damis put me in a terrible fright on your account. You saw I tried all I could to baffle his design and to calm his anger. In fact I was so confused that the thought of denying what he said never occurred to me; but, nevertheless, thank heaven, it was all for the best and things are on a surer footing. The esteem in which you are held has dispelled the storm, and my husband cannot be offended with you. He wishes us to be together constantly, the better to set at defiance the spiteful remarks which people spread abroad, and that is the reason why I may be shut up here alone with you, without fear of being blamed. This justifies me in opening my heart to you, a little too readily, perhaps, in response to your love.

TARTUFFE. This language, Madam, is a little difficult to comprehend. You spoke but lately in a different strain.

ELMIRE. Ah! if such a refusal has offended you, how very little you know a woman's heart, how little you understand what we mean when we defend ourselves so feebly. At such times our modesty always struggles with any tender sentiments we may feel. Whatever reasons we may find for the love which conquers us, there is always a little shame in the avowal of it. We resist at first, but from our manner it can easily be seen our heart surrenders, that our words oppose our wishes for the sake of honor, and that we refuse in such a way as to promise everything. I am making a very free confession to you, to be sure, and I am not sparing woman's modesty; but, since these words have at last escaped me, should I have been anxious to restrain Damis, should I, I ask you, have listened to you so long and with so much patience, when you offered me your heart, should I have taken the thing as I did, if the offer of your heart had not given me pleasure? What could you infer from such an action when I myself tried to make you renounce the proposed marriage, if it were not that I took an interest in you, and that I should have been grieved if such a marriage had taken place and you had in the least divided that affection which I wanted to be wholly mine?

TARTUFFE. It is certainly, Madam, extremely pleasant to hear such words from the lips one loves. Their honey generously diffuses through all my senses a sweetness which I never before knew. The happiness of pleasing you is my supreme study, and it is the delight of my heart to carry out your wishes, but, with your leave, my heart presumes still to doubt a little of its felicity. It may be that these words are a plausible stratagem to compel me to break off the approaching marriage; and, if I must speak candidly to you, I shall not trust in these tender words until I am assured they mean what they say by a few of those favors for which I sigh, which will establish in my heart a firm belief in the kindly sentiments you bear towards me.

ELMIRE. [*She coughs to warn her husband.*] What? would you proceed so fast and exhaust the kindness of my heart all at once? I commit myself in making such a tender admission; yet that is not enough for you. Will nothing satisfy you but to push things to their furthest extremity?

TARTUFFE. The less a blessing is merited the less one ventures to hope for it. Our love can hardly be satisfied with words. A condition full-fraught with happiness is difficult to realise and we wish to enjoy it before we believe in it. I so little deserve your favors that I doubt the success of my boldness; and I shall not believe anything, Madam, until you have satisfied my passion by real proofs.

ELMIRE. Good Heavens! How very tyrannical is your love, and into what strange agitation it throws me! What an irresistible power it exercises over the heart, and how violently it clamors for what it desires! What? Is there no avoiding your pursuit? Will you not give me time to breathe? Is it decent to be so very exacting, to insist without quarter upon those things which you demand, and, by your pressing ardor, thus to take advantage of the weakness which you see is felt for you?

TARTUFFE. But if you look upon my address with a favorable eye, why refuse me convincing proofs?

ELMIRE. How can I comply with your desires without offending that heaven of which you constantly speak?

TARTUFFE. If heaven is the only thing which opposes my wishes I can easily remove such an obstacle; that need not be any restraint upon your love.

ELMIRE. But the judgments of heaven are terrifying.

TARTUFFE. I can dispel these absurd fears from you, Madam; I know the art of removing scruples. Heaven, it is true, forbids certain gratifications; but there are ways of compounding with it. It is a science to stretch the strings of our conscience according to divers needs and to rectify the immorality of the act with the purity of our intention. I can initiate you into these secrets, Madam; you have only to allow yourself to be led. Satisfy my desire, and do not be afraid: I will be answerable for you in everything, and I will take the sin upon myself. You cough a good deal, Madam.

ELMIRE. Yes, it racks me.

TARTUFFE. Would you please to take a piece of this liquorice?

ELMIRE. It is a troublesome cold, to be sure; and I very much fear all the liquorice in the world will not do it any good now.

TARTUFFE. It is certainly very tiresome.

ELMIRE. Yes, more than I can say.

TARTUFFE. In short your scruple is easily overcome. You may be sure the secret will be well kept here, and no harm is done unless the thing is noised abroad. The scandal of the world is what makes the offence, and to sin in secret is not to sin at all.

ELMIRE. [*After having coughed again.*] Well, I see I must make up my mind to yield: that I must consent to grant you everything: and that with less than this I ought not to expect you should be satisfied, or convinced. It is indeed very hard to come to this, and it is greatly against my will that I venture so far, but, since people persist in driving me to this; since they will not believe anything that is said to them, and since they wish for more convincing testimony, one must even resolve upon it and satisfy them. If this gratification carries any offense in it, so much the worse for those who force me to this violence; the fault, assuredly, is not mine.

TARTUFFE. Yes, Madam, I take it upon myself, and the thing itself . . .

ELMIRE. Open the door a little, and pray, look if my husband is not in that passage.

TARTUFFE. Why need you trouble yourself so much about him? Between ourselves, he is a man to be led by the nose. He is inclined to be proud of our intercourse, and I have brought him so far as to see everything without believing anything.

ELMIRE. Nevertheless, pray, go out for a moment and look carefully everywhere outside.

SCENE VI
ORGON, ELMIRE

ORGON. [*Coming from under the table.*] Well! he is an abominable man, I admit. I cannot get over it, it has stunned me.

ELMIRE. What? you come out so soon? You make fools of people. Go back under the table-cloth, it is not time yet; stay to the end to make sure of things, and do not trust to mere conjectures.

ORGON. No: no one more wicked ever came out of hell.

ELMIRE. Good Heavens! You ought not to believe things too easily: let yourself be fully convinced before you give in, and do not hurry, lest you should be mistaken. [*She pushes her husband behind her.*]

SCENE VII
TARTUFFE, ELMIRE, ORGON

TARTUFFE. Everything conspires, Madam, to my satisfaction. I have looked everywhere, there is no one here; and my ravished soul . . .

ORGON. [*Stopping him.*] Gently, you are too eager in your amorous wishes; you ought not to be so impetuous. Ah! ah! my good man, you want to rob me of my wife. How your soul is led away by temptations! You would marry my daughter and covet my wife. I have very much doubted for a long time whether you were in earnest, and I always thought you would change your tone. But the proof has gone quite far enough: I am satisfied, and for my part I do not want any more.

ELMIRE. [*To* TARTUFFE.] The part I have played is contrary to my inclinations, but I was obliged to the necessity of treating you thus.

TARTUFFE. What? Do you believe . . .?

ORGON. Come, pray, no more talk, leave this place, and without ceremony.

TARTUFFE. I intended . . .

ORGON. Your speeches are no longer in season. You must quit this house immediately.

TARTUFFE. It is for you to leave, you who speak as though you were the master of it. The house belongs to me, and I will make you know it. I will show you plainly it is useless to resort to these cowardly tricks in order to pick a quarrel with me. You have made a great mistake in insulting me. I have it in my power to confound and to punish imposture, to avenge an offended heaven, and to make those repent who talk of turning me away.

SCENE VIII
ELMIRE, ORGON

ELMIRE. What talk is this? What does he mean?

ORGON. Alas! I am ashamed; it is no laughing matter.

ELMIRE. Why?

ORGON. I see my fault by what he says, and the deed of gift troubles my mind.

ELMIRE. The deed of gift . . .

ORGON. Yes, the thing is done, but there is still something else which makes me anxious.

Elmire. What is that?

Orgon. You shall know all, but let us see first if a particular box is still upstairs.

END OF ACT IV

ACT V

SCENE I
Orgon, Cléante

Cléante. Where are you going so fast?

Orgon. Indeed, I do not know.

Cléante. It seems to me the first thing to be done is to consult together concerning what steps we can take in this matter.

Orgon. This box troubles me greatly; it distresses me more than anything else.

Cléante. Then it contains an important secret?

Orgon. It is a trust that Argas himself, my unfortunate friend, put secretly into my hands: he selected me for this, when he fled. And, from what he told me, on these papers depend his life and his fortune.

Cléante. Then why did you trust them to any other hands?

Orgon. It was from a conscientious motive. I went straight away to that wretch in utter confidence, and his arguments persuaded me it was better to give him the box to keep, so that, in case of enquiry, I could deny having it. I might have the help of a subterfuge in readiness, by which my conscience might be quite safe in swearing against the truth.

Cléante. If one may judge by appearances, you are in a bad case. The deed of gift and this trust are, to speak frankly, steps taken with little consideration. You may be carried great lengths by such pledges. Since this man has these advantages over you, it is still greater imprudence in you to irritate him: you ought to seek some gentler method.

Orgon. What? To conceal such a false heart and such a wicked soul under so fair an appearance of ardent zeal! And I, who received him as a beggar and penniless ... It is all over, I renounce all pious people: I shall hold them henceforth in utter abhorrence, and shall become worse to them than the devil.

Cléante. Is not that just like your hasty ways? You never judge anything calmly. You never keep in due reason. You always rush from one extreme to the other. You see your error, and you realise you have been imposed upon by a false piety. But is it reasonable that, in order to correct one mistake, you should commit a greater, and not make any difference between the heart of a perfidious rascal and that of a good man? What? because a villain has shamelessly imposed upon you, under the pompous mask of austerity, would you have it that all men are like him, and that there is not a sincere worshipper to be found now-a-days? Leave these foolish deductions to unbelievers; distinguish between virtue and the appearance of it; do not bestow your esteem so rashly; and keep in this the rightful middle course. Do not honor imposture, if you can avoid doing so, but at the same time, do not attack true virtue. If you must fall into an extremity, err, rather, on the other side.

SCENE II
DAMIS, ORGON, CLÉANTE

DAMIS. Is it true, father, that this scoundrel threatens you, that he has forgotten every benefit he has received, and that his cowardly and shameless arrogance turns your goodness to him into arms against you?

ORGON. Yes, my son, and it causes me inexpressible grief.

DAMIS. Leave him to me, I will crop his two ears for him: you must not flinch before his insolence. I will rid you of him at a stroke, and, to put an end to the matter, I will put an end to him.

CLÉANTE. That is exactly how a mere boy talks. Try to moderate these violent outbursts. We live under a government, and in an age in which violence only makes matters worse.

SCENE III
MADAME PERNELLE, MARIANE, ELMIRE, DORINE, DAMIS, ORGON, CLÉANTE

MME. PERNELLE. What is the matter? What are these dreadful, mysterious reports I hear?

ORGON. They are of things which I have seen with my own eyes, and you see how I am paid for my kindness. I eagerly take in a man out of charity, I shelter him, and treat him as my own brother. I heap benefits upon him every day, I give him my daughter and everything I possess, and, all the while, the villain, the traitor, harbors the black design of seducing my wife. Not content even with this vile attempt, he dares to threaten me with my own gifts; and, in order to ruin me, he intends to use the advantage he has obtained through my unwise good nature to drive me out of my estate which I made over to him, and to reduce me to the same condition from which I rescued him.

DORINE. Poor man!

MME. PERNELLE. I can never believe, my son, that he would commit so black a deed.

ORGON. Why?

MME. PERNELLE. Good people are always envied.

ORGON. What do you mean by that, mother?

MME. PERNELLE. Why, there are strange goings-on in your house. It is very plain to see the ill-will they bear him.

ORGON. What has this hatred to do with what I have just told you?

MME. PERNELLE. When you were a child I told you a hundred times that in this world virtue is ever persecuted, and that the envious may die, but envy never.

ORGON. But what has this speech to do with what has happened today?

MME. PERNELLE. They have most likely fabricated a hundred idle stories against him for your benefit.

ORGON. I have already told you I have seen everything myself.

MME. PERNELLE. The spite of slanderers is great.

ORGON. You would drive me mad, mother. I tell you I saw with my own eyes this monstrous crime.

MME. PERNELLE. Tongues are always ready to spit venom: nothing here below is proof against them.

ORGON. That remark seems to lack common sense. I have seen it, I tell you, seen it, with my own eyes, seen it, what people call seen it. Must I drum it in your ears a hundred times and shout at the top of my voice?

MME. PERNELLE. Well, appearances deceive more often than not: you must not always judge by what you see.

ORGON. I'm furious.

MME. PERNELLE. We are naturally subject to false suspicions, and a bad construction is often put on a good deed.

ORGON. Must I regard his desire to kiss my wife as charitable?

MME. PERNELLE. You should have just cause before you accuse people. You ought to have waited until you were sure you saw these things.

ORGON. How the devil could I better satisfy myself? Ought I then to have waited, mother, until before my eyes he had ... You will make me say something obscene.

MME. PERNELLE. Indeed I am sure his soul burns with too pure a zeal; I cannot possibly believe he would attempt the things of which people accuse him.

ORGON. Enough! If you were not my mother I do not know what I might say to you, you make me so angry.

DORINE. Such is the just reward of acts in this world, Monsieur. You would not believe and now you are not believed.

CLÉANTE. We waste time in mere trifles which we ought to use in taking measures. We ought not to sleep when a knave threatens.

DAMIS. What? would his effrontery go to such lengths?

ELMIRE. For my part, I do not believe he can possibly make out a case: his ingratitude would be too glaring.

CLÉANTE. You must not trust to that. He will find means to justify his actions against you: for less than this a powerful party has involved people in sad troubles. I tell you again, armed as he is, you ought never to have driven him thus far.

ORGON. That is true, but what could I do? I was not the master of my feelings when I saw the insolence of this traitor.

CLÉANTE. I wish, with all my heart, we could arrange for even the shadow of peace between you two.

ELMIRE. If I had known he had such weapons in his hands I would not have made so much noise about the matter, and my ...

ORGON. What does that man want? Go quickly, and see. A nice condition I am in for seeing anybody.

SCENE IV
MONSIEUR LOYAL, MADAM PERNELLE, ORGON, DAMIS,
MARIANE, DORINE, ELMIRE, CLÉANTE

M. LOYAL. Good-morning, my dear sister, pray let me speak to your master.

DORINE. He is engaged with friends, and I doubt whether he can see anyone at present.

M. LOYAL. I do not want to be intrusive in his own house. I do not think my presence concerns anything that will distress him. I have come upon a matter which will please him.

DORINE. What is your name?

M. LOYAL. Simply tell him I come, on behalf of Monsieur Tartuffe, for his good.

DORINE. He is a man who comes with a civil message from Monsieur Tartuffe, concerning a matter which he says will please you.

CLÉANTE. You must see who this man is, and what he can want.

ORGON. Perhaps he comes here to reconcile us. In what way shall I behave to him?

CLÉANTE. You ought not to show your resentment; and if he speaks of an agreement you ought to listen to him?

M. LOYAL. Your servant, Monsieur. May heaven destroy those who wish you harm, and may it be as favorable to you as I wish.

ORGON. This civil beginning bears out my opinion, and augurs already some reconciliation.

M. LOYAL. I was your father's servant, and your whole household has ever been dear to me.

ORGON. I am greatly ashamed, Monsieur, and I beg your pardon in that I do not know you or your name.

M. LOYAL. My name is Loyal, I am a native of Normandy, and, in spite of envious people, a bailiff. Thanks to heaven, I have had, for the last forty years, the happiness of holding this office with much credit. I have come to you, Monsieur, by your leave, to serve a writ of a certain kind . . .

ORGON. What? are you here . . . ?

M. LOYAL. Calm yourself, Sir. It is nothing but a summons, an order to remove you and yours hence, to take your furniture away, and to make way for others, without delay or remission, as hereby decreed.

ORGON. I to leave this house?

M. LOYAL. Yes, Monsieur, if it please you. The house, at present, as you well know, belongs unquestionably to good Monsieur Tartuffe. Henceforth, of all your goods he is lord and master, by virtue of a contract which I have with me. It is in due form and nothing can be said against it.

DAMIS. Truly I admire this impudence: it is colossal.

M. LOYAL. Monsieur, I have not any business with you. It is with this gentleman. He is both reasonable and civil, and he knows the duty of a sensible man too well to wish to resist what is in any way just.

ORGON. But . . .

M. LOYAL. Yes, Monsieur, I know you would not rebel for a million, and that you will, like a gentleman, allow me to execute here the orders which have been given me.

DAMIS. Monsieur Bailiff, it may happen that you will here get the stick laid across your black gown.

M. LOYAL. Order your son to be silent or withdraw, Monsieur. I should be sorry to have to put your name down in my official report.

DORINE. This Monsieur Loyal has a very disloyal air.

M. LOYAL. I have much sympathy with all worthy people, and I would not have burdened myself, Monsieur, with these documents save to oblige you and to do you service, to take away in this manner the chance of someone else being chosen who, not having for you the esteem I have, would have proceeded in a less gentle manner.

ORGON. What can be worse than to order people out of their own house?

M. LOYAL. Monsieur, you are given time, and I will suspend proceedings under the writ until tomorrow, I will simply come to pass the night here, with ten of my men, without scandal and without noise. For the sake of form, you will be so good as to bring me the keys of your door before you go to bed. I will take care not to disturb your repose, and not to allow anything unseemly. But tomorrow, early in the morning, you must be ready to clear the house even to the smallest utensil. My men will help you. I have chosen strong fellows, so that they can assist you to take everything away. It is not possible to act better than I am acting, I feel sure, and, since I treat you with great consideration, Monsieur, I beg that on your part you will treat me properly and that you will not annoy me in any way in the execution of the duties of my office.

ORGON. With the best heart in the world would I give just now a hundred of the brightest louis d'or[7] that are left me could I have the pleasure of giving one of the soundest clouts possible on his beak.

CLÉANTE. Be quiet, do not make matters worse.

DAMIS. I can hardly contain myself. My hand itches at this monstrous impertinence.

DORINE. Upon my word, Monsieur Loyal, a drubbing with a stick would not sit ill on your broad back.

M. LOYAL. We could easily punish those shameful words, my girl; women, also, are answerable to the law.

CLÉANTE. Let us end all this, Monsieur, there has been enough of it. Give up this paper, for goodness' sake, quickly, and leave us.

M. LOYAL. Good-bye for the present. May Heaven keep you all in happiness!

ORGON. May it confound you and him who sent you!

SCENE V

ORGON, CLÉANTE, MARIANE, ELMIRE, MADAME PERNELLE, DORINE, DAMIS

ORGON. Ah! well. You see now, mother, I was right, and you can judge of the rest by the warrant. Do you acknowledge his treachery at last?

MME. PERNELLE. I am quite thunderstruck: I feel as though I had dropped from the clouds!

DORINE. You have not any reason to complain, or to blame him. His pious designs are confirmed by this. His virtue reaches its consummation in the love of his neighbor. He knows that riches very often corrupt a man, and, out of pure charity, he would take away from you everything which could become an obstacle in the way of your salvation.

ORGON. Hold your tongue. I am continually telling you to be quiet.

CLÉANTE. Let us see what course we ought to follow.

ELMIRE. Go and expose the ungrateful wretch's audacity. His proceeding destroys the validity of the contract. His disloyalty will appear too black to allow him to gain the success he expects.

SCENE VI

VALÈRE, ORGON, CLÉANTE, ELMIRE, MARIANE, *etc.*

VALÈRE. I am very sorry, Monsieur, that I come to trouble you, but I am forced to it by the urgency of the danger. A friend who is united to me by the closest ties, and who knows the interest I take in you, has, by a hazardous step, violated for my sake the secrecy due to affairs of state and has just sent me some intelligence in consequence of which you will be compelled to make a sudden flight. About an hour ago, the knave, who has imposed upon you for so long, thought proper to accuse you to the king, and, amongst the charges which he brings against you, he has put into his hands the important documents of a state criminal whose guilty secret he says you have kept in contempt of the duty of a subject. I do not know the details of the crime with which you are charged, but a warrant

[7] Gold coins issued during the reigns of Louis XIII through Louis XVI—that is, from 1610 through 1792.

is out against your person, and the better to execute it, he himself is appointed to accompany the person who is to arrest you.

CLÉANTE. His pretensions are now armed, and it is by this means that the traitor seeks to render himself master of your property.

ORGON. I tell you the fellow is a vile brute.

VALÈRE. The least delay may be fatal to you. My coach is at the door to take you away, and I have brought you a thousand louis d'or. Do not let us lose any time; the bolt is shot, and this is one of those blows which must be parried by flight. I myself offer to conduct you to a safe retreat, and I will accompany you even to the end of your flight.

ORGON. Alas! what do I not owe to your thoughtful care? I must thank you another time. I beg that heaven will be propitious enough to enable me to acknowledge some day this generous service. Farewell. The rest of you be careful . . .

CLÉANTE. Go quickly, brother, we will see to everything necessary.

LAST SCENE
A POLICE OFFICER, TARTUFFE, VALÈRE, ORGON, ELMIRE, MARIANE, *etc.*

TARTUFFE. Gently, Monsieur, gently, do not run so fast. You will not have to go very far in order to find your lodging; we take you prisoner in the King's name.

ORGON. Wretch! You have kept this shaft for the last. This is the blow, villain, by which you dispatch me, and it crowns all your evil deeds.

TARTUFFE. Your abuse has no power to disturb me; I am accustomed to endure all things for the sake of heaven.

CLÉANTE. Your moderation is great, to be sure.

DAMIS. How impudently the villain plays with heaven!

TARTUFFE. All your abuse cannot move me. I do not think of anything but of doing my duty.

MARIANE. You may aspire to great glory from *this* duty. And this task is a very proper one for *you* to undertake.

TARTUFFE. A task cannot but be glorious when it proceeds from the power which sends me to this place.

ORGON. Ungrateful wretch, do you remember that it was my charitable hand which raised you from a miserable condition?

TARTUFFE. Yes, I know what assistance I had from you, but the interest of the King is my first duty. The imperative obligation of that sacred duty stifles all gratitude in my heart, and I would sacrifice friend, wife, parents and myself with them to so powerful a bond.

ELMIRE. The hypocrite!

DORINE. How well and artfully he knows how to make himself a fine cloak out of all that men hold sacred.

CLÉANTE. But if this zeal which fills you, and upon which you plume yourself, is as perfect as you say it is, why did it not appear before he happened to surprise you soliciting his wife? Why did you not think to denounce him until his honor obliged him to turn you away? I do not say the gift of all his property he recently made you should have prevented you from doing your duty, but why did you agree to take anything of his when you intended to treat him as a criminal today?

TARTUFFE. [*To the* POLICE OFFICER.] Pray, Monsieur, deliver me from this clamor, and be so good as to execute your warrant.

POLICE OFFICER. Certainly. We have delayed the execution too long, without doubt.

Your words aptly remind me to fulfil it. My warrant will be executed if you follow me directly to the prison which is assigned you for your dwelling.

TARTUFFE. Who? I, Monsieur.

POLICE OFFICER. Yes, you.

TARTUFFE. Why, then, to prison?

POLICE OFFICER. I have no account to render to you. Compose yourself, Monsieur, after so great an alarm. We live under a king who is an enemy to fraud, a king whose eyes look into the depths of all hearts, and who cannot be deceived by the most artful imposter. Gifted with a fine discernment, his lofty soul at all times sees things in the right light. He is never betrayed into exaggeration, and his sound judgment never falls into any excess. He confers an everlasting glory upon men of worth; but this zeal does not radiate blindly: his esteem for the sincere does not close his heart to the horror aroused by those who are treacherous. Even this person was not the man to overreach him: he has guarded himself against more subtle snares. From the first his quick perception pierced through all the vileness coiled round that man's heart, who, coming to accuse you, betrayed himself, and by a righteous act of divine justice revealed himself to the King as a notorious rogue, of whose deeds, under another name, the King was aware. His life is one long series of utterly black actions, of which volumes might be written. In short, the monarch detested his vile ingratitude and his disloyalty towards you; to his other misdeeds he has added this crime; and I am placed in this matter under his orders, so that the lengths to which his impudence would carry him might be seen, and in order to make him give you entire satisfaction. Yes, I am instructed to take away from the wretch all your documents of which he declares he is the owner, and to place them in your hands. By his sovereign power he annuls the terms of the contract which made over to that man all your wealth, and, finally, he pardons you the secret offense into which the flight of a friend caused you to fall. This is the reward he bestows for the zeal which he formerly saw you display in the support of his rights, to show that his heart knows, when least suspected, how to recompense a good action, that merit is never ignored by him, and that he remembers good much better than evil.

DORINE. Heaven be praised!

MADAME PERNELLE. Now I breathe again.

ELMIRE. What a happy end to our troubles!

MARIANE. Who would have dared to foretell this?

ORGON. [*To* TARTUFFE.] Ah! well, there you go, traitor!

CLÉANTE. Ah! my brother, stay, do not descend to abuse. Leave the wretch to his evil fate, and do not add to the remorse which overwhelms him. Much rather hope his heart may today make a happy return to the bosom of virtue; that he may reform his life in detesting his crime, and thus cause our glorious King to temper justice; whilst you throw yourself on your knees in return for his lenity and render the thanks such mild treatment demands.

ORGON. Yes, it is well said. Let us joyfully throw ourselves at his feet and praise the goodness which his heart has shown to us. Then, having acquitted ourselves a little of this first duty, let us apply ourselves to the pressing claims of another, and by a happy wedding let us crown in Valère the ardor of a generous and sincere lover.

END

[1667]

Henrik Ibsen   *1828–1906*

HEDDA GABLER

Translated by William Archer and Sir Edmund Gosse

CHARACTERS

GEORGE TESMAN	JUDGE BRACK
HEDDA TESMAN, *his wife*	EILERT LÖVBORG
MISS JULIANA TESMAN, *his aunt*	BERTA, *servant at the Tesmans'*
MRS. ELVSTED	

SCENE:

TESMAN'S *villa, in the west end of Christiania.*

ACT I

A spacious, handsome and tastefully furnished drawing-room, decorated in dark colors. In the back, a wide doorway with curtains drawn back, leading into a smaller room decorated in the same style as the drawing-room. In the right-hand wall of the front room, a folding door leading out to the hall. In the opposite wall, on the left, a glass door, also with curtains drawn back. Through the panes can be seen part of a verandah outside, and trees covered with autumn foliage. An oval table, with a cover on it, and surrounded by chairs, stands well forward. In front, by the wall on the right, a wide stove of dark porcelain, a high-backed arm-chair, a cushioned foot-rest, and two foot-stools. A settee, with a small round table in front of it, fills the upper right-hand corner. In front, on the left, a little way from the wall, a sofa. Farther back than the glass door, a piano. On either side of the doorway at the back a whatnot with terra-cotta and majolica ornaments.[1] —Against the back wall of the inner room a sofa, with a table, and one or two chairs. Over the sofa hangs the portrait of a handsome elderly man in a General's uniform. Over the table a hanging lamp, with an opal glass shade. —A number of bouquets are arranged about the drawing-room, in vases and glasses. Others lie upon the tables. The floors in both rooms are covered with thick carpets. — Morning light. The sun shines in through the glass door.

MISS JULIANA TESMAN, with her bonnet on and carrying a parasol, comes in from the hall, followed by BERTA, who carries a bouquet wrapped in paper. MISS TESMAN is a comely and pleasant-looking lady of about sixty-five. She is nicely but simply dressed in a gray walking-costume. BERTA is a middle-aged woman of plain and rather countrified appearance.

MISS TESMAN [*stops close to the door, listens, and says softly*]. Upon my word, I don't believe they are stirring yet!

BERTA [*also softly*]. I told you so, Miss. Remember how late the steamboat got in last night. And then, when they got home!—good Lord, what a lot the young mistress had to unpack before she could get to bed.

MISS TESMAN. Well, well—let them have their sleep out. But let us see that they get

---

[1] A *whatnot* is a stand with shelves for small decorative articles. *Terra-cotta* is a brownish-red clay used in pottery, and *majolica* is a kind of glazed and richly decorated pottery from Italy.

a good breath of the fresh morning air when they do appear. [*She goes to the glass door and throws it open.*]

BERTA [*beside the table, at a loss what to do with the bouquet in her hand*]. I declare there isn't a bit of room left. I think I'll put it down here, Miss. [*She places it on the piano.*]

MISS TESMAN. So you've got a new mistress now, my dear Berta. Heaven knows it was a wrench to me to part with you.

BERTA [*on the point of weeping*]. And do you think it wasn't hard for me too, Miss? After all the blessed years I've been with you and Miss Rina.

MISS TESMAN. We must make the best of it, Berta. There was nothing else to be done. George can't do without you, you see—he absolutely can't. He has had you to look after him ever since he was a little boy.

BERTA. Ah, but, Miss Julia, I can't help thinking of Miss Rina lying helpless at home there, poor thing. And with only that new girl, too! She'll never learn to take proper care of an invalid.

MISS TESMAN. Oh, I shall manage to train her. And of course, you know, I shall take most of it upon myself. You needn't be uneasy about my poor sister, my dear Berta.

BERTA. Well, but there's another thing, Miss. I'm so mortally afraid I shan't be able to suit the young mistress.

MISS TESMAN. Oh, well—just at first there may be one or two things—

BERTA. Most like she'll be terrible grand in her ways.

MISS TESMAN. Well, you can't wonder at that—General Gabler's daughter! Think of the sort of life she was accustomed to in her father's time. Don't you remember how we used to see her riding down the road along with the General? In that long black habit—and with feathers in her hat?

BERTA. Yes, indeed—I remember well enough—! But good Lord, I should never have dreamt in those days that she and Master George would make a match of it.

MISS TESMAN. Nor I.—But, by-the-bye, Berta—while I think of it: in future you musn't say Master George. You must say Dr. Tesman.

BERTA. Yes, the young mistress spoke of that too—last night—the moment they set foot in the house. Is it true, then, Miss?

MISS TESMAN. Yes, indeed it is. Only think, Berta—some foreign university has made him a doctor—while he has been abroad, you understand. I hadn't heard a word about it, until he told me himself upon the pier.

BERTA. Well, well, he's clever enough for anything, he is. But I didn't think he'd have gone in for doctoring people too.

MISS TESMAN. No, no, it's not that sort of doctor he is. [*Nods significantly.*] But let me tell you, we may have to call him something still grander before long.

BERTA. You don't say so! What can that be, Miss?

MISS TESMAN [*smiling*]. H'm—wouldn't you like to know! [*With emotion.*] Ah, dear, dear— if my poor brother could only look up from his grave now, and see what his little boy has grown into! [*Looks around.*] But bless me, Berta—why have you done this? Taken the chintz[2] covers off all the furniture?

BERTA. The mistress told me to. She can't abide covers on the chairs, she says.

MISS TESMAN. Are they going to make this their everyday sitting-room then?

BERTA. Yes, that's what I understood—from the mistress. Master George—the doctor—he said nothing.

[2] A printed cotton fabric.

[GEORGE TESMAN *comes from the right into the inner room, humming to himself, and carrying an unstrapped empty portmanteau.*[3] *He is a middle-sized, young-looking man of thirty-three, rather stout, with a round, open, cheerful face, fair hair and beard. He wears spectacles, and is somewhat carelessly dressed in comfortable indoor clothes.*]

MISS TESMAN. Good morning, good morning, George.

TESMAN [*in the doorway between the rooms*]. Aunt Julia! Dear Aunt Julia! [*Goes up to her and shakes hands warmly.*] Come all this way—so early! Eh?

MISS TESMAN. Why of course I had to come and see how you were getting on.

TESMAN. In spite of your having had no proper night's rest?

MISS TESMAN. Oh, that makes no difference to me.

TESMAN. Well, I suppose you got home all right from the pier? Eh?

MISS TESMAN. Yes, quite safely, thank goodness. Judge Brack was good enough to see me right to my door.

TESMAN. We were so sorry we couldn't give you a seat in the carriage. But you saw what a pile of boxes Hedda had to bring with her.

MISS TESMAN. Yes, she had certainly plenty of boxes.

BERTA [*to* TESMAN]. Shall I go in and see if there's anything I can do for the mistress?

TESMAN. No thank you, Berta—you needn't. She said she would ring if she wanted anything.

BERTA [*going towards the right*]. Very well.

TESMAN. But look here—take this portmanteau with you.

BERTA [*taking it*]. I'll put it in the attic.

[*She goes out by the hall door.*]

TESMAN. Fancy, Auntie—I had the whole of that portmanteau chock full of copies of documents. You wouldn't believe how much I have picked up from all the archives I have been examining—curious old details that no one has had any idea of—

MISS TESMAN. Yes, you don't seem to have wasted your time on your wedding trip, George.

TESMAN. No, that I haven't. But do take off your bonnet, Auntie. Look here! Let me untie the strings—eh?

MISS TESMAN [*while he does so*]. Well, well—this is just as if you were still at home with us.

TESMAN [*with the bonnet in his hand, looks at it from all sides*]. Why, what a gorgeous bonnet you've been investing in!

MISS TESMAN. I bought it on Hedda's account.

TESMAN. On Hedda's account? Eh?

MISS TESMAN. Yes, so that Hedda needn't be ashamed of me if we happened to go out together.

TESMAN [*patting her cheek*]. You always think of everything, Aunt Julia. [*Lays the bonnet on a chair beside the table.*] And now, look here—suppose we sit comfortably on the sofa and have a little chat, till Hedda comes.

[*They seat themselves. She places her parasol*[4] *in the corner of the sofa.*]

MISS TESMAN [*takes both his hands and looks at him*]. What a delight it is to have you again, as large as life, before my very eyes, George! My George—my poor brother's own boy!

TESMAN. And it's a delight for me, too, to see you again, Aunt Julia! You, who have been father and mother in one to me.

---

[3] A leather trunk.   [4] A flimsy sun umbrella.

MISS TESMAN. Oh, yes, I know you will always keep a place in your heart for your old aunts.

TESMAN. And what about Aunt Rina? No improvement—eh?

MISS TESMAN. Oh, no—we can scarcely look for any improvement in her case, poor thing. There she lies, helpless, as she has lain for all these years. But heaven grant I may not lose her yet awhile! For if I did, I don't know what I should make of my life, George—especially now that I haven't you to look after any more.

TESMAN [*patting her back*]. There, there, there—!

MISS TESMAN [*suddenly changing her tone*]. And to think that here you are a married man, George!—And that you should be the one to carry off Hedda Gabler, the beautiful Hedda Gabler! Only think of it—she, that was so beset with admirers!

TESMAN [*hums a little and smiles complacently*]. Yes, I fancy I have several good friends about town who would like to stand in my shoes—eh?

MISS TESMAN. And then this fine long wedding-tour you have had! More than five—nearly six months—

TESMAN. Well, for me it has been a sort of tour of research as well. I have had to do so much grubbing among old records—and to read no end of books too, Auntie.

MISS TESMAN. Oh, yes, I suppose so. [*More confidentially, and lowering her voice a little.*] But listen now, George—have you nothing—nothing special to tell me?

TESMAN. As to our journey?

MISS TESMAN. Yes.

TESMAN. No, I don't know of anything except what I have told you in my letters. I had a doctor's degree conferred on me—but that I told you yesterday.

MISS TESMAN. Yes, yes, you did. But what I mean is—haven't you any—any—expectations?

TESMAN. Expectations?

MISS TESMAN. Why, you know, George—I'm your old auntie!

TESMAN. Why, of course I have expectations.

MISS TESMAN. Ah!

TESMAN. I have every expectation of being a professor one of these days.

MISS TESMAN. Oh, yes, a professor—

TESMAN. Indeed, I may say I am certain of it. But my dear Auntie—you know all about that already!

MISS TESMAN [*laughing at herself*]. Yes, of course I do. You are quite right there. [*Changing the subject.*] But we were talking about your journey. It must have cost a great deal of money, George?

TESMAN. Well, you see—my handsome traveling-scholarship went a good way.

MISS TESMAN. But I can't understand how you can have made it go far enough for two.

TESMAN. No, that's not so easy to understand—eh?

MISS TESMAN. And especially traveling with a lady—they tell me that makes it ever so much more expensive.

TESMAN. Yes, of course—it makes it a little more expensive. But Hedda had to have this trip, Auntie! She really had to. Nothing else would have done.

MISS TESMAN. No, no, I suppose not. A wedding-tour seems to be quite indispensable nowadays.—But tell me now—have you gone thoroughly over the house yet?

TESMAN. Yes, you may be sure I have. I have been afoot ever since daylight.

MISS TESMAN. And what do you think of it all?

TESMAN. I'm delighted! Quite delighted! Only I can't think what we are to do with the two empty rooms between the inner parlor and Hedda's bedroom.

MISS TESMAN [*laughing*]. Oh, my dear George, I dare say you may find some use for them—in the course of time.

TESMAN. Why of course you are quite right, Aunt Julia! You mean as my library increases—eh?

MISS TESMAN. Yes, quite so, my dear boy. It was your library I was thinking of.

TESMAN. I am specially pleased on Hedda's account. Often and often, before we were engaged, she said that she would never care to live anywhere but in Secretary Falk's villa.

MISS TESMAN. Yes, it was lucky that this very house should come into the market, just after you had started.

TESMAN. Yes, Aunt Julia, the luck was on our side, wasn't it—eh?

MISS TESMAN. But the expense, my dear George! You will find it very expensive, all this.

TESMAN [*looks at her, a little cast down*]. Yes, I suppose I shall, Aunt!

MISS TESMAN. Oh, frightfully!

TESMAN. How much do you think? In round numbers? —Eh?

MISS TESMAN. Oh, I can't even guess until all the accounts come in.

TESMAN. Well, fortunately, Judge Brack has secured the most favorable terms for me,—so he said in a letter to Hedda.

MISS TESMAN. Yes, don't be uneasy, my dear boy. —Besides, I have given security for the furniture and all the carpets.

TESMAN. Security? You? My dear Aunt Julia—what sort of security could you give?

MISS TESMAN. I have given a mortgage on our annuity.

TESMAN [*jumps up*]. What! On your—and Aunt Rina's annuity!

MISS TESMAN. Yes, I knew of no other plan, you see.

TESMAN [*placing himself before her*]. Have you gone out of your senses, Auntie! Your annuity—it's all that you and Aunt Rina have to live upon.

MISS TESMAN. Well, well, don't get so excited about it. It's only a matter of form you know—Judge Brack assured me of that. It was he that was kind enough to arrange the whole affair for me. A mere matter of form, he said.

TESMAN. Yes, that may be all very well. But nevertheless—

MISS TESMAN. You will have your own salary to depend upon now. And, good heavens, even if we did have to pay up a little—! To eke things out a bit at the start—! Why, it would be nothing but a pleasure to us.

TESMAN. Oh, Auntie—will you never be tired of making sacrifices for me!

MISS TESMAN [*rises and lays her hands on his shoulders*]. Have I had any other happiness in this world except to smooth your way for you, my dear boy? You, who have had neither father nor mother to depend on. And now we have reached the goal, George! Things have looked black enough for us, sometimes; but, thank heaven, now you have nothing to fear.

TESMAN. Yes, it is really marvelous how everything has turned out for the best.

MISS TESMAN. And the people who opposed you—who wanted to bar the way for you—now you have them at your feet. They have fallen, George. Your most dangerous rival—his fall was the worst. —And now he has to lie on the bed he has made for himself—poor misguided creature.

TESMAN. Have you heard anything of Eilert? Since I went away, I mean.

MISS TESMAN. Only that he is said to have published a new book.

TESMAN. What! Eilert Lövborg! Recently—eh?

MISS TESMAN. Yes, so they say. Heaven knows whether it can be worth anything! Ah, when your new book appears—that will be another story, George! What is it to be about?

TESMAN. It will deal with the domestic industries of Brabant during the Middle Ages.

MISS TESMAN. Fancy—to be able to write on such a subject as that!

TESMAN. However, it may be some time before the book is ready. I have all these collections to arrange first, you see.

MISS TESMAN. Yes, collecting and arranging—no one can beat you at that. There you are my poor brother's own son.

TESMAN. I am looking forward eagerly to setting to work at it; especially now that I have my own delightful home to work in.

MISS TESMAN. And, most of all, now that you have got the wife of your heart, my dear George.

TESMAN [*embracing her*]. Oh, yes, yes, Aunt Julia. Hedda—she is the best part of all! [*Looks towards the doorway.*] I believe I hear her coming—eh?

[HEDDA *enters from the left through the inner room. She is a woman of nine-and-twenty. Her face and figure show refinement and distinction. Her complexion is pale and opaque. Her steel-gray eyes express a cold, unruffled repose. Her hair is of an agreeable medium brown, but not particularly abundant. She is dressed in a tasteful, somewhat loose-fitting morning-gown.*]

MISS TESMAN [*going to meet* HEDDA]. Good morning, my dear Hedda! Good morning, and a hearty welcome.

HEDDA [*holds out her hand*]. Good morning, dear Miss Tesman! So early a call! This is kind of you.

MISS TESMAN [*with some embarrassment*]. Well—has the bride slept well in her new home?

HEDDA. Oh yes, thanks. Passably.

TESMAN [*laughing*]. Passably! Come, that's good, Hedda! You were sleeping like a stone when I got up.

HEDDA. Fortunately. Of course one has always to accustom one's self to new surroundings, Miss Tesman—little by little. [*Looking towards the left.*] Oh—there the servant has gone and opened the verandah door, and let in a whole flood of sunshine.

MISS TESMAN [*going towards the door*]. Well, then, we will shut it.

HEDDA. No, no, not that! Tesman, please draw the curtains. That will give a softer light.

TESMAN [*at the door*]. All right—all right. There now, Hedda, now you have both shade and fresh air.

HEDDA. Yes, fresh air we certainly must have, with all these stacks of flowers—But—won't you sit down, Miss Tesman?

MISS TESMAN. No, thank you. Now that I have seen that everything is all right here—thank heaven!—I must be getting home again. My sister is lying longing for me, poor thing.

TESMAN. Give her my very best love, Auntie; and say I shall look in and see her later in the day.

MISS TESMAN. Yes, yes, I'll be sure to tell her. But by-the-bye, George—[*feeling in her dress pocket*]—I have almost forgotten—I have something for you here.

TESMAN. What is it, Auntie? Eh?

MISS TESMAN [*produces a flat parcel wrapped in newspaper and hands it to him*]. Look here, my dear boy.

TESMAN [*opening the parcel*]. Well, I declare! Have you really saved them for me, Aunt Julia! Hedda, isn't this touching—eh?

HEDDA [*beside the whatnot on the right*]. Well, what is it?

TESMAN. My old morning-shoes! My slippers.

HEDDA. Indeed. I remember you often spoke of them while we were abroad.

TESMAN. Yes, I missed them terribly. [*Goes up to her.*] Now you shall see them, Hedda!

HEDDA [*going towards the stove*]. Thanks, I really don't care about it.

TESMAN [*following her*]. Only think—ill as she was, Aunt Rina embroidered these for me. Oh you can't think how many associations cling to them.

HEDDA [*at the table*]. Scarcely for me.

MISS TESMAN. Of course not for Hedda, George.

TESMAN. Well, but now that she belongs to the family, I thought—

HEDDA [*interrupting*]. We shall never get on with this servant, Tesman.

MISS TESMAN. Not get on with Berta?

TESMAN. Why, dear, what puts that in your head? Eh?

HEDDA [*pointing*]. Look there! She has left her old bonnet lying about on a chair.

TESMAN [*in consternation, drops the slippers on the floor*]. Why, Hedda—

HEDDA. Just fancy, if any one should come in and see it.

TESMAN. But Hedda—that's Aunt Julia's bonnet.

HEDDA. Is it!

MISS TESMAN [*taking up the bonnet*]. Yes, indeed it's mine. And what's more, it's not old, Madame Hedda.

HEDDA. I really did not look closely at it, Miss Tesman.

MISS TESMAN [*trying on the bonnet*]. Let me tell you it's the first time I have worn it—the very first time.

TESMAN. And a very nice bonnet it is too—quite a beauty!

MISS TESMAN. Oh, it's no such great thing, George. [*Looks around her.*] My parasol—? Ah, here. [*Takes it.*] For this is mine too—[*mutters*]—not Berta's.

TESMAN. A new bonnet and a new parasol! Only think, Hedda!

HEDDA. Very handsome indeed.

TESMAN. Yes, isn't it? But Auntie, take a good look at Hedda before you go! See how handsome she is!

MISS TESMAN. Oh, my dear boy, there's nothing new in that. Hedda was always lovely. [*She nods and goes towards the right.*]

TESMAN [*following*]. Yes, but have you noticed what splendid condition she is in? How she has filled out on the journey?

HEDDA [*crossing the room*]. Oh, do be quiet—?

MISS TESMAN [*who has stopped and turned*]. Filled out?

TESMAN. Of course you don't notice it so much now that she has that dress on. But I, who can see—

HEDDA [*at the glass door, impatiently*]. Oh, you can't see anything.

TESMAN. It must be the mountain air in the Tyrol—

HEDDA [*curtly, interrupting*]. I am exactly as I was when I started.

TESMAN. So you insist; but I'm quite certain you are not. Don't you agree with me, Auntie?

MISS TESMAN [*who has been gazing at her with folded hands*]. Hedda is lovely—lovely—lovely. [*Goes up to her, takes her head between both hands, draws it downwards, and kisses her hair*]. God bless and preserve Hedda Tesman—for George's sake.

HEDDA [*gently freeing herself*]. Oh—! Let me go.

MISS TESMAN [*in quiet emotion*]. I shall not let a day pass without coming to see you.

TESMAN. No you won't, will you, Auntie? Eh?

MISS TESMAN. Good-bye—good-bye!

[*She goes out by the hall door.* Tesman *accompanies her. The door remains half open.* TESMAN *can be heard repeating his message to Aunt Rina and his thanks for the slippers. In the meantime,* HEDDA *walks about the room raising her arms and clenching her hands as if in desperation. Then she flings back the curtains from the glass door, and stands there looking out.*

Presently TESMAN *returns and closes the door behind him.*]

TESMAN [*picks up the slippers from the floor*]. What are you looking at, Hedda?

HEDDA [*once more calm and mistress of herself*]. I am only looking at the leaves. They are so yellow—so withered.

TESMAN [*wraps up the slippers and lays them on the table*]. Well you see, we are well into September now.

HEDDA [*again restless*]. Yes, to think of it!—Already in—in September.

TESMAN. Don't you think Aunt Julia's manner was strange, dear? Almost solemn? Can you imagine what was the matter with her? Eh?

HEDDA. I scarcely know her, you see. Is she often like that?

TESMAN. No, not as she was today.

HEDDA [*leaving the glass door*]. Do you think she was annoyed about the bonnet?

TESMAN. Oh, scarcely at all. Perhaps a little, just at the moment—

HEDDA. But what an idea, to pitch her bonnet about in the drawing-room! No one does that sort of thing.

TESMAN. Well you may be sure Aunt Julia won't do it again.

HEDDA. In any case, I shall manage to make my peace with her.

TESMAN. Yes, my dear, good Hedda, if you only would.

HEDDA. When you call this afternoon, you might invite her to spend the evening here.

TESMAN. Yes, that I will. And there's one thing more you could do that would delight her heart.

HEDDA. What is it?

TESMAN. If you could only prevail on yourself to say *du*[5] to her. For my sake, Hedda? Eh?

HEDDA. No, no, Tesman—you really mustn't ask that of me. I have told you so already. I shall try to call her "Aunt"; and you must be satisfied with that.

TESMAN. Well, well. Only I think now that you belong to the family, you—

HEDDA. H'm—I can't in the least see why—

[*She goes up towards the middle doorway.*]

TESMAN [*after a pause*]. Is there anything the matter with you, Hedda? Eh?

HEDDA. I'm only looking at my old piano. It doesn't go at all well with all the other things.

TESMAN. The first time I draw my salary, we'll see about exchanging it.

HEDDA. No, no—no exchanging. I don't want to part with it. Suppose we put it there in the inner room, and then get another here in its place. When it's convenient, I mean.

TESMAN [*a little taken aback*]. Yes—of course we could do that.

HEDDA [*takes up the bouquet from the piano*]. These flowers were not here last night when we arrived.

---

[5] Like the French and the Germans, Norwegians reserve the familiar form of the pronoun "you" (*du*) for conversations between lovers and intimate friends; the more formal *de* is used between strangers and casual acquaintances.

TESMAN. Aunt Julia must have brought them for you.

HEDDA [*examining the bouquet*]. A visiting-card. [*Takes it out and reads.*] "Shall return later in the day." Can you guess whose card it is?

TESMAN. No. Whose? Eh?

HEDDA. The name is "Mrs. Elvsted."

TESMAN. Is it really? Sheriff Elvsted's wife? Miss Rysing that was.

HEDDA. Exactly. The girl with the irritating hair, that she was always showing off. An old flame of yours, I've been told.

TESMAN [*laughing*]. Oh, that didn't last long; and it was before I knew you, Hedda. But fancy her being in town!

HEDDA. It's odd that she should call upon us. I have scarcely seen her since we left school.

TESMAN. I haven't seen her either for—heaven knows how long. I wonder how she can endure to live in such an out-of-the-way hole—eh?

HEDDA [*after a moment's thought says suddenly*]. Tell me, Tesman—isn't it somewhere near there that he—that—Eilert Lövborg is living?

TESMAN. Yes, he is somewhere in that part of the country.

   [BERTA *enters by the hall door.*]

BERTA. That lady, ma'am, that brought some flowers a little while ago, is here again. [*Pointing.*] The flowers you have in your hand, ma'am.

HEDDA. Ah, is she? Well, please show her in.

   [BERTA *opens the door for* MRS. ELVSTED, *and goes out herself.* —MRS. ELVSTED *is a woman of fragile figure, with pretty, soft features. Her eyes are light blue, large, round, and somewhat prominent, with a startled, inquiring expression. Her hair is remarkably light, almost flaxen, and unusually abundant and wavy. She is a couple of years younger than* HEDDA. *She wears a dark visiting dress, tasteful, but not quite in the latest fashion.*]

HEDDA [*receives her warmly*]. How do you do, my dear Mrs. Elvsted? It's delightful to see you again.

MRS. ELVSTED [*nervously, struggling for self-control*]. Yes, it's a very long time since we met.

TESMAN [*gives her his hand*]. And we too—eh?

HEDDA. Thanks for your lovely flowers—

MRS. ELVSTED. Oh, not at all—I would have come straight here yesterday afternoon; but I heard that you were away—

TESMAN. Have you just come to town? Eh?

MRS. ELVSTED. I arrived yesterday, about midday. Oh, I was quite in despair when I heard that you were not at home.

HEDDA. In despair! How so?

TESMAN. Why, my dear Mrs. Rysing—I mean Mrs. Elvsted—

HEDDA. I hope that you are not in any trouble?

MRS. ELVSTED. Yes, I am. And I don't know another living creature here that I can turn to.

HEDDA [*laying the bouquet on the table*]. Come—let us sit here on the sofa—

MRS. ELVSTED. Oh, I am too restless to sit down.

HEDDA. Oh no, you're not. Come here. [*She draws* MRS. ELVSTED *down upon the sofa and sits at her side.*]

TESMAN. Well? What is it, Mrs. Elvsted?

HEDDA. Has anything particular happened to you at home?

MRS. ELVSTED. Yes—and no. Oh—I am so anxious you should not misunderstand me—

HEDDA. Then your best plan is to tell us the whole story, Mrs. Elvsted.

TESMAN. I suppose that's what you have come for—eh?

MRS. ELVSTED. Yes, yes—of course it is. Well then, I must tell you—if you don't already know—that Eilert Lövborg is in town, too.

HEDDA. Lövborg—!

TESMAN. What! Has Eilert Lövborg come back? Fancy that, Hedda!

HEDDA. Well, well—I hear it.

MRS. ELVSTED. He has been here a week already. Just fancy—a whole week! In this terrible town, alone! With so many temptations on all sides.

HEDDA. But my dear Mrs. Elvsted—how does he concern you so much?

MRS. ELVSTED [*looks at her with a startled air, and says rapidly*]. He was the children's tutor.

HEDDA. Your children's?

MRS. ELVSTED. My husband's. I have none.

HEDDA. Your step-children's, then?

MRS. ELVSTED. Yes.

TESMAN [*somewhat hesitatingly*]. Then was he—I don't know how to express it—was he—regular enough in his habits to be fit for the post? Eh?

MRS. ELVSTED. For the last two years his conduct has been irreproachable.

TESMAN. Has it indeed? Fancy that, Hedda!

HEDDA. I hear it.

MRS. ELVSTED. Perfectly irreproachable, I assure you! In every respect. But all the same—now that I know he is here—in this great town—and with a large sum of money in his hands—I can't help being in mortal fear for him.

TESMAN. Why did he not remain where he was? With you and your husband? Eh?

MRS. ELVSTED. After his book was published he was too restless and unsettled to remain with us.

TESMAN. Yes, by-the-bye, Aunt Julia told me he had published a new book.

MRS. ELVSTED. Yes, a big book, dealing with the march of civilization—in broad outline, as it were. It came out about a fortnight ago. And since it has sold so well, and been so much read—and made such a sensation—

TESMAN. Has it indeed? It must be something he has had lying by since his better days.

MRS. ELVSTED. Long ago, you mean?

TESMAN. Yes.

MRS. ELVSTED. No, he has written it all since he has been with us—within the last year.

TESMAN. Isn't that good news, Hedda? Think of that.

MRS. ELVSTED. Ah, yes, if only it would last!

HEDDA. Have you seen him here in town?

MRS. ELVSTED. No, not yet. I have had the greatest difficulty in finding out his address. But this morning I discovered it at last.

HEDDA [*looks searchingly at her*]. Do you know, it seems to me a little odd of your husband—h'm—

MRS. ELVSTED [*starting nervously*]. Of my husband! What?

HEDDA. That he should send you to town on such an errand—that he does not come himself and look after his friend.

MRS. ELVSTED. Oh, no, no—my husband has no time. And besides, I—I had some shopping to do.

HEDDA [*with a slight smile*]. Ah, that is a different matter.

MRS. ELVSTED [*rising quickly and uneasily*]. And now I beg and implore you, Mr. Tesman—receive Eilert Lövborg kindly if he comes to you! And that he is sure to do. You see you were such great friends in the old days. And then you are interested in the same studies—the same branch of science—so far as I can understand.

TESMAN. We used to be, at any rate.

MRS. ELVSTED. That is why I beg so earnestly that you—you too—will keep a sharp eye upon him. Oh, you will promise me that, Mr. Tesman—won't you?

TESMAN. With the greatest of pleasure, Mrs. Rysing—

HEDDA. Elvsted.

TESMAN. I assure you I shall do all I possibly can for Eilert. You may rely upon me.

MRS. ELVSTED. Oh, how very, very kind of you! [*Presses his hands.*] Thanks, thanks, thanks! [*Frightened.*] You see, my husband is very fond of him!

HEDDA [*rising*]. You ought to write to him, Tesman. Perhaps he may not care to come to you of his own accord.

TESMAN. Well, perhaps it would be the right thing to do, Hedda? Eh?

HEDDA. And the sooner the better. Why not at once?

MRS. ELVSTED [*imploringly*]. Oh, if you only would!

TESMAN. I'll write this moment. Have you his address, Mrs.—Mrs. Elvsted?

MRS. ELVSTED. Yes. [*Takes a slip of paper from her pocket, and hands it to him.*] Here it is.

TESMAN. Good, good. Then I'll go in—[*Looks about him.*] By-the-bye,—my slippers? Oh, here. [*Takes the packet, and is about to go.*]

HEDDA. Be sure you write him a cordial, friendly letter. And a good long one too.

TESMAN. Yes, I will.

MRS. ELVSTED. But please, please don't say a word to show that I have suggested it.

TESMAN. No, how could you think I would? Eh?

[*He goes out to the right, through the inner room.*]

HEDDA [*goes up to* MRS. ELVSTED, *smiles, and says in a low voice*]. There. We have killed two birds with one stone.

MRS. ELVSTED. What do you mean?

HEDDA. Could you not see that I wanted him to go?

MRS. ELVSTED. Yes, to write the letter—

HEDDA. And that I might speak to you alone.

MRS. ELVSTED [*confused*]. About the same thing?

HEDDA. Precisely.

MRS. ELVSTED [*apprehensively*]. But there is nothing more, Mrs. Tesman! Absolutely nothing!

HEDDA. Oh, yes, but there is. There is a great deal more—I can see that. Sit here —and we'll have a cosy, confidential chat. [*She forces* MRS. ELVSTED *to sit in the easy-chair beside the stove, and seats herself on one of the foot-stools.*]

MRS. ELVSTED [*anxiously, looking at her watch*]. But, my dear Mrs. Tesman—I was really on the point of going.

HEDDA. Oh, you can't be in such a hurry.—Well? Now tell me something about your life at home.

MRS. ELVSTED. Oh, that is just what I care least to speak about.

HEDDA. But to me, dear—? Why, weren't we school-fellows?

MRS. ELVSTED. Yes, but you were in the class above me. Oh, how dreadfully afraid of you I was then!

HEDDA. Afraid of me?

MRS. ELVSTED. *Yes,* dreadfully. For when we met on the stairs you used always to pull my hair.

HEDDA. Did I, really?

MRS. ELVSTED. Yes, and once you said you would burn it off my head.

HEDDA. Oh, that was all nonsense, of course.

MRS. ELVSTED. Yes, but I was so silly in those days.—And since then, too—we have drifted so far—far apart from each other. Our circles have been so entirely different.

HEDDA. Well, then, we must try to drift together again. Now listen! At school we said *du* to each other; and we called each other by our Christian names—

MRS. ELVSTED. No, I am sure you must be mistaken.

HEDDA. No, not at all! I can remember quite distinctly. So now we are going to renew our old friendship. [*Draws the foot-stool closer to* MRS. ELVSTED.] There now! [*Kisses her cheek.*] You must say *du* to me and call me Hedda.

MRS. ELVSTED [*presses and pats her hands*]. Oh, how good and kind you are! I am not used to such kindness.

HEDDA. There, there, there! And I shall say *du* to you, as in the old days, and call you my dear Thora.

MRS. ELVSTED. My name is Thea.

HEDDA. Why, of course! I meant Thea. [*Looks at her compassionately.*] So you are not accustomed to goodness and kindness, Thea? Not in your own home?

MRS. ELVSTED. Oh, if I only had a home! But I haven't any; I have never had a home.

HEDDA [*looks at her for a moment*]. I almost suspected as much.

MRS. ELVSTED [*gazing helplessly before her*]. Yes—yes—yes.

HEDDA. I don't quite remember—was it not as housekeeper that you first went to Mr. Elvsted's?

MRS. ELVSTED. I really went as governess. But his wife—his late wife—was an invalid, —and rarely left her room. So I had to look after the housekeeping as well.

HEDDA. And then—at last—you became mistress of the house.

MRS. ELVSTED [*sadly*]. Yes, I did.

HEDDA. Let me see—about how long ago was that?

MRS. ELVSTED. My marriage?

HEDDA. Yes.

MRS. ELVSTED. Five years ago.

HEDDA. To be sure; it must be that.

MRS. ELVSTED. Oh, those five years—! Or at all events the last two or three of them! Oh, if you could only imagine—

HEDDA [*giving her a little slap on the hand*]. De?[6] Fie, Thea!

MRS. ELVSTED. Yes, yes, I will try—Well if—you could only imagine and understand—

HEDDA [*lightly*]. Eilert Lövborg has been in your neighborhood about three years, hasn't he?

MRS. ELVSTED [*looks at her doubtfully*]. Eilert Lövborg? Yes—he has.

HEDDA. Had you known him before, in town here?

MRS. ELVSTED. Scarcely at all. I mean—I knew him by name of course.

HEDDA. But you saw a good deal of him in the country?

MRS. ELVSTED. Yes, he came to us every day. You see, he gave the children lessons; for in the long run I couldn't manage it all myself.

HEDDA. No, that's clear.—And your husband—? I suppose he is often away from home?

MRS. ELVSTED. Yes. Being Sheriff, you know, he has to travel about a good deal in his district.

---

[6] *De* is the formal second-person pronoun. Hedda wishes Thea to use the more intimate pronoun *du*.

HEDDA [*leaning against the arm of the chair*]. Thea—my poor, sweet Thea—now you must tell me everything—exactly as it stands.

MRS. ELVSTED. Well then, you must question me.

HEDDA. What sort of a man is your husband, Thea? I mean—you know—in everyday life. Is he kind to you?

MRS. ELVSTED [*evasively*]. I am sure he means well in everything.

HEDDA. I should think he must be altogether too old for you. There is at least twenty years' difference between you, is there not?

MRS. ELVSTED [*irritably*]. Yes, that is true, too. Everything about him is repellent to me! We have not a thought in common. We have no single point of sympathy— he and I.

HEDDA. But is he not fond of you all the same? In his own way?

MRS. ELVSTED. Oh, I really don't know. I think he regards me simply as a useful property. And then it doesn't cost much to keep me. I am not expensive.

HEDDA. That is stupid of you.

MRS. ELVSTED [*shakes her head*]. It cannot be otherwise—not with him. I don't think he really cares for any one but himself—and perhaps a little for the children.

HEDDA. And for Eilert Lövborg, Thea.

MRS. ELVSTED [*looking at her*]. For Eilert Lövborg? What puts that into your head?

HEDDA. Well, my dear—I should say, when he sends you after him all the way to town—[*smiling almost imperceptibly*]. And besides, you said so yourself, to Tesman.

MRS. ELVSTED [*with a little nervous twitch*]. Did I? Yes, I suppose I did. [*Vehemently, but not loudly.*] No—I may just as well make a clean breast of it at once! For it must all come out in any case.

HEDDA. Why, my dear Thea—?

MRS. ELVSTED. Well, to make a long story short: My husband did not know that I was coming.

HEDDA. What! Your husband didn't know it!

MRS. ELVSTED. No, of course not. For that matter, he was away from home himself— he was traveling. Oh, I could bear it no longer, Hedda! I couldn't indeed—so utterly alone as I should have been in future.

HEDDA. Well? And then?

MRS. ELVSTED. So I put together some of my things—what I needed most—as quietly as possible. And then I left the house.

HEDDA. Without a word?

MRS. ELVSTED. Yes—and took the train straight to town.

HEDDA. Why, my dear, good Thea—to think of you daring to do it!

MRS. ELVSTED [*rises and moves about the room*]. What else could I possibly do?

HEDDA. But what do you think your husband will say when you go home again?

MRS. ELVSTED [*at the table, looks at her*]. Back to him?

HEDDA. Of course.

MRS. ELVSTED. I shall never go back to him again.

HEDDA [*rising and going towards her*]. Then you have left your home—for good and all?

MRS. ELVSTED. Yes. There was nothing else to be done.

HEDDA. But then—to take flight so openly.

MRS. ELVSTED. Oh, it's impossible to keep things of that sort secret.

HEDDA. But what do you think people will say of you, Thea?

MRS. ELVSTED. They may say what they like for aught *I* care. [*Seats herself wearily and sadly on the sofa.*] I have done nothing but what I had to do.

HEDDA [*after a short silence*]. And what are your plans now? What do you think of doing?

MRS. ELVSTED. I don't know yet. I only know this, that I must live here, where Eilert Lövborg is—if I am to live at all.

HEDDA [*takes a chair from the table, seats herself beside her, and strokes her hands*]. My dear Thea—how did this—this friendship—between you and Eilert Lövborg come about?

MRS. ELVSTED. Oh, it grew up gradually. I gained a sort of influence over him.

HEDDA. Indeed?

MRS. ELVSTED. He gave up his old habits. Not because I asked him to, for I never dared do that. But of course he saw how repulsive they were to me; and so he dropped them.

HEDDA [*concealing an involuntary smile of scorn*]. Then you have reclaimed him—as the saying goes—my little Thea.

MRS. ELVSTED. So he says himself, at any rate. And he, on his side, has made a real human being of me—taught me to think, and to understand so many things.

HEDDA. Did he give you lessons too, then?

MRS. ELVSTED. No, not exactly lessons. But he talked to me—talked about such an infinity of things. And then came the lovely, happy time when I began to share in his work—when he allowed me to help him!

HEDDA. Oh, he did, did he?

MRS. ELVSTED. Yes! He never wrote anything without my assistance.

HEDDA. You were two good comrades, in fact?

MRS. ELVSTED [*eagerly*]. Comrades! Yes, fancy, Hedda—that is the very word he used!—Oh, I ought to feel perfectly happy; and yet I cannot; for I don't know how long it will last.

HEDDA. Are you no surer of him than that?

MRS. ELVSTED [*gloomily*]. A woman's shadow stands between Eilert Lövborg and me.

HEDDA [*looks at her anxiously*]. Who can that be?

MRS. ELVSTED. I don't know. Some one he knew in his—in his past. Some one he has never been able wholly to forget.

HEDDA. What has he told you—about this?

MRS. ELVSTED. He has only once—quite vaguely—alluded to it.

HEDDA. Well! And what did he say?

MRS. ELVSTED. He said that when they parted, she threatened to shoot him with a pistol.

HEDDA [*with cold composure*]. Oh, nonsense! No one does that sort of thing here.

MRS. ELVSTED. No. And that is why I think it must have been that red-haired singing woman whom he once—

HEDDA. Yes, very likely.

MRS. ELVSTED. For I remember they used to say of her that she carried loaded firearms.

HEDDA. Oh—then of course it must have been she.

MRS. ELVSTED [*wringing her hands*]. And now just fancy, Hedda—I hear that this singing-woman—that she is in town again! Oh, I don't know what to do—

HEDDA [*glancing towards the inner room*]. Hush! Here comes Tesman. [*Rises and whispers.*] Thea—all this must remain between you and me.

MRS. ELVSTED [*springing up*]. Oh, yes, yes! for heaven's sake—!

[*George Tesman, with a letter in his hand, comes from the right through the inner room.*]

TESMAN. There now—the epistle is finished.

HEDDA. That's right. And now Mrs. Elvsted is just going. Wait a moment—I'll go with you to the garden gate.

TESMAN. Do you think Berta could post the letter, Hedda dear?

HEDDA [*takes it*]. I will tell her so.

[BERTA *enters from the hall.*]

BERTA. Judge Brack wishes to know if Mrs. Tesman will receive him.

HEDDA. Yes, ask Judge Brack to come in. And look here—put this letter in the post.

BERTA [*taking the letter*]. Yes, ma'am.

[*She opens the door for* JUDGE BRACK *and goes out herself.* BRACK *is a man of forty-five; thick-set, but well-built and elastic in his movements. His face is roundish with an aristocratic profile. His hair is short, still almost black, and carefully dressed. His eyes are lively and sparkling. His eyebrows thick. His moustaches are also thick, with short-cut ends. He wears a well-cut walking-suit, a little too youthful for his age. He uses an eye-glass, which he now and then lets drop.*]

JUDGE BRACK [*with his hat in his hand, bowing*]. May one venture to call so early in the day?

HEDDA. Of course one may.

TESMAN [*presses his hand*]. You are welcome at any time. [*Introducing him.*] Judge Brack—Miss Rysing—

HEDDA. Oh—!

BRACK [*bowing*]. Ah—delighted—

HEDDA [*looks at him and laughs*]. It's nice to have a look at you by daylight, Judge!

BRACK. Do you find me—altered?

HEDDA. A little younger, I think.

BRACK. Thank you so much.

TESMAN. But what do you think of Hedda—eh? Doesn't she look flourishing? She has actually—

HEDDA. Oh, do leave me alone. You haven't thanked Judge Brack for all the trouble he has taken—

BRACK. Oh, nonsense—it was a pleasure to me—

HEDDA. Yes, you are a friend indeed. But here stands Thea all impatience to be off—so *au revoir,* Judge. I shall be back again presently. [*Mutual salutations.* MRS. ELVSTED *and* HEDDA *go out by the hall door.*]

BRACK. Well,—is your wife tolerably satisfied—

TESMAN. Yes, we can't thank you sufficiently. Of course she talks of a little rearrangement here and there; and one or two things are still wanting. We shall have to buy some additional trifles.

BRACK. Indeed!

TESMAN. But we won't trouble you about these things. Hedda says she herself will look after what is wanting.—Shan't we sit down? Eh?

BRACK. Thanks, for a moment. [*Seats himself beside the table.*] There is something I wanted to speak to you about, my dear Tesman.

TESMAN. Indeed? Ah, I understand! [*Seating himself.*] I suppose it's the serious part of the frolic that is coming now. Eh?

BRACK. Oh, the money question is not so very pressing; though, for that matter, I wish we had gone a little more economically to work.

TESMAN. But that would never have done, you know! Think of Hedda, my dear fellow! You, who know her so well—. I couldn't possibly ask her to put up with a shabby style of living!

BRACK. No, no—that is just the difficulty.

TESMAN. And then—fortunately—it can't be long before I receive my appointment.

BRACK. Well, you see—such things are often apt to hang fire for a time.

TESMAN. Have you heard anything definite? Eh?

BRACK. Nothing exactly definite—[*interrupting himself*]. But by-the-bye—I have one piece of news for you.

TESMAN. Well?

BRACK. Your old friend, Eilert Lövborg, has returned to town.

TESMAN. I know that already.

BRACK. Indeed! How did you learn it?

TESMAN. From that lady who went out with Hedda.

BRACK. Really? What was her name? I didn't quite catch it.

TESMAN. Mrs. Elvsted.

BRACK. Aha—Sheriff Elvsted's wife? Of course—he has been living up in their regions.

TESMAN. And fancy—I'm delighted to hear that he is quite a reformed character!

BRACK. So they say.

TESMAN. And then he has published a new book—eh?

BRACK. Yes, indeed he has.

TESMAN. And I hear it has made some sensation!

BRACK. Quite an unusual sensation.

TESMAN. Fancy—isn't that good news! A man of such extraordinary talents—I felt so grieved to think that he had gone irretrievably to ruin.

BRACK. That was what everybody thought.

TESMAN. But I cannot imagine what he will take to now! How in the world will he be able to make his living? Eh?

[*During the last words,* HEDDA *has entered by the hall door.*]

HEDDA [*to* BRACK, *laughing with a touch of scorn*]. Tesman is forever worrying about how people are to make their living.

TESMAN. Well, you see, dear—we were talking about poor Eilert Lövborg.

HEDDA [*glancing at him rapidly*]. Oh, indeed? [*Seats herself in the arm-chair beside the stove and asks indifferently.*] What is the matter with him?

TESMAN. Well—no doubt he has run through all his property long ago; and he can scarcely write a new book every year—eh? So I really can't see what is to become of him.

BRACK. Perhaps I can give you some information on that point.

TESMAN. Indeed!

BRACK. You must remember that his relations have a good deal of influence.

TESMAN. Oh, his relations, unfortunately have entirely washed their hands of him.

BRACK. At one time they called him the hope of the family.

TESMAN. At one time, yes! But he has put an end to all that.

HEDDA. Who knows? [*With a slight smile.*] I hear they have reclaimed him up at Sheriff Elvsted's—

BRACK. And then this book that he has published—

TESMAN. Well, well, I hope to goodness they may find something for him to do. I have just written to him. I asked him to come and see us this evening, Hedda dear.

BRACK. But, my dear fellow, you are booked for my bachelors' party this evening. You promised on the pier last night.

HEDDA. Had you forgotten, Tesman?

TESMAN. Yes, I had utterly forgotten.

BRACK. But it doesn't matter, for you may be sure he won't come.

TESMAN. What makes you think that? Eh?

BRACK [*with a little hesitation, rising and resting his hands on the back of his chair*]. My
  dear Tesman—and you too, Mrs. Tesman—I think I ought not to keep you in
  the dark about something that—that—
TESMAN. That concerns Eilert—?
BRACK. Both you and him.
TESMAN. Well, my dear Judge, out with it.
BRACK. You must be prepared to find your appointment deferred longer than you
  desired or expected.
TESMAN [*jumping up uneasily*]. Is there some hitch about it? Eh?
BRACK. The nomination may perhaps be made conditional on the result of a
  competition—
TESMAN. Competition! Think of that, Hedda!
HEDDA [*leans farther back in the chair*]. Aha—aha!
TESMAN. But who can my competitor be? Surely not—?
BRACK. Yes, precisely—Eilert Lövborg.
TESMAN [*clasping his hands*]. No, no—it's quite inconceivable! Quite impossible!
  Eh?
BRACK. H'm—that is what it may come to, all the same.
TESMAN. Well but, Judge Brack—it would show the most incredible lack of consid-
  eration for me. [*Gesticulates with his arms.*] For—just think—I'm a married man.
  We have been married on the strength of these prospects, Hedda and I; and run
  deep into debt; and borrowed money from Aunt Julia too. Good heavens, they
  had as good as promised me the appointment. Eh?
BRACK. Well, well, well—no doubt you will get it in the end; only after a contest.
HEDDA [*immovable in her arm-chair*]. Fancy, Tesman, there will be a sort of sporting
  interest in that.
TESMAN. Why, my dearest Hedda, how can you be so indifferent about it?
HEDDA [*as before*]. I am not at all indifferent. I am most eager to see who wins.
BRACK. In any case, Mrs. Tesman, it is best that you should know how matters stand.
  I mean—before you set about the little purchases I hear you are threatening.
HEDDA. This can make no difference.
BRACK. Indeed! Then I have no more to say. Good-bye! [*To* TESMAN.] I shall look in
  on my way back from my afternoon walk, and take you home with me.
TESMAN. Oh yes, yes—your news has quite upset me.
HEDDA [*reclining, holds out her hand*]. Good-bye, Judge; and be sure you call in the
  afternoon.
BRACK. Many thanks. Good-bye, good-bye!
TESMAN [*accompanying him to the door*]. Good-bye, my dear Judge! You must really
  excuse me—
[JUDGE BRACK *goes out by the hall door.*]
TESMAN [*crosses the room*]. Oh, Hedda—one should never rush into adventures. Eh?
HEDDA [*looks at him, smiling*]. Do you do that?
TESMAN. Yes, dear—there is no denying—it was adventurous to go and marry and
  set up house upon mere expectations.
HEDDA. Perhaps you are right there.
TESMAN. Well—at all events, we have our delightful home, Hedda! Fancy, the home
  we both dreamed of—the home we were in love with, I may almost say. Eh?
HEDDA [*rising slowly and wearily*]. It was part of our compact that we were to go into
  society—to keep open house.
TESMAN. Yes, if you only knew how I had been looking forward to it! Fancy—to see
  you as hostess—in a select circle? Eh? Well, well, well—for the present we shall

have to get on without society, Hedda—only to invite Aunt Julia now and then.—Oh, I intended you to lead such an utterly different life, dear—!

HEDDA. Of course I cannot have my man in livery just yet.

TESMAN. Oh no, unfortunately. It would be out of the question for us to keep a footman, you know.

HEDDA. And the saddle-horse I was to have had—

TESMAN [*aghast*]. The saddle-horse!

HEDDA. —I suppose I must not think of that now.

TESMAN. Good heavens, no!—that's as clear as daylight.

HEDDA [*goes up the room*]. Well, I shall have one thing at least to kill time with in the meanwhile.

TESMAN [*beaming*]. Oh, thank heaven for that! What is it, Hedda? Eh?

HEDDA [*in the middle doorway, looks at him with covert scorn*]. My pistols, George.

TESMAN [*in alarm*]. Your pistols!

HEDDA [*with cold eyes*]. General Gabler's pistols.

[*She goes out through the inner room, to the left.*]

TESMAN [*rushes up to the middle doorway and calls after her.*] No, for heaven's sake, Hedda darling—don't touch those dangerous things! For my sake, Hedda! Eh?

ACT II

The room at the TESMANS' *as in the first act, except that the piano has been removed, and an elegant little writing-table with bookshelves put in its place. A smaller table stands near the sofa at the left. Most of the bouquets have been taken away.* MRS. ELVSTED's *bouquet is upon the large table in front. — It is afternoon.*

HEDDA, *dressed to receive callers, is alone in the room. She stands by the open glass door, loading a revolver. The fellow to it lies in an open pistol-case on the writing-table.*

HEDDA [*looks down the garden, and calls*]. So you are here again, Judge!

BRACK [*is heard calling from a distance*]. As you see, Mrs. Tesman!

HEDDA [*raises the pistol and points*]. Now I'll shoot you, Judge Brack!

BRACK [*calling unseen*]. No, no, no! Don't stand aiming at me!

HEDDA. This is what comes of sneaking in by the back way. [*She fires.*]

BRACK [*nearer*]. Are you out of your senses—!

HEDDA. Dear me—did I happen to hit you?

BRACK [*still outside*]. I wish you would let these pranks alone!

HEDDA. Come in then, Judge.

[JUDGE BRACK, *dressed as though for a men's party, enters by the glass door. He carries a light overcoat over his arm.*]

BRACK. What the deuce—haven't you tired of that sport, yet? What are you shooting at?

HEDDA. Oh, I am only firing in the air.

BRACK [*gently takes the pistol out of her hand*]. Allow me, madam! [*Looks at it.*] Ah—I know this pistol well! [*Looks around.*] Where is the case? Ah, here it is. [*Lays the pistol in it, and shuts it.*] Now we won't play at that game any more today.

HEDDA. Then what in heaven's name would you have me do with myself?

BRACK. Have you had no visitors?

HEDDA [*closing the glass door*]. Not one. I suppose all our set are still out of town.

BRACK. And is Tesman not at home either?

HEDDA [*at the writing-table, putting the pistol-case in a drawer which she shuts*]. No. He rushed off to his aunt's directly after lunch; he didn't expect you so early.

BRACK. H'm—how stupid of me not to have thought of that!

HEDDA [*turning her head to look at him*]. Why stupid?

BRACK. Because if I had thought of it I should have come a little—earlier.

HEDDA [*crossing the room*]. Then you would have found no one to receive you; for I have been in my room changing my dress ever since lunch.

BRACK. And is there no sort of little chink that we could hold a parley through?

HEDDA. You have forgotten to arrange one.

BRACK. That was another piece of stupidity.

HEDDA. Well, we must just settle down here—and wait. Tesman is not likely to be back for some time yet.

BRACK. Never mind; I shall not be impatient.

[HEDDA *seats herself in the corner of the sofa.* BRACK *lays his overcoat over the back of the nearest chair, and sits down, but keeps his hat in his hand. A short silence. They look at each other.*]

HEDDA. Well?

BRACK [*in the same tone*]. Well?

HEDDA. I spoke first.

BRACK [*bending a little forward*]. Come, let us have a cosy little chat, Mrs. Hedda.

HEDDA [*leaning further back in the sofa*]. Does it not seem like a whole eternity since our last talk? Of course I don't count those few words yesterday evening and this morning.

BRACK. You mean since our last confidential talk? Our last *tête-à-tête*?[7]

HEDDA. Well, yes—since you put it so.

BRACK. Not a day has passed but I have wished that you were home again.

HEDDA. And I have done nothing but wish the same thing.

BRACK. You? Really, Mrs. Hedda? And I thought you had been enjoying your tour so much!

HEDDA. Oh, yes, you may be sure of that!

BRACK. But Tesman's letters spoke of nothing but happiness.

HEDDA. Oh, Tesman! You see, he thinks nothing so delightful as grubbing in libraries and making copies of old parchments, or whatever you call them.

BRACK [*with a spice of malice*]. Well, that is his vocation in life—or part of it at any rate.

HEDDA. Yes, of course; and no doubt when it's your vocation—But *I!* Oh, my dear Mr. Brack, how mortally bored I have been.

BRACK [*sympathetically*]. Do you really say so? In downright earnest?

HEDDA. Yes, you can surely understand it—! To go for six whole months without meeting a soul that knew anything of our circle, or could talk about the things we are interested in.

BRACK. Yes, yes—I too should feel that a deprivation.

HEDDA. And then, what I found most intolerable of all—

BRACK. Well?

HEDDA. —was being everlastingly in the company of—one and the same person—

BRACK [*with a nod of assent*]. Morning, noon, and night, yes—at all possible times and seasons.

HEDDA. I said "everlastingly."

BRACK. Just so. But I should have thought, with our excellent Tesman, one could—

HEDDA. Tesman is—a specialist, my dear Judge.

BRACK. Undeniably.

---

[7] Private conversation.

HEDDA. And specialists are not at all amusing to travel with. Not in the long run at any rate.

BRACK. Not even—the specialist one happens to love?

HEDDA. Faugh—don't use that sickening word!

BRACK [*taken aback*]. What do you say, Mrs. Hedda?

HEDDA [*half laughing, half irritated*]. You should just try it! To hear of nothing but the history of civilization, morning, noon, and night—

BRACK. Everlastingly.

HEDDA. Yes, yes, yes! And then all this about the domestic industry of the middle ages—! That's the most disgusting part of it!

BRACK [*looks searchingly at her*]. But tell me—in that case, how am I to understand your—? H'm—

HEDDA. My accepting George Tesman, you mean?

BRACK. Well, let us put it so.

HEDDA. Good heavens, do you see anything so wonderful in that?

BRACK. Yes and no—Mrs. Hedda.

HEDDA. I had positively danced myself tired, my dear Judge. My day was done— [*With a slight shudder.*] Oh no—I won't say that; nor think it either!

BRACK. You have assuredly no reason to.

HEDDA. Oh, reasons—[*Watching him closely.*] And George Tesman—after all, you must admit that he is correctness itself.

BRACK. His correctness and respectability are beyond all question.

HEDDA. And I don't see anything absolutely ridiculous about him.—Do you?

BRACK. Ridiculous? N—no—I shouldn't exactly say so—

HEDDA. Well—and his powers of research, at all events, are untiring.—I see no reason why he should not one day come to the front, after all.

BRACK [*looks at her hesitatingly*]. I thought that you, like every one else, expected him to attain the highest distinction.

HEDDA [*with an expression of fatigue*]. Yes, so I did.—And then, since he was bent, at all hazards, on being allowed to provide for me—I really don't know why I should not have accepted his offer?

BRACK. No—if you look at it in that light—

HEDDA. It was more than my other adorers were prepared to do for me, my dear Judge.

BRACK [*laughing*]. Well, I can't answer for all the rest; but as for myself, you know quite well that I have always entertained a—a certain respect for the marriage tie—for marriage as an institution, Mrs. Hedda.

HEDDA [*jestingly*]. Oh, I assure you I have never cherished any hopes with respect to you.

BRACK. All I require is a pleasant and intimate interior, where I can make myself useful in every way, and am free to come and go as—a trusted friend—

HEDDA. Of the master of the house, do you mean?

BRACK [*bowing*]. Frankly—of the mistress first of all; but of course of the master, too, in the second place. Such a triangular friendship—if I may call it so—is really a great convenience for all parties, let me tell you.

HEDDA. Yes, I have many a time longed for some one to make a third on our travels. Oh—those railway-carriage *tête-à-têtes*—!

BRACK. Fortunately your wedding journey is over now.

HEDDA [*shaking her head*]. Not by a long—long way. I have only arrived at a station on the line.

BRACK. Well, then the passengers jump out and move about a little, Mrs. Hedda.

HEDDA. I never jump out.

BRACK. Really?

HEDDA. No—because there is always some one standing by to—

BRACK [*laughing*]. To look at your ankles, do you mean?

HEDDA. Precisely.

BRACK. Well but, dear me—

HEDDA [*with a gesture of repulsion*]. I won't have it. I would rather keep my seat where I happen to be—and continue the *tête-à-tête*.

BRACK. But suppose a third person were to jump in and join the couple.

HEDDA. Ah—that is quite another matter!

BRACK. A trusted, sympathetic friend—

HEDDA. —with a fund of conversation on all sorts of lively topics—

BRACK. —and not the least bit of a specialist!

HEDDA [*with an audible sigh*]. Yes, that would be a relief indeed.

BRACK [*hears the front door open, and glances in that direction*]. The triangle is completed.

HEDDA [*half aloud*]. And on goes the train.

[GEORGE TESMAN, *in a gray walking-suit, with a soft felt hat, enters from the hall. He has a number of unbound books under his arm and in his pockets.*]

TESMAN [*goes up to the table beside the corner settee*]. Ouf—what a load for a warm day—all these books. [*Lays them on the table.*] I'm positively perspiring, Hedda. Hallo—are you there already, my dear Judge? Eh? Berta didn't tell me.

BRACK [*rising*]. I came in through the garden.

HEDDA. What books have you got here?

TESMAN [*stands looking them through*]. Some new books on my special subjects— quite indispensable to me.

HEDDA. Your special subjects?

BRACK. Yes, books on his special subjects, Mrs. Tesman. [BRACK *and* HEDDA *exchange a confidential smile.*]

HEDDA. Do you need still more books on your special subjects?

TESMAN. Yes, my dear Hedda, one can never have too many of them. Of course one must keep up with all that is written and published.

HEDDA. Yes, I suppose one must.

TESMAN [*searching among his books*]. And look here—I have got hold of Eilert Lövborg's new book too. [*Offering it to her.*] Perhaps you would like to glance through it, Hedda? Eh?

HEDDA. No, thank you. Or rather—afterwards perhaps.

TESMAN. I looked into it a little on the way home.

BRACK. Well, what do you think of it—as a specialist?

TESMAN. I think it shows quite remarkable soundness of judgment. He never wrote like that before. [*Putting the books together.*] Now I shall take all these into my study. I'm longing to cut the leaves—! And then I must change my clothes. [*To* BRACK.] I suppose we needn't start just yet? Eh?

BRACK. Oh, dear no—there is not the slightest hurry.

TESMAN. Well then, I will take my time. [*Is going with his books, but stops in the doorway and turns.*] By-the-bye, Hedda—Aunt Julia is not coming this evening.

HEDDA. Not coming? Is it that affair of the bonnet that keeps her away?

TESMAN. Oh, not at all. How could you think such a thing of Aunt Julia? Just fancy—! The fact is, Aunt Rina is very ill.

HEDDA. She always is.

TESMAN. Yes, but today she is much worse than usual, poor dear.

HEDDA. Oh, then it's only natural that her sister should remain with her. I must bear my disappointment.

TESMAN. And you can't imagine, dear, how delighted Aunt Julia seemed to be—because you had come home looking so flourishing!

HEDDA [*half aloud, rising*]. Oh, those everlasting aunts!

TESMAN. What?

HEDDA [*going to the glass door*]. Nothing.

TESMAN. Oh, all right.

[*He goes through the inner room, out to the right.*]

BRACK. What bonnet were you talking about?

HEDDA. Oh, it was a little episode with Miss Tesman this morning. She had laid down her bonnet on the chair there—[*looks at him and smiles*]. —And I pretended to think it was the servant's.

BRACK [*shaking his head*]. Now my dear Mrs. Hedda, how could you do such a thing? To that excellent old lady, too!

HEDDA [*nervously crossing the room*]. Well, you see—these impulses come over me all of a sudden; and I cannot resist them. [*Throws herself down in the easy-chair by the stove.*] Oh, I don't know how to explain it.

BRACK [*behind the easy-chair*]. You are not really happy—that is at the bottom of it.

HEDDA [*looking straight before her*]. I know of no reason why I should be—happy. Perhaps you can give me one?

BRACK. Well—amongst other things, because you have got exactly the home you had set your heart on.

HEDDA [*looks up at him and laughs*]. Do you too believe in that legend?

BRACK. Is there nothing in it, then?

HEDDA. Oh, yes, there is something in it.

BRACK. Well?

HEDDA. There is this in it, that I made use of Tesman to see me home from evening parties last summer—

BRACK. I, unfortunately, had to go quite a different way.

HEDDA. That's true. I know you were going a different way last summer.

BRACK [*laughing*]. Oh fie, Mrs. Hedda! Well, then—you and Tesman—?

HEDDA. Well, we happened to pass here one evening; Tesman, poor fellow, was writhing in the agony of having to find conversation; so I took pity on the learned man—

BRACK [*smiles doubtfully*]. You took pity? H'm—

HEDDA. Yes, I really did. And so—to help him out of his torment—I happened to say, in pure thoughtlessness, that I should like to live in this villa.

BRACK. No more than that?

HEDDA. Not that evening.

BRACK. But afterwards?

HEDDA. Yes, my thoughtlessness had consequences, my dear Judge.

BRACK. Unfortunately that too often happens, Mrs. Hedda.

HEDDA. Thanks! So you see it was this enthusiasm for Secretary Falk's villa that first constituted a bond of sympathy between George Tesman and me. From that came our engagement and our marriage, and our wedding journey, and all the rest of it. Well, well, my dear Judge—as you make your bed so you must lie, I could almost say.

BRACK. This is exquisite! And you really cared not a rap about it all the time?

HEDDA. No, heaven knows I didn't.

BRACK. But now? Now that we have made it so homelike for you?

HEDDA. Uh—the rooms all seem to smell of lavender and dried rose-leaves. —But perhaps it's Aunt Julia that has brought that scent with her.

BRACK [*laughing*]. No, I think it must be a legacy from the late Mrs. Secretary Falk.

HEDDA. Yes, there is an odor of mortality about it. It reminds me of a bouquet—the day after the ball. [*Clasps her hands behind her head, leans back in her chair and looks at him.*] Oh, my dear Judge—you cannot imagine how horribly I shall bore myself here.

BRACK. Why should not you, too, find some sort of vocation in life, Mrs. Hedda?

HEDDA. A vocation—that should attract me?

BRACK. If possible, of course.

HEDDA. Heaven knows what sort of a vocation that could be. I often wonder whether—[*breaking off*]. But that would never do either.

BRACK. Who can tell? Let me hear what it is.

HEDDA. Whether I might not get Tesman to go into politics, I mean.

BRACK [*laughing*]. Tesman? No, really now, political life is not the thing for him— not at all in his line.

HEDDA. No, I daresay not. —But if I could get him into it all the same?

BRACK. Why—what satisfaction could you find in that? If he is not fitted for that sort of thing, why should you want to drive him into it?

HEDDA. Because I am bored, I tell you! [*After a pause.*] So you think it quite out of the question that Tesman should ever get into the ministry?

BRACK. H'm—you see, my dear Mrs. Hedda—to get into the ministry, he would have to be a tolerably rich man.

HEDDA [*rising impatiently*]. Yes, there we have it! It is this genteel poverty I have managed to drop into—! [*Crosses the room.*] That is what makes life so pitiable! So utterly ludicrous! —For that's what it is.

BRACK. Now *I* should say the fault lay elsewhere.

HEDDA. Where, then?

BRACK. You have never gone through any really stimulating experience.

HEDDA. Anything serious, you mean?

BRACK. Yes, you may call it so. But now you may perhaps have one in store.

HEDDA [*tossing her head*]. Oh, you're thinking of the annoyances about this wretched professorship! But that must be Tesman's own affair. I assure you I shall not waste a thought upon it.

BRACK. No, no. I daresay not. But suppose now that what people call—in elegant language—a solemn responsibility were to come upon you? [*Smiling.*] A new responsibility, Mrs. Hedda?

HEDDA [*angrily*]. Be quiet! Nothing of that sort will ever happen!

BRACK [*warily*]. We will speak of this again a year hence—at the very outside.

HEDDA [*curtly*]. I have no turn for anything of the sort, Judge Brack. No responsibilities for me!

BRACK. Are you so unlike the generality of women as to have no turn for duties which—?

HEDDA [*beside the glass door*]. Oh, be quiet, I tell you!—I often think there is only one thing in the world I have any turn for.

BRACK [*drawing near to her*]. And what is that, if I may ask?

HEDDA [*stands looking out*]. Boring myself to death. Now you know it. [*Turns, looks towards the inner room, and laughs.*] Yes, as I thought! Here comes the Professor.

BRACK [*softly, in a tone of warning*]. Come, come, come, Mrs. Hedda!

[GEORGE TESMAN, *dressed for the party, with his gloves and hat in his hand, enters from the right through the inner room.*]

TESMAN. Hedda, has no message come from Eilert Lövborg? Eh?

HEDDA. No.

TESMAN. Then you'll see he'll be here presently.

BRACK. Do you really think he will come?

TESMAN. Yes, I am almost sure of it. For what you were telling us this morning must have been a mere floating rumor.

BRACK. You think so?

TESMAN. At any rate, Aunt Julia said she did not believe for a moment that he would ever stand in my way again. Fancy that!

BRACK. Well then, that's all right.

TESMAN [*placing his hat and gloves on a chair on the right*]. Yes, but you must really let me wait for him as long as possible.

BRACK. We have plenty of time yet. None of my guests will arrive before seven or half-past.

TESMAN. Then meanwhile we can keep Hedda company, and see what happens. Eh?

HEDDA [*placing* BRACK's *hat and overcoat upon the corner settee*]. And at the worst Mr. Lövborg can remain here with me.

BRACK [*offering to take his things*]. Oh, allow me, Mrs. Tesman!—What do you mean by "At the worst"?

HEDDA. If he won't go with you and Tesman.

TESMAN [*looks dubiously at her*]. But, Hedda dear—do you think it would quite do for him to remain with you? Eh? Remember, Aunt Julia can't come.

HEDDA. No, but Mrs. Elvsted is coming. We three can have a cup of tea together.

TESMAN. Oh, yes, that will be all right.

BRACK [*smiling*]. And that would perhaps be the safest plan for him.

HEDDA. Why so?

BRACK. Well, you know, Mrs. Tesman, how you used to gird at my little bachelor parties. You declared they were adapted only for men of the strictest principles.

HEDDA. But no doubt Mr. Lövborg's principles are strict enough now. A converted sinner—

[BERTA *appears at the hall door.*]

BERTA. There's a gentleman asking if you are at home, ma'am—

HEDDA. Well, show him in.

TESMAN [*softly*]. I'm sure it is he! Fancy that!

[EILERT LÖVBORG *enters from the hall. He is slim and lean; of the same age as* TESMAN, *but looks older and somewhat worn-out. His hair and beard are of a blackish brown, his face long and pale, but with patches of color on the cheek-bones. He is dressed in a well-cut black visiting suit, quite new. He has dark gloves and a silk hat. He stops near the door, and makes a rapid bow, seeming somewhat embarrassed.*]

TESMAN [*goes up to him and shakes him warmly by the hand*]. Well, my dear Eilert—so at last we meet again!

ELERT LÖVBORG [*speaks in a subdued voice*]. Thanks for your letter, Tesman. [*Approaching* HEDDA.] Will you too shake hands with me, Mrs. Tesman?

HEDDA [*taking his hand*]. I am glad to see you, Mr. Lövborg. [*With a motion of her hand.*] I don't know whether you two gentlemen—?

LÖVBORG [*bowing slightly*]. Judge Brack, I think.

BRACK [*doing likewise*]. Oh, yes,—in the old days—

TESMAN [*to* LÖVBORG, *with his hands on his shoulders*]. And now you must make yourself entirely at home, Eilert! Mustn't he, Hedda?—For I hear you are going to settle in town again? Eh?

LÖVBORG. Yes, I am.

TESMAN. Quite right, quite right. Let me tell you, I have got hold of your new book; but I haven't had time to read it yet.

LÖVBORG. You may spare yourself the trouble.

TESMAN. Why so?

LÖVBORG. Because there is very little in it.

TESMAN. Just fancy—how can you say so?

BRACK. But it has been very much praised, I hear.

LÖVBORG. That was what I wanted; so I put nothing into the book but what every one would agree with.

BRACK. Very wise of you.

TESMAN. Well but, my dear Eilert—!

LÖVBORG. For now I mean to win myself a position again—to make a fresh start.

TESMAN [*a little embarrassed*]. Ah, that is what you wish to do? Eh?

LÖVBORG [*smiling, lays down his hat, and draws a packet, wrapped in paper, from his coat pocket*]. But when this one appears, George Tesman, you will have to read it. For this is the real book—the book I have put my true self into.

TESMAN. Indeed? And what is it?

LÖVBORG. It is the continuation.

TESMAN. The continuation? Of what?

LÖVBORG. Of the book.

TESMAN. Of the new book?

LÖVBORG. Of course.

TESMAN. Why, my dear Eilert—does it not come down to our own days?

LÖVBORG. Yes, it does; and this one deals with the future.

TESMAN. With the future! But, good heavens, we know nothing of the future!

LÖVBORG. No; but there is a thing or two to be said about it all the same. [*Opens the packet.*] Look here—

TESMAN. Why, that's not your handwriting.

LÖVBORG. I dictated it. [*Turning over the pages.*] It falls into two sections. The first deals with the civilizing forces of the future. And here is the second—[*running through the pages towards the end*]—forecasting the probable line of development.

TESMAN. How odd now! I should never have thought of writing anything of that sort.

HEDDA [*at the glass door, drumming on the pane*]. H'm—I daresay not.

LÖVBORG [*replacing the manuscript in its paper and laying the packet on the table*]. I brought it, thinking I might read you a little of it this evening.

TESMAN. That was very good to you, Eilert. But this evening—? [*Looking at* BRACK.] I don't quite see how we can manage it—

LÖVBORG. Well then, some other time. There is no hurry.

BRACK. I must tell you, Mr. Lövborg—there is a little gathering at my house this evening—mainly in honor of Tesman, you know—

LÖVBORG [*looking for his hat*]. Oh—then I won't detain you—

BRACK. No, but listen—will you not do me the favor of joining us?

LÖVBORG [*curtly and decidedly*]. No, I can't—thank you very much.

BRACK. Oh, nonsense—do! We shall be quite a select little circle. And I assure you we shall have a "lively time," as Mrs. Hed—as Mrs. Tesman says.

LÖVBORG. I have no doubt of it. But nevertheless—

BRACK. And then you might bring your manuscript with you, and read it to Tesman at my house. I could give you a room to yourselves.

TESMAN. Yes, think of that, Eilert,—why shouldn't you? Eh?

HEDDA [*interposing*]. But, Tesman, if Mr. Lövborg would really rather not! I am sure Mr. Lövborg is much more inclined to remain here and have supper with me.

LÖVBORG [*looking at her*]. With you, Mrs. Tesman?

HEDDA. And with Mrs. Elvsted.

LÖVBORG. Ah—[*Lightly.*] I saw her for a moment this morning.

HEDDA. Did you? Well, she is coming this evening. So you see you are almost bound to remain, Mr. Lövborg, or she will have no one to see her home.

LÖVBORG. That's true. Many thanks, Mrs. Tesman—in that case I will remain.

HEDDA. Then I have one or two orders to give the servant—

[*She goes to the hall door and rings.* BERTA *enters.* HEDDA *talks to her in a whisper, and points towards the inner room.* BERTA *nods and goes out again.*]

TESMAN [*at the same time, to* LÖVBORG]. Tell me, Eilert—is it this new subject—the future—that you are going to lecture about?

LÖVBORG. Yes.

TESMAN. They told me at the bookseller's, that you are going to deliver a course of lectures this autumn.

LÖVBORG. That is my intention. I hope you won't take it ill, Tesman.

TESMAN. Oh no, not in the least! But—?

LÖVBORG. I can quite understand that it must be disagreeable to you.

TESMAN [*cast down*]. Oh, I can't expect you, out of consideration for me, to—

LÖVBORG. But I shall wait till you have received your appointment.

TESMAN. Will you wait? Yes, but—yes, but—are you not going to compete with me? Eh?

LÖVBORG. No; it is only the moral victory I care for.

TESMAN. Why, bless me—then Aunt Julia was right after all! Oh yes—I knew it! Hedda! Just fancy—Eilert Lövborg is not going to stand in our way!

HEDDA [*curtly*]. Our way? Pray leave me out of the question.

[*She goes up towards the inner room, where* BERTA *is placing a tray with decanters and glasses on the table.* HEDDA *nods approval, and comes forward again.* BERTA *goes out.*]

TESMAN [*at the same time*]. And you, Judge Brack—what do you say to this? Eh?

BRACK. Well, I say that a moral victory—h'm—may be all very fine—

TESMAN. Yes, certainly. But all the same—

HEDDA [*looking at* TESMAN *with a cold smile*]. You stand there looking as if you were thunderstruck—

TESMAN. Yes—so I am—I almost think—

BRACK. Don't you see, Mrs. Tesman, a thunderstorm has just passed over?

HEDDA [*pointing towards the inner room*]. Will you not take a glass of cold punch, gentlemen?

BRACK [*looking at his watch*]. A stirrup-cup? Yes, it wouldn't come amiss.

TESMAN. A capital idea, Hedda! just the thing! Now that the weight has been taken off my mind—

HEDDA. Will you not join them, Mr. Lövborg?

LÖVBORG [*with a gesture of refusal*]. No, thank you. Nothing for me.

BRACK. Why, bless me—cold punch is surely not poison.

LÖVBORG. Perhaps not for every one.

HEDDA. I will keep Mr. Lövborg company in the meantime.

TESMAN. Yes, yes, Hedda dear, do.

[*He and* BRACK *go into the inner room, seat themselves, drink punch, smoke cigarettes, and carry on a lively conversation during what follows.* EILERT LÖVBORG *remains beside the stove.* HEDDA *goes to the writing-table.*]

HEDDA [*raising her voice a little*]. Do you care to look at some photographs, Mr. Lövborg? You know Tesman and I made a tour in the Tyrol[8] on our way home?

[*She takes up an album, and places it on the table beside the sofa, in the further corner of which she seats herself.* EILERT LÖVBORG *approaches, stops, and looks at her. Then he takes a chair and seats himself at her left, with his back towards the inner room.*]

HEDDA [*opening the album*]. Do you see this range of mountains, Mr. Lövborg? It's the Ortler group. Tesman has written the name underneath. Here it is: "The Ortler group near Meran."

LÖVBORG [*who has never taken his eyes off her, says softly and slowly*]. Hedda—Gabler!

HEDDA [*glancing hastily at him*]. Ah! Hush!

LÖVBORG [*repeats softly*]. Hedda Gabler!

HEDDA [*looking at the album*]. That was my name in the old days—when we two knew each other.

LÖVBORG. And I must teach myself never to say Hedda Gabler again—never, as long as I live.

HEDDA [*still turning over the pages*]. Yes, you must. And I think you ought to practice in time. The sooner the better, I should say.

LÖVBORG [*in a tone of indignation*]. Hedda Gabler married? And married to—George Tesman!

HEDDA. Yes—so the world goes.

LÖVBORG. Oh, Hedda, Hedda—how could you[9] throw yourself away!

HEDDA [*looks sharply at him*]. What? I can't allow this!

LÖVBORG. What do you mean? [TESMAN *comes into the room and goes towards the sofa.*]

HEDDA [*hears him coming and says in an indifferent tone*]. And this is a view from the Val d'Ampezzo, Mr. Lövborg. Just look at these peaks! [*Looks affectionately up at* TESMAN.] What's the name of these curious peaks, dear?

TESMAN. Let me see? Oh, those are the Dolomites.

HEDDA. Yes, that's it—Those are the Dolomites, Mr. Lövborg.

TESMAN. Hedda dear,—I only wanted to ask whether I shouldn't bring you a little punch after all? For yourself at any rate—eh?

HEDDA. Yes, do, please; and perhaps a few biscuits.

TESMAN. No cigarettes?

HEDDA. No.

TESMAN. Very well.

[*He goes into the inner room and out to the right.* BRACK *sits in the inner room, and keeps an eye from time to time on* HEDDA *and* LÖVBORG.]

LÖVBORG [*softly, as before*]. Answer me, Hedda—how could you go and do this?

HEDDA [*apparently absorbed in the album*]. If you continue to say *du* to me I won't talk to you.

LÖVBORG. May I not say *du* when we are alone?

HEDDA. No. You may think it: but you mustn't say it.

LÖVBORG. Ah, I understand. It is an offense against George Tesman, whom you[10] —love.

HEDDA [*glances at him and smiles*]. Love? What an idea!

---

[8] The Tyrolese mountains discussed in the subsquent exchanges are all in Northern Italy near the Austrian border.
[9] Lövborg uses the intimate pronoun *du*.
[10] Here Lövborg begins using the formal pronoun *de*.

Lövborg. You don't love him then!

Hedda. But I won't hear of any sort of unfaithfulness! Remember that.

Lövborg. Hedda—answer me one thing—

Hedda. Hush!

[Tesman *enters with a small tray from the inner room.*]

Tesman. Here you are! Isn't this tempting? [*He puts the tray on the table.*]

Hedda. Why do you bring it yourself?

Tesman [*filling the glasses*]. Because I think it's such fun to wait upon you, Hedda.

Hedda. But you have poured out two glasses. Mr. Lövborg said he wouldn't have any—

Tesman. No, but Mrs. Elvsted will soon be here, won't she?

Hedda. Yes, by-the-bye—Mrs. Elvsted—

Tesman. Had you forgotten her? Eh?

Hedda. We were so absorbed in these photographs. [*Shows him a picture.*] Do you remember this little village?

Tesman. Oh, it's that one just below the Brenner Pass. It was there we passed the night—

Hedda. —and met that lively party of tourists.

Tesman. Yes, that was the place. Fancy—if we could only have had you with us, Eilert! Eh? [*He returns to the inner room and sits beside* Brack.]

Lövborg. Answer me this one thing, Hedda—

Hedda. Well?

Lövborg. Was there no love in your friendship for me either? Not a spark—not a tinge of love in it?

Hedda. I wonder if there was? To me it seems as though we were two good comrades—two thoroughly intimate friends. [*Smilingly.*] You especially were frankness itself.

Lövborg. It was you that made me so.

Hedda. As I look back upon it all, I think there was really something beautiful, something fascinating—something daring—in—in that secret intimacy—that comradeship which no living creature so much as dreamed of.

Lövborg. Yes, yes, Hedda! Was there not?—When I used to come to your father's in the afternoon—and the General sat over at the window reading his papers— with his back towards us—

Hedda. And we two on the corner sofa—

Lövborg. Always with the same illustrated paper before us—

Hedda. For want of an album, yes.

Lövborg. Yes, Hedda, and when I made my confessions to you—told you about myself, things that at that time no one else knew! There I would sit and tell you of my escapades—my days and nights of devilment. Oh, Hedda—what was the power in you that forced me to confess these things?

Hedda. Do you think it was any power in me?

Lövborg. How else can I explain it? And all those—those roundabout questions you used to put to me—

Hedda. Which you understood so particularly well—

Lövborg. How could you sit and question me like that? Question me quite frankly—

Hedda. In roundabout terms, please observe.

Lövborg. Yes, but frankly nevertheless. Cross-question me about—all that sort of thing?

Hedda. And how could you answer, Mr. Lövborg?

LÖVBORG. Yes, that is just what I can't understand—in looking back upon it. But tell me now, Hedda—was there not love at the bottom of our friendship? On your side, did you not feel as though you might purge my stains away if I made you my confessor? Was it not so?

HEDDA. No, not quite.

LÖVBORG. What was your motive, then?

HEDDA. Do you think it quite incomprehensible that a young girl—when it can be done—without any one knowing—

LÖVBORG. Well?

HEDDA. —should be glad to have a peep, now and then, into a world which—

LÖVBORG. Which—?

HEDDA. —which she is forbidden to know anything about?

LÖVBORG. So that was it?

HEDDA. Partly. Partly—I almost think.

LÖVBORG. Comradeship in the thirst for life. But why should not that, at any rate, have continued?

HEDDA. The fault was yours.

LÖVBORG. It was you that broke with me.

HEDDA. Yes, when our friendship threatened to develop into something more serious. Shame upon you, Eilert Lövborg! How could you think of wronging your—your frank comrade?

LÖVBORG [*clenching his hands*]. Oh, why did you not carry out your threat? Why did you not shoot me down?

HEDDA. Because I have such a dread of scandal.

LÖVBORG. Yes, Hedda, you are a coward at heart.

HEDDA. A terrible coward. [*Changing her tone.*] But it was a lucky thing for you. And now you have found ample consolation at the Elvsteds'.

LÖVBORG. I know what Thea has confided to you.

HEDDA. And perhaps you have confided to her something about us?

LÖVBORG. Not a word. She is too stupid to understand anything of that sort.

HEDDA. Stupid?

LÖVBORG. She is stupid about matters of that sort.

HEDDA. And I am cowardly. [*Bends over towards him, without looking him in the face, and says more softly—*] But now I will confide something to you.

LÖVBORG [*eagerly*]. Well?

HEDDA. The fact that I dared not shoot you down—

LÖVBORG. Yes!

HEDDA. —that was not my most arrant cowardice—that evening.

LÖVBORG [*looks at her a moment, understands, and whispers passionately*]. Oh, Hedda! Hedda Gabler! Now I begin to see a hidden reason beneath our comradeship! You and I—! After all, then, it was your craving for life—

HEDDA [*softly, with a sharp glance*]. Take care! Believe nothing of the sort!

[*Twilight has begun to fall. The hall door is opened from without by* BERTA.]

HEDDA [*closes the album with a bang and calls smilingly*]. Ah, at last! My darling Thea, —come along!

[MRS. ELVSTED *enters from the hall. She is in evening dress. The door is closed behind her.*]

HEDDA [*on the sofa, stretches out her arms towards her*]. My sweet Thea—you can't think how I have been longing for you!

[MRS. ELVSTED, *in passing, exchanges slight salutations with the gentlemen in the inner room, then goes up to the table and gives* HEDDA *her hands.* EILERT LÖVBORG *has risen. He and* MRS. ELVSTED *greet each other with a silent nod.*]

MRS. ELVSTED. Ought I to go in and talk to your husband for a moment?

HEDDA. Oh, not at all. Leave those two alone. They will soon be going.

MRS. ELVSTED. Are they going out?

HEDDA. Yes, to a supper-party.

MRS. ELVSTED [*quickly, to* LÖVBORG]. Not you?

LÖVBORG. No.

HEDDA. Mr. Lövborg remains with us.

MRS. ELVSTED [*takes a chair and is about to seat herself at his side*]. Oh, how nice it is here!

HEDDA. No, thank you, my little Thea! Not there! You'll be good enough to come over here to me. I will sit between you.

MRS. ELVSTED. Yes, just as you please.

[*She goes round the table and seats herself on the sofa on* HEDDA'*s right.* LÖVBORG *re-seats himself on his chair.*]

LÖVBORG [*after a short pause, to* HEDDA]. Is not she lovely to look at?

HEDDA [*lightly stroking her hair*]. Only to look at?

LÖVBORG. Yes. For we two—she and I—we are two real comrades. We have absolute faith in each other; so we can sit and talk with perfect frankness—

HEDDA. Not round about, Mr. Lövborg?

LÖVBORG. Well—

MRS. ELVSTED [*softly, clinging close to* HEDDA]. Oh, how happy I am, Hedda; for, only think, he says I have inspired him too.

HEDDA [*looks at her with a smile*]. Ah! Does he say that, dear?

LÖVBORG. And then she is so brave, Mrs. Tesman!

MRS. ELVSTED. Good heavens—am I brave?

LÖVBORG. Exceedingly—where your comrade is concerned.

HEDDA. Ah, yes—courage! If one only had that!

LÖVBORG. What then? What do you mean?

HEDDA. Then life would perhaps be liveable, after all. [*With a sudden change of tone.*] But now, my dearest Thea, you really must have a glass of cold punch.

MRS. ELVSTED. No, thanks—I never take anything of that kind.

HEDDA. Well then, you, Mr. Lövborg.

LÖVBORG. Nor I, thank you.

MRS. ELVSTED. No, he doesn't either.

HEDDA [*looks fixedly at him*]. But if I say you shall?

LÖVBORG. It would be no use.

HEDDA [*laughing*]. Then I, poor creature, have no sort of power over you?

LÖVBORG. Not in that respect.

HEDDA. But seriously, I think you ought to—for your own sake.

MRS. ELVSTED. Why, Hedda—!

LÖVBORG. How so?

HEDDA. Or rather on account of other people.

LÖVBORG. Indeed?

HEDDA. Otherwise people might be apt to suspect that—in your heart of hearts— you did not feel quite secure—quite confident of yourself.

MRS. ELVSTED [*softly*]. Oh please, Hedda—

LÖVBORG. People may suspect what they like—for the present.

MRS. ELVSTED [*joyfully*]. Yes, let them!

HEDDA. I saw it plainly in Judge Brack's face a moment ago.

LÖVBORG. What did you see?

HEDDA. His contemptuous smile, when you dared not go with them into the inner room.

LÖVBORG. Dared not? Of course I preferred to stop here and talk to you.

MRS. ELVSTED. What could be more natural, Hedda?

HEDDA. But the Judge could not guess that. And I saw, too, the way he smiled and glanced at Tesman when you dared not accept his invitation to this wretched little supper-party of his.

LÖVBORG. Dared not! Do you say I dared not?

HEDDA. *I* don't say so. But that was how Judge Brack understood it.

LÖVBORG. Well, let him.

HEDDA. Then you are not going with them?

LÖVBORG. I will stay here with you and Thea.

MRS. ELVSTED. Yes, Hedda—how can you doubt that?

HEDDA [*smiles and nods approvingly to* LÖVBORG]. Firm as a rock! Faithful to your principles, now and forever! Ah, that is how a man should be! [*Turns to* MRS. ELVSTED *and caresses her.*] Well now, what did I tell you, when you came to us this morning in such a state of distraction—

LÖVBORG [*surprised*]. Distraction!

MRS. ELVSTED [*terrified*]. Hedda—oh Hedda—!

HEDDA. You can see for yourself; you haven't the slightest reason to be in such mortal terror—[*interrupting herself*]. There! Now we can all three enjoy ourselves!

LÖVBORG [*who has given a start*]. Ah—what is all this, Mrs. Tesman?

MRS. ELVSTED. Oh my God, Hedda! What are you saying? What are you doing?

HEDDA. Don't get excited! That horrid Judge Brack is sitting watching you.

LÖVBORG. So she was in mortal terror! On my account!

MRS. ELVSTED [*softly and piteously*]. Oh, Hedda—now you have ruined everything!

LÖVBORG [*looks fixedly at her for a moment. His face is distorted*]. So that was my comrade's frank confidence in me?

MRS. ELVSTED [*imploringly*]. Oh, my dearest friend—only let me tell you—

LÖVBORG [*takes one of the glasses of punch, raises it to his lips, and says in a low, husky voice*]. Your health, Thea!

[*He empties the glass, puts it down, and takes the second.*]

MRS. ELVSTED [*softly*]. Oh, Hedda, Hedda—how could you do this?

HEDDA. *I* do it? *I?* Are you crazy?

LÖVBORG. Here's your health, too, Mrs. Tesman. Thanks for the truth. Hurrah for the truth! [*He empties the glass and is about to re-fill it.*]

HEDDA [*lays her hand on his arm*]. Come, come—no more for the present. Remember you are going out to supper.

MRS. ELVSTED. No, no, no!

HEDDA. Hush! They are sitting watching you.

LÖVBORG [*putting down the glass*]. Now. Thea—tell me the truth—

MRS. ELVSTED. Yes.

LÖVBORG. Did your husband know that you had come after me?

MRS. ELVSTED [*wringing her hands*]. Oh, Hedda—do you hear what he is asking?

LÖVBORG. Was it arranged between you and him that you were to come to town and look after me? Perhaps it was the Sheriff himself that urged you to come? Aha, my dear—no doubt he wanted my help in his office! Or was it at the card-table that he missed me?

MRS. ELVSTED [*softly, in agony*]. Oh, Lövborg, Lövborg—!

LÖVBORG [*seizes a glass and is on the point of filling it*]. Here's a glass for the old Sheriff too!

HEDDA [*preventing him*]. No more just now. Remember, you have to read your manuscript to Tesman.

LÖVBORG [*calmly, putting down the glass*]. It was stupid of me all this, Thea—to take it in this way, I mean. Don't be angry with me, my dear, dear comrade. You shall see—both of you and the others—that if I was fallen once—now I have risen again! Thanks to you, Thea.

MRS. ELVSTED [*radiant with joy*]. Oh, heaven be praised—!

[BRACK *has in the meantime looked at his watch. He and* TESMAN *rise and come into the drawing-room.*]

BRACK [*takes his hat and overcoat*]. Well, Mrs. Tesman, our time has come.

HEDDA. I suppose it has.

LÖVBORG [*rising*]. Mine too, Judge Brack.

MRS. ELVSTED [*softly and imploringly*]. Oh, Lövborg, don't do it!

HEDDA [*pinching her arm*]. They can hear you!

MRS. ELVSTED [*with a suppressed shriek*]. Ow!

LÖVBORG [*to* BRACK]. You were good enough to invite me.

BRACK. Well, are you coming after all?

LÖVBORG. Yes, many thanks.

BRACK. I'm delighted—

LÖVBORG [*to* TESMAN, *putting the parcel of MS. in his pocket*]. I should like to show you one or two things before I send it to the printer's.

TESMAN. Fancy—that will be delightful. But, Hedda dear, how is Mrs. Elvsted to get home? Eh?

HEDDA. Oh, that can be managed somehow.

LÖVBORG [*looking towards the ladies*]. Mrs. Elvsted? Of course, I'll come again and fetch her. [*Approaching.*] At ten or thereabouts, Mrs. Tesman? Will that do?

HEDDA. Certainly. That will do capitally.

TESMAN. Well, then, that's all right. But you must not expect me so early, Hedda.

HEDDA. Oh, you may stop as long—as long as ever you please.

MRS. ELVSTED [*trying to conceal her anxiety*]. Well then, Mr. Lövborg—I shall remain here until you come.

LÖVBORG [*with his hat in his hand*]. Pray do, Mrs. Elvsted.

BRACK. And now off goes the excursion train, gentlemen! I hope we shall have a lively time, as a certain fair lady puts it.

HEDDA. Ah, if only the fair lady could be present unseen—!

BRACK. Why unseen?

HEDDA. In order to hear a little of your liveliness at first hand, Judge Brack.

BRACK [*laughing*]. I should not advise the fair lady to try it.

TESMAN [*also laughing*]. Come, you're a nice one, Hedda! Fancy that!

BRACK. Well, good-bye, good-bye, ladies.

LÖVBORG [*bowing*]. About ten o'clock, then.

[BRACK, LÖVBORG, *and* TESMAN *go out by the hall door. At the same time* BERTA *enters from the inner room with a lighted lamp, which she places on the dining-room table; she goes out by the way she came.*]

MRS. ELVSTED [*who has risen and is wandering restlessly about the room*]. Hedda—Hedda—what will come of all this?

HEDDA. At ten o'clock—he will be here. I can see him already—with vine-leaves in his hair[11]—flushed and fearless—

MRS. ELVSTED. Oh, I hope he may.

---

[11] Bacchus, the Greek and Roman god of wine and revelry, was often portrayed with vine leaves in his hair.

HEDDA. And then, you see—then he will have regained control over himself. Then he will be a free man for all his days.

MRS. ELVSTED. Oh God!—if he would only come as you see him now!

HEDDA. He will come as I see him—so, and not otherwise! [*Rises and approaches* THEA.] You may doubt him as long as you please; I believe in him. And now we will try—

MRS. ELVSTED. You have some hidden motive in this, Hedda!

HEDDA. Yes, I have. I want for once in my life to have power to mold a human destiny.

MRS. ELVSTED. Have you not the power?

HEDDA. I have not—and have never had it.

MRS. ELVSTED. Not your husband's?

HEDDA. Do you think that is worth the trouble? Oh, if you could only understand how poor I am. And fate has made you so rich! [*Clasps her passionately in her arms.*] I think I must burn your hair off, after all.

MRS. ELVSTED. Let me go! Let me go! I am afraid of you, Hedda!

BERTA [*in the middle doorway*]. Tea is laid in the dining-room, ma'am.

HEDDA. Very well. We are coming.

MRS. ELVSTED. No, no, no! I would rather go home alone! At once.

HEDDA. Nonsense! First you shall have a cup of tea, you little stupid. And then—at ten o'clock—Eilert Lövborg will be here—with vine-leaves in his hair. [*She drags* MRS. ELVSTED *almost by force towards the middle doorway.*]

ACT III

The room at the TESMANS'. *The curtains are drawn over the middle doorway, and also over the glass door. The lamp, half turned down and with a shade over it, is burning on the table. In the stove, the door of which stands open, there has been a fire, which is now nearly burnt out.*

MRS. ELVSTED, *wrapped in a large shawl, and with her feet upon a foot-rest, sits close to the stove, sunk back in the arm-chair.* HEDDA, *fully dressed, lies sleeping upon the sofa, with a sofa-blanket over her.*

MRS. ELVSTED [*after a pause, suddenly sits up in her chair, and listens eagerly. Then she sinks back again wearily, moaning to herself*]. Not yet!—Oh God—oh God—not yet! [BERTA *slips in by the hall door. She has a letter in her hand.*]

MRS. ELVSTED [*turns and whispers eagerly*]. Well—has any one come?

BERTA [*softly*]. Yes, a girl has brought this letter.

MRS. ELVSTED [*quickly, holding out her hand*]. A letter! Give it to me!

BERTA. No, it's for Dr. Tesman, ma'am.

MRS. ELVSTED. Oh, indeed.

BERTA. It was Miss Tesman's servant that brought it. I'll lay it here on the table.

MRS. ELVSTED. Yes, do.

BERTA [*laying down the letter*]. I think I had better put out the lamp. It's smoking.

MRS. ELVSTED. Yes, put it out. It must soon be daylight now.

BERTA [*putting out the lamp*]. It is daylight already, ma'am.

MRS. ELVSTED. Yes, broad day! And no one come back yet—!

BERTA. Lord bless you, ma'am! I guessed how it would be.

MRS. ELVSTED. You guessed?

BERTA. Yes, when I saw that a certain person had come back to town—and that he went off with them. For we've heard enough about that gentleman before now.

MRS. ELVSTED. Don't speak so loud! You will waken Mrs. Tesman.

BERTA [*looks towards the sofa and sighs*]. No, no—let her sleep, poor thing. Shan't I put some wood on the fire?

MRS. ELVSTED. Thanks, not for me.

BERTA. Oh, very well. [*She goes softly out by the hall door.*]

HEDDA [*is awakened by the shutting of the door, and looks up*]. What's that—?

MRS. ELVSTED. It was only the servant—

HEDDA [*looking about her*]. Oh, we're here—! Yes, now I remember. [*Sits erect upon the sofa, stretches herself, and rubs her eyes.*] What o'clock is it, Thea?

MRS. ELVSTED [*looks at her watch*]. It's past seven.

HEDDA. When did Tesman come home?

MRS. ELVSTED. He has not come.

HEDDA. Not come home yet?

MRS. ELVSTED [*rising*]. No one has come.

HEDDA. Think of our watching and waiting here till four in the morning—

MRS. ELVSTED [*wringing her hands*]. And how I watched and waited for him!

HEDDA [*yawns, and says with her hand before her mouth*]. Well, well—we might have spared ourselves the trouble.

MRS. ELVSTED. Did you get a little sleep?

HEDDA. Oh yes; I believe I have slept pretty well. Have you not?

MRS. ELVSTED. Not for a moment. I couldn't, Hedda!—not to save my life.

HEDDA [*rising and goes towards her*]. There, there, there! There's nothing to be so alarmed about. I understand quite well what has happened.

MRS. ELVSTED. Well, what do you think? Won't you tell me?

HEDDA. Why, of course it has been a very late affair at Judge Brack's—

MRS. ELVSTED. Yes, yes, that is clear enough. But all the same—

HEDDA. And then, you see, Tesman hasn't cared to come home and ring us up in the middle of the night. [*Laughing.*] Perhaps he wasn't inclined to show himself either—immediately after a jollification.

MRS. ELVSTED. But in that case—where can he have gone?

HEDDA. Of course he has gone to his aunts' and slept there. They have his old room ready for him.

MRS. ELVSTED. No, he can't be with them; for a letter has just come for him from Miss Tesman. There it lies.

HEDDA. Indeed? [*Looks at the address.*] Why yes, it's addressed in Aunt Julia's own hand. Well then, he has remained at Judge Brack's. And as for Eilert Lövborg —he is sitting, with vine-leaves in his hair, reading his manuscript.

MRS. ELVSTED. Oh Hedda, you are just saying things you don't believe a bit.

HEDDA. You really are a little blockhead, Thea.

MRS. ELVSTED. Oh yes, I suppose I am.

HEDDA. And how mortally tired you look.

MRS. ELVSTED. Yes, I am mortally tired.

HEDDA. Well then, you must do as I tell you. You must go into my room and lie down for a little while.

MRS. ELVSTED. Oh no, no—I shouldn't be able to sleep.

HEDDA. I am sure you would.

MRS. ELVSTED. Well, but your husband is certain to come soon now; and then I want to know at once—

HEDDA. I shall take care to let you know when he comes.

MRS. ELVSTED. Do you promise me, Hedda?

HEDDA. Yes, rely upon me. Just you go in and have a sleep in the meantime.

MRS. ELVSTED. Thanks; then I'll try to. [*She goes off through the inner room.*]

[HEDDA *goes up to the glass door and draws back the curtains. The broad daylight streams into the room. Then she takes a little hand-glass from the writing-table, looks at herself in it, and arranges her hair. Next she goes to the hall door and presses the bell-button.* BERTA *presently appears at the hall door.*]

BERTA. Did you want anything, ma'am?

HEDDA. Yes; you must put some more wood in the stove. I am shivering.

BERTA. Bless me—I'll make up the fire at once. [*She rakes the embers together and lays a piece of wood upon them; then stops and listens.*] That was a ring at the front door, ma'am.

HEDDA. Then go to the door. I will look after the fire.

BERTA. It'll soon burn up. [*She goes out by the hall door.*]

[HEDDA *kneels on the foot-rest and lays some more pieces of wood in the stove. After a short pause,* GEORGE TESMAN *enters from the hall. He looks tired and rather serious. He steals on tiptoe towards the middle doorway and is about to slip through the curtains.*]

HEDDA [*at the stove, without looking up*]. Good morning.

TESMAN [*turns*]. Hedda! [*Approaching her.*] Good heavens—are you up so early? Eh?

HEDDA. Yes, I am up very early this morning.

TESMAN. And I never doubted you were still sound asleep! Fancy that, Hedda!

HEDDA. Don't speak so loud. Mrs. Elvsted is resting in my room.

TESMAN. Has Mrs. Elvsted been here all night?

HEDDA. Yes, since no one came to fetch her.

TESMAN. Ah, to be sure.

HEDDA [*closes the door of the stove and rises*]. Well, did you enjoy yourself at Judge Brack's?

TESMAN. Have you been anxious about me? Eh?

HEDDA. No, I should never think of being anxious. But I asked if you had enjoyed yourself.

TESMAN. Oh, yes,—for once in a way. Especially the beginning of the evening; for then Eilert read me part of his book. We arrived more than an hour too early —fancy that! And Brack had all sorts of arrangements to make—so Eilert read to me.

HEDDA [*seating herself by the table on the right*]. Well? Tell me, then—

TESMAN [*sitting on a foot-stool near the stove*]. Oh Hedda, you can't conceive what a book that is going to be! I believe it is one of the most remarkable things that have ever been written. Fancy that!

HEDDA. Yes, yes; I don't care about that—

TESMAN. I must make a confession to you, Hedda. When he had finished reading— a horrid feeling came over me.

HEDDA. A horrid feeling?

TESMAN. I felt jealous of Eilert for having had it in him to write such a book. Only think, Hedda!

HEDDA. Yes, yes, I am thinking!

TESMAN. And then how pitiful to think that he—with all his gifts—should be irreclaimable after all.

HEDDA. I suppose you mean that he has more courage than the rest?

TESMAN. No, not at all—I mean that he is incapable of taking his pleasures in moderation.

HEDDA. And what came of it all—in the end?

TESMAN. Well, to tell the truth, I think it might best be described as an orgy, Hedda.

HEDDA. Had he vine-leaves in his hair?

TESMAN. Vine-leaves? No, I saw nothing of the sort. But he made a long, rambling speech in honor of the woman who had inspired him in his work—that was the phrase he used.

HEDDA. Did he name her?

TESMAN. No, he didn't; but I can't help thinking he meant Mrs. Elvsted. You may be sure he did.

HEDDA. Well—where did you part from him?

TESMAN. On the way to town. We broke up—the last of us at any rate—all together; and Brack came with us to get a breath of fresh air. And then, you see, we agreed to take Eilert home; for he had had far more than was good for him.

HEDDA. I daresay.

TESMAN. But now comes the strange part of it, Hedda; or, I should rather say, the melancholy part of it. I declare I am almost ashamed—on Eilert's account—to tell you—

HEDDA. Oh, go on—!

TESMAN. Well, as we were getting near town, you see, I happened to drop a little behind the others. Only for a minute or two—fancy that!

HEDDA. Yes, yes, yes, but—?

TESMAN. And then, as I hurried after them—what do you think I found by the wayside? Eh?

HEDDA. Oh, how should I know!

TESMAN. You mustn't speak of it to a soul, Hedda! Do you hear! Promise me, for Eilert's sake. [*Draws a parcel, wrapped in paper, from his coat pocket.*] Fancy, dear—I found this.

HEDDA. Is not that the parcel he had with him yesterday?

TESMAN. Yes, it is the whole of his precious, irreplaceable manuscript! And he had gone and lost it, and knew nothing about it. Only fancy, Hedda! So deplorably—

HEDDA. But why did you not give him back the parcel at once?

TESMAN. I didn't dare to—in the state he was then in—

HEDDA. Did you not tell any of the others that you had found it?

TESMAN. Oh, far from it! You can surely understand that, for Eilert's sake, I wouldn't do that.

HEDDA. So no one knows that Eilert Lövborg's manuscript is in your possession?

TESMAN. No. And no one must know it.

HEDDA. Then what did you say to him afterwards?

TESMAN. I didn't talk to him again at all; for when we got in among the streets, he and two or three of the others gave us the slip and disappeared. Fancy that!

HEDDA. Indeed! They must have taken him home then.

TESMAN. Yes, so it would appear. And Brack, too, left us.

HEDDA. And what have you been doing with yourself since?

TESMAN. Well, I and some of the others went home with one of the party, a jolly fellow, and took our morning coffee with him; or perhaps I should rather call it our night coffee—eh? But now, when I have rested a little, and given Eilert, poor fellow, time to have his sleep out, I must take this back to him.

HEDDA [*holds out her hand for the packet*]. No—don't give it to him! Not in such a hurry, I mean. Let me read it first.

TESMAN. No, my dearest Hedda, I mustn't, I really mustn't.

HEDDA. You must not?

TESMAN. No—for you can imagine what a state of despair he will be in when he awakens and misses the manuscript. He has no copy of it, you must know! He told me so.

HEDDA [*looking searchingly at him*]. Can such a thing not be reproduced? Written over again?

TESMAN. No, I don't think that would be possible. For the inspiration, you see—

HEDDA. Yes, yes—I suppose it depends on that. [*Lightly.*] But, by-the-bye—here is a letter for you.

TESMAN. Fancy—!

HEDDA [*handing it to him*]. It came early this morning.

TESMAN. It's from Aunt Julia! What can it be? [*He lays the packet on the other foot-stool, opens the letter, runs his eye through it, and jumps up*]. Oh, Hedda—she says that poor Aunt Rina is dying!

HEDDA. Well, we were prepared for that.

TESMAN. And that if I want to see her again, I must make haste. I'll run in to them at once.

HEDDA [*suppressing a smile*]. Will you run?

TESMAN. Oh, dearest Hedda—if you could only make up your mind to come with me! Just think!

HEDDA [*rises and says wearily, repelling the idea*]. No, no, don't ask me. I will not look upon sickness and death. I loathe all sorts of ugliness.

TESMAN. Well, well, then—! [*Bustling around.*] My hat—My overcoat—? Oh, in the hall—I do hope I mayn't come too late, Hedda! Eh?

HEDDA. Oh, if you run—

[BERTA *appears at the hall door.*]

BERTA. Judge Brack is at the door, and wishes to know if he may come in.

TESMAN. At this time! No, I can't possibly see him.

HEDDA. But I can. [*To* BERTA.] Ask Judge Brack to come in.

[BERTA *goes out.*]

HEDDA [*quickly whispering*]. The parcel, Tesman! [*She snatches it up from the stool.*]

TESMAN. Yes, give it to me!

HEDDA. No, no, I will keep it till you come back.

[*She goes to the writing-table and places it in the book-case.* TESMAN *stands in a flurry of haste, and cannot get his gloves on.* JUDGE BRACK *enters from the hall.*]

HEDDA [*nodding to him*]. You are an early bird, I must say.

BRACK. Yes, don't you think so? [*To* TESMAN.] Are you on the move, too?

TESMAN. Yes, I must rush off to my aunts'. Fancy—the invalid one is lying at death's door, poor creature.

BRACK. Dear me, is she indeed? Then on no account let me detain you. At such a critical moment—

TESMAN. Yes, I must really rush—Good-bye! Good-bye!

[*He hastens out by the hall door.*]

HEDDA [*approaching*]. You seem to have made a particularly lively night of it at your rooms, Judge Brack.

BRACK. I assure you I have not had my clothes off, Mrs. Hedda.

HEDDA. Not you, either?

BRACK. No, as you may see. But what has Tesman been telling you of the night's adventures?

HEDDA. Oh, some tiresome story. Only that they went and had coffee somewhere or other.

BRACK. I have heard about that coffee-party already. Eilert Lövborg was not with them, I fancy?

HEDDA. No, they had taken him home before that.

BRACK. Tesman, too?

HEDDA. No, but some of the others, he said.

BRACK [*smiling*]. George Tesman is really an ingenuous creature, Mrs. Hedda.

HEDDA. Yes, heaven knows he is. Then is there something behind all this?

BRACK. Yes, perhaps there may be.

HEDDA. Well then, sit down, my dear Judge, and tell your story in comfort.

[*She seats herself to the left of the table.* BRACK *sits near her, at the long side of the table.*]

HEDDA. Now then?

BRACK. I had special reasons for keeping track of my guests—or rather of some of my guests—last night.

HEDDA. Of Eilert Lövborg among the rest, perhaps?

BRACK. Frankly, yes.

HEDDA. Now you make me really curious—

BRACK. Do you know where he and one or two of the others finished the night, Mrs. Hedda?

HEDDA. If it is not quite unmentionable, tell me.

BRACK. Oh no, it's not at all unmentionable. Well, they put in an appearance at a particularly animated soirée.[12]

HEDDA. Of the lively kind?

BRACK. Of the very liveliest—

HEDDA. Tell me more of this, Judge Brack—

BRACK. Lövborg, as well as the others, had been invited in advance. I knew all about it. But he had declined the invitation; for now, as you know, he has become a new man.

HEDDA. Up at the Elvsteds', yes. But he went after all, then?

BRACK. Well, you see, Mrs. Hedda—unhappily the spirit moved him at my rooms last evening—

HEDDA. Yes, I hear he found inspiration.

BRACK. Pretty violent inspiration. Well, I fancy, that altered his purpose; for we men folk are unfortunately not always so firm in our principles as we ought to be.

HEDDA. Oh, I am sure you are an exception, Judge Brack. But as to Lövborg—?

BRACK. To make a long story short—he landed at last in Mademoiselle Diana's rooms.

HEDDA. Mademoiselle Diana's?

BRACK. It was Mademoiselle Diana that was giving the soirée to a select circle of her admirers and her lady friends.

HEDDA. Is she a red-haired woman?

BRACK. Precisely.

HEDDA. A sort of a—singer?

BRACK. Oh yes—in her leisure moments. And moreover a mighty huntress—of men—Mrs. Hedda. You have no doubt heard of her. Eilert Lövborg was one of her most enthusiastic protectors—in the days of his glory.

HEDDA. And how did all this end?

BRACK. Far from amicably, it appears. After a most tender meeting, they seem to have come to blows—

---

[12] An evening party.

HEDDA. Lövborg and she?

BRACK. Yes. He accused her or her friends of having robbed him. He declared that his pocket-book had disappeared—and other things as well. In short, he seems to have made a furious disturbance.

HEDDA. And what came of it all?

BRACK. It came to a general scrimmage, in which the ladies as well as the gentlemen took part. Fortunately the police at last appeared on the scene.

HEDDA. The police too?

BRACK. Yes. I fancy it will prove a costly frolic for Eilert Lövborg, crazy being that he is.

HEDDA. How so?

BRACK. He seems to have made a violent resistance—to have hit one of the constables on the head and torn the coat off his back. So they had to march him off to the police-station with the rest.

HEDDA. How have you learnt all this?

BRACK. From the police themselves.

HEDDA [*gazing straight before her*]. So that is what happened. Then he had no vine-leaves in his hair.

BRACK. Vine-leaves, Mrs. Hedda?

HEDDA [*changing her tone*]. But tell me now, Judge—what is your real reason for tracking out Eilert Lövborg's movements so carefully?

BRACK. In the first place, it could not be entirely indifferent to me if it should appear in the police-court that he came straight from my house.

HEDDA. Will the matter come into court, then?

BRACK. Of course. However, I should scarcely have troubled so much about that. But I thought that, as a friend of the family, it was my duty to supply you and Tesman with a full account of his nocturnal exploits.

HEDDA. Why so, Judge Brack?

BRACK. Why, because I have a shrewd suspicion that he intends to use you as a sort of blind.

HEDDA. Oh, how can you think such a thing!

BRACK. Good heavens, Mrs. Hedda—we have eyes in our head. Mark my words! This Mrs. Elvsted will be in no hurry to leave town again.

HEDDA. Well, even if there should be anything between them, I suppose there are plenty of other places where they could meet.

BRACK. Not a single home. Henceforth, as before, every respectable house will be closed against Eilert Lövborg.

HEDDA. And so ought mine to be, you mean?

BRACK. Yes. I confess it would be more than painful to me if this personage were to be made free of your house. How superfluous, how intrusive, he would be, if he were to force his way into—

HEDDA. —into the triangle?

BRACK. Precisely. It would simply mean that I should find myself homeless.

HEDDA [*looks at him with a smile*]. So you want to be the one cock in the basket—that is your aim.

BRACK [*nods slowly and lowers his voice*]. Yes, that is my aim. And for that I will fight —with every weapon I can command.

HEDDA [*her smile vanishing*]. I see you are a dangerous person—when it comes to the point.

BRACK. Do you think so?

HEDDA. I am beginning to think so. And I am exceedingly glad to think—that you have no sort of hold over me.

BRACK [*laughing equivocally*]. Well, well, Mrs. Hedda—perhaps you are right there. If I had, who knows what I might be capable of?

HEDDA. Come, come now, Judge Brack. That sounds almost like a threat.

BRACK [*rising*]. Oh, not at all! The triangle, you know, ought, if possible, to be spontaneously constructed.

HEDDA. There I agree with you.

BRACK. Well, now I have said all I had to say; and I had better be getting back to town. Good-bye, Mrs. Hedda. [*He goes towards the glass door.*]

HEDDA [*rising*]. Are you going through the garden?

BRACK. Yes, it's a short cut for me.

HEDDA. And then it is the back way, too.

BRACK. Quite so. I have no objection to back ways. They may be piquant enough at times.

HEDDA. When there is ball practice going on, you mean?

BRACK [*in the doorway, laughing to her*]. Oh, people don't shoot their tame poultry, I fancy.

HEDDA [*also laughing*]. Oh no, when there is only one cock in the basket—

[*They exchange laughing nods of farewell. He goes. She closes the door behind him.* HEDDA, *who has become quite serious, stands for a moment looking out. Presently she goes and peeps through the curtain over the middle doorway. Then she goes to the writing-table, takes* LÖVBORG'S *packet out of the book-case, and is on the point of looking through its contents.* BERTA *is heard speaking loudly in the hall.* HEDDA *turns and listens. Then she hastily locks up the packet in the drawer, and lays the key on the inkstand.* EILERT LÖVBORG, *with his great coat on and his hat in his hand, tears open the hall door. He looks somewhat confused and irritated.*]

LÖVBORG [*looking towards the hall*]. And I tell you I must and will come in! There!
[*He closes the door, turns and sees* HEDDA, *at once regains his self-control, and bows.*]

HEDDA [*at the writing-table*]. Well, Mr. Lövborg, this is rather a late hour to call for Thea.

LÖVBORG. You mean rather an early hour to call on you. Pray pardon me.

HEDDA. How do you know that she is still here?

LÖVBORG. They told me at her lodgings that she had been out all night.

HEDDA [*going to the oval table*]. Did you notice anything about the people of the house when they said that?

LÖVBORG [*looks inquiringly at her*]. Notice anything about them?

HEDDA. I mean, did they seem to think it odd?

LÖVBORG [*suddenly understanding*]. Oh yes, of course! I am dragging her down with me! However, I didn't notice anything.—I suppose Tesman is not up yet?

HEDDA. No—I think not—

LÖVBORG. When did he come home?

HEDDA. Very late.

LÖVBORG. Did he tell you anything?

HEDDA. Yes, I gathered that you had had an exceedingly jolly evening at Judge Brack's.

LÖVBORG. Nothing more?

HEDDA. I don't think so. However, I was so dreadfully sleepy—
[MRS. ELVSTED *enters through the curtains of the middle doorway.*]

MRS. ELVSTED [*going towards him*]. Ah, Lövborg! At last—!

LÖVBORG. Yes, at last. And too late!

MRS. ELVSTED [*looks anxiously at him*]. What is too late?

LÖVBORG. Everything is too late now. It is all over with me.

MRS. ELVSTED. Oh no no—don't say that!

LÖVBORG. You will say the same when you hear—

MRS. ELVSTED. I won't hear anything!

HEDDA. Perhaps you would prefer to talk to her alone! If so, I will leave you.

LÖVBORG. No, stay—you too. I beg you to stay.

MRS. ELVSTED. Yes, but I won't hear anything, I tell you.

LÖVBORG. It is not last night's adventures that I want to talk about.

MRS. ELVSTED. What is it then—?

LÖVBORG. I want to say that now our ways must part.

MRS. ELVSTED. Part!

HEDDA [*involuntarily*]. I knew it!

LÖVBORG. You can be of no more service to me, Thea.

MRS. ELVSTED. How can you stand there and say that! No more service to you! Am I not to help you now, as before? Are we not to go on working together?

LÖVBORG. Henceforward I shall do no work.

MRS. ELVSTED [*despairingly*]. Then what am I to do with my life?

LÖVBORG. You must try to live your life as if you had never known me.

MRS. ELVSTED. But you know I cannot do that!

LÖVBORG. Try if you cannot, Thea. You must go home again—

MRS. ELVSTED [*in vehement protest*]. Never in this world! Where you are, there will I be also! I will not let myself be driven away like this! I will remain here! I will be with you when the book appears.

HEDDA [*half aloud, in suspense*]. Ah yes—the book!

LÖVBORG [*looks at her*]. My book and Thea's; for that is what it is.

MRS. ELVSTED. Yes, I feel that it is. And that is why I have a right to be with you when it appears! I will see with my own eyes how respect and honor pour in upon you afresh. And the happiness—the happiness—oh, I must share it with you!

LÖVBORG. Thea—our book will never appear.

HEDDA. Ah!

MRS. ELVSTED. Never appear!

LÖVBORG. Can never appear.

MRS. ELVSTED [*in agonized foreboding*]. Lövborg—what have you done with the manuscript?

HEDDA [*looks anxiously at him*]. Yes, the manuscript—?

MRS. ELVSTED. Where is it?

LÖVBORG. Oh Thea—don't ask me about it!

MRS. ELVSTED. Yes, yes I will know. I demand to be told at once.

LÖVBORG. The manuscript—Well then—I have torn the manuscript into a thousand pieces.

MRS. ELVSTED [*shrieks*]. Oh no, no—!

HEDDA [*involuntarily*]. But that's not—

LÖVBORG [*looks at her*]. Not true, you think?

HEDDA [*collecting herself*]. Oh well, of course—since you say so. But it sounded so improbable—

LÖVBORG. It is true, all the same.

MRS. ELVSTED [*wringing her hands*]. Oh God—oh God, Hedda—torn his own work to pieces!

LÖVBORG. I have torn my own life to pieces. So why should I not tear my life-work too—?

MRS. ELVSTED. And you did this last night?

LÖVBORG. Yes, I tell you! Tore it into a thousand pieces and scattered them on the fiord—far out. There there is cool sea-water at any rate—let them drift upon it—drift with the current and the wind. And then presently they will sink—deeper and deeper—as I shall, Thea.

MRS. ELVSTED. Do you know, Lövborg, that what you have done with the book—I shall think of it to my dying day as though you had killed a little child.

LÖVBORG. Yes, you are right. It is a sort of child-murder.

MRS. ELVSTED. How could you, then—! Did not the child belong to me too?

HEDDA [*almost inaudibly*]. Ah, the child—

MRS. ELVSTED [*breathing heavily*]. It is all over then. Well, well, now I will go, Hedda.

HEDDA. But you are not going away from town?

MRS. ELVSTED. Oh, I don't know what I shall do. I see nothing but darkness before me. [*She goes out by the hall door.*]

HEDDA [*stands waiting for a moment*]. So you are not going to see her home, Mr. Lövborg?

LÖVBORG. I? Through the streets? Would you have people see her walking with me?

HEDDA. Of course I don't know what else may have happened last night. But is it so utterly irretrievable?

LÖVBORG. It will not end with last night—I know that perfectly well. And the thing is that now I have no taste for that sort of life either. I won't begin it anew. She has broken my courage and my power of braving life out.

HEDDA [*looking straight before her*]. So that pretty little fool has had her fingers in a man's destiny. [*Looks at him.*] But all the same, how could you treat her so heartlessly?

LÖVBORG. Oh, don't say that it was heartless!

HEDDA. To go and destroy what has filled her whole soul for months and years. You do not call that heartless!

LÖVBORG. To you I can tell the truth, Hedda.

HEDDA. The truth?

LÖVBORG. First promise me—give me your word—that what I now confide to you Thea shall never know.

HEDDA. I give you my word.

LÖVBORG. Good. Then let me tell you that what I said just now was untrue.

HEDDA. About the manuscript?

LÖVBORG. Yes. I have not torn it to pieces—nor thrown it into the fiord.

HEDDA. No, no—But—where is it then?

LÖVBORG. I have destroyed it none the less—utterly destroyed it, Hedda!

HEDDA. I don't understand.

LÖVBORG. Thea said that what I had done seemed to her like a child-murder.

HEDDA. Yes, so she said.

LÖVBORG. But to kill his child—that is not the worst thing a father can do to it.

HEDDA. Not the worst?

LÖVBORG. No. I wanted to spare Thea from hearing the worst.

HEDDA. Then what is the worst?

LÖVBORG. Suppose now, Hedda, that a man—in the small hours of the morning—came home to his child's mother after a night of riot and debauchery, and said: "Listen—I have been here and there—in this place and in that. And I have taken our child with me—to this place and to that. And I have lost the child—

utterly lost it. The devil knows into what hands it may have fallen—who may have had their clutches on it."

HEDDA. Well—but when all is said and done, you know—that was only a book—

LÖVBORG. Thea's pure soul was in that book.

HEDDA. Yes, so I understand.

LÖVBORG. And you can understand, too, that for her and me together no future is possible.

HEDDA. What path do you mean to take then?

LÖVBORG. None. I will only try to make an end of it all—the sooner the better.

HEDDA [a step nearer to him]. Eilert Lövborg—listen to me. Will you not try to—to do it beautifully?

LÖVBORG. Beautifully? [Smiling.] With vine-leaves in my hair, as you used to dream in the old days—?

HEDDA. No, no. I have lost my faith in the vine-leaves. But beautifully, nevertheless! For once in a way!—Good-bye! You must go now—and do not come here any more.

LÖVBORG. Good-bye, Mrs. Tesman. And give George Tesman my love. [He is on the point of going.]

HEDDA. No, wait! I must give you a memento to take with you.

[She goes to the writing-table and opens the drawer and the pistol-case; then returns to LÖVBORG with one of the pistols.]

LÖVBORG [looks at her]. This? Is this the memento?

HEDDA [nodding slowly]. Do you recognize it? It was aimed at you once.

LÖVBORG. You should have used it then.

HEDDA. Take it—and do you use it now.

LÖVBORG [puts the pistol in his breast pocket]. Thanks!

HEDDA. And beautifully, Eilert Lövborg. Promise me that!

LÖVBORG. Good-bye, Hedda Gabler. [He goes out by the hall door.]

[HEDDA listens for a moment at the door. Then she goes up to the writing-table, takes out the packet of manuscript, peeps under the cover, draws a few of the sheets half out, and looks at them. Next she goes over and seats herself in the arm-chair beside the stove, with the packet in her lap. Presently she opens the stove door, and then the packet.]

HEDDA [throws one of the quires into the fire and whispers to herself]. Now I am burning your child, Thea!—Burning it, curly-locks! [Throwing one or two more quires into the stove.] Your child and Eilert Lövborg's. [Throws the rest in.] I am burning—I am burning your child.

ACT IV

The same rooms at the TESMANS'. It is evening. The drawing-room is in darkness. The back room is lighted by the hanging lamp over the table. The curtains over the glass door are drawn close.

HEDDA, dressed in black, walks to and fro in the dark room. Then she goes into the back room and disappears for a moment to the left. She is heard to strike a few chords on the piano. Presently she comes in sight again, and returns to the drawing-room. BERTA enters from the right, through the inner room, with a lighted lamp, which she places on the table in front of the corner settee in the drawing-room. Her eyes are red with weeping, and she has black ribbons in her cap. She goes quietly and circumspectly out to the right. HEDDA goes up to the glass door, lifts the curtain a little aside, and looks out into the darkness. Shortly afterwards, MISS TESMAN, in mourning, with a bonnet and veil on, comes in from the hall. HEDDA goes towards her and holds out her hand.

MISS TESMAN. Yes, Hedda, here I am, in mourning and forlorn; for now my poor sister has at last found peace.

HEDDA. I have heard the news already, as you see. Tesman sent me a card.

MISS TESMAN. Yes, he promised me he would. But nevertheless I thought that to Hedda here—in the house of life—I ought myself to bring the tidings of death.

HEDDA. That was very kind of you.

MISS TESMAN. Ah, Rina ought not to have left us just now. This is not the time for Hedda's house to be a house of mourning.

HEDDA [*changing the subject*]. She died quite peacefully, did she not, Miss Tesman?

MISS TESMAN. Oh, her end was so calm, so beautiful. And then she had the unspeakable happiness of seeing George once more—and bidding him good-bye. —Has he come home yet?

HEDDA. No. He wrote that he might be detained. But won't you sit down?

MISS TESMAN. No thank you, my dear, dear Hedda. I should like to, but I have so much to do. I must prepare my dear one for her rest as well as I can. She shall go to her grave looking her best.

HEDDA. Can I not help you in any way?

MISS TESMAN. Oh, you must not think of it! Hedda Tesman must have no hand in such mournful work. Nor let her thoughts dwell on it either—not at this time.

HEDDA. One is not always mistress of one's thoughts—

MISS TESMAN [*continuing*]. Ah yes, it is the way of the world. At home we shall be sewing a shroud; and here there will soon be sewing too, I suppose—but of another sort, thank God!

[GEORGE TESMAN *enters by the hall door.*]

HEDDA. Ah, you have come at last!

TESMAN. You here, Aunt Julia? With Hedda? Fancy that!

MISS TESMAN. I was just going, my dear boy. Well, have you done all you promised?

TESMAN. No; I'm really afraid I have forgotten half of it. I must come to you again tomorrow. Today my brain is all in a whirl. I can't keep my thoughts together.

MISS TESMAN. Why, my dear George, you mustn't take it in this way.

TESMAN. Mustn't—? How do you mean?

MISS TESMAN. Even in your sorrow you must rejoice, as I do—rejoice that she is at rest.

TESMAN. Oh yes, yes—you are thinking of Aunt Rina.

HEDDA. You will feel lonely now, Miss Tesman.

MISS TESMAN. Just at first, yes. But that will not last very long, I hope. I daresay I shall soon find an occupant for poor Rina's little room.

TESMAN. Indeed? Who do you think will take it? Eh?

MISS TESMAN. Oh, there's always some poor invalid or other in want of nursing, unfortunately.

HEDDA. Would you really take such a burden upon you again?

MISS TESMAN. A burden! Heaven forgive you, child—it has been no burden to me.

HEDDA. But suppose you had a total stranger on your hands—

MISS TESMAN. Oh, one soon makes friends with sick folks; and it's such an absolute necessity for me to have some one to live for. Well, heaven be praised, there may soon be something in this house, too, to keep an old aunt busy.

HEDDA. Oh, don't trouble about anything here.

TESMAN. Yes, just fancy what a nice time we three might have together, if—?

HEDDA. If—?

TESMAN [*uneasily*]. Oh, nothing. It will all come right. Let us hope so—eh?

MISS TESMAN. Well, well, I daresay you two want to talk to each other. [*Smiling.*] And perhaps Hedda may have something to tell you too, George. Good-bye! I must go home to Rina. [*Turning at the door.*] How strange it is to think that now Rina is with me and with my poor brother as well!

TESMAN. Yes, fancy that, Aunt Julia! Eh?

[MISS TESMAN *goes out by the hall door.*]

HEDDA [*follows* TESMAN *coldly and searchingly with her eyes*]. I almost believe your Aunt Rina's death affects you more than it does your Aunt Julia.

TESMAN. Oh, it's not that alone. It's Eilert I am so terribly uneasy about.

HEDDA [*quickly*]. Is there anything new about him?

TESMAN. I looked in at his rooms this afternoon, intending to tell him the manuscript was in safe keeping.

HEDDA. Well, did you not find him?

TESMAN. No. He wasn't at home. But afterwards I met Mrs. Elvsted, and she told me he had been here early this morning.

HEDDA. Yes, directly after you had gone.

TESMAN. And he said that he had torn his manuscript to pieces—eh?

HEDDA. Yes, so he declared.

TESMAN. Why, good heavens, he must have been completely out of his mind! And I suppose you thought it best not to give it back to him, Hedda?

HEDDA. No, he did not get it.

TESMAN. But of course you told him that we had it?

HEDDA. No. [*Quickly.*] Did you tell Mrs. Elvsted?

TESMAN. No; I thought I had better not. But you ought to have told him. Fancy, if, in desperation, he should go and do himself some injury! Let me have the manuscript, Hedda! I will take it to him at once. Where is it?

HEDDA [*cold and immovable, leaning on the arm-chair*]. I have not got it.

TESMAN. Have not got it? What in the world do you mean?

HEDDA. I have burnt it—every line of it.

TESMAN [*with a violent movement of terror*]. Burnt! Burnt Eilert's manuscript!

HEDDA. Don't scream so. The servant might hear you.

TESMAN. Burnt! Why, good God—! No, no, no! It's impossible!

HEDDA. It is so, nevertheless.

TESMAN. Do you know what you have done, Hedda? It's unlawful appropriation of lost property. Fancy that! Just ask Judge Brack, and he'll tell you what it is.

HEDDA. I advise you not to speak of it—either to Judge Brack, or to any one else.

TESMAN. But how could you do anything so unheard-of? What put it into your head? What possessed you? Answer me that—eh?

HEDDA [*suppressing an almost imperceptible smile*]. I did it for your sake, George.

TESMAN. For my sake!

HEDDA. This morning, when you told me about what he had read to you—

TESMAN. Yes, yes—what then?

HEDDA. You acknowledged that you envied his work.

TESMAN. Oh, of course I didn't mean that literally.

HEDDA. No matter—I could not bear the idea that any one should throw you into the shade.

TESMAN [*in an outburst of mingled doubt and joy*]. Hedda! Oh, is this true? But—but— I never knew you to show your love like that before. Fancy that!

HEDDA. Well, I may as well tell you that—just at this time—[*impatiently, breaking off*]. No, no; you can ask Aunt Julia. She will tell you, fast enough.

TESMAN. Oh, I almost think I understand you, Hedda! [*Clasps his hands together.*] Great heavens! do you really mean it! Eh?

HEDDA. Don't shout so. The servant might hear.

TESMAN [*laughing in irrepressible glee*]. The servant! Why, how absurd you are, Hedda. It's only my old Berta! Why, I'll tell Berta myself.

HEDDA [*clenching her hands together in desperation*]. Oh, it is killing me,—it is killing me, all this!

TESMAN. What is, Hedda? Eh?

HEDDA [*coldly, controlling herself*]. All this—absurdity—George.

TESMAN. Absurdity! Do you see anything absurd in my being overjoyed at the news! But after all perhaps I had better not say anything to Berta.

HEDDA. Oh—why not that too?

TESMAN. No, no, not yet! But I must certainly tell Aunt Julia. And then that you have begun to call me George too! Fancy that! Oh, Aunt Julia will be so happy— so happy.

HEDDA. When she hears that I have burnt Eilert Lövborg's manuscript—for your sake?

TESMAN. No, by-the-bye—that affair of the manuscript—of course nobody must know about that. But that you love me so much, Hedda—Aunt Julia must really share my joy in that! I wonder, now, whether this sort of thing is usual in young wives? Eh?

HEDDA. I think you had better ask Aunt Julia that question too.

TESMAN. I will indeed, some time or other. [*Looks uneasy and downcast again.*] And yet the manuscript—the manuscript! Good God! it is terrible to think what will become of poor Eilert now.

[MRS. ELVSTED, *dressed as in the first act, with hat and cloak, enters by the hall door.*]

MRS. ELVSTED [*greets them hurriedly, and says in evident agitation*]. Oh, dear Hedda, forgive my coming again.

HEDDA. What is the matter with you, Thea?

TESMAN. Something about Eilert Lövborg again—eh?

MRS. ELVSTED. Yes! I am dreadfully afraid some misfortune has happened to him.

HEDDA [*seizes her arm*]. Ah,—do you think so?

TESMAN. Why, good Lord—what makes you think that, Mrs. Elvsted?

MRS. ELVSTED. I heard them talking of him at my boarding-house—just as I came in. Oh, the most incredible rumors are afloat about him today.

TESMAN. Yes, fancy, so I heard too! And I can bear witness that he went straight home to bed last night. Fancy that!

HEDDA. Well, what did they say at the boarding-house?

MRS. ELVSTED. Oh, I couldn't make out anything clearly. Either they knew nothing definite, or else—They stopped talking when they saw me; and I did not dare to ask.

TESMAN [*moving about uneasily*]. We must hope—we must hope that you misunderstood them, Mrs. Elvsted.

MRS. ELVSTED. No, no; I am sure it was of him they were talking. And I heard something about the hospital or—

TESMAN. The hospital?

HEDDA. No—surely that cannot be!

MRS. ELVSTED. Oh, I was in such mortal terror! I went to his lodgings and asked for him there.

HEDDA. You could make up your mind to that, Thea!

MRS. ELVSTED. What else could I do? I really could bear the suspense no longer.

TESMAN. But you didn't find him either—eh?

MRS. ELVSTED. No. And the people knew nothing about him. He hadn't been home since yesterday afternoon, they said.

TESMAN. Yesterday! Fancy, how could they say that?

MRS. ELVSTED. Oh, I am sure something terrible must have happened to him.

TESMAN. Hedda dear—how would it be if I were to go and make inquiries—?

HEDDA. No, no—don't you mix yourself up in this affair.

[JUDGE BRACK, *with his hat in his hand, enters by the hall door, which* BERTA *opens, and closes behind him. He looks grave and bows in silence.*]

TESMAN. Oh, is that you, my dear Judge? Eh?

BRACK. Yes. It was imperative I should see you this evening.

TESMAN. I can see you have heard the news about Aunt Rina.

BRACK. Yes, that among other things.

TESMAN. Isn't it sad—eh?

BRACK. Well, my dear Tesman, that depends on how you look at it.

TESMAN [*looks doubtfully at him*]. Has anything else happened?

BRACK. Yes.

HEDDA [*in suspense*]. Anything sad, Judge Brack?

BRACK. That, too, depends on how you look at it, Mrs. Tesman.

MRS. ELVSTED [*unable to restrain her anxiety*]. Oh! it is something about Eilert Lövborg!

BRACK [*with a glance at her*]. What makes you think that, Madam? Perhaps you have already heard something—?

MRS. ELVSTED [*in confusion*]. No, nothing at all, but—

TESMAN. Oh, for heaven's sake, tell us!

BRACK [*shrugging his shoulders*]. Well, I regret to say Eilert Lövborg has been taken to the hospital. He is lying at the point of death.

MRS. ELVSTED [*shrieks*]. Oh God! Oh God—

TESMAN. To the hospital! And at the point of death.

HEDDA [*involuntarily*]. So soon then—

MRS. ELVSTED [*wailing*]. And we parted in anger, Hedda!

HEDDA [*whispers*]. Thea—Thea—be careful!

MRS. ELVSTED [*not heeding her*]. I must go to him! I must see him alive!

BRACK. It is useless, Madam. No one will be admitted.

MRS. ELVSTED. Oh, at least tell me what has happened to him? What is it?

TESMAN. You don't mean to say that he has himself—Eh?

HEDDA. Yes, I am sure he has.

TESMAN. Hedda, how can you—?

BRACK [*keeping his eyes fixed upon her*]. Unfortunately you have guessed quite correctly, Mrs. Tesman.

MRS. ELVSTED. Oh, how horrible!

TESMAN. Himself, then! Fancy that!

HEDDA. Shot himself!

BRACK. Rightly guessed again, Mrs. Tesman.

MRS. ELVSTED [*with an effort at self-control*]. When did it happen, Mr. Brack?

BRACK. This afternoon—between three and four.

TESMAN. But, good Lord, where did he do it? Eh?

BRACK [*with some hesitation*]. Where? Well—I suppose at his lodgings.

MRS. ELVSTED. No, that cannot be; for I was there between six and seven.

BRACK. Well, then, somewhere else. I don't know exactly. I only know that he was found—. He had shot himself—in the breast.

MRS. ELVSTED. Oh, how terrible! That he should die like that!

HEDDA [*to* BRACK]. Was it in the breast?

BRACK. Yes—as I told you.

HEDDA. Not in the temple?

BRACK. In the breast, Mrs. Tesman.

HEDDA. Well, well—the breast is a good place, too.

BRACK. How do you mean, Mrs. Tesman?

HEDDA [*evasively*]. Oh, nothing—nothing.

TESMAN. And the wound is dangerous, you say—eh?

BRACK. Absolutely mortal. The end has probably come by this time.

MRS. ELVSTED. Yes, yes, I feel it. The end! The end! Oh, Hedda—!

TESMAN. But tell me, how have you learnt all this?

BRACK [*curtly*]. Through one of the police. A man I had some business with.

HEDDA [*in a clear voice*]. At last a deed worth doing!

TESMAN [*terrified*]. Good heavens, Hedda! what are you saying?

HEDDA. I say there is beauty in this.

BRACK. H'm, Mrs. Tesman—

TESMAN. Beauty! Fancy that!

MRS. ELVSTED. Oh, Hedda, how can you talk of beauty in such an act!

HEDDA. Eilert Lövborg has himself made up his account with life. He has had the courage to do—the one right thing.

MRS. ELVSTED. No, you must never think that was how it happened! It must have been in delirium that he did it.

TESMAN. In despair!

HEDDA. That he did not. I am certain of that.

MRS. ELVSTED. Yes, yes! In delirium! Just as when he tore up our manuscript.

BRACK [*starting*]. The manuscript? Has he torn that up?

MRS. ELVSTED. Yes, last night.

TESMAN [*whispers softly*]. Oh, Hedda, we shall never get over this.

BRACK. H'm, very extraordinary.

TESMAN [*moving about the room*]. To think of Eilert going out of the world in this way! And not leaving behind him the book that would have immortalized his name—

MRS. ELVSTED. Oh, if only it could be put together again!

TESMAN. Yes, if it only could! I don't know what I would not give—

MRS. ELVSTED. Perhaps it can, Mr. Tesman.

TESMAN. What do you mean?

MRS. ELVSTED [*searches in the pocket of her dress*]. Look here. I have kept all the loose notes he used to dictate from.

HEDDA [*a step forward*]. Ah—!

TESMAN. You have kept them, Mrs. Elvsted! Eh?

MRS. ELVSTED. Yes, I have them here. I put them in my pocket when I left home. Here they still are—

TESMAN. Oh, do let me see them!

MRS. ELVSTED [*hands him a bundle of papers*]. But they are in such disorder—all mixed up.

TESMAN. Fancy, if we could make something out of them, after all! Perhaps if we two put our heads together—

MRS. ELVSTED. Oh, yes, at least let us try—

TESMAN. We will manage it! We must! I will dedicate my life to this task.

HEDDA. You, George? Your life?

TESMAN. Yes, or rather all the time I can spare. My own collections must wait in the meantime. Hedda—you understand, eh? I owe this to Eilert's memory.

HEDDA. Perhaps.

TESMAN. And so, my dear Mrs. Elvsted, we will give our whole minds to it. There is no use in brooding over what can't be undone—eh? We must try to control our grief as much as possible, and—

MRS. ELVSTED. Yes, yes, Mr. Tesman, I will do the best I can.

TESMAN. Well then, come here. I can't rest until we have looked through the notes. Where shall we sit? Here? No, in there, in the back room. Excuse me, my dear Judge. Come with me, Mrs. Elvsted.

MRS. ELVSTED. Oh, if only it were possible!

[TESMAN *and* MRS. ELVSTED *go into the back room. She takes off her hat and cloak. They both sit at the table under the hanging lamp, and are soon deep in an eager examination of the papers.* HEDDA *crosses to the stove and sits in the arm-chair. Presently* BRACK *goes up to her.*]

HEDDA [*in a low voice*]. Oh, what a sense of freedom it gives one, this act of Eilert Lövborg's.

BRACK. Freedom. Mrs. Hedda? Well, of course, it is a release for him—

HEDDA. I mean for me. It gives me a sense of freedom to know that a deed of deliberate courage is still possible in this world,—a deed of spontaneous beauty.

BRACK [*smiling*]. H'm—my dear Mrs. Hedda—

HEDDA. Oh, I know what you are going to say. For you are a kind of a specialist too, like—you know!

BRACK [*looking hard at her*]. Eilert Lövborg was more to you than perhaps you are willing to admit to yourself. Am I wrong?

HEDDA. I don't answer such questions. I only know Eilert Lövborg has had the courage to live his life after his own fashion. And then—the last great act, with its beauty! Ah! that he should have the will and the strength to turn away from the banquet of life—so early.

BRACK. I am sorry, Mrs. Hedda,—but I fear I must dispel an amiable illusion.

HEDDA. Illusion?

BRACK. Which could not have lasted long in any case.

HEDDA. What do you mean?

BRACK. Eilert Lövborg did not shoot himself voluntarily.

HEDDA. Not voluntarily?

BRACK. No. The thing did not happen exactly as I told it.

HEDDA [*in suspense*]. Have you concealed something? What is it?

BRACK. For poor Mrs. Elvsted's sake I idealized the facts a little.

HEDDA. What are the facts?

BRACK. First, that he is already dead.

HEDDA. At the hospital?

BRACK. Yes—without regaining consciousness.

HEDDA. What more have you concealed?

BRACK. This—the event did not happen at his lodgings.

HEDDA. Oh, that can make no difference.

BRACK. Perhaps it may. For I must tell you—Eilert Lövborg was found shot in—in Mademoiselle Diana's boudoir.

HEDDA [*makes a motion as if to rise, but sinks back again*]. That is impossible, Judge Brack! He cannot have been there again today.

BRACK. He was there this afternoon. He went there, he said, to demand the return of something which they had taken from him. Talked wildly about a lost child—

HEDDA. Ah—so that was why—

BRACK. I thought probably he meant his manuscript; but now I hear he destroyed that himself. So I suppose it must have been his pocket-book.

HEDDA. Yes, no doubt. And there—there he was found?

BRACK. Yes, there. With a pistol in his breastpocket, discharged. The ball had lodged in a vital part.

HEDDA. In the breast—yes.

BRACK. No—in the bowels.

HEDDA [*looks up at him with an expression of loathing*]. That too! Oh, what curse is it that makes everything I touch turn ludicrous and mean?

BRACK. There is one point more, Mrs. Hedda—another disagreeable feature in the affair.

HEDDA. And what is that?

BRACK. The pistol he carried—

HEDDA [*breathless*]. Well? What of it?

BRACK. He must have stolen it.

HEDDA [*leaps up*]. Stolen it! That is not true! He did not steal it!

BRACK. No other explanation is possible. He must have stolen it—Hush!

[TESMAN *and* MRS. ELVSTED *have risen from the table in the back room, and come into the drawing-room.*]

TESMAN [*with the papers in both his hands*]. Hedda dear, it is almost impossible to see under that lamp. Think of that!

HEDDA. Yes, I am thinking.

TESMAN. Would you mind our sitting at your writing-table—eh?

HEDDA. If you like. [*Quickly.*] No, wait! Let me clear it first!

TESMAN. Oh, you needn't trouble, Hedda. There is plenty of room.

HEDDA. No, no; let me clear it, I say! I will take these things in and put them on the piano. There! [*She has drawn out an object, covered with sheet music, from under the book-case, places several other pieces of music upon it, and carries the whole into the inner room, to the left.* TESMAN *lays the scraps of paper on the writing-table, and moves the lamp there from the corner table,* HEDDA *returns.*]

HEDDA [*behind* MRS. ELVSTED'S *chair, gently ruffling her hair*]. Well, my sweet Thea,— how goes it with Eilert Lövborg's monument?

MRS. ELVSTED [*looks dispiritedly up at her*]. Oh, it will be terribly hard to put in order.

TESMAN. We must manage it. I am determined. And arranging other people's papers is just the work for me.

[HEDDA *goes over to the stove, and seats herself on one of the foot-stools.* BRACK *stands over her, leaning on the arm-chair.*]

HEDDA [*whispers*]. What did you say about the pistol?

BRACK [*softly*]. That he must have stolen it.

HEDDA. Why stolen it?

BRACK. Because every other explanation ought to be impossible, Mrs. Hedda.

HEDDA. Indeed?

BRACK [*glances at her*]. Of course Eilert Lövborg was here this morning. Was he not?

HEDDA. Yes.

BRACK. Were you alone with him?

HEDDA. Part of the time.

BRACK. Did you not leave the room whilst he was here?

HEDDA. No.

BRACK. Try to recollect. Were you not out of the room a moment?

HEDDA. Yes, perhaps just a moment—out in the hall.

BRACK. And where was your pistol-case during that time?

HEDDA. I had it locked up in—

BRACK. Well, Mrs. Hedda?

HEDDA. The case stood there on the writing-table.

BRACK. Have you looked since, to see whether both the pistols are there?

HEDDA. No.

BRACK. Well, you need not. I saw the pistol found in Lövborg's pocket, and I knew it at once as the one I had seen yesterday—and before, too.

HEDDA. Have you it with you?

BRACK. No; the police have it.

HEDDA. What will the police do with it?

BRACK. Search till they find the owner.

HEDDA. Do you think they will succeed?

BRACK [bends over her and whispers]. No, Hedda Gabler—not so long as I say nothing.

HEDDA [looks frightened at him]. And if you do not say nothing,—what then?

BRACK [shrugs his shoulders]. There is always the possibility that the pistol was stolen.

HEDDA [firmly]. Death rather than that.

BRACK [smiling]. People say such things—but they don't do them.

HEDDA [without replying]. And supposing the pistol wasn't stolen, and the owner is discovered? What then?

BRACK. Well, Hedda—then comes the scandal.

HEDDA. The scandal!

BRACK. Yes, the scandal—of which you are mortally afraid. You will, of course, be brought before the court—both you and Mademoiselle Diana. She will have to explain how the thing happened—whether it was an accidental shot or murder. Did the pistol go off as he was trying to take it out of his pocket, to threaten her with? Or did she tear the pistol out of his hand, shoot him, and push it back into his pocket? That would be quite like her; for she is an able-bodied young person, this same Mademoiselle Diana.

HEDDA. But *I* have nothing to do with all this repulsive business.

BRACK. No. But you will have to answer the question: Why did you give Eilert Lövborg the pistol? And what conclusions will people draw from the fact that you did give it to him?

HEDDA [lets her head sink]. That is true. I did not think of that.

BRACK. Well, fortunately, there is no danger, so long as I say nothing.

HEDDA [looks up at him]. So I am in your power, Judge Brack. You have me at your beck and call, from this time forward.

BRACK [whispers softly]. Dearest Hedda—believe me—I shall not abuse my advantage.

HEDDA. I am in your power none the less. Subject to your will and your demands. A slave, a slave then! [Rises impetuously.] No, I cannot endure the thought of that! Never!

BRACK [looks half-mockingly at her]. People generally get used to the inevitable.

HEDDA [returns his look]. Yes, perhaps. [She crosses to the writing-table. Suppressing an involuntary smile, she imitates TESMAN's intonations.] Well? Are you getting on, George? Eh?

TESMAN. Heaven knows, dear. In any case it will be the work of months.

HEDDA [as before]. Fancy that? [Passes her hands softly through MRS. ELVSTED's hair.] Doesn't it seem strange to you, Thea? Here are you sitting with Tesman—just as you used to sit with Eilert Lövborg?

MRS. ELVSTED. Ah, if I could only inspire your husband in the same way.

HEDDA. Oh, that will come too—in time.

TESMAN. Yes, do you know, Hedda—I really think I begin to feel something of the sort. But won't you go and sit with Brack again?

HEDDA. Is there nothing I can do to help you two?

TESMAN. No, nothing in the world. [*Turning his head.*] I trust to you to keep Hedda company, my dear Brack.

BRACK [*with a glance at* HEDDA]. With the very greatest of pleasure.

HEDDA. Thanks. But I am tired this evening. I will go in and lie down a little on the sofa.

TESMAN. Yes, do dear—eh?

[HEDDA *goes into the back room and draws the curtains. A short pause. Suddenly she is heard playing a wild dance on the piano.*]

MRS. ELVSTED [*starts from her chair*]. Oh—what is that?

TESMAN [*runs to the doorway*]. Why, my dearest Hedda—don't play dance music tonight! Just think of Aunt Rina! And of Eilert too!

HEDDA [*puts her head out between the curtains*]. And of Aunt Julia. And of all the rest of them. —After this, I will be quiet. [*Closes the curtains again.*]

TESMAN [*at the writing-table*]. It's not good for her to see us at this distressing work. I'll tell you what, Mrs. Elvsted,—you shall take the empty room at Aunt Julia's, and then I will come over in the evenings, and we can sit and work there—eh?

HEDDA [*in the inner room*]. I hear what you are saying, Tesman. But how am *I* to get through the evenings out here?

TESMAN [*turning over the papers*]. Oh, I daresay Judge Brack will be so kind as to look in now and then, even though I am out.

BRACK [*in the arm-chair, calls out gaily*]. Every blessed evening, with all the pleasure in life, Mrs. Tesman! We shall get on capitally together, we two!

HEDDA [*speaking loud and clear*]. Yes, don't you flatter yourself we will, Judge Brack? Now that you are the one cock in the basket—

[*A shot is heard within.* TESMAN, MRS. ELVSTED, *and* BRACK *leap to their feet.*]

TESMAN. Oh, now she is playing with those pistols again.

[*He throws back the curtains and runs in, followed by* MRS. ELVSTED. HEDDA *lies stretched on the sofa, lifeless. Confusion and cries.* BERTA *enters in alarm from the right.*]

TESMAN [*shrieks to* BRACK]. Shot herself! Shot herself in the temple! Fancy that!

BRACK [*half-fainting in the arm-chair*]. Good God!—people don't do such things.

[1890]

Anton Pavlovich Chekhov   *1860–1904*

THE CHERRY ORCHARD

Translated by David Magarshack

CHARACTERS

LYUBOV (LYUBA) ANDREYEVNA RANEVSKY, *a landowner*

ANYA, *her daughter, aged seventeen*

VARYA, *her adopted daughter, aged twenty-four*

LEONID ANDREYEVICH GAYEV, *Mrs. Ranevsky's brother*

YERMOLAY ALEXEYEVICH LOPAKHIN, *a businessman*

PETER (PYOTR) SERGEYEVICH TROFIMOV, *a student*

BORIS BORISOVICH SIMEONOV-PISHCHIK, *a landowner*

CHARLOTTE IVANOVNA, *a governess*

SIMON PANTELEYEVICH YEPIKHODOV, *a clerk*

DUNYASHA, *a maid*

FIRS, *a manservant, aged eighty-seven*

YASHA, *a young manservant*

A HIKER

A STATIONMASTER

A POST OFFICE CLERK

GUESTS *and* SERVANTS

SCENE:
The action takes place on MRS. RANEVSKY'S *estate.*

ACT I

A room which is still known as the nursery. One of the doors leads to ANYA'S *room. Daybreak; the sun will be rising soon. It is May. The cherry trees are in blossom, but it is cold in the orchard. Morning frost. The windows of the room are shut. Enter* DUNYASHA, *carrying a candle, and* LOPAKHIN *with a book in his hand.*

LOPAKHIN. The train's arrived, thank goodness. What's the time?

DUNYASHA. Nearly two o'clock, sir. [*Blows out the candle.*] It's light already.

LOPAKHIN. How late was the train? Two hours at least. [*Yawns and stretches.*] What a damn fool I am! Came here specially to meet them at the station and fell asleep. . . . Sat down in a chair and dropped off. What a nuisance! Why didn't you wake me?

DUNYASHA. I thought you'd gone, sir. [*Listens.*] I think they're coming.

LOPAKHIN [*listening*]. No. . . . I should have been there to help them with the luggage and so on. [*Pause.*] Mrs. Ranevsky's been abroad for five years. I wonder what she's like now. . . . She's such a nice person. Simple, easy-going. I remember when I was a lad of fifteen, my late father—he used to keep a shop in the village—punched me in the face and made my nose bleed. We'd gone into the yard to fetch something, and he was drunk. Mrs. Ranevsky—I remember it as if it happened yesterday, she was such a young girl then and so slim—took me to the washstand in this very room, the nursery. "Don't cry, little peasant," she said, "it won't matter by the time you're wed." [*Pause.*] Little peasant. . . . It's quite true my father was a peasant, but here I am wearing a white waistcoat and brown shoes. A dirty peasant in a fashionable shop. . . . Except, of course, that

I'm a rich man now, rolling in money. But, come to think of it, I'm a plain peasant still. . . . [*Turns the pages of his book.*] Been reading this book and haven't understood a word. Fell asleep reading it.
[*Pause.*]

DUNYASHA. The dogs have been awake all night; they know their masters are coming.

LOPAKHIN. What's the matter, Dunyasha? Why are you in such a state?

DUNYASHA. My hands are shaking. I think I'm going to faint.

LOPAKHIN. A little too refined, aren't you, Dunyasha? Quite the young lady. Dress, hair. It won't do, you know. Remember your place!

[*Enter* YEPIKHODOV *with a bunch of flowers; he wears a jacket and brightly polished high-boots which squeak loudly; on coming in, he drops the flowers.*]

YEPIKHODOV [*picking up the flowers*]. The gardener sent these. Said to put them in the dining room. [*Hands the flowers to* DUNYASHA.]

LOPAKHIN. Bring me some kvass[1] while you're about it.

DUNYASHA. Yes, sir. [*Goes out.*]

YEPIKHODOV. Thirty degrees, morning frost, and the cherry trees in full bloom. Can't say I think much of our climate, sir. [*Sighs.*] Our climate isn't particularly accommodating, is it, sir? Not when you want it to be, anyway. And another thing. The other day I bought myself this pair of boots, and believe me, sir, they squeak so terribly that it's more than a man can endure. Do you happen to know of something I could grease them with?

LOPAKHIN. Go away. You make me tired.

YEPIKHODOV. Every day, sir, I'm overtaken by some calamity. Not that I mind. I'm used to it. I just smile. [DUNYASHA *comes in and hands* LOPAKHIN *the kvass.*] I'll be off. [*Bumps into a chair and knocks it over.*] There you are, sir. [*Triumphantly.*] You see, sir, pardon the expression, this sort of circumstance . . . I mean to say . . . Remarkable! Quite remarkable. [*Goes out.*]

DUNYASHA. I simply must tell you, sir: Yepikhodov has proposed to me.

LOPAKHIN. Oh?

DUNYASHA. I really don't know what to do, sir. He's ever such a quiet fellow, except that sometimes he starts talking and you can't understand a word he says. It sounds all right and it's ever so moving, only you can't make head or tail of it. I like him a little, I think. I'm not sure though. He's madly in love with me. He's such an unlucky fellow, sir. Every day something happens to him. Everyone teases him about it. They've nicknamed him Twenty-Two Calamities.

LOPAKHIN [*listens*]. I think I can hear them coming.

DUNYASHA. They're coming! Goodness, I don't know what's the matter with me. I've gone cold all over.

LOPAKHIN. Yes, they are coming all right. Let's go and meet them. Will she recognize me? We haven't seen each other for five years.

DUNYASHA [*agitated*]. I'm going to faint. Oh dear, I'm going to faint!

Two carriages can be heard driving up to the house. LOPAKHIN *and* DUNYASHA *go out quickly. The stage is empty. People can be heard making a noise in the adjoining rooms.* FIRS, *who has been to meet* MRS. RANEVSKY *at the station, walks across the stage hurriedly, leaning on a stick. He wears an old-fashioned livery coat and a top hat; he keeps muttering to himself, but it is impossible to make out a single word. The noise offstage becomes louder. A voice is heard: "Let's go through here."* MRS. RANEVSKY, ANYA, *and* CHARLOTTE, *with a lap dog on*

---

[1] An alcoholic beverage somewhat like beer.

a little chain, all wearing traveling clothes, VARYA, *wearing an overcoat and a head scarf,* GAYEV, SIMEONOV-PISHCHIK, LOPAKHIN, DUNYASHA, *carrying a bundle and an umbrella, and other* SERVANTS *with luggage walk across the stage.*

ANYA. Let's go through here. Remember this room, Mother?

MRS. RANEVSKY [*joyfully, through tears*]. The nursery!

VARYA. It's so cold. My hands are quite numb. [*To* MRS. RANEVSKY.] Your rooms, the white one and the mauve one, are just as you left them, Mother dear.

MRS. RANEVSKY. The nursery! My dear, my beautiful room! I used to sleep here when I was a little girl. [*Cries.*] I feel like a little girl again now. [*Kisses her brother and* VARYA, *and then her brother again.*] Varya is the same as ever. Looks like a nun. And I also recognize Dunyasha. [*Kisses* DUNYASHA.]

GAYEV. The train was two hours late. How do you like that? What a way to run a railway!

CHARLOTTE [*to* PISHCHIK]. My dog also eats nuts.

PISHCHIK [*surprised*]. Good Lord!

[*All, except* ANYA *and* DUNYASHA, *go out.*]

DUNYASHA. We thought you'd never come. [*Helps* ANYA *off with her coat and hat.*]

ANYA. I haven't slept for four nights on our journey. Now I'm chilled right through.

DUNYASHA. You left before Easter. It was snowing and freezing then. It's different now, isn't it? Darling Anya! [*Laughs and kisses her.*] I've missed you so much, my darling, my precious! Oh, I must tell you at once! I can't keep it to myself a minute longer. . . .

ANYA [*apathetically*]. What is it this time?

DUNYASHA. Our clerk, Yepikhodov, proposed to me after Easter.

ANYA. Always the same. [*Tidying her hair.*] I've lost all my hairpins. [*She is so tired, she can hardly stand.*]

DUNYASHA. I don't know what to think. He loves me so much, so much!

ANYA [*tenderly, looking through the door into her room*]. My own room, my own windows, just as if I'd never been away! I'm home again! As soon as I get up in the morning, I'll run out into the orchard. . . . Oh, if only I could sleep. I didn't sleep all the way back, I was so worried.

DUNYASHA. Mr. Trofimov arrived the day before yesterday.

ANYA [*joyfully*]. Peter!

DUNYASHA. He's asleep in the bathhouse. He's been living there. Afraid of being a nuisance, he says. [*Glancing at her watch.*] I really ought to wake him, except that Miss Varya told me not to. "Don't you dare wake him!" she said.

[VARYA *comes in with a bunch of keys at her waist.*]

VARYA. Dunyasha, coffee quick! Mother's asking for some.

DUNYASHA. I won't be a minute! [*Goes out.*]

VARYA. Well, thank goodness you're all back. You're home again, my darling. [*Caressing her.*] My darling is home again! My sweet child is home again!

ANYA. I've had such an awful time!

VARYA. I can imagine it.

ANYA. I left before Easter. It was terribly cold then. All the way Charlotte kept talking and doing her conjuring tricks. Why did you force Charlotte on me?

VARYA. But you couldn't have gone alone, darling, could you? You're only seventeen!

ANYA. In Paris it was also cold and snowing. My French is awful. I found Mother living on the fourth floor. When I got there, she had some French visitors, a few ladies and an old Catholic priest with a book. The place was full of tobacco smoke and terribly uncomfortable. Suddenly I felt sorry for Mother, so sorry that I took her head in my arms, held it tightly, and couldn't let go. Afterwards Mother was very sweet to me. She was crying all the time.

VARYA [*through tears*]. Don't go on, Anya. Please don't.

ANYA. She'd already sold her villa near Mentone. She had nothing left. Nothing! I hadn't any money, either. There was hardly enough for the journey. Mother just won't understand! We had dinner at the station and she would order the most expensive things and tip the waiters a ruble each. Charlotte was just the same. Yasha, too, demanded to be given the same kind of food. It was simply awful! You see, Yasha is Mother's manservant. We've brought him back with us.

VARYA. Yes, I've seen the scoundrel.

ANYA. Well, what's been happening? Have you paid the interest on the mortgage?

VARYA. Heavens, no!

ANYA. Dear, oh dear . . .

VARYA. The estate will be up for sale in August.

ANYA. Oh dear!

LOPAKHIN [*puts his head through the door and bleats*]. Bah-h-h! [*Goes out.*]

VARYA [*through tears*]. Oh, I'd like to hit him! [*Shakes her fist.*]

ANYA [*gently embracing* VARYA]. Varya, has he proposed to you? [VARYA *shakes her head.*] But he loves you. Why don't you two come to an understanding? What are you waiting for?

VARYA. I don't think anything will come of it. He's so busy. He can't be bothered with me. Why, he doesn't even notice me. I wish I'd never known him. I can't stand the sight of him. Everyone's talking about our wedding, everyone's congratulating me, while there's really nothing in it. It's all so unreal. Like a dream. [*In a different tone of voice.*] You've got a new brooch. Like a bee, isn't it?

ANYA [*sadly*]. Yes, Mother bought it. [*Goes to her room, talking quite happily, like a child.*] You know, I went up in a balloon in Paris!

VARYA. My darling's home again! My dearest one's home again! [DUNYASHA *has come back with a coffeepot and is making coffee;* VARYA *is standing at the door of* ANYA'*s room.*] All day long, darling, I'm busy about the house, and all the time I'm dreaming, dreaming. If only we could find a rich husband for you! My mind would be at rest then. I'd go into a convent and later on a pilgrimage to Kiev . . . to Moscow. Just keep going from one holy place to another. On and on. . . . Wonderful!

ANYA. The birds are singing in the orchard. What's the time?

VARYA. It's past two. It's time you were asleep, darling. [*Goes into* ANYA'*s room.*] Wonderful!

[*Enter* YASHA *with a traveling rug and a small bag.*]

YASHA [*crossing the stage, in an affected genteel voice*]. May I be permitted to go through here?

DUNYASHA. I can hardly recognize you, Yasha. You've changed so much abroad.

YASHA. Hmmm . . . And who are you, may I ask?

DUNYASHA. When you left, I was no bigger than this. [*Shows her height from the floor with her hand.*] I'm Dunyasha, Fyodor Kozoedov's daughter. Don't you remember me?

YASHA. Mmmm . . . Juicy little cucumber! [*Looks round, then puts his arms around her; she utters a little scream and drops a saucer.* YASHA *goes out hurriedly.*]

VARYA [*in the doorway, crossly*]. What's going on there?

DUNYASHA [*in tears*]. I've broken a saucer.

VARYA. That's lucky.

ANYA [*coming out of her room*]. Mother must be told Peter's here.

VARYA. I gave orders not to wake him.

ANYA [*pensively*]. Father died six years ago. A month after our brother, Grisha, was
drowned in the river. Such a pretty little boy. He was only seven. Mother took
it badly. She went away, went away never to come back. [*Shudders.*] Peter Trofimov was Grisha's tutor. He might remind her . . .
[FIRS *comes in, wearing a jacket and a white waistcoat.*]
FIRS [*walks up to the coffeepot anxiously*]. Madam will have her coffee here. [*Puts on
white gloves.*] Is the coffee ready? [*Sternly, to* DUNYASHA.] You there! Where's the
cream?
DUNYASHA. Oh dear! [*Goes out quickly.*]
FIRS [*fussing round the coffeepot*]. The nincompoop! [*Muttering to himself.*] She's
come from Paris. . . . Master used to go to Paris. . . . Aye, by coach. . . . [*Laughs.*]
VARYA. What are you talking about, Firs?
FIRS. Sorry, what did you say? [*Joyfully.*] Madam is home again! Home at last! I can
die happy now. [*Weeps with joy.*]

Enter MRS. RANEVSKY, GAYEV, *and* SIMEONOV-PISHCHIK, *the last one wearing a Russian
long-waisted coat of expensive cloth and wide trousers. As he enters,* GAYEV *moves his arms
and body as if he were playing billiards.*

MRS. RANEVSKY. How does it go now? Let me think. Pot the red in the corner.
Double into the middle pocket.
GAYEV. And straight into the corner! A long time ago, Lyuba, you and I slept in this
room. Now I'm fifty-one. . . . Funny, isn't it!
LOPAKHIN. Aye, time flies.
GAYEV. I beg your pardon?
LOPAKHIN. "Time flies," I said.
GAYEV. The place reeks of patchouli.[2]
ANYA. I'm off to bed. Good night, Mother. [*Kisses her mother.*]
MRS. RANEVSKY. My sweet little darling! [*Kisses her hands.*] You're glad to be home,
aren't you? I still can't believe it.
ANYA. Good night, Uncle.
GAYEV [*kissing her face and hands*]. God bless you. You're so like your mother! [*To
his sister.*] You were just like her at that age, Lyuba.
[ANYA *shakes hands with* LOPAKHIN *and* PISHCHIK. *Goes out and shuts the door behind
her.*]
MRS. RANEVSKY. She's terribly tired.
PISHCHIK. It was a long journey.
VARYA [*to* LOPAKHIN *and* PISHCHIK.]. Well, gentlemen, it's past two o'clock. You
mustn't outstay your welcome, must you?
MRS. RANEVSKY [*laughs*]. You're just the same, Varya. [*Draws* VARYA *to her and kisses
her.*] Let me have my coffee first and then we'll all go. [FIRS *puts a little cushion
under her feet.*] Thank you, Firs dear. I've got used to having coffee. I drink it day
and night. Thank you, Firs, thank you, my dear old man. [*Kisses* FIRS.]
VARYA. I'd better make sure they've brought all the things in. [*Goes out.*]
MRS. RANEVSKY. Is it really me sitting here? [*Laughs.*] I feel like jumping about,
waving my arms. [*Covers her face with her hands.*] And what if it's all a dream? God
knows, I love my country. I love it dearly. I couldn't look out of the train for
crying. [*Through tears.*] But, I suppose I'd better have my coffee. Thank you, Firs,
thank you, dear old man. I'm so glad you're still alive.

[2] A plant from the mint family, at that time a popular fragrance.

FIRS. The day before yesterday . . .

GAYEV. He's a little deaf.

LOPAKHIN. At five o'clock I've got to leave for Kharkov. What a nuisance! I wish I could have had a good look at you, a good talk with you. You're still as magnificent as ever. . . .

PISHCHIK [*breathing heavily*]. Lovelier, I'd say. Dressed in the latest Paris fashion. If only I were twenty years younger—ho-ho-ho!

LOPAKHIN. This brother of yours says that I'm an ignorant oaf, a tightfisted peasant, but I don't mind. Let him talk. All I want is that you should believe in me as you used to, that you should look at me as you used to with those wonderful eyes of yours. Merciful heavens! My father was a serf of your father and your grandfather, but you, you alone, did so much for me in the past that I forgot everything, and I love you just as if you were my own flesh and blood, more than my own flesh and blood.

MRS. RANEVSKY. I can't sit still, I can't. . . . [*Jumps up and walks about the room in great agitation.*] This happiness is more than I can bear. Laugh at me if you like. I'm making such a fool of myself. Oh, my darling little bookcase . . . [*Kisses the bookcase.*] My sweet little table . . .

GAYEV. You know, of course, that Nanny died here while you were away.

MRS. RANEVSKY [*sits down and drinks her coffee*]. Yes, God rest her soul. They wrote to tell me about it.

GAYEV. Anastasy, too, is dead. Boss-eyed Peter left me for another job. He's with the Police Superintendent in town now. [*Takes a box of fruit drops out of his pocket and sucks one.*]

PISHCHIK. My daughter Dashenka—er—wishes to be remembered to you.

LOPAKHIN. I'd like to say something very nice and cheerful to you. [*Glances at his watch.*] I shall have to be going in a moment and there isn't much time to talk. As you know, your cherry orchard's being sold to pay your debts. The auction is on the twenty-second of August. But there's no need to worry, my dear. You can sleep soundly. There's a way out. Here's my plan. Listen carefully, please. Your estate is only about twelve miles from town, and the railway is not very far away. Now, all you have to do is break up your cherry orchard and the land along the river into building plots and lease them out for country cottages. You'll then have an income of at least twenty-five thousand a year.

GAYEV. I'm sorry, but what utter nonsense!

MRS. RANEVSKY. I don't quite follow you, Lopakhin.

LOPAKHIN. You'll be able to charge your tenants at least twenty-five rubles a year for a plot of about three acres. I bet you anything that if you advertise now, there won't be a single plot left by the autumn. They will all be snapped up. In fact, I congratulate you. You are saved. The site is magnificent and the river is deep enough for bathing. Of course, the place will have to be cleared, tidied up. . . . I mean, all the old buildings will have to be pulled down, including, I'm sorry to say, this house, but it isn't any use to anybody any more, is it? The old cherry orchard will have to be cut down.

MRS. RANEVSKY. Cut down? My dear man, I'm very sorry but I don't think you know what you're talking about. If there's anything of interest, anything quite remarkable, in fact, in the whole county, it's our cherry orchard.

LOPAKHIN. The only remarkable thing about this orchard is that it's very large. It only produces a crop every other year, and even then you don't know what to do with the cherries. Nobody wants to buy them.

GAYEV. Why, you'll find our orchard mentioned in the encyclopedia.

LOPAKHIN [*glancing at his watch*]. If we can't think of anything and if we can't come to any decision, it won't be only your cherry orchard but your whole estate that will be sold at auction on the twenty-second of August. Make up your mind. I tell you, there is no other way. Take my word for it. There isn't.

FIRS. In the old days, forty or fifty years ago, the cherries used to be dried, preserved, made into jam, and sometimes—

GAYEV. Do shut up, Firs.

FIRS. —and sometimes cartloads of dried cherries were sent to Moscow and Kharkov. Fetched a lot of money, they did. Soft and juicy, those cherries were. Sweet and such a lovely smell . . . They knew the recipe then. . . .

MRS. RANEVSKY. And where's the recipe now?

FIRS. Forgotten. No one remembers it.

PISHCHIK [*to* MRS. RANEVSKY]. What was it like in Paris? Eh? Eat any frogs?

MRS. RANEVSKY. I ate crocodiles.

PISHCHIK. Good Lord!

LOPAKHIN. Till recently there were only the gentry and the peasants in the country. Now we have holiday-makers. All our towns, even the smallest, are surrounded by country cottages. I shouldn't be surprised if in twenty years the holiday-maker multiplies enormously. All your holiday-maker does now is drink tea on the veranda, but it's quite in the cards that if he becomes the owner of three acres of land, he'll do a bit of farming on the side, and then your cherry orchard will become a happy, prosperous, thriving place.

GAYEV [*indignantly*]. What nonsense!

[*Enter* VARYA *and* YASHA.]

VARYA. I've got two telegrams in here for you, Mother dear. [*Picks out a key and unlocks the old-fashioned bookcase with a jingling noise.*] Here they are.

MRS. RANEVSKY. They're from Paris. [*Tears the telegrams up without reading them.*] I've finished with Paris.

GAYEV. Do you know how old this bookcase is, Lyuba? Last week I pulled out the bottom drawer and saw some figures burned into it. This bookcase was made exactly a hundred years ago. What do you think of that? Eh? We ought really to celebrate its centenary. An inanimate object, but say what you like, it's a bookcase after all.

PISHCHIK [*amazed*]. A hundred years! Good Lord!

GAYEV. Yes, indeed. It's quite something. [*Feeling round the bookcase with his hands.*] Dear, highly esteemed bookcase, I salute you. For over a hundred years you have devoted yourself to the glorious ideals of goodness and justice. Throughout the hundred years your silent appeal to fruitful work has never faltered. It sustained [*through tears*] in several generations of our family, their courage and faith in a better future and fostered in us the ideals of goodness and social consciousness.

[*Pause.*]

LOPAKHIN. Aye. . . .

MRS. RANEVSKY. You haven't changed a bit, have you, darling Leonid?

GAYEV [*slightly embarrassed*]. Off the right into a corner! Pot into the middle pocket!

LOPAKHIN [*glancing at his watch*]. Well, afraid it's time I was off.

YASHA [*handing* MRS. RANEVSKY *her medicine*]. Your pills, ma'am.

PISHCHIK. Never take any medicines, dear lady. I don't suppose they'll do you much harm, but they won't do you any good either. Here, let me have 'em, my dear lady. [*Takes the box of pills from her, pours the pills into the palm of his hand, blows on them, puts them all into his mouth, and washes them down with kvass.*] There!

MRS. RANEVSKY [*alarmed*]. You're mad!

PISHCHIK. Swallowed the lot.

LOPAKHIN. The glutton!

[*All laugh.*]

FIRS. He was here at Easter, the gentleman was. Ate half a bucketful of pickled cucumbers, he did.... [*Mutters.*]

MRS. RANEVSKY. What is he saying?

VARYA. He's been muttering like that for the last three years. We've got used to it.

YASHA. Old age!

[CHARLOTTE, *in a white dress, very thin and tightly laced, a lorgnette*³ *dangling from her belt, crosses the stage.*]

LOPAKHIN. I'm sorry, Miss Charlotte, I haven't had the chance of saying how-do-you-do to you. [*Tries to kiss her hand.*]

CHARLOTTE [*snatching her hand away*]. If I let you kiss my hand, you'll want to kiss my elbow, then my shoulder ...

LOPAKHIN. It's not my lucky day. [*They all laugh.*] My dear Charlotte, show us a trick, please.

MRS. RANEVSKY. Yes, do show us a trick, Charlotte.

CHARLOTTE. I won't. I'm off to bed. [*Goes out.*]

LOPAKHIN. We'll meet again in three weeks. [*Kisses* MRS. RANEVSKY'*s hand.*] Good-bye for now. I must go. [*To* GAYEV.] So long. [*Embraces* PISHCHIK.] So long. [*Shakes hands with* VARYA *and then with* FIRS *and* YASHA.] I wish I didn't have to go. [*To* MRS. RANEVSKY.] Let me know if you make up your mind about the country cottages. If you decide to go ahead, I'll get you a loan of fifty thousand or more. Think it over seriously.

VARYA [*angrily*]. For goodness' sake, go!

LOPAKHIN. I'm going, I'm going.... [*Goes out.*]

GAYEV. The oaf! However, I'm sorry. Varya's going to marry him, isn't she? He's Varya's intended.

VARYA. Don't say things you'll be sorry for, Uncle.

MRS. RANEVSKY. But why not, Varya? I should be only too glad. He's a good man.

PISHCHIK. A most admirable fellow, to tell the truth. My Dashenka—er—also says that—er—says all sorts of things. [*Drops off and snores, but wakes up immediately.*] By the way, my dear lady, you will lend me two hundred and forty rubles, won't you? Must pay the interest on the mortgage tomorrow.

VARYA [*terrified*]. We have no money; we haven't!

MRS. RANEVSKY. We really haven't any, you know.

PISHCHIK. Have a good look around—you're sure to find it. [*Laughs.*] I never lose hope. Sometimes I think it's all over with me, I'm done for, then—hey presto—they build a railway over my land and pay me for it. Something's bound to turn up, if not today, then tomorrow. I'm certain of it. Dashenka might win two hundred thousand. She's got a ticket in the lottery, you know.

MRS. RANEVSKY. Well, I've finished my coffee. Now to bed.

FIRS [*brushing* GAYEV'*s clothes admonishingly*]. Put the wrong trousers on again, sir. What am I to do with you?

VARYA [*in a low voice*]. Anya's asleep. [*Opens a window quietly.*] The sun has risen. It's no longer cold. Look, Mother dear. What lovely trees! Heavens, what wonderful air! The starlings are singing.

GAYEV [*opens another window*]. The orchard's all white. Lyuba, you haven't forgotten, have you? The long avenue there—it runs on and on, straight as an arrow. It gleams on moonlit nights. Remember? You haven't forgotten, have you?

³ A pair of eyeglasses with a handle instead of earpieces.

MRS. RANEVSKY [*looking through the window at the orchard*]. Oh, my childhood, oh, my innocence! I slept in this nursery. I used to look out at the orchard from here. Every morning happiness used to wake with me. The orchard was just the same in those days. Nothing has changed. [*Laughs happily.*] White, all white! Oh, my orchard! After the dark, rainy autumn and the cold winter, you're young again, full of happiness; the heavenly angels haven't forsaken you. If only this heavy load could be lifted from my heart; if only I could forget my past!

GAYEV. Well, and now they're going to sell the orchard to pay our debts. Funny, isn't it?

MRS. RANEVSKY. Look! Mother's walking in the orchard in . . . a white dress! [*Laughs happily.*] It *is* Mother!

GAYEV. Where?

VARYA. Really, Mother dear, what are you saying?

MRS. RANEVSKY. There's no one there. I just imagined it. Over there, on the right, near the turning to the summer house, a little white tree's leaning over. It looks like a woman. [*Enter* TROFIMOV. *He is dressed in a shabby student's uniform and wears glasses.*] What an amazing orchard! Masses of white blossom. A blue sky . . .

TROFIMOV. I say, Mrs. Ranevsky . . . [*She looks round at him.*] I've just come to say hello. I'll go at once. [*Kisses her hand warmly.*] I was told to wait till morning, but I—I couldn't. I couldn't.

[MRS. RANEVSKY *gazes at him in bewilderment.*]

VARYA [*through tears*]. This is Peter Trofimov.

TROFIMOV. Peter Trofimov. Your son Grisha's old tutor. I haven't changed so much, have I?

[MRS. RANEVSKY *embraces him and weeps quietly.*]

GAYEV [*embarrassed*]. There, there, Lyuba.

VARYA [*cries*]. I did tell you to wait till tomorrow, didn't I, Peter?

MRS. RANEVSKY. Grisha, my . . . little boy. Grisha . . . my son.

VARYA. It can't be helped, Mother. It was God's will.

TROFIMOV [*gently, through tears*]. Now, now . . .

MRS. RANEVSKY [*weeping quietly*]. My little boy died, drowned. Why? Why, my friend? [*More quietly.*] Anya's asleep in there and here I am shouting, making a noise. . . . Well, Peter? You're not as good-looking as you were, are you? Why not? Why have you aged so much?

TROFIMOV. A peasant woman in a railway carriage called me "a moth-eaten gentleman."

MRS. RANEVSKY. You were only a boy then. A charming young student. Now you're growing thin on top, you wear glasses. . . . You're not still a student, are you? [*Walks toward the door.*]

TROFIMOV. I expect I shall be an eternal student.

MRS. RANEVSKY [*kisses her brother and then* VARYA]. Well, go to bed now. You, Leonid, have aged too.

PISHCHIK [*following her*]. So, we're off to bed now, are we? Oh dear, my gout! I think I'd better stay the night here. Now, what about letting me have the—er—two hundred and forty rubles tomorrow morning, dear lady? Early tomorrow morning. . . .

GAYEV. He does keep on, doesn't he?

PISHCHIK. Two hundred and forty rubles—to pay the interest on the mortgage.

MRS. RANEVSKY. But I haven't any money, my dear man.

PISHCHIK. I'll pay you back, dear lady. Such a trifling sum.

MRS. RANEVSKY. Oh, all right. Leonid will let you have it. Let him have it, Leonid.

GAYEV. Let him have it? The hell I will.

MRS. RANEVSKY. What else can we do? Let him have it, please. He needs it. He'll pay it back.

[MRS. RANEVSKY, TROFIMOV, PISHCHIK, *and* FIRS *go out.* GAYEV, VARYA, *and* YASHA *remain.*]

GAYEV. My sister hasn't got out of the habit of throwing money about. [*To* YASHA.] Out of my way, fellow. You reek of the hen house.

YASHA [*grins*]. And you, sir, are the same as ever.

GAYEV. I beg your pardon? [*To* VARYA.] What did he say?

VARYA [*to* YASHA]. Your mother's come from the village. She's been sitting in the servant's quarters since yesterday. She wants to see you.

YASHA. Oh, bother her!

VARYA. You shameless bounder!

YASHA. I don't care. She could have come tomorrow, couldn't she? [*Goes out.*]

VARYA. Dear Mother is just the same as ever. Hasn't changed a bit. If you let her, she'd give away everything.

GAYEV. I suppose so. [*Pause.*] When a lot of remedies are suggested for an illness, it means that the illness is incurable. I've been thinking, racking my brains; I've got all sorts of remedies, lots of them, which, of course, means that I haven't got one. It would be marvelous if somebody left us some money. It would be marvelous if we found a very rich husband for Anya. It would be marvelous if one of us went to Yaroslavl to try out luck with our great-aunt, the Countess. She's very rich, you know. Very rich.

VARYA [*crying*]. If only God would help us.

GAYEV. Don't howl! Our aunt is very rich, but she doesn't like us. First, because my sister married a lawyer and not a nobleman. . . . [ANYA *appears in the doorway.*] She did not marry a nobleman, and she has not been leading an exactly blameless life, has she? She's a good, kind, nice person. I love her very much. But, however much you try to make allowances for her, you have to admit that she is an immoral woman. You can sense it in every movement she makes.

VARYA [*in a whisper*]. Anya's standing in the doorway.

GAYEV. I beg your pardon? [*Pause.*] Funny thing, there's something in my right eye. Can't see properly. On Thursday, too, in the district court . . .
[ANYA *comes in.*]

VARYA. Why aren't you asleep, Anya?

ANYA. I can't sleep, I can't.

GAYEV. My little darling. [*Kisses* ANYA'*s face and hands.*] My dear child! [*Through tears.*] You're not my niece, you're my angel. You're everything to me. Believe me. Do believe me.

ANYA. I believe you, Uncle. Everyone loves you, everyone respects you, but, dear Uncle, you shouldn't talk so much. What were you saying just now about Mother, about your own sister? What did you say it for?

GAYEV. Well, yes, yes. [*He takes her hand and covers his face with it.*] You're quite right. It was dreadful. Dear God, dear God, help me! That speech I made to the bookcase today—it was so silly. The moment I finished it, I realized how silly it was.

VARYA. It's quite true, Uncle dear. You oughtn't to talk so much. Just don't talk, that's all.

ANYA. If you stopped talking, you'd feel much happier yourself.

GAYEV. Not another word. [*Kisses* ANYA's *and* VARYA's *hands.*] Not another word. Now to business. Last Thursday I was at the county court, and, well—er—I met a lot of people there, and we started talking about this and that, and—er—it would seem that we might manage to raise some money on a promissory note and pay the interest to the bank.

VARYA. Oh, if only God would help us!

GAYEV. I shall be there again on Tuesday, and I'll have another talk. [*To* VARYA.] For goodness' sake, don't howl! [*To* ANYA.] Your mother will have a talk with Lopakhin. I'm sure he won't refuse her. After you've had your rest, you'll go to Yaroslavl to see your great-aunt, the Countess. That's how we shall tackle the problem from three different sides, and I'm sure we'll get it settled. The interest we shall pay. Of that I'm quite sure. [*Puts a fruit drop in his mouth.*] I give you my word of honor, I swear by anything you like, the estate will not be sold! [*Excitedly.*] Why, I'll stake my life on it! Here's my hand; call me a rotten scoundrel if I allow the auction to take place. I stake my life on it!

ANYA [*has regained her composure; she looks happy*]. You're so good, Uncle dear! So clever! [*Embraces him.*] I'm no longer worried now. Not a bit worried. I'm happy. [*Enter* FIRS.]

FIRS [*reproachfully*]. Have you no fear of God, sir? When are you going to bed?

GAYEV. Presently, presently. Go away, Firs. Never mind, I'll undress this time. Well, children, bye-bye now. More about it tomorrow. Now you must go to bed. [*Kisses* ANYA *and* VARYA.] I'm a man of the eighties. People don't think much of that time, but let me tell you, I've suffered a great deal for my convictions during my life. It's not for nothing that the peasants love me. You have to know your peasant, you have to know how to—

ANYA. There you go again, Uncle.

VARYA. Please, Uncle dear, don't talk so much.

FIRS [*angrily*]. Sir!

GAYEV. I'm coming, I'm coming. You two go to bed. Off two cushions into the middle. Pot the white!

[GAYEV *goes out*, FIRS *shuffling off after him.*]

ANYA. I'm not worried any longer now. I don't feel like going to Yaroslavl. I don't like my great-aunt, but I'm no longer worried. I ought to thank Uncle for that. [*Sits down.*]

VARYA. I ought to go to bed, and I shall be going in a moment, I must tell you first that something unpleasant happened here while you were away. You know, of course, that only a few old servants live in the old servants' quarters: Yefimushka, Polia, Evstigney, and, well, also Karp. They had been letting some tramps sleep there, but I didn't say anything about it. Then I heard that they were telling everybody that I'd given orders for them to be fed on nothing but dried peas. I'm supposed to be a miser, you see. It was all that Evstigney's doing. Well, I said to myself, if that's how it is, you just wait! So I sent for Evstigney. [*Yawns.*] He comes. "What do you mean," I said, "Evstigney, you silly old fool?" [*Looks at* ANYA.] Darling! [*Pause.*] Asleep ... [*Takes* ANYA *by the arm.*] Come to bed, dear. ... Come on! [*Leads her by the arm.*] My darling's fallen asleep. Come along. [*They go out. A shepherd's pipe is heard playing from far away on the other side of the orchard.* TROFIMOV *walks across the stage and, catching sight of* VARYA *and* ANYA, *stops.*] Shh! She's asleep, asleep. Come along, my sweet.

ANYA [*softly, half asleep*]. I'm so tired. ... I keep hearing harness bells. Uncle ... dear ... Mother and Uncle ...

VARYA. Come on, my sweet, come on. . . .

[*They go into* ANYA'*s room.*]

TROFIMOV [*deeply moved*]. My sun! My spring!

CURTAIN

ACT II

Open country. A small tumbledown wayside chapel. Near it, a well, some large stones, which look like old gravestones, and an old bench. A road can be seen leading to GAYEV'*s estate. On one side, a row of tall dark poplars; it is there that the cherry orchard begins. In the distance, some telegraph poles, and far, far away on the horizon, the outlines of a large town that is visible only in very fine, clear weather. The sun is about to set.* CHAR-LOTTE, YASHA, *and* DUNYASHA *are sitting on the bench;* YEPIKHODOV *is standing nearby and is playing a guitar; they all sit sunk in thought.* CHARLOTTE *wears a man's old peaked hat; she has taken a shotgun from her shoulder and is adjusting the buckle on the strap.*

CHARLOTTE [*pensively*]. I haven't a proper passport, I don't know how old I am, and I can't help thinking that I'm still a young girl. When I was a little girl, my father and mother used to travel the fairs and give performances—very good ones. I used to do the *salto mortale*[4] and all sorts of other tricks. When Father and Mother died, a German lady adopted me and began educating me. Very well. I grew up and became a governess, but where I came from and who I am, I do not know. Who my parents were, I do not know either. They may not even have been married. I don't know. [*Takes a cucumber out of her pocket and starts eating it.*] I don't know anything. [*Pause.*] I'm longing to talk to someone, but there is no one to talk to. I haven't anyone. . . .

YEPIKHODOV [*plays his guitar and sings*]. "What care I for the world and its bustle? What care I for my friends and my foes?" . . . Nice to play a mandolin.

DUNYASHA. It's a guitar, not a mandolin. [*She looks at herself in a hand mirror and powders her face.*]

YEPIKHODOV. To a madman in love, it's a mandolin. [*Sings softly.*] "If only my heart was warmed by the fire of love requited."

[YASHA *joins in.*]

CHARLOTTE. How terribly these people sing! Ugh! Like hyenas.

DUNYASHA [*to* YASHA]. All the same, you're ever so lucky to have been abroad.

YASHA. Why, of course. Can't help agreeing with you there. [*Yawns, then lights a cigar.*]

YEPIKHODOV. Stands to reason. Abroad, everything's in excellent complexion. Been like that for ages.

YASHA. Naturally.

YEPIKHODOV. I'm a man of some education, I read all sorts of remarkable books, but what I simply can't understand is where it's all leading to. I mean, what do I really want—to live or to shoot myself? In any case, I always carry a revolver. Here it is. [*Shows them his revolver.*]

CHARLOTTE. That's done. Now I can go. [*Puts the shotgun over her shoulder.*] You're a very clever man, Yepikhodov. You frighten me to death. Women must be

---

[4] Death-leap.

madly in love with you. Brrr! [*Walking away.*] These clever people are all so stupid. I've no one to talk to. Always alone, alone, I've no one, and who I am and what I am for is a mystery. [*Walks off slowly.*]

YEPIKHODOV. Strictly speaking, and apart from all other considerations, what I ought to say about myself, among other things, is that Fate treats me without mercy, like a storm a small boat. Even supposing I'm mistaken, why in that case should I wake up this morning and suddenly find a spider of quite enormous dimensions on my chest? As big as that. [*Uses both hands to show the spider's size.*] Or again, I pick up a jug of kvass and there's something quite outrageously indecent in it, like a cockroach. [*Pause.*] Have you ever read Buckle's *History of Civilization?* [5] [*Pause.*] May I have a word or two with you, Dunyasha?

DUNYASHA. Oh, all right. What is it?

YEPIKHODOV. I'd be very much obliged if you'd let me speak to you in private. [*Sighs.*]

DUNYASHA [*embarrassed*]. All right, only first bring me my cape, please. It's hanging near the wardrobe. It's so damp here.

YEPIKHODOV. Very well, I'll fetch it. . . . Now I know what to do with my revolver. [*Picks up his guitar and goes out strumming it.*]

YASHA. Twenty-two Calamities! A stupid fellow, between you and me. [*Yawns.*]

DUNYASHA. I hope to goodness he won't shoot himself. [*Pause.*] I'm ever so nervous. I can't help being worried all the time. I was taken into service when I was a little girl, and now I can't live like a peasant any more. See my hands? They're ever so white, as white as a young lady's. I've become so nervous, so sensitive, so like a lady. I'm afraid of everything. I'm simply terrified. So if you deceived me, Yasha, I don't know what would happen to my nerves.

YASHA [*kisses her*]. Little cucumber! Mind you, I expect every girl to be respectable. What I dislike most is for a girl to misbehave herself.

DUNYASHA. I've fallen passionately in love with you, Yasha. You're so educated. You can talk about anything
[*Pause.*]

YASHA [*yawning*]. You see, in my opinion, if a girl is in love with somebody, it means she's immoral. [*Pause.*] It is so pleasant to smoke a cigar in the open air. [*Listens.*] Someone's coming. It's them. . . . [DUNYASHA *embraces him impulsively.*] Please go home and look as if you've been down to the river for a swim. Take that path or they'll think I had arranged to meet you here. Can't stand that sort of thing.

DUNYASHA [*coughing quietly*]. Your cigar has given me an awful headache. [*Goes out.*]
[YASHA *remains sitting near the chapel. Enter* MRS. RANEVSKY, GAYEV, *and* LOPAKHIN.]

LOPAKHIN. You must make up your minds once and for all. There's not much time left. After all, it's quite a simple matter. Do you agree to lease your land for country cottages or don't you? Answer me in one word: yes or no. Just one word.

MRS. RANEVSKY. Who's been smoking such horrible cigars here? [*Sits down.*]

GAYEV. Now that they've built the railway, things are much more convenient. [*Sits down.*] We've been to town for lunch—pot the red in the middle! I really should have gone in to have a game first.

MRS. RANEVSKY. There's plenty of time.

LOPAKHIN. Just one word. [*Imploringly.*] Please give me your answer!

GAYEV [*yawns*]. I beg your pardon?

---

[5] Henry Thomas Buckle (1821–1862) is best known for his *History of Civilization in England* (1857–1861).

MRS. RANEVSKY [*looking in her purse*]. Yesterday I had a lot of money, but I've hardly any left today. My poor Varya! Tries to economize by feeding everybody on milk soup and the old servants in the kitchen on peas, and I'm just throwing money about stupidly. [*Drops her purse, scattering some gold coins.*] Goodness gracious, all over the place! [*She looks annoyed.*]

YASHA. Allow me to pick 'em up, madam. It won't take a minute. [*Starts picking up the coins.*]

MRS. RANEVSKY. Thank you, Yasha. Why on earth did I go out to lunch? That disgusting restaurant of yours with its stupid band, and those tablecloths smelling of soap. Why did you have to drink so much, Leonid? Or eat so much? Or talk so much? You did talk a lot again in the restaurant today and all to no purpose. About the seventies and the decadents[6] . . . And who to? Talking about the decadents to waiters!

LOPAKHIN. Aye. . . .

GAYEV [*waving his arm*]. I'm incorrigible, that's clear. [*Irritably to* YASHA.] What are you hanging around here for?

YASHA [*laughs*]. I can't hear your voice without laughing, sir.

GAYEV [*to his sister*]. Either he or I.

MRS. RANEVSKY. Go away, Yasha. Run along.

YASHA [*returning the purse to* MRS. RANEVSKY]. At once, madam. [*Is hardly able to suppress his laughter.*] This very minute. [*Goes out.*]

LOPAKHIN. The rich merchant Deriganov is thinking of buying your estate. I'm told he's coming to the auction himself.

MRS. RANEVSKY. Where did you hear that?

LOPAKHIN. That's what they're saying in town.

GAYEV. Our Yaroslavl great-aunt has promised to send us money, but when and how much we do not know.

LOPAKHIN. How much will she send? A hundred thousand? Two hundred?

MRS. RANEVSKY. Well, I hardly think so. Ten or fifteen thousand at most. We must be thankful for that.

LOPAKHIN. I'm sorry, but such improvident people as you, such peculiar, unbusinesslike people, I've never met in my life! You're told in plain language that your estate's going to be sold, and you don't seem to understand.

MRS. RANEVSKY. But what are we to do? Tell us, please.

LOPAKHIN. I tell you every day. Every day I go on repeating the same thing over and over again. You must let out the cherry orchard and the land for country cottages, and you must do it now, as quickly as possible. The auction is on top of you! Try to understand! The moment you decide to let your land, you'll be able to raise as much money as you like, and you'll be saved.

MRS. RANEVSKY. Country cottages, holiday-makers—I'm sorry, but it's so vulgar.

GAYEV. I'm of your opinion entirely.

LOPAKHIN. I shall burst into tears or scream or have a fit. I can't stand it. You've worn me out! [*To* GAYEV.] You're a silly old woman!

GAYEV. I beg your pardon?

LOPAKHIN. A silly old woman! [*He gets up to go.*]

MRS. RANEVSKY [*in dismay*]. No, don't go. Please stay. I beg you. Perhaps we'll think of something.

LOPAKHIN. What is there to think of?

---

[6] A name adopted by a group of French and English writers of the late nineteenth century because of their admiration for the decadent period in Roman civilization.

MRS. RANEVSKY. Please don't go. I beg you. Somehow I feel so much more cheerful with you here. [*Pause.*] I keep expecting something to happen, as though the house was going to collapse on top of us.

GAYEV [*deep in thought*]. Cannon off the cushion. Pot into the middle pocket. . . .

MRS. RANEVSKY. I'm afraid we've sinned too much—

LOPAKHIN. You sinned!

GAYEV [*putting a fruit drop into his mouth*]. They say I squandered my entire fortune on fruit drops. [*Laughs.*]

MRS. RANEVSKY. Oh, my sins! . . . I've always thrown money about aimlessly, like a madwoman. Why, I even married a man who did nothing but pile up debts. My husband died of champagne. He drank like a fish. Then, worse luck, I fell in love with someone, had an affair with him, and it was just at that time—it was my first punishment, a blow that nearly killed me—that my boy was drowned in the river here. I went abroad, never to come back, never to see that river again. I shut my eyes and ran, beside myself, and *he* followed me—pitilessly, brutally. I bought a villa near Mentone because *he* had fallen ill. For the next three years I knew no rest, nursing him day and night. He wore me out. Everything inside me went dead. Then, last year, I had to sell the villa to pay my debts. I left for Paris, where he robbed me, deserted me, and went to live with another woman. I tried to poison myself. Oh, it was all so stupid, so shaming. . . . It was then that I suddenly felt an urge to go back to Russia, to my homeland, to my daughter. [*Dries her eyes.*] Lord, O Lord, be merciful! Forgive me my sins! Don't punish me any more! [*Takes a telegram from her pocket.*] I received this telegram from Paris today. He asks me to forgive him. He implores me to go back. [*Tears up the telegram.*] What's that? Music? [*Listens intently.*]

GAYEV. That's our famous Jewish band. Remember? Four fiddles, a flute, and a double bass.

MRS. RANEVSKY. Does it still exist? We ought to arrange a party and have them over to the house.

LOPAKHIN [*listening*]. I don't hear anything. [*Sings quietly.*] "And the Germans, if you pay 'em, will turn a Russian into a Frenchman." [*Laughs.*] I saw an excellent play at the theatre last night. It was very amusing.

MRS. RANEVSKY. I don't suppose it was amusing at all. You shouldn't be watching plays, but should be watching yourselves more often. What dull lives you live. What nonsense you talk.

LOPAKHIN. Perfectly true. Let's admit quite frankly that the life we lead is utterly stupid. [*Pause.*] My father was a peasant, an idiot. He understood nothing. He taught me nothing. He just beat me when he was drunk and always with a stick. As a matter of fact, I'm just as big a blockhead and an idiot myself. I never learnt anything, and my handwriting is so abominable that I'm ashamed to let people see it.

MRS. RANEVSKY. You ought to get married, my friend.

LOPAKHIN. Yes. That's true.

MRS. RANEVSKY. Married to our Varya. She's a nice girl.

LOPAKHIN. Aye. . . .

MRS. RANEVSKY. Her father was a peasant too. She's a hard-working girl, and she loves you. That's the important thing. Why, you've been fond of her for a long time yourself.

LOPAKHIN. Very well. I've no objection. She's a good girl.

[*Pause.*]

GAYEV. I've been offered a job in a bank. Six thousand a year. Have you heard, Lyuba?

MRS. RANEVSKY. You in a bank! You'd better stay where you are.

[*FIRS comes in carrying an overcoat.*]

FIRS [*to* GAYEV]. Please put it on, sir. It's damp out here.

GAYEV [*putting on the overcoat*]. You're a damned nuisance, my dear fellow.

FIRS. Come along, sir. Don't be difficult. . . . This morning, too, you went off without saying a word. [*Looks him over.*]

MRS. RANEVSKY. How you've aged, Firs!

FIRS. What's that, ma'am?

LOPAKHIN. Your mistress says you've aged a lot.

FIRS. I've been alive a long time. They were trying to marry me off before your dad was born. . . . [*Laughs.*] When freedom⁷ came, I was already chief valet. I refused to accept freedom and stayed on with my master. [*Pause.*] I well remember how glad everyone was, but what they were glad about, they did not know themselves.

LOPAKHIN. It wasn't such a bad life before, was it? At least, they flogged you.

FIRS [*not hearing him*]. I should say so. The peasants stuck to their masters and the masters to their peasants. Now everybody does what he likes. You can't understand nothing.

GAYEV. Shut up, Firs. I have to go to town tomorrow. I've been promised an introduction to a general who might lend us some money on a promissory note.

LOPAKHIN. Nothing will come of it. You won't pay the interest, either. You may be sure of that.

MRS. RANEVSKY. Oh, he's just imagining things. There aren't any generals.

[*Enter* TROFIMOV, ANYA, *and* VARYA.]

GAYEV. Here they are at last.

ANYA. There's Mother.

MRS. RANEVSKY [*affectionately*]. Come here, come here, my dears. [*Embracing* ANYA *and* VARYA.] If you only knew how much I love you both. Sit down beside me. That's right.

[*All sit down.*].

LOPAKHIN. Our eternal student is always walking about with the young ladies.

TROFIMOV. Mind your own business.

LOPAKHIN. He's nearly fifty and he's still a student.

TROFIMOV. Do drop your idiotic jokes.

LOPAKHIN. Why are you so angry, you funny fellow?

TROFIMOV. Well, stop pestering me.

LOPAKHIN [*laughs*]. Tell me, what do you think of me?

TROFIMOV. Simply this: You're a rich man and you'll soon be a millionaire. Now, just as a beast of prey devours everything in its path and so helps to preserve the balance of nature, so you, too, perform a similar function.

[*They all laugh.*]

VARYA. You'd better tell us about the planets, Peter.

MRS. RANEVSKY. No, let's carry on with what we were talking about yesterday.

TROFIMOV. What was that?

GAYEV. Pride.

---

⁷ The emancipation of the Russian serfs took place in 1861.

TROFIMOV. We talked a lot yesterday, but we didn't arrive at any conclusion. As you see it, there's something mystical about the proud man. You may be right for all I know. But try to look at it simply, without being too clever. What sort of pride is it, is there any sense in it, if, physiologically, man is far from perfect? If, in fact, he is, in the vast majority of cases, coarse, stupid, and profoundly unhappy? It's time we stopped admiring ourselves. All we must do is—work!

GAYEV. We're going to die all the same.

TROFIMOV. Who knows? And what do you mean by "we're going to die"? A man may possess a hundred senses. When he dies, he loses only the five we know. The other ninety-five live on.

MRS. RANEVSKY. How clever you are, Peter!

LOPAKHIN [*ironically*]. Oh, frightfully!

TROFIMOV. Mankind marches on, perfecting its powers. Everything that is incomprehensible to us now, will one day become familiar and comprehensible. All we have to do is to work and do our best to assist those who are looking for truth. Here in Russia only a few people are working so far. The vast majority of the educated people I know, do nothing. They aren't looking for anything. They are quite incapable of doing any work. They call themselves intellectuals, but speak to their servants as inferiors and treat the peasants like animals. They're not particularly keen on their studies, they don't do any serious reading, they are bone idle, they merely talk about science, and they understand very little about art. They are all so solemn, they look so very grave, they talk only of important matters, they philosophize. Yet anyone can see that our workers are abominably fed, sleep on bare boards, thirty and forty to a room—bedbugs everywhere, stench, damp, moral turpitude. It's therefore obvious that all our fine phrases are merely a way of deluding ourselves and others. Tell me, where are all those children's crèches people are talking so much about? Where are the reading rooms? You find them only in novels. Actually, we haven't any. All we have is dirt, vulgarity, brutality. I dislike and I'm frightened of all these solemn countenances, just as I'm frightened of all serious conversations. Why not shut up for once?

LOPAKHIN. Well, I get up at five o'clock in the morning. I work from morning till night, and I've always lots of money on me—mine and other people's—and I can see what the people around me are like. One has only to start doing something to realize how few honest, decent people there are about. Sometimes when I lie awake, I keep thinking; Lord, you've given us vast forests, boundless plains, immense horizons, and living here, we ourselves ought really to be giants—

MRS. RANEVSKY. You want giants, do you? They're all right only in fairy tales. Elsewhere they frighten me. [YEPIKHODOV *crosses the stage in the background, playing his guitar. Pensively.*] There goes Yepikhodov.

ANYA [*pensively*]. There goes Yepikhodov.

GAYEV. The sun's set, ladies and gentlemen.

TROFIMOV. Yes.

GAYEV [*softly, as though declaiming*]. Oh, nature, glorious nature! Glowing with eternal radiance, beautiful and indifferent, you, whom we call Mother, uniting in yourself both life and death, you—life-giver and destroyer . . .

VARYA [*imploringly*]. Darling uncle!

ANYA. Uncle, again!

TROFIMOV. You'd far better pot the red in the middle.

GAYEV. Not another word! Not another word!

They all sit deep in thought. Everything is still. The silence is broken only by the subdued muttering of FIRS. *Suddenly a distant sound is heard. It seems to come from the sky, the sound of a breaking string, slowly dying away, melancholy.*

MRS. RANEVSKY. What's that?

LOPAKHIN. I don't know. I expect a bucket must have broken somewhere far away in a coal mine, but somewhere a very long distance away.

GAYEV. Perhaps it was a bird, a heron or something.

TROFIMOV. Or an eagle-owl.

MRS. RANEVSKY [*shudders*]. It makes me feel dreadful for some reason.
    [*Pause.*]

FIRS. Same thing happened before the misfortune: the owl hooted and the samovar[8] kept hissing.

GAYEV. Before what misfortune?

FIRS. Before they gave us our freedom.
    [*Pause.*]

MRS. RANEVSKY. Come, let's go in, my friends. It's getting dark. [*To* ANYA.] There are tears in your eyes. What's the matter, darling. [*Embraces her.*]

ANYA. It's nothing, Mother. Nothing.

TROFIMOV. Someone's coming.

[*A* HIKER *appears. He wears a shabby white peaked cap and an overcoat; he is slightly drunk.*]

HIKER. Excuse me, is this the way to the station?

GAYEV. Yes, follow that road.

HIKER. I'm greatly obliged to you sir. [*Coughs.*] Glorious weather ... [*Declaiming.*] Brother, my suffering brother, come to the Volga, you whose groans[9] ... [*To* VARYA.] Mademoiselle, won't you give thirty kopecks to a starving Russian citizen?

[VARYA, *frightened, utters a little scream.*]

LOPAKHIN [*angrily*]. There's a limit to the most disgraceful behavior.

MRS. RANEVSKY [*at a loss*]. Here, take this. [*Looks for some money in her purse.*] No silver. Never mind, have this gold one.

HIKER. Profoundly grateful to you, ma'am. [*Goes out.*]
    [*Laughter.*]

VARYA [*frightened*]. I'm going away. I'm going away. Good heavens, Mother dear, there's no food for the servants in the house, and you gave him a gold sovereign!

MRS. RANEVSKY. What's to be done with a fool like me? I'll give you all I have when we get home. You'll lend me some more money, Lopakhin, won't you?

LOPAKHIN. With pleasure.

MRS. RANEVSKY. Let's go in. It's time. By the way, Varya, we've found you a husband here. Congratulations.

VARYA [*through tears*]. This isn't a joking matter, Mother.

LOPAKHIN. Okhmelia, go to a nunnery![10]

GAYEV. Look at my hands. They're shaking. It's a long time since I had a game of billiards.

---

[8] A metal urn used in Russia for making tea.

[9] The hiker is quoting from poems by Syomon Nadson (1862–1887) and Nikolay Nekrasov (1821–1878).

[10] Here, and below, Lopakhin alludes imprecisely to Hamlet's address to Ophelia in Act 3, Scene 1, lines 89–90 and 121.

LOPAKHIN. Okhmelia, O nymph, remember me in your prayers!

MRS. RANEVSKY. Come along, come along, it's almost supper time.

VARYA. That man frightened me. My heart's still pounding.

LOPAKHIN. Let me remind you, ladies and gentlemen: The cherry orchard is up for sale on the twenty-second of August. Think about it! Think!

[*They all go out except* TROFIMOV *and* ANYA.]

ANYA [*laughing*]. I'm so glad the hiker frightened Varya. Now we are alone.

TROFIMOV. Varya's afraid we might fall in love. That's why she follows us around for days on end. With her narrow mind she cannot grasp that we are above love. The whole aim and meaning of our life is to bypass everything that is petty and illusory, that prevents us from being free and happy. Forward! Let us march on irresistibly toward the bright star shining there in the distance! Forward! Don't lag behind, friends!

ANYA [*clapping her hands excitedly*]. You talk so splendidly! [*Pause.*] It's so heavenly here today!

TROFIMOV. Yes, the weather is wonderful.

ANYA. What have you done to me, Peter? Why am I no longer as fond of the cherry orchard as before? I loved it so dearly. I used to think there was no lovelier place on earth than our orchard.

TROFIMOV. The whole of Russia is our orchard. The earth is great and beautiful. There are lots of lovely places on it. [*Pause.*] Think, Anya: your grandfather, your greatgrandfather, and all your ancestors owned serfs. They owned living souls. Can't you see human beings looking at you from every cherry tree in your orchard, from every leaf and every tree trunk? Don't you hear their voices? To own living souls—that's what has changed you all so much, you who are living now and those who lived before you. That's why your mother, you yourself, and your uncle no longer realize that you are living on borrowed capital, at other people's expense, at the expense of those whom you don't admit farther than your entrance hall. We are at least two hundred years behind the times. We haven't got anything at all. We have no definite attitude toward our past. We just philosophize, complain of depression, or drink vodka. Isn't it abundantly clear that before we start living in the present, we must atone for our past, make an end of it? And atone for it we can only by suffering, by extraordinary, unceasing labor. Understand that, Anya.

ANYA. The house we live in hasn't really been ours for a long time. I'm going to leave it. I give you my word.

TROFIMOV. If you have the keys of the house, throw them into the well and go away. Be free as the wind.

ANYA [*rapturously*]. How well you said it!

TROFIMOV. Believe me, Anya, believe me! I'm not yet thirty, I'm young, I'm still a student, but I've been through hell more than once. I'm driven from pillar to post. In winter I'm half-starved, I'm ill, worried, poor as a beggar. You can't imagine the terrible places I've been to! And yet, always, every moment of the day and night, my heart was full of ineffable visions of the future. I feel, I'm quite sure, that happiness is coming, Anya. I can see it coming already.

ANYA [*pensively*]. The moon is rising.

YEPIKHODOV *can be heard playing the same sad tune as before on his guitar. The moon rises. Somewhere near the poplars* VARYA *is looking for* ANYA *and calling, "Anya, where are you?"*

TROFIMOV. Yes, the moon is rising. [*Pause.*] There it is—happiness! It's coming nearer and nearer. Already I can hear its footsteps, and if we never see it, if we never know it, what does it matter? Others will see it.

VARYA [*offstage*]. Anya, where are you?

TROFIMOV. That Varya again! [*Angrily.*] Disgusting!

ANYA. Never mind, let's go to the river. It's lovely there.

TROFIMOV. Yes, let's.

[*They go out.*]

VARYA [*offstage*]. Anya! Anya!

CURTAIN

ACT III

The drawing room, separated by an archway from the ballroom. A candelabra is alight. The Jewish band can be heard playing in the entrance hall. It is the same band that is mentioned in Act Two. Evening. In the ballroom people are dancing the Grande Ronde. SIMEONOV-PISHCHIK's voice van be heard crying out, "Promenade à une paire!"[11] *They all come out into the drawing room;* PISHCHIK *and* CHARLOTTE *the first couple,* TROFIMOV *and* MRS. RANEVSKY *the second,* ANYA *and a* POST OFFICE CLERK *the third,* VARYA *and the* STATIONMASTER *the fourth, and so on.* VARYA *is quietly crying and dries her eyes as she dances. The last couple consists of* DUNYASHA *and a partner. They walk across the drawing room.* PISHCHIK *shouts, "Grande Ronde balancez!"*[12] *and "Les cavaliers à genoux et remerciez vos dames!"*[13] FIRS, *wearing a tailcoat, brings in soda water on a tray.* PISHCHIK *and* TROFIMOV *come into the drawing room.*

PISHCHIK. I've got high blood-pressure. I've had two strokes already, and I find dancing hard work. But, as the saying goes, if you're one of a pack, wag your tail, whether you bark or not. As a matter of fact, I'm as strong as a horse. My father, may he rest in peace, liked his little joke, and speaking about our family pedigree, he used to say that the ancient Simeonov-Pishchiks came from the horse that Caligula had made a senator.[14] [*Sits down.*] But you see, the trouble is that I have no money. A hungry dog believes only in meat. [*Snores, but wakes up again at once.*] I'm just the same. All I can think of is money.

TROFIMOV. There really is something horsy about you.

PISHCHIK. Well, a horse is a good beast. You can sell a horse.

[*From an adjoining room comes the sound of people playing billiards.* VARYA *appears in the ballroom under the archway.*]

TROFIMOV [*teasing her*]. Mrs. Lopakhin! Mrs. Lopakhin!

VARYA [*angrily*]. Moth-eaten gentleman!

TROFIMOV. Well, I am a moth-eaten gentleman and proud of it.

VARYA [*brooding bitterly*]. We've hired a band, but how we are going to pay for it, I don't know. [*Goes out.*]

TROFIMOV [*to* PISHCHIK]. If the energy you have wasted throughout your life looking

---

[11] "March in a pair!"

[12] "Grand circle, pause!"

[13] "Gentlemen on your knees and thank your ladies!"

[14] The mad emperor Caligula (A.D. 12–41) appointed a horse to serve in the Roman Senate.

for money to pay the interest on your debts had been spent on something else, you'd most probably have succeeded in turning the world upside down.

PISHCHIK. Nietzsche[15] the famous philosopher—a great man, a man of great intellect—says in his works that there's nothing wrong about forging bank notes.

TROFIMOV. Have you read Nietzsche?

PISHCHIK. Well, actually, Dashenka told me about it. I don't mind telling you, though, that in my present position I might even forge bank notes. The day after tomorrow I've got to pay three hundred and ten rubles. I've already got one hundred and thirty. [*Feels his pockets in alarm.*] My money's gone, I've lost my money! [*Through tears.*] Where is it? [*Happily.*] Ah, here it is, in the lining. Lord the shock brought me out in a cold sweat!

[*Enter* MRS. RANEVSKY *and* CHARLOTTE.]

MRS. RANEVSKY [*hums a popular Georgian dance tune*]. Why is Leonid so late? What's he doing in town? [*To* DUNYASHA.] Offer the band tea, please.

TROFIMOV. I don't suppose the auction has taken place.

MRS. RANEVSKY. What a time to have a band! What a time to have a party! Oh, well, never mind. [*Sits down and hums quietly.*]

CHARLOTTE [*hands* PISHCHIK *a pack of cards*]. Here's a pack of cards. Think of a card.

PISHCHIK. All right.

CHARLOTTE. Now shuffle the pack. That's right. Now give it to me. Now, then, my dear Mr. Pishchik, *eins, zwei, drei!*[16] Look in your breast pocket. Is it there?

PISHCHIK [*takes the card out of his breast pocket*]. The eight of spades! Absolutely right! [*Surprised.*] Good Lord!

CHARLOTTE [*holding a pack of cards on the palm of her hand, to* TROFIMOV]. Tell me, quick, what's the top card?

TROFIMOV. Well, let's say the queen of spades.

CHARLOTTE. Here it is. [*To* PISHCHIK.]. What's the top card now?

PISHCHIK. The ace of hearts.

CHARLOTTE. Here you are! [*Claps her hands and the pack of cards disappears.*] What lovely weather we've having today. [*A mysterious female voice, which seems to come from under the floor, answers. "Oh yes, glorious weather, madam!"*] You're my ideal, you're so nice! [*The voice: "I like you very much too, madam."*]

STATIONMASTER [*clapping his hands*]. Bravo, Madam Ventriloquist!

PISHCHIK [*looking surprised*]. Good Lord! Enchanting, Miss Charlotte, I'm simply in love with you.

CHARLOTTE. In love! Are you sure you can love? *Guter Mensch, aber schlecter Musikant.*[17]

TROFIMOV [*claps* PISHCHIK *on the shoulder*]. Good old horse!

CHARLOTTE. Attention, please. One more trick. [*She takes a rug from a chair.*] Here's a very good rug. I'd like to sell it. [*Shaking it.*] Who wants to buy it?

PISHCHIK [*surprised*]. Good Lord!

CHARLOTTE. *Eins, zwei, drei!* [*Quickly snatching up the rug, which she had let fall, she reveals* ANYA *standing behind it.* ANYA *curtseys, runs to her mother, embraces her, and runs back to the ballroom, amid general enthusiasm.*]

MRS. RANEVSKY [*applauding*]. Bravo, bravo!

CHARLOTTE. Now, once more. *Eins, zwei, drei!* [*Lifts the rug; behind it stands* VARYA, *who bows.*]

---

[15] Friedrich Wilhelm Nietzsche (1844–1900), a German philosopher.

[16] "One, two, three!"

[17] "A good man, but a bad musician." A line by Heinrich Heine (1799–1856), a German poet.

PISHCHIK [*surprised*]. Good Lord!

CHARLOTTE. The end! [*Throws the rug over* PISHCHIK, *curtseys, and runs off to the ball-room.*]

PISHCHIK [*running after her*]. The hussy! What a woman, eh? What a woman! [*Goes out.*]

MRS. RANEVSKY. Still no Leonid. I can't understand what he can be doing in town all this time. It must be over now. Either the estate has been sold or the auction didn't take place. Why keep us in suspense so long?

VARYA [*trying to comfort her*]. I'm certain Uncle must have bought it.

TROFIMOV [*sarcastically*]. Oh, to be sure!

VARYA. Our great-aunt sent him power of attorney to buy the estate in her name and transfer the mortgage to her. She's done it for Anya's sake. God will help us and Uncle will buy it. I'm sure of it.

MRS. RANEVSKY. Your great-aunt sent fifteen thousand to buy the estate in her name. She doesn't trust us—but the money wouldn't even pay the interest. [*She covers her face with her hands.*] My whole future is being decided today, my future. . . .

TROFIMOV [*teasing* VARYA]. Mrs. Lopakhin!

VARYA [*crossly*]. Eternal student! Expelled twice from the university, weren't you?

MRS. RANEVSKY. Why are you so cross, Varya? He's teasing you about Lopakhin. Well, what of it? Marry Lopakhin if you want to. He is a nice, interesting man. If you don't want to, don't marry him. Nobody's forcing you, darling.

VARYA. I regard such a step seriously, Mother dear. I don't mind being frank about it: He is a nice man, and I like him.

MRS. RANEVSKY. Well, marry him. What are you waiting for? That's what I can't understand.

VARYA. But, Mother dear, I can't very well propose to him myself, can I? Everybody's been talking to me about him for the last two years. Everyone! But he either says nothing or makes jokes. I quite understand. He's making money. He has his business to think of, and he hasn't time for me. If I had any money, just a little, a hundred rubles, I'd give up everything and go right away as far as possible. I'd have gone into a convent.

TROFIMOV. Wonderful!

VARYA [*to* TROFIMOV]. A student ought to be intelligent! [*In a gentle voice, through tears.*] How plain you've grown, Peter! How you've aged! [*To* MRS. RANEVSKY, *no longer crying.*] I can't live without having something to do, Mother! I must be doing something all the time.

[*Enter* YASHA.]

YASHA [*hardly able to restrain his laughter*]. Yepikhodov's broken a billiard cue! [*Goes out.*]

VARYA. What's Yepikhodov doing here? Who gave him permission to play billiards? Can't understand these people! [*Goes out.*]

MRS. RANEVSKY. Don't tease her, Peter. Don't you see she is unhappy enough already?

TROFIMOV. She's a bit too conscientious. Pokes her nose into other people's affairs. Wouldn't leave me and Anya alone all summer. Afraid we might have an affair. What business is it of hers? Besides, the idea never entered my head. Such vulgarity is beneath me. We are above love.

MRS. RANEVSKY. So, I suppose I must be beneath love. [*In great agitation.*] Why isn't Leonid back? All I want to know is: Has the estate been sold or not? Such a calamity seems so incredible to me that I don't know what to think. I'm completely at a loss. I feel like screaming, like doing something silly. Help me, Peter. Say something. For God's sake, say something!

TROFIMOV. What does it matter whether the estate's been sold today or not? The estate's been finished and done with long ago. There's no turning back. The road to it is closed. Stop worrying, my dear. You mustn't deceive yourself. Look the truth straight in the face for once in your life.

MRS. RANEVSKY. What truth? You can see where truth is and where it isn't, but I seem to have gone blind. I see nothing. You boldly solve all important problems, but tell me, dear boy, isn't it because you're young, isn't it because you haven't had the time to live through the consequences of any of your problems? You look ahead boldly, but isn't it because you neither see nor expect anything terrible to happen to you, because life is still hidden from your young eyes? You're bolder, more honest, you see much deeper than any of us, but think carefully, try to understand our position, be generous even a little, spare me. I was born here, you know. My father and mother lived here, and my grandfather also. I love this house. Life has no meaning for me without the cherry orchard, and if it has to be sold, then let me be sold with it. [*Embraces* TROFIMOV *and kisses him on the forehead.*] Don't you see, my son was drowned here. [*Weeps.*] Have pity on me, my good, kind friend.

TROFIMOV. You know I sympathize with you with all my heart.

MRS. RANEVSKY. You should have put it differently. [*Takes out her handkerchief. A telegram falls on the floor.*] My heart is so heavy today. You can't imagine how heavy. I can't bear this noise. The slightest sound makes me shudder. I'm trembling all over. I'm afraid to go to my room. I'm terrified to be alone. . . . Don't condemn me, Peter. I love you as my own son. I'd gladly let Anya marry you, I swear I would. Only, my dear boy, you must study, you must finish your course at the university. You never do anything. You just drift from one place to another. That's what's so strange. Isn't that so? Isn't it? And you should do something about your beard. Make it grow, somehow. [*Laughs.*] You are funny!

TROFIMOV [*picking up the telegram*]. I have no wish to be handsome.

MRS. RANEVSKY. That telegram's from Paris. I get one every day. Yesterday and today. That wild man is ill again, in trouble again. He asks me to forgive him. He begs me to come back to him, and I really think I ought to be going back to Paris to be near him for a bit. You're looking very stern, Peter. But what's to be done, my dear boy? What am I to do? He's ill. He's lonely. He's unhappy. Who'll look after him there? Who'll stop him from doing something silly? Who'll give him his medicine at the right time? And, why hide it? Why be silent about it? I love him. That's obvious. I love him. I love him. He's a millstone round my neck and he's dragging me down to the bottom with him, but I love the millstone, and I can't live without it. [*Presses* TROFIMOV'*s hand.*] Don't think badly of me, Peter. Don't say anything. Don't speak.

TROFIMOV [*through tears*]. For God's sake—forgive my being so frank, but he left you penniless!

MRS. RANEVSKY. No, no, no! You mustn't say that. [*Puts her hands over her ears.*]

TROFIMOV. Why, he's a scoundrel, and you're the only one who doesn't seem to know it. He's a petty scoundrel, a nonentity.

MRS. RANEVSKY [*angry but restraining herself*]. You're twenty-six or twenty-seven, but you're still a schoolboy—a sixth-grade schoolboy!

TROFIMOV. What does that matter?

MRS. RANEVSKY. You ought to be a man. A person of your age ought to understand people who are in love. You ought to be in love yourself. You ought to fall in love. [*Angrily.*] Yes! Yes! And you're not so pure either. You're just a prude, a ridiculous crank, a freak!

TROFIMOV [*horrified*]. What is she saying?

MRS. RANEVSKY. "I'm above love!" You're not above love, you're simply what Firs calls a nincompoop. Not have a mistress at your age!

TROFIMOV [*horrified*]. This is terrible! What is she saying? [*Walks quickly into the ballroom, clutching his head.*] It's dreadful! I can't! I'll go away! [*Goes out but immediately comes back.*] All is at an end between us! [*Goes out into the hall.*]

MRS. RANEVSKY [*shouting after him*]. Peter, wait! You funny boy, I was only joking. Peter!

[*Someone can be heard running rapidly up the stairs and then suddenly falling down-stairs with a crash. ANYA and VARYA scream, followed immediately by laughter.*]

MRS. RANEVSKY. What's happened?

ANYA [*laughing, runs in*]. Peter's fallen down the stairs! [*Runs out.*]

MRS. RANEVSKY. What an eccentric! [*The STATIONMASTER stands in the middle of the ballroom and recites "The Fallen Woman" by Alexey Tolstoy.*[18] *The others listen. But he has hardly time to recite a few lines when the sound of a waltz comes from the entrance hall, and the recitation breaks off. Everybody dances. TROFIMOV, ANYA, VARYA, and MRS. RANEVSKY enter from the hall.*] Well, Peter dear, you pure soul, I'm sorry. . . . Come, let's dance. [*Dances with TROFIMOV.*]

[*ANYA and VARYA dance together. FIRS comes in and stands his walking stick near the side door. YASHA has also come in from the drawing room and is watching the dancing.*]

YASHA. Well, Grandpa!

FIRS. I'm not feeling too well. We used to have generals, barons, and admirals at our dances before, but now we send for the post office clerk and the station-master. Even they are not too keen to come. Afraid I'm getting weak. The old master, the mistress's grandfather that is, used to give us powdered sealing wax for medicine. It was his prescription for all illnesses. I've been taking sealing wax every day for the last twenty years or more. That's perhaps why I'm still alive.

YASHA. You make me sick, Grandpa. [*Yawns.*] I wish you was dead.

FIRS. Ugh, you nincompoop! [*Mutters.*]

[*TROFIMOV and MRS. RANEVSKY dance in the ballroom and then in the drawing room.*]

MRS. RANEVSKY. *Merci.*[19] I think I'll sit down a bit. [*Sits down.*] I'm tired.

[*Enter ANYA.*]

ANYA [*agitated*]. A man in the kitchen said just now that the cherry orchard has been sold today.

MRS. RANEVSKY. Sold? Who to?

ANYA. He didn't say. He's gone away now.

[*ANYA dances with TROFIMOV; both go off to the ballroom.*]

YASHA. Some old man gossiping, madam. A stranger.

FIRS. Master Leonid isn't here yet. Hasn't returned. Wearing his light autumn overcoat. He might catch cold. Oh, these youngsters!

MRS. RANEVSKY. I shall die! Yasha, go and find out who bought it.

YASHA. But he's gone, the old man has. [*Laughs.*]

MRS. RANEVSKY [*a little annoyed*]. Well, what are you laughing at? What are you so pleased about?

YASHA. Yepikhodov's a real scream. Such a fool. Twenty-two Calamities!

[18] Alexey Tolstoy (1817–1875) was a popular Russian poet and playwright. He is not Leo Tolstoy (1828–1910), Russian novelist, author of *War and Peace.*

[19] "Thank you."

MRS. RANEVSKY. Firs, where will you go if the estate's sold?

FIRS. I'll go wherever you tell me, ma'am.

MRS. RANEVSKY. You look awful! Are you ill? You'd better go to bed.

FIRS. Me to bed, ma'am? [*Ironically.*] If I goes to bed, who's going to do the waiting? Who's going to look after everything? I'm the only one in the whole house.

YASHA [*to* MRS. RANEVSKY.]. I'd like to ask you a favor, madam. If you go back to Paris, will you take me with you? It's quite impossible for me to stay here. [*Looking round, in an undertone.*] You know perfectly well yourself what an uncivilized country this is—the common people are so immoral—and besides, it's so boring here, the food in the kitchen is disgusting, and on top of it, there's that old Firs wandering about, muttering all sorts of inappropriate words. Take me with you, madam, please!

[*Enter* PISHCHIK.]

PISHCHIK. May I have the pleasure of a little dance, fair lady? [MRS. RANEVSKY *goes with him.*] I'll have one hundred and eighty rubles off you all the same, my dear, charming lady.... I will, indeed. [*They dance.*] One hundred and eighty rubles....

[*They go into the ballroom.*]

YASHA [*singing softly*]. "Could you but feel the agitated beating of my heart."

[*In the ballroom a woman in a gray top hat and check trousers can be seen jumping about and waving her arms. Shouts of "Bravo, Charlotte! Bravo!"*]

DUNYASHA [*stops to powder her face*]. Miss Anya told me to join the dancers because there are lots of gentlemen and very few ladies. But dancing makes me dizzy and my heart begins beating so fast. I say, Firs, the post office clerk said something to me just now that quite took my breath away.

[*The music becomes quieter.*]

FIRS. What did he say to you?

DUNYASHA. "You're like a flower," he said.

YASHA [*yawning*]. What ignorance! [*Goes out.*]

DUNYASHA. Like a flower! I'm ever so delicate, and I love people saying nice things to me!

FIRS. You'll come to a bad end, my girl. Mark my words.

[*Enter* YEPIKHODOV.]

YEPIKHODOV. You seem to avoid me, Dunyasha. Just as if I was some insect. [*Sighs.*] Oh, life!

DUNYASHA. What do you want?

YEPIKHODOV. No doubt you may be right. [*Sighs.*] But, of course, if one looks at things from a certain point of view, then, if I may say so and if you'll forgive my frankness, you have reduced me absolutely to a state of mind. I know what Fate has in store for me. Every day some calamity overtakes me, but I got used to it so long ago that I just look at my Fate and smile. You gave me your word, and though I—

DUNYASHA. Let's talk about it some other time. Leave me alone now. Now, I am dreaming. [*Plays with her fan.*]

YEPIKHODOV. Every day some calamity overtakes me, and I—let me say it quite frankly—why, I just smile, laugh even.

[*Enter* VARYA *from the ballroom.*]

VARYA. Are you still here, Simon! What an ill-mannered fellow you are, to be sure! [*To* DUNYASHA.] Be off with you, Dunyasha. [*To* YEPIKHODOV.] First you go and play billiards and break a cue, and now you wander about the drawing room as if you were a guest.

YEPIKHODOV. It's not your place to reprimand me, if you don't mind my saying so.

VARYA. I'm not reprimanding you. I'm telling you. All you do is drift about from one place to another without ever doing a stroke of work. We're employing an office clerk, but goodness knows why.

YEPIKHODOV [*offended*]. Whether I work or drift about, whether I eat or play billiards, is something which only people older than you, people who know what they're talking about, should decide.

VARYA. How dare you talk to me like that? [*Flaring up.*] How dare you? I don't know what I'm talking about, don't I? Get out of here! This instant!

YEPIKHODOV [*cowed*]. Express yourself with more delicacy, please.

VARYA [*beside herself*]. Get out of here this minute! Out! [*He goes toward the door, and she follows him.*] Twenty-two Calamities! Don't let me see you here again! Never set foot here again! [YEPIKHODOV *goes out. He can be heard saying behind the door. "I'll lodge a complaint."*] Oh, so you're coming back, are you? [*Picks up the stick which* FIRS *has left near the door.*] Come on, come on, I'll show you! Coming are you? Well, take that! [*Swings the stick as* LOPAKHIN *comes in.*]

LOPAKHIN. Thank you very much!

VARYA [*angrily and derisively*]. I'm so sorry!

LOPAKHIN. It's quite all right. Greatly obliged to you for the kind reception.

VARYA. Don't mention it. [*Walks away, then looks round and inquires gently.*] I didn't hurt you, did I?

LOPAKHIN. Oh no, not at all. There's going to be an enormous bump on my head for all that.

[*Voices in the ballroom:* "LOPAKHIN's *arrived.* LOPAKHIN!"]

PISHCHIK. Haven't heard from you or seen you for ages, my dear fellow! [*Embraces* LOPAKHIN.] Do I detect a smell of brandy, dear boy? We're doing very well here, too.

[*Enter* MRS. RANEVSKY.]

MRS. RANEVSKY. Is it you, Lopakhin? Why have you been so long? Where's Leonid?

LOPAKHIN. He came back with me. He'll be here in a moment.

MRS. RANEVSKY [*agitated*]. Well, what happened? Did the auction take place? Speak, for heaven's sake!

LOPAKHIN [*embarrassed, fearing to betray his joy*]. The auction was over by four o'clock. We missed our train and had to wait till half past nine. [*With a deep sigh.*] Oh dear, I'm afraid I feel a little dizzy.

[*Enter* GAYEV. *He carries some parcels in his right hand and wipes away his tears with his left.*]

MRS. RANEVSKY. What's the matter, Leonid? Well! [*Impatiently, with tears.*] Quick, tell me for heaven's sake!

GAYEV [*doesn't answer, only waves his hands resignedly; to* FIRS, *weeping*]. Here, take these—anchovies, Kerch herrings. . . I've had nothing to eat all day. I've had a terrible time. [*The door of the billiard room is open; the click of billiard balls can be heard and* YASHA's *voice: "Seven and eighteen!"* GAYEV's *expression changes. He is no longer crying.*] I'm awfully tired. Come and help me change, Firs.

[GAYEV *goes off through the ballroom to his own room, followed by* FIRS.]

PISHCHIK. Well, what happened at the auction? Come, tell us!

MRS. RANEVSKY. Has the cherry orchard been sold?

LOPAKHIN. It has.

MRS. RANEVSKY. Who bought it?

LOPAKHIN. I bought it. [*Pause.* MRS. RANEVSKY *is crushed; she would have collapsed on the floor if she had not been standing near an armchair.* VARYA *takes the keys from her belt, throws them on the floor in the center of the drawing room, and goes out.*] I bought it! One moment, please, ladies and gentlemen. I feel dazed. I can't talk. . . . [*Laughs.*] Deriganov was already there when we got to the auction. Gayev had only fifteen thousand, and Deriganov began his bidding at once with thirty thousand over and above the mortgage. I realized the position at once and took up his challenge. I bid forty. He bid forty-five. He kept raising his bid by five thousand and I by adding another ten thousand. Well, it was soon over. I bid ninety thousand on top of the arrears, and the cherry orchard was knocked down to me. Now the cherry orchard is mine! Mine! [*Laughs loudly.*] Merciful heavens, the cherry orchard's mine! Come on, tell me, tell me I'm drunk. Tell me I'm out of my mind. Tell me I'm imagining it all. [*Stamps his feet.*] Don't laugh at me! If my father and my grandfather were to rise from their graves and see what's happened, see how their Yermolay, their beaten and half-literate Yermolay, Yermolay who used to run around barefoot in winter, see how that same Yermolay bought this estate, the most beautiful estate in the world! I've bought the estate where my father and grandfather were slaves, where they weren't even allowed inside the kitchen. I must be dreaming. I must be imagining it all. It can't be true. It's all a figment of your imagination, shrouded in mystery. [*Picks up the keys, smiling affectionately.*] She's thrown down the keys. Wants to show she's no longer the mistress here. [*Jingles the keys.*] Oh well, never mind. [*The band is heard tuning up.*] Hey you, musicians, play something! I want to hear you. Come, all of you! Come and watch Yermolay Lopakhin take an axe to the cherry orchard. Watch the trees come crashing down. We'll cover the place with country cottages, and our grandchildren and great-grandchildren will see a new life springing up here. Strike up the music! [*The band plays.* MRS. RANEVSKY *has sunk into a chair and is weeping bitterly. Reproachfully.*] Why did you not listen to me? You poor dear, you will never get it back now. [*With tears.*] Oh, if only all this could be over soon, if only our unhappy, disjointed life could somehow be changed soon.

PISHCHIK [*takes his arm, in an undertone*]. She's crying. Let's go into the ballroom. Let's leave her alone. Come on. [*Takes his arm and leads him away to the ballroom.*]

LOPAKHIN. What's the matter? You there in the band, play up, play up! Let's hear you properly. Let's have everything as I want it now. [*Ironically.*] Here comes the new landowner, the owner of the cherry orchard! [*Knocks against a small table accidentally and nearly knocks over the candelabra.*] I can pay for everything!

LOPAKHIN *goes out with* PISHCHIK. *There is no one left in the ballroom except* MRS. RANEVSKY, *who remains sitting in a chair, hunched up and crying bitterly. The band plays quietly.* ANYA *and* TROFIMOV *come in quickly.* ANYA *goes up to her mother and kneels in front of her.* TROFIMOV *remains standing by the entrance to the ballroom.*

ANYA. Mother, Mother, why are you crying? My dear, good, kind Mother, my darling Mother, I love you; God bless you, Mother. The cherry orchard is sold. It's gone. That's true, quite true, but don't cry, Mother. You still have your life ahead of you, and you've still got your kind and pure heart. . . . Come with me, darling. Come. Let's go away from here. We shall plant a new orchard, an orchard more splendid than this one. You will see it, you will understand, and joy, deep, serene joy, will steal into your heart, sink into it like the sun in the evening, and you will smile, Mother! Come, darling! Come!

CURTAIN

ACT IV

The scene is the same as in the first act. There are no curtains at the windows or pictures on the walls. Only a few pieces of furniture are left. They have been stacked in one corner as if for sale. There is a feeling of emptiness. Near the front door and at the back of the stage, suitcases, traveling bags, etc., are piled up. The door on the left is open and the voices of VARYA *and* ANYA *can be heard.* LOPAKHIN *stands waiting.* YASHA *is holding a tray with glasses of champagne. In the entrance hall* YEPIKHODOV *is tying up a box. There is a constant murmur of voices offstage, the voices of peasants who have come to say good-bye.* GAYEV'S *voice is heard: "Thank you, my dear people, thank you."*

YASHA. The peasants have come to say good-bye. In my opinion, sir, the peasants are decent enough fellows, but they don't understand a lot.

[*The murmur of voices dies away.* MRS. RANEVSKY *and* GAYEV *come in through the entrance hall; she is not crying, but she is pale. Her face is quivering. She cannot speak.*]

GAYEV. You gave them your purse, Lyuba. You shouldn't. You really shouldn't.

MRS. RANEVSKY. I—I couldn't help it. I just couldn't help it.

[*Both go out.*]

LOPAKHIN [*calling through the door after them*]. Please take a glass of champagne. I beg you. One glass each before we leave. I forgot to bring any from town, and I could find only one bottle at the station. Please! [*Pause.*] Why, don't you want any? [*Walks away from the door.*] If I'd known, I wouldn't have bought it. Oh well, I don't think I'll have any, either. [YASHA *puts the tray down carefully on a chair.*] You'd better have some, Yasha.

YASHA. Thank you, sir. To those who're going away! And here's to you, sir, who're staying behind! [*Drinks.*] This isn't real champagne. Take it from me, sir.

LOPAKHIN. Paid eight rubles a bottle. [*Pause.*] Damn cold here.

YASHA. The stoves haven't been lit today. We're leaving, anyway. [*Laughs.*]

LOPAKHIN. What's so funny?

YASHA. Oh, nothing. Just feeling happy.

LOPAKHIN. It's October, but it might just as well be summer: it's so sunny and calm. Good building weather. [*Glances at his watch and calls through the door.*] I say, don't forget the train leaves in forty-seven minutes. In twenty minutes we must start for the station. Hurry up!

[TROFIMOV *comes in from outside, wearing an overcoat.*]

TROFIMOV. I think it's about time we were leaving. The carriages are at the door. Where the blazes could my galoshes have got to? Disappeared without a trace. [*Through the door.*] Anya, I can't find my galoshes! Can't find them!

LOPAKHIN. I've got to go to Kharkov. I'll leave with you on the same train. I'm spending the winter in Kharkov. I've been hanging about here too long. I'm worn out with having nothing to do. I can't live without work. Don't know what to do with my hands. They just flop about as if they belonged to someone else.

TROFIMOV. Well, we'll soon be gone and then you can resume your useful labors.

LOPAKHIN. Come on, have a glass of champagne.

TROFIMOV. No, thank you.

LOPAKHIN. So you're off to Moscow, are you?

TROFIMOV. Yes. I'll see them off to town, and I'm off to Moscow tomorrow.

LOPAKHIN. I see. I suppose the professors have stopped lecturing while you've been away. They're all waiting for you to come back.

TROFIMOV. Mind your own business.

LOPAKHIN. How many years have you been studying at the university?

TROFIMOV. Why don't you think of something new for a change? This is rather old, don't you think?—and stale. [*Looking for his galoshes.*] I don't suppose we shall ever meet again, so let me give you a word of advice as a farewell gift: Don't wave your arms about. Get rid of the habit of throwing your arms about. And another thing: To build country cottages in the hope that in the fullness of time vacationers will become landowners is the same as waving your arms about. Still, I like you in spite of everything. You've got fine sensitive fingers, like an artist's, and you have a fine sensitive soul.

LOPAKHIN [*embraces him*]. My dear fellow, thanks for everything. Won't you let me lend you some money for your journey? You may need it.

TROFIMOV. Need it? Whatever for?

LOPAKHIN. But you haven't any, have you?

TROFIMOV. Oh, but I have. I've just got some money for a translation. Got it here in my pocket. [*Anxiously.*] Where could those galoshes of mine have got to?

VARYA [*from another room*]. Oh, take your filthy things! [*Throws a pair of galoshes onto the stage.*]

TROFIMOV. Why are you so cross, Varya? Good heavens, these are not my galoshes!

LOPAKHIN. I had about three thousand acres of poppy sown last spring. Made a clear profit of forty thousand. When my poppies were in bloom, what a beautiful sight they were! Well, so you see, I made forty thousand and I'd be glad to lend you some of it because I can afford to. So why be so high and mighty? I'm a peasant. . . . I'm offering it to you without ceremony.

TROFIMOV. Your father was a peasant, my father was a pharmacist, all of which proves exactly nothing. [LOPAKHIN *takes out his wallet.*] Put it back! Put it back! If you offered me two hundred thousand, I wouldn't accept it. I'm a free man. Everything you prize so highly, everything that means so much to all of you, rich or poor, has no more power over me than a bit of fluff blown about in the air. I can manage without you. I can pass you by. I'm strong and proud. Mankind is marching toward a higher truth, toward the greatest happiness possible on earth, and I'm in the front ranks!

LOPAKHIN. Will you get there?

TROFIMOV. I will. [*Pause.*] I will get there or show others the way to get there.

[*The sound of an axe striking a tree can be heard in the distance.*]

LOPAKHIN. Well, good-bye, my dear fellow. Time to go. You and I are trying to impress one another, but life goes on regardless. When I work hard for hours on end, I can think more clearly, and then I can't help feeling that I, too, know what I live for. Have you any idea how many people in Russia exist goodness only knows why? However, no matter. It isn't they who make the world go round. I'm told Gayev has taken a job at the bank at six thousand a year. He'll never stick to it. Too damn lazy.

ANYA [*in the doorway*]. Mother asks you not to begin cutting the orchard down till she's gone.

TROFIMOV. Really, haven't you any tact at all? [*Goes out through the hall.*]

LOPAKHIN. Sorry, I'll see to it at once, at once! The damned idiots! [*Goes out after* TROFIMOV.]

ANYA. Has Firs been taken to the hospital?

YASHA. I told them to this morning. They must have taken him, I should think.

ANYA [*to* YEPIKHODOV, *who is crossing the ballroom*]. Please find out if Firs has been taken to the hospital.

YASHA [*offended*]. I told Yegor this morning. I haven't got to tell him a dozen times, have I?

YEPIKHODOV. Old man Firs, if you want my final opinion, is beyond repair, and it's high time he was gathered to his fathers. So far as I'm concerned, I can only envy him. [*Puts a suitcase on a hatbox and squashes it.*] There, you see! I knew it. [*Goes out.*]

YASHA [*sneeringly*]. Twenty-two Calamities!

VARYA [*from behind the door*]. Has Firs been taken to the hospital?

ANYA. He has.

VARYA. Why didn't they take the letter for the doctor?

ANYA. We'd better send it on after him. [*Goes out.*]

VARYA [*from the next room*]. Where's Yasha? Tell him his mother's here. She wants to say good-bye to him.

YASHA [*waves his hand impatiently*]. Oh, that's too much!

[*All this time* DUNYASHA *has been busy with the luggage. Now that* YASHA *is alone, she goes up to him.*]

DUNYASHA. You haven't even looked at me once, Yasha. You're going away, leaving me behind. [*Bursts out crying and throws her arms around his neck.*]

YASHA. Must you cry? [*Drinks champagne.*] I'll be back in Paris in a week. Tomorrow we catch the express and off we go! That's the last you'll see of us. I can hardly believe it, somehow. *Vive la France!*[20] I hate it here. It doesn't suit me at all. It's not the kind of life I like. I'm afraid it can't be helped. I've had enough of all this ignorance. More than enough. [*Drinks champagne.*] So what's the use of crying? Behave yourself and you won't end up crying.

DUNYASHA [*powdering her face, looking in a hand mirror*]. Write to me from Paris, please. I did love you, Yasha, after all. I loved you so much. I'm such an affectionate creature, Yasha.

YASHA. They're coming here. [*Busies himself around the suitcases, humming quietly.*]

[*Enter* MRS. RANEVSKY, GAYEV, ANYA, *and* CHARLOTTE.]

GAYEV. We ought to be going. There isn't much time left. [*Looking at* YASHA.] Who's smelling of pickled herrings here?

MRS. RANEVSKY. In another ten minutes we ought to be getting into the carriages. [*Looks round the room.*] Good-bye, dear house, good-bye, old grandfather house! Winter will pass, spring will come, and you won't be here any more. They'll have pulled you down. The things these walls have seen! [*Kisses her daughter affectionately.*] My precious one, you look radiant. Your eyes are sparkling like diamonds. Happy? Very happy?

ANYA. Oh yes, very! A new life is beginning, Mother!

GAYEV [*gaily*]. It is, indeed. Everything's all right now. We were all so worried and upset before the cherry orchard was sold, but now, when everything has been finally and irrevocably settled, we have all calmed down and even cheered up. I'm a bank official now, a financier. Pot the red in the middle. As for you, Lyuba, say what you like, but you too are looking a lot better. There's no doubt about it.

MRS. RANEVSKY. Yes, my nerves are better, that's true. [*Someone helps her on with her*

---

[20] "Long live France!"

hat and coat.] I sleep well. Take my things out, Yasha. It's time. [*To* ANYA.] We'll soon be seeing each other again, darling. I'm going to Paris. I'll live there on the money your great-aunt sent from Yaroslavl to buy the estate—three cheers for Auntie!—but the money won't last long, I'm afraid.

ANYA. You'll come home soon, Mother, very soon. I'm going to study, pass my school exams, and then I'll work and help you. We shall read all sorts of books together, won't we, Mother? [*Kisses her mother's hands.*] We shall read during the autumn evenings. We'll read lots and lots of books, and a new, wonderful world will open up to us. [*Dreamily.*] Oh, do come back, Mother!

MRS. RANEVSKY. I'll come back, my precious. [*Embraces her daughter.*]

[*Enter* LOPAKHIN. CHARLOTTE *quietly hums a tune.*]

GAYEV. Happy Charlotte! She's singing!

CHARLOTTE [*picks up a bundle that looks like a baby in swaddling clothes*]. My darling baby, go to sleep, my baby. [*A sound of a baby crying is heard.*] Hush, my sweet, my darling boy. [*The cry is heard again.*] Poor little darling, I'm so sorry for you! [*Throws the bundle down.*] So you will find me another job, won't you? I can't go on like this.

LOPAKHIN. We'll find you one, don't you worry.

GAYEV. Everybody's leaving us. Varya's going away. All of a sudden, we're no longer wanted.

CHARLOTTE. I haven't anywhere to live in town. I must go away. [*Sings quietly.*] It's all the same to me. . . .

[*Enter* PISHCHIK.]

LOPAKHIN. The nine days' wonder!

PISHCHIK [*out of breath*]. Oh dear, let me get my breath back! I'm all in. Dear friends . . . a drink of water, please.

GAYEV. Came to borrow some money, I'll be bound. Not from me this time. Better make myself scarce. [*Goes out.*]

PISHCHIK. Haven't seen you for ages, dearest lady. [*To* LOPAKHIN.] You here too? Glad to see you . . . man of immense intellect. . . . Here, that's for you, take it. [*Gives* LOPAKHIN *money.*] Four hundred rubles. That leaves eight hundred and forty I still owe you.

LOPAKHIN [*puzzled, shrugging his shoulders*]. I must be dreaming. Where did you get it?

PISHCHIK. One moment . . . Terribly hot . . . Most extraordinary thing happened. Some Englishmen came to see me. They found some kind of white clay on my land. [*To* MRS. RANEVSKY.] Here's four hundred for you too, beautiful ravishing lady. [*Gives her the money.*] The rest later. [*Drinks some water.*] Young fellow in the train just now was telling me that some—er—great philosopher advises people to jump off roofs. "Jump!" he says, and that'll solve all your problems. [*With surprise.*] Good Lord! More water, please.

LOPAKHIN. Who were these Englishmen?

PISHCHIK. I let them a plot of land with the clay on a twenty-four years' lease. And now you must excuse me, my friends. I'm in a hurry. Must be rushing off somewhere else. To Znoykov's, to Kardamonov's . . . Owe them all money. [*Drinks.*] Good-bye. I'll look in on Thursday.

MRS. RANEVSKY. We're just leaving for town. I'm going abroad tomorrow.

PISHCHIK. What? [*In a worried voice.*] Why are you going to town? Oh! I see! The furniture, the suitcases . . . Well, no matter. [*Through tears.*] No matter. Men of immense intellect, these Englishmen. . . . No matter. . . . No matter. I wish you all the best. May God help you. . . . No matter. Everything in this world comes to an end. [*Kisses* MRS. RANEVSKY'*s hand.*] When you hear that my end has come, remember the—er—old horse and say: Once there lived a man called Simeonov-Pishchik; may he rest in peace. Remarkable weather we've been having. . . . Yes. [*Goes out in great embarrassment, but immediately comes back and says, standing in the doorway.*] My Dashenka sends her regards. [*Goes out.*]

MRS. RANEVSKY. Well, we can go now. I'm leaving with two worries on my mind. One concerns Firs. He's ill. [*With a glance at her watch.*] We still have about five minutes.

ANYA. Firs has been taken to the hospital, Mother. Yasha sent him off this morning.

MRS. RANEVSKY. My other worry concerns Varya. She's used to getting up early and working. Now that she has nothing to do, she's like a fish out of water. She's grown thin and pale, and she's always crying, poor thing. [*Pause.*] You must have noticed it, Lopakhin. As you very well know, I'd always hoped to see her married to you. Indeed, everything seemed to indicate that you two would get married. [*She whispers to* ANYA, *who nods to* CHARLOTTE, *and they both go out.*] She loves you, you like her, and I simply don't know why you two always seem to avoid each other. I don't understand it.

LOPAKHIN. To tell you the truth, neither do I. The whole thing's odd somehow. If there's still time, I'm ready even now. . . . Let's settle it at once and get it over. I don't feel I'll ever propose to her without you here.

MRS. RANEVSKY. Excellent! Why, it shouldn't take more than a minute. I'll call her at once.

LOPAKHIN. And there's champagne here too. Appropriate to the occasion. [*Looks at the glasses.*] They're empty. Someone must have drunk it. [YASHA *coughs.*] Lapped it up, I call it.

MRS. RANEVSKY [*excitedly*]. Fine! We'll go out, Yasha, *allez!*[21] I'll call her. [*Through the door.*] Varya, leave what you're doing and come here for a moment. Come on. [MRS. RANEVSKY *goes out with* YASHA.]

LOPAKHIN [*glancing at his watch*]. Aye. . . .

  [*Pause. Behind the door suppressed laughter and whispering can be heard. Enter* VARYA.]

VARYA [*spends a long time examining the luggage*]. Funny, can't find it.

LOPAKHIN. What are you looking for?

VARYA. Packed it myself, and can't remember.

  [*Pause.*]

LOPAKHIN. Where are you going now, Varya?

VARYA. Me? To the Ragulins'. I've agreed to look after their house—to be their housekeeper, I suppose.

LOPAKHIN. In Yashnevo, isn't it? About fifty miles from here. [*Pause.*] Aye. . . . So life's come to an end in this house.

VARYA [*examining the luggage*]. Where can it be? Must have put it in the trunk. Yes, life's come to an end in this house. It will never come back.

LOPAKHIN. I'm off to Kharkov by the same train. Lots to see to there. I'm leaving Yepikhodov here to keep an eye on things. I've given him the job.

VARYA. Have you?

LOPAKHIN. This time last year it was already snowing, you remember. Now it's calm and sunny. A bit cold, though. Three degrees of frost.

VARYA. I haven't looked. [*Pause.*] Anyway, our thermometer's broken.

  [*Pause. A voice from outside, through the door:* "Mr. LOPAKHIN!"]

LOPAKHIN [*as though he had long been expecting this call*]. Coming! [*Goes out quickly.*]

[21] "Let's go!"

[VARYA *sits down on the floor, lays her head on a bundle of clothes, and sobs quietly. The door opens and* MRS. RANEVSKY *comes in cautiously.*]

MRS. RANEVSKY. Well? [*Pause.*] We must go.

VARYA [*no longer crying, dries her eyes*]. Yes, it's time, Mother dear. I'd like to get to the Ragulins' today, I only hope we don't miss the train.

MRS. RANEVSKY [*calling through the door*]. Anya, put your things on.

[*Enter* ANYA, *followed by* GAYEV *and* CHARLOTTE. GAYEV *wears a warm overcoat with a hood.* SERVANTS *and* COACHMEN *come in.* YEPIKHODOV *is busy with the luggage.*]

MRS. RANEVSKY. Now we can be on our way.

ANYA [*joyfully*]. On our way. Oh, yes!

GAYEV. My friends, my dear, dear friends, leaving this house for good, how can I remain silent, how can I, before parting from you, refrain from expressing the feelings which now pervade my whole being—

ANYA [*imploringly*]. Uncle!

VARYA. Uncle dear, please don't.

GAYEV [*dejectedly*]. Double the red into the middle. . . . Not another word!

[*Enter* TROFIMOV, *followed by* LOPAKHIN.]

TROFIMOV. Well, ladies and gentlemen, it's time to go.

LOPAKHIN. Yepikhodov, my coat!

MRS. RANEVSKY. Let me sit down a minute. I feel as though I've never seen the walls and ceilings of this house before. I look at them now with such eagerness, with such tender emotion. . . .

GAYEV. I remember when I was six years old sitting on this window sill on Trinity Sunday and watching Father going to church.

MRS. RANEVSKY. Have all the things been taken out?

LOPAKHIN. I think so. [*To* YEPIKHODOV *as he puts on his coat.*] Mind, everything's all right here, Yepikhodov.

YEPIKHODOV [*in a hoarse voice*]. Don't you worry, sir.

LOPAKHIN. What's the matter with your voice?

YEPIKHODOV. I've just had a drink of water and I must have swallowed something.

YASHA [*contemptuously*]. What ignorance!

MRS. RANEVSKY. There won't be a soul left in this place when we've gone.

LOPAKHIN. Not till next spring.

[VARYA *pulls an umbrella out of a bundle of clothes with such force that it looks as if she were going to hit someone with it;* LOPAKHIN *pretends to be frightened.*]

VARYA. Good heavens, you didn't really think that—

TROFIMOV. Come on, let's get into the carriages! It's time. The train will be in soon.

VARYA. There are your galoshes, Peter. By that suitcase. [*Tearfully.*] Oh, how dirty they are, how old. . . .

TROFIMOV [*putting on his galoshes*]. Come along, ladies and gentlemen.

[*Pause.*]

GAYEV [*greatly put out, afraid of bursting into tears*]. Train . . . station . . . in off into the middle pocket . . . double the white into the corner.

MRS. RANEVSKY. Come along!

LOPAKHIN. Is everyone here? No one left behind? [*Locks the side door on the left.*] There are some things in there. I'd better keep it locked. Come on!

ANYA. Good-bye, old house! Good-bye, old life!

TROFIMOV. Welcome new life!

[TROFIMOV *goes out with* ANYA. VARYA *casts a last look round the room and goes out unhurriedly.* YASHA *and* CHARLOTTE, *carrying her lap dog, go out.*]

LOPAKHIN. So, it's till next spring. Come along, ladies and gentlemen. Till we meet again. [*Goes out.*]

[MRS. RANEVSKY *and* GAYEV *are left alone. They seem to have been waiting for this moment. They fling their arms around each other, sobbing quietly, restraining themselves, as though afraid of being overheard.*]

GAYEV [*in despair*]. My sister! My sister!

MRS. RANEVSKY. Oh, my dear, my sweet, my beautiful orchard! My life, my youth, my happiness, good-bye! . . .

ANYA [*offstage, happily, appealingly*]. Mo-ther!

TROFIMOV [*offstage, happily, excited*]. Where are you?

MRS. RANEVSKY. One last look at the walls and the windows. Mother loved to walk in this room.

GAYEV. My sister, my sister!

ANYA [*offstage*]. Mo-ther!

TROFIMOV [*offstage*]. Where are you?

MRS. RANEVSKY. We're coming.

They go out. The stage is empty. The sound of all the doors being locked is heard, then of carriages driving off. It grows quiet. The silence is broken by the muffled noise of an axe striking a tree, sounding forlorn and sad. Footsteps can be heard. FIRS *appears from the door on the right. He is dressed, as always, in a jacket and white waistcoat. He is wearing slippers. He looks ill.*

FIRS [*walks up to the door and tries the handle*]. Locked! They've gone. [*Sits down on the sofa.*] Forgot all about me. Never mind. Let me sit down here for a bit. Forgotten to put on his fur coat, the young master has. Sure of it. Gone off in his light overcoat. [*Sighs anxiously.*] I should have seen to it. . . . Oh, these youngsters! [*Mutters something which cannot be understood.*] My life's gone just as if I'd never lived. . . . [*Lies down.*] I'll lie down a bit. No strength left. Nothing's left. Nothing. Ugh, you—nincompoop! [*Lies motionless.*]

A distant sound is heard, which seems to come from the sky, the sound of a breaking string, slowly dying away, melancholy. It is followed by silence, broken only by the sound of an axe striking a tree far away in the orchard.

CURTAIN

[1904]

Bernard Shaw   *1856–1950*

PYGMALION

CHARACTERS

CLARA EYNSFORD-HILL	HENRY HIGGINS
MRS EYNSFORD-HILL	A SARCASTIC BYSTANDER
A BYSTANDER	MRS PEARCE
FREDDY EYNSFORD-HILL	ALFRED DOOLITTLE
ELIZA DOOLITTLE	MRS HIGGINS
COLONEL PICKERING	PARLORMAID

Period—The Present
ACT I
The Portico of St. Paul's,
Covent Garden 11:15 P.M.
ACT II
Professor Higgins's Phonetic Laboratory, Wimpole
Street. Next day. 11 A.M.
ACT III
The Drawing Room in Mrs Higgins's Flat on
Chelsea Embankment. Several Months Later.
At-Home Day
ACT IV
The Same as Act II. Several Months Later. Midnight
ACT V
The Same as Act III. The Following Morning

Note for Technicians: A complete representation of the play as printed for the first time in this edition is technically possible only on the cinema screen or on stages furnished with exceptionally elaborate machinery. For ordinary theatrical use the scenes separated by rows of asterisks are to be omitted.

In the dialogue an *e* upside down indicates the indefinite vowel, sometimes called obscure or neutral, for which, though it is one of the commonest sounds in English speech, our wretched alphabet has no letter.

PREFACE TO PYGMALION
A PROFESSOR OF PHONETICS

As will be seen later on, Pygmalion needs, not a preface, but a sequel, which I have supplied in its due place.

The English have no respect for their language, and will not teach their children to speak it. They spell it so abominably that no man can teach himself what it sounds like. It is impossible for an Englishman to open his mouth without making some other Englishman hate or despise him. German and Spanish are accessible to foreigners: English is not accessible even to Englishmen. The reformer England needs today is an energetic phonetic enthusiast: that is why I have made such a one the hero of a popular play. There have been heroes of that kind crying in the wilderness for many years past. When I became interested in the subject towards the end of the eighteen-seventies, the illustrious Alexander Melville Bell, the inventor of Visible Speech, had emigrated to Canada, where his son invented the telephone; but Alexander J. Ellis was still a London patriarch, with an impressive head always covered by a velvet skull cap, for which he would apologize to public meetings in a very courtly manner. He and Tito Pagliardini, another phonetic veteran, were men whom it was impossible to dislike. Henry Sweet, then a young man, lacked their sweetness of character: he was about as conciliatory to conventional mortals as Ibsen or Samuel Butler. His great ability as a phonetician (he was, I think the best of them all at his job) would have entitled him to high official recognition, and perhaps enabled him to popularize his subject, but for his Satanic contempt for all academic dignitaries and persons in general who thought more of Greek than of phonetics. Once, in the days when the Imperial Institute rose in South Kensington, and Joseph Chamberlain was booming the Empire, I induced the editor of a leading monthly review to commission an article from Sweet on the imperial importance of his subject. When it arrived, it contained nothing but a savagely derisive attack on a professor of language and literature whose chair Sweet regarded as proper to a phonetic expert only. The article, being libellous, had to be returned as impossible; and I had to renounce my dream of dragging its author into the limelight. When I met him afterwards, for the first time for many years, I found to my astonishment that he, who had been a quite tolerably presentable young man, had actually managed by sheer scorn to alter his personal appearance until he had become a sort of walking repudiation of Oxford and all its traditions. It must have been largely in his own despite that he was squeezed into something called a Readership of phonetics there. The future of phonetics rests probably with his pupils, who all swore by him; but nothing could bring the man himself into any sort of compliance with the university to which he nevertheless clung by divine right in an intensely Oxonian way. I daresay his papers, if he has left any, include some satires that may be published without too destructive results fifty years hence. He was, I believe, not in the least an ill-natured man: very much the opposite, I should say; but he would not suffer fools gladly.

Those who knew him will recognize in my third act the allusion to the patent shorthand in which he used to write postcards, and which may be acquired from a four and sixpenny manual published by the Clarendon Press. The postcards which Mrs Higgins describes are such as I have received from Sweet. I would decipher a sound which a cockney would represent by *zerr*, and a Frenchman by *seu*, and then write demanding with some heat what on earth it meant. Sweet, with boundless contempt for my stupidity, would reply that it not only meant but obviously was the word Result, as no other word containing that sound, and capable of making sense with the context, existed in any language spoken on earth. That less expert mortals should require fuller indications was beyond Sweet's patience. Therefore, though the whole point of his current Shorthand is that it can express every sound in the language perfectly, vowels as well as consonants, and that your hand has to make no stroke except the easy and current ones with which you write m, n, and u, l, p, and q, scribbling them at whatever angle comes easiest to you, his unfortunate determination to make this remarkable and quite legible script serve also as a shorthand reduced it in his own practice to the most inscrutable of cryptograms. His true objective was the provision of a full, accurate, legible script for our noble but ill-dressed language; but he was led past that by his contempt for the popular Pitman system of shorthand, which he called the Pitfall system. The triumph of Pitman was a triumph of business organization: there was a weekly paper to persuade you to learn Pitman: there were cheap textbooks and exercise books and transcripts of speeches for you to copy, and schools where experienced teachers coached you up to the necessary proficiency. Sweet could not organize his market in that fashion. He might as well have been the Sybil who tore up the leaves of prophecy that nobody would attend to. The four and sixpenny manual, mostly in his lithographed handwriting, that was never vulgarly advertized, may perhaps some day be taken up by a syndicate and pushed upon the public as the Times pushed the Encyclopædia Britannica; but until then it will certainly not prevail against Pitman. I have bought three copies of it during my lifetime; and I am informed by the publishers that its cloistered existence is still a steady and healthy one. I actually learned the system too several times; and yet the shorthand in which I am writing these lines is Pitman's. And the reason is, that my secretary cannot transcribe Sweet, having been perforce taught in the schools of Pitman. Therefore, Sweet railed at Pitman as vainly as Thersites railed at Ajax: his raillery, however it may have eased his soul, gave no popular vogue to Current Shorthand.

Pygmalion Higgins is not a portrait of Sweet, to whom the adventure of Eliza Doolittle would have been impossible; still, as will be seen, there are touches of Sweet in the play. With Higgins's physique and temperament Sweet might have set the Thames on fire. As it was, he impressed himself professionally on Europe to an extent that made his comparative personal obscurity, and the failure of Oxford to do justice to his eminence, a puzzle to foreign specialists in his subject. I do not blame Oxford, because I think Oxford is quite right in demanding a certain social amenity from its nurslings (heaven knows it is not exorbitant in its requirements!); for although I well know how hard it is for a man of genius with a seriously underrated subject to maintain serene and kindly relations with the men who underrate it, and who keep all the best places for less important subjects which they profess without originality and sometimes without much capacity for them, still, if he overwhelms them with wrath and disdain, he cannot expect them to heap honors on him.

Of the later generations of phoneticians I know little. Among them towers the Poet Laureate, to whom perhaps Higgins may owe his Miltonic sympathies, though here again I must disclaim all portraiture. But if the play makes the public aware that there are such people as phoneticians, and that they are among the most important people in England at present, it will serve its turn.

I wish to boast that Pygmalion has been an extremely successful play all over Europe and North America as well as at home. It is so intensely and deliberately didactic, and its subject is esteemed so dry, that I delight in throwing it at the heads of the wiseacres who repeat the parrot cry that art should never be didactic. It goes to prove my contention that art should never be anything else.

Finally, and for the encouragement of people troubled with accents that cut them off from all high employment, I may add that the change wrought by Professor Higgins in the flower-girl is neither impossible nor uncommon. The modern concierge's daughter who fulfils her ambition by playing the Queen of Spain in Ruy Blas at the Théâtre Français is only one of many thousands of men and women who have sloughed off their native dialects and acquired a new tongue. But the thing has to be done scientifically, or the last state of the aspirant may be worse than the first. An honest and natural slum dialect is more tolerable than the attempt of a phonetically untaught person to imitate the vulgar dialect of the golf club; and I am sorry to say that in spite of the efforts of our Royal Academy of Dramatic Art, there is still too much sham golfing English on our stage, and too little of the noble English of Forbes Robertson.

BERNARD SHAW

ACT I

London at 11:15 P.M. Torrents of heavy summer rain. Cab whistles blowing frantically in all directions. Pedestrians running for shelter into the portico of St. Paul's church (not Wrench's cathedral but Inigo Jones's church[1] in Covent Garden vegetable market), among

---

[1] Inigo Jones (1573–1652), who introduced the classical style of architecture in England, is noted for designing Queen's House at Greenwich and the Royal Banqueting Hall at Whitehall, as well as his masterpiece, St. Paul's Church at Covent Gardens. Sir Christopher Wren (1632–1723) was perhaps

them a lady and her daughter in evening dress. All are peering out gloomily at the rain,
except one man with his back turned to the rest, wholly preoccupied with a notebook in which
he is writing.

The church clock strikes the first quarter.

THE DAUGHTER [*in the space between the central pillars, close to the one on her left*]. I'm
getting chilled to the bone. What can Freddy be doing all this time? He's been
gone twenty minutes.

THE MOTHER [*on her daughter's right*]. Not so long. But he ought to have got us a cab
by this.

A BYSTANDER [*on the lady's right*]. He wont[2] get no cab not until half-past eleven,
missus, when they come back after dropping their theatre fares.

THE MOTHER. But we must have a cab. We cant stand here until half-past eleven. It's
too bad.

THE BYSTANDER. Well, it aint my fault, missus.

THE DAUGHTER. If Freddy had a bit of gumption, he would have got one at the
theatre door.

THE MOTHER. What could he have done, poor boy?

THE DAUGHTER. Other people got cabs. Why couldnt he?

[FREDDY *rushes in out of the rain from the Southhampton Street side, and comes between*
them closing a dripping umbrella. He is a young man of twenty, in evening dress, very wet
round the ankles.]

THE DAUGHTER. Well, havnt you got a cab?

FREDDY. Theres not one to be had for love or money.

THE MOTHER. Oh, Freddy, there must be one. You cant have tried.

THE DAUGHTER. It's too tiresome. Do you expect us to go and get one ourselves?

FREDDY. I tell you theyre all engaged. The rain was so sudden: nobody was prepared; and everybody had to take a cab. Ive been to Charing Cross one way and
nearly to Ludgate Circus the other; and they were all engaged.

THE MOTHER. Did you try Trafalgar Square?

FREDDY. There wasnt one at Trafalgar Square.

THE DAUGHTER. Did you try?

FREDDY. I tried as far as Charing Cross Station. Did you expect me to walk to
Hammersmith?

THE DAUGHTER. You havnt tried at all.

THE MOTHER. You really are very helpless, Freddy. Go again; and dont come back
until you have found a cab.

FREDDY. I shall simply get soaked for nothing.

THE DAUGHTER. And what about us? Are we to stay here all night in this draught,
with next to nothing on? You selfish pig—

FREDDY. Oh, very well: I'll go, I'll go. [*He opens his umbrella and dashes off Strand-*
wards,[3] *but comes into collision with a flower girl who is hurrying in for shelter, knocking*
her basket out of her hands. A blinding flash of lightning, followed instantly by a rattling
peal of thunder, orchestrates the incident.]

THE FLOWER GIRL. Nah then, Freddy: look wh' y' gowin, deah.

FREDDY. Sorry [*he rushes off*].

England's greatest architect, designing fifty-two different churches in London following the Great
Fire of 1666. St. Paul's Cathedral was his most notable achievement.

[2] Shaw advocated a number of reforms in spelling and typography. Thus, in this play apostrophes are
omitted from many contractions ("wont" for "won't," "dont" for "don't") and periods are omitted
after most abbreviations ("Mrs" for "Mrs.").

[3] I.e., toward the Strand.

THE FLOWER GIRL [*picking up her scattered flowers and replacing them in the basket*]. Theres menners f' yer! Tə-oo branches o voylets trod into the mad. [*She sits down on the plinth of the column, sorting her flowers, on the lady's right. She is not at all a romantic figure. She is perhaps eighteen, perhaps twenty, hardly older. She wears a little sailor hat of black straw that has long been exposed to the dust and soot of London and has seldom if ever been brushed. Her hair needs washing rather badly: its mousy color can hardly be natural. She wears a shoddy black coat that reaches nearly to her knees and is shaped to her waist. She has a brown skirt with a coarse apron. Her boots are much the worse for wear. She is no doubt as clean as she can afford to be; but compared to the ladies she is very dirty. Her features are no worse than theirs; but their condition leaves something to be desired; and she needs the services of a dentist.*]

THE MOTHER. How do you know that my son's name is Freddy, pray?

THE FLOWER GIRL. Ow, eez yə-ooa san, is e? Wal, fewd dan y' də-ooty bawmz a mather should, eed now bettern to spawl a pore gel's flahrzn than ran awy athaht pyin. Will ye-oo py me f'them? [*Here, with apologies, this desperate attempt to represent her dialect without a phonetic alphabet must be abandoned as unintelligible outside London.*]

THE DAUGHTER. Do nothing of the sort, mother. The idea!

THE MOTHER. Please allow me, Clara. Have you any pennies?

THE DAUGHTER. No. Ive nothing smaller than sixpence.

THE FLOWER GIRL [*hopefully*]. I can give you change for a tanner,[4] kind lady.

THE MOTHER [*to* CLARA]. Give it to me. [CLARA *parts reluctantly.*] Now [*to* THE GIRL]. This is for your flowers.

THE FLOWER GIRL. Thank you kindly, lady.

THE DAUGHTER. Make her give you the change. These things are only a penny a bunch.

THE MOTHER. Do hold your tongue, Clara. [*To* THE GIRL] You can keep the change.

THE FLOWER GIRL. Oh, thank you, lady.

THE MOTHER. Now tell me how you know that young gentleman's name.

THE FLOWER GIRL. I didnt.

THE MOTHER. I heard you call him by it. Dont try to deceive me.

THE FLOWER GIRL [*protesting*]. Who's trying to deceive you? I called him Freddy or Charlie same as you might yourself if you was talking to a stranger and wished to be pleasant.

THE DAUGHTER. Sixpence thrown away! Really, mamma, you might have spared Freddy that. [*She retreats in disgust behind the pillar.*]

[*An elderly gentleman of the amiable military type rushes into the shelter, and closes a dripping umbrella. He is in the same plight as* FREDDY, *very wet about the ankles. He is in evening dress, with a light overcoat. He takes the place left vacant by the daughter.*]

THE GENTLEMAN. Phew!

THE MOTHER [*to* THE GENTLEMAN]. Oh sir, is there any sign of its stopping?

THE GENTLEMAN. I'm afraid not. It started worse than ever about two minutes ago [*he goes to the plinth beside the flower girl; puts up his foot on it; and stoops to turn down his trouser ends*].

THE MOTHER. Oh dear! [*She retires sadly and joins her daughter*].

THE FLOWER GIRL [*taking advantage of the military gentleman's proximity to establish friendly relations with him*]. If it's worse, it's a sign it's nearly over. So cheer up, Captain; and buy a flower off a poor girl.

THE GENTLEMAN. I'm sorry. I havnt any change.

THE FLOWER GIRL. I can give you change, Captain.

---

[4] "Tanner": a coin worth six pence.

THE GENTLEMAN. For a sovereign?[5] Ive nothing less.

THE FLOWER GIRL. Garn! Oh do buy a flower off me, Captain. I can change half-a-crown.[6] Take this for tuppence.

THE GENTLEMAN. Now dont be troublesome: theres a good girl. [*Trying his pockets*] I really havnt any change—Stop: heres three hapence, if thats any use to you [*he retreats to the other pillar*].

THE FLOWER GIRL [*disappointed, but thinking three half-pence better than nothing*]. Thank you, sir.

THE BYSTANDER [*to* THE GIRL]. You be careful: give him a flower for it. Theres a bloke here behind taking down every blessed word youre saying. [*All turn to the man who is taking notes.*]

THE FLOWER GIRL [*springing up terrified*]. I aint done nothing wrong by speaking to the gentleman. Ive a right to sell flowers if I keep off the kerb.[7] [*Hysterically*] I'm a respectable girl: so help me, I never spoke to him except to ask him to buy a flower off me.

General hubbub, mostly sympathetic to the flower girl, but deprecating her excessive sensibility. Cries of Dont start hollerin. Who's hurting you? Nobody's going to touch you. Whats the good of fussing? Steady on. Easy easy, etc., come from the elderly staid spectators, who pat her comfortingly. Less patient ones bid her shut her head, or ask her roughly what is wrong with her. A remoter group, not knowing what the matter is, crowd in and increase the noise with question and answer: Whats the row? What-she do? Where is he? A tec[8] taking her down. What! him? Yes: him over there: Took money off the gentleman, etc.

THE FLOWER GIRL [*breaking through them to* THE GENTLEMAN, *crying wildly*]. Oh, sir, dont let him charge me. You dunno what it means to me. Theyll take away my character and drive me on the streets for speaking to gentlemen. They—

THE NOTE TAKER [*coming forward on her right, the rest crowding after him*]. There! there! there! there! who's hurting you, you silly girl? What do you take me for?

THE BYSTANDER. It's aw rawt: e's a gentleman: look at his bə-oots. [*Explaining to* THE NOTE TAKER] She thought you was a copper's nark, sir.

THE NOTE TAKER [*with quick interest*]. Whats a copper's nark?

THE BYSTANDER [*inept at definition*]. It's a—well, it's a copper's nark, as you might say. What else would you call it? A sort of informer.

THE FLOWER GIRL [*still hysterical*]. I take my Bible oath I never said a word—

THE NOTE TAKER [*overbearing but good-humored*]. Oh, shut up, shut up. Do I look like a policeman?

THE FLOWER GIRL [*far from reassured*]. Then what did you take down my words for? How do I know whether you took me down right? You just shew me what youve wrote about me. [THE NOTE TAKER *opens his book and holds it steadily under her nose though the pressure of the mob trying to read it over his shoulders would upset a weaker man.*] Whats that? That aint proper writing. I cant read that.

THE NOTE TAKER. I can. [*Reads, reproducing her pronunciation exactly*] "Cheer ap, Keptin; n' baw ya flahr orf a pore gel."

THE FLOWER GIRL [*much distressed*]. It's because I called him Captain. I meant no harm. [*To* THE GENTLEMAN] Oh, sir, dont let him lay a charge agen me for a word like that. You—

THE GENTLEMAN. Charge! I make no charge. [*To* THE NOTE TAKER] Really, sir, if

---

[5] "Sovereign": one pound sterling (worth twenty shillings or 240 pence).
[6] "Half a crown": worth 2½ shillings.
[7] "Kerb": curb.
[8] "Tec": detective.

you are a detective, you need not begin protecting me against molestation by young women until I ask you. Anybody could see that the girl meant no harm.

THE BYSTANDERS GENERALLY [*demonstrating against police espionage*]. Course they could. What business is it of yours? You mind your own affairs. He wants promotion, he does. Taking down people's words! Girl never said a word to him. What harm if she did? Nice thing a girl cant shelter from the rain without being insulted, etc., etc., etc. [*She is conducted by the more sympathetic demonstrators back to her plinth, where she resumes her seat and struggles with her emotion*].

THE BYSTANDER. He aint a tec. He's a blooming busybody: thats what he is. I tell you, look at his bo-oots.

THE NOTE TAKER [*turning on him genially*]. And how are all your people down at Selsey?

THE BYSTANDER [*suspiciously*]. Who told you my people come from Selsey?

THE NOTE TAKER. Never you mind. They did. [*To* THE GIRL] How do you come to be up so far east? You were born in Lisson Grove.

THE FLOWER GIRL [*appalled*]. Oh, what harm is there in my leaving Lisson Grove? It wasnt fit for a pig to live in; and I had to pay four-and-six a week. [*In tears*] Oh, boo—hoo—oo—

THE NOTE TAKER. Live where you like; but stop that noise.

THE GENTLEMAN [*to* THE GIRL]. Come, come! he cant touch you: you have a right to live where you please.

A SARCASTIC BYSTANDER [*thrusting himself between* THE NOTE TAKER *and* THE GENTLEMAN]. Park Lane, for instance. I'd like to go into the Housing Question with you, I would.

THE FLOWER GIRL [*subsiding into a brooding melancholy over her basket, and talking very low-spiritedly to herself*]. I'm a good girl, I am.

THE SARCASTIC BYSTANDER [*not attending to her*]. Do you know where *I* come from?

THE NOTE TAKER [*promptly*]. Hoxton.

[*Titterings. Popular interest in* THE NOTE TAKER*'s performance increases*.]

THE SARCASTIC ONE [*amazed*]. Well, who said I didnt? Bly me! you know everything, you do.

THE FLOWER GIRL [*still nursing her sense of injury*]. Aint no call to meddle with me, he aint.

THE BYSTANDER [*to her*]. Of course he aint. Dont you stand it from him. [*To* THE NOTE TAKER] See here: what call have you to know about people what never offered to meddle with you?

THE FLOWER GIRL. Let him say what he likes. I dont want to have no truck with him.

THE BYSTANDER. You take us for dirt under your feet, dont you? Catch you taking liberties with a gentleman!

THE SARCASTIC BYSTANDER. Yes: tell him where he come from if you want to go fortune-telling.

THE NOTE TAKER. Cheltenham, Harrow, Cambridge, and India.

THE GENTLEMAN. Quite right.

[*Great laughter. Reaction in* THE NOTE TAKER*'s favor. Exclamations of* He knows all about it. Told him proper. Hear him tell the toff [9] where he come from? etc.]

THE GENTLEMAN. May I ask, sir, do you do this for your living at a music hall?

THE NOTE TAKER. I've thought of that. Perhaps I shall some day.

[*The rain has stopped; and the persons on the outside of the crowd begin to drop off.*]

---

[9] "Toff": slang for a stylishly dressed gentleman.

THE FLOWER GIRL [*resenting the reaction*]. He's no gentleman, he aint, to interfere with a poor girl.

THE DAUGHTER [*out of patience, pushing her way rudely to the front and displacing* THE GENTLEMAN, *who politely retires to the other side of the pillar*]. What on earth is Freddy doing? I shall get pneumownia if I stay in this draught any longer.

THE NOTE TAKER [*to himself, hastily making a note of her pronunciation of "monia"*]. Earlscourt.

THE DAUGHTER [*violently*]. Will you please keep your impertinent remarks to yourself.

THE NOTE TAKER. Did I say that out loud? I didnt mean to. I beg your pardon. Your mother's Epsom, unmistakeably.

THE MOTHER [*advancing between her daughter and* THE NOTE TAKER]. How very curious! I was brought up in Largelady Park, near Epsom.

THE NOTE TAKER [*uproariously amused*]. Ha! ha! What a devil of a name! Excuse me. [*To* THE DAUGHTER] You want a cab, do you?

THE DAUGHTER. Dont dare speak to me.

THE MOTHER. Oh, please, please, Clara. [*Her daughter repudiates her with an angry shrug and retires haughtily.*] We should be so grateful to you, sir, if you found us a cab. [THE NOTE TAKER *produces a whistle.*] Oh, thank you. [*She joins her daughter.*] [THE NOTE TAKER *blows a piercing blast.*]

THE SARCASTIC BYSTANDER. There! I knowed he was a plainclothes copper.

THE BYSTANDER. That aint a police whistle: thats a sporting whistle.

THE FLOWER GIRL [*still preoccupied with her wounded feelings*]. He's no right to take away my character. My character is the same to me as any lady's.

THE NOTE TAKER. I dont know whether youve noticed it; but the rain stopped about two minutes ago.

THE BYSTANDER. So it has. Why didnt you say so before? and us losing our time listening to your silliness. [*He walks off towards the Strand.*]

THE SARCASTIC BYSTANDER. I can tell where you come from. You come from Anwell. Go back there.

THE NOTE TAKER [*helpfully*]. *H*anwell.

THE SARCASTIC BYSTANDER [*affecting great distinction of speech*]. Thenk you, teacher. Haw haw! So long [*he touches his hat with mock respect and strolls off*].

THE FLOWER GIRL. Frightening people like that! How would he like it himself?

THE MOTHER. It's quite fine now, Clara. We can walk to a motor bus. Come. [*She gathers her skirts above her ankles and hurries off towards the Strand.*]

THE DAUGHTER. But the cab—[*her mother is out of hearing*]. Oh, how tiresome! [*She follows angrily.*]

[*All the rest have gone except* THE NOTE TAKER, THE GENTLEMAN, *and* THE FLOWER GIRL, *who sits arranging her basket, and still pitying herself in murmurs.*]

THE FLOWER GIRL. Poor girl! Hard enough for her to live without being worried and chivied.[10]

THE GENTLEMAN [*returning to his former place on* THE NOTE TAKER's *left*]. How do you do it, if I may ask?

THE NOTE TAKER. Simply phonetics. The science of speech. Thats my profession: also my hobby. Happy is the man who can make a living by his hobby! You can spot an Irishman or a Yorkshireman by his brogue. *I* can place any man within six miles. I can place him within two miles in London. Sometimes within two streets.

---

[10] "Chivied": chased.

THE FLOWER GIRL. Ought to be ashamed of himself, unmanly coward!

THE GENTLEMAN. But is there a living in that?

THE NOTE TAKER. Oh yes. Quite a fat one. This is an age of upstarts. Men begin in Kentish Town with £80 a year, and end in Park Lane with a hundred thousand. They want to drop Kentish Town; but they give themselves away every time they open their mouths. Now I can teach them—

THE FLOWER GIRL. Let him mind his own business and leave a poor girl—

THE NOTE TAKER [*explosively*]. Woman: cease this detestable boohooing instantly; or else seek the shelter of some other place of worship.

THE FLOWER GIRL [*with feeble defiance*]. Ive a right to be here if I like, same as you.

THE NOTE TAKER. A woman who utters such depressing and disgusting sounds has no right to be anywhere—no right to live. Remember that you are a human being with a soul and the divine gift of articulate speech: that your native language is the language of Shakespear and Milton and The Bible; and dont sit there crooning like a bilious pigeon.

THE FLOWER GIRL [*quite overwhelmed, looking up at him in mingled wonder and deprecation without daring to raise her head*]. Ah-ah-ah-ow-ow-ow-oo!

THE NOTE TAKER [*whipping out his book*]. Heavens! what a sound! [*He writes; then holds out the book and reads, reproducing her vowels exactly*] Ah-ah-ah-ow-ow-ow-oo!

THE FLOWER GIRL [*tickled by the performance, and laughing in spite of herself*]. Garn!

THE NOTE TAKER. You see this creature with her kerbstone English: the English that will keep her in the gutter to the end of her days. Well, sir, in three months I could pass that girl off as a duchess at an ambassador's garden party. I could even get her a place as lady's maid or shop assistant, which requires better English.

THE FLOWER GIRL. What's that you say?

THE NOTE TAKER. Yes, you squashed cabbage leaf, you disgrace to the noble architecture of these columns, you incarnate insult to the English language: I could pass you off as the Queen of Sheba. [*To* THE GENTLEMAN] Can you believe that?

THE GENTLEMAN. Of course I can. I am myself a student of Indian dialects; and—

THE NOTE TAKER [*eagerly*]. Are you? Do you know Colonel Pickering, the author of Spoken Sanscrit?

THE GENTLEMAN. I am Colonel Pickering. Who are you?

THE NOTE TAKER. Henry Higgins, author of Higgins's Universal Alphabet.

PICKERING [*with enthusiasm*]. I came from India to meet you.

HIGGINS. I was going to India to meet you.

PICKERING. Where do you live?

HIGGINS. 27A Wimpole Street. Come and see me tomorrow.

PICKERING. I'm at the Carlton. Come with me now and lets have a jaw over some supper.

HIGGINS. Right you are.

THE FLOWER GIRL [*to* PICKERING, *as he passes her*]. Buy a flower, kind gentleman. I'm short for my lodging.

PICKERING. I really havnt any change. I'm sorry [*he goes away*].

HIGGINS [*shocked at* THE GIRL's *mendacity*]. Liar. You said you could change half-a-crown.

THE FLOWER GIRL [*rising in desperation*]. You ought to be stuffed with nails, you ought. [*Flinging the basket at his feet*] Take the whole blooming basket for six-pence.

[*The church clock strikes the second quarter.*]

HIGGINS [*hearing in it the voice of God, rebuking him for his Pharisaic*[11] *want of charity to the poor girl*]. A reminder. [*He raises his hat solemnly; then throws a handful of money into the basket and follows* PICKERING.]

THE FLOWER GIRL [*picking up a half-crown*]. Ah-ow-ooh! [*Picking up a couple of florins*] Aaah-ow-ooh! [*Picking up several coins*] Aaaaaah-ow-ooh! [*Picking up a half-sovereign*] Aaaaaaaaaaaah-ow-ooh!!!

FREDDY [*springing out of a taxicab*]. Got one at last. Hallo! [*To* THE GIRL] Where are the two ladies that were here?

THE FLOWER GIRL. They walked to the bus when the rain stopped.

FREDDY. And left me with a cab on my hands! Damnation!

THE FLOWER GIRL [*with grandeur*]. Never mind, young man. I'm going home in a taxi. [*She sails off to the cab. The driver puts his hand behind him and holds the door firmly shut against her. Quite understanding his mistrust, she shews him her handful of money.*] A taxi fare aint no object to me, Charlie. [*He grins and opens the door.*] Here. What about the basket?

THE TAXIMAN. Give it here. Tuppence extra.

LIZA. No: I dont want nobody to see it. [*She crushes it into the cab and gets in, continuing the conversation through the window.*] Goodbye, Freddy.

FREDDY [*dazedly raising his hat*]. Goodbye.

TAXIMAN. Where to?

LIZA. Bucknam Pellis [Buckingham Palace].

TAXIMAN. What d'ye mean—Bucknam Pellis?

LIZA. Dont you know where it is? In the Green Park, where the King lives. Goodbye, Freddy. Dont let me keep you standing there. Goodbye.

FREDDY. Goodbye. [*He goes.*]

TAXIMAN. Here? Whats this about Bucknam Pellis? What business have you at Bucknam Pellis?

LIZA. Of course I havnt none. But I wasnt going to let him know that. You drive me home.

TAXIMAN. And wheres home?

LIZA. Angel Court, Drury Lane, next Meiklejohn's oil shop.

TAXIMAN. That sounds more like it, Judy. [*He drives off.*]

*   *   *

Let us follow the taxi to the entrance to Angel Court, a narrow little archway between two shops, one of them Meiklejohn's oil shop. When it stops there, ELIZA *gets out, dragging her basket with her.*

LIZA. How much?

TAXIMAN [*indicating the taximeter*]. Cant you read? A shilling.

LIZA. A shilling for two minutes!!

TAXIMAN. Two minutes or ten: it's all the same.

LIZA. Well, I dont call it right.

TAXIMAN. Ever been in a taxi before?

LIZA [*with dignity*]. Hundreds and thousands of times, young man.

TAXIMAN [*laughing at her*]. Good for you, Judy. Keep the shilling, darling, with best love from all at home. Good luck! [*He drives off.*]

LIZA [*humiliated*]. Impidence!

[11] "Pharisaic": self-righteous or hypocritical.

She picks up the basket and trudges up the alley with it to her lodging: a small room with very old wall paper hanging loose in the damp places. A broken pane in the window is mended with paper. A portrait of a popular actor and a fashion plate[12] of ladies' dresses, all wildly beyond poor ELIZA*'s means, both torn from newspapers, are pinned up on the wall. A birdcage hangs in the window; but its tenant died long ago: it remains as a memorial only.*

These are the only visible luxuries: the rest is the irreducible minimum of poverty's needs: a wretched bed heaped with all sorts of coverings that have any warmth in them, a draped packing case with a basin and jug on it and a little looking glass over it, a chair and table, the refuse of some suburban kitchen, and an American alarum clock on the shelf above the unused fireplace: the whole lighted with a gas lamp with a penny in the slot meter. Rent: four shillings a week.

Here, ELIZA, *chronically weary, but too excited to go to bed, sits, counting her new riches and dreaming and planning what to do with them, until the gas goes out, when she enjoys for the first time the sensation of being able to put in another penny without grudging it. This prodigal mood does not extinguish her gnawing sense of the need for economy sufficiently to prevent her from calculating that she can dream and plan in bed more cheaply and warmly than sitting up without a fire. So she takes off her shawl and skirt and adds them to the miscellaneous bedclothes. Then she kicks off her shoes and gets into bed without any further change.*

ACT II

Next day at 11 *A.M.* HIGGINS*'s laboratory in Wimpole Street. It is a room on the first floor, looking on the street, and was meant for the drawing room. The double doors are in the middle of the back wall; and persons entering find in the corner to their right two tall file cabinets at right angles to one another against the walls. In this corner stands a flat writing-table, on which are a phonograph, a laryngoscope,[13] a row of tiny organ pipes with a bellows, a set of lamp chimneys for singing flames with burners attached to a gas plug in the wall by an indiarubber tube, several tuning-forks of different sizes, a life-size image of half a human head, shewing in section the vocal organs, and a box containing a supply of wax cylinders for the phonograph.*

Further down the room, on the same side, is a fireplace, with a comfortable leather-covered easy-chair at the side of the hearth nearest the door, and a coal-scuttle. There is a clock on the mantle-piece. Between the fireplace and the phonograph table is a stand for newspapers.

On the other side of the central door, to the left of the visitor, is a cabinet of shallow drawers. On it is a telephone and the telephone directory. The corner beyond, and most of the side wall, is occupied by a grand piano, with the keyboard at the end furthest from the door, and a bench for the player extending the full length of the keyboard. On the piano is a dessert dish heaped with fruit and sweets, mostly chocolates.

The middle of the room is clear. Besides the easy-chair, the piano bench, and two chairs at the phonograph table, there is one stray chair. It stands near the fireplace. On the walls, engravings: mostly Piranesis and mezzotint portraits. No paintings.

PICKERING *is seated at the table, putting down some cards and a tuning-fork which he has been using.* HIGGINS *is standing up near him, closing two or three file drawers which are hanging out. He appears in the morning light as a robust, vital, appetizing sort of man of forty or thereabouts, dressed in a professional-looking black frock-coat with a white linen collar and*

---

[12] A fashion plate is an advertisement depicting a woman in fine clothing. Before the advent of photography and color printing, the outlines of the figures in fashion plates were printed in black ink and then colored by hand.

[13] "Laryngoscope": an instrument for looking at the vocal chords in the throat.

black silk tie. He is of the energetic, scientific type, heartily, even violently interested in every-
thing that can be studied as a scientific subject, and careless about himself and other people,
including their feelings. He is, in fact, but for his years and size, rather like a very impetuous
baby "taking notice" eagerly and loudly, and requiring almost as much watching to keep him
out of unintended mischief. His manner varies from genial bullying when he is in a good
humor to stormy petulance when anything goes wrong; but he is so entirely frank and void of
malice that he remains likeable even in his least reasonable moments.

HIGGINS [*as he shuts the last drawer*]. Well, I think thats the whole show.
PICKERING. It's really amazing. I havnt taken half of it in, you know.
HIGGINS. Would you like to go over any of it again?
PICKERING [*rising and coming to the fireplace, where he plants himself with his back to the*
fire]. No, thank you: not now. I'm quite done up for this morning.
HIGGINS [*following him, and standing beside him on his left*]. Tired of listening to
sounds?
PICKERING. Yes. It's a fearful strain. I rather fancied myself because I can pronounce
twenty-four distinct vowel sounds; but your hundred and thirty beat me. I cant
hear a bit of difference between most of them.
HIGGINS [*chuckling, and going over to the piano to eat sweets*]. Oh, that comes with
practice. You hear no difference at first; but you keep on listening, and presently you find theyre all as different as A from B. [MRS PEARCE *looks in: she is*
HIGGINS'*s housekeeper.*] Whats the matter?
MRS PEARCE [*hesitating, evidently perplexed*]. A young woman asks to see you, sir.
HIGGINS. A young woman! What does she want?
MRS PEARCE. Well, sir, she says youll be glad to see her when you know what she's
come about. She's quite a common girl, sir. Very common indeed. I should
have sent her away, only I thought perhaps you wanted her to talk into your
machines. I hope Ive not done wrong; but really you see such queer people
sometimes—youll excuse me, I'm sure, sir—
HIGGINS. Oh, thats all right, Mrs Pearce. Has she an interesting accent?
MRS PEARCE. Oh, something dreadful, sir, really. I dont know how you can take an
interest in it.
HIGGINS [*to* PICKERING]. Lets have her up. Shew her up, Mrs. Pearce [*he rushes across*
to his working table and picks out a cylinder to use on the phonograph].
MRS PEARCE [*only half resigned to it*]. Very well, sir. It's for you to say. [*She goes*
downstairs.]
HIGGINS. This is rather a bit of luck. I'll shew you how I make records. We'll set her
talking; and I'll take it down first in Bell's Visible Speech; then in broad Romic;
and then we'll get her on the phonograph so that you can turn her on as often
as you like with the written transcript before you.
MRS PEARCE [*returning*]. This is the young woman.

THE FLOWER GIRL *enters in state. She has a hat with three ostrich feathers, orange, sky-blue,*
and red. She has a nearly clean apron, and the shoddy coat has been tidied a little. The pathos
of this deplorable figure, with its innocent vanity and consequential air, touches PICKERING,
who has already straightened himself in the presence of MRS PEARCE. *But as to* HIGGINS, *the*
only distinction he makes between men and women is that when he is neither bullying nor
exclaiming to the heavens against some feather-weight cross, he coaxes women as a child coaxes
its nurse when it wants to get anything out of her.

HIGGINS [*brusquely, recognizing her with unconcealed disappointment, and at once, baby-*
like, making an intolerable grievance of it]. Why, this is the girl I jotted down last

night. She's no use: Ive got all the records I want of the Lisson Grove lingo; and I'm not going to waste another cylinder on it. [*To* THE GIRL] Be off with you: I dont want you.

THE FLOWER GIRL. Dont you be so saucy. You aint heard what I come for yet. [*To* Mrs Pearce, *who is waiting at the door for further instructions*]. Did you tell him I come in a taxi?

MRS PEARCE. Nonsense, girl! what do you think a gentleman like Mr Higgins cares what you came in?

THE FLOWER GIRL. Oh, we are proud! He aint above giving lessons, not him: I heard him say so. Well, I aint come here to ask for any compliment; and if my money's not good enough I can go elsewhere.

HIGGINS. Good enough for what?

THE FLOWER GIRL. Good enough for yə-oo. Now you know, dont you? I'm come to have lessons, I am. And to pay for em tə-oo: make no mistake.

HIGGINS [*stupent*[14]]. Well!!! [*Recovering his breath with a gasp*] What do you expect me to say to you?

THE FLOWER GIRL. Well, if you was a gentleman, you might ask me to sit down, I think. Dont I tell you I'm bringing you business?

HIGGINS. Pickering: shall we ask this baggage to sit down, or shall we throw her out of the window?

THE FLOWER GIRL [*running away in terror to the piano, where she turns at bay*]. Ah-ah-oh-ow-ow-ow-oo! [*Wounded and whimpering.*] I wont be called a baggage when Ive offered to pay like any lady.

[*Motionless, the two men stare at her from the other side of the room, amazed.*]

PICKERING [*gently*]. But what is it you want?

THE FLOWER GIRL. I want to be a lady in a flower shop stead of sellin at the corner of Tottenham Court Road. But they wont take me unless I can talk more genteel. He said he could teach me. Well, here I am ready to pay him—not asking any favor—and he treats me zif I was dirt.

MRS PEARCE. How can you be such a foolish ignorant girl as to think you could afford to pay Mr Higgins?

THE FLOWER GIRL. Why shouldnt I? I know what lessons cost as well as you do; and I'm ready to pay.

HIGGINS. How much?

THE FLOWER GIRL [*coming back to him, triumphant*]. Now youre talking! I thought youd come off it when you saw a chance of getting back a bit of what you chucked at me last night. [*Confidentially*] Youd had a drop in, hadnt you?

HIGGINS [*peremptorily*]. Sit down.

THE FLOWER GIRL. Oh, if youre going to make a compliment of it—

HIGGINS [*thundering at her*]. Sit down.

MRS PEARCE [*severely*]. Sit down, girl. Do as youre told.

THE FLOWER GIRL. Ah-ah-ah-ow-ow-oo! [*She stands, half rebellious, half bewildered.*]

PICKERING [*very courteous*]. Wont you sit down? [*He places the stray chair near the hearthrug between himself and* HIGGINS.]

LIZA [*coyly*]. Dont mind if I do. [*She sits down.* PICKERING *returns to the hearthrug.*]

HIGGINS. Whats your name?

THE FLOWER GIRL. Liza Doolittle.

HIGGINS [*declaiming gravely*].

---

[14] "Stupent": stupefied or amazed.

> Eliza, Elizabeth, Betsy and Bess,
> They went to the woods to get a bird's nes':

PICKERING. They found a nest with four eggs in it:

HIGGINS. They took one apiece, and left three in it.

> [*They laugh heartily at their own fun.*]

LIZA. Oh, dont be silly.

MRS PEARCE [*placing herself behind* ELIZA*'s chair*]. You mustnt speak to the gentleman like that.

LIZA. Well, why wont he speak sensible to me?

HIGGINS. Come back to business. How much do you propose to pay me for the lessons?

LIZA. Oh, I know whats right. A lady friend of mine gets French lessons for eighteenpence an hour from a real French gentleman. Well, you wouldn't have the face to ask me the same for teaching me my own language as you would for French; so I wont give more than a shilling. Take it or leave it.

HIGGINS [*walking up and down the room, rattling his keys and his cash in his pockets*]. You know, Pickering, if you consider a shilling, not as a simple shilling, but as a percentage of this girl's income, it works out as fully equivalent to sixty or seventy guineas from a millionaire.

PICKERING. How so?

HIGGINS. Figure it out. A millionaire has about £150 a day. She earns about half-a-crown.

LIZA [*haughtily*]. Who told you I only—

HIGGINS [*continuing*]. She offers me two-fifths of her day's income for a lesson. Two-fifths of a millionaire's income for a day would be somewhere about £60. It's handsome. By George, it's enormous! it's the biggest offer I ever had.

LIZA [*rising, terrified*]. Sixty pounds! What are you talking about? I never offered you sixty pounds. Where would I get—

HIGGINS. Hold your tongue.

LIZA [*weeping*]. But I aint got sixty pounds. Oh—

MRS PEARCE. Don't cry, you silly girl. Sit down. Nobody is going to touch your money.

HIGGINS. Somebody is going to touch you, with a broomstick, if you dont stop snivelling. Sit down.

LIZA [*obeying slowly*]. Ah-ah-ah-ow-oo-o! One would think you was my father.

HIGGINS. If I decide to teach you, I'll be worse than two fathers to you. Here [*he offers her his silk handkerchief!*]

LIZA. What's that for?

HIGGINS. To wipe your eyes. To wipe any part of your face that feels moist. Remember: thats your handkerchief; and thats your sleeve. Dont mistake the one for the other if you wish to become a lady in a shop.

> [LIZA, *utterly bewildered, stares helplessly at him.*]

MRS PEARCE. It's no use talking to her like that, Mr Higgins: she doesnt understand you. Besides, youre quite wrong: she doesnt do it that way at all [*she takes the handkerchief*].

LIZA [*snatching it*]. Here! You give me that handkerchief. He gev it to me, not to you.

PICKERING [*laughing*]. He did. I think it must be regarded as her property, Mrs Pearce.

MRS PEARCE [*resigning herself*] Serve you right, Mr Higgins.

PICKERING. Higgins: I'm interested. What about the ambassador's garden party? I'll say youre the greatest teacher alive if you make that good. I'll bet you all the expenses of the experiment you cant do it. And I'll pay for the lessons.

LIZA. Oh, you are real good. Thank you, Captain.

HIGGINS [*tempted, looking at her*]. It's almost irresistible. She's so deliciously low—so horribly dirty—

LIZA [*protesting extremely*]. Ah-ah-ah-ah-ow-ow-oo-oo!!! I aint dirty: I washed my face and hands afore I come, I did.

PICKERING. Youre certainly not going to turn her head with flattery, Higgins.

MRS PEARCE [*uneasy*]. Oh, dont say that, sir: theres more ways than one of turning a girl's head; and nobody can do it better than Mr Higgins, though he may not always mean it. I do hope, sir, you wont encourage him to do anything foolish.

HIGGINS [*becoming excited as the idea grows on him*]. What is life but a series of inspired follies? The difficulty is to find them to do. Never lose a chance: it doesnt come every day. I shall make a duchess of this draggletailed guttersnipe.

LIZA [*strongly deprecating this view of her*]. Ah-ah-ah-ow-ow-oo!

HIGGINS [*carried away*]. Yes: in six months—in three if she has a good ear and a quick tongue—I'll take her anywhere and pass her off as anything. We'll start today: now! this moment. Take her away and clean her, Mrs Pearce. Monkey Brand,[15] if it wont come off any other way. Is there a good fire in the kitchen?

MRS PEARCE [*protesting*]. Yes; but—

HIGGINS [*storming on*]. Take all her clothes off and burn them. Ring up Whiteley or somebody for new ones. Wrap her up in brown paper til they come.

LIZA. Youre no gentleman, youre not, to talk of such things. I'm a good girl, I am; and I know what the like of you are, I do.

HIGGINS. We want none of your Lisson Grove prudery here, young woman. Youve got to learn to behave like a duchess. Take her away, Mrs Pearce. If she gives you any trouble, wallop her.

LIZA [*springing up and running between* PICKERING *and* MRS PEARCE *for protection*]. No! I'll call the police, I will.

MRS PEARCE. But Ive no place to put her.

HIGGINS. Put her in the dustbin.

LIZA. Ah-ah-ah-ow-ow-oo!

PICKERING. Oh come, Higgins! be reasonable.

MRS PEARCE [*resolutely*]. You must be reasonable, Mr Higgins: really you must. You cant walk over everybody like this.

[HIGGINS, *thus scolded, subsides. The hurricane is succeeded by a zephyr of amiable surprise.*]

HIGGINS [*with professional exquisiteness of modulation*]. *I* walk over everybody! My dear Mrs Pearce, my dear Pickering, I never had the slightest intention of walking over anyone. All I propose is that we should be kind to this poor girl. We must help her to prepare and fit herself for her new station in life. If I did not express myself clearly it was because I did not wish to hurt her delicacy, or yours.

[LIZA, *reassured, steals back to her chair.*]

MRS PEARCE [*to* PICKERING]. Well, did you ever hear anything like that, sir?

PICKERING [*laughing heartily*]. Never, Mrs Pearce: never.

HIGGINS [*patiently*]. Whats the matter?

MRS PEARCE. Well, the matter is, sir, that you can't take a girl up like that as if you were picking up a pebble on the beach.

---

[15] "Monkey Brand": a British cleaning product similar to Ajax.

HIGGINS. Why not?

MRS PEARCE. Why not! But you dont know anything about her. What about her parents? She may be married.

LIZA. Garn!

HIGGINS. There! As the girl very properly says, Garn! Married indeed! Dont you know that a woman of that class looks a worn out drudge of fifty a year after she's married?

LIZA. Whood marry me?

HIGGINS [*suddenly resorting to the most thrillingly beautiful low tones in his best elocutionary style*]. By George, Eliza, the streets will be strewn with the bodies of men shooting themselves for your sake before Ive done with you.

MRS PEARCE. Nonsense, sir. You mustnt talk like that to her.

LIZA [*rising and squaring herself determinedly*]. I'm going away. He's off his chump,[16] he is. I dont want no balmies[17] teaching me.

HIGGINS [*wounded in his tenderest point by her insensibility to his elocution*]. Oh, indeed! I'm mad, am I? Very well, Mrs Pearce: you neednt order the new clothes for her. Throw her out.

LIZA [*whimpering*]. Nah-ow. You got no right to touch me.

MRS PEARCE. You see now what comes of being saucy. [*Indicating the door*] This way, please.

LIZA [*almost in tears*]. I didn't want no clothes. I wouldn't have taken them [*she throws away the handkerchief*]. I can buy my own clothes.

HIGGINS [*deftly retrieving the handkerchief and intercepting her on her reluctant way to the door*]. Youre an ungrateful wicked girl. This is my return for offering to take you out of the gutter and dress you beautifully and make a lady of you.

MRS PEARCE. Stop, Mr Higgins. I wont allow it. It's you that are wicked. Go home to your parents, girl; and tell them to take better care of you.

LIZA. I aint got no parents. They told me I was big enough to earn my own living and turned me out.

MRS PEARCE. Wheres your mother?

LIZA. I aint got no mother. Her that turned me out was my sixth stepmother. But I done without them. And I'm a good girl, I am.

HIGGINS. Very well, then, what on earth is all this fuss about? The girl doesnt belong to anybody—is no use of anybody but me. [*He goes to* MRS PEARCE *and begins coaxing.*] You can adopt her, Mrs Pearce: I'm sure a daughter would be a great amusement to you. Now dont make any more fuss. Take her downstairs; and—

MRS PEARCE. But whats to become of her? Is she to be paid anything? Do be sensible, sir.

HIGGINS. Oh, pay her whatever is necessary: put it down in the housekeeping book. [*Impatiently*] What on earth will she want with money? She'll have her food and her clothes. She'll only drink if you give her money.

LIZA [*turning on him*]. Oh you are a brute. It's a lie: nobody ever saw the sign of liquor on me. [*To* PICKERING] Oh, sir: youre a gentleman: dont let him speak to me like that.

PICKERING [*in good-humored remonstrance*]. Does it occur to you, Higgins, that the girl has some feelings?

HIGGINS [*looking critically at her*]. Oh no, I dont think so. Not any feelings that we need bother about. [*Cheerily*] Have you, Eliza?

LIZA. I got my feelings same as anyone else.

---

[16] "Off his chump": out of his mind.
[17] "Balmies": madmen.

HIGGINS [*to* PICKERING, *reflectively*]. You see the difficulty?

PICKERING. Eh? What difficulty?

HIGGINS. To get her to talk grammar. The mere pronunciation is easy enough.

LIZA. I dont want to talk grammar. I want to talk like a lady in a flower-shop.

MRS PEARCE. Will you please keep to the point, Mr Higgins. I want to know on what terms the girl is to be here. Is she to have any wages? And what is to become of her when youve finished your teaching? You must look ahead a little.

HIGGINS [*impatiently*]. Whats to become of her if I leave her in the gutter? Tell me that, Mrs Pearce.

MRS PEARCE. Thats her own business, not yours, Mr Higgins.

HIGGINS. Well, when Ive done with her, we can throw her back into the gutter; and then it will be her own business again; so thats all right.

LIZA. Oh, youve no feeling heart in you; you dont care for nothing but yourself. [*She rises and takes the floor resolutely.*] Here! Ive had enough of this. I'm going [*making for the door*]. You ought to be ashamed of yourself, you ought.

HIGGINS [*snatching a chocolate cream from the piano, his eyes suddenly beginning to twinkle with mischief*]. Have some chocolates, Eliza.

LIZA [*halting, tempted*]. How do I know what might be in them? Ive heard of girls being drugged by the likes of you.

[HIGGINS *whips out his penknife; cuts a chocolate in two; puts one half into his mouth and bolts it; and offers her the other half.*]

HIGGINS. Pledge of good faith, Eliza. I eat one half: you eat the other. [LIZA *opens her mouth to retort: he pops the half chocolate into it.*] You shall have boxes of them, barrels of them, every day. You shall live on them. Eh?

LIZA [*who has disposed of the chocolate after being nearly choked by it*]. I wouldn't have ate it, only I'm too ladylike to take it out of my mouth.

HIGGINS. Listen, Eliza. I think you said you came in a taxi.

LIZA. Well, what if I did? Ive as good a right to take a taxi as anyone else.

HIGGINS. You have, Eliza; and in future you shall have as many taxis as you want. You shall go up and down and round the town in a taxi every day. Think of that, Eliza.

MRS PEARCE. Mr Higgins: youre tempting the girl. It's not right. She should think of the future.

HIGGINS. At her age! Nonsense! Time enough to think of the future when you havent any future to think of. No, Eliza: do as this lady does: think of other people's futures; but never think of your own. Think of chocolates, and taxis, and gold, and diamonds.

LIZA. No: I dont want no gold and no diamonds. I'm a good girl, I am. [*She sits down again, with an attempt at dignity.*]

HIGGINS. You shall remain so, Eliza, under the care of Mrs Pearce. And you shall marry an officer in the Guards, with a beautiful moustache: the son of a marquis, who will disinherit him for marrying you, but will relent when he sees your beauty and goodness—

PICKERING. Excuse me, Higgins; but I really must interfere. Mrs Pearce is quite right. If this girl is to put herself in your hands for six months for an experiment in teaching, she must understand thoroughly what she's doing.

HIGGINS. How can she? She's incapable of understanding anything. Besides, do any of us understand what we are doing? If we did, would we ever do it?

PICKERING. Very clever, Higgins; but not to the present point. [*To* ELIZA] Miss Doolittle—

LIZA [*overwhelmed*]. Ah-ah-ow-oo!

HIGGINS. There! Thats all youll get out of Eliza. Ah-ah-ow-oo! No use explaining. As a military man you ought to know that. Give her her orders: thats enough for her. Eliza: you are to live here for the next six months, learning how to speak beautifully, like a lady in a florist's shop. If youre good and do whatever youre told, you shall sleep in a proper bedroom, and have lots to eat, and money to buy chocolates and take rides in taxis. If youre naughty and idle you will sleep in the back kitchen among the black beetles, and be walloped by Mrs Pearce with a broomstick. At the end of six months you shall go to Buckingham Palace in a carriage, beautifully dressed. If the King finds out youre not a lady, you will be taken by the police to the Tower of London, where your head will be cut off as a warning to other presumptuous flower girls. If you are not found out, you shall have a present of seven-and-sixpence[18] to start life with as a lady in a shop. If you refuse this offer you will be a most ungrateful wicked girl; and the angels will weep for you. [*To* PICKERING] Now are you satisfied, Pickering? [*To* MRS PEARCE] Can I put it more plainly and fairly, Mrs Pearce?

MRS PEARCE [*patiently*]. I think youd better let me speak to the girl properly in private. I dont know that I can take charge of her or consent to the arrangement at all. Of course I know you dont mean her any harm; but when you get what you call interested in people's accents, you never think or care what may happen to them or you. Come with me, Eliza.

HIGGINS. Thats all right. Thank you, Mrs Pearce. Bundle her off to the bath-room.

LIZA [*rising reluctantly and suspiciously*]. Youre a great bully, you are. I wont stay here if I dont like. I wont let nobody wallop me. I never asked to go to Bucknam Palace, I didnt. I was never in trouble with the police, not me. I'm a good girl—

MRS PEARCE. Dont answer back, girl. You dont understand the gentleman. Come with me. [*She leads the way to the door, and holds it open for* ELIZA.]

LIZA [*as she goes out*]. Well, what I say is right. I wont go near the King, not if I'm going to have my head cut off. If I'd known what I was letting myself in for, I wouldn't have come here. I always been a good girl; and I never offered to say a word to him; and I dont owe him nothing; and I dont care; and I wont be put upon; and I have my feelings the same as anyone else—

[MRS PEARCE *shuts the door; and* ELIZA*'s plaints are no longer audible.*]

* * *

ELIZA *is taken upstairs to the third floor greatly to her surprise; for she expected to be taken down to the scullery. There* MRS PEARCE *opens a door and takes her into a spare bedroom.*

MRS PEARCE. I will have to put you here. This will be your bedroom.

LIZA. O-h, I couldnt sleep here, missus. It's too good for the likes of me. I should be afraid to touch anything. I aint a duchess yet, you know.

MRS PEARCE. You have got to make yourself as clean as the room: then you wont be afraid of it. And you must call me Mrs Pearce, not missus. [*She throws open the door of the dressingroom, now modernized as a bathroom.*]

LIZA. Gawd! whats this? Is this where you wash clothes? Funny sort of copper[19] I call it.

MRS PEARCE. It is not a copper. This is where we wash ourselves, Eliza, and where I am going to wash you.

LIZA. You expect me to get into that and wet myself all over! Not me. I should catch my death. I knew a woman did it every Saturday night; and she died of it.

---

[18] "Seven-and-sixpence": seven shillings and sixpence—approximately one dollar.
[19] "Copper": slang for a laundry basin.

Mrs Pearce. Mr Higgins has the gentlemen's bathroom downstairs; and he has a
bath every morning, in cold water.

Liza. Ugh! He's made of iron, that man.

Mrs Pearce. If you are to sit with him and the Colonel and be taught you will have
to do the same. They wont like the smell of you if you dont. But you can have
the water as hot as you like. There are two taps: hot and cold.

Liza [weeping]. I couldnt. I dursnt. Its not natural: it would kill me. Ive never had
a bath in my life: not what youd call a proper one.

Mrs Pearce. Well, dont you want to be clean and sweet and decent, like a lady? You
know you cant be a nice girl inside if youre a dirty slut outside.

Liza. Boohoo!!!!

Mrs Pearce. Now stop crying and go back into your room and take off all your
clothes. Then wrap yourself in this [Taking down a gown from its peg and handing
it to her] and come back to me. I will get the bath ready.

Liza [all tears]. I cant. I wont. I'm not used to it. Ive never took off all my clothes
before. It's not right: it's not decent.

Mrs Pearce. Nonsense, child. Dont you take off all your clothes every night when
you go to bed?

Liza [amazed]. No. Why should I? I should catch my death. Of course I take off my
skirt.

Mrs Pearce. Do you mean that you sleep in the underclothes you wear in the
daytime?

Liza. What else have I to sleep in?

Mrs Pearce. You will never do that again as long as you live here. I will get you a
proper nightdress.

Liza. Do you mean change into cold things and lie awake shivering half the night?
You want to kill me, you do.

Mrs Pearce. I want to change you from a frowzy slut to a clean respectable girl fit
to sit with the gentlemen in the study. Are you going to trust me and do what
I tell you or be thrown out and sent back to your flower basket?

Liza. But you dont know what the cold is to me. You dont know how I dread it.

Mrs Pearce. Your bed wont be cold here: I will put a hot water bottle in it. [Pushing
her into the bedroom] Off with you and undress.

Liza. Oh, if only I'd a known what a dreadful thing it is to be clean I'd never have
come. I didnt know when I was well off. I—

Mrs Pearce pushes her through the door, but leaves it partly open lest her prisoner should
take to flight.

Mrs Pearce puts on a pair of white rubber sleeves, and fills the bath, mixing hot and cold,
and testing the result with the bath thermometer. She perfumes it with a handful of bath salts
and adds a palmful of mustard. She then takes a formidable looking long handled scrubbing
brush and soaps it profusely with a ball of scented soap.

Eliza comes back with nothing on but the bath gown huddled tightly round her, a piteous
spectacle of abject terror.

Mrs Pearce. Now come along. Take that thing off.

Liza. Oh I couldn't, Mrs Pearce: I reely couldn't. I never done such a thing.

Mrs Pearce. Nonsense. Here: step in and tell me whether its hot enough for you.

Liza. Ah-oo! Ah-oo! It's too hot.

Mrs Pearce [deftly snatching the gown away and throwing Eliza down on her back]. It
wont hurt you. [She sets to work with the scrubbing brush.]

[ELIZA's *screams are heartrending.*]

* * *

Meanwhile, the COLONEL *has been having it out with* HIGGINS *about* ELIZA. PICKERING *has come from the hearth to the chair and seated himself astride of it with his arms on the back to cross-examine him.*

PICKERING. Excuse the straight question, Higgins. Are you a man of good character where women are concerned?

HIGGINS [*moodily*]. Have you ever met a man of good character where women are concerned?

PICKERING. Yes: very frequently.

HIGGINS [*dogmatically, lifting himself on his hands to the level of the piano, and sitting on it with a bounce*]. Well, I havnt. I find that the moment I let a woman make friends with me, she becomes jealous, exacting, suspicious, and a damned nuisance. I find that the moment I let myself make friends with a woman, I become selfish and tyrannical. Women upset everything. When you let them into your life, you find that the woman is driving at one thing and youre driving at another.

PICKERING. At what, for example?

HIGGINS [*coming off the piano restlessly*]. Oh, Lord knows! I suppose the woman wants to live her own life; and the man wants to live his; and each tries to drag the other on to the wrong track. One wants to go north and the other south; and the result is that both have to go east, though they both hate the east wind. [*He sits down on the bench at the keyboard.*] So here I am, a confirmed old bachelor, and likely to remain so.

PICKERING [*rising and standing over him gravely*]. Come, Higgins! You know what I mean. If I'm to be in this business I shall feel responsible for that girl. I hope it's understood that no advantage is to be taken of her position.

HIGGINS. What! That thing! Sacred, I assure you. [*Rising to explain*] You see, she'll be a pupil; and teaching would be impossible unless pupils were sacred. Ive taught scores of American millionairesses how to speak English: the best looking women in the world. I'm seasoned. They might as well be blocks of wood. *I* might as well be a block of wood. It's—

[MRS PEARCE *opens the door. She has* ELIZA's *hat in her hand.* PICKERING *retires to the easy-chair at the hearth and sits down.*]

HIGGINS [*eagerly*]. Well, Mrs Pearce: is it all right?

MRS PEARCE [*at the door*]. I just wish to trouble you with a word, if I may, Mr Higgins.

HIGGINS. Yes, certainly. Come in. [*She comes forward.*] Dont burn that, Mrs Pearce. I'll keep it as a curiosity. [*He takes the hat.*]

MRS PEARCE. Handle it carefully, sir, please. I had to promise her not to burn it; but I had better put it in the oven for a while.[20]

HIGGINS [*putting it down hastily on the piano*]. Oh! thank you. Well, what have you to say to me?

PICKERING. Am I in the way?

MRS PEARCE. Not at all, sir. Mr Higgins: will you please be very particular what you say before the girl?

---

[20] Mrs. Pearce intends to sterilize the hat in order to kill any lice on it.

HIGGINS [*sternly*]. Of course. I'm always particular about what I say. Why do you say this to me?

MRS PEARCE [*unmoved*]. No sir: youre not at all particular when youve mislaid anything or when you get a little impatient. Now it doesnt matter before me: I'm used to it. But you really must not swear before the girl.

HIGGINS [*indignantly*]. *I* swear! [*Most emphatically*] I never swear. I detest the habit. What the devil do you mean?

MRS PEARCE [*stolidly*]. Thats what I mean, sir. You swear a great deal too much. I dont mind your damning and blasting, and what the devil and where the devil and who the devil—

HIGGINS. Mrs Pearce: this language from your lips! Really!

MRS PEARCE [*not to be put off*]. —but there is a certain word I must ask you not to use. The girl used it herself when she began to enjoy the bath. It begins with the same letter as bath. She knows no better: she learnt it at her mother's knee. But she must not hear it from your lips.[21]

HIGGINS [*loftily*]. I cannot charge myself with having ever uttered it, Mrs Pearce. [*She looks at him steadfastly. He adds, hiding an uneasy conscience with a judicial air.*] Except perhaps in a moment of extreme and justifiable excitement.

MRS PEARCE. Only this morning, sir, you applied it to your boots, to the butter, and to the brown bread.

HIGGINS. Oh, that! Mere alliteration, Mrs Pearce, natural to a poet.

MRS PEARCE. Well, sir, whatever you choose to call it, I beg you not to let the girl hear you repeat it.

HIGGINS. Oh, very well, very well. Is that all?

MRS PEARCE. No, sir. We shall have to be very particular with this girl as to personal cleanliness.

HIGGINS. Certainly. Quite right. Most important.

MRS PEARCE. I mean not to be slovenly about her dress or untidy in leaving things about.

HIGGINS [*going to her solemnly*]. Just so. I intended to call your attention to that. [*He passes on to* PICKERING, *who is enjoying the conversation immensely.*] It is these little things that matter, Pickering. Take care of the pence and the pounds will take care of themselves is as true of personal habits as of money. [*He comes to anchor on the hearthrug, with the air of a man in an unassailable position.*]

MRS PEARCE. Yes, sir. Then might I ask you not to come down to breakfast in your dressing-gown, or at any rate not to use it as a napkin to the extent you do, sir. And if you would be so good as not to eat everything off the same plate, and to remember not to put the porridge saucepan out of your hand on the clean tablecloth, it would be a better example to the girl. You know you nearly choked yourself with a fishbone in the jam only last week.

HIGGINS [*routed from the hearthrug and drifting back to the piano*]. I may do these things sometimes in absence of mind; but surely I dont do them habitually. [*Angrily*] By the way: my dressing-gown smells most damnably of benzine.

MRS PEARCE. No doubt it does, Mr. Higgins. But if you will wipe your fingers—

HIGGINS [*yelling*]. Oh very well, very well: I'll wipe them in my hair in future.

MRS PEARCE. I hope youre not offended, Mr. Higgins.

HIGGINS [*shocked at finding himself thought capable of an unamiable sentiment*]. Not at all, not at all. Youre quite right, Mrs Pearce: I shall be particularly careful before the girl. Is that all?

---

[21] Mrs. Pearce is alluding to the British intensive adverb "bloody." The derivation of the word is unclear, but it is now considered an obscenity by polite Britons.

MRS PEARCE. No, sir. Might she use some of those Japanese dresses you brought from abroad? I really cant put her back into her old things.

HIGGINS. Certainly. Anything you like. Is that all?

MRS PEARCE. Thank you, sir. Thats all. [*She goes out.*]

HIGGINS. You know, Pickering, that woman has the most extraordinary ideas about me. Here I am, a shy, diffident sort of man. Ive never been able to feel really grown-up and tremendous, like other chaps. And yet she's firmly persuaded that I'm an arbitrary overbearing bossing kind of person. I cant account for it. [MRS PEARCE *returns.*]

MRS PEARCE. If you please, sir, the trouble's beginning already. Theres a dustman downstairs, Alfred Doolittle, wants to see you. He says you have his daughter here.

PICKERING [*rising*]. Phew! I say!

HIGGINS [*promptly*]. Send the blackguard up.

MRS PEARCE. Oh, very well, sir. [*She goes out.*]

PICKERING. He may not be a blackguard, Higgins.

HIGGINS. Nonsense. Of course he's a blackguard.

PICKERING. Whether he is or not, I'm afraid we shall have some trouble with him.

HIGGINS [*confidently*]. Oh no: I think not. If theres any trouble he shall have it with me, not I with him. And we are sure to get something interesting out of him.

PICKERING. About the girl?

HIGGINS. No. I mean his dialect.

PICKERING. Oh!

MRS PEARCE [*at the door*]. Doolittle, sir. [*She admits* DOOLITTLE *and retires.*]

ALFRED DOOLITTLE *is an elderly but vigorous dustman, clad in the costume of his profession, including a hat with a back brim covering his neck and shoulders. He has well marked and rather interesting features, and seems equally free from fear and conscience. He has a remarkably expressive voice, the result of a habit of giving vent to his feelings without reserve. His present pose is that of wounded honor and stern resolution.*

DOOLITTLE [*at the door, uncertain which of the two gentlemen is his man*]. Professor Iggins?

HIGGINS. Here. Good morning. Sit down.

DOOLITTLE. Morning, Governor. [*He sits down magisterially*] I come about a very serious matter, Governor.

HIGGINS [*to* PICKERING]. Brought up in Hounslow. Mother Welsh, I should think. [DOOLITTLE *opens his mouth, amazed.* HIGGINS *continues*] What do you want, Doolittle?

DOOLITTLE [*menacingly*]. I want my daughter: thats what I want. See?

HIGGINS. Of course you do. Youre her father, arnt you? You dont suppose anyone else wants her, do you? I'm glad to see you have some spark of family feeling left. She's upstairs. Take her away at once.

DOOLITTLE [*rising, fearfully taken aback*]. What!

HIGGINS. Take her away. Do you suppose I'm going to keep your daughter for you?

DOOLITTLE [*remonstrating*]. Now, now, look here, Governor. Is this reasonable? Is it fairity to take advantage of a man like this? The girl belongs to me. You got her. Where do I come in? [*He sits down again.*]

HIGGINS. Your daughter had the audacity to come to my house and ask me to teach her how to speak properly so that she could get a place in a flower shop. This gentleman and my housekeeper have been here all the time. [*Bullying him*] How dare you come here and attempt to blackmail me? You sent her here on purpose.

DOOLITTLE [*protesting*]. No, Governor.

HIGGINS. You must have. How else could you possibly know that she is here?

DOOLITTLE. Don't take a man up like that, Governor.

HIGGINS. The police shall take you up. This is a plant—a plot to extort money by threats. I shall telephone for the police [*he goes resolutely to the telephone and opens the directory*].

DOOLITTLE. Have I asked you for a brass farthing? I leave it to the gentleman here: have I said a word about money?

HIGGINS [*throwing the book aside and marching down on* DOOLITTLE *with a poser*]. What else did you come for?

DOOLITTLE [*sweetly*]. Well, what would a man come for? Be human, Governor.

HIGGINS [*disarmed*]. Alfred: did you put her up to it?

DOOLITTLE. So help me, Governor, I never did. I take my Bible oath I aint seen the girl these two months past.

HIGGINS. Then how did you know she was here?

DOOLITTLE [*"most musical, most melancholy"*]. I'll tell you, Governor, if youll only let me get a word in. I'm willing to tell you. I'm wanting to tell you. I'm waiting to tell you.

HIGGINS. Pickering: this chap has a certain natural gift of rhetoric. Observe the rhythm of his native woodnotes wild. "I'm willing to tell you: I'm wanting to tell you: I'm waiting to tell you." Sentimental rhetoric! thats the Welsh strain in him. It also accounts for his mendacity and dishonesty.

PICKERING. Oh, please, Higgins: I'm west country myself. [*To* DOOLITTLE] How did you know the girl was here if you didnt send her?

DOOLITTLE. It was like this, Governor. The girl took a boy in the taxi to give him a jaunt. Son of her landlady, he is. He hung about on the chance of her giving him another ride home. Well, she sent him back for her luggage when she heard you was willing for her to stop here. I met the boy at the corner of Long Acre and Endell Street.

HIGGINS. Public house. Yes?

DOOLITTLE. The poor man's club, Governor: why shouldnt I?

PICKERING. Do let him tell his story, Higgins.

DOOLITTLE. He told me what was up. And I ask you, what was my feelings and my duty as a father? I says to the boy, "You bring me the luggage," I says—

PICKERING. Why didnt you go for it yourself?

DOOLITTLE. Landlady wouldn't have trusted me with it, Governor. She's that kind of woman: you know. I had to give the boy a penny afore he trusted me with it, the little swine. I brought it to her just to oblige you like, and make myself agreeable. Thats all.

HIGGINS. How much luggage?

DOOLITTLE. Musical instrument, Governor. A few pictures, a trifle of jewelry, and a bird-cage. She said she didnt want no clothes. What was I to think from that, Governor? I ask you as a parent what was I to think?

HIGGINS. So you came to rescue her from worse than death, eh?

DOOLITTLE [*appreciatively: relieved at being so well understood*]. Just so, Governor. Thats right.

PICKERING. But why did you bring her luggage if you intended to take her away?

DOOLITTLE. Have I said a word about taking her away? Have I now?

HIGGINS [*determinedly*]. Youre going to take her away, double quick. [*He crosses to the hearth and rings the bell.*]

DOOLITTLE [*rising*]. No, Governor. Dont say that. I'm not the man to stand in my girl's light. Heres a career opening for her, as you might say; and—

[MRS PEARCE *opens the door and awaits orders.*]

Higgins. Mrs Pearce: this is Eliza's father. He has come to take her away. Give her to him. [*He goes back to the piano, with an air of washing his hands of the whole affair.*]

Doolittle. No. This is a misunderstanding. Listen here—

Mrs Pearce. He cant take her away, Mr. Higgins: how can he? You told me to burn her clothes.

Doolittle. Thats right. I cant carry the girl through the streets like a blooming monkey, can I? I put it to you.

Higgins. You have put it to me that you want your daughter. Take your daughter. If she has no clothes go out and buy her some.

Doolittle [*desperate*]. Wheres the clothes she came in? Did I burn them or did your missus here?

Mrs Pearce. I am the housekeeper, if you please. I have sent for some clothes for your girl. When they come you can take her way. You can wait in the kitchen. This way, please.

[Doolittle, *much troubled, accompanies her to the door; then hesitates; finally turns confidentially to* Higgins.]

Doolittle. Listen here, Governor. You and me is men of the world aint we?

Higgins. Oh! Men of the world, are we? Youd better go, Mrs Pearce.

Mrs Pearce. I think so, indeed, sir. [*She goes, with dignity*].

Pickering. The floor is yours, Mr Doolittle.

Doolittle [*to* Pickering]. I thank you, Governor. [*To* Higgins, *who takes refuge on the piano bench, a little overwhelmed by the proximity of his visitor; for* Doolittle *has a professional flavour of dust around him.*] Well, the truth is, Ive taken a sort of fancy to you, Governor; and if you want the girl, I'm not so set on having her back home again but what I might be open to an arrangement. Regarded in the light of a young woman, she's a fine handsome girl. As a daughter she's not worth her keep; and so I tell you straight. All I ask is my rights as a father; and youre the last man alive to expect me to let her go for nothing; for I can see youre one of the straight sort, Governor. Well, whats a five-pound note to you? and whats Eliza to me? [*He turns on his chair and sits down judicially.*]

Pickering. I think you ought to know, Doolittle, that Mr Higgins's intentions are entirely honorable.

Doolittle. Course they are, Governor. If I thought they wasn't, I'd ask fifty.

Higgins [*revolted*]. Do you mean to say that you would sell your daughter for £50?

Doolittle. Not in a general way I wouldn't; but to oblige a gentleman like you I'd do a good deal, I do assure you.

Pickering. Have you no morals, man?

Doolittle [*unabashed*]. Cant afford them, Governor. Neither could you if you was as poor as me. Not that I mean any harm, you know. But if Liza is going to have a bit out of this, why not me too?

Higgins [*troubled*]. I dont know what to do, Pickering. There can be no question that as a matter of morals it's a positive crime to give this chap a farthing. And yet I feel a sort of rough justice in his claim.

Doolittle. Thats it, Governor. Thats all I say. A father's heart, as it were.

Pickering. Well, I know the feeling; but really it seems hardly right—

Doolittle. Dont say that, Governor. Dont look at it that way. What am I, Governors both? I ask you, what am I? I'm one of the undeserving poor: thats what I am. Think of what that means to a man. It means that he's up agen middle class morality all the time. If theres anything going, and I put in for a bit of it, it's always the same story: "Youre undeserving; so you cant have it." But my needs is as great as the most deserving widow's that ever got money out of six different charities in one week for the death of the same husband. I dont need less than a deserving man: I need more. I dont eat less hearty than him; and I drink a lot more. I want a bit of amusement, cause I'm a thinking man. I want cheerfulness and a song and a band when I feel low. Well, they charge me just the same for everything as they charge the deserving. What is middle class morality? Just an excuse for never giving me anything. Therefore, I ask you, as two gentlemen, not to play that game on me. I'm playing straight with you. I aint pretending to be deserving. I'm undeserving; and I mean to go on being undeserving. I like it; and thats the truth. Will you take advantage of a man's nature to do him out of the price of his own daughter what he's brought up and fed and clothed by the sweat of his brow until she's growed big enough to be interesting to you two gentlemen? Is five pounds unreasonable? I put it to you; and I leave it to you.

HIGGINS [*rising, and going over to* PICKERING]. Pickering: if we were to take this man in hand for three months, he could choose between a seat in the Cabinet and a popular pulpit in Wales.

PICKERING. What do you say to that, Doolittle?

DOOLITTLE. Not me, Governor, thank you kindly. Ive heard all the preachers and all the prime ministers—for I'm a thinking man and game for politics or religion or social reform same as all the other amusements—and I tell you it's a dog's life any way you look at it. Undeserving poverty is my line. Taking one station in society with another, it's—it's—well, it's the only one that has any ginger in it, to my taste.

HIGGINS. I suppose we must give him a fiver.

PICKERING. He'll make a bad use of it, I'm afraid.

DOOLITTLE. Not me, Governor, so help me I wont. Don't you be afraid that I'll save it and spare it and live idle on it. There wont be a penny of it left by Monday: I'll have to go to work same as if I'd never had it. It wont pauperize me, you bet. Just one good spree for myself and the missus, giving pleasure to ourselves and employment to others, and satisfaction to you to think it's not been throwed away. You couldnt spend it better.

HIGGINS [*taking out his pocket book and coming between* DOOLITTLE *and the piano*]. This is irresistible. Lets give him ten. [*He offers two notes to the dustman.*]

DOOLITTLE. No, Governor. She wouldnt have the heart to spend ten; and perhaps I shouldnt neither. Ten pounds is a lot of money: it makes a man feel prudent like; and then goodbye to happiness. You give me what I ask you, Governor: not a penny more, and not a penny less.

PICKERING. Why dont you marry that missus of yours? I rather draw the line at encouraging that sort of immorality.

DOOLITTLE. Tell her so, Governor: tell her so. *I*'m willing. It's me that suffers by it. Ive no hold on her. I got to be agreeable to her. I got to give her presents. I got to buy her clothes something sinful. I'm a slave to that woman, Governor, just because I'm not her lawful husband. And she knows it too. Catch her marrying me! Take my advice, Governor: marry Eliza while she's young and dont know no better. If you dont youll be sorry for it after. If you do, she'll be sorry for it after; but better her than you, because youre a man, and she's only a woman and dont know how to be happy anyhow.

HIGGINS. Pickering: if we listen to this man another minute, we shall have no convictions left. [*To* DOOLITTLE] Five pounds I think you said.

DOOLITTLE. Thank you kindly, Governor.

HIGGINS. Youre sure you wont take ten?

DOOLITTLE. Not now. Another time, Governor.

HIGGINS [*handing him a five-pound note*]. Here you are.

DOOLITTLE. Thank you, Governor. Good morning. [*He hurries to the door, anxious to get away with his booty. When he opens it he is confronted with a dainty and exquisitely clean young Japanese lady in a simple blue cotton kimono printed cunningly with small white jasmine blossoms. MRS PEARCE is with her. He gets out of her way deferentially and apologizes.*] Beg pardon, miss.

THE JAPANESE LADY. Garn! Dont you know your own daughter?

DOOLITTLE	*Exclaiming*	Bly me! it's Eliza!
HIGGINS	*simultaneously*	Whats that! This!
PICKERING		By Jove!

LIZA. Dont I look silly?

HIGGINS. Silly?

MRS PEARCE [*at the door*]. Now, Mr. Higgins, please dont say anything to make the girl conceited about herself.

HIGGINS [*conscientiously*]. Oh! Quite right, Mrs Pearce. [*To* ELIZA] Yes: damned silly.

MRS PEARCE. Please, sir.

HIGGINS [*correcting himself*]. I mean extremely silly.

LIZA. I should look all right with my hat on. [*She takes up her hat; puts it on; and walks across the room to the fireplace with a fashionable air.*]

HIGGINS. A new fashion, by George! And it ought to look horrible!

DOOLITTLE [*with fatherly pride*]. Well, I never thought she'd clean up as good looking as that, Governor. She's a credit to me, aint she?

LIZA. I tell you, it's easy to clean up here. Hot and cold water on tap, just as much as you like, there is. Woolly towels, there is; and a towel horse so hot, it burns your fingers. Soft brushes to scrub yourself, and a wooden bowl of soap smelling like primroses. Now I know why ladies is so clean. Washing's a treat for them. Wish they could see what it is for the like of me!

HIGGINS. I'm glad the bathroom met with your approval.

LIZA. It didnt: not all of it; and I dont care who hears me say it. Mrs Pearce knows.

HIGGINS. What was wrong, Mrs Pearce?

MRS PEARCE [*blandly*]. Oh, nothing, sir. It doesnt matter.

LIZA. I had a good mind to break it. I didnt know which way to look. But I hung a towel over it, I did.

HIGGINS. Over what?

MRS PEARCE. Over the looking-glass, sir.

HIGGINS. Doolittle: you have brought your daughter up too strictly.

DOOLITTLE. Me! I never brought her up at all, except to give her a lick of a strap now and again. Dont put it on me, Governor. She aint accustomed to it, you see: thats all. But she'll soon pick up your free-and-easy ways.

LIZA. I'm a good girl, I am; and I wont pick up no free-and-easy ways.

HIGGINS. Eliza: if you say again that youre a good girl, your father shall take you home.

LIZA. Not him. You dont know my father. All he come here for was to touch you for some money to get drunk on.

DOOLITTLE. Well, what else would I want money for? To put into the plate in church, I suppose. [*She puts out her tongue at him. He is so incensed by this that* PICKERING *presently finds it necessary to step between them.*] Dont you give me none of your lip; and dont let me hear you giving this gentleman any of it neither, or youll hear from me about it. See?

HIGGINS. Have you any further advice to give her before you go, Doolittle? Your blessing, for instance.

DOOLITTLE. No, Governor: I aint such a mug as to put up my children to all I know myself. Hard enough to hold them in without that. If you want Eliza's mind improved, Governor, you do it yourself with a strap. So long, gentlemen. [*He turns to go.*]

HIGGINS [*impressively*]. Stop. Youll come regularly to see your daughter. It's your duty, you know. My brother is a clergyman; and he could help you in your talks with her.

DOOLITTLE [*evasively*]. Certainly, I'll come, Governor. Not just this week, because I have a job at a distance. But later on you may depend on me. Afternoon, gentlemen. Afternoon, maam. [*He touches his hat to* MRS PEARCE, *who disdains the salutation and goes out. He winks at* HIGGINS, *thinking him probably a fellow sufferer from* MRS PEARCE*'s difficult disposition, and follows her.*]

LIZA. Dont you believe the old liar. He'd as soon you set a bulldog on him as a clergyman. You wont see him again in a hurry.

HIGGINS. I dont want to, Eliza. Do you?

LIZA. Not me. I dont want never to see him again, I dont. He's a disgrace to me, he is, collecting dust, instead of working at his trade.

PICKERING. What is his trade, Eliza?

LIZA. Talking money out of other people's pockets into his own. His proper trade's a navvy;[22] and he works at it sometimes too—for exercise—and earns good money at it. Aint you going to call me Miss Doolittle any more?

PICKERING. I beg your pardon, Miss Doolittle. It was a slip of the tongue.

LIZA. Oh, I dont mind; only it sounded so genteel. I should just like to take a taxi to the corner of Tottenham Court Road and get out there and tell it to wait for me, just to put the girls in their place a bit. I wouldnt speak to them, you know.

PICKERING. Better wait til we get you something really fashionable.

HIGGINS. Besides, you shouldnt cut your old friends now that you have risen in the world. Thats what we call snobbery.

LIZA. You dont call the like of them my friends now, I should hope. Theyve took it out of me often enough with their ridicule when they had the chance; and now I mean to get a bit of my own back. But if I'm to have fashionable clothes, I'll wait. I should like to have some. Mrs Pearce says youre going to give me some to wear in bed at night different to what I wear in the daytime; but it do seem a waste of money when you could get something to shew. Besides, I never could fancy changing into cold things on a winter night.

MRS PEARCE [*coming back*]. Now, Eliza. The new things have come for you to try on.

LIZA. Ah-ow-oo-ooh! [*She rushes out.*]

MRS PEARCE [*following her*]. Oh, dont rush about like that, girl. [*She shuts the door behind her.*]

HIGGINS. Pickering: we have taken on a stiff job.

PICKERING [*with conviction*]. Higgins: we have.

*   *   *

There seems to be some curiosity as to what HIGGINS*'s lessons to* ELIZA *were like. Well, here is a sample: the first one.*

Picture ELIZA, *in her new clothes, and feeling her inside put out of step by a lunch, dinner, and breakfast of a kind to which it is unaccustomed, seated with* HIGGINS *and the* COLONEL *in the study, feeling like a hospital out-patient at a first encounter with the doctors.*

---

[22] "Navvy": a ditch-digger.

HIGGINS, *constitutionally unable to sit still, discomposes her still more by striding restlessly about. But for the reassuring presence and quietude of her friend the* COLONEL *she would run for her life, even back to Drury Lane.*

HIGGINS. Say your alphabet.

LIZA. I know my alphabet. Do you think I know nothing? I dont need to be taught like a child.

HIGGINS [*thundering*]. Say your alphabet.

PICKERING. Say it, Miss Doolittle. You will understand presently. Do what he tells you; and let him teach you in his own way.

LIZA. Oh well, if you put it like that—Ahyee, bəyee, cəyee, dəyee—

HIGGINS [*with the roar of a wounded lion*]. Stop. Listen to this, Pickering. This is what we pay for as elementary education. This unfortunate animal has been locked up for nine years in school at our expense to teach her to speak and read the language of Shakespear and Milton. And the result is Ahyee, Bə-yee, Cə-yee, Də-yee. [*To* ELIZA] Say A, B, C, D.

LIZA [*almost in tears*]. But I'm sayin it. Ahyee, Bəyee, Cəyee—

HIGGINS. Stop. Say a cup of tea.

LIZA. A cappətə-ee.

HIGGINS. Put your tongue forward until it squeezes against the top of your lower teeth. Now say cup.

LIZA. C-c-c—I cant. C-Cup.

PICKERING. Good. Splendid, Miss Doolittle.

HIGGINS. By Jupiter, she's done it at the first shot. Pickering: we shall make a duchess of her. [*To* ELIZA] Now do you think you could possibly say tea? Not tə-yee, mind: if you ever say bə-yee cə-yee də-yee again you shall be dragged round the room three times by the hair of your head. [*Fortissimo*] T, T, T, T.

LIZA [*weeping*]. I cant hear no difference cep that it sounds more genteel-like when you say it.

HIGGINS. Well, if you can hear that difference, what the devil are you crying for? Pickering: give her a chocolate.

PICKERING. No, no. Never mind crying a little, Miss Doolittle: you are doing very well; and the lessons wont hurt. I promise you I wont let him drag you round the room by your hair.

HIGGINS. Be off with you to Mrs Pearce and tell her about it. Think about it. Try to do it by yourself: and keep your tongue well forward in your mouth instead of trying to roll it up and swallow it. Another lesson at half-past four this afternoon. Away with you.

[ELIZA, *still sobbing, rushes from the room.*]

And that is the sort of ordeal poor ELIZA *has to go through for months before we meet her again on her first appearance in London society of the professional class.*

ACT III

It is MRS HIGGINS's *at-home day. Nobody has yet arrived. Her drawing room, in a flat on Chelsea Embankment, has three windows looking on the river; and the ceiling is not so lofty as it would be in an older house of the same pretension. The windows are open, giving access to a balcony with flowers in pots. If you stand with your face to the windows, you have the fireplace on your left and the door in the right-hand wall close to the corner nearest the windows.*

Mrs Higgins *was brought up on Morris and Burne Jones;*[23] *and her room, which is very unlike her son's room in Wimpole Street, is not crowded with furniture and little tables and nicknacks. In the middle of the room there is a big ottoman; and this, with the carpet, the Morris wall-papers, and the Morris chintz window curtains and brocade covers of the ottoman and its cushions, supply all the ornament, and are much too handsome to be hidden by odds and ends of useless things. A few good oil-paintings from the exhibitions in the Grosvenor Gallery thirty years ago (the Burne Jones, not the Whistler*[24] *side of them) are on the walls. The only landscape is a Cecil Lawson on the scale of a Rubens. There is a portrait of* Mrs Higgins *as she was when she defied fashion in her youth in one of the beautiful Rossettian costumes which, when caricatured by people who did not understand, led to the absurdities of popular estheticism in the eighteen-seventies.*

In the corner diagonally opposite the door Mrs Higgins, *now over sixty and long past taking the trouble to dress out of the fashion, sits writing at an elegantly simple writing-table with a bell button within reach of her hand. There is a Chippendale chair further back in the room between her and the window nearest her side. At the other side of the room, further forward, is an Elizabethan chair roughly carved in the taste of Inigo Jones. On the same side a piano in a decorated case. The corner between the fireplace and the window is occupied by a divan cushioned in Morris chintz.*

It is between four and five in the afternoon.

The door is opened violently; and Higgins *enters with his hat on.*

Mrs Higgins [*dismayed*]. Henry! [*Scolding him*] What are you doing here today! It is my at-home day: you promised not to come. [*As he bends to kiss her, she takes his hat off, and presents it to him.*]

Higgins. Oh bother! [*He throws the hat down on the table.*]

Mrs Higgins. Go home at once.

Higgins [*kissing her*]. I know, mother. I came on purpose.

Mrs Higgins. But you mustnt. I'm serious, Henry. You offend all my friends: they stop coming whenever they meet you.

Higgins. Nonsense! I know I have no small talk; but people dont mind. [*He sits on the settee.*]

Mrs Higgins. Oh! dont they? Small talk indeed! What about your large talk? Really, dear, you mustnt stay.

Higgins. I must. Ive a job for you. A phonetic job.

Mrs Higgins. No use, dear. I'm sorry; but I cant get round your vowels; and though I like to get pretty postcards in your patent shorthand, I always have to read the copies in ordinary writing you so thoughtfully send me.

Higgins. Well, this isn't a phonetic job.

Mrs Higgins. You said it was.

Higgins. Not your part of it. Ive picked up a girl.

Mrs Higgins. Does that mean that some girl has picked you up?

Higgins. Not at all. I dont mean a love affair.

Mrs Higgins. What a pity!

Higgins. Why?

---

[23] "Morris and Burne Jones": William Morris (1834–1896) and Sir Edward Coley Burne-Jones (1833–1898) were key members of the Pre-Raphaelite movement in the arts. Morris was famous as a poet and artist, but Shaw is here referring to his work as a designer who set up his own company to create wallpaper, furniture, carpet, and other home furnishings. Burne-Jones was primarily a painter, but he also created stained-glass windows for Morris's company.

[24] James Abbott McNeill Whistler (1834–1903), an American painter who lived in London and Paris, advocated a simplicity of design that was quite different from the Pre-Raphaelite style.

MRS HIGGINS. Well, you never fall in love with anyone under forty-five. When will you discover that there are some rather nice-looking young women about?

HIGGINS. Oh, I cant be bothered with young women. My idea of a lovable woman is somebody as like you as possible. I shall never get into the way of seriously liking young women: some habits lie too deep to be changed. [*Rising abruptly and walking about, jingling his money and his keys in his trouser pockets*] Besides, theyre all idiots.

MRS HIGGINS. Do you know what you would do if you really loved me, Henry?

HIGGINS. Oh bother! What? Marry, I suppose.

MRS HIGGINS. No. Stop fidgeting and take your hands out of your pockets. [*With a gesture of despair, he obeys and sits down again.*] Thats a good boy. Now tell me about the girl.

HIGGINS. She's coming to see you.

MRS HIGGINS. I dont remember asking her.

HIGGINS. You didnt. *I* asked her. If youd known her you wouldnt have asked her.

MRS HIGGINS. Indeed! Why?

HIGGINS. Well, it's like this. She's a common flower girl. I picked her off the kerbstone.

MRS HIGGINS. And invited her to my at-home!

HIGGINS [*rising and coming to her to coax her*]. Oh, thatll be all right. Ive taught her to speak properly; and she has strict orders as to her behavior. She's to keep to two subjects: the weather and everybody's health—Fine day and How do you do, you know—and not to let herself go on things in general. That will be safe.

MRS HIGGINS. Safe! To talk about our health! about our insides! perhaps about our outsides! How could you be so silly, Henry?

HIGGINS [*impatiently*]. Well, she must talk about something. [*He controls himself and sits down again.*] Oh, she'll be all right: dont you fuss. Pickering is in it with me. Ive a sort of bet on that I'll pass her off as a duchess in six months. I started on her some months ago; and she's getting on like a house on fire. I shall win my bet. She has a quick ear; and she's been easier to teach than my middle-class pupils because she's had to learn a complete new language. She talks English almost as you talk French.

MRS HIGGINS. Thats satisfactory, at all events.

HIGGINS. Well, it is and it isnt.

MRS HIGGINS. What does that mean?

HIGGINS. You see, Ive got her pronunciation all right; but you have to consider not only how a girl pronounces, but what she pronounces; and that's where—

[*They are interrupted by* THE PARLORMAID, *announcing guests.*]

THE PARLORMAID. Mrs and Miss Eynsford Hill. (*She withdraws.*)

HIGGINS. Oh Lord! [*He rises; snatches his hat from the table; and makes for the door; but before he reaches it his mother introduces him.*]

MRS *and* MISS EYNSFORD HILL *are the mother and daughter who sheltered from the rain in Covent Garden. The mother is well bred, quiet, and has the habitual anxiety of straitened means. The daughter has acquired a gay air of being very much at home in society: the bravado of genteel poverty.*

MRS EYNSFORD HILL [*to* MRS HIGGINS]. How do you do? [*They shake hands.*]

MISS EYNSFORD HILL. How d'you do? [*She shakes.*]

MRS HIGGINS [*introducing*]. My son Henry.

MRS EYNSFORD HILL. Your celebrated son! I have so longed to meet you, Professor Higgins.

HIGGINS [*glumly, making no movement in her direction*]. Delighted. [*He backs against the piano and bows brusquely.*]

MISS EYNSFORD HILL [*going to him with confident familiarity*]. How do you do?

HIGGINS [*staring at her*]. Ive seen you before somewhere. I havent the ghost of a notion where; but Ive heard your voice. [*Drearily*] It doesnt matter. Youd better sit down.

MRS HIGGINS. I'm sorry to say that my celebrated son has no manners. You mustnt mind him.

MISS EYNSFORD HILL [*gaily*]. I dont. [*She sits in the Elizabethan chair.*]

MRS EYNSFORD HILL [*a little bewildered*]. Not at all. [*She sits on the ottoman between her daughter and* MRS HIGGINS, *who has turned her chair away from the writing-table.*]

HIGGINS. Oh, have I been rude? I didnt mean to be.

He goes to the central window, through which, with his back to the company, he contemplates the river and the flowers in Battersea Park on the opposite bank as if they were a frozen desert. THE PARLORMAID *returns, ushering in* PICKERING.]

THE PARLORMAID. Colonel Pickering. [*She withdraws.*]

PICKERING. How do you do, Mrs Higgins?

MRS HIGGINS. So glad youve come. Do you know Mrs Eynsford Hill—Miss Eynsford Hill? [*Exchange of bows. The* COLONEL *brings the Chippendale chair a little forward between* MRS HILL *and* MRS HIGGINS, *and sits down.*]

PICKERING. Has Henry told you what weve come for?

HIGGINS [*over his shoulder*]. We were interrupted: damn it!

MRS HIGGINS. Oh Henry, Henry, really!

MRS EYNSFORD HILL [*half rising*]. Are we in the way?

MRS HIGGINS [*rising and making her sit down again*]. No, no. You couldnt have come more fortunately: we want you to meet a friend of ours.

HIGGINS [*turning hopefully*]. Yes, by George! We want two or three people. Youll do as well as anybody else.

[THE PARLORMAID *returns, ushering* FREDDY.]

THE PARLORMAID. Mr Eynsford Hill.

HIGGINS [*almost audibly, past endurance*]. God of Heaven! another of them.

FREDDY [*shaking hands with* MRS HIGGINS]. Ahdedo?

MRS HIGGINS. Very good of you to come. [*Introducing*] Colonel Pickering.

FREDDY [*bowing*]. Ahdedo?

MRS HIGGINS. I dont think you know my son, Professor Higgins.

FREDDY [*going to* HIGGINS]. Ahdedo?

HIGGINS [*looking at him much as if he were a pick-pocket*]. I'll take my oath Ive met you before somewhere. Where was it?

FREDDY. I don't think so.

HIGGINS [*resignedly*]. It dont matter, anyhow. Sit down.

[*He shakes* FREDDY's *hand, and almost slings him on to the ottoman with his face to the windows; then comes round to the other side of it.*]

HIGGINS. Well, here we are, anyhow! [*He sits down on the ottoman next* MRS EYNSFORD HILL *on her left.*] And now what the devil are we going to talk about until Eliza comes?

MRS HIGGINS. Henry: you are the life and soul of the Royal Society's soirées;[25] but really youre rather trying on more commonplace occasions.

---

[25] "Royal Society's soirées": Founded in the 1640s, the Royal Society of London for the Improvement of Natural Knowledge is probably the most famous and distinguished scientific society in the world.

HIGGINS. Am I? Very sorry. [*Beaming suddenly.*] I suppose I am, you know. [*Uproariously*] Ha, ha!

MISS EYNSFORD HILL [*who considers* HIGGINS *quite eligible matrimonially*]. I sympathize. *I* havnt any small talk. If people would only be frank and say what they really think!

HIGGINS [*relapsing into gloom*]. Lord forbid!

MRS EYNSFORD HILL [*taking up her daughter's cue*]. But why?

HIGGINS. What they think they ought to think is bad enough Lord knows; but what they really think would break up the whole show. Do you suppose it would be really agreeable if I were to come out now with what *I* really think?

MISS EYNSFORD HILL [*gaily*]. Is it so very cynical?

HIGGINS. Cynical! Who the dickens said it was cynical? I mean it wouldn't be decent.

MRS EYNSFORD HILL [*seriously*]. Oh! I'm sure you dont mean that, Mr Higgins.

HIGGINS. You see, we're all savages, more or less. We're supposed to be civilized and cultured—to know all about poetry and philosophy and art and science, and so on; but how many of us know even the meanings of these names? [*To* MISS HILL] What do you know of poetry? [*To* MRS HILL] What do you know of science? [*Indicating* FREDDY] What does he know of art or science or anything else? What the devil do you imagine I know of philosophy?

MRS HIGGINS [*warningly*]. Or of manners, Henry?

THE PARLORMAID [*opening the door*]. Miss Doolittle. [*She withdraws.*]

HIGGINS [*rising hastily and running to* MRS HIGGINS]. Here she is, mother. [*He stands on tiptoe and makes signs over his mother's head to* ELIZA *to indicate to her which lady is her hostess.*]

ELIZA, *who is exquisitely dressed, produces an impression of such remarkable distinction and beauty as she enters that they all rise, quite fluttered. Guided by* HIGGINS*'s signals, she comes to* MRS HIGGINS *with studied grace.*

LIZA [*speaking with pedantic correctness of pronunciation and great beauty of tone*]. How do you do, Mrs Higgins? [*She gasps slightly in making sure of the H in Higgins, but is quite successful.*] Mr Higgins told me I might come.

MRS HIGGINS [*cordially*]. Quite right: I'm very glad indeed to see you.

PICKERING. How do you do, Miss Doolittle?

LIZA [*shaking hands with him*]. Colonel Pickering, is it not?

MRS EYNSFORD HILL. I feel sure we have met before, Miss Doolittle. I remember your eyes.

LIZA. How do you do? [*She sits down on the ottoman graceful in the place just left vacant by* HIGGINS.]

MRS EYNSFORD HILL [*introducing*]. My daughter Clara.

LIZA. How do you do?

CLARA [*impulsively*]. How do you do? [*She sits down on the ottoman beside* ELIZA, *devouring her with her eyes.*]

FREDDY [*coming to their side of the ottoman*]. Ive certainly had the pleasure.

MRS EYNSFORD HILL [*introducing*]. My son Freddy.

LIZA. How do you do?

[FREDDY *bows and sits down in the Elizabethan chair, infatuated.*]

HIGGINS [*suddenly*]. By George, yes: it all comes back to me! [*They stare at him.*] Covent Garden! [*Lamentably*] What a damned thing!

MRS HIGGINS. Henry, please! [*He is about to sit on the edge of the table*] Dont sit on my writing table: youll break it.

HIGGINS [*sulkily*]. Sorry.

He goes to the divan, stumbling into the fender and over the fire-irons on his way; extricating himself with muttered imprecations; and finishing his disastrous journey by throwing himself so impatiently on the divan that he almost breaks it. MRS HIGGINS *looks at him, but controls herself and says nothing. A long and painful pause ensues.*

MRS HIGGINS [*at last, conversationally*]. Will it rain, do you think?

LIZA. The shallow depression in the west of these islands is likely to move slowly in an easterly direction. There are no indications of any great change in the barometrical situation.

FREDDY. Ha! ha! how awfully funny!

LIZA. What is wrong with that, young man? I bet I got it right.

FREDDY. Killing!

MRS EYNSFORD HILL. I'm sure I hope it wont turn cold. There so much influenza about. It runs right through our whole family regularly every spring.

LIZA [*darkly*]. My aunt died of influenza: so they said.

MRS EYNSFORD HILL [*clicks her tongue sympathetically*]. ! ! !

LIZA [*in the same tragic tone*]. But it's my belief they done the old woman in.

MRS HIGGINS [*puzzled*]. Done her in?

LIZA. Y-e-e-e-es, Lord love you! Why should she die of influenza? She come through diphtheria right enough the year before. I saw her with my own eyes. Fairly blue with it, she was. They all thought she was dead; but my father he kept ladling gin down her throat til she came to so sudden that she bit the bowl off the spoon.

MRS EYNSFORD HILL [*startled*]. Dear me!

LIZA [*piling up the indictment*]. What call would a woman with that strength in her have to die of influenza? What become of her new straw hat that should have come to me? Somebody pinched it; and what I say is, them as pinched it done her in.

MRS EYNSFORD HILL. What does doing her in mean?

HIGGINS [*hastily*]. Oh, thats the new small talk. To do a person in means to kill them.

MRS EYNSFORD HILL [*To* ELIZA, *horrified*]. You surely dont believe that your aunt was killed?

LIZA. Do I not! Them she lived with would have killed her for a hat-pin, let alone a hat.

MRS EYNSFORD HILL. But it cant have been right for your father to pour spirits down her throat like that. It might have killed her.

LIZA. Not her. Gin was mother's milk to her. Besides, he'd poured so much down his own throat that he knew the good of it.

MRS EYNSFORD HILL. Do you mean that he drank?

LIZA. Drank! My word! Something chronic.

MRS EYNSFORD HILL. How dreadful for you!

LIZA. Not a bit. It never did him no harm what I could see. But then he did not keep it up regular. [*Cheerfully*] On the burst, as you might say, from time to time. And always more agreeable when he had a drop in. When he was out of work, my mother used to give him fourpence and tell him to go out and not come back until he'd drunk himself cheerful and loving-like. Theres lots of women has to make their husbands drunk to make them fit to live with. [*Now quite at her ease*] You see, it's like this. If a man has a bit of a conscience, it always takes him when he's sober; and then it makes him low-spirited. A drop of booze just takes that off and makes him happy. [*To* FREDDY, *who is in convulsions of suppressed laughter.*] Here! what are you sniggering at?

FREDDY. The new small talk. You do it so awfully well.

LIZA. If I was doing it proper, what was you laughing at? [*To* HIGGINS] Have I said anything I oughtnt?

MRS HIGGINS [*interposing*]. Not at all, Miss Doolittle.

LIZA. Well, thats a mercy, anyhow. [*Expansively*] What I always say is—

HIGGINS [*rising and looking at his watch*]. Ahem!

LIZA [*looking round at him; taking the hint; and rising*]. Well: I must go. [*They all rise. FREDDY goes to the door.*] So pleased to have met you. Goodbye. [*She shakes hands with MRS HIGGINS.*]

MRS HIGGINS. Goodbye.

LIZA. Goodbye, Colonel Pickering.

PICKERING. Goodbye, Miss Doolittle. [*They shake hands.*]

LIZA [*nodding to the others*]. Goodbye, all.

FREDDY [*opening the door for her*]. Are you walking across the Park, Miss Doolittle? If so—

LIZA [*with perfectly elegant diction*]. Walk! Not bloody likely. [*Sensation.*] I am going in a taxi. [*She goes out.*]

[PICKERING *gasps and sits down.* FREDDY *goes out on the balcony to catch another glimpse of* ELIZA.]

MRS EYNSFORD HILL [*suffering from shock*]. Well, I really cant get used to the new ways.

CLARA [*throwing herself discontentedly into the Elizabethan chair*]. Oh, it's all right, mamma, quite right. People will think we never go anywhere or see anybody if you are so old-fashioned.

MRS EYNSFORD HILL. I daresay I am very old-fashioned; but I do hope you wont begin using that expression, Clara. I have got accustomed to hearing you talking about men as rotters, and calling everything filthy and beastly; though I do think it horrible and unladylike. But this last is really too much. Dont you think so, Colonel Pickering?

PICKERING. Dont ask me. Ive been away in India for several years; and manners have changed so much that I sometimes dont know whether I'm at a respectable dinner-table or in a ship's forecastle.

CLARA. It's all a matter of habit. Theres no right or wrong in it. Nobody means anything by it. And it's so quaint, and gives such a smart emphasis to things that are not in themselves very witty. I find the new small talk delightful and quite innocent.

MRS EYNSFORD HILL [*rising*]. Well, after that, I think it's time for us to go.

[PICKERING *and* HIGGINS *rise.*]

CLARA [*rising*]. Oh yes: we have three at-homes to go to still. Goodbye, Mrs Higgins. Goodbye, Colonel Pickering. Goodbye, Professor Higgins.

HIGGINS [*coming grimly at her from the divan, and accompanying her to the door*]. Goodbye. Be sure you try on that small talk at the three at-homes. Don't be nervous about it. Pitch it in strong.

CLARA [*all smiles*]. I will. Goodbye. Such nonsense, all this early Victorian prudery!

HIGGINS [*tempting her*]. Such damned nonsense!

CLARA. Such bloody nonsense!

MRS EYNSFORD HILL [*convulsively*]. Clara!

CLARA. Ha! ha! [*She goes out radiant, conscious of being thoroughly up to date, and is heard descending the stairs in a stream of silvery laughter.*]

FREDDY [*to the heavens at large*]. Well, I ask you— [*He gives it up, and comes to* MRS HIGGINS.] Goodbye.

MRS HIGGINS [*shaking hands*]. Goodbye. Would you like to meet Miss Doolittle again?

FREDDY [*eagerly*]. Yes, I should, most awfully.

MRS HIGGINS. Well, you know my days.

FREDDY. Yes, Thanks awfully. Goodbye. [*He goes out.*]

MRS EYNSFORD HILL. Goodbye, Mr Higgins.

HIGGINS. Goodbye. Goodbye.

MRS EYNSFORD HILL [*to* PICKERING]. It's no use. I shall never be able to bring myself to use that word.

PICKERING. Dont. It's not compulsory, you know. Youll get on quite well without it.

MRS EYNSFORD HILL. Only, Clara is so down on me if I am not positively reeking with the latest slang. Goodbye.

PICKERING. Goodbye. [*They shake hands.*]

MRS EYNSFORD HILL [*to* MRS HIGGINS]. You mustnt mind Clara. [PICKERING, *catching from her lowered tone that this is not meant for him to hear, discreetly joins* HIGGINS *at the window.*] We're so poor! and she gets so few parties, poor child! She doesnt quite know. [MRS HIGGINS, *seeing that her eyes are moist, takes her hand sympathetically and goes with her to the door.*] But the boy is nice. Dont you think so?

MRS HIGGINS. Oh, quite nice. I shall always be delighted to see him.

MRS EYNSFORD HILL. Thank you, dear. Goodbye. [*She goes out.*]

HIGGINS [*eagerly*]. Well? Is Eliza presentable? [*he swoops on his mother and drags her to the ottoman, where she sits down in* ELIZA*'s place with her son on her left.* PICKERING *returns to his chair on her right.*]

MRS HIGGINS. You silly boy, of course she's not presentable. She's a triumph of your art and of her dressmaker's; but if you suppose for a moment that she doesnt give herself away in every sentence she utters, you must be perfectly cracked about her.

PICKERING. But dont you think something might be done? I mean something to eliminate the sanguinary element from her conversation.

MRS HIGGINS. Not as long as she is in Henry's hands.

HIGGINS [*aggrieved*]. Do you mean that my language is improper?

MRS HIGGINS. No, dearest: it would be quite proper—say on a canal barge; but it would not be proper for her at a garden party.

HIGGINS [*deeply injured*]. Well I must say—

PICKERING [*interrupting him*]. Come, Higgins: you must learn to know yourself. I havnt heard such language as yours since we used to review the volunteers in Hyde Park twenty years ago.

HIGGINS [*sulkily*]. Oh, well, if you say so, I suppose I dont always talk like a bishop.

MRS HIGGINS [*quieting* HENRY *with a touch*]. Colonel Pickering: will you tell me what is the exact state of things in Wimpole Street?

PICKERING [*cheerfully: as if this completely changed the subject*]. Well, I have come to live there with Henry. We work together at my Indian Dialects; and we think it more convenient—

MRS HIGGINS. Quite so. I know all about that: it's an excellent arrangement. But where does this girl live?

HIGGINS. With us, of course. Where should she live?

MRS HIGGINS. But on what terms? Is she a servant? If not, what is she?

PICKERING [*slowly*]. I think I know what you mean, Mrs Higgins.

HIGGINS. Well, dash me if *I* do! Ive had to work at the girl every day for months to get her to her present pitch. Besides, she's useful. She knows where my things are, and remembers my appointments and so forth.

MRS HIGGINS. How does your housekeeper get on with her?

HIGGINS. Mrs Pearce? Oh, she's jolly glad to get so much taken off her hands; for before Eliza came, she used to have to find things and remind me of my appointments. But she's got some silly bee in her bonnet about Eliza. She keeps saying "You dont think, sir": doesnt she, Pick?

PICKERING. Yes: thats the formula. "You dont think, sir." Thats the end of every conversation about Eliza.

HIGGINS. As if I ever stop thinking about the girl and her confounded vowels and consonants. I'm worn out, thinking about her, and watching her lips and her teeth and her tongue, not to mention her soul, which is the quaintest of the lot.

MRS HIGGINS. You certainly are a pretty pair of babies, playing with your live doll.

HIGGINS. Playing! The hardest job I ever tackled: make no mistake about that, mother. But you have no idea how frightfully interesting it is to take a human being and change her into a quite different human being by creating a new speech for her. It's filling up the deepest gulf that separates class from class and soul from soul.

PICKERING [*drawing his chair closer to* MRS HIGGINS *and bending over to her eagerly*]. Yes: it's enormously interesting. I assure you, Mrs Higgins, we take Eliza very seriously. Every week—every day almost—there is some new change. [*Closer again*] We keep records of every stage—dozens of gramophone disks and photographs—

HIGGINS [*assailing her at the other ear*]. Yes, by George: it's the most absorbing experiment I ever tackled. She regularly fills our lives up: doesnt she, Pick?

PICKERING. We're always talking Eliza.

HIGGINS. Teaching Eliza.

PICKERING. Dressing Eliza.

MRS HIGGINS. What!

HIGGINS. Inventing new Elizas.

HIGGINS	[*speaking together*]	You know, she has the most extra-ordinary quickness of ear:
PICKERING		I assure you, my dear Mrs Higgins, that girl
HIGGINS		just like a parrot. Ive tried her with every
PICKERING		is a genius. She can play the piano quite beautifully.
HIGGINS		possible sort of sound that a human being can make
PICKERING		We have taken her to classical concerts and to music
HIGGINS		Continental dialects, African dialects, Hottentot
PICKERING		halls; and it's all the same to her: she plays everything
HIGGINS		clicks, things it took me years to get hold of; and
PICKERING		she hears right off when she comes home, whether it's
HIGGINS		she picks them up like a shot, right away, as if she had
PICKERING		Beethoven and Brahms or Lehar and Lionel Monckton;[26]

---

[26] In addition to the famous classical composers, Ludwig van Beethoven (1770–1827) and Johannes Brahms (1833–1897), Pickering is alluding to the contemporary composers of operettas, Franz Lehar (1870–1948) and Lionel Monckton (1861–1924).

HIGGINS ⎫   ⎰ been at it all her life.
           ⎬   ⎱ though six months ago, she'd never
PICKERING ⎭   as much as touched a piano—

Mrs HIGGINS [*putting her fingers in her ears, as they are by this time shouting one another down with an intolerable noise*]. Sh-sh-sh—sh! [*They stop.*]

PICKERING. I beg your pardon. [*He draws his chair back apologetically.*]

HIGGINS. Sorry. When Pickering starts shouting nobody can get a word in edgeways.

Mrs HIGGINS. Be quiet, Henry. Colonel Pickering: dont you realize that when Eliza walked into Wimpole Street, something walked in with her?

PICKERING. Her father did. But Henry soon got rid of him.

Mrs HIGGINS. It would have been more to the point if her mother had. But as her mother didnt something else did.

PICKERING. But what?

Mrs HIGGINS [*unconsciously dating herself by the word*]. A problem.

PICKERING. Oh, I see. The problem of how to pass her off as a lady.

HIGGINS. I'll solve that problem. Ive half solved it already.

Mrs HIGGINS. No, you two infinitely stupid male creatures: the problem of what is to be done with her afterwards.

HIGGINS. I dont see anything in that. She can go her own way, with all the advantages I have given her.

Mrs HIGGINS. The advantages of that poor woman who was here just now! The manners and habits that disqualify a fine lady from earning her own living without giving her a fine lady's income! Is that what you mean?

PICKERING [*indulgently, being rather bored*]. Oh, that will be all right, Mrs Higgins. [*He rises to go.*]

HIGGINS [*rising also*]. We'll find her some light employment.

PICKERING. She's happy enough. Don't you worry about her. Goodbye. [*He shakes hands as if he were consoling a frightened child, and makes for the door.*]

HIGGINS. Anyway, theres no good bothering now. The thing's done. Goodbye, mother. [*He kisses her, and follows* PICKERING].

PICKERING [*turning for a final consolation*]. There are plenty of openings. We'll do whats right. Goodbye.

HIGGINS [*to* PICKERING *as they go out together*]. Lets take her to the Shakespear exhibition at Earls Court.

PICKERING. Yes: lets. Her remarks will be delicious.

HIGGINS. She'll mimic all the people for us when we get home.

PICKERING. Ripping. [*Both are heard laughing as they go downstairs.*]

Mrs HIGGINS [*rises with an impatient bounce, and returns to her work at the writing-table. She sweeps a litter of disarranged papers out of her way; snatches a sheet of paper from her stationery case; and tries resolutely to write. At the third line she gives it up; flings down her pen; grips the table angrily and exclaims*]. Oh, men! men!! men!!!

*   *   *

    Clearly ELIZA *will not pass as a duchess yet; and* HIGGINS*'s bet remains unwon. But the six months are not yet exhausted; and just in time* ELIZA *does actually pass as a princess. For a glimpse of how she did it imagine an Embassy in London one summer evening after dark. The hall door has an awning and a carpet across the sidewalk to the kerb, because a grand reception is in progress. A small crowd is lined up to see the guests arrive.*

    A Rolls-Royce car drives up. PICKERING *in evening dress, with medals and orders, alights, and hands out* ELIZA, *in opera cloak, evening dress, diamonds, fan, flowers and all acces-*

sories. HIGGINS *follows. The car drives off; and the three go up the steps and into the house, the door opening for them as they approach.*

Inside the house they find themselves in a spacious hall from which the grand staircase rises. On the left are the arrangements for the gentlemen's cloaks. The male guests are depositing their hats and wraps there.

On the right is a door leading to the ladies' cloakroom. Ladies are going in cloaked and coming out in splendor. PICKERING *whispers to* ELIZA *and points out the ladies' room. She goes into it.* HIGGINS *and* PICKERING *take off their overcoats and take tickets for them from the attendant.*

One of the guests, occupied in the same way, has his back turned. Having taken his ticket, he turns round and reveals himself as an important looking young man with an astonishingly hairy face. He has an enormous moustache, flowing out into luxuriant whiskers. Waves of hair cluster on his brow. His hair is cropped closely at the back, and glows with oil. Otherwise he is very smart. He wears several worthless orders. He is evidently a foreigner, guessable as a whiskered Pandour[27] from Hungary; but in spite of the ferocity of his moustache he is amiable and genially voluble.

Recognizing HIGGINS, *he flings his arms wide apart and approaches him enthusiastically.*

WHISKERS. Maestro, maestro [*he embraces* HIGGINS *and kisses him on both cheeks*]. You remember me?

HIGGINS. No I dont. Who the devil are you?

WHISKERS. I am your pupil: your first pupil, your best and greatest pupil. I am little Nepommuck, the marvellous boy. I have made your name famous throughout Europe. You teach me phonetic. You cannot forget ME.

HIGGINS. Why dont you shave?

NEPOMMUCK. I have not your imposing appearance, your chin, your brow. Nobody notice me when I shave. Now I am famous: they call me Hairy Faced Dick.

HIGGINS. And what are you doing here among all these swells?

NEPOMMUCK. I am interpreter. I speak 32 languages. I am indispensable at these international parties. You are great cockney specialist: you place a man anywhere in London the moment he open his mouth. I place any man in Europe.

[*A footman hurries down the grand staircase and comes to* NEPOMMUCK.]

FOOTMAN. You are wanted upstairs. Her Excellency cannot understand the Greek gentleman.

NEPOMMUCK. Thank you, yes, immediately.

[*The* FOOTMAN *goes and is lost in the crowd.*]

NEPOMMUCK [*to* HIGGINS]. This Greek diplomatist pretends he cannot speak nor understand English. He cannot deceive me. He is the son of a Clerkenwell watchmaker. He speaks English so villainously that he dare not utter a word of it without betraying his origin. I help him to pretend; but I make him pay through the nose. I make them all pay. Ha Ha! [*He hurries upstairs.*]

PICKERING. Is this fellow really an expert? Can he find out Eliza and blackmail her?

HIGGINS. We shall see. If he finds her out I lose my bet.

[ELIZA *comes from the cloakroom and joins them.*]

PICKERING. Well, Eliza, now for it. Are you ready?

LIZA. Are you nervous, Colonel?

PICKERING. Frightfully. I feel exactly as I felt before my first battle. It's the first time that frightens.

---

[27] The Croatian Pandours of Baron Trenck in the 1740s were soldiers infamous for their unrestrained ferocity.

LIZA. It is not the first time for me, Colonel. I have done this fifty times—hundreds of times—in my little piggery in Angel Court in my day-dreams. I am in a dream now. Promise me not to let Professor Higgins wake me; for if he does I shall forget everything and talk as I used to in Drury Lane.

PICKERING. Not a word, Higgins. [*To* ELIZA] Now, ready?

LIZA. Ready.

PICKERING. Go.

[*They mount the stairs,* HIGGINS *last.* PICKERING *whispers to the* FOOTMAN *on the first landing.*]

FIRST LANDING FOOTMAN. Miss Doolittle, Colonel Pickering, Professor Higgins.

SECOND LANDING FOOTMAN. Miss Doolittle, Colonel Pickering, Professor Higgins.

[*At the top of the staircase the Ambassador and his wife, with* NEPOMMUCK *at her elbow, are receiving.*]

HOSTESS [*taking* ELIZA's *hand*]. How d'ye do?

HOST [*same play*]. How d'ye do? How d'ye do, Pickering?

LIZA [*with a beautiful gravity that awes her hostess*]. How do you do? [*She passes on to the drawingroom.*]

HOSTESS. Is that your adopted daughter, Colonel Pickering? She will make a sensation.

PICKERING. Most kind of you to invite her for me. [*He passes on.*]

HOSTESS [*to* NEPOMMUCK]. Find out all about her.

NEPOMMUCK [*bowing*]. Excellency—[*he goes into the crowd*].

HOST. How d'ye do, Higgins? You have a rival here tonight. He introduced himself as your pupil. Is he any good?

HIGGINS. He can learn a language in a fortnight—knows dozens of them. A sure mark of a fool. As a phonetician, no good whatever.

HOSTESS. How d'ye do, Professor?

HIGGINS. How do you do? Fearful bore for you this sort of thing. Forgive my part in it. [*He passes on.*]

In the drawingroom and its suite of salons the reception is in full swing. ELIZA *passes through. She is so intent on her ordeal that she walks like a somnambulist in a desert instead of a débutante in a fashionable crowd. They stop talking to look at her, admiring her dress, her jewels, and her strangely attractive self. Some of the younger ones at the back stand on their chairs to see.*

The HOST *and* HOSTESS *come in from the staircase and mingle with their guests.* HIGGINS, *gloomy and contemptuous of the whole business, comes into the group where they are chatting.*

HOSTESS. Ah, here is Professor Higgins: he will tell us. Tell us all about the wonderful young lady, Professor.

HIGGINS [*almost morosely*]. What wonderful young lady?

HOSTESS. You know very well. They tell me there has been nothing like her in London since people stood on their chairs to look at Mrs Langtry.[28]

[NEPOMMUCK *joins the group, full of news.*]

HOSTESS. Ah, here you are at last, Nepommuck. Have you found out all about the Doolittle lady?

NEPOMMUCK. I have found out all about her. She is a fraud.

HOSTESS. A fraud! Oh no.

NEPOMMUCK. YES, yes. She cannot deceive me. Her name cannot be Doolittle.

---

[28] Lillie Langtry (1853–1929) was a famous beauty, a celebrated actress, and the mistress of King Edward VII.

HIGGINS. Why?

NEPOMMUCK. Because Doolittle is an English name. And she is not English.

HOSTESS. Oh, nonsense! She speaks English perfectly.

NEPOMMUCK. Too perfectly. Can you shew me any English woman who speaks English as it should be spoken? Only foreigners who have been taught to speak it speak it well.

HOSTESS. Certainly she terrified me by the way she said How d'ye do. I had a schoolmistress who talked like that; and I was mortally afraid of her. But if she is not English what is she?

NEPOMMUCK. Hungarian.

ALL THE REST. Hungarian!

NEPOMMUCK. Hungarian. And of royal blood. I am Hungarian. My blood is royal.

HIGGINS. Did you speak to her in Hungarian?

NEPOMMUCK. I did. She was very clever. She said "Please speak to me in English: I do not understand French." French! She pretends not to know the difference between Hungarian and French. Impossible: she knows both.

HIGGINS. And the blood royal? How did you find that out?

NEPOMMUCK. Instinct, maestro, instinct. Only the Magyar[29] races can produce that air of the divine right, those resolute eyes. She is a princess.

HOST. What do you say, Professor?

HIGGINS. I say an ordinary London girl out of the gutter and taught to speak by an expert. I place her in Drury Lane.

NEPOMMUCK. Ha ha ha! Oh, maestro, maestro, you are mad on the subject of cockney dialects. The London gutter is the whole world for you.

HIGGINS [*to the* HOSTESS]. What does your Excellency say?

HOSTESS. Oh, of course I agree with Nepommuck. She must be a princess at least.

HOST. Not necessarily legitimate, of course. Morganatic[30] perhaps. But that is undoubtedly her class.

HIGGINS. I stick to my opinion.

HOSTESS. Oh, you are incorrigible.

[*The group breaks up, leaving* HIGGINS *isolated.* PICKERING *joins him.*]

PICKERING. Where is Eliza? We must keep an eye on her.

[ELIZA *joins them.*]

LIZA. I dont think I can bear much more. The people all stare so at me. An old lady has just told me that I speak exactly like Queen Victoria. I am sorry if I have lost your bet. I have done my best; but nothing can make me the same as these people.

PICKERING. You have not lost it, my dear. You have won it ten times over.

HIGGINS. Let us get out of this. I have had enough of chattering to these fools.

PICKERING. Eliza is tired; and I am hungry. Let us clear out and have supper somewhere.

ACT IV

The Wimpole Street laboratory. Midnight. Nobody in the room. The clock on the mantelpiece strikes twelve. The fire is not alight: it is a summer night.

Presently HIGGINS *and* PICKERING *are heard on the stairs.*

---

[29] The Magyars were nomadic Hungarian warriors.

[30] "Morganatic": The offspring of a "left-handed marriage" in which a man of noble blood marries a woman from a lower class with the proviso that their children will not inherit their father's rank or privileges.

HIGGINS [*calling down to* PICKERING]. I say, Pick: lock up, will you? I shant be going out again.

PICKERING. Right. Can Mrs Pearce go to bed? We dont want anything more, do we?

HIGGINS. Lord, no!

ELIZA *opens the door and is seen on the lighted landing in all the finery in which she has just won* HIGGINS*'s bet for him. She comes to the hearth, and switches on the electric lights there. She is tired: her pallor contrasts strongly with her dark eyes and hair; and her expression is almost tragic. She takes off her cloak; puts her fan and gloves on the piano; and sits down on the bench, brooding and silent.* HIGGINS, *in evening dress, with overcoat and hat, comes in, carrying a smoking jacket which he has picked up downstairs. He takes off the hat and overcoat; throws them carelessly on the newspaper stand; disposes of his coat in the same way; puts on the smoking jacket; and throws himself wearily into the easy-chair at the hearth.* PICKERING, *similarly attired, comes in. He also takes off his hat and overcoat, and is about to throw them on* HIGGINS*'s when he hesitates.*

PICKERING. I say: Mrs Pearce will row[31] if we leave these things lying about in the drawing room.

HIGGINS. Oh, chuck them over the bannisters into the hall. She'll find them there in the morning and put them away all right. She'll think we were drunk.

PICKERING. We are, slightly. Are there any letters?

HIGGINS. I didnt look. [PICKERING *takes the overcoats and hats and goes downstairs.* HIGGINS *begins half singing half yawning an air from* La Fanciulla del Golden West. *Suddenly he stops and exclaims*] I wonder where the devil my slippers are!

ELIZA *looks at him darkly; then rises suddenly and leaves the room.* HIGGINS *yawns again, and resumes his song.* PICKERING *returns, with the contents of the letter-box in his hand.*

PICKERING. Only circulars, and this coroneted billet-doux[32] for you. [*He throws the circulars into the fender, and posts himself on the hearthrug, with his back to the grate.*]

HIGGINS [*glancing at the billet-doux*]. Money-lender. [*He throws the letter after the circulars.*]

[ELIZA *returns with a pair of large down-at-heel slippers. She places them on the carpet before* HIGGINS *and sits as before without a word.*]

HIGGINS [*yawning again*]. Oh Lord! What an evening! What a crew! What a silly tomfoolery! [*He raises his shoe to unlace it, and catches sight of the slippers. He stops unlacing and looks at them as if they had appeared there of their own accord.*] Oh! theyre there, are they?

PICKERING [*stretching himself*]. Well, I feel a bit tired. It's been a long day. The garden party, a dinner party, and the reception! Rather too much of a good thing. But youve won your bet, Higgins. Eliza did the trick, and something to spare, eh?

HIGGINS [*fervently*]. Thank God it's over!

[ELIZA *flinches violently; but they take no notice of her; and she recovers herself and sits stonily as before.*]

PICKERING. Were you nervous at the garden party? *I* was. Eliza didnt seem a bit nervous.

HIGGINS. Oh, she wasnt nervous. I knew she'd be all right. No: it's the strain of

---

[31] "Row": quarrel noisily.

[32] "Coroneted billet-doux": literally, a crowned love letter—evidently an advertisement that was addressed as if it were personal mail.

putting the job through all these months that has told on me. It was interesting enough at first, while we were at the phonetics; but after that I got deadly sick of it. If I hadnt backed myself to do it I should have chucked the whole thing up two months ago. It was a silly notion: the whole thing has been a bore.

PICKERING. Oh come! the garden party was frightfully exciting. My heart began beating like anything.

HIGGINS. Yes, for the first three minutes. But when I saw we were going to win hands down, I felt like a bear in a cage, hanging about doing nothing. The dinner was worse: sitting gorging there for over an hour, with nobody but a damned fool of a fashionable woman to talk to! I tell you, Pickering, never again for me. No more artificial duchesses. The whole thing has been simple purgatory.

PICKERING. Youve never been broken in properly to the social routine. [*Strolling over to the piano*] I rather enjoy dipping into it occasionally myself: it makes me feel young again. Anyhow, it was a great success: an immense success. I was quite frightened once or twice because Eliza was doing it so well. You see, lots of the real people cant do it at all: theyre such fools that they think style comes by nature to people in their position; and so they never learn. Theres always something professional about doing a thing superlatively well.

HIGGINS. Yes: thats what drives me mad: the silly people dont know their own silly business. [*Rising*] However, it's over and done with; and now I can go to bed at last without dreading tomorrow.

[ELIZA's *beauty becomes murderous.*]

PICKERING. I think I shall turn in too. Still, it's been a great occasion: a triumph for you. Goodnight. [*He goes.*]

HIGGINS [*following him*]. Goodnight. [*Over his shoulder, at the door*] Put out the lights, Eliza; and tell Mrs Pearce not to make coffee for me in the morning: I'll take tea. [*He goes out.*]

ELIZA *tries to control herself and feel indifferent as she rises and walks across to the hearth to switch off the lights. By the time she gets there she is on the point of screaming. She sits down in* HIGGINS's *chair and holds on hard to the arms. Finally she gives way and flings herself furiously on the floor, raging.*

HIGGINS [*in despairing wrath outside*]. What the devil have I done with my slippers? [*He appears at the door.*]

LIZA [*snatching up the slippers, and hurling them at him one after the other with all her force*]. There are your slippers. And there. Take your slippers; and may you never have a day's luck with them!

HIGGINS [*astounded*]. What on earth——! [*He comes to her.*] Whats the matter? Get up. [*He pulls her up.*] Anything wrong?

LIZA [*breathless*]. Nothing wrong—with you. Ive won your bet for you, havnt I? Thats enough for you. *I* dont matter, I suppose.

HIGGINS. You won my bet! You! Presumptuous insect! *I* won it. What did you throw those slippers at me for?

LIZA. Because I wanted to smash your face. I'd like to kill you, you selfish brute. Why didnt you leave me where you picked me out of—in the gutter? You thank God it's all over, and that now you can throw me back again there, do you? [*She crisps her fingers frantically*]

HIGGINS [*looking at her in cool wonder*]. The creature is nervous, after all.

LIZA [*gives a suffocated scream of fury, and instinctively darts her nails at his face*]. !!

HIGGINS [*catching her wrists*]. Ah! would you? Claws in, you cat. How dare you shew your temper to me? Sit down and be quiet. [*He throws her roughly into the easy-chair.*]

LIZA [*crushed by superior strength and weight*]. Whats to become of me? Whats to become of me?

HIGGINS. How the devil do I know whats to become of you? What does it matter what becomes of you?

LIZA. You dont care. I know you dont care. You wouldnt care if I was dead. I'm nothing to you—not so much as them slippers.

HIGGINS [*thundering*]. Those slippers.

LIZA [*with bitter submission*]. Those slippers. I didnt think it made any difference now.

[*A pause. ELIZA hopeless and crushed. HIGGINS a little uneasy.*]

HIGGINS [*in his loftiest manner*]. Why have you begun going on like this? May I ask whether you complain of your treatment here?

LIZA. No.

HIGGINS. Has anybody behaved badly to you? Colonel Pickering? Mrs Pearce? Any of the servants?

LIZA. No.

HIGGINS. I presume you dont pretend that *I* have treated you badly?

LIZA. No.

HIGGINS. I am glad to hear it. [*He moderates his tone.*] Perhaps youre tired after the strain of the day. Will you have a glass of champagne? [*He moves towards the door.*]

LIZA. No. [*Recollecting her manners.*] Thank you.

HIGGINS [*good-humored again*]. This has been coming on you for some days. I suppose it was natural for you to be anxious about the garden party. But thats all over now. [*He pats her kindly on the shoulder. She writhes.*] Theres nothing more to worry about.

LIZA. No. Nothing more for you to worry about. [*She suddenly rises and gets away from him by going to the piano bench, where she sits and hides her face.*] Oh God! I wish I was dead.

HIGGINS [*staring after her in sincere surprise*]. Why? In heaven's name, why? [*Reasonably, going to her*] Listen to me, Eliza. All this irritation is purely subjective.

LIZA. I dont understand. I'm too ignorant.

HIGGINS. It's only imagination. Low spirits and nothing else. Nobody's hurting you. Nothing's wrong. You go to bed like a good girl and sleep it off. Have a little cry and say your prayers: that will make you comfortable.

LIZA. I heard your prayers. "Thank God it's all over!"

HIGGINS [*impatiently*]. Well, dont you thank God it's all over? Now you are free and can do what you like.

LIZA [*pulling herself together in desperation*]. What am I fit for? What have you left me fit for? Where am I to go? What am I to do? Whats to become of me?

HIGGINS [*enlightened, but not at all impressed*]. Oh, thats whats worrying you, is it? [*He thrusts his hands into his pockets, and walks about in his usual manner, rattling the contents of his pockets, as if condescending to a trivial subject out of pure kindness.*] I shouldnt bother about it if I were you. I should imagine you wont have much difficulty in settling yourself somewhere or other, though I hadn't quite realized that you were going away. [*She looks quickly at him: he does not look at her, but examines the dessert stand on the piano and decides that he will eat an apple.*] You might marry, you know. [*He bites a large piece out of the apple and munches it noisily.*] You see, Eliza, all men are not confirmed old bachelors like me and the Colonel. Most men are the marrying sort (poor devils!); and youre not bad-looking: it's quite a pleasure to look at you sometimes—not now, of course, because youre crying and looking as ugly as the very devil; but when youre all right and quite yourself, youre what I should call attractive. That is, to the people in the marrying line, you understand. You go to bed and have a good nice rest; and then get up and look at yourself in the glass; and you wont feel so cheap.

[ELIZA *again looks at him, speechless, and does not stir. The look is quite lost on him: he eats his apple with a dreamy expression of happiness, as it is quite a good one.*]

HIGGINS [*a genial afterthought occurring to him*]. I daresay my mother could find some chap or other who would do very well.

LIZA. We were above that at the corner of Tottenham Court Road.

HIGGINS [*waking up*]. What do you mean?

LIZA. I sold flowers. I didnt sell myself. Now youve made a lady of me I'm not fit to sell anything else. I wish youd left me where you found me.

HIGGINS [*slinging the core of the apple decisively into the grate*]. Tosh, Eliza. Dont you insult human relations by dragging all this cant[33] about buying and selling into it. You neednt marry the fellow if you dont like him.

LIZA. What else am I to do?

HIGGINS. Oh, lots of things. What about your old idea of a florist's shop? Pickering could set you up in one: he has lots of money. [*Chuckling*] He'll have to pay for all those togs[34] you have been wearing today; and that, with the hire of the jewellery, will make a big hole in two hundred pounds. Why, six months ago you would have thought it the millennium to have a flower shop of your own. Come! youll be all right. I must clear off to bed: I'm devilish sleepy. By the way, I came down for something: I forget what it was.

LIZA. Your slippers.

HIGGINS. Oh yes, of course. You shied them at me. [*He picks them up, and is going out when she rises and speaks to him.*]

LIZA. Before you go, sir—

HIGGINS [*dropping the slippers in his surprise at her calling him Sir*]. Eh?

LIZA. Do my clothes belong to me or to Colonel Pickering?

HIGGINS [*coming back into the room as if her question were the very climax of unreason*]. What the devil use would they be to Pickering?

LIZA. He might want them for the next girl you pick up to experiment on.

HIGGINS [*shocked and hurt*]. Is that the way you feel towards us?

LIZA. I dont want to hear anything more about that. All I want to know is whether anything belongs to me. My own clothes were burnt.

HIGGINS. But what does it matter? Why need you start bothering about that in the middle of the night?

LIZA. I want to know what I may take away with me. I dont want to be accused of stealing.

HIGGINS [*now deeply wounded*]. Stealing! You shouldnt have said that, Eliza. That shews a want of feeling.

LIZA. I'm sorry. I'm only a common ignorant girl; and in my station I have to be careful. There cant be any feelings between the like of you and the like of me. Please will you tell me what belongs to me and what doesnt?

HIGGINS [*very sulky*]. You may take the whole damned houseful if you like. Except the jewels. Theyre hired. Will that satisfy you? [*He turns on his heel and is about to go in extreme dudgeon.*]

LIZA [*drinking in his emotion like nectar, and nagging him to provoke a further supply*]. Stop, please. [*She takes off her jewels.*] Will you take these to your room and keep them safe? I dont want to run the risk of their being missing.

---

[33] "Cant": pious platitudes.
[34] "Togs": clothes.

HIGGINS [*furious*]. Hand them over. [*She puts them into his hands.*] If these belonged
  to me instead of to the jeweller, I'd ram them down your ungrateful throat. [*He
  perfunctorily thrusts them into his pockets, unconsciously decorating himself with the
  protruding ends of the chains.*]
LIZA [*taking a ring off*]. This ring isnt the jeweller's: it's the one you bought me in
  Brighton. I dont want it now. [HIGGINS *dashes the ring violently into the fireplace, and
  turns on her so threateningly that she crouches over the piano with her hands over her face
  and exclaims*] Dont you hit me.
HIGGINS. Hit you! You infamous creature, how dare you accuse me of such a thing?
  It is you who have hit me. You have wounded me to the heart.
LIZA [*thrilling with hidden joy*]. I'm glad. Ive got a little of my own back, anyhow.
HIGGINS [*with dignity, in his finest professional style*]. You have caused me to lose my
  temper: a thing that has hardly ever happened to me before. I prefer to say
  nothing more tonight. I am going to bed.
LIZA [*pertly*]. Youd better leave a note for Mrs Pearce about the coffee; for she wont
  be told by me.
HIGGINS [*formally*]. Damn Mrs Pearce; and damn the coffee; and damn you; and
  [*wildly*] damn my own folly in having lavished my hard-earned knowledge and
  the treasure of my regard and intimacy on a heartless guttersnipe. [*He goes out
  with impressive decorum, and spoils it by slamming the door savagely.*]

  ELIZA *goes down on her knees on the hearthrug to look for the ring. When she finds it she
considers for a moment what to do with it. Finally she flings it down on the dessert stand and
goes upstairs in a tearing rage.*

                              *   *   *

  The furniture of ELIZA's *room has been increased by a big wardrobe and a sumptuous
dressing table. She comes in and switches on the electric light. She goes to the wardrobe; opens
it; and pulls out a walking dress, a hat, and a pair of shoes, which she throws on the bed.
She takes off her evening dress and shoes; then takes a padded hanger from the wardrobe;
adjusts it carefully in the evening dress; and hangs it in the wardrobe, which she shuts with
a slam. She puts on her walking shoes, her walking dress, and hat. She takes her wrist watch
from the dressing-table and fastens it on. She pulls on her gloves; takes her vanity bag; and
looks into it to see that her purse is there before hanging it on her wrist. She makes for the door.
Every movement expresses her furious resolution.*
  She takes a last look at herself in the glass.
  *She suddenly puts out her tongue at herself; then leaves the room, switching off the electric
light at the door.*
  Meanwhile, in the street outside, FREDDY EYNSFORD HILL, *lovelorn, is gazing up at the
second floor, in which one of the windows is still lighted.*
  The light goes out.

FREDDY. Goodnight, darling, darling, darling.
  [ELIZA *comes out, giving the door a considerable bang behind her.*]
LIZA. Whatever are you doing here?
FREDDY. Nothing. I spend most of my nights here. It's the only place where I'm
  happy. Don't laugh at me, Miss Doolittle.
LIZA. Don't you call me Miss Doolittle, do you hear? Liza's good enough for me.
  [*She breaks down and grabs him by the shoulders*] Freddy: you dont think I'm a
  heartless guttersnipe, do you?
FREDDY. Oh no, no, darling: how can you imagine such a thing? You are the
  loveliest, dearest—

[*He loses all self-control and smothers her with kisses. She, hungry for comfort, responds. They stand there in one another's arms. An elderly police constable arrives.*]

CONSTABLE [*scandalized*]. Now then! Now then!! Now then!!!

[*They release one another hastily.*]

FREDDY. Sorry, constable. Weve only just become engaged. [*They run away.*]

THE CONSTABLE *shakes his head, reflecting on his own courtship and on the vanity of human hopes. He moves off in the opposite direction with slow professional steps.*

The flight of the lovers takes them to Cavendish Square. There they halt to consider their next move.

LIZA [*out of breath*]. He didnt half give me a fright, that copper. But you answered him proper.

FREDDY. I hope I havent taken you out of your way. Where were you going?

LIZA. To the river.

FREDDY. What for?

LIZA. To make a hole in it.

FREDDY [*horrified*]. Eliza, darling. What do you mean? What's the matter?

LIZA. Never mind. It doesnt matter now. There's nobody in the world now but you and me, is there?

FREDDY. Not a soul.

[*They indulge in another embrace, and are again surprised by a much younger constable.*]

SECOND CONSTABLE. Now then, you two! What's this? Where do you think you are? Move along here, double quick.

FREDDY. As you say, sir, double quick.

[*They run away again, and are in Hanover Square before they stop for another conference.*]

FREDDY. I had no idea the police were so devilishly prudish.

LIZA. It's their business to hunt girls off the streets.

FREDDY. We must go somewhere. We cant wander about the streets all night.

LIZA. Cant we? I think it'd be lovely to wander about for ever.

FREDDY. Oh, darling.

[*They embrace again, oblivious of the arrival of a crawling taxi. It stops.*]

TAXIMAN. Can I drive you and the lady anywhere, sir?

[*They start asunder.*]

LIZA. Oh, Freddy, a taxi. The very thing.

FREDDY. But, damn it, I've no money.

LIZA. I have plenty. The Colonel thinks you should never go out without ten pounds in your pocket. Listen. We'll drive about all night; and in the morning I'll call on old Mrs Higgins and ask her what I ought to do. I'll tell you all about it in the cab. And the police wont touch us in there.

FREDDY. Righto! Ripping. [*To the* TAXIMAN] Wimbledon Common [*They drive off.*]

ACT V

MRS HIGGINS'S *drawing room. She is at her writing-table as before.* THE PARLORMAID *comes in.*

THE PARLORMAID [*at the door*]. Mr Henry, maam, is downstairs with Colonel Pickering.

MRS HIGGINS. Well, shew them up.

THE PARLORMAID. Theyre using the telephone, maam. Telephoning to the police, I think.

MRS HIGGINS. What!

THE PARLORMAID [*coming further in and lowering her voice*]. Mr Henry is in a state, maam. I thought I'd better tell you.

MRS HIGGINS. If you had told me that Mr Henry was not in a state it would have been more surprising. Tell them to come up when theyve finished with the police. I suppose he's lost something.

THE PARLORMAID. Yes, maam [*going*].

MRS HIGGINS. Go upstairs and tell Miss Doolittle that Mr Henry and the Colonel are here. Ask her not to come down til I send for her.

THE PARLORMAID. Yes, maam.

[HIGGINS *bursts in. He is, as* THE PARLORMAID *has said, in a state.*]

HIGGINS. Look here, mother: heres a confounded thing!

MRS HIGGINS. Yes, dear. Good morning. [*He checks his impatience and kisses her, whilst* THE PARLORMAID *goes out.*] What is it?

HIGGINS. Eliza's bolted.

MRS HIGGINS [*calmly continuing her writing*]. You must have frightened her.

HIGGINS. Frightened her! nonsense! She was left last night, as usual, to turn out the lights and all that; and instead of going to bed she changed her clothes and went right off: her bed wasnt slept in. She came in a cab for her things before seven this morning; and that fool Mrs Pearce let her have them without telling me a word about it. What am I to do?

MRS HIGGINS. Do without, I'm afraid, Henry. The girl has a perfect right to leave if she chooses.

HIGGINS [*wandering distractedly across the room*]. But I cant find anything. I dont know what appointments Ive got. I'm—[PICKERING *comes in.* MRS HIGGINS *puts down her pen and turns away from the writing-table.*]

PICKERING [*shaking hands*]. Good morning, Mrs Higgins. Has Henry told you? [*He sits down on the ottoman.*]

HIGGINS. What does that ass of an inspector say? Have you offered a reward?

MRS HIGGINS [*rising in indignant amazement*]. You dont mean to say you have set the police after Eliza.

HIGGINS. Of course. What are the police for? What else could we do? [*He sits in the Elizabethan chair.*]

PICKERING. The inspector made a lot of difficulties. I really think he suspected us of some improper purpose.

MRS HIGGINS. Well, of course he did. What right have you to go to the police and give the girl's name as if she were a thief, or a lost umbrella, or something? Really! [*She sits down again, deeply vexed.*]

HIGGINS. But we want to find her.

PICKERING. We cant let her go like this, you know, Mrs. Higgins. What were we to do?

MRS HIGGINS. You have no more sense, either of you, than two children. Why—

[THE PARLORMAID *comes in and breaks off the conversation.*]

THE PARLORMAID. Mr Henry: a gentleman wants to see you very particular. He's been sent on from Wimpole Street.

HIGGINS. Oh, bother! I cant see anyone now. Who is it?

THE PARLORMAID. A Mr Doolittle, sir.

PICKERING. Doolittle! Do you mean the dustman?

THE PARLORMAID. Dustman! Oh no, sir: a gentleman.

HIGGINS [*springing up excitedly*]. By George, Pick, it's some relative of hers that she's gone to. Somebody we know nothing about. [*To* THE PARLORMAID] Send him up, quick.

THE PARLORMAID. Yes, sir. [*She goes.*]

HIGGINS [*eagerly, going to his mother*]. Genteel relatives! now we shall hear something. [*He sits down in the Chippendale chair.*]

MRS HIGGINS. Do you know any of her people?

PICKERING. Only her father: the fellow we told you about.

THE PARLORMAID [*announcing*]. Mr Doolittle. [*She withdraws.*]

DOOLITTLE *enters. He is resplendently dressed as for a fashionable wedding, and might, in fact, be the bridegroom. A flower in his buttonhole, a dazzling silk hat, and patent leather shoes complete the effect. He is too concerned with the business he has come on to notice* MRS HIGGINS. *He walks straight to* HIGGINS. *and accosts him with vehement reproach.*

DOOLITTLE [*indicating his own person*]. See here! Do you see this? You done this.

HIGGINS. Done what, man?

DOOLITTLE. This, I tell you. Look at it. Look at this hat. Look at this coat.

PICKERING. Has Eliza been buying you clothes?

DOOLITTLE. Eliza! not she. Why would she buy me clothes?

MRS HIGGINS. Good morning, Mr Doolittle. Wont you sit down?

DOOLITTLE [*taken aback as he becomes conscious that he has forgotten his hostess*]. Asking your pardon, maam. [*He approaches her and shakes her proffered hand.*] Thank you. [*He sits down on the ottoman, on* PICKERING'*s right.*] I am that full of what has happened to me that I cant think of anything else.

HIGGINS. What the dickens has happened to you?

DOOLITTLE. I shouldnt mind if it had only happened to me: anything might happen to anybody and nobody to blame but Providence, as you might say. But this is something that you done to me: yes, you, Enry Iggins.

HIGGINS. Have you found Eliza?

DOOLITTLE. Have you lost her?

HIGGINS. Yes.

DOOLITTLE. You have all the luck, you have. I aint found her; but she'll find me quick enough now after what you done to me.

MRS HIGGINS. But what has my son done to you, Mr Doolittle?

DOOLITTLE. Done to me! Ruined me. Destroyed my happiness. Tied me up and delivered me into the hands of middle class morality.

HIGGINS [*rising intolerantly and standing over* DOOLITTLE]. Youre raving. Youre drunk. Youre mad. I gave you five pounds. After that I had two conversations with you, at half-a-crown an hour. Ive never seen you since.

DOOLITTLE. Oh! Drunk am I? Mad am I? Tell me this. Did you or did you not write a letter to an old blighter in America that was giving five millions to found Moral Reform Societies all over the world, and that wanted you to invent a universal language for him?

HIGGINS. What! Ezra D. Wannafeller! He's dead. [*He sits down again carelessly.*]

DOOLITTLE. Yes: he's dead; and I'm done for. Now did you or did you not write a letter to him to say that the most original moralist at present in England, to the best of your knowledge, was Alfred Doolittle, a common dustman?

HIGGINS. Oh, after your first visit I remember making some silly joke of the kind.

DOOLITTLE. Ah! you may well call it a silly joke. It put the lid on me right enough.

Just give him the chance he wanted to shew that Americans is not like us: that
they reckonize and respect merit in every class of life, however humble. Them
words is in his blooming will, in which, Henry Higgins, thanks to your silly
joking, he leaves me a share in his Predigested Cheese Trust worth three thousand a year on condition that I lecture for his Wannafeller Moral Reform World
League as often as they ask me up to six times a year.

HIGGINS. The devil he does! Whew! [*Brightening suddenly*] What a lark!

PICKERING. A safe thing for you, Doolittle. They wont ask you twice.

DOOLITTLE. It aint the lecturing I mind. I'll lecture them blue in the face, I will, and
not turn a hair. It's making a gentleman of me that I object to. Who asked him
to make a gentleman of me? I was happy. I was free. I touched pretty nigh everybody for money when I wanted it, same as I touched you, Enry Iggins. Now I am
worrited;[35] tied neck and heels; and everybody touches me for money. It's a fine
thing for you, says my solicitor. Is it? says I. You mean it's a good thing for you,
I says. When I was a poor man and had a solicitor once when they found a pram
in the dust cart,[36] he got me off, and got shut of me and got me shut of him as
quick as he could. Same with the doctors: used to shove me out of the hospital
before I could hardly stand on my legs, and nothing to pay. Now they finds out
that I'm not a healthy man and cant live unless they looks after me twice a day.
In the house I'm not let do a hand's turn for myself: somebody else must do it
and touch me for it. A year ago I hadnt a relative in the world except two or three
that wouldnt speak to me. Now Ive fifty, and not a decent week's wages among
the lot of them. I have to live for others and not for myself: thats middle class
morality. You talk of losing Eliza. Dont you be anxious: I bet she's on my doorstep
by this: she that could support herself easy by selling flowers if I wasnt respectable.
And the next one to touch me will be you, Enry Iggins. I'll have to learn to speak
middle class language from you, instead of speaking proper English. Thats where
youll come in; and I daresay thats what you done it for.

MRS HIGGINS. But, my dear Mr Doolittle, you need not suffer all this if you are really
in earnest. Nobody can force you to accept this bequest. You can repudiate it.
Isnt that so, Colonel Pickering?

PICKERING. I believe so.

DOOLITTLE [*softening his manner in deference to her sex*]. Thats the tragedy of it, maam.
It's easy to say chuck it; but I havnt the nerve. Which of us has? We're all
intimidated. Intimidated, maam: thats what we are. What is there for me if I
chuck it but the workhouse in my old age? I have to dye my hair already to keep
my job as a dustman. If I was one of the deserving poor, and had put by a bit,
I could chuck it; but then why should I, acause the deserving poor might as well
be millionaires for all the happiness they ever has. They dont know what happiness is. But I, as one of the undeserving poor, have nothing between me and
the pauper's uniform but this here blasted three thousand a year that shoves me
into the middle class. (Excuse the expression, maam; youd use it yourself if you
had my provocation.) Theyve got you every way you turn: it's a choice between
the Skilly[37] of the workhouse and the Char Bydis of the middle class; and I
havent the nerve for the workhouse. Intimidated: thats what I am. Broke.
Bought up. Happier men than me will call for my dust, and touch me for their

---

[35] "Worrited": worried.

[36] "Pram in the dust cart": baby carriage in the trash can.

[37] Doolittle is referring to Scylla and Charybdis, mythological monsters in *The Iliad*. Ulysses was forced
to choose between sailing close to Scylla, a huge snake-like monster with six heads, and Charybdis,
a dreaded whirlpool.

tip; and I'll look on helpless, and envy them. And thats what your son has brought me to. [*He is overcome by emotion.*]

Mrs Higgins. Well, I'm very glad youre not going to do anything foolish, Mr Doolittle. For this solves the problem of Eliza's future. You can provide for her now.

Doolittle [*with melancholy resignation*]. Yes, maam: I'm expected to provide for everyone now, out of three thousand a year.

Higgins [*jumping up*]. Nonsense! he cant provide for her. He shant provide for her. She doesnt belong to him. I paid him five pounds for her. Doolittle: either youre an honest man or a rogue.

Doolittle [*tolerantly*]. A little of both, Henry, like the rest of us: a little of both.

Higgins. Well, you took that money for the girl; and you have no right to take her as well.

Mrs Higgins. Henry: dont be absurd. If you want to know where Eliza is, she is upstairs.

Higgins [*amazed*]. Upstairs!!! Then I shall jolly soon fetch her downstairs. [*He makes resolutely for the door.*]

Mrs Higgins [*rising and following him*]. Be quiet, Henry. Sit down.

Higgins. I—

Mrs Higgins. Sit down, dear; and listen to me.

Higgins. Oh very well, very well, very well. [*He throws himself ungraciously on the ottoman, with his face towards the windows.*] But I think you might have told us this half an hour ago.

Mrs Higgins. Eliza came to me this morning. She told me of the brutal way you two treated her.

Higgins [*bounding up again*]. What!

Pickering [*rising also*]. My dear Mrs Higgins, she's been telling you stories. We didnt treat her brutally. We hardly said a word to her; and we parted on particularly good terms. [*Turning on* Higgins] Higgins: did you bully her after I went to bed?

Higgins. Just the other way about. She threw my slippers in my face. She behaved in the most outrageous way. I never gave her the slightest provocation. The slippers came bang into my face the moment I entered the room—before I had uttered a word. And used perfectly awful language.

Pickering [*astonished*]. But why? What did we do to her?

Mrs Higgins. I think I know pretty well what you did. The girl is naturally rather affectionate, I think. Isnt she, Mr Doolittle?

Doolittle. Very tender-hearted, maam. Takes after me.

Mrs Higgins. Just so. She had become attached to you both. She worked very hard for you, Henry. I dont think you quite realize what anything in the nature of brain work means to a girl of her class. Well, it seems that when the great day of trial came, and she did this wonderful thing for you without making a single mistake, you two sat there and never said a word to her, but talked together of how glad you were that it was all over and how you had been bored with the whole thing. And then you were surprised because she threw your slippers at you! *I* should have thrown the fire-irons at you.

Higgins. We said nothing except that we were tired and wanted to go to bed. Did we, Pick?

Pickering [*shrugging his shoulders*]. That was all.

Mrs Higgins [*ironically*]. Quite sure?

Pickering. Absolutely. Really, that was all.

Mrs Higgins. You didnt thank her, or pet her, or admire her, or tell her how splendid she'd been.

HIGGINS [*impatiently*]. But she knew all about that. We didnt make speeches to her, if thats what you mean.

PICKERING [*conscience stricken*]. Perhaps we were a little inconsiderate. Is she very angry?

MRS HIGGINS [*returning to her place at the writing-table*]. Well, I'm afraid she wont go back to Wimpole Street, especially now that Mr Doolittle is able to keep up the position you have thrust on her; but she says she is quite willing to meet you on friendly terms and to let bygones be bygones.

HIGGINS [*furious*]. Is she, by George? Ho!

MRS HIGGINS. If you promise to behave yourself, Henry, I'll ask her to come down. If not, go home; for you have taken up quite enough of my time.

HIGGINS. Oh, all right. Very well, Pick: you behave yourself. Let us put on our best Sunday manners for this creature that we picked out of the mud. [*He flings himself sulkily into the Elizabethan chair.*]

DOOLITTLE [*remonstrating*]. Now, now, Enry Iggins! Have some consideration for my feelings as a middle class man.

MRS HIGGINS. Remember your promise, Henry. [*She presses the bell-button on the writing-table.*] Mr Doolittle: will you be so good as to step out on the balcony for a moment. I dont want Eliza to have the shock of your news until she has made it up with these two gentlemen. Would you mind?

DOOLITTLE. As you wish, lady. Anything to help Henry to keep her off my hands. [*He disappears through the window.*]

[THE PARLORMAID *answers the bell.* PICKERING *sits down in* DOOLITTLE's *place.*]

MRS HIGGINS. Ask Miss Doolittle to come down, please.

THE PARLORMAID. Yes, maam. [*She goes out.*]

MRS HIGGINS. Now, Henry: be good.

HIGGINS. I am behaving myself perfectly.

PICKERING. He is doing his best, Mrs Higgins.

[*A pause.* HIGGINS *throws back his head; stretches out his legs; and begins to whistle.*]

MRS HIGGINS. Henry, dearest, you dont look at all nice in that attitude.

HIGGINS [*pulling himself together.*]. I was not trying to look nice, mother.

MRS HIGGINS. It doesnt matter, dear. I only wanted to make you speak.

HIGGINS. Why?

MRS HIGGINS. Because you cant speak and whistle at the same time.

[HIGGINS *groans. Another very trying pause.*]

HIGGINS [*springing up, out of patience*]. Where the devil is that girl? Are we to wait here all day?

[ELIZA *enters, sunny, self-possessed, and giving a staggeringly convincing exhibition of ease of manner. She carries a little work-basket, and is very much at home.* PICKERING *is too much taken aback to rise.*]

LIZA. How do you do, Professor Higgins? Are you quite well?

HIGGINS [*choking*]. Am I—[*He can say no more.*]

LIZA. But of course you are: you are never ill. So glad to see you again, Colonel Pickering. [*He rises hastily; and they shake hands.*] Quite chilly this morning, isnt it? [*She sits down on his left. He sits beside her.*]

HIGGINS. Dont you dare try this game on me. I taught it to you; and it doesnt take me in. Get up and come home; and dont be a fool.

[ELIZA *takes a piece of needlework from her basket, and begins to stitch at it, without taking the least notice of this outburst.*]

MRS HIGGINS. Very nicely put, indeed, Henry. No woman could resist such an invitation.

HIGGINS. You let her alone, mother. Let her speak for herself. You will jolly soon see whether she has an idea that I havnt put into her head or a word that I havnt put into her mouth. I tell you I have created this thing out of the squashed cabbage leaves of Covent Garden; and now she pretends to play the fine lady with me.

Mrs Higgins [*placidly*]. Yes, dear; but youll sit down, wont you?

[Higgins *sits down again, savagely.*]

Liza [*to* Pickering, *taking no apparent notice of* Higgins, *and working away deftly*]. Will you drop me altogether now that the experiment is over, Colonel Pickering?

Pickering. Oh dont. You mustnt think of it as an experiment. It shocks me, somehow.

Liza. Oh, I'm only a squashed cabbage leaf—

Pickering [*impulsively*]. No.

Liza [*continuing quietly*]. —but I owe so much to you that I should be very unhappy if you forgot me.

Pickering. It's very kind of you to say so, Miss Doolittle.

Liza. It's not because you paid for my dresses. I know you are generous to everybody with money. But it was from you that I learnt really nice manners, and that is what makes one a lady, isnt it? You see it was so very difficult for me with the example of Professor Higgins always before me. I was brought up to be just like him, unable to control myself, and using bad language on the slightest provocation. And I should never have known that ladies and gentlemen didnt behave like that if you hadnt been there.

Higgins. Well!!

Pickering. Oh, thats only his way, you know. He doesnt mean it.

Liza. Oh, *I* didnt mean it either, when I was a flower girl. It was only my way. But you see I did it; and thats what makes the difference after all.

Pickering. No doubt. Still, he taught you to speak; and I couldnt have done that, you know.

Liza [*trivially*]. Of course: that is his profession.

Higgins. Damnation!

Liza [*continuing*]. It was just like learning to dance in the fashionable way: there was nothing more than that in it. But do you know what began my real education?

Pickering. What?

Liza [*stopping her work for a moment*]. Your calling me Miss Doolittle that day when I first came to Wimpole Street. That was the beginning of self-respect for me. [*She resumes her stitching.*] And there were a hundred little things you never noticed, because they came naturally to you. Things about standing up and taking off your hat and opening doors—

Pickering. Oh, that was nothing.

Liza. Yes: things that shewed you thought and felt about me as if I were something better than a scullery-maid; though of course I know you would have been just the same to a scullery-maid if she had been let into the drawing room. You never took off your boots in the dining room when I was there.

Pickering. You mustnt mind that. Higgins takes off his boots all over the place.

Liza. I know. I am not blaming him. It is his way, isnt it? But it made such a difference to me that you didnt do it. You see, really and truly, apart from the things anyone can pick up (the dressing and the proper way of speaking, and so on), the difference between a lady and a flower girl is not how she behaves, but how she's treated. I shall always be a flower girl to Professor Higgins, because he always treats me as a flower girl, and always will; but I know I can be a lady to you, because you always treat me as a lady, and always will.

Mrs Higgins. Please dont grind your teeth, Henry.

Pickering. Well, this is really very nice of you, Miss Doolittle.

Liza. I should like you to call me Eliza, now, if you would.

PICKERING. Thank you, Eliza, of course.

LIZA. And I should like Professor Higgins to call me Miss Doolittle.

HIGGINS. I'll see you damned first.

MRS HIGGINS. Henry! Henry!

PICKERING [*laughing*]. Why dont you slang back at him? Dont stand it. It would do him a lot of good.

LIZA. I cant. I could have done it once; but now I cant go back to it. You told me, you know, that when a child is brought to a foreign country, it picks up the language in a few weeks, and forgets its own. Well, I am a child in your country. I have forgotten my own language, and can speak nothing but yours. Thats the real break-off with the corner of Tottenham Court Road. Leaving Wimpole Street finishes it.

PICKERING [*much alarmed*]. Oh! but youre coming back to Wimpole Street, arnt you? Youll forgive Higgins?

HIGGINS [*rising*]. Forgive! Will she, by George! Let her go. Let her find out how she can get on without us. She will relapse into the gutter in three weeks without me at her elbow.

> [DOOLITTLE *appears at the centre window. With a look of dignified reproach at* HIGGINS, *he comes slowly and silently to his daughter, who, with her back to the window, is unconscious of his approach.*]

PICKERING. He's incorrigible, Eliza. You wont relapse, will you.

LIZA. No: not now. Never again. I have learnt my lesson. I dont believe I could utter one of the old sounds if I tried. [DOOLITTLE *touches her on her left shoulder. She drops her work, losing her self-possession utterly at the spectacle of her father's splendor*] A-a-a-a-a-ah-ow-ooh!

HIGGINS [*with a crow of triumph*]. Aha! Just so. A-a-a-a-ahowooh! A-a-a-a-ahowooh! A-a-a-a-ahowooh! Victory! victory! [*He throws himself on the divan, folding his arms, and spraddling arrogantly.*]

DOOLITTLE. Can you blame the girl? Dont look at me like that, Eliza. It aint my fault. Ive come into some money.

LIZA. You must have touched a millionaire this time, dad.

DOOLITTLE. I have. But I'm dressed something special today. I'm going to St. George's, Hanover Square. Your stepmother is going to marry me.

LIZA [*angrily*]. Youre going to let yourself down to marry that low common woman!

PICKERING [*quietly*]. He ought to, Eliza. [*To* DOOLITTLE] Why has she changed her mind?

DOOLITTLE [*sadly*]. Intimidated, Governor. Intimidated. Middle class morality claims its victim. Wont you put on your hat, Liza, and come and see me turned off?

LIZA. If the Colonel says I must, I—I'll [*almost sobbing*] I'll demean myself. And get insulted for my pains, like enough.

DOOLITTLE. Dont be afraid: she never comes to words with anyone now, poor woman! respectability has broke all the spirit out of her.

PICKERING [*squeezing* ELIZA's *elbow gently*]. Be kind to them, Eliza. Make the best of it.

LIZA [*forcing a little smile for him through her vexation*]. Oh well, just to shew theres no ill feeling. I'll be back in a moment. [*She goes out.*]

DOOLITTLE [*sitting down beside* PICKERING]. I feel uncommon nervous about the ceremony, Colonel. I wish youd come and see me through it.

PICKERING. But youve been through it before, man. You were married to Eliza's mother.

DOOLITTLE. Who told you that, Colonel?

PICKERING. Well, nobody told me. But I concluded—naturally—

DOOLITTLE. No: that aint the natural way, Colonel; it's only the middle class way. My way was always the undeserving way. But dont say nothing to Eliza. She dont know: I always had a delicacy about telling her.

PICKERING. Quite right. We'll leave it so, if you dont mind.

DOOLITTLE. And youll come to the church, Colonel, and put me through straight?

PICKERING. With pleasure. As far as a bachelor can.

MRS HIGGINS. May I come, Mr Doolittle? I should be very sorry to miss your wedding.

DOOLITTLE. I should indeed be honored by your condescension, maam; and my poor old woman would take it as a tremenjous compliment. She's been very low, thinking of the happy days that are no more.

MRS HIGGINS [*rising*]. I'll order the carriage and get ready. [*The men rise, except* HIGGINS] I shant be more than fifteen minutes. [*As she goes to the door* ELIZA *comes in, hatted and buttoning her gloves.*] I'm going to the church to see your father married, Eliza. You had better come in the brougham with me. Colonel Pickering can go on with the bridegroom.

[MRS HIGGINS *goes out.* ELIZA *comes to the middle of the room between the centre window and the ottoman.* PICKERING *joins her.*]

DOOLITTLE. Bridegroom! What a word! It makes a man realize his position, somehow. [*He takes up his hat and goes towards the door.*]

PICKERING. Before I go, Eliza, do forgive Higgins and come back to us.

LIZA. I dont think dad would allow me. Would you, dad?

DOOLITTLE [*sad but magnanimous*]. They played you off very cunning, Eliza, them two sportsmen. If it had been only one of them, you could have nailed him. But you see, there was two; and one of them chaperoned the other, as you might say. [*To* PICKERING] It was artful of you, Colonel; but I bear no malice: I should have done the same myself. I been the victim of one woman after another all my life; and I dont grudge you two getting the better of Eliza. I shant interfere. It's time for us to go, Colonel. So long, Henry. See you in St George's, Eliza. [*He goes out.*]

PICKERING [*coaxing*]. Do stay with us, Eliza. [*He follows* DOOLITTLE.]

ELIZA *goes out on the balcony to avoid being alone with* HIGGINS. *He rises and joins her there. She immediately comes back into the room and makes for the door; but he goes along the balcony quickly and gets his back to the door before she reaches it.*

HIGGINS. Well, Eliza, youve had a bit of your own back, as you call it. Have you had enough? and are you going to be reasonable? Or do you want any more?

LIZA. You want me back only to pick up your slippers and put up with your tempers and fetch and carry for you.

HIGGINS. I havnt said I wanted you back at all.

LIZA. Oh, indeed. Then what are we talking about?

HIGGINS. About you, not about me. If you come back I shall treat you just as I have always treated you. I cant change my nature; and I dont intend to change my manners. My manners are exactly the same as Colonel Pickering's.

LIZA. Thats not true. He treats a flower girl as if she was a duchess.

HIGGINS. And I treat a duchess as if she was a flower girl.

LIZA. I see. [*She turns away composedly, and sits on the ottoman, facing the window.*] The same to everybody.

HIGGINS. Just so.

LIZA. Like father.

HIGGINS [*grinning, a little taken down*]. Without accepting the comparison at all points, Eliza, it's quite true that your father is not a snob, and that he will be quite at home in any station of life to which his eccentric destiny may call him. [*Seriously*] The great secret, Eliza, is not having bad manners or good manners or any other particular sort of manners, but having the same manners for all human souls: in short, behaving as if you were in Heaven, where there are no third-class carriages, and one soul is as good as another.

LIZA. Amen. You are a born preacher.

HIGGINS [*irritated*]. The question is not whether I treat you rudely, but whether you ever heard me treat anyone else better.

LIZA [*with sudden sincerity*]. I dont care how you treat me. I dont mind your swearing at me. I shouldnt mind a black eye: Ive had one before this. But [*standing up and facing him*] I wont be passed over.

HIGGINS. Then get out of my way; for I wont stop for you. You talk about me as if I were a motor bus.

LIZA. So you are a motor bus: all bounce and go, and no consideration for anyone. But I can do without you: dont think I cant.

HIGGINS. I know you can. I told you you could.

LIZA [*wounded, getting away from him to the other side of the ottoman with her face to the hearth*]. I know you did, you brute. You wanted to get rid of me.

HIGGINS. Liar.

LIZA. Thank you. [*She sits down with dignity.*]

HIGGINS. You never asked yourself, I suppose, whether *I* could do without you.

LIZA [*earnestly*]. Dont you try to get round me. Youll have to do without me.

HIGGINS [*arrogant*]. I can do without anybody. I have my own soul: my own spark of divine fire. But [*with sudden humility*] I shall miss you, Eliza. [*He sits down near her on the ottoman.*] I have learnt something from your idiotic notions: I confess that humbly and gratefully. And I have grown accustomed to your voice and appearance. I like them, rather.

LIZA. Well, you have both of them on your gramophone and in your book of photographs. When you feel lonely without me, you can turn the machine on. It's got no feelings to hurt.

HIGGINS. I cant turn your soul on. Leave me those feelings; and you can take away the voice and the face. They are not you.

LIZA. Oh, you are a devil. You can twist the heart in a girl as easy as some could twist her arms to hurt her. Mrs Pearce warned me. Time and again she has wanted to leave you; and you always got round her at the last minute. And you dont care a bit for her. And you dont care a bit for me.

HIGGINS. I care for life, for humanity; and you are a part of it that has come my way and been built into my house. What more can you or anyone ask?

LIZA. I wont care for anybody that doesnt care for me.

HIGGINS. Commercial principles, Eliza. Like [*reproducing her Covent Garden pronunciation with professional exactness*] s'yollin voylets [selling violets], isn't it?

LIZA. Dont sneer at me. It's mean to sneer at me.

HIGGINS. I have never sneered in my life. Sneering doesnt become either the human face or the human soul. I am expressing my righteous contempt for Commercialism. I dont and wont trade in affection. You call me a brute because you couldnt buy a claim on me by fetching my slippers and finding my spectacles. You were a fool: I think a woman fetching a man's slippers is a disgusting sight: did I ever fetch your slippers? I think a good deal more of you for throwing them in my face. No use slaving for me and then saying you want to be cared for: who cares for a slave? If you come back, come back for the sake of good fellowship; for youll get nothing else. Youve had a thousand times as much out of me as I have out of you; and if you dare to set up your little dog's tricks of fetching and carrying slippers against my creation of a Duchess Eliza, I'll slam the door in your silly face.

LIZA. What did you do it for if you didnt care for me?

HIGGINS [*heartily*]. Why, because it was my job.

LIZA. You never thought of the trouble it would make for me.

HIGGINS. Would the world ever have been made if its maker had been afraid of making trouble? Making life means making trouble. Theres only one way of escaping trouble; and thats killing things. Cowards, you notice, are always shrieking to have troublesome people killed.

LIZA. I'm no preacher: I dont notice things like that. I notice that you dont notice me.

HIGGINS [*jumping up and walking about intolerantly*]. Eliza: youre an idiot. I waste the treasures of my Miltonic mind by spreading them before you. Once for all, understand that I go my way and do my work without caring twopence what happens to either of us. I am not intimidated, like your father and your stepmother. So you can come back or go to the devil: which you please.

LIZA. What am I to come back for?

HIGGINS [*bouncing up on his knees on the ottoman and leaning over it to her*]. For the fun of it. Thats why I took you on.

LIZA [*with averted face*]. And you may throw me out tomorrow if I dont do everything you want me to?

HIGGINS. Yes; and you may walk out tomorrow if I dont do everything you want me to.

LIZA. And live with my stepmother?

HIGGINS. Yes, or sell flowers.

LIZA. Oh! if I only could go back to my flower basket! I should be independent of both you and father and all the world! Why did you take my independence from me? Why did I give it up? I'm a slave now, for all my fine clothes.

HIGGINS. Not a bit. I'll adopt you as my daughter and settle money on you if you like. Or would you rather marry Pickering?

LIZA [*looking fiercely round at him*]. I wouldnt marry you if you asked me; and youre nearer my age than what he is.

HIGGINS [*gently*]. Than he is: not "than what he is."

LIZA [*losing her temper and rising*]. I'll talk as I like. Youre not my teacher now.

HIGGINS [*reflectively*]. I dont suppose Pickering would, though. He's as confirmed an old bachelor as I am.

LIZA. Thats not what I want; and dont you think it. Ive always had chaps enough wanting me that way. Freddy Hill writes to me twice and three times a day, sheets and sheets.

HIGGINS [*disagreeably surprised*]. Damn his impudence! [*He recoils and finds himself sitting on his heels.*]

LIZA. He has a right to if he likes, poor lad. And he does love me.

HIGGINS [*getting off the ottoman*]. You have no right to encourage him.

LIZA. Every girl has a right to be loved.

HIGGINS. What! By fools like that?

LIZA. Freddy's not a fool. And if he's weak and poor and wants me, may be he'd make me happier than my betters that bully me and dont want me.

HIGGINS. Can he make anything of you? Thats the point.

LIZA. Perhaps I could make something of him. But I never thought of us making anything of one another; and you never think of anything else. I only want to be natural.

HIGGINS. In short, you want me to be as infatuated about you as Freddy? Is that it?

LIZA. No I dont. That's not the sort of feeling I want from you. And dont you be too sure of yourself or of me. I could have been a bad girl if I'd liked. Ive seen more of some things than you, for all your learning. Girls like me can drag gentlemen down to make love to them easy enough. And they wish each other dead the next minute.

HIGGINS. Of course they do. Then what in thunder are we quarrelling about?

LIZA [*much troubled*]. I want a little kindness. I know I'm a common ignorant girl, and you a book-learned gentleman; but I'm not dirt under your feet. What I done [*correcting herself*] what I did was not for the dresses and the taxis: I did it because we were pleasant together and I come—came—to care for you; not to want you to make love to me, and not forgetting the difference between us, but more friendly like.

HIGGINS. Well, of course. Thats just how I feel. And how Pickering feels. Eliza: youre a fool.

LIZA. Thats not a proper answer to give me [*She sinks on the chair at the writing-table in tears*].

HIGGINS. It's all youll get until you stop being a common idiot. If youre going to be a lady, youll have to give up feeling neglected if the men you know dont spend half their time snivelling over you and the other half giving you black eyes. If you cant stand the coldness of my sort of life, and the strain of it, go back to the gutter. Work til youre more a brute than a human being; and then cuddle and squabble and drink til you fall asleep. Oh, it's a fine life, the life of the gutter. It's real: it's warm: it's violent: you can feel it through the thickest skin: you can taste it and smell it without any training or any work. Not like Science and Literature and Classical Music and Philosophy and Art. You find me cold, unfeeling, selfish, dont you? Very well: be off with you to the sort of people you like. Marry some sentimental hog or other with lots of money, and a thick pair of lips to kiss you with and a thick pair of boots to kick you with. If you cant appreciate what youve got, youd better get what you can appreciate.

LIZA [*desperate*]. Oh, you are a cruel tyrant. I cant talk to you: you turn everything against me: I'm always in the wrong. But you know very well all the time that youre nothing but a bully. You know I cant go back to the gutter, as you call it, and that I have no real friends in the world but you and the Colonel. You know well I couldnt bear to live with a low common man after you two; and it's wicked and cruel of you to insult me by pretending I could. You think I must go back to Wimpole Street because I have nowhere else to go but father's. But dont you be too sure that you have me under your feet to be trampled on and talked down. I'll marry Freddy, I will, as soon as I'm able to support him.

HIGGINS [*thunderstruck*]. Freddy!!! that young fool! That poor devil who couldn't get a job as an errand boy even if he had the guts to try for it! Woman: do you not understand that I have made you a consort for a king?

LIZA. Freddy loves me: that makes him king enough for me. I dont want him to work: he wasnt brought up to it as I was. I'll go and be a teacher.

HIGGINS. Whatll you teach, in heaven's name?

LIZA. What you taught me. I'll teach phonetics.

HIGGINS. Ha! ha! ha!

LIZA. I'll offer myself as an assistant to that hairy-faced Hungarian.

HIGGINS [*rising in a fury*]. What! That imposter! that humbug! that toadying igno-ramus! Teach him my methods! my discoveries! You take one step in his direc-tion and I'll wring your neck. [*He lays hands on her.*] Do you hear?

LIZA [*defiantly non-resistant*]. Wring away. What do I care? I knew youd strike me some day. [*He lets her go, stamping with rage at having forgotten himself, and recoils so hastily that he stumbles back into his seat on the ottoman.*] Aha! Now I know how to deal with you. What a fool I was not to think of it before! You cant take away the knowledge you gave me. You said I had a finer ear than you. And I can be civil and kind to people, which is more than you can. Aha! [*Purposely dropping her aitches to annoy him.*] Thats done you, Enry Iggins, it az. Now I dont care that [*snapping her fingers*] for your bullying and your big talk. I'll advertize it in the papers that your duchess is only a flower girl that you taught, and that she'll teach anybody to be a duchess just the same in six months for a thousand guineas. Oh, when I think of myself crawling under your feet and being trampled on and called names, when all the time I had only to lift up my finger to be as good as you, I could just kick myself.

HIGGINS [*wondering at her*]. You damned impudent slut, you! But it's better than snivelling; better than fetching slippers and finding spectacles, isn't it. [*Rising*] By George, Eliza, I said I'd make a woman of you; and I have. I like you like this.

LIZA. Yes: you turn round and make up to me now that I'm not afraid of you, and can do without you.

HIGGINS. Of course I do, you little fool. Five minutes ago you were like a millstone round my neck. Now youre a tower of strength: a consort battleship. You and I and Pickering will be three old bachelors together instead of only two men and a silly girl.

[MRS HIGGINS *returns, dressed for the wedding.* ELIZA *instantly becomes cool and elegant.*]

MRS HIGGINS. The carriage is waiting, Eliza. Are you ready?

LIZA. Quite. Is the Professor coming?

MRS HIGGINS. Certainly not. He cant behave himself in church. He makes remarks out loud all the time on the clergyman's pronunciation.

LIZA. Then I shall not see you again, Professor. Goodbye. [*She goes to the door.*]

MRS HIGGINS [*coming to* HIGGINS]. Goodbye, dear.

HIGGINS. Goodbye, mother. [*He is about to kiss her, when he recollects something.*] Oh, by the way, Eliza, order a ham and a Stilton cheese, will you? And buy me a pair of reindeer gloves, number eights, and a tie to match that new suit of mine. You can choose the color. [*His cheerful, careless, vigorous voice shews that he is incorrigible.*]

LIZA [*disdainfully*]. Number eights are too small for you if you want them lined with lamb's wool. You have three new ties that you have forgotten in the drawer of your washstand. Colonel Pickering prefers double Gloucester to Stilton; and you dont notice the difference. I telephoned Mrs Pearce this morning not to forget the ham. What you are to do without me I cannot imagine. [*She sweeps out.*]

MRS HIGGINS. I'm afraid youve spoilt that girl, Henry. I should be uneasy about you and her if she were less fond of Colonel Pickering.

HIGGINS. Pickering! Nonsense: she's going to marry Freddy. Ha ha! Freddy! Freddy!! Ha ha ha ha ha!!!!! [*He roars with laughter as the play ends.*]

* * *

[1914; revised ed., 1941]

Susan Glaspell   *1882–1948*

TRIFLES

CHARACTERS

COUNTY ATTORNEY
MRS. PETERS, *the sheriff's wife*
SHERIFF HENRY PETERS

MR. HALE, *a neighbor*
MRS. HALE

Scene: The kitchen in the now abandoned farmhouse of JOHN WRIGHT, *a gloomy kitchen, and left without having been put in order—unwashed pans under the sink, a loaf of bread outside the breadbox, a dish towel on the table—other signs of incompleted work. At the rear the outer door opens, and the* SHERIFF *comes in, followed by the* COUNTY ATTORNEY *and* HALE. *The* SHERIFF *and* HALE *are men in middle life, the* COUNTY ATTORNEY *is a young man; all are much bundled up and go at once to the stove. They are followed by the two women—the* SHERIFF'S WIFE *first; she is a slight wiry woman, a thin nervous face.* MRS. HALE *is larger and would ordinarily be called more comfortable looking, but she is disturbed now and looks fearfully about as she enters. The women have come in slowly and stand close together near the door.*

COUNTY ATTORNEY [*rubbing his hands*]. This feels good. Come up to the fire, ladies.

MRS. PETERS [*after taking a step forward*]. I'm not—cold.

SHERIFF [*unbuttoning his overcoat and stepping away from the stove as if to mark the beginning of official business*]. Now, Mr. Hale, before we move things about, you explain to Mr. Henderson just what you saw when you came here yesterday morning.

COUNTY ATTORNEY. By the way, has anything been moved? Are things just as you left them yesterday?

SHERIFF [*looking about*]. It's just the same. When it dropped below zero last night, I thought I'd better send Frank out this morning to make a fire for us—no use getting pneumonia with a big case on; but I told him not to touch anything except the stove—and you know Frank.

COUNTY ATTORNEY. Somebody should have been left here yesterday.

SHERIFF. Oh—yesterday. When I had to send Frank to Morris Center for that man who went crazy—I want you to know I had my hands full yesterday. I knew you could get back from Omaha by today, and as long as I went over everything here myself—

COUNTY ATTORNEY. Well, Mr. Hale, tell just what happened when you came here yesterday morning.

HALE. Harry and I had started to town with a load of potatoes. We came along the road from my place; and as I got here, I said, "I'm going to see if I can't get John Wright to go in with me on a party telephone." I spoke to Wright about it once before, and he put me off, saying folks talked too much anyway, and all he asked was peace and quiet—I guess you know about how much he talked himself; but I thought maybe if I went to the house and talked about it before his wife, though I said to Harry that I didn't know as what his wife wanted made much difference to John—

1498

COUNTY ATTORNEY. Let's talk about that later, Mr. Hale. I do want to talk about that, but tell now just what happened when you got to the house.

HALE. I didn't hear or see anything; I knocked at the door, and still it was all quiet inside. I knew they must be up, it was past eight o'clock. So I knocked again, and I thought I heard somebody say, "Come in." I wasn't sure, I'm not sure yet, but I opened the door—this door [*indicating the door by which the two women are still standing*], and there in that rocker—[*pointing to it*] sat Mrs. Wright.

[*They all look at the rocker.*]

COUNTY ATTORNEY. What—was she doing?

HALE. She was rockin' back and forth. She had her apron in her hand and was kind of—pleating it.

COUNTY ATTORNEY. And how did she—look?

HALE. Well, she looked queer.

COUNTY ATTORNEY. How do you mean—queer?

HALE. Well, as if she didn't know what she was going to do next. And kind of done up.

COUNTY ATTORNEY. How did she seem to feel about your coming?

HALE. Why, I don't think she minded—one way or other. She didn't pay much attention. I said, "How do, Mrs. Wright, it's cold, ain't it?" And she said, "Is it?"—and went on kind of pleating at her apron. Well, I was surprised; she didn't ask me to come up to the stove, or to set down, but just sat there, not even looking at me, so I said, "I want to see John." And then she—laughed. I guess you would call it a laugh. I thought of Harry and the team outside, so I said a little sharp: "Can't I see John?" "No," she says, kind o' dull like. "Ain't he home?" says I. "Yes," says she, "he's home." "Then why can't I see him?" I asked her, out of patience. " 'Cause he's dead," says she. *"Dead?"* says I. She just nodded her head, not getting a bit excited, but rockin' back and forth. "Why—where is he?" says I, not knowing what to say. She just pointed upstairs—like that [*himself pointing to the room above*]. I got up, with the idea of going up there. I walked from there to here—then I says, "Why, what did he die of?" "He died of a rope around his neck," says she, and just went on pleatin' at her apron. Well, I went out and called Harry. I thought I might—need help. We went upstairs, and there he was lyin'—

COUNTY ATTORNEY. I think I'd rather have you go into that upstairs, where you can point it all out. Just go on now with the rest of the story.

HALE. Well, my first thought was to get that rope off. I looked . . . [*Stops, his face twitches.*] . . . but Harry, he went up to him, and he said, "No, he's dead all right, and we'd better not touch anything." So we went back downstairs. She was still sitting that same way. "Has anybody been notified?" I asked. "No," says she, unconcerned. "Who did this, Mrs. Wright?" said Harry. He said it business-like—and she stopped pleatin' of her apron. "I don't know," she says. "You don't *know?*" says Harry. "No," says she. "Weren't you sleepin' in the bed with him?" says Harry. "Yes," says she, "but I was on the inside." "Somebody slipped a rope round his neck and strangled him, and you didn't wake up?" says Harry. "I didn't wake up," she said after him. We must 'a looked as if we didn't see how that could be, for after a minute she said, "I sleep sound." Harry was going to ask her more questions, but I said maybe we ought to let her tell her story first to the coroner, or the sheriff, so Harry went fast as he could to Rivers' place, where there's a telephone.

COUNTY ATTORNEY. And what did Mrs. Wright do when she knew that you had gone for the coroner?

HALE. She moved from that chair to this over here . . . [*Pointing to a small chair in the corner.*] . . . and just sat there with her hands held together and looking down. I got a feeling that I ought to make some conversation, so I said I had come in to see if John wanted to put in a telephone, and at that she started to laugh, and then she stopped and looked at me—scared. [*The* COUNTY ATTORNEY, *who has had his notebook out, makes a note.*] I dunno, maybe it wasn't scared. I wouldn't like to say it was. Soon Harry got back, and then Dr. Lloyd came, and you, Mr. Peters, and so I guess that's all I know that you don't.

COUNTY ATTORNEY [*looking around*]. I guess we'll go upstairs first—and then out to the barn and around there. [*To the* SHERIFF.] You're convinced that there was nothing important here—nothing that would point to any motive?

SHERIFF. Nothing here but kitchen things.

[*The* COUNTY ATTORNEY, *after again looking around the kitchen, opens the door of a cupboard closet. He gets up on a chair and looks on a shelf. Pulls his hand away, sticky.*]

COUNTY ATTORNEY. Here's a nice mess.

[*The women draw nearer.*]

MRS. PETERS [*to the other woman*]. Oh, her fruit; it did freeze. [*To the* LAWYER.] She worried about that when it turned so cold. She said the fir'd go out and her jars would break.

SHERIFF. Well, can you beat the women! Held for murder and worryin' about her preserves.

COUNTY ATTORNEY. I guess before we're through she may have something more serious than preserves to worry about.

HALE. Well, women are used to worrying over trifles.

[*The two women move a little closer together.*]

COUNTY ATTORNEY [*with the gallantry of a young politician*]. And yet, for all their worries, what would we do without the ladies? [*The women do not unbend. He goes to the sink, takes a dipperful of water from the pail and, pouring it into a basin, washes his hands. Starts to wipe them on the roller towel, turns it for a cleaner place.*] Dirty towels! [*Kicks his foot against the pans under the sink.*] Not much of a housekeeper, would you say, ladies?

MRS. HALE [*stiffly*]. There's a great deal of work to be done on a farm.

COUNTY ATTORNEY. To be sure. And yet . . . [*With a little bow to her.*] . . . I know there are some Dickson county farmhouses which do not have such roller towels. [*He gives it a pull to expose its full length again.*]

MRS. HALE Those towels get dirty awful quick. Men's hands aren't always as clean as they might be.

COUNTY ATTORNEY. Ah, loyal to your sex, I see. But you and Mrs. Wright were neighbors. I suppose you were friends, too.

MRS. HALE [*shaking her head*]. I've not seen much of her of late years. I've not been in this house—it's more than a year.

COUNTY ATTORNEY. And why was that? You didn't like her?

MRS. HALE. I liked her all well enough. Farmers' wives have their hands full, Mr. Henderson. And then—

COUNTY ATTORNEY. Yes—?

MRS. HALE [*looking about*]. It never seemed a very cheerful place.

COUNTY ATTORNEY. No—it's not cheerful. I shouldn't say she had the homemaking instinct.

Mrs. Hale. Well, I don't know as Wright had, either.

County Attorney. You mean that they didn't get on very well?

Mrs. Hale. No, I don't mean anything. But I don't think a place'd be any cheerfuler for John Wright's being in it.

County Attorney. I'd like to talk more of that a little later. I want to get the lay of things upstairs now. [*He goes to the left, where three steps lead to a stair door.*]

Sheriff. I suppose anything Mrs. Peters does'll be all right. She was to take in some clothes for her, you know, and a few little things. We left in such a hurry yesterday.

County Attorney. Yes, but I would like to see what you take, Mrs. Peters, and keep an eye out for anything that might be of use to us.

Mrs. Peters. Yes, Mr. Henderson.

[*The women listen to the men's steps on the stairs, then look about the kitchen.*]

Mrs. Hale. I'd hate to have men coming into my kitchen, snooping around and criticizing. [*She arranges the pans under sink which the* Lawyer *had shoved out of place.*]

Mrs. Peters. Of course it's no more than their duty.

Mrs. Hale. Duty's all right, but I guess that deputy sheriff that came out to make the fire might have got a little of this on. [*Gives the roller towel a pull.*] Wish I'd thought of that sooner. Seems mean to talk about her for not having things slicked up when she had to come away in such a hurry.

Mrs. Peters [*Who has gone to a small table in the left rear corner of the room, and lifted one end of a towel that covers a pan*]. She had bread set. [*Stands still.*]

Mrs. Hale [*eyes fixed on a loaf of bread beside the breadbox, which is on a low shelf at the other side of the room. Moves slowly toward it*]. She was going to put this in there. [*Picks up loaf, then abruptly drops it. In a manner of returning to familiar things.*] It's a shame about her fruit. I wonder if it's all gone. [*Gets up on the chair and looks.*] I think there's some here that's all right, Mrs. Peters. Yes—here; [*Holding it toward the window.*] this is cherries, too. [*Looking again.*] I declare I believe that's the only one. [*Gets down, bottle in her hand. Goes to the sink and wipes it off on the outside.*] She'll feel awful bad after all her hard work in the hot weather. I remember the afternoon I put up my cherries last summer. [*She puts the bottle on the big kitchen table, center of the room, front table. With a sigh, is about to sit down in the rocking chair. Before she is seated realizes what chair it is; with a slow look at it, steps back. The chair, which she has touched, rocks back and forth.*]

Mrs. Peters. Well, I must get those things from the front-room closet. [*She goes to the door at the right, but after looking into the other room steps back.*] You coming with me, Mrs. Hale? You could help me carry them.

[*They go into the other room; reappear,* Mrs. Peters *carrying a dress and skirt,* Mrs. Hale *following with a pair of shoes.*]

Mrs. Peters. My, it's cold in there. [*She puts the cloth on the big table, and hurries to the stove.*]

Mrs. Hale [*examining the skirt*]. Wright was close. I think maybe that's why she kept so much to herself. She didn't even belong to the Ladies' Aid. I suppose she felt she couldn't do her part, and then you don't enjoy things when you feel shabby. She used to wear pretty clothes and be lively, when she was Minnie Foster, one of the town girls singing in the choir. But that—oh, that was thirty years ago. This all you was to take in?

Mrs. Peters. She said she wanted an apron. Funny thing to want, for there isn't much to get you dirty in jail, goodness knows. But I suppose just to make her feel more natural. She said they was in the top drawer in this cupboard. Yes, here. And then her little shawl that always hung behind the door. [*Opens stair door and looks.*] Yes, here it is. [*Quickly shuts door leading upstairs.*]

MRS. HALE [*abruptly moving towards her*]. Mrs. Peters?

MRS. PETERS. Yes, Mrs. Hale?

MRS. HALE. Do you think she did it?

MRS. PETERS [*in a frightened voice*]. Oh, I don't know.

MRS. HALE. Well, I don't think she did. Asking for an apron and her little shawl. Worrying about her fruit.

MRS. PETERS [*starts to speak, glances up, where footsteps are heard in the room above. In a low voice*]. Mr. Peters says it looks bad for her. Mr. Henderson is awful sarcastic in a speech, and he'll make fun of her sayin' she didn't wake up.

MRS. HALE. Well, I guess John Wright didn't wake when they was slipping that rope under his neck.

MRS. PETERS. No, it's strange. It must have been done awful crafty and still. They say it was such a—funny way to kill a man, rigging it all up like that.

MRS. HALE. That's just what Mr. Hale said. There was a gun in the house. He says that's what he can't understand.

MRS. PETERS. Mr. Henderson said coming out that what was needed for the case was a motive; something to show anger, or—sudden feeling.

MRS. HALE [*who is standing by the table*]. Well, I don't see any signs of anger around here. [*She puts her hand on the dish towel which lies on the table, stands looking down at the table, one half of which is clean, the other half messy.*] It's wiped here. [*Makes a move as if to finish work, then turns and looks at loaf of bread outside the breadbox. Drops towel. In that voice of coming back to familiar things.*] Wonder how they are finding things upstairs? I hope she had it a little more red-up there. You know, it seems kind of *sneaking*. Locking her up in town and then coming out here and trying to get her own house to turn against her!

MRS. PETERS. But, Mrs. Hale, the law is the law.

MRS. HALE. I s'pose 'tis. [*Unbuttoning her coat.*] Better loosen up your things, Mrs. Peters. You won't feel them when you go out.

[MRS. PETERS *takes off her fur tippet,*[1] *goes to hang it on hook at back of room, stands looking at the under part of the small corner table.*]

MRS. PETERS. She was piecing a quilt. [*She brings the large sewing basket, and they look at the bright pieces.*]

MRS. HALE. It's log cabin pattern. Pretty, isn't it? I wonder if she was goin' to quilt or just knot it?

[*Footsteps have been heard coming down the stairs. The* SHERIFF *enters, followed by* HALE *and the* COUNTY ATTORNEY.]

SHERIFF. They wonder if she was going to quilt it or just knot it. [*The men laugh, the women look abashed.*]

COUNTY ATTORNEY [*rubbing his hands over the stove*]. Frank's fire didn't do much up there, did it? Well, let's go out to the barn and get that cleared up.

[*The men go outside.*]

MRS. HALE [*resentfully*]. I don't know as there's anything so strange, our takin' up our time with little things while we're waiting for them to get the evidence. [*She sits down at the big table, smoothing out a block with decision.*] I don't see as it's anything to laugh about.

[1] A small scarf.

MRS. PETERS [*apologetically*]. Of course they've got awful important things on their minds. [*Pulls up a chair and joins* MRS. HALE *at the table.*]

MRS. HALE [*examining another block.*]. Mrs. Peters, look at this one. Here, this is the one she was working on, and look at the sewing! All the rest of it has been so nice and even. And look at this! It's all over the place! Why, it looks as if she didn't know what she was about! [*After she has said this, they look at each other, then start to glance back at the door. After an instant* MRS. HALE *has pulled at a knot and ripped the sewing.*]

MRS. PETERS. Oh, what are you doing, Mrs. Hale?

MRS. HALE [*mildly*]. Just pulling out a stitch or two that's not sewed very good. [*Threading a needle.*] Bad sewing always made me fidgety.

MRS. PETERS [*nervously*]. I don't think we ought to touch things.

MRS. HALE. I'll just finish up this end. [*Suddenly stopping and leaning forward.*] Mrs. Peters?

MRS. PETERS. Yes, Mrs. Hale?

MRS. HALE. What do you suppose she was so nervous about?

MRS. PETERS. Oh—I don't know. I don't know as she was nervous. I sometimes sew awful queer when I'm just tired. [MRS. HALE *starts to say something, looks at* MRS. PETERS, *then goes on sewing.*] Well, I must get these things wrapped up. They may be through sooner than we think. [*Putting apron and other things together.*] I wonder where I can find a piece of paper, and string.

MRS. HALE. In that cupboard, maybe.

MRS. PETERS [*looking in cupboard*]. Why, here's a birdcage. [*Holds it up.*] Did she have a bird, Mrs. Hale?

MRS. HALE. Why, I don't know whether she did or not—I've not been here for so long. There was a man around last year selling canaries cheap, but I don't know as she took one; maybe she did. She used to sing real pretty herself.

MRS. PETERS [*glancing around*]. Seems funny to think of a bird here. But she must have had one, or why should she have a cage? I wonder what happened to it?

MRS. HALE. I s'pose maybe the cat got it.

MRS. PETERS. No, she didn't have a cat. She's got that feeling some people have about cats—being afraid of them. My cat got in her room, and she was real upset and asked me to take it out.

MRS. HALE. My sister Bessie was like that. Queer, ain't it?

MRS. PETERS [*examining the cage*]. Why, look at this door. It's broke. One hinge is pulled apart.

MRS. HALE [*looking, too*]. Looks as if someone must have been rough with it.

MRS. PETERS. Why, yes. [*She brings the cage forward and puts it on the table.*]

MRS. HALE. I wish if they're going to find any evidence they'd be about it. I don't like this place.

MRS. PETERS. But I'm awful glad you came with me, Mrs. Hale. It would be lonesome for me sitting here alone.

MRS. HALE. It would, wouldn't it? [*Dropping her sewing.*] But I tell you what I do wish, Mrs. Peters. I wish I had come over sometimes when *she* was here. I—[*Looking around the room.*]—wish I had.

MRS. PETERS. But of course you were awful busy, Mrs. Hale—your house and your children.

MRS. HALE. I could've come. I stayed away because it weren't cheerful—and that's why I ought to have come. I—I've never liked this place. Maybe because it's down in a hollow, and you don't see the road. I dunno what it is, but it's a lonesome place and always was. I wish I had come over to see Minnie Foster sometimes. I can see now—[*shakes her head*].

Mrs. Peters. Well, you mustn't reproach yourself, Mrs. Hale. Somehow we just don't see how it is with other folks until—something comes up.

Mrs. Hale. Not having children makes less work—but it makes a quiet house, and Wright out to work all day, and no company when he did come in. Did you know John Wright, Mrs. Peters?

Mrs. Peters. Not to know him; I've seen him in town. They say he was a good man.

Mrs. Hale. Yes—good; he didn't drink, and kept his word as well as most, I guess, and paid his debts. But he was a hard man, Mrs. Peters. Just to pass the time of day with him. [*Shivers.*] Like a raw wind that gets to the bone. [*Pauses, her eye falling on the cage.*] I should think she would 'a wanted a bird. But what do you suppose went with it?

Mrs. Peters. I don't know, unless it got sick and died. [*She reaches over and swings the broken door, swings it again; both women watch it.*]

Mrs. Hale. You weren't raised round here, were you? [Mrs. Peters *shakes her head.*] You didn't know—her?

Mrs. Peters. Not till they brought her yesterday.

Mrs. Hale. She—come to think of it, she was kind of like a bird herself—real sweet and pretty, but kind of timid and—fluttery. How—she—did—change. [*Silence; then as if struck by a happy thought and relieved to get back to everyday things.*] Tell you what, Mrs. Peters, why don't you take the quilt in with you? It might take up her mind.

Mrs. Peters. Why, I think that's a real nice idea, Mrs. Hale. There couldn't possibly be any objection to it, could there? Now, just what would I take? I wonder if her patches are in here—and her things. [*They look in the sewing basket.*]

Mrs. Hale. Here's some red. I expect this has got sewing things in it. [*Brings out a fancy box.*] What a pretty box. Looks like something somebody would give you. Maybe her scissors are in here. [*Opens box. Suddenly puts her hand to her nose.*] Why—[Mrs. Peters *bends nearer, then turns her face away.*] There's something wrapped up in this piece of silk.

Mrs. Peters. Why, this isn't her scissors.

Mrs. Hale [*lifting the silk*]. Oh, Mrs. Peters—it's—[Mrs. Peters *bends closer.*]

Mrs. Peters. It's the bird.

Mrs. Hale [*jumping up*]. But, Mrs Peters—look at it. Its neck! Look at its neck! It's all—other side *to*.

Mrs. Peters. Somebody—wrung—its neck.

[*Their eyes meet. A look of growing comprehension of horror. Steps are heard outside.* Mrs. Hale *slips box under quilt pieces, and sinks into her chair. Enter* Sheriff *and* County Attorney. Mrs. Peters *rises.*]

County Attorney [*as one turning from serious things to little pleasantries*]. Well, ladies, have you decided whether she was going to quilt it or knot it?

Mrs. Peters. We think she was going to—knot it.

County Attorney. Well, that's interesting, I'm sure. [*Seeing the birdcage.*] Has the bird flown?

Mrs. Hale [*putting more quilt pieces over the box*]. We think the—cat got it.

County Attorney [*preoccupied*]. Is there a cat?

[Mrs. Hale *glances in a quick covert way at* Mrs. Peters.]

Mrs. Peters. Well, not now. They're superstitious, you know. They leave.

County Attorney [*to* Sheriff Peters, *continuing an interrupted conversation*]. No sign at all of anyone having come from the outside. Their own rope. Now let's go up again and go over it piece by piece. [*They start upstairs.*] It would have to have been someone who knew just the—

[MRS. PETERS *sits down. The two women sit there not looking at one another, but as if peering into something and at the same time holding back. When they talk now, it is in the manner of feeling their way over strange ground, as if afraid of what they are saying, but as if they cannot help saying it.*]

MRS. HALE. She liked the bird. She was going to bury it in that pretty box.

MRS. PETERS [*in a whisper*]. When I was a girl—my kitten—there was a boy took a hatchet, and before my eyes—and before I could get there—[*Covers her face an instant*]. If they hadn't held me back, I would have—[*Catches herself, looks upstairs where steps are heard, falters weakly*]—hurt him.

MRS. HALE [*with a slow look around her*]. I wonder how it would seem never to have had any children around. [*Pause.*] No, Wright wouldn't like the bird—a thing that sang. She used to sing. He killed that, too.

MRS. PETERS [*moving uneasily*]. We don't know who killed the bird.

MRS. HALE. I knew John Wright.

MRS. PETERS. It was an awful thing was done in this house that night, Mrs. Hale. Killing a man while he slept, slipping a rope around his neck that choked the life out of him.

MRS. HALE. His neck. Choked the life out of him.

[*Her hand goes out and rests on the birdcage.*]

MRS. PETERS [*with rising voice*]. We don't know who killed him. We don't *know.*

MRS. HALE [*her own feeling not interrupted*]. If there'd been years and years of nothing, then a bird to sing to you, it would be awful—still, after the bird was still.

MRS. PETERS [*something within her speaking*]. I know what stillness is. When we homesteaded in Dakota, and my first baby died—after he was two years old, and me with no other then—

MRS. HALE [*moving*]. How soon do you suppose they'll be through, looking for evidence?

MRS. PETERS. I know what stillness is. [*Pulling herself back.*] The law has got to punish crime, Mrs. Hale.

MRS. HALE [*not as if answering that*]. I wish you'd seen Minnie Foster when she wore a white dress with blue ribbons and stood up there in the choir and sang. [*A look around the room.*] Oh, I *wish* I'd come over here once in a while! That was a crime! That was a crime! Who's going to punish that?

MRS. PETERS [*looking upstairs*]. We mustn't—take on.

MRS. HALE. I might have known she needed help! I know how things can be—for women. I tell you, it's queer, Mrs. Peters. We live close together, and we live far apart. We all go through the same things—it's all just a different kind of the same thing. [*Brushes her eyes, noticing the bottle of fruit, reaches out for it.*] If I was you, I wouldn't tell her her fruit was gone. Tell her it *ain't.* Tell her it's all right. Take this in to prove it to her. She—she may never know whether it was broke or not.

MRS. PETERS [*takes the bottle, looks about for something to wrap it in; takes petticoat from the clothes brought from the other room, very nervously begins winding this around the bottle. In a false voice*]. My, it's a good thing the men couldn't hear us. Wouldn't they just laugh! Getting all stirred up over a little thing like a—dead canary. As if that could have anything to do with—with—wouldn't they *laugh!*

[*The men are heard coming downstairs.*],

MRS. HALE [*under her breath*]. Maybe they would—maybe they wouldn't.

COUNTY ATTORNEY. No, Peters, it's all perfectly clear except a reason for doing it. But you know juries when it comes to women. If there was some definite thing. Something to show—something to make a story about—a thing that would connect up with this strange way of doing it.

[*The women's eyes meet for an instant. Enter* HALE *from outer door.*]

HALE. Well, I've got the team around. Pretty cold out there.

COUNTY ATTORNEY. I'm going to stay here awhile by myself. [*To the* SHERIFF.] You can send Frank out for me, can't you? I want to go over everything. I'm not satisfied that we can't do better.

SHERIFF. Do you want to see what Mrs. Peters is going to take in?

[*The* LAWYER *goes to the table, picks up the apron, laughs.*]

COUNTY ATTORNEY. Oh, I guess they're not very dangerous things the ladies have picked up. [*Moves a few things about, disturbing the quilt pieces which cover the box. Steps back.*] No, Mrs. Peters doesn't need supervising. For that matter, a sheriff's wife is married to the law. Ever think of it that way, Mrs. Peters?

MRS. PETERS. Not—just that way.

SHERIFF [*chuckling*]. Married to the law. [*Moves toward the other room.*] I just want you to come in here a minute, George. We ought to take a look at these windows.

COUNTY ATTORNEY [*scoffingly*]. Oh, windows!

SHERIFF. We'll be right out, Mr. Hale.

[HALE *goes outside. The* SHERIFF *follows the* COUNTY ATTORNEY *into the other room. Then* MRS. HALE *rises, hands tight together, looking intensely at* MRS. PETERS, *whose eyes take a slow turn, finally meeting* MRS. HALE'S. *A moment* MRS. HALE *holds her, then her own eyes point the way to where the box is concealed. Suddenly* MRS. PETERS *throws back quilt pieces and tries to put the box in the bag she is wearing. It is too big. She opens box, starts to take bird out, cannot touch it, goes to pieces, stands there helpless. Sound of a knob turning in the other room.* MRS. HALE *snatches the box and puts it in the pocket of her big coat. Enter* COUNTY ATTORNEY *and* SHERIFF.]

COUNTY ATTORNEY [*facetiously*]. Well, Henry, at least we found out that she was not going to quilt it. She was going to—what is it you call it, ladies?

MRS. HALE [*her hand against her pocket*]. We call it—knot it, Mr. Henderson.

[1916]

Eugene O'Neill   *1888-1953*

DESIRE UNDER THE ELMS

CHARACTERS

EPHRAIM CABOT
SIMEON ⎫
PETER ⎬ *His sons*
EBEN ⎭
ABBIE PUTNAM

YOUNG GIRL, TWO FARMERS, THE FIDDLER, A SHERIFF,
AND OTHER FOLK FROM THE NEIGHBORING FARMS.

The action of the entire play takes place in, and immediately outside of, the Cabot farmhouse in New England, in the year 1850. The south end of the house faces front to a stone wall with a wooden gate at center opening on a country road. The house is in good condition but in need of paint. Its walls are a sickly grayish, the green of the shutters faded. Two enormous elms are on each side of the house. They bend their trailing branches down over the roof. They appear to protect and at the same time subdue. There is a sinister maternity in their aspect, a crushing, jealous absorption. They have developed from their intimate contact with the life of man in the house an appalling humaneness. They brood oppressively over the house. They are like exhausted women resting their sagging breasts and hands and hair on its roof, and when it rains their tears trickle down monotonously and rot on the shingles.

There is a path running from the gate around the right corner of the house to the front door. A narrow porch is on this side. The end wall facing us has two windows in its upper story, two larger ones on the floor below. The two upper are those of the father's bedroom and that of the brothers. On the left, ground floor, is the kitchen—on the right, the parlor, the shades of which are always drawn down.

PART I
SCENE I

Exterior of the farmhouse. It is sunset of a day at the beginning of summer in the year 1850. There is no wind and everything is still. The sky above the roof is suffused with deep colors, the green of the elms glows, but the house is in shadow, seeming pale and washed out by contrast.

A door opens and EBEN CABOT *comes to the end of the porch and stands looking down the road to the right. He has a large bell in his hand and this he swings mechanically, awakening a deafening clangor. Then he puts his hands on his hips and stares up at the sky. He sighs with a puzzled awe and blurts out with halting appreciation.*

EBEN. God! Purty! [*His eyes fall and he stares about him frowningly. He is twenty-five, tall and sinewy. His face is well-formed, good-looking, but its expression is resentful and defensive. His defiant, dark eyes remind one of a wild animal's in captivity. Each day is a cage in which he finds himself trapped but inwardly unsubdued. There is a fierce repressed vitality about him. He has black hair, mustache, a thin curly trace of beard. He is dressed in rough farm clothes.*]

He spits on the ground with intense disgust, turns and goes back into the house. SIMEON *and*
PETER *come in from their work in the fields. They are tall men, much older than their
half-brother [*SIMEON *is thirty-nine and* PETER *thirty-seven], built on a squarer, simpler
model, fleshier in body, more bovine and homelier in face, shrewder and more practical. Their
shoulders stoop a bit from years of farm work. They clump heavily along in their clumsy
thick-soled boots caked with earth. Their clothes, their faces, hands, bare arms and throats are
earth-stained. They smell of earth. They stand together for a moment in front of the house
and, as if with the one impulse, stare dumbly up at the sky, leaning on their hoes. Their faces
have a compressed, unresigned expression. As they look upward, this softens.*

SIMEON. [*grudgingly*] Purty.
PETER. Ay-eh.
SIMEON. [*suddenly*] Eighteen year ago.
PETER. What?
SIMEON. Jenn. My woman. She died.
PETER. I'd fergot.
SIMEON. I rec'lect—now an' agin. Makes it lonesome. She'd hair long's a hoss'
    tail—an' yaller like gold!
PETER. Waal—she's gone. [*This with indifferent finality—then after a pause*] They's
    gold in the West, Sim.
SIMEON. [*still under the influence of sunset—vaguely*] In the sky?
PETER. Waal—in a manner o' speakin'—thar's the promise. [*Growing excited*] Gold
    in the sky—in the West—Golden Gate—Californi-a!—Goldest West!—fields o'
    gold!
SIMEON. [*excited in his turn*] Fortunes layin' just atop o' the ground waitin' t' be
    picked! Solomon's mines,[1] they says! [*For a moment they continue looking up at the
    sky—then their eyes drop.*]
PETER. [*with sardonic bitterness*] Here—it's stones atop o' the ground—stones atop
    o' stones—makin' stone walls—year atop o' year—him 'n' yew 'n' me 'n' then
    Eben—makin' stone walls fur him to fence us in!
SIMEON. We've wuked. Give our strength. Give our years. Plowed 'em under in the
    ground—[*he stamps rebelliously*]—rottin'—makin' soil for his crops! [*A pause*]
    Waal—the farm pays good for hereabouts.
PETER. If we plowed in Californi-a, they'd be lumps o' gold in the furrow!
SIMEON. Californi-a's t'other side o' earth, a'most. We got t' calc'late—
PETER. [*after a pause*] 'Twould be hard fur me, too, to give up what we've 'arned
    here by our sweat. [*A pause.* EBEN *sticks his head out of the dining-room window,
    listening.*]
SIMEON. Ay-eh. [*A pause*] Mebbe—he'll die soon.
PETER. [*doubtfully*] Mebbe.
SIMEON. Mebee—fur all we knows—he's dead now.
PETER. Ye'd need proof.
SIMEON. He's been gone two months—with no word.
PETER. Left us in the fields an evenin' like this. Hitched up an' druv off into the
    West. That's plum onnateral. He hain't never been off this farm 'ceptin' t' the
    village in thirty year or more, not since he married Eben's maw. [*A pause.
    Shrewdly*] I calc'late we might git him declared crazy by the court.

---

[1] According to legend, the fabulous wealth of Solomon (king of Israel in the tenth century B.C.) was
extracted from rich gold and silver mines.

Simeon. He skinned 'em too slick. He got the best o' all on 'em. They'd never b'lieve him crazy. [*A pause*] We got t' wait—till he's under ground.

Eben. [*with a sardonic chuckle*] Honor thy father! [*They turn, startled, and stare at him. He grins, then scrowls*] I pray he's died. [*They stare at him. He continues matter-of-factly*] Supper's ready.

Simeon *and* Peter. [*together*] Ayeh.

Eben. [*gazing up at the sky*] Sun's downin' purty.

Simeon *and* Peter. [*together*] Ay-eh. They's gold in the West.

Eben. Ay-eh. [*Pointing*] Yonder atop o' the hill pasture, ye mean?

Simeon *and* Peter. [*together*] In Californi-a!

Eben. Hunh? [*Stares at them indifferently for a second, then drawls*] Waal—supper's gittin' cold. [*He turns back into kitchen.*]

Simeon. [*startled—smacks his lips*] I air hungry!

Peter. [*sniffing*] I smells bacon!

Simeon. [*with hungry appreciation*] Bacon's good!

Peter. [*in same tone*] Bacon's bacon! [*They turn, shouldering each other, their bodies bumping and rubbing together as they hurry clumsily to their food, like two friendly oxen toward their evening meal. They disappear around the right corner of house and can be heard entering the door.*]

CURTAIN

SCENE II

The color fades from the sky. Twilight begins. The interior of the kitchen is now visible. A pine table is at center, a cookstove in the right rear corner, four rough wooden chairs, a tallow candle on the table. In the middle of the rear wall is fastened a big advertising poster with a ship in full sail and the word "California" in big letters. Kitchen utensils hang from nails. Everything is neat and in order but the atmosphere is of a men's camp kitchen rather than that of a home.

Places for three are laid. Eben *takes boiled potatoes and bacon from the stove and puts them on the table, also a loaf of bread and a crock of water.* Simeon *and* Peter *shoulder in, slump down in their chairs without a word.* Eben *joins them. The three eat in silence for a moment, the two elder as naturally unrestrained as beasts of the field,* Eben *picking at his food without appetite, glancing at them with a tolerant dislike.*

Simeon. [*suddenly turns to* Eben] Looky here! Ye'd oughtn't t' said that, Eben.

Peter. 'Twa'n't righteous.

Eben. What?

Simeon. Ye prayed he'd died.

Eben. Waal—don't yew pray it? [*A pause.*]

Peter. He's our Paw.

Eben. [*violently*] Not mine!

Simeon. [*dryly*] Ye'd not let no one else say that about yer Maw! Ha! [*He gives one abrupt sardonic guffaw.* Peter *grins.*]

Eben. [*very pale*] I meant—I hain't his'n—I hain't like him—he hain't me!

Peter. [*dryly*] Wait till ye've growed his age!

Eben. [*intensely*] I'm Maw—every drop o' blood! [*A pause. They stare at him with indifferent curiosity.*]

Peter. [*reminiscently*] She was good t' Sim 'n' me. A good Stepmaw's scurse.

SIMEON. She was good t' everyone.

EBEN. [*greatly moved, gets to his feet and makes an awkward bow to each of them—stammering*] I be thankful t' ye. I'm her—her heir. [*He sits down in confusion.*]

PETER. [*after a pause—judicially*] She was good even t' him.

EBEN. [*fiercely*] An' fur thanks he killed her!

SIMEON. [*after a pause*] No one never kills nobody. It's allus somethin'. That's the murderer.

EBEN. Didn't he slave Maw t' death?

PETER. He's slaved himself t' death. He's slaved Sim 'n' me 'n' yew t' death—on'y none o' us hain't died—yit.

SIMEON. It's somethin'—drivin' him—t' drive us!

EBEN. [*vengefully*] Waal—I hold him t' jedgment! [*Then scornfully*] Somethin'! What's somethin'?

SIMEON. Dunno.

EBEN. [*sardonically*] What's drivin' yew to Californi-a, mebbe? [*They look at him in surprise*] Oh, I've heerd ye! [*Then, after a pause*] But ye'll never go t' the gold fields!

PETER. [*assertively*] Mebbe!

EBEN. Whar'll ye git the money?

PETER. We kin walk. It's an a'mighty ways—Californi-a—but if yew was t' put all the steps we've walked on this farm end t' end we'd be in the moon!

EBEN. The Injuns'll skulp ye on the plains.

SIMEON. [*with grim humor*] We'll mebbe make 'em pay a hair fur a hair!

EBEN. [*decisively*] But t'aint that. Ye won't never go because ye'll wait here fur yer share o' the farm, thinkin' allus he'll die soon.

SIMEON. [*after a pause*] We've a right.

PETER. Two-thirds belongs t'us.

EBEN. [*jumping to his feet*] Ye've no right! She wa'n't yewr Maw! It was her farm! Didn't he steal it from her? She's dead. It's my farm.

SIMEON. [*sardonically*] Tell that t'Paw—when he comes! I'll bet ye a dollar he'll laugh—fur once in his life. Ha! [*He laughs himself in one single mirthless bark.*]

PETER. [*amused in turn, echoes his brother*] Ha!

SIMEON. [*after a pause*] What've ye got held agin us, Eben? Year arter year it's skulked in yer eye—somethin'.

PETER. Ay-eh.

EBEN. Ay-eh. They's somethin'. [*Suddenly exploding*] Why didn't ye never stand between him 'n' my Maw when he was slavin' her to her grave—t' pay her back fur the kindness she done t' yew? [*There is a long pause. They stare at him in surprise.*]

SIMEON. Waal—the stock'd got t' be watered.

PETER. 'R they was woodin' t' do.

SIMEON. 'R plowin'.

PETER. 'R hayin'.

SIMEON. 'R spreadin' manure.

PETER. 'R weedin'.

SIMEON. 'R prunin'.

PETER. 'R milkin'.

EBEN. [*breaking in harshly*] An' makin' walls—stone atop o' stone—makin' walls till yer heart's a stone ye heft up out o' the way o' growth onto a stone wall t' wall in yer heart!

SIMEON. [*matter-of-factly*] We never had no time t' meddle.

PETER. [*to* EBEN] Yew was fifteen afore yer Maw died—an' big fur yer age. Why didn't ye never do nothin'?

EBEN. [*harshly*] They was chores t' do, wa'n't they? [*A pause—then slowly*] It was on'y arter she died I come to think o' it. Me cookin'—doin' her work—that made me know her, suffer her sufferin'—she'd come back t' help—come back t' bile potatoes—come back t' fry bacon—come back t' bake biscuits—come back all cramped up t' shake the fire, an' carry ashes, her eyes weepin' an' bloody with smoke an' cinders same's they used t' be. She still comes back—stands by the stove thar in the evenin'—she can't find it nateral sleepin' an' restin' in peace. She can't git used t' bein' free—even in her grave.

SIMEON. She never complained none.

EBEN. She'd got too tired. She'd got too used t' bein' too tired. That was what he done. [*With vengeful passion*] An' sooner'r later, I'll meddle. I'll say the thin's I didn't say then t' him! I'll yell 'em at the top o' my lungs. I'll see t' it my Maw gits some rest an' sleep in her grave! [*He sits down again, relapsing into a brooding silence. They look at him with a queer indifferent curiosity.*]

PETER. [*after a pause*] Whar in tarnation d'ye s'pose he went, Sim?

SIMEON. Dunno. He druv off in the buggy, all spick an' span, with the mare all breshed an' shiny, druv off clackin' his tongue an' wavin' his whip. I remember it right well. I was finishin' plowin', it was spring an' May an' sunset, an' gold in the West, an' he druv off into it. I yells "Whar ye goin', Paw?" an' he hauls up by the stone wall a jiffy. His old snake's eyes was glitterin' in the sun like he'd been drinkin' a jugful an' he says with a mule's grin: "Don't ye run away till I come back!"

PETER. Wonder if he knowed we was wantin' fur Californi-a?

SIMEON. Mebbe. I didn't say nothin' and he says, lookin' kinder queer an' sick: "I been hearin' the hens cluckin' an' the roosters crowin' all the durn day. I been listenin' t' the cows lowin' an' everythin' else kickin' up till I can't stand it no more. It's spring an' I'm feelin' damned," he says. "Damned like an old bare hickory tree fit on'y fur burnin'," he says. An' then I calc'late I must've looked a mite hopeful, fur he adds real spry and vicious: "But don't git no fool idee I'm dead. I've sworn t' live a hundred an' I'll do it, if on'y t' spite yer sinful greed! An' now I'm ridin' out t' learn God's message t' me in the spring, like the prophets done. An' yew git back t' yer plowin'," he says. An' he druv off singin' a hymn. I thought he was drunk—'r I'd stopped him goin'.

EBEN. [*scornfully*] No, ye wouldn't! Ye're scared o' him. He's stronger—inside—than both o' ye put together!

PETER. [*sardonically*] An' yew—be yew Samson?[2]

EBEN. I'm gittin' stronger. I kin feel it growin' in me growin'—an' growin'—till it'll bust out—! [*He gets up and puts on his coat and a hat. They watch him, gradually breaking into grins.* EBEN *avoids their eyes sheepishly*] I'm goin' out fur a spell—up the road.

PETER. T' the village?

SIMEON. T' see Minnie?

EBEN. [*defiantly*] Ay-eh!

PETER. [*jeeringly*] The Scarlet Woman!

SIMEON. Lust—that's what's growin' in ye!

---

[2] An Israelite noted for his great strength. He was ultimately betrayed by his mistress Delilah. See the Bible, Judges, Chapters 13–16.

EBEN. Waal—she's purty!

PETER. She's been purty fur twenty year!

SIMEON. A new coat o' paint'll make a heifer out of forty.

EBEN. She hain't forty!

PETER. If she hain't, she's teeterin' on the edge.

EBEN. [*desperately*] What d'yew know—

PETER. All they is . . . Sim knew her—an' then me arter—

SIMEON. An' Paw kin tell yew somethin' too! He was fust!

EBEN. D'ye mean t' say he . . .?

SIMEON. [*with a grin*] Ay-eh! We air his heirs in everythin'!

EBEN. [*intensely*] That's more to it! That grows on it! It'll bust soon! [*Then violently*] I'll go smash my fist in her face! [*He pulls open the door in rear violently.*]

SIMEON. [*with a wink at* PETER—*drawlingly*] Mebbe—but the night's wa'm— purty—by the time ye git thar mebbe ye'll kiss her instead!

PETER. Sart'n he will! [*They both roar with coarse laughter.* EBEN *rushes out and slams the door—then the outside front door—comes around the corner of the house and stands still by the gate, staring up at the sky.*]

SIMEON. [*looking after him*] Like his Paw.

PETER. Dead spit an' image!

SIMEON. Dog'll eat dog!

PETER. Ay-eh. [*Pause. With yearning*] Mebbe a year from now we'll be in Californi-a.

SIMEON. Ay-eh. [*A pause. Both yawn*] Let's git t'bed. [*He blows out the candle. They go out door in rear.* EBEN *stretches his arms up to the sky—rebelliously.*]

EBEN. Waal—thar's a star, an' somewhar's they's him, an' here's me, an' thar's Min up the road—in the same night. What if I does kiss her? She's like t'night, she's soft 'n' wa'm, her eyes kin wink like a star, her mouth's wa'm, her arms're wa'm, she smells like a wa'm plowed field, she's purty . . . Ay-eh! By God A'mighty she's purty, an' I don't give a damn how many sins she's sinned afore mine or who she's sinned 'em with, my sin's as purty as any one on 'em! [*He strides off down the road to the left.*]

SCENE III

It is the pitch darkness just before dawn. EBEN *comes in from the left and goes around to the porch, feeling his way, chuckling bitterly and cursing half-aloud to himself.*

EBEN. The cussed old miser! [*He can be heard going in the front door. There is a pause as he goes upstairs, then a loud knock on the bedroom door of the brothers*] Wake up!

SIMEON. [*startledly*] Who's thar?

EBEN. [*pushing open the door and coming in, a lighted candle in his hand. The bedroom of the brothers is revealed. Its ceiling is the sloping roof. They can stand upright only close to the center dividing wall of the upstairs.* SIMEON *and* PETER *are in a double bed, front.* EBEN's *cot is to the rear.* EBEN *has a mixture of silly grin and vicious scowl on his face*] I be!

PETER. [*angrily*] What in hell's-fire . . .?

EBEN. I got news fur ye! Ha! [*He gives one abrupt sardonic guffaw.*]

SIMEON. [*angrily*] Couldn't ye hold it 'til we'd got our sleep?

EBEN. It's nigh sunup. [*Then explosively*] He's gone an' married agen!

SIMEON *and* PETER. [*explosively*] Paw!

EBEN. Got himself hitched to a female 'bout thirty-five—an' purty, they says . . .

SIMEON. [*aghast*] It's a durn lie!

PETER. Who says?

SIMEON. They been stringin' ye!

EBEN. Think I'm a dunce, do ye? The hull village says. The preacher from New Dover, he brung the news—told it t' our preacher—New Dover, that's whar the old loon got himself hitched—that's whar the woman lived—

PETER. [*no longer doubting—stunned*] Waal . . . !

SIMEON. [*the same*] Waal . . . !

EBEN. [*sitting down on a bed—with vicious hatred*] Ain't he a devil out o' hell? It's jest t' spite us—the damned old mule!

PETER. [*after a pause*] Everythin'll go t' her now.

SIMEON. Ay-eh. [*A pause—dully*] Waal—if it's done—

PETER. It's done us. [*Pause—then persuasively*] They's gold in the fields o' Californi-a, Sim. No good a-stayin' here now.

SIMEON. Jest what I was a-thinkin'. [*Then with decision*] S'well fust's last! Let's light out and git this mornin'.

PETER. Suits me.

EBEN. Ye must like walkin'.

SIMEON. [*sardonically*] If ye'd grow wings on us we'd fly thar!

EBEN. Ye'd like ridin' better—on a boat, wouldn't ye? [*Fumbles in his pocket and takes out a crumpled sheet of foolscap*] Waal, if ye sign this ye kin ride on a boat. I've had it writ out an' ready in case ye'd ever go. It says fur three hundred dollars t' each ye agree yewr shares o' the farm is sold t' me. [*They look suspiciously at the paper. A pause.*]

SIMEON. [*wonderingly*] But if he's hitched agen—

PETER. An' whar'd yew git that sum o' money, anyways?

EBEN. [*cunningly*] I know whar it's hid. I been waitin'—Maw told me. She knew whar it lay fur years, but she was waitin' . . . It's her'n—the money he hoarded from her farm an' hid from Maw. It's my money by rights now.

PETER. Whar's it hid?

EBEN. [*cunningly*] Whar yew won't never find it without me. Maw spied on him—'r she'd never knowed. [*A pause. They look at him suspiciously, and he at them*] Waal, is it fa'r trade?

SIMEON. Dunno.

PETER. Dunno.

SIMEON. [*looking at window*] Sky's grayin'.

PETER. Ye better start the fire, Eben.

SIMEON. An' fix some vittles.

EBEN. Ay-eh. [*Then with a forced jocular heartiness*] I'll git ye a good one. If ye're startin' t' hoof it t' Californi-a ye'll need somethin' that'll stick t' yer ribs. [*He turns to the door, adding meaningly*] But ye kin ride on a boat if ye'll swap. [*He stops at the door and pauses. They stare at him.*]

SIMEON. [*suspiciously*] Whar was ye all night?

EBEN. [*defiantly*] Up t' Min's. [*Then slowly*] Walkin' thar, fust I felt 's if I'd kiss her; then I got a-thinkin' o' what ye'd said o' him an' her an' I says, I'll bust her nose fur that! Then I got t' the village an' heerd the news an' I got madder'n hell an' run all the way t' Min's not knowin' what I'd do—[*He pauses—then sheepishly but more defiantly*] Waal—when I seen her, I didn't hit her—nor I didn't kiss her nuther—I begun t' beller like a calf an' cuss at the same time, I was durn mad—an' she got scared—an' I jest grabbed holt an' tuk her—[*Proudly*] Yes, sirree! I tuk her. She may've been his'n—an' your'n, too—but she's mine now!

SIMEON. [*dryly*] In love, air yew?

EBEN. [*with lofty scorn*] Love! I don't take no stock in sech slop!

PETER. [*winking at SIMEON*] Mebbe Eben's aimin' t' marry, too.

SIMEON. Min'd make a true faithful he'pmeet! [*They snicker.*]

EBEN. What do I care fur her—'ceptin' she's round an' wa'm? The p'int is she was his'n—an' now she b'longs t' me! [*He goes to the door—then turns—rebelliously*] An' Min hain't sech a bad un. They's worse'n Min in the world, I'll bet ye! Wait'll we see this cow the Old Man's hitched t'! She'll beat Min, I got a notion! [*He starts to go out.*]

SIMEON. [*suddenly*] Mebbe ye'll try t' make her your'n, too?

PETER. Ha! [*He gives a sardonic laugh of relish at this idea.*]

EBEN. [*spitting with disgust*] Her—here—sleepin' with him—stealin' my Maw's farm! I'd as soon pet a skunk 'r kiss a snake! [*He goes out. The two stare after him suspiciously. A pause. They listen to his steps receding.*]

PETER. He's startin' the fire.

SIMEON. I'd like t' ride t' Californi-a—but—

PETER. Min might o' put some scheme in his head.

SIMEON. Mebbe it's all a lie 'bout Paw marryin'. We'd best wait an' see the bride.

PETER. An' don't sign nothin' till we does!

SIMEON. Nor till we've tested it's good money. [*Then with a grin*] But if Paw's hitched we'd be sellin' Eben somethin we'd never git nohow!

PETER. We'll wait an' see. [*Then with sudden vindictive anger*] An' till he comes, let's yew 'n' me not wuk a lick, let Eben tend to thin's if he's a mind t', let's us jest sleep an' eat an' drink likker, an' let the hull damned farm go t' blazes!

SIMEON. [*excitedly*] By God, we've 'arned a rest! We'll play rich fur a change. I hain't a-going to stir outa bed till breakfast's ready.

PETER. An' on the table!

SIMEON. [*after a pause—thoughtfully*] What d'ye calc'late she'll be like—our new Maw? Like Eben thinks?

PETER. More'n' likely.

SIMEON. [*vindictively*] Waal—I hope she's a she-devil that'll make him wish he was dead an' living in the pit o' hell fur comfort!

PETER. [*fervently*] Amen!

SIMEON. [*imitating his father's voice*] "I'm ridin' out t' learn God's message t' me in the spring like the prophets done," he says. I'll bet right then an' thar he knew plumb well he was goin' whorin', the stinkin' old hypocrite!

SCENE IV

Same as Scene ii—shows the interior of the kitchen with a lighted candle on table. It is gray dawn outside. SIMEON *and* PETER *are just finishing their breakfast.* EBEN *sits before his plate of untouched food, brooding frowningly.*

PETER. [*glancing at him rather irritably*] Lookin' glum don't help none.

SIMEON. [*sarcastically*] Sorrowin' over his lust o' the flesh!

PETER. [*with a grin*] Was she yer fust?

EBEN. [*angrily*] None o' yer business. [*A pause*] I was thinkin' o' him. I got a notion he's gittin' near—I kin feel him comin' on like yew kin feel malaria chill afore it takes ye.

PETER. It's too early yet.

SIMEON. Dunno. He'd like t' catch us nappin'—jest t' have somthin' t' hoss us 'round over.

PETER. [*mechanically gets to his feet.* SIMEON *does the same*] Waal—let's git t'wuk. [*They both plod mechanically toward the door before they realize. Then they stop short.*]

SIMEON. [*grinning*] Ye're a cussed fool, Peter—and I be wuss! Let him see we hain't wukin'! We don't give a durn!

PETER. [*as they go back to the table*] Not a damned durn! It'll serve t' show him we're done with him. [*They sit down again.* EBEN *stares from one to the other with surprise.*]

SIMEON. [*grins at him*] We're aimin' t' start bein' lilies o' the field.[3]

PETER. Nary a toil 'r spin 'r lick o' wuk do we put in!

SIMEON. Ye're sole owner—till he comes—that's what ye wanted. Waal, ye got t' be sole hand, too.

PETER. The cows air bellerin'. Ye better hustle at the milkin'.

EBEN. [*with excited joy*] Ye mean ye'll sign the paper?

SIMEON. [*dryly*] Mebbe.

PETER. Mebbe.

SIMEON. We're considerin'. [*Peremptorily*] Ye better git t' wuk.

EBEN. [*with queer excitement*] It's Maw's farm agen! It's my farm! Them's my cows! I'll milk my durn fingers off fur cows o' mine! [*He goes out door in rear, they stare after him indifferently.*]

SIMEON. Like his Paw.

PETER. Dead spit 'n' image!

SIMEON. Waal—let dog eat dog! [EBEN *comes out of front door and around the corner of the house. The sky is beginning to grow flushed with sunrise.* EBEN *stops by the gate and stares around him with glowing, possessive eyes. He takes in the whole farm with his embracing glance of desire.*]

EBEN. It's purty! It's damned purty! It's mine! [*He suddenly throws his head back boldly and glares with hard, defiant eyes at the sky*] Mine, d'ye hear? Mine! [*He turns and walks quickly off left, rear, toward the barn. The two brothers light their pipes.*]

SIMEON. [*putting his muddy boots up on the table, tilting back his chair, and puffing defiantly*] Waal—this air solid comfort—fur once.

PETER. Ay-eh. [*He follows suit. A pause. Unconsciously they both sigh.*]

SIMEON. [*suddenly*] He never was much o' a hand at milkin', Eben wa'n't.

PETER. [*with a snort*] His hands air like hoofs! [*A pause.*]

SIMEON. Reach down the jug thar! Let's take a swaller. I'm feelin' kind o' low.

PETER. Good idee! [*He does so—gets two glasses—they pour out drinks of whisky*] Here's t' the gold in Californi-a!

SIMEON. An' luck t' find it! [*They drink—puff resolutely—sigh—take their feet down from the table.*]

PETER. Likker don't pear t' sot right.

SIMEON. We hain't used t' it this early. [*A pause. They become very restless.*]

PETER. Gittin' close in this kitchen.

SIMEON. [*with immense relief*] Let's git a breath o' air. [*They arise briskly and go out rear —appear around house and stop by the gate. They stare up at the sky with a numbed appreciation.*]

PETER. Purty!

SIMEON. Ay-eh. Gold's t' the East now.

PETER. Sun's startin' with us fur the Golden West.

SIMEON. [*staring around the farm, his compressed face tightened, unable to conceal emotion*] Waal—it's our last mornin'—mebbe.

PETER. [*the same*] Ay-eh.

---

[3] See Matthew 6:34: "Consider the lilies of the field, how they grow; they toil not, neither do they spin."

SIMEON. [*stamps his foot on the earth and addresses it desperately*] Waal—ye've thirty year
o' me buried in ye—spread out over ye—blood an' bone an' sweat—rotted away
—fertilizin' ye—richin' yer soul—prime manure, by God, that's what I been t'
ye!

PETER. Ay-eh! An' me!

SIMEON. An' yew, Peter. [*He sighs—then spits*] Waal—no use'n cryin' over spilt milk.

PETER. They's gold in the West—an' freedom, mebbe. We been slaves t' stone walls
here.

SIMEON. [*defiantly*] We hain't nobody's slaves from this out—nor nothin's slave
nuther. [*A pause—restlessly*] Speaking o' milk, wonder how Eben's managin'?

PETER. I s'pose he's managin'.

SIMEON. Mebbe we'd ought t' help—this once.

PETER. Mebbe. The cows knows us.

SIMEON. An' likes us. They don't know him much.

PETER. An' the hosses, an' pigs, an' chickens. They don't know him much.

SIMEON. They knows us like brothers—an' likes us! [*Proudly.*] Hain't we raised 'em
t' be fust-rate, number one prize stock?

PETER. We hain't—not no more.

SIMEON. [*dully*] I was fergittin'. [*Then resignedly*] Waal, let's go help Eben a spell an'
git waked up.

PETER. Suits me. [*They are starting off down left, rear, for the barn when* EBEN *appears from
there hurrying toward them, his face excited.*]

EBEN. [*breathlessly*] Waal—har they be! The old mule an' the bride! I seen 'em from
the barn down below at the turnin'.

PETER. How could ye tell that far?

EBEN. Hain't I as far-sight as he's near-sight? Don't I know the mare 'n' buggy, an'
two people settin' in it? Who else . . . ? An' I tell ye I kin feel 'em a-comin', too!
[*He squirms as if he had the itch.*]

PETER. [*beginning to be angry*] Waal—let him do his own unhitchin'!

SIMEON. [*angry in his turn*] Let's hustle in an' git our bundles an' be a-goin' as he's
a-comin'. I don't want never t' step inside the door agen arter he's back. [*They
both start back around the corner of the house.* EBEN *follows them.*]

EBEN. [*anxiously*] Will ye sign it afore ye go?

PETER. Let's see the color o' the old skinflint's money an' we'll sign. [*They disappear
left. The two brothers clump upstairs to get their bundles.* EBEN *appears in the kitchen,
runs to window, peers out, comes back and pulls up a strip of flooring in under stove,
takes out a canvas bag and puts it on table, then sets the floorboard back in place. The
two brothers appear a moment after. They carry old carpet bags.*]

EBEN. [*puts his hand on bag guardingly*] Have ye signed?

SIMEON. [*shows paper in his hand*] Ay-eh. [*Greedily*] Be that the money?

EBEN. [*opens bag and pours out pile of twenty-dollar gold pieces*] Twenty-dollar pieces
—thirty on 'em. Count 'em. [*Peter does so, arranging them in stacks of five, biting one
or two to test them.*]

PETER. Six hundred. [*He puts them in bag and puts it inside his shirt carefully.*]

SIMEON. [*handing paper to* EBEN] Har ye be.

EBEN. [*after glance, folds it carefully and hides it under his shirt—gratefully*] Thank yew.

PETER. Thank yew fur the ride.

SIMEON. We'll send ye a lump o' gold fur Christmas. [*A pause.* EBEN *stares at them and
they at him.*]

PETER. [*awkwardly*] Waal—we're a-goin'.

SIMEON. Comin' out t' the yard?

EBEN. No. I'm waitin' in here a spell. [*Another silence. The brothers edge awkwardly to door in rear—then turn and stand.*]

SIMEON. Waal—good-by.

PETER. Good-by.

EBEN. Good-by. [*They go out. He sits down at the table, faces the stove and pulls out the paper. He looks from it to the stove. His face, lighted up by the shaft of sunlight from the window, has an expression of trance. His lips move. The two brothers come out to the gate.*]

PETER. [*looking off toward barn*] Thar he be—unhitchin'.

SIMEON. [*with a chuckle*] I'll bet ye he's riled!

PETER. An' thar she be.

SIMEON. Let's wait 'n' see what our new Maw looks like.

PETER. [*with a grin*] An' give him our partin' cuss!

SIMEON. [*grinning*] I feel like raisin' fun. I feel light in my head an' feet.

PETER. Me, too. I feel like laffin' till I'd split up the middle.

SIMEON. Reckon it's the likker?

PETER. No. My feet feel itchin' t' walk an' walk—an' jump high over thin's—an'. . . .

SIMEON. Dance? [*A pause.*]

PETER. [*puzzled*] It's plumb onnateral.

SIMEON. [*a light coming over his face*] I calc'late it's 'cause school's out. It's holiday. Fur once we're free!

PETER. [*dazedly*] Free?

SIMEON. The halter's broke—the harness is busted—the fence bars is down—the stone walls air crumblin' an' tumblin'! We'll be kickin' up an' tearin' away down the road!

PETER. [*drawing a deep breath—oratorically*] Anybody that wants this stinkin' old rock-pile of a farm kin hev it. T'ain't our'n, no sirree!

SIMEON. [*takes the gate off its hinges and puts it under his arm*] We harby 'bolishes shet gates, an' open gates, an' all gates, by thunder!

PETER. We'll take it with us fur luck an' let 'er sail free down some river.

SIMEON. [*as a sound of voices comes from left, rear*] Har they comes! [*The two brothers congeal into two stiff, grim-visaged statues.* EPHRAIM CABOT *and* ABBIE PUTNAM *come in.* CABOT *is seventy-five, tall and gaunt, with great, wiry, concentrated power, but stoop-shouldered from toil. His face is as hard as if it were hewn out of a boulder, yet there is a weakness in it, a petty pride in its own narrow strength. His eyes are small, close together, and extremely near-sighted, blinking continually in the effort to focus on objects, their stare having a straining, ingrowing quality. He is dressed in his dismal black Sunday suit.* ABBIE *is thirty-five, buxom, full of vitality. Her round face is pretty but marred by its rather gross sensuality. There is strength and obstinacy in her jaw, a hard determination in her eyes, and about her whole personality the same unsettled, untamed, desperate quality which is so apparent in* EBEN.]

CABOT. [*as they enter—a queer strangled emotion in his dry cracking voice*] Har we be t' hum, Abbie.

ABBIE. [*with lust for the word*] Hum! [*Her eyes gloating on the house without seeming to see the two stiff figures at the gate*] It's purty—purty! I can't b'lieve it's r'ally mine.

CABOT. [*sharply*] Yewr'n? Mine! [*He stares at her penetratingly. She stares back. He adds relentingly*] Our'n—mebbe! It was lonesome too long. I was growin' old in the spring. A hum's got t' hev a woman.

ABBIE. [*her voice taking possession*] A woman's got t' hev a hum!

CABOT. [*nodding uncertainly*] Ay-eh. [*Then irritably*] Whar be they? Ain't thar nobody about—'r wukin'—r' nothin'?

ABBIE. [*sees the brothers. She returns their stare of cold appraising contempt with interest—slowly*] Thar's two men loafin' at the gate an' starin' at me like a couple o' strayed hogs.

CABOT. [*straining his eyes*] I kin see 'em—but I can't make out. . . .

SIMEON. It's Simeon.

PETER. It's Peter.

CABOT. [*exploding*]. Why hain't ye wukin'?

SIMEON. [*dryly*] We're waitin' t' welcome ye hum—yew an' the bride!

CABOT. [*confusedly*] Huh? Waal—this be yer new Maw, boys. [*She stares at them and they at her.*]

SIMEON. [*turns away and spits contemptuously*] I see her!

PETER. [*spits also*] An' I see her!

ABBIE. [*with the conqueror's conscious superiority*] I'll go in an' look at *my* house. [*She goes slowly around to porch.*]

SIMEON. [*with a snort*] *Her* house!

PETER. [*calls after her*] Ye'll find Eben inside. Ye better not tell him it's *yewr* house.

ABBIE. [*mouthing the name*] Eben. [*Then quietly*] I'll tell Eben.

CABOT. [*with a contemptuous sneer*] Ye needn't heed Eben. Eben's a dumb fool—like his Maw—soft an' simple!

SIMEON. [*with his sardonic burst of laughter*] Ha! Eben's a chip o' yew—spit 'n' image—hard 'n' bitter's a hickory tree! Dog'll eat dog. He'll eat ye yet, old man!

CABOT. [*commandingly*] Ye git t' wuk!

SIMEON. [*as ABBIE disappears in house—winks at PETER and says tauntingly*] So that thar's our new Maw, be it? Whar in hell did ye dig her up? [*He and PETER laugh.*]

PETER. Ha! Ye'd better turn her in the pen with the other sows. [*They laugh uproariously, slapping their thighs.*]

CABOT. [*so amazed at their effrontery that he stutters in confusion*] Simeon! Peter! What's come over ye? Air ye drunk?

SIMEON. We're free, old man—free o' yew an' the hull damned farm! [*They grow more and more hilarious and excited.*]

PETER. An' we're startin' out fur the gold fields o' Californi-a!

SIMEON. Ye kin take this place an' burn it!

PETER. An' bury it—fur all we cares!

SIMEON. We're free, old man! [*He cuts a caper.*]

PETER. Free! [*He gives a kick in the air.*]

SIMEON. [*in a frenzy*] Whoop!

PETER. Whoop! [*They do an absurd Indian war dance about the old man who is petrified between rage and the fear that they are insane.*]

SIMEON. We're free as Injuns! Lucky we don't skulp ye!

PETER. An' burn yer barn an' kill the stock!

SIMEON. An' rape yer new woman! Whoop! [*He and PETER stop their dance, holding their sides, rocking with wild laughter.*]

CABOT. [*edging away*] Lust fur gold—fur the sinful, easy gold o' Californi-a! It's made ye mad!

SIMEON. [*tauntingly*] Wouldn't ye like us to send ye back some sinful gold, ye old sinner?

PETER. They's gold besides what's in Californi-a! [*He retreats back beyond the vision of the old man and takes the bag of money and flaunts it in the air above his head, laughing.*]

SIMEON. And sinfuller, too!

PETER. We'll be voyagin' on the sea! Whoop! [*He leaps up and down.*]

SIMEON. Livin' free! Whoop! [*He leaps in turn.*]

CABOT. [*suddenly roaring with rage*] My cuss on ye!

SIMEON. Take our'n in trade fur it! Whoop!

CABOT. I'll hev ye both chained up in the asylum!

PETER. Ye old skinflint! Good-by!

SIMEON. Ye old blood sucker! Good-by!

CABOT. Go afore I . . . !

PETER. Whoop! [*He picks a stone from the road.* SIMEON *does the same.*]

SIMEON. Maw'll be in the parlor.

PETER. Ay-eh! One! Two!

CABOT. [*frightened*] What air ye . . . ?

PETER. Three! [*They both throw, the stones hitting the parlor window with a crash of glass, tearing the shade.*]

SIMEON. Whoop!

PETER. Whoop!

CABOT. [*in a fury now, rushing toward them*] If I kin lay hands on ye—I'll break yer bones fur ye! [*But they beat a capering retreat before him,* SIMEON *with the gate still under his arm.* CABOT *comes back, panting with impotent rage. Their voices as they go off take up the song of the gold-seekers to the old tune of "Oh, Susannah!"*]

> "I jumped aboard the Liza ship,
> And traveled on the sea,
> And every time I thought of home
> I wished it wasn't me!
> Oh! Californi-a,
> That's the land fur me!
> I'm off to Californi-a!
> With my wash bowl on my knee."

[*In the meantime, the window of the bedroom on right is raised and* ABBIE *sticks her head out. She looks down at* CABOT *with a sigh of relief.*]

ABBIE. Waal—that's the last o' them two, hain't it? [*He doesn't answer. Then in possessive tones*] This here's a nice bedroom, Ephraim. It's a r'al nice bed. Is it my room, Ephraim?

CABOT. [*grimly—without looking up*] Our'n! [*She cannot control a grimace of aversion and pulls back her head slowly and shuts the window. A sudden horrible thought seems to enter* CABOT'S *head*] They been up to somethin'! Mebbe—mebbe they've pizened the stock—r' somethin'! [*He almost runs off down toward the barn. A moment later the kitchen door is slowly pushed open and* ABBIE *enters. For a moment she stands looking at* EBEN. *He does not notice her at first. Her eyes take him in penetratingly with a calculating appraisal of his strength as against hers. But under this her desire is dimly awakened by his youth and good looks. Suddenly he becomes conscious of her presence and looks up. Their eyes meet. He leaps to his feet, glowering at her speechlessly.*]

ABBIE. [*in her most seductive tones which she uses all through this scene*] Be you—Eben? I'm Abbie—[*She laughs*] I mean, I'm yer new Maw.

EBEN. [*viciously*] No, damn ye!

ABBIE. [*as if she hadn't heard—with a queer smile*] Yer Paw's spoke a lot o' yew. . . .

EBEN. Ha!

ABBIE. Ye mustn't mind him. He's an old man. [*A long pause. They stare at each other*] I don't want t' pretend playin' Maw t' ye, Eben. [*Admiringly*] Ye're too big an' too strong fur that. I want t' be frens with ye. Mebbe with me fur a fren ye'd find ye'd like livin' here better. I kin make it easy fur ye with him, mebbe. [*With a scornful sense of power*] I calc'late I kin git him t' do most anythin' fur me.

EBEN. [*with bitter scorn*] Ha! [*They stare again,* EBEN *obscurely moved, physically attracted to her—in forced stilted tones*] Yew kin go t' the devil!

ABBIE. [*calmly*] If cussin' me does ye good, cuss all ye've a mind t'. I'm all prepared t' have ye agin me—at fust. I don't blame ye nuther. I'd feel the same at any stranger comin' t' take my Maw's place. [*He shudders. She is watching him carefully*] Yew must've cared a lot fur yewr Maw, didn't ye? My Maw died afore I'd growed. I don't remember her none. [*A pause*] But yew won't hate me long, Eben. I'm not the wust in the world—an' yew an' me've got a lot in common. I kin tell that by lookin' at ye. Waal—I've had a hard life, too—oceans o' trouble an' nuthin' but wuk fur reward. I was a orphan early an' had t' wuk fur others in other folks' hums. Then I married an' he turned out a drunken spreer an' so he had to wuk fur others an' me too agen in other folks' hums, an' the baby died, an' my husband got sick an' died too, an' I was glad sayin' now I'm free fur once, on'y I diskivered right away all I was free fur was t' wuk agen in other folks' hums, doin' other folks' wuk till I'd most give up hope o' ever doin' my own wuk in my own hum, an' then your Paw come. . . . [CABOT *appears returning from the barn. He comes to the gate and looks down the road the brothers have gone. A faint strain of their retreating voices is heard:* "Oh, Californi-a! That's the place for me." *He stands glowering, his fist clenched, his face grim with rage.*]

EBEN. [*fighting against his growing attraction and sympathy—harshly*] An' bought yew —like a harlot! [*She is stung and flushes angrily. She has been sincerely moved by the recital of her troubles. He adds furiously*] An' the price he's payin' ye—this farm— was my Maw's, damn ye!—an' mine now!

ABBIE. [*with a cool laugh of confidence*] Yewr'n? We'll see 'bout that! [*Then strongly*] Waal—what if I did need a hum? What else'd I marry an old man like him fur?

EBEN. [*maliciously*] I'll tell him ye said that!

ABBIE. [*smiling*] I'll say ye're lyin' a-purpose—an' he'll drive ye off the place!

EBEN. Ye devil!

ABBIE. [*defying him*] This be my farm—this be my hum—this be my kitchen—!

EBEN. [*furiously, as if he were going to attack her*] Shut up, damn ye!

ABBIE. [*walks up to him—a queer coarse expression of desire in her face and body—slowly*] An' upstairs—that be my bedroom—an' my bed! [*He stares into her eyes, terribly confused and torn. She adds softly*] I hain't bad nor mean—'ceptin' fur an enemy— but I got t' fight fur what's due me out o' life, if I ever 'spect t' git it. [*Then putting her hand on his arm—seductively*] Let's yew 'n' me be frens, Eben.

EBEN. [*stupidly—as if hypnotized*] Ay-eh. [*Then furiously flinging off her arm*] No, ye durned old witch! I hate ye! [*He rushes out the door.*]

ABBIE. [*looks after him smiling satisfiedly—then half to herself, mouthing the word*] Eben's nice. [*She looks at the table, proudly*] I'll wash up *my* dishes now. [EBEN *appears outside, slamming the door behind him. He comes around corner, stops on seeing his father, and stands staring at him with hate.*]

CABOT. [*raising his arms to heaven in the fury he can no longer control*] Lord God o' Hosts, smite the undutiful sons with Thy wust cuss!

EBEN. [*breaking in violently*] Yew 'n' yewr God! Allus cussin' folks—allus naggin' 'em!

CABOT. [*oblivious to him—summoningly*] God o' the old! God o' the lonesome!

EBEN. [*mockingly*] Naggin' His sheep t' sin! T' hell with yewr God! [CABOT *turns. He and* EBEN *glower at each other.*]

CABOT. [*harshly*] So it's yew. I might've knowed it. [*Shaking his finger threateningly at him*] Blasphemin' fool! [*Then quickly*] Why hain't ye t' wuk?

EBEN. Why hain't yew? They've went. I can't wuk it all alone.

CABOT. [*contemptuously*] Nor noways! I'm wuth ten o' ye yit, old's I be! Ye'll never be more'n half a man! [*Then, matter-of-factly*] Waal—let's get t' the barn. [*They go. A last faint note of the "Californi-a" song is heard from the distance.* ABBIE *is washing her dishes.*]

CURTAIN

PART II

SCENE I

The exterior of the farmhouse, as in Part I—a hot Sunday afternoon two months later. ABBIE, *dressed in her best, is discovered sitting in a rocker at the end of the porch. She rocks listlessly, enervated by the heat, staring in front of her with bored, half-closed eyes.*

EBEN *sticks his head out of his bedroom window. He looks around furtively and tries to see—or hear—if anyone is on the porch, but although he has been careful to make no noise,* ABBIE *has sensed his movement. She stops rocking, her face grows animated and eager, she waits attentively.* EBEN *seems to feel her presence, he scowls back his thoughts of her and spits with exaggerated disdain—then withdraws back into the room.* ABBIE *waits, holding her breath as she listens with passionate eagerness for every sound within the house.*

EBEN *comes out. Their eyes meet; his falter. He is confused, he turns away and slams the door resentfully. At this gesture,* ABBIE *laughs tantalizingly, amused but at the same time piqued and irritated. He scowls, strides off the porch to the path and starts to walk past her to the road with a grand swagger of ignoring her existence. He is dressed in his store suit, spruced up, his face shines from soap and water.* ABBIE *leans forward on her chair, her eyes hard and angry now, and, as he passes her, gives a sneering, taunting chuckle.*

EBEN. [*stung—turns on her furiously*] What air yew cacklin' 'bout?

ABBIE. [*triumphant*] Yew!

EBEN. What about me?

ABBIE. Ye look all slicked up like a prize bull.

EBEN. [*with a sneer*] Waal—ye hain't so durned purty yerself, be ye? [*They stare into each other's eyes, his held by hers in spite of himself, hers glowingly possessive. Their physical attraction becomes a palpable force quivering in the hot air.*]

ABBIE. [*softly*] Ye don't mean that, Eben. Ye may think ye mean it, mebbe, but ye don't. Ye can't. It's agin nature, Eben. Ye been fightin' yer nature ever since the day I come—tryin t' tell yerself I hain't purty t'ye. [*She laughs a low humid laugh without taking her eyes from his. A pause—her body squirms desirously—she murmurs languorously*] Hain't the sun strong an' hot? Ye kin feel it burnin' into the earth—Nature—makin' thin's grow—bigger 'n' bigger—burnin' inside ye— makin' ye want t' grow—into somethin' else—till ye're jined with it—an' it's your'n—but it owns ye, too— an' makes ye grow bigger—like a tree—like them elums—[*She laughs again softly, holding his eyes. He takes a step toward her, compelled against his will*] Nature'll beat ye, Eben. Ye might's well own up t' it fust 's last.

EBEN. [*trying to break from her spell—confusedly*] If Paw'd hear ye goin' on.... [*Resentfully*] But ye've made such a damned idjit out o' the old devil...! [ABBIE *laughs.*]

ABBIE. Waal—hain't it easier fur yew with him changed softer?

EBEN. [*defiantly*] No. I'm fightin' him—fightin' yew—fightin' fur Maw's rights t'
her hum! [*This breaks her spell for him. He glowers at her*] An' I'm onto ye. Ye hain't
foolin' me a mite. Ye're aimin' t' swaller up everythin' an' make it your'n. Waal,
you'll find I'm a heap sight bigger hunk nor yew kin chew! [*He turns from her with
a sneer.*]

ABBIE. [*trying to regain her ascendancy—seductively*] Eben!

EBEN. Leave me be! [*He starts to walk away.*]

ABBIE. [*more commandingly*] Eben!

EBEN. [*stops—resentfully*] What d'ye want?

ABBIE. [*trying to conceal a growing excitement*] Whar air ye goin'?

EBEN. [*with malicious nonchalance*] Oh—up the road a spell.

ABBIE. T' the village?

EBEN. [*airily*] Mebbe.

ABBIE. [*excitedly*] T' see that Min, I s'pose?

EBEN. Mebbe.

ABBIE. [*weakly*] What d'ye want t' waste time on her fur?

EBEN. [*revenging himself now—grinning at her*] Ye can't beat Nature, didn't ye say?
[*He laughs and again starts to walk away.*]

ABBIE. [*bursting out*] An ugly old hake!

EBEN. [*with a tantalizing sneer*] She's purtier'n yew be!

ABBIE. That every wuthless drunk in the country has. . . .

EBEN. [*tauntingly*] Mebbe—but she's better'n yew. She owns up fa'r 'n' squar' t'
her doin's.

ABBIE. [*furiously*] Don't ye dare compare. . . .

EBEN. She don't go sneakin' an' stealin'—what's mine.

ABBIE. [*savagely seizing on his weak point*] Your'n? Yew mean—my farm?

EBEN. I mean the farm yew sold yerself fur like any other old whore—my farm!

ABBIE. [*stung—fiercely*] Ye'll never live t' see the day when even a stinkin' weed on
it'll belong t' ye! [*Then in a scream*] Git out o' my sight! Go on t' yer slut—
disgracin' yer Paw 'n' me! I'll git yer Paw t' horsewhip ye off the place if I want
t'! Ye're only livin' here 'cause I tolerate ye! Git along! I hate the sight o' ye! [*She
stops, panting and glaring at him.*]

EBEN. [*returning her glance in kind*] An' I hate the sight o' yew! [*He turns and strides
off up the road. She follows his retreating figure with concentrated hate. Old* CABOT
*appears coming up from the barn. The hard, grim expression of his face has changed. He
seems in some queer way softened, mellowed. His eyes have taken on a strange, incongruous dreamy quality. Yet there is no hint of physical weakness about him—rather he
looks more robust and younger.* ABBIE *sees him and turns away quickly with unconcealed
aversion. He comes slowly up to her.*]

CABOT. [*mildly*] War yew an' Eben quarrelin' agen?

ABBIE. [*shortly*] No.

CABOT. Ye was talkin' a'mighty loud. [*He sits down on the edge of porch.*]

ABBIE. [*snappishly*] If ye heerd us they hain't no need askin' questions.

CABOT. I didn't hear what ye said.

ABBIE. [*relieved*] Waal—it wa'n't nothin' t' speak on.

CABOT. [*after a pause*] Eben's queer.

ABBIE. [*bitterly*] He's the dead spit 'n' image o' yew!

CABOT. [*queerly interested*] D'ye think so, Abbie? [*After a pause, ruminatingly*] Me 'n'
Eben's allus fit 'n' fit. I never could b'ar him noways. He's so thunderin'
soft—like his Maw.

ABBIE. [*scornfully*] Ay-eh! 'Bout as soft as yew be!

Cabot. [*as if he hadn't heard*] Mebbe I been too hard on him.

Abbie. [*jeeringly*] Waal—ye're gittin' soft now—soft as slop! That's what Eben was sayin'.

Cabot. [*his face instantly grim and ominous*] Eben was sayin'? Waal, he'd best not do nothin' t' try me 'r he'll soon diskiver. . . . [*A pause. She keeps her face turned away. His gradually softens. He stares up at the sky*] Purty, hain't it?

Abbie. [*crossly*] I don't see nothin' purty.

Cabot. The sky. Feels like a wa'm field up thar.

Abbie. [*sarcastically*] Air yew aimin' t' buy up over the farm too? [*She snickers contemptuously.*]

Cabot. [*strangely*] I'd like t' own my place up thar. [*A pause*] I'm gittin' old, Abbie. I'm gittin' ripe on the bough. [*A pause. She stares at him mystified. He goes on*] It's allus lonesome cold in the house—even when it's bilin' hot outside. Hain't yew noticed?

Abbie. No.

Cabot. It's wa'm down t' the barn—nice smellin' an' warm—with the cows. [*A pause*] Cows is queer.

Abbie. Like yew?

Cabot. Like Eben. [*A pause*] I'm gittin' t' feel resigned t' Eben—jest as I got t' feel 'bout his Maw. I'm gittin' t' learn to b'ar his softness—jest like her'n I calc'late I c'd a'most take t' him—if he wa'n't sech a dumb fool! [*A pause*] I s'pose it's old age a-creepin' in my bones.

Abbie. [*indifferently*] Waal—ye hain't dead yet.

Cabot. [*roused*] No, I hain't, yew bet—not by a hell of a sight—I'm sound 'n' tough as hickory! [*Then moodily*] But arter three score and ten the Lord warns ye t' prepare. [*A pause*] That's why Eben's come in my head. Now that his cussed sinful brothers is gone their path t' hell, they's no one left but Eben.

Abbie. [*resentfully*] They's me, hain't they? [*Agitatedly*] What's all this sudden likin' ye've tuk to Eben? Why don't ye say nothin' 'bout me? Hain't I yer lawful wife?

Cabot. [*simply*] Ay-eh. Ye be. [*A pause—he stares at her desirously—his eyes grow avid—then with a sudden movement he seizes her hands and squeezes them, declaiming in a queer camp meeting preacher's tempo*] Yew air my Rose o' Sharon![4] Behold, yew air fair; yer eyes air doves; yer lips air like scarlet; yer two breasts air like two fawns; yer navel be like a round goblet; yer belly be like a heap o' wheat. . . . [*He covers her hand with kisses. She does not seem to notice. She stares before her with hard angry eyes.*]

Abbie. [*jerking her hands away—harshly*] So ye're plannin' t' leave the farm t' Eben, air ye?

Cabot. [*dazedly*] Leave . . . ? [*Then with resentful obstinacy*] I hain't a-givin' it t' no one!

Abbie. [*remorselessly*] Ye can't take it with ye.

Cabot. [*thinks a moment—then reluctantly*] No, I calc'late not. [*After a pause—with a strange passion*] But if I could, I would, by the Eternal! 'R if I could, in my dyin' hour, I'd set it afire an' watch it burn—this house an' every ear o' corn an' every tree down t' the last blade o' hay! I'd sit an' know it was all a'dying with me an' no one else'd ever own what was mine, what I'd made out o' nothin' with my own sweat 'n' blood! [*A pause—then he adds with a queer affection*] 'Ceptin' the cows. Them I'd turn free.

---

[4] Here, and in the following lines, Cabot is echoing the Song of Solomon in the Bible, one of the most impassioned love poems in all of literature.

ABBIE. [*harshly*] An' me?

CABOT. [*with a queer smile*] Ye'd be turned free, too.

ABBIE. [*furiously*] So that's the thanks I git fur marryin' ye—t' have ye change kind to Eben who hates ye, an' talk o' turnin' me out in the road.

CABOT. [*hastily*] Abbie! Ye know I wa'n't. . . .

ABBIE. [*vengefully*] Just let me tell ye a thing or two 'bout Eben! Whar's he gone? T' see that harlot, Min! I tried fur t' stop him. Disgracin' yew an' me—on the Sabbath, too!

CABOT. [*rather guiltily*] He's a sinner—nateral-born. It's lust eatin' his heart.

ABBIE. [*enraged beyond endurance—wildly vindictive*] An' his lust fur me! Kin ye find excuses fur that?

CABOT. [*stares at her—after a dead pause*] Lust—fur yew?

ABBIE. [*defiantly*] He was tryin' t' make love t' me—when ye heerd us quarrelin'.

CABOT. [*stares at her—then a terrible expression of rage comes over his face—he springs to his feet shaking all over*] By the A'mighty God—I'll end him!

ABBIE. [*frightened now for* EBEN] No! Don't ye!

CABOT. [*violently*] I'll git the shotgun an' blow his soft brains t' the top o' them elums!

ABBIE. [*throwing her arms around him*] No, Ephraim!

CABOT. [*pushing her away violently*] I will, by God!

ABBIE. [*in a quieting tone*] Listen, Ephraim. 'Twa'n't nothin' bad—on'y a boy's foolin'—'twa'n't meant serious—jest jokin' an' teasin'. . . .

CABOT. Then why did ye say—lust?

ABBIE. It must hev sounded wusser'n I meant. An' I was mad at thinkin'—ye'd leave him the farm.

CABOT. [*quieter but still grim and cruel*] Waal then, I'll horsewhip him off the place if that much'll content ye.

ABBIE. [*reaching out and taking his hand*] No. Don't think o' me! Ye mustn't drive him off. 'Tain't sensible. Who'll ye get to help ye on the farm? They's no one hereabouts.

CABOT. [*considers this—then nodding his appreciation.*] Ye got a head on ye. [*Then irritably*] Waal, let him stay. [*He sits down on the edge of the porch. She sits beside him. He murmurs contemptuously*] I oughtn't t' git riled so—at that 'ere fool calf. [*A pause*] But har's the p'int. What son o' mine'll keep on here t' the farm—when the Lord does call me? Simeon an' Peter air gone t' hell—an' Eben's follerin' 'em.

ABBIE. They's me.

CABOT. Ye're on'y a woman.

ABBIE. I'm yewr wife.

CABOT. That hain't me. A son is me—my blood—mine. Mine ought t' git mine. An' then it's still mine—even though I be six foot under. D'ye see?

ABBIE. [*giving him a look of hatred*] Ay-eh. I see. [*She becomes very thoughtful, her face growing shrewd, her eyes studying* CABOT *craftily.*]

CABOT. I'm gittin' old—ripe on the bough. [*Then with a sudden forced reassurance*] Not but what I hain't a hard nut t' crack even yet—an' fur many a year t' come! By the Etarnal, I kin break most o' the young fellers' backs at any kind o' work any day o' the year!

ABBIE. [*suddenly*] Mebbe the Lord'll give *us* a son.

CABOT. [*turns and stares at her eagerly*] Ye mean—a son—t' me 'n' yew?

ABBIE. [*with a cajoling smile*] Ye're a strong man yet, hain't ye? 'Tain't noways impossible, be it? We know that. Why d'ye stare so? Hain't ye never thought o' that afore? I been thinkin' o' it all along. Ay-eh—an' I been prayin' it'd happen, too.

CABOT. [*his face growing full of joyous pride and a sort of religious ecstasy*] Ye been prayin', Abbie?—fur a son?—t' us?

ABBIE. Ay-eh. [*With a grim resolution*] I want a son now.

CABOT. [*excitedly clutching both of her hands in his*] It'd be the blessin' o' God Abbie —the blessin' o' God A'mighty on me—in my old age—in my lonesomeness! They hain't nothin' I wouldn't do fur ye then, Abbie. Ye'd hev on'y t' ask it—anythin' ye'd a mind t'!

ABBIE. [*interrupting*] Would ye will the farm t' me then—t' me an' it . . .?

CABOT. [*vehemently*] I'd do anythin' ye axed, I tell ye! I swar it! May I be everlastin' damned t' hell if I wouldn't! [*He sinks to his knees pulling her down with him. He trembles all over with the fervor of his hopes*] Pray t' the Lord agen, Abbie. It's the Sabbath! I'll jine ye! Two prayers air better nor one. "An' God hearkened unto Rachel"![5] An' God hearkened unto Abbie! Pray, Abbie! Pray fur him to hear-ken! [*He bows his head, mumbling. She pretends to do likewise but gives him a side glance of scorn and triumph.*]

SCENE II

About eight in the evening. The interior of the two bedrooms on the top floor is shown. EBEN *is sitting on the side of his bed in the room on the left. On account of the heat he has taken off everything but his undershirt and pants. His feet are bare. He faces front, brooding moodily, his chin propped on his hands, a desperate expression on his face.*

In the other room CABOT *and* ABBIE *are sitting side by side on the edge of their bed, an old four-poster with feather mattress. He is in his night shirt, she in her nightdress. He is still in the queer, excited mood into which the notion of a son has thrown him. Both rooms are lighted dimly and flickeringly by tallow candles.*

CABOT. The farm needs a son.

ABBIE. I need a son.

CABOT. Ay-eh. Sometimes ye air the farm an' sometimes the farm be yew. That's why I clove t' ye in my lonesomeness. [*A pause. He pounds his knee with his fist*] Me an' the farm has got t' beget a son!

ABBIE. Ye'd best go t' sleep. Ye're gittin' thin's all mixed.

CABOT. [*with an impatient gesture*] No, I hain't. My mind's clear's a well. Ye don't know me, that's it. [*He stares hopelessly at the floor.*]

ABBIE. [*indifferently*] Mebbe. [*In the next room* EBEN *gets up and paces up and down distractedly.* ABBIE *hears him. Her eyes fasten on the intervening wall with concentrated attention.* EBEN *stops and stares. Their hot glances seem to meet through the wall. Unconsciously he stretches out his arms for her and she half rises. Then aware, he mutters a curse at himself and flings himself face downward on the bed, his clenched fists above his head, his face buried in the pillow.* ABBIE *relaxes with a faint sigh but her eyes remain fixed on the wall; she listens with all her attention for some movement from* EBEN.]

CABOT. [*suddenly raises his head and looks at her—scornfully*] Will ye ever know me—'r will any man 'r woman? [*Shaking his head*] No. I calc'late 't wa'n't t' be. [*He turns away.* ABBIE *looks at the wall. Then, evidently unable to keep silent about his thoughts, without looking at his wife, he puts out his hand and clutches her knee. She starts*

---

[5] The allusion is to Genesis 30:22. Rachel, the wife of Jacob, remained barren for many years until "God hearkened to her" and she bore Jacob a son in his old age.

violently, looks at him, sees he is not watching her, concentrates again on the wall and pays no attention to what he says] Listen, Abbie. When I come here fifty odd year ago—I was jest twenty an' the strongest an' hardest ye ever seen—ten times as strong an' fifty times as hard as Eben. Waal—this place was nothin' but fields o' stones. Folks laughed when I tuk it. They couldn't know what I knowed. When ye kin make corn sprout out o' stones, God's livin' in yew! They wa'n't strong enuf fur that! They reckoned God was easy. They laughed. They don't laugh no more. Some died here abouts. Some went West an' died. They're all under ground—fur follerin' arter an easy God. God hain't easy. [*He shakes his head slowly*] An' I growed hard. Folks kept allus sayin' he's a hard man like 'twas sinful t' be hard, so's at last I said back at 'em: Waal then, by thunder, ye'll git me hard an' see how ye like it! [*Then suddenly*] But I give in t' weakness once. 'Twas arter I'd been here two year. I got weak—despairful—they was so many stones. They was a party leavin', givin' up, goin' West. I jined 'em. We tracked on 'n on. We come t' broad medders, plains, whar the soil was black an' rich as gold. Nary a stone. Easy. Ye'd on'y to plow an' sow an' then set an' smoke yer pipe an' watch thin's grow. I could o' been a rich man—but somethin' in me fit me an' fit me—the voice o' God sayin': "This hain't wuth nothin' t' Me. Git ye back t' hum!" I got afeerd o' that voice an' I lit out back t' hum here, leavin' my claim an' crops t' whoever'd a mind t' take 'em. Ay-eh. I actoolly give up what was rightful mine! God's hard, not easy! God's in the stones! Build my church on a rock—out o' stones an' I'll be in them! That's what He meant t' Peter![6] [*He sighs heavily—a pause*] Stones. I picked 'em up an' piled 'em into walls. Ye kin read the years of my life in them walls, every day a hefted stone, climbin' over the hills up and down, fencin' in the fields that was mine, whar I'd make thin's grow out o' nothin'—like the will o' God, like the servant o' His hand. It wa'n't easy. It was hard an' He made me hard fur it. [*He pauses*] All the time I kept gittin' lonesomer. I tuk a wife. She bore Simeon an' Peter. She was a good woman. She wuked hard. We was married twenty year. She never knowed me. She helped but she never knowed what she was helpin'. I was allus lonesome. She died. After that it wa'n't so lonesome fur a spell. [*A pause*] I lost count o' the years. I had no time t' fool away countin' 'em. Sim an' Peter helped. The farm growed. It was all mine! When I thought o' that I didn't feel lonesome. [*A pause*] But ye can't hitch yer mind t' one thin' day an' night. I tuk another wife—Eben's Maw. Her folks was contestin' me at law over my deeds t' the farm—my farm! That's why Eben keeps a-talkin' his fool talk o' this bein' his Maw's farm. She bore Eben. She was purty—but soft. She tried t' be hard. She couldn't. She never knowed me nor nothin'. It was lonesomer 'n hell with her. After a matter o' sixteen odd years, she died. [*A pause*] I lived with the boys. They hated me 'cause I was hard. I hated them 'cause they was soft. They coveted the farm without knowin' what it meant. It made me bitter 'n wormwood. It aged me—them coveting what I'd made fur mine. Then this spring the call come—the voice o' God cryin' in my wilderness, in my lonesomeness—t' go out an' seek an' find! [*Turning to her with strange passion*] I sought ye an' I found ye! Yew air my Rose o' Sharon! Yer eyes air like. . . . [*She has turned a blank face, resentful eyes to his. He stares at her for a moment—then harshly*] Air ye any the wiser fur all I've told ye?

ABBIE. [*confusedly*] Mebbe.

---

[6] "Upon this rock I will build my church"—Matthew 16:18.

CABOT. [*pushing her away from him—angrily*] Ye don't know nothin'—nor never will. If ye don't hev a son t' redeem ye. . . . [*This in a tone of cold threat.*]

ABBIE. [*resentfully*] I've prayed, hain't I?

CABOT. [*bitterly*] Pray agen—fur understandin'!

ABBIE. [*a veiled threat in her tone*] Ye'll have a son out o' me, I promise ye.

CABOT. How kin ye promise?

ABBIE. I got second-sight mebbe. I kin foretell. [*She gives a queer smile.*]

CABOT. I believe ye have. Ye give me the chills sometimes. [*He shivers*] It's cold in this house. It's oneasy. They's thin's pokin' about in the dark—in the corners. [*He pulls on his trousers, tucking in his night shirt, and pulls on his boots.*]

ABBIE. [*surprised*] Whar air ye goin'?

CABOT. [*queerly*] Down whar it's restful—whar it's warm—down t' the barn. [*Bitterly*] I kin talk t' the cows. They know. They know the farm an' me. They'll give me peace. [*He turns to go out the door.*]

ABBIE. [*a bit frightenedly*] Air ye ailin' tonight, Ephraim?

CABOT. Growin'. Growin' ripe on the bough. [*He turns and goes, his boots clumping down the stairs. EBEN sits up with a start, listening. ABBIE is conscious of his movement and stares at the wall. CABOT comes out of the house around the corner and stands by the gate, blinking at the sky. He stretches up his hands in a tortured gesture*] God A'mighty, call from the dark! [*He listens as if expecting an answer. Then his arms drop, he shakes his head and plods off toward the barn. EBEN and ABBIE stare at each other through the wall. EBEN sighs heavily and ABBIE echoes it. Both become terribly nervous, uneasy. Finally ABBIE gets up and listens, her ear to the wall. He acts as if he saw every move she was making, he becomes resolutely still. She seems driven into a decision—goes out the door in rear determinedly. His eyes follow her. Then as the door of his room is opened softly, he turns away, waits in an attitude of strained fixity. ABBIE stands for a second staring at him, her eyes burning with desire. Then with a little cry she runs over and throws her arms about his neck, she pulls his head back and covers his mouth with kisses. At first, he submits dumbly; then he puts his arms about her neck and returns her kisses, but finally, suddenly aware of his hatred, he hurls her away from him, springing to his feet. They stand speechless and breathless, panting like two animals.*]

ABBIE. [*at last—painfully*] Ye shouldn't, Eben—ye shouldn't—I'd make ye happy!

EBEN. [*harshly*] I don't want t' be happy—from yew!

ABBIE. [*helplessly*] Ye do, Eben! Ye do! Why d'ye lie?

EBEN. [*viciously*] I don't take t'ye, I tell ye! I hate the sight o' ye!

ABBIE. [*with an uncertain troubled laugh*] Waal, I kissed ye anyways—an' ye kissed back—yer lips was burnin'—ye can't lie 'bout that! [*Intensely*] If ye don't care, why did ye kiss me back—why was yer lips burnin'?

EBEN. [*wiping his mouth*] It was like pizen on 'em. [*Then tauntingly*] When I kissed ye back, mebbe I thought 'twas someone else.

ABBIE. [*wildly*] Min?

EBEN. Mebbe.

ABBIE. [*torturedly*] Did ye go t' see her? Did ye r'ally go? I thought ye mightn't. Is that why ye throwed me off jest now?

EBEN. [*sneeringly*] What if it be?

ABBIE. [*raging*] Then ye're a dog, Eben Cabot!

EBEN. [*threateningly*] Ye can't talk that way t' me!

ABBIE. [*with a shrill laugh*] Can't I? Did ye think I was in love with ye—a weak thin' like yew? Not much! I on'y wanted ye fur a purpose o' my own—an' I'll hev ye fur it yet 'cause I'm stronger'n yew be!

EBEN. [*resentfully*] I knowed well it was on'y part o' yer plan t' swaller everythin'!

ABBIE. [*tauntingly*] Mebbe!

EBEN. [*furious*] Git out o' my room!

ABBIE. This air my room an' ye're on'y hired help!

EBEN. [*threateningly*] Git out afore I murder ye!

ABBIE. [*quite confident now*] I hain't a mite afeerd. Ye want me, don't ye? Yes, ye do! An' yer Paw's son'll never kill what he wants! Look at yer eyes! They's lust fur me in 'em, burnin' 'em up! Look at yer lips now! They're tremblin' an' longin' t' kiss me, an' yer teeth t' bite! [*He is watching her now with a horrible fascination. She laughs a crazy triumphant laugh*] I'm a-goin' t' make all o' this hum my hum! They's one room hain't mine yet, but it's a-goin' t' be tonight. I'm a-goin' down now an' light up! [*She makes him a mocking bow*] Won't ye come courtin' me in the best parlor, Mister Cabot?

EBEN. [*staring at her—horribly confused—dully*] Don't ye dare! It hain't been opened since Maw died an' was laid out thar! Don't ye . . . ! [*But her eyes are fixed on his so burningly that his will seems to wither before hers. He stands swaying toward her helplessly.*]

ABBIE. [*holding his eyes and putting all her will into her words as she backs out the door*] I'll expect ye afore long, Eben.

EBEN. [*stares after her for a while, walking toward the door. A light appears in the parlor window. He murmurs*] In the parlor? [*This seems to arouse connotations, for he comes back and puts on his white shirt, collar, half ties the tie mechanically, puts on coat, takes his hat, stands barefooted looking about him in bewilderment, mutters wonderingly*] Maw! Whar air yew? [*Then goes slowly toward the door in rear.*]

SCENE III

A few minutes later. The interior of the parlor is shown. A grim, repressed room like a tomb in which the family has been interred alive. ABBIE *sits on the edge of the horsehair sofa. She has lighted all the candles and the room is revealed in all its preserved ugliness. A change has come over the woman. She looks awed and frightened now, ready to run away.*

The door is opened and EBEN *appears. His face wears an expression of obsessed confusion. He stands staring at her, his arms hanging disjointedly from his shoulders, his feet bare, his hat in his hand.*

ABBIE. [*after a pause—with a nervous, formal politeness*] Won't ye set?

EBEN. [*dully*] Ay-eh. [*Mechanically he places his hat carefully on the floor near the door and sits stiffly beside her on the edge of the sofa. A pause. They both remain rigid, looking straight ahead with eyes full of fear.*]

ABBIE. When I fust come in—in the dark—they seemed somethin' here.

EBEN. [*simply*] Maw.

ABBIE. I kin still feel—somethin'. . . .

EBEN. It's Maw.

ABBIE. At fust I was feered o' it. I wanted t' yell an' run. Now—since yew come— seems like it's growin' soft an' kind t' me. [*Addressing the air—queerly*] Thank yew.

EBEN. Maw allus loved me.

ABBIE. Mebbe it knows I love yew, too. Mebbe that makes it kind t' me.

EBEN. [*dully*] I dunno. I should think she'd hate ye.

ABBIE. [*with certainty*] No. I kin feel it don't—not no more.

EBEN. Hate ye fur stealin' her place—here in her hum—settin' in her parlor whar she was laid—[*He suddenly stops, staring stupidly before him.*]

ABBIE. What is it, Eben?

EBEN. [*in a whisper*] Seems like Maw didn't want me t' remind ye.

ABBIE. [*excitedly*] I knowed, Eben! It's kind t' me! It don't b'ar me no grudges fur
  what I never knowed an' couldn't help!

EBEN. Maw b'ars him a grudge.

ABBIE. Waal, so does all o' us.

EBEN. Ay-eh. [*With passion*] I does, by God!

ABBIE. [*taking one of his hands in hers and patting it*] Thar! Don't git riled thinkin' o'
  him. Think o' yer Maw who's kind t' us. Tell me about yer Maw, Eben.

EBEN. They hain't nothin' much. She was kind. She was good.

ABBIE. [*putting one arm over his shoulder. He does not seem to notice—passionately*] I'll be
  kind an' good t' ye!

EBEN. Sometimes she used t' sing fur me.

ABBIE. I'll sing fur ye!

EBEN. This was her hum. This was her farm.

ABBIE. This is my hum! This is my farm!

EBEN. He married her t' steal 'em. She was soft an' easy. He couldn't 'preciate her.

ABBIE. He can't 'preciate me!

EBEN. He murdered her with his hardness.

ABBIE. He's murderin' me!

EBEN. She died. [*A pause*] Sometimes she used to sing fur me. [*He bursts into a fit
  of sobbing.*]

ABBIE. [*both her arms around him—with wild passion*] I'll sing fur ye! I'll die fur ye! [*In
  spite of her overwhelming desire for him, there is a sincere maternal love in her manner
  and voice—a horribly frank mixture of lust and mother love*] Don't cry, Eben! I'll take
  yer Maw's place! I'll be everythin' she was t' ye! Let me kiss ye, Eben! [*She pulls
  his head around. He makes a bewildered pretense of resistance. She is tender*] Don't be
  afeered! I'll kiss ye pure, Eben—same 's if I was a Maw t' ye—an' ye kin kiss me
  back 's if yew was my son—my boy—sayin' good-night t' me! Kiss me, Eben.
  [*They kiss in restrained fashion. Then suddenly wild passion overcomes her. She kisses
  him lustfully again and again and he flings his arms about her and returns her kisses.
  Suddenly, as in the bedroom, he frees himself from her violently and springs to his feet. He
  is trembling all over, in a strange state of terror.* ABBIE *strains her arms toward him with
  fierce pleading*] Don't ye leave me, Eben! Can't ye see it hain't enuf—lovin' ye
  like a Maw—can't ye see it's got t' be that an' more—much more—a hundred
  times more—fur me t' be happy—fur yew t' be happy?

EBEN. [*to the presence he feels in the room*] Maw! Maw! What d'ye want? What air ye
  tellin' me?

ABBIE. She's tellin' ye t' love me. She knows I love ye an' I'll be good t' ye. Can't
  ye feel it? Don't ye know? She's tellin' ye t' love me, Eben!

EBEN. Ay-eh. I feel—mebbe she—but—I can't figger out—why—when ye've stole
  her place—here in her hum—in the parlor whar she was—

ABBIE. [*fiercely*] She knows I love ye!

EBEN. [*his face suddenly lighting up with a fierce, triumphant grin*] I see it! I sees why.
  It's her vengeance on him—so's she kin rest quiet in her grave!

ABBIE. [*wildly*] Vengeance o' God on the hull o' us! What d'we give a durn? I love
  ye, Eben! God knows I love ye! [*She stretches out her arms for him.*]

EBEN. [*throws himself on his knees beside the sofa and grabs her in his arms—releasing
  all his pent-up passion*] An' I love ye, Abbie!—now I kin say it! I been dyin' fur
  want o' ye—every hour since ye come! I love ye! [*Their lips meet in a fierce,
  bruising kiss.*]

SCENE IV

Exterior of the farmhouse. It is just dawn. The front door at right is opened and EBEN *comes out and walks around to the gate. He is dressed in his working clothes. He seems changed. His face wears a bold and confident expression, he is grinning to himself with evident satisfaction. As he gets near the gate, the window of the parlor is heard opening and the shutters are flung back and* ABBIE *sticks her head out. Her hair tumbles over her shoulders in disarray, her face is flushed, she looks at* EBEN *with tender, langourous eyes and calls softly.*]

ABBIE. Eben. [*As he turns—playfully*] Jest one more kiss afore ye go. I'm goin' to miss ye fearful all day.

EBEN. An' me yew, ye kin bet! [*He goes to her. They kiss several times. He draws away, laughingly*] Thar. That's enuf, hain't it? Ye won't hev none left fur next time.

ABBIE. I got a million o' 'em left fur yew! [*Then a bit anxiously*] D'ye r'ally love me, Eben?

EBEN. [*emphatically*] I like ye better'n any gal I ever knowed! That's gospel!

ABBIE. Likin' hain't lovin'.

EBEN. Waal then—I love ye. Now air yew satisfied?

ABBIE. Ay-eh, I be. [*She smiles at him adoringly.*]

EBEN. I better git t' the barn. The old critter's liable t' suspicion an' come sneakin' up.

ABBIE. [*with a confident laugh*] Let him! I kin allus pull the wool over his eyes. I'm goin' t' leave the shutters open and let in the sun 'n' air. This room's been dead long enuf. Now it's goin' t' be my room!

EBEN. [*frowning*] Ay-eh.

ABBIE. [*hastily*] I meant—our room.

EBEN. Ay-eh.

ABBIE. We made it our'n last night, didn't we? We give it life—our lovin' did. [*A pause.*]

EBEN. [*with a strange look*] Maw's gone back t' her grave. She kin sleep now.

ABBIE. May she rest in peace! [*Then tenderly rebuking*] Ye oughtn't t' talk o' sad thin's —this mornin'.

EBEN. It jest come up in my mind o' itself.

ABBIE. Don't let it. [*He doesn't answer. She yawns*] Waal, I'm a-goin' t' steal a wink o' sleep. I'll tell the Old Man I hain't feelin' pert. Let him git his own vittles.

EBEN. I see him comin' from the barn. Ye better look smart an' git upstairs.

ABBIE. Ay-eh. Good-by. Don't ferget me. [*She throws him a kiss. He grins—then squares his shoulders and awaits his father confidently.* CABOT *walks slowly up from the left, staring up at the sky with a vague face.*]

EBEN. [*jovially*] Mornin', Paw. Star-gazin' in daylight?

CABOT. Purty, hain't it?

EBEN. [*looking around him possessively*] It's a durned purty farm.

CABOT. I mean the sky.

EBEN. [*grinning*] How d'ye know? Them eyes o' your'n can't see that fur. [*This tickles his humor and he slaps his thigh and laughs*] Ho-ho! That's a good un!

CABOT. [*grimly sarcastic*] Ye're feelin' right chipper, hain't ye? Whar'd ye steal the likker?

EBEN. [*good-naturedly*] 'Tain't likker. Jest life. [*Suddenly holding out his hand—soberly*] Yew 'n' me is quits. Let's shake hands.

CABOT. [*suspiciously*] What's come over ye?

EBEN. Then don't. Mebbe it's jest as well. [*A moment's pause*] What's come over me? [*Queerly*] Didn't ye feel her passin'—goin' back t' her grave?

CABOT. [*dully*] Who?

EBEN. Maw. She kin rest now an' sleep content. She's quits with ye.

CABOT. [*confusedly*] I rested. I slept good—down with the cows. They know how t' sleep. They're teachin' me.

EBEN. [*suddenly jovial again*] Good fur the cows! Waal—ye better git t' work.

CABOT. [*grimly amused*] Air yew bossin' me, ye calf?

EBEN. [*beginning to laugh*] Ay-eh! I'm bossin' yew! Ha-ha-ha! See how ye like it. Ha-ha-ha! I'm the prize rooster o' this roost. Ha-ha-ha! [*He goes off toward the barn laughing.*]

CABOT. [*looks after him with scornful pity*] Soft-headed. Like his Maw. Dead spit 'n' image. No hope in him! [*He spits with contemptuous disgust*] A born fool! [*Then matter-of-factly*] Waal—I'm gittin' peckish. [*He goes toward the door.*]

CURTAIN

PART III

SCENE I

A night in late spring the following year. The kitchen and the two bedrooms upstairs are shown. The two bedrooms are dimly lighted by a tallow candle in each. EBEN *is sitting on the side of the bed in his room, his chin propped on his fists, his face a study of the struggle he is making to understand his conflicting emotions. The noisy laughter and music from below where a kitchen dance is in progress annoy and distract him. He scowls at the floor.*

In the next room a cradle stands beside the double bed.

In the kitchen all is festivity. The stove has been taken down to give more room to the dancers. The chairs, with wooden benches added, have been pushed back against the walls. On these are seated, squeezed in tight against one another, farmers and their wives and their young folks of both sexes from the neighboring farms. They are all chattering and laughing loudly. They evidently have some secret joke in common. There is no end of winking, of nudging, of meaning nods of the head toward CABOT *who, in a state of extreme hilarious excitement increased by the amount he has drunk, is standing near the rear door where there is a small keg of whisky and serving drinks to all the men. In the left corner, front, dividing the attention with her husband,* ABBIE *is sitting in a rocking chair, a shawl wrapped about her shoulders. She is very pale, her face is thin and drawn, her eyes are fixed anxiously on the open door in rear as if waiting for someone.*

The musician is tuning up his fiddle, seated in the far right corner. He is a lanky young fellow with a long, weak face. His pale eyes blink incessantly and he grins about him slyly with a greedy malice.

ABBIE. [*suddenly turning to a young girl on her right*] Whar's Eben?

YOUNG GIRL. [*eying her scornfully*] I dunno, Mrs. Cabot. I hain't seen Eben in ages. [*Meaningly*] Seems like he's spent most o' his time t' hum since yew come.

ABBIE. [*vaguely*] I tuk his Maw's place.

YOUNG GIRL. Ay-eh. So I've heerd. [*She turns away to retail this bit of gossip to her mother sitting next to her.* ABBIE *turns to her left to a big stoutish middle-aged man whose flushed face and starting eyes show the amount of "likker" he has consumed.*]

ABBIE. Ye hain't seen Eben, hev ye?

MAN. No, I hain't. [*Then he adds with a wink*] If yew hain't, who would?

ABBIE. He's the best dancer in the county. He'd ought t' come an' dance.

MAN. [*with a wink*] Mebbe he's doin' the dutiful an' walkin' the kid t' sleep. It's a boy, hain't it?

ABBIE. [*nodding vaguely*] Ay-eh—born two weeks back—purty's a picter.

MAN. They all is—t' their Maws. [*Then in a whisper, with a nudge and a leer*] Listen, Abbie—if ye ever git tired o' Eben, remember me! Don't fergit now! [*He looks at her uncomprehending face for a second—then grunts disgustedly*] Waal—guess I'll likker agin. [*He goes over and joins* CABOT *who is arguing noisily with an old farmer over cows. They all drink.*]

ABBIE. [*This time appealing to nobody in particular*] Wonder what Eben's a-doin'? [*Her remark is repeated down the line with many a guffaw and titter until it reaches the fiddler. He fastens his blinking eyes on* ABBIE.]

FIDDLER. [*raising his voice*] Bet I kin tell ye, Abbie, what Eben's doin'! He's down t' the church offerin' up prayers o' thanksgivin'. [*They all titter expectantly.*]

A MAN. What fur? [*Another titter.*]

FIDDLER. 'Cause unto him a—[*He hesitates just long enough*] brother is born! [*A roar of laughter. They all look from* ABBIE *to* CABOT. *She is oblivious, staring at the door.* CABOT, *although he hasn't heard the words, is irritated by the laughter and steps forward, glaring about him. There is an immediate silence.*]

CABOT. What're ye all bleatin' about—like a flock o' goats? Why don't ye dance, damn ye? I axed ye here t' dance—t' eat, drink an' be merry—an' thar ye set cacklin' like a lot o' wet hens with the pip! Ye've swilled my likker an' guzzled my vittles like hogs, hain't ye? Then dance fur me, can't ye? That's fa'r an' squar', hain't it? [*A grumble of resentment goes around but they are all evidently in too much awe of him to express it openly.*]

FIDDLER. [*slyly*] We're waitin' fur Eben. [*A suppressed laugh.*]

CABOT. [*with a fierce exultation*] T'hell with Eben! Eben's done fur now! I got a new son! [*His mood switching with drunken suddenness*] But ye needn't t' laugh at Eben, none o' ye! He's my blood, if he be a dumb fool. He's better nor any o' yew! He kin do a day's work a'most up t' what I kin—an' that'd put any o' yew pore critters t' shame!

FIDDLER. An' he kin do a good night's work, too! [*A roar of laughter.*]

CABOT. Laugh, ye damn fools! Ye're right jist the same, Fiddler. He kin work day an' night too, like I kin, if need be!

OLD FARMER. [*from behind the keg where he is weaving drunkenly back and forth—with great simplicity*] They hain't many t' touch ye, Ephraim—a son at seventy-six. That's a hard man fur ye! I be on'y sixty-eight an' I couldn't do it. [*A roar of laughter in which* CABOT *joins uproariously.*]

CABOT. [*slapping him on the back*] I'm sorry fur ye, Hi. I'd never suspicion sech weakness from a boy like yew!

OLD FARMER. An' I never reckoned yew had it in ye nuther, Ephraim. [*There is another laugh.*]

CABOT. [*suddenly grim*] I got a lot in me—a hell of a lot—folks don't know on. [*Turning to the fiddler*] Fiddle 'er up, durn ye! Give 'em somethin' t' dance t'! What air ye, an ornament? Hain't this a celebration? Then grease yer elbow an' go it!

FIDDLER. [*seizes a drink which the* OLD FARMER *holds out to him and downs it*] Here goes! [*He starts to fiddle "Lady of the Lake." Four young fellows and four girls form in two lines and dance a square dance. The* FIDDLER *shouts directions for the different movements, keeping his words in the rhythm of the music and interspersing them with jocular personal remarks to the dancers themselves. The people seated along the walls stamp their feet and*] *clap their hands in unison.* CABOT *is especially active in this respect. Only* ABBIE *remains apathetic, staring at the door as if she were alone in a silent room.*]

FIDDLER. Swing your partner t' the right! That's it, Jim! Give her a b'ar hug. Her Maw hain't lookin'. [*Laughter*] Change partners! That suits ye, don't it, Essie, now ye got Reub afore ye? Look at her redden up, will ye? Waal, life is short an' so's love, as the feller says. [*Laughter.*]

CABOT. [*excitedly, stamping his foot*] Go it, boys! Go it, gals!

FIDDLER. [*with a wink at the others*] Ye're the spryest seventy-six ever I sees, Ephraim! Now if ye'd on'y good eye-sight . . . ! [*Suppressed laughter. He gives* CABOT *no chance to retort but roars*] Promenade! Ye're walkin' like a bride down the aisle, Sarah! Waal, while they's life they's allus hope, I've heerd tell. Swing your partner to the left! Gosh A'mighty, look at Johnny Cook high-steppin'! They hain't goin' t' be much strength left fur howin' in the corn lot t'morrow. [*Laughter.*]

CABOT. Go it! Go it! [*Then suddenly, unable to restrain himself any longer, he prances into the midst of the dancers, scattering them, waving his arms about wildly*] Ye're all hoofs! Git out o' my road! Give me room! I'll show ye dancin'. Ye're all too soft! [*He pushes them roughly away. They crowd back toward the walls, muttering, looking at him resentfully.*]

FIDDLER. [*jeeringly*] Go it, Ephraim! Go it! [*He starts "Pop, Goes the Weasel," increasing the tempo with every verse until at the end he is fiddling crazily as fast as he can go.*]

CABOT. [*starts to dance, which he does very well and with tremendous vigor. Then he begins to improvise, cuts incredibly grotesque capers, leaping up and cracking his heels together, prancing around in a circle with body bent in an Indian war dance, then suddenly straightening up and kicking as high as he can with both legs. He is like a monkey on a string. And all the while he intersperses his antics with shouts and derisive comments*] Whoop! Here's dancin' fur ye! Whoop! See that! Seventy-six, if I'm a day! Hard as iron yet! Beatin' the young 'uns like I allus done! Look at me! I'd invite ye t' dance on my hundredth birthday on'y ye'll all be dead by then. Ye're a sickly generation! Yer hearts air pink, not red! Yer veins is full o' mud an' water! I be the on'y man in the county! Whoop! See that! I'm a Injun! I've killed Injuns in the West afore ye was born—an' skulped 'em too! They's a arrer wound on my backside I c'd show ye! The hull tribe chased me. I outrun 'em all—with the arrer stuck in me! An' I tuk vengeance on 'em. Ten eyes fur an eye, that was my motter! Whoop! Look at me! I kin kick the ceilin' off the room! Whoop!

FIDDLER. [*stops playing—exhaustedly*] God A'mighty, I got enuf. Ye got the devil's strength in ye.

CABOT. [*delightedly*] Did I beat yew, too? Waal, ye played smart. Hev a swig. [*He pours whisky for himself and* FIDDLER. *They drink. The others watch* CABOT *silently with cold, hostile eyes. There is a dead pause. The* FIDDLER *rests.* CABOT *leans against the keg, panting, glaring around him confusedly. In the room above,* EBEN *gets to his feet and tiptoes out the door in rear, appearing a moment later in the other bedroom. He moves silently, even frightenedly, toward the cradle and stands there looking down at the baby. His face is as vague as his reactions are confused, but there is a trace of tenderness, of interested discovery. At the same moment that he reaches the cradle* ABBIE *seems to sense something. She gets up weakly and goes to* CABOT]

ABBIE. I'm goin' up t' the baby.

CABOT. [*with real solicitation*] Air ye able fur the stairs? D'ye want me t' help ye, Abbie?

ABBIE. No. I'm able. I'll be down agen soon.

CABOT. Don't ye git wore out! He needs ye, remember—our son does! [*He grins affectionately, patting her on the back. She shrinks from his touch.*]

ABBIE. [*dully*] Don't—tech me. I'm goin'—up. [*She goes.* CABOT *looks after her. A*

whisper goes around the room. CABOT *turns. It ceases. He wipes his forehead steaming
with sweat. He is breathing pantingly.*]

CABOT. I'm a-goin' out t' git fresh air. I'm feelin' a mite dizzy. Fiddle up thar!
Dance, all o' ye! Here's likker fur them as wants it. Enjoy yerselves. I'll be back.
[*He goes, closing the door behind him.*]

FIDDLER. [*sarcastically*] Don't hurry none on our account! [*A supressed laugh. He
imitates* ABBIE]. Whar's Eben? [*More laughter.*]

A WOMAN. [*loudly*] What's happened in this house is plain as the nose on yer face!
[ABBIE *appears in the doorway upstairs and stands looking in surprise and adoration at*
EBEN *who does not see her.*]

A MAN. Ssshh! He's li'ble t' be listenin' at the door. That'd be like him. [*Their
voices die to an intensive whispering. Their faces are concentrated on this gossip. A noise
as of dead leaves in the wind comes from the room.* CABOT *has come out from the porch
and stands by the gate, leaning on it, staring at the sky blinkingly.* ABBIE *comes across the
room silently.* EBEN *does not notice her until quite near.*]

EBEN. [*starting*] Abbie!

ABBIE. Ssshh! [*She throws her arms around him. They kiss—then bend over the cradle
together*] Ain't he purty?—dead spit 'n' image o' yew!

EBEN. [*pleased*] Air he? I can't tell none.

ABBIE. E-zactly like!

EBEN. [*frowningly*] I don't like this. I don't like lettin' on what's mine's his'n. I been
doin' that all my life. I'm gittin' t' the end o' b'arin' it!

ABBIE. [*putting her finger on his lips*] We're doin' the best we kin. We got t' wait.
Somethin's bound t' happen. [*She puts her arms around him*] I got t' go back.

EBEN. I'm goin' out. I can't b'ar it with the fiddle playin' an the laughin'.

ABBIE. Don't git feelin' low. I love ye, Eben. Kiss me. [*He kisses her. They remain in
each other's arms.*]

CABOT. [*at the gate, confusedly*] Even the music can't drive it out—somethin'. Ye kin
feel it droppin' off the elums, climbin' up the roof, sneakin' down the chimney,
pokin' in the corners! They's no peace in houses, they's no rest livin' with folks.
Somethin's always livin' with ye. [*With a deep sigh*] I'll go t' the barn an' rest a
spell. [*He goes wearily toward the barn.*]

FIDDLER. [*tuning up*] Let's celebrate the old skunk gittin' fooled! We kin have some
fun now he's went. [*He starts to fiddle "Turkey in the Straw." There is real merriment
now. The young folks get up to dance.*]

SCENE II

*A half hour later—Exterior—*EBEN *is standing by the gate looking up at the sky, an
expression of dumb pain bewildered by itself on his face.* CABOT *appears, returning from the
barn, walking wearily, his eyes on the ground. He sees* EBEN *and his whole mood immediately
changes. He becomes excited, a cruel, triumphant grin comes to his lips, he strides up and
slaps* EBEN *on the back. From within comes the whining of the fiddle and the noise of
stamping feet and laughing voices.*

CABOT. So har ye be!

EBEN. [*startled, stares at him with hatred for a moment—then dully*] Ay-eh.

CABOT. [*surveying him jeeringly*] Why hain't ye been in t' dance? They was all axin'
fur ye.

EBEN. Let 'em ax!

CABOT. They's a hull passel o' purty gals.

EBEN. T' hell with 'em!

CABOT. Ye'd ought t' be marryin' one o' 'em soon.

EBEN. I hain't marryin' no one.

CABOT. Ye might 'arn a share o' a farm that way.

EBEN. [*with a sneer*] Like yew did, ye mean? I hain't that kind.

CABOT. [*stung*] Ye lie! 'Twas yer Maw's folks aimed t' steal my farm from me.

EBEN. Other folks don't say so. [*After a pause—defiantly*] An' I got a farm, anyways!

CABOT. [*derisively*] Whar?

EBEN. [*stamps a foot on the ground*] Har!

CABOT. [*throws his head back and laughs coarsely*] Ho-ho! Ye hev, hev ye? Waal, that's a good un!

EBEN. [*controlling himself—grimly*] Ye'll see!

CABOT. [*stares at him suspiciously, trying to make him out—a pause—then with scornful confidence*] Ay-eh. I'll see. So'll ye. It's ye that's blind—blind as a mole underground. [EBEN *suddenly laughs, one short sardonic bark: "Ha." A pause.* CABOT *peers at him with renewed suspicion*] What air ye hawin' 'bout? [EBEN *turns away without answering.* CABOT *grows angry*] God A'mighty, yew air a dumb dunce! They's nothin' in that thick skull o' your'n but noise—like a empty keg it be! [EBEN *doesn't seem to hear.* CABOT's *rage grows*] Yewr farm! God A'mighty! If ye wa'n't a born donkey ye'd know ye'll never own stick nor stone on it, specially now arter him bein' born. It's his'n, I tell ye—his'n arter I die—but I'll live a hundred jest t' fool ye all—an' he'll be growed then—yewr age a'most! [EBEN *laughs again his sardonic "Ha." This drives* CABOT *into a fury*] Ha? Ye think ye kin git 'round that someways, do ye? Waal, it'll be her'n, too—Abbie's—ye won't git 'round her—she knows yer tricks—she'll be too much fur ye—she wants the farm her'n—she was afeerd o' ye—she told me ye was sneakin' 'round tryin' t' make love t' her t' git her on yer side ... ye ... ye mad fool, ye! [*He raises his clenched fists threateningly.*]

EBEN. [*is confronting him, choking with rage*] Ye lie, ye old skunk! Abbie never said no sech thing!

CABOT. [*suddenly triumphant when he sees how shaken* EBEN *is*] She did. An' I says, I'll blow his brains t' the top o' them elums—an' she says no, that hain't sense, who'll ye git t' help ye on the farm in his place—an' then she says yew'n me ought t' have a son—I know we kin, she says—an' I says, if we do, ye kin have anythin' I've got ye've a mind t'. An' she says, I wants Eben cut off so's this farm'll be mine when ye die! [*With terrible gloating*] An' that's what's happened, hain't it? An' the farm's her'n! An' the dust o' the road—that's you'rn! Ha! Now who's hawin'?

EBEN. [*has been listening, petrified with grief and rage—suddenly laughs wildly and brokenly*] Ha-ha-ha! So that's her sneakin' game—all along!—like I suspicioned at fust—t' swaller it all—an' me, too ... ! [*Madly*] I'll murder her! [*He springs toward the porch but* CABOT *is quicker and gets in between.*]

CABOT. No, ye don't!

EBEN. Git out o' my road! [*He tries to throw* CABOT *aside. They grapple in what becomes immediately a murderous struggle. The old man's concentrated strength is too much for* EBEN. CABOT *gets one hand on his throat and presses him back across the stone wall. At the same moment,* ABBIE *comes out on the porch. With a stifled cry she runs toward them.*]

ABBIE. Eben! Ephraim! [*She tugs at the hand on* EBEN's *throat*] Let go, Ephraim! Ye're chokin' him!

CABOT. [*removes his hand and flings* EBEN *sideways full length on the grass, gasping and choking. With a cry,* ABBIE *kneels beside him trying to take his head on her lap, but he pushes her away.* CABOT *stands looking down with fierce triumph*] Ye needn't t've fret, Abbie, I wa'n't aimin' t' kill him. He hain't wuth hangin' fur—not by a hell of a sight! [*More and more triumphantly*] Seventy-six an' him not thirty yit—an' look whar he be fur thinkin' his Paw was easy! No, by God, I hain't easy! An' him upstairs, I'll raise him t' be like me! [*He turns to leave them*] I'm goin' in an' dance!—sing an' celebrate! [*He walks to the porch—then turns with a great grin*] I don't calc'late it's left in him, but if he gits pesky, Abbie, ye jest sing out. I'll come a-runnin' an' by the Etarnal, I'll put him across my knee an' birch him! Ha-ha-ha! [*He goes into the house laughing. A moment later his loud "whoop" is heard.*]

ABBIE. [*tenderly*] Eben. Air ye hurt? [*She tries to kiss him but he pushes her violently away and struggles to a sitting position.*]

EBEN. [*gaspingly*] T'hell—with ye!

ABBIE. [*not believing her ears*] It's me, Eben—Abbie—don't ye know me?

EBEN. [*glowering at her with hatred*] Ay-eh—I know ye—now! [*He suddenly breaks down, sobbing weakly.*]

ABBIE. [*fearfully*] Eben—what's happened t' ye—why did ye look at me 's if ye hated me?

EBEN. [*violently, between sobs and gasps*] I do hate ye! Ye're a whore—a damn trickin' whore!

ABBIE. [*shrinking back horrified*] Eben! Ye don't know what ye're sayin'!

EBEN. [*scrambling to his feet and following her—accusingly*] Ye're nothin' but a stinkin' passel o' lies! Ye've been lyin' t' me every word ye spoke, day an' night, since we fust—done it. Ye've kept sayin' ye loved me. . . .

ABBIE. [*frantically*] I do love ye! [*She takes his hand but he flings hers away.*]

EBEN. [*unheeding*] Ye've made a fool o' me—a sick, dumb fool—a-purpose! Ye've been on'y playin' yer sneakin', stealin' game all along—gittin' me t' lie with ye so's ye'd hev a son he'd think was his'n, an' makin' him promise he'd give ye the farm and let me eat dust, if ye did git him a son! [*Staring at her with anguished, bewildered eyes*] They must be a devil livin' in ye! T'ain't human t' be as bad as that be!

ABBIE. [*stunned—dully*] He told yew . . . ?

EBEN. Hain't it true? It hain't no good in yew lyin'.

ABBIE. [*pleadingly*] Eben, listen—ye must listen—it was long ago—afore we done nothin'—yew was scornin' me—goin' t' see Min—when I was lovin' ye—an' I said it t' him t' git vengeance on ye!

EBEN. [*unheedingly. With tortured passion*] I wish ye was dead! I wish I was dead along with ye afore this come! [*Ragingly*] But I'll git my vengeance too! I'll pray Maw t' come back t' help me—t' put her cuss on yew an' him!

ABBIE. [*brokenly*] Don't ye, Eben! Don't ye! [*She throws herself on her knees before him, weeping*] I didn't mean t' do bad t' ye! Fergive me, won't ye?

EBEN. [*not seeming to hear her—fiercely*] I'll git squar' with the old skunk—an' yew! I'll tell him the truth 'bout the son he's so proud o'! Then I'll leave ye here t' pizen each other—with Maw comin' out o' her grave at nights—an' I'll go t' the gold fields o' Californi-a whar Sim an' Peter be!

ABBIE. [*terrified*] Ye won't leave me? Ye can't!

EBEN. [*with fierce determination*] I'm a-goin', I tell ye! I'll git rich thar an' come back an' fight him fur the farm he stole—an' I'll kick ye both out in the road—t' beg an' sleep in the woods—an' yer son along with ye—t' starve an' die! [*He is hysterical at the end.*]

ABBIE. [*with a shudder—humbly*] He's yewr son, too, Eben.

EBEN. [*torturedly*] I wish he never was born! I wish he'd die this minit! I wish I'd

never sot eyes on him! It's him—yew havin' him—a-purpose t' steal—that's
changed everythin'!

ABBIE. [*gently*] Did ye believe I loved ye—afore he come?

EBEN. Ay-eh—like a dumb ox!

ABBIE. An' ye don't believe no more?

EBEN. B'lieve a lyin' thief! Ha!

ABBIE. [*shudders—then humbly*] An' did ye r'ally love me afore?

EBEN. [*brokenly*] Ay-eh—an' ye was trickin' me!

ABBIE. An' ye don't love me now!

EBEN. [*violently*] I hate ye, I tell ye!

ABBIE. An' ye're truly goin' West—goin' t' leave me—all account o' him being
born?

EBEN. I'm a-goin' in the mornin'—or may God strike me t' hell!

ABBIE. [*after a pause—with a dreadful cold intensity—slowly*] If that's what his comin's
done t' me—killin' yewr love—takin' yew away—my on'y joy—the on'y joy I ever
knowed—like heaven t' me—purtier'n heaven—then I hate him, too, even if I
be his Maw!

EBEN. [*bitterly*] Lies! Ye love him! He'll steal the farm fur ye! [*Brokenly*] But t'ain't
the farm so much—not no more—it's yew foolin' me—gittin' me t' love ye—
lyin' yew loved me—jest t' git a son t' steal!

ABBIE. [*distractedly*] He won't steal! I'd kill him fust! I do love ye! I'll prove t' ye . . .!

EBEN. [*harshly*] T'ain't no use lyin' no more. I'm deaf t' ye! [*He turns away*] I hain't
seein' ye agen. Good-by!

ABBIE. [*pale with anguish*] Hain't ye even goin' t' kiss me—not once—arter all we
loved?

EBEN. [*in a hard voice*] I hain't wantin' t' kiss ye never agen! I'm wantin' t' forgit I
ever sot eyes on ye!

ABBIE. Eben!—ye mustn't—wait a spell—I want t' tell ye. . . .

EBEN. I'm a-goin' in t' git drunk. I'm a-goin' t' dance.

ABBIE. [*clinging to his arm—with passionate earnestness*] If I could make it—'s if he'd
never come up between us—if I could prove t' ye I wa'n't schemin' t' steal from
ye—so's everythin' could be jest the same with us, lovin' each other jest the
same, kissin' an' happy the same's we've been happy afore he come—if I could
do it—ye'd love me agen, wouldn't ye? Ye'd kiss me agen? Ye wouldn't never
leave me, would ye?

EBEN. [*moved*] I calc'late not. [*Then shaking her hand off his arm—with a bitter smile*]
But ye hain't God, be ye?

ABBIE. [*exultantly*] Remember ye've promised! [*Then with strange intensity*] Mebbe I
kin take back one thin' God does!

EBEN. [*peering at her*] Ye're gittin' cracked, hain't ye? [*Then going towards door*] I'm
a-goin' t' dance.

ABBIE. [*calls after him intensely*] I'll prove t' ye! I'll prove I love ye better'n. . . . [*He
goes in the door, not seeming to hear. She remains standing where she is looking after
him—then she finishes desperately*] Better'n everythin' else in the world!

SCENE III

Just before dawn in the morning—shows the kitchen and CABOT's *bedroom. In the kitchen,
by the light of a tallow candle on the table,* EBEN *is sitting, his chin propped on his hands,
his drawn face blank and expressionless. His carpetbag is on the floor beside him. In the
bedroom, dimly lighted by a small whale-oil lamp,* CABOT *lies asleep.* ABBIE *is bending over*

the cradle, listening, her face full of terror yet with an undercurrent of desperate triumph.
Suddenly, she breaks down and sobs, appears about to throw herself on her knees beside the
cradle; but the old man turns restlessly, groaning in his sleep, and she controls herself, and,
shrinking away from the cradle with a gesture of horror, backs swiftly toward the door in rear
and goes out. A moment later she comes into the kitchen and, running to EBEN, *flings her*
arms about his neck and kisses him wildly. He hardens himself, he remains unmoved and
cold, he keeps his eyes straight ahead.

ABBIE. [*hysterically*] I done it, Eben! I told ye I'd do it! I've proved I love ye—
    better'n everythin'—so's ye can't never doubt me no more!
EBEN. [*dully*] Whatever ye done, it hain't no good now.
ABBIE. [*wildly*] Don't ye say that! Kiss me, Eben, won't ye? I need ye t' kiss me arter
    what I done! I need ye t' say ye love me!
EBEN. [*kisses her without emotion—dully*] That's fur good-by. I'm a-goin' soon.
ABBIE. No! No! Ye won't go—not now!
EBEN. [*going on with his own thoughts*] I been a-thinkin'—an' I hain't goin' t' tell Paw
    nothin'. I'll leave Maw t' take vengeance on ye. If I told him, the old skunk'd jest
    be stinkin' mean enuf to take it out on that baby. [*His voice showing emotion in
    spite of him*] An' I don't want nothin' bad t' happen t' him. He hain't t' blame
    fur yew. [*He adds with a certain queer pride*] An' he looks like me! An' by God, he's
    mine! An' some day I'll be a-comin' back an' . . . !
ABBIE. [*too absorbed in her own thoughts to listen to him—pleadingly*] They's no cause fur
    ye t' go now—they's no sense—it's all the same's it was—they's nothin' come
    b'tween us now—arter what I done!
EBEN. [*something in her voice arouses him. He stares at her a bit frightenedly*] Ye look mad,
    Abbie. What did ye do?
ABBIE. I—I killed him, Eben.
EBEN. [*amazed*] Ye killed him?
ABBIE. [*dully*] Ay-eh.
EBEN. [*recovering from his astonishment—savagely*] An' serves him right! But we got t'
    do somethin' quick t' make it look s'if the old skunk'd killed himself when he
    was drunk. We kin prove by 'em all how drunk he got.
ABBIE. [*wildly*] No! No! Not him! [*Laughing distractedly*] But that's what I ought t'
    done, hain't it? I oughter killed him instead! Why didn't ye tell me?
EBEN. [*appalled*] Instead? What d'ye mean?
ABBIE. Not him.
EBEN. [*his face grown ghastly*] Not—not that baby!
ABBIE. [*dully*] Ay-eh!
EBEN. [*falls to his knees as if he'd been struck—his voice trembling with horror*] Oh, God
    A'mighty! A'mighty God! Maw, whar was ye, why didn't ye stop her?
ABBIE. [*simply*] She went back t' her grave that night we fust done it, remember?
    I hain't felt her about since. [*A pause.* EBEN *hides his head in his hands, trembling
    all over as if he had the ague. She goes on dully*] I left the piller over his little face.
    Then he killed himself. He stopped breathin'. [*She begins to weep softly.*]
EBEN. [*rage beginning to mingle with grief*] He looked like me. He was mine, damn ye!
ABBIE. [*slowly and brokenly*] I didn't want t' do it. I hated myself fur doin' it. I loved
    him. He was so purty—dead spit 'n' image o' yew. But I loved yew more—an'
    yew was goin' away—far off whar I'd never see ye agen, never kiss ye, never feel
    ye pressed agin me agen—an' ye said ye hated me fur havin' him—ye said ye
    hated him an' wished he was dead—ye said if it hadn't been fur him comin' it'd
    be the same's afore between us.

EBEN. [*unable to endure this, springs to his feet in a fury, threatening her, his twitching fingers seeming to reach out for her throat*] Ye lie! I never said—I never dreamed ye'd—I'd cut off my head afore I'd hurt his finger!

ABBIE. [*piteously, sinking on her knees*] Eben, don't ye look at me like that—hatin' me—not after what I done fur ye—fur us—so's we could be happy agen—

EBEN. [*furiously now*] Shut up, or I'll kill ye! I see yer game now—the same old sneakin' trick—ye're aimin' t' blame me fur the murder ye done!

ABBIE. [*moaning—putting her hands over her ears*] Don't ye, Eben! Don't ye! [*She grasps his legs.*]

EBEN. [*his mood suddenly changing to horror, shrinks away from her*] Don't ye tech me! Ye're pizen! How could ye—t' murder a pore little critter—Ye must've swapped yer soul t' hell! [*Suddenly raging*] Ha! I kin see why ye done it! Not the lies ye jest told—but 'cause ye wanted t' steal agen—steal the last thin' ye'd left me—my part o' him—no, the hull o' him—ye saw he looked like me—ye knowed he was all mine—an' ye couldn't b'ar it—I know ye! Ye killed him fur bein' mine! [*All this has driven him almost insane. He makes a rush past her for the door—then turns—shaking both fists at her, violently*] But I'll take vengeance now! I'll git the Sheriff! I'll tell him everythin'! Then I'll sing "I'm off to Californi-a!" an' go—gold—Golden Gate—gold sun—fields o' gold in the West! [*This last he half shouts, half croons incoherently, suddenly breaking off passionately*] I'm a-goin' fur the Sheriff t' come an' git ye! I want ye tuk away, locked up from me! I can't stand t' luk at ye! Murderer an' thief 'r not, ye still tempt me! I'll give ye up t' the Sheriff! [*He turns and runs out, around the corner of house, panting and sobbing, and breaks into a swerving sprint down the road.*]

ABBIE. [*struggling to her feet, runs to the door, calling after him*] I love ye, Eben! I love ye! [*She stops at the door weakly, swaying, about to fall*] I don't care what ye do—if ye'll on'y love me agen—[*She falls limply to the floor in a faint.*]

SCENE IV

About an hour later. Same as Scene iii. Shows the kitchen and CABOT's *bedroom. It is after dawn. The sky is brilliant with the sunrise. In the kitchen,* ABBIE *sits at the table, her body limp and exhausted, her head bowed down over her arms, her face hidden. Upstairs,* CABOT *is still asleep but awakens with a start. He looks toward the window and gives a snort of surprise and irritation—throws back the covers and begins hurriedly pulling on his clothes. Without looking behind him, he begins talking to* ABBIE *whom he supposes beside him.*

CABOT. Thunder 'n' lightin', Abbie! I hain't slept this late in fifty year! Looks 's if the sun was full riz a'most. Must've been the dancin' an' likker. Must be gittin' old. I hope Eben's t' wuk. Ye might've tuk the trouble t' rouse me, Abbie. [*He turns—sees no one there—surprised*] Waal—whar air she? Gittin' vittles, I calc'late. [*He tiptoes to the cradle and peers down—proudly*] Mornin', sonny. Purty's a picter! Sleepin' sound. He don't beller all night like most o' 'em. [*He goes quietly out the door in rear—a few moments later enters kitchen—sees* ABBIE —*with satisfaction*] So thar ye be. Ye got any vittles cooked?

ABBIE. [*without moving*] No.

CABOT. [*coming to her, almost sympathetically*] Ye feelin' sick?

ABBIE. No.

CABOT. [*pats her on shoulder. She shudders*] Ye'd best lie down a spell. [*Half jocularly*] Yer son'll be needin' ye soon. He'd ought t' wake up with a gnashin' appetite, the sound way he's sleepin'.

ABBIE. [*shudders—then in a dead voice*] He hain't never goin' t' wake up.

CABOT. [*jokingly*] Takes after me this mornin'. I hain't slept so late in . . .

ABBIE. He's dead.

CABOT. [*stares at her—bewilderedly*] What. . . .

ABBIE. I killed him.

CABOT. [*stepping back from her—aghast*] Air ye drunk—'r crazy—'r . . . !

ABBIE. [*suddenly lifts her head and turns on him—wildly*] I killed him, I tell ye! I
   smothered him. Go up an' see if ye don't b'lieve me! [CABOT *stares at her a second,
   then bolts out the rear door, can be heard bounding up the stairs, and rushes into the
   bedroom and over to the cradle.* ABBIE *has sunk back lifelessly into her former position.*
   CABOT *puts his hand down on the body in the crib. An expression of fear and horror comes
   over his face.*]

CABOT. [*shrinking away—tremblingly*] God A'mighty! God A'mighty. [*He stumbles out
   the door—in a short while returns to the kitchen—comes to* ABBIE, *the stunned expression
   still on his face—hoarsely*] Why did ye do it? Why? [*As she doesn't answer, he grabs
   her violently by the shoulder and shakes her*] I ax ye why ye done it! Ye'd better tell
   me 'r . . . !

ABBIE. [*gives him a furious push which sends him staggering back and springs to her
   feet—with wild rage and hatred*] Don't ye dare tech me! What right hev ye t'
   question me 'bout him? He wa'n't yewr son! Think I'd have a son by yew? I'd
   die fust! I hate the sight o' ye an' allus did! It's yew I should've murdered, if I'd
   had good sense! I hate ye! I love Eben. I did from the fust. An' he was Eben's
   son—mine an' Eben's—not your'n!

CABOT. [*stands looking at her dazedly—a pause—finding his words with an effort—dully*]
   That was it—what I felt—pokin' round the corners—while ye lied—holdin'
   yerself from me—sayin' ye'd a'ready conceived—*He lapses into crushed silence—
   then with a strange emotion*] He's dead, sart'n. I felt his heart. Pore little critter!
   [*He blinks back one tear, wiping his sleeve across his nose.*]

ABBIE. [*hysterically*] Don't ye! Don't ye! [*She sobs unrestrainedly.*]

CABOT. [*with a concentrated effort that stiffens his body into a rigid line and hardens his
   face into a stony mask—through his teeth to himself*] I got t' be—like a stone—a rock
   o' jedgment! [*A pause. He gets complete control over himself—harshly*] If he was
   Eben's, I be glad he air gone! An' mebbe I suspicioned it all along. I felt they
   was somethin' onnateral —somewhars—the house got so lonesome—an' cold—
   drivin' me down t' the barn—t' the beasts o' the field. . . . Ay-eh. I must've
   suspicioned—somethin'. Ye didn't fool me—not altogether, leastways—I'm too
   old a bird—growin' ripe on the bough. . . . [*He becomes aware he is wandering,
   straightens again, looks at* ABBIE *with a cruel grin*] So ye'd liked t' hev murdered me
   'stead o' him, would ye? Waal, I'll live to be a hundred! I'll live t' see ye hung!
   I'll deliver ye up t' the jedgment o' God an' the law! I'll git the Sheriff now.
   [*Starts for the door.*]

ABBIE. [*dully*] Ye needn't. Eben's gone fur him.

CABOT. [*amazed*] Eben—gone fur the Sheriff?

ABBIE. Ay-eh.

CABOT. T' inform agen ye?

ABBIE. Ay-eh.

CABOT. [*considers this—a pause—then in a hard voice*] Waal, I'm thankful fur him
   savin' me the trouble. I'll git t' wuk. [*He goes to the door—then turns—in a voice full
   of strange emotion*] He'd ought t' been my son, Abbie. Ye'd ought t' loved me. I'm
   a man. If ye'd loved me, I'd never told no Sheriff on ye no matter what ye did,
   if they was t' brile me alive!

ABBIE. [*defensively*] They's more to it nor yew know, makes him tell.

CABOT. [*dryly*] Fur yewr sake, I hope they be. [*He goes out—comes around to the gate—stares up at the sky. His control relaxes. For a moment he is old and weary. He murmurs despairingly*] God A'mighty, I be lonesomer'n ever! [*He hears running footsteps from the left, immediately is himself again.* EBEN *runs in, panting exhaustedly, wild-eyed and mad looking. He lurches through the gate.* CABOT *grabs him by the shoulder.* EBEN *stares at him dumbly*] Did ye tell the Sheriff?

EBEN. [*nodding stupidly*] Ay-eh.

CABOT. [*gives him a push away that sends him sprawling—laughing with withering contempt*] Good fur ye! A prime chip o' yer Maw ye be! [*He goes toward the barn, laughing harshly.* EBEN *scrambles to his feet. Suddenly* CABOT *turns—grimly threatening*] Git off this farm when the Sheriff takes her—or, by God, he'll have t' come back an' git me fur murder, too! [*He stalks off.* EBEN *does not appear to have heard him. He runs to the door and comes into the kitchen.* ABBIE *looks up with a cry of anguished joy.* EBEN *stumbles over and throws himself on his knees beside her sobbing brokenly.*]

EBEN. Fergive me!

ABBIE. [*happily*] Eben! [*She kisses him and pulls his head over against her breast.*]

EBEN. I love ye! Fergive me!

ABBIE. [*ecstatically*] I'd fergive ye all the sins in hell fur sayin' that! [*She kisses his head, pressing it to her with a fierce passion of possession.*]

EBEN. [*brokenly*] But I told the Sheriff. He's comin' fur ye!

ABBIE. I kin b'ar what happens t' me—now!

EBEN. I woke him up. I told him. He says, wait 'til I git dressed. I was waiting. I got to thinkin' o' yew. I got to thinkin' how I'd loved ye. It hurt like somethin' was bustin' in my chest an' head. I got t' cryin'. I knowed sudden I loved ye yet, an' allus would love ye!

ABBIE. [*caressing his hair—tenderly*] My boy, hain't ye!

EBEN. I begun t' run back. I cut across the fields an' through the woods. I thought ye might have time t' run away—with me—an' . . .

ABBIE. [*shaking her head*] I got t' take my punishment—t' pay fur my sin.

EBEN. Then I want t' share it with ye.

ABBIE. Ye didn't do nothin'.

EBEN. I put it in yer head. I wisht he was dead! I as much as urged ye t' do it!

ABBIE. No. It was me alone!

EBEN. I'm as guilty as yew be! He was the child o' our sin.

ABBIE. [*lifting her head as if defying God*] I don't repent that sin! I hain't askin' God t' fergive that!

EBEN. Nor me—but it led up t' the other—an' the murder ye did, ye did 'count o' me—an' it's my murder, too, I'll tell the Sheriff—an' if ye deny it, I'll say we planned it t'gether—an' they'll all b'lieve me, fur they suspicion everythin' we've done, an' it'll seem likely an' true to 'em. An' it is true—way down. I did help ye—somehow.

ABBIE. [*laying her head on his—sobbing*] No! I don't want yew t' suffer!

EBEN. I got t' pay fur my part o' the sin! An' I'd suffer wuss leavin' ye, goin' West, thinkin' o' ye day an' night, bein' out when yew was in—[*Lowering his voice*] 'r bein' alive when yew was dead. [*A pause*] I want t' share with ye, Abbie—prison 'r death 'r hell 'r anythin'! [*He looks into her eyes and forces a trembling smile*] If I'm sharin' with ye, I won't feel lonesome, leastways.

ABBIE. [*weakly*] Eben! I won't let ye! I can't let ye!

EBEN. [*kissing her—tenderly*] Ye can't he'p yerself. I got ye beat fur once!

ABBIE. [*forcing a smile—adoringly*] I hain't beat—s'long's I got ye!

EBEN. [*hears the sound of feet outside*] Ssshh! Listen! They've come t' take us!

ABBIE. No, it's him. Don't give him no chance to fight ye, Eben. Don't say noth-in'—no matter what he says. An' I won't neither. [*It is* CABOT. *He comes up from the barn in a great state of excitement and strides into the house and then into the kitchen.* EBEN *is kneeling beside* ABBIE, *his arm around her, hers around him. They stare straight ahead.*]

CABOT. [*stares at them, his face hard. A long pause—vindictively*] Ye make a slick pair o' murderin' turtle doves! Ye'd ought t' be both hung on the same limb an' left thar t' swing in the breeze an' rot—a warnin' t' old fools like me t' b'ar their lonesomeness alone—an' fur young fools like ye t' hobble their lust. [*A pause. The excitement returns to his face, his eyes snap, he looks a bit crazy*] I couldn't work today. I couldn't take no interest. T' hell with the farm! I'm leavin' it! I've turned the cows an' other stock loose! I've druv 'em into the woods whar they kin be free! By freein' 'em, I'm freein' myself! I'm quittin' here today! I'll set fire t' house an' barn an' watch 'em burn, an' I'll leave yer Maw t' haunt the ashes, an' I'll will the fields back t' God, so that nothin' human kin never touch 'em! I'll be a-goin' to Californi-a—t' jine Simeon an' Peter—true sons o' mine if they be dumb fools—an' the Cabots'll find Solomon's Mines t'gether! [*He suddenly cuts a mad caper*] Whoop! What was the song they sung? "Oh, Californi-a! That's the land fur me." [*He sings this—then gets on his knees by the floor-board under which the money was hid*] An' I'll sail thar on one o' the finest clippers I kin find! I've got the money! Pity ye didn't know whar this was hidden so's ye could steal. . . . [*He has pulled up the board. He stares—feels—stares again. A pause of dead silence. He slowly turns, slumping into a sitting position on the floor, his eyes like those of a dead fish, his face the sickly green of an attack of nausea. He swallows painfully several times—forces a weak smile at last*] So—ye did steal it!

EBEN. [*emotionlessly*] I swapped it t' Sim an' Peter fur their share o' the farm—t' pay their passage t' Californi-a.

CABOT. [*with one sardonic*] Ha! [*He begins to recover. Gets slowly to his feet—strangely*] I calc'late God give it to 'em—not yew! God's hard, not easy! Mebbe they's easy gold in the West but it hain't God's gold. It hain't fur me. I kin hear His voice warnin' me agen t' be hard an' stay on my farm. I kin see his hand usin' Eben t' steal t' keep me from weakness. I kin feel I be in the palm o' His hand, His fingers guidin' me. [*A pause—then he mutters sadly*] It's a-goin' t' be lonesomer now than ever it war afore—an' I'm gittin' old, Lord—ripe on the bough. . . . [*Then stiffening*] Waal—what d'ye want? God's lonesome, hain't He? God's hard an' lonesome! [*A pause. The* SHERIFF *with two men comes up the road from the left. They move cautiously to the door. The* SHERIFF *knocks on it with the butt of his pistol.*]

SHERIFF. Open in the name o' the law. [*They start.*]

CABOT. They've come fur ye. [*He goes to the rear door*] Come in, Jim! [*The three men enter.* CABOT *meets them in doorway*] Jest a minit, Jim. I got 'em safe here. [*The* SHERIFF *nods. He and his companions remain in the doorway.*]

EBEN. [*suddenly calls*] I lied this mornin', Jim. I helped her to do it. Ye kin take me, too.

ABBIE. [*brokenly*] No!

CABOT. Take 'em both. [*He comes forward—stares at* EBEN *with a trace of grudging admiration*] Purty good—fur yew! Waal, I got t' round up the stock. Good-by.

EBEN. Good-by.

ABBIE. Good-by. [CABOT *turns and strides past the men—comes out and around the corner of the house, his shoulders squared, his face stony, and stalks grimly toward the barn. In the meantime the* SHERIFF *and men have come into the room.*]

SHERIFF. [*embarrassedly*] Waal—we'd best start.

ABBIE. Wait. [*Turns to* EBEN] I love ye, Eben.

EBEN. I love ye, Abbie. [*They kiss. The three men grin and shuffle embarrassedly.* EBEN *takes* ABBIE'S *hand. They go out the door in rear, the men following, and come from the house, walking hand in hand to the gate.* EBEN *stops there and points to the sunrise sky*] Sun's a-rizin'. Purty, hain't it?

ABBIE. Ay-eh. [*They both stand for a moment looking up raptly in attitudes strangely aloof and devout.*]

SHERIFF. [*looking around at the farm enviously—to his companions*] It's a jim-dandy farm, no denyin'. Wished I owned it!

CURTAIN

[1924]

Tennessee Williams *1911–1983*

THE GLASS MENAGERIE

Scene:
An Alley in St. Louis

Part I. Preparation for a Gentleman Caller.
Part II. The Gentleman calls.

Time: *Now and the Past*

THE CHARACTERS

AMANDA WINGFIELD (*the mother*). A little woman of great but confused vitality clinging frantically to another time and place. Her characterization must be carefully created, not copied from type. She is not paranoiac, but her life is paranoia. There is much to admire in Amanda, and as much to love and pity as there is to laugh at. Certainly she has endurance and a kind of heroism, and though her foolishness makes her unwittingly cruel at times, there is tenderness in her slight person.

LAURA WINGFIELD (*her daughter*). Amanda, having failed to establish contact with reality, continues to live vitally in her illusions, but Laura's situation is even graver. A childhood illness has left her crippled, one leg slightly shorter than the other, and held in a brace. This defect need not be more than suggested on the stage. Stemming from this, Laura's separation increases till she is like a piece of her own glass collection, too exquisitely fragile to move from the shelf.

TOM WINGFIELD (*her son and the narrator of the play*). A poet with a job in a warehouse. His nature is not remorseless, but to escape from a trap he has to act without pity.

JIM O'CONNOR (*the gentleman caller*). A nice, ordinary, young man.

PRODUCTION NOTES

Being a "memory play," *The Glass Menagerie* can be presented with unusual free-dom of convention. Because of its considerably delicate or tenuous material, atmospheric touches and subtleties of direction play a particularly important part. Expressionism and all other unconventional techniques in drama have only one valid aim, and that is a closer approach to truth. When a play employs unconven-tional techniques, it is not, or certainly shouldn't be, trying to escape its respon-sibility of dealing with reality, or interpreting experience, but is actually or should be attempting to find a closer approach, a more penetrating and vivid expression of things as they are. The straight realistic play with its genuine Frigidaire and authentic ice-cubes, its characters who speak exactly as its audience speaks, cor-responds to the academic landscape and has the same virtue of a photographic

1544

likeness. Everyone should know nowadays the unimportance of the photographic in art: that truth, life, or reality is an organic thing which the poetic imagination can represent or suggest, in essence, only through transformation, through changing into other forms than those which were merely present in appearance.

These remarks are not meant as a preface only to this particular play. They have to do with a conception of a new, plastic theatre which must take the place of the exhausted theatre of realistic conventions if the theatre is to resume vitality as a part of our culture.

The Screen Device:

There is *only one important difference between the original and the acting version of the play* and that is the *omission* in the latter of the device that I tentatively included in my *original* script. This device was the use of a screen on which were projected magic-lantern slides bearing images or titles. I do not regret the omission of this device from the original Broadway production. The extraordinary power of Miss Taylor's[1] performance made it suitable to have the utmost simplicity in the physical production. But I think it may be interesting to some readers to see how this device was conceived. So I am putting it into the published manuscript. These images and legends, projected from behind, were cast on a section of wall between the front-room and dining-room areas, which should be indistinguishable from the rest when not in use.

The purpose of this will probably be apparent. It is to give accent to certain values in each scene. Each scene contains a particular point (or several) which is structurally the most important. In an episodic play, such as this, the basic structure or narrative line may be obscured from the audience; the effect may seem fragmentary rather than architectural. This may not be the fault of the play so much as the lack of attention in the audience. The legend or image upon the screen will strengthen the effect of what is merely allusion in the writing and allow the primary point to be made more simply and lightly than if the entire responsibility were on the spoken lines. Aside from this structural value, I think the screen will have a definite emotional appeal, less definable but just as important. An imaginative producer or director may invent many other uses for this device than those indicated in the present script. In fact the possibilities of the device seem much larger to me than the instance of this play can possibly utilize.

The Music:

Another extra-literary accent in this play is provided by the use of music.[2] A single recurring tune, "The Glass Menagerie," is used to give emotional emphasis to suitable passages. This tune is like circus music, not when you are on the grounds or in the immediate vicinity of the parade, but when you are at some distance and very likely thinking of something else. It seems under those circumstances to continue almost interminably and it weaves in and out of your preoccupied consciousness; then it is the lightest, most delicate music in the world and perhaps the saddest. It expresses the surface vivacity of life with the underlying strain of immutable and inexpressible sorrow. When you look at a piece of delicately spun glass you think of two things: how beautiful it is and how easily it can be broken.

---

[1] Laurette Taylor (1884–1946) played the part of Amanda in the original production of the play.
[2] Paul Bowles (1910–   ) composed the music for the first production.

Both of those ideas should be woven into the recurring tune, which dips in and out of the play as if it were carried on a wind that changes. It serves as a thread of connection and allusion between the narrator with his separate point in time and space and the subject of his story. Between each episode it returns as reference to the emotion, nostalgia, which is the first condition of the play. It is primarily Laura's music and therefore comes out most clearly when the play focuses upon her and the lovely fragility of glass which is her image.

The Lighting:

The lighting in the play is not realistic. In keeping with the atmosphere of memory, the stage is dim. Shafts of light are focused on selected areas or actors, sometimes in contradistinction to what is the apparent center. For instance, in the quarrel scene between Tom and Amanda, in which Laura has no active part, the clearest pool of light is on her figure. This is also true of the supper scene, when her silent figure on the sofa should remain the visual center. The light upon Laura should be distinct from the others, having a peculiar pristine clarity such as light used in early religious portraits of female saints or madonnas. A certain correspondence to light in religious paintings, such as El Greco's,[3] where the figures are radiant in atmosphere that is relatively dusky, could be effectively used throughout the play. (It will also permit a more effective use of the screen.) A free, imaginative use of light can be of enormous value in giving a mobile, plastic quality to plays of a more or less static nature.

Tennessee Williams

SCENE I

The Wingfield apartment is in the rear of the building, one of those vast hive-like conglomerations of cellular living-units that flower as warty growths in overcrowded urban centers of lower middle-class population and are symptomatic of the impulse of this largest and fundamentally enslaved section of American society to avoid fluidity and differentiation and to exist and function as one interfused mass of automatism.

The apartment faces an alley and is entered by a fire escape, a structure whose name is a touch of accidental poetic truth, for all of these huge buildings are always burning with the slow and implacable fires of human desperation. The fire escape is part of what we see — that is, the landing of it and steps descending from it.

The scene is memory and is therefore nonrealistic. Memory takes a lot of poetic license. It omits some details; others are exaggerated, according to the emotional value of the articles it touches, for memory is seated predominantly in the heart. The interior is therefore rather dim and poetic.

At the rise of the curtain, the audience is faced with the dark, grim rear wall of the Wingfield tenement. This building is flanked on both sides by dark, narrow alleys which run into murky canyons of tangled clotheslines, garbage cans, and the sinister latticework of neighboring fire escapes. It is up and down these side alleys that exterior entrances and exits are made during the play. At the end of TOM'S *opening commentary, the dark tenement wall slowly becomes transparent and reveals the interior of the ground-floor Wingfield apartment.*

Nearest the audience is the living room which also serves as a sleeping room for LAURA, *the sofa unfolding to make her bed. Just beyond, separated from the living room by a wide arch*

---

[3] El Greco (1541–1614) was born in Crete but painted primarily in Spain. His paintings are noted for their elongated human shapes, their odd color schemes, and their eerie lighting.

or second proscenium with transparent faded portieres (or second curtain), is the dining room. In an old-fashioned whatnot[4] in the living room are seen scores of transparent glass animals. A blown-up photograph of the father hangs on the wall of the living room, to the left of the archway. It is the face of a very handsome young man in a doughboy's[5] First World War cap. He is gallantly smiling, ineluctably smiling, as if to say "I will be smiling forever."

Also hanging on the wall, near the photograph, are a typewriter keyboard chart and a Gregg shorthand diagram. An upright typewriter on a small table stands beneath the charts.

The audience hears and sees the opening scene in the dining room through both the transparent fourth wall of the building and the transparent gauze portieres of the dining-room arch. It is during this revealing scene that the fourth wall slowly ascends, out of sight. This transparent exterior wall is not brought down again until the very end of the play, during TOM's final speech.

The narrator is an undisguised convention of the play. He takes whatever license with dramatic convention is convenient to his purposes.

TOM enters, dressed as a merchant sailor, and strolls across to the fire escape. There he stops and lights a cigarette. He addresses the audience.

TOM. Yes, I have tricks in my pocket, I have things up my sleeve. But I am the opposite of a stage magician. He gives you illusion that has the appearance of truth. I give you truth in the pleasant disguise of illusion.

To begin with, I turn back time. I reverse it to that quaint period, the thirties, when the huge middle class of America was matriculating in a school for the blind. Their eyes had failed them, or they had failed their eyes, and so they were having their fingers pressed forcibly down on the fiery Braille alphabet of a dissolving economy.

In Spain there was revolution.[6] Here there was only shouting and confusion. In Spain there was Guernica. Here there were disturbances of labor, sometimes pretty violent, in otherwise peaceful cities such as Chicago, Cleveland, Saint Louis . . . This is the social background of the play.

[*Music begins to play.*]

The play is memory. Being a memory play, it is dimly lighted, it is sentimental, it is not realistic. In memory everything seems to happen to music. That explains the fiddle in the wings.

I am the narrator of the play, and also a character in it. The other characters are my mother, Amanda, my sister, Laura, and a gentleman caller who appears in the final scenes. He is the most realistic character in the play, being an emissary from a world of reality that we were somehow set apart from. But since I have a poet's weakness for symbols, I am using this character also as a symbol; he is the long-delayed but always expected something that we live for.

There is a fifth character in the play who doesn't appear except in this larger-than-life-size photograph over the mantel. This is our father who left us a long time ago. He was a telephone man who fell in love with long distances; he gave up his job with the telephone company and skipped the light fantastic out of town . . .

---

[4] A stand with shelves for decorative articles.   [5] An American infantryman.
[6] The Spanish Civil War (1936–1939) pitted the Nationalist forces of Francisco Franco against a coalition of socialists, anarchists, and communists. Guernica in northern Spain was heavily damaged in 1937 by German bombers supporting Franco.

The last we heard of him was a picture postcard from Mazatlan, on the Pacific coast of Mexico, containing a message of two words: "Hello—Goodbye!" and no address.

I think the rest of the play will explain itself. . . .

[AMANDA's *voice becomes audible through the portieres.*]

[*Legend on screen:* "Ou sont les neiges."[7]]

[*TOM divides the portieres and enters the dining room.* AMANDA *and* LAURA *are seated at a drop-leaf table. Eating is indicated by gestures without food or utensils.* AMANDA *faces the audience.* TOM *and* LAURA *are seated in profile. The interior has lit up softly and through the scrim*[8] *we see* AMANDA *and* LAURA *seated at the table.*]

AMANDA [*calling*]. Tom?

TOM. Yes, Mother.

AMANDA. We can't say grace until you come to the table!

TOM. Coming, Mother. [*He bows slightly and withdraws, reappearing a few moments later in his place at the table.*]

AMANDA [*to her son*]. Honey, don't *push* with your *fingers.* If you have to push with something, the thing to push with is a crust of bread. And chew—chew! Animals have secretions in their stomachs which enable them to digest food without mastication, but human beings are supposed to chew their food before they swallow it down. Eat food leisurely, son, and really enjoy it. A well-cooked meal has lots of delicate flavors that have to be held in the mouth for appreciation. So chew your food and give your salivary glands a chance to function!

[*TOM deliberately lays his imaginary fork down and pushes his chair back from the table.*]

TOM. I haven't enjoyed one bite of this dinner because of your constant directions on how to eat it. It's you that make me rush through meals with your hawklike attention to every bite I take. Sickening—spoils my appetite—all this discussion of—animals' secretion—salivary glands—mastication!

AMANDA [*lightly*]. Temperament like a Metropolitan star![9]

[*TOM rises and walks toward the living room.*]

You're not excused from the table.

TOM. I'm getting a cigarette.

AMANDA. You smoke too much.

[*LAURA rises.*]

LAURA. I'll bring in the blanc mange.[10]

[*TOM remains standing with his cigarette by the portieres.*]

AMANDA [*rising*]. No, sister, no sister—you be the lady this time and I'll be the darky.

LAURA. I'm already up.

AMANDA. Resume your seat, little sister—I want you to stay fresh and pretty—for gentlemen callers!

LAURA [*sitting down*]. I'm not expecting any gentlemen callers.

AMANDA [*crossing out to the kitchenette, airily*]. Sometimes they come when they are least expected! Why, I remember one Sunday afternoon in Blue Mountain—

[*She enters the kitchenette.*]

TOM. I know what's coming!

---

[7] "Where are the snows [of yesteryear]," a line from a poem by François Villon (1431–1461?).

[8] A thin fabric curtain or screen which can be transparent or opaque, depending on the lighting.

[9] I.e., an opera star.

[10] A sweet pudding made with milk and cornstarch.

LAURA. Yes. But let her tell it.

TOM. Again?

LAURA. She loves to tell it.

[AMANDA *returns with a bowl of dessert.*]

AMANDA. One Sunday afternoon in Blue Mountain—your mother received—*seventeen!*—gentlemen callers! Why, sometimes there weren't chairs enough to accommodate them all. We had to send the nigger over to bring in folding chairs from the parish house.

TOM [*remaining at the portieres*]. How did you entertain those gentlemen callers?

AMANDA. I understood the art of conversation!

TOM. I bet you could talk.

AMANDA. Girls in those days *knew* how to talk, I can tell you.

TOM. Yes?

[*Image on screen:* AMANDA *as a girl on a porch, greeting callers.*]

AMANDA. They knew how to entertain their gentlemen callers. It wasn't enough for a girl to be possessed of a pretty face and a graceful figure—although I wasn't slighted in either respect. She also needed to have a nimble wit and a tongue to meet all occasions.

TOM. What did you talk about?

AMANDA. Things of importance going on in the world! Never anything coarse or common or vulgar.

[*She addresses* TOM *as though he were seated in the vacant chair at the table though he remains by the portieres.*[11] *He plays this scene as though reading from a script.*]

My callers were gentlemen—all! Among my callers were some of the most prominent young planters of the Mississippi Delta—planters and sons of planters!

[TOM *motions for music and a spot light on* AMANDA. *Her eyes lift, her face glows, her voice becomes rich and elegiac.*]

[*Screen legend:* "Ou sont les neiges d'antan?"]

There was young Champ Laughlin who later became vice-president of the Delta Planters Bank. Hadley Stevenson who was drowned in Moon Lake and left his widow one hundred and fifty thousand in Government bonds. There were the Cutrere brothers, Wesley and Bates. Bates was one of my bright particular beaux! He got in a quarrel with that wild Wainwright boy. They shot it out on the floor of Moon Lake Casino. Bates was shot through the stomach. Died in the ambulance on his way to Memphis. His widow was also well provided-for, came into eight or ten thousand acres, that's all. She married him on the rebound—never loved her—carried my picture on him the night he died! And there was that boy that every girl in the Delta had set her cap for! That beautiful, brilliant young Fitzhugh boy from Greene County!

TOM. What did he leave his widow?

AMANDA. He never married! Gracious, you talk as though all of my old admirers had turned up their toes to the daisies!

TOM. Isn't this the first you've mentioned that still survives?

AMANDA. That Fitzhugh boy went North and made a fortune—came to be known as the Wolf of Wall Street! He had the Midas touch, whatever he touched turned to gold! And I could have been Mrs. Duncan J. Fitzhugh, mind you! But—I picked your *father!*

---

[11] Curtains in a doorway.

LAURA [*rising*]. Mother, let me clear the table.

AMANDA. No, dear, you go in front and study your typewriter chart. Or practice your shorthand a little. Stay fresh and pretty!—It's almost time for our gentlemen callers to start arriving. [*She flounces girlishly toward the kitchenette.*] How many do you suppose we're going to entertain this afternoon?

[TOM *throws down the paper and jumps up with a groan.*]

LAURA [*alone in the dining room*]. I don't believe we're going to receive any, Mother.

AMANDA [*reappearing, airily*]. Why? No one—not one? You must be joking!

[LAURA *nervously echoes her laugh. She slips in a fugitive manner through the half-open portieres and draws them gently behind her. A shaft of very clear light is thrown on her face against the faded tapestry of the curtains. Faintly the music of "The Glass Menagerie" is heard as she continues, lightly.*]

Not one gentleman caller? It can't be true! There must be a flood, there must have been a tornado!

LAURA. It isn't a flood, it's not a tornado, Mother. I'm just not popular like you were in Blue Mountain. . . .

[TOM *utters another groan.* LAURA *glances at him with a faint, apologetic smile. Her voice catches a little:*]

Mother's afraid I'm going to be an old maid.

[*The scene dims out with the "Glass Menagerie" music.*]

SCENE II

On the dark stage the screen is lighted with the image of blue roses. Gradually LAURA'*s figure becomes apparent and the screen goes out. The music subsides.*

LAURA *is seated in the delicate ivory chair at the small claw-foot table. She wears a dress of soft violet material for a kimono—her hair is tied back from her forehead with a ribbon. She is washing and polishing her collection of glass.* AMANDA *appears on the fire escape steps. At the sound of her ascent,* LAURA *catches her breath, thrusts the bowl of ornaments away, and seats herself stiffly before the diagram of the typewriter keyboard as though it held her spellbound. Something has happened to* AMANDA. *It is written in her face as she climbs to the landing: a look that is grim and hopeless and a little absurd. She has on one of those cheap or imitation velvety-looking cloth coats with imitation fur collar. Her hat is five or six years old, one of those dreadful cloche[12] hats that were worn in the late Twenties, and she is clutching an enormous black patent-leather pocketbook with nickel clasps and initials. This is her full-dress outfit, the one she usually wears to the D.A.R.[13] Before entering she looks through the door. She purses her lips, opens her eyes very wide, rolls them upward and shakes her head. Then she slowly lets herself in the door. Seeing her mother's expression* LAURA *touches her lips with a nervous gesture.*

LAURA. Hello, Mother, I was— [*She makes a nervous gesture toward the chart on the wall.* AMANDA *leans against the shut door and stares at* LAURA *with a martyred look.*]

AMANDA. Deception? Deception? [*She slowly removes her hat and gloves, continuing the sweet suffering stare. She lets the hat and gloves fall on the floor—a bit of acting.*]

LAURA [*shakily*]. How was the D.A.R. meeting?

[AMANDA *slowly opens her purse and removes a dainty white handkerchief which she shakes out delicately and delicately touches to her lips and nostrils.*]

Didn't you go to the D.A.R. meeting, Mother?

[12] A bell-shaped, close-fitting hat.
[13] Daughters of the American Revolution, an organization for women whose ancestors fought the British in the Revolutionary War.

AMANDA [*faintly, almost inaudibly*]. —No.—No. [*then more forcibly:*] I did not have the strength—to go to the D.A.R. In fact, I did not have the courage! I wanted to find a hole in the ground and hide myself in it forever! [*She crosses slowly to the wall and removes the diagram of the typewriter keyboard. She holds it in front of her for a second, staring at it sweetly and sorrowfully—then bites her lips and tears it in two pieces.*]

LAURA [*faintly*]. Why did you do that, Mother?

[AMANDA *repeats the same procedure with the chart of the Gregg Alphabet.*]

Why are you—

AMANDA. Why? Why? How old are you, Laura?

LAURA: Mother, you know my age.

AMANDA. I thought that you were an adult; it seems that I was mistaken. [*She crosses slowly to the sofa and sinks down and stares at* LAURA.]

LAURA. Please don't stare at me, Mother.

[AMANDA *closes her eyes and lowers her head. There is a ten-second pause.*]

AMANDA. What are we going to do, what is going to become of us, what is the future?

[*There is another pause.*]

LAURA. Has something happened, Mother? [AMANDA *draws a long breath, takes out the handkerchief again, goes through the dabbing process.*] Mother, has—something happened?

AMANDA. I'll be all right in a minute, I'm just bewildered—[*She hesitates.*]—by life. . . .

LAURA. Mother, I wish that you would tell me what's happened!

AMANDA. As you know, I was supposed to be inducted into my office at the D.A.R. this afternoon.

[*Screen image:* A swarm of typewriters.]

But I stopped off at Rubicam's Business College to speak to your teacher about your having a cold and ask them what progress they thought you were making down there.

LAURA. Oh. . . .

AMANDA. I went to the typing instructor and introduced myself as your mother. She didn't know who you were. "Wingfield," she said, "We don't have any such student enrolled at the school!"

I assured her she did, that you had been going to classes since early in January.

"I wonder," she said, "If you could be talking about that terribly shy little girl who dropped out of school after only a few days' attendance?"

"No," I said, "Laura, my daughter, has been going to school every day for the past six weeks!"

"Excuse me," she said. She took the attendance book out and there was your name, unmistakably printed, and all the dates you were absent until they decided that you had dropped out of school.

I still said, "No, there must have been some mistake! There must have been some mix-up in the records!"

And she said, "No—I remember her perfectly now. Her hands shook so that she couldn't hit the right keys! The first time we gave a speed test, she broke down completely—was sick at the stomach and almost had to be carried into the wash room! After that morning she never showed up any more. We phoned the house but never got any answer"—While I was working at Famous–Barr, I suppose, demonstrating those—

[*She indicates a brassiere with her hands.*]

Oh! I felt so weak I could barely keep on my feet! I had to sit down while they got me a glass of water! Fifty dollars' tuition, all of our plans—my hopes and ambitions for you—just gone up the spout, just gone up the spout like that. [LAURA *draws a long breath and gets awkwardly to her feet. She crosses to the Victrola*[14] *and winds it up.*] What are you doing?

LAURA. Oh! [*She releases the handle and returns to her seat.*]

AMANDA. Laura, where have you been going when you've gone out pretending that you were going to business college?

LAURA. I've just been going out walking.

AMANDA. That's not true.

LAURA. It is. I just went walking.

AMANDA. Walking? Walking? In winter? Deliberately courting pneumonia in that light coat? Where did you walk to, Laura?

LAURA. All sorts of places—mostly in the park.

AMANDA. Even after you'd started catching that cold?

LAURA. It was the lesser of two evils, Mother.

[*Screen image:* Winter scene in a park.]

I couldn't go back there. I—threw up—on the floor!

AMANDA. From half past seven till after five every day you mean to tell me you walked around the park, because you wanted to make me think that you were still going to Rubicam's Business College?

LAURA. It wasn't as bad as it sounds. I went inside places to get warmed up.

AMANDA. Inside where?

LAURA. I went in the art museum and the bird houses at the Zoo. I visited the penguins every day! Sometimes I did without lunch and went to the movies. Lately I've been spending most of my afternoons in the Jewel Box, that big glass house where they raise the tropical flowers.

AMANDA. You did all this to deceive me, just for deception? [LAURA *looks down.*] Why?

LAURA. Mother, when you're disappointed, you get that awful suffering look on your face, like the picture of Jesus' mother in the museum!

AMANDA. Hush!

LAURA. I couldn't face it.

[*There is a pause. A whisper of strings is heard. Legend on screen:* "The Crust of Humility."]

AMANDA [*hopelessly fingering the huge pocketbook*]. So what are we going to do the rest of our lives? Stay home and watch the parades go by? Amuse ourselves with the glass menagerie, darling? Eternally play those worn-out phonograph records your father left as a painful reminder of him? We won't have a business career— we've given that up because it gave us nervous indigestion! [*She laughs wearily.*] What is there left but dependency all our lives? I know so well what becomes of unmarried women who aren't prepared to occupy a position. I've seen such pitiful cases in the South—barely tolerated spinsters living upon the grudging patronage of sister's husband or brother's wife!—stuck away in some little mousetrap of a room—encouraged by one in-law to visit another—little birdlike women without any nest—eating the crust of humility all their life!

Is that the future that we've mapped out for ourselves? I swear it's the only alternative I can think of! [*She pauses.*] It isn't a very pleasant alternative, is it?

---

[14] A brand name that is often used generically for an early record player.

[*She pauses again.*] Of course—some girls *do marry.*

[LAURA *twists her hands nervously.*]

Haven't you ever liked some boy?

LAURA. Yes. I liked one once. [*She rises.*] I came across his picture a while ago.

AMANDA [*with some interest*]. He gave you his picture?

LAURA. No, it's in the yearbook.

AMANDA [*disappointed*]. Oh—a high school boy.

[*Screen image:* Jim as the high school hero bearing a silver cup.]

LAURA. Yes. His name was Jim. [*She lifts the heavy annual from the claw-foot table.*] Here he is in *The Pirates of Penzance.*[15]

AMANDA [*absently*]. The what?

LAURA. The operetta the senior class put on. He had a wonderful voice and we sat across the aisle from each other Mondays, Wednesdays and Fridays in the Aud. Here he is with the silver cup for debating! See his grin?

AMANDA [*absently*]. He must have had a jolly disposition.

LAURA. He used to call me—Blue Roses.

[*Screen image:* Blue roses.]

AMANDA. Why did he call you such a name as that?

LAURA. When I had that attack of pleurosis—he asked me what was the matter when I came back. I said pleurosis—he thought that I said Blue Roses! So that's what he always called me after that. Whenever he saw me, he'd holler, "Hello, Blue Roses!" I didn't care for the girl that he went out with. Emily Meisenbach. Emily was the best-dressed girl at Soldan. She never struck me, though, as being sincere . . . It says in the Personal Section—they're engaged. That's—six years ago! They must be married by now.

AMANDA. Girls that aren't cut out for business careers usually wind up married to some nice man. [*She gets up with a spark of revival.*] Sister, that's what you'll do!

[LAURA *utters a startled, doubtful laugh. She reaches quickly for a piece of glass.*]

LAURA. But, Mother—

AMANDA. Yes? [*She goes over to the photograph.*]

LAURA [*in a tone of frightened apology*]. I'm—crippled!

AMANDA. Nonsense! Laura, I've told you never, never to use that word. Why, you're not crippled, you just have a little defect—hardly noticeable, even! When people have some slight disadvantage like that, they cultivate other things to make up for it—develop charm—and vivacity—and—*charm!* That's all you have to do! [*She turns again to the photograph.*] One thing your father had *plenty of*—was *charm!*

[*The scene fades out with music.*]

SCENE III

Legend on screen: "After the fiasco—"

TOM *speaks from the fire escape landing.*

TOM. After the fiasco at Rubicam's Business College, the idea of getting a gentleman caller for Laura began to play a more and more important part in Mother's calculations. It became an obsession. Like some archetype of the universal

---

[15] A comic opera written in 1879 by Sir William Schwenck Gilbert (1836–1911) and Sir Arthur Sullivan (1842–1900).

unconscious, the image of the gentleman caller haunted our small apartment. . . .

[*Screen image:* A young man at the door of a house with flowers.]

An evening at home rarely passed without some allusion to this image, this specter, this hope. . . . Even when he wasn't mentioned, his presence hung in Mother's preoccupied look and in my sister's frightened, apologetic manner—hung like a sentence passed upon the Wingfields!

Mother was a woman of action as well as words. She began to take logical steps in the planned direction. Late that winter and in the early spring—realizing that extra money would be needed to properly feather the nest and plume the bird—she conducted a vigorous campaign on the telephone, roping in subscribers to one of those magazines for matrons called *The Homemaker's Companion,* the type of journal that features the serialized sublimations of ladies of letters who think in terms of delicate cuplike breasts, slim, tapering waists, rich, creamy thighs, eyes like wood smoke in autumn, fingers that soothe and caress like strains of music, bodies as powerful as Etruscan sculpture.[16]

[*Screen image:* The cover of a glamor magazine.]

[AMANDA *enters with the telephone on a long extension cord. She is spotlighted in the dim stage.*]

AMANDA. Ida Scott? This is Amanda Wingfield! We *missed* you at the D.A.R. last Monday! I said to myself: She's probably suffering with that sinus condition! How is that sinus condition?

Horrors! Heaven have mercy!—You're a Christian matryr, yes, that's what you are, a Christian martyr!

Well, I just now happened to notice that your subscription to the *Companion's* about to expire! Yes, it expires with the next issue, honey!—just when that wonderful new serial by Bessie Mae Hopper is getting off to such an exciting start. Oh, honey, it's something that you can't miss! You remember how *Gone with the Wind* took everybody by storm? You simply couldn't go out if you hadn't read it. All everybody *talked* was Scarlett O'Hara. Well, this is a book that critics already compare to *Gone with the Wind*. It's the *Gone with the Wind* of the post-World-War generation!—What?—Burning?—Oh, honey, don't let them burn, go take a look in the oven and I'll hold the wire! Heavens—I think she's hung up!

[*The scene dims out.*]

[*Legend on screen:* "You think I'm in love with Continental Shoemakers?"]

[*Before the lights come up again, the violent voices of* TOM *and* AMANDA *are heard. They are quarreling behind the portieres. In front of them stands* LAURA *with clenched hands and panicky expression. A clear pool of light is on her figure throughout this scene.*]

TOM. What in Christ's name am I—

AMANDA [*shrilly*]. Don't you use that—

TOM. —supposed to do!

AMANDA. —expression! Not in my—

TOM. Ohhh!

AMANDA. —presence! Have you gone out of your senses?

TOM. I have, that's true, *driven* out!

AMANDA. What is the matter with you, you—big—big—IDIOT!

TOM. Look!—I've got *no thing*, no single thing—

[16] The Etruscans who dominated central Italy in the fifth century B.C. were noted for their naturalistic sculpture.

AMANDA. Lower your voice!

TOM. —in my life here that I can call my OWN! Everything is—

AMANDA. Stop that shouting!

TOM. Yesterday you confiscated my books! You had the nerve to—

AMANDA. I took that horrible novel back to the library—yes! That hideous book by that insane Mr. Lawrence.[17]

[TOM *laughs wildly.*]

I cannot control the output of diseased minds or people who cater to them—

[TOM *laughs still more wildly.*]

BUT I WON'T ALLOW SUCH FILTH BROUGHT INTO MY HOUSE! No, no, no, no, no!

TOM. House, house! Who pays rent on it, who makes a slave of himself to—

AMANDA [*fairly screeching*]. Don't you DARE to—

TOM. No, no, *I* mustn't say things! *I've* got to just—

AMANDA. Let me tell you—

TOM. I don't want to hear any more!

[*He tears the portieres open. The dining-room area is lit with a turgid smoky red glow. Now we see* AMANDA; *her hair is in metal curlers and she is wearing a very old bathrobe, much too large for her slight figure, a relic of the faithless Mr. Wingfield. The upright typewriter now stands on the drop-leaf table, along with a wild disarray of manuscripts. The quarrel was probably precipitated by* AMANDA*'s interruption of* TOM*'s creative labor. A chair lies overthrown on the floor. Their gesticulating shadows are cast on the ceiling by the fiery glow.*]

AMANDA. You *will* hear more, you—

TOM. No, I won't hear more, I'm going out!

AMANDA. You come right back in—

TOM. Out, out, out! Because I'm—

AMANDA. Come back here, Tom Wingfield! I'm not through talking to you!

TOM. Oh, go—

LAURA [*desperately*]. —Tom!

AMANDA. You're going to listen, and no more insolence from you! I'm at the end of my patience!

[*He comes back toward her.*]

TOM. What do you think I'm at? Aren't I supposed to have any patience to reach the end of, Mother? I know, I know. It seems unimportant to you, what I'm *doing*—what I *want* to do—having a little *difference* between them! You don't think that—

AMANDA. I think you've been doing things that you're ashamed of. That's why you act like this. I don't believe that you go every night to the movies. Nobody goes to the movies night after night. Nobody in their right minds goes to the movies as often as you pretend to. People don't go to the movies at nearly midnight, and movies don't let out at two A.M. Come in stumbling. Muttering to yourself like a maniac! You get three hours' sleep and then go to work. Oh, I can picture the way you're doing down there. Moping, doping, because you're in no condition.

TOM [*wildly*]. No, I'm in no condition!

AMANDA. What right have you got to jeopardize your job? Jeopardize the security of us all? How do you think we'd manage if you were—

TOM. Listen! You think I'm crazy about the *warehouse*? [*He bends fiercely toward her*

---

[17] D.H. Lawrence (1885–1930) was a poet and novelist who openly advocated eroticism and sexual freedom.

slight figure.] You think I'm in love with the Continental Shoemakers? You think I want to spend fifty-five *years* down there in that—*celotex interior!* with—*fluorescent—tubes!* Look! I'd rather somebody picked up a crowbar and battered out my brains—than go back mornings! I *go!* Every time you come in yelling that Goddamn *"Rise and Shine!" "Rise and Shine!"* I say to myself, "How *lucky dead* people are!" But I get up. I *go!* For sixty-five dollars a month I give up all that I dream of doing and being *ever!* And you say self—*self's* all I ever think of. Why, listen, if self is what I thought of, Mother, I'd be where he is—GONE! [*He points to his father's picture.*] As far as the system of transportation reaches! [*He starts past her. She grabs his arm.*] Don't grab at me, Mother!

AMANDA. Where are you going?

TOM. I'm going to the *movies!*

AMANDA. I don't believe that lie!

[TOM *crouches toward her, overtowering her tiny figure. She backs away, gasping.*]

TOM. I'm going to opium dens! Yes, opium dens, dens of vice and criminals' hangouts, Mother. I've joined the Hogan Gang, I'm a hired assassin, I carry a tommy gun in a violin case! I run a string of cat houses in the Valley! They call me Killer, Killer Wingfield, I'm leading a double-life, a simple, honest warehouse worker by day, by night a dynamic *czar* of the *underworld, Mother.* I go to gambling casinos, I spin away fortunes on the roulette table! I wear a patch over one eye and a false mustache, sometimes I put on green whiskers. On those occasions they call me—*El Diablo!* Oh, I could tell you many things to make you sleepless! My enemies plan to dynamite this place. They're going to blow us all sky-high some night! I'll be glad, very happy, and so will you! You'll go up, up on a broomstick, over Blue Mountain with seventeen gentlemen callers! You ugly—babbling old—*witch....* [*He goes through a series of violent, clumsy movements, seizing his overcoat, lunging to the door, pulling it fiercely open. The women watch him, aghast. His arm catches in the sleeve of the coat as he struggles to pull it on. For a moment he is pinioned by the bulky garment. With an outraged groan he tears the coat off again, splitting the shoulder of it, and hurls it across the room. It strikes against the shelf of* LAURA*'s glass collection, and there is a tinkle of shattering glass.* LAURA *cries out as if wounded.*]

[*Music.*]

[*Screen legend:* "The Glass Menagerie."]

LAURA [*shrilly*]. My *glass!*—menagerie.... [*She covers her face and turns away.*]

[*But* AMANDA *is still stunned and stupefied by the "ugly witch" so that she barely notices this occurrence. Now she recovers her speech.*]

AMANDA [*in an awful voice*]. I won't speak to you—until you apologize!

[*She crosses through the portieres and draws them together behind her.* TOM *is left with* LAURA. LAURA *clings weakly to the mantel with her face averted.* TOM *stares at her stupidly for a moment. Then he crosses to the shelf. He drops awkwardly on his knees to collect the fallen glass, glancing at* LAURA *as if he would speak but couldn't.*]

[*"The Glass Menagerie" music steals in as the scene dims out.*]

SCENE IV

The interior of the apartment is dark. There is a faint light in the alley. A deep-voiced bell in a church is tolling the hour of five.

TOM *appears at the top of the alley. After each solemn boom of the bell in the tower, he shakes a little noisemaker or rattle as if to express the tiny spasm of man in contrast to the sustained power and dignity of the Almighty. This and the unsteadiness of his advance make it evident that he has been drinking. As he climbs the few steps to the fire escape landing light steals up inside.* LAURA *appears in the front room in a nightdress. She notices that* TOM*'s bed is empty.* TOM *fishes in his pockets for his door key, removing a motley assortment of articles in the search, including a shower of movie ticket stubs and an empty bottle. At last he finds the key, but just as he is about to insert it, it slips from his finger. He strikes a match and crouches below the door.*

TOM [*bitterly*]. One crack—and it falls through!
 [LAURA *opens the door.*]
LAURA. Tom! Tom, what are you doing?
TOM. Looking for a door key.
LAURA. Where have you been all this time?
TOM. I have been to the movies.
LAURA. All this time at the movies?
TOM. There was a very long program. There was a Garbo[18] picture and a Mickey Mouse and a travelogue and a newsreel and a preview of coming attractions. And there was an organ solo and a collection for the Milk Fund—simultaneously—which ended up in a terrible fight between a fat lady and an usher!
LAURA [*innocently*]. Did you have to stay through everything?
TOM. Of course! And, oh, I forgot! There was a big stage show! The headliner on this stage show was Malvolio the Magician. He performed wonderful tricks, many of them, such as pouring water back and forth between pitchers. First it turned to wine and then it turned to beer and then it turned to whisky. I know it was whisky it finally turned into because he needed somebody to come up out of the audience to help him and I came up—both shows! It was Kentucky Straight Bourbon. A very generous fellow, he gave souvenirs. [*He pulls from his back pocket a shimmering rainbow-colored scarf.*] He gave me this. This is his magic scarf. You can have it, Laura. You wave it over a canary cage and you get a bowl of goldfish. You wave it over the goldfish bowl and they fly away canaries. . . . But the wonderfullest trick of all was the coffin trick. We nailed him into a coffin and he got out of the coffin without removing one nail. [*He has come inside.*] There is a trick that would come in handy for me—get me out of this two-by-four situation! [*He flops onto the bed and starts removing his shoes.*]
LAURA. Tom—shhh!
TOM. What're you shushing me for?
LAURA. You'll wake up Mother.
TOM. Goody, goody! Pay 'er back for all those "Rise an' Shines." [*He lies down, groaning.*] You know it don't take much intelligence to get yourself into a nailed-up coffin, Laura. But who in hell ever got himself out of one without removing one nail?
 [*As if in answer, the father's grinning photograph lights up. The scene dims out.*]
 [*Immediately following, the church bell is heard striking six. At the sixth stroke the alarm clock goes off in* AMANDA*'s room, and after a few moments we hear her calling: "Rise and Shine! Rise and Shine!* LAURA*, go tell your brother to rise and shine!"*]
TOM [*sitting up slowly*]. I'll rise—but I won't shine.
 [*The light increases.*]
AMANDA. Laura, tell your brother his coffee is ready.

---

[18] Greta Garbo (1905–1990) a Swedish film actress renowned for her beauty and her aura of detachment.

[LAURA *slips into the front room.*]

LAURA. Tom!—It's nearly seven. Don't make Mother nervous.

[*He stares at her stupidly.*]

[*beseechingly:*] Tom, speak to Mother this morning. Make up with her, apologize, speak to her!

TOM. She won't to me. It's her that started not speaking.

LAURA. If you just say you're sorry she'll start speaking.

TOM. Her not speaking—is that such a tragedy?

LAURA. Please—please!

AMANDA [*calling from the kitchenette*]. Laura, are you going to do what I asked you to do, or do I have to get dressed and go out myself?

LAURA. Going, going—soon as I get on my coat!

[*She pulls on a shapeless felt hat with a nervous, jerky movement, pleadingly glancing at TOM. She rushes awkwardly for her coat. The coat is one of AMANDA's, inaccurately made-over, the sleeves too short for LAURA.*]

Butter and what else?

AMANDA [*entering from the kitchenette*]. Just butter. Tell them to charge it.

LAURA. Mother, they make such faces when I do that.

AMANDA. Sticks and stones can break our bones, but the expression on Mr. Garfinkel's face won't harm us! Tell your brother his coffee is getting cold.

LAURA [*at the door*]. Do what I asked you, will you, will you, Tom?

[*He looks sullenly away.*]

AMANDA. Laura, go now or just don't go at all!

LAURA [*rushing out*]. Going—going!

[*A second later she cries out. TOM springs up and crosses to the door. TOM opens the door.*]

TOM. Laura?

LAURA. I'm all right. I slipped, but I'm all right.

AMANDA [*peering anxiously after her*]. If anyone breaks a leg on those fire-escape steps, the landlord ought to be sued for every cent he possesses! [*She shuts the door. Now she remembers she isn't speaking to TOM and returns to the other room.*]

[*As TOM comes listlessly for his coffee, she turns her back to him and stands rigidly facing the window on the gloomy gray vault of the areaway. Its light on her face with its aged but childish features is cruelly sharp, satirical as a Daumier* [19] *print.*]

[*The music of "Ave Maria" is heard softly.*]

[*TOM glances sheepishly but sullenly at her averted figure and slumps at the table. The coffee is scalding hot; he sips it and gasps and spits it back in the cup. At his gasp, AMANDA catches her breath and half turns. Then she catches herself and turns back to the window. TOM blows on his coffee, glancing sidewise at his mother. She clears her throat. TOM clears his. He starts to rise, sinks back down again, scratches his head, clears his throat again. AMANDA coughs. TOM raises his cup in both hands to blow on it, his eyes staring over the rim of it at his mother for several moments. Then he slowly sets the cup down and awkwardly and hesitantly rises from the chair.*]

TOM [*hoarsely*]. Mother. I—I apologize, Mother.

[AMANDA *draws a quick, shuddering breath. Her face works grotesquely. She breaks into childlike tears.*]

I'm sorry for what I said, for everything that I said, I didn't mean it.

AMANDA [*sobbingly*]. My devotion has made me a witch and so I make myself hateful to my children!

TOM. *No*, you *don't*.

[19] Honoré Daumier (1808–1879), a French lithographer, painter, and sculptor whose satirical prints often lampooned politicians.

AMANDA. I worry so much, don't sleep, it makes me nervous!

TOM [*gently*]. I understand that.

AMANDA. I've had to put up a solitary battle all these years. But you're my right-hand bower![20] Don't fall down, don't fail!

TOM [*gently*]. I try, Mother.

AMANDA [*with great enthusiasm*]. Try and you will *succeed!* [*The notion makes her breathless.*] Why, you—you're just *full* of natural endowments! Both my children—they're *unusual* children! Don't you think I know it? I'm so—*proud!* Happy and—feel I've—so much to be thankful for but—promise me one thing, son!

TOM. What, Mother?

AMANDA. Promise, son, you'll—never be a drunkard!

TOM [*turns to her grinning*]. I will never be a drunkard, Mother.

AMANDA. That's what frightened me so, that you'd be drinking! Eat a bowl of Purina!

TOM. Just coffee, Mother.

AMANDA. Shredded wheat biscuit?

TOM. No. No, Mother, just coffee.

AMANDA. You can't put in a day's work on an empty stomach. You've got ten minutes—don't gulp! Drinking too-hot liquids makes cancer of the stomach. . . . Put cream in.

TOM. No, thank you.

AMANDA. To cool it.

TOM. No! No, thank you, I want it black.

AMANDA. I know, but it's not good for you. We have to do all that we can to build ourselves up. In these trying times we live in, all that we have to cling to is—each other. . . . That's why it's so important to—Tom, I—I sent out your sister so I could discuss something with you. If you hadn't spoken I would have spoken to you. [*She sits down.*]

TOM [*gently*]. What is it, Mother, that you want to discuss?

AMANDA. *Laura!*

[*TOM puts his cup down slowly.*]

[*Legend on screen:* "Laura." *Music:* "*The Glass Menagerie.*"]

TOM. —Oh.—Laura . . .

AMANDA [*touching his sleeve*]. You know how Laura is. So quiet but—still water runs deep! She notices things and I think she—broods about them.

[TOM *looks up.*]

A few days ago I came in and she was crying.

TOM. What about?

AMANDA. You.

TOM. Me?

AMANDA. She has an idea that you're not happy here.

TOM. What gave her that idea?

AMANDA. What gives her any idea? However, you do act strangely. I—I'm not criticizing, understand *that!* I know your ambitions do not lie in the warehouse, that like everybody in the whole wide world—you've had to—make sacrifices, but—Tom—Tom—life's not easy, it calls for—Spartan endurance! There's so many things in my heart that I cannot describe to you! I've never told you but I—*loved* your father. . . .

TOM [*gently*]. I know that, Mother.

[20] The Jack of trumps, the highest card in certain card games.

AMANDA. And you—when I see you taking after his ways! Staying out late—and—
well, you *had* been drinking the night you were in that—terrifying condition!
Laura says that you hate the apartment and that you go out nights to get away
from it! Is that true, Tom?

TOM. No. You say there's so much in your heart that you can't describe to me.
That's true of me, too. There's so much in my heart that I can't describe to *you!*
So let's respect each other's—

AMANDA. But, why—*why,* Tom—are you always so *restless?* Where do you *go* to,
nights?

TOM. I—go to the movies.

AMANDA. Why do you go to the movies so much, Tom?

TOM. I go to the movies because—I like adventure. Adventure is something I don't
have much of at work, so I go to the movies.

AMANDA. But, Tom, you go to the movies *entirely* too *much!*

TOM. I like a lot of adventure.

[AMANDA *looks baffled, then hurt. As the familiar inquisition resumes,* TOM *becomes hard
and impatient again.* AMANDA *slips back into her querulous attitude toward him.*]

[*Image on screen:* A sailing vessel with Jolly Roger.]

AMANDA. Most young men find adventure in their careers.

TOM. Then most young men are not employed in a warehouse.

AMANDA. The world is full of young men employed in warehouses and offices and
factories.

TOM. Do all of them find adventure in their careers?

AMANDA. They do or they do without it! Not everybody has a craze for adventure.

TOM. Man is by instinct a lover, a hunter, a fighter, and none of those instincts are
given much play at the warehouse!

AMANDA. Man is by instinct! Don't quote instinct to me! Instinct is something that
people have got away from! It belongs to animals! Christian adults don't want
it!

TOM. What do Christian adults want, then, Mother?

AMANDA. Superior things! Things of the mind and the spirit! Only animals have to
satisfy instincts! Surely your aims are somewhat higher than theirs! Than monkeys—pigs—

TOM. I reckon they're not.

AMANDA. You're joking. However, that isn't what I wanted to discuss.

TOM [*rising*]. I haven't much time.

AMANDA [*pushing his shoulders*]. Sit down.

TOM. You want me to punch in red at the warehouse, Mother?

AMANDA. You have five minutes. I want to talk about Laura.

[*Screen legend:* "Plans and Provisions."]

TOM. All right! What about Laura?

AMANDA. We have to be making some plans and provisions for her. She's older than
you, two years, and nothing has happened. She just drifts along doing nothing.
It frightens me terribly how she just drifts along.

TOM. I guess she's the type that people call home girls.

AMANDA. There's no such type, and if there is, it's a pity! That is unless the home
is hers, with a husband!

TOM. What?

AMANDA. Oh, I can see the handwriting on the wall as plain as I see the nose in
front of my face! It's terrifying! More and more you remind me of your father!
He was out all hours without explanation!—Then *left! Goodbye!* And me with the
bag to hold. I saw that letter you got from the Merchant Marine. I know what

you're dreaming of. I'm not standing here blindfolded. [*She pauses.*] Very well, then. Then *do* it! But not till there's somebody to take your place.

TOM. What do you mean?

AMANDA. I mean that as soon as Laura has got somebody to take care of her, married, a home of her own, independent—why, then you'll be free to go wherever you please, on land, on sea, whichever way the wind blows you! But until that time you've got to look out for your sister. I don't say me because I'm old and don't matter! I say for your sister because she's young and dependent.

I put her in business college—a dismal failure! Frightened her so it made her sick at the stomach. I took her over to the Young People's League at the church. Another fiasco. She spoke to nobody, nobody spoke to her. Now all she does is fool with those pieces of glass and play those worn-out records. What kind of life is that for a girl to lead?

TOM. What can I do about it?

AMANDA. Overcome selfishness! Self, self, self is all that you ever think of!

[TOM *springs up and crosses to get his coat. It is ugly and bulky. He pulls on a cap with earmuffs.*]

Where is your muffler? Put your wool muffler on!

[*He snatches it angrily from the closet, tosses it around his neck and pulls both ends tight.*]

Tom! I haven't said what I had in mind to ask you.

TOM. I'm too late to—

AMANDA [*catching his arm—very importunately; then shyly*]. Down at the warehouse, aren't there some—nice young men?

TOM. No!

AMANDA. There *must* be—*some* . . .

TOM. Mother—[*He gestures.*]

AMANDA. Find out one that's clean-living—doesn't drink and ask him out for sister!

TOM. What?

AMANDA. For *sister!* To *meet!* Get *acquainted!*

TOM [*stamping to the door*]. Oh, my *go-osh!*

AMANDA. Will you? [*He opens the door. She says, imploringly:*] Will you? [*He starts down the fire escape.*] Will you? *Will* you, dear?

TOM [*calling back*]. Yes!

[AMANDA *closes the door hesitantly and with a troubled but faintly hopeful expression.*]

[*Screen image:* The cover of a glamor magazine.]

[*The spotlight picks up* AMANDA *at the phone.*]

AMANDA. Ella Cartwright? This is Amanda Wingfield! How are you, honey? How is that kidney condition?

[*There is a five-second pause.*]

Horrors!

[*There is another pause.*]

You're a Christian martyr, yes, honey, that's what you are, a Christian matryr! Well, I just now happened to notice in my little red book that your subscription to the *Companion* has just run out! I knew that you wouldn't want to miss out on the wonderful serial starting in this new issue. It's by Bessie May Hopper, the first thing she's written since *Honeymoon for Three.* Wasn't that a strange and interesting story? Well, this one is even lovelier, I believe. It has a sophisticated, society background. It's all about the horsey set on Long Island!

[*The light fades out.*]

SCENE V

Legend on the screen: "Annunciation."
Music is heard as the light slowly comes on.
    It is early dusk of a spring evening. Supper has just been finished in the Wingfield *apartment.* AMANDA *and* LAURA, *in light-colored dresses, are removing dishes from the table* *in the dining room, which is shadowy, their movements formalized almost as a dance or* *ritual, their moving forms as pale and silent as moths.* TOM, *in white shirt and trousers, rises* *from the table and crosses toward the fire escape.*

AMANDA [*as he passes her*]. Son, will you do me a favor?
TOM. What?
AMANDA. Comb your hair! You look so pretty when your hair is combed!
    [TOM *slouches on the sofa with the evening paper. Its enormous headline reads: "Franco*[21] *Triumphs."*]
    There is only one respect in which I would like you to emulate your father.
TOM. What respect is that?
AMANDA. The care he always took of his appearance. He never allowed himself to
    look untidy.
    [*He throws down the paper and crosses to the fire escape.*]
    Where are you going?
TOM. I'm going out to smoke.
AMANDA. You smoke too much. A pack a day at fifteen cents a pack. How much
    would that amount to in a month? Thirty times fifteen is how much, Tom?
    Figure it out and you will be astounded at what you could save. Enough to give
    you a night-school course in accounting at Washington U.! Just think what a
    wonderful thing that would be for you, son!
    [TOM *is unmoved by the thought.*]
TOM. I'd rather smoke. [*He steps out on the landing, letting the screen door slam.*]
AMANDA [*sharply*]. I know! That's the tragedy of it. . . . [*Alone, she turns to look at her*
    husband's picture.]
    [*Dance music: "The World Is Waiting for the Sunrise!"*]
TOM [*to the audience*]. Across the alley from us was the Paradise Dance Hall. On
    evenings in spring the windows and doors were open and the music came
    outdoors. Sometimes the lights were turned out except for a large glass sphere
    that hung from the ceiling. It would turn slowly about and filter the dusk with
    delicate rainbow colors. Then the orchestra played a waltz or a tango, some-
    thing that had a slow and sensuous rhythm. Couples would come outside, to the
    relative privacy of the alley. You could see them kissing behind ash pits and
    telephone poles. This was the compensation for lives that passed like mine,
    without any change or adventure. Adventure and change were imminent in this
    year. They were waiting around the corner for all these kids. Suspended in the
    mist over Berchtesgaden,[22] caught in the folds of Chamberlain's[23] umbrella. In
    Spain there was Guernica! But here there was only hot swing music and liquor,
    dance halls, bars, and movies, and sex that hung in the gloom like a chandelier

---

[21] General Francisco Franco (1892–1975), the leader of the Nationalist forces during the Spanish
    Civil War. His forces triumphed in 1939.
[22] A town in the German Alps, the site of Adolf Hitler's vacation villa.
[23] Neville Chamberlain (1869–1940) was the prime minister of Great Britain who sought to avoid war
    with Hitler through a policy of appeasement.

and flooded the world with brief, deceptive rainbows. . . . All the world was waiting for bombardments!

[AMANDA *turns from the picture and comes outside.*]

AMANDA [*sighing*]. A fire escape landing's a poor excuse for a porch. [*She spreads a newspaper on a step and sits down, gracefully and demurely as if she were settling into a swing on a Mississippi veranda.*] What are you looking at?

TOM. The moon.

AMANDA. Is there a moon this evening?

TOM. It's rising over Garfinkel's Delicatessen.

AMANDA. So it is! A little silver slipper of a moon. Have you made a wish on it yet?

TOM. Um-hum.

AMANDA. What did you wish for?

TOM. That's a secret.

AMANDA. A secret, huh? Well, I won't tell mine either. I will be just as mysterious as you.

TOM. I bet I can guess what yours is.

AMANDA. Is my head so transparent?

TOM. You're not a sphinx.

AMANDA. No, I don't have secrets. I'll tell you what I wished for on the moon. Success and happiness for my precious children! I wish for that whenever there's a moon, and when there isn't a moon, I wish for it, too.

TOM. I thought perhaps you wished for a gentleman caller.

AMANDA. Why do you say that?

TOM. Don't you remember asking me to fetch one?

AMANDA. I remember suggesting that it would be nice for your sister if you brought home some nice young man from the warehouse. I think that I've made that suggestion more than once.

TOM. Yes, you have made it repeatedly.

AMANDA. Well?

TOM. We are going to have one.

AMANDA. *What?*

TOM. A gentleman caller!

[*The annunciation is celebrated with music.*]

[AMANDA *rises.*]

[*Image on screen:* A caller with a bouquet.]

AMANDA. You mean you have asked some nice young man to come over?

TOM. Yep. I've asked him to dinner.

AMANDA. You really did?

TOM. I did!

AMANDA. You did, and did he—*accept?*

TOM. He did!

AMANDA. Well, well—well, well! That's—lovely!

TOM. I thought that you would be pleased.

AMANDA. It's definite then?

TOM. Very definite.

AMANDA. Soon?

TOM. Very soon.

AMANDA. For heaven's sake, stop putting on and tell me some things, will you?

TOM. What things do you want me to tell you?

AMANDA. *Naturally* I would like to know when he's *coming!*

TOM. He's coming tomorrow.

AMANDA. *Tomorrow?*

TOM. Yep. Tomorrow.

AMANDA. But, Tom!

TOM. Yes, Mother?

AMANDA. Tomorrow gives me no time!

TOM. Time for what?

AMANDA. Preparations! Why didn't you phone me at once, as soon as you asked him, the minute that he accepted? Then, don't you see, I could have been getting ready!

TOM. You don't have to make any fuss.

AMANDA. Oh, Tom, Tom, Tom, of course I have to make a fuss! I want things nice, not sloppy! Not thrown together. I'll certainly have to do some fast thinking, won't I?

TOM. I don't see why you have to think at all.

AMANDA. You just don't know. We can't have a gentleman caller in a pigsty! All my wedding silver has to be polished, the monogrammed table linen ought to be laundered! The windows have to be washed and fresh curtains put up. And how about clothes? We have to *wear* something, don't we?

TOM. Mother, this boy is no one to make a fuss over!

AMANDA. Do you realize he's the first young man we've introduced to your sister? It's terrible, dreadful, disgraceful that poor little sister has never received a single gentleman caller! Tom, come inside! [*She opens the screen door.*]

TOM. What for?

AMANDA. I want to ask you some things.

TOM. If you're going to make such a fuss, I'll call it off, I'll tell him not to come!

AMANDA. You certainly won't do anything of the kind. Nothing offends people worse than broken engagements. It simply means I'll have to work like a Turk! We won't be brilliant, but we will pass inspection. Come on inside.

[TOM *follows her inside, groaning.*]

Sit down.

TOM. Any particular place you would like me to sit?

AMANDA. Thank heavens I've got that new sofa! I'm also making payments on a floor lamp I'll have sent out! And put the chintz covers on, they'll brighten things up! Of course I'd hoped to have these walls re-papered.... What is the young man's name?

TOM. His name is O'Connor.

AMANDA. That, of course, means fish—tomorrow is Friday! I'll have that salmon loaf—with Durkee's dressing! What does he do? He works at the warehouse?

TOM. Of course! How else would I—

AMANDA. Tom, he—doesn't drink?

TOM. Why do you ask me that?

AMANDA. Your father *did!*

TOM. Don't get started on that!

AMANDA. He *does* drink, then?

TOM. Not that I know of!

AMANDA. Make sure, be certain! The last thing I want for my daughter's a boy who drinks!

TOM. Aren't you being a little bit premature? Mr. O'Connor has not yet appeared on the scene!

AMANDA. But will tomorrow. To meet your sister, and what do I know about his character? Nothing! Old maids are better off than wives of drunkards!

TOM. Oh, my God!

AMANDA. Be still!

TOM [*leaning forward to whisper*]. Lots of fellows meet girls whom they don't marry!

AMANDA. Oh, talk sensibly, Tom—and don't be sarcastic! [*She has gotten a hair-brush.*]

TOM. What are you doing?

AMANDA. I'm brushing that cowlick down! [*She attacks his hair with the brush.*] What is this young man's position at the warehouse?

TOM [*submitting grimly to the brush and the interrogation*]. This young man's position is that of a shipping clerk, Mother.

AMANDA. Sounds to me like a fairly responsible job, the sort of a job *you* would be in if you just had more *get-up*. What is his salary? Have you any idea?

TOM. I would judge it to be approximately eighty-five dollars a month.

AMANDA. Well—not princely, but—

TOM. Twenty more than I make.

AMANDA. Yes, how well I know! But for a family man, eighty-five dollars a month is not much more than you can just get by on. . . .

TOM. Yes, but Mr. O'Connor is not a family man.

AMANDA. He might be, mightn't he? Some time in the future?

TOM. I see. Plans and provisions.

AMANDA. You are the only young man that I know of who ignores the fact that the future becomes the present, the present the past, and the past turns into ever-lasting regret if you don't plan for it!

TOM. I will think that over and see what I can make of it.

AMANDA. Don't be supercilious with your mother! Tell me some more about this—what do you call him?

TOM. James D. O'Connor. The D. is for Delaney.

AMANDA. Irish on *both* sides! *Gracious!* And doesn't drink?

TOM. Shall I call him up and ask him right this minute?

AMANDA. The only way to find out about those things is to make discreet inquiries at the proper moment. When I was a girl in Blue Mountain and it was suspected that a young man drank, the girl whose attentions he had been receiving, if any girl *was,* would sometimes speak to the minister of his and sort of feel him out on the young man's character. That is the way such things are discreetly handled to keep a young woman from making a tragic mistake!

TOM. Then how did you happen to make a tragic mistake?

AMANDA. That innocent look of your father's had everyone fooled! He *smiled*—the world was *enchanted!* No girl can do worse than put herself at the mercy of a handsome appearance! I hope that Mr. O'Connor is not too good-looking.

TOM. No, he's not too good-looking. He's covered with freckles and hasn't too much of a nose.

AMANDA. He's not right-down homely, though?

TOM. Not right-down homely. Just medium homely, I'd say.

AMANDA. Character's what to look for in a man.

TOM. That's what I've always said, Mother.

AMANDA. You've never said anything of the kind and I suspect you would never give it a thought.

TOM. Don't be so suspicious of me.

AMANDA. At least I hope he's the type that's up and coming.

TOM. I think he really goes in for self-improvement.

AMANDA. What reason have you to think so?

TOM. He goes to night school.

AMANDA [*beaming*]. Splendid! What does he do, I mean study?

TOM. Radio engineering and public speaking!

AMANDA. Then he has visions of being advanced in the world! Any young man who studies public speaking is aiming to have an executive job some day! And radio engineering? A thing for the future! Both of these facts are very illuminating. Those are the sort of things that a mother should know concerning any young man who comes to call on her daughter. Seriously or—not.

TOM. One little warning. He doesn't know about Laura. I didn't let on that we had dark ulterior motives. I just said, why don't you come and have dinner with us? He said okay and that was the whole conversation.

AMANDA. I bet it was! You're eloquent as an oyster. However, he'll know about Laura when he gets here. When he sees how lovely and sweet and pretty she is, he'll thank his lucky stars he was asked to dinner.

TOM. Mother, you mustn't expect too much of Laura.

AMANDA. What do you mean?

TOM. Laura seems all those things to you and me because she's ours and we love her. We don't even notice she's crippled any more.

AMANDA. Don't say crippled! You know that I never allow that word to be used!

TOM. But face facts, Mother. She is and—that's not all—

AMANDA. What do you mean "not all?"

TOM. Laura is very different from other girls.

AMANDA. I think the difference is all to her advantage.

TOM. Not quite all—in the eyes of others—strangers—she's terribly shy and lives in a world of her own and those things make her seem a little peculiar to people outside the house.

AMANDA. Don't say peculiar.

TOM. Face the facts. She is.

[*The dance hall music changes to a tango that has a minor and somewhat ominous tone.*]

AMANDA. In what way is she peculiar—may I ask?

TOM [*gently*]. She lives in a world of her own—a world of little glass ornaments, Mother....

[*He gets up.* AMANDA *remains holding the brush, looking at him, troubled.*]

She plays old phonograph records and—that's about all—[*He glances at himself in the mirror and crosses to the door.*]

AMANDA [*sharply*]. Where are you going?

TOM. I'm going to the movies. [*He goes out the screen door.*]

AMANDA. Not to the movies, every night to the movies! [*She follows quickly to the screen door.*] I don't believe you always go to the movies!

[*He is gone.* AMANDA *looks worriedly after him for a moment. Then vitality and optimism return and she turns from the door, crossing to the portieres.*]

Laura, Laura!

[LAURA *answers from the kitchenette.*]

LAURA. Yes, Mother.

AMANDA. Let those dishes go and come in front!

[LAURA *appears with a dish towel.* AMANDA *speaks to her gaily.*]

Laura, come here and make a wish on the moon!

[*Screen image:* The Moon.]

LAURA [*entering*]. Moon—moon?

AMANDA. A little silver slipper of a moon. Look over your left shoulder, Laura, and make a wish!

[LAURA *looks faintly puzzled as if called out of sleep.* AMANDA *seizes her shoulders and turns her at an angle by the door.*]

Now! Now, darling, *wish!*

LAURA. What shall I wish for, Mother?

AMANDA [*her voice trembling and her eyes suddenly filling with tears*]. Happiness! Good fortune!

[*The sound of the violin rises and the stage dims out.*]

SCENE VI

The light comes up on the escape landing. TOM *is leaning against the grill, smoking.*

[*Screen image:* The high school hero.]

TOM. And so the following evening I brought Jim home to dinner. I had known Jim slightly in high school. In high school Jim was a hero. He had tremendous Irish good nature and vitality with the scrubbed and polished look of white chinaware. He seemed to move in a continual spotlight. He was a star in basketball, captain of the debating club, president of the senior class and the glee club and he sang the male lead in the annual light operas. He was always running or bounding, never just walking. He seemed always at the point of defeating the law of gravity. He was shooting with such velocity through his adolescence that you would logically expect him to arrive at nothing short of the White House by the time he was thirty. But Jim apparently ran into more interference after his graduation from Soldan. His speed had definitely slowed. Six years after he left high school he was holding a job that wasn't much better than mine.

[*Screen image:* THE CLERK.]

He was the only one at the warehouse with whom I was on friendly terms. I was valuable to him as someone who could remember his former glory, who had seen him win basketball games and the silver cup in debating. He knew of my secret practice of retiring to a cabinet of the washroom to work on poems when business was slack in the warehouse. He called me Shakespeare. And while the other boys in the warehouse regarded me with suspicious hostility, Jim took a humorous attitude toward me. Gradually his attitude affected the others, their hostility wore off and they also began to smile at me as people smile at an oddly fashioned dog who trots across their path at some distance.

I knew that Jim and Laura had known each other at Soldan, and I had heard Laura speak admiringly of his voice. I didn't know if Jim remembered her or not. In high school Laura had been as unobtrusive as Jim had been astonishing. If he did remember Laura, it was not as my sister, for when I asked him to dinner, he grinned and said, "You know, Shakespeare, I never thought of you as having folks!"

He was about to discover that I did. . . .

[*Legend on screen:* "The accent of a coming foot."]

[*The light dims out on* TOM *and comes up in the Wingfield living room—a delicate lemony light. It is about five on a Friday evening of late spring which comes "scattering poems in the sky."*]

[AMANDA *has worked like a Turk in preparation for the gentleman caller. The results are astonishing. The new floor lamp with its rose silk shade is in place, a colored paper lantern conceals the broken light fixture in the ceiling, new billowing white curtains are at the windows, chintz covers are on the chairs and sofa, a pair of new sofa pillows make their initial appearance. Open boxes and tissue paper are scattered on the floor.*]

[LAURA *stands in the middle of the room with lifted arms while* AMANDA *crouches before her, adjusting the hem of a new dress, devout and ritualistic. The dress is colored and designed by memory. The arrangement of* LAURA*'s hair is changed; it is softer and more becoming. A fragile, unearthly prettiness has come out in* LAURA: *she is like a piece of translucent glass touched by light, given a momentary radiance, not actual, not lasting.*]

AMANDA [*impatiently*]. Why are you trembling?

LAURA. Mother, you've made me so nervous!

AMANDA. How have I made you nervous?

LAURA. By all this fuss! You make it seem so important!

AMANDA. I don't understand you, Laura. You couldn't be satisfied with just sitting home, and yet whenever I try to arrange something for you, you seem to resist it. [*She gets up.*] Now take a look at yourself. No, wait! Wait just a moment—I have an idea!

LAURA. What is it now?

[AMANDA *produces two powder puffs which she wraps in handkerchiefs and stuffs in* LAURA*'s bosom.*]

LAURA. Mother, what are you doing?

AMANDA. They call them "Gay Deceivers"!

LAURA. I won't wear them!

AMANDA. You will!

LAURA. Why should I?

AMANDA. Because, to be painfully honest, your chest is flat.

LAURA. You make it seem like we were setting a trap.

AMANDA. All pretty girls are a trap, a pretty trap, and men expect them to be.

[*Legend on screen:* "A pretty trap."]

Now look at yourself, young lady. This is the prettiest you will ever be! [*She stands back to admire* LAURA.] I've got to fix myself now! You're going to be surprised by your mother's appearance!

[AMANDA *crosses through the portieres, humming gaily.* LAURA *moves slowly to the long mirror and stares solemnly at herself. A wind blows the white curtains inward in a slow, graceful motion and with a faint, sorrowful sighing.*]

AMANDA [*from somewhere behind the portieres*]. It isn't dark enough yet.

[LAURA *turns slowly before the mirror with a troubled look.*]

[*Legend on screen:* "This is my sister: Celebrate her with strings!" *Music plays.*]

AMANDA [*laughing, still not visible*]. I'm going to show you something. I'm going to make a spectacular appearance!

LAURA. What is it, Mother?

AMANDA. Possess your soul in patience—you will see! Something I've resurrected from that old trunk! Styles haven't changed so terribly much after all. . . . [*She parts the portieres.*] Now just look at your mother! [*She wears a girlish frock of yellowed voile with a blue silk sash. She carries a bunch of jonquils—the legend of her youth is nearly revived. Now she speaks feverishly:*] This is the dress in which I led the cotillion. Won the cakewalk twice at Sunset Hill, wore one Spring to the Governor's Ball in Jackson! See how I sashayed around the ballroom, Laura? [*She raises her skirt and does a mincing step around the room.*] I wore it on Sundays for my gentleman callers! I had it on the day I met your father. . . . I had malaria fever all that Spring. The change of climate from East Tennessee to the Delta— weakened resistance. I had a little temperature all the time—not enough to be serious—just enough to make me restless and giddy! Invitations poured in—

parties all over the Delta! "Stay in bed," said Mother, "you have a fever!"—but
I just wouldn't. I took quinine but kept on going, going! Evenings, dances!
Afternoons, long, long rides! Picnics—lovely! So lovely, that country in May—all
lacy with dogwood, literally flooded with jonquils! That was the spring I had the
craze for jonquils. Jonquils became an absolute obsession. Mother said, "Honey,
there's no more room for jonquils." And still I kept on bringing in more
jonquils. Whenever, wherever I saw them, I'd say, "Stop! Stop! I see jonquils!"
I made the young men help me gather the jonquils! It was a joke, Amanda and
her jonquils. Finally there were no more vases to hold them, every available
space was filled with jonquils. No vases to hold them? All right, I'll hold them
myself! And then I—[*She stops in front of the picture. Music plays.*] met your father!
Malaria fever and jonquils and then—this—boy.... [*She switches on the rose-
colored lamp.*] I hope they get here before it starts to rain. [*She crosses the room and
places the jonquils in a bowl on the table.*] I gave your brother a little extra change
so he and Mr. O'Connor could take the service car home.

LAURA [*with an altered look*]. What did you say his name was?

AMANDA. O'Connor.

LAURA. What is his first name?

AMANDA. I don't remember. Oh, yes, I do. It was—Jim!

[LAURA *sways slightly and catches hold of a chair.*]

[*Legend on screen:* "Not Jim!"]

LAURA [*faintly*]: Not—Jim!

AMANDA. Yes, that was it, it was Jim! I've never known a Jim that wasn't nice!

[*The music becomes ominous.*]

LAURA. Are you sure his name is Jim O'Connor?

AMANDA. Yes. Why?

LAURA. Is he the one that Tom used to know in high school?

AMANDA. He didn't say so. I think he just got to know him at the warehouse.

LAURA. There was a Jim O'Connor we both knew in high school—[*then, with effort*]
If that is the one that Tom is bringing to dinner—you'll have to excuse me, I
won't come to the table.

AMANDA. What sort of nonsense is this?

LAURA. You asked me once if I'd ever liked a boy. Don't you remember I showed
you this boy's picture?

AMANDA. You mean the boy you showed me in the yearbook?

LAURA. Yes, that boy.

AMANDA. Laura, Laura, were you in love with that boy?

LAURA. I don't know, Mother. All I know is I couldn't sit at the table if it was him!

AMANDA. It won't be him! It isn't the least bit likely. But whether it is or not, you
will come to the table. You will not be excused.

LAURA. I'll have to be, Mother.

AMANDA. I don't intend to humor your silliness, Laura. I've had too much from you
and your brother, both! So just sit down and compose yourself till they come.
Tom has forgotten his key so you'll have to let them in, when they arrive.

LAURA [*panicky*]. Oh, Mother—*you* answer the door!

AMANDA [*lightly*]. I'll be in the kitchen—busy!

LAURA. Oh, Mother, please answer the door, don't make me do it!

AMANDA [*crossing into the kitchenette*]. I've got to fix the dressing for the salmon. Fuss,
fuss—silliness!—over a gentleman caller!

[*The door swings shut.* LAURA *is left alone.*]

[*Legend on screen:* "Terror!"]

[*She utters a low moan and turns off the lamp—sits stiffly on the edge of the sofa, knotting her fingers together.*]

[*Legend on screen:* "The Opening of a Door!"]

[*Tom and Jim appear on the fire escape steps and climb to the landing. Hearing their approach, Laura rises with a panicky gesture. She retreats to the portieres. The doorbell rings. Laura catches her breath and touches her throat. Low drums sound.*]

AMANDA [*calling*]. Laura, sweetheart! The door!

[*Laura stares at it without moving.*]

JIM. I think we just beat the rain.

TOM. Uh-huh. [*He rings again, nervously. Jim whistles and fishes for a cigarette.*]

AMANDA [*very, very gaily*]. Laura, that is your brother and Mr. O'Connor! Will you let them in, darling?

[*Laura crosses toward the kitchenette door.*]

LAURA [*breathlessly*]. Mother—you go to the door! [*Amanda steps out of the kitchenette and stares furiously at Laura. She points imperiously at the door.*]

LAURA. Please, please!

AMANDA [*in a fierce whisper*]. What is the matter with you, you silly thing?

LAURA [*desperately*]. Please, you answer it, *please!*

AMANDA. I told you I wasn't going to humor you, Laura. Why have you chosen this moment to lose your mind?

LAURA. Please, please, please, you go!

AMANDA. You'll have to go to the door because I can't!

LAURA [*despairingly*]. I can't either!

AMANDA. *Why?*

LAURA. I'm *sick!*

AMANDA. I'm sick, too—of your nonsense! Why can't you and your brother be normal people? Fantastic whims and behavior! [*Tom gives a long ring.*] Preposterous goings on! Can you give me one reason—[*She calls out lyrically.*] Coming! Just one second!—why you should be afraid to open a door? Now you answer it, Laura!

LAURA. Oh, oh, oh . . . [*She returns through the portieres, darts to the Victrola, winds it frantically and turns it on.*]

AMANDA. Laura Wingfield, you march right to that door!

LAURA. *Yes—yes, Mother!*

[*A faraway, scratchy rendition of "Dardanella" softens the air and gives her strength to move through it. She slips to the door and draws it cautiously open. Tom enters with the caller, Jim O'Connor.*]

TOM. Laura, this is Jim. Jim, this is my sister, Laura.

JIM [*stepping inside*]. I didn't know that Shakespeare had a sister!

LAURA [*retreating, stiff and trembling, from the door*]. How—how do you do?

JIM [*heartily, extending his hand*]. Okay!

[*Laura touches it hesitantly with hers.*]

JIM. Your hand's *cold,* Laura!

LAURA. Yes, well—I've been playing the Victrola. . . .

JIM. Must have been playing classical music on it! You ought to play a little hot swing music to warm you up!

LAURA. Excuse me—I haven't finished playing the Victrola. . . . [*She turns awkwardly and hurries into the front room. She pauses a second by the Victrola. Then she catches her breath and darts through the portieres like a frightened deer.*]

JIM [*grinning*]. What was the matter?

TOM. Oh—with Laura? Laura is—terribly shy.

JIM. Shy, huh? It's unusual to meet a shy girl nowadays. I don't believe you ever mentioned you had a sister.

TOM. Well, now you know. I have one. Here is the *Post Dispatch.* You want a piece of it?

JIM. Uh-huh.

TOM. What piece? The comics?

JIM. Sports! [*He glances at it.*] Ole Dizzy Dean is on his bad behavior.

TOM [*uninterested*]. Yeah? [*He lights a cigarette and goes over to the fire-escape door.*]

JIM. Where are *you* going?

TOM. I'm going out on the terrace.

JIM [*going after him*]. You know, Shakespeare—I'm going to sell you a bill of goods!

TOM. What goods?

JIM. A course I'm taking.

TOM. Huh?

JIM. In public speaking! You and me, we're not the warehouse type.

TOM. Thanks—that's good news. But what has public speaking got to do with it?

JIM. It fits you for—executive positions!

TOM. Awww.

JIM. I tell you it's done a helluva lot for me.

[*Image on screen:* Executive at his desk.]

TOM. In what respect?

JIM. In every! Ask yourself what is the difference between you an' me and men in the office down front? Brains?—No!—Ability?—No! Then what? Just one little thing—

TOM. What is that one little thing?

JIM. Primarily it amounts to—social poise! Being able to square up to people and hold your own on any social level!

AMANDA [*from the kitchenette*]. Tom?

TOM. Yes, Mother?

AMANDA. Is that you and Mr. O'Connor?

TOM. Yes, Mother.

AMANDA. Well, you just make yourselves comfortable in there.

TOM. Yes, Mother.

AMANDA. Ask Mr. O'Connor if he would like to wash his hands.

JIM. Aw, no—no—thank you—I took care of that at the warehouse. Tom—

TOM. Yes?

JIM. Mr. Mendoza was speaking to me about you.

TOM. Favorably?

JIM. What do you think?

TOM. Well—

JIM. You're going to be out of a job if you don't wake up.

TOM. I am waking up—

JIM. You show no signs.

TOM. The signs are interior.

[*Image on screen:* The sailing vessel with the Jolly Roger again.]

TOM. I'm planning to change. [*He leans over the fire-escape rail, speaking with quiet exhilaration. The incandescent marquees and signs of the first-run movie houses light his face from across the alley. He looks like a voyager.*] I'm right at the point of committing myself to a future that doesn't include the warehouse and Mr. Mendoza or even a night-school course in public speaking.

JIM. What are you gassing about?

TOM. I'm tired of the movies.

JIM. Movies!

TOM. Yes, movies! Look at them—[*a wave toward the marvels of Grand Avenue*] All of those glamorous people—having adventures—hogging it all, gobbling the whole thing up! You know what happens? People go to the *movies* instead of *moving!* Hollywood characters are supposed to have all the adventures for everybody in America, while everybody in America sits in a dark room and watches them have them! Yes, until there's a war. That's when adventure becomes available to the masses! *Everyone's* dish, not only Gable's![24] Then the people in the dark room come out of the dark room to have some adventures themselves—goody, goody! It's our turn now, to go to the South Sea Island—to make a safari—to be exotic, far-off! But I'm not patient. I don't want to wait till then. I'm tired of the *movies* and I am *about to move!*

JIM [*incredulously*]. Move?

TOM. Yes.

JIM. When?

TOM. Soon!

JIM. Where? Where?

[*The music seems to answer the question, while* TOM *thinks it over. He searches in his pockets.*]

TOM. I'm starting to boil inside. I know I seem dreamy, but inside—well, I'm boiling! Whenever I pick up a shoe, I shudder a little thinking how short life is and what I am doing! Whatever that means, I know it doesn't mean shoes—except as something to wear on a traveler's feet! [*He finds what he has been searching for in his pockets and holds out a paper to* JIM.] Look—

JIM. What?

TOM. I'm a member.

JIM [*reading*]. The Union of Merchant Seamen.

TOM. I paid my dues this month, instead of the light bill.

JIM. You will regret it when they turn the lights off.

TOM. I won't be here.

JIM. How about your mother?

TOM. I'm like my father. The bastard son of a bastard! Did you notice how he's grinning in his picture in there? And he's been absent going on sixteen years!

JIM. You're just talking, you drip. How does your mother feel about it?

TOM. Shhh! Here comes Mother! Mother is not acquainted with my plans!

AMANDA [*coming through the portieres*]. Where are you all?

TOM. On the terrace, Mother.

[*They start inside. She advances to them.* TOM *is distinctly shocked at her appearance. Even* JIM *blinks a little. He is making his first contact with girlish Southern vivacity and in spite of the night-school course in public speaking is somewhat thrown off the beam by the unexpected outlay of social charm. Certain responses are attempted by* JIM *but are swept aside by* AMANDA*'s gay laughter and chatter.* TOM *is embarrassed but after the first shock* JIM *reacts very warmly. He grins and chuckles, is altogether won over.*]

[*Image on screen:* Amanda as a girl.]

[24] Clark Gable (1901–1960), the famous leading man in such films as *Gone With the Wind* (1940) and *The Misfits* (1960).

AMANDA [*coyly smiling, shaking her girlish ringlets*]. Well, well, well, so this is Mr. O'Connor. Introductions entirely unnecessary. I've heard so much about you from my boy. I finally said to him, Tom—good gracious!—why don't you bring this paragon to supper? I'd like to meet this nice young man at the warehouse!—instead of just hearing him sing your praises so much! I don't know why my son is so stand-offish—that's not Southern behavior!

Let's sit down and—I think we could stand a little more air in here! Tom, leave the door open. I felt a nice fresh breeze a moment ago. Where has it gone to? Mmm, so warm already! And not quite summer, even. We're going to burn up when summer really gets started. However, we're having—we're having a very light supper. I think light things are better fo' this time of year. The same as light clothes are. Light clothes an' light food are what warm weather calls fo'. You know our blood gets so thick during th' winter—it takes a while fo' us to *adjust* ou'selves!—when the season changes . . . It's come so quick this year. I wasn't prepared. All of a sudden—heavens! Already summer! I ran to the trunk an' pulled out this light dress—terribly old! Historical almost! But feels so good—so good an' co-ol, y' know. . . .

TOM. Mother—

AMANDA. Yes, honey?

TOM. How about—supper?

AMANDA. Honey, you go ask Sister if supper is ready! You know that Sister is in full charge of supper! Tell her you hungry boys are waiting for it. [*to* JIM] Have you met Laura?

JIM. She—

AMANDA. Let you in? Oh, good, you've met already! It's rare for a girl as sweet an' pretty as Laura to be domestic! But Laura is, thank heavens, not only pretty but also very domestic. I'm not at all. I never was a bit. I never could make a thing but angel-food cake. Well, in the South we had so many servants. Gone, gone, gone. All vestige of gracious living! Gone completely! I wasn't prepared for what the future brought me. All of my gentleman callers were sons of planters and of course I assumed that I would be married to one and raise my family on a large piece of land with plenty of servants. But man proposes—and woman accepts the proposal! To vary that old, old saying[25] a little bit—I married no planter! I married a man who worked for the telephone company! That gallantly smiling gentleman over there! [*She points to the picture.*] A telephone man who—fell in love with long-distance! Now he travels and I don't even know where! But what am I going on for about my—tribulations? Tell me yours—I hope you don't have any! Tom?

TOM [*returning*]. Yes, Mother?

AMANDA. Is supper nearly ready?

TOM. It looks to me like supper is on the table.

AMANDA. Let me look—[*She rises prettily and looks through the portieres.*] Oh, lovely! But where is Sister?

TOM. Laura is not feeling well and she says that she thinks she'd better not come to the table.

AMANDA. What? Nonsense! Laura? Oh, Laura!

LAURA [*from the kitchenette, faintly*]. Yes, Mother.

AMANDA. You really must come to the table. We won't be seated until you come to the table! Come in, Mr. O'Connor. You sit over there, and I'll . . . Laura? Laura

---

[25] The old saying is, "Man proposes, but God disposes."

Wingfield! You're keeping us waiting, honey! We can't say grace until you come to the table!

[*The kitchenette door is pushed weakly open and* LAURA *comes in. She is obviously quite faint, her lips trembling, her eyes wide and staring. She moves unsteadily toward the table.*]

[*Screen legend:* "Terror!"]

[*Outside a summer storm is coming on abruptly. The white curtains billow inward at the windows and there is a sorrowful murmur from the deep blue dusk.*]

[LAURA *suddenly stumbles; she catches at a chair with a faint moan.*]

TOM. Laura!

AMANDA. Laura!

[*There is a clap of thunder.*]

[*Screen legend:* "Ah!"]

[*despairingly*] Why, Laura, you *are* ill, darling! Tom, help your sister into the living room, dear! Sit in the living room, Laura—rest on the sofa. Well! [*to* JIM *as* TOM *helps his sister to the sofa in the living room*] Standing over the hot stove made her ill! I told her that it was just too warm this evening, but— [TOM *comes back to the table.*] Is Laura all right now?

TOM. Yes.

AMANDA. What *is* that? Rain? A nice cool rain has come up! [*She gives* JIM *a frightened look.*] I think we may—have grace—now ...

[TOM *looks at her stupidly.*] Tom, honey—you say grace!

TOM. Oh ... "For these and all thy mercies—"

[*They bow their heads,* AMANDA *stealing a nervous glance at* JIM. *In the living room* LAURA, *stretched on the sofa, clenches her hand to her lips, to hold back a shuddering sob.*]

God's Holy Name be praised—

[*The scene dims out.*]

SCENE VII

It is half an hour later. Dinner is just being finished in the dining room, LAURA *is still huddled upon the sofa, her feet drawn under her, her head resting on a pale blue pillow, her eyes wide and mysteriously watchful. The new floor lamp with its shade of rose-colored silk gives a soft, becoming light to her face, bringing out the fragile, unearthly prettiness which usually escapes attention. From outside there is a steady murmur of rain, but it is slackening and soon stops; the air outside becomes pale and luminous as the moon breaks through the clouds. A moment after the curtain rises, the lights in both rooms flicker and go out.*

JIM. Hey, there, Mr. Light Bulb!

[AMANDA *laughs nervously.*]

[*Legend on screen:* "Suspension of a public service."]

AMANDA. Where was Moses when the lights went out? Ha-ha. Do you know the answer to that one, Mr. O'Connor?

JIM. No, Ma'am, what's the answer?

AMANDA. In the dark! [JIM *laughs appreciatively.*] Everybody sit still. I'll light the candles. isn't it lucky we have them on the table? Where's a match? Which of you gentleman can provide a match?

JIM. Here.

AMANDA. Thank you, Sir.

JIM. Not at all, Ma'am!

AMANDA [*as she lights the candles*]. I guess the fuse has burned out. Mr. O'Connor, can you tell a burnt-out fuse? I know I can't and Tom is a total loss when it comes to mechanics.

[*They rise from the table and go into the kitchenette, from where their voices are heard.*] Oh, be careful you don't bump into something. We don't want our gentleman caller to break his neck. Now wouldn't that be a fine howdy-do?

JIM. Ha-ha! Where is the fuse-box?

AMANDA. Right here next to the stove. Can you see anything?

JIM. Just a minute.

AMANDA. Isn't electricity a mysterious thing? Wasn't it Benjamin Franklin who tied a key to a kite? We live in such a mysterious universe, don't we? Some people say that science clears up all the mysteries for us. In my opinion it only creates more! Have you found it yet?

JIM. No, Ma'am. All these fuses look okay to me.

AMANDA. Tom!

TOM. Yes, Mother?

AMANDA. That light bill I gave you several days ago. The one I told you we got the notices about?

[*Legend on screen:* "Ha!"]

TOM. Oh—yeah.

AMANDA. You didn't neglect to pay it by any chance?

TOM. Why, I—

AMANDA. Didn't! I might have known it!

JIM. Shakespeare probably wrote a poem on that light bill, Mrs. Wingfield.

AMANDA. I might have known better than to trust him with it! There's such a high price for negligence in this world!

JIM. Maybe the poem will win a ten-dollar prize.

AMANDA. We'll just have to spend the remainder of the evening in the nineteenth century, before Mr. Edison made the Mazda lamp!

JIM. Candlelight is my favorite kind of light.

AMANDA. That shows you're romantic! But that's no excuse for Tom. Well, we got through dinner. Very considerate of them to let us get through dinner before they plunged us into everlasting darkness, wasn't it, Mr. O'Connor?

JIM. Ha-ha!

AMANDA. Tom, as a penalty for your carelessness you can help me with the dishes.

JIM. Let me give you a hand.

AMANDA. Indeed you will not!

JIM. I ought to be good for something.

AMANDA. Good for something! [*Her tone is rhapsodic.*] *You?* Why, Mr. O'Connor, nobody, *nobody's* given me this much entertainment in years—as you have!

JIM. Aw, now, Mrs. Wingfield!

AMANDA. I'm not exaggerating, not one bit! But Sister is all by her lonesome. You go keep her company in the parlor! I'll give you this lovely old candelabrum that used to be on the altar at the Church of the Heavenly Rest. It was melted a little out of shape when the church burnt down. Lightning struck it one spring. Gypsy Jones was holding a revival at the time and he intimated that the church was destroyed because the Episcopalians gave card parties.

JIM. Ha-ha.

AMANDA. And how about you coaxing Sister to drink a little wine? I think it would be good for her! Can you carry both at once?

JIM. Sure. I'm Superman!

AMANDA. Now, Thomas, get into this apron!

[JIM *comes into the dining room, carrying the candelabrum, its candles lighted, in one hand and a glass of wine in the other. The door of the kitchenette swings closed on* AMANDA*'s gay laughter; the flickering light approaches the portieres.* LAURA *sits up nervously as* JIM *enters. She can hardly speak from the almost intolerable strain of being alone with a stranger.*]

[*Screen legend:* "I don't suppose you remember me at all!"]

[*At first, before* JIM*'s warmth overcomes her paralyzing shyness,* LAURA*'s voice is thin and breathless, as though she had just run up a steep flight of stairs.* JIM*'s attitude is gently humorous. While the incident is apparently unimportant, it is to* LAURA *the climax of her secret life.*]

JIM. Hello there, Laura.

LAURA [*faintly*]. Hello.

[*She clears her throat.*]

JIM. How are you feeling now? Better?

LAURA. Yes. Yes, thank you.

JIM. This is for you. A little dandelion wine. [*He extends the glass toward her with extravagant gallantry.*]

LAURA. Thank you.

JIM. Drink it—but don't get drunk!

[*He laughs heartily.* LAURA *takes the glass uncertainly; she laughs shyly.*]
Where shall I set the candles?

LAURA. Oh—oh, anywhere . . .

JIM. How about here on the floor? Any objections?

LAURA. No.

JIM. I'll spread a newspaper under to catch the drippings. I like to sit on the floor. Mind if I do?

LAURA. Oh, no.

JIM. Give me a pillow?

LAURA. What?

JIM. A pillow!

LAURA. Oh . . . [*She hands him one quickly.*]

JIM. How about you? Don't you like to sit on the floor?

LAURA. Oh—yes.

JIM. Why don't you, then?

LAURA. I—will.

JIM. Take a pillow!

[LAURA *does. He sits on the floor on the other side of the candelabrum.* JIM *crosses his legs and smiles engagingly at her.*] I can't hardly see you sitting way over there.

LAURA. I can—see you.

JIM. I know, but that's not fair, I'm in the limelight.

[LAURA *moves her pillow closer.*]
Good! Now I can see you! Comfortable?

LAURA. Yes.

JIM. So am I. Comfortable as a cow! Will you have some gum?

LAURA. No, thank you.

JIM. I think that I will indulge, with your permission. [*He musingly unwraps a stick of gum and holds it up.*] Think of the fortune made by the guy that invented the first piece of chewing gum. Amazing, huh? The Wrigley Building is one of the sights of Chicago—I saw it when I went up to the Century of Progress. Did you take in the Century of Progress?[26]

---

[26] The byname of the 1933–1934 World's Fair in Chicago.

LAURA. No, I didn't.

JIM. Well, it was quite a wonderful exposition. What impressed me most was the Hall of Science. Gives you an idea of what the future will be in America, even more wonderful than the present time is! [*There is a pause.* JIM *smiles at her.*] Your brother tells me you're shy. Is that right, Laura?

LAURA. I—don't know.

JIM. I judge you to be an old-fashioned type of girl. Well, I think that's a pretty good type to be. Hope you don't think I'm being too personal—do you?

LAURA [*hastily, out of embarrassment*]. I believe I *will* take a piece of gum, if you— don't mind. [*clearing her throat*] Mr. O'Connor, have you—kept up with your singing?

JIM. Singing? Me?

LAURA. Yes, I remember what a beautiful voice you had.

JIM. When did you hear me sing?

[LAURA *does not answer, and in the long pause which follows a man's voice is heard singing offstage.*]

> VOICE:
> O blow, ye winds, heigh-ho,
> A-roving, I will go!
> I'm off to my love
> With a boxing glove—
> Ten thousand miles away!

JIM. You say you've heard me sing?

LAURA. Oh, yes! Yes, very often . . . I—don't suppose—you remember me—at all?

JIM [*smiling doubtfully*]. You know I have an idea I've seen you before. I had that idea soon as you opened the door. It seemed almost like I was about to remember your name. But the name that I started to call you—wasn't a name! And so I stopped myself before I said it.

LAURA. Wasn't it—Blue Roses?

JIM [*springing up, grinning*]. Blue Roses! By gosh, yes—Blue Roses! That's what I had on my tongue when you opened the door! Isn't it funny what tricks your memory plays? I didn't connect you with high school somehow or other. But that's where it was; it was high school. I didn't even know you were Shakespeare's sister! Gosh, I'm sorry.

LAURA. I didn't expect you to. You—barely knew me!

JIM. But we did have a speaking acquaintance, huh?

LAURA. Yes, we—spoke to each other.

JIM. When did you recognize me?

LAURA. Oh, right away!

JIM. Soon as I came in the door?

LAURA. When I heard your name I thought it was probably you. I knew that Tom used to know you a little in high school. So when you came in the door—well, then I was—sure.

JIM. Why didn't you *say* something, then?

LAURA [*breathless*]. I didn't know what to say, I was—too surprised!

JIM. For goodness' sakes! You know, this sure is funny!

LAURA. Yes! Yes, isn't it, though . . .

JIM. Didn't we have a class in something together?

LAURA. Yes, we did.

JIM. What class was that?

LAURA. It was—singing—chorus!

JIM. Aw!

LAURA. I sat across the aisle from you in the Aud.

JIM. Aw.

LAURA. Mondays, Wednesdays, and Fridays.

JIM. Now I remember—you always came in late.

LAURA. Yes, it was so hard for me, getting upstairs. I had that brace on my leg—it clumped so loud!

JIM. I never heard any clumping.

LAURA [*wincing at the recollection*]. To me it sounded like—thunder!

JIM. Well, well, well, I never even noticed.

LAURA. And everybody was seated before I came in. I had to walk in front of all those people. My seat was in the back row. I had to go clumping all the way up the aisle with everyone watching!

JIM. You shouldn't have been self-conscious.

LAURA. I know, but I was. It was always such a relief when the singing started.

JIM. Aw, yes, I've placed you now! I used to call you Blue Roses. How was it that I got started calling you that?

LAURA. I was out of school a little while with pleurosis. When I came back you asked me what was the matter. I said I had pleurosis—you thought I said *Blue Roses*. That's what you always called me after that!

JIM. I hope you didn't mind.

LAURA. Oh, no—I liked it. You see, I wasn't acquainted with many—people. . . .

JIM. As I remember you sort of stuck by yourself.

LAURA. I—I—never have had much luck at—making friends.

JIM. I don't see why you wouldn't.

LAURA. Well, I—started out badly.

JIM. You mean being—

LAURA. Yes, it sort of—stood between me—

JIM. You shouldn't have let it!

LAURA. I know, but it did, and—

JIM. You were shy with people!

LAURA. I tried not to be but never could—

JIM. Overcome it?

LAURA. No, I—I never could!

JIM. I guess being shy is something you have to work out of kind of gradually.

LAURA [*sorrowfully*]. Yes—I guess it—

JIM. Takes time!

LAURA. Yes—

JIM. People are not so dreadful when you know them. That's what you have to remember! And everybody has problems, not just you, but practically everybody has got some problems. You think of yourself as having the only problems, as being the only one who is disappointed. But just look around you and you will see lots of people as disappointed as you are. For instance, I hoped when I was going to high school that I would be further along at this time, six years later, than I am now. You remember that wonderful write-up I had in *The Torch*?

LAURA. Yes! [*She rises and crosses to the table.*]

JIM. It said I was bound to succeed in anything I went into!

[LAURA *returns with the high school yearbook.*]

Holy Jeez! *The Torch!*

[*He accepts it reverently. They smile across the book with mutual wonder.* LAURA *crouches beside him and they begin to turn the pages. LAURA's shyness is dissolving in his warmth.*]

LAURA. Here you are in *The Pirates of Penzance!*

JIM [*wistfully*]. I sang the baritone lead in that operetta.

LAURA [*raptly*]. So—*beautifully!*

JIM [*protesting*]. Aw—

LAURA. Yes, yes—beautifully—beautifully!

JIM. You heard me?

LAURA. All three times!

JIM. No!

LAURA. Yes!

JIM. All three performances?

LAURA [*looking down*]. Yes.

JIM. Why?

LAURA. I—wanted to ask you to—autograph my program. [*She takes the program from the back of the yearbook and shows it to him.*]

JIM. Why didn't you ask me to?

LAURA. You were always surrounded by your own friends so much that I never had a chance to.

JIM. You should have just—

LAURA. Well, I—thought you might think I was—

JIM. Thought I might think you was—what?

LAURA. Oh—

JIM [*with reflective relish*]. I was beleaguered by females in those days.

LAURA. You were terribly popular!

JIM. Yeah—

LAURA. You had such a—friendly way—

JIM. I was spoiled in high school.

LAURA. Everybody—liked you!

JIM. Including you?

LAURA. I—yes, I—did, too—[*She gently closes the book in her lap.*]

JIM. Well, well, well! Give me that program, Laura.

[*She hands it to him. He signs it with a flourish.*]

There you are—better late than never!

LAURA. Oh, I—what a—surprise!

JIM. My signature isn't worth very much right now. But some day—maybe—it will increase in value! Being disappointed is one thing and being discouraged is something else. I am disappointed but I am not discouraged. I'm twenty-three years old. How old are you?

LAURA. I'll be twenty-four in June.

JIM. That's not old age!

LAURA. No, but—

JIM. You finished high school?

LAURA [*with difficulty*]. I didn't go back.

JIM. You mean you dropped out?

LAURA. I made bad grades in my final examinations. [*She rises and replaces the book and the program on the table. Her voice is strained.*] How is—Emily Meisenbach getting along?

JIM. Oh, that kraut-head!

LAURA. Why do you call her that?

JIM. That's what she was.

LAURA. You're not still—going with her?

JIM. I never see her.

LAURA. It said in the "Personal" section that you were—engaged!

JIM. I know, but I wasn't impressed by that—propaganda!

LAURA. It wasn't—the truth?

JIM. Only in Emily's optimistic opinion!

LAURA. Oh—

[*Legend:* "What have you done since high school?"]

[JIM *lights a cigarette and leans indolently back on his elbows smiling at* LAURA *with a warmth and charm which lights her inwardly with altar candles. She remains by the table, picks up a piece from the glass menagerie collection, and turns it in her hands to cover her tumult.*]

JIM [*after several reflective puffs on his cigarette*]. What have you done since high school?

[*She seems not to hear him.*]

Huh?

[LAURA *looks up.*]

I said what have you done since high school, Laura?

LAURA. Nothing much.

JIM. You must have been doing something these six long years.

LAURA. Yes.

JIM. Well, then, such as what?

LAURA. I took a business course at business college—

JIM. How did that work out?

LAURA. Well, not very—well—I had to drop out, it gave me—indigestion—

[JIM *laughs gently.*]

JIM. What are you doing now?

LAURA. I don't do anything—much. Oh, please don't think I sit around doing nothing! My glass collection takes up a good deal of time. Glass is something you have to take good care of.

JIM. What did you say—about glass?

LAURA. Collection I said—I have one—[*She clears her throat and turns away again, acutely shy.*]

JIM [*abruptly*]. You know what I judge to be the trouble with you? Inferiority complex! Know what that is? That's what they call it when someone low-rates himself! I understand it because I had it, too. Although my case was not so aggravated as yours seems to be. I had it until I took up public speaking, developed my voice, and learned that I had an aptitude for science. Before that time I never thought of myself as being outstanding in any way whatsoever! Now I've never made a regular study of it, but I have a friend who says I can analyze people better than doctors that make a profession of it. I don't claim that to be necessarily true, but I can sure guess a person's psychology, Laura! [*He takes out his gum.*] Excuse me, Laura. I always take it out when the flavor is gone. I'll use this scrap of paper to wrap it in. I know how it is to get it stuck on a shoe. [*He wraps the gum in paper and puts it in his pocket.*] Yep—that's what I judge to be your principal trouble. A lack of confidence in yourself as a person. You don't have the proper amount of faith in yourself. I'm basing that fact on a number of your remarks and also on certain observations I've made. For instance that clumping you thought was so awful in high school. You say that you even dreaded to walk into class. You see what you did? You dropped out of school, you gave up an education because of a clump, which as far as I know was practically non-existent! A little physical defect is what you have. Hardly noticeable even! Magnified thousands of times by imagination! You know what my strong advice to you is? Think of yourself as *superior* in some way!

LAURA. In what way would I think?

JIM. Why, man alive, Laura! Just look about you a little. What do you see? A world full of common people! All of 'em born and all of 'em going to die! Which of them has one-tenth of your good points! Or mine! Or anyone else's, as far as that goes—gosh! Everybody excels in some one thing. Some in many! [*He unconsciously glances at himself in the mirror.*] All you've got to do is discover in *what!* Take me, for instance. [*He adjusts his tie at the mirror.*] My interest happens to lie in electro-dynamics. I'm taking a course in radio engineering at night school, Laura, on top of a fairly responsible job at the warehouse. I'm taking that course and studying public speaking.

LAURA. Ohhhh.

JIM. Because I believe in the future of television! [*turning his back to her.*] I wish to be ready to go up right along with it. Therefore I'm planning to get in on the ground floor. In fact I've already made the right connections and all that remains is for the industry itself to get under way! Full steam—[*His eyes are starry.*] *Knowledge*—Zzzzzp! *Money*—Zzzzzp!—*Power!* That's the cycle democracy is built on!

[*His attitude is convincingly dynamic.* LAURA *stares at him, even her shyness eclipsed in her absolute wonder. He suddenly grins.*]

I guess you think I think a lot of myself!

LAURA. No—o-o-o, I—

JIM. Now how about you? Isn't there something you take more interest in than anything else?

LAURA. Well, I do—as I said—have my—glass collection—

[*A peal of girlish laughter rings from the kitchenette.*]

JIM. I'm not right sure I know what you're talking about. What kind of glass is it?

LAURA. Little articles of it, they're ornaments mostly! Most of them are little animals made out of glass, the tiniest little animals in the world. Mother calls them a glass menagerie! Here's an example of one, if you'd like to see it! This one is one of the oldest. It's nearly thirteen.

[*Music:* "The Glass Menagerie."]

[*He stretches out his hand.*]

Oh, be careful—if you breathe, it breaks!

JIM. I'd better not take it. I'm pretty clumsy with things.

LAURA. Go on, I trust you with him! [*She places the piece in his palm.*] There now—you're holding him gently! Hold him over the light, he loves the light! You see how the light shines through him?

JIM. It sure does shine!

LAURA. I shouldn't be partial, but he is my favorite one.

JIM. What kind of thing is this one supposed to be?

LAURA. Haven't you noticed the single horn on his forehead?

JIM. A unicorn, huh?

LAURA. Mmmm-hmmm!

JIM. Unicorns—aren't they extinct in the modern world?

LAURA. I know!

JIM. Poor little fellow, he must feel sort of lonesome.

LAURA [*smiling*]. Well, if he does, he doesn't complain about it. He stays on a shelf with some horses that don't have horns and all of them seem to get along nicely together.

JIM. How do you know?

LAURA [*lightly*]. I haven't heard any arguments among them!

JIM [*grinning*]. No arguments, huh? Well, that's a pretty good sign! Where shall I set him?

LAURA. Put him on the table. They all like a change of scenery once in a while!

JIM. Well, well, well, well—[*He places the glass piece on the table, then raises his arms and stretches.*] Look how big my shadow is when I stretch!

LAURA. Oh, oh, yes—it stretches across the ceiling!

JIM [*crossing to the door*]. I think it's stopped raining. [*He opens the fire-escape door and the background music changes to a dance tune.*] Where does the music come from?

LAURA. From the Paradise Dance Hall across the alley.

JIM. How about cutting a rug a little, Miss Wingfield?

LAURA. Oh, I—

JIM. Or is your program filled up? Let me have a look at it. [*He grasps an imaginary card.*] Why, every dance is taken! I'll just have to scratch some out.
[*Waltz music: "La Golondrina."*]
Ahhh, a waltz! [*He executes some sweeping turns by himself, then holds his arms toward Laura.*]

LAURA [*breathlessly*]. I—can't dance!

JIM. There you go, that inferiority stuff!

LAURA. I've never danced in my life!

JIM. Come on, try!

LAURA. Oh, but I'd step on you!

JIM. I'm not made out of glass.

LAURA. How—how—how do we start?

JIM. Just leave it to me. You hold your arms out a little.

LAURA. Like this?

JIM [*taking her in his arms*]. A little bit higher. Right. Now don't tighten up, that's the main thing about it—relax.

LAURA [*laughing breathlessly*]. It's hard not to.

JIM. Okay.

LAURA. I'm afraid you can't budge me.

JIM. What do you bet I can't? [*He swings her into motion.*]

LAURA. Goodness, yes, you can!

JIM. Let yourself go, now Laura, just let yourself go.

LAURA. I'm—

JIM. Come on!

LAURA. —trying!

JIM. Not so stiff—easy does it!

LAURA. I know but I'm—

JIM. Loosen th' backbone! There now, that's a lot better.

LAURA. Am I?

JIM. Lots, lots better! [*He moves her about the room in a clumsy waltz.*]

LAURA. Oh, my!

JIM. Ha-ha!

LAURA. Oh, my goodness!

JIM. Ha-ha-ha!
[*They suddenly bump into the table, and the glass piece on it falls to the floor.* JIM *stops the dance.*]
What did we hit on?

LAURA. Table.

JIM. Did something fall off it? I think—

LAURA. Yes.

JIM. I hope that it wasn't the little glass horse with the horn!

LAURA. Yes [*She stoops to pick it up.*]

JIM. Aw, aw, aw. Is it broken?

LAURA. Now it is just like all the other horses.

JIM. It's lost its—

LAURA. Horn! It doesn't matter. Maybe it's a blessing in disguise.

JIM. You'll never forgive me. I bet that that was your favorite piece of glass.

LAURA. I don't have favorites much. It's no tragedy, Freckles. Glass breaks so easily. No matter how careful you are. The traffic jars the shelves and things fall off them.

JIM. Still I'm awfully sorry that I was the cause.

LAURA [*smiling*]. I'll just imagine he had an operation. The horn was removed to make him feel less—freakish!

[*They both laugh.*]

Now he will feel more at home with the other horses, the ones that don't have horns. . . .

JIM. Ha-ha, that's very funny! [*Suddenly he is serious.*] I'm glad to see that you have a sense of humor. You know—you're—well—very different! Surprisingly different from anyone else I know! [*His voice becomes soft and hesitant with a genuine feeling.*] Do you mind me telling you that?

[LAURA *is abashed beyond speech.*]

I mean it in a nice way—

[LAURA *nods shyly, looking away.*]

You make me feel sort of—I don't know how to put it! I'm usually pretty good at expressing things, but—this is something that I don't know how to say!

[LAURA *touches her throat and clears it — turns the broken unicorn in her hands. His voice becomes softer.*]

Has anyone ever told you that you were pretty?

[*There is a pause, and the music rises slightly.* LAURA *looks up slowly, with wonder, and shakes her head.*]

Well, you are! In a very different way from anyone else. And all the nicer because of the difference, too.

[*His voice becomes low and husky.* LAURA *turns away, nearly faint with the novelty of her emotions.*]

I wish that you were my sister. I'd teach you to have some confidence in yourself. The different people are not like other people, but being different is nothing to be ashamed of. Because other people are not such wonderful people. They're one hundred times one thousand. You're one times one! They walk all over the earth. You just stay here. They're common as—weeds, but—you—well, you're—*Blue Roses!*

[*Image on screen:* Blue Roses.]

[*The music changes.*]

LAURA. But blue is wrong for—roses. . . .

JIM. It's right for you! You're—pretty!

LAURA. In what respect am I pretty?

JIM. In all respects—believe me! Your eyes—your hair—are pretty! Your hands are pretty! [*He catches hold of her hand.*] You think I'm making this up because I'm invited to dinner and have to be nice. Oh, I could do that! I could put on an act for you, Laura, and say lots of things without being very sincere. But this time

I am. I'm talking to you sincerely. I happened to notice you had this inferiority complex that keeps you from feeling comfortable with people. Somebody needs to build your confidence up and make you proud instead of shy and turning away and—blushing. Somebody—ought to—*kiss* you, Laura!

[*His hand slips slowly up her arm to her shoulder as the music swells tumultuously. He suddenly turns her about and kisses her on the lips. When he releases her,* LAURA *sinks on the sofa with a bright, dazed look.* JIM *backs away and fishes in his pocket for a cigarette.*]

[*Legend on screen:* "A souvenir."]

Stumblejohn!

[*He lights the cigarette, avoiding her look. There is a peal of girlish laughter from* AMANDA *in the kitchenette.* LAURA *slowly raises and opens her hand. It still contains the little broken glass animal. She looks at it with a tender, bewildered expression.*]

Stumblejohn! I shouldn't have done that—that was way off the beam. You don't smoke, do you?

[*She looks up, smiling, not hearing the question. He sits beside her rather gingerly. She looks at him speechlessly—waiting. He coughs decorously and moves a little farther aside as he considers the situation and senses her feelings, dimly, with perturbation. He speaks gently.*]

Would you—care for a—mint?

[*She doesn't seem to hear him but her look grows brighter even.*]

Peppermint? Life Saver? My pocket's a regular drugstore—wherever I go. . . .

[*He pops a mint in his mouth. Then he gulps and decides to make a clean breast of it. He speaks slowly and gingerly.*] Laura, you know, if I had a sister like you, I'd do the same thing as Tom. I'd bring out fellows and—introduce her to them. The right type of boys—of a type to—appreciate her. Only—well—he made a mistake about me. Maybe I've got no call to be saying this. That may not have been the idea in having me over. But what if it was? There's nothing wrong with that. The only trouble is that in my case—I'm not in a situation to—do the right thing. I can't take down your number and say I'll phone. I can't call up next week and—ask for a date. I thought I had better explain the situation in case you—misunderstood it and—I hurt your feelings. . . .

[*There is a pause. Slowly, very slowly,* LAURA*'s look changes, her eyes returning slowly from his to the glass figure in her palm.* AMANDA *utters another gay laugh in the kitchenette.*]

LAURA [*faintly*]. You—won't—call again?

JIM. No, Laura, I can't. [*He rises from the sofa.*] As I was just explaining, I've—got strings on me. Laura, I've—been going steady! I go out all the time with a girl named Betty. She's a home-girl like you, and Catholic, and Irish, and in a great many ways we—get along fine. I met her last summer on a moonlight boat trip up the river to Alton, on the *Majestic*. Well—right away from the start it was—love!

[*Legend:* Love!]

[LAURA *sways slightly forward and grips the arm of the sofa. He fails to notice, now enrapt in his own comfortable being.*]

Being in love has made a new man of me!

[*Leaning stiffly forward, clutching the arm of the sofa,* LAURA *struggles visibly with her storm. But* JIM *is oblivious; she is a long way off.*]

The power of love is really pretty tremendous! Love is something that—changes the whole world, Laura!

[*The storm abates a little and* LAURA *leans back. He notices her again.*]

It happened that Betty's aunt took sick, she got a wire and had to go to Centralia. So Tom—when he asked me to dinner—I naturally just accepted the invitation, not knowing that you—that he—that I—[*He stops awkwardly.*] Huh— I'm a stumblejohn!

[*He flops back on the sofa. The holy candles on the altar of* LAURA's *face have been snuffed out. There is a look of almost infinite desolation.* JIM *glances at her uneasily.*]

I wish that you would—say something.

[*She bites her lip which was trembling and then bravely smiles. She opens her hand again on the broken glass figure. Then she gently takes his hand and raises it level with her own. She carefully places the unicorn in the palm of his hand, then pushes his fingers closed upon it.*]

What are you—doing that for? You want me to have him? Laura?

[*She nods.*]

What for?

LAURA. A—souvenir. . . .

[*She rises unsteadily and crouches beside the Victrola to wind it up.*]

[*Legend on screen:* "Things have a way of turning out so badly!" *Or image:* "Gentleman caller waving goodbye—gaily."]

[*At this moment* AMANDA *rushes brightly back into the living room. She bears a pitcher of fruit punch in an old-fashioned cut-glass pitcher, and a plate of macaroons. The plate has a gold border and poppies painted on it.*]

AMANDA. Well, well, well! Isn't the air delightful after the shower? I've made you children a little liquid refreshment.

[*She turns gaily to* JIM.] Jim, do you know that song about lemonade?

>   "Lemonade, lemonade
>   Made in the shade and stirred with a spade—
>   Good enough for any old maid!"

JIM [*uneasily*]. Ha-ha! No—I never heard it.

AMANDA. Why, Laura! You look so serious!

JIM. We were having a serious conversation.

AMANDA. Good! Now you're better acquainted!

JIM [*uncertainly*]. Ha-ha! Yes.

AMANDA. You modern young people are much more serious-minded than my generation. I was so gay as a girl!

JIM. You haven't changed, Mrs. Wingfield.

AMANDA. Tonight I'm rejuvenated! The gaiety of the occasion, Mr. O'Connor! [*She tosses her head with a peal of laughter, spilling some lemonade.*] Ooo! I'm baptizing myself!

JIM. Here—let me—

AMANDA [*setting the pitcher down*]. There now. I discovered we had some maraschino cherries. I dumped them in, juice and all!

JIM. You shouldn't have gone to that trouble, Mrs. Wingfield.

AMANDA. Trouble, trouble? Why, it was loads of fun! Didn't you hear me cutting up in the kitchen? I bet your ears were burning! I told Tom how outdone with him I was for keeping you to himself so long a time! He should have brought you over much, much sooner! Well, now that you've found your way, I want you to be a very frequent caller! Not just occasional but all the time. Oh, we're going to have a lot of gay times together! I see them coming! Mmm, just breath that air! So fresh, and the moon's so pretty! I'll skip back out—I know where my place is when young folks are having a—serious conversation!

JIM. Oh, don't go out, Mrs. Wingfield. The fact of the matter is I've got to be going.

AMANDA. Going, now? You're joking! Why, it's only the shank of the evening, Mr. O'Connor!

JIM. Well, you know how it is.

AMANDA. You mean you're a young workingman and have to keep workingmen's hours. We'll let you off early tonight. But only on the condition that next time you stay later. What's the best night for you? Isn't Saturday night the best night for you workingmen?

JIM. I have a couple of time-clocks to punch, Mrs. Wingfield. One at morning, another one at night!

AMANDA. My, but you *are* ambitious! You work at night, too?

JIM. No, Ma'am, not work but—Betty!

[*He crosses deliberately to pick up his hat. The band at the Paradise Dance Hall goes into a tender waltz.*]

AMANDA. Betty? Betty? Who's—Betty!

[*There is an ominous cracking sound in the sky.*]

JIM. Oh, just a girl. The girl I go steady with!

[*He smiles charmingly. The sky falls.*]

[*Legend:* "The Sky Falls."]

AMANDA [*a long-drawn exhalation*]. Ohhh . . . Is it a serious romance, Mr. O'Connor?

JIM. We're going to be married the second Sunday in June.

AMANDA. Ohhhh—how nice! Tom didn't mention that you were engaged to be married.

JIM. The cat's not out of the bag at the warehouse yet. You know how they are. They call you Romeo and stuff like that. [*He stops at the oval mirror to put on his hat. He carefully shapes the brim and the crown to give a discreetly dashing effect.*] It's been a wonderful evening, Mrs. Wingfield. I guess this is what they mean by Southern hospitality.

AMANDA. It really wasn't anything at all.

JIM. I hope it don't seem like I'm rushing off. But I promised Betty I'd pick her up at the Wabash depot, an' by the time I get my jalopy down there her train'll be in. Some women are pretty upset if you keep 'em waiting.

AMANDA. Yes, I know—the tyranny of women! [*She extends her hand.*] Goodbye, Mr. O'Connor. I wish you luck—and happiness—and success! All three of them, and so does Laura! Don't you, Laura?

LAURA. Yes!

JIM [*taking* LAURA's *hand*]. Goodbye, Laura. I'm certainly going to treasure that souvenir. And don't you forget the good advice I gave you. [*He raises his voice to a cheery shout.*] So long, Shakespeare! Thanks again, ladies. Good night!

[*He grins and ducks jauntily out. Still bravely grimacing,* AMANDA *closes the door on the gentleman caller. Then she turns back to the room with a puzzled expression. She and* LAURA *don't dare to face each other.* LAURA *crouches beside the Victrola to wind it.*]

AMANDA [*faintly*]. Things have a way of turning out so badly. I don't believe that I would play the Victrola. Well, well—well! Our gentleman caller was engaged to be married! [*She raises her voice.*] Tom!

TOM [*from the kitchenette*]. Yes, Mother?

AMANDA. Come in here a minute. I want to tell you something awfully funny.

TOM [*entering with a macaroon and a glass of lemonade*]. Has the gentleman caller gotten away already?

AMANDA. The gentleman caller has made an early departure. What a wonderful joke you played on us!

TOM. How do you mean?

AMANDA. You didn't mention that he was engaged to be married.

TOM. Jim? Engaged?

AMANDA. That's what he just informed us.

TOM. I'll be jiggered! I didn't know about that.

AMANDA. That seems very peculiar.

TOM. What's peculiar about it?

AMANDA. Didn't you call him your best friend down at the warehouse?

TOM. He is, but how did I know?

AMANDA. It seems extremely peculiar that you wouldn't know your best friend was going to be married!

TOM. The warehouse is where I work, not where I know things about people!

AMANDA. You don't know things anywhere! You live in a dream; you manufacture illusions!

[*He crosses to the door.*]

Where are you going?

TOM. I'm going to the movies.

AMANDA. That's right, now that you've had us make such fools of ourselves. The effort, the preparations, all the expense! The new floor lamp, the rug, the clothes for Laura! All for what? To entertain some other girl's fiancé! Go to the movies, go! Don't think about us, a mother deserted, an unmarried sister who's crippled and has no job! Don't let anything interfere with your selfish pleasure! Just go, go, go—to the movies!

TOM. All right, I will! The more you shout about my selfishness to me the quicker I'll go, and I won't go to the movies!

AMANDA. Go, then! Go to the moon—you selfish dreamer!

[*TOM smashes his glass on the floor. He plunges out on the fire escape, slamming the door. LAURA screams in fright. The dance-hall music becomes louder. TOM stands on the fire escape, gripping the rail. The moon breaks through the storm clouds, illuminating his face.*]

[*Legend on screen:* "And so goodbye . . ."]

[*TOM's closing speech is timed with what is happening inside the house. We see, as though through soundproof glass, that AMANDA appears to be making a comforting speech to LAURA, who is huddled upon the sofa. Now that we cannot hear the mother's speech, her silliness is gone and she has dignity and tragic beauty. LAURA's hair hides her face until, at the end of the speech, she lifts her head to smile at her mother. AMANDA's gestures are slow and graceful, almost dancelike, as she comforts her daughter. At the end of her speech she glances a moment at the father's picture—then withdraws through the portieres. At the close of TOM's speech, LAURA blows out the candles, ending the play.*]

TOM. I didn't go to the moon, I went much further—for time is the longest distance between two places. Not long after that I was fired for writing a poem on the lid of a shoe-box. I left Saint Louis. I descended the steps of this fire escape for a last time and followed, from then on, in my father's footsteps, attempting to find in motion what was lost in space. I traveled around a great deal. The cities swept about me like dead leaves, leaves that were brightly colored but torn away from the branches. I would have stopped, but I was pursued by something. It always came upon me unawares, taking me altogether by surprise. Perhaps it was a familiar bit of music. Perhaps it was only a piece of transparent glass. Perhaps I am walking along a street at night, in some strange city, before I have found companions. I pass the lighted window of a shop where perfume is sold. The window is filled with pieces of colored glass, tiny transparent bottles in delicate colors, like bits of a shattered rainbow. Then all at once my sister touches my shoulder. I turn around and look into her eyes. Oh, Laura, Laura, I tried to leave you behind me, but I am more faithful than I intended to be! I reach for a cigarette, I cross the street, I run into the movies or a bar, I buy a drink, I speak to the nearest stranger—anything that can blow your candles out!

[LAURA *bends over the candles.*]

For nowadays the world is lit by lightning! Blow out your candles, Laura—and so goodbye. . . .

[*She blows the candles out.*]

[1944]

Lorraine Hansberry   *1930–1965*

A RAISIN IN THE SUN

CHARACTERS

RUTH YOUNGER
TRAVIS YOUNGER
WALTER LEE YOUNGER (BROTHER)
BENEATHA YOUNGER
LENA YOUNGER (MAMA)

JOSEPH ASAGAI
GEORGE MURCHISON
KARL LINDNER
BOBO
MOVING MEN

The action of the play is set in Chicago's Southside, sometime between World War II and the present.

ACT I

SCENE I:
Friday morning.

SCENE II:
The following morning.

ACT II

SCENE I:
Later, the same day.

SCENE II:
Friday night, a few weeks later.

SCENE III:
Moving day, one week later.

ACT III

An hour later.

ACT I

SCENE I

The YOUNGER *living room would be a comfortable and well-ordered room if it were not for a number of indestructible contradictions to this state of being. Its furnishings are typical and undistinguished and their primary feature now is that they have clearly had to accommodate the living of too many people for too many years—and they are tired. Still, we can see that at some time, a time probably no longer remembered by the family (except perhaps for* MAMA), *the furnishings of this room were actually selected with care and love and even hope—and brought to this apartment and arranged with taste and pride.*

That was a long time ago. Now the once loved pattern of the couch upholstery has to fight to show itself from under acres of crocheted doilies and couch covers which have themselves finally come to be more important than the upholstery. And here a table or a chair has been moved to disguise the worn places in the carpet; but the carpet has fought back by showing its weariness, with depressing uniformity, elsewhere on its surface.

Weariness has, in fact, won in this room. Everything has been polished, washed, sat on, used, scrubbed too often. All pretenses but living itself have long since vanished from the very atmosphere of this room.

Moreover, a section of this room, for it is not really a room unto itself, though the landlord's lease would make it seem so, slopes backward to provide a small kitchen area, where the family prepares the meals that are eaten in the living room proper, which must also serve as dining room. The single window that has been provided for these "two" rooms is located in this kitchen area. The sole natural light the family may enjoy in the course of a day is only that which fights its way through this little window.

At left, a door leads to a bedroom which is shared by MAMA *and her daughter,* BENEATHA. *At right, opposite, is a second room (which in the beginning of the life of this apartment was probably a breakfast room) which serves as a bedroom for* WALTER *and his wife,* RUTH.

Time: Sometime between World War II and the present.

Place: Chicago's Southside.

At Rise: It is morning dark in the living room. TRAVIS *is asleep on the make-down bed at center. An alarm clock sounds from within the bedroom at right, and presently* RUTH *enters from that room and closes the door behind her. She crosses sleepily toward the window. As she passes her sleeping son she reaches down and shakes him a little. At the window she raises the shade and a dusky Southside morning light comes in feebly. She fills a pot with water and puts it on to boil. She calls to the boy, between yawns, in a slightly muffled voice.*

RUTH *is about thirty. We can see that she was a pretty girl, even exceptionally so, but now it is apparent that life has been little that she expected, and disappointment has already begun to hang in her face. In a few years, before thirty-five even, she will be known among her people as a "settled woman."*

She crosses to her son and gives him a good, final, rousing shake.

RUTH. Come on now, boy, it's seven thirty! [*Her son sits up at last, in a stupor of sleepiness.*] I say hurry up, Travis! You ain't the only person in the world got to use a bathroom! [*The child, a sturdy, handsome little boy of ten or eleven, drags himself out of the bed and almost blindly takes his towels and "today's clothes" from drawers and a closet and goes out to the bathroom, which is in an outside hall and which is shared by another family or families on the same floor.* RUTH *crosses to the bedroom door at right and opens it and calls in to her husband.*] Walter Lee! . . . It's after seven thirty! Lemme see you do some waking up in there now! [*She waits.*] You better get up from there, man! It's after seven thirty I tell you. [*She waits again.*] All right, you just go ahead and lay there and next thing you know Travis be finished and Mr. Johnson'll be in there and you'll be fussing and cussing round here like a mad man! And be late too! [*She waits, at the end of patience.*] Walter Lee—it's time for you to get up!

[*She waits another second and then starts to go into the bedroom, but is apparently satisfied that her husband has begun to get up. She stops, pulls the door to, and returns to the kitchen area. She wipes her face with a moist cloth and runs her fingers through her sleep-disheveled hair in a vain effort and ties an apron around her housecoat. The bedroom door at right opens and her husband stands in the doorway in his pajamas, which are rumpled and mismated. He is a lean, intense young man in his middle thirties, inclined to quick nervous movements and erratic speech habits—and always in his voice there is a quality of indictment.*]

WALTER. Is he out yet?

RUTH. What you mean *out*? He ain't hardly got in there good yet.

WALTER [*Wandering in, still more oriented to sleep than to a new day*]. Well, what was you doing all that yelling for if I can't even get in there yet? [*Stopping and thinking.*] Check coming today?

RUTH. They *said* Saturday and this is just Friday and I hopes to God you ain't going to get up here first thing this morning and start talking to me 'bout no money— 'cause I 'bout don't want to hear it.

WALTER. Something the matter with you this morning?

RUTH. No—I'm just sleepy as the devil. What kind of eggs you want?

WALTER. Not scrambled. [RUTH *starts to scramble eggs.*] Paper come? [RUTH *points impatiently to the rolled up* Tribune *on the table, and he gets it and spreads it out and vaguely reads the front page.*] Set off another bomb yesterday.

RUTH [*maximum indifference*]. Did they?

WALTER [*Looking up*]. What's the matter with you?

RUTH. Ain't nothing the matter with me. And don't keep asking me that this morning.

WALTER. Ain't nobody bothering you. [*Reading the news of the day absently again.*] Say Colonel McCormick is sick.

RUTH [*Affecting tea-party interest*]. Is he now? Poor thing.

WALTER [*Sighing and looking at his watch*]. Oh, me. [*He waits.*] Now what is that boy doing in the bathroom all this time? He just going to have to start getting up earlier. I can't be being late to work on account of him fooling around in there.

RUTH [*Turning on him*]. Oh, no he ain't going to be getting up no earlier no such thing! It ain't his fault that he can't get to bed no earlier nights 'cause he got a bunch of crazy good-for-nothing clowns sitting up running their mouths in what is supposed to be his bedroom after ten o'clock at night . . .

WALTER. That's what you mad about, ain't it? The things I want to talk about with my friends just couldn't be important in your mind, could they?

[*He rises and finds a cigarette in her handbag on the table and crosses to the little window and looks out, smoking and deeply enjoying this first one.*]

RUTH [*Almost matter of factly, a complaint too automatic to deserve emphasis*]. Why you always got to smoke before you eat in the morning?

WALTER [*At the window*]. Just look at 'em down there . . . Running and racing to work . . . [*He turns and faces his wife and watches her a moment at the stove, and then, suddenly.*] You look young this morning, baby.

RUTH [*Indifferently*]. Yeah?

WALTER. Just for a second—stirring them eggs. It's gone now—just for a second it was—you looked real young again. [*Then, drily.*] It's gone now—you look like yourself again.

RUTH. Man, if you don't shut up and leave me alone.

WALTER [*Looking out to the street again*]. First thing a man ought to learn in life is not to make love to no colored woman first thing in the morning. You all some evil people at eight o'clock in the morning.

[TRAVIS *appears in the hall doorway, almost fully dressed and quite wide awake now, his towels and pajamas across his shoulders. He opens the door and signals for his father to make the bathroom in a hurry.*]

TRAVIS [*Watching the bathroom*]. Daddy, come on!

[WALTER *gets his bathroom utensils and flies out to the bathroom.*]

RUTH. Sit down and have your breakfast, Travis.

TRAVIS. Mama, this is Friday. [*Gleefully.*] Check coming tomorrow, huh?

RUTH. You get your mind off money and eat your breakfast.

TRAVIS [*Eating*]. This is the morning we supposed to bring the fifty cents to school.

RUTH. Well, I ain't got no fifty cents this morning.

TRAVIS. Teacher say we have to.

RUTH. I don't care what teacher say. I ain't got it. Eat your breakfast, Travis.

TRAVIS. I *am* eating.

RUTH. Hush up now and just eat!

[*The boy gives her an exasperated look for her lack of understanding, and eats grudgingly.*]

TRAVIS. You think Grandmama would have it?

RUTH. No! And I want you to stop asking your grandmother for money, you hear me?

TRAVIS [*Outraged*]. Gaaaleee! I don't ask her, she just gimme it sometimes!

RUTH. Travis Willard Younger—I got too much on me this morning to be—

TRAVIS. Maybe Daddy—

RUTH. *Travis!*

[*The boy hushes abruptly. They are both quiet and tense for several seconds.*]

TRAVIS [*Presently*]. Could I maybe go carry some groceries in front of the supermarket for a little while after school then?

RUTH. Just hush, I said. [*Travis jabs his spoon into his cereal bowl viciously, and rests his head in anger upon his fists.*] If you through eating, you can get over there and make up your bed.

[*The boy obeys stiffly and crosses the room, almost mechanically, to the bed and more or less carefully folds the covering. He carries the bedding into his mother's room and returns with his books and cap.*]

TRAVIS [*Sulking and standing apart from her unnaturally*]. I'm gone.

RUTH [*Looking up from the stove to inspect him automatically.*] Come here. [*He crosses to her and she studies his head.*] If you don't take this comb and fix this here head, you better! [TRAVIS *puts down his books with a great sigh of oppression, and crosses to the mirror. His mother mutters under her breath about his "stubbornness."*] 'Bout to march out of here with that head looking just like chickens slept in it! I just don't know where you get your stubborn ways ... And get your jacket, too. Looks chilly out this morning.

TRAVIS [*With conspicuously brushed hair and jacket*]. I'm gone.

RUTH. Get carfare and milk money—[*Waving one finger.*]— and not a single penny for no caps, you hear me?

TRAVIS [*With sullen politeness*]. Yes'm.

[*He turns in outrage to leave. His mother watches after him as in his frustration he approaches the door almost comically. When she speaks to him, her voice has become a very gentle tease.*]

RUTH [*Mocking; as she thinks he would say it*]. Oh, Mama makes me so mad sometimes, I don't know what to do! [*She waits and continues to his back as he stands stock-still in front of the door.*] I wouldn't kiss that woman good-bye for nothing in this world this morning! [*The boy finally turns around and rolls his eyes at her, knowing the mood has changed and he is vindicated; he does not, however, move toward her yet.*] Not for nothing in this world! [*She finally laughs aloud at him and holds out her arms to him and we see that it is a way between them, very old and practiced. He crosses to her and allows her to embrace him warmly but keeps his face fixed with masculine rigidity. She holds him back from her presently and looks at him and runs her fingers over the features of his face. With utter gentleness—.*] Now—whose little old angry man are you?

TRAVIS [*The masculinity and gruffness start to fade at last*]. Aw gaalee—Mama . . .

RUTH [*Mimicking*]. Aw—gaaaaalleeeee, Mama! [*She pushes him, with rough playfulness and finality, toward the door.*] Get on out of here or you going to be late.

TRAVIS [*In the face of love, new aggressiveness*]. Mama, could I *please* go carry groceries?

RUTH. Honey, it's starting to get so cold evenings.

WALTER [*Coming in from the bathroom and drawing a make-believe gun from a make-believe holster and shooting at his son*]. What is it he wants to do?

RUTH. Go carry groceries after school at the supermarket.

WALTER. Well, let him go . . .

TRAVIS [*Quickly, to the ally*]. I *have* to—she won't gimme the fifty cents . . .

WALTER [*To his wife only*]. Why not?

RUTH [*Simply, and with flavor*]. 'Cause we don't have it.

WALTER [*To* RUTH *only*]. What you tell the boy things like that for? [*Reaching down into his pants with a rather important gesture.*] Here, son—

[*He hands the boy the coin, but his eyes are directed to his wife's.* TRAVIS *takes the money happily.*]

TRAVIS. Thanks, Daddy.

[*He starts out,* RUTH *watches both of them with murder in her eyes.* WALTER *stands and stares back at her with defiance, and suddenly reaches into his pocket again on an afterthought.*]

WALTER [*Without even looking at his son, still staring hard at his wife*]. In fact, here's another fifty cents . . . Buy yourself some fruit today—or take a taxi cab to school or something!

TRAVIS. Whoopee—

[*He leaps up and clasps his father around the middle with his legs, and they face each other in mutual appreciation; slowly* WALTER LEE *peeks around the boy to catch the violent rays from his wife's eyes and draws his head back as if shot.*]

WALTER. You better get down now—and get to school, man.

TRAVIS [*At the door*]. O.K. Good-bye.

[*He exits.*]

WALTER [*After him, pointing with pride*]. That's *my* boy. [*She looks at him in disgust and turns back to her work.*] You know what I was thinking 'bout in the bathroom this morning?

RUTH. No.

WALTER. How come you always try to be so pleasant!

RUTH. What is there to be pleasant 'bout!

WALTER. You want to know what I was thinking 'bout in the bathroom or not!

RUTH. I know what you was thinking 'bout.

WALTER [*Ignoring her*]. 'Bout what me and Willy Harris was talking about last night.

RUTH [*Immediately—a refrain*]. Willy Harris is a good-for-nothing loud mouth.

WALTER. Anybody who talks to me has got to be a good-for-nothing loud mouth, ain't he? And what you know about who is just a good-for-nothing loud mouth? Charlie Atkins was just a "good-for-nothing loud mouth" too, wasn't he! When he wanted me to go in the dry-cleaning business with him. And now—he's grossing a hundred thousand a year. A hundred thousand dollars a year! You still call *him* a loud mouth!

RUTH [*Bitterly*]. Oh, Walter Lee . . .

[*She folds her head on her arms over on the table.*]

WALTER [*Rising and coming to her and standing over her*]. You tired, ain't you? Tired of everything. Me, the boy, the way we live—this beat-up hole—everything. Ain't you? [*She doesn't look up, doesn't answer.*] So tired—moaning and groaning all the time, but you wouldn't do nothing to help, would you? You couldn't be on my side that long for nothing, could you?

RUTH. Walter, please leave me alone.

WALTER. A man needs for a woman to back him up . . .

RUTH. Walter—

WALTER. Mama would listen to you. You know she listen to you more than she do me and Bennie. She think more of you. All you have to do is just sit down with her when you drinking your coffee one morning and talking 'bout things like you do and—[*He sits down beside her and demonstrates graphically what he thinks her methods and tone should be.*]—you just sip your coffee, see, and say easy like that you been thinking 'bout that deal Walter Lee is so interested in, 'bout the store and all, and sip some more coffee, like what you saying ain't really that important to you— And the next thing you know, she be listening good and asking you questions and when I come home—I can tell her the details. This ain't no fly-by-night proposition, baby. I mean we figured it out, me and Willy and Bobo.

RUTH [*With a frown*]. Bobo?

WALTER. Yeah. You see, this little liquor store we got in mind cost seventy-five thousand and we figured the initial investment on the place be 'bout thirty thousand, see. That be ten thousand each. Course, there's a couple of hundred you got to pay so's you don't spend your life just waiting for them clowns to let your license get approved—

RUTH. You mean graft?

WALTER [*Frowning impatiently*]. Don't call it that. See there, that just goes to show you what women understand about the world. Baby, don't *nothing* happen for you in this world 'les you pay *somebody* off!

RUTH. Walter, leave me alone! [*She raises her head and stares at him vigorously—then says, more quietly.*] Eat your eggs, they gonna be cold.

WALTER [*Straightening up from her and looking off*]. That's it. There you are. Man say to his woman: I got me a dream. His woman say: Eat your eggs. [*Sadly, but gaining in power.*] Man say: I got to take hold of this here world, baby! And a woman will say: Eat your eggs and go to work. [*Passionately now.*] Man say: I got to change my life, I'm choking to death, baby! And his woman say—[*In utter anguish as he brings his fists down on his thighs.*]—Your eggs is getting cold!

RUTH [*Softly*]. Walter, that ain't none of our money.

WALTER [*Not listening at all or even looking at her*]. This morning, I was lookin' in the mirror and thinking about it . . . I'm thirty-five years old; I been married eleven years and I got a boy who sleeps in the living room—[*Very, very quietly*]—and all I got to give him is stories about how rich white people live . . .

RUTH. Eat your eggs, Walter.

WALTER. *Damn my eggs . . . damn all the eggs that ever was!*

RUTH. Then go to work.

WALTER [*Looking up at her*]. See—I'm trying to talk to you 'bout myself—[*Shaking his head with the repetition*]—and all you can say is eat them eggs and go to work.

RUTH [*Wearily*]. Honey, you never say nothing new. I listen to you every day, every night and every morning, and you never say nothing new. [*Shrugging.*] So you would rather *be* Mr. Arnold than be his chauffeur. So—I would *rather* be living in Buckingham Palace.[1]

---

[1] The residence of the British royal family in London.

WALTER. That is just what is wrong with the colored woman in this world . . . Don't understand about building their men up and making 'em feel like they somebody. Like they can do something.

RUTH [*Drily, but to hurt*]. There *are* colored men who do things.

WALTER. No thanks to the colored woman.

RUTH. Well, being a colored woman, I guess I can't help myself none.

[*She rises and gets the ironing board and sets it up and attacks a huge pile of rough-dried clothes, sprinkling them in preparation for the ironing and then rolling them into tight fat balls.*]

WALTER [*Mumbling*]. We one group of men tied to a race of women with small minds.

[*His sister* BENEATHA *enters. She is about twenty, as slim and intense as her brother. She is not as pretty as her sister-in-law, but her lean, almost intellectual face has a handsomeness of its own. She wears a bright-red flannel nightie, and her thick hair stands wildly about her head. Her speech is a mixture of many things; it is different from the rest of the family's insofar as education has permeated her sense of English—and perhaps the Midwestern rather than the South has finally—at last—won out in her inflection; but not altogether, because over all of it is a soft slurring and transformed use of vowels which is the decided influence of the Southside. She passes through the room without looking at either* RUTH *or* WALTER *and goes to the outside door and looks, a little blindly, out to the bathroom. She sees that it has been lost to the Johnsons. She closes the door with a sleepy vengeance and crosses to the table and sits down a little defeated*].

BENEATHA. I am going to start timing those people.

WALTER. You should get up earlier.

BENEATHA [*Her face in her hands. She is still fighting the urge to go back to bed*]. Really— would you suggest dawn? Where's the paper?

WALTER [*Pushing the paper across the table to her as he studies her almost clinically, as though he has never seen her before*]. You a horrible-looking chick at this hour.

BENEATHA [*Drily*]. Good morning, everybody.

WALTER [*Senselessly*]. How is school coming?

BENEATHA [*In the same spirit*]. Lovely. Lovely. And you know, biology is the greatest. [*Looking up at him.*] I dissected something that looked just like you yesterday.

WALTER. I just wondered if you've made up your mind and everything.

BENEATHA [*Gaining in sharpness and impatience*]. And what did I answer yesterday morning—and the day before that?

RUTH [*From the ironing board, like someone disinterested and old*]. Don't be so nasty, Bennie.

BENEATHA [*Still to her brother*]. And the day before that and the day before that!

WALTER [*Defensively*]. I'm interested in you. Something wrong with that? Ain't many girls who decide—

WALTER AND BENEATHA [*In unison*]. —"to be a doctor." [*Silence.*]

WALTER. Have we figured out yet just exactly how much medical school is going to cost?

RUTH. Walter Lee, why don't you leave that girl alone and get out of here to work?

BENEATHA [*Exits to the bathroom and bangs and bangs on the door*]. Come on out of there, please! [*She comes back into the room.*]

WALTER [*Looking at his sister intently*]. You know the check is coming tomorrow.

BENEATHA [*Turning on him with a sharpness all her own*]. That money belongs to

Mama, Walter, and it's for her to decide how she wants to use it. I don't care if she wants to buy a house or a rocket ship or just nail it up somewhere and look at it. It's hers. Not ours—*hers*.

WALTER [*Bitterly*]. Now ain't that fine! You just got your mother's interest at heart, ain't you, girl? You such a nice girl—but if Mama got that money she can always take a few thousand and help you through school too—can't she?

BENEATHA. I have never asked anyone around here to do anything for me!

WALTER. No! And the line between asking and just accepting when the time comes is big and wide—ain't it!

BENEATHA [*With fury*]. What do you want from me, Brother—that I quit school or just drop dead, which!

WALTER. I don't want nothing but for you to stop acting holy 'round here. Me and Ruth done made some sacrifices for you—why can't you do something for the family?

RUTH. Walter, don't be dragging me in it.

WALTER. You are in it—Don't you get up and go work in somebody's kitchen for the last three years to help put clothes on her back?

RUTH. Oh, Walter—that's not fair . . .

WALTER. It ain't that nobody expects you to get on your knees and say thank you, Brother; thank you, Ruth; thank you, Mama—and thank you, Travis, for wearing the same pair of shoes for two semesters—

BENEATHA [*Dropping to her knees*]. Well—I *do*—all right?—thank everybody . . . and forgive me for ever wanting to be anything at all . . . forgive me, forgive me!

RUTH. Please stop it! Your mama'll hear you.

WALTER. Who the hell told you you had to be a doctor? If you so crazy 'bout messing 'round with sick people—then go be a nurse like other women—or just get married and be quiet . . .

BENEATHA. Well—you finally got it said . . . It took you three years but you finally got it said. Walter, give up; leave me alone—it's Mama's money.

WALTER. *He was my father, too!*

BENEATHA. So what? He was mine, too—and Travis' grandfather—but the insurance money belongs to Mama. Picking on me is not going to make her give it to you to invest in any liquor stores—[*Underbreath, dropping into a chair*]—and I for one say, God bless Mama for that!

WALTER [*To* RUTH]. See—did you hear? Did you hear!

RUTH. Honey, please go to work.

WALTER. Nobody in this house is ever going to understand me.

BENEATHA. Because you're a nut.

WALTER. Who's a nut?

BENEATHA. You—you are a nut. Thee is mad, boy.

WALTER [*Looking at his wife and his sister from the door, very sadly*]. The world's most backward race of people, and that's a fact.

BENEATHA [*Turning slowly in her chair*]. And then there are all those prophets who would lead us out of the wilderness—[WALTER *slams out of the house*]—into the swamps!

RUTH. Bennie, why you always gotta be pickin' on your brother? Can't you be a little sweeter sometimes?

[*Door opens.* WALTER *walks in.*]

WALTER [*To* RUTH]. I need some money for carfare.

RUTH [*Looks at him, then warms; teasing, but tenderly*]. Fifty cents? [*She goes to her bag and gets money.*] Here, take a taxi.

[WALTER *exits.* MAMA *enters. She is a woman in her early sixties, full-bodied and strong. She is one of those women of a certain grace and beauty who wear it so unobtrusively that it takes a while to notice. Her dark-brown face is surrounded by the total whiteness of her hair, and, being a woman who has adjusted to many things in life and overcome many more, her face is full of strength. She has, we can see, wit and faith of a kind that keep her eyes lit and full of interest and expectancy. She is, in a word, a beautiful woman. Her bearing is perhaps most like the noble bearing of the women of the Hereros of Southwest Africa—rather as if she imagines that as she walks she still bears a basket or a vessel upon her head. Her speech, on the other hand, is as careless as her carriage is precise—she is inclined to slur everything—but her voice is perhaps not so much quiet as simply soft.*]

MAMA. Who that 'round here slamming doors at this hour?

[*She crosses through the room, goes to the window, opens it, and brings in a feeble little plant growing doggedly in a small pot on the window sill. She feels the dirt and puts it back out.*]

RUTH. That was Walter Lee. He and Bennie was at it again.

MAMA. My children and they tempers. Lord, if this little old plant don't get more sun than it's been getting it ain't never going to see spring again. [*She turns from the window.*] What's the matter with you this morning, Ruth? You looks right peaked. You aiming to iron all them things? Leave some for me. I'll get to 'em this afternoon. Bennie honey, it's too drafty for you to be sitting 'round half dressed. Where's your robe?

BENEATHA. In the cleaners.

MAMA. Well, go get mine and put it on.

BENEATHA I'm not cold, Mama, honest.

MAMA. I know—but you so thin . . .

BENEATHA [*Irritably*]. Mama, I'm not cold.

MAMA [*Seeing the make-down bed as* TRAVIS *has left it.*] Lord have mercy, look at that poor bed. Bless his heart—he tries, don't he?

[*She moves to the bed* TRAVIS *has sloppily made up.*]

RUTH. No—he don't half try at all 'cause he knows you going to come along behind him and fix everything. That's just how come he don't know how to do nothing right now—you done spoiled that boy so.

MAMA. Well—he's a little boy. Ain't supposed to know 'bout housekeeping. My baby, that's what he is. What you fix for his breakfast this morning?

RUTH [*Angrily*]. I feed my son, Lena!

MAMA. I ain't meddling—[*Underbreath; busy-bodyish*] I just noticed all last week he had cold cereal, and when it starts getting chilly in the fall a child ought to have some hot grits or something when he goes out in the cold—

RUTH [*Furious*]. I gave him hot oats—is that all right!

MAMA. I ain't meddling. [*Pause.*] Put a lot of nice butter on it? [RUTH *shoots an angry look and does not reply.*] He likes lots of butter.

RUTH [*Exasperated*]. Lena—

MAMA [*To* BENEATHA. MAMA *is inclined to wander conversationally sometimes*]. What was you and your brother fussing 'bout this morning?

BENEATHA. It's not important, Mama.

[*She gets up and goes to look out at the bathroom, which is apparently free, and she picks up her towels and rushes out.*]

MAMA. What was they fighting about?

RUTH. Now you know as well as I do.

MAMA [*Shaking her head*]. Brother still worrying hisself sick about that money?

RUTH. You know he is.

MAMA. You had breakfast?

RUTH. Some coffee.

MAMA. Girl, you better start eating and looking after yourself better. You almost as thin as Travis.

RUTH. Lena—

MAMA. Uh-hunh?

RUTH. What are you going to do with it?

MAMA. Now don't you start, child. It's too early in the morning to be talking about money. It ain't Christian.

RUTH. It's just that he got his heart set on that store—

MAMA. You mean that liquor store that Willy Harris want him to invest in?

RUTH. Yes—

MAMA. We ain't no business people, Ruth. We just plain working folks.

RUTH. Ain't nobody business people till they go into business. Walter Lee say colored people ain't never going to start getting ahead till they start gambling on some different kinds of things in the world—investments and things.

MAMA. What done got into you, girl? Walter Lee done finally sold you on investing.

RUTH. No. Mama, something is happening between Walter and me. I don't know what it is—but he needs something—something I can't give him any more. He needs this chance, Lena.

MAMA [Frowning deeply]. But liquor, honey—

RUTH. Well—like Walter say—I spec people going to always be drinking themselves some liquor.

MAMA. Well—whether they drinks it or not ain't none of my business. But whether I go into business selling it to 'em is, and I don't want that on my ledger this late in life. [Stopping suddenly and studying her daughter-in-law.] Ruth Younger, what's the matter with you today? You look like you could fall right over.

RUTH. I'm tired.

MAMA. Then you better stay home from work today.

RUTH. I can't stay home. She'd be calling up the agency and screaming at them, "My girl didn't come in today—send me somebody! My girl didn't come in!" Oh, she just have a fit . . .

MAMA. Well, let her have it. I'll just call her up and say you got the flu—

RUTH [Laughing.] Why the flu?

MAMA. 'Cause it sounds respectable to 'em. Something white people get, too. They know 'bout the flu. Otherwise they think you been cut up or something when you tell 'em you sick.

RUTH. I got to go in. We need the money.

MAMA. Somebody would of thought my children done all but starved to death the way they talk about money here late. Child, we got a great big old check coming tomorrow.

RUTH [Sincerely, but also self-righteously]. Now that's your money. It ain't got nothing to do with me. We all feel like that—Walter and Bennie and me—even Travis.

MAMA [Thoughtfully, and suddenly very far away]. Ten thousand dollars—

RUTH. Sure is wonderful.

MAMA. Ten thousand dollars.

RUTH. You know what you should do, Miss Lena? You should take yourself a trip somewhere. To Europe or South America or someplace—

MAMA [Throwing up her hands at the thought]. Oh, child!

RUTH. I'm serious. Just pack up and leave! Go on away and enjoy yourself some. Forget about the family and have yourself a ball for once in your life—

MAMA [*Drily*]. You sound like I'm just about ready to die. Who'd go with me? What I look like wandering 'round Europe by myself?

RUTH. Shoot—these here rich white women do it all the time. They don't think nothing of packing up they suitcases and piling on one of them big steamships and—swoosh!—they gone, child.

MAMA. Something always told me I wasn't no rich white woman.

RUTH. Well—what are you going to do with it then?

MAMA. I ain't rightly decided. [*Thinking. She speaks now with emphasis.*] Some of it got to be put away for Beneatha and her schoolin'—and ain't nothing going to touch that part of it. Nothing. [*She waits several seconds, trying to make up her mind about something, and looks at* RUTH *a little tentatively before going on.*] Been thinking that we maybe could meet the notes on a little old two-story somewhere, with a yard where Travis could play in the summertime, if we use part of the insurance for a down payment and everybody kind of pitch in. I could maybe take on a little day work again, a few days a week—

RUTH [*Studying her mother-in-law furtively and concentrating on her ironing, anxious to encourage without seeming to.*] Well, Lord knows, we've put enough rent into this here rat trap to pay for four houses by now . . .

MAMA [*Looking up at the words "rat trap" and then looking around and leaning back and sighing—in a suddenly reflective mood—*]. "Rat trap"—yes, that's all it is. [*Smiling.*] I remember just as well the day me and Big Walter moved in here. Hadn't been married but two weeks and wasn't planning on living here no more than a year. [*She shakes her head at the dissolved dream.*] We was going to set away, little by little, don't you know, and buy a little place out in Morgan Park. We had even picked out the house. [*Chuckling a little.*] Looks right dumpy today. But Lord, child, you should know all the dreams I had 'bout buying that house and fixing it up and making me a little garden in the back—[*She waits and stops smiling.*] And didn't none of it happen.

[*Dropping her hands in a futile gesture.*]

RUTH [*Keeps her head down, ironing*]. Yes, life can be a barrel of disappointments, sometimes.

MAMA. Honey, Big Walter would come in here some nights back then and slump down on that couch there and just look at the rug, and look at me and look at the rug and then back at me—and I'd know he was down then . . . really down. [*After a second very long and thoughtful pause; she is seeing back to times that only she can see.*] And then, Lord, when I lost that baby—little Claude—I almost thought I was going to lose Big Walter too. Oh, that man grieved hisself! He was one man to love his children.

RUTH. Ain't nothin' can tear at you like losin' your baby.

MAMA. I guess that's how come that man finally worked hisself to death like he done. Like he was fighting his own war with this here world that took his baby from him.

RUTH. He sure was a fine man, all right. I always liked Mr. Younger.

MAMA. Crazy 'bout his children! God knows there was plenty wrong with Walter Younger—hard-headed, mean, kind of wild with women—plenty wrong with him. But he sure loved his children. Always wanted them to have something—be something. That's where Brother gets all these notions, I reckon. Big Walter used to say, he'd get right wet in the eyes sometimes, lean his head back with the water standing in his eyes and say, "Seem like God didn't see fit to give the black man nothing but dreams—but He did give us children to make them dreams seem worth while." [*She smiles.*] He could talk like that, don't you know.

RUTH. Yes, he sure could. He was a good man, Mr. Younger.

MAMA. Yes, a fine man—just couldn't never catch up with his dreams, that's all. [BENEATHA *comes in, brushing her hair and looking up to the ceiling, where the sound of a vacuum cleaner has started up.*]

BENEATHA. What could be so dirty on that woman's rugs that she has to vacuum them every single day?

RUTH. I wish certain young women 'round here who I could name would take inspiration about certain rugs in a certain apartment I could also mention.

BENEATHA [*Shrugging*]. How much cleaning can a house need, for Christ's sake.

MAMA [*Not liking the Lord's name used thus*]. Bennie!

RUTH. Just listen to her—just listen!

BENEATHA. Oh, God!

MAMA. If you use the Lord's name just one more time—

BENEATHA [*A bit of a whine.*] Oh, Mama—

RUTH. Fresh—just fresh as salt, this girl!

BENEATHA [*Drily*]. Well—if the salt loses its savor—

MAMA. Now that will do. I just ain't going to have you 'round here reciting the scriptures in vain—you hear me?

BENEATHA. How did I manage to get on everybody's wrong side by just walking into a room?

RUTH. If you weren't so fresh—

BENEATHA. Ruth, I'm twenty years old.

MAMA. What time you be home from school today?

BENEATHA. Kind of late [*With enthusiasm.*] Madeline is going to start my guitar lessons today.

[MAMA *and* RUTH *look up with the same expression.*]

MAMA. Your *what* kind of lessons?

BENEATHA. Guitar.

RUTH. O, Father!

MAMA. How come you done taken it in your mind to learn to play the guitar?

BENEATHA. I just want to, that's all.

MAMA [*Smiling*]. Lord, child, don't you know what to do with yourself? How long it going to be before you get tired of this now—like you got tired of that little play-acting group you joined last year? [*Looking at* RUTH.] And what was it the year before that?

RUTH. The horseback-riding club for which she bought that fifty-five-dollar riding habit that's been hanging in the closet ever since!

MAMA [*To* BENEATHA]. Why you got to flit so from one thing to another, baby?

BENEATHA [*Sharply*]. I just want to learn to play the guitar. Is there anything wrong with that?

MAMA. Ain't nobody trying to stop you. I just wonders sometimes why you has to flit so from one thing to another all the time. You ain't never done nothing with all that camera equipment you brought home—

BENEATHA. I don't flit! I—I experiment with different forms of expression—

RUTH. Like riding a horse?

BENEATHA. —People have to express themselves one way or another.

MAMA. What is it you want to express?

BENEATHA [*Angrily*]. Me! [MAMA *and* RUTH *look at each other and burst into raucous laughter.*] Don't worry—I don't expect you to understand.

MAMA [*To change the subject*]. Who you going out with tomorrow night?

BENEATHA [*With displeasure*]. George Murchison again.

MAMA [*Pleased*]. Oh—you getting a little sweet on him?

RUTH. You ask me, this child ain't sweet on nobody but herself—[*Underbreath.*] Express herself!

[*They laugh.*]

BENEATHA. Oh—I like George all right, Mama. I mean I like him enough to go out with him and stuff, but—

RUTH [*For devilment*]. What does *and stuff* mean?

BENEATHA. Mind your own business.

MAMA. Stop picking at her now, Ruth. [*A thoughtful pause, and then a suspicious sudden look at her daughter as she turns in her chair for emphasis.*] What *does* it mean?

BENEATHA [*Wearily*]. Oh, I just mean I couldn't ever really be serious about George. He's—he's so shallow.

RUTH. Shallow—what do you mean he's shallow? He's *Rich!*

MAMA. Hush, Ruth.

BENEATHA. I know he's rich. He knows he's rich, too.

RUTH. Well—what other qualities a man got to have to satisfy you, little girl?

BENEATHA. You wouldn't even begin to understand. Anybody who married Walter could not possibly understand.

MAMA [*Outraged*]. What kind of way is that to talk about your brother?

BENEATHA. Brother is a flip—let's face it.

MAMA [*To* RUTH, *helplessly*]. What's a flip?

RUTH [*Glad to add kindling*]. She's saying he's crazy.

BENEATHA. Not crazy. Brother isn't really crazy yet—he—he's an elaborate neurotic.

MAMA. Hush your mouth!

BENEATHA. As for George. Well. George looks good—he's got a beautiful car and he takes me to nice places and, as my sister-in-law says, he is probably the richest boy I will ever get to know and I even like him sometimes—but if the Youngers are sitting around waiting to see if their little Bennie is going to tie up the family with the Murchisons, they are wasting their time.

RUTH. You mean you wouldn't marry George Murchison if he asked you someday? That pretty, rich thing? Honey, I knew you was odd—

BENEATHA. No I would not marry him if all I felt for him was what I feel now. Besides, George's family wouldn't really like it.

MAMA. Why not?

BENEATHA. Oh, Mama—the Murchisons are honest-to-God-real-*live*-rich colored people, and the only people in the world who are more snobbish than rich white people are rich colored people. I thought everybody knew that. I've met Mrs. Murchison. She's a scene!

MAMA. You must not dislike people 'cause they well off, honey.

BENEATHA. Why not? It makes just as much sense as disliking people 'cause they are poor, and lots of people do that.

RUTH [*A wisdom-of-the-ages manner, to* MAMA]. Well, she'll get over some of this—

BENEATHA. Get over it? What are you talking about, Ruth? Listen, I'm going to be a doctor. I'm not worried about who I'm going to marry yet—if I ever get married.

MAMA *and* RUTH. *If!*

MAMA. Now, Bennie—

BENEATHA. Oh, I probably will . . . but first I'm going to be a doctor, and George, for one, still thinks that's pretty funny. I couldn't be bothered with that. I am going to be a doctor and everybody around here better understand that!

MAMA [*Kindly*]. 'Course you going to be a doctor, honey, God willing.

BENEATHA [*Drily*]. God hasn't got a thing to do with it.

MAMA. Beneatha—that just wasn't necessary.

BENEATHA. Well—neither is God. I get sick of hearing about God.

MAMA. Beneatha!

BENEATHA. I mean it! I'm just tired of hearing about God all the time. What has He got to do with anything? Does he pay tuition?

MAMA. You 'bout to get your fresh little jaw slapped!

RUTH. That's just what she needs, all right!

BENEATHA. Why? Why can't I say what I want to around here, like everybody else?

MAMA. It don't sound nice for a young girl to say things like that—you wasn't brought up that way. Me and your father went to trouble to get you and Brother to church every Sunday.

BENEATHA. Mama, you don't understand. It's all a matter of ideas, and God is just one idea I don't accept. It's not important. I am not going out and be immoral or commit crimes because I don't believe in God. I don't even think about it. It's just that I get tired of Him getting credit for all the things the human race achieves through its own stubborn effort. There simply is no blasted God— there is only man and it is he who makes miracles!

[MAMA *absorbs this speech, studies her daughter and rises slowly and crosses to* BENEATHA *and slaps her powerfully across the face. After, there is only silence and the daughter drops her eyes from her mother's face, and* MAMA *is very tall before her.*]

MAMA. Now—you say after me, in my mother's house there is still God. [*There is a long pause and* BENEATHA *stares at the floor wordlessly.* MAMA *repeats the phrase with precision and cool emotion.*] In my mother's house there is still God.

BENEATHA. In my mother's house there is still God.

[*A long pause.*]

MAMA [*Walking away from* BENEATHA, *too disturbed for triumphant posture. Stopping and turning back to her daughter*]. There are some ideas we ain't going to have in this house. Not long as I am at the head of this family.

BENEATHA. Yes, ma'am.

[MAMA *walks out of the room.*]

RUTH [*Almost gently, with profound understanding*]. You think you a woman, Bennie—but you still a little girl. What you did was childish—so you got treated like a child.

BENEATHA. I see. [*Quietly.*] I also see that everybody thinks it's all right for Mama to be a tyrant. But all the tyranny in the world will never put a God in the heavens!

[*She picks up her books and goes out.*]

RUTH [*Goes to* MAMA'S *door*]. She said she was sorry.

MAMA [*Coming out, going to her plant*]. They frightens me, Ruth. My children.

RUTH. You got good children, Lena. They just a little off sometimes—but they're good.

MAMA. No—there's something come down between me and them that don't let us understand each other and I don't know what it is. One done almost lost his mind thinking 'bout money all the time and the other done commence to talk about things I can't seem to understand in no form or fashion. What is it that's changing, Ruth?

RUTH [*Soothingly, older than her years*]. Now . . . you taking it all too seriously. You just got strong-willed children and it takes a strong woman like you to keep 'em in hand.

MAMA [*Looking at her plant and sprinkling a little water on it*]. They spirited all right,

my children. Got to admit they got spirit—Bennie and Walter. Like this little old plant that ain't never had enough sunshine or nothing—and look at it . . .
[*She has her back to* RUTH, *who has had to stop ironing and lean against something and put the back of her hand to her forehead.*]

RUTH [*Trying to keep* MAMA *from noticing*]. You . . . sure . . . loves that little old thing, don't you? . . .

MAMA. Well, I always wanted me a garden like I used to see sometimes at the back of the houses down home. This plant is close as I ever got to having one. [*She looks out of the window as she replaces the plant.*] Lord, ain't nothing as dreary as the view from this window on a dreary day, is there? Why ain't you singing this morning, Ruth? Sing that "No Ways Tired." That song always lifts me up so—[*She turns at last to see that* RUTH *has slipped quietly into a chair, in a state of semiconsciousness.*] Ruth! Ruth honey—what's the matter with you . . . Ruth!

CURTAIN

SCENE II

It is the following morning; a Saturday morning, and house cleaning is in progress at the YOUNGERS. *Furniture has been shoved hither and yon and* MAMA *is giving the kitchen-area walls a washing down.* BENEATHA, *in dungarees, with a handkerchief tied around her face, is spraying insecticide into the cracks in the walls. As they work, the radio is on and a Southside disk-jockey program is inappropriately filling the house with a rather exotic saxophone blues.* TRAVIS, *the sole idle one, is leaning on his arms, looking out the window.*

TRAVIS. Grandmama, that stuff Bennie is using smells awful. Can I go downstairs, please?

MAMA. Did you get all them chores done already? I ain't seen you doing much.

TRAVIS. Yes'm—finished early. Where did Mama go this morning?

MAMA [*Looking at* BENEATHA]. She had to go on a little errand.

TRAVIS. Where?

MAMA. To tend to her business.

TRAVIS. Can I go outside then?

MAMA. Oh, I guess so. You better stay right in front of the house, though . . . and keep a good lookout for the postman.

TRAVIS. Yes'm. [*He starts out and decides to give his* AUNT BENEATHA *a good swat on the legs as he passes her.*] Leave them poor little old cockroaches alone, they ain't bothering you none.
[*He runs as she swings the spray gun at him both viciously and playfully.* WALTER *enters from the bedroom and goes to the phone.*]

MAMA. Look out there, girl, before you be spilling some of that stuff on that child!

TRAVIS [*Teasing*]. That's right—look out now!
[*He exits.*]

BENEATHA [*Drily*]. I can't imagine that it would hurt him—it has never hurt the roaches.

MAMA. Well, little boys' hides ain't as tough as Southside roaches.

WALTER [*Into phone*]. Hello—Let me talk to Willy Harris.

MAMA. You better get over there behind the bureau. I seen one marching out of there like Napoleon yesterday.

WALTER. Hello, Willy? It ain't come yet. It'll be here in a few minutes. Did the
    lawyer give you the papers?
BENEATHA. There's really only one way to get rid of them, Mama—
MAMA. How?
BENEATHA. Set fire to this building.
WALTER. Good. Good. I'll be right over.
BENEATHA. Where did Ruth go, Walter?
WALTER. I don't know.
    [*He exits abruptly.*]
BENEATHA. Mama, where did Ruth go?
MAMA [*Looking at her with meaning*]. To the doctor, I think.
BENEATHA. The doctor? What's the matter. [*They exchange glances.*] You don't
    think—
MAMA [*With her sense of drama*]. Now I ain't saying what I think. But I ain't never
    been wrong 'bout a woman neither.
    [*The phone rings*].
BENEATHA [*At the phone*]. Hay-lo . . . [*Pause, and a moment of recognition.*] Well—when
    did you get back! . . . And how was it? . . . Of course I've missed you—in my way
    . . . This morning? No . . . house cleaning and all that and Mama hates it if I let
    people come over when the house is like this . . . You *have?* Well, that's different
    . . . What is it—Oh, what the hell, come on over . . . Right, see you then.
    [*She hangs up.*]
MAMA [*Who has listened vigorously, as is her habit*]. Who is that you inviting over here
    with this house looking like this? You ain't got the pride you was born with!
BENEATHA. Asagai doesn't care how houses look, Mama—he's an intellectual.
MAMA. *Who?*
BENEATHA. Asagai—Joseph Asagai. He's an African boy I met on campus. He's been
    studying in Canada all summer.
MAMA. What's his name?
BENEATHA. Asagai, Joseph. Ah-sah-guy . . . He's from Nigeria.
MAMA. Oh, that's the little country that was founded by slaves way back . . .
BENEATHA. No, Mama—that's Liberia.
MAMA. I don't think I never met no African before.
BENEATHA. Well, do me a favor and don't ask him a whole lot of ignorant questions
    about Africans. I mean, do they wear clothes and all that—
MAMA. Well, now, I guess if you think we so ignorant 'round here maybe you
    shouldn't bring your friends here—
BENEATHA. It's just that people ask such crazy things. All anyone seems to know
    about when it comes to Africa is Tarzan—
MAMA [*Indignantly*]. Why should I know anything about Africa?
BENEATHA. Why do you give money at church for the missionary work?
MAMA. Well, that's to help save people.
BENEATHA. You mean save them from *heathenism*—
MAMA [*Innocently*]. Yes.
BENEATHA. I'm afraid they need more salvation from the British and the French.
    [RUTH *comes in forlornly and pulls off her coat with dejection. They both turn to look at
    her.*]
RUTH [*Dispiritedly*]. Well, I guess from all the happy faces—everybody knows.
BENEATHA. You pregnant?
MAMA. Lord have mercy, I sure hope it's a little old girl. Travis ought to have a
    sister.

[BENEATHA *and* RUTH *give her a hopeless look for this grandmotherly enthusiasm.*]

BENEATHA. How far along are you?

RUTH. Two months.

BENEATHA. Did you mean to? I mean did you plan it or was it an accident?

MAMA. What do you know about planning or not planning?

BENEATHA. Oh, Mama.

RUTH [*Wearily*]. She's twenty years old, Lena.

BENEATHA. Did you plan it, Ruth?

RUTH. Mind your own business.

BENEATHA. It is my business—where is he going to live, on the *roof?* [*There is silence following the remark as the three women react to the sense of it.*] Gee—I didn't mean that, Ruth, honest. Gee, I don't feel like that at all. I—I think it is wonderful.

RUTH [*Dully*]. Wonderful.

BENEATHA. Yes—really.

MAMA [*Looking at* RUTH, *worried*]. Doctor say everything going to be all right?

RUTH [*Far away*]. Yes—she says everything is going to be fine . . .

MAMA [*Immediately suspicious*]. "She"—What doctor you went to?

[RUTH *folds over, near hysteria.*]

MAMA [*Worriedly hovering over* RUTH]. Ruth honey—what's the matter with you—you sick?

[RUTH *has her fists clenched on her thighs and is fighting hard to suppress a scream that seems to be rising in her.*]

BENEATHA. What's the matter with her, Mama?

MAMA [*Working her fingers in* RUTH'S *shoulder to relax her*]. She be all right. Women gets right depressed sometimes when they get her way. [*Speaking softly, expertly, rapidly.*] Now you just relax. That's right . . . just lean back, don't think 'bout nothing at all . . . nothing at all—

RUTH. I'm all right . . .

[*The glassy-eyed look melts and then she collapses into a fit of heavy sobbing. The bell rings.*]

BENEATHA. Oh, my God—that must be Asagai.

MAMA [*To* RUTH]. Come on now, honey. You need to lie down and rest awhile . . . then have some nice hot food.

[*They exit,* RUTH'S *weight on her mother-in-law.* BENEATHA *herself profoundly disturbed, opens the door to admit a rather dramatic-looking young man with a large package.*]

ASAGAI. Hello, Alaiyo—

BENEATHA [*Holding the door open and regarding him with pleasure*]. Hello . . . [*Long pause.*] Well—come in. And please excuse everything. My mother was very upset about my letting anyone come here with the place like this.

ASAGAI [*Coming into the room*]. You look disturbed too . . . Is something wrong?

BENEATHA [*Still at the door, absently*]. Yes . . . we've all got acute ghetto-itus. [*She smiles and comes toward him, finding a cigarette and sitting.*] So—sit down! How was Canada?

ASAGAI [*A sophisticate*]. Canadian.

BENEATHA [*Looking at him*]. I'm very glad you are back.

ASAGAI [*Looking back at her in turn*]. Are you really?

BENEATHA. Yes—very.

ASAGAI. Why—you were quite glad when I went away. What happened?

BENEATHA. You went away.

ASAGAI. Ahhhhhhhh.

BENEATHA. Before—you wanted to be so serious before there was time.

ASAGAI. How much time must there be before one knows what one feels?

BENEATHA [*Stalling this particular conversation. Her hands pressed together, in a deliberately childish gesture*]. What did you bring me?

ASAGAI [*Handing her the package*]. Open it and see.

BENEATHA [*Eagerly opening the package and drawing out some records and the colorful robes of a Nigerian woman*]. Oh, Asagai! . . . You got them for me! . . . How beautiful . . . and the records too! [*She lifts out the robes and runs to the mirror with them and holds the drapery up in front of herself.*]

ASAGAI [*Coming to her at the mirror*]. I shall have to teach you how to drape it properly. [*He flings the material about her for the moment and stands back to look at her*]. Ah—Oh-pay-gay-day, oh-gbah-mu-shay. [*A Yoruba exclamation for admiration.*] You wear it well . . . very well . . . mutilated hair and all.

BENEATHA [*Turning suddenly*]. My hair—what's wrong with my hair?

ASAGAI [*Shrugging*]. Were you born with it like that?

BENEATHA [*Reaching up to touch it*]. No . . . of course not.

[*She looks back to the mirror, disturbed*].

ASAGAI [*Smiling*]. How then?

BENEATHA. You know perfectly well how — as crinkly as yours . . . that's how.

ASAGAI. And it is ugly to you that way?

BENEATHA [*Quickly*]. Oh, no—not ugly . . . [*More slowly, apologetically.*] But it's so hard to manage when it's, well—raw.

ASAGAI. And so to accommodate that—you mutilate it every week?

BENEATHA. It's not mutilation!

ASAGAI [*Laughing aloud at her seriousness*]. Oh . . . please! I am only teasing you because you are so very serious about these things. [*He stands back from her and folds his arms across his chest as he watches her pulling at her hair and frowning in the mirror.*] Do you remember the first time you met me at school? . . . [*He laughs.*] You came up to me and you said—and I thought you were the most serious little thing I had ever seen—you said: [*He imitates her.*] "Mr. Agasai—I want very much to talk with you. About Africa. You see, Mr. Asagai, I am looking for my identity!"

[*He laughs.*]

BENEATHA [*Turning to him, not laughing*]. Yes—

[*Her face is quizzical, profoundly disturbed.*]

ASAGAI [*Still teasing and reaching out and taking her face in his hands and turning her profile to him*]. Well . . . it is true that this is not so much a profile of a Hollywood queen as perhaps the queen of the Nile—[*A mock dismissal of the importance of the question.*] But what does it matter? Assimilationism is so popular in your country.

BENEATHA [*Wheeling, passionately, sharply*]. I am not an assimilationist!

ASAGAI [*The protest hangs in the room for a moment and* ASAGAI *studies her, his laughter fading*]. Such a serious one. [*There is a pause.*] So—you like the robes? You must take excellent care of them—they are from my sister's personal wardrobe.

BENEATHA [*With incredulity*]. You—you sent all the way home—for me?

ASAGAI [*With charm*]. For you—I would do much more . . . Well, that is what I came for. I must go.

BENEATHA. Will you call me Monday?

ASAGAI. Yes . . . We have a great deal to talk about. I mean about identity and time and all that.

BENEATHA. Time?

ASAGAI. Yes. About how much time one needs to know what one feels.

BENEATHA. You never understood that there is more than one kind of feeling which can exist between a man and a woman—or, at least, there should be.

ASAGAI [*Shaking his head negatively but gently*]. No. Between a man and a woman there need be only one kind of feeling. I have that for you ... Now even ... right this moment ...

BENEATHA. I know—and by itself—it won't do. I can find that anywhere.

ASAGAI. For a woman it should be enough.

BENEATHA. I know—because that's what it says in all the novels that men write. But it isn't. Go ahead and laugh—but I'm not interested in being someone's little episode in America or—[*With feminine vengeance*]—one of them! [ASAGAI *has burst into laughter again.*] That's funny as hell, huh!

ASAGAI. It's just that every American girl I have known has said that to me. White— black—in this you are all the same. And the same speech, too!

BENEATHA [*Angrily*]. Yuk, yuk, yuk!

ASAGAI. It's how you can be sure that the world's most liberated women are not liberated at all. You all talk about it too much!

[MAMA *enters and is immediately all social charm because of the presence of a guest.*]

BENEATHA. Oh—Mama—this is Mr. Asagai.

MAMA. How do you do?

ASAGAI [*Total politeness to an elder*]. How do you do, Mrs. Younger. Please forgive me for coming at such an outrageous hour on a Saturday.

MAMA. Well, you are quite welcome. I just hope you understand that our house don't always look like this. [*Chatterish.*] You must come again. I would love to hear all about—[*Not sure of the name*]—your country. I think it's so sad the way our American Negroes don't know nothing about Africa 'cept Tarzan and all that. And all that money they pour into these churches when they ought to be helping you people over there drive out them French and Englishmen done taken away your land.

[*The mother flashes a slightly superior look at her daughter upon completion of the recitation.*]

ASAGAI [*Taken aback by this sudden and acutely unrelated expression of sympathy*]. Yes ... yes ...

MAMA [*Smiling at him suddenly and relaxing and looking him over*]. How many miles is it from here to where you come from?

ASAGAI. Many thousands.

MAMA [*Looking at him as she would* WALTER]. I bet you don't half look after yourself, being away from your mama either. I spec you better come 'round here from time to time and get yourself some decent home-cooked meals ...

ASAGAI [*Moved*]. Thank you. Thank you very much. [*They are all quiet, then—.*] Well ... I must go. I will call you Monday, Alaiyo.

MAMA. What's that he call you?

ASAGAI. Oh—"Alaiyo." I hope you don't mind. It is what you would call a nick-name, I think. It is a Yoruba[2] word. I am a Yoruba.

MAMA [*Looking at* BENEATHA]. I—I thought he was from—

ASAGAI [*Understanding*]. Nigeria is my country. Yoruba is my tribal origin—

BENEATHA. You didn't tell us what Alaiyo means ... for all I know, you might be calling me Little Idiot or something ...

ASAGAI. Well ... let me see ... I do not know how just to explain it ... The sense of a thing can be so different when it changes languages.

BENEATHA. You're evading.

---

[2] The Yoruba tribe is prevalent in southwest Nigeria. Yoruba culture is rich and varied, particularly renown for the sculpture of the Bénin dynasty (ca. 1400–1897).

ASAGAI. No—really it is difficult . . . [*Thinking.*] It means . . . it means One for
   Whom Bread—Food—Is Not Enough. [*He looks at her.*] Is that all right?
BENEATHA [*Understanding, softly*]. Thank you.
MAMA [*Looking from one to the other and not understanding any of it*]. Well . . . that's
   nice . . . You must come see us again—Mr.—
ASAGAI. Ah-sah-guy . . .
MAMA. Yes . . . Do come again.
ASAGAI. Good-bye.
   [*He exits.*]
MAMA [*After him*]. Lord, that's a pretty thing just went out here! [*Insinuatingly, to
   her daughter.*] Yes, I guess I see why we done commence to get so interested in
   Africa 'round here. Missionaries my aunt Jenny!
   [*She exits.*]
BENEATHA. Oh, Mama! . . .
   [*She picks up the Nigerian dress and holds it up to her in front of the mirror again.
   She sets the headdress on haphazardly and then notices her hair again and clutches at
   it and then replaces the headdress and frowns at herself. Then she starts to wriggle in
   front of the mirror as she thinks a Nigerian woman might.* TRAVIS *enters and regards
   her.*]
TRAVIS. You cracking up?
BENEATHA. Shut up.
   [*She pulls the headdress off and looks at herself in the mirror and clutches at her hair
   again and squinches her eyes as if trying to imagine something. Then, suddenly, she gets
   her raincoat and kerchief and hurriedly prepares for going out.*]
MAMA [*Coming back into the room*]. She's resting now. Travis, baby, run next door
   and ask Miss Johnson to please let me have a little kitchen cleanser. This here
   can is empty as Jacob's kettle.
TRAVIS. I just came in.
MAMA. Do as you told. [*He exits and she looks at her daughter.*] Where you going?
BENEATHA [*Halting at the door*]. To become a queen of the Nile!
   [*She exits in a breathless blaze of glory.* RUTH *appears in the bedroom doorway.*]
MAMA. Who told you to get up?
RUTH. Ain't nothing wrong with me to be lying in no bed for. Where did Bennie
   go?
MAMA [*Drumming her fingers*]. Far as I could make out—to Egypt. [RUTH *just looks at
   her.*] What time is it getting to?
RUTH. Ten twenty. And the mailman going to ring that bell this morning just like
   he done every morning for the last umpteen years.
   [TRAVIS *comes in with the cleanser can.*]
TRAVIS. She say to tell you that she don't have much.
MAMA [*Angrily*]. Lord, some people I could name sure is tight-fisted! [*Directing her
   grandson.*] Mark two cans of cleanser down on the list there. If she that hard up
   for kitchen cleanser, I sure don't want to forget to get her none!
RUTH. Lena—maybe the woman is just short on cleanser—
MAMA [*Not listening*]. —Much baking powder as she done borrowed from me all
   these years, she could of done gone into the baking business!
   [*The bell sounds suddenly and sharply and all three are stunned—serious and silent—
   mid-speech. In spite of all the other conversations and distractions of the morning, this is
   what they have been waiting for, even* TRAVIS, *who looks helplessly from his mother to his
   grandmother.* RUTH *is the first to come to life again.*]
RUTH [*To* TRAVIS]. Get down them steps, boy!

[TRAVIS *snaps to life and flies out to get the mail.*]

MAMA [*Her eyes wide, her hand to her breast*]. You mean it done really come?

RUTH [*Excited*]. Oh, Miss Lena!

MAMA [*Collecting herself*]. Well . . . I don't know what we all so excited about 'round here for. We known it was coming for months.

RUTH. That's a whole lot different from having it come and being able to hold it in your hands . . . a piece of paper worth ten thousand dollars . . . [TRAVIS *bursts back into the room. He holds the envelope high above his head, like a little dancer, his face is radiant and he is breathless. He moves to his grandmother with sudden slow ceremony and puts the envelope into her hands. She accepts it, and then merely holds it and looks at it.*] Come on! Open it . . . Lord have mercy, I wish Walter Lee was here!

TRAVIS. Open it, Grandmama!

MAMA [*Staring at it*]. Now you all be quiet. It's just a check.

RUTH. Open it . . .

MAMA [*Still staring at it*]. Now don't act silly . . . We ain't never been no people to act silly 'bout no money—

RUTH [*Swiftly*]. We ain't never had none before—*open it!*

[MAMA *finally makes a good strong tear and pulls out the thin blue slice of paper and inspects it closely. The boy and his mother study it raptly over* MAMA's *shoulders.*]

MAMA. Travis! [*She is counting off with doubt.*] Is that the right number of zeros?

TRAVIS. Yes'm . . . ten thousand dollars. Gaalee, Grandmama, you rich.

MAMA [*She holds the check away from her, still looking at it. Slowly her face sobers into a mask of unhappiness*]. Ten thousand dollars. [*She hands it to* RUTH.] Put it away somewhere, Ruth. [*She does not look at* RUTH; *her eyes seem to be seeing something somewhere very far off.*] Ten thousand dollars they give you. Ten thousand dollars.

TRAVIS [*To his mother, sincerely*]. What's the matter with Grandmama—don't she want to be rich?

RUTH [*Distractedly*]. You go out and play now, baby. [TRAVIS *exits.* MAMA *starts wiping dishes absently, humming intently to herself.* RUTH *turns to her, with kind exasperation.*] You've gone and got yourself upset.

MAMA [*Not looking at her*]. I spec if it wasn't for you all . . . I would just put that money away or give it to the church or something.

RUTH. Now what kind of talk is that. Mr. Younger would just be plain mad if he could hear you talking foolish like that.

MAMA [*Stopping and staring off*]. Yes. . . . he sure would. [*Sighing.*] We got enough to do with that money, all right. [*She halts then, and turns and looks at her daughter-in-law hard;* RUTH *avoids her eyes and* MAMA *wipes her hands with finality and starts to speak firmly to* RUTH.] Where did you go today, girl?

RUTH. To the doctor.

MAMA [*Impatiently*]. Now, Ruth . . . you know better than that. Old Doctor Jones is strange enough in his way but there ain't nothing 'bout him make somebody slip and call him "she"—like you done this morning.

RUTH. Well, that's what happened—my tongue slipped.

MAMA. You went to see that woman, didn't you?

RUTH [*Defensively, giving herself away*]. What woman you talking about?

MAMA [*Angrily*]. That woman who—

[WALTER *enters in great excitement.*]

WALTER. Did it come?

MAMA [*Quietly*]. Can't you give people a Christian greeting before you start asking about money?

WALTER [*To* RUTH]. Did it come? [RUTH *unfolds the check and lays it quietly before him, watching him intently with thoughts of her own.* WALTER *sits down and grasps it close and counts off the zeros.*] Ten thousand dollars—[*He turns suddenly, frantically to his mother and draws some papers out of his breast pocket.*] Mama—look. Old Willy Harris put everything on paper—

MAMA. Son—I think you ought to talk to your wife . . . I'll go on out and leave you alone if you want—

WALTER. I can talk to her later—Mama, look—

MAMA. Son—

WALTER. WILL SOMEBODY PLEASE LISTEN TO ME TODAY!

MAMA [*Quietly*]. I don't 'low no yellin' in this house, Walter Lee, and you know it—[WALTER *stares at them in frustration and starts to speak several times.*] And there ain't going to be no investing in no liquor stores. I don't aim to have to speak on that again.
[*A long pause.*]

WALTER. Oh—so you don't aim to have to speak on that again? So *you* have decided . . . [*Crumpling his papers.*] Well, *you* tell that to my boy tonight when you put him to sleep on the living-room couch . . . [*Turning to* MAMA *and speaking directly to her.*] Yeah—and tell it to my wife, Mama, tomorrow when she has to go out of here to look after somebody else's kids. And tell it to *me*, Mama, every time we need a new pair of curtains and I have to watch *you* go out and work in somebody's kitchen. Yeah, you tell me then!
[WALTER *starts out.*]

RUTH. Where you going?

WALTER. I'm going out!

RUTH. Where?

WALTER. Just out of this house somewhere—

RUTH [*Getting her coat*]. I'll come too.

WALTER. I don't want you to come!

RUTH. I got something to talk to you about, Walter.

WALTER. That's too bad.

MAMA [*Still quietly*]. Walter Lee—[*She waits and he finally turns and looks at her.*] Sit down.

WALTER. I'm a grown man, Mama.

MAMA. Ain't nobody said you wasn't grown. But you still in my house and my presence. And as long as you are—you'll talk to your wife civil. Now sit down.

RUTH [*Suddenly*]. Oh, let him go on out and drink himself to death! He makes me sick to my stomach! [*She flings her coat against him.*]

WALTER [*Violently*]. And you turn mine too, baby! [RUTH *goes into their bedroom and slams the door behind her.*] That was my greatest mistake—

MAMA [*Still quietly*]. Walter, what is the matter with you?

WALTER. Matter with me? Ain't nothing the matter with *me!*

MAMA. Yes there is. Something eating you up like a crazy man. Something more than me not giving you this money. The past few years I been watching it happen to you. You get all nervous acting and kind of wild in the eyes—[WALTER *jumps up impatiently at her words.*] I said sit there now, I'm talking to you!

WALTER. Mama—I don't need no nagging at me today.

MAMA. Seem like you getting to a place where you always tied up in some kind of knot about something. But if anybody ask you 'bout it you just yell at 'em and bust out the house and go out and drink somewheres. Walter Lee, people can't live with that. Ruth's a good, patient girl in her way—but you getting to be too much. Boy, don't make the mistake of driving that girl away from you.

WALTER. Why—what she do for me?

MAMA. She loves you.

WALTER. Mama—I'm going out. I want to go off somewhere and be by myself for a while.

MAMA. I'm sorry 'bout your liquor store, son. It just wasn't the thing for us to do. That's what I want to tell you about—

WALTER. I got to go out, Mama—
[*He rises.*]

MAMA. It's dangerous, son.

WALTER. What's dangerous?

MAMA. When a man goes outside his home to look for peace.

WALTER [*Beseechingly*]. Then why can't there never be no peace in this house then?

MAMA. You done found it in some other house?

WALTER. No—there ain't no woman! Why do women always think there's a woman somewhere when a man gets restless. [*Coming to her.*] Mama—Mama—I want so many things . . .

MAMA. Yes, son—

WALTER. I want so many things that they are driving me kind of crazy . . . Mama— look at me.

MAMA. I'm looking at you. You a good-looking boy. You got a job, a nice wife, a fine boy and—

WALTER. A job. [*Looks at her.*] Mama, a job? I open and close car doors all day long. I drive a man around in his limousine and I say, "Yes, sir; no, sir; very good, sir; shall I take the Drive, sir?" Mama, that ain't no kind of job . . . that ain't nothing at all. [*Very quietly.*] Mama, I don't know if I can make you understand.

MAMA. Understand what, baby?

WALTER [*Quietly*]. Sometimes it's like I can see the future stretched out in front of me—just plain as day. The future, Mama. Hanging over there at the edge of my days. Just waiting for me—a big, looming blank space—full of *nothing*. Just waiting for *me*. [*Pause.*] Mama—sometimes when I'm downtown and I pass them cool, quiet-looking restaurants where them white boys are sitting back and talking 'bout things . . . sitting there turning deals worth millions of dollars . . . sometimes I see guys don't look much older than me—

MAMA. Son—how come you talk so much 'bout money?

WALTER [*With immense passion*]. Because it is life, Mama!

MAMA [*Quietly*]. Oh—[*Very quietly.*] So now it's life. Money is life. Once upon a time freedom used to be life—now it's money. I guess the world really do change . . .

WALTER. No—it was always money, Mama. We just didn't know about it.

MAMA. No . . . something has changed. [*She looks at him.*] You something new, boy. In my time we was worried about not being lynched and getting to the North if we could and how to stay alive and still have a pinch of dignity too . . . Now here come you and Beneatha—talking 'bout things we ain't never even thought about hardly, me and your daddy. You ain't satisfied or proud of nothing we done. I mean that you had a home; that we kept you out of trouble till you was grown; that you don't have to ride to work on the back of nobody's streetcar— You my children—but how different we done become.

WALTER. You just don't understand, Mama, you just don't understand.

MAMA. Son—do you know your wife is expecting another baby? [WALTER *stands, stunned, and absorbs what his mother has said.*] That's what she wanted to talk to you about. [WALTER *sinks down into a chair.*] This ain't for me to be telling—but you ought to know. [*She waits.*] I think Ruth is thinking 'bout getting rid of that child.

WALTER [*Slowly understanding*]. No—no—Ruth wouldn't do that.

MAMA. When the world gets ugly enough—a woman will do anything for her family. *The part that's already living.*

WALTER. You don't know Ruth, Mama, if you think she would do that.

[RUTH *opens the bedroom door and stands there a little limp.*]

RUTH [*Beaten*]. Yes I would too, Walter. [*Pause.*] I gave her a five-dollar down payment.

[*There is total silence as the man stares at his wife and the mother stares at her son.*]

MAMA [*Presently*]. Well—[*Tightly.*] Well—son, I'm waiting to hear you say something . . . I'm waiting to hear how you be your father's son. Be the man he was . . . [*Pause.*] Your wife say she going to destroy your child. And I'm waiting to hear you talk like him and say we a people who give children life, not who destroys them—[*She rises.*] I'm waiting to see you stand up and look like your daddy and say we done give up one baby to poverty and that we ain't going to give up nary another one . . . I'm waiting.

WALTER. Ruth—

MAMA. If you a son of mine, tell her! [WALTER *turns, looks at her and can say nothing. She continues, bitterly.*] You . . . you are a disgrace to your father's memory. Somebody get me my hat.

CURTAIN

ACT II

SCENE I

TIME: *Later the same day.*

At rise: RUTH *is ironing again. She has the radio going. Presently* BENEATHA'S *bedroom door opens and* RUTH'S *mouth falls and she puts down the iron in fascination.*

RUTH. What have we got on tonight!

BENEATHA [*Emerging grandly room from the doorway so that we can see her thoroughly robed in the costume Asagai brought*]. You are looking at what a well-dressed Nigerian woman wears—[*She parades for* RUTH, *her hair completely hidden by the headdress; she is coquettishly fanning herself with an ornate oriental fan, mistakenly more like Butterfly than any Nigerian that ever was.*] Isn't it beautiful? [*She promenades to the radio and, with an arrogant flourish, turns off the good loud blues that is playing.*] Enough of this assimilationist junk! [RUTH *follows her with her eyes as she goes to the phonograph and puts on a record and turns and waits ceremoniously for the music to come up. Then, with a shout*—] OCOMOGOSIAY!

[RUTH *jumps. The music comes up, a lovely Nigerian melody.* BENEATHA *listens, enraptured, her eyes far away*—"*back to the past.*" *She begins to dance.* RUTH *is dumfounded.*]

RUTH. What kind of dance is that?

BENEATHA. A folk dance.

RUTH [*Pearl Bailey*]. What kind of folks do that, honey?

BENEATHA. It's from Nigeria. It's a dance of welcome.

RUTH. Who you welcoming?

BENEATHA. The men back to the village.

RUTH. Where they been?

BENEATHA. How should I know—out hunting or something. Anyway, they are coming back now . . .

RUTH. Well, that's good.

BENEATHA [*with the record*].

Alundi, alundi
Alundi alunya
Jop pu a jeepua
Ang gu sooooooooooo

Ai yai yae . . .
Ayehaye—alundi . . .

[WALTER *comes in during this performance; he has obviously been drinking. He leans against the door heavily and watches his sister, at first with distaste. Then his eyes look off— "back to the past"—as he lifts both his fists to the roof, screaming.*]

WALTER. YEAH . . . AND ETHIOPIA STRETCH FORTH HER HANDS AGAIN! . . .

RUTH [*Drily, looking at him*]. Yes—and Africa sure is claiming her own tonight. [*She gives them both up and starts ironing again.*]

WALTER [*All in a drunken, dramatic shout*]. Shut up! . . . I'm digging them drums . . . them drums move me! . . . [*He makes his weaving way to his wife's face and leans in close to her.*] In my *heart of hearts*—[*he thumps his chest*]—I am much warrior!

RUTH [*Without even looking up*]. In your heart of hearts you are much drunkard.

WALTER [*Coming away from her and starting to wander around the room, shouting*]. Me and Jomo . . . [*Intently, in his sister's face. She has stopped dancing to watch him in this unknown mood.*] That's my man, Kenyatta.[3] [*Shouting and thumping his chest.*] FLAMING SPEAR! HOT DAMN! [*He is suddenly in possession of an imaginary spear and actively spearing enemies all over the room.*] OCOMOGOSIAY . . . THE LION IS WAKING . . . OWIMOWEH! [*He pulls his shirt open and leaps up on a table and gestures with his spear. The bell rings. RUTH goes to answer.*]

BENEATHA [*To encourage WALTER, thoroughly caught up with this side of him*]. OCOMOGOSIAY, FLAMING SPEAR!

WALTER [*On the table, very far gone, his eyes pure glass sheets. He sees what we cannot, that he is a leader of his people, a great chief, a descendant of Chaka, and that the hour to march has come*]. Listen my black brothers—

BENEATHA. OCOMOGOSIAY!

WALTER. —Do you hear the waters rushing against the shores of the coastlands—

BENEATHA. OCOMOGOSIAY!

WALTER. —Do you hear the screeching of the cocks in yonder hills beyond where the chiefs meet in council for the coming of the mighty war—

BENEATHA. OCOMOGOSIAY!

WALTER. —Do you hear the beating of the wings of the birds flying low over the mountains and the low places of our land—

---

[3] Jomo Kenyatta (1893?–1978) was a leader in the struggle of the Kenyans to gain independence from Great Britain. Imprisoned for terrorism in 1953 and then exiled, he became the president of independent Kenya from 1964–1978, consolidating his power by suppressing and banning all political opposition.

[Ruth *opens the door.* George Murchison *enters.*]

BENEATHA. OCOMOGOSIAY!

WALTER. —Do you hear the singing of the women, singing the war songs of our fathers to the babies in the great houses . . . singing the sweet war songs? OH, DO YOU HEAR, MY BLACK BROTHERS!

BENEATHA [*Completely gone*]. We hear you, Flaming Spear—

WALTER. Telling us to prepare for the greatness of the time—[*To* George.] Black Brother!

[*He extends his hand for the fraternal clasp.*]

GEORGE. Black Brother, hell!

RUTH [*Having had enough, and embarrassed for the family*]. Beneatha, you got company—what's the matter with you? Walter Lee Younger, get down off that table and stop acting like a fool . . .

[WALTER *comes down off the table suddenly and makes a quick exit to the bathroom.*]

RUTH. He's had a little to drink . . . I don't know what her excuse is.

GEORGE [*To* BENEATHA]. Look honey, we're going *to* the theatre—we're not going to be *in* it . . . so go change, huh?

RUTH. You expect this boy to go out with you looking like that?

BENEATHA [*Looking at* GEORGE]. That's up to George. If he's ashamed of his heritage—

GEORGE. Oh, don't be so proud of yourself, Bennie—just because you look eccentric.

BENEATHA. How can something that's natural be eccentric?

GEORGE. That's what being eccentric means—being natural. Get dressed.

BENEATHA. I don't like that, George.

RUTH. Why must you and your brother make an argument out of everything people say?

BENEATHA. Because I hate assimilationist Negroes!

RUTH. Will somebody please tell me what assimila-whoever means!

GEORGE. Oh, it's just a college girl's way of calling people Uncle Toms—but that isn't what it means at all.

RUTH. Well, what does it mean?

BENEATHA [*Cutting* GEORGE *off and staring at him as she replies to* RUTH]. It means someone who is willing to give up his own culture and submerge himself completely in the dominant, and in this case, *oppressive* culture!

GEORGE. Oh, dear, dear, dear! Here we go! A lecture on the African past! On our Great West African Heritage! In one second we will hear all about the great Ashanti empires;[4] the great Songhay civilizations; and the great sculpture of Bénin—and then some poetry in Bantu—and the whole monologue will end with the word *heritage!* [*Nastily.*] Let's face it, baby, your heritage is nothing but a bunch of raggedy-assed spirituals and some grass huts!

BENEATHA. *Grass huts!* [RUTH *crosses to her and forcibly pushes her toward the bedroom.*] See there . . . you are standing there in your splendid ignorance talking about people who were the first to smelt iron on the face of the earth! [RUTH *is pushing her through the door.*] The Ashanti were performing surgical operations when the English—[RUTH *pulls the door to, with* BENEATHA *on the other side, and smiles graciously at* GEORGE. BENEATHA *opens the door and shouts the end of the sentence defiantly*

---

[4] The Ashanti empire prospered during the 18th century in what is now Ghana; the Songhay empire dominated West Central Africa in the fifteenth century; the Bénin dynasty ruled the coastal region near the mouth of the Niger River from about 1400 until the end of the nineteenth century; the Bantu language is spoken by most Africans living south of the equator.

at George.]—were still tatooing themselves with blue dragons . . . [*She goes back inside.*]

RUTH. Have a seat, George. [*They both sit,* RUTH *folds her hands rather primly on her lap, determined to demonstrate the civilization of the family.*] Warm, ain't it? I mean for September. [*Pause.*] Just like they always say about Chicago weather: If it's too hot or cold for you, just wait a minute and it'll change. [*She smiles happily at this cliché of clichés.*] Everybody say it's got to do with them bombs and things they keep setting off. [*Pause.*] Would you like a nice cold beer?

GEORGE. No, thank you. I don't care for beer. [*He looks at his watch.*] I hope she hurries up.

RUTH. What time is the show?

GEORGE. It's an eight-thirty curtain. That's just Chicago, though. In New York standard curtain time is eight-forty.

[*He is rather proud of this knowledge.*]

RUTH [*Properly appreciating it*]. You get to New York a lot?

GEORGE [*Offhand*]. Few times a year.

RUTH. Oh—that's nice. I've never been to New York.

[WALTER *enters. We feel he has relieved himself, but the edge of unreality is still with him.*]

WALTER. New York ain't got nothing Chicago ain't. Just a bunch of hustling people all squeezed up together—being "Eastern."

[*He turns his face into a screw of displeasure.*]

GEORGE. Oh—you've been?

WALTER. *Plenty* of times.

RUTH [*Shocked at the lie*]. Walter Lee Younger!

WALTER [*Staring her down*]. Plenty! [*Pause.*] What we got to drink in this house? Why don't you offer this man some refreshment. [*To* GEORGE.] They don't know how to entertain people in this house, man.

GEORGE. Thank you—I don't really care for anything.

WALTER [*Feeling his head; sobriety coming*]. Where's Mama?

RUTH. She ain't come back yet.

WALTER [*Looking* MURCHISON *over from head to toe, scrutinizing his carefully casual tweed sports jacket over cashmere V-neck sweater over soft eyelet shirt and tie, and soft slacks, finished off with white buckskin shoes*]. Why all you college boys wear them fairyish-looking white shoes?

RUTH. Walter Lee!

[GEORGE MURCHISON *ignores the remark.*]

WALTER [*To* RUTH]. Well, they look crazy as hell—white shoes, cold as it is.

RUTH [*Crushed*]. You have to excuse him—

WALTER. No he don't! Excuse me for what? What you always excusing me for! I'll excuse myself when I needs to be excused! [*A pause.*] They look as funny as them black knee socks Beneatha wears out of here all the time.

RUTH. It's the college *style*, Walter.

WALTER. Style, hell. She looks like she got burnt legs or something!

RUTH. Oh, Walter—

WALTER [*An irritable mimic*]. Oh, Walter! Oh, Walter! [*To* MURCHISON.] How's your old man making out? I understand you all going to buy that big hotel on the Drive?[5] [*He finds a beer in the refrigerator, wanders over to* MURCHISON, *sipping and wiping his lips with the back of his hand, and straddling a chair backwards to talk to the*

---

[5] Lake Shore Drive is a very prosperous strip of hotels and condominiums in Chicago along the shore of Lake Michigan.

other man.] Shrewd move. Your old man is all right, man. [*Tapping his head and half winking for emphasis.*] I mean he knows how to operate. I mean he thinks *big,* you know what I mean, I mean for a *home,* you know? But I think he's kind of running out of ideas now. I'd like to talk to him. Listen, man, I got some plans that could turn this city upside down. I mean I think like he does. *Big.* Invest big, gamble big, hell, lose *big* if you have to, you know what I mean. It's hard to find a man on this whole Southside who understands my kind of thinking—you dig? [*He scrutinizes* MURCHISON *again, drinks his beer, squints his eyes and leans in close, confidential, man to man.*] Me and you ought to sit down and talk sometimes, man. Man, I got me some ideas . . .

MURCHISON [*With boredom*]. Yeah—sometimes we'll have to do that, Walter.

WALTER [*Understanding the indifference, and offended*]. Yeah—well, when you get the time, man. I know you a busy little boy.

RUTH. Walter, please—

WALTER [*Bitterly, hurt*]. I know ain't nothing in this world as busy as you colored college boys with your fraternity pins and white shoes . . .

RUTH [*Covering her face with humiliation*]. Oh, Walter Lee—

WALTER. I see you all all the time—with the books tucked under your arms—going to your [*British A—a mimic*] "clahsses." And for what! What the hell you learning over there? Filling up your heads—[*Counting off on his fingers*]—with the sociology and the psychology—but they teaching you how to be a man? How to take over and run the world? They teaching you how to run a rubber plantation or a steel mill? Naw—just to talk proper and read books and wear white shoes . . .

GEORGE [*Looking at him with distaste, a little above it all*]. You're all wacked up with bitterness, man.

WALTER [*Intently, almost quietly, between the teeth, glaring at the boy*]. And you—ain't you bitter, man? Ain't you just about had it yet? Don't you see no stars gleaming that you can't reach out and grab? You happy?—you contented son-of-a-bitch—you happy? You got it made? Bitter? Man, I'm a volcano. Bitter? Here I am a giant—surrounded by ants! Ants who can't even understand what it is the giant is talking about.

RUTH [*Passionately and suddenly*]. Oh, Walter—ain't you with nobody!

WALTER [*Violently*]. No! 'Cause ain't nobody with me! Not even my own mother!

RUTH. Walter, that's a terrible thing to say!

[BENEATHA *enters, dressed for the evening in a cocktail dress and earrings.*]

GEORGE. Well—hey, you look great.

BENEATHA. Let's go, George. See you all later.

RUTH. Have a nice time.

GEORGE. Thanks. Good night. [*To* WALTER, *sarcastically.*] Good night, *Prometheus.*[6]

[BENEATHA *and* GEORGE *exit.*]

WALTER [*To* RUTH]. Who is Prometheus?

RUTH. I don't know. Don't worry about it.

WALTER [*In fury, pointing after* GEORGE.] See there, they get to a point where they can't insult you man to man—they got to go talk about something ain't nobody never heard of!

RUTH. How do you know it was an insult? [*To humor him.*] Maybe Prometheus is a nice fellow.

---

[6] In Greek mythology, Prometheus was one of the Titans. He is known as the supreme trickster and also as the god who gave fire to humanity.

WALTER. Prometheus! I bet there ain't even no such thing! I bet that simple-minded clown—

RUTH. Walter—

[*She stops what she is doing and looks at him.*]

WALTER [*Yelling*]. Don't start!

RUTH. Start what?

WALTER. Your nagging! Where was I? Who was I with? How much money did I spend?

RUTH [*Plaintively*]. Walter Lee—why don't we just try to talk about it . . .

WALTER [*Not listening*]. I been out talking with people who understand me. People who care about the things I got on my mind.

RUTH [*Wearily*]. I guess that means people like Willy Harris.

WALTER. Yes, people like Willy Harris.

RUTH [*With a sudden flash of impatience*]. Why don't you all just hurry up and go into the banking business and stop talking about it!

WALTER. Why? You want to know why? 'Cause we all tied up in a race of people that don't know how to do nothing but moan, pray and have babies!

[*The line is too bitter even for him and he looks at her and sits down.*]

RUTH. Oh, Walter . . . [*Softly.*] Honey, why can't you stop fighting me?

WALTER [*Without thinking*]. Who's fighting you? Who even cares about you?

[*This line begins the retardation of his mood.*]

RUTH. Well—[*She waits a long time, and then with resignation starts to put away her things.*] I guess I might as well go on to bed . . . [*More or less to herself*] I don't know where we lost it . . . but we have . . . [*Then, to him*] I—I'm sorry about this new baby, Walter. I guess maybe I better go on and do what I started . . . I guess I just didn't realize how bad things was with us . . . I guess I just didn't really realize—[*She starts out to the bathroom and stops.*] You want some hot milk?

WALTER. Hot milk?

RUTH. Yes—hot milk.

WALTER. Why hot milk?

RUTH. 'Cause after all that liquor you come home with you ought to have something hot in your stomach.

WALTER. I don't want no milk.

RUTH. You want some coffee then?

WALTER. No, I don't want no coffee. I don't want nothing hot to drink. [*Almost plaintively.*] Why you always trying to give me something to eat?

RUTH [*Standing and looking at him helplessly*]. What else can I give you, Walter Lee Younger?

[*She stands and looks at him and presently turns to go out again. He lifts his head and watches her going away from him in a new mood which began to emerge when he asked her "Who cares about you?".*]

WALTER. It's been rough, ain't it, baby? [*She hears and stops but does not turn around and he continues to her back.*] I guess between two people there ain't never as much understood as folks generally thinks there is. I mean like between me and you—[*She turns to face him.*] How we gets to the place where we scared to talk softness to each other. [*He waits, thinking hard himself.*] Why you think it got to be like that? [*He is thoughtful, almost as a child would be.*] Ruth, what is it gets into people ought to be close?

RUTH. I don't know, honey. I think about it a lot.

WALTER. On account of you and me, you mean? The way things are with us. The way something done come down between us.

RUTH. There ain't so much between us, Walter . . . Not when you come to me and try to talk to me. Try to be with me . . . a little even.

WALTER [*Total honesty*]. Sometimes . . . sometimes . . . I don't even know how to try.

RUTH. Walter—

WALTER. Yes?

RUTH [*Coming to him, gently and with misgiving, but coming to him*]. Honey . . . life don't have to be like this. I mean sometimes people can do things so that things are better . . . You remember how we used to talk when Travis was born . . . about the way we were going to live . . . the kind of house . . . [*She is stroking his head.*] Well, it's all starting to slip away from us . . .

[MAMA *enters, and* WALTER *jumps up and shouts at her.*]

WALTER. Mama, where have you been?

MAMA. My—them steps is longer than they used to be. Whew! [*She sits down and ignores him.*] How you feeling this evening, Ruth?

[RUTH *shrugs, disturbed some at having been prematurely interrupted and watching her husband knowingly.*]

WALTER. Mama, where have you been all day?

MAMA [*Still ignoring him and leaning on the table and changing to more comfortable shoes*]. Where's Travis?

RUTH. I let him go out earlier and he ain't come back yet. Boy, is he going to get it!

WALTER. Mama!

MAMA [*As if she has heard him for the first time*]. Yes, son?

WALTER. Where did you go this afternoon?

MAMA. I went down town to tend to some business that I had to tend to.

WALTER. What kind of business?

MAMA. You know better than to question me like a child, Brother.

WALTER [*Rising and bending over the table*]. Where were you, Mama? [*Bringing his fists down and shouting.*] Mama, you didn't go do something with that insurance money, something crazy?

[*The front door opens slowly, interrupting him, and* TRAVIS *peeks his head in, less than hopefully.*]

TRAVIS [*To his mother*]. Mama, I—

RUTH. "Mama I" nothing! You're going to get it, boy! Get on in that bedroom and get yourself ready!

TRAVIS. But I—

MAMA. Why don't you all never let the child explain hisself.

RUTH. Keep out of it now, Lena.

[MAMA *clamps her lips together, and* RUTH *advances toward her son menacingly.*]

RUTH. A thousand times I have told you not to go off like that—

MAMA [*Holding out her arms to her grandson*]. Well—at least let me tell him something. I want him to be the first one to hear . . . Come here, Travis. [*The boy obeys, gladly.*] Travis—[*She takes him by the shoulders and looks into his face.*]—you know that money we got in the mail this morning?

TRAVIS. Yes'm—

MAMA. Well—what you think your grandmama gone and done with that money?

TRAVIS. I don't know, Grandmama.

MAMA [*Putting her finger on his nose for emphasis*]. She went out and she bought you a house! [*The explosion comes from* WALTER *at the end of the revelation and he jumps up and turns away from all of them in a fury.* MAMA *continues, to* TRAVIS.]

You glad about the house? It's going to be yours when you get to be a man.

TRAVIS. Yeah—I always wanted to live in a house.

MAMA. All right, gimme some sugar then—[TRAVIS *puts his arms around her neck as she watches her son over the boy's shoulder. Then, to* TRAVIS, *after the embrace.*] Now when you say your prayers tonight, you thank God and your grandfather— 'cause it was him who give you the house—in his way.

RUTH [*Taking the boy from* MAMA *and pushing him toward the bedroom*]. Now you get out of here and get ready for your beating.

TRAVIS. Aw, Mama—

RUTH. Get on in there—[*Closing the door behind him and turning radiantly to her mother-in-law.*] So you went and did it!

MAMA [*Quietly, looking at her son with pain*]. Yes, I did.

RUTH [*Raising both arms classically*]. Praise God! [*Looks at* WALTER *a moment, who says nothing. She crosses rapidly to her husband.*] Please, honey—let me be glad . . . you be glad too. [*She has laid her hands on his shoulders, but he shakes himself free of her roughly, without turning to face her.*] Oh, Walter . . . a home . . . *a home.* [*She comes back to* MAMA.] Well—where is it? How big is it? How much is it going to cost?

MAMA. Well—

RUTH. When we moving?

MAMA [*Smiling at her*]. First of the month.

RUTH [*Throwing back her head with jubilance*]. Praise God!

MAMA [*Tentatively, still looking at her son's back turned against her and* RUTH.] It's—it's a nice house too . . . [*She cannot help speaking directly to him. An imploring quality in her voice, her manner, makes her almost like a girl now.*] Three bedrooms—nice big one for you and Ruth. . . . Me and Beneatha still have to share our room, but Travis have one of his own—and—[*With difficulty*] I figures if the—new baby—is a boy, we could get one of them double-decker outfits . . . And there's a yard with a little patch of dirt where I could maybe get to grow me a few flowers . . . And a nice big basement . . .

RUTH. Walter honey, be glad—

MAMA [*Still to his back, fingering things on the table*]. 'Course I don't want to make it sound fancier than it is . . . It's just a plain little old house—but it's made good and solid—and it will be *ours.* Walter Lee—it makes a difference in a man when he can walk on floors that belong to *him* . . .

RUTH. Where is it?

MAMA [*Frightened at this telling*]. Well—well—it's out there in Clybourne Park— [RUTH's *radiance fades abruptly, and* WALTER *finally turns slowly to face his mother with incredulity and hostility.*]

RUTH. Where?

MAMA [*Matter-of-factly*]. Four o six Clybourne Street, Clybourne Park.

RUTH. Clybourne Park? Mama, there ain't no colored people living in Clybourne Park.

MAMA [*Almost idiotically*]. Well, I guess there's going to be some now.

WALTER [*Bitterly*]. So that's the peace and comfort you went out and bought for us today!

MAMA [*Raising her eyes to meet his finally*]. Son—I just tried to find the nicest place for the least amount of money for my family.

RUTH [*Trying to recover from the shock*]. Well—well—'course I ain't one never been 'fraid of no crackers,[7] mind you—but—well, wasn't there no other houses nowhere?

MAMA. Them houses they put up for colored in them areas way out all seem to cost twice as much as other houses. I did the best I could.

RUTH [*Struck senseless with the news, in its various degrees of goodness and trouble, she sits a moment, her fists propping her chin in thought, and then she starts to rise, bringing her fists down with vigor, the radiance spreading from cheek to cheek again*]. Well—well!— All I can say is—if this is my time in life—*my time*—to say good-bye—[*And she builds with momentum as she starts to circle the room with an exuberant, almost tear-fully happy release*]—to these God-damned cracking walls!—[*She pounds the walls*]—and these marching roaches!—[*She wipes at an imaginary army of march-ing roaches*]—and this cramped little closet which ain't now or never was no kitchen! . . . then I say it loud and good, *Hallelujah! and good-bye misery . . . I don't never want to see your ugly face again!* [*She laughs joyously, having practically destroyed the apartment, and flings her arms up and lets them come down happily, slowly, reflec-tively, over her abdomen, aware for the first time perhaps that the life therein pulses with happiness and not despair.*] Lena?

MAMA [*Moved, watching her happiness*]. Yes, honey?

RUTH [*Looking off*]. Is there—is there a whole lot of sunlight?

MAMA [*Understanding*]. Yes, child, there's a whole lot of sunlight.
[*Long pause.*]

RUTH [*Collecting herself and going to the door of the room* TRAVIS *is in*]. Well—I guess I better see 'bout Travis. [*To* MAMA.] Lord, I sure don't feel like whipping nobody today!
[*She exits.*]

MAMA [*The mother and son are left alone now and the mother waits a long time, considering deeply, before she speaks*]. Son—you—you understand what I done, don't you? [WALTER *is silent and sullen.*] I—I just seen my family falling apart today . . . just falling to pieces in front of my eyes . . . We couldn't of gone on like we was today. We was going backwards 'stead of forwards—talking 'bout killing babies and wishing each other was dead . . . When it gets like that in life—you just got to do something different, push on out and do something bigger . . . [*She waits.*] I wish you say something, son . . . I wish you'd say how deep inside you you think I done the right thing—

WALTER [*Crossing slowly to his bedroom door and finally turning there and speaking measuredly*]. What you need me to say you done right for? *You* the head of the family. You run our lives like you want to. It was your money and you did what you wanted with it. So what you need for me to say it was all right for? [*Bitterly, to hurt her as deeply as he knows is possible.*] So you butchered up a dream of mine—you—who always talking 'bout your children's dreams . . .

MAMA. Walter Lee—
[*He just closes the door behind him.* MAMA *sits alone, thinking heavily.*]

CURTAIN

SCENE II

TIME: *Friday night. A few weeks later.*
At rise: *Packing crates mark the intention of the family to move.* BENEATHA *and* GEORGE *come in, presumably from an evening out again.*

---

[7] A disparaging term generally applied to lower-class, white Southerners.

GEORGE. O.K. . . . O.K., whatever you say . . . [*They both sit on the couch. He tries to kiss her. She moves away.*] Look, we've had a nice evening; let's not spoil it, huh? . . . [*He again turns her head and tries to nuzzle in and she turns away from him, not with distaste but with momentary lack of interest; in a mood to pursue what they were talking about.*]

BENEATHA. I'm *trying* to talk to you.

GEORGE. We always talk.

BENEATHA. Yes—and I love to talk.

GEORGE [*Exasperated; rising*]. I know it and I don't mind it sometimes . . . I want you to cut it out, see— The moody stuff, I mean. I don't like it. You're a nice-looking girl . . . all over. That's all you need, honey, forget the atmosphere. Guys aren't going to go for the atmosphere—they're going to go for what they see. Be glad for that. Drop the Garbo[8] routine. It doesn't go with you. As for myself, I want a nice—[*Groping.*]—simple—[*Thoughtfully.*]—sophisticated girl . . . not a poet— O.K.?

[*She rebuffs him again and he starts to leave.*]

BENEATHA. Why are you angry?

GEORGE. Because this is stupid! I don't go out with you to discuss the nature of "quiet desperation" or to hear all about your thoughts—because the world will go on thinking what it thinks regardless—

BENEATHA. Then why read books? Why go to school?

GEORGE [*With artificial patience, counting on his fingers*]. It's simple. You read books—to learn facts—to get grades—to pass the course—to get a degree. That's all—it has nothing to do with thoughts.

[*A long pause.*]

BENEATHA. I see. [*A longer pause as she looks at him.*] Good night, George.

[GEORGE *looks at her a little oddly, and starts to exit. He meets* MAMA *coming in.*]

GEORGE. Oh—hello, Mrs. Younger.

MAMA. Hello, George, how you feeling?

GEORGE. Fine—fine, how are you?

MAMA. Oh, a little tired. You know them steps can get you after a day's work. You all have a nice time tonight?

GEORGE. Yes—a fine time. Well, good night.

MAMA. Good night. [*He exits.* MAMA *closes the door behind her.*] Hello, honey. What you sitting like that for?

BENEATHA. I'm just sitting.

MAMA. Didn't you have a nice time?

BENEATHA. No.

MAMA. No? What's the matter?

BENEATHA. Mama, George is a fool—honest. [*She rises.*]

MAMA [*Hustling around unloading the packages she has entered with. She stops*]. Is he, baby?

BENEATHA. Yes.

[BENEATHA *makes up* TRAVIS' *bed as she talks.*]

MAMA. You sure?

BENEATHA. Yes.

MAMA. Well—I guess you better not waste your time with no fools.

[BENEATHA *looks up at her mother, watching her put groceries in the refrigerator. Finally*

---

[8] Greta Garbo (1905–1990), a Swedish actress who became famous for her air of remote sophistication in such films as *Grand Hotel* (1932) and *Anna Karenina* (1935).

she gathers up her things and starts into the bedroom. At the door she stops and looks back at her mother.]

BENEATHA. Mama—

MAMA. Yes, baby—

BENEATHA. Thank you.

MAMA. For what?

BENEATHA. For understanding me this time.

[*She exits quickly and the mother stands, smiling a little, looking at the place where* BENEATHA *just stood.* RUTH *enters.*]

RUTH. Now don't you fool with any of this stuff, Lena—

MAMA. Oh, I just thought I'd sort a few things out.

[*The phone rings.* RUTH *answers.*]

RUTH [*At the phone*]. Hello—Just a minute. [*Goes to door.*] Walter, it's Mrs. Arnold. [*Waits. Goes back to the phone. Tense.*] Hello. Yes, this is his wife speaking . . . He's lying down now. Yes . . . well, he'll be in tomorrow. He's been very sick. Yes—I know we should have called, but we were so sure he'd be able to come in today. Yes—yes, I'm very sorry. Yes . . . Thank you very much. [*She hangs up.* WALTER *is standing in the doorway of the bedroom behind her.*] That was Mrs. Arnold.

WALTER [*Indifferently*]. Was it?

RUTH. She said if you don't come in tomorrow that they are getting a new man . . .

WALTER. Ain't that sad—ain't that crying sad.

RUTH. She said Mr. Arnold has had to take a cab for three days . . . Walter, you ain't been to work for three days! [*This is a revelation to her.*] Where you been, Walter Lee Younger? [WALTER *looks at her and starts to laugh.*] You're going to lose your job.

WALTER. That's right . . .

RUTH. Oh, Walter, and with your mother working like a dog every day—

WALTER. That's sad too—Everything is sad.

MAMA. What you been doing for these three days, son?

WALTER. Mama—you don't know all the things a man what got leisure can find to do in this city . . . What's this—Friday night? Well—Wednesday I borrowed Willy Harris' car and I went for a drive . . . just me and myself and I drove and drove . . . Way out . . . way past South Chicago, and I parked the car and I sat and looked at the steel mills all day long. I just sat in the car and looked at them big black chimneys for hours. Then I drove back and I went to the Green Hat. [*Pause.*] And Thursday—Thursday I borrowed the car again and I got in it and I pointed it the other way and I drove the other way—for hours—way, way up to Wisconsin, and I looked at the farms. I just drove and looked at the farms. Then I drove back and I went to the Green Hat. [*Pause.*] And today—today I didn't get the car. Today I just walked. All over the Southside. And I looked at the Negroes and they looked at me and finally I just sat down on the curb at Thirty-ninth and South Parkway and I just sat there and watched the Negroes go by. And then I went to the Green Hat. You all sad? You all depressed? And you know where I am going right now—

[RUTH *goes out quietly.*]

MAMA. Oh, Big Walter, is this the harvest of our days?

WALTER. You know what I like about the Green Hat? [*He turns the radio on and a steamy, deep blues pours into the room.*] I like this little cat they got there who blows a sax . . . He blows. He talks to me. He ain't but 'bout five feet tall and he's got a conked head and his eyes is always closed and he's all music—

MAMA [*Rising and getting some papers out of her handbag*]. Walter—

WALTER. And there's this other guy who plays the piano . . . and they got a sound. I mean they can work on some music . . . They got the best little combo in the world in the Green Hat . . . You can just sit there and drink and listen to them three men play and you realize that don't nothing matter worth a damn, but just being there—

MAMA. I've helped do it to you, haven't I, son? Walter, I been wrong.

WALTER. Naw—you ain't never been wrong about nothing, Mama.

MAMA. Listen to me, now. I say I been wrong, son. That I been doing to you what the rest of the world been doing to you. [*She stops and he looks up slowly at her and she meets his eyes pleadingly.*] Walter—what you ain't never understood is that I ain't got nothing, don't own nothing, ain't never really wanted nothing that wasn't for you. There ain't nothing as precious to me . . . There ain't nothing worth holding on to, money, dreams, nothing else—if it means—if it means it's going to destroy my boy. [*She puts her papers in front of him and he watches her without speaking or moving.*] I paid the man thirty-five hundred dollars down on the house. That leaves sixty-five hundred dollars. Monday morning I want you to take this money and take three thousand dollars and put it in a savings account for Beneatha's medical schooling. The rest you put in a checking account—with your name on it. And from now on any penny that comes out of it or that go in it is for you to look after. For you to decide. [*She drops her hands a little helplessly.*] It ain't much, but it's all I got in the world and I'm putting it in your hands. I'm telling you to be the head of the family from now on like you supposed to be.

WALTER [*Stares at the money*]. You trust me like that, Mama?

MAMA. I ain't never stop trusting you. Like I ain't never stop loving you.

[*She goes out, and* WALTER *sits looking at the money on the table as the music continues in its idiom, pulsing in the room. Finally, in a decisive gesture, he gets up and, in a furious action, flings the bedclothes wildly from his son's makeshift bed to all over the floor—with a cry of desperation. Then he picks up the money and goes out in a hurry.*]

CURTAIN

SCENE III

TIME: *Saturday, moving day, one week later.*

Before the curtain rises, RUTH's *voice, a strident, dramatic church alto, cuts through the silence.*

It is, in the darkness, a triumphant surge, a penetrating statement of expectation: "Oh, Lord, I don't feel no ways tired! Children, oh, glory hallelujah!"

As the curtain rises we see that RUTH *is alone in the living room, finishing up the family's packing. It is moving day. She is nailing crates and tying cartons.* BENEATHA *enters, carrying a guitar case, and watches her exuberant sister-in-law.*

RUTH. Hey!

BENEATHA [*Putting away the case*]. Hi.

RUTH [*Pointing at a package*]. Honey—look in that package there and see what I found on sale this morning at the South Center. [RUTH *gets up and moves to the package and draws out some curtains.*] Lookahere—hand-turned hems!

BENEATHA. How do you know the window size out there?

RUTH [*Who hadn't thought of that*]. Oh—Well, they bound to fit something in the whole house. Anyhow, they was too good a bargain to pass us. [RUTH *slaps her*

head, suddenly remembering something.] Oh, Bennie—I meant to put a special note
on that carton over there. That's your mama's good china and she wants 'em to
be very careful with it.

BENEATHA. I'll do it.

[BENEATHA *finds a piece of paper and starts to draw large letters on it.*]

RUTH. You know what I'm going to do as soon as I get in that new house?

BENEATHA. What?

RUTH. Honey—I'm going to run me a tub of water up to here . . . [*With her fingers
practically up to her nostrils.*] And I'm going to get in it—and I am going to sit . . .
and sit . . . and sit in that hot water and the first person who knocks to tell *me*
to hurry up and come out—

BENEATHA. Gets shot at sunrise.

RUTH [*Laughing happily*]. You said it, sister! [*Noticing how large* BENEATHA *is absent-
mindedly making the note.*] Honey, they ain't going to read that from no airplane.

BENEATHA [*Laughing herself*]. I guess I always think things have more emphasis if
they are big, somehow.

RUTH [*Looking up at her and smiling*]. You and your brother seem to have that as a
philosophy of life. Lord, that man—done changed so 'round here. You know—
you know what we did last night? Me and Walter Lee?

BENEATHA. What?

RUTH [*Smiling to herself*]. We went to the movies. [*Looking at* BENEATHA *to see if she
understands.*] We went to the movies. You know the last time me and Walter went
to the movies together?

BENEATHA. No.

RUTH. Me neither. That's how long it been. [*Smiling again.*] But we went last night.
The picture wasn't much good, but that didn't seem to matter. We went—and
we held hands.

BENEATHA. Oh, Lord!

RUTH. We held hands—and you know what?

BENEATHA. What?

RUTH. When we come out of the show it was late and dark and all the stores and
things was closed up . . . and it was kind of chilly and there wasn't many people
on the streets . . . and we was still holding hands, me and Walter.

BENEATHA. You're killing me.

[WALTER *enters with a large package. His happiness is deep in him; he cannot keep still
with his new-found exuberance. He is singing and wiggling and snapping his fingers. He
puts his package in a corner and puts a phonograph record, which he has brought in with
him, on the record player. As the music comes up he dances over to* RUTH *and tries to get
her to dance with him. She gives in at last to his raunchiness and in a fit of giggling
allows herself to be drawn into his mood and together they deliberately burlesque an old
social dance of their youth.*]

BENEATHA [*Regarding them a long time as they dance, then drawing in her breath for a
deeply exaggerated comment which she does not particularly mean*]. Talk about—
olddddddddddd-fashionedddddddd—Negroes!

WALTER [*Stopping momentarily*]. What kind of Negroes?

[*He says this in fun. He is not angry with her today, nor with anyone. He starts to dance
with his wife again.*]

BENEATHA. Old-fashioned.

WALTER [*As he dances with* RUTH]. You know, when these *New Negroes* have their
convention—[*Pointing at his sister*]—that is going to be the chairman of the

Committee on Unending Agitation. [*He goes on dancing, then stops.*] Race, race, race! . . . Girl, I do believe you are the first person in the history of the entire human race to successfully brainwash yourself. [BENEATHA *breaks up and he goes on dancing. He stops again, enjoying his tease.*] Damn, even the N double A C P takes a holiday sometimes! [BENEATHA *and* RUTH *laugh. He dances with* RUTH *some more and starts to laugh and stops and pantomines someone over an operating table.*] I can just see that chick someday looking down at some poor cat on an operating table before she starts to slice him, saying . . . [*Pulling his sleeves back maliciously*] "By the way, what are your views on civil rights down there? . . ."

[*He laughs at her again and starts to dance happily. The bell sounds.*]

BENEATHA. Sticks and stones may break my bones but . . . words will never hurt me!

[BENEATHA *goes to the door and opens it as* WALTER *and* RUTH *go on with the clowning.* BENEATHA *is somewhat surprised to see a quiet-looking middle-aged white man in a business suit holding his hat and a briefcase in his hand and consulting a small piece of paper.*]

MAN. Uh—how do you do, miss. I am looking for Mrs.—[*he looks at the slip of paper*] Mrs. Lena Younger?

BENEATHA [*Smoothing her hair with slight embarrassment*]. Oh—yes, that's my mother. Excuse me. [*She closes the door and turns to quiet the other two.*] Ruth! Brother! Somebody's here. [*Then she opens the door. The man casts a curious quick glance at all of them.*] Uh—come in please.

MAN [*Coming in*]. Thank you.

BENEATHA. My mother isn't here just now. Is it business?

MAN. Yes . . . well, of a sort.

WALTER [*Freely, the Man of the House*]. Have a seat. I'm Mrs. Younger's son. I look after most of her business matters.

[RUTH *and* BENEATHA *exchange amused glances.*]

MAN [*Regarding* WALTER, *and sitting*]. Well—My name is Karl Lindner . . .

WALTER [*Stretching out his hand*]. Walter Younger. This is my wife—[RUTH *nods politely*]—and my sister.

LINDNER. How do you do.

WALTER [*Amiably, as he sits himself easily on a chair, leaning with interest forward on his knees and looking expectantly into the newcomer's face*]. What can we do for you, Mr. Lindner!

LINDNER [*Some minor shuffling of the hat and briefcase on his knees*]. Well—I am a representative of the Clybourne Park Improvement Association—

WALTER [*Pointing*]. Why don't you sit your things on the floor?

LINDNER. Oh—yes. Thank you. [*He slides the briefcase and hat under the chair.*] And as I was saying—I am from the Clybourne Park Improvement Association and we have had it brought to our attention at the last meeting that you people—or at least your mother—has bought a piece of residential property at—[*He digs for the slip of paper again*]—four o six Clybourne Street . . .

WALTER. That's right. Care for something to drink? Ruth, get Mr. Lindner a beer.

LINDNER [*Upset for some reason*]. Oh—no, really. I mean thank you very much, but no thank you.

RUTH [*Innocently*]. Some coffee?

LINDNER. Thank you, nothing at all.

[BENEATHA *is watching the man carefully.*]

LINDNER. Well, I don't know how much you folks know about our organization. [*He is a gentle man; thoughtful and somewhat labored in his manner.*] It is one of these

community organizations set up to look after—oh, you know, things like block
upkeep and special projects and we also have what we call our New Neighbors
Orientation Committee . . .

BENEATHA [*Drily*]. Yes—and what do they do?

LINDNER [*Turning a little to her and then returning the main force to* WALTER]. Well—it's
what you might call a sort of welcoming committee, I guess. I mean they, we, I'm
the chairman of the committee—go around and see the new people who move
into the neighborhood and sort of give them the lowdown on the way we do
things out in Clybourne Park.

BENEATHA [*With appreciation of the two meanings, which escape* RUTH *and* WALTER].
Un-huh.

LINDNER. And we also have the category of what the association calls—[*He looks
elsewhere*]—uh—special community problems . . .

BENEATHA. Yes—and what are some of those?

WALTER. Girl, let the man talk.

LINDNER [*With understated relief*]. Thank you. I would sort of like to explain this
thing in my own way. I mean I want to explain to you in a certain way.

WALTER. Go ahead.

LINDNER. Yes. Well, I'm going to try to get right to the point. I'm sure we'll all
appreciate that in the long run.

BENEATHA. Yes.

WALTER. Be still now!

LINDNER. Well—

RUTH [*Still innocently*]. Would you like another chair—you don't look comfortable.

LINDNER [*More frustrated than annoyed*]. No, thank you very much. Please. Well—to
get right to the point I—[*A great breath, and he is off at last*] I am sure you people
must be aware of some of the incidents which have happened in various parts
of the city when colored people have moved into certain areas—[BENEATHA
exhales heavily and starts tossing a piece of fruit up and down in the air.] Well—
because we have what I think is going to be a unique type of organization in
American community life—not only do we deplore that kind of thing—but we
are trying to do something about it. [BENEATHA *stops tossing and turns with a new
and quizzical interest to the man.*] We feel—[*gaining confidence in his mission because
of the interest in the faces of the people he is talking to*]—we feel that most of the
trouble in this world, when you come right down to it—[*He hits his knee for
emphasis*]—most of the trouble exists because people just don't sit down and
talk to each other.

RUTH [*Nodding as she might in church, pleased with the remark*]. You can say that again,
mister.

LINDNER [*More encouraged by such affirmation*]. That we don't try hard enough in this
world to understand the other fellow's problem. The other guy's point of view.

RUTH. Now that's right.

[BENEATHA *and* WALTER *merely watch and listen with genuine interest.*]

LINDNER. Yes—that's the way we feel out in Clybourne park. And that's why I was
elected to come here this afternoon and talk to you people. Friendly like, you
know, the way people should talk to each other and see if we couldn't find some
way to work this thing out. As I say, the whole business is a matter of *caring* about
the other fellow. Anybody can see that you are a nice family of folks, hard
working and honest I'm sure. [BENEATHA *frowns slightly, quizzically, her head tilted*

regarding him.] Today everybody knows what it means to be on the outside of *something.* And of course, there is always somebody who is out to take the advantage of people who don't always understand.

WALTER. What do you mean?

LINDNER. Well—you see our community is made up of people who've worked hard as the dickens for years to build up that little community. They're not rich and fancy people; just hard-working, honest people who don't really have much but those little homes and a dream of the kind of community they want to raise their children in. Now, I don't say we are perfect and there is a lot wrong in some of the things they want. But you've got to admit that a man, right or wrong, has the right to want to have the neighborhood he lives in a certain kind of way. And at the moment the overwhelming majority of our people out there feel that people get along better, take more of a common interest in the life of the community, when they share a common background. I want you to believe me when I tell you that race prejudice simply doesn't enter into it. It is a matter of the people of Clybourne Park believing, rightly or wrongly, as I say, that for the happiness of all concerned that our Negro families are happier when they live in their *own* communities.

BENEATHA [*With a grand and bitter gesture*]. This, friends, is the Welcoming Committee!

WALTER [*Dumfounded, looking at* LINDNER]. Is this what you came marching all the way over here to tell us?

LINDNER. Well, now we've been having a fine conversation. I hope you'll hear me all the way through.

WALTER [*Tightly*]. Go ahead, man.

LINDNER. You see—in the face of all things I have said, we are prepared to make your family a very generous offer . . .

BENEATHA. Thirty pieces and not a coin less!

WALTER. Yeah?

LINDNER [*Putting on his glasses and drawing a form out of the briefcase*]. Our association is prepared, through the collective effort of our people, to buy the house from you at a financial gain to your family.

RUTH. Lord have mercy, ain't this the living gall!

WALTER. All right, you through?

LINDNER. Well, I want to give you the exact terms of the financial arrangement—

WALTER. We don't want to hear no exact terms of no arrangements. I want to know if you got any more to tell us 'bout getting together?

LINDNER [*Taking off his glasses*]. Well—I don't suppose that you feel . . .

WALTER. Never mind how I feel—you got any more to say 'bout how people ought to sit down and talk to each other? . . . Get out of my house, man.

[*He turns his back and walks to the door.*]

LINDNER [*Looking around at the hostile faces and reaching and assembling his hat and briefcase*]. Well—I don't understand why you people are reacting this way. What do you think you are going to gain by moving into a neighborhood where you just aren't wanted and where some elements—well—people can get awful worked up when they feel that their whole way of life and everything they've ever worked for is threatened.

WALTER. Get out.

LINDNER [*At the door, holding a small card*]. Well—I'm sorry it went like this.

WALTER. Get out.

LINDNER [*Almost sadly regarding* WALTER]. You just can't force people to change their hearts, son.

[*He turns and puts his card on a table and exits.* WALTER *pushes the door to with stinging hatred, and stands looking at it.* RUTH *just sits and* BENEATHA *just stands. They say nothing.* MAMA *and* TRAVIS *enter.*]

MAMA. Well—this all the packing got done since I left out of here this morning. I testify before God that my children got all the energy of the dead. What time the moving men due?

BENEATHA. Four o'clock. You had a caller, Mama.

[*She is smiling, teasingly.*]

MAMA. Sure enough—who?

BENEATHA [*Her arms folded saucily*]. The Welcoming Committee.

[WALTER *and* RUTH *giggle.*]

MAMA [*Innocently*]. Who?

BENEATHA. The Welcoming Committee. They said they're sure going to be glad to see you when you get there.

WALTER [*Devilishly*]. Yeah, they said they can't hardly wait to see your face.

[*Laughter.*]

MAMA [*Sensing their facetiousness*]. What's the matter with you all?

WALTER. Ain't nothing the matter with us. We just telling you 'bout the gentleman who came to see you this afternoon. From the Clybourne Park Improvement Association.

MAMA. What he want?

RUTH [*In the same mood as* BENEATHA *and* WALTER]. To welcome you, honey.

WALTER. He said they can't hardly wait. He said the one thing they don't have, that they just *dying* to have out there is a fine family of colored people! [*To* RUTH *and* BENEATHA.] Ain't that right!

RUTH *and* BENEATHA [*Mockingly*]. Yeah! He left his card in case—

[*They indicate the card, and* MAMA *picks it up and throws it on the floor—understanding and looking off as she draws her chair up to the table on which she has put her plant and some sticks and some cord.*]

MAMA. Father, give us strength. [*Knowingly—and without fun.*] Did he threaten us?

BENEATHA. Oh—Mama—they don't do it like that any more. He talked Brotherhood. He said everybody ought learn how to sit down and hate each other with good Christian fellowship.

[*She and* WALTER *shake hands to ridicule the remark.*]

MAMA [*Sadly*]. Lord, protect us . . .

RUTH. You should hear the money those folks raised to buy the house from us. All we paid and then some.

BENEATHA. What they think we going to do—eat 'em?

RUTH. No, honey, marry 'em.

MAMA [*Shaking her head*]. Lord, Lord, Lord . . .

RUTH. Well—that's the way the crackers crumble. Joke.

BENEATHA [*Laughingly noticing what her mother is doing*]. Mama, what are you doing?

MAMA. Fixing my plant so it won't get hurt none on the way . . .

BENEATHA. Mama, you going to take *that* to the new house?

MAMA. Un-huh.

BENEATHA. That raggedy-looking old thing?

MAMA [*Stopping and looking at her*]. It expresses *me*.

RUTH [*With delight, to* BENEATHA]. So there, Miss Thing!

[WALTER *comes to* MAMA *suddenly and bends down behind her and squeezes her in his arms with all his strength. She is overwhelmed by the suddenness of it and, though delighted, her manner is like that of* RUTH *with* TRAVIS.]

MAMA. Look out now, boy! You make me mess up my thing here!

WALTER [*His face lit, he slips down on his knees beside her, his arms still about her*]. Mama . . . you know what it means to climb up in the chariot?

MAMA [*Gruffly, very happy*]. Get on away from me now . . .

RUTH [*Near the gift-wrapped package, trying to catch* WALTER'S *eye*]. Psst—

WALTER. What the old song say, Mama . . .

RUTH. Walter—Now?

[*She is pointing to the package.*]

WALTER [*Speaking the lines, sweetly, playfully, in his mother's face*].

I got wings . . . you got wings. . .
All God's children got wings . . .

MAMA. Boy—get out of my face and do some work . . .

WALTER.

When I get to heaven gonna put on my wings,
Gonna fly all over God's heaven . . .

BENEATHA [*Teasingly, from across the room*]. Everybody talking 'bout heaven ain't going there!

WALTER [*To* RUTH, *who is carrying the box across to them*]. I don't know, you think we ought to give her that . . . Seems to me she ain't been very appreciative around here.

MAMA [*Eying the box, which is obviously a gift*]. What is that?

WALTER [*Taking it from* RUTH *and putting it on the table in front of* MAMA]. Well—what you all think. Should we give it to her?

RUTH. Oh—she was pretty good today.

MAMA. I'll good you—

[*She turns her eyes to the box again.*]

BENEATHA. Open it, Mama.

[*She stands up, looks at it, turns and looks at all of them, and then presses her hands together and does not open the package.*]

WALTER [*Sweetly*]. Open it, Mama. It's for you. [MAMA *looks in his eyes. It is the first present in her life without its being Christmas. Slowly she opens her package and lifts out, one by one, a brand-new sparkling set of gardening tools.* WALTER *continues, prodding.*] Ruth made up the note—read it . . .

MAMA [*Picking up the card and adjusting her glasses*]. "To our own Mrs. Miniver— Love from Brother, Ruth and Beneatha." Ain't that lovely . . .

TRAVIS [*Tugging at his father's sleeve*]. Daddy, can I give her mine now?

WALTER. All right, son. [TRAVIS *flies to get his gift.*] Travis didn't want to go in with the rest of us, Mama. He got his own. [*Somewhat amused.*] We don't know what it is . . .

TRAVIS [*Racing back in the room with a large hatbox and putting it in front of his grandmother*]. Here!

MAMA. Lord have mercy, baby. You done gone and bought your grandmother a hat?

TRAVIS [*Very proud*]. Open it!

[*She does and lifts out an elaborate, but very elaborate, wide gardening hat, and all the adults break up at the sight of it.*]

RUTH. Travis, honey, what is that?

TRAVIS [*Who thinks it is beautiful and appropriate*]. It's a gardening hat! Like the ladies always have on in the magazines when they work in their gardens.

BENEATHA [*Giggling fiercely*]. Travis—we were trying to make Mama Mrs. Miniver—not Scarlett O'Hara!

MAMA [*Indignantly*]. What's the matter with you all! This here is a beautiful hat! [*Absurdly.*] I always wanted me one just like it!

[*She pops it on her head to prove it to her grandson, and the hat is ludicrous and considerably oversized.*]

RUTH. Hot dog! Go, Mama!

WALTER [*Doubled over with laughter*]. I'm sorry, Mama—but you look like you ready to go out and chop you some cotton sure enough!

[*They all laugh except* MAMA, *out of deference to* TRAVIS' *feelings*]

MAMA [*Gathering the boy up to her*]. Bless your heart—this is the prettiest hat I ever owned—[WALTER, RUTH *and* BENEATHA *chime in—noisily, festively and insincerely congratulating* TRAVIS *on his gift.*] What are we all standing around here for? We ain't finished packin' yet. Bennie, you ain't packed one book.

[*The bell rings.*]

BENEATHA. That couldn't be the movers . . . it's not hardly two good yet—

[BENEATHA *goes into her room.* MAMA *starts for door.*]

WALTER [*Turning, stiffening*]. Wait—wait—I'll get it.

[*He stands and looks at the door.*]

MAMA. You expecting company, son?

WALTER [*Just looking at the door*]. Yeah—yeah . . .

[MAMA *looks at* RUTH, *and they exchange innocent and unfrightened glances.*]

MAMA [*Not understanding*]. Well, let them in, son.

BENEATHA [*From her room*]. We need some more string.

MAMA. Travis—you run to the hardware and get me some string cord.

[MAMA *goes out and* WALTER *turns and looks at* RUTH. TRAVIS *goes to a dish for money.*]

RUTH. Why don't you answer the door, man?

WALTER [*Suddenly bounding across the floor to her*]. 'Cause sometimes it hard to let the future begin! [*Swooping down in her face.*]

I got wings! You got wings!

All God's children got wings!

[*He crosses to the door and throws it open. Standing there is a very slight little man in a not too prosperous business suit and with haunted frightened eyes and a hat pulled down tightly, brim up, around his forehead.* TRAVIS *passes between the men and exits.* WALTER *leans deep in the man's face, still in his jubilance.*]

When I get to heaven gonna put on my wings,

Gonna fly all over God's heaven . . .

[*The little man just stares at him.*]

Heaven—

[*Suddenly he stops and looks past the little man into the empty hallway.*] Where's Willy, man?

BOBO. He ain't with me.

WALTER [*Not disturbed*]. Oh—come on in. You know my wife.

BOBO [*Dumbly, taking off his hat*]. Yes—h'you, Miss Ruth.

RUTH [*Quietly, a mood apart from her husband already, seeing* BOBO]. Hello, Bobo.

WALTER. You right on time today . . . Right on time. That's the way! [*He slaps* BOBO *on his back.*] Sit down . . . lemme hear.

[RUTH *stands stiffly and quietly in back of them, as though somehow she senses death, her eyes fixed on her husband.*]

BOBO [*His frightened eyes on the floor, his hat in his hands*]. Could I please get a drink of water, before I tell you about it, Walter Lee?

[WALTER *does not take his eyes off the man.* RUTH *goes blindly to the tap and gets a glass of water and brings it to* BOBO.]

WALTER. There ain't nothing wrong, is there?

BOBO. Lemme tell you—

WALTER. Man—didn't nothing go wrong?

BOBO. Lemme tell you—Walter Lee. [*Looking at* RUTH *and talking to her more than to* WALTER.] You know how it was. I got to tell you how it was. I mean first I got to tell you how it was all the way . . . I mean about the money I put in, Walter Lee . . .

WALTER [*With taut agitation now*]. What about the money you put in?

BOBO. Well—it wasn't much as we told you—me and Willy— [*He stops.*] I'm sorry, Walter. I got a bad feeling about it. I got a real bad feeling about it . . .

WALTER. Man, what you telling me about all this for? . . . Tell me what happened in Springfield . . .

BOBO. Springfield.

RUTH [*Like a dead woman*]. What was supposed to happen in Springfield?

BOBO [*To her*]. This deal that me and Walter went into with Willy—Me and Willy was going to go down to Springfield and spread some money 'round so's we wouldn't have to wait so long for the liquor license . . . That's what we were going to do. Everybody said that was the way you had to do, you understand, Miss Ruth?

WALTER. Man—what happened down there?

BOBO [*A pitiful man, near tears*]. I'm trying to tell you, Walter.

WALTER [*Screaming at him suddenly*]. THEN TELL ME, GODDAMNIT . . . WHAT'S THE MATTER WITH YOU?

BOBO. Man . . . I didn't go to no Springfield, yesterday.

WALTER [*Halted, life hanging in the moment*]. Why not?

BOBO [*The long way, the hard way to tell*]. 'Cause I didn't have no reasons to . . .

WALTER. Man, what are you talking about!

BOBO. I'm talking about the fact that when I got to the train station yesterday morning—eight o'clock like we planned . . . Man—*Willy didn't never show up.*

WALTER. Why . . . where was he . . . where is he?

BOBO. That's what I'm trying to tell you . . . I don't know . . . I waited six hours . . . I called his house . . . and I waited . . . six hours . . . I waited in that train station six hours . . . [*Breaking into tears.*] That was all the extra money I had in the world . . . [*Looking up at* WALTER *with the tears running down his face.*] Man, *Willy is gone.*

WALTER. Gone, what you mean Willy is gone? Gone where? You mean he went by himself. You mean he went off to Springfield by himself—to take care of getting the license—[*Turns and looks anxiously at* RUTH.] You mean maybe he didn't want too many people in on the business down there? [*Looks to* RUTH *again, as before.*] You know Willy got his own ways. [*Looks back to* BOBO.] Maybe you was late yesterday and he just went on down there without you. Maybe—maybe—he's been callin' you at home tryin' to tell you what happened or something. Maybe—maybe—he just got sick. He's somewhere—he's got to be somewhere. We just got to find him—me and you got to find him. [*Grabs* BOBO *senselessly by the collar and starts to shake him.*] We got to!

BOBO [*In sudden angry, frightened agony*]. What's the matter with you, Walter! *When a cat take off with your money he don't leave you no maps!*

WALTER [*Turning madly, as though he is looking for* WILLY *in the very room*]. Willy! . . . Willy . . . don't do it . . . Please don't do it . . . Man, not with that money . . . Man, please, not with that money . . . Oh, God . . . Don't let it be true . . . [*He is *wandering around, crying out for Willy and looking for him or perhaps for help from God.*] Man . . . I trusted you . . . Man, I put my life in your hands . . . [*He starts to crumple down on the floor as* RUTH *just covers her face in horror.* MAMA *opens the door and comes into the room, with* BENEATHA *behind her.*] Man . . . [*He starts to pound the floor with his fists, sobbing wildly*] That money is made out of my father's flesh . . .

BOBO [*Standing over him helplessly*]. I'm sorry, Walter . . . [*Only* WALTER's *sobs reply.* BOBO *puts on his hat*] I had my life staked on this deal, too . . . [*He exits.*]

MAMA [*To* WALTER]. Son—[*She goes to him, bends down to him, talks to his bent head.*] Son . . . Is it gone? Son, I gave you sixty-five hundred dollars. Is it gone? All of it? Beneatha's money too?

WALTER [*Lifting his head slowly*]. Mama . . . I never . . . went to the bank at all . . .

MAMA [*Not wanting to believe him*]. You mean . . . your sister's school money . . . you used that too . . . Walter? . . .

WALTER. Yessss! . . . All of it . . . It's all gone . . .

[*There is total silence.* RUTH *stands with her face covered with her hands;* BENEATHA *leans forlornly against a wall, fingering a piece of red ribbon from the mother's gift.* MAMA *stops and looks at her son without recognition and then, quite without thinking about it, starts to beat him senselessly in the face.* BENEATHA *goes to them and stops it.*]

BENEATHA. Mama!

[MAMA *stops and looks at both of her children and rises slowly and wanders vaguely, aimlessly away from them.*]

MAMA. I seen . . . him . . . night after night . . . come in . . . and look at that rug . . . and then look at me . . . the red showing in his eyes . . . the veins moving in his head . . . I seen him grow thin and old before he was forty . . . working and working and working like somebody's old horse . . . killing himself . . . and you—you give it all away in a day . . .

BENEATHA. Mama—

MAMA. Oh, God . . . [*She looks up to Him.*] Look down here—and show me the strength.

BENEATHA. Mama—

MAMA [*Folding over*]. Strength . . .

BENEATHA [*Plaintively*]. Mama . . .

MAMA. Strength!

CURTAIN

ACT III

TIME: *An hour later.*

At curtain, there is a sullen light of gloom in the living room, gray light not unlike that which began the first scene of Act I. At left we can see WALTER *within his room, alone with himself. He is stretched out on the bed, his shirt out and open, his arms under his head. He does not smoke, he does not cry out, he merely lies there, looking up at the ceiling, much as if he were alone in the world.*

In the living room BENEATHA *sits at the table, still surrounded by the now almost ominous packing crates. She sits looking off. We feel that this is a mood struck perhaps an hour before, and it lingers now, full of the empty sound of profound disappointment. We see on a line from her brother's bedroom the sameness of their attitudes. Presently the bell rings and* BENEATHA *rises without ambition or interest in answering. It is* ASAGAI, *smiling broadly, striding into the room with energy and happy expectation and conversation.*

ASAGAI. I came over ... I had some free time. I thought I might help with the packing. Ah, I like the look of packing crates! A household in preparation for a journey! It depresses some people ... but for me ... it is another feeling. Something full of the flow of life, do you understand? Movement, progress ... It makes me think of Africa.

BENEATHA. Africa!

ASAGAI. What kind of a mood is this? Have I told you how deeply you move me?

BENEATHA, He gave away the money, Asagai ...

ASAGAI. Who gave away what money?

BENEATHA. The insurance money. My brother gave it away.

ASAGAI. Gave it away?

BENEATHA. He made an investment! With a man even Travis wouldn't have trusted.

ASAGAI. And it's gone?

BENEATHA. Gone!

ASAGAI. I'm very sorry ... And you, now?

BENEATHA. Me? ... Me? ... Me I'm nothing ... Me. When I was very small ... we used to take our sleds out in the wintertime and the only hills we had were the ice-covered stone steps of some houses down the street. And we used to fill them in with snow and make them smooth and slide down them all day ... and it was very dangerous you know ... far too steep ... and sure enough one day a kid named Rufus came down too fast and hit the sidewalk ... and we saw his face just split open right there in front of us ... And I remember standing there looking at his bloody open face thinking that was the end of Rufus. But the ambulance came and they took him to the hospital and they fixed the broken bones and they sewed it all up ... and the next time I saw Rufus he had just a little line down the middle of his face ... I never got over that ...

ASAGAI. What?

BENEATHA. That that was what one person could do for another, fix him up—sew up the problem, make him all right again. That was the most marvelous thing in the world ... I wanted to do that. I always thought it was the one concrete thing in the world that a human being could do. Fix up the sick, you know—and make them whole again. This was truly being God ...

ASAGAI. You wanted to be God?

BENEATHA. No—I wanted to cure. It used to be so important to me. I wanted to cure. It used to matter. I used to care. I mean about people and how their bodies hurt ...

ASAGAI. And you've stopped caring?

BENEATHA. Yes—I think so.

ASAGAI. Why?

BENEATHA. Because it doesn't seem deep enough, close enough to the truth.

ASAGAI. Truth? Why is it that you despairing ones always think that only you have the truth? I never thought to see *you* like that. You! Your brother made a stupid, childish mistake—and you are grateful to him. So that now you can give up the ailing human race on account of it. You talk about what good is struggle; what good is anything? Where are we all going? And why are we bothering?

BENEATHA. *And you cannot answer it!* All your talk and dreams about Africa and Independence. Independence and then what? What about all the crooks and petty thieves and just plain idiots who will come into power to steal and plunder the same as before—only now they will be black and do it in the name of the new Independence— You cannot answer that.

ASAGAI [*Shouting over her*]. *I live the answer!* [*Pause.*] In my village at home it is the exceptional man who can even read a newspaper . . . or who ever *sees* a book at all. I will go home and much of what I will have to say will seem strange to the people of my village . . . But I will teach and work and things will happen, slowly and swiftly. At times it will seem that nothing changes at all . . . and then again . . . the sudden dramatic events which make history leap into the future. And then quiet again. Retrogression even. Guns, murder, revolution. And I even will have moments when I wonder if the quiet was not better than all that death and hatred. But I will look about my village at the illiteracy and disease and ignorance and I will not wonder long. And perhaps . . . perhaps I will be a great man . . . I mean perhaps I will hold on to the substance of truth and find my way always with the right course . . . and perhaps for it I will be butchered in my bed some night by the servants of empire . . .

BENEATHA. *The martyr!*

ASAGAI. . . . or perhaps I shall live to be a very old man respected and esteemed in my new nation . . . And perhaps I shall hold office and this is what I'm trying to tell you, Alaiyo; perhaps the things I believe now for my country will be wrong and outmoded, and I will not understand and do terrible things to have things my way or merely to keep my power. Don't you see that there will be young men and women, not British soldiers then, but my own black countrymen . . . to step out of the shadows some evening and slit my then useless throat? Don't you see they have always been there . . . that they always will be. And that such a thing as my own death will be an advance? They who might kill me even . . . actually replenish me!

BENEATHA. Oh, Asagai, I know all that.

ASAGAI. Good! Then stop moaning and groaning and tell me what you plan to do.

BENEATHA. Do?

ASAGAI. I have a bit of a suggestion.

BENEATHA. What?

ASAGAI [*Rather quietly for him*]. That when it is all over—that you come home with me—

BENEATHA [*Slapping herself on the forehead with exasperation born of misunderstanding*]. Oh—Asagai—at this moment you decide to be romantic!

ASAGAI [*Quickly understanding the misunderstanding*]. My dear, young creature of the New World—I do not mean across the city—I mean across the ocean; home—to Africa.

BENEATHA [*Slowly understanding and turning to him with murmured amazement*]. To—to Nigeria?

ASAGAI. Yes! . . . [*Smiling and lifting his arms playfully.*] Three hundred years later the African Prince rose up out of the seas and swept the maiden back across the middle passage over which her ancestors had come—

BENEATHA [*Unable to play*]. Nigeria?

ASAGAI. Nigeria. Home. [*Coming to her with genuine romantic flippancy.*] I will show you our mountains and our stars; and give you cool drinks from gourds and teach you the old songs and the ways of our people—and, in time, we will pretend that—[*Very softly*]—you have only been away for a day—

[*She turns her back to him, thinking. He swings her around and takes her full in his arms in a long embrace which proceeds to passion.*]

BENEATHA [*Pulling away*]. You're getting me all mixed up—

ASAGAI. Why?

BENEATHA. Too many things—too many things have happened today. I must sit down and think. I don't know what I feel about anything right this minute.

[*She promptly sits down and props her chin on her fist.*]

ASAGAI [*Charmed*]. All right, I shall leave you. No—don't get up. [*Touching her, gently, sweetly.*] Just sit awhile and think . . . Never be afraid to sit awhile and think. [*He goes to door and looks at her.*] How often I have looked at you and said, "Ah—so this is what the New World hath finally wrought . . ."

[*He exits.* BENEATHA *sits on alone. Presently* WALTER *enters from his room and starts to rummage through things, feverishly looking for something. She looks up and turns in her seat.*]

BENEATHA [*Hissing*]. Yes—just look at what the New World hath wrought! . . . Just look! [*She gestures with bitter disgust.*] There he is! *Monsieur le petit bourgeois noir—* himself! There he is—Symbol of a Rising Class! Entrepreneur! Titan of the system! [WALTER *ignores her completely and continues frantically and destructively looking for something and hurling things to floor and tearing things out of their place in his search.* BENEATHA *ignores the eccentricity of his actions and goes on with the monologue of insult.*] Did you dream of yachts on Lake Michigan, Brother? Did you see yourself on the Great Day sitting down at the Conference Table, surrounded by all the mighty bald-headed men in America? All halted, waiting, breathless, waiting for your pronouncements on industry? Waiting for you—Chairman of the Board? [WALTER *finds what he is looking for—a small piece of white paper—and pushes it in his pocket and puts on his coat and rushes out without ever having looked at her. She shouts after him.*] I look at you and I see the final triumph of stupidity in the world!

[*The door slams and she returns to just sitting again.* RUTH *comes quickly out of* MAMA'S *room.*]

RUTH. Who was that?

BENEATHA. Your husband.

RUTH. Where did he go?

BENEATHA. Who knows—maybe he has an appointment at U.S. Steel.

RUTH [*Anxiously, with frightened eyes*]. You didn't say nothing bad to him, did you?

BENEATHA. Bad? Say anything bad to him? No—I told him he was a sweet boy and full of dreams and everything is strictly peachy keen, as the ofay[9] kids say!

[MAMA *enters from her bedroom. She is lost, vague, trying to catch hold, to make some sense of her former command of the world, but it still eludes her. A sense of waste overwhelms her gait; a measure of apology rides on her shoulders. She goes to her plant, which has remained on the table, looks at it, picks it up and takes it to the window sill and sits it outside, and she stands and looks at it a long moment. Then she closes the window, straightens her body with effort and turns around to her children.*]

MAMA. Well—ain't it a mess in here, though? [*A false cheerfulness, a beginning of something.*] I guess we all better stop moping around and get some work done. All this unpacking and everything we got to do. [RUTH *raises her head slowly in response to the sense of the line; and* BENEATHA *in similar manner turns very slowly to look at her mother.*] One of you all better call the moving people and tell 'em not to come.

RUTH. Tell 'em not to come?

MAMA. Of course, baby. Ain't no need in 'em coming all the way here and having

---

[9] A slang word for *white.*

to go back. They charges for that too. [*She sits down, fingers to her brow, thinking.*]
Lord, ever since I was a little girl, I always remembers people saying, "Lena—
Lena Eggleston, you aims too high all the time. You needs to slow down and see
life a little more like it is. Just slow down some." That's what they always used
to say down home—"Lord, that Lena Eggleston is a high-minded thing. She'll
get her due one day!"

RUTH. No, Lena . . .

MAMA. Me and Big Walter just didn't never learn right.

RUTH. Lena, no! We gotta go. Bennie—tell her . . . [*She rises and crosses to* BENEATHA
with her arms outstretched. BENEATHA *doesn't respond.*] Tell her we can still move . . .
the notes ain't but a hundred and twenty five a month. We got four grown
people in this house—we can work . . .

MAMA [*To herself*]. Just aimed too high all the time—

RUTH [*Turning and going to* MAMA *fast—the words pouring out with urgency and desperation*]. Lena—I'll work . . . I'll work twenty hours a day in all the kitchens in
Chicago . . . I'll strap my baby on my back if I have to and scrub all the floors
in America and wash all the sheets in America if I have to—but we got to move
. . . We got to get out of here . . .

[MAMA *reaches out absently and pats* RUTH'S *hand.*]

MAMA. No—I sees things differently now. Been thinking 'bout some of the things
we could do to fix this place up some. I seen a second-hand bureau over on
Maxwell Street just the other day that could fit right there. [*She points to where the
new furniture might go.* RUTH *wanders away from her.*] Would need some new
handles on it and then a little varnish and then it look like something brand-
new. And—we can put up them new curtains in the kitchen . . . Why this place
be looking fine. Cheer us all up so that we forget trouble ever came . . . [*To
RUTH.*] And you could get some nice screens to put up in your room round the
baby's basinet . . . [*She looks at both of them, pleadingly.*] Sometimes you just got to
know when to give up some things . . . and hold on to what you got.

[WALTER *enters from the outside, looking spent and leaning against the door, his coat
hanging from him.*]

MAMA. Where you been, son?

WALTER [*Breathing hard*]. Made a call.

MAMA. To who, son?

WALTER. To The Man.

MAMA. What man, baby?

WALTER. The Man, Mama. Don't you know who The Man is?

RUTH. Walter Lee?

WALTER. *The Man.* Like the guys in the streets say—The Man. Captain Boss—
Mistuh Charley . . . Old Captain Please Mr. Bossman . . .

BENEATHA [*Suddenly*]. Lindner!

WALTER. That's right! That's good. I told him to come right over.

BENEATHA [*Fiercely, understanding*]. For what? What do you want to see him for!

WALTER [*Looking at his sister*]. We going to do business with him.

MAMA. What you talking 'bout, son?

WALTER. Talking 'bout life, Mama. You all always telling me to see life like it is.
Well—I laid in there on my back today . . . and I figured it out. Life just like it
is. Who gets and who don't get. [*He sits down with his coat on and laughs.*] Mama,
you know it's all divided up. Life is. Sure enough. Between the takers and the
"tooken." [*He laughs.*] I've figured it out finally. [*He looks around at them.*] Yeah.

Some of us always getting "tooken." [*He laughs.*] People like Willy Harris, they don't never get "tooken." And you know why the rest of us do? 'Cause we all mixed up. Mixed up bad. We get to looking 'round for the right and the wrong; and we worry about it and cry about it and stay up nights trying to figure out 'bout the wrong and the right of things all the time . . . And all the time, man, them takers is out there operating, just taking and taking. Willy Harris? Shoot— Willy Harris don't even count. He don't even count in the big scheme of things. But I'll say one thing for old Willy Harris . . . he's taught me something. He's taught me to keep my eye on what counts in this world. Yeah—[*Shouting out a little.*] Thanks, Willy!

RUTH. What did you call that man for, Walter Lee?

WALTER. Called him to tell him to come on over to the show. Gonna put on a show for the man. Just what he wants to see. You see, Mama, the man came here today and he told us that them people out there where you want us to move—well they so upset they willing to pay us not to move out there. [*He laughs again.*] And—and oh, Mama—you would of been proud of the way me and Ruth and Bennie acted. We told him to get out . . . Lord have mercy! We told the man to get out. Oh, we was some proud folks this afternoon, yeah. [*He lights a cigarette.*] We were still full of that old-time stuff . . .

RUTH [*Coming toward him slowly*]. You talking 'bout taking them people's money to keep us from moving in that house?

WALTER. I ain't just talking 'bout it, baby—I'm telling you that's what's going to happen.

BENEATHA. Oh, God! Where is the bottom! Where is the real honest-to-God bottom so he can't go any farther!

WALTER. See—that's the old stuff. You and that boy that was here today. You all want everybody to carry a flag and a spear and sing some marching songs, huh? You wanna spend your life looking into things and trying to find the right and wrong part, huh? Yeah. You know what's going to happen to that boy some-day—he'll find himself sitting in a dungeon, locked in forever—and the takers will have the key! Forget it, baby! There ain't no causes—there ain't nothing but taking in this world, and he who takes most is smartest—and it don't make a damn bit of difference *how.*

MAMA. You making something inside me cry, son. Some awful pain inside me.

WALTER. Don't cry, Mama. Understand. That white man is going to walk in that door able to write checks for more money than we ever had. It's important to him and I'm going to help him . . . I'm going to put on the show, Mama.

MAMA. Son—I come from five generations of people who was slaves and share-croppers—but ain't nobody in my family never let nobody pay 'em no money that was a way of telling us we wasn't fit to walk the earth. We ain't never been that poor. [*Raising her eyes and looking at him.*] We ain't never been that dead inside.

BENEATHA. Well—we are dead now. All the talk about dreams and sunlight that goes on in this house. All dead.

WALTER. What's the matter with you all! I didn't make this world! It was give to me this way! Hell, yes, I want me some yachts someday! Yes, I want to hang some real pearls 'round my wife's neck. Ain't she supposed to wear no pearls? Some-body tell me—tell me, who decides which women is suppose to wear pearls in this world. I tell you I am a *man*—and I think my wife should wear some pearls in this world!

[*This last line hangs a good while and* WALTER *begins to move about the room. The word "Man" has penetrated his consciousness; he mumbles it to himself repeatedly between strange agitated pauses as he moves about.*]

MAMA. Baby, how you going to feel on the inside?

WALTER. Fine! . . . Going to feel fine . . . a man . . .

MAMA. You won't have nothing left then, Walter Lee.

WALTER [*Coming to her*]. I'm going to feel fine, Mama. I'm going to look that son-of-a-bitch in the eyes and say—[*he falters*]—and say, "All right, Mr. Lindner—[*He falters even more*]—that's your neighborhood out there. You got the right to keep it like you want. You got the right to have it like you want. Just write the check and—the house is yours." And, and I am going to say —[*His voice almost breaks.*] And you—you people just put the money in my hand and you won't have to live next to this bunch of stinking niggers! . . . [*He straightens up and moves away from his mother, walking around the room.*] Maybe—maybe I'll just get down on my black knees . . . [*He does so;* RUTH *and* BENNIE *and* MAMA *watch him in frozen horror.*] Captain, Mistuh, Bossman. [*He starts crying.*] A-hee-hee-hee! [*Wringing his hands in profoundly anguished imitation.*] Yasssssuh! Great White Father, just gi' ussen de money, fo' God's sake, and we's ain't gwine come out deh and dirty up yo' white folks neighborhood . . .

[*He breaks down completely, then gets up and goes into the bedroom.*]

BENEATHA. That is not a man. That is nothing but a toothless rat.

MAMA. Yes—death done come in this here house. [*She is nodding, slowly, reflectively.*] Done come walking in my house. On the lips of my children. You what supposed to be my beginning again. You—what supposed to be my harvest. [*To* BENEATHA] You—you mourning your brother?

BENEATHA. He's no brother of mine.

MAMA. What you say?

BENEATHA. I said that that individual in that room is no brother of mine.

MAMA. That's what I thought you said. You feeling like you better than he is today? [BENEATHA *does not answer.*] Yes? What you tell him a minute ago? That he wasn't a man? Yes? You give him up for me? You done wrote his epitaph too—like the rest of the world? Well, who give you the privilege?

BENEATHA. Be on my side for once! You saw what he just did, Mama! You saw him—down on his knees. Wasn't it you who taught me—to despise any man who would do that. Do what he's going to do.

MAMA. Yes—I taught you that. Me and your daddy. But I thought I taught you something else too . . . I thought I taught you to love him.

BENEATHA. Love him? There is nothing left to love.

MAMA. There is always something left to love. And if you ain't learned that, you ain't learned nothing. [*Looking at her.*] Have you cried for that boy today? I don't mean for yourself and for the family 'cause we lost the money. I mean for him; what he been through and what it done to him. Child, when do you think is the time to love somebody the most; when they done good and made things easy for everybody? Well then, you ain't through learning—because that ain't the time at all. It's when he's at his lowest and can't believe in hisself 'cause the world done whipped him so. When you starts measuring somebody, measure him right, child, measure him right. Make sure you done taken into account what hills and valleys he come through before he got to wherever he is.

[TRAVIS *bursts into the room at the end of the speech, leaving the door open.*]

TRAVIS. Grandmama—the moving men are downstairs! The truck just pulled up.

MAMA [*Turning and looking at him*]. Are they, baby? They downstairs?

[*She sighs and sits.* LINDNER *appears in the doorway. He peers in and knocks lightly, to gain attention, and comes in. All turn to look at him.*]

LINDNER [*Hat and briefcase in hand*]. Uh—hello . . .

[RUTH *crosses mechanically to the bedroom door and opens it and lets it swing open freely and slowly as the lights come up on* WALTER *within, still in his coat, sitting at the far corner of the room. He looks up and out through the room to* LINDNER]

RUTH. He's here.

[*A long minute passes and* WALTER *slowly gets up.*]

LINDNER [*Coming to the table with efficiency, putting his briefcase on the table and starting to unfold papers and unscrew fountain pens*]. Well, I certainly was glad to hear from you people. [WALTER *has begun the trek out of the room, slowly and awkwardly, rather like a small boy, passing the back of his sleeve across his mouth from time to time.*] Life can really be so much simpler than people let it be most of the time. Well—with whom do I negotiate? You, Mrs. Younger, or your son here? [MAMA *sits with her hands folded on her lap and her eyes closed as* WALTER *advances.* TRAVIS *goes close to* LINDNER *and looks at the papers curiously.*] Just some official papers, sonny.

RUTH. Travis, you go downstairs.

MAMA [*Opening her eyes and looking into* WALTER'S]. No. Travis, you stay right here. And you make him understand what you doing, Walter Lee. You teach him good. Like Willy Harris taught you. You show where our five generations done come to. Go ahead, son—

WALTER [*Looks down into his boy's eyes.* TRAVIS *grins at him merrily and* WALTER *draws him beside him with his arm lightly around his shoulder*]. Well, Mr. Lindner. [BENEATHA *turns away.*] We called you—[*There is a profound, simple groping quality in his speech*]—because, well, me and my family [*He looks around and shifts from one foot to the other.*] Well—we are very plain people . . .

LINDNER. Yes—

WALTER. I mean—I have worked as a chauffeur most of my life—and my wife here, she does domestic work in people's kitchens. So does my mother. I mean—we are plain people . . .

LINDNER. Yes, Mr. Younger—

WALTER [*Really like a small boy, looking down at his shoes and then up at the man*]. And—uh—well, my father, well, he was a laborer most of his life.

LINDNER [*Absolutely confused*]. Uh, yes—

WALTER [*Looking down at his toes once again*]. My father almost beat a man to death once because this man called him a bad name or something, you know what I mean?

LINDNER. No, I'm afraid I don't.

WALTER [*Finally straightening up*]. Well, what I mean is that we come from people who had a lot of pride. I mean—we are very proud people. And that's my sister over there and she's going to be a doctor—and we are very proud—

LINDNER. Well—I am sure that is very nice, but—

WALTER [*Starting to cry and facing the man eye to eye*]. What I am telling you is that we called you over here to tell you that we are very proud and that this is—this is my son, who makes the sixth generation of our family in this country, and that we have all thought about your offer and we have decided to move into our house because my father—my father—he earned it. [MAMA *has her eyes closed and is rocking back and forth as though she were in church, with her head nodding the amen yes.*] We don't want to make no trouble for nobody or fight no causes—but we will try to be good neighbors. That's all we got to say. [*He looks the man absolutely in the eyes.*] We don't want your money.

[*He turns and walks away from the man.*]

LINDNER [*Looking around at all of them*]. I take it then that you have decided to occupy.

BENEATHA. That's what the man said.

LINDNER [*To* MAMA *in her reverie*]. Then I would like to appeal to you, Mrs. Younger. You are older and wiser and understand things better I am sure . . .

MAMA [*Rising*]. I am afraid you don't understand. My son said we was going to move and there ain't nothing left for me to say. [*Shaking her head with double meaning.*] You know how these young folks is nowadays, mister. Can't do a thing with 'em. Good-bye.

LINDNER [*Folding up his materials*]. Well—if you are that final about it . . . There is nothing left for me to say. [*He finishes. He is almost ignored by the family, who are concentrating on* WALTER LEE. *At the door* LINDNER *halts and looks around.*] I sure hope you people know what you're doing.

[*He shakes his head and exits.*]

RUTH [*Looking around and coming to life*]. Well, for God's sake—if the moving men are here—LET'S GET THE HELL OUT OF HERE!

MAMA [*Into action*]. Ain't it the truth! Look at all this here mess. Ruth put Travis' good jacket on him . . . Walter Lee, fix your tie and tuck your shirt in, you look just like somebody's hoodlum. Lord have mercy, where is my plant? [*She flies to get it amid the general bustling of the family, who are deliberately trying to ignore the nobility of the past moment.*] You all start on down . . . Travis child, don't go empty handed . . . Ruth, were did I put that box with my skillets in it? I want to be in charge of it myself . . . I'm going to make us the biggest dinner we ever ate tonight . . . Beneatha, what's the matter with them stockings? Pull them things up, girl . . .

[*The family starts to file out as two moving men appear and begin to carry out the heavier pieces of furniture, bumping into the family as they move about.*]

BENEATHA. Mama, Asagai—asked me to marry him today and go to Africa—

MAMA [*In the middle of her getting-ready activity*]. He did? You ain't old enough to marry nobody—[*Seeing the moving men lifting one of her chairs precariously.*] Darling, that ain't no bale of cotton, please handle it so we can sit in it again. I had that chair twenty-five years . . .

[*The movers sigh with exasperation and go on with their work.*]

BENEATHA [*Girlishly and unreasonably trying to pursue the conversation*]. To go to Africa, Mama—be a doctor in Africa . . .

MAMA [*Distractedly*]. Yes, baby—

WALTER. Africa! What he want you to go to Africa for?

BENEATHA. To practice there . . .

WALTER. Girl, if you don't get all them silly ideas out your head! You better marry yourself a man with some loot . . .

BENEATHA [*Angrily, precisely as in the first scene of the play*]. What have you got to do with who I marry!

WALTER. Plenty. Now I think George Murchison—

[*He and* BENEATHA *go out yelling at each other vigorously;* BENEATHA *is heard saying that she would not marry* GEORGE MURCHISON *if he were Adam and she were Eve, etc. The anger is loud and real till their voices diminish.* RUTH *stands at the door and turns to* MAMA *and smiles knowingly.*]

MAMA [*Fixing her hat at last*]. Yeah—they something all right, my children . . .

RUTH. Yeah—they're something. Let's go, Lena.

MAMA [*Stalling, starting to look around at the house*]. Yes—I'm coming. Ruth—

RUTH. Yes?

MAMA [*Quietly, woman to woman*]. He finally come into his manhood today, didn't he? Kind of like a rainbow after the rain . . .

RUTH [*Biting her lip lest her own pride explode in front of* MAMA]. Yes, Lena.

[WALTER'S *voice calls for them raucously*.]

MAMA [*Waving* RUTH *out vaguely*]. All right, honey—go on down. I be down directly.

[RUTH *hesitates, then exits.* MAMA *stands, at last alone in the living room, her plant on the table before her as the lights start to come down. She looks around at all the walls and ceilings and suddenly, despite herself, while the children call below, a great heaving thing rises in her and she puts her fist to her mouth, takes a final desperate look, pulls her coat about her, pats her hat and goes out. The lights dim down. The door opens and she comes back in, grabs her plant, and goes out for the last time.*]

CURTAIN

[1959]

Wole Soyinka 1934–

THE STRONG BREED

CHARACTERS

EMAN, *a stranger*

SUNMA, *Jaguna's daughter*

IFADA, *an idiot*

A GIRL

JAGUNA

OROGE

ATTENDANT STALWARTS. *The villagers*

from Eman's past:

OLD MAN, *his father*

OMAE, *his betrothed*

TUTOR

PRIEST

ATTENDANTS. *The villagers*

The scenes are described briefly, but very often a darkened stage with lit areas will not only suffice but is necessary. Except for the one indicated place, there can be no break in the action. A distracting scene-change would be ruinous.

A mud house, with space in front of it. EMAN, *in light buba*[1] *and trousers stands at the window, looking out. Inside,* SUNMA *is clearing the table of what looks like a modest clinic, putting the things away in a cupboard. Another rough table in the room is piled with exercise books, two or three worn text-books, etc.* SUNMA *appears agitated. Outside, just below the window crouches* IFADA. *He looks up with a shy smile from time to time, waiting for* EMAN *to notice him.*

SUNMA [*hesitant*]. You will have to make up your mind soon Eman. The lorry[2] leaves very shortly.

[*As* EMAN *does not answer,* SUNMA *continues her work, more nervously. Two villagers, obvious travellers, pass hurriedly in front of the house, the man has a small raffia*[3] *sack, the woman a cloth-covered basket, the man enters first, turns and urges the woman who is just emerging to hurry.*]

SUNMA [*seeing them, her tone is more intense*]. Eman, are we going or aren't we? You will leave it till too late.

EMAN [*quietly*]. There is still time—if you want to go.

SUNMA. If I want to go . . . and you?

[EMAN *makes no reply.*]

SUNMA [*bitterly*]. You don't really want to leave here. You never want to go away— even for a minute.

[IFADA *continues his antics.* EMAN *eventually pats him on the head and the boy grins happily. Leaps up suddenly and returns with a basket of oranges which he offers to* EMAN.]

EMAN. My gift for today's festival enh?

[IFADA *nods, grinning.*]

EMAN. They look ripe—that's a change.

SUNMA [*she has gone inside the room. Looks round the door*]. Did you call me?

---

[1] A traditional shirt worn by Africans of the Yoruba tribe.
[2] A passenger vehicle constructed on a large truck frame.
[3] A fiber made from palm leaves.

EMAN. No. [*She goes back.*] And what will you do tonight Ifada? Will you take part in the dancing? Or perhaps you will mount your own masquerade?[4]

[IFADA *shakes his head, regretfully.*]

EMAN. You won't? So you haven't any? But you would like to own one.

[IFADA *nods eagerly.*]

EMAN. Then why don't you make your own?

[IFADA *stares, puzzled by this idea.*]

EMAN. Sunma will let you have some cloth you know. And bits of wool . . .

SUNMA [*coming out*]. Who are you talking to Eman?

EMAN. Ifada. I am trying to persuade him to join the young maskers.

SUNMA [*losing control*]. What does he want here? Why is he hanging around us?

EMAN [*amazed*]. What . . . ? I said Ifada, Ifada.

SUNMA. Just tell him to go away. Let him go and play somewhere else!

EMAN. What is this? Hasn't he always played here?

SUNMA. I don't want him here. [*Rushes to the window.*] Get away idiot. Don't bring your foolish face here any more, do you hear? Go on, go away from here . . .

EMAN [*restraining her*]. Control yourself Sunma. What on earth has got into you?

[IFADA, *hurt and bewildered, backs slowly away.*]

SUNMA. He comes crawling round here like some horrible insect. I never want to lay my eyes on him again.

EMAN. I don't understand. It *is* Ifada you know. Ifada! The unfortunate one who runs errands for you and doesn't hurt a soul.

SUNMA. I cannot bear the sight of him.

EMAN. You can't do what? It can't be two days since he last fetched water for you.

SUNMA. What else can he do except that? He is useless. Just because we have been kind to him . . . Others would have put him in an asylum.

EMAN. You are not making sense. He is not a madman, he is just a little more unlucky than other children. [*Looks keenly at her.*] But what is the matter?

SUNMA. It's nothing. I only wish we had sent him off to one of those places for creatures like him.

EMAN. He is quite happy here. He doesn't bother anyone and he makes himself useful.

SUNMA. Useful! Is that one of any use to anybody? Boys of his age are already earning a living but all he can do is hang around and drool at the mouth.

EMAN. But he does work. You know he does a lot for you.

SUNMA. Does he? And what about the farm you started for him! Does he ever work on it? Or have you forgotten that it was really for Ifada you cleared that bush. Now you have to go and work it yourself. You spend all your time on it and you have no room for anything else.

EMAN. That wasn't his fault. I should first have asked him if he was fond of farming.

SUNMA. Oh, so he can choose? As if he shouldn't be thankful for being allowed to live.

EMAN. Sunma!

SUNMA. He does not like farming but he knows how to feast his dumb mouth on the fruits.

EMAN. But I want him to. I encourage him.

SUNMA. Well keep him. I don't want to see him any more.

EMAN [*after some moments*]. But why? You cannot be telling all the truth. What has he done?

[4] A ritual festival in which masked dancers invoke supernatural spirits.

SUNMA. The sight of him fills me with revulsion.

EMAN [*goes to her and holds her*]. What really is it?

[SUNMA *avoids his eyes.*] It is almost as if you are forcing yourself to hate him. Why?

SUNMA. That is not true. Why should I?

EMAN. Then what is the secret? You've even played with him before.

SUNMA. I have always merely tolerated him. But I cannot any more. Suddenly my disgust won't take him any more. Perhaps . . . perhaps it is the new year. Yes, yes, it must be the new year.

EMAN. I don't believe that.

SUNMA. It must be. I am a woman, and these things matter. I don't want a mis-shape near me. Surely for one day in the year, I may demand some wholesomeness.

EMAN. I do not understand you.

[SUNMA *is silent.*]

It was cruel of you. And to Ifada who is so helpless and alone. We are the only friends he has.

SUNMA. No, just you. I have told you, with me it has always been only an act of kindness. And now I haven't any pity left for him.

EMAN. No. He is not a wholesome being.

[*He turns back to looking through the window.*]

SUNMA [*half-pleading*]. Ifada can rouse your pity. And yet if anything, I need more kindness from you. Every time my weakness betrays me, you close your mind against me . . . Eman . . . Eman . . .

[*A* GIRL *comes in view, dragging an effigy by a rope attached to one of its legs. She stands for a while gazing at* EMAN. IFADA, *who has crept back shyly to his accustomed position, becomes somewhat excited when he sees the effigy. The* GIRL *is unsmiling. She possesses in fact, a kind of inscrutability which does not make her hard but is unsettling.*]

GIRL. Is the teacher in?

EMAN. [*smiling*]. No.

GIRL. Where is he gone?

EMAN. I don't really know. Shall I ask?

GIRL. Yes, do.

EMAN [*turning slightly*]. Sunma, a girl outside wants to know . . .

[SUNMA *turns away, goes into the inside room.*]

EMAN. Oh. [*Returns to the* GIRL, *but his slight gaiety is lost.*] There is no one at home who can tell me.

GIRL. Why are you not in?

EMAN. I don't really know. Maybe I went somewhere.

GIRL. All right. I will wait until you get back.

[*She pulls the effigy to her, sits down.*]

EMAN [*slowly regaining his amusement*]. So you are all ready for the new year.

GIRL [*without turning round*]. I am not going to the festival.

EMAN. Then why have you got that?

GIRL. Do you mean my carrier? I am unwell you know. My mother says it will take away my sickness with the old year.

EMAN. Won't you share the carrier with your playmates?

GIRL. Oh, no. Don't you know I play alone? The other children won't come near me. Their mothers would beat them.

EMAN. But I have never seen you here. Why don't you come to the clinic?

GIRL. My mother said No.

[*Gets up, begins to move off.*]

EMAN. You are not going away?

GIRL. I must not stay talking to you. If my mother caught me . . .

EMAN. All right, tell me what you want before you go.

GIRL [*stops. For some moments she remains silent*]. I must have some clothes for my carrier.

EMAN. Is that all? You wait a moment.

[SUNMA *comes out as he takes down a buba from the wall. She goes to the window and glares almost with hatred at the* GIRL. *The* GIRL *retreats hastily, still impassive.*]

By the way Sunma, do you know who that girl is?

SUNMA. I hope you don't really mean to give her that.

EMAN. Why not? I hardly ever use it.

SUNMA. Just the same don't give it to her. She is not a child. She is as evil as the rest of them.

EMAN. What has got into you today?

SUNMA. All right, all right. Do what you wish.

[*She withdraws. Baffled,* EMAN *returns to the window.*]

EMAN. Here . . . will this do? Come and look at it.

GIRL. Throw it.

EMAN. What is the matter? I am not going to eat you.

GIRL. No one lets me come near them.

EMAN. But I am not afraid of catching your disease.

GIRL. Throw it.

[EMAN *shrugs and tosses the buba. She takes it without a word and slips it on the effigy, completely absorbed in the task.* EMAN *watches for a while, then joins* SUNMA *in the inner room.*]

GIRL [*after a long, cool survey of* IFADA]. You have a head like a spider's egg, and your mouth dribbles like a roof. But there is no one else. Would you like to play?

[IFADA *nods eagerly, quite excited.*]

GIRL. You will have to get a stick.

[IFADA *rushes around, finds a big stick and whirls it aloft, bearing down on the carrier.*]

GIRL. Wait. I don't want you to spoil it. If it gets torn I shall drive you away. Now, let me see how you are going to beat it.

[IFADA *hits it gently.*]

GIRL. You may hit harder than that. As long as there is something left to hang at the end.

[*She appraises him up and down.*]

You are not very tall . . . will you be able to hang it from a tree?

[IFADA *nods, grinning happily.*]

GIRL. You will hang it up and I will set fire to it. [*Then, with surprising venom*] But just because you are helping me, don't think it is going to cure you. I am the one who will get well at midnight, do you understand? It is my carrier and it is for me alone.

[*She pulls at the rope to make sure that it is well attached to the leg.*]

Well don't stand there drooling. Let's go.

[*She begins to walk off, dragging the effigy in the dust.* IFADA *remains where he is for some moments, seemingly puzzled. Then his face breaks into a large grin and he leaps after the procession, belabouring the effigy with all his strength. The stage remains empty for some moments. Then the horn of a lorry is sounded and* SUNMA *rushes out. The hooting continues for some time with a rhythmic pattern.* EMAN *comes out.*]

EMAN. I am going to the village . . . I shan't be back before nightfall.

SUNMA [*blankly*]. Yes.

EMAN [*hesitates*]. Well what do you want me to do?

SUNMA. The lorry was hooting just now.

EMAN. I didn't hear it.

SUNMA. It will leave in a few minutes. And you did promise we could go away.

EMAN. I promised nothing. Will you go home by yourself or shall I come back for you?

SUNMA. You don't even want me here?

EMAN. But you have to go home haven't you?

SUNMA. I had hoped we would watch the new year together—in some other place.

EMAN. Why do you continue to distress yourself?

SUNMA. Because you will not listen to me. Why do you continue to stay where nobody wants you?

EMAN. That is not true.

SUNMA. It is. You are wasting your life on people who really want you out of their way.

EMAN. You don't know what you are saying.

SUNMA. You think they love you? Do you think they care at all for what you—or I—do for them?

EMAN. *Them?* These are your own people. Sometimes you talk as if you were a stranger too.

SUNMA. I wonder if I really sprang from here. I know they are evil and I am not. From the oldest to the smallest child, they are nourished in evil and unwholesomeness in which I have no part.

EMAN. You knew this when you returned?

SUNMA. You reproach me then for trying at all?

EMAN. I reproach you with nothing? But you must leave me out of your plans. I can have no part in them.

SUNMA [*nearly pleading*]. Once I could have run away. I would have gone and never looked back.

EMAN. I cannot listen when you talk like that.

SUNMA. I swear to you, I do not mind what happens afterwards. But you must help me tear myself away from here. I can no longer do it by myself . . . It is only a little thing. And we have worked so hard this past year . . . surely we can go away for a week . . . even a few days would be enough.

EMAN. I have told you Sunma . . .

SUNMA [*desperately*]. Two days Eman. Only two days.

EMAN [*distressed*]. But I tell you I have no wish to go.

SUNMA [*suddenly angry*]. Are you so afraid then?

EMAN. Me? Afraid of what?

SUNMA. You think you will not want to come back.

EMAN [*pitying*]. You cannot dare me that way.

SUNMA. Then why won't you leave here, even for an hour? If you are so sure that your life is settled here, why are you afraid to do this thing for me? What is so wrong that you will not go into the next town for a day or two?

EMAN. I don't want to. I do not have to persuade you, or myself about anything. I simply have no desire to go away.

SUNMA [*His quiet confidence appears to incense her*]. You are afraid. You accuse me of losing my sense of mission, but you are afraid to put yours to the test.

EMAN. You are wrong Sunma. I have no sense of mission. But I have found peace here and I am content with that.

SUNMA. I haven't. For a while I thought that too, but I found there could be no peace in the midst of so much cruelty. Eman, tonight at least, the last night of the old year . . .

EMAN. No Sunma. I find this too distressing; you should go home now.

SUNMA. It is the time for making changes in one's life Eman. Let's breathe in the new year away from here.

EMAN. You are hurting yourself.

SUNMA. Tonight. Only tonight. We will come back tomorrow, as early as you like. But let us go away for this one night. Don't let another year break on me in this place . . . you don't know how important it is to me, but I will tell you, I will tell you on the way . . . but we must not be here today, Eman, do this one thing for me.

EMAN [*sadly*]. I cannot.

SUNMA [*suddenly calm*]. I was a fool to think it would be otherwise. The whole village may use you as they will but for me there is nothing. Sometimes I think you believe that doing anything for me makes you unfaithful to some part of your life. If it was a woman then I pity her for what she must have suffered. [EMAN *winces and hardens slowly.* SUNMA *notices nothing.*] Keeping faith with so much is slowly making you inhuman. [*Seeing the change in* EMAN.] Eman. Eman. What is it?

[*As she goes towards him,* EMAN *goes into the house.*]

SUNMA [*apprehensive, follows him*]. What did I say? Eman, forgive me, forgive me please. [EMAN *remains facing into the slow darkness of the room.* SUNMA, *distressed, cannot decide what to do.*] I swear I didn't know . . . I would not have said it for all the world.

[*A lorry is heard taking off somewhere nearby. The sound comes up and slowly fades away into the distance.* SUNMA *starts visibly, goes slowly to the window.*]

SUNMA [*as the sound dies off, to herself*]. What happens now?

EMAN [*joining her at the window*]. What did you say?

SUNMA. Nothing.

EMAN. Was that not the lorry going off?

SUNMA. It was.

EMAN. I am sorry I couldn't help you.

[SUNMA, *about to speak, changes her mind.*]

EMAN. I think you ought to go home now.

SUNMA. No, don't send me away. It's the least you can do for me. Let me stay here until all the noise is over.

EMAN. But are you not needed at home? You have a part in the festival.

SUNMA. I have renounced it; I am Jaguna's eldest daughter only in name.

EMAN. Renouncing one's self is not so easy—surely you know that.

SUNMA. I don't want to talk about it. Will you at least let us be together tonight?

EMAN. But . . .

SUNMA. Unless you are afraid my father will accuse you of harbouring me.

EMAN. All right, we will go out together.

SUNMA. Go out? I want us to stay here.

EMAN. When there is so much going on outside?

SUNMA. Some day you will wish that you went away when I tried to make you.

EMAN. Are we going back to that?

SUNMA. No. I promise you I will not recall it again. But you must know that it was also for your sake that I tried to get us away.

EMAN. For me? How?

SUNMA. By yourself you can do nothing here. Have you not noticed how tightly we shut out strangers? Even if you lived here for a lifetime, you would remain a stranger.

EMAN. Perhaps that is what I like. There is peace in being a stranger.

SUNMA. For a while perhaps. But they would reject you in the end. I tell you it is only I who stand between you and contempt. And because of this you have earned their hatred. I don't know why I say this now, except that somehow, I feel that it no longer matters. It is only I who have stood between you and much humiliation.

EMAN. Think carefully before you say any more. I am incapable of feeling indebted to you. This will make no difference at all.

SUNMA. I ask for nothing. But you must know it all the same. It is true I hadn't the strength to go by myself. And I must confess this now, if you had come with me, I would have done everything to keep you from returning.

EMAN. I know that.

SUNMA. You see, I bare myself to you. For days I had thought it over, this was to be a new beginning for us. And I placed my fate wholly in your hands. Now the thought will not leave me, I have a feeling which will not be shaken off, that in some way, you have tonight totally destroyed my life.

EMAN. You are depressed, you don't know what you are saying.

SUNMA. Don't think I am accusing you. I say all this only because I cannot help it.

EMAN. We must not remain shut up here. Let us go and be part of the living.

SUNMA. No. Leave them alone.

EMAN. Surely you don't want to stay indoors when the whole town is alive with rejoicing.

SUNMA. Rejoicing! Is that what it seems to you? No, let us remain here. Whatever happens I must not go out until all this is over.

[*There is silence. It has grown much darker.*]

EMAN. I shall light the lamp.

SUNMA [*eager to do something*]. No, let me do it.

[*She goes into the inner room.*

EMAN *paces the room, stops by a shelf and toys with the seeds in an 'ayo'[5] board, takes down the whole board and places it on a table, playing by himself.*

The GIRL *is now seen coming back, still dragging her 'carrier'.* IFADA *brings up the rear as before. As he comes round the corner of the house two men emerge from the shadows. A sack is thrown over* IFADA'*s head, the rope is pulled tight rendering him instantly helpless. The* GIRL *has reached the front of the house before she turns round at the sound of scuffle. She is in time to see* IFADA *thrown over the shoulders and borne away. Her face betraying no emotion at all, the* GIRL *backs slowly away, turns and flees, leaving the 'carrier' behind.*

SUNMA *enters, carrying two kerosene lamps. She hangs one up from the wall.*]

EMAN. One is enough.

SUNMA. I want to leave one outside.

[*She goes out, hangs the lamp from a nail just above the door. As she turns she sees the effigy and gasps.* EMAN *rushes out.*]

EMAN. What is it? Oh, is that what frightened you?

SUNMA. I thought . . . I didn't really see it properly.

[EMAN *goes towards the object, stoops to pick it up.*]

---

[5] Ayo is a game played on a wooden board with sixteen holes arranged in two parallel columns of eight holes apiece. Seeds are placed in these holes according to fixed rules. The object is to get four seeds in a hole.

EMAN. It must belong to that sick girl.

SUNMA. Don't touch it.

EMAN. Let's keep it for her.

SUNMA. Leave it alone. Don't touch it Eman.

EMAN [*shrugs and goes back*]. You are very nervous.

SUNMA. Let's go in.

EMAN. Wait. [*He detains her by the door, under the lamp.*] I know there is something more than you've told me. What are you afraid of tonight?

SUNMA. I was only scared by that thing. There is nothing else.

EMAN. I am not blind Sunma. It is true I would not run away when you wanted me to, but that doesn't mean I do not feel things. What does tonight really mean that it makes you so helpless?

SUNMA. It is only a mood. And your indifference to me . . . let's go in.

[EMAN *moves aside and she enters; he remains there for a moment and then follows.*
She fiddles with the lamp, looks vaguely round the room, then goes and shuts the door, bolting it. When she turns, it is to meet EMAN's *eyes, questioning.*]

SUNMA. There is a cold wind coming in.

[EMAN *keeps his gaze on her.*]

SUNMA. It *was* getting cold.

[*She moves guiltily to the table and stands by the 'ayo' board, rearranging the seeds.* EMAN *remains where he is a few moments, then brings a stool and sits opposite her. She sits down also and they begin to play in silence.*]

SUNMA. What bought you here at all, Eman? And what makes you stay?

[*There is another silence.*]

SUNMA. I am not trying to share your life. I know you too well by now. But at least we have worked together since you came. Is there nothing at all I deserve to know?

EMAN. Let me continue a stranger—especially to you. Those who have much to give fulfil themselves only in total loneliness.

SUNMA. Then there is no love in what you do.

EMAN. There is. Love comes to me more easily with strangers.

SUNMA. That is unnatural.

EMAN. Not for me. I know I find consummation only when I have spent myself for a total stranger.

SUNMA. It seems unnatural to me. But then I am a woman. I have a woman's longings and weaknesses. And the ties of blood are very strong in me.

EMAN [*smiling*]. You think I have cut loose from all these—ties of blood.

SUNMA. Sometimes you are so inhuman.

EMAN. I don't know what that means. But I am very much my father's son.

[*They play in silence. Suddenly* EMAN *pauses listening.*]

EMAN. Did you hear that?

SUNMA [*quickly*]. I heard nothing . . . it's your turn.

EMAN. Perhaps some of the mummers are coming this way.

[EMAN *about to play, leaps up suddenly.*]

SUNMA. What is it? Don't you want to play any more?

[EMAN *moves to the door.*]

SUNMA. No. Don't go out Eman.

EMAN. If it's the dancers I want to ask them to stay. At least we won't have to miss everything.

SUNMA. No, no. Don't open the door. Let us keep out everyone tonight.

[*A terrified and disordered figure bursts suddenly round the corner, past the window and begins hammering at the door. It is* IFADA. *Desperate with terror, he pounds madly at the door, dumb-moaning all the while.*]

EMAN. Isn't that Ifada?

SUNMA. They are only fooling about. Don't pay any attention.

EMAN [*looks round the window*]. That is Ifada. [*Begins to unbolt the door.*]

SUNMA [*pulling at his hands*]. It is only a trick they are playing on you. Don't take any notice Eman.

EMAN. What are you saying? The boy is out of his senses with fear.

SUNMA. No, no. Don't interfere Eman. For God's sake don't interfere.

EMAN. Do you know something of this then?

SUNMA. You are a stranger here Eman. Just leave us alone and go your own way. There is nothing you can do.

EMAN [*He tries to push her out of the way but she clings fiercely to him*]. Have you gone mad? I tell you the boy must come in.

SUNMA. Why won't you listen to me Eman? I tell you it's none of your business. For your own sake do as I say.

[EMAN *pushes her off, unbolts the door.* IFADA *rushes in, clasps* EMAN *round the knees, dumb-moaning against his legs.*]

EMAN [*manages to re-bolt the door*]. What is it Ifada? What is the matter?

[*Shouts and voices are heard coming nearer the house.*]

SUNMA. Before it's too late, let him go. For once Eman, believe what I tell you. Don't harbour him or you will regret it all your life.

[EMAN *tries to calm* IFADA *who becomes more and more abject as the outside voices get nearer.*]

EMAN. What have they done to him? At least tell me that. What is going on Sunma?

SUNMA [*with sudden venom*]. Monster! Could you not take yourself somewhere else?

EMAN. Stop talking like that.

SUNMA. He could have run into the bush couldn't he? Toad! Why must he follow us with his own disasters!

VOICES OUTSIDE. It's here . . . Round the back . . . Spread, spread . . . this way . . . no, head him off . . . use the bush path and head him off . . . get some more lights . . .

[EMAN *listens. Lifts* IFADA *bodily and carries him into the inner room. Returns at once, shutting the door behind him.*]

SUNMA [*slumps into a chair, resigned*]. You always follow your own way.

JAGUNA [*comes round the corner followed by* OROGE *and three men, one bearing a torch*]. I knew he would come here.

OROGE. I hope our friend won't make trouble.

JAGUNA. He had better not. You, recall all the men and tell them to surround the house.

OROGE. But he may not be in the house after all.

JAGUNA. I know he is here . . . [*to the men*] . . . go on, do as I say. [*He bangs on the door.*] Teacher, open your door . . . you two stay by the door. If I need you I will call you.

[EMAN *opens the door.*]

JAGUNA [*speaks as he enters*]. We know he is here.

EMAN. Who?

JAGUNA. Don't let us waste time. We are grown men, teacher. You understand me and I understand you. But we must take back the boy.

EMAN. This is my house.

JAGUNA. Daughter, you'd better tell your friend. I don't think he quite knows our ways. Tell him why he must give up the boy.

SUNMA. Father, I . . .

JAGUNA. Are you going to tell him or aren't you?

SUNMA. Father, I beg you, leave us alone tonight . . .

JAGUNA. I thought you might be a hindrance. Go home then if you will not use your sense.

SUNMA. But there are other ways . . .

JAGUNA [*turning to the men*]. See that she gets home. I no longer trust her. If she gives trouble carry her. And see that the women stay with her until all this is over.

[SUNMA *departs, accompanied by one of the men.*]

JAGUNA. Now teacher . . .

OROGE [*restrains him*]. You see, Mister Eman, it is like this. Right now, nobody knows that Ifada has taken refuge here. No one except us and our men—and they know how to keep their mouths shut. We don't want to have to burn down the house you see, but if the word gets around, we would have no choice.

JAGUNA. In fact, it may be too late already. A carrier should end up in the bush, not in a house. Anyone who doesn't guard his door when the carrier goes by has himself to blame. A contaminated house should be burnt down.

OROGE. But we are willing to let it pass. Only, you must bring him out quickly.

EMAN. All right. But at least you will let me ask you something.

JAGUNA. What is there to ask? Don't you understand what we have told you?

EMAN. Yes. But why did you pick on a helpless boy. Obviously he is not willing.

JAGUNA. What is the man talking about? Ifada is a godsend. Does he have to be willing?

EMAN. In my home, we believe that a man should be willing.

OROGE. Mister Eman, I don't think you quite understand. This is not a simple matter at all. I don't know what you do, but here, it is not a cheap task for anybody. No one in his senses would do such a job. Why do you think we give refuge to idiots like him? We don't know where he came from. One morning, he is simply there, just like that. From nowhere at all. You see, there is a purpose in that.

JAGUNA. We only waste time.

OROGE. Jaguna, be patient. After all, the man has been with us for some time now and deserves to know. The evil of the old year is no light thing to load on any man's head.

EMAN. I know something about that.

OROGE. You do? [*Turns to* JAGUNA *who snorts impatiently.*] You see I told you so didn't I? From the moment you came I saw you were one of the knowing ones.

JAGUNA. Then let him behave like a man and give back the boy.

EMAN. It is you who are not behaving like men.

JAGUNA [*advances aggressively*]. That is a quick mouth you have . . .

OROGE. Patience Jaguna . . . if you want the new year to cushion the land there must be no deeds of anger. What did you mean my friend?

EMAN. It is a simple thing. A village which cannot produce its own carrier contains no men.

JAGUNA. Enough. Let there be no more talk or this business will be ruined by some rashness. You . . . come inside. Bring the boy out, he must be in the room there.

EMAN. Wait.

[*The men hesitate.*]

JAGUNA [*hitting the nearer one and propelling him forward*]. Go on. Have you changed masters now that you listen to what he says?

OROGE [*sadly*]. I am sorry you would not understand Mister Eman. But you ought to know that no carrier may return to the village. If he does, the people will stone him to death. It has happened before. Surely it is too much to ask a man to give up his own soil.

EMAN. I know others who have done more.

[IFADA *is brought out, abjectly dumb-moaning.*]

EMAN. You can see him with your own eyes. Does it really have meaning to use one as unwilling as that?

OROGE [*smiling*]. He shall be willing. Not only willing but actually joyous. I am the one who prepares them all, and I have seen worse. This one escaped before I began to prepare him for the event. But you will see him later tonight, the most joyous creature in the festival. Then perhaps you will understand.

EMAN. Then it is only a deceit. Do you believe the spirit of a new year is so easily fooled?

JAGUNA. Take him out. [*The men carry out* IFADA.] You see, it is so easy to talk. You say there are no men in this village because they cannot provide a willing carrier. And yet I heard Oroge tell you we only use strangers. There is only one other stranger in the village, but I have not heard him offer himself [*spits.*] It is so easy to talk is it not?

[*He turns his back on him. They go off, taking* IFADA *with them, limp and silent. The only sign of life is that he strains his neck to keep his eyes on* EMAN *till the very moment that he disappears from sight.* EMAN *remains where they left him, staring after the group.*]

A black-out lasting no more than a minute. The lights come up slowly and IFADA *is seen returning to the house. He stops at the window and looks in. Seeing no one, he bangs on the sill. Appears surprised that there is no response. He slithers down on his favourite spot, then sees the effigy still lying where the* GIRL *had dropped it in her flight. After some hesitation, he goes towards it, begins to strip it of the clothing. Just then the* GIRL *comes in.*

GIRL. Hey, leave that alone. You know it's mine.

[IFADA *pauses, then speeds up his action.*]

GIRL. I said it is mine. Leave it where you found it.

[*She rushes at him and begins to struggle for possession of the carrier.*]

GIRL. Thief! Thief! Let it go, it is mine. Let it go. You animal, just because I let you play with it. Idiot! Idiot!

[*The struggle becomes quite violent. The* GIRL *is hanging to the effigy and* IFADA *lifts her with it, flinging her all about. The* GIRL *hangs on grimly.*]

GIRL. You are spoiling it . . . why don't you get your own? Thief! Let it go you thief!

[SUNMA *comes in walking very fast, throwing apprehensive glances over her shoulder. Seeing the two children, she becomes immediately angry. Advances on them.*]

SUNMA. So you've made this place your playground. Get away you untrained pigs. Get out of here.

[IFADA *flees at once, the* GIRL *retreats also, retaining possession of the 'carrier'.*

   SUNMA *goes to the door. She has her hand on the door when the significance of* IFADA'*s presence strikes her for the first time. She stands rooted to the spot, then turns slowly round.*]

SUNMA. Ifada! What are you doing here? [IFADA *is bewildered.* SUNMA *turns suddenly and rushes into the house, flying into the inner room and out again.*] Eman! Eman!

Eman! [*She rushes outside.*] Where did he go? Where did they take him? [IFADA *distressed, points.* SUNMA *seizes him by the arm, drags him off.*] Take me there at once. God help you if we are too late. You loathsome thing, if you have let him suffer . . .

[*Her voice fades into other shouts, running footsteps, banged tins, bells, dogs, etc., rising in volume.*]

It is a narrow passage-way between two mud-houses. At the far end one man after another is seen running across the entry, the noise dying off gradually.

About half-way down the passage, EMAN *is crouching against the wall, tense with apprehension. As the noise dies off, he seems to relax, but the alert hunted look is still in his eyes which are ringed in a reddish colour. The rest of his body has been whitened with a floury substance. He is naked down to the waist, wears a baggy pair of trousers, calf-length, and around both feet are bangles.*

EMAN. I will simply stay here till dawn. I have done enough.

[*A window is thrown open and a woman empties some slop from a pail. With a startled cry* EMAN *leaps aside to avoid it and the woman puts out her head.*]

WOMAN. Oh, my head. What have I done! Forgive me neighbour. . . . Eh, it's the carrier! [*Very rapidly she clears her throat and spits on him, flings the pail at him and runs off, shouting.*] He's here. The carrier is hiding in the passage. Quickly, I have found the carrier!

[*The cry is taken up and* EMAN *flees down the passage. Shortly afterwards his pursuers come pouring down the passage in full cry. After the last of them come* JAGUNA *and* OROGE.]

OROGE. Wait, wait. I cannot go so fast.

JAGUNA. We will rest a little then. We can do nothing anyway.

OROGE. If only he had let me prepare him.

JAGUNA. They are the ones who break first, these fools who think they were born to carry suffering like a hat. What are we to do now?

OROGE. When they catch him I must prepare him.

JAGUNA. He? It will be impossible now. There can be no joy left in that one.

OROGE. Still, it took him by surprise. He was not expecting what he met.

JAGUNA. Why then did he refuse to listen? Did he think he was coming to sit down to a feast. He had not even gone through one compound before he bolted. Did he think he was taken round the people to be blessed? A woman, that is all he is.

OROGE. No, no. He took the beating well enough. I think he is the kind who would let himself be beaten from night till dawn and not utter a sound. He would let himself be stoned until he dropped dead.

JAGUNA. Then what made him run like a coward?

OROGE. I don't know. I don't really know. It is a night of curses Jaguna. It is not many unprepared minds will remain unhinged under the load.

JAGUNA. We must find him. It is a poor beginning for a year when our own curses remain hovering over our homes because the carrier refused to take them.

[*They go. The scene changes.* EMAN *is crouching beside some shrubs, torn and bleeding.*]

EMAN. They are even guarding my house . . . as if I would go there, but I need water . . . they could at least grant me that . . . I can be thirsty too . . . [*he pricks his ears*] . . . there must be a stream nearby . . . [*As he looks round him, his eyes widen at a scene he encounters.*]

[*An* OLD MAN, *short and vigorous-looking, is seated on a stool. He also is wearing calf-length baggy trousers, white. On his head, a white cap. An* ATTENDANT *is engaged in rubbing his body with oil. Round his eyes two white rings have already been marked.*]

OLD MAN. Have they prepared the boat?

ATTENDANT. They are making the last sacrifice.

OLD MAN. Good. Did you send for my son?

ATTENDANT. He's on his way.

OLD MAN. I have never met the carrying of the boat with such a heavy heart. I hope nothing comes of it.

ATTENDANT. The gods will not desert us on that account.

OLD MAN. A man should be at his strongest when he takes the boat my friend. To be weighed down inside and out is not a wise thing. I hope when the moment comes I shall have found my strength.

[*Enter* EMAN, *a wrapper round his waist and a 'danski'*[6] *over it.*]

OLD MAN. I meant to wait until after my journey to the river, but my mind is so burdened with my own grief and yours I could not delay it. You know I must have all my strength. But I sit here, feeling it all eaten slowly away by my unspoken grief. It helps to say it out. It even helps to cry sometimes. [*He signals to the attendant to leave them.*] Come nearer . . . we will never meet again son. Not on this side of the flesh. What I do not know is whether you will return to take my place.

EMAN. I will never come back.

OLD MAN. Do you know what you are saying? Ours is a strong breed my son. It is only a strong breed that can take this boat to the river year after year and wax stronger on it. I have taken down each year's evils for over twenty years. I hoped you would follow me.

EMAN. My life here died with Omae.

OLD MAN. Omae died giving birth to your child and you think the world is ended. Eman, my pain did not begin when Omae died. Since you sent her to stay with me son, I lived with the burden of knowing that this child would die bearing your son.

EMAN. Father . . .

OLD MAN. Don't you know it was the same with you? And me? No woman survives the bearing of the strong ones. Son, it is not the mouth of the boaster that says he belongs to the strong breed. It is the tongue that is red with pain and black with sorrow. Twelve years you were away my son, and for those twelve years I knew the love of an old man for his daughter and the pain of a man helplessly awaiting his loss.

EMAN. I wish I had stayed away. I wish I never came back to meet her.

OLD MAN. It had to be. But you know now what slowly ate away my strength. I awaited your return with love and fear. Forgive me then if I say that your grief is light. It will pass. This grief may drive you now from home. But you must return.

EMAN. You do not understand. It is not grief alone.

OLD MAN. What is it then? Tell me, I can still learn.

EMAN. I was away twelve years. I changed much in that time.

OLD MAN. I am listening.

EMAN. I am unfitted for your work father. I wish to say no more. But I am totally unfitted for your call.

[6] A brief Yoruba attire.

OLD MAN. It is only time you need son. Stay longer and you will answer the urge of your blood.

EMAN. That I stayed at all was because of Omae. I did not expect to find her waiting. I would have taken her away, but hard as you claim to be, it would have killed you. And I was a tired man. I needed peace. Because Omae was peace, I stayed. Now nothing holds me here.

OLD MAN. Other men would rot and die doing this task year after year. It is strong medicine which only we can take. Our blood is strong like no other. Anything you do in life must be less than this, son.

EMAN. That is not true father.

OLD MAN. I tell you it is true. Your own blood will betray you son, because you cannot hold it back. If you make it do less than this, it will rush to your head and burst it open. I say what I know my son.

EMAN. There are other tasks in life father. This one is not for me. There are even greater things you know nothing of.

OLD MAN. I am very sad. You only go to give to others what rightly belongs to us. You will use your strength among thieves. They are thieves because they take what is ours, they have no claim of blood to it. They will even lack the knowledge to use it wisely. Truth is my companion at this moment my son. I know everything I say will surely bring the sadness of truth.

EMAN. I am going father.

OLD MAN. Call my attendant. And be with me in your strength for this last journey. A-ah, did you hear that? It came out without my knowing it; this is indeed my last journey. But I am not afraid.

[EMAN *goes out. A few moments later, the attendant enters.*]

ATTENDANT. The boat is ready.

OLD MAN. So am I.

[*He sits perfectly still for several moments. Drumming begins somewhere in the distance, and the old man sways his head almost imperceptibly. Two men come in bearing a miniature boat, containing an indefinable mound. They rush it in and set it briskly down near the* OLD MAN, *and stand well back. The* OLD MAN *gets up slowly, the* ATTENDANT *watching him keenly. He signs to the men, who lift the boat quickly onto the* OLD MAN'*s head. As soon as it touches his head, he holds it down with both hands and runs off, the men give him a start, then follow at a trot.*

As the last man disappears OROGE *limps in and comes face to face with* EMAN—*as carrier—who is now seen still standing beside the shrubs, staring into the scene he has just witnessed.* OROGE, *struck by the look on* EMAN'*s face, looks anxiously behind him to see what has engaged* EMAN'*s attention.* EMAN *notices him then, and the pair stare at each other.* JAGUNA *enters, sees him and shouts, 'Here he is', rushes at* EMAN *who is whipped back to the immediate and flees,* JAGUNA *in pursuit. Three or four others enter and follow them.* OROGE *remains where he is, thoughtful.*]

JAGUNA [*re-enters*]. They have closed in on him now, we'll get him this time.

OROGE. It is nearly midnight.

JAGUNA. You were standing there looking at him as if he was some strange spirit. Why didn't you shout?

OROGE. You shouted didn't you? Did that catch him?

JAGUNA. Don't worry. We have him now. But things have taken a bad turn. It is no longer enough to drive him past every house. There is too much contamination about already.

OROGE [*not listening*]. He saw something. Why may I not know what it was?

JAGUNA. What are you talking about?

OROGE. Hm. What is it?

JAGUNA. I said there is too much harm done already. The year will demand more from this carrier than we thought.

OROGE. What do you mean?

JAGUNA. Do we have to talk with the full mouth?

OROGE. S-sh . . . look!

[JAGUNA *turns just in time to see* SUNMA *fly at him, clawing at his face like a crazed tigress.*]

SUNMA. Murderer! What are you doing to him. Murderer! Murderer!

[JAGUNA *finds himself struggling really hard to keep off his daughter, he succeeds in pushing her off and striking her so hard on the face that she falls to her knees. He moves on her to hit her again.*]

OROGE [*comes between*]. Think what you are doing Jaguna, she is your daughter.

JAGUNA. My daughter! Does this one look like my daughter? Let me cripple the harlot for life.

OROGE. That is a wicked thought Jaguna.

JAGUNA. Don't come between me and her.

OROGE. Nothing in anger—do you forget what tonight is?

JAGUNA. Can you blame me for forgetting?

[*Draws his hand across his cheek—it is covered with blood.*]

OROGE. This is an unhappy night for us all. I fear what is to come of it.

JAGUNA. Let's go. I cannot restrain myself in this creature's presence. My own daughter . . . and for a stranger . . .

[*They go off,* IFADA, *who came in with* SUNMA *and had stood apart, horror-stricken, comes shyly forward. He helps* SUNMA *up. They go off, he holding* SUNMA *bent and sobbing.*]

[*Enter* EMAN —*as carrier. He is physically present in the bounds of this next scene, a side of a round thatched hut. A young girl, about fourteen runs in, stops beside the hut. She looks carefully to see that she is not observed, puts her mouth to a little hole in the wall.*]

OMAE. Eman . . . Eman . . .

[EMAN —*as carrier—responds, as he does throughout the scene, but they are unaware of him.*]

EMAN [*from inside*]. Who is it?

OMAE. It is me, Omae.

EMAN. How dare you come here!

[*Two hands appear at the hole and pushing outwards, create a much larger hole through which* EMAN *puts out his head. It is* EMAN *as a boy, the same age as the girl.*]

Go away at once. Are you trying to get me into trouble!

OMAE. What is the matter?

EMAN. You. Go away.

OMAE. But I came to see you.

EMAN. Are you deaf? I say I don't want to see you. Now go before my tutor catches you.

OMAE. All right. Come out.

EMAN. Do what!

OMAE. Come out.

EMAN. You must be mad.

OMAE [*sits on the ground*]. All right, if you don't come out I shall simply stay here until your tutor arrives.

EMAN [*about to explode, thinks better of it and the head disappears. A moment later he emerges from behind the hut.*] What sort of a devil has got into you?

OMAE. None. I just wanted to see you.

EMAN [*His mimicry is nearly hysterical*]. 'None. I just wanted to see you.' Do you think this place is the stream where you can go and molest innocent people?

OMAE [*coyly*]. Aren't you glad to see me?

EMAN. I am not.

OMAE. Why?

EMAN. Why? Do you really ask me why? Because you are a woman and a most troublesome woman. Don't you know anything about this at all? We are not meant to see any woman. So go away before more harm is done.

OMAE [*flirtatious*]. What is so secret about it anyway? What do they teach you?

EMAN. Nothing any woman can understand.

OMAE. Ha ha. You think we don't know eh? You've all come to be circumcised.

EMAN. Shut up. You don't know anything.

OMAE. Just think, all this time you haven't been circumcised, and you dared make eyes at us women.

EMAN. Thank you—woman. Now go.

OMAE. Do they give you enough to eat?

EMAN [*testily*]. No. We are so hungry that when silly girls like you turn up, we eat them.

OMAE [*feigning tears*]. Oh, oh, oh, he's abusing me. He's abusing me.

EMAN [*alarmed*]. Don't try that here. Go quickly if you are going to cry.

OMAE. All right, I won't cry.

EMAN. Cry or no cry, go away and leave me alone. What do you think will happen if my tutor turns up now.

OMAE. He won't.

EMAN [*mimicking*]. 'He won't.' I suppose you are his wife and he tells you where he goes. In fact this is just the time he comes round to our huts. He could be at the next hut this very moment.

OMAE. Ha-ha. You're lying. I left him by the stream, pinching the girls' bottoms. Is that the sort of thing he teaches you?

EMAN. Don't say anything against him or I shall beat you. Isn't it you loose girls who tease him, wiggling your bottoms under his nose?

OMAE [*going tearful again*]. A-ah, so I am one of the loose girls eh?

EMAN. Now don't start accusing me of things I didn't say.

OMAE. But you said it. You said it.

EMAN. I didn't. Look Omae, someone will hear you and I'll be in disgrace. Why don't you go before anything happens.

OMAE. It's all right. My friends have promised to hold your old rascal tutor till I get back.

EMAN. Then you go back right now. I have work to do. [*Going in.*]

OMAE [*runs after and tries to hold him. EMAN leaps back, genuinely scared*]. What is the matter? I was not going to bite you.

EMAN. Do you know what you nearly did? You almost touched me!

OMAE. Well?

EMAN. Well! Isn't it enough that you let me set my eyes on you? Must you now totally pollute me with your touch? Don't you understand anything?

OMAE. Oh, that.

EMAN [*nearly screaming*]. It is not 'oh that'. Do you think this is only a joke or a little visit like spending the night with your grandmother? This is an important period of my life. Look, these huts, we built them with our own hands. Every boy builds his own. We learn things, do you understand? And we spend much time just thinking. At least, I do. It is the first time I have had nothing to do except think. Don't you see, I am becoming a man. For the first time, I understand that I have a life to fulfill. Has that thought ever worried you?

OMAE. You are frightening me.

EMAN. There. That is all you can say. And what use will that be when a man finds himself alone—like that? [*Points to the hut.*] A man must go on his own, go where no one can help him, and test his strength. Because he may find himself one day sitting alone in a wall as round as that. In there, my mind could hold no other thought. I may never have such moments again to myself. Don't dare to come and steal any more of it.

OMAE [*this time, genuinely tearful*]. Oh, I know you hate me. You only want to drive me away.

EMAN [*impatiently*]. Yes, yes, I know I hate you—but go.

OMAE [*going, all tears. Wipes her eyes, suddenly all mischief*]. Eman.

EMAN. What now?

OMAE. I only want to ask one thing ... do you promise to tell me?

EMAN. Well, what is it?

OMAE [*gleefully*]. Does it hurt?

[*She turns instantly and flees, landing straight into the arms of the returning tutor.*]

TUTOR. Te-he-he ... what have we here? What little mouse leaps straight into the beak of the wise old owl eh?

[OMAE *struggles to free herself, flies to the opposite side, grimacing with distaste.*]

TUTOR. I suppose you merely came to pick some fruits eh? You did not sneak here to see any of my children.

OMAE. Yes, I came to steal your fruits.

TUTOR. Te-he-he ... I thought so. And that dutiful son of mine over there. He saw you and came to chase you off my fruit trees didn't he? Te-he-he ... I'm sure he did, isn't that so my young Eman?

EMAN. I was talking to her.

TUTOR. Indeed you were. Now be good enough to go into your hut until I decide your punishment. [EMAN *withdraws.*] Te-he-he ... now now my little daughter, you need not be afraid of me.

OMAE [*spiritedly*]. I am not.

TUTOR. Good. Very good. We ought to be friendly. [*His voice becomes leering.*] Now this is nothing to worry you my daughter ... a very small thing indeed. Although of course if I were to let it slip that your young Eman had broken a strong taboo, it might go hard on him you know. I am sure you would not like that to happen, would you?

OMAE. No.

TUTOR. Good. You are sensible my girl. Can you wash clothes?

OMAE. Yes.

TUTOR. Good. If you will come with me now to my hut, I shall give you some clothes to wash, and then we will forget all about this matter eh? Well, come on.

OMAE. I shall wait here. You go and bring the clothes.

TUTOR. Eh? What is that? Now now, don't make me angry. You should know better than to talk back at your elders. Come now.

[*He takes her by the arm, and tries to drag her off.*]

OMAE. No no, I won't come to your hut. Leave me. Leave me alone you shameless old man.

TUTOR. If you don't come I shall disgrace the whole family of Eman, and yours too.

[EMAN *re-enters with a small bundle.*]

EMAN. Leave her alone. Let us go Omae.

TUTOR. And where do you think you are going?

EMAN. Home.

TUTOR. Te-he-he . . . As easy as that eh? You think you can leave here any time you please? Get right back inside that hut!

[EMAN *takes* OMAE *by the arm and begins to walk off.*]

TUTOR. Come back at once.

[*He goes after him and raises his stick.* EMAN *catches it, wrenches it from him and throws it away.*]

OMAE [*hopping delightedly*]. Kill him. Beat him to death.

TUTOR. Help! Help! He is killing me! Help!

[*Alarmed,* EMAN *clamps his hand over his mouth.*]

EMAN. Old tutor, I don't mean you any harm, but you mustn't try to harm me either. [*He removes his hand.*]

TUTOR. You think you can get away with your crime. My report shall reach the elders before you ever get into town.

EMAN. You are afraid of what I will say about you? Don't worry. Only if you try to shame me, then I will speak. I am not going back to the village anyway. Just tell them I have gone, no more. If you say one word more than that I shall hear of it the same day and I shall come back.

TUTOR. You are telling me what to do? But don't think to come back next year because I will drive you away. Don't think to come back here even ten years from now. And don't send your children.

[*Goes off with threatening gestures.*]

EMAN. I won't come back.

OMAE. Smoked vulture! But Eman, he says you cannot return next year. What will you do?

EMAN. It is a small thing one can do in the big towns.

OMAE. I thought you were going to beat him that time. Why didn't you crack his dirty hide?

EMAN. Listen carefully Omae . . . I am going on a journey.

OMAE. Come on. Tell me about it on the way.

EMAN. No, I go that way. I cannot return to the village.

OMAE. Because of that wretched man? Anyway you will first talk to your father.

EMAN. Go and see him for me. Tell him I have gone away for some time. I think he will know.

OMAE. But Eman . . .

EMAN. I haven't finished. You will go and live with him till I get back. I have spoken to him about you. Look after him!

OMAE. But what is this journey? When will you come back?

EMAN. I don't know. But this is a good moment to go. Nothing ties me down.

OMAE. But Eman, you want to leave me.

EMAN. Don't forget all I said. I don't know how long I will be. Stay in my father's house as long as you remember me. When you become tired of waiting, you must do as you please. You understand? You must do as you please.

OMAE. I cannot understand anything Eman. I don't know where you are going or why. Suppose you never came back! Don't go Eman. Don't leave me by myself.

EMAN. I must go. Now let me see you on your way.

OMAE. I shall come with you.

EMAN. Come with me! And who will look after you? Me? You will only be in my way, you know that! You will hold me back and I shall desert you in a strange place. Go home and do as I say. Take care of my father and let him take care of you.

[*He starts going but* OMAE *clings to him.*]

OMAE. But Eman, stay the night at least. You will only lose your way. Your father Eman, what will he say? I won't remember what you said . . . come back to the village . . . I cannot return alone Eman . . . come with me as far as the cross-roads.

[*His face set,* EMAN *strides off and* OMAE *loses balance as he increases his pace. Falling, she quickly wraps her arms around his ankle, but* EMAN *continues unchecked, dragging her along.*]

OMAE. Don't go Eman . . . Eman, don't leave me, don't leave me . . . don't leave your Omae . . . don't go Eman . . . don't leave your Omae . . .

[EMAN — *as carrier* — *makes a nervous move as if he intends to go after the vanished pair. He stops but continues to stare at the point where he last saw them. There is stillness for a while. Then the* GIRL *enters from the same place and remains looking at* EMAN. *Startled,* EMAN *looks apprehensively round him. The* GIRL *goes nearer but keeps beyond arm's length.*]

GIRL. Are you the carrier?

EMAN. Yes. I am Eman.

GIRL. Why are you hiding?

EMAN. I really came for a drink of water . . . er . . . is there anyone in front of the house?

GIRL. No.

EMAN. But there might be people in the house. Did you hear voices?

GIRL. There is no one here.

EMAN. Good. Thank you. [*He is about to go, stops suddenly.*] Er . . . would you . . . you will find a cup on the table. Could you bring me the water out here? The water-pot is in a corner.

[*The* GIRL *goes. She enters the house, then, watching* EMAN *carefully, slips out and runs off.*]

EMAN [*sitting*]. Perhaps they have all gone home. It will be good to rest. [*He hears voices and listens hard.*] Too late. [*Moves cautiously nearer the house.*] Quickly girl, I can hear people coming. Hurry up. [*Looks through the window.*] Where are you? Where is she? [*The truth dawns on him suddenly and he moves off, sadly.*]

[*Enter* JAGUNA *and* OROGE, *led by the* GIRL.]

GIRL [*pointing*]. He was there.

JAGUNA. Ay, he's gone now. He is a sly one is your friend. But it won't save him for ever.

OROGE. What was he doing when you saw him?

GIRL. He asked me for a drink of water.

JAGUNA, OROGE } Ah! [*They look at each other.*]

OROGE. We should have thought of that.

JAGUNA. He is surely finished now. If only we had thought of it earlier.

OROGE. It is not too late. There is still an hour before midnight.

JAGUNA. We must call back all the men. Now we need only wait for him—in the right place.

OROGE. Everyone must be told. We don't want anyone heading him off again.

JAGUNA. And it works so well. This is surely the help of the gods themselves Oroge. Don't you know at once what is on the path to the stream?

OROGE. The sacred trees.

JAGUNA. I tell you it is the very hand of the gods. Let us go.

[*An overgrown part of the village.* EMAN *wanders in, aimlessly, seemingly uncaring of discovery. Beyond him, an area lights up, revealing a group of people clustered round a spot, all the heads are bowed. One figure stands away and separate from them. Even as* EMAN *looks, the group breaks up and the people disperse, coming down and past him. Only three people are left, a man (*EMAN*) whose back is turned, the village priest and the isolated one. They stand on opposite sides of the grave, the man on the mound of earth. The priest walks round to the man's side and lays a hand on his shoulder.*]

PRIEST. Come.

EMAN. I will. Give me a few moments here alone.

PRIEST. Be comforted.

[*They fall silent.*]

EMAN. I was gone twelve years but she waited. She whom I thought had too much of the laughing child in her. Twelve years I was a pilgrim, seeking the vain shrine of secret strength. And all the time, strange knowledge, this silent strength of my child-woman.

PRIEST. We all saw it. It was a lesson to us; we did not know that such goodness could be found among us.

EMAN. Then why? Why the wasted years if she had to perish giving birth to my child? [*They are both silent.*] I do not really know for what great meaning I searched. When I returned, I could not be certain I had found it. Until I reached my home and I found her a full-grown woman, still a child at heart. When I grew to believe it, I thought, this, after all, is what I sought. It was here all the time. And I threw away my new-gained knowledge. I buried the part of me that was formed in strange places. I made a home in my birthplace.

PRIEST. That was as it should be.

EMAN. Any truth of that was killed in the cruelty of her brief happiness.

PRIEST [*looks up and sees the figure standing away from them, the child in his arms. He is totally still*]. Your father—he is over there.

EMAN. I knew he would come. Has he my son with him?

PRIEST. Yes.

EMAN. He will let no one take the child. Go and comfort him priest. He loved Omae like a daughter, and you all know how well she looked after him. You see how strong we really are. In his heart of hearts the old man's love really awaited a daughter. Go and comfort him. His grief is more than mine.

[*The* PRIEST *goes. The* OLD MAN *has stood well away from the burial group. His face is hard and his gaze unswerving from the grave. The* PRIEST *goes to him, pauses, but sees that he can make no dent in the man's grief. Bowed, he goes on his way.*]

[EMAN, *as carrier, walking towards the graveside, the other* EMAN *having gone. His feet sink into the mound and he breaks slowly on to his knees, scooping up the sand in his hands and pouring it on his head. The scene blacks out slowly.*]

[*Enter* JAGUNA *and* OROGE.]

OROGE. We have only a little time.

JAGUNA. He will come. All the wells are guarded. There is only the stream left him. The animal must come to drink.

OROGE. You are sure it will not fail—the trap I mean.

JAGUNA. When Jaguna sets the trap, even elephants pay homage—their trunks downwards and one leg up in the sky. When the carrier steps on the fallen twigs, it is up in the sacred trees with him.

OROGE. I shall breathe again when this long night is over.

[*They go out.*]

[*Enter* EMAN—*as carrier—from the same direction as the last two entered. In front of him is a still figure, the* OLD MAN *as he was, carrying the dwarf boat.*]

EMAN [*joyfully*]. Father.

[*The figure does not turn round.*]

EMAN. It is your son. Eman. [*He moves nearer.*] Don't you want to look at me? It is I, Eman. [*He moves nearer still.*]

OLD MAN. You are coming too close. Don't you know what I carry on my head?

EMAN. But Father, I am your son.

OLD MAN. Then go back. We cannot give the two of us.

EMAN. Tell me first where you are going.

OLD MAN. Do *you* ask that? Where else but to the river?

EMAN [*visibly relieved*]. I only wanted to be sure. My throat is burning. I have been looking for the stream all night.

OLD MAN. It is the other way.

EMAN. But you said . . .

OLD MAN. I take the longer way, you know how I must do this. It is quicker if you take the other way. Go now.

EMAN. No, I will only get lost again. I shall go with you.

OLD MAN. Go back my son. Go back.

EMAN. Why? Won't you even look at me?

OLD MAN. Listen to your father. Go back.

EMAN. But father!

[*He makes to hold him. Instantly the* OLD MAN *breaks into a rapid trot.* EMAN *hesitates, then follows, his strength nearly gone.*]

EMAN. Wait father. I am coming with you . . . wait . . . wait for me father . . .

[*There is a sound of twigs breaking, of a sudden trembling in the branches. Then silence.*]

[*The front of* EMAN'*s house. The effigy is hanging from the sheaves.*[7] *Enter* SUNMA, *still supported by* IFADA, *she stands transfixed as she sees the hanging figure.* IFADA *appears to go mad, rushes at the object and tears it down.* SUNMA, *her last bit of will gone, crumbles against the wall. Some distance away from them, partly hidden, stands the* GIRL, *impassively watching.* IFADA *hugs the effigy to him, stands above* SUNMA. *The* GIRL *remains where she is, observing.*

Almost at once, the villagers begin to return, subdued and guilty. They walk across the front, skirting the house as widely as they can. No word is exchanged. JAGUNA *and* OROGE *eventually appear.* JAGUNA *who is leading, sees* SUNMA *as soon as he comes in view. He stops at once, retreating slightly.*]

OROGE [*almost whispering*]. What is it?

JAGUNA. The viper.

[OROGE *looks cautiously at the woman.*]

OROGE. I don't think she will even see you.

---

[7] The overhanging edge of the roof, or eaves.

JAGUNA. Are you sure? I am in no frame of mind for another meeting with her.

OROGE. Let's go home.

JAGUNA. I am sick to the heart of the cowardice I have seen tonight.

OROGE. That is the nature of men.

JAGUNA. Then it is a sorry world to live in. We did it for them. It was all for their own common good. What did it benefit me whether the man lived or died. But did you see them? One and all they looked up at the man and words died in their throats.

OROGE. It was no common sight.

JAGUNA. Women could not have behaved so shamefully. One by one they crept off like sick dogs. Not one could raise a curse.

OROGE. It was not only him they fled. Do you see how unattended we are?

JAGUNA. There are those who will pay for this night's work!

OROGE. Ay, let us go home.

[*They go off.* SUNMA, IFADA *and* GIRL *remain as they are, the light fading slowly on them.*]

THE END

[1964]

Alice Childress   *1920–*

WINE IN THE WILDERNESS

CHARACTERS

BILL JAMESON, *an artist aged thirty-three*
OLDTIMER, *an old roustabout character in his sixties*
SONNY-MAN, *a writer aged twenty-seven*

CYNTHIA, *a social worker aged twenty-five,* SONNY-MAN'S WIFE.
TOMMY, *a woman factory worker aged thirty*

Time: The summer of 1964. Night of a riot.

Place: Harlem, New York City, New York, U.S.A.

Scene: A one room apartment in a Harlem Tenement. It used to be a three room apartment but the tenant has broken out walls and is half finished with a redecorating job. The place is now only partly reminiscent of its past tawdry days, plaster broken away and lathing exposed right next to a new brick-faced portion of wall. The kitchen is now a part of the room. There is a three-quarter bed covered with an African throw, a screen is placed at the foot of the bed to insure privacy when needed. The room is obviously black dominated, pieces of sculpture, wall hangings, paintings. An artist's easel is standing with a drapery thrown across it so the empty canvas beneath it is hidden. Two other canvases the same size are next to it, they too are covered and conceal paintings. The place is in a beautiful, rather artistic state of disorder. The room also reflects an interest in other darker peoples of the world . . . A Chinese incense-burner Buddha, an American Indian feathered war helmet, a Mexican serape, a Japanese fan, a West Indian travel poster. There is a kitchen table, chairs, floor cushions, a couple of box crates, books, bookcases, plenty of artist's materials. There is a small raised platform for model posing. On the platform is a backless chair. The tail end of a riot is going on out in the street. Noise and screaming can be heard in the distance. . . . running feet, voices shouting over loudspeakers.

OFFSTAGE VOICES. Offa the street! Into your homes! Clear the street! [*The whine of a bullet is heard.*] Cover that roof! It's from the roof! [BILL *is seated on the floor with his back to the wall, drawing on a large sketch pad with charcoal pencil. He is very absorbed in his task but flinches as he hears the bullet sound, ducks and shields his head with upraised hand . . . then resumes sketching. The telephone rings, he reaches for phone with caution, pulls it toward him by the cord in order to avoid going near window or standing up.*]
BILL. Hello? Yeah, my phone is on. How the hell I'm gonna be talkin' to you if it's not on? [*Sound of glass breaking in the distance.*] I could lose my damn life answerin' the phone. Sonny-man, what the hell you callin' me up for! I thought you and Cynthia might be downstairs dead. I banged on the floor and hollered down the air-shaft, no answer. No stuff! Thought yall was dead. I'm sittin' here drawin' a picture in your memory. In a bar! Yall sittin' in a bar? See there, you done blew the picture that's in your memory . . . No kiddin', they wouldn't let you in the block? Man, they can't keep you outta your own house. Found? You found who? Model? What model? Yeah, yeah, thanks, . . . but I like to find my

own models. No! Don't bring nobody up here in the middle of a riot . . . Hey, Sonny-man! Hey! [*Sound of yelling and rushing footsteps in the hall.*]

WOMAN'S VOICE [*offstage*]. Damnit, Bernice! The riot is over! What you hidin' in the hall for? I'm in the house, your father's in the house, . . . and you out there hidin' in the hall!

GIRL'S VOICE [*offstage*]. The house might burn down!

BILL. Sonny-man, I can't hear you!

WOMAN'S VOICE [*offstage*]. If it do burn down, what the hell you gon' do, run off and leave us to burn up by ourself? The riot is over. The police say it's over! Get back in the house!

[*Sound of running feet and a knock on the door.*]

BILL. They say it's over. Man, they oughta let you on your own block, in your own house . . . Yeah, we still standin', this seventy year old house got guts. Thank you, yeah, thanks but I like to pick my own models. You drunk? Can't you hear when I say not to . . . Okay, all right, bring her . . . [*Frantic knocking at the door.*] I gotta go. Yeah, yeah, bring her. I gotta go . . . [*Hangs up phone and opens the door for* OLDTIMER. *The old man is carrying a haul of loot . . . two or three bottles of liquor, a ham, a salami and a suit with price tags attached.*] What's this! Oh, no, no, no, Oldtimer, not here . . . [*Faint sound of a police whistle.*] The police after you? What you bring that stuff in here for?

OLDTIMER [*Runs past* BILL *to center as he looks for a place to hide the loot*]. No, no, they not really after me but . . . I was in the basement so I could stash this stuff, . . . but a fella told me they pokin' round down there . . . in the back yard pokin' round . . . the police doin' a lotta pokin' round.

BILL. If the cops are searchin' why you wanna dump your troubles on me?

OLDTIMER. I don't wanna go to jail. I'm too old to go to jail. What we gonna do?

BILL. We can throw it the hell outta the window. Didn't you think of just throwin it away and not worry 'bout jail?

OLDTIMER. I can't do it. It's like . . . I'm Oldtimer but my hands and arms is somebody else that I don' know-a-tall. [BILL *pulls stuff out of* OLDTIMER'*s arms and places loot on the kitchen table.* OLDTIMER'*s arms fall to his sides.*] Thank you, son.

BILL. Stealin' ain't worth a bullet through your brain, is it? You wanna get shot down and drown in your own blood, . . . for what? A suit, a bottle of whiskey? Gonna throw your life away for a damn ham?

OLDTIMER. But I ain' really stole nothin', Bill, cause I ain' no thief. Them others, . . . they smash the windows, they run in the stores and grab and all. Me, I pick up what they left scatter in the street. Things they drop . . . things they trample underfoot. What's in the street ain' like stealin'. This is leavin's. What I'm gon' do if the police come?

BILL [*starts to gather the things in the tablecloth that is on the table*]. I'll throw it out the air-shaft window.

OLDTIMER [*places himself squarely in front of the air-shaft window*]. I be damn. Uh-uh, can't let you do it, Bill-Boy. [*Grabs the liquor and holds on.*]

BILL [*wraps the suit, the ham and the salami in the tablecloth and ties the ends together in a knot*]. Just for now, then you can go down and get it later.

OLDTIMER [*getting belligerent*]. I say I ain' gon' let you do it.

BILL. Sonny-man calls this "The people's revolution." A revolution should not be looting and stealing. Revolutions are for liberation. [OLDTIMER *won't budge from before the window.*] Okay, man, you win, it's all yours. [*Walks away from* OLDTIMER *and prepares his easel for sketching.*]

OLDTIMER. Don't be mad with me, Bill-Boy, I couldn't help myself.

BILL [*at peace with the old man*]. No hard feelin's.

OLDTIMER [*as he uncorks bottle*]. I don't blame you for bein' fed up with us, . . . fella like you oughta be fed up with your people sometime. Hey, Billy, let's you and me have a little taste together.

BILL. Yeah, why not.

OLDTIMER [*at table pouring drinks*]. You mustn't be too hard on me. You see, you talented, you got somethin' on the ball, you gonna make it on past these white folk, . . . but not me, Billy-boy, it's too late in the day for that. Time, time, time, . . . time done put me down. Father Time is a bad white cat. Whatcha been paintin' and drawin' lately? You can paint me again if you wanta, . . . no charge. Paint me 'cause that might be the only way I get to stay in the world after I'm dead and gone. Somebody'll look up at your paintin' and say, . . . "Who's that?" And you say, . . . "That's Oldtimer." [BILL *joins* OLDTIMER *at table and takes one of the drinks.*] Well, here's lookin' at you and goin' down me. [*Gulps drink down.*]

BILL [*raising his glass*]. Your health, Oldtimer.

OLDTIMER. My day we didn't have all this grants and scholarship like now. Whatcha been doin'?

BILL. I'm working on the third part of a triptych.

OLDTIMER. A what tick?

BILL. A triptych.

OLDTIMER. Hot-damn, that calls for another drink. Here's to the trip-tick. Down the hatch. What is one-a-those?

BILL. It's three paintings that make one work . . . three paintings that make one subject.

OLDTIMER. Goes together like a new outfit . . . hat, shoes and suit.

BILL. Right. The title of my triptych is . . . "Wine in the Wilderness" . . . Three canvases on black womanhood. . . .

OLDTIMER [*eyes light up*]. Are they naked pitchers?

BILL [*crosses to paintings*]. No, all fully clothed.

OLDTIMER [*wishing it was a naked picture*]. Man, ain' nothin' dirty 'bout naked pitchers. That's art. What you call artistic.

BILL. Right, right, right, but these are with clothes. That can be artistic too. [*Uncovers one of the canvases and reveals painting of a charming little girl in Sunday dress and hair ribbon.*] I call her . . . "Black girlhood."

OLDTIMER. Awwwww, that's innocence! Don't know what it's all about. Ain't that the little child that live right down the street? Yeah. That call for another drink.

BILL. Slow down, Oldtimer, wait till you see this. [*Covers the painting of the little girl, then uncovers another canvas and reveals a beautiful woman, deep mahogany complexion, she is cold but utter perfection, draped in startling colors of African material, very "Vogue" looking. She wears a golden head-dress sparkling with brilliants and sequins applied over the paint.*] There she is . . . "Wine In The Wilderness" . . . Mother Africa, regal, black womanhood in her noblest form.

OLDTIMER. Hot damn. I'd die for her, no stuff, . . . oh, man. "Wine In The Wilderness."

BILL. Once, a long time ago, a poet named Omar[1] told us what a paradise life could be if a man had a loaf of bread, a jug of wine and . . . a woman singing

---

[1] Omar Khayyám (ca. 1048–1122) was the author of *The Rubáiyát*, which was given its most famous translation into English by Edward Fitzgerald in 1859.

to him in the wilderness. She is the woman, she is the bread, she is the wine, she is the singing. This Abyssinian maiden[2] is paradise, . . . perfect black woman-hood.

OLDTIMER [*pours for* BILL *and himself*]. To our Abyssinian maiden.

BILL. She's the Sudan, the Congo River, the Egyptian Pyramids . . . Her thighs are African Mahogany . . . she speaks and her words pour forth sparkling clear as the waters . . . Victoria Falls.

OLDTIMER. Ow! Victoria Falls! She got a pretty name.

BILL [*covers her up again*]. Victoria Falls is a waterfall not her name. Now, here's the one that calls for a drink. [*Snatches cover from the empty canvas.*]

OLDTIMER [*stunned by the empty canvas*]. Your . . . your pitcher is gone.

BILL. Not gone . . . she's not painted yet. This will be the third part of the triptych. This is the unfinished third of "Wine In The Wilderness." She's gonna be the kinda chick that is grass roots, . . . no, not grass roots, . . . I mean she's under-neath the grass roots. The lost woman, . . . what the society has made out of our women. She's as far from my African queen as a woman can get and still be female, she's as close to the bottom as you can get without crackin' up . . . she's ignorant, unfeminine, coarse, rude . . . vulgar . . . a poor, dumb chick that's had her behind kicked until it's numb . . . and the sad part is . . . she ain't together, you know . . . there's no hope for her.

OLDTIMER. Oh, man, you talkin 'bout my first wife.

BILL. A chick that ain' fit for nothin' but to . . . to . . . just pass her by.

OLDTIMER. Yeah, later for her. When you see her, cross over to the other side of the street.

BILL. If you had to sum her up in one word it would be nothin'!

OLDTIMER [*roars with laughter*]. That call for a double!

BILL [*beginning to slightly feel the drinks. He covers the canvas again*]. Yeah, that's a double! The kinda woman that grates on your damn nerves. And Sonny-man just called to say he found her runnin' round in the middle-a this riot. Sonny-man say she's the real thing from underneath them grass roots. A back-country chick right outa the wilds of Mississippi, . . . but she ain't never been near there. Born in Harlem, raised right here in Harlem, . . . but back country. Got the picture?

OLDTIMER [*full of laughter*]. When . . . when . . . when she get here let's us stomp her to death.

BILL. Not till after I paint her. Gonna put her right here on this canvas. [*Pats the canvas, walks in a strut around the table.*] When she gets put down on canvas, . . . then triptych will be finished.

OLDTIMER [*joins him in the strut*]. Trip-tick will be finish . . . trip-tick will be finish . . .

BILL. Then "Wine In The Wilderness" will go up against the wall to improve the view of some post office . . . or some library . . . or maybe a bank . . . and I'll win a prize . . . and the queen, my black queen will look down from the wall so the messed up chicks in the neighborhood can see what a woman oughta be . . . and the innocent child on one side of her and the messed up chick on the other side of her . . . MY STATEMENT.

OLDTIMER [*turning the strut into a dance*]. Wine in the wilderness . . . up against the wall . . . wine in the wilderness . . . up against the wall . . .

[2] Abyssinia was a kingdom in Africa. Bill may be alluding to the Abyssinian maiden praised in Samuel Taylor Coleridge's poem "Kubla Khan" (1816).

WOMAN FROM UPSTAIRS APT [*offstage*]. What's the matter! The house on fire?

BILL [*calls upstairs through the air-shaft window*]. No, baby! We down here paintin' pictures! [*Sound of police siren in distance.*]

WOMAN FROM UPSTAIRS APT [*offstage*]. So much-a damn noise! Cut out the noise! [*To her husband hysterically.*] Percy! Percy! You hear a police siren! Percy! That a fire engine?!

BILL. Another messed up chick. [*Gets a rope and ties it to* OLDTIMER*'s bundle.*] Got an idea. We'll tie the rope to the bundle, . . . then . . . [*Lowers bundle out of window.*] lower the bundle outta the window . . . and tie it to this nail here behind the curtain. Now! Nobody can find it except you and me . . . Cops come, there's no loot. [*Ties rope to nail under curtain.*]

OLDTIMER. Yeah, yeah, loot long gone 'til I want it. [*Makes sure window knot is secure.*] It'll be swingin' in the breeze free and easy. [*There is knocking on the door.*]

SONNY-MAN. Open up! Open up! Sonny-man and company.

BILL [*putting finishing touches on securing knot to nail*]. Wait, wait, hold on. . . .

SONNY-MAN. And-a here we come! [*Pushes the door open. Enters room with his wife* CYNTHIA *and* TOMMY. SONNY-MAN *is in high spirits. He is in his late twenties, his wife* CYNTHIA *is a bit younger. She wears her hair in a natural style, her clothing is tweedy and in good, quiet taste.* SONNY-MAN *is wearing slacks and a dashiki over a shirt.* TOMMY *is dressed in a mis-matched skirt and sweater, wearing a wig that is not comical, but is wiggy looking. She has the habit of smoothing it every once in a while, patting to make sure it's in place. She wears sneakers and bobby sox, carries a brown paper sack.*]

CYNTHIA. You didn't think it was locked, did you?

BILL. Door not locked? [*Looking over* TOMMY.]

TOMMY. You oughta run him outta town, pushin' open people's door.

BILL. Come right on in.

SONNY-MAN [*standing behind* TOMMY *and pointing down at her to draw* BILL*'s attention*]. Yes, sireeeeee.

CYNTHIA. Bill, meet a friend-a ours . . . This is Miss Tommy Fields. Tommy, meet a friend-a ours . . . this is Bill Jameson . . . Bill, Tommy.

BILL. Tommy, if I may call you that . . .

TOMMY [*likes him very much*]. Help yourself, Bill. It's a pleasure. Bill Jameson, well, all right.

BILL. The pleasure is all mine. Another friend-a ours. Oldtimer.

TOMMY [*with respect and warmth*]. How are you, Mr. Timer?

BILL [*laughs along with others,* OLDTIMER *included*]. What you call him, baby?

TOMMY. Mr. Timer, . . . ain't that what you say? [*They all laugh expansively.*]

BILL. No, sugar pie, that's not his name, . . . we just say . . . "Oldtimer," that's what everybody call him. . . .

OLDTIMER. Yeah, they all call me that . . . everybody say that . . . Oldtimer.

TOMMY. That's cute, . . . but what's your name?

BILL. His name is . . . er . . . er . . . What is your name?

SONNY-MAN. Dog-bite, what's your name, man? [*There is a significant moment of self-consciousness as* CYNTHIA, SONNY-MAN *and* BILL *realize they don't know* OLDTIMER*'s name.*]

OLDTIMER. Well, it's . . . Edmond L. Matthews.

TOMMY. Edmond *L*. Matthews. What's the L for?

OLDTIMER. Lorenzo, . . . Edmond Lorenzo Matthews.

BILL AND SONNY-MAN. Edmond Lorenzo Matthews.

TOMMY. Pleased to meetcha, Mr. Matthews.

OLDTIMER. Nobody call me that in a long, long time.

TOMMY. I'll call you Oldtimer like the rest but I like to know who I'm meetin'. [OLDTIMER *gives her a chair.*] There you go. He's a gentleman too. Bet you can tell my feet hurt. I got one corn, . . . and that one is enough. Oh, it'll ask you for somethin'. [*General laughter.* BILL *indicates to* SONNY-MAN *that* TOMMY *seems right.* CYNTHIA *and* OLDTIMER *take seats near* TOMMY.]

BILL. You rest yourself, baby, er . . . er . . . Tommy. You did say Tommy.

TOMMY. I cut it to Tommy . . . Tommy-Marie, I use both of 'em sometime.

BILL. How 'bout some refreshment?

SONNY-MAN. Yeah, how 'bout that. [*Pouring drinks.*]

TOMMY. Don't yall carry me too fast, now.

BILL [*indicating liquor bottles*]. I got what you see and also some wine . . . couple-a cans-a beer.

TOMMY. I'll take the wine.

BILL. Yeah, I knew it.

TOMMY. Don't wanta start nothin' I can't keep up. [OLDTIMER *slaps his thigh with pleasure.*]

BILL. That's all right, baby, you just a wine-o.

TOMMY. You the one that's got the wine, not me.

BILL. I use it for cookin'.

TOMMY. You like to get loaded while you cook? [OLDTIMER *is having a ball.*]

BILL [*as he pours wine for* TOMMY]. Oh, baby, you too much.

OLDTIMER [*admiring* TOMMY]. Oh, Lord, I wish, I wish, I wish I was young again.

TOMMY [*flirtatiously*]. Lively as you are, . . . I don't know what we'd do with you if you got any younger.

OLDTIMER. Oh, hush now!

SONNY-MAN [*whispering to* BILL *and pouring drinks*]. Didn't I tell you! Know what I'm talkin' about. You dig? All the elements, man.

TOMMY [*worried about what the whispering means*]. Let's get somethin' straight. I didn't come bustin' in on the party . . . I was asked. If you married and any wives or girl-friends round here . . . I'm innocent. Don't wanna get shot at, or jumped on. Cause I wasn't doin' a thing but mindin' my business! . . . [*Saying the last in loud tones to be heard in other rooms.*]

OLDTIMER. Jus' us here, that's all.

BILL. I'm single, baby. Nobody wants a poor artist.

CYNTHIA. Oh, honey, we wouldn't walk you into a jealous wife or girl friend.

TOMMY. You paint all-a these pitchers? [BILL *and* SONNY-MAN *hand out drinks.*]

BILL. Just about. Your health, baby, to you.

TOMMY [*lifts her wine glass*]. All right, and I got one for you. . . . Like my grampaw used-ta say, . . . Here's to the men's collars and the women's skirts, . . . may they never meet. [*General laughter.*]

OLDTIMER. But they ain't got far to go before they do.

TOMMY [*suddenly remembers her troubles*]. Niggers, niggers . . . niggers, . . . I'm sick-a niggers, ain't you? A nigger will mess up everytime . . . Lemmie tell you what the niggers done . . .

BILL. Tommy, baby, we don't use that word around here. We can talk about each other a little better than that.

CYNTHIA. Oh, she doesn't mean it.

TOMMY. What must I say?

BILL. Try Afro-Americans.

TOMMY. Well, . . . the Afro-Americans burnt down my house.

OLDTIMER. Oh, no they didn't!

Tommy. Oh, yes they did . . . it's almost burn down. Then the firemen nailed up my
    door . . . the door to my room, nailed up shut tight with all I got in the world.
Oldtimer. Shame, what a shame.
Tommy. A *damn* shame. My clothes . . . Everything gone. This riot blew my life. All
    I got is gone like it never was.
Oldtimer. I know it.
Tommy. My transistor radio . . . that's gone.
Cynthia. Ah, gee.
Tommy. The transistor . . . and a brand new pair-a shoes I never had on one time
    . . . [*Raises her right hand.*] If I never move, that's the truth . . . new shoes gone.
Oldtimer. Child, when hard luck fall it just keep fallin'.
Tommy. And in my top dresser drawer I got a my-on-ase jar with forty-one dollars
    in it. The fireman would not let me in to get it . . . And it was a Afro-American
    fireman, don'tcha know.
Oldtimer. And you ain't got no place to stay. [Bill *is studying her for portrait possi-*
    bilities.]
Tommy [*rises and walks around room*]. That's a lie. I always got some place to go. I
    don't wanta boast but I ain't never been no place that I can't go back the second
    time. Woman I use to work for say . . . "Tommy, any time, any time you want a
    sleep-in place you come right here to me." . . . And that's Park Avenue, my own
    private bath and T.V. set. . . . But I don't want that . . . so I make it on out here
    to the dress factory. I got friends . . . not a lot of 'em . . . but a few *good* ones. I
    call my friend—girl and her mother . . . they say . . . "Tommy, you come here,
    bring yourself over here." So Tommy got a roof with no sweat. [*Looks at torn*
    walls.] Looks like the Afro-Americans got to you too. Breakin' up, breakin'
    down, . . . that's all they know.
Bill. No, Tommy, . . . I'm redecorating the place . . .
Tommy. You mean you did this to yourself?
Cynthia. It's gonna be wild . . . brick-face walls . . . wall to wall carpet.
Sonny-man. She was breakin'up everybody in the bar . . . had us all laughin' . . .
    crackin' us up. In the middle of a riot . . . she's gassin' everybody!
Tommy. No need to cry. It's sad enough. They hollerin' whitey, whitey . . . but who
    they burn out? Me.
Bill. The brothers and sisters are tired, weary of the endless get-no-where struggle.
Tommy. I'm standin' there in the bar . . . tellin' like it is . . . next thing I know they
    talkin' bout bringin' me to meet you. But you know what I say? Can't nobody
    pick nobody for nobody else. It don't work. And I'm standin' there in a mis-
    match skirt and top and these sneaker-shoes. I just went to put my dresses in the
    cleaner . . . Oh, Lord, wonder if they burn down the cleaner. Well, no matter,
    when I got back it was all over . . . They went in the grocery store, rip out the
    shelves, pull out all the groceries . . . the hams . . . the . . . the . . . the can goods
    . . . everything . . . and then set fire . . . Now who you think live over the grocery?
    Me, that's who. I don't even go to the store lookin' this way . . . but this would
    be the time, when . . . folks got a fella they want me to meet.
Bill [*suddenly self-conscious*]. Tommy, they thought . . . they thought I'd like to
    paint you . . . that's why they asked you over.
Tommy [*pleased by the thought but she can't understand it*]. Paint me? For what? If he
    was gonna paint somebody seems to me it'd be one of the pretty girls they show
    in the beer ads. They even got colored on television now, . . . brushin' their
    teeth and smokin' cigarettes, . . . some of the prettiest girls in the world. He
    could get them, . . . couldn't you?

BILL. Sonny-man and Cynthia were right. I want to paint you.

TOMMY [*suspiciously*]. Naked, with no clothes on?

BILL. No, baby, dressed just as you are now.

OLDTIMER. Wearin' clothes is also art.

TOMMY. In the cleaner I got a white dress with a orlon sweater to match it, maybe I can get it out tomorrow and pose in that. [CYNTHIA, OLDTIMER *and* SONNY-MAN *are eager for her to agree.*]

BILL. No, I will paint you today, Tommy, just as you are, holding your brown paper bag.

TOMMY. Mmmmmm, me holdin' the damn bag, I don't know 'bout that.

BILL. Look at it this way, tonight has been a tragedy.

TOMMY. Sure in hell has.

BILL. And so I must paint you tonight, . . . Tommy in her moment of tragedy.

TOMMY. I'm tired.

BILL. Damn, baby, all you have to do is sit there and rest.

TOMMY. I'm hungry.

SONNY-MAN. While you're posin' Cynthia can run down to our house and fix you some eggs.

CYNTHIA [*gives her husband a weary look*]. Oh, Sonny, that's such a lovely idea.

SONNY-MAN. Thank you, darlin', I'm in there, . . . on the beam.

TOMMY [*ill at ease about posing*]. I don't want no eggs. I'm goin' to find me some Chinee food.

BILL. I'll go. If you promise to stay here and let me paint you, . . . I'll get you anything you want.

TOMMY [*brightening up*]. Anything I want. Now, how he sound? All right, you comin' on mighty strong there. "Anything you want." When last you heard somebody say that? . . . I'm warnin' you, now, . . . I'm free, single and disengage, . . . so you better watch yourself.

BILL [*keeping her away from ideas of romance*]. Now this is the way the program will go down. First I'll feed you, then I'll paint you.

TOMMY. Okay, I'm game, I'm a good sport. First off, I want me some Chinese food.

CYNTHIA. Order up, Tommy, the treat's on him.

TOMMY. How come it is you never been married? All these girls runnin' round Harlem lookin' for husbands. [*To* CYNTHIA.] I don't blame 'em, 'cause I'm lookin' for somebody myself.

BILL. I've been married, married and divorced, she divorced me, Tommy, so maybe I'm not much of a catch.

TOMMY. Look at it this-a-way. Some folks got bad taste. That woman had bad taste. [*All laugh except* BILL *who pours another drink.*] Watch it, Bill, you gonna rust the linin' of your stomach. Ain't this a shame? The riot done wipe me out and I'm sittin' here havin' me a ball. Sittin' here ballin'! [*As* BILL *refills her glass.*] Hold it, that's enough. Likker ain' my problem.

OLDTIMER. I'm havin' me a good time.

TOMMY. Know what I say 'bout divorce. [*Slaps her hands together in a final gesture.*] Anybody don' wantcha, . . . later, let 'em go. That's bad taste for you.

BILL. Tommy, I don't wanta ever get married again. It's me and my work, I'm not gettin' serious about anybody. . . .

TOMMY. He's spellin' at me, now. Nigger . . . I mean Afro-American . . . I ain' ask you nothin'. You hinkty, I'm hinkty too. I'm independent as a hog on ice, . . . and a hog on ice is dead, cold, well-preserved . . . and don't need a mother-grabbin' thing. [*All laugh heartily except* BILL *and* CYNTHIA.] I know models get paid. I ain' no square but this is a special night and so this one'll be on the house. Show you my heart's in the right place.

BILL. I'll be glad to pay you, baby.

TOMMY. You don't really like me, do you? That's all right, sometime it happen that way. You can't pick for *nobody*. Friends get to matchin' up friends and they mess up everytime. Cynthia and Sonny-man done messed up.

BILL. I like you just fine and I'm glad and grateful that you came.

TOMMY. Good enough. [*Extends her hand. They slap hands together.*] You 'n me friends?

BILL. Friends, baby, friends. [*Putting rock record on.*]

TOMMY [*trying out the model stand*]. Okay. Dad! Let's see 'bout this *anything I want* jive. Want me a bucket-a Egg Foo Yong, and you get you a shrimp-fry rice, we split that and each have some-a both. Make him give you the soy sauce, the hot mustard and the duck sauce too.

BILL. Anything else, baby?

TOMMY. Since you ask, yes. If your money hold out, get me a double order egg roll. And a half order of the sweet and sour spare ribs.

BILL [*to* OLDTIMER *and* SONNY-MAN]. Come on, come on. I need some strong men to help me bring back your order, baby.

TOMMY [*going into her dance . . . simply standing and going through some boo-ga-loo motions*]. Better go get it 'fore I think up some more to go 'long with it. [*The men laugh and vanish out of the door. Steps heard descending stairs.*] Turn that off. [CYNTHIA *turns off record player.*] How could I forget your name, good as you been to me this day. Thank you. Cynthia, thank you. I *like* him. Oh, I *like* him. But I don't wanta push him too fast. Oh, I got to play these cards right.

CYNTHIA [*a bit uncomfortable*]. Oh, Honey, . . . Tommy, you don't want a poor artist.

TOMMY. Tommy's not lookin' for a meal ticket. I been doin' for myself all my life. It takes two to make it in this high-price world. A black man see a hard way to go. The both of you gotta pull together. That way you accomplish.

CYNTHIA. I'm a social worker . . . and I see so many broken homes. Some of these men! Tommy, don't be in a rush about the marriage thing.

TOMMY. Keep it to yourself, . . . but I was thirty my last birthday and haven't ever been married. I coulda been. Oh, yes, indeed, coulda been. But I don't want any and everybody. What I want with a no-good piece-a nothin'? I'll never forget what the Reverend Martin Luther King said . . . "I have a dream." I liked him sayin' it 'cause truer words have never been spoke. [*Straightening the room.*] I have a dream, too. Mine is to find a man who'll treat me just half-way decent . . . just to meet me half-way is all I ask, to smile, be kind to me. Somebody in my corner. Not to wake up by myself in the mornin' and face this world all alone.

CYNTHIA. About Bill, it's best not to ever count on anything, anything at all, Tommy.

TOMMY [*this remark bothers her for a split second but she shakes it off*]. Of course, Cynthia, that's one of the foremost rules of life. Don't count on *nothin'*!

CYNTHIA. Right, don't be too quick to put your trust in these men.

TOMMY. You put your trust in one and got yourself a husband.

CYNTHIA. Well, yes, but what I mean is . . . Oh, you know. A man is a man and Bill is also an artist and his work comes before all else and there are other factors . . .

TOMMY [*sits facing* CYNTHIA]. What's wrong with me?

CYNTHIA. I don't know what you mean.

TOMMY. Yes you do. You tryin' to tell me I'm aimin' too high by lookin' at Bill.

CYNTHIA. Oh, no, my dear.

TOMMY. Out there in the street, in the bar, you and your husband were so sure that he'd *like* me and want to paint my picture.

CYNTHIA. But he does want to paint you, he's very eager to . . .

TOMMY. But why? Somethin' don't fit right.

CYNTHIA [*feeling sorry for* TOMMY]. If you don't want to do it, just leave and that'll be that.

TOMMY. Walk out while he's buyin' me what I ask for, spendin' his money on me? That'd be too dirty. [*Looks at books. Takes one from shelf.*] Books, books, books everywhere. "Afro-American History." I like that. What's wrong with me, Cynthia? Tell me, I won't get mad with you, I swear. If there's somethin' wrong that I can change, I'm ready to do it. Eighth grade, that's all I had of school. You a social worker, I know that means college. I come from poor people. [*Examining the book in her hand.*] Talkin' 'bout poverty this and poverty that and studyin' it. When you in it you don' be studyin' 'bout it. Cynthia, I remember my mother tyin' up her stockin's with strips-a rag 'cause she didn't have no garters. When I get home from school she'd say, . . . "Nothin' much here to eat." Nothin' much might be grits, or bread and coffee. I got sick-a all that, got me a job. Later for school.

CYNTHIA. The Matriarchal Society.

TOMMY. What's that?

CYNTHIA. A Matriarchal Society is one in which the women rule . . . the women have the power . . . the women head the house.

TOMMY. We didn't have nothin' to rule over, not a pot nor a window. And my papa picked hisself up and run off with some finger-poppin' woman and we never hear another word 'til ten, twelve years later when a undertaker call up and ask if Mama wanta come claim his body. And don'cha know, mama went on over and claim it. A woman need a man to claim, even if it's a dead one. What's wrong with me? Be honest.

CYNTHIA. You're a fine person . . .

TOMMY. Go on, I can take it.

CYNTHIA. You're too brash. You're too used to looking out for yourself. It makes us lose our femininity . . . It makes us hard . . . it makes us seem very hard. We do for ourselves too much.

TOMMY. If I don't, who's gonna do for me?

CYNTHIA. You have to let the black man have his manhood again. You have to give it back, Tommy.

TOMMY. I didn't take it from him, how I'm gonna give it back? What else is the matter with me? You had school, I didn't. I respect that.

CYNTHIA. Yes, I've had it, the degree and the whole bit. For a time I thought I was about to move into another world, the so-called "integrated" world, a place where knowledge and know-how could set you free and open all the doors, but that's a lie. I turned away from that idea. The first thing I did was give up dating white fellas.

TOMMY. I never had none to give up. I'm not soundin' on you. White folks nothin' happens when I look at 'em. I don't hate 'em, don't love 'em . . . just nothin' shakes a-tall. The dullest people in the world. The way they talk . . . "Oh, hotty, hooty, hoo" . . . Break it down for me to A, B, C's. That Bill . . . I like him, with his black, uppity, high-handed ways. What do you do to get a man you want? A social worker oughta tell you things like that.

CYNTHIA. Don't chase him . . . at least don't let it look that way. Let him pursue you.

TOMMY. What if he won't? Men don't chase me much, not the kind I like.

CYNTHIA [*rattles off instructions glibly*]. Let him do the talking. Learn to listen. Stay in the background a little. Ask his opinion . . . "What do you think, Bill?"

TOMMY. Mmmmm, "Oh, hooty, hooty, hoo."

CYNTHIA. But why count on him? There are lots of other nice guys.

TOMMY. You don't think he'd go for me, do you?

CYNTHIA [*trying to be diplomatic*]. Perhaps you're not really his type.

TOMMY. Maybe not, but he's mine. I'm so lonesome . . . I'm *lonesome* . . . I want somebody to love. Somebody to say . . . "That's all right," when the World treats me mean.

CYNTHIA. Tommy, I think you're too good for Bill.

TOMMY. I don't wanta hear that. The last man that told me I was too good for him . . . was trying' to get away. He's good enough for me. [*Straightening room.*]

CYNTHIA. Leave the room alone. What we need is a little more sex appeal and a little less washing, cooking and ironing. [TOMMY *puts down the room straightening.*] One more thing . . . do you have to wear that wig?

TOMMY [*a little sensitive*]. I like how your hair looks. But some of the naturals I don't like. Can see all the lint caught up in the hair like it hasn't been combed since know not when. You a Muslim?[3]

CYNTHIA. No.

TOMMY. I'm just sick-a hair, hair, hair. Do it this way, don't do it, leave it natural, straighten it, process, no process. I get sick-a hair and talkin' 'bout it and foolin' with it. That's why I wear the wig.

CYNTHIA. I'm sure your own must be just as nice or nicer than that.

TOMMY. It oughta be. I only paid nineteen ninety five for this.

CYNTHIA. You ought to go back to usin' your own.

TOMMY [*tensely*]. I'll be givin' that some thought.

CYNTHIA. You're pretty nice people just as you are. Soften up, Tommy. You might surprise yourself.

TOMMY. I'm listenin'.

CYNTHIA. Expect more. Learn to let men open doors for you . . .

TOMMY. What if I'm standin' there and they don't open it?

CYNTHIA [*trying to level with her*]. You're a fine person. He wants to paint you, that's all. He's doing a kind of mural thing and we thought he would enjoy painting you. I'd hate to see you expecting more out of the situation than what's there.

TOMMY. Forget it, sweetie-pie, don' nothin' happen that's not suppose to. [*Sound of laughter in the hall.* BILL, OLDTIMER *and* SONNY-MAN *enter.*]

BILL. No Chinese restaurant left, baby! It's wiped out. Gone with the revolution.

SONNY-MAN [*to* CYNTHIA]. Baby, let's move, split the scene, get on with it, time for home.

BILL. The revolution is here. Whatta you do with her? You paint her!

SONNY-MAN. You write her . . . you write the revolution. I'm gonna write the revolution into a novel nine hundred pages long.

BILL. Dance it! Sing it! "Down in the cornfield Hear dat mournful sound . . . [SONNY-MAN *and* OLDTIMER *harmonize.*] Dear old Massa am-a sleepin' A-sleepin' in

---

[3] The Muslims are believers in Islam, a monotheistic religion founded by the prophet Mohammed in the seventh century. The Black Muslims were established in the United States beginning in the 1930s under such leaders as Elijah Muhammad (1897–1975) and Malcolm X (1925–1965). They advocate racial separation and a very strict moral code involving, among other things, the subservience of women to men.

the cold, cold ground." Now for "Wine In The Wilderness!" Triptych will be finished.

CYNTHIA [*in* BILL*'s face*]. "Wine In The Wilderness," huh? Exploitation!

SONNY-MAN. Upstairs, all out, come on, Oldtimer. Folks can't create in a crowd. Cynthia, move it, baby.

OLDTIMER [*starting toward the window*]. My things! I got a package.

SONNY-MAN [*heads him off*]. Up and out. You don't have to go home, but you have to get outta here. Happy paintin', yall. [*One backward look and they are all gone.*]

BILL. Whatta night, whatta night, whatta night, baby. It will be painted, written, sung and discussed for generations.

TOMMY [*notices nothing that looks like Chinese food; he is carrying a small bag and a container*]. Where's the Foo-Yong?

BILL. They blew the restaurant, baby. All I could get was a couple-a franks and a orange drink from the stand.

TOMMY [*tersely*]. You brought me a frank-footer? That's what you think-a me, a frank-footer?

BILL. Nothin' to do with what I think. Place is closed.

TOMMY [*quietly surly*]. This is the damn City-a New York, any hour on the clock they sellin' the chicken in the basket, barbecue ribs, pizza pie, hot pastrami samitches; and you brought me a frank-footer?

BILL. Baby, don't break bad over somethin' to eat. The smart set, the jet, the beautiful people, kings and queens eat frankfurters.

TOMMY. If a queen sent you out to buy her a bucket-a Foo Yong, you wouldn't come back with no lonely-ass frank-footer.

BILL. Kill me 'bout it, baby! Go 'head and shoot me six times. That's the trouble with our women, yall always got your mind on food.

TOMMY. Is that our trouble? [*Laughs.*] Maybe you right. Only two things to do. Either eat the frankfooter or walk on outta here. You got any mustard?

BILL [*gets mustard from the refrigerator*]. Let's face it, our folks are not together. The brothers and sisters have busted up Harlem . . . no plan, no nothin'. There's your black revolution, heads whipped, hospital full and we still in the same old bag.

TOMMY [*seated at the kitchen table*]. Maybe what everybody need is somebody like you, who know how things oughta go, to get on out there and start some action.

BILL. You still mad about the frankfurter?

TOMMY. No. I keep seein' pitchers of what was in my room and how it all must be spoiled now. [*Sips the orange drink.*] A orange never been near this. Well, it's cold. [*Looking at an incense burner.*] What's that?

BILL. An incense burner, was given to me by the Chinese guy, Richard Lee. I'm sorry they blew his restaurant.

TOMMY. Does it help you to catch the number?

BILL. No, baby, I just burn incense sometime.

TOMMY. For what?

BILL. Just 'cause I feel like it. Baby, ain't you used to nothin'?

TOMMY. Ain't used to burnin' incent for nothin'.

BILL [*laughs*]. Burnin' what?

TOMMY. That stuff.

BILL. What did you call it?

TOMMY. Incent.

BILL. It's not incent, baby. It's incense.

TOMMY. Like the sense you got in your head. In-sense. Thank you. You're a very correctable person, ain't you?

BILL. Let's put you on canvas.

TOMMY [*stubbornly*]. I have to eat first.

BILL. That's another thing 'bout black women, they wanta eat 'fore they do anything else. Tommy. . . . Tommy, . . . I bet your name is Thomasina. You look like a Thomasina.

TOMMY. You could sit there and guess til your eyes pop out and you never would guess my first name. You might could guess the middle name but not the first one.

BILL. Tell it to me.

TOMMY. My name is Tomorrow.

BILL. How's that?

TOMMY. Tomorrow, . . . like yesterday and *tomorrow,* and the middle name is just plain Marie. That's what my father name me. Tomorrow Marie. My mother say he thought it had a pretty sound.

BILL. Crazy! I never met a girl named Tomorrow.

TOMMY. They got to callin' me Tommy for short, so I stick with that. Tomorrow Marie, . . . Sound like a promise that can never happen.

BILL [*straightens chair on stand; he is very eager to start painting*]. That's what Shakespeare said, . . . "Tomorrow and tomorrow and tomorrow." Tomorrow, you will be on this canvas.

TOMMY [*still uneasy about being painted*]. What's the hurry? Rome wasn't built in a day, . . . that's another saying.

BILL. If I finish in time, I'll enter you in the exhibition.

TOMMY [*loses interest in the food. Examines the room. Looks at portrait on the wall*]. He looks like somebody I know or maybe saw before.

BILL. That's Frederick Douglass.[4] A man who used to be a slave. He escaped and spent his life trying to make us all free. He was a great man.

TOMMY. Thank you, Mr. Douglass. Who's the light colored man? [*Indicates a frame next to the Douglass.*]

BILL. He's white. That's John Brown.[5] They killed him for tryin' to shoot the country outta the slavery bag. He dug us, you know. Old John said, "Hell no, slavery must go."

TOMMY. I heard all about him. Some folks say he was crazy.

BILL. If he had been shootin' at *us* they wouldn't have called him a nut.

TOMMY. School wasn't a great part-a my life.

BILL. If it was you wouldn't-a found out too much 'bout black history cause the books full-a nothin' but whitey, . . . all except the white ones who dug us, . . . they not there either. Tell me, . . . who was Elijah Lovejoy?[6]

TOMMY. Elijah Lovejoy, . . . Mmmmmmm. I don't know. Have anything to do with the Bible?

BILL. No, that's another white fella, . . . Elijah had a printin' press and the main thing he printed was "Slavery got to go." Well the man moved in on him,

---

[4] Frederick Douglass (1817–1895) is best known for his autobiographical *Narrative of the Life of Frederick Douglass, an American Slave* (1845).

[5] John Brown (1800–1859) was hung after leading an attack on a government arsenal at Harpers Ferry, Virginia, in the hope of provoking a slave revolt.

[6] Elijah Parish Lovejoy (1802–1837), the founder and editor of an antislavery newspaper, was tarred and feathered and later shot to death by pro-slavery extremists in Alton, Illinois.

smashed his press time after time . . . but he kept puttin' it back together and doin' his thing. So, one final day, they came in a mob and burned him to death.

TOMMY [*blows her nose with sympathy as she fights tears*]. That's dirty.

BILL [*as TOMMY glances at titles in book case*]. Who was Monroe Trotter?[7]

TOMMY. Was he white?

BILL. No, soul brother. Spent his years tryin' to make it all right. Who was Harriet Tubman?[8]

TOMMY. I heard-a her. But don't put me through no test, Billy. [*Moving around studying pictures and books.*] This room is full-a things I don' know nothin' about. How'll I get to know?

BILL. Read, go to the library, book stores, ask somebody.

TOMMY. Okay, I'm askin'. Teach me things.

BILL. Aw, baby, why torment yourself? Trouble with our women, . . . they all wanta be great brains. Leave somethin' for a man to do.

TOMMY [*eager to impress him*]. What you think-a Martin Luther King?

BILL. A great guy. But it's too late in the day for the singin' and prayin' now.

TOMMY. What about Malcolm X?[9]

BILL. Great cat . . . but there again . . . Where's the program?

TOMMY. What about Adam Powell?[10] I voted for him. That's one thing bout me. I vote. Maybe if everybody vote for the right people . . .

BILL. The ballot box. It would take me all my life to straighten you on that hype.

TOMMY. I got the time.

BILL. You gonna wind up with a king size headache. The Matriarchy gotta go. Yall throw them suppers together, keep your husband happy, raise the kids.

TOMMY. I don't have a husband. Course, that could be fixed. [*Leaving the unspoken proposal hanging in the air.*]

BILL. You know the greatest thing you could do for your people? Sit up there and let me put you down on canvas.

TOMMY. Bein' married and havin' a family might be good for your people as a race, but I was thinkin' bout myself a little.

BILL. Forget yourself sometime, sugar. On that canvas you'll be givin' and givin' and givin' . . . That's where you can do you thing best. What you stallin' for?

TOMMY [*returns to table and sits in chair*]. I . . . I don't want to pose in this outfit.

BILL [*patience is wearing thin*]. Why, baby, why?

TOMMY. I don't feel proud-a myself in this.

BILL. Art, baby, we are talkin' art. Whatcha want . . . Ribbons? Lace? False eyelashes?

TOMMY. No, just my white dress with the orlon sweater, . . . or anything but this what I'm wearin'. You oughta see me in that dress with my pink linen shoes. Oh, hell, the shoes are gone. I forgot 'bout the fire . . .

BILL. Oh, stop fightin' me! Another thing . . . our women don't know a damn thing bout bein' feminine. *Give in* sometime. It won't kill you. You tellin' me how to

---

[7] [William] Monroe Trotter (1872–1934) was the founder and editor of the Boston *Guardian* (1902–1934) and a militant civil rights activist in the first two decades of the twentieth century.

[8] Harriet Tubman (1820–1913) escaped from slavery herself and then helped 300 others to escape through the Underground Railroad.

[9] Malcolm X, born Malcolm Little (1925–1965), was a militant Black Muslim leader before his assassination in 1965.

[10] Adam Clayton Powell, Jr. (1908–1972) represented the residents of Harlem in the U.S. Congress for over twenty years in the period from 1945–1969.

paint? Maybe you oughta hang out your shingle and give art lessons! You too damn opinionated. You gonna pose or you not gonna pose? Say somethin'!

TOMMY. You makin' me nervous! Hollerin' at me. My mama never holler at me. Hollerin'.

BILL. But I'll soon be too tired to pick up the brush, baby.

TOMMY [*eye catches picture of white woman on the wall*]. That's a white woman! Bet you never hollered at her and I bet she's your girlfriend . . . too, and when she posed for her pitcher I bet yall was laughin' . . . and you didn't buy her no frankfooter!

BILL [*feels a bit smug about his male prowess*]. Awww, come on, cut that out, baby. That's a little blonde, blue-eyed chick who used to pose for me. That aint' where it's at. This is a new day, the deal is goin' down different. This is the black moment, doll. Black, black, black is bee-yoo-tee-full. Got it? *Black is beautiful.*

TOMMY. Then how come it is that I don't *feel* beautiful when you *talk* to me?!!

BILL. That's your hang-up, not mine. You supposed to stretch forth your wings like Ethiopia, shake off them chains that been holdin' you down. Langston Hughes[11] said let 'em see how beautiful you are. But you determined not to ever be beautiful. Okay, that's what makes you Tommy.

TOMMY. Do you have a girl friend? And who is she?

BILL [*now enjoying himself to the utmost*]. Naw, naw, naw, doll. I *know* people, but none-a this "tie-you-up-and-I-own-you" jive. I ain't mistreatin' nobody and there's enough-a me to go around. That's another thing with our women, . . . they wanta *latch* on. Learn to play it by ear, roll with the punches, cut down on some-a this "got-you-to-the-grave" kinda relationship. Was today all right? Good, be glad, . . . take what's at hand because tomorrow never comes, it's always today. [*She begins to cry.*] Awwww, I didn't mean it that way . . . I forgot your name. [*He brushes her tears away.*] You act like I belong to you. You're jealous of a picture?

TOMMY. That's how women are, always studyin' each other and wonderin' how they look up 'gainst the next person.

BILL [*a bit smug*]. That's human nature. Whatcha call healthy competition.

TOMMY. You think she's pretty?

BILL. She was, perhaps still is. Long, silky hair. She could sit on her hair.

TOMMY [*with bitter arrogance*]. Doesn't *everybody?*

BILL. You got a head like a rock and gonna have the last word if it kills you. Baby, I bet you could knock out Mohamud Ali in the first round, then rare back and scream like Tarzan . . . "Now, I am the greatest!" [*He is very close to her and is amazed to feel a great sense of physical attraction.*] What we arguin' bout? [*Looks her over as she looks away. He suddenly wants to put the conversation on a more intimate level. His eye is on the bed.*] Maybe tomorrow would be a better time for paintin'. Wanna freshen up, take a bath, baby? Water's nice n' hot.

TOMMY [*knows the sound and turns to check on the look; notices him watching the bed; starts weeping*]. No, I don't! Nigger!

BILL. Was that nice? What the hell, let's paint the picture. Or are you gonna hold that back too?

TOMMY. I'm posin'. Shall I take off the wig?

BILL. No, it's a part of your image, ain't it? You must have a reason for wearin' it. [TOMMY *snatches up her orange drink and sits in the model's chair.*]

---

[11] Langston Hughes (1902–1967) was one of the most important poets of the twentieth century and a leading member of the Harlem Renaissance, a period of great creativity by black writers during the 1920s and 1930s.

TOMMY [*with defiance*]. Yes, I wear it cause you and those like you go for long, silky hair, and this is the only way I can have some without burnin' my mother-grabbin' brains out. Got it? [*She accidentally knocks over container of orange drink into her lap.*] Hell, I can't wear this. I'm soaked through. I'm not gonna catch no double pneumonia sittin' up here wringin' wet while you paint and holler at me.

BILL. Bitch!

TOMMY. You must be talkin' bout your mama!

BILL. Shut up! Aw, shut-up! [*Phone rings. He finds an African throw-cloth and hands it to her.*] Put this on. Relax, don't go way mad, and all the rest-a that jazz. Change, will you? I apologize. I'm sorry. [*He picks up phone.*] Hello, survivor of a riot speaking. Who's calling? [TOMMY *retires behind the screen with the throw. During the conversation she undresses and wraps the throw around her. We see* TOMMY *and* BILL *but they can't see each other.*] Sure, told you not to worry. I'll be ready for the exhibit. If you don't dig it, don't show it. Not time for you to see it yet. Yeah, yeah, next week. You just make sure your exhibition room is big enough to hold the crowds that's gonna congregate to see this fine chick I got here. [*This perks* TOMMY's *ears up.*] You oughta see her. The finest black woman in the world . . . No, . . . the finest *any* woman in the world . . . This gorgeous satin chick is . . . is . . . black velvet moonlight . . . an ebony queen of the universe . . . [TOMMY *can hardly believe her ears.*] One look at her and you go back to Spice Islands . . . She's Mother Africa . . . You flip, double flip. She has come through everything that has been put on her . . . [*He unveils the gorgeous woman he has painted . . . "Wine In The Wilderness."* TOMMY *believes he is talking about her.*] Regal . . . grand . . . magnificent, fantastic . . . You would vote her the woman you'd most like to meet on a desert island, or around the corner from anywhere. She's here with me now . . . and I don't know if I want to show her to you or anybody else . . . I'm beginnin' to have this deep attachment . . . She sparkles, man, Harriet Tubman, Queen of the Nile . . . sweetheart, wife, mother, sister, friend . . . The night . . . a black diamond . . . A dark, beautiful dream . . . A cloud with a silvery lining . . . Her wrath is a storm over the Bahamas. "Wine In The Wilderness" . . . The memory of Africa . . . The *now* of things . . . but best of all and most important . . . She's tomorrow . . . she's my tomorrow . . . [TOMMY *is dressed in the African wrap. She is suddenly awakened to the feeling of being loved and admired. She removes the wig and fluffs her hair. Her hair under the wig must not be an accurate, well-cut Afro . . . but should be rather attractive natural hair. She studies herself in a mirror. We see her taller, more relaxed and sure of herself. Perhaps braided hair will go well with Afro robe.*] Aw, man, later. You don't believe in nothin'! [*He covers "Wine In The Wilderness." Is now in a glowing mood.*] Baby, whenever you ready. [*She emerges from behind the screen. Dressed in the wrap, sans wig. He is astounded.*] Baby, what . . . ? Where . . . where's the wig?

TOMMY. I don't think I want to wear it, Bill.

BILL. That is very becoming . . . the drape thing.

TOMMY. Thank you.

BILL. I don't know what to say.

TOMMY. It's time to paint. [*Steps up on the model stand and sits in the chair. She is now a queen, relaxed and smiling her appreciation for his past speech to the art dealer. Her feet are bare.*]

BILL [*mystified by the change in her; tries to do a charcoal sketch*]. It is quite late.

TOMMY. Makes me no difference if it's all right with you.

BILL [*wants to create the other image*]. Could you put the wig back on?

TOMMY. You don't really like wigs, do you?

BILL. Well, no.

TOMMY. Then let's have things the way you like.

BILL [*has no answer for this. He makes a haphazard line or two as he tries to remember the other image*]. Tell me something about yourself, . . . anything.

TOMMY [*now on sure ground*]. I was born in Baltimore, Maryland and raised here in Harlem. My favorite flower is "Four O'clocks," that's a bush flower. My wearin' flower, corsage flower, is pink roses. My mama raised me, mostly by herself, God rest the dead. Mama belonged to "The Eastern Star." Her father was a "Mason." If a man in the family is a "Mason" any woman related to him can be an "Eastern Star." My grandfather was a member of "The Prince Hall Lodge." I had a uncle who was an "Elk," . . . a member of "The Improved Benevolent Protective Order of Elks of the World": "The Henry Lincoln Johnson Lodge." You know, the white "Elks" are called "The Benevolent Protective Order of Elks" but the black "Elks" are called "The *Improved* Benevolent Protective Order of Elks of the World." That's because the black "Elks" got the copyright first but the white "Elks" took us to court about it to keep us from usin' the name. Over fifteen hundred black folk went to jail for wearin' the "Elk" emblem on their coat lapel. Years ago, . . . that's what you call history.

BILL. I didn't know about that.

TOMMY. Oh, it's understandable. Only way I heard bout John Brown was because the black "Elks" bought his farmhouse where he trained his men to attack the government.

BILL. The black "Elks" bought the John Brown Farm? What did they do with it?

TOMMY. They built a outdoor theatre and put a perpetual light in his memory, . . . and they buildin' cottages there, one named for each state in the union and . . .

BILL. How do you know about it?

TOMMY. Well, our "Elks" helped my cousin go through school with a scholarship. She won a speaking contest and wrote a composition titled "Onward and Upward, O, My Race." That's how she won the scholarship. Coreen knows all that Elk history.

BILL [*seeing her with new eyes*]. Tell me some more about you, Tomorrow Marie. I bet you go to church.

TOMMY. Not much as I used to. Early in life I pledged myself in the A.M.E. Zion Church.

BILL [*studying her face, seeing her for the first time*]. A.M.E.

TOMMY. A.M.E. That's African Methodist Episcopal. We split off from the white Methodist Episcopal and started our own in the year Seventeen hundred and ninety six. We built our first buildin' in the year 1800. How bout that?

BILL. That right?

TOMMY. Oh, I'm just showin' off. I taught Sunday School for two years and you had to know the history of A.M.E. Zion . . . or else you couldn't teach. My great, great grandparents was slaves.

BILL. Guess everybody's was.

TOMMY. Mine was slaves in a place called Sweetwater Springs, Virginia. We tried to look it up one time but somebody at Church told us that Sweetwater Springs had become a part of Norfolk . . . so we didn't carry it any further . . . As it would be a expense to have a lawyer trace your people.

BILL [*throws charcoal pencil across room*]. No good! It won't work! I can't work anymore.

TOMMY. Take a rest. Tell me about you.

BILL [*sits on bed*]. Everybody in my family worked for the Post Office. They bought a home in Jamaica, Long Island. Everybody on that block bought an aluminum screen door with a duck on it, . . . or was it a swan? I guess that makes my favorite flower crab grass and hedges. I have a lot of bad dreams. [TOMMY *massages his temples and the back of his neck.*] A dream like suffocating, dying of suffocation. The worst kinda dream. People are standing in a weird looking art gallery, they're looking and laughing at everything I've ever done. My work begins to fade off the canvas, right before my eyes. Everything I've ever done is laughed away.

TOMMY. Don't be so hard on yourself. If I was smart as you I'd wake up singin' every mornin'. [*There is the sound of thunder. He kisses her.*] When it thunders that's the angels in heaven playin' with their hoops, rollin' their hoops and bicycle wheels in the rain. My Mama told me that.

BILL. I'm glad you're here. Black is beautiful, you're beautiful, A.M.E. Zion, Elks, pink roses, bush flower, . . . blooming out of the slavery of Sweetwater Springs, Virginia.

TOMMY. I'm gonna take a bath and let the riot and the hell of living go down the drain with the bath water.

BILL. Tommy, Tommy, Tomorrow Marie, let's save each other, let's be kind and good to each other while it rains and the angels roll those hoops and bicycle wheels. [*They embrace. The sound of rain.*]

[*Music in as lights come down. As lights fade down to darkness, music comes in louder. There is a flash of lightning. We see* TOMMY *and* BILL *in each other's arms. It is very dark. Music up louder, then softer and down to very soft. Music is mixed with the sound of rain beating against the window. Music slowly fades as gray light of dawn shows at window. Lights go up gradually. The bed is rumpled and empty.* BILL *is in the bathroom.* TOMMY *is at the stove turning off the coffee pot. She sets table with cups and saucers, spoons.* TOMMY*'s hair is natural, she wears another throw draped around her. She sings and hums a snatch of a joyous spiritual.*]

TOMMY. "Great day, Great day, the world's on fire, Great day . . . " [*Calling out to* BILL *who is in bath.*] Honey, I found the coffee, and it's ready. Nothin' here to go with it but a cucumber and a Uneeda biscuit.

BILL [*offstage; joyous yell from offstage*]. Tomorrow and tomorrow and tomorrow! Good mornin', Tomorrow!

TOMMY [*more to herself than to* BILL]. "Tomorrow and tomorrow." That's Shakespeare. [*Calls to* BILL.] You say that was Shakespeare?

BILL [*offstage*]. Right, baby, right!

TOMMY. I bet Shakespeare was black! You know how we love poetry. That's what give him away. I bet he was passin'. [*Laughs.*]

BILL [*offstage*]. Just you wait, one hundred years from now all the honkys gonna claim our poets just like they stole our blues. They gonna try to steal Paul Lawrence Dunbar and LeRoi and Margaret Walker.[12]

TOMMY [*to herself*]. God moves in a mysterious way, even in the middle of a riot. [*A knock on the door.*] Great day, great day the world's on fire . . . [*Opens the door.* OLDTIMER *enters. He is soaking wet. He does not recognize her right away.*]

OLDTIMER. 'Scuse me, I must be in the wrong place.

TOMMY [*patting her hair*]. This is me. Come on in, Edmond Lorenzo Matthews. I took off my hair-piece. This is me.

---

[12] Paul Lawrence Dunbar (1872–1906), LeRoi Jones (Imamu Amiri Baraka, 1934–), and Margaret Walker (1915–) are prominent black poets.

OLDTIMER [*very distracted and worried*]. Well, howdy-do and good mornin'. [*He has had a hard night of drinking and sleeplessness.*] Where Bill-boy? It pourin' down some rain out there. [*Makes his way to the window.*]

TOMMY. What's the matter?

OLDTIMER [*raises the window and starts pulling in the cord, the cord is weightless and he realizes there is nothing on the end of it*]. No, no, it can't be. Where is it? It's gone! [*Looks out the window.*]

TOMMY. You gonna catch your death. You wringin' wet.

OLDTIMER. Yall take my things in? It was a bag-a loot. A suit and some odds and ends. It was my loot. Yall took it in?

TOMMY. No. [*Realizes his desperation. She calls to* BILL *through the closed bathroom door.*] Did you take in any loot that was outside the window?

BILL [*offstage*]. No.

TOMMY. He said "no."

OLDTIMER [*yells out window*]. Thieves, . . . dirty thieves . . . lotta good it'll do you . . .

TOMMY [*leads him to a chair, dries his head with a towel*]. Get outta the wet things. You smell just like a whiskey still. Why don't you take care of yourself. [*Dries off his hands.*]

OLDTIMER. Drinkin' with the boys. Likker was everywhere all night long.

TOMMY. You got to be better than this.

OLDTIMER. Everything I ever put my hand and mind to do, it turn out wrong, . . . Nothin' but mistakes . . . When you don' know, you don' know. I don't know nothin'. I'm ignorant.

TOMMY. Hush that talk . . . You know lotsa things, everybody does. [*Helps him remove wet coat.*]

OLDTIMER. Thanks. How's the trip-tick?

TOMMY. The what?

OLDTIMER. *Trip-tick*. That's a paintin'.

TOMMY. See there, you know more about art than I do. What's a trip-tick? Have some coffee and explain me a trip-tick.

OLDTIMER [*proud of his knowledge*]. Well, I tell you, . . . a trip-tick is a paintin' that's in three parts . . . but they all belong together to be looked at all at once. Now . . . this is the first one . . . a little innocent girl . . . [*Unveils picture.*]

TOMMY. She's sweet.

OLDTIMER. And this is "Wine In The Wilderness" . . . The Queen of the Universe . . . the finest chick in the world.

TOMMY [*Tommy is thoughtful as he unveils the second picture*]. That's not me.

OLDTIMER. No, you gonna be this here last one. The worst gal in town. A messed-up chick that—that—[*He unveils the third canvas and is face to face with the almost blank canvas, then realizes what he has said. He turns to see the stricken look on* TOMMY'S *face.*]

TOMMY. The messed-up chick, *that's* why they brought me here, ain't it? That's why he wanted to paint me! Say it!

OLDTIMER. No, I'm lyin'. I didn't mean it. It's the society that messed her up. Awwwwww, Tommy, don't look that-a-way. It's art, . . . it's only art . . . He couldn't mean you . . . it's art . . . [*The door opens.* CYNTHIA *and* SONNY-MAN *enter.*]

SONNY-MAN. Any body want a ride down . . . down . . . down . . . downtown? What's wrong? Excuse me . . . [*Starts back out.*]

TOMMY [*blocking the exit to* CYNTHIA *and* SONNY-MAN]. No, come on in. Stay with it . . . "Brother" . . . "Sister." Tell 'em what a trip-tick is, Oldtimer.

CYNTHIA [*very ashamed*]. Oh, no.

TOMMY. You don't have to tell 'em. They already know. The messed-up chick! How come you didn't pose for that, my sister? The messed-up chick lost her home last night, ... burnt out with no place to go. You and Sonny-man gave me comfort, you cheered me up and took me in ... *took me in!*

CYNTHIA. Tommy, we didn't know you, we didn't mean ...

TOMMY. It's all right! I was lost but now I'm found! Yeah, the blind can see! [*She dashes behind the screen and puts on her clothing, sweater, skirt etc.*]

OLDTIMER [*goes to bathroom door*]. Billy, come out!

SONNY-MAN. Billy, step out here, please! [BILL *enters shirtless, wearing dungarees.*] Oldtimer let it out 'bout the triptych.

BILL. The rest of you move on.

TOMMY [*looking out from behind screen*]. No, don't go a step. You brought me here, see me out!

BILL. Tommy, let me explain it to you.

TOMMY [*coming out from behind screen*]. I gotta check out my apartment and my clothes and money. Cynthia, ... I can't wait for anybody to open the door or look out for me and all that kinda crap you talk. A bunch-a liars!

BILL. Oldtimer, why you ...

TOMMY. Leave him the hell alone. He ain't said nothin' that ain't so!

SONNY-MAN. Explain to the sister that some mistakes have been made.

BILL. Mistakes have been made, baby. The mistakes were yesterday, this is today ...

TOMMY. Yeah, and I'm Tomorrow, remember? Trouble is I was Tommin' to you, to all of you, ... "Oh, maybe they gon' like me." ... I was your fool, thinkin' writers and painters know moren' me, that maybe a little bit of you would rub off on me.

CYNTHIA. We are wrong. I knew it yesterday. Tommy, I told you not to expect anything out of this ... this arrangement.

BILL. This is a relationship, not an arrangement.

SONNY-MAN. Cynthia, I tell you all the time, keep outta other people's business. What the hell you got to do with who's gonna get what outta what? You and Oldtimer, yakkin' and yakkin'. [*To* OLDTIMER.] Man, your mouth gonna kill you.

BILL. It's me and Tommy. Clear the room.

TOMMY. Better not, I'll kill him! The "black people" this and the "Afro-American" ... that ... You ain't got no use for none-a us. Oldtimer, you their fool too. Till I got here they didn't even know your damn name. There's something inside-a me that says I ain' suppose to let *nobody* play me cheap. Don't care how much they know! [*She sweeps some of the books to the floor.*]

BILL. Don't you have any forgiveness in you? Would I be beggin' you if I didn't care? Can't you be generous enough ...

TOMMY. Nigger, I been too damn generous with you, already. All-a these people know I wasn't down here all night posin' for no pitcher, nigger!

BILL. Cut that out, Tommy, and you not going anywhere!

TOMMY. You wanna bet? Nigger!

BILL. Okay, you called it, baby, I did act like a low, degraded person ...

TOMMY [*combing out her wig with her fingers while holding it*]. Didn't call you no low, degraded person. Nigger! [*To* CYNTHIA *who is handing her a comb.*] "Do you have to wear a wig?" Yes! To soften the blow when yall go upside-a my head with a baseball bat. [*Going back to taunting* BILL *and ignoring* CYNTHIA'S *comb.*] Nigger!

BILL. That's enough-a that. You right and you're wrong too.

TOMMY. Ain't a-one-a us you like that's alive and walkin' by you on the street ... you don't like flesh and blood niggers.

BILL. Call me that, baby, but don't call yourself. That what you think of yourself?

TOMMY. If a black somebody is in a history book, or printed on a pitcher, or drawed on a paintin', . . . or if they're a statue, . . . dead, and outta the way, and can't talk back, then you dig 'em and full-a so much-a damn admiration and talk 'bout "our" history. But when you run into us livin' and breathin' ones, with the life's blood still pumpin' through us, . . . then you comin' on 'bout how we ain' never together. You hate us, that's what! *You hate black me!*

BILL [*stung to the heart, confused and saddened by the half truth which applies to himself*]. I never hated you, I never will, no matter what you or any of the rest of you do to *make* me hate you. I won't! Hell, woman, why do you say that! Why would I hate you??

TOMMY. Maybe I look too much like the mother that gave birth to you. Like the Ma and Pa that worked in the post office to buy you a house and a screen door with a damn duck on it. And you so ungrateful you didn't even like it.

BILL. No, I didn't, baby. I don't like screen doors with ducks on 'em.

TOMMY. You didn't like who was livin' behind them screen doors. Phoney Nigger!

BILL. That's all! Damnit! don't go there no more!

TOMMY. Hit me, so I can tear this place down and scream bloody murder.

BILL [*somewhere between laughter and tears*]. Looka here, baby, I'm willin' to say I'm wrong, even in fronta the room fulla people . . .

TOMMY [*through clenched teeth*]. Nigger.

SONNY-MAN. The sister is upset.

TOMMY. And you stop callin' me "the" sister, . . . if you feelin' so brotherly why don't you say "my" sister? Ain't no we-ness in your talk. "The" Afro-American, "the" black man, there's no we-ness in you. Who you think you are?

SONNY-MAN. I was talkin' in general er . . . *my* sister, 'bout the masses.

TOMMY. There he go again. "The" masses. Tryin' to make out like we pitiful and you got it made. You the masses your damn self and don't even know it. [*Another angry look at* BILL.] Nigger.

BILL [*pulls dictionary from shelf*]. Let's get this ignorant "nigger" talk squared away. You can stand some education.

TOMMY. You *treat* me like a nigger, that's what. I'd rather be called one than treated that way.

BILL [*questions* TOMMY]. What is a nigger? [*Talks as he is trying to find word.*] A nigger is a low, degraded person, *any* low degraded person. I learned that from my teacher in the fifth grade.

TOMMY. Fifth grade is a liar! Don't pull that dictionary crap on me.

BILL [*pointing to the book*]. Webster's New World Dictionary of The American Language, College Edition.

TOMMY. I don't need to find out what no college white folks say nigger is.

BILL. I'm tellin' you it's a low, degraded person. Listen. [*Reads from the book.*] Nigger, N-i-g-g-e-r, . . . A Negro . . . A member of any dark-skinned people . . . Damn. [*Amazed by dictionary description.*]

SONNY-MAN. Brother Malcolm *said* that's what they meant, . . . nigger is a Negro, Negro is a nigger.

BILL [*slowly finishing his reading*]. A vulgar, offensive term of hostility and contempt. Well, so much for the fifth grade teacher.

SONNY-MAN. No, they do not call low, degraded white folks niggers. Come to think of it, did you ever hear whitey call Hitler a nigger? Now if some whitey digs us, . . . the others might call him a nigger-*lover*, but they don't call him no nigger.

OLDTIMER. No, they don't.

TOMMY [*near tears*]. When they say "nigger," just dry-long-so, they mean educated you and uneducated me. They hate you and call you "nigger," I called you "nigger" but I love you. [*There is dead silence in the room for a split second.*]

SONNY-MAN [*trying to establish peace*]. There you go. There you go.

CYNTHIA [*cautioning* SONNY-MAN]. Now is not the time to talk, darlin'.

BILL. You love me? Tommy, that's the greatest compliment you could . . .

TOMMY [*sorry she said it*]. You must be runnin' a fever, nigger, I ain' said nothin' 'bout lovin' you.

BILL [*in a great mood*]. You did, yes, you did.

TOMMY. Well, you didn't say it to *me*.

BILL. Oh, Tommy, . . .

TOMMY [*cuts him off abruptly*]. And don't you dare say it now. I'm tellin' you, . . . it ain't to be said now. [*Checks through her paper bag to see if she has everything. Starts to put on the wig, changes her mind, holds it to end of scene. Turns to the others in the room.*] Oldtimer, . . . my brothers and my sister.

OLDTIMER. I wish I was a thousand miles away. I'm so sorry. [*He sits at the foot of the model stand.*]

TOMMY. I don't stay mad, it's here today and gone tomorrow. I'm sorry your feelin's got hurt, . . . but when I'm hurt I turn and hurt back. Somewhere, in the middle of last night, I thought the old me was gone, . . . lost forever, and gladly. But today was flippin' time, so back I flipped. Now it's "turn the other cheek" time. If I can go through life other-cheekin' the white folk, . . . guess yall can be other-cheeked too. But I'm goin' back to the nitty-gritty crowd, where the talk is we-ness and us-ness. I hate to do it but I have to thank you cause I'm walkin' out with much more than I brought in. [*Goes over and looks at the queen in the "Wine In The Wilderness" painting.*] Tomorrow-Marie had such a lovely yesterday. [BILL *takes her hand, she gently removes it from his grasp.*] Bill, I don't have to wait for anybody's by-your-leave to be a "Wine In The Wilderness" woman. I can be if I wanta, . . . and I *am*. I am. I am. I'm not the one you made up and painted, the very pretty lady who can't talk back, . . . but I'm "Wine In The Wilderness" . . . alive and kickin', me . . . Tomorrow-Marie, cussin' and fightin' and lookin' out for my damn self cause ain' nobody else 'round to do it, dontcha know. And, Cynthia, if my hair is straight, or if it's natural, or if I wear a wig, or take it off, . . . that's all right; because wigs . . . shoes . . . hats . . . bags . . . and even this . . . [*She picks up the African throw she wore a few moments before . . . fingers it.*] They're just what you call . . . access . . . [*Fishing for the word.*] . . . like what you wear with your Easter outfit . . .

CYNTHIA. Accessories.

TOMMY. Thank you, my sister. Accessories. Somethin' you add on or take off. The real thing is takin' place on the inside . . . that's where the action is. That's "Wine In The Wilderness," . . . a woman that's a real one and a good one. And yall just better believe I'm it. [*She proceeds to the door.*]

BILL. Tommy. [*She turns. He takes the beautiful queen, "Wine In The Wilderness" from the easel.*] She's not it at all, Tommy. This chick on the canvas, . . . nothin' but accessories, a dream. I drummed up outta the junk room of my mind. [*Places the "queen" to one side.*] *You* are and . . . [*Points to* OLDTIMER] . . . Edmond Lorenzo Matthews . . . the real beautiful people, . . . Cynthia . . .

CYNTHIA [*bewildered and unbelieving*]. Who? Me?

BILL. Yeah, honey, you and Sonny-man, don't know how beautiful you are. [*Indicates the other side of model stand.*] Sit there.

SONNY-MAN [*places cushions on the floor at the foot of the model stand*]. Just sit here and be my beautiful self. [*To* CYNTHIA]. Turn on, baby, we gonna get our picture took. [CYNTHIA *smiles.*]

BILL. Now there's Oldtimer, the guy who was here before there were scholarships and grants and stuff like that, the guy they kept outta the schools, the man the factories wouldn't hire, the union wouldn't let him join . . .

SONNY-MAN. Yeah, yeah, rap to me. Where you goin' with it, man? Rap on.

BILL. I'm makin' a triptych.

SONNY-MAN. Make it, man.

BILL. [*indicating* CYNTHIA *and* SONNY-MAN]. On the other side, Young Man and Woman, workin' together to do our thing.

TOMMY [*quietly*]. I'm goin' now.

BILL. But you belong up there in the center, "Wine In The Wilderness" . . . that's who you are. [*Moves the canvas of "the little girl" and places a sketch pad on the easel.*] The nightmare, about all that I've done disappearing before my eyes. It was a good nightmare. I was painting in the dark, all head and no heart. I couldn't see until you came, baby. [*To* CYNTHIA, SONNY-MAN *and* OLDTIMER.] Look at Tomorrow. She came through the biggest riot of all, . . . somethin' called "Slavery," and she's even comin' through the "now" scene, . . . folks laughin' at her, even her own folks laughin' at her. And look *how* . . . with her head high like she's poppin' her fingers at the world. [*Takes up charcoal pencil and tears old page off sketch pad so he can make a fresh drawing.*] Aw, let me put it down, Tommy. "Wine In The Wilderness," you gotta let me put it down so all the little boys and girls can look up and see you on the wall. And you know what they're gonna say? "Hey, don't she look like somebody we know?" [TOMMY *slowly returns and takes her seat on the stand.* TOMMY *is holding the wig in her lap. Her hands are very graceful looking against the texture of the wig.*] And they'll be right, you're somebody they know . . . [*He is sketching hastily. There is a sound of thunder and the patter of rain.*] Yeah, roll them hoops and bicycle wheels. [*Music in low. Music up higher as* BILL *continues to sketch.*]

CURTAIN

[1969]

Sam Shepard   *1943–*

TRUE WEST

CHARACTERS

AUSTIN, *early thirties, light blue sports shirt, light tan cardigan sweater, clean blue jeans, white tennis shoes*

LEE, *his older brother, early forties, filthy white t-shirt, tattered brown overcoat covered with dust, dark blue baggy suit pants from the Salvation Army, pink suede belt, pointed black forties dress shoes scuffed up, holes in the soles, no socks, no hat, long pronounced sideburns, "Gene Vincent" hairdo, two days' growth of beard, bad teeth*

SAUL KIMMER, *late forties, Hollywood producer, pink and white flower print sports shirt, white sports coat with matching polyester slacks, black and white loafers*

MOM, *early sixties, mother of the brothers, small woman, conservative white skirt and matching jacket, red shoulder bag, two pieces of matching red luggage*

SCENE: *All nine scenes take place on the same set; a kitchen and adjoining alcove of an older home in a Southern California suburb, about 40 miles east of Los Angeles. The kitchen takes up most of the playing area to stage left. The kitchen consists of a sink, upstage center, surrounded by counter space, a wall telephone, cupboards, and a small window just above it bordered by neat yellow curtains. Stage left of sink is a stove. Stage right, a refrigerator. The alcove adjoins the kitchen to stage right. There is no wall division or door to the alcove. It is open and easily accessible from the kitchen and defined only by the objects in it: a small round glass breakfast table mounted on white iron legs, two matching white iron chairs set across from each other. The two exterior walls of the alcove which prescribe a corner in the upstage right are composed of many small windows, beginning from a solid wall about three feet high and extending to the ceiling. The windows look out to bushes and citrus trees. The alcove is filled with all sorts of house plants in various pots, mostly Boston ferns hanging in planters at different levels. The floor of the alcove is composed of green synthetic grass.*

All entrances and exits are made stage left from the kitchen. There is no door. The actors simply go off and come onto the playing area.

NOTE ON SET AND COSTUME: *The set should be constructed realistically with no attempt to distort its dimensions, shapes, objects, or colors. No objects should be introduced which might draw special attention to themselves other than the props demanded by the script. If a stylistic "concept" is grafted onto the set design it will only serve to confuse the evolution of the characters' situation, which is the most important focus of the play.*

Likewise, the costumes should be exactly representative of who the characters are and not added onto for the sake of making a point to the audience.

NOTE ON SOUND: *The Coyote of Southern California has a distinct yapping, dog-like bark, similar to a Hyena. This yapping grows more intense and maniacal as the pack grows in numbers, which is usually the case when they lure and kill pets from suburban yards. The sense of growing frenzy in the pack should be felt in the background, particularly in Scenes*

*VII and VIII. In any case, these Coyotes never make the long, mournful, solitary howl of the
Hollywood stereotype.*

The sound of Crickets can speak for itself.

*These sounds should also be treated realistically even though they sometimes grow in
volume and numbers.*

ACT I

SCENE I

Night. Sound of crickets in dark. Candlelight appears in alcove, illuminating AUSTIN, *seated
at glass table hunched over a writing notebook, pen in hand, cigarette burning in ashtray,
cup of coffee, typewriter on table, stacks of paper, candle burning on table.*

Soft moonlight fills kitchen illuminating LEE, *beer in hand, six-pack on counter behind
him. He's leaning against the sink, mildly drunk; takes a slug of beer.*

LEE. So, Mom took off for Alaska, huh?

AUSTIN. Yeah.

LEE. Sorta' left you in charge.

AUSTIN. Well, she knew I was coming down here so she offered me the place.

LEE. You keepin' the plants watered?

AUSTIN. Yeah.

LEE. Keepin' the sink clean? She don't like even a single tea leaf in the sink ya'
know.

AUSTIN [*trying to concentrate on writing*]. Yeah, I know.
     [*Pause.*]

LEE. She gonna' be up there a long time?

AUSTIN. I don't know.

LEE. Kinda' nice for you, huh? Whole place to yourself.

AUSTIN. Yeah, it's great.

LEE. Ya' got crickets anyway. Tons a' crickets out there. [*looks around kitchen.*] Ya'
got groceries? Coffee?

AUSTIN [*looking up from writing*]. What?

LEE. You got coffee?

AUSTIN. Yeah.

LEE. At's good. [*short pause.*] Real coffee? From the bean?

AUSTIN. Yeah. You want some?

LEE. Naw. I brought some uh— [*motions to beer.*]

AUSTIN. Help yourself to whatever's— [*motions to refrigerator.*]

LEE. I will. Don't worry about me. I'm not the one to worry about. I mean I can
uh— [*pause.*] You always work by candlelight?

AUSTIN. No—uh—Not always.

LEE. Just sometimes?

AUSTIN [*puts pen down, rubs his eyes*]. Yeah. Sometimes it's soothing.

LEE. Isn't that what the old guys did?

AUSTIN. What old guys?

LEE. The Forefathers. You know.

AUSTIN. Forefathers?

LEE. Isn't that what they did? Candlelight burning into the night? Cabins in the
wilderness.

AUSTIN [*rubs hand through his hair*]. I suppose.

LEE. I'm not botherin' you am I? I mean I don't wanna break into yer uh—concentration or nothin'.

AUSTIN. No, it's all right.

LEE. That's good. I mean I realize that yer line a' work demands a lota' concentration.

AUSTIN. It's okay.

LEE. You probably think that I'm not fully able to comprehend somethin' like that, huh?

AUSTIN. Like what?

LEE. That stuff yer doin'. That art. You know. Whatever you call it.

AUSTIN. It's just a little research.

LEE. You may not know it but I did a little art myself once.

AUSTIN. You did?

LEE. Yeah! I did some a' that. I fooled around with it. No future in it.

AUSTIN. What'd you do?

LEE. Never mind what I did! Just never mind about that. [*pause.*] It was ahead of its time.
   [*pause.*]

AUSTIN. So, you went out to see the old man, huh?

LEE. Yeah, I seen him.

AUSTIN. How's he doing?

LEE. Same. He's doin' just about the same.

AUSTIN. I was down there too, you know.

LEE. What d'ya' want, an award? You want some kinda' medal? You were down there. He told me all about you.

AUSTIN. What'd he say?

LEE. He told me. Don't worry.
   [*pause.*]

AUSTIN. Well—

LEE. You don't have to say nothin'.

AUSTIN. I wasn't.

LEE. Yeah, you were gonna' make somethin' up. Somethin' brilliant.
   [*pause.*]

AUSTIN. You going to be down here very long, Lee?

LEE. Might be. Depends on a few things.

AUSTIN. You got some friends down here?

LEE [*laughs*]. I know a few people. Yeah.

AUSTIN. Well, you can stay here as long as I'm here.

LEE. I don't need your permission do I?

AUSTIN. No.

LEE. I mean she's my mother too, right?

AUSTIN. Right.

LEE. She might've just as easily asked me to take care of her place as you.

AUSTIN. That's right.

LEE. I mean I know how to water plants.
   [*long pause.*]

AUSTIN. So you don't know how long you'll be staying then?

LEE. Depends mostly on houses, ya' know.

AUSTIN. Houses?

LEE. Yeah. Houses. Electric devices. Stuff like that. I gotta' make a little tour first.

[*short pause.*]

AUSTIN. Lee, why don't you just try another neighborhood, all right?

LEE [*laughs*]. What'sa' matter with this neighborhood? This is a great neighborhood. Lush. Good class a' people. Not many dogs.

AUSTIN. Well, our uh—Our mother just happens to live here. That's all.

LEE. Nobody's gonna' know. All they know is somethin's missing. That's all. She'll never even hear about it. Nobody's gonna' know.

AUSTIN. You're going to get picked up if you start walking around here at night.

LEE. Me? I'm gonna' git picked up? What about you? You stick out like a sore thumb. Look at you. You think yer regular lookin'?

AUSTIN. I've got too much to deal with here to be worrying about—

LEE. Yer not gonna' have to worry about me! I've been doin' all right without you. I haven't been anywhere near you for five years! Now isn't that true?

AUSTIN. Yeah.

LEE. So you don't have to worry about me. I'm a free agent.

AUSTIN. All right.

LEE. Now all I wanna' do is borrow yer car.

AUSTIN. No!

LEE. Just fer a day. One day.

AUSTIN. No!

LEE. I won't take it outside a twenty mile radius. I promise ya'. You can check the speedometer.

AUSTIN. You're not borrowing my car! That's all there is to it.

[*pause.*]

LEE. Then I'll just take the damn thing.

AUSTIN. Lee, look—I don't want any trouble, all right?

LEE. That's a dumb line. That is a dumb fuckin' line. You git paid fer dreamin' up a line like that?

AUSTIN. Look, I can give you some money if you need money.

[LEE *suddenly lunges at* AUSTIN, *grabs him violently by the shirt and shakes him with tremendous power.*]

LEE. Don't you say that to me! Don't you ever say that to me! [*just as suddenly he turns him loose, pushes him away and backs off.*] You may be able to git away with that with the Old Man. Git him tanked up for a week! Buy him off with yer Hollywood blood money, but not me! I can git my own money my own way. Big money!

AUSTIN. I was just making an offer.

LEE. Yeah, well keep it to yourself! [*long pause*]. Those are the most monotonous fuckin' crickets I ever heard in my life.

AUSTIN. I kinda' like the sound.

LEE. Yeah. Supposed to be able to tell the temperature by the number a' pulses. You believe that?

AUSTIN. The temperature?

LEE. Yeah. The air. How hot it is.

AUSTIN. How do you do that?

LEE. I don't know. Some woman told me that. She was a Botanist. So I believed her.

AUSTIN. Where'd you meet her?

LEE. What?

AUSTIN. The woman Botanist?

LEE. I met her on the desert. I been spendin' a lota' time on the desert.

AUSTIN. What were you doing out there?

LEE [*pause, stares in space*]. I forgit. Had me a Pit Bull there for a while but I lost him.

AUSTIN. Pit Bull?

LEE. Fightin' dog. Damn I made some good money off that little dog. Real good money.

[*pause.*]

AUSTIN. You could come up north with me, you know.

LEE. What's up there?

AUSTIN. My family.

LEE. Oh, that's right, you got the wife and kiddies now don't ya'. The house, the car, the whole slam. That's right.

AUSTIN. You could spend a couple days. See how you like it. I've got an extra room.

LEE. Too cold up there.

[*pause.*]

AUSTIN. You want to sleep for a while?

LEE [*pause, stares at* AUSTIN]. I don't sleep.

[*lights to black.*]

SCENE II

Morning. AUSTIN *is watering plants with a vaporizer,* LEE *sits at glass table in alcove drinking beer.*

LEE. I never realized the old lady was so security-minded.

AUSTIN. How do you mean?

LEE. Made a little tour this morning. She's got locks on everything. Locks and double-locks and chain locks and— What's she got that's so valuable?

AUSTIN. Antiques I guess. I don't know.

LEE. Antiques? Brought everything with her from the old place, huh. Just the same crap we always had around. Plates and spoons.

AUSTIN. I guess they have personal value to her.

LEE. Personal value. Yeah. Just a lota' junk. Most of it's phony anyway. Idaho decals. Now who in the hell wants to eat offa' plate with the State of Idaho starin' ya' in the face. Every time ya' take a bite ya' get to see a little bit more.

AUSTIN. Well it must mean something to her or she wouldn't save it.

LEE. Yeah, well personally I don't wann' be invaded by Idaho when I'm eatin'. When I'm eatin' I'm home. Ya' know what I'm sayin'? I'm not driftin', I'm home. I don't need my thoughts swept off to Idaho. I don't need that!

[*pause.*]

AUSTIN. Did you go out last night?

LEE. Why?

AUSTIN. I thought I heard you go out.

LEE. Yeah, I went out. What about it?

AUSTIN. Just wondered.

LEE. Damn coyotes kept me awake.

AUSTIN. Oh yeah, I heard them. They must've killed somebody's dog or something.

LEE. Yappin' their fools head off. They don't yap like that on the desert. They howl. These are city coyotes here.

AUSTIN. Well, you don't sleep anyway do you?

[*pause,* LEE *stares at him.*]

LEE: You're pretty smart aren't ya?

AUSTIN. How do you mean?

LEE. I mean you never had any more on the ball than I did. But here you are gettin' invited into prominent people's houses. Sittin' around talkin' like you know somethin'.

AUSTIN. They're not so prominent.

LEE. They're a helluva' lot more prominent than the houses I get invited into.

AUSTIN. Well you invite yourself.

LEE. That's right. I do. In fact I probably got a wider range a' choices than you do, come to think of it.

AUSTIN. I wouldn't doubt it.

LEE. In fact I been inside some pretty classy places in my time. And I never even went to an Ivy League school either.

AUSTIN. You want some breakfast or something?

LEE. Breakfast?

AUSTIN. Yeah. Don't you eat breakfast?

LEE. Look, don't worry about me pal. I can take care a' myself. You just go ahead as though I wasn't even here, all right?

[AUSTIN *goes into kitchen, makes coffee.*]

AUSTIN. Where'd you walk to last night?

[*pause.*]

LEE. I went up in the foothills there. Up in the San Gabriels.[1] Heat was drivin' me crazy.

AUSTIN. Well, wasn't it hot out on the desert?

LEE. Different kinda' heat. Out there it's clean. Cools off at night. There's a nice little breeze.

AUSTIN. Where were you, the Mojave?[2]

LEE. Yeah. The Mojave. That's right.

AUSTIN. I haven't been out there in years.

LEE. Out past Needles[3] there.

AUSTIN. Oh yeah.

LEE. Up here it's different. This country's real different.

AUSTIN. Well, it's been built up.

LEE. Built up? Wiped out is more like it. I don't even hardly recognize it.

AUSTIN. Yeah. Foothills are the same though, aren't they?

LEE. Pretty much. It's funny goin' up in there. The smells and everything. Used to catch snakes up there, remember?

AUSTIN. You caught snakes.

LEE. Yeah. And you'd pretend you were Geronimo[4] or some damn thing. You used to go right out to lunch.

AUSTIN. I enjoyed my imagination.

LEE. That what you call it? Looks like yer still enjoyin' it.

AUSTIN. So you just wandered around up there, huh?

LEE. Yeah. With a purpose.

---

[1] The San Gabriel Mountains are located just to the north of greater Los Angeles.

[2] The Mojave Desert, located northeast of Los Angeles, receives about six inches of rain per year with summer temperatures of over 120°F.

[3] Needles is a town east–northeast of Los Angeles on the California–Arizona border.

[4] Geronimo (1829–1909) was a chief of the Apache Indians who led his people in ten years of war against the white settlers in Arizona.

AUSTIN. See any houses?

[*pause.*]

LEE. Couple. Couple a' real nice ones. One of 'em didn't even have a dog. Walked right up and stuck my head in the window. Not a peep. Just a sweet kinda' suburban silence.

AUSTIN. What kind of a place was it?

LEE. Like a paradise. Kinda' place that sorta' kills ya' inside. Warm yellow lights. Mexican tile all around. Copper pots hangin' over the stove. Ya' know like they got in the magazines. Blonde people movin' in and outa' the rooms, talkin' to each other. [*pause.*] Kinda' place you wish you sorta' grew up in, ya' know.

AUSTIN. That's the kind of place you wish you'd grown up in?

LEE. Yeah, why not?

AUSTIN. I thought you hated that kind of stuff.

LEE. Yeah, well you never knew too much about me did ya'?

[*pause.*]

AUSTIN. Why'd you go out to the desert in the first place?

LEE. I was on my way to see the old man.

AUSTIN. You mean you just passed through there?

LEE. Yeah. That's right. Three months of passin' through.

AUSTIN. Three months?

LEE. Somethin' like that. Maybe more. Why?

AUSTIN. You lived on the Mojave for three months?

LEE. Yeah. What'sa' matter with that?

AUSTIN. By yourself?

LEE. Mostly. Had a couple a' visitors. Had that dog for a while.

AUSTIN. Didn't you miss people?

LEE [*laughs*]. People?

AUSTIN. Yeah. I mean I go crazy if I have to spend three nights in a motel by myself.

LEE. Yer not in a motel now.

AUSTIN. No, I know. But sometimes I have to stay in motels.

LEE. Well, they got people in motels don't they?

AUSTIN. Strangers.

LEE. Yer friendly aren't ya'? Aren't you the friendly type?

[*pause.*]

AUSTIN. I'm going to have somebody coming by here later, Lee.

LEE. Ah! Lady friend?

AUSTIN. No, a producer.

LEE. Aha! What's he produce?

AUSTIN. Film. Movies. You know.

LEE. Oh, movies. Motion Pictures! A Big Wig huh?

AUSTIN. Yeah.

LEE. What's he comin' by here for?

AUSTIN. We have to talk about a project.

LEE. Whadya' mean, "a project"? What's "a project"?

AUSTIN. A script.

LEE. Oh. That's what yer doin' with all these papers?

AUSTIN. Yeah.

LEE. Well, what's the project about?

AUSTIN. We're uh—it's a period piece.

LEE. What's "a period piece"?

AUSTIN. Look, it doesn't matter. The main thing is we need to discuss this alone. I mean—

LEE. Oh, I get it. You want me outa' the picture.

AUSTIN. Not exactly. I just need to be alone with him for a couple of hours. So we can talk.

LEE. Yer afraid I'll embarrass ya' huh?

AUSTIN. I'm not afraid you'll embarrass me!

LEE. Well, I tell ya' what—Why don't you just gimme the keys to yer car and I'll be back here around six o'clock or so. That give ya' enough time?

AUSTIN. I'm not loaning you my car, Lee.

LEE. You want me to just git lost huh? Take a hike? Is that it? Pound the pavement for a few hours while you bullshit yer way into a million bucks.

AUSTIN. Look, it's going to be hard enough for me to face this character on my own without—

LEE. You don't know this guy?

AUSTIN. No I don't know— He's a producer. I mean I've been meeting with him for months but you never get to know a producer.

LEE. Yer tryin' to hustle him? Is that it?

AUSTIN. I'm not trying to hustle him! I'm trying to work out a deal! It's not easy.

LEE. What kinda' deal?

AUSTIN. Convince him it's a worthwhile story.

LEE. He's not convinced? How come he's comin' over here if he's not convinced? I'll convince him for ya'.

AUSTIN. You don't understand the way things work down here.

LEE. How do things work down here?

[*pause.*]

AUSTIN. Look, if I loan you my car will you have it back here by six?

LEE. On the button. With a full tank a' gas.

AUSTIN [*digging in his pocket for keys*]. Forget about the gas.

LEE. Hey, these days gas is gold, old buddy. [AUSTIN *hands the keys to* LEE.] You remember that car I used to loan you?

AUSTIN. Yeah.

LEE. Forty Ford. Flathead.

AUSTIN. Yeah.

LEE. Sucker hauled ass didn't it?

AUSTIN. Lee, it's not that I don't want to loan you my car—

LEE. You are loanin' me yer car.

[LEE *gives* AUSTIN *a pat on the shoulder, pause.*]

AUSTIN. I know. I just wish—

LEE. What? You wish what?

AUSTIN. I don't know. I wish I wasn't—I wish I didn't have to be doing business down here. I'd like to just spend some time with you.

LEE. I thought it was "Art" you were doin'.

[LEE *moves across kitchen toward exit, tosses keys in his hand.*]

AUSTIN. Try to get it back here by six, okay?

LEE. No sweat. Hey, ya' know, if that uh—story of yours doesn't go over with the guy—tell him I got a couple a' "projects" he might be interested in. Real commercial. Full a' suspense. True-to-life stuff.

[LEE *exits,* AUSTIN *stares after* LEE *then turns, goes to papers at table, leafs through pages, lights fade to black.*]

SCENE III

Afternoon. Alcove, SAUL KIMMER *and* AUSTIN *seated across from each other at table.*

SAUL. Well, to tell you the truth Austin, I have never felt so confident about a project in quite a long time.

AUSTIN. Well, that's good to hear, Saul.

SAUL. I am absolutely convinced we can get this thing off the ground. I mean we'll have to make a sale to television and that means getting a major star. Somebody bankable. But I think we can do it. I really do.

AUSTIN. Don't you think we need a first draft before we approach a star?

SAUL. No, no, not at all. I don't think it's necessary. Maybe a brief synopsis. I don't want you to touch the typewriter until we have some seed money.

AUSTIN. That's fine with me.

SAUL. I mean it's a great story. Just the story alone. You've really managed to capture something this time.

AUSTIN. I'm glad you like it, Saul.

[LEE *enters abruptly into kitchen carrying a stolen television set, short pause.*]

LEE. Aw shit, I'm sorry about that. I am really sorry Austin.

AUSTIN [*standing*]. That's all right.

LEE [*moving toward them*]. I mean I thought it was way past six already. You said to have it back here by six.

AUSTIN. We were just finishing up. [*To Saul.*] This is my, uh—brother, Lee.

SAUL [*standing*]. Oh, I'm very happy to meet you.

[LEE *sets T.V. on sink counter, shakes hands with* SAUL.]

LEE. I can't tell ya' how happy I am to meet you sir.

SAUL. Saul Kimmer.

LEE. Mr. Kipper.

SAUL. Kimmer.

AUSTIN. Lee's been living out on the desert and he just uh—

SAUL. Oh, that's terrific! [*To* LEE.] Palm Springs?

LEE. Yeah. Yeah, right. Right around in that area. Near uh—Bob Hope Drive there.

SAUL. Oh I love it out there. I just love it. The air is wonderful.

LEE. Yeah. Sure is. Healthy.

SAUL. And the golf. I don't know if you play golf, but the golf is just about the best.

LEE. I play a lota' golf.

SAUL. Is that right?

LEE. Yeah. In fact I was hoping I'd run into somebody out here who played a little golf. I've been lookin' for a partner.

SAUL. Well, I uh—

AUSTIN. Lee's just down for a visit while our mother's in Alaska.

SAUL. Oh, your mother's in Alaska?

AUSTIN. Yes. She went up there on a little vacation. This is her place.

SAUL. I see. Well isn't that something. Alaska.

LEE. What kinda' handicap do ya' have, Mr. Kimmer?

SAUL. Oh I'm just a Sunday duffer really. You know.

LEE. That's good 'cause I haven't swung a club in months.

SAUL. Well we ought to get together sometime and have a little game. Austin, do you play?

[SAUL *mimes a Johnny Carson golf swing for* AUSTIN.]

Austin. No. I don't uh—I've watched it on T.V.

Lee [*to* Saul]. How 'bout tomorrow morning? Bright and early. We could get out there and put in eighteen holes before breakfast.

Saul. Well, I've got uh—I have several appointments—

Lee. No, I mean real early. Crack a'dawn. While the dew's still thick on the fairway.

Saul. Sounds really great.

Lee. Austin could be our caddie.

Saul. Now that's an idea. [*laughs.*]

Austin. I don't know the first thing about golf.

Lee. There's nothing' to it. Isn't that right, Saul? He'd pick it up in fifteen minutes.

Saul. Sure. Doesn't take long. 'Course you have to play for years to find your true form. [*chuckles.*]

Lee [*to* Austin]. We'll give ya' a quick run-down on the club faces. The irons, the woods. Show ya' a couple pointers on the basic swing. Might even let ya' hit the ball a couple times. Whadya' think, Saul?

Saul. Why not. I think it'd be great. I haven't had any exercise in weeks.

Lee. 'At's the spirit! We'll have a little orange juice right afterwards.
  [*pause.*]

Saul. Orange juice?

Lee. Yeah! Vitamin C! Nothin' like a shot a' orange juice after a round a' golf. Hot shower. Snappin' towels at each other's privates. Real sense a' fraternity.

Saul [*smiles at* Austin]. Well, you make it sound very inviting, I must say. It really does sound great.

Lee. Then it's a date.

Saul. Well, I'll call the country club and see if I can arrange something.

Lee. Great! Boy, I sure am sorry that I busted in on ya' all in the middle of yer meeting.

Saul. Oh that's quite all right. We were just about finished anyway.

Lee. I can wait out in the other room if you want.

Saul. No really—

Lee. Just got Austin's color T.V. back from the shop. I can watch a little amateur boxing now.
  [Lee *and* Austin *exchange looks.*]

Saul. Oh—Yes.

Lee. You don't fool around in Television, do you Saul?

Saul. Uh—I have in the past. Produced some T.V. Specials. Network stuff. But it's mainly features now.

Lee. That's where the big money is, huh?

Saul. Yes. That's right.

Austin. Why don't I call you tomorrow, Saul and we'll get together. We can have lunch or something.

Saul. That'd be terrific.

Lee. Right after the golf.
  [*pause.*]

Saul. What?

Lee. You can have lunch right after the golf.

Saul. Oh, right.

Lee. Austin was tellin' me that yer interested in stories.

Saul. Well, we develop certain projects that we feel have commercial potential.

Lee. What kinda' stuff do ya' go in for?

SAUL. Oh, the usual. You know. Good love interest. Lots of action. [*chuckles at* AUSTIN.]

LEE. Westerns?

SAUL. Sometimes.

AUSTIN. I'll give you a ring, Saul.

[AUSTIN *tries to move* SAUL *across the kitchen but* LEE *blocks their way.*]

LEE. I got a Western that'd knock yer lights out.

SAUL. Oh really?

LEE. Yeah. Contemporary Western. Based on a true story. 'Course I'm not a writer like my brother here. I'm not a man of the pen.

SAUL. Well—

LEE. I mean I can tell ya' a story off the tongue but I can't put it down on paper. That don't make any difference though does it?

SAUL. No, not really.

LEE. I mean plenty a' guys have stories don't they? True-life stories. Musta' been a lota' movies made from real life.

SAUL. Yes. I suppose so.

LEE. I haven't seen a good Western since "Lonely Are the Brave." You remember that movie?

SAUL. No, I'm afraid I—

LEE. Kirk Douglas. Helluva' movie. You remember that movie, Austin?

AUSTIN. Yes.

LEE [*to* SAUL]. The man dies for the love of a horse.

SAUL. Is that right.

LEE. Yeah. Ya' hear the horse screamin' at the end of it. Rain's comin' down. Horse is screamin'. Then there's a shot. BLAM! Just a single shot like that. Then nothin' but the sound of rain. And Kirk Douglas is ridin' in the ambulance. Ridin' away from the scene of the accident. And when he hears that shot he knows that his horse has died. He knows. And you see his eyes. And his eyes die. Right inside his face. And then his eyes close. And you know that he's died too. You know that Kirk Douglas has died from the death of his horse.

SAUL [*eyes* AUSTIN *nervously*]. Well, it sounds like a great movie. I'm sorry I missed it.

LEE. Yeah, you shouldn't a' missed that one.

SAUL. I'll have to try to catch it some time. Arrange a screening or something. Well, Austin, I'll have to hit the freeway before rush hour.

AUSTIN [*ushers him toward exit*]. It's good seeing you, Saul.

[AUSTIN *and* SAUL *shake hands.*]

LEE. So ya' think there's room for a real Western these days? A true-to-life Western?

SAUL. Well, I don't see why not. Why don't you uh—tell the story to Austin and have him write a little outline.

LEE. You'd take a look at it then?

SAUL. Yes. Sure. I'll give it a read-through. Always eager for new material. [*smiles at* AUSTIN].

LEE. That's great! You'd really read it then huh?

SAUL. It would just be my opinion of course.

LEE. That's all I want. Just an opinion. I happen to think it has a lota' possibilities.

SAUL. Well, it was great meeting you and I'll—

[SAUL *and* LEE *shake.*]

LEE. I'll call you tomorrow about the golf.

SAUL. Oh. Yes, right.

LEE. Austin's got your number, right?

SAUL. Yes.

LEE. So long Saul. [*gives* SAUL *a pat on the back.*]

[SAUL *exits,* AUSTIN *turns to* LEE, *looks at T.V. then back to* LEE.]

AUSTIN. Give me the keys.

[AUSTIN *extends his hand toward* LEE, LEE *doesn't move, just stares at* AUSTIN, *smiles, lights to black.*]

SCENE IV

Night. Coyotes in distance, fade, sound of typewriter in dark, crickets, candlelight in alcove, dim light in kitchen, lights reveal AUSTIN *at glass table typing,* LEE *sits across from him, foot on table, drinking beer and whiskey, the T.V. is still on sink counter,* AUSTIN *types for a while, then stops.*

LEE. All right, now read it back to me.

AUSTIN. I'm not reading it back to you, Lee. You can read it when we're finished. I can't spend all night on this.

LEE. You got better things to do?

AUSTIN. Let's just go ahead. Now what happens when he leaves Texas?

LEE. Is he ready to leave Texas yet? I didn't know we were that far along. He's not ready to leave Texas.

AUSTIN. He's right at the border.

LEE [*sitting up*]. No, see, this is one a' the crucial parts. Right here. [*taps paper with beer can.*] We can't rush through this. He's not right at the border. He's a good fifty miles from the border. A lot can happen in fifty miles.

AUSTIN. It's only an outline. We're not writing an entire script now.

LEE. Well ya' can't leave things out even if it is an outline. It's one a' the most important parts. Ya' can't go leavin' it out.

AUSTIN. Okay, okay. Let's just—get it done.

LEE. All right. Now. He's in the truck and he's got his horse trailer and his horse.

AUSTIN. We've already established that.

LEE. And he sees this other guy comin' up behind him in another truck. And that truck is pullin' a gooseneck.

AUSTIN. What's a gooseneck?

LEE. Cattle trailer. You know the kind with a gooseneck, goes right down in the bed a' the pick-up.

AUSTIN. Oh. All right. [*types.*]

LEE. It's important.

AUSTIN. Okay. I got it.

LEE. All these details are important.

[AUSTIN *types as they talk.*]

AUSTIN. I've got it.

LEE. And this other guy's got his horse all saddled up in the back a' the gooseneck.

AUSTIN. Right.

LEE. So both these guys have got their horses right along with 'em, see.

AUSTIN. I understand.

LEE. Then this first guy suddenly realizes two things.

AUSTIN. The guy in front?

LEE. Right. The guy in front realizes two things almost at the same time. Simultaneous.

AUSTIN. What were the two things?

LEE. Number one, he realizes that the guy behind him is the husband of the woman he's been—

[LEE *makes gesture of screwing by pumping his arm.*]

AUSTIN [*sees* LEE*'s gesture.*] Oh. Yeah.

LEE. And number two, he realizes he's in the middle of Tornado Country.

AUSTIN. What's "Tornado Country"?

LEE. Panhandle.

AUSTIN. Panhandle?

LEE. Sweetwater. Around in that area. Nothin'. Nowhere. And number three—

AUSTIN. I thought there was only two.

LEE. There's three. There's a third unforeseen realization.

AUSTIN. And what's that?

LEE. That he's runnin' outa' gas.

AUSTIN [*stops typing*]. Come on, Lee.

[AUSTIN *gets up, moves to kitchen, gets a glass of water.*]

LEE. Whadya' mean, "come on"? That's what it is. Write it down! He's runnin' outa' gas.

AUSTIN. It's too—

LEE. What? It's too what? It's too real! That's what ya' mean isn't it? It's too much like real life!

AUSTIN. It's not like real life! It's not enough like real life. Things don't happen like that.

LEE. What! Men don't fuck other men's women?

AUSTIN. Yes. But they don't end up chasing each other across the Panhandle. Through "Tornado Country."

LEE. They do in this movie!

AUSTIN. And they don't have horses conveniently along with them when they run out of gas! And they don't run out of gas either!

LEE. These guys run outa' gas! This is my story and one a' these guys runs outa' gas!

AUSTIN. It's just a dumb excuse to get them into a chase scene. It's contrived.

LEE. It is a chase scene! It's already a chase scene. They been chasin' each other fer days.

AUSTIN. So now they're supposed to abandon their trucks, climb on their horses and chase each other into the mountains?

LEE [*standing suddenly*]. There aren't any mountains in the Panhandle! It's flat!

[LEE *turns violently toward windows in alcove and throws beer can at them.*]

LEE. Goddamn these crickets! [*yells at crickets.*] Shut up out there! [*pause, turns back toward table.*] This place is like a fuckin' rest home here. How're you supposed to think!

AUSTIN. You wanna' take a break?

LEE. No, I don't wanna' take a break! I wanna' get this done! This is my last chance to get this done.

AUSTIN [*moves back into alcove*]. All right. Take it easy.

LEE. I'm gonna' be leavin' this area. I don't have time to mess around here.

AUSTIN. Where are you going?

LEE. Never mind where I'm goin'! That's got nothin' to do with you. I just gotta'

get this done. I'm not like you. Hangin' around bein' a parasite offa' other
fools. I gotta' do this thing and get out.

[*pause.*]

AUSTIN. A parasite? Me?

LEE. Yeah, you!

AUSTIN. After you break into people's houses and take their televisions?

LEE. They don't need their televisions! I'm doin' them a service.

AUSTIN. Give me back my keys, Lee.

LEE. Not until you write this thing! You're gonna' write this outline thing for me
or that car's gonna' wind up in Arizona with a different paint job.

AUSTIN. You think you can force me to write this? I was doing you a favor.

LEE. Git off yer high horse will ya'! Favor! Big favor. Handin' down favors from the
mountain top.

AUSTIN. Let's just write it, okay? Let's sit down and not get upset and see if we can
just get through this.

[AUSTIN *sits at typewriter.*]

[*long pause.*]

LEE. Yer not gonna' even show it to him, are ya'?

AUSTIN. What?

LEE. This outline. You got no intention of showin' it to him. Yer just doin' this
'cause yer afraid a' me.

AUSTIN. You can show it to him yourself.

LEE. I will, boy! I'm gonna' read it to him on the golf course.

AUSTIN. And I'm not afraid of you either.

LEE. Then how come yer doin' it?

AUSTIN [*pause*]. So I can get my keys back.

[*pause as* LEE *takes keys out of his pocket slowly and throws them on table, long pause,*
AUSTIN *stares at keys.*]

LEE. There. Now you got yer keys back.

[AUSTIN *looks up at* LEE *but doesn't take keys.*]

LEE. Go ahead. There's yer keys. [AUSTIN *slowly takes keys off table and puts them back
in his own pocket.*] Now what're you gonna' do? Kick me out?

AUSTIN. I'm not going to kick you out, Lee.

LEE. You couldn't kick me out, boy.

AUSTIN. I know.

LEE. So you can't even consider that one. [*pause.*] You could call the police. That'd
be the obvious thing.

AUSTIN. You're my brother.

LEE. That don't mean a thing. You go down to the L.A. Police Department there
and ask them what kinda' people kill each other the most. What do you think
they'd say?

AUSTIN. Who said anything about killing?

LEE. Family people. Brothers. Brothers-in-law. Cousins. Real American-type people. They kill each other in the heat mostly. In the Smog-Alerts. In the Brush
Fire Season. Right about this time a' year.

AUSTIN. This isn't the same.

LEE. Oh no? What makes it different?

AUSTIN. We're not insane. We're not driven to acts of violence like that. Not over
a dumb movie script. Now sit down.

[*long pause,* LEE *considers which way to go with it.*]

LEE. Maybe not. [*He sits back down at table across from* AUSTIN.] Maybe you're right. Maybe we're too intelligent, huh? [*pause.*] We got our heads on our shoulders. One of us has even got a Ivy League diploma. Now that means somethin' don't it? Doesn't that mean somethin'?

AUSTIN. Look, I'll write this thing for you, Lee. I don't mind writing it. I just don't want to get all worked up about it. It's not worth it. Now, come on. Let's just get through it, okay?

LEE. Nah. I think there's easier money. Lotsa' places I could pick up thousands. Maybe millions. I don't need this shit. I could go up to Sacramento Valley and steal me a diesel. Ten thousand a week dismantling one a' those suckers. Ten thousand a week!

[LEE *opens another beer, puts his foot back up on table.*]

AUSTIN. No, really, look, I'll write it out for you. I think it's a great idea.

LEE. Nah, you got yer own work to do. I don't wanna' interfere with yer life.

AUSTIN. I mean it'd be really fantastic if you could sell this. Turn it into a movie. I mean it.

[*pause.*]

LEE. Ya' think so huh?

AUSTIN. Absolutely. You could really turn your life around, you know. Change things.

LEE. I could get me a house maybe.

AUSTIN. Sure you could get a house. You could get a whole ranch if you wanted to.

LEE [*laughs*]. A ranch? I could get a ranch?

AUSTIN. 'Course you could. You know what a screenplay sells for these days?

LEE. No. What's it sell for?

AUSTIN. A lot. A whole lot of money.

LEE. Thousands?

AUSTIN. Yeah. Thousands.

LEE. Millions?

AUSTIN. Well—

LEE. We could get the old man outa' hock then.

AUSTIN. Maybe.

LEE. Maybe? Whadya' mean, maybe?

AUSTIN. I mean it might take more than money.

LEE. You were just tellin' me it'd change my whole life around. Why wouldn't it change his?

AUSTIN. He's different.

LEE. Oh, he's of a different ilk huh?

AUSTIN. He's not gonna' change. Let's leave the old man out of it.

LEE. That's right. He's not gonna' change but I will. I'll just turn myself right inside out. I could be just like you then, huh? Sittin' around dreamin' stuff up. Gettin' paid to dream. Ridin' back and forth on the freeway just dreamin' my fool head off.

AUSTIN. It's not all that easy.

LEE. It's not, huh?

AUSTIN. No. There's a lot of work involved.

LEE. What's the toughest part? Deciding whether to jog or play tennis?

[*long pause.*]

AUSTIN. Well, look. You can stay here—do whatever you want to. Borrow the car.

Come in and out. Doesn't matter to me. It's not my house. I'll help you write
this thing or—not. Just let me know what you want. You tell me.

LEE. Oh. So now suddenly you're at my service. Is that it?

AUSTIN. What do you want to do Lee?

[*long pause,* LEE *stares at him then turns and dreams at windows.*]

LEE: I tell ya' what I'd do if I still had that dog. Ya' wanna' know what I'd do?

AUSTIN. What?

LEE. Head to Ventura.[5] 'Cook up a little match. God that little dog could bear
down. Lota' money in dog fightin'. Big money.

[*pause.*]

AUSTIN. Why don't we try to see this through, Lee. Just for the hell of it. Maybe
you've really got something here. What do you think?

[*pause,* LEE *considers.*]

LEE. Maybe so. No harm in tryin' I guess. You think it's such a hot idea. Besides,
I always wondered what'd be like to be you.

AUSTIN. You did?

LEE. Yeah, sure. I used to picture you walkin' around some campus with yer arms
fulla' books. Blondes chasin' after ya'.

AUSTIN. Blondes? That's funny.

LEE. What's funny about it?

AUSTIN. Because I always used to picture you somewhere.

LEE. Where'd you picture me?

AUSTIN. Oh, I don't know. Different places. Adventures. You were always on some
adventure.

LEE. Yeah.

AUSTIN. And I used to say to myself, 'Lee's got the right idea. He's out there in the
world and here I am. What am I doing?'

LEE. Well you were settin' yourself up for somethin'.

AUSTIN. I guess.

LEE. We better get started on this thing then.

AUSTIN. Okay.

[AUSTIN *sits up at typewriter, puts new paper in.*]

LEE. Oh. Can I get the keys back before I forget? [AUSTIN *hesitates.*] You said I could
borrow the car if I wanted, right? Isn't that what you said?

AUSTIN. Yeah. Right.

[AUSTIN *takes keys out of his pocket, sets them on table,* LEE *takes keys slowly, plays with
them in his hand.*]

LEE. I could get a ranch, huh?

AUSTIN. Yeah. We have to write it first though.

LEE. Okay. Let's write it. [*lights start dimming slowly to end of scene as* AUSTIN *types,* LEE
speaks.] So they take off after each other straight into an endless black prairie.
The sun is just comin' down and they can feel the night on their backs. What
they don't know is that each one of 'em is afraid, see. Each one separately thinks
that he's the only one that's afraid. And they keep ridin' like that straight into
the night. Not knowing. And the one who's chasin' doesn't know where the
other one is taking him. And the one who's being chased doesn't know where
he's going.

[*lights to black, typing stops in the dark, crickets fade.*]

---

[5] Ventura is a beach community about fifty miles northwest of Los Angeles.

ACT II

SCENE V

Morning. LEE *at the table in alcove with a set of golf clubs in a fancy leather bag,* AUSTIN *at sink washing a few dishes.*

AUSTIN. He really liked it, huh?

LEE. He wouldn't a' gave me these clubs if he didn't like it.

AUSTIN. He gave you the clubs?

LEE. Yeah. I told ya' he gave me the clubs. The bag too.

AUSTIN. I thought he just loaned them to you.

LEE. He said it was part a' the advance. A little gift like. Gesture of his good faith.

AUSTIN. He's giving you an advance?

LEE. Now what's so amazing about that? I told ya' it was a good story. You even said it was a good story.

AUSTIN. Well that is really incredible Lee. You know how many guys spend their whole lives down here trying to break into this business? Just trying to get in the door?

LEE [*pulling clubs out of bag, testing them*]. I got no idea. How many?

[*pause.*]

AUSTIN. How much of an advance is he giving you?

LEE. Plenty. We were talkin' big money out there. Ninth hole is where I sealed the deal.

AUSTIN. He made a firm commitment?

LEE. Absolutely.

AUSTIN. Well, I know Saul and he doesn't fool around when he says he likes something.

LEE. I thought you said you didn't know him.

AUSTIN. Well, I'm familiar with his tastes.

LEE. I let him get two up on me goin' into the back nine. He was sure he had me cold. You shoulda' seen his face when I pulled out the old pitching wedge and plopped it pin-high, two feet from the cup. He 'bout shit his pants. "Where'd a guy like you ever learn how to play golf like that?," he says.

[LEE *laughs,* AUSTIN *stares at him.*]

AUSTIN. 'Course there's no contract yet. Nothing's final until it's on paper.

LEE. It's final, all right. There's no way he's gonna' back out of it now. We gambled for it.

AUSTIN. Saul, gambled?

LEE. Yeah, sure. I mean he liked the outline already so he wasn't risking that much. I just guaranteed it with my short game.

[*pause.*]

AUSTIN. Well, we should celebrate or something. I think Mom left a bottle of champagne in the refrigerator. We should have a little toast.

[AUSTIN *gets glasses from cupboard, goes to refrigerator, pulls out bottle of champagne.*]

LEE. You shouldn't oughta' take her champagne, Austin. She's gonna' miss that.

AUSTIN. Oh, she's not going to mind. She'd be glad we put it to good use. I'll get her another bottle. Besides, it's perfect for the occasion.

[*pause.*]

LEE. Yer gonna' get a nice fee fer writin' the script a' course. Straight fee.

[AUSTIN *stops, stares at* LEE, *puts glasses and bottle on table, pause.*]

AUSTIN. I'm writing the script?

LEE. That's what he said. Said we couldn't hire a better screenwriter in the whole town.

AUSTIN. But I'm already working on a script. I've got my own project. I don't have time to write two scripts.

LEE. No, he said he was gonna' drop that other one.

[*pause.*]

AUSTIN. What? You mean mine? He's going to drop mine and do yours instead?

LEE [*smiles*]. Now look, Austin, it's jest beginner's luck ya' know. I mean I sank a fifty foot putt for this deal. No hard feelings.

[AUSTIN *goes to phone on wall, grabs it, starts dialing.*]

He's not gonna' be in, Austin. Told me he wouldn't be in 'till late this afternoon.

AUSTIN [*stays on phone, dialing, listens*]. I can't believe this. I just can't believe it. Are you sure he said that? Why would he drop mine?

LEE. That's what he told me.

AUSTIN. He can't do that without telling me first. Without talking to me at least. He wouldn't just make a decision like that without talking to me!

LEE. Well I was kinda' surprised myself. But he was real enthusiastic about my story.

[AUSTIN *hangs up phone violently, paces.*]

AUSTIN. What'd he say! Tell me everything he said!

LEE. I been tellin' ya'! He said he liked the story a whole lot. It was the first authentic Western to come along in a decade.

AUSTIN. He liked that story! Your story?

LEE. Yeah! What's so surprisin' about that?

AUSTIN. It's stupid! It's the dumbest story I ever heard in my life.

LEE. Hey, hold on! That's my story yer talkin' about!

AUSTIN. It's a bullshit story! It's idiotic. Two lamebrains chasing each other across Texas! Are you kidding? Who do you think's going to see a film like that?

LEE. It's not a film! It's a movie. There's a big difference. That's somethin' Saul told me.

AUSTIN. Oh he did, huh?

LEE. Yeah, he said, "In this business we make movies, American movies. Leave the films to the French."

AUSTIN. So you got real intimate with old Saul huh? He started pouring forth his vast knowledge of Cinema.

LEE. I think he liked me a lot, to tell ya' the truth. I think he felt I was somebody he could confide in.

AUSTIN. What'd you do, beat him up or something?

LEE [*stands fast*]. Hey, I've about had it with the insults buddy! You think yer the only one in the brain department here? Yer the only one that can sit around and cook things up? There's other people got ideas too, ya' know!

AUSTIN. You must've done something. Threatened him or something. Now what'd you do Lee?

LEE. I convinced him!

[LEE *makes sudden menacing lunge toward* AUSTIN, *wielding golf club above his head, stops himself, frozen moment, long pause,* LEE *lowers club.*]

AUSTIN. Oh, Jesus. You didn't hurt him did you? [*long silence,* LEE *sits back down at the table.*] Lee! Did you hurt him?

LEE. I didn't do nothin' to him! He liked my story. Pure and simple. He said it was the best story he's come across in a long, long time.

AUSTIN. That's what he told me about my story! That's the same thing he said to me.

LEE. Well, he musta' been lyin'. He musta' been lyin' to one of us anyway.

AUSTIN. You can't come into this town and start pushing people around. They're gonna' put you away!

LEE. I never pushed anybody around! I beat him fair and square. [*pause.*] They can't touch me anyway. They can't put a finger on me. I'm gone. I can come in through the window and go out through the door. They never knew what hit 'em. You, yer stuck. Yer the one that's stuck. Not me. So don't be warnin' me what to do in this town.

[*pause,* AUSTIN *crosses to table, sits at typewriter, rests.*]

AUSTIN. Lee, come on, level with me will you? It doesn't make any sense that suddenly he'd throw my idea out the window. I've been talking to him for months. I've got too much at stake. Everything's riding on this project.

LEE. What's yer idea?

AUSTIN. It's just a simple love story.

LEE. What kinda' love story?

AUSTIN [*stands, crosses into kitchen*]. I'm not telling you!

LEE. Ha! 'Fraid I'll steal it huh? Competition's gettin' kinda' close to home isn't it?

AUSTIN. Where did Saul say he was going?

LEE. He was gonna' take my story to a couple studios.

AUSTIN. That's *my* outline you know! I wrote that outline! You've got no right to be peddling it around.

LEE. You weren't ready to take credit for it last night.

AUSTIN. Give me my keys!

LEE. What?

AUSTIN. The keys! I want my keys back!

LEE. Where you goin'?

AUSTIN. Just give me my keys! I gotta' take a drive. I gotta' get out of here for a while.

LEE. Where you gonna' go, Austin?

AUSTIN [*pause*]. I might just drive out to the desert for a while. I gotta think.

LEE. You can think here just as good. This is the perfect set-up for thinkin'. We got some writin' to do here, boy. Now let's just have us a little toast. Relax. We're partners now.

[LEE *pops the cork of the champagne bottle, pours two drinks as the lights fade to black.*]

SCENE VI

Afternoon. LEE *and* SAUL *in kitchen,* AUSTIN *in alcove.*

LEE. Now you tell him. You tell him, Mr. Kipper.

SAUL. Kimmer.

LEE. Kimmer. You tell him what you told me. He don't believe me.

AUSTIN. I don't want to hear it.

SAUL. It's really not a big issue, Austin. I was simply amazed by your brother's story and—

AUSTIN. Amazed? You lost a bet! You gambled with my material!

SAUL. That's really beside the point, Austin. I'm ready to go all the way with your brother's story. I think it has a great deal of merit.

AUSTIN. I don't want to hear about it, okay? Go tell it to the executives! Tell it to somebody who's going to turn it into a package deal or something. A T.V. series. Don't tell it to me.

SAUL. But I want to continue with your project too, Austin. It's not as though we can't do both. We're big enough for that aren't we?

AUSTIN. "We"? *I* can't do both! I don't know about "we."

LEE [*to* SAUL]. See, what'd I tell ya'. He's totally unsympathetic.

SAUL. Austin, there's no point in our going to another screenwriter for this. It just doesn't make sense. You're brothers. You know each other. There's a familiarity with the material that just wouldn't be possible otherwise.

AUSTIN. There's no familiarity with the material! None! I don't know what "Tornado Country" is. I don't know what a "gooseneck" is. And I don't want to know! [*pointing to* LEE.] He's a hustler! He's a bigger hustler than you are! If you can't see that, then—

LEE [*to* AUSTIN]. Hey, now hold on. I didn't have to bring this bone back to you, boy. I persuaded Saul here that you were the right man for the job. You don't have to go throwin' up favors in my face.

AUSTIN. Favors! I'm the one who wrote the fuckin' outline! You can't even spell.

SAUL [*to* AUSTIN]. Your brother told me about the situation with your father.
[*pause.*]

AUSTIN. What? [*Looks at* LEE.]

SAUL. That's right. Now we have a clear-cut deal here, Austin. We have big studio money standing behind this thing. Just on the basis of your outline.

AUSTIN [*to* SAUL]. What'd he tell you about my father?

SAUL. Well—that he's destitute. He needs money.

LEE. That's right. He does.
[AUSTIN *shakes his head, stares at them both.*]

AUSTIN [*to* LEE]. And this little assignment is supposed to go toward the old man? A charity project? Is that what this is? Did you cook this up on the ninth green too?

SAUL. It's a big slice, Austin.

AUSTIN [*to* LEE]. I gave him money! I already gave him money. You know that. He drank it all up!

LEE. This is a different deal here.

SAUL. We can set up a trust for your father. A large sum of money. It can be doled out to him in parcels so he can't misuse it.

AUSTIN. Yeah, and who's doing the doling?

SAUL. Your brother volunteered.
[AUSTIN *laughs.*]

LEE. That's right. I'll make sure he uses it for groceries.

AUSTIN [*to* SAUL]. I'm not doing this script! I'm not writing this crap for you or anybody else. You can't blackmail me into it. You can't threaten me into it. There's no way I'm doing it. So just give it up. Both of you.
[*long pause.*]

SAUL. Well, that's it then. I mean this is an easy three hundred grand. Just for a first draft. It's incredible, Austin. We've got three different studios all trying to cut each other's throats to get this material. In one morning. That's how hot it is.

AUSTIN. Yeah, well you can afford to give me a percentage of the outline then. And you better get the genius here an agent before he gets burned.

LEE. Saul's gonna' be my agent. Isn't that right, Saul?

SAUL. That's right. [*to* AUSTIN.] Your brother has really got something, Austin. I've been around too long not to recognize it. Raw talent.

AUSTIN. He's got a lota' balls is what he's got. He's taking you right down the river.

SAUL. Three hundred thousand, Austin. Just for a first draft. Now you've never been offered that kind of money before.

AUSTIN. I'm not writing it.

[*pause.*]

SAUL. I see. Well—

LEE. We'll just go to another writer then. Right, Saul? Just hire us somebody with some enthusiasm. Somebody who can recognize the value of a good story.

SAUL. I'm sorry about this, Austin.

AUSTIN. Yeah.

SAUL. I mean I was hoping we could continue both things but now I don't see how it's possible.

AUSTIN. So you're dropping my idea altogether. Is that it? Just trade horses in midstream? After all these months of meetings.

SAUL. I wish there was another way.

AUSTIN. I've got everything riding on this, Saul. You know that. It's my only shot. If this falls through—

SAUL. I have to go with what my instincts tell me—

AUSTIN. Your instincts!

SAUL. My gut reaction.

AUSTIN. You lost! That's your gut reaction. You lost a gamble. Now you're trying to tell me you like his story? How could you possibly fall for that story? It's as phony as Hoppalong Cassidy.[6] What do you see in it? I'm curious.

SAUL. It has the ring of truth, Austin.

AUSTIN [*laughs*]. Truth?

LEE. It is true.

SAUL. Something about the real West.

AUSTIN. Why? Because it's got horses? Because it's got grown men acting like little boys?

SAUL. Something about the land. Your brother is speaking from experience.

AUSTIN. So am I!

SAUL. But nobody's interested in love these days, Austin. Let's face it.

LEE. That's right.

AUSTIN [*to* SAUL]. He's been camped out on the desert for three months. Talking to cactus. What's he know about what people wanna' see on the screen! I drive on the freeway every day. I swallow the smog. I watch the news in color. I shop in the Safeway. I'm the one who's in touch! Not him!

SAUL. I have to go now, Austin.

[SAUL *starts to leave.*]

AUSTIN. There's no such thing as the West anymore! It's a dead issue! It's dried up, Saul, and so are you.

[SAUL *stops and turns to* AUSTIN.]

SAUL. Maybe you're right. But I have to take the gamble, don't I?

AUSTIN. You're a fool to do this, Saul.

---

[6] The character of Hoppalong Cassidy was created by William Boyd in a series of low-budget films during the 1930s and 1940s. In the early 1950s the televised *Hoppalong Cassidy* show was a hit on NBC.

SAUL. I've always gone on my hunches. Always. And I've never been wrong. [*to* LEE]. I'll talk to you tomorrow, Lee.

LEE. All right, Mr. Kimmer.

SAUL. Maybe we could have some lunch.

LEE. Fine with me. [*smiles at* AUSTIN.]

SAUL. I'll give you a ring.

[SAUL *exits, lights to black as brothers look at each other from a distance.*]

SCENE VII

Night. Coyotes, crickets, sound of typewriter in dark, candlelight up on LEE *at typewriter struggling to type with one finger system,* AUSTIN *sits sprawled out on kitchen floor with whiskey bottle, drunk.*

AUSTIN [*singing, from floor*].

> "Red sails in the sunset
> Way out on the blue
> Please carry my loved one
> Home safely to me
>
> Red sails in the sunset—"

LEE [*slams fist on table*]. Hey! Knock it off will ya'! I'm tryin' to concentrate here.

AUSTIN [*laughs*]. You're tryin' to concentrate?

LEE. Yeah. That's right.

AUSTIN. Now you're tryin' to concentrate.

LEE. Between you, the coyotes and the crickets a thought don't have much of a chance.

AUSTIN. "Between me, the coyotes and the crickets." What a great title.

LEE. I don't need a title! I need a thought.

AUSTIN [*laughs*]. A thought! Here's a thought for ya'—

LEE. I'm not askin' fer yer thoughts! I got my own. I can do this thing on my own.

AUSTIN. You're going to write an entire script on your own?

LEE. That's right.

[*pause.*]

AUSTIN. Here's a thought. Saul Kimmer—

LEE. Shut up will ya'!

AUSTIN. He thinks we're the same person.

LEE. Don't get cute.

AUSTIN. He does! He's lost his mind. Poor old Saul. [*giggles.*] Thinks we're one and the same.

LEE. Why don't you ease up on that champagne.

AUSTIN [*holding up bottle*]. This isn't champagne any more. We went through the champagne a long time ago. This is serious stuff. The days of champagne are long gone.

LEE. Well, go outside and drink it.

AUSTIN. I'm enjoying your company, Lee. For the first time since your arrival I am finally enjoying your company. And now you want me to go outside and drink alone?

LEE. That's right.

[LEE *reads through paper in typewriter, makes an erasure.*]

AUSTIN. You think you'll make more progress if you're alone? You might drive yourself crazy.

LEE. I could have this thing done in a night if I had a little silence.

AUSTIN. Well you'd still have the crickets to contend with. The coyotes. The sounds of the Police Helicopters prowling above the neighborhood. Slashing their searchlights down through the streets. Hunting for the likes of you.

LEE. I'm a screenwriter now! I'm legitimate.

AUSTIN [*laughing*]. A screenwriter!

LEE. That's right. I'm on salary. That's more'n I can say for you. I got an advance coming.

AUSTIN. This is true. This is very true. An advance. [*pause*]. Well, maybe I oughta' go out and try my hand at your trade. Since you're doing so good at mine.

LEE. Ha!

[LEE *attempts to type some more but gets the ribbon tangled up, starts trying to re-thread it as they continue talking.*]

AUSTIN. Well why not? You don't think I've got what it takes to sneak into people's houses and steal their T.V.s?

LEE. You couldn't steal a toaster without losin' yer lunch.

[AUSTIN *stands with a struggle, supports himself by the sink.*]

AUSTIN. You don't think I could sneak into somebody's house and steal a toaster?

LEE. Go take a shower or somethin' will ya!

[LEE *gets more tangled up with the typewriter ribbon, pulling it out of the machine as though it was fishing line.*]

AUSTIN. You really don't think I could steal a crumby toaster? How much you wanna' bet I can't steal a toaster! How much? Go ahead! You're a gambler aren't you? Tell me how much yer willing to put on the line. Some part of your big advance? Oh, you haven't got that yet have you. I forgot.

LEE. All right. I'll bet you your car that you can't steal a toaster without gettin' busted.

AUSTIN. You already got my car!

LEE. Okay, your house then.

AUSTIN. What're you gonna' give me! I'm not talkin' about my house and my car, I'm talkin' about what are you gonna' give me. You don't have nothin' to give me.

LEE. I'll give you—shared screen credit. How 'bout that? I'll have it put in the contract that this was written by the both of us.

AUSTIN. I don't want my name on that piece of shit! I want something of value. You got anything of value? You got any tidbits from the desert? Any Rattlesnake bones? I'm not a greedy man. Any little personal treasure will suffice.

LEE. I'm gonna' just kick yer ass out in a minute.

AUSTIN. Oh, so now you're gonna' kick me out! Now I'm the intruder. I'm the one who's invading your precious privacy.

LEE. I'm trying to do some screenwriting here!!

[LEE *stands, picks up typewriter, slams it down hard on table, pause, silence except for crickets.*]

AUSTIN. Well, you got everything you need. You got plenty a' coffee? Groceries. You got a car. A contract. [*pause.*] Might need a new typewriter ribbon but other than that you're pretty well fixed. I'll just leave ya' alone for a while.

[AUSTIN *tries to steady himself to leave,* LEE *makes a move toward him.*]

LEE. Where you goin'?

AUSTIN. Don't worry about me. I'm not the one to worry about.

[AUSTIN *weaves toward exit, stops.*]

LEE. What're you gonna' do? Just go wander out into the night?

AUSTIN. I'm gonna' make a little tour.

LEE. Why don't ya' just go to bed for Christ's sake. Yer makin' me sick.

AUSTIN. I can take care a' myself. Don't worry about me.

[AUSTIN *weaves badly in another attempt to exit, he crashes to the floor,* LEE *goes to him but remains standing.*]

LEE. You want me to call your wife for ya' or something?

AUSTIN [*from floor*]. My wife?

LEE. Yeah. I mean maybe she can help ya' out. Talk to ya' or somethin'.

AUSTIN [*struggles to stand again*]. She's five hundred miles away. North. North of here. Up in the North country where things are calm. I don't need any help. I'm gonna' go outside and I'm gonna' steal a toaster. I'm gonna' steal some other stuff too. I might even commit bigger crimes. Bigger than you ever dreamed of. Crimes beyond the imagination!

[AUSTIN *manages to get himself vertical, tries to head for exit again.*]

LEE. Just hang on a minute, Austin.

AUSTIN. Why? What for? You don't need my help, right? You got a handle on the project. Besides, I'm lookin' forward to the smell of the night. The bushes. Orange blossoms. Dust in the driveways. Rain bird sprinklers. Lights in people's houses. You're right about the lights, Lee. Everybody else is livin' the life. Indoors. Safe. This is a Paradise down here. You know that? We're livin' in a Paradise. We've forgotten about that.

LEE. You sound just like the old man now.

AUSTIN. Yeah, well we all sound alike when we're sloshed. We just sorta' echo each other.

LEE. Maybe if we could work on this together we could bring him back out here. Get him settled down some place.

[AUSTIN *turns violently toward* LEE, *takes a swing at him, misses and crashes to the floor again,* LEE *stays standing.*]

AUSTIN. I don't want him out here! I've had it with him! I went all the way out there! I went out of my way. I gave him money and all he did was play Al Jolson[7] records and spit at me! I gave him money!

[*pause.*]

LEE. Just help me a little with the characters, all right? You know how to do it, Austin.

AUSTIN [*on floor, laughs*]. The characters!

LEE. Yeah. You know. The way they talk and stuff. I can hear it in my head but I can't get it down on paper.

AUSTIN. What characters?

LEE. The guys. The guys in the story.

AUSTIN. Those aren't characters.

LEE. Whatever you call 'em then. I need to write somethin' out.

AUSTIN. Those are illusions of characters.

LEE. I don't give a damn what ya' call 'em! You know what I'm talkin' about!

AUSTIN. Those are fantasies of a long lost boyhood.

LEE. I gotta' write somethin' out on paper!!

[*pause.*]

---

[7] Al Jolson (1888–1950), a comedian and singer, was born in Russia as Asa Yoelson, but became famous in the United States for his song-and-dance routines in blackface.

AUSTIN. What for? Saul's gonna' get you a fancy screenwriter isn't he?

LEE. I wanna' do it myself!

AUSTIN. Then do it! Yer on your own now, old buddy. You bulldogged yer way into contention. Now you gotta' carry it through.

LEE. I will but I need some advice. Just a couple a' things. Come on, Austin. Just help me get 'em talkin' right. It won't take much.

AUSTIN. Oh, now you're having a little doubt huh? What happened? The pressure's on, boy. This is it. You gotta' come up with it now. You don't come up with a winner on your first time out they just cut your head off. They don't give you a second chance ya' know.

LEE. I got a good story! I know it's a good story. I just need a little help is all.

AUSTIN. Not from me. Not from yer little old brother. I'm retired.

LEE. You could save this thing for me, Austin. I'd give ya' half the money. I would. I only need half anyway. With this kinda' money I could be a long time down the road. I'd never bother ya' again. I promise. You'd never even see me again.

AUSTIN [*still on floor*]. You'd disappear?

LEE. I would for sure.

AUSTIN. Where would you disappear to?

LEE. That don't matter. I got plenty a' places.

AUSTIN. Nobody can disappear. The old man tried that. Look where it got him. He lost his teeth.

LEE. He never had any money.

AUSTIN. I don't mean that. I mean his teeth! His real teeth. First he lost his real teeth, then he lost his false teeth. You never knew that did ya'? He never confided in you.

LEE. Nah, I never knew that.

AUSTIN. You wanna' drink?

[AUSTIN *offers bottle to* LEE, LEE *takes it, sits down on kitchen floor with* AUSTIN, *they share the bottle.*]

Yeah, he lost his real teeth one at a time. Woke up every morning with another tooth lying on the mattress. Finally, he decides he's gotta' get 'em all pulled out but he doesn't have any money. Middle of Arizona with no money and no insurance and every morning another tooth is lying on the mattress. [*takes a drink.*] So what does he do?

LEE. I dunno'. I never knew about that.

AUSTIN. He begs the government. G.I. Bill or some damn thing. Some pension plan he remembers in the back of his head. And they send him out the money.

LEE. They did?

[*They keep trading the bottle between them, taking drinks.*]

AUSTIN. Yeah. They send him the money but it's not enough money. Costs a lot to have all yer teeth yanked. They charge by the individual tooth, ya' know. I mean one tooth isn't equal to another tooth. Some are more expensive. Like the big ones in the back—

LEE. So what happened?

AUSTIN. So he locates a Mexican dentist in Juarez who'll do the whole thing for a song. And he takes off hitchhiking to the border.

LEE. Hitchhiking?

AUSTIN. Yeah. So how long you think it takes him to get to the border? A man his age.

LEE. I dunno.

AUSTIN. Eight days it takes him. Eight days in the rain and the sun and every day he's droppin' teeth on the blacktop and nobody'll pick him up 'cause his mouth's full a' blood. [*pause, they drink.*] So finally he stumbles into the dentist. Dentist takes all his money and all his teeth. And there he is, in Mexico, with his gums sewed up and his pockets empty.

[*long silence,* AUSTIN *drinks.*]

LEE. That's it?

AUSTIN. Then I go out to see him, see. I go out there and I take him out for a nice Chinese dinner. But he doesn't eat. All he wants to do is drink Martinis outa' plastic cups. And he takes his teeth out and lays 'em on the table 'cause he can't stand the feel of 'em. And we ask the waitress for one a' those doggie bags to take the Chop Suey home in. So he drops his teeth in the doggie bag along with the Chop Suey. And then we go out to hit all the bars up and down the highway. Says he wants to introduce me to all his buddies. And in one a' those bars, in one a' those bars up and down the highway, he left that doggie bag with his teeth laying in the Chop Suey.

LEE. You never found it?

AUSTIN. We went back but we never did find it. [*pause.*] Now that's a true story. True to life.

[*They drink as lights fade to black.*]

SCENE VIII

Very early morning, between night and day. No crickets, coyotes yapping feverishly in distance before light comes up, a small fire blazes up in the dark from alcove area, sound of LEE *smashing typewriter with a golf club, lights coming up,* LEE *seen smashing typewriter methodically then dropping pages of his script into a burning bowl set on the floor of alcove, flames leap up,* AUSTIN *has a whole bunch of stolen toasters lined up on the sink counter along with* LEE's *stolen T.V., the toasters are of a wide variety of models, mostly chrome,* AUSTIN *goes up and down the line of toasters, breathing on them and polishing them with a dish towel, both men are drunk, empty whiskey bottles and beer cans litter floor of kitchen, they share a half empty bottle on one of the chairs in the alcove,* LEE *keeps periodically taking deliberate ax-chops at the typewriter using a nine-iron as* AUSTIN *speaks, all of their mother's house plants are dead and drooping.*

AUSTIN [*polishing toasters*]. There's gonna' be a general lack of toast in the neighborhood this morning. Many, many unhappy, bewildered breakfast faces. I guess it's best not to even think of the victims. Not to even entertain it. Is that the right psychology?

LEE [*pauses*]. What?

AUSTIN. Is that the correct criminal psychology? Not to think of the victims?

LEE. What victims?

[LEE *takes another swipe at typewriter with nine-iron, adds pages to the fire.*]

AUSTIN. The victims of crime. Of breaking and entering. I mean is it a prerequisite for a criminal not to have a conscience?

LEE. Ask a criminal.

[*pause,* LEE *stares at* AUSTIN.]

What're you gonna' do with all those toasters? That's the dumbest thing I ever saw in my life.

AUSTIN. I've got hundreds of dollars worth of household appliances here. You may not realize that.

Lee. Yeah, and how many hundreds of dollars did you walk right past?

Austin. It was toasters you challenged me to. Only toasters. I ignored every other temptation.

Lee. I never challenged you! That's no challenge. Anybody can steal a toaster.

[Lee *smashes typewriter again.*]

Austin. You don't have to take it out on my typewriter ya' know. It's not the machine's fault that you can't write. It's a sin to do that to a good machine.

Lee. A sin?

Austin. When you consider all the writers who never even had a machine. Who would have given an eyeball for a good typewriter. Any typewriter.

[Lee *smashes typewriter again.*]

Austin [*polishing toasters*]. All the ones who wrote on matchbook covers. Paper bags. Toilet paper. Who had their writing destroyed by their jailers. Who persisted beyond all odds. Those writers would find it hard to understand your actions.

[Lee *comes down on typewriter with one final crushing blow of the nine-iron then collapses in one of the chairs, takes a drink from bottle, pause.*]

Austin [*after pause*]. Not to mention demolishing a perfectly good golf club. What about all the struggling golfers? What about Lee Trevino? What do you think he would've said when he was batting balls around with broomsticks at the age of nine. Impoverished.

[*pause.*]

Lee. What time is it anyway?

Austin. No idea. Time stands still when you're havin' fun.

Lee. Is it too late to call a woman? You know any women?

Austin. I'm a married man.

Lee. I mean a local woman.

[Austin *looks out at light through window above sink.*]

Austin. It's either too late or too early. You're the nature enthusiast. Can't you tell the time by the light in the sky? Orient yourself around the North Star or something?

Lee. I can't tell anything.

Austin. Maybe you need a little breakfast. Some toast! How 'bout some toast?

[Austin *goes to cupboard, pulls out loaf of bread and starts dropping slices into every toaster, Lee stays sitting, drinks, watches Austin.*]

Lee. I don't need toast. I need a woman.

Austin. A woman isn't the answer. Never was.

Lee. I'm not talkin' about permanent. I'm talkin' about temporary.

Austin [*putting toast in toasters*]. We'll just test the merits of these little demons. See which brands have a tendency to burn. See which one can produce a perfectly golden piece of fluffy toast.

Lee. How much gas you got in yer car?

Austin. I haven't driven my car for days now. So I haven't had an opportunity to look at the gas gauge.

Lee. Take a guess. You think there's enough to get me to Bakersfield?[8]

Austin. Bakersfield? What's in Bakersfield?

Lee. Just never mind what's in Bakersfield! You think there's enough goddamn gas in the car!

---

[8] Bakersfield is an inland city about one hundred miles north and slightly east of Los Angeles.

AUSTIN. Sure.

LEE. Sure. You could care less, right. Let me run outa' gas on the Grapevine. You could give a shit.

AUSTIN. I'd say there was enough gas to get you just about anywhere, Lee. With your determination and guts.

LEE. What the hell time is it anyway?

[LEE *pulls out his wallet, starts going through dozens of small pieces of paper with phone numbers written on them, drops some on the floor, drops others in the fire.*]

AUSTIN. Very early. This is the time of morning when the coyotes kill people's cocker spaniels. Did you hear them? That's what they were doing out there. Luring innocent pets away from their homes.

LEE [*searching through his papers*]. What's the area code for Bakersfield? You know?

AUSTIN. You could always call the operator.

LEE. I can't stand that voice they give ya'.

AUSTIN. What voice?

LEE. That voice that warns you that if you'd only tried harder to find the number in the phone book you wouldn't have to be calling the operator to begin with.

[LEE *gets up, holding a slip of paper from his wallet, stumbles toward phone on wall, yanks receiver, starts dialing.*]

AUSTIN. Well I don't understand why you'd want to talk to anybody else anyway. I mean you can talk to me. I'm your brother.

LEE [*dialing*]. I wanna' talk to a woman. I haven't heard a woman's voice in a long time.

AUSTIN. Not since the Botanist?

LEE. What?

AUSTIN. Nothing. [*Starts singing as he tends toast.*]

> "Red sails in the sunset
> Way out on the blue
> Please carry my loved one
> Home safely to me"

LEE. Hey, knock it off will ya'! This is long distance here.

AUSTIN. Bakersfield?

LEE. Yeah, Bakersfield. It's Kern County.

AUSTIN. Well, what County are *we* in?

LEE. You better get yourself a 7-Up, boy.

AUSTIN. One County's as good as another.

[AUSTIN *hums "Red Sails" softly as* LEE *talks on phone.*]

LEE [*to phone*]. Yeah, operator look—first off I wanna' know the area code for Bakersfield. Right. Bakersfield! Okay. Good. Now I wanna' know if you can help me track somebody down. [*pause.*] No, no I mean a phone number. Just a phone number. Okay. [*holds a piece of paper up and reads it.*] Okay, the name is Melly Ferguson. Melly. [*pause.*] I dunno'. Melly. Maybe. Yeah. Maybe Melanie. Yeah. Melanie Ferguson. Okay. [*pause.*] What? I can't hear ya' so good. Sounds like yer under the ocean. [*pause.*] You got ten Melanie Fergusons? How could that be? Ten Melanie Fergusons in Bakersfield? Well gimme all of 'em then. [*pause.*] What d'ya' mean? Gimmie all ten Melanie Fergusons! That's right. Just a second. [*to* AUSTIN.] Gimme a pen.

AUSTIN. I don't have a pen.

LEE. Gimme a pencil then!

AUSTIN. I don't have a pencil.

LEE [*to phone*]. Just a second, operator. [*to* AUSTIN.] Yer a writer and ya' don't have a pen or a pencil!

AUSTIN. I'm not a writer. You're a writer.

LEE. I'm on the phone here! Get me a pen or a pencil.

AUSTIN. I gotta' watch the toast.

LEE [*to phone*]. Hang on a second, operator.

[LEE *lets the phone drop then starts pulling all the drawers in the kitchen out on the floor and dumping the contents, searching for a pencil,* AUSTIN *watches him casually.*]

LEE [*crashing through drawers, throwing contents around kitchen*]. This is the last time I try to live with people, boy! I can't believe it. Here I am! Here I am again in a desperate situation! This would never happen out on the desert. I would never be in this kinda' situation out on the desert. Isn't there a pen or a pencil in this house! Who lives in this house anyway!

AUSTIN. Our mother.

LEE. How come she don't have a pen or a pencil! She's a social person isn't she? Doesn't she have to make shopping lists? She's gotta' have a pencil. [*finds a pencil.*] Aaha! [*He rushes back to phone, picks up receiver.*] All right operator. Operator? Hey! Operator! Goddamnit!

[LEE *rips the phone off the wall and throws it down, goes back to chair and falls into it, drinks, long pause.*]

AUSTIN. She hung up?

LEE. Yeah, she hung up. I knew she was gonna' hang up. I could hear it in her voice.

[LEE *starts going through his slips of paper again.*]

AUSTIN. Well, you're probably better off staying here with me anyway. I'll take care of you.

LEE. I don't need takin' care of! Not by you anyway.

AUSTIN. Toast is almost ready.

[AUSTIN *starts buttering all the toast as it pops up.*]

LEE. I don't want any toast!

[*long pause.*]

AUSTIN. You gotta' eat something. Can't just drink. How long have we been drinking, anyway?

LEE [*looking through slips of paper.*] Maybe it was Fresno. What's the area code for Fresno? How could I have lost that number! She was beautiful.

[*pause.*]

AUSTIN. Why don't you just forget about that, Lee. Forget about the woman.

LEE. She had green eyes. You know what green eyes do to me?

AUSTIN. I know but you're not gonna' get it on with her now anyway. It's dawn already. She's in Bakersfield for Christ's sake.

[*long pause,* LEE *considers the situation.*]

LEE. Yeah. [*looks at windows.*] It's dawn?

AUSTIN. Let's just have some toast and—

LEE. What is this bullshit with the toast anyway! You make it sound like salvation or something. I don't want any goddamn toast! How many times I gotta' tell ya'!

[LEE *gets up, crosses upstage to windows in alcove, looks out,* AUSTIN *butters toast.*]

AUSTIN. Well it is like salvation sort of. I mean the smell. I love the smell of toast. And the sun's coming up. It makes me feel like anything's possible. Ya' know?

LEE [*back to* AUSTIN, *facing windows upstage.*] So go to church why don't ya'.

AUSTIN. Like a beginning. I love beginnings.

LEE. Oh yeah. I've always been kinda' partial to endings myself.

AUSTIN. What if I come with you, Lee?

LEE [*pause as* LEE *turns toward* AUSTIN]. What?

AUSTIN. What if I come with you out to the desert?

LEE. Are you kiddin'?

AUSTIN. No. I'd just like to see what it's like.

LEE. You wouldn't last a day out there pal.

AUSTIN. That's what you said about the toasters. You said I couldn't steal a toaster either.

LEE. A toaster's got nothin' to do with the desert.

AUSTIN. I could make it, Lee. I'm not that helpless. I can cook.

LEE. Cook?

AUSTIN. I can.

LEE. So what! You can cook. Toast.

AUSTIN. I can make fires. I know how to get fresh water from condensation.

[AUSTIN *stacks buttered toast up in a tall stack on plate.*]

[LEE *slams table.*]

LEE. It's not somethin' you learn out of a Boy Scout handbook!

AUSTIN. Well how do you learn it then! How're you supposed to learn it!

[*pause.*]

LEE. Ya' just learn it, that's all. Ya' learn it 'cause ya' have to learn it. You don't *have* to learn it.

AUSTIN. You could teach me.

LEE [*stands*]. What're you, crazy or somethin'? You went to college. Here, you are down here, rollin' in bucks. Floatin' up and down in elevators. And you wanna' learn how to live on the desert!

AUSTIN. I do, Lee. I really do. There's nothin' down here for me. There never was. When we were kids here it was different. There was a life here then. But now—I keep comin' down here thinkin' it's the fifties or somethin'. I keep finding myself getting off the freeway at familiar landmarks that turn out to be unfamiliar. On the way to appointments. Wandering down streets I thought I recognized that turn out to be replicas of streets I remember. Streets I misremember. Streets I can't tell if I lived on or saw in a postcard. Fields that don't even exist anymore.

LEE. There's no point cryin' about that now.

AUSTIN. There's nothin' real down here, Lee! Least of all me!

LEE. Well I can't save you from that!

AUSTIN. You can let me come with you.

LEE. No dice, pal.

AUSTIN. You could let me come with you, Lee!

LEE. Hey, do you actually think I chose to live out in the middle a' nowhere? Do ya'? Ya' think it's some kinda' philosophical decision I took or somethin'? I'm livin' out there 'cause I can't make it here! And yer bitchin' to me about all yer success!

AUSTIN. I'd cash it all in in a second. That's the truth.

LEE [*pause, shakes his head*]. I can't believe this.

AUSTIN. Let me go with you.

LEE. Stop sayin' that will ya'! Yer worse than a dog.

[AUSTIN *offers out the plate of neatly stacked toast to* LEE.]

AUSTIN. You want some toast?

[LEE *suddenly explodes and knocks the plate out of* AUSTIN's *hand, toast goes flying, long frozen moment where it appears* LEE *might go all the way this time when* AUSTIN *breaks it by slowly lowering himself to his knees and begins gathering the scattered toast from the floor and stacking it back on the plate.* LEE *begins to circle* AUSTIN *in a slow, predatory way, crushing pieces of toast in his wake, no words for a while,* AUSTIN *keeps gathering toast, even the crushed pieces.*]

LEE. Tell ya' what I'll do, little brother. I might just consider makin' you a deal. Little trade. [AUSTIN *continues gathering toast as* LEE *circles him through this.*] You write me up this screenplay thing just like I tell ya'. I mean you can use all yer usual tricks and stuff. Yer fancy language. Yer artistic hocus pocus. But ya' gotta' write everything like I say. Every move. Every time they run outa' gas, they run outa' gas. Every time they wanna' jump on a horse, they do just that. If they wanna' stay in Texas, by God they'll stay in Texas! [*Keeps circling.*] And you finish the whole thing up for me. Top to bottom. And you put my name on it. And I own all the rights. And every dime goes in my pocket. You do all that and I'll sure enough take ya' with me to the desert. [LEE *stops, pause, looks down at* AUSTIN.] How's that sound?

[*pause as* AUSTIN *stands slowly holding plate of demolished toast, their faces are very close, pause.*]

AUSTIN. It's a deal.

[LEE *stares straight into* AUSTIN*'s eyes, then he slowly takes a piece of toast off the plate, raises it to his mouth and takes a huge crushing bite never taking his eyes off* AUSTIN*'s, as* LEE *crunches into the toast the lights black out.*]

SCENE IX

Mid-day. No sound, blazing heat, the stage is ravaged; bottles, toasters, smashed typewriter, ripped out telephone, etc. All the debris from previous scene is now starkly visible in intense yellow light, the effect should be like a desert junkyard at high noon, the coolness of the preceding scenes is totally obliterated. AUSTIN *is seated at table in alcove, shirt open, pouring with sweat, hunched over a writing notebook, scribbling notes desperately with a ballpoint pen.* LEE *with no shirt, beer in hand, sweat pouring down his chest, is walking a slow circle around the table, picking his way through the objects, sometimes kicking them aside.*

LEE [*as he walks*]. All right, read it back to me. Read it back to me!

AUSTIN [*scribbling at top speed*]. Just a second.

LEE. Come on, come on! Just read what ya' got.

AUSTIN. I can't keep up! It's not the same as if I had a typewriter.

LEE. Just read what we got so far. Forget about the rest.

AUSTIN. All right. Let's see—okay—[*wipes sweat from his face, reads as* LEE *circles.*] Luke says uh—

LEE. Luke?

AUSTIN. Yeah.

LEE. His name's Luke? All right, all right—we can change the names later. What's he say? Come on, come on.

AUSTIN. He says uh—[*reading.*] "I told ya' you were a fool to follow me in here. I know this prairie like the back a' my hand."

LEE. No, no, no! That's not what I said. I never said that.

AUSTIN. That's what I wrote.

LEE. It's not what I said. I never said "like the back a' my hand." That's stupid. That's one a' those—whadya' call it? Whadya' call that?

AUSTIN. What?

LEE. Whadya' call it when somethin's been said a thousand times before. Whadya' call that?

AUSTIN. Um—a cliché?

LEE. Yeah. That's right. Cliché. That's what that is. A cliché. "The back a' my hand." That's stupid.

AUSTIN. That's what you said.

LEE. I never said that! And even if I did, that's where yer supposed to come in. That's where yer supposed to change it to somethin' better.

AUSTIN. Well how am I supposed to do that and write down what you say at the same time?

LEE. Ya' just do, that's all! You hear a stupid line you change it. That's yer job.

AUSTIN. All right. [*makes more notes.*]

LEE. What're you changin' it to?

AUSTIN. I'm not changing it. I'm just trying to catch up.

LEE. Well change it! We gotta' change that, we can't leave that in there like that. "... the back a' my hand." That's dumb.

AUSTIN [*stops writing, sits back*]. All right.

LEE [*pacing*]. So what'll we change it to?

AUSTIN. Um—How 'bout—"I'm on intimate terms with this prairie."

LEE [*to himself considering line as he walks*]. "I'm on intimate terms with this prairie." Intimate terms, intimate terms. Intimate—that means like uh—sexual right?

AUSTIN. Well—yeah—or—

LEE. He's on sexual terms with the prairie? How dya' figure that?

AUSTIN. Well it doesn't necessarily have to mean sexual.

LEE. What's it mean then?

AUSTIN. It means uh—close—personal—

LEE. All right. How's it sound? Put it into the uh—the line there. Read it back. Let's see how it sounds. [*to himself.*] "Intimate terms."

AUSTIN [*scribbles in notebook*]. Okay. It'd go something like this: [*reads.*] "I told ya' you were a fool to follow me in here. I'm on intimate terms with this prairie."

LEE. That's good. I like that. That's real good.

AUSTIN. You do?

LEE. Yeah. Don't you?

AUSTIN. Sure.

LEE. Sounds original now. "Intimate terms." That's good. Okay. Now we're cookin'! That has a real ring to it.

[AUSTIN *makes more notes,* LEE *walks around, pours beer on his arms and rubs it over his chest feeling good about the new progress, as he does this* MOM *enters unobtrusively down left with her luggage, she stops and stares at the scene still holding luggage as the two men continue, unaware of her presence,* AUSTIN *absorbed in his writing,* LEE *cooling himself off with beer.*]

LEE [*continues*]. "He's on intimate terms with this prairie." Sounds real mysterious and kinda' threatening at the same time.

AUSTIN [*writing rapidly*]. Good.

LEE. Now—[LEE *turns and suddenly sees* MOM, *he stares at her for a while, she stares back,* AUSTIN *keeps writing feverishly, not noticing,* LEE *walks slowly over to* MOM *and takes a closer look, long pause.*]

LEE. Mom?

[AUSTIN *looks up suddenly from his writing, sees* MOM, *stands quickly, long pause,* MOM *surveys the damage.*]

AUSTIN. Mom. What're you doing back?

MOM. I'm back.

LEE. Here, lemme take those for ya.

[LEE *sets beer on counter then takes both her bags but doesn't know where to set them down in the sea of junk so he just keeps holding them.*]

AUSTIN. I wasn't expecting you back so soon. I thought uh— How was Alaska?

MOM. Fine.

LEE. See any igloos?

MOM. No. Just glaciers.

AUSTIN. Cold huh?

MOM. What?

AUSTIN. It must've been cold up there?

MOM. Not really.

LEE. Musta' been colder than this here. I mean we're havin' a real scorcher here.

MOM. Oh? [*she looks at damage.*]

LEE. Yeah. Must be in the hundreds.

AUSTIN. You wanna' take your coat off, Mom?

MOM. No. [*pause, she surveys space.*] What happened in here?

AUSTIN. Oh um— Me and Lee were just sort of celebrating and uh—

MOM. Celebrating?

AUSTIN. Yeah. Uh—Lee sold a screenplay. A story, I mean.

MOM. Lee did?

AUSTIN. Yeah.

MOM. Not you?

AUSTIN. No. Him.

MOM [*to* LEE]. You sold a screenplay?

LEE. Yeah. That's right. We're just sorta' finishing it up right now. That's what we're doing here.

AUSTIN. Me and Lee are going out to the desert to live.

MOM. You and Lee?

AUSTIN. Yeah. I'm taking off with Lee.

MOM [*she looks back and forth at each of them, pause*]. You gonna go live with your father?

AUSTIN. No. We're going to a different desert Mom.

MOM. I see. Well, you'll probably wind up on the same desert sooner or later. What're all these toasters doing here?

AUSTIN. Well—we had kind of a contest.

MOM. Contest?

LEE. Yeah.

AUSTIN. Lee won.

MOM. Did you win a lot of money, Lee?

LEE. Well not yet. It's comin' in any day now.

MOM [*to* LEE]. What happened to your shirt?

LEE. Oh. I was sweatin' like a pig and I took it off.

[AUSTIN *grabs* LEE*'s shirt off the table and tosses it to him,* LEE *sets down suitcases and puts his shirt on.*]

MOM. Well it's one hell of a mess in here isn't it?

AUSTIN. Yeah, I'll clean it up for you, Mom. I just didn't know you were coming back so soon.

MOM. I didn't either.

AUSTIN. What happened?

MOM. Nothing. I just started missing all my plants.

[*she notices dead plants.*]

AUSTIN. Oh.

MOM. Oh, they're all dead aren't they. [*She crosses toward them, examines them closely.*] You didn't get a chance to water I guess.

AUSTIN. I was doing it and then Lee came and—

LEE. Yeah I just distracted him a whole lot here, Mom. It's not his fault.

[*pause, as* MOM *stares at plants.*]

MOM. Oh well, one less thing to take care of I guess. [*turns toward brothers.*] Oh, that reminds me— You boys will probably never guess who's in town. Try and guess.

[*long pause, brothers stare at her.*]

AUSTIN. Whadya' mean, Mom?

MOM. Take a guess. Somebody very important has come to town. I read it, coming down on the Greyhound.

LEE. Somebody very important?

MOM. See if you can guess. You'll never guess.

AUSTIN. Mom—we're trying to uh—[*points to writing pad.*]

MOM. Picasso. [*pause*] Picasso's in town. Isn't that incredible? Right now.

[*pause.*]

AUSTIN. Picasso's dead, Mom.

MOM. No, he's not dead. He's visiting the museum. I read it on the bus. We have to go down there and see him.

AUSTIN. Mom—

MOM. This is the chance of a lifetime. Can you imagine? We could all go down and meet him. All three of us.

LEE. Uh—I don't think I'm really up fer meetin' anybody right now. I'm uh— What's his name?

MOM. Picasso! Picasso! You've never heard of Picasso? Austin, you've heard of Picasso.

AUSTIN. Mom, we're not going to have time.

MOM. It won't take long. We'll just hop in the car and go down there. An opportunity like this doesn't come along every day.

AUSTIN. We're gonna' be leavin' here, Mom!

[*pause.*]

MOM. Oh.

LEE. Yeah.

[*pause.*]

MOM. You're both leaving?

LEE [*looks at* AUSTIN]. Well we were thinkin' about that before but now I—

AUSTIN. No, we are! We're both leaving. We've got it all planned.

MOM [*to* AUSTIN]. Well you can't leave. You have a family.

AUSTIN. I'm leaving. I'm getting out of here.

LEE [*to* MOM]. I don't really think Austin's cut out for the desert do you?

MOM. No. He's not.

AUSTIN. I'm going with you, Lee!

MOM. He's too thin.

LEE. Yeah, he'd just burn up out there.

AUSTIN [*to* LEE]. We just gotta' finish this screenplay and then we're gonna' take off. That's the plan. That's what you said. Come on, let's get back to work, Lee.

LEE. I can't work under these conditions here. It's too hot.

AUSTIN. Then we'll do it on the desert.

LEE. Don't be tellin' me what we're gonna do!

MOM. Don't shout in the house.

LEE. We're just gonna' have to postpone the whole deal.

AUSTIN. I can't postpone it! It's gone past postponing! I'm doing everything you said. I'm writing down exactly what you tell me.

LEE. Yeah, but you were right all along see. It is a dumb story. "Two lamebrains chasin' each other across Texas." That's what you said, right?

AUSTIN. I never said that.

[LEE *sneers in* AUSTIN'*s face then turns to* MOM.]

LEE. I'm gonna' just borrow some a' your antiques, Mom. You don't mind do ya'? Just a few plates and things. Silverware.

[LEE *starts going through all the cupboards in kitchen pulling out plates and stacking them on counter as* MOM *and* AUSTIN *watch.*]

MOM. You don't have any utensils on the desert?

LEE. Nah, I'm fresh out.

AUSTIN [*to* LEE]. What're you doing?

MOM. Well some of those are very old. Bone china.

LEE. I'm tired of eatin' outa' my bare hands, ya' know. It's not civilized.

AUSTIN [*to* LEE]. What're you doing? We made a deal!

MOM. Couldn't you borrow the plastic ones instead? I have plenty of plastic ones.

LEE [*as he stacks plates*]. It's not the same. Plastic's not the same at all. What I need is somethin' authentic. Somethin' to keep me in touch. It's easy to get outa' touch out there. Don't worry I'll get em' back to ya'.

[AUSTIN *rushes up to* LEE, *grabs him by shoulders.*]

AUSTIN. You can't just drop the whole thing, Lee!

[LEE *turns, pushes* AUSTIN *in the chest knocking him backwards into the alcove,* MOM *watches numbly,* LEE *returns to collecting the plates, silverware, etc.*]

MOM. You boys shouldn't fight in the house. Go outside and fight.

LEE. I'm not fightin'. I'm leavin'.

MOM. There's been enough damage done already.

LEE [*his back to* AUSTIN *and* MOM, *stacking dishes on counter*]. I'm clearin' outa' here once and for all. All this town does is drive a man insane. Look what it's done to Austin there. I'm not lettin' that happen to me. Sell myself down the river. No sir. I'd rather be a hundred miles from nowhere than let that happen to me.

[*During this* AUSTIN *has picked up the ripped-out phone from the floor and wrapped the cord tightly around both his hands. He lunges at* LEE *whose back is still to him, wraps the cord around* LEE'*s neck, plants a foot in* LEE'*s back and pulls back on the cord, tightening it,* LEE *chokes desperately, can't speak and can't reach* AUSTIN *with his arms,* AUSTIN *keeps applying pressure on* LEE'*s back with his foot, bending him into the sink,* MOM *watches.*]

AUSTIN [*tightening cord*]. You're not goin' anywhere! You're not takin' anything with you. You're not takin' my car! You're not takin' the dishes! You're not takin' anything! You're stayin' right here!

MOM. You'll have to stop fighting in the house. There's plenty of room outside to fight. You've got the whole outdoors to fight in.

[LEE *tries to tear himself away, he crashes across the stage like an enraged bull dragging* AUSTIN *with him, he snorts and bellows but* AUSTIN *hangs on and manages to keep clear of* LEE'*s attempts to grab him, they crash into the table, to the floor,* LEE *is face down thrashing wildly and choking,* AUSTIN *pulls cord tighter, stands with one foot planted on* LEE'*s back and the cord stretched taut.*]

AUSTIN [*holding cord.*] Gimme back my keys, Lee! Take the keys out! Take 'em out!

[LEE *desperately tries to dig in his pockets, searching for the car keys,* MOM *moves closer.*]

MOM [*calmly to* AUSTIN]. You're not killing him are you?

AUSTIN. I don't know. I don't know if I'm killing him. I'm stopping him. That's all. I'm just stopping him.

[LEE *thrashes but* AUSTIN *is relentless.*]

MOM. You oughta' let him breathe a little bit.

AUSTIN. Throw the keys out, Lee!

[LEE *finally gets keys out and throws them on floor but out of* AUSTIN*'s reach,* AUSTIN *keeps pressure on cord, pulling* LEE*'s neck back,* LEE *gets one hand to the cord but can't relieve the pressure.*]

Reach me those keys would ya', Mom.

MOM [*not moving*]. Why are you doing this to him?

AUSTIN. Reach me the keys!

MOM. Not until you stop choking him.

AUSTIN. I can't stop choking him! He'll kill me if I stop choking him!

MOM. He won't kill you. He's your brother.

AUSTIN. Just get me the keys would ya'!

[*pause.* MOM *picks keys up off floor, hands them to* AUSTIN.]

AUSTIN [*to* MOM]. Thanks.

MOM. Will you let him go now?

AUSTIN. I don't know. He's not gonna' let me get outa' here.

MOM. Well you can't kill him.

AUSTIN. I can kill him! I can easily kill him. Right now. Right here. All I gotta' do is just tighten up. See? [*He tightens cord,* LEE *thrashes wildly,* AUSTIN *releases pressure a little, maintaining control.*] Ya' see that?

MOM. That's a savage thing to do.

AUSTIN. Yeah well don't tell me I can't kill him because I can. I can just twist. I can just keep twisting. [AUSTIN *twists the cord tighter,* LEE *weakens, his breathing changes to a short rasp.*]

MOM. Austin!

[AUSTIN *relieves pressure,* LEE *breathes easier but* AUSTIN *keeps him under control.*]

AUSTIN [*eyes on* LEE, *holding cord*]. I'm goin' to the desert. There's nothing stopping me. I'm going by myself to the desert.

[MOM *moving toward her luggage.*]

MOM. Well, I'm going to go check into a motel. I can't stand this anymore.

AUSTIN. Don't go yet!

[MOM *pauses.*]

MOM. I can't stay here. This is worse than being homeless.

AUSTIN. I'll get everything fixed up for you, Mom. I promise. Just stay for a while.

MOM [*picking up luggage*]. You're going to the desert.

AUSTIN. Just wait!

[LEE *thrashes,* AUSTIN *subdues him,* MOM *watches holding luggage, pause.*]

MOM. It was the worst feeling being up there. In Alaska. Staring out a window. I never felt so desperate before. That's why when I saw that article on Picasso I thought—

AUSTIN. Stay here, Mom. This is where you live.

[*She looks around the stage.*]

MOM. I don't recognize it at all.

[*She exits with luggage,* AUSTIN *makes a move toward her but* LEE *starts to struggle and* AUSTIN *subdues him again with cord, pause.*]

AUSTIN [*holding cord*]. Lee? I'll make ya' a deal. You let me get outa' here. Just let me get to my car. All right, Lee? Gimme a little headstart and I'll turn you loose. Just gimme a little headstart. All right?

[LEE *makes no response,* AUSTIN *slowly releases tension on cord, still nothing from* LEE.]

AUSTIN. Lee?

[LEE *is motionless,* AUSTIN *very slowly begins to stand, still keeping a tenuous hold on the cord and his eyes riveted to* LEE *for any sign of movement,* AUSTIN *slowly drops the cord and stands, he stares down at* LEE *who appears to be dead.*]

AUSTIN [*whispers*]. Lee?

[*pause.* AUSTIN *considers, looks toward exit, back to* LEE, *then makes a small movement as if to leave. Instantly* LEE *is on his feet and moves toward exit, blocking* AUSTIN*'s escape. They square off to each other, keeping a distance between them. Pause, a single coyote heard in distance, lights fade softly into moonlight. The figures of the brothers now appear to be caught in a vast desert-like landscape, they are very still but watchful for the next move. Lights go slowly to black as the after-image of the brothers pulses in the dark, coyote fades.*]

[1980]

Beth Henley *1952–*

AM I BLUE?

First Produced in New York City by Circle Repertory Company

CHARACTERS

JOHN POLK, *seventeen*
ASHBE, *sixteen*
HILDA, *a waitress, thirty-five*

STREET PEOPLE: BARKER, WHORE, BUM, CLAREECE

SCENE: *A bar, the street, the living room of a run-down apartment.*
TIME: *Fall 1968*

The scene opens on a street in the New Orleans French Quarter on a rainy, blue bourbon night. Various people—a WHORE, BUM, STREET BARKER, CLAREECE *—appear and disappear along the street. The scene then focuses on a bar where a piano is heard from the back room playing softly and indistinctly "Am I Blue?" The lights go up on* JOHN POLK, *who sits alone at a table. He is seventeen, a bit overweight and awkward. He wears nice clothes, perhaps a navy sweater with large white monograms. His navy raincoat is slung over an empty chair. While drinking* JOHN POLK *concentrates on the red and black card that he holds in his hand. As soon as the scene is established,* ASHBE *enters from the street. She is sixteen, wears a flowered plastic raincoat, a white plastic rain cap, red galoshes, a butterfly barrette, and jeweled cat-eye glasses. She is carrying a bag full of stolen goods. Her hair is very curly.* ASHBE *makes her way cautiously to* JOHN POLK'S *table. As he sees her coming, he puts the card into his pocket. She sits in the empty chair and pulls his raincoat over her head.*

ASHBE. Excuse me ... do you mind if I sit here please?
JOHN POLK [*looks up at her—then down into his glass*]. What are you doing hiding under my raincoat? You're getting it all wet.
ASHBE. Well, I'm very sorry, but after all it is a raincoat. [*He tries to pull off coat*]. It was rude of me I know, but look I just don't want them to recognize me.
JOHN POLK [*looking about*]. Who to recognize you?
ASHBE. Well, I stole these two ash trays from the Screw Inn, ya know right down the street. [*She pulls out two glass commercial ash trays from her white plastic bag.*] Anyway, I'm scared the manager saw me. They'll be after me I'm afraid.
JOHN POLK. Well, they should be. Look, do you mind giving me back my raincoat? I don't want to be found protecting any thief.
ASHBE [*coming out from under coat*]. Thief—would you call Robin Hood a thief?
JOHN POLK. Christ.
ASHBE [*back under coat*]. No, you wouldn't. He was valiant—all the time stealing from the rich and giving to the poor.
JOHN POLK. But your case isn't exactly the same, is it? You're stealing from some crummy little bar and keeping the ash trays for yourself. Now give me back my coat.
ASHBE [*throws coat at him*]. Sure, take your old coat. I suppose I should have explained—about Miss Marcey. [*Silence.*] Miss Marcey, this cute old lady with a

1724

little hump in her back. I always see her in her sun hat and blue print dress. Miss
Marcey lives in the apartment building next to ours. I leave all the stolen goods,
as gifts on her front steps.

JOHN POLK. Are you one of those kleptomaniacs? [*He starts checking his wallet.*]

ASHBE. You mean when people all the time steal and they can't help it?

JOHN POLK. Yeah.

ASHBE. Oh, no. I'm not a bit careless. Take my job tonight, my very first night job,
if you want to know. Anyway, I've been planning it for two months, trying to
decipher which bar most deserved to be stolen from. I finally decided on the
Screw Inn. Mainly because of the way they're so mean to Mr. Groves. He works
at the magazine rack at Diver's Drugstore and is really very sweet, but he has a
drinking problem. I don't think that's fair to be mean to people simply because
they have a drinking problem—and, well, anyway, you see I'm not just stealing
for personal gain. I mean, I don't even smoke.

JOHN POLK. Yeah, well, most infants don't, but then again, most infants don't hang
around bars.

ASHBE. I don't see why not, Toulouse-Latrec[1] did.

JOHN POLK. They'd throw me out.

ASHBE. Oh, they throw me out too, but I don't accept defeat. [*Slowly moves into
him.*] Why it's the very same with my pickpocketing.

[JOHN POLK *sneers, turns away.*]

ASHBE. It's a very hard art to master. Why every time I've done it, I've been caught.

JOHN POLK. That's all I need, is to have some slum kid tell me how good it is to steal.
Everyone knows it's not.

ASHBE [*about his drink*]. That looks good. What is it?

JOHN POLK. Hey, would you mind leaving me alone—I just wanted to be alone.

ASHBE. Okay. I'm sorry. How about if I'm quiet?

[JOHN POLK *shrugs. He sips drink, looks around, catches her eye, she smiles and sighs.*]

ASHBE. I was just looking at your pin. What fraternity are you in?

JOHN POLK. S.A.E.

ASHBE. Is it a good fraternity?

JOHN POLK. Sure, it's the greatest.

ASHBE. I bet you have lots of friends.

JOHN POLK. Tons.

ASHBE. Are you serious?

JOHN POLK. Yes.

ASHBE. Hmm. Do they have parties and all that?

JOHN POLK. Yeah, lots of parties, booze, honking horns, it's exactly what you would
expect.

ASHBE. I wouldn't expect anything. Why did you join?

JOHN POLK. I don't know. Well, my brother . . . I guess it was my brother . . . he told
me how great it was, how the fraternity was supposed to get you dates, make you
study, solve all your problems.

ASHBE. Gee, does it?

JOHN POLK. Doesn't help you study.

ASHBE. How about dates? Do they get you a lot of dates?

JOHN POLK. Some.

ASHBE. What were the girls like?

---

[1] Henri Toulouse-Latrec (1864-1901) was a French painter and graphic artist who was famous for
depicting the decadent nightlife in Parisian bars.

JOHN POLK. I don't know—they were like girls.

ASHBE. Did you have a good time?

JOHN POLK. I had a pretty good time.

ASHBE. Did you make love to any of them?

JOHN POLK [*to self*]. Oh, Christ . . .

ASHBE. I'm sorry . . . I just figured that's why you had the appointment with the whore . . . cause you didn't have anyone else . . . to make love to.

JOHN POLK. How did you know I had the, ah, the appointment?

ASHBE. I saw you put the red card in your pocket when I came up. Those red cards are pretty familiar around here. The house is only about a block or so away. It's one of the best though, really very plush. Only two murders and a knifing in its whole history. Do you go there often?

JOHN POLK. Yeah, I like to give myself a treat.

ASHBE. Who do you have?

JOHN POLK. What do you mean?

ASHBE. I mean which girl. [JOHN POLK *gazes into his drink*.] Look, I just thought I might know her is all.

JOHN POLK. Know her, ah, how would you know her?

ASHBE. Well, some of the girls from my high school go there to work when they get out.

JOHN POLK. G.G., her name is G.G.

ASHBE. G.G. . . . Hmm, well, how does she look?

JOHN POLK. I don't know.

ASHBE. Oh, you've never been with her before?

JOHN POLK. No.

ASHBE [*confidentially*]. Are you one of those kinds that likes a lot of variety?

JOHN POLK. Variety? Sure, I guess I like variety.

ASHBE. Oh, yes, now I remember.

JOHN POLK. What?

ASHBE. G.G., that's just her working name. Her real name is Myrtle Reims, she's Kay Reims' older sister. Kay is in my grade at school.

JOHN POLK. Myrtle? Her name is Myrtle?

ASHBE. I never liked the name either.

JOHN POLK. Myrtle, oh, Christ. Is she pretty?

ASHBE [*matter of fact*]. Pretty, no she's not real pretty.

JOHN POLK. What does she look like?

ASHBE. Let's see . . . she's, ah, well, Myrtle had acne and there are a few scars left. It's not bad. I think they sort of give her character. Her hair's red, only I don't think it's really red. It sort of fizzles out all over her head. She's got a pretty good figure . . . big top . . . but the rest of her is kind of skinny.

JOHN POLK. I wonder if she has a good personality.

ASHBE. Well, she was a senior when I was a freshman; so I never really knew her. I remember she used to paint her finger nails lots of different colors . . . pink, orange, purple. I don't know, but she kind of scares me. About the only time I ever saw her true personality was around a year ago. I was over at Kay's making a health poster for school. Anyway, Myrtle comes busting in, screaming about how she can't find her spangled bra anywhere. Kay and I just sat on the floor cutting pictures of food out of magazines while she was storming about slamming drawers and swearing. Finally, she found it. It was pretty garish—red with black and gold sequined G's on each cup. That's how I remember the name—G.G.

[*As* Ashbe *illustrates the placement of the G's she spots* Hilda, *the waitress, approaching.* Ashbe *pulls the raincoat over her head and hides on the floor.* Hilda *enters through the beaded curtains spilling her tray.* Hilda *is a woman of few words.*]

Hilda. Shit, damn curtain. Nuther drink?

John Polk. Mam?

Hilda [*points to drink*]. Vodka coke?

John Polk. No, thank you. I'm not quite finished yet.

Hilda. Napkin's clean.

[Ashbe *pulls her bag off the table.* Hilda *looks at* Ashbe *then to* John Polk. *She walks around the table, as* Ashbe *is crawling along the floor to escape.* Ashbe *runs into* Hilda's *toes.*]

Ashbe. Are those real gold?

Hilda. You again. Out.

Ashbe. She wants me to leave. Why should a paying customer leave? [*Back to* Hilda.] Now I'll have a mint julep and easy on the mint.

Hilda. This pre-teen with you?

John Polk. Well, I . . . No . . . I . . .

Hilda. I.D.'s

Ashbe. Certainly, I always try to cooperate with the management.

Hilda [*looking at* John Polk's *I.D.*]. I.D., 11-12-50. Date: 11-11-68.

John Polk. Yes, but . . . well, 11-12 is less than two hours away.

Hilda. Back in two hours.

Ashbe. I seem to have left my identification in my gold lamé bag.

Hilda. Well, boo-hoo. [*Motions for* Ashbe *to leave with a minimum of effort. She goes back to table.*] No tip.

Ashbe. You didn't tip her?

John Polk. I figured the drinks were so expensive . . . I just didn't . . .

Hilda. No tip!

John Polk. Look, Miss, I'm sorry. [*Going through his pockets.*] Here would you like a . . . nickel . . . wait, wait, here's a quarter.

Hilda. Just move ass, sonny. You too, Barbie.

Ashbe. Ugh, I hate public rudeness. I'm sure I'll refrain from ever coming here again.

Hilda. Think I'll go in the back room and cry.

[Ashbe *and* John Polk. *exit.* Hilda *picks up tray and exits through the curtain, tripping again.*]

Hilda. Shit, Damn curtain.

[Ashbe *and* John Polk *are now standing outside under the awning of the bar.*]

Ashbe. Gee, I didn't know it was your birthday tomorrow. Happy birthday! Don't be mad. I thought you were at least twenty or twenty-one, really.

John Polk. It's o.k. Forget it.

[*As they begin walking, various blues are heard coming from the near-by bars.*]

Ashbe. It's raining.

John Polk. I know.

Ashbe. Are you going over to the house now?

John Polk. No, not till twelve.

Ashbe. Yeah, the red and black cards—they mean all night. Midnight till morning.

[*At this point a street barker beckons the couple into his establishment. Perhaps he is accompanied by a whore.*]

Barker. Hey mister, bring your baby on in, buy her a few drinks, maybe tonight ya get lucky.

Ashbe. Keep walking.

John Polk. What's wrong with the place?

Ashbe. The drinks are watery rot gut, and the show girls are boys . . .

Barker. Up yours, punk!

John Polk [*who has now sat down on a street bench*]. Look, just tell me where a cheap bar is. I've got to stay drunk, but I just don't have much money left.

Ashbe. Yikes, there aren't too many cheap bars around here, and a lot of them check I.D.'s.

John Polk. Well, do you know of any that don't?

Ashbe. No, not for sure.

John Polk. Oh, God, I need to get drunk.

Ashbe. Aren't you?

John Polk. Some, but I'm losing ground fast.

[*By this time a bum who has been traveling drunkenly down the street falls near the couple and begins throwing up.*]

Ashbe. Oh, I know! You can come to my apartment. It's just down the block. We keep one bottle of rum around. I'll serve you a grand drink, three or four if you like.

John Polk [*fretfully*]. No, thanks.

Ashbe. But look, we're getting all wet.

John Polk. Sober too, wet and sober.

Ashbe. Oh, come on! Rain's blurring my glasses.

John Polk. Well, how about your parents? What would they say?

Ashbe. Daddy's out of town and Mama lives in Atlanta; so I'm sure they won't mind. I think we have some cute, little marshmallows. [*Pulling on him.*] Won't you really come?

John Polk. You've probably got some gang of muggers waiting to kill me. Oh, all right . . . what the hell, let's go.

Ashbe. Hurrah! Come on. It's this way. [*She starts across the stage, stops, and picks up an old hat.*] Hey, look at this hat. Isn't it something! Here, wear it to keep off the rain.

John Polk [*throwing hat back onto street*]. No, thanks, you don't know who's worn it before.

Ashbe [*picking hat back up*]. That makes it all the more exciting. Maybe it was a butcher who slaughtered his wife or a silver pirate with a black bird on his throat. Who do you guess?

John Polk. I don't know. Anyway what's the good of guessing? I mean you'll never really know.

Ashbe [*trying the hat on*]. Yeah, probably not.

[*At this point* Ashbe *and* John Polk *reach the front door.*]

Ashbe. Here we are.

[Ashbe *begins fumbling for her key.* Clareece, *a teeny-bopper, walks up to* John Polk.]

Clareece. Hey, man, got any spare change?

John Polk [*looking through his pockets*]. Let me see . . . I . . .

Ashbe [*Coming up between them, giving* Clareece *a shove*]. Beat it, Clareece. He's my company.

Clareece [*walks away and sneers.*] Oh, shove it, Frizzels.

Ashbe. A lot of jerks live around here. Come on in.

[*She opens the door. Lights go up on the living room of a run-down apartment in a run-down apartment house. Besides being merely run-down the room is a malicious pig sty*] *with colors, paper hats, paper dolls, masks, torn up stuffed animals, dead flowers and leaves, dress-up clothes, etc., thrown all about.*]

My bones are cold. Do you want a towel to dry off?

JOHN POLK. Yes, thank you.

ASHBE [*she picks up a towel off the floor and tosses it to him*]. Here. [*He begins drying off, as she takes off her rain things; then she begins raking things off the sofa.*] Please do sit down. [*He sits.*] I'm sorry the place is disheveled, but my father's been out of town. I always try to pick up and all before he gets in. Of course, he's pretty used to messes. My mother never was too good at keeping things clean.

JOHN POLK. When's he coming back?

ASHBE. Sunday, I believe. Oh, I've been meaning to say . . .

JOHN POLK. What?

ASHBE. My name's Ashbe Williams.

JOHN POLK. Ashbe?

ASHBE. Yeah, Ashbe.

JOHN POLK. My name's John Polk Richards.

ASHBE. John Polk? They call you John Polk?

JOHN POLK. It's family.

ASHBE [*putting on socks*]. These are my favorite socks, the red furry ones. Well, here's some books and magazines to look at while I fix you something to drink. What do you want in your rum?

JOHN POLK. Coke's fine.

ASHBE. I'll see if we have any. I think I'll take some hot Kool-Aid myself.
[*She exits to the kitchen.*]

JOHN POLK. Hot Kool-Aid?

ASHBE. It's just Kool-Aid that's been heated, like hot chocolate or hot tea.

JOHN POLK. Sounds great.

ASHBE. Well, I'm used to it. You get so much for your dime, it makes it worth your while. I don't buy presweetened, of course, it's better to sugar your own.

JOHN POLK. I remember once I threw up a lot of grape Kool-Aid when I was a kid. I've hated it ever since. Hey, would you check on the time?

ASHBE [*she enters carrying a tray with several bottles of food coloring, a bottle of rum, and a huge glass*]. I'm sorry we don't have Coke. I wonder if rum and Kool-Aid is good? Oh, we don't have a clock either.

[*She pours a large amount of rum into the large glass.*]

JOHN POLK. I'll just have it with water then.

ASHBE [*she finds an almost empty glass of water somewhere in the room and dumps it in with the rum*]. Would you like food coloring in the water? It makes a drink all the more aesthetic. Of course, some people don't care for aesthetics.

JOHN POLK. No, thank you, just plain water.

ASHBE. Are you sure? The taste is entirely the same. I put it in all my water.

JOHN POLK. Well . . .

ASHBE. What color do you want?

JOHN POLK. I don't know.

ASHBE. What's your favorite color?

JOHN POLK. Blue, I guess.
[*She puts a few blue drops into the glass. As she has nothing to stir with, she blows into the glass turning the water blue.*]

JOHN POLK. Thanks.

ASHBE [*exits. She screams from the kitchen*]. Come on, say come on, cat, eat your fresh, good milk.

JOHN POLK. You have a cat?

ASHBE [*off*]. No.

JOHN POLK. Oh.

ASHBE [*she enters carrying a tray with a cup of hot Kool-Aid and Cheerios and colored marshmallows*]. Here are some Cheerios and some cute, little, colored marsh-mallows to eat with your drink.

JOHN POLK. Thanks.

ASHBE. I one time smashed all the big white marshmallows in the plastic bag at the grocery store.

JOHN POLK. Why did you do that?

ASHBE. I was angry. Do you like ceramics?

JOHN POLK. Yes.

ASHBE. My mother makes them. It's sort of her hobby. She is very talented.

JOHN POLK. My mother never does anything. Well, I guess she can shuffle the bridge deck okay.

ASHBE. Actually, my mother is a dancer. She teaches at a school in Atlanta. She's really very talented.

JOHN POLK [*indicates ceramics*]. She must be to do all these.

ASHBE. Well, Madeline, my older sister, did the blue one. Madeline gets to live with Mama.

JOHN POLK. And you live with your father.

ASHBE. Yeah, but I get to go visit them sometimes.

JOHN POLK. You do ceramics too?

ASHBE. No, I never learned . . . but I have this great potholder set. [*Gets up to show him.*] See, I make lots of multicolored potholders and send them to Mama and Madeline. I also make paper hats. [*Gets material to show him.*] I guess they're more creative, but making potholders is more relaxing. Here would you like to make a hat?

JOHN POLK. I don't know, I'm a little drunk.

ASHBE. It's not hard a bit. [*Hands him material.*] Just draw a real pretty design on the paper. It really doesn't have to be pretty, just whatever you want.

JOHN POLK. It's kind of you to give my creative drives such freedom.

ASHBE. Ha, ha, ha. I'll work on my potholder set a bit.

JOHN POLK. What time is it? I've really got to check on the time.

ASHBE. I know. I'll call the operator.

[*She goes to the phone.*]

JOHN POLK. How do you get along without a clock?

ASHBE. Well, I've been late for school a lot. Daddy has a watch. It's 11:03.

JOHN POLK. I've got a while yet. [ASHBE *twirls back to her chair, drops, and sighs.*] Are you a dancer, too?

ASHBE [*delighted*]. I can't dance a bit, really. I practice a lot is all, at home in the afternoon. I imagine you go to a lot of dances.

JOHN POLK. Not really, I'm a terrible dancer. I usually get bored or drunk.

ASHBE. You probably drink too much.

JOHN POLK. No, it's just since I've come to college. All you do there is drink more beer and write more papers.

ASHBE. What are you studying for to be?

JOHN POLK. I don't know.

ASHBE. Why don't you become a rancher?

JOHN POLK. Dad wants me to help run his soybean farm.

ASHBE. Soybean farm. Yikes, that's really something. Where is it?

JOHN POLK. Well, I live in the Delta, Hollybluff, Mississippi. Anyway, Dad feels I should go to business school first; you know, so I'll become, well, management-minded. Pass the blue.

ASHBE. Is that what you really want to do?

JOHN POLK. I don't know. It would probably be as good as anything else I could do. Dad makes good money. He can take vacations whenever he wants. Sure it'll be a ball.

ASHBE. I'd hate to have to be management-minded. [JOHN POLK *shrugs.*] I don't mean to hurt your feelings, but I would really hate to be a management mind. [*She starts walking on her knees, twisting her fists in front of her eyes, and making clicking sounds as a management mind would make.*]

JOHN POLK. Cut it out. Just forget it. The farm could burn down, and I wouldn't even have to think about it.

ASHBE [*after a pause*]. Well, what do you want to talk about?

JOHN POLK. I don't know.

ASHBE. When was the last dance you went to?

JOHN POLK. Dances. That's a great subject. Let's see, oh, I don't really remember—it was probably some blind date. God, I hate dates.

ASHBE. Why?

JOHN POLK. Well, they always say that they don't want popcorn, and they wind up eating all of yours.

ASHBE. You mean, you hate dates just because they eat your popcorn? Don't you think that's kind of stingy?

JOHN POLK. It's the principle of the thing. Why can't they just say, yes, I'd like some popcorn when you ask them. But, no, they're always so damn coy.

ASHBE. I'd tell my date if I wanted popcorn. I'm not that immature.

JOHN POLK. Anyway, it's not only the popcorn. It's a lot of little things. I've finished coloring. What do I do now?

ASHBE. Now you have to fold it. Here . . . like this. [*She explains the process with relish.*] Say, that's really something.

JOHN POLK. It's kind of funny looking. [*Putting the hat on.*] Yeah, I like it, but you could never wear it anywhere.

ASHBE. Well, like what anyway?

JOHN POLK. Huh?

ASHBE. The things dates do to you that you don't like, the little things.

JOHN POLK. Oh, well, just the way, they wear those false eyelashes and put their hand on your knee when you're trying to parallel park, and keep on giggling and going off to the bathroom with their girl friends. It's obvious they don't want to go out with me. They just want to go out so that they can wear their new clothes and won't have to sit on their ass in the dormitory. They never want to go out with me. I can never even talk to them.

ASHBE. Well, you can talk to me, and I'm a girl.

JOHN POLK. Well, I'm really kind of drunk, and you're a stranger . . . well, I probably wouldn't be able to talk to you tomorrow. That makes a difference.

ASHBE. Maybe it does. [*A bit of a pause and then extremely pleased by the idea she says.*] You know we're alike because I don't like dances either.

JOHN POLK. I thought you said you practiced . . . in the afternoons.

ASHBE. Well, I like dancing. I just don't like dances. At least not like . . . well, not like the one our school was having tonight . . . they're so corny.

JOHN POLK. Yeah, most dances are.

ASHBE. All they serve is potato chips and fruit punch, and then this stupid baby band plays and everybody dances around thinking they're so hot. I frankly wouldn't dance there. I would prefer to wait till I am invited to an exclusive ball. It doesn't really matter which ball, just one where they have huge, golden chandeliers and silver fountains, and serve delicacies of all sorts and bubble blue champagne. I'll arrive in a pink silk cape [*laughing.*] I want to dance in pink!

JOHN POLK. You're mixed up. You're probably one of those people that live in a fantasy world.

ASHBE. I do not. I accept reality as well as anyone. Anyway you can talk to me, remember. I know what you mean by the kind of girls it's hard to talk to. There are girls a lot that way in the small clique at my school. Really tacky and mean. They expect everyone to be as stylish as they are, and they won't even speak to you in the hall. I don't mind if they don't speak to me, but I really love the orphans, and it hurts my feelings when they are so mean to them.

JOHN POLK. What do you mean—they're mean to the "orpheens?" [*Giggles to himself at the wordplay.*]

ASHBE. Oh, well, they sometimes snicker at the orphans' dresses. The orphans usually have hand-me-down, drab, ugly dresses. Once Shelly Maxwell wouldn't let Glinda borrow her pencil, even though she had two. It hurt her feelings.

JOHN POLK. Are you best friends with these orphans?

ASHBE. I hardly know them at all. They're really shy. I just like them a lot. They're the reason I put spells on the girls in the clique.

JOHN POLK. Spells, what do you mean, witch spells?

ASHBE. Witch spells? Not really, mostly just voodoo.

JOHN POLK. Are you kidding? Do you really do voodoo?

ASHBE. Sure, here I'll show you my doll. [*Goes to get doll, comes back with straw voodoo doll. Her air as she returns is one of frightening mystery.*] I know a lot about the subject. Cora, she used to wash dishes in the Moonlight Cafe, told me all about voodoo. She's a real expert on the subject, went to all the meetings and everything. Once she caused a man's throat to rot away and turn almost totally black. She's moved to Chicago now.

JOHN POLK. It doesn't really work. Does it?

ASHBE. Well, not always. The thing about voodoo is that both parties have to believe in it for it to work.

JOHN POLK. Do the girls in school believe in it?

ASHBE. Not really, I don't think. That's where my main problem comes in. I have to make the clique believe in it, yet I have to be very subtle. Mainly, I give reports in English class or Speech.

JOHN POLK. Reports?

ASHBE. On voodoo.

JOHN POLK. That's really kind of sick, you know.

ASHBE. Not really. I don't cast spells that'll do any real harm. Mainly, just the kind of thing to make them think . . . to keep them on their toes. [*Blue-drink intoxication begins to take over and* JOHN POLK *begins laughing.*] What's so funny?

JOHN POLK. Nothing. I was just thinking what a mean little person you are.

ASHBE. Mean! I'm not mean a bit.

JOHN POLK. Yes, you are mean ... [*picking up color*] ... and green too.

ASHBE. Green?

JOHN POLK. Yes, green with envy of those other girls; so you play all those mean little tricks.

ASHBE. Envious of those other girls, that stupid, close-minded little clique!

JOHN POLK. Green as this marshmallow. [*Eats marshmallow.*]

ASHBE. You think I want to be in some group ... a sheep like you? A little sheep like you that does everything when he's supposed to do it!

JOHN POLK. Me a sheep ... I do what I want!

ASHBE. Ha! I've known you for an hour and already I see you for the sheep you are!

JOHN POLK. Don't take your green meanness out on me.

ASHBE. Not only are you a sheep, you are a NORMAL sheep. Give me back my colors! [*Begins snatching colors away.*]

JOHN POLK [*pushing colors at her*]. Green and mean! Green and mean! Green and mean!

ASHBE [*throwing marshmallows at him*]. That's the reason you're in a fraternity and the reason you're going to manage your mind. And dates ... you go out on dates merely because it's expected of you even though you have a terrible time. That's the reason you go to the whorehouse to prove you're a normal man. Well, you're much too normal for me.

JOHN POLK. Infant bitch. You think you're really cute.

ASHBE. That really wasn't food coloring in your drink, it was poison! [*She laughs, he picks up his coat to go, and she stops throwing marshmallows at him.*] Are you going? I was only kidding. For Christ sake, it wasn't really poison. Come on, don't go. Can't you take a little friendly criticism?

JOHN POLK. Look, did you have to bother me tonight? I had enough problems without ...

[*Phone rings. Both look at phone, it rings for the third time. He stands undecided.*]

ASHBE. Look, wait, we'll make it up. [*She goes to answer phone.*] Hello ... Daddy. How are you? ... I'm fine ... Dad, you sound funny ... What? ... Come on, Daddy, you know she's not here. [*Pause.*] Look, I told you I wouldn't call anymore. You've got her number in Atlanta. [*Pause, as she sinks to the floor.*] Why have you started again? ... Don't say that. I can tell it. I can. Hey, I have to go to bed now, I don't want to talk anymore, okay? [*Hangs up phone, then softly to self.*] Goddamnit.

JOHN POLK [*he has heard the conversation and is taking off his coat*]. Hey, Ashbe ... [*She looks at him blankly, her mind far away.*] You want to talk?

ASHBE. No. [*slight pause.*] Why don't you look at my shell collection? I have this special shell collection. [*She shows him collection.*]

JOHN POLK. They're beautiful, I've never seen colors like this. [ASHBE *is silent, he continues to himself.*] I used to go to Biloxi[2] a lot when I was a kid ... One time my brother and I, we camped out on the beach. The sky was purple. I remember it was really purple. We ate pork and beans out of a can. I'd always kinda wanted to do that. Every night for about a week after I got home, I dreamt about these waves foaming over my head and face. It was funny. Did you find these shells or buy them?

ASHBE. Some I found, some I bought. I've been trying to decipher their meaning. Here, listen, do you hear that?

---

[2] Biloxi, Mississippi, is located on the Gulf of Mexico about 100 miles east of New Orleans.

JOHN POLK. Yes.

ASHBE. That's the soul of the sea. [*She listens.*] I'm pretty sure it's the soul of the sea. Just imagine when I decipher the language. I'll know all the secrets of the world.

JOHN POLK. Yeah, probably you will. [*Looking into the shell.*] You know, you were right.

ASHBE. What do you mean?

JOHN POLK. About me, you were right. I am a sheep, a normal one. I've been trying to get out of it, but now I'm as big a sheep as ever.

ASHBE. Oh, it doesn't matter. You're company. It was rude of me to say.

JOHN POLK. No, because it was true. I really didn't want to go into a fraternity, I didn't even want to go to college, and I sure as hell don't want to go back to Hollybluff and work the soybean farm till I'm eighty.

ASHBE. I still say you could work on a ranch.

JOHN POLK. I don't know. I wanted to be a minister or something good, but I don't even know if I believe in God.

ASHBE. Yeah.

JOHN POLK. I never used to worry about being a failure. Now I think about it all the time. It's just I need to do something that's . . . fulfilling.

ASHBE. Fulfilling, yes, I see what you mean. Well, how about college? Isn't it fulfilling? I mean, you take all those wonderful classes, and you have all your very good friends.

JOHN POLK. Friends, yeah, I have some friends.

ASHBE. What do you mean?

JOHN POLK. Nothing . . . well, I do mean something. What the hell, let me try to explain. You see it was my "friends," the fraternity guys that set me up with G.G., excuse me, Myrtle, as a gift for my eighteenth birthday.

ASHBE. You mean, you didn't want the appointment?

JOHN POLK. No, I didn't want it. Hey, ah, were did my blue drink go?

ASHBE [*as she hands him the drink*]. They probably thought you really wanted to go.

JOHN POLK. Yeah, I'm sure they gave a damn what I wanted. They never even asked me. Hell, I would have told them a handkerchief, a pair of argyle socks, but, no, they have to get me a whore just because it's a cool-ass thing to do. They make me sick. I couldn't even stay at the party they gave. All the sweaty T-shirts, and moron sex stories . . . I just couldn't take it.

ASHBE. Is that why you were at the Blue Angel so early?

JOHN POLK. Yeah, I needed to get drunk, but not with them. They're such creeps.

ASHBE. Gosh, so you really don't want to go to Myrtle's?

JOHN POLK. No, I guess not.

ASHBE. Then are you going?

JOHN POLK [*pause*]. Yes.

ASHBE. That's wrong. You shouldn't go just to please them.

JOHN POLK. Oh, that's not the point anymore, maybe at first it was, but it's not anymore. Now I have to go for myself . . . to prove to myself that I'm not afraid.

ASHBE. Afraid? [*Slowly, as she begins to grasp his meaning.*] You mean, you've never slept with a girl before?

JOHN POLK. Well, I've never been in love.

ASHBE [*in amazement*]. You're a virgin?

JOHN POLK. Oh, God.

ASHBE. No, don't feel bad, I am too.

JOHN POLK. I thought I should be in love . . .

ASHBE. Well, you're certainly not in love with Myrtle. I mean, you haven't even met her.

JOHN POLK. I know, but, God, I thought maybe I'd never fall in love. What then? You should experience everything ... shouldn't you? Oh, what's it matter, everything's so screwed.

ASHBE. Screwed? Yeah, I guess it is. I mean, I always thought it would be fun to have a lot of friends who gave parties and go to dances all dressed up. Like the dance tonight ... it might have been fun.

JOHN POLK. Well, why didn't you go?

ASHBE. I don't know. I'm not sure it would have been fun. Anyway, you can't go ... alone.

JOHN POLK. Oh, you need a date?

ASHBE. Yeah, or something.

JOHN POLK. Say, Ashbe, ya wanna dance here?

ASHBE. No, I think we'd better discuss your dilemma.

JOHN POLK. What dilemma?

ASHBE. Myrtle. It doesn't seem right you should ...

JOHN POLK. Let's forget Myrtle for now. I've got a while yet. Here have some more of this blue-moon drink.

ASHBE. You're only trying to escape through artificial means.

JOHN POLK. Yeah, you got it. Now come on. Would you like to dance? Hey, you said you liked to dance.

ASHBE. You're being ridiculous.

JOHN POLK [*winking at her*]. Dance?

ASHBE. John Polk, I just thought ...

JOHN POLK. Hmm?

ASHBE. How to solve your problem ...

JOHN POLK. Well ...

ASHBE. Make love to me!

JOHN POLK. What?

ASHBE. It all seems logical to me. It would prove you weren't scared, and you wouldn't be doing it just to impress others.

JOHN POLK. Look, I ... I mean, I hardly know you ...

ASHBE. But we've talked. It's better this way, really. I won't be so apt to point out your mistakes.

JOHN POLK. I'd feel great, stripping a twelve-year-old of her virginity.

ASHBE. I'm sixteen! Anyway, I'd be stripping you of yours just as well. I'll go put on some Tiger Claw perfume. [*She runs out.*]

JOHN POLK. Hey, come back! Tiger Claw perfume, Christ.

ASHBE [*entering*]. I think one should have different scents for different moods.

JOHN POLK. Hey, stop spraying that! You know I'm not going to ... well, you'd get neurotic, or pregnant, or some damn thing. Stop spraying, will you!

ASHBE. Pregnant? You really think I could get pregnant?

JOHN POLK. Sure, it'd be a delightful possibility.

ASHBE. It really wouldn't be bad. Maybe I would get to go to Tokyo for an abortion. I've never been to the Orient.

JOHN POLK. Sure getting cut on is always a real treat.

ASHBE. Anyway, I might just want to have my dear baby. I could move to Atlanta with Mama and Madeline. It'd be wonderful fun. Why I could take him to the supermarket, put him in one of those little baby seats to stroll him about. I'd buy peach baby food and feed it to him with a tiny golden spoon. Why I could take colored pictures of him and send them to you through the mail. Come on . . . [*Starts putting pillows onto the couch.*] Well, I guess you should kiss me for a start. It's only etiquette, everyone begins with it.

JOHN POLK. I don't think I could even kiss you with a clear conscience. I mean, you're so small with those little cat-eye glasses and curly hair . . . I couldn't even kiss you.

ASHBE. You couldn't even kiss me? I can't help it if I have to wear glasses. I got the prettiest ones I could find.

JOHN POLK. Your glasses are fine. Let's forget it, okay?

ASHBE. I know, my lips are too purple, but if I eat carrots, the dye'll come off and they'll be orange.

JOHN POLK. I didn't say anything about your lips being too purple.

ASHBE. Well, what is it? You're just plain chicken, I suppose . . .

JOHN POLK. Sure, right, I'm chicken, totally chicken. Let's forget it. I don't know how, but, somehow, this is probably all my fault.

ASHBE. You're darn right it's all your fault! I want to have my dear baby or at least get to Japan. I'm so sick of school I could smash every marshmallow in sight! [*She starts smashing.*] Go on to your skinny pimple whore. I hope the skinny whore laughs in your face, which she probably will because you have an easy face to laugh in.

JOHN POLK. You're absolutely right, she'll probably hoot and howl her damn fizzle red head off. Maybe you can wait outside the door and hear her, give you lots of pleasure, you sadistic, little thief.

ASHBE. Thief! Was Robin Hood . . . Oh, what's wrong with this world? I just wasn't made for it, is all. I've probably been put in the wrong world, I can see that now.

JOHN POLK. You're fine in this world.

ASHBE. Sure, everyone just views me as an undesirable lump.

JOHN POLK. Who?

ASHBE. You, for one.

JOHN POLK [*pause*]. You mean because I wouldn't make love to you?

ASHBE. It seems clear to me.

JOHN POLK. But you're wrong, you know.

ASHBE [*to self, softly*]. Don't pity me.

JOHN POLK. The reason I wouldn't wasn't that . . . it's just that . . . well, I like you too much to.

ASHBE. You like me?

JOHN POLK. Undesirable lump, Jesus. Your cheeks they're . . . they're . . .

ASHBE. My cheeks? They're what?

JOHN POLK. They're rosy.

ASHBE. My cheeks are rosy?

JOHN POLK. Yeah, your cheeks, they're really rosy.

ASHBE. Well, they're natural, you know. Say, would you like to dance?

JOHN POLK. Yes.

ASHBE. I'll turn on the radio. [*She turns on radio. Ethel Waters is heard singing "Honey in the Honeycomb." ASHBE begins snapping her fingers.*] Yikes, let's jazz it out.

[*They dance.*]

JOHN POLK. Hey, I'm not good or anything . . .

ASHBE. John Polk.

JOHN POLK. Yeah?
ASHBE. Baby, I think you dance fine!

[*They dance on, laughing, saying what they want till end of song. Then a radio announcer comes on and says the 12:00 news will be in five minutes. Billie Holiday or Terry Pierce, begins singing, "Am I Blue?"*]

JOHN POLK. Dance?
ASHBE. News in five minutes.
JOHN POLK. Yeah.
ASHBE. That means five minutes till midnight.
JOHN POLK. Yeah, I know.
ASHBE. Then you're not . . .
JOHN POLK. Ashbe, I've never danced all night. Wouldn't it be something to . . . to dance all night and watch the rats come out of the gutter?
ASHBE. Rats?
JOHN POLK. Don't they come out at night? I hear New Orleans has lots of rats.
ASHBE. Yeah, yeah, it's got lots of rats.
JOHN POLK. Then let's dance all night and wait for them to come out.
ASHBE. All right . . . but, how about our feet?
JOHN POLK. Feet?
ASHBE. They'll hurt.
JOHN POLK. Yeah.
ASHBE. [*smiling*]. Okay, then let's dance.
[*He takes her hand, and they dance as lights black out and the music soars and continues to play.*]

END

[1982]

A Handbook for
Literary Study

❧❧❧❧❧❧

ABBREVIATIONS: Common abbreviations encountered in literary study include the following.

anon. anonymous
app. appendix
art., arts. article(s)
b. born
biblio. bibliography, bibliographer
bk., bks. book(s)
bull. bulletin
ca. (or *c.*) "about," used to indicate an approximate date; for example, ca. 1776
ch., chs. chapter(s)
col., cols. column(s)
coll. college
comp. compiler, compiled by
d. died
dept. department
diss. Ph.D dissertation
doc., docs. document(s)
ed., eds. editor(s), edited by
e.g. (*exempli gratia*) "for example"—set off by commas
esp. especially
et al. (*et alii*) "and others"
etc. (*et cetera*) "and so forth"
ex., exs. example(s)
f., ff. page or pages following a specific reference; for example, p. 12ff.
fig., figs. figure(s)
front. frontispiece
ibid. (*ibidem*) "in the same place"; that is, the title cited in the immediately preceding note
i.e. (*id est*) "that is," preceded and followed by a comma
illus. illustrator, illustrated by, illustration(s)
intro., introd. introduction, introduced by
jour. journal
l., ll. line(s)
loc. cit. (*loco citato*) "in the place (or passage) cited"
mag., mags. magazine(s)
ms, mss manuscript, capitalized and followed by a period when referring to a specific manuscript.

n., nn. note(s)
n.d. no date; for example, on the title page of a book
no., nos. number(s)
n.p. no place of publication cited
p., pp. page(s)
par., pars. paragraph(s)
passim "here and there throughout the work"; for example, p. 23 et passim
pref. preface
pseud. pseudonym
pt., pts. part(s)
pub., pubs. published by, publication(s)
rev. revised or revised by; reviewed or reviewed by
rpt. reprint, reprinted
sc. scene
sec., secs. section(s)
sic "thus"; placed in square brackets [sic] to indicate that there is an error in the
    quoted passage and that the passage in question has been quoted accurately,
st., sts. stanza(s)
tr., trans. translator, translated by
univ. university
v., vs. verse(s)
vol., vols. volume(s)

ABRIDGEMENT: A condensed or shortened version of a work.

ABSTRACT: The opposite of *concrete*; used to describe a word or group of words
    representing attitudes, generalities, ideas, or qualities that cannot be perceived
    directly through the senses. Language is best seen as forming a continuous
    ladder ranging from earthily concrete at its base to airily abstract at its top. On
    this ladder the word *insect* is relatively abstract while *spittle bug* is quite concrete.

ABSURD, THEATRE OF THE: A type of modern drama (often associated with Ed-
    ward Albee, Samuel Beckett, Jean Genet, Eugène Ionesco, Arthur Kopit, and
    Harold Pinter) that attempts to convey the playwright's vision of an absurd,
    frustrating, illogical, and essentially meaningless human condition by ignoring
    or distorting the usual conventions of plot, characterization, structure, setting,
    and dialogue. While drawing philosophically upon existentialism, the absurdist
    playwrights often use the techniques of surrealism and expressionism.

ACCENT (PP. 724–725): Used in English poetry to describe the stress or emphasis
    accorded to certain syllables. When a pronounced syllable receives no stress or
    emphasis, it is, by contrast, referred to as unaccented. In English poetry, *meter*
    depends on the pattern of accented and unaccented syllables. For example, in
    the following couplet from Byron's "Don Juan" (1819), the meter is iambic
    pentameter and the stresses fall on the even numbered syllables:

> There's NOT a SEA the PASSenGER e'er PUKES in,
> Turns UP more DANG'rous BREAKers THAN the EUXine.

ACROSTIC (P. 771): A poem in which certain letters (ordinarily the first in each
    line) spell out a word or words.

ACT (P. 1061): A major division of a play; sometimes subdivided into a number
    of separate *scenes*.

ACTION: The events or incidents that take place within a literary work which, taken together, provide the *plot*. See *plot*.

ADAGE: A wise saying or proverb familiar to most people. For example, "Honey catches more flies than vinegar."

ADAPTATION: The recasting of a work from one medium of art to another (as, for example, when a novel is made into a film).

ADVENTURE STORY: A story (or novel) in which action—usually physical action—provides the primary interest.

AESTHETIC DISTANCE: See *psychic distance*.

AESTHETICS: The study of the beautiful. A branch of philosophy that attempts to define the nature of art and the criteria by which it may be judged.

AFFECTIVE FALLACY: A term employed in modern criticism to describe the sup posed error of judging a literary work by its effect—usually its emotional effect—upon the reader.

AGON: A Greek word for "contest." The part of a Greek play in which two characters, each aided and supported by half the *chorus*, argue with one another.

AGONIST: A participant in the *agon*, a major character in a play or (by extension) a novel. Hence, a *protagonist* is a primary character; an *antagonist* is an opposing major character; and a *deuteragonist* is a secondary, or minor, character.

ALEXANDRINE (P. 766): A line of poetry of twelve syllables, consisting of six iambic feet (iambic hexameter). Example: "Virtue gives her selfe light, through darknesse for to wade" (Edmund Spenser, *The Faerie Queene*, 1590, I.i).

> A needless Alexandrine ends the song,
> That, like a wounded snake, drags it slow length along.
>
> (Alexander Pope,
> from *An Essay on Criticism*, 1711)

ALLEGORY (PP. 705–708): A type of narrative that attempts to reinforce its thesis by making its characters (and sometimes its events and setting, as well) represent specific abstract ideas or qualities; see *fable*, *parable*, and *symbol*.

ALLITERATION (PP. 753–755): The repetition in two or more nearby words of initial consonant sounds. See also *assonance* and *consonance*. Alliteration is what gives punch to Abraham Lincoln's contention that "the ballot is stronger than the bullet."

ALLITERATIVE VERSE (PP. 741–743): A metrical system in which each line contains a fixed number of accented syllables (emphasized by alliteration) and a variable number of unaccented ones.

ALLUSION (PP. 661–664): A reference, generally brief, to a person, place, thing, or event with which the reader is presumably familiar. Allusion is a device that allows a writer to compress a great deal of meaning into a very few words. Allusions "work" to the extent they are recognized and understood; when they are not, they tend to confuse.

AMBIGUITY (PP. 668–671): The use of a word or phrase in such a way as to give it two or more competing meanings. Example: "Nowadays we are all so hard up that the only pleasant things to pay are compliments. They're the only things we can pay" (Oscar Wilde, from *Lady Windemere's Fan*, 1892).

AMBIVALENCE: The existence of two mutually opposed or contradictory feelings about a given issue, idea, person, or object. You feel ambivalent, for example, when you want to celebrate St. Patrick's Day with plenty of green beer, but you also want to pass your accounting test the next morning.

AMERICAN LITERATURE, GUIDES TO: Bibliographic guides to the study of American literature and authors include Patricia P. Havlice, ed., *Index to American Author Bibliographies* (Metuchen, N.J.: Scarecrow Press, 1971); Clarence L. Ghodes and Sandford Marovitz, *Bibliographical Guide to the Study of the Literature of the U.S.A.* (Durham, N.C.: Duke UP, 1984); Lewis Leary, ed., *American Literature: A Study and Research Guide* (New York: St. Martin's Press, 1976); Howard Mumford Jones and Richard M. Ludwig, *Guide to American Literature and Its Background Since 1890* (Cambridge, Mass.: Harvard UP, 1972); Charles Nilon, *Bibliography of Bibliographies in American Literature* (New York: R. R. Bowker, 1970); Valmai Kirkham Fenster, *Guide to American Literature* (Littleton, Colo.: Libraries Unlimited, 1983); and the bibliographical volume of the *Literary History of the United States* (New York: Macmillan, 1974). These can be supplemented by Lewis Leary, ed., *Articles on American Literature, 1900–50* (Durham, N.C.: Duke UP, 1954), supplements 1970, 1979; James L. Woodress and J. Albert Robbins, eds., *American Literary Scholarship* (Durham, N.C.: Duke UP), published annually; *American Literature* (Durham, N.C.: Duke UP), published quarterly; *MLA International Bibliography of Books and Articles on the Modern Languages and Literature* (New York: Modern Language Association); *Year's Work in Modern Language Studies* (Leeds, Eng.: Modern Humanities Research Assoc.); *Abstracts of English Studies* (Calgary, Alberta, Canada: U of Calgary P), published quarterly; *Humanities Index* (New York: H. W. Wilson Company). See also *English and American literature, guides to.*

AMERICAN NOVEL, GUIDES TO: See Donna L. Gerstenberger and George Hendrick, eds., Vol. 1: *The American Novel 1789–1959: A Checklist of Twentieth-Century Criticism* (Denver: Alan Swallow, 1961); Vol. 2: *The American Novel: A Checklist of Twentieth-Century Criticism on Novels Written Since 1789; Criticism Written, 1960–1968* (Chicago: Alan Swallow, 1970).

ANACHRONISM: A person or thing that is chronologically out of place.

ANAGNORISIS: The scene of recognition or discovery that leads to a reversal. The term was first used by Aristotle in his discussion of *tragedy.*

ANAGRAM: A word, name, or phrase made by rearranging the letters of another. For example, *eat* is an anagram of *tea.* Samuel Butler's *Erewhon* (nowhere), published in 1872, is an example of an anagram used as the title of a novel.

ANALOGY: A comparison, usually imaginative, of two essentially unlike things which nonetheless share one or more common features. Writers use analogies as a method of exploring familiar subjects in new and fresh ways or as a method of exploring difficult ideas by comparing them to things known and familiar.

ANALYSIS (PP. 9–13): An attempt to study one element or part of a literary work. See *criticism.*

ANAPEST (ANAPESTIC) (PP. 737–739): A foot of two unaccented syllables followed by an accented one. Example: "It was MANy and MANy a YEAR aGO" (Edgar Allan Poe, "Annabelle Lee," 1850).

ANECDOTE: A brief unadorned narrative about a particular person or incident. Short stories differ from anecdotes by virtue of their greater length and the deliberate artistic arrangement of their elements.

ANGST: A German word for "anxiety" or "anguish." The term is often applied to the plight of the characters of existential post–World War II literature. See *existentialism*.

ANIMISM (PP. 702–703): A poetic figure of speech in which an idea or inanimate object is described as though it were living, without attributing human traits to it; see also *personification*. Example: "The fog comes on little cat feet" (Carl Sandburg, "Fog," 1916).

ANNOTATED BIBLIOGRAPHY: A bibliography that includes a brief summary or description of each title included.

ANNOTATION: The explanatory note (or notes) that an author or editor supplies for a given text.

ANTAGONIST (PP. 60–61, 1096): The rival or opponent against whom the major character (the *protagonist* or *hero*) is contending.

ANTECEDENT EVENTS: Events that have taken place before the plot of a story, novel, or play begins, but which are somehow important to that plot.

ANTHOLOGY: A collection of essays, short stories, poems, and/or plays written by a number of different authors. This text is an anthology.

ANTICLIMAX: A sudden transition from the important (or serious) to the trivial (or ludicrous). We speak of something being anticlimactic when it occurs after the *crisis* (or *climax*) of the plot has been reached. In most cases the Republican and Democratic National Conventions are anticlimactic because the candidates and the major planks of the platform have been decided well in advance.

ANTIHERO: A *protagonist* whose distinctive qualities are directly opposite to, or incompatible with, those associated with the traditional hero. Such an opposition by no means implies that the character is evil or villainous, but it often tends to reflect the author's belief that modern life no longer tolerates or produces individuals capable of genuine heroism in its classic sense. In Joseph Heller's *Catch-22* (1961), Yossarian is an antihero as is Lysistrata in the famous play by Aristophanes (411 B.C.).

ANTINOVEL (ANTI-STORY): A type of experimental novel (or short story), usually associated with the contemporary French school of Alain Robbe-Grillet, that attempts to convey to the reader the experience of objective reality without authorial direction by dispensing with the traditional aspects of realistic ("mimetic") fiction, e.g., plot, character, theme, dialogue.

APHORISM: A short, pithy saying, usually by a known author. Example: "Fortune favors the brave" (Virgil, *The Aeneid,* X).

APOLLONIAN: A term similar in meaning to classicism and implying the qualities of reason, clarity, and morality that were characteristics of the Greek god Apollo. The term was first used by Friedrich Nietzsche in *The Birth of Tragedy.* See the opposite term, *Dionysian.*

APOLOGY: In literature a term meaning a justification or a defense.

APOSTROPHE (P. 701): A figure of speech in which a person (usually not present) or a personified quality or object is addressed as if present. Example: "Judge of nations, spare us yet,/ Lest we forget—lest we forget" (Rudyard Kipling, "Recessional," 1897).

APOTHEGM: A pithy, witty saying. E.g., Iago's definition of jealousy in *Othello*: "It is the green-eyed monster, which doth mock/ The meat it feeds on."

APRON STAGE: A stage that projects out into the audience. In traditional theaters the apron is that part of the stage in front of the proscenium arch. See *proscenium arch.*

ARCHAISM: Obsolete words, phrases, syntax, or spelling. Example:

> Winter is icumen in,
> Lhude sing Goddamm,
> Raineth drop and staineth slop,
> And how the wind doth ramm!
>
> (Ezra Pound,
> from "Ancient Music," 1926)

ARCHETYPE (PP. 81, 707): Used in literary analysis to describe certain basic and recurrent patterns of plot, character, or theme; see also *symbol.*

ARENA STATE/ARENA THEATER (P. 1083): A theater with seating surrounding, or nearly surrounding, the stage. See *theater in the round.*

ARGUMENT: A summary statement of the content or thesis of a literary work.

ASIDE (PP. 1076–1077): A dramatic convention in which the lines addressed by a character to the audience are presumed to go unheard by the other characters. Example: "IAGO [*Aside*]. O, you are well tuned now!/ But I'll set down the pegs that make this music/ As honest as I am" (Shakespeare, *Othello,* 1604, II.i).

ASSONANCE (PP. 753–755): The repetition in two or more nearby words of similar vowel sounds; see also *consonance* and *alliteration.* Example: ". . . the ch*a*lk w*a*ll f*a*lls" (W. H. Auden, "Look Stranger," 1936).

ATMOSPHERE (PP. 68–69): The mood or feeling pervading a literary work. Example: The gloomy melancholy in Edgar Allan Poe's "The Fall of the House of Usher" (1839).

AUGUSTAN PERIOD: The period in English literature between about 1700 and 1750, when English writers deliberately set out to imitate ideals of restraint and balance in the reign of Roman Emperor Caesar Augustus (27 B.C.–A.D.14). Major writers include Addison, Pope, Steele, and Swift.

AUTOBIOGRAPHY: The story of a person's life written by the subject himself or herself.

AVANT-GARDE: New, innovative, or experimental art; a work whose subject matter, style, or form places it at the forefront of a literary or artistic trend or movement.

BAD QUARTOS: A term for a number of inaccurate or garbled early editions of Shakespeare's plays.

BALLAD (PP. 763–765): A narrative poem consisting of a series of four-line stanzas, originally sung or recited as part of the oral traditions of an unsophisticated rural folk society. Ballads that are the genuine products of a folk society are sometimes referred to as "popular," "folk," or "traditional" ballads as opposed to "literary" ballads deliberately composed by educated poets in imitation of the form and spirit of those originals. See also *broadside ballad* and *Child ballad.*

BARD: Originally an ancient order of Celtic minstrel-poets who composed and sang (usually accompanied on a harp) verses celebrating the deeds of their warriors and chiefs; now chiefly used as a synonym for poet.

BATHOS: A ludicrous appearance of the trivial or mundane within a context of supposed sublimity. Here is an example of bathos from "The Ode to Stephen Dowling Bots, De'd" in Mark Twain's *Adventures of Huckleberry Finn* (1885):

> Despised love struck not with woe
>   That head of curly knots
> Nor stomach troubles laid him low,
>   Young Stephen Dowling Bots.
>
> O no. Then list with tearful eye,
>   Whilst I his fate do tell.
> His soul did from this cold world fly,
>   By falling down a well.

BELLES LETTRES: A French expression denoting artistic literature. As an adjective it is spelled *belletristic.*

BIBLIOGRAPHY: A list of books, articles, and other references on a particular subject.

BIBLIOGRAPHY OF BIBLIOGRAPHIES: See Theodore Besterman, *A World Bibliography of Bibliographies, and of Bibliographical Catalogues, Calendars, Abstracts, Digests, and the Like,* 4 vols. and index (Lausanne: Soc. Bibliographica, 1965). Supplement, 1964–1974, Alice F. Toomey, ed., 2 vols. (Totowa, N.J.: 1977); Charles H. Nilon, *Bibliography of Bibliographies in American Literature* (New York: R. R. Bowker, 1970); Eugene P. Sheehy, *Guide to Reference Books* (Chicago: American Library Assoc., 1986), supplement 1992. For recent bibliographies see *Bibliographical Index: A Cumulative Bibliography of Bibliographies* (New York: H. H. Wilson), published twice a year and cumulatively in December.

BILDUNGSROMAN: A novel that traces the initiation, development, and education of a young person. From the terms *bildung* ("formation") and *roman* ("novel").

BIOGRAPHICAL FALLACY: The error of interpreting a literary work too exclusively in terms of the life of its author.

BIOGRAPHICAL REFERENCE WORKS: A list of frequently used directories of biographical information includes the *Dictionary of National Biography* (DNB); *Dictionary of American Biography* (DAB); *Who's Who in America; Current Biography; New York Times Index; Webster's Biographical Dictionary; McGraw-Hill Encyclopedia of World Biography; Author Biographies Master Index: A Consolidated Guide to Biographical Information Concerning Authors Living and Dead; Dictionary of Literary Biography; Twentieth-Century Authors; Contemporary Authors; American Authors; British Authors; World Authors; The Writer's Directory.*

BIOGRAPHY: The written history or account of a person's life. See also *literary biography.*

BLACK HUMOR: Humor which is the product of a morbid, alienated, or pessimistic view of the world. Black humor is often associated with the *antinovel* (*antistory*) and the *theater of the absurd.* Black humor is exemplified in the folk expression, "Been down so long it looks like up to me."

BLANK VERSE (P. 761): Lines of unrhymed iambic pentameter, as, for example, in Shakespeare's *Othello* (1604) or Milton's *Paradise Lost* (1667).

BLOCKING: The pattern of the actors' position and movement on the stage. Sometimes this pattern is made an explicit part of the playwright's script.

BLURB: A publisher's or reviewer's enthusiastic comment or description on a ʋook's dust jacket or cover. Example: John Ciardi's comment on a recent book of poetry, "This is a master work, a book that adds a voice and presence to American poetry. It is no passing book, but one to go on the master shelf and remain there." (But the cynic wonders, will it ever be taken down from the shelf and read?)

BOMBAST: Language that is inflated, extravagant, verbose, and insincere.

BON MOT: Literally a "good word," a witty remark. Example: Calvin Coolidge's response when asked why he was always so taciturn: "If you don't say anything, you won't be called on to repeat it."

BOOK REVIEWS: See the annual volumes of *Book Review Digest* (New York: H. W. Wilson) and *Book Review Index* (Detroit: Gale Research).

BOOKS IN PRINT: *Books in Print* (New York: R. R. Bowker) offers an annual compilation in volumes arranged by author, title, and subject. Bowker also anticipates new books in its *Forthcoming Books,* published five times a year.

BOURGEOISE TRAGEDY: See *domestic tragedy.*

BOWDLERIZE: To gut a piece of writing in the interest of morality or decorum. The word originated in 1818 when Thomas Bowdler (1754–1825), an Englishman, published his attempt at an inoffensive, expurgated edition of Shakespeare.

BOX SET: A realistic stage setting consisting of a room with a ceiling and three walls. The fourth (imaginary) wall exists between the actors and the audience.

BRITISH MUSEUM CATALOG: *The British Museum's General Catalogue of Printed Books,* 263 vols. (London: Trustees of the BM, 1965) and its supplements provides a list of all the books owned by the British Library (formerly called the British Museum). See *National Union Catalog.*

BROADSIDE BALLAD: A ballad printed on a single sheet and sold in the streets. See *ballad.*

BURLESQUE: A form of humor that ridicules persons, attitudes, actions, or things by means of distortion and exaggeration. Burlesque of a particular literary work or style is referred to as *parody. Caricature,* on the other hand, creates humor by distorting or exaggerating an individual's prominent physical features; see also *satire.* Tom Stoppard's *The Real Inspector Hound* (1968), for example, burlesques the conventions of theatrical murder mysteries.

CACOPHONY: See *euphony.*

CADENCE: The rhythmical "tune" established in verse or prose by patterns of stressed and unstressed syllables, or the inflection of a speaker's voice. Great speeches like Lincoln's "Gettysburg Address" are said to have cadence, as, of course, does great poetry.

CAESURA (PP. 728–729): A pause or break occurring near the middle of a line of poetry, customarily marked by a double slash in scansion. Example:

> Treason doth never prosper;//what's the reason?
> For if it prosper,//none dare call it treason.

> (Sir John Harington, "Of Treason," 1612)

CALL NUMBER: The set of numbers assigned to a library book in order to help in locating it on the shelf.

CANON: An established body of accepted writing. The term *literary canon* refers to the major works within a given national literature.

CANTO: A section or division of a long poem.

CARICATURE: Humor or ridicule created by the distortion of a character's physical features. Political cartoonists often create caricatures of the dignitaries they lampoon. See *burlesque.*

CAROLINE PERIOD: The period in English literature coinciding with the reign of Charles I (1625–1649). Major writers include the Cavalier poets Carew, Herrick, Lovelace, and Suckling. See *Cavalier poets.*

CARPE DIEM: A Latin phrase meaning "seize the day," generally applied to lyric poems that urge the celebration of the fleeting present. See, for example, Robert Herrick's "To the Virgins to Make Much of Time" (1648).

CATASTROPHE: A form of *conclusion* (or *dénouement*), usually tragic in its outcome.

CATHARSIS (P. 1102): A term used by Aristotle to describe the psychological feeling of relief and release (the purgation of such emotions as pity and fear) experienced by the audience through their exposure to tragedy. See *classical tragedy.*

CAVALIER POETS: A group of poets—including Carew, Herrick, Lovelace, and Suckling—associated with the court of Charles I of England (1625–1649), whose supporters were known as Cavaliers. The Cavalier poets were known for their light and amorous verse. See *Caroline period.*

CHANCE AND COINCIDENCE: *Chance* refers to events or "happenings" within a plot that occur without sufficient preparation; *coincidence* to the accidental occurrence of two (or more) events that have a certain correspondence.

CHARACTER (PP. 60–67, 1095–1098): An individual within a literary work. Characters may be complex and well developed (*round characters*) or undifferentiated and one-dimensional (*flat characters*); they may change in the course of the plot (*dynamic characters*) or remain essentially the same (*static characters*).

CHARACTERIZATION: The process by which an author creates, develops, and presents a character.

CHAUCERIAN STANZA: See *rhyme royal.*

CHILD BALLAD: The name given to one of the 305 ballads brought together and published by Francis J. Child in his five-volume collection *English and Scottish Popular Ballads* (1882–1898). These ballads are frequently cited by the number assigned them by Child.

CHRONICLE PLAY: A form of Elizabethan drama that drew its subject matter from history, particularly the *Chronicles* (1577) of Raphael Holinshed and various continuations by his imitators. Shakespeare's histories are good examples of chronicle plays.

CHORUS (PP. 1072–1073): In Greek drama the chorus was a group of singers and dancers who sometimes served as actors to comment on or interpret the significance of the action.

CHRONICLE: A record of events set down in their historical order.

CHRONOLOGICAL: A pattern of organization or presentation that introduces events or things in their normal time sequence.

\.QUAIN: A five-line stanza, particularly as popularized by Adelaide Crapsey (1878–1914). Example:

> These be
> Three silent things
> The falling snow . . . the hour
> Before the dawn . . . the mouth of one
> Just dead.
>
> ("Cinquain, Triad," 1915)

CITATION INDEXES: Guides to book and journal articles that have been cited by other authors (in their text, footnotes, or bibliography) during the previous year. See *Arts and Humanities Citation Index.*

CLASSIC: A piece of literature that by common agreement of readers and critics has come to be regarded as a major work.

CLASSICAL: Refers to Greek and Roman literature; for example to Sophocles' *King Oedipus* (c. 429 B.C.) or Aristophanes' *Lysistrata* (411 B.C.).

CLASSICAL TRAGEDY (P. 1102): Refers to Greek and Roman tragedies or plays written imitating their subjects or conventions.

CLICHÉ: A trite, worn-out expression that has lost its original vitality and freshness. Examples: "sharp as a tack," "dumb as a doorknob," "boring as a bump on a log." As Alexander Pope explains in "An Essay on Criticism" (1711), a writer indulges in predictable clichés at his or her peril:

> Where'er you find "the cooling western breeze,"
> In the next line, it "whispers through the trees";
> If crystal streams "with pleasing murmers creep,"
> The reader's threatened (not in vain) with "sleep."

CLIMAX: See *crisis.*

CLOAK AND DAGGER: A type of literary work dealing with espionage and intrigue.

CLOAK AND SWORD: A type of literary work containing swashbuckling action, gallant heroes, and plots filled with adventure.

CLOSED COUPLET (P. 761): See *couplet.*

CLOSET DRAMA (P. 1065): A drama written to be read rather than staged and acted. Examples: *Samson Agonistes* by Milton, *Cain* by Byron, and *Prometheus Unbound* by Shelley.

CLOWN: A comic character of rustic origins. Example: the profanely punning clown in Act III, Scene i, of *Othello.*

COHERENCE: A principle that insists that the various parts of a literary work be related to one another in a clear and logical manner.

COINCIDENCE: See *chance and coincidence.*

COLLATION: A close, word-by-word, comparison of texts with a record of the variations discovered.

COLLOQUIAL LANGUAGE: Language that is informal and conversational. For example, Samuel L. Clemens's "The Celebrated Jumping Frog of Calaveras County" (1865) is filled with the colloquial language of the nineteenth-century American West.

COMEDY (PP. 1103–1105): Broadly, any literary work designed to amuse. The term is usually reserved for plays that have a lighthearted and humorous tone, that are amusing, and that have a happy ending. See *comedy of humours, comedy of manners, comedy of situation, farce, new comedy, old comedy, romantic comedy.*

COMEDY OF HUMOURS: A type of comedy derived from the medieval physiological theory of the "four humours," the four identifiable elements believed to determine and control individual temperament and personality. When these humours became imbalanced the result was a lopsided, eccentric personality whose actions became a fit subject for comedy. Examples: *Every Man in His Humor* (1598) and *Every Man Out of His Humor* (1599) by Ben Jonson.

COMEDY OF MANNERS: A type of realistic, often satiric, comedy concerned with the behavior of men and women who violate the manners, norms, and conventions of polite, sophisticated upper-class society. Also referred to as *drawing room comedy.* Examples: *She Stoops to Conquer* (1773) by Goldsmith, *The School for Scandal* (1777) by Sheridan, and *The Importance of Being Earnest* (1895) by Wilde.

COMEDY OF SITUATION: A type of comedy whose chief interest lies in the ingenuity and twists and turns of the plot. The term sitcom is used now in reference to popular TV programs and movies of this type.

COMIC RELIEF: A comic scene introduced into an otherwise serious or tragic fictional or dramatic work, usually to relieve, if only momentarily, the tension of the plot. It often heightens, by contrast, the emotional intensity of the work. Example: the clown scene in *Othello* (III. i).

COMMEDIA DEL L'ARTE: An early Italian form of improvised comedy that draws much of its humor from the buffoonery of stock characters (the harlequin or the pantaloon). It is most significant for its influence upon the comedies of Shakespeare and Moliere.

COMPLICATION (PP. 34–35, 1092): That part of the plot in which the conflict is developed and intensified; sometimes referred to as the *rising action.*

COMPUTERIZED LITERATURE SEARCH: An on-line computerized search of bibliographic data bases offered by commercial and nonprofit organizations. For availability and charges consult your librarian.

CONCEIT: Usually refers to a startling, ingenious, perhaps even farfetched, metaphor establishing an analogy or comparison between two apparently incongruous things. Examples: John Donne's "The Flea" (1633), George Herbert's "The Pulley" (1633), Andrew Marvell's "The Definition of Love" (1681).

CONCLUSION: See *resolution.*

CONCORDANCE: An alphabetical index of the words used in a given text or in the work of a given author.

CONCRETE: Opposite of *abstract.* Language referring directly to what we see, hear, touch, taste, or smell is concrete. Most literature uses concrete language and expresses even abstract concepts concretely through images and metaphors.

CONFESSIONAL LITERATURE: A literary work in which the author reveals or "confesses" events or feelings that are normally concealed. Examples: Sylvia Plath's "Morning Song" (1961), Anne Sexton's "The Truth the Dead Know" (1962).

CONFIDANT/CONFIDANTE (P. 1096): The individual, often a minor character, to whom a major character reveals or "confesses" his or her private thoughts

...d feelings. Playwrights use the confidante as a device to communicate necessary information to the reader and audience.

CONFLICT (PP. 33–36): The struggle or encounter within the plot of two opposing forces that serves to create reader or audience interest and suspense.

CONNOTATION (PP. 657–660): The ideas associated with or suggested by a given word or phrase, as opposed to its literal meaning. A word's connotations are the product of its common usage and emotional overtones, not of its simple definition. Thus, owning a Porsche carries connotations of wealth, flashiness, and conspicuous consumption that are quite different from the connotation of stodgy aristocracy associated with owning an equally expensive Rolls Royce or Bentley. See *denotation*.

CONSISTENCY: The internal coherence of the various parts and the tone of a literary work.

CONSONANCE (PP. 753–755): The repetition in two or more nearby words of similar consonant sounds preceded by different accented vowels, e.g., "pl*uck*" and "kn*ock*." When it occurs at the end of lines, consonance often serves as a substitute for *end rhyme;* see *alliteration*.

CONTEMPORARY LITERATURE: Literature written since the end of World War II (1945). See *post-modern*.

CONTROLLING IMAGE: The image or metaphor that runs throughout a literary work and determines its structure or nature. For example, the white whale in Melville's *Moby-Dick* (1851) or the wallpaper in Charlotte Perkins Gilman's story "The Yellow Wall-Paper" (1892).

CONVENTION: Any literary device, technique, style, or form, or any aspect of subject matter, characterization, or theme that has become recognized and accepted by authors and audiences through repeated use. By convention, for example, the open stage in the Greek theater could represent any public locale and by convention the male characters in Greek comedies were equipped with enormous artificial phalluses.

COPYRIGHT: The legal right that protects an author's exclusive ownership and control of his or her own work. Under the Copyright Act of 1976 (effective January 1, 1978), new works by American authors are protected for the life of the author plus fifty years, and existing works are protected for seventy-five years from the date of original publication. The English Copyright Act of 1911, like the American Copyright Act of 1976, protects a work for the author's life plus fifty years.

COPY TEXT: The text used by an editor as the source for the edition of a work. See *edition*.

CORPUS CHRISTI PLAYS: See *mystery play*.

COSMIC IRONY: A form of irony of situation in which an individual's insignificance and powerlessness are exposed by being juxtaposed against an uncaring and infinite universe. See *irony of situation*. Thomas Hardy's poetry often exemplifies the use of cosmic irony, particularly in "Hap" and "The Convergence of the Twain."

COUNTERPLOT: See *subplot*.

COUP DE THÉÂTRE: French for "stroke of theater"—i.e., a striking effect.

COUPLET (P. 761): A single pair of rhymed lines. When they form a complete thought or statement they are referred to as a *closed couplet*. Example of a closed couplet:

> What's Fame? a fanc'd life in others' breath,
> A thing beyond us, ev'n before our death.

CRISIS (PP. 1092–1093): That point during the plot when the action reaches its turning point; also called the *climax;* see *anticlimax.*

CRITIC: An individual who evaluates and passes judgment on the quality and worth of a literary work. The critic who writes about contemporary works is also known as a reviewer and tends to be much maligned by authors. In this context Richard Le Gallienne has said that "a critic is a man created to praise greater men than himself, but he is never able to find them."

CRITICISM: The description, analysis, interpretation, or evaluation of a literary work of art; see also *deconstruction, historical criticism, new criticism, psychological/ psychoanalytic criticism, reader response criticism, structuralism, textual criticism, theoretical criticism,* and *practical criticism.* Perhaps Pope's comment in his *Essay on Criticism* (1711) is still as relevant as ever:

> Some are bewilder'd in the maze of schools,
> And some made coxcombs nature meant but fools.

CRITIQUE: A critical examination of a work of art.

CRUELTY, THEATER OF: A theory about theater formulated by Antonin Artaud in the 1930s. Artaud wished to give modern theater the power of early religious ritual by using shocking or horrifying events to underscore the basic cruelty of life. Jean Genet, Peter Weiss, and Peter Shaffer are important playwrights influenced by Artaud's ideas.

CURTAIN LINE: Line or lines that come just before the curtain falls ending a scene or act. Especially good examples occur in Ibsen's *Hedda Gabler* (1890).

CURTAIN RAISER: A brief play performed as a prelude to a more substantial work.

DACTYL (PP. 735–737): A foot of one accented syllable followed by two unaccented syllables. Example: DIFFicult.

DECONSTRUCTION: A contemporary critical movement greatly indebted to French theorist Jacques Derrida that holds that there is an inherently unstable relationship between words and meaning. A deconstructionist critic objectively examines each element of the literary text for its internal signification in order to demonstrate that every text finally generates innumerable, contradictory, and ultimately indeterminate meanings. Major texts include Derrida's *Of Grammatology* (tr. 1976), *Writing and Difference* (tr. 1978), and *Acts of Literature* (tr. 1992); Paul De Man's *Allegories of Reading* (1979) and *Blindness and Insight* (1981); and Jonathan Culler's *On Deconstruction* (1982).

DECORUM: The idea, derived from classical theory and thus at times approaching the status of doctrine, that all the elements of a literary work (i.e., setting, character, action, style) must be appropriately related to one another.

DEDUCTION: A method of reasoning that moves from the general to the specific.

DENOTATION (PP. 654–657): The literal, dictionary meaning of a given word or phrase. See *connotation.*

ᴇᴍᴇɴᴛ (ᴘᴘ. 34, 1094): From the French word meaning "unknotting" or "untying." A term sometimes used for the final *resolution* of the conflict or complications of the plot.

ᴅᴇᴛᴇʀᴍɪɴɪsᴍ: The belief or theory that human actions and events are controlled by and result from causes that determine them. According to Karl Marx, that determinism results from the economic environment; according to Charles Darwin, it results from the scientific laws governing evolution; according to Sigmund Freud, it results from the human unconscious; and, according to some religions and theologians, it results from the will of a god or gods. Characters who illustrate determinism act without free will in accordance with forces beyond their control. *Existentialism,* by contrast, invests human beings with direct control over and responsibility for their lives. See *existentialism.*

ᴅᴇᴜs ᴇx ᴍᴀᴄʜɪɴᴀ: "God from the machine." Derived from a practice in Greek drama whereby an impersonation of a god was mechanically lowered onto the stage to intervene in and solve the issues of the play. Commonly used today to describe any apparently contrived or improbable device used by an author to resolve the difficulties of plot. The intervention of the King at the end of *Tartuffe* can, in this sense, be said to illustrate the use of deus ex machina.

ᴅɪᴀʟᴇᴄᴛ: Language used by a particular geographic, social, or ethnic group and differing from the norm in pronunciation, diction, and grammar. Lampito uses a southern dialect in Douglass Parker's translation of *Lysistrata,* and all of the characters in *Desire Under the Elms* use a country dialect.

ᴅɪᴀʟᴏɢᴜᴇ (ᴘᴘ. 1085–1090): The conversation that goes on between or among characters in a literary work.

ᴅɪᴄᴛɪᴏɴ (ᴘ. 85): The author's choice or selection of words (vocabulary). The artistic arrangement of those words constitutes *style.*

ᴅɪᴅᴀᴄᴛɪᴄ: Literature designed more to teach a lesson or instruct the reader or audience than to present an experience objectively. In a didactic work *theme* is generally the most important element. Alexander Pope's *Essay on Criticism* (1711) and Edmund Spenser's *The Faerie Queene* (1590) are good examples of didactic poetry.

ᴅɪɢʀᴇssɪᴏɴ: The insertion into a work of material that is not closely related to its main subject.

ᴅɪᴍᴇᴛᴇʀ: A line of poetry consisting of two metrical feet; see *foot.* See, for example, Robert Frost's "Dust of Snow" (1923).

ᴅɪᴏɴʏsɪᴀɴ: A term similar in meaning to romanticism and implying the qualities of emotionalism, irrationality, and inspiration that were associated with the Greek god Dionysus. See the opposite term, *Apollonian.*

ᴅɪsᴄᴏᴠᴇʀʏ: A sudden exposure of facts in a tragedy, precipitating the reversal of fortune of the protagonist. In *Oedipus* the discovery occurs when Oedipus finally learns his parentage and thus that he has married his own mother and slain his father.

ᴅɪssᴏɴᴀɴᴄᴇ: See *euphony and cacophony.*

ᴅɪsᴛᴀɴᴄᴇ: The degree of detachment achieved by the reader and audience from the people and events of a literary work.

ᴅᴏɢɢᴇʀᴇʟ: A deprecatory term for inferior poetry.

ᴅᴏᴍᴇsᴛɪᴄ ᴛʀᴀɢᴇᴅʏ: A type of tragedy (originating in the eighteenth century as a reflection of its growing middle-class society) in which an ordinary middle-class (or lower-class) protagonist suffers ordinary (although by no means insignificant) disasters; also called *bourgeoise tragedy*. In this text, Eugene O'Neill's *Desire Under the Elms* (1924) is an example of domestic tragedy.

DOUBLE ENTENDRE (PP. 673–674): A form of pun in which one of the two meanings is risqué or sexually suggestive.

DOUBLE RHYME: See *masculine and feminine rhyme*.

DOWNSTAGE/UPSTAGE (PP. 1076–1077): *Downstage* is a stage direction referring to the front half of the stage, the part nearest to the audience; *upstage* refers to the back half of the stage. Thus, in theater jargon, an actor who moves farther back on stage during dialogue is *upstaging*, or forcing the other actor to face away from the audience while speaking. See *upstage*.

DRAMA CRITICISM: Useful bibliographies include *Drama Criticism: A Checklist of Interpretation Since 1940 of English and American Plays* (Denver: Alan Swallow, 1966); *Drama Criticism: A Checklist of Interpretation Since 1940 of Classical and Continental Plays* (Chicago: Alan Swallow, 1971); Stanley J. Wells, ed., *English Drama (excluding Shakespeare): Select Bibliographical Guides* (London: Oxford UP, 1975); Charles A. Carpenter, ed., *Modern British Drama* (Arlington Heights, Ill.: AHM Press, 1979) and *Modern Drama Scholarship and Criticism 1966–1980* (Toronto: U of Toronto P, 1986); Edward H. Mikhail, ed., *English Drama, 1900–1950: A Guide to Information Sources* (Detroit: Gale Research, 1977); Paul F. Breed and Florence M. Sniderman, eds., *Dramatic Criticism Index: A Bibliography of Commentaries on Playwrights from Ibsen to the Avant-Garde* (Detroit: Gale Research, 1972); Irving Adelman and Rita Dworkin, eds., *Modern Drama: A Checklist of Critical Literature on 20th Century Plays* (Metuchen, N.J.: Scarecrow Press, 1967); Edward Mikhail, ed., *Contemporary British Drama, 1950–1976: An Annotated Critical Bibliography* (Totowa, N.J.: Rowman, 1976); Helen H. Palmer, ed., *European Drama Criticism, 1900–1975* (Hamden, Conn.: Shoe String Press, 1977). See also the annual bibliography in the quarterly journal *Modern Drama* and the MLA *International Bibliography of Books and Articles on the Modern Languages and Literature* (New York: Modern Language Association).

DRAMA REVIEWS: For reviews of American plays see the annual volumes of *New York Theatre Critics' Reviews* (New York: Critics' Theatre Reviews) and *New York Times Theatre Reviews, 1870–1980*, 20 vols. (New York: Arno Press, 1980).

DRAMATIC IRONY: See *irony*.

DRAMATIC MONOLOGUE (P. 760): A type of poem in which a character, at some specific critical moment, addresses an identifiable but silent audience, thereby unintentionally revealing his or her essential temperament and personality. Classic examples are Robert Browning's "Porphyria's Lover" (1836), "My Last Duchess" (1842), and "Soliloquy of the Spanish Cloister" (1842).

DRAMATIS PERSONAE: A play's cast of characters.

DRAWING ROOM COMEDY: A light *comedy of manners* featuring upper-class characters, so named because the frequent setting of the action is aristocratic drawing rooms. Oscar Wilde's *The Importance of Being Earnest* (1895) is a good example.

DUMB SHOW: A pantomime occurring commonly in an Elizabethan play.

DYNAMIC AND STATIC CHARACTERS: See *character*.

EDITION: A single version of a book, remaining essentially unchanged in its re-

ings. Thus a second (or later) edition of a book indicates significant au-
orial changes. The word *edition* can also be used to mean the total number of
copies of a book printed from a single set of type. See *printing*.

EDWARDIAN PERIOD: The literary period between the death of Queen Victoria in
1901 and the beginning of World War I in 1914. Named for King Edward VII,
who occupied the throne from 1901 to 1910. Major writers include Conrad,
Joyce, Kipling, Shaw, Wells, and Yeats.

EFFECT: The total impression or impact of a work upon the reader or audience.

ELEGY: In its more modern usage, a poem that laments or solemnly mediates on
death, loss, or the passing of things of value. See, for example, Theodore
Roethke's "Elegy for Jane: My Student, Thrown by a Horse" (1953).

ELIZABETHAN PERIOD: The literary period coinciding with the reign of Elizabeth
I of England, 1558–1603. Major writers include Marlowe, Shakespeare, Sidney,
and Spenser.

EMPATHY: The state of entering into and actually participating in the emotional,
mental, or physical life of an object, person, or literary character.

EMPHASIS: The weight or stress that an author gives to one or more of the
elements of the work. For example, most writers of popular western fiction
place their primary emphasis upon plot.

END RHYME: Rhyme that occurs at the end of lines of poetry; also called terminal
rhyme; see *masculine and feminine rhyme*.

END-STOPPED LINE (PP. 728–729): A line of poetry that concludes with a pause.
For example:

> A little learning is a dangerous thing;
> Drink deep, or taste not the Pierian spring:
>
> (from "An Essay on Criticism"
> Alexander Pope, 1711)

ENGLISH AND AMERICAN LITERATURE, GUIDES TO: Bibliographic guides to the
study of English and American literature include Richard D. Altick and Andrew
Wright, *Selective Bibliography for the Study of English and American Literature* (New
York: Macmillan, 1979); Robert C. Schweik and Dieter Riesner, *Reference Sources
in English and American Literature: An Annotated Bibliography* (New York: W. W.
Norton, 1977); Frederick W. Bateson and Harrison T. Meserole, eds., *Guide to
English and American Literature* (London: Longman, 1976); John L. Somer and
Barbara Eck Cooper, *American and British Literature, 1945–1975: An Annotated
Bibliography of Contemporary Scholarship* (Lawrence, Kans.: Regents Press, 1980);
Nancy Baker, *A Research Guide for Undergraduate Students* (New York: Modern
Language Association, 1989).

ENGLISH LITERATURE, GUIDES TO: Bibliographic guides to the study of English
literature and authors include George Watson, ed., *New Cambridge Bibliography of
English Literature* (New CBEL), 4 vols. (Cambridge, Eng.: Cambridge UP, 1969–
1976); and David E. Pownall, ed., *Articles on Twentieth-Century Literature: An
Annotated Bibliography, 1954–1970*, 7 vols. (Millwood, N.Y.:Kraus-Thomson Org.,
1973–1980). Trevor Howard-Hill, *Bibliography of British Literary Bibliographies* (Oxford: Clarendon, 1987); Michael Marcuse, *A Reference Guide for English Studies*
(Berkeley: U of California P, 1990). These can be supplemented by the annual

volumes of the *MLA International Bibliography of Books and Articles on the Modern Languages and Literature* (New York: Modern Language Association) and the *Year's Work in Modern Language Studies* (Leeds, Eng.: Modern Humanities Research Assoc.), and by *Abstracts of English Studies* (Calgary, Alberta, Canada: U of Calgary P), published quarterly. See also *English and American literature, guides to.*

ENGLISH NOVEL, GUIDES TO: Bibliographic guides to the English novel include Helen H. Palmer and Anne J. Dyson, eds., *English Novel Explication: Criticisms to 1972* (Hamden, Conn.: Shoe String Press, 1973) and supplements; Inglis F. Bell and Donald Baird, eds., *The English Novel, 1578–1956: A Checklist of Twentieth-Century Criticisms* (Hamden, Conn.: Shoe String Press, 1974); Anthony E. Dyson, ed., *The English Novel: Select Bibliographical Guides* (London: Oxford UP, 1974); Paul Schlueter and June Schlueter, eds., *English Novel: Twentieth Century Criticism* (Athens, Ohio: Ohio UP, 1982).

ENGLISH SONNET: See *sonnet.*

ENJAMBMENT (PP. 728–729): A line of poetry that carries its idea or thought over to the next line without a grammatical pause; also called a *run-on line.*

ENTR'ACTE: The interval between two acts of a play, especially when enlivened by music or dance.

EPIC: A long narrative poem, elevated and dignified in theme, tone, and style, celebrating heroic deeds and historically (at times cosmically) important events; usually focuses on the adventures of a hero who has qualities that are super-human or divine and on whose fate very often depends the destiny of a tribe, a nation, or even the whole of the human race. *The Iliad, The Odyssey,* and *The Aeneid* are the most important epics in western world literature.

EPIGRAM (P. 762): A short, pointed, and witty statement, either constituting an entire poem (often in the form of a two-line couplet) or "buried" within a larger one. Here, for example, is a short, savage epigram by John Wilmot, Earl of Rochester, entitled "On King Charles":

> We have a pretty witty king
> And whose word no man relies on:
> He never said a foolish thing,
> And never did a wise one.

To which Charles II replied: "This is very true: for my words are my own, and my actions are my ministers'."

EPIGRAPH: A quotation prefacing a literary work, often containing a clue to the writer's intention. Consider, for example, the epigraph from Dante's *Inferno* that precedes T. S. Eliot's "The Love Song of J. Alfred Prufrock" (1917).

EPILOGUE: The final, concluding section of a literary work, usually a play, offered in summation, to point a lesson or moral, or to thank the audience (reader) for its indulgence; see *prologue.*

EPIPHANY: Applied to literature by James Joyce to describe a sudden revelation, or "showing forth," of the essential truth about a character, situation, or experience. See Joyce's "Araby" (1914) in this text.

EPISODE (PP. 36–37, 1095): A single, unified *incident* within a narrative that may or may not advance the plot. Plots containing a series of episodes, arranged chronologically, are said to be "episodic."

EPISTOLARY NOVEL: A type of novel in which the narrative is carried on by means of a series of letters. Samuel Richardson's *Pamela* (1740) and *Clarissa Harlowe* (1748) are among the best-known epistolary novels.

EPITAPH: Verses written to commemorate the dead. Most epitaphs are laudatory, as in Alexander Pope's lines on Sir Isaac Newton:

> Nature and nature's laws lay hid in night:
> God said, "Let Newton be!" and all was light.
>
> ("Epitaph," 1730)

Some, however, are bitter and intemperate, as in these lines by Byron on Lord Castlereagh, the British Foreign Secretary who helped reestablish monarchies in Europe following the downfall of Napoleon:

> Posterity will ne'er survey
> A nobler grave than this:
> Here lie the bones of Castlereagh:
> Stop, traveller————
>
> ("Epitaph," 1820)

EPITHALAMION/EPITHALAMIUM: A song or poem celebrating a wedding, from the Greek meaning "poem upon or at the bridal chamber." Edmund Spenser's *Epithalamion* (1595) is the most famous example of such poetry.

EPITHET: A word or phrase that characterizes a person or thing. Literary epithets include phrases like Homer's "rosy-fingered dawn" or Shakespeare's "honest Iago." Vulgar insults are also known as epithets, as in Earle Birney's alliterative poem, "Anglosaxon Street" (1942):

> Here is a ghetto   gotten for goyim
> O with care denuded   of nigger and kike

ERRATA: Errors and misprints that are discovered only after the work has been printed. A list of errata is sometimes glued into the front of the book.

ESCAPE LITERATURE: Any kind of writing whose main purpose is to entertain, to allow the reader to "escape" from the everyday concerns of his or her world. Margaret Mitchell's novel of the American Civil War, *Gone With the Wind* (1936), is a good example.

ETYMOLOGICAL DICTIONARY: A dictionary that traces the historical development of individual words. The standard etymological dictionary for the English language is the 13 volume *Oxford English Dictionary* (OED) and its supplements (Oxford, Eng.: Oxford UP, 1933; rev. ed., 1988), which compiles every word used from the earliest times to the present. An etymological dictionary is a vital tool for close textual analysis, which often requires an understanding of how the meanings of certain words have changed over time.

EULOGY: A formal and dignified speech or piece of writing praising a person or thing (often the deceased).

EUPHONY AND CACOPHONY (PP. 753–754): *Euphony* describes language that is harmonious, smooth, and pleasing to the ear. Harsh, nonharmonious, and discordant language is *cacophony;* cacophony is also referred to as *dissonance.* For an example of the effective use of euphony and cacophony examine Robert Herrick's quatrain "Upon Julia's Voice" (1648). Note particularly the hard, cacophonous consonants describing the damned in line 2 and the euphonious *m* and *l* sounds in the final image of Julia's voice:

> So smooth, so sweet, so silvery is thy voice,
> As, could they hear, the Damned would make no noise,
> But listen to thee (walking in thy chamber)
> Melting melodious words to Lutes of Amber.

EVALUATION: A judgment about the particular merits or success of a given work.

EVIDENCE: The facts, examples, or arguments given in support of a writer's assertion or thesis. Literary analysis invariably requires the amassing of evidence from the work itself.

EYE RHYME: See *visual rhyme*.

EXISTENTIALISM: A post–World War II philosophy, associated most frequently with the Frenchman Jean Paul Sartre (1905–1980), which posits a meaningless, absurd, and alienating world in which a person must deliberately create his or her own meaning and affirmation through personal choices. Albert Camus's "The Guest" (1957) is an example of an existential short story.

EXPATRIATE WRITER: A writer who lives for a prolonged period in a country other than his or her own. Some of the better known expatriate writers include Joseph Conrad, Henry James, and Ernest Hemingway.

EXPLICATION (PP. 5–9): A detailed word-by-word and line-by-line attempt to explain the entire meaning of a literary work. From a Latin word meaning "unfolding."

EXPOSITION (PP. 34–36, 1091–1092): The part of a work that provides necessary background information.

EXPRESSIONISM: A movement in revolt against realism that attempts to objectify inner experience by using nonrealistic techniques. The movement first achieved importance in the plays of Strindberg, particularly in *A Dream Play* (1902). Expressionism also exerted an influence on Pirandello, Lorca, Eugene O'Neill, Arthur Miller, and Tennessee Williams.

FABLE: A story with a moral lesson, often employing animals who talk and act like human beings: see *allegory*.

FALLING ACTION (PP. 34–36, 1093–1095): The part of a dramatic plot that follows the *crisis* (or *climax*) and precedes the *resolution* (or *dénouement*).

FALSE RHYME (P. 751): Rhyme pairing the sounds of accented and unaccented syllables, e.g., "tennis" and "remiss."

FANTASY: A work of fiction that deliberately sets aside everyday reality. There are strong elements of fantasy in Gabriel García Márquez's story "A Very Old Man with Enormous Wings" (1968). Critics have identified the fantasy technique used by Márquez and others as "magical realism."

FARCE: A type of comedy that achieves its effect through ridiculous and exaggerated situations, broad, often crude, verbal humor, and various kinds of buffoonery and physical horseplay. There are strong elements of farce in both Aristophanes' *Lysistrata* (411 B.C.) and in Anton Chekhov's *The Cherry Orchard* (1904).

FATALISM: A theory and belief that future events are predetermined and will take place regardless of the choices, decisions, or actions we make in the present. The Swede in Stephen Crane's "The Blue Hotel" (1898) is a good example of a character haunted by a fatalistic sense of doom.

FEMININE RHYME: See *masculine and feminine rhyme.*

FEMINIST CRITICISM: Literary criticism written from the perspective of women, reflecting feminist attitudes, concerns, and values. Feminist criticism is concerned both with how the meaning of a literary work is affected when read from a woman's perspective and how female characters and women in general are treated within the work. This literary movement grows out of (and is part of) the feminist movement that since the late 1960s has attempted to improve equal rights and equal opportunities for women by identifying and removing the political, social, and psychological obstacles that prevent women from achieving their full possibilities as human beings. Major texts include Elaine Showalter, *A Literature of Their Own* (1977) and *The New Feminist Criticism* (1985); Judith Fetterley, *The Resistant Reader* (1978); Sandra M. Gilbert and Susan Gubar's *The Madwoman in the Attic* (1979); and Nina Baym, *Feminism and American Literary History* (1992).

FESTSCHRIFT: A collection of essays by a series of authors, written to honor a distinguished scholar. From the German meaning "celebration writing."

FICTION: A prose narrative that is the product of the imagination.

FIGURATIVE LANGUAGE (PP. 692–708): Language used imaginatively and non literally. Figurative language is composed of such figures of speech (or tropes) as *metaphor, simile, personification, metonymy, synecdoche, apostrophe, hyperbole, symbol, irony,* and *paradox.*

FILM CRITICISM: Criticism that attempts to explain, analyze, and evaluate a motion picture film. See *criticism.*

FILM REVIEWS: See *New York Times Film Reviews, 1913–1980* (New York: Arno Press, 1981), a twelve-volume set with supplements every two years, and *Film Review Digest Annual* (Millwood, N.Y.: KTO).

FIN DE SIÈCLE: "End of the century," usually applied to the 1890s, a period noted for rapid social change, estheticism, and decadence.

FIRST DRAFT: A writer's first unrevised and unedited version of a complete work. Also called the *rough draft.* When the manuscript is in the author's handwriting it is called a *holograph.*

FLASHBACK (P. 37): The interruption of a narrative plotline in order to present an earlier scene or episode; a technique of *exposition.* As young Robin waits outside the darkened church in Hawthorne's "My Kinsman, Major Molineux" (1832), the reader is presented with a flashback providing information about his home and family.

FOIL (PP. 62, 1096): A character who provides a direct contrast to another character. Dr. Watson is a foil to Sherlock Holmes: "When I hear you give your reasons . . . ," he tells the great detective in "A Scandal in Bohemia" (1891), "the thing always appears to me to be so ridiculously simple that I could easily do it myself, though at each successive instance of your reasoning I am baffled, until you explain your process."

FOLK BALLAD: See *ballad.*

FOLKTALE: A short narrative or story of unknown authorship handed down (and modified) through oral tradition from one generation to the next. Many fairy tales and mythological legends originated as folktales.

FOOT (PP. 723–726): The basic metrical or rhythmical unit within a line of poetry. A foot of poetry generally consists of an accented syllable and one or more unaccented syllables arranged in a variety of patterns; see *scansion*.

FORESHADOWING: A device by means of which the author hints at something to follow. Young Goodman Brown's rendezvous with the devil in Hawthorne's story (1835) is foreshadowed by a number of elements in the plot, not the least of which is the crooked staff carried by his companion "which bore the likeness of a great black snake."

FOREWORD: A short introductory statement designed to orient the reader to the work that follows. It is often written by someone other than the author.

FORM: A term used either as a synonym for literary *genre* or type, or to describe the essential organizational structure of a work of art.

FORMAT: The physical makeup of a book, journal, or other type of publication, including its page size, typeface, margins, paper, binding, and cover.

FOURTEENERS: Lines of poetry with fourteen syllables (seven iambic feet).

FRAME NARRATIVE/FRAME STORY: A narrative (or story) that encloses one or more other narratives (or stories) to produce a "story within a story." *The Arabian Nights*, Boccaccio's *Decameron* (*ca.* 1350), and Chaucer's *Canterbury Tales* (*ca.* 1390) are familiar examples.

FREE VERSE (PP. 745–747): A type of poetry that deliberately seeks to free itself from the restrictions imposed by traditionally fixed conventions of meter, rhyme, and stanza. Free verse is now often called poetry in open forms. T. S. Eliot's "The Love Song of J. Alfred Prufrock" (1917) and the various poems from Walt Whitman's *Leaves of Grass* (1855) are good examples of free verse.

FREYTAG'S TRIANGLE: A way of describing (and diagramming) the standard plot structure of *exposition, complication, crisis, falling action,* and *resolution*. This structure for a five-act play was analyzed by Gustav Freytag in his *Technik des Dramas* (1863).

FUSTIAN: Bombastic, pretentious speech.

GENRE: A form, class, or type of literary work—e.g., the short story, novel, poem, play, or essay; often used to denote such literary subclassifications as the detective story, the gothic novel, the pastoral elegy, or the revenge tragedy.

GLOSS: An explanation of a difficult word or passage, often by means of a footnote.

GLOSSARY: A list of words followed by definitions or explanations—usually at the rear of a book.

GOTHIC: The term originally referred to the Germanic tribe of Goths and later to things medieval (especially in its barbaric and supernatural aspects). It is now generally applied to literature dealing with the strange, mysterious, and supernatural designed to invoke suspense and terror in the reader (or audience). Gothic literature invariably exploits ghosts and monsters and settings such as castles, dungeons, and graveyards, which impart a suitably sinister and terrifying atmosphere.

Haiku (pp. 767–768): A Japanese form of poetry; three lines of five, seven, and five syllables, respectively, present a single concentrated image or emotion. Here, for example, is a haiku by the Japanese poet Issa (1763–1827):

> only one guy and
> only one fly trying to
> make the guest room do
>
> (translated by Cid Corman)

Hamartia: The error or frailty that leads to the destruction of a tragic hero. See *tragic flaw.*

Harlequin: The conventional *clown* or buffoon in *commedia del l'arte,* usually masked and dressed in parti-colored tights. A *harlequinade* is a play or skit in which the harlequin stars.

Heightening: The deliberate intensification of the dramatic action. In Stephen Crane's "The Blue Hotel" (1898), for example, the card game clearly heightens the conflict between and among the various characters.

Heptameter: A line of poetry consisting of seven metrical feet; see *foot.*

Hermeneutics: A synonym for the theory or art of criticism.

Hero/Heroine (p. 60): The central character in a literary work; also often referred to as the *protagonist.*

Heroic Couplet: A pair of rhymed iambic pentameter lines; a stanza composed of two heroic couplets is called a *heroic quatrain.* Example:

> Men must be taught as if you taught them not,
> And things unknown proposed as things forgot.
>
> (Alexander Pope,
> from *An Essay on Criticism,* 1711)

Heroic Line: The term given to iambic pentameter because it is so often associated with epic or heroic poetry.

Hexameter: A line of poetry consisting of six metrical feet; see *foot.* See, for example, Ernest Dowson's "Non Sum Qualis Eram Bonae Sub Regno Cynarae" (1896), which begins

> Last night, ah, yesternight, betwixt her lips and mine
> There fell thy shadow, Cynara! thy breath was shed
> Upon my soul between the kisses and the wine;

High Comedy and Low Comedy: Any type of highly verbal comedy whose appeal is mainly intellectual and sophisticated, often with a basic seriousness of purpose, is *high comedy* (e.g., a *comedy of manners*). *Low comedy* is nonintellectual and lacks serious purpose (e.g., a *farce*).

High Style and Low Style (p. 1090): *High style* is a formal and elevated literary style rich in poetic devices. Percy Bysshe Shelley's "Ode to the West Wind" (1820) is a good example of a poem written in the high style. *Low style* is casual and conversational. "Nobody Loses All the Time" (1923) by e. e. cummings is written in the low style.

HISTORICAL CRITICISM: Seeks to understand and explain a literary work in terms of the author's life and the historical context and circumstances in which it was written.

HUBRIS: The excessive pride, arrogance, or self-confidence that results in the defeat or downfall of the hero; see *tragic flaw.*

HYPERBOLE (P. 681): A figure of speech that achieves emphasis and heightened effect (either serious or comic) through deliberate exaggeration. Consider, for example, Byron's hyperbolic claim that

> Man, being reasonable, must get drunk;
>   The best of life is but intoxication:
> Glory, the grape, love, gold, in these are sunk
>   The hopes of all men, and of every nation;

> (from *Don Juan,* 1819, Canto 2, CLXXIX)

IAMB (IAMBIC) (PP. 725–729): A foot composed of an unaccented syllable followed by an accented one, as in the word "em*bark.*"

IDENTICAL RHYME: Rhyme achieved through the repetition of the same word or two words that have the same sound but are spelled differently and have different meanings; e.g., "sight" and "cite."

ILLUSTRATION: The use of examples to develop a generalization.

IMAGERY (PP. 685–691): Most commonly refers to visual pictures produced verbally through literal or figurative language, although it is often defined more broadly to include sensory experience other than the visual.

IMITATION: A concept, originating in classical criticism with Aristotle's *Poetics,* that all art is a form of imitation.

IMPLIED AUTHOR: The critical assumption that present somewhere in every literary work is an authorial personality (an "implied author") who mediates or intervenes in some way between the text and the reader. The implied author is always a creation or persona—an idealized, created version of the real author— and is not to be confused with that real author. For further discussion see Wayne Booth, *The Rhetoric of Fiction* (1961).

IMPLIED READER: The critical assumption that every text has a hypothetical (or "implied") reader who embodies all the predispositions necessary for the text to have its full effect. For further discussion see Wolfgang Iser, *The Implied Reader: Patterns of Communication in Prose Fiction From Bunyan to Beckett* (tr. 1974).

IMPRESSION: See *printing.*

INCIDENT: See *episode.*

INCONGRUITY (P. 676): A word, phrase, or idea that is out of keeping, inconsistent, or inappropriate in its context. There is considerable incongruity, for example, in Tom Stoppard's *The Real Inspector Hound* (1968) when the inspector shows up wearing inflatable pontoon boots and a flashing miner's helmet at a scene where no crime has been discovered, reported, or presumably even perpetrated.

INDEX/ABSTRACT: A book or set of books containing listings of articles. For example, *Humanities Index, Abstract of English Studies, Reader's Guide to Periodical Literature.* Indexes and abstracts provide the quickest way to find articles on specific topics in journals and newspapers. Instructions for the use of these reference tools will be found in the front of each volume.

INDUCTION: The method of reasoning that moves from the consideration of specifics or particulars to a conclusion about them.

INITIATION STORY: Commonly used to describe a narrative focussing on a young person's movement from innocence toward maturity as a result of experience; see *bildungsroman*. Hawthorne's "My Kinsman, Major Molineux" (1832) and Faulkner's "Barn Burning" (1939) are excellent examples of the story of initiation.

IN MEDIAS RES (PP. 36, 1091): Latin for a narrative that begins "in the middle of things." Hemingway's "Hills Like White Elephants" (1927) begins *in medias res*.

INTENTIONAL FALLACY: A term employed in modern criticism to describe the error of interpreting the meaning of a literary work as if the stated purpose or intention of its author resolves all doubts about its meaning. See *new criticism*.

INTERIOR MONOLOGUE: See *monologue*.

INTERLUDE: From the Latin meaning "between the play," the interlude developed in the late fifteenth and early sixteenth centuries as a type of brief stage entertainment produced between the acts of a longer play or between courses of a feast.

INTERNAL RHYME (P. 750): Rhyme within a line of poetry; also called *middle rhyme;* e.g., "For the moon never *beams* without bringing me *dreams*/Of the beautiful Annabel Lee" (from "Annabel Lee," 1850, by Edgar Allan Poe).

INTRIGUE: A scheme that one character devises to entrap another, thus providing impetus for the plot.

INVECTIVE: Insulting or abusive language. Here, for example, is a good example of invective from James Stephens's poem, "A Glass of Beer" (1918):

> May the devil grip the whey-faced slut by the hair,
> And beat bad manners out of her skin for a year.

INVOCATION: An appeal to a deity for help or support usually occurring at the beginning of a long poem or play. See, for example, the opening lines of John Milton's *Paradise Lost* (1667).

IRONY (PP. 679–684): Refers to some contrast or discrepancy between appearance and reality. Irony takes a number of special forms: in *verbal irony* there is a contrast between what is literally said and what is actually meant; in *dramatic irony* the state of affairs known to the reader (or audience) is the reverse of what its participants suppose it to be; in *situational irony* a set of circumstances turns out to be the reverse of what is expected or is appropriate.

ISBN—INTERNATIONAL STANDARD BOOK NUMBER: The number assigned each book to facilitate its identification in placing orders. The ISBN is printed with the other publication data on the back of the title page of each copy. In paperback editions it is also frequently printed together with a bar code on the back cover.

ISSN—INTERNATIONAL STANDARD SERIAL NUMBER: The number assigned each serial by title as an aid to identification. Like the ISBN above, it is usually located with other publication data on the back of the title page.

ITALIAN SONNET: See *sonnet*.

JACOBEAN PERIOD: The period coinciding with the reign of James I of England, 1603–1625 (*Jacobus* is Latin for "James"). Major writers include Jonson, Beaumont and Fletcher, Shakespeare, and Donne.

JOURNAL: A personal memoir recording events and impressions, memories, and reflections; a form of autobiography. Some writers choose to write fiction in the guise of purported journal entries, as Charlotte Perkins Gilman does in her short story, "The Yellow Wall-Paper" (1892). The term is also applied to certain periodical publications.

JUVENALIA: Writings produced during an author's youth, usually characterized by immaturity and lack of polish.

JUXTAPOSITION (PP. 695–696): A form of implied comparison or contrast created by placing two items side by side. In John Crowe Ransom's "Piazza Piece" (1927), for example, the words of the "gentleman in a dustcoat" and the "lady young in beauty" are juxtaposed to create a dramatic and ironic contrast.

KABUKI PLAYS: Popular and highly theatrical Japanese plays combining dance, musical theater, and stage spectacle. The acting is formal and stylized instead of realistic.

LAMENT: A song of complaint, often expressing grief.

LEGEND: A story or narrative handed down from the past. Legends differ from myths on the basis of the elements of historical truth they contain. One speaks, for example, of Arthurian *legend* because there is some historical evidence of Arthur's existence. In speaking of the *myth* of Sisyphus, in contrast, one is aware that no such person actually existed. See *myth*.

LEITMOTIF: A word, phrase, or *theme* that recurs in a literary work.

LETTERS: The name sometimes given to literature.

LIGHT VERSE: Poems, usually short, that are humorous and witty. The following lines by Bert Leston Taylor are light verse:

> Whenas galoshed my Julia goes,
> Unbuckled all from top to toes,
> How swift the poem becometh prose!
>
> (from "Upon Julia's Arctics")

LIMERICK (P. 768): A light, humorous (and often scurrilous and pornographic) verse form composed of five anapestic lines, rhyming AABBA: lines one, two, and five contain three feet (trimeter), lines three and four contain two (dimeter). Most limericks are anonymous. The following poem by Morris Bishop (1893-1973) is a limerick about limericks:

> The limerick is furtive and mean;
> You must keep her in close quarantine
>   Or she sneaks to the slums
>   And promptly becomes
> Disorderly, drunk and obscene.

LITERAL: Accurate, exact, and concrete language, i.e., nonfigurative language; see *figurative language*.

LITERARY BALLAD: See *ballad.*

LITERARY BIOGRAPHY: See Patricia P. Havlice, ed., *Index to Literary Biography,* 2 vols. (Metuchen, N.J.: Scarecrow Press, 1975), supplement 1983.

LITERARY HISTORY, ENGLAND: Basic surveys include Albert C. Baugh et al., *A Literary History of England* (New York: Prentice-Hall, 1967), Hardin Craig et al., *A History of English Literature,* 4 vols. (London: Collier-Macmillan, 1962), and the individual volumes of the *Oxford History of English Literature* (OHEL) (Oxford: Oxford UP, 1945–). Also Allardyce Nicoll, *A History of English Drama, 1660–1900,* 6 vols. (Cambridge, Eng.: Cambridge UP, 1952–1959) and Reginald A. Foakes, ed., *Routledge History of English Poetry,* 6 vols. (Boston: Routledge, 1977–). See also Margaret Drabble, *Oxford Companion to English Literature* (Oxford: Clarendon Press, 1985).

LITERARY HISTORY, UNITED STATES: The basic survey is Robert E. Spiller, ed., *Literary History of the United States* (LHUS), 2 vols. (New York: Macmillan, 1974). See also James D. Hart, *Oxford Companion to American Literature* (New York: Oxford UP, 1984); Max J. Herzberg et al., *The Reader's Encyclopedia of American Literature* (New York: Thomas Y. Crowell, 1962).

LITERARY RESEARCH, GUIDES TO: The single most complete guide to literary research is Margaret C. Patterson, *Literary Research Guide* (New York: Modern Language Association, 1983). For discussion of the purposes and methods of literary research in English and American literature see Richard D. Altick, *The Art of Literary Research* (New York: W. W. Norton, 1982).

LITTLE MAGAZINES: Literary journals with small circulations and limited budgets. Many little magazines are *avant-garde* and experimental in their choice of material. They often provide an outlet for lesser known authors.

LOCAL COLOR WRITERS: The name given to authors who realistically and sympathetically treat the rural life of a particular geographical region and, not infrequently, employ regional dialects, settings, and folk materials in their work.

LOCALE: See *setting.*

LONG MEASURE: A stanza that consists of four lines of iambic tetrameter, rhyming either ABCB or ABAB.

LOW COMEDY: See *high comedy and low comedy.*

LYRIC (P. 760): A short, songlike poem, by a single speaker on a single subject, expressing a personal thought, mood, or feeling.

MALAPROPISM: A comic misuse of words, from the Latin meaning "ill-suited to the purpose." The term derives from Mrs. Malaprop, a character in Richard Brinsley Sheridan's comedy *The Rivals* (1775), whose garbled exhortations are often quite funny. At one point, for example, she argues that an educated young lady must speak correctly and "be mistress of orthodoxy, that she might not mis-spell and mispronounce words so shamefully as girls usually do; and likewise that she might reprehend the true meaning of what she is saying."

MANNERS: The prevailing code of social conduct or behavior; see *comedy of manners.*

MARCHEN: The German word for *folktale* or fairy tale.

MASCULINE AND FEMININE RHYME (P. 750): The most common kinds of end rhyme. *Masculine end rhyme,* predominant in English poetry, consists of accented words of one syllable or polysyllabic words where the final syllable is accented;

for example, *"fond"* and *"despond."* *Feminine end rhyme* (or *double rhyme*) consists of rhyming words of two syllables in which the accent falls on the first syllable; e.g., *"wooings"* and *"cooings."* A variation of feminine rhyme, called *triple rhyme*, occurs when there is a correspondence of sound in the final three syllables, an accented syllable followed by two unaccented ones; e.g., *"glorious"* and *"uxorious."* (These examples, by the way, are taken from three successive stanzas of Byron's *Don Juan* (1821). See Canto 3, stanzas vi–viii.)

MASQUE: An elaborate form of court entertainment—a mixture of drama, music, song, and dance—developed in Renaissance Italy and transported to England during Elizabethan times. The speaking characters, who were often courtiers, wore masks. *Comus* (1634) by John Milton is probably the most important masque in English literature.

MEASURE: A synonym for *meter.*

MELODRAMA: In its original Greek sense, a "melodrama" meant a play with music (*melos* means "song"). But by the mid–nineteenth century the term had become synonymous with a highly conventionalized type of sensationalistic plot pitting stereotypic hero and villain against one another in a series of suspense-ridden, emotion-charged, and violence-filled scenes. The term *melodramatic* is used generally to describe sensational, emotional, and action-oriented writings, e.g., the cowboy western or the gothic novel.

MEMOIRS: A form of autobiographical writing, usually dealing with the recollections of significant events in the lives of significant people other than the author.

METAFICTION: A literary work in which the central focus is on the nature of fiction itself or on the way in which fiction establishes and asserts its meaning.

METAPHOR (PP. 694–695): A figure of speech in which two unlike objects are implicitly compared without the use of *like* or *as;* see also *conceit* and *simile.* Most readers of poetry take delight in discovering fresh metaphors, such as Sylvia Plath's description of a nurse who walks on "two erasers" in "Lullaby" (1960) or Dylan Thomas's reference to his own poems as "spindrift pages" in "In My Craft or Sullen Art" (1946).

METAPHYSICAL POETRY: A kind of realistic, often ironic and witty, verse combining intellectual ingenuity and psychological insight. Metaphysical poetry was written partly in reaction to the conventions of Elizabethan love poetry by such seventeenth-century poets as John Donne, George Herbert, and Andrew Marvell. One of its hallmarks is the metaphysical *conceit*, a particularly interesting and ingenious type of metaphor.

METER: See *rhythm and meter.*

METONYMY (P. 695): A figure of speech in which one object or idea takes the place of another with which it is closely associated. We sometimes refer, for example, to the White House when we actually mean the president. In the same way we speak of the crown when we mean the reigning monarch.

METRICS: A synonym for *prosody.* See *prosody.*

MICROFILM/MICROFICHE/MICROCARD: 16mm or 35mm microfilm (on reel or cartridge), 4 × 6 microfiche sheets, and 6 × 9 microcards provide a convenient and inexpensive way of preserving and using multiple pages of print material. Machines needed to read these various kinds of microtext are available in most libraries.

MIDDLE ENGLISH LITERATURE: The literature of medieval England, from about 1150 to 1500.

MILIEU: The environment or surroundings in which an author lives or in which a work is written.

MIMESIS: The Greek word for *imitation*. Because of the influence of Eric Auerbach's seminal study, *Mimesis: The Representation of Reality in Western Literature* (trans. by Willard Trask. Princeton: Princeton UP, 1953), the word *mimesis* generally means the imitation of reality in literature. See *realism*.

MINOR PLOT: See *subplot*.

MIRACLE PLAY: A medieval religious play concerned with the life and martyrdom of a saint.

MIXED METAPHOR (P. 716): Two or more metaphors combined together in such a way as to be incongruous, illogical, or even ludicrous. Example: That rat cheats on his honey with every vixen in the neighborhood.

MODERN: A term applied to works written in the twentieth century. In the sense that it connotes *new*, the term *modern* often implies a break with tradition and a rejection of past ideas, values, assumptions, and techniques.

MODERN DRAMA: A period in the history of drama that is usually said to have begun with the first performance of Henrik Ibsen's *A Doll's House* in 1879. Modern drama rejected the romanticized heroes and poetic style of prior drama and instead made use of everyday characters and ordinary prose. From an initial emphasis on *realism* and *naturalism*, modern drama quickly evolved in the more experimental direction of *expressionism*.

MONODY: An elegy for the dead recited or delivered by a single speaker. See *elegy*.

MONOGRAPH: A scholarly study of a single subject; a monograph is longer than an article and usually shorter than a book.

MONOLOGUE: An extended speech delivered by a single speaker, alone or in the presence of others. In a general sense, *asides, dramatic monologues*, and *soliloquies* are all types of monologues. When the monologue serves to reveal a character's internal thoughts and feelings, it is sometimes referred to as an *interior monologue*. A good example is Othello's speech at the beginning of Act V, Scene ii, in which he reflects on the incipient murder of Desdemona.

MONOMETER: A line of poetry consisting of a single metrical foot; see *foot*. In George Herbert's "Easter Wings" (1633), for example, each stanza narrows to two monometer lines at its exact midpoint.

MOOD: See *atmosphere*.

MORALITY PLAY: A form of allegorical medieval drama in which personified virtues and vices struggle for the human soul. *Everyman* (*ca.* 1470) is the most famous morality play.

MOTIF: An idea, theme, character, situation, or element that recurs in literature or folklore; see *archetype, convention, stock character, stock situation*. For example, one may discuss the revenge motif in *Othello* (1604) or the jungle motif in Joseph Conrad's "Heart of Darkness" (1899).

MOTIVE (P. 66): The cause that moves a character to act.

MS (MSS): The abbreviation for manuscript(s), an author's handwritten or typed copy of a text prepared and submitted for publication.

MUSES: The Greek goddesses presiding over the arts, including history, music, drama, dance, and poetry.

MYSTERY PLAY: A medieval religious play based on stories from the Old and New Testaments to which the author often added comic scenes. Also referred to as Corpus Christi plays because they were frequently performed on Corpus Christi day (the first Thursday after Trinity Sunday). The plays eventually came to be sponsored by the various trade guilds and were staged on movable wagons which could be drawn to various locations in large English towns such as York, Chester, Coventry, and Wakefield. Cycles of forty or more mystery plays covered the complete biblical history from the creation through the resurrection. The *Second Shepherds' Play* (*ca.* 1400) is one of the best of the mystery plays.

MYTH: Broadly, any idea or belief to which a number of people subscribe; see *legend.*

NARRATION: A form of exposition that retells an event or series of related events in order to make a point.

NARRATIVE: A series of unified events; see *plot* and *action.*

NARRATIVE POEM (PP. 759–760): A poem that tells a story.

NARRATIVE SEQUENCE: The order in which events are recounted.

NARRATIVE TECHNIQUE: The author's methods of presenting or telling a story.

NARRATOR: The character or voice that tells the story; see *point of view* and *persona.*

NATIONAL UNION CATALOG: The *National Union Catalog,* 685 vols. (London: Mansell, 1968), and its supplements provide a cumulative author list of the holdings of the Library of Congress and some one thousand other libraries in the United States and Canada. See *British Museum Catalog.*

NATURALISM: A post-Darwinian movement of the late nineteenth century that tried to apply the "laws" of scientific determinism to fiction. The naturalist went beyond the realist's insistence on the objective presentation of the details of everyday life to insist that the materials of literature should be arranged to reflect a deterministic universe in which a person is a biological creature controlled by environment and heredity. Major writers include Crane, Dreiser, Norris, and O'Neill in America; Zola in France; and Hardy and Gissing in England. Crane's "The Blue Hotel" (1898) is perhaps the best example in this text of a naturalistic short story. See also *realism.*

NEOCLASSICAL PERIOD: English literature written between 1660, the year that Charles II regained the throne, and 1798, the year that Wordsworth and Coleridge published *Lyrical Ballads* and announced the arrival of *Romanticism.* Major neoclassical poets include John Dryden, Thomas Gray, Alexander Pope, and Jonathan Swift.

NEW COMEDY: A type of *comedy of manners,* featuring *stock characters* and conventional plots, which in the fourth and third century B.C. replaced the *Old Comedy* of Aristophanes. See *old comedy.*

NEW CRITICISM: The New Criticism refers to a type or "school" of criticism that seeks to analyze and study a literary work as autonomous, without reference to the author's intention, the impact or effect on the reader, the historical or cultural period in which the work was written (see *historical criticism*), or the validity of the ideas that may be extrapolated from it. Its method is based on the close reading and analysis of the verbal elements of the text, although its leading exponents and practitioners (academic critics such as John Crowe Ransom, I. A. Richards, Cleanth Brooks, Robert Penn Warren, Allen Tate, R. P. Blackmur, Yvor Winters, and Kenneth Burke) often disagree on just how this analysis is to be undertaken. The term originates from the title of John Crowe Ransom's book *The New Criticism* (1941) and is "new" in the sense that it constituted a deliberate break with the older subjective and impressionistic theories of art that allowed extrinsic rather than solely intrinsic considerations to influence evaluation.

NOH PLAYS: A formal and lofty form of Japanese drama written between 1300 and 1600.

NOM DE PLUME: French meaning "pen name."

NOVEL: The name generally applied to any long fictional prose narrative.

NOVELETTE: A longish prose narrative, not long enough to be regarded as a novel but too long to be a short story. Joseph Conrad's "Heart of Darkness" (1899) and Leo Tolstoy's "The Death of Ivan Ilych" (1886) are examples of novelettes. Also called a short novel.

OBJECTIVE: See *subjective*.

OBLIGATORY SCENE (PP. 1092–1093): A scene whose circumstances are so fully anticipated by the audience as the plot develops that the playwright is "obliged" to provide it.

OCCASIONAL VERSE: Poetry written to celebrate or commemorate a particular event or occasion. For example, "Alexander's Feast" by John Dryden was commissioned in 1697 for the celebration of St. Cecilia's Day.

OCTAMETER: A line of poetry consisting of eight metrical feet; see *foot*.

OCTAVE: See *sonnet*.

OCTET: A synonym for *octave;* see *sonnet*.

ODE (P. 767): A long lyric poem, serious and dignified in subject, tone, and style, sometimes with an elaborate stanzaic structure, often written to commemorate or celebrate an event or individual. Among the better-known odes in this text are "Alexander's Feast" (1697) by John Dryden, "Ode on a Grecian Urn" (1820) by John Keats, and "Ode to the West Wind" (1820) by Percy Bysshe Shelley.

OLD COMEDY (P. 1104): Greek comedies of the fifth century B.C. (represented in this text by Aristophanes' *Lysistrata*, 411 B.C.) that combined religious ceremony with satire and farce. See *new comedy*.

OLD ENGLISH LITERATURE: Literature written from about 450 to 1150: from the Anglo-Saxon invasion of England to the beginning of the Middle English period. Old English is a Germanic language greatly different from Middle English and modern English.

ONOMATOPOEIA (P. 755): A word (or a group of words) whose sound has the effect of suggesting or reinforcing its denotative meaning. Words like *buzz* and *pop* are said to be onomatopoetic.

OPÉRA BOUFFE: A French term for light comic opera.

OPERETTA: A comic opera or musical comedy.

ORATION: An elaborate speech delivered in a formal and dignified manner.

ORGANIZATION: The overall plan or design which shapes the work.

OTTAVA RIMA (P. 766): A stanza of Italian origin consisting of eight iambic pentameter lines rhyming ABABABCC. The stanza is most famous in English because of its use in Byron's *Don Juan* (1819-1824).

OUTLINE: A plan that the writer develops to guide the composing of his or her first draft, in which the constituent parts are clearly labelled. Outlines may take the form of an informal list of the major points the writer wishes to make or of a formal plan (using roman numerals, letters, and arabic numerals) that presents in detailed order all the material that the writer intends to present. Outlines can also be made during the revision process to check the work's structure and make certain that all the relevant points have been covered.

OXYMORON: A figure of speech, used for rhetorical effect, that brings together and combines antithetical, paradoxical, or contradictory terms, e.g., "living death," "wise fool," "sweet sorrow." Other, more cynical examples might include "military intelligence" and "business ethics."

PANTOMIME: Silent acting: a form of drama that is acted without speech by means of facial expressions, gestures, and body movement.

PARABLE (P. 707): A story designed to convey or illustrate a moral lesson. For example, the biblical story of "The Good Samaritan." See *allegory* and *fable*.

PARADOX (PP. 674–676): A self-contradictory and absurd statement that turns out to be, in some sense at least, actually true and valid. There is, for example, a startling paradox when John Donne cries out to God in "Batter My Heart, Three-Personed God" (1633):

> . . . for I,
> Except you enthrall me, never shall be free;
> Nor ever chaste, except you ravish me.

PARAPHRASE (PP. 715–716): A restatement, using different words, of the essential ideas or argument of a piece or passage of writing. To paraphrase a poem is to restate its ideas in prose.

PARODY: See *burlesque*.

PASSION PLAY: A play dealing with the events in the life of Christ before the resurrection. See *mystery play*.

PASTORAL: A literary work dealing with, and often celebrating, a rural world and a way of life lived close to nature. Pastoral denotes subject matter rather than form; hence, the terms *pastoral lyric, pastoral ode, pastoral elegy, pastoral drama, pastoral epic,* and *pastoral novel.* A good example of pastoral poetic conventions occurs in Christopher Marlowe's "The Passionate Shepherd to His Love" (1599).

PATHETIC FALLACY: A form of *personification*, which attributes human qualities or feelings to inanimate objects. Although first used disapprovingly by John Ruskin in *Modern Painters* (1856), the phrase no longer necessarily carries with it Ruskin's negative connotation; see *personification*. For example, Coleridge refers in "Christabel" (1816) to

> The one red leaf, the last of its clan,
> That dances as often as dance it can.

PATHOS: The quality in a literary work that evokes a feeling of pity, tenderness, and sympathy from the reader or audience. Overdone or misused pathos becomes mere *sentimentality*. There is considerable pathos, for example, in the undeserving death of Desdemona in Shakespeare's *Othello* (1604).

PENTAMETER: A line of poetry consisting of five metrical feet; see *foot*. Here, for example, is a fine epigram in iambic pentameter by Thomas Bancroft:

> Weapons in peace grow hungry, and will eat
> Themselves with rust; but war allows them meat.

PERFECT AND IMPERFECT RHYME (PP. 750–751): In *perfect rhyme* (also called full rhyme or true rhyme) the vowel and any succeeding consonant sounds are identical and the preceding consonant sounds different; e.g., "true" and "blue." Some poets, particularly modern ones, deliberately alternate perfect rhyme with *imperfect rhyme*, in which the correspondence of sound is inexact, approximate, and "imperfect." Imperfectly rhymed words generally end with identical vowels or identical consonants, but not both; for example, "blue" and "boot." Imperfect rhyme is also referred to as *approximate rhyme, half-rhyme, near rhyme, oblique rhyme,* or *slant rhyme. Alliteration, assonance,* and *consonance* are types of imperfect rhyme.

PERIPETEIA: The unexpected reversal of fortune or circumstances. For example, the messenger in *Oedipus,* expecting to cheer the king by revealing that Polybus and Merope were not really his parents, actually convinces Oedipus that he has murdered his father and married his mother.

PERSONA (P.: PERSONAE): The voice or mask the author adopts for the purpose of telling the story or "speaking" the words of a lyric poem. The term *persona* is a way of reminding us that the narrator of the work is not to be confused with the author, and should be regarded as another of the author's creations or fictions. See *implied author*.

PERSONIFICATION (PP. 700–701): A figure of speech in which an idea or thing is given human attributes or feelings or is spoken of as if it were human; see also *pathetic fallacy*. For instance, in the poem "Ex-Basketball Player" (1957), John Updike writes of how the former high school star Flick Webb is reduced to playing pinball at Mae's luncheonette before the "bright applauding tiers/ Of Necco Wafers, Nibs, and Juju Beads."

PHILOLOGY: The study of language and literature.

PICARESQUE NOVEL: Derived from the Spanish word *picaro,* meaning "rogue" or "rascal," the term *picaresque novel* generally refers to a basically realistic and often satiric work of fiction chronicling the career of an engaging, lower-class rogue-hero, who takes to the road for a series of loose, episodic adventures, sometimes in the company of a sidekick. A well-known example of the picaresque novel is Miguel de Cervantes's *Don Quixote* (1605). The earlier, anonymous classic of the genre is *Lazarillo de Tormes* (1554).

PICTURE POEM (P. 770): A poem printed in such a way as to create a visual image of the object or idea described. See George Herbert's "Easter Wings" (1633) for an example.

PIÈCE BIEN FAITE: See *well-made play*.

PIRATED EDITION: An unauthorized edition of an author's work, involving the infringement of *copyright*. Usually this consists of the publication and sale of the works of an author in one country, without the permission of the author and the payment of royalties in another.

PLAGIARISM: The act of borrowing the words or ideas of someone else without appropriate attribution.

PLOT (PP. 33–38, 1091–1095): The patterned arrangement of the events in a narrative or play. See also *exposition, complication, crisis, falling action, anticlimax,* and *resolution.*

POETIC DICTION: Words deliberately chosen because of their poetic quality.

POETIC JUSTICE: The doctrine (now generally discredited in theory and practice) that good should be rewarded and evil punished—that characters in the end should reap their just rewards. See the student essay by Deborah Chappel for a discussion of poetic justice in Chaucer's "The Miller's Tale" (*ca.* 1390).

POETIC LICENSE: Used to describe (and justify) literary experimentation: a writer's deliberate departure from conventions of form and language—and at times even the departure from logic and fact.

POETICS: A theory or set of theories about the nature of poetry. The most famous example is Aristotle's *Poetics* (*ca.* 335 B.C.).

POET LAUREATE: Originally a court poet, maintained by the royal family to give literary expression to their accomplishments. Since the late seventeenth century the position in England has become a formal title conferred by the monarch and carrying with it national distinction. Recent Poet Laureates have included John Masefield (1930–1967), Cecil Day Lewis (1968–1972), Sir John Betjeman (1973–1984), and Ted Hughes (1984–   ).

POETRY CRITICISM: The single most important bibliography of poetry criticism is Joseph M. Kuntz and Nancy C. Martinez, eds., *Poetry Explication: A Checklist of Interpretation since 1925 of British and American Poems Past and Present* (Boston: G. K. Hall, 1980). See also Gloria S. Cline and Jeffrey A. Baker, comps., *Index to Criticisms of British and American Poetry* (Metuchen, N.J.: Scarecrow Press, 1973); Phillis Gershator, ed., *A Bibliographical Guide to the Literature of Contemporary American Poetry, 1970–1975* (Metuchen, N.J.: Scarecrow Press, 1976); George Hendrick and Donna Gerstenberger, eds., *American and British Poetry: A Guide to the Criticism, 1925–1978* (Athens, Ohio: Ohio UP, 1984).

POETRY INDEX: See *Columbia Granger's Index to Poetry* (New York: Columbia UP, 1990). Lists by title, first line, author, and subject poems appearing in anthologies. Earlier editions cover earlier anthologies. This standard guide can be supplemented by *Index of American Periodical Verse* (Metuchen, N.J.: Scarecrow Press), published annually.

POINT OF ATTACK: That point in the play at which the main action of the plot begins.

POINT OF VIEW (PP. 70–76): The angle or perspective from which a story is told.

POLEMIC: A work vigorously setting forth the author's point of view, usually on a controversial subject.

POPULAR BALLAD: See *ballad.*

POST-MODERN: A term used to describe contemporary writing (roughly since 1965) that is experimental in nature.

PRACTICAL CRITICISM: See *theoretical criticism and practical criticism*.

PRÉCIS: An abstract or concise summary that provides, in the same order as the original, the essential points, statements, or facts of a work.

PREFACE: The author's or editor's introduction, in which the writer states his or her purposes and assumptions and makes any acknowledgments.

PRELUDE: A short poem introducing a longer one.

PRIMARY AND SECONDARY SOURCES: *Primary sources* are the original documents; *secondary sources* are those that comment on or analyze those original documents.

PRINTING: All the copies of a work run off at one time on the same typesetting (also called an *impression*). See *edition*.

PRIVATE THEATERS: The smaller indoor theaters of the English Renaissance— for example, Blackfriars, The Inns of Court, or the Court. Private theaters attracted a higher class of audience than the *public theaters* and presented *masques* and performances by troupes of child actors as well as more typical Renaissance plays.

PROBLEM PLAY: A play that explores a controversial social issue of its day. *Ghosts* (1881), by Henrik Ibsen, is a good example since it explores the implications of widespread syphilis in the sexually hypocritical Victorian age. See also *thesis play*.

PROLOGUE: A prefatory statement or speech beginning a literary work, usually a play, preparing the audience for what is to follow; see *epilogue* and *preface*.

PROMPT BOOK: A copy of a play containing stage directions and other details needed to stage the work.

PROOFREADING: The stage in the process of revision in which the author checks for typographical errors or for basic errors in spelling, grammar, and punctuation.

PROSCENIUM (PP. 1071–1072): In modern stagecraft the proscenium is the forward part of the stage between the curtain and the orchestra. The arch from which the curtain hangs is the *proscenium arch*. The area in front of the proscenium is sometimes also referred to as the *apron*.

PROSODY: The description and study of the underlying principles of poetry, e.g., its meter, rhyme, and stanzaic form.

PROTAGONIST (PP. 60, 1096): The chief character of a literary work. Also commonly referred to as the *hero* or *heroine;* see *antagonist*.

PSEUDONYM: A fictitious name assumed by an author; also referred to as a *pen name* or (French) *nom de plume*. The most famous example of a pseudonym in American literature is Samuel L. Clemens's choice of "Mark Twain."

PSYCHIC DISTANCE: The necessary emotional distance or detachment that readers must achieve if they are to regard a literary work objectively. Implicit in achieving psychic distance is the realization that literature is not life. Also called *aesthetic distance*.

PSYCHOLOGICAL/PSYCHOANALYTIC CRITICISM: The use of a psychological and psychoanalytic theory to interpret a writer's work or to understand the personality of the writer. Interpretations based on the theories of Sigmund Freud (1856–1939) are called Freudian and tend to focus on subconscious conflicts—

particularly those involving Freud's hypothesis that children develop through oral, anal, Oedipal, and phallic stages. Freud's interpretation of the Oedipal conflict in *The Interpretation of Dreams* (1900) is particularly famous. The psychoanalytic theories of Freud's disciple Carl Jung (1875–1961) are also popular among critics. Jung postulated that human beings share a "collective unconscious" of common myths and archetypes.

PUBLIC THEATERS: The large open-air theaters of the English Renaissance such as the Fortune and the Globe. See *private theaters*.

PULITZER PRIZE: Prizes awarded annually since 1917 by the School of Journalism and the Board of Trustees of Columbia University for achievement in the fields of literature, music, and journalism. The awards are named after their donor, American journalist Joseph Pulitzer (1847–1911).

PULP MAGAZINES: Magazines printed on inexpensive pulp paper, usually enclosed in a provocative cover, and containing melodramatic adventure stories (love stories, crime stories, or western stories). The "pulps" had their heyday during the 1920s and 1930s.

PUN (PP. 673–674): A play on words, involving words with similar or identical sounds but with different meanings. Puns are usually humorous, but not always. In George Herbert's devoutly religious poem, "The Pulley" (1633), much of the significance arises from Herbert's playful punning on the meanings of the "rest" that God denies humans while granting so many other blessings. The word here means "remainder," "repose," and "freedom from troubles."

PURPLE PROSE: Prose that is emotionally charged and usually not terribly artistic or in good taste.

PURPOSE: The author's basic reason for writing; the goal or objective that the author sets out to achieve.

QUANTITATIVE METER (P. 745): A metrical system (used in Greek and Latin verse) in which units are measured not by stress but by the length of time it takes to pronounce long and short syllables.

QUATRAIN (PP. 763–765): A four-line stanza employing a variety of rhyme schemes.

QUOTATIONS, SOURCE OF: The standard dictionaries used for attributing quotations are *The Oxford Dictionary of Quotations* (New York: Oxford UP, 1992) and *Bartlett's Familiar Quotations* (Boston: Little, Brown, 1968). See also *The Macmillan Dictionary of Quotations* (New York: Macmillan, 1989).

RAISONNEUR: (French for "reasoner.") A character in a play, usually someone who is detached from the main action and is not a central figure, who personifies reason and objectivity. Like the confidant or confidante in the novel, and the chorus in Greek drama, the raisonneur often serves to express the questions in the audience's mind and to deliver the judgments of the author. In Moliere's *Tartuffe* (1667), Cleante serves as a *raisonneur*.

READER RESPONSE CRITICISM: A critical approach (also referred to as "reception theory," "subjective criticism," or "the phenomenology of reading") that begins by assuming that texts are meant to be read; that a text does not really exist until it is in fact read; and that, to some extent at least, the meaning of a text is created or produced by the reader. Reader response criticism examines those elements and features of the work that arouse and shape the response of a hypothetical or *implied reader* whose presence can be derived or implied from the work itself. See *implied reader.* Major texts include Norman Holland, *The Dynamics of Literary Response* (1968); Walter J. Slatoff, *With Respect to Readers: The Dimension of Literary Response* (1970); Louise M. Rosenblatt, *The Reader, the Text, the Poem: The Transactional Theory of the Literary Work* (1978); Wolfgang Iser, *The Act of Reading: A Theory of Aesthetic Response* (tr. 1978); David Bleich, *Subjective Criticism* (1978); Jane Tompkins, ed., *Reader-Response Criticism* (1980); Susan R. Suleiman and Inge Crossman, eds. *The Reader in the Text: Essays on Audience and Interpretation* (1980).

READER'S THEATER: A form of theater where the players read from a script.

REALISM: The nineteenth-century literary movement that reacted to romanticism by insisting on a faithful, objective presentation of the details of everyday life; see *naturalism.* In American literature the realistic period is generally assigned to the years between 1865, the end of the Civil War, and 1900, the beginning of the modern period, which has a literature and art of its own. Major writers include Chekhov, Conrad, James, Maupassant, and Tolstoy.

RECOGNITION SCENE: The moment in a fictional or dramatic work in which one of the characters makes an important (and often decisive) discovery that determines his or her subsequent course of action. See *discovery.*

REFRAIN (PP. 666–668): A line, in whole or in part, or a group of lines that recur, sometimes with slight variation, in a poem or song, at the close of a stanza and help establish meter, sustain mood, or add emphasis. In a song the refrain is usually called the chorus and listeners are expected to join in. For an especially effective use of the refrain see Joni Mitchell's popular song "Both Sides Now" (1967).

REJOINDER: A reply to a reply; a comeback.

RENAISSANCE PERIOD: The period in England beginning about 1500 (with the end of the middle ages) and ending with the establishment of the Commonwealth by Oliver Cromwell in 1649. The Renaissance in England, which took much of its direction from the Renaissance that swept Italy a century before, was characterized by a new interest in humanistic learning, which flowered in the works of Sidney, Spenser, Shakespeare, Donne, and Milton.

REPARTEE: A witty or ingenious reply. Here, for example, is a brief bit of repartee (involving both a *riposte* and a *rejoinder*) between the poet Ben Jonson (1572–1637) and one John Sylvester, who challenged him to match his impromptu rhymes. Sylvester began,

> I, John Sylvester,
> Lay with your sister.

To this, Jonson promptly replied,

> And I, Ben Jonson,
> Slept with your wife.

When Sylvester objected that Jonson's endwords did not rhyme, Jonson replied, "Ah yes, but they are true!"

RESEARCH, GUIDES TO: See *literary research, guides to.*

RESEARCH PAPER: See *style manuals.*

RESOLUTION (PP. 34–35, 1094–1095): The final section of the plot in which the major conflict, issue, or problem is resolved; also referred to as the *conclusion* or *dénouement.*

RESTORATION PERIOD: The period in English literature that begins with the restoration of the monarchy (Charles II) and the end of the Commonwealth in 1660 and ends about 1700. Major writers include Bunyan, Congreve, Dryden, Milton, and Wycherley.

REVENGE TRAGEDY: A type of tragedy (popularized in Elizabethan England by Thomas Kyd's *The Spanish Tragedy*, 1592) that turns on the motive of revenge, revels in violence, horror, and other forms of sensationalism, and typically has a bloody ending. Shakespeare's *Hamlet* (1604) is probably the most famous example of a revenge tragedy.

REVERSAL: The *protagonist's* change of fortune.

REVIEW: A critical appraisal of a play, book, film, or performance published in a periodical.

REVUE: A loose series of musical skits and songs, often satirizing contemporary events.

RHETORICAL QUESTION: A question asked for effect, to which no response or reply is expected.

RHYME (PP. 748–753): The repetition at regular intervals in a line or lines of poetry of similar or identical sounds based on a correspondence between the vowels and succeeding consonants of accented syllables; see also *end rhyme, false rhyme, identical rhyme, internal rhyme, masculine and feminine rhyme, perfect and imperfect rhyme,* and *visual rhyme;* also *alliteration, assonance,* and *consonance.*

RHYME ROYAL (PP. 765–766): A stanza of seven iambic pentameter lines rhyming ABABBCC.

RHYME SCHEME (P. 752): The pattern of end rhymes within a given stanza of poetry.

RHYTHM AND METER (PP. 721–747): Rhythm is the general term given to the measured repetition of accent or beats in units of poetry or prose. In English poetry, rhythm is generally established by manipulating both the pattern of accent and the number of syllables in a given line. Meter refers to the predominant rhythmic pattern within any given line (or lines) of poetry.

RIPOSTE: A rapid, biting reply. See *repartee.*

RISING ACTION: See *complication.*

ROMANTIC COMEDY: A type of comedy which turns on the adventures and misadventures of lovers and ends happily.

ROMANTICISM: See *romantic period.*

ROMANTIC PERIOD: The period in English literature that began in 1798 with the publication of *Literary Ballads* by Wordsworth and Coleridge and ended with the passage of the Reform Bill of 1832. The dominant spirit or intellectual climate of the period, *romanticism,* defies easy generalizations. It is usually said to include the optimistic belief in the natural goodness and perfectibility of humanity, the celebration of the organic relationship between people and nature, and the high priority given to imagination and intuition as opposed to reason. Major writers include Wordsworth, Coleridge, Byron, Keats, and Shelley. In

American literature, the romantic period is usually assigned the years between 1820 and 1865 and includes the works of Bryant, Irving, Cooper, Poe, Thoreau, Emerson, Hawthorne, Melville, Longfellow, and Whitman.

RONDEAU, RONDEL, AND ROUNDEL: These terms are sometimes used interchangeably and may refer to a variety of short, fixed-form poems. Characteristic of them all is the use of a limited number of rhymes (usually only two) and of a refrain formed of the beginning words or lines. The repetitions of the refrain "round" the poem to its conclusion and thus give rise to the name used to describe it. See Leigh Hunt's "Rondeau," Algernon Swinburne's "Roundel," and Amy Jo Schoonover's "Rondeau: An Un-Love Song."

ROUND AND FLAT CHARACTERS: See *character*.

RUBAIS (P. 763): An iambic pentameter quatrain in which the first two lines rhyme with the last one, AAXA. The form was popularized by Edward FitzGerald in his free translation of *The Rubáiyát of Omar Khayyám* (1895). Here is a typical rubais:

> They say the Lion and the Lizard keep
> The Courts where Jamshyd gloried and drank deep:
> And Bahram, the great Hunter—the Wild Ass
> Stamps o'er his Head, but cannot break his Sleep.

RUN-ON LINE: See *enjambment*.

SARCASM (P. 681): A form of verbal irony delivered in a derisive, caustic, and bitter manner to belittle or ridicule its subject. In John Updike's "A&P" (1962), for example, there is considerable sarcasm when Sammy, the young checkout teller, describes the typical customers as "houseslaves in pin curlers," "sheep," and "scared pigs in a chute."

SATIRE (P. 681): A type of writing that holds up persons, ideas, or things to varying degrees of amusement, ridicule, or contempt in order, presumably, to improve, correct, or bring about some desirable change.

SATYR PLAY: An ancient Greek play of comic relief that followed an author's trilogy of tragedies. Euripides's *Cyclops* is the only complete example of a satyr play.

SCANSION (PP. 723–729): The analysis of a poem's metrical pattern.

SCENARIO: The brief outline of a plot, providing the key details of scenes, situations, and characters.

SCENE (PP. 1060–1061): A self-contained segment of a work of fiction or drama; also used as a synonym for setting. See *act*.

SCIENCE FICTION: A form of fantasy literature that speculatively extrapolates known facts of science or its possibilities into the future. Ray Bradbury's "August 2002: Night Meeting" (1950) is an example of good science fiction.

SEMIOTICS: The study of signs (including words, sounds, gestures, postures, facial expressions and other communication signals). According to Jonathan Culler, semiotics is "A program . . . which seeks to identify the conventions and operations by which any signifying practice (such as literature) produces its observable effects of meaning."

SENSUOUS: In literature, sensuous refers to writing that appeals to one or more of the reader's five senses.

SENTIMENTALITY: The presence of emotion or feeling that seems excessive or unjustified in terms of the circumstances; see *pathos.*

SEPTET (PP. 765–766): A seven-line stanza employing a variety of rhyme schemes. Adrienne Rich's "Storm Warnings" (1951), Theodore Roetke's "I Knew a Woman" (1958), and Anne Sexton's "Her Kind" (1960) are good examples of poems in septets.

SEQUEL: A work that continues the characters and plot of a preceding work.

SERIAL: The publication of a work in periodic installments.

SERIALS, GUIDE TO: The most complete guide to periodicals published in the United States since 1900 is the *Reader's Guide to Periodical Literature* (New York: H. W. Wilson).

SESTET: (P. 765) A six-line stanza. Robert Graves's "The Naked and the Nude" (1957), Henry Reed's "Naming of Parts" (1947), and W. D. Snodgrass's "April Inventory" (1959) are examples of poems in sestets.

SESTINA: A fixed verse form (originally French) consisting of six sestets and a tercet. Instead of using rhyme, a sestina uses the final word in each line of the first sestet to conclude a line in each subsequent sestet. In the following scheme, each letter represents the word ending a line; each row of letters represents a stanza:

$$
\begin{array}{cccccc}
a & b & c & d & e & f \\
f & a & e & b & d & c \\
c & f & d & a & b & e \\
e & c & b & f & a & d \\
d & e & a & c & f & b \\
b & d & f & e & c & a \\
  &   & e & c & a &   \\
\end{array}
$$

Often, the final tercet includes all six end-words, with two words used per line.

SETTING (PP. 67–70): The time and place in which the action of a story, poem, or play occurs; physical setting alone is often referred to as the *locale.*

SHAKESPEAREAN SONNET: See *sonnet.*

SHORT STORY: A short work of narrative prose fiction. The distinction between the short story and novel is mainly one of length.

SHORT STORY CRITICISM: The standard print bibliographies—Thurston Jarvis, ed., *Short Fiction Criticism: A Checklist of Interpretation since 1925 of Stories and Novelettes* (Denver: Alan Swallow, 1960); Warren S. Walker, ed., *Twentieth-Century Short Story Explication,* 3rd ed. (Hamden, Conn.: Shoe String Press, 1977. Supplement I, 1980; supplement II, 1984); Joe Weixlmann, ed., *American Short-Fiction Criticism and Scholarship, 1959–1977: A Checklist* (Chicago: Alan Swallow, 1982)—can be supplemented by the annual bibliography of short-fiction criticism that appears in each summer issue of *Studies in Short Fiction* (Newberry, S.C.: Newberry College).

SHORT STORY HISTORY: Discussions of the historical development of the short story include the following: Walter Allen, *The Short Story in English* (1980); Thomas Owen Beachcroft, *The Modest Art: A Survey of the Short Story in English* (1968); Eugene Current-Garcia, *The American Short Story Before 1850: A Critical History* (1985); Joseph M. Flora, ed., *The English Short Story, 1880–1945* (1985);

Albert J. George, *Short Fiction in France, 1800–1850* (1964); Clare Hanson, *Short Stories and Short Fictions, 1880–1980* (1985); Wendall V. Harris, *British Short Fiction in the 19th Century* (1979); James Kilroy, ed., *The Irish Short Story: A Critical History* (1984); Harold Oren, *The Victorian Short Story: Development and Triumph of a Literary Genre* (1986); William Peden, *The American Short Story: Continuity and Change, 1940–1975* (1975); Philip Stevick, ed., *The American Short Story, 1900– 1945: A Critical History* (1984); Dennis Vannatta, *The English Short Story, 1945– 1980: A Critical History* (1985); Arthur Voss, *The American Short Story: A Critical Survey* (1973); Gordon Weaver, *The American Short Story, 1945–1980: A Critical History* (1983).

Short Story Index: The standard source to short stories published since 1900 in major periodicals is *Short Story Index: An Index to Stories in Collections and Periodicals* (SSI) (New York: H. W. Wilson). Published since 1913 in five-year cumulations plus annual supplements.

Simile (pp. 694–695): A figure of speech in which two essentially dissimilar objects are expressly compared with one another by the use of *like* or *as*; see *metaphor* and *figurative language*. Gerard Manley Hopkins (1844–1889), for example, uses a simile when he writes that God's grandeur "will shine out, like shining from shook foil."

Situation: Either the basic set of circumstances in which a group of characters find themselves at some point during the plot, or the set of circumstances in effect at the beginning of the plot before the action begins.

Situational Irony (Irony of Situation): See *irony*.

Slapstick: Low comedy characterized by physical action, horseplay, and practical jokes.

Soliloquy: A dramatic convention in which a character, alone on stage (*solus*), speaks aloud and thus shares his or her thoughts with the audience. See *aside* and *monologue*. Iago's soliloquy at the end of Act I, Scene iii, in *Othello* (1604) is a good example.

Song: A lyric poem set to music.

Sonnet (pp. 768–769): A poem of 14 iambic pentameter lines expressing a single thought or idea and utilizing one of several established rhyme scenes. The sonnet in English generally follows one of two basic patterns: the *Italian sonnet* (or *Petrarchan sonnet* named after the Italian Renaissance poet Petrarch) consists of an eight-line *octave*, rhyming ABBAABBA, followed by a six-line *sestet*, rhyming variously CDECDE, CDCCDC, etc.; and the *English sonnet* (or *Shakespearean sonnet*) consists of three four-line *quatrains* and a concluding *couplet*, rhyming ABAB CDCD EFEF GG. A variant of the English sonnet, the *Spenserian sonnet* (named after English poet Edmund Spenser), links its quatrains by employing the rhyme scheme ABAB BCBC CDCD EE. This text includes numerous sonnets by Shakespeare, as well as others by Spenser, Drayton, Sidney, Donne, Milton, Wordsworth, Shelley, E. B. Browning, and Frost.

Spenserian Sonnet: See *sonnet*.

Spenserian Stanza (p. 766): A nine-line stanza consisting of eight lines of iambic pentameter and a concluding line of iambic hexameter, rhyming ABABBCBCC—made famous by the English poet Edmund Spenser in the *Faerie Queene* (1590–1596).

Spondee (Spondaic) (p. 739): A foot of two accented syllables; e.g., "dew-drop."

Stanza (pp. 761–767): A group of lines forming a structural unit or division of a poem. Stanzas may be units of form established through similarity in the number of lines, length of lines, meter and rhyme scheme; or stanzas may exist as logical units determined by their thought or content.

Stock Character: A character who conventionally appears in certain forms of literature and art and who is easily recognizable on that basis. For example, the rich uncle of domestic comedy; the hard-boiled detective of the pulp magazines; the female confidante of soap opera; the cruel stepmother of the fairy tale; and the mustachioed villain of nineteenth-century melodrama. Also referred to as a *type character*.

Stock Situation: A situation or incident that occurs so frequently in literature as to become at once familiar: e.g., the family feud, the missing heir, the love triangle, the case of mistaken identity.

Strategy: The method an author chooses to achieve his or her purpose or ends.

Stream of Consciousness: The narrative method of capturing and representing the inner workings of a character's mind. The term was first used by William James in his *Principles of Psychology* (1890).

Stress: The accent or emphasis given certain syllables in the scansion of verse.

Strong Curtain: A powerful ("strong") conclusion to an act of a play. See Ibsen's *Hedda Gabler* (1890) for good instances of strong curtain lines.

Structuralism: A critical approach, utilizing methodology of anthropology and linguistics, that attempts to analyze literature in terms of its underlying structural patterns. In critic Jonathan Culler's words, "Structuralists take linguistics as a model and attempt to develop grammars . . . that would account for the form and meaning of literary works." Major texts include Culler's *Structuralist Poetics* (1973); Robert Scholes, *Structuralism in Literature: An Introduction* (1974); Terence Hawkes, *Structuralism and Semiotics* (1977); John Sturrock, ed., *Structuralism and Since: From Levi-Strauss to Derrida* (1979).

Structure: The overall pattern or design of a literary work.

Style (pp. 84–89): The author's characteristic manner of expression; style includes the author's diction, syntax, sentence patterns, punctuation, and spelling, as well as the use made of such devices as sound, rhythm, imagery, and figurative language.

Style, Manuals of: The most widely used manuals of style or style sheets for information on the most widely accepted conventions for such matters as footnotes, bibliography, punctuation, quotations, abbreviations and the presentation of research include the *MLA Handbook for Writers of Research Papers, Theses, and Dissertations,* Joseph Gibaldi and Walter S. Achtert, eds. (New York: Modern Language Association, 1988); Kate L. Turabian, *Student's Guide for Writing College Papers* (Chicago: U of Chicago P, 1982); *A Manual of Style: For Authors, Editors, and Copywriters* (Chicago: U of Chicago P, 1982).

Stylistics: The study of the *style* of literary texts.

Subjective: In literary criticism, judgments based on personal or emotional beliefs are subjective, as opposed to those based on criteria that are objective and impersonal.

Subplot (p. 36): The subplot (also called the *minor plot* or *underplot*) is a secondary action or complication within a fictional or dramatic work that often serves to reinforce or contrast to the main plot.

SUMMARY: A brief overview of the ideas and information already developed.

SUPPORT: The evidence or proof that an author marshals to back up his or her argument.

SUSPENSE: The psychological tension or anxiety resulting from the reader's or audience's uncertainty or just how a situation or conflict is likely to end.

SWASHBUCKLER: A type of literary work containing gallant heroes, beautiful maidens, and plenty of sword fights.

SYLLABIC METER (PP. 743–745): A metrical system (common to Japanese and Romance verse but rare in English) in which units are measured by the number of syllables in a line.

SYMBOL (PP. 79–82, 705–708): Literally, something that stands for something else. In literature, any word, object, action, or character that embodies and evokes a range of additional meaning and significance. In Anton Chekkov's *The Cherry Orchard* (1904), for example, the lovely but unproductive orchard is a symbol of the fading and effete aristocratic way of life. See also *allegory*.

SYNECDOCHE (P. 695): A figure of speech in which a part is used to signify the whole or, less frequently, the whole is used to signify the part; e.g., "greaser" for a youth affecting the tough-guy look of the 1950s.

SYNESTHESIA: From the Greek meaning "perceiving together." The simultaneous experiencing of two or more senses when only one of them is being stimulated, as, for example, when color is attributed to sound ("blue note").

SYNOPSIS: A summary or résumé of a piece of writing.

TABLEAU/TABLEAUX: A momentary pause or interlude during the scene of a play (often just before the curtain) during which the actors freeze in position.

TALE: A short and simple narrative in prose or verse. Though *tale* was once used as a synonym for short story, the term *short story* is now reserved for short fictional narratives that demonstrate a conscious artistry in their design.

TERCET (P. 762): A stanza of three lines. Hardy's "The Convergence of the Twain" (1912) is an interesting example of a poem in tercets.

TERMINAL RHYME: See *end rhyme*.

TERZA RIMA (P. 762): A verse form composed of interlocking three-line stanzas, or *tercets*, rhyming ABA BCB CDC, etc. Shelley's "Ode to the West Wind" (1820) and Frost's "Acquainted with the Night" (1928) are good examples.

TETRAMETER: A line of poetry consisting of four metrical feet. Some well-known poems in tetrameter include Marlowe's "The Passionate Shepherd to His Love" (1599), Raleigh's "The Nymph's Reply to the Shepherd" (1600), Donne's "A Valediction: Forbidding Mourning" (1633), and Marvell's "To His Coy Mistress" (1681).

TEXTUAL CRITICISM: The kind of scholarship that attempts to establish through reconstruction the "correct" and authoritative text of a literary work as its author originally wrote it. The standard introduction to the theory and practice of textual criticism is James Thorpe, *Principles of Textual Criticism* (1972).

THALIA: The Greek muse or goddess of comedy.

THEATER IN THE ROUND: Plays presented on a stage that is surrounded by the audience. See *arena stage/arena theater.*

THEME (PP. 76–79, 717–718): The controlling idea or meaning of a work of art.

THEORETICAL CRITICISM AND PRACTICAL CRITICISM: Theoretical criticism is concerned with identifying and establishing the general, underlying principles of art; *practical criticism* (or *applied criticism*) concerns itself with the study and analysis of specific individual works.

THESIS: The assertion or proposition that unifies and controls the entire work.

THESIS NOVEL/PLAY: A novel or play that deals with a specific problem and advocates a "thesis" in the form of a solution; also called a problem novel or *problem play.*

THREE UNITIES: Three rules or absolutes of sixteenth-and seventeenth-century Italian and French drama, broadly adapted from Aristotle's *Poetics*: the Unity of Time, which limits a play to a single day; the Unity of Place, which limits a play's setting to a single location; and the Unity of Action, which limits a play to a single story line.

TONE (PP. 89–90, 716–717): The author's attitude toward the subject or audience.

TOUR DE FORCE: A feat of skill and ingenuity.

TRADITIONAL BALLAD: A synonym for folk ballad; see *ballad.*

TRAGEDY (PP. 1101–1103): Broadly, any serious literary work in which the protagonist suffers a major reversal of fortune, often leading to his or her downfall or death; see *classical tragedy, domestic tragedy, revenge tragedy, tragicomedy.*

TRAGICOMEDY: A type of drama (most often associated with Elizabethan and Jacobean drama) that mixes the conventions of tragedy and comedy and in which the *protagonist*, although subject to a series of crises (often including the threat of death), manages to escape to celebrate a happy (and frequently highly contrived) ending. Shakespeare's *Cymbeline* (*ca.* 1608) and Dryden's *Love Triumphant* (1693) are examples of the genre.

TRAGIC FLAW (P. 1102): The principal defect in character or judgment that leads to the downfall of the *tragic hero.* In Greek tragedy this flaw is often *hubris,* the hero's excessive pride or self-confidence. The hubris of Oedipus, for example, leads him to ignore well-intentioned warnings by Tiresias, Creon, Jocasta, and the Herdsman in his effort to discover the murderer of King Laius.

TRAGIC HERO (PP. 1102–1103): The name sometimes given to the protagonist of a tragedy, if he or she has the qualities of greatness. Thus Oedipus is both a protagonist and a tragic hero, while Willy Loman in Arthur Miller's *Death of a Salesman* (1949) is only the former.

TRAVESTY: A work that is made humorous by a ridiculous treatment of a serious subject.

TRILOGY: A literary work in three parts, each of which is capable of standing alone.

TRIMETER: A line of poetry consisting of three metrical feet; see *foot.*

TRIPLE RHYME: See *masculine and feminine rhyme.*

TRIPLET (P. 762): A stanza of three lines rhyming AAA. See *tercet.*

TROCHEE (TROCHAIC) (PP. 733–735): A foot composed of an accented syllable followed by an unaccented one; e.g., *tur*key."

TROPE: Another name for *figure of speech.*

TYPE CHARACTER: See *stock character.*

"UBI SUNT" MOTIF: The theme which laments the vanished past. The Latin phrase means "where are."

UNDERPLOT: See *subplot.*

UNDERSTATEMENT: A figure of speech in which what is literally said falls considerably short (or "under") the magnitude or seriousness of what is being discussed. Understatement thus has the effect of emphasizing the very thing it apparently tries to minimize. For example, the speaker in T. S. Eliot's "Journey of the Magi" (1927) uses understatement when he says of the birth of Christ, "it was (you may say) satisfactory."

UNITY: The quality of a work of art in which every element or part clearly and effectively relates to the accomplishment of a complete and independent whole. Unity in a literary work requires the presence of some central organizing principle to which all the parts are necessarily related, making the work an organic whole. See also *three unities.*

UNRELIABLE NARRATOR: A narrator whose knowledge and judgments about characters or events is sufficiently incomplete or flawed to render him or her an unreliable guide to the author's intentions. In this sense most of the narrators in Robert Browning's monlogues are unreliable. See particularly Browning's "My Last Duchess" (1842).

UPSTAGE (PP. 1076–1077): *Upstage* is a stage direction that refers to the back half of the stage; *downstage* refers to the front half of the stage, the part nearest to the audience. Thus, in theater jargon, an actor who moves farther back on the stage during dialogue is *upstaging* the other actor by forcing them to face away from the audience while speaking. The term *upstaging* now refers to any showy or theatrical behavior that denies due attention to the other actors.

VANITY PRESS: A publishing house that charges its authors for the privilege of seeing their works in print. The implication is that such works lack artistic and commercial value and are being published only because of their authors' vanity.

VARIORUM EDITION: An edition of a work that contains all the possible variant readings of the text together with notes and commentary.

VERBAL IRONY: See *irony.*

VERISIMILITUDE: The quality of being lifelike or true to actuality.

VERSIFICATION: An all-inclusive term for the art and practice of writing poetry.

VILLANELLE: A fixed verse form (originally French) consisting of five three-line stanzas (or *tercets*) followed by a *quatrain,* rhyming ABA ABA ABA ABA ABA BBAA. The first line of the poem is repeated in lines 6, 12, and 18; the third line is repeated in lines 9, 15, and 19. See Dylan Thomas's "Do Not Go Gentle into That Good Night" and Theodore Roethke's "The Waking."

VICTORIAN PERIOD: The literary period coinciding with the long reign of England's Queen Victoria, 1837–1901. Major writers include Arnold, Browning, Dickens, George Eliot, Hardy, Thackeray, and Tennyson.

VISUAL RHYME (P. 751): Words that rhyme to the eye but not to the ear; their spelling is similar, but they are pronounced differently: "plow" and "blow."

WELL-MADE PLAY (PIÈCE BIEN FAITE) (P. 1095): A type of play, written according to formula, characterized by a tightly structured, suspenseful plot that turns on a secret; quickly rising action; and a series of reversals, inevitably leading to a climactic scene that reveals the secret and allows the hero to triumph.

ZEUGMA: A figure of speech in which a single verb takes on different meanings with different objects (e.g., He drank her beauty and her wine) or in which a single adjective takes on different meanings with two different nouns (e.g., Although the room was bright, the students were not).

THEMATIC
CONTENTS

Literature is of enduring interest in part because it is capable of exploring with great forcefulness the central themes raised in the very process of living. The thematic classification that follows is but one of many possible ways of categorizing the works in this anthology. Some works, of course, explore several themes simultaneously; others resist classification entirely. Probably no system of thematic classification is adequate to the task, but in the pages that follow we hope at least to have given you a useful starting point for thinking about and discussing some of the key themes embodied in the works of great authors.

INNOCENCE AND EXPERIENCE

CARPE DIEM

LOVE, HATE, AND JEALOUSY

SUCCESS AND FAILURE

DYING, DEATH, AND GRIEF

THE INDIVIDUAL AND THE SOCIETY

RELIGION AND THE SUPERNATURAL

PAST, PRESENT, AND FUTURE

PREJUDICE, BONDAGE, AND REBELLION

MAN AND NATURE

ART AND THE ARTIST

INDEX TO AUTHORS, TITLES, AND FIRST LINES

❧❧❧❧❧❧❧

Note: First lines are set in roman type; all
titles are italicized except titles of poems listed under authors' names.

A

A & P, 516
Abortions will not let you forget, 996
About suffering they were never wrong, 981
According to Brueghel, 954
Acquainted with the Night, 945
Advice, 976
Advice to My Son, 1038
After Apple-Picking, 942
After Great Pain, A Formal Feeling Comes, 907
Afternoon on a Hill, 965
Against Love, 835
A little learning is a dangerous thing, 842
All Nature seems at work. Slugs leave their
 lair—, 868
All night it fell around us, 1011
All night, this headland, 1004
The Altar, 770
Amarantha sweet and fair, 832
American Poetry, 651
Am I Blue?, 1724
Among the other things that do not matter,
 1044
Ancient Music, 955
And here face down beneath the sun, 966
Anecdote of the Jar, 951
Angelou, Maya
 The Health Food Diner, 1024
 My Arkansas, 1024
 On the Pulse of Morning, 1025
Anglosaxon Street, 742
Annabel Lee, 738

Announced by all the trumpets of the sky,
 888
Anthem for Doomed Youth, 719
anyone lived in a pretty how town, 971
Apparently with No Surprise, 703
The apparition of these faces in the crowd,
 955
Applauding youths laughed with young prosti-
 tutes, 963
April Inventory, 1015
Araby, 303
Aristophanes
 Lysistrata, 1130
The Armadillo, 985
Arnold, Matthew
 Dover Beach, 904
Ars Poetica, 650
As I came to the edge of the woods, 946
As I sd to my, 1014
The Assyrian came down like the wolf on the
 fold, 737, 870
The Astronomer's Wife, 406
As virtuous men pass mildly away, 694, 821
At noon in the desert a panting lizard, 993
At the Bomb Testing Site, 993
At the Edge, 1010
Atwood, Margaret
 Landcrab, 698
 You Fit into Me, 1046
Auden, W. H.
 Look, Stranger, 751
 Musée des Beaux Arts, 981
 The Unknown Citizen, 982